WHAT FANTASTIC FICTION

DO I READ NEXT?

A Reader's Guide to Recent Fantasy, Horror and Science Fiction

WHAT FANTASTIC FICTION

DO I READ NEXT?

A Reader's Guide to Recent Fantasy, Horror and Science Fiction

NEIL BARRON

GALE

Detroit
New York
Toronto
London

Neil Barron
Contributors: Stefan Dziemianowicz and Scott Imes

Gale Research Staff:
Coordinating Editors: Lydia Fink and Charles B. Montney
Contributing Editors: Victoria A. Coughlin, Paula Cutcher-Jackson, Kathleen Dallas, Shelly Dickey, Nancy Franklin, William Harmer, Prindle LaBarge, Debra M. Kirby, Sharon McGilvray, Dana Shonta, Kelly Sprague
Managing Editor: Ann V. Evory

Production Director: MaryBeth Trimper
External Production Assistant: Shanna P. Heilveil
Product Design Manager: Cynthia Baldwin
Senior Art Director: Mary Krzewinski

Manager, Data Entry Services: Eleanor Allison
Data Entry Supervisor: Ken D. Benson, Jr.
Data Entry Associates: Shanitta Watkins

Manager, Technical Support Services: Theresa Rocklin
Programmer/Analyst: Joshua E. Cohen

Library of Congress Cataloging-in-Publication Data
What fantastic fiction do I read next? : a reader's guide to fantasy,
   horror, and science fiction / [edited by] Neil Barron.
       p.   cm.
     Lists 4800 books published between 1989-1997 taken from What do I
read next?
   Includes bibliographical references and index.
   ISBN 0-7876-1866-7 (alk. paper)
    1. Fantastic fiction--Bibliography. 2. Fantastic fiction--History
and criticism. 3. Horror tales--Bibliography. 4. Horror tales-
-History and criticism. 5. Science Fiction--Bibliography.
6. Science Fiction--History and criticism. I. Barron, Neil, 1934-

Z5917.F3W3 1997
[PN3435]
016.80883'87--dc21   97-33418
                                             CIP

This book is printed on acid-free paper that meets the minimum requirements of American National Standard for Information Sciences—Permanent Paper for Printed Library Materials, ANSI Z39.48-1984.

ISBN 0-7876-1866-7

Printed in the United States of America
10 9 8 7 6 5 4 3 2 1

Contents

Introduction

Fantasy, horror, and science fiction can easily be found, whether on the big screen in the form of a Steven Spielberg production, on television as a mini-series, on bestseller lists, or on the shelves of a library. It's no wonder, either—the fantastic provides great action, philosophical issues, humor, and even comments on the human condition. Indeed, dragons, monsters, invaders, magicians, and aliens have in stories as old as history. There's no question fantastic fiction is important; the true question for readers, from the avid "Star Trek" fan to the reader who has read it all, is "What do I read next?"

Designed as a tool to assist in the exploration of fantastic fiction, *What Fantastic Fiction Do I Read Next?* guides the reader to both current and classic recommendations in the widely read genres of fantasy, horror, and science fiction. Collecting entries from previous volumes of Gale's *What Do I Read Next?* annual, *What Fantastic Fiction Do I Read Next?* allows readers quick and easy access to specific data on recent titles in these popular genres. In addition, each entry provides alternate reading selections, coming to the rescue of librarians and booksellers who may be unfamiliar with these genres yet must answer the frequently posed question "What fantastic fiction do I read next?"

About the Contributors

Neil Barron, an expert in the field of fantastic fiction, coordinates the compilation of fantasy, horror, and science fiction titles for *What Do I Read Next?*. He is the editor of three reader guides: *Fantasy Literature* and *Horror Literature* (both Garland, 1990) and *Anatomy of Wonder: A Critical Guide to Science Fiction* (Bowker, 4th ed., 1995).

Assisting Mr. Barron through the years of *What Do I Read Next?* have been two other experts in fantastic fiction. **Scott Imes** has managed the well-known Twin Cities specialty fantastic fiction bookstore, Uncle Hugo's, for 20 years, where he has developed a vast knowledge of the fantasy and science fiction genres as well as a vast collection of titles. **Stefan Dziemianowicz** is an editor for a New York law book publisher. His horror credentials include co-editing the quarterly journal, *Necrofile*, and writing the definitive study, *The Annotated Guide to Unknown and Unknown Worlds* (Starmont House, 1991). He has co-edited numerous anthologies and recently compiled *A Whisper in the Dark: 12 Thrilling Tales by Louisa May Alcott* (Barnes and Noble, 1996). The authors have been ably assisted by numerous contributors throughout the years.

Details on over 4,800 Titles

What Fantastic Fiction Do I Read Next? contains more than 4,800 entries for fantasy, horror, and science fiction titles published in the past eight years. The criteria for inclusion of specific titles vary somewhat from genre to genre, but for the most part, the experts have attempted to select the recently published books they consider the best.

The entries are listed alphabetically by main author. Most provide the following information:

- **Author or editor's name** and real name if a pseudonym is used. Co-authors, co-editors, and illustrators are also listed where applicable.

- **Book title.**

- **Date and place of publication; name of publisher.**

- **Series name.**

- **Story type:** Genre and specific categories within each genre, identified by the compiling expert. Definitions of these types are listed in the "Key to Story Types" section following the Introduction.

- **Major characters:** Names and brief descriptions of up to three characters featured in the title.

- **Time period:** When the story takes place.

- **Locale:** Where the story takes place.

- **What the book is about:** A brief plot summary.

- **Other books you might like:** Titles by other authors written on a similar theme or in a similar style. Readers use these titles to delve more deeply into fantasy, horror, or science fiction.

Indexes Answer Readers' Questions

The eight indexes in *What Fantastic Fiction Do I Read Next?*, used separately or in conjunction with each other, create many pathways to the featured recommended titles, answering general questions or locating specific titles. For example:

"Are there any new *Star Wars* books?"

The SERIES INDEX lists entries by the name of the series of which they are a part, helping readers locate books in a series they enjoy.

"I like Sword and Sorcery books. Can you recommend any new ones?"

The STORY TYPE INDEX breaks each genre into story types or more specialized areas. In the Fantasy genre, for example, there is a story type heading "Sword and Sorcery." This index allows readers to focus on titles that fall in a category they particularly enjoy. For the definitions of genre terms, see the "Key to Story Types" beginning on page ix.

"I'm looking for a fantasy set in Wales..."

The GEOGRAPHIC INDEX lists titles by their locale, helping readers pinpoint an area in which they have a particular interest, such as their hometown, a distant country, or even Cyberspace.

"Do you know of any horror stories set during the 18th century?"

The TIME PERIOD INDEX is a chronological listing of titles by time period, allowing readers to find stories set in a time period—past or future—that interests them or to find a book whose title they do not remember, except that it's set during World War II.

"What titles are available that feature vampires?"

The CHARACTER DESCRIPTION INDEX identifies the major characters by occupation (e.g. Accountant, Editor, Librarian) or persona (e.g. Cyborg, Noblewoman, Stowaway). This index, for example, allows a reader who enjoys books featuring mythical creatures to find them easily.

"Has anyone written any new books with Merlin (the magician) in them?"

The CHARACTER NAME INDEX lists the major characters named in the entries, which can help readers who remember some information about a book, but not an author or title, locate it. It can also point them to more books about a famous character such as Alice in Wonderland.

"What has Dean Koontz written recently?"

The AUTHOR INDEX contains the names of all authors featured in the entries and those listed under "Other books you might like," pointing readers to an extensive list of an author's works.

"What books are like *Red Mars*?"

The TITLE INDEX includes all main entry titles and all titles recommended under "Other books you might like" in one alphabetical listing. Thus readers can find a specific title they know, new or old, and go to that entry to find out what titles are similar.

The indexes can also be used together to narrow down or broaden choices. A reader interested in horror set in England during the late 19th century would consult the TIME PERIOD INDEX and GEOGRAPHIC INDEX to see which titles appear in both. Detectives abound in mystery fiction, but may be found in other genres as well. Searching for Detective in the CHARACTER DESCRIPTION INDEX enables a mystery reader to cross over into previously unknown realms of reading experiences, perhaps as far as a detective story set on Mars! And with the AUTHOR and TITLE indexes, which include all books listed under "Other books you might like," it is easy to compile an extensive list of recommended reading, beginning with a recently published title or a classic from the past.

Suggestions Are Welcome

The editors welcome any comments and suggestions for enhancing and improving *What Fantastic Fiction Do I Read Next?*. Please address correspondence to:

Editors
What Do I Read Next?
Gale Research
645 Griswold St.
Detroit, MI 48226-4094
Phone: 313-961-2242
Toll-free: 800-347-4253
Fax: 313-961-6083

Key to Story Types

The following is a list of terms used to classify the story type of each title included in *What Fantastic Fiction Do I Read Next?* along with brief definitions of the terms. To find books that fall under a particular story type heading, see the Story Type Index.

Fantasy Story Types

Adventure: The character(s) must face a series of obstacles, which may include monsters, conflict with other travellers, war, interference by supernatural elements, interference by nature, and so on.

Alternate History: Using history as a backdrop, the author adds fantastic elements to build the story.

Alternate Universe: More accurately, in most cases, alternate history, in which the South won the American Civil War, the Nazis triumphed, etc. The idea is a venerable one in SF.

Alternate World: The story starts out in the everyday world, but the main character is transported to an alternate/parallel world by supernatural means and generally must go on an Adventure or Quest in order to find a way home.

Anthology: A collection of short fiction by different authors usually related in theme or setting.

Collection: A book of short stories by a single author.

Contemporary: The story is set in the everyday world, but elements of the fantastic begin to intrude (e.g., a unicorn appears or the character suddenly has the ability to perform magic).

Contemporary Realism: Stories in which the fantasy elements are part of a muted background and a "mundane" or "realistic" tone predominates.

Historical: This sub-genre could also be called Alternate History. Using history as a backdrop, the author adds fantastic elements to build the story.

Horror: Although the story has been classified as Fantasy in this section, there are strong elements of horror (e.g., psychological, supernatural, etc.).

Humor: Fantasy in which humor, from cerebral to slapstick, is prominent.

Legend: A story based on a legend, myth, or fairy tale that has been rewritten.

Light Fantasy: There is a great deal of humor throughout the story and it is almost guaranteed to have a happy ending.

Literary: Usually refers to novels not published as fantasy and sometimes incorporating unconventional narrative techniques.

Magic Conflict: The main conflict of the story stems from magical interference. Protagonists may be caught in the middle of a conflict between sorcerers or may themselves be engaged in conflict with other sorcerers.

Military: Stories that can range from space wars (compare Space Opera under Science Fiction) to more local battles; most such stories tend to glorify military virtues.

Mystery: Although the story has been classified as Fantasy in this section, there are strong elements of Mystery (e.g., suspense, detectives, etc.).

Political: The novel deals with political issues that are skewed by the use and presence of fantastic elements.

Post-Disaster: Story set in a much degraded environment, frequently involving a reduction in population and the resulting loss of access to processes, resources, technology, etc.

Psychic Powers: Parapsychological or paranormal powers believed by some to be credible, e.g., telepathy, telekinesis, etc.

Quest: The character embarks on a journey to achieve a specific goal, such as retrieving a jewel from an evil wizard.

Religious: Religion of any sort plays a primary role in the plot.

Romance: The main characters are in love, but separated by internal motivations or external interference. Elements of the fantastic may add to or help solve the problem.

Satire: With an ironic and/or detached point of view, the author is writing on a particular theme (such as religion) using elements of the fantastic to exaggerate and explore the theme.

Science Fiction: Although the story has been classified as Fantasy in this section, there are strong elements of Science Fiction.

Sword and Sorcery: The tried and true formula of this subgenre has a muscle-bound swordsman, who is innocent of thought and common sense, up against evil sorcerers and sorceresses, who naturally lose in the end because they are evil. However, Sword and Sorcery continues to be updated, with heroines instead of heroes and a bit of thought prior to action.

Time Travel: In Science Fiction Time Travel, there is a rational explanation rooted in science for the character's ability to move through time. In Fantasy Time Travel, the rational explanation is rooted in the supernatural.

Urban: Story featuring a city setting and having strong urban themes such as group identification and the resulting interactions.

Young Adult: A story that is either geared towards young adults or may be of interest to teenage readers. This subgenre frequently involves a child or teenager maturing by accepting responsibility for self-determined goals and discovering strategies to achieve those goals.

Horror Story Types

Alternate World: Generally, any imagined world in science fiction, fantasy, or horror. In horrific worlds, supernatural laws or beings are often assumed, commonly with hostile or terrifying implications.

Ancient Evil Unleashed: The evils may take familiar forms, like vampires undead for centuries, or malevolent ancient gods released from bondage by careless humans, or ancient prophecies wreaking havoc on today's world. The so-called *Cthulhu Mythos* originated by H.P. Lovecraft, in which *Cthulhu* is prominent among a pantheon of ancient evil gods, is a specific variation of this.

Anthology: A collection of short fiction by different authors, usually related in theme or setting.

Apocalyptic Horror: Traditionally, horrors that signal or presage the end of the world, or the world of the characters, and the establishment of a new, possibly very sinister order.

Black Magic: Magic directed toward malevolent ends, as distinct from white magic, which is directed toward benevolent ends. Witchcraft is commonly thought of as a black art. Voodoo consists of mysterious rites and practices including sorcery, magic and conjuration and often has evil goals. Compare Satanism and Curse.

Carnival-Circus Horror: Derived from its setting, especially the freakish world of the sideshow, in which the distorted or horrific is the norm and is sometimes used as a distorting mirror to reveal hidden selves.

Child-in-Peril: The innocence of childhood is often used to heighten the intensity and unpredictability of evil.

Collection: A book of short stories by a single author.

Coming-of-Age: A story in which the growth and development of a young character, typically a teenager, is portrayed, often by showing how obstacles are overcome and maturity achieved. The literary term is *Bildungsroman*, literally an education novel.

Curse: The words said when someone wishes evil or harm on someone or something, such as a witch's or prophet's curse. Compare Black Magic.

Doppelganger: A double or alter ego, popularized in the works of E.T.A. Hoffmann, Edgar Allan Poe, and Robert Louis Stevenson.

Erotic Horror: Some have contended that sexuality and horror are inextricably linked, as in Bram Stoker's *Dracula* and Sheridan Le Fanu's "Carmilla," although others have argued that they are antithetical. Sexuality became increasingly explicit in the 1980s, sometimes verging on the pornographic, as in Bret Easton Ellis' *American Psycho*.

Evil Children: The presumed innocence of a child is replaced with adult-like malevolence and cunning, contradicting the reader's usual expectations.

Fantasy: A narrative describing events the reader believes to be impossible and for which no explanation is offered; magic is often employed.

Femme Fatale: A seductress for whom men abandon careers, families and responsibilities and who feels no pity or compunction in return; a common figure in history and literature.

Gay/Lesbian Fiction: In which the homosexuality of one or more characters is integral to the plot of the story.

Ghost Story: Involces the spirits of the dead, who can be benevolent, as in Charles Dickens, or malevolent, as in the tales of M.R. James.

Gothic Family Chronicle: A story often covering several generations of a family, many of whose members are typically evil, perverted, or loathsome, and in which family violence is common. The family may live in a decaying mansion suggestive of those in eighteenth century Gothic novels.

Haunted House: Literally, a house visited by ghosts, usually with evil intentions in horror fiction, but sometimes the subject of comedy.

Historical: Using history as a backdrop, the author adds fantastic elements to build the story. Historical figures are often portrayed as figures in supernatural dramas, and fantastic explanations are sometimes given for historical events.

Literary: Usually refers to novels not published as horror and sometimes incorporating unconventional narrative techniques. Metafictional narratives take as their subject matter the nature of fiction itself and are often therefore self-referential.

Mystery: A story in which the identity of evildoers is often concealed and suspense therefore heightened. Psychic detective tales are often mysteries.

Nature in Revolt: Tales in which normally docile plants or animals suddenly turn against humankind, sometimes transformed (giant crabs resulting from radioactivity, predatory rats, plagues, blobs that threaten London or Miami, etc.).

Occult: An adjective suggesting fiction based on a mystical or secret doctrine, but sometimes referring to supernatural fiction generally. Implies that there is a reality beyond the perceived world that only adepts can penetrate. Black Magic may or may not be part of an occult world.

Possession: Domination, usually of humans, by evil spirits, demons, aliens, or other agencies in which one's own volition is replaced by an outside force.

Psychological Suspense: Tales often not supernatural in nature in which the psychological exploration and quirks of characters, rather than outside creations, generate suspense and plot.

Reanimated Dead: These can take many forms, such as mummies and zombies (often the result of Voodoo).

Reincarnation: The rebirth of a soul in a new body, such as that of a poet in the body of Archy, the cockroach in Don Marquis's witty tales, although the tone is darker in horror fiction.

Satanism: Suggests worship of evil rather than benevolent gods, the antithesis of conventional theism, whether Christianity or other religions. Evil demons are Satan writ small and usually lack the awful majesty of their parent.

Satire: A tale embodying wit, mockery, or irony to attack ideas or customs judged wrong-headed by the author; uncommon in horror fiction.

Science Fiction: Stories in which supernatural or fantastic elements are absent and some degree of "rational" explanation is present. The science fiction surface of the film *Alien* is disrupted by the horror of the alien monster.

Serial Killer: A multiple murderer, going back to Bluebeard and up to Ed Gein, who inspired Robert Bloch's *Psycho*.

Small Town Horror: The coziness and intimacy of a small community is disrupted by some sort of horrific happening, suggesting an unjustified placidity and complacency on the part of the citizens.

Supernatural Vengeance: Punishment inflicted by God or a godlike creature, whether justly or capriciously; contrast Apocalyptic Horror and Ancient Evil Unleashed.

Time Travel: An uncommon mechanism in horror fiction, standard in science fiction.

Techno-Horror: Suggests a catastrophe with horrific elements resulting from a scientific miscalculation or technological hubris; for example, Victor Frankenstein's unnamed monster or a plague resulting from a laboratory mishap.

Vampire Story: Based on mythical bloodsucking creatures possessing supernatural powers and various forms, both animal and human. The concept can be traced far back in history, long before Bram Stoker's famous novel, *Dracula*.

Werewolf Story: *Were* is Old English for man, suggesting the ancient lineage of a creature that once dominated a world in which witches and sorcerers were equally feared. Sometimes used to refer to a shape shifter in the form of any animal.

Wild Talents: The phrase comes from Charles Fort's writings and usually refers to parapsychological powers such as telepathy, psychokinesis, and precognition, collectively called psychic or psi phenomena.

Witchcraft: Characters either profess to be or are stigmatized as witches or warlocks, and practitioners of magic associated with witchcraft. This can include black magic (see Black Magic) or white magic (e.g. wicca).

Science Fiction Story Types

Adventure: Suggests a novel or short fiction filled with a rapid sequence of incidents but little character development; Space Opera is a specialized form of adventure fiction.

Alternate History: A story dealing with how society might have evolved if a specific historical event had happened differently, e.g. if the South had won the American Civil War.

Alternate Intelligence: Story featuring an entity with a sense of identity the ability to determine its own goals and actions. The natural or manufactured entity results from a synergy, generally unpredictable, of individual elements. This subgenre frequently involves a computer-type intelligence.

Alternate Universe: More accurately, in most cases, alternate history, in which the South won the American Civil War, the Nazis triumphed, etc. The idea is a venerable one in SF.

Anthology: A collection of short fiction, ranging from short stories to novellas, written by different authors.

Arts: Stories incorporating themes related to music, painting, drama, and the arts generally.

Collection: A book of short stories written by a single author.

Contemporary Realism: Stories in which the science fictional elements are part of a muted background and a "mundane" or "realistic" tone predominates.

Cyberpunk: Usually applied to the stories by a group of writers who became prominent in the mid-1980s, such as William Gibson author of *Neuromancer* (1984). The "cyber" is derived from cybernetics, nominally the study of control and communications in machines. These stories also share a downbeat, punk sensibility reminiscent of the hardboiled school of detective fiction writers.

Disaster: A tale recounting some event or events seriously disruptive of the social fabric but not as serious as a holocaust; see Post-Holocaust.

Dystopian: The antonym of utopian, sometimes called anti-utopian, in which traditionally positive utopian themes are treated satirically or ironically and the mood is downbeat or satiric.

End of the World: Such a tale concentrates on the last events following a Disaster but preceding the Post-Holocaust period, although there may be some chronological or thematic overlap.

Espionage Thriller: Analogous to Mystery, in which espionage replaces the narrower world of the private investigator.

Family Saga: Usually refers to any large scale narrative extending over time and involving many related individuals.

Fantasy: A narrative describing events the reader believes to be impossible and for which no scientific or pseudoscientific explanation is offered; magic is usually substituted for scientific laws. Contrast Science Fantasy.

First Contact: Any story about the initial meeting or communication of humans with extraterrestrials or aliens. The term may take its name from the eponymous 1945 story by Murray Leinster.

Future Shock: A journalistic term derived from Alvin Toffler's 1970 book of the same name; refers to the alleged disorientation resulting from rapid technological change.

Gay/Lesbian Fiction: In which the homosexuality of one or more characters is integral to the plot.

Generation Starship: A story in which the time required for interstellar travel encompasses many human generations; assumes that pseudoscientific explanations involving faster-than-light drives are rejected.

Genetic Manipulation: Sometimes called genetic engineering, this assumes that the knowledge exists to shape creatures, human or otherwise, using genetic means, as in *Brave New World* (1932).

Hard Science Fiction: Stories in which the author adheres with varying degrees of rigor to scientific principles believed to be true at the time of writing, principles derived from hard (physical, biological) rather than soft (social) sciences.

Horror: Refers to stories in which interest in the events, the intellectual puzzle characteristic of much SF, is subordinated to a feeling of terror or horror by the reader, which could result from a Disaster, Invasion of Earth, or other causes.

Humor: SF in which humor, from cerebral to slapstick, is prominent. Early SF was sometimes unintentionally humorous; some modern work is deliberately, and sometimes successfully, so. Compare Satire and Parody.

Immortality: Usually includes extreme longevity, resulting from fountains of youth, elixirs, or something with a pseudoscientific basis.

Invasion of Earth: An extremely common theme, often paralleling historical events and reflecting fears of the time. Most invasions are depicted as malign, only occasionally benign.

Literary: Usually refers to novels not published as SF and sometimes incorporating unconventional narrative techniques. Metafictional narratives take as their subject matter the nature of fiction itself and are often therefore self-referential.

Lost Colony: Stories centering around a colony on another world that loses contact with or is abandoned by its parent civilization and the type of society that evolves under those conditions. Conflict usually arises when contact is re-established between the colony and its home world.

Medical: Stories in which medical themes are dominant; compare Genetic Manipulation, a specialized form of medical narrative.

Military: Stories that can range from space wars (compare Space Opera) to more local battles; most such stories tend to glorify military virtues.

Mystery: SF to which traditional mystery/detective structures have been grafted, not always successfully, and in which private eyes go down many mean galaxies; a distant relative of Cyberpunk.

Mystical: Suggesting a body of esoteric knowledge known to few and which can have a transforming effect on those possessing it.

Parody: A narrative that follows the form of the original but usually changes its sense to nonsense, thus making fun of the original or its ideas. Compare Humor.

Political: Narratives in which themes of power are paramount, whether on a local or galactic scale.

Post-Disaster: Story set in a much degraded environment, frequently involving a reduction in population and the resulting loss of access to processes, resources, technology, etc.

Post-Holocaust: The events following a world-wide disaster, often the result of human folly rather than natural events (collision with a meteor, etc.).

Post-Nuclear Holocaust: The events following a world-wide nuclear disaster.

Psychic Powers: Parapsychological or paranormal powers believed by some to be credible, e.g., telepathy, telekinesis, etc.

Robot Fiction: From the Jewish Golem to the traditional clanking bucket of bolts to the human-like android, robots in various guises have been among us for centuries. The term comes from Karel Capek's play, *R.U.R.*, which stands for Rossum's Universal Robots. Robots are often surrogates for humans and may be treated seriously or comically.

Romance: A somewhat elastic term sometimes used to distinguish it from the traditional (realistic, naturalistic) novel but more commonly referring to any narrative in which the world or characters are somewhat idealized. Before the phrase science fiction was introduced in the early 1930s, scientific romance was the most common term.

Satire: With an ironic and/or detached point of view, the author is writing on a particular theme (such as religion) using elements of the fantastic to exaggerate and explore the theme.

Science Fantasy: A somewhat vague term in which there are "rational" elements from SF and "magical" or "fanciful" elements from fantasy, which hopefully cohere in a plausible story. Many Adventures are Science Fantasy.

Space Colony: A permanent space station, usually orbiting Earth but generally located in deep space or near other planets or stars.

Space Opera: Intergalactic adventures; westerns in space; a specialized form of Adventure.

TechnoThriller: Stories in which a technological development, such as an invention, is linked to a series of suspenseful ("thrilling") events.

Theological: Stories in which religion or religious belief plays an important role.

Time Travel: An ancient tradition in SF, whether the traveller goes forward or backward, and replete with paradoxes.

UFO: Unidentified Flying Objects literally, although sometimes used more generally to refer to any object of mysterious origin or intent. A cliche today in First Contact and Invasion of Earth stories.

Utopian: A large, often influential, story type that takes its name from Thomas More's 1516 book *Utopia*. Usually refers to a society considered "better" by the author, even if not perfect. Aldous Huxley's *Island* (1962) is a utopia, whereas his more famous *Brave New World* (1932) is a dark twin, a dystopia.

Young Adult: A story that is either geared towards young adults or may be of interest to teenage readers, this subgenre involves a child or teenager testing his or her skills against adversity to achieve a greater degree of maturity and self-awareness.

Award Winners

World Fantasy Award

For this award, fantasy is defined to include both fantasy and horror fiction. Reader ballots generate a list of candidates, and a panel of judges selects additional candidates and the winners, which are announced at the World Fantasy Convention held over Halloween weekend each year.

Best Novel

1989 - *Koko* by Peter Straub
Runners-up: *The Last Coin* by James P. Blaylock; *Sleeping in Flame* by Jonathan Carroll; *Fade* by Robert Cormier; *The Silence of the Lambs* by Thomas Harris; and *The Drive-In* by Joe R. Lansdale

1990 - *Lyonesse: Madouc* by Jack Vance
Runners-up: *A Child Across the Sky* by Jonathan Carroll; *In a Dark Dream* by Charles L. Grant; *The Stress of Her Regard* by Tim Powers; *Carrion Comfort* by Dan Simmons; *Soldier of Arete* by Gene Wolfe

1991 - *Only Begotten Daughter* by James Morrow
Runners-up: *Tigana* by Guy Gavriel Kay; *Thomas the Rhymer* by Ellen Kushner; *Good Omens* by Terry Pratchett and Neil Gaiman; *Mary Reilly* by Valerie Martin

1992 - *Boy's Life* by Robert R. McCammon
Runners-up: *Hunting the Ghost Dancer* by A.A. Attanasio; *The Paper Grail* by James P. Blaylock; *Bone Dance* by Emma Bull; *Outside the Dog Museum* by Jonathan Carroll; *The Little Country* by Charles de Lint

1993 - *Last Call* by Tim Powers
Runners-up: *Anno Dracula* by Kim Newman; *Was* by Geoff Ryman; *Photographing Fairies* by Steve Szilagyi; *Briar Rose* by Jane Yolen

1994 - *Glimpses* by Lewis Shiner
Runners-up: *The Innkeeper's Song* by Peter S. Beagle; *Drawing Blood* by Poppy Z. Brite; *Skin* by Kathe Koja; *The Throat* by Peter Straub; *The Iron Dragon's Daughter* by Michael Swanwick; *Lord of the Two Lands* by Judith Tarr

1995 - *Towing Jehovah* by James Morrow
Runners-up: *Brittle Innings* by Michael Bishop; *From the Teeth of Angels* by Jonathan Carroll; *Love and Sleep* by John Crowley; *Waking the Moon* by Elizabeth Hand; *The Circus of the Earth and the Air* by Brooke Stevens

1996 - *The Prestige* by Christopher Priest
Runners-up: *All the Bells on Earth* by James P. Blaylock; *Red Earth, Pouring Rain* by Vikram Chandra; *The Silent Strength of Stones* by Nina Kiriki Hoffman; *Requiem* by Graham Joyce; *Expiration Date* by Tim Powers

Best Collection

1989 - *Storeys From the Old Hotel* by Gene Wolfe
Runners-up: *Cabal* by Clive Barker; *Charles*

Beaumont: Selected Stories by Charles Beaumont; *The Blood Kiss* by Dennis Etchison; *Angry Candy* by Harlan Ellison; *The Knight and Knave of Swords* by Fritz Leiber

1990 - *Richard Matheson: Collected Stories* by Richard Matheson

Runners-up: *Novelty* by John Crowley; *Harlan Ellison's Watching* by Harlan Ellison; *By Bizarre Hands* by Joe R. Lansdale; *Blue World and Other Stories* by Robert R. McCammon

1991 - *The Start of the End of It All and Other Stories* by Carol Emshwiller

Runners-up: *The Brains of Rats* by Michael Blumlein; *The Leiber Chronicles* by Fritz Leiber; *Prayers to Broken Stones* by Dan Simmons; *Houses Without Doors* by Peter Straub

1992 - *The Ends of the Earth* by Lucius Shephard

Runners-up: *More Shapes than One* by Fred Chappell; *The Bone Forest* by Robert Holdstock; *Lafferty in Orbit* by R.A. Lafferty; *Grimscribe: His Lives and Works* by Thomas Ligotti; *Night of the Cooters: More Neat Stories* by Howard Waldrop

1993 - *The Sons of Noah and Other Stories* by Jack Cady

Runners-up: *Bear's Fantasies* by Greg Bear; *Lord Kelvin's Machine* by James P. Blaylock; *Spiritwalk* by Charles de Lint; *Meeting in Infinity* by John Kessel; *Mr. Fox and Other Feral Tales* by Norman Partridge

1994 - *Alone with the Horrors* by Ramsey Campbell

Runners-up: *Antiquities* by John Crowley; *Dreams Underfoot* by Charles de Lint; *Angels & Visitations: A Miscellany* by Neil Gaiman; *Hogfoot Right and Bird-Hands* by Garry Kilworth; *Under the Crust* by Terry Lamsley; *Transients and Other Disquieting Stories* by Darrell Schweitzer

1995 - *The Calvin Coolidge Home for Dead Comedians* and *A Conflagration Artist* by Bradley Denton

Runners-up: *The Early Fears* by Robert Bloch; *Travelers in Magic* by Lisa Goldstein; *The Earth Wire & Other Stories* by Joel Lane; *Haunted: Tales of the Grotesque* by Joyce Carol Oates

1996 - *Seven Tales and a Fable* by Gwyneth Jones

Runners-up: *The Secret of This Book* by Brian Aldiss; *The Panic Hand* by Jonathan Carroll; *Death Stalks the Night* by Hugh B. Cave; *The Ivory and the Horn* by Charles de Lint

Best Anthology

1989 - *The Year's Best Fantasy: First Annual Collection*, edited by Ellen Datlow and Terri Windling

Runners-up: *Night Visions 6*, edited anonymously;

Silver Scream, edited by David Schow; *Prime Evil*, edited by Douglas Winter

1990 - *The Year's Best Fantasy: Second Annual Collection*, edited by Ellen Datlow and Terri Windling

Runners-up: *Blood Is Not Enough*, edited by Ellen Datlow; *Razored Saddles*, edited by Joe R. Lansdale and Pat LoBrutto; *Book of the Dead*, edited by John Skipp and Craig Spector

1991 - *Best New Horror*, edited by Stephen Jones and Ramsey Campbell

Runners-up: *The Walls of Fear*, edited by Kathryn Cramer; *Alien Sex*, edited by Ellen Datlow; *The Year's Best Fantasy & Horror: 3rd Annual Collection*, edited by Ellen Datlow and Terri Windling; *Borderlands*, edited by Thomas F. Monteleone; *Dark Voices 2*, edited by David Sutton and Stephen Jones

1992 - *The Year's Best Fantasy & Horror: Fourth Annual Collection*, edited by Ellen Datlow and Terri Windling

Runners-up: *A Whisper of Blood*, edited by Ellen Datlow; *Famous Fantastic Mysteries*, edited by Stefan Dziemianowicz, Martin H. Greenberg, and Robert Weinberg; *Final Shadows*, edited by Charles L. Grant; *After the King*, edited by Martin H. Greenberg; *When the Music's Over*, edited by Lewis Shiner

1993 - *Metahorror*, edited by Dennis Etchison

Runners-up: *Narrow Houses*, edited by Peter Crowther; *Grails: Quests, Visitations, and Other Occurrences*, edited by Richard Gilliam, Martin H. Greenberg, and Edward E. Kramer; *Northern Frights*, edited by Don Hutchinson; *Freak Show*, edited by F. Paul Wilson

1994 - *Full Spectrum 4*, edited by Lou Aronica, Amy Stout, and Betsy Mitchell

Runners-up: *Snow White, Blood Red*, edited by Ellen Datlow and Terri Windling; *The Year's Best Fantasy and Horror #6*, edited by Ellen Datlow and Terri Windling; *Christmas Forever*, edited by David G. Hartwell; *Sinestre*, edited by George Hatch; *The Oxford Book of Modern Fairy Tales*, edited by Alison Lurie

1995 - *Little Deaths*, edited by Ellen Datlow

Runners-up: *Love in Vein*, edited by Poppy Z. Brite and Martin H. Greenberg; *Black Thorn, White Rose*, edited by Ellen Datlow and Terri Windling; *Shadows over Innsmouth*, edited by Stephen Jones

1996 - *The Penguin Book of Modern Fantasy by Women*, edited by A. Susan Williams and Richard Glyn Jones

Runners-up: *Dark Love*, edited by Nancy A. Collins,

Edward E. Kramer, and Martin H. Greenberg; *Dark Terrors*, edited by Stephen Jones and David Sutton; *She's Fantastical*, edited by Lucy Sussex and Judith Buckrich; *High Fantastic*, edited by Steve Rasnic Tem

Life Achievement Award
1989 - Evangeline Walton
1990 - R.A. Lafferty
1991 - Ray Russell
1992 - Edd Cartier
1993 - Harlan Ellison
1994 - Jack Williamson
1995 - Ursula K. Le Guin
1996 - Gene Wolfe

Mythopoeic Society Fantasy Award
The Mythopoeic Awards are chosen each year by committees composed of volunteer Mythopoeic Society members and are presented at Mythcon. The award is a statuette of a seated lion, after Aslan from the Chronicles of Narnia. Since 1992, fantasy awards have been given in two categories: adult and children's literature.

Fantasy Award
1989 - *Unicorn Mountain* by Michael Bishop
1990 - *The Stress of Her Regard* by Tim Powers
1991 - *Thomas the Rhymer* by Ellen Kushner

Adult Fantasy Award
1992 - *A Woman of the Iron People* by Eleanor Arnason
1993 - *Briar Rose* by Jane Yolen
1994 - *The Porcelain Dove* by Delia Sherman
1995 - *Something Rich and Strange* by Patricia A. McKillip
1996 - *Waking the Moon* by Elizabeth Hand

Children's Fantasy Award
1992 - *Haroun and the Sea of Stories* by Salman Rushdie
1993 - *Knight's Wyrd* by Debra Doyle and James D. Macdonald
1994 - *The Kingdom of Kevin Malone* by Suzy McKee Charnas
1995 - *Owl in Love* by Patrice Kindl
1996 - *The Crown of Dalemark* by Diana Wynne Jones

Bram Stoker Award
Named after the author of *Dracula*, this award is voted upon by active members of the Horror Writers Association at an annual summer conference. See also the World Fantasy Awards above.

Best Novel
1989 - *The Silence of the Lambs* by Thomas Harris
Runners-up: *Stinger* by Robert R. McCammon; *Black Wind* by F. Paul Wilson; *The Drive-In* by Joe R. Lansdale; *Queen of the Damned* by Anne Rice; *Flesh*

by Richard Laymon.

1990 - *Carrion Comfort* by Dan Simmons
Runners-up: *Geek Love* by Katherine Dunn; *In a Dark Dream* by Charles L. Grant; *Midnight* by Dean R. Koontz; *The Wolf's Hour* by Robert R. McCammon

1991 - *Mine* by Robert R. McCammon
Runners-up: *Funland* by Richard Layman; *Reign* by Chet Williamson; *Savage Season* by Joe R. Lansdale

1992 - *Boy's Life* by Robert R. McCammon
Runners-up: *The M.D.* by Thomas M. Disch; *Needful Things* by Stephen King; *Dark Tower III: The Waste Lands* by Stephen King; *Summer of Night* by Dan Simmons

1993 - *Blood of the Lamb* by Thomas F. Monteleone
Runners-up: *Homecoming* by Matthew Costello; *Deathgrip* by Brian Hodge; *Hideaway* by Dean Koontz; *Children of the Night* by Dan Simmons

1994 - *The Throat* by Peter Straub
Runners-up: *Anno Dracula* by Kim Newman; *Blackburn* by Bradley Denton; *Drawing Blood* by Poppy Z. Brite; *The Summoning* by Bentley Little

1995 - *Dead in the Water* by Nancy Holder
Runners-up: *The Alienist* by Caleb Carr; *From the Teeth of Angels* by Jonathan Carroll; *Insomnia* by Stephen King; *The Butcher Boy* by Patrick McCabe

1996 - *Zombie* by Joyce Carol Oates
Runners-Up: *Widow* by Billie Sue Mosiman; *deadrush* by Yvonne Navarro; *Bone Music* by Alan Rodgers

1997 - *The Green Mile* by Stephen King
Runners-up: *Exquisite Corpse* by Poppy Z. Brite; *Crota* by Owl Goingback; *The Hellfire Club* by Peter Straub

Best First Novel
1989 - *The Suiting* by Kelley Wilde
1990 - *Sunglasses After Dark* by Nancy A. Collins
1991 - *The Revelation* by Bentley Little
1992 - *The Cipher* by Kathe Koja and *Prodigal* by Melanie Tem
1993 - *Sineater* by Elizabeth Massie
1994 - *The Thread That Binds the Bones* by Nina Kiriki Hoffman
1995 - *Grave Markings* by Michael Arnzen
1996 - *The Safety of Unknown Cities* by Lucy Taylor
1997 - *Crota* by Owl Goingback

Best Collection
1989 - *Charles Beaumont: Selected Stories* by Charles Beaumont

1990 - *Richard Matheson: Collected Stories* by Richard Matheson
Runners-up: *Blue World and Other Stories* by Robert R. McCammon; *By Bizarre Hands* by Joe R.

Lansdale; *Patterns* by Pat Cadigan; *Soft and Others* by F. Paul Wilson

1991 - *Four Past Midnight* by Stephen King
Runners-up: *Houses Without Doors* by Peter Straub; *Prayers to Broken Stones* by Dan Simmons; *The Brains of Rats* by Michael Blumlein

1992 - *Prayers to Broken Stones* by Dan Simmons
Runners-up: *Waking Nightmares* by Ramsey Campbell; *Sexpunks & Savage Sagas* by Richard Sutphen; *The Naked Flesh of Feeling* by J.N. Williamson

1993 - *Mr. Fox and Other Feral Tales* by Norman Partridge
Runners-up: *Nightmare Flower* by Elizabeth Engstrom; *Fantastic Tales* by I.U. Tarchetti

1994 - *Alone with the Horrors* by Ramsey Campbell
Runners-up: *Close to the Bone* by Lucy Taylor; *A Good, Secret Place* by Richard Laymon; *Lovedeath* by Dan Simmons; *Nightmares & Dreamscapes* by Stephen King

1995 - *The Early Fears* by Robert Bloch
Runners-up: *Writer of the Purple Rage* by Joe R. Lansdale; *The Flesh Artist* by Lucy Taylor; *Born Bad* by Andrew Vachss

1996 - *The Panic Hand* by Jonathan Carroll
Runners-up: *Cages* by Ed Gorman; *The Black Carousel* by Charles L. Grant; *Strange Highways* by Dean R. Koontz

1997 - *The Nightmare Factory* by Thomas Ligotti
Runners-up: *The Convulsion Factory* by Brian Hodge; *Shadow Dreams* by Elizabeth Massie; *With Wounds Still Wet* by Wayne Allen Sallee; *The Pavilion of Frozen Women* by S.P. Somtow

Lifetime Achievement Award
1989 - Ray Bradbury; Ronald Chetwynd-Hayes
1990 - Robert Bloch
1991 - Hugh B. Cave; Richard Matheson
1992 - Gahan Wilson
1993 - Ray Russell
1994 - Joyce Carol Oates
1995 - Christopher Lee
1996 - Harlan Ellison
1997 - Ira Levin; Forrest J. Ackerman

Hugo Award
The Hugos, named for Hugo Gernsback, founding editor of *Amazing Stories*, are given at the world SF conventions (worldcons) held over Labor Day each year and are chosen by the votes of those attending or supporting the convention.

Best Novel
1989 - *Cyteen* by C.J. Cherryh
Runners-up: *Red Prophet* by Orson Scott Card; *Falling Free* by Lois McMaster Bujold; *Islands in the Net* by Bruce Sterling; *Mona Lisa Overdrive* by William Gibson

1990 - *Hyperion* by Dan Simmons
Runners-up: *The Boat of a Million Years* by Poul Anderson; *Prentice Alvin* by Orson Scott Card; *A Fire in the Sun* by George Alec Effinger; *Grass* by Sheri S. Tepper

1991 - *The Vor Game* by Lois McMaster Bujold
Runners-up: *Earth* by David Brin; *The Fall of Hyperion* by Dan Simmons; *The Quiet Pools* by M.P. Kube-McDowell; and *Queen of Angels* by Greg Bear

1992 - *Barrayar* by Lois McMaster Bujold
Runners-up: *Bone Dance* by Emma Bull; *All the Weyrs of Pern* by Anne McCaffrey; *The Summer Queen* by Joan Vinge; *Xenocide* by Orson Scott Card; *Stations of the Tide* by Michael Swanwick

1993 - *A Fire upon the Deep* by Vernor Vinge and *Doomsday Book* by Connie Willis
Runners-up: *Red Mars* by Kim Stanley Robinson; *China Mountain Zhang* by Maureen F. McHugh; *Steel Beach* by John Varley

1994 - *Green Mars* by Kim Stanley Robinson
Runners-up: *Moving Mars* by Greg Bear; *Glory Season* by David Brin; *Virtual Light* by William Gibson; *Beggars in Spain* by Nancy Kress

1995 - *Mirror Dance* by Lois McMaster Bujold
Runners-up: *Mother of Storms* by John Barnes; *Brittle Innings* by Michael Bishop; *Beggars and Choosers* by Nancy Kress; *Towing Jehovah* by James Morrow

1996 - *The Diamond Age* by Neal Stephenson
Runners-up: *The Time Ships* by Stephen Baxter; *Brightness Reef* by David Brin; *The Terminal Experiment* by Robert J. Sawyer; *Remake* by Connie Willis

John W. Campbell Award (Best New Writer)
1989 - Michaela Roessner
1990 - Kristine Kathryn Rusch
1991 - Julia Ecklar
1992 - Ted Chiang
1993 - Laura Resnick
1994 - Amy Thomson
1995 - Jeff Noon
1996 - David Feintuch

Nebula Award

Given by the Science Fiction and Fantasy Writers of America, an organization of about 1,300 members, of whom about a third vote. The awards, in four fiction categories of varying length, are announced several months before the Hugos and probably influence the voting for them. Because of the Nebula rules, some candidates are published prior to the immediately preceding year.

Best Novel

1989 - *The Healer's War* by Elizabeth Ann Scarborough
Runners-up: *The Boat of a Million Years* by Poul Anderson; *Prentice Alvin* by Orson Scott Card; *Good News From Outer Space* by John Kessel; *Ivory* by Mike Resnick; *Sister Light, Sister Dark* by Jane Yolen

1990 - *Tehanu: The Last Book of Earthsea* by Ursula K. Le Guin
Runners-up: *Mary Reilly* by Valerie Martin; *Only Begotten Daughter* by James Morrow; *The Fall of Hyperion* by Dan Simmons; *Redshift Rendezvous* by John E. Stith; *White Jenna* by Jane Yolen

1991 - *Stations of the Tide* by Michael Swanwick
Runners-up: *Orbital Resonance* by John Barnes; *Barrayar* by Lois McMaster Bujold; *Bone Dance* by Emma Bull; *The Difference Engine* by William Gibson and Bruce Sterling

1992 - *Doomsday Book* by Connie Willis
Runners-up: *A Million Open Doors* by John Barnes; *Sarah Canary* by Karen Joy Fowler; *China Mountain Zhang* by Maureen McHugh; *A Fire Upon the Deep* by Vernor Vinge; *Briar Rose* by Jane Yolen

1993 - *Red Mars* by Kim Stanley Robinson
Runners-up: *Assemblers of Infinity* by Kevin J. Anderson and Doug Beason; *Hard Landing* by A.J. Budrys; *Beggars in Spain* by Nancy Kress; *Nightside the Long Sun* by Gene Wolfe

1994 - *Moving Mars* by Greg Bear
Runners-up: *Parable of the Sower* by Octavia Butler; *Gun, with Occasional Music* by Jonathan Lethem; *Temporary Agency* by Rachel Pollack; *Green Mars* by Kim Stanley Robinson; *A Night in the Lonesome October* by Roger Zelazny

1995 - *The Terminal Experiment* by Robert J. Sawyer
Runners-up: *Mother of Storms* by John Barnes; *Beggars and Choosers* by Nancy Kress; *Celestis* by Paul Park; *Metropolitan* by Walter Jon Williams; *Calde of the Long Sun* by Gene Wolfe

1996 - *Slow River* by Nicola Griffith
Runners-up: *The Silent Strength of Stones* by Nina Kiriki Hoffman; *Winter Rose* by Patricia McKillip; *Expiration Date* by Tim Powers; *The Diamond Age* by Neal Stephenson; *Starplex* by Robert J. Sawyer

Grand Master

1990 - Lester del Ray
1992 - Frederik Pohl
1994 - Damon Knight
1995 - A.E. Van Vogt
1996 - Jack Vance

Arthur C. Clarke Award

The Arthur C. Clarke Award honors the best British science fiction novel from the previous year.

Best Novel

1989 - *Unquenchable Fire* by Rachel Pollack
1990 - *The Child Garden* by Geoff Ryman
1991 - *Take Back Plenty* by Colin Greenland
1992 - *Synners* by Pat Cadigan
1993 - *Body of Glass* by Marge Piercy (U.S. title: *He, She and It*)
1994 - *Vurt* by Jeff Noon
1995 - *Fools* by Pat Cadigan

WHAT FANTASTIC FICTION

DO I READ NEXT?

A Reader's Guide to
Recent Fantasy,
Horror and
Science Fiction

Fantastic Fiction Titles

PATRICIA AAKHUS

The Voyage of Mael Duin's Curragh

(Santa Cruz: Storyline Press, 1989)

Story type: Fantasy (Legend)
Major character(s): Mael Duin, Outcast, Wanderer
Time period(s): Indeterminate
Locale(s): At Sea (Heading for Viking territory)

Summary: Mael Duin sets out in a curragh on a sea quest to avenge the murder of his father. Caught in a storm, the curragh drifts from the shore, landing on strange and magical islands. On one Mael Duin is captivated by the witch, Epona. Story explores the Celtic legend from *The Book of the Dun Cow*.

Other books you might like:
Kenneth C. Flint, *Isle of Destiny*,
R.A. MacAvoy, *The Book of Kells*, 1989
Robin McKinley, *The Outlaws of Sherwood*, 1989
Mickey Zucker Reichert, *Dragonrank Master*, 1989
Mickey Zucker Reichert, *Godslayer*, 1987
    Book 1-The Bifrost Guardians
Gene Wolfe, *Soldier of Arete*, 1989

DONALD AAMODT

A Name to Conjure With

(New York: Avon, 1989)

Story type: Fantasy (Light Fantasy)
Series: Sandy MacGregor
Major character(s): Sandy MacGregor, Hero, Wizard; Zhadnoboth, Sorcerer
Time period(s): 1980s
Locale(s): Zarathandra, Alternate Universe

Summary: Sandy MacGregor is summoned, by way of an elevator shaft turned portal, to the world of Zarathandra, in a parallel universe. Here he is ordered by the Veiled Goddess to accompany the inept and greedy sorcerer Zhadnoboth and two revenge-seeking berserkers on a quest to loot the mountain stronghold of her nemesis, the evil god Kels Zalkir. In his quest, Sandy discovers that his ''name'' in this world commands unknown magical and often times uncontrollable powers.

Other books you might like:
Mayer Alan Brenner, *Catastrophe's Spell*, 1989
Brad Strickland, *Nul's Quest*, 1989

DONALD AAMODT

A Troubling Along the Border

(New York: Avon, 1991)

Story type: Fantasy (Light Fantasy; Adventure)
Series: Sandy MacGregor
Major character(s): Sandy MacGregor, Hero (reluctant), Wizard; Zhadnoboth, Sorcerer
Time period(s): Indeterminate
Locale(s): Zarathandra, Alternate Universe

Summary: Stuck on the planet Zarathandra, Sandy MacGregor remains the unwilling tool of the goddess of love who now sends him to a realm between worlds to battle an ancient demon.

Other books you might like:
Isaac Asimov, *The Gods Themselves*, 1972
Mayer Alan Brenner, *Catastrophe's Spell*, 1989
Jo Clayton, *Wild Magic*, 1991
Pamela Dean, *The Hidden Land*, 1986
Pamela Dean, *The Secret Country*, 1985
Pamela Dean, *The Whim of the Dragon*, 1989
David Eddings, *The Sapphire Rose*, 1991
P.C. Hodgell, *Dark of the Moon*, 1985
P.C. Hodgell, *God Stalk*, 1982
Brad Strickland, *Nul's Quest*, 1989

4

SHALE AARON

Virtual Death

(New York: HarperPrism, 1995)

Story type: Science Fiction (Satire; Arts)
Major character(s): Lydia Melmoth, Artist (death artist), Fugitive; Frankly Adams, Artist (depressionist), Fugitive; Stamen Melmoth, Government Official, Fugitive
Time period(s): 21st Century
Locale(s): New York, New York; Philadelphia, Pennsylvania

Summary: When authorities identify Lydia's mother as a ''Banjo'' terrorist, Lydia goes underground to escape arrest. Lydia soon discovers that everyone around her selfishly wants her to resume her career as the greatest death artist in the world. First novel.

Other books you might like:
Jonathan Carroll, *From the Teeth of Angels*, 1994
William Gibson, *Neuromancer*, 1984
Parke Godwin, *Waiting for the Galactic Bus*, 1988
Shariann Lewitt, *Memento Mori*, 1995
John Varley, *Steel Beach*, 1992

5

DAFYDD AB HUGH

Arthur War Lord

(New York: AvoNova, 1994)

Story type: Fantasy (Time Travel; Legend)
Series: Arthur War Lord
Major character(s): Peter Smythe, Time Traveller, Military Personnel (major); Cors Cant Ewin, Minstrel (bard); Anlawdd, Royalty (princess), Criminal (assassin)
Time period(s): 1990s; 5th century
Locale(s): Caer Camlann Castle, England

Summary: Sent to investigate possible IRA involvement in a top-secret British military research project, Peter Smythe wakes one night and discovers that one of the scientists, using the project's time machine to send her mind to the 5th century A.D., has changed the present through her actions in the past. Smythe follows, hoping to undo the damage, and finds his consciousness inside the mind of Lancelot at King Arthur's court. Now he must figure out which of the other minds harbors the IRA agent, and whether she intends to kill King Arthur or save him.

Other books you might like:
Poul Anderson, *The Shield of Time*, 1990
Gordon R. Dickson, *The Dragon and the George*, 1976
Phyllis Eisenstein, *Shadow of Earth*, 1979
Katherine Kurtz, *The Lodge of the Lynx*, 1992
    Deborah Turner Harris, co-author
Robert Silverberg, *Letters From Atlantis*, 1990

6

DAFYDD AB HUGH

Balance of Power

(New York: Pocket, 1995)

Story type: Science Fiction (Space Opera; Political)
Series: Star Trek: The Next Generation
Major character(s): Wesley Crusher, Student—College, Military Personnel; Jean-Luc Picard, Spaceship Captain, Military Personnel; Geordi La Forge, Engineer, Military Personnel
Time period(s): 24th century
Locale(s): *U.S.S. Enterprise*, Spaceship; San Francisco, California; United Federation of Planets, Interstellar Empire/Federation

Summary: When a Federation scientist dies and his inventions go up for auction, various members of the *Enterprise* crew receive authorization to bid on them, particularly a photonic pulse cannon. Meanwhile, at Starfleet Academy, Wesley Crusher's best friend has found a way to counterfeit gold-pressed latinum. When Wesley tries to stop the theft of the counterfeiting device, a Ferengi outlaw kidnaps him as well. At the auction the Ferengi will outbid everyone with their counterfeit latinum, unless Wesley can figure out a way to escape his captors, keep the cannon out of Cardassian hands, and avoid expulsion from the Academy as AWOL.

Other books you might like:
Robert Asprin, *Phule's Paradise*, 1992
Diane Carey, *Battlestations!*, 1986
Carolyn Clowes, *The Pandora Principle*, 1990
John M. Ford, *How Much for Just the Planet?*, 1987
William R. Thompson, *Debtors' Planet*, 1994

7

DAFYDD AB HUGH

Fallen Heroes

(New York: Pocket, 1994)

Story type: Science Fiction (Space Opera; Time Travel)
Series: Star Trek: Deep Space Nine
Major character(s): Benjamin Sisko, Leader, Military Personnel; Quark, Alien (Ferengi), Saloon Keeper/Owner; Odo, Alien (shapeshifter), Security Officer
Time period(s): 24th century
Locale(s): Deep Space Nine, Space Station (Bajoran)

Summary: When warriors determined to save a comrade attack Deep Space Nine, Benjamin Sisko and his crew struggle to save the station and its personnel. However, Quark and Odo, thrown three days forward in time by a Gamma Quadrant device, find a deserted Deep Space Nine and must unravel the invasion's cause and discover a way to return to the past and save the station.

Other books you might like:
Esther Friesner, *Warchild*, 1994
K.W. Jeter, *Bloodletter*, 1993
Sandy Schofield, *The Big Game*, 1993
Lois Tilton, *Betrayal*, 1994

John Vornholt, *Antimatter*, 1994

8
DAFYDD AB HUGH

The Final Fury
(New York: Pocket, 1996)

Story type: Science Fiction (Space Opera)
Series: Star Trek: Voyager
Major character(s): Kathryn Janeway, Spaceship Captain, Space Explorer; B'Elanna Torres, Engineer, Alien (half-Klingon); Neelix, Alien (Talaxian), Cook
Time period(s): 24th century
Locale(s): *U.S.S. Voyager*, Spaceship; Planet—Imaginary; Delta Quadrant, Outer Space

Summary: *Voyager*'s crew intercepts a Starfleet distress call in the Delta quadrant. The signal leads them to a nightmarish planet filled with demonic-looking aliens and a Federation pilot held captive on it. Captain Janeway and her Away Team free the pilot, but must determine how they can stop an invasion force of 27 billion preparing to mount an assault against the Alpha Quadrant. Concludes the four-part Invasion! Series which spans all four Star Trek television series.

Other books you might like:
James Blish, *Cities in Flight*, 1970
Diane Carey, *First Strike*, 1996
Alan Dean Foster, *Aliens*, 1986
L.A. Graf, *Time's Enemy*, 1996
Barbara Paul, *The Three-Minute Universe*, 1988
Dean Wesley Smith, *The Soldiers of Fear*, 1996
    Kristine Kathryn Rusch, co-author

9
DAFYDD AB HUGH

Warriorwards
(New York: Baen, 1990)

Story type: Fantasy (Magic Conflict)
Series: Jiana
Major character(s): Jiana, Warrior; Radience, Slave; Toq, Mythical Creature (Boy-God)
Time period(s): Indeterminate
Locale(s): Bay Bay, Alternate Earth

Summary: Jiana, an unemployed warrior adept, wants to free the enslaved Radience. Unfortunately, slaves can become free only by freeing themselves, so Jiana must become a slave to set an example for Radience. Jiana is hampered by interference from her alter egos, the boy-god Toq, and the memories she continually must suppress.

Other books you might like:
C.J. Cherryh, *Wizard Spawn*, 1989
    Nancy Asire, co-author
C.J. Cherryh, *The Paladin*, 1988
Elizabeth Moon, *Sheepfarmer's Daughter*, 1988
Kate Wilhelm, *Cambio Bay*, 1990
Gene Wolfe, *Soldier of Arete*, 1989
Gene Wolfe, *Soldier of the Mist*, 1986

10
LYNN ABBEY

Beneath the Web
(New York: Ace, 1994)

Story type: Fantasy (Magic Conflict; Romance)
Major character(s): Berika Ingoldesdaughter, Shepherd, Sorceress; Rinchen "Wolf" sorRodion, Royalty (prince); Driskolt "Dart" sorMeklan, Nobleman
Time period(s): Indeterminate
Locale(s): Walensor, Fictional Country; Eyerlon, Fictional City

Summary: Now the mistress of a nobleman, Berika treads a precarious path among the factions in Eyerlon. When enemies attack the network of power, the Web, Berika must choose her allies with care if she hopes to save Walensor. Sequel to *The Wooden Sword*.

Other books you might like:
C.J. Cherryh, *Angel with the Sword*, 1985
Phyllis Eisenstein, *In the Red Lord's Reach*, 1989
Simon R. Green, *Blue Moon Rising*, 1991
Barbara Hambly, *Dog Wizard*, 1993
Patricia C. Wrede, *Shadow Magic*, 1982

11
LYNN ABBEY

The Brazen Gambit
(Lake Geneva, Wisconsin: TSR, 1994)

Story type: Fantasy (Political; Adventure)
Series: Dark Sun: Chronicles of Athas
Major character(s): Pavek of Urik, Religious (templar), Adventurer
Time period(s): Indeterminate
Locale(s): Athas, Planet—Imaginary

Summary: After discovering a plot, Pavek flees the city of Urik for the desert lest he die at the hands of people he formerly trusted. Game tie-in and first of a series.

Other books you might like:
Troy Denning, *The Crimson Legion*, 1992
Troy Denning, *The Verdant Passage*, 1991
Simon Hawke, *The Outcast*, 1993
Simon Hawke, *The Seeker*, 1994
Ryan Hughes, *The Darkness Before the Dawn*, 1995

12
LYNN ABBEY
ROBERT ASPRIN, Co-Author

Catwoman
(New York: Warner, 1992)

Story type: Science Fiction (Adventure)
Series: Batman
Major character(s): Selena "Catwoman" Kyle, Criminal, Heroine; Bruce "Batman" Wayne, Hero, Detective—Amateur; Eddie "Tiger" Lobb, Criminal

Time period(s): 1990s
Locale(s): Gotham City (New York City)

Summary: Catwoman appeals to the Wilderness Warriors for assistance in dealing with Eddie Lobb, an unscrupulous collector of tiger pelts. As she tries to bring Lobb to justice, Catwoman crosses paths with Batman, who is following the trail of illegal arms sales to members of the former Soviet Union.

Other books you might like:
Craig Shaw Gardner, *Batman*, 1989
Craig Shaw Gardner, *The Batman Murders*, 1990
Craig Shaw Gardner, *Batman Returns*, 1992
Martin H. Greenberg, *The Further Adventures of Batman*, 1989
    editor
Martin H. Greenberg, *The Further Adventures of Batman 2: Featuring the Penguin*, 1992
    editor
Martin H. Greenberg, *The Further Adventures of the Joker*, 1990
    editor
Simon Hawke, *Batman: To Stalk a Specter*, 1991
Joe R. Lansdale, *Batman: Captured by the Engines*, 1991

13

LYNN ABBEY

Cinnabar Shadows

(Lake Geneva, Wisconsin: TSR, 1995)

Story type: Fantasy (Magic Conflict)
Series: Dark Sun: Chronicles of Athas
Major character(s): Kakzim, Religious (brother), Mythical Creature (halfling); Mahtra, Genetically Altered Being; Pavek of Urik, Religious, Adventurer
Time period(s): Indeterminate
Locale(s): Athas, Planet—Imaginary

Summary: The insane Brother Kakzim wants to fulfill the Black Tree brethren's goals by destroying the city of Urik. The first steps of his most recent plan leave Mahtra homeless and alone, while vengeance and greed may destroy everything.

Other books you might like:
M.A.R. Barker, *Man of Gold*, 1984
Steven Brust, *Jhereg*, 1983
Glen Cook, *The Black Company*, 1984
Anne Logston, *Shadow*, 1991
Julian May, *The Many-Colored Land*, 1981

14

LYNN ABBEY

The Forge of Virtue

(New York: Popular Library Questar, 1991)

Story type: Fantasy (Quest)
Series: Ultima Saga
Major character(s): Jordan Hawson, Knight; Althea, Gentlewoman; Drumon, Artisan (farrier)

Time period(s): Indeterminate Past
Locale(s): Brittania, Fictional Country

Summary: Lord British, ruler of Brittania, has disappeared and the members of the Council of Mages are in hiding. Althea's brother Balthan, amanuensis to Mage Felespar of the Council, is also missing, and the only clue to his fate is a magic talisman that points to Britain City. Althea persuades Jordan and Drumon to help her find her brother. As they meet and overcome various perils, it becomes apparent that there is more at stake than one young magician's life.

Other books you might like:
Eleanor Arnason, *The Sword Smith*, 1978
Phyllis Eisenstein, *The Crystal Palace*, 1988
Elizabeth Ann Scarborough, *The Christening Quest*, 1985
J.R.R. Tolkien, *The Hobbit*, 1938
Patricia C. Wrede, *Shadow Magic*, 1982

15

LYNN ABBEY

The Temper of Wisdom

(New York: Warner Questar, 1992)

Story type: Fantasy (Quest; Magic Conflict)
Series: Ultima Saga
Major character(s): Jordan Hawson, Knight, Handicapped; Balthan Wanderson, Magician
Time period(s): Indeterminate Past
Locale(s): Brittania, Fictional Country

Summary: Jordan, his companions, and the rescued Balthan return home to find Hawksnest enthralled by the corrupt Inquisitor Lohgrin. Balthan, accused as a traitor, must flee the castle. In order to free Hawksnest, the companions must find a way to destroy Lohgrin's sorcery.

Other books you might like:
Robin Wayne Bailey, *Night Watch*, 1990
C.J. Cherryh, *The Tree of Swords and Jewels*, 1983
Stephen R. Donaldson, *Lord Foul's Bane*, 1977
Randall Garrett, *Too Many Magicians*, 1967
Katherine Kurtz, *Deryni Rising*, 1970
Elizabeth Marie Pope, *The Perilous Gard*, 1974

16

LYNN ABBEY

The Wooden Sword

(New York: Ace, 1991)

Story type: Fantasy (Adventure; Mystery)
Major character(s): Berika Ingoldesdaughter, Shepherd, Runaway; Dart, Nobleman, Amnesiac; Hirmin, Farmer, Fiance(e)
Time period(s): Indeterminate
Locale(s): Walensor, Fictional Country

Summary: When Berika prays to the gods to show her a way to escape the village of Gorge and her impending marriage to the sadistic Hirmin, she opens her eyes and sees Dart, who brings with him a magic harp, but no memory. When Dart helps Berika escape, Hirmin pursues the runaways, but is killed with a wooden sword which the forest goddess, Weycha, provides. Dart and Berika try to make their way to Eyerlon, the capital, while avoiding detection by the government's sorcerers and discovery of Dart's identity and mission.

Other books you might like:
C.J. Cherryh, *Rusalka*, 1989
Phyllis Eisenstein, *Born to Exile*, 1978
Ursula K. Le Guin, *A Wizard of Earthsea*, 1968
Patricia A. McKillip, *The Riddle-Master of Hed*, 1976
Elizabeth Moon, *Sheepfarmer's Daughter*, 1988
J.R.R. Tolkien, *The Fellowship of the Ring*, 1954

17

KOBO ABE

The Face of Another
(New York: Kodansha, 1992)

Story type: Horror (Psychological Suspense)
Major character(s): Doctor K, Doctor (dermatologist)
Time period(s): 1960s
Locale(s): Japan (Osaka region)

Summary: Told in the form of three diaries, this outstanding meditation on the conflict of identity and appearance tells of a scientist disfigured in a laboratory experiment who fashions a synthetic, life-like face mask to conceal his deformity. When his conduct becomes increasingly more uninhibited as a result of his new identity, he finds himself incapable of determining whether he is being overwhelmed by a new person or simply confronting buried aspects of his character that refuse to stay hidden. This novel was originally published in 1962 and translated by E. Dale Saunders.

Other books you might like:
Randall Boyll, *Darkman*, 1990
Ariel Dorfman, *Mascara*, 1989
Gaston Leroux, *The Phantom of the Opera*, 1911
Robert Louis Stevenson, *The Strange Case of Dr. Jekyll and Mr. Hyde*, 1888
Oscar Wilde, *The Picture of Dorian Gray*, 1891

18

ALEX ABELLA

The Killing of the Saints
(New York: Crown, 1991)

Story type: Horror (Occult)
Major character(s): Charlie Morrell, Lawyer; Ramon Valdez, Religious (priest of Santeria)
Time period(s): 1990s
Locale(s): Los Angeles, California

Summary: Appointed to defend a priest of the Afro-Hispanic religion Santeria following the man's grisly killings during a jewelry heist, lawyer Charlie Morrell finds himself pitted against occult forces beyond his understanding and forced to confront his own ambivalence regarding his Cuban heritage.

Other books you might like:
Hugh B. Cave, *Disciples of Dread*, 1988
Nicholas Conde, *The Religion*, 1982

John Farris, *All Heads Turn When the Hunt Goes By*, 1977
William Hjortsberg, *Falling Angel*, 1978

19

PETER ACKROYD

The Trial of Elizabeth Cree
(New York: Nan A. Talese/Doubleday, 1995)

Story type: Horror (Literary)
Major character(s): Elizabeth Cree, Actress; John Cree, Actor; Dan Leno, Actor
Time period(s): 1880s (1880)
Locale(s): London, England (Limehouse District)

Summary: Published in England in 1994 as *Dan Leno and the Limehouse Golem*, this novel traces the dismal lives of music hall actress Elizabeth Cree and her husband John, a frustrated actor who turns his penchant for artistic expression into a series of inventive murders and dismemberments that the popular press blames on a golem, until Elizabeth poisons him. The Crees' lives unfold against a vividly realized background portrait of Victorian England in which Karl Marx, George Gissing and other historical figures are characters.

Other books you might like:
Caleb Carr, *The Alienist*, 1994
E.L. Doctorow, *The Waterworks*, 1994
William Hjortsberg, *Nevermore*, 1994
Paul West, *The Women of Whitechapel and Jack the Ripper*, 1992

20

MARK ACRES

Dark Divide
(New York: Ace, 1991)

Story type: Fantasy (Adventure)
Series: Runesword
Major character(s): Caltus "Cal" Talienson, Warrior; Elizebith of Morea, Sorceress; Malendor, Vampire, Mythical Creature (dark elf)
Time period(s): Indeterminate
Locale(s): Trondholm, Fictional Country

Summary: Cal and his companions must save the Kingdom of Trondholm when a vampire looses his zombie hordes on the land of the living to secure the region for his Dark Lord.

Other books you might like:
Stephen Billias, *Horrible Humes*, 1991
Clayton Emery, *Outcasts*, 1990
Rose Estes, *Skryling's Blade*, 1990
    Tom Wham, co-author
J.F. Rivkin, *The Dreamstone*, 1991
Christopher Stasheff, *King Kobold Revived*, 1984
Margaret Weis, *Fire Sea*, 1991
    Tracy Hickman, co-author

21

MARK ACRES

Dragonspawn

(New York: AvoNova, 1994)

Story type: Fantasy (Magic Conflict; Adventure)
Major character(s): Bagsby, Thief; Shulana, Wizard, Mythical Creature (elf); Valdaimon, Wizard
Time period(s): Indeterminate
Locale(s): Heileshein, Fictional Country

Summary: The Black Prince, Ruprecht, and the wizard Valdaimon plot to control all the Land between the Rivers, while a thief and wizard attempt a daring theft that will defeat this plan. These competing schemes could resolve a 5000-year-old conflict.

Other books you might like:
Glen Cook, *The Black Company*, 1984
Barbara Hambly, *Dragonsbane*, 1987
Guy Gavriel Kay, *The Summer Tree*, 1985
Dennis L. McKiernan, *Dragondoom*, 1990
Melanie Rawn, *Stronghold*, 1990

22

DOUGLAS ADAMS

The Illustrated Hitchhiker's Guide to the Galaxy

(New York: Harmony, 1994)

Story type: Science Fiction (Humor; Space Opera)
Series: Hitchhiker's Guide to the Galaxy
Major character(s): Arthur Dent, Traveller; Ford Prefect, Writer, Alien; Zaphod Beeblebrox, Political Figure (President of the Galaxy), Fugitive
Time period(s): 1980s
Locale(s): *Heart of Gold*, Spaceship (experimental); Outer Space

Summary: When construction of an interstellar bypass destroys the Earth, Ford Prefect saves Arthur Dent by surreptitiously hitching a lift with the construction fleet. When the captain discovers the stowaways, he deposits them into the vacuum of space without the benefit of space suits. A highly improbable rescue by the stolen *Heart of Gold* propels Arthur and Ford into a series of zany adventures. Folio reprint of the 1980 edition lavishly illustrated with digitally modified photographs.

Other books you might like:
Harlan Ellison, *I, Robot: The Illustrated Screenplay*, 1994
  Isaac Asimov, co-author
James Gurney, *Dinotopia*, 1992
Harry Harrison, *Planet Story*, 1979
Terry Jones, *Lady Cottington's Pressed Fairy Book*, 1994
  Brian Froud, co-author
Robert Anton Wilson, *Reality Is What You Can Get Away With: An Illustrated Screenplay*, 1992

23

DOUGLAS ADAMS

The Long Dark Tea-Time of the Soul

(New York: Simon and Schuster, 1989)

Story type: Science Fiction (Satire)
Series: The Adventures of Dirk Gently
Major character(s): Dirk Gently, Detective—Private, Psychic; Kate Schechter, Heroine
Time period(s): 1980s

Summary: An explosion occurs at Heathrow Airport just as Dirk Gently, psychic detective, is about to board a plane for Oslo. He and Kate Schechter, another survivor of the explosion, soon become enmeshed in a baffling, often rather silly attempt to discover the perpetrators of the crime. Eventually they uncover evidence that the ancient Norse Gods are involved.

Other books you might like:
Piers Anthony, *Castle Roogna*, 1979
Piers Anthony, *The Source of Magic*, 1979
Piers Anthony, *A Spell for Chameleon*, 1977
Ron Goulart, *The Prisoner of Blackwood Castle*, 1984
Ron Goulart, *Starpirate's Brain*, 1987
Ron Goulart, *Upside Downside*, 1982
Keith Laumer, *Retief's Ransom*, 1971
Keith Laumer, *The Return of Retief*, 1985
Keith Laumer, *Reward for Retief*, 1989

24

DOUGLAS ADAMS

Mostly Harmless

(New York: Harmony Books, 1992)

Story type: Science Fiction (Humor; Space Opera)
Series: Hitchhiker's Guide to the Galaxy
Major character(s): Arthur Dent, Traveller; Ford Prefect, Writer, Alien
Time period(s): Indeterminate
Locale(s): Lamuella, Planet—Imaginary; Mythical Place (Offices of *The Hitchhiker's Guide to the Galaxy*)

Summary: As Ford investigates the often moved publishing offices of *The Hitchhiker's Guide to the Galaxy*, Arthur searches for a home to replace his beloved Earth, destroyed during construction of a hyperspace bypass, while characters from previous books pop into and out of the plot.

Other books you might like:
John DeChancie, *Paradox Alley*, 1987
John DeChancie, *Red Limit Freeway*, 1984
John DeChancie, *Starrigger*, 1983
Alan Dean Foster, *To the Vanishing Point*, 1988
Mel Gilden, *Surfing Samurai Robots*, 1988
Parke Godwin, *Waiting for the Galactic Bus*, 1988
Robert Rankin, *Armageddon: The Musical*, 1990
Robert Reed, *Down the Bright Way*, 1991
Neal Stephenson, *Snow Crash*, 1992

25

RICHARD ADAMS

Tales From Watership Down
(New York: Knopf, 1996)

Story type: Fantasy (Collection; Young Adult)
Major character(s): El-ahrairah, Animal (rabbit), Leader; Rabscuttle, Animal (rabbit); Dandilion, Animal (rabbit), Storyteller
Time period(s): Indeterminate
Locale(s): Land of Yesterday, Mythical Place; The Down, Mythical Place

Summary: Dandilion relates generally upbeat adventures of the mythical rabbit hero, El-ahrairah, and his companion, Rabscuttle, and stories of the rabbits and life at the Down. Includes a three-page lapine glossary and a brief introduction discussing the 20 original stories' relationship to characters and events in *Watership Down*.

Other books you might like:
Mary Brown, *The Unlikely Ones*, 1986
Kenneth Grahame, *The Wind in the Willows*, 1908
William Horwood, *Duncton Wood*, 1980
Brian Jacques, *Mariel of Redwall*, 1992
Brian Jacques, *Martin the Warrior*, 1994
Garry Kilworth, *The Foxes of Firstdark*, 1990
Tad Williams, *Tailchaser's Song*, 1985

26

ROBERT ADAMS

Of Beginnings and Endings
(New York: NAL Signet, 1989)

Story type: Science Fiction (Alternate Universe)
Series: Castaways in Time
Major character(s): Bass Foster, Time Traveller, Warrior; Harold Kenmore, Scientist, Time Traveller
Time period(s): 15th century (1489)
Locale(s): Alternate Earth (America and England)

Summary: Bass Foster and his companions must make places for themselves in fifteenth-century England and America. Meanwhile, mysterious and superpowerful beings have become aware of the castaways.

Other books you might like:
Daniel Da Cruz, *Mixed Doubles*, 1989
Simon Hawke, *The Argonaut Affair*, 1987
    Time Wars, No. 7
Simon Hawke, *The Kyber Connection*, 1986
    Time Wars, No. 6
Leo Frankowski, *The Flying Warlord*, 1989
Leo Frankowski, *The High-Tech Knight*, 1989
Leo Frankowski, *The Radiant Warrior*, 1989

27

TERRY A. ADAMS

The Master of Chaos
(New York: DAW Books, 1989)

Story type: Science Fiction (First Contact)
Major character(s): Hanna, Telepath, Diplomat
Time period(s): Indeterminate Future
Locale(s): Uskos, Planet—Imaginary

Summary: Lady Hanna is assigned to make first contact with a friendly alien race, the Uskosians, but is kidnapped and tortured by space pirates who kill the Uskosians. Rescued, she vows revenge and, at the same time, attempts to salvage some form of peaceful contact with the aliens.

Other books you might like:
Gregory Benford, *Tides of Light*, 1989
David Alexander Smith, *Rendezvous*, 1988
Sheri S. Tepper, *Grass*, 1989
James Tiptree Jr., *Brightness Falls From the Air*, 1985

28

WILLIAM ADAMS
CECIL BROOKS, Co-Author

The Unwound Way
(New York: Ballantine/Del Rey, 1991)

Story type: Science Fiction (Political; Arts)
Major character(s): Evan Larkspur, Actor, Fugitive; Ariel Nimitz, Administrator; Ken Mishima, Martial Arts Expert
Time period(s): Indeterminate Future
Locale(s): Nexus, Planet—Imaginary (Nexus University); Newcount Two, Planet—Imaginary; *Barbarossa*, Spaceship

Summary: Close to 100 years have passed since Evan Larkspur's naval operation on the spaceship *Barbarossa* went awry. He returns to normal space and the plays he had written before he left are now classics, and his Old Rite Kanalist compatriots have been eliminated or corrupted in his absence. Trapped by Maximillian Conde into impersonating a government official, what he finds on Newcount Two will challenge all his talents and require his classical education to avert disaster for himself and his companions.

Other books you might like:
C.J. Cherryh, *Forty Thousand in Gehenna*, 1983
Glen Cook, *The Dragon Never Sleeps*, 1988
Alan Dean Foster, *Cyber Way*, 1990
Diana G. Gallagher, *The Alien Dark*, 1990
Frank Herbert, *Dune*, 1965
Steve Miller, *Carpe Diem*, 1989
    Sharon Lee, co-author
Sheri S. Tepper, *Raising the Stones*, 1990
David Weber, *Mutineers' Moon*, 1991

29

PATRICK H. ADKINS

Sons of the Titans

(New York: Ace, 1990)

Story type: Fantasy (Legend; Adventure)
Series: Titans
Major character(s): Kronis, Nobleman (Lord of the Titans); Zeus, Royalty (King-to-be)
Time period(s): Indeterminate Past (ancient Hellenic era)
Locale(s): Greece

Summary: Zeus struggles against his Titan father to assume the throne of the King of the Gods.

Other books you might like:
Tom Holt, *Expecting Someone Taller*, 1987
Thomas Burnett Swann, *The Gods Abide*, 1976
Howard Waldrop, *A Dozen Tough Jobs*, 1989
Roger Zelazny, *Creatures of Light and Darkness*, 1969

30

JACK ADRIAN, Editor

Strange Tales from the Strand

(New York: Oxford University Press, 1992)

Story type: Horror (Anthology)

Summary: Twenty-nine tales of madness, murder, melodrama, revenants, superbeasts, unnatural disasters, and fantasy that appeared in the long-running British popular fiction periodical *The Strand* between 1891 and 1950. Included are Graham Greene's gruesome ghost story "All But Empty" (a.k.a. "A Little Place Off the Edgeware Road"); Hugh Walpole's tale of vengeance from beyond the grave, "The Tarn"; W. L. George's grisly mistaken identity story, "Waxworks"; Villiers de l'Isle-Adam's *conte cruel* "Torture by Hope"; C. J. Cutcliffe Hyne's tale of an accidentally revived prehistoric behemoth, "Lizard"; the comic "Queer Story of Brownlow's Newspaper" by H. G. Wells; and three stories by Arthur Conan Doyle: "How it Happened," "The Silver Mirror," and "The Horror of the Heights."

Other books you might like:
Isaac Asimov, *Isaac Asimov Presents the Best Horror and Supernatural Tales of the 19th Century*, 1983
    Charles G. Waugh and Martin H. Greenberg, co-editors
Sam Moskowitz, *Ghostly by Gaslight*, 1971
    Alden H. Norton, co-editor
Sam Moskowitz, *Great Untold Stories of Fantasy and Horror*, 1969
    Alden H. Norton, co-editor
Sam Moskowitz, *Science Fiction by Gaslight*, 1968
    editor

31

AESOP

Aesop's Fables

(New York: Signet Classic, 1992)

Story type: Fantasy (Collection; Legend)

Summary: Contains two pages of notes on the text, an eight-page afterword discussing Aesop and the structure and development of the fable as literary form with examples, a two-page bibliography, a three-page index plus 203 fables selected and adapted by Zipes from Reverend Thomas James's *Aesop's Fables: A New Version, Chiefly From Original Sources* (1848) to which Zipes has added modernized language and idioms and, for a few fables, created new morals more relevant to the contemporary reader. Includes "The Ants and the Grasshopper," "The Country Mouse and the City Mouse," "The Hare and the Tortoise" and "The Shepherd Boy and the Wolf."

Other books you might like:
Richard Erdoes, *American Indian Myths and Legends*, 1984
    Alfonso Ortiz, co-editor
Garry Kilworth, *The Foxes of Firstdark*, 1990
Dean R. Koontz, *Oddkins*, 1988
Barry Lopez, *Crow and Weasel*, 1990
Howard Norman, *Northern Tales: Traditional Stories of Eskimo and Indian Peoples*, 1990

32

PHYLLIS CAROL AGINS

Suisan

(New York: Baen, 1992)

Story type: Fantasy (Legend)
Major character(s): Suisan, Maiden; Cwenn, Royalty (queen), Step-Parent; Allard, Mythical Creature (dwarf), Miner
Time period(s): Indeterminate Past
Locale(s): The City, Mythical Place; The Forest, Mythical Place

Summary: Happy in the mines where they find and work metals and gems, seven little men discover through a vision that a beautiful young girl will be coming to them. Suisan, the Snow White Cwenn sent with the hunter to die, lives with the miners and their visions. The dwarves secretly build a wonderful growing crystal casket but cannot forsee why she will need it. Author's first book.

Other books you might like:
Steven Brust, *The Sun, the Moon, and the Stars*, 1987
Kara Dalkey, *The Nightingale*, 1988
Charles de Lint, *Jack, the Giant-Killer*, 1987
Pamela Dean, *Tam Lin*, 1991
Sheri S. Tepper, *Beauty*, 1991
Patricia C. Wrede, *Snow White and Rose Red*, 1989

33

MARJORIE AGOSIN, Editor

The Secret Weavers: Stories of the Fantastic by Latin American Women

(Fredonia, New York: White Pine Press, 1991)

Story type: Fantasy (Anthology)
Major character(s): Luz, Teenager, Psychic; Erzsebet, Noble-woman (countess), Vampire; Segismundo Linares, Maintenance Worker (janitor)
Time period(s): 20th century; Indeterminate Past
Locale(s): South America; Mythical Place

Summary: This volume contains 45 stories written from the 1930s to the present by 18 women from Argentina and Chile. This is the first English translation for most of the stories which are about the Fantastic, taken as a matter of fact as in "The Compulsion Dreamer" by Silvian Ocampo, about a young woman whose dreams come true, a situation she accepts and works into the fabric of her life. There is a lengthy introduction, with notes on the authors and translators following the stories.

Other books you might like:
Samuel R. Delany, *Dhalgren*, 1975
Greer Ilene Gilman, *Moonwise*, 1990
Lisa Goldstein, *The Dream Years*, 1985
Tanith Lee, *The Book of the Damned*, 1990
Pat Murphy, *The City, Not Long After*, 1989
Jack Zipes, *Don't Bet on the Prince*, 1986
    editor

34

JERRY AHERN

The Struggle

(New York: Zebra, 1989)

Story type: Science Fiction (Post-Nuclear Holocaust)
Series: Survivalist
Major character(s): John T. Rourke, Military Personnel (Soldier), Spy; Colonel Antonovich, Military Personnel
Time period(s): 21st century
Locale(s): Pacific Ocean

Summary: In a half-destroyed, post-nuclear holocaust world, Russia and the United States continue to oppose each other. Rourke, an ex-CIA operative, must contain Colonel Antonovich's attempt to gain world dominance for Russia.

Other books you might like:
Richard Austin, *Devil's Deal*, 1989
    The Guardians. Vol. 13
James Axler, *Red Equinox*, 1989
    Deathlands 9
Bob Ham, *Tennessee Terror*, 1989
    The Overlord 4
William W. Johnstone, *Trapped in the Ashes*, 1989
James Rouch, *Civilian Slaughter*, 1989
    The Zone 8

35

JOAN AIKEN

The Haunting of Lamb House

(New York: St. Martin's, 1993)

Story type: Horror (Haunted House; Literary)
Major character(s): Toby Lamb, Child; Henry James, Writer, Historical Figure; E.F. Benson, Writer, Historical Figure
Time period(s): 19th century; 20th century
Locale(s): Rye, England

Summary: The journal of Toby Lamb, a sensitive and mistreated young boy living at the end of the 18th century, falls into the hands of two later tenants of Lamb House, writers Henry James and E.F. Benson, each of whose literary involvement with the diary causes the spirits of Lamb House to manifest. Told in the form of three interlocking novellas, this homage to the classic British ghost story was first published in England in 1992.

Other books you might like:
Jonathan Aycliffe, *Whispers in the Dark*, 1993
E.F. Benson, *The Collected Ghost Stories of E.F. Benson*, 1992
Henry James, *Stories of the Supernatural*, 1970

36

JIM AIKIN

The Wall at the Edge of the World

(New York: Ace, 1993)

Story type: Science Fiction (Post-Holocaust; Psychic Powers)
Major character(s): Danlo Ree, Telepath, Traveller; Ainne Murrinder, Telepath; Linnie, Teacher
Time period(s): Indeterminate Future
Locale(s): Sacramento, California; Ranoima, Fictional City

Summary: Despite the easy life as part of the Body of Harmony, Danlo Ree defeats the Guidance put on him by the Joddies after his wife's Cleansing. He could work as a Joddie, utilizing his talent of surrepticiously influencing other minds and mentally partitioning his own thoughts. However, after Linnie's band of women from outside the wall kidnap Danlo, he comes to realize that he must stop the killing, whatever the cost.

Other books you might like:
Emma Bull, *Bone Dance*, 1991
Marjorie Bradley Kellogg, *Harmony*, 1991
Pat Murphy, *The City, Not Long After*, 1989
Frank M. Robinson, *The Power*, 1956
Jean Stewart, *Return to Isis*, 1992
Vernor Vinge, *A Fire upon the Deep*, 1992
Paul O. Williams, *The Breaking of Northwall*, 1980

PETER ALBANO

Assault of the Super Carrier
(New York: Zebra, 1996)

Story type: Science Fiction (Military)
Series: Seventh Carrier
Major character(s): Brent Ross, Military Personnel; Yoshi Matsuhara, Military Personnel; Hiroshi Fujito, Military Personnel
Time period(s): 1990s
Locale(s): *Yonaga*, At Sea; *Edo*, At Sea; Japan

Summary: Brent accompanies *Edo* on its shakedown cruise, looking for a possible pirate ship which preys on fishing vessels. After a deadly encounter, and prior to *Yonaga*'s setting out for the Middle East, Brent takes leave, as ordered, only to find anti-military sentiment which could easily prove lethal.

Other books you might like:
David Alexander, *Nomad*, 1992
Daniel Da Cruz, *Texas on the Rocks*, 1987
Daniel Da Cruz, *Texas Triumphant*, 1987
John Dalmas, *The Yngling*, 1971
G. Harry Stine, *Warbots*, 1988

PETER ALBANO

Ordeal of the Seventh Carrier
(New York: Zebra, 1992)

Story type: Science Fiction (Military)
Series: Seventh Carrier
Major character(s): Yoshi Matsuhara, Military Personnel
Time period(s): 1990s
Locale(s): *Yonaga*, At Sea

Summary: The *Yonaga* prepares for a bloody showdown with the Arab battle group directed against Japan by the fanatic Libyan terrorist bent on extending his influence in the Pacific.

Other books you might like:
Daniel Da Cruz, *The Ayes of Texas*, 1982
Daniel Da Cruz, *Texas on the Rocks*, 1987
Daniel Da Cruz, *Texas Triumphant*, 1987
G. Harry Stine, *Force of Arms*, 1990
G. Harry Stine, *Warbots*, 1988

39

PETER ALBANO

Revenge of the Seventh Carrier
(New York: Zebra, 1992)

Story type: Science Fiction (Military)
Series: Seventh Carrier
Major character(s): Yoshi Matsuhara, Military Personnel; Brent Ross, Military Personnel; Arlene Spencer, Journalist
Time period(s): 1990s
Locale(s): *Yonaga*, At Sea

Summary: When a Libyan madman assembles an army of fanatics and naval forces able to attack major cities with poison gas weapons, the Japanese aircraft carrier *Yonanga* with its indomitable Samurai crew and their comrades, brave airmen from around the world, must stop the disaster.

Other books you might like:
Daniel Da Cruz, *The Ayes of Texas*, 1982
Daniel Da Cruz, *Texas on the Rocks*, 1987
Daniel Da Cruz, *Texas Triumphant*, 1987
G. Harry Stine, *Operation Iron Fist*, 1989
G. Harry Stine, *Warbots*, 1988

PETER ALBANO

Super Carrier: The Ultimate Secret Weapon
(New York: Zebra, 1994)

Story type: Science Fiction (Military)
Series: Seventh Carrier
Major character(s): Hiroshi Fujito, Military Personnel (admiral); Brent Ross, Military Personnel (commander)
Time period(s): 1990s
Locale(s): *Yonaga*, At Sea; Marianas Islands, Trust Territory of the Pacific Islands

Summary: To prevent the success of a Libyan jihad, the super carrier *Yonaga*, armed with a secret weapon, engages the enemy in the Pacific and the Middle East.

Other books you might like:
David Alexander, *Nomad*, 1992
Daniel Da Cruz, *Texas on the Rocks*, 1987
Daniel Da Cruz, *Texas Triumphant*, 1987
John Dalmas, *The Yngling*, 1971
G. Harry Stine, *Warbots*, 1988

KATHLEEN ALCALA

Mrs. Vargas and the Dead Naturalist
(Corvallis, Oregon: Calyx Books, 1992)

Story type: Fantasy (Collection)

Summary: Six original and eight stories slightly revised from 1985-1991 appearances in periodicals and anthologies. Themes of these fantasy and magical realism stories include romance, nature and Roman Catholicism.

Other books you might like:
Marjorie Agosin, *The Secret Weavers: Stories of the Fantastic by Latin American Women*, 1991
editor
Pauline Melville, *Shape-Shifter: Stories by Pauline Melville*, 1991
Susanna J. Sturgis, *Magic Realism by Women: Dreams in a Minor Key*, 1991
editor

42

BRIAN W. ALDISS

Common Clay: 20 Odd Stories

(New York: St. Martin's, 1996)

Story type: Fantasy (Collection; Science Fiction)

Summary: This collection contains individual commentaries to one story from a 1987 conference program book, seven original and 12 stories reprinted from periodicals and anthologies 1992-1995, with one revised, "Her Toes Were Beautiful on the Mountains." The commentary loosely links the stories into chapters of a "chronicle novel," discussing life, death, and transformation in tones ranging from darkly humorous to horrific, with some suggestions of a happier existence. The British edition is titled *The Secret of This Book*.

Other books you might like:
Alfred Bester, *Star Light, Star Bright*, 1976
Philip K. Dick, *The Collected Stories of Philip K. Dick*, 1987
    five volumes
Cordwainer Smith, *The Rediscovery of Man*, 1993
Marc Stiegler, *The Gentle Seduction*, 1990
Theodore Sturgeon, *The Ultimate Egoist*, 1994
John Varley, *Blue Champagne*, 1986

43

BRIAN W. ALDISS

Dracula Unbound

(New York: HarperCollins, 1991)

Story type: Horror (Science Fiction)
Major character(s): Joe Bodeland, Scientist; Bram Stoker, Writer (author of *Dracula*), Historical Figure; Count Dracula, Vampire
Time period(s): 1990s (1999)
Locale(s): Utah

Summary: In this semi-sequel to the author's *Frankenstein Unbound*, the discovery of a 65-million-year-old tomb in Utah sends space/time manipulator Joe Bodeland investigating. Through a process not unlike the "time sink" he has developed for disposing of toxic waste, Bodeland hops a ghost train from the past that rides through the tomb site and there discovers that the immortal Count Dracula has planned a future in which he will enslave all mankind.

Other books you might like:
Fred Saberhagen, *The Dracula Tape*, 1975
John Shirley, *Dracula in Love*, 1979
Dan Simmons, *Carrion Comfort*, 1989
Peter Tremayne, *Dracula Unborn*, 1977
Chelsea Quinn Yarbro, *Out of the House of Life*, 1990

44

BRIAN W. ALDISS

Last Orders

(New York: Carroll and Graf, 1989)

Story type: Science Fiction (Collection)

Summary: This volume contains nine short stories and five pieces the author calls Enigmas. Publication dates range from 1973 through 1977. The best known stories in the collection are "Last Orders," "Creatures of Apogee," "The Monster of Ingratitude IV," and "The Aperture Moment."

Other books you might like:
J.G. Ballard, *Billenium and Other Stories*, 1962
J.G. Ballard, *The Drowned World*, 1962
J.G. Ballard, *Terminal Beach*, 1964
J.G. Ballard, *Vermilion Sands*, 1971
Paul Park, *Soldiers of Paradise*, 1987
Paul Park, *Sugar Rain*, 1989
Keith Roberts, *Kiteworld*, 1985
Keith Roberts, *The Passing of the Dragons*, 1977

45

BRIAN W. ALDISS

Man in His Time: The Best Science Fiction Stories of Brian W. Aldiss

(New York: Atheneum, 1989)

Story type: Science Fiction (Collection)

Summary: This volume contains twenty-two stories, ranging in original publication date from 1955 to 1986. Among the earliest are "Outside" (1955), "The Failed Men" (1957), "Poor Little Warrior!" (1958), and "Who Can Replace Man?" (1958), the cumulative excellence of which earned Aldiss a special award at the 1959 World Science Fiction Convention as Most Promising New Author. Other outstanding stories included are "The Saliva Tree" (1965), which won a Nebula Award, "Heresies of the Huge God" (1966), "Last Orders" (1976), "The Gods in Flight" (1984), "My Country 'Tis Not Only of Thee" (1986), and "The Difficulties Involved in Photographing Nix Olympica" (1986).

Other books you might like:
J.G. Ballard, *Billenium and Other Stories*, 1962
J.G. Ballard, *The Drowned World*, 1962
J.G. Ballard, *Terminal Beach*, 1964
J.G. Ballard, *Vermilion Sands*, 1971
Paul Park, *Soldiers of Paradise*, 1987
Paul Park, *Sugar Rain*, 1989
Keith Roberts, *Kiteworld*, 1985
Keith Roberts, *The Passing of the Dragons*, 1977

46

BRIAN W. ALDISS

Non-Stop

(New York: Carroll & Graf, 1989)

Story type: Science Fiction (Generation Starship)
Major character(s): Roy Complain, Hunter; Henry Marapper, Religious (Priest)
Time period(s): Indeterminate Future
Locale(s): *Big Dog*, Spaceship

Summary: Roy Complain has grown up in a primitive jungle world, but he has never been satisfied with the reasons the priests give for his people's boring and confined life. He wants explanations for the odd legends he's learned. Who are the Giants who supposedly built his world? Who are the people who live beyond Quarters in the place called Forwards? What lies beyond the metal walls that have always surrounded him? Eventually Complain decides to find out.

Other books you might like:
Ronald Anthony Cross, *Prisoners of Paradise*, 1988
Harry Harrison, *Captive Universe*, 1969
Robert A. Heinlein, *Orphans of the Sky*, 1963
Fritz Leiber, *Ship of Shadows*, 1988
Harry Martinson, *Aniara*, 1956

47

BRIAN W. ALDISS

A Romance of the Equator: The Best Fantasy Stories of Brian W. Aldiss

(New York: Atheneum, 1990)

Story type: Fantasy (Collection)
Time period(s): Indeterminate

Summary: This collection contains 26 short stories and an introduction in which Aldiss reveals his personal favorites to the reader. The stories include "Old Hundredth," "The Worm That Flies," "Lies," "The Small Stones of Tu Fu" and others published between 1960 and 1989. This book is a companion volume to *Man in his Time: The Best Science Fiction Stories of Brian W. Aldiss* (1989).

Other books you might like:
J.G. Ballard, *Terminal Beach*, 1964
J.G. Ballard, *Vermilion Sands*, 1971
Anthony Boucher, *Far and Away*, 1955
Ellen Datlow, *The Year's Best Fantasy and Horror: Third Annual Collection*, 1990
    Terri Windling, co-editor
Chad Oliver, *Another Kind*, 1954
Chad Oliver, *The Edge of Forever*, 1971

48

BRIAN W. ALDISS

Somewhere East of Life

(New York: Carroll & Graf, 1994)

Story type: Science Fiction (Contemporary Realism)
Major character(s): Burnell, Amnesiac, Activist
Time period(s): 21st century
Locale(s): Turkmenistan; Georgia

Summary: As Burnell travels around Asia documenting destructive forces' effects on architecture, he tries to locate and reacquire the 10 years of memories stolen from him, some of which have been sold as soft core pornography.

Other books you might like:
Pat Cadigan, *Fools*, 1992
Pat Cadigan, *Mindplayers*, 1987
Katharine Kerr, *Resurrection*, 1992
Nancy Kress, *Brain Rose*, 1990
Michael Swanwick, *Vacuum Flowers*, 1987

49

BRIAN W. ALDISS

A Tupelov Too Far and Other Stories

(New York: St. Martin's Press, 1994)

Story type: Science Fiction (Collection)

Summary: Contains an original poem, "Short Stories," and 12 stories published in periodicals and anthologies 1967-1992. Frequently philosophical, some stories feature terrestrial settings such as "Three Degrees Over" with its orgy in an Oxford garden, while others take place light years away and one is set in the Afterworld. Aldiss exhibits dark humor in "Better Morphosis," a twist on Kafka's work, and a humorless revisiting of his Frankenstein myth in "Summertime Was Nearly Over."

Other books you might like:
J.G. Ballard, *The Best Short Stories of J.G. Ballard*, 1978
Gardner Dozois, *Geodesic Dreams: The Best Short Fiction of Gardner Dozois*, 1992
Damon Knight, *One Side Laughing: Stories Unlike Other Stories*, 1991
John Varley, *Blue Champagne*, 1986
Gene Wolfe, *Endangered Species*, 1989

50

RAY ALDRIDGE

Emperor of Everything

(New York: Bantam Spectra, 1992)

Story type: Science Fiction (Adventure)
Series: Emancipator
Major character(s): Ruiz Aw, Slave (former), Agent; Corean Heiclaro, Trader (slave); Nisa, Slave (escaped), Royalty
Time period(s): Indeterminate Future
Locale(s): Sook, Planet—Imaginary

Summary: Shepherding a band of escaped slaves across the planet Sook, Ruiz reaches Seastack. In a desperate gamble to gain safety, he accepts a job as a hired assassin at the risk of being captured and "genched"—mentally re-conditioned.

Other books you might like:
Marion Zimmer Bradley, *The Shattered Chain*, 1976
Emma Bull, *Bone Dance*, 1991
Robert A. Heinlein, *Citizen of the Galaxy*, 1957
Anne McCaffrey, *Sassinak*, 1990
    Elizabeth Moon, co-author
Jack Williamson, *The Reefs of Space*, 1964
    Frederik Pohl, co-author

51

RAY ALDRIDGE

The Pharaoh Contract

(New York: Bantam Spectra, 1991)

Story type: Science Fiction (Adventure)
Series: Emancipator

Major character(s): Ruiz Aw, Agent, Martial Arts Expert; Nacker the Teach, Health Care Professional (minddriver); Nisa, Royalty (princess of Pharaoh), Slave
Time period(s): Indeterminate Future
Locale(s): *Vigia*, Spaceship; Pharaoh, Planet—Imaginary; Sook, Planet—Imaginary (pirate base)

Summary: Ruiz Aw, born a slave, is an enforcer for the Arts League, the corporation which provides slaves for the Pangalac Worlds. He has Nacker loosen the Death Net which the Arts League installed along with a compulsion to complete his mission. Nacker's technique changes Ruiz Aw, but is successful in preventing the device from activating.

Other books you might like:
Allan Cole, *Sten*, 1984
    Chris Bunch, co-author
Stephen Goldin, *Jade Darcy and the Affair of Honor*, 1988
    Mary Mason, co-author
Steve Perry, *The Man Who Never Missed*, 1985
Carol Severance, *Reefsong*, 1991
Michael Swanwick, *Vacuum Flowers*, 1987
Sydney J. Van Scyoc, *Deepwater Dreams*, 1991

52

BUZZ ALDRIN
JOHN BARNES, Co-Author

Encounter with Tiber
(New York: Warner Aspect, 1996)

Story type: Science Fiction (Family Saga; First Contact)
Major character(s): Chris Terrence, Astronaut; Zahmekoses, Alien (Tiberian), Space Explorer; Diehrenn, Alien (Tiberian), Writer
Time period(s): 21st century; 73rd century B.C.
Locale(s): Outer Space

Summary: The alien Tiberians mount an expensive voyage to explore and possibly settle Earth, leaving encyclopedias for humans to discover on the Moon and Mars when colonization proves impossible. A message alerting humanity to the encyclopedias spurs human space exploration in the 2000s, resulting in an unsuccessful lunar recovery attempt and the need for a multinational effort to recover the Martian encyclopedia.

Other books you might like:
John Barnes, *A Million Open Doors*, 1992
John Barnes, *Mother of Storms*, 1994
John Barnes, *Orbital Resonance*, 1991
Robert L. Forward, *Rocheworld*, 1990
Diana G. Gallagher, *The Alien Dark*, 1990
David Alexander Smith, *Marathon*, 1982
David Alexander Smith, *Rendezvous*, 1988
Allen Steele, *The Tranquility Alternative*, 1996

53

DAVID ALEXANDER

Desert Fire
(New York: Worldwide Gold Eagle, 1993)

Story type: Science Fiction (Time Travel; Political)

Series: Nomad
Major character(s): Quinn ''Nomad'', Time Traveller, Warrior; Lux Vadim, Religious, Scientist
Time period(s): 2030s (2035); 1990s (1991)
Locale(s): Los Angeles, California; Sunyata, Space Station; New York, New York

Summary: When a psychotic religious leader, Lux Vadim, escapes prison and implements lethal plans to control the power of the ancients, Quinn must follow Vadim back in time and stop him from changing the outcome of the U.S. invasion of Iraq.

Other books you might like:
Poul Anderson, *The Time Patrol*, 1991
Keith William Andrews, *Sink the Armada*, 1990
Roger L. DiSilvestro, *Living with the Reptiles*, 1990
Randall Frakes, *The Terminator*, 1985
    Bill Wisher, co-author
Robert Charles Wilson, *A Bridge of Years*, 1991

54

DAVID ALEXANDER

Nomad
(New York: Worldwide Gold Eagle, 1992)

Story type: Science Fiction (Adventure; Techno-Thriller)
Series: Nomad
Major character(s): Quinn ''Nomad'', Warrior, Spy; Ramsey, Spy (double agent); Bill Bruckner, Spy, Criminal (assassin)
Time period(s): 2030s (2030)
Locale(s): Earth; Outer Space (near Earth orbit)

Summary: Quinn's assignment, protecting the remaining unassassinated scientists connected with the Prometheus Project and discovering the force behind the assassination, proves difficult since Quinn's boss works for the enemy.

Other books you might like:
Jack L. Chalker, *War of Shadows*, 1979
Burt Cole, *The Quick*, 1989
Daniel Da Cruz, *Texas on the Rocks*, 1987
William R. Forstchen, *A Darkness upon the Ice*, 1985
Brian Stableford, *Optiman*, 1980
Walter Jon Williams, *Hardwired*, 1986
Timothy Zahn, *The Backlash Mission*, 1986

55

LLOYD ALEXANDER

The Arkadians
(New York: Dutton, 1995)

Story type: Fantasy (Young Adult; Adventure)
Major character(s): Lucian, Adventurer, Fugitive; Joy-in-the-Dance, Adventurer; Fronto, Animal (talking donkey), Writer (poet)
Time period(s): Indeterminate Past
Locale(s): Arkadia, Ancient Civilization (Greek); Greece

Summary: To escape soothsayers and the king's murderous intent, Lucian flees with Fronto, who seeks restoration to human form. Soon the mysterious Joy-in-the-Dance joins them, proving useful to the dangerous quest.

Other books you might like:
Gillian Bradshaw, *The Land of Gold*, 1992
Mary Brown, *The Unlikely Ones*, 1986
Tom Holt, *Goatsong*, 1990
Mary James, *Shoebag*, 1990
Sherwood Smith, *Wren to the Rescue*, 1990
Robert Watson, *Whilom*, 1990

56

LLOYD ALEXANDER

The Remarkable Journey of Prince Jen
(New York: Dutton, 1991)

Story type: Fantasy (Quest; Young Adult)
Major character(s): Jen, Royalty (prince); Mafoo, Servant; Voyaging Moon, Musician
Time period(s): Indeterminate Past
Locale(s): China

Summary: Before Prince Jen sets off to find the legendary court of T'ien-kuo, a strange old man gives him six rather ordinary objects to take with him. Not appreciating a future need for the objects, Jen loses a saddle and most of his retinue almost immediately. Undaunted, Jen continues his journey, learning about himself and his responsibilities before he learns the true value of the gifts.

Other books you might like:
William Goldman, *The Princess Bride*, 1973
Kathryn Grant, *The Willow Garden*, 1989
Barry Hughart, *Bridge of Birds*, 1984
Barry Hughart, *Eight Skilled Gentlemen*, 1990
Jeanne Larsen, *Silk Road*, 1989
Andre Norton, *Imperial Lady*, 1989
   Susan Shwartz, co-author
Laurence Yep, *Tongues of Jade*, 1991

57

ATHENA ALEXIS

Along Came a Spider
(New York: Dell, 1991)

Story type: Horror (Gothic Family Chronicle)
Major character(s): Alice McNamara, Teenager; Daria Broderick, Child (Alice's half-sister); Jeremy Woolcott, Teenager (Alice's cousin by marriage)
Time period(s): 1990s
Locale(s): Congreve, Georgia

Summary: In this first novel written in the grand gothic tradition of V.C. Andrews, Alice McNamara and her beloved mother, stepfather, and half-sister Daria inherit her stepgrandfather's family fortune with the provision that they relocate from New York to the family mansion in Georgia. Once there, Alice runs afoul of family matriarch Aunt Thelma, walks in fear of a mysterious old woman kept locked in the attic, fends off the advances of her lewd cousin Bubba, and develops a general disdain for those eccentricities of extended

southern families that make it possible for the rest of us to feel much better about ourselves.

Other books you might like:
V.C. Andrews, *Flowers in the Attic*, 1979
Robert R. McCammon, *Usher's Passing*, 1984
Michael McDowell, *Blackwater*, 1983
Andrew Neiderman, *Sister, Sister*, 1992

58

KATINA ALEXIS

Souls
(New York: Pocket, 1992)

Story type: Horror (Occult)
Major character(s): Maria Demos, Real Estate Agent; Vince De Luca, Detective—Police; Taylor Caroline Shedian, FBI Agent
Time period(s): 1990s
Locale(s): Chaseburn, Florida

Summary: A pair of determined millionaires with occult connections plot to recall the soul of 18th century witch Maria Trapnell from the spirit realm, reinstate it in the body of her lineal descendant, Maria Demos, and help her resume the reign of terror she and her coven of followers initiated centuries before.

Other books you might like:
D.A. Fowler, *The Devil's End*, 1992
Marcy Heidish, *The Torching*, 1992

59

ALICE ALFONSI, Editor
JOHN SCOGNAMIGLIO, Co-Editor

Dark Seductions
(New York: Zebra, 1993)

Story type: Horror (Anthology)

Summary: The fifteen authors who contributed fourteen stories to this collection of erotic horror are better known as novelists for Zebra Books. Richard Lee Byers' "Gloves" tells of a paraplegic model who so desires to make love again that she submits to a bizarre prosthetic process, with terrifying results. Ric Hautala's "Cousin's Curse" is a vampire tale and Ronald Kelly's "Whorehouse Hollow" an exercise in southern grotesque. Stephen George's "Hard" and Scott Ciencin's "The Victim" both probe the underside of the entertainment profession, respectively porno films and method acting. And Tamara Thorne's "Good Vibrations" is about a marital aid with a mind of its own.

Other books you might like:
Ellen Datlow, *Alien Sex*, 1990
Jeff Gelb, *Hot Blood: Tales of Provocative Horror*, 1989
   Lonn Friend, co-editor
Jeff Gelb, *Hotter Blood: More Tales of Erotic Horror*, 1991
   Michael Garrett, co-editor
Jeff Gelb, *Hottest Blood: The Ultimate in Erotic Horror*, 1993
   Michael Garrett, co-editor

Margaret L. Carter, *Demon Lovers and Strange Seductions*, 1973

JUDITH ALGUIRE

Zeta Base

(Tallahassee: Naiad, 1991)

Story type: Science Fiction (Gay/Lesbian Fiction; Disaster)
Major character(s): Jordan "Antiquity" Thyme, Scientist, Computer Expert; Morgan Quade, Artist; Jaffey, Engineer, Computer Expert
Time period(s): Indeterminate Future (500th year of galactic civilization)
Locale(s): Earth

Summary: Antiquity, an expert on SOLCOM, the ancient computer monitoring the Sun, announces ominous findings about the Sun's output. Gathered for the galaxy's half-millennium celebration, Antiquity's three proteges struggle with a rekindled love triangle as one of them, Jaffey, performs the SOLCOM systems-check needed to verify Antiquity's findings which indicate tragedy for the earth. A first novel.

Other books you might like:
Perry Brass, *Mirage*, 1991
Lauren Wright Douglas, *In the Blood*, 1989
Nancy Tyler Glenn, *Clicking Stones*, 1989
Camarin Grae, *Stranded*, 1991
Robert Leininger, *Black Sun*, 1991
Lynda Lyons, *Priorities*, 1990

61

MARY ELIZABETH ALLEN

All Hallow's Eve: Tales of Love and the Supernatural

(New York: Walker, 1992)

Story type: Fantasy (Anthology)
Summary: These sixteen original stories written in the Regency romance tradition are mostly tales of liaisons between mortal women and ghostly lovers. The best stories include S. N. Lewitt's "Pipe Dreams," about a rock musician who summons Mary Shelley's ghost for inspiration; Andre Norton's tale of ghostly revenge, "The Nabob's Gift"; and Caroline Stevermer's "Waiting for Harry," about a family ghost that predicts death. The volume also includes stories by Joan Aiken, Marvin Kaye, and Morgan Llywellyn.

Other books you might like:
Don Congdon, *Tales of Love and Horror*, 1961
Ellen Datlow, *Alien Sex*, 1990
Jeff Gelb, *Hot Blood: Tales of Provocative Horror*, 1990
    Michael Garret, co-editor
Jeff Gelb, *Hottest Blood: The Ultimate in Erotic Horror*, 1993
    Michael Garret, co-editor
Jeff Gelb, *Hotter Blood: More Tales of Erotic Horror*, 1990
    Michael Garret, co-editor
Michel Parry, *Devil's Kisses*, 1976
    editor

Michele Slung, *I Shudder at Your Touch*, 1991
editor

62

ROGER MACBRIDE ALLEN

Ambush at Corellia

(New York: Bantam Spectra, 1995)

Story type: Science Fiction (Space Opera; Political)
Series: Star Wars: The Corellian Trilogy
Major character(s): Leia Organa Solo, Royalty, Leader (New Republic Head of State); Han Solo, Spaceship Captain, Warrior; Luke Skywalker, Martial Arts Expert, Hero
Time period(s): Indeterminate Past
Locale(s): Corellia, Planet—Imaginary; Interstellar Empire/Federation

Summary: A trade summit with a government completely isolated since the Imperial/Alliance war seems the perfect opportunity for Han and Leia to work in a family vacation, showing the children their father's homeland. Their plans, however, originally did not include a compromised intelligence operation, a megalomaniac dictator, or a device capable of destroying stars! First of a trilogy.

Other books you might like:
Kevin J. Anderson, *Jedi Search*, 1994
Brian Daley, *The Han Solo Adventures*, 1992
Alan Dean Foster, *Splinter of the Mind's Eye*, 1978
Barbara Hambly, *Children of the Jedi*, 1995
George Lucas, *The Star Wars Trilogy*, 1987
    Donald F. Glut, James Kahn, co-authors
L. Neil Smith, *The Lando Calrissian Adventures*, 1994
Timothy Zahn, *Heir to the Empire*, 1991

63

ROGER MACBRIDE ALLEN

Caliban

(New York: Ace, 1993)

Story type: Science Fiction (Robot Fiction; Mystery)
Series: Isaac Asimov's Caliban
Major character(s): CBN-001 "Caliban", Robot; Alvar Kresh, Lawman (sheriff); Fredda Leving, Computer Expert, Engineer (robot engineer)
Time period(s): Indeterminate Future
Locale(s): Inferno, Planet—Imaginary

Summary: Coming to awareness in a pool of blood with a woman lying at its feet, Caliban decides to leave and explore the city. Sheriff Kresh realizes Caliban acts differently than other robots and may have assaulted Fredda Leving. While all attempts to capture or destroy Caliban fail, Fredda Leving's ideas on the Three Laws of Robotics cause a riot.

Other books you might like:
Isaac Asimov, *The Caves of Steel*, 1954
Isaac Asimov, *The Naked Sun*, 1957
Philip K. Dick, *Blade Runner*, 1982
Robert A. Heinlein, *The Moon Is a Harsh Mistress*, 1966
Lisa Mason, *Arachne*, 1990

Victor Milan, *The Cybernetic Samurai*, 1986
Cordwainer Smith, *Norstrilia*, 1975
Amy Thomson, *Virtual Girl*, 1993
John Varley, *Steel Beach*, 1993

64

ROGER MACBRIDE ALLEN

Inferno

(New York: Ace, 1994)

Story type: Science Fiction (Robot Fiction; Mystery)
Series: Isaac Asimov's Caliban
Major character(s): Caliban, Robot, Revolutionary; Prospero, Robot; Alvar Kresh, Lawman (sheriff)
Time period(s): Indeterminate Future
Locale(s): Inferno, Planet—Imaginary

Summary: A politician's murder creates suspicion of Caliban, the only robot not bound by the protective Laws of Robotics. However, Caliban's actions could send revolutionary reverberations through society.

Other books you might like:
Isaac Asimov, *The Complete Robot*, 1982
Isaac Asimov, *The Robots of Dawn*, 1983
Michael P. Kube-McDowell, *Odyssey*, 1987
Mike McQuay, *Suspicion*, 1987
William F. Wu, *Predator*, 1993

65

ROGER MACBRIDE ALLEN

The Modular Man

(New York: Bantam Sepctra, 1992)

Story type: Science Fiction (Cyberpunk; Political)
Series: Next Wave
Major character(s): David "Herbert" Clancy Bailey, Robot (human imprinted), Inventor; Samantha "Sam" Crandall, Journalist (*The Washington Post*); Phillipe "Phil" Montoya Sanders, Police Officer, Computer Expert (amateur)
Time period(s): 21st century
Locale(s): Washington, District of Columbia

Summary: When Bailey moves his personality into a machine hoping to avoid death, forces move to declare him legally dead and power down the hardware, intending to avoid a world populated by rich immortals and poverty-struck mortal humans. Includes a 12-page article by Isaac Asimov on intelligent robots.

Other books you might like:
Greg Bear, *Heads*, 1991
David Brin, *Earth*, 1990
Pat Cadigan, *Mindplayers*, 1987
Philip K. Dick, *Blade Runner*, 1982
Robert A. Heinlein, *The Moon Is a Harsh Mistress*, 1966
Victor Milan, *The Cybernetic Samurai*, 1986
Rudy Rucker, *Software*, 1982
Rudy Rucker, *Wetware*, 1988
Melissa Scott, *Dreamships*, 1992

Michael Swanwick, *Vacuum Flowers*, 1987
Thomas T. Thomas, *ME: A Novel of Self Discovery*, 1991
John Varley, *Steel Beach*, 1992
Vernor Vinge, *A Fire upon the Deep*, 1992
Walter Jon Williams, *Voice of the Whirlwind*, 1987

66

ROGER MACBRIDE ALLEN

The Ring of Charon

(New York: Tor, 1990)

Story type: Science Fiction (Hard Science Fiction; Disaster)
Series: Hunted Earth
Major character(s): Larry O'Shawnessy Chao, Scientist (gravity researcher); Dianne Steiger, Spaceship Captain; Frank Barlow, Spaceman
Time period(s): Indeterminate Future
Locale(s): Gravities Research Station, Pluto; Earth; Outer Space

Summary: When the remote gravity research facility's funding is threatened, Larry Chao sneaks in an unauthorized experiment on the gravity generator, the Ring of Charon. His new configuration allows the first strong gravity waves to be generated in Sol Space, awakening automatic equipment quiescent for millenia. The automatic equipment triggered includes a device which transports the Earth, but not the Moon, out of Sol Space. Other equipment begins breaking up and moving other astronomical bodies. The humans remaining must find out how to stop this disaster while those on Earth must find how to survive in their new location.

Other books you might like:
David Brin, *Startide Rising*, 1983
Robert L. Forward, *Dragon's Egg*, 1980
Dan Simmons, *The Fall of Hyperion*, 1990
Dan Simmons, *Hyperion*, 1989
John E. Stith, *Redshift Rendezvous*, 1990

67

ROGER MACBRIDE ALLEN

The Shattered Sphere

(New York: Tor, 1994)

Story type: Science Fiction (First Contact; Space Opera)
Series: Hunted Earth
Major character(s): Sianna Colette, Scientist (gravitational physicist), Student; Wally Sturgis, Computer Expert (Multisystem Research Institute), Student (doctoral candidate); Larry O'Shawnessy Chao, Scientist (gravitational physicist)
Time period(s): 25th century (2430s)
Locale(s): Naked Purple Habitat, Space Station (former L5 colony); *Terra Nova*, Spaceship; Earth (displaced to the Multisystem)

Summary: Earth loses contact with the colonized Solar System after Larry Chao's experiment with gravity awakens an ancient mechanism which transports the Earth through a wormhole into an artificial planetary system with several stars orbiting a Dyson sphere, all held in orbits utilizing colossal gravity forces. Five years later, Larry Chao searches alien artifacts on the Moon for direction in his quest to recover the stolen Earth, while Sianna and Wally struggle to understand the alien technology until a monstrous invader threatens to destroy all. Sequel to *The Ring of Charon*.

Other books you might like:
Stephen Baxter, *Raft*, 1991
Glen Cook, *The Dragon Never Sleeps*, 1988
Robert L. Forward, *Dragon's Egg*, 1980
Vonda N. McIntyre, *Metaphase*, 1992
Vonda N. McIntyre, *Transition*, 1991
John E. Stith, *Redshift Rendezvous*, 1990
Vernor Vinge, *A Fire upon the Deep*, 1992

68

ROGER MACBRIDE ALLEN
ERIC KOTANI, Co-Author

Supernova

(New York: Avon, 1991)

Story type: Science Fiction (Hard Science Fiction; Disaster)
Major character(s): George Prescott, Scientist, Student; Desmond Miller, Doctor; Jessica Talmadge, Scientist, Student
Time period(s): 1990s; 2000s
Locale(s): Arizona; California; Japan

Summary: George Prescott, studying supernova formation, focuses in on Sirius. His models predict that this star is indeed a candidate for a supernova. When he announces this at an amateur astronomy meeting, others start studying Sirius. Meanwhile Desmond, who has just lost his family because of a madman's deed, joins a millennialist cult, the Christriders, and sees in the Sirius supernova data the proof of the end of the world. Millennialists are prevented from blowing up Los Angeles' water supply and the worst supernova effects are averted, with warning, giving the world about 100 years to prepare for the hard radiation that will shower on them from the Sirius supernova.

Other books you might like:
Piers Anthony, *Rings of Ice*, 1974
Greg Bear, *The Forge of God*, 1987
David Brin, *Earth*, 1990
Fred Hoyle, *The Inferno*, 1973
    Geoffrey Hoyle, co-author
Eric Kotani, *Between the Stars*, 1988
    John Maddox Roberts, co-author
Eric Kotani, *The Island Worlds*, 1987
    John Maddox Roberts, co-author
Larry Niven, *Lucifer's Hammer*, 1977
    Jerry Pournelle, co-author

69

ROGER MACBRIDE ALLEN

Utopia

(New York: Ace, 1996)

Story type: Science Fiction (Robot Fiction)
Series: Isaac Asimov's Caliban
Major character(s): Alvar Kresh, Political Figure (governor); Davlo Lentrall, Scientist; Caliban, Robot
Time period(s): Indeterminate Future
Locale(s): Inferno, Planet—Imaginary

Summary: To prevent the planet Inferno from dying, residents plan to drop a comet on it, creating a polar sea and a whole new ecology. However, many people do not want to see any change in their cozy lives, especially robots that will not allow any danger to humans, even if it costs Inferno its future. But for one, the fall of the comet provides a chance to exact vengeance.

Other books you might like:
Isaac Asimov, *Robots and Empire*, 1985
Arthur C. Clarke, *The Hammer of God*, 1993
James P. Hogan, *Code of the Lifemaker*, 1983
Anne McCaffrey, *The City Who Fought*, 1993
    S.M. Stirling, co-author
Frederik Pohl, *Mining the Oort*, 1992
L. Neil Smith, *The Venus Belt*, 1981
William F. Wu, *Predator*, 1993

70

SHEILA ROSALYND ALLEN

The Meddlesome Ghost

(New York: Walker, 1989)

Story type: Fantasy (Romance)
Series: Lovers of Steadford Abbey
Major character(s): Sir Harry Steadford, Spirit, Nobleman
Time period(s): 19th century
Locale(s): England

Summary: Doomed to be a ghost until he atones for his past, Sir Harry decides to play matchmaker for each heir to Steadford Abbey. The latest heir is paralyzed and bed-ridden by a recent wound and already has a fiancee; but, that doesn't stop Harry from trying to fix him up with his nurse.

Other books you might like:
Rebecca Brandewyne, *Passion Moon Rising*, 1989
Lindsay Clarke, *The Chymical Wedding*, 1989
Dean Wesley Smith, *Laying the Music to Rest*, 1989

71

AARON ALLSTON

Doc Sidhe

(New York: Baen, 1995)

Story type: Fantasy (Alternate World; Adventure)
Major character(s): Harris Greene, Sports Figure (kickboxing), Martial Arts Expert (tae kwon do); Desmond

''Doc Sidhe'' MaqqRee, Hero (crime-fighting superhero); Gabriela ''Gaby'' Donohue, Experimental Subject, Girlfriend
Time period(s): 1990s; Indeterminate
Locale(s): New York, New York; Alternate Earth

Summary: When Harris interrupts a strange trio's attempt to kidnap Gaby, a conjuring circle transports Harris to New York City, seemingly of the 1930s, but with many differences in the familiar environment. Harris soon meets Doc Sidhe who helps Harris locate Gaby and unravel the mystery surrounding her supressed magical abilities while deadly foes of various species plot against both universes.

Other books you might like:
Robin Wayne Bailey, *Brothers of the Dragon*, 1993
Gordon R. Dickson, *The Dragon and the George*, 1976
Philip Jose Farmer, *Escape From Loki*, 1991
Alis A. Rasmussen, *The Labyrinth Gate*, 1988
Kenneth Robeson, *Doc Savage Omnibus #1*, 1986
   pseudonym of Will Murray
Kenneth Robeson, *White Eyes*, 1992
   pseudonym of Will Murray

72

AARON ALLSTON

Double Jeopardy
(New York: Tor, 1994)

Story type: Science Fiction (Humor)
Series: Car Warriors
Major character(s): James ''Spark'' Parker, Insurance Investigator; Bojake ''Buffalo'' Lincoln, Insurance Investigator; E. ''Pif'' Heiligmann, Detective
Time period(s): 21st century
Locale(s): Texas

Summary: While trying to solve a case for Reunion Insurance Company, Spark, Buffalo, and Pif run afoul of the powerful Medcorp, needing their training as skilled combat drivers and investigators to stay alive and clear their names.

Other books you might like:
John DeChancie, *Starrigger*, 1983
John DeChancie, *Paradox Alley*, 1987
John DeChancie, *Red Limit Freeway*, 1984
David Drake, *The Square Deal*, 1992
Roger Zelazny, *Damnation Alley*, 1986

73

AARON ALLSTON

Galatea in 2-D
(New York: Baen, 1993)

Story type: Fantasy (Contemporary; Magic Conflict)
Major character(s): Roger Simmons, Artist; Elsie, Mythical Creature (nymph); Kevin Matthews, Artist, Criminal
Time period(s): 1990s
Locale(s): Earth

Summary: When Roger Simmons discovers the ability of bringing forth characters from his paintings, Kevin Matthews,

another artist adept at animating characters from paintings, decides he must quash Roger's ability and, if necessary, his life.

Other books you might like:
Chester Anderson, *The Butterfly Kid*, 1967
Charles de Lint, *The Little Country*, 1991
Michael Ende, *The Neverending Story*, 1983
Philip Jose Farmer, *Red Orc's Rage*, 1991
Tim Powers, *Last Call*, 1992
Clifford D. Simak, *Out of Their Minds*, 1970
Wm. Mark Simmons, *When Dreams Collide*, 1992
Vivian Vande Velde, *User Unfriendly*, 1991
Oscar Wilde, *The Picture of Dorian Gray*, 1891

74

DAVID AMBROSE

The Man Who Turned into Himself
(New York: St. Martin's, 1994)

Story type: Horror (Doppelganger)
Major character(s): Rick Hamilton, Publisher (magazine); Harold Allison, Lawyer; Emma Todd, Doctor (psychiatrist)
Time period(s): 1990s (1994)
Locale(s): Devon, Connecticut

Summary: After an accident, magazine publisher Rick Hamilton awakens to find himself trapped inside the consciousness of his alter ego, real-estate developer Richard Hamilton, who lives in the world of the alter egos of everyone else Rick knows. Rick must convince Richard that he is not merely a psychotic aspect of Richard, but a legitimate personality who wants to return to his own world. This is the author's first novel.

Other books you might like:
David Ely, *Seconds*, 1963
Richard Matheson, *7 Seconds to Midnight*, 1993
T.L. Parkinson, *The Man Upstairs*, 1991
Daniel Quinn, *Dreamer*, 1989

75

J. EDWARD AMES

The Death Crystal
(New York: Leisure, 1990)

Story type: Horror (Serial Killer)
Major character(s): Harlan Perry, Maintenance Worker (janitor); Stevie Lasalle, Psychologist, Teacher (self-defense); Neal Bryce, Police Officer
Time period(s): 1990s
Locale(s): New Orleans, Louisiana

Summary: Under the influence of his schizophrenic alter ego Johnny Law, and with the help of the magic Tuoai Stone of Atlantis, homicidal Vietnam veteran Harlan Perry commits a series of brutal murders that have an infectious influence on the city of New Orleans.

Other books you might like:
Peter Straub, *Koko*, 1988

76

J. EDWARD AMES

Spellcaster

(New York: Zebra, 1989)

Story type: Horror (Black Magic)
Major character(s): Alexey Zverkov, Psychic (Possessor of an "evil eye"); Alan Breaux, Detective—Police
Time period(s): 1980s (During Mardi Gras)
Locale(s): New Orleans, Louisiana (French Quarter)

Summary: Vowing revenge for the death of his lover-sister, Alexey Zverkov develops his "evil eye" to the point where he can wreak unbelievable havoc at will, a power he plans to unleash at the height of the Mardi Gras celebration. Led by Detective Breaux, a small group follows a series of murders to track Zverkov, penetrate his disguise, and thwart his evil plans.

Other books you might like:
Dennis Wheatley, *Strange Conflict*, 1941

77

JOHN EDWARD AMES

The Asylum

(New York: Zebra, 1994)

Story type: Horror (Mystery)
Major character(s): Reno Sloan, Detective—Private (former lawyer); Malachi Feldman, Scientist (chemist); Erin Kirby, Detective—Police
Time period(s): 1990s (1994)
Locale(s): New Orleans, Louisiana (Cypress Island)

Summary: Disbarred lawyer Reno Sloan uncovers a plot among the administrators of the Cypress Island Clinic to feed a newly-invented hallucinogenic drug to the children of local rich families, and "treat" them for the psychoses it induces at significant expense once they are admitted into the clinic.

Other books you might like:
Robin Cook, *Coma*, 1977
Stephen King, *Firestarter*, 1980
Kathe Koja, *Bad Brains*, 1992
Karl Edward Wagner, "The Fourth Seal", 1984
   in *In a Lonely Place*
F. Paul Wilson, *The Select*, 1994

 78

MEL D. AMES

Tales of Titillation and Terror

(Oakville, Ontario/Buffalo, New York: Mosaic Press, 1996)

Story type: Horror (Collection)

Summary: This collection brings together 15 stories of mystery and supernatural horror by a Canadian writer. "The Messiah of Soul" is a homage to Edgar Allan Poe, and "The Embryo" a blend of horror and science fiction concerned with psychological and physical regression. "The Polargeist" and "Sasquatch" both draw their brooding atmosphere from their Canadian wilderness settings while "The Ghost Walker" and "The Promise of His Coming" employ unreliable, and possibly psychologically unbalanced, narrators. "The Enigma of Andrew Marler" and "No Sirens for Jonathan" are revenge stories with O Henry-type twists. Don Hutchison and Peter Sellers both supply introductions.

Other books you might like:
S. Darnbrook Colson, *People of the Night*, 1994
Christopher Fowler, *Sharper Knives*, 1992
Brian Hopkins, *Something Haunts Us All*, 1995
Elizabeth Massie, *Shadow Dreams*, 1996
David Niall Wilson, *The Fall of the House of Escher and Other Illusions*, 1995

79

MARTIN AMIS

London Fields

(New York: Harmony Books, 1990)

Story type: Science Fiction (Literary)
Major character(s): Samson Young, Writer; Nicola Six, Girlfriend
Time period(s): Indeterminate Future
Locale(s): England

Summary: As the world nears environmental collapse, Sam Young, an American writer dying, perhaps of radiation poisoning, moves to London and rents the flat of the dramatist and sexual athlete Mark Asprey. Young is writing a murder mystery based on the lives of those around him, including Asprey and his girlfriend Nicola Six. The events of Young's life mirror in curious fashion those of the ongoing environmental collapse.

Other books you might like:
Doris Lessing, *The Fifth Child*, 1988
James Morrow, *This Is the Way the World Ends*, 1986
Kim Stanley Robinson, *The Gold Coast*, 1988
Fay Weldon, *The Cloning of Joanna May*, 1990

80

MARTIN AMIS

Time's Arrow

(New York: Harmony Books, 1991)

Story type: Science Fiction (Literary; Time Travel)
Major character(s): Tod T. Friendly, Doctor, Criminal
Time period(s): 1940s; 1950s
Locale(s): New York, New York; Auschwitz, Poland; Munich, Germany

Summary: Tod T. Friendly's life unfolds backward in time as the symbiote infecting him progressively works its way through memories from his recent life as a physician in America to earlier memories of atrocities committed and life surrounding his duties as a doctor at Auschwitz, to earliest memories of his childhood in pre-Hitler Germany.

Other books you might like:
Piers Anthony, *Bearing an Hourglass*, 1984

Philip K. Dick, *Ubik*, 1969
Ken Grimwood, *Replay*, 1986
Dan Simmons, *The Fall of Hyperion*, 1990
Dan Simmons, *Hyperion*, 1989
Kurt Vonnegut Jr., *The Sirens of Titan*, 1959
Kurt Vonnegut Jr., *Slaughterhouse Five*, 1969
T.H. White, *The Once and Future King*, 1958

81

BETH AMOS

Cold White Fury

(New York: HarperPaperbacks, 1996)

Story type: Horror (Wild Talents)
Major character(s): Jennifer Bolton, Teacher; Tanner Bolton, Child (Jennifer's 8-year-old son); Eric Singleton, Doctor
Time period(s): 1990s (1995)
Locale(s): Hillenberg, Virginia

Summary: A routine MRI scan reacts with a metal sliver lodged in young Tanner Bolton's head, activating his extra-sensory perception and psychic powers. Tanner and his mother learn their lives are endangered when Tanner's conversations with the ghost of his father, formerly a geneticist, reveal that people close to the Bolton family are involved in a conspiracy to use lower class people as human guinea pigs in genetic experiments. First novel.

Other books you might like:
Douglas Clegg, *Eye of the Needle*, 1994
John Farris, *The Fury*, 1976
Stephen King, *Firestarter*, 1980
Dean R. Koontz, *Lightning*, 1988
Michael Kurland, *Button Bright*, 1990
David B. Silva, *Disappeared*, 1995

82

DANA ANDERSON
CHARLES DE LINT, Co-Author
RAY GARTON, Co-Author

Cafe Purgatorium

(New York: Tor, 1991)

Story type: Horror (Anthology)
Summary: Three novellas of horror and fantasy. The title story by Dana Anderson is concerned with a love that persists from beyond the grave. Charles de Lint's "Death Leaves an Echo" is a horror tale of a dead man forced to choose between horrible alternatives. Ray Garton's "Dr. Krusadian's Methods" tells of a unique type of therapy given to curb the child-abusing tendencies of two parents.

Other books you might like:
Mervyn Peake, *Sometime, Never*, 1954
   William Golding and John Wyndham, co-authors
Lucius Shepard, *Nantucket Slayrides*, 1990
   Robert Frazer, co-author
Lucius Shepard, *The Night Visions Series*, 1984-1992
   no author on *Night Visions* series, changing editor with each of the 10 volumes

83

KEVIN J. ANDERSON
DOUG BEASON, Co-Author

Assemblers of Infinity

(New York: Bantam Spectra, 1993)

Story type: Science Fiction (Invasion of Earth; Hard Science Fiction)
Major character(s): Celeste McConnell, Administrator (director of US Space Agency), Psychic (esper); Jason Dvorak, Administrator (director of Columbus Base), Architect; Erika Trace, Scientist (nanotechnology)
Time period(s): 2020s
Locale(s): Columbus Base, Moon (Earth's); Antarctica; Daedalus Crater, Moon (Earth's)

Summary: When a routine check of the array at Dedalus on the far side of the Moon discovers a large alien construction site which kills the investigating crew, Celeste McConnell sends nanotechnologist Erika Trace to research the phenomenon in isolation at the Sim-Mars station which waited unoccupied to train the upcoming Mars expedition. Fears over the nanocritters' possible threat to Earth forces McConnell to prevent any personnel returning from the Moon, but, unfortunately nanocritters may already contaminate the Earth.

Other books you might like:
Roger MacBride Allen, *The Ring of Charon*, 1990
Greg Bear, *Blood Music*, 1985
David Brin, *Earth*, 1990
Octavia E. Butler, *Dawn*, 1987
Michael Flynn, *The Nanotech Chronicles*, 1991
Diana G. Gallagher, *The Alien Dark*, 1990
Janet Kagan, *Mirabile*, 1991

84

KEVIN J. ANDERSON

Blindfold

(New York: Warner Aspect, 1995)

Story type: Science Fiction (Psychic Powers; Political)
Major character(s): Kalliana, Telepath (truthsayer); Troy Boren, Accountant, Outlaw; Tharion, Telepath (Truthsayer Guild master)
Time period(s): Indeterminate
Locale(s): Atlas, Planet—Imaginary; OrbLab2, Space Station

Summary: When the Truthsayer Kalliana falsely convicts Troy Boren of murder, Guild Master Tharion learns that someone has tampered with the telepathy-inducing drug Veritas, thereby undermining the entire judicial system on Atlas.

Other books you might like:
Karen Haber, *The War Minstrels*, 1995
Karen Haber, *Woman Without a Shadow*, 1995
Anne McCaffrey, *Damia*, 1992
Anne McCaffrey, *Pegasus in Flight*, 1990
Anne McCaffrey, *The Rowan*, 1990
Anne McCaffrey, *To Ride Pegasus*, 1973
Joanna Russ, *And Chaos Died*, 1970

85

KEVIN J. ANDERSON

Climbing Olympus

(New York: Warner Aspect, 1994)

Story type: Science Fiction (Space Colony; Hard Science Fiction)

Major character(s): Rachel Dycek, Doctor; Boris Tiban, Criminal, Genetically Altered Being; Cora Marisovna, Criminal, Genetically Altered Being

Time period(s): 21st century

Locale(s): Mars

Summary: As genetically altered colonists terraform Mars, the rebellious leader of the severely modified humans, Boris Tiban, tries to destroy everything to avenge the wrongs done to him. As he rages, Rachel Dycek and Cora Marisovna, mother of his Earth-normal child, take refuge at a sanctuary until they can begin rebuilding and lobbying for the terraforming project and the rights of the colonists.

Other books you might like:
Greg Bear, *Moving Mars*, 1993
Ben Bova, *Mars*, 1992
Kim Stanley Robinson, *Red Mars*, 1993
Allen Steele, *Labyrinth of Night*, 1992
S.C. Sykes, *Red Genesis*, 1991

86

KEVIN J. ANDERSON

Darksaber

(New York: Bantam Spectra, 1995)

Story type: Science Fiction (Mystical; Space Opera)

Series: Star Wars

Major character(s): Luke Skywalker, Martial Arts Expert (Jedi Knight), Hero; Leia Organa Solo, Royalty, Leader; Callista, Martial Arts Expert (Jedi Knight), Pilot (spaceship)

Time period(s): Indeterminate Past

Locale(s): New Republic, Interstellar Empire/Federation

Summary: In search of a means to restore Jedi abilities to his love, Callista, Luke Skywalker revisits Tatooine to contact Obi-Wan Kenobi's spirit. There he discovers a plan among the galaxy's criminal warlords to reconstruct a superweapon, the Death Star. Meanwhile, surviving Imperial forces plan to crush the New Republic.

Other books you might like:
Roger MacBride Allen, *Ambush at Corellia*, 1995
Brian Daley, *The Han Solo Adventures*, 1992
Barbara Hambly, *Children of the Jedi*, 1995
Vonda N. McIntyre, *The Crystal Star*, 1994
L. Neil Smith, *The Lando Calrissian Adventures*, 1994
Timothy Zahn, *Heir to the Empire*, 1991

87

KEVIN J. ANDERSON

Game's End

(New York: Roc, 1990)

Story type: Fantasy (Alternate World)

Series: Gamearth

Major character(s): Melanie, Student, Sports Figure (fantasy gameplayer); David, Student, Sports Figure (fantasy gameplayer)

Time period(s): 1990s (1990)

Locale(s): Earth; Gamearth, Planet—Imaginary

Summary: Gamearth has become real for Melanie and David. As the last Sorcerers on Gamearth work to free their world from the Players' control, David continues to try to destroy it. This time Gamearth has learned how to fight back.

Other books you might like:
M.A.R. Barker, *Man of Gold*, 1984
Steven Brust, *Jhereg*, 1983
Geary Gravel, *A Key for the Nonesuch*, 1990
Joel Rosenberg, *The Sleeping Dragon*, 1983
Will Shetterly, *The Tangled Lands*, 1989

88

KEVIN J. ANDERSON

Gameplay

(New York: Signet, 1989)

Story type: Fantasy (Alternate World)

Series: Gamearth

Major character(s): David, Student, Sports Figure (Fantasy gameplayer); Melanie, Student, Sports Figure (Fantasy gameplayer)

Time period(s): Indeterminate

Locale(s): Earth; Gamearth, Planet—Imaginary

Summary: Though David failed in his first attempt to destroy Gamearth, he has not given up. His creation of Scartis threatens the world of Gamearth if the players cannot find a way to defeat him. Unfortunately, the fantasy characters have taken on a life of their own and even ''Rulewoman'' Melanie's secret map changes may not save the game.

Other books you might like:
Barbara Hambly, *The Silent Tower*, 1988
Joel Rosenberg, *Guardians of the Flame: The Warriors*, 1983-1985
Will Shetterly, *The Tangled Lands*, 1989
Sheri S. Tepper, *Marianne, the Matchbox and the Malachite Mouse*, 1989

89

KEVIN J. ANDERSON

Ground Zero

(New York: HarperPrism, 1995)

Story type: Horror (Science Fiction)

Series: X-Files

Major character(s): Fox Mulder, FBI Agent; Dana Scully, FBI Agent, Doctor; Matthew Bradoukis, Military Personnel (general)
Time period(s): 1990s (1995)
Locale(s): Pleasonton, California; Washington, District of Columbia

Summary: Based on the popular television show "The X-Files," about a pair of special FBI agents assigned to crack cases too weird for regular field operatives. This novel take agents Mulder and Scully to a laboratory in California to investigate the disintegrated remains of Dr. Emil Gregory, a nuclear physicist whose project "Bright Anvil" has produced a nuclear weapon that can kill on a small scale without creating fallout. When other people around the country begin dying as Gregory did, Mulder and Scully must find out who, or what, has acquired Gregory's secret weapon.

Other books you might like:
Charles L. Grant, *Goblins*, 1994
Charles L. Grant, *Whirlwind*, 1995
Jeff Rice, *The Night Stalker*, 1973
Jeff Rice, *The Night Strangler*, 1974

90

KEVIN J. ANDERSON
DOUG BEASON, Co-Author

Ill Wind

(New York: Forge, 1995)

Story type: Science Fiction (Disaster)
Major character(s): Spencer Lockwood, Scientist (physicist), Administrator (solar-satellite project); Connor Brooks, Sailor, Criminal; Todd Severyn, Engineer (petroleum)
Time period(s): 1990s
Locale(s): California; New Mexico; Southwest

Summary: When a supertanker's oil spill in San Francisco Bay leads officials to employ unproven, oil-eating bacteria in the cleanup, petroleum-based modern technology suffers collapse. Scientists then race to deploy solar power satellites to avert worldwide chaos.

Other books you might like:
John Barnes, *Mother of Storms*, 1994
David Brin, *Earth*, 1990
Larry Niven, *Footfall*, 1985
  Jerry Pournelle, co-author
Larry Niven, *Lucifer's Hammer*, 1977
  Jerry Pournelle, co-author
Kit Pedler, *Mutant 59, The Plastic Eater*, 1972
  Gerry Davis, co-author
Neal Stephenson, *Snow Crash*, 1992

91

KEVIN J. ANDERSON

Jedi Search

(New York: Bantam Spectra, 1994)

Story type: Science Fiction (Space Opera)
Series: Star Wars: Jedi Academy Trilogy

Major character(s): Luke Skywalker, Martial Arts Expert (Jedi Knight), Hero; Han Solo, Spaceship Captain, Warrior; Chewbacca, Alien (Wookie), Adventurer
Time period(s): Indeterminate Past
Locale(s): Coruscant, Planet—Imaginary; Kessel, Planet—Imaginary; New Republic, Interstellar Empire/Federation

Summary: While Luke Skywalker begins setting up a new training center for Jedi Knights on Coruscant, Han Solo and Chewbacca break out of prison on Kessel, fleeing to a secret Imperial research laboratory. When Luke seeks his friends, he discovers a new weapon, more powerful than even the old emperor's Death Star.

Other books you might like:
Brian Daley, *The Han Solo Adventures*, 1992
Vonda N. McIntyre, *The Crystal Star*, 1994
Kathy Tyers, *The Truce at Bakura*, 1994
Dave Wolverton, *The Courtship of Princess Leia*, 1994
Timothy Zahn, *Heir to the Empire*, 1991

92

KEVIN J. ANDERSON
DOUG BEASON, Co-Author

Lifeline

(New York: Bantam Spectra, 1990)

Story type: Science Fiction (Post-Holocaust; Political)
Major character(s): Ramis Barrera, Settler (colonist); Anna Tripolk, Scientist (biologist); Duncan McLaris, Manufacturer, Administrator
Time period(s): 21st century
Locale(s): Kibalchick, Space Station; Orbitech, Space Station; Clavius Base, Moon (Earth's)

Summary: After Earth self-destructs, the L5 colonies and Moon Base must survive. Aguinaldo has adequate food, but only gets it to Orbitech after much of the population has been spaced. The leader of Kibalchick thinks it is her duty to destroy all the American colonies. Ramis Barrera takes food to Orbitech and manages to defuse the weapons on Kibalchick set to blow up Orbitech. He ends up joining the Russians in colonizing Mars.

Other books you might like:
Ben Bova, *Test of Fire*, 1982
Philip Jose Farmer, *Tongues of the Moon*, 1964
Andrew Stephenson, *Nightwatch*, 1979

93

KEVIN J. ANDERSON

Ruins

(New York: HarperPrism, 1996)

Story type: Horror (Science Fiction)
Series: X-Files
Major character(s): Dana Scully, FBI Agent, Doctor; Fox Mulder, FBI Agent; Cassandra Rubicon, Archaeologist
Time period(s): 1990s (1996)
Locale(s): Xitaclan, Mexico

Summary: In this fourth novel based on the popular television series, agents Mulder and Scully, specialists in investigating paranormal phenomena are sent to a dig site at the Pyramid of Kukulkan on the Yucatan peninsula to find a missing university archaeology expedition. Their discoveries bring them into conflict with Central American drug lords, tomb looters, the United States military, and possibly supernatural and extraterrestrial powers that seem to be attracted to the pyramid.

Other books you might like:
Randall Boyll, *Darkman #4: The Face of Death*, 1994
Charles L. Grant, *Goblins*, 1984
Charles L. Grant, *Whirlwind*, 1995
Jeff Rice, *The Night Stalker*, 1973

94

KEVIN J. ANDERSON
LARRY DICKISON, Illustrator

Shifting the Boundaries: The Selected Works of Kevin J. Anderson

(Concord, California: Dark Regions Press, 1995)

Story type: Horror (Collection)

Summary: Eight stories blend elements of fantasy, horror and science fiction in the author's first collection. ''A Glimpse of the Ankou'' and ''Dark Angel, Archangel'' offer two different visions of death incarnate. In ''Drilling Deep,'' drilling into the stratas beneath a farm transforms the landscape into a forest primeval. ''Final Performance'' suggests ghostly revenge as the reason for the burning of Shakespeare's Globe Theatre, while ''Scarecrow'' tells of the rather strange gods to whom a psychotic farm woman pays her obeisance. Doug Beason supplies the introduction.

Other books you might like:
Kim Antieau, *Trudging to Eden*, 1994
Michael A. Arnzen, *Needles and Sins*, 1993
Elizabeth Massie, *Southern Discomfort: Selected Works of Elizabeth Massie*, 1993
Ardath Mayhar, *Mean Little Old Lady at Work*, 1993
Stephen Mark Rainey, *Fugue Devil and Other Weird Horrors*, 1992

95

KEVIN J. ANDERSON, Editor

Tales From Jabba's Palace

(New York: Bantam Spectra, 1996)

Story type: Science Fiction (Anthology; Space Opera)
Series: Star Wars
Major character(s): Jabba the Hutt, Organized Crime Figure, Alien
Time period(s): Indeterminate Past
Locale(s): Tatooine, Planet—Imaginary; Galactic Empire, Interstellar Empire/Federation

Summary: Contains a two-page introduction, seven pages of authors' biographies, a five-page epilog, and 19 original stories featuring the shady characters from Jabba's Palace in *The Return of the Jedi*. Authors include Kevin J. Anderson, M.

Shayne Bell, John Gregory Betancourt, A.C. Crispin, George Alec Effinger, Kenneth C. Flint, Esther M. Friesner, Barbara Hamby, Judith and Garfield Reeves-Stevens, Jennifer Roberson, Kathy Tyers, Deborah Wheeler, Dave Wolverton, William Wu, and Timothy Zahn.

Other books you might like:
Roger MacBride Allen, *Ambush at Corellia*, 1995
Barbara Hambly, *Children of the Jedi*, 1995
James Kahn, *Return of the Jedi*, 1983
Michael P. Kube-McDowell, *Before the Storm*, 1996
George Lucas, *The Star Wars Trilogy*, 1987
    Donald F. Glut, James Kahn, co-authors
Timothy Zahn, *Heir to the Empire*, 1991

96

KEVIN J. ANDERSON, Editor

Tales From the Mos Eisley Cantina

(New York: Bantam Spectra, 1995)

Story type: Science Fiction (Anthology; Adventure)
Series: Star Wars
Time period(s): Indeterminate Past
Locale(s): Interstellar Empire/Federation; Tatooine, Planet—Imaginary (Mos Eisley spaceport)

Summary: Contains seven pages of authors' biographies and 16 original stories utilizing a multitude of characters and familiar settings from George Lucas' *Star Wars* (1976) milieu. The 18 authors include Kevin J. Anderson, Doug Beason, M. Shayne Bell, David Bischoff, A.C. Crispin, Kenneth C. Flint, Barbara Hambly, Daniel Keys Moran, Jennifer Roberson, Kathy Tyers, Dave Wolverton, and Timothy Zahn.

Other books you might like:
Roger MacBride Allen, *Ambush at Corellia*, 1995
Arthur C. Clarke, *Tales From the White Hart*, 1957
Brian Daley, *The Han Solo Adventures*, 1992
Spider Robinson, *Callahan and Company*, 1987
L. Neil Smith, *The Lando Calrissian Adventures*, 1994

97

KEVIN J. ANDERSON
DOUG BEASON, Co-Author

The Trinity Paradox

(New York: Bantam Spectra, 1991)

Story type: Science Fiction (Alternate Universe; Time Travel)
Major character(s): Elizabeth Devane, Activist, Time Traveller
Time period(s): 1990s; 1940s
Locale(s): Los Alamos, New Mexico

Summary: While sabotaging an exotic weapon at Los Alamos National Laboratory, anti-nuclear activist Elizabeth Devane helps trigger a disastrous explosion that throws her nearly fifty years into the past. Her 1970s college degree in physics and subsequent work in nuclear physics afford Elizabeth enough background to join the Manhattan Project in hopes of stopping the development of nuclear weapons.

Other books you might like:
Keith William Andrews, *Search and Destroy*, 1990
Michael Flynn, *In the Country of the Blind*, 1990
Robert A. Heinlein, *Farnham's Freehold*, 1964
Dan Simmons, *The Fall of Hyperion*, 1990
Dan Simmons, *Hyperion*, 1989
Wilson Tucker, *The Time Masters*, 1971
    revised
John Varley, *Millennium*, 1983
Walter Jon Williams, *Days of Atonement*, 1991

98

KEVIN J. ANDERSON
DOUG BEASON, Co-Author

Virtual Destruction
(New York: Ace, 1996)

Story type: Science Fiction (Techno-Thriller; Mystery)
Major character(s): Hal Michaelson, Computer Expert, Leader; Gary Lesserac, Computer Expert; Craig Kreident, FBI Agent
Time period(s): 1990s
Locale(s): Livermore, California; Washington, District of Columbia

Summary: Hal develops a new virtual reality system while secretly developing a second use for it. Specializing in high tech crime, Craig investigates Hal's death in the V.R. lab.

Other books you might like:
Bruce Bethke, *Headcrash*, 1995
Terry Bisson, *Johnny Mnemonic*, 1995
Alan Dean Foster, *Cyber Way*, 1990
Marc Laidlaw, *Neon Lotus*, 1988
Fred Saberhagen, *Octagon*, 1981
Neal Stephenson, *Snow Crash*, 1992
John E. Stith, *Redshift Rendezvous*, 1990

99

KEVIN J. ANDERSON, Editor

War of the Worlds: Global Dispatches
(New York: Bantam Spectra, 1996)

Story type: Science Fiction (Anthology; Invasion of Earth)
Summary: Contains 19 original stories and essays and one, Howard Waldrop's "Night of the Cooters," reprinted from a 1987 *Omni*. Stories present H.G. Wells' *The War of the Worlds'* Martian invasion as if seen through the eyes of different journalists and notables worldwide, such as Edgar Rice Burroughs, Emily Dickinson, Henry James, Rudyard Kipling, Jack London, Percival Lowell, Pablo Picasso, Joseph Pulitzer, Teddy Roosevelt, Leo Tolstoy, Mark Twain, and Jules Verne. Other authors include Kevin J. Anderson, Doug Beason, M. Shayne Bell, Gregory Benford, Janet Berliner, David Brin, George Alec Effinger, Barbara Hambly, Mike Resnick, Robert Silverberg, Allen Steele, Walter Jon Williams, Connie Willis, and Dave Wolverton.

Other books you might like:
Steven R. Boyett, *Treks Not Taken*, 1996

Randall Garrett, *Takeoff!*, 1979
Randall Garrett, *Takeoff, Too!*, 1986
Manly Wade Wellman, *Sherlock Holmes's War of the Worlds*, 1975
    Wade Wellman, co-author
H.G. Wells, *The War of the Worlds*, 1898

100

MARGARET J. ANDERSON

The Druid's Gift
(New York: Knopf, 1989)

Story type: Fantasy (Time Travel)
Major character(s): Caitlin, Young Woman (Rebellious)
Time period(s): 10th century B.C.; 18th century
Locale(s): St. Kilda Islands, Scotland (Islands off the coast)

Summary: New Druid settlements on the nearby mainland upset the harmony and order of several simple Scottish villages. The villagers fear and distrust the strange Druids and their mysterious ways of magic and music and grow increasingly hostile towards them. Despite the animosity, Caitlin persists in her quest to learn the secret ways of the Druids. With the aid of Druid magic and her own visionary powers, Caitlin travels in spirit form to the future in order to reconcile the fate of her native villagers with that of the Druids.

Other books you might like:
Diana Wynne Jones, *A Tale of Time City*, 1987
Welwyn Wilton Katz, *The Third Magic*, 1988
Richard Peck, *Voices After Midnight*, 1989
William Sleator, *Strange Attractors*, 1990

101

MARGARET J. ANDERSON

The Ghost Inside the Monitor
(New York: Knopf/Bullseye, 1990)

Story type: Fantasy (Time Travel; Young Adult)
Major character(s): Sarah Pearce, Child, Computer Expert; Pascale, Spirit (Ghost)
Time period(s): 20th century
Locale(s): Dixon Landing

Summary: After she turns off her computer screen, 11-year-old Sarah sees the ghost of a child who died in the early years of the century. Then she's pulled through the computer into the ghost's own era.

Other books you might like:
Pam Conrad, *Stonewords: A Ghost Story*, 1990
Gilbert B. Cross, *A Witch Across Time*, 1990
Penelope Lively, *The Ghost of Thomas Kempe*, 1973
Patricia A. McKillip, *The House on Parchment Street*, 1973
Kit Pearson, *Handful of Time*, 1988
Elizabeth Marie Pope, *The Sherwood Ring*, 1958

102

POUL ANDERSON

All One Universe

(New York: Tor, 1996)

Story type: Science Fiction (Collection)

Summary: Contains a two-page introduction plus individual introductions to four essays and 14 stories reprinted from periodicals and anthologies 1978-1993, with most from the last decade. Varying in tone from somber to light, with settings on and off Earth, the stories explore diverse themes such as hard science and scientific advancement, ecology, alternate histories, prehistoric society, and branching realities.

Other books you might like:
Brian W. Aldiss, *Man in His Time: The Best Science Fiction Stories of Brian W. Aldiss*, 1989
Larry Niven, *N-Space*, 1990
Charles Sheffield, *Dancing with Myself*, 1993
Marc Stiegler, *The Gentle Seduction*, 1990
Connie Willis, *Impossible Things*, 1994

103

POUL ANDERSON

The Armies of Elfland

(New York: Tor, 1992)

Story type: Fantasy (Collection)

Summary: Contains a three-page foreward in which Anderson indicates that all stories herein share a romantic vein in the Middle Ages sense of ''a tale full of color and imagination.'' The stories, reprinted from periodicals and books, include one collaboration with Karen Anderson, ''A Feast for the Gods''; one Hugo Award and Nebula Award winner, ''The Queen of Air and Darkness''; and six other stories.

Other books you might like:
David Brin, *The River of Time*, 1986
Orson Scott Card, *Maps in a Mirror*, 1990
John Varley, *Blue Champagne*, 1986
Kurt Vonnegut Jr., *Welcome to the Monkey House*, 1968

104

POUL ANDERSON

The Boat of a Million Years

(New York: Tor, 1989)

Story type: Science Fiction (Immortality)
Major character(s): Hanno, Immortal, Sailor; Rufus, Immortal
Locale(s): Europe; Outer Space

Summary: Hanno, an ancient Phoenician, discovers himself to be immortal and spends more than 2,000 years seaching for others of his kind. Eventually he and the other immortals he discovers leave Earth for the eternal adventure of space exploration.

Other books you might like:
Joe Haldeman, *Buying Time*, 1989

Robert A. Heinlein, *Time Enough for Love*, 1973
Clifford D. Simak, *Way Station*, 1963
Norman Spinrad, *Bug Jack Barron*, 1969
Roger Zelazny, *This Immortal*, 1966

105

POUL ANDERSON

Harvest of Stars

(New York: Tor, 1993)

Story type: Science Fiction (Political; Theological)
Major character(s): Anson Guthrie, Businessman, Disembodied Personality; Kyra Davis, Pilot (spaceship), Spaceman (space colonist); Eiko Tamura, Technician, Spacewoman (space colonist)
Time period(s): Indeterminate Future
Locale(s): Earth; Moon (Earth's); Demeter, Planet—Imaginary

Summary: Trying to expand the Avantists' power beyond North America, Enrique Sayre uses a spare Download of Anson Guthrie, a brilliant entrepreneur and politician, to do the planning. However, Kyra and the Underground have the original Download and get it to the Moon where, with the aid of Rinndalir, Selenarch of Luna, they resist the power of the Avantists. Selected humans who desire freedom colonize Demeter with the aid of a planet-wide intelligence.

Other books you might like:
Greg Bear, *Eon*, 1985
Greg Bear, *Queen of Angels*, 1990
Gordon R. Dickson, *Necromancer*, 1962
Joe Haldeman, *Worlds: A Novel of the Near Future*, 1981
Robert A. Heinlein, *Methuselah's Children*, 1958
Donald Kingsbury, *The Moon Goddess and the Son*, 1986
Michael P. Kube-McDowell, *The Quiet Pools*, 1990
Pamela Sargent, *Venus of Dreams*, 1986
Allen Steele, *Clarke County, Space*, 1990

106

POUL ANDERSON

Harvest the Fire

(New York: Tor, 1995)

Story type: Science Fiction (Political; Alternate Intelligence)
Series: Harvest of Stars
Major character(s): Jesse Nicol, Spaceship Captain, Writer (poet); Lucas ''Venator'' Mthembu, Artificial Intelligence, Robot; Lirion, Genetically Altered Being (Selenarch), Revolutionary (Scaine Croi)
Time period(s): 28th century
Locale(s): Argentina; Hydra Square, Moon (Earth's); *Verdea*, Spaceship

Summary: A poet searching for understanding, Nicol leaves Earth to work for the lunar based transportation which still employs human pilots. Sympathetic to the genetically manipulated Selenarchs, the Scaine Croi recruits him to pilot a ship to Proserpina. Resurrected from the Terramind as a Peace

Force robot, Venator finds himself outmaneuvered by Lirion and unable to foil the Scaine Croi plot.

Other books you might like:
Jack C. Haldeman II, *High Steel*, 1993
    Jack Dann, co-author
Fred Saberhagen, *Berserker*, 1967
George Turner, *Genetic Soldier*, 1994
John Varley, *Steel Beach*, 1992
Jack Williamson, *The Humanoids*, 1949

107

POUL ANDERSON

Inconstant Star

(New York: Baen, 1991)

Story type: Science Fiction (Adventure; Military)
Series: Man-Kzin Wars
Major character(s): Eric Saxtorph, Spaceship Captain (owner-tramp spaceship); Ulf Reichstein Markham, Administrator (commissioner of Space Station); Tyra Nordbo, Writer, Noblewoman (Wunderland)
Time period(s): 23rd century
Locale(s): Wunderland, Planet—Imaginary; Outer Space

Summary: Eric Saxtorph wants to investigate a mysterious star that originated outside the galaxy. Commissioner Markham blocks this until he can come along as he is a Kzin agent. After Saxtorph's return, Tyra Nordbo charters the ship to clear her father of the charge of being in Kzin pay. She discovers a black hole and makes a further discovery that it is her brother who is the Kzin agent. This volume collects two short pieces, *Iron*, published originally in *The Man-Kzin Wars* (1988), and *Inconstant Star*, published originally in *The Man-Kzin Wars III* (1990).

Other books you might like:
Dean Ing, *Cathouse*, 1991
Larry Niven, *Tales of Known Space*, 1975
H. Beam Piper, *Space Viking*, 1963
Jerry Pournelle, *Prince of Mercenaries*, 1989
L. Neil Smith, *Contact and Commune*, 1990
Sheri S. Tepper, *Grass*, 1989

108

POUL ANDERSON
STEVEN POPKES, Co-Author

The Longest Voyage/Slow Lightning

(New York: Tor, 1991)

Story type: Science Fiction (First Contact)
Major character(s): Val Nira, Space Explorer (marooned); Gray, Alien (Spatien); Gnoza, Alien
Time period(s): Indeterminate Future; 21st century (2019-2035)
Locale(s): Hisagazi Yarzik Island, Moon—Imaginary; *Proud Mary*, Spaceship

Summary: Poul Anderson's "The Longest Voyage" received the Hugo Award after its publication in *Analog* (Dec. 1960). In the story, Rovic moves precipitously to protect what he

perceives as his society's right to develop at its own pace when he is confronted with changes he foresees through Val Nira's contact. Previously unpublished, Steven Popkes' "Slow Lightning" suggests a future in which humans help extraterrestrials determine if humanity is to be considered intelligent or just food for the truly intelligent residents of the galaxy.

Other books you might like:
Isaac Asimov, *The Ugly Little Boy/The Widget, the Wadget, and Boff*, 1989
    Theodore Sturgeon, co-author
David Brin, *Startide Rising*, 1983
Gordon R. Dickson, *Naked to the Stars/The Alien Way*, 1990
John M. Ford, *Fugue State/The Death of Dr. Island*, 1990
    Gene Wolfe, co-author
Vonda N. McIntyre, *Screwtop/The Girl Who Was Plugged In*, 1989
    James Tiptree, Jr., co-author
Steven Popkes, *Caliban Landing*, 1987
John Varley, *Press Enter/Hawksbill Station*, 1990
    Robert Silverberg, co-author
John Varley, *Tango Charlie and Foxtrot Charlie/The Star Pit*, 1989
    Samuel R. Delany, co-author

109

POUL ANDERSON

The Shield of Time

(New York: Tor, 1990)

Story type: Science Fiction (Time Travel)
Series: Time Patrol
Major character(s): Manse Everard, Agent (Time Patrol); Wanda Tamberly, Agent (Time Patrol)
Time period(s): Indeterminate Past; 1990s (1990)
Locale(s): Earth

Summary: The delicate underpinnings of reality seem to be unravelling as Manse and Wanda strive to keep matters in balance. However, each time change can lead to unforeseen consequences, and when your change fails to restore the course of events, life gets interesting.

Other books you might like:
Gordon R. Dickson, *The Dragon Knight*, 1990
Gordon R. Dickson, *Time Storm*, 1977
Gordon R. Dickson, *The Dragon and the George*, 1976
Barbara Hambly, *Those Who Hunt the Night*, 1988
Larry Niven, *The Flight of the Horse*, 1973

110

POUL ANDERSON

Space Folk

(New York: Baen Books, 1989)

Story type: Science Fiction (Collection)

Summary: This volume reprints eleven short stories, an essay, and a poem. The fiction originally appeared between 1953 and 1985 in such magazines as *Amazing, Analog, Galaxy, Fantas-*

tic Universe, and *Boys' Life*, and such original anthologies as *Far Frontiers* and *Infinity*. Among the best known stories are ''Pride'' (1985), ''Hunter's Moon'' (1978), and ''Deathwomb'' (1983).

Other books you might like:
David Brin, *The River of Time*, 1986
David Brin, *Startide Rising*, 1983
David Brin, *The Uplift War*, 1987
Gordon R. Dickson, *The Forever Man*, 1986
Gordon R. Dickson, *Lost Dorsai*, 1980
Gordon R. Dickson, *Way of the Pilgrim*, 1987
Larry Niven, *The Integral Trees*, 1984
Larry Niven, *The Mote in God's Eye*, 1974
   Jerry Pournelle, co-author
Larry Niven, *Protector*, 1973
Larry Niven, *Ringworld*, 1970

111

POUL ANDERSON

The Stars Are Also Fire

(New York: Tor, 1994)

Story type: Science Fiction (Alternate Intelligence; Genetic Manipulation)
Major character(s): Ian Kenmuir, Spaceship Captain, Revolutionary; Dagny Beynac, Political Figure (mayor of the Moon), Parent; Lilisaire, Political Figure, Genetically Altered Being
Time period(s): 21st century; 28th century
Locale(s): Port Bowen, Moon (Earth's); Zamok Vysoki, Moon (Earth's)

Summary: While humans colonize the Moon and Alpha Centauri, computers and Earth develop intelligence, creating Teramind, a conjoining of all free cyber minds. The Teramind controls the Solar System and has its own goals, which do not include human space exploration and development. Fortunately, Demeter Mother, the AI at Alpha Centauri based on human personality downloads rather than pure mechanical constructs, distracts the Teramind from human beings and their genetically manipulated cohorts and friends.

Other books you might like:
Helen Collins, *Mutagenesis*, 1993
Robert A. Heinlein, *The Moon Is a Harsh Mistress*, 1966
Kim Stanley Robinson, *Green Mars*, 1994
Joan Slonczewski, *A Door into Ocean*, 1986
Norman Spinrad, *Deus X*, 1993
Allen Steele, *Clarke County, Space*, 1990
John Varley, *Steel Beach*, 1992
Jack Williamson, *The Humanoids*, 1949

112

POUL ANDERSON

The Time Patrol

(New York: Tor, 1991)

Story type: Science Fiction (Time Travel; Collection)
Series: Time Patrol

Major character(s): Manse Everard, Agent (Time Patrol)
Locale(s): Earth

Summary: This omnibus volume collects the adventures of Time Patrol Unattached Agent Manse Everard as he journeys here and there in time to keep the course of history intact. Included are *The Guardians of Time* (1981), ''Time Patrolmen'' (1983), and *The Year of the Ransom* (1988). It also includes the little-known prequel to last year's *Shield of Time* and a new novella, ''Star of the Sea.''

Other books you might like:
David Gerrold, *The Man Who Folded Himself*, 1991
Barbara Hambly, *Those Who Hunt the Night*, 1988
Robert A. Heinlein, *Glory Road*, 1963
Robert A. Heinlein, *The Number of the Beast*, 1979
Larry Niven, *The Flight of the Horse*, 1973
Robert Silverberg, *The Gate of Worlds*, 1967
Robert Charles Wilson, *A Bridge of Years*, 1991

113

C. DEAN ANDERSSON

Buried Screams

(New York: Zebra, 1992)

Story type: Horror (Ancient Evil Unleashed)
Major character(s): Karl Thomas Clayburn, Writer; Beth Ann Simpson, Undertaker; Erik Robert Lindholm, Worker (gravedigger)
Time period(s): 1990s
Locale(s): Stoneridge, Kentucky

Summary: A mysterious force that came to earth in a meteorite in prehistoric times and became entombed beneath the ground that now serves as the Stoneridge graveyard gradually takes over the townsfolk one by one. The burden of rescuing Stoneridge falls to three citizens, each of whom lived through an abusive childhood and thus is better equipped to face the onslaught of horrors unleashed upon them.

Other books you might like:
Douglas Clegg, *Goat Dance*, 1989
Jack Finney, *The Body Snatchers*, 1955
Stephen King, *The Tommyknockers*, 1987
T.E.D. Klein, *The Ceremonies*, 1984

114

C. DEAN ANDERSSON

Fiend

(New York: Zebra, 1994)

Story type: Horror (Supernatural Vengeance; Witchcraft)
Major character(s): Joe Clark, Student—College; T.T. Dyson, Serial Killer; Medea, Witch
Time period(s): 1990s (1994)
Locale(s): Dallas, Texas

Summary: At a Dallas comic book convention comic book writer neophyte Joe Clark encounters a woman who teaches him how to access his muse through sex magic. Alas, Joe's muse is the inspiration for his comic book character Toxique, a superhero avenger whose spirit reanimates the body of a dead serial killer and begins wreaking havoc at the convention.

Other books you might like:
Sean Costello, *The Cartoonist*, 1991
Ron Dee, *Succumb*, 1994
Richard Christian Matheson, *Created By*, 1993

115

C. DEAN ANDERSSON

I Am Dracula
(New York: Zebra, 1993)

Story type: Horror (Vampire Story)
Major character(s): Vlad Tepes, Vampire; Tzigane, Witch
Time period(s): 15th century
Locale(s): Transylvania

Summary: This historically accurate novel tells an altered account of Count Dracula's vampiric origins, portraying him as a disenchanted Wallachian noble whose disdain for humanity leads him into a liaison with a witch woman, and an introduction to Satanism that he eventually regrets.

Other books you might like:
Mara McCuniff, *The Vampire Memoirs*, 1990
Michael Romkey, *I, Vampire*, 1990
Fred Saberhagen, *Bram Stoker's Dracula*, 1992
    James V. Hart, co-author
Bram Stoker, *Dracula*, 1895

116

C. DEAN ANDERSSON

I Am Frankenstein
(New York: Zebra, 1996)

Story type: Horror (Reanimated Dead)
Major character(s): Gunthar Thunnar Frankenstein, Scientist; Katiasi, Young Woman; Anton Gorobec, Reanimated Dead
Time period(s): 1800s

Summary: A woman from the future visits Victor Frankenstein shortly after he has reanimated a dead human being to inform him that he and she are both pawns in the hands of Secret Masters, possibly extraterrestrial beings who are manipulating their fates to serve their own inscrutable ends.

Other books you might like:
Brian W. Aldiss, *Frankenstein Unbound*, 1973
Stephen Jones, *The Mammoth Book of Frankenstein*, 1994
    editor
Michel Parry, *Rivals of Frankenstein*, 1977
    editor
Fred Saberhagen, *The Frankenstein Papers*, 1986
Mary Shelley, *Frankenstein*, 1818

117

KEITH WILLIAM ANDREWS

Search and Destroy
(New York: Berkley, 1990)

Story type: Science Fiction (Time Travel; Military)
Series: Freedom's Rangers
Major character(s): Travis Hunter, Military Personnel (lieutenant); Rachel Stein, Scientist (mathematician), Agent (Chronos Project)
Time period(s): 1770s (1777)
Locale(s): North America (Dominion of British North America)

Summary: The Army's Chronos Project aims at countering the effects of the KGB's time travel project which threatens to wipe out the 20th century American enemy by altering historical events so that America never produces a United States. After saving George Washington from an assassination attempt, Lt. Hunter must try to prevent the colonial army's defeat by the enemy armed with weapons from the future while Rachel is held by Soviet time travel agents.

Other books you might like:
Roger L. DiSilvestro, *Living with the Reptiles*, 1990
Warren Norwood, *Stranded!*, 1989
    Mel Odom, co-author
Warren Norwood, *Trapped!*, 1989
Warren Norwood, *Vanished*, 1988
H. Beam Piper, *Lord Kalvan of Otherwhen*, 1965
L. Neil Smith, *The Gallatin Divergence*, 1985
John Varley, *Millennium*, 1983

118

KEITH WILLIAM ANDREWS

Sink the Armada
(New York: Berkley, 1990)

Story type: Science Fiction (Time Travel; Military)
Series: Freedom's Rangers
Major character(s): Travis Hunter, Military Personnel (lieutenant); Greg King, Military Personnel (sergeant)
Time period(s): 16th century (1588)
Locale(s): Caribbean; At Sea

Summary: KGB time commandos have planned to prevent the birth of the United States of America by arming the Spanish Armada sufficiently well to defeat England before England colonizes America. Free America's Chronos Project must stop the interference if the United States is to come about.

Other books you might like:
Roger L. DiSilvestro, *Living with the Reptiles*, 1990
Phyllis Eisenstein, *Shadow of Earth*, 1979
Randall Frakes, *The Terminator*, 1985
    Bill Wisher, co-author
H. Beam Piper, *Lord Kalvan of Otherwhen*, 1965
L. Neil Smith, *The Gallatin Divergence*, 1985
L. Neil Smith, *The Nagasaki Vector*, 1983
John Varley, *Millennium*, 1983

`119`

KEITH WILLIAM ANDREWS

Treason in Time
(New York: Berkley, 1990)

Story type: Science Fiction (Time Travel; Military)
Series: Freedom's Rangers
Major character(s): Travis Hunter, Military Personnel (lieutenant); Greg King, Military Personnel (sergeant)
Time period(s): 1910s (1918)
Locale(s): Europe

Summary: Hoping to halt the development of the USSR before it comes into being, the Joint Chiefs have formulated Operation Backlash in which time travellers will support White Russian Admiral Aleksandr V. Kolchak to defeat the Reds, stopping the Russian Revolution before the Soviets can consolidate power.

Other books you might like:
Roger L. DiSilvestro, *Living with the Reptiles*, 1990
Randall Frakes, *The Terminator*, 1985
    Bill Wisher, co-author
Warren Norwood, *Vanished*, 1988
H. Beam Piper, *Lord Kalvan of Otherwhen*, 1965
L. Neil Smith, *The Nagasaki Vector*, 1983
John Varley, *Millennium*, 1983

`120`

V.C. ANDREWS (Pseudonym of Andrew Neiderman)

Dawn
(New York: Pocket, 1990)

Story type: Horror (Coming-of-Age)
Major character(s): Dawn Longchamp, Teenager; Jimmy Longchamp, Child (Dawn's younger brother); Philip Cutler, Teenager
Time period(s): 1990s (1990)
Locale(s): Washington, District of Columbia

Summary: Dawn Longchamp's idyllic life is shattered when the death of her mother brings to light secrets about the family's past and Dawn's identity. Placed with a foster family, she fights to preserve her innocence and be reunited with her younger brother Jimmy.

Other books you might like:
Angela Carter, *The Magic Toyshop*, 1967

`121`

V.C. ANDREWS (Pseudonym of Andrew Neiderman)

Gates of Paradise
(New York: Poseidon Books, 1989)

Story type: Horror (Gothic Family Chronicle)
Series: Castell Family
Major character(s): Annie Casteel Stonewall, Handicapped; Luke Casteel Jr., Relative (Annie's half-brother)
Time period(s): 1980s (Present)

Locale(s): Boston, Massachusetts (Farthinggale Manor, family estate)

Summary: Although physically weak and isolated at Farthinggale Manor, Annie searches through the tangled Casteel family history to unearth the secrets that have cursed all the Casteels, while at the same time falling hopelessly into a "forbidden" love with her half-brother, Luke. (Most of this novel was written by Andrew Neideerman.)

Other books you might like:
Michael McDowell, *Blackwater*, 1983
Joyce Carol Oates, *Bellefleur*, 1980

`122`

V.C. ANDREWS (Pseudonym of Andrew Neiderman)

Secrets of the Morning
(New York: Pocket, 1991)

Story type: Horror (Gothic Family Chronicle)
Series: New Series of the Cutler Family
Major character(s): Dawn Longchamp, Student, Musician; Michael Sutton, Teacher (Dawn's music teacher); Jimmy Longchamp, Military Personnel (Dawn's foster brother)
Time period(s): 1990s
Locale(s): New York, New York

Summary: Having recovered from the abuse she suffered at the hands of her mother's family in *Dawn*, following the revelation that she is an adopted child, Dawn Longchamp attends the Bernhardt School of Performing Arts in New York in the hope of breaking clean of her family heritage. While there, however, she falls for music teacher Michael Sutton, and teeters on the brink of repeating the same error her real mother made.

Other books you might like:
Athena Alexis, *Along Came a Spider*, 1991

`123`

V.C. ANDREWS (Pseudonym of Andrew Neiderman)

Web of Dreams
(New York: Pocket Books, 1990)

Story type: Horror (Gothic Family Chronicle)
Series: Castell Family
Major character(s): Leigh Van Voreen, Young Woman; Luke Casteel Jr., Young Man
Time period(s): 20th century
Locale(s): Boston, Massachusetts (Farthinggale Manor); Willies, West Virginia

Summary: Attending her father's funeral, Annie Casteel discovers her grandmother's diary and reads the story of Leigh's dark secret and her rescue and restoration by Luke Casteel.

Other books you might like:
Michael McDowell, *Blackwater*, 1983
Joyce Carol Oates, *Bellefleur*, 1980

124

RODERICK ANSCOMBE

The Secret Life of Laszlo, Count Dracula
(New York: Hyperion, 1994)

Story type: Horror (Serial Killer)
Major character(s): Laszlo, Count Dracula, Nobleman; Elizabeth, Spouse (Laszlo's wife); Gregory, Religious (priest)
Time period(s): 1860s (1866); 1880s (1887)
Locale(s): Paris, France; Transylvania

Summary: While working as an assistant to the renowned psychiatrist Jean Martin Charcot, Laszlo is driven by jealousy to murder a female patient and drink her blood. Twenty years later, having succeeded his deceased brother George as the new Count Dracula and married George's widow Elizabeth, Laszlo struggles with his drive to murder and drink the blood of victims, committing acts that give rise among the townspeople to the legends of the legendary supernatural vampire. This psychoanalytical rendering of the Dracula legend is the author's first novel.

Other books you might like:
Anne Rice, *The Vampire Lestat*, 1985
Michael Romkey, *The Vampire Papers*, 1994
Bram Stoker, *Dracula*, 1897

125

MARK ANTHONY
ELLEN PORATH, Co-Author

Kindred Spirits
(Lake Geneva, Wisconsin: TSR, 1991)

Story type: Fantasy (Mystery)
Series: Dragonlance: The Meetings Sextet
Major character(s): Flint Fireforge, Mythical Creature (dwarf), Artisan (metalsmith); Tanis Half-Elvin, Mythical Creature (elf)
Time period(s): Indeterminate
Locale(s): Qualinesti, Fictional Country

Summary: When Tanis stands accused of murdering a pompous elf lord, Flint must prove his innocence to avoid Tanis's permanent banishment. This is the author's first published book. A game tie-in novel.

Other books you might like:
Tina Daniell, *Dark Heart*, 1992
Mary Kirchoff, *Wanderlust*, 1991
   Steve Winter, co-author
Richard A. Knaak, *Kaz the Minotaur*, 1990
Barbara Siegel, *Tanis, the Shadow Years*, 1990
   Scott Siegel, co-author
Margaret Weis, *Dragons of Autumn Twilight*, 1984
   Tracy Hickman, co-author

126

MARK ANTHONY

Tower of Doom
(Lake Geneva, Wisconsin: TSR, 1994)

Story type: Horror (Reanimated Dead)
Series: Ravenloft
Major character(s): Wort, Handicapped (hunchback); Baron Caidin, Nobleman; Mika, Doctor
Time period(s): Indeterminate
Locale(s): Ravenloft, Fictional Country

Summary: Wort, the hunchbacked half-brother of the Baron Caidin, discovers a magic talisman that allows him to exact supernatural vengeance against his persecutors. Meanwhile, the baron resorts to a similar necromancy to create a zombie army that builds a tower he needs to defend himself against neighboring enemies.

Other books you might like:
Elaine Bergstrom, *Tapestry of Dark Souls*, 1993
P.N. Elrod, *I, Strahd*, 1993
Christie Golden, *Dance of the Dead*, 1992
Christie Golden, *The Enemy Within*, 1994
J. Robert King, *Carnival of Fear*, 1993
Brian Thomsen, *Tales of Ravenloft*, 1994
   editor
Chet Williamson, *Mordenheim*, 1994

127

PATRICIA ANTHONY

Brother Termite
(New York: Harcourt Brace, 1993)

Story type: Science Fiction (Invasion of Earth; Satire)
Major character(s): Reem ''First Cousin Brother'', Alien (Cousin), Political Figure (White House chief of staff); Jeff Womack, Political Figure (President of the United States), Human; Tali, Alien (Cousin), Political Figure (Cousin Brother Conscience)
Time period(s): 21st century
Locale(s): Washington, District of Columbia

Summary: In control of the United States government for a century, half of it overtly, aliens stop human advancement in the sciences and begin an ominous breeding program while the decline in human births precipitates a crisis in the baby food industry. Reem acts as troubleshooter despite Washington plotting and difficulties with his own kind and within himself.

Other books you might like:
Octavia E. Butler, *Dawn*, 1987
Arthur C. Clarke, *Childhood's End*, 1953
Parke Godwin, *Waiting for the Galactic Bus*, 1988
W.A. Harbinson, *Dream Maker*, 1992
Robert A. Heinlein, *The Puppet Masters*, 1991
   revised edition
John Kessel, *Good News From Outer Space*, 1989
Robert Rankin, *Armageddon: The Musical*, 1990
David Alexander Smith, *In the Cube*, 1993

128

PATRICIA ANTHONY

Cold Allies

(New York: Harcourt Brace Jovanovich, 1993)

Story type: Science Fiction (Military; First Contact)
Major character(s): Gordon Means, Military Personnel (sergeant); Valentin Baranyk, Military Personnel (lieutenant general); Jerry Casey, Teenager, Refugee
Time period(s): 2010s
Locale(s): Colorado; Pyrenees, Europe; Poland

Summary: The American, European, Russian alliance battles the Arab nations moving north into Europe looking for food and a place to settle. Sent via his robot tank to protect the only remaining communication and observation satellite, Gordon picks up an alien little blue light which seems to like him. The Americans decide to use the aliens in the war effort despite the inability of the military to establish communication with them. A first novel.

Other books you might like:
Jean Mark Gawron, *Dream of Glass*, 1993
Jack C. Haldeman II, *High Steel*, 1993
    Jack Dann, co-author
Gwyneth Jones, *White Queen*, 1993
Ursula K. Le Guin, *The Lathe of Heaven*, 1971
Garfield Reeves-Stevens, *Nighteyes*, 1989

129

PATRICIA ANTHONY

Cradle of Splendor

(New York: Ace, 1996)

Story type: Science Fiction (First Contact; Political)
Major character(s): Dolores Sims, Artist (painter), Spy (CIA agent); Ana Maria Bonfim, Political Figure (Presidente of Brazil); Edson Carvalho, Spy (Brazilian)
Time period(s): 1990s
Locale(s): Brazil

Summary: Ana Maria becomes the presidente of Brazil through treachery and the help of the CIA and labors to bring Brazil's technology to a more advanced state. When the first space launch almost fails, but then succeeds, every spy tries to discover why.

Other books you might like:
Alan Dean Foster, *Cyber Way*, 1990
Mark Leyner, *My Cousin, My Gastroenterologist*, 1990
Linda Nagata, *Tech-Heaven*, 1995
Neal Stephenson, *The Diamond Age*, 1995

130

PATRICIA ANTHONY

Happy Policeman

(New York: Harcourt Brace, 1994)

Story type: Science Fiction (Mystery; Contemporary Realism)

Major character(s): DeWitt Dawson, Police Officer; Bodeen Woodruff, Police Officer; Seresen, Alien (Torku)
Time period(s): 1990s
Locale(s): Coomey, Texas

Summary: Coomey, Texas has existed in a Torku-created bubble for six years. After Loretta Harper's murder and her sons' disappearance, DeWitt Dawson sets out to investigate, only to find the aliens have destroyed evidence and answer all his questions with riddles.

Other books you might like:
Isaac Asimov, *The Caves of Steel*, 1953
Richard Bowker, *Dover Beach*, 1987
John Brunner, *The Squares of the City*, 1965
D.G. Compton, *Chronocules*, 1970
Edmund Cooper, *Seahorse in the Sky*, 1969
Philip K. Dick, *A Maze of Death*, 1970
Brad Ferguson, *The World Next Door*, 1990
Joan Slonczewski, *The Wall Around Eden*, 1989

131

PIERS ANTHONY

Alien Plot

(New York: Tor, 1992)

Story type: Science Fiction (Collection)

Summary: Contains a brief autobiographical sketch, "Faces," an article, "Think of the Reader," plus 16 stories, 7 original and 11 from periodicals and anthologies 1970-1991. The stories display a wide variety of fantasy and science fiction themes with several involving the problems writers have with editors.

Other books you might like:
David Brin, *The River of Time*, 1986
Orson Scott Card, *Maps in a Mirror*, 1990
Larry Niven, *N-Space*, 1990
John Varley, *Blue Champagne*, 1986
John Varley, *The Persistence of Vision*, 1978
Kurt Vonnegut Jr., *Welcome to the Monkey House*, 1968

132

PIERS ANTHONY

And Eternity

(New York: Morrow, 1990)

Story type: Fantasy (Contemporary; Magic Conflict)
Series: Incarnations of Immortality
Major character(s): Orlene, Spirit (ghost); Jolie, Spirit (ghost); Vita, Prostitute
Time period(s): Indeterminate Future
Locale(s): Earth; Hell; Heaven

Summary: Orlene, the mortal daughter of Gaea has finally died, after being overwhelmed with a succession of tragedies. In Afterlife, she is protected by Gaea's companion Jolie, herself the sometime-consort of Satan. Together, Orlene and Jolie seek out and are joined by Vita, contemporary mortal with her own share of troubles, her own compelling attractions and her own unsettling moral code. In a world where the

Incarnation of Good seems to have fallen asleep, these three women form a triumvirate and pursue a great quest that takes them through a succession of trials as numerous and mysterious as the Incarnations themselves. This is the seventh and concluding volume in this unusual allegorical series which has personified good, evil, nature, war, fate, time and death.

Other books you might like:
Poul Anderson, *Operation Chaos*, 1971
Orson Scott Card, *Seventh Son*, 1987
Brian Daley, *The Doomfarers of Coramonde*, 1977
Robert A. Heinlein, *Waldo and Magic, Inc.*, 1950
Roger Zelazny, *Nine Princes in Amber*, 1970

133

PIERS ANTHONY

But What of Earth?

(New York: Tor, 1989)

Story type: Science Fiction (End of the World)
Major character(s): Scott Krebs, Student; Lucy, Thief
Time period(s): Indeterminate Future

Summary: Earth's civilization is on the verge of collapse due to overpopulation and the depletion of resources when practical matter transmitters are invented and increasing numbers of people emigrate to new worlds. Those few who either can't or won't leave Earth must deal with a near total breakdown of law and order. This volume includes Anthony's previously unpublished version of this novel which was published in butchered form by Laser Books in 1976. Also included are two short essays describing the background to the book's publication and nearly seventy pages of notes detailing all of the changes suggested by a series of Laser editors.

Other books you might like:
Neal Barrett Jr., *Dawn's Uncertain Light*, 1989
Neal Barrett Jr., *Through Darkest America*, 1987
Jerry Earl Brown, *Earthfall*, 1989
Keith Laumer, *The Stars Must Wait*, 1990

134

PIERS ANTHONY
ROBERT E. MARGROFF, Co-Author

The Caterpillar's Question

(New York: Ace, 1992)

Story type: Fantasy (Alternate World; Contemporary)
Major character(s): Tappuah "Tappy" Concord, Orphan, Mythical Creature (Imago); Jack, Artist, Companion; Malva, Alien (Gaol)
Time period(s): 1990s
Locale(s): United States

Summary: Hidden from the alien Gaol as a maimed, blind, mute, thirteen-year-old girl, Tappy, the Imago, finds her way to a rock which leads to an alternate world. The alien honkers protect her until the Agents of the Imago rescue Tappy. If she does not realize her power as the Imago, the Agents of the Imago will kill Tappy before allowing her capture by the Gaol.

Other books you might like:
Glen Cook, *The Black Company*, 1984
Charles de Lint, *The Little Country*, 1991
Philip Jose Farmer, *The Maker of Universes*, 1965
Philip Jose Farmer, *Red Orc's Rage*, 1991
Alan Dean Foster, *Cyber Way*, 1990
Robert Jordan, *The Eye of the World*, 1989
Meredith Ann Pierce, *The Pearl of the Soul of the World*, 1990
Jim Shepard, *Lights Out in the Reptile House*, 1990
Karen Wehrstein, *Lion's Heart*, 1991
Roger Zelazny, *Nine Princes in Amber*, 1970

135

PIERS ANTHONY

Chaos Mode

(New York: Ace/Putnam, 1993)

Story type: Fantasy (Adventure; Quest)
Series: Virtual Mode
Major character(s): Colene, Teenager, Adventurer; Burgess, Animal (invertebrate); Seqiro, Animal (horse), Telepath
Time period(s): 21st century; Indeterminate
Locale(s): Earth; Shale, Alternate Earth

Summary: Colene, Seqiro, Darius and Nona arrive in a world where vertebrates never developed and meet Burgess, a floater of the triramous phylum, who has been exiled from his people as contaminated by selfishness. They travel along the Virtual Mode to Julia where society has become ugly through the change from Animus to Anima.

Other books you might like:
Jack L. Chalker, *When the Changewinds Blow*, 1987
Cynthia Felice, *Godsfire*, 1978
Alan Dean Foster, *To the Vanishing Point*, 1988
Alan Garner, *Elidor*, 1967
Harry Harrison, *West of Eden*, 1984
Ward Hawkins, *Red Flame Burning*, 1985
Diana Wynne Jones, *The Homeward Bounders*, 1981
L. Neil Smith, *Contact and Commune*, 1980
Timothy Zahn, *Triplet*, 1987

136

PIERS ANTHONY
ROBERT E. MARGROFF, Co-Author

Chimaera's Copper

(New York: Tor, 1990)

Story type: Fantasy (Adventure; Magic Conflict)
Series: Kelvin of Rud
Major character(s): Kelvin Knight Hackleberry, Hero; Rowforth, Royalty (King-Usurper); Heln, Spouse
Time period(s): 1990s
Locale(s): Rud, Fictional Country; Alternate Earth

Summary: Kelvin with his brother and father, are trapped in an unknown alternate universe by the Chimaera, while Heln is threatened by Kelvin's old enemies and his unborn child is cursed. Only Kelvin can save his family, but will he be able to free himself from the Chimaera in time?

Other books you might like:
John DeChancie, *Castle Perilous*, 1988
Charles de Lint, *Drink Down the Moon*, 1990
John Deakins, *Barrow*, 1990
Ellen Kushner, *Thomas the Rhymer*, 1990
Alis A. Rasmussen, *The Labyrinth Gate*, 1988

137

PIERS ANTHONY

The Color of Her Panties
(New York: Morrow, 1992)

Story type: Fantasy (Light Fantasy; Quest)
Series: Xanth
Major character(s): Mela Merwoman, Mythical Creature (mermaid), Widow(er); Gwenny Goblin, Mythical Creature (goblin), Feminist; Okra Ogress, Mythical Creature (ogre), Runaway
Time period(s): Indeterminate
Locale(s): Xanth, Fictional Country

Summary: Gwenny Goblin, accompanied by Che Centaur and Jenny Elf, go to the Good Magician to discover how Gwenny can become chief of the Goblins. Meanwhile, Mela Merwoman, seeking a husband, Okra Ogress, trying to become a main character, and Ida Human, trying to discover her destiny, also seek out the Good Magician and wind up helping Gwenny.

Other books you might like:
Robert Asprin, *Another Fine Myth*, 1978
Kyle Crocco, *Heroes, Inc.*, 1991
Suzette Haden Elgin, *Twelve Fair Kingdoms*, 1981
Alan Dean Foster, *Spellsinger*, 1983
Pamela F. Service, *Weirdos of the Universe, Unite!*, 1992
Christopher Stasheff, *The Warlock in Spite of Himself*, 1969

138

PIERS ANTHONY

Demons Don't Dream
(New York: Tor, 1993)

Story type: Fantasy (Light Fantasy; Quest)
Series: Xanth
Major character(s): Dug, Teenager, Adventurer; Kim, Teenager; Jenny Elf, Mythical Creature (elf), Guide
Time period(s): Indeterminate
Locale(s): Xanth, Fictional Country

Summary: The first players to try a new computer fantasy game allowing entry to Xanth, Kim and Dug compete to achieve their most cherished desire while utilizing a chosen and possibly traitorous companion. The pair help several other inhabitants find what they want most, while saving the magic in Xanth.

Other books you might like:
Robert Asprin, *Another Fine Myth*, 1978
Diane Duane, *So You Want to Be a Wizard?*, 1983

Alan Dean Foster, *Spellsinger*, 1983
Gillian Rubinstein, *Space Demons*, 1988
William Sleator, *Interstellar Pig*, 1984
Christopher Stasheff, *The Warlock in Spite of Himself*, 1969
Patricia C. Wrede, *Talking to Dragons*, 1985

139

PIERS ANTHONY

Firefly
(New York: Morrow, 1990)

Story type: Horror (Erotic Horror)
Major character(s): Geode Demerit, Maintenance Worker; Oenone Brown, Housewife; Frank Tishner, Police Officer
Time period(s): 1990s
Locale(s): Middle Kingdom Ranch, Florida

Summary: A monster has taken over the grounds of the remote Middle Kingdom Ranch, attracting its human victims with sexually stimulating pheromones and then draining them of their bodily fluids.

Other books you might like:
Ray Russell, *Incubus*, 1976

140

PIERS ANTHONY

Fractal Mode
(New York: Ace/Putnam, 1992)

Story type: Fantasy (Quest; Adventure)
Series: Virtual Mode
Major character(s): Colene, Teenager, Adventurer; Darius, Ruler (Cyng of Pwer); Nona, Heroine, Heiress—Dispossessed
Time period(s): 1990s
Locale(s): Oklahoma, Alternate Universe

Summary: Nona, the ninth daughter in the ninth generation, is destined to change the rule of her fractal universe from Animus to Anima. While seeking out the Megaplayers, she meets Colene, Darius, Seqiro and Provos. They help her by enlisting the aid of Angus, a giant, while Colene talks to a math professor to find the exact spot where the change must occur. She also rescues a sexually abused child who Provos adopts as her own. They finally get Nona to the exact predetermined spot for the change from Animus to Anima. After accomplishing that, the band, plus Nona, set out again along the Virtual Mode.

Other books you might like:
Jack L. Chalker, *When the Changewinds Blow*, 1987
Alan Dean Foster, *To the Vanishing Point*, 1988
Alan Garner, *Elidor*, 1967
Diana Wynne Jones, *Eight Days of Luke*, 1988
Michael Reaves, *The Shattered World*, 1984

141

PIERS ANTHONY

Geis of the Gargoyle

(New York: Tor, 1995)

Story type: Fantasy (Light Fantasy; Quest)
Series: Xanth
Major character(s): Gary Gargoyle, Mythical Creature (gargoyle); Iris, Royalty (queen); D. Mentia, Demon
Time period(s): Indeterminate
Locale(s): Xanth, Fictional Country

Summary: Gary Gargoyle asks the Good Magician Humfrey for a way to purify the Swan Knee River and release the gargoyles from their geis. Transformed into a man, Gary must also tutor the child, Surprise, and teach her control over her magic.

Other books you might like:
Robert Asprin, *Another Fine Myth*, 1978
Robert N. Charrette, *Never Trust an Elf*, 1992
Susan Cooper, *Silver on the Tree*, 1977
Susan Dexter, *The Wizard's Shadow*, 1993
Alan Dean Foster, *Spellsinger at the Gate*, 1983
Laurell K. Hamilton, *Nightseer*, 1992
Brian Stableford, *The Last Days of the Edge of the World*, 1985
Christopher Stasheff, *The Warlock in Spite of Himself*, 1969

142

PIERS ANTHONY

Hard Sell

(Houston, Texas: Tafford, 1990)

Story type: Science Fiction (Humor)
Major character(s): Fisk Center, Businessman (sucker)
Time period(s): 21st century
Locale(s): Earth

Summary: Fisk Center, bilked of all his money by Mars, Ltd., must find some way to survive. He finds a job which he soon discovers is for an illegal adoption agency and ends up with an eleven-year-old daughter who proceeds to take over his life.

Other books you might like:
Steven Brust, *Cowboy Feng's Space Bar and Grille*, 1990
Lois McMaster Bujold, *Borders of Infinity*, 1989
Alan Dean Foster, *Quozl*, 1989
Mel Gilden, *Outer Space and All That Junk*, 1989
Harry Harrison, *Bill, the Galactic Hero: The Planet of the Robot Slaves*, 1989
Keith Laumer, *Reward for Retief*, 1989

143

PIERS ANTHONY

Harpy Thyme

(New York: Tor, 1994)

Story type: Fantasy (Light Fantasy; Quest)

Series: Xanthe
Major character(s): Gloha Harpy-Goblin, Mythical Creature (winged goblin); Trent, Magician; Graeboe, Mythical Creature (giant)
Time period(s): Indeterminate
Locale(s): Xanth, Fictional Country

Summary: With no others like her, Gloha Harpy-Goblin seeks her ideal man. When the Good Magician Humphrey will not help her, a rejuvenated Trent and the skeleton, Marrow Bones, accompany her on the search. Although Gloha helps the demon, Metria, find happiness, she requires Trent's advice and magical assistance to achieve her own goal.

Other books you might like:
Douglas W. Clark, *Alchemy Unlimited*, 1990
Suzette Haden Elgin, *Twelve Fair Kingdoms*, 1981
Diana Wynne Jones, *Howl's Moving Castle*, 1986
Terry Pratchett, *The Colour of Magic*, 1983
Patricia C. Wrede, *Dealing with Dragons*, 1990

144

PIERS ANTHONY
MERCEDES LACKEY, Co-Author

If I Pay Thee Not in Gold

(New York: Baen, 1993)

Story type: Fantasy (Magic Conflict; Quest)
Major character(s): Xylina, Orphan, Young Woman; Faro, Slave; Ware, Demon
Time period(s): Indeterminate (Age of the Mazonians)
Locale(s): Mazonia, Fictional Country

Summary: In Mazonia, women conjure and rule but men have no magical abilities and serve as slaves. Though poor, Xylina possesses more magical talents than most women, and after gaining a slave in her womanhood initiation rites, begins to improve her fortunes with his shrewd advice. But a secret enemy manages to thwart their efforts with disasters, both natural and magical. With Xylina near bankruptcy, Ware offers her the choice of becoming his lover or accepting the Queen's offer to repay the debt if Xylina will undertake the quest to retrieve a shard of a magic crystal that can make the wearer immortal.

Other books you might like:
C.J. Cherryh, *Angel with the Sword*, 1985
Phyllis Eisenstein, *Born to Exile*, 1978
Mercedes Lackey, *Arrows of the Queen*, 1987
Mercedes Lackey, *By the Sword*, 1991
Mack Reynolds, *Amazon Planet*, 1975
Jack Vance, *Emphyrio*, 1969
Joan D. Vinge, *The Snow Queen*, 1980
Patricia C. Wrede, *Caught in Crystal*, 1987
Patricia C. Wrede, *Shadow Magic*, 1982

145

PIERS ANTHONY

Isle of View
(New York: Avon, 1990)

Story type: Fantasy (Light Fantasy; Romance)
Series: Xanth
Major character(s): Dolph, Royalty (Prince of Xanth); Che Centaur, Mythical Creature (Winged-Centaur); Jenny Elf, Mythical Creature (Elf)
Time period(s): 1990s
Locale(s): Xanth, Fictional Country

Summary: Che Centaur has been kidnapped by goblins. Jenny Elf, a visitor from the world of Two Moons, comforts him even as she tries to find a way back to her home. Prince Dolph leads an expedition to rescue Che, knowing that he must also decide which woman he will marry. Finally Che, Jenny and the Goblin princess go to live with the centaurs, while Dolph marries Electra to save her from certain death and finds he loves her after all.

Other books you might like:
Robert Asprin, *Another Fine Myth*, 1978
Steven R. Boyett, *Ariel*, 1983
Linda Haldeman, *The Lastborn of Elvinwood*, 1978
Christopher Stasheff, *The Warlock in Spite of Himself*, 1969

146

PIERS ANTHONY

Isle of Woman
(New York: Tor, 1993)

Story type: Fantasy (Historical)
Major character(s): Blaze, Blacksmith; Ember, Parent (mother), Leader; Stone, Artisan
Time period(s): 20000th century B.C.; 2020s (2021)
Locale(s): Earth

Summary: A series of vignettes details the rise of humanity from the plains of Africa through post-disaster America as seen through a group of people in several reincarnations. Blaze, always a fireworker, finds his true love, Ember, repeatedly denied him or known only through dreams, while their families perpetually win despite the odds.

Other books you might like:
Poul Anderson, *The Boat of a Million Years*, 1989
Jean M. Auel, *Clan of the Cave Bear*, 1990
John Brunner, *The Tides of Time*, 1984
W. Michael Gear, *People of the Wolf*, 1990
    Kathleen O'Neal Gear, co-author
Crawford Kilian, *The Empire of Time*, 1978
Robert Silverberg, *Gilgamesh the King*, 1984
L. Neil Smith, *The Crystal Empire*, 1986
Roger Welsch, *Touching the Fire*, 1992

147

PIERS ANTHONY

Killobyte
(New York: Ace/Putnam, 1993)

Story type: Fantasy (Contemporary; Adventure)
Major character(s): Walter Toland, Adventurer, Handicapped; Baal Curran, Handicapped, Teenager; Phreak, Computer Expert, Criminal
Time period(s): 1990s
Locale(s): United States; Virtual Reality, Cyberspace

Summary: While playing the virtual reality computer game, Killobyte, Walter Toland and Baal Curran discover that another player, a dangerous psychotic, has learned how to trap them in the game to kill them repeatedly. As the game continues, Walter and Baal begin to suspect the evil player can expand his influence to the realm outside the game.

Other books you might like:
Philip Jose Farmer, *Red Orc's Rage*, 1991
Will Shetterly, *The Tangled Lands*, 1989
Wm. Mark Simmons, *When Dreams Collide*, 1992
Vivian Vande Velde, *User Unfriendly*, 1991

148

PIERS ANTHONY

Man From Mundania
(New York: Avon, 1989)

Story type: Fantasy (Light Fantasy)
Series: Xanth
Major character(s): Ivy, Royalty (princess), Sorceress; Grey Murphy, Student—College, Sorcerer (apprentice)
Time period(s): 1980s
Locale(s): Xanth, Planet—Imaginary; Mundania, Fictional Country (Earth world)

Summary: Princess Ivy is sent to Mundania by evil Compewter. She meets Grey Murphy and the two travel back to Xanth in order to fight Com-pewter.

Other books you might like:
Robert Asprin, *Myth-Nomers and Im-Pervections*, 1988
Mercedes Lackey, *Knight of Ghosts and Shadows*, 1990
Terry Pratchett, *Sourcery*, 1989
Will Shetterly, *The Tangled Lands*, 1990
Christopher Stasheff, *The Warlock in Spite of Himself*, 1969

149

PIERS ANTHONY

Mercycle
(Houston: Tafford Publishing, Inc., 1991)

Story type: Science Fiction (Adventure)
Major character(s): Don Kestle, Archaeologist; Eleph, Alien
Time period(s): Indeterminate Future
Locale(s): Earth

Summary: Recruited by a mysterious alien force not limited by time and space, five adventurers engage in a difficult and dangerous secret mission. The individuals are subjected to a process which renders them out of phase with the normal world, allowing them a lengthy journey across the bottom of the sea. As they overcome obstacles, they find their mission involves saving the entire world.

Other books you might like:
David Brin, *Startide Rising*, 1983
Vonda N. McIntyre, *Superluminal*, 1983
Carol Severance, *Reefsong*, 1991
Joan Slonczewski, *A Door into Ocean*, 1986
Allen Steele, *Orbital Decay*, 1989
John E. Stith, *Redshift Rendezvous*, 1990

150
PIERS ANTHONY
ROBERT E. MARGROFF, Co-Author

Mouvar's Magic
(New York: Tor, 1992)

Story type: Fantasy (Adventure; Magic Conflict)
Series: Kelvin of Rud
Major character(s): Kelvin Knight Hackleberry, Hero; Zady, Witch; Horace, Mythical Creature (dragon), Telepath
Time period(s): 1990s
Locale(s): Kelvinia, Fictional Country; Alternate Earth

Summary: In a final desperate attempt to rend the empire asunder, Devale employs Zady to defeat Kelvin's efforts to save the alliance. Kelvin lays waste to orcs, giants and other foes with the aid of a dragon and magic implements supplied by Mouvar which allow Kelvin to discover his own magic-wielding ability. Concluding volume of the five book series.

Other books you might like:
John DeChancie, *Castle Perilous*, 1988
Stephen R. Donaldson, *Lord Foul's Bane*, 1977
Melanie Rawn, *Stronghold*, 1990
Christopher Rowley, *Bazil Broketail*, 1992

151
PIERS ANTHONY

Orc's Opal
(New York: Tor, 1990)

Story type: Fantasy (Quest; Magic Conflict)
Series: Kelvin of Rud
Major character(s): Kelvin Knight Hackleberry, Hero; Zady, Witch
Time period(s): 1990s
Locale(s): Kelvinia, Fictional Country; Alternate Earth

Summary: Kelvin is home with his family recuperating from his last adventure when the evil Zady swears to get even by taking the lives of his children. In the many worlds of the multiverse, the Prophesy of Mouvar is unfolding as predicted, and now the children must find the Orc's Opal.

Other books you might like:
John DeChancie, *Castle Perilous*, 1988

Charles de Lint, *Drink Down the Moon*, 1990
John Deakins, *Barrow*, 1990
Ellen Kushner, *Thomas the Rhymer*, 1990
Alis A. Rasmussen, *The Labyrinth Gate*, 1988
Nancy Springer, *Red Wizard*, 1990

152
PIERS ANTHONY

Phaze Doubt
(New York: Ace/Putnam, 1990)

Story type: Fantasy (Light Fantasy)
Series: Apprentice Adept
Major character(s): Nepe/Flach, Mythical Creature (unicorn), Animal (shapechanger); Brown, Lesbian, Magician (adept); Lysander, Android, Agent
Time period(s): Indeterminate Future
Locale(s): Phaze, Planet—Imaginary

Summary: Hectare is invading Phaze, and Lysander is one of their agents. He is the subject of a prophecy that he will save Phaze, so Nepe/Flach takes him with her as she works to save Phaze. Lysander finds himself more and more sympathetic to Phaze until the planet makes a quarter turn and he turns into one of them and they expel the Hectare. Lysander marries Oche and they all live happily ever after.

Other books you might like:
Robert Asprin, *Another Fine Myth*, 1978
Steven R. Boyett, *Ariel*, 1983
Suzette Haden Elgin, *Twelve Fair Kingdoms*, 1983
Dale Estey, *A Lost Tale*, 1980
Alan Dean Foster, *Spellsinger*, 1983
Christopher Stasheff, *The Warlock in Spite of Himself*, 1969

153
PIERS ANTHONY

Question Quest
(New York: Avon, 1991)

Story type: Fantasy (Quest; Light Fantasy)
Series: Xanth
Major character(s): Lacuna, Housewife, Agent; Humfrey, Magician; Rose, Sorceress, Royalty (princess)
Time period(s): Indeterminate
Locale(s): Xanth, Fictional Country

Summary: Lacuna, feeling life has passed her by, goes to the Good Magician Grey to learn what she can do about it. He sends her to Hell to comfort Humfrey, the former Magician who is trying to rescue his wife, Rose. While waiting he tells Lacuna his history and that of Xanth. Then Humfrey must decide which of his former wives, all in Hell, he wishes to rescue. Taking turns, Humfrey ends up returning to Xanth with MareAnn. Lacuna returns to a changed Xanth, one where she is married with children, thus finding her purpose.

Other books you might like:
Robert Asprin, *Another Fine Myth*, 1978
Suzette Haden Elgin, *And Then There'll Be Fireworks*, 1981
Suzette Haden Elgin, *The Grand Jubilee*, 1981

Suzette Haden Elgin, *Twelve Fair Kingdoms*, 1981
Alan Dean Foster, *Spellsinger*, 1983
Christopher Stasheff, *The Warlock in Spite of Himself*, 1969

Crawford Kilian, *The Empire of Time*, 1978
Garry Kilworth, *Split Second*, 1985
Harry Turtledove, *A Different Flesh*, 1988

154

PIERS ANTHONY

Roc and a Hard Place

(New York: Tor, 1995)

Story type: Fantasy (Light Fantasy)
Series: Xanth
Major character(s): Metria "Woe Betide", Demon; Grossclout, Professor, Demon; Roxanne Roc, Mythical Creature (roc)
Time period(s): Indeterminate
Locale(s): Emerald Mountains, Mythical Place; Xanth, Fictional Country

Summary: Consulting with the Good Magician Humfrey on a way to get the stork to heed her summons, Metria must first assemble the judge and jury to try Roxanne Roc for breaking the Adult Conspiracy. After solving some problems along the way and travelling to Mundania, the trial begins with Professor Grossclout as judge.

Other books you might like:
Robert Asprin, *Myth-ing Persons*, 1984
C. Dale Brittain, *A Bad Spell in Yurt*, 1991
Suzette Haden Elgin, *Twelve Fair Kingdoms*, 1981
Alan Dean Foster, *Son of Spellsinger*, 1993
Diana Wynne Jones, *Castle in the Air*, 1991
Andre Norton, *Dragon Magic*, 1972
Terry Pratchett, *Witches Abroad*, 1993

155

PIERS ANTHONY

Shame of Man

(New York: Tor, 1994)

Story type: Science Fiction (Family Saga; Adventure)
Series: Geodyssey
Major character(s): Hu "Hugh", Musician, Parent; Ann "Annai", Dancer, Parent; Minnie "Miin", Psychic, Child
Time period(s): Indeterminate Past
Locale(s): Earth

Summary: Hu, Ann and their children experience love, hate and betrayal at the hands of Bub and Sis in their many guises from 8,000,000 B.C. to 2050 A.D. The separate incidents in different times and places yield the story of how Hugh and his family manage to determine that humanity's appetites need curbing to save the Earth.

Other books you might like:
Brian W. Aldiss, *Cryptozoic*, 1968
Roger MacBride Allen, *Orphan of Creation*, 1988
Poul Anderson, *The Boat of a Million Years*, 1989
Neal Barrett Jr., *Dawn's Uncertain Light*, 1989
Michael Bishop, *No Enemy but Time*, 1982
John Brunner, *The Tides of Time*, 1982
Philip Jose Farmer, *Traitor to the Living*, 1973

156

PIERS ANTHONY, Editor
RICHARD GILLIAM, Co-Editor

Tales From the Great Turtle

(New York: Tor, 1994)

Story type: Fantasy (Anthology; Legend)

Summary: Contains a three-page introduction by Anthony, a two-page afterword by Gilliam, three pages of biographical notes on the authors, two reprinted and 27 original stories all sharing native American themes. Authors include Piers Anthony, Jack Dann, Esther M. Friesner, Ed Gorman, Brad Linaweaver, Mike Resnick, Kristine Kathryn Rusch, William Sanders, Pamela Sargent, Steve Rasnic Tem and Jane Yolen.

Other books you might like:
Richard Erdoes, *American Indian Myths and Legends*, 1984
    Alfonso Ortiz, co-author
Alan Dean Foster, *Cyber Way*, 1990
Richard Gilliam, *Grails: Quests of the Dawn*, 1994
    Martin H. Greenberg, Edward E. Kramer, co-editors
Barry Lopez, *Crow and Weasel*, 1990
Howard Norman, *Northern Tales: Traditional Stories of Eskimo and Indian Peoples*, 1980
Gerald Vizenor, *Dead Voices: Natural Agonies in the Real World*, 1992
Roger Welsch, *Touching the Fire*, 1992

157

PIERS ANTHONY

Tatham Mound

(New York: Morrow, 1991)

Story type: Fantasy (Quest; Historical)
Major character(s): Tale Teller, Indian (Tocobaga), Companion (translator); Hernando De Soto, Historical Figure, Explorer
Time period(s): 16th century (1510s & 1540s)
Locale(s): Florida; South

Summary: Wounded, Hotfoot is visited by an ancestor, Dead Eagle, who reveals to him a sacred mission. He takes the name Throatshot, and becomes apprenticed to a trader. In his wanderings he learns languages and takes the name, Tale Teller. His linguistic skill leads to his accompanying Hernando De Soto as translator while De Soto explores.

Other books you might like:
Orson Scott Card, *Seventh Son*, 1987
Sue Harrison, *Mother Earth, Father Sky*, 1990
J. Alison James, *Sing for a Gentle Rain*, 1990
William Sarabande, *Beyond the Sea of Ice*, 1987
Robert Shea, *Shaman*, 1991
Catherine Wells, *The Earth Is All That Lasts*, 1991
Roger Zelazny, *Bridge of Ashes*, 1976

158

PIERS ANTHONY
ROBERT KORNWISE, Co-Author

Through the Ice

(Lancaster, PA: Underwood-Miller, 1989)

Story type: Fantasy (Alternate World)
Major character(s): Seth Warner, Hero
Time period(s): 1990s
Locale(s): Earth; Alternate Earth (Parellel plane of existence)

Summary: Trying to escape from punks about to beat him up, Seth falls into a world populated by fairies, trolls and elves. He joins a band of heroes (the Chosen) who are trying to defeat the evil sorceror, Nefarious, and save Earth's planes of existence.

Other books you might like:
Ray Garton, *Methods of Madness*, 1990
Peni R. Griffin, *Otto From Otherwhere*, 1990
Shirley Rousseau Murphy, *Medallion of the Black Hound*, 1989
  Welch Suggs, co-author
J. Michael Straczynski, *OtherSyde*, 1990

159

PIERS ANTHONY

Total Recall

(New York: William Morrow, 1989)

Story type: Science Fiction (Adventure)
Major character(s): Douglas Quail, Construction Worker; Melina, Prostitute
Time period(s): Indeterminate Future
Locale(s): Earth; Mars

Summary: Douglas Quail is a construction worker with a boring job and a beautiful wife, but he keeps dreaming about having adventures on Mars. Hoping to come to terms with these disturbing dreams, he goes to Rekall, a corporation which creates artificial memories. An ersatz vacation on Mars, with all the tourist trimmings, will, he hopes, satisfy whatever buried urge is behind the dreams. Something goes wrong, however, and Quail discovers that his dreams are terribly real. Film novelization based on Philip K. Dick's "We Can Remember It for you Wholesale."

Other books you might like:
Philip K. Dick, *Do Androids Dream of Electric Sheep?*, 1968
Philip K. Dick, *Flow My Tears, the Policeman Said*, 1974
Philip K. Dick, *A Scanner Darkly*, 1977
Philip K. Dick, *Time Out of Joint*, 1959
Sharon Webb, *The Halflife*, 1989

160

PIERS ANTHONY

Virtual Mode

(New York: Ace/Putnam, 1991)

Story type: Fantasy (Quest)

Series: Virtual Mode
Major character(s): Colene, Teenager, Adventurer; Darius, Ruler (Cyng of Pwer); Seqiro, Animal (intelligent horse), Telepath
Time period(s): 1990s
Locale(s): Oklahoma, Alternate Universe

Summary: Colene, an unhappy 14-year-old who has tried suicide, rescues Darius. As she nurses him back to health she is happy, but does not believe his claim that he comes from another dimension until he disappears. While he tries to search for her by creating a path between the two dimensions, Colene sets off to find him and finds Seqiro instead. The two travel until captured by Ddwng. During Darius' search, he also gets captured by Ddwng and is forced to complete an interplanetary mission before he can claim Colene. Once united the two set off and are hailed by Nona in a strange dimension.

Other books you might like:
Jack L. Chalker, *The River of Dancing Gods*, 1984
C.J. Cherryh, *Rusalka*, 1989
Alan Dean Foster, *Spellsinger*, 1983
Diana Wynne Jones, *Fire and Hemlock*, 1984
Christopher Stasheff, *Her Majesty's Wizard*, 1986

161

PIERS ANTHONY
ALFRED TELLA, Co-Author

The Willing Spirit

(New York: Tor, 1996)

Story type: Fantasy (Legend; Quest)
Major character(s): Hari, Religious (Brahmin), Adventurer; Mohini, Deity; Ravana, Deity, Demon
Time period(s): Indeterminate Past
Locale(s): India

Summary: The Immortals Mohini and Ravana play a game. If Mohini, in the persona of a mortal woman, can seduce Hari seven times, she wins and Ravana earns banishment for a century. If Ravana, through mortal men, can kill Hari, he wins and Mohini must provide him with a century of erotic frenzy. Meanwhile, Hari wishes only to see a bit of the world. Based on Indian myths and legends.

Other books you might like:
John Brunner, *The Traveller in Black*, 1971
Kara Dalkey, *Goa*, 1996
L. Sprague de Camp, *The Golden Wind*, 1969
Rudyard Kipling, *Famous Tales of India*, 1962
Mack Reynolds, *Space Search*, 1984
Chelsea Quinn Yarbro, *The Path of the Eclipse*, 1981
Roger Zelazny, *Lord of Light*, 1967

162

PIERS ANTHONY

Yon Ill Wind

(New York: Tor, 1996)

Story type: Fantasy (Light Fantasy; Quest)

Series: Xanth
Major character(s): X(A/N)[th] ''Nimby'', Demon, Handicapped (mute); Chlorine, Runaway, Adventurer; Sean Baldwin, Teenager, Vacationer
Time period(s): Indeterminate
Locale(s): Xanth, Fictional Country

Summary: As they return from vacation, a hurricane blows the Baldwin family into Xanth where they encounter Nimby, travelling in mortal form because of a bet, along with his human companion, Chlorine. Chlorine must escort the Baldwins safely out of Xanth after harnessing the hurricane which has followed the Baldwins there.

Other books you might like:
Robert Asprin, *Another Fine Myth*, 1978
K.B. Bogen, *Go Quest, Young Man*, 1993
Susan Cooper, *Silver on the Tree*, 1977
Alan Dean Foster, *Spellsinger*, 1983
Diana Wynne Jones, *Hexwood*, 1994
Andre Norton, *Here Abide Monsters*, 1973
Terry Pratchett, *Reaper Man*, 1992
Christopher Stasheff, *M'Lady Witch*, 1994

163

KIM ANTIEAU

The Jigsaw Woman
(New York: Roc, 1996)

Story type: Fantasy (Legend; Time Travel)
Major character(s): Keelie, Reanimated Dead, Psychic; Victor Beaufort, Scientist; Lee, Abuse Victim
Time period(s): Indeterminate Past
Locale(s): Earth

Summary: Dr. Victor Beaufort creates Keelie from the body parts of three women and brings her to life. Not content to remain his companion, Keelie searches for her true identity, and learns that she has encountered the same three women and her creator continually throughout human history. First novel.

Other books you might like:
Michael Bishop, *Brittle Innings*, 1994
Amarantha Knight, *The Darker Passions: Frankenstein*, 1995
Jamil Nasir, *The Higher Space*, 1996
Christopher Pike, *The Season of Passage*, 1992
Christopher Pike, *The Starlight Crystal*, 1996
Mary Shelley, *Frankenstein*, 1818

164

KIM ANTIEAU

Trudging to Eden
(Woodinville, Washington: Silver Salamander Press, 1994)

Story type: Horror (Collection)

Summary: This first collection by a writer of fantasy, horror, and science fiction brings together 12 stories, six original to the volume. ''Listening for the General'' blends horror with magic realism in its tale of a woman's revenge on a banana republic military officer. In ''Cycles,'' an Appalachian family shows a strange fecundity that spans the generations. ''Frac-

tures'' tells of a multiple personality created by a woman's absorption of ghosts, and ''Lab Rats'' reflects on the near-future possibilities of laboratory animal experimentation. ''Mark of the Beast'' is a variation on the werewolf story, and ''The Girl with No Hair'' on a tale of witchcraft. Charles de Lint supplies an introduction.

Other books you might like:
Jack Cady, *The Sons of Noah and Other Stories*, 1993
Nina Kiriki Hoffman, *Common Threads*, 1995
Steve Rasnic Tem, *Celestial Inventory*, 1991
Chet Williamson, *The House of Fear*, 1989

165

ALLEN APPEL

Till the End of Time
(New York: Doubleday, 1990)

Story type: Fantasy (Contemporary; Time Travel)
Series: Alex Balfour
Major character(s): Alex Balfour, Historian; Molly Glenn, Journalist
Time period(s): 1990s; 1940s
Locale(s): New York, New York; Japan

Summary: Alex, like his father and grandfather, is fascinated with the past. This time Alex finds himself drawn physically to December 7, 1941, Pearl Harbor, Hawaii. When Alex tries to convince President Roosevelt not to drop the bomb on Japan, the President sends Alex there to find out what is really happening in that part of the world. Meanwhile, in 1990, Molly Glenn, his girlfriend, is in Japan working on a story. ALA Best Books For Young Adults title.

Other books you might like:
Alan Brennert, *Time and Chance*, 1990
Philip K. Dick, *The Man in the High Castle*, 1963
Ken Grimwood, *Replay*, 1986
David Wingrove, *The Middle Kingdom*, 1990

166

KEN APPLEBY

The Voice of Cepheus
(New York: Ballantine/Del Rey, 1989)

Story type: Science Fiction (First Contact)
Major character(s): Sheilagh Mathews, Student, Astronaut; Adrian Holdsworth, Scientist (Astronomer)
Time period(s): 21st century (2001)
Locale(s): *Unity*, Spaceship

Summary: Signals are received from an alien race in the direction of the star Cepheus. Once interpreted, the signals provide information that leads to a technological revolution. Humanity sends a spacecraft to contact the aliens, but it is disabled. The marooned crew establishes contact with the friendly Cepheans and a utopian age of exploration begins. This is Appleby's first novel.

Other books you might like:
Arthur C. Clarke, *Childhood's End*, 1953
Edward Gibson, *Reach*, 1989

Jack McDevitt, *The Hercules Text*, 1986
Carl Sagan, *Contact*, 1985
David Alexander Smith, *Rendezvous*, 1988

167

RISA ARATYR

Hunter of the Light

(New York: HarperPrism, 1995)

Story type: Fantasy (Legend; Adventure)
Major character(s): Blackthorn, Minstrel (bard), Hero
Time period(s): Indeterminate Past
Locale(s): Ireland (Eirinn)

Summary: More comfortable as entertainer than as warrior, Blackthorn, now chosen champion, must stalk and kill the white dream-stag to preserve the balance between light and dark. Author's first novel.

Other books you might like:
Greg Bear, *Songs of Earth and Power*, 1994
Charles de Lint, *Greenmantle*, 1988
Charles de Lint, *Moonheart: A Romance*, 1984
Kenneth C. Flint, *Riders of the Sidhe*, 1984
Casey Flynn, *Most Ancient Song*, 1991
Morgan Llywelyn, *Bard*, 1984
Patricia A. McKillip, *The Book of Atrix Wolfe*, 1995

168

JOHN ARBUCCI

Blood of Innocents

(New York: Onyx, 1991)

Story type: Horror (Wild Talents)
Major character(s): Jack Rigger, Child; Clark Ashton, Doctor; Francis Chapin, Teacher
Time period(s): 1990s (1991)
Locale(s): Brookline, Massachusetts

Summary: The discovery that young Jack Rigger can hurt and heal himself at will is a godsend for Dr. Clark Ashton, who hopes to use the boy's talent to rehabilitate his flagging bioengineering company. What Ashton doesn't know is that Jack can also inflict his talents on those persons whom he does not like. This is the author's first novel.

Other books you might like:
John Farris, *The Fury*, 1976

169

NATHAN ARCHER (Pseudonym of Lawrence Watt-Evans)

Martian Deathtrap

(New York: Ballantine Del Rey, 1996)

Story type: Science Fiction (Invasion of Earth)
Series: Mars Attacks
Major character(s): Bud Garcia, Resistance Fighter; Katie Winters, Child, Resistance Fighter; Quisaz Hadrak, Alien (Martian), Military Personnel
Time period(s): 1990s

Locale(s): United States

Summary: When Bud hides under the trees to avoid an attack, Martians release powerful bioactive agents which produce unforeseen results, giant insects which threaten humans and Martians alike, as Bud and others struggle to repel the invaders. Film and comic book tie-in originating from rare 1962 Topps trading cards.

Other books you might like:
Kevin J. Anderson, *War of the Worlds: Global Dispatches*, 1996
  editor
David Brin, *Earth*, 1990
Jonathan Gems, *Mars Attacks!*, 1996
Ray W. Murrill, *War Dogs of the Golden Horde*, 1996
Larry Niven, *Footfall*, 1985
  Jerry Pournelle, co-author
H.G. Wells, *The War of the Worlds*, 1898

170

NATHAN ARCHER (Pseudonym of Lawrence Watt-Evans)

Ragnarok

(New York: Pocket, 1995)

Story type: Science Fiction (Space Opera)
Series: Star Trek: Voyager
Major character(s): Kathryn Janeway, Spaceship Captain, Military Personnel; Tuvok, Security Officer, Alien (Vulcan); Chakotay, Military Personnel (commander), Indian
Time period(s): 24th century
Locale(s): *U.S.S. Voyager*, Spaceship; Outer Space

Summary: The *Voyager* crew detects a tetryon beam that may originate in a device capable of transporting them back to the Federation. As they approach the site, they find themselves in the midst of a battle between two species which has raged for hundreds of years. Hoping to negotiate a peace that would allow them to examine the source of the tetryon beam, Janeway attempts to communicate with the warring sides, but succeeds only in attracting the hostile fire from ships on both sides.

Other books you might like:
Gordon R. Dickson, *Soldier, Ask Not*, 1967
David Drake, *Ranks of Bronze*, 1986
Brad Ferguson, *The Last Stand*, 1995
Joe Haldeman, *The Forever War*, 1974
Robert A. Heinlein, *Starship Troopers*, 1959
Lawrence Watt-Evans, *Crosstime Traffic*, 1992
Lawrence Watt-Evans, *Out of This World*, 1994
Susan Wright, *Violations*, 1995

171

MICHAEL ARMSTRONG

Agviq

(New York: Popular Library Questar, 1990)

Story type: Science Fiction (Post-Nuclear Holocaust; Contemporary Realism)

Major character(s): Claudia, Scientist, Anthropologist; Rob, Student—College
Time period(s): 1990s
Locale(s): Barrow, Alaska; Utqiagvik, Alaska

Summary: Claudia and Rob are on a dig studying the old Innuit culture. When a radio broadcast warns them that a nuclear holocaust has occurred, they take shelter in the Innuit home they've uncovered. When they come out three weeks later they must survive in a world heading for nuclear winter without the support of a technological society. This novel was expanded from the 1985 short story, "Going After Arvig."

Other books you might like:
Suzy McKee Charnas, *Motherlines*, 1979
Suzy McKee Charnas, *Walk to the End of the World*, 1974
Gordon R. Dickson, *Wolf and Iron*, 1990
W. Michael Gear, *People of the Wolf*, 1990
    Kathleen O'Neal Gear, co-author
Donald E. McQuinn, *Warrior*, 1990
R.M. Meluch, *Chicago Red*, 1990
Paul O. Williams, *The Breaking of Northwall*, 1981

172

MICHAEL ARMSTRONG

The Hidden War
(Lake Geneva, Wisconsin: TSR, 1994)

Story type: Science Fiction (Military; Arts)
Major character(s): Krim, Military Personnel, Spaceman (pilot)
Time period(s): Indeterminate Future
Locale(s): Earth; *Jeanne Kirkpatrick*, Spaceship

Summary: After serving half of his 30-year sentence for opposing Earth forces' attack of the Jack, a free asteroid settlement based on beat poetry, Krim receives a "hide," a protective outer skin, and an early release with the request that he fight for the new Solarian Alliance against the Terrorons, invaders from light years distant. Aboard the *Jeanne Kirkpatrick*, Krim learns more about the covert aspects of the space forces.

Other books you might like:
Glen Cook, *The Dragon Never Sleeps*, 1988
Marjorie Bradley Kellogg, *Harmony*, 1991
Melisa C. Michaels, *First Battle*, 1985
Janet Morris, *Dream Dancer*, 1981
Clifford D. Simak, *Shakespeare's Planet*, 1976

173

ELEANOR ARNASON

Ring of Swords
(New York: Tor, 1993)

Story type: Science Fiction (Gay/Lesbian Fiction; Military)
Major character(s): Anna Perez, Diplomat, Scientist; Ettin Gwarha, Diplomat (First Defenders), Alien (Hwarhath); Nicholas Sanders, Linguist
Time period(s): 22nd century
Locale(s): Planet—Imaginary; Space Station

Summary: After Anna Perez acts honorably toward them, Hwarhath negotiators demand that she attend talks which will determine humanity's status as intelligent beings, a discussion with culture-shattering potential. Little prepared for diplomacy by her scientific education, Anna discovers she and a perceived traitor, Nicholas Sanders, represent humanity's best hope of avoiding destruction.

Other books you might like:
David Brin, *Glory Season*, 1993
Octavia E. Butler, *Survivor*, 1978
Helen Collins, *Mutagenesis*, 1993
Diana G. Gallagher, *The Alien Dark*, 1990
Nicola Griffith, *Ammonite*, 1993
Joan Slonczewski, *Daughter of Elysium*, 1993
Joan Slonczewski, *A Door into Ocean*, 1986
David Alexander Smith, *Homecoming*, 1990

174

ELEANOR ARNASON

A Woman of the Iron People
(New York: Morrow, 1991)

Story type: Science Fiction (First Contact)
Major character(s): Nia, Alien; Li Lixia, Linguist, Sociologist
Time period(s): 23rd century
Locale(s): Sigma Draconis II, Planet—Imaginary

Summary: After the remaining countries on Earth recover from the devastation left by the 20th century, they send out an interstellar exploratory expedition which finds intelligent, humanoid, furry aliens on an Earth-like planet. Lixia is one of a dozen social scientists dropped on different parts of the planet who contact the local inhabitants and learn their customs, languages and cultures. Since the potentially dangerous, mature, breeding males do not live in the alien villages, male humans have difficulty interacting with the villagers.

Other books you might like:
Ursula K. Le Guin, *Always Coming Home*, 1987
Ursula K. Le Guin, *The Left Hand of Darkness*, 1969
Judith Moffett, *Pennterra*, 1987
Joan Slonczewski, *The Wall Around Eden*, 1989
Joan Slonczewski, *A Door into Ocean*, 1986
Joan Slonczewski, *Still Forms on Foxfield*, 1980
L. Neil Smith, *Contact and Commune*, 1990

175

MICHAEL A. ARNZEN

Grave Markings
(New York: Dell/Abyss, 1994)

Story type: Horror (Serial Killer)
Major character(s): Mark Michael Kilpatrick, Artist (tattoo artist), Serial Killer; Roy Roberts, Journalist; John Lockerman, Police Officer
Time period(s): 1990s (1994)
Locale(s): Colorado Springs, Colorado

Summary: A handful of concerned citizens band together to rid Colorado Springs of a bizarre serial killer who leaves his victims covered with full-body tattoos. Alternating between omniscient and subjective viewpoints, this first novel details the twisted mind of Mark Michael Kilpatrick, a tattoo artist who never overcame his abuse as a child and now vents it through destructive creativity.

Other books you might like:
Poppy Z. Brite, *Drawing Blood*, 1993
Michael Cadnum, *Skyscape*, 1994
Kathe Koja, *Skin*, 1993
Kathe Koja, *Strange Angels*, 1994
Jessica Amanda Salmonson, *Anthony Shriek*, 1991

176

MICHAEL A. ARNZEN
MARGE B. SIMON, Illustrator

Needles and Sins

(Concord, California: Dark Regions Press, 1993)

Story type: Horror (Collection)

Summary: This chapbook collects 11 stories, three of which are original to the book. ''An Eye for An Eye,'' ''Marked'' and ''Copycats'' share the common theme of the strange clients of tattoo artists, while ''Counterpoint,'' ''Phrenological Love,'' and ''Spring Ahead, Fall Back'' are about psychopaths masquerading as normal human beings. ''The Spirit of the Bayonet'' follows the escapades of a soldier driven crazy by boot camp. The stories are introduced by Karl Edward Wagner. This is the author's first book.

Other books you might like:
Edward Bryant, *Darker Passions*, 1992
Adam-Troy Castro, *Lost in Booth Nine*, 1993
Lucy Taylor, *Unnatural Acts*, 1992

177

LOU ARONICA

Full Spectrum 2

(New York: Bantam Spectra, 1990)

Story type: Science Fiction (Anthology)
Series: Full Spectrum
Time period(s): Indeterminate

Summary: This collection of 27 short stories aims at investigating the entire realm of new ''speculative fiction.'' Some of this book's better-known authors include Greg Bear, David Brin, Edward Bryant, Vonda N. McIntyre, Patricia A. McKillip, Kim Stanley Robinson, Michaela Roessner and Michael Swanwick. Some of the newer authors include Carolyn Ives Gilman, Karen Haber and Elizabeth Hand. Reprint of 1989 Doubleday Foundation hardcover edition.

Other books you might like:
Isaac Asimov, *Isaac Asimov Presents the Great SF Stories: 21 (1959)*, 1990
    Martin H. Greenberg, co-editor
Groff Conklin, *The Best of Science Fiction*, 1946
Gardner Dozois, *The Year's Best Science Fiction: Seventh Annual Collection*, 1990
Harlan Ellison, *Dangerous Visions*, 1967

Raymond J. Healy, *Famous Science Fiction Stories: Adventures in Time and Space*, 1946
    J. Francis McComas, co-editor
Robert Silverberg, *The Science Fiction Hall of Fame, Volume 1*, 1970
Donald A. Wollheim, *The 1990 Annual World's Best Science Fiction*, 1990
    Arthur W. Saha, co-editor

178

LOU ARONICA, Editor
AMY STOUT, Co-Editor
BETSY MITCHELL, Co-Editor

Full Spectrum 3

(New York: Doubleday Foundation, 1991)

Story type: Science Fiction (Anthology)
Series: Full Spectrum

Summary: This volume contains an introduction by Lou Aronica plus 23 stories original to this anthology whose themes range from magical realism to hard science fiction. Better-known authors herein include Poul Anderson, Gregory Benford, Michael Bishop, Ursula K. Le Guin, Barry N. Malzberg, James Morrow and Norman Spinrad. Some notable authors newer to the genres include Kevin J. Anderson, Karen Joy Fowler, Elizabeth Hand, Peg Kerr, Jack McDevitt, Kristine Kathryn Rusch, Nancy Willard and David Zindell. One story, ''Desert Rain,'' is a collaborative effort by Mark L. Van Name and Pat Murphy. Two stories originally written in foreign languages appear herein. Kim Stanley Robinson translated Joelle Wintrebert's ''Transfusion'' from French and Sally Schiller and Anne Calveley translated Wolfgang Jeschke's ''Loitering at Death's Door'' from German.

Other books you might like:
Michael Bishop, *Nebula Awards 25*, 1991
    editor
Ellen Datlow, *The Year's Best Fantasy and Horror: Fourth Annual Collection*, 1991
    Terri Windling, co-editor
Gardner Dozois, *The Year's Best Science Fiction: Eighth Annual Collection*, 1991
    editor
Harlan Ellison, *Dangerous Visions*, 1967
    editor
Robert Silverberg, *The Science Fiction Hall of Fame, Volume 1*, 1970
    editor
Donald A. Wollheim, *The 1990 Annual World's Best Science Fiction*, 1990
    Arthur W. Saha, co-editor
George Zebrowski, *Nebula Awards 22*, 1988
    editor

179

LOU ARONICA, Editor
AMY STOUT, Co-Editor
BETSY MITCHELL, Co-Editor

Full Spectrum 4
(New York: Bantam Spectra, 1993)

Story type: Science Fiction (Anthology)
Series: Full Spectrum

Summary: Includes one poem by Ursula K. Le Guin, six pages of biographical notes about the authors and editors plus 19 original stories, several with themes of a sexual nature and several about aliens; other themes include nanotechnology, psychology and terraforming. Authors include Ray Aldridge, Kevin J. Anderson, David Brin, Stephen R. Donaldson, Gregory Feeley, Elizabeth Hand, Nancy Kress, Dave Smeds and Martha Soukup.

Other books you might like:
Ellen Datlow, *Omni Best Science Fiction Three*, 1993
    editor
Gardner Dozois, *The Year's Best Science Fiction: Tenth Annual Collection*, 1993
    editor
James Morrow, *Nebula Awards 27*, 1993
    editor
Kristine Kathryn Rusch, *The Best of Pulphouse: The Hardback Magazine*, 1991
    editor
Robert Silverberg, *Universe 2*, 1992
    Karen Haber, co-editor

180

BRUCE D. ARTHURS, Editor

Copper Star
(Tempe, Arizona: 1991 World Fantasy Convention, 1991)

Story type: Horror (Anthology)

Summary: This special anthology for the 1991 World Fantasy Convention brings together 16 original stories and poems of horror and fantasy with a southwestern orientation. Included are Mike Newland's tale of a ghostly encounter in the desert, "Carrion Eaters"; Ed Bryant's satire on the difference between the horror of country and city life, "Country Mouse"; Norman Partridge's story of a boxer's mystic origins, "The Cut Man"; and Jeanette M. Hopper's tale of a midwife's horrifying experience delivering a child born in desert heat, "Swelter."

Other books you might like:
Stephen Jones, *Gaslight and Ghosts*, 1988
    Jo Fletcher, co-editor
Joe R. Lansdale, *Razored Saddles*, 1989
    Pat LoBrutto, co-editor
Joe R. Lansdale, *The New Frontier*, 1989
Kathryn Ptacek, *Women of the West*, 1990
Frank D. McSherry Jr., *Western Ghosts*, 1990
    Charles G. Waugh and Martin H. Greenberg, co-editors

181

CATHERINE ASARO

Catch the Lightning
(New York: Tor, 1996)

Story type: Science Fiction (Adventure; Genetic Manipulation)
Series: Skolian Empire
Major character(s): Akushtina "Tina" Santis Pulivok, Waiter/Waitress, Psychic; Althor, Military Personnel (Jagernaut Secondary), Psychic; Kryx Iquar, Alien, Psychic
Time period(s): 1980s (1987); Indeterminate Future
Locale(s): Los Angeles, California; The Cylinder, Space Station

Summary: Tina meets a weird man on the way home from work, discovering that he comes not only from another planet, but another universe and another time. Recognizing a psychic connection, she helps Althor escape from her government and universe, only to find far more subtle dangers in his universe.

Other books you might like:
Marion Zimmer Bradley, *The Forbidden Tower*, 1977
Emma Bull, *Bone Dance*, 1991
Anne McCaffrey, *The Rowan*, 1990
K.D. Wentworth, *Moonspeaker*, 1994
Walter Jon Williams, *Metropolitan*, 1995

182

CATHERINE ASARO

Primary Inversion
(New York: Tor, 1995)

Story type: Science Fiction (Political; Psychic Powers)
Major character(s): Sauscony Valdoria, Genetically Altered Being (esper); Rex Blackstone, Military Personnel, Pilot (spaceship); J'briol Qox, Genetically Altered Being (esper), Heir
Time period(s): Indeterminate Future
Locale(s): Delos, Planet—Imaginary; Foreshires Hold, Planet—Imaginary; Allied Worlds of Earth, Interstellar Empire/Federation

Summary: While on the Earth Alliance world, Delos, Sauscony of Skolia discovers J'briol, supposedly Aristo, heir to the Trader empire. Once enslaved by an Aristo, she recognizes he lacks the empathic void of a true Aristo when they discover a psychic bond. J'briol refuses to accept the truth about the Aristos, risking his life and sanity and a potential end to the war between the Skolians and the Traders. First novel.

Other books you might like:
Jeffrey A. Carver, *Dragons in the Stars*, 1992
Michelle Shirey Crean, *Dancer of the Sixth*, 1993
Jacqueline Lichtenberg, *House of Zeor*, 1974
Alis A. Rasmussen, *A Passage of Stars*, 1990
Dan Simmons, *Hyperion*, 1989
David Weber, *Path of the Fury*, 1992

183
FRANK ASCH
Journey to Terezor
(New York: Holiday House, 1989)

Story type: Science Fiction (Young Adult)
Major character(s): Matt Hilton, Teenager; Ryan Morrison, Scientist
Time period(s): 1980s
Locale(s): S-15, Planet—Imaginary (The planetary system of Terezor)

Summary: Matt Hilton and his family are kidnapped by aliens and brought to the Earth colony on another planet. Determined to regain their freedom, he and two other teenagers hatch a desperate plot to escape the colony.

Other books you might like:
Grace Chetwin, *Collidescope*, 1990
John Christopher, *The City of Gold and Lead*, 1967
John Christopher, *The Pool of Fire*, 1968
John Christopher, *The White Mountains*, 1967
Jo Dereske, *The Lone Sentinel*, 1989

184
CONSTANCE ASH
The Stalking Horse
(New York: Ace, 1990)

Story type: Fantasy (Political)
Major character(s): Glennys Eve, Dancer (Ballerina), Horse Trainer
Time period(s): Indeterminate
Locale(s): St. Lucien, Fictional Country

Summary: In a world where political intrigue and social change are predominant, Glennys hopes to make the leap from horse trainer to ballerina. But she must be careful to guard the secret of her ability to communicate mind-to-mind with the horses, which are a part of the ballet company.

Other books you might like:
Anne McCaffrey, *Dragonflight*, 1981
Anne McCaffrey, *The White Dragon*, 1986
Jack Vance, *Suldrun's Garden*, 1983

185
CONSTANCE ASH
The Stallion Queen
(New York: Ace, 1992)

Story type: Fantasy (Adventure)
Series: Horsegirl Saga
Major character(s): Glennys Eve, Leader, Telepath (animal); Leon, Royalty (prince)
Time period(s): Indeterminate
Locale(s): Saquave Wilderness, Fictional Country (desert)

Summary: Hoping to leave corruption behind with the court life, Glennys and her followers have established themselves in the Saquave Wilderness, adopting a life style compatible with nature and the environment. When, 10 winters later, Prince Leon appears, the future of the settlement comes into question.

Other books you might like:
Mary H. Herbert, *Dark Horse*, 1990
Mary H. Herbert, *Lightning's Daughter*, 1991
Peter Morwood, *The Horse Lord*, 1987
Mary Stanton, *The Heavenly Horse From the Outermost West*, 1988
Mary Stanton, *Piper at the Gate*, 1989

186
MIKE ASHLEY, Editor
The Camelot Chronicles
(New York: Carroll & Graf, 1992)

Story type: Fantasy (Anthology; Legend)
Major character(s): Arthur, Royalty (King of the Britons); Guenevere, Royalty, Spouse; Merlin, Magician
Time period(s): 5th century
Locale(s): England

Summary: Contains a 2-page introduction by the editor, 7-page guide to Arthurian characters, 9-page appendix, "Mountain Madness" by Theordore Goodridge Roberts plus 18 stories written this century, 10 since 1980, all sharing themes which involve King Arthur and his knights. Authors of the 8 original stories and 10 stories reprinted from books and periodicals include Vera Chapman, Phyllis Ann Karr, Howard Pyle, Darrell Schweitzer, Keith Taylor, Peter Tremayne, P. G. Wodehouse and Jane Yolen, with the story, "John, the Knight of the Lion," listed as traditional. Companion volume to *The Pendragon Chronicles*.

Other books you might like:
Marion Zimmer Bradley, *The Mists of Avalon*, 1983
Gillian Bradshaw, *Hawk of May*, 1980
Courtway Jones, *In the Shadow of the Oak King*, 1991
Sharan Newman, *Guinevere*, 1981
Howard Pyle, *The Story of King Arthur and His Knights*, 1903
Howard Pyle, *The Story of the Champions of the Round Table*, 1905
Persia Woolley, *Guinevere: The Legend in Autumn*, 1991

187
MIKE ASHLEY, Editor
The Mammoth Book of Short Horror Novels
(New York: Carroll & Graf, 1994)

Story type: Horror (Anthology)

Summary: The ten short novels collected in this anthology span 100 years and cover such subjects as a demonically possessed toy (Stephen King's "The Monkey"), psychic possession (Arthur Conan Doyle's "The Parasite"), ghostly visitations (Russell Kirk's "There's a Long, Long Trail A-Winding"), nature in revolt (Lucius Shepard's "How the Wind Spoke at Madaket"), manmade monsters (T.E.D. Klein's

''Nadelman's God''), vampirism (John Metcalfe's ''The Feasting Dead'') and ancient family curses (David Case's ''Fengriffen''). Included as well are stories by Algernon Blackwood, A.C. Benson, and Oliver Onions. This volume was originally published in 1988.

Other books you might like:
David G. Hartwell, *The Dark Descent*, 1987
    editor
David G. Hartwell, *Foundations of Fear*, 1993
    editor
Tim Haydock, *The Mammoth Book of Classic Chillers*, 1986
    editor
Stephen Jones, *The Mammoth Book of Terror*, 1991
    editor
Charles G. Waugh, *13 Short Horror Novels*, 1987
    Martin H. Greenberg, co-editor

188

MIKE ASHLEY, Editor

The Merlin Chronicles

(New York: Carroll & Graf, 1995)

Story type: Fantasy (Anthology; Legend)
Major character(s): Merlin, Magician
Time period(s): 5th century
Locale(s): Camelot, England

Summary: Subtitled, ''Magic and Adventure From the Age of Legend,'' this volume contains a seven-page guide to Arthurian characters, a 15-page introduction and individual introductions to 10 original and 12 stories reprinted from anthologies, collections, and periodicals. The stories vary in tone from light to serious and feature Merlin and other famous characters and life at Arthur's Camelot. Authors include Marion Zimmer Bradley, Vera Chapman, Charles de Lint, Esther Friesner, Robert Holdstock, Phyllis Ann Karr, Tanith Lee, William Morris, H. Warner Munn, Jennifer Roberson, Jessica Amanda Salmonson, Darrell Schweitzer, Peter Tremayne, and Jane Yolen.

Other books you might like:
Marion Zimmer Bradley, *The Mists of Avalon*, 1983
Simon Hawke, *The Wizard of 4th Street*, 1987
Andrea Hopkins, *Chronicles of King Arthur*, 1994
    editor
Courtway Jones, *In the Shadow of the Oak King*, 1991
Stephen R. Lawhead, *Merlin*, 1988
Mary Stewart, *The Crystal Cave*, 1970

189

PAULINE ASHWELL

Project Farcry

(New York: Tor, 1995)

Story type: Science Fiction (Psychic Powers; First Contact)
Major character(s): Big Sword, Alien, Telepath; John James Jordan, Spaceman, Leader; Richard ''Rivername'' Jordan, Telepath, Teenager
Time period(s): Indeterminate Future

Locale(s): Lambda, Planet—Imaginary

Summary: Before discovering that his son, Richard, can read minds, John takes his son with him on the Second Lambdan Exploratory Expedition. Called ''Rivername'' by Big Sword, Richard acts as intermediary between the aliens and the scientists who now recognize that the aliens are intelligent. Unfortunately, Richard must return to Earth with his father, leaving no one to develop relationships with the aliens.

Other books you might like:
Orson Scott Card, *Speaker for the Dead*, 1986
A.C. Crispin, *Serpent's Gift*, 1992
    Deborah A. Marshall, co-author
H.M. Hoover, *Only Child*, 1992
Janet Kagan, *Hellspark*, 1988
H. Beam Piper, *Little Fuzzy*, 1962

190

PAULINE ASHWELL

Unwillingly to Earth

(New York: Tor, 1992)

Story type: Science Fiction (Adventure)
Major character(s): Lysistrata ''Lizzie'' Lee, Student, Teenager; D. J. McClare, Professor, Scientist; B Leydon, Student, Companion
Time period(s): Indeterminate Future
Locale(s): Russett, Earth (Interplanetary College of the Humanities); Excenus 23, Planet—Imaginary; Incognita, Planet—Imaginary

Summary: Because of Lizzie's gift for Cultural Engineering and innate stubbornness, she attends college on Earth, despite her hidden inherited inability to use reading machines which tremendously increase reading speed. Lizzie overcomes her handicap in the nick of time, enabling her to continue her education and incidentally acquire experience in her field of study. Author's first novel.

Other books you might like:
Lois McMaster Bujold, *The Warrior's Apprentice*, 1986
A.C. Crispin, *Starbridge*, 1989
Tara K. Harper, *Lightwing*, 1992
Frank Herbert, *Dune*, 1965
Laura J. Mixon, *Glass Houses*, 1992
Rebecca Ore, *Becoming Alien*, 1988
Kathy Tyers, *Shivering World*, 1991

191

ISAAC ASIMOV

The Asimov Chronicles: Fifty Years of Isaac Asimov

(Arlington Heights: Dark Harvest, 1989)

Story type: Science Fiction (Collection)
Summary: This retrospective collection, edited by Martin H. Greenberg and heavily illustrated by Ron Lindahn and Val Lakey Lindahn, includes fifty short stories, one from each year of Isaac Asimov's enormously productive career, plus

some essays. Beginning with the early "Marooned Off Vesta" (1939) and ending with the recent "I Love Little Pussy" (1988), the book includes Asimov's Hugo and Nebula Award winning "The Bicentenial Man" (1977) and such classic works as "Nightfall" (1941), "Evidence" (1946), "Little Lost Robot" (1947), "The Martian Way" (1952), "The Ugly Little Boy" (1958), and ."". That Thou Art Mindful of Him" (1974).

Other books you might like:
James Blish, *Cities in Flight*, 1970
    Revised edition
Martin H. Greenberg, *Foundation's Friends*, 1989
    Editer
Jack Williamson, *The Humanoids*, 1949

192

ISAAC ASIMOV

The Complete Stories - Volume 1
(New York: Doubleday Foundation, 1990)

Story type: Science Fiction (Collection; Science Fiction)

Summary: This book collects the complete contents of three previous collections: *Earth Is Room Enough, Nine Tomorrows,* and *Nightfall and Other Stories,* comprising 46 stories with an additional brief introduction. Dr. Asimov's personal favorite, "The Last Question," is included in this volume as is "Nightfall," voted best science fiction story of all time by the Science Fiction Writers of America.

Other books you might like:
Alfred Bester, *Star Light, Star Bright*, 1976
James Blish, *The Best of James Blish*, 1979
Larry Niven, *Tales of Known Space*, 1975
Cordwainer Smith, *The Best of Cordwainer Smith*, 1975
    pseudonym of Paul Myron Anthony Linebarger
Theodore Sturgeon, *Caviar*, 1955
William Tenn, *The Seven Sexes*, 1968
John Varley, *The Persistence of Vision*, 1978

193

ISAAC ASIMOV

The Complete Stories - Volume 2
(New York: Doubleday Foundation, 1992)

Story type: Science Fiction (Collection)

Summary: These 40 stories, published 1941-1976, reprise Asimov's early prime years. His personal favorite of the group, "The Bicentennial Man" (1976), received both Hugo and Nebula Awards.

Other books you might like:
Alfred Bester, *Star Light, Star Bright*, 1976
James Blish, *The Best of James Blish*, 1979
Arthur C. Clarke, *Tales From Planet Earth*, 1990
Larry Niven, *Tales of Known Space*, 1975
Robert Sheckley, *The Collected Robert Sheckley*, 1991
    5 volumes
Theodore Sturgeon, *Caviar*, 1955
William Tenn, *The Seven Sexes*, 1968

John Varley, *Blue Champagne*, 1986
John Varley, *The Persistence of Vision*, 1978

194

ISAAC ASIMOV, Editor
MARTIN H. GREENBERG, Co-Editor
CHARLES G. WAUGH, Co-Editor

Faeries
(New York: Roc, 1991)

Story type: Fantasy (Anthology)
Series: Isaac Asimov's Magical Worlds of Fantasy

Summary: This volume includes a three-page introduction plus 18 reprinted stories about fairies. Most appeared in magazines and anthologies during the past 40 years, but two are from early this century, H.C. Bailey's "The Fairy Prince" and Lord Dunsany's "The Kith of Elf Folk." One story, Poul Anderson's "Queen of Air and Darkness," received both Hugo and Nebula Awards. Other authors include Isaac Asimov, Richard McKenna, Andre Norton, Jessica Amanda Salmonson, Henry Slesar, Thomas Burnett Swann and Robert F. Young.

Other books you might like:
Emma Bull, *War for the Oaks*, 1987
Andrew Lang, *The Blue Fairy Book*, 1889
    editor
Andrew Lang, *The Red Fairy Book*, 1890
    editor
Jody Lynn Nye, *Mythology 101*, 1990
James D. Priest, *Kirins: The Spell of No'an*, 1990
Will Shetterly, *Elsewhere*, 1991
Terri Windling, *Borderland*, 1986
    Mark Alan Arnold, co-editor
Terri Windling, *Bordertown*, 1986
    Mark Alan Arnold, co-editor
Terri Windling, *Faery*, 1984
    editor
Terri Windling, *Life on the Border*, 1991
    editor

195

ISAAC ASIMOV

Forward the Foundation
(New York: Doubleday Foundation, 1993)

Story type: Science Fiction (Political; Robot Fiction)
Series: Foundation
Major character(s): Hari Seldon, Scientist (mathematician); Dors Venabili, Scientist, Martial Arts Expert; R. Daneel "Eto Demerzel" Olivaw, Robot
Time period(s): Indeterminate Future
Locale(s): Trantor, Planet—Imaginary

Summary: R. Daneel Olivaw, in the persona of Eto Demerzel, encourages Hari Seldon to complete his work on psychohistory and develop a device called the Prime Radiant which displays the resulting equations.

Other books you might like:
Ben Bova, *Sam Gunn, Unlimited*, 1993
Robert L. Forward, *Timemaster*, 1992
Charles Sheffield, *One Man's Universe*, 1993
Joan Slonczewski, *Daughter of Elysium*, 1993
John Varley, *Steel Beach*, 1992
Vernor Vinge, *A Fire upon the Deep*, 1992

196

ISAAC ASIMOV

Gold: The Final Science Fiction Collection
(New York: HarperPrism, 1995)

Story type: Science Fiction (Collection)
Summary: Contains 15 previously uncollected stories, 18 essays on science fiction, plus 20 essays on writing science fiction. The tone varies from humorous to serious with themes including computers, robots, future society, ecology, the performing arts, and writing.

Other books you might like:
Robert L. Forward, *Indistinguishable From Magic*, 1995
Larry Niven, *N-Space*, 1990
Larry Niven, *Playgrounds of the Mind*, 1991
Charles Sheffield, *Dancing with Myself*, 1993
Gene Wolfe, *Castle of Days*, 1992

197

ISAAC ASIMOV
MARTIN H. GREENBERG, Co-Author

Isaac Asimov Presents the Great SF Stories: 20 (1958)
(New York: DAW, 1990)

Story type: Science Fiction (Anthology)
Series: Isaac Asimov Presents the Great SF Stories
Time period(s): Indeterminate

Summary: This collection contains an introduction plus 12 stories featuring some of the best short fiction from 1958. Notable stories include Isaac Asimov's "The Feeling of Power," perhaps even more timely than when written, James Gunn's "The Immortals," Clifford D. Simak's "The Big Front Yard," and Cordwainer Smith's "The Burning of the Brain," a glimpse into Smith's extensive Instrumentality of Mankind series (1964-1979). Other excellent authors include Poul Anderson, C.M. Kornbluth, Robert Silverberg and Robert Sheckley.

Other books you might like:
Lou Aronica, *Full Spectrum 2*, 1990
    Shawna McCarthy, Amy Stout, Patrick LoBruto, co-editors
Groff Conklin, *The Best of Science Fiction*, 1946
Gardner Dozois, *The Year's Best Science Fiction: Seventh Annual Collection*, 1990
Harlan Ellison, *Dangerous Visions*, 1967
Raymond J. Healy, *Famous Science Fiction Stories: Adventures in Time and Space*, 1946
    J. Francis McComas, co-editor

Robert Silverberg, *The Science Fiction Hall of Fame, Volume 1*, 1970
Donald A. Wollheim, *The 1990 Annual World's Best Science Fiction*, 1990
    Arthur W. Saha, co-editor

198

ISAAC ASIMOV
MARTIN H. GREENBERG, Co-Author

Isaac Asimov Presents the Great SF Stories: 21 (1959)
(New York: DAW, 1990)

Story type: Science Fiction (Anthology)
Series: Isaac Asimov Presents the Great SF Stories
Time period(s): Indeterminate

Summary: Among the more memorable 1959 stories here are Alfred Bester's "The Pi Man," Carol Emswiller's "Day at the Beach," Philip Jose Farmer's "The Alley Man," Clifford D. Simak's "A Death in the House," Cordwainer Smith's "No, No, Not Rogov!," occurring early in Smith's Instrumentality of Mankind series (1964-1979), and Theodore Sturgeon's "The Man Who Lost the Sea." Other notable authors include Marion Zimmer Bradley, Damon Knight, Robert Sheckley and William Tenn.

Other books you might like:
Lou Aronica, *Full Spectrum 2*, 1990
    Shawna McCarthy, Amy Stout, Patrick LoBruto, co-editors
Groff Conklin, *The Best of Science Fiction*, 1946
Harlan Ellison, *Dangerous Visions*, 1967
Raymond J. Healy, *Famous Science Fiction Stories: Adventures in Time and Space*, 1946
    J. Francis McComas, co-editor
Robert Silverberg, *The Science Fiction Hall of Fame, Volume 1*, 1970
Donald A. Wollheim, *The 1990 Annual World's Best Science Fiction*, 1990
    Arthur W. Saha, co-editor

199

ISAAC ASIMOV, Editor
MARTIN H. GREENBERG, Co-Editor

Isaac Asimov Presents the Great SF Stories: 22 (1959)
(New York: DAW, 1991)

Story type: Science Fiction (Anthology)
Series: Isaac Asimov Presents the Great SF Stories

Summary: This volume contains a six-page introduction by Isaac Asimov plus 11 stories judged to be the best of 1960 including Christopher Anvil's "Mind Partner," J.G. Ballard's "The Voices of Time," Arthur C. Clarke's "I Remember Babylon," Damon Knight's "The Handler," Fritz Leiber's "Mariana," Frederik Pohl's "The Day the Icicle Works Closed," Rick Raphael's "Make

Mine. . .Homogenized'' and Cordwainer Smith's ''The Lady Who Sailed the Soul,'' from Smith's Instrumentality of Mankind series (1964-1979).

Other books you might like:

Anthony Boucher, *The Best From Fantasy and Science Fiction: 7*, 1958
editor

Groff Conklin, *Science Fiction Oddities*, 1966
editor

Groff Conklin, *The Science Fiction Omnibus*, 1956
editor

Groff Conklin, *12 Great Classics of Science Fiction*, 1963
editor

Harry Harrison, *S.F.: Author's Choice*, 1968
editor

Judith Merril, *5th Annual of the Year's Best S-F*, 1960
editor

Judith Merril, *SF: 59, The Year's Greatest Science Fiction and Fantasy*, 1959
editor

200

ISAAC ASIMOV, Editor
MARTIN H. GREENBERG, Co-Editor

Isaac Asimov Presents the Great SF Stories: 23 (1961)
(New York: DAW, 1991)

Story type: Science Fiction (Anthology)
Series: Isaac Asimov Presents the Great SF Stories

Summary: This volume contains a five-page introduction plus 13 stories judged best from 1961 including Brian Aldiss' Hugo Award winning story, ''Hothouse.'' One story, ''The Quaker Cannon,'' is a collaboration between Frederik Pohl and C.M. Kornbluth. Other stories include Poul Anderson's ''Hiding Place,'' Isaac Asimov's ''What Is This Thing Called Love?,'' Arthur C. Clarke's ''Death and the Senator,'' Randall Garrett's ''The Highest Treason,'' R.A. Lafferty's ''Rainbird,'' Jack Vance's ''The Moon Moth'' and Cordwainer Smith's ''A Planet Named Shayol,'' a story occurring late in the chronology of Smith's Instrumentality of Mankind series (1964-1979).

Other books you might like:

Anthony Boucher, *The Best From Fantasy and Science Fiction: 8*, 1959
editor

Groff Conklin, *Another Part of the Galaxy*, 1966
editor

Groff Conklin, *Giants Unleashed*, 1965
editor

Groff Conklin, *Science Fiction Adventures in Dimension*, 1953
editor

Judith Merril, *7th Annual of the Year's Best S-F*, 1962
editor

Judith Merril, *6th Annual of the Year's Best S-F*, 1961
editor

Frederik Pohl, *The Best Science Fiction From If*, 1964
editor

Robert Silverberg, *The Science Fiction Hall of Fame, Volume 1*, 1970
editor

201

ISAAC ASIMOV, Editor
MARTIN H. GREENBERG, Co-Editor

Isaac Asimov Presents the Great SF Stories: 24 (1962)
(New York: DAW, 1992)

Story type: Science Fiction (Anthology)
Series: Isaac Asimov Presents the Great SF Stories

Summary: Contains a 6-page introduction plus introductions to each of the 13 stories reprinted from 1962 periodicals including one Hugo Award nominee, ''When You Care, When You Love,'' by Theodore Sturgeon, in addition to ''Kings Who Die'' by Poul Anderson, ''The Insane Ones'' by J. G. Ballard, ''Roofs of Silver'' by Gordon R. Dickson, ''Earthlings Go Home!'' by Mack Reynolds and ''The Ballad of Lost C'mell'' by Cordwainer Smith. Other authors include Christopher Anvil, Harry Harrison, R. A. Lafferty and James White.

Other books you might like:

Kingsley Amis, *Spectrum 2*, 1963
Robert Conquest, co-editor

Groff Conklin, *17 X Infinity*, 1963
editor

Avram Davidson, *The Best From Fantasy and Science Fiction: 12*, 1963
editor

Judith Merril, *8th Annual of the Year's Best S-F*, 1963
editor

Frederik Pohl, *The Seventh Galaxy Reader*, 1964
editor

Cordwainer Smith, *The Best of Cordwainer Smith*, 1975

202

ISAAC ASIMOV, Editor
MARTIN H. GREENBERG, Co-Editor

Isaac Asimov Presents the Great SF Stories: 25 (1963)
(New York: DAW, 1992)

Story type: Science Fiction (Anthology)
Series: Isaac Asimov Presents the Great SF Stories

Summary: Contains a 4-page introduction plus introductions to each of the 13 stories reprinted from 1963 periodicals including the Hugo Award winner, ''No Truce with Kings'' by Poul Anderson, and one Hugo Award nominee, ''A Rose for Ecclesiastes'' by Roger Zelazny in addition to ''They Don't Make Life Like They Used To'' by Alfred Bester and ''Bernie the Faust'' by William Tenn. Other authors include Christopher Anvil, John Brunner, Hal Clement, Philip K.

Dick, Fred Saberhagen, Robert Silverberg and Clifford D. Simak.

Other books you might like:
Kingsley Amis, *Spectrum 3*, 1964
  Robert Conquest, co-editor
Alfred Bester, *Star Light, Star Bright*, 1976
Groff Conklin, *Great Stories of Space Travel*, 1963
Avram Davidson, *The Best From Fantasy and Science Fiction: 13*, 1964
  editor
Judith Merril, *9th Annual of the Year's Best S-F*, 1964
  editor
Frederik Pohl, *The Eighth Galaxy Reader*, 1965
  editor
William Tenn, *The Seven Sexes*, 1968

203

ISAAC ASIMOV

Magic: The Final Fantasy Collection

(New York: HarperPrism, 1996)

Story type: Fantasy (Collection)

Summary: This volume contains a two-page introduction by the publishers, 11 uncollected fantasy stories, 13 commentaries and critiques, and nine essays on writing fantasy. Eight of the 11 stories utilizing puns and jokes share the *Azazel* milieu, while one features the Black Widowers and Batman and two others present light fables.

Other books you might like:
Brian W. Aldiss, *A Romance of the Equator: The Best Fantasy Stories of Brian W. Aldiss*, 1990
David Brin, *The River of Time*, 1986
Orson Scott Card, *Maps in a Mirror*, 1990
Larry Niven, *N-Space*, 1990
Charles Sheffield, *Dancing with Myself*, 1993
Gene Wolfe, *Castle of Days*, 1992

204

ISAAC ASIMOV, Editor
CHARLES G. WAUGH, Co-Editor
MARTIN H. GREENBERG, Co-Editor

The Mammoth Book of Fantastic Science Fiction

(New York: Carroll & Graf, 1992)

Story type: Science Fiction (Anthology)

Summary: Contains 10 notable novelettes and novellas first published in the 1970s including Poul Anderson's "The Queen of Air and Darkness," Donald Kingsbury's "The Moon Goddess and the Sun," Frederik Pohl's "In the Problem Pit," Robert Silverberg's "Born with the Dead," Norman Spinrad's "Riding the Torch," and John Varley's "The Persistence of Vision" plus stories by Gordon R. Dickson, Larry Niven, Joan D. Vinge and Edward Wellen.

Other books you might like:
Terry Carr, *The Science Fiction Hall of Fame, Volume 4*, 1986
  editor
James Gunn, *Nebula Award Stories 10*, 1975
  editor
Ursula K. Le Guin, *Nebula Award Stories 11*, 1977
  editor
Frederik Pohl, *The Best Science Fiction for 1972*, 1972
  editor
Frederik Pohl, *Nebula Winners 14*, 1980
  editor
Frederik Pohl, *The Science Fiction Roll of Honor*, 1975
  editor

205

ISAAC ASIMOV, Editor
CHARLES G. WAUGH, Co-Editor
MARTIN H. GREENBERG, Co-Editor

The Mammoth Book of Modern Science Fiction: Short Novels of the 1980s

(New York: Carroll & Graf, 1993)

Story type: Science Fiction (Anthology)

Summary: 10 short novels originally published in periodicals and anthologies including the Hugo and Nebula Award winning stories "The Saturn Game" by Poul Anderson, "Hardfought" by Greg Bear, "Trinity" by Nancy Kress, "The Blind Geometer" by Kim Stanley Robinson and "Sailing to Byzantium" by Robert Silverberg. Other authors are Gregory Benford, Suzy McKee Charnas, Barry N. Malzberg, James Tiptree, Jr., and Walter Jon Williams.

Other books you might like:
Michael Bishop, *Nebula Awards 24*, 1990
  editor
Terry Carr, *The Science Fiction Hall of Fame, Volume 4*, 1986
  editor
Gardner Dozois, *Modern Classics of Science Fiction*, 1992
  editor
Gardner Dozois, *The Year's Best Science Fiction Series*, 1984-1993
  editor
Ursula K. Le Guin, *The Norton Book of Science Fiction: North American Science Fiction, 1960-1990*, 1993
  Brian Attebery, co-editor
Tom Shippey, *The Oxford Book of Science Fiction Stories*, 1992
  editor
George Zebrowski, *Nebula Awards 22*, 1988
  editor

206

ISAAC ASIMOV

Nemesis

(New York: Doubleday/Foundation, 1989)

Story type: Science Fiction (Space Opera)
Major character(s): Janus Pitt, Ruler; Marlene, Teenager
Time period(s): 23rd century (2236)
Locale(s): Earth; Rotor, Planet—Imaginary

Summary: Human beings have established a renegade colony, Rotor, circling Earth's recently discovered neighbor, the star Nemesis. The colony's ruler, Janus Pitt, is hostile to Earth, but a young Rotorian discovers that Nemesis poses a dire threat to life on both Earth and Rotor.

Other books you might like:
Arthur C. Clarke, *Rama II*, 1989
Frederik Pohl, *Gateway*, 1977
Bob Shaw, *Orbitsville*, 1975

207

ISAAC ASIMOV
ROBERT SILVERBERG, Co-Author

Nightfall

(New York: Doubleday Foundation, 1990)

Story type: Science Fiction (End of the World)
Major character(s): Sheerin 501, Scientist, Psychologist; Beenay 25, Scientist (astronomer); Theremon 762, Journalist
Time period(s): Indeterminate
Locale(s): Kalgash, Planet—Imaginary

Summary: Inspired by a quote from Emerson, Kalgash is a world on the edge of chaos, torn between the madness of religious fanaticism and the unyielding rationalism of science. Lurking beneath it all is a collective, instinctual fear of the Darkness, because Kalgash is a world of perpetual daylight. Only a handful of people on the planet are prepared to face the truth—five of their six suns are setting while the remaining one is about to be eclipsed for the first time in over 2,000 years. Based on Asimov's 1941 story of the same name.

Other books you might like:
Poul Anderson, *A Stone in Heaven*, 1979
Larry Niven, *Lucifer's Hammer*, 1977
    Jerry Pournelle, co-author
Larry Niven, *The Mote in God's Eye*, 1974
    Jerry Pournelle, co-author
Frederik Pohl, *Jem*, 1979
Gene Wolfe, *The Shadow of the Torturer*, 1980

208

ISAAC ASIMOV
ROBERT SILVERBERG, Co-Author

The Positronic Man

(New York: Doubleday Foundation, 1993)

Story type: Science Fiction (Robot Fiction)

Major character(s): Andrew Martin, Robot, Revolutionary
Time period(s): 22nd century; 23rd century
Locale(s): California

Summary: Gerald Martin purchases prototype domestic service robot NDR-113 but his children immediately name the robot ''Andrew'' and learn how to divert it from their father's tasks to play with them. When the manufacturer discovers Andrew's unique learning and emotional abilities, the company unsuccessfully attempts to recall NDR-113. During a century of service to the Martin family, Andrew's emancipation and demands for self-determination propel legal reformation. Based on Asimov's 1976 story, ''The Bicentennial Man.''

Other books you might like:
Philip K. Dick, *Blade Runner*, 1982
David Gerrold, *When HARLIE Was One: Release 2.0*, 1988
Rudy Rucker, *Wetware*, 1988
Joan Slonczewski, *Daughter of Elysium*, 1993
Thomas T. Thomas, *ME: A Novel of Self Discovery*, 1991
John Varley, *Steel Beach*, 1992
Jack Williamson, *The Humanoids*, 1949

209

ISAAC ASIMOV
ROBERT SILVERBERG, Co-Author

The Ugly Little Boy

(New York: Doubleday Foundation, 1992)

Story type: Science Fiction (Contemporary Realism; Romance)
Major character(s): Edith Fellowes, Nurse; Timmie, Prehistoric Human (Neanderthal); Gerald Hoskins, Scientist
Time period(s): 21st century; 380th century B.C.
Locale(s): New York

Summary: This novel expands the 1958 short story by Isaac Asimov about Timmie, a Neanderthal boy brought 40,000 years forward to be studied at Stasis Technologies, Ltd. where Miss Fellowes recognizes him as a human child.

Other books you might like:
Eleanor Arnason, *A Woman of the Iron People*, 1991
David Brin, *The Uplift War*, 1987
Orson Scott Card, *Ender's Game*, 1985
Robert Reed, *Down the Bright Way*, 1991
Cordwainer Smith, *Norstrilia*, 1975
Dave Wolverton, *Serpent Catch*, 1991

210

JANET ASIMOV

Murder at the Galactic Writers' Society

(New York: DAW, 1995)

Story type: Science Fiction (Mystery; Robot Fiction)
Major character(s): Arda, Android, Spy; Fortizak ''Zak'', Writer; Smith, Government Official
Time period(s): Indeterminate Future
Locale(s): Terran Federation, Interstellar Empire/Federation; New York, New York

Summary: Passing as a human being, Arda constantly faces prejudice against positronic intelligence. Assigned to prevent embarrassment of Earth while protecting the alien and human writers attending the Galactic Writers' Society meeting hosted on Earth by Zak, Arda must prevent the robbery of Princess Vush's ruulogem, reportedly the largest in the universe. Failure could lead to interplanetary disaster.

Other books you might like:
Wilhelmina Baird, *Crashcourse*, 1993
Hal Clement, *Fossil*, 1993
Janet O. Jeppson, *The Last Immortal*, 1981
    pseuodnym of Janet Asimov
Janet O. Jeppson, *The Second Experiment*, 1974
    pseudonym of Janet Asimov
Sharyn McCrumb, *Bimbos of the Death Sun*, 1987
Laura J. Mixon, *Glass Houses*, 1992

211

JANET ASIMOV
ISAAC ASIMOV, Co-Author

Norby and the Court Jester

(New York: Walker, 1991)

Story type: Science Fiction (Young Adult; Robot Fiction)
Series: Norby
Major character(s): Norby, Robot; Jeff Wells, Student, Teenager
Time period(s): Indeterminate Future
Locale(s): Izz, Planet—Imaginary

Summary: Jeff Wells and Norby take advantage of Space Academy spring break to visit a toy and game fair and their friends, Princess Rinda and her robot, Pera. On Izz, Jeff and Norby search for the missing Pera and the person who has sabotaged the planetary computer system.

Other books you might like:
Eleanor Cameron, *The Wonderful Flight to the Mushroom Planet*, 1954
Thomas M. Disch, *The Brave Little Toaster: A Bedtime Story for Small Appliances*, 1986
Thomas M. Disch, *The Brave Little Toaster Goes to Mars*, 1988
Paul W. Fairman, *The Runaway Robot*, 1964
    as Lester del Rey
Clifford D. Simak, *City*, 1952

212

JANET ASIMOV
ISAAC ASIMOV, Co-Author

Norby and the Oldest Dragon

(New York: Walker, 1990)

Story type: Science Fiction (Robot Fiction)
Series: Norby
Major character(s): Jeff Wells, Teenager (space cadet); Norby, Robot
Time period(s): Indeterminate Future
Locale(s): Jamya, Planet—Imaginary

Summary: Jeff and Norby attend the birthday party of the Grand Dragon of Jamya, a supposedly routine event, and find themselves and the planet in enormous danger, threatened by a gigantic cloud creature. For children.

Other books you might like:
Isaac Asimov, *The Caves of Steel*, 1954
Isaac Asimov, *I, Robot*, 1950
Isaac Asimov, *The Naked Sun*, 1957
Isaac Asimov, *The Rest of the Robots*, 1964
Isaac Asimov, *Robot Dreams*, 1986
John Bellairs, *The Eyes of the Killer Robot*, 1986
H.M. Hoover, *Orvis*, 1987
Jane Yolen, *The Robot and Rebecca and the Missing Owser*, 1981

213

JANET ASIMOV
ISAAC ASIMOV, Co-Author

Norby and Yobo's Great Adventure

(New York: Walker, 1989)

Story type: Science Fiction (Robot Fiction; Time Travel)
Series: Norby
Major character(s): Jeff Wells, Teenager (space cadet); Norby, Robot
Time period(s): Indeterminate Future; Indeterminate Past
Locale(s): Mars; Earth

Summary: Norby and Jeff accompany their commander, Admiral Yobo, on a time travel adventure into the pre-historic past as the Admiral attempts to trace the history of an ancient family heirloom—a carved ivory tusk. For children.

Other books you might like:
Isaac Asimov, *The Caves of Steel*, 1954
Isaac Asimov, *I, Robot*, 1950
Isaac Asimov, *The Naked Sun*, 1957
Isaac Asimov, *The Rest of the Robots*, 1964
Isaac Asimov, *Robot Dreams*, 1986
John Bellairs, *The Eyes of the Killer Robot*, 1986
H.M. Hoover, *Orvis*, 1987
Jane Yolen, *The Robot and Rebecca and the Missing Owser*, 1981

214

JANET ASIMOV
ISAAC ASIMOV, Co-Author

Norby Down to Earth

(New York: Walker, 1989)

Story type: Science Fiction (Robot Fiction)
Series: Norby
Major character(s): Jeff Wells, Teenager (space cadet); Norby, Robot
Time period(s): Indeterminate Future
Locale(s): Terran Federation, Interstellar Empire/Federation

Summary: Jeff and Norby visit the independent nation of Manhattan on the planet Earth and find themselves smack in the middle of a mystery. Someone is zapping small robots with an electronic gun that apparently does no lasting damage while someone else is stealing computer parts. Eventually they uncover a complex and dastardly plot.

Other books you might like:
Isaac Asimov, *The Caves of Steel*, 1954
Isaac Asimov, *I, Robot*, 1950
Isaac Asimov, *The Naked Sun*, 1957
Isaac Asimov, *The Rest of the Robots*, 1964
Isaac Asimov, *Robot Dreams*, 1986
John Bellairs, *The Eyes of the Killer Robot*, 1986
H.M. Hoover, *Orvis*, 1987
Jane Yolen, *The Robot and Rebecca and the Missing Owser*, 1981

215

NANCY ASIRE

Tears of Time

(New York: Baen, 1993)

Story type: Fantasy (Sword and Sorcery)
Major character(s): Kahsir, Royalty (prince), Warrior; Iowyn, Royalty (princess), Warrior; Tsingar, Military Personnel (General)
Time period(s): Indeterminate
Locale(s): Vyjenor, Fictional Country; Dramujh, Fictional City

Summary: Carrying on the centuries-long warfare of his people, the Krotanya, Kahsir leads his army against the invading armies of the evil Leishoranya, who use their psychic powers to kill and enslave. In a desperate fight to rescue his sister, Iowyn, Kahsir uses his own psychic powers to kill Leishoranyan soldiers, contrary to the ethics of his people. As the Krotanya refugees flee their villages and his own soldiers try to defend their borders, Kahsir also wrestles with his conscience. Sequel to *Twilight's Kingdom*.

Other books you might like:
Marion Zimmer Bradley, *Stormqueen!*, 1978
C.J. Cherryh, *A Dirge for Stabis*, 1989
    Leslie J. Fish, co-author
C.J. Cherryh, *Wizard Spawn*, 1989
    Nancy Asire, co-author
Barbara Hambly, *The Armies of Daylight*, 1983
Katherine Kurtz, *Deryni Checkmate*, 1972
Katherine Kurtz, *Deryni Rising*, 1970
Katherine Kurtz, *High Deryni*, 1973
J.R.R. Tolkien, *The Two Towers*, 1955

216

NANCY ASIRE

To Fall Like Stars

(New York: Baen, 1996)

Story type: Fantasy (Military; Psychic Powers)
Major character(s): Kashir, Royalty (prince), Warrior; Tsingar, Military Personnel (general); Lorhaiden, Warrior
Time period(s): Indeterminate
Locale(s): Hvalkir, Fictional City; Vyjenor, Fictional Country

Summary: Staking the survival of the Krotanya on one great battle, the High King leads his army against the Leishoranya hoping to distract the powers of Darkness while his people use the Mind-Gates to flee to comparative safety in the mountains. When, a generation later, the Leishoranya again menace the Krotanyan remnant, Lorhaiden searches for a forbidden mind weapon that can save his people, but destroy the wielder of the weapon.

Other books you might like:
C.J. Cherryh, *Well of Shiuan*, 1978
Phyllis Eisenstein, *In the Red Lord's Reach*, 1989
Barbara Hambly, *The Armies of Daylight*, 1983
Robert Jordan, *The Fires of Heaven*, 1993
Patricia A. McKillip, *Harpist in the Wind*, 1979
J.R.R. Tolkien, *The Return of the King*, 1956

217

ROBERT ASPRIN

M.Y.T.H. Inc.

(Norfolk, Virginia: Donning Starblaze, 1990)

Story type: Fantasy (Light Fantasy)
Series: M.Y.T.H.
Major character(s): Guido, Bodyguard; Nunzio, Bodyguard
Time period(s): Indeterminate
Locale(s): Klah, Alternate Universe

Summary: Guido and Nunzio of the M.Y.T.H. Inc. crew have joined the army of Queen Hemlock in an effort to undermine its effectiveness.

Other books you might like:
Brian Daley, *A Tapestry of Magics*, 1983
Poul Anderson, *Hoka!*, 1984
    Gordon R. Dickson, co-author
Fritz Leiber, *Swords and Deviltry*, 1970
Will Shetterly, *Cats Have No Lord*, 1985
Christopher Stasheff, *The Warlock Unlocked*, 1982

218

ROBERT ASPRIN

Phule's Company

(New York: Ace, 1990)

Story type: Science Fiction (Humor; Military)
Series: Phule's Company
Major character(s): Willard Phule, Military Personnel; Beeker, Servant (butler)
Time period(s): Indeterminate Future
Locale(s): Haskin's Planet, Planet—Imaginary

Summary: A megamillionaire playboy with an eye for opportunity takes command of a unit of the worst misfits in the generally rakish Space Legion. Their first mission is guarding the swamp miners of Haskin's Planet.

Other books you might like:
Lois McMaster Bujold, *Borders of Infinity*, 1989
Lois McMaster Bujold, *The Warrior's Apprentice*, 1986
Brian Daley, *Fall of the White Ship Avatar*, 1987
Brian Daley, *Jinx on a Terran Inheritance*, 1985

Brian Daley, *Requiem for a Ruler of Worlds*, 1985
Harry Harrison, *Bill, the Galactic Hero*, 1965

219

ROBERT ASPRIN

Phule's Paradise

(New York: Ace, 1991)

Story type: Science Fiction (Humor; Military)
Series: Phule's Company
Major character(s): Willard Phule, Military Personnel; Tusk-Anini, Military Personnel; Maxine Pruet, Organized Crime Figure, Businesswoman
Time period(s): Indeterminate Future
Locale(s): Haskin's Planet, Planet—Imaginary; Lorelei, Space Station

Summary: Willard Phule and his company of misfits are sent to Space Station Lorelei where they are to protect a casino owner with more money than sense from being taken over by organized crime. Some legionnaires with criminal pasts infiltrate the local crime scene and some man the hotel, while Phule hires computer experts to debug the slot machines. After firing all those in cahoots with the local crime boss, Phule manages to open the casino and prevent a takeover.

Other books you might like:
Brian Daley, *Fall of the White Ship Avatar*, 1987
Brian Daley, *Jinx on a Terran Inheritance*, 1985
Brian Daley, *Requiem for a Ruler of Worlds*, 1985
Harry Harrison, *Bill, the Galactic Hero*, 1965
George H. Smith, *Kar Kaballa*, 1969
Walter Jon Williams, *The Crown Jewels*, 1987

220

ROBERT ASPRIN

Sweet MYTH-tery of Life

(Virginia Beach, Virginia: Donning, 1994)

Story type: Fantasy (Light Fantasy)
Series: M.Y.T.H.
Major character(s): Skeeve, Magician; Hemlock, Royalty (queen), Ruler; Cassandra, Vampire
Time period(s): Indeterminate
Locale(s): Klah, Planet—Imaginary

Summary: Given one month by Queen Hemlock to decide whether to marry her or rule alone when she abdicates, Skeeve decides to research the institution of marriage, including a date with Cassandra at a vampire night club.

Other books you might like:
Kyle Crocco, *Heroes Wanted*, 1991
George Alec Effinger, *Maureen Birnbaum, Barbarian Swordsperson: The Complete Stories*, 1993
Neil Gaiman, *Good Omens: The Nice and Accurate Prophecies of Agnes Nutter, Witch*, 1990
   Terry Pratchett, co-author
Laurell K. Hamilton, *Guilty Pleasures*, 1993
John Moore, *Slay and Rescue*, 1993

221

ROBERT ASPRIN
LINDA EVANS, Co-Author

Time Scout

(New York: Baen, 1995)

Story type: Science Fiction (Time Travel)
Major character(s): Kenneth "Kit" Carson, Time Traveller (time scout), Aged Person; Margo van Wyyck, Time Traveller; Malcolm Moore, Time Traveller, Guide
Time period(s): 1880s; 1st century (47)
Locale(s): Shangri-la, Space Station (time nexus); London, England; Roman Empire

Summary: Hoping to thwart his granddaughter's desire to become the first female time scout, Kit Carson abandons his retirement to guide Margo around Victorian London and 1st century Roman Syria.

Other books you might like:
Poul Anderson, *The Time Patrol*, 1991
L. Sprague de Camp, *Rivers of Time*, 1993
Linda Evans, *Sleipnir*, 1994
Spider Robinson, *Callahan and Company*, 1987
Clifford D. Simak, *Way Station*, 1963
John Varley, *Millennium*, 1983

222

ROBERT ASPRIN
LINDA EVANS, Co-Author

Wagers of Sin

(New York: Baen, 1996)

Story type: Science Fiction (Time Travel)
Series: Time Scout
Major character(s): Skeeter Jackson, Con Artist, Time Traveller; Marcus, Saloon Keeper/Owner, Slave; Goldie Morran, Businesswoman
Time period(s): 1st century; 1880s (1885)
Locale(s): Roman Empire; Denver, Colorado

Summary: Time Terminal 86's resident con man, Skeeter Jackson, makes a wager with Goldie Morran concerning who can con the most money out of others. However, an even greater thief robs Goldie while Skeeter must stand combat in the arenas of ancient Rome in the vague hope of remaining alive long enough to rescue a friend from slavery.

Other books you might like:
Poul Anderson, *The Time Patrol*, 1991
L. Sprague de Camp, *Rivers of Time*, 1993
Linda Evans, *Far Edge of Darkness*, 1996
Crawford Kilian, *Rogue Emperor*, 1988
Lisa Mason, *The Golden Nineties*, 1995
Sam Merwin Jr., *The House of Many Worlds*, 1951
Robert Silverberg, *Up the Line*, 1969
Harry Turtledove, *Agent of Byzantium*, 1987
Chelsea Quinn Yarbro, *Blood Games*, 1980

223

PETER ATKINS

Morningstar
(New York: HarperCollins, 1992)

Story type: Horror (Serial Killer; Vampire Story)
Major character(s): Donovan Moon, Journalist; Jonathan Frost, Businessman (Real estate developer); T. Astare, Vampire
Time period(s): 1990s (1992)
Locale(s): San Francisco, California
Summary: Down-and-out freelance reporter Donovan Moon is hired to assist Jonathan Frost in his work as a vampire hunter, a trade he plies under the guise of a serial killer who signs his handiwork ''Morningstar.'' This is the author's first novel.

Other books you might like:
Pat Cadigan, *The Power and the Passion*, 1989
   short story in *Patterns*
Barbara Hambly, *Those Who Hunt the Night*, 1987
Kim Newman, *Bad Dreams*, 1990

224

A.A. ATTANASIO

The Dragon and the Unicorn
(New York: HarperPrism, 1996)

Story type: Fantasy (Legend; Science Fiction)
Major character(s): Uther Pendragon, Leader, Warrior; Merlinus ''Myrddin/Lailoken'' Ambrosius, Wizard, Demon; Morgeu, Royalty, Demon
Time period(s): Indeterminate Past
Locale(s): England (Britain); Avalon, Mythical Place
Summary: The eternal struggle for immortality yields the unicorn and dragon and leads to the human manifestation of strife and harmony, King Arthur of Britain. First of a series, and first published in the U.K. in 1994.

Other books you might like:
Mike Ashley, *The Pendragon Chronicles*, 1990
   editor
Marion Zimmer Bradley, *The Forest House*, 1994
Andrea Hopkins, *Chronicles of King Arthur*, 1994
   editor
Courtway Jones, *In the Shadow of the Oak King*, 1991
Morgan Llywelyn, *Druids*, 1991
T.H. White, *The Once and Future King*, 1958
Jack Whyte, *The Skystone*, 1996

225

A.A. ATTANASIO

Hunting the Ghost Dancer
(New York: Harper Collins Publishers, 1991)

Story type: Fantasy (Quest)
Major character(s): Timov, Child; Hamr, Hunter, Wanderer; Baat, Monster
Time period(s): 480th century B.C.

Locale(s): Earth
Summary: In the distant past, a small group of people are forced to leave their diseased and dying tribe. They set out to find and kill one of the last of the Ghost Dancers, immensely powerful spirits with an appetite for destruction.

Other books you might like:
Jean M. Auel, *Clan of the Cave Bear*, 1980
W. Michael Gear, *People of the Wolf*, 1990
   Kathleen O'Neal Gear, co-author
Jack London, *Before Adam*, 1906
Dave Wolverton, *Serpent Catch*, 1991

226

A.A. ATTANASIO

Kingdom of the Grail
(New York: HarperCollins, 1992)

Story type: Fantasy (Historical; Legend)
Major character(s): Ailena Valaise, Noblewoman, Parent (Guy Lanfranc's); Rachel Tibbon, Imposter; Guy Lanfranc, Nobleman
Time period(s): 12th century
Locale(s): Wales
Summary: Guy Lanfranc sends his elderly mother, Ailena, from her castle to venture forth on a religious pilgrimage. When Ailena meets Rachel who looks like Ailena in her youth, Ailena arranges to have Rachel return to Wales as Ailena with her youth miraculously restored through use of the Grail. Rachel's appearance in Wales forces a crisis of faith, forcing Rachel to join the Welsh rebellion.

Other books you might like:
Frans G. Bengtsson, *The Long Ships*, 1954
Parke Godwin, *Sherwood*, 1991
Frances Mary Hendry, *Quest for a Maid*, 1990
Robert Rice, *The Last Pendragon*, 1991
Persia Woolley, *Guinevere: The Legend in Autumn*, 1992

227

A.A. ATTANASIO

The Last Legends of Earth
(New York: Doubleday/Foundation, 1989)

Story type: Science Fiction (Space Opera)
Series: Radix Tetrad
Major character(s): Chan-ti Beppu, Wanderer; Ned O'Tennis, Pilot
Time period(s): Indeterminate Future
Locale(s): Chalco-Doror, Planet—Imaginary
Summary: Millennia after the Earth was destroyed in a nova, a super-powerful alien known as the Rimstalker resurrects humankind on the planets of a distant star system. It does this not out of kindness, but to use humanity as bait to attract its ancient enemies, the spider-like zotl, which feed on the psychic pain of intelligent life forms. Humanity must struggle against both the Rimstalker and the zotl.

Other books you might like:
Philip Jose Farmer, *To Your Scattered Bodies Go*, 1971
Dan Simmons, *Hyperion*, 1989
E.E. "Doc" Smith, *Galactic Patrol*, 1950
E.E. "Doc" Smith, *Gray Lensman*, 1951
E.E. "Doc" Smith, *The Skylark of Space*, 1946
E.E. "Doc" Smith, *Skylark of Valeron*, 1949
E.E. "Doc" Smith, *Triplanetary*, 1948

228

A.A. ATTANASIO

The Moon's Wife: A Hystery
(New York: HarperCollins, 1993)

Story type: Fantasy (Contemporary Realism)
Major character(s): Sigrid Lindo, Accountant; Daniel Schel, Deity; Glendil, Witch
Time period(s): 1990s (1993)
Locale(s): Arcadia, New York; New York, New York

Summary: After a wildly orgasmic seizure in a supermarket, Sigrid Lindo begins to hear the moon asking her to marry him. She quickly ends up in a mental hospital where she must confront her sanity. If she decides she truly can hear the moon, she must cope with the effect that decision will have on her life and, possibly, the whole world.

Other books you might like:
Eleanor Arnason, *Daughter of the Bear King*, 1987
Peter S. Beagle, *A Fine and Private Place*, 1960
Emma Bull, *War for the Oaks*, 1987
John Crowley, *Little, Big*, 1981
Robert Holdstock, *Mythago Wood*, 1984

229

A.A. ATTANASIO

Solis
(New York: HarperCollins, 1994)

Story type: Science Fiction (Alternate Intelligence; Dystopian)
Major character(s): Charles "Mr. Charlie" Outis, Disembodied Personality, Reanimated Dead; Munk, Android (androne), Revolutionary; Mei Nili, Revolutionary
Time period(s): 120th century
Locale(s): Mars; Outer Space

Summary: Returning to consciousness after 1000 years, Charles Outis discovers a demand for his memories and the need for his brain as mechanical controller in an asteroid mining operation. After Munk and Mei Nili salvage Mr. Charlie, a meeting of the artificial intelligences, the Maat Pashalik, attempts to assign ownership of the brain as property. However, Munk's programmed love of human beings forces it to abscond with Mr. Charlie and attempt the dangerous trek to Solis where they may find sanctuary.

Other books you might like:
Greg Bear, *Heads*, 1991
Gregory Benford, *Great Sky River*, 1987
Rudy Rucker, *Live Robots*, 1994

Dan Simmons, *The Fall of Hyperion*, 1990
Jim Starlin, *Lady El*, 1992
Diana Graziaunas, co-author

230

MARGARET ATWOOD

Good Bones and Simple Murders
(New York: Doubleday, 1994)

Story type: Fantasy (Collection; Science Fiction)

Summary: Contains 35 stories, parables, monologues, prose poems and other short works reprinted from periodicals and collections or broadcast on the BBC program, "Anthology." The tone varies from whimsical to dark with themes including memories and views of a reincarnated bat, new slants on rewritten fairy tales, a few words from Gertrude to Hamlet, various recipes for making a man, techniques and rewards of tree stump hunting, the view of humanity by intelligent extra-terrestrial moths and futures with gender-role reversal and computer control.

Other books you might like:
James Finn Garner, *Politically Correct Bedtime Stories*, 1994
Ursula K. Le Guin, *Buffalo Gals and Other Animal Presences*, 1987
Ursula K. Le Guin, *A Fisherman of the Inland Sea*, 1994
Connie Willis, *Impossible Things*, 1994
Jack Zipes, *The Outspoken Princess and the Gentle Knight*, 1994
editor

231

JEAN M. AUEL

The Plains of Passage
(New York: Crown, 1990)

Story type: Fantasy (Romance; Historical)
Series: Earth's Children
Major character(s): Ayla, Prehistoric Human, Shaman; Jondalar, Prehistoric Human, Hunter
Time period(s): Indeterminate Past (Late Pleistocene Epoch)
Locale(s): Europe

Summary: As they cross the continent in their search for home, Ayla and Jondalar make friends and enemies while amazing everyone with their control over wild animals.

Other books you might like:
W. Michael Gear, *People of the Fire*, 1991
Kathleen O'Neal Gear, co-author
W. Michael Gear, *People of the Wolf*, 1990
Kathleen O'Neal Gear, co-author
Richard Herley, *The Stone Arrow*, 1978
J.H. Rosny, *Quest for Fire*, 1967
1909
William Sarabande, *Beyond the Sea of Ice*, 1987

232

NINA AUERBACH, Editor
U.C. KNOEPFLMACHER, Co-Editor

Forbidden Journeys: Fairy Tales and Fantasies by Victorian Women Writers
(Chicago: The University of Chicago Press, 1992)

Story type: Fantasy (Anthology; Legend)

Summary: Contains 11 stories, frequently dark and angry, divided into four parts with scholarly and interpretive introductions illustrating the revision of traditional fairy tale material, the creation of subversive text, the expansion of that subversion and the undercutting of underlying assumptions. Includes three tales by Christina Rossetti and a full-length fantasy novel with a startling feminist reversal by Jean Ingelow, "Mopsa the Fairy." Other authors include Frances Hodgson Burnett, Julia Horatia Ewing, Maria Molesworth, Edith Nesbit and Anne Thackeray Ritchie.

Other books you might like:
Michael Patrick Hearn, *The Victorian Fairy Tale Book*, 1988
    editor
Ethel Johnston Phelps, *Tatterhood and Other Tales*, 1978
    editor
Jack Zipes, *Beauties, Beasts and Enchantments*, 1989
    editor
Jack Zipes, *Don't Bet on the Prince*, 1986
    editor
Jack Zipes, *Spells of Enchantment*, 1991
    editor

233

RICHARD AUSTIN (Pseudonym of Victor Milan)

Devil's Deal
(New York: Jove, 1989)

Story type: Science Fiction (Post-Nuclear Holocaust)
Series: Guardians
Major character(s): McKay, Military Personnel; McKendree, Racist
Time period(s): Indeterminate Future
Locale(s): Wyoming

Summary: The Guardians, a well-armed special forces group that works for the President of the United States, is sent to Wyoming to deal with a post-nuclear war version of the racist Aryan Brotherhood. Bullets fly and bloody bodies pile up quickly.

Other books you might like:
Jerry Ahern, *Final Rain*, 1989
    The Survivalist 19
James Axler, *Red Equinox*, 1989
    Deathlands 9
Neal Barrett Jr., *Dawn's Uncertain Light*, 1989
Neal Barrett Jr., *Through Darkest America*, 1987
Algis Budrys, *Some Will Not Die*, 1961

234

JAMES AXLER

Deep Trek
(New York: Worldwide Library Gold Eagle, 1994)

Story type: Science Fiction (Post-Holocaust)
Series: Earth Blood
Major character(s): Jim Hilton, Military Personnel; Nanci Simms, Teacher (retired), Warrior; Henderson McGill, Military Personnel
Time period(s): 2040s (2040)
Locale(s): California; Nevada

Summary: Reunited after attempting to locate family and friends, the survivors of *Aquila*'s crew undertake a perilous journey toward a California rendezvous to search for a rumored secret military base.

Other books you might like:
Jerry Ahern, *The Quest*, 1981
Octavia E. Butler, *Dawn*, 1987
J.M. Morgan, *Beyond Eden*, 1992
David Robbins, *The Fox Run*, 1986
Paul O. Williams, *The Breaking of Northwall*, 1981

235

JONATHAN AYCLIFFE (Pseudonym of Denis MacEoin)

The Lost
(New York: HarperPrism, 1996)

Story type: Horror (Vampire Story)
Major character(s): Michael Feraru, Teacher; Liliana Popescu, Lawyer; Elena Vlaicu, Maintenance Worker (caretaker)
Time period(s): 1990s (1996)
Locale(s): Castel Vlaicu, Romania

Summary: Michael Feraru returns to his family home in Romania after the fall of the Ceausescu dictatorship to reclaim his family's old castle in the hope of turning it into an orphange. But the deeper he penetrates into the country the more informed he becomes of the legacy of vampirism surrounding his family name and the more irreversibly he succumbs to it.

Other books you might like:
Elaine Bergstrom, *Shattered Glass*, 1989
Andrei Codrescu, *Blood Countess*, 1995
Jeanne Kalogridis, *Children of the Vampire*, 1995
Shawn Ryan, *Nocturnas*, 1995
Dan Simmons, *Children of the Night*, 1992
Bram Stoker, *Dracula*, 1897

236

JONATHAN AYCLIFFE (Pseudonym of Denis MacEoin)

The Matrix
(New York: Harper, 1995)

Story type: Horror (Occult)
Major character(s): Andrew Macleod, Professor (of sociology); Duncan Mylne, Sorcerer; Ramsey Maclean, Doctor

Time period(s): 1990s (1995)
Locale(s): Edinburgh, Scotland

Summary: While investigating local occult groups as part of his academic research in sociology, Andrew Macleod encounters the Fraternity of the Old Path and its mysterious adherent, Duncan Mylne. Mylne quickly takes Andrew under his wing and begins instructing him in the practice of ritual magic that will eventually lead him to try to resurrect his deceased beloved wife, Catriona.

Other books you might like:
Ramsey Campbell, *The Influence*, 1988
Fritz Leiber, *Conjure Wife*, 1953
Peter Straub, *Mrs. God*, 1991

237

JONATHAN AYCLIFFE (Pseudonym of Denis MacEoin)

Naomi's Room
(New York: Harper Paperbacks, 1992)

Story type: Horror (Ghost Story)
Major character(s): Charles Hillenbrand, Professor (at Cambridge University); Laura Hillenbrand, Spouse (of Charles); Dafydd Lewis, Photographer
Time period(s): 1970s (1970)
Locale(s): Cambridge, England

Summary: The haunting of Charles Hillenbrand and his wife by the specter of his horribly mutilated daughter Naomi leads to the discovery of a sealed attic in their house, and within it the legacy of the previous owner whose curious life and horrible fate seem to mirror Charles's own.

Other books you might like:
Judith Hawkes, *Julian's House*, 1989
Shirley Jackson, *The Haunting of Hill House*, 1959
Richard Matheson, *Hell House*, 1971
Chet Williamson, *Soulstorm*, 1986

238

JONATHAN AYCLIFFE (Pseudonym of Denis MacEoin)

The Vanishment
(New York: HarperCollins, 1994)

Story type: Horror (Haunted House)
Major character(s): Peter Clare, Writer; Susannah Adderstone, Young Woman; Rachel Wigram, Child (4-year-old)
Time period(s): 1990s (1994)
Locale(s): Tredannack, England (Petherick House)

Summary: Peter Clare's wife disappears while they are vacationing at remote Petherick House, a building with a reputation among the local townspeople for being haunted. As Peter digs into its century-old history of parricide and fatal sibling rivalry to solve the mystery of his wife's vanishment, he touches upon the eerie possibility that the house's grisly past is being repeated by himself and his small circle of friends and acquaintances.

Other books you might like:
Ramsey Campbell, *The Influence*, 1988

Judith Hawkes, *Julian's House*, 1989
Shirley Jackson, *The Haunting of Hill House*, 1959
Stephen King, *The Shining*, 1977
Roland Topor, *The Tenant*, 1966

239

JONATHAN AYCLIFFE (Pseudonym of Denis MacEoin)

Whispers in the Dark
(New York: Harper, 1993)

Story type: Horror (Child-in-Peril)
Major character(s): Charlotte Metcalf, Child, Orphan; Antony Aryton, Nobleman; Antonia Aryton, Noblewoman
Time period(s): 1890s
Locale(s): Kirkwhelpington, England (Barras Lodge)

Summary: Strongly influenced by the writing of M.R. James, this novel tells of orphaned Charlotte Metcalf, who seeks help from her mother's estranged relatives at Barras Lodge. While there, she is visited by the ghostly figures of children who warn her to leave before she falls victim to the curse implicit in the family motto, "They shall inherit it forever."

Other books you might like:
Richard Dalby, *Ghosts and Scholars*, 1987
    Rosemary Pardoe, co-editor
James Herbert, *Haunted*, 1988
M.R. James, *Casting the Runes and Other Ghost Stories*, 1987
Daniel Rhodes, *Next, After Lucifer*, 1988
Robert Westall, *Antique Dust*, 1989

240

RICHARD BACHMAN (Pseudonym of Stephen King)

The Regulators
(New York: Dutton, 1996)

Story type: Horror (Wild Talents)
Major character(s): Seth Garin, Child (6-year-old); Johnny Marinville, Writer; Collie Entragion, Police Officer (former)
Time period(s): 1990s (1996)
Locale(s): Wentworth, Ohio

Summary: The peace of a small middle-American town is shattered when a disembodied entity invades the mind of an autistic boy and begins turning the violent fantasies spawned by his television-watching into horrifying reality. This novel shares characters and themes with *Desperation*, which bears the Stephen King byline and was released at approximately the same time under one of the publisher's other imprints.

Other books you might like:
Ramsey Campbell, *Incarnate*, 1983
Dennis Etchison, *Shadow Man*, 1993
Charles L. Grant, *In a Dark Dream*, 1989
Dean R. Koontz, *Dragon Tears*, 1992
Kim Newman, *Bad Dreams*, 1990

241

ROBIN W. BAILEY

The Lost City of Zork

(New York: Avon, 1991)

Story type: Fantasy (Light Fantasy; Quest)
Series: Infocom
Major character(s): Caspar Wartsworth, Adventurer, Barbarian
Time period(s): Indeterminate
Locale(s): Borphee, Fictional City

Summary: Arrested and sent to war as a galley slave, Caspar survives when his ship is wrecked. He then assembles a group of adventurers who hope to free the Borphee Guild of Wizards by defeating King Duncanthrax and recovering their leader, Berknip. This book ties into the Zork computer gaming universe.

Other books you might like:
Arthur Byron Cover, *Planetfall*, 1989
Arthur Byron Cover, *Stationfall*, 1988
George Alec Effinger, *The Zork Chronicles*, 1990
Craig Shaw Gardner, *Wishbringer*, 1988

242

ROBIN WAYNE BAILEY

Brothers of the Dragon

(New York: Roc, 1993)

Story type: Fantasy (Alternate World; Adventure)
Series: Brothers of the Dragon
Major character(s): Eric Podlowski, Martial Arts Expert, Teacher; Robert Podlowski, Martial Arts Expert, Waiter/Waitress
Time period(s): 1990s; Indeterminate
Locale(s): Catskill Mountains, New York; Palenoc, Mythical Place

Summary: Drawn by a glowing light, Eric and Robert go through a waterfall and find themselves in a strange and dangerous land where their martial arts skills allow the pair to survive and begin investigating the world. Before long, Eric and Robert become involved in an ancient power struggle in the parallel land. First of a series.

Other books you might like:
Gael Baudino, *Dragonsword*, 1988
Pamela Dean, *The Secret Country*, 1985
Gordon R. Dickson, *The Dragon and the George*, 1976
Carole Nelson Douglas, *Cup of Clay*, 1991
Rick Shelley, *The Hero King*, 1992

243

ROBIN WAYNE BAILEY

Flames of the Dragon

(New York: Roc, 1994)

Story type: Fantasy (Alternate World; Magic Conflict)
Series: Brothers of the Dragon

Major character(s): Eric Podlowski, Martial Arts Expert, Leader; Robert Podlowski, Martial Arts Expert, Writer; Katherine "Katy" Dowd, Librarian, Adventurer
Time period(s): 1990s; Indeterminate
Locale(s): Palenoc, Mythical Place; Catskill Mountains, New York; Dowdsville, New York

Summary: Katy's library research allows her to bring Eric from Palenoc to prove Robert innocent of murdering Eric in Dowdsville. Katy returns to Palenoc with the pair where Robert's search for the fate of his friend, Scott, yields insight into mysterious deaths as they encounter forces of the Heart of Darkness and the Dark Lord.

Other books you might like:
David Eddings, *Pawn of Prophecy*, 1982
David Gemmell, *Morningstar*, 1993
Terry Goodkind, *Wizard's First Rule*, 1994
Robert Jordan, *The Eye of the World*, 1989

244

ROBIN WAYNE BAILEY

Night Watch

(Lake Geneva, Wisconsin: TSR, 1990)

Story type: Fantasy (Mystery; Magic Conflict)
Major character(s): Garett Starlen, Police Officer (Captain); Burge, Police Officer; Blossom, Police Officer
Time period(s): Indeterminate Past
Locale(s): Greyhawk, Mythical Place; Mist Marsh, Fictional Country

Summary: Five seers of Greyhawk have been killed in one night by their own instruments of divination. Garett, as commander of the night shift of the City Watch, is assigned to investigate. He discovers evidence that this is the work of the Horned Society and acquires a magic sword that is the only weapon capable of fighting their powers.

Other books you might like:
Steven Brust, *Jhereg*, 1983
C.J. Cherryh, *Angel with the Sword*, 1985
Barbara Hambly, *The Dark Hand of Magic*, 1990
Barbara Hambly, *The Ladies of Mandrigyn*, 1984
Barbara Hambly, *The Witches of Wenshar*, 1987
Janet Morris, *Beyond Sanctuary*, 1985
Patricia C. Wrede, *Daughter of Witches*, 1983

245

ROBIN WAYNE BAILEY

Shadowdance

(Clarkston, Georgia: White Wolf Borealis, 1996)

Story type: Fantasy (Quest)
Major character(s): Innowen, Handicapped, Dancer; Minarik, Military Personnel, Leader; Razkili, Military Personnel (soldier)
Time period(s): Indeterminate
Locale(s): Ispor, Fictional Country; Parendur, Fictional City

Summary: Paralyzed and helpless, Innowen deals with a witch to allow him to walk during the dark hours, for which he must dance every night. This seems ideal, but Innowen's dancing allows and forces viewers to succumb to their dark impulses. Ashamed and horrified, he sets out to find the witch and discover her reasons for the curse.

Other books you might like:
Scott Baker, *Drink the Fire From the Flames*, 1987
Glen Cook, *The Black Company*, 1984
Simon R. Green, *Hawk & Fisher*, 1990
Ellen Kushner, *Swordspoint*, 1987
Fritz Leiber, *Ill Met in Lankhmar*, 1995

246

SHARON BAINBRIDGE

Blood and Roses

(New York: Diamond, 1994)

Story type: Horror (Vampire Story)
Major character(s): Sir Geoffrey, Nobleman, Vampire; Elaine Portland, Young Woman; William R. Praisegood, Doctor
Time period(s): 19th century (late)
Locale(s): High Grimmire, England

Summary: Sir Geoffrey, who contracts vampirism shortly after Count Dracula arrives on English soil, meets his match in William Praisegood, a doctor whose scientific method and incomplete skepticism make him a formidable match against those who prey upon his patients.

Other books you might like:
Traci Briery, *The Vampire Journals*, 1993
P.N. Elrod, *Red Death*, 1993
Kim Newman, *Anno Dracula*, 1992
Michael Romkey, *I, Vampire*, 1990
Bram Stoker, *Dracula*, 1897

247

WILHELMINA BAIRD

Chaos Come Again

(New York: Ace, 1996)

Story type: Science Fiction (Alternate Intelligence; Psychic Powers)
Series: Crashcourse
Major character(s): Desi "Daisy Smeet" Smith, Doctor, Psychic; Jeremiah "Jonesy" Jones, Journalist, Psychic; Ice, Divorced Person, Villain
Time period(s): Indeterminate Future
Locale(s): *Windrunner/Windy*, Spaceship

Summary: After encountering an intelligent alien symbiont, the human race acquires many new abilities which sweep through the population like wildfire. Many groups of humans reject the symbs, causing a period of warfare. Desi searches for her brilliant, insane ex-husband with the help of a lonely planetary intelligence, a stowaway reporter, and her neurotic, intelligent spaceship, human enough to have a symb of her own.

Other books you might like:
Stephen Goldin, *Jade Darcy and the Zen Pirates*, 1990
    Mary Mason, co-author

Anne McCaffrey, *Powers That Be*, 1993
    Elizabeth Ann Scarborough, co-author
Robert J. Sawyer, *Starplex*, 1996
Dan Simmons, *Hyperion*, 1989
Sheri S. Tepper, *Raising the Stones*, 1990
David Weber, *Path of the Fury*, 1992

248

WILHELMINA BAIRD

Clipjoint

(New York: Ace, 1994)

Story type: Science Fiction (Arts; Mystery)
Series: Crashcourse
Major character(s): Cassandra "Cass" Blaine, Actress, Thief; Hans-Bjorn "Mokey/Moke" Eklunk, Artist (sculptor), Actor; Dribble, Genetically Altered Being
Time period(s): 21st century
Locale(s): Never, Space Station; Virginity, Planet—Imaginary

Summary: Cass and Moke feel compelled to leave their comfortable new lives and return to Never when they receive a vidclip which seems to feature the deceased actor, Dosh. With the help of her friends, Cass uncovers proof of Coelacanth Productions' criminal activities.

Other books you might like:
Greg Bear, *Queen of Angels*, 1990
Pat Cadigan, *Synners*, 1991
Emily Devenport, *Shade*, 1991
Philip K. Dick, *A Scanner Darkly*, 1977
Laura J. Mixon, *Glass Houses*, 1992

249

WILHELMINA BAIRD

Crashcourse

(New York: Ace, 1993)

Story type: Science Fiction (Cyberpunk; Arts)
Series: Crashcourse
Major character(s): Cassandra "Cass" Blaine, Actress, Thief; Doshky "Dosh", Prostitute, Actor; Hans-Bjorn "Mokey/ Moke" Eklunk, Artist, Actor
Time period(s): 21st century
Locale(s): Chicago, Illinois; Never, Space Station

Summary: Desperate to earn enough money to get off-planet, Cassie, Dosh and Moke agree to participate as actors in a production to be filmed without their reading scripts, to promote spontaneous reactions felt by the audience through cyber links. Problems arise as the actors experience difficulty distinguishing real events from scripted actions. First novel.

Other books you might like:
David Brin, *Earth*, 1990
Pat Cadigan, *Synners*, 1991
William C. Dietz, *Matrix Man*, 1990
Neal Stephenson, *Snow Crash*, 1992
Robert Charles Wilson, *Memory Wire*, 1987

250

WILHELMINA BAIRD

Psykosis

(New York: Ace, 1995)

Story type: Science Fiction (First Contact; Alternate Intelligence)
Series: Crashcourse
Major character(s): Cassandra ''Cass'' Blaine, Criminal (burglar), Companion; McLaren ''Swordfish'' DeLorn, Diplomat (ambassador), Military Personnel; Hans-Bjorn ''Mokey/Moke'' Eklunk, Artist (sculptor), Genius
Time period(s): 21st century
Locale(s): *Hercules*, Spaceship; Outer Space; Resurrection, Planet—Imaginary

Summary: Retaining the atomic heart and enhanced bones and nervous system from the last war with the aliens, Swordfish volunteers to attempt a meeting with them to avert yet another war. When the meeting with the telepathic toadstools on Resurrection ends with humans taken hostage, Swordfish, Cass, and Moke rush to rescue the hostages before the Navy slags the planet.

Other books you might like:
David Brin, *Brightness Reef*, 1995
Octavia E. Butler, *Dawn*, 1987
L. Warren Douglas, *Cannon's Orb*, 1994
Larry Niven, *The Mote in God's Eye*, 1974
    Jerry Pournelle, co-author
S. Andrew Swann, *Specters of the Dawn*, 1994
Sheri S. Tepper, *Grass*, 1989
David Weber, *Path of the Fury*, 1992

251

MIKE BAKER, Editor

Young Blood

(New York: Zebra, 1994)

Story type: Horror (Anthology)
Summary: The 29 stories collected in this volume all were written by authors under the age of 30, many of whom had not published professionally before. Of the handful of supernatural stories, the stand-out is Clark Perry's ''Little Black Bags,'' about a monster found inside the body of a doctor's backwoods patient. Most fall within the realm of psychological horror, including Gordon van Gelder's tale of a man's alienation from his family, ''Something More''; Tim Waggoner's psycho tale of childhood neuroses that become adult psychoses, ''Mr. Punch''; and Brian Everson's gruesomely humorous ''Hebe Kills Jerry.'' One third of the book is taken up with classic reprints by Ramsey Campbell, Robert Bloch, Edgar Allan Poe, Robert E. Howard, and Stephen King, all published before the authors turned 30.

Other books you might like:
Peter Enfantino, *Quick Chills*, 1989
    Bob Morrish, co-editor
Peter Enfantino, *Quick Chills II*, 1991
    Bob Morrish, co-editor

Joy Oestreicher, *Air Fish*, 1992
    Richard Singer, co-editor

252

NANCY BAKER

The Night Inside

(New York: Fawcett Columbine, 1994)

Story type: Horror (Vampire Story)
Major character(s): Ardeth Alexander, Student; Dimitri Rozokov, Vampire; Ambrose Dale, Businessman
Time period(s): 1990s (1994); 1890s (1898)
Locale(s): Toronto, Ontario, Canada

Summary: In an unusual buddy story Ardeth Alexander, a student abducted to feed vampire Dimitri Rozokov, pools resources and knowledge with the sympathetic vampire to free him from imprisonment by pornographers who use him in snuff films. Together they discover the link binding Rozokov's current captors with the man who first began persecuting him a century before. This is the author's first novel.

Other books you might like:
Tanya Huff, *Blood Pact*, 1993
Roxanne Longstreet, *The Undead*, 1993
Yvonne Navarro, *Afterage*, 1993
Anne Rice, *The Vampire Lestat*, 1985

253

NICHOLSON BAKER

The Fermata

(New York: Random House, 1994)

Story type: Science Fiction (Psychic Powers; Humor)
Major character(s): Arnold Strine, Writer, Criminal; Joyce Collier, Businesswoman; Marian, Librarian
Time period(s): 1990s
Locale(s): Boston, Massachusetts

Summary: When he learns to halt the progression of events and, in effect, stop the passage of time while remaining unaffected, Arnold begins taking unnatural liberties with acquaintances and strangers. He indulges his fantasies by undressing and redressing women and creating anomalies in normal existence from within the spaces between moments of time, maintaining throughout a fractured moral perspective.

Other books you might like:
Jeff Gelb, *Hot Blood: Tales of Provocative Horror*, 1989
    Lonn Friend, co-editor
Steven Gould, *Jumper*, 1992
Robert A. Heinlein, *The Number of the Beast*, 1980
Alan Lightman, *Einstein's Dreams*, 1993
John D. MacDonald, *The Girl, the Gold Watch, and Everything*, 1962

`254`

SCOTT BAKER

Ancestral Hungers
(New York: Tor, 1995)

Story type: Horror (Vampire Story)
Major character(s): David Bathory, Drug Dealer; Dara, Wanderer; Michael Bathory, Businessman (David's brother)
Time period(s): 1990s (1995)
Locale(s): Illinois

Summary: In this expansion of his 1982 novel, *Dhampire*, the author chronicles the life of David Bathory, a lineal descendant of Count Dracula, who is forced to come to terms with his family roots after the murder of his wife. Returning to his family homestead, David finds himself drawn into a struggle with his family that mandates he draw on his inherited traits as a "dhampire," or being capable of mastering his vampire relatives.

Other books you might like:
Christopher Golden, *Of Saints and Shadows*, 1994
Tanith Lee, *Darkness, I*, 1995
Kim Newman, *Anno Dracula*, 1992
Brian Stableford, *Young Blood*, 1991
Robert Weinberg, *Bloodwar*, 1995

`255`

SCOTT BAKER

Webs
(New York: Tor, 1989)

Story type: Horror (Psychological Suspense)
Major character(s): Brian Gerard, Professor (college); Karen Attercop, Student (spider fancier), Lover (Brian's)
Time period(s): 1980s
Locale(s): Point Marsh Key, Florida (Aubrey Estate, the Florida coast)

Summary: His wife confined to a mental hosiptal, Brian Gerard accepts a teaching job in Florida that includes free use of a large estate. Soon he finds himself plagued by an army of huge spiders and begins an affair with a pretty young student, whose expertise with spiders may rescue him from his infestation—unless she is behind it.

Other books you might like:
K.W. Jeter, *Soul Eater*, 1983

`256`

ROBERT T. BAKKER

Raptor Red
(New York: Bantam, 1995)

Story type: Fantasy (Adventure; Science Fiction)
Major character(s): Raptor Red, Animal (dinosaur)
Time period(s): Indeterminate Past (early Cretaceous)
Locale(s): Asia; North America

Summary: Raptor Red tragically loses her mate while hunting and must flee predators and natural disasters as she searches for a comfortable environment and a new mate.

Other books you might like:
Arthur Conan Doyle, *The Lost World*, 1912
James Gurney, *Dinotopia*, 1992
Garry Kilworth, *The Foxes of Firstdark*, 1990
Stephen Leigh, *Ray Bradbury Presents: Dinosaur World*, 1992

`257`

CHRIS BALDICK, Editor

The Oxford Book of Gothic Tales
(New York: Oxford University Press, 1992)

Story type: Horror (Anthology)

Summary: This superb omnibus pulls together 37 classic and contemporary stories of horror and the supernatural that define the gloomy and antiquated atmosphere of the Gothic mode. Included are seven excessively morbid fragments of early-Gothic horror from the late-eighteenth and early-nineteenth centuries; late-Gothic masterpieces of doomed families such as Poe's "The Fall of the House of Usher" and Nathaniel Hawthorne's "Rappacini's Daughter"; early-modern Gothic tales from the pulp era including H. P. Lovecraft's Poe pastiche, "The Outsider," and Clark Ashton Smith's vampire tale, "A Rendezvous in Averoigne"; and contemporary examples of the southern gothic (William Faulkner's "A Rose for Emily") and satiric Gothic (Patrick McGrath's "Blood Disease").

Other books you might like:
Peter Haining, *Gothic Tales of Terror*, 1972
   editor
Peter Haining, *The Shilling Shockers*, 1978
   editor
Bradford Morrow, *The New Gothic*, 1991
   Patrick McGrath, co-editor
Patricia L. Skarda, *The Evil Image: Two Centuries of Gothic Short Fiction and Poetry*, 1981
   Nora Crowe, co-editor

`258`

BILL BALDWIN

Canby's Legion
(New York: Warner Aspect, 1995)

Story type: Science Fiction (Space Opera; Military)
Major character(s): Gordon Canby, Spaceship Captain, Mercenary; Nikolai Kobir, Spaceship Captain, Pirate; Sadir, Nobleman (First Earl of Relando)
Time period(s): 27th century (2681-2692)
Locale(s): United States (East Coast); Khalife, Planet—Imaginary

Summary: Gordon Canby, a retired war hero, unites a group of fellow veterans into a mercenary unit called Canby's Legion. Hired by the First Earl of Renaldo to destroy the Kirskian pirates, Canby hunts a man named Nikolai Kobir, whom he once faced as an enemy starship captain.

Other books you might like:
John Dalmas, *The Regiment*, 1987
Gordon R. Dickson, *Dorsai!*, 1976
David Drake, *At Any Price*, 1985
David Drake, *Igniting the Reaches*, 1994
David Drake, *Through the Breach*, 1995
Jerry Pournelle, *The Mercenary*, 1977
Jerry Pournelle, *Prince of Mercenaries*, 1989

259
BILL BALDWIN

The Defenders
(New York: Questar, 1992)

Story type: Science Fiction (Military; Space Opera)
Series: Helmsman
Major character(s): Wilf Brim, Military Personnel, Spaceship Captain; Onrad, Ruler (emperor)
Time period(s): 520th century
Locale(s): Avalon, Planet—Imaginary (center of galactic civilization); Interstellar Empire/Federation

Summary: Wilf Brim and his young emperor must assemble defenses for Avalon when the League of Dark Stars attacks the heart of galactic civiliztion.

Other books you might like:
David Brin, *Startide Rising*, 1983
Lois McMaster Bujold, *The Vor Game*, 1990
Allan Cole, *Sten*, 1984
    Chris Bunch, co-author
Glen Cook, *The Dragon Never Sleeps*, 1988
Brian Daley, *Requiem for a Ruler of Worlds*, 1985
Alis A. Rasmussen, *Revolution's Shore*, 1990
E.E. "Doc" Smith, *The Lensman Series*, 1948-1954
Vernor Vinge, *A Fire upon the Deep*, 1992

260
BILL BALDWIN

The Defiance
(New York; Warner Aspect, 1996)

Story type: Science Fiction (Military)
Series: Helmsman
Major character(s): Wilf Brim, Military Personnel
Time period(s): 521st century
Locale(s): Atalanta, Fictional City; Interstellar Empire/Federation; Outer Space

Summary: As the League of Dark Stars continues its war with the Empire, Admiral Wilf Brim must lead a siegebreaking of Atalanta, then capture Gontor, a vast alien fortress built into an asteroid.

Other books you might like:
Lois McMaster Bujold, *The Warrior's Apprentice*, 1986
Glen Cook, *The Dragon Never Sleeps*, 1988
Gordon R. Dickson, *Dorsai!*, 1976

Debra Doyle, *The Price of the Stars*, 1992
    James D. Macdonald, co-author
Robert A. Heinlein, *Starship Troopers*, 1959
Sherwood Smith, *The Phoenix in Flight*, 1993
    Dave Trowbridge, co-author
David Weber, *On Basilisk Station*, 1993

261
BILL BALDWIN

The Mercenaries
(New York: Warner Questar, 1991)

Story type: Science Fiction (Space Opera)
Series: Helmsman
Major character(s): Wilf Brim, Military Personnel, Spaceship Captain (Starfury); Nadia Tissaurd, Military Personnel
Time period(s): 520th century
Locale(s): *Starfury*, Spaceship (prototype); Fluvanna, Interstellar Empire/Federation (Magor, the capital)

Summary: With most of the fleet in mothballs due to the Treaty of Garak, Wilf Brim takes *Starfury* to Fluvanna to protect raw materials needed to construct a new imperial fleet.

Other books you might like:
David Brin, *Startide Rising*, 1983
Lois McMaster Bujold, *Brothers in Arms*, 1989
Glen Cook, *The Dragon Never Sleeps*, 1988
Melisa C. Michaels, *Skirmish*, 1985
Alis A. Rasmussen, *The Price of Ransom*, 1990

262
BILL BALDWIN

The Siege
(New York: Warner Questar, 1994)

Story type: Science Fiction (Space Opera; Military)
Series: Helmsman
Major character(s): Wilf Brim, Military Personnel (admiral); Nikolai Yanuarievich Ursis, Military Personnel
Time period(s): 520th century
Locale(s): *Alexasander Grobkin*, Spaceship; Avalon, Planet—Imaginary; Interstellar Empire/Federation

Summary: The League of Dark Stars once again attempts to invade the Sodeskayan Worlds. Wilf's ground troops need space support but his superiors expect the Sodeskayans to provide most of the ships. Unfortunately, the Sodeskayan shipyards have barely begun spaceship production.

Other books you might like:
Allan Cole, *Sten*, 1984
    Chris Bunch, co-author
Michelle Shirey Crean, *Dancer of the Sixth*, 1993
Brian Daley, *Requiem for a Ruler of Worlds*, 1985
David Drake, *The Warrior*, 1991
David Weber, *The Honor of the Queen*, 1993

263

MARGARET BALL

Changeweaver

(New York: Baen, 1993)

Story type: Fantasy (Historical; Magic Conflict)
Major character(s): Tamai, Shaman (Flameweaver), Heroine; Charles Francis Carrington, Traveller, Writer; Louisa McAusland, Diplomat, Shaman
Time period(s): 1880s (1887)
Locale(s): Gandhara, Fictional City; Kashgar, Ancient Civilization (Silk Road); Peking, China

Summary: Carrington arrives in Gandhara en route to Peking to achieve a trade agreement with the Chin Empire. There he meets his guide, Tamai, who reluctantly accompanies him over the Pamirs to Kashgar and across the Great Desert. Adopting a daughter and facing physical dangers, Tamai gains the control she had always lacked, unaware that the fate of the Chin Empire resides in her hands. Sequel to *Flameweaver.*

Other books you might like:
Marion Zimmer Bradley, *Hawkmistress!*, 1982
Carol Chase, *Hawk's Flight*, 1991
Marc Laidlaw, *Neon Lotus*, 1988
Jeanne Larsen, *Silk Road*, 1989
Catherine Lyndell, *Stolen Dreams*, 1989
    pseudonym of Margaret Ball
Anne McCaffrey, *PartnerShip*, 1992
    Margaret Ball, co-author
Elizabeth Ann Scarborough, *Nothing Sacred*, 1991

264

MARGARET BALL

Flameweaver

(New York: Baen, 1991)

Story type: Fantasy (Magic Conflict; Alternate History)
Major character(s): Tamai, Psychic; Louisa Westbrook, Gentlewoman, Psychic; James McAusland, Military Personnel (Lieutenant)
Time period(s): 1880s (1884)
Locale(s): Gandhara, Fictional City; India

Summary: Because she is unable to have children, Tamai's psychic powers, though strong, are undisciplined and dangerous. When invaders come from the north, she goes south with her cousin and a trained eagle to bargain for rifles from the legendary ''Angrez.'' Tamai's psychic battle to protect her traveling companions nearly kills her, but Louisa Westbrook nurses her back to health while Tamai helps Louisa develop her latent powers.

Other books you might like:
Poul Anderson, *A Midsummer Tempest*, 1984
Marion Zimmer Bradley, *Hawkmistress!*, 1982
C.J. Cherryh, *A Dirge for Stabis*, 1989
    Leslie Fish, co-author
John M. Ford, *The Dragon Waiting*, 1983
Lisa Goldstein, *The Red Magician*, 1982

Rudyard Kipling, *Kim*, 1901
Ursula K. Le Guin, *Tehanu: The Last Book of Earthsea*, 1990
Elizabeth Ann Scarborough, *Nothing Sacred*, 1991
Patricia C. Wrede, *Sorcery and Cecelia*, 1988
    Caroline Stevermer, co-author

265

MARGARET BALL

Lost in Translation

(New York: Baen, 1995)

Story type: Fantasy (Light Fantasy; Alternate World)
Major character(s): Allie, Student—College; Domerc, Student—College, Wizard; Aigar, Wizard, Professor
Time period(s): Indeterminate
Locale(s): Coindra, Fictional Country; Alternate Earth

Summary: Sent against her will to a university in southern France, Allie arrives instead in a strange place where students study the art of magic. With the help of fellow students, she must prevent Aigar from using magic to raise deadly Landmonsters from the earth.

Other books you might like:
Carolyn Cushman, *Witch and Wombat*, 1994
Brett Davis, *The Faery Convention*, 1995
Anne McCaffrey, *PartnerShip*, 1992
    Margaret Ball, co-author
Caroline Stevermer, *A College of Magics*, 1994
Sheri S. Tepper, *Marianne, the Magus, and the Manticore*, 1985

266

MARGARET BALL

Mathemagics

(New York: Baen, 1996)

Story type: Fantasy (Light Fantasy; Alternate World)
Series: Chicks in Chainmail
Major character(s): Rivakonneva ''Riva'', Warrior, Parent; Dennis ''Dennis Dithrovvu'' Withrow, Scientist (mathematician), Teacher; Mikhalevviko ''Mikh'', Wizard, Criminal
Time period(s): 1990s; Indeterminate
Locale(s): Austin, Texas; Dazau, Planet—Imaginary

Summary: Riva spends most of her time on Earth studying mathematics and allowing her daughter to study while Riva commutes to work as Bronze Bra Guild fighter and bodyguard on Dazau. When Mikhalevviko joins forces with a self-aggrandizing Bible thumper intent on wiping out all secular literature on Earth, Riva and Dennis travel to Dazau, where Dennis' mathematical formulas translate to magic spells. The pair must rescue Riva's daughter and her friends and restore Earth's books by eliminating the ensorcelled literary characters created on Dazau.

Other books you might like:
Marion Zimmer Bradley, *The Sword and Sorceress Series*, 1984-1996
    editor

George Alec Effinger, *Maureen Birnbaum, Barbarian Swordsperson: The Complete Stories*, 1993
Esther Friesner, *Chicks in Chainmail*, 1995
    editor
Holly Lisle, *Minerva Wakes*, 1994
Sharyn McCrumb, *Bimbos of the Death Sun*, 1987
Jessica Amanda Salmonson, *Amazons!*, 1979
    editor

267

MARGARET BALL

The Shadow Gate
(New York: Baen, 1991)

Story type: Fantasy (Alternate World; Magic Conflict)
Major character(s): Lisa, Secretary; Judith Templeton, Computer Expert; Count Berengar, Nobleman, Mythical Creature (elf)
Time period(s): 1990s (1991); Indeterminate Past
Locale(s): Austin, Texas; Duchy of Aquitaine, France

Summary: Berengar, the elvish Count of the Garronais, is trying to call the former Queen of the Middle Realm, Sybille, back from where she has fled so that she can restore the power of the Stones of Jura. Instead, three humans connected with the New Age Psychic Research Center are transported from Austin, Texas to the Duchy of Aquitaine in a world where elf and human co-exist (uneasily) and magic works (weakly). Despite the interference of the elf-hating Durandine monks, they reach the Stones and one of the mortals proves to be the one who can find Sybille and restore elvish magic.

Other books you might like:
Emma Bull, *War for the Oaks*, 1987
Barbara Hambly, *The Silent Tower*, 1986
Barbara Hambly, *The Silicon Mage*, 1988
R.A. MacAvoy, *The Book of Kells*, 1985
Elizabeth Marie Pope, *The Perilous Gard*, 1974

268

BETTY BALLANTINE

The Secret Oceans
(New York: Ballantine, 1994)

Story type: Science Fiction (First Contact)
Major character(s): Katerina ''Kate'' Kominsky, Sea Captain, Scientist; David Schlessinger, Activist (environmental), Scientist
Time period(s): 2000s
Locale(s): *Turtle*, Submarine; At Sea

Summary: On *Turtle*'s maiden voyage the crew discovers an ancient species hidden in the ocean which has surreptitiously observed human beings and society for a long time. Extensive illustrations.

Other books you might like:
David Bischoff, *seaQuest DSV: The Ancient*, 1994
Orson Scott Card, *The Abyss*, 1989
Arthur C. Clarke, *The Deep Range*, 1957
Arthur C. Clarke, *Dolphin Island*, 1963

David Kirschner, *The Pagemaster*, 1993
    Ernie Contreras, co-author
James Gurney, *Dinotopia*, 1992
Kathryn Lasky, *Shadows in the Water*, 1992
Roy Meyers, *Dolphin Boy*, 1967
Theodore Sturgeon, *Voyage to the Bottom of the Sea*, 1961

269

J.G. BALLARD

The Atrocity Exhibition
(San Francisco, California: RE/SEARCH Publications, 1990)

Story type: Science Fiction (Collection)
Major character(s): Ronald Reagan, Political Figure
Time period(s): 1970s (1970)
Locale(s): Earth

Summary: This is the ''revised, expanded, illustrated edition'' of a book that was printed and suppressed before release by Doubleday in 1970. It was later issued by Grove as *Love and Napalm: Export USA*. Short, vivid vignettes mix surrealism, politics, sex, popular culture, medicine and technology. This edition has extensive margin notes by the author that explain references and expand on his ideas.

Other books you might like:
Iain M. Banks, *The Bridge*, 1946
Michael Blumlein, *The Brains of Rats*, 1990
William S. Burroughs, *Naked Lunch*, 1959
Brian Byson, *Have to Go: Planet R-101*, 1982
Mark Leyner, *My Cousin, My Gastroenterologist*, 1990

270

J.G. BALLARD

Running Wild
(New York: Farrar, Straus & Giroux, 1989)

Story type: Horror (Serial Killer)
Major character(s): Richard Greville, Doctor (Psychiatrist, police advisor); Payne, Police Officer (Sergeant; Reading CID)
Time period(s): 1980s (1988)
Locale(s): Pangbourne Village (Exclusive ''planned community'')

Summary: On June 25, 1988, thirty-two adult residents of Pangbourne Village are quickly and efficiently murdered and thirteen children vanish. Greville's scrupulous analysis of the incident leads him to a terrifying and provocative conclusion.

Other books you might like:
Lawrence Block, *Ariel*, 1980
Stephen King, *''The Children of the Corn''*, 1977
William March, *The Bad Seed*, 1954

271

J.G. BALLARD

War Fever

(New York: Farrar, Straus, Giroux, 1991)

Story type: Science Fiction (Collection)

Summary: 14 stories written between 1975 and 1991 and originally published in periodicals and anthologies in the United States and Great Britain. Frequent humor and thorny satire appear within the themes of war, politics, media manipulation, pollution and human nature. In "The Secret History of World War 3," reports of a brief nuclear war are slipped into continuous reports of every medical detail of third-term U.S. President Ronald Reagan. Some of the short stories are presented in a non-traditional format including "The Index" which looks at 20th century literature through the index to an unpublished biography of an unknown but influential figure. "Answers to a Questionnaire," labelled 1-100, provide a look into the assassination of the Messiah during His Second Coming on Earth. In "Notes Towards a Mental Breakdown" Dr. Robert Loughlin depicts, through footnotes, events surrounding his breakdown.

Other books you might like:
Alfred Bester, *The Light Fantastic*, 1976
Alfred Bester, *Star Light, Star Bright*, 1976
Philip K. Dick, *The Best of Philip K. Dick*, 1977
R.A. Lafferty, *Lafferty in Orbit*, 1991
Kim Stanley Robinson, *Remaking History*, 1991
Cordwainer Smith, *The Best of Cordwainer Smith*, 1975
Kurt Vonnegut Jr., *Welcome to the Monkey House*, 1968
Gene Wolfe, *Endangered Species*, 1989

272

IAIN M. BANKS

Against a Dark Background

(New York: Bantam Spectra, 1993)

Story type: Science Fiction (Space Opera)
Series: Culture
Major character(s): Lady Sharrow, Thief, Warrior
Time period(s): 100th century
Locale(s): *Solo*, Spaceship; Golter, Planet—Imaginary

Summary: Lady Sharrow pursues her quest of finding the sole remaining Lazy Gun, a fabled weapon lost among the worlds of the Thrial star system. Killers from the Huhsz cult of assassins search for her while flashbacks to horrors in her life haunt her.

Other books you might like:
David Brin, *Startide Rising*, 1983
Glen Cook, *The Dragon Never Sleeps*, 1988
Alan Dean Foster, *The Tar-Aiym Krang*, 1972
Vonda N. McIntyre, *Metaphase*, 1992
Charles Sheffield, *Transcendence*, 1992
Vernor Vinge, *A Fire upon the Deep*, 1992

273

IAIN M. BANKS

Canal Dreams

(New York: Doubleday, 1991)

Story type: Science Fiction (Contemporary Realism)
Series: The Culture
Major character(s): Hisako Onado, Musician; Philippe, Military Personnel; Sucre, Revolutionary
Time period(s): Indeterminate Future
Locale(s): Gatun Lake, Panama; *Nakedo*, At Sea

Summary: An unexpected war traps Hisako Onodo, an internationally renowned cellist, in the Panama Canal. She forms a liaison with an officer on another ship, and keeps herself distracted with diving and parties. When the war engulfs her, she must find a way to live in a world rapidly and violently falling apart. Originally published in England in 1989.

Other books you might like:
J.G. Ballard, *Concrete Island*, 1985
Lisa Goldstein, *The Dream Years*, 1985
Pat Murphy, *The City, Not Long After*, 1989
Lucius Shepard, *Life During Wartime*, 1987
Lewis Shiner, *Slam*, 1990

274

IAIN M. BANKS

Feersum Endjinn

(New York: Bantam Spectra, 1995)

Story type: Science Fiction (Literary)
Major character(s): Alandre Sessine VII, Nobleman; Ergates, Animal (ant); Hortis Gadfium, Scientist
Time period(s): Indeterminate Future
Locale(s): Great Hall, Fictional City

Summary: After Count Sessine's final material life ends by treachery, bizarre digital violence begins to end his virtual post-death lives. While a barely literate boy befriends a talking ant, Horis Gadfium tries to understand the gigantic structure she inhabits.

Other books you might like:
Russell Hoban, *Riddley Walker*, 1980
Ian McDonald, *Terminal Cafe*, 1994
Mervyn Peake, *Gormenghast*, 1950
Lucius Shepard, *The Golden*, 1993
John Varley, *The Ophiuchi Hotline*, 1977

275

IAIN M. BANKS

The Player of Games

(New York: St. Martin's Press, 1989)

Story type: Science Fiction (Political)
Major character(s): Jernau Gurgeh, Sports Figure (Gameplayer); Flere-Imsaho, Robot
Time period(s): Indeterminate Future

Locale(s): The Culture, Interstellar Empire/Federation (various artificial worlds); Empire of Azad, Interstellar Empire/Federation (various planets)

Summary: Gurgeh, one of the greatest of the Culture's game players, is recruited to journey to the Empire of Azad, an intensely xenophobic and potentially hostile neighboring power. Political office and indeed all power in Azad is gained through winning an incredibly complex game. Gurgeh must master the game and gain the respect of Nicosar, the Emperor of Azad, in order to avoid armed conflict.

Other books you might like:
Greg Bear, *Eon*, 1985
Greg Bear, *Eternity*, 1988
David Brin, *The Uplift War*, 1987
C.J. Cherryh, *Cyteen*, 1988
Michael Moorcock, *An Alien Heat*, 1972

276

IAIN M. BANKS

The State of the Art
(Shingleton, CA: Ziesing, 1989)

Story type: Science Fiction (First Contact)
Series: The Culture
Major character(s): Diziet Sma, Alien; Dervley Linter, Alien (Deserter)
Time period(s): 1970s (1977)
Locale(s): Earth

Summary: The starship Arbitrary enters Earth orbit and a truly eccentric group of humanoid aliens and their accompanying artificial intelligence make first contact with humanity. The aliens, who look just like us, use this similarity to move invisibly through our world, weighing and evaluating. They may choose to help us, remain aloof, or, if we warrant it, reduce Earth to a singularity.

Other books you might like:
Octavia E. Butler, *Dawn*, 1987
John Kessel, *Good News From Outer Space*, 1989
Joan Slonczewski, *The Wall Around Eden*, 1989

277

IAIN M. BANKS

Use of Weapons
(New York: Bantam Spectra, 1992)

Story type: Science Fiction (Space Opera; Political)
Series: The Culture
Major character(s): Cheradenine Zakalwe, Spy, Mercenary; Diziet Sma, Spy; Skaffen-Amtiskaw, Artificial Intelligence
Time period(s): Indeterminate Future
Locale(s): *Xenophobe*, Spaceship; Voerenhutz, Planet—Imaginary; The Culture, Interstellar Empire/Federation

Summary: The Culture, in its efforts to stabilize a galactic civilization on the Culture's periphery, needs to find and hire Zakalwe, a master agent retired for some years. As Sma finds out, discovering his whereabouts proves easier than insuring

that he does the job. Zakalwe, haunted by his past and unsure of his own motivations, may explode.

Other books you might like:
Glen Cook, *The Dragon Never Sleeps*, 1988
Ian McDonald, *Desolation Road*, 1988
Dan Simmons, *Hyperion*, 1989
Bruce Sterling, *Schismatrix*, 1985
F. Paul Wilson, *The LaNague Chronicles*, 1992

278

LYNNE REID BANKS

The Adventures of King Midas
(New York: Morrow, 1992)

Story type: Fantasy (Young Adult; Legend)
Major character(s): Midas, Royalty (king); Nandan, Magician; The Mumbo, Mythical Creature (baby dragon)
Time period(s): Indeterminate Past
Locale(s): Fictional Country

Summary: When Nandan grants King Midas the power to turn whatever he touches to gold, it takes the king only a single day to discover that golden food and a golden daughter do not provide much fulfilment. Nandan cannot reverse the spell, but he sets the king on a quest to a talking rock, a witch and a dragon who all have a part in returning life to normal.

Other books you might like:
Grace Chetwin, *Gom on Windy Mountain*, 1986
Susan Fletcher, *Dragon's Milk*, 1989
Judith Gorog, *Winning Scheherazade*, 1991
Norton Juster, *Alberic the Wise and Other Journeys*, 1965
Phyllis McGinley, *The Plain Princess*, 1945
Jane Resh Thomas, *The Princess in the Pigpen*, 1989
Nancy Willard, *Uncle Terrible: More Adventures of Anatole*, 1982
Patricia C. Wrede, *Dealing with Dragons*, 1990
Patricia C. Wrede, *Searching for Dragons*, 1991
Jane Yolen, *Wizard's Hall*, 1991

279

LYNNE REID BANKS

The Secret of the Indian
(New York: Avon Camelot, 1990)

Story type: Fantasy (Time Travel; Young Adult)
Series: Indian in the Cupboard
Major character(s): Omri, Child, Student; Patrick, Friend; Little Bear, Indian
Time period(s): 1980s; 19th century (Old West)
Locale(s): England; West

Summary: Once again the secret of Little Bear, a plastic toy figurine that comes to life through the magic cupboard, is at risk of discovery as Omri and Patrick must borrow and animate toy plastic doctors to save the wounded in Little Bear's own time and place. Reprint of the 1989 Doubleday hardcover.

Other books you might like:
Pauline Clarke, *The Return of the Twelves*, 1964

Edward Eager, *Knight's Castle*, 1956
Richard Kennedy, *Amy's Eyes*, 1985
Elisabeth Mace, *Under Siege*, 1990
E. Nesbit, *Story of the Amulet*, 1907

280

NICK BANTOCK

The Golden Mean

(San Francisco: Chronicle Books, 1993)

Story type: Fantasy (Contemporary; Romance)
Series: Griffin & Sabine
Major character(s): Griffin Moss, Artist (postcard designer); Sabine Strohem, Artist (stamp designer); Victor Frolatti, Journalist (scientific)
Time period(s): 1990s
Locale(s): Sicmon Islands, Fictional Country; Devon, England; Kenya

Summary: The third and final Griffin & Sabine book also consists of actual postcards and letters. The romance between the correspondents heats up as they move toward the resolution of the mystery and their meeting in the flesh. However, a menacing journalist may sever the lovers' tenuous bonds. An intriguing multi-media novel.

Other books you might like:
A.S. Byatt, *Possession: A Romance*, 1990
John Crowley, *Little, Big*, 1981
Umberto Eco, *Foucault's Pendulum*, 1989
Lisa Goldstein, *The Dream Years*, 1985
Pat Murphy, *The City, Not Long After*, 1989

281

NICK BANTOCK

Sabine's Notebook

(San Francisco: Chronicle, 1992)

Story type: Fantasy (Contemporary; Romance)
Series: Griffin & Sabine
Major character(s): Griffin Moss, Artist (postcard designer); Sabine Strohem, Artist (stamp designer)
Time period(s): 1990s
Locale(s): London, England; Alexandria, Egypt; Brisbane, Australia

Summary: Griffin flees his studio to avoid meeting the mysterious, alluring and possibly imaginary Sabine. He begins to write to her at his address, and their correspondence continues. The emotional connection between these two strange individuals increases even as the mystery between them deepens. Sequel to *Griffin & Sabine* and composed of actual letters and postcards.

Other books you might like:
John Crowley, *Little, Big*, 1981
Umberto Eco, *Foucault's Pendulum*, 1989
Greer Ilene Gilman, *Moonwise*, 1990
Lisa Goldstein, *The Dream Years*, 1985
Pat Murphy, *The City, Not Long After*, 1989

282

NICK BANTOCK

The Venetian's Wife: A Strangely Sensual Tale of a Renaissance Explorer, a Computer, and a Metamorphosis

(San Francisco: Chronicle Books, 1996)

Story type: Fantasy (Contemporary)
Major character(s): Niccolo Dei Conti, Explorer, Collector; Sara Wolfe, Artist (painter)
Time period(s): 1990s; 15th century
Locale(s): New Orleans, Louisiana; Venice, Italy

Summary: Bored with her job, Sara Wolfe receives an offer to do research for a mysterious employer who communicates only by e-mail. She begins to collect art objects, to experience odd events, and to fear she's losing her mind. Profusely illustrated with images of art objects, as well as reproductions of letters, diaries, and e-mail.

Other books you might like:
A.S. Byatt, *Possession: A Romance*, 1990
John Crowley, *Little, Big*, 1981
Lisa Goldstein, *The Dream Years*, 1985
Karen Elizabeth Gordon, *Paris out of Hand*, 1996
Barbara Hodgson, *The Tattooed Map*, 1995

283

CLIVE BARKER

Cabal

(New York: Poseidon, 1988)

Story type: Horror (Collection)

Summary: In "Cabal," (filmed as *Nightbreed*) Boone, a psychotic murder suspect, flees to Midian, a town filled with monsters, where he becomes one of them. Other stories include "Twilight at the Towers," a combination spy and werewolf story, and "The Life of Death," in which a girl falls in love with death.

Other books you might like:
Thomas M. Disch, *Getting into Death*, 1976

284

CLIVE BARKER

Everville

(New York: HarperCollins, 1995)

Story type: Horror (Apocalyptic Horror)
Series: Book of the Art Trilogy
Major character(s): Tesla Bombeck, Biker; Nathan Grillo, Computer Expert; Phoebe Cobb, Receptionist
Time period(s): 1990s (1995)
Locale(s): Everville, Oregon

Summary: In this sequel to the author's 1989 novel *The Great and Secret Show*, the struggle resumes between two mortals who have attained mystical transcendance to control The Art, a magic that permits manipulation of time and space. The battle is fought on an epic scale that spans a century of earth time, back to America's frontier days, and extends from the mundane world into the Quiddity, a dreamworld that separates daily life from the realm of mystical experience.

Other books you might like:
Raymond E. Feist, *Faerie Tale*, 1988
Stephen King, *The Stand*, 1978
Robert R. McCammon, *Swan Song*, 1987
Alan Rodgers, *Night*, 1991

285

CLIVE BARKER

Forms of Heaven
(New York: HarperPrism, 1996)

Story type: Horror (Collection)
Summary: Never before collected, the three early plays gathered here contain a number of themes that dominate the author's mature work. "Crazyface" mixes the comic and grotesque in its account of a clown's travels through the plague-ravaged Europe of the Middle Ages. "Paradise Street" anticipates the author's fantasy novel *Weaveworld* with a portrait of contemporary Liverpool transformed into an idyllic dreamscape. The sea of dreams in which the imagination continually refreshes itself is the subject of "Subtle Bodies," a drama whose concepts inform the novels *Everville* and *The Great and Secret Show*.

Other books you might like:
Hamilton Deane, *Dracula: The Ultimate Illustrated Edition of the World-Famous Vampire Play*, 1993
    John L. Balderston, co-author
Marvin Kaye, *Thirteen Plays of Ghosts and the Supernatural*, 1990
    editor
Arch Oboler, *The Oboler Omnibus*, 1945

286

CLIVE BARKER

The Great and Secret Show
(New York: Harper and Row, 1990)

Story type: Horror (Apocalyptic Horror)
Series: Book of the Art Trilogy
Major character(s): Randolph Jaffe, Postal Worker; Richard Wesley Fletcher, Scientist
Time period(s): 1990s
Locale(s): Palomo Grove, California
Summary: Soon after Randolph Jaffe discovers the key to the "Secret Art" and shares it with his friend Richard Wesley Fletcher, the two men become enemies as their quests for the Secret Art launch a protracted, apocalyptic conflict between Good and Evil that is violent, raw, extravagant, vulgar, visceral, and wildly metaphysical.

Other books you might like:
Stephen King, *The Stand*, 1978
    Complete and uncut edition published in 1990
Stephen King, *The Dark Tower: The Gunslinger*,

Stephen King, *The Talisman*, 1984
    Peter Straub, co-author
Robert R. McCammon, *Swan Song*, 1987

287

CLIVE BARKER

The Hellbound Heart
(New York: Harper, 1991)

Story type: Horror (Haunted House)
Major character(s): Frank, Demon; Rory, Businessman (Frank's brother); Julia, Housewife, Spouse (Rory's)
Time period(s): 1980s
Locale(s): England
Summary: This short novel of love and obsession originally published in 1986 tells of thrill-seeking Frank, whose dealings with the extradimensional Cenobites leave him destroyed physically and trapped spiritually between dimensions. His only hope for resurrection is to seduce Julia, his sister-in-law, who has moved with big brother Frank into the house that imprisons him and who is easily persuaded to supply him with the blood and flesh of victims he needs to return to the earthly plane. Filmed as *Hellraiser*.

Other books you might like:
Lisa Cantrell, *Torments*, 1990
Tom Elliott, *The Dwelling*, 1989
H.P. Lovecraft, *The Lurker at the Threshold*, 1945
    August Derleth, co-author
Al Sarrantonio, *House Haunted*, 1991

288

CLIVE BARKER

Imajica
(New York: HarperCollins, 1991)

Story type: Horror (Apocalyptic Horror)
Major character(s): John Furie "Gentle" Zacharias, Artist; Judith O'Dell, Heroine; Pie 'oh' Pah, Mythical Creature (Mystif)
Time period(s): 1990s
Locale(s): London, England; New York, New York
Summary: The failed assassination of Judith O'Dell brings her back together with former lover "Gentle" Zacharias. Their reunion precipitates the couple on a quest to help the earthly plane (known as the Fifth Dominion) become reconciled with the other four extradimensional dominions and repair the sundered (and metaphorical) federation of the Imajica, split apart two centuries ago by forces that are continuing to work against its reunion.

Other books you might like:
Raymond E. Feist, *Faerie Tale*, 1988
Stephen King, *The Dark Tower Series*, 1982-1992
Stephen King, *The Stand: The Complete and Uncut Edition*, 1990
Robert R. McCammon, *Swan Song*, 1987
Alan Rodgers, *Fire*, 1990

289

CLIVE BARKER

Incarnations

(New York: HarperPrism, 1995)

Story type: Horror (Collection)

Summary: The author, a talented playwright as well as writer of macabre fiction, collects three plays written for small production companies in the 1980s. "Colossus" is set during the Age of Napoleon and attempts to forge a link between the paintings of Goya and the real-life horrors of war that inspired them. In "Frankenstein in Love," Joseph Frankenstein resurrects corpses in a third world country in the throes of revolution, and the reanimated dead look upon their situation as not unlike the fate of mortals living in a godless universe. In "The History of the Devil," Satan is tried in court by a jury of mortals and lesser demons to determine whether his exile from Heaven can be revoked if he can prove that his time on Earth has not adversely affected the normal course of events. Barker supplies an introduction and illustrations.

Other books you might like:
Hamilton Deane, *Dracula: The Ultimate Illustrated Edition of the World-Famous Vampire Play*, 1993
   John L. Balderston, co-author
Marvin Kaye, *Thirteen Plays of Ghosts and the Supernatural*, 1990
   editor
Arch Oboler, *The Oboler Omnibus*, 1945

290

CLIVE BARKER

Sacrament

(New York: HarperCollins, 1996)

Story type: Horror (Occult)
Major character(s): Will Rabjohns, Photographer; Rosa McGee, Supernatural Being; Jacob Steep, Supernatural Being
Time period(s): 1990s (1996)
Locale(s): San Francisco, California; Burnt Yarley, England

Summary: While in a coma that results from his mauling by a polar bear, nature photographer Will Rabjohns recalls his childhood encounter with Rosa McGee and Jacob Steep, two characters whom he now realizes represent the yin and yang of nature's cycle of life and death. Will grasps that what he has learned from the couple has bearing on his understanding of the AIDS epidemic's toll on his friends in the gay community of San Francisco, and he travels back to his native England to come to terms with his life and the many deaths that have affected him.

Other books you might like:
Jonathan Carroll, *After Silence*, 1995
Jay B. Laws, *The Unfinished*, 1993
Jonathan Nasaw, *The World on Blood*, 1996

291

CLIVE BARKER

Tapping the Vein: Books One and Two

(Forestville, California: Eclipse Books, 1989)

Story type: Horror (Collection)

Summary: Four graphic versions of stories taken from Barker's *Books of Blood*: "Human Remains," "Pig Blood Blues." (I) "Skins of the Fathers," "In the Hills, the Cities" (II). Imaginative illustrations vividly and accurately convey the sense of the original stories.

Other books you might like:
Steve Niles, *Saturday Mourning Fly in My Eye*, 1989

292

CLIVE BARKER

The Thief of Always

(New York: HarperCollins, 1992)

Story type: Horror (Coming-of-Age)
Major character(s): Harvey Swick, Child (10-year-old boy); Rictus, Mythical Creature (messenger); Mrs. Griffin, Housekeeper
Time period(s): 1990s (1992)
Locale(s): Alternate Universe (Mr. Hood's Holiday House)

Summary: Bored by the dreary February weather, Harvey Swick follows the six-inch tall Rictus on a celestial journey to Mr. Hood's Holiday House, a wish-fulfilling fantasyland where he must learn to sort out those experiences with potentially nasty side effects from those of more positive substance.

Other books you might like:
Ray Bradbury, *Something Wicked This Way Comes*, 1962
Stephen King, *The Eyes of the Dragon*, 1987
Stephen King, *The Talisman*, 1984
   Peter Straub, co-author
Dean R. Koontz, *Oddkins*, 1989

293

ROBERT H. BARLOW

The Hoard of the Wizard Beast and One Other

(West Warwick, Rhode Island: Necronomicon Press, 1994)

Story type: Horror (Collection)

Summary: This chapbook contains two recently discovered stories of the author, a disciple of H.P. Lovecraft who eventually became his literary executor. "The Hoard of the Wizard Beast" is about a lackey sent to replenish the coffers of the ruler of the world of Zeth from the treasures guarded by a strange creature and the grisly fate that befalls him. "The Slaying of the Monster" is a tongue-in-cheek fantasy about the cowardice of a band of men sent out to slay a dragon menacing their town. S.T. Joshi supplies the introduction. The booklet also reproduces in holograph the original manuscript pages with Lovecraft's hand-written corrections to Barlow's original writing.

Other books you might like:
Lord Dunsany, *Ghosts of the Heaviside Layer and Other Fantasies*, 1980
Clark Ashton Smith, *The Vaults of Yoh-Vombis*, 1988
Clark Ashton Smith, *The Dweller in the Gulf*, 1987
Clark Ashton Smith, *Mother of Toads*, 1987

294
JOHN BARNES

Kaleidoscope Century
(New York: Tor, 1995)

Story type: Science Fiction (Dystopian; Techno-Thriller)
Major character(s): Joshua Ali Quare, Experimental Subject; Sadi, Mercenary, Immortal
Time period(s): 22nd century (2109)
Locale(s): Earth; Red Sands City, Mars

Summary: Waking from Transit in a shack on Mars, Quare explores his returning memories, some conflicting but all true. Born to a Communist family in 1969, he escapes a violent, alcoholic father by joining "The Organization," then the KGB, and helping suppress research into closed timelike curves and life extension. Innoculated with an experimental virus, agents become longlifers, transiting every 15 years to become more youthful and losing all memories. Quare remembers participating in many violent wars, culminating with Earth controlled by the winning artificial intelligence. A message waits for his attention, probably from Sadi, but perhaps from the Organization, and Quare must decide if he wants to comply.

Other books you might like:
Brian W. Aldiss, *Somewhere East of Life*, 1994
Stephen Bury, *Interface*, 1994
Joe Haldeman, *The Forever War*, 1975
James Patrick Kelly, *Wildlife*, 1994
Nancy Kress, *Brain Rose*, 1990

295
JOHN BARNES

A Million Open Doors
(New York: Tor, 1992)

Story type: Science Fiction (Political; Arts)
Major character(s): Giraut Leones, Teacher; Aimeric "Ambrose Cruthers" de Sanha Marsao, Diplomat (ambassador); Margaret, Student, Revolutionary
Time period(s): Indeterminate Future (3rd Millennium)
Locale(s): Wilson, Planet—Imaginary; Nansen, Planet—Imaginary

Summary: Giraut Leones accompanies Aimeric de Sanha Marsao to Caledony to prepare it for wider galactic contact. Once there, Giraut finds the culture stifling and decides to open a school to teach the gracious Nou Occitan lifestyle. After a revolution and the discovery of an earlier civilization on Nansen, he begins to travel throughout the galaxy studying

cross cultural influences along with his new wife, Margaret, a former student.

Other books you might like:
Michael Bishop, *Eyes of Fire*, 1980
John Brunner, *Born Under Mars*, 1967
Gordon R. Dickson, *The Chantry Guild*, 1988
Cynthia Felice, *Double Nocturne*, 1986
Raymond Harris, *Shadows of the White Sun*, 1988
R.A. MacAvoy, *The Third Eagle: Lessons Along a Minor String*, 1989
Michael McCollum, *Antares Dawn*, 1986
Jerry Pournelle, *King David's Spaceship*, 1980
Melissa Scott, *The Kindly Ones*, 1987
Norman Spinrad, *A World Between*, 1979
Walter Jon Williams, *Ambassador of Progress*, 1984

296
JOHN BARNES

Mother of Storms
(New York: Tor, 1994)

Story type: Science Fiction (Disaster; Political)
Major character(s): Jesse Callare, Teacher, Student—College; Mary Ann "Synthi Venture" Waterhouse, Actress, Television Personality (XV); Louie Tynan, Astronaut
Time period(s): 2020s (2028)
Locale(s): Earth; Outer Space

Summary: The UN bombing of a weapons cache in the Arctic releases so much methane that the ocean temperature rises sufficiently to spawn a monstrous hurricane, destroying Hawaii. Instead of dissipating, it calfs and sends out other gigantic storms, one of which travels across the Yucatan Peninsula into the Caribbean where it devastates the islands and Florida. The only hope to stop this storm involves Louie Tynan's travelling to the Oort Cloud for a comet whose ice will seed and cool the atmosphere.

Other books you might like:
Roger MacBride Allen, *Supernova*, 1991
    Eric Kotani, co-author
Piers Anthony, *Rings of Ice*, 1974
J.G. Ballard, *The Drowned World*, 1962
David Brin, *Earth*, 1990
Fred Hoyle, *The Inferno*, 1973
    Geoffrey Hoyle, co-author
D.F. Jones, *Denver Is Missing*, 1974
Fritz Leiber, *The Wanderer*, 1964
Larry Niven, *Lucifer's Hammer*, 1977
    Jerry Pournelle, co-author
Bruce Sterling, *Heavy Weather*, 1994
James Sutherland, *Stormtrack*, 1974

297
JOHN BARNES

One for the Morning Glory
(New York: Tor, 1996)

Story type: Fantasy (Light Fantasy; Quest)

Major character(s): Amatus, Royalty (prince); Calliope, Royalty (princess), Heir—Dispossessed; Cedric, Military Personnel, Political Figure (prime minister)
Time period(s): Indeterminate Past
Locale(s): The Kingdom, Fictional Country

Summary: Drinking the wine of the gods, Prince Amatus finds himself only half a person, the right half. He obtains four guardians and begins performing the tasks needed to regain his left half.

Other books you might like:
Piers Anthony, *Wielding a Red Sword*, 1986
Tom Holt, *Expecting Someone Taller*, 1988
Diana Wynne Jones, *Castle in the Air*, 1991
Andre Norton, *The Year of the Unicorn*, 1965
Terry Pratchett, *The Light Fantastic*, 1988
Clifford D. Simak, *The Fellowship of the Talisman*, 1978

298

JOHN BARNES

Orbital Resonance

(New York: Tor, 1991)

Story type: Science Fiction (Post-Holocaust)
Major character(s): Melpomene Murray, Student, Writer; Randomly Distributed ''Randy'' Schwartz, Student; Theophilius ''Ted'' Harrison, Student, Immigrant
Time period(s): 2020s
Locale(s): *Flying Dutchman*, Spaceship (converted asteroid)

Summary: Ordered to write a book which will allow survivors on Earth to understand life on *Flying Dutchman*, Melpomene struggles to tell of her friends, their activities, their growing into adulthood, and the complications which arise when an immigrant from dying Earth joins the group of spaceborn adolescents.

Other books you might like:
James Blish, *A Life for the Stars*, 1962
Lois McMaster Bujold, *Falling Free*, 1988
Alan Dean Foster, *Glory Lane*, 1987
Melisa C. Michaels, *Skirmish*, 1985
Alis A. Rasmussen, *A Passage of Stars*, 1990
Alis A. Rasmussen, *The Price of Ransom*, 1990
Alis A. Rasmussen, *Revolution's Shore*, 1990
Allen Steele, *Clarke County, Space*, 1990

299

JOHN BARNES

Union Fires

(New York: Worldwide Gold Eagle, 1992)

Story type: Fantasy (Time Travel)
Series: Time Raider
Major character(s): Daniel ''Dan'' Samson, Martial Arts Expert, Time Traveller; Prescott ''Sean Toole'' Heller, Military Personnel, Spy; Caroline ''Sarah'' Carelias, Spy, Time Traveller
Time period(s): 1860s (1864)
Locale(s): Virginia

Summary: Freed to travel the Wind Between Time in search of heroic battles, Dan finds himself inhabiting the body of a double agent, Sean Toole. Toole had planned to betray the underground railroad which brings slaves north to freedom, but Dan's eternal quest to right the wrongs of errant warriors again transforms matters. Through mystic discussions with Master Xi who started Dan on his journey through time, Dan discovers his fate entwines with his companions' throughout history.

Other books you might like:
Marc Laidlaw, *Neon Lotus*, 1988
Fritz Leiber, *The Big Time*, 1961
Kevin D. Randle, *Remember Gettysburg*, 1988
    Robert J. Cornett, co-author
Robert Reed, *Down the Bright Way*, 1991
Barry Sadler, *Casca: The Eternal Mercenary*, 1979
Harry Turtledove, *The Guns of the South*, 1992

300

JOHN BARNES

Wartide

(New York: Worldwide Gold Eagle, 1992)

Story type: Fantasy (Time Travel)
Series: Time Raider
Major character(s): Daniel ''Dan'' Samson, Martial Arts Expert, Time Traveller; Jackson Houston, Military Personnel (possessed by Dan); Turenne, Military Personnel
Time period(s): 1990s (1992); 1940s
Locale(s): Italy

Summary: Rescued from death by Master Xi after a lethal heroic act, Dan finds himself presented with the opportunity to fight heroic battles in another time. Transporting his own spirit into Jackson Houston, Dan helps defeat a German war effort which resulted in the secret development of a new poison gas.

Other books you might like:
Keith William Andrews, *Freedom's Rangers*, 1989
Fritz Leiber, *The Big Time*, 1961
Jerry Pournelle, *Janissaries*, 1979
Robert Reed, *Down the Bright Way*, 1991
Barry Sadler, *Casca: The Eternal Mercenary*, 1979
Barry Sadler, *Casca: Panzer Soldier*, 1980
Richard Sapir, *The Destroyer #1: Created, the Destroyer*, 1971

301

STEVEN BARNES

Firedance

(New York: Tor, 1994)

Story type: Science Fiction (Adventure)
Series: Aubrey Knight
Major character(s): Aubrey Knight, Martial Arts Expert, Spouse; Promise, Dancer, Spouse
Time period(s): 2030s (2033)
Locale(s): Los Angeles, California; Africa

Summary: While powerful enemies utilize trained assassins, clones of Aubrey Knight, Knight travels to Africa to kill the dictator of United Africa, unaware that others consider him expendable. Exploring his mysterious past, Knight must face his own clones to save himself and his family.

Other books you might like:
George Alec Effinger, *When Gravity Fails*, 1987
Stephen Goldin, *Jade Darcy and the Affair of Honor*, 1988
    Mary Mason, co-author
Stephen Goldin, *Jade Darcy and the Zen Pirates*, 1990
    Mary Mason, co-author
Larry Niven, *Achilles' Choice*, 1991
    Steven Barnes, co-author
Larry Niven, *Dream Park*, 1981
    Steven Barnes, co-author

302

STEVEN BARNES

Gorgon Child
(New York: Tor, 1989)

Story type: Science Fiction (Adventure)
Series: Streetlethal
Major character(s): Aubrey Knight, Martial Arts Expert, Sports Figure; Promise, Dancer
Time period(s): 21st century (2028)
Locale(s): Los Angeles, California

Summary: Aubry Knight, martial artist, former professional athlete turned crusader, must save America from enslavement at the hands of a fanatical religious leader who plots to use genetically enhanced super-soldiers to overthrow the government.

Other books you might like:
Richard Kadrey, *Metrophage*, 1988
Daniel Keys Moran, *The Long Run*, 1989
W.T. Quick, *Dreams of Flesh and Sand*, 1988
W.T. Quick, *Dreams of Gods and Men*, 1989
W.T. Quick, *Systems*, 1989

303

CHARLES BARNITZ

The Deepest Sea
(New York: Roc, 1996)

Story type: Fantasy (Historical; Adventure)
Major character(s): Bran Snorrison, Hero, Immortal; Caitria, Companion (ghost), Spirit; Frydys, Girlfriend
Time period(s): 8th century (792-795)
Locale(s): Ireland; England

Summary: Hoping to win gold, glory, and the woman he loves, Bran joins a band of Vikings from his hometown for an autumn of trading and looting. Separated from his crewmates, Bran meets Caitria, spends a winter in Lindisfarne Monastery just before the Danes attack it, slays a dragon, and fights his way across England. Older, richer, and immortal from the effects of the dragon's blood, he returns to his kin in Ireland. First novel.

Other books you might like:
Poul Anderson, *Hrolf Kraki's Saga*, 1973
Frans G. Bengtsson, *The Long Ships*, 1954
Parke Godwin, *A Memory of Lions*, 1976
Harry Harrison, *The Hammer and the Cross*, 1993
R.A. MacAvoy, *The Book of Kells*, 1985
Diana L. Paxson, *The Wolf and the Raven*, 1993
Robert Silverberg, *Gilgamesh the King*, 1984

304

SUE HOLLISTER BARR

Twisted
(New York: Leisure, 1992)

Story type: Horror (Curse)
Major character(s): Simba, Musician; Ronna Parsons, Vagrant; Officer Parsons, Police Officer
Time period(s): 1960s (1966)
Locale(s): Berkeley, California

Summary: Cross-country pursuit by Officer Parsons catalyzes the memories of previous lives lived by a van full of hippies and revealed to them following sexual romps and drug-induced dreams. The closer Parsons draws to his quarry, the closer all parties involved come to acting out a scenario lived through by their nineteenth century predecessors, one that ended in bloodshed and dismemberment.

Other books you might like:
Paddy Chayefsky, *Altered States*, 1978
Tom Elliott, *The Dwelling*, 1990
Ruby Jean Jensen, *Baby Doll*, 1991

305

NEAL BARRETT JR.

Dawn's Uncertain Light
(New York: NAL Signet, 1989)

Story type: Science Fiction (Post-Nuclear Holocaust)
Major character(s): Howie Ryder, Teenager; Ritcher Jones, Religious, Adventurer
Time period(s): 21st century
Locale(s): North America

Summary: Having previously discovered the horrible secret his entire civilization is based on, that the meat animals everyone raises and eats are actually human beings just like himself, Howie Ryder sets off across country in an attempt to save his sister Caroline, who has been taken by the government to be used in a forced breeding program.

Other books you might like:
David Brin, *The Postman*, 1985
Edgar Pangborn, *The Company of Glory*, 1975
Edgar Pangborn, *Davy*, 1964
Edgar Pangborn, *The Judgment of Eve*, 1966
Joan Slonczewski, *The Wall Around Eden*, 1989

306

NEAL BARRETT JR.

Judge Dredd
(New York: St. Martin's, 1995)

Story type: Science Fiction (Dystopian; Adventure)
Major character(s): Joseph "Judge" Dredd, Police Officer (Judge), Fugitive; Herman D. "Fergie" Ferguson, Criminal, Computer Expert; Hershey, Police Officer (Judge)
Time period(s): 22nd century (2139)
Locale(s): Mega-City One, New York (New York City); Aspen Prison, Colorado

Summary: Framed and wrongly convicted of murder, Judge Dredd requires help from Fergie and Judge Hershey to clear his name and uncover the plot by his clone brother to overturn the system of Judges. Novelizes the film.

Other books you might like:
Philip K. Dick, *Blade Runner*, 1982
Craig Shaw Gardner, *Batman*, 1989
Ed Naha, *Robocop 2*, 1990
Richard Osborne, *Demolition Man*, 1993
Robert Tine, *Universal Soldier*, 1992

307

NEAL BARRETT JR.

The Touch of Your Shadow, the Whisper of Your Name
(New York: Dell, 1996)

Story type: Science Fiction (Adventure; Space Opera)
Series: Babylon 5
Major character(s): Michael Garibaldi, Security Officer (Spaceman); John Sheridan, Leader, Spaceman; Susan Ivanova, Leader, Spacewoman
Time period(s): 23rd century (2260)
Locale(s): Babylon 5, Space Station; Interstellar Empire/Federation

Summary: As nightmares plague everyone aboard Babylon 5, riots and individual fights become common, while the approach of a huge apparition brings fear of invasion. Garibaldi and Sheridan must find the cause before strife sunders the League of Non-Aligned Worlds. Television tie-in set before the episode, "A Day in the Strife."

Other books you might like:
Jim Mortimore, *Clarke's Law*, 1996
S.M. Stirling, *Betrayals*, 1996
Lois Tilton, *Accusations*, 1995
John Vornholt, *Blood Oath*, 1995
John Vornholt, *Voices*, 1995

308

T.A. BARRON

The Ancient One
(New York: Philomel, 1992)

Story type: Fantasy (Time Travel; Young Adult)
Major character(s): Kate, Time Traveller, Teenager
Time period(s): 1990s; 15th century (1490s)
Locale(s): Cronon's Crater, Oregon

Summary: While helping her Great Aunt Melanie in her attempt to preserve a redwood forest from logging, Kate travels 500 years into the past where a magical race's battle against Gashra and the evil lizard people who wish to destroy the forest parallels the battle between environmentalists and loggers in Kate's time. Companion volume to *Heartlight*.

Other books you might like:
J. Alison James, *Sing for a Gentle Rain*, 1990
C.S. Lewis, *The Lion, the Witch, and the Wardrobe*, 1950
C.S. Lewis, *Prince Caspian*, 1951
C.S. Lewis, *The Voyage of the Dawn Treader*, 1952
J.R.R. Tolkien, *The Hobbit*, 1938

309

T.A. BARRON

The Lost Years of Merlin
(New York: Philomel, 1996)

Story type: Fantasy (Legend; Young Adult)
Major character(s): Emrys, Child, Psychic; Branwen, Step-Parent; Rhia, Child, Psychic
Time period(s): 6th century
Locale(s): Isle of Fincayra, Mythical Place

Summary: Washed ashore then raised by Branwen as her own, Emrys must leave home. He runs away to the Isle of Fincayra to discover his identity and magical abilities. On the enchanted isle, Emrys meets Rhia and finds his fate entwined with Fincayra's.

Other books you might like:
Mike Ashley, *The Merlin Chronicles*, 1995
    editor
Ann Curry, *The Book of Brendan*, 1990
T.H. White, *The Sword in the Stone*, 1939
Jane Yolen, *The Hobby*, 1996
Jane Yolen, *Passager*, 1996

310

T.A. BARRON

The Merlin Effect
(New York: Philomel, 1994)

Story type: Fantasy (Young Adult; Adventure)
Major character(s): Kate Gordon, Teenager, Adventurer; Geoffrey Bardsey, Religious (monk), Immortal; Nimue, Sorceress
Time period(s): 1990s; Indeterminate
Locale(s): Pacific Ocean; Baja California, Mexico

Summary: When Kate Gordon investigates a giant whirlpool, the current traps her kayak, pulling her into an undersea world. There she discovers Geoffrey Bardsey and the battle between the legendary wizard, Merlin, and his ancient enemy, Nimue.

Other books you might like:
Susan Cooper, *The Dark Is Rising*, 1973
Susan Cooper, *Greenwitch*, 1974
Susan Cooper, *The Grey King*, 1975
Ursula K. Le Guin, *A Wizard of Earthsea*, 1968
Madeleine L'Engle, *An Acceptable Time*, 1990

311

SCOTT IAN BARRY

The Streeter
(New York: Tor, 1994)

Story type: Horror (Nature in Revolt)
Major character(s): Adams Shaws, Guard (of the Amsterdam Starpark); Gilbert Becker, Administrator (Bureau of Animal Affairs); Andrew Stern, Professor (Chair, Psychology Dept. SUNY), Psychologist
Time period(s): 1990s (1994)
Locale(s): New York, New York (Queens)

Summary: Enraged by their ingestion of toxic chemicals at a nearby waste dump, a pack of homeless dogs known as "streeters" roam the grounds of the Amsterdam Starpark, mauling and eating those foolish enough to walk its grounds alone.

Other books you might like:
William Dantz, *Hunger*, 1992
David Dvorkin, *Ursus*, 1989
Ronald Kelly, *Pitfall*, 1990
T.J. Kirby, *Deadly Breed*, 1992
Dean R. Koontz, *Watchers*, 1987
Barry Porter, *Junkyard*, 1989
Whitley Strieber, *The Wolfen*, 1978

312

JOHN BARTH

The Last Voyage of Somebody the Sailor
(Boston: Little Brown, 1991)

Story type: Fantasy (Legend; Time Travel)
Major character(s): Simon William Behler, Journalist, Adventurer; Sinbad the Sailor, Businessman, Adventurer
Time period(s): 1980s (1980); Indeterminate Past
Locale(s): Baghdad, Middle East

Summary: While attempting to retrace the legendary voyages of Sinbad the Sailor, Simon Behler is lost at sea. He survives and eventually finds himself in ancient Baghdad and even in Sinbad's own house where Sinbad is involved in raising venture capital for his forthcoming seventh voyage. Simon challenges Sinbad to a storytelling marathon hoping to discover a solution to his plight and a way home to his own time.

Other books you might like:
Richard F. Burton, *The Book of the Thousand Nights and a Night. A Plain and Literal Translation of the Arabian Nights Entertainments*, 1885-1886
10 volumes
Patricia Daniels, *Sinbad the Sailor*, 1980
Craig Shaw Gardner, *The Other Sinbad*, 1991
Stephen Goldin, *Shrine of the Desert Mage*, 1988
Andrew Lang, *The Arabian Nights Entertainments*, 1969
editor
Jeanne Larsen, *Bronze Mirror*, 1991
Salman Rushdie, *Haroun and the Sea of Stories*, 1990
Susan Shwartz, *Arabesques: More Tales of the Arabian Nights*, 1988
editor
Susan Shwartz, *Arabesques II*, 1989
editor
Paul B. Thompson, *Red Sands*, 1988
Tonya R. Carter, co-author
Jack Zipes, *Arabian Nights: The Marvels and Wonders of the Thousand and One Nights*, 1991
(editor)

313

DONALD BARTHELME

The King
(New York: Harper and Row, 1990)

Story type: Fantasy (Legend; Humor)
Major character(s): Arthur, Royalty (King); Guinevere, Royalty (Queen); Launcelot, Knight
Time period(s): 1940s
Locale(s): England

Summary: This Retelling of Le Morte d'Arthur occurs during world War II. Arthur, Guinevere and Launcelot's classic triangle evolves while the Knights of the Round Table struggle to fit into the war effort and Mordred plots to take over the government. This novel was published posthumously.

Other books you might like:
Steven Brust, *The Sun, the Moon, and the Stars*, 1987
Kara Dalkey, *The Nightingale*, 1988
Pamela Dean, *Tam Lin*, 1991
Charles de Lint, *Jack, the Giant-Killer*, 1987
Patricia C. Wrede, *Snow White and Rose Red*, 1989

314

DAN BARTON

Relife
(New York: Pocket, 1991)

Story type: Horror (Mystery)
Major character(s): Thomas F. Maxwell, Lawyer; Maureen Maxwell, Real Estate Agent, Spouse (Thomas's wife); Scott Maxwell, Addict (Thomas's son)
Time period(s): 1990s
Locale(s): Los Angeles, California

Summary: Suffering from amnesia after a severe car accident, Tom Maxwell begins trying to put the pieces of his broken life back together, starting with a reconciliation with his estranged family. When he discovers he never sustained the serious injuries he was presumed to have suffered, he finds himself in a race against time to find out who he really is and why his caretakers have lied to him before he is overwhelmed by the excessive aging of different parts of his body.

Other books you might like:
David Ely, *Seconds*, 1963
Ken Grimwood, *Replay*, 1986
Dean R. Koontz, *Hideaway*, 1992
Dean R. Koontz, *The House of Thunder*, 1982

315

WILLIAM BARTON

Dark Sky Legion

(New York: Bantam Spectra, 1992)

Story type: Science Fiction (Political; Space Opera)
Major character(s): Maaron Denturian, Immortal, Government Official (Televox); Odin, Artificial Intelligence (*Naglfar*); Sessiri-wohnith, Alien (Hoda)
Time period(s): Indeterminate Future
Locale(s): Olam, Planet—Imaginary; Earth; *Naglfar*, Spaceship

Summary: Using matter transmitters, humans were dispersed from Earth, many sent unwillingly by Cpaht during the Red Millennium. After more than forty thousand years the Metastable Order maintains human society by sending out duplicates of its Senators who reincarnate when they arrive at a planet. Maaron Denturian arrives at Olam finding his long experience and extraordinary powers as a Televox of the Metastable Order necessary to meet the challenge to his beliefs and purpose.

Other books you might like:
Roger MacBride Allen, *The Ring of Charon*, 1990
John Brunner, *The World Swappers*, 1959
Octavia E. Butler, *Dawn*, 1987
Timothy A. Madden, *Outbanker*, 1990
Robert Silverberg, *Recalled to Life*, 1962
Sheri S. Tepper, *Sideshow*, 1992
A.E. van Vogt, *The World of Null-A*, 1948
David Weber, *Mutineers' Moon*, 1991

316

WILLIAM BARTON
MICHAEL CAPOBIANCO, Co-Author

Fellow Traveller

(New York: Bantam Spectra, 1991)

Story type: Science Fiction (Techno-Thriller)
Major character(s): Mikhail Sergeevich Gorbachev, Political Figure, Historical Figure; Vladimir ''Volodya'' Alekseevich Manarov, Astronaut; Miroslav Ilyich Bronstein, Astronaut
Time period(s): 1990s; 21st century (2000-2017)

Locale(s): Earth; Asteroid (the asteroid belt)

Summary: The Soviets have embarked on a bold gamble to regain world leadership and ensure economic prosperity by trying to move an asteroid into Earth orbit to harvest its ores for industry. The more reactionary elements in the United States see the project as a potential weapon and are willing to risk the destruction of life on Earth to stop the Soviets.

Other books you might like:
Michael Capobianco, *Burster*, 1990
Arthur C. Clarke, *Rendezvous with Rama*, 1973
Gordon R. Dickson, *The Far Call*, 1978
Robert A. Heinlein, *Farmer in the Sky*, 1950
Dean McLaughlin, *The Man Who Wanted Stars*, 1965
Carl Sagan, *Contact*, 1985

317

WILLIAM BARTON
MICHAEL CAPOBIANCO, Co-Author

Iris

(New York: Doubleday Foundation, 1990)

Story type: Science Fiction (Hard Science Fiction)
Major character(s): Brendan Sealock, Engineer, Scientist; Demogorgon, Computer Expert
Time period(s): 21st century (2097)
Locale(s): *Deepstar*, Spaceship; Ocypete, Moon—Imaginary (Moon of the planet Iris)

Summary: Iris, a wandering planet, enters the solar system and is visited by an oddball group of artists, scientists and computer hackers who pass near it while on their way to colonize Triton. They discover an alien artifact. Meanwhile the backgrounds and the complex interactions of the members of the exploration team are examined in detail.

Other books you might like:
Greg Bear, *Eon*, 1985
Greg Bear, *Eternity*, 1988
Gregory Benford, *Heart of the Comet*, 1986
    David Brin, co-author
Arthur C. Clarke, *Rendezvous with Rama*, 1973
Arthur C. Clarke, *2001: A Space Odyssey*, 1968
Arthur C. Clarke, *2010: Odyssey Two*, 1982
Arthur C. Clarke, *2061: Odyssey Three*, 1987

318

WILLIAM BARTON

The Transmigration of Souls

(New York: Warner Aspect, 1996)

Story type: Science Fiction (First Contact; Alternate Universe)
Major character(s): Astrid Kincaid, Military Personnel, Space Explorer; Ahmad Zeq, Space Explorer; Ling Erhsham, Space Explorer
Time period(s): Indeterminate Future
Locale(s): Moon (Earth's); Outer Space; Alternate Universe

Summary: While Fortress America pursues a policy of extreme isolation, Chinese and Arab astronauts, followed by American soldiers, explore an ancient alien artifact whose ability to access alternate realities may annihilate the known universe.

Other books you might like:
Roger MacBride Allen, *The Ring of Charon*, 1990
Roger MacBride Allen, *The Shattered Sphere*, 1994
Greg Bear, *Eon*, 1985
David Brin, *Earth*, 1990
Vernor Vinge, *A Fire upon the Deep*, 1992
David Weber, *Mutineers' Moon*, 1991
George Zebrowski, *Stranger Suns*, 1991

319

WILLIAM BARTON

When Heaven Fell

(New York: Warner Aspect, 1995)

Story type: Science Fiction (Invasion of Earth; Military)
Major character(s): Athol Morrison, Mercenary; Alexandra "Alix" Moreno, Companion, Traveller
Time period(s): 22nd century
Locale(s): Earth; Planet—Imaginary

Summary: Having served the Masters with distinction, Athol returns for a visit to a vanquished Earth, now repopulated with numerous extraterrestrial races and a development nexus for the Masters' new frontier. Athol reacquaints himself with family and friends and tours Earth, finding general subjugation with only small pockets of resistance to the fate of humanity.

Other books you might like:
Roger MacBride Allen, *The Shattered Sphere*, 1994
Octavia E. Butler, *Dawn*, 1987
David Gerrold, *A Matter for Men*, 1989
  revised edition
Robert A. Heinlein, *The Puppet Masters*, 1991
  revised edition
Anne McCaffrey, *Freedom's Landing*, 1995
Tim Sullivan, *The Parasite War*, 1989

320

GRAEME BASE

The Discovery of Dragons

(New York: Abrams, 1996)

Story type: Fantasy (Collection; Legend)
Major character(s): Bjorn of Bromme, Warrior (Viking), Adventurer; Soong Mei Ying, Traveller, Adventurer; E.F. Libermann, Cartographer, Scientist (amphibiologist)
Time period(s): 9th century; 13th century
Locale(s): Europe; Asia; Africa

Summary: Through letters, Bjorn of Bromme, Soong Mei Ying and E.F. Libermann relate discoveries of many different types of dragons they encounter as they travel through three continents. Lavishly illustrated.

Other books you might like:
James C. Christensen, *Voyage of the Basset*, 1996
  Renwick St. James, Alan Dean Foster, co-authors
James Gurney, *Dinotopia*, 1992

James Gurney, *The World Beneath*, 1995
Michael Hague, *The Book of Dragons*, 1995
  editor
Terry Jones, *The Goblin Companion*, 1996
  Brian Froud, co-author

321

DON BASSINGTHWAITE
NANCY KILPATRICK, Co-Author

As One Dead

(Clarkston, Georgia: White Wolf, 1996)

Story type: Horror (Vampire Story)
Series: Vampire: The Masquerade
Major character(s): Bianka, Vampire; Lot, Vampire; DeWinter, Vampire
Time period(s): 1990s (1996)
Locale(s): Toronto, Ontario, Canada

Summary: Bianka, the hybrid offspring of two vampire clans, hopes to lead the restrained Apollonian members of the Camarilla sect in revolt against the Dionysian Sabbat vampires, who have restricted the Camarilla to living in a small Toronto ghetto called The Box. This novel is set in the publisher's "Vampire: The Masquerade" gaming world, in which vampire clans are enjoined by the law of their species to mingle unobtrusively with mortals and keep their supernatural identities secret.

Other books you might like:
Nancy A. Collins, *A Dozen Black Roses*, 1996
Brian Herbert, *Blood on the Sun*, 1996
  Marie Landis, co-author
Robert Weinberg, *Bloodwar*, 1995
Robert Weinberg, *The Unbeholden*, 1996
Robert Weinberg, *Unholy Allies*, 1995
Robert Weinberg, *Vampire Diary: The Embrace*, 1995
  Mark Rein-Hagen, co-author

322

JOHN CALVIN BATCHELOR

Peter Nevsky and the True Story of the Russian Moon Landing

(New York: Henry Holt, 1993)

Story type: Science Fiction (Political; Alternate Universe)
Major character(s): Peter Nevsky, Orphan, Spaceman; Alexander Oryolin, Spaceman, Hero; Dmitry Zhukovsky, Spaceman, Hero
Time period(s): 1960s (1968-1969)
Locale(s): Starry Town, Union of Soviet Socialist Republics (manned space center); Moscow, Russia

Summary: Arriving at Starry Town ready to begin cosmonaut training, Peter Nevsky becomes embroiled in the intrigues of his heroes, three World War II flying aces, now the core of the Russian space program which aims at a Soviet Moon landing at the time of *Apollo 11*. Related as memoirs of an aged Nevsky.

Other books you might like:
William Barton, *Fellow Traveller*, 1991
　　Michael Capobianco, co-author
Gordon R. Dickson, *The Far Call*, 1978
Edward Gibson, *Reach*, 1989
Dan Simmons, *Phases of Gravity*, 1989
Norman Spinrad, *Russian Spring*, 1991

323

GAEL BAUDINO

Branch and Crown
(New York: Roc, 1996)

Story type: Fantasy (Religious; Historical)
Series: Water
Major character(s): Obadiah Jenkins, Religious, Diplomat; Sari, Traveller (pilgrim), Healer (herbalist)
Time period(s): Indeterminate
Locale(s): The Three Kingdoms, Fictional Country; Great Library of Kanez, Fictional City

Summary: The story of the diplomats from the Righteous States of America comes to a close. The Great Library stores much information which shed, disturbing light on the origins of the religions of the Three Kingdoms.

Other books you might like:
James P. Blaylock, *The Paper Grail*, 1991
Jack Cady, *The Off Season*, 1995
Orson Scott Card, *Seventh Son*, 1987
Barbara Hambly, *The Witches of Wenshar*, 1987
Rachel Pollack, *Temporary Agency*, 1994

324

GAEL BAUDINO

Dragon Death
(New York: Roc, 1992)

Story type: Fantasy (Magic Conflict)
Series: Dragonsword
Major character(s): Suzanne "Alouzon" Helling, Student, Guardian; Silbakor, Mythical Creature (dragon); Helen "Kyria" Addams, Sorceress
Time period(s): 1990s
Locale(s): Los Angeles, California; Gryylth, Fictional Country

Summary: Alouzon struggles to defeat the enemy which followed her to Los Angeles then returns to Gryylth to overcome the treacherous subversion of a young sorcerer and prevent the war which threatens to lay waste to Gryylth.

Other books you might like:
Kevin J. Anderson, *Gamearth*, 1989
Nick Pollotta, *Bureau 13*, 1991
Mickey Zucker Reichert, *By Chaos Cursed*, 1991
Mickey Zucker Reichert, *Godslayer*, 1987

325

GAEL BAUDINO

Duel of Dragons
(New York: Roc, 1991)

Story type: Fantasy (Alternate World)
Series: Dragonsword
Major character(s): Suzanne "Alouzon" Helling, Student, Guardian; Helen "Kyria" Addams, Scholar, Sorceress; Silbakor, Mythical Creature (dragon)
Time period(s): 1990s; Indeterminate Past (equivalent-5th century)
Locale(s): Los Angeles, California; Gryylth, Fictional Country; Vaylle, Fictional Country

Summary: When Silbakor transports Suzanne and Helen, now Alouzon and Kyria, to Gryylth, they find that the land created by a now-dead medieval history professor, Helen's ex-husband, is being laid waste by 20th century weapons and supernatural creatures. Silbakor must battle the White Worm while Kyria must hold weapons, creatures and Helen's bitterness at bay. Alouzon finds that her own creation, Vaylle, is similarly beset, the devastation arising from her own memories of the Vietnam War era.

Other books you might like:
Kevin J. Anderson, *Gamearth*, 1989
Pamela Dean, *Tam Lin*, 1991
Tom Deitz, *Windmaster's Bane*, 1986
Barbara Hambly, *The Time of the Dark*, 1982
Guy Gavriel Kay, *The Summer Tree*, 1985
Mickey Zucker Reichert, *Godslayer*, 1987
Joel Rosenberg, *The Sleeping Dragon*, 1983

326

GAEL BAUDINO

Gossamer Axe
(New York: Roc, 1990)

Story type: Fantasy (Time Travel; Romance)
Major character(s): Christa Cruitaire, Teacher (Harp), Musician; Melinda Moore, Musician; Monica Sanchez, Musician
Time period(s): 20th century
Locale(s): Denver, Colorado

Summary: Separated from her lover by hundreds of years, the Celtic bard Chairiste Ni Cummen, now known as Christa Cruitaire, must find a way to rescue Siudb from both the Sidh's endless twilight and the royal bard, Orfide. When Christa finds that rock music can be used to free her lover, she forms an all-girl rock band with which to challenge the power of the gods.

Other books you might like:
Isaac Asimov, *Foundation and Empire*, 1952
Steven Brust, *Cowboy Feng's Space Bar and Grille*, 1990
Emma Bull, *War for the Oaks*, 1987
Patricia Kennealy, *The Silver Branch*, 1988
Patricia Kennealy, *The Throne of Scone*, 1986
Patricia Kennealy, *The Copper Crown*, 1984

Mercedes Lackey, *Knight of Ghosts and Shadows*, 1990
  Ellen Guon, co-author

327

GAEL BAUDINO

Maze of Moonlight

(New York: Roc, 1993)

Story type: Fantasy (Historical; Romance)
Major character(s): Christopher delAurvre, Nobleman (Baron of Aurverelle); Vanessa, Mythical Creature (elf); Natil, Mythical Creature (elf), Minstrel
Time period(s): 14th century (1399-1400)
Locale(s): Adria, Fictional Country

Summary: Three years after the crushing defeat of the Christian armies by the Turks at Nicopolis, Christopher, emaciated, ragged and apparently insane, finally reaches his castle. After months of reclusiveness, he rescues Vanessa, a peasant girl with unusual abilities inherited from her half-elf father. Christopher learns that elves still share the world with humans and that he must accept their help as he attempts to unite the squabbling barons of Adria and repel invading mercenary armies.

Other books you might like:
Emma Bull, *War for the Oaks*, 1987
C.J. Cherryh, *The Dreamstone*, 1983
C.J. Cherryh, *Rusalka*, 1989
Gordon R. Dickson, *The Dragon Knight*, 1990
Barbara Hambly, *The Silent Tower*, 1986
Katherine Kurtz, *Deryni Rising*, 1970
Elizabeth Marie Pope, *The Perilous Gard*, 1974
Elizabeth Ann Scarborough, *Phantom Banjo*, 1991
Elizabeth Ann Scarborough, *Song of Sorcery*, 1982
Barbara W. Tuchman, *A Distant Mirror*, 1978
  non-fiction
Patricia C. Wrede, *Shadow Magic*, 1982

328

GAEL BAUDINO

O Greenest Branch!

(New York: Roc, 1995)

Story type: Fantasy (Historical; Religious)
Series: Water
Major character(s): Sari, Abuse Victim (spousal), Traveller (pilgrim); Aeid, Royalty (crown prince), Adventurer; Obadiah Jenkins, Religious (minister), Diplomat (ambassador)
Time period(s): Indeterminate
Locale(s): The Three Kingdoms, Fictional Country; Africa; Nuhr, Fictional City

Summary: The Reverend Ambassador Jenkins and his diplomatic entourage from the Righteous States of America seem unable to convince Kin Inwa Kabir and his ministers that they have anything to offer the drought-ridden lands of the Three Kingdoms. Desperate for change, Crown Prince Aeid tries to steer his father away from his fanatically religious court and

toward negotiations with the strangers who want to station troops there to halt French conquest of northern Africa. Meanwhile, Sari, an old woman who has finally rid herself of her abusive husband, makes a pilgrimage back to the land of her youth to atone for her abandonment of her goddess and start a new life.

Other books you might like:
Maya Kaathryn Bohnhoff, *The Meri*, 1992
Octavia E. Butler, *Wild Seed*, 1980
Orson Scott Card, *Red Prophet*, 1988
Orson Scott Card, *Seventh Son*, 1987
Barbara Hambly, *The Witches of Wenshar*, 1987
Simon Hawke, *The Seeker*, 1994
Rosemary Kirstein, *The Steerswoman*, 1989
Paul O. Williams, *The Breaking of Northwall*, 1981
Paul O. Williams, *The Ends of the Circle*, 1981

329

GAEL BAUDINO

Strands of Sunlight

(New York: Roc, 1994)

Story type: Fantasy (Urban; Religious)
Series: Strands of Starlight
Major character(s): Natil Summerson, Mythical Creature (elf), Immortal; Sandy "Sana" Joy, Musician (harpist), Psychic (healer); Theodore "TK" Karlington Winters, Veteran, Mythical Creature (elf)
Time period(s): 1990s (1991-1992)
Locale(s): Denver, Colorado; Elvenhome, Colorado

Summary: As sole surviving Firstborn Elf, Natil strives to guide her friends through their changes into Elves bound to compassionately aid humanity. Sana uses her harp to focus healing energies while TK battles against drug dealers in the neighborhood after meeting the Elves of Denver who seek to reestablish connection to the Creatrix. Third in series.

Other books you might like:
Maya Kaathryn Bohnhoff, *The Meri*, 1992
Maya Kaathryn Bohnhoff, *Taminy*, 1993
Mercedes Lackey, *Knight of Ghosts and Shadows*, 1990
Mercedes Lackey, *When the Bough Breaks*, 1993
  Holly Lisle, co-author
Susan Palwick, *Flying in Place*, 1992
Will Shetterly, *Elsewhere*, 1991

330

STEPHEN BAXTER

Anti-Ice

(New York: HarperPrism, 1994)

Story type: Science Fiction (Techno-Thriller; Alternate Universe)
Major character(s): Josiah Traveller, Inventor, Engineer; Ned Vicars, Adventurer, Diplomat
Time period(s): 1870s (1870)
Locale(s): Manchester, England; *Phaeton*, Spaceship

Summary: Ned learns about the horrors of Anti-Ice (naturally occurring anti-matter) from his brother's experience in the Crimean War where Professor Traveller used some to construct a fearsome bomb. The Professor must invent as many peaceful uses for Anti-Ice as possible to prevent the limited resource from being used in superior explosive weapons.

Other books you might like:
William Gibson, *The Difference Engine*, 1991
  Bruce Sterling, co-author
Joe Haldeman, *The Forever War*, 1975
Robert J. Sawyer, *Far-Seer*, 1992
Jules Verne, *Twenty Thousand Leagues under the Sea*, 1870
Jules Verne, *From the Earth to the Moon*, 1874

331

STEPHEN BAXTER

Flux

(New York: HarperPrism, 1995)

Story type: Science Fiction (Hard Science Fiction; Political)
Major character(s): Dura, Genetically Altered Being, Settler (Human Being); Hork, Genetically Altered Being, Government Official; Adda, Genetically Altered Being, Patient
Time period(s): Indeterminate Future
Locale(s): The Star, Outer Space (neutron star); Parz City, Fictional City

Summary: As a neutron star's rotation slows, glitches occur more frequently, endangering the environment. The Human Beings living in the mantle of the star remember technology from before the War with the colonists. Dura, her brother Farr, and the elderly, critically wounded Adda find medical help in Parz City, anchored at the pole. Unfortunately, the residents of Parz City no longer possess any knowledge of the ancient technology, forcing them to retain the help of Human Beings, before the glitches destroy everything.

Other books you might like:
Greg Bear, *Eon*, 1985
Gregory Benford, *Furious Gulf*, 1994
James Blish, *The Seedling Stars*, 1956
Megan Lindholm, *Alien Earth*, 1992
Roger Zelazny, *Flare*, 1992
  Thomas T. Thomas, co-author

332

STEPHEN BAXTER

Raft

(New York: Roc, 1992)

Story type: Science Fiction (Space Colony; Hard Science Fiction)
Major character(s): Rees, Teenager, Scientist; Sheen, Miner; Pallas, Pilot
Time period(s): Indeterminate Future
Locale(s): Outer Space

Summary: A ship had been caught in a Bolder Ring, a gateway to another universe, and disabled. 500 years after it reached the universe, the descendants of the crew were divided by the lack of essential supplies. The universe in which they found themselves had a force of gravity a billion times stronger than Earth's and the nebula in which humans had been living since their arrival was collapsing in on itself. Rees, unhappy as a miner, stows away on a tree-ship to the Raft where he begins to get enough education to believe a solution to the ultimate death of the colony could be discovered. This is the author's first novel.

Other books you might like:
Roger MacBride Allen, *The Ring of Charon*, 1990
James Blish, *They Shall Have Stars*, 1957
David Brin, *Sundiver*, 1979
Hal Clement, *Mission of Gravity*, 1978
Robert L. Forward, *Dragon's Egg*, 1980
Robert L. Forward, *Starquake*, 1985
Larry Niven, *The Integral Trees*, 1984
Vernor Vinge, *Marooned in Realtime*, 1986

333

STEPHEN BAXTER

Ring

(New York: HarperPrism, 1996)

Story type: Science Fiction (Hard Science Fiction; Post-Holocaust)
Series: Xeelee
Major character(s): Lieserl, Human, Experimental Subject; Louise Ye Armonk, Engineer (starship designer), Leader; Spinner-of-Rope, Pilot, Space Explorer
Time period(s): 22nd century; Indeterminate Future (50,000th century)
Locale(s): Earth; *Great Northern*, Spaceship (starship); Outer Space

Summary: When Lieserl plunges into the heart of the sun, she discovers an instability that will destroy it within ten thousand years. Hired in a desperate attempt to save the human race after finding the rest of the universe slowly succumbing to the same fate, Louise and her crew agree to take the *Great Northern* through a wormhole into the distant future seeking an immense alien artifact which may hold the key to their survival. Author's brief note details the Xeelee sequence chronology and bibliography.

Other books you might like:
Roger MacBride Allen, *The Ring of Charon*, 1990
Greg Bear, *The Forge of God*, 1987
Gregory Benford, *Far Futures*, 1995
  editor
James Blish, *Cities in Flight*, 1970
Arthur C. Clarke, *Childhood's End*, 1953
John E. Stith, *Redshift Rendezvous*, 1990
Vernor Vinge, *A Fire upon the Deep*, 1992

334

STEPHEN BAXTER

The Time Ships

(New York: HarperPrism, 1996)

Story type: Science Fiction (Time Travel; Alternate History)
Major character(s): The Writer, Writer, Time Traveller; Nebogipfel, Mutant (Morlock), Time Traveller; Weena, Mutant (Eloi), Young Woman
Time period(s): Indeterminate Past; Indeterminate Future
Locale(s): Richmond, England; The Sphere, Underground Environment; Palace of Green Porcelain, Mythical Place

Summary: Consumed with guilt over abandoning Weena to a grisly death at the hands of the Morlocks, the Writer resolves to return to A.D. 802,701 and attempt to rescue her. Stopping short of his goal, however, he realizes that his first journey through time drastically changed history, with horrifying results. Accidently joining forces with Nebogipfel, a Morlock scientist, they journey from the beginning to the end of time searching for the key to their own history. Sequel to H.G. Wells' *The Time Machine*.

Other books you might like:
Greg Bear, *Eon*, 1985
Paul Di Filippo, *The Steampunk Trilogy*, 1995
Gordon R. Dickson, *Time Storm*, 1977
R. Garcia y Robertson, *The Virgin and the Dinosaur*, 1996
K.W. Jeter, *Morlock Night*, 1979
Alex McDonough, *Scorpio*, 1990
H.G. Wells, *The Time Machine*, 1895

335

STEPHEN BAXTER

Timelike Infinity

(New York: Roc, 1993)

Story type: Science Fiction (Hard Science Fiction)
Series: Xeelee
Major character(s): Jasoft Parz, Diplomat, Time Traveller; Michael Poole, Scientist; Shira, Time Traveller, Revolutionary (Friends of Wigner)
Time period(s): Indeterminate Future
Locale(s): *Hermit Crab*, Spaceship; *The Spline*, Spaceship (Qax)

Summary: Michael Poole leaves the Oort Cloud where he studies quark nuggets, to rescue a member of the team who returns through the time portal Michael helped develop. When he finds her on the Friends of Wigner's Earthship orbiting Jupiter, he learns that 1500 years in the future, the Qax control the solar system, forbidding longevity treatment. However, the Friends' hidden agenda prevents them from contacting humanity or warning of the impending Qax invasion.

Other books you might like:
James Blish, *The Triumph of Time*, 1958
David Brin, *Startide Rising*, 1983
Octavia E. Butler, *Dawn*, 1987
Robert L. Forward, *Starquake*, 1985
Robert L. Forward, *Timemaster*, 1992
Megan Lindholm, *Alien Earth*, 1992
Vonda N. McIntyre, *Metaphase*, 1992
Dan Simmons, *The Fall of Hyperion*, 1990
Dan Simmons, *Hyperion*, 1989

336

PETER S. BEAGLE

The Folk of the Air

(New York: Del Rey, 1988)

Story type: Fantasy (Magic Conflict)
Major character(s): Farrell, Hippie (Medieval Anachronist)
Time period(s): 1980s
Locale(s): Earth

Summary: Farrell helps fight an evil man called out of his own time by a witch.

Other books you might like:
Adrienne Martine-Barnes, *The Rainbow Sword*, 1988

337

PETER S. BEAGLE

The Innkeeper's Song

(New York: Roc, 1993)

Story type: Fantasy (Quest; Literary)
Major character(s): ''Lal'' Lalkhamsin-Khamsolal, Sailor; Nyateneri, Religious, Fugitive; Karsh, Innkeeper
Time period(s): Indeterminate Past
Locale(s): Corcorva, Fictional City

Summary: Three women, all unusual, all marked by their pasts and secrets, meet on the road. At an inn, they reveal some secrets as they plot to rescue a wizard to whom each owes a debt. Several additional characters add their voices to this quilted novel where everyone gains insight while the world threatens to crash down around them.

Other books you might like:
Eleanor Arnason, *The Sword Smith*, 1978
John M. Ford, *Casting Fortune*, 1989
Barry Hughart, *Bridge of Birds*, 1984
Ellen Kushner, *Swordspoint*, 1987
Patricia A. McKillip, *The Riddle-Master of Hed*, 1976

338

PETER S. BEAGLE, Editor
JANET BERLINER, Co-Editor

Peter S. Beagle's Immortal Unicorn

(New York: HarperPrism, 1995)

Story type: Fantasy (Anthology; Legend)
Summary: Contains a two-page preface, a five-page foreword, and 27 original stories with individual introductions by both editors and a brief biography of each author. The tone varies from dark to humorous with themes involving unicorns in diverse settings. Authors include the editors and Edward Bry-

ant, Charles de Lint, Karen Joy Fowler, Ellen Kushner, Eric Lustbader, Lisa Mason, Elizabeth Ann Scarborough, Robert Sheckley, Will Shetterly, Susan Shwartz, Dave Smeds, S.P. Smotow, Judith Tarr, Melanie Tem, Nancy Willard, Tad Williams, and Dave Wolverton.

Other books you might like:

David Copperfield, *David Copperfield's Tales of the Impossible*, 1995
  Janet Berliner, co-editor
Bruce Coville, *The Unicorn Treasury*, 1988
  editor
Jack Dann, *Unicorns!*, 1982
  Gardner Dozois, co-editor
Jack Dann, *Unicorns II*, 1992
  Gardner Dozois, co-editor
Pamela Dean, *The Secret Country*, 1985
Jane Yolen, *Here There Be Unicorns*, 1994

339

PETER S. BEAGLE

The Unicorn Sonata

(Atlanta: Turner Publishing, 1996)

Story type: Fantasy (Alternate World; Young Adult)
Major character(s): Josephine ''Joey'' Rivera, Musician, Teenager; Indigo, Musician, Teenager; Touriq, Mythical Creature (unicorn)
Time period(s): 1990s; Indeterminate
Locale(s): Los Angeles, California; Shei'rah, Alternate Earth

Summary: Joey follows Indigo's haunting music through the mobile border to the land of Shei'rah, populated by unicorns, satyrs, water nymphs, dragons, and phoenixes. Travelling back and forth to Shei'rah, Joey may prove the key to reversing the affliction blinding elderly unicorns.

Other books you might like:

Bruce Coville, *The Unicorn Treasury*, 1988
  editor
Jack Dann, *Unicorns!*, 1982
  Gardner Dozois, co-editor
Jack Dann, *Unicorns II*, 1992
  Gardner Dozois, co-editor
Pamela Dean, *The Secret Country*, 1985
Jane Yolen, *Here There Be Unicorns*, 1994

340

GREG BEAR

Anvil of Stars

(New York: Warner Questar, 1992)

Story type: Science Fiction (First Contact; Hard Science Fiction)
Major character(s): Martin ''Marty'' Gordon, Leader (Pan of the Watch), Spaceman; Ariel Hawthorn, Spaceman; Eye on Sky, Alien, Spaceman
Time period(s): 23rd century
Locale(s): *Dawn Trader*, Spaceship (Ship of Law); Buttercup Star System, Outer Space

Summary: After killer machines wipe out the Earth, surviving humans find out from their saviors that galactic civilization now expects the remaining humans to follow the Law, a galactic code, and wipe out the race which attacked humanity. A small group of humans set out in a wondrous spaceship to carry out the mission of revenge. When they find a civilization which may be the source of the killer technology, the humans must face the difficult questions surrounding their fitness to judge the aliens and propriety of the human destruction of those intelligent beings. Sequel to *The Forge of God*.

Other books you might like:

David Brin, *Earth*, 1990
Orson Scott Card, *Ender's Game*, 1985
Larry Niven, *Footfall*, 1985
  Jerry Pournelle, co-author
Dan Simmons, *The Fall of Hyperion*, 1990
Dan Simmons, *Hyperion*, 1989
Vernor Vinge, *A Fire upon the Deep*, 1992

341

GREG BEAR

Bear's Fantasies

(Newark, New Jersey: The Wildside Press, 1992)

Story type: Fantasy (Collection)

Summary: Published by the Philadelphia Science Fiction Society, this book contains a two-page introduction with five stories first published in periodicals and anthologies 1973-1985 plus one, ''Sleepside Story,'' first appearing in a 1988 limited edition from Cheap Street Press. Some stories share a dark tone surrounding themes of religion or crime while others present traditional themes as in ''Webster,'' in which a dictionary helps a woman focus her thoughts into powerful magical tools, and ''Sleepside Story,'' in which a young man plans to rescue his mother from a witch/prostitute, but comes away from the situation with an unexpected inheritance.

Other books you might like:

Brian W. Aldiss, *A Romance of the Equator: The Best Fantasy Stories of Brian W. Aldiss*, 1990
David Brin, *The River of Time*, 1986
Orson Scott Card, *Maps in a Mirror*, 1990
Robert Holdstock, *The Bone Forest*, 1992
Kate Wilhelm, *And the Angels Sing*, 1992
Gene Wolfe, *Storeys From the Old Hotel*, 1992

342

GREG BEAR

Eon

(New York: Tor Books, 1989)

Story type: Science Fiction (Hard Science Fiction)
Major character(s): Judith Hoffman, Scientist; Garry Lanier, Engineer
Time period(s): 21st century
Locale(s): Thistledown, Asteroid

Summary: When an asteroid miraculously appears out of nowhere and enters Earth orbit, NASA, NATO, and the UN send explorers. They discover the stone is hollow and appears to have once been inhabited by human beings from our future, now all mysteriously vanished. Then an even more startling discovery is made. This precursor to *Eternity* was originally published in 1985.

Other books you might like:
Gregory Benford, *Great Sky River*, 1987
Gregory Benford, *Tides of Light*, 1989
Arthur C. Clarke, *Rendezvous with Rama*, 1973
Larry Niven, *Ringworld*, 1970
Larry Niven, *Ringworld Engineers*, 1980
Dan Simmons, *The Fall of Hyperion*, 1990
Dan Simmons, *Hyperion*, 1989

343
GREG BEAR

Heads
(New York: St. Martins Press, 1991)

Story type: Science Fiction (Political; Hard Science Fiction)
Major character(s): Mickey Sandoval, Researcher; Rho Sandoval, Businessman
Time period(s): 22nd century
Locale(s): Moon (Earth's)

Summary: When Mickey arranges to take possession of 410 cryogenically frozen heads, Rho and Mickey trigger a furor over removal of cultural and anthropological artifacts from their proper setting. They find themselves at the focus of an attempt by Logologists and religious activists to exert influence on Luna.

Other books you might like:
Pat Cadigan, *Mindplayers*, 1987
Pat Cadigan, *Synners*, 1991
Diana G. Gallagher, *The Alien Dark*, 1990
Robert A. Heinlein, *The Moon Is a Harsh Mistress*, 1966
Fritz Leiber, *The Silver Eggheads*, 1962
Rudy Rucker, *Wetware*, 1988
Robert Silverberg, *Recalled to Life*, 1962
Michael D. Weaver, *My Father Immortal*, 1989

344
GREG BEAR

Legacy
(New York: Tor, 1995)

Story type: Science Fiction (Lost Colony; First Contact)
Series: Eon
Major character(s): Olmy Ap Sennon, Adventurer (Hexamon agent), Sailor; Frederik Ry Ornis, Technician (gate opener); Able Lenk, Leader (Naderite)
Time period(s): Indeterminate Future
Locale(s): *Thistledown*, Spaceship; Lamarkia, Planet— Imaginary; *Vigilant*, At Sea

Summary: Young and bored, Olmy divorces his Naderite wife and volunteers for a mission to retrieve the missing key stolen by Lenk and observe the effect on Lamarkia, the protected planet on the Way colonized by Lenk and his followers.

Although seemingly diverse, life on Lamarkia remains simple, with few individuals stealing characteristics from each other to develop new forms, but without DNA, making the planet unsuitable for human beings. Unfortunately, Olmy cannot complete his mission and leave the planet until he finds the missing key, now on another continent. Prequel to *Eon*.

Other books you might like:
L. Warren Douglas, *Cannon's Orb*, 1994
Harry Harrison, *The Deathworld Trilogy*, 1976
Rosemary Kirstein, *The Outskirter's Secret*, 1992
Anne McCaffrey, *Freedom's Landing*, 1995
Charles Sheffield, *Godspeed*, 1993

345
GREG BEAR

Moving Mars
(New York: Tor, 1993)

Story type: Science Fiction (Hard Science Fiction; Political)
Major character(s): Casseia Majamdar, Political Figure; Charles Franklin, Scientist (theoretical physicist); Ti Sandra Erzul, Political Figure (first President of Mars)
Time period(s): 22nd century (2171-2184)
Locale(s): Earth; Mars

Summary: Casseia Majamdar, a young Martian with political ambitions, finds herself attracted to Charles Franklin, whose focused interest in unlocking the secrets of the universe leads to a breakthrough in theoretical physics. Alarmed factions on Earth threaten to subdue Mars by any means necessary, eventually relying on the harshest possible method and generating unexpected resistance.

Other books you might like:
Roger MacBride Allen, *The Ring of Charon*, 1990
Ben Bova, *Mars*, 1992
Arthur C. Clarke, *The Sands of Mars*, 1952
D.G. Compton, *Farewell, Earth's Bliss*, 1971
Gordon R. Dickson, *The Pritcher Mass*, 1972
Robert A. Heinlein, *Red Planet*, 1949
Eric Kotani, *Between the Stars*, 1988
    John Maddox Roberts, co-author
Frederik Pohl, *Mining the Oort*, 1992
Jerry Pournelle, *Birth of Fire*, 1976
Kim Stanley Robinson, *Red Mars*, 1992
Allen Steele, *Labyrinth of Night*, 1992
S.C. Sykes, *Red Genesis*, 1991

346
GREG BEAR, Editor
MARTIN H. GREENBERG, Co-Editor

New Legends
(New York: Tor, 1995)

Story type: Science Fiction (Anthology)
Summary: Contains a five-page general introduction, brief individual introductions, a one-page afterword, one article considering the influence of science fiction on the real world, Gregory Benford's ''Old Legends,'' and 15 original stories

having "great soul," with one story set on the world of *The Left Hand of Darkness* (1969), Ursula K. Le Guin's "Coming of Age in Karhide." Bear divides this volume into six sections, "Choices," "Growing Up," "Them and Us," "Win, Lose, or Draw," "Redemption," and "Cyphers," with themes which include genetic manipulation, hard science, time travel, and future society. Other authors include Poul Anderson, George Alec Effinger, Greg Egan, Geoffrey A. Landis, Paul J. McAuley, Mary Rosenblum, Robert Sheckley, and Robert Silverberg.

Other books you might like:

Isaac Asimov, *Isaac Asimov Presents the Great SF Stories*, 1979-1992
 Martin H. Greenberg, co-editor
Gardner Dozois, *Modern Classics of Science Fiction*, 1992
 editor
Martin H. Greenberg, *After the King: Stories in Honor of J.R.R. Tolkien*, 1992
 editor
David G. Hartwell, *The Ascent of Wonder: The Evolution of Hard SF*, 1994
 Kathryn Cramer, co-editor
Raymond J. Healy, *Adventures in Time and Space*, 1946
 J. Frances McComas, co-editor
Ursula K. Le Guin, *The Norton Book of Science Fiction: North American Science Fiction, 1960-1990*, 1993
 Brian Attebery, co-editor
Tom Shippey, *The Oxford Book of Science Fiction Stories*, 1992
 editor

347

GREG BEAR

Queen of Angels
(New York: Warner, 1990)

Story type: Science Fiction (Cyberpunk; Techno-Thriller)
Major character(s): Mary Choy, Police Officer; Richard Fettle, Writer (aspiring); Martin Burke, Psychologist
Time period(s): 21st century
Locale(s): Hispaniola, Caribbean; Los Angeles, California

Summary: Mary Choy, searching for a murderer, gets caught in international intrigue. While Richard Fettle tries to understand the murderer, Martin Burke tries to cure him, and all three try to keep him from a vigilante organization.

Other books you might like:

Gregory Benford, *Tides of Light*, 1989
Gregory Benford, *Great Sky River*, 1987
Dan Simmons, *The Fall of Hyperion*, 1990
Dan Simmons, *Hyperion*, 1989
Bruce Sterling, *Crystal Express*, 1989

348

GREG BEAR

Songs of Earth and Power
(New York: Tor, 1994)

Story type: Fantasy (Alternate World; Urban)
Major character(s): Michael Perrin, Adventurer; Eleuth, Mythical Creature (sidhe-human), Magician; Kristine Pendeers, Professor, Researcher
Time period(s): 1980s; Indeterminate
Locale(s): Los Angeles, California; Realm of the Sidhe, Mythical Place

Summary: This omnibus edition contains slightly rewritten versions of *The Infinity Concerto* (1984) and its sequel, *The Serpent Mage* (1986). When a magical song opens the way, Michael Perrin travels to the fairy realm where he finds himself involved in a struggle which could destroy the Earthly realm as well as the magical one. Returning to Los Angeles, Michael must research a powerful magical song to save the Earth.

Other books you might like:

Emma Bull, *Finder*, 1994
Emma Bull, *War for the Oaks*, 1987
Charles de Lint, *The Little Country*, 1991
Barbara Hambly, *The Silent Tower*, 1986
Elizabeth Ann Scarborough, *Phantom Banjo*, 1991

349

GREG BEAR

Tangents
(New York: Warner, 1989)

Story type: Science Fiction (Collection)

Summary: This collection of nine short stories and an article includes the original novelette, "Sisters," which has been nominated for the 1989 Nebula Award. Among the better reprint stories included are the award-winning "Tangents" and "Blood Music" (source of Bear's novel of that name), "Webster," "Dead Run," "Sleepside Story," and "Schroedinger's Plague."

Other books you might like:

Gregory Benford, *In Alien Flesh*, 1986
David Brin, *The River of Time*, 1986
Bruce Sterling, *Crystal Express*, 1989
Vernor Vinge, *Threats. . .and Other Promises*, 1988
Roger Zelazny, *Frost and Fire*, 1989

350

WARREN NEWTON BEATH

Bloodletter
(New York: Tor, 1994)

Story type: Horror (Serial Killer)
Major character(s): Steven Albright, Writer; Eva LaPorte, Doctor (psychiatrist); Diver Dan, Serial Killer
Time period(s): 1990s (1994)

Locale(s): Hollywood, California

Summary: Against the backdrop of Hollywood, where nothing is as it seems, Steven Albright, author of the popular Bloodletter vampire novels now being adapted to the screen, becomes convinced that his fictional character is real and out to destroy him. Ultimately, Albright's delusion is shared by his psychiatrist, who becomes romantically involved with him, and "Diver Dan," an obsessive fan of the Bloodletter series who is compelled to commit murders at the bidding of his vampire master.

Other books you might like:
Robert Bloch, *Psycho II*, 1992
Stephen King, *The Dark Half*, 1990
Richard Christian Matheson, *Created By*, 1993
David J. Schow, *The Kill Riff*, 1988

351
WARREN NEWTON BEATH

Shock Lines
(New York: Zebra, 1993)

Story type: Horror (Ancient Evil Unleashed)
Major character(s): Philip Strayhorn, Teacher (high school); Regina Dentata, Teenager; Leslie Strayhorn, Spouse (Philip's wife)
Time period(s): 1990s (1993)
Locale(s): Oildorado, California

Summary: Earthquake activity along the San Andreas fault releases the Trickster, an evil spirit of Indian lore who incarnates itself as a teenage girl to bring misery to the people of a small oil town in California.

Other books you might like:
Chris Curry, *Trickster*, 1993
    Lisa Dean, co-author
G. Wayne Miller, *Thunder Rise*, 1988
Kathryn Ptacek, *Ghost Dance*, 1990
Patrick Whalen, *Deathwalker*, 1993
Chet Williamson, *Dreamthorp*, 1989

352
WARREN NEWTON BEATH

Who Killed James Dean?
(New York: Tor, 1995)

Story type: Horror (Occult)
Major character(s): Lou Ehlers, Student (of comparative religions); Cleveland Carroll Devereaux, Writer (biographer); Cherie Lowe, Young Woman (James Dean fan)
Time period(s): 1990s (1995); 1950s (1955)
Locale(s): Westwood, California

Summary: While studying the cult-like nature of the fans of the deceased movie star James Dean, comparative religions scholar Lou Ehlers discovers that Dean's untimely death may have been a consequence of the actor's dabblings in the occult. As the fortieth anniversary of Dean's death approaches, Ehlers, who bears a physical resemblance to the actor, gets the uneasy feeling that he has been chosen to play a part in a ritual re-enactment of the actor's death to help resurrect him.

Other books you might like:
Clive Barker, *Sex, Death and Starshine*, 1984
    in *Books of Blood 1*
David Darke, *Horrorshow*, 1994
Norman Partridge, *Spyder*, 1995
Theodore Roszak, *Flicker*, 1993

353
CHARLES BEAUMONT

The Howling Man
(New York: Tor, 1992)

Story type: Horror (Collection)

Summary: Originally published in 1988 under the title *Charles Beaumont: Selected Stories*, this collection of 29 tales (one in collaboration with Chad Oliver; five never before published) and an excerpt from the 1959 novel, *The Intruder*, written by the second most prolific writer for the "Twilight Zone" television series, includes some of the most provocative horror fiction produced in the early postwar years. Included are tales of twisted sexuality such as "Miss Gentilbelle," "The Dark Music," and "The New People"; the vampire stories "Last Rites" and "Place of Meeting"; the dark fantasies "The Jungle," "The Vanishing American" and "Free Dirt"; and Beaumont's classic of a possessed jazz musician, "Dark Country." Eighteen writers and editors have contributed tributes.

Other books you might like:
Ray Bradbury, *The Stories of Ray Bradbury*, 1980
Dennis Etchison, *The Dark Country*, 1982
Richard Matheson, *Collected Stories*, 1989
William Relling Jr., *The Infinite Man and Other Stories*, 1989

354
MICHAEL BEDARD

Painted Devil
(New York: Atheneum, 1994)

Story type: Fantasy (Young Adult; Horror)
Major character(s): Alice Higginson, Teenager, Actor (puppeteer); Mr. Dwyer, Librarian
Time period(s): 1990s
Locale(s): Caledon, Canada

Summary: Alice agrees to help Mr. Dwyer stage a puppet show using old Punch and Judy puppets and a rare script held by the library. As practice progresses, a dark ambience seems to envelop the town, extending to Alice's Aunt Emily who returns to Caledon to aid Alice's mother during her difficult pregnancy. Aunt Emily finds a similarity between today's events and those of 28 years earlier.

Other books you might like:
Pauline Clarke, *The Return of the Twelves*, 1963
Lynne Reid Banks, *The Indian in the Cupboard*, 1981
Sylvia Waugh, *The Mennyms*, 1994

355

CLARE BELL

People of the Sky
(New York: Tor, 1989)

Story type: Science Fiction (First Contact)
Major character(s): Kesbe Temiya, Indian; Sahacat, Indian, Shaman
Time period(s): 23rd century
Locale(s): Oneway, Planet—Imaginary

Summary: Two hundred years ago the Pueblo Indians, following a prophecy, emigrated to Oneway, a planet circling a star light years from Earth. There they found an intelligent race of alien flyers, the Aronans, and joined them in a symbiotic relationship in the isolation of Barranca canyon. Now their existence has been almost forgotten by those who live in Oneway's high-tech enclaves. Then Kesbe rediscovers the lost colony of the People of the Sky when her airplane is forced down in a storm over Barranca canyon. They, however, refuse to help her unless she becomes one of them, joining in symbiosis with an Aronan.

Other books you might like:
Charles de Lint, *Svaha*, 1989
R.A. MacAvoy, *The Third Eagle: Lessons Along a Minor String*, 1989
Andre Norton, *Beast Master*, 1959
Andre Norton, *The Sioux Space Man*, 1960
Dan Simmons, *Phases of Gravity*, 1989

356

CLARE BELL

Ratha and Thistle-Chaser
(New York: Margaret K. McElderry Books/Macmillan, 1990)

Story type: Fantasy (Adventure; Young Adult)
Series: Ratha
Major character(s): Thakur, Animal, Teacher; Ratha, Animal, Leader (Clan); Newt, Animal
Time period(s): Indeterminate Past (25 million years ago)
Locale(s): Alternate Earth

Summary: A Clan of intelligent wild cats must move to new territory when drought threatens the herdbeasts they use for food. Thakur is both fascinated by, and wary of, Newt who has strange ways and talents. This is a 1991 ALA Best Books For Young Adults title.

Other books you might like:
Richard Adams, *Watership Down*, 1972
William Horwood, *Duncton Wood*, 1980
Tad Williams, *Tailchaser's Song*, 1985

357

DOUGLAS BELL

Mojo and the Pickle Jar
(New York: Tor, 1991)

Story type: Fantasy (Contemporary; Religious)

Major character(s): Joseph ''Mojo'' Birdsong, Criminal; Roger K. ''RK'' Narn, Lawman (Texas Ranger); Juanita Vasquez, Smuggler
Time period(s): 1990s
Locale(s): Southwest

Summary: Mojo and Juanita are in big trouble by the time they meet Grandmother Montoya. Juanita's pickle jar contains an object much more precious than the demon she believes is there. Instead it contains the stolen heart of a saint. They must survive a demon's trying to kill them and retrieve the heart to save the world. First novel.

Other books you might like:
Jon Cohen, *Max Lakeman and the Beautiful Stranger*, 1990
Alan Dean Foster, *Cyber Way*, 1990
Parke Godwin, *The Snake Oil Wars*, 1989
Parke Godwin, *Waiting for the Galactic Bus*, 1988
Simon Hawke, *The Wizard of 4th Street*, 1989
Marc Laidlaw, *Neon Lotus*, 1988
James Morrow, *Only Begotten Daughter*, 1988

358

M. SHAYNE BELL

Nicoji
(New York: Baen, 1991)

Story type: Science Fiction (Disaster; Adventure)
Major character(s): Sam, Hunter; Jake, Hunter; Eloise, Hunter
Time period(s): Indeterminate Future
Locale(s): Nicoji, Planet—Imaginary

Summary: Trapped on an alien planet by a ruthlessly exploitive company, Sam and Jake decide to escape. Following rumors of a newer, more fair company, they set out into the swamps that cover the planet. Unfortunately, the planet is about to go through a major upheaval, both economic and biological, and Sam and Jake are soon fighting just to survive.

Other books you might like:
Hal Clement, *Cycle of Fire*, 1957
Frank Herbert, *Dune*, 1965
Barry B. Longyear, *Enemy Mine*, 1985
   David Gerrold, co-author
H. Beam Piper, *Little Fuzzy*, 1962

359

M. SHAYNE BELL, Editor

Washed by a Wave of Wind
(Salt Lake City, Utah: Signature Books, 1993)

Story type: Science Fiction (Anthology; Theological)

Summary: Contains a five-page introduction by the editor, ''Toward a Science Fiction From the West''; an 11-page prologue by Barbara R. Hume, ''Strange Bedfellows: A History of Science Fiction in the Corridor''; plus three reprinted and 18 original stories by writers from the (Mormon) Corridor who share beliefs concerning the nature of good life and how to achieve it. Stories feature Western impressions and underlying Western frontier values as characters face threats to individual and artistic freedom. Authors include the editor, Elizabeth H. Boyer, Orson Scott Card and Dave Wolverton.

Other books you might like:
Ray Bradbury, *The Martian Chronicles*, 1950
David Brin, *The Postman*, 1985
Orson Scott Card, *The Folk of the Fringe*, 1989
Orson Scott Card, *Maps in a Mirror*, 1990
Orson Scott Card, *Seventh Son*, 1987
Robert A. Heinlein, *Farnham's Freehold*, 1964
Clifford D. Simak, *All Flesh Is Grass*, 1965
L. Neil Smith, *Pallas*, 1993
Sheri S. Tepper, *Raising the Stones*, 1990

360
RENE BELLETTO

Machine
(New York: Grove Press, 1993)

Story type: Horror (Science Fiction)
Major character(s): Marc Lacroix, Doctor (psychiatrist); Marie Lacroix, Housewife; Michael Zyto, Serial Killer
Time period(s): 1990s (1990)
Locale(s): Paris, France

Summary: Originally published in France in 1990, this novel tells of the horrifying backfire that occurs when Marc Lacroix tries to look into the mind of a serial killer by means of a machine that will exchange some of his psychic energy with the murderer's, but which accidentally switches their personalities completely. Translated by Lanie Goodman.

Other books you might like:
Harlan Ellison, *Mefisto in Onyx*, 1993
Damon Knight, *Mind Switch*, 1963
H.P. Lovecraft, *The Thing on the Doorstep*, 1963
   in *The Dunwich Horror and Others*
Curt Siodmak, *Gabriel's Body*, 1988
F. Paul Wilson, *Sibs*, 1993

361
HANS BEMMANN

The Broken Goddess
(New York: Roc, 1994)

Story type: Fantasy (Alternate World)
Major character(s): I, Writer; Rana Bressanone, Mythical Creature
Time period(s): 1990s; Indeterminate
Locale(s): Munich, Germany; Mythical Place (fairy realm)

Summary: When challenged about his beliefs concerning fairy tales at a conference, a young academic follows his questioner. His search for her leads to a realm where she reveals her true form to him and he discovers the importance of faith. Translated by Anthea Bell from the 1990 German edition.

Other books you might like:
John Crowley, *Little, Big*, 1981
Charles de Lint, *Memory and Dream*, 1994
Barbara Hambly, *The Silent Tower*, 1986
Robert Holdstock, *Mythago Wood*, 1984

R.A. Salvatore, *The Woods out Back*, 1993

362
PETER BENCHLEY

Beast
(New York: Random House, 1991)

Story type: Horror (Nature in Revolt)
Major character(s): William Somers "Whip" Darling, Fisherman; Marcus Sharp, Military Personnel (Navy lieutenant); Herbert Talley, Professor (marine biologist)
Time period(s): 1990s
Locale(s): Bermuda

Summary: It's summertime and that means fishermen, swimmers, smugglers and anyone else foolish enough to go in the waters off Bermuda are fair game for *Architeuthis dux*, a ravenous monster squid that wreaks havoc on tourism and scientific research and causes no end of turmoil for its human pursuers in this rewrite of Benchley's 1974 blockbuster, *Jaws*.

Other books you might like:
Orson Scott Card, *The Abyss*, 1989
Matthew J. Costello, *Wurm*, 1991
Michael Crichton, *Sphere*, 1987
Jules Verne, *Twenty Thousand Leagues under the Sea*, 1873

363
PETER BENCHLEY

White Shark
(New York: Random House, 1994)

Story type: Horror (Science Fiction)
Major character(s): Simon Chase, Scientist (oceanographer); Max Chase, Child (Simon's 10 year old son); Tall Man Palmer, Sailor
Time period(s): 1990s (1996)
Locale(s): Osprey Island, Massachusetts

Summary: Simon Chase thinks his worst troubles are trying to keep his impoverished oceanographic research center afloat and money-hungry poachers from turning the great white shark into a member of the endangered species list—that is, until the product of a biological experiment from Nazi Germany is liberated from the hold of a ship that sank off the American shore some 50 years ago and begins decimating sea life and human life in nearby waters.

Other books you might like:
Matthew J. Costello, *Wurm*, 1991
William Dantz, *Hunger*, 1992
Elizabeth Forrest, *Dark Tide*, 1993
J.M. Morgan, *Between the Devil and the Deep*, 1992

364

GREGORY BENFORD, Editor
MARTIN H. GREENBERG, Co-Editor

Alternate Americas

(New York: Bantam Spectra, 1992)

Story type: Science Fiction (Anthology; Alternate Universe)
Series: What Might Have Been

Summary: Contains a three-page introduction by Gregory Benford plus 14 short stories commissioned for this volume with five originally appearing in 1992 periodicals and one in an anthology. Several stories feature Columbus's voyages while others present the Americas comparably explored and settled from various directions, some stories successfully employing comic twists. Authors include A. A. Attanasio, L. Sprague de Camp, Esther M. Friesner, James Morrow, Kim Stanley Robinson, Pamela Sargent, Robert Silverberg, Harry Turtledove and George Zebrowski.

Other books you might like:
Orson Scott Card, *Seventh Son*, 1987
Glen Cook, *A Matter of Time*, 1985
Phyllis Eisenstein, *Shadow of Earth*, 1979
Michael Flynn, *In the Country of the Blind*, 1990
Katharine Kerr, *Resurrection*, 1992
Frank D. McSherry Jr., *The Fantastic Civil War*, 1991
   editor
Ward Moore, *Bring the Jubilee*, 1953
Mike Resnick, *Alternate Kennedys*, 1992
   editor
Mike Resnick, *Alternate Presidents*, 1992
   editor
John Maddox Roberts, *King of the Wood*, 1983
S.M. Stirling, *Marching through Georgia*, 1988

365

GREGORY BENFORD, Editor
MARTIN H. GREENBERG, Co-Editor

Alternate Wars

(New York: Bantam Spectra, 1991)

Story type: Science Fiction (Anthology; Alternate Universe)
Series: What Might Have Been

Summary: This anthology of stories about alternate wars throughout human history includes an introduction by Gregory Benford and 12 stories, including "If Lee Had Not Won the Battle of Gettysburg" by the Right Honorable Winston S. Churchill, M.P. The remaining 11 stories are all by science fiction authors including Poul Anderson, F.M. Busby, Nancy Kress, Allen Steele, Harry Turtledove and George Zebrowski.

Other books you might like:
J.G. Ballard, *The Atrocity Exhibition*, 1990
Arthur C. Clarke, *Tales From Planet Earth*, 1990
Philip K. Dick, *The Man in the High Castle*, 1962
Michael Flynn, *In the Country of the Blind*, 1990
William Gibson, *The Difference Engine*, 1990
   Bruce Sterling, co-author
Brad Linaweaver, *Moon of Ice*, 1988

Jack McDevitt, *A Talent for War*, 1989
Frank D. McSherry Jr., *The Fantastic Civil War*, 1991
   editor
Ward Moore, *Bring the Jubilee*, 1953

366

GREGORY BENFORD, Editor

Far Futures

(New York: Tor, 1995)

Story type: Science Fiction (Anthology; Science Fiction)
Time period(s): Indeterminate Future

Summary: This book contains a 12-page introduction and brief individual introductions with biographies for five novellas, written with the purpose of dealing with "truly grand perspectives in time." Poul Anderson, Greg Bear, Joe Haldeman, Donald Kingsbury, and Charles Sheffield project events from 1600 to several billion years in the future.

Other books you might like:
Poul Anderson, *The Stars Are Also Fire*, 1994
Poul Anderson, *Tau Zero*, 1970
James Blish, *Cities in Flight*, 1970
Arthur C. Clarke, *The City and the Stars*, 1956
Larry Niven, *A World Out of Time*, 1976
Cordwainer Smith, *The Rediscovery of Man*, 1993
Olaf Stapledon, *Last and First Men*, 1930
Olaf Stapledon, *Star Maker*, 1937

367

GREGORY BENFORD

Furious Gulf

(New York: Bantam Spectra, 1994)

Story type: Science Fiction (Hard Science Fiction)
Series: Great Sky River
Major character(s): Killeen Bishop, Spaceship Captain, Genetically Altered Being; Toby Bishop, Refugee, Genetically Altered Being; Quath'jutt'kkal'thon "Quath", Alien (Myriapodia), Revolutionary
Time period(s): 280th century
Locale(s): *Argo*, Spaceship; Outer Space (galactic center)

Summary: Pursued by mechs, Family Bishop continues toward True Center with help from Quath and the Magnetic Mind. The *Argo* encounters many intelligences on its trip into the black hole and the Esty, condensed space time, they find there.

Other books you might like:
Roger MacBride Allen, *The Ring of Charon*, 1990
Stephen Baxter, *Raft*, 1992
Greg Bear, *Eon*, 1985
Larry Niven, *Neutron Star*, 1968
Frederik Pohl, *Gateway*, 1977
Dan Simmons, *Hyperion*, 1989
Joan Slonczewski, *Daughter of Elysium*, 1993

368

GREGORY BENFORD

Matter's End

(New York: Bantam Spectra, 1995)

Story type: Science Fiction (Collection)

Summary: The 21 stories in this collection include Benford's first published work, "Stand-In" (1965), and exhibit a wide range of length and theme. The tone varies from humorous to dark with stories individually emphasizing setting, character, or science, according to the six-page afterword.

Other books you might like:
David G. Hartwell, *The Ascent of Wonder: The Evolution of Hard SF*, 1990
   Kathryn Cramer, co-editor
Judith Merril, *The Best of Judith Merril*, 1976
Marc Stiegler, *The Gentle Seduction*, 1990
Theodore Sturgeon, *The Complete Egoist*, 1994
John Varley, *The Persistence of Vision*, 1978

369

GREGORY BENFORD

Sailing Bright Eternity

(New York: Bantam Spectra, 1995)

Story type: Science Fiction (Hard Science Fiction; Robot Fiction)
Series: Galactic Center
Major character(s): Nigel Walmsley, Astronaut, Immortal; Toby Bishop, Wanderer; Killeen, Parent, Wanderer
Time period(s): Indeterminate Future
Locale(s): Galcen, Mythical Place (The Lair Labyrinth)

Summary: Toby learns that he, his father, and grandfather hold the key to the ultimate destruction of the Mechs. Unable to believe that happiness could be their undoing, the Mechs actively search for the key, while ancient forces aid the humans.

Other books you might like:
Roger MacBride Allen, *The Ring of Charon*, 1990
Stephen Baxter, *Raft*, 1992
Frederik Pohl, *Gateway*, 1977
Robert Reed, *Down the Bright Way*, 1991
Dan Simmons, *Hyperion*, 1989
Dan Simmons, *The Fall of Hyperion*, 1990

370

GREGORY BENFORD

Tides of Light

(New York: Bantam, 1989)

Story type: Science Fiction (Hard Science Fiction)
Major character(s): Killeen, Spaceship Captain (Captain of Family Bishop); Quath'jutt'kkal'thon "Quath", Alien, Revolutionary
Time period(s): Indeterminate Future
Locale(s): *Argo*, Spaceship; Abraham's Star, Outer Space

Summary: Fleeing the mechs who infest their home planet, Family Bishop has stolen a starship and journeyed to Abraham's Star. On a planet of that star they find other human beings fighting a battle against yet another hostile civilization, the half-alien/half-machine cybers. Cap'n Killeen must find a place for his Family, despite the hostility of cybers, mechs, and other human beings.

Other books you might like:
David Brin, *Startide Rising*, 1983
David Brin, *The Uplift War*, 1987
Edward Gibson, *Reach*, 1989
David Alexander Smith, *Rendezvous*, 1988

371

MARCIA J. BENNETT

Seeking the Dream Brother

(New York: Ballantine/Del Rey, 1989)

Story type: Science Fiction (Adventure)
Series: Ni-Lach
Major character(s): Dhalvad, Alien, Psychic; Theon, Human
Time period(s): Indeterminate Future
Locale(s): Lach, Planet—Imaginary

Summary: The Ni-lach Dhalvad has fled humanity and returned to his own people because humans fear his ability to heal and teleport. Now, however, he's called on a dangerous dream quest to rescue his long lost brother.

Other books you might like:
David Brin, *The Uplift War*, 1987
Leslie Gadallah, *Cat's Gambit*, 1989
H. Beam Piper, *Fuzzies and Other People*, 1984
H. Beam Piper, *Little Fuzzy*, 1962
H. Beam Piper, *The Other Human Race*, 1964

372

E.F. BENSON

The Collected Ghost Stories of E.F. Benson

(New York: Carroll & Graf, 1992)

Story type: Horror (Collection)

Summary: A landmark omnibus that collects all the major supernatural fiction of an Edwardian writer (1867-1940) better known for his comedies of manners. Included among the 54 stories are the classic vampire tales "The Room in the Tower" and "Mrs. Amworth"; the Christmas ghost story, "How Fear Departed from the Long Gallery"; a tale of a ghostly manifestation of a disease, "Caterpillars"; a story of precognition, "The Bus-Conductor"; and the tale of a slug-like horror that haunts the grounds of a former churchyard, "Negotium Perambulans." Editor Richard Dalby has also included "The Clonmel Witch Burning," an early essay in which Benson recounts the horrible torture of a suspected 19th century Irish witch.

Other books you might like:
Hugh Benson, *The Light Invisible*, 1907

Algernon Blackwood, *Best Ghost Stories of Algernon Blackwood*, 1973
A.M. Burrage, *Warning Whispers*, 1988
William Fryer Harvey, *Midnight Tales*, 1946

373

NANCY VARIAN BERBERICK

A Child of Elvish
(New York: Ace, 1992)

Story type: Fantasy (Quest)
Major character(s): Kicva, Mythical Creature (elf), Adventurer; Joze, Adventurer; Islief the Watcher, Mythical Creature (First People)
Time period(s): Indeterminate
Locale(s): Elfland, Mythical Place

Summary: When Islief's lady appears to Kicva and Joze as a ghost to request help overturning an evil sorcerer's plotting, they agree to find and bring back to the spirit the child of mixed Mannish and Elvin heritage who can safely wield the ancient magic and correct the upset balance of forces. Sequel to *The Jewels of Elvish*.

Other books you might like:
Sheila Gilluly, *The Boy From the Burren*, 1990
Robert Jordan, *The Eye of the World*, 1989
Andre Norton, *The Elvenbane*, 1991
    Mercedes Lackey, co-author
Michael Scott Rohan, *The Forge in the Forest*, 1989
Margaret Weis, *Dragon Wing*, 1990
    Tracy Hickman, co-author

374

NANCY VARIAN BERBERICK

The Panther's Hoard
(New York: Ace, 1994)

Story type: Fantasy (Sword and Sorcery)
Major character(s): Garrock, Warrior, Mythical Creature (dwarf)
Time period(s): 7th century
Locale(s): England; Wales; Mythical Place

Summary: The sole surviving member of the ancient race of dwarves leads human warriors to battle the elder-gods in their own realm. Sequel to *Shadow of the Seventh Moon*.

Other books you might like:
Patrick H. Adkins, *Sons of the Titans*, 1990
Linda Evans, *Sleipnir*, 1994
Jason Henderson, *The Spawn of Loki*, 1994
Mark C. Perry, *Morigu: The Dead*, 1990
Elizabeth Ann Scarborough, *Last Refuge*, 1992

375

NANCY VARIAN BERBERICK

Shadow of the Seventh Moon
(New York: Ace, 1991)

Story type: Fantasy (Historical)
Major character(s): Garroc, Warrior, Mythical Creature (dwarf); Lydi, Witch; Dyfed, Warrior
Time period(s): 7th century (630)
Locale(s): England

Summary: Garroc, the last of the Dwarves, tells his story to the human woman Sif, daughter of Garroc's human fosterling Hinthan. Garroc was scout and soldier for Halfdan and his son Erich War Hawk, Saxon lords who held the borderland between Saxons and Welsh in the century after King Arthur's death. As kings battle each other and Erich seeks revenge on Vorgund, the slayer of Halfdan, Garroc finds his own destiny.

Other books you might like:
Lynn Abbey, *Unicorn and Dragon*, 1987
C.J. Cherryh, *The Tree of Swords and Jewels*, 1983
Parke Godwin, *The Last Rainbow*, 1985
Rudyard Kipling, *Puck of Pook's Hill*, 1988
Andre Norton, *Merlin's Mirror*, 1975

376

DAVID BERGANTINO

Wes Craven's New Nightmare
(New York: Tor, 1994)

Story type: Horror (Supernatural Vengeance)
Major character(s): Heather Lagenkamp, Actress, Historical Figure; Wes Craven, Director (film), Historical Figure; Dylan Porter, Child (Heather's 5-year-old son)
Time period(s): 1990s (1994)
Locale(s): Los Angeles, California

Summary: A series of grisly deaths in the manner of the *Nightmare on Elm Street* series of movies plagues the set of director Wes Craven's newest horror film. Craven and his leading actress discover that they are the doings of the spiritual force embodied by "Nightmares" heavy Freddy Krueger, and that in order to contain it they must make another movie that brings his character back to life. This book is a novelization of the 1994 Wes Craven film of the same title.

Other books you might like:
Jonathan Carroll, *A Child Across the Sky*, 1989
David Darke, *Horrorshow*, 1994
Martin H. Greenberg, *Nightmares on Elm Street: Freddy Krueger's Seven Sweetest Dreams*, 1991
    editor
Dale Hoover, *65mm*, 1994
Brad Strickland, *Shadowshow*, 1988

377

EDWARD P. BERGLUND, Editor

Disciples of Cthulhu

(Oakland, California: Chaosium, 1996)

Story type: Horror (Anthology)

Summary: A revision of a 1976 paperback original, this volume collects nine homages to the Cthulhu Mythos fiction of H.P. Lovecraft, including Brian Lumley's ''The Fairground Horror,'' in which a travelling carnival brings Lovecraftian horrors to the town it visits; Ramsey Campbell's ''The Tugging,'' in which quirks of astronomy induce nightmares of universal doom; and Fritz Leiber's ''The Horror From the Depths,'' in which a man's attempt to reconcile himself with his personal demons parallels his pursuit of forbidden occult knowledge. Robert M. Price's ''Dope War of the Black Tong,'' is a pastiche of Robert E. Howard in which a detective grapples with Lovecraftian monstrosities, is new to this edition. Robert Bloch supplies the introduction.

Other books you might like:
Lin Carter, *The Spawn of Cthulhu*, 1991
     editor
H.P. Lovecraft, *Tales of the Cthulhu Mythos: Golden Anniversary Anthology*, 1990
Robert M. Price, *The Azathoth Cycle*, 1995
     editor
Robert M. Price, *The Hastur Cycle*, 1993
     editor
Robert M. Price, *The New Lovecraft Circle*, 1996
     editor
Robert M. Price, *The Shub Niggurath Cycle*, 1994
     editor
Robert M. Price, *Tales of the Lovecraft Mythos*, 1992
     editor
Thomas M.K. Stratman, *Cthulhu's Heirs*, 1994
James Turner, *Cthulhu 2000*, 1995
     editor

378

ELAINE BERGSTROM

Blood Alone

(New York: Jove, 1990)

Story type: Horror (Vampire Story)
Major character(s): Paul Stodard, Artisan; Laurence Austra, Vampire; Gregory Hunter, Military Personnel
Time period(s): 1940s
Locale(s): Europe

Summary: During the tense months prior to the beginning of World War II, members of the Austra family strive to protect their business (creating stained glass for religious shrines) and keep secret the fact that they're vampires as they combat insane Nazi doctors and hordes of spies. This novel is a sequel to *Shattered Glass*.

Other books you might like:
Marc Eliot, *How Dear the Dawn*, 1987
Robert R. McCammon, *The Wolf's Hour*, 1988

Dan Simmons, *Carrion Comfort*, 1989
Robert Weinberg, *The Armageddon Box*, 1991

379

ELAINE BERGSTROM

Daughter of the Night

(New York: Jove, 1992)

Story type: Horror (Vampire Story)
Series: Chronicles of the Austra Family
Major character(s): Elizabeth Bathori, Noblewoman, Historical Figure; Catherine Austra, Vampire; Charles, Nobleman (Wallachian lord), Vampire
Time period(s): 16th century (1563); 17th century (1609-1610)
Locale(s): Transylvania

Summary: This novel presents a fictional rendering of the historical figure Elizabeth Bathori, who gained renown in Eastern Europe of the late sixteenth and early seventeenth century for bathing in the blood of more than 600 female victims. Here, the author surmises that Elizabeth's ghastly habits began following her association with a Wallachian vampire lady, Catherine Austra, during the same tribal wars between Turkey and Transylvania that yielded the legends of Vlad Tepes, Count Dracula.

Other books you might like:
Les Daniels, *The Black Castle*, 1978
Brian Lumley, *Vamphyri!*, 1987
Anne Rice, *The Vampire Lestat*, 1985
Michael Romkey, *I, Vampire*, 1990
Brian Stableford, *The Empire of Fear*, 1988
Chelsea Quinn Yarbro, *The Palace*, 1978

380

ELAINE BERGSTROM

Tapestry of Dark Souls

(Geneva, Wisconsin: TSR, 1993)

Story type: Horror (Occult)
Series: Ravenloft
Major character(s): Leith, Werewolf; Jonathan, Young Man (Leith's son); Sondra, Young Woman
Time period(s): Indeterminate
Locale(s): Ravenloft, Fictional Country

Summary: In the imaginary world of Ravenloft, the Guardians keep watch over a tapestry with the power to absorb and amplify evil. As their numbers dwindle, they hope that the stalwart young Jonathan, entrusted to their care, will spend his life keeping the tapestry from the hands of those who would use it for evil. But Jonathan's mother was herself infected by the tapestry while she bore her son, raising doubts as to whether Jonathan himself can be trusted.

Other books you might like:
P.N. Elrod, *I, Strahd*, 1993
Christie Golden, *Dance of the Dead*, 1992
J. Robert King, *Carnival of Fear*, 1993

381

JANET BERLINER
GEORGE GUTHRIDGE, Co-Author

Child of the Journey

(Clarkston, Georgia: White Wolf Borealis, 1996)

Story type: Fantasy (Magic Conflict; Historical)
Series: Madagascar Manifesto
Major character(s): Solomon Freund, Psychic; Miriam Rathenau, Singer, Spouse; Erich ''Erich Alois'' Weser, Telepath, Animal Trainer
Time period(s): 1930s (1938-1939)
Locale(s): Netherlands; Berlin, Germany; *Sogne*, At Sea

Summary: Solomon searches for his beloved Miriam, while Miriam pledges her body, if not her heart, to Erich, expecting thus to protect Solomon. When Erich leads a mission to occupy Madagascar, Miriam uses the little time available to speak with Solomon onboard the ship and share hopes for some positive change. Sequel to *Child of the Light*.

Other books you might like:
Martin Amis, *Time's Arrow*, 1991
Peter S. Beagle, *Peter S. Beagle's Immortal Unicorn*, 1995
    Janet Berliner, co-editor
Janet Gluckman, *Child of the Light*, 1992
    George Guthridge, co-author
Lisa Goldstein, *The Red Magician*, 1982
Robin Hobb, *Royal Assassin*, 1995
Jane Yolen, *Briar Rose*, 1992

382

JANET BERLINER, Editor
UWE LUSERKE, Co-Editor
MARTIN H. GREENBERG, Co-Editor

Desire Burn: Women's Stories from the Dark Side of Passion

(New York: Carroll & Graf, 1995)

Story type: Horror (Anthology)

Summary: Twenty reprinted stories by twenty women authors explore issues of female sexuality in a horror context. In Lois Tilton's ''The Other Woman'' and Diedra Cox's ''Remnants,'' obsessive passions keep women and their partners alive after death. Both Dawn Dunn in ''The Lonely Heart'' and Nancy Holder in ''Heat'' link sexuality to pain. Poppy Z. Brite's ''The Sixth Sentinel'' is a ghost story, Esther Friesner's ''Do I Dare to Ask Your Name?'' a vampire story, and Jan Barrette's ''Patent Pending'' and Katherine Dunn's ''Near Flesh'' science fiction stories. Cynthia Ward's ''Midwife'' and Joyce Carol Oates' ''Love, Letter'' are exercises in psychological horror, and Berliner's own ''Castoff'' is a tale of supernatural revenge.

Other books you might like:
Marvin Kaye, *Angels of Darkness*, 1995
    editor
Kathryn Ptacek, *Women of Darkness*, 1988
    editor
Kathryn Ptacek, *Women of Darkness II*, 1990
    editor
Lisa Tuttle, *Skin of the Soul*, 1990
    editor

383

MICHAEL BERLYN

The Eternal Enemy

(New York: Morrow, 1990)

Story type: Science Fiction (First Contact; Space Opera)
Major character(s): Markos, Scientist (exobiologist); Van Pelt, Spaceship Captain
Time period(s): Indeterminate Future
Locale(s): *Paladin*, Spaceship; Outer Space; Gandji, Planet—Imaginary

Summary: Markos is sent to Gandji, a planet circling Tau Ceti, with a mission to find and rescue a lost probe ship scout, and to study the local sentient life. Van Pelt believes the Habers are dangerous and decides to wipe them out over Markos' objections that the Habers are completely non-violent. Markos, killed in the attempt to warn or help the Habers, finds himself changed, but alive, and continues his campaign to prevent the elimination of the Habers.

Other books you might like:
David Brin, *The Uplift War*, 1987
Octavia E. Butler, *Imago*, 1989
Octavia E. Butler, *Adulthood Rites*, 1988
Octavia E. Butler, *Dawn*, 1987
Orson Scott Card, *Ender's Game*, 1985
David Alexander Smith, *Homecoming*, 1990

384

ELUKI BES SHAHAR

Archangel Blues

(New York: DAW, 1993)

Story type: Science Fiction (Space Opera; Political)
Series: Hellflower
Major character(s): Butterfly St. Cyr, Smuggler (darktrader), Spaceship Captain; Paladin, Artificial Intelligence; Baijon ''Tiggy'' Stardust, Knight (Hellflower)
Time period(s): Indeterminate Future
Locale(s): *Ghost Dance*, Spaceship; Palaceoid Morningstar, Planet—Imaginary; Phoenix Empire, Interstellar Empire/Federation

Summary: Paladin's acting up impedes Butterly St. Cyr's goal of finding and destroying Governor-General Mallorum Archangel before he can plunge the Phoenix Empire into war.

Other books you might like:
Glen Cook, *The Dragon Never Sleeps*, 1988
Cheryl J. Franklin, *Fire Crossing*, 1991
Neal Stephenson, *Snow Crash*, 1992
Vernor Vinge, *A Fire upon the Deep*, 1992
David Weber, *Path of the Fury*, 1992

385
ELUKI BES SHAHAR

Darktraders
(New York: DAW, 1992)

Story type: Science Fiction (Political; Space Opera)
Series: Hellflower
Major character(s): Butterfly St. Cyr, Smuggler (darktrader), Spaceship Captain; Paladin, Artificial Intelligence; Baijon "Tiggy" Stardust, Knight (Hellflower)
Time period(s): Indeterminate Future
Locale(s): Imperial Mikasa, Planet—Imaginary; *Woebegone*, Spaceship

Summary: While Butterfly tries to return Tiggy to Kenner, his Hellflower father, Imperial Prince Archangel schemes to use illegal Old Federation technology to gain control of the universe and kill Tiggy. Starflower honor prevents Butterfly's execution until after replacement of the arm she loses saving Tiggy's life. Tiggy's honor forces Butterfly to become embroiled in Starflower politics while they try to prevent the destruction of the Empire.

Other books you might like:
Glen Cook, *The Dragon Never Sleeps*, 1988
Cheryl J. Franklin, *Fire Crossing*, 1991
James P. Hogan, *Entoverse*, 1991
Dan Simmons, *Hyperion*, 1989
Neal Stephenson, *Snow Crash*, 1992
Michael Swanwick, *Stations of the Tide*, 1991
George Zebrowski, *Stranger Suns*, 1991

386
ELUKI BES SHAHAR

Hellflower
(New York: DAW, 1991)

Story type: Science Fiction (Adventure)
Major character(s): Butterfly St. Cyr, Smuggler (darktrader), Spaceship Captain; Paladin, Artificial Intelligence
Time period(s): Indeterminate Future
Locale(s): Wanderweb, Planet—Imaginary; *Firecat*, Spaceship

Summary: Butterfly's partner, Paladin, now installed in her spaceship, had been an abandoned library of the Federation, all of whose technology is now illegal. While having a constant communication device installed for Paladin, Butterfly rescues a Hellflower, a man from one of the worlds where honor is complex and primary.

Other books you might like:
Emma Bull, *Bone Dance*, 1991
Glen Cook, *The Dragon Never Sleeps*, 1988
Brian Daley, *Requiem for a Ruler of Worlds*, 1985
William C. Dietz, *Drifter*, 1991
Alis A. Rasmussen, *A Passage of Stars*, 1990
David Alexander Smith, *Marathon*, 1982

387
ALEXANDER BESHER

Rim: A Novel of Virtual Reality
(New York: HarperCollins West, 1994)

Story type: Science Fiction (Post-Disaster; Techno-Thriller)
Major character(s): Frank Gobi, Professor, Computer Expert
Time period(s): 2020s (2027)
Locale(s): Tokyo, Japan; Berkeley, California

Summary: Facing cutthroat industrial warfare, Satori Corp. struggles to hold its market share of the virtual reality entertainment market with its shared reality computer system housing millions of human psyches. When the system crashes, Gobi must locate a missing Satori Corp. executive and algorithm to save his son, who is trapped inside virtual reality.

Other books you might like:
Ben Bova, *Death Dream*, 1994
Victor Milan, *The Cybernetic Samurai*, 1985
Will Shetterly, *The Tangled Lands*, 1989
Neal Stephenson, *Snow Crash*, 1992
Vivian Vande Velde, *User Unfriendly*, 1991
Dave Wolverton, *On My Way to Paradise*, 1989

388
ALFRED BESTER

The Demolished Man
(New York: Vintage, 1996)

Story type: Science Fiction (Psychic Powers; Mystery)
Major character(s): Ben Reich, Businessman, Murderer; Augustus "Gus" Tate, Psychic (esper), Doctor (psychiatrist); Lincoln Powell, Psychic (esper), Police Officer
Time period(s): 24th century
Locale(s): New York, New York

Summary: Although is has been 87 years since the last successful premediated murder. Ben Reich believes he can commit the perfect crime. He discovers a method for hiding his thoughts which may prove undetectable and unbreakable, no matter the strength of the telepath. Lincoln Powell, a master telepathic detective, may solve the case, but the Man With No Face could prove Reich's undoing. Revised reissue of the 1953 Hugo Award winning novel.

Other books you might like:
Isaac Asimov, *The Caves of Steel*, 1953
Greg Bear, *Queen of Angels*, 1990
Katharine Kerr, *Polar City Blues*, 1990
Lee Killough, *Deadly Silents*, 1981
David Alexander Smith, *In the Cube*, 1993

389
ALFRED BESTER

The Stars My Destination
(New York: Vintage, 1996)

Story type: Science Fiction (Science Fiction; Psychic Powers)

Major character(s): Gulliver ''Gully'' Foyle, Spaceman, Psychic (jaunter); Olivia Presteign, Handicapped, Businesswoman; Presteign, Businessman
Time period(s): 24th century
Locale(s): Earth; Outer Space; Sargasso Asteroid, Asteroid

Summary: Abandoned rather than rescued by a passing ship, the marooned Gully Foyle focuses all his energy on survival so he can destroy those who ignored him. Heroic self-rescue and an attack on the offensive ship lead Gully to imprisonment in a lightless prison until another daring self-rescue allows Gully to a continue his search for vengeance. Originally published in 1956.

Other books you might like:
Roger MacBride Allen, *The Ring of Charon*, 1990
Orson Scott Card, *Ender's Game*, 1985
Glen Cook, *The Dragon Never Sleeps*, 1988
Robert A. Heinlein, *The Moon Is a Harsh Mistress*, 1966
Dan Simmons, *Hyperion*, 1989
David Alexander Smith, *In the Cube*, 1993
Vernor Vinge, *A Fire upon the Deep*, 1992

390

JOHN BETANCOURT, Editor

The Best of Weird Tales
(New York: Barnes & Noble, 1995)

Story type: Horror (Anthology)

Summary: The 27 stories collected represent the best fantasy and horror tales published in the revived (1988-1993) *Weird Tales*. Included are ''Midnight Mass,'' F. Paul Wilson's vision of a world run by vampires, and Thomas Ligotti's ''Lost Art of Twilight,'' in which a young artist is vampirized by his family. David Schow's ''Night Bloomer'' and Brian Lumley's ''Fruiting Bodies'' are tales of gruesome vegetation that takes over human beings, and William F. Nolan's ''At Diamond Lake'' and Ramsey Campbell's ''The Same in Any Language'' are grisly revenge tales. A final ghost story collaboration between Henry Kuttner and Robert Bloch, intended for the original *Weird Tales*, in the 1930s, is also included.

Other books you might like:
Robert Weinberg, *100 Wild Little Weird Tales*, 1993
　Stefan Dziemianowicz, Martin H. Greenberg, co-editors
Stefan Dziemianowicz, *Weird Tales: 32 Unearthed Terrors*, 1987
　Robert Weinberg, Martin H. Greenberg, co-editors
Peter Haining, *Weird Tales*, 1976
　editor
Marvin Kaye, *Weird Tales, The Magazine That Never Dies*, 1988
　editor
Robert Weinberg, *The Eighth Green Man and Other Strange Folk*, 1989
　editor
Robert Weinberg, *Far Below and Other Horrors*, 1974
　editor

391

JOHN BETANCOURT

Rememory
(New York: Popular Library Questar, 1990)

Story type: Science Fiction (Genetic Manipulation; Adventure)
Major character(s): Slash, Genetically Altered Being (Catman), Thief; Hangman, Genetically Altered Being, Sidekick
Time period(s): Indeterminate Future
Locale(s): Fishtown The Sprawl, North America

Summary: When their latest theft from the dogmen turns out to be a shipment of top secret spyeyes, Slash and Hangman are suddenly caught up in political intrigue between catmen, dogmen and government agents. Only their familiarity with the underworld of the Sprawl allows them to stay one step ahead of everyone else.

Other books you might like:
Ben Bova, *Cyberbooks*, 1989
George Alec Effinger, *When Gravity Fails*, 1987
William Gibson, *Neuromancer*, 1984
Joan D. Vinge, *Catspaw*, 1988
Walter Jon Williams, *Hardwired*, 1986

392

BRUCE BETHKE

Headcrash
(New York: Warner Aspect, 1995)

Story type: Science Fiction (Cyberpunk; Satire)
Major character(s): Jack ''MAX—KOOL'' Burroughs, Computer Expert; Joseph ''Gunnar Savage'' LeMat, Computer Expert
Time period(s): 2000s
Locale(s): St. Paul, Minnesota; Heaven, Cyberspace (computer virtual reality nightclub)

Summary: Administratively suspended from work, Jack's limited employment opportunities lead to a questionable consulting contract. His research material includes experimental interface hardware, the use of which allows dangerous manipulation of virtual reality computer space and attracts attention from similarly empowered individuals. First novel.

Other books you might like:
Douglas Adams, *The Hitchhiker's Guide to the Galaxy*, 1980
Alexander Besher, *Rim: A Novel of Virtual Reality*, 1994
Ed Blome, *Title Deleted for Security Reasons*, 1993
Pat Cadigan, *Synners*, 1991
Michael Flynn, *In the Country of the Blind*, 1990
Lisa Mason, *Cyberweb*, 1995
Nick Pollotta, *Illegal Aliens*, 1989
　Phil Foglio, co-author
Neal Stephenson, *Snow Crash*, 1992

393
BRUCE BETHKE

Maverick
(New York: Ace, 1990)

Story type: Science Fiction (Robot Fiction)
Series: Isaac Asimov's Robot City: Robots and Aliens
Major character(s): David "Derec" Avery, Computer Expert; Janet Anastasi, Scientist (roboticist); Maverick, Alien
Time period(s): Indeterminate Future
Locale(s): Tau Puppis IV, Planet—Imaginary; Outer Space

Summary: The robots on Tau Puppis IV have built a city, but have no humans to serve, as they are programmed to do. Perhaps, they reason, the indigenous people, a race of wolf-like intelligent creatures who call themselves the Kin, can be defined as human. Meanwhile, Dr. Janet Anastasi is seeking her three "Learning Machines," robots capable of imprinting on intelligent beings and taking on their forms. Her son Derec and his father are fleeing from a dangerous enemy. And some of the Kin regard the Learning Machine called Silversides as a goddess.

Other books you might like:
Isaac Asimov, *Robots and Empire*, 1985
Isaac Asimov, *The Robots of Dawn*, 1983
Jerry Oltion, *Isaac Asimov's Robot City/Robots and Aliens Book 4: Alliance*, 1990
Clifford D. Simak, *A Heritage of Stars*, 1977
Thea Von Harbou, *Metropolis*, 1927

394
AMBROSE BIERCE

Poems of Ambrose Bierce
(Lincoln: University of Nebraska Press, 1995)

Story type: Horror (Collection)

Summary: Editer M.E. Grenander supplements the 98 previously collected poems of this great writer of fantastic and realistic fiction at the turn of the century with another eight previously uncollected poems and 12 essays, prefaces and reviews on poetic craft. Bierce's concerns in his poetry reflect those of his fiction, including the morbid (*A Vision of Doom*), life during wartime (*The Death of Grant, The Confederate Flag*), the philosophy of cynicism (*Cynic Perforce From Studying Mankind*), and the politics of his day (*The Mormon Question, The Statesmen*). All are informed by his caustic wit.

Other books you might like:
William Hope Hodgson, *Beyond the Dawning: The Poems of William Hope Hodgson*, 1995
Neil Gaiman, *Now We Are Sick*, 1993
    Neil Gaiman, co-author
H.P. Lovecraft, *Collected Poems*, 1963

395
STEPHEN BILLIAS

Horrible Humes
(New York: Ace, 1991)

Story type: Fantasy (Adventure; Quest)
Series: Runesword
Major character(s): Caltus "Cal" Talienson, Warrior; Hathor, Mythical Creature (troll), Revolutionary (vegetarian); Queen of Ice, Ruler (land beyond Mistwall)
Time period(s): Indeterminate
Locale(s): Steadfast-by-Sea, Fictional City; Country of the Wind Websters, Fictional Country

Summary: Hoping to preserve her power by preventing flesh-eating creatures from becoming peaceful vegetarians, the Queen of Ice launches her attack on Hathor. Hathor is captured as he and Cal, with their sworn companions, Bith, a sorceress, and Endril, an elf, journey north to repair a rift in the Mistwall.

Other books you might like:
Mark Acres, *Dark Divide*, 1991
Tom Deitz, *Stoneskin's Revenge*, 1991
Clayton Emery, *Outcasts*, 1990
Rose Estes, *Skryling's Blade*, 1990
    Tom Wham, co-author
Robert Jordan, *The Eye of the World*, 1989
J.F. Rivkin, *The Dreamstone*, 1991
J.R.R. Tolkien, *The Fellowship of the Ring*, 1954
J.R.R. Tolkien, *The Return of the King*, 1956
J.R.R. Tolkien, *The Two Towers*, 1955

396
PATRICK BILLINGS (Pseudonym of Earl Murray)

The Quiet
(New York: Tor, 1989)

Story type: Horror (Serial Killer)
Major character(s): Amy Ellerman, Student (plant ecology grad student); John Tanner, Ranger (game warden); Martin Linders, Ranger (bear specialist)
Time period(s): 1990s (1994)
Locale(s): Yellowstone National Park, Wyoming

Summary: Game wardens at Yellowstone National Park find their hands full when a bizarre murderer deliberately baits bears to kill people and help him attain his communion with a native American bear god.

Other books you might like:
Scott Ian Barry, *The Streeter*, 1994
David Dvorkin, *Ursus*, 1989
T.J. Kirby, *Deadly Breed*, 1992
Dean R. Koontz, *Watchers*, 1987

397

ANNE BILLSON

Suckers
(New York: Atheneum, 1993)

Story type: Horror (Vampire Story; Satire)
Major character(s): Dora Rosamund Vale, Businesswoman (fashion consultant); Duncan Fender, Photographer; Rose Murasaki, Editor (magazine), Vampire
Time period(s): 1990s (1993)
Locale(s): London, England

Summary: Thirteen years ago, Dora Vale and Duncan Fender destroyed Duncan's lover Violet Westron, after discovering that she was a vampire. But Violet returns and, under the alias Rose Murasaki, begins editing *Bellini*, a hot fashion magazine that promotes the lifestyle of the undead as a fashion trend.

Other books you might like:
Poppy Z. Brite, *Lost Souls*, 1992
Nancy A. Collins, *Sunglasses After Dark*, 1990
Ray Garton, *Live Girls*, 1987
Anne Rice, *The Vampire Lestat*, 1985
John Skipp, *The Light at the End*, 1986
    Craig Spector, co-author
S.P. Somtow, *Vampire Junction*, 1984

398

MARGARET BINGLEY

Seeds of Evil
(New York: Carroll and Graf, 1990)

Story type: Horror (Evil Children)
Major character(s): Meg Marshall, Housewife; Olivia Marshall, Child, Twin; Orlando Marshall, Child, Twin
Time period(s): 1980s (1988)
Locale(s): England

Summary: Olivia and Orlando, twins born to an artificially inseminated mother, share an unnatural rapport and a talent for viciousness. Meg Marshall's search for the anonymous sperm donor culminates in the shocking revelation of why her children are so badly misbehaved. First published 1988.

Other books you might like:
Jean Paiva, *The Lilith Factor*, 1989
Thomas Tryon, *The Other*, 1972
John Wyndham, *The Midwich Cuckoos*, 1957

399

DAVID BISCHOFF

Hunter's Planet
(New York: Bantam Spectra, 1994)

Story type: Science Fiction (Techno-Thriller; Adventure)
Series: Aliens vs. Predator
Major character(s): Machiko Naguchi, Warrior, Guide; Attila, Android, Martial Arts Expert; Livermore Evanston, Businessman, Criminal
Time period(s): Indeterminate Future

Locale(s): Hunter's Planet, Planet—Imaginary

Summary: After years of hunting with a Predator pack as an honored warrior, Machiko Naguchi accepts a position as guide on Hunter's Planet, prepared for big game hunting by Livermore Evanston. Machiko and Attila soon discover that the planet houses a secret facility designed to promote Evanston's insane and deadly research into controlling aggressive life forms.

Other books you might like:
Alan Dean Foster, *Alien*, 1979
Alan Dean Foster, *Alien 3*, 1992
Alan Dean Foster, *Aliens*, 1986
Simon Hawke, *Predator 2*, 1990
Paul Monette, *Predator*, 1987
Steve Perry, *Aliens: Earth Hive*, 1992
Steve Perry, *Aliens: The Female War*, 1993
    Stephanie Perry, co-author
Steve Perry, *Aliens: Nightmare Asylum*, 1993
Steve Perry, *Prey*, 1994
    Stephanie Perry, co-author

400

DAVID BISCHOFF

Night of the Living Shark!
(New York: Ace, 1991)

Story type: Science Fiction (Humor; Young Adult)
Series: Daniel M. Pinkwater's Melvinge of the Megaverse
Major character(s): Melvinge, Hero, Werewolf; Harlan, Animal, Disembodied Personality (Grabovnikon's); Grabovnikon "Grab", Artificial Intelligence
Time period(s): Indeterminate
Locale(s): Megaverse Mall, Mythical Place; *Grabovnikon*, Spaceship

Summary: Melvinge and Harlan use the Grabovnikon to travel through time and space in search of Megaverse Mall and a parking place despite threats from gypsy werewolves, Sdark the Loan Shark and deadly puns. This book contains an afterword by Daniel M. Pinkwater whose guidelines form the basis for the Melvinge of the Megaverse Series.

Other books you might like:
Douglas Adams, *The Restaurant at the End of the Universe*, 1980
John DeChancie, *Paradox Alley*, 1987
John DeChancie, *Red Limit Freeway*, 1984
John DeChancie, *Starrigger*, 1983
Debra Doyle, *Night of the Living Rat!*, 1992
    James D. Macdonald, co-author
Alan Dean Foster, *Glory Lane*, 1987
T. Jackson King, *Retread Shop*, 1988
Somtow Sucharitkul, *Mallworld*, 1981

401

MICHAEL BISHOP

Apartheid, Superstrings, and Mordecai Thubana

(Eugene, OR: Axolotl Press, 1989)

Story type: Science Fiction (Political)
Major character(s): Mordecai Thubana, Construction Worker (African); Gerrit Myburgh, Businessman (Afrikaner)
Time period(s): 1990s
Locale(s): South Africa

Summary: Myburgh, an upper-class Afrikaner, is in a car accident out on the Veldt. Afterwards he finds himself stuck in an odd sort of shadow existence, invisible to other white South Africans. Myburgh is picked up by a bus taking blacks to work in Pretoria and meets Thubana, a self-educated roofer who studies such aspects of modern physics as the Grand Unified Theory and superstring. Thubana uses this knowledge to explain what has happened to Myburgh. Then they fall into the clutches of the notorious police department Special Branch.

Other books you might like:
Terry Bisson, *Fire on the Mountain*, 1988
Pat Murphy, *The City, Not Long After*, 1989
Mike Resnick, *Ivory: A Legend of Past and Future*, 1988
Mike Resnick, *Paradise: A Chronicle of a Distant World*, 1989

402

MICHAEL BISHOP

At the City Limits of Fate

(Cambridge, Massachusetts: Edgewood Press, 1996)

Story type: Fantasy (Collection; Religious)

Summary: Contains 15 stories reprinted from periodicals and anthologies 1982-1996. The stories vary in tone from humorous to downbeat with theological themes including Genesis, a plague of butterflies, post-disaster life, fate, St. Augustine's religious agony, child abuse, televangelism, and the trial of Judas Iscariot.

Other books you might like:
Gwyneth Jones, *Seven Tales and a Table*, 1995
Garry Kilworth, *Hogfoot Right and Bird-Hands*, 1993
James Morrow, *Bible Stories for Adults*, 1996
Nancy Springer, *Damnbanna*, 1992
Cherry Wilder, *Dealers in Light and Darkness*, 1995
Kate Wilhelm, *State of Grace*, 1991

403

MICHAEL BISHOP

Brittle Innings

(New York: Bantam, 1994)

Story type: Horror (Coming-of-Age)

Major character(s): Danny Boles, Sports Figure (baseball player), Indian; Henry Clerval, Sports Figure (baseball player), Reanimated Dead; Buck Hoey, Sports Figure (baseball player)
Time period(s): 1940s (Summer, 1943)
Locale(s): Chattahooche Valley, Georgia

Summary: Native American baseball scout Danny Boles tells the story of his thwarted baseball career, which included rooming with a fellow minor league player who, unbeknownst to his teammates, was the original Frankenstein's monster. This gentle fantasy with a serious moral is essentially about people trying to fit into societies hostile to their existence. Sequel to Mary Shelley's *Frankenstein*.

Other books you might like:
Brian W. Aldiss, *Frankenstein Unbound*, 1973
Emmanuel Carrere, *Gothic Romance*, 1990
Mary Shelley, *Frankenstein*, 1818

404

MICHAEL BISHOP

Count Geiger's Blues

(New York: Tor, 1992)

Story type: Science Fiction (Arts; Alternate Universe)
Major character(s): Xavier Thaxton, Journalist, Hero (comic book superhero); Mikhail ''the Mick'' Geoffrey Menaker, Teenager; Bari Carlisle, Designer (fashion), Girlfriend (Xavier's)
Time period(s): 1990s
Locale(s): Oconee (fictional state bordering Tennessee and Georgia)

Summary: Stuffy, culture-encrusted Xavier Thaxton relates with difficulty to his new roommate, the Mick, Xavier's nephew who revels in popular culture. As Xavier's accident with radioactive waste changes Xavier into a comic book superhero, Xavier's relationship with the Mick improves while the change to superhero threatens Xavier's relationship with his girlfriend, Bari.

Other books you might like:
William Borden, *Superstoe*, 1968
Richard Brautigan, *The Hawkline Monster*, 1974
Mark Jacobson, *Gojiro*, 1991
Michael Kandel, *Captain Jack Zodiac*, 1992
George R.R. Martin, *Wild Cards*, 1987
    editor
Greg Snow, *That's All, Folks!*, 1992
Michael D. Weaver, *My Father Immortal*, 1989

405

MICHAEL BISHOP

Nebula Awards 24

(New York: Harcourt Brace Jovanovich, 1990)

Story type: Science Fiction (Anthology)
Series: Nebula Awards
Time period(s): Indeterminate

Summary: This collection from the Science Fiction Writers of America features articles, stories, poetry and memorials appearing during 1988. Michael Bishop contributed the introduction, with articles by Paul De Filippo, Bill Warren and Ian Watson and memorials to Clifford D. Simak by Gordon R. Dickson and to Robert A. Heinlein by Frank M. Robinson. Excerpts from novels are contributed by Lois McMaster Bujold and Jane Yolen. Stories appear by Neal Barrett, Jr., George Alec Effinger, Connie Willis and Gene Wolfe. This volume also continues the tradition of showcasing Rhysling Award winners' poetry, among others, Suzette Haden Elgin and Lucius Shepard.

Other books you might like:
Lou Aronica, *Full Spectrum 2*, 1990
    Shawna McCarthy, Amy Stout, Patrick LoBruto, co-editors
Gardner Dozois, *The Year's Best Science Fiction: Seventh Annual Collection*, 1990
Frank Herbert, *Nebula Winners 15*, 1981
Damon Knight, *Nebula Award Stories: 1965*, 1966
Robert Silverberg, *The Science Fiction Hall of Fame, Volume 1*, 1970
Donald A. Wollheim, *The 1990 Annual World's Best Science Fiction*, 1990
    Arthur W. Saha, co-editor
George Zebrowski, *Nebula Awards 22*, 1988

406

MICHAEL BISHOP, Editor

Nebula Awards 25

(New York: Harcourt Brace Jovanovich, 1991)

Story type: Science Fiction (Anthology)
Series: Nebula Awards

Summary: Subtitled, *SFWA's Choices for the Best Science Fiction 1989*, this volume contains an introduction by Michael Bishop plus articles, fiction nominated for Nebula Awards and three Rhysling Award winning poems by Bruce Boston, John M. Ford and Robert Frazier. Nebula Award winning fiction includes stories by Lois McMaster Bujold, Geoffrey A. Landis, Connie Willis and an excerpt from a novel by Elizabeth Scarborough. Other fiction includes stories by Michael Bishop, John Crowley, Gardner Dozois, and Mike Resnick. Ian Watson looks at fantasy and science fiction novels of 1989, Bill Warren writes of science fiction films of 1989 and Paul Di Filippo looks at SFWA's Annual "Nebula Award Mania." In other essays, founder and first president of SFWA, Damon Knight, asks "What is Science Fiction?," Orson Scott Card presents a speech delivered in 1989 to the Indiana Humanities Council and Richard Grant discusses the writing process. Appendixes include an article about the Nebula Awards and a list of Nebula Award winners 1965-1988.

Other books you might like:
Lou Aronica, *Full Spectrum*, 1988
    Shawna McCarthy, co-editor
Terry Carr, *Terry Carr's Best Science Fiction and Fantasy of the Year #16*, 1987
    editor

Gardner Dozois, *The Year's Best Science Fiction: Seventh Annual Collection*, 1990
    editor
Harlan Ellison, *Dangerous Visions*, 1967
    editor
Raymond J. Healy, *Adventures in Time and Space*, 1946
    J. Francis McComas, co-editor
Frank Herbert, *Nebula Winners 15*, 1981
    editor
Damon Knight, *Nebula Award Stories 1965*, 1966
    editor
Robert Silverberg, *The Science Fiction Hall of Fame, Volume 1*, 1970
    editor
Donald A. Wollheim, *The 1990 Annual World's Best Science Fiction*, 1990
    Arthur W. Saha, co-editor
George Zebrowski, *Nebula Awards 21*, 1987
    editor
George Zebrowski, *Nebula Awards 22*, 1988
    editor

407

MICHAEL BISHOP

No Enemy but Time

(New York: Bantam Spectra, 1989)

Story type: Science Fiction (Time Travel)
Major character(s): Joshua Kampa, Time Traveller; Helen, Prehistoric Human (Habiline)
Time period(s): 1980s; Indeterminate Past (Pleistocene period)
Locale(s): Africa

Summary: In this Nebula Award-winning novel, Joshua Kampa, a black American, travels into the Pleistocene past and takes up life with the near-human habilines he meets there. Originally published in 1982.

Other books you might like:
Roger MacBride Allen, *Orphan of Creation*, 1988
William Golding, *The Inheritors*, 1955
Elizabeth Marshall Thomas, *Reindeer Moon*, 1987

408

TERRY BISSON

Bears Discover Fire

(New York: Tor, 1993)

Story type: Science Fiction (Collection)

Summary: Contains all 19 of Bisson's short stories reprinted from 1990s periodicals. Includes the Hugo Award and Nebula Award-winning title story plus a Hugo Award nominee, "Press Ann," and a Nebula Award nominee, "They're Made Out of Meat." Stories vary in tone from humor to horror and reflect themes including first contact, time travel and environmental awareness. Concludes with a four-page afterword in which Bisson indicates his intent and the genesis of individual stories.

Other books you might like:
Damon Knight, *One Side Laughing: Stories Unlike Other Stories*, 1991
Nancy Kress, *The Aliens of Earth*, 1993
Spider Robinson, *Antinomy*, 1980
Spider Robinson, *Melancholy Elephants*, 1984
Michael Swanwick, *Gravity's Angels*, 1991
John Varley, *Blue Champagne*, 1986
John Varley, *The Persistence of Vision*, 1978

409

TERRY BISSON

Johnny Mnemonic
(New York: Pocket, 1995)

Story type: Science Fiction (Cyberpunk; Adventure)
Major character(s): Johnny, Courier (mnemonic), Fugitive
Time period(s): 2020s (2021)
Locale(s): Newark, New Jersey; Cyberspace; New York, New York

Summary: Immediately after Johnny transfers a computer file to his wetwired computer storage system, Yakuza assassins kill his employers and fragment the download key needed to rid him of the lethal file. Johnny flees to Newark where he hopes to unload the valuable file and collect his generous fee, if he can avoid the dragnet of well-armed thugs enthusiastically searching for him. Novelizes the film, based on William Gibson's short story.

Other books you might like:
Bruce Bethke, *Headcrash*, 1995
Pat Cadigan, *Fools*, 1992
Pat Cadigan, *Mindplayers*, 1987
George Alec Effinger, *When Gravity Fails*, 1987
William Gibson, *Neuromancer*, 1984
Neal Stephenson, *Snow Crash*, 1992
Michael Swanwick, *Vacuum Flowers*, 1987

410

TERRY BISSON

Pirates of the Universe
(New York; Tor, 1996)

Story type: Science Fiction (Adventure; Future Shock)
Major character(s): Gunther ''Gun'' Ryder, Spaceman (Space Ranger); Gordon Ryder, Fugitive; Donna, Girlfriend
Time period(s): 21st century
Locale(s): Orlando, Florida; Overworld, Space Station

Summary: Gunther Ryder has only one goal, to win a coveted spot in the Disney-Windows live-in theme park, ''Pirates of the Universe,'' for himself and his girlfriend Donna. To do so, he must complete one more ''Petey Hunt,'' in which Space Rangers seize the valuable skin of mysterious alien ship/creatures, which has replaced gold as the new world economic currency.

Other books you might like:
Shale Aaron, *Virtual Death*, 1995

Kevin J. Anderson, *Ill Wind*, 1995
  Doug Beason, co-author
David R. Bunch, *Moderan*, 1971
Mary Rosenblum, *The Stone Garden*, 1995
Robert Sheckley, *Journey Beyond Tomorrow*, 1962
Kurt Vonnegut Jr., *Player Piano*, 1952

411

TERRY BISSON

Virtuosity
(New York: Pocket, 1995)

Story type: Science Fiction (Alternate Intelligence; Techno-Thriller)
Major character(s): Sid 6.7, Artificial Intelligence, Criminal; Parker Barnes, Police Officer, Experimental Subject
Time period(s): 1990s (1999)
Locale(s): Los Angeles, California

Summary: When a computer program composed of serial killer personalities manifests itself in reality, Parker Barnes must find it and neutralize the deadly threat. Novelizes the film.

Other books you might like:
Piers Anthony, *Killobyte*, 1993
Ben Bova, *Death Dream*, 1994
Philip Jose Farmer, *Red Orc's Rage*, 1991
Cole Perriman, *Terminal Games*, 1994
Robert J. Sawyer, *The Terminal Experiment*, 1995
Vivian Vande Velde, *User Unfriendly*, 1991

412

TERRY BISSON

Voyage to the Red Planet
(New York: William Morrow, 1990)

Story type: Science Fiction (Adventure; Arts)
Major character(s): Natasha Alyosha Katerina Kirov, Spaceship Captain; Rocket Man Bass, Pilot (spaceship); S.C. Jeffries, Doctor
Time period(s): Indeterminate Future
Locale(s): *Mary Poppins*, Spaceship; Mars

Summary: When a never-used, mothballed spaceship becomes available to a renegade independent movie producer, he arranges for a ship's crew and the necessary movie-making equipment and personnel to travel to Mars to film on location. Once there, the group must not only film their movie, but also overcome the problem threatening to keep them on Mars forever.

Other books you might like:
James Blish, *The Triumph of Time*, 1958
Harry Harrison, *The Technicolor Time Machine*, 1967
John Varley, *Demon*, 1984
Ian Watson, *Chekhov's Journey*, 1989

413

GARY L. BLACKWOOD

Beyond the Door

(New York: Atheneum, 1991)

Story type: Science Fiction (Young Adult; Political)
Major character(s): Walter Scott Shaffer Jr., Student, Adventurer; Tomeas, Outcast, Scientist; Tallulah ''Tulley'' Bankhead, Student, Adventurer
Time period(s): 1990s
Locale(s): Earth; Gale'tin, Planet—Imaginary

Summary: In his local library, Scott discovers a door which leads to another world, Gale'tin, which is beginning to develop modern technology. There he meets Tomeas who seems to be trying to help bring higher technology to his world. After Tulley also ventures to Gale'tin, Scott and Tulley discover the darker truth, that Tomeas pursues dangerous experiments, hoping to increase his control over his universe's emerging technology.

Other books you might like:
David Brin, *Earth*, 1990
Cheryl J. Franklin, *Fire Crossing*, 1991
Alexander Key, *The Forgotten Door*, 1965
Madeleine L'Engle, *A Wrinkle in Time*, 1962
Margaret Weis, *Fire Sea*, 1991
  Tracy Hickman, co-author
Robert Charles Wilson, *A Bridge of Years*, 1991

414

GARY L. BLACKWOOD

The Dying Sun

(New York: Atheneum, 1989)

Story type: Science Fiction (Young Adult)
Major character(s): James, Teenager; Robert, Teenager (James' best friend)
Time period(s): 21st century (2050)
Locale(s): Missouri

Summary: A new ice age has driven most of the population of the United States south into Mexico where they live in newly-built but horribly overcrowded cities along the border. The native Mexicans, hating this gringo invasion, are becoming increasingly violent and James' family decides to move back to Missouri, even though it is now little more than a frozen wasteland. James stays behind but, as the violence escalates, decides that he too must travel north.

Other books you might like:
Bruce Brooks, *No Kidding*, 1989
John Christopher, *The Long Winter*, 1962
John Christopher, *Wild Jack*, 1974
Michael Moorcock, *The Ice Schooner*, 1969

415

JOHN BLAIR

Bright Angel

(New York: Ballantine/Del Rey, 1991)

Story type: Science Fiction (First Contact; Disaster)
Major character(s): James Harris, Settler (colonist); Song Lan, Scientist; Hugh Carney, Doctor
Time period(s): 21st century (2063-2071)
Locale(s): Earth; Outer Space

Summary: James Harris should have died with the rest of the human colony on Comfort, but instead, he appeared in Antarctica, twelve light years away. The moment of his return to Earth coincided with the beginning of a cooling trend, just like the climate change which had killed the colony on Comfort. After years of living incognito, Harris must face his past in order to save himself and Earth.

Other books you might like:
C.J. Cherryh, *Voyager in Night*, 1984
Arthur C. Clarke, *2001: A Space Odyssey*, 1968
Arthur C. Clarke, *2010: Odyssey Two*, 1982
Arthur C. Clarke, *2061: Odyssey Three*, 1987
Ursula K. Le Guin, *The Lathe of Heaven*, 1971
Alice Sheldon, *Up the Walls of the World*, 1978
  as James Tiptree, Jr.

416

JOHN BLAIR

A Landscape of Darkness

(New York: Ballantine, 1990)

Story type: Science Fiction (Military; Psychic Powers)
Major character(s): John Sebastian Clay, Mercenary; Howard S. Rankin, Military Personnel (colonel); Tind, Warrior (assassin)
Time period(s): Indeterminate Future
Locale(s): Earth; Ithavoll, Planet—Imaginary

Summary: John Clay is recruited for a secret mission to destroy a suspected alien weapon on a backward planet. The Mission leads him and three companions into a series of violent and bloody encounters culminating in Clay's confrontation with a dead ''god.'' This is the author's first novel.

Other books you might like:
Robert Asprin, *The Bug Wars*, 1979
C.J. Cherryh, *The Faded Sun: Kesrith*, 1978
Gordon R. Dickson, *Dorsai!*, 1959
Gordon R. Dickson, *Soldier, Ask Not*, 1968
Joe Haldeman, *The Forever War*, 1975

417

KATHERINE BLAKE

The Interior Life

(New York: Baen, 1990)

Story type: Fantasy (Romance; Alternate World)

Major character(s): Sue, Housewife, Parent (mother); Lady Amalia, Noblewoman (mistress of Fendarath)
Time period(s): Indeterminate Past; 1990s (1990)
Locale(s): Fendarath, Fictional Country

Summary: A bored housewife's daydreams and fantasies tap into an alternate world. The bond between Sue and the inhabitants of Fendarath enables her to help Amalia become queen and shows Sue the necessity of becoming involved with others. This is the author's first novel.

Other books you might like:
Marion Zimmer Bradley, *The House Between the Worlds*, 1980
Stephen R. Donaldson, *The Mirror of Her Dreams*, 1986
Suzette Haden Elgin, *The Grand Jubilee*, 1981
Suzette Haden Elgin, *Twelve Fair Kingdoms*, 1981
Suzette Haden Elgin, *And Then There'll Be Fireworks*, 1981
Marge Piercy, *Woman on the Edge of Time*, 1976

418

JAY D. BLAKENEY

The Goda War

(New York: Ace Books, 1989)

Story type: Science Fiction (Military)
Major character(s): Dire-Lord Brock, Nobleman, Warrior; Kezi Falmah-Al, Warrior (Colonel)
Time period(s): Indeterminate Future
Locale(s): Held Empire, Interstellar Empire/Federation

Summary: As two powerful empires battle, Brock, dire-lord of the Held, whose side is losing, vows to activate the long dormant goddas, planet-sized killing machines. Also searching for the goddas is Colonel Kezi Falmah-Al. She too seeks to turn the machines to military advantage.

Other books you might like:
Jack McDevitt, *A Talent for War*, 1989
Fred Saberhagen, *Berserker*, 1967
Fred Saberhagen, *Berserker Man*, 1979
Fred Saberhagen, *The Berserker Throne*, 1985
Fred Saberhagen, *The Berserker Wars*, 1981
Fred Saberhagen, *Berserker's Planet*, 1975
Fred Saberhagen, *Earth Descended*, 1982
Fred Saberhagen, *The Ultimate Enemy*, 1979

419

JAY D. BLAKENEY

Requiem for Anthi

(New York: Ace Books, 1990)

Story type: Science Fiction (Space Opera)
Series: Anthi
Major character(s): Asan, Alien, Nobleman; Zaula, Alien, Noblewoman
Time period(s): Indeterminate Future
Locale(s): Ruantl, Planet—Imaginary

Summary: On a dying planet, the few survivors of an alien race fight for rule. Then the earthmen come, members of the Galactic Space Institute, eager to despoil the planet of its little

remaining wealth. The lord Asan swears to fight them off, even if it means reawakening the goddess Anthi herself.

Other books you might like:
Emma Bull, *Falcon*, 1989
C.J. Cherryh, *The Faded Sun: Kesrith*, 1978
A.C. Crispin, *Starbridge*, 1989
Mary Gentle, *Ancient Light*, 1989
Mary Gentle, *Golden Witchbreed*, 1983
Melisa C. Michaels, *Far Harbor*, 1989

420

JAMES P. BLAYLOCK

All the Bells on Earth

(New York: Ace, 1995)

Story type: Fantasy (Contemporary Realism)
Major character(s): Walt Stebbins, Salesman (mail order); Roger Argyle, Businessman; Ivy Stebbins, Real Estate Agent
Time period(s): 1990s (1995)
Locale(s): Orange, California

Summary: While somebody defaces churches in peaceful Orange, good-hearted but eccentric catalog salesman Walt Stebbins gets hold of an extremely weird talisman, a dead bird in a jar. When the events come together, Walt's decisions mean the difference between life and damnation for a surprisingly large number of people.

Other books you might like:
Ray Bradbury, *Something Wicked This Way Comes*, 1962
Jack Cady, *The Off Season*, 1995
John Crowley, *Aegypt*, 1987
Robertson Davies, *What's Bred in the Bone*, 1985
Tim Powers, *Last Call*, 1992

421

JAMES P. BLAYLOCK

The Last Coin

(New York: Ace, 1988)

Story type: Fantasy (Religious)
Major character(s): Pennyman, Fortune Hunter (Rare coin collector); Andrew, Young Man (Amiable idler, unwitting hero)
Time period(s): 1980s
Locale(s): California (Guest House)

Summary: Story revolves around the thirty coins Judas Iscariot was given in exchange for the betrayal of Christ. One man has come close to collecting all thirty; if successful, he will possess a vast supernatural power.

Other books you might like:
Michael Frayn, *Sweet Dreams*, 1974
Barry B. Longyear, *The God Box*,
Rudy Rucker, *White Light, or What Is Cantor's Continuum Problem*,

422

JAMES P. BLAYLOCK

Lord Kelvin's Machine

(Sauk City, Wisconsin: Arkham House, 1992)

Story type: Fantasy (Quest; Historical)
Major character(s): Langdon St. Ives, Scientist, Explorer; Ignatio Narbando, Scientist; Jack Owlesby, Artisan (toymaker)
Time period(s): 19th century
Locale(s): London, England; At Sea (under the North Sea)

Summary: Langdon St. Ives, introduced in *Homunculus*, is pursuing Dr. Ignatio Narbando to get revenge for the murder of his wife. He travels to South America, Norway, beneath the North Sea, high in the air and back in time, dodging a bizarre cast of lunatics and ne'er-do-wells the whole way. Eventually, the salvation of the world and his soul hinge on St. Ives' moral choices and the fabulous machine of Lord Kelvin. Illustrated by J.K. Potter.

Other books you might like:
John Bellairs, *The Face in the Frost*, 1969
William Gibson, *The Difference Engine*, 1991
   Bruce Sterling, co-author
K.W. Jeter, *Infernal Devices*, 1987
Tim Powers, *The Anubis Gates*, 1983
Howard Waldrop, *Night of the Cooters*, 1990

423

JAMES P. BLAYLOCK

Night Relics

(New York: Ace, 1994)

Story type: Horror (Ghost Story)
Major character(s): Peter Travers, Architect; Lance Klein, Businessman (real estate developer); Bernard Pomeroy, Businessman (salesman)
Time period(s): 1990s (1994)
Locale(s): Trabuco Canyon, California

Summary: The disapearance of his ex-wife Amanda and son David in the land surrounding his house spurs Peter Travers to action. In the course of his actions, he examines his life and finds that current events may dovetail horribly with an act of murder that resulted in the house being haunted for over 70 years.

Other books you might like:
Jonathan Aycliffe, *Naomi's Room*, 1991
Stephen King, *The Shining*, 1977
T.M. Wright, *Little Boy Lost*, 1992

424

JAMES P. BLAYLOCK

The Paper Grail

(New York: Ace, 1991)

Story type: Fantasy (Quest; Contemporary)

Major character(s): Howard Barton, Museum Curator; Roy Barton, Construction Worker (builder of haunted houses); Mr. Jimmers, Companion (eccentric)
Time period(s): 1990s
Locale(s): California

Summary: Hoping to acquire a promised sketch by legendary Japanese artist Hoku-sai, Howard journeys to Northern California. Upon his arrival, eccentric behavior by acquaintances and family turn the simple task into a confusing quest for the artwork, that turns out to be a magic talisman with which the skilled wielder can control the elements.

Other books you might like:
Charles de Lint, *The Little Country*, 1990
Tom Deitz, *Soulsmith*, 1991
Roger L. DiSilvestro, *Living with the Reptiles*, 1990
Alan Dean Foster, *Cyber Way*, 1990
Marc Laidlaw, *Neon Lotus*, 1988
Stephen Leigh, *The Abraxis Marvel Circus*, 1990

425

JAMES P. BLAYLOCK

The Stone Giant

(New York: Ace, 1989)

Story type: Fantasy (Light Fantasy)
Major character(s): Theophile Escargot, Cook (baker of pies), Adventurer (exiled); Leta, Young Woman (beautiful companion of Theophi)
Time period(s): Indeterminate
Locale(s): Twombly Town, Earth (Quasi modern town)

Summary: Theophile is kicked out of his marriage and leaves Twombly Town, only to find himself on a series of adventures. Elves, faeries, witches and goblins are a part of the supporting cast.

Other books you might like:
Avram Davidson, *Marco Polo and the Sleeping Beauty*, 1988
L. Sprague de Camp, *The Honorable Barbarian*, 1989
R.A. Lafferty, *The Devil Is Dead*, 1988

426

JAMES BLISH

The Devil's Day

(New York: Baen, 1989)

Story type: Horror (Apocalyptic Horror)
Series: After Such Knowledge Trilogy
Major character(s): Father Domenico, Religious (Jesuit priest), Magician (White magician); Theron Ware, Magician (Black magician)
Time period(s): 1960s
Locale(s): Italy; United States

Summary: Black magician Theron Ware, urged on by Baines, a billionaire industrialist, releases eighty demons from hell for one night. This triggers the appearance of Dis, capital of Hell, in Death Valley, the Devil himself, and the onslaught of Armageddon, while a handful of men fight to keep Satan from final and total victory. Originally published as *Black Easter* in 1968 and as *The Day After Judgment* in 1971.

Other books you might like:
Stephen King, *The Stand*, 1978
Robert R. McCammon, *Swan Song*, 1987

427

JAMES BLISH
J.A. LAWRENCE, Co-Author

Star Trek: The Classic Episodes 1
(New York: Bantam Spectra, 1991)

Story type: Science Fiction (Space Opera; Collection)
Series: Star Trek
Major character(s): James T. Kirk, Spaceship Captain; Spock, Scientist, Alien (Vulcan); Leonard McCoy, Doctor
Time period(s): 23rd century
Locale(s): *U.S.S. Enterprise*, Spaceship; Outer Space

Summary: This volume includes a 12-page introduction by D.C. Fontana plus all 8 prefaces originally appearing in Blish's *Star Trek 3, 4, 5, 6, 9, 10, 11 & 12*, the forward to *Star Trek 12*, plus Blish's story versions of all 27 episodes aired during *Star Trek's* original first television season (1966-1967) and appearing previously in Blish's numbered Star Trek Series (1967-1977). Stories include two from Hugo Award winning episodes, "The Menagerie" by series creator Gene Roddenberry, and "The City on the Edge of Forever" by Harlan Ellison. Other notable stories include the prequel to *Star Trek II: The Wrath of Khan* titled "Space Seed," plus Theodore Sturgeon's "Shore Leave" and Robert Bloch's "What Are Little Girls Made Of?"

Other books you might like:
Margaret Wander Bonanno, *Strangers From the Sky*, 1987
Lee Correy, *The Abode of Life*, 1982
Gene DeWeese, *Chain of Attack*, 1987
Diane Duane, *Doctor's Orders*, 1990
John M. Ford, *How Much for Just the Planet?*, 1987
Alan Dean Foster, *Star Trek Log Ten*, 1978
J.A. Lawrence, *Mudd's Angels*, 1978
Jean Lorrah, *The IDIC Epidemic*, 1988
Vonda N. McIntyre, *Enterprise*, 1986
Vonda N. McIntyre, *The Entropy Effect*, 1981
Vonda N. McIntyre, *Star Trek II: The Wrath of Khan*, 1982
Melinda M. Snodgrass, *The Tears of the Singers*, 1984
Howard Weinstein, *The Covenant of the Crown*, 1981

428

JAMES BLISH

Star Trek: The Classic Episodes 2
(New York: Bantam Spectra, 1991)

Story type: Science Fiction (Space Opera; Collection)
Series: Star Trek
Major character(s): James T. Kirk, Spaceship Captain; Spock, Scientist, Alien (Vulcan); Leonard McCoy, Doctor
Time period(s): 23rd century
Locale(s): *U.S.S. Enterprise*, Spaceship; Outer Space

Summary: This volume contains a 14-page introduction by David Gerrold plus Blish's story versions of the 25 episodes aired during *Star Trek's* original second television season (1967-1968). Stories include three from episodes receiving Hugo Award nominations, Theodore Sturgeon's "Amok Time," Norman Spinrad's "The Doomsday Machine," and David Gerrold's "The Trouble with Tribbles." Other notable stories include two from Robert Bloch's episodes, "Catspaw" and "Wolf in the Fold."

Other books you might like:
Greg Bear, *Corona*, 1984
Margaret Wander Bonanno, *Dwellers in the Crucible*, 1985
A.C. Crispin, *Time for Yesterday*, 1988
A.C. Crispin, *Yesterday's Son*, 1983
Alan Dean Foster, *Star Trek Log One*, 1974
Janet Kagan, *Uhura's Song*, 1985
J.A. Lawrence, *Mudd's Angels*, 1978
Jean Lorrah, *The Vulcan Academy Murders*, 1984
Sondra Marshak, *Star Trek: The New Voyages*, 1976
    Myrna Culbreath, co-author
Sondra Marshak, *Star Trek: The New Voyages II*, 1978
    Myrna Culbreath, co-author
Vonda N. McIntyre, *The Search for Spock*, 1984
Robert E. Vardeman, *The Klingon Gambit*, 1981

429

JAMES BLISH
J.A. LAWRENCE, Co-Author

Star Trek: The Classic Episodes 3
(New York: Bantam Spectra, 1991)

Story type: Science Fiction (Space Opera; Collection)
Series: Star Trek
Major character(s): James T. Kirk, Spaceship Captain; Spock, Scientist, Alien (Vulcan); Leonard McCoy, Doctor
Time period(s): 23rd century
Locale(s): *U.S.S. Enterprise*, Spaceship; Outer Space

Summary: This volume contains a 16-page introduction by Norman Spinrad plus Blish's story version of each of the 24 episodes aired during *Star Trek's* original third television season (1968-1969). The stories appear in Blish's numbered Star Trek Series (1967-1977).

Other books you might like:
Margaret Wander Bonanno, *Strangers From the Sky*, 1987
A.C. Crispin, *Yesterday's Son*, 1983
Diane Duane, *The Wounded Sky*, 1983
John M. Ford, *The Final Reflection*, 1984
Jack C. Haldeman II, *Perry's Planet*, 1980
Joe Haldeman, *Planet of Judgment*, 1977
Joe Haldeman, *World Without End*, 1979
Barbara Hambly, *Ishmael*, 1985
J.A. Lawrence, *Mudd's Angels*, 1978
Jean Lorrah, *The Night of the Twin Moons*, 1976
M.S. Murdock, *Web of the Romulans*, 1983
Kathleen Sky, *Vulcan!*, 1978
Robert E. Vardeman, *Mutiny on the Enterprise*, 1983

430

ROBERT BLOCH

The Complete Stories of Robert Bloch, Volume 2: Bitter Ends
(New York: Citadel Twilight, 1990)

Story type: Horror (Collection)

Summary: Thirty-one tales of horror, suspense and science fiction, originally published between 1956 and 1960. Stories such as "Betsy Blake Will Live Forever" and "Terror over Hollywood" display Bloch's fascination with the gulf between Hollywood images and reality. "The Screaming People," a tale of paranoia, and "The Real Bad Friend," with its schizophrenic narrator, reveal Bloch's interest in psychological horror. The witty puns of "Crime in Rhyme" and poetic justice of "Sock Finish" are characteristic trademarks of Bloch's short fiction. Originally published in 1987 as *The Selected Stories*, this reprint is mistitled, as it is not a complete collection.

Other books you might like:
Charles Beaumont, *Selected Stories*, 1988
Fredric Brown, *The Best of Fredric Brown*, 1976
Henry Kuttner, *The Best of Henry Kuttner*, 1975
Richard Matheson, *Collected Stories*, 1989

431

ROBERT BLOCH

The Complete Stories of Robert Bloch, Volume 3: Last Rites
(New York: Citadel Twilight, 1991)

Story type: Horror (Collection)

Summary: This final volume of the mistitled reprint of *The Selected Stories of Robert Bloch* brings together 39 tales of horror, suspense and science fiction published between 1960 and 1979. Included are the gruesome tale of ventriloquism, "Final Performance"; a future story of Jack of Ripper, "A Toy for Juliette"; a fantasy of a horrifying cliche come to life, "A Case of the Stubborns"; and three stories set at the carnival: "Double Whammy," "Freak Show" and "The Animal Fair." All selections are leavened with Bloch's morbid wit.

Other books you might like:
Charles Beaumont, *Selected Stories*, 1988
Fredric Brown, *The Best of Fredric Brown*, 1976
Henry Kuttner, *The Best of Henry Kuttner*, 1975
Richard Matheson, *Collected Stories*, 1989
William Relling Jr., *The Infinite Man*, 1989

432

ROBERT BLOCH

The Complete Stories of Robert Bloch. Volume 1: Final Reckonings
(New York: Citadel, 1990)

Story type: Horror (Collection)

Summary: Thirty-one stories first published between 1939 and 1956. Bloch's sense of the horror tradition is evident in "The Skull of the Marquis de Sade" and "The Man Who Collected Poe." His fascination with psychological obsession is illustrated in "The Head Man," his interest in split personality with "Lucy Comes to Stay," his concern with persecution and madness in "Terror in the Night," and his ironical humor in "The Pin." Originally published in 1987 as *The Selected Stories...*, this reprint is mistitled, as it is not a complete collection.

Other books you might like:
Charles Beaumont, *Charles Beaumont: Selected Stories*, 1988
Richard Matheson, *Richard Matheson: Collected Stories*, 1989

433

ROBERT BLOCH

The Early Fears
(Minneapolis, Minnesota: Fedogan & Bremer, 1994)

Story type: Horror (Collection)

Summary: This omnibus collects the contents of *The Opener of the Way* (1945) and *Pleasant Dreams* (1962), and adds three recently published tales to boost the story count to 39. The stories are a virtual roadmap to themes and approaches that have dominated Bloch's work for 61 years, including Lovecraftian horror ("The Mannikin" and "The Shambler From the Stars"), psychological horror ("Yours Truly, Jack the Ripper" and "Enoch"), juvenile delinquency ("Sweets to the Sweet" and "Sweet Sixteen"), and deals with the devil ("Fiddler's Fee" and "That Hellbound Train"). Included are collaborations with Edgar Allan Poe ("The Lighthouse") and Henry Kuttner ("The Grab Bag"). Bloch has supplied a new introduction.

Other books you might like:
Charles Beaumont, *Collected Stories*, 1988
Ray Bradbury, *The Stories of Ray Bradbury*, 1980
Richard Matheson, *Collected Stories*, 1989
William F. Nolan, *Things Beyond Midnight*, 1984

434

ROBERT BLOCH

Fear and Trembling
(New York: Tor, 1989)

Story type: Horror (Collection)

Summary: Thirteen stories that span most of Bloch's career from the earliest, "The Brood of Bubastis," a 1937 chiller in the Lovecraft mode to "Horror Scope," a gory 1989 tale of a serial killer with a taste for dismemberment. The typical Bloch mix of wit, gore, cynicism, irony, and a touch of sentimentality. Lively writing, vivid scenes, and Bloch's trademark twist endings.

Other books you might like:
Charles Beaumont, *Selected Stories*, 1988
Charles Birkin, *My Name Is Death*, 1966
Richard Matheson, *Collected Stories*, 1989

435
ROBERT BLOCH
ANDRE NORTON, Co-Author

The Jekyll Legacy
(New York: Tor, 1990)

Story type: Horror (Mystery)
Major character(s): Hester Lane, Writer; Gertrude Kirby, Child-Care Giver; Alfred Prothore, Political Figure
Time period(s): 1880s
Locale(s): London, England

Summary: On assignment in London to investigate the founding of the Salvation Army, Canadian writer Hester Lane moves into the house of her recently deceased uncle Henry Jekyll. There she becomes embroiled in an intrigue involving white slavers who appear to have been influenced by Jekyll's former associate, the mysterious Edward Hyde.

Other books you might like:
Robert Bloch, *Night of the Ripper*, 1985
Valerie Martin, *Mary Reilly*, 1990
Robert Louis Stevenson, *The Strange Case of Dr. Jekyll and Mr. Hyde*, 1886

436
ROBERT BLOCH

Lori
(New York: Tor, 1989)

Story type: Horror (Mystery)
Major character(s): Lori Holmes, Young Woman (Beautiful); Anthony Leverett, Doctor (Psychiatrist)
Time period(s): 1980s
Locale(s): Los Angeles, California

Summary: A mysterious phone call and the picture of a long dead girl—her exact double—send Lori on a search for the truth about her own tangled, forgotten past, a search that threatens her sanity and even her life.

Other books you might like:
John Farris, *When Michael Calls*, 1967

437
ROBERT BLOCH

Midnight Pleasures
(New York: Tor, 1991)

Story type: Horror (Collection)

Summary: A reprint of a 1987 collection of 14 stories of horror and suspense by one of the masters of the modern horror story. Included are "The Rubber Room," a tale of psychological horror; "The Night Before Christmas," a grim exercise in adultery and revenge; "Everybody Needs a Little Love," about an obsession taken to extremes; and "The Totem Pole," a story of an Indian curse from the author's early *Weird Tales* fiction.

Other books you might like:
Charles Beaumont, *Selected Stories*, 1988
Hugh B. Cave, *Murgunstrumm and Others*, 1977
Richard Matheson, *Collected Stories*, 1989
William Relling Jr., *The Infinite Man*, 1989
Manly Wade Wellman, *Worse Things Waiting*, 1973

438
ROBERT BLOCH, Editor

Monsters in Our Midst
(New York: Tor, 1993)

Story type: Horror (Anthology)

Summary: This second collection of non-supernatural horror stories is a follow-up to Bloch's previous anthology *Psycho Paths* (Tor, 1991), and pursues the same agenda of psychological horror fiction that the author has promulgated since he wrote *Psycho* in 1959. The best of the 17 stories includes Ramsey Campbell's "For You to Judge," about a man who becomes "infected" by the spirit of a vicious murderer; Jonathan Carroll's "The Lick of Time," concerned with a woman who creates an alternate identity on her answering machine; Bloch's own "It Takes One to Know One," in which a disgruntled author fulfills a pact he and his friends made years before; and Ray Bradbury's "Fee Fie Fo Fum," about an elderly woman who sees murderous intentions in a young man but can convince no one of his true nature.

Other books you might like:
Richard T. Chizmar, *Cold Blood*, 1991
Ed Gorman, *Dark Crimes II: Modern Masters of Noir*, 1992 editor
Ed Gorman, *Stalkers*, 1990
Martin H. Greenberg, co-editor

439
ROBERT BLOCH

The Mysteries of the Worm
(Oakland, California: Chaosium, 1993)

Story type: Horror (Collection)

Summary: An expansion of Robert Bloch's 1981 volume of the same title, this book collects 17 stories written in homage to the mythic underpinnings of H.P. Lovecraft's stories, dubbed the Cthulhu Mythos. Included are ''The Shambler From the Stars,'' which inspired Lovecraft's own classic ''The Haunter of the Dark''; ''The Mannikin,'' about a hunchback whose deformity is more than a physical hindrance; ''The Creeper in the Crypt,'' which fuses horror and hard-boiled crime fiction; and several stories steeped in Egyptian mythology, including ''The Secret of Sebek,'' ''The Faceless God,'' and ''Fane of the Black Pharoah.'' Series editor Robert Price supplies an introduction, and Bloch and the late Lin Carter afterwords.

Other books you might like:
Ramsey Campbell, *Cold Print*, 198
August Derleth, *Tales of the Cthulhu Mythos*, 1969
    editor
H.P. Lovecraft, *The Watchers out of Time*, 1974
    August Derleth, co-author

440
ROBERT BLOCH

Psycho
(New York: Tor, 1989)

Story type: Horror (Serial Killer)
Major character(s): Norman Bates, Innkeeper (Motel Owner), Murderer (Lunatic); Mary Crane, Thief
Time period(s): 1950s
Locale(s): Fairvale, Texas (Bates Motel)

Summary: Fleeing with $40,000 in stolen money, Mary Crane stops off—permanently—at the Bates Motel. A private detective, Mary's boyfriend, Sam Loomis, and her sister, Lila, subsequently track Mary to the motel where they, too, encounter Norman's vengeful ''Mother.'' Originally published in 1959.

Other books you might like:
Ramsey Campbell, *The Face That Must Die*, 1979

441
ROBERT BLOCH

Psycho II
(New York: Tor, 1989)

Story type: Horror (Mystery)
Major character(s): Norman Bates, Murderer (Escaped lunatic); Adam Claiborne, Doctor (Norman's psychiatrist)
Time period(s): 1980s
Locale(s): Fairvale, Texas; Hollywood, California

Summary: Norman escapes from confinement and heads for Hollywood, where a film of his career is being made. Shortly thereafter, deaths begin to occur on the studio backlot which may—or may not—be Norman's fault. Originally published in 1982.

Other books you might like:
Ramsey Campbell, *The Doll Who Ate His Mother*, 1976

442
ROBERT BLOCH

Psycho House
(New York: Tor, 1990)

Story type: Horror (Mystery)
Major character(s): Amelia ''Amy'' Haines, Writer (True crime novels); Hank Gibbs, Journalist, Publisher (Fairvale's sole newspaper)
Time period(s): 1990s
Locale(s): Fairvale, Texas

Summary: The Bates Motel and adjoining house is rebuilt as a tourist attraction, but before opening day it becomes the site of multiple murders. While researching a book on Bates' original crimes, Amy Haines finds herself both a suspect in the new killings and a potential victim of Bates' ''successor.''

Other books you might like:
Nina Romberg, *The Spirit Stalker*, 1989

443
ROBERT BLOCH
MARTIN H. GREENBERG, Co-Author

Psycho-Paths
(New York: Tor, 1991)

Story type: Horror (Anthology)

Summary: Seventeen tales of non-supernatural horror, collected by the author of *Psycho*. Most of the stories fall into the subgenre of psychological horror, and are offered as an antidote to horror fiction that caters to tastes for gore and supernatural special effects. The best include Steve Rasnic Tem's ''Jesse,'' Charles Grant's ''Kin'' and Edward D. Hoch's ''The Secret Blade.''

Other books you might like:
Alfred Hitchcock, *Alfred Hitchcock Presents: Stories Not for the Nervous*, 1965
Alfred Hitchcock, *Alfred Hitchcock Presents: Stories My Mother Never Told Me*, 1963
Alfred Hitchcock, *Alfred Hitchcock Presents: Stories for Late at Night*, 1961
Joan Kahn, *Hanging by a Thread*, 1969
Joan Kahn, *The Edge of the Chair*, 1967

444
FRANCESCA LIA BLOCK

Baby Be-Bop
(New York: HarperCollins, 1995)

Story type: Fantasy (Contemporary; Young Adult)
Series: Weetzie Bat
Major character(s): Dirk McDonald, Teenager, Homosexual; Grandma Fifi, Grandparent, Dancer; Pop, Teenager
Time period(s): 1970s
Locale(s): Los Angeles, California

Summary: Dirk lives in a little cottage with his grandmother and her pets. As he grows up, he slowly discovers his homosexuality and what that means to society. With the help of the ghosts of his father and great-grandmother, Dirk learns to love himself and others.

Other books you might like:
Marion Dane Bauer, *Am I Blue?*, 1994
   editor
James P. Blaylock, *Land of Dreams*, 1987
Diana Wynne Jones, *Aunt Maria*, 1991
Daniel Manus Pinkwater, *Young Adults*, 1991
Will Shetterly, *Elsewhere*, 1991

445

FRANCESCA LIA BLOCK

Cherokee Bat and the Goat Guys

(New York: HarperCollins, 1992)

Story type: Fantasy (Young Adult; Contemporary)
Series: Weetzie Bat
Major character(s): Cherokee Bat, Teenager, Musician; Coyote, Shaman; Witch Baby, Musician (drummer), Witch
Time period(s): 1990s
Locale(s): Los Angeles, California

Summary: Weetzie Bat and her friends have gone to South America to shoot a film, leaving the teenaged children under the care of Coyote. Left to their own devices, the teenagers form a band and begin to grapple with the attractions and perils of adulthood. Magic gifts from Coyote give the band confidence, but also inspire them to recklessness. Written in an exotic style, this novel, like its predecessors, deals frankly, but not graphically, with adult problems such as sex and drug use.

Other books you might like:
James P. Blaylock, *Land of Dreams*, 1987
Emma Bull, *War for the Oaks*, 1987
Diana Wynne Jones, *Aunt Maria*, 1991
Daniel Manus Pinkwater, *Young Adults*, 1991
Will Shetterly, *Elsewhere*, 1991
Terri Windling, *Bordertown*, 1986
   Mark Alan Arnold, co-editor

446

FRANCESCA LIA BLOCK

Ecstasia

(New York: Roc, 1993)

Story type: Fantasy (Romance)
Major character(s): Rafe, Musician (drummer), Orphan; Calliope, Psychic, Orphan; Lily, Sports Figure (acrobat), Addict
Time period(s): Indeterminate Future
Locale(s): Elysia, Fictional City

Summary: In Elysia, a city of eternal youth populated only by the young, Rafe drums for Ecstasia, Elysia's hottest band. Rafe falls in love with a doomed woman whose addiction and loss drag her Under, where old people go. Perhaps love, even in this exotic world, can beat age and death.

Other books you might like:
Poppy Z. Brite, *Drawing Blood*, 1993
John Crowley, *Little, Big*, 1981
Jonathan Littell, *Bad Voltage*, 1989
Ian McDonald, *Desolation Road*, 1988
Pat Murphy, *The City, Not Long After*, 1989

447

FRANCESCA LIA BLOCK

The Hanged Man

(New York: HarperCollins, 1994)

Story type: Fantasy (Contemporary Realism)
Major character(s): Laurel, Psychic; Jack, Addict; Claudia, Addict
Time period(s): 1990s
Locale(s): Los Angeles, California

Summary: While waiting in the hospital room for her father to die, Laurel meets Jack, a mysterious junkie. Overwhelmed by her abusive childhood, Laurel begins to sink into a half-remembered world of dreams and regrets. The book takes its structure from a tarot reading with cards indicating the changes Laurel must make to survive.

Other books you might like:
Poppy Z. Brite, *Lost Souls*, 1992
William S. Burroughs, *Junky*, 1953
Pat Cadigan, *Synners*, 1991
Kathe Koja, *Skin*, 1993
Alexander Trocchi, *Cain's Book*, 1960

448

FRANCESCA LIA BLOCK

Missing Angel Juan

(New York: HarperCollins, 1993)

Story type: Fantasy (Young Adult; Contemporary)
Series: Weetzie Bat
Major character(s): Witch Baby, Teenager, Musician (drummer); Angel Juan, Teenager, Musician (bass guitar); Charlie Bat, Spirit, Grandparent
Time period(s): 1990s
Locale(s): Los Angeles, California; New York, New York

Summary: When Angel Juan leaves warm and sunny California for New York, Witch Baby follows him. Searching for her missing lover, the strange young woman finds out about life and herself. Like Block's other books, this stylistically exotic novel deals frankly, although not graphically, with adult issues such as sex and drug abuse.

Other books you might like:
James P. Blaylock, *Land of Dreams*, 1987
Emma Bull, *War for the Oaks*, 1987
Suzy McKee Charnas, *The Bronze King*, 1985
Daniel Manus Pinkwater, *Young Adults*, 1991
Will Shetterly, *Elsewhere*, 1991

449

FRANCESCA LIA BLOCK

Primavera

(New York: Roc, 1994)

Story type: Fantasy (Literary; Adventure)
Series: Elysia
Major character(s): Primavera, Singer; Calliope, Parent, Psychic; Gunn, Peddler, Businessman (pimp)
Time period(s): Indeterminate Future
Locale(s): Elysia, Fictional City; Paradise, Fictional Country

Summary: At the end of *Ecstasia*, the band retires to Paradise, the Desert they reclaimed, to raise Primavera. The city of youth, Elysia, has a long reach, seducing Primavera into its lotus-eater world. She must learn her parents' lessons and a few hard ones of her own if she wants to escape.

Other books you might like:
James P. Blaylock, *Land of Dreams*, 1987
Storm Constantine, *Wraeththu*, 1993
John Crowley, *Little, Big*, 1981
Ian McDonald, *Desolation Road*, 1988
Pat Murphy, *The City, Not Long After*, 1989

450

FRANCESCA LIA BLOCK

Witch Baby

(New York: HarperCollins, 1991)

Story type: Fantasy (Contemporary; Young Adult)
Major character(s): Witch Baby, Teenager, Foundling; Dirk McDonald, Teenager, Homosexual; My Secret Agent Lover Man, Filmmaker
Time period(s): 1990s
Locale(s): Los Angeles, California; Santa Cruz, California

Summary: Witch Baby, the mysterious half-child of My Secret Agent Lover Man, doesn't fit into her odd extended family. Attempting to fit in, she causes disruption and confusion all around her. Eventually she runs away to find out who she really is and where she belongs. Enjoyable for adults, this book deals with difficult, mature themes in an off-beat way. Sequel to *Weetzie Bat*.

Other books you might like:
James P. Blaylock, *Land of Dreams*, 1987
Diana Wynne Jones, *Aunt Maria*, 1991
Daniel Manus Pinkwater, *Young Adults*, 1991
Will Shetterly, *Elsewhere*, 1991
Terri Windling, *Bordertown*, 1986
　　Mark Alan Arnold, co-editor

451

ED BLOME

Title Deleted for Security Reasons

(Honesdale, Pennsylvania: West End Books, 1993)

Story type: Science Fiction (Alternate Intelligence; Humor)
Series: Paranoia

Major character(s): James-B-OND-1, Clone, Security Officer; Claude, Robot (foundrybot), Sidekick; Frank-I-STN-4, Administrator, Clone
Time period(s): Indeterminate Future (After the Big Oops)
Locale(s): Alpha Complex, Earth (Washington D.C. area)

Summary: Through luck and regular, traitorous computer hacking, James-B-OND-1 survives to acquire a potentially lethal assignment, rooting out traitorous leadership within the Troubleshooter Bureau. James-B-OND-1 faces additional danger when the Computer deletes its memory of the assignment for security reasons. Game tie-in.

Other books you might like:
Douglas Adams, *The Hitchhiker's Guide to the Galaxy*, 1980
Jack L. Chalker, *The Red Tape War*, 1991
　　Mike Resnick, George Alec Effinger, co-authors
Harry Harrison, *Bill, the Galactic Hero: The Planet of the Robot Slaves*, 1989
Larry Niven, *Fallen Angels*, 1991
　　Jerry Pournelle, Michael Flynn, co-authors
Ken Rolston, *Extreme Paranoia: Nobody Knows the Trouble I've Shot*, 1991
Neal Stephenson, *Snow Crash*, 1992

452

BRITTON BLOOM

Matrix Cubed

(Lake Geneva, Wisconsin: TSR, 1991)

Story type: Science Fiction (Political)
Series: Buck Rogers: The Inner Planets Trilogy
Major character(s): Kemal Gavilan, Royalty
Time period(s): 25th century
Locale(s): Mercury

Summary: Kemal Gavilan struggles to solve his father's murder, the result of family treachery. Mercury's survival is further threatened by an upcoming RAM operation against Earth and Mercury. This is the author's first published novel and a sequel to *First Power Play* and *Prime Squared*.

Other books you might like:
Frank Herbert, *Dune*, 1965
Richard A. Lupoff, *Buck Rogers in the 25th Century*, 1978
　　as Addison E. Steele
Richard A. Lupoff, *That Man on Beta II*, 1978
　　as Addison E. Steele
John Miller, *First Power Play*, 1990
M.S. Murdock, *Armageddon Off Vesta*, 1989
M.S. Murdock, *Hammer of Mars*, 1989
M.S. Murdock, *Prime Squared*, 1990
M.S. Murdock, *Rebellion 2456*, 1989
Philip Francis Nowlan, *Armageddon 2419 A.D.*, 1962
John Silbersack, *Roger's Rangers*, 1983

453

MICHAEL BLUMLEIN

The Brains of Rats

(Los Angeles: Scream/Press, 1989)

Story type: Horror (Collection)

Summary: Twelve stories, five original to this volume. The tension between Blumlein's precise, stripped down, almost clinically detached prose and his extreme, visceral, grotesque scenes and situations provokes disturbing reactions in the reader. A practicing M.D., his stories are glutted with body parts and surgical descriptions. Especially unnerving are the title story, a complex meditation on the tensions between the sexes, and ''Tissue Ablation and Variant Regeneration: A Case Report,'' a visceral, darkly comedic description of an operation on ''Mr. Reagan'' to remove body parts for regeneration to feed Third World countries.

Other books you might like:
J.G. Ballard, *Love and Napalm: Export U.S.A.*, 1969
Dennis Etchison, *The Blood Kiss*, 1988
Joe R. Lansdale, *By Bizarre Hands*, 1989
David J. Skal, *Antibodies*, 1988
John Shirley, *Heatseeker*, 1989

454

GILES BLUNT

Cold Eye

(New York: Avon, 1990)

Story type: Horror (Doppelganger)
Major character(s): Nicholas Hood, Artist (painter); Andre Bellisle, Businessman (art patron); Gary Lauzon, Detective—Police
Time period(s): 1980s (1989)
Locale(s): New York, New York

Summary: When Andre Bellisle begins steering Nicholas Hood to scenes of carnage for inspiration, Hood's paintings become wildly successful. But Hood finds himself increasingly attracted to the violence that gives rise to his work. This first novel was first published in 1989.

Other books you might like:
Pars Lagerkvist, *The Dwarf*, 1945
Oscar Wilde, *The Picture of Dorian Gray*, 1891

455

K.B. BOGEN

Go Quest, Young Man

(Lake Geneva, Wisconsin: TSR, 1994)

Story type: Fantasy (Quest; Light Fantasy)
Major character(s): Erwyn, Sorcerer, Royalty
Time period(s): Indeterminate
Locale(s): Fictional Country

Summary: To avoid an enforced marriage, Erwyn enters the Sorcerer's Apprentice School. Completing formal instruction, Journeyman Sorcerer Erwyn begins a four year wandering internship equipped for guidance with his copy of the *Sorcerers Almanac*. First novel.

Other books you might like:
C. Dale Brittain, *A Bad Spell in Yurt*, 1991
Esther Friesner, *Wishing Season*, 1993
John Moore, *Slay and Rescue*, 1993
S.P. Somtow, *The Wizard's Apprentice*, 1993
Caroline Stevermer, *A College of Magics*, 1994

456

NANCY BOGEN

Bagatelle—Guinevere

(New York: Twickenham, 1995)

Story type: Fantasy (Science Fiction; Contemporary Realism)
Major character(s): Felice Rothman, Writer (poet); Nancy Bogen, Editor; Laleekh, Alien
Time period(s): 1970s (1976)
Locale(s): New York, New York; X, Planet—Imaginary

Summary: After failing to sell her well-received prose poem, Felice volunteers for a secret NASA mission to the nearby, newly discovered planet X. There she searches out the local humanoid natives who kidnap her into a vast underground city, believing her a construct of a neighboring underground city.

Other books you might like:
Piers Anthony, *The Caterpillar's Question*, 1992
    Philip Jose Farmer, co-author
Eleanor Arnason, *A Woman of the Iron People*, 1991
Jesse Browner, *Conglomeros*, 1992
Jane M. Lindskold, *Brother to Dragons, Companion to Owls*, 1994
Sheri S. Tepper, *A Plague of Angels*, 1993

457

TIMOTHY BOGGS

By the Sword

(New York: Berkley Boulevard, 1996)

Story type: Fantasy (Legend; Adventure)
Series: Hercules: The Legendary Journeys
Major character(s): Hercules, Hero, Warrior
Time period(s): Indeterminate Past
Locale(s): Ancient Civilization; Ithaca, Greece

Summary: When marauders steal a magical sword forged by Hephaestos for Zeus, Hercules promises his half-brother Hermes that he will recover the magical weapon. First of a television tie-in series.

Other books you might like:
Kyle Crocco, *Heroes, Inc.*, 1991
Ru Emerson, *The Empty Throne*, 1996
Ru Emerson, *Masques*, 1990
Barbara Hambly, *Beauty and the Beast*, 1989
Jason Henderson, *Highlander: The Element of Fire*, 1995
Barry Hughart, *Bridge of Birds*, 1984
John Moore, *Slay and Rescue*, 1993

458

MAYA KAATHRYN BOHNHOFF

The Crystal Rose

(New York: Baen, 1995)

Story type: Fantasy (Political; Religious)
Series: Meri
Major character(s): Daimhin Feich, Political Figure (regent); Taminy-a-Cuinn, Religious, Psychic; Ren Catahn, Leader
Time period(s): Indeterminate
Locale(s): Halig-liath, Fictional City (religious center); Creiddylad, Fictional City; Airdnasheen, Fictional City

Summary: While helping Airleas mature into the good king he wishes to become, Taminy must defeat the evil Daimhin Feich without compromising her principles. Ren Catahn provides a home for the refugees, including the prince and his mother, while Feich plots to control the government and the church.

Other books you might like:
Suzette Haden Elgin, *Twelve Fair Kingdoms*, 1981
C.S. Friedman, *When True Night Falls*, 1993
Mercedes Lackey, *The Lark and the Wren*, 1991
Marc Laidlaw, *Neon Lotus*, 1988
Elizabeth Ann Scarborough, *Nothing Sacred*, 1991

459

MAYA KAATHRYN BOHNHOFF

The Meri

(New York: Baen, 1992)

Story type: Fantasy (Quest; Religious)
Major character(s): Meredydd a-Lagan, Orphan, Student; Osraed Bevol, Guardian, Teacher; Lealbhallain, Student
Time period(s): Indeterminate
Locale(s): Halig-liath, Mythical Place (academy)

Summary: Adopted by Osraed Bevol after seeing her family murdered, Meredydd becomes the only female to study at Halig-liath. A gifted student, Meredydd must overcome traditional attitudes against female mages to become apprenticed to the Meri, the bridge between the world and the Infinite. She must reconcile her conflicting goals of revenge and service before she can attain her destiny. Author's first novel.

Other books you might like:
Margaret J. Anderson, *The Druid's Gift*, 1989
John Desjarlais, *The Throne of Tara*, 1990
Sue Harrison, *Mother Earth, Father Sky*, 1990
Ursula K. Le Guin, *A Wizard of Earthsea*, 1968
Morgan Llywelyn, *The Horse Goddess*, 1982

460

MAYA KAATHRYN BOHNHOFF

The Spirit Gate

(New York: Baen, 1996)

Story type: Fantasy (Religious; Psychic Powers)

Major character(s): Kassia Telek, Witch, Widow(er); Lukasha, Sorcerer; Damek, Assistant (sorcerer's)
Time period(s): Indeterminate
Locale(s): Polia, Fictional Country

Summary: Blamed for the floods which killed her husband and father, Kassia has a hard time supporting her son. When her sister can no longer offer housing, Kassia tries to earn enough money by telling futures until, realizing that she cannot continue, Kassia applies to the local school for training. Damek takes an instant dislike to Kassia, but Lukasha recognizes her power and realizes he can use her to help save the king from the Frankish bishop's foreign religion.

Other books you might like:
Barbara Hambly, *The Time of the Dark*, 1982
Marc Laidlaw, *Neon Lotus*, 1988
Thomas K. Martin, *A Matter of Honor*, 1994
Andre Norton, *Witch World*, 1963
Elizabeth Ann Scarborough, *Nothing Sacred*, 1991

461

MAYA KAATHRYN BOHNHOFF

Taminy

(New York: Baen, 1993)

Story type: Fantasy (Political; Religious)
Series: Meri
Major character(s): Taminy-a-Cuinn, Religious, Psychic; Israed Bevol, Teacher, Psychic; Wyth, Religious
Time period(s): Indeterminate
Locale(s): Halig-liath, Mythical Place (academy); Nairne, Fictional City; Creiddylad, Fictional City

Summary: After Meredydd replaces Taminy as vessel for the Meri, Taminy returns to Halig-laith with Bevol. Accused of practicing Wicke, Taminy passes every test of purity to no avail. Charged by the Meri to open Halig-liath to female students, Wyth finds his fellows closed to the Meri's request, perhaps endangering Halig-laith.

Other books you might like:
Margaret J. Anderson, *The Druid's Gift*, 1989
Margaret Ball, *Flameweaver*, 1991
Adrian Cole, *Mother of Storms*, 1992
Tom Deitz, *Soulsmith*, 1991
Carole Nelson Douglas, *Cup of Clay*, 1991
Suzette Haden Elgin, *Twelve Fair Kingdoms*, 1981
Sean Russell, *The Initiate Brother*, 1991
Elizabeth Ann Scarborough, *Last Refuge*, 1992

462

JOHANNA BOLTON

Mission: Tori

(New York: Ballantine/Del Rey, 1990)

Story type: Science Fiction (First Contact; Espionage Thriller)
Major character(s): Mier Silver, Spy (Special Intelligence Agency), Psychic (limited); Hac, Android (Human Analog Computer); Ttar Began, Spy (consortium)
Time period(s): Indeterminate Future

Locale(s): Tori, Planet—Imaginary; Earth; Outer Space

Summary: Mier Silver is sent to investigate why agents have disappeared or gone insane on Tori, a planet with rich mineral deposits. While on route, she and Hac are targets for murder. The victim's so-called brother, Ttar, catches up with the two just before they land on Tori. On the planet, they are taken over by a parasite, but there is a cure. They find out that the head of the SIA is a traitor. Hac is not an android, but human. He and Mier team up.

Other books you might like:
Harry Harrison, *Planet of the Damned*, 1962
Robert A. Heinlein, *The Puppet Masters*, 1990
Brian Stableford, *The Castaways of Tanagar*, 1981
Brian Stableford, *The City of the Sun*, 1978
Timothy Zahn, *Spinneret*, 1985

463

MARGARET WANDER BONANNO

The Others

(New York: St. Martin's Press, 1990)

Story type: Science Fiction (Political; Psychic Powers)
Major character(s): Lingri, Historian, Writer (poet)
Time period(s): Indeterminate
Locale(s): Planet—Imaginary

Summary: An advanced civilization on an isolated archipelago has been contacted by the more primitive intelligent species on the planet. When contact is made, the more numerous, more aggressive 'People' declare the pacifistic people of the archipelago the 'Others'. Lingri, of the Others, is charged with chronicling the eradication of the Others by the People after 80 years of contact. At the same time, Lingri also describes the Others' long history.

Other books you might like:
C.J. Cherryh, *Forty Thousand in Gehenna*, 1984
Mary Gentle, *Golden Witchbreed*, 1984
Edgar Pangborn, *A Mirror for Observers*, 1954
James D. Priest, *Kirins: The Spell of No'an*, 1990
A.E. van Vogt, *Slan*, 1951

464

MARGARET WANDER BONANNO

OtherWhere

(New York: St. Martins Press, 1991)

Story type: Science Fiction (Political; Psychic Powers)
Series: Others
Major character(s): Lingri, Historian (chronicler), Writer; Joreth, Genetically Altered Being (Intermix); Dwiri, Telepath
Time period(s): Indeterminate
Locale(s): Planet—Imaginary

Summary: Having been rescued at the last possible moment by Lingri's son, Joreth, and his crew of Intermixes and People, the Others set out on a journey to their potential new home. During the trip, Lingri recalls events and circumstances which led to the deaths of almost all the Others and forced her to abandon her son and his father. This book opens with a brief summary of *The Others*.

Other books you might like:
Eleanor Arnason, *A Woman of the Iron People*, 1991
Octavia E. Butler, *Dawn*, 1987
Orson Scott Card, *Ender's Game*, 1985
Robert N. Charrette, *Choose Your Enemies Carefully*, 1990
C.J. Cherryh, *Cyteen*, 1988
Frank Herbert, *Dune*, 1965
Ken Kato, *Yamato: A Rage in Heaven*, 1990
Dan Simmons, *Hyperion*, 1989
Joan Slonczewski, *A Door into Ocean*, 1986
Sheri S. Tepper, *Raising the Stones*, 1990

465

MARGARET WANDER BONANNO

OtherWise

(New York: St. Martin's Press, 1993)

Story type: Science Fiction (Post-Holocaust; Psychic Powers)
Series: Others
Major character(s): Lingri, Historian, Writer (poet); Joreth, Musician; Chior, Leader, Scientist (meteorologist)
Time period(s): Indeterminate
Locale(s): The World, Planet—Imaginary

Summary: In telepathic contact with the Others in the Iceworld, Lingri travels with her half-People son Joreth, to investigate the message that the Patriots no longer control the People, that some Others still live on the mainland, and that transportation for the Others to leave the world still exists in the Hidden. While evading the remaining guard patrols, Lingri meets many friends on the devastated continent where she continues to develop as an empath. Chior faces the results of his disastrous meddling which spurred the Holocaust.

Other books you might like:
David Brin, *Sundiver*, 1980
C.J. Cherryh, *Cyteen*, 1988
Samuel R. Delany, *They Fly at Ciron*, 1993
Mary Gentle, *Golden Witchbreed*, 1984
Frank Herbert, *Dune*, 1965
Rosemary Kirstein, *The Outskirter's Secret*, 1992
Edgar Pangborn, *A Mirror for Observers*, 1954
A.E. van Vogt, *Slan*, 1946
Gene Wolfe, *Nightside the Long Sun*, 1993

466

MARGARET WANDER BONANNO

Preternatural

(New York: Tor, 1996)

Story type: Science Fiction (First Contact; Alternate Intelligence)
Major character(s): Karen Rohmer Guerreri, Writer; Max Neimark, Actor, Director; Laurence ''Larry'' Koster, Actor
Time period(s): 1990s
Locale(s): New York, New York; Los Angeles, California

Summary: Science fiction writer Karen Gu erreri discovers that the alien telepathic jellyfish characters in her novel-in-progress actually exist and communicate with humans, including famous actors Max Neimark (a thinly-disguised Leonard Nimoy) and Larry Koster (William Shatner).

Other books you might like:
Philip K. Dick, *The Three Stigmata of Palmer Eldritch*, 1965
Nancy Kress, *Brain Rose*, 1990
Sharyn McCrumb, *Bimbos of the Death Sun*, 1988
Nichelle Nichols, *Saturn's Child*, 1995
     Margaret Wander Bonanno, co-author
Patrick O'Leary, *Door Number Three*, 1995
Christopher Pike, *The Eternal Enemy*, 1993
Christopher Pike, *The Starlight Crystal*, 1996

467

MARGARET WANDER BONANNO

Probe

(New York: Pocket Books, 1992)

Story type: Science Fiction (Space Opera)
Series: Star Trek
Major character(s): James T. Kirk, Spaceship Captain; Spock, Scientist, Alien (Vulcan); Tiam, Diplomat (ambassador), Alien (Romulan)
Time period(s): 23rd century
Locale(s): *U.S.S. Enterprise*, Spaceship (Federation); *Galtizh*, Spaceship (Romulan); Temaris, Planet—Imaginary

Summary: Engaging in a joint archaeological excavation of Temaris with Romulan scientists, the *Enterprise* crew takes part in cultural exchanges until the reappearance of an alien probe and Romulan defections seed new distrust amo ng treacherous Romulans, leaving the Enterprise as everyone's only hope, if the *Enterprise* can quickly learn to communicate with the probe. Sequel to *Star Trek IV: Voyage Home*. Extensive unauthorized changes made to the author's text.

Other books you might like:
Diane Duane, *Doctor's Orders*, 1990
Barbara Hambly, *Ishmael*, 1985
Janet Kagan, *Uhura's Song*, 1985
Vonda N. McIntyre, *Star Trek IV: The Voyage Home*, 1986
V.E. Mitchell, *Enemy Unseen*, 1990
Peter Morwood, *Rules of Engagement*, 1990

468

JAY R. BONANSINGA

The Black Mariah

(New York: Warner, 1994)

Story type: Horror (Curse)
Major character(s): Lucas Hynde, Truck Driver; Sophie Cohen, Truck Driver; Vanessa DeGeaux, Aged Person
Time period(s): 1990s (1994)
Locale(s): Georgia; Tennessee

Summary: Lucas Hynde and Sophie Cohen are unsuccessful in their efforts to help refuel a car in transit driven by someone who claims he has been cursed by a voodoo practitioner to keep his car in motion. When the driver dies of spontaneous combustion after his car runs out of fuel, the curse is passed to Lucas and Sophie. This variation on the legend of the Flying Dutchman is the author's first novel.

Other books you might like:
Eric Flanders, *Night Blood*, 1993
Ray Garton, *Lot Lizards*, 1991
Billie Sue Mosiman, *Night Cruise*, 1993
Stephen Wright, *Going Native*, 1994

469

JAY R. BONANSINGA

Sick

(New York: Warner, 1995)

Story type: Horror (Wild Talents)
Major character(s): Sarah Brandis, Dancer (exotic); Henry Decker, Psychologist; Frank Moon, Detective—Police
Time period(s): 1990s (1995)
Locale(s): Chicago, Illinois

Summary: Sarah Brandis's visualization technique for dealing with her rage and anger give her a means for focusing her emotions into a power that transforms her physically into a vicious avenger against her supposed persecutors.

Other books you might like:
Paddy Chayefsky, *Altered States*, 1972
Douglas Clegg, *Dark of the Eye*, 1994
Dean R. Koontz, *Dragon Tears*, 1993

470

WILLIAM BORNEFELD

Time and Light

(Clarkston, Georgia: White Wolf Borealis, 1996)

Story type: Science Fiction (Dystopian; Post-Holocaust)
Major character(s): Noreen, Scientist; Martine, Girlfriend; Hayes, Scientist, Administrator
Time period(s): Indeterminate Future
Locale(s): Fullerton, Fictional City; Outside, Fictional Country

Summary: The Family of Man, the remnants of the human race, live in a beautiful city in the center of a radioactive wastleland. One day Dr. Noreen goes outside for samples and discovers an empty, but living, world. In the Outside, he finds some photographs that unhinge his life, leading him to question everything. Includes an essay by the author discussing the specific photographic images.

Other books you might like:
Aldous Huxley, *Brave New World*, 1932
Walter M. Miller Jr., *A Canticle for Leibowitz*, 1960
William F. Nolan, *Logan's Run*, 1967
     George Clayton Johnson, co-author
Charles Oberndorf, *Sheltered Lives*, 1992
George Orwell, *1984*, 1949

DOUGLAS BORTON

Deathsong
(New York: NAL Onyx, 1989)

Story type: Horror (Ancient Evil Unleashed)
Major character(s): Billy Lee Kidd, Singer (country music); Kuruk, Cult Member (high priest of Antarok cult)
Time period(s): 1980s
Locale(s): Los Angeles, California

Summary: Billy Lee is granted the dubious gift of singing the ''Deathsong'' that opens the Door for the dark forces of Antarok. But she also has the power to close the Door and save the world if she can find and use it in time—and before she, herself, is sacrificed to Antarok.

Other books you might like:
George R.R. Martin, *The Armageddon Rag*, 1983
Anne Rice, *The Queen of the Damned*, 1988

DOUGLAS BORTON

Kane
(New York: Onyx, 1990)

Story type: Horror (Serial Killer; Psychological Suspense)
Major character(s): Kane, Murderer; Bill Needham, Businessman (service-station owner)
Time period(s): 1990s (1990)
Locale(s): Tuskett, California

Summary: One warm summer evening, a mysterious man named Kane walks into Tuskett, California, an aging, decaying small town at the edge of the Mojave desert. Indestructible, inexplicable, possessed of extreme strength and the ability to hypnotize, the black-clad stranger intends, for reasons known only to him, to destroy the entire population of Tuskett—23 people—in one long night.

Other books you might like:
Robert Bloch, *Psycho*, 1959
Stephen King, *The Dark Tower: The Gunslinger*, 1982
Robert R. McCammon, *Stinger*, 1988

DOUGLAS BORTON

Shadow Dance
(New York: Signet, 1991)

Story type: Horror (Ancient Evil Unleashed)
Major character(s): Timothy Cutter, Child; Rachel Weiss, Psychologist; Robert Thorn, Drifter
Time period(s): 1990s
Locale(s): Los Angeles, California

Summary: No one believes Timothy Cutter when he tells them that his parents were killed by the Runa, an ancient disembodied force that claims people sensitive to its presence for its own. But now the Runa has taken over Robert Thorn, who will stop at nothing to find Timothy.

Other books you might like:
G. Wayne Miller, *Thunder Rise*, 1988

ANTHONY BOUCHER

The Compleat Werewolf and Other Tales of Fantasy and Science Fiction
(New York: Carroll and Graf, 1990)

Story type: Horror (Collection)

Summary: Title novella and nine short stories first published between 1941 and 1945 that mix horror, humor, and fantasy. Especially notable are the title novella about a college professor who acquires the power to exploit his previously hidden wereworlf tendencies, ''We Print the Truth,'' about a newspaper owner who must face unexpected consequences when his casual wish to always print ''only the truth'' is granted, and ''The Ghost of Me,'' in which the ghost of a murder victim returns too soon—before the murder has been committed.

Other books you might like:
Charles Beaumont, *Charles Beaumont: Selected Stories*, 1988

ALINE BOUCHER-KAPLAN

World Spirits
(New York: Baen, 1991)

Story type: Science Fiction (Theological; Political)
Series: Khyren
Major character(s): Raunn ni Obradi san Derrith, Agent; Verrer ni Rimmani san Derrith, Alien (Tulkan); Auriel il Tarz, Trader, Agent
Time period(s): Indeterminate Future
Locale(s): Chennidur, Planet—Imaginary

Summary: Chennidur is an enigma to the interstellar Trading Family which has its contract. Auriel il Tarz is sent to learn about the locals who believe technological devices to be evil and against the religion which is so important there. Auriel meets Raunn who is in a position to introduce her to clan society where she witnesses some of the detrimental effects of the spacer's imports.

Other books you might like:
Emma Bull, *Falcon*, 1989
Mary Gentle, *Golden Witchbreed*, 1984
Frank Herbert, *Dune*, 1965
Rosemary Kirstein, *The Steerswoman*, 1989
Ursula K. Le Guin, *The Word for World Is Forest*, 1972
Steve Perry, *The 97th Step*, 1989
Joan Slonczewski, *A Door into Ocean*, 1986

476

BEN BOVA

Brothers

(New York: Bantam, 1996)

Story type: Science Fiction (Medical)
Major character(s): Arthur Marshak, Doctor, Researcher; Jessie Marshak, Doctor; Julia Marshak, Spouse
Time period(s): 1990s
Locale(s): Washington, District of Columbia

Summary: Brothers Arthur and Jessie Marshak take opposite sides in a nationally-publicized argument over whether controvesial medical experiments, using cancer to regenerate organs within the body, should continue.

Other books you might like:
Robin Cook, *Godplayer*, 1983
Michael Crichton, *Jurassic Park*, 1990
Michael Crichton, *The Terminal Man*, 1972
James Gunn, *The Immortals*, 1962
Linda Nagata, *Tech-Heaven*, 1995

477

BEN BOVA

Cyberbooks

(New York: Tor, 1989)

Story type: Science Fiction (Humor)
Major character(s): Carl Lewis, Inventor; Scarlet Dean, Editor
Time period(s): 1980s
Locale(s): New York, New York

Summary: An inventor attempts to interest a major publisher in his revolutionary new electronic book. Meanwhile, a variety of odd and amusing characters attempt to steal or buy it.

Other books you might like:
Frederik Pohl, *The Coming of the Quantum Cats*, 1986
Spider Robinson, *Callahan's Crosstime Saloon*, 1977
Kate Wilhelm, *Crazy Time*, 1988

478

BEN BOVA

Death Dream

(New York: Bantam, 1994)

Story type: Science Fiction (Cyberpunk; Techno-Thriller)
Major character(s): Dan Santorini, Computer Expert, Engineer; Jason Lowrey, Inventor, Genius; Angie Santorini, Child
Time period(s): 21st century
Locale(s): Florida; Virtual Reality, Cyberspace

Summary: Dan Santorini accepts a job with ParaReality, Inc., to create the virtual reality theme park, Cyber World, with his old friend, Jason Lowrey, a wizard in creating cyberspace reality. Disaster among program uses, a threat to Dan's daughter from a co-worker and sabotage to the theme park bring Dan and Jason into direct conflict.

Other books you might like:
Piers Anthony, *Killobyte*, 1993
Greg Bear, *Queen of Angels*, 1990
Edmund Cooper, *Prisoner of Fire*, 1976
Alan Dean Foster, *The I Inside*, 1984
Stephen Goldin, *And Not Make Dreams Your Master*, 1981
Andrew M. Greeley, *God Game*, 1986
Nancy Kress, *Brain Rose*, 1990
James Morrow, *The Continent of Lies*, 1984
Mack Reynolds, *Perchance to Dream*, 1977
Norman Spinrad, *The Void Captain's Tale*, 1983

479

BEN BOVA

Empire Builders

(New York: Tor, 1993)

Story type: Science Fiction (Political)
Series: Privateers
Major character(s): Dan Randolph, Businessman, Fugitive; Jane Scanwell, Political Figure, Organized Crime Figure; Rafaelo Gaetano, Political Figure, Organized Crime Figure
Time period(s): 21st century
Locale(s): Earth; Moon (Earth's)

Summary: When scientists predict that the Greenhouse Effect will rapidly escalate in 10 years, leaders suppress the news until the Global Economic Council formulates a solution. Forced underground because his knowledge presents too great a threat, Dan Randolph teams with some Council members and economic rivals to defeat Rafaelo Gaetano's scheme of Mafia takeover.

Other books you might like:
Poul Anderson, *The Psychotechnic League*, 1981
C.J. Cherryh, *Hellburner*, 1992
Barney Cohen, *Blood on the Moon*, 1984
Alan Dean Foster, *The Man Who Used the Universe*, 1983
Alexis A. Gilliland, *The Revolution From Rosinante*, 1981
Donald Kingsbury, *The Moon Goddess and the Son*, 1986
Eric Kotani, *Act of God*, 1985
   John Maddox Roberts, co-author
Mack Reynolds, *Trojan Orbit*, 1985
Allen Steele, *Orbital Decay*, 1989

480

BEN BOVA

Future Crime

(New York: Tor, 1990)

Story type: Science Fiction (Collection)
Time period(s): Indeterminate Future
Locale(s): Earth

Summary: Seven short stories and a 1976 novella *City of Darkness* dealing with crime in the future. It ranges from extrapolating current trends to depicting wholly new crimes.

Other books you might like:
Isaac Asimov, *Tales of the Black Widowers*, 1974

Larry Niven, *The Long Arm of Gil Hamilton*, 1976
Larry Niven, *N-Space*, 1990
Larry Niven, *Oath of Fealty*, 1981
    Jerry Pournelle, co-author
Larry Niven, *The Patchwork Girl*, 1980
L.A. Taylor, *Blossom of Erda*, 1986
    pseudonym of Laurie Sparer

481
BEN BOVA

Mars
(New York: Bantam Spectra, 1992)

Story type: Science Fiction (Political; Hard Science Fiction)
Major character(s): James "Jamie" Fox Waterman, Indian (Navaho), Scientist (geologist); Joanna Brumado, Scientist (biologist); Mikhail Andreivitch Vosnesensky, Spaceman, Leader
Time period(s): 21st century
Locale(s): Earth; Mars

Summary: Resented from the beginning, Jamie Waterman wins a position on the first manned Mars expedition only after one man gets sick and another black-balled. When he doesn't follow the script, American politicians fear his becoming too popular. On Mars, Jamie thinks he sees a city in the Vallis Marineris and goes to explore. When the expedition leaves, the team expects follow-up missions.

Other books you might like:
Isaac Asimov, *The Martian Way*, 1955
Arthur C. Clarke, *The Sands of Mars*, 1952
D.G. Compton, *Farewell, Earth's Bliss*, 1971
Philip K. Dick, *Martian Time-Slip*, 1964
Gordon R. Dickson, *The Far Call*, 1978
Robert A. Heinlein, *Red Planet*, 1949
Sterling E. Lanier, *Menace Under Marwood*, 1983
Frederik Pohl, *Man Plus*, 1976
Kim Stanley Robinson, *Red Mars*, 1993
Allen Steele, *Labyrinth of Night*, 1992
Jack Williamson, *Beachhead*, 1992

482
BEN BOVA

Moonrise
(New York: Avon, 1996)

Story type: Science Fiction (Political; Hard Science Fiction)
Major character(s): Paul Stavenger, Astronaut (retired), Businessman; Joanna Masterson Stavenger, Businesswoman; Douglas Stavenger, Experimental Subject, Teenager
Time period(s): 21st century
Locale(s): Moonbase, Moon (Earth's); Earth; Outer Space

Summary: Privatization of the space program brings the possibility of rapid technological development, if Masterson Aerospace's corporate infighting over Moonbase and anti-technological religious fanatics do not spell disaster for the fragile site.

Other books you might like:
Kevin J. Anderson, *Assemblers of Infinity*, 1993
    Doug Beason, co-author
Robert A. Heinlein, *The Moon Is a Harsh Mistress*, 1966
Allen Steele, *Lunar Descent*, 1991
Allen Steele, *The Tranquility Alternative*, 1996
John Varley, *Steel Beach*, 1992

483
BEN BOVA

Orion Among the Stars
(New York: Tor, 1995)

Story type: Science Fiction (Military; Immortality)
Series: Orion
Major character(s): Orion, Immortal, Warrior; Aten, Immortal; Frede, Military Personnel, Health Care Professional (medic)
Time period(s): Indeterminate Future
Locale(s): Lunga, Planet—Imaginary; Loris, Planet—Imaginary

Summary: Orion awakens in the far future where he and a team of professional soldiers must take and hold a planet for the Commonwealth, at war with the Hegemony. On Lunga, ancient marine dwellers who deplore humankind's bellicosity contact Orion in hopes of stopping the space/time disruptions which threaten everyone's existence.

Other books you might like:
Roger MacBride Allen, *The Torch of Honor*, 1985
John Dalmas, *The Regiment*, 1987
Gordon R. Dickson, *Dorsai!*, 1976
Stephen Goldin, *The Eternity Brigade*, 1980
Joe Haldeman, *The Forever War*, 1975
Robert A. Heinlein, *Starship Troopers*, 1959
Joel Rosenberg, *Not for Glory*, 1988
Timothy Zahn, *Cobra*, 1985

484
BEN BOVA

Orion and the Conqueror
(New York: Tor, 1994)

Story type: Science Fiction (Alternate Universe; Fantasy)
Series: Orion
Major character(s): Orion, Immortal, Warrior; Hera, Immortal, Deity; Philip of Macedon, Ruler, Historical Figure
Time period(s): 4th century B.C.
Locale(s): Macedonia; Athens, Greece

Summary: Arriving in Macedonia without knowledge of his past, Orion becomes part of a complicated plot among Philip of Macedon, his wife and his son, who is impatient to inherit the throne. When his memory slowly returns, Orion wants to find Anya but must obey Hera and Aten, who plan Philip's assassination.

Other books you might like:
Poul Anderson, *The Boat of a Million Years*, 1989
Piers Anthony, *Steppe*, 1985

Greg Bear, *Eternity*, 1988
Raymond Harris, *The Schizogenic Man*, 1990
Crawford Kilian, *Rogue Emperor*, 1988
Fritz Leiber, *The Big Time*, 1961
Kirk Mitchell, *Procurator*, 1984
Melissa Scott, *A Choice of Destinies*, 1986
Roger Zelazny, *Roadmarks*, 1979

485

BEN BOVA

Orion in the Dying Time
(New York: Tor, 1990)

Story type: Science Fiction (Science Fantasy; Theological)
Series: Orion
Major character(s): Orion, Immortal, Warrior; Anya, Warrior; Set, Alien
Time period(s): 80th century B.C.
Locale(s): Shaydan, Egypt (ancient)

Summary: In prehistoric Egypt, Orion and Anya encounter dinosaurs who rule humans. In trying to unite them, he causes a holocaust that allows Set to colonize the area with Shaydanians, reptilian beings. Then with the aid of Aten, a being evolved beyond man, Orion leads Subotai and his mongol horde back through time to Egypt where they rout the Shaydanians. Before returning to stasis, Orion learns that Aten is man's enemy as well as that of the Shaydanians and has other dastardly plots in reserve.

Other books you might like:
Poul Anderson, *The Boat of a Million Years*, 1989
Michael Crichton, *Jurassic Park*, 1990
Harry Harrison, *Return to Eden*, 1988
Harry Harrison, *West of Eden*, 1984
Harry Harrison, *Winter in Eden*, 1986
Roger Zelazny, *Lord of Light*, 1967

486

BEN BOVA

Sam Gunn, Unlimited
(New York: Bantam Spectra, 1993)

Story type: Science Fiction (Collection)
Major character(s): Sam Gunn, Businessman; Jane ''Jade'' Avril Inconnu, Journalist
Time period(s): Indeterminate Future
Locale(s): Space Station; Asteroid Belt, Outer Space

Summary: Fascinated as a youth by tales about the famous entrepreneur Sam Gunn, Jade locates Sam's acquaintances and records events in Sam's adult life as seen by those who had known him. Much new material with some stories reprinted from 1980s and 1990s periodicals.

Other books you might like:
Poul Anderson, *Harvest of Stars*, 1993
Robert L. Forward, *Timemaster*, 1992
Robert A. Heinlein, *The Man Who Sold the Moon*, 1950
Frederik Pohl, *The Space Merchants*, 1953
   C.M. Kornbluth, co-author

L. Neil Smith, *The Nagasaki Vector*, 1983
L. Neil Smith, *Tom Paine Maru*, 1984
L. Neil Smith, *The Venus Belt*, 1983
F. Paul Wilson, *The LaNague Chronicles*, 1992

487

BEN BOVA

Star Brothers
(New York: Tor, 1990)

Story type: Science Fiction (Science Fiction)
Series: Voyagers
Major character(s): Keith Stoner, Astronaut, Hero; Jo Camerata, Industrialist
Time period(s): 21st century
Locale(s): Earth; Moon (Earth's)

Summary: Former astronaut Keith Stoner, the first man to live through cryonic sleep and the first man to meet an alien, draws upon his alien friend's powers in a desperate effort to save the world from political chaos and a plague that could destroy all life on Earth.

Other books you might like:
Octavia E. Butler, *Dawn*, 1987
Arthur C. Clarke, *Childhood's End*, 1953
Damon Knight, *CV*, 1987
Damon Knight, *The Observers*, 1988

488

BEN BOVA
A.J. AUSTIN, Co-Author

To Fear the Light
(New York: Tor, 1994)

Story type: Science Fiction (Political; First Contact)
Series: To Save the Sun
Major character(s): Adela de Montgarde, Scientist; Jephthah, Activist (rabble rouser); Ettalira, Alien (Gatanni), Explorer
Time period(s): Indeterminate Future
Locale(s): Earth; Tsing IV, Planet—Imaginary

Summary: Awakened after two centuries in cryosleep to oversee the end of her project to save Earth's sun, the dismayed Adela de Montgarde finds xenophobia, particularly against the Sarpan, whipped up by Jephthah using untraceable transmissions. After the discovery of intelligent life on another planet, Jephthah plots to murder the scouting party and imperial family who travel to the system.

Other books you might like:
John Brunner, *A Maze of Stars*, 1991
Gordon R. Dickson, *None but Man*, 1969
Ursula K. Le Guin, *Planet of Exile*, 1966
Chad Oliver, *Unearthly Neighbors*, 1960
Mike Resnick, *Second Contact*, 1990
James H. Schmitz, *The Demon Breed*, 1968

489

BEN BOVA
A.J. AUSTIN, Co-Author

To Save the Sun
(New York: Tor, 1992)

Story type: Science Fiction (Science Fiction)
Major character(s): Nicholas, Royalty (Emperor of the Hundred Worlds); Adela de Montgarde, Scientist; Javas, Royalty (Prince of the Hundred Worlds)
Time period(s): Indeterminate Future
Locale(s): Corinth, Planet—Imaginary; Luna, Moon (Earth's); Hundred Worlds, Interstellar Empire/Federation

Summary: Adela convinces Nicholas that he can save the sun and leave Earth's population in place to continue as a genetic baseline to control genetic drift in the Hundred Worlds. Important individuals in the government disapprove of the plan as expensive, surrealistic and unnecessary for their goals. Nicholas moves the government to Earth's moon, giving the project his strong support and arranging the event of his death to promote the success of the project.

Other books you might like:
Stephen Baxter, *Raft*, 1992
David Brin, *Earth*, 1990
Gregory Feeley, *The Oxygen Barons*, 1990
Michael Flynn, *In the Country of the Blind*, 1990
Robert L. Forward, *Martian Rainbow*, 1991
Larry Niven, *Protector*, 1973
Allen Steele, *Lunar Descent*, 1991

490

BEN BOVA
BILL POGUE, Co-Author

The Trikon Deception
(New York: Tor, 1992)

Story type: Science Fiction (Techno-Thriller)
Major character(s): Hugh O'Donnell, Scientist; Dan Tighe, Leader; Lance Muncie, Spaceman
Time period(s): 1990s (1998)
Locale(s): Trikon Station, Space Station; United States

Summary: Trikon, a space station funded by North America, Japan, and United Europe, has been designed as a risk-free environment for controversial genetic experiments. When Trikon's survival becomes threatened by espionage and sabotage, Hugh O'Donnell must save the space station from the sabotage he stands accused of.

Other books you might like:
Roger MacBride Allen, *The Ring of Charon*, 1990
Gordon R. Dickson, *The Far Call*, 1978
James P. Hogan, *Endgame Enigma*, 1987
Larry Niven, *Fallen Angels*, 1991
　Jerry Pournelle and Michael Flynn, co-authors
Allen Steele, *Lunar Descent*, 1991
Allen Steele, *Orbital Decay*, 1989
Walter Jon Williams, *Voice of the Whirlwind*, 1987

491

BEN BOVA

Triumph
(New York: Tor, 1993)

Story type: Science Fiction (Alternate Universe; Political)
Major character(s): Winston Churchill, Historical Figure, Political Figure; Franklin Delano Roosevelt, Historical Figure, Political Figure; Adolf Hitler, Historical Figure, Political Figure
Time period(s): 1940s (April 1945)
Locale(s): London, England; Berlin, Germany; Moscow, Union of Soviet Socialist Republics

Summary: Fearing Joseph Stalin's post-war influence, Winston Churchill plots to poison Stalin with plutonium.

Other books you might like:
Len Deighton, *SS-GB*, 1978
Philip K. Dick, *The Man in the High Castle*, 1962
Michael Flynn, *In the Country of the Blind*, 1990
Robert Harris, *Fatherland*, 1992
Fritz Leiber, *The Big Time*, 1961
Harry Turtledove, *The Guns of the South*, 1992

492

GARY BOWEN

Diary of a Vampire
(New York: Rhinoceros, 1995)

Story type: Horror (Vampire Story)
Major character(s): Rafael Guitierrez, Vampire; Michael Duran, Artist; James Flannagan, Businessman
Time period(s): 1990s (1991)
Locale(s): Baltimore, Maryland

Summary: Rafael, a vampire much older than his youthful appearance would indicate, awakens in the 1990s after a 15-year sleep and begins adjusting to a world that the AIDS virus and various political, social, and political changes have made vastly different from the world he used to know. This erotic tale is the author's first novel.

Other books you might like:
Poppy Z. Brite, *Lost Souls*, 1993
Nancy A. Collins, *Sunglasses After Dark*, 1990
John Peyton Cooke, *Out for Blood*, 1991
Mark Ivanhoe, *Virgintooth*, 1991
Jonathan Nasaw, *The World on Blood*, 1996
Anne Rice, *The Vampire Lestat*, 1985

493

DAVID BOWKER

The Death Prayer
(Clarkston, Georgia: White Wolf, 1996)

Story type: Horror (Black Magic)
Major character(s): Vernon Laverne, Police Officer (detective superintendant); Lyn Savage, Detective—Police; Hugo Prince, Religious (black magic priest)

Time period(s): 1990s (1995)

Summary: A series of killings improbably committed by the risen dead points to Hugo Prince, leader of the cultish Quest for the Higher Self, and a Kahuna who kills his enemies by simply uttering the death prayer. In the course of his investigations of Prince, Detective Superintendant Vernon Laverne discovers that he has latent psychic talents that can put a stop to Prince's evil. The novel was first published in England in 1995.

Other books you might like:
Garry Kilworth, *Angel*, 1993
Dean R. Koontz, *The Bad Place*, 1990
Stephen Laws, *Macabre*, 1994
Graham Masterton, *Burial*, 1994
Guy N. Smith, *The Black Fedora*, 1991

494

ELIZABETH H. BOYER

The Clan of the Warlord
(New York: Ballantine Del Rey, 1992)

Story type: Fantasy (Quest; Magic Conflict)
Major character(s): Mistislaus, Wizard; Skylda "Skyla", Orphan, Witch; Guthrum, Mythical Creature (dwarf)
Time period(s): Indeterminate
Locale(s): Fairholm, Fictional Country; Rangfara, Fictional Country

Summary: After Rangfara falls to the Krypplinger, a peasant brings the infant Skyla to Mistilaus, who recognizes her abilities as a witch almost immediately. Before long Skyla dresses like a boy and spends much of her time in the woods. Many people, including a pack of wild boys, escaped slaves who could be her cousins, believe Skyla can lead them to the lost treasure of her forebears.

Other books you might like:
Jo Clayton, *Wild Magic*, 1991
Louise Cooper, *The Pretender*, 1991
C.S. Friedman, *Black Sun Rising*, 1991
Melanie Rawn, *The Star Scroll*, 1989
Michelle Sagara, *Into the Dark Lands*, 1991
R.A. Salvatore, *Sojourn*, 1991
Elizabeth Ann Scarborough, *Phantom Banjo*, 1991

495

ELIZABETH H. BOYER

The Dragon's Carbuncle
(New York: Ballantine/Del Rey, 1990)

Story type: Fantasy (Sword and Sorcery; Legend)
Series: Wizard's War
Major character(s): Leifr, Adventurer; Thurid, Wizard
Time period(s): Indeterminate Past
Locale(s): Djofullhol, Scandinavia

Summary: Misfit Leifr, a Scipling in Alfar must try to rescue his friend Thurid from the Fire Wizards' Inquistion, and Ljosa, his beloved who is held by his old enemy Sorkvir. With the help of his Rhbu sword, Endalaus Daudi, Leifr faces seemingly impossible tasks.

Other books you might like:
Mayer Alan Brenner, *Catastrophe's Spell*, 1989
Suzy McKee Charnas, *The Golden Thread*, 1989
Glen Cook, *Tower of Fear*, 1989
Diane Duane, *High Wizardry*, 1989
Peni R. Griffin, *Otto From Otherwhere*, 1990
Jane Resh Thomas, *The Princess in the Pigpen*, 1989

496

ROBERT H. BOYER, Editor
KENNETH J. ZAHORSKI, Co-Editor

Visions & Imaginings: Classic Fantasy Fiction
(Chicago: Academy Chicago, 1992)

Story type: Fantasy (Anthology)

Summary: Recollects 17 of the best stories from the editors' five anthologies published 1977-1981 which presented classic fantasy stories by prominent writers from the past 150 years. The stories chosen include Joan Aiken's "The Harp of Fishbones," Lloyd Alexander's "The Foundling," Peter S. Beagle's "Lila the Werewolf," Lord Dunsany's "The Bridge of the Man-Horse," Ursula K. Le Guin's "April in Paris," George MacDonald's "The Light Princess," Kenneth Morris' "Red Peach Blossom Inlet," Frank Stockton's "The Accomodating Circumstance," Evangeline Walton Ensley's "The Mistress of Kaer-Mor" and T.H. White's "The Troll."

Other books you might like:
Lin Carter, *Discoveries in Fantasy*, 1972
  editor
Lin Carter, *Golden Cities, Far*, 1970
  editor
Lin Carter, *Great Short Novels of Adult Fantasy 1*, 1972
  editor
Lin Carter, *Great Short Novels of Adult Fantasy 2*, 1973
  editor
Lin Carter, *New Worlds for Old*, 1971
  editor
Lester del Rey, *Once upon a Time: A Treasury of Modern Fairy Tales*, 1991
  Risa Kessler, co-editor
Martin H. Greenberg, *After the King: Stories in Honor of J.R.R. Tolkien*, 1992
  editor

497

STEVEN R. BOYETT

Treks Not Taken
(Burbank, California: Sneaker Press/Midnight Graffiti Press, 1996)

Story type: Science Fiction (Collection; Parody)
Major character(s): Jean-Alex Pickhard, Spaceship Captain; Datum, Android, Space Explorer; Troi Rogers, Socialite, Spacewoman
Time period(s): 24th century

Locale(s): *U.S.S. Enterprise,* Spaceship

Summary: Contains a six-page introduction and 20 teleplay outlines for ''Star Trek: The Next Generation'' as if written by literary greats including Anthony Burgess, Tom Clancy, Michael Crichton, Joseph Heller, Ernest Hemmingway, Jack Kerouac, Ken Kesey, Stephen King, Herman Melville, Anne Rice, Tom Robbins, J.D. Salinger, Dr. Seuss, and Kurt Vonnegut, Jr.

Other books you might like:
Kevin J. Anderson, *War of the Worlds: Global Dispatches,* 1996
    editor
John M. Ford, *How Much for Just the Planet?,* 1987
Randall Garrett, *Takeoff!,* 1979
Randall Garrett, *Takeoff, Too!,* 1986
Leah Rewolinski, *Star Wreck: The Generation Gap,* 1990
Leah Rewolinski, *Star Wreck II: The Attack of the Jargonites,* 1991

498

JOSEPHINE BOYLE

Holy Terror

(New York: St. Martin's, 1995)

Story type: Horror (Haunted House)
Major character(s): Emily Wakelin, Artisan (does embroidery); John Wakelin, Accountant; Lady Abigail Curran, Aged Person
Time period(s): 1990s (1993)
Locale(s): Little Hocking, England (in Essex)

Summary: Emily Wakelin's strange visions and feelings of dread while visiting her next-door neighbors convince her that the legendary ghost who haunts their home is real, and that its manifestations are somehow bound up with her work to help commemorate the martyrdom of a local hero in the sixteenth century. This novel was first published in England in 1993.

Other books you might like:
Jonathan Aycliffe, *The Vanishment,* 1993
James P. Blaylock, *Night Relics,* 1994
Bernard Taylor, *Sweetheart, Sweetheart,* 1977

499

RANDALL BOYLL

After Sundown

(New York: Charter, 1989)

Story type: Horror (Ghost Story)
Major character(s): Mark Butler, Parent (Mormon father); Robin Pruett, Child
Time period(s): 1980s
Locale(s): Salt Lake City, Utah; Spike Mountain, Utah

Summary: Following the death of a Pruett daughter, the two families travel for solace to Spike Mountain only to find themselves isolated and thrust into madness and death as the evil of a violent incident in 1896 is released. This is Boyll's first novel.

Other books you might like:
John Christopher, *The Possessors,* 1964
Stephen King, *The Shining,* 1977

500

RANDALL BOYLL

Chiller

(New York: Jove, 1992)

Story type: Horror (Science Fiction)
Major character(s): Peter Kaye, Student—Graduate (in mathematics); Darbi Kaye, Child (Peter's six-year-old daughter); Kim Marden, Hotel Worker
Time period(s): 1990s
Locale(s): St. Charles, Missouri (and points across America)

Summary: Though his daughter Darbi has officially died of cancer, graduate student Peter Kaye packs her scientifically-reanimated body in ice and takes her on a cross-country bankrobbing spree to raise money for her admission to a secret cryogenics clinic in Wyoming.

Other books you might like:
Daniel H. Gower, *The Orpheus Process,* 1992
Stephen King, *Firestarter,* 1980

501

RANDALL BOYLL

Darkman

(New York: Jove, 1990)

Story type: Horror (Science Fiction)
Major character(s): Peyton Westlake, Scientist (Darkman); Julie Hastings, Lawyer
Time period(s): 1980s
Locale(s): Detroit, Michigan (Wayne State University)

Summary: Gangsters seeking evidence to local political corruption blow up the laboratory of a scientist who had been developing artificial skin. Grotesquely scarred by the explosion, the scientist establishes a secret laboratory from which he uses his artificial skin, which in sunlight only retains its consistency for 99 minutes, to wreak revenge on the men who destroyed his life. This book is a novelization of the Sam Raimi film, based on the screenplay by Raimi, Chuck Pfarrer, Ivan Raimi, Daniel Goldin, and Joshua Goldin.

Other books you might like:
Sean Costello, *Captain Quad,* 1991
Craig Shaw Gardner, *Batman,* 1989
Gaston Leroux, *The Phantom of the Opera,* 1910
H.G. Wells, *The Invisible Man,* 1897

502

RANDALL BOYLL

Darkman #1: The Hangman

(New York: Pocket, 1994)

Story type: Horror (Mystery)
Series: Darkman

Major character(s): Peyton Westlake, Scientist (Darkman); Penny Larsen, Secretary—Legal; Danny "Mouse" Frakes, Child
Time period(s): 1990s (1994)
Locale(s): Detroit, Michigan

Summary: Disfigured horribly by thugs, Peyton Westlake uses the artificial skin he has developed to walk the streets as a shadowy avenger known as "Darkman." In this first adventure in the series inspired by the 1990 film by Sam Raimi, Darkman fights a street gang run by a latter-day Fagin, who recruits juveniles to do his dirty work.

Other books you might like:
Craig Shaw Gardner, *Batman*, 1991
Ric Meyers, *Fear Itself*, 1991
Ric Meyers, *Living Hell*, 1991
Ric Meyers, *Worst Nightmare*, 1992

503

RANDALL BOYLL

Darkman #2: The Price of Fear
(New York: Pocket, 1994)

Story type: Horror (Mystery)
Series: Darkman
Major character(s): Peyton Westlake, Scientist (Darkman); Julie Hastings, Lawyer; Martin Clayborne, Businessman (real estate developer)
Time period(s): 1990s (1994)
Locale(s): Detroit, Michigan

Summary: With the help of a synthetic skin he has developed, Peyton Westlake impersonates one of the assailants who brutally disfigured him and infiltrates his gang of thugs. Westlake discovers that the gang has been hired to terrorize citizens of the Eastview Estates development into selling their homes cheaply, and that the mastermind behind it, Martin Clayborne, has engaged the services of Westlake's former fiancee, Julie Hastings, under the pretense that he is trying to help out the Eastview Estates residents. This is the second novel spun off from Sam Raimi's 1990 film, *Darkman*.

Other books you might like:
Craig Shaw Gardner, *Batman*, 1991
Ric Meyers, *Fear Itself*, 1991
Ric Meyers, *Living Hell*, 1991
Ric Meyers, *Worst Nightmare*, 1992

504

RANDALL BOYLL

Darkman #3: The Gods of Hell
(New York: Pocket, 1994)

Story type: Horror (Mystery)
Series: Darkman
Major character(s): Peyton Westlake, Scientist (Darkman); Norman Hopewell, Religious (evangelist); Edgar P. Fritz, Criminal
Time period(s): 1990s (1994)
Locale(s): Detroit, Michigan

Summary: In his latest adventure, disfigured scientist Peyton Westlake, who has become a master of disguise through his development of synthetic flesh, encounters a fake faith, the Church of Eternal Youth and Beauty, whose guiding prophet ensures his aging congregation of immortality and ageless beauty by extorting exorbitant tithes and permitting them to gang rape virgins abducted for their regular services. Westlake must not only dissolve the church, but find a way to save their newest potential sacrifice, the niece of his former fiancee. This is the third adventure spun off from Sam Raimi's 1990 film *Darkman*.

Other books you might like:
Craig Shaw Gardner, *Batman*, 1991
Ric Meyers, *Fear Itself*, 1991
Ric Meyers, *Living Hell*, 1991

505

RANDALL BOYLL

Darkman #4: The Face of Death
(New York: Pocket, 1995)

Story type: Horror (Mystery)
Series: Darkman
Major character(s): Peyton Westlake, Scientist (Darkman); Harold "Rondo" Ferguson, Spy (CIA agent); Jennifer "Darla" Dalton, Young Woman
Time period(s): 1990s (1995)
Locale(s): Detroit, Michigan

Summary: Based on the 1990 Sam Raimi film *Darkman*, this is the fourth adventure of Peyton Westlake, a scientist disfigured in a fire set by criminals who uses a short-lived synthetic flesh to restore his normal appearance and fight the criminals whose lives intersect with his. In this novel, Westlake crosses paths with Rondo, a rogue CIA agent with psychopathic tendencies, who hopes to use the synthetic flesh to impersonate the president of the United States and set the country back on the militaristic agenda of the Cold War years.

Other books you might like:
Craig Shaw Gardner, *Batman*, 1991
Ric Meyers, *Fear Itself*, 1991
Ric Meyers, *Living Hell*, 1991
Ric Meyers, *Worst Nightmare*, 1992

506

RANDALL BOYLL

Mongster
(New York: Berkley, 1991)

Story type: Horror (Reanimated Dead)
Major character(s): Frank "Weasel" Whipple, Automechanic; Arnold White, Child (stepson of Frank Whipple); Jack Cumberland, Thief
Time period(s): 1990s (1990)
Locale(s): Wabash Heights, Indiana

Summary: Only young Arnold, a victim of child abuse, knows the whereabouts of the sarcophagus buried beneath his home town—and the magic words that will awaken the creature within to avenge him—in this Stephen King influenced novel. And he needs all the help he can get, for his stepfather and the son of the man from whom the sarcophagus was stolen have joined forces against him.

Other books you might like:
David Case, *The Third Grave*, 1981
Charles L. Grant, *The Long Night of the Grave*, 1986
Robert E. Howard, *Skull-Face*, 1946
Stephen King, *It*, 1986
Anne Rice, *The Mummy, or Ramses the Damned*, 1989

507
RANDALL BOYLL

Tales From the Crypt: Demon Knight
(New York: Pocket, 1995)

Story type: Horror (Ancient Evil Unleashed)
Major character(s): Silas Brayker, Thief; The Salesman, Demon; Jeryline A. Bascombe, Servant
Time period(s): 1990s (1995)
Locale(s): Wormwood, New Mexico

Summary: The citizens of Wormwood team up with mysterious stranger Silas Brayker to fight a demon horde that has followed him to their town in the hope of retrieving a magic talisman in his possession that will allow the powers of darkness to take over the universe. This book is a novelization of a screenplay by Ethan Reiff, Cyrus Voris and Mark Bishop written for a film spun off from the popular cable television series based on the E.C. comics of the 1950s.

Other books you might like:
Joe R. Lansdale, *Dead in the West*, 1986
Robert R. McCammon, *Stinger*, 1988
Christopher Moore, *Practical Demonkeeping*, 1993

508
RAY BRADBURY

Death Is a Lonely Business
(New York: Bantam, 1992)

Story type: Horror (Mystery)
Major character(s): The Crazy, Writer; Elmo Crumley, Detective—Private; Constance Rattigan, Actress (former)
Time period(s): 1940s
Locale(s): Venice Beach, California

Summary: The narrator, a writer of weird tales known only by his nickname, The Crazy, enlists the aid of a private detective and a fading movie star to help him find out why his grotesque but lovable friends are suddenly dying from unknown causes. This novel was originally published in 1985.

Other books you might like:
Robert Bloch, *The Star Stalker*, 1968
William Hjortsberg, *Falling Angel*, 1978

509
RAY BRADBURY

A Graveyard for Lunatics
(New York: Knopf, 1990)

Story type: Horror (Mystery)
Major character(s): Roy Holdstrom, Filmmaker (special effects); Fritz Wong, Director (film director); Manny Leiber, Director (film director)
Time period(s): 1950s (1954)
Locale(s): Hollywood, California

Summary: Hired by Maximus Films to script science fiction movies, the unnamed narrator finds himself caught up in a backlot intrigue that begins when he stumbles upon the corpse of a Hollywood executive supposedly 20 years dead and his friend in the special effects department creates a monster that so disturbs the studio he is fired from his job. This is a sequel to *Death Is a Lonely Business*.

Other books you might like:
Robert Bloch, *Psycho II*, 1982
Robert Bloch, *The Star Stalker*, 1968
Jonathan Carroll, *A Child Across the Sky*, 1989

510
RAY BRADBURY

The Martian Chronicles
(New York: Doubleday, 1990)

Story type: Science Fiction (First Contact; Space Colony)
Major character(s): Wilder, Spaceship Captain; Hathaway, Spaceman
Time period(s): 20th century; 21st century
Locale(s): Mars; Earth

Summary: The 40th anniversary hardcover reprint edition of the 1950 classic collection of short stories about the colonization of Mars. War and hardship on Earth have people emigrating to Mars after four ill-fated exploratory expeditions.

Other books you might like:
Hal Clement, *Needle*, 1950
Mary Gentle, *Golden Witchbreed*, 1983
Walter S. Tevis, *The Man Who Fell to Earth*, 1963
Wynne Whiteford, *Lake of the Sun*, 1989
Gene Wolfe, *Endangered Species*, 1989

511
RAY BRADBURY

The October Country
(New York: Del Rey, 1996)

Story type: Horror (Collection)

Summary: First published in 1955, this classic collection brings together 19 stories that blur the boundary between supernatural and mainstream fiction. Included are Bradbury's modern reworkings of Gothic horror themes, ''Skeleton'' and ''The Scythe,'' and his poignant tale of a love that endures beyond death, "The Lake." "The Emissary" and the vampire tale "The Man Upstairs" both feature children whose imaginations endow them with a sensitivity to the dark side of life. "Uncle Einar" and "The Homecoming" are loosely linked stories concerned with a family of supernatural creatures trying to live unobtrusively as normal human beings. "The Dwarf," "The Next in Line," and "The Jar" are stories of psychological suspense in which the emotional needs of characters prove as powerful and dangerous as supernatural forces.

Other books you might like:
Charles Beaumont, *Selected Stories*, 1988
Dennis Etchison, *The Dark Country*, 1982
Charles L. Grant, *Tales From the Nightside*, 1981
Shirley Jackson, *The Lottery, or the Adventures of James Harris*, 1949
Richard Matheson, *Collected Stories*, 1989

512

RAY BRADBURY

Quicker than the Eye
(New York: Avon, 1996)

Story type: Science Fiction (Collection; Fantasy)

Summary: Contains nine original and 12 stories reprinted from periodicals and anthologies 1955-1996. Frequently upbeat in tone with a strong sense of setting, the stories' themes include a cross-time encounter, ghosts, time travel, a dystopian future, an Irish tall tale, earthquakes, magic on a submarine, and molecular rejuvenation. A five-page afterword discusses the stories.

Other books you might like:
Brian W. Aldiss, *Man in His Time: The Best Science Fiction Stories of Brian W. Aldiss*, 1989
J.G. Ballard, *The Best Short Stories of J.G. Ballard*, 1978
Alfred Bester, *Star Light, Star Bright*, 1976
Nancy Kress, *The Aliens of Earth*, 1993
Henry Kuttner, *The Best of Henry Kuttner*, 1975
Clifford D. Simak, *Skirmish: The Great Short Fiction of Clifford D. Simak*, 1977
John Varley, *Blue Champagne*, 1986
Kurt Vonnegut Jr., *Welcome to the Monkey House*, 1968

513

RAY BRADBURY

The Toynbee Convector
(New York: Bantam Spectra, 1989)

Story type: Science Fiction (Collection)

Summary: The twenty-three stories contained in this latest collection originally appeared in such magazines as *Omni, Twilight Zone, Gallery*, and *Weird Tales*, as well as the anthology *Dark Forces*. Among the stories included are "On the Orient, North," "At Midnight, in the Month of June," "The Toynbee Convector," "A Touch of Petulance," "The Tombstone," "The Thing at the Top of the Stairs," and

"Colonel Stonesteel's Genuine Home-made Truly Egyptian Mummy."

Other books you might like:
Robert Bloch, *The Selected Stories of Robert Bloch*, 1988
Harlan Ellison, *Angry Candy*, 1988
George R.R. Martin, *Portraits of His Children*, 1987
Theodore Sturgeon, *A Touch of Sturgeon*, 1987
Gene Wolfe, *Endangered Species*, 1989

514

SCOTT BRADFIELD

Dream of the Wolf
(New York: Knopf, 1990)

Story type: Horror (Collection)

Summary: The author's first collection brings together 13 stories, most of which are centered around social misfits or outsiders whose alienation induces them to seek escape into fantasy. The best selections include the title story, in which a man's obsessive dreams about life as a wolf begin to interfere with his humdrum daily life, "Ghost Guessed" in which a failed suicide is haunted by the ghost he would have become, and "The Wind Box," in which a man searching for meaning in his life finds that his emotional turmoil causes earthquakes. A shorter version was published in England in 1988 as *The Secret Life of Houses*.

Other books you might like:
Ron Hansen, *Nebraska*, 1989
Shirley Jackson, *The Lottery, or the Adventures of James Harris*, 1949
Eric McCormack, *Inspecting the Vaults*, 1987
Ian McEwan, *In Between the Sheets*, 1979
Joyce Carol Oates, *Night-Side*, 1980

515

SCOTT BRADFIELD

What's Wrong with America
(New York: St. Martin's, 1994)

Story type: Horror (Satire)
Major character(s): Emma Delaney O'Hallahan, Widow(er), Abuse Victim; Marvin O'Hallahan, Aged Person; Donald Sullivan, Banker
Time period(s): 1990s (1994)
Locale(s): Los Angeles, California

Summary: After killing her abusive husband, Emma O'Hallahan tries to live a good life but finds herself haunted by his slovenly ghost, nosy neighbors and relatives, and a variety of opportunistic social and political parasites "sympathetic" to her position. Their quirky behaviors sum up the wry title the author has given this subtle satire of life in modern America. This novel was first published in England.

Other books you might like:
Thomas M. Disch, *The Businessman: A Tale of Terror*, 1984
Thomas M. Disch, *The M.D.: A Horror Story*, 1991
Thomas M. Disch, *The Priest: A Gothic Romance*, 1994
Patrick McGrath, *The Grotesque*, 1989

Gus Weill, *Flesh*, 1990

516

MARION ZIMMER BRADLEY, Editor

The Best of Marion Zimmer Bradley's Fantasy Magazine

(New York: Warner Aspect, 1994)

Story type: Fantasy (Anthology)

Summary: Contains a three-page introduction plus individual introductions to 18 stories reprinted from *Marion Zimmer Bradley's Fantasy Magazine* 1988-1991, with one Nebula Award finalist, Mary C. Aldridge's "The Adinkra Cloth." Mercedes Lackey's "Nightside" features the protagonist from her Diana Tregarde series and Phyllis Ann Karr's "The Truth about the Lady of the Lake" features her novels' protagonists, the sorceress Frostflower and the woman warrior Thorn. The tone varies from humorous to dark with themes such as magic conflict, war with extraterrestrials, sword and sorcery and adventure. Other authors include Lynne Armstrong-Jones, Jo Clayton, Tanya Huff, Jacqueline Lichtenberg, Diana L. Paxson, Jennifer Roberson, L.A. Taylor, Elisabeth Waters and Lawrence Watt-Evans.

Other books you might like:
Kristine Kathryn Rusch, *The Best of Pulphouse: The Hardback Magazine*, 1991
  editor
Jessica Amanda Salmonson, *Amazons!*, 1979
  editor
Jessica Amanda Salmonson, *Heroic Visions*, 1983
  editor
Pamela Sargent, *Women of Wonder: Science Fiction Stories by Women about Women*, 1975
  editor
Jane Yolen, *Xanadu*, 1993
  editor

517

MARION ZIMMER BRADLEY, Editor
ELISABETH WATERS, Co-Editor

The Best of Marion Zimmer Bradley's Fantasy Magazine, Volume II

(New York: Warner Aspect, 1995)

Story type: Fantasy (Anthology)

Summary: Contains a two-page introduction and individual introductions to 15 stories reprinted from *Marion Zimmer Bradley's Fantasy Magazine*. The tone varies from ominous to light with themes such as high fantasy, martial arts, mythical creatures, vampirism, Merlin the Magician, and psychic detection with Dana Tregarde in "Satanic, Versus" by Mercedes Lackey. Other authors include George Barr, Jo Clayton, Janet Kagan, Phyllis Ann Karr, Jennifer Roberson, eluki bes shahar, Brad Strickland, Elisabeth Waters, and Deborah Wheeler.

Other books you might like:
Kristine Kathryn Rusch, *The Best From Fantasy and Science Fiction: A 45th Anniversary Anthology*, 1994
  Edward L. Ferman, co-editor
Kristine Kathryn Rusch, *The Best of Pulphouse: The Hardback Magazine*, 1991
  editor
Jessica Amanda Salmonson, *Amazons!*, 1979
  editor
Jessica Amanda Salmonson, *Heroic Visions*, 1979
  editor
A. Susan Williams, *The Lifted Veil: The Book of Fantastic Literature by Women*, 1993
  editor

518

MARION ZIMMER BRADLEY
JULIAN MAY, Co-Author
ANDRE NORTON, Co-Author

Black Trillium

(New York: Doubleday Foundation, 1990)

Story type: Fantasy (Quest; Magic Conflict)
Major character(s): Haramis, Royalty (princess); Kadiya, Royalty (princess); Anigel, Royalty (princess)
Time period(s): Indeterminate
Locale(s): Ruwenda, Fictional Country

Summary: After their parents are killed by the invading Labornok soldiers, princesses Haramis, Kadiya and Anigel must each seek out a talisman to defeat the Archmage Orogastus and regain the kingdom. On the quest Anigel must overcome her timidity, Kadiya her recklessness and Haramis her arrogance. Working together, they defeat Orogastus. Haramis becomes Archmage, Kadiya ambassador to the Wild Ones and Anigel, who marries Prince Antar of Labornok, becomes queen of both kingdoms.

Other books you might like:
Robert Asprin, *Thieves' World*, 1979
Jack L. Chalker, *The River of the Dancing Gods*, 1984
Katherine Kurtz, *Deryni Rising*, 1981
Will Shetterly, *Liavek*, 1985
  Emma Bull, co-editor
Clifford D. Simak, *The Fellowship of the Talisman*, 1978
Jack Vance, *Lyonesse*, 1983
Terri Windling, *Borderland*, 1986
  Mark Arnold, co-editor

519

MARION ZIMMER BRADLEY

Domains of Darkover

(New York: DAW, 1990)

Story type: Science Fiction (Anthology)
Series: Darkover
Time period(s): Indeterminate Future
Locale(s): Darkover, Planet—Imaginary

Summary: 17 stories from various times in Darkover history. Both new readers and those familiar with Bradley's universe will enjoy Mercedes Lackey's story, "An Object Lesson," about the Free Amazons of Darkover. Dorothy J. Heydt also submitted a strong mystery story, "Death in Thendara."

Other books you might like:
C.J. Cherryh, *Angel with the Sword*, 1985
C.J. Cherryh, *The Faded Sun: Kesrith*, 1978
L. Sprague de Camp, *The Hand of Zei*, 1963
Stephen Goldin, *Jade Darcy and the Affair of Honor*, 1988
Elizabeth Moon, *Sheepfarmer's Daughter*, 1988
Jack Vance, *City of the Chasch*, 1968

520

MARION ZIMMER BRADLEY

Exile's Song

(New York: DAW, 1996)

Story type: Science Fiction (Science Fantasy; Family Saga)
Series: Darkover
Major character(s): Margaret Alton, Musician, Psychic; Mikhail Lanart-Hastur, Nobleman, Psychic; Lew Alton, Diplomat, Psychic
Time period(s): Indeterminate Future
Locale(s): Darkover, Planet—Imaginary

Summary: Margaret Alton comes to Darkover to research music. Instead she finds herself treated with awe while unknown relatives keep popping up and expecting her to fulfill a role she doesn't want. When she starts getting visions, she must decide just what a planet she hardly remembers really means to her.

Other books you might like:
Octavia E. Butler, *Mind of My Mind*, 1977
Paula E. Downing, *Rinn's Star*, 1990
Cheryl J. Franklin, *The Light of Exile*, 1990
Anne McCaffrey, *Powers That Be*, 1993
    Elizabeth Ann Scarborough, co-author
Andre Norton, *Ice Crown*, 1970
James H. Schmitz, *The Telzey Toy*, 1973
Jack Vance, *Madouc*, 1990
Timothy Zahn, *A Coming of Age*, 1985

521

MARION ZIMMER BRADLEY

The Forest House

(New York: Viking, 1994)

Story type: Fantasy (Historical; Religious)
Major character(s): Eilan, Religious (druid high priestess), Parent; Gaius Macellius Severus Siluricus, Military Personnel (Roman/British); Caillean, Religious (druid priestess)
Time period(s): 1st century (70s)
Locale(s): Deva, England; Vernematon, England (the Forest House); Roman Empire

Summary: Caillean tells her novices the story of Eilan, last Lady of Vernemation, and Gaius, the forbidden Roman sol-

dier she loved during the time of the Forest House and the Roman occupation of the country, which leads to their sharing the misty island with the Nazarene monks who shelter there.

Other books you might like:
Margaret Ball, *Flameweaver*, 1991
Frans G. Bengtsson, *The Long Ships*, 1954
Maya Kaathryn Bohnhoff, *The Meri*, 1992
Jack Holland, *The Fire Queen*, 1992
Morgan Llywelyn, *Druids*, 1991
Bridget Wood, *Wolfking*, 1992

522

MARION ZIMMER BRADLEY

Ghostlight

(New York: Tor, 1995)

Story type: Fantasy (Contemporary; Magic Conflict)
Major character(s): Truth Jourdemayne, Researcher; Julian Pilgrim, Magician; Thorne Blackburn, Magician, Parent
Time period(s): 1990s
Locale(s): Shadowkill, New York

Summary: Three decades after Truth's mother dies in a bizarre magical ritual and her father vanishes, the aunt who raised her gives Truth some magical artifacts belonging to her father. When Truth decides to write her father's biography, her research leads her to an old house called Shadow Gate and to a meeting with Julian Pilgrim, the handsome new owner who plans to recreate the same ritual that killed her mother.

Other books you might like:
Margaret Ball, *The Shadow Gate*, 1991
Emma Bull, *War for the Oaks*, 1987
R.A. MacAvoy, *Tea with the Black Dragon*, 1983
Elizabeth Ann Scarborough, *Phantom Banjo*, 1991

523

MARION ZIMMER BRADLEY
HOLLY LISLE, Co-Author

Glenraven

(New York: Baen, 1996)

Story type: Fantasy (Magic Conflict; Adventure)
Major character(s): Jay Jay Bennington, Writer, Traveller; Sophie Cortiss, Traveller; Matthiall, Wizard
Time period(s): 1990s
Locale(s): Glenraven, Fictional Country (between France and Italy); Europe

Summary: Jay Jay Bennington, facing her third divorce, and Sophie Cortiss, unable to come to terms with the death of her daughter, travel to Glenraven, a mysterious Alpine country under the rule of a semi-immortal tyrant. As the country reaches out for a hero, the tyrant and her servants expect beings of immense power, not two ordinary women from North Carolina.

Other books you might like:
Poul Anderson, *Three Hearts and Three Lions*, 1961
Greg Bear, *The Infinity Concerto*, 1984
Jack L. Chalker, *The River of Dancing Gods*, 1984

Alan Dean Foster, *Spellsinger*, 1983
Barbara Hambly, *The Time of the Dark*, 1982
Diana Wynne Jones, *Hexwood*, 1994
Clifford D. Simak, *Special Deliverance*, 1982
Christopher Stasheff, *The Witch Doctor*, 1994

524

MARION ZIMMER BRADLEY

The Heirs of Hammerfell

(New York: DAW Books, 1989)

Story type: Science Fiction (Science Fantasy)
Series: Darkover
Major character(s): Alastair, Heir, Twin; Conn, Heir, Twin
Time period(s): Indeterminate
Locale(s): Darkover, Planet—Imaginary

Summary: During the planet Darkover's dark ages, bloody clan warfare is the order of the day. When clan Storn wipes out clan Hammerfell, the twin heirs of Hammerfell survive and grow up separated from each other, each convinced the other is dead. Eventually both return to fight for their inheritance and to be reunited.

Other books you might like:
Katherine Kurtz, *The Harrowing of Gwynedd*, 1989
Katherine Kurtz, *The Quest for Saint Camber*, 1986
Anne McCaffrey, *Dragonsdawn*, 1988
Anne McCaffrey, *Nerilka's Story*, 1986
Anne McCaffrey, *The Renegades of Pern*, 1989
Andre Norton, *The Gate of the Cat*, 1987
Andre Norton, *Sorceress of the Witch World*, 1968
Andre Norton, *'Ware Hawk*, 1983

525

MARION ZIMMER BRADLEY

Lady of the Trillium

(New York: Bantam Spectra, 1995)

Story type: Fantasy (Psychic Powers; Magic Conflict)
Series: Trillium
Major character(s): Haramis, Magician, Recluse; Mikayla, Royalty (princess), Student (magic); Fiolon, Nobleman, Musician
Time period(s): Indeterminate
Locale(s): Ruwenda, Fictional Country; Labornok, Fictional Country

Summary: In choosing a successor to Archmage, Haramis chooses Mikayla, who remains unenthusiastic about everything save her betrothal to Lord Fiolon. Haramis' magical attempt to sever the couple's telepathic link has disastrous results.

Other books you might like:
Jo Clayton, *Dancer's Rise*, 1993
Diane Duane, *So You Want to Be a Wizard?*, 1983
Sharon Green, *Silver Princess, Golden Knight*, 1993
Monica Hughes, *The Promise*, 1992
Julian May, *Blood Trillium*, 1992
Andre Norton, *Golden Trillium*, 1993

Pamela F. Service, *Winter of Magic's Return*, 1985
Mary Frances Zambreno, *Journeyman Wizard*, 1994

526

MARION ZIMMER BRADLEY, Editor

Leroni of Darkover

(New York: DAW, 1991)

Story type: Science Fiction (Anthology; Psychic Powers)
Series: Darkover
Time period(s): Indeterminate Future
Locale(s): Darkover, Planet—Imaginary

Summary: This volume contains 22 stories about Darkovans with the psychic gifts of 'laran.' Stories include historical background on the first settlers in "The Tower at New Skye" by Priscilla W. Armstrong, some unusual uses of 'laran' in "Food for the Worms" by Roxana Pierson and a Terran with psychic powers in "The Speaking Touch" by Margaret Carter. "A Meeting of Minds" by Elisabeth Waters is a short, humorous piece.

Other books you might like:
Suzette Haden Elgin, *Communipath Worlds*, 1980
Suzette Haden Elgin, *Native Tongue*, 1984
Anne McCaffrey, *To Ride Pegasus*, 1973
Vonda N. McIntyre, *Dreamsnake*, 1978
A.E. van Vogt, *Slan*, 1946
Patricia C. Wrede, *Caught in Crystal*, 1987

527

MARION ZIMMER BRADLEY
MERCEDES LACKEY, Co-Author

Rediscovery: A Novel of Darkover

(New York: DAW, 1993)

Story type: Science Fiction (Lost Colony; Psychic Powers)
Series: Darkover
Major character(s): Leonie Hastur, Telepath; Elizabeth Macintosh, Spacewoman, Telepath; Kermiak Alderan, Royalty, Telepath
Time period(s): Indeterminate Future
Locale(s): *Minnesota*, Spaceship; Darkover, Planet— Imaginary

Summary: An exploratory mission from Earth discovers an inhospitably cold planet deficient in heavy metals and sends down a landing party. Far away, Leonie Hastur finds herself in an alien mind after the Terrans' shuttle crashes in a storm and becomes fascinated by the strange minds before losing contact. The two known telepaths on the crew, Elizabeth and David, soon communicate with the natives. While listening to local entertainment, Elizabeth realizes their language, Gaelic, indicates Terran origin.

Other books you might like:
Margaret Wander Bonanno, *The Others*, 1990
Diana G. Gallagher, *The Alien Dark*, 1990
Kris Jensen, *Mentor*, 1991
Mercedes Lackey, *Wing Commander: Freedom Flight*, 1992
  Ellen Guon, co-author

Anne McCaffrey, *The Rowan*, 1990
Anne McCaffrey, *The Ship Who Searched*, 1992
  Mercedes Lackey, co-author
Joan Slonczewski, *A Door into Ocean*, 1986

528

MARION ZIMMER BRADLEY, Editor

Renunciates of Darkover
(New York: DAW, 1991)

Story type: Science Fiction (Anthology)
Series: Darkover
Time period(s): Indeterminate Future
Locale(s): Darkover, Planet—Imaginary

Summary: In this collection of 22 stories about the Order of Renunciates, "Carlina's Calling" by Patricia D. Novak, tells how the Sisterhood of the Sword and the Priestesses of Avarra joined to form the Order of Reununciates, popularly known as the Free Amazons. Several stories involve Renunciates with 'laran' powers including "Strife" by Chel Avery. Some stories, such as "Amazon Fragment" by Marion Zimmer Bradley, tell of internal Guild conflicts while others tell of Darkovan political intrigue, as in "Set a Thief" by Mercedes Lackey. One story, "The Honor of the Guild" by Joan Marie Verba, is a murder mystery, and others provide historical background development as in "Dalereuth Guild House" by Priscilla W. Armstrong.

Other books you might like:
C.J. Cherryh, *Gate of Ivrel*, 1976
Barbara Hambly, *The Ladies of Mandrigyn*, 1984
Elizabeth A. Lynn, *The Dancers of Arun*, 1979
Elizabeth A. Lynn, *The Northern Girl*, 1980
C.L. Moore, *Jirel of Joiry*, 1969

529

MARION ZIMMER BRADLEY, Editor

Sword and Sorceress VIII
(New York: DAW, 1991)

Story type: Fantasy (Anthology; Sword and Sorcery)
Series: Sword and Sorceress

Summary: 22 original stories about women warriors with a three-page introduction by the editor plus brief introductions with biographical sketches of the author for each story. Authors whose first professional sale appears here include Deborah Burros, Jere Dunham, Margaret Howes, Stephanie Shaver and Cynthia Ward. Other authors include Laurell K. Hamilton, Mercedes Lackey, Diana L. Paxson, Jennifer Roberson, Eluki bes Shahar, Josepha Sherman and Dave Smeds.

Other books you might like:
Ellen Datlow, *The Year's Best Fantasy and Horror: Fourth Annual Collection*, 1991
  Terri Windling, co-editor
Ellen Kushner, *Basilisk*, 1980
  editor
Will Shetterly, *Liavek*, 1985
  Emma Bull, co-editor

Will Shetterly, *Liavek: Spells of Binding*, 1988
  Emma Bull, co-editor
Terri Windling, *Borderland*, 1986
  Mark Alan Arnold, co-editor
Terri Windling, *Life on the Border*, 1991
  editor

530

MARION ZIMMER BRADLEY, Editor

Sword and Sorceress IX
(New York: DAW, 1992)

Story type: Fantasy (Anthology; Sword and Sorcery)
Series: Sword and Sorcery
Time period(s): Indeterminate Past

Summary: 26 original stories which revolve around women as primary actors in and initiators of adventure plus a trenchant three-page introduction by the editor and introductions to each story. Authors whose first professional sale appears here include Tanya Beaty, Lisa Deason, Eric Haines, Lee Ann Martins and Leslie Ann Miller. Other authors include Mercedes Lackey, Diana Paxson, Josepha Sherman and Dave Smeds.

Other books you might like:
C.J. Cherryh, *Festival Moon*, 1987
  editor
Ellen Datlow, *The Year's Best Fantasy and Horror: Third Annual Collection*, 1990
  Terri Windling, co-editor
Ellen Kushner, *Basilisk*, 1980
  editor
Will Shetterly, *Liavek*, 1985
  Emma Bull, co-editor
Terri Windling, *Borderland*, 1986
  Mark Alan Arnold, co-editor
Terri Windling, *Elsewhere*, 1981
  Mark Alan Arnold, co-editor

531

MARION ZIMMER BRADLEY, Editor

Sword and Sorceress XI
(New York: DAW, 1994)

Story type: Fantasy (Anthology; Sword and Sorcery)
Series: Sword and Sorceress

Summary: Contains a two-page introduction and individual introductions with biographical sketches of the authors of 33 original stories featuring sword wielding heroines in diverse settings and situations. Authors include Lynne Armstrong-Jones, Jo Clayton, Diana L. Paxson, Dave Smeds and Deborah Wheeler.

Other books you might like:
Nina Auerbach, *Forbidden Journeys: Fairy Tales and Fantasies by Victorian Women Writers*, 1992
  U.C. Knoepflmacher, co-editor
George Alec Effinger, *Maureen Birnbaum, Barbarian Swordsperson: The Complete Stories*, 1993

Jessica Amanda Salmonson, *Amazons!*, 1979
editor
Terri Windling, *Life on the Border*, 1991
editor
Jack Zipes, *Don't Bet on the Prince*, 1986
editor

532

MARION ZIMMER BRADLEY, Editor

Sword and Sorceress XII

(New York: DAW, 1995)

Story type: Fantasy (Anthology; Sword and Sorcery)
Series: Sword and Sorceress

Summary: Contains a four-page introduction plus individual introductions to 22 original stories including one collaboration, ''A Dragon in Distress,'' by Mercedes Lackey and Elisabeth Waters. The tone varies from somber and ominous to light and whimsical with themes including high fantasy, music and a rewritten version of ''Cinderella.'' Other authors include Lynne Armstrong-Jones, Diana L. Paxson, Jennifer Roberson, L.S. Silverthorne, and Deborah Wheeler.

Other books you might like:
George Alec Effinger, *Maureen Birnbaum, Barbarian Swordsperson: The Complete Stories*, 1993
Esther Friesner, *Chicks in Chainmail*, 1995
editor
C.L. Moore, *Jirel of Joiry*, 1969
Kathleen M. Massie-Ferch, *Ancient Enchantresses*, 1995
Martin H. Greenberg, Richard Gilliam, co-editors
Jessica Amanda Salmonson, *Amazons!*, 1979
editor

533

MARION ZIMMER BRADLEY

Sword and Sorceress XIII

(New York: DAW, 1996)

Story type: Fantasy (Anthology; Sword and Sorcery)
Series: Sword and Sorceress

Summary: This anthology contains a two-page introduction plus individual introductions to 22 original stories, frequently somber to ominous in tone, with themes including shapeshifting, dream quests, biography, magic conflict, martial arts, and mythical creatures. Authors include Jo Clayton, Cynthia McQuillin, Diana L. Paxson, Marella Sands, Charles M. Saplak, Laura J. Underwood, and Deborah Wheeler.

Other books you might like:
George Alec Effinger, *Maureen Birnbaum, Barbarian Swordsperson: The Complete Stories*, 1993
Esther Friesner, *Chicks in Chainmail*, 1995
editor
C.L. Moore, *Jirel of Joiry*, 1969
Kathleen M. Massie-Ferch, *Ancient Enchantresses*, 1995
Martin H. Greenberg, Richard Gilliam, co-editors
Jessica Amanda Salmonson, *Amazons!*, 1979
editor

534

MARION ZIMMER BRADLEY
ANDRE NORTON, Co-Author
MERCEDES LACKEY, Co-Author

Tiger Burning Bright

(New York: Morrow/AvoNova, 1995)

Story type: Fantasy (Magic Conflict; Political)
Major character(s): Shelyra ''Raymonda'', Royalty (princess); Leopold, Royalty (prince), Military Personnel; Apolon, Magician
Time period(s): Indeterminate
Locale(s): Merina, Fictional City (city-state)

Summary: When Merina falls to Balthasar, the three former rulers, Dowager Queen Adele, Queen Lydana and Princess Shelyra, assume alternate identities to avoid Balthasar's grasp. Masquerading as a gypsy, Shelyra bonds with Balthasar's son, Leopold, as opposition to the harsh rule and Apolon's necromancy builds.

Other books you might like:
Piers Anthony, *For Love of Evil*, 1988
Jack L. Chalker, *Demons of the Dancing Gods*, 1984
L. Sprague de Camp, *Land of Unreason*, 1942
Fletcher Pratt, co-author
John M. Ford, *The Dragon Waiting*, 1983
Fritz Leiber, *Gather, Darkness!*, 1950
James H. Schmitz, *The Witches of Karres*, 1966
Melinda M. Snodgrass, *Queen's Gambit Declined*, 1989
Christopher Stasheff, *King Kobold Revived*, 1984

535

MARION ZIMMER BRADLEY, Editor

Towers of Darkover

(New York: DAW, 1993)

Story type: Fantasy (Anthology; Psychic Powers)
Series: Darkover
Time period(s): Indeterminate Future
Locale(s): Darkover, Planet—Imaginary

Summary: Contains a five-page editorial and individual introductions to 20 original stories focusing on life around the citadels occupied by those developing their psychic abilities, some to master natural forces and others to forward goals of domination. Set at various times, some stories feature characters developed in novels of Bradley's Darkover Series (1962-1993) and utilize diverse themes. Authors include Emily Alward, Lynne Armstrong Jones, Marion Zimmer Bradley, Patricia B. Cirone, Patricia Duffy Novak, Diann Partridge, Diana L. Paxson, Joan Marie Verba, Elisabeth Waters and Deborah Wheeler.

Other books you might like:
Margaret Wander Bonanno, *The Others*, 1990
Suzette Haden Elgin, *Communipath Worlds*, 1980
Elizabeth A. Lynn, *The Dancers of Arun*, 1979
Anne McCaffrey, *The Rowan*, 1990
Elizabeth Ann Scarborough, *Last Refuge*, 1992
Theodore Sturgeon, *More than Human*, 1953

536

MARION ZIMMER BRADLEY

Witch Hill
(New York: Tor, 1990)

Story type: Horror (Black Magic)
Major character(s): Sarah Latimer, Student (art student drop out), Witch; Brian Standish, Doctor; Matthew Hay, Religious (Leader—Church of the Antique)
Time period(s): 1970s (1971)
Locale(s): Arkham, Massachusetts (Witch Hill)

Summary: Following the death of her family, Sarah Latimer seeks refuge at her father's family home, Witch Hill. All too soon, her dark family legacy asserts itself and Sarah is trapped in the web of an occult mystery perpetuated by preceding generations of Latimers, each of which produced a woman named Sarah who practiced witchcraft.

Other books you might like:
John Farris, *All Heads Turn When the Hunt Goes By*, 1977
Anne Rice, *The Witching Hour*, 1990

537

MARION ZIMMER BRADLEY

Witchlight
(New York: Tor, 1996)

Story type: Fantasy (Contemporary; Magic Conflict)
Major character(s): Winter Musgrave, Amnesiac; Truth Jourdemayne, Researcher (paranormal); Hunter "Grey" Greyson, Magician
Time period(s): 1990s
Locale(s): Taghkanic College, New York; San Francisco, California

Summary: Unable to remember much of her past, Winter Musgrave finds herself fleeing from an unseen force that plays tricks—including mutilating small animals—wherever she goes. Desperate, Winter seeks help from Truth Jourdemayne, who studies paranormal phenomena, and gradually uncovers her missing memories. A loose sequel to *Ghostlight*.

Other books you might like:
Jonathan Carroll, *Bones of the Moon*, 1988
John Crowley, *Love and Sleep*, 1994
Dean R. Koontz, *Cold Fire*, 1991
Marc Laidlaw, *The 37th Mandala*, 1996
Christopher Pike, *Whisper of Death*, 1991

538

WILL BRADLEY (Pseudonym of Brad Strickland)

Ark Liberty
(New York: Roc, 1992)

Story type: Science Fiction (Post-Nuclear Holocaust; Alternate Intelligence)
Major character(s): Stefan Li, Scientist, Disembodied Personality (computer imprint); Carin Hawk, Explorer
Time period(s): 2080s (2084); 24th century

Locale(s): Liberty, Undersea Environment/Habitat; Atlantic Ocean; North America

Summary: Fearing universal destruction of Earth society, Stefan Li defies orders when he begins to fill *Liberty* with people to prepare *Liberty* for survival without contact from the outside world. When officials try to stop him, Stefan Li foils their plans, costing Li his corporeal existence. Friends salvage his personality and memories by imprinting them onto *Liberty*'s computer. Centuries later, after they attempt to seed Earth's atmosphere with beneficial bacteria, survivers from *Liberty* explore a ruined North America hoping to discover signs of recovery, but finding instead a threat to *Liberty*'s survival.

Other books you might like:
David Brin, *Earth*, 1990
Octavia E. Butler, *Dawn*, 1987
Daniel F. Galouye, *Dark Universe*, 1961
Marjorie Bradley Kellogg, *Harmony*, 1991
Rosemary Kirstein, *The Outskirter's Secret*, 1992
Vonda N. McIntyre, *Starfarers*, 1989
Vonda N. McIntyre, *Transition*, 1991
Donald E. McQuinn, *Warrior*, 1990
J.M. Morgan, *Desert Eden*, 1991
Michael D. Weaver, *My Father Immortal*, 1989
Catherine Wells, *The Earth Is All That Lasts*, 1991
Paul O. Williams, *The Breaking of Northwall*, 1980

539

GILLIAN BRADSHAW

Horses of Heaven
(New York: Doubleday, 1991)

Story type: Fantasy (Historical; Romance)
Major character(s): Mauakes, Ruler; Heliokleia, Royalty (princess)
Time period(s): 2nd century B.C.
Locale(s): Ferghana, Asia; Bactria, Asia

Summary: Mauakes, ruler of Ferghana where the natives raise flying stallions, marries Heliokleia of the elephant masters. Their marriage is difficult as Helioka is an intelligent, independent person and Mauakes expects women to serve and obey.

Other books you might like:
David Cook, *Horselords*, 1990
Morgan Llywelyn, *Bard*, 1987
Morgan Llywelyn, *The Horse Goddess*, 1982
Josepha Sherman, *The Horse of Flame*, 1990
David Wingrove, *The Middle Kingdom*, 1990

540

GILLIAN BRADSHAW

The Land of Gold
(New York: Greenwillow, 1992)

Story type: Fantasy (Young Adult; Quest)
Major character(s): Kandaki, Royalty (princess of Nubia), Heiress—Dispossessed; Hathor, Mythical Creature (dragon); Prahotep, Adventurer

Time period(s): Indeterminate Past
Locale(s): Nubia, Ancient Civilization; Africa

Summary: Shabako usurps her parents' throne and leaves Kandaki to die in the swamp, but Prahotep and his companions rescue her and agree to join forces to defeat Shabako. The group travels a dangerous waterway to Napata where, recognized as Queen of Nubia, Kandaki organizes a force to overthrow Shabako. Sequel to *The Dragon and the Thief.*

Other books you might like:
Lloyd Alexander, *The High King*, 1968
John Christopher, *Beyond the Burning Lands*, 1971
Peter Dickinson, *The Blue Hawk*, 1976
Frances Mary Hendry, *Quest for a Maid*, 1990
Andre Norton, *The Crystal Gryphon*, 1992
Robert Silverberg, *Letters From Atlantis*, 1990
Robert Silverberg, *Thebes of the Hundred Gates*, 1991

541
CHRISTOPHER BRAM

Father of Frankenstein
(New York: Dutton, 1995)

Story type: Horror (Literary)
Major character(s): James Whale, Director (movie), Homosexual; Clayton Boone, Gardener; Boris Karloff, Actor, Historical Figure
Time period(s): 1950s (1957)
Locale(s): Santa Monica, California

Summary: In the last month of his life James Whale, director of the films *Frankenstein* and *Bride of Frankenstein*, is afflicted with a series of strokes that affect his ability to discriminate between past and present, and real life and the movies. In this flashback-studded novel, the gay director initially repels and then earns the affection of his homophobic ex-Marine gardener, and the two develop a relationship that begins to resemble the one between Victor Frankenstein and his creation.

Other books you might like:
Emmanuel Carrere, *Gothic Romance*, 1984
Kim Newman, *Anno Dracula*, 1992
Theodore Roszak, *The Memoirs of Elizabeth Frankenstein*, 1995

542
GARY BRANDNER

Doomstalker
(New York: Fawcett, 1989)

Story type: Horror (Satanism)
Major character(s): Brian Kettering, Detective—Police; Doomstalker, Demon
Time period(s): 1980s (Prologue in 1951)
Locale(s): California

Summary: As a six year old, Brian Kettering sees his father killed in a duel with the Doomstalker, a demon. As a grown man, Kettering again faces the Doomstalker, with his friends, family, and his own soul at stake.

Other books you might like:
William Peter Blatty, *The Exorcist*, 1971
Dean R. Koontz, *Darkfall*, 1984

543
PERRY BRASS

Mirage
(Ridgefield, Connecticut: Belhue Press, 1991)

Story type: Science Fiction (Gay/Lesbian Fiction)
Major character(s): Greeland, Homosexual, Criminal; Enkidu, Homosexual, Boyfriend
Time period(s): 1990s
Locale(s): Ki, Planet—Imaginary; New York, New York

Summary: When Greeland kills and defiles Enkidu's estranged brother, a priestess informs Greeland he must forfeit his life and innocent Enkidu must forfeit his third testicle, the "Egg of the Infinite Eye," source of power and identification among Same Sex men who mate with each other rather than with women. To maintain the balance of their world, Greeland and Enkidu must use the power of their third testicles to travel to Earth in search of a man who would return to Ki to take the place of the murdered man. This is the author's first novel.

Other books you might like:
Judith Alguire, *Zeta Base*, 1991
Lauren Wright Douglas, *In the Blood*, 1989
Jack Finney, *The Body Snatchers*, 1955
  as Jack Finney
Nancy Tyler Glenn, *Clicking Stones*, 1989
Camarin Grae, *Stranded*, 1991
Lynda Lyons, *Priorities*, 1990

544
JEFF BREDENBERG

The Dream Vessel
(New York: AvoNova, 1992)

Story type: Science Fiction (Post-Nuclear Holocaust)
Major character(s): Gregory, Revolutionary, Government Official; Big Tom, Businessman (slave trader); Pec-Pec, Magician, Religious (Rastsa thief/trickster)
Time period(s): Indeterminate Future
Locale(s): Blue Ridge Mountains, North America; Thomas Island, Caribbean

Summary: Hundreds of years after a nuclear holocaust which destroyed civilization, survivors have overthrown the repressive dictator in control of the former United States. Rebel leader Rosenthal Webb sends Gregory to the Caribbean to investigate the possibility of shipmakers there constructing a huge ship to carry the message of freedom to other continents. Ignoring Webb's intent, Gregory arranges for Big Tom to begin construction of the giant ship.

Other books you might like:
Will Bradley, *Ark Liberty*, 1992
David Brin, *Earth*, 1990
Octavia E. Butler, *Dawn*, 1987

Daniel F. Galouye, *Dark Universe*, 1961
Rosemary Kirstein, *The Outskirter's Secret*, 1992
Sterling E. Lanier, *Hiero's Journey*, 1973

545

JEFF BREDENBERG

The Man in the Moon Must Die

(New York: AvoNova, 1993)

Story type: Science Fiction (Techno-Thriller; Robot Fiction)
Major character(s): Benito Funcitti, Government Official (Mayor of Fun City); Elvis, Robot, Spouse; Blanche, Artificial Intelligence
Time period(s): Indeterminate Future
Locale(s): Earth; Fun City, Moon (Earth's)

Summary: After "sending" a traveller to the Moon, a matter transmitter fails to destroy the original Benito Funcitti after creating a new Funcitti on the Moon. Now recognized as an illegal redundancy, the Earthbound Funcitti takes Elvis and flees destruction, working to change the system to allow him the right of existence.

Other books you might like:
Roger MacBride Allen, *The Modular Man*, 1992
Greg Bear, *Heads*, 1991
Algis Budrys, *Rogue Moon*, 1960
Joan Slonczewski, *Daughter of Elysium*, 1993
John Varley, *The Persistence of Vision*, 1978
Kate Wilhelm, *The Mile-Long Spaceship*, 1963

546

J.H. BRENNAN

Shiva Accused: An Adventure of the Ice Age

(New York: HarperCollins, 1991)

Story type: Fantasy (Historical; Young Adult)
Series: Shiva
Major character(s): Shiva, Prehistoric Human, Teenager; Hiram, Prehistoric Human; Crone, Shaman
Time period(s): Indeterminate Past (Ice Age)
Locale(s): Europe

Summary: In this sequel to *Shiva: An Adventure of the Ice Age*, the Barradik tribe seizes Shiva, whom they accuse of murdering the spiritual leader of their tribe. Hiram, who loves Shiva, and Crone, a powerful shaman, resolve to rescue her.

Other books you might like:
Eleanor Arnason, *The Sword Smith*, 1978
Jean M. Auel, *Clan of the Cave Bear*, 1980
Jean M. Auel, *The Mammoth Hunters*, 1985
Jean M. Auel, *The Valley of Horses*, 1982
Elizabeth Marshall Thomas, *Reindeer Moon*, 1987

547

J.H. BRENNAN

Shiva's Challenge: An Adventure of the Ice Age

(New York: HarperCollins, 1992)

Story type: Fantasy (Young Adult; Historical)
Series: Shiva
Major character(s): Shiva, Prehistoric Human (Cro-Magnon), Teenager; Hiram, Prehistoric Human (Cro-Magnon); Thag, Prehistoric Human (Neanderthal), Chieftain
Time period(s): Indeterminate Past (Ice Age)
Locale(s): Europe; Mamar's Kingdom, Mythical Place

Summary: To determine her fitness to act as shaman, Shiva must survive potentially deadly tests of poison followed by a journey through the frozen lands to the North. When Hiram returns from a successful hunt to find Shiva gone, he sets out to find her.

Other books you might like:
Jean M. Auel, *Clan of the Cave Bear*, 1980
Sue Harrison, *Mother Earth, Father Sky*, 1990
Meredith Ann Pierce, *The Woman Who Loved Reindeer*, 1989
William Sarabande, *Beyond the Sea of Ice*, 1987
Elizabeth Marshall Thomas, *Reindeer Moon*, 1987

548

J.H. BRENNAN

Shiva: An Adventure of the Ice Age

(New York: Lippincott, 1990)

Story type: Fantasy (Historical; Adventure)
Series: Shiva
Major character(s): Shiva, Prehistoric Human (Cro-Magnon), Teenager; Hiram, Prehistoric Human (Cro-Magnon); Doban, Prehistoric Human (Neanderthal), Child
Time period(s): Indeterminate
Locale(s): Europe

Summary: Shiva, an orphan teenager adopts a lost ogre child, Doban, despite the disapproval of her tribe. Assisted by Hiram, they encounter adventures and dire prophecies along the way to restoring Doban to his own ogre (Neanderthal) tribe.

Other books you might like:
Eleanor Arnason, *The Sword Smith*, 1978
Jean M. Auel, *Clan of the Cave Bear*, 1980
Jean M. Auel, *The Mammoth Hunters*, 1985
Jean M. Auel, *The Plains of Passage*, 1990
Jean M. Auel, *The Valley of Horses*, 1982

549

JOSEPH PAYNE BRENNAN

The Adventures of Lucius Leffing

(Hampton Falls, NH: Donald M. Grant, 1990)

Story type: Horror (Collection)

Series: Lucius Leffing
Major character(s): Lucius Leffing, Paranormal Investigator; Joseph Payne Brennan, Sidekick
Time period(s): 1980s
Locale(s): New Haven, Connecticut

Summary: Thirteen stories, featuring Leffing, written in the "classical detective story" formula: a problem, usually supernatural, is presented; Leffing investigates; Leffing solves the problem to the continuing amazement of his confidant, "Brennan." Clever, cozy, deliberately old fashioned tales.

Other books you might like:
Algernon Blackwood, *John Silence*, 1908
William Hope Hodgson, *Carnacki the Ghost Finder*, 1913
Seabury Quinn, *The Phantom Fighter*, 1966

550
MAYER ALAN BRENNER

Catastrophe's Spell
(New York: DAW, 1989)

Story type: Fantasy (Light Fantasy)
Series: Dance of the Gods
Major character(s): Maximillian, Sorcerer; Zalzyn Shaa, Magician
Time period(s): Indeterminate Future
Locale(s): Earth

Summary: Max tries to get a friend out of an enchanted castle. Zalzyn tries to help a young man free his father and sister from a dungeon.

Other books you might like:
Donald Aamodt, *A Name to Conjure With*, 1989
Piers Anthony, *Man From Mundania*, 1989
Piers Anthony, *A Spell for Chameleon*, 1977
Robert Asprin, *Myth-ing Persons*, 1986
    Myth Adventure Series
Craig Shaw Gardner, *An Excess of Enchantments*, 1989
Anne McCaffrey, *Alchemy and Academe*, 1970
Lawrence Watt-Evans, *With a Single Spell*,

551
MAYER ALAN BRENNER

Spell of Apocalypse
(New York: DAW, 1994)

Story type: Fantasy (Light Fantasy; Magic Conflict)
Series: Dance of the Gods
Major character(s): Maximillian, Sorcerer; The Great Karlini, Sorcerer; The Creeping Sword, Handicapped, Sorcerer
Time period(s): Indeterminate
Locale(s): Peridol, Fictional City

Summary: Forces gather in Peridol as all sides prepare for a final battle for power among the gods, humans and non-humans.

Other books you might like:
Susan Dexter, *The Wizard's Shadow*, 1993

Neil Gaiman, *Good Omens: The Nice and Accurate Prophecies of Agnes Nutter, Witch*, 1990
    Terry Pratchett, co-author
Mary Gentle, *Rats and Gargoyles*, 1991
P.C. Hodgell, *God Stalk*, 1982
Harry Turtledove, *The Case of the Toxic Spell Dump*, 1993

552
MAYER ALAN BRENNER

Spell of Fate
(New York: DAW, 1992)

Story type: Fantasy (Magic Conflict; Political)
Series: Dance of the Gods
Major character(s): Maximillian, Sorcerer; Zalzyn Shaa, Adventurer
Time period(s): Indeterminate
Locale(s): Peridol, Fictional City (imperial city)

Summary: To complete the overthrow of the rule of gods, Max and his companions must master the proper kind of magic needed. Mortals and gods assemble in Peridol to attend an imperial coronation, but busy themselves in intrigue, making and breaking alliances in their unofficial war, while the return of one long-absent will determine the eventual winner.

Other books you might like:
Donald Aamodt, *A Troubling Along the Border*, 1991
Jo Clayton, *Wild Magic*, 1991
Jo Clayton, *Wildfire*, 1992
Mary Gentle, *Rats and Gargoyles*, 1991
Laurell K. Hamilton, *Nightseer*, 1992
P.C. Hodgell, *Dark of the Moon*, 1985
P.C. Hodgell, *God Stalk*, 1982
Elizabeth Moon, *Surrender None: The Legacy of Gird*, 1990

553
ALAN BRENNERT

Her Pilgrim Soul
(New York: Tor, 1990)

Story type: Horror (Collection)

Summary: Eight tales of fantasy, science fiction and horror centered around people grappling with feelings of loneliness and emotional suffering. The best include "Jamie's Smile," about the psychological scars of the family of a child with birth defects, and "Healer," about a petty criminal's struggle to accomodate his new personality after he acquires the miraculous power to heal.

Other books you might like:
Michael Blumlein, *The Brains of Rats*, 1990
David Drake, *The Heart of Darkness*, 1983
Fritz Leiber, *The Leiber Chronicles*, 1989
Lucius Shepard, *The Jaguar Hunter*, 1987
Theodore Sturgeon, *E Pluribus Unicorn*, 1953

554

ALAN BRENNERT

Ma Qui and Other Phantoms
(Eugene, Oregon: Pulphouse, 1991)

Story type: Horror (Collection)
Series: Author's Choice Monthly

Summary: Four stories (one original to the volume) concerned with literal and metaphoric ghosts. The title story tells of a horrifying afterlife for dead MIAs left in Vietnam. ''Futures'' is a delicate tale of an aging man whose extraordinary affliction forces him to come to terms with his own mortality.

Other books you might like:
Michael Blumlein, *The Brains of Rats*, 1990
David Drake, *The Heart of Darkness*, 1983
Fritz Leiber, *The Leiber Chronicles*, 1989
Lucius Shepard, *The Jaguar Hunter*, 1987

555

ALAN BRENNERT

Time and Chance
(New York: Tor, 1990)

Story type: Fantasy (Contemporary)
Major character(s): Richard Cochrane, Actor (First reality); Rick Cochrane, Insurance Agent (Second reality; doppelganger)
Time period(s): 1990s
Locale(s): New York, New York

Summary: On a visit to his hometown, successful actor Richard Cochrane is given a chance to see what his life might have been had he married his pregnant girl friend thirteen years before. When he meets his double from a parellel world, the two decide to switch places.

Other books you might like:
Piers Anthony, *Split Infinity*, 1981
Lisa Goldstein, *The Dream Years*, 1985
Ken Grimwood, *Replay*, 1986

556

GRENDEL BRIARTON (Pseudonym of Reginald Bretnor)

The Collected Feghoot
(Eugene, Oregon: Pulphouse Publishing, 1992)

Story type: Science Fiction (Humor; Collection)
Series: Ferdinand Feghoot

Summary: Includes an introduction plus a 1989 essay by Reginald Bretnor who wrote most of the included science fiction short stories lavishly decorated with punnish wordplay. Expands earlier books reprinting stories from 1950s-1960s periodicals.

Other books you might like:
Piers Anthony, *Castle Roogna*, 1979
Piers Anthony, *Centaur Aisle*, 1981
Piers Anthony, *The Source of Magic*, 1979

Piers Anthony, *A Spell for Chameleon*, 1977
Reginald Bretnor, *The Schimmelhorn File*, 1979
Reginald Bretnor, *Schimmelhorn's Gold*, 1986
Italo Calvino, *Cosmicomics*, 1968
Italo Calvino, *T Zero*, 1969
Larry Niven, *Fallen Angels*, 1991
    Jerry Pournelle and Michael Flynn, co-authors
Spider Robinson, *Callahan's Crosstime Saloon*, 1977

557

TRACI BRIERY

The Vampire Journals
(New York: Zebra, 1993)

Story type: Horror (Vampire Story)
Major character(s): Maria Theresa Allogiamento, Vampire; Antonio da Clovina, Vampire; Gloria, Vampire
Time period(s): 18th century; 1990s (1993)
Locale(s): Sicily, Italy; Los Angeles, California

Summary: In this semi-sequel to the author's *The Vampire Memoirs* (1991), vampire Maria Theresa Allogiamento recounts how she chose vampirism in order to overcome the plight of the average woman in the 18th century, and how she has survived for 200 years to fit in with the current scene in Los Angeles and scoff at mortal poseurs fascinated with the vampire lifestyle.

Other books you might like:
C. Dean Andersson, *I Am Dracula*, 1993
Anne Rice, *The Vampire Lestat*, 1985
Michael Romkey, *I, Vampire*, 1990
Chelsea Quinn Yarbro, *The Olivia Trilogy*, 1987-1989

558

TRACI BRIERY

The Werewolf Chronicles
(New York: Zebra, 1995)

Story type: Horror (Werewolf Story)
Major character(s): Loraine ''Phyllis'' Turner, Dancer, Werewolf; Roxanne, Dancer; Tamara Taylor, Singer
Time period(s): 1990s (1995)
Locale(s): Los Angeles, California

Summary: While recuperating on her uncle's llama farm in Wisconsin from the hectic life of a Hollywood hopeful, Phyllis Turner is mauled by a wolf. Back in California, she learns to cope with her regular transformations into a werewolf, but finds she is being stalked by mysterious figures who kill her friends and leave her to take the rap for their murders.

Other books you might like:
Crosland Brown, *Tombley's Walk*, 1991
Nancy A. Collins, *Wild Blood*, 1994
Dennis Danvers, *Wilderness*, 1992
Whitley Strieber, *The Wild*, 1991
Whitley Strieber, *The Wolfen*, 1978

559

TRACI BRIERY

Wolfsong

(New York: Zebra, 1996)

Story type: Horror (Werewolf Story)
Major character(s): Loraine ''Phyllis'' Turner, Dancer, Werewolf; Peter Thomas, Police Officer; Tamara Taylor, Singer
Time period(s): 1990s (1996)
Locale(s): Los Angeles, California

Summary: In this sequel to *The Werewolf Chronicles*, shapeshifter Loraine Turner searches for the killer of her roommate, a crime of which she has been wrongly accused. At the same time, she struggles to come to terms with ''Jan,'' the werewolf persona that has awakened her and invites her to run with the pack.

Other books you might like:
Crosland Brown, *Tombley's Walk*, 1991
Nancy A. Collins, *Wild Blood*, 1994
Dennis Danvers, *Wilderness*, 1993
Pat Murphy, *Nadya: The Wolf Chronicles*, 1996
Whitley Strieber, *The Wild*, 1991

560

PATRICIA BRIGGS

Masques

(New York: Ace, 1993)

Story type: Fantasy (Magic Conflict; Political)
Major character(s): Geoffrey ae'Magi, Magician; Wolf, Magician, Warrior; Aralorn, Mythical Creature (shapechanger), Martial Arts Expert
Time period(s): Indeterminate
Locale(s): Reth, Fictional Country

Summary: The evil and beguiling magician, Geoffrey ae'Magi, will overcome Reth with hordes of undead unless stopped by the few warriors who can resist him. Captured and held at ae'Magi's castle, Aralorn faces death by torture if Wolf cannot negotiate the maze and rescue her.

Other books you might like:
Terry Brooks, *The Talismans of Shannara*, 1993
Teresa Edgerton, *The Grail and the Ring*, 1994
Laurell K. Hamilton, *Nightseer*, 1992
Tanya Huff, *Gate of Darkness, Circle of Light*, 1989
Margaret Weis, *Fire Sea*, 1991
  Tracy Hickman, co-author
Margaret Weis, *Into the Labyrinth*, 1991
  Tracy Hickman, co-author

561

PATRICIA BRIGGS

Steal the Dragon

(New York: Ace, 1995)

Story type: Fantasy (Political; Adventure)

Major character(s): Rialla, Horse Trainer, Spy; Tris, Healer, Traitor
Time period(s): Indeterminate
Locale(s): Darran, Fictional Country

Summary: Aware that detection as a spy in Darran would mean her return to slavery, Rialla travels there hoping to foil an assassination plot aimed at killing a leader who wishes to eliminate slavery. In Darran, Tris aids the cause, despite personal danger.

Other books you might like:
Robin Hobb, *Assassin's Apprentice*, 1995
P.C. Hodgell, *God Stalk*, 1982
Mercedes Lackey, *The Eagle and the Nightingales*, 1995
L.E. Modesitt Jr., *Of Tangible Ghosts*, 1994
Patricia C. Wrede, *The Raven Ring*, 1994

562

DAVID BRIN

Brightness Reef

(New York: Bantam Spectra, 1995)

Story type: Science Fiction (Political; First Contact)
Series: Uplift
Major character(s): Hph-wayuo ''Alvin'', Alien (hoon), Student; Sara, Scientist; Sax/Ewasx, Alien (traeki/Jophur)
Time period(s): Indeterminate Future
Locale(s): Jijo, Planet—Imaginary

Summary: Abandoned on the fallow planet Jijo, the six intelligent species illegally resident on the Slope hope to follow to innocence the path of the once intelligent glavers. Meanwhile, the last species to arrive, humans, bring many acceptable innovations, including paper and books, completely disposable without difficulty. While prepared for the eventual appearance of the galactics, an unexpected visit by criminals intent on stealing from Jijo may shatter the accord of the Six's Common.

Other books you might like:
Eleanor Arnason, *Ring of Swords*, 1993
Gregory Benford, *Furious Gulf*, 1994
C.J. Cherryh, *Foreigner*, 1994
L. Warren Douglas, *Cannon's Orb*, 1994
Jack McDevitt, *The Engines of God*, 1994
Alis A. Rasmussen, *Revolution's Shore*, 1990
Vernor Vinge, *A Fire upon the Deep*, 1992

563

DAVID BRIN

Earth

(New York: Bantam Spectra, 1990)

Story type: Science Fiction (Hard Science Fiction; Contemporary Realism)
Major character(s): Alex Lustig, Scientist (physicist); George Hutton, Engineer, Industrialist; Jen Wolling, Scientist (behavioral/biological), Scholar (founder of Modern Gaianism)
Time period(s): 2030s (2039)

Locale(s): Earth (from crust to core); North Island, New Zealand; Kuwenezi Canton Kuwenezi, South Africa

Summary: A mob has released a black hole built by Alex Lustig and it drops into the Earth. Investigating whether it will dissipate or grow, destroying the planet from the inside out as it develops, Alex enlists the financial and scientific aid of multi-billionaire George Hutton and others, including his grandmother, Nobel Prize winner Jen Wolling. The project takes on global proportions to the background of life on a 21st century Earth in which the growth of industry, technology and population is matched by a growth of conscience toward the environment's future.

Other books you might like:
Roger MacBride Allen, *The Ring of Charon*, 1990
Greg Bear, *The Forge of God*, 1987
Octavia E. Butler, *Adulthood Rites*, 1988
Octavia E. Butler, *Dawn*, 1987
Octavia E. Butler, *Imago*, 1989
John Varley, *Titan*, 1979

564

DAVID BRIN

Glory Season
(New York: Bantam Spectra, 1993)

Story type: Science Fiction (Genetic Manipulation; Lost Colony)
Major character(s): Maia Lamai, Teenager, Traveller; Leie Lamai, Teenager, Twin; Renna, Spaceman, Diplomat (ambassador)
Time period(s): Indeterminate Future
Locale(s): Stratos, Planet—Imaginary

Summary: Stratos' colonists left the human interstellar federation, the Phylum, to develop an ideal society in which most conceptions, sparked by men, result in genetic clones of the mothers, while children conceived in Summer, the vars, receive genetic material from both parents. An alien human frontman from the Phylum arrives to let Stratos know that waves of colonists will move through the sector, turning Stratos society into turmoil. Forced out of Lamai at 15, as usual for vars, Maia travels around Stratos trying to find a place for herself. She realizes the inadequacy of her education while learning about men through the alien she befriends before discovering his gender.

Other books you might like:
Eleanor Arnason, *Ring of Swords*, 1993
Eleanor Arnason, *A Woman of the Iron People*, 1991
Octavia E. Butler, *Dawn*, 1987
M.J. Engh, *Rainbow Man*, 1993
Ursula K. Le Guin, *Always Coming Home*, 1987
Joan Slonczewski, *Daughter of Elysium*, 1993
Joan Slonczewski, *A Door into Ocean*, 1986
Sheri S. Tepper, *Grass*, 1989
Sheri S. Tepper, *Raising the Stones*, 1990
Sheri S. Tepper, *Sideshow*, 1992

565

DAVID BRIN

Infinity's Shore
(New York: Bantram Spectra, 1996)

Story type: Science Fiction (First Contact; Political)
Series: Uplift
Major character(s): Kaa, Genetically Altered Being (dolphin), Pilot (spaceship); Hph-wayuo "Alvin", Alien (hoon), Teenager; Asx/Ewasx, Alien (traeki/Jophur)
Time period(s): Indeterminate Future
Locale(s): Jijo, Planet—Imaginary; *Streaker*, Spaceship; *Polkjhy*, Spaceship (Jophur)

Summary: Vanquishing the Rothen gene thieves, the Six Races face a truly giant spaceship, as the Jophur had followed the Rothens to Jijo looking for the *Streaker*. Forced to flee the Old Ones after trying to turn over to them the dead alien, "Herbie," and the location of the derelict fleet, *Streaker* plunges deep into Jijo's ocean just in time to rescue Alvin and his friends from their demolished submarine. Meanwhile, the Jophur attempt to annihilate the g'Keks, perhaps the last of their ancient enemies still living.

Other books you might like:
C.J. Cherryh, *Foreigner*, 1994
L. Warren Douglas, *Cannon's Orb*, 1994
Larry Niven, *Protector*, 1973
Frederik Pohl, *The Other End of Time*, 1996
Alis A. Rasmussen, *A Passage of Stars*, 1990
Vernor Vinge, *A Fire upon the Deep*, 1992

566

DAVID BRIN

Otherness
(New York: Bantam Spectra, 1994)

Story type: Science Fiction (Collection)

Summary: Contains 13 stories and exerpts from novels plus eight essays, some with notes about the fiction, divided into "Transitions," "Contact," "Continuity," "Cosmos" and "Otherness." Themes include biology, medicine, societal ideology and first contact. One story, "Bonding to the Genji," set the scene for the shared-universe volume, *Murasaki*.

Other books you might like:
Robert Silverberg, *Murasaki*, 1992
    Martin H. Greenberg, co-editor
Cordwainer Smith, *The Rediscovery of Man*, 1993
Marc Stiegler, *The Gentle Seduction*, 1990
John Varley, *Blue Champagne*, 1986
Connie Willis, *Impossible Things*, 1994

567

JANE BRINDLE

The Tallow Image
(London: Orion, 1995)

Story type: Horror (Witchcraft)
Major character(s): Matthew Slater, Horse Trainer (breeder); Cathy Barrington, Young Woman (Matt's wife); Rebecca Norman, Witch
Time period(s): 1880s (1880); 1980s (1988)
Locale(s): Fremantle, Australia; Bedford, England

Summary: The night before her execution, witch Rebecca Norman presents jailer Ralph Ryan with one of two dolls she has fashioned from candlewax. More than a century later, Ryan's lineal descendant, Ralph Slater, finds his life a shambles after his bride, Cathy, comes into possession of the second doll while the couple is honeymooning in Australia, and begins acting as though possessed of a wonton woman's spirit. The pseudonymous author first published this novel in 1994. Distributed by Trafalgar Square, Pomfort, Vermont.

Other books you might like:
Leigh Clark, *Evil Reincarnate*, 1994
Basil Copper, *The Black Death*, 1993
Kathryn Meyer Griffith, *Witches*, 1994
Ruby Jean Jensen, *Baby Doll*, 1991
Anne Rice, *The Witching Hour*, 1990
Guy N. Smith, *Witch Spell*, 1994

568

POPPY Z. BRITE

Drawing Blood
(New York: Delacorte, 1993)

Story type: Horror (Haunted House)
Major character(s): Trevor McGee, Artist (a.k.a. Trevor Black); Zachary Busch, Computer Expert; Kinsey Hummingbird, Mechanic
Time period(s): 1970s (1972); 1990s (1992)
Locale(s): Missing Mile, North Carolina

Summary: Under the alias Trevor Black, Trevor McGee returns to the small North Carolina town where his artist father murdered Trevor's mother and brother before killing himself 20 years before. Fortified by the love of his soulmate Zachary Busch, Trevor seeks to understand his father's actions and, in so doing, breaks through to Birdland, a spirit realm that fuels his artistic skills but also exposes him to the same madness that destroyed his father.

Other books you might like:
Giles Blunt, *Cold Eye*, 1988
Jessica Amanda Salmonson, *Anthony Shriek*, 1992

569

POPPY Z. BRITE

Exquisite Corpse
(New York: Simon & Schuster, 1996)

Story type: Horror (Serial Killer)
Major character(s): Lysander "Jay" Byrne, Serial Killer; Andrew Compton, Serial Killer, Homosexual; Lucas Ransom, Writer (a.k.a. Lush Rimbaud)
Time period(s): 1990s (1996)
Locale(s): New Orleans, Louisiana

Summary: Andrew Compton, a gay serial killer modeled on real-life sociopath Jeffrey Dahmer, escapes from prison in London and flees to New Orleans. There, he meets and befriends Jay Byrne, a serial killer who has preyed for years on young men in the French Quarter, and the two express their emotions toward each other through an act of ritual murder and cannibalism.

Other books you might like:
Dennis Cooper, *Frisk*, 1991
Brett Easton Ellis, *American Psycho*, 1991
Thomas Harris, *The Silence of the Lambs*, 1988
Rick R. Reed, *Obsessed*, 1991

570

POPPY Z. BRITE

Lost Souls
(New York: Delacorte, 1992)

Story type: Horror (Vampire Story)
Major character(s): Nothing, Teenager; Ghost, Musician (lead singer of Lost Souls); Zillah, Vampire
Time period(s): 1990s
Locale(s): New Orleans, Louisiana; Missing Mile, North Carolina

Summary: The author's first novel is a prose poem on adolescent angst, embodied in the character of Nothing, a child of mortal and vampire parents. Nothing runs away from his home in Maryland to missing Mile, North Carolina, home of the band Lost Souls? whose music speaks profoundly to him, but along the way encounters a van full of punk vampires and spends the rest of the story torn between their world of hedonistic excess and the world of misunderstood mortal teenagers.

Other books you might like:
Nancy A. Collins, *Sunglasses After Dark*, 1989
Nancy A. Collins, *Tempter*, 1990
Ray Garton, *Crucifax*, 1988
Anne Rice, *The Vampire Lestat*, 1985
John Skipp, *The Light at the End*, 1986
   Craig Spector, co-author
S.P. Somtow, *Vampire Junction*, 1983

571

POPPY Z. BRITE, Editor

Love in Vein

(New York: HarperCollins, 1994)

Story type: Horror (Anthology; Vampire Story)

Summary: The 20 stories written originally for this volume all fall within the subgenre of erotic vampire fiction. Included are Norman Partridge's "Do Not Hasten to Bid Me Adieu," a variation on the Dracula legend as seen through the eyes of an American character from Bram Stoker's novel; Douglas Clegg's "White Chapel," about a being who feeds on human pain and suffering; Brian Hodge's "The Alchemy of the Throat," concerning a castrato who falls in with vampire society; Mike Baker's "Love Me Forever," featuring a shapeshifting vampire; A.R. Morlan's ".'.And the Horses Rise at Midnight," about a tattooed vampire in a carnival side-show; Elizabeth Engstrom's "Elixir," about a color-blind man who draws his capacity to see normally from an unusually endowed hooker; and Robert Devereaux's "A Slow Red Whisper of Sand," which mixes vampires into a tableau of love and death in California.

Other books you might like:

Ellen Datlow, *Blood Is Not Enough*, 1989
   editor
Ellen Datlow, *A Whisper of Blood*, 1991
   editor
Amarantha Knight, *Love Bites*, 1995
   editor
Cecilia Tan, *Blood Kiss: Vampire Erotica*, 1994
   editor

572

POPPY Z. BRITE

Swamp Foetus

(Baltimore, Maryland: Borderlands Press, 1993)

Story type: Horror (Collection)

Summary: Twelve stories of provocative horror fiction, often with strong sexual content. Several draw strongly on the southern Gothic tradition, among them "His Mouth Shall Taste of Wormwood," an updating of H.P. Lovecraft's potboiler, "The Hound," and the coming of age tale, "A Georgia Story." "Angels" and "How to Get Ahead in New York" involve characters from the eponymous rock band of the author's first novel, *Lost Souls*. The best offerings are the World Fantasy Award nominated tales "The Ash of Memory, the Dust of Desire," and a harrowing tale of zombies in India, "Calcutta, Lord of Nerves." This book was released only in a signed limited edition.

Other books you might like:

Ramsey Campbell, *Scared Stiff*, 1987
Scott Edelman, *Suicide Art*, 1992
Ray Garton, *Methods of Madness*, 1990
Robert R. McCammon, *Blue World*, 1990
David J. Schow, *Seeing Red*, 1990

573

C. DALE BRITTAIN

A Bad Spell in Yurt

(New York: Baen, 1991)

Story type: Fantasy (Light Fantasy)
Series: Daimbert
Major character(s): Daimbert, Wizard (Royal)
Time period(s): Indeterminate
Locale(s): Yurt, Fictional Country; Alternate Earth

Summary: A mediocre wizard's school student, Daimbert finds he has much left to learn when he becomes Royal Wizard. With the king in danger, Daimbert searches for the person using black magic. When a dragon shows up and terrorizes people at the royal castle, Daimbert requires help from the retired Royal Wizard to defeat it.

Other books you might like:

Robert Don Hughes, *Prophet of Lamath*, 1979
Tanith Lee, *Black Unicorn*, 1991
Christopher Stasheff, *The Warlock Unlocked*, 1982
Michael C. Staudinger, *The Falcon Rises*, 1991
Jane Yolen, *Wizard's Hall*, 1990
Mary Frances Zambreno, *A Plague of Sorcerers*, 1991

574

C. DALE BRITTAIN

Daughter of Magic

(New York: Baen, 1996)

Story type: Fantasy (Light Fantasy; Adventure)
Series: Daimbert
Major character(s): Daimbert, Wizard (royal); Theodora, Witch; Antonia, Witch, Child
Time period(s): Indeterminate
Locale(s): Yurt, Fictional Country; Caelrhon, Fictional Country

Summary: After Daimbert takes charge of his daughter, Antonia, she begins to exhibit distressing independence and use of magic, while Daimbert's undead enemy, Vlad, again attacks.

Other books you might like:

Carolyn Cushman, *Witch and Wombat*, 1994
Rose Estes, *Troll-Taken*, 1993
Holly Lisle, *Minerva Wakes*, 1994
James H. Schmitz, *The Witches of Karres*, 1966
Christopher Stasheff, *King Kobold*, 1971
Patricia C. Wrede, *Talking to Dragons*, 1993
   revised edition

575

C. DALE BRITTAIN

Voima

(New York: Baen, 1995)

Story type: Fantasy (Magic Conflict)

Major character(s): Roric No-man's Son, Warrior, Adventurer; Karin, Royalty, Adventurer; Valmar, Royalty, Adventurer
Time period(s): Indeterminate
Locale(s): Fictional Country

Summary: When the time of changes grows near, the immortal Wanderers find humans to help repair the damage caused by misuse of voima, the magic force of life and renewal. Meanwhile, many work against the Wanderers' influences as strife threatens the human kingdoms.

Other books you might like:
David Eddings, *Pawn of Prophecy*, 1982
Terry Goodkind, *Wizard's First Rule*, 1994
Barbara Hambly, *The Rainbow Abyss*, 1991
Katharine Kerr, *Daggerspell*, 1986
Mark C. Perry, *Morigu: The Dead*, 1990

576

C. DALE BRITTAIN

The Witch and the Cathedral
(New York: Baen, 1995)

Story type: Fantasy (Religious; Magic Conflict)
Series: Daimbert
Major character(s): Daimbert, Wizard (royal); Theodora, Witch
Time period(s): Indeterminate
Locale(s): Caelrhon, Fictional Country

Summary: Unhappy at his lot in love and events in Yurt, Daimbert travels to Caelrhon where he meets Theodora and finds himself instantly attracted to her. However, despite threats to the kingdom's cathedral by magical creatures, Daimbert's help seems unwanted by any of Caelrhon's powerful groups, leading Daimbert to suspect a plot against wizardry as an institution.

Other books you might like:
Mercedes Lackey, *The Eagle and the Nightingales*, 1995
Mercedes Lackey, *The Robin and the Kestrel*, 1993
Christopher Stasheff, *The Warlock in Spite of Himself*, 1969
Paula Volsky, *Illusion*, 1992

577

C. DALE BRITTAIN

The Wood Nymph and the Cranky Saint
(New York: Baen, 1993)

Story type: Fantasy (Quest; Light Fantasy)
Series: Daimbert
Major character(s): Daimbert, Wizard (royal); Joachim, Religious (royal chaplain), Adventurer
Time period(s): Indeterminate
Locale(s): Yurt, Fictional Country; Alternate Earth

Summary: Left in charge during the King of Yurt's vacation, Daimbert travels with Joachim to investigate the sighting of a wood nymph and complaints surrounding a saint's shrine. Daimbert unexpectedly finds himself called upon to act as judge in a question of royal honor.

Other books you might like:
Douglas W. Clark, *Whirlwind Alchemy*, 1993
Alexis A. Gilliland, *Lord of the Troll-Bats*, 1992
Nick Pollotta, *Bureau 13*, 1991
Christopher Stasheff, *The Warlock Heretical*, 1987
Christopher Stasheff, *The Warlock Rock*, 1990

578

JOHN BRIZZOLARA

Empire's Horizon
(New York: DAW, 1989)

Story type: Science Fiction (Theological)
Major character(s): Martin Cain, Journalist
Time period(s): Indeterminate Future
Locale(s): Darkath, Planet—Imaginary

Summary: Famous journalist Martin Cain has travelled from planet to planet reporting the news, but always hoping to find God. Arriving on Darkath, a remote outpost of the failing Terran Empire, he becomes embroiled in the religious controversies of the world's two native races and discovers a strange sort of redemption.

Other books you might like:
James Blish, *A Case of Conscience*, 1958
Mary Gentle, *Ancient Light*, 1987
Mary Gentle, *Golden Witchbreed*, 1985
Frank Herbert, *Children of Dune*, 1976
Frank Herbert, *Dune*, 1965
Frank Herbert, *Dune Messiah*, 1965
Robert Silverberg, *Downward to the Earth*, 1970

579

BRUCE BROOKS

No Kidding
(New York: Harper & Row, 1989)

Story type: Science Fiction (Young Adult)
Major character(s): Sam, Teenager; Ollie, Child (Sam's younger brother)
Time period(s): 21st century
Locale(s): Washington, District of Columbia

Summary: More than half the adult population of the United States is addicted to alcohol and children as young as twelve now have the legal right to have their alcoholic parents committed. Sam, a teenage boy with a compulsion to control others, has his mother committed and then, upon her release, has himself named her guardian.

Other books you might like:
Gary L. Blackwood, *The Dying Sun*, 1989
Robert Cormier, *Fade*, 1988
Leigh Kennedy, *The Journal of Nicholas the American*, 1986

580
TERRY BROOKS

The Druid of Shannara
(New York: Del Rey, 1991)

Story type: Fantasy (Quest)
Series: Heritage of Shannara
Major character(s): Walker Boh, Adventurer; Morgan Leah, Adventurer; Pe Ell, Murderer
Time period(s): Indeterminate
Locale(s): The Four Lands, Mythical Place

Summary: Walker Boh, Morgan Leah and Pe Ell journey with Quickening, a creature created by the King of the Silver River, a being as old as mankind. They seek the Black Elfstone, which Walker needs to discharge his duty to restore Paranor, the lost Druid's Keep.

Other books you might like:
Dennis L. McKiernan, *The Dark Tide*, 1984
Dennis L. McKiernan, *Shadows of Doom*, 1984
J.R.R. Tolkien, *The Return of the King*, 1956
J.R.R. Tolkien, *The Two Towers*, 1955
J.R.R. Tolkien, *The Fellowship of the Ring*, 1954

581
TERRY BROOKS

The Elf Queen of Shannara
(New York: Ballantine/Del Rey, 1992)

Story type: Fantasy (Quest)
Series: Heritage of Shannara
Major character(s): Wren Ohmsford, Mythical Creature (elf), Adventurer
Time period(s): Indeterminate
Locale(s): The Four Lands, Fictional Country; Morrowindl Island, Fictional Country

Summary: Carrying out the Druid, Allanon's, charge to Wren, that of finding and returning elves to the world of men, Wren and Garth travel westward. When Wren consults a Seer, the Addershag, she directs Wren to an island, Morrowindl, to which all Land Elves emigrated. Continuing their journey, they meet and receive assistance from mythical and fantastic creatures as Wren grows aware of her elvish nature and her ability to wield magical forces.

Other books you might like:
Dennis L. McKiernan, *The Dark Tide*, 1984
Andre Norton, *The Elvenbane*, 1991
   Mercedes Lackey, co-author
J.R.R. Tolkien, *The Fellowship of the Ring*, 1954
J.R.R. Tolkien, *The Hobbit*, 1938
J.R.R. Tolkien, *The Return of the King*, 1956
J.R.R. Tolkien, *The Two Towers*, 1955
Terri Windling, *Life on the Border*, 1991
   editor

582
TERRY BROOKS

First King of Shannara
(New York: Ballantine Del Rey, 1996)

Story type: Fantasy (Magic Conflict; Adventure)
Series: Shannara
Major character(s): Bremen, Wizard, Adventurer; Kinson Ravenloft, Scout, Adventurer
Time period(s): Indeterminate
Locale(s): The Four Lands, Fictional Country

Summary: When hoards of Trolls invade the Four Lands, Bremen, Kinson Ravenloft and their small company must find a means of defeating their evil leader, the corrupted Druid, Brona. Set after events in *The Talismans of Shannara* and prior to *The Sword of Shannara*.

Other books you might like:
Dave Duncan, *The Cutting Edge*, 1992
David Eddings, *Belgarath the Sorcerer*, 1995
   Leigh Eddings, co-author
Terry Goodkind, *Wizard's First Rule*, 1994
Robert Jordan, *The Eye of the World*, 1990
L.E. Modesitt Jr., *The Magic of Recluce*, 1991

583
TERRY BROOKS

Hook
(New York: Fawcett Columbine, 1992)

Story type: Fantasy (Adventure; Quest)
Major character(s): James Hook, Pirate, Sea Captain; Peter ''Peter Pan'' Banning, Lawyer, Adventurer; Tinkerbell, Mythical Creature (fairy)
Time period(s): 1990s
Locale(s): Neverland, Mythical Place

Summary: To lure Peter Pan into a final battle, Captain Hook kidnaps Peter's children from Wendy's London home. Tinkerbell then returns Peter to Neverland, working to restore Peter's suppressed memories and credibility among the Lost Boys, Peter's former followers. Novelizes the film.

Other books you might like:
J.M. Barrie, *Peter Pan*, 1904
Stephen R. Donaldson, *Lord Foul's Bane*, 1977
Michael Ende, *The Neverending Story*, 1983
William Goldman, *The Princess Bride*, 1973
James Kahn, *Indiana Jones and the Temple of Doom*, 1984
J.R.R. Tolkien, *The Hobbit*, 1938

584
TERRY BROOKS

The Scions of Shannara
(New York: Del Rey, 1990)

Story type: Fantasy (Quest)
Series: Heritage of Shannara

Major character(s): Par Ohmsford, Heir—Lost, Magician; Coll Ohmsford, Adventurer
Time period(s): Indeterminate
Locale(s): The Four Lands, Mythical Place

Summary: Three hundred years after events in the Sword of Shannara Series, Par Ohmsford and his brother Coll search to find Par's lost legacy, the fabled sword of Shannara.

Other books you might like:
Dennis L. McKiernan, *The Dark Tide*, 1984
Dennis L. McKiernan, *Shadows of Doom*, 1984
J.R.R. Tolkien, *The Return of the King*, 1956
J.R.R. Tolkien, *The Two Towers*, 1955
J.R.R. Tolkien, *The Fellowship of the Ring*, 1954

585

TERRY BROOKS

The Talismans of Shannara

(New York: Ballantine Del Rey, 1993)

Story type: Fantasy (Quest; Magic Conflict)
Series: Heritage of Shannara
Major character(s): Par Ohmsford, Mythical Creature (elf), Adventurer; Walker Boh, Magician (Druidic), Warrior; Wren Elessedil, Mythical Creature (elf), Ruler (Queen)
Time period(s): Indeterminate
Locale(s): The Four Lands, Fictional Country

Summary: Despite completing their quests, the descendants of the House of Shannara remain plagued by Shadowen dark magic and Rimmer Dall's determination to separate the family. Par can alleviate the problems, but only if he can master the legendary Sword of Shannara. Concludes the series.

Other books you might like:
Patricia Briggs, *Masques*, 1993
Dave Duncan, *The Cutting Edge*, 1992
David Eddings, *Pawn of Prophecy*, 1982
Robert Jordan, *The Eye of the World*, 1989
J.R.R. Tolkien, *The Fellowship of the Ring*, 1954
Margaret Weis, *Fire Sea*, 1991
    Tracy Hickman, co-author
Margaret Weis, *Into the Labyrinth*, 1993
    Tracy Hickman, co-author

586

TERRY BROOKS

The Tangle Box

(New York: Ballantine Del Rey, 1994)

Story type: Fantasy (Magic Conflict)
Series: Magic Kingdom of Landover
Major character(s): Ben Holiday, Ruler (King of Landover), Parent; Willow, Royalty (Queen of Landover); Horris Kew, Magician, Criminal
Time period(s): Indeterminate
Locale(s): Landover, Fictional Country

Summary: When Ben Holiday initiates the repatriation to Landover of the outcasts Horris and Biggar, Ben falls victim to the plot of an evil sorcerer, Gorse, who plans revenge and

conquest in Landover. Imprisoned with comrades in the labyrinthine Tangle Box, Ben must rely on rescue from the Lady Willow whose mysterious mission yields hints of Ben's plight.

Other books you might like:
Patricia Briggs, *Masques*, 1993
Susan Dexter, *The Wizard's Shadow*, 1993
Barbara Hambly, *The Silent Tower*, 1986
Barbara Hambly, *The Time of the Dark*, 1982
A.C.H. Smith, *Labyrinth*, 1986
Martha Wells, *The Element of Fire*, 1993
Elizabeth Willey, *The Well-Favored Man: The Tale of the Sorcerer's Nephew*, 1993

587

TERRY BROOKS

Witches' Brew

(New York: Ballantine Del Rey, 1995)

Story type: Fantasy (Magic Conflict; Adventure)
Series: Magic Kingdom of Landover
Major character(s): Ben Holiday, Ruler, Parent; Questor Thews, Wizard, Adventurer; Abernathy, Animal (dog), Adventurer
Time period(s): Indeterminate
Locale(s): Landover, Fictional Country

Summary: Ben Holiday wishes for continuing peaceful times in Landover so he can enjoy his magical daughter's childhood. However, King Rydall desires control of Landover and sends seven champions, each of a different form, which Ben must defeat before Rydall will abandon his claims to Landover.

Other books you might like:
Dave Duncan, *The Cutting Edge*, 1993
Holly Lisle, *Mind of the Magic*, 1995
Margaret Weis, *Dragon Wing*, 1990
    Tracy Hickman, co-author
Martha Wells, *The Element of Fire*, 1993
Elizabeth Willey, *The Well-Favored Man: The Tale of the Sorcerer's Nephew*, 1993

588

JOHN BROSNAN

The Sky Lords

(New York: St. Martins Press, 1991)

Story type: Science Fiction (Genetic Manipulation; Post-Holocaust)
Major character(s): Jan Dorvin, Fugitive; Milo, Genetically Altered Being, Immortal
Time period(s): Indeterminate Future
Locale(s): Minerva, Fictional Country (feminist); Sky Lord Pangloth, Alternate Earth (giant dirigible)

Summary: In the 800 years since the Genetic Wars, the Sky Lords, giant dirigibles, have come to control the ground over which they fly, and the people who still survive there. The aftermath of the Genetic Wars, the Blight, is gradually destroying what viable surface remains, and the science which could have solved the Earth's problems has been forgotten. Jan Darvin, the last woman from Minerva, joins forces with Milo, a strange genetically altered man, who promises Jan revenge on the Sky Lord Pangloth which destroyed Minerva.

Other books you might like:
Steven Barnes, *Gorgon Child*, 1989
Charles Ingrid, *The Marked Man*, 1989
Donald E. McQuinn, *Warrior*, 1990
Joan Slonczewski, *The Wall Around Eden*, 1989
Sheri S. Tepper, *The Gate to Women's Country*, 1988
Michael D. Weaver, *My Father Immortal*, 1989
Paul O. Williams, *The Breaking of Northwall*, 1980

`589`
JOHN BROSNAN

The War of the Sky Lords
(New York: St. Martin's Press, 1992)

Story type: Science Fiction (Post-Holocaust; Adventure)
Series: Sky Lords
Major character(s): Jan Dorvin, Administrator (Minervan); Ryn ''Robin'', Runaway; Andrea Du Lucent, Royalty (princess)
Time period(s): Indeterminate Future
Locale(s): Minerva, Fictional Country; *Sky Angel*, At Sea (giant dirigible); Shangri La, Undersea Environment/Habitat

Summary: In a habitat deep under Antarctica the Eloi protect Ryn from the diseases and Sky Lords of the outer world. When the renegade fleet of Sky Lords searching for the habitat arrives in the Antarctic, Ryn escapes to the Lord Mordred, trading his support of the Duke Du Lucent for sex with the Princess Andrea. Meanwhile in the north, Jan Dorvin works at eliminating the blight and developing a new, healthy society.

Other books you might like:
John Crowley, *Beasts*, 1976
Marjorie Bradley Kellogg, *Harmony*, 1991
Donald E. McQuinn, *Warrior*, 1990
Pat Murphy, *The City, Not Long After*, 1989
Sheri S. Tepper, *The Gate to Women's Country*, 1988
Joan D. Vinge, *The Summer Queen*, 1991
Paul O. Williams, *The Breaking of Northwall*, 1980

`590`
CROSLAND BROWN

Tombley's Walk
(New York: Avon, 1991)

Story type: Horror (Werewolf Story)
Major character(s): Bud Turner, Fugitive (alias James Ernest Rigler); Melody Parker, Lawyer; Justin Barker, Banker
Time period(s): 1980s (1986)
Locale(s): Tombley's Walk, Texas

Summary: At the height of a rabies epidemic in rural Texas, a series of strange maulings occurs. Some leave the victims

dead, but others leave the victims alive and ravenous in their appetites for food, sex, and mayhem. This is the author's first novel.

Other books you might like:
Ron Dee, *Dusk*, 1991
Chelsea Quinn Yarbro, *Beastnights*, 1989
Gary Brandner, *The Howling*, 1983

`591`
JERRY EARL BROWN

Earthfall
(New York: Ace Books, 1990)

Story type: Science Fiction (Post-Nuclear Holocaust)
Major character(s): Chia Swann, Spaceship Captain; O'Rourke, Wanderer
Time period(s): 22nd century
Locale(s): Outer Space (In Earth orbit)

Summary: More than one hundred years after a nuclear war nearly ended all life on Earth, primitive humanity still clings to survival on the desolate, mutant-infested planet. Meanwhile, a high-tech human civilization flourishes in Earth-orbit and beyond. Travel to the Earth's surface is prohibited, the interdiction strictly enforced by deadly EarthWatch sentinels. One woman, Chia Swann, determines to brave both the dangers on Earth and those in Earth-orbit to save the human beings who still survive on the planet's surface.

Other books you might like:
Walter M. Miller Jr., *A Canticle for Leibowitz*, 1960
Robert Silverberg, *At Winter's End*, 1988
Robert Silverberg, *The New Springtime*, 1989
Michael D. Weaver, *My Father Immortal*, 1989

`592`
JERRY EARL BROWN

Snowmen
(New York: Pocket, 1991)

Story type: Science Fiction (Genetic Manipulation; Adventure)
Major character(s): Neil Freese, Guide; Dennis Gall, Guide
Time period(s): 1990s
Locale(s): Nepal

Summary: As Gall and Freese rush to save a climber from death, they uncover the remains of Operation Snowman, a biological experiment using criminals that has gone horribly wrong.

Other books you might like:
Philip Jose Farmer, *Escape From Loki*, 1991
Marc Laidlaw, *Neon Lotus*, 1988
Kim Stanley Robinson, *Escape From Kathmandu*, 1989
Elizabeth Ann Scarborough, *Nothing Sacred*, 1991
Ryder Syvertson, *Fortress of Forbidden Destiny*, 1991

593

MARY BROWN

Master of Many Treasures

(New York: Baen, 1995)

Story type: Fantasy (Quest)
Series: Unlikely Ones
Major character(s): Summer, Telepath, Traveller; Growch, Animal (dog), Companion; Jason, Mythical Creature (dragon), Human
Time period(s): Indeterminate
Locale(s): Venice, Italy; Middle East; Blue Mountain, Mythical Place

Summary: With a magic ring to protect her and foster communication through telepathy with animals, Summer realizes she must follow her one true love, now a dragon most of the time, and achieve her destiny. Sequel to *Pigs Don't Fly*.

Other books you might like:
Lois McMaster Bujold, *The Spirit Ring*, 1992
Don Callander, *Dragon Companion*, 1994
Robert N. Charrette, *Never Deal with a Dragon*, 1990
Thorarinn Gunnarsson, *Dragon's Domain*, 1993
Angus Wells, *Lords of the Sky*, 1994

594

MARY BROWN

Pigs Don't Fly

(New York: Baen, 1994)

Story type: Fantasy (Light Fantasy; Quest)
Major character(s): Summer, Orphan, Guide; Gilman, Knight, Handicapped; The Wimperling, Animal
Time period(s): Indeterminate Past (medieval)
Locale(s): Fictional City; Evreux, Fictional City; Fictional Country (on the road)

Summary: When Summer's mother dies, she finds herself alone in a hostile village. She flees with only her dowry and a magic ring that permits her to understand the speech of animals. Out of love and pity, she seeks to guide a chance-met knight, recently blinded and suffering from amnesia, to his home with the aid of a dog, a horse, a pigeon and a pig.

Other books you might like:
Peter S. Beagle, *The Folk of the Air*, 1986
Lois McMaster Bujold, *The Spirit Ring*, 1992
Barbara Hambly, *Dragonsbane*, 1986
Patricia A. McKillip, *The Forgotten Beasts of Eld*, 1976
Patricia C. Wrede, *Sorcery and Cecelia*, 1988
    Caroline Stevermer, co-author

595

JESSE BROWNER

Conglomeros

(New York: Random House, 1992)

Story type: Fantasy (Satire; Contemporary)

Major character(s): Aaron X, Heir, Smuggler; Conglomeros, Monster; Victor Brauner, Artist (deceased)
Time period(s): 1990s
Locale(s): New York, New York; Piatra Neamt, Romania

Summary: While at an exhibition of Victor Brauner's life works, Aaron encounters a statue of the Conglomeros. That night he dreams of the statue and, upon awakening, recognizes it from a description in his grandfather's diary. Convinced that the Conglomeros exists in an innocent state, Aaron decides after much research to find it and protect it from harm. Unfortunately, despite their best efforts, humans frequently destroy what they love. Author's first novel.

Other books you might like:
Orson Scott Card, *Songmaster*, 1980
Jeff Collignon, *Her Monster*, 1992
Samuel R. Delany, *Tales of Neveryon*, 1979
Mark Jacobson, *Gojiro*, 1991
Whitley Strieber, *The Wild*, 1991
Donald E. Westlake, *Humans*, 1991

596

VICTORIA BROWNWORTH, Editor

Night Bites: Vampire Stories by Women

(Seattle: Seal Press, 1996)

Story type: Horror (Anthology; Vampire Story)

Summary: This volume contains 16 original and frequently erotic stories by female authors featuring vampires. Victoria Brownworth's ''Twelfth Night'' is concerned with a vampire journalist who uses the world beat she covers to conceal her feeding habits. Judith M. Redding's ''Unexpurgated Notes from a Homicide'' tells of vampires who seek an antidote for the AIDS-infected blood they have consumed. Nikki Baker's ''Backlash'' concerns a female detective in pursuit of a vampiric killer, and Judith Katz's ''Anita, Polish Vampire, Holds Forth at the Jewish Cafe of the Dead,'' a vampire koffee-klatsch. In Lisa D. Williamson's ''Best of Friends,'' a teenager mistakes her burgeoning vampirism for an unwanted pregnancy, and in Mabel Maney's ''Almost the Color of the Summer Sky,'' a young girl fascinated by a vampire movie is oblivious to the existence of a vampire in her immediate family.

Other books you might like:
Martin H. Greenberg, *Vamps*, 1987
    Charles G. Waugh, co-editor
Barbara Hambly, *Sisters of the Night*, 1995
    Martin H. Greenberg, co-editor
Pam Keesey, *Dark Angels: Lesbian Vampire Stories*, 1995
    editor
Pam Keesey, *Daughters of Darkness: Lesbian Vampire Stories*, 1993
    editor
Robert Weinberg, *Girls' Night Out*, 1997
    Stefan Dziemianowicz and Martin H. Greenberg, co-editors

597

JOSEPH BRUCHAC

Dawn Land

(Golden, Colorado: Fulcrum Publishing, 1993)

Story type: Fantasy (Quest; Legend)
Major character(s): Young Hunter, Prehistoric Human (Abenaki Indian), Teenager; Medicine Plant, Psychic (seer), Indian (Abenaki Indian); Talker, Shaman, Prehistoric Human (Abenaki Indian)
Time period(s): 80th century B.C.
Locale(s): Adirondack Mountains, North America; Hudson River Valley, North America

Summary: While out hunting food for his tribe, Young Hunter is bitten by a snake. Unharmed by the bite, he returns to tell the tribal elders of the incident. Talker, the shaman, recognizes this as a spiritual event; Young Hunter has been chosen by the snake to be the protector of his people. And a menace soon appears, one that will challenge all of Young Hunter's strength, both physical and spiritual, in a fight for the survival of the Only People.

Other books you might like:
Jean M. Auel, *Clan of the Cave Bear*, 1980
W. Michael Gear, *People of the River*, 1992
    Kathleen O'Neal Gear, co-author
Betsy James, *Dark Heart*, 1992
Lynn Armistead McKee, *Woman of the Mists*, 1991
William Sarabande, *Thunder in the Sky*, 1992
Roger Welsch, *Touching the Fire*, 1992

598

J.V. BRUMMELS

Deus Ex Machina

(New York: Bantam Spectra, 1989)

Story type: Science Fiction (End of the World)
Major character(s): David Jones, Writer
Time period(s): 21st century
Locale(s): New City, Earth

Summary: Environmental problems and over-population have brought the world to a state of near collapse and now everything seems likely to be destroyed as the sun goes nova. A small number of people must decide whether to perish with the rest of humanity or leave the planet using an experimental teleportation device. This is Brummels' first novel.

Other books you might like:
Vonda N. McIntyre, *Starfarers*, 1989
Philip Wylie, *When Worlds Collide*, 1933
    Edwin Balmer, co-author

599

JOHN BRUNNER

Children of the Thunder

(New York: Ballantine Del Rey, 1989)

Story type: Science Fiction (Psychic Powers)

Major character(s): Peter Levin, Writer (Science writer); Claudia Morris, Sociologist
Time period(s): 1990s
Locale(s): England

Summary: Claudia Morris's research into juvenile delinquency seems to point to a pattern. Brilliant children are committing crimes of greater or lesser magnitude, and getting away with them. Peter Levin's reporter's sense tells him that something important is going on. Working together, they make a discovery that could change the world.

Other books you might like:
Roger MacBride Allen, *Orphan of Creation*, 1988
Daniel Keys Moran, *Emerald Eyes*, 1988
Daniel Keys Moran, *The Long Run*, 1989
A.E. van Vogt, *Slan*, 1946
John Wyndham, *The Midwich Cuckoos*, 1957

600

JOHN BRUNNER

A Maze of Stars

(New York: Ballantine/Del Rey, 1991)

Story type: Science Fiction (Alternate Intelligence; Adventure)
Major character(s): Ship, Artificial Intelligence; Stripe, Passenger; Volar, Passenger
Time period(s): Indeterminate Future
Locale(s): Milky Way Galaxy, Outer Space

Summary: The Ship which brought colonists to the worlds of the Arm makes repeated sweeps to see how they are doing, but these sweeps are muddled in time so that this latest sweep is the earliest as far as the settlers are concerned. Ship has passengers from time to time who comment on the planets it visits, each leaving the Ship at a world of their choosing. Some colonists are advanced enough to build their own starships while others have reverted to cannibalism or changed into something inhuman. Still the Ship must continue its sweeps lest it feels the all too human emotion of boredom.

Other books you might like:
Poul Anderson, *The Boat of a Million Years*, 1989
James Blish, *Earthman, Come Home*, 1955
James Blish, *A Life for the Stars*, 1962
Glen Cook, *The Dragon Never Sleeps*, 1988
Keith Laumer, *Star Colony*, 1981
Anne McCaffrey, *The Ship Who Sang*, 1969
Frederik Pohl, *The World at the End of Time*, 1990
Robert J. Sawyer, *Golden Fleece*, 1990
David Alexander Smith, *Homecoming*, 1990
Norman Spinrad, *The Void Captain's Tale*, 1983

601

JOHN BRUNNER

Muddle Earth

(New York: Ballantine Del Rey, 1993)

Story type: Science Fiction (Satire; Adventure)

Major character(s): Rinpoche Gibbs, Time Traveller, Adventurer; Nixy Anangaranga-Jones, Tourist, Adventurer; Sherlock Holmes, Detective—Private, Teenager
Time period(s): 24th century
Locale(s): Earth

Summary: Revived from cryogenic suspended animation and cured of disease, Rinpoche Gibbs discovers an Earth now run by aliens as a tourist attraction and fraught with science fiction cliches. As usual with wealthy resurrectees, authorities omit the standard orientation and allow Gibbs to reeducate himself. When he immediately runs afoul of authorities and organized crime, Gibbs must seek help from an adolescent Sherlock Holmes in a Victorian London reenactment zone.

Other books you might like:
Douglas Adams, *The Hitchhiker's Guide to the Galaxy*, 1980
Chester Anderson, *The Butterfly Kid*, 1967
Ron Goulart, *After Things Fell Apart*, 1970
Ron Goulart, *When the Waker Sleeps*, 1975
Larry Niven, *Fallen Angels*, 1991
  Jerry Pournelle, Michael Flynn, co-authors
Mike Resnick, *Inside the Funhouse*, 1992
  editor
Ken Rolston, *Extreme Paranoia: Nobody Knows the Trouble I've Shot*, 1991
H.G. Wells, *When the Sleeper Wakes*, 1899

602
JOHN BRUNNER

The Shockwave Rider
(New York: Ballantine/Del Rey, 1990)

Story type: Science Fiction (Future Shock)
Major character(s): Nickie Haflinger, Experimental Subject
Time period(s): 21st century
Locale(s): United States

Summary: A massive computerized data-net controls virtually everything and the majority of Americans suffer periodic nervous breakdowns caused by future shock. Nickie Haflinger lives at Tarnover, a mysterious institution which has trained him from childhood to handle large quantities of data without falling prey to future shock. Eventually, however, Nickie discovers that Tarnover has its darker side. The scientists there are doing experiments in genetic manipulation which result in children who are deformed but even more capable of manipulating data than Nickie is. Nickie flees the institution and begins to search for a way to destroy both it and the out-of-control data-net which has enslaved humanity. Originally published in 1975.

Other books you might like:
William Gibson, *Neuromancer*, 1984
Kim Stanley Robinson, *The Gold Coast*, 1988
Norman Spinrad, *Little Heroes*, 1987
Bruce Sterling, *Islands in the Net*, 1988

603
KAREN BRUSH

Demon Pig
(New York: Avon, 1991)

Story type: Fantasy (Magic Conflict; Light Fantasy)
Major character(s): Quadroped, Animal (pig)
Time period(s): Indeterminate
Locale(s): Nine Kingdoms, Fictional Country

Summary: When the Queen of the Dead enlists the help of a trickster god to start a new war, Quadroped and his strange friends must restore peace to the Nine Kingdoms while rescuing his people and stopping the forces of evil.

Other books you might like:
Kenneth Grahame, *The Wind in the Willows*, 1908
Brian Jacques, *Mattimeo*, 1990
Brian Jacques, *Mossflower*, 1988
Brian Jacques, *Redwall*, 1987
Garry Kilworth, *The Foxes of Firstdark*, 1990
Margery Sharp, *The Rescuers*, 1959
Tad Williams, *Tailchaser's Song*, 1985
David Henry Wilson, *The Coachman Rat*, 1985

604
STEVEN BRUST

Agyar
(New York: Tor, 1993)

Story type: Fantasy (Urban; Horror)
Major character(s): Janos "Jack" Agyar, Vampire; Jim, Spirit; Susan Pfahl, Student
Time period(s): 1990s
Locale(s): Lakota, Ohio

Summary: Jack is compelled by Laura Kellem to come to Lakota to take the fall for the deaths she caused. While her scheme develops, though, Jack finds friendship with a ghost, satisfaction in writing, sustenance and power with Jill and a bond with Susan that leads him to overthrow all of it.

Other books you might like:
Suzy McKee Charnas, *The Vampire Tapestry*, 1980
Storm Constantine, *Burying the Shadow*, 1992
Charles de Lint, *Mulengro: A Romany Tale*, 1985
John M. Ford, *The Dragon Waiting*, 1983
Megan Lindholm, *Wizard of the Pigeons*, 1986

605
STEVEN BRUST

Athyra
(New York: Ace, 1993)

Story type: Fantasy (Adventure)
Series: Vlad Taltos
Major character(s): Vlad Taltos, Sorcerer, Martial Arts Expert (retired assassin); Saun, Apprentice, Healer
Time period(s): Indeterminate Future
Locale(s): Smallcliff, Fictional City

Summary: On his way to a lesson with his master, Saun encounters a mysterious easterner named Vlad and becomes curious over Vlad's background and the possibility of Vlad teaching Saun witchcraft.

Other books you might like:
Jonathan Carroll, *Sleeping in Flame*, 1988
Glen Cook, *The Black Company*, 1984
Barbara Hambly, *The Rainbow Abyss*, 1991
Tanya Huff, *Child of the Grove*, 1988
Mickey Zucker Reichert, *The Legend of Nightfall*, 1993

606

STEVEN BRUST

Cowboy Feng's Space Bar and Grille

(New York: Ace Books, 1990)

Story type: Science Fiction (Humor)
Major character(s): Billy, Musician; Jamie, Musician
Time period(s): Indeterminate Future; Indeterminate Past
Locale(s): Moon (Earth's); Outer Space

Summary: A time-travelling bar, owned by a very strange proprietor and full of eccentric patrons, leaps across space and time to avoid a nuclear war, voyaging first to the moon and later to other solar systems altogether.

Other books you might like:
Spider Robinson, *Callahan's Crosstime Saloon*, 1977
Spider Robinson, *Callahan's Lady*, 1989
Spider Robinson, *Callahan's Secret*, 1986
Spider Robinson, *Time Travelers Strictly Cash*, 1981

607

STEVEN BRUST

Five Hundred Years After

(New York: Tor, 1994)

Story type: Fantasy (Political; Adventure)
Series: Khaavren Romances
Major character(s): Khaavren of House Tiassa, Military Personnel (Imperial Guard); Pel of House Yendi, Nobleman (Duke of Galstan); Aliera e'Kieron, Royalty
Time period(s): Indeterminate Past (350 years prior to *Jhereg*)
Locale(s): Dragaera, Planet—Imaginary

Summary: Five hundred years after events in *The Phoenix Guards*, Khaavren and his companions must foil the uprising and conspiracy which threatens to destroy the Imperial Orb and the very fabric of Dragaeran society. Pays homage to Alexandre Dumas' *Twenty Years After*.

Other books you might like:
Alexandre Dumas, *Twenty Years After*, 1845
Katharine Kerr, *Daggerspell*, 1986
Mercedes Lackey, *Magic's Promise*, 1990
Sheri S. Tepper, *King's Blood Four*, 1983
Chelsea Quinn Yarbro, *A Candle for D'Artagnan*, 1989

608

STEVEN BRUST
MEGAN LINDHOLM, Co-Author

The Gypsy

(New York: Tor, 1992)

Story type: Fantasy (Mystery; Urban)
Major character(s): Cigany, Gypsy; Mike Stepovich, Police Officer
Time period(s): 1990s
Locale(s): Lakota, Indiana

Summary: Nothing in Mike Stepovich's life makes sense any more, what with seeing his new partner as a jerk, losing touch with his kids since his divorce and hating being single. Now, against all evidence and sense, he believes the arrested Gypsy innocent. Despite Mike's efforts, people still die. For his part, the Gypsy slowly remembers his purpose in Lakota and his role in fighting the Fair Lady.

Other books you might like:
Emma Bull, *Bone Dance*, 1991
Charles de Lint, *Mulengro: A Romany Tale*, 1985
Heather Gladney, *Teot's War*, 1987
Lisa Goldstein, *A Mask for the General*, 1987
Megan Lindholm, *Cloven Hooves*, 1991
Megan Lindholm, *Wizard of the Pigeons*, 1986
Pat Murphy, *The Falling Woman*, 1986

609

STEVEN BRUST

Orca

(New York: Ace, 1996)

Story type: Fantasy (Adventure; Political)
Series: Vlad Taltos
Major character(s): Vlad Taltos, Sorcerer, Martial Arts Expert (assassin); Kiera, Thief; Loftis, Detective (Imperial Investigator)
Time period(s): Indeterminate Future
Locale(s): Dragaera, Planet—Imaginary

Summary: By befriending a woman in Northport, Vlad involves himself with an investigation into the death of a merchant, Fyres. The investigation grows to encompass the Empress and the house of Orca, represented by Loftis and a variety of others. Although very talented, Vlad enlists Kiera's talents for theft to unravel the mystery surrounding Fryes' vanishing companies and holdings.

Other books you might like:
Marion Zimmer Bradley, *Lythande*, 1986
Lois McMaster Bujold, *The Vor Game*, 1990
Glen Cook, *The Black Company*, 1984
Simon R. Green, *Hawk & Fisher*, 1990

610

STEVEN BRUST

Phoenix

(New York: Ace, 1990)

Story type: Fantasy (Adventure)
Major character(s): Vlad Taltos, Sorcerer, Martial Arts Expert; Loiosh, Animal (jhereg), Mythical Creature (dragon)
Time period(s): Indeterminate Future
Locale(s): Adrilankha, Fictional Country; Greensere, Fictional Country

Summary: Vlad's patron goddess, Yerra, has a job for him—to assassinate the king of Greensere. Unfortunately, the consequences are almost certainly war, forced conscription of humans, revolution of humans against Dragaerans, and further strain on Vlad and Cawti's marriage. But you can't say no to a goddess.

Other books you might like:
Samuel R. Delany, *Tales of Neveryon*, 1979
George Alec Effinger, *When Gravity Fails*, 1987
Barry Hughart, *Bridge of Birds*, 1984
Melisa C. Michaels, *Skirmish*, 1985
Roger Zelazny, *Nine Princes in Amber*, 1970

611

STEVEN BRUST

The Phoenix Guards

(New York: Tor, 1991)

Story type: Fantasy (Adventure)
Series: Khaavren Romances
Major character(s): Khaavren of House Tiassa, Gentleman; Aerich of House Lyorn, Gentleman; Tazendra of House Dzur, Gentlewoman
Time period(s): Indeterminate Past (850 years prior to *Jhereg*)
Locale(s): Dragaera, Planet—Imaginary

Summary: Khaavren is a landless son of fallen nobility, possessor of a good sword and "tolerably well acquainted with its use." Along with his loyal friends, he enthusiastically seeks adventure and romance, while pledged to the service of the Emperor at the very end of the reign of the Athyra. But as the cycle moves on and the throne passes to the House of the Phoenix, Khaavren's life and the future of Dragaera depend on his wariness. A tribute to Alexandre Dumas's *The Three Musketeers*.

Other books you might like:
Brian Daley, *A Tapestry of Magics*, 1983
Alexandre Dumas, *The Three Musketeers*, 1846
Barbara Hambly, *The Rainbow Abyss*, 1991
Joel Rosenberg, *D'Shai*, 1991
Roger Zelazny, *Nine Princes in Amber*, 1970

612

EDWARD BRYANT

Aqua Sancta

(Arvada, Colorado: Roadkill Press, 1994)

Story type: Horror (Vampire Story)
Major character(s): Father Callahan, Religious (Catholic priest); The Vampire, Vampire
Time period(s): 1990s (1994)
Locale(s): United States

Summary: This beautifully designed and illustrated short-short story in chapbook form tells of a priest captured by a ravenous vampire, and the ingenious method he devises to dispatch the creature in the nick of time.

Other books you might like:
Poppy Z. Brite, *Love in Vein*, 1994
  editor
Martin H. Greenberg, *Dracula: Prince of Darkness*, 1994
  editor
Brian Hodge, *Shrines and Desecrations*, 1994
Nancy Kilpatrick, *Sex and the Single Vampire*, 1994

613

EDWARD BRYANT

Fetish

(Eugene, Oregon: Axolotl/Pulphouse, 1991)

Story type: Horror (Black Magic)
Major character(s): Angela Black, Witch; Conway Delacroix, Writer
Time period(s): 1990s
Locale(s): Arroyo Hondo, New Mexico

Summary: When white witch Angela Black responds to a call for help from her old lover, Conway Delacroix, she becomes caught up in a scheme to retrieve a Zuni Indian fetish from the murderer who killed Delacroix's friends, and to find out why the fetish means so much to so many people.

Other books you might like:
Kathryn Ptacek, *Ghost Dance*, 1990
Anne Rice, *The Witching Hour*, 1990
Sarban, *The Doll Maker and Other Tales of the Uncanny*, 1953
John Updike, *The Witches of Eastwick*, 1984

614

JOHN BUCHAN

Witchwood

(New York: Caroll & Graf, 1989)

Story type: Fantasy (Religious)
Time period(s): 17th century
Locale(s): Scotland

Summary: A young minister, newly assigned to an isolated village, discovers a coven of witches praticing the old ways in the woods surrounding the village. His efforts to abolish the group are thwarted by the villagers and by his superiors, who don't believe him.

Other books you might like:
Gael Baudino, *Strands of Starlight*, 1989
Katherine Kurtz, *The Harrowing of Gwynedd*, 1989
    Vol 1 - The Heirs of St. Camber
Frank E. Peretti, *This Present Darkness*, 1986

615

RAYMOND BUCKLAND

Cardinal's Sin
(Minneapolis: Llewellyn, 1996)

Story type: Horror (Black Magic)
Series: Committee
Major character(s): Duncan Webster, Writer; Patrizio Ganganelli, Religious (cardinal); Tanya Demidas, Witch
Time period(s): 1990s (1993)
Locale(s): Vatican City; Washington, District of Columbia

Summary: In this second adventure of The Committee, Duncan Webster reconvenes his multicultural team of psychically endowed specialists to battle Cardinal Ganganelli, a Vatican aspirant who has discovered black magic texts in the Vatican library. Still incensed by the ill treatment his mother received from American GIs in World War II, Ganganelli has unleashed demonic forces that have upset weather patterns throughout the world.

Other books you might like:
Katherine Kurtz, *The Adept*, 1991
    Deborah Turner Harris, co-author
Brian Lumley, *Psychomech*, 1984
Thomas F. Monteleone, *The Blood of the Lamb*, 1992
Robert Morgan, *The Things That Are Not There*, 1992
Dennis Wheatley, *The Devil Rides Out*, 1935

616

RAYMOND BUCKLAND

The Committee
(St. Paul, Minnesota: Llewellyn, 1993)

Story type: Horror (Wild Talents)
Major character(s): Duncan Webster, Writer; Bill Highland, Political Figure (senator); Earl Stratford, Paranormal Investigator
Time period(s): 1990s (1993)
Locale(s): Washington, District of Columbia

Summary: In what is advertised as a psi-tech suspense thriller, Duncan Webster joins with a covert group of psychically-endowed operatives to thwart an international cabal that is destroying American spy satellites by psychokinesis. This is the author's first novel.

Other books you might like:
Steven M. Krauzer, *Brainstorm*, 1991
Brian Lumley, *Psychamok*, 1985
Brian Lumley, *Psychomech*, 1984
Brian Lumley, *Psychosphere*, 1984
Jack Martin, *Scanners*, 1979

617

ALGIS BUDRYS

Hard Landing
(New York: Warner Questar, 1993)

Story type: Science Fiction (Invasion of Earth; Mystery)
Major character(s): Dothan Stablits, Police Officer; Jack Mullica, Alien; William Henshaw, Veterinarian
Time period(s): 1940s
Locale(s): Shoreview, Illinois

Summary: Dothan Stablits' investigation of an accidental death discovers no unusual aspects, but when the pathologist notifies the National Register of Pathological Anomalies, Dr. William Henshaw performs a second autopsy and confirms the discovery of aliens on Earth. Abandoned by policy, the stranded aliens follow a standard defensive scenario including no interference with natives and no contact with each other.

Other books you might like:
Greg Bear, *The Forge of God*, 1987
David Brin, *Earth*, 1990
Alan Dean Foster, *Cyber Way*, 1990
Rebecca Ore, *Becoming Alien*, 1987
David Weber, *Mutineers' Moon*, 1991
George Zebrowski, *Stranger Suns*, 1991

618

ALGIS BUDRYS, Editor

L. Ron Hubbard Presents Writers of the Future, Volume VII
(Los Angeles: Bridge Publications, 1991)

Story type: Science Fiction (Anthology)
Series: Writers of the Future

Summary: 15 original stories chosen from the winners and finalists of the ongoing L. Ron Hubbard Writers of the Future Contest, open only to emerging writers.

Other books you might like:
George R.R. Martin, *The John W. Campbell Awards, Volume 5*, 1984
    editor
George R.R. Martin, *New Voices I-IV*, 1977-1981
    editor

619

ALGIS BUDRYS, Editor
DAVE WOLVERTON, Co-Editor

L. Ron Hubbard Presents Writers of the Future, Volume VIII
(Los Angeles: Bridge Publications, 1992)

Story type: Science Fiction (Anthology)
Series: Writers of the Future

Summary: Includes a two-page introduction by Dave Wolverton; articles on writing by Algis Budrys, Lois McMaster Bujold, R. Garcia y Robertson and L. Ron Hubbard; one article by Edd Cartier, "Notes to the New Artist"; a five-page article by Dave Wolverton, "More Than a Contest"; five pages describing the Writers of the Future rules and deadlines plus 17 stories from winners and finalists and illustrations from a dozen contest winning illustrators. Stories include the grand prize winner, Alan Burt's "The Last Indian War" and other quarterly winners, Michael Paul Metzger's "Anne of a Thousand Years"; M.C. Sumner's "Surrogate"; and Steven Woodworth's "Scary Monsters." One story, Nicholas A. DiChario's "The Winterberry," appeared first in Mike Resnick's *Alternate Kennedys*.

Other books you might like:
Lou Aronica, *Full Spectrum*, 1988
   Shawna McCarthy, co-editor
George R.R. Martin, *The John W. Campbell Awards, Volume 5*, 1984
   editor
George R.R. Martin, *New Voices I-IV*, 1977-1981
   editor
Kristine Kathryn Rusch, *The Best of Pulphouse: The Hardback Magazine*, 1991
   editor

620

LOIS MCMASTER BUJOLD

Barrayar
(New York: Baen, 1991)

Story type: Science Fiction (Political; Family Saga)
Series: Adventures of Miles Vorkosigan
Major character(s): Cordelia Naismith, Noblewoman (Lady Vorkosigan); Aral Vorkosigan, Nobleman (Lord Vorkosigan), Ruler (regent); Bothari, Bodyguard, Murderer
Locale(s): Barrayar, Planet—Imaginary

Summary: Cordelia and Aral move into the Vorkosigan family home on feudal Barrayar where Cordelia conceives a son. Aral, the new regent to the throne, is forced to make decisions which are unpopular among some of the Vor who Aral must rule. When an attack on Aral is safely avoided, Cordelia remains unable to put aside her fears for her husband. *Barrayar* is a direct sequel to *Shards of Honor* (1986) and contains an afterword with a chronology of the Miles Naismith universe.

Other books you might like:
Emma Bull, *Falcon*, 1989
C.J. Cherryh, *Forty Thousand in Gehenna*, 1983
Stephen Goldin, *Jade Darcy and the Affair of Honor*, 1988
   Mary Mason, co-author
Frank Herbert, *Dune*, 1965
Steve Perry, *The Man Who Never Missed*, 1985
Alis A. Rasmussen, *A Passage of Stars*, 1990

621

LOIS MCMASTER BUJOLD

Borders of Infinity
(New York: Baen Books, 1989)

Story type: Science Fiction (Humor)
Series: Adventures of Miles Vorkosigan
Major character(s): Miles Vorkosigan, Military Personnel, Diplomat
Time period(s): Indeterminate Future
Locale(s): Barryaran Empire, Interstellar Empire/Federation

Summary: This volume contains three episodes from the life of Miles Vorkosigan, a puny aristocrat who prefers to use wit rather than military might when it comes to solving problems. "The Mountains of Mourning" from this collection is a Nebula Award nominee.

Other books you might like:
Anne McCaffrey, *Sassinak*, 1989
   Elizabeth Moon, co-author
Rebecca Ore, *Becoming Alien*, 1987
Rebecca Ore, *Being Alien*, 1989
Allen Steele, *Orbital Decay*, 1989

622

LOIS MCMASTER BUJOLD

Cetaganda
(New York: Baen, 1996)

Story type: Science Fiction (Mystery; Political)
Series: Adventures of Miles Vorkosigan
Major character(s): Miles Vorkosigan, Nobleman, Military Personnel (lieutenant); Ivan Vorpatril, Nobleman, Diplomat; Mia Maz, Diplomat (protocol)
Time period(s): Indeterminate Future
Locale(s): Eta Ceta IV, Planet—Imaginary; Cetaganda, Interstellar Empire/Federation

Summary: Sent to Cetaganda with Ivan as Vor representatives to the Dowager Empress' funeral, Miles finds a fight, perhaps accidentally, before they can dock. Now possessing an illegal weapon, Miles convinces Ivan they should investigate the circumstances of the attack, which leads to questions about the Dowager Empress' death and the highest, most secret parts of Cetagandan society.

Other books you might like:
Eleanor Arnason, *Ring of Swords*, 1993
L. Warren Douglas, *Stepwater*, 1995
Mary Gentle, *Golden Witchbreed*, 1984
Jack Vance, *Alastor*, 1995
Joan D. Vinge, *The Summer Queen*, 1991

623

LOIS MCMASTER BUJOLD

Dreamweaver's Dilemma
(Framingham, Massachusetts: NESFA Press, 1996)

Story type: Science Fiction (Collection)

Summary: Contains a six-page preface by Lillian Stewart Carl, author's biography and bibliography, five pages of timeline of Barrayaran and human history, two original and four stories reprinted from periodicals 1985-1989, three original and four generally biographical essays reprinted from 1990-1992 periodicals and 16 pages by Suford Lewis on pronunciation of terms and genealogy of the Vorkosigan line. Frequently upbeat in tone, the stories' themes include Sherlock Holmes, bartering between a non-human and a homemaker, cats, urban life, dream composing, and one Miles Vorkosigan adventure.

Other books you might like:
Joe Haldeman, *Vietnam and Other Alien Worlds*, 1993
Zenna Henderson, *Ingathering: The Complete People Stories of Zenna Henderson*, 1995
James H. Schmitz, *The Best of James H. Schmitz*, 1991
Cordwainer Smith, *The Rediscovery of Man*, 1993
James White, *The White Papers*, 1996

624

LOIS MCMASTER BUJOLD

Memory

(New York: Baen, 1996)

Story type: Science Fiction (Mystery; Political)
Series: Adventures of Miles Vorkosigan
Major character(s): Miles Vorkosigan, Nobleman, Military Personnel (retired); Simon Illyan, Government Official (Imperial Security); Ivan Vorpatril, Nobleman, Military Personnel
Time period(s): Indeterminate Future
Locale(s): Barrayar, Planet—Imaginary

Summary: Discovered covering up the seizures still recurring since his recovery from death, Miles loses his commission and the Dendarii Mercenaries to a medical discharge. Before he can even think about what to do with his life, Miles must discover what happened to Illyan's memory chip and prevent Illyan's death.

Other books you might like:
Greg Bear, *Queen of Angels*, 1990
C.J. Cherryh, *Heavy Time*, 1991
Katharine Kerr, *Polar City Blues*, 1990
Steve Perry, *The Man Who Never Missed*, 1985
Allen Steele, *The Jericho Iteration*, 1994

625

LOIS MCMASTER BUJOLD

Mirror Dance

(New York: Baen, 1994)

Story type: Science Fiction (Family Saga; Political)
Series: Adventures of Miles Vorkosigan
Major character(s): Miles Vorkosigan, Nobleman, Military Personnel (admiral); Mark Pierre Vorkosigan, Clone
Time period(s): Indeterminate Future
Locale(s): Escobar, Planet—Imaginary; Jackson's Whole, Planet—Imaginary; *Ariel*, Spaceship

Summary: Impersonating Miles, Mark steals the *Ariel* and sets off for Jackson's Whole to free House Bharaputra's clones on his own. When the plan goes awry, Miles attempts a rescue, dying in the effort. After the loss of the stasis box preserving Miles' body and with precious little time to act, Mark must first travel to Barrayar and convince the family to trust him and support his plan.

Other books you might like:
Pauline Ashwell, *Unwillingly to Earth*, 1992
F.M. Busby, *Rissa Kerguelen*, 1977
C.J. Mills, *Brander's Book*, 1992
C.J. Mills, *Winter World*, 1988
Alis A. Rasmussen, *A Passage of Stars*, 1990
Karen Ripley, *The Tenth Class*, 1991
Joan D. Vinge, *The Summer Queen*, 1991

626

LOIS MCMASTER BUJOLD

The Spirit Ring

(New York: Baen, 1992)

Story type: Fantasy (Political; Light Fantasy)
Major character(s): Fiametta Beneforte, Magician, Fugitive; Thur Ochs, Miner, Spy (Abbot Monreal's)
Time period(s): Indeterminate
Locale(s): Montefoglia, Fictional Country (European dukedom); Alternate Earth

Summary: Although imperfectly understanding the nature of the spell, Fiametta correctly utilizes a magic spell while casting a ring without the supervision of her father who had apprenticed her without benefit of sanction by proper authorities. The ring's unexpected and undesired catch leads to the official notice of Fiametta's magical abilities and her enlistment in Abbot Monreal's plan to expose Lord Uberto Ferrante as a user of forbidden magic. Fiametta and Thur also provide the assistance needed to free the spirit of Fiametta's deceased father.

Other books you might like:
Laurell K. Hamilton, *Nightseer*, 1992
Marc Laidlaw, *Neon Lotus*, 1988
Robin McKinley, *The Blue Sword*, 1982
Robin McKinley, *The Hero and the Crown*, 1984
Patricia C. Wrede, *Mairelon the Magician*, 1991

627

LOIS MCMASTER BUJOLD

The Vor Game

(New York: Baen, 1990)

Story type: Science Fiction (Humor; Adventure)
Series: Adventures of Miles Vorkosigan
Major character(s): Miles Vorkosigan, Military Personnel, Diplomat; Gregor Vorbarra, Ruler (Emperor)
Time period(s): Indeterminate Future
Locale(s): Barrayaran Empire, Interstellar Empire/Federation

Summary: Miles Vorkosigan's misadventures while on his first assignment as a newly commissioned ensign lead to an undercover assignment and action with his cousin, the Emperor, and the mercenary soldiers who consider Miles their leader.

Other books you might like:

Anne McCaffrey, *Sassinak*, 1989
  Elizabeth Moon, co-author
Rebecca Ore, *Human to Human*, 1990
Rebecca Ore, *Being Alien*, 1989
Rebecca Ore, *Becoming Alien*, 1987
Allen Steele, *Orbital Decay*, 1989

628

LOIS MCMASTER BUJOLD, Editor
ROLAND J. GREEN, Co-Editor

Women at War
(New York: Tor, 1995)

Story type: Science Fiction (Anthology; Military)

Summary: Contains a two-page introduction by Bujold, a one-page introduction by Green, and brief introductions by Bujold to 17 original stories with diverse military themes written by women. Jane Yolen sets "The One-Armed Queen" on the world of *Sister Light, Sister Dark* (1988), while Holly Lisle's "A Few Good Men" features her character, Medwind Song, introduced in *Fire in the Mist* (1992). Other authors include Margaret Ball, P.J. Beese, Juanita Coulson, P.N. Elrod, P.M. Griffin, Adrienne Martine-Barnes, R.M. Meluch, Elizabeth Moon, Mickey Zucker Reichert, Elizabeth Ann Scarborough, and Judith Tarr.

Other books you might like:

Marion Zimmer Bradley, *Sword and Sorceress I-XII*, 1984-1995
  editor
Janrae Frank, *New Eves: Science Fiction about the Extraordinary Women of Today and Tomorrow*, 1994
  Jean Stine, Forrest J. Ackerman, co-editors
Esther Friesner, *Chicks in Chainmail*, 1995
  editor
Jessica Amanda Salmonson, *Amazons!*, 1979
  editor
Pamela Sargent, *Women of Wonder, the Classic Years: Science Fiction by Women From the 1940s to the 1970s*, 1995
  editor
Pamela Sargent, *Women of Wonder, the Contemporary Years: Science Fiction by Women From the 1970s to the 1990s*, 1995
  editor

629

EMMA BULL

Bone Dance
(New York: Ace, 1991)

Story type: Science Fiction (Post-Holocaust)
Major character(s): Sparrow, Trader, Troubleshooter; Sharrea, Psychic
Time period(s): Indeterminate Future

Locale(s): Minneapolis, Minnesota

Summary: When Sparrow woke up broke, in a ditch, with no memory of how she got there, she made her way to visit Sharrea. Sharrea read the cards. Sparrow received definite, but unhelpful, advice and warnings which did not deter her search for the legendary videotape of *The Horses*. The mind-control weapons which had turned the tide in war—the Horses—are dead, but their legacy remains.

Other books you might like:

Margaret Wander Bonanno, *The Others*, 1990
Pat Cadigan, *Synners*, 1991
Ernest Hogan, *Cortez on Jupiter*, 1990
Pat Murphy, *The City, Not Long After*, 1989
Walter Jon Williams, *Hardwired*, 1986

630

EMMA BULL
WILL SHETTERLY, Co-Author

Double Feature
(Framingham, Massachusetts: NESFA Press, 1994)

Story type: Fantasy (Collection; Urban)

Summary: Contains a two-page introduction by Patrick and Teresa Nielsen Hayden, individual introductions by the authors, a three-page bibliography and biography of Emma Bull, a two-page bibliography and biography of Will Shetterly, two essays on writing by Bull, the authors' sole published collaborative story, one original poem and four reprinted stories by Bull plus one original and three reprinted stories by Shetterly. Material reprinted from 1985-1992 periodicals includes five stories from the Liavek shared-world anthology series (1985-1990) and one story which gave rise to novels from each author set in Terri Windling's Borderlands milieu.

Other books you might like:

John M. Ford, *Casting Fortune*, 1989
Will Shetterly, *Elsewhere*, 1991
Will Shetterly, *Liavek*, 1985
  Emma Bull, co-editor
Will Shetterly, *Liavek: Festival Week*, 1990
Will Shetterly, *Liavek: Wizard's Row*, 1987
  Emma Bull, co-editor
Will Shetterly, *Nevernever*, 1993
Terri Windling, *Borderland*, 1986
  Mark Alan Arnold, co-editor
Terri Windling, *Life on the Border*, 1991
  editor

631

EMMA BULL

Falcon
(New York: Ace, 1989)

Story type: Science Fiction (Space Opera)
Major character(s): Nikki Falcon, Royalty (Prince), Pilot; Jacob, Spy
Time period(s): Indeterminate Future

Locale(s): Cymru, Planet—Imaginary; Bellmakers World, Planet—Imaginary

Summary: Dominic Glyndwr, nephew of the ruler of Cymru, realizes that his planet appears headed for revolution, but is unable to stop it. Fleeing for his life, and later adopting the name Nikki Falcon, he becomes a gestalt pilot, a dangerous profession which eventually kills those who follow it.

Other books you might like:
C.J. Cherryh, *Rimrunners*, 1989
Daniel Keys Moran, *The Long Run*, 1989
Walter Jon Williams, *Angel Station*, 1989
David Zindell, *Neverness*, 1988

| 632 |

EMMA BULL

Finder
(New York: Tor, 1994)

Story type: Fantasy (Urban; Psychic Powers)
Series: Borderland
Major character(s): Finder Orient, Psychic; Tick-Tick, Mythical Creature (elf), Mechanic (motorcycle); Alexandra "Sunny" Rico, Detective—Police
Time period(s): Indeterminate Future
Locale(s): Bordertown, Fictional City; Borderland, Mythical Place

Summary: Able to unerringly locate objects through a sixth sense, Finder tracks clues in a police murder investigation pointing to a new drug which could drive a permanent wedge between human and elf residents of Bordertown.

Other books you might like:
Simon R. Green, *Guard Against Dishonor*, 1991
Will Shetterly, *Elsewhere*, 1991
Will Shetterly, *The Liavek Series*, 1985-1990
  Emma Bull, co-editor
Will Shetterly, *Nevernever*, 1993
Terri Windling, *Borderland*, 1986
  Mark Alan Arnold, co-editor
Terri Windling, *Bordertown*, 1986
  Mark Alan Arnold, co-editor
Terri Windling, *Life on the Border*, 1991
  editor

| 633 |

DAVID R. BUNCH

Bunch!
(Cambridge, Massachusetts: Broken Mirrors Press, 1993)

Story type: Science Fiction (Collection)

Summary: Contains a four-page introduction by Barry N. Malzberg, one original story, "Control," plus 31 stories reprinted from periodicals 1957-1984. The stories, frequently dark in tone, contain a strong sense of American setting and explore themes surrounding human interrelationships and the human condition in a changed or changing world.

Other books you might like:
David Brin, *The River of Time*, 1986
Michael Flynn, *The Nanotech Chronicles*, 1991
Garry Kilworth, *Hogfoot Right and Bird-Hands*, 1993
Nancy Kress, *The Aliens of Earth*, 1993
Rebecca Ore, *Alien Bootlegger and Other Stories*, 1993
Michael Swanwick, *Gravity's Angels*, 1991
John Varley, *Blue Champagne*, 1986

| 634 |

DONALD BURLESON
ROBERT M. KNOX, Illustrator

Beyond the Lamplight
(Lockport, New York: Jack O'Lantern Press, 1996)

Story type: Horror (Collection)

Summary: This compilation of 34 stories encapsulates a decade of work by a writer whose stories range in theme from Lovecraftian terror to tales of psychological horror. More traditional horror stories include "The Interview," about a practical joke that escalates into an encouter with supernatural horror, and "Kokopelli," about a creature of Native American mythology still very much alive in contemporary times. A number of stories, including "Walkie-Talkie," "The Treehouse," "Uncle Neddy's Chair," and "Jigsaw," feature inanimate objects that become agents of supernatural dread. A trio of tales—"Down in the Mouth," "Family Dentistry," and "Gums"—extracts horror from the unlikely theme of dental care. Ramsey Campbell supplies an introduction.

Other books you might like:
Christopher Fowler, *Sharper Knives*, 1992
David Langford, *Irrational Numbers*, 1993
Mark Morris, *Close to the Bone*, 1995
Jeffrey Osier, *Driftglider and Other Stories*, 1994
Stephen Mark Rainey, *Fugue Devil and Other Weird Horrors*, 1993

| 635 |

DONALD BURLESON

Four Shadowings
(West Warwick, Rhode Island: Necronomicon Press, 1994)

Story type: Horror (Collection)

Summary: The four stories in this chapbook display the diverse talents of a writer best known as a Lovecraft scholar and poststructuralist critic. "A Student of Geometry" is a tale of psychological horror whose point of view character is slowly driven mad by her family and school life, while "The Wind at the Top of the Tree" is a traditional ghost story. "Blue Luke" tells of a family demon who continues to exert his control over a girl who gave up her belief in it long before, and "One-Night Strand" is a perversely chilling story about what a visitor to a fleapit hotel finds goes on after hours.

Other books you might like:
Michael A. Arnzen, *Needles and Sins*, 1993
Joe R. Lansdale, *By Bizarre Hands*, 1989
Jeffrey Osier, *Driftglider and Other Stories*, 1994

Stephen Mark Rainey, *Fugue Devil and Other Weird Horrors*, 1993
David J. Schow, *Seeing Red*, 1990

636

DONALD BURLESON

Lemon Drops and Other Horrors
(Bristol, Rhode Island: Hobgoblin Press, 1993)

Story type: Horror (Collection)

Summary: This first collection by a well-known Lovecraft scholar and controversial critic brings together 20 stories that range from the subtle to the gruesome. Among the former are "Snow Cancellations," about an endless snowfall and its implications, and "English 303," in which an English teacher lecturing on Joyce's *Finnegan's Wake* finds that time itself has become endlessly cyclical. Among the latter are "Milk," about the repulsive consequences of drinking spoiled milk; "Extractions," about the passions of a masochist; and "Connections," in which a young boy takes his grandfather's analogy of himself to an aging tree a little too far. Seven stories, including "Dark Brother," about a demonic presence in a house that only the family cat can see, are original to the book.

Other books you might like:
Ed Gorman, *Prisoners and Other Stories*, 1992
Stephen King, *Skeleton Crew*, 1985
Joe R. Lansdale, *By Bizarre Hands*, 1989
F. Paul Wilson, *Soft and Others*, 1989

637

WILLIAM S. BURROUGHS

Ghost of Chance
(New York: Serpent's Tail, 1995)

Story type: Science Fiction (Literary)
Major character(s): Mission, Pirate, Leader (captain); Ghost, Animal (lemur)
Time period(s): 17th century; Indeterminate
Locale(s): Madagascar

Summary: An elaborate short novella with 13 footnotes details the story of Captain Mission and his Museum of Lost Species. When the Board destroys Mission and his anti-control paradise, strange diseases live on, hidden in the Museum, changing life utterly. Interwoven with the story, Burroughs expresses views on religion, ecology, viruses, morality, and lemurs. First published as a limited edition by the Library Fellows of the Whitney Museum of American Art in 1991.

Other books you might like:
Kathy Acker, *Pussy, King of the Pirates*, 1996
J.G. Ballard, *Crash*, 1973
Richard Calder, *Dead Girls*, 1995
William T. Vollmann, *You Bright and Risen Angels*, 1987
Monique Wittig, *Les Guerilleres*, 1971

638

STEPHEN BURY (Pseudonym of Neal Stephenson and J. Frederick George)

Interface
(New York: Bantam, 1994)

Story type: Science Fiction (Political; Techno-Thriller)
Major character(s): William Anthony Cozzano, Political Figure, Experimental Subject; Cyrus "Cy" Ogle, Public Relations; Eleanor Boxwood Richmond, Political Figure
Time period(s): 1990s (1995)
Locale(s): Springfield, Illinois; Washington, District of Columbia

Summary: Cozzano suffers a severe stroke just as the president announces that forgiveness of the National Debt will form the basis of his new economic policy. The Network, an organization of interests who find this intolerable, decides to elect a president they control. A suddenly available technology allowing installation of a computer chip in a stroke victim's brain to bypass damage permits Cozzano to run for president. The Network manages Cozzano's campaign and, without his consent or knowledge, controls his chip, bringing instantaneous response to polled reactions.

Other books you might like:
Pat Cadigan, *Synners*, 1991
Michael Flynn, *In the Country of the Blind*, 1990
Edward Gibson, *In the Wrong Hands*, 1992
George Orwell, *Nineteen Eighty-Four*, 1949
Neal Stephenson, *Snow Crash*, 1992

639

F.M. BUSBY

Arrow From Earth
(New York: AvoNova, 1995)

Story type: Science Fiction (Political; Family Saga)
Series: Slow Freight
Major character(s): Clarence Engels "Clancy" Allaird, Spaceship Captain, Parent; Margaret "Marnie" Allaird, Stowaway, Teenager; Anne Portaris, Inventor, Spacewoman
Time period(s): 21st century
Locale(s): Glen Springs, Colorado; *Arrow*, Spaceship; Outer Space

Summary: Forced to leave home to avoid molestation by her mother's boyfriend, Marnie Allaird sneaks onto *Arrow* before the crew arrives, hoping to stay for the whole trip, or until she comes of legal age. While aboard *Arrow*, Marnie and the crew must deal with marauders from Earth, mutineers from *Starfinder*, and a strange being from the Aleph Continuum.

Other books you might like:
John Barnes, *Orbital Resonance*, 1991
Gregory Benford, *Timescape*, 1980
David Drake, *Starliner*, 1992
John M. Ford, *Growing Up Weightless*, 1993
George Zebrowski, *Stranger Suns*, 1991

640

F.M. BUSBY

Islands of Tomorrow
(New York: AvoNova, 1994)

Story type: Science Fiction (Time Travel; Political)
Major character(s): Lucian ''Luke'' Tabor, Student— Graduate, Time Traveller; Jay Rozak, Time Traveller, Revolutionary; Karen Cecile ''Casey'' Collins, Student, Time Traveller
Time period(s): 1990s; Indeterminate Future
Locale(s): Pullman, Washington (Washington State University)

Summary: Recruited by Jay, Luke becomes involved in a political demonstration against unfair taxes and treatment of students. During the demonstration and his subsequent arrest, Luke realizes that impossible events continue while he and all the other arrested students find themselves kidnapped to an unpleasant future. They must not only locate a way home but also prevent the future they discover.

Other books you might like:
Greg Bear, *Eternity*, 1988
Matthew J. Costello, *Day of the Snake*, 1992
Robert Silverberg, *The Gate of Worlds*, 1967
Dan Simmons, *Hyperion*, 1989
L. Neil Smith, *The Nagasaki Vector*, 1983
Sheri S. Tepper, *Beauty*, 1991
Connie Willis, *Doomsday Book*, 1992

641

F.M. BUSBY

The Singularity Project
(New York: Tor, 1993)

Story type: Science Fiction (Mystery; Techno-Thriller)
Major character(s): Mitch Banning, Engineer (communications), Writer; Gudrun ''Dauna'' Haig, Journalist; Elihu ''Emil Storchesson'' Coogan, Agent, Criminal
Time period(s): 21st century
Locale(s): Seattle, Washington

Summary: When Mitch decides to check out the potential story lead his girlfriend, Dauna, hears at work, it leads to employment on a secret project to construct a matter transmitter. Mitch doubts the transmitter because he recognizes Coogan as a con artist but continues with the project as an engineer because it seems that it could actually work. However, a man calling himself the Hornet tries to sabotage the project.

Other books you might like:
Roger MacBride Allen, *The Ring of Charon*, 1990
Greg Bear, *Eon*, 1989
Philip K. Dick, *The Unteleported Man*, 1983
  revised
Alan Dean Foster, *Cyber Way*, 1990
Laura J. Mixon, *Glass Houses*, 1992
Kim Stanley Robinson, *Red Mars*, 1993
Sheri S. Tepper, *Sideshow*, 1992

A.E. van Vogt, *The Weapon Makers*, 1946

642

F.M. BUSBY

Slow Freight
(New York: Bantam Spectra, 1991)

Story type: Science Fiction (First Contact)
Major character(s): Habeggar, Professor, Inventor; Rance Collier, Public Relations; Cassandra Monlux, Scientist, Agent (liaison)
Time period(s): 21st century
Locale(s): United States; *Starfinder*, Spaceship; *Environ*, Spaceship (alien)

Summary: Two recent discoveries, the Traction drive and the Habgate pipeline, make interstellar travel practical. The system has one minor logistical problem; there is a two year delay between entry and exit from the Habgate which, fortunately, does not age whatever is in the pipeline. Transit seems instantaneous. Coincidentally, Environ, containing all remaining Liij, is heading for the solar system.

Other books you might like:
Greg Bear, *Eon*, 1989
Michael Berlyn, *The Eternal Enemy*, 1990
Orson Scott Card, *Ender's Game*, 1985
Jeffrey A. Carver, *From a Changeling Star*, 1989
C.J. Cherryh, *Forty Thousand in Gehenna*, 1983
Harry Harrison, *The Deathworld Trilogy*, 1976
Janet Kagan, *Hellspark*, 1988
Sheri S. Tepper, *Grass*, 1989

643

F.M. BUSBY

The Triad Worlds
(New York: AvoNova, 1996)

Story type: Science Fiction (Political; First Contact)
Series: Slow Freight
Major character(s): Irtuk-Saa, Alien (Maghan), Ruler; Samuel ''Sam'' Hall Gowdy, Spaceship Captain; Sydnie ''Charel Secour'' Lightner, Spacewoman, Criminal (retired)
Time period(s): Indeterminate Future
Locale(s): Magh, Planet—Imaginary; *Romer*, Spaceship; Eamn, Planet—Imaginary

Summary: The crew of the *Romer* realizes that they will not be setting up a colony in the new, inhabited system they reach. When a raid captures several of *Romer*'s crew, Sam attempts to rescue the kidnappees as an ''Inspections Committee'' gets aboard and takes control of *Romer*. Sydnie recognizes her old gang boss and warns Sam.

Other books you might like:
Greg Bear, *Eon*, 1985
David Brin, *Brightness Reef*, 1995
C.J. Cherryh, *Foreigner*, 1994
Jane M. Lindskold, *Marks of Our Brothers*, 1995
David Weber, *Mutineers' Moon*, 1991
George Zebrowski, *Stranger Suns*, 1991

644

ANNE KELLEHER BUSH

Children of Enchantment

(New York: Warner Aspect, 1996)

Story type: Fantasy (Post-Disaster; Psychic Powers)
Series: Power and the Pattern
Major character(s): Roderic Ridenau, Royalty, Leader; Annadale Farhallen, Empath
Time period(s): 28th century
Locale(s): North America; Meriga, Fictional Country (Balkanized United States)

Summary: The disappearance of King Abelard Ridenau thrusts Prince Roderic into regency, forcing him to continue his father's plan to reunite shattered Meriga through alliances and military action against the Mutens and Harleyriders while some of his siblings surreptitiously vie for individual power. Unfortunately, events and prophecy drive Roderic and Annadale together despite Roderic's desire for another.

Other books you might like:
Shirley Meier, *Shadow's Daughter*, 1991
Shirley Meier, *Shadow's Son*, 1991
    S.M. Stirling, Karen Wehrstein, co-authors
S.M. Stirling, *Saber & Shadow*, 1991
    Shirley Meier, co-author
S.M. Stirling, *Snowbrother*, 1992
    expanded
Karen Wehrstein, *Lion's Heart*, 1991
Karen Wehrstein, *Lion's Soul*, 1991
Paul O. Williams, *The Breaking of Northwall*, 1981

645

ANNE KELLEHER BUSH

Daughter of Prophecy

(New York: Warner Aspect, 1995)

Story type: Fantasy (Post-Disaster; Psychic Powers)
Major character(s): Nydia Farhallen, Psychic; Abelard Ridenau, Ruler (king); Phineas, Military Personnel (captain)
Time period(s): 28th century (2714-2724)
Locale(s): United States (Meriga)

Summary: Abelard rescues Nydia from immolation as a witch in Tennessy Fall and escorts her to his capital in Ahga City. Unsafe among the court intrigues because of her psychic powers, Nydia accompanies Abelard on his campaign to subdue the Harleyriders. Her knowledge of the old Magic helps him evade treachery in Senifay and defeat the traitorous Senador of Vada. Even though she loves him, Nydia fears the consequences if she uses the old Magic to give him a son to inherit the kingdom. First novel.

Other books you might like:
Margaret Wander Bonanno, *The Others*, 1990
David Brin, *The Postman*, 1985
Octavia E. Butler, *Parable of the Sower*, 1993
Ursula K. Le Guin, *The Lathe of Heaven*, 1971
Anne McCaffrey, *To Ride Pegasus*, 1973

Walter M. Miller Jr., *A Canticle for Leibowitz*, 1960

646

JACK BUTLER

Nightshade

(New York: The Atlantic Monthly Press, 1989)

Story type: Science Fiction (Horror)
Major character(s): John Shade, Vampire, Rancher; Mandrake, Robot
Time period(s): 22nd century
Locale(s): Mars

Summary: Born in America's Old West of seemingly normal parents, Jack Shade is a vampire who has lived on into the age of space colonization and now resides on Mars where he quietly earns his living as a rancher and occasional secret agent. Mars's complex social order is facing imminent collapse, however, as several political blocs compete for power. Shade is drawn into the conflict, becoming a leader of the revolution.

Other books you might like:
Poul Anderson, *The Boat of a Million Years*, 1989
Michael Bishop, *The Secret Ascension*, 1987
Katherine Dunn, *Geek Love*, 1989
William Gibson, *Neuromancer*, 1984
Norman Spinrad, *Little Heroes*, 1987
Roger Zelazny, *This Immortal*, 1966

647

OCTAVIA E. BUTLER

Bloodchild and Other Stories

(New York: Four Walls Eight Windows, 1995)

Story type: Science Fiction (Collection)

Summary: Contains two autobiographical essays and all five of Butler's short stories published 1971-1993 in periodicals and anthologies, with one Hugo Award and Nebula Award winning story, ''Bloodchild''; one Hugo Award winner, ''Speech Sounds''; and her first published story, ''Crossover.'' Themes include gender role reversal, issues of oppression and empowerment, and the strength of women which allows them to endure the unbearable.

Other books you might like:
Nancy Kress, *The Aliens of Earth*, 1993
Ursula K. Le Guin, *The Compass Rose*, 1982
C.L. Moore, *The Best of C.L. Moore*, 1975
Pat Murphy, *Points of Departure*, 1990
L.A. Taylor, *Women's Work*, 1995
James Tiptree Jr., *Her Smoke Rose Up Forever*, 1990
Connie Willis, *Impossible Things*, 1994

648

OCTAVIA E. BUTLER

Imago

(New York: Warner, 1989)

Story type: Science Fiction (Post-Nuclear Holocaust)
Series: Xenogenesis
Major character(s): Jodahs, Genetically Altered Being (alien-human construct); Lilith, Parent (Jodahs' mother)
Time period(s): 21st century
Locale(s): Earth

Summary: The alien Oankali have continued their efforts, first described in *Dawn* and *Adulthood Rites*, to establish a civilization populated by Oankali-human hybrids on a revitalized Earth which had been all but destroyed by nuclear war. Jodahs, half human, half alien, and possessed of enormous power to do both good and evil, must make a place for himself, despite the hostility of both races.

Other books you might like:
Gardner Dozois, *Strangers*, 1978
Bruce Sterling, *Involution Ocean*, 1977

649

OCTAVIA E. BUTLER

Parable of the Sower

(New York: Four Walls Eight Windows, 1993)

Story type: Science Fiction (Theological; Adventure)
Major character(s): Lauren Oya Olamina, Teenager, Religious; Joanne Garfield, Teenager, Slave; Harry Balter, Teenager, Traveller
Time period(s): 2020s (2025-2027)
Locale(s): Robledos, California; Los Angeles, California; Oregon

Summary: Growing up in Robledos, a middle class, racially mixed, walled neighborhood, Lauren recognizes the wall as a temporary solution to the poverty and violence surrounding them. Born a hyper-empath as a result of legal, intelligence-enhancement drugs which killed her mother, Lauren suffers others' discomfort. Her father, a Baptist minister, teaches her to live with the pain and hide her condition. Unwilling to hurt her father, Lauren develops her own religion, Earthseed, secretly, compiling a book of her inspirations. Prepared for years, when Robledos unexpectedly burns, Lauren sets off as a man to find a place where she can work for pay and found an Earthseed community.

Other books you might like:
Eleanor Arnason, *A Woman of the Iron People*, 1991
David Brin, *Earth*, 1990
David Brin, *The Postman*, 1985
Nicola Griffith, *Ammonite*, 1993
Marjorie Bradley Kellogg, *Harmony*, 1991
Pat Murphy, *The City, Not Long After*, 1989
Joan Slonczewski, *A Door into Ocean*, 1986
Neal Stephenson, *Snow Crash*, 1992
Vernor Vinge, *A Fire upon the Deep*, 1992

Eric Vinicoff, *The Weigher*, 1992
Marcia Martin, co-author

650

RICHARD LEE BYERS

Dark Fortune

(New York: Diamond, 1993)

Story type: Horror (Occult)
Major character(s): Tom Carpenter, Religious (minister); Rebecca Carpenter, Spouse (Tom's wife); Willie Harper, Teenager
Time period(s): 1990s (1993)
Locale(s): Corona City, Florida

Summary: When the fallen Reverend Carpenter reshapes his life with the help of a tarot deck, it gives him the power to heal others. But those whom he heals begin to reveal a dark side that suggests the powers of darkness are using the minister as their conduit.

Other books you might like:
John Byrne, *Whipping Boy*, 1992
Brian Hodge, *Deathgrip*, 1992
Stephen King, *The Dead Zone*, 1979

651

RICHARD LEE BYERS

Dead Time

(New York: Zebra, 1992)

Story type: Horror (Serial Killer)
Major character(s): Jack Stone, Martial Arts Expert; Cheryl Stone, Prostitute; Vadoma Petalo, Gypsy
Time period(s): 1990s (1991)
Locale(s): Tampa, Florida

Summary: Jack Stone finds himself mystically transported back in time three weeks, with just enough time to prevent the murder of his sister. Before he can do so, though, he must determine how his time travel was made possible and who the shadowy entity is that dogs his trail and repeatedly tries to stop him.

Other books you might like:
Ken Grimwood, *Replay*, 1987
Lisa Tuttle, *Lost Futures*, 1992

652

RICHARD LEE BYERS

The Ebon Mask

(Clarkston, Georgia: White Wolf, 1996)

Story type: Horror (Occult)
Series: Wraith: The Oblivion; Dark Kingdoms Trilogy
Major character(s): James Graham, Nobleman (Marquis of Montrose); Frank Bellamy, FBI Agent; Jim Dunn, FBI Agent
Time period(s): 1990s (1996)

Locale(s): St. Louis, Missouri; Stygia, Mythical Place (The Afterlife)

Summary: Intrigue among factions in the Shadowlands beyond death dovetails with a murder spree perpetrated by the Atheist in the world of the living. Synchronization of events in both worlds points the way to a possible resolution of their problems. This novel is set in the publisher's "Wraith: The Oblivion" gaming scenario, in which the Shadowlands of the Afterlife abut our own world.

Other books you might like:
Sam Chupp, *Sins of the Fathers*, 1995
Rick Hautala, *Beyond the Shroud*, 1996

653

RICHARD LEE BYERS

Netherworld

(New York: HarperPaperbacks, 1995)

Story type: Horror (Vampire Story)
Series: World of Darkness: Vampire
Major character(s): Zane Tyler, Salesman; Alexander Blake, Vampire; Sartak, Vampire
Time period(s): 1990s (1995)
Locale(s): Tampa, Florida

Summary: Arrested on the suspicion that he murdered his girlfriend, Rose, Zane Tyler escapes from prison with the help of a hulking vampire named Sartak. With Sartak's help, Zane penetrates into the world of the Vampire Masquerade, in which numerous clans of vampires live scretly among human beings, and discovers that his girlfriend's disappearance is linked to a power struggle between the vampire clans and other supernatural beings fighting for dominance. This novel is set against the backdrop of a gaming scenario created by White Wolf.

Other books you might like:
Keith Herber, *Prince of the City*, 1994
James A. Moore, *The House of Secrets*, 1995
   Kevin Murphy, co-author
Robert Weinberg, *Bloodwar*, 1995
Robert Weinberg, *Unholy Allies*, 1995

654

RICHARD LEE BYERS

The Vampire's Apprentice

(New York: Zebra, 1992)

Story type: Horror (Vampire Story)
Major character(s): David Brent, Vampire; Carter Cavanaugh, Vampire; Liz Scarbrough, Clerk (bookstore worker)
Time period(s): 1990s
Locale(s): Tampa, Florida

Summary: Nerdy David Brent seeks prestige and respect by becoming an Olympian—i.e. a vampire—but spends most of his new existence struggling to obtain his next meal and wrestling with his conscience over the moral questions that come with being a member of the Undead.

Other books you might like:
Poppy Z. Brite, *Lost Souls*, 1992
Nancy A. Collins, *Sunglasses After Dark*, 1989
John Peyton Cooke, *Out for Blood*, 1991
Mark Ivanhoe, *Virgintooth*, 1991
Anne Rice, *Interview with the Vampire*, 1976

655

JOHN BYRNE

Whipping Boy

(New York: Dell/Abyss, 1992)

Story type: Horror (Wild Talents)
Major character(s): Paul Trayne, Teenager; Robert Trayne, Religious (evangelical preacher), Parent (Paul's father); Walker Stone, Journalist
Time period(s): 1990s
Locale(s): Faulkner, Illinois

Summary: Preacher Robert Trayne tours the country with his son Paul, nicknamed "The Whipping Boy" because his laying on of hands absorbs guilt feelings from all who come in contact with him. But Paul's touch also relieves recipients of their inhibitions, initiating a spree of debauchery that an informal posse of citizens in Faulkner, Illinois decides to put a stop to.

Other books you might like:
James Herbert, *The Fog*, 1975
Brian Hodge, *Deathgrip*, 1992
Stephen King, *The Dead Zone*, 1979
Dean R. Koontz, *Midnight*, 1989

656

PAT CADIGAN

Dirty Work

(Shingletown, California: Mark V. Ziesing, 1993)

Story type: Science Fiction (Collection)
Summary: Contains a four-page introduction by Storm Constantine and individual story introductions by Cadigan to 17 stories reprinted from periodicals and anthologies and one, "Lost Girls," written for this volume. Stories utilize diverse themes from cyberpunk as in the title story which features a character, Deadpan Alley, from *Mindplayers* to alternative history, featured in several stories, while Cadigan's tone varies from dark to humorous.

Other books you might like:
David Brin, *The River of Time*, 1990
Gardner Dozois, *Geodesic Dreams: The Best Short Fiction of Gardner Dozois*, 1992
Michael Flynn, *The Nanotech Chronicles*, 1991
Nancy Kress, *The Aliens of Earth*, 1993
Cordwainer Smith, *The Best of Cordwainer Smith*, 1975
Bruce Sterling, *Crystal Express*, 1989
Bruce Sterling, *Mirrorshades: The Cyberpunk Anthology*, 1986
   editor
Marc Stiegler, *The Gentle Seduction*, 1990

John Varley, *Blue Champagne*, 1986
John Varley, *The Persistence of Vision*, 1978

657

PAT CADIGAN

Fools

(New York: Bantam Spectra, 1992)

Story type: Science Fiction (Cyberpunk; Alternate Intelligence)
Major character(s): Marceline, Police Officer (Brain Police), Imposter (memory junkie); Savoy, Actor, Disembodied Personality
Time period(s): Indeterminate Future
Locale(s): United States

Summary: Disoriented after a post-mindplay fugue state, Marceline decides she must have contracted with an escort service to perform especially unsavory work, hoping to satisfy her needs as a memory junkie. Her confusion deepens into fear as she discovers disturbing memories, too much cash in her pockets and a sense of being manipulated. Additional mindplay experiences lead her to believe she has involved herself illegally in an operation which franchises or bootlegs personalities, perhaps acquired using a highly illegal mindsuck. Beseeched by a victim's wife, Marceline agrees to help find or reconstruct the husband's personality. Contemporaneous with *Mindplayers*.

Other books you might like:
Piers Anthony, *Total Recall*, 1989
Samuel R. Delany, *Dhalgren*, 1975
Philip K. Dick, *A Maze of Death*, 1970
Philip K. Dick, *A Scanner Darkly*, 1977
George Alec Effinger, *When Gravity Fails*, 1987
Peter R. Emshwiller, *The Host*, 1991
Peter R. Emshwiller, *Short Blade*, 1992
Mick Farren, *The Feelies*, 1990
Katharine Kerr, *Polar City Blues*, 1990
Neal Stephenson, *Snow Crash*, 1992
Michael Swanwick, *Vacuum Flowers*, 1987
Walter Jon Williams, *Voice of the Whirlwind*, 1987

658

PAT CADIGAN

Mindplayers

(New York: Bantam Spectra, 1991)

Story type: Science Fiction (Cyberpunk; Future Shock)
Major character(s): Alexandria Victoria Haas, Psychologist (Reality Affixer), Counselor; Paolo Segretti, Lawyer, Psychologist
Time period(s): Indeterminate Future
Locale(s): United States

Summary: The Brain Police picked Allie up from being dry cleaned. She was now a mind criminal charged with possessing an illegal psychosis. Segretti asked if anyone had approached her about the unusual organization of her mind before he affixed her reality for the first time. The terms of her

probation included mindplayer training. This book is a reissue of the 1987 edition.

Other books you might like:
Gregory Benford, *Great Sky River*, 1987
David Brin, *Earth*, 1990
Jeffrey A. Carver, *The Rapture Effect*, 1987
George Alec Effinger, *When Gravity Fails*, 1987
Victor Milan, *The Cybernetic Samurai*, 1986
Rudy Rucker, *Software*, 1982
Theodore Sturgeon, *Case and the Dreamer*, 1974

659

PAT CADIGAN

Patterns

(Kansas City: Ursus Imprints, 1989)

Story type: Science Fiction (Collection)

Summary: This collection includes one original short story, "The Power and the Passion," and eleven reprints. Among the best of these are "Pretty Boy Crossover," "It Was the Heat," "Angel" and "Rock On."

Other books you might like:
Patricia A. McKillip, *Fool's Run*, 1989
John Shirley, *Heatseeker*, 1989
Bruce Sterling, *Crystal Express*, 1989

660

PAT CADIGAN

Synners

(New York: Bantam Spectra, 1991)

Story type: Science Fiction (Arts; Cyberpunk)
Major character(s): Gina Aiesa, Artist; Mark "Visual Mark" Zamiatin, Artist; Cassandra "Sam" Ludovic, Artist
Time period(s): 21st century
Locale(s): Los Angeles, California

Summary: Over a score of years big business has moved into and taken over the production of synthesized videos, removing much of the individual control held by video artists called synners. Scientists have developed the first artificial neural cell which allows a direct human-computer interface. Synners and video production executives scramble for control of the new technology.

Other books you might like:
Gregory Benford, *Great Sky River*, 1987
David Brin, *Earth*, 1990
Jeffrey A. Carver, *The Rapture Effect*, 1987
George Alec Effinger, *When Gravity Fails*, 1987
Richard Kadrey, *Metrophage*, 1988
Victor Milan, *The Cybernetic Samurai*, 1986
Rudy Rucker, *Software*, 1982

661

MICHAEL CADNUM

Ghostwright

(New York: Carroll & Graf, 1992)

Story type: Horror (Doppelganger)
Major character(s): Hamilton Speke, Writer (playwright); Timothy Asquith, Alcoholic; Clara Speke, Housewife (Hamilton's wife)
Time period(s): 1990s (1992)
Locale(s): San Francisco, California

Summary: When Timothy Asquith promises to tell the world that his old friend, renowned playwright Hamilton Speke, stole all his ideas from Timothy, Speke murders him. But Timothy is endowed with powers that the grave cannot contain, forcing Speke not only to defend himself but to ponder the curious creative bond the two men share.

Other books you might like:
Stephen King, *The Dark Half*, 1989
Stephen King, *Misery*, 1987
Richard Laymon, *The Stake*, 1990
T. Lucien Wright, *Blood Brothers*, 1992

662

MICHAEL CADNUM

Horses of the Night

(New York: Carroll & Graf, 1993)

Story type: Horror (Black Magic)
Major character(s): Stratton Fields, Architect; Nona Lyle, Doctor (psychiatrist); Tyson De Vere, Architect
Time period(s): 1990s (1993)
Locale(s): San Francisco, California

Summary: Underappreciated architect Stratton Fields makes a pact with dark forces to protect himself and his interests. When those he loves, as well as his enemies, come to harm, he begins to doubt his supposed benefactors and himself.

Other books you might like:
Scott Baker, *Webs*, 1988
Charles L. Grant, *The Pet*, 1986
Patrick McGrath, *Spider*, 1991

663

MICHAEL CADNUM

The Judas Glass

(New York: Carroll & Graf, 1996)

Story type: Horror (Vampire Story)
Major character(s): Richard Stirling, Lawyer, Vampire; Rebecca Pennant, Musician; Sam Opal, Doctor
Time period(s): 1990s (1996)
Locale(s): San Francisco, California

Summary: A cut from an antique glass mirror endows Richard Stirling with vampiric appetites, powers, and a new sensual appreciation for a world unknown to him as a mortal. Richard resurrects his murdered lover Rebecca to share his new existence with him and becomes the object of a statewide manhunt.

Other books you might like:
Brett Easton Ellis, *The Informers*, 1994
Jonathan Nasaw, *The World on Blood*, 1996
Anne Rice, *Interview with the Vampire*, 1976
Lucius Shepard, *The Golden*, 1993
Brian Stableford, *Young Blood*, 1992

664

MICHAEL CADNUM

Nightlight

(New York: St. Martin's, 1989)

Story type: Horror (Mystery)
Major character(s): Paul Wright, Journalist, Critic (restaurant); Mary Lewis, Widow(er) (Paul's aunt); Leonard Lewis, Photographer (Mary's son)
Time period(s): 1980s (1989)
Locale(s): Berkeley, California

Summary: Desperate for a break from his newspaper job, Paul Wright accedes to his Aunt Mary's request that he search for his missing cousin, a morbid young man whose main interest is photographing cemeteries. When Paul arrives at the secluded cabin that was his cousin's last known abode, he finds that it is the setting of a recurring nightmare that has plagued him for months.

Other books you might like:
Ramsey Campbell, *Incarnate*, 1983
Daniel Quinn, *Dreamer*, 1988

665

MICHAEL CADNUM

Skyscape

(New York: Carroll & Graf, 1994)

Story type: Horror (Psychological Suspense)
Major character(s): Curtis Newns, Artist (painter); Margaret Newns, Writer; Red Patterson, Doctor (psychiatrist)
Time period(s): 1990s (1995)
Locale(s): San Francisco, California; Mojave Desert, California

Summary: Blocked creatively after the destruction of his masterpiece, "Skyscape," painter Curtis Newns agrees to undergo treatment with charismatic television psychiatrist Red Patterson at his remote facility in the Mojave Desert. Once there, Newns and his wife, Margaret, become involved in a struggle for identity with Patterson, who seeks not only to create vicariously through Newns, but to dominate and usurp his personality, at any cost.

Other books you might like:
Kathe Koja, *Bad Brains*, 1992
Kathe Koja, *Strange Angels*, 1994
Thomas Tessier, *The Dreams of Dr. Ladybank*, 1991
   in *Night Visions 9*

666

MICHAEL CADNUM

Sleepwalker

(New York: St. Martins, 1991)

Story type: Horror (Reanimated Dead)
Major character(s): Davis Lowry, Anthropologist; Peter Chambers, Anthropologist; Irene Sarnii, Anthropologist
Time period(s): 1990s (1991)
Locale(s): York, England

Summary: An archaeological dig in England turns up the mummified body of the eighth century Skeldergate Man, but a series of mysterious deaths among the expedition's members suggests that the exhumed body is not dead.

Other books you might like:
Peter Ackroyd, *First Light*, 1989
David Case, *The Third Grave*, 1981

667

MICHAEL CADNUM

St. Peter's Wolf

(New York: Carroll & Graf)

Story type: Horror (Werewolf Story)
Major character(s): Benjamin Byrd, Psychologist; Johanna Fisher, Linguist (translator); Jacob Zinser, Collector (art)
Time period(s): 1990s
Locale(s): San Francisco, California

Summary: Given a set of antique silver fangs by a fellow art connoisseur, psychologist Benjamin Byrd comes to know satisfaction he has never known before as, under their influence, he begins to experience nightly transformation into a werewolf who lives, loves and feeds without inhibition.

Other books you might like:
Scott Bradfield, *Dream of the Wolf*, 1990
Crosland Brown, *Tombley's Walk*, 1991
Dennis Danvers, *Wilderness*, 1991

668

JACK CADY

Inagehi

(Seattle: Broken Moon Press, 1994)

Story type: Horror (Mystery)
Major character(s): Harriette Johnson, Teacher (music teacher); Johnny Whitcomb, Worker; Lewis Corey, Artisan
Time period(s): 1950s
Locale(s): North Carolina

Summary: Harriette Johnson returns to her family homestead in North Carolina on a quest to unravel her father's unsolved murder. As she probes into her family's past, she uncovers the truth about how her father acquired the family land and realizes that her father's death was a means of atoning for past indiscretions and making peace with his Cherokee heritage and mystical understanding of life.

Other books you might like:
Fred Chappell, *I Am One of You Forever*, 1991
G. Wayne Miller, *Thunder Rise*, 1988
Manly Wade Wellman, *Who Fears the Devil?*, 1962

669

JACK CADY

The Off Season

(New York: St. Martin's, 1995)

Story type: Fantasy (Contemporary Realism)
Major character(s): Joel-Andrew, Religious, Wanderer; Kune, Doctor; Obed, Animal (cat), Linguist
Time period(s): 1970s (1973); 1880s (1888)
Locale(s): Point Vestal, Oregon

Summary: In a small town where ghosts exist beside the living and the present sometimes reflects one year, sometimes another, Joel-Andrew, a travelling prophet, and a cat arrive one day, upsetting certain balances.

Other books you might like:
James P. Blaylock, *Land of Dreams*, 1987
John Crowley, *Little, Big*, 1981
Robert Holdstock, *Mythago Wood*, 1984
Ian McDonald, *Desolation Road*, 1988
Pat Murphy, *The City, Not Long After*, 1989

670

JACK CADY

The Sons of Noah and Other Stories

(Seattle, Washington: Broken Moon Press, 1992)

Story type: Horror (Collection)

Summary: The seven stories collected in this booklet reveal one of the most talented writers of psychological and supernatural horror working today. The best are the title story, about a land development scheme that unleashes an uncontrollable elemental force, and the Conradian "By Reason of Darkness," which tells of a Vietnam vet who brings the war home, and the army buddies who must help him fight it.

Other books you might like:
Michael Blumlein, *The Brains of Rats*, 1989
Fred Chappell, *More Shapes than One*, 1991
Lucius Shepard, *The Jaguar Hunter*, 1987
Dan Simmons, *Prayers to Broken Stones*, 1990

671

JACK CADY

Street

(New York: St. Martin's, 1994)

Story type: Horror (Serial Killer)
Major character(s): Silk, Streetperson; Symptomatic Nerve Gas, Streetperson; Elgin, Streetperson

Time period(s): 1990s (1994)
Locale(s): Seattle, Washington

Summary: A group of homeless people, the flotsam of disillusionment with the American establishment and tragically misspent lives, band together to track down a serial killer preying on the homeless and runaways in their town. Their investigations take them on an odyssey of self-understanding and redemption.

Other books you might like:
George C. Chesbro, *Bone*, 1989
Gordon Linzner, *The Troupe*, 1988
David Martin, *Bring Me Children*, 1992
Rick R. Reed, *Penance*, 1993
Wayne Allen Sallee, *The Holy Terror*, 1992

672

MARTIN CAIDIN

Beamriders!

(New York: Baen Books, 1989)

Story type: Science Fiction (Adventure)
Major character(s): Kim Seavers, Sports Figure, Spy; Caleb Massey, Scientist
Time period(s): Indeterminate Future
Locale(s): Moon (Earth's)

Summary: Breakthroughs in laser technology lead to the development of teleportation. Beamriding, as it is called, remains enormously dangerous, however, and is only used for emergency situations. A small cadre of tough and talented beamriders is developed. They are called on whenever a daring rescue is needed or an impossible mission must be accomplished.

Other books you might like:
Ben Bova, *Voyagers III: Star Brothers*, 1990
Ben Bova, *Voyagers II: The Alien Within*, 1986
John Cramer, *Twistor*, 1989
John Varley, *Millennium*, 1983

673

MARTIN CAIDIN

Indiana Jones and the Sky Pirates

(New York: Bantam, 1993)

Story type: Fantasy (Adventure; Psychic Powers)
Series: Indiana Jones
Major character(s): Indiana "Indy" Jones, Archaeologist; Willard Cromwell, Martial Arts Expert, Adventurer
Time period(s): 1930s
Locale(s): Africa; Europe; Southwest

Summary: When Indy and his companions investigate reports of monstrous flying machines believed to fly through use of psychokinetic levitation, they uncover a plot to control international commerce and military power.

Other books you might like:
Campbell Black, *Raiders of the Lost Ark*, 1981
James Kahn, *Indiana Jones and the Temple of Doom*, 1984

Rob MacGregor, *Indiana Jones and the Dance of the Giants*, 1991
Rob MacGregor, *Indiana Jones and the Genesis Deluge*, 1992
Rob MacGregor, *Indiana Jones and the Interior World*, 1992
Rob MacGregor, *Indiana Jones and the Last Crusade*, 1989
Rob MacGregor, *Indiana Jones and the Peril at Delphi*, 1991
Rob MacGregor, *Indiana Jones and the Seven Veils*, 1991
Rob MacGregor, *Indiana Jones and the Unicorn's Legacy*, 1992

674

MARTIN CAIDIN

Indiana Jones and the White Witch

(New York: Bantam, 1994)

Story type: Fantasy (Adventure; Quest)
Series: Indiana Jones
Major character(s): Indiana "Indy" Jones, Archaeologist; Gale Parker, Archaeologist; Caitlin St. Brendan, Religious (Wicca), Magician
Time period(s): 1930s
Locale(s): England

Summary: When thieves steal an incomplete map leading to an ancient hoard of gold, Indy, Gale and Caitlin, who wields Merlin's legendary sword, undertake a perilous worldwide search for the treasure.

Other books you might like:
Campbell Black, *Raiders of the Lost Ark*, 1981
James Kahn, *Indiana Jones and the Temple of Doom*, 1984
Rob MacGregor, *Indiana Jones and the Dance of the Giants*, 1991
Rob MacGregor, *Indiana Jones and the Genesis Deluge*, 1992
Rob MacGregor, *Indiana Jones and the Interior World*, 1992
Rob MacGregor, *Indiana Jones and the Last Crusade*, 1989
Rob MacGregor, *Indiana Jones and the Peril at Delphi*, 1991
Rob MacGregor, *Indiana Jones and the Seven Veils*, 1991
Rob MacGregor, *Indiana Jones and the Unicorn's Legacy*, 1992

675

MARTIN CAIDIN

A Life in the Future

(Lake Geneva, Wisconsin: TSR, 1995)

Story type: Science Fiction (Adventure; Time Travel)
Series: Buck Rogers
Major character(s): Buck Rogers, Pilot, Experimental Subject; Wilma Deering, Pilot, Psychologist
Time period(s): 1990s (1996); 25th century
Locale(s): *Io*, Submarine; Pacific Ocean

Summary: When Buck Rogers crashes at an air show, his irreparable injuries lead experimenters to send the dying Buck 400 years into the future. Snatched from death by advanced technology, Buck's knowledge of Chile proves vital in overcoming Chileans aided by extraterrestrial survivors from Atlantis.

Other books you might like:
John Miller, *First Power Play*, 1990
M.S. Murdock, *Prime Squared*, 1990
M.S. Murdock, *Rebellion 2456*, 1989
Philip Francis Nowlan, *Armageddon 2419 A.D.*, 1962
John Silbersack, *Roger's Rangers*, 1983

676

MARTIN CAIDIN

Prison Ship
(New York: Baen, 1989)

Story type: Science Fiction (First Contact)
Major character(s): Jake Marden, Criminal, Computer Expert; Arbok, Alien, Pilot
Time period(s): 21st century
Locale(s): Earth; Outer Space

Summary: Six alien criminals, all of different species, all on the run, end up on Earth and join forces with a group of equally despicable human criminals.

Other books you might like:
Rick Cook, *Limbo System*, 1989
L. Ron Hubbard, *The Doomed Planet*, 1987
Larry Niven, *Man-Kzin Wars*, 1988
Larry Niven, *Man-Kzin Wars II*, 1989
Rebecca Ore, *Becoming Alien*, 1987
Rebecca Ore, *Being Alien*, 1989

677

ROBERT CAIN

Cybernarc
(New York: HarperCollins, 1991)

Story type: Science Fiction (Adventure; Robot Fiction)
Series: Cybernarc
Major character(s): RAMROD Mark I "Rod", Robot, Artificial Intelligence; Christopher Drake, Military Personnel (Seal)
Time period(s): 21st century
Locale(s): Colombia; United States

Summary: A product of CIA Project RAMROD, ROD survives initial testing and is teamed up with Christopher Drake for advanced field testing in Operation Amber Harvest aimed at capturing Colombian drug lord Luis Delgado-Valasquez.

Other books you might like:
Philip K. Dick, *The Three Stigmata of Palmer Eldritch*, 1965
Alan Dean Foster, *Outland*, 1981
Ernest Hogan, *High Aztec*, 1992
Ed Naha, *Robocop*, 1987
Ed Naha, *Robocop 2*, 1990
William Shatner, *TekLab*, 1991
William Shatner, *TekWar*, 1989
G. Harry Stine, *Warbots*, 1988
Thomas T. Thomas, *ME: A Novel of Self Discovery*, 1991

678

ROBERT CAIN

Endgame
(New York: Harper Paperbacks, 1993)

Story type: Science Fiction (Robot Fiction; Adventure)
Series: Cybernarc
Major character(s): RAMROD Mark I "Rod", Robot, Artificial Intelligence; Christopher Drake, Martial Arts Expert, Teacher
Time period(s): 21st century
Locale(s): Colombia

Summary: When Rod rebels against orders and attacks a drug lord's army and captures a leader, a drug kingpin declares vengeance on cybernarc. Meanwhile, U.S. forces launch a covert worldwide operation against the illegal drug trade.

Other books you might like:
David Alexander, *Nomad*, 1992
Isaac Asimov, *The Caves of Steel*, 1954
Isaac Asimov, *The Naked Sun*, 1957
Philip K. Dick, *A Scanner Darkly*, 1977
Michael Kandel, *Captain Jack Zodiac*, 1992
Ed Naha, *Robocop*, 1987
Ed Naha, *Robocop 2*, 1990
L.S. Riker, *Kill Crazy*, 1993
G. Harry Stine, *Sierra Madre*, 1988

679

ROBERT CAIN

Gold Dragon
(New York: HarperCollins, 1991)

Story type: Science Fiction (Adventure; Robot Fiction)
Series: Cybernarc
Major character(s): RAMROD Mark I "Rod", Robot, Artificial Intelligence; Christopher Drake, Military Personnel (Seal); Feng Hwa Chung, Drug Dealer
Time period(s): 21st century
Locale(s): Thailand; Myanmar; *Zhang-Zhou*, At Sea

Summary: ROD and Christopher Drake are sent to the Golden Triangle to find the heroin laboratory of Chinese drug lord Feng Hwa Chung, who supplies drugs to Bangkok and Hong Kong. Their mission is complicated when Drake is captured and ROD must find and free him.

Other books you might like:
Alan Dean Foster, *Outland*, 1981
Ed Naha, *Robocop*, 1987
Ed Naha, *Robocop 2*, 1990
William Shatner, *TekLords*, 1991
Ben Sloane, *Outland Strip*, 1991
Ben Sloane, *Ultimate Weapon*, 1991
G. Harry Stine, *The Lost Battalion*, 1989
G. Harry Stine, *Sierra Madre*, 1988

680
GEOFFREY CAINE

Curse of the Vampire
(New York: Diamond, 1991)

Story type: Horror (Vampire Story)
Series: Adventures of Abraham Stroud
Major character(s): Abraham Hale Stroud, Detective—Private, Psychic; Louis P. Cage, Archaeologist; Oliver Banaker, Doctor, Vampire
Time period(s): 1990s
Locale(s): Andover, Illinois

Summary: Psychically sensitive private detective Abraham Stroud runs afoul of the powerbrokers of Andover when his investigation of the disappearance of several of Andover's children and the discovery of a boneyard on the outskirts of town points to the town's leading citizens and their abnormal taste for blood. Before he can prevent more disappearances though, he must overcome the townspeoples' prejudices toward his family, who were long regarded as sorcerers and murderers.

Other books you might like:
Charles L. Grant, *The Hour of the Oxrun Dead*, 1977
Barbara Hambly, *Those Who Hunt the Night*, 1988
Stephen King, *Salem's Lot*, 1975
Robert Weinberg, *The Armageddon Box*, 1991

681
GEOFFREY CAINE

Legion of the Dead
(New York: Diamond, 1992)

Story type: Horror (Reanimated Dead)
Series: Adventures of Abraham Stroud
Major character(s): Abraham Hale Stroud, Detective—Private, Psychic; Dr. Leonard Wisnewski, Museum Curator (New York Museum of Antiquities); Dr. Kendra Cline, Doctor (epidemiologist)
Time period(s): 1990s (1992)
Locale(s): New York, New York

Summary: In this third adventure of psychic detective Abraham Stroud, the uncovering of a buried Etruscan ship in a Manhattan construction site releases a malignant force that sends scores of New Yorkers into comas, from which they awaken as zombified shock troops prepared to do its evil bidding.

Other books you might like:
Nigel Kneale, *Quatermass and the Pit*, 1968
William Relling Jr., *New Moon*, 1988
Robert Weinberg, *The Dead Man's Kiss*, 1992

682
GEOFFREY CAINE

Wake of the Werewolf
(New York: Diamond, 1991)

Story type: Horror (Werewolf Story)
Series: Adventures of Abraham Stroud
Major character(s): Abraham Hale Stroud, Detective—Private, Psychic; Anna Laughing More, Police Officer; John Kerac, Prisoner (escaped convict), Indian
Time period(s): 1990s
Locale(s): Merrimac, Michigan

Summary: In this second adventure of Abraham Stroud, ex-cop turned psychic investigator, the escape from a Michigan penitentiary of an Indian who partially ate his captors brings Stroud into contact with the remains of the Ojibway tribe, who are convinced that the prisoner, John Kerac, has been bitten by an elemental spirit called the Wendigo, and been turned into a shape-shifting monster.

Other books you might like:
Charles L. Grant, *The Nestling*, 1982
T. Chris Martindale, *Where the Chill Waits*, 1991
S.P. Somtow, *Moon Dance*, 1989

683
RICHARD CALDER

Dead Boys
(New York: St. Martin's, 1996)

Story type: Science Fiction (Cyberpunk; Literary)
Series: Dead Girls
Major character(s): Ignatz Zwakh, Addict, Refugee; Vanity, Android (Lilim), Prostitute; Dagon, Android (Elohim), Murderer
Time period(s): 21st century
Locale(s): Bangkok, Thailand; Paris, Mars

Summary: Short-time companion to Primavera, the now-dead android assassin, Ignatz Zwakh wanders Bangkok, sinking into decay. Meanwhile, on Mars, the Elohim and Dead Girls carry on a cladestine war in a strange future where metaphysical viruses corrupt reality.

Other books you might like:
Greg Bear, *Blood Music*, 1985
Philip K. Dick, *Do Androids Dream of Electric Sheep?*, 1965
Elizabeth Hand, *AEstival Tide*, 1992
Jonathan Littell, *Bad Voltage*, 1989
Ian McDonald, *Terminal Cafe*, 1994

684
RICHARD CALDER

Dead Girls
(New York: St. Martin's, 1995)

Story type: Science Fiction (Cyberpunk)
Series: Dead Girls

Major character(s): Ignatz Zwakh, Fugitive; Primavera, Android (Lilim), Murderer; Jack Morganstern, Spy
Time period(s): 21st century
Locale(s): Bangkok, Thailand

Summary: A machine-infected killer in a teenage body, Primavera, and her human lover find themselves set up in an elaborate series of betrayals, part of the dirty politics of a ruined world. To survive, they must crack Primavera's secrets and find their true enemies. First novel.

Other books you might like:
J.G. Ballard, *Hello America*, 1981
Philip K. Dick, *Bladerunner*, 1982
Jonathan Littell, *Bad Voltage*, 1989
Ian McDonald, *Terminal Cafe*, 1994
Amy Thomson, *Virtual Girl*, 1993

`685`

DON CALLANDER

Aquamancer
(New York: Ace, 1993)

Story type: Fantasy (Quest; Magic Conflict)
Series: Pyromancer
Major character(s): Douglas Brightglade, Wizard (journeyman pyromancer), Fiance(e); Myrn Manstar, Apprentice (aquamancer), Fiance(e)
Time period(s): Indeterminate Past
Locale(s): Old Kingdom, Fictional Country; Choin, Fictional Country

Summary: For his required Journeying, Douglas Brightglade receives Master Flarman Flowerstalk's assignment to utilize his craft to investigate a coven of evil witches in the Old Kingdom. When Myrn Manstar grows concerned over the lack of communication from Douglas, Myrn convinces her master to allow her, as apprentice, to follow and help Douglas.

Other books you might like:
Lois McMaster Bujold, *The Spirit Ring*, 1992
Gordon R. Dickson, *The Dragon Knight*, 1990
Alexis A. Gilliland, *Lord of the Troll-Bats*, 1992
Laurell K. Hamilton, *Nightseer*, 1992
Martha Wells, *The Element of Fire*, 1993

`686`

DON CALLANDER

Dragon Companion
(New York: Ace, 1994)

Story type: Fantasy (Alternate World; Adventure)
Major character(s): Tom Whitehead, Librarian, Adventurer; Retruance Constable, Mythical Creature (dragon); Murdan of Overhall, Leader (High Historian)
Time period(s): Indeterminate
Locale(s): Carolna, Fictional Country

Summary: When suddenly transported to another world, Tom Whitehead finds himself befriended by an intelligent dragon and immediately joins Murdan's forces as a Dragon Companion, so proclaimed by Retruance Constable.

Other books you might like:
Gordon R. Dickson, *The Dragon and the George*, 1976
Gordon R. Dickson, *The Dragon at War*, 1992
Anne McCaffrey, *Dragonriders of Pern*, 1988
Christopher Rowley, *Bazil Broketail*, 1992
Lawrence Watt-Evans, *The Blood of a Dragon*, 1991

`687`

DON CALLANDER

Dragon Rescue
(New York: Ace, 1995)

Story type: Fantasy (Adventure; Quest)
Major character(s): Alix Amanda Trusslo, Royalty (princess), Adventurer; Murdan of Overhall, Companion (Arbitrance's); Arbitrance Constable, Mythical Creature (dragon)
Time period(s): Indeterminate
Locale(s): Carolna, Fictional Country

Summary: Arbitrance's family becomes concerned over his ten-year absence, not especially lengthy for the species. When his family and Murdan of Overhall search for Arbitrance, they little expect to find him kidnapping small children to play with them before returning them safely. Sequel to *Dragon Companion*.

Other books you might like:
Gael Baudino, *Duel of Dragons*, 1991
Gordon R. Dickson, *The Dragon and the George*, 1976
Anne McCaffrey, *Dragonriders of Pern*, 1988
Christopher Rowley, *Bazil Broketail*, 1992
Patricia C. Wrede, *Searching for Dragons*, 1991
Laurence Yep, *Dragon of the Lost Sea*, 1982

`688`

DON CALLANDER

Geomancer
(New York: Ace, 1994)

Story type: Fantasy (Magic Conflict)
Series: Pyromancer
Major character(s): Douglas Brightglade, Wizard, Fiance(e); Myrn Manstar, Wizard, Fiance(e); Marbleheart, Animal (sea otter), Companion (wizard's familiar)
Time period(s): Indeterminate Past
Locale(s): Dukedom, Fictional Country; Choin, Fictional Country

Summary: Douglas, Myrn and Marbleheart come to the aid of ensorcelled Stone Warriors, victims of an ancient geomancy. Douglas and Myrn's romance continues as Douglas prepares for the examination which will determine his fitness as Master Wizard.

Other books you might like:
Patricia Briggs, *Masques*, 1993
Douglas W. Clark, *Whirlwind Alchemy*, 1993
Phyllis Eisenstein, *In the Red Lord's Reach*, 1989

Mercedes Lackey, *The Robin and the Kestrel*, 1993
Christopher Stasheff, *The Warlock in Spite of Himself*, 1969

689

DON CALLANDER

Pyromancer

(New York: Ace, 1992)

Story type: Fantasy (Magic Conflict; Quest)
Major character(s): Flarman Flowerstalk, Wizard, Magician; Douglas Brightblade, Apprentice, Teenager; Bryarmote, Mythical Creature (dwarf), Royalty
Time period(s): Indeterminate Past
Locale(s): Wizard's High, Mythical Place

Summary: The owl door knocker recognizes the perfect apprentice and encourages Douglas to apply for the position. After both student and mage sign the contract, Douglas, with the help of the Owl and Blue Tea Kettle, grows to understand the operation of Wizard's High and its interaction with the neighbors and surrounding community. Eventually Douglas' studies might lead to his father, lost at sea and assumed to be dead. Author's first novel.

Other books you might like:
Debra Doyle, *School of Wizardry*, 1990
   James D. Macdonald, co-author
Diane Duane, *So You Want to Be a Wizard?*, 1983
Simon Hawke, *The Reluctant Sorcerer*, 1992
Diana Wynne Jones, *Castle in the Air*, 1991
Meredith Ann Pierce, *The Pearl of the Soul of the World*, 1990
Jane Yolen, *Wizard's Hall*, 1991

690

ITALO CALVINO

Italian Folktales

(New York: Harcourt Brace Jovanovich, 1992)

Story type: Fantasy (Legend; Collection)

Summary: Includes acknowledgements by translator George Martin, an 18-page introduction by Calvino translated by Catherine Hill, 200 folktales selected and retold by Calvino with 43 pages of notes and a five-page bibliography. From all areas having an Italian linguistic base, Calvino chose folktales of every variety including religious and local legends, short stories, animal fables, jokes and anecdotes.

Other books you might like:
Giambattista Basile, *Pentameron or Entertainment for the Little Ones*, 1893
   Sir Richard Burton, translator
Richard Erdoes, *American Indian Myths and Legends*, 1984
   Alfonso Ortiz, co-editor
Charles Perrault, *Complete Fairy Tales*, 1961
   A.E. Johnson, et al., translators
Ethel Johnston Phelps, *Tatterhood and Other Tales*, 1978
   editor
A.K. Ramanujan, *Folktales From India*, 1991
   editor

Moss Roberts, *Chinese Fairy Tales and Fantasies*, 1979
   editor
Jane Yolen, *Favorite Folktales From around the World*, 1986
   editor
Jack Zipes, *Beauties, Beasts and Enchantments*, 1989
   editor
Jack Zipes, *The Brothers Grimm: From Enchanted Forests to the Modern World*, 1988
   editor
Jack Zipes, *Spells of Enchantment*, 1991
   editor

691

ITALO CALVINO

Numbers in the Dark and Other Stories

(New York: Pantheon, 1995)

Story type: Science Fiction (Collection)

Summary: Contains a three-page preface by Esther Calvino and 37 stories, fables, and impossible interviews, 21 written 1943-1958 and 16 written 1968-1984 with several original to this volume. The tone of some stories tends toward horror, but most stories explore the human condition with wry humor and irony using themes which include computer-generated literature, a 35,000-year-old Neanderthal Man, alternate societal structures, the quest for truth, politics, and the results of mindless application of technology. Translated from Italian by Tim Parks.

Other books you might like:
Alfred Bester, *Star Light, Star Bright*, 1976
David G. Hartwell, *The World Treasury of Science Fiction*, 1989
   editor
Stanislaw Lem, *The Cyberiad*, 1974
Stanislaw Lem, *Mortal Engines*, 1977
Cordwainer Smith, *The Rediscovery of Man*, 1993
Marc Stiegler, *The Gentle Seduction*, 1990
Theodore Sturgeon, *E Pluribus Unicorn*, 1953
John Varley, *Blue Champagne*, 1986
Kurt Vonnegut Jr., *Welcome to the Monkey House*, 1968

692

RAMSEY CAMPBELL

Alone with the Horrors

(Sauk City, Wisconsin: Arkham House, 1993)

Story type: Horror (Collection)

Summary: The 39 stories in this book are presented as the best short fiction from the first 30 years of work by the best living writer of horror fiction. Included are homages to the work of H.P. Lovecraft ("The Room in the Castle," "Cold Print"), tales of urban horror ("The Depths," "Mackintosh Willy"), gruesome tales in the E.C. comics tradition ("Call First," "Heading Home"), stories of erotic terror ("Loveman's Comeback") and cosmic horror ("The Voice of the Beach"), and stories that demonstrate how humor and horror are simply opposite sides of the same coin ("Seeing the World," "End of the Line''). This book is an indispensable cornerstone of any weird fiction library.

Other books you might like:
Robert Aickman, *The Wine-Dark Sea*, 1988
T.E.D. Klein, *Dark Gods*, 1985
Thomas Ligotti, *Songs of a Dead Dreamer*, 1990

693
RAMSEY CAMPBELL

Ancient Images
(New York: Scribner's, 1989)

Story type: Horror (Mystery)
Major character(s): Sandy Allen, Television (film editor); Roger Stone, Historian (film historian)
Time period(s): 1980s
Locale(s): London, England (Suburb of Redfield)

Summary: Following the mysterious death of a friend, Allen searches for *Tower of Fear*, a long suppressed Karloff/Lugosi film that reveals a terrible secret about the aristocratic Redfield family.

Other books you might like:
Edmund Copper, *The Amber Print*, 1973
Edmund Copper, *From Evil's Pillow*, 1973
Robin Hardy, *The Wicker Man*, 1978

694
RAMSEY CAMPBELL

The Count of Eleven
(New York: Tor, 1992)

Story type: Horror (Serial Killer)
Major character(s): Jack Orchard, Businessman (video salesman); Julia Orchard, Computer Expert (programmer), Spouse (Jack's wife); Laura Orchard, Child (Jack and Julia's daughter)
Time period(s): 1990s (1990)
Locale(s): Liverpool, England

Summary: In bad need of good luck after his video store burns down, amateur numerologist Jack Orchard receives a chain letter promising him improved luck if only he will help maintain the chain. When his luck fails to improve, Jack takes it upon himself to force other recipients of the letter to keep the chain going under penalty of death. Originally published in England in 1991.

Other books you might like:
Ken Greenhall, *Deathchain*, 1991
Ruby Jean Jensen, *Chain Letter*, 1987

695
RAMSEY CAMPBELL, Editor

Deathport
(New York: Pocket, 1993)

Story type: Horror (Anthology)

Summary: This third anthology of stories by members of the Horror Writers of America collects 28 tales centered around the Dry Plains International Airport in Texas, each chronicling a strange event attributable to the airport's being built over an Indian burial ground. Les Daniels' ''The Man in the Mirror'' and Dan Perez's ''The Smoking Mirror'' both deal with the revenge of Aztec warriors on visitors to the airport, and Chet Williamson's ''Scalps'' with the strange effect the airport's atmosphere has on a serial killer. Ron Dee and P.D. Cacek's ''Jet Lag'' imagines a unique way to refuel airplanes, and Lawrence Watt-Evans' ''Beneath the Tarmac'' tells of a monster living under the airport runway.

Other books you might like:
Robert R. McCammon, *Under the Fang*, 1991
  editor
F. Paul Wilson, *Freak Show*, 1992
  editor

696
RAMSEY CAMPBELL

Demons by Daylight
(New York: Carroll and Graf, 1990)

Story type: Horror (Collection)

Summary: Fifteen stories divided into three sections: ''Nightmares,'' ''Errol Undercliffe: a Tribute,'' and ''Relationships.'' Except for the Lovecraftian Undercliffe pieces, the stories are characterized by vivid dramatic vignettes, extreme compression, suppressed or nonexistent transitions, and a blurring of the lines between the rational and the insane, and the real and the nightmarish. Noteworthy stories include ''Potential,'' in which a conventional man's dark potential is unleashed, ''The Sentinenals,'' about a sinister group of rocks which may or may not come to life, and ''The Telephones,'' a sexually charged doppelganger story. Originally published in 1973.

Other books you might like:
Clive Barker, *Books of Blood Series*, 1984-1985

697
RAMSEY CAMPBELL

Far Away and Never
(West Warwick, Rhode Island: Necronomicon Press, 1996)

Story type: Horror (Collection)

Summary: The complete sword and sorcery fiction of an author better known as a writer of contemporary urban horror totals seven dark tales of magic and mystery. Six are set on the planet Tond, and four of these feature the heroic warrior Ryre, who battles a sentient plant in ''The Sustenance of Hoak,'' a man who steals identities in ''The Changer of Names,'' winged monsters in ''The Pit of Wings,'' and a man-eating cavern in ''The Mouths of Light.'' Included as well is ''The Ways of Chaos,'' a previously unpublished chapter written for the round-robin novel *Genseric's Fifth-Born Son*, written in the 1970s and based on a fragment left by Robert E. Howard at his death. The author supplies an introduction.

Other books you might like:
David Drake, *Vettius and His Friends*, 1989
Robert E. Howard, *Solomon Kane*, 1995
Brian Lumley, *Iced on Aran and Other Dream Quests*, 1992
Michael Shea, *Nifft the Lean*, 1982
Karl Edward Wagner, *The Book of Kane*, 1985

698

RAMSEY CAMPBELL

The Influence
(New York: Tor, 1989)

Story type: Horror (Possession)
Major character(s): Rowan, Child (seven year old girl); Queenie, Spirit (Rowan's deceased aunt)
Time period(s): 1980s
Locale(s): Mount Pleasant, England (A suburb of London)

Summary: After Queenie leaves her house to her niece, Alisoun, strange things begin happening, especially to Alisoun's daughter, Rowan. Is Queenie's spirit, as personified in Vicky, a mysterious little girl, animating the house and threatening to possess Rowan?

Other books you might like:
Thomas Tessier, *Phantom*, 1982

699

RAMSEY CAMPBELL

The Long Lost
(New York: Tor Books, 1994)

Story type: Horror (Wild Talents)
Major character(s): David Owain, Businessman (owner of a home repair company); Joelle Owain, Businesswoman (David's wife and partner); Gwendolyn Owain, Aged Person
Time period(s): 1990s (1994)
Locale(s): Chester, England

Summary: While on holiday in Wales, David and Joelle Owain encounter Gwendolyn, an old woman living by herself on an island off the coast who claims to be a distant relative. When they bring Gwendolyn back with them to stay in Chester, her presence ignites tensions that have been simmering beneath the town's placid social veneer, turning neighbors against one another and leaving the reader to wonder exactly who Gendolyn really is. This book was first published in England in 1993.

Other books you might like:
Douglas Clegg, *Goat Dance*, 1989
Stephen King, *Needful Things*, 1991
Elizabeth Massie, *Sineater*, 1992

700

RAMSEY CAMPBELL

Midnight Sun
(New York: Tor, 1991)

Story type: Horror (Ancient Evil Unleashed)
Major character(s): Ben Sterling, Writer (Ellen's husband); Ellen Sterling, Artist (book illustrator); Johnny Sterling, Child (Ben and Ellen's son)
Time period(s): 1990s
Locale(s): Yorkshire, England

Summary: Orphaned while a young boy, Ben Sterling is raised by his aunt at his family's ancestral home. It was here that Ben's great grandfather returned from the Arctic years before, and died under mysterious circumstances no one wishes to discuss. When Ben inherits the estate years later, he discovers the secret of what his grandfather instilled in the surrounding Sterling Forest, and the terrible sacrifice he and his family will be forced to make if they are to keep it from running amok.

Other books you might like:
Douglas Clegg, *Goat Dance*, 1989
T.E.D. Klein, *The Ceremonies*, 1984
Graham Masterton, *The Manitou*, 1975
Thomas Tryon, *Harvest Home*, 1973

701

RAMSEY CAMPBELL

The One Safe Place
(New York: Tor, 1996)

Story type: Horror (Psychological Suspense)
Major character(s): Susanne Travis, Teacher; Marshall Travis, Child (Susanne's 12-year-old son); Darren Fancy, Child (12-year-old)
Time period(s): 1990s (1996)
Locale(s): Manchester, England

Summary: A minor altercation between lowlife criminal Phil Fancy and bookseller Don Travis leads to Don's death and the Fancy family terrorizing the Travises. Most of this scathing critique of the modern judicial system's blindness chronicles the kidnapping of 12-year-old Marshall Travis by Phil Fancy's son, Darren, and the torments Darren subjects Marshall to in order to win the esteem of his family. This novel was published in England in 1995.

Other books you might like:
Anthony Burgess, *A Clockwork Orange*, 1962
William Golding, *Lord of the Flies*, 1954
K.W. Jeter, *The Night Man*, 1989
Joe R. Lansdale, *The Nightrunners*, 1987
Patrick McCabe, *The Butcher Boy*, 1992

702

RAMSEY CAMPBELL

The Parasite

(New York: Tor, 1989)

Story type: Horror (Possession)

Major character(s): Rose Tierney, Critic (film reviewer), Psychic; Peter Grace, Spirit (black magician)

Time period(s): 1980s

Locale(s): New York, New York; Munich, Germany; Liverpool, England

Summary: After a mugging releases latent psychic abilities, Rose finds herself endangered by strange external and internal forces: a mysterious baldheaded man, a sinister psychiatrist, occultists, hallucinations, frightening out-of-body trips, and, most scary, an internal ''parasite'' which may be the spirit of Peter Grace, a deceased black magician. Originally published in 1980.

Other books you might like:
Ira Levin, *Rosemary's Baby*, 1967

703

RAMSEY CAMPBELL

Strange Things and Stranger Places

(New York: Tor, 1993)

Story type: Horror (Collection)

Summary: This book collects 10 hitherto uncollected stories, including the haunted house tale ''Cat and Mouse''; the science fiction novella, ''Medusa''; several homages to the E.C. horror comics including ''Wrapped Up'' and ''Rising Generation''; two stories that take place in carnival fairgrounds, ''Little Man,'' and ''The Next Sideshow''; and the profoundly disturbing novella, ''Needing Ghosts,'' about a man's tenuous grip on reality. The author supplies an introduction on the origins of the stories.

Other books you might like:
Robert Aickman, *The Wine-Dark Sea*, 1988
Dennis Etchison, *The Dark Country*, 1982
T.E.D. Klein, *Dark Gods*, 1985
Thomas Ligotti, *Grimscribe: His Lives and Works*, 1992
Thomas Ligotti, *Songs of a Dead Dreamer*, 1990

704

RAMSEY CAMPBELL

Two Obscure Tales

(West Warwick, Rhode Island: Necronomicon Press, 1993)

Story type: Horror (Collection)

Summary: As the title implies, these are two somewhat opaque stories, written in the early 1970s when the author was establishing a trademark style of ambiguity that would distinguish the stories of his groundbreaking collection *Demons by Daylight*. ''The Void'' concerns a car accident victim trying to sort out his life after the trauma. ''The Urge'' records an encounter between a writer and a young man who discuss their different metaphysical approaches to life. Campbell has supplied an amusing introduction.

Other books you might like:
Robert Aickman, *The Wine-Dark Sea*, 1988
Dennis Etchison, *The Dark Country*, 1982
Thomas Ligotti, *Songs of a Dead Dreamer*, 1990

705

RAMSEY CAMPBELL

Waking Nightmares

(New York: Tor, 1991)

Story type: Horror (Collection)

Summary: Nineteen stories by the master of implied (but nonetheless gruesome) horror. Stories range in approach from ''The Guide,'' an homage to the subtle fiction of M.R. James, to ''It Helps if You Sing,'' a grisly satire on religious fundamentalism. There is one ingenious vampire tale (''Jack in the Box'') and two stories concerned with one of Campbell's favorite themes, the relation of fiction to life: ''Meeting the Author'' and ''Next Time You'll Know Me.''

Other books you might like:
Robert Aickman, *The Wine-Dark Sea*, 1988
Dennis Etchison, *The Dark Country*, 1987
Thomas Ligotti, *Grimscribe: His Lives and Works*, 1992
Thomas Ligotti, *Songs of a Dead Dreamer*, 1989
T.E.D. Klein, *Dark Gods*, 1985

706

MARK CANTER

Ember From the Sun

(New York: Delacorte, 1996)

Story type: Science Fiction (Mystical; Science Fiction)

Major character(s): Yute Nahadeh, Anthropologist (paleoanthropologist), Indian (Caiyuh); Ember Ozette, Prehistoric Human (Neanderthal), Psychic (healer); Nika Nahadeh, Psychic, Relative (sister)

Time period(s): 1990s

Locale(s): Whaler Bay, Washington; Kantishna Hills, Alaska

Summary: A bookworm from early childhood, Yute never learns the ways of his people. While documenting his father's hunting with primitive weapons, Yute spends the night in an ice cave and discovers a frozen, pregnant Neanderthal woman whose embryo, implanted in a surrogate mother, becomes a Neanderthal infant. Visions compel an older Ember Ozette to search for the last survivors of her race, who are now facing genocide. First novel.

Other books you might like:
Michael Armstrong, *Agviq*, 1990
Jean M. Auel, *Clan of the Cave Bear*, 1980
Kathleen O'Neal Gear, *Song of the Wolf*, 1992
    W. Michael Gear, co-author
Sue Harrison, *Mother Earth, Father Sky*, 1990
Jack McDevitt, *Ancient Shores*, 1996

707

LISA CANTRELL

Boneman

(New York: Tor, 1992)

Story type: Horror (Mystery; Reanimated Dead)
Major character(s): J. J. Coley, Journalist; Dallas Reid, Detective—Police; Jackie Swann, Detective—Police
Time period(s): 1990s (1992)
Locale(s): Phoenix City, North Carolina

Summary: When a group of murderous, seemingly indestructible Haitian drug dealers begin taking over the narcotics trade in Phoenix City, rumors begin circulating that they are the zombie minions of a legendary supernatural bogeyman known as ''The Boneman.''

Other books you might like:
Hugh B. Cave, *Disciples of Dread*, 1988
K.W. Jeter, *Wolf Flow*, 1992
David J. Schow, *The Shaft*, 1990
Robert Weinberg, *The Black Lodge*, 1991

708

LISA CANTRELL

The Ridge

(New York: Tor, 1989)

Story type: Horror (Literary)
Major character(s): Nick Vear, Spy (Government hit-man); Sara Vear, Child (Vear's catatonic daughter)
Time period(s): 1980s
Locale(s): North Carolina

Summary: In the Ridge, an old house atop a cliff, four of five people—Vear's ex-wife's family—die mysteriously, the sole survivor being Vear's catatonic seven year old daughter, Sara. The search for the killer leads Vear into conflicts with the police, the mob, his ex-wife's family, Sara, and, finally, with an ancient, malevolent power that could threaten mankind.

Other books you might like:
John Farris, *The Fury*, 1977

709

LISA CANTRELL

Torments

(New York: Tor, 1990)

Story type: Horror (Haunted House)
Major character(s): Vince Colletti, Businessman; Sonny O'Hara, Businessman (construction consultant); Jennifer Clark, Artist (interior designer)
Time period(s): 1980s (1989)
Locale(s): Merrillville, North Carolina

Summary: In this sequel to the author's Bram Stoker Award-winning first novel, *The Manse*, the destruction of Merrillville's haunted house appears to have had little effect on the supernatural influence that pervades its grounds. The condo-miniums erected on the old site are plagued with mysterious construction problems, the dead are walking once more, and the survivors of the conflagration that consumed the old mansion are being summoned home to confront the fate they barely escaped two years before.

Other books you might like:
Tom Elliott, *The Dwelling*, 1989
Shirley Jackson, *The Haunting of Hill House*, 1959

710

KAREL CAPEK

War With the Newts

(Highland Park: Catbird Press, 1990)

Story type: Science Fiction (Literary)
Major character(s): Van Toch, Explorer (Captain); Bondy, Businessman
Time period(s): 1930s
Locale(s): Prague (The Dutch East Indies)

Summary: Captain Van Toch has discovered a rare form of intelligent salamander and offers to provide them to the capitalist Bondy to sell as servants and proletarian workers. Equipped with tools and weapons, however, the salamanders soon multiply enormously and eventually take over the world. Originally published in 1936.

Other books you might like:
Eleanor Arnason, *To the Resurrection Station*, 1986
David Brin, *Startide Rising*, 1983
David Brin, *The Uplift War*, 1987
John Brunner, *Children of the Thunder*, 1989
Clifford D. Simak, *City*, 1952
H.G. Wells, *The Food of the Gods*, 1904
H.G. Wells, *The Island of Doctor Moreau*, 1896

711

MICHAEL CAPOBIANCO

Burster

(New York: Bantam Spectra, 1990)

Story type: Science Fiction (Generation Starship; Space Colony)
Major character(s): Peter Zolotin, Student—Graduate, Spaceman; Traveler, Artificial Intelligence; Eugenia Taranga, Spaceship Captain
Time period(s): 23rd century
Locale(s): *Asia*, Spaceship; *Quiet Earth*, Spaceship; Mars

Summary: Starship Asia, 14 years out on its colonizing mission in the Epsilon Indi system, scans a burst of radiation near Sol. At the same time, all communications with Earth are cut off. Peter Zolotin is chosen to journey back to Earth to ascertain its fate with the aid of Traveler, an advanced artificial intelligence system designed to gather data and which also has a sentient personality. While Peter is gone, Captain Taranga and the scientists on *Asia* argue bitterly about what type of planet will best support life while mutiny is swiftly forming.

Other books you might like:
David Brin, *The Uplift War*, 1987
Octavia E. Butler, *Imago*, 1989
Octavia E. Butler, *Mind of My Mind*, 1977
Octavia E. Butler, *Wild Seed*, 1980
David R. Palmer, *Emergence*, 1984
Alis A. Rasmussen, *A Passage of Stars*, 1990
Alis A. Rasmussen, *The Price of Ransom*, 1990
Alis A. Rasmussen, *Revolution's Shore*, 1990

▮**712**

MARY CARAKER

The Faces of Ceti
(Boston: Houghton Miflin, 1991)

Story type: Science Fiction (First Contact; Young Adult)
Major character(s): Maya Gart, Teenager, Settler; Brock Magnus, Teenager, Settler; Carlos Vega, Leader, Settler
Time period(s): 22nd century
Locale(s): Ceti, Planet—Imaginary (Tau Ceti System)

Summary: Maya Gart, a nonconformist among colonists settling the Tau Ceti System, ends up on Ceti where the plant life is poisonous. Only the Hlur, animals who may be sentient, are edible. The Arcadian leader demands that Cetians contribute more to the common cause or go without supplies. Maya and Brock then take a trip in which they contact the Hlur and learn how to make the plant life nutritious. They find many surprises on their return.

Other books you might like:
Eleanor Arnason, *A Woman of the Iron People*, 1990
F.M. Busby, *Rebel's Seed*, 1986
Janet Kagan, *Hellspark*, 1988
Garry Kilworth, *The Night of Kadar*, 1980
Ursula K. Le Guin, *The Eye of the Heron*, 1983
Larry Niven, *A Gift from Earth*, 1968

▮**713**

MARY CARAKER

The Snows of Jaspre
(Boston: Houghton Mifflin, 1989)

Story type: Science Fiction (Young Adult)
Major character(s): Anders Ahlwen, Psychic; Morgan Farraday, Administrator (School administrator)
Time period(s): 24th century
Locale(s): Jaspre, Planet—Imaginary

Summary: Morgan Farraday and her daughter Dee, new settlers on the icy planet Jaspre, face difficulties on a colonial world, not the least of which is the charismatic Anders Ahlwen, leader of a group of psychics who live in a mysterious city under the ice.

Other books you might like:
Clare Bell, *People of the Sky*, 1989
Jo Dereske, *The Lone Sentinel*, 1989
H.M. Hoover, *The Bell Tree*, 1982
H.M. Hoover, *Children of Morrow*, 1973
H.M. Hoover, *Treasures of Morrow*, 1976

▮**714**

JACK CARAVELA

The Gifted
(New York: Zebra, 1991)

Story type: Horror (Wild Talents)
Major character(s): Rob Endicott, Telepath, Worker (gas station attendant); Tom Naufts, Criminal (assassin), Telepath; Brian Corman, Businessman (head of the Alliance)
Time period(s): 1990s
Locale(s): Mesa, New Mexico

Summary: Paranormally endowed with the telepathic power to read and influence minds, Rob Endicott flees his foster father, Brian Corman, who hopes to train him to kill people with thoughts and serve as a secret weapon for the shadowy business consortium known as the Alliance. Not easily thwarted, Corman sends telepath assassin Tom Naufts to track Rob down.

Other books you might like:
John Arbucci, *Blood of Innocents*, 1991
John Farris, *The Fury*, 1976
Stephen King, *Firestarter*, 1980
Jack Martin, *Scanners*, 1981

▮**715**

ORSON SCOTT CARD

Alvin Journeyman
(New York: Tor, 1995)

Story type: Fantasy (Psychic Powers; Historical)
Series: Tales of Alvin Maker
Major character(s): Alvin Maker, Blacksmith (journeyman), Psychic (maker); Margaret "Peggy" Larner, Psychic (torch), Activist (anti-slavery); Calvin Miller, Psychic (criminal), Relative (Alvin's brother)
Time period(s): Indeterminate
Locale(s): Alternate Earth

Summary: To build the city of his vision and help preserve peace in the spreading colonies, Alvin must defeat his ancient enemy, the Unmaker, whose deadly plots have threatened Alvin's life at every turn. Alvin and his young friend, Arthur Stuart, flee a false scandal in Vigor Church and travel to Hatrack River, only to find that the Unmaker has already spread lies and accusations through the hearts of those ready to believe them. While Alvin stands trial for his life in the town of his apprenticeship, his jealous brother, Calvin, hones his own particular talents to bring about Alvin's downfall.

Other books you might like:
Jean M. Auel, *Clan of the Cave Bear*, 1990
Octavia E. Butler, *Wild Seed*, 1980
William Sarabande, *The Edge of the World*, 1993
Harry Turtledove, *The Guns of the South*, 1992
Paul O. Williams, *The Breaking of Northwall*, 1981

716
ORSON SCOTT CARD
The Call of Earth
(New York: Tor, 1993)

Story type: Science Fiction (Political)
Series: Homecoming
Major character(s): Rasa, Teacher, Parent; Vozmuzhalnoy "Moozh" Vozmozho, Military Personnel (General); Nafai, Teenager
Time period(s): Indeterminate Future
Locale(s): Harmony, Planet—Imaginary

Summary: While General Vozmuzhalnoy Vozmozho attacks Basilica, hoping to marry influentially to keep his conquest as bloodless as possible, Nafai, led by the Oversoul, gathers a group of men and their wives in preparation for the journey to Earth.

Other books you might like:
Piers Anthony, *If I Pay Thee Not in Gold*, 1993
    Mercedes Lackey, co-author
Isaac Asimov, *Foundation and Earth*, 1986
John Brunner, *Catch a Falling Star*, 1968
Raymond Harris, *Shadows of the White Sun*, 1988
Colin Kapp, *The Wizard of Anharitte*, 1973
Michael McCollum, *Antares Dawn*, 1986
Melissa Scott, *Five-Twelfths of Heaven*, 1985
Robert Silverberg, *Lord Valentine's Castle*, 1980
Clifford D. Simak, *A Heritage of Stars*, 1977

717
ORSON SCOTT CARD
Children of the Mind
(New York: Tor, 1996)

Story type: Science Fiction (Family Saga; First Contact)
Series: Ender Wiggin
Major character(s): Jane, Artificial Intelligence, Deity; Peter Wiggin, Reincarnated Person; Malu, Philosopher, Deity
Time period(s): Indeterminate Future
Locale(s): Lusitania, Planet—Imaginary; Pacifica, Planet—Imaginary

Summary: Joining his wife in seclusion, Ender loses interest in young Val, giving Jane permission to take Val's body if she can. With the Starways Congress shutting down all ansibles and computers to eliminate her, Jane needs a new place to stay in order to continue the rescue of the Hive Queen and the pequeninos before the fleet can destroy Lusitania and all its residents. As the descolada virus no longer poses a risk to the human race, Jane continues to move ships instantaneously, dispersing the Buggers and Piggies to many planets, preventing another xenocide. Direct sequel to *Xenocide*.

Other books you might like:
Glen Cook, *The Dragon Never Sleeps*, 1988
Dan Simmons, *The Fall of Hyperion*, 1989
Sheri S. Tepper, *Grass*, 1989
Jack Vance, *Alastor*, 1995
Vernor Vinge, *A Fire upon the Deep*, 1992

718
ORSON SCOTT CARD
Earthborn
(New York: Tor, 1995)

Story type: Science Fiction (Political; Theological)
Series: Homecoming
Major character(s): Akma, Rebel (heretic), Abuse Victim; Shedemei, Historian, Immortal; Edhadeya, Royalty (princess), Teacher
Time period(s): Indeterminate Future
Locale(s): Darakemba, Fictional Country; Chelem, Fictional Country

Summary: After 500 years on Earth, the descendants of Nafai and Elemak continue their progenitors' feud, as Shedemei's search for Earth's guardian computer to aid Oversoul seems fruitless. Akma's disbelief in Oversoul and influence over others may catalyze a revolution if Shedemei cannot effect a repair. Fifth, concluding volume in the series, which is based on *The Book of Mormon*.

Other books you might like:
Brian W. Aldiss, *Helliconia Summer*, 1983
Poul Anderson, *The Boat of a Million Years*, 1989
Lloyd Biggle, *Monument*, 1974
James Blish, *Midsummer Century*, 1972
Robert Silverberg, *At Winter's End*, 1988
Clifford D. Simak, *The Fellowship of the Talisman*, 1978
Jack Vance, *The Brave Free Men*, 1973

719
ORSON SCOTT CARD
Earthfall
(New York: Tor, 1995)

Story type: Science Fiction (Family Saga; First Contact)
Series: Homecoming
Major character(s): Nafai, Leader, Spaceship Captain (navigator); Elemak, Linguist, Renegade; Oykib, Teacher, Telepath
Time period(s): Indeterminate Future
Locale(s): Harmony, Planet—Imaginary; Outer Space; Earth

Summary: During the long space voyage to Earth to find help for the ailing Oversoul, political machinations continue until Elemak and Nafai suspend their struggle pending their father's death. On Earth they find two mutated, inimical symbiotic species, winged angels and subterranean diggers. While Elemak allies the diggers to his cause against Nafai, Nafai leads away all who wish to join him in founding a community where all three species will live peacefully. Fourth in the series, which is based on *The Book of Mormon*.

Other books you might like:
Isaac Asimov, *Foundation and Earth*, 1986
Ben Bova, *As on a Darkling Plain*, 1972
John Brunner, *Catch a Falling Star*, 1968
John Dalmas, *Homecoming*, 1984
Harry Harrison, *Return to Eden*, 1988
Clifford D. Simak, *Cemetery World*, 1973

Brian Stableford, *The Castaways of Tanagar*, 1981

720

ORSON SCOTT CARD

The Folk of the Fringe

(West Bloomfield, Michigan: Phantasia Press, 1989)

Story type: Science Fiction (Post-Nuclear Holocaust)
Major character(s): Jamie Teague, Adventurer; Herman Deaver, Religious
Time period(s): 21st century
Locale(s): Utah

Summary: This series of five interconnected stories, which originally appeared between 1985 and 1987 in *Isaac Asimov's Science Fiction Magazine* and elsewhere, tells the story of a loosely-knit group of survivors of a nuclear war, and the gradual growth of a Mormon nation on the shores of Great Salt Lake.

Other books you might like:
Neal Barrett Jr., *Dawn's Uncertain Light*, 1989
Neal Barrett Jr., *Through Darkest America*, 1987
David Brin, *The Postman*, 1985
Edgar Pangborn, *The Company of Glory*, 1975
Edgar Pangborn, *Davy*, 1964
Edgar Pangborn, *The Judgment of Eve*, 1966

721

ORSON SCOTT CARD, Editor

Future on Fire

(New York: Tor, 1991)

Story type: Science Fiction (Anthology)
Time period(s): Indeterminate Future

Summary: This collection of 15 stories from the 1980s, each briefly introduced by Orson Scott Card, contains an 11-page introduction in which he explains that the stories selected are not necessarily comfortable to read, but are important and wonderful. Among the authors included are Michael Bishop, Pat Cadigan, James Patrick Kelly, Ursula K. Le Guin, Pat Murphy, Kim Stanley Robinson, Lucius Shepard, Bruce Sterling and Connie Willis.

Other books you might like:
Lou Aronica, *Full Spectrum*, 1988
    Shawna McCarthy, co-editor
Michael Bishop, *Nebula Awards 24*, 1990
    editor
Gardner Dozois, *The Year's Best Science Fiction: Seventh Annual Collection*, 1990
    editor
David G. Hartwell, *The World Treasury of Science Fiction*, 1989
    editor
Kristine Kathryn Rusch, *Pulphouse, Issue 8: Science Fiction*, 1990
    editor

Donald A. Wollheim, *The 1990 Annual World's Best Science Fiction*, 1990
Arthur W. Saha, co-editor

722

ORSON SCOTT CARD

Lost Boys

(New York: HarperCollins, 1992)

Story type: Fantasy (Contemporary Realism; Religious)
Major character(s): Step Fletcher, Computer Expert, Religious (Mormon); Stevie Fletcher, Child; DeAnne Fletcher, Housewife
Time period(s): 1980s (1983)
Locale(s): Steuben, North Carolina

Summary: When Step and DeAnne Fletcher move with their three children to Steuben, North Carolina, their withdrawn eight-year-old Stevie becomes sensitive to the presence of "the lost boys" — the ghosts of townschildren who died at the hands of a murderer who now appears to be stalking Stevie. This novel is an expansion of the author's controversial 1989 short story of the same name.

Other books you might like:
Douglas Bell, *Mojo and the Pickle Jar*, 1991
Alan Dean Foster, *Cyber Way*, 1990
Katharine Kerr, *Polar City Blues*, 1990
Mercedes Lackey, *Children of the Night*, 1990
Elizabeth Ann Scarborough, *Nothing Sacred*, 1991
Kate Wilhelm, *Death Qualified: A Mystery of Chaos*, 1991

723

ORSON SCOTT CARD
KATHRYN H. KIDD, Co-Author

Lovelock

(New York: Tor, 1994)

Story type: Science Fiction (Political; Science Fiction)
Series: Mayflower Trilogy
Major character(s): Lovelock, Animal (capuchin monkey), Genetically Altered Being; Carol Jeanne Cocciolone, Scientist (Gaiologist), Genius; Redmond "Red" Eugene Todd, Spouse, Psychologist
Time period(s): 21st century
Locale(s): *Ark*, Spaceship (Mayflower Village)

Summary: As witness for Carol Jeanne, Lovelock accompanies her and her dysfunctional family on the *Ark* where Carol Jeanne, Chief Gaiologist, plans for the safety and health of the colony. The stress of changes brought about by the move to the *Ark* and small town life aboard it force Lovelock to recognize that although his enhanced intelligence permits him to effectively complement Carol Jeanne, his conditioning and lack of speech make him only a tool or a slave, rather than a beloved friend as he previously believed.

Other books you might like:
David Brin, *Startide Rising*, 1983
Thomas A. Easton, *Sparrowhawk*, 1990
James H. Schmitz, *The Demon Breed*, 1968

Joan Slonczewski, *Daughter of Elysium*, 1993
Cordwainer Smith, *The Best of Cordwainer Smith*, 1975
Amy Thomson, *Virtual Girl*, 1993
Vernor Vinge, *A Fire upon the Deep*, 1992
Gene Wolfe, *Nightside the Long Sun*, 1993

724

ORSON SCOTT CARD

Maps in a Mirror
(New York: Tor, 1990)

Story type: Horror (Collection)

Summary: A mammoth collection of 46 fantasy, horror, and science fiction stories by one of the most important writers of imaginative fiction to emerge in the 1980s. Of particular interest are ''Lost Boys,'' a poignant tale of a young boy's alienation from his family; ''Fat Farm,'' about a unique weight loss program; ''Deep Breathing Exercises,'' in which a man develops an uncanny ability to predict when disaster will strike; and ''Memories of My Head,'' the one story original to the volume, in which a suicide pens his farewell note *after* his death.

Other books you might like:
Ray Bradbury, *The Stories of Ray Bradbury*, 1980
Fritz Leiber, *The Leiber Chronicles*, 1989
Harlan Ellison, *The Essential Ellison: A 35-Year Retrospective*, 1987

725

ORSON SCOTT CARD

The Memory of Earth
(New York: Tor, 1992)

Story type: Science Fiction (Space Colony; Political)
Series: Homecoming
Major character(s): Nafai, Student, Child; Rasa, Teacher, Parent; Volemak, Leader, Parent
Time period(s): Indeterminate Future
Locale(s): Harmony, Planet—Imaginary

Summary: For 40 million years the Oversoul, an artificial intelligence located in orbit above the planet of Harmony, has banned advanced technology to prevent the catastrophies that had destroyed humanity on Earth. Now, needing repair, the Oversoul decides to speak through visions and dreams to those most sensitive to its communications so that they can learn about space travel and bring the Oversoul to interface with the Keeper of Earth.

Other books you might like:
Isaac Asimov, *Foundation*, 1951
Marion Zimmer Bradley, *Two to Conquer*, 1980
C.J. Cherryh, *Angel with the Sword*, 1985
C.J. Cherryh, *Forty Thousand in Gehenna*, 1983
Robert A. Heinlein, *The Moon Is a Harsh Mistress*, 1966
Anne McCaffrey, *Dragonflight*, 1968

726

ORSON SCOTT CARD

Pastwatch: The Redemption of Christopher Columbus
(New York: Tor, 1996)

Story type: Science Fiction (Time Travel; Alternate History)
Major character(s): Diko, Time Traveller; Hunahpu Matamoros, Time Traveller; Christopher Columbus, Historical Figure, Explorer
Time period(s): 22nd century; 15th century (1492-1493)
Locale(s): Africa; Hispaniola, Caribbean

Summary: On an ecologically devastated Earth, a small group of Time Watchers records history. In researching Columbus, they discover changes in the past and decide to go back in time to try to mold a new history.

Other books you might like:
Kevin J. Anderson, *The Trinity Paradox*, 1991
  Doug Beason, co-author
Poul Anderson, *The Shield of Time*, 1990
Ben Bova, *Triumph*, 1993
Jack L. Chalker, *Downtiming the Night Side*, 1985
L. Sprague de Camp, *Lest Darkness Fall*, 1941
Michael Flynn, *In the Country of the Blind*, 1990
Crawford Kilian, *The Empire of Time*, 1978
Robert Charles Wilson, *Mysterium*, 1994

727

ORSON SCOTT CARD

Prentice Alvin
(New York: Tor Books, 1989)

Story type: Fantasy (Magic Conflict)
Series: Tales of Alvin Maker
Major character(s): Alvin Miller Jr., Apprentice; Peggy Guester, Mythical Creature (A Torch)
Time period(s): Indeterminate
Locale(s): Alternate Earth

Summary: Alvin returns to his birthplace to become a blacksmith's apprentice. With the help of the Torch, Peggy, he will also learn to become a Maker.

Other books you might like:
Stephen R. Donaldson, *Chronicles of Thomas Covenant*,
Mark Helprin, *Winter's Tale*, 1983
Tom Reamy, *Blind Voices*, 1978
Bob Skimin, *Gray Victory*, 1988

728

ORSON SCOTT CARD

The Ships of Earth
(New York: Tor, 1994)

Story type: Science Fiction (Alternate Intelligence; Family Saga)
Series: Homecoming

Major character(s): Nafai, Student, Hunter; Elemak, Leader, Rogue; Luet, Psychic, Spouse
Time period(s): Indeterminate Future
Locale(s): Harmony, Planet—Imaginary

Summary: Exiled to the desert, the descendants of Rasa and Volemak must travel to find the port of embarkation to Earth. Elemak, the oldest, resents Nafai, seeing him as a threat to his leadership, but also fears the protection the Oversoul gives Nafai. Inevitable conflict between the two follows when Nafai penetrates the ancient starport and becomes Starmaster.

Other books you might like:
Ben Bova, *As on a Darkling Plain*, 1972
Paula E. Downing, *Rinn's Star*, 1990
Cynthia Felice, *Double Nocturne*, 1986
William R. Forstchen, *Ice Prophet*, 1983
H. Beam Piper, *The Cosmic Computer*, 1964
Melissa Scott, *Five-Twelfths of Heaven*, 1985
Cordwainer Smith, *Quest of the Three Worlds*, 1966
Jack Vance, *Big Planet*, 1957
James White, *The Dream Millennium*, 1974

729

ORSON SCOTT CARD

Treasure Box

(New York: HarperCollins, 1996)

Story type: Horror (Witchcraft)
Major character(s): Quentin Fears, Computer Expert; Sally Sannazarro, Nurse; Mike Bolt, Police Officer (chief)
Time period(s): 1990s (1996)
Locale(s): Mixinick, New York; Washington, District of Columbia

Summary: Quentin Fears discovers that his wife Madeleine and her entire extended family are all phantoms created by a young witch who hopes to trick Quentin into opening a magic box. This will release a creature that will increase her supernatural powers at the expense of Quentin's life.

Other books you might like:
Ramsey Campbell, *Incarnate*, 1983
Jonathan Carroll, *A Child Across the Sky*, 1988
Jonathan Carroll, *From the Teeth of Angels*, 1994
Mark A. Clements, *The Land of Nod*, 1995
Lisa Tuttle, *Pillow Friend*, 1996

730

ORSON SCOTT CARD

Xenocide

(New York: Tor, 1991)

Story type: Science Fiction (Space Colony; Theological)
Series: Ender Wiggin
Major character(s): Andrew Wiggin, Warrior, Psychologist; Wang-mu, Servant, Genetically Altered Being; Jane, Artificial Intelligence
Time period(s): Indeterminate Future
Locale(s): Lusitania, Planet—Imaginary; Path, Planet—Imaginary

Summary: The descolada virus threatens to destroy human life on Lusitania as scientists' vaccines barely stay ahead of the rapidly changing pathogen, which could be permanently destroyed by the colonists. Because other intelligent life on Lusitania would be devastated and then destroyed without the descolada virus, the scientists refuse to employ the drastic solution readily available if time allows a gentler treatment.

Other books you might like:
Octavia E. Butler, *Xenogenesis Series*, 1987-1989
James H. Schmitz, *The Demon Breed*, 1968
Dan Simmons, *The Fall of Hyperion*, 1990
Dan Simmons, *Hyperion*, 1989
Joan Slonczewski, *A Door into Ocean*, 1986
Sheri S. Tepper, *Grass*, 1989

731

DIANE CAREY

Best Destiny

(New York: Pocket, 1992)

Story type: Science Fiction (Space Opera)
Series: Star Trek
Major character(s): George Samuel Kirk, Parent (James T. Kirk's), Spaceman (Starfleet); James T. "Jimmy" Kirk, Teenager, Adventurer
Time period(s): 23rd century
Locale(s): *U.S.S. Enterprise*, Spaceship; Outer Space

Summary: Jimmy's efforts to gain respect lead to trouble until George ignites Jimmy's enthusiasm by taking him on a shakedown voyage of the just-completed *Enterprise*. After pirates attack their shuttle, George forces Jimmy into a jury-rigged life support capsule, expecting everyone else to die. However, Jimmy decides to rebel by ramming the capsule into the pirate vessel then sabotaging the ship, allowing the Starfleet crew to rescue themselves. Sequel to *Final Frontier*.

Other books you might like:
Margaret Wander Bonanno, *Dwellers in the Crucible*, 1985
Diane Duane, *Doctor's Orders*, 1990
Barbara Hambly, *Ghost Walker*, 1991
Vonda N. McIntyre, *Enterprise*, 1986
Della Van Hise, *Killing Time*, 1985

732

DIANE CAREY
JAMES I. KIRKLAND, Co-Author

First Frontier

(New York: Pocket, 1995)

Story type: Science Fiction (Time Travel; Alternate Universe)
Series: Star Trek
Major character(s): James T. Kirk, Spaceship Captain; Spock, Scientist, Alien (Vulcan); Leonard McCoy, Doctor
Time period(s): Indeterminate Past (65 million years ago); 23rd century
Locale(s): Earth; *U.S.S. Enterprise*, Spaceship

Summary: While testing a new shielding technology, the *Enterprise* finds only a lush wilderness where human life never evolved when they return to Earth. Romulans and Klingons subjugate most other space-faring races and now fight each other to the death. Marooned in this alternate history, Kirk leads a landing party back in time through the Guardian of Forever. Realizing that someone has prevented the asteroid impact that drove the dinosaurs to extinction, they must ensure that the asteroid strikes so that mammals inherit the Earth.

Other books you might like:
Margaret Wander Bonanno, *Strangers From the Sky*, 1987
Michael Crichton, *Jurassic Park*, 1991
A.C. Crispin, *Time for Yesterday*, 1988
Dana Kramer-Rolls, *Home Is the Hunter*, 1990
Judith Reeves-Stevens, *Federation*, 1994
   Garfield Reeves-Stevens, co-author

733

DIANE CAREY

First Strike

(New York: Pocket, 1996)

Story type: Science Fiction (Space Opera; First Contact)
Series: Star Trek
Major character(s): James T. Kirk, Spaceship Captain; Spock, Scientist, Alien (Vulcan); Zennor, Alien, Spaceship Captain
Time period(s): 23rd century
Locale(s): *U.S.S. Enterprise*, Spaceship; Outer Space; Interstellar Empire/Federation

Summary: When a mysterious spaceship invades Klingon space and resists all efforts to destroy it, the Klingon commander resorts to desperate measures, asking James Kirk of the Federation for help. To the Klingons' disgust, Kirk first insists on negotiating with the invaders, terrifying aliens whom Klingon myths call the Havoc and human mythology, the Furies. Since the Furies believe that they must reclaim their own territory from the evil Conquerors who drove out their ancestors millenia before, even the *Enterprise* may not be able to stop them. First of the four part Invasion! Series which spans all four of the Star Trek television series and continues in *The Soldiers of Fear*.

Other books you might like:
Dafydd ab Hugh, *The Final Fury*, 1996
   Invasion! Series, part 4
Orson Scott Card, *Ender's Game*, 1985
Gene DeWeese, *Chain of Attack*, 1987
Brad Ferguson, *The Last Stand*, 1995
L.A. Graf, *Time's Enemy*, 1996
   Invasion! Series, part 3
Barbara Paul, *The Three-Minute Universe*, 1988
Dean Wesley Smith, *The Soldiers of Fear*, 1996
   Kristine Kathryn Rusch, co-author; Invasion! Series, part 2
David Weber, *Path of the Fury*, 1992

734

LEONARD CARPENTER

Conan of the Red Brotherhood

(New York: Tor, 1993)

Story type: Fantasy (Sword and Sorcery)
Series: Conan the Barbarian
Major character(s): Conan, Barbarian, Warrior; Sulula ''Philiope'', Servant, Imposter (noblewoman); Yildiz, Ruler (emperor)
Time period(s): Indeterminate Past
Locale(s): Turan, Fictional Country; Aghrapur, Fictional City; At Sea

Summary: As Conan carves out a pirate empire, Emperor Yildiz plots his destruction.

Other books you might like:
Roland J. Green, *Conan the Relentless*, 1992
Robert E. Howard, *Bran Mak Morn*, 1969
Robert E. Howard, *Conan the Barbarian*, 1955
Robert E. Howard, *Hour of the Dragon*, 1977
Robert E. Howard, *King Conan*, 1953
Robert Jordan, *Conan the Invincible*, 1985
Steve Perry, *Conan the Formidable*, 1990

735

LEONARD CARPENTER

Conan the Gladiator

(New York: Tor, 1995)

Story type: Fantasy (Sword and Sorcery; Adventure)
Series: Conan the Barbarian
Major character(s): Conan, Barbarian, Warrior; Sathilda, Entertainer (acrobat)
Time period(s): Indeterminate Past
Locale(s): Stygia, Fictional Country; Luxur, Fictional City

Summary: After he joins Sathilda's troupe for diversion, Conan runs afoul of officials and must fight exotic warriors and wild beasts in the Arena of Luxur.

Other books you might like:
Roland J. Green, *Conan at the Demon's Gate*, 1994
Robert E. Howard, *Conan the Barbarian*, 1955
Robert E. Howard, *Hour of the Dragon*, 1977
Robert E. Howard, *King Conan*, 1953
John Maddox Roberts, *Conan and the Manhunters*, 1994
Karl Edward Wagner, *Darkness Weaves*, 1978
   revised edition

736

LEONARD CARPENTER

Conan the Outcast

(New York: Tor, 1991)

Story type: Fantasy (Sword and Sorcery)
Series: Conan the Barbarian
Major character(s): Conan, Barbarian, Warrior
Time period(s): Indeterminate Past

Locale(s): Qjara, Fictional City

Summary: Queen Regula declares Conan an outcast, but when the high priest, Khumanos, plans to sacrifice Qjara in hopes of returning Lord Votantha and glory to the City of Sark, Conan represents Qjara's only hope of survival.

Other books you might like:
Roland J. Green, *Conan the Guardian*, 1991
Robert Jordan, *Conan the Invincible*, 1985
Robert Jordan, *Conan the Victorious*, 1984
Steve Perry, *Conan the Formidable*, 1990
John Maddox Roberts, *Conan the Bold*, 1989
John Maddox Roberts, *Conan the Champion*, 1987

737

LEONARD CARPENTER

Conan the Savage

(New York: Tor, 1992)

Story type: Fantasy (Sword and Sorcery)
Series: Conan the Barbarian
Major character(s): Conan, Barbarian, Warrior; Songa, Hunter, Warrior
Time period(s): Indeterminate Past
Locale(s): Brythunia, Fictional Country

Summary: After Conan escapes from the "unescapable" prison mine pits of Brythunia and flees into the wilderness, he discovers Songa and her people, the Atupans, and gains acceptance among them. When raiders abduct Songa, Conan follows and wreaks vengeance on the kidnappers, then confronts the demon goddess gaining power in Brythunia.

Other books you might like:
Roland J. Green, *Conan the Guardian*, 1991
Robert E. Howard, *Conan the Barbarian*, 1955
Robert E. Howard, *Conan the Conqueror*, 1950
Robert E. Howard, *King Conan*, 1953
Robert Jordan, *Conan the Invincible*, 1985
Robert Jordan, *Conan the Victorious*, 1984
Steve Perry, *Conan the Formidable*, 1990

738

LEONARD CARPENTER

Conan, Scourge of the Bloody Coast

(New York: Tor, 1994)

Story type: Fantasy (Sword and Sorcery)
Series: Conan the Barbarian
Major character(s): Conan, Barbarian, Warrior; Crotalus, Wizard
Time period(s): Indeterminate Past (Hyperborean Age)
Locale(s): Vilayet Sea, Fictional Country; Turan, Fictional Country

Summary: Setting mainland empires against each other, Conan and his band of pirates attempt to recover a sunken treasure of gold and gems while avoiding Crotalus' deadly machinations.

Other books you might like:
Roland J. Green, *Conan at the Demon's Gate*, 1994
Robert E. Howard, *Conan the Barbarian*, 1955
Steve Perry, *Conan the Formidable*, 1990
John Maddox Roberts, *Conan and the Manhunters*, 1994
Karl Edward Wagner, *Darkness Weaves*, 1978
  revised edition

739

A.A. CARR

Eye Killers

(Norman: University of Oklahoma Press, 1995)

Story type: Horror (Vampire Story)
Major character(s): Michael Roanhorse, Shepherd; Falke, Vampire; Diana Logan, Teacher (of high school English)
Time period(s): 1990s (1995)
Locale(s): Albuquerque, New Mexico

Summary: This first novel by a talented Native American film director draws from his own Navajo roots. When a European vampire named Falke seduces Michael Roanhorse's daughter, Melissa, to become one of his followers, Michael embarks on a quest to reacquaint himself with his native heritage and harness the mystical powers that will show him how to defeat this enemy. Michael's efforts to enlist Caucasian English teacher Diana Logan to fight the European Falke recapitulate in miniature the clash of the Anglo-American and Native American cultures.

Other books you might like:
Muriel Gray, *Trickster*, 1994
Colin Kersey, *Soul Catcher*, 1995
G. Wayne Miller, *Thunder Rise*, 1988
Adam Niswander, *The Charm*, 1993
Kathryn Ptacek, *Ghost Dance*, 1990

740

EMMANUEL CARRERE

Gothic Romance

(New York: Scribners, 1990)

Story type: Horror (Mystery)
Major character(s): Ann, Writer (modern gothic romance writer); Robert Walton, Publisher; Mary Shelley, Writer (wrote *Frankenstein*), Historical Figure
Time period(s): 1990s (1990); 1810s (1814)
Locale(s): London, England; Lake Geneva, Switzerland

Summary: While John Polidori tells the story of how Mary Shelley wrote her Gothic masterpiece, *Frankenstein*, Ann, a modern writer of Gothic romances, becomes involved in a series of mysterious experiences that suggest a correspondence between her own life and that of Mary Shelley almost 200 years before. This is a revision, translated by Lanie Goodman, of *Bravoure*, 1984.

Other books you might like:
Brian W. Aldiss, *Frankenstein Unbound*, 1973
Tim Powers, *The Stress of Her Regard*, 1989
Kathryn Ptacek, *In Silence Sealed*, 1988

741

JERRY JAY CARROLL

Top Dog

(New York: Ave, 1996)

Story type: Fantasy (Alternate World; Satire)
Major character(s): William ''Bogey'' Ingersol, Business-man, Animal (dog); Helmish, Artisan, Inventor
Time period(s): 1990s; Indeterminate
Locale(s): Planet—Imaginary

Summary: Although surprised to find himself in a dog's body on another world rather than waiting to serve prison time for violating SEC rules, Bogey quickly learns to use his new abilities, integrating his Earthly business skills. Brought to help with the battle between good and evil for the Fair Lands, Bogey must decide whom to support in the conflict. First novel.

Other books you might like:
Carolyn Cushman, *Witch and Wombat*, 1994
Gordon R. Dickson, *The Dragon and the George*, 1976
Barbara Hambly, *The Silver Tower*, 1986
William Kotzwinkle, *The Bear Went over the Mountain*, 1996
Mark E. Rogers, *The Adventures of Samurai Cat*, 1984
J.R.R. Tolkien, *The Fellowship of the Ring*, 1954

742

JONATHAN CARROLL

After Silence

(New York: Doubleday, 1993)

Story type: Horror (Mystery)
Major character(s): Max Fischer, Artist (cartoonist); Lily Aaron, Restaurateur; Lincoln Aaron, Teenager
Time period(s): 1980s; 1990s (1993)
Locale(s): Los Angeles, California

Summary: Max Fischer discovers that his girlfriend Lily has lied to him about having a husband, and that her son Lincoln is actually a child whom she kidnapped while an infant. Although Max forgives Lily and tries to establish a stable family, Lincoln's discovery of the truth years later precipitates all three of them on a path toward dissolution and death.

Other books you might like:
Dennis Etchison, *Darkside*, 1986
Ronald Kelly, *Father's Little Helper*, 1992
Dean R. Koontz, *Hideaway*, 1991
Bernard Taylor, *Mother's Boys*, 1987

743

JONATHAN CARROLL

A Child Across the Sky

(New York: Doubleday, 1990)

Story type: Horror (Mystery)
Major character(s): Weber Greston, Director (film director); Philip Strayhorn, Director (recently deceased); Cullen James, Writer (Weber's former lover)

Time period(s): 1990s (1990)
Locale(s): New York, New York; Los Angeles, California

Summary: Distinguished film director Weber Greston agrees to finish a horror film by his friend Philip Strayhorn, left incomplete at Philip's suicide. Through his association with mutual acquaintances, he begins to suspect that Philip was privy to dark truths that he translated into the imagery of his wildly successful ''Midnight'' film series.

Other books you might like:
Steven R. Boyett, *The Answer Tree*, 1988
    in David Schow, *Silver Scream*, 1988
Ramsey Campbell, *Ancient Images*, 1988

744

JONATHAN CARROLL

From the Teeth of Angels

(New York: Doubleday, 1994)

Story type: Horror (Mystery)
Major character(s): Wyatt Leonard, Actor (children's television star), Homosexual; Arlen Ford, Actress; Leland Zivic, Photographer
Time period(s): 1990s (1994)
Locale(s): Vienna, Austria

Summary: A handful of celebrities whose paths cross in Vienna discuss their lives and fear of impending death with one another, unaware that death personified is among their company.

Other books you might like:
Charles L. Grant, *For Fear of the Night*, 1988
Stephen King, *It*, 1986

745

JONATHAN CARROLL

Outside the Dog Museum

(New York: Doubleday, 1992)

Story type: Fantasy (Contemporary)
Major character(s): Harry Radcliffe, Architect
Time period(s): 20th century
Locale(s): Los Angeles, California; Republic of Saru, Fictional Country

Summary: Harry Radcliffe, world-famous architect and jerk, goes mad. With the help of Venasque, a shaman who appears in Carroll's last two books, he eventually regains his sanity and takes a commission to build a Museum for the Sultan of Saru, a small Middle Eastern country. The commission, however, is more than it seems, and Harry's world goes through some very strange changes before the story ends.

Other books you might like:
James P. Blaylock, *The Paper Grail*, 1991
John Crowley, *Little, Big*, 1981
Lisa Goldstein, *The Dream Years*, 1985
Robert Holdstock, *Mythago Wood*, 1984
James Patrick Kelly, *Look into the Sun*, 1989
Pat Murphy, *The City, Not Long After*, 1989

746

JONATHAN CARROLL

The Panic Hand

(New York: St. Martin's, 1996)

Story type: Horror (Collection)

Summary: Featuring stories in which real life sits cheek-by-jowl with the fantastic and the comic frequently nosedives into horror, this first collection is considerably expanded from its first appearance in Germany nearly a decade ago and its British publication in 1995. In the World Fantasy Award-winning "Man's Best Dog," a child learns of an imminent animal revolt from her beloved pet. "Flash in the Pants" tells of a house that weeps for the departure of its tenants, and "The Sadness of Detail" of a woman confronted by a man who shows future photographs of her family to prove she can change the future for them. "The Jane Fonda Room" and "Postgraduate" are concerned with private hells in the afterlife and personal forms of damnation. The novellas "Uh-Oh City" and "The Black Cocktail" are concerned with the divided self and feature characters who are, respectively, fractions of the gods and fragments of the narrator.

Other books you might like:

Angela Carter, *Burning Your Boats: The Collected Short Stories*, 1996
Rachel Ingalls, *The End of Tragedy*, 1987
Ian McEwan, *In Between the Sheets*, 1978
Stephen Millhauser, *The Barnum Museum*, 1991

747

ANGELA CARTER

Burning Your Boats: The Collected Short Stories

(New York: Holt, 1996)

Story type: Horror (Collection)

Summary: This omnibus volume collects 42 tales, assembling the contents of four short fiction collections plus six previously uncollected works by a writer who consciously evoked the Gothic in her work and specialized in reworking classic fairy tales into contemporary parables. Included are "The Company of Wolves," a riff on the tale of Little Red Riding Hood, and "Lady of the House of Love," a continuation of Bram Stoker's *Dracula*, both of which explore the sexual subcurrents of their source material. Fantastic representations of female empowerment are the core of "The Courtship of Mr. Lyon" and "The Tiger's Bride," while "The Fall River Axe Murders" explores a different sort of empowerment in the examination of the Lizzie Borden case. "The Cabinet of Edgar Allan Poe" recreates the childhood of its subject in an effort to understand his morbid literary vision. Salman Rushdie supplies an introduction. This book was first published in England in 1995.

Other books you might like:

Thomas Ligotti, *Songs of a Dead Dreamer*, 1990
Patrick McGrath, *Blood and Water and Other Tales*, 1988
Stephen Millhauser, *In the Penny Arcade*, 1986

Joyce Carol Oates, *Haunted: Tales of the Grotesque*, 1994

748

CARMEN CARTER

The Devil's Heart

(New York: Pocket, 1993)

Story type: Science Fiction (Space Opera; Psychic Powers)
Series: Star Trek: The Next Generation
Major character(s): Jean-Luc Picard, Spaceship Captain, Military Personnel; Data, Android, Military Personnel; Guinan, Alien (Listener), Saloon Keeper/Owner
Time period(s): 24th century
Locale(s): *U.S.S. Enterprise*, Spaceship

Summary: Sent to investigate reports of problems in an isolated archaeological outpost, the *Enterprise* crew finds only one survivor, whose dying words speak of the legendary Ko N'ya, or Devil's Heart, a stone with reputed powers to make wishes come true—at a price. Recovering the artifact from the Ferengi marauders who have taken it from the outpost, Picard takes custody of it then dreams disturbingly of the lives and deaths of others who have held the stone. Obsessed with the stone, Picard acquires power to alter events—even past events.

Other books you might like:

Campbell Black, *Raiders of the Lost Ark*, 1981
Marion Zimmer Bradley, *Sharra's Exile*, 1981
C.J. Cherryh, *Exile's Gate*, 1988
A.C. Crispin, *Time for Yesterday*, 1988
A.C. Crispin, *Yesterday's Son*, 1983
J.R.R. Tolkien, *The Return of the King*, 1956
Della Van Hise, *Killing Time*, 1985

749

CARMEN CARTER
PETER DAVID, Co-Author
MICHAEL JAN FRIEDMAN, Co-Author

Doomsday World

(New York: Pocket Books, 1990)

Story type: Science Fiction (Space Opera; Espionage Thriller)
Series: Star Trek: The Next Generation
Major character(s): Data, Android, Military Personnel; Geordi La Forge, Engineer, Military Personnel; Worf, Military Personnel, Security Officer
Time period(s): 24th century
Locale(s): Kirlos, Planet—Imaginary; *U.S.S. Enterprise*, Spaceship

Summary: The Federation and the K'vin Hegemony have co-existed for years on the artificial planet Kirlos, created by the vanished Ariantu people. Assigned to assist an archaeological team in uncovering the ruins on Kirlos, Data, Geordi and Worf find themselves cut off from the *Enterprise* and under suspicion as perpetrators of a series of terrorist attacks. Then a descendant of the Ariantu activates their ancient doomsday weapon and the *Enterprise* crew must stop it.

Other books you might like:
Diane Carey, *Ghost Ship*, 1988
  Star Trek: The Next Generation 1
C.J. Cherryh, *Downbelow Station*, 1981
Gene DeWeese, *The Peacekeepers*, 1988
  Star Trek: The Next Generation 2
Clifford D. Simak, *Destiny Doll*, 1971

750

RAPHAEL CARTER

The Fortunate Fall
(New York: Tor, 1996)

Story type: Science Fiction (Cyberpunk; Post-Holocaust)
Major character(s): Maya Tayanichna Andreyeva, Journalist, Cyborg; Keishi Mirabara, Researcher, Technician; Pavel Sergeyevich Voskresenye, Activist, Cyborg
Time period(s): 23rd century
Locale(s): Leningrad, Russia; Arkhangelsk, Russia

Summary: As a camera, what Maya sees and feels, her on-line audience also sees and feels. While working on a documentary about the worst holocaust in living memory, Calinshchina, she stumbles on the interview of a lifetime, an interview with Pavel Voskresenye, an eye-witness to that atrocity. Dependent upon a new screener, Keishi Mirabara, who controls Maya's output to the net, Maya faces a tough day pursuing the story while being sought herself by officials. First novel.

Other books you might like:
Alfred Bester, *The Computer Connection*, 1975
Pat Cadigan, *Mindplayers*, 1987
John M. Ford, *Growing Up Weightless*, 1993
John M. Ford, *The Princes of Air*, 1982
William Gibson, *Burning Chrome*, 1986
Maureen F. McHugh, *China Mountain Zhang*, 1992
Rudy Rucker, *Live Robots*, 1994
Neal Stephenson, *Snow Crash*, 1993
Michael Swanwick, *Vacuum Flowers*, 1987
Gene Wolfe, *The Fifth Head of Cerberus*, 1972

751

JEFFREY A. CARVER

Down the Stream of Stars
(New York: Bantam Spectra, 1990)

Story type: Science Fiction (First Contact; Psychic Powers)
Series: Changeling Star
Major character(s): Claudi Melnik, Child; Lupo, Animal (half earth wolf, half picobear); Roald Thornekan, Spaceship Captain
Time period(s): Indeterminate Future (Year 269 of the Auricle Alliance)
Locale(s): *Charity*, Spaceship

Summary: When Claudi Melnik and Lupo seem to sense the presence of the Throg, an intelligent race hostile to humans, Captain Thornekan must decide how to best continue his interstellar flight.

Other books you might like:
Greg Bear, *Eon*, 1985
Gregory Benford, *Heart of the Comet*, 1986
  David Brin, co-author
C.J. Cherryh, *Cyteen*, 1988
Alis A. Rasmussen, *A Passage of Stars*, 1990
Vernor Vinge, *Marooned in Realtime*, 1986

752

JEFFREY A. CARVER

Dragon Rigger
(New York: Tor, 1993)

Story type: Science Fiction (Adventure; Science Fantasy)
Major character(s): Jael LaBrae, Pilot (spaceship), Heroine; Kan-Kon, Pilot (spaceship; retired); Windruth, Alien (dragon), Leader
Time period(s): Indeterminate Future
Locale(s): Dragon Realm, Mythical Place

Summary: Jael befriends Kan-Kon immediately before feeling called to the Dragon Realm where conditions worsen as the dragons lose battle after battle. According to the prophecy, Jael will save the Dragon Realm at the cost of her life. Sequel to *Dragons in the Stars*.

Other books you might like:
Sean Dalton, *Beyond the Void*, 1991
Debra Doyle, *The Price of the Stars*, 1992
  James D. Macdonald, co-author
Cheryl J. Franklin, *Fire Crossing*, 1991
Geary Gravel, *A Key for the Nonesuch*, 1990
Colin Greenland, *Take Back Plenty*, 1992
David Weber, *Path of the Fury*, 1992

753

JEFFREY A. CARVER

Dragons in the Stars
(New York: Tor, 1992)

Story type: Science Fiction (Adventure; Science Fantasy)
Major character(s): Jael LeBrae, Spacewoman, Teenager; Deuteronomous Mogurn, Spaceship Captain, Smuggler; "Ar" Rarberticandornan, Alien, Spaceman
Time period(s): Indeterminate Future
Locale(s): *Cassandra*, Spaceship; *Seneca*, Spaceship

Summary: Jael LeBrae, a qualified rigger, finally gets hired by Mogurn, who uses an illegal device to gain control over her. Her low self-esteem, already damaged by an unhappy childhood, causes her to blame her misfortunes on her deceased father. In the Flux, where riggers' mental images form the route through hyperspace, she feels happy but drawn to the Mountain Route, rumored to be inhabited by dragons and forbidden by Mogurn as too dangerous.

Other books you might like:
Greg Bear, *Eon*, 1985
Orson Scott Card, *Xenocide*, 1991
Stephen R. Donaldson, *The Gap into Vision: Forbidden Knowledge*, 1991

Cheryl J. Franklin, *Fire Get*, 1987
Eric Kotani, *Act of God*, 1985
    John Maddox Roberts, co-author
Alis A. Rasmussen, *A Passage of Stars*, 1990
Melissa Scott, *Dreamships*, 1992
Dan Simmons, *Hyperion*, 1989
Cordwainer Smith, *The Best of Cordwainer Smith*, 1975

754

JEFFREY A. CARVER

From a Changeling Star
(New York: Bantam Spectra, 1989)

Story type: Science Fiction (Hard Science Fiction)
Major character(s): Willard Ruskin, Scientist; Dax, Artificial Intelligence
Time period(s): Indeterminate Future (Year 178 of the Auricle Alliance)
Locale(s): Kantano's World, Planet—Imaginary; Starmuse Station, Space Station

Summary: Scientists on Starmuse Station breathlessly await the impending supernova of the star Betelgeuse, but Willard Ruskin, a scientist whose presence is vital to the project, is in difficulty on Kantano's World. Agents of the authoritarian Tandesko Triune have attempted to assassinate Ruskin. Someone else has infected him with nano-agents — microscopic, artificial intelligences, who protect his body from physical harm. Finally, Ruskin is suffering from partial amnesia. In order to save himself and Starmuse Station, Ruskin must discover who infected him with the nano-agents and why the Tandesko Triune wants him dead.

Other books you might like:
Greg Bear, *Eon*, 1985
Gregory Benford, *Heart of the Comet*, 1986
    David Brin, co-author
C.J. Cherryh, *Cyteen*, 1988
Vernor Vinge, *Marooned in Realtime*, 1986

755

JEFFREY A. CARVER

The Infinite Sea
(New York: Tor, 1996)

Story type: Science Fiction (First Contact; Space Opera)
Series: Chaos Chronicles
Major character(s): John Bandicut, Spaceman; Charlie/Charlene, Alien (quarx); Julie Stone, Spacewoman
Time period(s): Indeterminate Future
Locale(s): Triton, Neptune (moon of Neptune); Planet—Imaginary; Undersea Environment/Habitat

Summary: John and his companions arrive at their unknown destination, a community near the edge of an undersea vent. At war with the residents of the land above, the alien Neri imprison the crew until John heals one of the Neri with the help of Charlene, demonstrating their friendship. They realize they must prevent the Neri from destruction by the giant volcano and leaking radiation, both, perhaps, caused by the

crashed spaceship they work at salvaging. Meanwhile, on Triton, the translator informs Julie that the Earth again faces disaster.

Other books you might like:
Roger MacBride Allen, *The Ring of Charon*, 1990
Stephen Baxter, *Flux*, 1995
David Brin, *Brightness Reef*, 1995
C.J. Cherryh, *Foreigner*, 1994
David Weber, *Path of the Fury*, 1992

756

JEFFREY A. CARVER

Neptune Crossing
(New York: Tor, 1994)

Story type: Science Fiction (First Contact)
Series: Chaos Chronicles
Major character(s): John Bandicut, Spaceman, Miner; Charlie, Alien (quarx)
Time period(s): 22nd century (2164)
Locale(s): Triton, Neptune (moon of Neptune)

Summary: A spell of silence-fugue renders John Bandicut receptive to contact by Charlie, reanimated after millennia of inactivity. Linking to John's mind, Charlie informs him of an impending disaster for the solar system, which Charlie and John must work to avert, a goal hindered by John's lowly position in the mining operation's hierarchy.

Other books you might like:
Roger MacBride Allen, *The Ring of Charon*, 1990
Gordon R. Dickson, *The Alien Way*, 1965
L. Warren Douglas, *Cannon's Orb*, 1994
Diana G. Gallagher, *The Alien Dark*, 1990
Vernor Vinge, *A Fire upon the Deep*, 1992
David Weber, *Mutineers' Moon*, 1991

757

JEFFREY A. CARVER

Strange Attractors
(New York: Tor, 1995)

Story type: Science Fiction (Space Opera)
Series: Chaos Chronicles
Major character(s): John Bandicut, Spaceman; Charlie, Alien (quarx)
Time period(s): Indeterminate Future
Locale(s): Outer Space; The Metaworld, Mythical Place

Summary: John Bandicut's heroic act saves the Earth but results in Bandicut's transportation to the Metaworld, a vast array of interconnected habitats. There Bandicut and Charlie begin to ally themselves with the strange beings occupying the environment and work to thwart the attempts of a non-corporeal entity to destroy the entire structure. Sequel to *Neptune Crossing*.

Other books you might like:
Roger MacBride Allen, *The Ring of Charon*, 1990
Roger MacBride Allen, *The Shattered Sphere*, 1994
John E. Stith, *Manhattan Transfer*, 1993

Vernor Vinge, *A Fire upon the Deep*, 1992
David Weber, *Path of the Fury*, 1992

758
JACKIE CASSADA

Shadows on the Hill
(Clarkston, Georgia: White Wolf, 1996)

Story type: Fantasy (Contemporary; Quest)
Series: World of Darkness: Immortal Eyes Trilogy
Major character(s): Tor, Mythical Creature (troll), Warrior; Eleighanaran "Leigh", Mythical Creature (sidhe), Noblewoman; Rasputin, Mythical Creature (pooka)
Time period(s): 1990s
Locale(s): San Francisco, California; Hilo, Hawaii

Summary: The companions continue their attempt to find the magical eyes, racing against Yrtalien to open the mythical gate back to Arcadia. Led to Hawaii, the land of the mysterious fairy spirits of the Pacific Isles, the menehune, the companions must contend with the Forsworn Prince as an enemy, as well as a band of half-human Faerie Hunters who want the companions dead. Second in the trilogy.

Other books you might like:
Emma Bull, *War for the Oaks*, 1987
Charles de Lint, *Jack of Kinrowan*, 1995
Pamela Dean, *Tam Lin*, 1991
Tom Deitz, *Windmaster's Bane*, 1986
Robert Holdstock, *Mythago Wood*, 1984

759
MICHAEL CASSUTT

Dragon Season
(New York: Tor, 1991)

Story type: Fantasy (Religious; Contemporary)
Major character(s): Richard Earl Walsh, Military Personnel; Maia Chios, Student, Heiress
Time period(s): 1990s
Locale(s): Tucson, Arizona

Summary: Rick Walsh arrived from Guam expecting to be met by his mysterious girlfriend, Maia. Instead, she's disappeared, leaving behind her infant son, her wallet and her car. Detective Sanchez, investigating the report on Maia's disappearance, informs Rick that many young women have been discovered missing near Tucson and are frequently never found.

Other books you might like:
Alan Dean Foster, *Cyber Way*, 1990
Alan Dean Foster, *To the Vanishing Point*, 1988
P.C. Hodgell, *Dark of the Moon*, 1985
P.C. Hodgell, *God Stalk*, 1982
Marc Laidlaw, *Neon Lotus*, 1988
Elizabeth Moon, *Sheepfarmer's Daughter*, 1988
Elizabeth Moon, *Surrender None: The Legacy of Gird*, 1990

760
MORT CASTLE

Cursed Be the Child
(New York: Leisure, 1990)

Story type: Horror (Child-in-Peril; Possession)
Major character(s): Lissette, Child, Spirit; Melissa "Missy" Barringer, Child; Warren Barringer, Professor (English professor)
Time period(s): 1990s
Locale(s): Chicago, Illinois (Suburbs)

Summary: Though they could wish to be a little more settled in their new home, Warren and Vicki Barringer are thrilled that five-year-old Melissa has adapted so well. They're not at all perturbed when Melissa creates an imaginary playmate to go with the new surroundings—until they discover that "Lissette" has an unhealthy influence on their child, and that *who* she is is not nearly so frightening as *what* she is and what she means to do to their family.

Other books you might like:
William Peter Blatty, *The Exorcist*, 1971
Ramsey Campbell, *The Influence*, 1988
Ramsey Campbell, *The Nameless*, 1981
Stephen King, *Pet Sematary*, 1983

761
ADAM-TROY CASTRO

Lost in Booth Nine
(Woodinville, Washington: Silver Salamander Press, 1993)

Story type: Horror (Collection)

Summary: The author's first book, a quartet of novellas set in and around an imaginary peepshow called Les Girls XXX, critiques the attitudes toward sexuality that existence of such places implies. In "Peepshow," the female performers are vampires who exploit their exploitative customers. In "The Girl in Booth Nine," a peepshow patron's fantasies become reality. "The Pussy Expert" is a mordant character study, and "Miracle Drug" a hallucinatory tale of a squatter house that serves as a doorway to hell. Dean Wesley Smith and Kristine Kathryn Rusch provide an introduction.

Other books you might like:
Ramsey Campbell, *Scared Stiff*, 1987
Ray Garton, *Methods of Madness*, 1990
Dan Simmons, *Lovedeath*, 1993
Lucy Taylor, *Close to the Bone*, 1993

762
HUGH B. CAVE

Bitter/Sweet
(West Warwick, Rhode Island: Necronomicon Press, 1996)

Story type: Horror (Collection)

Summary: An author best known for his work in the pulp fiction magazines presents two original stories in which seemingly ominous problems are resolved happily. In "By Heaven!" the ghosts of literary figures renowned for their tastefulness mete out gentle but just desserts to rude and insensitive contemporary cultural figures. In "Aiyana and the Gallant Rider," a dream therapist helps two lonely people interpret their nightmares and overcome the fears that have inspired them.

Other books you might like:
Fred Chappell, *More Shapes than One*, 1991
R. Chetwynd-Hayes, *Tales From the Shadows*, 1986
Carl Jacobi, *Smoke of the Snake*, 1994
Frank Belknap Long, *Return to Tomorrow*, 1995
Manly Wade Wellman, *Worse Things Waiting*, 1973

763

HUGH B. CAVE

Death Stalks the Night
(Minneapolis: Fedogan & Bremer, 1995)

Story type: Horror (Collection)

Summary: The seventeen stories reprinted in this volume were published in the mid-1930s in the "shudder pulps." Shudder pulp tales traditionally subjected a hero and heroine to weird menaces of a seemingly supernatural nature before revealing them to be the handiwork of criminal masterminds. In "The Flame Fiend," the perpetrator of a series of gruesome murders is a man who dons an asbestos suit and, doused with gasoline, sets himself afire to smother his victims. In "A Modern Nero," a discredited film director uses a remote resort to film grisly tortures that will give his movies verisimilitude. The title of "The Crawling Ones" refers to a torture method used in Borneo where insects are used to devour the flesh of victims. Genuine supernaturalism can be found in "Death's Loving Arms," which features a feral woman brought to America by a research expedition, and "Tomb for the Living," where a submarine pierces through a maelstrom into a world beneath the ocean floor inhabited by primitive life forms. The late Karl Edward Wagner, who planned to bring this book out over a decade ago under the Carcosa House imprint, wrote the introduction.

Other books you might like:
Carl Jacobi, *Smoke of the Snake*, 1994
Sheldon Jaffery, *The Weirds*, 1987
    editor
E. Hoffman Price, *Far Lands Other Days*, 1975
Robert Weinberg, *Uncanny Tales*, 1974
    editor

764

HUGH B. CAVE

Disciples of Dread
(New York: Tor, 1989)

Story type: Horror (Black Magic)
Major character(s): Mark Donner, Young Man (American); Khargi, Religious (Voodoo priest)
Time period(s): 1980s

Locale(s): Jamaica

Summary: Mark Donner is stalked by the Disciples of Dread, an international terrorist organization led by Khargi, a voodoo practitioner, in a plot to trap Mark's psychically talented twin brother, an American spy.

Other books you might like:
John Farris, *The Fury*, 1976
Dennis Wheatley, *Strange Conflict*, 1941

765

HUGH B. CAVE

Lucifer's Eye
(New York: Tor, 1991)

Story type: Horror (Occult)
Major character(s): Peter Sheldon, Worker (plantation caretaker); Edith Craig, Heiress; Ma Jarrett, Psychic
Time period(s): 1990s
Locale(s): St. Albans, Caribbean

Summary: Talk about bad timing: Edith Craig arrives on St. Albans to take charge of her late father's coffee plantation at the same time the townspeople begin disappearing in the nearby Blackrock mountains. Exploration of the rumored Devil's Pit at the core of Blackrock Peak uncovers the secret of the green fog that turns the townspeople into automatons and the presence of a satanic terrorist squadron ready to overrun the island.

Other books you might like:
James Herbert, *The Dark*, 1980
James Herbert, *The Fog*, 1975
Peter Straub, *Floating Dragon*, 1982

766

MICHAEL CECILIONE

Deathscape
(New York: Diamond, 1992)

Story type: Horror (Wild Talents)
Major character(s): Laura Kane, Student; Neil Stone, Police Officer; Henry Kent, Doctor
Time period(s): 1990s (1992)
Locale(s): Groverton, New York

Summary: A near-drowning experience endows Laura Kane with the ability to foresee the deaths of others. It also opens the doorway between life and death to let in "The Croaker," a monstrous avatar of death responsible for all of the victims in Laura's visions.

Other books you might like:
Stephen King, *The Dead Zone*, 1979
Kathe Koja, *Bad Brains*, 1992
Dean R. Koontz, *Hideaway*, 1992
Joe R. Lansdale, *The Nightrunners*, 1987

767

MICHAEL CECILIONE

Domination
(New York: Zebra, 1993)

Story type: Horror (Vampire Story)
Major character(s): Kelly Mitchell, Journalist (investigative reporter); Eric Rossi, Police Officer; Ilana Florescu, Vampire
Time period(s): 1990s (1993)
Locale(s): New York, New York

Summary: Domination is the name of New York's hottest new nightclub and, as its victims become known all over Manhattan, a source of interest to investigative reporter Kelly Mitchell. In the course of her work, Kelly crosses paths with Ilana Florescu, a vampire who uses the domination subculture to literalize her superior relationship to her human prey.

Other books you might like:
Poppy Z. Brite, *Lost Souls*, 1992
Ray Garton, *Live Girls*, 1987
John Skipp, *The Light at the End*, 1986
    Craig Spector, co-author
S.P. Somtow, *Vampire Junction*, 1983

768

MICHAEL CECILIONE

Soul Snatchers
(New York: Diamond, 1992)

Story type: Horror (Black Magic)
Major character(s): Elaine Prescott, Journalist (crime reporter); Zachary Carver, Police Officer (sheriff); Reverend Isaac Prowier, Religious
Time period(s): 1990s (1992)
Locale(s): Edens Bluff, Massachusetts

Summary: Seeking respite from the stress of her job as a crime reporter in Manhattan, Elaine Prescott takes a leave of absence at the house of an aunt in a remote section of Massachusetts, only to discover that a bizarre sect of resurrectionists that came over with the town's founders in the days of the Pilgrims is busily reviving corpses of the recent dead.

Other books you might like:
Elizabeth Ergas, *Devil's Gate*, 1991
Patrick Whalen, *Out of the Night*, 1990
T.M. Wright, *The Island*, 1988

769

MICHAEL CECILIONE

Thirst
(New York: Zebra, 1996)

Story type: Horror (Vampire Story)
Major character(s): Cassandra Hall, Designer (fashion), Vampire; Julian Aragon, Vampire, Writer (poet); Rolando, Designer (fashion)
Time period(s): 1990s (1995)

Locale(s): New York, New York

Summary: Newly vampirized Cassandra Hall pines for the affections of her vampire initiator, Julian, who has turned her on to the vampire life through sexual ecstasy. Cassandra tries to live unobtrusively in the vampire subculture of Manhattan, taking blood from sexual clients and staying out of the path of a band of righteous vampire killers known as the Advocates.

Other books you might like:
Gary Bowen, *Diary of a Vampire*, 1995
Nancy A. Collins, *Sunglasses After Dark*, 1989
Ray Garton, *Live Girls*, 1987
John Skipp, *The Light at the End*, 1986
    Craig Spector, co-author
Karen E. Taylor, *Blood Secrets*, 1994

770

JACK L. CHALKER

The Cybernetic Walrus
(New York: Ballantine Del Rey, 1995)

Story type: Science Fiction (Techno-Thriller; Cyberpunk)
Series: Wonderland Gambit
Major character(s): Cory Maddox, Computer Expert (programmer), Adventurer; Riki Fresca, Artist
Time period(s): 21st century
Locale(s): United States; Cyberspace (computer virtual reality)

Summary: Recruited into a government program to design computer reality, Cory Maddox soon finds it impossible to distinguish virtual reality from genuine memory.

Other books you might like:
Piers Anthony, *The Caterpillar's Question*, 1992
    Philip Jose Farmer, co-author
C.J. Cherryh, *Wave Without a Shore*, 1981
Philip K. Dick, *Eye in the Sky*, 1957
Alan Dean Foster, *To the Vanishing Point*, 1988
Robert A. Heinlein, *The Number of the Beast*, 1980
Fritz Leiber, *The Sinful Ones*, 1953
Rebecca Ore, *The Illegal Rebirth of Billy the Kid*, 1991
Melissa Scott, *Trouble and Her Friends*, 1994

771

JACK L. CHALKER

The Demons at Rainbow Bridge
(New York: Ace Books, 1989)

Story type: Science Fiction (Adventure)
Series: Quintara Marathon
Major character(s): Jimmy McCray, Telepath; Modra Stryke, Empath
Time period(s): Indeterminate Future
Locale(s): Rainbow Bridge, Planet—Imaginary

Summary: Three hostile and radically different interstellar empires live in an uneasy balance. Then that balance is threatened by the discovery on the planet Rainbow Bridge of an odd horned lifeform which, somehow, resembles a creature found in the oldest legends of all three interstellar cultures.

Other books you might like:
Janet Kagan, *Hellspark*, 1988
Paul J. McAuley, *Four Hundred Billion Stars*, 1988
Dan Simmons, *The Fall of Hyperion*, 1990
Dan Simmons, *Hyperion*, 1989

772

JACK L. CHALKER

Echoes of the Well of Souls

(New York: Ballantine Del Rey, 1993)

Story type: Science Fiction (Adventure; Alternate Intelligence)
Series: Well World
Major character(s): Nathan Brazil, Immortal, Sea Captain; Mavra Chang, Immortal, Chieftain; Theresa "Terry" Perez, Journalist (television)
Time period(s): 21st century
Locale(s): Earth; Well World, Planet—Imaginary

Summary: When an asteroid crashes into the Amazon jungle, a chunk splits off and captures Nathan Brazil and two handicapped people near Rio de Janeiro. The main body of the meteor transports a scientific and photo journalist team, along with two army officers, to a mysterious planet primal to all life other than Markovian in this incarnation of the universe.

Other books you might like:
Piers Anthony, *Thousandstar*, 1980
Greg Bear, *Eon*, 1985
Philip Jose Farmer, *The Maker of Universes*, 1965
Michael P. Kube-McDowell, *Enigma*, 1986
Michael McCollum, *A Greater Infinity*, 1982
Brian Stableford, *Journey to the Center*, 1982
Jack Vance, *Planet of Adventure*, 1993
Joan D. Vinge, *The Summer Queen*, 1991
Timothy Zahn, *Spinneret*, 1985

773

JACK L. CHALKER

Gods of the Well of Souls

(New York: Ballantine Del Rey, 1994)

Story type: Science Fiction (Adventure)
Series: Well World
Major character(s): Nathan Brazil, Immortal; Mavra Chang, Immortal; Juana "Juan" Campos, Drug Dealer
Time period(s): 1990s
Locale(s): Well World, Planet—Imaginary

Summary: Mavra Chang's team arranges to rescue Mavra and Lori and bust up the drug cartel. When a volcanic eruption jolts Nathan Brazil and a very pregnant Terry off the island and Juana Campos, Lori and Mavra escape the cartel, all end up in the Well of Souls where Kraang, a megalomaniacal Markovian takes control.

Other books you might like:
Greg Bear, *Eon*, 1985
Jacqueline Lichtenberg, *Dushau*, 1985
Robert Silverberg, *Valentine Pontifex*, 1983

John Varley, *Titan*, 1979
Joan D. Vinge, *The Summer Queen*, 1991

774

JACK L. CHALKER

Horrors of the Dancing Gods

(New York: Ballantine Del Rey, 1995)

Story type: Fantasy (Quest; Adventure)
Series: Dancing Gods
Major character(s): Irving de Oro, Hero, Warrior; Marge, Mythical Creature (kauri); Larae Ngamuku, Young Woman
Time period(s): Indeterminate
Locale(s): Husaquahr, Fictional Country; Yuggoth, Fictional Country

Summary: The supposedly dead Boquillas stirs up ancient evil from the Sea of Dreams, which centers on the evil continent of Yuggoth. As Joe and a mysterious changeling have disappeared there, Joe's son Irving, Marge, and Poquah set out to rescue them and acquire a statue that will instantly grant any wish.

Other books you might like:
C.J. Cherryh, *The Goblin Mirror*, 1992
Elizabeth Forrest, *Dark Tide*, 1993
Tim Powers, *The Drawing of the Dark*, 1979
Clifford D. Simak, *The Fellowship of the Talisman*, 1978
Melinda M. Snodgrass, *Queen's Gambit Declined*, 1989
Christopher Stasheff, *The Secular Wizard*, 1995
Harry Turtledove, *The Case of the Toxic Spell Dump*, 1993
Jack Vance, *Lyonesse*, 1983

775

JACK L. CHALKER

The March Hare Network

(New York; Ballantine Del Rey, 1996)

Story type: Science Fiction (Techno-Thriller; Political)
Series: Wonderland Gambit
Major character(s): Cory Maddox, Computer Expert, Handicapped (quadriplegic); Korinna "Kori" Kassemi Ajani, Waiter/Waitress, Parent (mother)
Time period(s): 1990s
Locale(s): California; Washington

Summary: Cory Maddox, now Drew Maddox, achieves rebirth in a slightly more primitive world as a helpless quadriplegic. When he is delivered to his enemies, he amazingly becomes Kori, seemingly the feminine side of Cory, with everything depending on her, despite her nature and lack of education.

Other books you might like:
Kevin J. Anderson, *Virtual Destruction*, 1996
    Doug Beason, co-author
John Barnes, *Kaleidoscope Century*, 1995
Ben Bova, *Death Dream*, 1994
Philip K. Dick, *Eye in the Sky*, 1956
Tanith Lee, *The Electric Forest*, 1979
Rebecca Ore, *The Illegal Rebirth of Billy the Kid*, 1991

Walter Jon Williams, *Voice of the Whirlwind*, 1987

776

JACK L. CHALKER

The Ninety Trillion Fausts

(New York: Ace, 1991)

Story type: Science Fiction (Political; Military)
Series: Quintara Marathon
Major character(s): Gun Roh Chin, Spaceship Captain; Jimmy McCray, Telepath; Krishna the Holy Mendoro, Telepath, Religious
Time period(s): Indeterminate Future
Locale(s): Rainbow Bridge, Planet—Imaginary

Summary: Survivors of three teams get together and plan a common strategy against the Quintara knowing that otherwise they would all perish. Jimmy, Josef, Modra, and Krishna then discover by telepathic means whom they are fighting. This book is a sequel to *The Demons at Rainbow Bridge*.

Other books you might like:
Piers Anthony, *Cluster*, 1977
David Brin, *Startide Rising*, 1983
Dave Duncan, *Hero*, 1991
Alan Dean Foster, *Glory Lane*, 1987
James H. Schmitz, *The Demon Breed*, 1968

777

JACK L. CHALKER
MIKE RESNICK, Co-Author
GEORGE ALEC EFFINGER, Co-Author

The Red Tape War

(New York: Tor, 1991)

Story type: Science Fiction (Humor)
Major character(s): Millard Fillmore Pierce, Administrator (class 2 arbiter); XB223, Computer (navigational); Honeylou Emmyjane "Marshmallo" Goldberg, Runaway
Time period(s): 87th century
Locale(s): *Pete Rozelle*, Spaceship

Summary: Thanks to the quirky XB223, Pierce has become lost on his way to his latest assignment. Life is complicated further by arrivals of a lizard-like alien version of Millard Fillmore Pierce from an alternate universe and of Marshmallo who provides another host for Pierce's personality. In this "round robin"-type novel, each author attempts to leave an unresolvable situation at the end of his alternating chapter.

Other books you might like:
Douglas Adams, *The Hitchhiker's Guide to the Galaxy*, 1980
Douglas Adams, *The Restaurant at the End of the Universe*, 1981
John DeChancie, *Paradox Alley*, 1987
John DeChancie, *Red Limit Freeway*, 1984
John DeChancie, *Starrigger*, 1983
Frank Herbert, *The Dosadi Experiment*, 1977
Ken Rolston, *Extreme Paranoia: Nobody Knows the Trouble I've Shot*, 1991

778

JACK L. CHALKER

The Run to Chaos Keep

(New York: Ace, 1991)

Story type: Science Fiction (Adventure)
Series: Quintara Marathon
Major character(s): Jimmy McCray, Telepath (of the Exchange); Gun Roh Chin, Pilot (spaceship); Josef, Leader (Mycohl)
Time period(s): Indeterminate Future
Locale(s): Alternate Universe

Summary: Teams from each Empire—the Exchange, the Mycohl and the Mizlaplan—have entered a Demon-controlled tesseract bordering on another continuum which Jimmy McCray claims is Hell. After several temptations and battles, remnants of the teams enter Chaos Keep, a place of great evil where the three teams will be forced to fight each other by the demon-like Quintara.

Other books you might like:
Piers Anthony, *Vision of Tarot*, 1980
  pseudonym of Piers Anthony Dillingham Jacob
E.E.Y. Hales, *Chariot of Fire*, 1977
Michael Lahey, *Quest for Apollo*, 1989
Larry Niven, *Inferno*, 1976
  Jerry Pournelle, co-author

779

JACK L. CHALKER

Shadow of the Well of Souls

(New York: Ballantine Del Rey, 1994)

Story type: Science Fiction (Adventure)
Series: Well World
Major character(s): Nathan Brazil, Immortal; Mavra Chang, Immortal; Theresa "Terry" Perez, Journalist (television), Handicapped
Time period(s): 21st century
Locale(s): Well World, Planet—Imaginary

Summary: When Nathan Brazil, Mavra Chang and their teams head toward the Well of Souls, a shipwreck maroons them on an isolated island. Juan Campos, now a female Gloptian bent on revenge, captures Mavra and Lori and a dire fate awaits them. Still, the Well requires Nathan Brazil or Mavra Chang for repairs.

Other books you might like:
Philip Jose Farmer, *The Fabulous Riverboat*, 1971
Larry Niven, *Ringworld*, 1970
Robert Silverberg, *Lord Valentine's Castle*, 1980
John Varley, *Titan*, 1979
Joan D. Vinge, *The Summer Queen*, 1991

780

JACK L. CHALKER

Songs of the Dancing Gods

(New York: Ballantine/Del Rey, 1990)

Story type: Fantasy (Alternate World; Quest)
Series: Dancing Gods
Major character(s): Joe de Oro, Barbarian, Hero; Tiana, Slave, Dancer; Macero, Thief
Time period(s): 1990s
Locale(s): Husaquahr, Fictional Country

Summary: Joe, Marge and Tiana return to Husaquahr to discover that Sugasto, Master of the Dead, and Boquillas have joined forces to conquer Husaquahr. The three travel north where Macero, a thief with a fixation on "Gilligan's Island" joins them and shows them how to get to Sugasto's stronghold. There they vanquish the two, Joe becomes a wood nymph and Tiana must return to ruling Marquewood.

Other books you might like:
Poul Anderson, *Three Hearts and Three Lions*, 1961
Marion Zimmer Bradley, *The House Between the Worlds*, 1980
Alan Dean Foster, *To the Vanishing Point*, 1988
Elizabeth Moon, *Divided Allegiance*, 1988
Elizabeth Moon, *Oath of Gold*, 1989
Elizabeth Moon, *Sheepfarmer's Daughter*, 1988

781

FRED CHAPPELL

The Lodger

(West Warwick, Rhode Island: Necronomicon Press, 1993)

Story type: Horror (Possession)
Major character(s): Robert Ackley, Librarian; Lyman Scoresby, Writer (poet)
Time period(s): 1990s
Locale(s): Plattsborough, North Carolina (Bryan University)

Summary: Librarian Robert Ackley opens a can of worms when he opens a book of verse by the decadent, second-rate, 19th century poet Lyman Scoresby and becomes possessed by the self-important writer's soul. In an effort to divest himself of this unwanted "lodger," he indulges in a variety of experiences that he feels certain will offend the poet's tastes.

Other books you might like:
Ramsey Campbell, *Meeting the Author*, 1991
    in *Waking Nightmares*
Marcy Heidish, *The Torching*, 1992
Thomas Ligotti, *Vastarien*, 1990
    in *Songs of a Dead Dreamer*
Michael Stewart, *Belladonna*, 1992

782

FRED CHAPPELL

More Shapes than One

(New York: St. Martin's, 1991)

Story type: Horror (Collection)
Summary: Thirteen stories lightly touched with fantasy, and told with a mild southern accent. "The Somewhere Doors" is a science fiction tale of destiny, and "Mankind Journeys through Forests of Symbols" a metaphysical meditation on creativity. Two stories, "Weird Tales" and "The Adder," show the influence of the writings of H.P. Lovecraft. Some stories resemble mainstream fiction, but all are exquisitely crafted.

Other books you might like:
Robert R. McCammon, *Blue World*, 1989
Manly Wade Wellman, *The Valley So Low*, 1986

783

SUZY MCKEE CHARNAS

The Furies

(New York: Tor, 1994)

Story type: Science Fiction (Gay/Lesbian Fiction; Post-Holocaust)
Major character(s): Alldera, Leader; Sheel Torriner, Leader
Time period(s): Indeterminate Future
Locale(s): The Grasslands, Fictional Country (Red Sands Camp); Holdfast, Fictional City

Summary: Alldera of the Free Fems, escaped slaves from Holdfast, leads the escapees back to free the fems left behind and to find men to mate with to allow them to have children. Led by Sheel, the Riding Women, who have no need for men, follow to talk the Free Fems into returning with them, but instead become involved in the rescue. The response of the Free Fems to their old oppressors confuses and disrupts the Riding Women. Sequel to *Motherlines*.

Other books you might like:
Eleanor Arnason, *A Woman of the Iron People*, 1991
Margaret Atwood, *The Handmaid's Tale*, 1985
Orson Scott Card, *Lovelock*, 1994
    Kathryn H. Kidd, co-author
Suzette Haden Elgin, *Native Tongue*, 1984
Norma Marder, *An Eye for Dark Places*, 1993
Marge Piercy, *Woman on the Edge of Time*, 1976
Pamela Sargent, *The Shore of Women*, 1986
Joan Slonczewski, *A Door into Ocean*, 1986
Michael D. Weaver, *My Father Immortal*, 1989

784

SUZY MCKEE CHARNAS

The Golden Thread

(New York: Bantam, 1989)

Story type: Fantasy (Magic Conflict)
Series: Sorcery Hall

Major character(s): Valentine Marsh, Student—High School, Sorceress (apprentice); Bosanka Lonat, Student—Exchange, Sorceress (of another realm)
Time period(s): Indeterminate
Locale(s): Sorcery Hall, Earth

Summary: Valentine Marsh has inherited the family gift of sorcery from her ailing grandmother. At a New Year's Eve party, Valentine attempts to use her novice powers and she and her friends mistakenly summon a girl named Bosanka Lonat from her native realm. Bosanka is a sinister and manipulative girl who poses as a foreign exchange student. She desperately needs to assemble Valentine and her skeptical friends together again in order to conjure the necessary psychic powers for her to return to her native realm.

Other books you might like:
Diane Duane, *High Wizardry*, 1989
Tim Powers, *The Anubis Gates*, 1983
   6th Printing 1989
Jane Resh Thomas, *The Princess in the Pigpen*, 1989
Connie Willis, *Light Raid*, 1989
   Science Fiction. Cynthia Felice, co-author
Roger Zelazny, *Today We Choose Faces*, 1973
   re-issue 1989

785

SUZY MCKEE CHARNAS

The Kingdom of Kevin Malone
(New York: Harcourt Brace Jovanovich, 1993)

Story type: Fantasy (Alternate World; Young Adult)
Major character(s): Kevin Malone, Teenager, Abuse Victim; Amy, Teenager
Time period(s): 1990s; Indeterminate
Locale(s): New York, New York (Central Park); Fayre Farre, Mythical Place

Summary: After Kevin teases Amy, she chases him through Central Park's Willowdell Arch and finds herself with him in Fayre Farre, an imaginary world Kevin dreamed up to escape his abusive father. Although Prince Kevin sees himself as the Promised Champion, a prophecy indicates Amy and her friends must save Kevin's Kingdom.

Other books you might like:
Gary L. Blackwood, *Beyond the Door*, 1991
Philip Jose Farmer, *Red Orc's Rage*, 1991
Steven Gould, *Jumper*, 1992
Peni R. Griffin, *Hobkin*, 1992
Betty Levin, *Mercy's Mill*, 1992
Susan Palwick, *Flying in Place*, 1992
Will Shetterly, *Elsewhere*, 1991
Nancy Springer, *The Friendship Song*, 1992

786

ROBERT N. CHARRETTE

Choose Your Enemies Carefully
(New York: Roc, 1990)

Story type: Science Fiction (Alternate Universe; Science Fantasy)
Series: Secrets of Power
Major character(s): Samuel Verner, Outlaw; Dodger, Mutant, Computer Expert (outlaw)
Time period(s): 2050s (2051)
Locale(s): London, England

Summary: When magic returns to Earth, its power calls Sam Verner. As Sam searches for his sister, his quest leads him across the ocean to England where druids rule again. But all is not what it seems and Sam and his new friends are plunged into a maze of intrigue and madness. Only when Sam accepts his destiny as a shaman can he embrace the power he needs. But what waits for him in the final confrontation of technology and flesh is a secret much darker than anything he knew lay waiting in the shadows.

Other books you might like:
Emma Bull, *Bone Dance*, 1991
Randall Garrett, *Too Many Magicians*, 1967
Barbara Hambly, *Dragonsbane*, 1986
Larry Niven, *Dream Park*, 1981
   Steven Barnes, co-author
Walter Jon Williams, *Hardwired*, 1986
Terri Windling, *Borderland*, 1986
   Mark Alan Arnold, co-editor
Terri Windling, *Bordertown*, 1986
   Mark Alan Arnold, co-editor

787

ROBERT N. CHARRETTE

Find Your Own Truth
(New York: Roc, 1991)

Story type: Fantasy (Adventure)
Series: Secrets of Power
Major character(s): Samuel Verner, Shaman; Janice Verner, Monster; Dodger, Mutant, Computer Expert (pecker)
Time period(s): 21st century
Locale(s): Ayer's Rock, Australia; Seattle, Washington

Summary: Sam Verner continues trying to reverse his sister's transformation into a Wendigo by stealing a powerful talisman that allows an unfriendly totem into the Sixth World. Vernor requires the aid of all his friends and immense sacrifice to avoid Spider's webs trapping the whole world. Based on the Shadowrun game.

Other books you might like:
Nigel Findley, *2XS*, 1992
William Gibson, *Neuromancer*, 1984
Jonathan Littell, *Bad Voltage*, 1989
David Pringle, *Route 666*, 1990
   editor
Walter Jon Williams, *Hardwired*, 1986

788

ROBERT N. CHARRETTE

A King Beneath the Mountain
(New York: Warner Aspect, 1995)

Story type: Fantasy (Urban; Magic Conflict)
Series: Prince Among Men
Major character(s): John Reddy, Mythical Creature (elf), Adventurer; Quetzal, Immortal; Elizabeth Spae, Researcher (magic), Adventurer
Time period(s): 21st century
Locale(s): Massachusetts; France

Summary: With corporations responding to reemerging magical forces, human and non-human agents plot to control this powerful, ancient magic. An invitation from a mysterious messenger leads John Reddy to accept the call for help from the awakened King Arthur to help stop an evil force that appeared with the magic.

Other books you might like:
Dennis Lee Anderson, *Arthur, King*, 1995
Donald Barthelme, *The King*, 1990
Molly Cochran, *The Forever King*, 1992
   Warren Murphy, co-author
Elizabeth Forrest, *Phoenix Fire*, 1992
Simon Hawke, *The Wizard of 4th Street*, 1987
Simon Hawke, *The Wizard of Camelot*, 1993
Michael A. Stackpole, *Once a Hero*, 1994

789

ROBERT N. CHARRETTE

A Knight Among Knaves
(New York: Warner Aspect, 1995)

Story type: Fantasy (Urban; Magic Conflict)
Series: Prince Among Men
Major character(s): John Reddy, Mythical Creature (elf); Bennett, Nobleman, Mythical Creature (elf); Holger Kun, Military Personnel
Time period(s): 21st century
Locale(s): Providence, Rhode Island; Faery, Mythical Place

Summary: Human and inhuman legacies still tear at John Reddy as the Glittering Path attempts to summon another demon. All sides, human, Faery, Corporate, Squatter, ancient, and modern, must work together or everyone dies.

Other books you might like:
Emma Bull, *Bone Dance*, 1991
Charles de Lint, *Svaha*, 1989
Tom Deitz, *Windmaster's Bane*, 1986
Nigel Findley, *2XS*, 1992
Walter Jon Williams, *Voice of the Whirlwind*, 1987

790

ROBERT N. CHARRETTE

Never Trust an Elf
(New York: Roc, 1992)

Story type: Fantasy (Urban; Political)
Series: Shadowrun
Major character(s): Kham, Mythical Creature (orc), Leader (teenage gang)
Time period(s): 2050s (2053)
Locale(s): Seattle, Washington; Orktown, Fictional City

Summary: Kham and his fellow Shadowrunners unexpectedly involve themselves in power struggles when they acquire an elven crystal usable as a conduit for magic forces. Set in the universe of the game, *Shadowrun*.

Other books you might like:
Emma Bull, *Bone Dance*, 1991
Nigel Findley, *2XS*, 1992
K.W. Jeter, *Madlands*, 1991
Christopher Kubasik, *Changeling*, 1992
Will Shetterly, *Elsewhere*, 1991
Jordan K. Weisman, *Into the Shadows*, 1992
   editor
Terri Windling, *Life on the Border*, 1991
   editor

791

ROBERT N. CHARRETTE

A Prince Among Men
(New York: Warner Aspect, 1994)

Story type: Fantasy (Urban; Magic Conflict)
Series: Prince Among Men
Major character(s): John Reddy, Security Officer; Arthur "Artos", Ruler, Hero; Nym, Mythical Creature (elf)
Time period(s): 21st century
Locale(s): Massachusetts

Summary: When supernatural forces utilize powerful elven magic which could transform or destroy the world, John Reddy and Nym bring King Arthur out of stasis to save the human realm.

Other books you might like:
Dennis Lee Anderson, *Arthur, King*, 1995
Donald Barthelme, *The King*, 1990
Molly Cochran, *The Forever King*, 1992
   Warren Murphy, co-author
Susan Cooper, *Over Sea, Under Stone*, 1966
Simon Hawke, *The Wizard of Camelot*, 1993
Michael A. Stackpole, *Once a Hero*, 1994

792
ROBERT N. CHARRETTE

Shadowrun: Never Deal with a Dragon
(New York: Roc, 1990)

Story type: Science Fiction (Alternate Universe; Science Fantasy)
Series: Secrets of Power
Major character(s): Samuel Verner, Businessman (corporate researcher/salaryman); Dodger, Mutant, Computer Expert (outlaw)
Time period(s): 2050s (2051)
Locale(s): Seattle, Washington

Summary: In the near future, magic is on the rise and ancient races (orks, elves and dwarves) have re-emerged as humanoform mutants and many now work for the megacorporations.

Other books you might like:
Emma Bull, *Bone Dance*, 1991
Randall Garrett, *Too Many Magicians*, 1967
Barbara Hambly, *Dragonsbane*, 1986
Larry Niven, *Dream Park*, 1981
    Steven Barnes, co-author
Walter Jon Williams, *Hardwired*, 1986
Terri Windling, *Borderland*, 1986
    Mark Alan Arnold, co-editor
Terri Windling, *Bordertown*, 1986
    Mark Alan Arnold, co-editor

793
ROBERT N. CHARRETTE

Timespell
(New York: HarperPrism, 1996)

Story type: Fantasy (Adventure; Magic Conflict)
Series: Chronicles of Aelwyn
Major character(s): Yan Tanafres, Wizard; Peyto Lennuick, Scholar; Teletha Schonnegon, Military Personnel (airship captain)
Time period(s): Indeterminate Past
Locale(s): At Sea; Scothandir, Fictional Country

Summary: Discouraged and frustrated by his lack of success as an apprentice magician, Yan sets out from his provincial home to seek his fortune in the Imperial Capitol. Pirates, shipwreck, fishers, mercenaries, airship crews, and strange magic mold his trip to destiny.

Other books you might like:
Glen Cook, *The Swordbearer*, 1982
Diane Duane, *The Door into Fire*, 1979
Ursula K. Le Guin, *A Wizard of Earthsea*, 1968
Patricia A. McKillip, *The Riddle-Master of Hed*, 1976
Judith Tarr, *Ars Magica*, 1989

794
CAROL CHASE

Hawk's Flight
(New York: Baen, 1991)

Story type: Fantasy (Adventure; Political)
Major character(s): Taverik Zandro, Businessman (merchant); Marko Kastazi, Businesswoman (merchant), Heiress—Lost
Time period(s): Indeterminate
Locale(s): Pakajan Peninsula, Fictional Country

Summary: Coming to a fellow merchant's aid, Taverik Zandro does not expect the secrets he uncovers or the political intrigue into which he is subsequently swept.

Other books you might like:
Marc Laidlaw, *Neon Lotus*, 1988
Ron Miller, *Palaces and Prisons*, 1991
Ron Miller, *Silk and Steel*, 1992
Terry Pratchett, *Wyrd Sisters*, 1990
Cynthia Voigt, *On Fortune's Wheel*, 1990

795
C.J. CHERRYH

Chanur's Legacy
(New York: DAW, 1992)

Story type: Science Fiction (Science Fiction; Political)
Series: Chanur
Major character(s): Hilfy Chanur, Alien (Han), Spaceship Captain; No'shto-shti-stlen, Alien (Stsho), Diplomat (Ambassador); Vikktakkht, Alien (Kif), Spaceship Captain
Time period(s): Indeterminate Future
Locale(s): *Chanur's Legacy*, Spaceship; Meetpoint, Space Station; Compact Space, Interstellar Empire/Federation

Summary: Hilfy, niece of Pyanfur, Personage of Personages, finds a deal on Meetpoint that, while too good to be true, Hilfy can't refuse. Hilfy encounters increasing difficulty with the commission, to deliver a precious object to an individual. Wherever they travel, *Chanur's Legacy* and her crew become a political focus due to the belief that Hilfy's time on *The Pride of Chanur* left her an agent of Pyanfur. The peace Pyanfur imposed on Compact Space seems at risk.

Other books you might like:
David Brin, *The Uplift War*, 1987
Diana G. Gallagher, *The Alien Dark*, 1990
Stephen Goldin, *Jade Darcy and the Zen Pirates*, 1990
    Mary Mason, co-author
Stephen Leigh, *Alien Tongue*, 1991
Alis A. Rasmussen, *A Passage of Stars*, 1990
L. Neil Smith, *Their Majesties' Bucketeers*, 1981

796

C.J. CHERRYH

Chernevog

(New York: Del Rey, 1990)

Story type: Fantasy (Legend)
Series: Rusalka
Major character(s): Pyetr Kochevikov, Hero; Sasha Misurov, Wizard, Apprentice; Kavi Chernevog, Wizard
Time period(s): Indeterminate Past (Before 988)
Locale(s): Vojvoda, Russia (Pre-Christian Russia)

Summary: Trying to follow his wife on her mysterious quest, Pyetr Kochevikov and Sasha Misurov accidently release Kavi Chernevog from the spell which had confined him, protecting everyone else. Their further wandering yields soul searching and personal recriminations.

Other books you might like:
Kingsley Amis, *The Green Man*, 1969
Jo Clayton, *Drinker of Souls*, 1986
Dan McGirt, *Jason Cosmo*, 1989
Flann O'Brien, *The Third Policeman*, 1967
Christopher Priest, *The Glamour*, 1984

797

C.J. CHERRYH

Cloud's Rider

(New York: Warner Aspect, 1996)

Story type: Science Fiction (Psychic Powers; Lost Colony)
Major character(s): Danny Fisher, Telepath; Cloud, Animal (nighthorse), Telepath; Brionne Goss, Telepath
Time period(s): Indeterminate Future
Locale(s): Planet—Imaginary

Summary: Escorting the three surviving residents of Tarmin up the mountains in a winter storm, Danny and Cloud guide them to safety at the village of Evergreen. Although a riderless nighthorse has followed them, Danny fears to tell all he knows, especially about the unconscious Brionne whose madness might draw disaster on them again if she wakes. Inside the walls, the villagers see an opportunity to claim Tarmin as salvage, with the three children as pawns or obstacles, while outside something lurks in the Wild.

Other books you might like:
Gayle Greeno, *Mind-Speakers' Call*, 1994
Anne McCaffrey, *Dragonsdawn*, 1988
Lisanne Norman, *Turning Point*, 1993
Andre Norton, *Catseye*, 1961
Vernor Vinge, *A Fire upon the Deep*, 1992

798

C.J. CHERRYH

Cyteen

(New York: Popular Library Questar, 1989)

Story type: Science Fiction (Hard Science Fiction)

Major character(s): Ariane Emory, Scientist, Political Figure; Ari, Clone, Scientist
Time period(s): 24th century
Locale(s): Cyteen, Planet—Imaginary (Circling Pell's star)

Summary: Ariane Emory is the most powerful person on Cyteen, a brilliant scientist, a ruthless politician, a virtual monster. Reseune, the company she controls, creates clones, the workers and soldiers who run the planet. Ariane, however, is getting old and in order to gain a kind of immortality, she clones herself. After Ariane is murdered, her clone, Ari, must take over. Controlled by those who would turn her into another Ariane, she must struggle to become her own person. Three paperback volumes, *The Betrayal*, *The Rebirth*, and *The Vindication* were reprinted in 1989 from the 1988 original one-volume edition.

Other books you might like:
Isaac Asimov, *Foundation*, 1951
Isaac Asimov, *Foundation and Empire*, 1952
Isaac Asimov, *Foundation's Edge*, 1982
Isaac Asimov, *Robots and Empire*, 1985
Isaac Asimov, *Second Foundation*, 1953
Bruce Sterling, *Islands in the Net*, 1988
Walter Jon Williams, *Angel Station*, 1989

799

C.J. CHERRYH

Downbelow Station

(New York: DAW Books, 1989)

Story type: Science Fiction (Space Opera)
Series: Union/Alliance
Major character(s): Damon Konstantin, Administrator (Spacestation administrator); Signy Mallory, Spaceship Captain
Time period(s): 24th century (2352)
Locale(s): Downbelow, Planet—Imaginary; Downbelow, Space Station; *Norway*, Spaceship

Summary: This Hugo Award-winning novel, an early entry in Cherryh's Union/Alliance future history series, recounts the complex struggle, both military and political, for Downbelow Station, a key defensive position in the battle between Earth and its rebellious colonies. Originally published in 1981.

Other books you might like:
Greg Bear, *Eon*, 1985
Gregory Benford, *Great Sky River*, 1987
Gregory Benford, *Tides of Light*, 1989
Emma Bull, *Falcon*, 1989
Walter Jon Williams, *Angel Station*, 1989

800

C.J. CHERRYH, Editor

Endgame

(New York: DAW, 1991)

Story type: Science Fiction (Anthology)
Series: Merovingen Nights

Major character(s): Altair Jones, Trader (canaler); Tom Mondragon, Revolutionary (former), Refugee
Time period(s): Indeterminate Future
Locale(s): Merovingen, Fictional Country

Summary: All the forces operating in Merovingen reach the crisis point, as those who fancy themselves powerful try to direct the course of events before the Sharrh return and scour the planet. This "braided" format novel incorporates seven short stories by Lynn Abbey, Nancy Asire, C.J. Cherryh, Mercedes Lackey, Janet and Chris Morris and Bradley H. Sinor. 15 pages of indexed maps follow the text.

Other books you might like:
Robert Asprin, *Thieves' World*, 1979
    editor
Marion Zimmer Bradley, *Sharra's Exile*, 1981
Lois McMaster Bujold, *The Warrior's Apprentice*, 1986
Emma Bull, *Bone Dance*, 1991
George R.R. Martin, *Jokertown Shuffle*, 1991
    editor
Will Shetterly, *Liavek*, 1985
    Emma Bull, co-editor
S.M. Stirling, *The Cage*, 1989
    Shirley Meier, co-author
Terri Windling, *Borderland*, 1986
    Mark Alan Arnold, co-editor

801

C.J. CHERRYH

Faery in Shadow
(New York: Ballantine Del Rey, 1994)

Story type: Fantasy (Adventure)
Major character(s): Caith mac Sliabhin, Outlaw; Dubhain, Mythical Creature (pooka); Firinne, Farmer
Time period(s): Indeterminate Past
Locale(s): Gaugach, Mythical Place (stream); Gleann Fiain, Fictional Country

Summary: Doomed for his sins, Caith must travel alone except for his inhuman companion and keeper, Dubhain. Fleeing from danger and their own quarreling, they stumble across a farm tended by an unusual couple and soon find themselves caught up in a web of evil, past sins and Sidhe magic.

Other books you might like:
Eleanor Arnason, *The Sword Smith*, 1978
Peter S. Beagle, *The Folk of the Air*, 1986
Emma Bull, *War for the Oaks*, 1987
Julian May, *The Many-Colored Land*, 1981
Evangeline Walton, *The Prince of Annwn*, 1974

802

C.J. CHERRYH

Flood Tide
(New York: DAW, 1990)

Story type: Science Fiction (Anthology)
Series: Merovingen Nights
Time period(s): Indeterminate Future

Locale(s): Merovingen, Fictional Country

Summary: 11 stories surrounding a murder and political struggles in Merovingen. The texts, overlapping in time, are woven together so that the many authors' works appear in the form of the "braided novel" rather than the traditional anthology format. Among the notable authors included in this volume are Lynn Abbey, Nancy Asire, C.J. Cherryh and Mercedes Lackey. This book is the sixth anthology edited by Cherryh, which follows her *Angel with the Sword* (1985).

Other books you might like:
George R.R. Martin, *Ace in the Hole*, 1990
George R.R. Martin, *Down and Dirty*, 1988
Will Shetterly, *Liavek*, 1985
    Emma Bull, co-editor
Will Shetterly, *Liavek: Festival Week*, 1990
    Emma Bull, co-editor
Will Shetterly, *Liavek: The Players of Luck*, 1986
    Emma Bull, co-editor
Will Shetterly, *Liavek: Spells of Binding*, 1988
    Emma Bull, co-editor
Will Shetterly, *Liavek: Wizard's Row*, 1987
    Emma Bull, co-editor
Terri Windling, *Borderland*, 1986
    Mark Alan Arnold, co-editor
Terri Windling, *Bordertown*, 1986
    Mark Alan Arnold, co-editor

803

C.J. CHERRYH

Foreigner
(New York: DAW, 1994)

Story type: Science Fiction (First Contact; Political)
Series: Foreigner Universe
Major character(s): Manadgi, Alien (Atevi); Bren Cameron, Linguist, Diplomat; Ilisidi, Alien (Atevi)
Time period(s): Indeterminate Future
Locale(s): *Phoenix*, Spaceship; Planet—Imaginary (Mospheria Island colony)

Summary: When *Phoenix*, a colony ship, arrives at its destination, the crew expects to find a habitable planet previously discovered by robot probes. Unable to find any recognizable stars, the crew searches for the nearest habitable system only to find it already inhabited by intelligent aliens. Unwilling to remain on the station, some of the colonists parachute down to the planet, hoping to construct return craft after setting up a community. The Alien Atevi make contact and agree to interact with one human, allowing humans to stay if they pay with information. Abandoned by *Phoenix*, several hundred years later humans and Atevi must learn to better understand each other and cooperate to keep their independence from the returning ship.

Other books you might like:
Eleanor Arnason, *Ring of Swords*, 1993
David Brin, *The Uplift War*, 1987
Gordon R. Dickson, *The Alien Way*, 1965
Diana G. Gallagher, *The Alien Dark*, 1990
Mary Gentle, *Golden Witchbreed*, 1984

Kris Jensen, *Mentor*, 1991
Janet Kagan, *Hellspark*, 1988
Larry Niven, *The Gripping Hand*, 1993
   Jerry Pournelle, co-author
Vernor Vinge, *A Fire upon the Deep*, 1992

804

C.J. CHERRYH

Fortress in the Eye of Time

(New York: HarperPrism, 1995)

Story type: Fantasy (Magic Conflict; Political)
Major character(s): Mauryl Gestaurien, Wizard; Tristen, Foundling; Cefwyn, Royalty (prince)
Time period(s): Indeterminate
Locale(s): Ylesuin, Fictional Country; Ynefel, Fictional City; Amefel, Fictional Country

Summary: With the Sihhe gone from the land and the war long over, Mauryl shapes a boy and summons a soul to continue the old battle. Not what Mauryl shaped or called, the boy, Tristen, must play a central role in the battle without knowing his past or his fate.

Other books you might like:
Glen Cook, *The Black Company*, 1984
Patricia A. McKillip, *The Riddle-Master of Hed*, 1976
Mary Stewart, *The Crystal Cave*, 1970
J.R.R. Tolkien, *The Fellowship of the Ring*, 1954
Joan D. Vinge, *The Snow Queen*, 1980
Paula Volsky, *Illusion*, 1992

805

C.J. CHERRYH

The Goblin Mirror

(New York: Ballantine Del Rey, 1992)

Story type: Fantasy (Magic Conflict; Quest)
Major character(s): Tamas of Maggiar, Royalty (prince), Adventurer; Ela, Witch (apprentice), Adventurer; Azdra'ik, Mythical Creature (goblin), Royalty (prince)
Time period(s): Indeterminate
Locale(s): Maggiar, Mythical Place (kingdom); Over-mountain, Mythical Place

Summary: When she survives the goblin attack which kills her mistress, Ela sets out to find and confront the goblin queen utilizing the shard of a powerful magical mirror. Ela meets Tamas whose comrades scattered in a goblin attack on the group who had set out to discover the cause of increasing problems in the kingdom. After Azdra'ik rescues Tamas from ensorcellment, an unexpected alliance forms.

Other books you might like:
David Eddings, *Pawn of Prophecy*, 1982
Mary Gentle, *Rats and Gargoyles*, 1991
Barbara Hambly, *Dragonsbane*, 1987
Laurell K. Hamilton, *Nightseer*, 1992
Robert Jordan, *The Eye of the World*, 1989
Elizabeth Moon, *Sheepfarmer's Daughter*, 1988

806

C.J. CHERRYH

Heavy Time

(New York: Warner Questar, 1991)

Story type: Science Fiction (Space Colony; Political)
Series: Compact Space
Major character(s): Paul Dekker, Pilot, Prospector; Morris Bird, Pilot, Prospector; Ben Pollard, Pilot, Prospector
Time period(s): Indeterminate Future
Locale(s): Asteroid (Sol's asteroid belt)

Summary: Paul Dekker wakes one day with his ship stolen, his partner missing, his memory destroyed and his future gone. The ASTEX mining monopoly, Mama, accuses him of being negligent, crazy and a cold-blooded murderer. Only renegade miners Morris Bird and Ben Pollard can help Dekker learn the truth that somewhere in his mind lies a dark secret that can change the fate of worlds.

Other books you might like:
Alan Dean Foster, *Cyber Way*, 1990
Rebecca Ore, *The Illegal Rebirth of Billy the Kid*, 1991
Alis A. Rasmussen, *A Passage of Stars*, 1990
Walter Jon Williams, *Voice of the Whirlwind*, 1987
Roger Zelazny, *Doorways in the Sand*, 1976

807

C.J. CHERRYH

Hellburner

(New York: Warner, 1992)

Story type: Science Fiction (Adventure; Political)
Series: Compact Space
Major character(s): Ben Pollard, Pilot; Paul Dekker, Pilot; Meg Kady, Pilot
Time period(s): 24th century (2320s)
Locale(s): Sol II, Space Station

Summary: Sent back out to visit Paul, Ben soon realizes that his life will not continue as he had planned. After Meg and Sal appear on Earth II, Ben recognizes his involvement in a conspiracy and political intrigue reaching from Earth to beyond the Belt with the future of humanity in the balance.

Other books you might like:
Gordon R. Dickson, *Dorsai!*, 1976
Paula E. Downing, *Flare Star*, 1992
Tara K. Harper, *Lightwing*, 1992
Alis A. Rasmussen, *A Passage of Stars*, 1990
Allen Steele, *Orbital Decay*, 1989
Walter Jon Williams, *Voice of the Whirlwind*, 1987

808

C.J. CHERRYH

Inheritor

(New York: DAW, 1996)

Story type: Science Fiction (Political; First Contact)
Series: Foreigner Universe

Major character(s): Bren Cameron, Diplomat, Linguist; Ilisidi, Alien (Atevi), Ruler; Jason "Jase" Graham, Spaceman, Engineer
Time period(s): Indeterminate Future
Locale(s): *Phoenix*, Spaceship (in orbit); Shejidan, Fictional City; Mospheira, Fictional City (island)

Summary: A near accident mars the return flight from Bren's successful tour of the new Atevi space facilities. Already in crisis due to immersion in Atevi language, Jase hears of his father's accidental death on the *Phoenix*. Repairs to their borrowed apartment reach completion, leading to the return of the hostile owner, Ilisidi, powerful grandmother of the current ruler and, hopefully, ally in what Bren interprets as warfare.

Other books you might like:
Eleanor Arnason, *Ring of Swords*, 1993
Gordon R. Dickson, *The Alien Way*, 1996
Mary Gentle, *Golden Witchbreed*, 1984
Elizabeth Moon, *Remnant Population*, 1996
Larry Niven, *The Gripping Hand*, 1993
  Jerry Pournelle, co-author

809

C.J. CHERRYH

Invader

(New York: DAW, 1995)

Story type: Science Fiction (First Contact; Political)
Series: Foreigner Universe
Major character(s): Bren Cameron, Linguist, Diplomat; Tabini, Alien (Atevi), Royalty; Deana Hanks, Linguist, Government Official
Time period(s): Indeterminate Future
Locale(s): Planet—Imaginary (Mospheira Island human colony); *Phoenix*, Spaceship

Summary: As human official translator to the Atevi, Bren realizes that the policy determined on Mospheira can lead only to disaster. When the *Phoenix* returns after abandoning the human colony, the government attempts to replace Bren with a human chauvinist successor and to prevent the ship from dealing with the Atevi. Convinced that this course leads to disaster for all, Bren contacts the ship directly as representative of the Atevi. Attempting to destabilize Atevi society, Deana gives them the idea of faster-than-light spaceships, risking the breakdown of relations or even warfare between human and Atevi. Sequel to *Foreigner*.

Other books you might like:
David Brin, *Brightness Reef*, 1995
Gordon R. Dickson, *The Alien Way*, 1965
L. Warren Douglas, *Cannon's Orb*, 1994
Diana G. Gallagher, *The Alien Dark*, 1990
Janet Kagan, *Hellspark*, 1988

810

C.J. CHERRYH

Lois & Clark

(Rocklin, California: Prima Publishing, 1996)

Story type: Science Fiction (Adventure)
Series: Superman
Major character(s): Clark "Superman" Kent, Journalist, Alien (Kryptonian); Lois Lane, Journalist, Girlfriend
Time period(s): 1990s
Locale(s): Metropolis (New York City)

Summary: While Superman works to save a village in the Caucasus Mountains from disaster, a bomb devastates a Metropolis hotel near the *Daily Planet*. Lois rushes to help, resulting in her public recognition as a hero. Unfortunately, the subsequent notoriety may prove disastrous for the secret she shares with Clark, and even their relationship.

Other books you might like:
M.J. Friedman, *Deadly Games*, 1996
M.J. Friedman, *Exile*, 1996
M.J. Friedman, *Heat Wave*, 1996
Martin H. Greenberg, *The Further Adventures of Superman*, 1993
  editor
Elliot S. Maggin, *Superman: Last Son of Krypton*, 1978
Elliot S. Maggin, *Superman: Miracle Monday*, 1981
Roger Stern, *The Death and Life of Superman*, 1993

811

C.J. CHERRYH

Rider at the Gate

(New York: Warner Aspect, 1995)

Story type: Science Fiction (Psychic Powers; Lost Colony)
Major character(s): Danny Fisher, Telepath; Guil Stewart, Telepath; Cloud, Animal (Nighthorse), Telepath
Time period(s): Indeterminate Future
Locale(s): Planet—Imaginary

Summary: A Nighthorse Rider dies under suspicious conditions on the trail. When her lover, Guil Stewart, hears of it, his emotions broadcast through his own Nighthorse to the other horses and riders in town. Forced at gunpoint to leave the walled town, Guil and his stallion, Burn, ride into the winter blizzards, seeking the killer. Danny and the dead woman's kinsmen search for Guil, unaware of an enemy tracking them.

Other books you might like:
Gayle Greeno, *Finders-Seekers*, 1993
R.A. MacAvoy, *The Grey Horse*, 1987
Anne McCaffrey, *Dragonflight*, 1968
James H. Schmitz, *The Universe Against Her*, 1964
Tricia Sullivan, *Lethe*, 1995

812

C.J. CHERRYH

Rimrunners

(New York: Warner, 1989)

Story type: Science Fiction (Adventure)
Major character(s): Elizabeth Yeager, Spacewoman; Ramey, Spaceman
Time period(s): 24th century
Locale(s): *Loki*, Spaceship (The Hinder Stars)

Summary: A down and out spacer finds a berth on the starship *Loki* and, despite working hard, finds herself on the bad side of the ship's executive officer. She also discovers that the ship may be involved in illegal activities.

Other books you might like:
Larry Niven, *The Mote in God's Eye*, 1974
   Jerry Pournelle, co-author
Larry Niven, *Protector*, 1973
Larry Niven, *Ringworld*, 1970
Walter Jon Williams, *Angel Station*, 1989

813

C.J. CHERRYH

Rusalka

(New York: Del Rey, 1989)

Story type: Fantasy (Legend)
Series: Rusalka
Major character(s): Pyetr Kochevikov, Hero, Fugitive; Sasha Misurov, Wizard, Apprentice
Time period(s): Indeterminate Past (Before 988)
Locale(s): Vojvoda, Russia (Pre-Christian Russia)

Summary: Accused of killing a wealthy noble, Pyetr and his friend Sasha flee the village and make for Kiev. In an enchanted forest, the two stumble upon Vulamets, a powerful old wizard, who coerces them to assist in his attempts to bring his murdered daughter Eveshka back from the dead. She roams the forest as a ghostly Rusalka, an ill-fated spirit that must prey on living things in order to restore its life, but alas the evil wizard Kavi Chernevog continues to hold her life force in sway.

Other books you might like:
Kingsley Amis, *The Green Man*, 1969
Jo Clayton, *Drinker of Souls*,
   Drinker of Souls Trilogy. Bk. 1
Dan McGirt, *Jason Cosmo*, 1989
Flann O'Brien, *The Third Policeman*, 1967
Christopher Priest, *The Glamour*, 1984

814

C.J. CHERRYH

Tripoint

(New York: Warner Aspect, 1994)

Story type: Science Fiction (Family Saga; Adventure)

Major character(s): Thomas ''Tom'' Bowe-Hawkins, Spaceman, Prisoner; Marie Hawkins, Spacewoman (cargo master), Parent; Austin Bowe, Spaceship Captain, Parent
Time period(s): Indeterminate Future
Locale(s): *Sprite*, Spaceship; *Corinthian*, Spaceship; Viking, Space Station (E. Eridani system)

Summary: Raised by Marie on the family ship, *Sprite*, Tom never feels accepted as one of the family. When, against orders, Marie decides to check out *Corinthian*, her rapist's ship, Tom decides to again try getting close to her and helping, but instead gets kidnapped by his half-brother. Unfortunately, his mother had threatened Austin that when Tom grew up, she'd have him hurt Austin and everyone close to him, making it difficult for anyone on *Corinthian* to trust him. On *Corinthian* Tom discovers he has the rare ability to stay sane in transit without tranquilizers.

Other books you might like:
Stephen Baxter, *Raft*, 1991
James Blish, *A Life for the Stars*, 1962
Lois McMaster Bujold, *Mirror Dance*, 1994
Lois McMaster Bujold, *The Warrior's Apprentice*, 1986
F.M. Busby, *Rissa Kerguelen*, 1977
Alis A. Rasmussen, *A Passage of Stars*, 1990
Vernor Vinge, *A Fire upon the Deep*, 1992

815

C.J. CHERRYH
NANCY ASIRE, Co-Author

Wizard Spawn

(New York: Baen, 1989)

Story type: Fantasy (Magic Conflict)
Series: Sword of Knowledge
Time period(s): Indeterminate

Summary: A society opposed to the use of magic and weapons is invaded a brutal race. Only a few of the conquered have the ability and will to use magic and weapons to defend their home.

Other books you might like:
Marion Zimmer Bradley, *Thendara House*, 1983
Sharon Green, *Lady Blade, Lord Fighter*, 1987
Jennifer Roberson, *Sword-Dancer*, 1986

816

C.J. CHERRYH

Yvgenie

(New York: Ballantine/Del Rey, 1991)

Story type: Fantasy (Legend)
Series: Rusalka
Major character(s): Pyetr Kochevikov, Hero; Kavi Chernevog, Spirit; Eveshka, Wizard
Time period(s): Indeterminate Past
Locale(s): Russia (pre-Christian)

Summary: Pyetr and Eveshka have a daughter, Ilyana, born a wizard like her mother. After Ilyana is discovered in the arms of Kavi, she is told many disturbing facts about her mother's early life. Eveshka leaves, Ilyana is kidnapped and Pyetr, carrying Eveshka's heart, sets out to save his family.

Other books you might like:
Steven Brust, *The Sun, the Moon, and the Stars*, 1987
Charles de Lint, *Jack, the Giant-Killer*, 1987
Pamela Dean, *Tam Lin*, 1991
Alan Garner, *The Weirdstone of Brisingamen*, 1969
Roberto Pazzi, *The Princess and the Dragon*, 1990
   M.J. Fitzgerald, co-author
Angus Wells, *Wrath of Ashar*, 1990
Patricia C. Wrede, *Snow White and Rose Red*, 1989

817

GEORGE C. CHESBRO

Bone

(New York: Mysterious Press 1990)

Story type: Horror (Serial Killer)
Major character(s): Bone, Streetperson, Amnesiac (murder suspect); Anne Winchell, Social Worker (Bone's lover)
Time period(s): 1980s
Locale(s): New York, New York (including underground caverns)

Summary: Bone wakes up one morning in the middle of a field, devoid of identity or memory, accused of beheading twenty-eight street people. Aided by Anne, a compassionate social worker, and Zulu, a seven-foot black storyteller, Bone struggles to learn his own identity and the awful truth about the killings—even at the risk of confirming his own guilt.

Other books you might like:
John Skipp, *The Light at the End*, 1986
   Craig Spector, co-author

818

GEORGE C. CHESBRO

The Fear in Yesterday's Rings

(New York: Mysterious Press, 1991)

Story type: Horror (Werewolf Story)
Series: Mongo
Major character(s): Robert ''Mongo'' Frederickson, Detective—Private; Harper Rhys-Whitney, Entertainer (circus performer); Phil Statler, Businessman (former circus owner)
Time period(s): 1990s (1991)
Locale(s): Nebraska; Midwest

Summary: Mongo, a circus dwarf turned criminologist, is thwarted in his efforts to return the Statler Brothers Circus to its ousted owner when the new owners refuse to sell. It's not long before Mongo suspects that their reticence is somehow related to a string of vicious deaths that has followed the circus across the country and been attributed to a werewolf.

Other books you might like:
D.J. Donaldson, *Blood on the Bayou*, 1991
Whitley Strieber, *The Wolfen*, 1978
Les Whitten, *Moon of the Wolf*, 1967

819

DEBORAH CHESTER

Reign of Shadows

(New York: Ace, 1996)

Story type: Fantasy (Political; Magic Conflict)
Series: Shadows
Major character(s): Caelan E'non, Gladiator, Psychic; Elandra Albain, Noblewoman, Bastard Daughter; Kostimon, Ruler (emperor)
Time period(s): Indeterminate Past
Locale(s): Trav, Fictional Country; Imperia, Fictional City

Summary: Nearly a millennium after Emperor Kostimon deals for a thousand years of life with the Dark God, Beloth, his empire collapses, undermined internally and externally. In the chaos, Caelan and Elandra find their destinies.

Other books you might like:
Scott Baker, *Drink the Fire From the Flames*, 1987
Glen Cook, *The Black Company*, 1984
Terry Goodkind, *Wizard's First Rule*, 1994
Barbara Hambly, *The Time of the Dark*, 1982
Martha Wells, *The Element of Fire*, 1993

820

GRACE CHETWIN

Collidescope

(New York: Bradbury Press, 1990)

Story type: Science Fiction (Time Travel)
Major character(s): Hahn, Spaceman; Frankie, Teenager; Sky-fire-trail, Indian
Time period(s): 1990s; 15th century
Locale(s): New York, New York

Summary: Hahn, a time-traveling agent for the Intergalactic Society for Planetary Conservation, is bushwacked as his spaceship nears the planet Earth. Time jumping into the past in an attempt to escape, he accidentally draws Frankie, a twentieth-century teenager who has earned her brown belt in karate, and Sky-fire-trail, a pre-colonial Delaware Indian, into an exciting adventure in space and time.

Other books you might like:
Helen Cresswell, *Moondial*, 1987
Alan Garner, *The Owl Service*, 1967
Alan Garner, *Red Shift*, 1973
Andre Norton, *The Defiant Agents*, 1962
Andre Norton, *Operation Time Search*, 1967
Andre Norton, *Quest Crosstime*, 1965

821

GRACE CHETWIN

Friends in Time

(New York: Bradbury Press, 1992)

Story type: Fantasy (Time Travel; Young Adult)
Major character(s): Emma Gibson, Time Traveller, Child; Abigail Porterhouse Bentley, Time Traveller, Child

Time period(s): 1990s (1995); 1840s (1846)
Locale(s): Middletown, New York

Summary: In the abandoned Bentley mansion Emma discovers Abigail whose taking of a medicine man's doll precipitated a trip 150 years into the future. After Emma befriends Abigail and plans to show her modern times, Abigail wishes both girls back to Abigail's time where Abigail decides to strand Emma. The girls must resolve their feelings and work together to return Emma to her own time.

Other books you might like:
Pam Conrad, *Stonewords: A Ghost Story*, 1990
Gilbert B. Cross, *A Witch Across Time*, 1990
Enid Richemont, *The Time Tree*, 1990
Robert Silverberg, *Letters From Atlantis*, 1990
Vivian Vande Velde, *A Well-Timed Enchantment*, 1990

822

ROB CHILSON

Men Like Rats

(New York: Popular Library Questar, 1989)

Story type: Science Fiction (Invasion of Earth)
Major character(s): Richer the Quick, Scavenger, Hero; Loy Little, Scavenger
Time period(s): Indeterminate Future
Locale(s): Earth

Summary: Alien invaders have taken over the Earth, turning human beings into little more than vermin hiding in cracks and crevasses. Scavenging desperately for food, doing battle with alien life forms and Earth-born mutants, humanity gradually loses ground to the invaders until one brave man begins to organize the resistance.

Other books you might like:
Gregory Benford, *Big Sky River*, 1987
Gregory Benford, *Tides of Light*, 1989
Thomas M. Disch, *The Genocides*, 1965
Thomas M. Disch, *Mankind under the Leash*, 1966
William Tenn, *Of Men and Monsters*, 1968
Jack Vance, *The Dragon Masters*, 1963

823

RICHARD T. CHIZMAR, Editor

Chillers

(Baltimore, Maryland: CD Publications)

Story type: Horror (Anthology)

Summary: The four authors represented in this anthology of dark suspense fiction each contribute 20,000 words of writing in different forms. Rex Miller's short novel "Kowloon" resurrects his misanthropic sociopath Chaingang Bunkowski by way of Chaingang's son, who still takes after his father despite his adoption by dad's killer, police detective Jack Eichord. Ardath Mayhar also has a short novel, "Winter-Stalk," in which a crusader against corruption in government turns vengeful when the forces he is battling murder his wife. Nancy Collins is on hand with four stories that deal variously with rock 'n' roll, circus freaks, southern racism, and lack of a

good health care plan. Chet Williamson's dynamic duo includes the psychological horror story "Dusty Death" and a study of disintegrating social dynamics, "Watching the Burning." Joe Lansdale supplies an introduction.

Other books you might like:
Robert Bloch, *Monsters in Our Midst*, 1993
  editor
Robert Bloch, *Psycho-Paths*, 1991
  editor
Joe R. Lansdale, *Dark at Heart*, 1992
  Karen Lansdale, co-editor

824

RICHARD T. CHIZMAR, Editor

Cold Blood

(Shingletown, California: Mark Ziesing, 1991)

Story type: Horror (Anthology)

Summary: Twenty-five tales of dark suspense, in which horror occurs in non-supernatural scenarios. Among the selections are John Shirley's "Jody and Annie on TV," about a thrill-killing teenage couple; F. Paul Wilson's "Home Repairs," starring his equalizer hero Repairman Jack; Richard Laymon's "Saving Grace," about two boys who save a woman from a serial killer and its peculiar aftermath; and a chapter from Ramsey Campbell's "comic" serial-killer novel, *The Count of Eleven*.

Other books you might like:
Robert Bloch, *Psycho-Paths*, 1991
  Martin H. Greenberg, co-editor
Ed Gorman, *Stalkers*, 1989
  Martin H. Greenberg, co-editor
Alfred Hitchcock, *Alfred Hitchcock Presents: Stories Not for the Nervous*, 1965
  editor
Joan Kahn, *Hanging by a Thread*, 1969

825

RICHARD T. CHIZMAR, Editor

The Earth Strikes Back

(Shingletown, California: Mark Ziesing, 1994)

Story type: Horror (Anthology; Nature in Revolt)

Summary: The 20 stories collected here all spin ecological horror scenarios out of the irresponsibility of man toward his environment. Included are Dan Simmons' "My Copsa Micas," which imagines the world as an organism trying to dispose of man like a virus; Thomas Tessier's "I Remember Me (But I'm Not Sure about You)," about a future in which a virus has destroyed short-term memory and identity; Poppy Brite's "Toxi Wastrels," a variation on the theme of Edgar Allan Poe's "Fall of the House of Usher," about the degeneration of a family that owns a chemical industry in the Louisiana swamps; Gary A. Braunbeck's "The Dreaded Hobblobs," about a mutant who represents the future evolution of humanity in a toxically despoiled world; and Nancy Collins' "Cancer Alley," about the revenge of a polluted town against the businessman who destroyed it. The book also includes stories by Norman Partridge, Hugh Cave, Ed Gorman, Richard Laymon, Chelsea Quinn Yarbro, Ric Hautala, and Thomas Monteleone.

Other books you might like:
John Skipp, *The Bridge*, 1991
  Craig Spector, co-author

826

RICHARD T. CHIZMAR

Midnight Promises
(Springfield, Pennsylvania: Gauntlet Publications, 1996)

Story type: Horror (Collection)

Summary: The 17 stories collected here by the editor of the horror magazine, *Cemetery Dance*, freely blend the genres of supernatural horror and dark suspense. The title story and ''Heroes'' use horrific elements to explore the emotional impact of terminal illness. ''The Season of Giving'' (written with Norman Partridge) and ''The Silence of Sorrow'' both probe the theme of child abuse. ''The Sinner King'' refurbishes the theme of the Holy Grail for a contemporary tale set in the Canadian wilderness. In ''Grand Finale'' a man discovers that the pick-ups he secretly videotapes during lovemaking play out sequences on film in which they try to kill him. Ed Gorman supplies an introduction and Ray Garton an afterword to this first book.

Other books you might like:
Scott Edelman, *Suicide Art*, 1992
Ray Garton, *Pieces of Hate*, 1996
Ed Gorman, *Cages*, 1995
Norman Partridge, *Bad Intentions*, 1996
Andrew Vachss, *A Flash of White*, 1993

827

JAMES C. CHRISTENSEN
RENWICK ST. JAMES, Co-Author
ALAN DEAN FOSTER, Co-Author

Voyage of the Basset
(New York: Workman Artisan, 1996)

Story type: Fantasy (Adventure; Young Adult)
Major character(s): Cassandra Aisling, Child, Adventurer; Algernon Aisling, Professor, Adventurer; Miranda Aisling, Teenager, Adventurer
Time period(s): 1850s
Locale(s): *H.M.S. Basset*, At Sea

Summary: Professor Aisling and his daughters set sail on the magical *H.M.S. Basset*, searching for the subjects of ancient legends. Presented as a lavishly illustrated journal of a voyage of discovery.

Other books you might like:
Betty Ballantine, *The Secret Oceans*, 1994
Graeme Base, *The Discovery of Dragons*, 1996
Michael Green, *Quest: In Search of the Dragontooth*, 1994
James Gurney, *Dinotopia*, 1992
James Gurney, *The World Beneath*, 1995

828

DEBORAH CHRISTIAN

Mainline
(New York: Tor, 1996)

Story type: Science Fiction (Alternate Universe; Psychic Powers)
Major character(s): Reva, Genetically Altered Being, Criminal (assassin); Javobo, Alien, Bounty Hunter; Vask Kastlin, Psychic (esper), Police Officer (Imperial Security)
Time period(s): Indeterminate Future
Locale(s): Selmun III/R'debh, Planet—Imaginary

Summary: Reva discovers her talent by inadvertently moving through the Lines of the Multiverse, forever losing her home, family, and friends. She takes off on her own as soon as she turns 16, living alone and moving through the Lines to avoid getting caught. Unfortunately, she permits herself to make some friends, trapping her on her current Mainline, unable to disappear while taking care of her very dangerous business. First novel.

Other books you might like:
Geary Gravel, *A Key for the Nonesuch*, 1990
James P. Hogan, *Paths to Otherwhere*, 1996
Michaela Roessner, *Vanishing Point*, 1993
Deborah Wheeler, *Northlight*, 1995
George Zebrowski, *Stranger Suns*, 1991

829

DEBORAH CHURCHMAN

Cross a Dark Bridge
(Rockville, Maryland: Ariadne, 1996)

Story type: Horror (Mystery)
Major character(s): Nathan Deeters, Store Owner; Gilead Grason, Clerk (Nathan's wife); Missy Grason, Twin (Gilead's)
Time period(s): 1990s (1996)
Locale(s): Cambridge, Maryland

Summary: When Nathan Deeters marries shy Gilead Grason, he inherits her eccentric itinerant family. As Gilead's mood progresses from shy reserve to near catatonia in her relationship with her husband, Nathan begins to suspect that there is a dark secret behind all of the Grasons' peculiarities, and that it may be linked to the sudden death of Gilead's father, which first put the family on the road. This is the author's first novel.

Other books you might like:
Katherine Dunn, *Geek Love*, 1989
Lewis Gannett, *The Living One*, 1993
Stella Gibbons, *Cold Comfort Farm*, 1932
Ian McEwan, *The Cement Garden*, 1978
Gus Weill, *Flesh*, 1991

830

SCOTT CIENCIN

The Lotus and the Rose

(New York: Warner Questar, 1993)

Story type: Fantasy (Political; Quest)
Major character(s): Trevelyan Arayncourt, Businessman (merchant prince)
Time period(s): Indeterminate
Locale(s): Autumn, Planet—Imaginary

Summary: As Trevelyan Arayncourt gains mastery over the wolves, an evil tyrant seeks to overwhelm the country. To eliminate the threat of the deadly hordes and lethal magic, Trevelyan must sacrifice the life of his lost love.

Other books you might like:
Carol Chase, *Hawk's Flight*, 1991
David Eddings, *Pawn of Prophecy*, 1982
Barbara Hambly, *The Ladies of Mandrigyn*, 1984
Mary H. Herbert, *Valorian*, 1993
Mercedes Lackey, *Arrows of the Queen*, 1987

831

SCOTT CIENCIN

Parliament of Blood

(New York: Zebra, 1992)

Story type: Horror (Vampire Story)
Major character(s): Danielle ''Dani'' Walthers, Doctor; Samantha ''Sam'' Walthers, Detective—Private (Danielle's mother), Parent; Devin Tyler, Vampire
Time period(s): 1990s (1992)
Locale(s): Isleta, New Mexico; Las Vegas, Nevada

Summary: In this concluding book of the trilogy begun with *The Vampire Odyssey* (1992) and *The Wildlings* (1992), half-vampire Dani Walthers tries to work incognito as an air ambulance medic and keep the vengeful vampire Parliament, of which she has run afoul, away from herself and her pregnant adoptive mother, private eye Sam Walthers. But when her cover is blown, Dani flees with Sam to Las Vegas, a hotbed of vampire activity, where she is forced to make her final choice between the vampire and mortal sides of her nature.

Other books you might like:
Peter Atkins, *Morningstar*, 1992
Poppy Z. Brite, *Lost Souls*, 1992

832

SCOTT CIENCIN

The Vampire Odyssey

(New York: Zebra, 1992)

Story type: Horror (Vampire Story)
Major character(s): Danielle ''Dani'' Walthers, Teenager, Student; Samantha ''Sam'' Walthers, Detective—Private, Parent (Danielle's mother); Bill Yoshino, Vampire
Time period(s): 1990s (1992)

Locale(s): Beverly Hills, California

Summary: In this first book of a trilogy, Sam Walthers struggles to save her adoptive daughter Danielle when the two discover that Danielle, who was born half-vampire, has been charged with the task of making her first kill in order to join the Parliament of vampires.

Other books you might like:
Poppy Z. Brite, *Lost Souls*, 1992
Leigh Clark, *Blood Sabbath*, 1991
Richie Tankersley Cusick, *Buffy the Vampire Slayer*, 1992
John Skipp, *Fright Night*, 1986
   Craig Spector, co-author

833

SCOTT CIENCIN

The Ways of Magic

(New York: AvoNova, 1996)

Story type: Fantasy (Young Adult; Religious)
Series: Elven Ways
Major character(s): Travest Mulvihill, Tailor; Tom Keeper, Teenager; Aitan Anzelm, Angel
Time period(s): Indeterminate
Locale(s): Earth

Summary: The angels bring ''salvation'' to mankind and, in the process, change the way the world runs. A talented artist, Tom must hide his art because all artists must belong to the artists' academy. When Aitan comes to Tom's father's inn and discovers Tom's talents, Aitan asks Tom to join him so that he can help Tom develop his skill.

Other books you might like:
Jo Clayton, *Drum Warning*, 1996
Susan Cooper, *The Dark Is Rising*, 1973
Madeleine L'Engle, *An Acceptable Time*, 1989
Holly Lisle, *Minerva Wakes*, 1994

834

SCOTT CIENCIN

The Wildlings

(New York: Zebra, 1992)

Story type: Horror (Vampire Story)
Major character(s): Danielle ''Dani'' Walthers, Teenager, Student (Medical student); Samantha ''Sam'' Walthers, Detective—Private, Parent (Danielle's mother); Marissa Tomley, Vampire
Time period(s): 1990s (1992)
Locale(s): Beverly Hills, California

Summary: In this sequel to *The Vampire Odyssey*, half-vampire Danielle Walthers openly repudiates the demands for blood sacrifice of the Parliament of vampires, and is branded a ''wilding,'' a vampire who kills other vampires and thus must be destroyed.

Other books you might like:
Poppy Z. Brite, *Lost Souls*, 1992
Richie Tankersley Cusick, *Buffy the Vampire Slayer*, 1992

John Skipp, *Fright Night*, 1986
  Craig Spector, co-author

835

SCOTT CIENCIN

The Wolves of Autumn

(New York: Warner Quester, 1992)

Story type: Fantasy (Quest)
Major character(s): Trevelyan Arayncourt, Businessman (merchant prince); Shantow, Warrior; Ariodne, Witch
Time period(s): Indeterminate
Locale(s): Autumn, Planet—Imaginary

Summary: The wolves, masters of mankind on Autumn, choose Trevelyan to discover a way of defeating the Hollow, monsters born to women but lacking souls.

Other books you might like:
Don Callander, *Pyromancer*, 1992
Stephen R. Donaldson, *Lord Foul's Bane*, 1977
Mary Gentle, *Rats and Gargoyles*, 1991
Laurie J. Marks, *The Moonbane Mage*, 1990
Patricia A. McKillip, *The Sorceress and the Cygnet*, 1991

836

JOSEPH CITRO

Dark Twilight

(New York: Warner, 1990)

Story type: Horror (Small Town Horror; Ancient Evil Unleashed)
Major character(s): Harrison Allen, Businessman, Unemployed; Nancy Wells, Teacher; Cliff Ransom, Worker
Time period(s): 1990s
Locale(s): Friar's Island, Vermont

Summary: Unemployed and alone, Harrison Allen returns after 15 years to an island off northwestern Vermont in search of a monster and a new start for himself. Intending to track down the legendary monster in nearby Lake Champlain, Harrison doesn't bargain for the other mysteries he must face—for the island is a gateway to another dimension of reality, and in his home there is Something in the Attic. His only helpmate in confronting the unknown is lonely schoolteacher Nancy Wells, lust object of local degenerate Cliff Ransom.

Other books you might like:
Gregg Almquist, *Beast Rising*, 1987
Steve Rasnic Tem, *Excavation*, 1987

837

JOSEPH CITRO

Deus X

(Sparta, New Jersey: Twilight, 1994)

Story type: Horror (Apocalyptic Horror)
Major character(s): Jeff Chandler, Government Official; Karen Bradley, Doctor (psychiatrist); William T. Sullivan, Religious (priest)

Time period(s): 1990s (1993)
Locale(s): Hobston, Vermont

Summary: In the guise of divine supernatural emissaries, vicious beings from an alternate dimension open a portal into our own and begin wreaking havoc, forcing a small band of human beings to thwart them and save the world.

Other books you might like:
Jack Finney, *The Body Snatchers*, 1955
Stephen King, *The Tommyknockers*, 1987
Robert R. McCammon, *Stinger*, 1988
Whitley Strieber, *The Forbidden Zone*, 1993

838

JOSEPH CITRO

The Unseen

(New York: Warner, 1990)

Story type: Horror (Ancient Evil Unleashed)
Major character(s): Roger Newton, Saloon Keeper/Owner; Laura Drew, Saloon Hostess, Lover (Newton's)
Time period(s): 1990s
Locale(s): Vermont

Summary: A number of Vermonters—a barkeeper and his lover, a drunken power company lineman, a female archaeologist, a pair of young boys and their grizzled guide—are drawn to a sinister, mysterious secluded area called "the Gore," where they encounter bizarre and dangerous things including coydogs (coyote-dog mixes), an ancient rock with mysterious powers, and a lost tribe.

Other books you might like:
John Farris, *Wildwood*, 1987

839

CHRIS CLAREMONT
BETH FLEISHER, Co-Author

Dragon Moon

(New York: Bantam Spectra, 1994)

Story type: Fantasy (Contemporary)
Major character(s): Cassandra "Cass" Dunreith, Martial Arts Expert, Writer; Mharyon, Mythical Creature (Celtic Rider); Fieran, Martial Arts Expert, Leader (S.C.A. king)
Time period(s): 1990s
Locale(s): Pennsylvania

Summary: As Lady Siobhan of Craigsmere, Cass fights in the Society for Creative Anachronism's Pensic War, hoping to ascend to the kingship in the historical recreationists' next cycle. After Fieran cheats her out of victory, Cass discovers that Fieran has summoned deadly legendary Celtic Riders into her world and must learn more about her own nature and powers to find a way of reversing their threat.

Other books you might like:
Emma Bull, *War for the Oaks*, 1987
Charles de Lint, *Greenmantle*, 1988
Charles de Lint, *Moonheart: A Romance*, 1984
Richard A. Knaak, *King of the Grey*, 1993

Mary Monica Pulver, *Murder at the War*, 1987
Melanie Rawn, *Knights of the Morningstar*, 1994
Pamela F. Service, *All's Faire*, 1993

840

CHRIS CLAREMONT

Grounded!

(New York: Ace, 1991)

Story type: Science Fiction (Military; Political)
Series: Nicole Shea
Major character(s): Nicole Shea, Pilot (spaceship), Military Personnel (Lieutenant); Alex Cobri, Computer Expert; Kymri, Pilot, Alien
Time period(s): Indeterminate Future
Locale(s): Earth; Space Station

Summary: Lieutenant Shea has lost her astronaut rating and is assigned to ground duty at Edwards Air Force Base. Her assignment is to be liaison to a delegation of the Halyan't'a, a cat-like alien race which she had contacted on her first mission. But there are hidden powers at work, and Shea finds that successful cooperation with the aliens is endangered, and so is her own life.

Other books you might like:
Poul Anderson, *A Knight of Ghosts and Shadows*, 1975
C.J. Cherryh, *The Pride of Chanur*, 1982
Gordon R. Dickson, *Dorsai!*, 1976
Cynthia Felice, *Downtime*, 1985
Anne McCaffrey, *Sassinak*, 1989
    Elizabeth Moon, co-author
Melissa Scott, *Mighty Good Road*, 1990

841

CHRIS CLAREMONT

Sundowner

(New York: Ace, 1994)

Story type: Science Fiction (Military)
Series: Nicole Shea
Major character(s): Nicole Shea, Pilot (spaceship), Military Personnel; Raqella, Alien (Halyan't'a/Hal), Pilot; Amy Cobri, Businesswoman, Socialite
Time period(s): Indeterminate Future
Locale(s): *U.S.S. Constitution*, Spaceship; *Sundowner*, Spaceship; Outer Space

Summary: Assigned as Captain of the *U.S.S. Constitution*, the most advanced starship yet designed, Nicole Shea must curb the emerging anti-alien sentiments which threaten the success of the first human and alien joint mission.

Other books you might like:
Eleanor Arnason, *Ring of Swords*, 1993
C.J. Cherryh, *The Pride of Chanur*, 1982
Debra Doyle, *The Price of the Stars*, 1992
    James D. Macdonald, co-author
Mercedes Lackey, *Wing Commander: Freedom Flight*, 1992
    Ellen Guon, co-author
Melisa C. Michaels, *First Battle*, 1985

Melisa C. Michaels, *Last War*, 1986
Melisa C. Michaels, *Skirmish*, 1985
David Weber, *On Basilisk Station*, 1993

842

DOUGLAS W. CLARK

Rehearsal for a Renaissance

(New York: Avon, 1992)

Story type: Fantasy (Historical; Light Fantasy)
Major character(s): Sebastian, Apprentice; Corwyn, Magician (alchemist); Gwen, Girlfriend
Time period(s): 15th century
Locale(s): France; Italy

Summary: Hoping to bring the Renaissance to the backwater town of Pomme de Terre, Corwyn, the world's first aquatic alchemist, sets out for Venice with his inept apprentice Sebastian, and Gwen, the tavernkeeper's daughter. On their way, they fall in with a band of pilgrims, Sebastian tries to turn Gwen into a noble lady (with alarming success), Gwen helps Antonio elope with Shylock's daughter Jessica and Corwyn uses alchemy to thwart the diabolical schemes of Hydro Phobius to sink Venice into the sea.

Other books you might like:
Robert Asprin, *Another Fine Myth*, 1988
Geoffrey Chaucer, *The Canterbury Tales*, 1478
Gordon R. Dickson, *The Dragon Knight*, 1990
L. Sprague de Camp, *Lest Darkness Fall*, 1941
Suzette Haden Elgin, *Twelve Fair Kingdoms*, 1981
Terry Pratchett, *Wyrd Sisters*, 1990
Elizabeth Ann Scarborough, *Bronwyn's Bane*, 1983
William Shakespeare, *The Merchant of Venice*, 1596

843

LEIGH CLARK

Blood Sabbath

(New York: Zebra, 1991)

Story type: Horror (Black Magic)
Major character(s): Heather Roberts, Teenager; Karin Roberts, Museum Curator; Magda Prokash, Witch
Time period(s): 1990s
Locale(s): Encino, California

Summary: After attending a clandestine black magic ritual, high school student Heather Roberts accidentally becomes the emissary of Azgaroth, a hungry god who demands sacrifices and similar socially unacceptable activities. Smitten with guilt for spoiling her daughter rotten, Karin Roberts takes it upon herself to rescue Heather from the demon's clutches.

Other books you might like:
William Peter Blatty, *The Exorcist*, 1971
Ramsey Campbell, *To Wake the Dead*, 1980
Ray Garton, *Crucifax*, 1988

844

LEIGH CLARK

Evil Reincarnate

(New York: Tor, 1994)

Story type: Horror (Serial Killer)
Major character(s): Connie Stallman, Doctor (psychiatrist); Tod Jarrow, Serial Killer; Azrael, Sorcerer
Time period(s): 1990s (1994); 16th century (1594)
Locale(s): Hollywood, California; Venice, Italy

Summary: In a narrative that veers back and forth between the sixteenth and twentieth centuries, prison psychiatrist Connie Stallman discovers that her unusual fascination with serial killer Tod Jarrow stems from the fact that they were lovers in a previous life, and that Tod's affiliation with the black arts have stoked his bloodthirstiness and ensured his immortality over the centuries.

Other books you might like:
Max Ehrlich, *The Reincarnation of Peter Proud*, 1974
Barbara Erskine, *Midnight Is a Lonely Place*, 1994
Marcy Heidish, *The Torch*, 1992
Michael Stewart, *Belladonna*, 1992

845

LEIGH CLARK

The Feeding

(New York: Leisure, 1992)

Story type: Horror (Child-in-Peril)
Major character(s): Matt Brenner, Architect; Robin Brenner, Photographer; Joshua Brenner, Child (10-year-old boy)
Time period(s): 1980s (1988)
Locale(s): Black Cavern, California

Summary: Matt and Robin Brenner take a vacation at the mountain resort Kemmering House to save their marriage, unaware that the house is intimately connected with underlying caves that are home to "The People of the Dark," a society of cannibalistic neanderthals who plan to kidnap their son Joshua in the hope of spawning future generations. This book was originally published in 1988.

Other books you might like:
Jack Ketchum, *Offspring*, 1991
Richard Laymon, *Midnight's Lair*, 1988

846

LEIGH CLARK

Shock Radio

(New York: Tor, 1996)

Story type: Horror (Serial Killer)
Major character(s): Aaron "Sunset" Scott, Radio Personality (disk jockey); Samantha Collier, Television Personality (news); Leah Steinberg, Waiter/Waitress
Time period(s): 1990s (1996)
Locale(s): Los Angeles, California

Summary: In a novel that parallels the crude confrontational style of a radio shock jock and the sociopathy of a serial killer, brash talk show host Aaron Scott (nee Steinberg) inadvertently encourages a brutal serial slayer known as the Phantom with his abusive on-air responses to the man's telephone calls into the show, then takes it upon himself to help track the villain down.

Other books you might like:
Richard Bachman, *The Running Man*, 1982
Robert Bloch, *Psycho II*, 1982
David J. Schow, *The Kill Riff*, 1988
John Skipp, *The Cleanup*, 1986
　Craig Spector, co-author

847

ARTHUR C. CLARKE
GREGORY BENFORD, Co-Author

Beyond the Fall of Night

(New York: Ace/Putnam, 1990)

Story type: Science Fiction (Hard Science Fiction; Invasion of Earth)
Major character(s): Alvin, Explorer, Human (supra); Cley, Heroine, Human (Ur); Seeker After Patterns, Guide, Animal (intelligent raccoon)
Time period(s): Indeterminate Future
Locale(s): Diaspar, Earth; Lys, Earth; Outer Space

Summary: Alvin escapes the beautiful but confining walls of Diaspar, a huge city on desolated Earth, and finds Lys, another inhabited city on the other side of the world. In uniting the two peoples once again, Alvin and the rest of mankind start restoring the Earth and regain the ability to explore space. Later, in helping Cley to find other Ur-humans after her community is destroyed, Seeker After Patterns discovers that the Mad Mind, the entity that once drove mankind back to his native world to cower in the cities for millenia, has escaped from the warped space-time vortex where it had been imprisoned and is bent on revenge and destruction. This collaboration is the sequel to Arthur C. Clarke's *Against the Fall of Night*, originally published in 1948.

Other books you might like:
Octavia E. Butler, *Dawn*, 1987
Orson Scott Card, *Speaker for the Dead*, 1986
Orson Scott Card, *Ender's Game*, 1985
Dan Simmons, *The Fall of Hyperion*, 1990
Dan Simmons, *Hyperion*, 1989

848

ARTHUR C. CLARKE
GENTRY LEE, Co-Author

The Garden of Rama

(New York: Bantam Spectra, 1991)

Story type: Science Fiction (First Contact; Space Colony)
Series: Rama

Major character(s): Nicole des Jardins Wakefield, Doctor, Adventurer; Richard Wakefield, Scientist, Adventurer; Kenji Watanabe, Historian, Settler
Time period(s): 23rd century
Locale(s): *Rama II*, Spaceship; *Rama III*, Spaceship; Outer Space

Summary: *Rama II* takes the human survivors of an exploration group and other creatures trapped on *Rama II* on a multi-year deep space voyage during which Nicole begins a new family. When *Rama II* arrives at The Node, a large construction facility in space near Sirius, the Ramans transport Nicole's family to temporary quarters to facilitate their testing humans and reconstructing *Rama II* into *Rama III*, designed as a human space colony for an expected 2000 colonists. When *Rama III* departs for Earth, some of Nicole's family must remain with The Node to begin breeding other humans for Ramans to study.

Other books you might like:
Roger MacBride Allen, *The Ring of Charon*, 1990
James Blish, *Cities in Flight*, 1969
Octavia E. Butler, *Dawn*, 1987
John DeChancie, *Paradox Alley*, 1987
Vonda N. McIntyre, *Transition*, 1991
Larry Niven, *Protector*, 1973
Allen Steele, *Clarke County, Space*, 1990
John Varley, *Wizard*, 1980
Vernor Vinge, *Marooned in Realtime*, 1986

849

ARTHUR C. CLARKE

The Ghost From the Grand Banks
(New York: Bantam Spectra, 1990)

Story type: Science Fiction (Contemporary Realism)
Major character(s): Donald Craig, Computer Expert; Jason Bradley, Engineer (underwater); Rupert Parkinson, Sailor
Time period(s): 2000s; 2010s
Locale(s): Ireland; *Glomar Explorer*, At Sea (North Atlantic Ocean)

Summary: Support for another attempt at raising the *Titanic* has resulted in two competing salvage operations, both planning to raise parts of the ship on the same day, to an accompanying media circus. Unbeknownst to either salvage team the sunspot cycle has combined with the cumulative effects of humankind on the environment to severely challenge their efforts.

Other books you might like:
David Brin, *Earth*, 1990
David Brin, *Startide Rising*, 1983
Octavia E. Butler, *Dawn*, 1987
Melissa Scott, *Mighty Good Road*, 1990
Joan Slonczewski, *A Door into Ocean*, 1986

850

ARTHUR C. CLARKE

The Hammer of God
(New York: Bantam Spectra, 1993)

Story type: Science Fiction (Disaster)
Major character(s): Robert Singh, Spaceship Captain
Time period(s): 22nd century (2110s)
Locale(s): Moon (Earth's); *Goliath*, Spaceship (space tug); Kali, Asteroid

Summary: After an amateur astronomer discovers a wayward asteroid, scientists calculate it could strike the Earth. Officials then order *Goliath* to intercept the asteroid and deflect its path. Expands the 1992 *Time* magazine story and concludes with a 14-page "Sources and Acknowledgments."

Other books you might like:
Greg Bear, *The Forge of God*, 1987
Gregory Benford, *Shiva Descending*, 1980
    William Rotsler, co-author
James Blish, *A Torrent of Faces*, 1967
    Norman L. Knight, co-author
David Brin, *Earth*, 1990
Gregory Benford, *Heart of the Comet*, 1986
    David Brin, co-author
Larry Niven, *Footfall*, 1985
    Jerry Pournelle, co-author
Larry Niven, *Lucifer's Hammer*, 1977
    Jerry Pournelle, co-author

851

ARTHUR C. CLARKE
GENTRY LEE, Co-Author

Rama II
(New York: Bantam Spectra, 1989)

Story type: Science Fiction (First Contact)
Series: Rama
Major character(s): Richard Wakefield, Engineer; Nicole Des Jardins, Doctor
Time period(s): 22nd century
Locale(s): Earth; *Rama II*, Spaceship

Summary: In this sequel to *Rendezvous with Rama*, a second Raman spacecraft enters the solar system late in the twenty-second century. A top-flight crew is sent to intercept and explore the gigantic vehicle, armed with all the knowledge gained during the first Raman encounter. Although the alien craft is similar to its predecessor, the human explorers discover startling, even deadly differences.

Other books you might like:
Gregory Benford, *Across the Sea of Suns*, 1984
Gregory Benford, *In the Ocean of Night*, 1977
Gregory Benford, *Heart of the Comet*, 1986
    David Brin, co-author
Edward Gibson, *Reach*, 1989
David Alexander Smith, *Rendezvous*, 1988

852

ARTHUR C. CLARKE
GENTRY LEE, Co-Author

Rama Revealed
(New York: Bantam Spectra, 1994)

Story type: Science Fiction (First Contact; Space Colony)
Series: Rama
Major character(s): Nicole des Jardins Wakefield, Political Figure (ex-governor); Eleanor of Aquitaine, Robot; Max Puckett, Farmer
Time period(s): Indeterminate Future
Locale(s): *Rama III*, Spaceship; Outer Space

Summary: The night before her scheduled execution, Nicole, with the help of two small robots, escapes to Max's farm where she hides in a secret room until she can join her husband, Richard. Still in charge after destroying the neighboring sentients' colony, Nakamura will not stop until he controls all of *Rama III*. Concluding novel in series.

Other books you might like:
Colin Greenland, *Take Back Plenty*, 1992
Vonda N. McIntyre, *Metaphase*, 1992
Frank M. Robinson, *The Dark Beyond the Stars*, 1991
David Alexander Smith, *Homecoming*, 1990
Vernor Vinge, *A Fire upon the Deep*, 1992

853

ARTHUR C. CLARKE
MIKE MCQUAY, Co-Author

Richter 10
(New York: Bantam Spectra, 1996)

Story type: Science Fiction (Disaster; Hard Science Fiction)
Major character(s): Lewis Crane, Scientist (seismologist); Elena "Lanie" King, Computer Expert; Dan Newcombe, Scientist (geologist), Religious
Time period(s): 21st century (2024-2058)
Locale(s): San Gabriel Mountains, California

Summary: After an earthquake leaves him parentless, Lewis Crane dedicates his life to predicting earthquakes. His real goal, however, involves stopping earthquakes altogether by fusing the earth's tectonic plates together.

Other books you might like:
Arthur Herzog III, *Earthsound*, 1975
David Lippincott, *Tremor Violet*, 1975
Mike McQuay, *Jitterbug*, 1984
Mike McQuay, *Lifekeeper*, 1980
Alvah Reidah, *Fault Lines*, 1972

854

ARTHUR C. CLARKE

Tales From Planet Earth
(New York: Bantam Spectra, 1990)

Story type: Science Fiction (Science Fiction; Collection)
Time period(s): Indeterminate

Locale(s): Earth

Summary: These stories, primarily from the 1950's, are all set on, or are about, Earth. The book includes a new introduction for each story by the author. The settings range from the recent past to the far future.

Other books you might like:
Groff Conklin, *The Science Fiction Omnibus*, 1956
Groff Conklin, *A Treasury of Science Fiction*, 1948
Cordwainer Smith, *The Best of Cordwainer Smith*, 1975
    pseudonym of Paul Myron Anthony Linebarger
Theodore Sturgeon, *A Way Home*, 1955
John Varley, *The Persistence of Vision*, 1978

855

J. BRIAN CLARKE

The Expediter
(New York: DAW, 1990)

Story type: Science Fiction (First Contact)
Major character(s): Gia Mayland, Researcher (expediter), Explorer; Peter Digonness, Businessman (Deputy Director of Expediters); Davakinapwottapellazanzis, Alien (Phuili), Researcher
Time period(s): 25th century (2416)
Locale(s): The Shouter, Planet—Imaginary; Groombra Four, Planet—Imaginary; *Century*, Spaceship

Summary: The Phuili, discovered behind the Pleides Star Cluster, are studying humans while humans study the relics of a 3rd race, long vanished from the galaxy. The Phuili do not necessarily believe that humans are sentient; they think of them more as clever "animals." However, as human and alien work side-by-side, they discover that each race has technology and culture that complement one another. They must use this growing partnership when a reaction set off by the long-silent, ancient relics begins to awaken the Silver People, a deadly race devoted to destroying all other life forms occupying "their" space.

Other books you might like:
Orson Scott Card, *The Abyss*, 1989
Alan Dean Foster, *Alien Nation*, 1988
Mary Gentle, *Golden Witchbreed*, 1983
James Patrick Kelly, *Look into the Sun*, 1989
Rebecca Ore, *Being Alien*, 1989

856

LINDSAY CLARKE

The Chymical Wedding
(New York: Knopf, 1989)

Story type: Fantasy (Contemporary; Historical)
Major character(s): Alex Darker, Divorced Person; Edward Nesbit, Writer (poet); Lavra, Psychic
Time period(s): 1980s; 1840s (1849)
Locale(s): England

Summary: Alex Darker retreats to the country, where he befriends an odd pair of recluses. He is drawn into an alchemical experiment that parallels tragic events of 150 years earlier. This book was published in 1989, but was not released until 1990.

Other books you might like:
John Crowley, *Little, Big*, 1981
Umberto Eco, *Foucault's Pendulum*, 1989
Stuart Gordon, *Smile on the Void*, 1981
Melissa Scott, *The Armor of Light*, 1988
   Lisa A. Barnett, co-author
Robert Anton Wilson, *Masks of the Illuminati*, 1981

857

JO CLAYTON

Dancer's Rise
(New York: DAW, 1993)

Story type: Fantasy (Adventure; Political)
Series: Dancer Trilogy
Major character(s): Serroi, Warrior, Sorceress; Camnor Heslin, Diplomat, Spy; Adlayra Ryan-Turriy, Mythical Creature (shapechanger)
Time period(s): Indeterminate
Locale(s): Fictional Country

Summary: After escaping centuries' imprisonment by force of magic, Serroi discovers a land of city states in which her previous adventures have achieved mythic status. After agreeing to deliver a newly created device to a distant ruler, Serroi and her companions encounter many impediments before she discovers the true nature of her enemy, one who wishes to control her. First of a trilogy.

Other books you might like:
Elizabeth Ann Scarborough, *Last Refuge*, 1992
Julie Dean Smith, *Sage of Sare*, 1992
Deborah Talmadge-Bickmore, *The Apprentice*, 1990
Martha Wells, *The Element of Fire*, 1993
Elizabeth Willey, *The Well-Favored Man: The Tale of the Sorcerer's Nephew*, 1993

858

JO CLAYTON

Drum Warning
(New York: Tor, 1996)

Story type: Fantasy (Young Adult; Adventure)
Series: Drums of Chaos
Major character(s): Cymel, Mythical Creature; Lyonz, Heir; Dur, Sorcerer
Time period(s): Indeterminate (year 734 since settling Glandair)
Locale(s): Glandair, Planet—Imaginary; Iomard, Planet—Imaginary

Summary: The two worlds of Iomard and Glandair draw close once a century, allowing special people to travel between the worlds. Cymel and her aunt rescue Lyonz across the worlds and learn more about the joining and the prophecy about a young hero who will save Glandair. Another youth, Dur, runs away from the organized Domains and becomes a rogue tribal sorcerer with the potential to ignite a war on two worlds.

Other books you might like:
Brian Daley, *The Doomfarers of Coramonde*, 1977
Maggie Furey, *Aurian*, 1994
Barbara Hambly, *The Time of the Dark*, 1982
Anne McCaffrey, *Dragondrums*, 1979

859

JO CLAYTON

Fire in the Sky
(New York: DAW, 1995)

Story type: Science Fiction (Political)
Series: Shadowsong
Major character(s): Shadith, Psychic; Kurz, Alien, Spy
Time period(s): Indeterminate Future
Locale(s): Beluchad, Planet—Imaginary

Summary: Although Shadith adjusts to life outside the Diadem, troubles force her to take a job as diplomat to the planet Beluchad, inhabited by two races and suffering from the invasion of two more. Shadith must bring peace with her odd empathic and musical powers or her life after the Diadem will end quickly.

Other books you might like:
Iain M. Banks, *The Player of Games*, 1989
David Brin, *Startide Rising*, 1983
C.J. Cherryh, *The Faded Sun: Kesrith*, 1978
W. Michael Gear, *Relic of Empire*, 1992
S. Andrew Swann, *Profiteer*, 1995

860

JO CLAYTON

The Magic Wars
(New York: DAW, 1993)

Story type: Fantasy (Magic Conflict; Quest)
Series: Wild Magic
Major character(s): Faan "Fa" Hasmara, Sorceress, Orphan; Serroi, Warrior, Sorceress; Navarre, Magician, Adventurer
Time period(s): Indeterminate
Locale(s): Kaerubulan, Fictional Country

Summary: Having mastered her abilities as magician, Faan yet seeks reunion with her mother. Unfortunately, others also desire the use of Faan's skill and, after capturing her, force Faan to use her skills on their behalf in the Magic Wars.

Other books you might like:
Louise Cooper, *The Avenger*, 1992
Mary Gentle, *Rats and Gargoyles*, 1991
P.C. Hodgell, *Dark of the Moon*, 1985
P.C. Hodgell, *God Stalk*, 1982
Mark C. Perry, *Morigu: The Dead*, 1990
Angus Wells, *Wild Magic*, 1993

861

JO CLAYTON

Shadowkill

(New York: DAW, 1991)

Story type: Science Fiction (Adventure)
Series: Shadith's Quest
Major character(s): Shadith, Psychic; Kikun, Alien, Warrior; Ginbiryol Seyirshi, Filmmaker
Time period(s): Indeterminate Future
Locale(s): Bol Mutian, Planet—Imaginary; Outer Space

Summary: Shadith and Ginbiryol are both captured by the Institute and sold into slavery. They must set aside their hatred long enough to destroy their masters, then they can finish their feud once and for all.

Other books you might like:
C.J. Cherryh, *Serpent's Reach*, 1980
Louise Cooper, *Nemesis*, 1988
C.L. Moore, *Northwest Smith*, 1981
Elizabeth Ann Scarborough, *The Healer's War*, 1988

862

JO CLAYTON

Shadowplay

(New York: DAW, 1990)

Story type: Science Fiction (Adventure)
Series: Shadith's Quest
Major character(s): Shadith, Psychic; Kikun, Alien, Warrior; Ginbiryol Seyirshi, Filmmaker
Time period(s): Indeterminate Future
Locale(s): Kiskai, Planet—Imaginary

Summary: Shadith, recently returned to human form, has been captured by evil filmmaker Ginbiryol Seyirshi, who intends to use her two other captives to create yet another devastating war which he will film for profit. Shadith, Kikun and Rohant join with local revolutionaries to thwart Seyirshi's plot.

Other books you might like:
R.A. MacAvoy, *The Third Eagle: Lessons Along a Minor String*, 1989
Anne McCaffrey, *The Death of Sleep*, 1990
   Jody Lynn Nye, co-author
Anne McCaffrey, *Generation Warrior*, 1991
   Elizabeth Moon, co-author
Anne McCaffrey, *Sassinak*, 1990
   Elizabeth Moon, co-author
Andre Norton, *Beast Master*, 1959

863

JO CLAYTON

Shadowspeer

(New York: DAW, 1990)

Story type: Science Fiction (Adventure)
Series: Shadith's Quest

Major character(s): Shadith, Psychic; Kikun, Alien, Warrior; Ginbiryol Seyirshi, Filmmaker
Time period(s): Indeterminate Future
Locale(s): *Kezzedua Dinnyee*, Spaceship; Chissoku Bogmaks, Planet—Imaginary

Summary: Shadith, enraged by the pointless deaths caused by Ginbiryol's "films," vows to hunt him down. To get to the elusive producer, however, will be more complex and dangerous than she and her companions imagined.

Other books you might like:
F.M. Busby, *Young Rissa*, 1977
Sharon Green, *The Crystals of Mida*, 1982
Robert A. Heinlein, *Friday*, 1982
Anne McCaffrey, *Crystal Singer*, 1982
Janet Morris, *The High Couch of Silistra*, 1977

864

JO CLAYTON

Wild Magic

(New York: DAW, 1991)

Story type: Fantasy (Magic Conflict; Religious)
Series: Wild Magic
Major character(s): Faan Korispais Piyolss, Orphan, Agent; Reyna Hayaka, Guardian (Faan's), Businessman; Faharmoy, Agent
Time period(s): Indeterminate
Locale(s): Zam Fadogurum, Fictional Country

Summary: Stolen from her sorceress mother, Faan receives spotty magic education which does not fully prepare her for the roll she is to play as the goddess' pawn battling the god's pawn, Faharmoy. This book is set in the same universe as the Drinker of Souls trilogy (1986-1989).

Other books you might like:
Donald Aamodt, *A Name to Conjure With*, 1989
Donald Aamodt, *A Troubling Along the Border*, 1991
Steven Brust, *Phoenix*, 1990
Louise Cooper, *The Deceiver*, 1991
Louise Cooper, *The Pretender*, 1991
David Eddings, *The Sapphire Rose*, 1991
P.C. Hodgell, *Dark of the Moon*, 1985
P.C. Hodgell, *God Stalk*, 1982
Sheri S. Tepper, *Grass*, 1989

865

JO CLAYTON

Wildfire

(New York: DAW, 1992)

Story type: Fantasy (Magic Conflict; Political)
Series: Wild Magic
Major character(s): Faan "Fa" Hasmara, Sorceress, Orphan
Time period(s): Indeterminate
Locale(s): Savvalis, Fictional City; Kyatawat, Mythical Place

Summary: Searching for her true mother, an ensorcelled sorceress, Faan again finds herself involved as a pawn in the struggle between gods and magicians for control of her world.

Other books you might like:
Mary Gentle, *Rats and Gargoyles*, 1991
P.C. Hodgell, *Dark of the Moon*, 1985
P.C. Hodgell, *God Stalk*, 1982

866

MONA CLEE

Branch Point
(New York: Ace, 1996)

Story type: Science Fiction (Time Travel; Alternate Universe)
Major character(s): Anna Leah Fall-Levchenko, Time Travel-ler, Scholar; Lavrenti Borisovich Zorin, Military Person-nel, Revolutionary; Jeffrey Kharitonov, Time Traveller
Time period(s): 1960s; 19th century
Locale(s): Alternate Earth; United States; Union of Soviet Socialist Republics

Summary: Equipped with a portable time machine and ad-vanced technology, Anna and her team travel back to 1962, intending to do anything necessary to stop the coming nuclear holocaust and eventual human extinction. When events prove difficult to mold, Anna and Jeffrey must again travel to the past, attempting to influence events positively. First novel.

Other books you might like:
Poul Anderson, *The Time Patrol*, 1991
Gregory Benford, *Alternate Wars*, 1991
    Martin H. Greenberg, co-editor
Randall Frakes, *Terminator 2: Judgment Day*, 1991
Harry Turtledove, *The Guns of the South*, 1992
H.G. Wells, *The Time Machine*, 1895
Robert Charles Wilson, *A Bridge of Years*, 1991

867

DOUGLAS CLEGG

Breeder
(New York: Pocket, 1990)

Story type: Horror (Black Magic)
Major character(s): Rachel Adair, Lawyer; Hugh Adair, Law-yer, Spouse; Mattie Peru, Streetperson (nee Madeleine Perreau)
Time period(s): 1980s (1988)
Locale(s): Washington, District of Columbia

Summary: Following her traumatic miscarriage, Rachel Adair moves with her husband Hugh into Washington's historic Draper House, a gift from her father-in-law. Gradually, the couple discovers that the house has a history of evil and that the elder Adair has engineered their relocation as part of a bargain made years before to a voodoo priest.

Other books you might like:
Nicholas Conde, *The Religion*, 1982
John Farris, *All Heads Turn When the Hunt Goes By*, 1977
Stephanie Kegan, *The Baby*, 1990
Ira Levin, *Rosemary's Baby*, 1967

868

DOUGLAS CLEGG

The Children's Hour
(New York: Dell, 1995)

Story type: Horror (Small Town Horror)
Major character(s): Joe Gardner, Writer (novelist); Homer "Hopfrog" Petersen, Carpenter; Tad Petersen, Child (Ho-mer's son)
Time period(s): 1990s (1995)
Locale(s): Colony, West Virginia

Summary: Joe Gardner returns from Baltimore to his home-town in rural West Virginia and relives the memories of his past, including the death of his girlfriend in an automobile accident. The deaths of several local children, and the return of one who disappeared twenty years before, lead Joe to the realization that the trauma of his youth was related to an evil presence living beneath the town that is now threatening to break out.

Other books you might like:
Stephen King, *It*, 1987
Nina Mandelik, *Entity*, 1991
Steve Rasnic Tem, *Excavation*, 1987

869

DOUGLAS CLEGG

Dark of the Eye
(New York: Pocket, 1994)

Story type: Horror (Wild Talents; Science Fiction)
Major character(s): Hope Stewart, Child (11 years old), Ex-perimental Subject; Kate Stewart, Housewife; Stephen Grace, Criminal (assassin)
Time period(s): 1990s (1994)
Locale(s): Salinas, California

Summary: When Kate Stewart spirits her daughter Hope away from the research facility where her scientist husband has been experimenting on her with a bizarre virus, it initiates a series of events that will bring them to California, and put them in the clutches of a death cult formed from the dregs of the 1960s counterculture who plan to use Hope's experimen-tally-boosted capabilities to summon the god of pain and horror they worship.

Other books you might like:
Randall Boyll, *Chiller*, 1992
Daniel H. Gower, *The Orpheus Process*, 1992
Dean R. Koontz, *Hideaway*, 1992

870

DOUGLAS CLEGG

Goat Dance
(New York: Pocket, 1989)

Story type: Horror (Ancient Evil Unleashed)

Major character(s): Malcolm "Cup" Coffey, Teacher (Elementary school); Theodora "Teddy" Amory, Child (Possessed)
Time period(s): 1800s (1801); 1980s (1985-87)
Locale(s): Pontefract, Virginia

Summary: A series of increasingly bizarre occurrences in Pontefract, Virginia heralds the coming of the Eater of Souls, a terror that can be averted only if a small group of townspeople can dig into the dark past of Pontefract for the secret of the nature of the evil and the means to combat it.

Other books you might like:
T.E.D. Klein, *The Ceremonies*, 1984
Bentley Little, *The Revelation*, 1990

871

DOUGLAS CLEGG

Never Land
(New York: Pocket Books, 1991)

Story type: Horror (Evil Children)
Major character(s): Sumter Monroe, Child; Beauregard Jackson, Child; Rowena Wandigaux, Grandparent
Time period(s): 1990s
Locale(s): Gull Island, Georgia

Summary: Every summer the members of the Wandigaux family gather on Gull Island for a reunion. This summer, ten-year-olds Sumter and Beauregard are driven by boredom to play in an abandoned shack they christen Neverland, where they learn secrets of their family's guarded past and how it has manifested through both of them.

Other books you might like:
Ray Bradbury, *Something Wicked This Way Comes*, 1962
Arthur Machen, "*The White People*", 1991
 in *The Horror Hall of Fame*
Thomas Tryon, *The Other*, 1971

872

HAL CLEMENT

Fossil
(New York: DAW, 1993)

Story type: Science Fiction (Science Fiction)
Major character(s): Janice Cedar, Researcher, Spouse (Hugh's); Hugh Rock Cedar, Administrator, Engineer (safety); S'Nash, Alien (Naxian), Researcher
Time period(s): Indeterminate Future
Locale(s): Habranha, Planet—Imaginary

Summary: On inhospitable Habranha, six intelligent alien races cooperate to discover the secrets of ancient fossils which may prove another intelligent race native to Habranha or may indicate that the race did not evolve locally, but rather descended from a legendary Seventh Race. However, research results may fall prey to secret agendas. Based on a universe created by Isaac Asimov.

Other books you might like:
David Brin, *Startide Rising*, 1983

Jeffrey A. Carver, *Dragons in the Stars*, 1992
A.C. Crispin, *Serpent's Gift*, 1992
 Deborah A. Marshall, co-author
Robert L. Forward, *Marooned on Eden*, 1993
 Martha Dodson Forward, co-author
Joan Slonczewski, *Daughter of Elysium*, 1993
Vernor Vinge, *A Fire upon the Deep*, 1992

873

MARK A. CLEMENTS

Children of the End
(New York: Donald I. Fine, 1993)

Story type: Horror (Science Fiction)
Major character(s): Tony Garwood, Guard (ex-cop); Deborah Kosarek, Writer (technical writer); George Irving Pendergast, Scientist (geneticist)
Time period(s): 1990s (1993)
Locale(s): San Diego, California

Summary: Using illegal aliens smuggled into the United States, mad scientist George Irving Pendergast breeds a ravenous race of shapeshifters known as Loners, which he intends to use as a weapon in the battle to fight overpopulation in America. Fueled by the belief that a human-free earth is their manifest destiny, the Loners quickly become a threat to the well-being of humanity.

Other books you might like:
Dean R. Koontz, *Shadowfires*, 1987
Dean R. Koontz, *Watchers*, 1987

874

MARK A. CLEMENTS

The Land of Nod
(New York: Donald I. Fine)

Story type: Horror (Mystery)
Major character(s): Jeffry Dittimore, Lawyer; Timothy Kregler, Spirit; Gail Rohr, Spirit
Time period(s): 1990s (1995)
Locale(s): Middlefield, Indiana

Summary: Recovering from a nervous breakdown, Jeffry Dittimore returns to his home town of Middlefield, only to discover that dead childhood friends are still alive there. In order to escape their unnatural hold on him and come to terms with buried traumas of the past that threaten his current life, Jeffry is forced to enter the Land of Nod, an imaginative world of his and his friends' creation, where the real and unreal collide.

Other books you might like:
Jonathan Carroll, *A Child Across the Sky*, 1988
Dale Hoover, *65mm*, 1993
William Browning Spencer, *Zod Wallop*, 1995

875

MARK A. CLEMENTS

Lorelei

(New York: Donald I. Fine, 1994)

Story type: Horror (Serial Killer)
Major character(s): Stacy Westerman, Psychologist; Clyde McGammon, Detective—Private; Lorelei, Serial Killer
Time period(s): 1990s (1994)
Locale(s): Washington, District of Columbia; New Orleans, Louisiana

Summary: A private detective with psychological problems related to his work as a former FBI agent teams up with a woman whose husband was seduced and murdered by a femme fatale serial killer. Together they discover the secret of the murderess' allure and motive and put an end to a cycle of killing that traverses the United States.

Other books you might like:
Ron Dee, *Succumb*, 1994
Christopher Fowler, *Red Bride*, 1992
Kathryn Ptacek, *In Silence Sealed*, 1988
Karen E. Taylor, *Bitter Blood*, 1994

876

SHIRLEY CLIMO

T.J.'s Ghost

(New York: Crowell, 1989)

Story type: Horror (Ghost Story)
Major character(s): Theresa "T.J." DuMar Jr., Teenager (On vacation); Winston D. Osborn, Teenager (T.J.'s friend)
Time period(s): 1980s
Locale(s): Pidgeon Point, California

Summary: Stuck with her old Aunt Onion and Uncle Will while her parents vacation, T.J. hears a mysterious foghorn and meets an Australian boy who, she gradually learns, is the ghost of a stowaway who went down in a shipwreck 120 years earlier. With her friend Winston, T.J. tries to learn all about her ghost and the mysterious quest that has brought him back to life to roam the California beach.

Other books you might like:
Helen K. Passey, *Speak to the Rain*, 1989

877

LEONARD CLINE

The Lady of the Frozen Death and Other Weird Tales

(West Warwick, Rhode Island: Necronomicon Press, 1992)

Story type: Horror (Collection)

Summary: A collection of five stories, two unpublished and three that appeared originally in the horror and weird mystery pulps under the author's pseudonym Alan Forsyth. Included are the title story, about a seductive snow elemental who lures men to their deaths; "The Guilt of Weasel Garrott," about a

soul exchange between a university professor and a criminal; "The Vampire of Bedlam Hill," a tale of witchcraft; and "Shuffle-Thump, in the Dark," about a blind man pursued either by the ghost of a friend or his guilty conscience. Editor Douglas A. Anderson has supplied a bibliography of the author's pseudonymous and unpublished writings.

Other books you might like:
Hugh B. Cave, *Murgunstrumm and Others*, 1975
August Derleth, *Someone in the Dark*, 1941
Carl Jacobi, *Revelations in Black*, 1947
E. Hoffman Price, *Far Lands Other Days*, 1977

878

B.W. CLOUGH

An Impossible Summer

(New York: Walker, 1992)

Story type: Fantasy (Young Adult; Contemporary)
Major character(s): Marianne "Rianne" Buechner, Child; Shannon Buechner, Child; Impossumble, Animal (opossum), Magician
Time period(s): 1990s
Locale(s): Virginia

Summary: Shortly after moving to Virginia, Rianne rescues a magical opossum from captivity at the Pet Farm Park. The opossum brings luck, sometimes good and sometimes bad, during the summer Rianne spends with her new companion.

Other books you might like:
Deborah Howe, *Bunnicula: A Rabbit Tale of Mystery*, 1979
    James Howe, co-author
Tanith Lee, *Black Unicorn*, 1991
Robert C. O'Brien, *Mrs. Frisby and the Rats of NIMH*, 1971
E.B. White, *Charlotte's Web*, 1952

879

MOLLY COCHRAN
WARREN MURPHY, Co-Author

The Forever King

(New York: Tor, 1992)

Story type: Fantasy (Contemporary; Legend)
Major character(s): Hal Woczniak, FBI Agent (retired), Knight; Saladin, Immortal, Murderer; Arthur Blessing, Orphan, Heir
Time period(s): 1990s
Locale(s): New York, New York; Chicago, Illinois; England

Summary: Saladin, a homicidal maniac genius, orchestrates his escape from a maximum security mental institution. The Grail, his since childhood, falls into the hands of Arthur, who feels an instant resonance with it. After the cup saves his Aunt Emily's life, she and Arthur escape to England to find Arthur's legacy.

Other books you might like:
Donald Barthelme, *The King*, 1990
Marion Zimmer Bradley, *The Mists of Avalon*, 1983
Martin Caidin, *The Messiah Stone*, 1986
Parke Godwin, *Beloved Exile*, 1984

Patricia Kennealy, *The Hawk's Gray Feather*, 1990
T.H. White, *The Once and Future King*, 1958

880

MOLLY COCHRAN
WARREN MURPHY, Co-Author

World Without End
(New York: Tor, 1996)

Story type: Fantasy (Psychic Powers; Legend)
Major character(s): Darian McCabe, Psychic, Sailor; Cory Althorpe, Doctor (psychiatrist), Psychic; Sam Smith, Psychic, Diver (scuba)
Time period(s): 1990s; Indeterminate Past
Locale(s): Caribbean; Atlantis, Mythical Place

Summary: Sam dives too deep while following a psychic call which leads to a fabulous magic treasure and a case of the bends. At the hospital, Sam meets Dr. Cory Althorpe who introduces him to a group of psychics, the Rememberers. Sam's involvement becomes pivotal as he attempts to undermine the group's enemies by travelling to Atlantis to bring about a benign future for Atlantis.

Other books you might like:
Ronald Anthony Cross, *The Lost Guardian*, 1995
Umberto Eco, *Foucault's Pendulum*, 1989
Michael Flynn, *In the Country of the Blind*, 1990
Robert Shea, *The Illuminatus! Trilogy*, 1988
    Robert Anton Wilson, co-author
Edward Whittemore, *Jerusalem Poker*, 1978
Robert Anton Wilson, *The Schrodinger's Cat Trilogy*, 1988

881

ANDREI CODRESCU

Blood Countess
(New York: Simon & Schuster, 1995)

Story type: Horror (Literary)
Major character(s): Drake Bathory-Kereshtur, Journalist; Elizabeth Bathory, Noblewoman, Historical Figure; Andrei de Kreshtur, Student
Time period(s): 1990s (1995); 16th century
Locale(s): Budapest, Hungary

Summary: Drawing parallels between the savagery of the past and the present, this first novel by a well known essayist and political commentator recounts the tale of Drake Bathory-Kereshtur, a journalist lured back to Romania after the fall of communism, and who confesses to the murder of a young woman there. As Drake recounts the how he is seduced into becoming part of a political group interested in restoring the monarchy, his tale begins to parallel that of his ancestor, Elizabeth Bathory, a countess renowned for bathing in the blood of virgins.

Other books you might like:
Peter Ackroyd, *Hawksmoor*, 1985
Christopher Bram, *Father of Frankenstein*, 1995
Dan Simmons, *Carrion Comfort*, 1989

882

M.T. COFFIN (Pseudonym of George Edward Stanley)

Pet Store
(New York: Avon, 1996)

Story type: Horror (Nature in Revolt)
Series: Spinetinglers
Major character(s): Amber, Child; Dad, Guard; Mr. Pinscher, Animal (dog)
Time period(s): 1990s (1996)
Locale(s): Woofburg, Mythical Place

Summary: Amber's dad moves the family to Woofburg only to discover that the town is run by sentient dogs. The family struggles to escape from Woofburg before they become the pets of Dad's employer, Mr. Pinscher. This book is aimed at readers in the 8- to 12-year-old age group.

Other books you might like:
Christopher Pike, *The Creature in the Teacher*, 1996
R.L. Stine, *Monster Blood II*, 1994
R.L. Stine, *Say Cheese and Die*, 1992
Tom B. Stone, *The Fright Before Christmas*, 1996

883

JON COHEN

Max Lakeman and the Beautiful Stranger
(New York: Warner, 1990)

Story type: Fantasy (Contemporary)
Major character(s): Max Lakeman, Landscaper; Mrs. Zeno, Disembodied Personality (Figment of Max's imagination)
Time period(s): 1990s
Locale(s): Gramentown, Pennsylvania

Summary: Max is living a comfortable life with his loving family until a woman he imagines comes to life in his backyard and seduces him. Things get out of hand as both Max and his wife face different threats to their life together.

Other books you might like:
Esther Friesner, *Sphynxes Wild*, 1989
Tanya Huff, *Gate of Darkness, Circle of Light*, 1989
Christopher Priest, *The Glamour*, 1984

884

THOMAS COLCHIE, Editor

A Hammock Beneath the Mangoes
(New York: Dutton, 1991)

Story type: Horror (Anthology)

Summary: This indispensable collection of 26 Latin American stories from five different geographic regions, some never published before in English translations, contains a number of tales of magic realism and metaphysical terror, including Gabriel Garcia Marquez's stream of consciousness narrative of a boy's fascination with a mysterious ship, ''The Last Voyage of the Ghost Ship''; Jorge Luis Borges' tale of the interpenetration of dream and reality, ''The Circular Ruins'';

and Julio Cortazar's fable of a man who loses the ability to distinguish between his subjective and objective perceptions of reality, "Axolotl." The editor has supplied instructive biographical notes for each author and an introduction.

Other books you might like:
Alberto Manguel, *Black Water: The Book of Fantastic Literature*, 1983
Alberto Manguel, *Black Water 2: More Tales of the Fantastic*, 1990

885

ADRIAN COLE

The Gods in Anger
(New York: Avon, 1991)

Story type: Fantasy (Magic Conflict)
Series: Omaran Saga
Major character(s): Simon Wargallow, Leader (Deliverers')
Time period(s): Indeterminate Future
Locale(s): Omara, Mythical Place

Summary: Hoping to save the last refuge of humanity, Simon Wargallow and his companions secretly journey into forbidden lands to determine the true nature of the threat posed to the human race. Reprint of the 1988 British edition.

Other books you might like:
Philip Jose Farmer, *Red Orc's Rage*, 1991
John Lee, *The Unicorn Quest*, 1986
Margaret Weis, *Fire Sea*, 1991
   Tracy Hickman, co-author

886

ADRIAN COLE

Mother of Storms
(New York: AvoNova, 1992)

Story type: Fantasy (Political; Adventure)
Series: Star Requiem
Major character(s): Aru Casruel, Adventurer, Immigrant; Zellorian, Wizard; Ussemitus, Adventurer, Psychic
Time period(s): Indeterminate
Locale(s): Innasmorn, Planet—Imaginary

Summary: The Alien Csendook defeat humanity, forcing the Imperial contingent to leave normal space for the haven of Innasmorn. The local inhabitants there have long been forbidden the use of metals and expect disaster to follow the invaders/refugees. Zellorian, controlling the Emperor Elect, finds the path under reality using pain and death and uses torture and death to control and understand the forces unique to Innasmorn. Reprint of British 1989 edition. First in series.

Other books you might like:
Charles de Lint, *The Little Country*, 1990
Cheryl J. Franklin, *Fire Crossing*, 1991
Mary Gentle, *Golden Witchbreed*, 1984
Marvin Kaye, *The Masters of Solitude*, 1978
   Parke Godwin, co-author
Elizabeth Moon, *Oath of Gold*, 1989
Sean Russell, *The Initiate Brother*, 1991

Will Shetterly, *Elsewhere*, 1991

887

ADRIAN COLE

Warlord of Heaven
(New York: AvoNova, 1993)

Story type: Fantasy (Military; Science Fiction)
Series: Star Requiem
Major character(s): Pyramors, Political Figure (consul), Military Personnel; Auganzar, Alien (Gsendooh), Military Personnel (Supreme Sanguinary); Zellorian, Political Figure (Prime Consul), Scientist
Time period(s): Indeterminate Future
Locale(s): Innasmorn, Planet—Imaginary; Eannor, Planet—Imaginary

Summary: In a new dimension, Zellorian plots to enslave the remains of humanity while his enemy, Pyramors, returns to the conquered human universe for revenge. First published in England in 1990, third in the series.

Other books you might like:
Emma Bull, *Falcon*, 1989
Glen Cook, *The Black Company*, 1984
Frank Herbert, *Dune*, 1965
Michael Moorcock, *Elric of Melnibone*, 1976
Roger Zelazny, *Nine Princes in Amber*, 1970

888

ALLAN COLE
CHRIS BUNCH, Co-Author

Empire's End
(New York: Ballantine Del Rey, 1993)

Story type: Science Fiction (Adventure; Political)
Series: Sten
Major character(s): Sten, Military Personnel (admiral); Cind, Military Personnel, Girlfriend; Ecu, Alien, Diplomat
Time period(s): Indeterminate Future
Locale(s): Bohr, Planet—Imaginary (Lupis Cluster); Dusable, Planet—Imaginary; *Victory*, Spaceship

Summary: When the Gurkas tell Sten that they want to work for him, Sten realizes that the Rule of the Eternal Emperor has deteriorated beyond recovery and the Emperor, now dangerous and totally corrupt, must be killed. Unfortunately, Sten must first find and destroy the source of EM^2, the powerbase of the Emperor. This sequel to *Vortex* (1992) concludes the eight volume series.

Other books you might like:
Lois McMaster Bujold, *Brothers in Arms*, 1988
Glen Cook, *The Dragon Never Sleeps*, 1988
Brian Daley, *Fall of the White Ship Avatar*, 1987
Joe Haldeman, *The Forever War*, 1975
Frank Herbert, *Dune*, 1965
Kevin O'Donnell Jr., *Fire on the Border*, 1990
Alis A. Rasmussen, *Revolution's Shore*, 1990
A.E. van Vogt, *The Weapon Makers*, 1946

889
ALLAN COLE
CHRIS BUNCH, Co-Author

The Far Kingdoms
(New York: Ballantine Del Rey, 1993)

Story type: Fantasy (Adventure; Quest)
Major character(s): Amalric Antero, Adventurer, Teenager; Janos Greycloak, Military Personnel, Wizard
Time period(s): Indeterminate
Locale(s): Valaroi, Fictional Country; Vacaan, Fictional Country (the Far Kingdoms)

Summary: The time has come for Amalric Antero to make the traditional coming of age voyage which expands trading territory and aids in a young man's maturation. Janos Greycloak rescues Amalric and infects him with the vision of discovering the fabled Far Kingdoms. Their odyssey brings unexpected peril and reward.

Other books you might like:
Margaret Ball, *Changeweaver*, 1993
Frans G. Bengtsson, *The Long Ships*, 1954
David Brin, *Glory Season*, 1993
Phyllis Eisenstein, *Sorcerer's Son*, 1979
Andre Norton, *Imperial Lady*, 1989
   Susan Shwartz, co-author

890
ALLAN COLE
CHRIS BUNCH, Co-Author

Kingdoms of the Night
(New York: Ballantine Del Rey, 1995)

Story type: Fantasy (Adventure; Quest)
Series: Far Kingdoms
Major character(s): Amalric Antero, Adventurer; Janela Kether Greycloak, Adventurer
Time period(s): Indeterminate
Locale(s): At Sea; Tyrenia, Fictional Country (Kingdoms of the Night)

Summary: Janela Kether Greycloak raises Amalric Antero from his malaise with word of the real Far Kingdoms, which she claims he never reached on his first trip. Journeying farther, they discover Tyrenia and the evil forces which threatens Tyrenia and the entire world.

Other books you might like:
Frans G. Bengtsson, *The Long Ships*, 1954
Dave Duncan, *The Cutting Edge*, 1992
David Eddings, *Pawn of Prophecy*, 1992
Terry Goodkind, *Wizard's First Rule*, 1994
James Hilton, *Lost Horizon*, 1933
Edward Myers, *The Mountain Made of Light*, 1992
Judith Tarr, *Spear of Heaven*, 1994

891
ALLAN COLE
CHRIS BUNCH, Co-Author

The Return of the Emperor
(New York: Ballantine/Del Rey, 1990)

Story type: Science Fiction (Military; Political)
Series: Sten
Major character(s): Sten, Military Personnel (admiral); Ian Mahoney, Military Personnel (ex-fleet marshall); Ecu, Alien, Diplomat
Time period(s): Indeterminate Future
Locale(s): *Santana*, Spaceship; Newton, Planet—Imaginary

Summary: For more than 2000 years the Eternal Emperor had produced and allocated AM2, the fuel needed for space travel. Now that the emperor has been assassinated, the remaining AM2 has become extremely precious. Something must be done to find a replacement power source before the empire is destroyed by war and lack of power. Members of the Cult of the Eternal Emperor are not worried, however, and happily await his return.

Other books you might like:
Brian Daley, *Fall of the White Ship Avatar*, 1987
Brian Daley, *Jinx on a Terran Inheritance*, 1985
Brian Daley, *Requiem for a Ruler of Worlds*, 1985
Stephen Goldin, *Jade Darcy and the Affair of Honor*, 1988
   Mary Mason, co-author
Dan Simmons, *Hyperion*, 1989

892
ALLAN COLE
CHRIS BUNCH, Co-Author

Revenge of the Damned
(New York: Ballantine/Del Rey, 1989)

Story type: Science Fiction (Military)
Series: Sten
Major character(s): Sten, Spaceship Captain, Bodyguard; Alex Kilgour, Spaceman
Time period(s): Indeterminate Future
Locale(s): Planet—Imaginary (A Tahn POW Camp on an alien planet)

Summary: The alien Tahn are attacking and humanity's interstellar empire is in chaos. Just when the Emperor needs him most, Sten's ship is destroyed and the Commander finds himself in a supposedly escape-proof prisoner of war camp on a hostile alien world.

Other books you might like:
William C. Dietz, *Prison Planet*, 1989
Harry Harrison, *Deathworld*, 1960
Barry B. Longyear, *Infinity Hold*, 1989

893

ALLAN COLE
CHRIS BUNCH, Co-Author

Vortex
(New York: Ballantine Del Rey, 1992)

Story type: Science Fiction (Immortality; Political)
Series: Sten
Major character(s): Sten, Military Personnel, Diplomat (ambassader); Ian Mahoney, Military Personnel; Alex Kilgour, Royalty (Laird), Military Personnel
Time period(s): Indeterminate Future
Locale(s): Jochi, Planet—Imaginary; Prime, Planet—Imaginary

Summary: The Emperor has returned, rebuilt Arundel Castle and replaced all his guards with strangers. At first relieved, Sten becomes troubled by the changes in the Emperor and his policies. Having been a friend to the Emperor for so long, Sten must decide where his loyalty lies when even the Gurkas question the Emperor's actions. Sequel to *Return of the Emperor* (1990).

Other books you might like:
F.M. Busby, *Rissa Kerguelen*, 1977
Brian Daley, *Requiem for a Ruler of Worlds*, 1985
Frank Herbert, *Dune*, 1965
Larry Niven, *Achilles' Choice*, 1991
   Steven Barnes, co-author
Alis A. Rasmussen, *A Passage of Stars*, 1990
Alis A. Rasmussen, *The Price of Ransom*, 1990
Alis A. Rasmussen, *Revolution's Shore*, 1990
A.E. van Vogt, *The Weapon Makers*, 1946
Ian Watson, *Inquisitor*, 1990

894

ALLAN COLE

The Warrior Returns
(New York: Ballantine Del Rey, 1996)

Story type: Fantasy (Adventure; Magic Conflict)
Series: Far Kingdoms
Major character(s): Rali Emilie Antero, Wizard, Lesbian; Novari, Mythical Creature (succubus); Magon, Royalty, Pirate
Time period(s): Indeterminate Past
Locale(s): Orissa, Fictional City; At Sea

Summary: Nearly dead after escaping from the Bear-King, Rali sleeps away 50 years with her lover, only to be rudely awakened by the Goddess Maranonia. The Goddess, patron of Orissa, wants the city saved from Novari, Rali's foe. Although not interested in old grudges, Rali must act to save her family, also held hostage.

Other books you might like:
Scott Baker, *Drink the Fire From the Flames*, 1987
M.A.R. Barker, *Man of Gold*, 1984
Diane Duane, *The Door into Fire*, 1979
Fritz Leiber, *Ill Met in Lankhmar*, 1995
Michael Scott Rohan, *The Anvil of Ice*, 1986

895

ALLAN COLE
CHRIS BUNCH, Co-Author

The Warrior's Tale
(New York: Ballantine Del Rey, 1994)

Story type: Fantasy (Quest; Military)
Series: Far Kingdoms
Major character(s): Rali Emilie Antero, Military Personnel (Maranon Guard); Gamelan, Wizard; Archon of Lycanth, Ruler, Wizard
Time period(s): Indeterminate Past
Locale(s): Orissa, Fictional City; Lycanth, Fictional City

Summary: When the armies of Orissa finally crush their enemies, the Archeons of Lycanth, one escapes with a spell which could destroy everything. Captain Antero and her victorious but distrusted all-woman unit sail off in pursuit, beyond everything they know, to strange lands.

Other books you might like:
Glen Cook, *The Black Company*, 1984
David Drake, *Vettius and His Friends*, 1989
Katherine Kurtz, *Deryni Rising*, 1970
Elizabeth Moon, *Sheepfarmer's Daughter*, 1988
Elizabeth Ann Scarborough, *Last Refuge*, 1992

896

BURT COLE

The Quick
(New York: Morrow, 1989)

Story type: Science Fiction (Military)
Major character(s): Shaman, Mercenary; Friedkin, Scientist
Time period(s): 21st century
Locale(s): United States

Summary: Shaman lives for combat and makes his living as a mercenary, gun-runner and pirate. When a popular liberation front comes into open conflict with the U.S. government, Shaman joins the conflict on both sides. It's all a game to him, a form of solipcism, until Shaman realizes that someone else is playing too.

Other books you might like:
L. Ron Hubbard, *Final Blackout*, 1948
   Reprint 1989
Barry B. Longyear, *Infinity Hold*, 1989
Robert Mason, *Weapon*, 1989
Jerry Pournelle, *Prince of Mercenaries*, 1989

897

DAMARIS COLE

Token of Dragonsblood
(Lake Geneva, Wisconsin: TSR, 1991)

Story type: Fantasy (Quest; Magic Conflict)
Major character(s): Noressa, Empath, Heiress—Dispossessed; Bydawine, Companion; Felaya, Sorceress
Time period(s): Indeterminate

Locale(s): Sidra, Fictional Country; Yetel, Planet—Imaginary

Summary: Spirited away from her family's destruction, Noressa grows up ignorant of the strange destiny bequeathed to her. Deprived of a proper teacher, Noressa must attempt to master her Talent with assistance from a wizard, Medwyn, before Felaya takes control of Noressa's medallion, the key to vast power. This is the author's first published book.

Other books you might like:
Jo Clayton, *Wild Magic*, 1991
David Cook, *Beyond the Moons*, 1991
Nigel Findley, *Into the Void*, 1991
Anne McCaffrey, *Dragonflight*, 1968
Andre Norton, *The Elvenbane*, 1991
   Mercedes Lackey, co-author

898

JEFF COLLIGNON

Her Monster
(New York: Soho Press, 1992)

Story type: Horror (Mystery)
Major character(s): Edward "Eddie" Talbot, Writer (science fiction writer), Recluse; Annie Talbot, Parent (mother of Eddie), Aged Person; Katherine "Kat" Mancy, Friend, Teenager
Time period(s): 1990s (1992)
Locale(s): Idaho

Summary: Born hideously deformed, Eddie Talbot leads a hermetic existence but lives vicariously through the heroes of his science fiction novels. When he establishes a rapport with Kat Mancy, Eddie's jealous mother decides to let the girl know just how closely Eddie's life resembles his fiction. A first novel.

Other books you might like:
Susan Kay, *Phantom*, 1991
Gaston Leroux, *The Phantom of the Opera*, 1911
Steve Vance, *Spook*, 1990

899

HELEN COLLINS

Mutagenesis
(New York: Tor, 1993)

Story type: Science Fiction (Genetic Manipulation; Medical)
Major character(s): Mattine "Mattie" Manan, Scientist, Explorer; Elizabeth, Traveller
Time period(s): 27th century (2635)
Locale(s): Anu/Dagda, Planet—Imaginary

Summary: After abandoning the colony on Anu prior to viability 500 years earlier, Earth sends an expedition to recover any usable food grains, intending to restore some genetic diversity on Earth. Not expecting human survivors, they find on the Plains a very religious community where women do not speak, preventing Mattie from interacting with the colonists. Elizabeth, a colonial woman caught reading, also forbidden to women, escapes and travels with Mattie to find other Anunne survivors. First novel.

Other books you might like:
Eleanor Arnason, *Ring of Swords*, 1993
David Brin, *Glory Season*, 1993
Octavia E. Butler, *Dawn*, 1987
C.J. Cherryh, *Serpent's Reach*, 1980
Nicola Griffith, *Ammonite*, 1993
Joan Slonczewski, *A Door into Ocean*, 1986
Sheri S. Tepper, *Grass*, 1989

900

NANCY A. COLLINS, Editor
EDWARD E. KRAMER, Co-Editor
MARTIN H. GREENBERG, Co-Editor

Dark Love
(New York: Roc, 1995)

Story type: Horror (Anthology)

Summary: Twenty-two stories published here for the first time explore the dark side of love and romance. In Stephen King's "Lunch at the Gotham Cafe," a writer's discussion of divorce proceedings with his wife in a Manhattan restaurant are interrupted by a rampaging maitre d' whose madness manifests the writer's own smoldering emotions. In Kathe Koja's "Pas de Deux," a woman's obsessive dancing and the toll it takes on her body is an outward expression of her emotional starvation. Robert Weinberg's "Ro Erg" tells of a man who lives the hedonistic life of an alter ego created by a computer misprint of his name, and Ramsey Campbell's "Going Under" of a man on a charity walk who discovers that the chaos and confusion of a stampede in a tunnel symbolize his entrapment within his own crumbling personal life. Karl Edward Wagner's "Locked Away" is about a woman who discovers the repressed emotions of another woman unleashed through a locket she wore, and Douglas E. Winter's "Loop" profiles a man's obsessive morbid interest in a porn star's film career. Ted Klein supplies an introduction.

Other books you might like:
Ellen Datlow, *Little Deaths*, 1994
   editor
Jeff Gelb, *Hot Blood: Tales of Provocative Horror*, 1989
   Lonn Friend, co-editor
Marvin Kaye, *Lovers and Other Monsters*, 1992
   editor
Michele Slung, *I Shudder at Your Touch*, 1992
   editor
Michele Slung, *Shudder Again*, 1993

901

NANCY A. COLLINS

A Dozen Black Roses
(Clarkston, Georgia: White Wolf, 1995)

Story type: Horror (Vampire Story)
Series: Sonja Blue
Major character(s): Sonja Blue, Vampire; Sinjon, Vampire; Esher, Vampire
Time period(s): 1990s (1996)

Locale(s): Deadtown, Alternate Universe

Summary: Sonja Blue foments civil war between the leading vampire clans of Deadtown when she attempts to liberate the mother of a young boy who has been abducted as a plaything for one of the vampire princes. This supernatural riff on the spaghetti western is set in the publisher's World of Darkness gaming milieu, an alternate universe in which supernatural beings run the world.

Other books you might like:

Don Bassingthwaite, *As One Dead*, 1996
   Nancy Kilpatrick, co-author
Brian Herbert, *Blood on the Sun*, 1996
   Marie Landis, co-author
Robert Weinberg, *The Unbeholden*, 1996

902

NANCY A. COLLINS, Editor
EDWARD E. KRAMER, Co-Editor
MARTIN H. GREENBERG, Co-Editor

Forbidden Acts
(New York: Avon, 1995)

Story type: Horror (Anthology)

Summary: The twenty-one stories commissioned especially for this volume probe social and personal taboos for their horror potential. Among the areas covered are television programming in Alan Moore's ''Light of Thy Countenance'' and Howard Kaylan's ''The Energy Pals,'' family life in Steve Rasnic Tem's ''Blood Knot,'' medical research in Rob Hardin's ''Interrogator Frames,'' autoeroticism in Lucy Taylor's ''Choke Hold,'' lesbian vampirism in Danielle Willis's ''Happy Couple,'' and sadomasochism in David Aaron Clark's ''Stations of the Cross.'' Former B-movie film reviewer Joe Bob Briggs supplies the introduction.

Other books you might like:

Ellen Datlow, *Little Deaths*, 1995
   editor
Jeff Gelb, *Hot Blood: Tales of Provocative Horror*, 1989
   Lonn Friend, co-editor
Jeff Gelb, *Hotter Blood: More Tales of Erotic Horror*, 1991
   Michael Garrett, co-editor
Jeff Gelb, *Hottest Blood: The Ultimate in Erotic Horror*, 1993
   Michael Garrett, co-editor
Michele Slung, *I Shudder at Your Touch*, 1991
   editor
Michele Slung, *Shudder Again*, 1993
   editor

903

NANCY A. COLLINS

In the Blood
(New York: Roc, 1992)

Story type: Horror (Vampire Story)
Series: Sonja Blue
Major character(s): Sonja Blue, Vampire; William Palmer, Detective; Dr. Pangloss, Supernatural Being

Time period(s): 1990s
Locale(s): San Francisco, California

Summary: In this sequel to her Bram Stoker Award-winning novel *Sunglasses After Dark* (1989), Collins continues the saga of Sonja Blue, the vampirized debutante searching for the being who turned her into a member of the Pretenders, a race of supernatural creatures that masquerades as the underground life of the human species. Sonja joins forces with William Palmer, a detective originally hired by her pursuers, and tracks her vampire overlord Morgan to San Francisco's famous Ghost House for a showdown.

Other books you might like:

Poppy Z. Brite, *Lost Souls*, 1992
P.N. Elrod, *The Vampire Files Series*, 1989-1992
Barbara Hambly, *Those Who Hunt the Night*, 1988
Anne Rice, *Interview with the Vampire*, 1976

904

NANCY A. COLLINS

Midnight Blue: The Sonja Blue Collection
(Stone Mountain, Georgia: White Wolf, 1995)

Story type: Horror (Collection; Vampire Story)
Series: Sonja Blue
Major character(s): Sonja Blue, Vampire

Summary: This compilation collects three novels featuring punk vampire heroine Sonja Blue. In *Sunglasses After Dark* (1989), newly vampirized heiress Denise Thorne adopts the pseudonym Sonja Blue and is introduced into the world of The Pretenders, creatures of myth and fantasy who masquerade as the downtrodden and marginal among mortals. In *In the Blood* (1992), Sonja continues her quest to find her vampire initiator. *Paint It Black*, first published in England in 1995, chronicles Sonja's climactic encounter with Morgan, the vampire who converted her.

Other books you might like:

Poppy Z. Brite, *Lost Souls*, 1993
Gail Petersen, *The Making of a Monster*, 1994
Anne Rice, *The Vampire Lestat*, 1985
Jody Scott, *I, Vampire*, 1984
John Skipp, *The Light at the End*, 1987
   Craig Spector, co-author
S.P. Somtow, *Vanitas: Escape From Vampire Junction*, 1995

905

NANCY A. COLLINS

Nameless Sins
(Springfield, Pennsylvania: Gauntlet Press, 1994)

Story type: Horror (Collection)

Summary: This first collection of 24 stories assembles nearly all of the short fiction written to date by this Bram Stoker Award-winning writer. Reprints include ''Freaktent,'' about a photographer of carnival sideshows; ''Rant,'' which presents the world through the eyes of a psychotic; ''Iphigenia,'' a bizarre anti-war story; the horror western, ''The Tortuga Hill Gang's Last Ride''; the Civil War horror story, ''The Sunday

Go-to-Meeting Jaw''; and a strange tale of sexual fulfillment, "The Two-Headed Man." Three stories first published here include "Without Sin," an irreverent retelling of the biblical story of Christ's crucifixion and resurrection; "Binky Malomar and His Amazing Instant Pussy Kit," an amusing riff on Lovecraftian horror; and "Speed Freaks with Guns: The Novelization," the novelization of a film script about a naive young man's encounter with a paranoid psychotic in Manhattan. Joe Lansdale supplies an introduction and Neil Gaiman the afterword.

Other books you might like:
Poppy Z. Brite, *Swamp Foetus*, 1992
Joe R. Lansdale, *By Bizarre Hands*, 1989
Elizabeth Massie, *Southern Discomfort: Selected Works of Elizabeth Massie*, 1993

906

NANCY A. COLLINS

Sunglasses After Dark
(New York: NAL Onyx, 1989)

Story type: Horror (Vampire Story)
Series: Sonja Blue
Major character(s): Sonja Blue, Vampire; Catherine Wheele, Psychic, Religious (Evangelist)
Time period(s): 1960s (1969); 1980s
Locale(s): New York, New York

Summary: Sonja Blue struggles to come to terms with the nature, morality, and meaning of her life as a vampire, while attempting to stay out of the clutches of her primary adversary, a demented, psychic evangelist.

Other books you might like:
Suzy McKee Charnas, *The Vampire Tapestry*, 1980
Tanith Lee, *Sabella, Or, The Blood Stone*, 1980
George R.R. Martin, *Fevre Dream*, 1982
Anne Rice, *Interview with the Vampire*, 1976
S.P. Somtow, *Vampire Junction*, 1984

907

NANCY A. COLLINS

Tempter
(New York: Onyx 1990)

Story type: Horror (Black Magic)
Major character(s): Adam Rossiter, Singer (former rock star); Charlotte Calder, Accountant (yuppie); Ti Alice, Occultist (voodoo priestess)
Time period(s): 1990s
Locale(s): New Orleans, Louisiana

Summary: A 37-year-old has-been rock star's quest for mystic enlightenment leads to a voodoo initiation ritual where he meets a priestess. Later, in her home, he discovers, in a mysterious ancient book called the *Aegrisomnia,* a mandala that opens a doorway between his world and that of the gods of voodoo. Charlie Calder, on the rebound from a string of disastrous love affairs, takes up with Rossiter, unaware that he

is coming under the sway of the Tempter, an incredibly evil ancient spirit that seeks to return to this world.

Other books you might like:
Hugh B. Cave, *The Evil*, 1981
William Hjortsberg, *Falling Angel*, 1978
Dean R. Koontz, *Darkfall*, 1984
H.P. Lovecraft, *The Case of Charles Dexter Ward*, 1927
Anne Rice, *The Vampire Lestat*, 1985

908

NANCY A. COLLINS

Walking Wolf
(Shingleton, California: Ziesing, 1995)

Story type: Horror (Werewolf Story)
Major character(s): William "Billy" Skillet, Werewolf; Witchfinder Jones, Bounty Hunter; Digging Woman, Indian
Time period(s): 1860s
Locale(s): Southwest

Summary: The orphan child of a human mother and werewolf father, Billy Skillet is raised by the Comanches, who revere him as a skinwalker, or shapeshifter, named Walking Wolf. Billy's adventures eventually bring him into the white man's world, where he holds a variety of jobs that permit him to view the true bestiality of humanity in the white man's treatment of the Native American nations.

Other books you might like:
William Berger, *Little Big Man*, 1964
Joe R. Lansdale, *Dead in the West*, 1986
S.P. Somtow, *Moon Dance*, 1990

909

NANCY A. COLLINS

Wild Blood
(New York: Roc, 1994)

Story type: Horror (Werewolf Story)
Major character(s): Skinner Cade, Young Man, Werewolf; Jez, Werewolf; Rosie, Magician (coyotero)
Time period(s): 1990s (1994)
Locale(s): Los Lobos, Arizona

Summary: Newly orphaned, Skinner Cade goes searching for the truth about his origins and discovers that he is a *vargr,* or purebred werewolf. After angering the wolf clan that he at first hopes to join by spurning their inhumane treatment of their prey, Skinner is helped by other creatures of fantasy and legend who masquerade as humans.

Other books you might like:
Poppy Z. Brite, *Lost Souls*, 1992
Crosland Brown, *Tombley's Walk*, 1990
Ron Dee, *Dusk*, 1991
S.P. Somtow, *Moon Dance*, 1990

910

S. DARNBROOK COLSON

People of the Night

(Seattle, Washington: Three Stones Publications, 1994)

Story type: Horror (Collection)

Summary: This trilogy of stories offers stark, often macabre portraits of social outcasts. "Brotherhood of the Dark" tells of the relationship between a prostitute and a crippled derelict, "People of the Night" of gang life, and "Darksiders" about the subculture of the city streets at night. Wayne Allen Sallee supplies the introduction.

Other books you might like:
Joe R. Lansdale, *By Bizarre Hands*, 1989
Wayne Allen Sallee, *Pain-Grin*, 1993
David J. Schow, *Black Leather Required*, 1994
David J. Schow, *Lost Angels*, 1990
John Shirley, *New Noir*, 1993

911

MARYSE CONDE

I, Tituba, Black Witch of Salem

(Charlottesville, Virginia: University Press of Virginia, 1992)

Story type: Fantasy (Historical)
Major character(s): Tituba, Historical Figure, Witch (healer); Mama Yaya, Spirit, Healer; John Indian, Slave, Spouse (Tituba's)
Time period(s): 17th century (1690s)
Locale(s): Barbados; Salem, Massachusetts, American Colonies

Summary: Prophesied to have much pain in her life and to travel across the water and return, Tituba marries John Indian. The property of Samuel Parris who accepts a position as minister in Salem Township where black means satanic, Tituba, victimized by the children of Salem, confesses to satanism. Although one of the first arrested for witchcraft, she lives in prison until pardoned with the other accused two years later when the prison sells her to pay for her chains and fees. Translated by Richard Philcox.

Other books you might like:
Octavia E. Butler, *Kindred*, 1979
Orson Scott Card, *Lost Boys*, 1992
Nathaniel Hawthorne, *The Scarlet Letter*, 1850
Susan Palwick, *Flying in Place*, 1992
Marge Piercy, *Woman on the Edge of Time*, 1976
Elizabeth Ann Scarborough, *The Healer's War*, 1989

912

NICHOLAS CONDE

In the Deep Woods

(New York: St. Martin's, 1989)

Story type: Horror (Serial Killer)
Major character(s): Carol Warren, Writer (Children's books); Paul Miller, Detective—Amateur
Time period(s): 1980s
Locale(s): New York, New York

Summary: After a good friend is murdered by a serial killer, Carol Warren is further horrified when an obsessed private detective implicates her brother in the killings. Her attempts to clear her brother make Carol an increasingly attractive target for the progressively demented murderer.

Other books you might like:
Robert Bloch, *Psycho*, 1959
Ramsey Campbell, *The Doll Who Ate His Mother*, 1976
Friedrich Durrenmatt, *It Happened in Broad Daylight*,

913

JANE LESLIE CONLY

R-T, Margaret, and the Rats of NIMH

(New York: Harper, 1990)

Story type: Fantasy (Science Fiction; Young Adult)
Series: Rats of NIMH
Major character(s): R-T "Artie", Child, Handicapped; Margaret, Child (R-T's sister); Racso, Animal (intelligent talking rat)
Time period(s): 1980s
Locale(s): Thom Valley (North Woods)

Summary: Lost in the North Woods, R-T and his sister Margaret are rescued by Racso and the other intelligent rats of NIMH. When the children finally return to their family at the end of summer, they are unable to keep the rats a secret, and civilization and science close in on the secret rat community in Thom Valley.

Other books you might like:
Richard Adams, *Watership Down*, 1974
Lynne Reid Banks, *The Indian in the Cupboard*, 1980
Pauline Clarke, *The Return of the Twelves*, 1964
Mary Norton, *The Borrowers*, 1953
Robert C. O'Brien, *Mrs. Frisby and the Rats of NIMH*, 1971

914

MICHAEL CONNER

Archangel

(New York: Tor, 1995)

Story type: Science Fiction (Alternate Universe; Mystery)
Major character(s): Danny Constantine, Journalist; Simon Gray, Scientist, Doctor; Selena Crockett, Heiress
Time period(s): 1930s (1930)
Locale(s): Minneapolis, Minnesota

Summary: Minneapolis escapes some effects of a pandemic hemorrhagic fever due to the immunity of African-Americans, encouraged to immigrate to that city. Danny Constantine trails a killer whose victims seem slain by a vampire, while his newspaper ignores the story and new powers vie for control of the city.

Other books you might like:
Greg Bear, *Blood Music*, 1985
Terry Bisson, *Fire on the Mountain*, 1988

John Christopher, *Empty World*, 1978
Philip K. Dick, *Dr. Bloodmoney*, 1965
Brad Ferguson, *The World Next Door*, 1990
Frank Herbert, *The White Plague*, 1982
Wilson Tucker, *The Year of the Quiet Sun*, 1970
Chelsea Quinn Yarbro, *Time of the Fourth Horseman*, 1976

915

FLYNN CONNOLLY

The Rising of the Moon

(New York: Ballantine Del Rey, 1993)

Story type: Science Fiction (Political)
Major character(s): Nuala Maebh Dennehy, Teacher, Revolutionary; Igraine, Revolutionary
Time period(s): 21st century
Locale(s): Ireland

Summary: After teaching abroad for 15 years, Nuala Dennehy returns to Ireland to discover complete repression of women, now the property of men, through a structure supported by the isolationist Irish government and Catholic church. Nuala finds an underground movement striving to empower women by distributing revolutionary literature and contraceptives and soon runs afoul of authorities. Author's first novel.

Other books you might like:
Margaret Atwood, *The Handmaid's Tale*, 1985
Maya Kaathryn Bohnhoff, *The Meri*, 1992
Maya Kaathryn Bohnhoff, *Taminy*, 1993
Lester del Rey, *The Eleventh Commandment*, 1970 revised
Suzette Haden Elgin, *The Judas Rose*, 1987
Suzette Haden Elgin, *Native Tongue*, 1984

916

JOHN DAVID CONNOR (Pseudonym of John H. Way and David C. Miller)

Contagion

(New York: Diamond, 1992)

Story type: Horror (Mystery)
Major character(s): Howard Fletcher, Doctor; Byron Swinton, Doctor (epidemiologist); Robby Swinton, Teenager
Time period(s): 1990s
Locale(s): New Orleans, Louisiana

Summary: A high school science project runs amuck when the son of an epidemiologist working for the Centers for Disease Control tries his hand at infectious disease research by releasing a new, lethal strain of typhus on the unsuspecting celebrants of the Mardi Gras festival in New Orleans.

Other books you might like:
Michael Crichton, *The Andromeda Strain*, 1969
Pauline Dunn, *The Crawling Dark*, 1991
Christopher Hyde, *Jericho Falls*, 1986
Peter Straub, *Floating Dragon*, 1982

917

PAM CONRAD

Stonewords: A Ghost Story

(New York: Harper and Row, 1990)

Story type: Fantasy (Time Travel; Young Adult)
Major character(s): Zoe, Child (20th century); Zoe Louise, Child (19th century), Spirit (20th century)
Time period(s): 20th century; 19th century
Locale(s): United States

Summary: 11-year-old Zoe discovers that her house is occupied by the ghost of her namesake, who carries her back to 1870 to try to prevent her tragic death.

Other books you might like:
L.M. Boston, *The Stones of Green Knowe*, 1976
William Mayne, *Earthfasts*, 1967
Ruth Park, *Playing Beatie Bow*, 1980
Philippa Pearce, *Tom's Midnight Garden*, 1959

918

ROBERT CONROY

1901

(Novato, California: Presidio Press/Lyford Books, 1995)

Story type: Science Fiction (Alternate Universe; Political)
Major character(s): Patrick Mahan, Military Personnel; Theodore Roosevelt, Historical Figure, Political Figure
Time period(s): 1900s (1901)
Locale(s): United States

Summary: When President McKinley refuses Kaiser Wilhelm II's demand that the U.S. surrender Pacific and Caribbean territories, the Kaiser initiates an invasion of the United States, first striking Long Island. First novel.

Other books you might like:
William Gibson, *The Difference Engine*, 1991
    Bruce Sterling, co-author
Kim Newman, *Anno Dracula*, 1993
Mike Resnick, *Alternate Presidents*, 1992
    editor
John Maddox Roberts, *King of the Wood*, 1983
Harry Turtledove, *The Guns of the South*, 1992

919

STORM CONSTANTINE

Bewitchments of Love and Hate

(New York: Tor, 1990)

Story type: Science Fiction (Gay/Lesbian Fiction; Science Fantasy)
Series: Books of Wraeththu
Major character(s): Swift, Heir; Calanthe, Wanderer; Trerzian, Royalty
Time period(s): Indeterminate
Locale(s): Earth

Summary: Swift grows up as the pampered child of the leader of the Varrs, a warlike tribe of Wraeththu. When Cal comes into this closed world, Swift has to learn to separate the positive and negative qulities of the Varrs if they are to survive.

Other books you might like:
Angela Carter, *The Bloody Chamber*, 1979
Ellen Kushner, *Swordspoint*, 1987
Tanith Lee, *The Book of the Damned*, 1990
Tanith Lee, *Night's Master*, 1978
Anne Rice, *Interview with the Vampire*, 1976

920

STORM CONSTANTINE

The Enchantments of Flesh and Spirit
(New York: Tor, 1989)

Story type: Science Fiction (Psychic Powers)
Series: Books of Wraeththu
Major character(s): Pellaz, Mutant, Psychic; Calanthe, Mutant, Psychic
Time period(s): Indeterminate Future
Locale(s): England

Summary: In a near-future England collapsing into economic and environmental ruin, a new form of human being comes into existence. The Wraeththu, hermaphroditic and endowed with psychic powers, begin to contest with humanity for control of the world.

Other books you might like:
Marion Zimmer Bradley, *The Shattered Chain*, 1976
John Christopher, *Pendulum*, 1968
Ursula K. Le Guin, *The Left Hand of Darkness*, 1969
Doris Lessing, *The Fifth Child*, 1988
Doris Lessing, *The Memoirs of a Survivor*, 1974

921

STORM CONSTANTINE

The Fulfillments of Fate and Desire
(New York: Tor, 1991)

Story type: Science Fiction (Gay/Lesbian Fiction; Science Fantasy)
Series: Books of Wraeththu
Major character(s): Calanthe, Wanderer, Prostitute; Panthera, Heir, Prostitute; Thiede, Deity, Ruler
Time period(s): 21st century
Locale(s): Fallsend, Fictional Country; Immanira, Fictional Country

Summary: Cal has hit bottom at the start of the final Wraeththu book, scraping and working as a prostitute. Slowly, Cal's nature and events conspire to drive him to Immanira.

Other books you might like:
Angela Carter, *The Bloody Chamber*, 1979
Ellen Kushner, *Swordspoint*, 1987
Tanith Lee, *Red as Blood: Or Tales from the Sisters Grimmer*, 1983
Michael Shea, *Nifft the Lean*, 1982

Chelsea Quinn Yarbro, *Hotel Transylvania*, 1978

922

DAVID COOK

Beyond the Moons
(Lake Geneva, Wisconsin: TSR, 1991)

Story type: Fantasy (Quest)
Series: Cloakmaster Cycle
Major character(s): Teldin Moore, Adventurer; Herphan Gomja, Military Personnel, Alien (Giff)
Time period(s): Indeterminate
Locale(s): Krynn, Planet—Imaginary

Summary: When a spelljamming ship crashes, a dying alien presents Teldin with a magical cloak, one which Teldin inadvertently dons then cannot remove. As he searches for the secret to his cloak's power, he finds himself in unpleasantly high demand as he tries to take the cloak to the mysterious creators. This book is set in the Spelljammer gaming milieu.

Other books you might like:
Brian Daley, *Fall of the White Ship Avatar*, 1987
Brian Daley, *Jinx on a Terran Inheritance*, 1985
Brian Daley, *Requiem for a Ruler of Worlds*, 1985
John DeChancie, *Starrigger*, 1983
Nigel Findley, *Into the Void*, 1991
Alis A. Rasmussen, *The Price of Ransom*, 1990

923

DAVID COOK

Horselords
(Lake Geneva, Wisconsin: TSR, 1990)

Story type: Fantasy (Historical)
Series: Forgotten Realms: The Empire Trilogy
Major character(s): Koja, Religious (priest); Yamun, Royalty (Khahan)
Time period(s): 12th century
Locale(s): Quaraband, Asia (City of Tents)

Summary: Koja of Khazari, Priest of Furo, joins Khahan Yamun's entourage. Their relationship develops through treachery, intrigue, and the consolidation of an empire. Novel based on a game.

Other books you might like:
M. Coleman Easton, *Spirits of Cavern and Hearth*, 1989
Ken Kato, *Yamato: A Rage in Heaven*, 1990
Marc Laidlaw, *Neon Lotus*, 1988
Jeanne Larsen, *Silk Road*, 1989
David Wingrove, *The Middle Kingdom*, 1990

924

DAVID COOK

King Pinch
(Lake Geneva, Wisconsin: TSR, 1995)

Story type: Fantasy (Adventure; Magic Conflict)
Series: Forgotten Realms: The Nobles

Major character(s): Pinch "Janol", Thief, Orphan; Lissa, Religious (priestess); Cleedis, Warrior
Time period(s): Indeterminate
Locale(s): Ankhapur, Fictional City

Summary: Upon the death of Pinch's guardian, King Manferic III, Cleedis finds Pinch and implores him to return to Ankhapur, where potential rulers employ an ancient test of worthiness. Interrupted at his current gambit, Pinch turns his attention toward the throne and the potentially deadly trials arising from his new goal.

Other books you might like:
Dave Duncan, *Magic Casement*, 1990
James Lowder, *The Ring of Winter*, 1992
Michelle Sagara, *Into the Dark Lands*, 1991
R.A. Salvatore, *The Legacy*, 1992
Michael Williams, *A Forest Lord*, 1991
Tad Williams, *The Dragonbone Chair*, 1988

925

GLEN COOK

Bleak Seasons

(New York: Tor, 1996)

Story type: Fantasy (Military; Magic Conflict)
Series: Chronicles of the Black Company: Glittering Stone Trilogy
Major character(s): Murgen, Military Personnel; Longshadow, Wizard; Croaker, Military Personnel, Doctor
Time period(s): Indeterminate Past
Locale(s): Dejagore, Fictional City; Shadowcatch, Fictional City

Summary: De facto leader of the Black Company since Croaker's disappearance, Murgen tries to defend Dejagore against an army and traitors. Meanwhile, Croaker and Lady try to survive the plots against them and the Company. Elsewhere, Longshadow plots, hoping to survive and conquer. First book of the Glittering Stone trilogy and the seventh Black Company novel.

Other books you might like:
Brian Daley, *The Doomfarers of Coramonde*, 1977
Terry Goodkind, *Wizard's First Rule*, 1994
Barbara Hambly, *The Ladies of Mandrigyn*, 1984
Guy Gavriel Kay, *Tigana*, 1990
Fritz Leiber, *Ill Met in Lankhmar*, 1995
Michael Moorcock, *The Swords Trilogy*, 1977

926

GLEN COOK

Deadly Quicksilver Lies

(New York: Roc, 1994)

Story type: Fantasy (Mystery)
Series: Garrett Files
Major character(s): Garrett, Detective—Private; Winger, Detective—Private
Time period(s): Indeterminate Past

Locale(s): TunFaire, Fictional Country

Summary: When hired to locate a missing teenager, Garrett must find a king's illegitimate daughter hiding from more than her mother. Garrett, Winger and Saucerhead Thorpe must keep one step ahead of the Rainmaker in unraveling the trail of mayhem and magic to find the girl and stay alive.

Other books you might like:
Robert Asprin, *Thieves' World*, 1979
    editor
Emma Bull, *Finder*, 1984
Randall Garrett, *Too Many Magicians*, 1967
Simon R. Green, *Hawk & Fisher*, 1990
Will Shetterly, *Nevernever*, 1993

927

GLEN COOK

Dread Brass Shadows

(New York: Roc, 1990)

Story type: Fantasy (Mystery)
Series: Garrett Files
Major character(s): Garrett, Detective—Private; Tinnie, Girlfriend
Time period(s): Indeterminate Past
Locale(s): TunFaire, Fictional Country

Summary: In this latest installment, someone has tried to murder Garrett's girlfriend, Tinnie. Garrett sets out in search of the *Book of Shadows* to find out why Tinnie is a target.

Other books you might like:
Craig Shaw Gardner, *Bride of the Slime Monster*, 1990

928

GLEN COOK

Dreams of Steel

(New York: Tor, 1990)

Story type: Fantasy (Sword and Sorcery)
Series: Chronicles of the Black Company
Major character(s): Croaker, Military Personnel (soldier), Historian; Lady, Military Personnel (soldier), Sorcerer
Time period(s): Indeterminate Past
Locale(s): Taglios, Fictional City; Dejagore, Fictional City

Summary: After the defeat at Dejagore, Croaker is believed dead, though Soulcatcher has healed him and holds him captive in her revenge against Lady. Lady takes command of and starts rebuilding the Black Company, and allies with a secret cult of assassins who believes she will become the avatar of their goddess in order to carry on the fight against the remaining Shadowmasters, who once served her Empire.

Other books you might like:
Robert Asprin, *Thieves' World*, 1979
Heather Gladney, *Teot's War*, 1987
Barbara Hambly, *The Ladies of Mandrigyn*, 1984
Fred Saberhagen, *Woundhealer's Story: The First Book of Lost Swords*, 1983
Gene Wolfe, *The Shadow of the Torturer*, 1980

929

GLEN COOK

Old Tin Sorrows

(New York: NAL Signet, 1989)

Story type: Fantasy (Mystery)
Series: Garrett Files
Major character(s): Garrett, Detective—Private
Time period(s): Indeterminate Past
Locale(s): TunFaire, Fictional Country

Summary: Garrett is hired by a general, then finds himself caught in the middle of murder, madness and greed.

Other books you might like:
William Kotzwinkle, *Fata Morgana*, 1977
Michael Kurland, *A Study in Sorcery*, 1989
Mercedes Lackey, *Children of the Night*, 1990

930

GLEN COOK

Pretty Pewter Gods

(New York: Roc, 1995)

Story type: Fantasy (Mystery; Urban)
Series: Garrett Files
Major character(s): Garrett, Detective—Private; Dead Man, Mythical Creature (loghyr); Magodor, Deity
Time period(s): Indeterminate Past
Locale(s): Karenta, Fictional City

Summary: With real estate scarce on Temple Row, Garrett has three reasons to find the key to the last remaining temple: the two minor pantheons who demand his services and the possibility of war on a supernatural scale that could destroy all reality.

Other books you might like:
Robert Asprin, *Thieves' World*, 1979
    editor
Emma Bull, *Finder*, 1994
Randall Garrett, *Too Many Magicians*, 1967
Simon R. Green, *Hawk & Fisher*, 1990
Laurell K. Hamilton, *Guilty Pleasures*, 1993
Jonathan Lethem, *Gun, with Occasional Music*, 1994
Will Shetterly, *Nevernever*, 1993
Gary K. Wolf, *Who Censored Roger Rabbit?*, 1981

931

GLEN COOK

Red Iron Nights

(New York: Roc, 1991)

Story type: Fantasy (Mystery; Urban)
Series: Garrett Files
Major character(s): Garrett, Detective—Private; Dead Man, Sidekick, Genius
Time period(s): Indeterminate Past
Locale(s): TunFaire, Fictional City

Summary: The Watch finally comes to Garrett for help when someone kills young women who are well-enough connected to pressure the Watch for results. Gruesome even for TunFaire, the murders point to some sort of ritual compulsion. When Garrett lands the culprit, the murders mysteriously continue.

Other books you might like:
Robert Asprin, *Thieves' World*, 1979
    editor
George Alec Effinger, *When Gravity Fails*, 1987
Randall Garrett, *Too Many Magicians*, 1967
Simon R. Green, *Hawk & Fisher*, 1990
Lee Killough, *Spider Play*, 1986
Michael Kurland, *A Study in Sorcery*, 1989
Mercedes Lackey, *Burning Water*, 1989

932

GLEN COOK

Tower of Fear

(New York: Tor, 1989)

Story type: Fantasy (Sword and Sorcery)
Major character(s): Nakar, Wizard (High priest of the evil god), Ruler (Deposed ruler of Qushmarrah); Ala-eh-din Beyh, Wizard (High priest of the benevolent), Warrior (Ally of Herodians)
Time period(s): Indeterminate
Locale(s): Qushmarrah, Alternate Earth (Middle Eastern type city setting)

Summary: Ala-eh-din Beyh opposes Nakar's rule of the city of Qushmarrah in a fierce combat of sorcery. Nakar's wife, the Witch, however intervenes at a crucial point of the battle and induces a magical stasis upon the warriors. Ala-eh-din Beyh's nominal allies, the Herodians, and the desert nomad mercenary Partars, in the meantime, invade and conquer the city. Conflict abounds as the conquerers fight among themselves and a resistance group, "The Living" emerges and attempts to resurrect the sorcerers.

Other books you might like:
Adrian Cole, *A Place Among the Fallen*, 1986
    Book of the Omarian Saga
Barbara Hambly, *The Time of the Dark*, 1982
    Darwath Trilogy. Bk. 1
Robert E. Vardeman, *Phantoms on the Wind*, 1989
    Demon Crown 2
Melanie Rawn, *The Star Scroll*, 1989
Alida Van Gores, *Mermaid's Song*, 1989

933

HUGH COOK

Lords of the Sword

(New York: Roc, 1991)

Story type: Fantasy (Adventure)
Series: Wizard War Chronicles
Major character(s): Deldragon Drakedon "Drake" Douay, Teenager, Apprentice (swordmaker)

Time period(s): Indeterminate
Locale(s): *Argans*, Fictional Country; *Flying Fish*, At Sea; *Warfolf*, At Sea

Summary: In the aftermath of his 16th birthday celebration, Drake appears before the king who mercifully orders Drake taken out to sea and dumped overboard. His punishment allows Drake to join pirates and begin the life journey which will culminate in his becoming one of Argans' greatest heroes.

Other books you might like:
Glen Cook, *The Black Company*, 1984
Mike Jeffries, *The Road to Underfall*, 1990
Elizabeth Moon, *Divided Allegiance*, 1988
Elizabeth Moon, *Oath of Gold*, 1989
Elizabeth Moon, *Sheepfarmer's Daughter*, 1988
Elizabeth Moon, *Surrender None: The Legacy of Gird*, 1990
Lawrence Watt-Evans, *The Blood of a Dragon*, 1991

934

RICK COOK

Limbo System

(New York: Baen Books, 1989)

Story type: Science Fiction (First Contact)
Major character(s): Peter Jenkins, Spaceship Captain; Sukihara Takiuji, Scientist
Time period(s): 21st century
Locale(s): *Maxwell*, Spaceship; Alien Colony Circling Star AC, Planet—Imaginary

Summary: An interstellar vessel on an exploratory flight discovers an alien culture which is evidently not native to the star system where it currently resides. Apparently the aliens are the descendants of a starfaring colony isolated for a million years after its interstellar drive failed. The aliens are enormously hostile and will stop at nothing to gain the secret of the human stardrive.

Other books you might like:
John Dalmas, *The Lizard War*, 1989
Larry Niven, *Man-Kzin Wars*, 1988
Larry Niven, *Man-Kzin Wars II*, 1988
    Niven is editor
Larry Niven, *The Mote in God's Eye*, 1974

935

RICK COOK

Mall Purchase Night

(New York: Baen, 1993)

Story type: Fantasy (Urban; Light Fantasy)
Major character(s): Andy Westin, Security Officer
Time period(s): 1990s
Locale(s): Black Oak Mall, Mythical Place

Summary: Magic and mythical creatures complicate Andy's job at one of the world's largest shopping malls built on an elven power source and gateway to Faerie realms.

Other books you might like:
Emma Bull, *War for the Oaks*, 1987
Charles de Lint, *Moonheart: A Romance*, 1984
Charles de Lint, *Spiritwalk*, 1992
Elizabeth Forrest, *Phoenix Fire*, 1992
Alan Dean Foster, *Cyber Way*, 1990
Nick Pollotta, *Doomsday Exam*, 1992
Will Shetterly, *Elsewhere*, 1991
Harry Turtledove, *The Case of the Toxic Spell Dump*, 1993
Terri Windling, *Life on the Border*, 1991
    editor

936

RICK COOK

The Wizardry Consulted

(New York: Baen, 1995)

Story type: Fantasy (Light Fantasy; Alternate World)
Series: Wizardry
Major character(s): William Irving "Wiz" Zumwalt, Computer Expert, Wizard; Wurm, Mythical Creature (dragon); Malkin, Thief, Companion
Time period(s): Indeterminate
Locale(s): Alternate Earth; California

Summary: Dragons kidnap Wiz Zumwalt, hoping to gain salvation for dragonkind.

Other books you might like:
Gael Baudino, *Dragonsword*, 1988
Gordon R. Dickson, *The Dragon and the George*, 1976
Barbara Hambly, *The Silent Tower*, 1986
Ursula K. Le Guin, *A Wizard of Earthsea*, 1967
Will Shetterly, *The Tangled Lands*, 1989
Brad Strickland, *Wizard's Mole*, 1991

937

RICK COOK

The Wizardry Cursed

(New York: Baen, 1991)

Story type: Fantasy (Adventure; Alternate World)
Series: Wizardry
Major character(s): William Irving "Wiz" Zumwalt, Computer Expert, Wizard; Bal-Simba, Wizard, Adventurer; Moira, Witch
Time period(s): 1990s (1991)
Locale(s): Alternate Earth; San Jose, California

Summary: Third in a continuing series about programmers loose in a magical world, this book involves an invasion by a pair of programmers and wargamers. The war, for the first time, is fought using both magic and technology.

Other books you might like:
Tom Deitz, *Windmaster's Bane*, 1986
Barbara Hambly, *The Silent Tower*, 1986
Simon Hawke, *The Ivanhoe Gambit*, 1984
Joel Rosenberg, *The Sleeping Dragon*, 1983
Roger Zelazny, *Nine Princes in Amber*, 1970

938

RICK COOK

The Wizardry Quested
(New York: Baen, 1996)

Story type: Fantasy (Light Fantasy; Quest)
Series: Wizardry
Major character(s): William Irving "Wiz" Zumwalt, Computer Expert, Wizard; Bal-Simba, Wizard, Adventurer; Moira, Witch, Spouse
Time period(s): Indeterminate; 1990s
Locale(s): Alternate Earth; Wizard's Keep, Mythical Place; Las Vegas, Nevada

Summary: Wiz Zumwalt must find the key to reversing the magical code which folded Moira's consciousness into a pet dragon. Unfortunately, when Moira and her entourage escape to Nevada to work on the problem, the rescue mission encounters complications involving local officials, the Federal Court and the U.S. Air Force, sensitive about publicity and events occurring near Area 51.

Other books you might like:
Gordon R. Dickson, *The Dragon and the George*, 1976
Barbara Hambly, *The Silent Tower*, 1986
Joel Rosenberg, *The Sleeping Dragon*, 1983
Will Shetterly, *The Tangled Lands*, 1989
Harry Turtledove, *The Case of the Toxic Spell Dump*, 1993

939

ROBIN COOK

Harmful Intent
(New York: Putnam, 1990)

Story type: Science Fiction (Medical)
Major character(s): Jeffrey Rhodes, Doctor; Kelly Everson, Nurse
Time period(s): 1980s
Locale(s): New England

Summary: Anesthesiologist Dr. Jeffrey Rhodes's career is destroyed when a patient to whom he has administered routine anesthesia goes into convulsions and dies. Rhodes is sued and convicted of second-degree murder. Convinced that the patient's death was not his fault and was not an accident, the doctor goes underground in an attempt to track down those actually responsible for this murder and others. He uncovers a plot more terrifying than anything he had thought possible.

Other books you might like:
Peter Caine, *Virus*, 1989
Michael Crichton, *The Andromeda Strain*, 1969
Michael Crichton, *The Terminal Man*, 1972
Alan Engel, *Variant*, 1988
Chelsea Quinn Yarbro, *Time of the Fourth Horseman*, 1976

940

ROBIN COOK

Mutation
(New York: Putnam, 1989)

Story type: Science Fiction (Medical)
Major character(s): Victor Frank, Doctor, Scientist; VJ, Mutant
Time period(s): 1980s
Locale(s): United States

Summary: Learning that his wife is infertile, Dr. Victor Frank attempts a bold and dangerous experiment. Drawing on the techniques of both animal husbandry and molecular genetics, he fuses an egg from his wife with one of his own sperm and then implants the resulting embryo in a surrogate mother. The baby born of the experiment seems normal at first, but then begins to change into something horrible.

Other books you might like:
John Brunner, *Children of the Thunder*, 1989
John Gribbin, *Father to the Man*, 1990
James Morrow, *Only Begotten Daughter*, 1990
Hayford Peirce, *Phylum Monsters*, 1989
Robert Reed, *Black Milk*, 1989

941

JOHN PEYTON COOKE

Out for Blood
(New York: Avon, 1991)

Story type: Horror (Vampire Story)
Major character(s): Chris Callaway, Vampire, Homosexual; Beth, Vampire; Vasily "Temsik" Kirilovich, Vampire
Time period(s): 1990s
Locale(s): Chicago, Illinois; Madison, Wisconsin

Summary: Saved from imminent death by the bite of a beautiful vampire, gay leukemia victim Chris Callaway becomes a vampire himself and is indoctrinated into survival strategies that include pretending to eat food in the company of others, hypnotizing cheap bar pick-ups, remembering not to bite any victim more than three times to keep them from becoming vampires, and avoiding vampire hunters who mingle with urban night life the same way vampires do.

Other books you might like:
Richard Lee Byers, *The Vampire's Apprentice*, 1992
Scott Edelman, *The Gift*, 1990
Jeffrey N. McMahan, *Vampires Anonymous*, 1991
Anne Rice, *Interview with the Vampire*, 1975

942

ELEANOR COONEY
DANIEL ALTIERI, Co-Author

Shangri-La: The Return to the World of Lost Horizon

(New York: Morrow, 1996)

Story type: Fantasy (Religious; Contemporary Realism)
Major character(s): Zhang, Military Personnel (Supreme Commander), Explorer; Ma Li "Sister", Military Personnel (People's Liberation Army), Revolutionary; Hugh Conway, Diplomat (retired)
Time period(s): 1960s; 2000s
Locale(s): Tibet; Shangri-La, Fictional Country (Shambala)

Summary: While looting Tibet during the Cultural Revolution, General Zhang discovers evidence of the existence of Shambala, core of Tibetan culture and possible liberation. Ordered to investigate, Zhang's mission of discovery suffers setbacks when Ma Li's prophecied help alerts Hugh Conway to the possiblity of diverting Zhang from his deadly quest. Sequel to James Hilton's novel.

Other books you might like:
James Hilton, *Lost Horizon*, 1933
Marc Laidlaw, *Neon Lotus*, 1988
Edward Myers, *Fire and Ice*, 1922
Elizabeth Ann Scarborough, *Last Refuge*, 1992
Elizabeth Ann Scarborough, *Nothing Sacred*, 1991

943

DENNIS COOPER

Frisk

(New York: Grove, Weidenfeld, 1991)

Story type: Horror (Serial Killer)
Major character(s): Dennis, Murderer (narrator); Gypsy Pete, Store Owner (bookstore)
Time period(s): 20th century (1970s-1990s)
Locale(s): Amsterdam, Netherlands

Summary: Early exposure to monster movies and pornography, and a viewing of "snuff" photos in the backroom of an adult bookstore, embarks a disaffected gay youth on a quest for emotional fulfillment, which he is convinced can only be achieved through violent sex ending in mutilation and murder.

Other books you might like:
Brett Easton Ellis, *American Psycho*, 1991
Thomas Harris, *The Silence of the Lambs*, 1988
Paul Russell, *Boys of Life*, 1991

944

DENNIS COOPER

Wrong

(New York: Grove/Weidenfeld, 1992)

Story type: Horror (Collection)

Summary: Nine stories and an epilogue that explore the dark side of sexuality and death. Included are "A Herd," about an aging homosexual's sadistic murders of neighborhood children; "Introducing Horror Hospital," about a punk rock band forced to live up to its nihilistic credo; and the short novel, "Safe," concerned with a man who finds the ultimate sexual thrill in murder.

Other books you might like:
Ray Garton, *Methods of Madness*, 1991
Eric McCormack, *Inspecting the Vaults*, 1987
David J. Schow, *Lost Angels*, 1990

945

LOUISE COOPER

Aisling

(New York: Tor, 1994)

Story type: Fantasy (Quest; Magic Conflict)
Series: Indigo
Major character(s): Indigo, Outcast; Grimya, Animal (wolf), Telepath; Niahrin, Witch
Time period(s): Indeterminate Past
Locale(s): Southern Isles, Fictional Country

Summary: Injured during a shipwreck, Indigo loses her memory, subverting her goal of reunion with her lost love. The sole remaining unvanquished demon from the Tower of Regrets takes advantage of Indigo's situation, drawing her into an evil plot which only the enchanted tune, the Aisling, can overcome. Concludes the series of eight novels.

Other books you might like:
James P. Blaylock, *The Last Coin*, 1988
Terry Goodkind, *Wizard's First Rule*, 1994
Marc Laidlaw, *Neon Lotus*, 1988
Fred Saberhagen, *The Last Book of Swords: Shieldbreaker's Story*, 1994
Patricia C. Wrede, *The Raven Ring*, 1994

946

LOUISE COOPER

Avatar

(New York: Tor, 1992)

Story type: Fantasy (Quest)
Series: Indigo
Major character(s): Indigo, Outcast; Grimya, Animal (wolf), Telepath; Uluye, Religious (high priestess)
Time period(s): Indeterminate Past
Locale(s): Dark Isle, Fictional Country

Summary: Indigo and Grimya pursue the fifth demon of the seven she released many years previously. In the humid jungles of the Dark Isle, a cult of death-worshippers takes in the travellers and initiates Indigo as their oracle. Indigo believes that she has found the demon, but must defeat it before the terrors of her past destroy her.

Other books you might like:
C.J. Cherryh, *Gate of Ivrel*, 1976
Glen Cook, *The Black Company*, 1984

Barbara Hambly, *The Time of the Dark*, 1982
Michael Moorcock, *Elric of Melnibone*, 1976
Michael Scott Rohan, *The Forge in the Forest*, 1987

947

LOUISE COOPER

The Avenger
(New York: Bantam Spectra, 1992)

Story type: Fantasy (Adventure)
Series: Chaos Gate Trilogy
Major character(s): Strann, Minstrel; Karuth, Sorceress; Ygorla, Sorceress, Ruler
Time period(s): Indeterminate Past
Locale(s): Star Peninsula, Fictional Country; Summer Isle, Fictional Country

Summary: Events rush to a climax as plots, human, divine and semi-divine, move toward completion. If Ygorla wins, she traps the world in a net of change and senseless cruelty, but if the Lords of Order defeat her, humanity will belong to them. There is only a narrow line of free will between them.

Other books you might like:
C.J. Cherryh, *Well of Shiuan*, 1978
Barbara Hambly, *The Time of the Dark*, 1982
Katherine Kurtz, *Deryni Rising*, 1970
Patricia A. McKillip, *The Riddle-Master of Hed*, 1976
Michael Moorcock, *Elric of Melnibone*, 1976

948

LOUISE COOPER

The Deceiver
(New York: Bantam Spectra, 1991)

Story type: Fantasy (Magic Conflict)
Series: Chaos Gate Trilogy
Major character(s): Tirand, Sorcerer; Karuth, Sorceress (Tirand's sister); Ygorla, Demon (half-human)
Time period(s): Indeterminate
Locale(s): Star Peninsula, Fictional Country; Souther Chaun, Fictional Country

Summary: The delicate balance between the gods of Chaos and Order is threatened by the birth of Ygorla, daughter of Narid-na-Gost, demon of Chaos, and a human woman. The High Initiate Tirand does not recognize the danger, in spite of Karuth's warnings. Now Ygorla and her father have the soul stone of Yandros, Lord of Chaos. *The Pretender* (1991) continues this story.

Other books you might like:
Barbara Hambly, *The Armies of Daylight*, 1983
Barbara Hambly, *The Time of the Dark*, 1982
Barbara Hambly, *The Walls of Air*, 1983
Katherine Kurtz, *Deryni Checkmate*, 1972
Katherine Kurtz, *Deryni Rising*, 1970
Katherine Kurtz, *High Deryni*, 1973
Ursula K. Le Guin, *The Farthest Shore*, 1972
Ursula K. Le Guin, *Tehanu: The Last Book of Earthsea*, 1990
Ursula K. Le Guin, *The Tombs of Atuan*, 1971

Ursula K. Le Guin, *A Wizard of Earthsea*, 1968

949

LOUISE COOPER

Infanta
(New York: Tor, 1990)

Story type: Fantasy (Quest)
Series: Indigo
Major character(s): Indigo, Outcast; Grimya, Animal (wolf), Telepath
Time period(s): Indeterminate Past
Locale(s): Huon Parita, Fictional City

Summary: Indigo has been led to Huon Parita in search of the second demon she released from the Tower of Regrets and must destroy, and which she believes has taken the form of the city's new ruler. While she looks for proof and waits for a method and opportunity to fight, she takes a position as governess to the dispossessed heir who will marry the new ruler when she reaches her twelfth birthday.

Other books you might like:
C.J. Cherryh, *Rusalka*, 1989
Glen Cook, *A Shadow of All Night Falling*, 1979
Tara K. Harper, *Wolfwalker*, 1990
Shirley Meier, *The Cage*, 1989
  S.M. Stirling, co-author
Joan D. Vinge, *The Snow Queen*, 1980

950

LOUISE COOPER

Nemesis
(New York: Tor, 1989)

Story type: Fantasy (Quest)
Series: Indigo
Major character(s): Princess Anghara, Young Woman (Rebellious), Royalty; Earth Mother, Deity (Goddess)
Time period(s): Indeterminate Past
Locale(s): Southern Isles, Fictional Country

Summary: Princess Anghara enters the sacred and forbidden Tower of Regrets in direct violation of her parents and the law of the kingdom. As a consequence of her actions, seven evil supernatural beings are let loose upon the land. Upon the advice of the goddess Earth Mother, Anghara renounces her claim to the throne, assumes the new identity of Indigo and proceeds on a quest to battle and expel the evil beings and also to expiate the mortal sins she has committed.

Other books you might like:
Marion Zimmer Bradley, *Thendara House*, 1983
David Eddings, *Guardians of the West*, 1987
Ursula K. Le Guin, *Tehanu: The Last Book of Earthsea*, 1990
Patricia A. McKillip, *The Changeling Sea*, 1988
Paul Edwin Zimmer, *Blood of the Colyn Muir*, 1988

951

LOUISE COOPER

Revenant

(New York: Tor, 1993)

Story type: Fantasy (Quest)
Series: Indigo
Major character(s): Indigo, Outcast; Grimya, Animal (wolf), Telepath; The Benefactor, Deity
Time period(s): Indeterminate Past
Locale(s): Joyful Travail, Fictional City; Nation of Prosperity, Fictional Country

Summary: After the trauma of recent adventures, Indigo abandons her attempts to trap the last two demons, searching for her lost lover instead. Wandering, she comes to an utterly pragmatic town without any strong emotion at all. The town hides an old secret, the uncovering of which may grant Indigo her desire.

Other books you might like:
C.J. Cherryh, *Gate of Ivrel*, 1976
Glen Cook, *The Black Company*, 1984
Barbara Hambly, *The Time of the Dark*, 1982
Michael Moorcock, *Elric of Melnibone*, 1976
Michael Scott Rohan, *The Forge in the Forest*, 1987

952

LOUISE COOPER

The Sleep of Stone

(New York: Atheneum, 1991)

Story type: Fantasy (Romance; Magic Conflict)
Series: Dragonflight
Major character(s): Ghysla, Mythical Creature (shapechanger); Anyr, Fiance(e) (Sivorne's); Mornan, Wizard
Time period(s): Indeterminate
Locale(s): Caris, Fictional City

Summary: Motivated by jealousy and love, Ghysla uses ancient magic to change Anyr's betrothed, Sivorne, into stone. When Ghysla reveals her love and her true form to Anyr, he scorns her love and enlists the aid of Mornan to overcome Ghysla's sorcery.

Other books you might like:
Octavia E. Butler, *Imago*, 1989
Margaret Mahy, *The Changeover*, 1984
Patricia A. McKillip, *The Changeling*, 1988
Jennifer Roberson, *Legacy of the Sword*, 1986
Jennifer Roberson, *Shapechangers*, 1984
Jennifer Roberson, *The Song of Homana*, 1985
Charles Sheffield, *The Selkie*, 1982
    David Bischoff, co-author
Terri Windling, *Life on the Border*, 1991
    editor

953

LOUISE COOPER

Star Ascendant

(New York: Tor, 1995)

Story type: Fantasy (Adventure; Political)
Major character(s): Benetan Liss, Military Personnel; Vordegh, Magician, Leader (First Magus); Iselia Darrow, Religious (disciple of the Lords of Order)
Time period(s): Indeterminate
Locale(s): Planet—Imaginary (extra-dimensional)

Summary: While Chaos holds supremacy, the forces of Order rally and prepare to initiate the battle which will overturn the rule of Chaos. Prequel to The Time Master Trilogy (1985-1987).

Other books you might like:
Craig Shaw Gardner, *Dragon Sleeping*, 1994
Elizabeth Hand, *Waking the Moon*, 1995
L. Dean James, *Summerland*, 1994
L.E. Modesitt Jr., *The Order War*, 1995
Mark C. Perry, *Morigu: The Dead*, 1990
Roger Zelazny, *Nine Princes in Amber*, 1970

954

LOUISE COOPER

Troika

(New York: Tor, 1991)

Story type: Fantasy (Quest)
Series: Indigo
Major character(s): Indigo, Outcast; Grimya, Animal (wolf), Telepath
Time period(s): Indeterminate Past
Locale(s): The Redoubt, Fictional City; Mull Barya, Fictional City

Summary: Indigo and Grimya continue their hunt for the evils released by Indigo's errors. This time, their path leads them back to sites from Indigo's past, where she has to fight not only the demons, but also her own treacherous heart and memory.

Other books you might like:
Gael Baudino, *Gossamer Axe*, 1990
Emma Bull, *War for the Oaks*, 1987
Barbara Hambly, *The Time of the Dark*, 1982
Michael Moorcock, *Elric of Melnibone*, 1976
Roger Zelazny, *Nine Princes in Amber*, 1970

955

ALFRED COPPEL

Glory

(New York: Tor, 1993)

Story type: Science Fiction (Political; Space Colony)
Series: Goldenwing Cycle

Major character(s): Black Clavius, Spaceman, Wanderer; Eliana Ehrengraf Voerster, Noblewoman; Broni Voerster, Teenager, Handicapped
Time period(s): 35th century
Locale(s): Voerster, Planet—Imaginary; *Gloria "Glory" Coelis*, Spaceship

Summary: At Voerster to deliver frozen animal embryos ordered hundreds of years earlier, *Glory* catalyzes action in the Voerster political crisis between Black and White descendants of South African settlers. Without *Glory*'s advanced medical technology, Broni Voerster will die prematurely.

Other books you might like:
Poul Anderson, *The Queen of Air and Darkness*, 1973
John Brunner, *A Maze of Stars*, 1991
Arthur C. Clarke, *The Songs of Distant Earth*, 1986
John Dalmas, *The Walkaway Clause*, 1985
William R. Forstchen, *Into the Sea of Stars*, 1986
Robert Cham Gilman, *The Rebel of Rhada*, 1968
    pseudonym of Alfred Coppel
Lee Killough, *A Voice out of Ramah*, 1979
Michael McCollum, *Antares Passage*, 1987
Jerry Pournelle, *King David's Spaceship*, 1980
Eric Frank Russell, *The Great Explosion*, 1962
Brian Stableford, *Wildeblood's Empire*, 1977

956

ALFRED COPPEL

Glory's People

(New York: Tor, 1996)

Story type: Science Fiction (Military; Space Opera)
Series: Goldenwing Cycle
Major character(s): Duncan Kr, Spaceship Captain, Empath; Anya Amaya, Pilot (spaceship Sailing Master); Minamoto no Kami, Leader (shogun), Scientist (xenobiologist)
Time period(s): 26th century
Locale(s): Yamato, Planet—Imaginary; *Gloria "Glory" Coelis*, Spaceship; Interstellar Empire/Federation

Summary: *Glory*'s warning of impending threat to Yamoto's populace goes unheeded until a malevolent intergalactic entity attacks directly.

Other books you might like:
Roger MacBride Allen, *The Ring of Charon*, 1990
Roger MacBride Allen, *The Shattered Sphere*, 1984
Orson Scott Card, *Speaker for the Dead*, 1986
Jeffrey A. Carver, *Neptune Crossing*, 1994
Glen Cook, *The Dragon Never Sleeps*, 1988
Vernor Vinge, *A Fire upon the Deep*, 1992

957

ALFRED COPPEL

Glory's War

(New York: Tor, 1995)

Story type: Science Fiction (Military; Hard Science Fiction)
Series: Goldenwing Cycle

Major character(s): Ekaterina Alexandrova Volkova, Military Personnel (colonel), Noblewoman (Gospodina); Duncan Kr, Spaceship Captain, Empath; Peter Mornay, Religious (Sharia cleric), Government Official
Time period(s): Indeterminate Future
Locale(s): *Gloria "Glory" Coelis*, Spaceship (Goldenwing); Nineveh, Planet—Imaginary; Nimrud, Planet—Imaginary

Summary: Acting on instructions from Nineveh's leaders, Peter Mornay commissions Colonel Kat Volkova to capture *Glory* as it attempts to deliver its cargo to Nimrud, the only other planet in the Ross system and Nineveh's enemy for over 400 years. As Duncan Kr and his crew help *Glory* fend off the invading troops, they become aware of another menace so powerful and destructive that humanity's survival here depends on forcing the colonists to put aside their centuries of enmity and cooperate in the face of a common threat. Sequel to *Glory*.

Other books you might like:
Lois McMaster Bujold, *Shards of Honor*, 1986
C.J. Cherryh, *Forty Thousand in Gehenna*, 1983
Glen Cook, *The Dragon Never Sleeps*, 1988
Robert L. Forward, *Rocheworld*, 1990
William H. Keith Jr., *Warstrider: Netlink*, 1995
Michael P. Kube-McDowell, *Emprise*, 1985
Larry Niven, *The Mote in God's Eye*, 1974
    Jerry Pournelle, co-author
Steve Perry, *The Man Who Never Missed*, 1985
Dan Simmons, *The Fall of Hyperion*, 1990
Dan Simmons, *Hyperion*, 1989
Vernor Vinge, *A Fire upon the Deep*, 1992

958

BASIL COPPER

The Black Death

(Minneapolis, Minnesota: Fedogan & Bremer, 1992)

Story type: Horror (Occult)
Major character(s): John Carter, Architect; Fiona Hammond, Ward; David Sennen, Religious
Time period(s): 20th century (early)
Locale(s): Thornton Basset, England

Summary: John Carter embarks on a promising career as a partner in an architectural firm located in the insular rural town of Thornton Basset. But his investigations into legends of ghostly hunters who roam the moors at night and the mysterious "black death" which claims the lives of those foolish enough to go wandering the moors after sundown bring him face to face with a secret cult involving the town's leading citizens.

Other books you might like:
Charles L. Grant, *The Hour of the Oxrun Dead*, 1977
Stephen Gregory, *The Woodwitch*, 1989
Thomas Tryon, *Harvest Home*, 1973
Dennis Wheatley, *The Irish Witch*, 1973

959

DAVID COPPERFIELD, Editor
JANET BERLINER, Co-Editor

David Copperfield's Beyond Imagination
(New York: HarperPrism, 1996)

Story type: Fantasy (Anthology)

Summary: This volume contains a four-page preface by Raymond E. Feist, eight pages of authors' biographies, a brief introduction plus individual introductions by Copperfield to 17 original stories varying in tone and themes, such as arts, romance, family relations, extraterrestrial contact, Hollywood illusion, public relations, ghosts, detection, and inventions. Authors include each editor and Kevin J. Anderson, Peter S. Beagle, Greg Bear, Edward Bryant, Charles de Lint, Karen Joy Fowler, Neil Gaiman, George Guthridge, Eric Lustbader, Anne McCaffrey, Robert Silverberg, Steve Rasnic Tem, and Tad Williams.

Other books you might like:
K.W. Jeter, *Infernal Devices*, 1987
Christopher Priest, *The Prestige*, 1996
Tom Reamy, *Blind Voices*, 1978
Brooke Stevens, *The Circus of the Earth and Air*, 1994

960

DAVID COPPERFIELD, Editor
JANET BERLINER, Co-Editor

David Copperfield's Tales of the Impossible
(New York: HarperPrism, 1995)

Story type: Horror (Anthology)

Summary: The world famous magician David Copperfield lends his imprimatur to this anthology of eighteen original stories featuring magic and sleight-of-hand. Included are S.P. Somotow's "Diamond's Aren't Forever," a lampoon of Thai mysticism that extrapolates to an illogical extreme the notion that the material world is an illusion; a story by F. Paul Wilson (with an unreproducible title) about a magic word that proves a curse; Lucy Taylor's "Switch," in which a young girl discovers that her escape from one harsh world results in her imprisonment in another; David Smed's alternate rock history about John Lennon's death, "The Eight of December," and Bob Weinberg's "Dealing with the Devil," in which players in a card game with the devil find a way to outwit him. The book also includes stories by Ray Bradbury and Joyce Carol Oates, and Copperfield's own first published fiction, "Snow," about a young boy who finds a way to conjure snowflakes. Dean Koontz supplies an introduction.

Other books you might like:
Walter B. Gibson, *Norgil the Magician*, 1977
Walter B. Gibson, *Norgil, More Tales of Prestidigetection*, 1977
Edward E. Kramer, *Tombs*, 1995
   Peter Crowther, co-editor
Roger Zelazny, *Wheel of Fortune*, 1995
   Martin H. Greenberg, co-editor

961

ROBERT CORMIER

Fade
(New York: Delacorte, 1989)

Story type: Horror (Wild Talents)
Major character(s): Paul Moreaux, Writer; Susan, Relative (Paul Moreaux's cousin)
Time period(s): 1930s (1938); 1980s (1988)
Locale(s): Monument, Massachusetts

Summary: Teenage Paul Moreaux's life changes dramatically when he learns from his uncle Adelard that he, like his uncle, possesses the power to fade to invisibility. 50 years later, Paul, now a reclusive author, dies leaving behind a haunting manuscript of his life and his search for the nephew who is heir to the power. His agent Meredith and cousin Susan discover the manuscript and struggle with the possible reality or fiction of the story.

Other books you might like:
Robert Stallman, *The Orphan*, 1980
H.G. Wells, *The Invisible Man*, 1897

962

BERNARD CORNWELL

The Winter King
(New York: St. Martin's, 1996)

Story type: Fantasy (Historical; Legend)
Series: Warlord Chronicles
Major character(s): Arthur, Warrior, Bastard Son; Derfel Cadarn, Slave, Warrior; Nimue, Orphan, Sorceress
Time period(s): 6th century
Locale(s): England; Brittany, France

Summary: A Saxon reared since infancy in Merlin's household, Derfel longs to fight in Arthur's warband. Chosen as one of the regents to protect the infant king, his half-brother's son, Mordred, Arthur seeks to bring peace among the rival Celtic kingdoms so that they may fight their mutual enemies, the Saxons. Yet Arthur spurns a marital alliance with one king's daughter in order to marry Guinevere, bringing on war with his Celtic neighbors while the Saxons raid his borders.

Other books you might like:
Poul Anderson, *The King of Ys: Roma Mater*, 1986
   Karen Anderson, co-author
Marion Zimmer Bradley, *The Mists of Avalon*, 1983
Parke Godwin, *The Last Rainbow*, 1985
Harry Harrison, *The Hammer and the Cross*, 1993
   John Holm, co-author
Diana L. Paxson, *The White Raven*, 1988

963

MATTHEW J. COSTELLO
CRAIG SHAW GARDNER, Co-Author

The 7th Guest

(Rocklin, California: Prima, 1995)

Story type: Horror (Haunted House)
Major character(s): Edward Knox, Gambler; Brian Dutton, Businessman; Hamilton Temple, Magician
Time period(s): 1990s (1995)
Locale(s): New York (Upstate)

Summary: Six guests are invited to the old abandoned Stauf Mansion, a house with a legacy of evil. Once there, they find themselves locked inside, and are informed by their mysterious benefactor that only one will emerge the next day, with his or her heart's desire granted, if all fulfill the tasks set out for them. Who will survive, and the role played by a mysterious seventh guest, are just part of the evening's mysteries in this novel based on a popular CD-ROM game.

Other books you might like:
Tom Elliott, *The Dwelling*, 1989
Shirley Jackson, *The Haunting of Hill House*, 1959
Richard Matheson, *Hell House*, 1971
Al Sarrantonio, *House Haunted*, 1991
Chet Williamson, *Soulstorm*, 1986

964

MATTHEW J. COSTELLO

Beneath Still Waters

(New York: Berkley, 1989)

Story type: Horror (Supernatural Vengeance)
Major character(s): Susan Sloan, Journalist, Single Parent; Dan Elliot, Journalist
Time period(s): 1980s (1989)
Locale(s): Ellerton, New York (Near the Kenicut Reservoir)

Summary: As the celebration of the 50th anniversary of the Kenicut Reservoir nears, citizens begin disappearing into its dark waters. Investigating the disappearances, reporters Susan Sloan and Dan Elliot learn that a whole town, Gouldens Falls, home to a Crowley-like cult, was once inundated beneath the Reservoir's waters. Evil spirits are now coming back for vengeance.

Other books you might like:
Alan Ryan, *Dead White*, 1983
Dean Wesley Smith, *Laying the Music to Rest*, 1989

965

MATTHEW J. COSTELLO

Child's Play III

(New York: Jove, 1991)

Story type: Horror (Black Magic)
Major character(s): Chucky, Disembodied Personality (lives in a doll), Murderer; Andy Barclay, Student; Brett C. Shelton, Student

Time period(s): 1990s
Locale(s): United States

Summary: The saga of Chucky, the walking, talking Good Guys Doll who has become the vessel for the soul of slain mass murderer Charles Lee Ray, continues in this novelization of the second sequel to the hit 1988 movie, *Child's Play*. This time, the indestructible Chucky tracks his former owner Andy Barclay to military school, where he enlists the help of upper class bullies in his efforts to dispose of Andy before Andy tries yet again to dispose of him. Based on a screenplay by Don Mancini.

Other books you might like:
Pat Graversen, *Dollies*, 1990
Abraham Merritt, *Burn Witch, Burn*, 1933
Sarban, *The Doll Maker and Other Tales of the Uncanny*, 1953

966

MATTHEW J. COSTELLO

Darkborn

(New York: Diamond, 1992)

Story type: Horror (Black Magic)
Major character(s): Will Duinngan, Lawyer; Jim Kiff, Veteran; Joshua James, Professor (of theology)
Time period(s): 1960s (1965); 1990s (1992)
Locale(s): New York, New York

Summary: The efforts of a group of schoolboys from Jesuit-run St. Jerome's Preparatory School to raise the demon Astaroth with an incantation from *The Book of Enoch* go awry, resulting in the unintentional blood sacrifice of one of their friends and a threat to their lives 27 years later when the demon comes to claim his due.

Other books you might like:
Ramsey Campbell, *Obsession*, 1986
Ramsey Campbell, *To Wake the Dead*, 1980
Stephen King, *It*, 1986
Peter Straub, *Ghost Story*, 1979

967

MATTHEW J. COSTELLO

Day of the Snake

(New York: Roc, 1992)

Story type: Science Fiction (Time Travel)
Series: Time Warrior
Major character(s): Jim Tiber, Time Traveller; Alessandra "Ale" Moreau, Time Traveller, Student; Flynn Lindstrom, Historian
Time period(s): 1990s; 1940s (1941)
Locale(s): New York, New York; Pearl Harbor, Hawaii

Summary: Jim Tiber finds himself suddenly in a grimly altered present and knows that the sinister Iron Men have again tampered with history. He reaches his colleagues in the Time Lab, where he learns of the focal point of change: December 7, 1941. Using the time transference device, four time travellers shift their consciousness to bodies from that time, attempting to restore history, while the remaining three guard their unconscious bodies from the cannibalistic Packs.

Other books you might like:
Poul Anderson, *The Shield of Time*, 1990
Poul Anderson, *The Time Patrol*, 1991
Gregory Benford, *Alternate Wars*, 1991
  Martin H. Greenberg, co-editor
Gordon R. Dickson, *The Dragon and the George*, 1976
Phyllis Eisenstein, *Shadow of Earth*, 1979
Charles L. Harness, *Lurid Dreams*, 1990
L. Neil Smith, *The Nagasaki Vector*, 1983

968

MATTHEW J. COSTELLO

Garden

(Sparta, New Jersey: Twilight Publishing, 1993)

Story type: Horror (Nature in Revolt)
Major character(s): Michael Cross, Professor (director of the NY Aquarium); Jo Cross, Young Woman (Michael Cross's daughter); Louis Farrand, Religious (priest)
Time period(s): 1990s
Locale(s): New York, New York

Summary: Five years after a species of undersea worm has infested the inhabitants of New York, Manhattan has become a fenced-in island inhabited by carriers of the voracious parasite and an unlucky few survivors who have managed to avoid infestation. Failure to completely eradicate the worms according to plan sends the guardians of Manhattan onto the island, where they experience a variety of horrifying encounters while searching for overlooked clues to the creatures' vulnerability. This novella is a direct sequel to the author's 1991 novel, *Wurm*. F. Paul Wilson has supplied an introduction.

Other books you might like:
John W. Campbell, *Who Goes There?*, 1948
  Who Goes There?
Robert A. Heinlein, *The Puppet Masters*, 1951
F. Paul Wilson, *Midnight Mass*, 1990

969

MATTHEW J. COSTELLO

Homecoming

(New York: Berkley, 1992)

Story type: Horror (Serial Killer)
Major character(s): Simon Farrell, Businessman; Lizbeth Farrell, Secretary (at Hudson College); Jack Friedman, Police Officer
Time period(s): 1990s (1992)
Locale(s): White Plains, New York; New York, New York

Summary: Simon Farrell's homecoming from his years of being held hostage in the Middle East is spoiled by the homecoming of Donald Pick, a recently released convict who was never prosecuted for his gruesome "Meatman" murders of several years before but who intends to resume his bloody rampage starting with Farrell's family.

Other books you might like:
John D. MacDonald, *The Executioners*, 1957
Rex Miller, *Slob*, 1987
T.M. Wright, *The Place*, 1990

970

MATTHEW J. COSTELLO

Hour of the Scorpion

(New York: Roc, 1991)

Story type: Science Fiction (Military; Alternate Universe)
Series: Time Warrior
Major character(s): Jim Tiber, Time Traveller; Alessandra "Ale" Moreau, Time Traveller, Student; Clarence Howell, Military Personnel (Sergeant)
Time period(s): 1960s (1968)
Locale(s): Saigon, Vietnam

Summary: Jim Tiber sneaked into the Time Lab and got caught in an experiment which sent him back to World War II. When he returned it was revealed that another group of time travellers from behind the Iron Curtain, the Iron Men, was stealing art to finance a major change in American history. Jim is now in Saigon where he must foil the Iron Men's planned escalation of the Vietnam War.

Other books you might like:
Poul Anderson, *The Shield of Time*, 1990
Keith William Andrews, *Search and Destroy*, 1990
Keith William Andrews, *Treason in Time*, 1990
Phyllis Eisenstein, *Shadow of Earth*, 1979
Michael Flynn, *In the Country of the Blind*, 1990
William R. Forstchen, *Rally Cry!*, 1990
Randall Frakes, *The Terminator*, 1985
  Bell Wisher, co-author
Kim Stanley Robinson, *Remaking History*, 1991
L. Neil Smith, *The Nagasaki Vector*, 1983

971

MATTHEW J. COSTELLO

Midsummer

(New York: Diamond, 1990)

Story type: Horror (Science Fiction)
Major character(s): Alan Ward, Military Personnel (Navy lieutenant), Monster; Joshua Tyler, Child; Erica Tyler, Parent (Joshua's mother)
Time period(s): 1990s
Locale(s): Stonywood, New York

Summary: In this tribute to John W. Campbell's classic short story "Who Goes There?" young Josh Tyler is sent by his widowed mother to spend the summer with his grandmother in the peaceful town of Stonywood. He is unaware that a prehistoric monster capable of absorbing a human personality and assuming its shape has come to town in the person of a Navy lieutenant Alan Ward, recently returned from an Antarctic research station where he survived a massacre. Now the Thing is taking over the inhabitants of Stonywood.

Other books you might like:
Jack Finney, *The Body Snatchers*, 1955
Alan Dean Foster, *The Thing*, 1982
Stephen King, *The Tommyknockers*, 1987

972

MATTHEW J. COSTELLO

seaQuest DSV: Fire Below

(New York: Ace, 1994)

Story type: Science Fiction (Adventure)
Series: seaQuest DSV
Major character(s): Nathan Hale Bridger, Scientist, Sea Captain; Lucas Wolenczak, Computer Expert, Teenager; Terry McShane, Military Personnel (UEO)
Time period(s): 2010s (2018)
Locale(s): *seaQuest DSV*, Submarine; SousMer, Undersea Environment/Habitat; Atlantic Ocean

Summary: Terrorists threaten SousMer while an ocean worm, newly discovered by the Azores Deep Sea Research Station, presents a new and deadly biological threat. Television tie-in.

Other books you might like:
David Bischoff, *seaQuest DSV: The Ancient*, 1994
Orson Scott Card, *The Abyss*, 1989
Diane Duane, *seaQuest DSV: The Novel*, 1993
    Peter Morwood, co-author
G. Harry Stine, *Starsea Invaders: First Action*, 1993
Theodore Sturgeon, *Voyage to the Bottom of the Sea*, 1961

973

MATTHEW J. COSTELLO

Wurm

(New York: Diamond, 1991)

Story type: Horror (Apocalyptic Horror)
Major character(s): Michael Cross, Professor (director of the NY Aquarium); Paul Barron, Religious (evangelist)
Time period(s): 1990s
Locale(s): New York, New York; Gulf of Mexico, At Sea

Summary: When Michael Cross and the Woods Hole Oceanographic Institute investigate the aftermath of the ship *Achilles*' ill-fated deep sea expedition, they find the crew dead and a new species of undersea worm that evolves in a frighteningly unpredictable fashion. Can it be any coincidence that at approximately the same time lapsed evangelist Paul Barron begins to preach once more, disseminating a message of imminent armageddon?

Other books you might like:
Orson Scott Card, *The Abyss*, 1989
Michael Crichton, *Sphere*, 1987
Robert Serling, *Something's Alive on the Titanic*, 1990
Dean Wesley Smith, *Laying the Music to Rest*, 1989

974

SEAN COSTELLO

Captain Quad

(New York: Pocket, 1991)

Story type: Horror (Wild Talents)
Major character(s): Peter Gardner, Handicapped (Captain Quad); Sam Gardner, Student (Peter's brother); Kelly Wheeler, Teacher
Time period(s): 1980s; 1990s
Locale(s): Massachusetts

Summary: Paralyzed from the neck down by a car accident, former medical school hopeful and promising musician Peter Gardner comes to hate the world and his friends and family. When a near-death experience teaches him how to project his consciousness outside his body, he seeks revenge against those whom he feels have betrayed him.

Other books you might like:
Stephen King, *Carrie*, 1974

975

SEAN COSTELLO

The Cartoonist

(New York: Pocket, 1990)

Story type: Horror (Supernatural Vengeance)
Major character(s): Scott Bowman, Doctor (psychiatrist); Vince Bateman, Doctor (psychiatrist); Grandpa Rowe, Artist (cartoonist), Psychic
Time period(s): 1980s (1988)
Locale(s): Quebec, Canada

Summary: As teenagers, Scott Bowman and two friends are parties to a hit-and-run accident for which they are never held accountable. Years later, Scott encounters a mute psychiatric patient whose drawings forecast the near future and whose apparent knowledge of Scott's past deeds jeopardizes his family's welfare.

Other books you might like:
John Farris, *Fiends*, 1990
Giles Blunt, *Cold Eye*, 1989

976

SEAN COSTELLO

Eden's Eyes

(New York: Pocket, 1989)

Story type: Horror (Possession)
Major character(s): Karen Lockheart, Patient (Eye-transplant recipient); Eve Crowell, Parent (Eye-donor's mother; religious)
Time period(s): 1980s
Locale(s): Ottawa, Ontario, Canada

Summary: The gift of an eye-transplant to Karen becomes a curse when the vengeful spirit of the donor, helped by his demented mother, comes to "reclaim" the organs taken from his dead body.

Other books you might like:
Pierre Boileau, *Choice Cuts*, 1966
    Thomas Narcejac, co-author
Michael McDowell, *The Amulet*, 1979
Maurice Renard, *The Hands of Orlac*, 1920

977

GREG COSTIKYAN

Another Day, Another Dungeon
(New York: Tor, 1990)

Story type: Fantasy (Light Fantasy)
Series: Cups and Sorcery
Major character(s): Timaeus D'Asperge, Magician (fire), Nobleman (lord); Garni ben Grimi, Mythical Creature (dwarf), Adventurer; Sydney Stollitt, Businesswoman (expedition organizer)
Time period(s): Indeterminate
Locale(s): Urf Durfal, Fictional City; Caverns of Cytorax, Mythical Place

Summary: Timaeus D'Asperge, newly graduated Magister Igniti, decides to test his prowess and make his reputation by leading an expedition to the Caverns of Cytorax, where, despite the local orcs, the adventurers find a magical statue which they must somehow bring home safely.

Other books you might like:
Piers Anthony, *Man From Mundania*, 1989
    Pseudonym of Piers Anthony Dillingham Jacob
Mayer Alan Brenner, *Catastrophe's Spell*, 1989
John Deakins, *Barrow*, 1990
Craig Shaw Gardner, *Wishbringer*, 1988
Matt Ruff, *Fool on the Hill*, 1989

978

GREG COSTIKYAN

By the Sword
(New York: Tor, 1993)

Story type: Fantasy (Light Fantasy)
Series: Magic of the Plains
Major character(s): Nijon Oonitsaupivia, Hero, Barbarian; Mika Nashram, Magician, Con Artist; Nlavi, Royalty (princess)
Time period(s): Indeterminate
Locale(s): Fictional Country; Purasham, Fictional City

Summary: In order to pass his manhood initiation, Nijon must go out on the plains, with only his horse, Naenae, and an obsidian knife, and survive for 40 days and nights. Despite losing both knife and horse, Nijon does survive with the help of the god Mongoose and gains riches from a caravan of scheming city traders. Returning to the village with his half-brother, he faces trial for murder, one committed by rivals who have planted incriminating evidence against him. Exiled, he sets out for the cities of the north to make his fortune, find

adventure, and rescue a princess from a dragon. Computer game tie-in and first of a series.

Other books you might like:
Robert Asprin, *Thieves' World*, 1979
    editor
Jean M. Auel, *The Mammoth Hunters*, 1985
Gordon R. Dickson, *The Dragon and the George*, 1976
Simon R. Green, *Blue Moon Rising*, 1991
Barbara Hambly, *Dragonsbane*, 1987
Terry Pratchett, *Guards! Guards!*, 1991
Elizabeth Ann Scarborough, *The Drastic Dragon of Draco, Texas*, 1986
J.R.R. Tolkien, *The Hobbit*, 1938
Chelsea Quinn Yarbro, *A Baroque Fable*, 1986

979

GREG COSTIKYAN

One Quest, Hold the Dragons
(New York: Tor, 1995)

Story type: Fantasy (Light Fantasy; Sword and Sorcery)
Series: Cups and Sorcery
Major character(s): Timaeus D'Asperge, Magician, Nobleman; Sydney Stollitt, Businesswoman (expedition organizer); Kraki Kronarsson, Adventurer
Time period(s): Indeterminate
Locale(s): Hamsterburg, Fictional City

Summary: After unwanted stays in a dungeon and a fairy ring on the way to Arst-Kara-Morn, Timaeus and his companions must again rescue the statue of King Stantius, held in hopes of tilting the political power in Hamsterburg.

Other books you might like:
Robert Asprin, *Another Fine Myth*, 1978
James P. Blaylock, *The Stone Giant*, 1989
Kyle Crocco, *Heroes, Inc.*, 1991
John Moore, *Slay and Rescue*, 1993
Roger Zelazny, *Bring Me the Head of Prince Charming*, 1991
    Robert Sheckley, co-author

980

JUANITA COULSON

Legacy of Earth
(New York: Ballantine/Del Rey, 1989)

Story type: Science Fiction (Family Saga)
Series: Children of the Stars
Major character(s): Anthony Saunder, Clone; Yrae, Alien, Actress
Time period(s): 21st century
Locale(s): Procyon Four, Planet—Imaginary

Summary: Anthony Saunder, poor step-child of the fabulously wealthy Saunder clan, makes his living creating emoto-tapes. When he is asked by the alien Whimeds to direct a presentation for the upcoming Interspecies Conference, he finds himself caught in the middle of a complex struggle between that species and another alien race.

Other books you might like:
Rebecca Ore, *Becoming Alien*, 1987
Rebecca Ore, *Being Alien*, 1989
Frederik Pohl, *Narabedla, Ltd.*, 1988

| 981 |

JUANITA COULSON

The Past of Forever

(New York: Ballantine/Del Rey, 1989)

Story type: Science Fiction (Family Saga)
Series: Children of the Stars
Major character(s): Dan McKelvey, Castaway
Time period(s): 21st century
Locale(s): Planet of the N'lacs, Planet—Imaginary

Summary: McKelvey, a poor relative of the Saunder family who dominated the first two books in this series, is stranded on a world where archaeologists study the remains of a once-advanced alien race which has fallen back into a primitive state. Whatever destroyed the N'lacs' advanced culture may still be a danger to humanity.

Other books you might like:
John Brizzolara, *Empire's Horizon*, 1989
Mary Gentle, *Ancient Light*, 1987
Mary Gentle, *Golden Witchbreed*, 1985

| 982 |

JUANITA COULSON

Star Sister

(New York: Ballantine/Del Rey, 1990)

Story type: Science Fiction (Adventure)
Major character(s): Renee Amos, Feminist
Time period(s): 1990s
Locale(s): Niand, Planet—Imaginary

Summary: A politically liberal young woman is accidentally teleported to another planet by passing aliens known as the Arbiters whose purpose is to deal with that planet's oppressive matriarchal government and end discrimination against men. The young woman joins the masculine cause and helps defeat the evil female ruler who is endangering the entire galaxy.

Other books you might like:
L. Sprague de Camp, *Rogue Queen*, 1951
Joanna Russ, *The Female Man*, 1975
B.J. Salterberg, *The Outlander: Captivity*, 1989
Sheri S. Tepper, *The Gate to Women's Country*, 1988

| 983 |

VINCENT COURTNEY

Goblins

(New York: Zebra, 1994)

Story type: Horror (Curse; Evil Children)

Major character(s): Marty Martin, Child (six-year-old boy); Dan Martin, Director (film); Vicki Martin, Housewife (Dan's wife, Marty's mother)
Time period(s): 1990s (1994)
Locale(s): Scotland

Summary: Vicki Martin's miscarriage following her visit to the legend-cursed Castle Drochil seems a coincidence, but the birth of her strange first child is not. Vicki has fallen victim to the curse of the castle's evil builders, and her adopted son, Marty, can't convince his mother that his certainty that his little brother is a bona-fide goblin is anything but the fancy of a jealous imagination.

Other books you might like:
Ira Levin, *Rosemary's Baby*, 1967
Bernard Taylor, *The Godsend*, 1976
Thomas Tryon, *The Other*, 1972

| 984 |

VINCENT COURTNEY

Harvest of Blood

(New York: Pinnacle, 1992)

Story type: Horror (Vampire Story)
Major character(s): Christopher Blaze, Detective—Private, Vampire; Reggie Carver, Detective—Private; Sue Blaze, Doctor (Christopher's wife)
Time period(s): 1990s (1992)
Locale(s): Miami, Florida

Summary: Having recovered from his first adventure as a vampirized cop in *Vampire Beat* (1991), Christopher Blaze returns as a private detective and faces his most formidable challenge yet: a fellow vampire running a drug pipeline between Central America and the United States.

Other books you might like:
P.N. Elrod, *The Vampire Files Series*, 1989-1992
Lee Killough, *Blood Hunt*, 1988

| 985 |

VINCENT COURTNEY

Vampire Beat

(New York: Zebra/Pinnacle, 1991)

Story type: Horror (Vampire Story)
Major character(s): Christopher Blaze, Police Officer, Vampire; Sue Catledge, Doctor; Yosekaat Rakz, Vampire
Time period(s): 1990s
Locale(s): Miami, Florida

Summary: Cursed by a dying black magician to become a vampire, detective Chris Blaze finds himself uniquely suited to track down a vampire serial killer on the streets of Miami, all the while trying to hide his own nighttime blood-drinking habits to keep himself above the suspicion of his colleagues.

Other books you might like:
P.N. Elrod, *The Vampire Files Series*, 1989-1992
Lee Killough, *Blood Hunt*, 1988
Brian Lumley, *Necroscope*, 1988

986

VINCENT COURTNEY

Wake Up Screaming

(New York: Pinnacle, 1992)

Story type: Horror (Occult)
Major character(s): Derek Harris, Child (12-year-old boy); Dutch Harris, Farmer, Grandparent (Derek's grandfather); Petie Mattison, Teenager
Time period(s): 1990s
Locale(s): Sundova Beach, Florida

Summary: When Derek Harris and his friend Petie play with an ancient grimoire found in Dutch Harris's house, they unwittingly open the gateway to the spirit world in which Dutch's first wife, Katherine, has been trapped for almost half a century and scheming for vengeance against the former members of her satanic cult.

Other books you might like:
Ramsey Campbell, *To Wake the Dead*, 1980
Leigh Clark, *Blood Sabbath*, 1991
Penelope Banka Kreps, *Demon's Fright*, 1992
Peter Straub, *Ghost Story*, 1979

987

ARTHUR BYRON COVER

Stationfall

(New York: Avon Books, 1989)

Story type: Science Fiction (Humor)
Major character(s): Homer Hunter, Spaceman (Lieutenant); Oliver, Robot
Time period(s): Indeterminate Future
Locale(s): Aurelian, Space Station

Summary: In this sequel to *Planetfall*, Homer and Oliver find themselves accidentally caught up in a war being fought on the space station Aurelian. They deal more or less successfully with spies, terrorists, space vampires, and a robot's ghost.

Other books you might like:
Douglas Adams, *The Hitchhiker's Guide to the Galaxy*, 1979
Ron Goulart, *Big Bang*, 1982
Ron Goulart, *Hellquad*, 1984
Ron Goulart, *Skyrocket Steele*, 1980
Barry B. Longyear, *Naked Came the Robot*, 1988
Alexei Panshin, *Masque World*, 1969

988

BRUCE COVILLE

Goblins in the Castle

(New York: Pocket Minstrel, 1992)

Story type: Fantasy (Quest; Young Adult)
Major character(s): Igor, Handicapped, Adventurer; William, Orphan, Adventurer; Herky, Mythical Creature (goblin)
Time period(s): Indeterminate

Locale(s): Toad-in-a-Cage Castle, Mythical Place; Nilbog, Mythical Place (goblin's city)

Summary: William and Igor set out from Toad-in-a-Cage Castle to discover a solution to the castle's goblins, which may soon escape confinement and again visit their benign trickery on everyone. After goblins kidnap Igor, Granny Pinchbottom directs William to Nilbog equipped with a quest and a reward. Taken prisoner in Nilbog, William relies on Herky to help him and Igor escape the other goblins.

Other books you might like:
Lynne Reid Banks, *The Indian in the Cupboard*, 1980
L. Frank Baum, *The Master Key: An Electrical Fairy Tale*, 1901
Edward Eager, *Knight's Castle*, 1956
Kathryn Lasky, *Double Trouble Squared*, 1991
Daniel Manus Pinkwater, *Lizard Music*, 1976
Vivian Vande Velde, *User Unfriendly*, 1991
Laurence Yep, *Dragon of the Lost Sea*, 1982
Mary Frances Zambreno, *A Plague of Sorcerers*, 1991

989

BRUCE COVILLE

Into the Land of the Unicorns

(New York: Scholastic, 1994)

Story type: Fantasy (Young Adult; Quest)
Series: Unicorn Chronicles
Major character(s): Cara Diana Hunter, Adventurer; The Dimblethum, Mythical Creature; Lightfoot, Mythical Creature (unicorn), Animal
Time period(s): 1990s; Indeterminate
Locale(s): Land of Luster, Fictional Country

Summary: Bearing an amulet she has promised to safeguard, Cara travels to Luster where she finds herself important to the survival of unicorns.

Other books you might like:
Peter S. Beagle, *The Last Unicorn*, 1968
Jack Dann, *Unicorns II*, 1992
  Gardner Dozois, co-editor
Elizabeth Goudge, *The Little White Horse*, 1946
Tanith Lee, *Black Unicorn*, 1991
Jane Yolen, *Here There Be Unicorns*, 1994

990

BRUCE COVILLE

Jennifer Murdley's Toad

(New York: Harcourt Brace Jovanovich, 1992)

Story type: Fantasy (Contemporary; Young Adult)
Series: Magic Shop
Major character(s): Jennifer Murdley, Teenager, Student; S.H. Elives, Businessman
Time period(s): 1990s
Locale(s): Smokey Hollow, Fictional City

Summary: In a chance visit to the magic shop, Jennifer spends 75[cnt] for a toad which she hopes to use as the subject of her writing assignment. Jennifer finds that her toad speaks but disapproves of all the resulting trouble. After a series of extraordinary adventures, Jennifer realizes the importance of internal beauty and discovers her own.

Other books you might like:
Annie Dalton, *Out of the Ordinary*, 1990
Diana Wynne Jones, *Howl's Moving Castle*, 1986
Diana Wynne Jones, *The Ogre Downstairs*, 1974
Edward Ormondroyd, *David and the Phoenix*, 1957
Pat O'Shea, *The Hounds of the Morrigan*, 1986
Patricia C. Wrede, *Dealing with Dragons*, 1990
Patricia C. Wrede, *Talking to Dragons*, 1985

991
BRUCE COVILLE

Jeremy Thatcher, Dragon Hatcher
(New York: Harcourt Brace Jovanovich, 1991)

Story type: Fantasy (Young Adult; Quest)
Series: Magic Shop
Major character(s): Jeremy Thatcher, Child; Tiamat, Mythical Creature (dragon)
Time period(s): 1990s
Locale(s): Blodgett's Crossing, Mythical Place

Summary: At Elive's Magic Supplies, Jeremy purchases a beautiful marbled ball, discovering when he arrives home the instructions for hatching his dragon egg. Before long, Jeremy joins the shop owner and the librarian to provide a way for Tiamat to journey to the world of dragons.

Other books you might like:
Thorarinn Gunnarsson, *Make Way for Dragons!*, 1990
Ursula K. Le Guin, *A Wizard of Earthsea*, 1968
Anne McCaffrey, *Dragon Drums*, 1979
Anne McCaffrey, *Dragonsinger*, 1977
Anne McCaffrey, *Dragonsong*, 1976
Edward Ormondroyd, *David and the Phoenix*, 1957
Patricia C. Wrede, *Dealing with Dragons*, 1990
Laurence Yep, *Tongues of Jade*, 1991

992
BRUCE COVILLE

My Teacher Flunked the Planet
(New York: Pocket Minstrel, 1992)

Story type: Science Fiction (Young Adult; Invasion of Earth)
Series: My Teacher Is an Alien
Major character(s): Peter Thompson, Student, Hero; Broxholm, Alien; Kreeblim, Alien
Time period(s): 1990s
Locale(s): United States

Summary: Equipped by the aliens with universal translators, Peter and his companions return to Earth to help determine Earth's fate with the Interplanetary Council, worried since all civilized societies have abandoned warfare before venturing into space.

Other books you might like:
Alan Dean Foster, *Glory Lane*, 1987
Daniel Manus Pinkwater, *Borgel*, 1990

Terry Pratchett, *Diggers*, 1991
Terry Pratchett, *Truckers*, 1990
Terry Pratchett, *Wings*, 1991

993
BRUCE COVILLE

My Teacher Fried My Brains
(New York: Pocket Minstrel, 1991)

Story type: Science Fiction (First Contact; Young Adult)
Series: My Teacher Is an Alien
Major character(s): Duncan Dougal, Student; Betty Lou Karpou, Alien, Teacher; Susan Simmons, Student
Time period(s): 1990s
Locale(s): United States (small town, fictional city)

Summary: Bully Duncan Dougal becomes convinced that a second alien is present at his school, but no one believes him. When Miss Karpou and her jelly-like pet, Poot, capture Duncan, they use his brain to regain communication with the Interplanetary Council, which is about to make a decision on "The Earth Question"—what to do about the extremely intelligent, but uncivilized, humans?

Other books you might like:
Janet Asimov, *Norby, the Mixed-up Robot*, 1983
    Isaac Asimov, co-author
Daniel Manus Pinkwater, *Lizard Music*, 1978
    as D. Manus Pinkwater
Terry Pratchett, *Diggers*, 1991
Terry Pratchett, *Truckers*, 1990
Terry Pratchett, *Wings*, 1991

994
BRUCE COVILLE

My Teacher Glows in the Dark
(New York: Pocket Minstrel, 1991)

Story type: Science Fiction (First Contact; Young Adult)
Series: My Teacher Is an Alien
Major character(s): Peter Thompson, Student; Hoo-Lan, Alien
Time period(s): 1990s
Locale(s): New Jersey; Spaceship (alien)

Summary: Peter Thompson is hurled into the middle of the Interplanetary League's debate over what to do about Earth. In their 3,000-year history they have never seen another species that kills its members with such reckless abandon. The danger from this mass insanity is so great that they are considering quarantine or destruction.

Other books you might like:
Daniel Manus Pinkwater, *Borgel*, 1990
Daniel Manus Pinkwater, *The Snarkout Boys and the Avocado of Death*, 1982
Terry Pratchett, *Diggers*, 1991
Terry Pratchett, *Truckers*, 1990
Terry Pratchett, *Wings*, 1991

995

GREG COX
JOHN GREGORY BETANCOURT, Co-Author

Devil in the Sky
(New York: Pocket, 1995)

Story type: Science Fiction (Adventure; Space Opera)
Series: Star Trek: Deep Space Nine
Major character(s): Ttan, Parent, Alien (Horta); Benjamin Sisko, Military Personnel (commander); Kira Nerys, Military Personnel (major), Alien (Bajoran)
Time period(s): 24th century
Locale(s): Deep Space Nine, Space Station; Davonia, Moon—Imaginary

Summary: When the Cardassians capture a mother Horta en route to Bajor for a mining project, her 20 eggs, held in stasis, arrive safely at Deep Space Nine while Kira and Dax lead a rescue mission. Nog and Jake's tampering with the stasis field allows the eggs to hatch, releasing 20 hungry Horta to consume the station. The Bajoran government has changed its mind, however, and no longer wants the Horta on Bajoran soil. If the mother Horta does not return soon, Sisko faces the unpleasant alternative of killing the baby Hortas or letting them destroy the station.

Other books you might like:
C.J. Cherryh, *Downbelow Station*, 1981
A.C. Crispin, *Sarek*, 1994
Peter David, *Q-Squared*, 1994
Diane Duane, *The Romulan Way*, 1987
   Peter Morwood, co-author
Kij Johnson, *Dragon's Honor*, 1996
   Greg Cox, co-author
Gore Vidal, *Visit to a Small Planet*, 1956

996

GREG COX

Iron Man: The Armor Trap
(New York: Berkley Boulevard, 1995)

Story type: Science Fiction (Adventure)
Series: Iron Man
Major character(s): Tony "Iron Man" Stark, Scientist, Hero; Jim "War Machine" Rhodes, Hero
Time period(s): 21st century
Locale(s): San Francisco, California; Cyberspace

Summary: When enemies capture Tony Stark, hoping to force him into producing a copy of his high-tech armor, his corporation sends War Machine to negotiate his release while Stark navigates a cyberspace maze, attempting to retrieve his armor. Comic book tie-in.

Other books you might like:
Peter David, *What Savage Beast*, 1995
Diane Duane, *Spider-Man: The Venom Factor*, 1994
Stan Lee, *The Ultimate Spider-Man*, 1994
   editor
Neal Stephenson, *Snow Crash*, 1992

John Varley, *Superheroes*, 1995
Ricia Mainhardt, co-editor

997

GREG COX, Editor
T.K.F. WEISKOPF, Co-Editor

Tomorrow Bites
(New York: Baen, 1995)

Story type: Horror (Anthology; Werewolf Story)

Summary: The volume consists of 11 reprints and one original story that situate the werewolf of supernatural horror in science fiction scenarios. In Michael Flynn's "Werehouse," shape shifting with the help of nanotechnology becomes a form of cheap thrill seeking on a future earth. James Blish offers a scientific explanation for lycanthropy in "There Shall Be No Darkness," while Poul Anderson, in "Operation Afreet," imagines an alternate World War II as fought by werewolves and other supernatural entities. Larry Niven's "There's a Wolf in My Time Machine" sends a time traveller to an alternate Earth in which the dominant species evolved from wolves, while Clark Ashton Smith's "A Prophecy of Monsters" ruminates on the problems a werewolf might have getting dinner in the future. Gene Wolfe, in "The Hero as Werewolf," considers the needs that humans and werewolves share.

Other books you might like:
Brian J. Frost, *Book of the Werewolf*, 1973
Martin H. Greenberg, *Werewolves*, 1995
   editor
Stephen Jones, *The Mammoth Book of Werewolves*, 1994
   editor
Byron Preiss, *The Ultimate Werewolf*, 1992
   editor
Bill Pronzini, *Werewolf!*, 1979
   editor

998

GREG COX, Editor
T.K.F. WEISKOPF, Co-Editor

Tomorrow Sucks
(New York: Baen, 1994)

Story type: Horror (Anthology; Vampire Story)

Summary: The dozen reprints gathered here represent an underexamined yet rich and rewarding side of vampire fiction: vampires in science fiction. Among the selections that probe science fiction's interface with the supernatural are the Ray Bradbury's "Pillar of Fire," about a creature of the undead resurrected in a future where belief in his kind has been obliterated; Brian Stableford's "The Man Who Loved the Vampire Lady," a story set in an alternate universe in which the ruling elite of history are vampires; C.L. Moore's "Shambleau," the classic space opera of a man who finds the basis for the Medusa myth in a race of extraterrestrial vampires; Joe L. Hensley's "And Not Quite Human," a tale of interstellar armageddon and the unlikely survivors who emerge; Leslie Roy Carter's "Vanishing Breed," about a future where vampires have been so perfectly bred to fit in with normal human beings that they have forgotten their Gothic heritage; S.N. Dyer's "Born Again," about a biological experiment that isolates a virus responsible for vampirism; and Roger Zelazny's "The Stainless Steel Leech," in which a renegade robot and the last vampire on earth form a curious friendship.

Other books you might like:

Ellen Datlow, *Blood Is Not Enough*, 1989
  editor
Ellen Datlow, *A Whisper of Blood*, 1991
  editor
Alan Ryan, *Vampires: Two Centuries of Great Vampire Stories*, 1987
Robert Weinberg, *Weird Vampire Tales*, 1992
  Stefan Dziemianowice, Martin H. Greenberg, co-editors

999

MICHAEL COX, Editor

The Oxford Book of Twentieth Century Ghost Stories

(New York: Oxford University Press, 1996)

Story type: Horror (Anthology; Ghost Story)

Summary: Arranged in chronological order, the 33 stories by American and British writers assembled here span the years 1910 to 1994 and provide an overview of the ghost story tradition in the 20th century. The selections include E. Nesbit's "In the Dark," in which a man is haunted either by a friend he murdered or his own guilty conscience; Ellen Glasgow's "The Shadowy Third," in which a love triangle is catalyzed by the ghost of a young girl; M.R. James's "The Diary of Mr. Poynter," which recounts the death and gruesome manifestation thereafter of a dissolute man; May Sinclair's "The Nature of Evidence" and F. Scott Fitzgerald's "A Short Trip Home," both of which involve ghosts who try to seduce the living into romantic liaisons; Fritz Leiber's "Smoke Ghost," which reconceives the traditional gothic ghost for a contemporary urban environment; and the sentimental ghost story "The July Ghost" by A.S. Byatt.

Other books you might like:

Richard Dalby, *The Mammoth Book of Ghost Stories 2*, 1991
  editor
Richard Dalby, *The Mammoth Book of Ghost Stories*, 1990
  editor
Larry Dark, *The Literary Ghost*, 1991
  editor
Robert Phillips, *Triumph of the Night*, 1989
  editor

1000

MICHAEL COX, Editor
R.A. GILBERT, Co-Editor

Victorian Ghost Stories: An Oxford Anthology

(New York: Oxford, 1991)

Story type: Horror (Anthology; Ghost Story)

Summary: Thirty-five ghost stories spanning the years 1852 to 1908. Included are such well known classics as Charles Dickens' tale of ghostly revenge, "To Be Taken with a Grain of Salt"; Henry James' tale of clothes that retain the spirit of their former owner, "A Romance of Certain Old Clothes"; M.R. James' tale of a hideous secret recorded in a mouldering book, "Canon Alberic's Scrapbook"; and less familiar tales by Algernon Blackwood, Bernard Capes, J. Sheridan LeFanu and others.

Other books you might like:

E.F. Bleiler, *A Treasury of Victorian Ghost Stories*, 1981
  editor
Richard Dalby, *Victorian Ghost Stories by Eminent Women Writers*, 1988
  editor

1001

JOHN COYNE

Child of Shadows

(New York: Warner, 1990)

Story type: Horror (Evil Children)
Major character(s): Melissa Vaughn, Social Worker; Adam, Foundling; Connor Connaghan, Artisan, Landlord (Melissa's)
Time period(s): 1990s
Locale(s): Beaver Creek, North Carolina; New York, New York

Summary: Frustrated with her hopeless job, Manhattan social worker Melissa Vaughn moves to North Carolina with Adam, an autistic child found living in the tunnels beneath Grand Central Station. When Adam shows abnormal familiarity with Melissa's hidden past and becomes an object of veneration for a bizarre evangelical cult, Melissa begins to wonder if he is really the innocent child she took him for.

Other books you might like:

Dean R. Koontz, *Servants of Twilight*, 1984
John Saul, *Suffer the Children*, 1977
Bernard Taylor, *The Godsend*, 1976

1002

JOHN COYNE

Fury

(New York: Warner, 1989)

Story type: Horror (Reincarnation)

Major character(s): Jennifer Winters, Lawyer; Kathy Dart, Psychic (New Age evangelist and channel)
Time period(s): 1980s
Locale(s): New York, New York; Dart Commune, Minnesota

Summary: When Jennifer Winters begins to experience increasingly violent ''primitive'' episodes, she gradually realizes that identities and enemies from previous lives are taking over. With the help of a ''New Age Channeller''—who may be a friend or a foe—she attempts to probe her past lives to confront the evil that has intruded into her present one.

Other books you might like:
Max Erlich, *The Reincarnation of Peter Proud*, 1974
William Hallahan, *The Search for Joseph Tully*, 1974
Charles Maclean, *The Watcher*, 1983
Ramona Stewart, *The Possession of Joel Delaney*, 1970

1003

BRIAN CRAIG (Pseudonym of Brian Stableford)

Ghost Dancers

(Baltimore, Maryland: GW Books, 1991)

Story type: Science Fiction (Adventure; Alternate Universe)
Series: Dark Future
Major character(s): Kid Zero, Outlaw; Pasco, Agent; Carl Preston, Agent
Time period(s): 1990s
Locale(s): Southwest United States, Alternate Earth; Antarctica, Alternate Earth (Mitso-Makema Base)

Summary: Kid Zero has accidently come into possession of a very hot data disk. Everybody wants it: GenTech (the disk's owners), Mitso-Makema (their rivals), the Mafia, the Yakuza and even what's left of the U.S. Government. They all want Kid Zero, too, and they're even willing to take him alive.

Other books you might like:
Nigel Findley, *2XS*, 1992
William Gibson, *Neuromancer*, 1984
Jack Yeovil, *Demon Download*, 1990
Kim Newman, *Krokodil Tears*, 1991
  as Jack Yoevil
Mike Resnick, *Soothsayer*, 1991
Steve Wilson, *The Lost Traveller*, 1976
Roger Zelazny, *Damnation Alley*, 1969

1004

BRIAN CRAIG (Pseudonym of Brian Stableford)

Plague Demon

(Baltimore, Maryland: GW Books/Games Workshop, 1990)

Story type: Fantasy (Quest; Horror)
Series: Warhammer
Major character(s): Harmis Datz, Military Personnel; Nicodemus, Religious; Averil, Sorceress
Time period(s): 16th century
Locale(s): Alternate Earth

Summary: The second story told by Orfeo to his jailer is about Harmis Datz, a soldier in a small country threatened by a once-human servant of the Plague God. Datz and companions must unravel plots, fight monsters, and face their own best/worst natures before the kingdom can be saved.

Other books you might like:
Steven Brust, *Jhereg*, 1983
Glen Cook, *The Black Company*, 1984
Barbara Hambly, *The Time of the Dark*, 1982
Fritz Leiber, *Swords and Deviltry*, 1970
Michael Shea, *Nifft the Lean*, 1982

1005

BRIAN CRAIG (Pseudonym of Brian Stableford)

Storm Warriors

(Baltimore, Maryland: GW Books/Games Workshop, 1991)

Story type: Fantasy (Adventure; Horror)
Series: Warhammer
Major character(s): Orfeo, Minstrel; Trystan, Minstrel (bard); Herla, Royalty (king)
Time period(s): 16th century
Locale(s): Morien Wales, Alternate Earth

Summary: Orfeo's last tale tells the fate of a king in Morien who allows a band of elves to settle in his land. They are not quite what they seem, and chaos soon threatens everyone. Too powerful for combat, chaos must be fought with music and spirit. A game tie-in novel.

Other books you might like:
Steven Brust, *Jhereg*, 1983
Glen Cook, *The Black Company*, 1984
Casey Flynn, *Most Ancient Song*, 1991
Michael Moorcock, *The Chronicles of Corum*, 1978
Keith Taylor, *Bard*, 1981

1006

BRIAN CRAIG (Pseudonym of Brian Stableford)

Zaragoz

(Baltimore, Maryland: GW Books/Games Workshop, 1990)

Story type: Fantasy (Adventure; Horror)
Series: Warhammer
Major character(s): Orfeo, Minstrel, Writer (poet); Semjaza, Sorcerer; Arcangelo, Religious
Time period(s): 16th century
Locale(s): Alternate Earth

Summary: The Castle Zaragoz is unconquerable except by treachery. The minstrel, Orfeo, wanders into the net of treachery, sorcery, deception and counter-deception that surrounds two families' claims to control the citadel. He must face down plotters and demons to see justice done. The first in a series of novels presented as stories told by Orfeo while in jail.

Other books you might like:
Steven Brust, *Jhereg*, 1983
Charles de Lint, *Yarrow*, 1986
David Ferring, *Konrad*, 1990
Fritz Leiber, *Swords and Deviltry*, 1970
Michael Moorcock, *Elric of Melnibone*, 1976

1007

RALPH ADAMS CRAM

Black Spirits and White

(West Warwick, Rhode Island: Necronomicon Press, 1993)

Story type: Horror (Collection)

Summary: Originally published in 1895, this slim booklet of six stories, the author's only contribution to the field of weird fiction, is a classic. Four of the stories are ghost tales, "No. 252 Rue M. le Prince" being an almost comic account of the attempt of several skeptics to exorcise a haunted house, and "In Kropfsberg Keep," "The White Villa," and "Sister Madelena" being about art students who travel to foreign lands and invariably run afoul of the local ghost in the houses they put up in. "Notre Dame des Eaux" is a *conte cruel* about an escaped madman and "The Dead Valley" a masterpiece of atmospheric horror about two boys who stumble upon a desolate valley laid waste by a noxious mist.

Other books you might like:
E.F. Benson, *The Collected Ghost Stories of E.F. Benson*, 1992
Ambrose Bierce, *Ghost and Horror Stories*, 1964
Algernon Blackwood, *Best Ghost Stories of Algernon Blackwood*, 1973
M.R. James, *Casting the Runes and Other Ghost Stories*, 1987
William Chambers Morrow, *The Ape, The Idiot, and Other People*, 1897

1008

JOHN CRAMER

Twistor

(New York: William Morrow, 1989)

Story type: Science Fiction (Hard Science Fiction)
Major character(s): David Harrison, Scientist (Physicist); Jeffrey Ernst, Child
Time period(s): 20th century
Locale(s): Seattle, Washington; Alternate Universe

Summary: David Harrison, a brilliant young physicist, has made a breakthrough that will allow human beings to enter and explore alternate universes. When espionage agents from a private corporation attempt to steal the experimental apparatus, David and two small children find themselves transported into and stranded in one such alternate universe.

Other books you might like:
Gregory Benford, *Timescape*, 1980
Robert L. Forward, *Dragon's Egg*, 1980
Robert L. Forward, *The Flight of the Dragonfly*, 1984
Robert L. Forward, *Starquake*, 1985
James P. Hogan, *The Genesis Machine*, 1981
James P. Hogan, *The Proteus Operation*, 1985

1009

KATHRYN CRAMER

Walls of Fear

(New York: Morrow, 1990)

Story type: Horror (Anthology; Haunted House)

Summary: In this successor to *The Architecture of Fear* Kathryn Cramer collects 16 original haunted house stories by Chet Williamson, Gene Wolfe, Jonathan Carroll, and other writers. Several of the best of these stories show the influence of well-known writers (H.P. Lovecraft in Richard A. Lupoff's "The House of Rue Chartres") and filmmakers (Peter Weir in Karl Edward Wagner's "Cedar Lane") associated with the horror genre.

Other books you might like:
Charles G. Waugh, *House Shudders*, 1987
Martin H. Greenberg, co-author

1010

MELISSA CRANDALL

Earth 2

(New York: Ace, 1994)

Story type: Science Fiction (Post-Disaster; Adventure)
Major character(s): Danziger, Spaceman, Castaway; Devon Adair, Leader, Settler
Time period(s): 22nd century
Locale(s): G889, Planet—Imaginary

Summary: Colonists from Earth hope to populate a healthy new world on which they can thrive. When a malfunction sends the crew and colonists far from their intended landing spot, New Pacifica, Devon and her comrades find intelligent natives, previously unknown. Novelizes the teleplay.

Other books you might like:
Roger MacBride Allen, *The Ring of Charon*, 1990
Stephen Baxter, *Raft*, 1991
Helen Collins, *Mutagenesis*, 1993
J.M. Dillard, *Emissary*, 1993
Alan Dean Foster, *Alien Nation*, 1988
David Gerrold, *Encounter at Farpoint*, 1987
Harry Harrison, *The Deathworld Trilogy*, 1976
Megan Lindholm, *Alien Nation*, 1988
Anne McCaffrey, *Dragonsdawn*, 1988

1011

BETTY ANNE CRAWFORD

The Bushido Incident

(New York: DAW, 1992)

Story type: Science Fiction (Mystery; Political)
Major character(s): So Pak, Spaceship Captain; Matsuda, Businessman; Ewha Thompson, Doctor (ship's)
Time period(s): 2090s (2096)
Locale(s): Earth; Zeta Reticuli 2, Planet—Imaginary

Summary: Sent on a probe to discover what happened to the Korean and Japanese miners who died mysteriously on Zeta Reticuli years earlier, So Pak hears from the Japanese businessman who controls Iwaski Corporation, the most powerful on the planet, that So Pak will never return. On Zeta Reticuli, So Pak and Ewha Thompson learn that the Japanese stole the patent for ultrasound mining which made Iwaski Corporation rich and that its illegal testing of viruses invadvertently created the virus now killing off the first aliens contacted by humanity.

Other books you might like:
Poul Anderson, *Question and Answer*, 1978
Gregory Benford, *The Stars in Shroud*, 1978
Ben Bova, *As on a Darkling Plain*, 1972
John Brunner, *Total Eclipse*, 1974
A. Bertram Chandler, *Frontier of the Dark*, 1984
Gordon R. Dickson, *The Far Call*, 1978
Colin Kapp, *The Survival Game*, 1976
Kim Stanley Robinson, *Icehenge*, 1984
Brian Stableford, *Critical Threshold*, 1977
Brian Stableford, *The Gates of Eden*, 1983

1012

DAN CRAWFORD

Rouse a Sleeping Cat
(New York: Ace, 1993)

Story type: Fantasy (Mystery; Political)
Series: Nimnestl the Bodyguard
Major character(s): Nimnestl, Bodyguard (royal); Conan III, Royalty, Child
Time period(s): Indeterminate
Locale(s): Rossacotta, Fictional Country

Summary: Nimnestl must protect nine-year-old King Conan III against court intrigue and problems in Rossacotta including a cult of demon worshippers and deadly treason. First of a series. First novel.

Other books you might like:
Steven Brust, *The Gypsy*, 1992
    Megan Lindholm, co-author
Lois McMaster Bujold, *The Spirit Ring*, 1992
Charles de Lint, *Mulengro: A Romany Tale*, 1985
Susan Fletcher, *Flight of the Dragon Kyn*, 1993
Simon R. Green, *The Bones of Haven*, 1992
Paula Volsky, *Illusion*, 1992

1013

DAN CRAWFORD

The Sure Death of a Mouse
(New York: Ace, 1994)

Story type: Fantasy (Mystery)
Series: Nimnestl the Bodyguard
Major character(s): Nimnestl, Bodyguard (royal); Polijn, Servant, Minstrel; Kaftus, Sorcerer
Time period(s): Indeterminate
Locale(s): Rossacotta, Fictional Country

Summary: Nimnestl investigates a series of murders at the palace and finds a plethora of suspects among the courtiers. Sequel to *Rouse a Sleeping Cat*.

Other books you might like:
Glen Cook, *Red Iron Nights*, 1991
Mary Gentle, *The Architecture of Desire*, 1993
Simon R. Green, *Hawk & Fisher*, 1990
Gary Gygax, *The Anubis Murders*, 1992
Joel Rosenberg, *Hour of the Octopus*, 1994

1014

DAN CRAWFORD

A Wild Dog and Lone
(New York: Ace, 1995)

Story type: Fantasy (Mystery; Political)
Series: Nimnestl the Bodyguard
Major character(s): Conan III, Ruler (king); Polijn, Child, Apprentice, Minstrel; Nimnestl, Bodyguard (royal)
Time period(s): Indeterminate
Locale(s): Rossacotta, Fictional Country

Summary: Sweltering in an early summer, the court of Conan III plans the development of a university while readying to move north. Although everyone wants to join the king's retinue, not everyone receives the invitation. While the military resents this usurping of their function as educators, the early, very hot summer may account for the high murder rate. However, intrigue abounds. Third in the series.

Other books you might like:
Allan Cole, *The Far Kingdoms*, 1993
    Chris Bunch, co-author
Mary Gentle, *Rats and Gargoyles*, 1991
Simon R. Green, *Hawk & Fisher*, 1990
P.C. Hodgell, *God Stalk*, 1982
Paula Volsky, *Illusion*, 1992

1015

F. MARION CRAWFORD

For the Blood Is the Life and Other Stories
(Clarkston, Georgia: White Wolf, 1996)

Story type: Horror (Collection)

Summary: These eight stories, all but one of which were collected in *Wandering Ghosts* in 1911, represent the bulk of supernatural fiction by a writer best known for popular, romantic novels produced at the turn of the century. "The Upper Berth" and "Man Overboard" are strongly atmospheric tales of hauntings onboard ships. "The Dead Smile" is a tale of Gothic family intrigue and "The Screaming Skull" a tale of revenge from beyond the grave. The title story is a classic of vampire fiction, and "By the Waters of Paradise" a tale of romance curtailed by the whims of destiny. "The King's Messenger" treats death allegorically.

Other books you might like:
Robert W. Chambers, *The King in Yellow*, 1895

Robert Hichens, *Tongues of Conscience*, 1900
Oliver Onions, *The Collected Ghost Stories of Oliver Onions*, 1935
Hugh Walpole, *All Souls' Night*, 1933
Edward Lucas White, *Lukundoo and Other Stories*, 1927

1016

ROBERTA CRAY

The Sword and the Lion

(New York: DAW, 1993)

Story type: Fantasy (Religious; Political)
Major character(s): Breyd, Religious (initiate), Warrior (Dyaddi)
Time period(s): Indeterminate Past
Locale(s): Ghezrat, Fictional City (walled fortress)

Summary: Prophecy indicates Breyd must join with her father as Dyaddi, one of the warrior pairs able to utilize divine strength in defense of the city gates when invaders breach all barriers. Breyd's new career brings expected glorious battles and unanticipated complications in her personal life.

Other books you might like:
Marion Zimmer Bradley, *The Firebrand*, 1987
Laurell K. Hamilton, *Nightseer*, 1992
P.C. Hodgell, *God Stalk*, 1982
Elizabeth Moon, *Sheepfarmer's Daughter*, 1988
Sean Russell, *Gatherer of Clouds*, 1992
Elizabeth Ann Scarborough, *Last Refuge*, 1992
Martha Wells, *The Element of Fire*, 1993

1017

MICHELLE SHIREY CREAN

Dancer of the Sixth

(New York: Ballantine Del Rey, 1993)

Story type: Science Fiction (Political; Military)
Major character(s): Auglaise "Dancer" DeWellesthar, Spaceship Captain, Military Personnel; Makellen Darke, Genetically Altered Being (Auryx), Psychic (esper); Harla Davenger/Daven, Military Personnel, Imposter
Time period(s): Indeterminate Future
Locale(s): O'Brian's Stake, Planet—Imaginary; Lioth, Planet—Imaginary

Summary: Captured by the Karranganthian, Auglaise and her Fourth Service Dancer Flight provide amusement with their slow deaths by torture. Rescued by the legendary Sixth Service, Dancer recovers with the help of her new commander, Michael, despite the death of her constant companion, Makellen Darke, who Sixth Service Security claims never existed. Twelve years later a Fourth Service Show Team plane crashes with a drugged pilot and Dancer's double, perhaps foiling an impending war. Author's first novel.

Other books you might like:
Lois McMaster Bujold, *Shards of Honor*, 1986
F.M. Busby, *Rissa Kerguelen*, 1977
Orson Scott Card, *Ender's Game*, 1985

Allan Cole, *Sten*, 1984
  Chris Bunch, co-author
Frank Herbert, *Dune*, 1965
Charles Sheffield, *Cold as Ice*, 1992
Eric Vinicoff, *The Weigher*, 1992
  Marcia Martin, co-author
David Weber, *On Basilisk Station*, 1993

1018

MICHAEL CRICHTON

Jurassic Park

(New York: Alfred A. Knopf, 1990)

Story type: Science Fiction (Genetic Manipulation; Adventure)
Major character(s): John Hammond, Businessman; Alan Grant, Scientist (paleontologist), Professor; Ellie Sattler, Scientist (paleobotanist)
Time period(s): 1980s (1989)
Locale(s): Isla Nublar, Costa Rica

Summary: Planning to make a fortune in patent life forms by cloning dinosaurs from bits of prehistoric DNA, International Genetic Technologies, Inc. constructs a highly automated theme park and resort featuring cloned dinosaurs as centerpieces for the enterprise. Just before the park is scheduled to open, Biosyn Corp., a competitor, arranges to sabotage park barriers and alarms in order to steal dinosaur embryos. While John Hammond, Alan Grant and Ellie Sattler visit the nearly completed park, a computer failure allows dinosaurs to run amok. As the human food source diminishes, the dinosaurs appear to desire migration, threatening to begin a new Age of Dinosaurs. Alan, Ellie and the few survivors must find a way to stop the release.

Other books you might like:
David Brin, *Startide Rising*, 1983
Octavia E. Butler, *Adulthood Rites*, 1988
Octavia E. Butler, *Dawn*, 1987
Octavia E. Butler, *Imago*, 1989
Larry Niven, *The Flight of the Horse*, 1973
Dave Wolverton, *Serpent Catch*, 1991

1019

MICHAEL CRICHTON

The Lost World

(New York: Knopf, 1995)

Story type: Science Fiction (Genetic Manipulation; Adventure)
Major character(s): Ian Malcolm, Scientist (mathematician); Sarah Harding, Scientist (field biologist); Richard Levine, Scientist (paleobiologist)
Time period(s): 1990s
Locale(s): Costa Rica

Summary: Years after the destruction of the ill-fated Jurassic Park and its reconstructed dinosaur species, scientists locate and investigate a new population of dinosaurs growing from Jurassic Park survivors.

Other books you might like:
Robert T. Bakker, *Raptor Red*, 1995
James F. David, *Footprints of Thunder*, 1995
Arthur Conan Doyle, *The Lost World*, 1912
James Gurney, *Dinotopia*, 1992
Harry Adam Knight, *Carnosaur*, 1984

1020

CATHY CRIMMINS
TOM MAEDER, Co-Author

Revenge of the Christmas Box
(Los Angeles: Dove Books, 1996)

Story type: Fantasy (Satire; Collection)

Summary: This collection contains a two-page introduction, three pages of spurious sequels and television tie-ins, and 20 stories exploring humorous and frequently fantastic aspects of Christmas boxes, including an FAA inspection of Santa's sled's black box recorder, organized elves, a cryogenic baby, and several boxes with nasty surprises.

Other books you might like:
William J. Brooke, *Teller of Tales*, 1994
David Fisher, *Legally Correct Fairy Tales*, 1996
James Finn Garner, *Politically Correct Bedtime Stories*, 1994
James Finn Garner, *Politically Correct Holiday Stories*, 1995
Kristine Kathryn Rusch, *Pulphouse, Issue 10: Special Issue*, 1991
    editor

1021

A.C. CRISPIN
T. JACKSON KING, Co-Author

Ancestor's World
(New York: Ace, 1996)

Story type: Science Fiction (First Contact; Political)
Series: StarBridge
Major character(s): Mahree Burroughs, Diplomat (ambassador); Gordon Mitchell, Anthropologist; Krillen, Alien (Na-Dina), Detective
Time period(s): Indeterminate Future
Locale(s): Na-Dina, Planet—Imaginary

Summary: Replacing the brutally murdered Interrelator to Na-Dina, Mahree brings a large crew to help evacuate the soon to be flooded Valley of Life. Contacted by corporations from the Shadowed Sector, Na-Dina feels compelled to develop a modern military and industrial infrastructure in order to compete in galactic society. Unfortunately the project will destroy the archaeological history of the Na-Dina and cause disastrous social upheaval.

Other books you might like:
David Brin, *Brightness Reef*, 1995
C.J. Cherryh, *Foreigner*, 1994
T. Jackson King, *Retread Shop*, 1988
Anne McCaffrey, *Treaty at Doona*, 1994
    Jody Lynn Nye, co-author
Jack McDevitt, *The Engines of God*, 1994

Larry Niven, *Protector*, 1973

1022

A.C. CRISPIN

Sarek
(New York: Pocket, 1994)

Story type: Science Fiction (Space Opera; Political)
Series: Star Trek
Major character(s): Peter James Kirk, Student; Sarek, Diplomat, Alien (Vulcan); Spock, Scientist, Alien (Vulcan)
Time period(s): 23rd century
Locale(s): *U.S.S. Enterprise*, Spaceship; Vulcan, Planet—Imaginary; United Federation of Planets, Interstellar Empire/Federation

Summary: Leaving his wife's deathbed to carry out what he sees as his duty, Sarek risks destroying the newly-won rapport with his son, Spock. Yet after Amanda's death, Sarek and Spock must work together to rescue James Kirk's nephew from Klingon kidnappers and foil a plot that would destroy the Federation.

Other books you might like:
Margaret Wander Bonanno, *Dwellers in the Crucible*, 1985
Diane Duane, *Spock's World*, 1989
Brad Ferguson, *A Flag Full of Stars*, 1991
Jean Lorrah, *The Vulcan Academy Murders*, 1984
Jeri Taylor, *Unification*, 1991

1023

A.C. CRISPIN
DEBORAH A. MARSHALL, Co-Author

Serpent's Gift
(New York: Ace, 1992)

Story type: Science Fiction (Adventure; Young Adult)
Series: StarBridge
Major character(s): Robert Gable, Psychologist, Administrator; Serge LaRoche, Student, Musician; Heather Farley, Student, Telepath
Time period(s): Indeterminate Future
Locale(s): StarBridge Academy, Asteroid; Starbridge Station, Space Station

Summary: Heather Farley, an eleven-year-old computer whiz accepted at StarBridge Academy despite her age because of powerful telepathic abilities, becomes infatuated with Serge, an older student still traumatized by the accidental loss of his hands despite fully functional prosthetics. When the asteroid's rich neutronium deposit suddenly becomes unstable, monitors blame the anthropologists working at a local dig and recommend evacuation, which could lead to the dissolution of StarBridge.

Other books you might like:
David Brin, *The Uplift War*, 1987
Lois McMaster Bujold, *The Warrior's Apprentice*, 1986
T. Jackson King, *Retread Shop*, 1988
Larry Niven, *Protector*, 1973
Rebecca Ore, *Being Alien*, 1989

David R. Palmer, *Emergence*, 1984
Tim Sullivan, *Lords of Creation*, 1992
Sheri S. Tepper, *After Long Silence*, 1990

1024

A.C. CRISPIN
JANNEAN ELLIOTT, Co-Author

Shadow World
(New York: Ace, 1991)

Story type: Science Fiction (First Contact; Young Adult)
Series: StarBridge
Major character(s): Mark Kenner, Student (interrelater), Diplomat; Ri-El Eerin, Alien (Elpind); Cara Hendricks, Journalist, Teenager
Time period(s): Indeterminate Future
Locale(s): Starbridge Academy, Asteroid (school); Elseemar, Planet—Imaginary

Summary: After a Cooperative League of Systems ship made an emergency landing on Elseemar, discovering the Elspind, an exceedingly short-lived and intelligent people, a lab was set up to try extending the life-span of the Elspind. When Mark Kenner is paired with Eerin on a student project, he is compelled to exercise his skills as an interrelater to save his life and the lives of his companions.

Other books you might like:
Stephen Baxter, *Raft*, 1991
David Brin, *Startide Rising*, 1983
Stephen Goldin, *Jade Darcy and the Affair of Honor*, 1988
    Mary Mason, co-author
T. Jackson King, *Retread Shop*, 1988
Rebecca Ore, *Being Alien*, 1989
David R. Palmer, *Emergence*, 1984
Alis A. Rasmussen, *A Passage of Stars*, 1990
Pamela F. Service, *Under Alien Stars*, 1990

1025

A.C. CRISPIN
KATHLEEN O'MALLEY, Co-Author

Silent Dances
(New York: Ace, 1990)

Story type: Science Fiction (First Contact)
Series: StarBridge
Major character(s): Tesa "Good Eyes", Handicapped (deaf), Linguist; Taller, Leader, Alien (Grus); Sailor "Lightning", Alien (Grus)
Time period(s): Indeterminate Future
Locale(s): Trinity, Planet—Imaginary (StarBridge Academy)

Summary: Tesa, deaf since birth, is the perfect ambassador to the alien Grus, an avian race that resembles giant cranes, whose cries can shatter human eardrums. As "interrelator," her assignment is to cement the human-avian bond by helping rear a newly-hatched chick. But the Grus have powerful enemies on their world—not only the eagle-like Aquila, but human predators who kill them for their iridescent feathers.

Tesa finds she must establish contact with two intelligent species while foiling the poachers.

Other books you might like:
Suzette Haden Elgin, *Communipath Worlds*, 1980
Ursula K. Le Guin, *The Word for World Is Forest*, 1972
Anne McCaffrey, *Decision at Doona*, 1969
H. Beam Piper, *Little Fuzzy*, 1962
H. Beam Piper, *The Other Human Race*, 1964

1026

A.C. CRISPIN
KATHLEEN O'MALLEY, Co-Author

Silent Songs
(New York: Ace, 1994)

Story type: Science Fiction (First Contact)
Series: StarBridge
Major character(s): Ptesa "Tesa/Good Eyes" Wakandagi, Diplomat (interrelator), Indian; Atle, Military Personnel (First-in-Conquest), Spaceship Captain; Taller, Leader, Alien (Avian)
Time period(s): Indeterminate Future
Locale(s): Crane, Space Station; Trinity, Planet—Imaginary; Cooperative League of Systems, Interstellar Empire/Federation

Summary: When the amphibian aliens attempt to conquer Trinity, Tesa leads the native Gnus and the rest of the team, without any advanced weapons, in defense of the planet. Meanwhile, another intelligent telepathic species makes itself known on Trinity.

Other books you might like:
Eleanor Arnason, *Ring of Swords*, 1993
David Brin, *Startide Rising*, 1983
Anne McCaffrey, *Treaty at Doona*, 1994
    Jody Lynn Nye, co-author
Larry Niven, *Protector*, 1973
Vernor Vinge, *A Fire upon the Deep*, 1992

1027

A.C. CRISPIN

Starbridge
(New York: Ace, 1989)

Story type: Science Fiction (First Contact)
Series: StarBridge
Major character(s): Mahree Burroughs, Teenager; Robert Gable, Psychologist, Administrator
Time period(s): Indeterminate Future
Locale(s): *Desiree*, Spaceship

Summary: Earth's first contact with an alien race nearly turns to disaster, but teenager Mahree Burroughs and ship's doctor Robert Gable make friends with the alien Dhurrrkk, and the two races begin to find common ground.

Other books you might like:
C.J. Cherryh, *Rimrunners*, 1989
Robert A. Heinlein, *Podkayne of Mars*, 1963
Patricia A. McKillip, *Fool's Run*, 1988

Andre Norton, *Ordeal in Otherwhere*, 1964

1028
KYLE CROCCO

Heroes Wanted
(New York: Ace, 1991)

Story type: Fantasy (Adventure; Light Fantasy)
Series: Heroes, Inc.
Major character(s): Cilla, Heroine, Companion; Grover, Hero, Mercenary; Beogoat, Wizard
Time period(s): Indeterminate
Locale(s): Hoven Westerhoven, Fictional Country

Summary: Grover and Cilla are hired to impersonate King Phillip and his servant Voss until after Phillip's marriage to Winona unites all Westerhoven. However, the wizard neglected to tell the two a few things, such as the fact that Winona hates Phillip. Therefore Cilla has to prevent her from poisoning Grover. Winona's death at the wedding causes a war in which Cilla kills Hans, Phillip's major enemy, and Grover shatters the sacred stone.

Other books you might like:
Piers Anthony, *A Spell for Chameleon*, 1977
Robert Asprin, *Phule's Company*, 1990
Jack L. Chalker, *The River of Dancing Gods*, 1984
Diane Duane, *So You Want to Be a Wizard?*, 1983
Alan Dean Foster, *Glory Lane*, 1990

1029
KYLE CROCCO

Heroes, Inc.
(New York: Ace, 1991)

Story type: Fantasy (Light Fantasy; Adventure)
Series: Heroes, Inc.
Major character(s): Grover, Hero (reluctant), Mercenary; Cilla, Companion, Heroine
Time period(s): Indeterminate Future
Locale(s): Parda, Fictional City; Jolinstive, Fictional City

Summary: In order to secure his inheritance, Grover must immediately produce an heir, a task made difficult by his sudden impotence. To solve this problem, Grover must obtain the vital ingredient, dragon gonads. Everyone's desire to make Grover a hero and sign him to a contract with Heroes, Inc. makes Grover's quest especially hard. First novel.

Other books you might like:
Neil Gaiman, *Good Omens: The Nice and Accurate Prophecies of Agnes Nutter, Witch*, 1990
   Terry Pratchett, co-author
Craig Shaw Gardner, *Revenge of the Fluffy Bunnies*, 1990
Thorarinn Gunnarsson, *Make Way for Dragons!*, 1990
Barry Hughart, *Bridge of Birds*, 1984
Dan McGirt, *Jason Cosmo*, 1989
Christopher Stasheff, *The Warlock in Spite of Himself*, 1969

1030
ANN ELIOT CROMPTON

Merlin's Harp
(New York: Donald I. Fine, 1995)

Story type: Fantasy (Legend; Young Adult)
Major character(s): Niviene, Mythical Creature (fey), Apprentice (Merlin's); Merlin, Magician
Time period(s): Indeterminate
Locale(s): Camelot, England; World of the Fey, Mythical Place

Summary: To save Arthur's kingdom, Merlin requires help from Niviene, daughter of the Lady of the Lake.

Other books you might like:
Mike Ashley, *The Merlin Chronicles*, 1995
   editor
Marion Zimmer Bradley, *The Forest House*, 1994
Marion Zimmer Bradley, *The Mists of Avalon*, 1983
Andrea Hopkins, *Chronicles of King Arthur*, 1994
   editor
Mary Stewart, *The Crystal Cave*, 1970

1031
GILBERT B. CROSS

A Witch Across Time
(New York: Atheneum, 1990)

Story type: Fantasy (Time Travel; Young Adult)
Major character(s): Hannah Kincaid, Teenager; Greg Donohue, Boyfriend; Patience, Spirit (ghost)
Time period(s): 1980s
Locale(s): Martha's Vineyard, Massachusetts

Summary: After being discharged from a period of institutionalization for emotional imbalance, 15-year-old Hannah spends the summer with her great-aunt at Martha's Vineyard. Along with a handsome new boy, Greg, Hannah encounters the ghost of a young woman, who was falsely executed as a witch in 1692 and seeks to clear her name.

Other books you might like:
Pam Conrad, *Stonewords: A Ghost Story*, 1990
Penelope Lively, *The Ghost of Thomas Kempe*, 1973
Patricia A. McKillip, *The House on Parchment Street*, 1973
Pat Murphy, *The Falling Woman*, 1986
Christopher Pike, *See You Later*, 1990
Elizabeth Marie Pope, *The Sherwood Ring*, 1958

1032
RONALD ANTHONY CROSS

The Fourth Guardian
(New York: Tor, 1994)

Story type: Science Fiction (Alternate Universe; Mystical)
Series: Eternal Guardians
Major character(s): Elena, Apprentice, Sorcerer; Corbo O'Connor, Gladiator, Sorcerer; Drusilla, Sorceress
Time period(s): 1990s; Indeterminate Past

Locale(s): Mexico; California; Astral Plane, Mythical Place

Summary: Using the Four Stones of Power, ancient Romans surreptitiously control human events for millennia. In the present, Corbo and Elena battle the emergence of a demon and the attempts of one Eternal Guardian to consolidate the Stones' power.

Other books you might like:
Umberto Eco, *Foucault's Pendulum*, 1989
Simon Hawke, *The Wizard of 4th Street*, 1987
Tom Holt, *Who's Afraid of Beowulf?*, 1989
Robert Shea, *The Illuminatus! Trilogy*, 1988
    Robert Anton Wilson, co-editor
Robert Anton Wilson, *The Earth Will Shake*, 1982

1033

RONALD ANTHONY CROSS

The Lost Guardian

(New York: Tor, 1995)

Story type: Science Fiction (Alternate Universe; Mystical)
Series: Eternal Guardians
Major character(s): Corbo O'Connor, Gladiator, Sorcerer; Gumby, Psychic; Elena, Sorcerer
Time period(s): Indeterminate Past; 1990s
Locale(s): Europe; Zaire

Summary: Corbo and others continue to vie for control of four stones, powerful magical objects that can prevent alien interference in human affairs.

Other books you might like:
Umberto Eco, *Foucault's Pendulum*, 1989
Michael Flynn, *In the Country of the Blind*, 1990
Robert Shea, *The Illuminatus! Trilogy*, 1988
    Robert Anton Wilson, co-author
Edward Whittemore, *Jerusalem Poker*, 1978
Robert Anton Wilson, *The Schrodinger's Cat Trilogy*, 1988

1034

JOHN CROWLEY

Antiquities

(Seattle, Washington: Incunabula, 1993)

Story type: Fantasy (Collection; Science Fiction)
Time period(s): 19th century; 21st century
Locale(s): Greece; United States; Planet—Imaginary

Summary: Contains seven stories, originally published 1977-1993, displaying a broad range of setting and tone. The stories, both fantasy and science fiction, deal with the past, memories and how people deal with them. In one, "Missolonghi 1824," Lord Byron, on his deathbed, relates a strange story that highlights his adventurous and tragic life.

Other books you might like:
A.S. Byatt, *Possession: A Romance*, 1990
Greer Ilene Gilman, *Moonwise*, 1990
Mark Helprin, *Winter's Tale*, 1983
Tim Powers, *The Stress of Her Regard*, 1989
John Whitbourn, *Popes and Phantoms*, 1993

1035

JOHN CROWLEY

Love and Sleep

(New York: Bantam, 1994)

Story type: Fantasy (Literary; Contemporary Realism)
Series: AEgypt
Major character(s): Pierce Moffett, Researcher; Giordano Bruno, Religious (monk), Historical Figure; Madimi, Angel
Time period(s): 1990s; 16th century (1583)
Locale(s): New York; Cumberland Mountains, Kentucky; London, England

Summary: Pierce Moffett researches the strange novels of Fellowes Kraft and tracks the possibility of Kraft's mysterious treasure. The secrets pile up around Moffett as his longforgotten childhood meshes with the lives of Bruno and Dee. Sequel to *AEgypt*.

Other books you might like:
A.S. Byatt, *Possession: A Romance*, 1990
Robertson Davies, *What's Bred in the Bone*, 1985
Umberto Eco, *Foucault's Pendulum*, 1990
Tim Powers, *Last Call*, 1992
Brian Stableford, *The Werewolves of London*, 1992

1036

JOHN CROWLEY

Novelty

(New York: Doubleday Foundation, 1989)

Story type: Science Fiction (Collection)

Summary: This collection of four of Crowley's stories includes the original novella "Great Work of Time," a 1989 Nebula Award nominee, as well as "In Blue," "The Nightingale Sings at Night," and "Novelty."

Other books you might like:
Jonathan Carroll, *Bones of the Moon*, 1987
Jonathan Carroll, *A Child Across the Sky*, 1989
Jonathan Carroll, *Sleeping in Flame*, 1988
Richard Grant, *Rumors of Spring*, 1987
Richard Grant, *Views from the Oldest House*, 1989
Ian McDonald, *Empire Dreams*, 1988
Ian McDonald, *Out on Blue Six*, 1989

1037

PETER CROWTHER, Editor

Blue Motel

(Clarkston, Georgia: White Wolf, 1996)

Story type: Horror (Anthology)
Series: Narrow Houses

Summary: The third and final volume in the Narrow Houses series of stories based on superstitions contains eighteen stories and poems written exclusively for the volume. Included are Ed Gorman's "Curses," a revenge tale involving the evil eye; Jonathan Aycliffe's "The Reiver's Lament," about a superstition surrounding a murder committed at an old country inn; Conrad Williams's "The Burn," in which a man's disordered mind begins to manifest itself in physical phenomena; and Carl West and Katherine MacLean's "Isaac My Son," a reworking of the biblical tale of Jacob and Isaac for Native American folklore, concerning a father's sacrifice of, and for, his son. Dennis Etchison provides an introduction. This volume was first published in England in 1994.

Other books you might like:
Jeff Gelb, *Fear Itself*, 1996
    editor
Gary L. Raisor, *Obsessions*, 1991
    editor
Wendy Webb, *More Phobias*, 1995
    Ric Gilliam, Ed Kramer, and Martin H. Greenberg, co-editors
Wendy Webb, *Phobias: Stories of Your Deepest Fears*, 1994
    Ric Gilliam, Ed Kramer, and Martin H. Greenberg, co-editors

1038

PETER CROWTHER
EDWARD E. KRAMER, Co-Author

Dante's Disciples
(Clarkston, Georgia: White Wolf, 1996)

Story type: Horror (Anthology)

Summary: Inspired by Dante's *Inferno*, the editors asked 26 writers to write stories featuring modern visions of hell. The results include Douglas Clegg's "The Ripening Sweetness of Late Afternoon," about a homicidal preacher who lives in a personal hell; Harlan Ellison's "Chatting with Anubis," in which archaeologists discover the jackal god Anubis presiding over the tomb of a famous god-killer; Nancy Holder's "Hell Is for Children," in which a young girl creates a computer virus that creates virtual reality hells for systems infected with it; Rick Hautala's "Tunnels," in which a graffiti artist discovers a netherworld of horror in the subway tunnels; and Brian Lumley's "Hell Is a Personal Place," in which Adolf Hitler discovers that the afterlife is a Fourth Reich that has no use for him.

Other books you might like:
Basil Davenport, *Deals with the Devil*, 1959
    editor
Marvin Kaye, *Devils and Demons*, 1987
    editor
Janet Morris, *Heroes in Hell*, 1986
    editor
Maximilian Rudwin, *Devil Stories*, 1921

1039

PETER CROWTHER
JAMES LOVEGROVE, Co-Author

Escardy Gap
(New York: Tor, 1996)

Story type: Horror (Carnival/Circus Horror)
Major character(s): Jeremiah Rackstraw, Entertainer; Joshua Knight, Child; Mayor Mayor, Political Figure (Mayor)
Time period(s): 1950s
Locale(s): Escardy Gap, Midwest

Summary: A nameless writer struggling to overcome a writer's block begins spontaneously transcribing the tale of Escardy Gap, a quaint middle-American town visited by a supernaturally endowed troupe of evildoers who call themselves the Company. As the Company begins wreaking havoc about town, the writer finds himself pondering his relationship to the characters he has created and his responsibility for conjuring a moral for their travails. This is a first collaborative novel by a well-known editor and a fantasy writer.

Other books you might like:
Ray Bradbury, *Something Wicked This Way Comes*, 1962
Charles G. Finney, *The Circus of Dr. Lao*, 1935
Dean R. Koontz, *Twilight Eyes*, 1987
Thomas F. Monteleone, *The Magnificent Gallery*, 1987
Tom Reamy, *Blind Voices*, 1978

1040

PETER CROWTHER, Editor
MARTIN H. GREENBERG, Co-Editor

Heaven Sent: 18 Glorious Tales of the Angels
(New York: DAW, 1995)

Story type: Fantasy (Anthology; Religious)

Summary: Contains a three-page introduction plus 18 original stories with ethereal themes. The tone varies from dark to humorous as angels' roles vary from Angel of Death to savior. Authors include Michael Bishop, John Brunner, Storm Constantine, Charles de Lint, Ed Gorman, Nina Kiriki Hoffman, Garry Kilworth, Jane M. Lindskold, Judith Moffett, and Kristine Kathryn Rusch.

Other books you might like:
Jack Dann, *Angels!*, 1995
    Gardner Dozois, co-editor
Neil Gaiman, *Good Omens: The Nice and Accurate Prophecies of Agnes Nutter, Witch*, 1990
    Terry Pratchett, co-author
Edward E. Kramer, *Tombs*, 1995
    Peter Crowther, co-editor
Alan Ryan, *Perpetual Light*, 1982
    editor
Pamela Sargent, *Afterlives: An Anthology of Stories about Life After Death*, 1986
    Ian Watson, co-editor

1041

PETER CROWTHER, Editor

Narrow Houses

(New York: Warner, 1994)

Story type: Horror (Anthology)
Series: Narrow Houses

Summary: Originally published in England in 1992, this book collects 30 stories by diverse hands concerned with the superstitions that shape our behavior. Included are Nancy Collins' "The Needle-Men," which traces several urban folk tales from Louisiana to a common source; Robert Holdstock's "The Silvering," concerned with the legend of the selkie; Chet Williamson's "The Swing of the Knife," about a businessman obsessed with the talismanic qualities of a knife; Peter James' "Breaking the Chain," about the consequences of not sending a chain letter; Stephen Gallagher's "The Sluice," about a young man's refusal to accept the finality of death; and Kim Newman's "Three on a Match," which ponders a future that did not happen as a result of a World War I doughboy not lighting a third cigarette from the same matchstick. Douglas Winter supplies the book's introduction.

Other books you might like:
Charles L. Grant, *Fears*, 1983
    editor
Gary L. Raisor, *Obsessions*, 1991
    editor
Wendy Webb, *Phobias: Stories of Your Deepest Fears*, 1994
    Ric Gilliam, Ed Kramer, and Martin H. Greenberg, co-editors
Wendy Webb, *More Phobias*, 1995
    Ric Gilliam, Ed Kramer, and Martin H. Greenberg, co-editors

1042

PETER CROWTHER, Editor

Touch Wood

(Clarkston, Georgia: White Wolf, 1996)

Story type: Horror (Anthology)
Series: Narrow Houses

Summary: First published in England in 1993, this volume in the Narrow Houses series features 25 original stories and poems based on old and new superstitions. Charles Grant's "Holding Hands" spins a startling suicide scenario from a superstition about passing on to the afterlife. Karl Edward Wagner's "Little Lessons in Gardening" is a revenge tale cultivated from the legend of the mandrake root. Michael Marshall Smith's "The Owner" is about a woman who finds herself being displaced from her own life. Bentley Little's "The Woods Be Dark" resurrects a folk legend of evil. Thomas Monteleone tackles superstitions regarding premature burial in "The Wager." Stanley Wiater's "Mysteries of the Word," a fantasy about the misfortune that befalls a child who utters a forbidden word, is illustrated by Gahan Wilson. Ramsey Campbell supplies the introduction.

Other books you might like:
Jeff Gelb, *Fear Itself*, 1996
    editor
Gary L. Raisor, *Obsessions*, 1991
    editor
Wendy Webb, *More Phobias*, 1995
    Ric Gilliam, Ed Kramer, and Martin H. Greenberg, co-editors
Wendy Webb, *Phobias: Stories of Your Deepest Fears*, 1994
    Ric Gilliam, Ed Kramer, and Martin H. Greenberg, co-editors

1043

OUIDA CROZIER

Shadows After Dark

(New York: Rising Tide Press, 1993)

Story type: Fantasy (Alternate World; Quest)
Major character(s): Kathryn Hartell, Lesbian, Researcher (AIDS); Kyril Vertok, Alien (oupir), Vampire
Time period(s): 1980s
Locale(s): Kornagy, Planet—Imaginary; Minneapolis, Minnesota

Summary: To find a cause of death spreading on Kornagy, Kyril travels to Earth where she meets Kathryn. The two find a bond which transcends the differences between them and even Kathryn's cultural prejudice against vampirism. However, the strength of their passion may prove fatal to Kathryn as the pair travels to Kornagy where human health fails.

Other books you might like:
Elaine Bergstrom, *Daughter of the Night*, 1992
Steven Brust, *Agyar*, 1993
Suzy McKee Charnas, *The Vampire Tapestry*, 1980
Nancy A. Collins, *In the Blood*, 1992
Ellen Datlow, *A Whisper of Blood*, 1991
    editor
Katherine V. Forrest, *Dreams and Swords*, 1990
Jewelle Gomez, *The Gilda Stories*, 1991
Pam Keesey, *Daughters of Darkness: Lesbian Vampire Stories*, 1993
    editor
Anne Rice, *Interview with the Vampire*, 1976

1044

ELAINE CUNNINGHAM

Daughter of the Drow

(Lake Geneva, Wisconsin: TSR, 1995)

Story type: Fantasy (Quest; Adventure)
Series: Forgotten Realms
Major character(s): Liriel Baenre, Magician, Mythical Creature (dark elf); Fyodor of Rashemen, Warrior
Time period(s): Indeterminate
Locale(s): Menzoberranzan, Fictional City; The Underdark, Mythical Place; Planet—Imaginary

Summary: With Menzoberranzan forces defeated afar and strife at home expected soon, Princess Liriel Baenri finds a way to the surface to pursue her dark elf magic, hoping to discover a way to protect her society from the tyranny of Loth and her priestesses.

Other books you might like:
Richard Awlinson, *Shadowdale*, 1989
Troy Denning, *The Parched Sea*, 1991
James Lowder, *The Prince of Lies*, 1993
R.A. Salvatore, *The Legacy*, 1992
R.A. Salvatore, *Siege of Darkness*, 1994
R.A. Salvatore, *Starless Night*, 1994
Margaret Weis, *DragonLance Chronicles*, 1988
   Tracy Hickman, co-author

1045
ELAINE CUNNINGHAM

Elfshadow
(Lake Geneva, Wisconsin: TSR, 1991)

Story type: Fantasy (Adventure)
Series: Forgotten Realms: The Harpers
Major character(s): Arilyn Moonblade, Warrior, Spy; Danilo ''Dan'' Thann, Nobleman; Kymil Nimesin, Martial Arts Expert (sword), Mythical Creature (elf)
Time period(s): Indeterminate
Locale(s): Evereska, Fictional City; Waterdeep, Fictional City

Summary: Someone is killing members of the Harpers, a group dedicated to justice. The killings fall into a pattern uncomfortably close to that of Arilyn's assignments. Secrecy has always served the Harpers well, but now all the groups with pieces of the puzzle are making it difficult for Arilyn to find out who the assassin is and what is sought. A game tie-in novel.

Other books you might like:
Troy Denning, *The Parched Sea*, 1991
Sheila Gilluly, *Greenbriar Queen*, 1988
Katharine Kerr, *Daggerspell*, 1986
Guy Gavriel Kay, *The Summer Tree*, 1985
Judith Tarr, *The Isle of Glass*, 1985
Terri Windling, *Borderland*, 1986
   Mark Alan Arnold, co-editor

1046
ELAINE CUNNINGHAM

Elfsong
(Lake Geneva, Wisconsin: TSR, 1994)

Story type: Fantasy (Quest; Mystery)
Series: Forgotten Realms: The Harpers
Major character(s): Danilo ''Dan'' Thann, Musician (bard); Elaith Craulnober, Mythical Creature (elf)
Time period(s): Indeterminate
Locale(s): The High Forest, Mythical Place

Summary: Danilo Thann must confront the green dragon who holds the key to the rewritten memories of bards and the new tales appearing among their songs.

Other books you might like:
Scott Ciencin, *The Night Parade*, 1992

Troy Denning, *The Parched Sea*, 1991
James Lowder, *The Ring of Winter*, 1992
Jean Rabe, *Red Magic*, 1991
Elizabeth Ann Scarborough, *Phantom Banjo*, 1991

1047
ELAINE CUNNINGHAM

The Radiant Dragon
(Lake Geneva, Wisconsin: TSR, 1992)

Story type: Fantasy (Quest)
Series: Cloakmaster Cycle
Major character(s): Teldin Moore, Adventurer; Vallus, Mythical Creature (elf), Wizard; Estriss, Alien (Illithid), Spaceship Captain
Time period(s): Indeterminate
Locale(s): Armistice, Planet—Imaginary; *Nightstalker*, Spaceship

Summary: Teldin seeks a great ship,*Spelljammer*, which he and a radiant dragon could take command by using their combined forces. Meanwhile, elves try to enlist Teldin's help in the second Unhuman War, hoping to use the power vested in Teldin's magic cloak. Set in the milieu of the role-playing game, *Spelljammer*.

Other books you might like:
David Cook, *Beyond the Moons*, 1991
Nigel Findley, *Into the Void*, 1991
Roger E. Moore, *The Maelstrom's Eye*, 1992

1048
ELAINE CUNNINGHAM

Silver Shadows
(Lake Geneva, Wisconsin: TSR, 1996)

Story type: Fantasy (Adventure)
Series: Forgotten Realms: The Harpers
Major character(s): Arilyn Moonblade, Warrior, Spy; Foxfire, Mythical Creature (elf), Leader; Danilo ''Dan'' Thann, Musician (bard), Spy
Time period(s): Indeterminate
Locale(s): The Forest of Tethir, Fictional City

Summary: Lured by promises of information about her magic sword and her fate, Arilyn Moonblade becomes the agent of powers who move to protect the Elves of Tethir when threatened. On arriving at her destination, the half-elf finds the situation and the elves' leader more compelling than she imagines.

Other books you might like:
Eleanor Arnason, *The Sword Smith*, 1978
Steven Brust, *Jhereg*, 1983
Terry Goodkind, *Wizard's First Rule*, 1994
Guy Gavriel Kay, *Tigana*, 1990
Fritz Leiber, *Ill Met in Lankhmar*, 1995

1049

ANN CURRY

The Book of Brendan

(New York: Holiday House, 1990)

Story type: Fantasy (Legend; Young Adult)
Major character(s): Elric, Child; Father Brendan, Religious; Arthur, Royalty
Time period(s): 8th century (725)
Locale(s): Hobury Abbey, England; Bay of Wodin, England

Summary: Myrddin, the evil magician, enchants most of the monks of the Abbey in his pursuit of the newly completed, illuminated *Book of Brendan*. Left to oppose him are the aging Father Brendan and two children, Elric and Bridget, who are aided by Avis, the bird from the Paradise of Birds (from the legend of Brendan the Mariner) and magical beasts from the *Book of Brendan*. Then the children call in King Arthur, his Queen, and Merlin.

Other books you might like:
John Bellairs, *The House with a Clock in Its Walls*, 1973
Edward Eager, *Seven-Day Magic*, 1962
Michael Ende, *The Neverending Story*, 1983
Alan Garner, *The Weirdstone of Brisingamen*, 1969
Betty Levin, *The Sword of Culann*, 1973
John Masefield, *The Box of Delights, or, When the Wolves Were Running*, 1935
Pat O'Shea, *The Hounds of the Morrigan*, 1986
Robert Westall, *Wind Eye*, 1977

1050

CHRIS CURRY

Panic

(New York: Pocket, 1994)

Story type: Horror (Child-in-Peril)
Major character(s): Rick Piper, Journalist (television); Carmen Zapata, Housekeeper; Jade Ewebean, Aged Person
Time period(s): 1990s (1994)
Locale(s): Santa Verde, California

Summary: Against his wish, Rick Piper returns to his family home to slay some personal demons, but instead encounters real ones: greenjacks, creatures of Scottish folklore who stole the soul of his nasty twin brother while he was young, and who now threaten his two young children.

Other books you might like:
Leigh Clark, *The Feeding*, 1992
Stephen R. George, *Dark Reunion*, 1990

1051

CHRIS CURRY

Thunder Road

(New York: Pocket, 1995)

Story type: Horror (Science Fiction)

Major character(s): Tom Abernathy, Rancher; Justin Martin, Teenager; Alexander Manderley, Scientist (UFO researcher)
Time period(s): 1990s (1995)
Locale(s): Madelyn, California

Summary: UFO sightings in the small town of Madelyn bring out peculiar behavior in some of the residents, including military personnel trying to keep the sighting secret, a serial killer who hopes the disappearance of his victims will be blamed on extraterrestrial abductions, and an unscrupulous evangelist who exploits the inexplicable events that are occurring to preach the coming armageddon.

Other books you might like:
Donald Burleson, *Flute Song*, 1996
Joseph Citro, *Deus X*, 1995
Maxine O'Callaghan, *Dark Time*, 1992
Whitley Strieber, *Majestic*, 1989

1052

CHRIS CURRY
LISA DEAN, Co-Author

Trickster

(New York: Pocket, 1992)

Story type: Horror (Serial Killer)
Major character(s): Phil Waterman, Police Officer (Sergeant Detective, Seattle PD); Dori Gallagher, Journalist (newspaper reporter); Seth Shepherd, Collector (art collector)
Time period(s): 1990s (1992)
Locale(s): Seattle, Washington

Summary: Emulating the Trickster of Salish Indian lore, a serial killer commandeers the bodies of innocent victims to perpetrate his grisly crimes and uses the Seattle underground to elude the police.

Other books you might like:
G. Wayne Miller, *Thunder Rise*, 1988
Kathryn Ptacek, *Ghost Dance*, 1990
Chet Williamson, *Dreamthorp*, 1989

1053

JAMES ROBERTO CURTIS

Shango

(Houston: Arte Publico, 1996)

Story type: Horror (Occult)
Major character(s): Miguel Calderon, Student—College; Rosa Garcia-Mesa, Religious (Santeria priestess); Osvaldo Gutierrez, Police Officer (lieutenant)
Time period(s): 1990s (1995)
Locale(s): Miami, Florida

Summary: Miguel Calderon is thrilled that his anthropoligical research into the mystical religion Santeria is reacquainting him with his Cuban roots. What he doesn't know is that the priestess under whom he is studying is preparing him to become a blood sacrifice to Shango, one of the black *santos*, or darker saints. First novel.

Other books you might like:
Alex Abella, *The Killing of the Saints*, 1991
Hugh B. Cave, *The Lower Deep*, 1990
Nicholas Conde, *The Religion*, 1982
Don Davis, *The Gris-Gris Man*, 1996
Brian Hodge, *The Darker Saints*, 1994
Robert Weinberg, *The Black Lodge*, 1991

1054

CAROLYN CUSHMAN

Witch and Wombat

(New York: Warner Questar, 1994)

Story type: Fantasy (Light Fantasy)
Major character(s): Hali, Witch, Guide; Bernie, Companion (Hali's familiar), Animal (crow/wombat)
Time period(s): Indeterminate
Locale(s): Inner Worlds, Mythical Place (realm of magic)

Summary: To offset a depletion of the reservoir of magic within the Inner World, Bentwood initiates a trans-dimensional business that seems to link fantasy role-playing gamers in computer virtual reality, but actually transports them to the Inner World for adventure. Under contract to Bentwood, Hali and Bernie reluctantly lead the first group. First novel.

Other books you might like:
Michael Ende, *The Neverending Story*, 1983
Holly Lisle, *Minerva Wakes*, 1994
Larry Niven, *The Magic Goes Away*, 1978
James D. Priest, *Kirins: The Spell of No'an*, 1990
Lawrence Watt-Evans, *The Rebirth of Wonder*, 1992

1055

RICHIE TANKERSLEY CUSICK

Blood Roots

(New York: Pocket, 1992)

Story type: Horror (Gothic Family Chronicle)
Major character(s): Oilvia Crawford, Young Woman; Rosalie Deveraux, Aged Person, Grandparent; Skyler, Handyman (groundskeeper)
Time period(s): 1990s
Locale(s): Louisiana

Summary: Olivia Crawford runs away from her sluttish mother to go live with the maternal grandmother she has never met at the family plantation on the Louisiana bayou. There, she encounters the family legacy of voodoo horror, cannibalism, and sexual perversity extending back to the Civil War era that made her mother what she is today and threatens to do the same to her.

Other books you might like:
Athena Alexis, *Along Came a Spider*, 1992
V.C. Andrews, *The Dollanganger Saga*, 1979-1987
    Andrew Neiderman, co-author
Michael McDowell, *The Blackwater Series*, 1983
Joyce Carol Oates, *Bellefleur*, 1980

1056

RICHIE TANKERSLEY CUSICK

Buffy the Vampire Slayer

(New York: Pocket, 1992)

Story type: Horror (Vampire Story)
Major character(s): Buffy, Teenager; Merrick, Vampire Hunter; Lothos, Vampire
Time period(s): 1990s (1992)
Locale(s): Los Angeles, California

Summary: Buffy is distracted from her plans for the Hemery High senior prom when she is informed by the mysterious Mr. Merrick that she is a member of the Order, a secret lineage of vampire killers that has existed since the expulsion of Adam and Eve from Eden. It is her special task to track down and kill Lothos, the Vampire King responsible for a recent spate of deaths and disappearances among local high school teenagers. This book is a novelization of Joss Whedon's screenplay for the film of the same name.

Other books you might like:
Poppy Z. Brite, *Lost Souls*, 1992
Ray Garton, *Crucifax Autumn*, 1988
John Skipp, *The Light at the End*, 1986
    Craig Spector, co-author
S.P. Somtow, *Valentine*, 1992
William Tedford, *Liquid Diet*, 1992

1057

DANIEL DA CRUZ

Mixed Doubles

(New York: Ballantine/Del Rey, 1989)

Story type: Science Fiction (Time Travel)
Major character(s): Justin Pope, Composer, Thief; John Skardon, Scientist
Time period(s): 1990s; 1920s
Locale(s): California; Vienna, Austria

Summary: Justin Pope is a minimally talented composer who has made a name for himself by stealing the work of others more talented but less fortunate than himself. Then he discovers a time machine and sets out to steal from the great masters themselves.

Other books you might like:
Brian W. Aldiss, *Frankenstein Unbound*, 1973
Mike McQuay, *Memories*, 1987
Michael Moorcock, *Behold the Man*, 1969
Kim Stanley Robinson, *The Memory of Whiteness*, 1985

1058

ROALD DAHL, Editor

Roald Dahl's Book of Ghost Stories

(New York: Farrar, Strauss and Giroux, 1996)

Story type: Horror (Anthology; Ghost Story)

Summary: First published in 1983, this volume assembles 14 stories of ghosts and the supernatural chosen by a modern master of the macabre. Included are stories by A.M. Burrage, among them "The Sweeper," about a rich woman who is cursed to death by a beggar she turned from her door; L.P. Hartley's "W.S.," about a writer stalked by one of his fictional creations; Cynthia Asquith's "A Corner Shop," in which a man returns from the dead to redress a wrong he feels he has committed; F. Marion Crawford's "The Upper Berth," about a berth on an ocean-going ship haunted by a gruesome revenant; Rosemary Timperley's "Christmas Meeting," a ghost story in which it is difficult to distinguish the dead from the living; and Edith Wharton's "Afterward," a classic tale about a house haunting so subtle no one can determine who the ghost is.

Other books you might like:
Ramsey Campbell, *Uncanny Banquet*, 1992
  editor
Richard Dalby, *The Mammoth Book of Ghost Stories*, 1990
  editor
Larry Dark, *The Literary Ghost*, 1991
  editor
Hugh Lamb, *Forgotten Tales of Terror*, 1978
  editor
Robert Phillips, *Triumph of the Night*, 1989
  editor

1059

RICHARD DALBY

Chillers for Christmas
(New York: Gallery Books, 1990)

Story type: Horror (Anthology)

Summary: Twenty-seven horror and suspense stories that span the century and take Christmas or winter as their theme. Some, like L.P. Hartley's "The Waits" and Bernard Capes' "The Vanishing House" are tales of traditional yuletide haunts, while Eugene Johnson's "Just Before Dawn" and John Collier's "Back for Christmas" offer unique forms of poetic justice as holiday gifts. Rudyard Kipling's "The Strange Ride of Morrowbie Jukes" and Sarban's "A Christmas Story" are classic narratives that defy categorization. Six tales are original to the volume.

Other books you might like:
Kathryn Cramer, *Spirits of Christmas*, 1989
  David Hartwell, co-author
Kathryn Cramer, *Christmas Ghosts*, 1987
  David Hartwell, co-author

1060

RICHARD DALBY, Editor

Dracula's Brood
(New York: Barnes & Noble, 1987)

Story type: Horror (Anthology; Vampire Story)

Summary: The editor, a well-known scholar of horror and supernatural fiction, includes 30 stories of vampirism pub-lished before or near the 1897 appearance of Bram Stoker's *Dracula*. Included are Anne Crawford's "A Mystery of the Campagna" and Julian Hawthorne's "Ken's Mystery," in which vampire femmes fatales victimize male artists; Arthur Conan Doyle's tale of psychic vampirism, "The Parasite"; Mary Elizabeth Braddon's "Good Lady Ducayne," in which a vampiric old lady feeds symbolically on the vitality of her young travelling companions; Vernon Lee's "Marsyas in Flanders," concerned with a cursed religious relic; and M.R. James's "Wailing Well," about the vampiric fate that befalls a young boy who disobeys his elders.

Other books you might like:
Christopher Frayling, *The Vampire*, 1978
  editor
Alan Ryan, *Vampires: Two Centuries of Great Vampire Stories*, 1988
  editor
Leslie Shepard, *The Dracula Book of Great Vampire Stories*, 1977
  editor

1061

RICHARD DALBY

The Mammoth Book of Ghost Stories
(New York: Carroll & Graf, 1995)

Story type: Horror (Anthology; Ghost Story)

Summary: Fifty ghost stories by American and British authors, ranging from recognized classics (Ambrose Bierce's "An Inhabitant of Carcosa," Rudyard Kipling's "They") to less reprinted stories by classic authors (William Hope Hodgson's "The Valley of the Lost Children," M.R. James's "The Haunted Doll's House"), modern stories in the classic tradition (Robert Aickman's "Unsettled Dust," Ramsey Campbell's "The Guide"), pulp horror stories (Manly Wade Wellman's "Where Angels Fear") and contemporary ghost stories (Basil Copper's "The House by the Tarn," Karl Edward Wagner's "In the Pines").

Other books you might like:
Robert Aickman, *The Fontana Book of Ghost Stories Series*, 1964-1971
Bennett Cerf, *Famous Ghost Stories*, 1956
Michael Cox, *The Oxford Book of English Ghost Stories*, 1986
  R.A. Gilbert, co-author
J.A. Cuddon, *The Penguin Book of Ghost Stories*, 1985

1062

RICHARD DALBY, Editor

The Mammoth Book of Victorian and Edwardian Ghost Stories
(New York: Carroll & Graf, 1995)

Story type: Horror (Anthology; Ghost Story)

Summary: Through 42 stories by British and American authors, the editor, a renowned authority on ghost stories and tales of horror, captures the sensibility of the supernatural story in the late nineteenth and early twentieth centuries. Included are J. Sheridan Le Fanu's tale of an unscrupulous man who weds his niece to a dead man, "Schalken the Painter"; one of William Hope Hodgson's tales of his psychic detective, Carnacki, "The Gateway of the Monster"; W.C. Morrow's story of a unique ghostly visitation "An Original Revenge"; and Bram Stoker's story of a young student beset by the evil influence of the former owner of the house he has rented, "The Judge's House." In addition to these classics, the book contains a wealth of stories that have been reprinted rarely, if at all.

Other books you might like:
Anonymous, *A Century of Ghost Stories*, 1936
Anonymous, *Fifty Years of Ghost Stories*, 1935
Cynthia Asquith, *The Ghost Book*, 1927
  editor
Joseph Lewis French, *The Short Story Omnibus*, 1926
  editor
Alexander Laing, *The Haunted Omnibus*, 1937

1063

RICHARD DALBY, Editor

Mistletoe Mayhem
(New York: Castle, 1993)

Story type: Horror (Anthology)

Summary: Published in England in 1992 as *Horror for Christmas*, this book brings together 13 tales of horror and suspense set during the Christmas season. Included are a Basil Copper story original to the anthology, "Wish You Were Here," about a writer who receives Christmas cards from the dead; Robert Bloch's sardonic tale of marital infidelity, "The Night Before Christmas"; Sabine Baring Gould's deal-with-the-devil tale, "Mustapha"; ghost stories from Marjorie Bowen ("The Crown Derby Plate") and W.W. Jacobs ("Jerry Bundler"); and Stephen Gallagher's suspense tale of a journalist trapped in a newsroom by a homicidal maniac, "Dance by the Light of the Moon." Other contributors include Nigel Kneale, R. Chetwynd-Hayes, Robert Aickman, and Hugh Walpole.

Other books you might like:
Kathryn Cramer, *Christmas Ghosts*, 1988
  David Hartwell, co-editor
Kathryn Cramer, *Spirits of Christmas*, 1989
  David Hartwell, co-editor
Seon Manley, *Christmas Ghosts*, 1978
  Gogo Lewis, co-editor
Mike Resnick, *Christmas Ghosts*, 1993
  Martin H. Greenberg, co-editor

1064

RICHARD DALBY, Editor

Modern Ghost Stories by Eminent Women Writers
(New York: Carroll & Graf, 1992)

Story type: Horror (Anthology; Ghost Story)

Summary: This book collects 27 ghost stories by women writers, some of whom will be unfamiliar to readers steeped in the supernatural horror canon. The ghostly manifestations recounted here include the spectral landlord of Edith Wharton's "Afterward," the haunted automobiles of Rosemary Pardoe's "The Chauffer" and Lady Antonia Fraser's "Who's Been Sitting in My Car," the ghost who doesn't know she's a ghost in Jean Rhys' "I Used to Live Here Once," and the ghostly family of Mary Elizabeth Counselman's southern Gothic, "The House of Shadows."

Other books you might like:
Kathryn Ptacek, *Women of Darkness*, 1989
  editor
Alan Ryan, *Haunting Women*, 1988
  editor
Jessica Amanda Salmonson, *What Did Miss Darrington See?*, 1989
  editor

1065

RICHARD DALBY, Editor

Shivers for Christmas
(New York: St. Martin's, 1996)

Story type: Horror (Anthology)

Summary: Sixteen stories of the supernatural with a Christmas theme are chosen by an editor renowned for his knowledge of the horror genre. Included are Amelia B. Edwards' "The Discovery of the Treasure Isles," about a magic island that plays hob with time; Nathaniel Hawthorne's "The Christmas Banquet," in which a Christmas feast is the setting for a meeting of ten people whose misery effects uncanny transformations; Terry Lamsley's "Two Returns," in which a man is victimized by a haunted coat left by a former tenant; Stephen Gallagher's "Fancy That!," about a man who buys an unusual present for an even more unusual companion; and Alan McMurray's "It Will All Be Over by Christmas," in which a soldier of the first World War keeps his promise to be home by Christmas Eve, even though he has died.

Other books you might like:
Kathryn Cramer, *Christmas Ghosts*, 1988
  David Hartwell, co-editor
Seon Manley, *Christmas Ghosts*, 1978
  Gogo Lewis, co-editor
Mike Resnick, *Christmas Ghosts*, 1993
  Martin H. Greenberg, co-editor

1066

KARA DALKEY

Blood of the Goddess
(New York: Tor, 1996)

Story type: Fantasy (Religious; Horror)
Series: Goa
Major character(s): Thomas Chinnery, Sailor, Apothecary; Aditi, Deity (goddess), Widow(er); Brother Timoteo, Religious, Lawyer

Time period(s): 16th century (1597)
Locale(s): Goa, India

Summary: En route to Cathay, Thomas Chinnery meets a reputed sorcerer and a mysterious Hindu woman, Aditi, who have an elixir which kills the living and restores the dead. When captured by the Inquisition in Goa, Thomas gains a limited release by promising to lead the authorities to the source of the elixir.

Other books you might like:
Piers Anthony, *The Willing Spirit*, 1996
    Alfred Tella, co-author
M.A.R. Barker, *Flamesong*, 1985
M.A.R. Barker, *Man of Gold*, 1984
Tanith Lee, *Tamastara; or, The Indian Nights*, 1984
Chelsea Quinn Yarbro, *The Path of the Eclipse*, 1981
Roger Zelazny, *Lord of Light*, 1967

1067

KARA DALKEY

Little Sister

(New York: Harcourt Brace/Jane Yolen Books, 1996)

Story type: Fantasy (Young Adult; Legend)
Major character(s): Fujiwara "Little Puddle" no Mitsuko, Teenager, Heroine; Goranu, Mythical Creature (tengu shapeshifter), Demon
Time period(s): 12th century
Locale(s): Japan; Mythical Place (netherworld)

Summary: After outlaws attack her village, a young noblewoman seeks aid from a demon to retrieve her sister's soul, lost while searching for her murdered husband.

Other books you might like:
Grace Chetwin, *Out of the Dark World*, 1985
John Gordon, *The Edge of the World*, 1983
Eloise Jarvis McGraw, *The Moorchild*, 1996
Sherwood Smith, *Wren's Quest*, 1993

1068

JOHN DALMAS

The Kalif's War

(New York: Baen, 1991)

Story type: Science Fiction (Military; Political)
Series: Regiment
Major character(s): Chodrisei "Coso" Biilathkamoro, Ruler (Kalif of the Karghanik Empire); Tain Faronya, Prisoner (confederation); Sumbaa, Computer
Time period(s): 220th century
Locale(s): Karghanik Empire, Interstellar Empire/Federation

Summary: Coso Biilanthkamoro becomes Kalif after a coup. His immediate concern is to bring the Confederation into the Karghanik Empire. He also is enamoured with Tain Faronya, a Confederation prisoner, and marries her despite the misgivings of friends, prelates and the Diet. After many plots and attempted coups during which he and the Kalifa are wounded, they finally set off to fight the Confederation leaving his "trusted" friend Jilsomo as acting Kalif.

Other books you might like:
Gordon R. Dickson, *The Tactics of Mistake*, 1971
Jerry Pournelle, *Falkenberg's Legion*, 1990
Joel Rosenberg, *Not for Glory*, 1988
S.M. Stirling, *Marching through Georgia*, 1988
Timothy Zahn, *Cobra*, 1985

1069

JOHN DALMAS

The Lantern of God

(New York: Baen Books, 1989)

Story type: Science Fiction (Space Colony)
Major character(s): Elver Brokols, Diplomat (Ambassador); Juliassa Hanorissia, Royalty (Princess)
Time period(s): Indeterminate Future
Locale(s): Almeon Colony, Planet—Imaginary

Summary: Two thousand years earlier an interstellar cargo ship, fleeing a major war, had abandoned a group of pleasure androids on a deserted planet. Rather than dying out, the androids began to reproduce and created their own civilization, eventually losing all memory of their origins. They are now true human beings, but the descendents of the starship crew that abandoned them have returned for the property their forerunners left behind.

Other books you might like:
C.J. Cherryh, *Forty Thousand in Gehenna*, 1983
Mary Gentle, *Ancient Light*, 1989
Mary Gentle, *Golden Witchbreed*, 1983
F. Paul Wilson, *The Tery*, 1990

1070

JOHN DALMAS

The Lion of Farside

(New York: Baen, 1995)

Story type: Fantasy (Alternate World; Political)
Major character(s): Curtis Macurdy, Farmer, Warrior; Varia, Psychic, Spouse (Curtis Macurdy's); Melody, Warrior
Time period(s): 1930s
Locale(s): Indiana; Yuulith, Planet—Imaginary; Alternate Universe

Summary: Originally from Yuulith, Varia wants only to remain with Curtis Macurdy in Indiana, defying the orders of her Sisterhood. When the Sisterhood abducts Varia, Curtis follows her to Yuulith. At first enslaved, Curtis quickly advances as a military leader until he influences even the basic social order in his quest to recover Varia.

Other books you might like:
Piers Anthony, *Var the Stick*, 1973
Ben Bova, *Orion*, 1984
Gordon R. Dickson, *The Dragon and the George*, 1976
Philip Jose Farmer, *The Maker of Universes*, 1965
Julian May, *The Many-Colored Land*, 1981
Christopher Stasheff, *Her Majesty's Wizard*, 1986
Harry Turtledove, *The Misplaced Legion*, 1987
Paul O. Williams, *The Ends of the Circle*, 1981

1071

JOHN DALMAS

The Lizard War

(New York: Baen Books, 1989)

Story type: Science Fiction (Military)
Major character(s): Luis Raoul DenUyl, Warrior; Tom, Farmer
Time period(s): 30th century
Locale(s): North America

Summary: A thousand years ago Earth had nearly destroyed itself in a nuclear war. Now, its level of technology roughly late medieval, the planet has been conquered by lizard-like aliens. The only humans standing between Earth and complete subjugation are a sect of mystic warriors.

Other books you might like:
Poul Anderson, *The High Crusade*, 1960
Rick Cook, *Limbo System*, 1989
Kenneth Von Gunden, *StarSpawn*, 1990
F. Paul Wilson, *The Tery*, 1989

1072

JOHN DALMAS

The Regiment's War

(New York: Baen, 1993)

Story type: Science Fiction (Military; Political)
Series: Regiment
Major character(s): Artus Romlar, Military Personnel (Colonel), Mercenary; Kelmer Faronya, Journalist; Gulthar Kro, Criminal (assassin), Spy
Time period(s): 220th century
Locale(s): Smolen, Fictional Country; Komars, Fictional Country

Summary: The White T'swa get their first job, fighting for the Smoleni against the occupying Komarsi. When the Smoleni begin turning the tide, the king of Komars hires the original T'swa to fight for him. Moderate forces must take over and make peace between the two countries, then prepare to fight the approaching Imperials.

Other books you might like:
Roger MacBride Allen, *The Torch of Honor*, 1985
Neal Barrett Jr., *The Karma Corps*, 1984
Lois McMaster Bujold, *Borders of Infinity*, 1989
David Drake, *Hammer's Slammers*, 1979
Gordon R. Dickson, *The Tactics of Mistake*, 1971
M.A. Foster, *The Warriors of Dawn*, 1975
P.M. Griffin, *Jungle Assault*, 1991
Colin Kapp, *The Ion War*, 1978
Jerry Pournelle, *Falkenberg's Legion*, 1990
S.M. Stirling, *The Stone Dogs*, 1990
Timothy Zahn, *Cobra*, 1985

1073

JOHN DALMAS

The White Regiment

(New York: Baen, 1990)

Story type: Science Fiction (Military; Political)
Series: Regiment
Major character(s): Artus Romlar, Military Personnel, Mercenary; Lotta Alsnor, Counselor, Psychic; Igsat Tarimenloku, Military Personnel (Klestronu commodore)
Time period(s): 220th century
Locale(s): Iryala, Planet—Imaginary; Terfreya, Planet—Imaginary; Confederation, Interstellar Empire/Federation

Summary: A Klestronu scoutship discovers Confederation space and decides to annex it to the Empire. Meanwhile on Iryala, T'swa warriors are training the locals into a Regiment to see how much they can learn of T'swa military arts. A scientist discovers a means of teleportation, but only the mentally gifted can use it (many of whom are warriors). When the Klestronu invade at Terfreya, the Regiment and the new method of teleportation must prove themselves and carry the day. The Klestronu retreat, but vow to return someday.

Other books you might like:
Gordon R. Dickson, *The Tactics of Mistake*, 1971
David Drake, *The Forlorn Hope*, 1984
Robert A. Heinlein, *Starship Troopers*, 1959
Jerry Pournelle, *Falkenberg's Legion*, 1990
Joel Rosenberg, *Not for Glory*, 1988

1074

JOHN DALMAS

The Yngling and the Circle of Power

(New York: Baen, 1992)

Story type: Science Fiction (Adventure; Post-Holocaust)
Series: Yngling
Major character(s): Nils Jarnhann, Telepath, Warrior; Deodoro "Ted" Baver, Anthropologist (ethnologist); Songstan Gampo, Ruler (Emperor of China)
Time period(s): 29th century
Locale(s): Europe; Mongolia; China

Summary: Nils, mentally contacted by minds far to the East, sets off in that direction along with Hans, a saga writer, and Baver, a man returned from the stars. After journeying across Russia and Mongolia, they finally arrive in China where Baver is captured by the Emperor's soldiers. Demon-driven Yeti brings Nils to the Emperor and his Circle of Power, hoping to destroy it all.

Other books you might like:
Piers Anthony, *Battle Circle*, 1978
Leigh Brackett, *The Long Tomorrow*, 1955
Gordon R. Dickson, *Wolf and Iron*, 1990
Leo Frankowski, *The Cross-Time Engineer*, 1986
Marc Laidlaw, *Neon Lotus*, 1988
Elizabeth Ann Scarborough, *Nothing Sacred*, 1991

1075

JOHN DALMAS

The Yngling in Yamato

(New York: Baen, 1994)

Story type: Science Fiction (Adventure; Post-Holocaust)
Series: Yngling
Major character(s): Nils Jarnhann, Telepath, Warrior; Matsumura Shinji, Nobleman, Warrior; Hidaka Sataru, Thief (bandit), Wizard
Time period(s): 29th century
Locale(s): Japan

Summary: When Nils Jarnhann, Hans and their starship crew travel to Yamato to seek out a holy man, rebellion and civil war reflect the weakness of the Emperor and the restlessness of the samurai nobility. Adopted by an imperial loyalist, Matsumura, Nils discovers much of the plot against the Emperor and seeks help from the holy man during the rebellion.

Other books you might like:
Dennis Schmidt, *Kensho*, 1979
Brian Stableford, *The Castaways of Tanagar*, 1981
Eric Van Lustbader, *Dai-San*, 1978
Jack Vance, *Servants of the Wankh*, 1969
Paul O. Williams, *The Sword of Forebearance*, 1985

1076

ANNIE DALTON

Out of the Ordinary

(New York: Harper, 1990)

Story type: Fantasy (Magic Conflict; Young Adult)
Major character(s): Molly Gurney, Teenager, Child-Care Giver; Floris, Foundling, Heir—Lost; Icanus Tomkins, Musician
Time period(s): 1980s
Locale(s): England; Launde, Alternate Universe

Summary: Molly Gurney finds herself babysitting for the enchanting (and enchanted) beautiful four-year-old foster child, Floris, who is soon the object of a search by malevolent, destructive powers. Aided by Icarus, Molly must protect Floris from evil wizardry and through a series of adventures through both England and occasionally the alternate world of Launde and the Heartstone.

Other books you might like:
Susan Cooper, *The Dark Is Rising*, 1973
Susan Cooper, *The Grey King*, 1975
Alan Garner, *Elidor*, 1967
Astrid Lindgren, *Mio My Son*, 1956
Pat O'Shea, *The Hounds of the Morrigan*, 1986

1077

SEAN DALTON (Pseudonym of Deborah Chester)

Beyond the Void

(New York: Ace, 1991)

Story type: Science Fiction (Adventure; Military)

Series: Operation StarHawks
Major character(s): Bryan Kelly, Military Personnel (commander, Special Operations); Phila Mohatsa, Military Personnel (communications officer); Antoinette Beaulieu, Doctor
Time period(s): Indeterminate Future
Locale(s): Outer Space

Summary: When legendary invaders from another universe come through gates, attack the Earthship *Sounder* and take it with them, the Starhawks follow to rescue the crew.

Other books you might like:
Lois McMaster Bujold, *Shards of Honor*, 1986
Allan Cole, *Sten*, 1984
   Chris Bunch, co-author
Brian Daley, *Jinx on a Terran Inheritance*, 1985
Stephen Goldin, *Jade Darcy and the Affair of Honor*, 1988
   Mary Mason, co-author
Geary Gravel, *A Key for the Nonesuch*, 1990
Steve Perry, *Matadora*, 1986
Jerry Pournelle, *The Children's Hour*, 1991
   S.M. Stirling, co-author

1078

SEAN DALTON (Pseudonym of Deborah Chester)

Destination: Mutiny

(New York: Ace, 1991)

Story type: Science Fiction (Adventure; Military)
Series: Operation StarHawks
Major character(s): Bryan Kelly, Military Personnel (commander, Special Operations); Olaf Siggerson, Pilot (spaceship); Ouoji, Animal (alien mascot)
Time period(s): Indeterminate Future
Locale(s): Melthanus, Planet—Imaginary; *Blade*, Spaceship

Summary: Having lost a member of their crew of Salukan, the Starhawks rescue Kelly from detox, steal the *Blade*, and set off to rescue 41. The expectation that they'll be able to return and clear their names seems less likely as their adventure progresses.

Other books you might like:
Lois McMaster Bujold, *Borders of Infinity*, 1989
Allan Cole, *The Return of the Emperor*, 1990
   Chris Bunch, co-author
Geary Gravel, *A Key for the Nonesuch*, 1990
Melisa C. Michaels, *Skirmish*, 1985
Steve Perry, *The Man Who Never Missed*, 1985
Alis A. Rasmussen, *A Passage of Stars*, 1990
Melissa Scott, *Mighty Good Road*, 1990

1079

SEAN DALTON (Pseudonym of Deborah Chester)

The Salukan Gambit

(New York: Ace, 1992)

Story type: Science Fiction (Adventure; Political)
Series: Operation StarHawks

Major character(s): Bryan Kelly, Military Personnel; Operative 41, Alien (half Human/half Salukan), Spaceman; Antoinette Beaulieu, Doctor
Time period(s): Indeterminate Future
Locale(s): *Sabre*, Spaceship; Banqot, Fictional City; Minzan, Planet—Imaginary

Summary: The StarHawks rescue Melaethia and her infant triplets, but before the *Sabre* builds up speed, a Jostic pirate vessel with several Salukan Warriors on board disables the *Sabre*. Since one of the Salukans, Melaethia's brother, desperately wants to hurt Melaethia, the StarHawks must keep Melaethia and her children safe while regaining control of the *Sabre*.

Other books you might like:
Lois McMaster Bujold, *Shards of Honor*, 1986
C.J. Cherryh, *The Pride of Chanur*, 1982
Allan Cole, *Sten*, 1984
   Chris Bunch, co-author
A.C. Crispin, *Starbridge*, 1989
Brian Daley, *Jinx on a Terran Inheritance*, 1985
Vonda N. McIntyre, *Metaphase*, 1992
Steve Perry, *The Man Who Never Missed*, 1985
Vernor Vinge, *A Fire upon the Deep*, 1992

1080

BRIAN D'AMATO

Beauty

(New York: Delacorte, 1992)

Story type: Horror (Science Fiction)
Major character(s): Jamie Angelo, Artist, Student (medical); Jaishree/Minaz, Artist, Model; David Lowenstein, Doctor
Time period(s): 1990s (1992)
Locale(s): New York, New York

Summary: This critique of the Manhattan art scene and fashion world tells of artist Jamie Angelo, a modern Pygmalion who has perfected a sculpting material, PCS10, that he uses in unorthodox plastic surgery procedures to remake the faces of wealthy patients. Jamie lives a life of decadent riches until his operations begin breaking down in unforeseen ways with hideous results. This is the author's first novel.

Other books you might like:
Kobo Abe, *The Face of Another*, 1966
Randall Boyll, *Darkman*, 1990
Ariel Dorfman, *Mascara*, 1988
Steve Vance, *Spook*, 1990

1081

DON D'AMMASSA
ROBERT H. KNOW, Illustrator

Twisted Images

(West Warwick, Rhode Island: Necronomicon Press, 1995)

Story type: Horror (Occult)
Major character(s): Alan Sheridan, Worker (Eblis Manufacturing); Chen Li, Young Woman; Tao Tieh, Aged Person
Time period(s): 1990s (1995)

Locale(s): Providence, Rhode Island

Summary: In this short story chapbook, Alan Sheridan moves into an apartment whose previous owner, a murder victim, left an ornately decorated Oriental mirror on the wall. His friendship with a young Asian woman in the building makes him aware of a legend of a secret world on the other side of the mirror and unfortunate mortals on this side in danger of being absorbed into it.

Other books you might like:
Gordon Linzner, *The Oni*, 1986
Bentley Little, *The Summoning*, 1993
Robert Morgan, *Some Things Never Die*, 1993
Donald Wandrei, *The Painted Mirror*, 1944
   in *The Eye and the Finger*
Kelley Wilde, *Angel Kiss*, 1993

1082

TONY DANIEL

Warpath

(New York: Tor, 1993)

Story type: Science Fiction (First Contact; Immortality)
Major character(s): Will James, Immortal, Publisher; Thomas Fall, Indian, Wanderer; Janey Calhoun, Alien (half chocalaca), Settler
Time period(s): 26th century (2563)
Locale(s): Candle, Planet—Imaginary

Summary: Reconstituted on Candle 500 years after his transmission from Earth, Will publishes the *Cold Truth*, a local newspaper for both the settlement of Jackson and Doom, the Mississippi Indian village. His friend, Thomas, carries a bit of clay containing a chocalaca, Raej, who protects him and allows him to travel faster than light alone in his canoe as the Mississippi Indians have done in pairs since the 11th century. Half chocalaca, Janey manipulates real space directly but without much control, perhaps leading to war between the settlers and Indians then throughout the universe. Author's first novel.

Other books you might like:
William Barton, *Dark Sky Legion*, 1992
Greg Bear, *Eon*, 1985
Jeffrey A. Carver, *Dragons in the Stars*, 1992
John DeChancie, *Starrigger*, 1983
Jack C. Haldeman II, *High Steel*, 1993
   Jack Dann, co-author
Alis A. Rasmussen, *A Passage of Stars*, 1990
Robert Silverberg, *Recalled to Life*, 1962
Vernor Vinge, *A Fire upon the Deep*, 1992

1083

LES DANIELS

No Blood Spilled

(New York: Tor, 1990)

Story type: Horror (Vampire Story)
Series: Chronicles of Don Sebastian

Major character(s): Don Sebastian de Villanueva, Vampire; Reginald Calder, Mentally Ill Person; Christopher Hawke, Military Personnel
Time period(s): 1840s
Locale(s): India

Summary: Efforts by Don Sebastian de Villanueva to resurrect the Thuggee death cult of Kali worshipers are almost confounded by the deranged vengeance-seeking Reginald Calder, competing Thuggee leader Kalidas Sen, and Lt. Christopher Hawke of the 5th Fusiliers. Aiding Don Sebastian is a young Indian boy named Jamini who becomes his devoted servant. The conflict in this best of Daniels' Don Sebastian novels climaxes in an exciting finale set during a monsoon in the jungles north of Calcutta.

Other books you might like:
Dan Simmons, *Song of Kali*, 1985

| 1084 |

JACK DANN, Editor
GARDNER DOZOIS, Co-Editor

Angels!
(New York: Ace, 1995)

Story type: Fantasy (Anthology; Religious)

Summary: Contains 12 stories and two poems about divine agents reprinted from periodicals and anthologies, with the tone varying from light to dark. Authors include Pat Cadigan, Philip K. Dick, Esther M. Friesner, Lisa Goldstein, Robert Silverberg, Kate Wilhelm, Jane Yolen, and Roger Zelazny.

Other books you might like:
Peter Crowther, *Heaven Sent: 18 Glorious Tales of the Angels*, 1995
    editor
Gardner Dozois, *The Year's Best Science Fiction Series*, 1984-1994
    editor
Neil Gaiman, *Good Omens: The Nice and Accurate Prophecies of Agnes Nutter, Witch*, 1990
    Terry Pratchett, co-author
Andrew M. Greeley, *Angel Light*, 1995
Alan Ryan, *Perpetual Light*, 1982
    editor
Sean Stewart, *Resurrection Man*, 1995

| 1085 |

JACK DANN, Editor
GARDNER DOZOIS, Co-Editor

Little People!
(New York: Ace, 1991)

Story type: Fantasy (Anthology)

Summary: This thematic anthology contains brief introductions with 11 stories originally published in magazines and anthologies between 1939 and 1988. All stories feature mythical creatures thought of as short in stature such as elves, pixies, sprites, fairies, gremlins and leprechauns. Authors include Jack Dann, L. Sprague de Camp, Harlan Ellison, Hor-

ace L. Gold, Henry Kuttner, Theodore Sturgeon and Gene Wolfe. One story, "Send No Money," is a collaboration between Susan Casper and Gardner Dozois.

Other books you might like:
Robin McKinley, *Imaginary Lands*, 1985
    editor
Baird Searles, *Halflings, Hobbits, Warrows & Weefolk: A Collection of Tales of Heroes Short in Stature*, 1991
    Brian Thomsen, co-editor
Terri Windling, *Elsewhere*, 1981
    Mark Alan Arnold, co-editor
Terri Windling, *Elsewhere II*, 1982
    Mark Alan Arnold, co-editor
Terri Windling, *Elsewhere III*, 1984
    Mark Alan Arnold, co-editor
Terri Windling, *Faery*, 1984
    editor

| 1086 |

JACK DANN

The Memory Cathedral
(New York: Bantam, 1995)

Story type: Science Fiction (Alternate Universe; Political)
Major character(s): Leonardo da Vinci, Historical Figure, Inventor; Niccolo Machiavelli, Historical Figure, Apprentice; Sandro Botticelli, Historical Figure, Artist (painter)
Time period(s): 15th century
Locale(s): Florence, Italy; Middle East; Alternate Earth

Summary: As Leonardo da Vinci dies, he explores the carefully stored memories of a lifetime. He recalls a ruthless kidnapper forcing him to construct the fantastic machines he has designed, while employing them to an end which proves heartbreaking to the savant. Concludes with a four-page afterword by Dann.

Other books you might like:
Martin Amis, *Time's Arrow*, 1991
L. Sprague de Camp, *Lest Darkness Fall*, 1941
Leo Frankowski, *The Cross-Time Engineer*, 1986
Paul J. McAuley, *Pasquale's Angel*, 1995
Chelsea Quinn Yarbro, *Ariosto*, 1980

| 1087 |

JACK DANN, Editor
GARDNER DOZOIS, Co-Editor

Unicorns II
(New York: Ace, 1992)

Story type: Fantasy (Anthology; Legend)

Summary: Contains a two-page preface plus individual introductions to 10 stories reprinted from periodicals and anthologies from 1984 to 1991 and two originals, Jack C. Haldeman II's "Ghost Town" and Lawrence Watt-Evan's "Unicornicopia," all sharing the theme of the mythical unicorn. With Susan Casper and Gardner Dozois collaborating on one story, other authors include Michael Bishop, Jack Dann, Gregory Frost, Janet Kagan, Tanith Lee, Mike Resnick, Patricia C. Wrede and Jane Yolen. Concludes with a short bibliography.

Other books you might like:
Peter S. Beagle, *The Last Unicorn*, 1968
Michael Bishop, *Unicorn Mountain*, 1988
Bruce Coville, *The Unicorn Treasury*, 1988
  editor
Pamela Dean, *The Secret Country*, 1985
Mark S. Geston, *The Siege of Wonder*, 1976
Tanith Lee, *Black Unicorn*, 1991
Madeleine L'Engle, *A Swiftly Tilting Planet*, 1978
Mike Resnick, *Stalking the Unicorn: A Fable of Tonight*, 1987

1088

WILLIAM DANTZ (Pseudonym of Rodman Philbrick)

Hunger
(New York: Tor, 1992)

Story type: Horror (Nature in Revolt; Science Fiction)
Major character(s): Sally Hart, Sailor (charter boat captain); Thomas J. Hart, Sailor (charter boat captain); Vernon Speke, Scientist (marine biologist)
Time period(s): 1990s
Locale(s): Key West, Florida

Summary: The escape of a half-dozen ravenous, genetically-engineered great white sharks from the Sealife Research Institute into tourist-infested waters off the Florida Keys pits a pair of animal-loving skindivers against the scientist who has been training the sharks as a new weapon for the Department of Defense.

Other books you might like:
Peter Benchley, *Beast*, 1991
Peter Benchley, *Jaws*, 1974
T.J. Kirby, *Deadly Breed*, 1991
Dean R. Koontz, *Watchers*, 1987
J.M. Morgan, *Between the Devil and the Deep*, 1992

1089

WILLIAM DANTZ (Pseudonym of Rodman Philbrick)

Nine Levels Down
(New York: Tor, 1995)

Story type: Horror (Psychological Suspense)
Major character(s): Anna Kane, Psychologist; John Marlon, Criminal; Kevin McRay, Police Officer
Time period(s): 1990s (1995)
Locale(s): New York, New York

Summary: Psychologist Anna Kane has developed an implant device that can neutralize the worst psychopathic impulses in her murderous patients. It proves all for nought when criminal patient John Marlon abducts her into the New York subway system, where he has kidnapped numerous other victims whom he has tortured fiendishly.

Other books you might like:
Michael Crichton, *The Terminal Man*, 1972
Richard Laymon, *Midnight's Lair*, 1988

Chet Williamson, *Lowland Rider*, 1988
F. Paul Wilson, *Implant*, 1995

1090

DENNIS DANVERS

Wilderness
(New York: Poseidon, 1991)

Story type: Horror (Werewolf Story)
Major character(s): Alice White, Travel Agent, Werewolf; Erik Summers, Scientist (biologist), Professor; Luther Adams, Doctor (psychiatrist)
Time period(s): 1990s
Locale(s): Richmond, Virginia

Summary: This first novel about the sacrifices of love tells the poignant tale of Alice White, who risks her chance for romantic fulfillment and personal freedom when she confesses to her boyfriend not only that she is a werewolf, but that she has killed a man during her feral transformation.

Other books you might like:
Peter S. Beagle, *Lila the Werewolf*, 1969
Scott Bradfield, *Dream of the Wolf*, 1990
Michael Cadnum, *St. Peter's Wolf*, 1991
Charles de Lint, *Wolf Moon*, 1988
Dean R. Koontz, *Watchers*, 1987
Thomas Tessier, *The Nightwalker*, 1979

1091

LARRY DARK

The Literary Ghost
(New York: Atlantic Monthly Press, 1991)

Story type: Horror (Anthology; Ghost Story)

Summary: Twenty-eight classic and contemporary ghost stories by writers whose work falls largely outside the horror and fantasy genres. Included are Tim O'Brien's tale of the horrors of the Vietnam War, ''The Ghost Soldiers''; Graham Greene's gruesome shocker of a revelation in a movie theater, ''A Little Place Off the Edgware Road''; Joyce Carol Oates' tale of a strange ritual noted among evening commuters and other members of the living dead, ''The Others''; and Patrick McGrath's extraordinary Gothic pastiche ''Marmilion.''

Other books you might like:
Bradford Morrow, *The New Gothic*, 1992
  Patrick McGrath, co-author
Robert Phillips, *Triumph of the Night*, 1988

1092

DAVID DARKE (Pseudonym of Ron Dee)

Blind Hunger
(New York: Pinnacle, 1993)

Story type: Horror (Vampire Story)
Major character(s): Patty Hunsacker, Widow(er), Handicapped (blind); Matt Hunsacker, Vampire; Chris Mikel, Child

Time period(s): 1990s (1993)
Locale(s): Nesoho, Missouri

Summary: Mark, the supposed twin brother of Matt Hunsacker, comes to stay with Matt's blind wife Patty after the untimely and inexplicable death of her husband. But Patty's senses tell her that Mark is actually Matt, risen from the grave as a vampire and intent on using their house as a base of operations for his regular feedings.

Other books you might like:
Lee Weathersby, *Kiss of the Vampire*, 1992
T. Lucien Wright, *Blood Brothers*, 1992

1093

DAVID DARKE (Pseudonym of Ron Dee)

Horrorshow

(New York: Zebra, 1994)

Story type: Horror (Small Town Horror)
Major character(s): Greg Driver, Actor; Jim, Actor; Dennis "Druzeppa" Thudd, Actor
Time period(s): 1990s (1995)
Locale(s): Twainton

Summary: As part of their plan to launch their careers as actors, Greg and Jim use their Halloween show on the local Twainton television station to air the final tape of Druzeppa, a monster movie host who died under mysterious circumstances while on the air 20 years before. Their action brings Druzeppa back from the dead to continue the satanic mission he was prevented from fulfilling before his death: urging the townspeople on to a life of debauchery and mayhem.

Other books you might like:
Dale Hoover, *65mm*, 1994
Jack Martin, *Videodrome*, 1982
Theodore Roszak, *Flicker*, 1993
Brad Strickland, *Shadowshow*, 1988

1094

DAVID DARKE (Pseudonym of Ron Dee)

Last Rites

(New York: Zebra, 1996)

Story type: Horror (Black Magic)
Major character(s): Betsy Walker, Femme Fatale; Gary Carpenter, Businessman; Tonia Carpenter, Artist
Time period(s): 1990s (1996)
Locale(s): Tulsa, Oklahoma

Summary: Following their high school reunion, a group of friends agrees to revive the Necro Club, a black magic coven they joined as teenagers in order to resurrect the dead and see into the future. When their plans go awry, it results in a deadly power struggle among themselves.

Other books you might like:
Leigh Clark, *Blood Sabbath*, 1991
Ed Kelleher, *The School*, 1988
  Harriette Vidal, co-author
Mark Morris, *Stitch*, 1992

R.L. Stine, *Superstitious*, 1995
Tamara Thorne, *Moonfall*, 1996

1095

DAVID DARKE (Pseudonym of Ron Dee)

Shade

(New York: Zebra, 1994)

Story type: Horror (Vampire Story)
Major character(s): Scarlett Shade, Writer, Vampire
Time period(s): 1990s (1994)
Locale(s): Norman, Oklahoma

Summary: Bestselling writer of vampire fiction Scarlett Shade turns out to be a real vampire who feeds off the "scarlett fever" of amorality and sexual abandon that her novels inspire in her devoted fans.

Other books you might like:
Steven Brust, *Agyar*, 1993
Tanya Huff, *Blood Price*, 1991
Anne Rice, *The Vampire Lestat*, 1985
T. Lucien Wright, *Blood Brothers*, 1991

1096

DIANA DARLING

The Painted Alphabet

(New York: Houghton Mifflin, 1992)

Story type: Fantasy (Legend; Religious)
Major character(s): Siladri, Farmer; Mpu Dibiaja, Shaman; Dayu Datu, Witch
Time period(s): Indeterminate
Locale(s): Bali, Indonesia

Summary: In this modern first novel, based on an ancient Balinese epic poem, Siladri, a farmer with a loving, happy family, decides to go to the mountains to study with a spiritual advisor. He leaves his infant son with his brother and takes his infant niece at his brother's insistence. His wife, taken on an expedition to the mountains as a child, hates and fears the mountains and refuses to let Siladri go alone.

Other books you might like:
Maya Kaathryn Bohnhoff, *The Meri*, 1992
Charles de Lint, *The Little Country*, 1990
Monica Hughes, *Sandwriter*, 1988
Barry Lopez, *Crow and Weasel*, 1990
Robin Morgan, *The Mer-Child: A Legend for Children and Other Adults*, 1991
Antoine de Saint-Exupery, *The Little Prince*, 1943
Lucius Shepard, *Kalimantan*, 1992

1097

ELLEN DATLOW, Editor

Alien Sex

(New York: Dutton, 1990)

Story type: Horror (Anthology; Science Fiction)

Summary: Nineteen tales and poems of science fiction, fantasy and horror concerned with the sexuality of humans and non-humans and the alienating potential of sexual relationships between men and women. Best stories include K.W. Jeter's brilliant ''The First Time,'' about a young boy's rite of passage into adulthood; Lisa Tuttle's ''Husbands,'' an inquiry into the unbridgeable differences between men and women; and Lewis Shiner's ''Scales,'' about a lamia who brings about the destruction of a marriage. With author and editor notes for each story.

Other books you might like:
Margaret L. Carter, *Demon Lovers and Strange Seductions*, 1973
Don Congdon, *Tales of Love and Horror*, 1961
Jeff Gelb, *Hotter Blood: More Tales of Erotic Horror*, 1991
    Michael Garrett, co-author
Jeff Gelb, *Hot Blood: Tales of Provocative Horror*, 1989
    Lonn Friend, co-author
Michele Slung, *I Shudder at Your Touch*, 1991

1098

ELLEN DATLOW, Editor
TERRI WINDLING, Co-Editor

Black Thorn, White Rose
(New York: Tor, 1994)

Story type: Fantasy (Anthology; Legend)

Summary: Contains five pages of recommended reading, a six-page introduction by Datlow and Windling plus individual introductions to one poem, one unusual recipe and 16 original stories which retell cherished fairy tales utilizing a darker and sexier tone for adults. Authors include Michael Cadnum, Storm Constantine, Ann Elizabeth Downer, Michael Kandel, Nancy Kress, Daniel Quinn, Midori Snyder, Peter Straub, Howard Waldrop, Patricia C. Wrede, Jane Yolen and Roger Zelazny.

Other books you might like:
Lester del Rey, *Once upon a Time: A Treasury of Modern Fairy Tales*, 1991
    Risa Kessler, co-editor
Tanith Lee, *Red as Blood: Or Tales from the Sisters Grimmer*, 1983
Terri Windling, *Life on the Border*, 1991
    editor
Jane Yolen, *The Xanadu Series*, 1993-1995
    editor
Jack Zipes, *Beauties, Beasts and Enchantments*, 1989
    editor

1099

ELLEN DATLOW, Editor

Blood Is Not Enough
(New York: Berkley, 1990)

Story type: Horror (Anthology; Vampire Story)

Summary: Seventeen stories that expand the boundaries of the traditional vampire tale in their exploration of the relationship between the victim and the victimizer. Highlights include Fritz Leiber's classic of exploitative advertising, ''The Girl with the Hungry Eyes,'' Gardner Dozois and Jack Dann's controversial tale of the victims of a concentration camp vampire, ''Down Among the Dead Men,'' Gahan Wilson's nasty interpretation of Lewis Carroll, ''The Sea Was Wet as Wet Could Be,'' Tanith Lee's tale of debilitating illness, ''The Janfia Tree,'' and Dan Simmons' story of psychic vampirism, ''Carrion Comfort,'' which became the basis for his Bram Stoker Award-winning novel of the same title. Reprint of a 1989 hardcover.

Other books you might like:
Richard Dalby, *Dracula's Brood*, 1987
Martin H. Greenberg, *Vamps*, 1987
    Charles G. Waugh, co-author
Alan Ryan, *Vampires: Two Centuries of Great Vampire Stories*, 1987
Leslie Shepard, *The Dracula Book of Great Vampire Stories*, 1977

1100

ELLEN DATLOW, Editor

Little Deaths
(New York: Dell, 1995)

Story type: Horror (Anthology)

Summary: The sixteen tales of erotic horror collected here have been distilled from the British version of this anthology, which appeared earlier in 1995 and contained twenty-four stories. Included are Stephen Dedman's ''The Lady of Situations,'' and Lucy Taylor's ''Hungry Skin,'' both tales with sadomasochistic subtexts, and Nicholas Royle's ''The Swing,'' which metaphorically likens a relationship to the tethering of two individuals. Joel Lane, in ''The Pain Barrier,'' blurs the boundaries between film and reality in his tale of a man who discovers the film star he has fallen for lives in the same dwelling used as the backdrop for his transgressive films. Joyce Carol Oates' ''Fever Blisters'' is a nightmarish story of a couple trying to recapture the ecstacy of their first sexual experience years after they know the horrible consequences it has wrought. Jack Womack's ''That Old School Tie,'' concerns a teacher whose interest in a student's chaos theory of literature draws him into kinky escapades. In Richard Christian Matheson's ''Menage a Trois,'' a man and woman develop an unusual relationship with the knife they use in sadomasochistic rituals.

Other books you might like:
Jeff Gelb, *Hot Blood: Tales of Provocative Horror*, 1989
    Lonn Friend, co-editor
Jeff Gelb, *Deadly After Dark*, 1994
    Michael Garrett, co-editor
Jeff Gelb, *Seeds of Fear*, 1995
    Michael Garrett, co-editor
Jeff Gelb, *Stranger by Night*, 1995
    Michael Garrett, co-editor
Jeff Gelb, *Hotter Blood: More Tales of Erotic Horror*, 1991
    Michael Garrett, co-editor
Jeff Gelb, *Hottest Blood: The Ultimate in Erotic Horror*, 1993
    Michael Garrett, co-editor

Michele Slung, *I Shudder at Your Touch*, 1991
    editor
Michele Slung, *Shudder Again*, 1993
    editor

1101

ELLEN DATLOW, Editor

Off Limits: Tales of Alien Sex
(New York: St. Martin's Press, 1996)

Story type: Science Fiction (Anthology)

Summary: Contains a three-page foreword by Rober Silverberg, a three-page introduction plus individual introductions by Datlow and authors' afterwords to four stories reprinted from periodicals and anthologies 1970-1993, original poems by Joe Haldeman and Jane Yolen, and 15 original stories. Stories are frequently dark in tone, all focusing on sex, with other themes such as disease, prostitution, dystopias, communication, gender politics, and power. Other authors include Samuel R. Delany, Neil Gaiman, Elizabeth Hand, Simon Ings, Gwyneth Jones, Bruce McAllister, Joyce Carol Oates, Martha Soukup, and Lisa Tuttle.

Other books you might like:
Octavia E. Butler, *Dawn*, 1987
Joseph Elder, *Eros in Orbit*, 1973
    editor
Philip Jose Farmer, *Strange Relations*, 1960
Richard Glyn Jones, *Cybersex*, 1996
    editor
Ursula K. Le Guin, *The Left Hand of Darkness*, 1969
Thomas N. Scortia, *Strange Bedfellows: Sex and Science Fiction*, 1972
    editor
Dan Simmons, *Lovedeath*, 1993
Theodore Sturgeon, *Venus Plus X*, 1960

1102

ELLEN DATLOW, Editor

Omni Best Science Fiction One
(New York: Omni Books, 1992)

Story type: Science Fiction (Anthology)

Summary: Contains six original stories and four reprinted from *Omni*, 1986-1987, with themes including arts, cyberpunk, first contact, genetic manipulation, and satire. Original story authors include Richard Kadrey, Elizabeth A. Lynn, Paul Park, and Robert Silverberg. Reprinted stories appear by Neal Barrett, Jr., Suzy McKee Charnas, Jack Dann, and Tom Maddox, whose "Snake Eyes" expands the world of *Halo* (1991).

Other books you might like:
Lou Aronica, *Full Spectrum*, 1988
    Shawna McCarthy, co-editor
Lou Aronica, *Full Spectrum 2*, 1990
    Shawna McCarthy, co-editor
Lou Aronica, *Full Spectrum 3*, 1991
    Amy Stout and Betsy Mitchell, co-editors

Michael Bishop, *Nebula Awards 25*, 1991
    editor
Gardner Dozois, *The Year's Best Science Fiction: Eighth Annual Collection*, 1991
    editor
Kristine Kathryn Rusch, *The Best of Pulphouse: The Hardback Magazine*, 1991
    editor
Robert Silverberg, *Universe 1*, 1990
    Karen Haber, co-editor
Robert Silverberg, *Universe 2*, 1992
    Karen Haber, co-editor

1103

ELLEN DATLOW, Editor

Omni Best Science Fiction Three
(Greensborough, North Carolina: Omni Books, 1993)

Story type: Science Fiction (Anthology)
Series: Omni Best Science Fiction

Summary: Contains a two-page introduction, individual story introductions, Thomas M. Disch's story, "Palindrome," reprinted from *Omni* plus 10 original stories, many containing sexual themes, by authors including Pat Cadigan, John Crowley, Ursula K. Le Guin, Ian McDonald, Pat Murphy and Gahan Wilson.

Other books you might like:
Lou Aronica, *Full Spectrum 4*, 1993
    Amy Stout, Betsy Mitchell, co-editors
Gardner Dozois, *The Year's Best Science Fiction: Tenth Annual Collection*, 1993
    editor
Kristine Kathryn Rusch, *The Best of Pulphouse: The Hardback Magazine*, 1991
    editor
Robert Silverberg, *Universe 1*, 1990
    Karen Haber, co-editor
Robert Silverberg, *Universe 2*, 1992
    Karen Haber, co-editor

1104

ELLEN DATLOW, Editor

Omni Visions One
(Greensborough, North Carolina: Omni Books, 1993)

Story type: Science Fiction (Anthology)
Series: Omni Visions

Summary: Contains a one-page introduction plus individual introductions to an original Joyce Carol Oates story and nine stories published in *Omni* 1986-1989. Themes include alternate universes, fantasy, ecological disaster, early radio broadcasting, missed chances and human illness with many stories dark in tone. Authors include James P. Blaylock, William S. Burroughs, Octavia E. Butler, Marc Laidlaw, Michael Swanwick and Howard Waldrop.

Other books you might like:
Lou Aronica, *Full Spectrum*, 1988
  Shawna McCarthy, co-editor
Lou Aronica, *Full Spectrum 2*, 1990
  Shawna McCarthy, Amy Stout, Patrick LoBrutto, co-editors
Gardner Dozois, *The Year's Best Science Fiction: Tenth Annual Collection*, 1993
  editor
James Morrow, *Nebula Awards 27*, 1993
  editor
Kristine Kathryn Rusch, *The Best of Pulphouse: The Hardback Magazine*, 1991
  editor
Robert Silverberg, *Universe 1*, 1990
  Karen Haber, co-editor
Robert Silverberg, *Universe 2*, 1992
  Karen Haber, co-editor

1105

ELLEN DATLOW, Editor
TERRI WINDLING, Co-Editor

Ruby Slippers, Golden Tears
(New York: AvoNova/Morrow, 1995)

Story type: Fantasy (Anthology; Legend)
Series: Snow White, Blood Red

Summary: Contains eight pages of recommended reading, a seven-page introduction by Windling and Datlow plus individual introductions to three poems and 19 original literary fairy tales with themes including high fantasy, the complications of modern life and horror. Also included are familiar stories in new guises, such as "Rumplestiltskin," "Puss in Boots," "The Princess and the Pea," and "Snow White," as well as other tales from Asia, Europe, and North America. Authors include John Brunner, Michael Cadnum, Nancy A. Collins, Neil Gaiman, Lisa Goldstein, Joyce Carol Oates, Susan Palwick, Delia Sherman, Gahan Wilson, Gene Wolfe, and Jane Yolen.

Other books you might like:
Lester del Rey, *Once upon a Time: A Treasury of Modern Fairy Tales*, 1991
  Risa Kessler, co-editor
Tanith Lee, *Red as Blood: Or Tales from the Sisters Grimmer*, 1983
Vivian Vande Velde, *Tales From the Brothers Grimm and the Sisters Weird*, 1995
Terri Windling, *The Armless Maiden and Other Tales for Childhood's Survivors*, 1995
  editor
Jane Yolen, *The Xanadu Series*, 1993-1995
  editor
Jack Zipes, *Don't Bet on the Prince*, 1986
  editor
Jack Zipes, *The Outspoken Princess and the Gentle Knight*, 1994
  editor

1106

ELLEN DATLOW, Editor
TERRI WINDLING, Co-Editor

Snow White, Blood Red
(New York: Morrow AvoNova, 1993)

Story type: Fantasy (Anthology; Legend)
Series: Snow White, Blood Red

Summary: Emphasizing the roots and archetypal imagery of the ancient fairy tale tradition, this volume contains a 14-page introduction by Terri Windling, "White as Snow: Fairy Tale and Fantasy"; a six-page introduction by Ellen Datlow, "Red as Blood: Fairy Tales and Horror"; and individual introductions to 20 original stories, frequently dark in tone, by authors including Jack Dann, Charles de Lint, Esther M. Friesner, Gregory Frost, Neil Gaiman, Kathe Koja, Nancy Kress, Tanith Lee, Elizabeth A. Lynn, Patricia A. McKillip, Gahan Wilson and Jane Yolen.

Other books you might like:
Lester del Rey, *Once upon a Time: A Treasury of Modern Fairy Tales*, 1991
  Risa Kessler, co-editor
Terri Windling, *Borderland*, 1986
  Mark Alan Arnold, co-editor
Terri Windling, *Elsewhere*, 1981
  Mark Alan Arnold, co-editor
Terri Windling, *Elsewhere II*, 1982
  Mark Alan Arnold, co-editor
Terri Windling, *Faery*, 1984
Terri Windling, *Life on the Border*, 1991
  editor
Jane Yolen, *Xanadu*, 1993
  editor
Jack Zipes, *Spells of Enchantment*, 1991
  editor, translator

1107

ELLEN DATLOW, Editor

Twists of the Tale
(New York: Dell, 1996)

Story type: Horror (Anthology)

Summary: Cats and their interests feature in 20 original stories and two reprints in this compilation. Among the best stories are Michael Marshall Smith's "Not Waving," which frames a love triangle in terms of feline mythology; Kathe Koja and Barry Malzberg's "Homage to Custom," which concerns a derelict woman who develops a psychic link with a feline; Douglas Clegg's "The Five," a tale of family dysfunction in which cats become pawns in a game of cruelty between parents and children; Michael Cadnum's "The Man Who Did Cats Harm," about feline revenge on a man who has killed one of their number; Gahan Wilson's "Best Friends," which shows how cats actually own people as their pets; and Joyce Carol Oates' "Nobody Knows My Name," a riff on the superstition that cats can suck the breath from the living while they sleep.

Other books you might like:
Jack Dann, *Magicats!*, 1984
    Gardner Dozois, co-editor
Claire Necker, *Supernatural Cats*, 1972
    editor
Andre Norton, *Catfantastic*, 1989
    Martin H. Greenberg, co-editor
Michel Parry, *Beware of the Cat*, 1974
    editor

1108

ELLEN DATLOW, Editor

A Whisper of Blood
(New York: Morrow, 1991)

Story type: Horror (Anthology; Vampire Story)

Summary: This collection of eighteen stories—three reprints, the rest new—explores, as its predecessor, *Blood Is Not Enough* did, the theme of vampirism through a variety of original and unlikely applications. Included are David Schow's "A Week in the Unlife," about a vampire who feeds off of other vampires; Thomas Ligotti's "Mrs. Rinaldi's Angel," about the parasitical nature of dreams; two stories that look at the vampiric nature of parent/child relationships, K.W. Jeter's "True Love" and Elizabeth Massie's "M is for the Many Things"; Suzy McKee Charnas's ghost vampire tale, "Now I Lay Me Down to Sleep"; Chelsea Quinn Yarbro's powerful tale of paranoia, "Do I Dare to Eat a Peach"; and Robert Silverberg's classic of an empath who feeds off the misery of others, "The Warm Man."

Other books you might like:
Richard Dalby, *Dracula's Brood*, 1987
Martin H. Greenberg, *A Taste for Blood*, 1992
    Robert Weinberg and Stefan Dziemianowicz, co-editors
Martin H. Greenberg, *Vamps*, 1987
    Charles G. Waugh, co-editor
Alan Ryan, *Vampires: Two Centuries of Great Vampire Stories*, 1987
Leslie Shepard, *The Dracula Book of Great Vampire Stories*, 1977
    editor

1109

ELLEN DATLOW, Editor
TERRI WINDLING, Co-Editor

The Year's Best Fantasy and Horror: Fifth Annual Collection
(New York: St. Martin's Press, 1992)

Story type: Horror (Anthology; Fantasy)

Summary: The fifth annual installment of this World Fantasy Award-winning series includes 44 stories and 6 poems, 26 of which fall within the purview of the horror genre. Included are two stories each by Kathe Koja and S. P. Somtow; vampire tales by Robert Holdstock, Gary Kilworth, and K. W. Jeter; Thomas Ligotti's story of a haunted movie theater, "The Glamour"; Dennis Etchison's non-supernatural chiller,

"Call Home"; and Karl Edward Wagner's erotic horror story, "The Kind Men Like."

Other books you might like:
Stephen Jones, *Best New Horror*, 1990-1992
Robert Morrish, *Quick Chills*, 1989-1992
    Peter Enfantino, co-editor
Karl Edward Wagner, *The Year's Best Horror Stories Series*, 1980-1992
    editor

1110

ELLEN DATLOW, Editor
TERRI WINDLING, Co-Editor

The Year's Best Fantasy and Horror: Fourth Annual Collection
(New York: St. Martin's Press, 1991)

Story type: Fantasy (Anthology; Horror)

Summary: This volume includes 52 stories published in 1990 plus introductions and notes. Highlights include "The First Time" by K.W. Jeter, a brutal story about a young man's very different coming of age, and Charles de Lint's "Freewheeling" which mixes tragedy, whimsey, art and punk. As in previous collections, this volume presents a spectrum ranging from dark horror to whimsical, 'folksy' fantasy. Some major authors include Michael Bishop, Jonathan Carroll, Angela Carter, John Crowley, Karen Joy Fowler, T.E.D. Klein, Ellen Kushner, R.A. Lafferty, Joe Lansdale, Joyce Carol Oates and Lucius Shepard.

Other books you might like:
David G. Hartwell, *The Color of Evil*, 1987
    editor
Robert R. McCammon, *Under the Fang*, 1991
Kristine Kathryn Rusch, *The Best of Pulphouse: The Hardback Magazine*, 1991
    editor
Kristine Kathryn Rusch, *Pulphouse, Issue 6: Fantasy*, 1990
    editor
Kristine Kathryn Rusch, *Pulphouse, Issue 9: Dark Fantasy*, 1990
    editor
Karl Edward Wagner, *The Year's Best Horror Stories XIX*, 1991
    editor
Terri Windling, *Life on the Border*, 1991
    editor

1111

ELLEN DATLOW, Editor
TERRI WINDLING, Co-Editor

The Year's Best Fantasy and Horror: Ninth Annual Collection
(New York: St. Martin's, 1996)

Story type: Horror (Anthology; Fantasy)

Summary: Datlow, who covers the horror end, and Windling, who selects the fantasy, choose 35 stories and 11 poems representing the best to appear in 1995. Horror highlights include Stephen King's Bram Stoker Award-winning "Lunch in the Gotham Cafe," about a psychopathic *maitre'd* on the loose in a Manhattan restaurant; Douglas Winter's "Loop," in which a man's obsession with a film starlet turns psychopathological; Michael Marshall Smith's tale of Internet terror, "More Tomorrow"; David Schow's "Refrigerator Heaven," a torture tale of imprisonment; Terry Lamsley's "Screens," in which a man discovers a macabre other life occurring at the home of a neighbor; and Tanith Lee's "La Dame," an allegorical tale of a man and the sea in a vampiric relationship. Fantasy efforts include Nina Kiriki Hoffman's domestic magic tale, "Home for Christmas"; Midori Snyder's riff on an old folk theme, "King of Crows"; and Peter S. Beagle's talking rhinoceros tale, "Professor Gottesman and the Indian Rhinoceros." Each editor supplies an essay surveying her respective field for the year, Ed Bryant wraps up films for the year, and Jim Frenkel supplies obituaries for 1995.

Other books you might like:
Lin Carter, *The Year's Best Fantasy Stories Series*, 1974-1980
  editor
Stephen Jones, *The Mammoth Book of Best New Horror*, 1996
  editor
Arthur W. Saha, *The Year's Best Fantasy Stories*, 1981-1988
  editor
Karl Edward Wagner, *The Year's Best Horror Stories Series*, 1979-1994
  editor

1112

ELLEN DATLOW, Editor
TERRI WINDLING, Co-Editor

The Year's Best Fantasy and Horror: Seventh Annual Collection
(New York: St. Martin's, 1994)

Story type: Horror (Anthology; Fantasy)

Summary: The most recent installment in this World Fantasy Award-winning compilation of outstanding fantasy and horror fiction collects 54 stories from a wide range of mainstream and genre markets. Included are Fred Chappell's World Fantasy Award-winning "The Lodger," an amusing tale of a librarian possessed by the soul of a hack poet; John Coyne's psychological horror story, "Snow Man"; Elizabeth Hand's "The Erl King," which recasts the classic folk tale as a parable for the age of rock 'n' roll; Graham Masterton's "The Taking of Mr. Bill," Nicholas Royle's "The Crucian Pit," and Nancy Collins' "The Sunday-Go-to-Meeting Jaw," all zombie stories; Neil Gaiman's "Troll Bridge," a retelling of the story of the three Billy Goats gruff as a parable about aging gracelessly; Thomas Tessier's "The Last Crossing," a tale of marital infidelity and murder; and Robert Westall's "In Camera," a mystery story with supernatural overtones. The book is prefaced with overviews of the year in horror, fantasy and film.

Other books you might like:
Karl Edward Wagner, *The Year's Best Horror Stories XXII*, 1994

1113

ELLEN DATLOW, Editor
TERRI WINDLING, Co-Editor

The Year's Best Fantasy and Horror: Sixth Annual Collection
(New York: St. Martin's, 1993)

Story type: Horror (Anthology; Fantasy)

Summary: The sixth installment in this award-winning annual series brings together 53 tales of fantasy and horror chosen by the editors as the best in their respective fields. Included are Poppy Brite's tale of the living dead in India, "Calcutta, Lord of Nerves"; Neil Gaiman's retelling of the fall of Lucifer as a hardboiled mystery, "Murder Mysteries"; Joyce Carol Oates' allegory of rigidly enforced sexual roles, "Martyrdom"; Ed Gorman's sensitive story of the stigma of deformity, "The Ugly File"; Clive Barker's spectral fantasy, "Hermione and the Moon"; and Peter Straub's tale of the heart of darkness in Vietnam, "The Ghost Village." The editors and critic Ed Bryant provide invaluable overviews of the year in fantasy, horror and film.

Other books you might like:
Stephen Jones, *Best New Horror 4*, 1993
  Ramsey Campbell, co-editor
Karl Edward Wagner, *The Year's Best Horror Stories XXI*, 1993
  editor

1114

ELLEN DATLOW, Editor
TERRI WINDLING, Co-Editor

The Year's Best Fantasy and Horror: Third Annual Collection
(New York: St. Martin's, 1990)

Story type: Horror (Anthology; Fantasy)

Summary: Forty-seven tales of fantasy and horror representing the best short fiction from mainstream and genre publications for 1989. The outstanding horror selections include Gary Kilworth's mystical "White Noise"; Lisa Tuttle's coming-of-age tale "The Walled Garden"; Fred Chappell's witty addition to the Cthulhu Mythos "The Adder"; Jonathan Carroll's surprisingly nasty "Mr. Fiddlehead"; and Ramsey Campbell's even nastier "Meeting the Author."

Other books you might like:
Peter Enfantino, *Quick Chills*, 1990
Stephen Jones, *Best New Horror*, 1990
  Ramsey Campbell, co-author
Karl Edward Wagner, *The Year's Best Horror Stories XVIII*, 1990

1115

JAMES F. DAVID

Footprints of Thunder

(New York: Forge, 1995)

Story type: Science Fiction (Disaster; Science Fantasy)
Major character(s): Scott McIntyre, Political Figure (U.S. president); Petra Zalewski, Student—College, Adventurer; Colter Swenson, Student—College, Adventurer
Time period(s): 1990s
Locale(s): Oregon; Washington, District of Columbia; Florida

Summary: When the barrier of time breaks down and dinosaurs appear in the modern world, some common folk and politicians scramble to address the catastrophe while other people take advantage of the chaos.

Other books you might like:
Robert T. Bakker, *Raptor Red*, 1995
Michael Crichton, *Jurassic Park*, 1990
Michael Crichton, *The Lost World*, 1995
Arthur Conan Doyle, *The Lost World*, 1912
Harry Adam Knight, *Carnosaur*, 1984
Stephen Leigh, *Ray Bradbury Presents: Dinosaur World*, 1992

1116

PETER DAVID
MICHAEL JAN FRIEDMAN, Co-Author
ROBERT GREENBERGER, Co-Author

The Disinherited

(New York: Pocket, 1992)

Story type: Science Fiction (Space Opera)
Series: Star Trek
Major character(s): Uhura, Military Personnel (Starfleet lieutenant), Space Explorer; Pavel Chekov, Military Personnel (Starfleet ensign), Space Explorer; James T. Kirk, Spaceship Captain
Time period(s): 23rd century
Locale(s): Rithra, Planet—Imaginary; *U.S.S. Enterprise*, Spaceship

Summary: Starfleet sends the *Enterprise* to protect the remaining population of the Xaridian system, now devastated by surprise attacks on three of the planets by unknown spaceships. An over-eager Ensign Chekov finds himself confined to quarters, but regains his place on the bridge crew. On temporary assignment to assist in translating the language of the Rithrim people for a diplomatic mission, Lieutenant Uhura discovers secrets on Rithra that hold the key to dealing with the attacks on the Xaridian worlds.

Other books you might like:
Orson Scott Card, *Ender's Game*, 1985
C.J. Cherryh, *The Faded Sun: Kesrith*, 1978
Diane Duane, *Doctor's Orders*, 1990
Julia Ecklar, *The Kobayashi Maru*, 1989
Janet Kagan, *Uhura's Song*, 1985
Joan D. Vinge, *The Outcasts of Heaven Belt*, 1978

1117

PETER DAVID

Imzadi

(New York: Pocket, 1992)

Story type: Science Fiction (Space Opera; Alternate Universe)
Series: Star Trek: The Next Generation
Major character(s): Deanna Troi, Psychologist, Empath; William T. Riker, Military Personnel (Starfleet), Space Explorer; Data, Android, Military Personnel (Starfleet)
Time period(s): 25th century; 24th century
Locale(s): Betazed, Planet—Imaginary; Forever World, Planet—Imaginary; United Federation of Planets, Interstellar Empire/Federation

Summary: While temporarily assigned to a dirtball Federation embassy, young and lusty Lieutenant William Riker rescues Deanna Troi from a kidnapper then tumbles into a brief but torrid sexual relationship during which the pair merges souls, thus becoming *imzadi* and leaving them fully telepathic with each other. Later, Deanna's inexplicable death robs Will of zest for life and enjoyment of the subsequent 40 years of his Starfleet career. In charge of Starbase 86, "Starbase Dead End," and nearing retirement, Admiral Riker learns that the Guardian of Forever, an alternate intelligence time travel device, has isolated a minor 24th-century time anomaly centered around Deanna Troi, whereupon Riker threatens his entire timeline in a desperate leap back in time to save his *imzadi*.

Other books you might like:
A.C. Crispin, *Yesterday's Son*, 1983
Michael Jan Friedman, *Fortune's Light*, 1991
Barbara Hambly, *Ishmael*, 1985
Laurell K. Hamilton, *Nightshade*, 1992
Howard Weinstein, *Perchance to Dream*, 1991
Howard Weinstein, *Power Hungry*, 1989

1118

PETER DAVID

Q-in-Law

(New York: Pocket, 1991)

Story type: Science Fiction (Space Opera; Humor)
Series: Star Trek: The Next Generation
Major character(s): Jean-Luc Picard, Spaceship Captain, Military Personnel; Q, Alien; Lwaxana Troi, Telepath, Alien (Betazed)
Time period(s): 24th century
Locale(s): *U.S.S. Enterprise*, Spaceship; Outer Space

Summary: The *U.S.S. Enterprise* is the site of the marriage of Kerin and Sehra, whose joining will also unite their rival families. When a curious Q arrives to probe this human emotion, he and Lwaxana Troi find each other. Q's machinations cause emotions to run so high that a blood feud is declared.

Other books you might like:
Diane Carey, *Ghost Ship*, 1988
Carmen Carter, *The Children of Hamlin*, 1988

C.J. Cherryh, *The Pride of Chanur*, 1982
Gene DeWeese, *The Peacekeepers*, 1988
Diane Duane, *Spock's World*, 1989
James H. Schmitz, *The Witches of Karres*, 1966

1119

PETER DAVID

Q-Squared

(New York: Pocket, 1994)

Story type: Science Fiction (Space Opera; Psychic Powers)
Series: Star Trek: The Next Generation
Major character(s): Jean-Luc Picard, Spaceship Captain, Military Personnel; Jack Crusher, Spaceship Captain; Q, Alien
Time period(s): 24th century
Locale(s): *U.S.S. Enterprise*, Spaceship

Summary: Q takes on the job of teaching the young Trelane, another transcendently powerful being who has had dealings with the *Enterprise* crew in the past. But even Q has trouble keeping the rebellious youngster under control, and when Trelane's creation of temporal anomalies leads to the intersection of multiple alternate universes, Picard and Q join forces to save the universe.

Other books you might like:
Diane Duane, *Dark Mirror*, 1993
Barbara Hambly, *Ishmael*, 1985
Terry Pratchett, *Mort*, 1989
Della Van Hise, *Killing Time*, 1985
Gore Vidal, *Visit to a Small Planet*, 1956

1120

PETER DAVID

The Rift

(New York: Pocket, 1991)

Story type: Science Fiction (Space Opera; First Contact)
Series: Star Trek
Major character(s): Spock, Scientist, Alien (Vulcan); Christopher Pike, Spaceship Captain; James T. Kirk, Spaceship Captain
Time period(s): 23rd century
Locale(s): *U.S.S. Enterprise*, Spaceship; Calligar, Planet—Imaginary

Summary: The *Enterprise* encounters a "rift" in the fabric of space-time that is a gateway to a distant sector of the galaxy where the people of the Calligar Worldnet live. Captain Pike and his officers meet with the Calligar leaders, who are not sure they want to have close contact with the Federation. 33.4 years later, the *Enterprise*, now commanded by James Kirk, has returned to establish relations, a job made more difficult when the Federation delegation is held hostage by the Calligar.

Other books you might like:
Margaret Wander Bonanno, *Strangers From the Sky*, 1987
C.J. Cherryh, *Port Eternity*, 1982
Diane Duane, *The Wounded Sky*, 1983
D.C. Fontana, *Vulcan's Glory*, 1989

R.A. MacAvoy, *The Book of Kells*, 1985
Vonda N. McIntyre, *The Entropy Effect*, 1981
Della Van Hise, *Killing Time*, 1985

1121

PETER DAVID

Vendetta

(New York: Pocket, 1991)

Story type: Science Fiction (Space Opera)
Series: Star Trek: The Next Generation
Major character(s): Jean-Luc Picard, Spaceship Captain, Military Personnel; Guinan, Saloon Keeper/Owner, Alien; Geordi La Forge, Engineer, Military Personnel
Time period(s): 24th century
Locale(s): *U.S.S. Enterprise*, Spaceship

Summary: The machine-like Borg have nearly demolished the Penzatti homeworld when their fleet is annihilated by another ship. When the *Enterprise* is ordered to the scene, Picard meets Guinan's adopted sister, Delcara, the sole survivor of an earlier Borg attack. Delcara controls a planet-destroying weapon built by an extinct people for the purpose of exacting revenge on the Borg, who destroyed their race.

Other books you might like:
C.J. Cherryh, *Serpent's Reach*, 1980
Carolyn Clowes, *The Pandora Principle*, 1990
A.C. Crispin, *The Eyes of the Beholders*, 1990
Gordon R. Dickson, *The Forever Man*, 1986
Anne McCaffrey, *The Ship Who Sang*, 1970

1122

PETER DAVID

What Savage Beast

(New York: Putnam Boulevard, 1995)

Story type: Science Fiction (Alternate Universe; Adventure)
Series: Incredible Hulk
Major character(s): Robert Bruce "Incredible Hulk" Banner, Scientist; Elizabeth "Betty Tanner" Banner, Spouse; Leonard "Doc" Samson, Doctor (psychiatrist)
Time period(s): 1990s; 22nd century
Locale(s): Chicago, Illinois; The Crossroads, Mythical Place (time nexus); Alternate Earth

Summary: Desperate to escape his current circumstances, including harassment by the military and difficulty providing his wife with a normal life, Dr. Banner undergoes experimental surgery, not comprehending the problems it will cause for himself and for his offspring.

Other books you might like:
Greg Cox, *Iron Man: The Armor Trap*, 1995
Diane Duane, *Spider-Man: The Venom Factor*, 1994
Stan Lee, *The Ultimate Silver Surfer*, 1995
    editor
Stan Lee, *The Ultimate Spider-Man*, 1994
    editor
David Michelinie, *Spider-Man: Carnage in New York*, 1995
    Dean Wesley Smith, co-author

John Varley, *Superheroes*, 1995
  Ricia Mainhardt, co-editor
Len Wein, *Stalker From the Stars*, 1978
  Marv Wolfman, Joseph Silva, co-authors

1123
PETER DAVID

Worf's First Adventure
(New York: Pocket Minstrel, 1993)

Story type: Science Fiction (Young Adult; Adventure)
Series: Star Trek: The Next Generation—Starfleet Academy
Major character(s): Worf Rozhenko, Alien (Klingon), Student; Soleta, Alien (Vulcan), Student; Mark McHenry, Scientist (mathematician), Student
Time period(s): 24th century
Locale(s): San Francisco, California (Starfleet Academy)

Summary: As a new cadet, Worf Rozhenko experiences some difficulty adjusting to life at Starfleet Academy, but begins to form friendships with other cadets, both human and extraterrestrial. A disastrous raid by Romulans presents unexpected challenges to Worf during his first mission.

Other books you might like:
Bruce Coville, *My Teacher Flunked the Planet*, 1992
A.C. Crispin, *Shadow World*, 1991
  Jannean Elliott, co-author
A.C. Crispin, *Silent Dances*, 1990
  Kathleen O'Malley, co-author
A.C. Crispin, *Starbridge*, 1989
Paul Davids, *The Glove of Darth Vader*, 1992
  Hollace Davids, co-author
Paul Davids, *The Lost City of the Jedi*, 1992

1124
PAUL DAVIDS
HOLLACE DAVIDS, Co-Author

The Glove of Darth Vader
(New York: Bantam Skylark, 1992)

Story type: Science Fiction (Young Adult; Space Opera)
Series: Star Wars
Major character(s): Luke Skywalker, Martial Arts Expert (Jedi Knight), Hero; Trioculus, Imposter (emperor's son), Ruler (emperor); C-3PO, Robot, Adventurer
Time period(s): Indeterminate Past
Locale(s): Kessel, Planet—Imaginary; Calamari, Planet—Imaginary

Summary: Aided by trickery, Trioculus poses as the deceased Emperor's son and declares himself Emperor with the help of the Central Committee of Grand Moffs. Trioculus then travels to Calamari to recover Darth Vader's indestructable glove, the symbol of great power. On Calamari, Trioculus finds himself opposed by Luke Skywalker, who is involved in freeing the exploited Whaladons. Contains a seven-page glossary and four-page biography of authors and illustrators.

Other books you might like:
Bonnie Bogart, *The Ewoks Join the Fight*, 1983

Amy Ehrlich, *The Ewoks and the Lost Children*, 1985
James Howe, *How the Ewoks Saved the Trees: An Old Ewok Legend*, 1984
Joe Johnston, *The Adventures of Peebo: A Tale of Magic and Suspense*, 1984
Melinda Luke, *The Baby Ewok's Picnic Surprise*, 1984
Melinda Luke, *Wicket Finds a Way: An Ewok Adventure*, 1984

1125
PAUL DAVIDS
HOLLACE DAVIDS, Co-Author

The Lost City of the Jedi
(New York: Bantam Skylark, 1992)

Story type: Science Fiction (Young Adult; Space Opera)
Series: Star Wars
Major character(s): Luke Skywalker, Martial Arts Expert (Jedi Knight), Hero; Trioculus, Imposter (emperor's son), Ruler (emperor); Ken, Teenager, Student (Jedi Knight)
Time period(s): Indeterminate Past
Locale(s): Lost City of the Jedi, Fictional City; Yavin Four, Moon—Imaginary

Summary: Warned of the threat to his rule posed by a Jedi Prince living in the Lost City of the Jedi, Trioculus searches Yavin Four. Failing to find the entrance to the legendary Lost City, Trioculus releases weapons which ignite the rainforests of Yavin Four, source of thousands of medicines used throughout the galaxy. Utilizing an access code given him in a vision by Obi-Wan Kenobi, Luke activates a weather control system within the Lost City in an attempt to save the planet. Contains a five-page glossary and three-page biography of authors and illustrators.

Other books you might like:
Bonnie Bogart, *The Ewoks Join the Fight*, 1983
Amy Ehrlich, *The Ewoks and the Lost Children*, 1985
James Howe, *How the Ewoks Saved the Trees: An Old Ewok Legend*, 1984
Joe Johnston, *The Adventures of Peebo: A Tale of Magic and Suspense*, 1984
Melinda Luke, *The Baby Ewok's Picnic Surprise*, 1984
Melinda Luke, *Wicket Finds a Way: An Ewok Adventure*, 1984

1126
PAUL DAVIDS
HOLLACE DAVIDS, Co-Author

Zorba the Hutt's Revenge
(New York: Bantam Skylark, 1992)

Story type: Science Fiction (Young Adult; Space Opera)
Series: Star Wars
Major character(s): Leia Organa, Royalty (princess), Diplomat; Zorba the Hutt, Alien, Parent (Jabba the Hutt's); Trioculus, Imposter (emperor's son), Ruler (emperor)
Time period(s): Indeterminate Past

Locale(s): Cloud City, Fictional City; Tatooine, Planet—Imaginary

Summary: When Zorba the Hutt discovers that his son died at the hands of Princess Leia, he travels to Cloud City to exact revenge on the Princess. After he cheats Lando Calrissian to gain control of Cloud City, Zorba must acquire the Princess from Trioculus who hopes to make her his queen. Contains a five-page glossary of terms and three-page biography of authors and illustrators.

Other books you might like:

Bonnie Bogart, *The Ewoks Join the Fight*, 1983
Amy Ehrlich, *The Ewoks and the Lost Children*, 1985
James Howe, *How the Ewoks Saved the Trees: An Old Ewok Legend*, 1984
Joe Johnston, *The Adventures of Peebo: A Tale of Magic and Suspense*, 1984
Melinda Luke, *The Baby Ewok's Picnic Surprise*, 1984
Melinda Luke, *Wicket Finds a Way: An Ewok Adventure*, 1984

1127

ROBERTSON DAVIES

The Cornish Trilogy

(New York: Penguin, 1992)

Story type: Fantasy (Collection; Contemporary)
Major character(s): Francis Cornish, Artist, Philanthropist; Maria Magdalena Theotohy, Scholar; Simon Darcourt, Religious (Anglican priest), Scholar
Time period(s): 1980s
Locale(s): Mythical Place (College of St. John and the Holy Ghost); Germany; Toronto, Ontario, Canada

Summary: Originally published as *The Rebel Angels* (1982), *What's Bred in the Bone* (1986) and *The Lyre of Orpheus* (1989), this omnibus relates the complicated story of Francis Cornish and the foundation he endowed on his death. The story is full of mystery, scholarship, comedy, history, angels, spirits and a bizarre murder revolving around the lonely figure of Francis Cornish, a man whose life locked him in a shell of history. The narration wraps Cornish in a web of monks, gypsies, professors, artists and mountebanks showing the impact of one individual on a curious world.

Other books you might like:

James P. Blaylock, *The Paper Grail*, 1991
Lindsay Clarke, *The Chymical Wedding*, 1989
John Crowley, *Little, Big*, 1981
Umberto Eco, *Foucault's Pendulum*, 1989
Fay Weldon, *Letters to Alice on First Reading Jane Austen*, 1984

1128

BRETT DAVIS

The Faery Convention

(New York: Baen, 1995)

Story type: Fantasy (Light Fantasy; Political)

Major character(s): Joe Cork, Mythical Creature (half-elf), Government Official (Congressional investigator); Ellen King, Receptionist; Merlin, Wizard, Leader
Time period(s): 21st century
Locale(s): Washington, District of Columbia

Summary: A plot by shapeshifters threatens to foil the Grimm Accord, a Congressional Act establishing a homeland for supernatural creatures within Texas and Oklahoma. While Joe and Ellen investigate, Merlin advances the wizards' control of U.S. weaponry. First novel.

Other books you might like:

Charles de Lint, *Memory and Dream*, 1994
Laurell K. Hamilton, *Guilty Pleasures*, 1993
Nick Pollotta, *Bureau 13*, 1991
Clifford D. Simak, *Out of Their Minds*, 1970
Michael Swanwick, *In the Drift*, 1985
Sheri S. Tepper, *A Plague of Angels*, 1993
Harry Turtledove, *The Case of the Toxic Spell Dump*, 1993
Gary K. Wolf, *Who Censored Roger Rabbit?*, 1981

1129

DON DAVIS
JAY DAVIS, Co-Author

Bring on the Night

(New York: Tor, 1993)

Story type: Horror (Vampire Story)
Major character(s): Dennis Coglin, Detective—Police; Nathan Kane, Vampire; Corky Washburn, Morgue Attendant (Nathan's aide)
Time period(s): 1990s (1993)
Locale(s): Chicago, Illinois

Summary: Nathan Kane moves to Chicago and uses the tactics of a contemporary serial killer to cover up his regular vampiric feastings.

Other books you might like:

Charles L. Grant, *The Soft Whisper of the Dead*, 1982
Stephen King, *Salem's Lot*, 1975
Robert R. McCammon, *They Thirst*, 1981
Bram Stoker, *Dracula*, 1897
Les Whitten, *Progeny of the Adder*, 1965

1130

DON DAVIS
JAY DAVIS, Co-Author

Sins of the Flesh

(New York: Tor, 1989)

Story type: Horror (Serial Killer)
Major character(s): Stephen Sikes, Young Man; Jesse Sikes, Murderer (Stephen's uncle), Monster (Shape-changing Wendigo)
Time period(s): 1960s (1968); 1980s (1988)
Locale(s): Gideon, Missouri; Kennett, Missouri

Summary: A black magician's curse turns Jesse Sikes into a semi-human serial killer. For twenty years his mother's occult powers imprison him, but upon her death he is freed to terrorize the townspeople. His nephew Stephen, the last of the Sikes, is the only person with the knowledge and ability to stop Jesse—if he has the courage and resourcefulness.

Other books you might like:
Les Whitten, *Moon of the Wolf*, 1967

1131
JAKE DAVIS

Destination: Showdown
(New York: Berkley, 1993)

Story type: Science Fiction (Post-Holocaust)
Series: Last Rangers
Major character(s): Alamo Smith, Lawman; APU-805 "Bird Dog", Robot, Military Personnel
Time period(s): 2030s (2035)
Locale(s): Texas (southwest border badlands)

Summary: When the evil leaders of a post-disaster city-state discover the underground organization led by Alamo Smith, the freedom fighter and Bird Dog must rush to keep an ultimate weapon from the overlords.

Other books you might like:
David Alexander, *Death Race*, 1992
David Alexander, *Nomad*, 1992
David Brin, *The Postman*, 1985
Bill Dolan, *Afrikorps*, 1991
Bill Dolan, *Iron Horse*, 1991
Michael D. Weaver, *My Father Immortal*, 1989

1132
JAKE DAVIS

The Last Rangers
(New York: Berkley, 1992)

Story type: Science Fiction (Post-Holocaust; Adventure)
Major character(s): Alamo Smith, Lawman; APU-805 "Bird Dog", Robot, Military Personnel; Rima, Prostitute
Time period(s): 2030s (2035)
Locale(s): Texas (southwest border badlands)

Summary: After a devastating war with the Red Chinese and continued environmental degradation, law and order in the United States breaks down, leaving the people at the mercy of vicious gangs. In Texas, the underground force of high-tech avengers, the Last Rangers, provides some hope for justice to the deteriorating frontier society along the southern border.

Other books you might like:
Robert Cain, *Cybernarc*, 1991
Mark Grant, *Mutants Amok*, 1991
   pseudonym of David Bischoff
Ed Naha, *Robocop*, 1987
David Robbins, *Yellowstone Run*, 1990
William Shatner, *TekWar*, 1989
G. Harry Stine, *Sierra Madre*, 1988

1133
MARGARET DAVIS

Mind Light
(New York: Ballantine Del Rey, 1993)

Story type: Science Fiction (First Contact)
Major character(s): Kiley Michaelson, Businesswoman, Pilot (spaceship); Greg Lukas, Spaceman, Pilot (spaceship)
Time period(s): Indeterminate Future
Locale(s): *Widdon Galaxy*, Spaceship; Jeross, Space Station

Summary: Desperate for any relief pilot, Kiley Michaelson hires the intoxicated and apparently ill Greg Lukas as a temporary solution, fearful she has acquired new problems for the family's spaceship. The family soon realizes Greg's unusual piloting skills result from Space Academy training, but must remain curious about his subsequent court martial. When the Space Corps becomes interested in reopening Greg's case, *Widdon Galaxy* flees to the site of Greg's crimes, where the ship finds interest among the first aliens to contact humans. Author's first book.

Other books you might like:
Roger MacBride Allen, *The Ring of Charon*, 1990
Eleanor Arnason, *Ring of Swords*, 1993
Alis A. Rasmussen, *A Passage of Stars*, 1990
Alis A. Rasmussen, *The Price of Ransom*, 1990
Alis A. Rasmussen, *Revolution's Shore*, 1990
David Alexander Smith, *Homecoming*, 1990
David Alexander Smith, *Rendezvous*, 1988

1134
MARGARET DAVIS

Minds Apart
(New York: Ballantine Del Rey, 1994)

Story type: Science Fiction (First Contact)
Major character(s): Daniel Keenan, Doctor (psychiatrist); Sensar, Alien (Gan-Tir), Teacher; Greg Lukas, Spaceman, Pilot (spaceship)
Time period(s): Indeterminate Future
Locale(s): *Widdon Galaxy*, Spaceship

Summary: Wanting to deal only with Daniel Keenan, the newly contacted aliens, the Gan-Tir, hire the *Widdon Galaxy* to bring representatives into human space for a conference. Keenan hates and fears the Gan-Tir as well as fearing Greg Lukas' Quayla symbiont, who drains Lukas. When the Gan-Tir decide to return home without seeing human representatives, they become mired in a barrier and require Keenan's help.

Other books you might like:
Eleanor Arnason, *Ring of Swords*, 1993
Octavia E. Butler, *Adulthood Rites*, 1988
Jacqueline Lichtenberg, *House of Zeor*, 1974
Rebecca Ore, *Becoming Alien*, 1987
Jack Vance, *The Anome*, 1973

1135

CHET DAY

The Hacker

(New York: Pocket, 1989)

Story type: Horror (Techno-Horror)
Major character(s): Succubus, Computer Expert, Murderer; Dennis "Tunnel Rat" Conlick, Computer Expert (Head of "The Surgery" computer)
Time period(s): 1980s
Locale(s): New Orleans, Louisiana

Summary: The Surgery, a "network" of computer experts working on a secret government project, is broken into by the Succubus, a psychotic, vindictive computer genius, who begins to pick off the Surgery members one by one while he steals their discoveries in an attempt to turn himself into a "god."

Other books you might like:
Herbert Lieberman, *City of the Dead*, 1976
F. Paul Wilson, *The Touch*, 1986

1136

LOUIS DE BERNIERES

Senor Vivo and the Coca Lord

(New York: Morrow, 1992)

Story type: Fantasy (Contemporary; Quest)
Major character(s): Dionisio Vivo, Critic (social), Patriot; Ramon Dario, Police Officer; Anica, Girlfriend
Time period(s): 1990s
Locale(s): South America

Summary: A prominent lecturer, Dionisio Vivo, criticizes a system corrupted by illegal coca trade. When an assassination attempt fails, Ramon warns Dionisio of the perils of his behavior. Dionisio, however, remains driven to fight the corruption despite the adverse effects to his relationships and friends.

Other books you might like:
Marjorie Agosin, *The Secret Weavers: Stories of the Fantastic by Latin American Women*, 1991
editor
Philip K. Dick, *A Scanner Darkly*, 1977
Philip K. Dick, *The Three Stigmata of Palmer Eldritch*, 1965
editor
Gabriel Garcia Marquez, *One Hundred Years of Solitude*, 1970
Ben Okri, *The Famished Road*, 1992

1137

LOUIS DE BERNIERES

The War of Don Emmanuel's Nether Parts

(New York: Morrow, 1992)

Story type: Fantasy (Satire; Political)
Major character(s): Aurelio, Indian, Shaman; Constanza Evans, Socialite; Asado, Military Personnel, Criminal

Time period(s): 1990s
Locale(s): South America

Summary: Directionless revolutionaries attempt to overthrow the government, precipitating vicious and repressive tactics designed to maintain governmental authority while Constanza's excesses heat up revolutionary fire. His village destroyed, Aurelio escapes from the mountains to the jungle where he learns magical arts. After leading village resistance to government attacks, Aurelio sets off with the villagers to settle new territory and create a peaceful society accompanied by magical cats which improve the humor of anyone they meet. Author's first novel.

Other books you might like:
Marjorie Agosin, *The Secret Weavers: Stories of the Fantastic by Latin American Women*, 1991
editor
Gabriel Garcia Marquez, *One Hundred Years of Solitude*, 1970
editor
Ben Okri, *The Famished Road*, 1992
Elizabeth Ann Scarborough, *Nothing Sacred*, 1991
Kurt Vonnegut Jr., *Cat's Cradle*, 1963

1138

L. SPRAGUE DE CAMP, Editor
CHRISTOPHER STASHEFF, Co-Editor

The Enchanter Reborn

(New York: Baen, 1992)

Story type: Fantasy (Anthology; Light Fantasy)
Series: Harold Shea
Major character(s): Harold Shea, Psychologist, Adventurer; Reed Chalmers, Psychologist, Adventurer

Summary: Contains a six-page introduction and three stories by Christopher Stasheff plus two stories by Holly Lisle and John Maddox Roberts developed from outlines by de Camp and Stasheff. Featuring Harold Shea, each story visits the universe of myths and literary adventures including characters from the Buddhist pantheon, classical mythology, Oz and *Don Quixote*.

Other books you might like:
Craig Shaw Gardner, *Slaves of the Volcano God*, 1989
Holly Lisle, *Fire in the Mist*, 1992
Clifford D. Simak, *Out of Their Minds*, 1970
Christopher Stasheff, *Her Majesty's Wizard*, 1986
Christopher Stasheff, *The Warlock in Spite of Himself*, 1969

1139

L. SPRAGUE DE CAMP

The Hand of Zei

(New York: Baen Books, 1990)

Story type: Science Fiction (Adventure)
Series: Viagens Interplanetarias
Major character(s): Dirk Barnevelt, Writer; George Tangaloa, Scientist
Time period(s): Indeterminate Future

Locale(s): Krishna, Planet—Imaginary

Summary: Dirk Barnevelt, who for years has been chronicling the adventures of others on the wild and dangerous planet Krishna, finally gets a chance to go there himself when his boss, a famous explorer, disappears on an undercover mission. All advanced technology is prohibited on Krishna, so Barnevelt finds ample opportunity for swashbuckling, swordplay, and derring do. Originally published in 1963.

Other books you might like:
Edgar Rice Burroughs, *Pirates of Venus*, 1934
Edgar Rice Burroughs, *A Princess of Mars*, 1917
Edgar Rice Burroughs, *Synthetic Men of Mars*, 1940
Poul Anderson, *Hoka!*, 1983
   Gordon R. Dickson, co-author
Robert A. Heinlein, *Glory Road*, 1963
R.A. MacAvoy, *The Third Eagle: Lessons Along a Minor String*, 1989

1140

L. SPRAGUE DE CAMP

The Honorable Barbarian
(New York: Del Rey, 1989)

Story type: Fantasy (Adventure)
Series: Unbeheaded King
Major character(s): Kerin, Barbarian
Time period(s): Indeterminate
Locale(s): Alternate Universe

Summary: Found in an awkward situation with the daughter of a prominent man, Kerin is sent on an ocean voyage. Originally dispatched by his older brother the king to the east to learn the secret of a clock escapement, Kerin encounters many misadventures. These include an amorous captain's mistress, a hermit wizard on a desert isle, capture by pirates, a princess in need and at last a meeting with the Emperor of the East who believes Kerin to have an important secret to reveal.

Other books you might like:
David Drake, *The Sea Hag*, 1988
   Book 1-The World of Crystal Walls
Geoffrey Marsh, *Fangs and the Hooded Demon*, 1988

1141

L. SPRAGUE DE CAMP
CATHERINE CROOK DE CAMP, Co-Author

The Pixilated Peeress
(New York: Ballantine/Del Rey, 1991)

Story type: Fantasy (Adventure)
Major character(s): Thorolf Zigramson, Scholar, Military Personnel; Yvette of Grintz, Runaway, Noblewoman; Wok, Leader, Mythical Creature (troll)
Time period(s): Indeterminate
Locale(s): Rhaetia, Fictional Country

Summary: Sergeant Thorolf Zigramson encounters the fugitive Countess Yvette of Grintz who can think of nothing but regaining her estates and escaping her noble, would-be husband. Accidentally turned into an octopus, her only cure is to be possessed by a Delta and then imprisoned by Sophonomists. Thorolf, thoroughly smitten, seeks to rescue her but is captured by Trolls. He manages to forge an alliance with them and rescue Yvette, who spurns him. When Thorolf becomes a mercenary and weds a foreign bride, Yvette belatedly decides she loves him.

Other books you might like:
Piers Anthony, *On a Pale Horse*, 1983
Robert Asprin, *Another Fine Myth*, 1978
Alan Dean Foster, *Spellsinger*, 1983
Christopher Stasheff, *The Warlock Rock*, 1990
Sheri S. Tepper, *King's Blood Four*, 1983

1142

L. SPRAGUE DE CAMP

Rivers of Time
(New York: Baen, 1993)

Story type: Science Fiction (Collection; Time Travel)
Major character(s): Reginald Rivers, Guide, Time Traveller
Time period(s): Indeterminate Past (Paleocene; Pleistocene)
Locale(s): Earth

Summary: Contains two original stories, a newly revised version of "A Gun for Dinosaur," and six stories from 1990s periodicals and an anthology. Stories feature Reginald Rivers who leads deep-pocket clients in perilous pursuit of the biggest big game of all time.

Other books you might like:
Poul Anderson, *The Time Patrol*, 1991
Michael Crichton, *Jurassic Park*, 1990
Roger L. DiSilvestro, *Living with the Reptiles*, 1990
Arthur Conan Doyle, *The Lost World*, 1912
Stephen Leigh, *Dinosaur Samurai*, 1993
   John J. Miller, co-author
J.F. Rivkin, *Tyrannosaurus Rex*, 1992

1143

L. SPRAGUE DE CAMP
CATHERINE CROOK DE CAMP, Co-Author

The Swords of Zinjaban
(New York: Baen, 1991)

Story type: Science Fiction (Arts; Humor)
Series: Viagens Interplanetarias
Major character(s): Fergus Reith, Tour Guide, Divorced Person; Alicia "Lish" Dyckman, Producer (assistant), Divorced Person; Gilan "Gilan the Third" bad-Jam, Alien (Krishnan), Ruler (Dasht of Rue)
Time period(s): 22nd century
Locale(s): Krishna, Planet—Imaginary (Tau Ceti System)

Summary: This story begins 20 years after Alicia left Krishna when Reith would not accept a reconciliation for their marriage. Reith discovers his latest tour presents unusual problems. His former marriage to the Cosmic Productions' employee complicates filming the motion picture they've come to make, as does Reith's former marriage to a potential mate of Gilan the Third who, making matters worse, has imprisoned Reith. A two-page introduction by the co-author summarizes three previous Krishna books.

Other books you might like:
Terry Bisson, *Voyage to the Red Planet*, 1990
Pat Cadigan, *Synners*, 1991
Craig Shaw Gardner, *Slaves of the Volcano God*, 1989
Harry Harrison, *The Technicolor Time Machine*, 1967
John Varley, *Demon*, 1984
Ian Watson, *Chekhov's Journey*, 1989

1144

L. SPRAGUE DE CAMP
DAVID DRAKE, Co-Author

The Undesired Princess and the Enchanted Bunny

(New York: Baen, 1990)

Story type: Fantasy (Light Fantasy; Alternate World)
Major character(s): Rollin Hobart, Engineer (consulting); Joe Johnson, Writer (ghostwriter)
Time period(s): 1990s (1990); Indeterminate
Locale(s): Loggia, Fictional Country; Hamisch, Fictional Country

Summary: This book contains two separate stories on a theme. A contemporary American male finds himself suddenly and unexpectedly transported to. . .somewhere else. . .where magic works, where the technology and social structure are medieval (magical) creatures, swords, wagons, castles, kings, beautiful princesses, etc. There is a menace to be surmounted and the reluctant hero tries to use his modern knowledge to help and discovers things don't quite work the way they do back home, and must adjust. David Drake's story is an homage to L. Sprague de Camp's stories in this sub-genre.

Other books you might like:
Jack L. Chalker, *The River of the Dancing Gods*, 1984
Rick Cook, *Wizard's Bane*, 1989
Brian Daley, *The Doomfarers of Coramonde*, 1977
Alan Dean Foster, *Quozl*, 1989
Barbara Hambly, *The Silent Tower*, 1988
Eric Frank Russell, *The Space Willies*, 1958
Mark Twain, *A Connecticut Yankee in King Arthur's Court*, 1889
    Pseudonym of Samuel Clemens

1145

L. SPRAGUE DE CAMP

The Venom Trees of Sunga

(New York: Ballantine Del Rey, 1992)

Story type: Science Fiction (Humor; Adventure)
Major character(s): Kirk Salazar, Student, Traveller; Alexis Ritter, Religious (high priestess), Leader; George Cantemir, Businessman, Criminal (ecological)
Time period(s): Indeterminate Future
Locale(s): Sunga, Planet—Imaginary

Summary: While visiting Sunga to advance his study of the ecology of Sunga's venom tree forest, Kirk Salazar travels

with a tour group to save money. Salazar's studies suffer through the efforts of Alexis Ritter, who lusts after Salazar despite her cult's dedication to chastity, and by George Cantemir's arrangement with a local chieftain, that would furnish the entire forest for lumber.

Other books you might like:
Stephen Goldin, *Jade Darcy and the Zen Pirates*, 1990
    Mary Mason, co-author
Harry Harrison, *Bill, the Galactic Hero: On the Planet of Tasteless Pleasure*, 1991
    David Bischoff, co-author
Janet Kagan, *Mirabile*, 1991
James Luceno, *Illegal Alien*, 1990
Harry Turtledove, *Earthgrip*, 1992

1146

TOM DE HAVEN

The End-of-Everything Man

(New York: Doubleday, 1991)

Story type: Fantasy (Adventure)
Series: Chronicles of the King's Tramp
Major character(s): Peter Musik, Journalist; Jack, Traveller, Agent; Didge, Magician (dispeller)
Time period(s): Indeterminate
Locale(s): Lostwithal, Planet—Imaginary

Summary: Despite Jack and his allies' successes, the plans of the Mage of Four still threaten Lostwithal. Disasters and character flaws sink the travellers from Kemolo into misery and distraction. Everything will stop if Jack can't find out what's going on and save his allies.

Other books you might like:
Piers Anthony, *Split Infinity*, 1980
Ru Emerson, *The Calling of the Three*, 1990
Barbara Hambly, *The Time of the Dark*, 1982
Julian May, *The Many-Colored Land*, 1981
Tom Robbins, *Another Roadside Attraction*, 1971

1147

TOM DE HAVEN

The Last Human

(New York: Bantam Spectra, 1992)

Story type: Fantasy (Political; Quest)
Series: Chronicles of the King's Tramp
Major character(s): Jack, Traveller (Walker)
Time period(s): Indeterminate
Locale(s): Undermoment, Mythical Place (extra-dimensional meeting place)

Summary: Jack and his comrades work to defeat the deadly threat represented by the Last Human: the Queen of Noise, a creature which has escaped from another dimension to the Undermoment, while citizens of the three safe worlds meet in the Undermoment to achieve mutual understanding.

Other books you might like:
Philip Jose Farmer, *To Your Scattered Bodies Go*, 1971
Barbara Hambly, *The Time of the Dark*, 1982

Robert Jordan, *The Eye of the World*, 1989
Michael Moorcock, *The Fortress of the Pearl*, 1989
Margaret Weis, *Serpent Mage*, 1992
  Tracy Hickman, co-author

1148

TOM DE HAVEN

Walker of Worlds

(New York: Doubleday, 1990)

Story type: Fantasy (Contemporary)
Series: Chronicles of the King's Tramp
Major character(s): Jack, Traveller
Time period(s): Indeterminate
Locale(s): Earth

Summary: As elements of fantasy begin to intrude on the life of everyday people, the Walker begins his journeys between worlds.

Other books you might like:
Clive Barker, *Weaveworld*, 1987
John Crowley, *Little, Big*, 1981
Charles de Lint, *Drink Down the Moon*, 1990
Robert Holdstock, *Lavondyss: Journey to an Unknown Region*, 1989
Llywelyn Morgan, *The Isles of the Blest*, 1989

1149

CHARLES DE LINT

Dreams Underfoot

(New York: Tor, 1993)

Story type: Fantasy (Urban; Collection)

Summary: Contains two original and 17 stories reprinted from periodicals, anthologies and small press publications 1987-1993. The extra-natural elements in some stories infuse from outside the real world, while in others, elements intrinsic to the real world we know hide until pointed out. In yet others, the very concept of a "real" world comes into question.

Other books you might like:
Emma Bull, *Bone Dance*, 1991
Steven Brust, *Agyar*, 1993
Megan Lindholm, *Wizard of the Pigeons*, 1986
Terri Windling, *Elsewhere*, 1981
  Mark Alan Arnold, co-editor
Terri Windling, *Elsewhere II*, 1982
  Mark Alan Arnold, co-editor
Terri Windling, *Elsewhere III*, 1984
  Mark Alan Arnold, co-editor

1150

CHARLES DE LINT

Drink Down the Moon

(New York: Ace, 1990)

Story type: Fantasy (Contemporary)
Time period(s): 1990s

Locale(s): Earth
Summary: In this sequel to *Jack the Giant Killer*, the normal, everyday world comes in contact with an alternate world where magic works. The characters find themselves facing and dealing with far more than they ever thought they would.

Other books you might like:
Suzy McKee Charnas, *The Vampire Tapestry*, 1980
Tom De Haven, *Walker of Worlds*, 1990
Alan Dean Foster, *Spellsinger*, 1983
  Book 1 - Spellsinger Series
Esther Friesner, *Elf Defense*, 1988
Tanya Huff, *Gate of Darkness, Circle of Light*, 1989

1151

CHARLES DE LINT

Ghosts of Wind and Shadow

(Eugene, Oregon: Pulphouse Publishing, 1991)

Story type: Fantasy (Urban; Contemporary)
Major character(s): Meran Kelledy, Musician, Mythical Creature (faerie); Cerin Kelledy, Mythical Creature (faerie); Lesli Batterberry, Musician, Runaway
Time period(s): 1990s
Locale(s): California

Summary: When Lesli's mother notices and begins to discourage her belief in Faerie, Lesli runs away and then is abducted and imprisoned. Informed of Lesli's disappearance, Cerin sets out to find her using Faerie guidance.

Other books you might like:
Mercedes Lackey, *Bardic Voices*, 1991
Will Shetterly, *Elsewhere*, 1991
Will Shetterly, *Liavek: Wizard's Row*, 1987
  Emma Bull, co-editor
Terri Windling, *Borderland*, 1986
  Mark Alan Arnold, co-editor
Terri Windling, *Bordertown*, 1986
  Mark Alan Arnold, co-editor
Terri Windling, *Life on the Border*, 1991
  editor

1152

CHARLES DE LINT

Hedgework and Guessery

(Eugene, Oregon: Pulphouse Publishing, 1991)

Story type: Fantasy (Collection)
Series: Author's Choice Monthly

Summary: Issue 22 in the Author's Choice Monthly Series, this collection contains an introduction plus 7 poems (1978-1991) and 8 short stories (1986-1990), most having appeared in periodicals, anthologies, chapbooks and limited edition books.

Other books you might like:
Ellen Datlow, *The Year's Best Fantasy and Horror: Third Annual Collection*, 1990
  Terri Windling, co-editor

Ron Goulart, *Skyrocket Steele Conquers the Universe and Other Media Tales*, 1990
Damon Knight, *God's Nose*, 1991
Elizabeth A. Lynn, *Tales From a Vanished Country*, 1990
Judith Moffett, *Two That Came True*, 1991
Kim Stanley Robinson, *A Sensitive Dependence on Initial Conditions*, 1991
Spider Robinson, *True Minds*, 1990

1153

CHARLES DE LINT

The Hidden City

(New York: Bantam Spectra, 1990)

Story type: Fantasy (Alternate World; Adventure)
Series: Philip Jose Farmer's The Dungeon
Major character(s): Clive Folliot, Military Personnel
Time period(s): 1870s (1870); 1890s (1896)
Locale(s): Alternate Earth

Summary: The adventure of Clive Folliot through the nine levels of the Dungeon's computer game-like world are continued in the fifth volume.

Other books you might like:
Robin Bailey, *The Lake of Fire*, 1989
Bruce Coville, *The Dark Abyss*, 1989
Robert A. Heinlein, *Glory Road*, 1963
Richard A. Lupoff, *The Black Tower*, 1988
Richard A. Lupoff, *The Final Battle*, 1990
Gene Wolfe, *The Shadow of the Torturer*, 1980

1154

CHARLES DE LINT

Into the Green

(New York: Tor, 1993)

Story type: Fantasy (Adventure)
Major character(s): Angharad, Minstrel, Wanderer
Time period(s): Indeterminate
Locale(s): Kingdoms of the Green Isles, Fictional Country

Summary: Incorporates short stories reprinted from Marion Zimmer Bradley's *Sword and Sorceress* anthology series into the novel framework and portrays Angharad's travels and encounters with the kingdom's residents, some of whom exhibit prejudice toward those possessing unusual powers and one whose gruesome trade in body parts could not exist without the magically empowered. Concludes with four pages of musical notation for harp.

Other books you might like:
Gael Baudino, *Gossamer Axe*, 1990
Phyllis Eisenstein, *Born to Exile*, 1978
Phyllis Eisenstein, *In the Red Lord's Reach*, 1989
Mercedes Lackey, *Bardic Voices*, 1991
Andre Norton, *Songsmith*, 1992
 A.C. Crispin, co-author
Caroline Stevermer, *River Rats*, 1992

1155

CHARLES DE LINT

The Ivory and the Horn

(New York: Tor, 1995)

Story type: Fantasy (Collection; Urban)
Time period(s): 1990s
Locale(s): Newford, Canada

Summary: Contains one original and 14 stories reprinted from periodicals, anthologies and chapbooks 1992-1994. All are set in Newford, home to a wide variety of artists and site of many unusual occurrences as magic infuses the mundane world.

Other books you might like:
David Brin, *The River of Time*, 1986
John Crowley, *Antiquities*, 1993
Lisa Goldstein, *Travellers in Magic*, 1994
Robert Holdstock, *The Bone Forest*, 1992
Megan Lindholm, *Wizard of the Pigeons*, 1986
Pat Murphy, *Points of Departure*, 1990
Gene Wolfe, *Storeys From the Old Hotel*, 1992

1156

CHARLES DE LINT

The Little Country

(New York: Morrow, 1991)

Story type: Fantasy (Legend; Contemporary)
Major character(s): Janey Little, Musician (pipes and fiddle); Thomas Little, Aged Person (Janey's grandfather); Felix Gavin, Sailor, Musician
Time period(s): 1990s (1991)
Locale(s): Bodbury, England; Mousehole, England

Summary: Janey Little and her grandfather, Thomas, are hiding a very important book in their cottage. Although they only suspect that is has unusual properties, it seems that whenever it's opened, things begin to happen. As Janey reads the book, the adventures that befall the characters within the story begin to affect the lives of Janey, Thomas and the people around them.

Other books you might like:
Tom Deitz, *Sunshaker's War*, 1990
Michael Ende, *The Neverending Story*, 1983
Raymond E. Feist, *Faerie Tale*, 1988
William Goldman, *The Princess Bride*, 1973
Mercedes Lackey, *Knight of Ghosts and Shadows*, 1990
 Ellen Guon, co-author

1157

CHARLES DE LINT

Memory and Dream

(New York: Tor, 1994)

Story type: Fantasy (Contemporary; Horror)

Major character(s): Isabelle "Izzy" Copley, Artist (painter), Student—College; Katharine Mully, Writer, Lesbian; Vincent Adjani Rushkin, Artist (painter), Recluse
Time period(s): 1970s (1973-1979); 1990s (1992-1993)
Locale(s): Canada

Summary: Izzy studies under the master painter, Rushkin, despite his abusive, moody nature, learning his ability to create animated doppelgangers of some paintings' subjects, including characters from Katharine's stories. Despite premonitions and direct warnings, Izzy continues her affiliation with Rushkin as her career advances, little suspecting the dark future resulting from her actions.

Other books you might like:
Aaron Allston, *Galatea in 2-D*, 1993
Steven Brust, *Agyar*, 1993
Ben Okri, *The Famished Road*, 1992
Nancy Springer, *Larque on the Wing*, 1994
Sheri S. Tepper, *A Plague of Angels*, 1993

1158

CHARLES DE LINT

Our Lady of the Harbour

(Eugene, Oregon: Pulphouse Publishing, 1991)

Story type: Fantasy (Legend; Contemporary)
Major character(s): Matt Casey, Musician; Amy Scallan, Musician; Katrina, Mythical Creature (mermaid)
Time period(s): 1970s
Locale(s): Nowford, Fictional City

Summary: Matt Casey, a brilliant musician unable to relate to people, attracts the attention of a mermaid. She trades her tail for legs, but is cursed to die unless she can get him to love her. This story is a retelling of Hans Christian Andersen's "The Little Mermaid."

Other books you might like:
Gael Baudino, *Gossamer Axe*, 1990
Emma Bull, *War for the Oaks*, 1987
Pamela Dean, *Tam Lin*, 1991
Ellen Kushner, *Thomas the Rhymer*, 1990
Terri Windling, *Life on the Border*, 1991
  editor

1159

CHARLES DE LINT

Spiritwalk

(New York: Tor, 1992)

Story type: Fantasy (Collection; Urban)
Series: Tamson House
Time period(s): 1990s
Locale(s): Ottawa, Ontario, Canada

Summary: Combines "Merlin Dreams in the Mondrean Wood" plus *Ascian in Rose* (1987), *Westlin Wind* (1989) and *Ghostwood* (1990) relating events surrounding Tamson House, a huge and mysterious house containing paths to lands through which Native American and Celtic magic leaks into our world. Set in the universe of *Moonheart: A Romance*.

Other books you might like:
Gael Baudino, *Gossamer Axe*, 1990
Emma Bull, *War for the Oaks*, 1987
Mercedes Lackey, *Born to Run*, 1992
  Larry Dixon, co-author
Mercedes Lackey, *Summoned to Tourney*, 1992
  Ellen Guon, co-author
John Maddox Roberts, *King of the Wood*, 1983
Will Shetterly, *Elsewhere*, 1991
Terri Windling, *Borderland*, 1986
  Mark Alan Arnold, co-editor
Terri Windling, *Bordertown*, 1986
  Mark Alan Arnold, co-editor
Terri Windling, *Life on the Border*, 1991
  editor

1160

CHARLES DE LINT

Svaha

(New York: Ace, 1989)

Story type: Science Fiction (Cyberpunk)
Major character(s): Gahzee Animiki-Waewidum, Indian, Scientist; Shigehero Gorp, Criminal
Time period(s): 21st century
Locale(s): Canada

Summary: In the late twentieth century, most of western civilization collapsed beneath the weight of its own pollution and corruption. The Native American peoples made a series of scientific discoveries which allowed them, almost overnight, to transform their reservations into virtual walled utopias. Now, however, the gangsters and multinational corporations who run what's left of the western world, have set themselves to invade and destroy the Native American lands. The scientist-warrior Gahzee must leave his home and enter a hellish world of radioactive wastelands, cybernetic samurai, and deadly plots to counter their efforts.

Other books you might like:
Andre Norton, *Beast Master*, 1959
Andre Norton, *Lord of Thunder*, 1962
Craig Strete, *The Bleeding Man and Other Stories*, 1977
Craig Strete, *Death in the Spirit House*, 1988
Craig Strete, *Dreams That Burn in the Night*, 1982

1161

CHARLES DE LINT

Westlin Wind

(Seattle, WA: The Anxolotl Press, 1989)

Story type: Fantasy (Quest)
Major character(s): Emma, Young Woman; Esmeralda Foyan, Young Woman
Time period(s): Indeterminate
Locale(s): Ottawa, Ontario, Canada; Alternate Universe

Summary: The quest is to save a woman, Emma, who has been separated from her soul. A group of friends goes after her body, while Esmeralda, traveling alone, searches for the soul.

Other books you might like:
Jo Clayton, *Diadem from the Stars*, 1986
Bruce Fergusson, *The Mace of Souls*, 1989
Jennifer Roberson, *Sword-Singer*, 1988

1162

CHARLES DE LINT
BRIAN FROUD, Illustrator

The Wild Wood

(New York: Bantam Spectra, 1994)

Story type: Fantasy (Contemporary)
Series: Brian Froud's Faerielands
Major character(s): Eithnie Gerrows, Artist (painter); Albin, Mythical Creature
Time period(s): 1990s
Locale(s): Ontario, Canada; Arizona

Summary: When Eithnie retreats to her secluded cabin to paint, she discovers the fairy realm, now endangered by modern development. Illustrations and five-page introduction by Brian Froud. First of a new series.

Other books you might like:
Pamela Dean, *The Secret Country*, 1985
Robert Holdstock, *Mythago Wood*, 1984
Tanith Lee, *Black Unicorn*, 1991
Megan Lindholm, *Cloven Hooves*, 1991
Patricia A. McKillip, *Something Rich and Strange*, 1994

1163

CHARLES DE LINT

The Wishing Well

(Eugene, Oregon: Pulphouse Publishing Axolotl Press, 1993)

Story type: Fantasy (Contemporary)
Major character(s): Brenda Perry, Journalist, Businesswoman (advertising manager); Ellie Carter, Spirit, Businesswoman; Jilly Coppercorn, Artist
Time period(s): 1990s
Locale(s): North America

Summary: While driving, Brenda finds an abandoned motel where she discovers a mysterious resident and a well from which voices seem to emanate—voices that begin to fill her dreams. When Brenda's lack of self-esteem precipitates financial and personal crises in her life, she abandons her friends in favor of living at the abandoned motel. Alarmed at her unusual behavior, Brenda's friends initiate a search for her.

Other books you might like:
Peni R. Griffin, *Hobkin*, 1992
Katharine Kerr, *Resurrection*, 1992
Kristine Kathryn Rusch, *The Gallery of His Dreams*, 1991
Nancy Springer, *Damnbanna*, 1992
Nancy Springer, *The Friendship Song*, 1992
Kate Wilhelm, *Naming the Flowers*, 1992

1164

JOHN DEAKINS

Barrow

(New York: Roc, 1990)

Story type: Fantasy (Magic Conflict)
Major character(s): Fleetfox, Hero
Time period(s): Indeterminate
Locale(s): Barrow, Fictional Country

Summary: Good and evil magic have leaked into the town of Barrow, leaving Fleetfox and sundry others to cope with the new order of life.

Other books you might like:
Don Davis, *Sins of the Flesh*, 1989
  Jay Davis, co-author
Gordon R. Dickson, *The Earth Lords*, 1989
Mark C. Perry, *Morigu: The Dead*, 1990
Jack Yeovil, *Drachenfels*, 1989

1165

PAMELA DEAN

The Dubious Hills

(New York: Tor, 1994)

Story type: Fantasy (Magic Conflict; Mystery)
Series: Secret Country
Major character(s): Arry, Teenager, Empath; Oonan, Healer; Halver, Teacher, Werewolf
Time period(s): Indeterminate
Locale(s): The Dubious Hills, Fictional Country

Summary: Cooperating with others to solve the mystery behind unusual lupine behavior, Arry discovers tantalizing hints about the fate of her missing parents. Further investigation uncovers a surreptitious revolution which could transform her entire society. Set during the Spring of *The Whim of the Dragon*.

Other books you might like:
Jesse Browner, *Conglomeros*, 1992
Diane Duane, *The Door into Fire*, 1979
Diane Duane, *The Door into Shadow*, 1984
Nina Kiriki Hoffman, *The Thread That Binds the Bones*, 1993
Diana Wynne Jones, *Cart and Cwidder*, 1977
Diana Wynne Jones, *Drowned Ammet*, 1978
Diana Wynne Jones, *The Spellcoats*, 1979
Meredith Ann Pierce, *The Dark-Angel*, 1982

1166

PAMELA DEAN

Tam Lin

(New York: Tor, 1991)

Story type: Fantasy (Legend; Historical)
Series: Fairy Tales
Major character(s): Janet Carter, Student; Thomas Lane, Student; Nick Tooley, Student
Time period(s): 1970s

Locale(s): Blackstock College, Minnesota

Summary: Entering college, Janet Carter finds exciting classical education fraught with Shakespeare, Keats, Pope and Homer. Living in a dormitory, away from home for the first time, Janet's growing up is complicated by an unwanted pregnancy.

Other books you might like:
Steven Brust, *The Sun, the Moon, and the Stars*, 1987
Kara Dalkey, *The Nightingale*, 1988
Charles de Lint, *Jack, the Giant-Killer*, 1987
Patricia C. Wrede, *Snow White and Rose Red*, 1989

1167

PAMELA DEAN

The Whim of the Dragon
(New York: Ace, 1989)

Story type: Fantasy (Alternate World)
Series: Secret Country
Major character(s): Fence, Wizard
Time period(s): 1980s
Locale(s): Earth; Hidden Land, Alternate Universe

Summary: A children's game becomes real when the children are able to cross over to the Hidden Land. The conclusion answers questions raised in the first two books and ends with a battle.

Other books you might like:
Joy Chant, *Red Moon and Black Mountain*, 1970
Susan Cooper, *The Dark Is Rising*, 1983
　　Book 1 The Dark Is Rising Series
C.S. Lewis, *The Chronicles of Narnia*,
　　1951-1956

1168

HAMILTON DEANE

Dracula: The Ultimate Illustrated Edition of the World-Famous Vampire Play
(New York: St. Martin's, 1993)

Story type: Horror (Anthology; Vampire Story)

Summary: The editor collects for the first time two stage adaptations of Bram Stoker's *Dracula*: Hamilton Deane's version, which was written in 1924 and toured with great success in England, and John Balderston's 1927 revision of Deane's play, which ran on Broadway and launched the career of Bela Lugosi. Both plays are extensively illustrated with stills and drawings as well as annotated.

Other books you might like:
Marvin Kaye, *13 Plays of Ghosts and the Supernatural*, 1990
　　editor
Bram Stoker, *Dracula*, 1895

1169

DON H. DEBRANDT

The Quicksilver Screen
(New York: Ballantine Del Rey, 1992)

Story type: Science Fiction (Cyberpunk; Arts)
Major character(s): Virgil Jakobi, Artist; Thann Demetrios, Artist; Shan, Artist
Time period(s): 21st century
Locale(s): Earth

Summary: Infinite Range Television (IRTV) allows humanity to view transmissions from alternate realities, providing new frontiers of entertainment for everyone. Corporate America assigns researchers to view IRTV in search of solutions to problems and possible new money-making ideas. When one researcher, Virgil Jakobi, takes an unauthorized sabbatical to help prevent a suicide, he finds himself pursued by a reanimated mass murderer.

Other books you might like:
Pat Cadigan, *Fools*, 1992
Pat Cadigan, *Mindplayers*, 1987
Pat Cadigan, *Synners*, 1991
Ernest Hogan, *Cortez on Jupiter*, 1990
Marjorie Bradley Kellogg, *Harmony*, 1991
William F. Nolan, *William F. Nolan's Logan: A Trilogy*, 1992
Neal Stephenson, *Snow Crash*, 1992

1170

ELISA DECARLO

The Devil You Say
(New York: AvoNova, 1993)

Story type: Fantasy (Mystery; Psychic Powers)
Major character(s): Aubrey Arbuthnot, Detective—Private, Psychic; Anthony Hornchurch, Servant, Detective—Amateur
Time period(s): 1930s (1933)
Locale(s): London, England

Summary: Hired by a mysterious client to bid on an ancient occult text, *The Book of Shadows*, Aubrey Arbuthnot becomes embroiled in a satanic plot to acquire the powerful artifact. A competitor of the successful bidder turns his daughter into a Ming vase while trying to get the book. Humorous adventure ensues as Aubrey works to destroy the tome and prevent the world's destruction. Author's first novel.

Other books you might like:
Lois McMaster Bujold, *The Spirit Ring*, 1992
Mercedes Lackey, *Burning Water*, 1989
Mercedes Lackey, *Children of the Night*, 1990
Mercedes Lackey, *Jinx High*, 1991
R.A. MacAvoy, *Tea with the Black Dragon*, 1983

1171

ELISA DECARLO

Strong Spirits

(New York: AvoNova, 1994)

Story type: Fantasy (Mystery; Psychic Powers)
Major character(s): Aubrey Arbuthnot, Detective—Private, Psychic; Anthony Hornchurch, Servant, Detective—Amateur; Farquhar Arbuthnot, Nobleman, Spirit
Time period(s): 1920s (1928)
Locale(s): England

Summary: When Aubrey Arbuthnot attempts to banish the ghost of his father, his work with spiritualists and activity on the astral plane awaken his psychic abilities. Prequel to *The Devil You Say.*

Other books you might like:
Nancy Atherton, *Aunt Dimity and the Duke*, 1994
Lois McMaster Bujold, *The Spirit Ring*, 1992
Mercedes Lackey, *Burning Water*, 1989
R.A. MacAvoy, *Tea with the Black Dragon*, 1983
H.P.G. Wodehouse, *Scream for Jeeves: A Parody*, 1994
    pseudonym of Peter Cannon

1172

JOHN DECHANCIE

Bride of the Castle

(New York: Ace, 1994)

Story type: Science Fiction (Alternate Universe; Humor)
Series: Castle Perilous
Major character(s): Incarnadine, Royalty, Magician; Linda, Bride, Magician; Rance, Royalty, Wanderer
Time period(s): 1990s; Indeterminate
Locale(s): Castle Perilous, Planet—Imaginary (center of the Multiverse); New York, New York

Summary: Returning from vacation, the king conjures up his double and leaves. While finalizing the design of her wedding dress, Linda worries if Gene will find happiness when they marry. Barbarians trap Gene in a seemingly peaceful manner when he ducks out of his bachelor party, while Rance must rid himself of the curse he picked up while grave robbing.

Other books you might like:
Charles de Lint, *The Little Country*, 1991
Robert A. Heinlein, *Glory Road*, 1963
Michael Kandel, *Strange Invasion*, 1989
Ken Rolston, *Extreme Paranoia: Nobody Knows the Trouble I've Shot*, 1991
Will Shetterly, *The Tangled Lands*, 1989

1173

JOHN DECHANCIE

Castle Dreams

(New York: Ace, 1992)

Story type: Science Fiction (Alternate Universe; Humor)
Series: Castle Perilous

Major character(s): Incarnadine, Royalty (King of the Realms Perilous), Magician; Trent, Royalty (Prince of the Realms Perilous)
Time period(s): 1990s
Locale(s): Castle Perilous, Planet—Imaginary (center of the Multiverse)

Summary: When Incarnadine turns up missing, suspicion falls on the new King of Castle Perilous, the former King's brother. Two spot quizzes and a final exam test readers' attentiveness to the story and views on the author's style and the publishing industry.

Other books you might like:
Douglas Adams, *Dirk Gently's Holistic Detective Agency*, 1987
Douglas Adams, *The Hitchhiker's Guide to the Galaxy*, 1980
Philip K. Dick, *A Maze of Death*, 1970
Alan Dean Foster, *Glory Lane*, 1987
Robert A. Heinlein, *Glory Road*, 1963

1174

JOHN DECHANCIE

Castle Spellbound

(New York: Ace, 1992)

Story type: Science Fiction (Alternate Universe; Science Fantasy)
Series: Castle Perilous
Major character(s): Trent, Royalty (prince); Osmirik, Librarian, Magician; Kwip, Thief
Time period(s): Indeterminate
Locale(s): Castle Perilous, Planet—Imaginary (center of the multiverse); Hellas, Mythical Place

Summary: King Incarnadine sends Trent to oversee a military campaign. Meanwhile, two lazy apprentice sorcerers unintentionally unleash supernatural forces, sending them into Castle Perilous with the instructions to clean up the entire place, no matter what the cost.

Other books you might like:
Steven Brust, *Cowboy Feng's Space Bar and Grille*, 1990
Alan Dean Foster, *Quozl*, 1989
Alan Dean Foster, *To the Vanishing Point*, 1988
Stephen Goldin, *Jade Darcy and the Zen Pirates*, 1990
    Mary Mason, co-author
Michael Kandel, *Strange Invasion*, 1989
Nick Pollotta, *Illegal Aliens*, 1989
    Phil Foglio, co-author

1175

JOHN DECHANCIE

Castle War!

(New York: Ace, 1990)

Story type: Science Fiction (Alternate Universe; Science Fantasy)
Series: Castle Perilous

Major character(s): Jeremy Hochstader, Computer Expert; Incarnadine, Royalty (King of Castle Perilous), Magician; Gene Ferraro, Adventurer

Time period(s): 1990s

Locale(s): Castle Perilous, Planet—Imaginary (Center of the Multiverse); Merydion, Planet—Imaginary

Summary: After the interuniversal medium is disturbed by a previous disaster, the residents of Castle Perilous are taken by surprise when they are visited by their duplicates from the mirror Castle Perilous that has appeared next door. His portal had become unusable, leaving Lord Incarnadine stranded in another universe. Jeremy, with the help of an artificial intelligence, must restabilize the cosmos.

Other books you might like:
Douglas Adams, *The Hitchhiker's Guide to the Galaxy*, 1980
Alan Dean Foster, *Quozl*, 1989
Alan Dean Foster, *To the Vanishing Point*, 1988
Alan Dean Foster, *Glory Lane*, 1987

1176

JOHN DECHANCIE
DAVID BISCHOFF, Co-Author

Dr. Dimension

(New York: Roc, 1993)

Story type: Science Fiction (Space Opera; Humor)

Major character(s): Demetrios "Dr. Dimension" Demopoulos, Scientist, Inventor; Vivian Vernon, Scientist; Samuel Flitheimer, Philanthropist

Time period(s): 1930s (1939); Indeterminate

Locale(s): Flitheimer University, Nebraska; *Mudlark*, Spaceship

Summary: Dr. Demopoulos thinks he might lose his grant when he blows up the physics lab once again. Dr. Vernon hopes to get his grant, but Sam Flitheimer proves to be a fan of super-science literature, fascinated with the idea of a spaceship or even a time machine. As the deadline arrives, a mysterious package of strange parts allows the inventor to complete a spaceship. Leaving to keep the ship out of Nazi hands, the explorers find themselves involved with aliens who need aid from the humans.

Other books you might like:
Douglas Adams, *The Hitchhiker's Guide to the Galaxy*, 1980
David Bischoff, *Night of the Living Shark!*, 1991
Alan Dean Foster, *To the Vanishing Point*, 1988
Mel Gilden, *Hawaiian U.F.O. Aliens*, 1991
T. Jackson King, *Retread Shop*, 1988
Henry Kuttner, *Robots Have No Tails*, 1952

1177

JOHN DECHANCIE

From Prussia with Love

(Rocklin, California: Prima, 1996)

Story type: Fantasy (Historical; Magic Conflict)
Series: Castle Falkenstein

Major character(s): Thomas "Tom" Edward Olam, Time Traveller, Computer Expert; Ludwig Wittelsbach, Ruler (king); Ruggerio Zambelli, Scientist (rocket)

Time period(s): Indeterminate (1870s equivalent)

Locale(s): *Wagner*, in the Air (zeppelin); Europe, Alternate Earth

Summary: While on the *Wagner* in Victorian-era Bavaria, Tom observes a Russian missile crash into the Baltic Sea. He convinces Ludwig to start his own research progarm to prevent Chancellor Bismarck's steam-powered ballistic missiles from conquering New Europe. With the aid of an Italian fireworks designer who plans to build a ship to go to the moon and his dwarf engineer, Ludwig creates a countermissile for the defense of his kingdom, despite his reluctance to develop weapons of mass destruction. Computer game tie-in.

Other books you might like:
Orson Scott Card, *The Folk of the Fringe*, 1989
John Crowley, *Aegypt*, 1987
William Gibson, *The Difference Engine*, 1991
   Bruce Sterling, co-author
Paul J. McAuley, *Pasquale's Angel*, 1995
Tim Powers, *The Anubis Gates*, 1983
Harry Turtledove, *The Guns of the South*, 1992

1178

JOHN DECHANCIE

Innerverse

(New York: AvoNova, 1996)

Story type: Science Fiction (Dystopian; Political)

Major character(s): Frank Sutter, Spy (Special Forces), Experimental Subject; Alice, Revolutionary, Adventurer

Time period(s): 2020s

Locale(s): United States; The Republic, Fictional Country (eastern United States)

Summary: Use of Innerverse, a nanotechnology development, brings despotism and a 30-year silence from the eastern United States. Searching for insight into the new society, Frank Sutter ingests Innerverse and begins to explore the Republic, aided by Alice, a Republican resident with inactive Innerverse.

Other books you might like:
Raphael Carter, *The Fortunate Fall*, 1996
Jeffrey A. Carver, *From a Changeling Star*, 1989
Philip K. Dick, *The Unteleported Man*, 1983
   revised edition
Neal Stephenson, *The Diamond Age*, 1995
Sheri S. Tepper, *Grass*, 1989
Vernor Vinge, *A Fire upon the Deep*, 1992

1179

JOHN DECHANCIE

The Kruton Interface

(New York: Ace, 1993)

Story type: Science Fiction (Humor; Space Opera)

Major character(s): David L. Wanker, Military Personnel, Spaceship Captain
Time period(s): Indeterminate Future
Locale(s): *U.S.S. Repulse*, Spaceship; Kruton, Planet—Imaginary; Outer Space

Summary: When a race of lawyers sues the entire human race, Captain David Wanker rushes to the Human/Kruton border with *U.S.S. Repulse*, the worst crewed spaceship in the fleet, to save humanity from the litigious shapechangers.

Other books you might like:
Douglas Adams, *The Hitchhiker's Guide to the Galaxy*, 1980
Douglas Adams, *The Restaurant at the End of the Universe*, 1982
Jack L. Chalker, *The Red Tape War*, 1991
  Mike Resnick, George Alec Effinger, co-authors
John M. Ford, *How Much for Just the Planet?*, 1987
Leah Rewolinski, *Star Wreck: The Generation Gap*, 1990
Leah Rewolinski, *Star Wreck II: The Attack of the Jargonites*, 1991
Leah Rewolinski, *Star Wreck III: Time Warped*, 1992

1180

JOHN DECHANCIE

Living with Aliens

(New York: Ace, 1995)

Story type: Science Fiction (Invasion of Earth; Adventure)
Major character(s): Drew Hayes, Teenager; Zorg, Alien; Flez, Alien
Time period(s): 1990s
Locale(s): Keynesville, Ohio

Summary: During his summer vacation, aliens come to live with Drew Hayes, a normal 13-year-old. Although the aliens can control other people's minds, nothing conquers the curiosity of a teenage boy with nothing to do.

Other books you might like:
Robert A. Heinlein, *Have Spacesuit—Will Travel*, 1958
Zenna Henderson, *Ingathering: The Complete People Stories of Zenna Henderson*, 1995
Daniel Keyes, *Flowers for Algernon*, 1966
Rebecca Ore, *Becoming Alien*, 1987

1181

JOHN DECHANCIE

MagicNet

(New York: Morrow AvoNova, 1993)

Story type: Fantasy (Adventure; Contemporary)
Major character(s): Schuyler "Skye" King, Professor, Detective—Amateur; Lloyd Merlin Jones, Computer Expert, Warlock; Grant, Computer Expert, Disembodied Personality
Time period(s): 1990s
Locale(s): Los Angeles, California; MagicNet, Cyberspace

Summary: While speaking to Grant on the telephone, Skye hears him murdered. Following Grant's instructions, Skye later finds a computer artifact of Grant's personality within MagicNet, an amateur computer network. Skye learns that Grant's death might be the result of Merlin's programming that utilizes magic to allow psychic manipulation of virtual reality, and travels to Los Angeles to confront Merlin. There he discovers a bizarre landscape and perilous reality and virtual reality.

Other books you might like:
Aaron Allston, *Galatea in 2-D*, 1993
Piers Anthony, *Killobyte*, 1993
Rick Cook, *The Wizardry Cursed*, 1991
Philip Jose Farmer, *Red Orc's Rage*, 1991
Will Shetterly, *The Tangled Lands*, 1989
Wm. Mark Simmons, *In the Net of Dreams*, 1990
Vivian Vande Velde, *User Unfriendly*, 1991

1182

RON DEE

Blood

(New York: Pocket, 1993)

Story type: Horror (Vampire Story)
Major character(s): Debi Develos, Vampire, Experimental Subject; Fred Langston, Police Officer (former FBI agent); Trish Blaine, Doctor
Time period(s): 1990s (1993)
Locale(s): Atlanta, Georgia

Summary: Debi Develos agrees to an experimental form of medical therapy to help cure her brain tumor, unaware that the serum injected into her will break down her inhibitions and turn her and everyone she bites into a bloodthirsty vampire.

Other books you might like:
Kathryn Meyer Griffith, *The Last Vampire*, 1992
Robert R. McCammon, *They Thirst*, 1981
Dan Simmons, *Children of the Night*, 1992
Brian Stableford, *The Empire of Fear*, 1988

1183

RON DEE

Blood Lust

(New York: Dell, 1990)

Story type: Horror (Vampire Story)
Major character(s): Warren MacDonald, Religious; Emily Knox, Teenager; Benjamin Dixon, Vampire Hunter, Religious
Time period(s): 1990s
Locale(s): Valley View, Missouri (a suburb of St. Louis)

Summary: A plague of vampirism spreads like wildfire through the small town of Valley View, claiming the wife of Warren MacDonald and the entire family of Emily Knox. With the help of Benjamin Dixon, a preacher who has tracked the vampire scourge from his own town, the two fight against hopeless odds to save Valley View, and perhaps the entire country, from this inexorable doom.

Other books you might like:
Robert R. McCammon, *They Thirst*, 1981

1184

RON DEE

Descent

(New York: Dell Abyss, 1991)

Story type: Horror (Occult)
Major character(s): Sarah Finley, Doctor (psychiatrist); Vickie Laster, Young Woman; Garcia Efstathiou, Lover (a.k.a. Aleister C.)
Time period(s): 1990s
Locale(s): Stillwater, Oklahoma

Summary: Vickie Laster's one-night stand with a stranger to get back at her abusive husband turns out to have some peculiar consequences. For one thing, her lover proves to be a dead rock star who had embraced the Satanic and died at the site of their tryst years before. For another, Vickie has become pregnant, even though medically incapable of bearing a child, leaving her to wonder just what the child really is.

Other books you might like:
Douglas Clegg, *Breeder*, 1990
Nancy A. Collins, *Tempter*, 1990
Ira Levin, *Rosemary's Baby*, 1967

1185

RON DEE

Dusk

(New York: Dell Abyss, 1991)

Story type: Horror (Vampire Story)
Major character(s): Samantha Borden, Government Official (immigration officer); Sheriff Bill, Lawman (local sheriff); Jay Adwon, Lawman (deputy)
Time period(s): 1990s
Locale(s): Dallas, Texas

Summary: When a group of rambunctious young vampires indiscriminately blows the cover of a vampire stronghold near the Mexican border, it leads to a bloody war with all the mortals living between the border and Dallas.

Other books you might like:
Stephen King, *Salem's Lot*, 1975
Robert R. McCammon, *They Thirst*, 1981

1186

RON DEE
ROGER GERBERDING, Illustrator

Sex and Blood

(Leesburg, Virginia: TAL, 1994)

Story type: Horror (Collection; Vampire Story)

Summary: This book features three interconnected stories by an author who specializes in vampire fiction. In ''Blood Tithe,'' lonely loser John contacts an escort agency unaware that its promise of great sex includes vampirism. In ''Stakeout,'' John's ex-wife Rhonda searches for her missing husband and ends up in a nightclub catering to the undead. In ''Wholly Lust,'' Rhonda fights for her mortality against vampires who want to turn her into what John has become. This chapbook, which was not available until 1995, was issued in a signed limited edition of 1,000 copies.

Other books you might like:
S. Darnbrook Colson, *Snakes*, 1992
Brian Hodge, *Shrines and Desecrations*, 1994
Nancy Kilpatrick, *Sex and the Single Vampire*, 1994
Edward Lee, *Edward Lee's Quest for Sex, Truth and Reality*, 1992
Lucy Taylor, *Unnatural Acts*, 1992

1187

RON DEE

Succumb

(New York: Pocket, 1994)

Story type: Horror (Doppelganger)
Major character(s): Martin Paarman, Teacher (music); Leigh Paarman, Advertising (executive), Businesswoman; Jan ''Jeanette'' Fancy, Femme Fatale
Time period(s): 1990s (1994)
Locale(s): United States

Summary: Frustrated with the loss of direction in his life and his increasingly strained marriage, Martin Paarman starts an affair with Jan Fancy, a seductive bar pickup who fulfills Martin's every need, and whom he begins to suspect is simply the sum of all his desires made flesh.

Other books you might like:
Charles L. Grant, *For Fear of the Night*, 1988
Richard Matheson, *Earthbound*, 1981
Eric McCormack, *The Paradise Motel*, 1989
T.L. Parkinson, *The Man Upstairs*, 1991

1188

TOM DEITZ

Above the Lower Sky

(New York: AvoNova/Morrow, 1994)

Story type: Fantasy (Science Fiction; Psychic Powers)
Major character(s): Kevin Mauney, Writer (fantasy novelist); Fir, Mythical Creature (selkie); Thunderbird Devlin ''Bird'' O'Connor, Indian (Cherokee)
Time period(s): 2020s (2024)
Locale(s): County Offaly, Ireland (United Eire); Aztlan Free Zone, Mexico

Summary: Fir induces Kevin to travel to the sea during a hurricane. Followed by several large men who try to kill him, Kevin discovers that he and his estranged sister, along with an unknown third person, must join together against an as yet unknown danger to save humanity.

Other books you might like:
Don Callander, *Aquamancer*, 1993
Gordon R. Dickson, *Home From the Shore*, 1978
A.E. van Vogt, *The Silkie*, 1969
Joan D. Vinge, *The Summer Queen*, 1991
Lawrence Watt-Evans, *The Lure of the Basilisk*, 1980

1189
TOM DEITZ

Darkthunder's Way
(New York: Avon, 1989)

Story type: Fantasy (Quest)
Series: David Sullivan
Major character(s): David Sullivan, Student—College, Adventurer; Morwyne the Powershaper, Mythical Creature
Time period(s): 20th century
Locale(s): Western United States, Alternate Earth

Summary: David and his companion, the son of a medicine man, travel through the mythlands of the Cherokee Indians to help Morwyne find a way home from the land of the Sidhe. Together they fight against the evil magic of Finnvarra.

Other books you might like:
Greg Bear, *The Infinity Concerto*, 1987
M. Coleman Easton, *Spirits of Cavern and Hearth*, 1989
Michael Moorcock, *The Fortress of the Pearl*, 1989
Dave Smeds, *The Schemes of Dragons*, 1989
Craig Strete, *Death in the Spirit House*, 1988

1190
TOM DEITZ

Dreambuilder
(New York: AvoNova, 1992)

Story type: Fantasy (Contemporary; Religious)
Series: Soulsmith
Major character(s): Ronny Dillon, Artist (metalsmith), Telepath; Lewis Welch, Political Figure (master of Cardalba), Telepath; Brandy Wallace, Artist, Teacher
Time period(s): 1990s
Locale(s): Cordova, Georgia; Welch County, Georgia

Summary: Ronny graduates from college about five years after the events in *Soulsmith*. Reluctant to return home due to his intense memories and the deaths in his family, Ronny complies with Lewis's urgent request, as predicted by the radio. While in Welch County, Ronny gets involved with Brandy and her castle-building project.

Other books you might like:
Piers Anthony, *Virtual Mode*, 1991
Emma Bull, *War for the Oaks*, 1987
Charles de Lint, *The Little Country*, 1991
Greer Ilene Gilman, *Moonwise*, 1991
Megan Lindholm, *Cloven Hooves*, 1991
Ian McDonald, *King of Morning, Queen of Day*, 1991
Jody Lynn Nye, *Mythology 101*, 1990
Claudia Peck, *Spirit Crossings*, 1991

1191
TOM DEITZ

Dreamseeker's Road
(New York: Morrow/AvoNova, 1995)

Story type: Fantasy (Adventure; Alternate World)

Series: David Sullivan
Major character(s): David Sullivan, Student—College, Adventurer; Alec McLean, Student—College, Adventurer; Aikin Daniels, Student—College, Adventurer
Time period(s): 1990s; Indeterminate
Locale(s): Georgia; Faerie, Mythical Place

Summary: A hunting trip the day before Halloween leads David and his friends into danger as an ancient and evil force tracks them, while the barriers between the human realm and Faerie break down.

Other books you might like:
Aaron Allston, *Doc Sidhe*, 1995
Greg Bear, *Songs of Earth and Power*, 1994
Charles de Lint, *Memory and Dream*, 1994
Charles de Lint, *Moonheart: A Romance*, 1984
Patricia A. McKillip, *The Book of Atrix Wolfe*, 1995
Jane Yolen, *The Wild Hunt*, 1995

1192
TOM DEITZ

The Gryphon King
(New York: Avon, 1989)

Story type: Fantasy (Contemporary)
Major character(s): Jay Madison, Student—College, Relative (Rob's half brother); Rob Tolar, Student—College, Relative (Jay's half brother)
Time period(s): 1980s
Locale(s): Athens, Georgia (University of Georgia)

Summary: A play is found which has the power to raise the Devil and reunite the magic and human worlds. A group of human college students and magic beings try to prevent the play from being read.

Other books you might like:
Ramsey Campbell, *Ancient Images*, 1990
Daniel Da Cruz, *Mixed Doubles*, 1989
John M. Ford, *Casting Fortune*, 1989
Joe Haldeman, *The Hemingway Hoax*, 1990

1193
TOM DEITZ

Soulsmith
(New York: Avon, 1991)

Story type: Fantasy (Contemporary; Young Adult)
Series: Soulsmith
Major character(s): Ronny Dillon, Orphan, Student—High School; Lewis Welch, Bastard Son, Student—High School; Road Man, Traveller, Magician
Time period(s): 1990s
Locale(s): Cordova, Georgia

Summary: After Ronny Dillon shattered his kneecap and lost his adoptive parents, he went to live with his grandmother and her son, Lewis, in rural Georgia. Unable to reconcile himself with the changes in his life, and having discovered a talent for working with metal in shop class, Ronny put his energy into decorating his crutch. Before long he is forced to notice that the town and people around him present dangers he is not prepared to handle.

Other books you might like:
Emma Bull, *War for the Oaks*, 1987
Charles de Lint, *The Dreaming Place*, 1990
Hila Feil, *Blue Moon*, 1990
Christopher Pike, *See You Later*, 1990
Michael Scott Rohan, *Chase the Morning*, 1991

1194

TOM DEITZ

Stoneskin's Revenge

(New York: Avon, 1991)

Story type: Fantasy (Contemporary; Adventure)
Series: David Sullivan
Major character(s): Calvin McIntosh, Indian (Cherokee), Wanderer; Robyn, Runaway; Utlunta, Indian, Monster
Time period(s): 1990s (1991)
Locale(s): Whidden, Georgia; Galunlati, Fictional Country

Summary: After the war in *Sunshaker's War*, a door into the other world of Galunlati was left open, and a monster escaped into Georgia. Calvin McIntosh, mostly Cherokee and a part-time sorcerer, has to deal with the problem without the help of his friends.

Other books you might like:
Emma Bull, *War for the Oaks*, 1987
Guy Gavriel Kay, *The Summer Tree*, 1985
Patricia Kennealy, *The Copper Crown*, 1986
Alex McDonough, *Scorpio*, 1990
Morgan Llywelyn, *Druids*, 1991

1195

TOM DEITZ

Sunshaker's War

(New York: Avon, 1990)

Story type: Fantasy (Adventure; Contemporary)
Series: David Sullivan
Major character(s): David Sullivan, Student—College, Adventurer; Calvin McIntosh, Indian, Wanderer; Fionchadd mac Ailill, Mythical Creature (Elf)
Time period(s): 1980s
Locale(s): Enotah County, Georgia; Galunlati, Mythical Place; Faerie, Mythical Place

Summary: The borders between the mortal lands and Faerie have supposedly been sealed to prevent the war between Tir-Nan-Og and Erenn. Not only are the borders leaking, but Calvin discovers that the magic being worked to wage the war is unbalancing the sun and will destroy all three worlds if not stopped. David, Calvin and their friends decide the only way to stop the war is to find out where Fionchadd is being held prisoner, rescue him, and return him to his people.

Other books you might like:
Margaret Ball, *The Shadow Gate*, 1991
Charles de Lint, *Svaha*, 1989
Barbara Hambly, *The Time of the Dark*, 1982

R.A. MacAvoy, *Tea with the Black Dragon*, 1983
Patricia C. Wrede, *The Seven Towers*, 1984

1196

TOM DEITZ

Wordwright

(New York: AvoNova, 1993)

Story type: Fantasy (Contemporary; Psychic Powers)
Series: Soulsmith
Major character(s): Ronny Dillon, Artist, Telepath; Lewis Owen Welch, Telepath; Donson Gwent, Director, Writer (playwright)
Time period(s): 1990s
Locale(s): Welch County, Georgia

Summary: After Martha, the Welch family matriarch, dies, Lewis renounces his Mastership to search for his and Ronny's sister. Before long the folks in town notice that the Luck seems to have left, and since Lew left, they blame Ronny. Brandy decides to help the town by producing a play despite knowing the plot will greatly upset Ronny. The director sparks a fight which forces Ron to leave Brandy Hall and eventually learn about the Road Man and the Welch family Luck.

Other books you might like:
Piers Anthony, *The Caterpillar's Question*, 1992
   Philip Jose Farmer, co-author
Maya Kaathryn Bohnhoff, *The Meri*, 1992
Emma Bull, *War for the Oaks*, 1987
Charles de Lint, *The Little Country*, 1990
Nina Kiriki Hoffman, *The Thread That Binds the Bones*, 1993
   Larry Dixon, co-author
Alis A. Rasmussen, *A Passage of Stars*, 1990
Lawrence Watt-Evans, *The Rebirth of Wonder*, 1992

1197

LESTER DEL REY, Editor
RISA KESSLER, Co-Editor

Once upon a Time: A Treasury of Modern Fairy Tales

(New York: Ballantine/Del Rey, 1991)

Story type: Fantasy (Anthology; Legend)

Summary: This volume contains 10 fairy tales by well-known science fiction and fantasy authors. All stories are new for this anthology, but the authors use classic fairy tale themes and characters. The stories are aimed at adult readers, but can be enjoyed by the younger reader with good reading skills. Major authors include Isaac Asimov, Terry Brooks, C.J. Cherryh, Barbara Hambly, Katherine Kurtz and Anne McCaffrey.

Other books you might like:
Steven Brust, *The Sun, the Moon, and the Stars*, 1987
Kara Dalkey, *The Nightingale*, 1988
Charles de Lint, *Jack, the Giant-Killer*, 1987
Andrew Lang, *The Blue Fairy Book*, 1889
   editor

Andrew Lang, *The Red Fairy Book*, 1890
   editor
Sheri S. Tepper, *Beauty*, 1991
Patricia C. Wrede, *Snow White and Rose Red*, 1989
Jack Zipes, *Beauties, Beasts and Enchantments*, 1989
   edited, translated
Jack Zipes, *Spells of Enchantment*, 1991
   edited, translated

1198
SAMUEL R. DELANY

They Fly at Ciron
(Seattle, Washington: Incunabula Press, 1993)

Story type: Science Fiction (Political)
Major character(s): Rahn, Farmer, Wanderer; Kire, Military Personnel (lieutenant); Vortcir, Alien (Winged One)
Time period(s): Indeterminate
Locale(s): Ciron, Fictional City; Hi-Vator, Fictional City

Summary: Gone for a week, Rahn considers heading home to Ciron when he kills a mountain lion and is afraid by a Winged One overhead. Kire observes the kill and casually uses his powergun to shoot at the Winged One who spied on the Myetran mission to "conquer all in a line like blood running down a map." Rahn, a primitive, gives Kire the skin in thanks and friendship, not understanding that Myetra marches next to Ciron.

Other books you might like:
Richard Grant, *Through the Heart*, 1991
Nicola Griffith, *Ammonite*, 1993
Marjorie Bradley Kellogg, *Harmony*, 1991
Morgan Llywelyn, *The Elementals*, 1993
J.M. Morgan, *Desert Eden*, 1991
Sheri S. Tepper, *A Plague of Angels*, 1993
Gene Wolfe, *The Shadow of the Torturer*, 1980

1199
MARTIN DELRIO

Mortal Kombat
(New York: Tor, 1995)

Story type: Fantasy (Adventure)
Series: Mortal Kombat
Major character(s): Liu Kang, Religious, Martial Arts Expert; Sonya Blade, Military Personnel, Warrior; Goro, Warrior, Royalty
Time period(s): 1990s
Locale(s): Hong Kong; Outworld, Mythical Place

Summary: Mortal warriors compete in a tournament to determine their worthiness to defend humanity from the evil sorcerer, Shang Tsung. Novelizes the film based on the electronic game.

Other books you might like:
Dean Devlin, *StarGate*, 1994
   Roland Emmerich, co-author
Wayland Drew, *Willow*, 1988
William R. Forstchen, *Arena*, 1994

Paul Monette, *Predator*, 1987
Jeff Rovin, *Mortal Kombat*, 1995

1200
TROY DENNING

The Parched Sea
(Lake Geneva, Wisconsin: TSR, 1991)

Story type: Fantasy (Adventure; Sword and Sorcery)
Series: Forgotten Realms: The Harpers
Major character(s): Ruha, Widow(er), Sorceress; Lander, Revolutionary; Kadumi, Warrior
Time period(s): Indeterminate Past
Locale(s): Anauroch, Mythical Place (desert)

Summary: In Anauroch to help the desert tribes resist the efforts of the Zhentarim to enslave them, Lander is too late to stop Ruha and Kadumi's tribes from being slaughtered. The remaining tribes may agree to work together to fight the Zhentarim, if Ruha and Lander can convince the tribes that Ruha's magical abilities are not a curse on their efforts. A game tie-in novel.

Other books you might like:
Elaine Cunningham, *Elfshadow*, 1991
Doris Egan, *The Gate of Ivory*, 1989
Heather Gladney, *Teot's War*, 1987
Melanie Rawn, *Dragon Prince*, 1988
Jennifer Roberson, *Sword-Singer*, 1988

1201
TROY DENNING

The Verdant Passage
(Lake Geneva, Wisconsin: TSR, 1991)

Story type: Fantasy (Adventure; Sword and Sorcery)
Series: Prism Pentad
Major character(s): Agis, Political Figure (senator), Psychic (psionic); Sadira, Slave, Mythical Creature (half elf); Rikus, Warrior (gladiator), Mythical Creature (dwarf)
Time period(s): Indeterminate
Locale(s): Athas, Mythical Place

Summary: An unlikely trio comes together through a group leading a popular rebellion against an unethical King. Based on the Dark Sun game from TSR.

Other books you might like:
Elaine Cunningham, *Elfshadow*, 1991
Heather Gladney, *Teot's War*, 1987
Melanie Rawn, *Dragon Prince*, 1988
Jennifer Roberson, *Sword-Singer*, 1988

1202
CAROL L. DENNIS

Dragon's Queen
(New York: Warner Questar, 1991)

Story type: Fantasy (Alternate World)
Series: Dragon's Pawn

Major character(s): Lealor, Guardian (gatewarden); Fafleen, Mythical Creature (dragon)
Time period(s): Indeterminate
Locale(s): Widdershins, Planet—Imaginary

Summary: When Lealor and Fafleen find themselves stuck on Widdershins, a place where dragons are forbidden, they try to unite people and dragons as they search for a way home from the Shadowlord's realm.

Other books you might like:
Pamela Dean, *The Hidden Land*, 1986
Pamela Dean, *The Secret Country*, 1985
Pamela Dean, *The Whim of the Dragon*, 1989
Margaret Weis, *Fire Sea*, 1991
    Tracy Hickman, co-author
Patricia C. Wrede, *Dealing with Dragons*, 1990
Patricia C. Wrede, *Searching for Dragons*, 1991
Patricia C. Wrede, *Talking to Dragons*, 1985

1203

BRADLEY DENTON

Blackburn

(New York: St. Martin's, 1993)

Story type: Horror (Serial Killer)
Major character(s): Jimmy Blackburn, Drifter, Serial Killer; Jasmine Blackburn, Child (Jimmy's sister); Ernest Tompkins, Child
Time period(s): 20th century
Locale(s): Wontoda, Kansas; Southwest

Summary: This extraordinary novel intersperses accounts of murders committed by Jimmy Blackburn, a young drifter who travels around the country under a variety of aliases, with vignettes from his deprived childhood and adolescence, forging a link between his loveless and alienated past and the crimes he commits against those who lie to or betray him.

Other books you might like:
Ramsey Campbell, *The Count of Eleven*, 1991
Truman Capote, *In Cold Blood*, 1967
Davis Grubb, *The Night of the Hunter*, 1953
Norman Mailer, *The Executioner's Song*, 1979
William F. Nolan, *Helltracks*, 1991

1204

BRADLEY DENTON

Buddy Holly Is Alive and Well on Ganymede

(New York: William Morrow, 1991)

Story type: Science Fiction (Humor; Adventure)
Major character(s): Oliver Vale, Fugitive; Richter, Government Official
Time period(s): 1980s (1989)
Locale(s): Kansas; Oklahoma

Summary: Oliver Vale is shocked into flight on his motorcycle by the sudden appearance on all televisions in the world of Buddy Holly requesting someone to contact Vale for him.

Vale flees all manner of agents, FBI, Kansas Bureau of Investigations, pro-flesh and anti-flesh aliens, as he tries to get to Lubbock, Texas where Buddy Holly is buried and where Vale hopes to find the answers to his many questions.

Other books you might like:
John DeChancie, *Paradox Alley*, 1987
John DeChancie, *Red Limit Freeway*, 1984
John DeChancie, *Starrigger*, 1983
Robert Rankin, *Armageddon: The Musical*, 1990
Robert Silverberg, *Letters From Atlantis*, 1990
Steven Spielberg, *Close Encounters of the Third Kind*, 1977

1205

BRADLEY DENTON

Lunatics

(New York: St. Martin's, 1996)

Story type: Fantasy (Contemporary Realism; Light Fantasy)
Major character(s): Jack, Mentally Ill Person; Lily, Deity; Stephen, Professor
Time period(s): 1990s
Locale(s): Austin, Texas

Summary: When Jack's life falls apart, he begins seeing Lily, apparently a goddess from the moon. His friends have a little trouble with this, especially when Jack takes to running around naked every full moon. With the Moon and Lily embodying love, soon everybody acts like a lunatic.

Other books you might like:
A.A. Attanasio, *The Moon's Wife: A Hystery*, 1993
Eleanor Arnason, *Daughter of the Bear King*, 1987
Emma Bull, *War for the Oaks*, 1987
Robert Holdstock, *Ancient Echoes*, 1996
Thorne Smith, *The Night Life of the Gods*, 1931

1206

JO DERESKE

The Lone Sentinel

(New York: Atheneum, 1989)

Story type: Science Fiction (Young Adult)
Major character(s): Erik, Teenager; Willa, Runaway
Time period(s): Indeterminate Future
Locale(s): Azure, Planet—Imaginary

Summary: On the planet Azure, machines called Sentinels produce a beam of energy that protects biosote, a strange growth needed by the Helgatites, a superior alien race. Erik and his father have lived in isolation, guarding the Lone Sentinel for as long as he can remember. Now, however, Erik's father has died and the teenager decides to carry on the job alone. He knows that if he reports his father's death, Trust Control, which oversees the Sentinels, will replace him and send him back to live in the city. Erik gets along fine until two runaways, Willa and Augusta, appear at his isolated outpost.

Other books you might like:
Frank Asch, *Journey to Terezor*, 1989
Gordon R. Dickson, *Way of the Pilgrim*, 1987
David Gerrold, *Chess with a Dragon*, 1987

Rebecca Ore, *Becoming Alien*, 1987
Rebecca Ore, *Being Alien*, 1989

1207
AUGUST DERLETH

The Mask of Cthulhu
(New York: Carroll & Graf, 1996)

Story type: Horror (Collection)

Summary: These six stories were all originally published in the pulp magazine *Weird Tales* and are consciously modeled on H.P. Lovecraft's renderings of the mechanistic forces of entropy and chaos as extradimensional monsters wreaking havoc on human affairs. "The Return of Hastur," "The Whippoorwills in the Hills" and "The Sandwin Compact" all feature naive young men who inherit estates from family members only to discover that their relatives have accessed monstrous forces of evil that still lurk in the family bequest. "Something in Wood" features a curio that embodies unspeakable evil and "The Seal of R'lyeh" a family curse of inescapable genetic destiny. "The House in the Valley" is loosely modeled on Lovecraft's classic "The Dunwich Horror." This book was first published in 1958.

Other books you might like:
Robert Bloch, *The Early Fears*, 1994
Ramsey Campbell, *The Inhabitant of the Lake and Less Welcome Tenants*, 1964
Frank Belknap Long, *The Hounds of Tindalos*, 1946
Brian Lumley, *Dagon's Bell and Other Discords*, 1995
Clark Ashton Smith, *Out of Space and Time*, 1942
Donald Wandrei, *The Eye and the Finger*, 1944

1208
AUGUST DERLETH

The Trail of Cthulhu
(New York: Carroll & Graf, 1996)

Story type: Horror (Ancient Evil Unleashed)
Major character(s): Laban Shrewsbury, Professor; Andrew Phelan, Researcher; Abel Keane, Student (divinity)
Time period(s): 1940s
Locale(s): Boston, Massachusetts; Lima, Peru

Summary: This episodic novel is stitched together from five pastiches of the writings of H.P. Lovecraft that were first published in the pulp magazine *Weird Tales* in the 1940s and 1950s. Laban Shrewsbury, a folklorist and lecturer, recruits a succession of five young men to assist him in the suppression of cultish activities in a variety of geographic locales that foreshadow the summoning of Cthulhu, an extradimensional entity whose existence in the earthly plane portends the destruction of mankind. This novel was first published in 1962.

Other books you might like:
Robert Bloch, *Strange Eons*, 1978
Basil Copper, *The Great White Space*, 1974
Brian Lumley, *The Burrowers Beneath*, 1974
Michael Shea, *The Colour out of Time*, 1984
Richard Tierney, *The House of the Toad*, 1993

1209
JOHN DESJARLAIS

The Throne of Tara
(Wheaton, Illinois: Crossway, 1990)

Story type: Fantasy (Legend; Religious)
Major character(s): Columcille, Royalty (Prince), Religious
Time period(s): 6th century
Locale(s): Iona, Ireland; Scotland

Summary: A change is being felt in Ireland as conflict between the old ways and Christianity becomes more prevalent. When Columcille exiles himself in Scotland he realizes that conflict with the druids was inevitable.

Other books you might like:
Margaret J. Anderson, *The Druid's Gift*, 1989
Frans G. Bengtsson, *The Long Ships*, 1954
Marion Zimmer Bradley, *The Mists of Avalon*, 1983
Kenneth C. Flint, *Cromm*, 1990
Stephen R. Lawhead, *Arthur*, 1989
Mike McQuay, *The Nexus*, 1989

1210
DIANE DESROCHERS

Walker between the Worlds
(St. Paul, Minnesota: Llewellyn, 1995)

Story type: Fantasy (Science Fiction; Psychic Powers)
Major character(s): Alan Kolkey, Scientist, Psychic; Dawn LaSarde, Psychic; Garuda, Animal (eagle)
Time period(s): 2000s (2001)
Locale(s): Tabriz, Iran

Summary: For lifetimes Alan Kolkey avoids his obligations to the Mother Goddess, but now she forces him into action by drawing a comet toward the Earth. In addition to the physical challenge, Alan has buried his true self and talents under a modern, macho surface which he needs to shed to save Earth. First novel.

Other books you might like:
Scott Baker, *Dhampire*, 1982
Gael Baudino, *Gossamer Axe*, 1990
Emma Bull, *Bone Dance*, 1991
Charles de Lint, *Svaha*, 1989
Stuart Gordon, *Smile on the Void*, 1981
Starhawk, *The Fifth Sacred Thing*, 1993

1211
EMILY DEVENPORT

Eggheads
(New York: Roc, 1996)

Story type: Science Fiction (First Contact; Political)
Major character(s): An, Spacewoman, Linguist; Mohamonero, Doctor; Jo, Spaceman
Time period(s): Indeterminate Future
Locale(s): Storm, Planet—Imaginary; Cabar 4, Planet—Imaginary

Summary: Having left the poverty of Storm as a teenager, An accepts a DNA transplant to better find and translate glyphs left by the progenitor Earlies. Complicated by the attempt on her life by her lover, Jo, and interference by the alien Vorn, also searching for glyphs, An's search becomes more difficult as the DNA integrates with her consciousness. As her DNA implant takes hold, An discovers the true position of the Vorn and the meaning of the glyphs.

Other books you might like:
C.J. Cherryh, *Foreigner*, 1994
A.C. Crispin, *Ancestor's World*, 1996
    T. Jackson King, co-author
L. Warren Douglas, *Stepwater*, 1995
Anne McCaffrey, *Freedom's Landing*, 1995
Jack McDevitt, *The Engines of God*, 1994

1212

EMILY DEVENPORT

Larissa

(New York: Roc, 1993)

Story type: Science Fiction (Science Fiction)
Major character(s): Larissa, Teenager, Runaway; Hazaar, Alien (Q'rin); Knossus, Alien (Aesopian)
Time period(s): Indeterminate Future
Locale(s): Hook, Planet—Imaginary; Z'taruhn, Planet—Imaginary

Summary: Believing herself a murderer, Larissa flees Hook. Very tall and athletic, Larissa works as a bodyguard until her job terminates on Z'taruhn where she meets Shade and her Aesopian friends and learns of the Aesopian origins.

Other books you might like:
David Brin, *Startide Rising*, 1983
David Brin, *The Uplift War*, 1987
Lois McMaster Bujold, *Shards of Honor*, 1986
Debra Doyle, *The Price of the Stars*, 1992
    James D. Macdonald, co-author
Stephen Goldin, *Jade Darcy and the Affair of Honor*, 1988
    Mary Mason, co-author
Steve Perry, *The Man Who Never Missed*, 1985
Alis A. Rasmussen, *A Passage of Stars*, 1990

1213

EMILY DEVENPORT

Shade

(New York: Roc, 1991)

Story type: Science Fiction (Psychic Powers; Young Adult)
Major character(s): Shade, Runaway, Teenager; Knossus, Alien (Aesopian); Donokh, Alien (Q'rin)
Time period(s): Indeterminate Future
Locale(s): Los Angeles, California; Z'taruhn, Planet—Imaginary

Summary: After being abandoned by her parents, Shade decides to stow away on a spaceship and leave Earth behind. She is abandoned again and marooned on Z'taruhn, a gambling planet with no Earth embassy. Shade survives by using her empathic ability to pick winners and through her partnership with Knossus, the elephant man.

Other books you might like:
Douglas Adams, *The Hitchhiker's Guide to the Galaxy*, 1980
David Brin, *Startide Rising*, 1983
George Alec Effinger, *When Gravity Fails*, 1987
W. Michael Gear, *Starstrike*, 1990
Janet Kagan, *Hellspark*, 1988
Pamela F. Service, *Under Alien Stars*, 1990

1214

ROBERT DEVEREAUX

Deadweight

(New York: Dell/Abyss, 1994)

Story type: Horror (Wild Talents; Reanimated Dead)
Major character(s): Karin Tanner, Gardener; Danny Daniels, Reanimated Dead; Frank Tanner, Lawyer (Karin's husband)
Time period(s): 1990s (1994)
Locale(s): Roseville, California

Summary: Married to the dull but dependable defense attorney who cleared her of the murder of her abusive husband, Karin Tanner grapples with her ambivalence toward her life and self-esteem. Her powerful feelings uncannily amplify her gardener's green thumb, accidentally resurrecting the corpse of her husband, who intends to settle the score with her. This is the author's first novel.

Other books you might like:
Rick Hautala, *Ghost Light*, 1992
Ruby Jean Jensen, *Celia*, 1991
Dean R. Koontz, *Shadowfires*, 1987

1215

ROBERT DEVEREAUX

Walking Wounded

(New York: Dell, 1996)

Story type: Horror (Wild Talents)
Major character(s): Katt Galloway, Masseuse; Marcus Galloway, Professor (English); Sherry Feit, Professor
Time period(s): 1990s (1996)
Locale(s): Fort Collins, Colorado

Summary: Katt discovers that she has the power to cure or kill by touch at the same time that she falls in love with Sherry, her philandering husband's mistress. She determines to dispose of her husband by activating his still dormant Huntington's Chorea, but finds her relationship with Sherry complicated by a serial killer stalking the two of them.

Other books you might like:
John Byrne, *Whipping Boy*, 1992
Thomas F. Monteleone, *The Blood of the Lamb*, 1992
Thomas F. Monteleone, *The Resurrectionist*, 1995
Yvonne Navarro, *Deadrush*, 1995
F. Paul Wilson, *The Touch*, 1997

1216
DEAN DEVLIN
ROLAND EMMERICH, Co-Author
STEPHEN MOLSTAD, Co-Author

Independence Day
(New York: HarperPrism, 1996)

Story type: Science Fiction (Invasion of Earth; Military)
Major character(s): Thomas Whitmore, Political Figure; Constance ''Connie'' Spano, Public Relations (communications director); Steven Hiller, Military Personnel, Pilot
Time period(s): 1990s
Locale(s): Washington, District of Columbia; Area 51, Nevada

Summary: Worldwide interruption of communications precedes a violent invasion of extraterrestrials which could spell the end of civilization, if not the human race. As millions die, defenders construct a toxic computer program in a desperate attempt to halt the aliens. Novelizes the film.

Other books you might like:
A.C. Crispin, *V*, 1984
Jonathan Gems, *Mars Attacks!*, 1996
Robert A. Heinlein, *Starship Troopers*, 1951
Larry Niven, *Footfall*, 1985
   Jerry Pournelle, co-author
Judith Reeves-Stevens, *The Day of Descent*, 1993
   Garfield Reeves-Stevens, co-author
Robert Tine, *Chain Reaction*, 1996

1217
DEAN DEVLIN
ROLAND EMMERICH, Co-Author

StarGate
(New York: Signet, 1994)

Story type: Science Fiction (Adventure)
Major character(s): Jack O'Neil, Military Personnel, Leader (StarGate program); Daniel Jackson, Linguist, Scholar (Egyptologist); Ra-hotep-kan ''Ra'', Alien
Time period(s): 1990s (1994); Indeterminate
Locale(s): Planet—Imaginary; Colorado; Africa

Summary: After excavation reveals an alien device dubbed ''StarGate,'' which seems to relate to Egyptian astronomy and the deity Ra, scientists speculate the device could transport humans to another planet. When an advance recon team tests the device, they arrive at an unknown place with ancient Egyptian architecture and discover they may have no way home from the potentially deadly planet. Novelizes the movie.

Other books you might like:
Roger MacBride Allen, *The Ring of Charon*, 1990
Philip K. Dick, *The Unteleported Man*, 1983
   revised edition
Alan Dean Foster, *The Last Starfighter*, 1984
Frederik Pohl, *Gateway*, 1977
George Zebrowski, *Stranger Suns*, 1991

1218
GENE DEWEESE

King of the Dead
(Lake Geneva, Wisconsin: Berkley, 1996)

Story type: Horror (Alternate World)
Series: Ravenloft
Major character(s): Firan Zal'honan, Sorcerer; Oldar, Assistant; Lord Darcalus, Wizard
Time period(s): Indeterminate
Locale(s): Darkon, Mythical Place

Summary: In his avatar as Firan Zal'honan, Azalin, King of the Dead, mourns the death of his son Irik and ponders the course of events that have brought him to the world of Darkon, where his current incarnation plots the assassination of Lord Darcalus. This novel is set in the gaming world of Ravenloft, a gothic universe where sorcery and supernatural beings are commonplace.

Other books you might like:
Mark Anthony, *Tower of Doom*, 1994
P.N. Elrod, *I, Strahd*, 1993
Laurell K. Hamilton, *Death of a Darklord*, 1995
Tanya Huff, *Scholar of Decay*, 1995
Chet Williamson, *Mordenheim*, 1994

1219
GENE DEWEESE

Renegade
(New York: Pocket, 1991)

Story type: Science Fiction (Space Opera)
Series: Star Trek
Major character(s): James T. Kirk, Spaceship Captain; Leonard McCoy, Doctor; Spock, Scientist, Alien (Vulcan)
Time period(s): 23rd century
Locale(s): *U.S.S. Enterprise*, Spaceship; Chyrellka, Planet—Imaginary; Vancadia, Planet—Imaginary

Summary: During the last year of its original five-year mission, the *Enterprise* responds to broken relations between the rebelling colony world, Vancadia, and mother world Chyrellka. When Kirk sends Spock and McCoy to investigate rebel demands, their capture and apparent deaths devastate Kirk. His subsequent investigation into events uncovers a Klingon plot against the Federation.

Other books you might like:
Margaret Wander Bonanno, *Dwellers in the Crucible*, 1985
J.M. Dillard, *The Lost Years*, 1989
Brad Ferguson, *A Flag Full of Stars*, 1991
Barbara Hambly, *Ishmael*, 1985
Della Van Hise, *Killing Time*, 1985
Robert E. Vardeman, *The Klingon Gambit*, 1981

1220

SUSAN DEXTER

The Prince of Ill Luck

(New York: Ballantine Del Rey, 1994)

Story type: Fantasy (Light Fantasy; Magic Conflict)
Series: Warhorse of Esdragon
Major character(s): Leith, Royalty (Prince of the Isles), Psychic; Kessallia, Noblewoman; Valadan, Animal (horse)
Time period(s): Indeterminate
Locale(s): Esdragon, Fictional Country

Summary: As Leith wanders the hills of Esdragon searching to lift the curse of ill luck which seems to strike all those around him, he encounters and befriends Valadan, a stallion sired by the wind. They conquer a glass hill, foiling fair, fiery Kessallia's plan to keep her many suiters busy while she searches for her father and long lost witch queen mother. Leith joins her through caves, mountain perils and strife on a quest to lift his curse and free Kessallia from her vow.

Other books you might like:
Tom Deitz, *Soulsmith*, 1990
Nina Kiriki Hoffman, *The Thread That Binds the Bones*, 1993
John Moore, *Slay and Rescue*, 1993
Midori Snyder, *The Flight of Michael McBride*, 1994
Patricia C. Wrede, *Calling on Dragons*, 1993

1221

SUSAN DEXTER

The True Knight

(New York: Ballantine Del Rey, 1996)

Story type: Fantasy (Quest; Magic Conflict)
Series: Warhorse of Esdragon
Major character(s): Titch, Warrior, Adventurer; Wren, Apprentice, Magician; Valadan, Animal (horse)
Time period(s): Indeterminate
Locale(s): Esdragon, Fictional Country

Summary: Setting out to achieve knighthood, Titch suffers wounds which require Wren's attention. Separating, the pair reunite when the Red Queen demands that mages and wisewomen find her ensorcelled son and transform him from a swan back into a prince or suffer death.

Other books you might like:
Anne Kelleher Bush, *Children of Enchantment*, 1996
Terry Goodkind, *Wizard's First Rule*, 1994
Robin Hobb, *Assassin's Apprentice*, 1995
J.V. Jones, *The Baker's Boy*, 1995
Kristine Kathryn Rusch, *Traitors*, 1994

1222

SUSAN DEXTER

The Wizard's Shadow

(New York: Ballantine Del Rey, 1993)

Story type: Fantasy (Magic Conflict; Adventure)

Major character(s): Crocken, Peddler, Adventurer; The Shadow, Disembodied Personality
Time period(s): Indeterminate
Locale(s): Armyn, Fictional Country; Axe-Edge, Fictional City

Summary: Seeking revenge, a dying wizard casts off his shadow. Summoned to meet the shadow during an eclipse, then threatened, Crocken cedes use of his body to the shadow. Crocken's goal of profitable trade and the shadow's mission of vengeance advance rapidly when Crocken's mad act of heroism saves Princess Gloriet.

Other books you might like:
Alfred Bester, *The Stars My Destination*, 1956
Kara Dalkey, *The Curse of Sagamore*, 1986
Kara Dalkey, *The Sword of Sagamore*, 1989
Elizabeth Forrest, *Phoenix Fire*, 1992
Marc Laidlaw, *Neon Lotus*, 1988

1223

PAUL DI FILIPPO

Ribofunk

(New York: Four Walls Eight Windows, 1996)

Story type: Science Fiction (Collection; Hard Science Fiction)

Summary: Contains two original and 11 stories reprinted from periodicals and anthologies 1989-1995. Ranging from downbeat to humorous, the stories focus on diverse aspects of biology with other themes including renegade gene splicers, human chimeras, a sentient river, and a revolutionary Peter Rabbit.

Other books you might like:
Michael Flynn, *The Nanotech Chronicles*, 1991
Janet Kagan, *Mirabile*, 1991
Robert Silverberg, *Murasaki*, 1992
    Martin H. Greenberg, co-editor
Marc Stiegler, *The Gentle Seduction*, 1990
John Varley, *The Persistence of Vision*, 1978

1224

PAUL DI FILIPPO

The Steampunk Trilogy

(New York: Four Walls Eight Windows, 1995)

Story type: Science Fiction (Alternate History; Collection)
Major character(s): Cosmo Cowperthwait, Inventor, Naturalist; Emily Dickinson, Writer (poet), Historical Figure
Time period(s): 19th century
Locale(s): Alternate Earth; England; Massachusetts

Summary: Contains one original and two reprinted stories set in a very different Victorian Era: "Victoria" (*Amazing*, 1991) features a randy Queen Victoria clone and mysterious super science as Cosmo Cowperthwait investigates Victoria's disappearance; in "Hottentots" Lovecraftian horrors threaten historical characters; and "Walt and Emily" (*Interzone*, 1993) works poets' verse into the romance between Walt Whitman and Emily Dickinson.

Other books you might like:
Philip K. Dick, *The Man in the High Castle*, 1962
Randall Garrett, *Too Many Magicians*, 1967
William Gibson, *The Difference Engine*, 1991
   Bruce Sterling, co-author
Kim Newman, *Anno Dracula*, 1993
Neal Stephenson, *Snow Crash*, 1992
Harry Turtledove, *The Guns of the South*, 1992

1225
PHILIP K. DICK

The Collected Stories of Philip K. Dick, Volume One: The Short Happy Life of the Brown Oxford

(New York: Carol Publishing Group, 1990)

Story type: Science Fiction (Collection)
Series: Collected Stories of Philip K. Dick
Major character(s): The Brown Oxford, Experimental Subject; Doc Labyrinth, Scientist; Shadrach Jones, Clerk, Royalty
Time period(s): 1950s
Locale(s): United States

Summary: This is a collection of 25 stories written between 1953-1955. The title story recounts an attempt to make the inanimate animate by the Principle of Sufficient Irritation. The stories range from whimsical to chilling, sometimes within a single work. This book is a reprint of the 1987 Underwood-Miller edition subtitled *Beyond Lies the Wub*.

Other books you might like:
Michael Bishop, *The Secret Ascension*, 1987
James P. Blaylock, *The Paper Grail*, 1991
Pat Cadigan, *Mindplayers*, 1987
K.W. Jeter, *The Glass Hammer*, 1985
Tim Powers, *Dinner at Deviant's Palace*, 1985

1226
PHILIP K. DICK

The Collected Stories of Philip K. Dick, Volume Two: We Can Remember It for You Wholesale

(New York: Carol Publishing Group, 1990)

Story type: Science Fiction (Collection)
Series: Collected Stories of Philip K. Dick
Major character(s): Douglas Quail, Clerk, Spy; Mr. McClane, Psychologist
Time period(s): Indeterminate Future
Locale(s): Earth; Mars

Summary: This volume contains 27 stories written between 1953-1954 from the early years of Dick's career and includes the story that inspired the movie *Total Recall*. As usual for Dick, Quail finds reality breaking down when a trip to a memory-implanting clinic provides him with recollections of an assassination that he may or may not have actually committed. Reprint of the 1986 Underwood-Miller edition *Second*

Variety, in which the title story was replaced with the movie tie-in story.

Other books you might like:
Michael Bishop, *The Secret Ascension*, 1987
James P. Blaylock, *The Digging Leviathan*, 1989
Pat Cadigan, *Patterns*, 1989
K.W. Jeter, *The Glass Hammer*, 1985
Tim Powers, *The Anubis Gates*, 1983

1227
PHILIP K. DICK

Eye in the Sky

(New York: Macmillan Collier Nucleus, 1989)

Story type: Science Fiction (Alternate Universe)
Major character(s): Jack Hamilton, Engineer; Marsha Hamilton, Liberal
Time period(s): 1950s (1959)
Locale(s): California

Summary: When an experiment in high-energy physics goes wrong, eight people find themselves flung into a series of increasingly bizarre nightmares which seem to reflect their own paranoid fears. They seek desperately for a way of escape and are changed utterly by their experience. Originally published in 1957.

Other books you might like:
Michael Bishop, *The Secret Ascension*, 1987
Fredric Brown, *What Mad Universe*, 1949
Ursula K. Le Guin, *The Lathe of Heaven*, 1971
Robert Charles Wilson, *Gypsies*, 1989
Gene Wolfe, *There Are Doors*, 1988
Roger Zelazny, *The Dream Master*, 1966

1228
PHILIP K. DICK

The Penultimate Truth

(New York: Carroll & Graf, 1989)

Story type: Science Fiction (Post-Nuclear Holocaust)
Major character(s): Nicholas St. James, Government Official; Joseph Adams, Writer
Time period(s): 21st century
Locale(s): United States

Summary: War has raged for fifteen years and Americans have been living underground all that time building the weapons needed to keep the war going. There is evidence, however, that something strange is going on. The President of the United States, seen periodically on the news, doesn't appear to be aging. There are rumors that the war may in fact be a hoax. Nick St. James determines to find out the truth. Originally published in 1964.

Other books you might like:
Michael Bishop, *The Secret Ascension*, 1987
Michael Kandel, *Strange Invasion*, 1989
Leonard C. Lewin, *Report from Iron Mountain*, 1967
Mordecai Roshwald, *Level 7*, 1959

1229

PHILIP K. DICK

The Zap Gun
(New York: Carroll & Graf, 1989)

Story type: Science Fiction (Satire)
Major character(s): Lars Powderdry, Engineer (Weapons Designer); Lilo Topchek, Engineer (Weapons Designer)
Time period(s): 21st century (2004)
Locale(s): Wes-bloc, Fictional Country; Peep-East, Fictional Country

Summary: Lars Powderdry is the most respected and successful weapons designer in Wes-bloc. While under the influence of hallucinogenic drugs he creates dazzling weapons, weapons capable of spectacular, wholesale destruction. There's just one catch. None of them work. They're all cheap fakes, just like the weapons Peep-East comes up with, designed to fulfill the public's need for violence and macho posturing. Despite great wealth and fame, Powderdry knows he's a fake and this upsets him. He decides to do something about it. Originally published in 1967.

Other books you might like:
Michael Bishop, *The Secret Ascension*, 1987
Ursula K. Le Guin, *The Lathe of Heaven*, 1971
A.E. van Vogt, *The Weapon Shops of Isher*, 1951
Kurt Vonnegut Jr., *Player Piano*, 1952

1230

CHARLES DICKENS
CARLO FRUTTERO, Co-Author
FRANCO LUCENTINI, Co-Author

The D. Case: The Truth about the Mystery of Edwin Drood
(New York: Harcourt Brace Jovanovich, 1992)

Story type: Fantasy (Mystery; Satire)
Major character(s): Sherlock Holmes, Detective—Private; Philip Marlowe, Detective—Private; Nero Wolfe, Detective—Private
Time period(s): 1990s
Locale(s): Rome, Italy (Urbis et Orbis Hotel)

Summary: A forum on the Completion of Unfinished or Fragmentary Works in Music and Literature, an international conference sponsored by the Japanese, attracts the greatest detectives from literature, all interested in Charles Dickens' fragmentary novel, *The Mystery of Edwin Drood*. To finish and solve that mystery, detectives including Lew Archer, Father Brown, Sherlock Holmes, Jules Maigret, Philip Marlowe, Hercule Poirot and Nero Wolfe listen and consult mediums and computers as simultaneous translations present Dickens' novel a chapter at a time, yielding a mystery surrounding the author as well as the novel. Translated by Gregory Dowling. Originally published in Italy in 1989.

Other books you might like:
Milorad Pavic, *Landscape Painted with Tea*, 1990
Bill Pronzini, *Double*, 1984
    Marcia Muller, co-author

Fred Saberhagen, *The Holmes-Dracula File*, 1978
Manly Wade Wellman, *Sherlock Holmes's War of the Worlds*, 1975
    Wade Wellman, co-author
Gary K. Wolf, *Who Censored Roger Rabbit?*, 1981

1231

PETER DICKINSON

Eva
(New York: Delacorte Press, 1989)

Story type: Science Fiction (Young Adult)
Major character(s): Eva, Teenager; Dad, Scientist
Time period(s): Indeterminate Future
Locale(s): Earth

Summary: When thirteen year old Eva is in a serious automobile accident and isn't expected to survive, her father, a primate zoologist, has her mind transferred into the brain of a chimpanzee. Eva must learn to live in the chimp body and must also learn to cope with what's left of the chimp's memories and impulses.

Other books you might like:
Roger MacBride Allen, *Orphan of Creation*, 1988
Michael Bishop, *Ancient of Days*, 1985
Michael Bishop, *No Enemy but Time*, 1982
John Gribbin, *Father to the Man*, 1989
Pat Murphy, *Rachel in Love*, 1987

1232

PETER DICKINSON
EMMA CHICHESTER-CLARK, Illustrator

Time and the Clock Mice, Etcetera
(New York: Delacorte, 1994)

Story type: Fantasy (Young Adult; Psychic Powers)
Major character(s): I, Writer, Artisan (clockmaker); Tracy Dickory, Animal (mouse), Telepath
Time period(s): 1990s
Locale(s): Branton, England

Summary: After 99 years of operation, the Branton Town Hall Clock stops, threatening the tourist trade. When the clockmaker's grandson investigates, he discovers, living inside, families of fabulously intelligent, telepathic Clock Mice who help keep things running. As the clock undergoes detailed repairs, Dickinson presents insight into clockworks, bells, people, cats, mice and animal intelligence.

Other books you might like:
Michael Ende, *The Night of Wishes: or The Satanarchaeolidealcohellish Notion Potion*, 1992
Brian Jacques, *Redwall*, 1987
Barry Lopez, *Crow and Weasel*, 1990
Robert C. O'Brien, *Mrs. Frisby and the Rats of NIMH*, 1971
James Thurber, *The 13 Clocks*, 1950

1233

GORDON R. DICKSON

The Dragon and the Djinn

(New York: Ace, 1996)

Story type: Fantasy (Quest; Alternate World)
Series: Dragon Knight
Major character(s): Jim Eckert, Knight, Magician; Sir Brian Neville-Smythe, Knight, Fiance(e)
Time period(s): Indeterminate
Locale(s): England, Alternate Earth; Middle East, Alternate Earth

Summary: To turn his engagement into marriage, Brian must travel to the Middle East in search of his fiancee's missing father to acquire his blessing. For his journey, Brian secures James' aid, not realizing how useful the magician will prove when pirates, sea giants and a particularly dangerous djinn impede their progress.

Other books you might like:
Glen Cook, *Tower of Fear*, 1989
Stephen Goldin, *Shrine of the Desert Mage*, 1988
Ursula K. Le Guin, *A Wizard of Earthsea*, 1968
R.A. MacAvoy, *Tea with the Black Dragon*, 1983
Elizabeth Ann Scarborough, *The Harem of Aman Akbar*, 1984

1234

GORDON R. DICKSON

The Dragon at War

(New York: Ace, 1992)

Story type: Fantasy (Alternate World; Magic Conflict)
Series: Dragon Knight
Major character(s): Jim Eckert, Knight, Magician; Essessili, Mythical Creature (sea serpent)
Time period(s): 14th century
Locale(s): England, Alternate Earth; France, Alternate Earth

Summary: When the French ally themselves with mighty sea serpents in order to defeat the English, Jim and his companions travel to France to enlist the help of dragons to repel the invasion of sea serpents. Fourth in the series.

Other books you might like:
Phyllis Eisenstein, *In the Red Lord's Reach*, 1989
Phyllis Eisenstein, *Shadow of Earth*, 1979
Ursula K. Le Guin, *A Wizard of Earthsea*, 1968
Brad Strickland, *Wizard's Mole*, 1991

1235

GORDON R. DICKSON

The Dragon Knight

(New York: Tor, 1990)

Story type: Fantasy (Alternate World; Quest)
Series: Dragon Knight
Major character(s): Jim Eckert, Nobleman (Baron de Bois de Malencontri), Magician; Aargh, Animal (Wolf/Englishwolf)

Time period(s): 14th century
Locale(s): England, Alternate Earth

Summary: In this continuation of *The Dragon and the George* (1976), Jim Eckert, who had decided to stay in the magical kingdom a few months previous, awakes in the form of a dragon. He realizes that he has much to learn about his new situation, and it had better be soon. He must fulfill his obligations to his king—will he have time to get his magic under control?

Other books you might like:
L. Sprague de Camp, *The Incomplete Enchanter*, 1942
Robert Don Hughes, *Prophet of Lamath*, 1979
Fritz Leiber, *The Knight and Knave of Swords*, 1990
Larry Niven, *The Magic Goes Away*, 1979
Alis A. Rasmussen, *The Labyrinth Gate*, 1988
Mark Twain, *A Connecticut Yankee in King Arthur's Court*, 1889
   Pseudonym of Samuel Clemens
Michael Williams, *A Sorcerer's Apprentice*, 1990

1236

GORDON R. DICKSON

The Dragon on the Border

(New York: Ace, 1992)

Story type: Fantasy (Alternate World; Magic Conflict)
Series: Dragon Knight
Major character(s): Jim Eckert, Knight, Magician; Dafydd ap Hywel, Martial Arts Expert (bowman), Royalty (Prince of Merlon)
Time period(s): 14th century
Locale(s): England, Alternate Earth

Summary: As Sir Jim and friends ride North toward the Scottish border, strange apparitions attack their party. Swift action by Dafydd defeats the attack which seemed to come from armor occupied by invisible men mounted on invisible horses. Jim immediately involves himself in repelling the invasion of Hollow Men, ensorcelled warriors. Traditionally hostile groups unite to eliminate the Hollow Men, but Jim himself must meet the final challenge from a deadly worm. Third in the series.

Other books you might like:
Mark Acres, *Dark Divide*, 1991
Ursula K. Le Guin, *A Wizard of Earthsea*, 1968
Christopher Stasheff, *King Kobold Revived*, 1984
Margaret Weis, *Fire Sea*, 1991
   Tracy Hickman, co-author
Patricia C. Wrede, *Searching for Dragons*, 1991

1237

GORDON R. DICKSON

The Dragon, the Earl, and the Troll

(New York: Ace, 1994)

Story type: Fantasy (Magic Conflict; Alternate World)
Series: Dragon Knight

Major character(s): Jim Eckert, Knight, Magician; Sir Brian Neville-Smythe, Knight; Mnrogar, Mythical Creature (troll)

Time period(s): Indeterminate

Locale(s): England, Alternate Earth

Summary: After Jim and Angela survive an attack on their castle, Carolinus informs them that they will have to attend the lavish Christmas feast of the Earl of Somerset. When the Dark Powers plan a new offensive, Jim must foil the plot with help from old friends and new allies.

Other books you might like:
Poul Anderson, *Three Hearts and Three Lions*, 1961
Randall Garrett, *Too Many Magicians*, 1967
Barbara Hambly, *The Dark Hand of Magic*, 1990
Christopher Stasheff, *The Warlock in Spite of Himself*, 1969
Patricia C. Wrede, *Dealing with Dragons*, 1990

1238

GORDON R. DICKSON

The Harriers

(New York: Baen, 1991)

Story type: Science Fiction (Anthology; Military)

Series: War and Honor

Locale(s): The Magnificate, Interstellar Empire/Federation

Summary: A shared world-type anthology featuring the military forces which guard the Hub and its diplomats. The three stories included are ''Of War and Codes and Honor,'' a collaboration between Gordon R. Dickson and Chelsea Quinn Yarbro, plus Steve Perry's ''Into the Hot and Moist,'' and S.N. Lewitt's ''Tonight We Improvise.''

Other books you might like:
David Brin, *Startide Rising*, 1983
Allan Cole, *Sten*, 1982
    Chris Bunch, co-author
S.N. Lewitt, *Cyberstealth*, 1989
George R.R. Martin, *Wild Cards*, 1987
    editor
Larry Niven, *Man-Kzin Wars*, 1988
    editor
Steve Perry, *The Man Who Never Missed*, 1985
Chelsea Quinn Yarbro, *Hyacinths*, 1983

1239

GORDON R. DICKSON

The Magnificent Wilf

(New York: Baen, 1995)

Story type: Science Fiction (Humor; First Contact)

Major character(s): Tom Parent, Diplomat; Lucy Parent, Linguist; Rex, Animal (dog)

Time period(s): Indeterminate Future

Locale(s): Earth; Cayahno, Planet—Imaginary

Summary: Chosen as a ''typical'' couple to host a visiting Oprinkian diplomat, Tom and Lucy develop new abilities, including telepathic contact with their dog, Rex, and find themselves thrust into galactic politics. As representatives of

Earth, Tom, Lucy, and Rex free the Bulburs from Jaktal tyranny, correct a wobble in Wockii futures, and save the galaxy from invaders. Expands previously published short stories into a novel.

Other books you might like:
Poul Anderson, *Earthman's Burden*, 1957
    Gordon R. Dickson, co-author
John M. Ford, *How Much for Just the Planet?*, 1987
Harry Harrison, *Bill, the Galactic Hero*, 1965
Keith Laumer, *Retief at Large*, 1978
Alexei Panshin, *Star Well*, 1968
James H. Schmitz, *The Witches of Karres*, 1966
Connie Willis, *Uncharted Territory*, 1994

1240

GORDON R. DICKSON

Naked to the Stars/The Alien Way

(New York: Tor, 1991)

Story type: Science Fiction (First Contact; Military)

Major character(s): Cal Truant, Military Personnel, Government Official; Jason ''Jase'' Lee Barchar, Government Official, Experimental Subject; Kator Secondcousin Brutogas, Alien (Ruml)

Time period(s): Indeterminate Future

Locale(s): Paumons, Planet—Imaginary; Earth; Ruml Homeworld, Planet—Imaginary

Summary: In *Naked to the Stars* (1961), Cal Truant risks his mission and the lives of many in a desperate attempt to force a meeting as equals between leaders of the Terran invasion force and the native Paumons. In *The Alien Way* (1965), a human trap infects Kator Secondcousin with a virus which causes transmission of Kator's thoughts into Jason Barchar's mind, allowing humans to understand the enemy to whom humanity wishes to extend friendship. As Jason begins to understand Ruml ways, his superiors start acting as if Jason has become the enemy.

Other books you might like:
Roger MacBride Allen, *The Ring of Charon*, 1990
Jeffrey A. Carver, *The Rapture Effect*, 1987
C.J. Cherryh, *Forty Thousand in Gehenna*, 1983
Robert L. Forward, *Dragon's Egg*, 1980
Janet Kagan, *Hellspark*, 1988
Rebecca Ore, *Becoming Alien*, 1987
Robert Silverberg, *Letters From Atlantis*, 1990
David Alexander Smith, *Homecoming*, 1990
David Alexander Smith, *Rendezvous*, 1988

1241

GORDON R. DICKSON

Other

(New York: Tor, 1994)

Story type: Science Fiction (Political)

Series: Childe Cycle

Major character(s): Bleys Ahrens, Genius, Activist; Antonia ''Toni'' Lu, Activist, Assistant; Henry MacLean, Farmer

Time period(s): 24th century
Locale(s): Association, Planet—Imaginary; New Earth, Planet—Imaginary

Summary: Bleys Ahrens continues his plan to unify the Others, those humans neither Exotics, Dorsai, nor Old Earth. He extends his influence to the worlds of new Earth, Cassida and Newton. At the same time, he tries to find and capture Hal Mayne, whose mysterious powers make him a match for Bleys.

Other books you might like:
Isaac Asimov, *Foundation and Empire*, 1952
Lois McMaster Bujold, *Brothers in Arms*, 1988
C.J. Cherryh, *Cyteen*, 1988
Frank Herbert, *Dune Messiah*, 1969
David Wingrove, *The Middle Kingdom*, 1990

1242

GORDON R. DICKSON

Wolf and Iron

(New York: Tor Books, 1990)

Story type: Science Fiction (Post-Holocaust)
Major character(s): Jeeris Belamy "Jeebee" Walther, Professor; Paul Sanderson, Businessman, Wanderer; Merry Sanderson, Girlfriend
Time period(s): 20th century
Locale(s): South Dakota; Montana

Summary: An expansion of the 1974 short story, "In Iron Years." Jeebee is forced by the collapse of modern society to leave the university town where he resides to visit his brother. While learning to understand the wolf he befriends on his travels, he learns to survive in a non-technological world.

Other books you might like:
Jean M. Auel, *Clan of the Cave Bear*, 1980
Dean R. Koontz, *Watchers*, 1987
Donald E. McQuinn, *Warrior*, 1990
David R. Palmer, *Emergence*, 1984
Alexei Panshin, *Rite of Passage*, 1968

1243

GORDON R. DICKSON

Young Bleys

(New York: Tor, 1991)

Story type: Science Fiction (Political)
Series: Childe Cycle
Major character(s): Bleys Ahrens, Student, Activist; Dahno Ahrens, Activist
Time period(s): 24th century
Locale(s): Association, Planet—Imaginary

Summary: When Bleys Ahrens becomes a problem for his mother, she sends him to live with his uncle on the planet Association. There Bleys joins his brother, Dahno, in an interstellar organization of people whose parentage is mixed among the Three Splinter Cultures: the Exotics, the Friendlies and the Dorsai. Bleys eventually takes over the organization, hoping to further his goal of dominating many worlds.

Other books you might like:
Isaac Asimov, *The Foundation Trilogy*, 1951-1953
Lois McMaster Bujold, *Adventures of Miles Vorkosian*, 1986-
Harry Harrison, *The Deathworld Trilogy*, 1960-1968
Steve Perry, *The Man Who Never Missed Series*, 1985-1989

1244

WILLIAM C. DIETZ

Bodyguard

(New York: Ace, 1994)

Story type: Science Fiction (Military; Adventure)
Major character(s): Max Maxon, Bodyguard, Handicapped (brain damaged); Sasha Casad, Teenager; Norris, Military Personnel (corporate)
Time period(s): Indeterminate Future
Locale(s): Sea-Tac Urboplex, Washington (Seattle, Tacoma); Mars

Summary: Max Maxon accepts the job of protecting Sasha on her trip to Europa Station. After kidnappers take her from his apartment right in front of him, Max must rescue her and get them to Europa despite the apparent army of people out to kill or rape Sasha.

Other books you might like:
Lois McMaster Bujold, *Shards of Honor*, 1986
Brian Daley, *Jinx on a Terran Inheritance*, 1985
Stephen Goldin, *Jade Darcy and the Affair of Honor*, 1988
  Mary Mason, co-author
Elizabeth Moon, *Hunting Party*, 1993
Steve Perry, *The Man Who Never Missed*, 1985

1245

WILLIAM C. DIETZ

Drifter

(New York: Ace, 1991)

Story type: Science Fiction (Adventure; Theological)
Series: Pik Lando
Major character(s): Pik Lando, Smuggler, Spaceship Captain; Wendy Wendeen, Religious, Doctor
Time period(s): Indeterminate Future
Locale(s): *The Tinker's Damn*, Spaceship; Angel, Planet—Imaginary

Summary: When Lando agreed to smuggle fertilizer past Mega-Metals Corporation customs officers, he didn't anticipate becoming involved in a revolution which could change not only Angel's government but also the ecology of the entire planet.

Other books you might like:
Lois McMaster Bujold, *The Vor Game*, 1990
C.J. Cherryh, *The Pride of Chanur*, 1982
Marc Laidlaw, *Neon Lotus*, 1988
Melisa C. Michaels, *First Battle*, 1985
Melisa C. Michaels, *Skirmish*, 1985
Larry Niven, *Fallen Angels*, 1991
  Jerry Pournelle, Michael Flynn, co-authors
Alis A. Rasmussen, *Revolution's Shore*, 1990

Joan Slonczewski, *A Door into Ocean*, 1986
Michael Swanwick, *Vacuum Flowers*, 1987
Walter Jon Williams, *Hardwired*, 1986

1246

WILLIAM C. DIETZ

Drifter's Run

(New York: Ace, 1992)

Story type: Science Fiction (Adventure)
Series: Pik Lando
Major character(s): Pik Lando, Smuggler, Pilot (spaceship); Melissa Sorenson, Child, Businesswoman; Cy Borg, Cyborg, Engineer
Time period(s): Indeterminate Future
Locale(s): *Junk*, Spaceship; Outer Space

Summary: When Pik Lando hastily signs on as pilot on the *Junk*, he finds the skills acquired as a smuggler prove useful when his captain mixes drayage, salvage and his perpetual search for the missing luxury liner, *Star of Empire*.

Other books you might like:
Lois McMaster Bujold, *Brothers in Arms*, 1988
Lois McMaster Bujold, *The Warrior's Apprentice*, 1986
Alis A. Rasmussen, *A Passage of Stars*, 1990
Alis A. Rasmussen, *The Price of Ransom*, 1990
Alis A. Rasmussen, *Revolution's Shore*, 1990
Mike Resnick, *Soothsayer*, 1991

1247

WILLIAM C. DIETZ

Drifter's War

(New York: Ace, 1992)

Story type: Science Fiction (Adventure)
Series: Pik Lando
Major character(s): Pik Lando, Smuggler, Pilot; Cy Borg, Cyborg, Engineer
Time period(s): Indeterminate Future
Locale(s): NBHJ-43301-G, Planet—Imaginary

Summary: When Cy's companions rejoin him on the drifting alien spacecraft, they find themselves on an unexpected hyperspace voyage which leads to a world in which they represent the natives' only hope of surviving an alien invasion.

Other books you might like:
David Brin, *Startide Rising*, 1983
John DeChancie, *Red Limit Freeway*, 1984
Alis A. Rasmussen, *A Passage of Stars*, 1990
Alis A. Rasmussen, *The Price of Ransom*, 1990
Alis A. Rasmussen, *Revolution's Shore*, 1990

1248

WILLIAM C. DIETZ

The Final Battle

(New York: Ace, 1995)

Story type: Science Fiction (Military)

Series: Legion of the Damned
Major character(s): Natalie Norwood, Military Personnel (general); Max Meyers, Military Personnel (master sergeant); Poseen-Ka, Alien (Hudathan), Military Personnel
Time period(s): Indeterminate Future
Locale(s): Worber's World, Planet—Imaginary; Battle Station Alpha XIV, Space Station (Old Lady); Confederacy of Sentient Beings, Interstellar Empire/Federation

Summary: Orbiting Worber's World in the *Old Lady*, Norwood watches the Hudathans who survive on the destroyed planet. Despite great vigilance by the Confederacy of Sentient Beings, the Hudathans smuggle technology planetside, which allows resumption of the Hudathan war to eliminate all competition.

Other books you might like:
Bill Baldwin, *The Siege*, 1994
John Dalmas, *The Regiment*, 1987
Andrew Keith, *Cohort of the Damned*, 1993
Anne McCaffrey, *Treaty at Doona*, 1994
    Jody Lynn Nye, co-author
Jerry Pournelle, *Falkenberg's Legion*, 1990
David Weber, *On Basilisk Station*, 1993

1249

WILLIAM C. DIETZ

Legion of the Damned

(New York: Ace, 1993)

Story type: Science Fiction (Military; Political)
Major character(s): Paula Scolari, Military Personnel; Marianne Mosby, Military Personnel; Sergi Chien-Chu, Counselor (advisor to the throne)
Time period(s): Indeterminate Future
Locale(s): Earth; Algeron, Planet—Imaginary

Summary: Earth creates a deadly legion of cyborgs through reanimation, surgery and involuntary recruitment and training programs with a high failure rate. If they survive basic training, Algeron provides a mutually beneficial but lethal training ground for Legionnaires and a like-minded native race. Meanwhile, the Emperor and Legion struggle to counter assaults from the alien Hudatha Empire.

Other books you might like:
David Drake, *The Jungle*, 1991
David Drake, *The Warrior*, 1991
Dave Duncan, *Hero*, 1991
Stephen Goldin, *Jade Darcy and the Affair of Honor*, 1988
    Mary Mason, co-author
Andrew Keith, *March or Die*, 1992
    William H. Keith, Jr., co-author
Jerry Pournelle, *Janissaries*, 1979
Richard Sapir, *The Destroyer #1: Created, the Destroyer*, 1971
    Warren Murphy, co-author
Robert Tine, *Universal Soldier*, 1992

1250

WILLIAM C. DIETZ

Mars Prime

(New York: Roc, 1992)

Story type: Science Fiction (Adventure; Mystery)
Series: Rex Corvan
Major character(s): Rex Corvan, Journalist; Kim Corvan, Editor (broadcast news); Martin, Artificial Intelligence
Time period(s): Indeterminate Future
Locale(s): *Outward Bound*, Spaceship; Mars

Summary: Rex and Kim Corvan travel on the second colony ship to Mars. Along the way, a serial killer menaces everyone while protocol and security hamper the investigation. On Mars itself, the threats grow more complex. Even with the help of artificial intelligences, Kim and Rex find it difficult to survive more mysterious disappearances and a revolution.

Other books you might like:
Robert L. Forward, *Martian Rainbow*, 1991
Robert A. Heinlein, *The Moon Is a Harsh Mistress*, 1966
Spider Robinson, *Stardance*, 1979
    Jeanne Robinson, co-author
Richard Paul Russo, *Destroying Angel*, 1992
Allen Steele, *Orbital Decay*, 1989
John E. Stith, *Redshift Rendezvous*, 1990

1251

WILLIAM C. DIETZ

Matrix Man

(New York: Roc, 1990)

Story type: Science Fiction (Adventure; Techno-Thriller)
Series: Rex Corvan
Major character(s): Rex Corvan, Journalist (television correspondent)
Time period(s): 21st century
Locale(s): Seattle, Washington

Summary: Rex Corvan, 3-D television superstar, has unusual equipment; a camera in place of his right eye, allowing him to easily provide a second camera viewpoint. When a new device, the video matrix generator, allows easy modification of video and holographic images, the World Peace Organization decides to use it to take over the world. As Corvan investigates, he becomes a target of an assassin.

Other books you might like:
David Brin, *Earth*, 1990
Pat Cadigan, *Synners*, 1991
Orson Scott Card, *Xenocide*, 1991
Jeffrey A. Carver, *The Rapture Effect*, 1987
Robert J. Sawyer, *Golden Fleece*, 1990

1252

WILLIAM C. DIETZ

McCade's Bounty

(New York: Ace, 1990)

Story type: Science Fiction (Adventure; Military)
Series: Sam McCade
Major character(s): Sam McCade, Spaceship Captain, Bounty Hunter (former); Mustapha Pong, Pirate (space), Kidnapper; Molly McCade, Child (Sam's daughter)
Time period(s): Indeterminate Future
Locale(s): Alice, Planet—Imaginary; *Void Runner*, Spaceship

Summary: While Sam McCade was off picking up a load of fertilizer for his home planet, Alice, Mustapha Pong attacked it. Sam returns in his converted warship, *Void Runner*, to find Alice in ruins, many people dead, his wife seriously wounded, and 60 children kidnapped. Sam and his crew set off to rescue the children and punish the pirates.

Other books you might like:
Lois McMaster Bujold, *The Vor Game*, 1990
Allan Cole, *Sten*, 1984
    Chris Bunch, co-author
Melisa C. Michaels, *Pirate Prince*, 1987
Melisa C. Michaels, *Skirmish*, 1985
David R. Palmer, *Emergence*, 1984

1253

WILLIAM C. DIETZ

Prison Planet

(New York: Ace Books, 1989)

Story type: Science Fiction (Adventure)
Major character(s): Jonathan Renn, Prisoner; Marla Mendez, Cyborg, Prisoner
Time period(s): Indeterminate Future
Locale(s): Swamp, Planet—Imaginary (A prison planet)

Summary: Renn, framed for a crime he did not commit, is dumped on the dangerous prison planet Swamp. He immediately sets out to rescue Marla, escape, and seek revenge.

Other books you might like:
Allan Cole, *Revenge of the Damned*, 1989
    Chris Bunch, co-author
Harry Harrison, *Deathworld*, 1960
Barry B. Longyear, *Infinity Hold*, 1989

1254

WILLIAM C. DIETZ

Where the Ships Die

(New York; Ace, 1996)

Story type: Science Fiction (Political; Adventure)
Major character(s): Dorn Voss, Student, Teenager; Carnaby Orr, Businessman; Natalie Voss, Spacewoman
Time period(s): Indeterminate Future
Locale(s): New Hope, Planet—Imaginary; La-Tri, Planet—Imaginary; Mechnos, Planet—Imaginary

Summary: Forced to leave school due to lack of payments by his parents, Dorn falls into the hands of slavers. While a volcano erupts on La-Tri, killing all of the philosophers at once, on Mechnos, Natalie realizes that Carnaby Orr murdered her parents.

Other books you might like:
L. Warren Douglas, *Stepwater*, 1995
Debra Doyle, *The Price of the Stars*, 1992
    James D. Macdonald, co-author
Alan Dean Foster, *The Tar-Aiym Krang*, 1972
Alis A. Rasmussen, *A Passage of Stars*, 1990
David Weber, *Mutineers' Moon*, 1991

`1255`

J.M. DILLARD

Specters

(New York: Dell Abyss, 1991)

Story type: Horror (Psychological Suspense)
Major character(s): Jacob Feinman, Doctor; Avra Kallisti, Clerk (in a bookstore); Magdalen Kallisti, Teacher
Time period(s): 1990s (1990); 1930s (1936)
Locale(s): Tampa, Florida; Baltimore, Maryland

Summary: Unbeknownst to twins Avra and Magdalen Kallisti, the man who abused them as children and murdered their mother has come back under a guise they least suspect, still intent on exorcising the ghosts of his own miserable childhood by killing the two of them.

Other books you might like:
Thomas Harris, *The Silence of the Lambs*, 1988
Jack Martin, *Halloween*, 1978

`1256`

J.M. DILLARD

Star Trek VI: The Undiscovered Country

(New York: Pocket, 1991)

Story type: Science Fiction (Space Opera)
Series: Star Trek
Major character(s): James T. Kirk, Spaceship Captain; Leonard McCoy, Doctor
Time period(s): 23rd century
Locale(s): U.S.S. Enterprise, Spaceship; *Kronos One*, Spaceship; Rura Penthe, Planet—Imaginary

Summary: Kirk and the *U.S.S. Enterprise* crew unwillingly follow orders to escort Klingon High Council Chancellor Gorkon to a negotiation session aimed at dismantling space stations and starbases along the Klingon Neutral Zone. When the Chancellor's assassination leads to Kirk and McCoy's trial and sentencing to the Klingon prison planet, Rura Penthe, the *U.S.S. Enterprise* crew must rescue their officers and foil the conspiracy which threatens potential Federation peace with the Klingon Empire. Novelizes the sixth motion picture.

Other books you might like:
Diane Duane, *Doctor's Orders*, 1990
Barbara Hambly, *Ishmael*, 1985
Janet Kagan, *Uhura's Song*, 1985

Vonda N. McIntyre, *The Search for Spock*, 1984
Vonda N. McIntyre, *Transition*, 1991
Vonda N. McIntyre, *Star Trek IV: The Voyage Home*, 1986
Vonda N. McIntyre, *Star Trek II: The Wrath of Khan*, 1982
Gene Roddenberry, *Star Trek - The Motion Picture: A Novel*, 1979

`1257`

J.M. DILLARD

Star Trek: The Lost Years

(New York: Pocket Books, 1989)

Story type: Science Fiction (Space Opera)
Series: Star Trek
Major character(s): James T. Kirk, Spaceship Captain; Spock, Scientist, Alien
Time period(s): 23rd century (Stardate 6987)
Locale(s): Earth; *U.S.S. Enterprise*, Spaceship

Summary: Its five year mission over, the *Enterprise* returns to Earth and its crew is reassigned to other duties. Captain Kirk is promoted to Admiral and placed in charge of a specially created Starfleet division, while Mr. Spock accepts a teaching position on Vulcan, and Dr. McCoy goes off to do medical research. Each must struggle to achieve some form of stability in a life without the other two, but each soon finds himself immersed in a new and exciting adventure as well.

Other books you might like:
Greg Bear, *Eon*, 1985
David Brin, *Startide Rising*, 1983
Emma Bull, *Falcon*, 1989
Larry Niven, *The Mote in God's Eye*, 1974
    Jerry Pournelle, co-author
David Alexander Smith, *Rendezvous*, 1988

`1258`

BARBARA DILLON

My Stepfather Shrank!

(New York: HarperCollins, 1992)

Story type: Science Fiction (Young Adult)
Major character(s): Mallory, Child; Woody, Parent (stepfather), Lawyer; Peebles, Spouse (inventor's)
Time period(s): 1990s
Locale(s): Jefferson Village, Fictional City

Summary: Mallory's stepfather, Woody, shrinks to three inches tall when he eats a piece of candy containing Mr. Peebles' latest invention, the "Lose It Now" diet formula. A "kidnapping" by a crow, scaring off burglars and a wild time at the carnival ensue before Mr. Peebles can save Woody with another of his unpredictable inventions.

Other books you might like:
Bruce Coville, *Jeremy Thatcher, Dragon Hatcher*, 1991
Beatrice Gormley, *Mail-Order Wings*, 1981
Mary Norton, *The Borrowers*, 1953
Jenny Pausacker, *Fast Forward*, 1989
John Peterson, *The Littles*, 1967
Terry Pratchett, *Truckers*, 1989

1259

JENNIFER DIMARCO

Escape to the Wind

(New York: Castillo International Inc., 1993)

Story type: Science Fiction (Gay/Lesbian Fiction; Post-Nuclear Holocaust)
Series: Wind Trilogy
Major character(s): Tyger, Leader (Windriders), Lesbian; Christopher Jarth, Leader, Military Personnel; Ardyn, Lesbian
Time period(s): Indeterminate Future
Locale(s): New Seattle, North America

Summary: War between rival gangs and oppression by the dictatorial Patriarchy makes life miserable for unempowered New Seattle residents. Outside the protective dome a post-war phenomenon, the radioactive Wind kills most humans, metamorphosing the few survivors and all other animal life. Tyger and other Windriders seek to escape the tyranny and violence by fleeing to the unprotected wild, there discovering evidence of new Patriarchy atrocities.

Other books you might like:
Octavia E. Butler, *Imago*, 1989
Marjorie Bradley Kellogg, *Harmony*, 1991
Frances Lucas, *Cathy IV*, 1992
Vonda N. McIntyre, *Starfarers*, 1989
Severna Park, *Speaking Dreams*, 1992
Joan Slonczewski, *A Door into Ocean*, 1986

1260

THOMAS M. DISCH

The M.D.: A Horror Story

(New York: Knopf, 1991)

Story type: Horror (Satire)
Major character(s): William "Billy" Michaels, Doctor; Mercury, Deity (god of medical science); Judge Michaels, Young Man (Billy's son)
Time period(s): 1990s
Locale(s): Minneapolis, Minnesota

Summary: As a young boy, Billy Michaels is given a magic caduceus that can either heal or render illness, depending on Billy's inclinations. Billy uses his Faustian powers megalomaniacally, creating a virulent disease which he alone can cure in this satire on the absolute corruption that comes with absolute power.

Other books you might like:
Robin Cook, *Coma*, 1977
Cyril M. Kornbluth, "The Little Black Bag", 1990
in *Intensive Scare*
Mary Shelley, *Frankenstein*, 1818
Karl Edward Wagner, "The Fourth Seal", 1983
in *In a Lonely Place*
F. Paul Wilson, *The Touch*, 1986

1261

THOMAS M. DISCH

The Priest: A Gothic Romance

(New York: Knopf, 1995)

Story type: Horror (Satire)
Major character(s): Pat Bryce, Religious (Catholic priest); A.D. Boscage, Writer; Alison Sanders, Student
Time period(s): 1990s (1995)
Locale(s): Minneapolis, Minnesota

Summary: In this savage satire on the Catholic church (not to mention the writings of Whitley Streiber), Father Patrick Bryce is punished for his pedophilic tendencies by being made to preside over a concentration-camp-like establishment designed to prevent pregnant young women from having abortions. When taken over by the transmigrated soul of 13th-century Bishop Silvanus de Roquefort, a participant in the Spanish Inquistion, Bryce launches into his duties with savage and lusty glee.

Other books you might like:
Lewis Gannett, *The Living One*, 1993
William Browning Spencer, *Resume with Monsters*, 1995

1262

ROGER L. DISILVESTRO

Living with the Reptiles

(New York: Donald I. Fine, 1990)

Story type: Science Fiction (Time Travel; Humor)
Major character(s): Jackson Black, Adventurer; Ritz, Financier, Handicapped (paralyzed); Hunter Killdeer, Police Officer (time police captain)
Time period(s): 20th century; 9th century
Locale(s): South America (Amazon jungle); England

Summary: The Time Police have shot down a renegade time traveller in the 20th century. Mr. Ritz arranges to get Jackson Black's help in recovering the time travel device. The salvage operation mounted in the Amazon jungle yields a time traveller from 2075 and his downed chronocraft. Ritz takes the chronocraft back to the 9th century. Captain Killdeer arrives in the 20th century and takes Black to 2101, finding the disasterous results of Ritz's trip, results which must be reversed if human life is to survive on Earth.

Other books you might like:
Warren Norwood, *Stranded!*, 1989
Mel Odom, co-author
Warren Norwood, *Trapped!*, 1989
Warren Norwood, *Vanished*, 1988
H. Beam Piper, *Lord Kalvan of Otherwhen*, 1965
L. Neil Smith, *The Nagasaki Vector*, 1983
John Varley, *Millennium*, 1983

1263

E.L. DOCTOROW

The Waterworks

(New York: Random House, 1994)

Story type: Science Fiction (Literary; Medical)
Major character(s): Martin Pemberton, Journalist; McIlvane, Editor; Sartorius, Doctor, Inventor
Time period(s): 1870s (1871)
Locale(s): New York, New York

Summary: A freelance writer, Martin Pemberton, sees his deceased father in the streets of New York, confides this to a friend and disappears. The friend, McIlvane, follows Pemberton's trail through a city of corruption and mystery. As much a picture of a city as a story, *Waterworks* shows New York growing, for good or ill, into its current form, with the science fiction elements fantastic to the 1870s evolving into mostly common 1990s technology.

Other books you might like:
James P. Blaylock, *Homunculus*, 1986
G.K. Chesterton, *The Man Who Was Thursday*, 1908
William Hjortsberg, *Nevermore*, 1994
Tim Powers, *The Anubis Gates*, 1983

1264

BILL DOLAN

Afrikorps

(New York: Harper, 1991)

Story type: Science Fiction (Military; Post-Holocaust)
Series: Afrikorps
Major character(s): Abe "TC" Creighton, Military Personnel
Time period(s): 22nd century (2175)
Locale(s): Africa

Summary: In the wake of the "Green House" cataclysm of 2050, the offspring of Biosphere survivors struggle to reclaim the Earth. When Africa gives rise to vicious and evil new armies which invade Europe, a multinational military force, Afrikorps, organizes to clean up Africa. Captain Creighton leads his team on a violent mission for a mysterious leader hoping to win new allies for the Afrikorps.

Other books you might like:
Frank Herbert, *Dune*, 1965
J.M. Morgan, *Desert Eden*, 1991
G. Harry Stine, *The Bastard Rebellion*, 1988
G. Harry Stine, *Warbots*, 1988

1265

BILL DOLAN

Cobra Curse

(New York: Harper Paperbacks, 1993)

Story type: Science Fiction (Military; Post-Holocaust)
Series: Afrikorps
Major character(s): Abe "TC" Creighton, Military Personnel
Time period(s): 22nd century (2178)

Locale(s): Egypt; Africa

Summary: When Captain Abe Creighton leads his troops on a routine mission in Egypt, survivalist cultists capture them. Creighton escapes and discovers their plot to control the world involves a bacteriological weapons arsenal. Africorps must stop the Cult of the Cobra if they hope to return peace to Africa.

Other books you might like:
Jake Davis, *The Last Rangers*, 1992
David Drake, *The Jungle*, 1991
K.W. Jeter, *Madlands*, 1991
Mike Resnick, *Future Earths: Under African Skies*, 1993
　　Gardner Dozois, co-editor
John Sievert, *Suicide Attack*, 1990
G. Harry Stine, *The Bastard Rebellion*, 1988

1266

BILL DOLAN

Iron Horse

(New York: Harper, 1991)

Story type: Science Fiction (Military; Post-Holocaust)
Series: Afrikorps
Major character(s): Abe "TC" Creighton, Military Personnel
Time period(s): 22nd century (2175)
Locale(s): Africa

Summary: Ordered to provide security for the building of a train, Captain Creighton must respond to a warning from cryogenically frozen survivors of the "Green House" cataclysm, now revived, who tell of Marauders mounting an assault. Creighton and the Afrikorps must stop the Marauders, save the survivors from the past and safeguard the train which represents the key to future freedom.

Other books you might like:
J.M. Morgan, *Desert Eden*, 1991
G. Harry Stine, *Guts and Glory*, 1991
G. Harry Stine, *Warbots*, 1988
Michael D. Weaver, *My Father Immortal*, 1989

1267

BILL DOLAN

White Rhino

(New York: Harper, 1992)

Story type: Science Fiction (Military; Post-Holocaust)
Series: Afrikorps
Major character(s): Abe "TC" Creighton, Military Personnel; Benhaddou, Criminal
Time period(s): 22nd century (2176)
Locale(s): Africa

Summary: Hoping to again bring civilization to Africa, Creighton and the Afrikorps attempt to install a new communications system and establish a game preserve while a killer, escaped from prison, seeks Creighton with murder in mind.

Other books you might like:
Will Bradley, *Ark Liberty*, 1992

David Brin, *The Postman*, 1985
Octavia E. Butler, *Dawn*, 1987
J.M. Morgan, *Future Eden*, 1992
G. Harry Stine, *The Bastard Rebellion*, 1988
G. Harry Stine, *Warbots*, 1988
Michael D. Weaver, *My Father Immortal*, 1989

1268

D.J. DONALDSON

Blood on the Bayou

(New York: St. Martins, 1991)

Story type: Horror (Werewolf Story)
Major character(s): Andy Broussard, Doctor (Chief medical examiner); Kit Franklyn, Psychologist
Time period(s): 1990s (1991)
Locale(s): New Orleans, Louisiana

Summary: A series of brutal murders in the New Orleans area raises suspicions that it is the work of a werewolf. Doctors Andy Broussard and Kit Franklyn resist the temptation to accept this incredible possibility until Kit herself is stalked by the murderer.

Other books you might like:
George C. Chesbro, *The Fear in Yesterday's Rings*, 1991
Whitley Strieber, *The Wolfen*, 1978
Les Whitten, *Moon of the Wolf*, 1967

1269

STEPHEN R. DONALDSON

Forbidden Knowledge

(New York: Bantam Spectra, 1991)

Story type: Science Fiction (Space Opera)
Series: Gap
Major character(s): Morn Hyland, Police Officer (United Mining Corporation); Nick Succorso, Pirate, Spaceman (Captain's Fancy); Angus Thermopyle, Convict
Time period(s): Indeterminate Future
Locale(s): *Captain's Fancy*, Spaceship (in Forbidden Space)

Summary: Some pirates clandestinely allied to United Mining Corporation Police operate at the edge of the Forbidden Space where the alien Amnion hold sway. Morn is addicted to use of the illegal zone control which was planted in her head against her wishes by Angus Thermopyle. When she finally gains the control device she fights to regain her sanity and her future. *Forbidden Knowledge* is a sequel to *The Real Story* (1990) and is the first of a five book cycle.

Other books you might like:
Lois McMaster Bujold, *The Warrior's Apprentice*, 1986
F.M. Busby, *Rissa Kerguelen*, 1977
Orson Scott Card, *Songmaster*, 1980
Stephen Goldin, *Jade Darcy and the Affair of Honor*, 1988
    Mary Mason, co-author
Robert A. Heinlein, *Friday*, 1982
Alis A. Rasmussen, *A Passage of Stars*, 1990

1270

STEPHEN R. DONALDSON

The Gap into Conflict: The Real Story

(New York: Bantam Spectra, 1991)

Story type: Science Fiction (Adventure; Space Opera)
Major character(s): Morn Hyland, Police Officer; Angus Thermopyle, Pirate (space)
Time period(s): Indeterminate Future
Locale(s): Com-Mine Station, Space Station; Outer Space

Summary: Morn Hyland was an agent of the military police when she caused the accident which blew up the Starmaster, her family's spaceship. Morn was the only survivor. She was rescued by Angus Thermopyle who then implanted an illegal device in her brain which allowed him control over her body and mind. It made her a perfect crew member and victim for his abuse.

Other books you might like:
Brian Daley, *Fall of the White Ship Avatar*, 1987
Brian Daley, *Jinx on a Terran Inheritance*, 1985
Brian Daley, *Requiem for a Ruler of Worlds*, 1985
George Alec Effinger, *When Gravity Fails*, 1987
Stephen Goldin, *Jade Darcy and the Affair of Honor*, 1988
    Mary Mason, co-author
Stephen Goldin, *Jade Darcy and the Zen Pirates*, 1990
    Mary Mason, co-author

1271

STEPHEN R. DONALDSON

The Gap into Madness: Chaos and Order

(New York: Bantam Spectra, 1994)

Story type: Science Fiction (Space Opera; Political)
Series: Gap
Major character(s): Angus Thermopyle, Spaceship Captain, Cyborg; Morn Hyland, Police Officer (United Mining Corporation), Addict; Nick Succorso, Pirate, Spaceman
Time period(s): Indeterminate Future
Locale(s): Interstellar Empire/Federation; *Trumpet*, Spaceship; *Punisher*, Spaceship

Summary: Former enemies struggle to survive and control *Trumpet* as it flees UMC police, who have been ordered to capture or kill all aboard her.

Other books you might like:
Roger MacBride Allen, *The Ring of Charon*, 1990
Allan Cole, *Sten*, 1984
    Chris Bunch, co-author
Glen Cook, *The Dragon Never Sleeps*, 1988
Vernor Vinge, *A Fire upon the Deep*, 1992
David Wingrove, *The Middle Kingdom*, 1990

1272

STEPHEN R. DONALDSON

The Gap into Power: A Dark and Hungry God Arises
(New York: Bantam, 1992)

Story type: Science Fiction (Space Opera)
Series: Gap
Major character(s): Morn Hyland, Police Officer (United Mining Corp.); Holt "The Dragon" Fasner, Administrator; Angus Thermopyle, Spaceship Captain, Cyborg
Time period(s): Indeterminate Future
Locale(s): Billingate, Space Station; *Trumpet*, Spaceship

Summary: Holt discovers that Warden Dios of the UMC Police plans to shut down Billingate, thereby disrupting trade with the alien Amnion and interfering with piratical fencing transactions. Angus Thermopyle, now a cyborg programmed with loyalty to UMCP, also heads for Billingate. Someone must rescue Morn Hyland and her force-grown son from the Amnion before Billingate's destruction.

Other books you might like:
John Brunner, *A Planet of Your Own*, 1966
F.M. Busby, *Rissa Kerguelen*, 1977
Orson Scott Card, *Wyrms*, 1987
C.J. Cherryh, *Cyteen*, 1988
Alis A. Rasmussen, *A Passage of Stars*, 1990
Robert Reed, *Down the Bright Way*, 1991

1273

STEPHEN R. DONALDSON

The Gap into Ruin: This Day All Gods Die
(New York: Bantam Spectra, 1996)

Story type: Science Fiction (Space Opera; Political)
Series: Gap
Major character(s): Morn Hyland, Police Officer (United Mining Corporation); Angus Thermopyle, Spaceship Captain, Cyborg; Warden Dios, Police Officer (United Mining Corporation), Leader
Time period(s): Indeterminate Future
Locale(s): Interstellar Empire/Federation; *Trumpet*, Spaceship; Outer Space

Summary: When Warden Dios plans to expose the corrupt leadership of the United Mining Corporation, his action may precipitate total war. Meanwhile, Angus Thermopyle and Morn Hyland struggle to obtain an antidote to the enemy's virus which could destroy all of human kind. Concludes the series.

Other books you might like:
Roger MacBride Allen, *The Ring of Charon*, 1990
Allan Cole, *Sten*, 1984
　Chris Bunch, co-author
Glen Cook, *The Dragon Never Sleeps*, 1988
Vernor Vinge, *A Fire upon the Deep*, 1992
David Wingrove, *The Middle Kingdom*, 1990

1274

STEPHEN R. DONALDSON, Editor

Strange Dreams
(New York: Bantam Spectra, 1993)

Story type: Fantasy (Anthology)
Summary: Contains a three-page introduction plus 28 stories originally published in periodicals and anthologies during the past 50 years, a majority from the 1970s and 1980s with diverse themes and settings and all unforgettable to the editor. Authors include Michael Bishop, Jorge Luis Borges, Orson Scott Card, C.J. Cherryh, Harlan Ellison, John M. Ford, Franz Kafka, Rudyard Kipling, Nancy Kress, R.A. Lafferty, Patricia A. McKillip, Robin McKinley, Lucius Shepard, Theodore Sturgeon, Sheri S. Tepper, Jack Vance and John Varley.

Other books you might like:
Jorge Luis Borges, *The Book of Fantasy*, 1990
　editor
Robert H. Boyer, *Visions & Imaginings: Classic Fantasy Fiction*, 1992
　Kenneth J. Zahorski, co-editor
Lin Carter, *Discoveries in Fantasy*, 1972
　editor
Lester del Rey, *Once upon a Time: A Treasury of Modern Fairy Tales*, 1991
　Risa Kessler, co-editor
Martin H. Greenberg, *After the King: Stories in Honor of J.R.R. Tolkien*, 1992
　editor
Jack Zipes, *Spells of Enchantment*, 1991
　editor

1275

JAMES DOOHAN
S.M. STIRLING, Co-Author

The Rising
(New York: Baen Starline, 1996)

Story type: Science Fiction (Adventure; Mystery)
Series: Flight Engineer
Major character(s): Peter Raeder, Engineer, Spaceman; Cynthia Robbins, Military Personnel (lieutenant), Spacewoman; Paddy Casey, Engineer, Spaceman
Time period(s): Indeterminate Future
Locale(s): *Invincible*, Spaceship; Outer Space; Ontario Base, Moon (Earth's)

Summary: When injuries from the war with secessionists prevent Peter Raeder from continuing to pilot a spaceship, he accepts the assignment of engineer aboard *Invincible*. However, unless Peter can discover who murdered *Invincible*'s previous engineer, the traitor will continue to kill. Doohan's first novel and first of a series.

Other books you might like:
Nigel Bennett, *Keeper of the King*, 1997
　P.N. Elrod, co-author
Jonathan Frakes, *The Abductors: Conspiracy*, 1996
　Dean Wesley Smith, co-author

S.M. Stirling, *Marching through Georgia*, 1988
S.M. Stirling, *The Stone Dogs*, 1990
S.M. Stirling, *Under the Yoke*, 1989
John E. Stith, *Redshift Rendezvous*, 1990

1276

FRAN DORF

A Reasonable Madness

(New York: Birch Lane Press/Carol, 1990)

Story type: Horror (Mystery)
Major character(s): Laura Gardner Wade, Heiress; David Goldman, Doctor (psychiatrist); Zach Wade, Businessman (department store manager), Spouse (Laura's husband)
Time period(s): 1990s (1990)
Locale(s): New York, New York

Summary: Rich and beautiful Laura Wade confesses to the murder of Rita Harmon, even though she was nowhere near the scene of the crime and witnesses claim to have seen a man do the killing. Can Laura really kill, as she maintains, through her psychic powers? If not, then how does she know details about the murder only someone present at the scene of the crime could know? This is the author's first novel.

Other books you might like:
Owen Brookes, *Inheritance*, 1980
John Farris, *The Fury*, 1976
James Herbert, *Moon*, 1985
Geoffrey Household, *The Sending*, 1980
Barry Wood, *The Killing Gift*, 1975

1277

CAROLE NELSON DOUGLAS

Cup of Clay

(New York: Tor, 1991)

Story type: Fantasy (Alternate World)
Series: Taliswoman
Major character(s): Alison Carver, Journalist; Rowan Firemayne, Hero, Musician
Time period(s): 1990s (1991); Indeterminate
Locale(s): Minnesota; Veil, Planet—Imaginary

Summary: Having finished a lengthy and disgusting newspaper series on generational familial sexual abuse of children, journalist Alison Carver retreats with her dog to her rural island in Southern Minnesota hoping to find rest and recovery. At her campsite Alison awakens to find herself transported to a mountainous land in which society seems much different, with brutal men, the Takers, exploiting children mercilessly. Hoping to return to her own Earth, Alison sets out to discover more about her new environment with the help of Rowan, who hopes to achieve through song his quest to become Guardian of the Cup of Earth.

Other books you might like:
Eleanor Arnason, *A Woman of the Iron People*, 1991
Gael Baudino, *Gossamer Axe*, 1990
Orson Scott Card, *Seventh Son*, 1987
Orson Scott Card, *Songmaster*, 1980

Phyllis Eisenstein, *Born to Exile*, 1978
J. Alison James, *Sing for a Gentle Rain*, 1990
Mercedes Lackey, *Bardic Voices*, 1991
Andrea Shettle, *Flute Song Magic*, 1990

1278

CAROLE NELSON DOUGLAS

Seed upon the Wind

(New York: Tor, 1992)

Story type: Fantasy (Alternate World; Quest)
Series: Taliswoman
Major character(s): Alison Carver, Journalist, Shaman (Taliswoman); Rowan Firemayne, Hero, Musician; Mark McPherson, Journalist
Time period(s): Indeterminate; 1990s
Locale(s): Veil, Planet—Imaginary; St. Paul, Minnesota; Huntsville, Indiana

Summary: After seeing a redhead like Rowan, Alison returns to her island in northern Minnesota, keeping the Cup of Earth with her. Continuing to Veil, Alison learns that Veil suffers greatly from the loss of the Cup and may not survive the attack of the Crux even with the Cup of Earth.

Other books you might like:
Eleanor Arnason, *A Woman of the Iron People*, 1991
Douglas Bell, *Mojo and the Pickle Jar*, 1991
Charles de Lint, *The Little Country*, 1990
John DeChancie, *Castle Perilous*, 1988
Phyllis Eisenstein, *Born to Exile*, 1978
Ru Emerson, *The Two in Hiding*, 1991
Geary Gravel, *A Key for the Nonesuch*, 1990

1279

L. WARREN DOUGLAS

Cannon's Orb

(New York: Ballantine Del Rey, 1994)

Story type: Science Fiction (First Contact; Genetic Manipulation)
Major character(s): Ben Cannon, Student, Political Figure; Estelle "Lysistrata" Mason, Genetically Altered Being, Student; Ennnesstheh, Alien (psaatla)
Time period(s): 25th century (2486)
Locale(s): Phastillan, Planet—Imaginary; Cannon's Orb, Planet—Imaginary

Summary: Realizing that without the trade disturbed by the pirates who prey on young colonies, the metal-poor Cannon's Orb and her neighbors cannot survive, Jack Cannon signs a treaty with the psaatla and human colony on Phastillan. Cannon contracts with the psaatla to come and change the Orb and its inhabitants, allowing human survival. The female form of the psaatla, non-sentient "ksta," spread through the Orb's soil in preparation for an eventual joint colony. Although intelligent, psaatla unfortunately consist of a worm colony and too many humans find them intolerably alien.

Other books you might like:
Eleanor Arnason, *Ring of Swords*, 1993

Michael Berlyn, *The Eternal Enemy*, 1990
Octavia E. Butler, *Dawn*, 1987
Helen Collins, *Mutagenesis*, 1993
Paula E. Downing, *Fallway*, 1993
C.S. Friedman, *The Madness Season*, 1990
Nicola Griffith, *Ammonite*, 1993
Anne McCaffrey, *Treaty at Doona*, 1994
　Jody Lynn Nye, co-author
Larry Niven, *The Gripping Hand*, 1993
　Jerry Pournelle, co-author
Joan Slonczewski, *A Door into Ocean*, 1986
Vernor Vinge, *A Fire upon the Deep*, 1992

1280

L. WARREN DOUGLAS

A Plague of Change

(New York: Ballantine Del Rey, 1992)

Story type: Science Fiction (Genetic Manipulation; Political)
Major character(s): Vassily ''Bass'' James Cannon, Heir, Computer Expert; Sfalek-ni Swadeith, Alien (psaatla)
Time period(s): 25th century (2470)
Locale(s): Cannon's Orb, Planet—Imaginary; Phastillan, Planet—Imaginary

Summary: When human colonies expand into the Caprian Reef, a region lacking in heavy metals, brisk trading permits continued survival. Vikings and other human predators disturb trade, threatening the viability of many colonies. Betrayed by his childhood friends, Bass, whose father founded Cannon's Orb, gravitates toward Phastillan, where he expects to find a solution while working for the very alien psaatla. Author's first novel.

Other books you might like:
Michael Berlyn, *The Eternal Enemy*, 1990
David Brin, *Startide Rising*, 1983
Octavia E. Butler, *Dawn*, 1987
C.S. Friedman, *The Madness Season*, 1990
Diana G. Gallagher, *The Alien Dark*, 1990
Robert A. Heinlein, *Stranger in a Strange Land*, 1991
　revised edition
Rebecca Ore, *Becoming Alien*, 1987
Vernor Vinge, *A Fire upon the Deep*, 1992

1281

L. WARREN DOUGLAS

Stepwater

(New York: Roc, 1995)

Story type: Science Fiction (Genetic Manipulation; Political)
Series: Arbiter Tale
Major character(s): John Minder XXIII, Ruler (Arbiter); Barc Doresh, Genetically Altered Being (Bors), Heir; Girelf, Genetically Altered Being (Mantee), Heir
Time period(s): Indeterminate Future
Locale(s): Xarafeille Stream, Interstellar Empire/Federation; Newhome, Planet—Imaginary; Stepwater, Planet—Imaginary

Summary: John Minder, the hereditary ruler of the many planets of the Xarafeille Stream, must recover the data cubes taken by his older brother who disappears to avoid becoming Arbiter. Unable to recover the Arbiter set, John must locate and acquire the cubes from the seven planets which each have a copy of one, and from them find the location of the planets of Poletzai, which should be at his command. The seven varieties of humans, six developed as special workers and all requiring his support and leadership to interact, must not learn the Arbiter lost access to his tools. Barc acquires the first of the lost data blocks for him while rescuing Margak Steep and its environs from disaster and saving the forbidden relationship with his one true love, Girelf.

Other books you might like:
David Brin, *Glory Season*, 1993
Alis A. Rasmussen, *The Price of Ransom*, 1990
Melissa Scott, *Shadow Man*, 1995
Cordwainer Smith, *The Rediscovery of Man*, 1993
S. Andrew Swann, *Forests of the Night*, 1993

1282

L. WARREN DOUGLAS

The Wells of Phyre

(New York: Roc, 1996)

Story type: Science Fiction (Genetic Manipulation; Political)
Series: Arbiter Tale
Major character(s): John Minder XXIII, Ruler (Arbiter); Slith Wrasselty, Genetically Altered Being (Fard), Businessman; Bleth Wrasselty, Genetically Altered Being (Fard)
Time period(s): Indeterminate Future
Locale(s): Phyre, Planet—Imaginary; Newhome, Planet—Imaginary; Xarafeille Stream, Interstellar Empire/Federation

Summary: Having not yet recovered enough information to find his fleet and the military police, the Arbiter must solve disputes and prevent major wars using the knowledge acquired by his many subjects, luckily finding the people he needs. On Phyre, one of the many inhabited planets of the Xarafeille Stream, Slith's dangerous discovery could lead to major interstellar war, instead of just making him rich. However, his nursling befriends the Arbiter's Consul, giving John Minder the information he needs to prevent war on another planet in the Stream.

Other books you might like:
David Brin, *Brightness Reef*, 1995
Lois McMaster Bujold, *Falling Free*, 1988
C.J. Cherryh, *Foreigner*, 1994
Julia Ecklar, *Regenesis*, 1995
Janet Kagan, *Mirabile*, 1991
S. Andrew Swann, *Forests of the Night*, 1993

1283

LAUREN WRIGHT DOUGLAS

In the Blood

(Tallahassee: Naiad Press, 1989)

Story type: Science Fiction (Gay/Lesbian Fiction)
Major character(s): Hart, Scientist, Lesbian; Sandoval, Military Personnel, Lesbian
Time period(s): 21st century
Locale(s): Arizona; California

Summary: A near-future America has fragmented into smaller nations as a result of the death and destruction caused by an artificially-created virus, the Red Death. Solar-tech Hart, a free Arizonan, must accompany Dr. Ashe, creator of an experimental vaccine against the Red Death, to the California border. Not everyone wants the vaccine freely distributed, however, and Hart must overcome attempts at treachery, kidnapping, even murder.

Other books you might like:
Suzy McKee Charnas, *Motherlines*, 1979
Suzy McKee Charnas, *Walk to the End of the World*, 1974
Nancy Tyler Glenn, *Clicking Stones*, 1989
Joanna Russ, *The Female Man*, 1975
Joanna Russ, *We Who Are About To. . .*, 1977
Chelsea Quinn Yarbro, *Time of the Fourth Horseman*, 1976

1284

TOM DOWD

Night's Pawn

(New York: Roc, 1993)

Story type: Science Fiction (Adventure)
Series: Shadowrun
Major character(s): Jason Chase, Businessman (corporate liason), Martial Arts Expert; Caroline "Cara Deaver" Tara Villiers, Fugitive
Time period(s): 2050s (2053)
Locale(s): New York, New York; Denver, Colorado; Germany

Summary: Caroline Villiers approaches Jason Chase with the request that Jason protect his former employer, Caroline's father, from corporate assassins. However, Chase discovers his skills must protect Caroline from the terrorists trying to kill her. Game tie-in.

Other books you might like:
Robert N. Charrette, *Choose Your Enemies Carefully*, 1991
Robert N. Charrette, *Find Your Own Truth*, 1991
Robert N. Charrette, *Never Deal with a Dragon*, 1990
Robert N. Charrette, *Never Trust an Elf*, 1992
Nigel Findley, *2XS*, 1992
Nigel Findley, *Shadowplay*, 1993
Christopher Kubasik, *Changeling*, 1992
Carl Sargent, *Streets of Blood*, 1992
    Marc Gascoigne, co-author
Nyx Smith, *Striper Assassin*, 1993
Jordan K. Weisman, *Into the Shadows*, 1992
    editor

1285

ANN DOWNER

The Spellkey Trilogy

(New York: Baen, 1995)

Story type: Fantasy (Quest; Magic Conflict)
Series: Spellkey
Major character(s): Caitlin, Foundling, Witch; The Badger, Bastard Son, Companion; Elric, Knight
Time period(s): Indeterminate
Locale(s): Thirdmoon, Fictional Country; Otherworld, Mythical Place

Summary: Accused of witchcraft and exiled to the Abbey of Ninthstile, Caitlin travels through the Thirteen Kingdoms escorted by Badger, a ward of the Abbot of Thirdmoon See. Followed by a mysterious man, they meet a variety of characters who help or hinder them as they learn about the Spellkey and how their destinies intertwine. Omnibus edition combining the previously published *The Spellkey* (1987), *The Glass Salamander* (1989), and *The Books of the Keepers* (1993), here revised and with new material.

Other books you might like:
Eleanor Arnason, *The Sword Smith*, 1978
C.J. Cherryh, *Rusalka*, 1989
Robert Jordan, *The Eye of the World*, 1990
Patricia A. McKillip, *The Riddle-Master of Hed*, 1976
J.R.R. Tolkien, *The Fellowship of the Ring*, 1954

1286

PAULA E. DOWNING

Fallway

(New York: Ballantine Del Rey, 1993)

Story type: Science Fiction (First Contact; Space Colony)
Major character(s): Jahnel Alain, Leader; Koyil, Alien (Avelle), Ruler; Gregory Austin, Captive (hostage), Spaceman
Time period(s): Indeterminate Future
Locale(s): Quevi Ltir, Asteroid

Summary: Five hundred years after the alien Avelle colonize an asteroid as an emergency space dock, the Faon, descendants of rescued humans, begin to gain the acceptance of their hosts, paying their guest debt by joining Avelle wars. Captured by the enemy, a shocked Jahnel finds humans confused about why anyone would attack a rescue ship responding to the 80-year-old distress call of Jahnel's ancestors. Jahnel must convince the Avelle and her compatriot Faon that they belong on Quevi Ltir to prevent disaster for all.

Other books you might like:
Eleanor Arnason, *Ring of Swords*, 1993
Stephen Baxter, *Raft*, 1991
Octavia E. Butler, *Dawn*, 1987
Gordon R. Dickson, *Naked to the Stars/The Alien Way*, 1991
C.S. Friedman, *The Madness Season*, 1990
Janet Kagan, *Mirabile*, 1991
Paula King, *Mad Roy's Light*, 1990
    pseudonym of Paula E. Downing

Joan D. Vinge, *The Summer Queen*, 1991

1287

PAULA E. DOWNING

Flare Star

(New York: Ballantine Del Rey, 1992)

Story type: Science Fiction (Disaster; Science Fiction)
Major character(s): Jason Roarke, Spaceman, Hero; Magda Janozek, Teenager; Yves Marceau, Spaceship Captain
Time period(s): 23rd century
Locale(s): Colony Station Wolf II, Planet—Imaginary; *Ceti Flag*, Spaceship (freighter)

Summary: As *Ceti Flag* approaches Wolf 359 to refuel and drop off supplies, the star produces a long overdue flare large enough to destroy the electronic mental equipment of the Wolf II colony, sear anyone caught on the dayside surface and kill anyone in the top two levels of the underground complex. The survival of the remaining colonists depends upon the *Ceti Flag*, which has lost the colony and may decide to pass it by.

Other books you might like:
Michael Berlyn, *The Eternal Enemy*, 1990
David Brin, *Earth*, 1990
F.M. Busby, *Slow Freight*, 1991
Michael Capobianco, *Burster*, 1990
A.C. Crispin, *Silent Dances*, 1990
    Kathleen O'Malley, co-author
Gregory Feeley, *The Oxygen Barons*, 1990
Paula King, *Mad Roy's Light*, 1990
    pseudonym of Paula E. Downing
Rebecca Ore, *Becoming Alien*, 1987
Allen Steele, *Orbital Decay*, 1989

1288

PAULA E. DOWNING

A Whisper of Time

(New York: Ballantine Del Rey, 1994)

Story type: Science Fiction (First Contact; Political)
Major character(s): Medoret Douglas, Alien, Foundling; Samta Montes, Indian (Mayan), Archaeologist (xenorchaeologist); Sieyes, Psychologist
Time period(s): Indeterminate Future
Locale(s): Ariadan, Planet—Imaginary; Cebalrai, Planet—Imaginary

Summary: Discovered in a long deserted city on Cebalrai, Medoret cannot fit in despite all attempts. Given a chance to return to that city, others judge her too emotionally unstable to explore it. Escaping with the aid of Samta Montes, Medoret triggers a signal which brings her own people back to Cebalrai.

Other books you might like:
John Brunner, *Bedlam Planet*, 1968
Octavia E. Butler, *Survivor*, 1978
C.J. Cherryh, *Cuckoo's Egg*, 1985
Gordon R. Dickson, *Wolfling*, 1969
Garry Kilworth, *The Night of Kadar*, 1980

Paula King, *Mad Roy's Light*, 1990
    pseudonym of Paula E. Downing
Dean R. Koontz, *Beastchild*, 1970
Anne McCaffrey, *Decision at Doona*, 1969
Kris Neville, *Bettyann*, 1970
H. Beam Piper, *Little Fuzzy*, 1962
Sydney J. Van Scyoc, *Darkchild*, 1982
Vernor Vinge, *Tatja Grimm's World*, 1987

1289

ARTHUR CONAN DOYLE

The Best Horror Stories of Arthur Conan Doyle

(Chicago: Academy, 1989)

Story type: Horror (Collection)

Summary: Thirteen stories that mix horror, mystery, and science fiction. Important stories include ''The American Tale,'' about a man-eating plant, ''The Captain of the *Polestar*,'' a ghostly sea story, ''The Leather Funnel'' and ''The Silver Hatchet,'' two stories about haunted objects, and ''J. Habakuk Jephson's Statement,'' a tale based on the true incident of the mysteriously abandoned ship, the *Mary Celeste*.

Other books you might like:
Guy de Maupassant, *The Dark Side*, 1989

1290

ARTHUR CONAN DOYLE

The Horror of the Heights and Other Tales of Suspense

(San Francisco: Chronicle, 1992)

Story type: Horror (Collection)

Summary: Fourteen stories of mystery and horror by the Victorian master of suspense. Included are the classic reanimated mummy story, ''Lot 249''; the science-fantasy, ''The Los Amigos Fiasco''; a tale of psychic vengeance, ''The Parasite''; and the title story concerned with monsters of the upper atmosphere that lie in wait for aviators.

Other books you might like:
Charles Dickens, *The Complete Ghost Stories of Charles Dickens*, 1982
Edward Bulwer Lytton, *The Haunters and the Haunted; or, the House and the Brain*, 1905
William Chambers Morrow, *The Ape, The Idiot, and Other People*, 1897
H.G. Wells, *28 Science Fiction Stories*, 1982

1291

DEBRA DOYLE
JAMES D. MACDONALD, Co-Author

By Honor Betray'd
(New York: Tor, 1994)

Story type: Science Fiction (Psychic Powers; Family Saga)
Series: Mageworlds
Major character(s): Theio syn-Ricte sus-Airaalin, Military Personnel (Grand Admiral), Psychic (Mage Lord); Errec Ransome, Psychic (Master of Adepts' Guild); Beka Rosselin Metadi, Royalty (Domina of Entibor), Spaceship Captain
Time period(s): Indeterminate Future
Locale(s): Namport, Fictional City; Nammerin, Planet—Imaginary; *Warhammer*, Spaceship

Summary: The war between the Republic and the Mage Worlds reaches a climax as the murderer of the Domina of Entibor reveals himself. A new understanding may form between the Mage-Circles and The Guild.

Other books you might like:
Allan Cole, *Empire's End*, 1993
   Chris Bunch, co-author
Glen Cook, *The Dragon Never Sleeps*, 1988
Michelle Shirey Crean, *Dancer of the Sixth*, 1993
Frank Herbert, *Dune*, 1965
Andre Norton, *Brother to Shadows*, 1993
Alis A. Rasmussen, *Revolution's Shore*, 1990
David Weber, *On Basilisk Station*, 1993

1292

DEBRA DOYLE
JAMES D. MACDONALD, Co-Author

The Gathering Flame
(New York: Tor, 1995)

Story type: Science Fiction (Political; Adventure)
Series: Mageworlds
Major character(s): Jos Metadi, Spaceship Captain, Privateer; Errec Ransome, Psychic (esper), Spaceman; Perada "Rada" Rosselin, Ruler (Domina of Entibor)
Time period(s): Indeterminate Future
Locale(s): Galcen, Planet—Imaginary; *Warhammer*, Spaceship; Entibor, Planet—Imaginary

Summary: The uncrowned Domina of Entibor, Perada, finds mages to kill, while Metadi, now Consort, leads the fleet, protecting Entibor and hunting mages. Despite Perada's best efforts, political holdovers from the previous government conspire with the enemy, resulting in disaster. Set prior to events in the Mageworlds Trilogy (1992-1994).

Other books you might like:
Lois McMaster Bujold, *The Warrior's Apprentice*, 1986
L. Warren Douglas, *A Plague of Change*, 1992
Mary Gentle, *Ancient Light*, 1987
Alis A. Rasmussen, *A Passage of Stars*, 1990
David Weber, *Mutineers' Moon*, 1991

1293

DEBRA DOYLE
JAMES D. MACDONALD, Co-Author

Groogleman
(New York: Harcourt Brace/Jane Yolen Books, 1996)

Story type: Science Fiction (Post-Holocaust; Young Adult)
Major character(s): Daniel Henchard, Teenager, Apprentice (healer); Lezzie Johnson, Healer (weller), Teenager; Joshua, Guide
Time period(s): Indeterminate Future
Locale(s): United States; Dead Lands, Mythical Place

Summary: Lezzie notes Daniel's interest and skill in healing and undertakes his training. When Lezzie responds to the report of a plague, fearsome Grooglemen capture her. As Daniel and Lezzie's patient, Joshua, set out for the Dead Lands to rescue her, he displays unexpected knowledge of the Grooglemen.

Other books you might like:
Nancy Farmer, *The Ear, the Eye, and the Arm*, 1994
David R. Palmer, *Emergence*, 1984
Sherwood Smith, *Wren's Quest*, 1993
Caroline Stevermer, *River Rats*, 1992
Vivian Vande Velde, *User Unfriendly*, 1991

1294

DEBRA DOYLE
JAMES D. MACDONALD, Co-Author

Knight's Wyrd
(New York: Harcourt Brace Jovanovich, 1992)

Story type: Fantasy (Young Adult; Adventure)
Major character(s): William "Will" Odosson, Knight, Adventurer
Time period(s): Indeterminate
Locale(s): Anglia, Fictional Country

Summary: After an outstanding first tournament, newly knighted Will Odosson sets off to meet his betrothed with some trepidation since a prophecy about him seems to indicate his death in the immediate future. Nonetheless, Will survives his many dangerous encounters with trolls, dragons, ogres and wizards.

Other books you might like:
Lloyd Alexander, *The Book of Three*, 1964
Susan Cooper, *Over Sea, Under Stone*, 1966
Diana Wynne Jones, *The Lives of Christopher Chant*, 1988
J.R.R. Tolkien, *The Hobbit*, 1938
Jane Yolen, *Wizard's Hall*, 1991

1295

DEBRA DOYLE
JAMES D. MACDONALD, Co-Author

The Long Hunt
(New York: Tor, 1996)

Story type: Science Fiction (Psychic Powers; Family Saga)

Series: Mageworlds
Major character(s): Errec Ransome, Spirit (ghost), Psychic; Jens Metadi Jessan D'Rosselin, Teenager, Heir; Chakallakak "Chaka" ngha Chakallakak, Alien (Selvaur), Teenager
Time period(s): Indeterminate Future
Locale(s): Maraghai, Planet—Imaginary; Khesat, Planet—Imaginary

Summary: Jens, Chaka, and Jens' foster brother leave Maraghai in search of fame and glory. Steered toward Khesat after several attempts on their lives, Jens admits he intends to go there to discover the whereabouts of his missing parents and perhaps become the new Highest, planetary leader of Khesat.

Other books you might like:
Lois McMaster Bujold, *Mirror Dance*, 1994
F.M. Busby, *Arrow From Earth*, 1995
C.S. Friedman, *The Madness Season*, 1990
Andre Norton, *Brother to Shadows*, 1993
David Weber, *Path of the Fury*, 1992

1296

DEBRA DOYLE
JAMES D. MACDONALD, Co-Author

Night of the Living Rat!

(New York: Ace, 1992)

Story type: Science Fiction (Humor)
Series: Daniel M. Pinkwater's Melvinge of the Megaverse
Major character(s): Melvinge, Hero, Werewolf; Loola, Girlfriend, Mythical Creature (were-lizard); Harlan, Animal (dogoid)
Time period(s): Indeterminate
Locale(s): Megaverse Mall, Mythical Place; Neitherworld, Mythical Place

Summary: The saga continues as the Loan Shark pursues Ratner and Harlan to the parking lot of the Megaverse Mall. Melvinge finds death in the Neitherworld boring—until Sdark the Loan Shark finds him. The Sdark's attempts at killing Melvinge in the Neitherworld return him to his body in the Mall parking lot, and vice versa. At last everyone meets again at the Really Big Dance Hall. An afterword by Daniel M. Pinkwater throws further confusion on the origins of the Megaverse.

Other books you might like:
Douglas Adams, *The Restaurant at the End of the Universe*, 1981
Robert Asprin, *Little Myth Marker*, 1985
David Bischoff, *Night of the Living Shark!*, 1991
Lionel Fenn, *The Seven Spears of the W'dch'ck*, 1988
Craig Shaw Gardner, *Revenge of the Fluffy Bunnies*, 1990
Richard A. Lupoff, *Night of the Living 'Gator!*, 1992
Daniel Manus Pinkwater, *Borgel*, 1990
Terry Pratchett, *Reaper Man*, 1992
Somtow Sucharitkul, *Mallworld*, 1981

1297

DEBRA DOYLE
JAMES D. MACDONALD, Co-Author

The Price of the Stars

(New York: Tor, 1992)

Story type: Science Fiction (Adventure; Political)
Series: Mageworlds
Major character(s): Beka Rosselin Metadi, Spaceship Captain, Heiress; Jessen, Doctor, Military Personnel (Spaceforce); Lannan, Military Personnel (Spaceforce), Psychic
Time period(s): Indeterminate Future
Locale(s): Innish-Kyl, Planet—Imaginary (Waycross); *Warhammer*, Spaceship; Mandeyn, Planet—Imaginary (Embrig Spaceport)

Summary: After eight years in space Beka meets with her father who offers her his ship, the *Warhammer*, if she will find out the names of her mother the Empress's assassins. Forced to fake her death and change the name of her ship to save her life, Beka accepts the help and companionship of the family's old weapons master as the intrigue turns more deadly.

Other books you might like:
Ray Aldridge, *The Pharaoh Contract*, 1991
Lois McMaster Bujold, *Shards of Honor*, 1986
Allan Cole, *Sten*, 1984
　　Chris Bunch, co-author
Brian Daley, *Jinx on a Terran Inheritance*, 1985
Stephen Goldin, *Jade Darcy and the Affair of Honor*, 1988
　　Mary Mason, co-author
Steve Perry, *The 97th Step*, 1989
Alis A. Rasmussen, *A Passage of Stars*, 1990

1298

DEBRA DOYLE
JAMES D. MACDONALD, Co-Author

School of Wizardry

(Mahwah, New Jersey: Troll Associates, 1990)

Story type: Fantasy (Magic Conflict; Young Adult)
Series: Circle of Magic
Major character(s): Randall, Apprentice, Wizard
Time period(s): Indeterminate
Locale(s): Alternate Earth

Summary: Determined to become a wizard, 12-year-old Randall is delighted to be accepted into the famed School of Wizardry, but his apprenticeship is marred when he realizes that one of the master wizards is using evil spells to destroy the school and gain supreme power.

Other books you might like:
Diane Duane, *So You Want to Be a Wizard?*, 1983
Diana Wynne Jones, *The Lives of Christopher Chant*, 1988
Ursula K. Le Guin, *A Wizard of Earthsea*, 1967
Otfried Preussler, *The Satanic Mill*, 1972
Sherwood Smith, *Wren to the Rescue*, 1990
Jane Yolen, *Wizard's Hall*, 1991

1299
DEBRA DOYLE
JAMES D. MACDONALD, Co-Author

Starpilot's Grave
(New York: Tor, 1993)

Story type: Science Fiction (Adventure; Psychic Powers)
Series: Mageworlds
Major character(s): Beka Rosselin Metadi, Ruler, Spaceship Captain; Nyls Jessan, Doctor, Military Personnel (intelligence officer); Llannat, Military Personnel (Space Force), Psychic
Time period(s): Indeterminate Future
Locale(s): *Warhammer*, Spaceship; Namport, Planet—Imaginary; Galcen, Planet—Imaginary

Summary: In this direct sequel to *The Price of the Stars*, Beka and Nyls act as traders in the Mageworlds to gather information confirming that the Mage Lords again prepare for war. Suddenly given orders to investigate a derelict Mageworld fighter from the Magewar, Llannat finds herself drawn to it and discovers a message left there for her hundreds of years earlier. Rumors of a Mageworld fleet become realized as Beka races ahead of it to warn Galcen before it arrives.

Other books you might like:
C.J. Cherryh, *Cyteen*, 1988
Brian Daley, *Jinx on a Terran Inheritance*, 1985
Stephen Goldin, *Jade Darcy and the Affair of Honor*, 1988
  Mary Mason, co-author
Larry Niven, *The Gripping Hand*, 1993
  Jerry Pournelle, co-author
Alis A. Rasmussen, *A Passage of Stars*, 1990
Alis A. Rasmussen, *Revolution's Shore*, 1990
Joan D. Vinge, *The Summer Queen*, 1991

1300
GARDNER DOZOIS

Geodesic Dreams: The Best Short Fiction of Gardner Dozois
(New York: St. Martin's Press, 1992)

Story type: Science Fiction (Collection)
Summary: Contains a seven-page foreward by Robert Silverberg plus 14 stories published 1971-1990 in anthologies and periodicals. Two stories received Nebula Awards, "Peacemaker" and "Morning Child"; one story received nomination for a Nebula Award, "Disciples"; and three stories received Hugo Award nominations, "Chains of the Sea," "A Kingdom by the Sea" and "A Special Kind of Morning." Dozois collaborates with Jack C. Haldeman II in "Executive Clemency" and with Jack Dann in "Down Among the Dead" and "Slow Dancing with Jesus."

Other books you might like:
David Brin, *The River of Time*, 1986
Samuel R. Delany, *Driftglass: 10 Tales of Speculative Fiction*, 1971
Larry Niven, *Tales of Known Space*, 1975
Cordwainer Smith, *The Best of Cordwainer Smith*, 1975

Theodore Sturgeon, *Sturgeon Is Alive and Well*, 1971
John Varley, *Blue Champagne*, 1986
John Varley, *The Persistence of Vision*, 1978
Gene Wolfe, *Storeys From the Old Hotel*, 1992

1301
GARDNER DOZOIS, Editor
SHEILA WILLIAMS, Co-Editor

Isaac Asimov's Ghosts
(New York: Ace, 1995)

Story type: Horror (Anthology; Ghost Story)
Summary: The twelve stories by diverse hands are collected from *Isaac Asimov's Science Fiction Magazine* and all feature ghosts. Connie Willis's "Death on the Nile" is a wry account of Americans travelling abroad who may be dead and on their way to the underworld. In Kim Antieau's "Hauntings" and Jack Dann's "Visitors," people with medical conditions that have brought them close to death are subject to visions of the dead that no one else can see. Terry Bisson's comic "Dead Man's Curve" is about a dangerous bend in a road that transports joyriders into a dimension inhabited by a ghost, while Sharon Faber's "The July Ward" tells of a secret ward in a hospital that conceals spectres of a surgeon's guilt. In Lisa's Goldstein's "Alfred," a young girl meets the ghost of her grandfather, who died in a Nazi concentration camp.

Other books you might like:
Isaac Asimov, *Isaac Asimov's Magical Worlds of Fantasy #10: Ghosts*, 1988
  Charles G. Waugh, Martin H. Greenberg, co-editors
Paul F. Olson, *Post Mortem: New Tales of Ghostly Horror*, 1989
  David B. Silva, co-editor
Peter Straub, *Peter Straub's Ghosts*, 1995
  editor

1302
GARDNER DOZOIS, Editor
SHEILA WILLIAMS, Co-Editor

Isaac Asimov's Vampires
(New York: Ace, 1996)

Story type: Horror (Anthology; Vampire Story)
Summary: These eight stories, culled from the pages of *Asimov's Science Fiction* magazine, feature vampires in a variety of different guises. Connie Willis' "Jack," set during the London blitz, and Tanith Lee's "Winter Flowers," which takes place during medieval times, both feature vampires who use wartime bloodshed to camouflage their feedings. Susan Palwick reworks the fairy tale of Cinderella into a tale of the undead in "Ever After," while David Redd gives the vampire theme a science fiction top spin in "The Old Man of Munnington." Greg Frost's "Some Things Are Better Left," a mordant meditation on becoming middle-aged, uses a high school reunion as a springboard for his tale of vampiric immortality.

Other books you might like:

Greg Cox, *Tomorrow Sucks*, 1994
  T.K.F. Weiskopf, co-author
Ellen Datlow, *Blood Is Not Enough*, 1989
  editor
Martin H. Greenberg, *A Taste for Blood*, 1992
  editor
Stephen Jones, *The Mammoth Book of Vampires*, 1992
  editor

1303

GARDNER DOZOIS, Editor

Modern Classic Short Novels of Science Fiction

(New York: St. Martin's Press, 1994)

Story type: Science Fiction (Anthology)

Summary: Includes a four-page introduction plus individual introductions to 13 stories published in anthologies and periodicals 1958-1992, including Poul Anderson's "The Longest Voyage," Samuel R. Delany's "The Star Pit," Frederik Pohl's "The Merchants of Venus," Joanna Russ' "Souls," Cordwainer Smith's "On the Storm Planet" and Jack Vance's "The Miracle Workers." Other authors include Brian W. Aldiss, Nancy Kress, Robert Silverberg, Kate Wilhelm and Gene Wolfe.

Other books you might like:

Isaac Asimov, *Isaac Asimov Presents the Great SF Stories Series*, 1979-1992
  Martin H. Greenberg, co-editor
David G. Hartwell, *The World Treasury of Science Fiction*, 1989
  editor
Ursula K. Le Guin, *The Norton Book of Science Fiction: North American Science Fiction, 1960-1990*, 1993
  Brian Attebery, co-editor
Tom Shippey, *The Oxford Book of Science Fiction Stories*, 1992
  editor
Robert Silverberg, *The Science Fiction Hall of Fame, Volume 1*, 1970
  editor

1304

GARDNER DOZOIS, Editor

Modern Classics of Science Fiction

(New York: St. Martin's Press, 1992)

Story type: Science Fiction (Anthology)

Summary: Contains a six-page preface including lists of wonderful stories not contained herein plus 26 stories published 1955-1989 in periodicals and anthologies and a two-page afterword with additional recommendations of newer authors. One story, "The Moment of the Storm" by Roger Zelazny, received a Hugo Award nomination; two stories, "Particle Theory" by Edward Bryant and "Driftglass" by Samuel R. Delany, received Nebula Award nominations; and one story,

"The Ugly Chickens" by Howard Waldrop, won a Nebula Award. Other stories include "Narrow Valley" by R. A. Lafferty, "Mother Hitton's Littul Kittons" by Cordwainer Smith, "The Other Celia" by Theodore Sturgeon, "The Moon Moth" by Jack Vance and "The Fifth Head of Cerberus" by Gene Wolfe.

Other books you might like:

Isaac Asimov, *Isaac Asimov Presents the Great SF Stories Series*, 1979-1992
  Martin H. Greenberg, co-editor
Groff Conklin, *12 Great Classics of Science Fiction*, 1963
  editor
Groff Conklin, *Another Part of the Galaxy*, 1966
  editor
Groff Conklin, *Giants Unleashed*, 1965
  editor
Harlan Ellison, *Dangerous Visions*, 1967
  editor
Robert Silverberg, *The Science Fiction Hall of Fame, Volume 1*, 1970
  editor

1305

GARDNER DOZOIS

Slow Dancing through Time

(Kansas City, Missouri: Ursus Imprints, 1990)

Story type: Science Fiction (Collection)
Time period(s): 1940s; 1960s
Locale(s): Europe; United States

Summary: 14 stories, with introductions, written between 1980-1985 by Dozois in collaboration with Jack Dann, Michael Swanwich, Susan Casper and Jack C. Haldeman III. "Down Among the Dead Men," a Roman story about a vampire in a World War II death camp, is the best known and most controversial. Lighter in tone, "Slow Dancing with Roman Jesus," a transcribed dream, features an uncool girl, a prom, and Jesus Christ, and shows Dozois' range.

Other books you might like:

Pat Cadigan, *Patterns*, 1989
Harlan Ellison, *Partners in Wonder: Harlan Ellison in Collaboration with. . .*, 1971
Kim Newman, *The Night Mayor*, 1990
Tim Powers, *The Anubis Gates*, 1983
Howard Waldrop, *Night of the Cooters*, 1990

1306

GARDNER DOZOIS, Editor

The Year's Best Science Fiction: Eighth Annual Collection

(New York: St. Martin's Press, 1991)

Story type: Science Fiction (Anthology)
Series: Year's Best Science Fiction

Summary: This volume contains 25 stories originally published in periodicals and anthologies during 1990, six pages of honorable mentions, plus a 22-page summation of the 1990

Science Fiction milieu by the editor, Gardner Dozois, who received a Hugo Award for his editing of last year's *Best Science Fiction of the Year; Seventh Annual Collection*. Appearing here are two stories which received both Hugo and Nebula Awards, "The Hemingway Hoax" by Joe Haldeman and "Bears Discover Fire" by Terry Bisson, one story which received a Nebula Award, "Tower of Babylon" by Ted Chiang, one which is a collaboration, "The All-Consuming" by Lucius Shepard and Robert Frazier, and two stories by one author, Greg Egan. Other authors include John Brunner, Alexander Jablokov, James Patrick Kelly, John Kessel, Nancy Kress, Ursula K. Le Guin, Michael Moorcock, Pat Murphy, Charles Sheffield, Lewis Shiner, Robert Silverberg, Bruce Sterling, Kate Wilhelm and Connie Willis.

Other books you might like:

Lou Aronica, *Full Spectrum 2*, 1990
    Shawna McCarthy, Amy Stout and Patrick LoBruto, co-editors
Michael Bishop, *Nebula Awards 25*, 1991
    editor
Harlan Ellison, *Dangerous Visions*, 1967
    editor
Raymond J. Healy, *Adventures in Time and Space*, 1946
    J. Francis McComas, co-editor
Robert Silverberg, *The Science Fiction Hall of Fame, Volume 1*, 1970
    editor
Donald A. Wollheim, *The 1990 Annual World's Best Science Fiction*, 1990
    Arthur W. Saha, co-editor

1307

GARDNER DOZOIS, Editor

The Year's Best Science Fiction: Eleventh Annual Collection

(New York: St. Martin's Press, 1994)

Story type: Science Fiction (Anthology)
Series: Year's Best Science Fiction

Summary: Contains a 35-page summation of science fiction in 1993, six pages of honorable mentions and 23 stories. The stories include one Hugo and Nebula Award winner, Charles Sheffield's "Georgia on My Mind"; one Hugo Award winner and Nebula Award nominee, Connie Willis' "Death on the Nile"; one Hugo Award nominee and Nebula Award winner, Jack Cady's "The Night We Buried Road Dog"; one Hugo Award and Nebula Award nominee, G. David Nordley's "Into the Miranda Rift"; and two Nebula Award nominees, Nancy Kress' "Dancing on Air" and Walter Jon Williams' "Wall, Stone, Craft." Other authors include Brian W. Aldiss, Neal Barrett Jr., Stephen Baxter, Pat Cadigan, Joe Haldeman, Rebecca Ore, Robert Reed, Mike Resnick, Dan Simmons and Bruce Sterling.

Other books you might like:

Lou Aronica, *Full Spectrum 4*, 1993
    Amy Stout, Betsy Mitchell, co-editors

David G. Hartwell, *The Ascent of Wonder: The Evolution of Hard SF*, 1994
    Kathryn Cramer, co-editor
Ursula K. Le Guin, *The Norton Book of Science Fiction: North American Science Fiction, 1960-1990*, 1993
    Brian Attebery, co-editor
James Morrow, *Nebula Awards 28*, 1994
    editor
Robert Silverberg, *Universe 3*, 1994
    Karen Haber, co-editor

1308

GARDNER DOZOIS, Editor

The Year's Best Science Fiction: Ninth Annual Collection

(New York: St. Martin's Press, 1992)

Story type: Science Fiction (Anthology)
Series: Year's Best Science Fiction

Summary: Contains 28 stories, five pages of honorable mentions, plus a 27-page summation of the 1991 Science Fiction milieu by the editor. "Beggars in Spain" by Nancy Kress received both a Hugo Award and a Nebula Award, "A Walk in the Sun" by Geoffrey A. Landis received a Hugo Award, "The Gallery of His Dreams" by Kristine Kathryn Rusch received both Hugo and Nebula nominations and three stories received a Hugo nomination. Other authors include Brian W. Aldiss, Gregory Benford, Jack Dann, Karen Joy Fowler, William Gibson, Alexander Jablokov, James Patrick Kelly, Ian McDonald, Kim Newman, Robert Reed, Kim Stanley Robinson, Robert Silverberg and Walter Jon Williams.

Other books you might like:

Lou Aronica, *Full Spectrum 3*, 1991
    Amy Stout and Betsy Mitchell, co-editors
Michael Bishop, *Nebula Awards 25*, 1991
    editor
Harlan Ellison, *Dangerous Visions*, 1967
    editor
Raymond J. Healy, *Adventures in Time and Space*, 1946
    J. Francis McComas, co-editor
James Morrow, *Nebula Awards 26*, 1992
    editor
Robert Silverberg, *The Science Fiction Hall of Fame, Volume 1*, 1970
    editor
Robert Silverberg, *Universe 2*, 1992
    Karen Haber, co-editor
Donald A. Wollheim, *The 1990 Annual World's Best Science Fiction*, 1990
    Arthur W. Saha, co-editor

1309

GARDNER DOZOIS

The Year's Best Science Fiction: Seventh Annual Collection

(New York: St. Martin's Press, 1990)

Story type: Science Fiction (Anthology; Hard Science Fiction)
Series: Year's Best Science Fiction
Time period(s): Indeterminate

Summary: This book contains 25 stories, a fifteen-page summation of 1989 by the editor and a lenthy list of runners-up. Gregory Benford, Robert Silverberg, John Varley, Nancy Kress, Janet Kagan and Connie Willis are among the 24 authors represented.

Other books you might like:
Lou Aronica, *Full Spectrum*, 1988
   Shawna McCarthy, co-editor
Lou Aronica, *Full Spectrum 2*, 1989
   Shawna McCarthy, co-editor
Groff Conklin, *The Best of Science Fiction*, 1946
Raymond J. Healy, *Adventures in Time and Space*, 1946
   J. Francis McComas, co-editor
Donald A. Wollheim, *The 1990 Annual World's Best Science Fiction*, 1990
   Arthur W. Saha, co-editor

1310

GARDNER DOZOIS, Editor

The Year's Best Science Fiction: Tenth Annual Collection

(New York: St. Martin's Press, 1993)

Story type: Science Fiction (Anthology)
Series: Year's Best Science Fiction

Summary: Contains a 26-page summation of science fiction in 1992, six pages of honorable mentions and 24 stories. These include one Hugo and Nebula Award winner, Connie Willis' "Even the Queen"; three Hugo and Nebula Award nominees, Bradley Denton's "The Territory," Nancy Kress' "The Mountain to Mohammed" and Maureen McHugh's "Protection"; and one Nebula Award nominee, Michael Swanwick's "Griffin's Egg." Other authors include Neal Barrett, Jr., Terry Bisson, Pat Cadigan, Arthur C. Clarke, L. Sprague de Camp, Joe Haldeman, Kathe Koja, Frederik Pohl, Robert Silverberg, Ian Watson and Kate Wilhelm.

Other books you might like:
Lou Aronica, *Full Spectrum 4*, 1993
   Amy Stout, Betsy Mitchell, co-editors
Michael Bishop, *Nebula Awards 25*, 1991
   editor
Ellen Datlow, *Omni Best Science Fiction Three*, 1993
   editor
Ursula K. Le Guin, *The Norton Book of Science Fiction: North American Science Fiction, 1960-1990*, 1993
   Brian Attebery, co-editor

James Morrow, *Nebula Awards 27*, 1993
   editor
Robert Silverberg, *Universe 2*, 1992
   Karen Haber, co-editor

1311

GARDNER DOZOIS, Editor

The Year's Best Science Fiction: Thirteenth Annual Collection

(New York: St. Martin's Griffin, 1996)

Story type: Science Fiction (Anthology)
Series: Year's Best Science Fiction

Summary: Contains a 39-page summation of science fiction in 1995, six pages of honorable mentions, and 24 stories with introductions. The stories include two Hugo Award winners that received Nebula Award nominations, James Patrick Kelly's "Think Like a Dinosaur" and Maureen F. McHugh's "The Lincoln Train"; one Hugo Award winner, Allen Steele's "The Death of Captain Future"; two Hugo Award nominees, Greg Egan's "Luminous" and Ursula K. LeGuin's "A Woman's Libration"; and one Nebula Award nominee, Brian Stableford's "Mortimer Gray's *History of Death*." Other authors include Poul Anderson, Terry Bisson, Pat Cadigan, Michael F. Flynn, Joe Haldeman, John Kessel, Nancy Kress, Paul J. McAuley, Robert Reed, Mary Rosenblum, Jeff Ryman, William Sanders, Dan Simmons, and Michael Swanwick.

Other books you might like:
David G. Hartwell, *The Ascent of Wonder: The Evolution of Hard SF*, 1994
   Kathryn Cramer, co-editor
David G. Hartwell, *The Year's Best Science Fiction: Thirteenth Annual Collection*, 1996
   editor
Jennifer Hershey, *Full Spectrum 5*, 1995
   Tom Dupree, Janna Silverstein, co-editors
Ursula K. Le Guin, *The Norton Book of Science Fiction: North American Science Fiction, 1960-1990*, 1993
   Brian Attebery, co-author
Pamela Sargent, *Nebula Awards 29*, 1996
   editor
Robert Silverberg, *Universe 3*, 1994
   Karen Haber, co-editor

1312

GARDNER DOZOIS, Editor

The Year's Best Science Fiction: Twelfth Annual Collection

(New York: St. Martin's Griffin, 1995)

Story type: Science Fiction (Anthology)
Series: Year's Best Science Fiction

Summary: Contains a 36-page summation of science fiction in 1994, six pages of honorable mentions, and 23 stories. The stories include one Hugo and Nebula Award winner, Mike

Resnick's "Seven Views of Olduvai George"; one Hugo Award winner and Nebula Award nominee, Joe Haldeman's "None So Blind"; two Hugo and Nebula Award nominees, both by Ursula K. Le Guin, "Forgiveness Day" and "The Matter of Seggri"; four Hugo Award nominees, Michael Bishop's "Cri de Coeur," Greg Egan's "Cocoon," Michael F. Flynn's "Melodies of the Heart," and Brian Stableford's "Les Fleurs du Mal"; and one Nebula Award nominee, Maureen F. McHugh's "Necropolis." Other authors include Stephen Baxter, Terry Bisson, Pat Cadigan, Lisa Goldstein, Katharine Kerr, Nancy Kress, Robert Reed, Mary Rosenblum, Howard Waldrop, and Walter Jon Williams.

Other books you might like:
David G. Hartwell, *The Ascent of Wonder: The Evolution of Hard SF*, 1994
  Kathryn Cramer, co-editor
Jennifer Hershey, *Full Spectrum 5*, 1995
  Tom Dupree, Janna Silverstein, co-editors
Ursula K. Le Guin, *The Norton Book of Science Fiction: North American Science Fiction, 1960-1990*, 1993
  Brian Attebery, co-editor
Pamela Sargent, *Nebula Awards 29*, 1995
  editor
Robert Silverberg, *Universe 3*, 1994
  Karen Haber, co-editor

1313

ALISON DRAKE

Lagoon

(New York: Ballantine, 1990)

Story type: Horror (Nature in Revolt)
Major character(s): Scott Nash, Photojournalist; Fay Donovan, Doctor (coroner)
Time period(s): 1990s
Locale(s): Lagoon, Georgia

Summary: Scott Nash returns to the small northeast Georgia town of Lagoon to discover the reason his brother Ben went berserk during dinner one evening and gunned down twenty-nine people at the local inn. Nash discovers that prior to his rampage, Ben had begun to exhibit strange physical symptons—which seem inexplicably to coincide with weather anomalies, disappearances, cannibalistic assaults, mutant plants and animals in the vicinity, and a pervasive sense of "wrongness" that has settled over the area. Joining forces with local physician Fay Donovan, Nash discovers that nature itself is in revolt against the abuses humanity has perpetrated upon it.

Other books you might like:
Robert Charles, *Flowers of Evil*, 1982
Marilyn Harris, *The Portent*, 1980
Leslie Horvitz, *The Dying*, 1987
David J. Michael, *Death Tour*, 1978
Alan E. Nourse, *The Fourth Horseman*, 1983

1314

DAVID DRAKE
JANET MORRIS, Co-Author

Arc Riders

(New York: Warner Aspect, 1995)

Story type: Science Fiction (Time Travel; Military)
Major character(s): Rebecca Carnes, Military Personnel, Time Traveller; Nan Roebeck, Time Traveller; Tim Grainger, Time Traveller
Time period(s): 26th century (November 17, 2522); 250th century B.C.
Locale(s): Boston, Massachusetts; Vietnam; Superior, Minnesota

Summary: While attempting to return to Anti-Reversion Command Central at the end of a mission, the team barely escapes from an unexpected attack. The Arc Riders retreat to 25,000 B.C. to find and correct the revision. Needing more information to discover when the change occurred, the team recruits Rebecca Carnes from 1991, just prior to the detailed years stored in their computer, hoping she can help them restore their timeline and avoid perpetual war or nuclear desctuction.

Other books you might like:
Poul Anderson, *The Time Patrol*, 1991
Fritz Leiber, *The Big Time*, 1961
Janet Morris, *Heroes in Hell*, 1986
Janet Morris, *Threshold*, 1990
  Chris Morris, co-author
Andre Norton, *The Crossroads of Time*, 1956
H. Beam Piper, *Lord Kalvan of Otherwhen*, 1965

1315

DAVID DRAKE, Editor
BILL FAWCETT, Co-Editor

Battlestation

(New York: Ace, 1992)

Story type: Science Fiction (Anthology; Space Opera)
Series: Battlestation
Time period(s): Indeterminate Future
Locale(s): *Stephen Hawking*, Spaceship; Outer Space

Summary: An alien species which colonizes planets by consuming everything usable on them has already destroyed hundreds of species when survivors of four planets ask for help from humans. The resulting battlestation they construct sets out to turn back the invasion. 11 authors including Diane Duane, Janet Morris, Robert Sheckley and Christopher Stasheff chronicle different aspects of the battle and individuals involved.

Other books you might like:
Robert Asprin, *The Bug Wars*, 1979
James Blish, *Cities in Flight*, 1970
Orson Scott Card, *Ender's Game*, 1985
Bill Fawcett, *The Siege of Arista*, 1991
Joe Haldeman, *The Forever War*, 1975
Anne McCaffrey, *The Ship Who Sang*, 1969

Elizabeth Mitchell, *Alien Stars*, 1985
　editor
Larry Niven, *Man-Kzin Wars*, 1988
　editor

1316

DAVID DRAKE
WILLIAM C. DIETZ, Co-Author

Cluster Command
(New York: Baen Books, 1989)

Story type: Science Fiction (Military)
Series: Crisis of Empire
Major character(s): Anson Merikur, Military Personnel (Commander); Bethany Windsor, Heiress
Time period(s): Indeterminate Future
Locale(s): Harmony Star Cluster, Interstellar Empire/Federation

Summary: As the First Empire enters its final days, corrupt government officials scramble for all they can get. Commander Anson Merikur is an exception to this trend, an old-fashioned military man who will do anything to stem the tide of collapse, even if it means war.

Other books you might like:
Lois McMaster Bujold, *Borders of Infinity*, 1989
　with David Drake
Lois McMaster Bujold, *The Warrior's Apprentice*, 1986
Larry Niven, *The Mote in God's Eye*, 1974
　Jerry Pournelle, co-author
Jerry Pournelle, *Prince of Mercenaries*, 1989

1317

DAVID DRAKE
JANET MORRIS, Co-Author

The Fourth Rome
(New York: Warner Aspect, 1996)

Story type: Science Fiction (Time Travel; Adventure)
Series: ARC Riders
Major character(s): Nan Roebeck, Time Traveller, Leader; Pauli Weigand, Time Traveller; Tim Grainger, Time Traveller
Time period(s): 1st century (9 A.D.); 1990s (1992)
Locale(s): Germany; Moscow, Russia

Summary: Team 79 finds no trace of those they track when sent into the past to capture Russian revisionists who plan to ensure Roman conquest of the ancient Germans by preventing the massacre in the Teutoberg Forest that ended Roman expansion east of the Rhine. Pauli, Rebecca, and Gerd stay in 9 A.D. to find the revisionists and ensure that history remains unchanged, while Nan, Tim, and Quo go forward to 1992 Moscow, searching for the technology that allowed the time transplant. In 1992, Nan and her group discover interference by far future conspirators that may extend to the highest levels of the Anti-Revisionist Command.

Other books you might like:
Poul Anderson, *Guardians of Time*, 1960

Poul Anderson, *Time Patrolman*, 1983
C.J. Cherryh, *Exile's Gate*, 1988
L. Sprague de Camp, *Lest Darkness Fall*, 1941
Janet Morris, *Heroes in Hell*, 1986
　editor
Elizabeth Ann Scarborough, *The Healer's War*, 1988

1318

DAVID DRAKE
JIM KJELGAARD, Co-Author

The Hunter Returns
(New York: Baen, 1991)

Story type: Fantasy (Historical; Adventure)
Major character(s): Hawk, Prehistoric Human, Inventor; Wolf, Prehistoric Human, Hunter; Willow, Prehistoric Human
Time period(s): Indeterminate Past (Pleistocene)
Locale(s): Earth

Summary: Hawk, Chief Spear-Maker, accidently invented a throwing stick with which he attacked a sabre-tooth tiger, a taboo act for a Chief Spear-Maker. Game is scarce and Hawk's break with tradition is blamed for the tribe's difficulty acquiring meat. Willow, wounded by a tiger, and Hawk become a couple while Hawk invents new hunting techniques and a better lifestyle. Expanded from the 1951 novel, *Firehunter*, by Kjelgaard alone.

Other books you might like:
Michael Armstrong, *Agviq*, 1990
Jean M. Auel, *Clan of the Cave Bear*, 1980
J.H. Brennan, *Shiva: An Adventure of the Ice Age*, 1990
W. Michael Gear, *People of the Wolf*, 1990
　Kathleen O'Neal Gear, co-author
Richard Herley, *The Stone Arrow*, 1978
Elizabeth Marshall Thomas, *Reindeer Moon*, 1987

1319

DAVID DRAKE

Igniting the Reaches
(New York: Ace, 1994)

Story type: Science Fiction (Adventure; Military)
Major character(s): Stephen Gregg, Military Personnel (colonel); Piet Ricimer, Spaceman
Time period(s): Indeterminate Future (4th millennium)
Locale(s): Venus; Benisan, Planet—Imaginary

Summary: When humans travel again in deep space, a millenium after the human empire collapses, a pair of young men from Venus seek gold and glory. They face natural dangers, aliens and a hostile Earth in pursuit of their dream.

Other books you might like:
Poul Anderson, *Flandry of Terra*, 1965
Iain M. Banks, *The Player of Games*, 1989
Lois McMaster Bujold, *Barrayar*, 1991
Glen Cook, *The Dragon Never Sleeps*, 1988
H. Beam Piper, *Space Viking*, 1963

1320

DAVID DRAKE

The Jungle

(New York: Tor, 1991)

Story type: Science Fiction (Adventure; Military)
Major character(s): Brainard, Military Personnel (Free Companies ensign)
Time period(s): Indeterminate Future (380s As-After Settlement)
Locale(s): Venus

Summary: With Earth destroyed, the survivors of humanity are trying to terraform Venus while carrying on the war which wiped out life on Earth. When Ensign Brainard's craft is downed, the crew must battle Venus's hostile jungle to return to their home, an underwater dome. This novel is set in the same milieu as Henry Kuttner's, *Destination Infinity* (1958), a retitling of *Fury* (1950), and his novella, "Clash by Night," the latter included here along with Drake's note of explanation.

Other books you might like:
David Brin, *Startide Rising*, 1983
David Brin, *The Uplift War*, 1987
Octavia E. Butler, *Dawn*, 1987
Harry Harrison, *The Deathworld Trilogy*, 1976
James H. Schmitz, *The Demon Breed*, 1968
Dan Simmons, *The Fall of Hyperion*, 1990
Dan Simmons, *Hyperion*, 1989
John Varley, *Titan*, 1979

1321

DAVID DRAKE

Justice

(New York: Ace, 1992)

Story type: Science Fiction (Military)
Series: Northworld
Major character(s): Nils Hansen, Police Officer (former); Sparrow, Artisan (smith), Matchmaker; Venkatna, Royalty (king)
Time period(s): Indeterminate Future
Locale(s): Northworld, Planet—Imaginary; Eight Planes of the Matrix, Mythical Place

Summary: When King Venkatna wishes to rule everyone and everything in Northland, North gives him a Web which will grant his wish, although it obeys his commands literally and some people, such as Nils Hansen, who will fight Venkatna to the very end, possess immunity to the Web. Meanwhile, Sparrow travels through the planes determined to secure a wife for his master, Saburo.

Other books you might like:
Robert A. Heinlein, *Starship Troopers*, 1959
Fritz Leiber, *The Big Time*, 1961
Michael Moorcock, *The Runstaff*, 1977
Jerry Pournelle, *Janissaries*, 1979
Roger Zelazny, *Lord of Light*, 1967
Roger Zelazny, *Nine Princes in Amber*, 1970

1322

DAVID DRAKE

Northworld

(New York: Ace, 1990)

Story type: Science Fiction (Mystical; Political)
Series: Northworld
Major character(s): Nils Hansen, Police Officer (Consensus)
Time period(s): Indeterminate Future
Locale(s): Northworld, Planet—Imaginary

Summary: First the Consensus sent an exploration team led by Captain Rolls and then a crisis team led by Captain North had gone to Northworld. Neither had returned. Finally, when several more attempts had failed, the Consensus tapped Special Forces Commissioner Nils Hansen to go and investigate.

Other books you might like:
John Brunner, *Children of the Thunder*, 1989
Frank Herbert, *Dune*, 1965
Michael Moorcock, *Elric of Melnibone*, 1976
Roger Zelazny, *Nine Princes in Amber*, 1970
Roger Zelazny, *Creatures of Light and Darkness*, 1969

1323

DAVID DRAKE

Old Nathan

(New York: Baen, 1991)

Story type: Fantasy (Collection; Magic Conflict)
Major character(s): Old Nathan, Backwoodsman, Magician
Time period(s): 1820s
Locale(s): Tennessee

Summary: With dialog written in backwoods dialect, these five adventures tell of Old Nathan, frequently called upon to do magical odd jobs. "The Bull" first appeared in *Whispers* magazine and "The Fool" first appeared in *Whispers VI* (1987). Stories original to this collection are "The Gold," "The Bullhead" and "The Box."

Other books you might like:
Tom Deitz, *Soulsmith*, 1991
Manly Wade Wellman, *After Dark*, 1980
Manly Wade Wellman, *The Hanging Stones*, 1982
Manly Wade Wellman, *John the Balladeer*, 1988
Manly Wade Wellman, *The Lost and Lurking*, 1981
Manly Wade Wellman, *Who Fears the Devil?*, 1963

1324

DAVID DRAKE

Redliners

(New York: Baen, 1996)

Story type: Science Fiction (Military; Adventure)
Summary: Deemed too dangerous for civilian life following their mission on Stalleybrass, Strike Force Company C41 deploys to provide protection for colonists settling Bezant, a hell planet where all life seems dangerous to humans. Crash

landing in the most dangerous area on the planet, miles from the colony site, the Company must fight off the enemy and get the colonists to their colony site.

Other books you might like:
Orson Scott Card, *Ender's Game*, 1985
Gordon R. Dickson, *The Tactics of Mistake*, 1971
Joe Haldeman, *The Forever War*, 1975
Harry Harrison, *Deathworld*, 1960
Robert A. Heinlein, *Starship Troopers*, 1959
Colin Kapp, *The Survival Game*, 1976
Jerry Pournelle, *Go Tell the Spartans*, 1991
S.M. Stirling, *Marching through Georgia*, 1988

1325

DAVID DRAKE

Rolling Hot

(New York: Baen Books, 1989)

Story type: Science Fiction (Military)
Series: Hammer's Slammers
Major character(s): June Ranson, Mercenary (Captain); Dick Suilin, Journalist, Mercenary
Time period(s): Indeterminate Future (Third Millennium)
Locale(s): Prosperity, Planet—Imaginary

Summary: Captain Ranson thinks she's been handed an easy assignment, but then disaster strikes. Now she must lead her own mercenary tank force and a mixed bag of raw recruits three hundred miles to relieve the district capital or the war will be effectively over and Hammer's Slammers will be on the losing side.

Other books you might like:
Harold Coyle, *Team Yankee*, 1988
Edward P. Hughes, *Masters of the Fist*, 1989
Keith Laumer, *The Complete Bolo*, 1990
Keith Laumer, *The Stars Must Wait*, 1989
Ralph Peters, *Red Army*, 1989
Jerry Pournelle, *Janissaries*, 1979
Jerry Pournelle, *Prince of Mercenaries*, 1989

1326

DAVID DRAKE

The Sharp End

(New York: Baen, 1993)

Story type: Science Fiction (Adventure; Military)
Major character(s): Matthew Coke, Military Personnel, Leader; Sten Moden, Military Personnel; Mary Margulies, Military Personnel
Time period(s): Indeterminate Future
Locale(s): Cantilucca, Planet—Imaginary

Summary: The Frisian Defense Forces survey team encounter difficulty on Cantilucca, whose warlords regularly terrorize the peasantry. Set in the *Hammer's Slammers* milieu.

Other books you might like:
Simon R. Green, *Hellworld*, 1993
Harry Harrison, *The Deathworld Trilogy*, 1976
Janet Kagan, *Hellspark*, 1988

Rosemary Kirstein, *The Outskirter's Secret*, 1992
Sheri S. Tepper, *Grass*, 1989

1327

DAVID DRAKE

The Square Deal

(New York: Tor, 1992)

Story type: Science Fiction (Adventure; Techno-Thriller)
Series: Car Warriors
Major character(s): Brian Deal, Teenager, Adventurer; John "J.C." Deal, Adventurer, Warrior; Ditsy Wallace, Journalist, Adventurer
Time period(s): 21st century
Locale(s): Mannheim, New Mexico

Summary: Brian spends his time repairing wrecks and helping his friend, Ditsy, with television coverage of highway autoduelling until his brother returns to Mannheim driving a hot car. Shortly thereafter, Brian, Ditsy and J.C. become involved in a feud which includes Ditsy's father, a local rancher and a gang of pirates on motorcycles. Ties into the game, *Car Wars*, inspired by the Alan Dean Foster story, "Why Johnny Can't Speed."

Other books you might like:
Robert Silverberg, *Car Sinister*, 1979
   Martin H. Greenberg and Joseph D. Olander, co-editors
Joan D. Vinge, *Mad Max Beyond Thunderdome*, 1985
Walter Jon Williams, *Hardwired*, 1986
Roger Zelazny, *Damnation Alley*, 1968

1328

DAVID DRAKE

Starliner

(New York: Baen, 1992)

Story type: Science Fiction (Adventure; Science Fiction)
Major character(s): Randall "Ran" Colville, Spaceman (Trident Starlines); Wanda Holly, Spaceman (Trident Starlines); Lady Scour, Alien (Szgranian), Royalty
Time period(s): Indeterminate Future
Locale(s): *Empress of Earth*, Spaceship (starliner); Outer Space

Summary: The *Empress of Earth* and *Brasil*, with routes from Earth to Tblisi and back, carry first class passengers as well as cargo class freight. Randall Colville, a new officer of the *Empress of Earth*, recognizes its potential value if war erupts between Nevasa and Grantholm. On the trip to Tblisi, Ran rescues a Nevasan passenger from her Grantholm kidnappers, foils an attempt to steal the ship and an attempt to hijack it, and becomes an integral member of the *Empress'* crew shepherding interesting passengers from planet to planet.

Other books you might like:
Stephen Baxter, *Raft*, 1991
C.J. Cherryh, *The Pride of Chanur*, 1982
Glen Cook, *The Dragon Never Sleeps*, 1988
John DeChancie, *Starrigger*, 1983
Vonda N. McIntyre, *Transition*, 1991

Alis A. Rasmussen, *A Passage of Stars*, 1990
Frank M. Robinson, *The Dark Beyond the Stars*, 1991
David Weber, *Mutineers' Moon*, 1991

1329

DAVID DRAKE

Surface Action
(New York: Ace, 1990)

Story type: Science Fiction (Military; Young Adult)
Major character(s): John Gordon, Mercenary; Daniel Cooke, Mercenary (naval)
Time period(s): Indeterminate Future
Locale(s): Venus

Summary: Hundreds of years after Earth's final war, the Venus colonies live on as domes under the endless oceans. Disputes between the domes are fought by mercenaries on the surface as naval engagements. Every boy on Venus dreams of joining a mercenary fleet—of a warrior's life on the high seas—and John Gordon is no exception. Son of a senator and nephew of a prominent commander, Johnnie has trained his whole life for battle. Now the time has come to experience his first taste of surface action.

Other books you might like:
Gordon R. Dickson, *Dorsai!*, 1976
Larry Niven, *The Mote in God's Eye*, 1974
    Jerry Pournelle, co-author
Jerry Pournelle, *The Mercenary*, 1977
Paul Preuss, *Breaking Strain*, 1987

1330

DAVID DRAKE

Through the Breach
(New York: Ace, 1995)

Story type: Science Fiction (Military; Adventure)
Major character(s): Piet Ricimer, Spaceman (general commander), Pirate; Stephen Gregg, Pirate
Time period(s): Indeterminate Future ((4th millenium))
Locale(s): Venus; Landolph's Breach, Outer Space (the Mirror)

Summary: Leading the Venus Asteroid Expedition, Piet Ricimer and Stephen Gregg head for the Mirror, a weak point where the barrier to booty and power lies thinnest. Sequel to *Igniting the Reaches*.

Other books you might like:
Poul Anderson, *Trader to the Stars*, 1964
C.J. Cherryh, *The Pride of Chanur*, 1982
L. Warren Douglas, *Bright Islands in a Dark Sea*, 1993
Gordon Eklund, *Space Pirates*, 1979
    E.E. Smith, co-author
Jack Vance, *Space Pirate*, 1953

1331

DAVID DRAKE

Vengeance
(New York: Ace, 1990)

Story type: Science Fiction (Political; Mystical)
Series: Northworld
Major character(s): Nils Hansen, Police Officer (former); North, Military Personnel (former)
Time period(s): Indeterminate Future
Locale(s): Northworld, Planet—Imaginary

Summary: Having gained the ability to manipulate the Matrix like the other "gods" before him, Hansen finds himself engaged in a power struggle with North over the fate of Northworld.

Other books you might like:
John Brunner, *Children of the Thunder*, 1989
Frank Herbert, *Dune*, 1965
Michael Moorcock, *Elric of Melnibone*, 1976
Roger Zelazny, *Nine Princes in Amber*, 1970
Roger Zelazny, *Creatures of Light and Darkness*, 1969

1332

DAVID DRAKE

The Voyage
(New York: Tor, 1994)

Story type: Science Fiction (Lost Colony; Military)
Major character(s): Lissea Doorman, Spaceship Captain, Military Personnel; Ned Slade, Military Personnel; Toll Warson, Military Personnel
Time period(s): Indeterminate Future
Locale(s): *Swift*, Spaceship; Planet—Imaginary

Summary: Lissea Doorman handpicks a crew for the Pancahte expedition, intending to reestablish contact. The venture brings much opportunity for action along the way. Contains a three-page "Author's Note" comparing the voyage to that of Homer's Argonauts in *The Iliad*. Set in the *Hammer's Slammers* milieu.

Other books you might like:
Nicola Griffith, *Ammonite*, 1993
Simon Lang, *The Trumpets of Tagan*, 1992
Vonda N. McIntyre, *Starfarers*, 1989
Alis A. Rasmussen, *The Price of Ransom*, 1990
A.E. van Vogt, *The Voyage of the Space Beagle*, 1950

1333

DAVID DRAKE
ROGER MACBRIDE ALLEN, Co-Author

The War Machine
(New York: Baen Books, 1989)

Story type: Science Fiction (Military)
Series: Crisis of Empire
Major character(s): Allison Spencer, Military Personnel (Captain)

Time period(s): Indeterminate Future
Locale(s): First Empire, Interstellar Empire/Federation

Summary: Captain Allison Spencer's marriage was destroyed by government officials for reasons of state and he sank into a life of drug addiction. Now, however, a hostile alien race menaces the Empire and Spencer appears to be the only man who can stop them.

Other books you might like:
Lois McMaster Bujold, *Borders of Infinity*, 1989
Lois McMaster Bujold, *The Warrior's Apprentice*, 1986
Larry Niven, *The Mote in God's Eye*, 1974
   Jerry Pournelle, co-author
Jerry Pournelle, *Prince of Mercenaries*, 1989
David Drake, *An Honorable Defense*, 1988
   Crisis of Empire Book I. Thomas T. Thomas, co-author

1334
DAVID DRAKE

The Warrior
(New York: Baen, 1991)

Story type: Science Fiction (Military)
Series: Hammer's Slammers
Major character(s): Samuel "Slick" Des Grieux, Military Personnel (Sergeant); Alois Hammer, Military Personnel (Colonel)
Time period(s): Indeterminate Future
Locale(s): Fictional Country

Summary: Constant battle keeps the adrenaline high and demonstrates the superior skills of Hammer's Slammers.

Other books you might like:
Greg Bear, *The Forge of God*, 1987
David Brin, *Earth*, 1990
Gordon R. Dickson, *Dorsai!*, 1976
Robert A. Heinlein, *Starship Troopers*, 1959
Keith Laumer, *Rogue Bolo*, 1986
G. Harry Stine, *Blood Siege*, 1990
G. Harry Stine, *The Lost Battalion*, 1989
G. Harry Stine, *Sierra Madre*, 1985

1335
RICHARD DREYFUSS
HARRY TURTLEDOVE, Co-Author

The Two Georges
(New York: Tor, 1996)

Story type: Science Fiction (Alternate Universe; Mystery)
Major character(s): Thomas Bushell, Military Personnel (colonel), Detective; Kathleen Flannery, Museum Curator, Adventurer; Samuel Stanley, Military Personnel
Time period(s): 1990s (1996)
Locale(s): North American Union, Alternate Earth (Canada and continental United States of America)

Summary: When thieves, presumably the Sons of Liberty who advocate separation from Great Britain, steal Gainsborough's famous painting, "The Two Georges," on exhibition in North America, Colonel Thomas Bushell must recover it before

Charles III visits Victoria, capital of the North American Union.

Other books you might like:
John Christopher, *New Found Land*, 1983
Michael Flynn, *In the Country of the Blind*, 1990
Randall Garrett, *Too Many Magicians*, 1967
Harry Harrison, *Tunnel through the Deeps*, 1972
Keith Laumer, *Worlds of the Imperium*, 1962
Michael Moorcock, *The Warlord of the Air*, 1971
John Maddox Roberts, *King of the Wood*, 1983
L. Neil Smith, *The Probability Broach*, 1980
Harry Turtledove, *A Different Flesh*, 1988

1336
JOHN DRIVER

The Hunger of the Beast
(New York: Jove, 1991)

Story type: Horror (Psychological Suspense)
Major character(s): Esau Wilkinson, Young Man; Diana LaBianca, Producer (assistant in New York Theatre); Dennis O'Connor, Journalist
Time period(s): 1990s
Locale(s): Fenwick, Vermont

Summary: Diana LaBianca's vacation at Vermont's Wilkinson Inn turns into a nightmare when she is mistaken for someone snooping into the owners' background and is imprisoned at the mercy of Esau Wilkinson, the deformed half-wit progeny of the Wilkinson clan.

Other books you might like:
John Fowles, *The Collector*, 1963
Stephen R. George, *The Forgotten*, 1991

1337
DIANE DUANE

Dark Mirror
(New York: Pocket, 1993)

Story type: Science Fiction (Alternate Universe; Space Opera)
Series: Star Trek: The Next Generation
Major character(s): Jean-Luc Picard, Spaceship Captain, Military Personnel; Hwii ih'iie-u Ulak!ha', Alien (native of Triton Two), Scientist; Geordi La Forge, Engineer, Military Personnel
Time period(s): 24th century
Locale(s): *U.S.S. Enterprise*, Spaceship; *I.S.S. Enterprise*, Spaceship; United Empire of Planets, Interstellar Empire/ Federation

Summary: Snatched during their investigation into a disturbance in the hyperstring structure of the galaxy, the crew of the *U.S.S. Enterprise* find themselves in an alternate universe where the United Empire of Planets rules the galaxy with fear and violence. Picard, Troi and La Forge must transport to the *Imperial Star Ship Enterprise*, impersonate their amoral counterparts and avoid assassination attempts by ambitious junior officers in order to find the information they need to escape to their own universe and save the Federation from the transdimensional invasion that the Empire plans. Set in the universe of the ''Star Trek'' episode, Mirror, Mirror.'

Other books you might like:
James Blish, *Star Trek 3*, 1969
Peter David, *Imzadi*, 1992
Philip K. Dick, *The Man in the High Castle*, 1962
Phyllis Eisenstein, *Shadow of Earth*, 1979
Michael Jan Friedman, *Double, Double*, 1989
Barbara Hambly, *Ishmael*, 1985

1338

DIANE DUANE

Doctor's Orders
(New York: Pocket, 1990)

Story type: Science Fiction (Space Opera)
Series: Star Trek
Major character(s): Leonard McCoy, Doctor; James T. Kirk, Spaceship Captain; At, Alien
Time period(s): 23rd century
Locale(s): Flyspeck, Planet—Imaginary; Musca Constellation, Outer Space; *U.S.S. Enterprise*, Spaceship

Summary: The *Enterprise* is sent to open diplomatic relations with three species on a recently contacted planet. The mission is intriguing and seems safe so Kirk hands over the controls to McCoy, much to the doctor's chagrin. Then Kirk vanishes from the planet, Starfleet demands to know why McCoy is in command and the Klingons arrive. Suddenly Kirk's afternoon of turning the tables on the doctor has gotten out of hand.

Other books you might like:
Lloyd Biggle, *This Darkening Universe*, 1975
John M. Ford, *How Much for Just the Planet?*, 1984
   Star Trek 36
Keith Laumer, *Retief: Diplomat at Arms*, 1982

1339

DIANE DUANE

The Door into Sunset
(New York: Tor, 1993)

Story type: Fantasy (Magic Conflict; Religious)
Series: Tale of the Five
Major character(s): Freelorn ''Lorn'', Heir—Dispossessed, Royalty (Prince of Arlen); Herewiss, Magician, Religious; Segnbora, Sorceress, Martial Arts Expert
Time period(s): Indeterminate
Locale(s): Arlen, Fictional Country

Summary: To restore vitality to Arlen, Lorn and his companions strive to overthrow the usurper king. Pursuing his goal, Lorn must sneak back into his homeland and discover, then attempt to pass, the rites of Initiation.

Other books you might like:
C.J. Cherryh, *Gate of Ivrel*, 1976
Sheila Gilluly, *Greenbriar Queen*, 1988
Barbara Hambly, *The Time of the Dark*, 1982
Guy Gavriel Kay, *The Summer Tree*, 1985
Guy Gavriel Kay, *Tigana*, 1990

Patricia Kennealy, *The Copper Crown*, 1984
Katharine Kerr, *Daggerspell*, 1986
Mercedes Lackey, *Magic's Pawn*, 1989
Patricia A. McKillip, *The Riddle-Master of Hed*, 1976
Martha Wells, *The Element of Fire*, 1993

1340

DIANE DUANE
PETER MORWOOD, Co-Author

High Moon
(New York: Avon, 1992)

Story type: Science Fiction (Military; Space Opera)
Series: Spacecops
Major character(s): Evan Glyndower, Military Personnel (Solar Patrol); Joss O'Bannion, Military Personnel (Solar Patrol)
Time period(s): Indeterminate Future
Locale(s): Phobos, Mars (2nd moon of Mars)

Summary: Vacationing on Phobos, Joss attends the Triplanetary Video, Solid, and Holo Collectors Convention while Evan visits the weapon experts at FAF Sydanham Upper. After a mysterious attack, the partners, ordered into space to find the ship containing their prototype decoder, find themselves fighting the Red Dawn, a band of outlaws.

Other books you might like:
Lois McMaster Bujold, *Brothers in Arms*, 1988
David Drake, *Northworld*, 1990
Stephen Goldin, *Jade Darcy and the Affair of Honor*, 1988
   Mary Mason, co-author
Steve Perry, *The Man Who Never Missed*, 1989
Paul Preuss, *The Diamond Moon*, 1990
Alis A. Rasmussen, *A Passage of Stars*, 1990

1341

DIANE DUANE

High Wizardry
(New York: Delacorte, 1990)

Story type: Fantasy (Science Fiction)
Major character(s): Dairine, Wizard
Time period(s): Indeterminate Future
Locale(s): Outer Space

Summary: Dairine finds a manual of magic on her computer and sets off on an adventure. She is chased by a wide variety of aliens and agents before her adventure ends.

Other books you might like:
Kevin J. Anderson, *Game's End*, 1990
Barbara Hambly, *The Silent Tower*, 1988
Michael Kandel, *In between Dragons*, 1990
Susan Beth Pfeffer, *Rewind to Yesterday*, 1988
Will Shetterly, *The Tangled Lands*, 1989
Connie Willis, *Light Raid*, 1989
   Science Fiction. Cynthia Felice, co-author

1342

DIANE DUANE
PETER MORWOOD, Co-Author

Kill Station

(New York: AvoNova, 1992)

Story type: Science Fiction (Mystery)
Series: Spacecops
Major character(s): Evan Glyndower, Military Personnel (solar patrol); Joss O'Bannion, Military Personnel (solar patrol)
Time period(s): 22nd century
Locale(s): *Nosey*, Spaceship; Asteroid Belt, Outer Space

Summary: While investigating a series of piracies to space-going freighters, Evan and Joss discover a conspiracy which may present a threat throughout the solar system.

Other books you might like:
Alfred Bester, *The Stars My Destination*, 1956
Glen Cook, *The Dragon Never Sleeps*, 1988
Katharine Kerr, *Polar City Blues*, 1990
Melisa C. Michaels, *Skirmish*, 1985
Alis A. Rasmussen, *Revolution's Shore*, 1990
John Varley, *Steel Beach*, 1992
Vernor Vinge, *A Fire upon the Deep*, 1992

1343

DIANE DUANE
PETER MORWOOD, Co-Author

Mindblast

(New York: Avon, 1991)

Story type: Science Fiction (Mystery)
Series: Spacecops
Major character(s): Evan Glyndower, Military Personnel (Solar Patrol); Joss O'Bannion, Military Personnel (Solar Patrol)
Time period(s): 22nd century
Locale(s): Freedom, Space Station (at L5)

Summary: When Glyndower's partner is killed on Freedom, he's paired with O'Bannion, and the two of them are sent to continue the investigation and find the killer despite corrupt cops and budget cutbacks.

Other books you might like:
Barney Cohen, *The Taking of Satcon Station*, 1982
   Jim Baen, co-author
Glen Cook, *Sweet Silver Blues*, 1987
P.M. Griffin, *Star Commandos*, 1986
Lee Killough, *Spider Play*, 1986
Mercedes Lackey, *Burning Water*, 1989
Walter Jon Williams, *Days of Atonement*, 1991

1344

DIANE DUANE
PETER MORWOOD, Co-Author

seaQuest DSV: The Novel

(New York: Ace, 1993)

Story type: Science Fiction (Adventure; Techno-Thriller)
Series: seaQuest DSV
Major character(s): Nathan Hale Bridger, Scientist, Sea Captain; Darwin, Animal (dolphin); Marilyn Stark, Sea Captain, Criminal
Time period(s): 2010s
Locale(s): *seaQuest DSV*, Submarine; Atlantic Ocean

Summary: When Marilyn Stark washes out as captain of *seaQuest DSV*, United Earth/Oceans Organization searches out Nathan Bridger and coerces him into the submarine, hoping to entice its designer into accepting captaincy. Attempting to gain revenge, Marilyn Stark uses her knowledge of *seaQuest DSV* to sabotage the research vehicle, threatening the lives of military and scientific personnel. Novelizes the television pilot.

Other books you might like:
Harry Harrison, *The Daleth Effect*, 1970
Damon Knight, *CV*, 1985
Damon Knight, *The Observers*, 1988
Damon Knight, *A Reasonable World*, 1991
Theodore Sturgeon, *Voyage to the Bottom of the Sea*, 1961
Jules Verne, *Twenty Thousand Leagues under the Sea*, 1870

1345

DIANE DUANE

Spider-Man: The Venom Factor

(New York: G.P. Putnam's Sons, 1994)

Story type: Science Fiction (Adventure; Mystery)
Series: Spider-Man
Major character(s): Peter "Spider-Man" Parker, Hero, Detective—Amateur; Hobgoblin, Criminal; Venom, Alien
Time period(s): 1990s
Locale(s): New York, New York

Summary: When the murder of an innocent man during a mysterious crime points unexpectedly toward Venom, Spider-Man must investigate the crime while simultaneously outsmarting Hobgoblin to save the city.

Other books you might like:
Stan Lee, *The Ultimate Spider-Man*, 1994
   editor
Dennis O'Neil, *Batman: Knightfall*, 1993
Roger Stern, *The Death and Life of Superman*, 1993
John Varley, *Superheroes*, 1995
   Ricia Mainhardt, co-editor
Len Wein, *Mayhem in Manhattan*, 1978
   Marv Wolfman, co-author

1346

TANNARIVE DUE

The Between

(New York: HarperCollins, 1995)

Story type: Horror (Wild Talents)
Major character(s): Hilton James, Social Worker; Dede James, Judge (Hilton's wife); Raul Puerta, Psychologist (therapist)
Time period(s): 1990s (1995)
Locale(s): Miami, Florida

Summary: After being saved from drowning when he was eight years old, Hilton James builds a good life for himself and family over the next thirty years. But a sudden spate of bad experiences, including dreams of an alternate life so vivid that Hilton is unable to separate them from reality, begins to suggest that he may never have been intended to live as long as he has and that fate is trying to rectify the situation. This is the author's first novel.

Other books you might like:
Stephen King, *The Dead Zone*, 1979
Stephen King, *Insomnia*, 1994
Dean R. Koontz, *Hideaway*, 1993
Daniel Quinn, *Dreamer*, 1988

1347

LEE DUIGON

Mind Stealer

(New York: Pinnacle, 1990)

Story type: Horror (Occult)
Major character(s): Larry Donaldson, Businessman; Geoff Tagge, Professor, Anthropologist; Tanaka, Shaman
Time period(s): 1990s (1990)
Locale(s): New Jersey

Summary: When workaholic Larry Donaldson dies mysteriously after a secretive six-week business training program, his brother-in-law Geoff suspects dark forces may be involved.

Other books you might like:
Thomas M. Disch, *The Businessman: A Tale of Terror*, 1984
John Tigges, *Venom*, 1988

1348

DAVE DUNCAN

The Cursed

(New York: Ballantine Del Rey, 1995)

Story type: Fantasy (Political; Adventure)
Major character(s): Gwin Nien Solith, Innkeeper, Magician (Poulscath); Bulion Tharn, Leader; Niad, Magician (Ivielscath), Teenager
Time period(s): Indeterminate
Locale(s): Da Lam, Fictional Country; Wesran, Fictional Country; Raragash, Fictional Country

Summary: Gwin illegally shelters Niad who feels the effect of the Curse which brings forth magical abilities, for good or ill. After Gwin encourages Niad to cure Bulion Tharn's malady, Gwin and Bulion agree to wed. Seeking a more hospitable environment for magicians, they lead a band of Cursed who may help Bulion, the prophecied Renewer, bind together the fragments of the old empire and renew its glory.

Other books you might like:
Terry Goodkind, *Stone of Tears*, 1995
Laurell K. Hamilton, *Nightseer*, 1992
George R.R. Martin, *The Wild Cards Series*, 1987-1995
L.E. Modesitt Jr., *The Towers of the Sunset*, 1992
Elizabeth Moon, *Sheepfarmer's Daughter*, 1988
Julie Dean Smith, *Call of Madness*, 1990
Janny Wurts, *Curse of the Mistwraith*, 1994

1349

DAVE DUNCAN

The Cutting Edge

(New York: Ballantine Del Rey, 1992)

Story type: Fantasy (Magic Conflict; Political)
Series: Handful of Men
Major character(s): Rap, Ruler, Adventurer
Time period(s): Indeterminate
Locale(s): Pandemia, Fictional Country

Summary: After 3000 years of the Protocol, a ban on the political use of some types of magic, prophecies indicate that cataclysmic changes threaten Pandemia. After more than a decade of peace and security in his kingdom, Rap hesitantly accepts his role in upcoming events as heroes and heroines begin to assemble in preparation for the political and magical chaos looming on the horizon.

Other books you might like:
David Eddings, *Pawn of Prophecy*, 1982
Robert Jordan, *The Eye of the World*, 1989
Elizabeth Moon, *Sheepfarmer's Daughter*, 1988
J.R.R. Tolkien, *The Fellowship of the Ring*, 1954
Paula Volsky, *Illusion*, 1992

1350

DAVE DUNCAN

Emperor and Clown

(New York: Ballantine Del Rey, 1992)

Story type: Fantasy (Light Fantasy; Adventure)
Series: Man of His Word
Major character(s): Rap, Warrior, Psychic (seer); Inosolan "Inos", Royalty (queen); Azak, Mythical Creature (djinn), Leader
Time period(s): Indeterminate Past
Locale(s): Pandemia, Fictional Country; Cenmere, Fictional Country (capital district); Hub of the Impire, Fictional City

Summary: Having failed his mission to rescue Queen Inos from Azak, Rap awaits his dark future at the hands of Azak's torturers. However, Azak's intention to recover his losses and free himself from a curse yields unexpected results.

Other books you might like:
Harry Turtledove, *An Emperor for the Legion*, 1987
Harry Turtledove, *The Legion of Videssos*, 1987
Harry Turtledove, *The Misplaced Legion*, 1987
Paula Volsky, *Illusion*, 1992

1351

DAVE DUNCAN

Faery Lands Forlorn
(New York: Ballantine/Del Rey, 1991)

Story type: Fantasy (Adventure; Light Fantasy)
Series: Man of His Word
Major character(s): Inosolan "Inos", Royalty (queen); Rap, Worker (stableboy), Psychic (seer); Kadolan "Kade", Royalty (princess), Guardian (Inosolan's aunt)
Time period(s): Indeterminate Past
Locale(s): Zark, Fictional Country; Faerie, Fictional Country

Summary: When Krasnegar is overrun with invaders, Inos, Rap and Aunt Kade escape through the magic casement. Unfortunately, it sends them to opposite ends of Pandemia. Inos and Aunt Kade must outwit the sorceress who has taken control of Zark and its sultan, even though as women they have no standing in Zarkian society. Rap is flung to the Island of Faery and having a word of power seems woefully inadequate to help him reach Inos.

Other books you might like:
Leo Frankowski, *The Cross-Time Engineer*, 1986
Barry Hughart, *Bridge of Birds*, 1984
Diana Wynne Jones, *Howl's Moving Castle*, 1986
John Morressy, *The Questing of Kedrigern*, 1987

1352

DAVE DUNCAN

Hero
(New York: Ballantine/Del Rey, 1991)

Story type: Science Fiction (Genetic Manipulation; Military)
Major character(s): Vaun, Genetically Altered Being, Hero; Feirn, Television Personality; Roker, Military Personnel
Time period(s): Indeterminate Future (295th Century of the Empire)
Locale(s): Ult, Planet—Imaginary

Summary: An unwilling hero in Ult's first contact with the Brotherhood, Vaun finds himself again forced by Roker to save Ult from the Brotherhood's invasion.

Other books you might like:
Lois McMaster Bujold, *Barrayar*, 1991
Orson Scott Card, *Ender's Game*, 1985
George Alec Effinger, *When Gravity Fails*, 1987
Stephen Goldin, *Jade Darcy and the Affair of Honor*, 1988
　Mary Mason, co-author
Marc Laidlaw, *Neon Lotus*, 1988
Alis A. Rasmussen, *Revolution's Shore*, 1990
James H. Schmitz, *The Demon Breed*, 1968
Cordwainer Smith, *Norstrilia*, 1975

1353

DAVE DUNCAN

The Hunters' Haunt
(New York: Ballantine Del Rey, 1995)

Story type: Fantasy (Adventure)
Major character(s): Omar "Trader of Tales" Anglith of Arkraz, Writer, Traveller
Time period(s): Indeterminate Past
Locale(s): Middle East

Summary: To avoid ejection from Hunters' Haunt Inn into a deadly storm, Omar agrees to a story-telling contest in which his tales must prove more entertaining than those of the inn's guests.

Other books you might like:
Salman Rushdie, *Haroun and the Sea of Stories*, 1990
Susan Shwartz, *Arabesques: More Tales of the Arabian Nights*, 1988
　editor
Dan Simmons, *Hyperion*, 1989
John Vornholt, *The Fabulist*, 1993
Jack Zipes, *Arabian Nights: The Marvels and Wonders of the Thousand and One Nights*, 1991
　editor

1354

DAVE DUNCAN

The Living God
(New York: Ballantine Del Rey, 1994)

Story type: Fantasy (Adventure; Magic Conflict)
Series: Handful of Men
Major character(s): Rap, Nobleman, Psychic; Zinixo, Mythical Creature (dwarf), Wizard; Emshander V, Ruler (Imperator)
Time period(s): Indeterminate Past
Locale(s): The Impire, Fictional Country

Summary: The awesome power of Zinixo continues to grow as he tracks down the last free wizards and tightens his hold on the Impire. As the mad dwarf's power grows, the hopes of Rap and his outmatched dissidents fail. If they cannot accomplish the seemingly impossible task of revitalizing the Impire, their entire world faces doom.

Other books you might like:
Glen Cook, *The Black Company*, 1984
David Eddings, *Pawn of Prophecy*, 1982
Robert Jordan, *The Eye of the World*, 1989
Patricia A. McKillip, *The Riddle-Master of Hed*, 1976
Lawrence Watt-Evans, *The Lure of the Basilisk*, 1980

1355

DAVE DUNCAN

Magic Casement
(New York: Ballantine/Del Rey, 1990)

Story type: Fantasy (Light Fantasy; Adventure)

Series: Man of His Word
Major character(s): Inosolan "Inos", Royalty (princess); Rap, Worker (stableboy), Psychic (seer)
Time period(s): Indeterminate Past
Locale(s): Krasnegar, Fictional Country; Kinvale, Fictional Country

Summary: Inos's peaceful childhood and many friendships, especially with Rap, come to an end when she's sent to Kinvale to learn to be a lady. In the meantime, Rap finds himself ostracized for his new abilities as a seer, befriended only by a newcomer who's almost too charming to be true. When Rap discovers that Inos's father is dying, he and his friend set off for Kinvale, unprepared for the experiences and revelations to come.

Other books you might like:
Sheila Gilluly, *Greenbriar Queen*, 1987
Lyndon Hardy, *Master of the Five Magics*, 1980
Mickey Zucker Reichert, *Godslayer*, 1987
Elizabeth Ann Scarborough, *Bronwyn's Bane*, 1983
Will Shetterly, *Liavek*, 1985
    Emma Bull, co-editer

1356

DAVE DUNCAN

Past Imperative

(New York: AvoNova/Morrow, 1995)

Story type: Fantasy (Alternate World)
Major character(s): Edward Exeter, Student; Eleal Singer, Singer, Handicapped; Throng Impresario, Entertainer
Time period(s): 1910s (1914); Indeterminate
Locale(s): Nargh, Fictional City; Fallo, Mythical Place (public school); Alternate Earth

Summary: Authorities accuse Edward Exeter of a terrible crime the summer after graduation, while in another world Eleal Singer prays to the Trickster for healing as she travels to an Art Festival. The gods pull them together across the gap between their worlds, to take part in a game whose rules and stakes they don't quite understand.

Other books you might like:
Eleanor Arnason, *Daughter of the Bear King*, 1987
Robert A. Heinlein, *Glory Road*, 1993
Will Shetterly, *The Tangled Lands*, 1989
S.P. Somtow, *Riverrun*, 1991
Roger Zelazny, *Nine Princes in Amber*, 1970

1357

DAVE DUNCAN

Perilous Seas

(New York: Ballantine/Del Rey, 1991)

Story type: Fantasy (Light Fantasy; Adventure)
Series: Man of His Word
Major character(s): Inosolan "Inos", Royalty (queen); Rap, Worker (stableboy), Psychic (seer); Kadolan "Kade", Royalty (princess), Guardian (Inosolan's aunt)
Time period(s): Indeterminate Past

Locale(s): Zark, Fictional Country; Dragon Reach, Fictional Country

Summary: Inos and Aunt Kade have allied themselves with the true sultan of Zark in an attempt to escape the sorceress Rasha and present their plea to the four Wardens for restoration of Krasnegar and Zark to their rightful rulers. Meanwhile, Rap encounters the fulfillment of the first of three dire prophecies presented by the magic casement.

Other books you might like:
Elizabeth H. Boyer, *The Elves and the Otterskin*, 1981
Gordon R. Dickson, *The Dragon and the George*, 1976
Raymond E. Feist, *Magician*, 1982
Barbara Hambly, *Dragonsbane*, 1987
Robert Jordan, *The Eye of the World*, 1989
Patricia C. Wrede, *The Seven Towers*, 1984

1358

DAVE DUNCAN

Present Tense

(New York: Avon, 1996)

Story type: Fantasy (Alternate World)
Series: Great Game
Major character(s): Edward Exeter, Traveller; Julian Smedley, Military Personnel, Handicapped; Kammaeman, Military Personnel
Time period(s): 1910s (1917); Indeterminate
Locale(s): England; Alternate Earth

Summary: Edward Exeter escapes the perils of the strange world he entered three years earlier. Unfortunately, he returns to Europe during the First World War still wanted for murder. Even worse, the forces that have decreed his destiny want him back enough to kill anyone in two worlds to get him.

Other books you might like:
Eleanor Arnason, *Daughter of the Bear King*, 1987
Guy Gavriel Kay, *The Summer Tree*, 1985
Kim Newman, *The Bloody Red Baron*, 1995
Brian Stableford, *The Carnival of Destruction*, 1994
Roger Zelazny, *Nine Princes in Amber*, 1970

1359

DAVE DUNCAN

The Reaver Road

(New York: Ballantine Del Rey, 1992)

Story type: Fantasy (Adventure)
Major character(s): Omar "Trader of Tales" Anglith of Arkraz, Writer, Traveller; Thorian, Royalty (crown prince), Traveller; Jaxian Tharpit, Government Official, Leader (Zanadon)
Time period(s): Indeterminate
Locale(s): Zanadon, Fictional City; Spice Lands, Fictional Country

Summary: As Omar and Thorian travel together they tell each other fabulous heroic tales about themselves and the war in the Spice Lands.

Other books you might like:
Stephen Goldin, *Shrine of the Desert Mage*, 1988
Laurell K. Hamilton, *Nightseer*, 1992
Andrew Lang, *The Arabian Nights Entertainments*, 1969
    editor
Susan Shwartz, *Arabesques: More Tales of the Arabian Nights*, 1988
    editor
Jack Zipes, *Arabian Nights: The Marvels and Wonders of the Thousand and One Nights*, 1991
    editor

`1360`

DAVE DUNCAN

The Stricken Field
(New York: Ballantine Del Rey, 1993)

Story type: Fantasy (Adventure; Magic Conflict)
Series: Handful of Men
Major character(s): Rap, Nobleman, Psychic; Zinixo, Mythical Creature (dwarf), Wizard; Emshander V, Ruler (Imperor)
Time period(s): Indeterminate Past
Locale(s): The Impire, Fictional Country

Summary: Zinixo controls the Impire and almost every magician in the world. A small group of nobles and magicians that oppose him suffer many setbacks and few successes while hoping that help can be found before Zinixo rules everything.

Other books you might like:
Glen Cook, *The Black Company*, 1984
David Eddings, *Pawn of Prophecy*, 1982
Robert Jordan, *The Eye of the World*, 1989
Patricia A. McKillip, *The Riddle-Master of Hed*, 1976
Lawrence Watt-Evans, *The Lure of the Basilisk*, 1980

`1361`

DAVE DUNCAN

Strings
(New York: Ballantine/Del Rey, 1990)

Story type: Science Fiction (Adventure)
Major character(s): Cedric, Teenager; Princess Alya, Royalty
Time period(s): 21st century
Locale(s): Nauc, Earth

Summary: On an Earth stewing in its own pollution, scientists work on developing superstring transportation as a way of escaping the planet. Cedric is a hick from the sticks, but his grandmother is head of the planetary exploration project. Through her he meets the Princess Alya and together they attempt to escape Earth before it collapses.

Other books you might like:
Piers Anthony, *But What of Earth?*, 1976
    Revised 1989
Gregory Benford, *Tides of Light*, 1989
Vonda N. McIntyre, *Starfarers*, 1989

`1362`

DAVE DUNCAN

Upland Outlaws
(New York: Ballantine Del Rey, 1993)

Story type: Fantasy (Magic Conflict; Political)
Series: Handful of Men
Major character(s): Rap, Ruler, Psychic; Zinixo, Mythical Creature (dwarf), Wizard; Emshander IV, Ruler (Imperor)
Time period(s): Indeterminate Past
Locale(s): Hub of the Impire, Fictional City

Summary: Chaos and confusion settle on the capital as omens and strange actions warn of a plot against the Impire. When King Rap must go out again to battle the insane Zinixo, this time without his power, he and a small group including the deposed Imperor create a crazy plan that just might save the Millenium.

Other books you might like:
Glen Cook, *The Black Company*, 1984
David Eddings, *Pawn of Prophecy*, 1982
Robert Jordan, *The Eye of the World*, 1989
Patricia A. McKillip, *The Riddle-Master of Hed*, 1976
Michael Scott Rohan, *The Forge in the Forest*, 1987

`1363`

DAVE DUNCAN

West of January
(New York: Ballantine/Del Rey, 1989)

Story type: Science Fiction (Adventure)
Major character(s): Knobil, Wanderer
Time period(s): Indeterminate Future
Locale(s): Planet—Imaginary

Summary: On a strange planet which revolves every 264.6 days and rotates every 263.6 days lives a wide variety of races, cultures, and animals, all originally from Earth. Knobil, son of a herdswoman and, supposedly, an angel, wanders the planet having adventures, some of them exciting, some of them tragic, some of them rather sexy.

Other books you might like:
Ronald Anthony Cross, *Prisoners of Paradise*, 1988
R.A. MacAvoy, *The Third Eagle: Lessons Along a Minor String*, 1989
Jack Vance, *Big Planet*, 1957
Jack Vance, *Showboat World*, 1975

`1364`

J.R. DUNN

This Side of Judgment
(New York: Harcourt Brace, 1994)

Story type: Science Fiction (Alternate Intelligence; Mystery)
Major character(s): Ross Bohlen, Government Official; Jason Telford, Fugitive; Scott Page, Murderer
Time period(s): 21st century

Locale(s): Ironwood, Montana; Washington, District of Columbia

Summary: The recent war to prevent Cybernetically Enhanced Individuals, called CEIs or chipheads, from taking over the world succeeded, but with great loss of life and much destruction. Recognizing the pattern, Bohlen looks for one of the few remaining chipheads who he believes murdered a young girl, while attempting to prevent the death of any innocent CEIs. Unfortunately, all chipheads eventually show symptoms of Pelton's Syndrome from excessive use of the interface, leading to fatal information overload. First novel.

Other books you might like:
Alfred Bester, *The Demolished Man*, 1953
Pat Cadigan, *Fools*, 1992
Philip K. Dick, *A Scanner Darkly*, 1977
James Patrick Kelly, *Wildlife*, 1994
Katharine Kerr, *Polar City Blues*, 1990
Frederik Pohl, *The Voices of Heaven*, 1994
Kevin D. Randle, *Mind Slayer*, 1992
    Richard Driscoll, co-author

1365

KATHERINE DUNN

Geek Love
(New York: Warner, 1990)

Major character(s): Olympia Binewski, Parent, Genetically Altered Being; Miranda Binewski, Artist (Medical)
Time period(s): 1980s
Locale(s): United States

Summary: Arturo Binewski and his wife Crystal Lil save the Carnival Fabulon from ruin by breeding their own freaks, products of Lil's ingestion of drugs, insecticides, arsenic, radioactive isotopes, etc. The story of this bizarre, perverse, grotesque, humorous, but also loving and tender menage is told by the dwarfed daughter Olympia, focusing on her own secret maternal love for her vulnerable "normal" daughter, Miranda.

Other books you might like:
Angela Carter, *Nights at the Circus*, 1985
William Goyen, *Arcadio*, 1983
Todd Robbins, "*Spurs*", 1932

1366

PAULINE DUNN (Pseudonym of Susan Hartzell)

The Crawling Dark
(New York: Zebra, 1991)

Story type: Horror (Apocalyptic Horror)
Major character(s): Martin Bryant, Student; Sandra Bryant, Restaurateur; Richard O'Brien, Police Officer (sheriff)
Time period(s): 1990s
Locale(s): Rockville, Tennessee

Summary: Martin and Sandra Bryant return to their home town to attend to the burial of their recently deceased father but find all of the townspeople dead from a biologically peculiar organism that can reanimate corpses seemingly at will. Along with the police force of nearby Edgerton, the two become involved in an effort to stop not just what appears on the surface to be an infestation of unknown origin but what may actually be the beginning of the biblical apocalypse.

Other books you might like:
Michael Crichton, *The Andromeda Strain*, 1969
Dean R. Koontz, *Phantoms*, 1983

1367

LORD DUNSANY

The Hashish Man and Other Stories by Lord Dunsany
(San Francisco: Manic D Press, 1996)

Story type: Fantasy (Collection)

Summary: Contains a two-page introduction, the "Preface to The Last Book of Wonder" and 25 stories excerpted from *A Dreamer's Tales* (1910), *Fifty-One Tales* (1915) and *The Last Book of Wonder* (1916). The stories' tone generally varies from grim to creepy with themes including chess, dream travel, prophecy, mythology, hunting, and sea voyages.

Other books you might like:
Hugh B. Cave, *Murgunstrumm and Others*, 1977
H.P. Lovecraft, *The Best of H.P. Lovecraft: Bloodcurdling Tales of Horror and the Macabre*, 1982
E. Hoffman Price, *Far Lands Other Days*, 1975
Clark Ashton Smith, *Other Dimensions*, 1970
Clark Ashton Smith, *Tales of Zothique*, 1995
Howard Wandrei, *Time Burial*, 1995

1368

DORANNA DURGIN

Dun Lady's Jess
(New York: Baen, 1994)

Story type: Fantasy (Alternate World; Magic Conflict)
Major character(s): Carey, Courier; Dun Lady's Jess, Animal (horse), Young Woman; Jaime Cabot, Horse Trainer
Time period(s): 1990s; Indeterminate
Locale(s): Alternate Earth; Marion, Ohio

Summary: Fleeing pursuers who seek to misuse the dangerous spells he carries, Carey and his horse trigger a spell that brings them to an alternate world, along with their pursuers. Separated from Carey and transformed into a human, Jess finds refuge at the Dancing Equine Dressage Center with new friends who help her rescue Carey. But even if Carey finds a way to go back and defeat the evil Calandre, Jess may not want to be a horse again.

Other books you might like:
Eleanor Arnason, *Daughter of the Bear King*, 1987
Jude Deveraux, *A Knight in Shining Armor*, 1989
Gordon R. Dickson, *The Dragon and the George*, 1976
C.S. Lewis, *The Magician's Nephew*, 1955
R.A. MacAvoy, *The Grey Horse*, 1987

1369

DORANNA DURGIN

Touched by Magic

(New York: Baen, 1996)

Story type: Fantasy (Magic Conflict; Mystery)
Major character(s): Reandn, Guard (King's Wolf), Detective; Rethia, Healer; Farren, Wizard
Time period(s): Indeterminate
Locale(s): King's Keep, Mythical Place; Keland, Fictional Country

Summary: Reandn's investigation into missing children progresses until magical interference destroys Reandn's life. The key to the lost children and the return of the magic, thought long gone, may hinge on a former wizard and a healer familiar with unicorns who took the magic with them on leaving.

Other books you might like:
Pamela Dean, *The Dubious Hills*, 1994
Graham Edwards, *Dragoncharm*, 1996
Simon R. Green, *Hawk & Fisher*, 1990
Irene Radford, *The Glass Dragon*, 1994
Melissa Scott, *Point of Hopes*, 1995
　　Lisa A. Barnett, co-author

1370

DAVID DVORKIN

Insatiable

(New York: Pinnacle, 1993)

Story type: Horror (Vampire Story)
Major character(s): Richard Venneman, Assistant (laboratory), Vampire; Jill Kennedy, Office Worker; Harold "Dirty" Dinsmuir, Scientist (physicist)
Time period(s): 1990s (1993)
Locale(s): Denver, Colorado

Summary: Newly vampirized Richard Venneman tries to kill himself by exposing his body to radiation, but only succeeds in transforming himself into a vampire for whom blood tastes disgusting, and whose victims develop an unquenchable obsession for him.

Other books you might like:
Poppy Z. Brite, *Lost Souls*, 1992
Nancy A. Collins, *Sunglasses After Dark*, 1989
John Peyton Cooke, *Out for Blood*, 1991
John Skipp, *The Light at the End*, 1986
　　Craig Spector, co-author

1371

DAVID DVORKIN

Ursus

(New York: Franklin Watts, 1989)

Story type: Science Fiction (Horror)
Major character(s): Mark Adler, Government Official; Phyllis Ortiveda, Police Officer
Time period(s): 1980s

Locale(s): Piketon, Rocky Mountains

Summary: Vicious mini-bears terrorize the Rocky Mountain community of Piketon. The town government, corrupt through and through, seems helpless to stop the killing.

Other books you might like:
Stephen King, *Cujo*, 1981
Dean R. Koontz, *Watchers*, 1987

1372

STEFAN DZIEMIANOWICZ, Editor
ROBERT WEINBERG, Co-Editor
MARTIN H. GREENBERG, Co-Editor

100 Ghastly Little Ghost Stories

(New York: Barnes & Noble, 1993)

Story type: Horror (Anthology; Ghost Story)

Summary: The title notwithstanding, this volume contains 101 short-short ghost stories of 300 words or less written since the late-eighteenth century. Representative authors include M.R. James, J. Sheridan Le Fanu, E.F. Benson, H.P. Lovecraft, Henry S. Whitehead, August Derleth, Steve Rasnic Tem, William F. Nolan, and Chet Williamson. Nearly half of the stories were first published in the pages of *Weird Tales*, the premiere magazine of weird fiction between 1923 and 1954. Donald Burleson's "The Pedicab" appears in print for the first time.

Other books you might like:
Richard Dalby, *The Mammoth Book of Ghost Stories*, 1990
Richard Dalby, *The Mammoth Book of Ghost Stories 2*, 1991
Al Sarrantonio, *100 Hair-Raising Little Horror Stories*, 1993
　　Martin H. Greenberg, co-editor
Sebastian Wolfe, *The Little Book of Horrors*, 1992

1373

STEFAN DZIEMIANOWICZ, Editor
ROBERT WEINBERG, Co-Editor
MARTIN H. GREENBERG, Co-Editor

100 Wicked Little Witch Stories

(New York: Barnes & Noble, 1995)

Story type: Horror (Anthology; Witchcraft)

Summary: Most of these 100 stories of approximately 3000 words or less are original to the volume. Their different approaches to the witch theme include deep-sea witchcraft (Lois Gresh's "Fish Witch"), doll magic (Kathryn Ptacek's "Poppet"), a bewitched supermarket manager (Adam Niswander's "Bat's Blood for Flavor"), a variation on Cinderella's fairy godmother (Tina L. Jens' "The Princess and the Frog"), medieval witchcraft (Brian McNaughton's "The Conversion of St. Monocarp"), Caribbean witchcraft (Nancy Kilpatrick's "Heartbeat"), and the unexpected effects of magic curses (Nancy and Wayne Holder's "1-900-Witches").

Other books you might like:
Richard Dalby, *Tales of Witchcraft*, 1991
Peter Haining, *The Witchcraft Reader*, 1969

Marvin Kaye, *Witches and Warlocks: Tales of Black Magic Old and New*, 1990
Rod Serling, *Rod Serling's Triple W*, 1963
Charles G. Waugh, *Yankee Witches*, 1988
   Martin H. Greenberg, Frank McSherry, Jr., co-editors

1374

STEFAN DZIEMIANOWICZ, Editor
ROBERT WEINBERG, Co-Editor
MARTIN H. GREENBERG, Co-Editor

Famous Fantastic Mysteries
(New York: Gramercy, 1991)

Story type: Horror (Anthology; Mystery)

Summary: Thirty stories collected from the pulp magazines *Famous Fantastic Mysteries* and *Fantastic Novels*, both of which specialized in reprints of fantasies and scientific romances from the early pulp magazines but also published original fiction. Included are horror classics such as Arthur Machen's black magic story, ''The Novel of the White Powder,'' Robert W. Chamber's extended dreamy tale, ''The King in Yellow,'' and William Hope Hodgson's nautical nightmare, ''The Derelict.'' More modern tales include H.P. Lovecraft's ''The Music of Erich Zann,'' Arthur C. Clarke's ''The Guardian,'' Robert Bloch's ''The Man Who Collected Poe,'' and A. Merritt's rare lost race novella, ''The Face in the Abyss.''

Other books you might like:
Tony Goodstone, *The Pulps*, 1970
   editor
Sam Moskowitz, *Hauntings and Horrors*, 1969
   editor
Sam Moskowitz, *Horrors Unknown*, 1971
   editor
Sam Moskowitz, *Masters of Horror*, 1968
   editor
Sam Moskowitz, *Science Fiction by Gaslight*, 1968
   editor

1375

STEFAN DZIEMIANOWICZ, Editor
ROBERT WEINBERG, Co-Editor
MARTIN H. GREENBERG, Co-Editor

Nursery Crimes
(New York: Barnes & Noble, 1993)

Story type: Horror (Anthology; Child-in-Peril)

Summary: Thirty horror stories of children in peril published over the last century and a half, beginning with J. Sheridan Le Fanu's ''The Child Who Went with the Fairies'' and running to Steve and Melanie Tem's ''Resettling.'' The many threats posed to the children in these stories include war (Ambrose Bierce's ''Chickamauga''), schools (Ramsey Campbell's ''The Interloper''), families (Charles Grant's ''Everything to Live For''), extradimensional specters (Henry S. Whitehead's ''The Trap''), and other children (Stephen Gallagher's ''Magpie''). The editors also include two full novels, Henry

James' classic ghost story, *The Turn of the Screw*, and Sarban's *The Doll Maker*, reprinted for the first time in over 30 years.

Other books you might like:
Vic Ghidalia, *The Devil's Generation*, 1973
Vic Ghidalia, *Little Monsters*, 1969

1376

STEFAN DZIEMIANOWICZ, Editor
ROBERT WEINBERG, Co-Editor
MARTIN H. GREENBERG, Co-Editor

To Sleep, Perchance to Dream. . .Nightmare
(New York: Barnes & Noble, 1993)

Story type: Horror (Anthology)

Summary: This book collects 30 stories involving dreams or nightmares. The contents range from 19th century tales to contemporary ones. Included are J. Sheridan Le Fanu's ''The Drunkard's Dream,'' about a man who cannot distinguish between a dream and a possible vision of hell; Bram Stoker's ''A Dream of Red Hands,'' about a man whose guilt for a crime he commited manifests as a nightmare; and Wilkie Collins' ''The Dream Woman,'' about a recurrent a dream in which a man envisions his death at the hands of the woman he has married. Also included are to H.P. Lovecraft's ''Dreams in the Witch House''; Clark Ashton Smith's ''Ubbo Sathla''; Fritz Leiber's ''The Dreams of Albert Moreland''; Clive Barker's ''In the Flesh,'' in which dreamers find a way to penetrate other dimensions through their dreams; Thomas Ligotti's ''Dream of a Mannikin'' and Charles L. Grant's ''The Last Dreadful Hour,'' in which dreamers awaken to find themselves incapable of distinguishing whether the dream world is not actually the real world; Bruce McAllister's ''Dream Baby,'' in which dreams are harnessed as weapons in the Vietnam War; and Scott Bradfield's ''Dream of the Wolf,'' in which a man entrapped by the daily routine of his life finds liberation in his nightly dreams of running with a wolf pack.

Other books you might like:
Poul Anderson, *The Night Fantastic*, 1991
   Karen Anderson, co-author
Damon Knight, *Perchance to Dream*, 1973

1377

STEFAN DZIEMIANOWICZ, Editor
ROBERT WEINBERG, Co-Editor
MARTIN H. GREENBERG, Co-Editor

Virtuous Vampires
(New York: Barnes & Noble, 1996)

Story type: Horror (Anthology; Vampire Story)

Summary: Vampires are the good guys in the 18 reprinted stories assembled here. They apply their nocturnal skills to detective work in Tanya Huff's ''This Town Ain't Big Enough'' and heal with their bite in Sharon Farber's ''A Surfeit of Melancholic Humours'' and Spider Robinson's

"Pyotr's Story." They protect mortals from Jack the Ripper in Les Daniels' "Yellow Fog" and Harry Turtledove's "Gentlemen of the Shade," from an otherworldly menace in C.L. Moore's "Scarlet Dream," and from humanity's own decadent tendencies in Brian Stableford's "The Hunger and Ecstasy of Vampires." And they help with humor in Henry Kuttner's "Masquerade" and Robert Bloch's "The Cloak."

Other books you might like:
Ellen Datlow, *Blood Is Not Enough*, 1989
    editor
Ellen Datlow, *A Whisper of Blood*, 1992
    editor
Martin H. Greenberg, *Vampire Detectives*, 1995
    editor
Alan Ryan, *Vampires: Two Centuries of Great Vampire Stories*, 1988
    editor

`1378`

WILLIAM EAKINS

Key West 2720 A.D.

(Pound Ridge, NY: Knights Press, 1989)

Story type: Science Fiction (Gay/Lesbian Fiction)
Major character(s): Sam Phoe, Government Official, Homosexual; Gibb, Homosexual
Time period(s): 28th century (2720)
Locale(s): Key West, Florida

Summary: The world is run by gigantic corporations and nations have fragmented into city-states. Homosexuals have been excluded from most places, but Sam Phoe, the mayor of Key West, Florida, has given sanctuary to all gays in exile. Now, however, a number of hostile factions are working to bring an end to Sam's rule, some out of homophobia, some out of a simple desire for power.

Other books you might like:
Samuel R. Delany, *The Bridge of Lost Desire*, 1987
Samuel R. Delany, *Dhalgren*, 1975
Samuel R. Delany, *The Splendor and Misery of Bodies, of Cities*, 1985
Samuel R. Delany, *Stars in My Pocket Like Grains of Sand*, 1984
Samuel R. Delany, *Triton*, 1976
Lauren Wright Douglas, *In the Blood*, 1989
Joanna Russ, *The Female Man*, 1975
Theodore Sturgeon, *Venus Plus X*, 1960

`1379`

DANIEL EASTERMAN (Pseudonym of Denis MacEoin)

Name of the Beast

(New York: HarperCollins, 1992)

Story type: Horror (Apocalyptic Horror)
Major character(s): Aisha Manfaluti, Archaeologist (Egyptologist); Michael Hunt, Spy (former M15 agent); al-Qurtubi, Terrorist
Time period(s): 1990s (1999)

Locale(s): Cairo, Egypt

Summary: At the same time fundamentalist terrorist al-Qurtubi ascends to the presidency of Egypt a plague occurs, fulfilling biblical prophecy and reinforcing the rumors that he is the anti-Christ setting the stage for apocalypse in the coming millenium.

Other books you might like:
Thomas F. Monteleone, *The Blood of the Lamb*, 1992
Brian Stableford, *The Werewolves of London*, 1990
Robert Weinberg, *The Dead Man's Kiss*, 1992
F. Paul Wilson, *Nightworld*, 1992

`1380`

M. COLEMAN EASTON

Spirits of Cavern and Hearth

(New York: St. Martin's, 1989)

Story type: Fantasy (Quest)
Major character(s): Yarkol Dolmi, Doctor; Dzaminid, Shaman
Time period(s): Indeterminate
Locale(s): Alternate Universe

Summary: The southern Hakhan farmers are at odds with the nothern Chirudak nomads over lands which are increasingly unable to accommodate each society's growth and lifestyle. War is imminent and only one man, Yarkol Dolmi, can prevent it. Yarkol has attained a mysterious affliction that provides him with mystical powers and gateways to the realm of spirits. He must use his powers to outwit and defeat the underground cavern spirits that have sided with the Chirudak before a peace can be negotiated.

Other books you might like:
Vonda N. McIntyre, *Dreamsnake*, 1986
Jonathan Wylie, *Dreams Street*, 1989
Roger Zelazny, *Wizard World*, 1989

`1381`

THOMAS A. EASTON

Greenhouse

(New York: Ace, 1991)

Story type: Science Fiction (Genetic Manipulation)
Series: Sparrowhawk
Major character(s): Tom Cross, Genetically Altered Being, Businessman; Muffy Bowen, Dancer, Captive
Time period(s): 2080s (2084)
Locale(s): United States

Summary: Human genetic experimentation yields a crop of intelligent, aggressive plants with a desire to begin turning their cousins, human beings, into members of the plant kingdom.

Other books you might like:
Alfred Bester, *Golem* [100], 1980
Octavia E. Butler, *Adulthood Rites*, 1988
Octavia E. Butler, *Dawn*, 1987
Octavia E. Butler, *Imago*, 1989
Jack Finney, *The Body Snatchers*, 1955

Janet Kagan, *Mirabile*, 1991
Joan Slonczewski, *A Door into Ocean*, 1986
Cordwainer Smith, *The Best of Cordwainer Smith*, 1975
Cordwainer Smith, *Norstrilia*, 1975
Michael Swanwick, *Vacuum Flowers*, 1987

1382

THOMAS A. EASTON

Seeds of Destiny
(New York: Ace, 1994)

Story type: Science Fiction (Genetic Manipulation; Political)
Series: Sparrowhawk
Major character(s): Dotson Barbtail, Alien (Rac), Genetically Altered Being; Marcus Aurelius Hrecker, Scientist; Gypsy Blossom, Genetically Altered Being (plant)
Time period(s): 23rd century
Locale(s): Belt Center 83, Asteroid; First-Stop, Planet—Imaginary (Tau Ceti system); *Saladin*, Spaceship

Summary: With life in the Solar System bleak under the Engineer's rule, when the expedition returns from First-Stop with news of a possibly engineered intelligent species, an expedition to eliminate any abomination and take over First-Stop leaves almost immediately. The Racs at first believe their Remakers have returned but soon discover they must defend themselves.

Other books you might like:
Frank Herbert, *The White Plague*, 1982
Janet Kagan, *Mirabile*, 1991
Bill Ransom, *ViraVax*, 1993
Kim Stanley Robinson, *Green Mars*, 1994
Joan Slonczewski, *Daughter of Elysium*, 1993

1383

THOMAS A. EASTON

Sparrowhawk
(New York: Ace, 1990)

Story type: Science Fiction (Mystery; Genetic Manipulation)
Series: Sparrowhawk
Major character(s): Bernie Fischer, Detective—Police; Ralph Chowdhury, Scientist (genetic engineer); Emily Gilman, Scientist (genetic engineer)
Time period(s): 2040s (2044)
Locale(s): United States

Summary: To satisfy gambling debts Ralph Chowdhury is forced to secretly engineer devices for the underworld. When Bernie Fischer investigates an attack on commuters by a giant sparrow modified for use as a transport, one witness, Dr. Emily Gilman, proves especially helpful. As they track down the cause behind the suddenly dangerous equipment, Emily herself becomes an obvious target of Chowdhury's lethal constructs. A first novel.

Other books you might like:
David Brin, *Startide Rising*, 1983
David Brin, *The Uplift War*, 1987
Philip K. Dick, *Blade Runner*, 1982

Alan Dean Foster, *Cyber Way*, 1990
Katharine Kerr, *Polar City Blues*, 1990
Cordwainer Smith, *Norstrilia*, 1975

1384

THOMAS A. EASTON

Tower of the Gods
(New York: Ace, 1993)

Story type: Science Fiction (First Contact; Genetic Manipulation)
Series: Sparrowhawk
Major character(s): Pearl Angelica, Genetically Altered Being (Bot); Lois McAlois, Pilot (spaceship); Blacktop, Alien (Rac), Genetically Altered Being
Time period(s): 22nd century
Locale(s): Tau Ceti IV, Planet—Imaginary; *Gypsy*, Spaceship; Moon (Earth's)

Summary: Pearl Angelica dreams of going to Earth to find bees for *Gypsy* and free everyone from hand fertilizing all plants. After she travels to Earthspace, Engineer kidnappers take her to a barren Earth where they judge her too dangerous to remain. They transport Pearl to the Moon and cage her in public view as a hostage for the Q-drive, which Pearl realizes must be kept out of engineer hands.

Other books you might like:
Octavia E. Butler, *Adulthood Rites*, 1988
Octavia E. Butler, *Imago*, 1989
Janet Kagan, *Mirabile*, 1992
Megan Lindholm, *Alien Earth*, 1992
Vonda N. McIntyre, *Metaphase*, 1992
Larry Niven, *Protector*, 1973

1385

THOMAS A. EASTON

Woodsman
(New York: Ace, 1992)

Story type: Science Fiction (Genetic Manipulation)
Series: Sparrowhawk
Major character(s): Alice Bell, Genetically Altered Being (bot); Frederick Suida, Genetically Altered Being (pig), Human; Lois McAlois, Spaceship Captain
Time period(s): 2090s
Locale(s): United States; Probe Station, Space Station

Summary: Believing that a richer and safer humanity depends upon returning to the good old days of machines, the Engineers have taken over the government, which now ignores the increasing violence against genetically altered beings. Recognizing the imminent destruction of the environment and collapse of the infrastructure which maintains the modestly successful but highly over-populated planet, Earth's intelligent plants prepare their self defense while possible salvation orbits overhead.

Other books you might like:
Octavia E. Butler, *Adulthood Rites*, 1988
Octavia E. Butler, *Dawn*, 1987

Octavia E. Butler, *Imago*, 1989
Jack Finney, *The Body Snatchers*, 1955
   pseudonym of Walter Braden Finney
Janet Kagan, *Mirabile*, 1991
James Morrow, *City of Truth*, 1992
Cordwainer Smith, *The Best of Cordwainer Smith*, 1975
Vernor Vinge, *A Fire upon the Deep*, 1992

1386

JULIA ECKLAR

The Kobayashi Maru
(New York: Pocket Books, 1989)

Story type: Science Fiction (Space Opera)
Series: Star Trek
Major character(s): James T. Kirk, Spaceship Captain; Sulu, Military Personnel (Spaceship officer)
Time period(s): 23rd century
Locale(s): *Hailey*, Spaceship; Hohweyn System, Outer Space

Summary: A freak accident leaves Captain Kirk and a number of his officers adrift in a shuttlecraft. Hope of rescue is small. With no possibility of saving themselves, Kirk, Sulu, Scotty, and the others pass the time describing their experiences with the Kobayashi Maru, a complex, computer-simulated exam that every student at Starfleet Academy must pass to graduate. This is Ecklar's first novel.

Other books you might like:
J.M. Dillard, *Star Trek: The Lost Years*, 1989
J.M. Dillard, *Star Trek V: The Final Frontier*, 1989
Diane Duane, *My Enemy, My Ally*, 1984
   Star Trek 18
D.C. Fontana, *Vulcan's Glory*, 1989
   Star Trek 44

1387

JULIA ECKLAR

Regenesis
(New York: Ace, 1995)

Story type: Science Fiction (Genetic Manipulation; Adventure)
Major character(s): Rahel Tovin, Scientist (zoologist), Animal Lover; Paval Kuvasc, Apprentice, Scientist (zoologist)
Time period(s): Indeterminate Future
Locale(s): New Dallas, Planet—Imaginary; Reyson's Planet, Planet—Imaginary; Uriel, Planet—Imaginary

Summary: A proctor for the Noah's Ark project, Rahel travels to various planets to ensure that transplanted Earth species survive in their new homes.

Other books you might like:
David Brin, *Startide Rising*, 1983
David Brin, *The Uplift War*, 1987
Orson Scott Card, *Lovelock*, 1994
   Kathryn H. Kidd, co-author
Hal Clement, *Fossil*, 1993
Michael Crichton, *Jurassic Park*, 1990

L.A. Graf, *Caretaker*, 1995
   pseudonym of Julia Ecklar and Karen Rose
L.A. Graf, *Extreme Prejudice*, 1995
   pseudonym of Julia Ecklar and Karen Rose
L.A. Graf, *Traitor Winds*, 1990
   pseudonym of Julia Ecklar and Karen Rose
Janet Kagan, *Mirabile*, 1991

1388

DAVID EDDINGS
LEIGH EDDINGS, Co-Author

Belgarath the Sorcerer
(New York: Ballantine Del Rey, 1995)

Story type: Fantasy (Adventure)
Major character(s): Belgarath, Sorcerer, Adventurer
Time period(s): Indeterminate
Locale(s): Mallorea, Fictional Country; Arendia, Fictional Country; Sendaria, Fictional Country

Summary: Belgarath relates his early life and the events which led to his becoming the world's most powerful sorcerer. Set prior to events in *Paw of Prophecy*.

Other books you might like:
Steven Brust, *The Phoenix Guards*, 1991
Raymond E. Feist, *Magician*, 1982
Robert Jordan, *The Eye of the World*, 1989
Michael Scott Rohan, *The Anvil of Ice*, 1986
J.R.R. Tolkien, *The Silmarillion*, 1977

1389

DAVID EDDINGS

The Diamond Throne
(New York: Del Rey, 1989)

Story type: Fantasy (Quest)
Series: Elenium
Major character(s): Sparhawk, Knight (Queen's Champion); Sephrenia, Sorceress
Time period(s): Indeterminate
Locale(s): Elenia, Planet—Imaginary

Summary: After a 10 year absence, Sparhawk returns to Elenia, only to find his queen in a state near death. Sephrenia has enclosed the queen in crystal to slow her death, but she and Sparhawk have a limited amount of time to try and find a cure.

Other books you might like:
Carole Nelson Douglas, *Keepers of Edanvant*, 1989
   Book 3 - Sword and Circulate
Sharon Green, *Hellhound Magic*,
Peter Morwood, *The Horse Lord*, 1986
   Book 1 - The Book of Years Series
Jonathan Wylie, *Dreams of Stone*,
   Book 1 of Unbalanced Earth Series
Jonathan Wylie, *The Lightless Kingdom*, 1989
   Book 2 of Unbalanced Earth Series

1390

DAVID EDDINGS

Domes of Fire

(New York: Ballantine Del Rey, 1993)

Story type: Fantasy (Quest)
Series: Tamuli
Major character(s): Sparhawk, Knight; Ehlana, Royalty (queen)
Time period(s): Indeterminate
Locale(s): Elenia, Fictional Country; Tamul Empire, Fictional Country

Summary: When threats face Elenia and the Tamul Empire, Sparhawk journeys to Tamuli with a large entourage including family, Pandion Knights, government officials, warriors and the Tamuli Ambassador. Sequel to The Elenium Series (1989-1992).

Other books you might like:
Dave Duncan, *The Cutting Edge*, 1992
Dave Duncan, *Magic Casement*, 1990
Barbara Hambly, *Dragonsbane*, 1987
Barbara Hambly, *The Time of the Dark*, 1982
Robert Jordan, *The Eye of the World*, 1989
Elizabeth Moon, *Sheepfarmer's Daughter*, 1988
Roger Zelazny, *Nine Princes in Amber*, 1970

1391

DAVID EDDINGS

The Hidden City

(New York: Ballantine Del Rey, 1994)

Story type: Fantasy (Magic Conflict; Adventure)
Series: Tamuli
Major character(s): Sparhawk, Knight, Parent (Aphrael's); Aphrael, Deity, Child; Bhelliom "Blue Rose", Mythical Creature (elemental)
Time period(s): Indeterminate
Locale(s): Arjuna, Fictional Country; Natayos, Fictional City; Cyrga, Fictional City (the Hidden City)

Summary: To gain control of Bhelliom, the jewel of power, the deity, Cyrgon, directs his minions to kidnap Sparhawk's wife, Queen Ehlana, and brings back into the world the banished monster, Klael. While Bhelliom battles its opposite force, Klael, Sparhawk must personally defeat Cyrgon to gain the return of Ehlana.

Other books you might like:
Glen Cook, *The Black Company*, 1984
Dave Duncan, *The Cutting Edge*, 1992
Raymond E. Feist, *Magician*, 1982
Terry Goodkind, *Wizard's First Rule*, 1994
Robert Jordan, *The Eye of the World*, 1989

1392

DAVID EDDINGS

The Ruby Knight

(New York: Ballantine/Del Rey, 1991)

Story type: Fantasy (Quest)
Series: Elenium
Major character(s): Sparhawk, Knight (Queen's Champion); Sephrenia, Sorceress; Talen, Thief
Time period(s): Indeterminate
Locale(s): Elenia, Planet—Imaginary

Summary: When Ehlana, Queen of Elenia, was poisoned, a spell to sustain her life was fashioned. The protective spell's time was rapidly running out when Sparhawk discovered that Ehlana's cure is the Bhelliom, a great jewel lost five hundred years ago. Sparhawk and his company of adventurers set off to ask the ghosts of those who knew of the jewel where it could be found. As they search for the jewel, their way is obstructed by Azash, an evil god not sympathetic to their efforts.

Other books you might like:
Carole Nelson Douglas, *Keepers of the Edanvant*, 1989
Sharon Green, *Hellhound Magic*, 1989
Peter Morwood, *The Horse Lord*, 1986
Jonathan Wylie, *The Lightless Kingdom*, 1989
Jonathan Wylie, *Dreams of Stone*, 1987

1393

DAVID EDDINGS

The Sapphire Rose

(New York: Ballantine/Del Rey, 1990)

Story type: Fantasy (Adventure; Political)
Series: Elenium
Major character(s): Sparhawk, Knight; Ehlana, Royalty (queen)
Time period(s): Indeterminate
Locale(s): Elenia, Planet—Imaginary

Summary: Having secured Bhelliom, the magic jewel needed to free Queen Ehlana from her slow poisoning, Sparhawk discovers himself betrothed to Ehlana. After arranging for a home guard, Sparhawk and the Pandion Knights move to protect the Church's throne from takeover by the Primate, Annias. That completed, Sparhawk prepares to use Bhelliom to destroy the god Azash, while the goddess Aphrael makes new plans for Sparhawk and Ehlana.

Other books you might like:
Steven Brust, *Phoenix*, 1990
Marc Laidlaw, *Neon Lotus*, 1988
Elizabeth Moon, *Divided Allegiance*, 1988
Elizabeth Moon, *Oath of Gold*, 1989
Elizabeth Moon, *Sheepfarmer's Daughter*, 1988
Persia Woolley, *Guinevere: The Legend in Autumn*, 1991

1394

DAVID EDDINGS

The Seeress of Kell

(New York: Del Rey, 1991)

Story type: Fantasy (Quest)
Series: Malloreon
Major character(s): Garion, Wizard (Shape-Changer), Royalty (Rivan King); Zandramas, Sorceress
Time period(s): Indeterminate
Locale(s): Mallorea, Fictional Country; Kell, Fictional Country

Summary: Garion and his companions continue their quest to recover Garion's infant son and heir as time runs out. They overcome the minions of the dark forces, allowing a final confrontation between good and evil. Much time is spent tying up loose, but not too pressing, ends.

Other books you might like:
Raymond E. Feist, *Magician*, 1982
Elizabeth Moon, *Divided Allegiance*, 1989
Elizabeth Moon, *Oath of Gold*, 1988
Elizabeth Moon, *Sheepfarmer's Daughter*, 1988
J.R.R. Tolkien, *The Return of the King*, 1956
J.R.R. Tolkien, *The Two Towers*, 1955
J.R.R. Tolkien, *The Fellowship of the Ring*, 1954

1395

DAVID EDDINGS

Sorceress of Darshiva

(New York: Del Rey, 1989)

Story type: Fantasy (Quest)
Series: Malloreon
Major character(s): Garion, Wizard (Shape-changer), Royalty (Rivan King)
Time period(s): Indeterminate
Locale(s): Mallorea, Fictional Country; Kell, Fictional Country

Summary: Garion, Child of the Light, sets out to rescue his infant son, kidnapped by the sorceress Zandramas, Child of the Dark. He and his companions must battle their enemies as they race against time to rescue the child before Zandramas uses him in a ritual that will assure the dominance of the Dark Forces.

Other books you might like:
Louise Cooper, *Nemesis*, 1989
Guy Gavriel Kay, *The Summer Tree*, 1985
    1st Book - The Fionavar Tapestry
J.R.R. Tolkien, *Lord of the Rings Trilogy*,

1396

SCOTT EDELMAN

Suicide Art

(West Warwick, Rhode Island: Necronomicon Press, 1992)

Story type: Horror (Collection)

Summary: A pair of horror stories that reflect metafictionally on the ways in which horror writers seek to fulfill the expectations of readers. ''The Suicide Artist'' is a first person account of an abusive upbringing that blurs the boundaries between real and imagined terrors. ''The Unkindest Cut'' tells of a sex transplant recipient who experiences an unusual type of phantom limb phenomena.

Other books you might like:
Dennis Etchison, *Metahorror*, 1992
    editor
Eric Garber, *Embracing the Dark*, 1991
    editor

1397

TERESA EDGERTON

The Castle of the Silver Wheel

(New York: Ace, 1993)

Story type: Fantasy (Magic Conflict; Romance)
Major character(s): Gwenlliant, Wizard; Tryffin fab Maelgwyn, Royalty, Government Official (Governor of Mochdreff)
Time period(s): Indeterminate
Locale(s): Ynys Celydonn, Fictional Country

Summary: When Tryffin returns to Mochdreff with his new bride, Gwenlliant, human and magical forces begin attempting to tear them apart and destroy Gwenlliant. With her knowledge of the ancient Wild Magic and of herself, Gwenlliant works to overcome the sorcery she believes wrought by Tryffin's supposed mistress. First of a trilogy.

Other books you might like:
Marion Zimmer Bradley, *The Mists of Avalon*, 1983
L.E. Modesitt Jr., *The Towers of the Sunset*, 1992
Josepha Sherman, *Child of Faerie, Child of Earth*, 1992
Persia Woolley, *Queen of the Summer Stars*, 1990

1398

TERESA EDGERTON

The Gnome's Engine

(New York: Ace, 1991)

Story type: Fantasy (Adventure; Romance)
Series: Goblin Moon
Major character(s): Sera Vorder, Gentlewoman; Francis Skelbrooke, Adventurer, Rake; Haakon Skogskra, Nobleman, Monster
Time period(s): 18th century
Locale(s): Euterpe, Alternate Earth; The New World, Alternate Earth

Summary: A direct sequel to *Goblin Moon*, this novel continues the mix of Regency-style romance and adventure. Skelbrooke has a series of adventures, while the rest of the heroes flee from Euterpe to the New World to escape their enemies. The story comes to a climax with an attempt to raise the sunken land of Panterra using a strange blend of magic and science.

Other books you might like:
Emma Bull, *War for the Oaks*, 1987
Katherine Kurtz, *Deryni Rising*, 1970
Ursula K. Le Guin, *A Wizard of Earthsea*, 1968
Judith Tarr, *Alamut*, 1989
Patricia C. Wrede, *Mairelon the Magician*, 1991
Patricia C. Wrede, *Sorcery and Cecelia*, 1988
    Caroline Stevermer, co-author

1399

TERESA EDGERTON

Goblin Moon

(New York: Ace, 1991)

Story type: Fantasy (Political)
Series: Green Lion
Major character(s): Caleb Braun, Worker; Sera Vorder, Gentlewoman; Gottfried Jenk, Scholar
Time period(s): Indeterminate Past
Locale(s): Thornberry-on-the-Lunn, Alternate Earth

Summary: Caleb Braun finds a body floating on the river. The body, that of a magician who had his books with him, is brought to Gottfried Jenk, a collector of curiosities. Both the commoners and the aristocracy of Thornberry become magically threatened.

Other books you might like:
Constance Ash, *The Stalking Horse*, 1990
Elizabeth C. Gaskell, *Cranford*, 1976
Ursula K. Le Guin, *A Wizard of Earthsea*, 1968
Judith Tarr, *Ars Magica*, 1989
Jack Vance, *Madouc*, 1990

1400

TERESA EDGERTON

The Grail and the Ring

(New York: Ace, 1994)

Story type: Fantasy (Mystery; Alternate World)
Major character(s): Gwenlliant, Wizard
Time period(s): Indeterminate
Locale(s): Ynys Celydonn, Fictional Country; Shadow Land, Mythical Place

Summary: When the power of an ancient ring transports Gwenlliant and her infant son to the Shadow Realm, she discovers an evil predator of Celydonn children. To save herself and the children, Gwenlliant must unravel the mystery of the ring.

Other books you might like:
Pamela Dean, *The Secret Country*, 1985
Rose Estes, *Troll-Taken*, 1993
Terry Goodkind, *Wizard's First Rule*, 1994
Laurell K. Hamilton, *Nightseer*, 1992
Holly Lisle, *Minerva Wakes*, 1994

1401

TERESA EDGERTON

The Moon in Hiding

(New York: Ace, 1989)

Story type: Fantasy (Quest)
Series: Green Lion
Major character(s): Telerini Pendaron, Apprentice, Wizard
Time period(s): Indeterminate Past (Medieval)
Locale(s): Wales

Summary: A group of people come together to fight a menace that threatens their survival. The situation is more out of control than in the first novel and the people are less certain of their course of action.

Other books you might like:
Katherine Kurtz, *The Harrowing of Gwynedd*, 1989
Robert E. Vardeman, *Phantoms on the Wind*,
Margaret Weis, *The Lost King*, 1990

1402

TERESA EDGERTON

The Work of the Sun

(New York: Ace, 1990)

Story type: Fantasy (Quest)
Series: Green Lion
Major character(s): Teleri ni Pendaron, Sorceress; Ceilyn mac Cuel, Knight, Werewolf; Diaspad, Royalty
Time period(s): Indeterminate Past (Middle Ages)
Locale(s): Kingdom of Celydonn, Fictional Country (legendary Celtic kingdom)

Summary: The heroes msut stop the evil princess' last attempt to steal the throne of Calydonn, this time with the help of a powerful artifact. Strong alchemical themes run through the story, which pays close attention to the emotional and moral changes of its characters.

Other books you might like:
Orson Scott Card, *Seventh Son*, 1987
Lindsay Clarke, *The Chymical Wedding*, 1989
Monica Furlong, *Wise Child*, 1987
Barbara Hambly, *The Armies of Daylight*, 1983
Barbara Hambly, *The Time of the Dark*, 1982
Barbara Hambly, *The Walls of Air*, 1983

1403

ROSEMARY EDGHILL

The Cup of Morning Shadows

(New York: DAW, 1995)

Story type: Fantasy (Alternate World; Quest)
Series: Twelve Treasures
Major character(s): Ruth Marlowe, Librarian, Student; Nic Brightlaw, Librarian, Military Personnel; Rohannan Melior, Mythical Creature (elf), Nobleman
Time period(s): 1990s (1995)

Locale(s): Ippisiqua, New York; Elphame, Mythical Place; Elfland, Mythical Place

Summary: Once touched by the magical land of Elphame, Ruth finds her way back, this time followed by her boss. She wants to find Melior, the elf she loves, but Elphame's impending civil war interferes. Ruth's discovery of the power behind the turmoil only increases her problems.

Other books you might like:
Eleanor Arnason, *Daughter of the Bear King*, 1987
Peter S. Beagle, *The Folk of the Air*, 1986
Emma Bull, *War for the Oaks*, 1987
Gordon R. Dickson, *The Dragon and the George*, 1976
Barbara Hambly, *The Time of the Dark*, 1982

`1404`

ROSEMARY EDGHILL

The Sword of Maiden's Tears

(New York: DAW, 1994)

Story type: Fantasy (Quest)
Series: Twelve Treasures
Major character(s): Ruth Marlowe, Librarian, Student; Rohannan Melior, Mythical Creature (elf)
Time period(s): 1990s
Locale(s): New York, New York; Elphame, Mythical Place

Summary: When Ruth Marlowe finds Rohannan Melior after muggers have taken the magical sword entrusted to his family, Ruth and her friends help Melior recover the powerful tool which has enslaved its human wielder, turning him into a golem.

Other books you might like:
Peter S. Beagle, *The Folk of the Air*, 1986
Elizabeth Forrest, *Phoenix Fire*, 1992
Fred Saberhagen, *The Sixth Book of Lost Swords: Mindsword's Story*, 1990
Fred Saberhagen, *The Second Book of Swords*, 1983

`1405`

GRAHAM EDWARDS

Dragoncharm

(New York: HarperPrism, 1996)

Story type: Fantasy (Magic Conflict; Political)
Major character(s): Fortune, Mythical Creature (dragon), Adventurer; Scope, Mythical Creature (dragon), Adventurer; Cumber, Mythical Creature (dragon), Adventurer
Time period(s): Indeterminate
Locale(s): Covamere, Mythical Place (fortress); Fictional Country

Summary: As the predicted time of treachery and conflict between Natural and Charmed dragons approaches, Fortune seeks a missing companion before plunging into the strife which could spell the end of the dragons' presence in the world. First novel.

Other books you might like:
Gael Baudino, *Dragonsword*, 1988

Thorarinn Gunnarsson, *Dragon's Domain*, 1993
Irene Radford, *The Glass Dragon*, 1994
Christopher Rowley, *Bazil Broketail*, 1992
Lawrence Watt-Evans, *The Blood of a Dragon*, 1991

`1406`

GEORGE ALEC EFFINGER

The Exile Kiss

(New York: Doubleday Foundation, 1991)

Story type: Science Fiction (Mystery; Dystopian)
Series: Marid Audran
Major character(s): Marid Audran, Assistant, Bodyguard; Friedlander Bey, Businessman, Organized Crime Figure (vicelord)
Time period(s): 23rd century
Locale(s): Africa (Budayeen (red-light district), North Africa); Africa (Arabian Desert)

Summary: Marid and Friedlander Bey are betrayed by Shaykh Reda Abu Adil and sent into exile to die in the Arabian Desert. While living with the Bedouin on his journey back to his home, Marid learns harsh truths about himself and he returns to the Budayeen prepared to exact revenge on those who betrayed him.

Other books you might like:
Pat Cadigan, *Mindplayers*, 1987
William Gibson, *Neuromancer*, 1984
John Shirley, *Eclipse*, 1987
John Shirley, *Eclipse Penumbra*, 1988
John Shirley, *Total Eclipse*, 1990
Bruce Sterling, *Islands in the Net*, 1988
Walter Jon Williams, *Hardwired*, 1986

`1407`

GEORGE ALEC EFFINGER

A Fire in the Sun

(New York: Doubleday Foundation, 1989)

Story type: Science Fiction (Mystery)
Major character(s): Marid Audran, Police Officer, Bodyguard; Friedlander Bey, Criminal, Businessman
Time period(s): 21st century
Locale(s): Africa (Budayeen, the red-light district of a Middle-Eastern city)

Summary: Once a small-time hood living in the slums, Marid is now Friedlander Bey's eyes and ears in the local police department. His employer's power, however, seems to be crumbling. Chaos has disrupted the tightly-regulated graft and corruption of the Budayeen—a mad killer is loose and Friedlander Bey lies mysteriously ill. Abu Adil, a major rival, may be behind the trouble. Marid must get to the bottom of the mystery, though it may cost him his life.

Other books you might like:
Richard Bowker, *Dover Beach*, 1987
William Gibson, *Neuromancer*, 1984
Norman Spinrad, *Little Heroes*, 1987
F. Paul Wilson, *Dydeetown World*, 1989

1408

GEORGE ALEC EFFINGER

Maureen Birnbaum, Barbarian Swordsperson: The Complete Stories
(Austin, Texas: Swan Press, 1993)

Story type: Fantasy (Collection; Light Fantasy)
Major character(s): Maureen Birnbaum, Heroine, Martial Arts Expert

Summary: Contains a three-page introduction by Mike Resnick and individual introductions by Effinger to the eight stories, including one original, one revised and six reprinted from 1980s and 1990s periodicals and a conference program book. Stories feature a scantily clad, sword wielding heroine with a passion for shopping and settings devised by Robert Adams, Isaac Asimov, Edgar Rice Burroughs and H.P. Lovecraft and legends surrounding the Holy Grail and Robin Hood.

Other books you might like:
Jack L. Chalker, *The Red Tape War*, 1991
   Mike Resnick, George Alec Effinger, co-authors
Alan Dean Foster, *Glory Lane*, 1987
Randall Garrett, *Takeoff!*, 1979
Randall Garrett, *Takeoff, Too!*, 1986
Tom Holt, *Flying Dutch*, 1992
Larry Niven, *The Flight of the Horse*, 1973

1409

GEORGE ALEC EFFINGER, Editor

The Old Funny Stuff
(Eugene, Oregon: Pulphouse Publishing, 1989)

Story type: Science Fiction (Collection)
Series: Author's Choice Monthly

Summary: This slim volume includes an introduction by the author, one original work of fiction, ''CHESS.BAT: A New Wave Story,'' and five other short stories, all published between 1982 and 1985 in such magazines as *Twilight Zone*, *Isaac Asimov's Science Fiction Magazine*, and *The Magazine of Fantasy and Science Fiction*. The best known stories in the volume are probably ''Mars Needs Beatniks'' and ''The Aliens Who Knew, I Mean, Everything.''

Other books you might like:
Edward Bryant, *Neon Twilight*, 1989
   Author's Choice Monthly. Issue 7
Edward Bryant, *Particle Theory*, 1980
Philip K. Dick, *The Collected Stories of Philip K. Dick*, 1987
George R.R. Martin, *Portraits of His Children*, 1987
Robert Sheckley, *Is THAT What People Do? The Selected Short Stories of Robert Sheckley*, 1984

1410

GEORGE ALEC EFFINGER

The Zork Chronicles
(New York: Avon, 1990)

Story type: Science Fiction (Science Fantasy; Humor)
Series: Infocom
Major character(s): Glorian, Companion; Mirakles, Hero; Spike, Companion
Time period(s): Indeterminate
Locale(s): Great Underground Empire, Fictional Country

Summary: Mirakles, with his trusty magic sword, is off on a quest for the Dipped Switch. Prodded along by his companion Glorian, they make their way through the Great Underground Empire encountering the Dragon's Lair, the Wizard's Workroom, the Kimono Dragon and the Warm Boot of Frobozz.

Other books you might like:
Robin W. Bailey, *Enchanter*, 1989
Arthur Byron Cover, *Planetfall*, 1988
Arthur Byron Cover, *Stationfall*, 1989
Brian Daley, *The Doomfarers of Coramonde*, 1977
Brian Daley, *Starfollowers of Coramonde*, 1979
Robert A. Heinlein, *Glory Road*, 1963
Michael Moorcock, *Elric of Melnibone*, 1976

1411

DORIS EGAN

The Gate of Ivory
(New York: DAW Books, 1989)

Story type: Science Fiction (Science Fantasy)
Series: Ivory
Major character(s): Theodora of Pyrene, Student; Ran Cormallon, Wizard
Time period(s): Indeterminate Future
Locale(s): Ivory, Planet—Imaginary

Summary: Theodora, an anthropology student, is accidentally stranded on the planet Ivory and, in order to support herself, sets up as a reader of Tarot cards. She soon discovers, however, that not all the magic users on the planet are fakes, that magic and high technology appear to exist side by side. The wizard Ran Cormallon befriends her and the two set off on a series of adventures.

Other books you might like:
Marion Zimmer Bradley, *The Shattered Chain*, 1976
Marion Zimmer Bradley, *Thendara House*, 1983
Christopher Stasheff, *The Warlock in Spite of Himself*, 1969
Christopher Stasheff, *The Warlock Insane*, 1969
Christopher Stasheff, *The Warlock Wandering*, 1986
Roger Zelazny, *Jack of Shadows*, 1971

1412
DORIS EGAN

Guilt-Edged Ivory
(New York: DAW, 1992)

Story type: Science Fiction (Mystery; Science Fantasy)
Series: Ivory

Summary: When Theodora learned that her sister-in-law could be forced to accept a co-wife, she realized that she could not wait to discover Ivoran genetic compatibility with mainstream humans. When the oldest son drowns as a result of sorcery at a party given by the prospective bride's family, Ran, accused of the murder, contracts to prove his innocence while Theodora endeavors to find the murderer.

Other books you might like:
Lois McMaster Bujold, *Barrayar*, 1991
Lois McMaster Bujold, *Shards of Honor*, 1986
Cheryl J. Franklin, *Fire Crossing*, 1991
Rosemary Kirstein, *The Steerswoman*, 1989
Alis A. Rasmussen, *A Passage of Stars*, 1990

1413
DORIS EGAN

Two-Bit Heroes
(New York: DAW, 1992)

Story type: Science Fiction (Adventure; Science Fantasy)
Series: Ivory
Major character(s): Theodora of Pyrene, Scholar, Bride; Ran Cormallon, Wizard; Stereth Tar'krim, Outlaw
Time period(s): Indeterminate Future
Locale(s): Ivory, Planet—Imaginary

Summary: Theodora of Pyrene and her half-husband Ran Cormallon, sent to ferret out information about Vere Atvalid, are captured by the notorious bandit Stereth Tar'krim who Vere Atvalid's father is pursuing. While Ran sulks, Theodora gives direction to the outlaw band by telling them of Robin Hood. Eventually Theodora and Ran escape and work to affect solutions.

Other books you might like:
L. Sprague de Camp, *The Swords of Zinjaban*, 1991
    Catherine Crook de Camp, co-author
Cynthia Felice, *Double Nocturne*, 1986
M.A. Foster, *The Warriors of Dawn*, 1975
Mary Gentle, *Golden Witchbreed*, 1984
Colin Kapp, *The Wizard of Anharitte*, 1973
Lee Killough, *Liberty's World*, 1985
Melissa Scott, *The Kindly Ones*, 1987
Sydney J. Van Scyoc, *Feather Stroke*, 1989

1414
GREG EGAN

Permutation City
(New York: HarperPrism, 1995)

Story type: Science Fiction (Cyberpunk; Alternate Intelligence)
Major character(s): Paul Durham, Computer Expert; Maria Deluca, Computer Expert; Thomas Riemann, Disembodied Personality (cyberspace copy)
Time period(s): 2050s (2050)
Locale(s): Elysium, Cyberspace (computer virtual reality); Sydney, Australia

Summary: Trying to perfect and understand cyberspace, Paul Durham sends copies of himself there as experiments in continuous consciousness and sensory experience, sending the fourth copy after the first three bail out. Paul meets Maria who develops an evolutionary mutative process for computer life which results in alien inhabitants and personal flexibility in Elysium.

Other books you might like:
Jean Mark Gawron, *Dreams of Glass*, 1993
James P. Hogan, *Realtime Interrupt*, 1995
Mary Rosenblum, *Chimera*, 1993
Melissa Scott, *Trouble and Her Friends*, 1994
Neal Stephenson, *Snow Crash*, 1992
Thomas T. Thomas, *ME: A Novel of Self Discovery*, 1991

1415
GREG EGAN

Quarantine
(New York: Harper Prism, 1995)

Story type: Science Fiction (Cyberpunk; Post-Disaster)
Major character(s): Nick Stavrianos, Police Officer (retired), Detective—Private; Laura Andrews, Patient (mental)
Time period(s): 2060s (2067)
Locale(s): Perth, Australia; New Hong Kong, Australia

Summary: Bio-enhanced while he was a policeman and further supplemented after the death of his wife, Nick takes a job to find Laura, who has been kidnapped from a mental institution. Suspecting the Children of the Bubble, a group organized after a bubble formed around the solar system, Nick finds himself co-opted by the Ensemble who install a loyalty chip, with unexpected results. Reprint of 1992 British edition.

Other books you might like:
John Barnes, *Kaleidoscope Century*, 1995
Philip K. Dick, *Ubik*, 1969
George Alec Effinger, *When Gravity Fails*, 1987
James P. Hogan, *The Multiplex Man*, 1992
Robert Reed, *Beyond the Veil of Stars*, 1994

1416

EHREN M. EHLY

Star Prey

(New York: Zebra, 1992)

Story type: Horror (Serial Killer)
Major character(s): Adrian Finesse, Actor; Jose Fuentes, Police Officer; Tamsin Weatherby, Actress
Time period(s): 1990s (1992)
Locale(s): Hollywood, California

Summary: Down-and-out B-movie actor Adrian Finesse was clearly too convincing in his last performance as a spirit channeler at a house party—now, movie starletts are dying bloody deaths that only make sense if one assumes that he has summoned the spirit of Jack the Ripper to contemporary Hollywood.

Other books you might like:
Robert Bloch, *The Shooting Star*, 1956
Robert Bloch, *The Star Stalker*, 1968
Gardner Dozois, *Ripper!*, 1988
  Susan Casper, co-editor

1417

PHYLLIS EISENSTEIN

In the Red Lord's Reach

(New York: NAL Signet, 1989)

Story type: Fantasy (Sword and Sorcery)
Major character(s): Alaric, Minstrel, Warlock
Time period(s): Indeterminate
Locale(s): Mythical Place

Summary: In this sequel to *Born to Exile*, Alaric wanders into the Red Lord's valley, only to join up with a nomadic band of reindeer herders. He realizes that he must use his magic talents to overthrow the reign of the Red Lord and restore peace to the valley.

Other books you might like:
Marion Zimmer Bradley, *Lythandedeer People*, 1986
Esther Friesner, *The Water King's Laughter*, 1989
Megan Lindholm, *The Reindeer People*, 1988
Anne McCaffrey, *Drangonsinger*, 1977
Manly Wade Wellman, *John the Balladeer*,

1418

GORDON EKLUND

A Thunder on Neptune

(New York: Morrow, 1989)

Story type: Science Fiction (First Contact)
Major character(s): Danny Hawkins, Child, Explorer; Samuel Goble, Scientist
Time period(s): 21st century
Locale(s): Mars; Neptune

Summary: Human beings are transformed on a molecular level and sent to the planet Neptune in an attempt to contact a mysterious alien race. When the first expedition ends in disaster—one man disappears, the other is driven insane—a second expedition is mounted using children on the theory that they will be more easily able to adapt to a radically different environment.

Other books you might like:
Octavia E. Butler, *Adulthood Rites*, 1988
Robert A. Heinlein, *Farmer in the Sky*, 1950
Robert A. Heinlein, *Red Planet*, 1949
Frederik Pohl, *Jem*, 1979
Frederik Pohl, *Man Plus*, 1976

1419

SUZETTE HADEN ELGIN

Earthsong

(New York: DAW, 1994)

Story type: Science Fiction (Political)
Series: Native Tongue
Major character(s): Delina Meloran Chornyak, Linguist, Scientist; Will Bluecrane, Indian, Chieftain; Nazareth Joanna Chornyak, Disembodied Personality (deceased)
Time period(s): 24th century (2300s)
Locale(s): Ozarks; Meander, Arkansas

Summary: After the aliens leave and quarantine humanity for persistent use of violence, Delina contacts the recently deceased Nazareth through a PICOTA ritual. Delina learns that the women of the linguists' lines must marry PICOTA men and join PICOTA families and that humanity requires a cure for hunger to eliminate violence.

Other books you might like:
Octavia E. Butler, *Parable of the Sower*, 1993
Helen Collins, *Mutagenesis*, 1993
Nicola Griffith, *Ammonite*, 1993
Janet Kagan, *Mirabile*, 1992
Joan Slonczewski, *Daughter of Elysium*, 1993
Joan Slonczewski, *A Door into Ocean*, 1986
Sheri S. Tepper, *Raising the Stones*, 1990

1420

ELTON ELLIOTT, Editor

Nanodreams

(New York: Baen, 1995)

Story type: Science Fiction (Anthology; Hard Science Fiction)

Summary: Contains a three-page preface and a two-page afterword by the editor, a nine-page foreword by John G. Cramer, a four-page introduction by Dr. K. Eric Drexler, three essays, and seven original and five stories reprinted from periodicals 1983-1992. Frequently optimistic in tone, the stories explore possible and wondrous effects of nanotechnology. Authors include Kevin J. Anderson, Poul Anderson, Greg Bear, Richard E. Geis, Charles Sheffield, Dave Smeds, and Marc Stiegler.

Other books you might like:
Kevin J. Anderson, *Assemblers of Infinity*, 1993
  Doug Beason, co-author

Greg Bear, *Blood Music*, 1985
Michael Flynn, *The Nanotech Chronicles*, 1991
Robert L. Forward, *Rocheworld*, 1990
Marc Stiegler, *The Gentle Seduction*, 1990

1421

KATE ELLIOTT (Pseudonym of Alis A. Rasmussen)

An Earthly Crown
(New York: DAW, 1993)

Story type: Science Fiction (Arts; Adventure)
Series: Jaran
Major character(s): Ilyakoria "Ilya" Bakhtiian, Leader, Barbarian; Terese "Tess" Soerensen, Heiress, Linguist; Diana Brooke-Holt, Actress
Time period(s): Indeterminate Future
Locale(s): Rhui, Planet—Imaginary (Delta Pavonis); Earth

Summary: Failed revolutionary, now a duke in the alien Chapalii Empire which rules Earth, Charles Soerensen visits Rhui, a primitive world that constitutes part of the fiefdom granted him by the Emperor. Taking a theater company with him as cover, he goes to meet his sister, Tess, officially declared dead, who has secretly remained on Rhui to marry Ilya. The actors hide their advanced technology as they accompany Ilya and his people on their path of conquest, while Charles travels to an ancient site that contains information about the ancient activities of Chapalii on the planet, information which could help bring freedom for all humanity. The story continues in *His Conquering Sword*.

Other books you might like:
Octavia E. Butler, *Dawn*, 1987
C.J. Cherryh, *The Faded Sun: Kesrith*, 1978
Cynthia Felice, *The Khan's Persuasion*, 1991
Mary Gentle, *Golden Witchbreed*, 1984
Ursula K. Le Guin, *The Left Hand of Darkness*, 1969
Alis A. Rasmussen, *The Price of Ransom*, 1990
Alis A. Rasmussen, *Revolution's Shore*, 1990
Christopher Stasheff, *A Company of Stars*, 1991
Christopher Stasheff, *We Open on Venus*, 1994

1422

KATE ELLIOTT

Jaran
(New York: DAW, 1992)

Story type: Science Fiction (Adventure)
Major character(s): Terese "Tess" Soerensen, Scholar, Noblewoman; Ilyakoria "Ilya" Bakhtiian, Barbarian; Cha Ishil Hokokul, Alien (Chapelli)
Time period(s): Indeterminate Future
Locale(s): Rhui, Planet—Imaginary

Summary: An unexpected stop maroons Tess thousands of miles from her intended destination. Rescued by Ilya, Tess accompanies Ilya and his three companions on a nearly lethal journey. She is again saved by Ilya however, and falls in love with him. Author's first novel, set on the same world as *An Earthly Crown*.

Other books you might like:
L. Sprague de Camp, *The Hand of Zei*, 1963
Paula E. Downing, *Rinn's Star*, 1990
Cynthia Felice, *The Khan's Persuasion*, 1991
Jacqueline Lichtenberg, *Dushau*, 1985
Ann Maxwell, *Fire Dancer*, 1982
Anne McCaffrey, *Killashandra*, 1985
Kathy Tyers, *Firebird*, 1987
Ted White, *The Sorceress of Qar*, 1966

1423

KATE ELLIOTT (Pseudonym of Alis A. Rasmussen)

The Law of Becoming
(New York: DAW, 1994)

Story type: Science Fiction (Political; Adventure)
Series: Jaran
Major character(s): Terese "Tess" Soerensen, Ruler; Vasily "Vasha" Kireyevsky, Warrior, Bastard Son; Anatoly Sakhalin, Warrior, Nobleman
Time period(s): Indeterminate Future
Locale(s): Rhui, Planet—Imaginary; London, England

Summary: Eight years after her brother's "death" on the interdicted world of Rhui, Tess Soerensen rules her brother's lands and collects information for the hoped-for rebellion against the alien Chapalli Empire, while concealing the advanced technology she uses in her "library." Tess' husband Ilya expands his conquests and alliances on Rhui, while Vasha tries to earn his father's approval through military exploits, only proving his worth in captivity. Having left Rhui to join his wife, Anatoly Sakhalin experiences culture shock before exploring the virtual reality world of "nesh," leading Anatoly to a meeting with the Chapali Emperor and a new role in the Game of Princes.

Other books you might like:
C.J. Cherryh, *The Faded Sun: Shon'Jir*, 1978
Gordon R. Dickson, *Way of the Pilgrim*, 1987
Jane S. Fancher, *Harmonies of the 'Net*, 1992
Mary Gentle, *Ancient Light*, 1987
Alis A. Rasmussen, *A Passage of Stars*, 1990

1424

TOM ELLIOTT

The Dwelling
(New York: St. Martin's, 1989)

Story type: Horror (Haunted House)
Major character(s): Katy McClure, Photographer (Police photographer); Ben Thibodeaux, Aged Person
Time period(s): 1980s (Flashbacks to 1931, 1958, 1967)
Locale(s): Creque Bayou, Louisiana

Summary: Three individuals—a police photographer, a fugitive, and a disgraced ex-college professor—are drawn to an old house in rural Louisiana, where they are possessed by a revenge-obsessed entity. There they are all forced to confront not only their own foulest experiences and deepest fears, but also those of their corrupt fathers, who committed a terrible crime in the house over thirty years previously. This is Elliott's first novel.

Other books you might like:
Jack Cady, *The Well*, 1980
Richard Matheson, *Hell House*, 1971

1425

BRETT EASTON ELLIS

American Psycho

(New York: Vintage, 1990)

Story type: Horror (Serial Killer)
Major character(s): Patrick Bateman, Businessman, Serial Killer; Timothy Price, Businessman (Wall Street fast-tracker); Donald Kimball, Detective—Private
Time period(s): 1990s (1990)
Locale(s): New York, New York

Summary: By day privileged, fashion-conscious Patrick Bateman makes a killing on Wall Street. By night, he translates his predatory impulses into a string of brutal and sadistic murders.

Other books you might like:
Robert Bloch, *Psycho*, 1959
John Farris, *The Axman Cometh*, 1989
Ira Levin, *Sliver*, 1991
David J. Schow, *The Kill Riff*, 1988

1426

BRETT EASTON ELLIS

The Informers

(New York: Alfred A. Knopf, 1994)

Story type: Horror (Vampire Story)
Major character(s): Dirk Erickson, Vampire; Martin, Producer (video); Christie, Student
Time period(s): 1980s
Locale(s): Los Angeles, California

Summary: Graham, Christie, Martin, Bruce and Cheryl are twenty-something Los Angelenos who tan by day, eat at all the fashionable restaurants by evening, take designer drugs by night, have reckless and indifferent sex, and help shape a culture so amoral that the vampires they number among their friends seem no worse than they are.

Other books you might like:
Poppy Z. Brite, *Lost Souls*, 1992
Anne Rice, *The Vampire Lestat*, 1985
Dan Simmons, *Carrion Comfort*, 1989

1427

JACK ELLIS

Nightlife

(New York: Zebra, 1996)

Story type: Horror (Vampire Story)

Major character(s): Richard Carnitch, Vampire; Simon Babych, Clerk (in a bookstore); Becky Rutman, Administrator (homeless shelter manager)
Time period(s): 1990s (1996)
Locale(s): Minneapolis, Minnesota

Summary: Richard Carnitch, a vampire who consumes the entire bodies of his victims, preys on the homeless who live on the streets of Minneapolis. Outrage over his activities draws together various friends of the homeless, who act as an unlikely band of vampire hunters.

Other books you might like:
George C. Chesbro, *Bone*, 1989
Don Davis, *Bring on the Night*, 1993
    Jay Davis, co-author
Roxanne Longstreet, *The Undead*, 1993
Rick R. Reed, *Penance*, 1993
Wayne Allen Sallee, *The Holy Terror*, 1992
John Skipp, *The Light at the End*, 1986
    Craig Spector, co-author

1428

JACK ELLIS

Seeing Eye

(New York: Zebra, 1995)

Story type: Horror (Wild Talents; Psychological Suspense)
Major character(s): Campbell Knight, Businessman (car dealership owner); Hope Matheson, Animal Lover (humane society worker)
Time period(s): 1990s (1995)
Locale(s): Battle Lake, Minnesota

Summary: Campbell Knight agrees to undergo a radical experiment to restore his sight that entails hooking implants in his brain to the visual cortex of his seeing-eye dog, Shadow. When Campbell begins "seeing" visions in which a psychotic woman imprisons and abuses small children in her basement, he realizes that Shadow is privy to a world whose whereabouts he must discover and make known to the police.

Other books you might like:
H.B. Gilmour, *The Eyes of Laura Mars*, 1978
Stephen King, *The Dead Zone*, 1979
Dean R. Koontz, *The Vision*, 1977
Dean R. Koontz, *Watchers*, 1987

1429

TERRY ELLIS

Invasion of Willow Wood Springs

(Santa Monica, CA: Roundtable, 1989)

Story type: Fantasy (Adventure)
Series: Willow Wood Springs
Time period(s): 1980s (1989)
Locale(s): Alternate Earth (Reath (Fantasy version of Earth))

Summary: After Reath is invaded by evil beings who have the power of mind control, a group of juvenile friends set out on a dangerous journey to find allies to defeat the evil ones.

Other books you might like:
John Christopher, *The White Mountains*, 1967
    Vol 1 - The Tripods Trilogy
Tanya Huff, *Gate of Darkness, Circle of Light*, 1989
R.A. Salvatore, *Echoes of the Fourth Magic*, 1990

1430

HARLAN ELLISON

Angry Candy

(New York: NAL Plume, 1989)

Story type: Horror (Collection)

Summary: Seventeen stories published between 1980 and 1988, plus a moving meditation on the death of friends, "Introduction: The Wind Took Your Answer Away." Most impressive are "Palladin of the Lost Hour," a poignant story about an old man and a watch that freezes time (winner in its TV version of a Writers Guild Most Outstanding Teleplay Award), "Soft Monkey," about a bag lady stalked by mobsters in Manhattan, "Function of Dream Sleep" about a young man who wakes and sees a secret mouth filled with teeth opening in his skin, and "Laugh Track," a moving story about a young man's quest to release his aunt's soul, captured in her laugh, from imprisonment on the laugh tracks of bad sitcoms.

Other books you might like:
George R.R. Martin, *Songs the Dead Men Sing*, 1983
David J. Schow, *Seeing Red*, 1990

1431

HARLAN ELLISON

The City on the Edge of Forever

(Gulf Breeze, Florida: Borderlands Press, 1995)

Story type: Science Fiction (Space Opera; Time Travel)
Series: Star Trek
Major character(s): James T. Kirk, Spaceship Captain, Time Traveller; Spock, Scientist, Alien (Vulcan)
Time period(s): 23rd century; 1930s
Locale(s): Planet—Imaginary; Chicago, Illinois

Summary: Contains a spirited Ellison introduction, the original script for the Star Trek teleplay, two prefatory treatments and two scenes Ellison added at producer Gene Roddenberry's request, plus comments by four original *Star Trek* writers and four original cast members. Kirk and Spock must use an alien dimensional doorway to rescue the ship's doctor and repair unintentional damage to their time continuum.

Other books you might like:
Douglas Adams, *The Original Hitchhiker's Radio Scripts*, 1985
Roger Elwood, *Six Science Fiction Plays*, 1976
    editor
Kurt Vonnegut Jr., *Between Time and Timbuktu*, 1972
Kurt Vonnegut Jr., *Happy Birthday, Wanda June*, 1970
Robert Anton Wilson, *Reality Is What You Can Get Away With: An Illustrated Screenplay*, 1992

1432

HARLAN ELLISON
ISAAC ASIMOV, Illustrator
MARK ZUG, Illustrator

I, Robot: The Illustrated Screenplay

(New York: Warner Aspect, 1994)

Story type: Science Fiction (Robot Fiction)
Series: Robot
Major character(s): Susan Calvin, Computer Expert, Psychologist (robopsychologist); Robert Bratenahl, Journalist (*Cosmos* magazine); Norman Bogert, Reanimated Dead (cryonically frozen), Scientist
Time period(s): 21st century
Locale(s): Earth; Aldebaran-C XII, Planet—Imaginary; Galactic Federation, Interstellar Empire/Federation

Summary: Contains a three-page introduction by Asimov, a 10-page introduction by Ellison, a chronology of events 1952-2076 and the unproduced screenplay adapted by Ellison in 1978 from four Asimov stories, "Robbie," "Runaround," "Liar" and "Lenny," which offer glimpses into Susan Calvin's life and her relationships with robots. Illustrations include 16 color plates by Mark Zug with indication of the plates' locations within the text plus camera and viewpoint directions.

Other books you might like:
John Brunner, *Stand on Zanzibar*, 1968
Roger Elwood, *Six Science Fiction Plays*, 1976
    editor
Kurt Vonnegut Jr., *Between Time and Timbuktu*, 1972
Kurt Vonnegut Jr., *Happy Birthday, Wanda June*, 1970
Robert Anton Wilson, *Reality Is What You Can Get Away With: An Illustrated Screenplay*, 1992

1433

HARLAN ELLISON

Mefisto in Onyx

(Shingletown, California: Mark Ziesing, 1993)

Story type: Horror (Serial Killer; Wild Talents)
Major character(s): Rudy Pairis, Psychic (mind reader); Allison Roche, Lawyer (deputy district attorney); Henry Lake Spanning, Convict
Time period(s): 1990s (1993)
Locale(s): Atmore, Alabama (Holman Prison)

Summary: At the urging of his friend District Attorney Allison Roche, mindreader Rudy Pairis reluctantly agrees to "jaunt" into the mind of Henry Lake Spanning, a serial killer whom Allison helped put on death row but now believes is innocent of the crimes for which he was convicted. This novella appeared earlier in 1993 in *Omni* magazine.

Other books you might like:
Rene Belletto, *Machine*, 1993
Damon Knight, *Mind Switch*, 1963
Curt Siodmak, *Gabriel's Body*, 1988
F. Paul Wilson, *Sibs*, 1992

1434

HARLAN ELLISON
JACEK YERKA, Illustrator

Mind Fields: The Art of Jacek Yerka
(Beverly Hills, California: Morpheus International, 1994)

Story type: Fantasy (Collection; Horror)

Summary: Contains 33 original stories and a three-page "Afterthoughts" by Ellison, inspired by 33 surreal paintings by Yerka. Despite ironic humor, the tone of the stories reflect Yerka's dark vision, with themes including anti-Semitism as a historical and contemporary force, classical myth and urban life.

Other books you might like:
Richard Brautigan, *In Watermelon Sugar*, 1968
Harry Harrison, *Planet Story*, 1979
Marlen Haushofer, *The Wall*, 1991
    Shaun Whiteside, translator
Cordwainer Smith, *The Rediscovery of Man*, 1993
Jane Yolen, *Briar Rose*, 1992

1435

HARLAN ELLISON
JACK DANN, Co-Author
JACK C. HALDEMAN II, Co-Author

Run for the Stars/Echoes of Thunder
(New York: Tor, 1991)

Story type: Science Fiction (Horror; Hard Science Fiction)
Major character(s): Benno Tallant, Experimental Subject; John Stranger, Indian (Mohawk), Construction Worker (orbital)
Time period(s): Indeterminate Future
Locale(s): Deald's World, Planet—Imaginary; Space Station

Summary: This book contains "Run for the Stars" by Harlan Ellison plus "Echoes of Thunder" by Jack Dann and Jack C. Haldeman II. In "Run for the Stars," retreating Terran forces, desperate to stop the Kyben armada heading toward Earth, modify unlikely hero Benno Tallant by implanting a cataclysmic bomb inside his body then turning him loose to be found by the Kyben. In "Echoes of Thunder," a corporation exercises its option to draft John Stranger for orbital construction. In space he must try to preserve his Indian spirit despite an environment which pulls him toward the dominant culture.

Other books you might like:
Jack Dann, *The Man Who Melted*, 1984
Jack Dann, *Wandering Stars: An Anthology of Jewish Fantasy and Science Fiction*, 1974
    editor
Alan Dean Foster, *Cyber Way*, 1990
Jack C. Haldeman II, *Vector Analysis*, 1979
Allen Steele, *Clarke County, Space*, 1990

1436

LARRY ELMORE
ROBERT ELMORE, Co-Author

Runes of Autumn
(Lake Geneva, Wisconsin: TSR, 1996)

Story type: Fantasy (Adventure; Mystery)
Major character(s): Rafin, Police Officer; Maraakuks Oit-Makidom, Military Personnel; Alyna, Wizard
Time period(s): Indeterminate
Locale(s): Stridgenfel, Fictional City

Summary: The death and mutilation of two boys make some people think Ammak raiders have returned, while others think a bear did it. The village, however, receives aid, some requested and some not, in fighting the ancient legacy of evil. First novel.

Other books you might like:
Eleanor Arnason, *The Sword Smith*, 1978
Glen Cook, *The Swordbearer*, 1982
Robert Jordan, *The Eye of the World*, 1990
Caroline Stevermer, *A College of Magics*, 1994
Martha Wells, *The Element of Fire*, 1993

1437

P.N. ELROD

Blood on the Water
(New York: Ace, 1992)

Story type: Horror (Vampire Story)
Series: Vampire Files
Major character(s): Jack Fleming, Detective—Private, Vampire; Charles Escott, Detective—Private; Vaughan Kyler, Organized Crime Figure
Time period(s): 1930s
Locale(s): Chicago, Illinois

Summary: In this sixth and final adventure of Elrod's hardboiled depression-era vampire series, reporter-turned-vampire-private-eye Jack Fleming becomes a pawn in a war between racketeers, one of whom seems to have discovered his true identity.

Other books you might like:
Vincent Courtney, *Vampire Beat*, 1990
Barbara Hambly, *Those Who Hunt the Night*, 1988
Tanya Huff, *Blood Price*, 1991
Lee Killough, *Blood Links*, 1987

1438

P.N. ELROD

Bloodlist
(New York: Ace, 1990)

Story type: Horror (Vampire Story)
Series: Vampire Files
Major character(s): Jack Fleming, Journalist (investigative reporter), Vampire; Charles Escott, Detective—Private; Frank Paco, Organized Crime Figure

Time period(s): 1930s (the Depression)
Locale(s): Chicago, Illinois

Summary: Investigative reporter Jack Fleming embarks on a search for the woman who turned him into a vampire in the first of a new series of hardboiled crime/vampire novels. In this adventure, Jack plays cat-and-mouse with Frank Paco, the Chicago racketeer who killed him for stealing a list of blackmail victims.

Other books you might like:
Stephen Gallagher, *Valley of Lights*, 1988
Barbara Hambly, *Immortal Blood*, 1987
William Hjortsberg, *Falling Angel*, 1978
Lee Killough, *Blood Links*, 1988
Lee Killough, *Blood Hunt*, 1987

1439

P.N. ELROD

Dance of Death

(New York: Ace, 1996)

Story type: Horror (Vampire Story; Historical)
Series: Adventures of Jonathan Barrett
Major character(s): Jonathan Barrett, Vampire; Oliver Marling, Doctor; Nora Jones, Vampire
Time period(s): 1770s (1777)
Locale(s): London, England

Summary: While searching for the woman who turned him into a vampire, American colonist and royalist Jonathan Barrett assumes responsibility for four-year-old Richard, the boy he sired with the wife of a cousin. When assassins unaware of his vampire nature attempt to kill him, Jonathan discovers that a plot involving family members has been hatched to eliminate him and the embarrassment he has caused.

Other books you might like:
Traci Briery, *The Vampire Journals*, 1993
Les Daniels, *Citizen Vampire*, 1981
Fred Saberhagen, *A Sharpness on the Neck*, 1996
T. Lucien Wright, *Thirst of the Vampire*, 1992

1440

P.N. ELROD

Death Masque

(New York: Berkley, 1995)

Story type: Horror (Vampire Story; Historical)
Series: Adventures of Jonathan Barrett
Major character(s): Jonathan Barrett, Vampire; Elizabeth Barrett, Young Woman; Oliver Fonteyn, Cousin (of Jonathan and Elizabeth)
Time period(s): 1770s (1777)
Locale(s): London, England

Summary: Jonathan Barrett, the vampire son of a Tory family in Revolutionary War America, retraces the steps he took in *Red Death*, travelling from the United States back to England as his family prepares to flee from colonial hooligans on Long Island. While serching for Nora Jones, the vampire love he

left behind, Jonathan stumbles upon a plot by his estranged mother's side of the family to ruin the Barretts.

Other books you might like:
Traci Briery, *The Vampire Journals*, 1993
Les Daniels, *Citizen Vampire*, 1981
Anne Rice, *The Vampire Lestat*, 1985
Lee Weathersby, *Kiss of the Vampire*, 1981
T. Lucien Wright, *Thirst of the Vampire*, 1992
Chelsea Quinn Yarbro, *Hotel Transylvania*, 1978

1441

P.N. ELROD

Fire in the Blood

(New York: Ace, 1991)

Story type: Horror (Vampire Story)
Series: Vampire Files
Major character(s): Jack Fleming, Journalist, Vampire; Charles Escott, Detective—Private; Doreen Gray, Photographer
Time period(s): 1930s
Locale(s): Chicago, Illinois

Summary: In his fifth adventure, investigative-reporter-turned-vampire-detective Jack Fleming takes on the case of a millionaire anxious for the return of a missing family heirloom bracelet and stumbles into an adventure chock full of blackmailers, pornographers, bootleggers, bookies, and all those other social miscreants who helped make depression-era Chicago famous.

Other books you might like:
Tanya Huff, *Blood Price*, 1991
Lee Killough, *Blood Links*, 1987

1442

P.N. ELROD

I, Strahd

(Geneva, Wisconsin: TSR, 1993)

Story type: Horror (Vampire Story; Fantasy)
Series: Ravenloft
Major character(s): Rudolph Van Richten, Doctor; Strahd Von Zarovich, Ruler (of Barovia), Vampire; Tatyana, Vampire
Time period(s): Indeterminate
Locale(s): Barovia, Fictional Country

Summary: Set in the mythical kingdom of Barovia, this fantasy-horror genre blend recounts how the ruler Strahd Von Zarovich is bewitched by his brother's fiance, Tatyana, vampirized, and turned into a cruel ruler who lets his kingdom fall into disarray. The novel is the first of a projected trilogy.

Other books you might like:
Les Daniels, *The Black Castle*, 1978
Brian Stableford, *The Empire of Fear*, 1988
Chelsea Quinn Yarbro, *The Palace*, 1978

1443
P.N. ELROD
Red Death
(New York: Ace, 1993)

Story type: Horror (Vampire Story)
Series: Adventures of Jonathan Barrett
Major character(s): Jonathan Barrett, Student (law student); Nora Jones, Vampire; Oliver Fonteyn Marlin, Student (law student)
Time period(s): 1770s (1773-1776)
Locale(s): Cambridge, England; Long Island, New York

Summary: Sent by his mother against his wishes to study law in England, Jonathan Barrett falls under the influence of vampire Nora Jones. Upon his return to New York, his lust for blood becomes increasingly difficult to hide from British soldiers who overrun the British colonies preparatory to the American Revolution.

Other books you might like:
Traci Briery, *The Vampire Journals*, 1993
Anne Rice, *The Vampire Lestat*, 1985
Lee Weathersby, *Kiss of the Vampire*, 1992
T. Lucien Wright, *Thirst of the Vampire*, 1992

1444
P.N. ELROD, Editor
MARTIN H. GREENBERG, Co-Editor
The Time of the Vampires
(New York: DAW, 1996)

Story type: Horror (Anthology; Vampire Story)

Summary: Nineteen stories written originally for this volume feature vampires in historical settings and famous historical personalities whose adventures bring them into contact with, or reveal them to have been, vampires. P.N. Elrod's "The Devil's Mark" is set during the witch-hunting craze of 17th-century England, and Elaine Bergstrom's "The Ghost of St. Mark's" during the London blitz. Lois Tilton's "Vision of Darkness" features Socrates, Teresa Patterson's "The Gift" features King Arthur, and Tanya Huff's "What Manner of Man" and Lillian Stewart Carl's "The Blood of the Lamb" both feature associates of Henry VIII, all involved in vampire intrigues. Most of the contributors to this volume are distinguished writers of vampire novels.

Other books you might like:
Martin H. Greenberg, *Celebrity Vampires*, 1994
  editor
Martin H. Greenberg, *Dracula: Prince of Darkness*, 1992
  editor
Stephen Jones, *The Mammoth Book of Vampires*, 1993
  editor
Alan Ryan, *Vampires: Two Centuries of Great Vampire Stories*, 1987
  editor
Robert Weinberg, *Rivals of Dracula*, 1996
  Stefan Dziemianowicz, Martin H. Greenberg, co-editors

1445
ELVIRA
JOHN PARAGON, Co-Author
Elvira: Transylvania 90210
(New York: Berkley/Boulevard, 1996)

Story type: Horror (Vampire Story)
Major character(s): Elvira, Young Woman; Shannon Doheny, Teenager; Sevil Alucard, Vampire
Time period(s): 1990s (1996)
Locale(s): Beaver Hills, California

Summary: Elvira, whose Gothic attire and peculiar behavior leads many to mistake her for a witch, discovers that a genuine vampire has moved next door to her and plans to vampirize the students of Beaver Hills High. This campy spoof, the author's first novel, lampoons not only teen-targeted television shows but also the television persona of Elvira herself.

Other books you might like:
Anne Billson, *Suckers*, 1993
Richie Tankersley Cusick, *Buffy the Vampire Slayer*, 1992
Lionel Fenn, *The Mark of the Moderately Vicious Vampire*, 1992
Christopher Moore, *Bloodsucking Fiends: A Love Story*, 1995

1446
ROGER ELWOOD
Angelwalk: A Modern Fable
(Westchester, Illinois: Crossway Books, 1988)

Story type: Fantasy (Religious)
Major character(s): Darian, Angel
Time period(s): 1980s
Locale(s): Heaven; Earth

Summary: An angel is allowed to go to Earth by God to find out why Lucifer was thrown out of Heaven. During his visit, he sees all manner of horrible things on Earth in this Christian fantasy.

Other books you might like:
John Bunyan, *The Pilgrim's Progress*, 1984
Parke Godwin, *Waiting for the Galactic Bus*, 1989
Andrew M. Greeley, *Angel Fire*, 1988
C.S. Lewis, *The Chronicles of Narnia*, 1988
C.S. Lewis, *Perelanda: A Novel*, 1990
C.S. Lewis, *Pilgrim's Regress*, 1958
Mike McQuay, *The Nexus*, 1989

1447
ROGER ELWOOD
Sorcerers of Sodom
(Tarrytown, New York: Fleming H. Revell Company, 1991)

Story type: Horror (Black Magic)
Major character(s): Brian Loeffler, Religious (former pastor); Judson McClane, Administrator (college chancellor); Anita Carlsen, Journalist ("The New Age Columnist")

Time period(s): 1990s
Locale(s): Beverly Hills, California

Summary: This pretentiously self-important ''Christian horror'' novel sends the pastor Brian Loeffler, fresh from the spectacular destruction of his pastorage owing to a momentary lapse of faith, to Beverly Hills. There, in the Sodom of Southern California, he brings down divine retribution on drug addicts, pornographers, homosexuals, New Age believers, and anyone who does not follow the ''true'' way.

Other books you might like:
William Peter Blatty, *The Exorcist*, 1971
Joe R. Lansdale, *Dead in the West*, 1986

1448

DAVID ELY

A Journal of the Flood Year

(New York: Donald I. Fine, 1992)

Story type: Science Fiction (Techno-Thriller; Disaster)
Major character(s): William G. Fowke, Engineer, Outlaw
Time period(s): 21st century
Locale(s): United States

Summary: A technological marvel, The Wall, claimed new land from the Atlantic Ocean while converting energy from wave action. When Fowke reports leaks in The Wall to a bureaucrat, the official dismisses the complaint as disagreeing with the computer system analysis of The Wall's integrity. As Fowke complains further, his status changes from troublemaker to fugitive pursued by robotic trackers of the bureaucracy. Written in journal form.

Other books you might like:
David Brin, *Earth*, 1990
Jeffrey A. Carver, *The Rapture Effect*, 1987
Emily Devenport, *Shade*, 1991
Rosemary Kirstein, *The Outskirter's Secret*, 1992
Larry Niven, *Fallen Angels*, 1991
    Jerry Pournelle and Michael Flynn, co-authors
Frederik Pohl, *Gladiator-at-Law*, 1955
    C.M. Kornbluth, co-author
Ken Rolston, *Extreme Paranoia: Nobody Knows the Trouble I've Shot*, 1991
Neal Stephenson, *Snow Crash*, 1992
Kathy Tyers, *Shivering World*, 1991

1449

WINIFRED ELZE

The Changeling Garden

(New York: St. Martin's/Wyatt, 1995)

Story type: Horror (Occult)
Major character(s): Annie Carter, Housewife; David Carter, Child (Annie's five-year-old son); Mariah Fenton, Herbalist
Time period(s): 1990s (1995)
Locale(s): Southwest

Summary: Shortly after the Carter family moves into a house whose previous owner specifically selected them, Annie and her son David find they have a psychic rapport with the plants and animals inhabiting the garden. Annie spends most of her time trying to prevent her husband Mark from selling off part of the yard for development into a parking lot and fending off Harley Baer, Jr., a lowlife possessed by the spirit of an ancient Mayan warrior intent on destroying the human race. This ecologically-aware tale is the author's first novel.

Other books you might like:
Alison Drake, *Lagoon*, 1990
John Skipp, *The Bridge*, 1991
    Craig Spector, co-author
David van Meter Smith, *Trinity Grove*, 1990
John Wyndham, *The Day of the Triffids*, 1951

1450

JANE EMERSON

City of Diamond

(New York: DAW, 1996)

Story type: Science Fiction (Political; Space Opera)
Major character(s): Adrian Mercati, Ruler (diamond protector); Iolanthe ''Io'' Pelagia, Royalty (lady); Tal Diamond, Alien (Elaphite/Human halfbreed), Military Personnel (special officer)
Time period(s): Indeterminate Future
Locale(s): *City of Diamond*, Spaceship; Baret Two, Planet—Imaginary

Summary: Adrian Mercati, the charismatic but inexperienced Protector of the *City of Diamond*, marries Lady Iolanthe Pegalia of the *City of Opal* in an effort to promote peace between the rival city-ships. Secretly, however, Adrian attempts to gain power over the other ship by searching for the Sawyer Crown, a mysterious alien artifact.

Other books you might like:
L. Warren Douglas, *Stepwater*, 1995
Valerie J. Freireich, *Becoming Human*, 1995
Valerie J. Freireich, *Testament*, 1995
Frank Herbert, *Dune*, 1965
Sheri S. Tepper, *Grass*, 1989
Margaret Weis, *Sentinels*, 1996
    Tracy Hickman, co-author

1451

RU EMERSON

The Empty Throne

(New York: Berkley Boulevard, 1996)

Story type: Fantasy (Legend; Adventure)
Series: Xena: Warrior Princess
Major character(s): Xena, Warrior, Royalty; Gabrielle, Sidekick, Adventurer
Time period(s): Indeterminate Past
Locale(s): Ancient Civilization; Ithaca, Greece

Summary: Xena and Gabrielle discover a village whose men have vanished and where ruffians rule the street. The two must find the truth behind the events before they, too, disappear. First of a television tie-in series.

Other books you might like:

Marion Zimmer Bradley, *The Sword and Sorceress Series*, 1984-1996
editor
Timothy Boggs, *By the Sword*, 1996
Timothy Boggs, *Serpent's Shadow*, 1996
George Alec Effinger, *Maureen Birnbaum, Barbarian Swordsperson: The Complete Stories*, 1993
Esther Friesner, *Chicks in Chainmail*, 1995
editor
Barbara Hambly, *Beauty and the Beast*, 1989
Jason Henderson, *Highlander: The Element of Fire*, 1995
Jessica Amanda Salmonson, *Amazons!*, 1979
editor

1452
RU EMERSON

One Land, One Duke
(New York: Ace, 1992)

Story type: Fantasy (Alternate World; Adventure)
Series: Night-Threads
Major character(s): Jennifer Cray, Lawyer, Magician; Dahven, Nobleman; Aletto, Heir—Dispossessed
Time period(s): Indeterminate
Locale(s): Rhadaz, Fictional Country; Podhru, Fictional City; Zelharri, Fictional Country

Summary: Arriving in Podhru, the Crays, Aletto, Lialla and Dahven find betrayal. After Aletto escapes and Jennifer clears Dahven of murdering his father, they travel to Zelharri where Aletto seeks to regain his rightful dukedom.

Other books you might like:

Piers Anthony, *Man From Mundania*, 1989
Jack L. Chalker, *The River of Dancing Gods*, 1984
Joy Chant, *Red Moon and Black Mountain*, 1971
Brian Daley, *The Doomfarers of Coramonde*, 1977
L. Sprague de Camp, *Land of Unreason*, 1942
Kate Elliott, *Jaran*, 1992
Barbara Hambly, *The Time of the Dark*, 1982

1453
RU EMERSON

Spell Bound
(New York: Ace, 1990)

Story type: Fantasy (Historical)
Major character(s): Sophie, Young Woman (''Cinderella''); Fairy Godmother, Mythical Creature
Time period(s): 15th century
Locale(s): Germany

Summary: In this rewrite of ''Cinderella,'' the characters have been fleshed out and given personal histories. Sophie becomes the pawn of her fairy godmother, when her fairy godmother sets out to take revenge for a wrongful death.

Other books you might like:

Tanith Lee, *Red as Blood: Or Tales from the Sisters Grimmer*, 1983

Morgan Llywelyn, *The Isles of the Blest*, 1989
Howard Waldrop, *A Dozen Tough Jobs*, 1989
David Henry Wilson, *The Coachman Rat*,
Patricia C. Wrede, *Snow White and Rose Red*,

1454
RU EMERSON

The Two in Hiding
(New York: Ace, 1991)

Story type: Fantasy (Adventure; Alternate World)
Series: Night-Threads
Major character(s): Aletto, Heir—Dispossessed, Runaway; Robyn Cray, Single Parent, Mythical Creature (shapechanger); Jennifer Cray, Lawyer, Magician
Time period(s): Indeterminate
Locale(s): Rhadaz, Fictional Country

Summary: Three Americans, Chris, Jennifer and Robyn Cray, have been called into Rhadaz where they find themselves mixed up in a dynastic dispute between Jadek and his nephew Aletto, the rightful, though sickly, heir. While travelling across the desert, Robyn and Chris try to get Aletto into good shape and teach him martial arts. Coming to Bez, Jennifer rescues Dahven who was sold into slavery, then leaves quickly before Duke Jadek's men seize them.

Other books you might like:

Piers Anthony, *Man From Mundania*, 1989
Piers Anthony, *Split Infinity*, 1980
Jack L. Chalker, *The River of Dancing Gods*, 1984
Brian Daley, *The Doomfarers of Coramonde*, 1977
L. Sprague de Camp, *The Complete Compleat Enchanter*, 1989
Fletcher Pratt, co-author
Barbara Hambly, *The Time of the Dark*, 1982

1455
CLAYTON EMERY

Final Sacrifice
(New York: HarperPrism, 1995)

Story type: Fantasy (Magic Conflict)
Series: Magic: The Gathering
Major character(s): Gull, Leader, Revolutionary; Greensleeves, Wizard, Revolutionary; Immugio, Mythical Creature (giant/ogre), Wizard
Time period(s): Indeterminate Past
Locale(s): The Domains, Fictional Country

Summary: Greensleeves and Gull begin to win their long war against the wizards, but can they do it without becoming what they hate? Based on the popular card game.

Other books you might like:

Brian Daley, *The Doomfarers of Coramonde*, 1977
William R. Forstchen, *Arena*, 1994
Lisa Goldstein, *Summer King, Winter Fool*, 1994
Terry Goodkind, *Wizard's First Rule*, 1994
Patricia A. McKillip, *The Riddle-Master of Hed*, 1976
Michael Scott Rohan, *The Anvil of Ice*, 1986

1456

CLAYTON EMERY

Outcasts

(New York: Ace, 1990)

Story type: Fantasy (Quest)
Series: Runesword
Major character(s): Elizebith of Morea, Sorceress; Hathor, Mythical Creature (Ogre); Dark Lord, Wizard
Time period(s): Indeterminate
Locale(s): Alternate Earth

Summary: Elizebith, kidnapped from the home of a hated sorceress and then abandoned, sets herself up as a witch. When one of her cures proves fatal, Bith runs. She meets some fellow travelers and is contacted by a god who requires that she find the magic swords which were scattered around the Earth before the Dark Lord can drain their power for his own uses.

Other books you might like:
Adrienne Martine-Barnes, *The Rainbow Sword*, 1988
C.J. Cherryh, *The Paladin*, 1988
Rose Estes, *Skryling's Blade*, 1990
    Tom Wham, co-author
Rosemary Kirstein, *The Steerswoman*, 1989
Laurie J. Marks, *The Moonbane Mage*, 1990
Elizabeth Moon, *Sheepfarmer's Daughter*, 1988
J.F. Rivkin, *Runesword: The Dreamstone*, 1991
Paul Edwin Zimmer, *Blood of the Colyn Muir*, 1988
    Jon de Cles, co-author

1457

CLAYTON EMERY

Shattered Chains

(New York: HarperPrism, 1995)

Story type: Fantasy (Magic Conflict)
Series: Magic: The Gathering
Major character(s): Gull, Leader, Revolutionary; Greensleeves, Wizard, Revolutionary; Norreen, Military Personnel
Time period(s): Indeterminate Past
Locale(s): The Domains, Fictional Country

Summary: Siblings Gull and Greensleeves continue their war against the wizards. Greensleeves must master the sorcery she hates, and Gull must learn to lead an army to allow survival of themselves and their followers. Based on the popular card game.

Other books you might like:
Steven Brust, *The Phoenix Guards*, 1991
Glen Cook, *The Black Company*, 1984
Pamela Dean, *The Secret Country*, 1985
William R. Forstchen, *Arena*, 1994
Ursula K. Le Guin, *A Wizard of Earthsea*, 1968
Sheri S. Tepper, *King's Blood Four*, 1983

1458

CAROL EMSHWILLER

Carmen Dog

(San Francisco: Mercury House, 1990)

Story type: Fantasy (Satire)
Major character(s): Pooch, Animal (dog)
Time period(s): Indeterminate
Locale(s): New York, New York

Summary: Women are turning into beasts, and beasts are turning into women in this story. Pooch, once the family dog, has become a woman, and decides to escape to New York City to become an opera singer. Once there, she begins to explore the nature of relationships between men and women.

Other books you might like:
Margaret Atwood, *The Handmaid's Tale*, 1986
Eugene Ionesco, *Rhinoceros*, 1959
Ira Levin, *The Stepford Wives*, 1979
James Morrow, *Only Begotten Daughter*, 1990
George Orwell, *Animal Farm*, 1986

1459

CAROL EMSHWILLER

The Start of the End of It All

(San Francisco: Mercury House, 1991)

Story type: Science Fiction (Collection; Contemporary Realism)

Summary: These 18 stories written before 1990 mix realism, science fiction and magical realism, exploring the experience of emotionally marginalized women and men whose lives are changed by the fantastic. The title story presents an alien invasion force that works through kitchens and dislikes cats, while the story "Eclipse" deals with public embarrassment and fears of alienation.

Other books you might like:
Marjorie Agosin, *The Secret Weavers: Stories of the Fantastic by Latin American Women*, 1991
    editor
Angela Carter, *The Infernal Desire Machines of Dr. Hoffman*, 1982
Pat Murphy, *Points of Departure*, 1990
James Tiptree Jr., *Her Smoke Rose Up Forever*, 1990
Fay Weldon, *Lives and Loves of a She-Devil*, 1983

1460

PETER R. EMSHWILLER

The Host

(New York: Bantam Spectra, 1991)

Story type: Science Fiction (Political; Techno-Thriller)
Major character(s): Watly Caiper, Murderer (accused), Disembodied Personality; Alysess Tolnismer, Doctor; Ragman, Psychic, Revolutionary
Time period(s): Indeterminate Future
Locale(s): United Countries of America, Fictional Country

Summary: The only possibility for motherhood Watly Caiper could imagine was a job as Host for Alvedine Industries. With the high pay from this dangerous position he could afford the antiprophies allowing fertility, and could hire a female to carry his child. As a resident of Level One Manhattan, and earlier in Brooklyn, he had never seen a child younger than himself except on CV, but his only goal in life is to be a mother. This is the author's first novel.

Other books you might like:
Emma Bull, *Bone Dance*, 1990
Katharine Kerr, *Polar City Blues*, 1990
Frederik Pohl, *The Years of the City*, 1984
Dan Simmons, *Hyperion*, 1989
Michael A. Stackpole, *Evil Ascending*, 1991
Michael A. Stackpole, *A Gathering Evil*, 1991
Michael Swanwick, *Vacuum Flowers*, 1987
Lawrence Watt-Evans, *Newer York*, 1991
    editer

1461

PETER R. EMSHWILLER

Short Blade

(New York: Bantam Spectra, 1992)

Story type: Science Fiction (Dystopian; Political)
Major character(s): Watly Caiper, Businesswoman, Disembodied Personality; Noonie Caiper, Child (Watly's daughter); Alysess Tolnismer, Doctor, Revolutionary
Time period(s): Indeterminate Future
Locale(s): United Countries of America, Fictional Country

Summary: In this sequel to *The Host* Watly has realized his dream of becoming a mother, but he is "killed" while hosting in the body of Sentiva Alvedine. Meanwhile, Noonie, threatened by Sentiva, wonders about the identity of her real mother as Watly fights to retain control of Sentiva's body. Watly's need to live and act as Sentiva compromises his ability to help his compatriots from First Level Manhattan in the revolution against their oppressors from the Second Level.

Other books you might like:
Pat Cadigan, *Mindplayers*, 1987
George Alec Effinger, *When Gravity Fails*, 1987
Frederik Pohl, *The Years of the City*, 1984
Rudy Rucker, *Wetware*, 1988
Dan Simmons, *The Fall of Hyperion*, 1990
Dan Simmons, *Hyperion*, 1989
Michael A. Stackpole, *A Gathering Evil*, 1991
Vernor Vinge, *A Fire upon the Deep*, 1992
Walter Jon Williams, *Hardwired*, 1986

1462

MICHAEL ENDE

The Night of Wishes: or The Satanarchaeolidealcohellish Notion Potion

(New York: Farrar, Straus and Giroux, 1992)

Story type: Fantasy (Magic Conflict; Light Fantasy)

Major character(s): Morris "Mauricio di Mauro", Animal (cat), Spy (High Council of Animals); Jacob Scribble, Animal (raven), Spy (High Council of Animals); Beelzebub Preposteror, Sorcerer
Time period(s): 1990s
Locale(s): Villa Nightmare, Mythical Place (Preposteror's house)

Summary: Assigned by the High Council of Animals to spy on Preposteror and his aunt, Mauricio and Jacob witness the creation of a wishing potion which would allow both evil sorcerers to achieve their annual quota of dastardly deeds before midnight arrives to avoid cancellation of their magical powers and the subsequent penalty. With a bit of magical help from Father New Year, Mauricio and Jacob struggle to contaminate the brew and modify the potion's power. Translated from German by Heiki Schwarzbauer and Rick Takvorian.

Other books you might like:
Karen Brush, *Demon Pig*, 1991
Karen Brush, *The Pig, the Prince and the Unicorn*, 1987
Kenneth Grahame, *The Wind in the Willows*, 1908
Margery Sharp, *The Rescuers*, 1959
Roger Zelazny, *Bring Me the Head of Prince Charming*, 1991
    Robert Sheckley, co-author

1463

GUY ENDORE

The Werewolf of Paris

(New York: Citadel, 1992)

Story type: Horror (Werewolf Story)
Major character(s): Bertrand Caillet, Military Personnel (National Guard), Werewolf; Aymar Galliez, Writer; Josephine Caillet, Servant (Bertrand's mother)
Time period(s): 1870s (1870)
Locale(s): Paris, France

Summary: Although guardian Aymar Galliez tries his best to hide from young Bertrand Caillet the fact that his ward is a werewolf born of the unholy union of a servant girl and an accursed stranger, Bertrand finds it impossible to restrain his bestial side during the rapine and slaughter of the Paris Commune uprisings of 1870. This extraordinary allegory of the dark side of human nature was first published in 1933. Robert Bach has written a new foreword.

Other books you might like:
Michael Cadnum, *St. Peter's Wolf*, 1991
S.P. Somtow, *Moon Dance*, 1990
Whitley Strieber, *The Wolfen*, 1978
Melanie Tem, *Wilding*, 1992
Jack Williamson, *Darker than You Think*, 1948

1464

PETER ENFANTINO, Editor

Quick Chills

(San Jose, CA: Deadline Publications, 1990)

Story type: Horror (Anthology)

Summary: Fourteen stories by 13 authors, written for small press magazines between 1988 and 1989 and selected by the editor of the small press review magazine *The Scream Factory*. Stories with familiar themes, such as Ed Bryant's "While She Was Out" (a woman stalked by a homicidal maniac) and Joe Lansdale's "Not from Detroit" (a man's physical grapple with the specter of death) are balanced by tales with relatively unconventional topics, such as Bentley Little's "Survivalist" (the fate of the only couple in a southwestern town who do not subscribe to survivalism) and Ken Wisman's "On the Side of the Road" (the terrors of genetic engineering).

Other books you might like:
Jessica Amanda Salmonson, *Tales by Moonlight II*, 1989
Jessica Amanda Salmonson, *Tales by Moonlight*, 1984
Elizabeth A. Saunders, *When the Black Lotus Blooms*, 1990
Stuart David Schiff, *The Whispers Series*, 1977-1987
David B. Silva, *Best of The Horror Show*, 1987

1465

M.J. ENGH

Rainbow Man

(New York: Tor, 1993)

Story type: Science Fiction (Adventure; Political)
Major character(s): Trojan nine zero eight Liss, Spacewoman; Leona Porlock, Spacewoman; Doron, Religious (Selector)
Time period(s): Indeterminate Future
Locale(s): Bimran, Planet—Imaginary

Summary: Having decided to live on a planet, Liss chooses Bimran partly because it lacks laws, especially for visitors, but also for its high pressure oxygen atmosphere. Due to her voluntary surgical sterilization, Liss's Visitor Permit defines her as male, and the friendly locals greet her as Rainbow Man for her bright clothing. With the help of another outsider, Leona, a spaceshipper like herself, Liss gradually understands why Bimran requires no laws in its religious society. Unfortunately, Liss becomes too close to Doron, potentially leading to disaster for all her friends.

Other books you might like:
Eleanor Arnason, *Ring of Swords*, 1993
David Brin, *Glory Season*, 1993
Marge Piercy, *He, She and It*, 1991
Alis A. Rasmussen, *A Passage of Stars*, 1990
Joan Slonczewski, *A Door into Ocean*, 1986
Sheri S. Tepper, *Grass*, 1989
David Weber, *Path of the Fury*, 1992

1466

ELIZABETH ENGSTROM

Lizzie Borden

(New York: Tor, 1991)

Story type: Horror (Psychological Suspense; Gay/Lesbian Fiction)
Major character(s): Andrew Borden, Businessman (mill owner); Lizzie Borden, Heroine (Andrew's daughter), His-torical Figure; Emma Borden, Spinster (Lizzie's older sister)
Time period(s): 1890s (1892)
Locale(s): Fall River, Massachusetts

Summary: A novel based on the famous Lizzie Borden murder case. Repressed and frustrated by her life in the parsimonious Borden household, Lizzie finds comfort in romantic relationships with other women. Through her sexual awakening, and with the help of a book lent to her by a lover, Lizzie learns how to liberate the murderous and uncontrollable "Other Lizzie" inside her.

Other books you might like:
John Farris, *The Axman Cometh*, 1989
John R. Maxim, *Abel/Baker/Charley*, 1984
Ed McBain, *Lizzie*, 1986

1467

ELIZABETH ENGSTROM

Nightmare Flower

(New York: Tor, 1992)

Story type: Horror (Collection)

Summary: This volume collects nineteen stories and one short novel, most of which dwell on the dark side of human relationships and love. "Will Lunch Be Ready on Time" and "Grandma's Hobby" are both concerned with cannibalism, and the title story with a man-eating plant. "The Final Tale" works a variation on the old ghost story formula, while the lengthy "Project Stone" is a near-science fiction story in which an Arizona town's subtle plans for social engineering backfire with horrifying results.

Other books you might like:
Pat Cadigan, *Patterns*, 1989
Pat Murphy, *Points of Departure*, 1990
Jessica Amanda Salmonson, *John Collier and Fredric Brown Went Quarreling through My Head*, 1989
Lisa Tuttle, *Memories of the Body*, 1992
Lisa Tuttle, *A Nest of Nightmares*, 1986

1468

S.K. EPPERSON

Borderland

(New York: Donald I. Fine, 1992)

Story type: Horror (Small Town Horror)
Major character(s): Wulf Nolan, Fire Fighter; Vic Kimmler, Police Officer, Widow(er); Myra Callahan, Housekeeper
Time period(s): 1990s (1992)
Locale(s): Denke, Kansas

Summary: Widower Vic Kimmler returns to his family homestead in Denke, Kansas, unaware that the town still practices its legacy of murder and cannibalism.

Other books you might like:
Randall Boyll, *After Sundown*, 1989
Jack Ketchum, *Offspring*, 1991
Michael B. Sirota, *Demon Shadows*, 1990

1469

S.K. EPPERSON

Dumford Blood

(New York: St. Martin's, 1991)

Story type: Horror (Mystery)
Major character(s): Ben Portlock, Police Officer; Lura Taylor, Convict (ex-convict), Girlfriend (former); Portis Jackson, Banker (Ben's brother-in-law)
Time period(s): 1990s
Locale(s): Dumford, Kansas

Summary: The mutilation of several animals in the small town of Dumford coupled with the gruesome death of the local garbageman forces local officer Ben Portlock to draw on all of his investigative skills to solve the murder before someone pins the blame on his former girlfriend.

Other books you might like:
Susan Rogers Cooper, *Other People's Houses*, 1990
Bill Crider, *Shotgun Saturday Night*, 1987
Jean Hagar, *Nightwalker*, 1990
David Martin, *Lie to Me*, 1990
Sharyn McCrumb, *If Ever I Return, Pretty Peggy-O*, 1990
Jim Thompson, *Pop. 1280*, 1964
Anne Wingate, *The Eye of Anna*, 1990

1470

S.K. EPPERSON

Green Lake

(New York: Donald I. Fine, 1996)

Story type: Horror (Psychological Suspense)
Major character(s): Madeleine Heron, Anthropologist, Widow(er); Eris Renard, Government Official (conservation officer), Indian; Dale Russell, Government Official (conservation officer)
Time period(s): 1990s (1996)
Locale(s): Green Lake, Kansas

Summary: Madeleine Heron retreats to her sister's cabin in remote Green Lake to work through her grief over the suicide of her husband. While there she falls in love with Native American Eris Renard, arousing the hostility of Eris's tribal matriarch and setting the stage for a difficult relationship to be played out against the town's midwestern Gothic backdrop, which includes acts of child molesting, necrophilia, and murder.

Other books you might like:
Robert Bloch, *American Gothic*, 1974
Ed Gorman, *Shadow Games*, 1993
Joe R. Lansdale, *Mucho Mojo*, 1994
Peter Straub, *The Throat*, 1993
S.J. Strayhorn, *Black Night*, 1996

1471

S.K. EPPERSON

The Moons of Summer

(New York: Donald I. Fine, 1994)

Story type: Horror (Mystery)
Major character(s): Guy Driscoll, Journalist; Michael Bish, Police Officer; Vernon Diest, Undertaker
Time period(s): 1990s (1994)
Locale(s): Colson, Kansas

Summary: Journalist Guy Driscoll returns to his home town of Colson in the hope it will help settle his rebellious teenage daughter, but immediately he reuns afoul of the police through his coverage of local crime and stumbles upon a plot by the local undertaker to keep a steady stream of business flowing through the door whether people are dying naturally or not.

Other books you might like:
James Neal Harvey, *The Headsman*, 1991
Joe R. Lansdale, *Act of Love*, 1981
Joe R. Lansdale, *Cold in July*, 1989
Stephen Wright, *M31: A Family Romance*, 1988

1472

S.K. EPPERSON

Nightmare

(New York: Leisure, 1993)

Story type: Horror (Psychological Suspense)
Major character(s): Bryan Raleigh, Doctor (psychiatrist); David Raleigh, Journalist; Kate Berquist, Health Care Professional (occupational therapist)
Time period(s): 1990s (1992)
Locale(s): Flint Hills, Kansas

Summary: David Raleigh is goaded by his psychiatrist brother Bryan to move to Bryan's clinic for women with multiple personality disorders and write a book promoting his medical breakthroughs. Once there, David discovers that someone is inducing the alternate personas of the patients to kill one another. This novel was originally published in 1992.

Other books you might like:
Robin Cook, *Coma*, 1977
Robin Cook, *Godplayer*, 1983
Dean R. Koontz, *The House of Thunder*, 1982

1473

ELIZABETH ERGAS

Devil's Gate

(New York: Zebra/Pinnacle, 1991)

Story type: Horror (Occult)
Major character(s): Alison Crandall Fortune, Paralegal; Sam Chandler, Architect; Adrian Blaise, Businessman (real estate developer)
Time period(s): 1990s (1990)
Locale(s): Draconia, New Hampshire

Summary: Two hundred years ago the townspeople of New Hope, New Hampshire sold their collective souls to the Devil. Renamed Draconia, the town's 20th century version seems poised on the verge of making the same mistake once more when real estate developer Adrian Blaise offers its citizens newfound wealth in exchange for its innocent women and children.

Other books you might like:
John Burke, *The Devil's Footsteps*, 1976
Thomas Tryon, *Harvest Home*, 1973

1474
ELIZABETH ERGAS

Rage
(New York: Zebra, 1993)

Story type: Horror (Supernatural Vengeance)
Major character(s): Leah Gold, Aged Person; Janie Rose, Young Woman; Maxwell Marsh, Journalist
Time period(s): 1990s (1993)
Locale(s): Sawquid, New York

Summary: Leah Gold's favorite necklace is fashioned from volcanic rock imbued with the soul of an angry young woman trapped in a lava flow almost a century before. Motivated by their own rage, Leah and her elderly friends find it possible to liberate the woman's spirit from the necklace to take revenge against their supposed persecutors.

Other books you might like:
Robert Bloch, *There Is a Serpent in Eden*, 1979
Edward Bryant, *Fetish*, 1991
A.R. Morlan, *The Amulet*, 1991

1475
STEVE ERICKSON

Arc d'X
(New York: Poseidon, 1993)

Story type: Fantasy (Historical; Religious)
Major character(s): Sally Hemings, Slave; Thomas Jefferson, Diplomat, Historical Figure; Etcher, Thief
Time period(s): 18th century; 21st century
Locale(s): Paris, France; Los Angeles, California; Berlin, Germany

Summary: After killing her master, Sally Hemings burns at the stake and returns to life as Thomas Jefferson's slave and mistress, accompanying the ambassador to Paris where 18th century ideals conflict with convenience. In a dystopian 21st century, echoes of the master and slave resonate in residents of a Los Angeles run by religious fanatics and policed by mobs. However, the balance changes when Etcher steals magical books and begins rewriting events.

Other books you might like:
Octavia E. Butler, *Kindred*, 1979
Maryse Conde, *I, Tituba, Black Witch of Salem*, 1992
Charles de Lint, *The Little Country*, 1991
Philip K. Dick, *Ubik*, 1969
Cynthia Kadohata, *In the Heart of the Valley of Love*, 1992

Marge Piercy, *Woman on the Edge of Time*, 1976
Lewis Shiner, *Glimpses*, 1993
Starhawk, *The Fifth Sacred Thing*, 1993

1476
BARBARA ERSKINE

Midnight Is a Lonely Place
(New York: Dutton, 1994)

Story type: Horror (Supernatural Vengeance)
Major character(s): Kate Kennedy, Writer; Greg Lindsey, Artist; Alison Lindsey, Teenager
Time period(s): 1990s (1994)
Locale(s): Colchester, England

Summary: Kate Kennedy retires to a seaside refuge to take time out from a rocky romance and begin her new biography of Lord Byron. While there, the ocean erodes a cliff that has entombed for centuries the bodies of a druid priest and his lover, victims of a jealous husband, who begin exerting their terrifying powers through living agents once their bodies are washed free.

Other books you might like:
Jonathan Aycliffe, *Naomi's Room*, 1991
Emmanuel Carrere, *Gothic Romance*, 1984
Marcy Heidish, *The Torching*, 1992
Michael Stewart, *Belladonna*, 1992

1477
ROSE ESTES

Elfwood
(New York: Ace, 1992)

Story type: Fantasy (Sword and Sorcery)
Major character(s): Jaeme, Nobleman; Decutonius, Magician; Kirk, Orphan
Time period(s): Indeterminate
Locale(s): Albion, Fictional Country; Elfwood, Mythical Place; Castle Elfwood, Mythical Place

Summary: The peaceful order imposed on Albion from Castle Elfwood falls prey to human barbarians and orcs. Four youths must destroy the enemy threat or lose both human and faerie realms to chaos.

Other books you might like:
Emma Bull, *War for the Oaks*, 1987
Laurell K. Hamilton, *Nightseer*, 1992
Jackie Hyman, *Shadowlight*, 1989
Robert Jordan, *The Eye of the World*, 1989
Joel Rosenberg, *The Road to Ehvenor*, 1991
Will Shetterly, *Elsewhere*, 1991
Marilyn Singer, *Charmed*, 1990
Terri Windling, *Life on the Border*, 1991
　　editor

1478

ROSE ESTES

The Hunter on Arena
(New York: Warner Questar, 1991)

Story type: Science Fiction (Adventure)
Series: Hunter
Major character(s): Braldt, Prisoner, Warrior; Keri, Prisoner; Randi, Prisoner
Time period(s): Indeterminate Future
Locale(s): Rototara, Planet—Imaginary

Summary: Captured by a technologically advanced people who have a mining colony on his planet, Braldt is separated from his companions and sent to fight in the arena for the amusement of his captors. With a team of other beings from other worlds, Braldt battles other teams for the right to continue living while searching for a way to escape and rescue his friends.

Other books you might like:
Jean M. Auel, *Clan of the Cave Bear*, 1980
Gordon R. Dickson, *Wolf and Iron*, 1990
Geary Gravel, *A Key for the Nonesuch*, 1990
Simon R. Green, *Winner Takes All*, 1991
Robert E. Howard, *Conan the Conqueror*, 1950
Frederik Pohl, *Gladiator-at-Law*, 1955
    C.M. Kornbluth, co-author

1479

ROSE ESTES

Iron Dragons: Mountains and Madness
(New York: Baen, 1993)

Story type: Fantasy (Quest)
Major character(s): Tianna, Royalty (princess), Magician; Steffan, Mythical Creature (half-elf), Engineer
Time period(s): Indeterminate
Locale(s): Bright Kingdom, Fictional Country

Summary: To fend off economic collapse, Tianna agrees to the plan of an elf and dwarf to build a railroad using dragons transformed into smoke-billowing engines to bring their goods and produce to outside markets. She and Steffan must avert war, sorcery and treachery to save the Bright Kingdom. Game tie-in.

Other books you might like:
Robin W. Bailey, *Enchanter*, 1989
Robin W. Bailey, *The Lost City of Zork*, 1991
George Alec Effinger, *The Zork Chronicles*, 1990
Craig Shaw Gardner, *Wishbringer*, 1988
Mercedes Lackey, *Castle of Deception*, 1992
    Josepha Sherman, co-author
Mercedes Lackey, *Fortress of Frost and Fire*, 1993
    Ru Emerson, co-author
Mercedes Lackey, *Prison of Souls*, 1993
    Josepha Sherman, co-author
Josepha Sherman, *The Chaos Gate*, 1994

1480

ROSE ESTES
TOM WHAM, Co-Author

The Stone of Time
(New York: Ace, 1992)

Story type: Fantasy (Quest)
Series: Runesword
Major character(s): Caltus "Cal" Talienson, Warrior; Elizebith of Morea, Sorceress
Time period(s): Indeterminate
Locale(s): Westwoods, Mythical Place (kingdom)

Summary: When the Dark Lord again sends the goblin-led legions into Westwoods, this time to capture the Stone of Time, Cal and his companions venture to Abaton to secure for themselves the Stone of Time with which they intend to permanently annihilate the Dark Lord.

Other books you might like:
Mark Acres, *Dark Divide*, 1991
Stephen Billias, *Horrible Humes*, 1991
Clayton Emery, *Outcasts*, 1990
J.F. Rivkin, *The Dreamstone*, 1991

1481

ROSE ESTES

Troll-Quest
(New York: Ace, 1995)

Story type: Fantasy (Urban; Quest)
Major character(s): Katherine Sinclair, Parent, Adventurer; Crystal, Parent, Mythical Creature (troll); Benjamin Bosch, Doctor
Time period(s): 1990s (1995)
Locale(s): Chicago, Illinois; Mammoth Caves, Kentucky

Summary: Despite warfare between humans and Under Dwellers, Katherine, a human, and Crystal, a troll, don't care about the larger conflict, since they only want their beloved children back. But their efforts intertwine with the fate of both races, as the theft of their children reflects the larger issues that face both humans and trolls.

Other books you might like:
Peter S. Beagle, *The Folk of the Air*, 1986
Lois McMaster Bujold, *The Spirit Ring*, 1992
Emma Bull, *War for the Oaks*, 1987
Michael de Larrabeiti, *The Borribles*, 1978
R.A. MacAvoy, *Tea with the Black Dragon*, 1983
Will Shetterly, *Elsewhere*, 1991

1482

ROSE ESTES

Troll-Taken
(New York: Ace, 1993)

Story type: Fantasy (Contemporary)
Major character(s): Katherine Sinclair, Parent, Adventurer; Benjamin Bosch, Doctor, Adventurer

Time period(s): 1990s
Locale(s): Chicago, Illinois

Summary: When Katherine Sinclair discovers her child has been taken and a sickly infant left instead, she begins a desperate search for her child. The search leads her deep under Chicago where whe discovers a society experiencing terrible health problems among youngsters.

Other books you might like:
David Eddings, *Sorceress of Darshiva*, 1989
Teresa Edgerton, *The Grail and the Ring*, 1994
Barbara Hambly, *The Silent Tower*, 1986
Richard A. Knaak, *King of the Grey*, 1993
Jody Lynn Nye, *Higher Mythology*, 1993
Viido Polikarpus, *Down Town*, 1985
    Tappan King, co-author

1483

DENNIS ETCHISON

California Gothic
(New York: Dell/Abyss, 1995)

Story type: Horror (Psychological Suspense)
Major character(s): Dan Markham, Store Owner (bookstore); Evie Markham, Store Owner (bookstore); Judy Rios, Young Woman
Time period(s): 1990s (1995)
Locale(s): Los Angeles, California

Summary: Dan Markham and his family are menaced by his ex-girlfriend, Judy, a former radical and member of the Church of Satan the Redeemer. Judy supposedly killed herself decades ago before the authorities could catch her, but she reappears looking exactly as she did, and tries to ignite the passions Dan knew as a younger and more idealistic radical.

Other books you might like:
Douglas Clegg, *Dark of the Eye*, 1994
Joe R. Lansdale, *Savage Season*, 1989
Robert R. McCammon, *Mine*, 1990
Chet Williamson, *Second Chance*, 1994

1484

DENNIS ETCHISON, Editor

The Complete Masters of Darkness
(Lancaster, PA: Underwood-Miller, 1991)

Story type: Horror (Anthology)
Summary: A compilation of the three individual "Masters of Darkness" paperbacks, totaling 45 stories. All tales were chosen by the authors as their favorite works, explanations of which are given in individual afterwords. Selections range in variety from simple pulp gems like Ray Bradbury's "The Dead Man" and Manly Wade Wellman's "Up Under the Roof," to Joyce Carol Oates' post-holocaust spoof "Family" and Clive Barker's political allegory "In the Hills, The Cities." Also included are Richard Matheson's science fiction terror tale "Dance of the Dead," Whitley Strieber's sexually provocative "Perverts," Steve Rasnic Tem's dreamy "Preparations for the Game," George R.R. Martin's comically

grotesque "The Monkey Treatment," Stephen King's dark fantasy "The Woman in the Room," and a rare short story by James Herbert, "Hallowe'en Child."

Other books you might like:
David G. Hartwell, *The Dark Descent*, 1987
Leo Margulies, *My Best Science Fiction Story*, 1949
Kirby McCauley, *Night Chills*, 1975

1485

DENNIS ETCHISON

Darkside
(Chicago: America Fantasy/Airgedlamh Publications, 1996)

Story type: Horror (Child-in-Peril)
Major character(s): Doug Carson, Composer (film); Casey Carson, Housewife; Erin Carson, Teenager
Time period(s): 1980s (1986)
Locale(s): Los Angeles, California

Summary: Behind the sleek facades and glossy sheen of contemporary Los Angeles lurk the Lost Ones, a death cult of youngsters driven to the dark side of the counterculture through the emptiness of their lives. When his stepdaughter Erin becomes involved with the cult, Doug Carson must infiltrate the Underground where they live, and even risk passing over to the other side to save her. Published as a paperback original in 1986, this signed limited hardcover edition of the book presents the author's preferred text. Ramsey Campbell supplies the introduction.

Other books you might like:
Poppy Z. Brite, *Drawing Blood*, 1993
Ray Garton, *Crucifax Autumn*, 1988
Melanie Tem, *Prodigal*, 1991

1486

DENNIS ETCHISON, Editor

MetaHorror
(New York: Dell/Abyss, 1992)

Story type: Horror (Anthology)

Summary: Twenty-one original stories meant to expand the boundaries of the modern horror story. Among the best are Scott Edelman's tale of McCarthyan paranoia, "Are You Now"; Lisa Tuttle's meditation on the battle of the sexes, "Replacements"; Donald R. Burleson's story of schoolchildren with horrifyingly acute perception, "Ziggles"; Ramsey Campbell's seriocomedy about the implications of communication breakdown, "End of the Line"; Steve Rasnic Tem's potent exploration of terminal illness, "Underground"; and "The Ghost Village," an excerpt from Peter Straub's novel, *The Throat*.

Other books you might like:
Kirby McCauley, *Dark Forces*, 1980
Thomas F. Monteleone, *Borderlands 1*, 1990
J.N. Williamson, *The Best of Masques*, 1988

1487

DENNIS ETCHISON

Shadow Man

(New York: Dell/Abyss, 1993)

Story type: Horror (Serial Killer; Child-in-Peril)
Major character(s): Jack Martin, Artist; Christopher Buckley, Child; Lissa Shelby, Counselor (youth counselor)
Time period(s): 1990s (1993)
Locale(s): Shadow Bay, California; Eden Cove, California

Summary: In a tale laced with subtle criticism about the fraying of American society, Jack Martin and Lissa Shelby struggle to protect a young boy from becoming the next victim of a child murderer who stalks the town of Shadow Bay and who is linked in the minds of the local children to the horror movies they watch.

Other books you might like:
Samuel M. Key, *From a Whisper to a Scream*, 1992
John Saul, *Suffer the Children*, 1977
Whitley Strieber, *Billy*, 1990

1488

RUTLEDGE ETHERIDGE

The First Duelist

(New York: Ace, 1994)

Story type: Science Fiction (Military; Space Opera)
Major character(s): Simon Barrow, Martial Arts Expert, Teenager; Griffin Joyner, Military Personnel; Corinne Hernandez, Martial Arts Expert
Time period(s): 22nd century (2128-2166)
Locale(s): Mercator, Asteroid (prison); *Celeste*, Spaceship; *Serendipity*, Spaceship

Summary: Condemned to the prison asteroid, Mercator, for sabotaging Earth's first star ship, the *Utic Shinar*, Simon Barrow joins forces with the legendary General Joyner and Talon. Together, they fight the injustices of the established government and strive to regain space travel for the entire human race.

Other books you might like:
Eleanor Arnason, *Ring of Swords*, 1993
Emma Bull, *Bone Dance*, 1991
Joe Haldeman, *All My Sins Remembered*, 1977
Steve Miller, *Agent of Change*, 1988
    Sharon Lee, co-author
Steve Perry, *The Man Who Never Missed*, 1985
Alis A. Rasmussen, *Revolution's Shore*, 1990

1489

KEN EULO
JOE MAUCK, Co-Author

Claw

(New York: Simon & Schuster, 1994)

Story type: Horror (Nature in Revolt)

Major character(s): Meg Stewart, Veterinarian; Dan Dragelman, Police Officer; Philip Roueche, Zoo Keeper (curator of the Los Angeles Zoo)
Time period(s): 1990s (1994)
Locale(s): Los Angeles, California

Summary: The bloody escape of Rajah, a Siberian tiger who is one of the star attractions of the Los Angeles Zoo, leads veterinarian Meg Stewart to investigate why the animal has suddenly turned so vicious. Meg discovers that Rajah is part of a project funded by the Department of Defense to give tigers the thinking capacity of human beings for use as potential weapons.

Other books you might like:
Peter Benchley, *White Shark*, 1994
T.J. Kirby, *Deadly Breed*, 1991
Dean R. Koontz, *Watchers*, 1987
Bob Mayer, *Operation Synbat*, 1994

1490

KEN EULO

Manhattan Heat

(New York: Tor, 1991)

Story type: Horror (Occult)
Major character(s): Frank Caldwell, Police Officer; Caroline Caldwell, Child (Frank's daughter); Kate Reeling, Psychologist
Time period(s): 1990s
Locale(s): New York, New York

Summary: Manhattan cop Frank Caldwell's efforts to be a good father and ex-husband in the wake of a divorce are interrupted by his latest case, which involves a coven of the walking dead who inhabit New York City's underground and who may be related to the religious practices of a fringe group of the local Cuban community.

Other books you might like:
Alex Abella, *The Killing of the Saints*, 1991
Nicholas Conde, *The Religion*, 1982
Gordon Linzner, *The Troupe*, 1988
Chet Williamson, *Lowland Rider*, 1988

1491

DAVID EVANS

Time Station London

(New York: Ace, 1996)

Story type: Science Fiction (Time Travel)
Series: Time Station
Major character(s): Steven "Brian Moore" Whitefeather, Military Personnel (colonel), Time Traveller; Samatha Trillby, Military Personnel (lieutenant); Diana Basehart, Time Traveller
Time period(s): 1940s (1940); Indeterminate Future
Locale(s): London, England; Coventry, England

Summary: Assigned to the London Time Station during the Blitz, Steven takes on the identity of a British counterintelligence officer in order to find out who plans to kill

Winston Churchill and to stop the plan, thus keeping history unchanged. Yet his love for Samantha, a native of the 20th century, leads him to travel backward and forward in time to prevent her destined death.

Other books you might like:

Dennis Lee Anderson, *Arthur, King*, 1995
Poul Anderson, *Time Patrolman*, 1983
David Drake, *Arc Riders*, 1995
　　Janet Morris, co-author
Harlan Ellison, *The City on the Edge of Forever*, 1995
S.D. Perry, *Timecop*, 1994
John T. Phillifent, *The Man From U.N.C.L.E.: The Mad Scientist Affair*, 1966

1492

LINDA EVANS

Far Edge of Darkness
(New York: Baen, 1996)

Story type: Science Fiction (Time Travel; Political)
Major character(s): Charlie Flynn, Police Officer, Time Traveller; Sibyl Johnson, Student, Time Traveller; Tony "Antonius Caelerus" Bartlett, Time Traveller, Criminal
Time period(s): 1990s; 1st century (79 A.D.)
Locale(s): Alaska; Roman Empire

Summary: At different times and places, Charlie Flynn and Sybil Johnson anger the powerful Carreras family and end up as slaves in ancient Rome trying to survive the eruption of Mt. Vesuvius. Meanwhile, thrown four years into the future, Logan McKee stumbles upon a secret base in Alaska and soon must try a desperate time jump to survive at all.

Other books you might like:

Poul Anderson, *Guardians of Time*, 1960
Robert Asprin, *Time Scout*, 1995
　　Linda Evans, co-author
Robert Asprin, *Wagers of Sin*, 1996
　　Linda Evans, co-author
Greg Bear, *Eternity*, 1988
L. Sprague de Camp, *Rivers of Time*, 1993
David Drake, *Birds of Prey*, 1984
Crawford Kilian, *Rogue Emperor*, 1988
Sam Merwin Jr., *The House of Many Worlds*, 1951
Melissa Scott, *A Choice of Destinies*, 1986
William Wu, *Warrior*, 1993

1493

LINDA EVANS

Sleipnir
(New York: Baen, 1994)

Story type: Fantasy (Sword and Sorcery; Legend)
Major character(s): Randy Barnes, Military Personnel; Gary Vernon, Military Personnel; Odin, Deity
Time period(s): 1980s; Indeterminate
Locale(s): Germany; Nifflheim, Mythical Place (Norse underworld); Valhalla, Mythical Place

Summary: While guarding a U.S. Army base in Germany, Randy watches Odin's eight-legged horse, Sleipnir, carry the soul of his buddy, Gary Vernon, to Valhalla. When Gary's grandmother gives Randy a knife with magical properties, Randy seeks vengeance against Odin himself on a perilous journey into the depths of a Norwegian cave which leads him to Nifflheim, the domain of Hel, goddess of the dead, and eventually to personal combat with Odin in Valhalla. First novel.

Other books you might like:

Harry Harrison, *The Hammer and the Cross*, 1993
　　John Holm, co-author
P.C. Hodgell, *God Stalk*, 1982
Robert E. Howard, *Conan the Conqueror*, 1950
Victor Koman, *The Jehovah Contract*, 1987
John Myers Myers, *Silverlock*, 1949
Diana L. Paxson, *The Wolf and the Raven*, 1993

1494

KENNETH W. FAIG JR.

Tales of the Lovecraft Collectors
(West Warwick, Rhode Island: Necronomicon Press, 1995)

Story type: Horror (Collection)

Summary: In an original approach to the tale of Lovecraftian horror, the author, a renowned H.P. Lovecraft scholar and genealogist of the Lovecraft family, presents four stories of mystery, the supernatural and romance from the diary of antiquarian book collector David Parkes Boynton, in which Boynton's travels bring him into contact with Lovecraft collectors who have found interesting associations between Lovecraft's stories and events in his personal life. "Collector the First: Major Geoffrey Hopinkson Smith (1857-1943)" suggests that the Mexican Indian legends of Lovecraft's story "The Transition of Juan Romero" were drawn from fact. "Collector the Second: Dean Allen Edgerton Noble (1876-1959)" focuses on Lovecraft's father, and a possible association with the Lizzie Borden murders. "Collector the Third: Charles Wilson Hodap (1842-1944)" suggests a source for Lovecraft's prose poem "Nyarlathotep," while "Collector the Fourth and Fifth: David Parkes Boynton (1897-1956) and Another Gentleman of the Hope Club" speculates about events in Lovecraft's personal life that may have precipitated his nervous breakdown. These stories were first collected in 1989 in slightly different form.

Other books you might like:

Peter Cannon, *Pulptime*, 1984
Richard A. Lupoff, *Lovecraft's Book*, 1985
Robert M. Price, *Tales of the Providence Pales*, 1983
　　editor
Ralph Vaughan, *Sherlock Holmes in the Adventure of the Ancient Gods*, 1990

1495

MARGARET FALK

Darkscope
(New York: Pinnacle, 1990)

Story type: Horror (Supernatural Vengeance)
Major character(s): Chelsea McCord, Artist; Ben Fletcher, Horse Trainer; Bob McCord, Businessman (Chelsea's uncle)
Time period(s): 1980s (1986)
Locale(s): Bisbee, Arizona

Summary: Following the failure of her marriage, Chelsea McCord takes up residence in Bisbee, a town once controlled by her great-grandfather, a powerful mining magnate. When she accidentally releases a spirit that was trapped in an old box camera in her attic, she reignites the long-standing feud between the McCords and the Barries, a family that was exploited by the McCords and whose members, both living and dead, are bent on revenge.

Other books you might like:
Michael McDowell, *Cold Moon over Babylon*, 1980
Dean Wesley Smith, *Laying the Music to Rest*, 1989
Peter Straub, *If You Could See Me Now*, 1977

1496

JANE S. FANCHER

Ground-Ties
(New York: Warner Questar, 1991)

Story type: Science Fiction (Political)
Major character(s): Loren Cantrell, Spaceship Captain (admiral); Stephen Ridenour, Computer Expert; Anevai Tyeewapi, Scientist, Guide
Time period(s): Indeterminate Future
Locale(s): *Cetacean*, Spaceship; HuteNamid, Planet—Imaginary

Summary: Officially, Admiral Cantrell's mission is to convey young Stephen Ridenour to HuteNamid to investigate possible misuse of the Nexus ComNet, the interstellar computer network that links the people of the Alliance. Although Ridenour's repressed memories and conflicting loyalties threaten his sanity and safety, he may hold the key to the salvation, or destruction, of HuteNamid.

Other books you might like:
Alfred Bester, *The Computer Connection*, 1974
Emma Bull, *Bone Dance*, 1991
C.J. Cherryh, *Downbelow Station*, 1981
Diane Duane, *Spock's World*, 1989
Mary Gentle, *Golden Witchbreed*, 1984
Frank Herbert, *Dune*, 1965
Jim Young, *The Face of the Deep*, 1979

1497

JANE S. FANCHER

Harmonies of the 'Net
(New York: Warner Questar, 1992)

Story type: Science Fiction (Political)
Major character(s): Stephen Ridenour, Computer Expert; Jonathan Wesley Smith, Computer Expert; Loren Cantrell, Spaceship Captain
Time period(s): Indeterminate Future
Locale(s): HuteNamid, Planet—Imaginary; *Cetacean*, Spaceship

Summary: Loren Cantrell deals with representatives of the 'NetAT who want to take Stephen off his assignment. Wesley Smith, both attracted to and repelled by Stephen Ridenour, learns more about Stephen and seduces him. Stephen, gradually remembering more about his past experiences as Zivon Ryevanishov, seeks out the Cocheta library, where he interfaces directly with the 'Net and begins to repair it. Sequel to *Uplink*.

Other books you might like:
Marion Zimmer Bradley, *The Forbidden Tower*, 1977
C.J. Cherryh, *Heavy Time*, 1991
David Drake, *Northworld*, 1990
William Gibson, *Neuromancer*, 1984
Robert A. Heinlein, *Stranger in a Strange Land*, 1961
C.J. Mills, *Winter World*, 1988
Neal Stephenson, *Snow Crash*, 1992

1498

JANE S. FANCHER

Ring of Lightning
(New York: DAW, 1995)

Story type: Fantasy (Political; Magic Conflict)
Series: Dance of the Rings
Major character(s): Dymorin Rhomandi dunMheric, Royalty (Princeps of Rhomatum); Mikhyel Rhomandi dunMheric, Royalty (Princeps of Rhomatum); Nikaenor "Nikki" Rhomandi dunMheric, Royalty (Princeps of Rhomatum)
Time period(s): Indeterminate
Locale(s): Rhomatum, Fictional City (city-state)

Summary: To survive the threat from a neighboring city-state and allow Rhomatum to blossom as a democracy, Deymorin must cease feuding with his brothers and plan a coordinated assault on their great-aunt's control of the magical power of the leythium Rings, focus of Rhomatum society. First of a series.

Other books you might like:
Robert Jordan, *The Eye of the World*, 1989
Melanie Rawn, *Dragon Prince*, 1988
Kristine Kathryn Rusch, *Traitors*, 1994
Martha Wells, *The Element of Fire*, 1993
Janny Wurts, *Curse of the Mistwraith*, 1994
Roger Zelazny, *Nine Princes in Amber*, 1970

1499

JANE S. FANCHER

Uplink

(New York: Warner Questar, 1992)

Story type: Science Fiction (Political)
Major character(s): Stephen Ridenour, Computer Expert; Anevai Tyeewapi, Scientist, Guide; Jonathan Wesley Smith, Computer Expert
Time period(s): Indeterminate Future
Locale(s): *Cetacean*, Spaceship; HuteNamid, Planet—Imaginary

Summary: While Stephen recovers aboard the *Cetacean*, having suffered a brutal beating on HuteNamid, the ship's doctor discovers evidence of his past abuse and drug addiction, possibly part of some plan by bigoted politicans back at Vandereaux. Stephen returns to HuteNamid and makes contact, at first unwillingly, through a virtual reality ''library'' with the Cocheta, a mysterious alien race. Sequel to *Ground-Ties*.

Other books you might like:
C.J. Cherryh, *Cyteen*, 1988
C.J. Cherryh, *Downbelow Station*, 1981
A.C. Crispin, *Silent Dances*, 1990
    Kathleen O'Malley, co-author
Cynthia Felice, *Downtime*, 1985
William Gibson, *Neuromancer*, 1984

1500

NANCY FARMER

The Ear, the Eye, and the Arm

(New York: Orchard Books, 1994)

Story type: Fantasy (Mystery; Science Fiction)
Major character(s): Amadeus Matsika, Military Personnel (general); Tendai Matsika, Child
Time period(s): 22nd century (2194)
Locale(s): Harare, Zimbabwe

Summary: Fearing his enemies might harm his children, General Matsika keeps the youngsters sheltered in the home compound. After Tendai and his sister and brother sneak out of the house to bus across Harare for a scout merit badge, the Blue Monkey lures them into the clutches of Fist and Knife and then the She Elephant who forces them to mine plastic. Tendai attracts the spirit of Zimbabwe which helps the children survive while the three mutant detectives, the Eye, the Ear, and the Arm, effect their rescue.

Other books you might like:
Gillian Bradshaw, *The Land of Gold*, 1992
Barry Lopez, *Crow and Weasel*, 1990
Ben Okri, *The Famished Road*, 1992
Ben Okri, *Songs of Enchantment*, 1993
Mike Resnick, *Future Earths: Under African Skies*, 1993
    Gardner Dozois, co-editor

1501

NANCY FARMER

A Girl Named Disaster

(New York: Orchard Books, 1996)

Story type: Fantasy (Adventure; Quest)
Major character(s): Nhamo, Child, Adventurer
Time period(s): 1990s
Locale(s): Lake Cabora Bassa, Mozambique; Zimbabwe

Summary: Fleeing the impending marriage which would make her fourth wife to a cruel man, Nhamo sets out for Zimbabwe to search for her father. Swept to the uncharted Lake Cabora Bassa, Nhamo nearly drowns. Near-starvation puts her in contact with the spirit world, a contact that remains after Nhamo leaves the wilderness.

Other books you might like:
Gillian Bradshaw, *The Land of Gold*, 1992
Kara Dalkey, *Little Sister*, 1996
Garth Nix, *Sabriel*, 1996
Ben Okri, *The Famished Road*, 1992
Ben Okri, *Songs of Enchantment*, 1993
Mike Resnick, *Future Earths: Under African Skies*, 1993
    Gardner Dozois, co-editor

1502

PHILIP JOSE FARMER

Dayworld Breakup

(New York: Tor, 1990)

Story type: Science Fiction (Adventure; Political)
Series: Dayworld
Major character(s): William St.-George Duncan, Revolutionary; Panthea Snick, Revolutionary, Girlfriend
Time period(s): 31st century
Locale(s): Earth

Summary: William St.-George Duncan, an integrated multiple personality, and Panthea Snick sabotage the system in hopes of forcing the government to reveal the secrets of a life-extending drug and the decline in population. A lengthy pursuit results in their capture after which Duncan's individual personalities become a further problem.

Other books you might like:
Robert A. Heinlein, *Revolt in 2100*, 1953
Robert A. Heinlein, *Sixth Column*, 1949
Steve Perry, *The Man Who Never Missed*, 1985
Clifford D. Simak, *The Werewolf Principle*, 1967
David Alexander Smith, *Homecoming*, 1990
A.E. van Vogt, *The Weapon Shops of Isher*, 1951
A.E. van Vogt, *The Weapon Makers*, 1946

1503

PHILIP JOSE FARMER

Escape From Loki

(New York: Bantam Falcon, 1991)

Story type: Fantasy (Adventure)

Series: Doc Savage
Major character(s): Clark "Doc" Savage Jr., Adventurer, Military Personnel (pilot); von Hessel, Nobleman (baron), Military Personnel (Colonel)
Time period(s): 1910s (1918)
Locale(s): Germany

Summary: When shot down over Germany and captured by Baron von Hessel, 16-year-old Lieutenant Clark Savage escapes only to be recaptured and thrown into an escape-proof salt mine where the Baron experiments on human guinea pigs. Doc Savage must defeat the Baron to save the Allies from his new superweapon.

Other books you might like:
Lester Dent, *Doc Savage Omnibus #13*, 1990
    as Kenneth Robeson
Lester Dent, *Doc Savage Omnibus #12*, 1990
    as Kenneth Robeson
Lester Dent, *Doc Savage Omnibus #11*, 1990
    as Kenneth Robeson
Lester Dent, *Doc Savage Omnibus #10*, 1989
    as Kenneth Robeson
Lester Dent, *Doc Savage Omnibus #9*, 1989
Lester Dent, *Doc Savage Omnibus #1*, 1986
William Murray, *Python Isle*, 1991

1504

PHILIP JOSE FARMER

More than Fire

(New York: Tor, 1993)

Story type: Science Fiction (Adventure)
Series: World of Tiers
Major character(s): Kickaha, Adventurer; Red Orc, Immortal; Khruuz, Alien
Time period(s): 1990s; Indeterminate
Locale(s): World of Tiers, Planet—Imaginary; Earth; Earth II, Planet—Imaginary

Summary: Aided by Khruuz, lone survivor of his race, Kickaha and Anana must stop the mad Lord, Red Orc, from finding the secret of creating and destroying universes. Concludes the series.

Other books you might like:
Piers Anthony, *Kirlian Quest*, 1978
Greg Bear, *Eternity*, 1988
Ben Bova, *Orion*, 1984
Octavia E. Butler, *Adulthood Rites*, 1988
Jack L. Chalker, *The Run to Chaos Keep*, 1990
Alan Dean Foster, *Glory Lane*, 1987
Jack Vance, *The Five Gold Bands*, 1963
Roger Zelazny, *Nine Princes in Amber*, 1970

1505

PHILIP JOSE FARMER, Editor

Quest to Riverworld

(New York: Warner Questar, 1993)

Story type: Science Fiction (Anthology; Immortality)

Series: Riverworld
Time period(s): Indeterminate Future
Locale(s): Riverworld, Planet—Imaginary

Summary: Contains 14 stories all sharing Philip Jose Farmer's Riverworld setting with two stories by the series' creator and one collaboration by David Bischoff and Dean Wesley Smith. Other authors include John Gregory Betancourt, Jody Lynn Nye, Robert Sheckley, Brad Strickland, Lawrence Watt-Evans and Robert Weinberg.

Other books you might like:
Pamela Sargent, *Afterlives: An Anthology of Stories about Life After Death*, 1986
    Ian Watson, co-editor
William Shatner, *Believe: A Novel*, 1992
    Michael Tobias, co-author
Robert Silverberg, *To the Land of the Living*, 1990
Clifford D. Simak, *Out of Their Minds*, 1970
Joan Slonczewski, *Daughter of Elysium*, 1993
Robert Weinberg, *The Mists From Beyond*, 1993
    Stefan R. Dziemianowicz, Martin H. Greenberg, co-editors

1506

PHILIP JOSE FARMER

Red Orc's Rage

(New York: Tor, 1991)

Story type: Fantasy (Contemporary; Alternate World)
Series: World of Tiers
Major character(s): Jim Grimson, Teenager, Criminal; L. Robert Porsena, Doctor (psychiatrist); Orc, Teenager, Nobleman
Time period(s): 1970s (1979)
Locale(s): Belmont City, Ohio; Tiersian Universe, Fictional Country

Summary: Jim's life is a mess until he begins treatment under Dr. Porsena, who has adapted Farmer's World of Tiers series (1965-) for use as a therapeutic tool. Jim chooses the series' major villain, Orc, as the alter ego through which he will try to confront his problems and learn positive coping strategies. Some new problems arise when Jim becomes convinced that he actually occupies the body of his alter ego.

Other books you might like:
Pat Cadigan, *Mindplayers*, 1987
Charles de Lint, *The Little Country*, 1990
Gordon R. Dickson, *The Dragon and the George*, 1976
Rudy Rucker, *Software*, 1982
Robert Silverberg, *Letters From Atlantis*, 1990
Vivian Vande Velde, *User Unfriendly*, 1991
Roger Zelazny, *Bridge of Ashes*, 1976

1507

PHILIP JOSE FARMER

Riders of the Purple Wage

(New York: Tor, 1992)

Story type: Science Fiction (Collection)

Summary: Contains eight stories reprinted from periodicals and anthologies including one from *Dangerous Visions* (1967), the title story, which received a Nebula Award nomination and a Hugo Award. The mood of these stories varies from humor to emotional drama while Farmer's social commentary encompasses situations as disparate as a time-travelling saint in "St. Francis Kisses His Ass Goodbye" and the IRS's encounter with a UFO in "UFO Versus IRS."

Other books you might like:
Alfred Bester, *Star Light, Star Bright*, 1976
Orson Scott Card, *Maps in a Mirror*, 1990
Larry Niven, *Tales of Known Space*, 1975
Robert Silverberg, *The Science Fiction Hall of Fame, Volume 1*, 1970
    editor
Cordwainer Smith, *The Best of Cordwainer Smith*, 1975
Theodore Sturgeon, *Aliens 4*, 1959
Theodore Sturgeon, *E Pluribus Unicorn*, 1953
William Tenn, *The Human Angle*, 1956
William Tenn, *Of All Possible Worlds*, 1955
John Varley, *Blue Champagne*, 1986
John Varley, *The Persistence of Vision*, 1978

1508

PHILIP JOSE FARMER, Editor
MARTIN H. GREENBERG, Co-Editor

Tales of Riverworld
(New York: Warner Questar, 1992)

Story type: Science Fiction (Anthology; Immortality)
Series: Riverworld
Time period(s): Indeterminate
Locale(s): Riverworld, Planet—Imaginary

Summary: Contains a two-page foreword and nine stories all sharing the world of Farmer's award winning *River of Eternity* (1983) begun in the Hugo Award winning novel, *To Your Scattered Bodies Go* (1971). This book includes one story by the editor, "Crossing the River"; one collaboration by Mike Resnick and Barry Malzberg, "Every Man a God"; the first appearance by Dane Helstrom, "A Hole in Hell"; the first humorous Riverworld story, "Blandings on Riverworld," by Phillip C. Jennings; and the first science fiction story by horror writer Ed Gorman, "Fool's Paradise," plus stories by John Gregory Betancourt, Allen Steele, Harry Turtledove and Robert Weinberg.

Other books you might like:
Diana G. Gallagher, *The Alien Dark*, 1990
Joe Haldeman, *The Hemingway Hoax*, 1990
Frank M. Robinson, *The Dark Beyond the Stars*, 1991
Pamela Sargent, *Afterlives: An Anthology of Stories about Life After Death*, 1986
    Ian Watson, co-editor
William Shatner, *Believe: A Novel*, 1992
    Michael Tobias, co-author
Robert Silverberg, *To the Land of the Living*, 1990

1509

MICK FARREN

The Armageddon Crazy
(New York: Ballantine/Del Rey, 1989)

Story type: Science Fiction (Dystopian)
Major character(s): Harry Carlisle, Police Officer; Cynthia Kline, Spy
Time period(s): 21st century
Locale(s): United States

Summary: In a future America where fundamentalist Christianity rules with an iron hand, a group of people gather together to stage a revolution using spectacular special effects.

Other books you might like:
Margaret Atwood, *The Handmaid's Tale*, 1986
Michael Bishop, *A Little Knowledge*, 1977
Robert A. Heinlein, *Sixth Column*, 1949
John Kessel, *Good News From Outer Space*, 1989
James Morrow, *Only Begotten Daughter*, 1990

1510

MICK FARREN

The Feelies
(New York: Ballantine/Del Rey, 1990)

Story type: Science Fiction (Contemporary Realism; Techno-Thriller)
Major character(s): John Wilson Heffer, Vacationer; Wanda-Jean, Television Personality (gameshow contestant)
Time period(s): 21st century
Locale(s): United States

Summary: John Wilson Heffer got a special deal on a feelie, a total sensory experience in a life support chamber. He couldn't resist the offer, but then found himself stuck as Billy the Kid getting shot by Pat Garrett, over and over. When it was noticed that his machine was malfunctioning, he'd been dead for quite some time. Meanwhile, Wanda-Jean wanted to experience a feelie. Although she could never afford it, if she won on the TV Gameshow "Wildest Dreams," the first prize was a feelie contract. Revised from the 1978 British edition.

Other books you might like:
Piers Anthony, *Total Recall*, 1989
    pseudonym of Piers Anthony Dillingham Jacob
Pat Cadigan, *Mindplayers*, 1987
Pat Cadigan, *Synners*, 1991
Harry Harrison, *Make Room, Make Room*, 1966
Walter Dean Myers, *Brainstorm*, 1977

1511

MICK FARREN

The Last Stand of the DNA Cowboys
(New York: Ballantine/Del Rey, 1989)

Story type: Science Fiction (Adventure)
Series: DNA Cowboys

Major character(s): Minstrel Boy, Warrior (DNA Cowboy); Billy Oblivion, Warrior (DNA Cowboy)
Time period(s): Indeterminate Future
Locale(s): Earth

Summary: In a post-holocaust world with a strong flavoring of drugs, rock n' roll and the sixties, the DNA Cowboys do their best to hold things together and have a good time.

Other books you might like:
Samuel R. Delany, *The Einstein Intersection*, 1987
Michael Moorcock, *The Final Programme*, 1968
Michael Moorcock, *The Fireclown*, 1965
William F. Wu, *Hong on the Range*, 1989

1512

MICK FARREN

Mars—The Red Planet

(New York: Ballantine/Del Rey, 1990)

Story type: Science Fiction (Adventure)
Major character(s): Lech Hammond, Journalist
Time period(s): 21st century
Locale(s): Mars

Summary: The Martian Soviets have uncovered an alien artifact and ace TV reporter Lech Hammond goes to investigate. Mars is in chaos when he arrives due to the attacks of a vicious serial killer whose actions may be stimulated by the artifact.

Other books you might like:
W. Michael Gear, *The Artifact*, 1989
Ian McDonald, *Desolation Road*, 1988
Daniel Keys Moran, *The Armageddon Blues*, 1988
Paul Preuss, *Arthur C. Clarke's Venus Prime, Vol. 2: Maelstrom*, 1988

1513

MICK FARREN

Necrom

(New York: Ballantine/Del Rey, 1991)

Story type: Science Fiction (Alternate Universe; Fantasy)
Major character(s): Joe Ribson, Musician (rock); Nephredann, Demon; Gideon Windemere, Drug Dealer
Time period(s): 1990s
Locale(s): New York, New York; Hole in the Void Valley, Alternate Universe

Summary: Gibson, an alcoholic ex-rock star, tries to remember his life before being confined and drugged in an asylum. It seems he'd gotten involved in an interdimensional effort to save humanity from demonic forces and nuclear destruction, but the drugs keep his mind fuzzy. Nonetheless, the evening news convinces him that he is not in the New York where he belongs.

Other books you might like:
Pat Cadigan, *Mindplayers*, 1987
Geary Gravel, *A Key for the Nonesuch*, 1990
Marc Laidlaw, *Neon Lotus*, 1988

Michael Moorcock, *Elric of Melnibone*, 1976
Elizabeth Ann Scarborough, *Nothing Sacred*, 1991
Michael A. Stackpole, *A Gathering Evil*, 1991

1514

MICK FARREN

The Time of Feasting

(New York: Tor, 1996)

Story type: Horror (Vampire Story)
Major character(s): Victor Renquist, Vampire; Kurt Carfax, Vampire; Gideon Kelly, Religious (ex-priest)
Time period(s): 1990s (1996)
Locale(s): New York, New York

Summary: At the approach of the next Feasting, a period when vampires state their hungers and disguise the carnage as the handiwork of human malefactors, vampire patriarch Victor Renquist is challenged for the leadership of his Manhattan-based vampire enclave by Kurt Carfax, a brash young vampire who threatens to bring notice and destruction down upon the vampire brood. Renquist and Carfax are avidly watched by Gideon Kelly, a defrocked priest who hopes to redeem himself by destroying them.

Other books you might like:
Poppy Z. Brite, *Lost Souls*, 1993
Nancy A. Collins, *Sunglasses After Dark*, 1989
Robert R. McCammon, *They Thirst*, 1981
Anne Rice, *The Queen of the Damned*, 1988
Whitley Strieber, *The Hunger*, 1981

1515

JOHN FARRIS

The Axman Cometh

(New York: Tor, 1989)

Story type: Horror (Psychological Suspense)
Major character(s): Shannon Hill, Artist; Donald Carnes, Boyfriend
Time period(s): 1960s (1964); 1980s
Locale(s): Emerson, Kansas; New York, New York

Summary: Trapped in a darkened, disabled elevator, Shannon is tormented by a stranger claiming to be the "Axman" who killed her entire family 20 years earlier. Meanwhile her boyfriend, urged on by the ghost of Ernest Hemingway, attempts to go to her rescue.

Other books you might like:
Peter Straub, *If You Could See Me Now*, 1977

1516

JOHN FARRIS

Fiends

(Arlington Heights, IL: Dark Harvest, 1989)

Story type: Horror (Ancient Evil Unleashed)
Major character(s): Arne Horsfall, Patient (escaped mental patient); Enid Waller, Nurse (mental hospital worker)

Time period(s): 1900s (1906); 1970s
Locale(s): Sublimity, Tennessee (a suburb of Nashville)

Summary: Made dumb and half-insane by a mysterious quest with his father in 1906, Arne Horsfall escapes the hospital in 1970, becoming an unwilling emissary for a breed of winged semi-human monsters who are unleashed to terrorize the countryside and recruit new members.

Other books you might like:
Jere Cunningham, *The Abyss*, 1981
Bentley Little, *The Revelation*, 1990

1517

JOHN FARRIS
JOE R. LANSDALE, Co-Author
STEPHEN GALLAGHER, Co-Author

Night Visions 8

(Arlington Heights, IL: Dark Harvest, 1991)

Story type: Horror (Anthology)
Series: Night Visions

Summary: Each of the three writers contribute approximately 30,000 words of contemporary horror fiction. The stories range from the dark whimsey of Gallagher's "The Back of His Hand" to the terrifying woman-in-jeopardy story "Incident On and Off a Mountain Road" by Lansdale. Afterword by Robert R. McCammon.

Other books you might like:
Charles L. Grant, *Night Visions 2*, 1985
George R.R. Martin, *Night Visions 3*, 1986
Alan Ryan, *Night Visions 1*, 1984
Douglas E. Winter, *Night Visions 5*, 1988

1518

JOHN FARRIS

Sacrifice

(New York: Tor, 1994)

Story type: Horror (Mystery)
Major character(s): Greg Walker, Repairman (appliance); Sharissa Walker, Teenager (Greg's daughter); C.G. Butterbaugh, Detective
Time period(s): 1990s (1994)
Locale(s): Sky Valley, Georgia; Kan Peten, Guatemala

Summary: If Greg Walker seems a little overprotective of his teenage daughter and nosy about her sex life, it's with good reason. A near immortal survivor of the ancient Mayas who has endured centuries of physical wear and tear, he must ritually sacrifice a virgin at an ancient Mayan temple every generation in order to maintain his longevity. This novel is an expansion of Farris's 1990 novella, "Good Morning, Daddy."

Other books you might like:
Robert R. McCammon, *Mystery Walk*, 1984
Ashley McConnell, *Days of the Dead*, 1992
G. Wayne Miller, *Thunder Rise*, 1988
Adam Niswander, *The Charm*, 1993

Dan Simmons, *Song of Kali*, 1985

1519

JOHN FARRIS

Scare Tactics

(New York: Tor, 1989)

Story type: Horror (Collection)

Summary: One short novel and two stories. Most notable is the novel, *The Guardians*, in which a political rivalry erupts into violence and murder. Other excellent stories include "The Odor of Violets," in which a man commits murder to lay claim to the work of another, only to discover that "Fate" has made sure he receives justice, and "Horrorshow," in which the hero uses his supernatural powers to expose a brutal murderer. The paperback edition contains two additional stories, "Scare Tactics" and "I Scream. You Scream. We All Scream for Ice Cream."

Other books you might like:
Robert R. McCammon, *Blue World*, 1990
F. Paul Wilson, *Soft and Others*, 1989

1520

GREG FARSHTEY, Editor
GREG GORDEN, Co-Editor
ED STARK, Co-Editor

Strange Tales From the Nile Empire

(Honesdale, Pennsylvania: West End Games, 1992)

Story type: Fantasy (Anthology; Adventure)
Series: Torg: The Possibility Wars
Major character(s): Morbius, Criminal, Ruler (High Lord)
Time period(s): 21st century
Locale(s): Nile Empire, Alternate Earth

Summary: This volume contains a nine-page introduction, a five-page appendix by Greg Gorden plus eight stories by six authors set in a Middle East in which Dr. Morbius's reality-warping ability creates a cross between ancient Egypt and 1930s heroic pulp fiction. A game tie-in.

Other books you might like:
George Alec Effinger, *When Gravity Fails*, 1987
Douglas Kaufman, *Dragons over England*, 1992
    Ed Stark, co-editor
Christopher Kubasik, *Changeling*, 1992
Will Shetterly, *Liavek*, 1985
    Emma Bull, co-editor
Ed Stark, *Mysterious Cairo*, 1992
    Editor
Jordan K. Weisman, *Into the Shadows*, 1992

1521

JOE CLIFFORD FAUST

Desperate Measures

(New York: Ballantine/Del Rey, 1989)

Story type: Science Fiction (Space Opera)

Series: Angel's Luck
Major character(s): James May, Spaceship Captain
Time period(s): Indeterminate Future
Locale(s): *Angel's Luck*, Spaceship

Summary: James May is consistently unlucky. He can barely make the payments on his spaceship, he's got the authorities sniffing at his heels, his copilot just disappeared (taking the autopilot with him) and, last but not least, the crime syndicate wants to repossess his ship. Then there's the cargo of beef in his hold; what's he supposed to do with that? It's definitely time to take desperate measures.

Other books you might like:
C.J. Cherryh, *Merchanter's Luck*, 1982
Rory Harper, *Petrogypsies*, 1989
R.A. MacAvoy, *The Third Eagle: Lessons Along a Minor String*, 1989
Walter Jon Williams, *Angel Station*, 1989

1522

JOE CLIFFORD FAUST

Ferman's Devils

(New York: Bantam Spectra, 1996)

Story type: Science Fiction (Humor)
Major character(s): Boddekker, Advertising; Honniker, Advertising; Bainbridge, Advertising, Student—College
Time period(s): 21st century
Locale(s): New York, New York

Summary: A rising star at an advertising agency, Boddekker must attain wealth and a wife to qualify for a magnificent house outside New York City. His mugging by a street gang and the demands of the ad agency to develop a winning ad campaign for a new product present Boddekker with the opportunity for a bold original approach to selling laundry soap utilizing the street gang.

Other books you might like:
Mel Gilden, *Tubular Android Superheroes*, 1991
Frederik Pohl, *Midas World*, 1983
Frederik Pohl, *The Space Merchants*, 1953
   C.M. Kornbluth, co-author
Nick Pollotta, *Illegal Aliens*, 1989
   Phil Foglio, co-author

1523

JOE CLIFFORD FAUST

Precious Cargo

(New York: Ballantine/Del Rey Books, 1990)

Story type: Science Fiction (Space Opera)
Series: Angel's Luck
Major character(s): James May, Spaceship Captain
Time period(s): Indeterminate Future
Locale(s): *Angel's Luck*, Spaceship

Summary: Captain May's *Angel's Luck* continues to find trouble (and silliness) wherever it goes. Although they've survived—barely—a battle with the evil Yueh-shing, they're stranded in space. Then, almost worse than being stranded,

they're picked up by a ship captained by May's ex-wife Maggie, a ship chockful to the gills with argumentative aliens.

Other books you might like:
C.J. Cherryh, *Merchanter's Luck*, 1982
Rory Harper, *Petrogypsies*, 1989
R.A. MacAvoy, *The Third Eagle: Lessons Along a Minor String*, 1989
Walter Jon Williams, *Angel Station*, 1989

1524

RON FAUST

Lord of the Dark Lake

(New York: Tor/Forge, 1996)

Story type: Horror (Psychological Suspense)
Major character(s): Jay Chandler, Archaeologist; Alexander Krisos, Wealthy; Walter Von Rabenaue, Guard
Time period(s): 1990s (1996)
Locale(s): Krisos Island, Greece

Summary: While excavating the Temple of Poseidon, Jay Chandler is invited to attend the annual celebrity-studded summer party that his friend Alexander Krisos throws on the family island. A macabre turn of events leads to the systematic murders of the party guests, driving Jay into the catacombs under the island where he becomes a latter day Theseus, attempting to elude a Minotaur and determine who is killing the guests and why.

Other books you might like:
Michael Green, *The Jimjams*, 1994
Michael T. Hinkemeyer, *Order of the Arrow*, 1989
Stephen Laws, *Daemonic*, 1995
Richard Laymon, *Midnight's Lair*, 1988
Brian Lumley, *The House of Doors*, 1990

1525

BILL FAWCETT, Editor

Cats in Space and Other Places

(New York: Baen, 1992)

Story type: Science Fiction (Anthology)

Summary: Divided into two sections, "Cats" and "Alien Cats," this volume contains 17 stories, most reprinted from periodicals and anthologies 1939-1991, with two stories by Cordwainer Smith, "The Game of Rat and Dragon" and "The Ballad of Lost C'Mell" and two by Fritz Leiber, "Ship of Shadows" and "Space-Time for Springers." One story, "Chanur's Homecoming," first appeared as chapter twelve of C.J. Cherryh's *Chanur's Homecoming* (1986). Other influential stories include "Mouse" by Fredric Brown and "Black Destroyer" by A.E. van Vogt. Other authors include Greg Bear, Arthur C. Clarke, David Drake, Robert A. Heinlein, Ursula K. Le Guin, Anne McCaffrey and S.M. Stirling.

Other books you might like:
Clare Bell, *Clan Ground*, 1984
C.J. Cherryh, *The Pride of Chanur*, 1982
Alan Dean Foster, *Cat-A-Lyst*, 1991
Robert A. Heinlein, *The Door into Summer*, 1957

Andre Norton, *Catfantastic*, 1989
  Martin H. Greenberg, co-editor
Michael Peak, *Cat House*, 1989
Mark E. Rogers, *The Adventures of Samurai Cat*, 1984
Cordwainer Smith, *The Best of Cordwainer Smith*, 1975
Marti Steussy, *Forest of the Night*, 1987

1526

BILL FAWCETT, Editor

Honor of the Regiment

(New York: Baen, 1993)

Story type: Science Fiction (Anthology; Alternate Intelligence)
Series: Bolo
Time period(s): Indeterminate Future
Locale(s): Earth; Planet—Imaginary

Summary: Contains eight original stories by 10 authors providing glimpses into the history and evolution of Bolos, heavily armed and armored artificial intelligences built for human defense. Authors include Larry Dixon, David Drake, Mercedes Lackey, S.N. Lewitt, Barry N. Malzberg, Mike Resnick, Christopher Stasheff and S.M. Stirling.

Other books you might like:
Orson Scott Card, *Ender's Game*, 1985
David Drake, *The Fleet*, 1988
  Bill Fawcett, co-editor
David Drake, *Counter Attack*, 1988
  Bill Fawcett, co-editor
Keith Laumer, *Bolo: The Annals of the Dinochrome Brigade*, 1976
Keith Laumer, *The Complete Bolo*, 1990
Keith Laumer, *Rogue Bolo*, 1986
G. Harry Stine, *Warbots*, 1988
Jack Williamson, *The Humanoid Touch*, 1980

1527

GREGORY FEELEY

The Oxygen Barons

(New York: Ace, 1990)

Story type: Science Fiction (Hard Science Fiction; Political)
Major character(s): Galvanix Nagashima, Scientist; Beryl, Warrior
Time period(s): Indeterminate Future
Locale(s): Tycho South Shore, Moon (Earth's)

Summary: The moon had been in the process of developing a viable ecology with water sent from the asteroid belt and carbon dioxide sent from Venus, allowing free water and a breathable atmosphere to develop. In order to save the newly declared Lunar Republic, Galvanix and Beryl undertake a suicide mission to pulverize the last water ice comet before it hits the moon. This is the author's first book.

Other books you might like:
Roger MacBride Allen, *The Ring of Charon*, 1990
Greg Bear, *Eon*, 1986
David Brin, *Earth*, 1990

Vonda N. McIntyre, *Transition*, 1990
Vonda N. McIntyre, *Starfarers*, 1989
Larry Niven, *The Smoke Ring*, 1987
Larry Niven, *The Integral Trees*, 1984

1528

HILA FEIL

Blue Moon

(New York: Atheneum, 1990)

Story type: Fantasy (Contemporary; Young Adult)
Major character(s): Julia, Child-Care Giver, Teenager; Molly, Child; Sean, Artist
Time period(s): 1990s
Locale(s): Cape Cod, Massachusetts

Summary: Molly's stepmother, soap opera writer Cheryl, is ready to make some changes in the home of Molly's dead mother Maria, another artist whose ghost Molly believes is present.

Other books you might like:
C.S. Adler, *Ghost Brother*, 1990
Ruth Arthur, *The Autumn People*, 1973
Avi, *Something Upstairs: A Tale of Ghosts*, 1988
Madeleine L'Engle, *The Moon by Night*, 1963

1529

DAVID FEINTUCH

Challenger's Hope

(New York: Warner Aspect, 1995)

Story type: Science Fiction (Military; Alternate Intelligence)
Series: Nicholas Seafort Saga
Major character(s): Nicholas Seafort, Military Personnel; Philip Tyre, Military Personnel (midshipman), Spaceman
Time period(s): 22nd century (2197-2198)
Locale(s): Outer Space

Summary: New to command, Nicholas Seafort first faces an alien attack, then plague. On a hopeless rescue mission, he must overcome emergencies and pull together a functioning crew from passengers.

Other books you might like:
F.M. Busby, *Slow Freight*, 1991
A. Bertram Chandler, *The Big Black Mark*, 1975
C.J. Cherryh, *Tripoint*, 1994
Margaret Davis, *Mind Light*, 1993
Paula E. Downing, *Flare Star*, 1992
Robert A. Heinlein, *Starman Jones*, 1953
David Gerrold, *Voyage of the Star Wolf*, 1990
Norman Spinrad, *The Void Captain's Tale*, 1983

1530

DAVID FEINTUCH

Fisherman's Hope

(New York: Warner Aspect, 1996)

Story type: Science Fiction (Military; Political)

Series: Nicholas Seafort Saga
Major character(s): Nicholas Seafort, Military Personnel; Edgar "Eddie" Tolliver, Military Personnel (aide-de-camp)
Time period(s): 23rd century (2201)
Locale(s): Earth; Moon (Earth's); Outer Space

Summary: Assigned command of the Space Academy at Devon and at Farside on the Moon, Nicholas Seafort reminisces about his own days at the Academy. While Seafort learns to navigate amidst political rivalries to gain even minimum appropriations, alien warships arrive in the Solar System, attacking Earth with only Seafort and his cadets to save the day. Fourth in the series.

Other books you might like:
Poul Anderson, *Ensign Flandry*, 1966
Lois McMaster Bujold, *The Vor Game*, 1990
F.M. Busby, *Star Rebel*, 1984
A. Bertram Chandler, *The Big Black Mark*, 1975
David Gerrold, *A Matter for Men*, 1983
Robert A. Heinlein, *Space Cadet*, 1948
Jerry Pournelle, *Prince of Mercenaries*, 1989
Harry Turtledove, *Worldwar: In the Balance*, 1994
Timothy Zahn, *Cobra*, 1985

1531

DAVID FEINTUCH

Midshipman's Hope

(New York: Warner Aspect, 1994)

Story type: Science Fiction (Military)
Series: Nicholas Seafort Saga
Major character(s): Nicholas Seafort, Military Personnel; Vax Holser, Military Personnel
Time period(s): 22nd century (2194-2195)
Locale(s): *U.N.S. Hibernia*, Spaceship; Outer Space; Hope Nation, Planet—Imaginary

Summary: When *Hibernia*'s captain dies of illness, Midshipman Seafort becomes her new captain, and is quickly challenged by unexpected difficulties including the attempted pirating of the ship.

Other books you might like:
Lois McMaster Bujold, *The Warrior's Apprentice*, 1986
F.M. Busby, *The Demu Trilogy*, 1980
Debra Doyle, *The Price of the Stars*, 1992
    James D. Macdonald, co-author
Sherwood Smith, *The Phoenix in Flight*, 1993
    Dave Trowbridge, co-author
David Weber, *On Basilisk Station*, 1993

1532

DAVID FEINTUCH

Voices of Hope

(New York: Warner Aspect, 1996)

Story type: Science Fiction (Political; Dystopian)
Series: Nicholas Seafort Saga

Major character(s): Philip Seafort, Genius, Child; Jared Tenere, Computer Expert, Runaway; Pook, Streetperson, Kidnapper
Time period(s): 23rd century (2229)
Locale(s): New York, New York

Summary: When Jared, a rebellious and spoiled teenager, runs away from home, he plans to sell his story to a scandal sheet, but ends up on the squalid, dangerous streets of New York among the trannies—the transients. Philip Seafort, son of ex-SecGen Seafort, thinks he knows where to find Jared and follows him. As Jared and Philip's parents search for the boys, Jared gets revenge by using his computer skills to help the trannies bring down the towers of the wealthy Uppies, escalating a "rumble" into full-scale class war.

Other books you might like:
Algis Budrys, *Some Will Not Die*, 1978
Emma Bull, *Bone Dance*, 1991
William Gibson, *Virtual Light*, 1993
Robert A. Heinlein, *Citizen of the Galaxy*, 1957
Amy Thomson, *Virtual Girl*, 1993

1533

RAYMOND E. FEIST

The King's Buccaneer

(New York: Doubleday Foundation, 1992)

Story type: Fantasy (Adventure; Young Adult)
Series: Riftwar
Major character(s): Nicholas, Royalty (prince), Teenager; Harry, Companion (squire)
Time period(s): Indeterminate
Locale(s): Novindus, Mythical Place; Midkemia, Mythical Place; Kelewan, Planet—Imaginary

Summary: Sent to his uncle, the Duke of Crydee, to learn about the responsibility that accompanies his privileged position, Prince Nicholas must grow up quickly when enemies invade Castle Crydee and kidnap his heartthrob. Nicholas leads a rescue mission to the pirates' stronghold to foil his family's enemies and rescue Lady Abigail, the object of both Nicholas's and Harry's affection.

Other books you might like:
M.A.R. Barker, *Flamesong*, 1985
M.A.R. Barker, *Man of Gold*, 1984
David Eddings, *Magician's Gambit*, 1983
David Eddings, *Pawn of Prophecy*, 1982
David Eddings, *Queen of Sorcery*, 1982
Janny Wurts, *The Master of Whitestorm*, 1992

1534

RAYMOND E. FEIST
JANNY WURTS, Co-Author

Mistress of the Empire

(New York: Doubleday Foundation, 1992)

Story type: Fantasy (Political)
Series: Empire Trilogy
Major character(s): Mara, Royalty (House Acoma)

Time period(s): Indeterminate
Locale(s): Kelewan, Planet—Imaginary

Summary: Tragedy rocks Mara's secure and happy marriage when her oldest son dies at the hands of an assassin. Mara engages in battle with magicians and others as she attempts to gain safety for her family.

Other books you might like:
M.A.R. Barker, *Flamesong*, 1985
M.A.R. Barker, *Man of Gold*, 1984
Janny Wurts, *Keeper of the Keys*, 1988
Janny Wurts, *The Master of Whitestorm*, 1992
Janny Wurts, *Shadowfane*, 1988
Janny Wurts, *Stormwarden*, 1984

1535

RAYMOND E. FEIST

Prince of the Blood

(New York: Doubleday, 1989)

Story type: Fantasy (Adventure)
Series: Riftwar
Major character(s): Borric, Royalty (Prince); Erland, Royalty (Prince)
Time period(s): Indeterminate
Locale(s): Krondor, Planet—Imaginary; Kesh, Planet—Imaginary

Summary: Set in the same world as *The Riftwar Saga*, the story follows the adventures of Borric and Erland, twin sons of Arutha. The twins, twenty years old, travel to Kesh on a diplomatic mission, but Borric is kidnapped and Erland must continue on his own.

Other books you might like:
Barbara Hambly, *The Time of the Dark*, 1984
Melanie Rawn, *Dragon Prince*, 1988
Janny Wurts, *Stormwarden*, 1988

1536

RAYMOND E. FEIST

Rise of a Merchant Prince

(New York: Morrow, 1995)

Story type: Fantasy (Political)
Series: Serpentwar Saga
Major character(s): Rupert ''Roo'' Avery, Businessman; Erik von Darkmoor, Military Personnel, Nobleman
Time period(s): Indeterminate
Locale(s): Midkemia, Fictional Country; Krondor, Mythical Place

Summary: Through a dimensional breach serpentine Sauur invade and begin their ruthless conquest of Midkemia. Erik feels he best serves the Empire as a soldier, while his lifelong friend, Roo, sees the opportunity for power and profit as a merchant. While luck and a timely marriage provide a quick rise in business, Roo's passions may lead to his personal downfall and disaster for all.

Other books you might like:
M.A.R. Barker, *Flamesong*, 1985
M.A.R. Barker, *Man of Gold*, 1984
David Eddings, *Pawn of Prophecy*, 1982
Robert Jordan, *The Eye of the World*, 1990
Tad Williams, *The Dragonbone Chair*, 1988

1537

RAYMOND E. FEIST
JANNY WURTS, Co-Author

Servant of the Empire

(New York: Doubleday Foundation, 1990)

Story type: Fantasy (Political; Romance)
Series: Empire Trilogy
Major character(s): Mara, Royalty (House Acoma); Desio, Royalty (House Minwanabi)
Time period(s): Indeterminate
Locale(s): Kelewan, Planet—Imaginary

Summary: Mara, having demonstrated her political prowess in the Great Game of the Tsurani Court, faces a blood feud with Lord Desio. Mara must deal with magic, murder and treachery before the battle between House Acoma and House Minwanabi is decided.

Other books you might like:
M.A.R. Barker, *Flamesong*, 1985
M.A.R. Barker, *Man of Gold*, 1984

1538

RAYMOND E. FEIST

Shadow of a Dark Queen

(New York: William Morrow, 1994)

Story type: Fantasy (Adventure; Quest)
Series: Serpentwar Saga
Major character(s): Erik von Darkmoor, Bastard Son, Fugitive; Rupert ''Roo'' Avery, Fugitive; Calis, Mercenary, Mythical Creature (elf)
Time period(s): Indeterminate
Locale(s): Krondor, Fictional City; Novindus, Fictional Country; Midkemia, Mythical Place

Summary: Erik works as an apprentice blacksmith, hoping one day to have his own smithy. When a quarrel with his half-brother leads to murder, Erik and his friend flee their birthplace. Caught and convicted, they escape execution in exchange for accepting a secret mission against the invading serpent men of Pantathia.

Other books you might like:
Stephen R. Donaldson, *The Illearth War*, 1977
David Eddings, *Pawn of Prophecy*, 1982
Barbara Hambly, *The Time of the Dark*, 1982
Robert Jordan, *The Eye of the World*, 1989
Tad Williams, *The Dragonbone Chair*, 1988

1539

CYNTHIA FELICE

Iceman

(New York: Ace, 1991)

Story type: Science Fiction (Political; Romance)
Major character(s): Jacinta Renya, Noblewoman, Government Official (Corps of Means); Michael Jivar, Government Official (Corps of Means); Ramon Santos, Nobleman
Time period(s): 45th century (Ice Age)
Locale(s): Earth

Summary: Jacinta Renya, a Ballendian aristocrat, serves in the Corps of Means. After a shuttle crash on frozen Earth, she is saved by Michael Jivar, an Earthman serving in the Corps. When Jacinta's uncle pushes the two into a marriage to advance his political career, Jacinta goes along with it, not knowing Michael's main mission is to destroy the House of Santos.

Other books you might like:
Poul Anderson, *The Night Face*, 1978
Johanna Bolton, *Mission: Tori*, 1990
Lois McMaster Bujold, *Barrayar*, 1991
Lois McMaster Bujold, *Shards of Honor*, 1986
Anne McCaffrey, *Restoree*, 1967
C.J. Mills, *Kit's Book*, 1991

1540

CYNTHIA FELICE

The Khan's Persuasion

(New York: DAW, 1991)

Story type: Science Fiction (Romance; Adventure)
Major character(s): Sindon Liang, Linguist; Rukmani Khan, Chieftain, Empath; David Quarrels, Engineer, Fiance(e) (former)
Time period(s): Indeterminate Future
Locale(s): Cestry Prime, Planet—Imaginary

Summary: Rukmani Khan kidnaps Sindon Liang and tries to get her to forget her own people and stay with him because of his greater sexual powers. David Quarrels comes after Sindon hoping to rescue her while Rukmani Khan is equally determined to keep her. David finally wins out as Rukmani Khan cannot stand to be physically impaired and commits suicide.

Other books you might like:
Octavia E. Butler, *Survivor*, 1978
L. Sprague de Camp, *The Virgin of Zesh*, 1983
L. Sprague de Camp, *The Prisoner of Zhamanak*, 1982
Mary Gentle, *Golden Witchbreed*, 1984
Raymond Harris, *Shadows of the White Sun*, 1988

1541

LIONEL FENN (Pseudonym of Charles L. Grant)

668: The Neighbor of the Beast

(New York: Ace, 1992)

Story type: Horror (Satire)

Series: Kent Montana
Major character(s): Kent Montana, Actor, Laird; Chita Juarel, Young Woman; Howmaster Maclemmon, Businessman
Time period(s): 1990s (1992)
Locale(s): Hamtucket, New Hampshire

Summary: In this spoof of the writing of H. P. Lovecraft, actor-buffoon Kent Montana agrees to fulfill the terms of an inheritance left him by unscrupulous businessman Howmaster Maclemmon by spending the night in Maclemmon's former home in Hamtucket. Unknown to Montana, the house is the meeting place of cultists who plan to sacrifice him during a ritual described in the *Bingonomicron* for summoning the extra-dimensional deity Bog-Muggoth.

Other books you might like:
Christopher Moore, *Practical Demonkeeping*, 1992

1542

LIONEL FENN (Pseudonym of Charles L. Grant)

Kent Montana and the Really Ugly Thing From Mars

(New York: Ace, 1990)

Story type: Science Fiction (Parody; Invasion of Earth)
Series: Kent Montana
Major character(s): Kent Montana, Actor, Laird; Chita Juarel, Waiter/Waitress; Nicodemus Hooker, Scientist
Time period(s): 1990s (1990)
Locale(s): New Jersey

Summary: IT came from Mars and crashed near Gander Pond, New Jersey. Nothing can stop IT. Not the Army. Not the Scientist. Not the Preacher. Only Kent Montana, unemployed actor and Scottish Laird, can save the Earth. A pastiche of every invasion from outer space movie.

Other books you might like:
Douglas Adams, *The Hitchhiker's Guide to the Galaxy*, 1980
Douglas Adams, *Life, the Universe, and Everything*, 1982
Douglas Adams, *The Restaurant at the End of the Universe*, 1980
Douglas Adams, *So Long, and Thanks for All the Fish*, 1984
Ben Bova, *The Starcrossed*, 1975
John M. Ford, *How Much for Just the Planet?*, 1987 Star Trek #36
David Langford, *The Leaky Establishment*, 1984
John T. Sladek, *Mechasm*, 1968

1543

LIONEL FENN (Pseudonym of Charles L. Grant)

Kent Montana and the Reasonably Invisible Man

(New York: Ace, 1991)

Story type: Science Fiction (Parody)
Series: Kent Montana
Major character(s): Kent Montana, Actor, Laird; Janice Plase, Police Officer; Lizzy Howgath, Librarian
Time period(s): 1990s

Locale(s): Merkleton, England

Summary: When Kent Montana, out-of-work actor and Scottish laird, is first hit over the head by a mostly-invisible assailant, he does not recognize the sinister plot unfolding. A mad scientist, who is also an unemployed musician, has found a formula that makes him almost completely invisible and now plans to take his revenge on Kent Montana and the public at large. This novel is a pastiche of the mad scientist, "B" movie genre.

Other books you might like:
Douglas Adams, *Dirk Gently's Holistic Detective Agency*, 1987
Douglas Adams, *The Long Dark Tea-Time of the Soul*, 1988
Daniel Da Cruz, *Mixed Doubles*, 1989
Harry Harrison, *Bill, the Galactic Hero*, 1965
John T. Sladek, *Mechasm*, 1968

1544

LIONEL FENN (Pseudonym of Charles L. Grant)

The Mark of the Moderately Vicious Vampire
(New York: Ace, 1989)

Story type: Horror (Satire; Vampire Story)
Major character(s): Kent Montana, Actor, Laird; Roxanne Lott, Young Woman; Count Lamar de la von Zaguar, Vampire, Nobleman (count)
Time period(s): 1990s (1992)
Locale(s): Assyria, Maine

Summary: When people begin dying and coming back from the dead in the beachfront community of Assyria, the townsfolk go on the lookout for a vampire. Because his eccentricities immediately raise suspicions, visting actor Kent Montana is forced to track down the real vampire in order to clear his own name.

Other books you might like:
John Peyton Cooke, *Out for Blood*, 1991
Stephen King, *Salem's Lot*, 1975

1545

LIONEL FENN (Pseudonym of Charles L. Grant)

Time: The Semi-Final Frontier
(New York: Ace, 1994)

Story type: Science Fiction (Time Travel)
Series: Diego
Major character(s): Diego, Gunfighter, Time Traveller; Dirk Winslow, Military Personnel; Angel Lecotta, Revolutionary, Time Traveller
Time period(s): 26th century
Locale(s): *CISS Angus*, Spaceship; Gannet, Planet—Imaginary

Summary: The Fate of the Universe rests in the competent hands of Captain Dirk Winslow, proud representative of the Conglomeration of Independent Space States. The man they call Diego just wants to return to his own time, 1880, although

the incompetence of Virgil, who created the Time Thing, and Molly, who drives it, may very well make this impossible. But first they must join forces against the dreaded Space Avenger.

Other books you might like:
Douglas Adams, *The Hitchhiker's Guide to the Galaxy*, 1980
John M. Ford, *How Much for Just the Planet?*, 1987
Larry Niven, *Fallen Angels*, 1991
    Jerry Pournelle, Michael Flynn, co-authors
Nick Pollotta, *Illegal Aliens*, 1989
    Phil Foglio, co-author
Patricia C. Wrede, *Sorcery and Cecelia*, 1988
    Caroline Severmer, co-author

1546

BRAD FERGUSON

A Flag Full of Stars
(New York: Pocket, 1991)

Story type: Science Fiction (Space Opera)
Series: Star Trek
Major character(s): James T. Kirk, Spaceship Captain (Starfleet admiral); G'Dath, Alien (Klingon), Scientist (physicist); Kevin Riley, Military Personnel (Starfleet lieutenant commander)
Time period(s): 23rd century
Locale(s): San Francisco, California; New York, New York; Earth

Summary: Kirk's new life changes when he meets Klingon scientist G'Dath who has made an important discovery which could mean either tremendous strides in Federation technology or Klingon subjugation of countless worlds. This book is a sequel to J.M. Dillard's *The Lost Years*.

Other books you might like:
James Blish, *Spock Must Die*, 1970
J.M. Dillard, *The Lost Years*, 1989
Diane Duane, *Doctor's Orders*, 1990
    Star Trek 50
John M. Ford, *The Final Reflection*, 1984
    Star Trek 16
John M. Ford, *How Much for Just the Planet?*, 1987
    Star Trek 16
Barbara Hambly, *Ishmael*, 1985
    Star Trek 23

1547

BRAD FERGUSON

The Last Stand
(New York: Pocket, 1995)

Story type: Science Fiction (First Contact; Space Opera)
Series: Star Trek: The Next Generation
Major character(s): Jean-Luc Picard, Spaceship Captain, Military Personnel; Data, Military Personnel (lieutenant commander), Android; Deanna Troi, Psychologist, Alien (Betazoid)
Time period(s): 24th century

Locale(s): Nem Ma'ak Bratuna, Planet—Imaginary; *U.S.S. Enterprise*, Spaceship

Summary: On a routine stellar mapping mission, the *Enterprise* encounters a warp field pulse in an uncharted system. Investigating, Picard finds a civilization preparing to defend itself from an attack by enemies who have held a grudge for 6,000 years. Picard offers his services as negotiator to avert war, while Riker and Troi reconnoiter the invading ships and Data and Ro investigate the planet, where they find some puzzling inconsistencies.

Other books you might like:
Nathan Archer, *Ragnarok*, 1995
C.J. Cherryh, *The Faded Sun: Kutath*, 1979
Gene DeWeese, *Chain of Attack*, 1987
Ursula K. Le Guin, *The Dispossessed*, 1974
Barbara Paul, *The Three-Minute Universe*, 1988

1548
BRAD FERGUSON

The World Next Door
(New York: Tor, 1990)

Story type: Science Fiction (Alternate Universe; Post-Nuclear Holocaust)
Major character(s): Jake Garfield, Minstrel, Wanderer; Prosper Cross, Minstrel, Wanderer; Digger Digby, Mountain Man
Time period(s): 21st century
Locale(s): Adirondack Mountains, New York; McAndrew, New York

Summary: The few survivors of 1962's nuclear World War III have been rebuilding their meager world for decades. Suddenly the citizens of McAndrew begin having strange dreams of things only the oldest remember—televisions, computers, electricity. Another Earth is close by and the walls between the two are dissolving as nuclear holocaust threatens once again. Jake Garfield and Prosper Cross help to solve the mystery and keep the town from being overrun by war.

Other books you might like:
Jerry Ahern, *The Struggle*, 1989
David Brin, *The Postman*, 1984
Jerry Earl Brown, *Earthfall*, 1990
Octavia E. Butler, *Dawn*, 1987
David Mace, *Firelance*, 1989

1549
BRUCE FERGUSSON

The Mace of Souls
(New York: Morrow, 1989)

Story type: Fantasy (Quest)
Major character(s): Falca Breks, Thief (Extortionist); Amala Damarr, Noblewoman (Falca's Lover)
Time period(s): Indeterminate
Locale(s): Six Kingdoms, Fictional Country

Summary: A Spiritlifter captures Amala's soul in his crystal mace and she is devoid of personality. The story is about Falca's quest to regain and return Amala's soul.

Other books you might like:
Charles de Lint, *Westlin Wind*, 1989
Alfred Tella, *Sundered Soul*, 1990

1550
KEITH FERRARIO

Deadly Friend
(New York: Leisure, 1994)

Story type: Horror (Ghost Story; Supernatural Vengeance)
Major character(s): Peter Cowal, Child; Bobby Cowal, Child; Amanda Collins, Paranormal Investigator
Time period(s): 1990s (1994)
Locale(s): Fulton, Ohio

Summary: A bunch of malicious high school students hound young Bobby Cowal to his death, unaware that Bobby's "imaginary" playmate, Georgie, is the ghost of a young boy with a long history of exacting vengeance against those who upset him.

Other books you might like:
Anne Dillard, *Specters*, 1991
Stephen King, *Carrie*, 1974
Abigail McDaniels, *The Uprising*, 1994
Jean Simon, *Ghost Boy*, 1994

1551
DAVID FERRING

Konrad
(Baltimore, Maryland: GW Books/Games Workshop, 1990)

Story type: Fantasy (Adventure; Quest)
Series: Warhammer: Warblade
Major character(s): Konrad, Servant; Wolf, Mercenary; Elyssa, Sorceress
Time period(s): 16th century
Locale(s): Alternate Earth

Summary: Konrad, an abused orphan involved in a forbidden affair with his Lord's daughter, flees his home when it is destroyed by monsters. He becomes the squire of a cynical wanderer and learns how to survive in a hostile world.

Other books you might like:
Adrian Cole, *A Place Among the Fallen*, 1986
Glen Cook, *The Black Company*, 1984
Michael Moorcock, *Elric of Melnibone*, 1976
Michael Shea, *Nifft the Lean*, 1982
Jack Yeovil, *Drachenfels*, 1990
  Pseudonym of Kim Newman

1552

DAVID FERRING

Shadowbreed

(Baltimore, Maryland: GW Books/Games Workshop, 1990)

Story type: Fantasy (Adventure)
Series: Warhammer: Warblade
Major character(s): Konrad, Warrior; Kastring, Warrior; Litzenreich, Sorcerer
Time period(s): 16th century
Locale(s): Alternate Earth

Summary: Konrad's story continues as he is taken prisoner by a chaos cult and begins to learn about his possible destiny. Escaping, he falls in with an eccentric wizard, and discovers a plot that threatens every level of his society.

Other books you might like:
Scott Baker, *Drink the Fire From the Flames*, 1987
Glen Cook, *The Black Company*, 1984
Michael Moorcock, *Elric of Melnibone*, 1976
Michael Shea, *Nifft the Lean*, 1982
Jack Yeovil, *Drachenfels*, 1990
   Pseudonym of Kim Newman

1553

FREDERICK FICHMAN

SETI

(New York: Roc, 1990)

Story type: Science Fiction (First Contact)
Major character(s): Sam Alexander, Radio (technician), Student—High School
Time period(s): 1990s
Locale(s): Escondita, California

Summary: Even as a small child, Sam Alexander was a radio genius with a strong interest in NASA's SETI (Search for Extraterrestrial Intelligence) project where his father worked. When his parents' plane disappeared, Sam's interest intensified. As his Aunt Marion and Uncle Stu allowed him to control his inheritance, he could afford the necessary equipment, but when his patience is rewarded, who should be told?

Other books you might like:
Orson Scott Card, *Wyrms*, 1987
Alan Dean Foster, *Quozl*, 1989
David R. Palmer, *Emergence*, 1984
Garfield Reeves-Stevens, *Nighteyes*, 1989
Rebecca Ore, *Becoming Alien*, 1988

1554

MORGAN FIELDS

Shaman Woods

(New York: Zebra, 1990)

Story type: Horror (Ancient Evil Unleashed)
Major character(s): Worth Martin, Child; Paul Martin, Teacher, Parent (Worth's father); Zacxk White Eagle, Indian, Shaman

Time period(s): 1990s (1990)
Locale(s): Agate Creek, California

Summary: Four-and-a-half centuries after a devastating battle between the Shoshone Indians and Spanish conquistadors, a lumber company harvests the forest that has grown up on the battlefield, liberating the bloodthirsty spirits who inhabit it.

Other books you might like:
Douglas Clegg, *Goat Dance*, 1989
Chet Williamson, *Dreamthorp*, 1989

1555

MEG FILES

Meridian 144

(New York: Soho Press, 1991)

Story type: Science Fiction (Post-Nuclear Holocaust; Literary)
Major character(s): Kitty Manning, Teacher; Norio Onoda, Tourist; Rogelio Torres, Student
Time period(s): 1990s
Locale(s): Tano Island, Pacific Islands

Summary: While exploring a sunken ship, Kitty survived the fireball and shockwave which wrought destruction on Tano Island. She left her shelter after several days to rescue her dog. Although it seemed that she was the only living thing on the island, within a few days the vegetation showed some green and Kitty noticed evidence of at least one other living person. This is the author's first novel.

Other books you might like:
Octavia E. Butler, *Dawn*, 1987
Gordon R. Dickson, *Wolf and Iron*, 1990
J.M. Morgan, *Desert Eden*, 1991
Elizabeth Ann Scarborough, *Nothing Sacred*, 1991
Catherine Wells, *The Earth Is All That Lasts*, 1991
Kate Wilhelm, *Margaret and I*, 1971
Kate Wilhelm, *Where Late the Sweet Birds Sang*, 1976

1556

SHEILA FINCH

Shaper's Legacy

(New York: Bantam Spectra, 1989)

Story type: Science Fiction (Genetic Manipulation)
Series: Shaper Exile
Major character(s): Beryt, Royalty; ReAth, Nobleman
Time period(s): Indeterminate Future
Locale(s): Beta Orbis IV, Planet—Imaginary

Summary: Five hundred years ago the Venn bioengineers came to Beta Orbis IV with stolen human germ plasma and created three artificial races. Now two of those races, the intelligent Ganu and the shape-shifting Liani, have united to form one nation and have overthrown the immortal Venn. Complex political and military intrigue is a given, however, and the Venn continue their genetic manipulation in secret.

Other books you might like:
Marion Zimmer Bradley, *The Heritage of Hastur*, 1975
Mary Gentle, *Ancient Light*, 1989

Mary Gentle, *Golden Witchbreed*, 1983
Daniel Keys Moran, *Emerald Eyes*, 1987
Robert Reed, *Black Milk*, 1989

1557

SHEILA FINCH

Shaping the Dawn
(New York: Bantam Books, 1989)

Story type: Science Fiction (Genetic Manipulation)
Series: The Shaper Exile
Major character(s): Rivi, Young Woman; Tagak, Scientist
Time period(s): Indeterminate Future
Locale(s): Beta Orbis IV, Planet—Imaginary

Summary: The struggle for control continues on Beta Orbis IV. The Biblists, mutant religious fanatics, come to the planet to destroy the Venn scientists. Meanwhile, Rivi, a troubled young woman, loses two lovers, travels across the planet, faces many dangers, and finds a higher destiny than she had ever thought possible.

Other books you might like:
Marion Zimmer Bradley, *The Heritage of Hastur*, 1975
Mary Gentle, *Ancient Light*, 1989
Mary Gentle, *Golden Witchbreed*, 1983
Daniel Keys Moran, *Emerald Eyes*, 1987
Robert Reed, *Black Milk*, 1989

1558

NIGEL FINDLEY

2XS
(New York: Roc, 1992)

Story type: Fantasy (Mystery; Science Fiction)
Series: Shadowrun
Major character(s): Derek Montgomery, Detective; Jacques Barnard, Wizard, Businessman
Time period(s): 2050s (2052)
Locale(s): Seattle, Washington

Summary: Dirk Montgomery, wrongly implicated in a murder, searches to find the murderer and the connection between the addictive computer chip, 2XS, and a product manufactured by a legitimate business, Yamatetsu Corporation. Life becomes more difficult when Yamatetsu's Senior Vice President, Jacques Barnard, notices Dirk's interest.

Other books you might like:
Pat Cadigan, *Mindplayers*, 1987
Robert N. Charrette, *Choose Your Enemies Carefully*, 1990
Robert N. Charrette, *Find Your Own Truth*, 1991
Robert N. Charrette, *Never Deal with a Dragon*, 1990
Glen Cook, *Sweet Silver Blues*, 1987
Mel Gilden, *Hawaiian U.F.O. Aliens*, 1991
Mel Gilden, *Surfing Samurai Robots*, 1988
Mel Gilden, *Tubular Android Superheroes*, 1991
Brian Craig, *Ghost Dancers*, 1991

1559

NIGEL FINDLEY

House of the Sun
(New York: Roc, 1995)

Story type: Science Fiction (Cyberpunk; Science Fantasy)
Series: Shadowrun
Major character(s): Gordon Ho, Royalty; Dirk Montgomery, Cyborg, Detective—Private (retired); Scott, Driver, Mythical Creature (ork)
Time period(s): 2050s (2055)
Locale(s): Cheyenne, Wyoming; Hawaii

Summary: Pulled out of retirement, Dirk Montgomery receives an easy mission to the Kingdom of Hawai'i. The easy mission starts well, goes bad, gets deadly, and proceeds downhill from there. Soon Dirk uncovers a plot so terrible that it frightens even Insect Spirits.

Other books you might like:
Emma Bull, *Bone Dance*, 1991
Pat Cadigan, *Synners*, 1991
Charles de Lint, *Svaha*, 1989
William Gibson, *Neuromancer*, 1984
Walter Jon Williams, *Voice of the Whirlwind*, 1987

1560

NIGEL FINDLEY

Into the Void
(Lake Geneva, Wisconsin: TSR, 1991)

Story type: Fantasy (Quest)
Series: Cloakmaster Cycle
Major character(s): Teldin Moore, Warrior; Aelfred Silverhorn, Mercenary; Estriss, Alien (Illithid), Telepath (mind flayer)
Time period(s): Indeterminate
Locale(s): *Probe*, Spaceship; Toril, Planet—Imaginary

Summary: In the quest to learn more about the cloak given him by a mortally wounded spelljammer, Teldin confides in Estriss, who senses magic-using ability in Teldin. As they travel to Toril, Estriss teaches Teldin what he can of the spelljamming basics. This sequel to David Cook's *Beyond the Moons* is set in the Spelljammer gaming milieu.

Other books you might like:
Damaris Cole, *Token of Dragonsblood*, 1991
David Cook, *Beyond the Moons*, 1991
Brian Daley, *Requiem for a Ruler of Worlds*, 1985
Alis A. Rasmussen, *The Price of Ransom*, 1990
Margaret Weis, *Dragon Wing*, 1990
   Tracy Hickman, co-author

1561

NIGEL FINDLEY

No Limits
(New York: Roc, 1996)

Story type: Science Fiction (Adventure)

Series: Virtual World
Major character(s): Samantha ''Sam'' Dooley, Pilot; Renard Gilbert, Warrior; Jared Bloch, Teacher, Military Personnel
Time period(s): 1990s; Indeterminate (Alternate Universe A.D. 3052)
Locale(s): Gold Beach, Oregon; Elsewhen, Cyberspace

Summary: Samantha Dooley leaves her granfather's deathbed wondering about the mystery of the Virtual Georgraphic League. Her search leads her to Elsewhen, a virtual world where she can exist in a desolate war zone of giant battle robots as the warrior she always wanted to be.

Other books you might like:
Iain M. Banks, *The Player of Games*, 1989
Robert N. Charrette, *Wolves on the Border*, 1989
Keith Laumer, *Bolo: The Annals of the Dinochrome Brigade*, 1976
G. Harry Stine, *Warbots*, 1988
Robert Thurston, *Robot Jox*, 1989

1562

TIMOTHY FINDLEY

Headhunter

(New York: Crown, 1994)

Story type: Horror (Psychological Suspense)
Major character(s): Lilah Kemp, Psychic (spiritualist); Rupert Kurtz, Doctor (psychiatrist); Charles Marlow, Doctor (psychiatrist)
Time period(s): 1990s (1994)
Locale(s): Toronto, Ontario, Canada

Summary: New to the Parkin Institute of Psychiatric Research, Doctor Charles Marlow discovers a ghastly plot by head psychiatrist Rupert Kurtz to cater to the perversions of his wealthy patients by controlling local youth with drugs and psychiatric techniques to turn them into therapeutic playthings.

Other books you might like:
John Edward Ames, *The Asylum*, 1994
Robin Cook, *Coma*, 1977
Kathe Koja, *Bad Brains*, 1992
Thomas Tessier, *The Dreams of Dr. Ladybank*, 1991
in *Night Visions 9*
F. Paul Wilson, *The Select*, 1994

1563

JON STEPHEN FINK

Further Adventures

(New York: St. Martin's Press, 1993)

Story type: Fantasy (Contemporary; Literary)
Major character(s): Reuven Agranovsky, Aged Person, Actor (radio); Amelia, Fugitive; Uncle Jake, Criminal, Fugitive
Time period(s): 1930s; 1990s
Locale(s): New York, New York

Summary: A mostly literate ex-radio actor contemplating suicide relates a strange and convoluted story which flips back

and forth between the past, when he secretly played the voice of The Green Ray, a radio hero, and the present, where he becomes involved in a strange kidnapping plot. First novel.

Other books you might like:
Lin Carter, *Invisible Death*, 1975
Tom De Haven, *Freak's Amour*, 1979
Philip Jose Farmer, *Doc Savage: His Apocalyptic Life*, 1973
Kenneth Robeson, *The Frightened Fish*, 1992
Grant Stockbridge, *The Spider #1: The Spider and the Pain Master/Secret City of Crime*, 1991

1564

JACK FINNEY (Pseudonym of Walter Braden Finney)

From Time to Time

(New York: Simon & Schuster, 1995)

Story type: Science Fiction (Time Travel; Alternate Universe)
Major character(s): Simon ''Si'' Morley, Time Traveller; E.E. Danziger, Scientist (physicist); Rube Prien, Military Personnel, Researcher
Time period(s): 1880s; 1990s
Locale(s): New York, New York

Summary: Happily settled in the New York City of 1888 with his wife, Julia, and young son, Willie, Si decides to return to the 1990s to check on the time travel project, now headed by Rube Prien. Convinced to return to 1912 despite Dr. Danziger's misgivings, Si attempts to prevent World War I. This sequel to *Time and Again* includes many photographs and illustrations of late 19th century and early 20th century New York City.

Other books you might like:
Poul Anderson, *The Time Patrol*, 1991
Gordon R. Dickson, *Time Storm*, 1977
Randall Frakes, *The Terminator*, 1985
Bill Wisher, co-author
Harry Turtledove, *The Guns of the South*, 1992
Connie Willis, *Doomsday Book*, 1992

1565

DAVID FISHER

Legally Correct Fairy Tales

(New York; Warner, 1996)

Story type: Fantasy (Collection; Legend)
Summary: Contains 14 familiar fairy tales and children's rhymes, humorously rewritten as if they form the basis for legal action. Includes ''Hansel and Gretel,'' ''Sleeping Beauty,'' ''Snow White,'' ''Pinocchio,'' ''Cinderella,'' ''Beauty and the Beast,'' ''Little Red Riding Hood,'' and ''Goldilocks.''

Other books you might like:
Margaret Atwood, *Good Bones and Simple Murders*, 1994
William J. Brooke, *Teller of Tales*, 1994
James Finn Garner, *Once upon a More Enlightened Time*, 1995
James Finn Garner, *Politically Correct Bedtime Stories*, 1994
James Finn Garner, *Politically Correct Holiday Stories*, 1995

1566

ERIC FLANDERS

The Forever Children

(New York: Zebra, 1992)

Story type: Horror (Science Fiction)
Major character(s): Warren Hubert Barry, Doctor; Dawn Henderson, Child; William Wesley, Child
Time period(s): 1990s
Locale(s): Jamay Lake, Indiana

Summary: To all outward appearances, Jamay Lake is an insular religious community that keeps to itself. In fact, the town is a huge experimental laboratory in which Dr. Warren Hubert Barry, the town's founder, strives to arrest the development of children between the ages of six and ten, in an effort to solve the world's overpopulation problem and help break the cycle of child abuse that comes from families having more children than they can reasonably hope to support.

Other books you might like:
Ira Levin, *The Stepford Wives*, 1972
John Saul, *Creature*, 1990
John Saul, *Darkness*, 1991

1567

ERIC FLANDERS

Night Blood

(New York: Zebra, 1993)

Story type: Horror (Vampire Story)
Major character(s): Val Romero, Vampire; Elaine Trent, Businesswoman; Jonathan Drew, Police Officer (FBI agent)
Time period(s): 1990s (1993)
Locale(s): Lansom, Texas

Summary: Footloose vampire Val Romero is tracked across the southwest by a group of different people whose lives have been adversely changed by contact with him. None are aware that their actions are being clandestinely observed and choreographed by a band of vampire hunters pursuing their own unusual agenda.

Other books you might like:
Peter Atkins, *Morningstar*, 1992
Poppy Z. Brite, *Lost Souls*, 1992
Ron Dee, *Blood Lust*, 1990
Ron Dee, *Dusk*, 1991
Gary L. Raisor, *Less than Human*, 1992

1568

ROBERT C. FLEET

Last Mountain

(New York: Ace, 1994)

Story type: Fantasy (Urban; Adventure)
Major character(s): Annunciata ''Nancy'' del Rio, Child; The Unicorn, Mythical Creature; Karus, Companion
Time period(s): 1990s; 16th century
Locale(s): Los Angeles, California; San Gabriel Mountains, California

Summary: Annunciata struggles to help unite the Unicorn with Karus, the Unicorn Rider, to bring a proper finale to the Unicorn's long life. However the Dreambreaker and other Border Patrol agents seek Annunicata for deportation.

Other books you might like:
Peter S. Beagle, *The Last Unicorn*, 1968
Bruce Coville, *The Unicorn Treasury*, 1988
  editor
John Lee, *The Unicorn Quest*, 1986
Tanith Lee, *Black Unicorn*, 1991
Jane Yolen, *Here There Be Unicorns*, 1994

1569

ROBERT C. FLEET

White Horse, Dark Dragon

(New York: Ace, 1993)

Story type: Fantasy (Contemporary; Adventure)
Major character(s): Jim Marlowe, Scientist; Frank Brown, Industrialist; Alta, Psychic
Time period(s): 1990s
Locale(s): Karistan, Fictional Country

Summary: Jim Marlowe travels to the small Balkan country of Karistan to prepare an environmental impact statement for a proposed mining project, a seemingly simple assignment. A local bureaucracy, a psychic, a blind woman, Marlowe's son and dog, and a dragon complicate matters. When the statement does not go as planned, mercenaries make the mystery a little more interesting. A first novel.

Other books you might like:
Emma Bull, *War for the Oaks*, 1987
Charles de Lint, *Moonheart: A Romance*, 1984
Tom Deitz, *Windmaster's Bane*, 1986
Guy Gavriel Kay, *The Summer Tree*, 1985
Michael Scott Rohan, *Chase the Morning*, 1991

1570

SID FLEISCHMAN

The Midnight Horse

(New York: Greenwillow, 1990)

Story type: Fantasy (Contemporary; Young Adult)
Major character(s): Great Chaffalo, Spirit, Magician; Touch, Orphan, Child
Time period(s): 1990s
Locale(s): Cricklewood, New Hampshire

Summary: On his way to meet his great uncle, Touch sees the Great Chaffalo for the first time. Later, when he is fleeing from his uncle, Touch convinces the ghost to change a bundle of straw into a horse for him. This is an ALA Best Books for Middle Readers title.

Other books you might like:
Alan Dean Foster, *Orphan Star*, 1977
Robert A. Heinlein, *Citizen of the Galaxy*, 1957

1571

SUSAN FLETCHER

Flight of the Dragon Kyn

(New York: Atheneum, 1993)

Story type: Fantasy (Quest; Young Adult)
Major character(s): Kara, Adventurer, Teenager
Time period(s): Indeterminate
Locale(s): Mythical Place

Summary: When Kara answers King Orrik's summons to help rid the kingdom of its dragon plague, Kara finds herself between the King and his brother in their power struggle. Kara's hazardous efforts in carrying out the King's orders take her into the dragons' lair where she suddenly recalls a previous visit. Prequel to *Dragon's Milk*.

Other books you might like:
Andre Norton, *Beast Master*, 1959
Andre Norton, *The Elvenbane*, 1992
  Mercedes Lackey, co-author
Vivian Vande Velde, *Dragon's Bait*, 1992
Patricia C. Wrede, *Dealing with Dragons*, 1990
Patricia C. Wrede, *Searching for Dragons*, 1991

1572

LYNN FLEWELLING

Luck in the Shadows

(New York: Bantam Spectra, 1996)

Story type: Fantasy (Magic Conflict; Political)
Series: Nightrunner
Major character(s): Alec of Kerry, Woodsman, Spy (Watcher); Nysander, Wizard (High Thaumaturgist), Spy (Watcher); Seregil, Spy (Watcher), Musician
Time period(s): Indeterminate
Locale(s): Rhiminee, Fictional City; Skala, Fictional Country

Summary: Seregil engineers Alec of Kerry's escape from captivity then, on a reconnaissance foray, steals a magic token which quickly renders him delusional then unconscious. With difficulty, Alec returns Seregil to Nysander who reverses the damage, recruits Alec as a spy and sets him to uncover the details of a plot to oust Skala's queen. First of a series.

Other books you might like:
Terry Goodkind, *Wizard's First Rule*, 1994
Robin Hobb, *Assassin's Apprentice*, 1995
J.V. Jones, *The Baker's Boy*, 1995
Mercedes Lackey, *Arrows of the Queen*, 1987
J.R.R. Tolkien, *The Fellowship of the Ring*, 1954
Paula Volsky, *Illusion*, 1992

1573

DENNY MARTIN FLINN

The Fearful Summons

(New York: Pocket, 1995)

Story type: Science Fiction (Space Opera)
Series: Star Trek

Major character(s): James T. Kirk, Spaceship Captain, Aged Person; Hikaru Sulu, Spaceship Captain; Maldari, Spaceship Captain, Alien (Thraxian)
Time period(s): 23rd century
Locale(s): *U.S.S. Enterprise*, Spaceship; Beta Prometheus, Planet—Imaginary; United Federation of Planets, Interstellar Empire/Federation

Summary: A Thraxian starship captain tricks Sulu and a landing party into coming aboard his vessel, then holds time hostage and demands advanced weaponry as ransom. When Federation negotiators refuse, Kirk and some of his former crew go to the rescue on board a borrowed space yacht.

Other books you might like:
Margaret Wander Bonanno, *Dwellers in the Crucible*, 1985
J.M. Dillard, *Recovery*, 1995
Michael Jan Friedman, *Legacy*, 1991
Vonda N. McIntyre, *Star Trek III: The Search for Spock*, 1984
Peter Morwood, *Rules of Engagement*, 1990

1574

KENNETH C. FLINT

Cromm

(New York: Doubleday, 1990)

Story type: Fantasy (Contemporary)
Major character(s): Colin McMahon, Artist (Graphic)
Time period(s): 1990s; 4th century
Locale(s): United States; Ireland

Summary: Colin's nightmares of a bloodthirsty 4th century Celtic god become all too real when he travels to Ireland, where the past and present merge into a dangerous adventure for him. He is forced to finish a fight in which his ancestor, another Colin, fought centuries ago. Explores Celtic folklore and mythology.

Other books you might like:
Clive Barker, *Weaveworld*, 1987
Lloyd Arthur Eshbach, *The Land Beyond the Gate*, 1988
R.A. MacAvoy, *The Book of Kells*, 1985
Keith Taylor, *The Cauldron of Plenty*, 1989
  The Damans, No. 2

1575

KENNETH C. FLINT

Legends Reborn

(New York: Bantam Spectra, 1992)

Story type: Fantasy (Quest; Urban)
Major character(s): Michael Kean, Businessman; Caitlin Bawn, Traveller, Immortal; Rury O'Mor, Chieftain, Immortal
Time period(s): 1990s
Locale(s): New York, New York (Manhattan); Ireland; Sidh, Mythical Place

Summary: While visiting Ireland, Michael Kean meets Caitlin Bawn in a glen where her world intersects the mortal realm. Excited by the difference of the mortal realm, Caitlin accompanies Michael, which brings Rury O'Mor to the mortal realm to find and return Caitlin to Sidh.

Other books you might like:
Gael Baudino, *Gossamer Axe*, 1990
Emma Bull, *War for the Oaks*, 1987
Charles de Lint, *Moonheart: A Romance*, 1984
Charles de Lint, *Spiritwalk*, 1992
Alan J. Lerner, *Brigadoon: A Musical Play in Two Acts*, 1947
Will Shetterly, *Elsewhere*, 1991
Terri Windling, *Life on the Border*, 1991
    Editor

1576

KENNETH C. FLINT

Otherworld

(New York: Bantam/Spectra, 1991)

Story type: Horror (Apocalyptic Horror)
Major character(s): Robert Cassiday, Government Official; Richard Jordan, Professor; Ann Archer, Teacher
Time period(s): 1990s
Locale(s): Denver, Colorado

Summary: Agent Robert Cassiday's investigation of the death of a friend at the hands of a mass murderer is repeatedly thwarted by annoying supernatural events. But Cassiday knows something his associates don't: that the tide of senseless violence increasing as we approach the millenium indicates forces from the supernatural Otherworld are threatening to break loose into our own.

Other books you might like:
Roger Elwood, *Sorcerers of Sodom*, 1991
Dan Simmons, *Carrion Comfort*, 1989

1577

CASEY FLYNN (Pseudonym of Kenneth C. Flint)

The Enchanted Isles

(New York: Bantam Spectra, 1991)

Story type: Fantasy (Legend; Quest)
Series: Gods of Ireland
Major character(s): Danu, Royalty (queen); Nuada, Leader, Immigrant; Dagda, Immigrant, Adventurer
Time period(s): Indeterminate Past
Locale(s): Ireland

Summary: Searching for a new homeland, the surviving people of Nemed arrive on a remote island where they receive succor and are told that they must acquire permission from Queen Danu to immigrate. On their dangerous journey to see Danu, the Nemedians are tested to see if they will be appropriate neighbors. This book is a sequel to *Most Ancient Song* (1991).

Other books you might like:
Marion Zimmer Bradley, *The Mists of Avalon*, 1983
Guy Gavriel Kay, *Tigana*, 1990
Patricia Kennealy, *The Silver Branch*, 1988
Morgan Llywelyn, *The Isles of the Blest*, 1989
Morgan Llywelyn, *Red Branch*, 1988

Ian McDonald, *King of Morning, Queen of Day*, 1991
Andrew J. Offutt, *Sword of the Gael*, 1975
Andrew J. Offutt, *When Death Birds Fly*, 1980
    Keith Taylor, co-author
Keith Taylor, *Bard*, 1981
Terri Windling, *Life on the Border*, 1991
    editor

1578

CASEY FLYNN (Pseudonym of Kenneth C. Flint)

Most Ancient Song

(New York: Bantam Spectra, 1991)

Story type: Fantasy (Legend; Quest)
Series: Gods of Ireland
Major character(s): Nuada, Leader, Immigrant; Dagda, Immigrant, Adventurer
Time period(s): Indeterminate Past
Locale(s): Ireland

Summary: Driven from home, the peaceful Nemedians have sailed in search of a new homeland. When they find a magnificent green isle, they decide to settle in the single beautiful valley they find ready for occupation. There they are attacked by the Formor, defenders of the new land who wield powerful magical devices. The Nemedians, unprepared for battle, are defended by strangers whose motives are unclear.

Other books you might like:
Marion Zimmer Bradley, *The Mists of Avalon*, 1983
Patricia Kennealy, *The Copper Crown*, 1984
Morgan Llywelyn, *Bard*, 1987
Morgan Llywelyn, *The Horse Goddess*, 1982
Michael Moorcock, *The Swords Trilogy*, 1977
Keith Taylor, *Bard*, 1981
Keith Taylor, *Search for the Starblade*, 1990
Keith Taylor, *The Sorcerer's Sacred Isle*, 1989
Evangeline Walton, *The Island of the Mighty*, 1970

1579

MICHAEL FLYNN

Firestar

(New York: Tor, 1996)

Story type: Science Fiction (Hard Science Fiction; Political)
Major character(s): Mariesa Gorley van Huyten, Heiress, Businesswoman; Barry Fast, Teacher; Ned DuBois, Astronaut
Time period(s): 1990s (1999); 2000s (2000-2007)
Locale(s): North Orange, New Jersey; Mir, Space Station

Summary: Dismayed by the government's failures in public education and space exploration, Mariesa van Huyten uses her inherited fortune to fund her personal education and space exploration dreams, battling corrupt government officials and saboteurs every step of the way.

Other books you might like:
Arthur C. Clarke, *Richter 10*, 1996
    Mike McQuay, co-author
G.C. Edmondson, *The Man Who Corrupted Earth*, 1980

Robert A. Heinlein, *Time Enough for Love*, 1973
Larry Niven, *Fallen Angels*, 1991
　Jerry Pournelle, Michael Flynn, co-authors
Charles Sheffield, *Higher Education*, 1996
　Jerry Pournelle, co-author
Charles Sheffield, *How to Save the World*, 1995
　editor

1580

MICHAEL FLYNN

The Nanotech Chronicles

(New York: Baen, 1991)

Story type: Science Fiction (Hard Science Fiction; Collection)
Major character(s): Pavel Denisovitch, Teacher
Time period(s): 21st century
Locale(s): L4, Space Station; Brazil; New York, New York

Summary: The six stories contained herein have been previously published in *Analog* and *New Destinies* magazines. The stories tie together as examples used by Pavel Denisovitch to explain development of nanotechnology necessary to life in orbiting space complexes. An urban arts theme runs through "Soul of the City," while "The Washer at the Ford" points out the necessity of radiation resistance to people in space. "Remember'd Kisses" presents one less benign aspect with horrifying overtones.

Other books you might like:
Octavia E. Butler, *Dawn*, 1987
Pat Cadigan, *Mindplayers*, 1987
Jeffrey A. Carver, *From a Changeling Star*, 1989
George Alec Effinger, *When Gravity Fails*, 1987
Robert L. Forward, *Rocheworld*, 1990
Janet Kagan, *Mirabile*, 1991
Rudy Rucker, *Wetware*, 1988
Marc Stiegler, *The Gentle Seduction*, 1990
Michael Swanwick, *Vacuum Flowers*, 1987

1581

JOHN FOGARTY

The Haunt

(New York: Popular Library, 1990)

Story type: Horror (Haunted House)
Major character(s): Mike O'Sullivan, Professor (Former); Mary McGiven, Girlfriend
Time period(s): 1990s
Locale(s): County Cork, Ireland (Puxley Estate)

Summary: Recovering from a traumatic encounter with a serial murderer, Mike O'Sullivan and his lover Mary McGiven, journey to Ireland to explore Puxley Estate, Mike's inherited estate. After they settle in, Mike becomes increasingly absorbed with the violent history of the surroundings and of his own family, until he can no longer distinguish between the real and the unreal, the past and the present, sanity and madness. This is Fogarty's first novel.

Other books you might like:
Stephen King, *The Shining*, 1977

1582

D.C. FONTANA

Vulcan's Glory

(New York: Pocket Book, 1989)

Story type: Science Fiction (Space Opera)
Series: Star Trek
Major character(s): Spock, Scientist, Alien; T'Pris, Alien
Time period(s): 23rd century (Prior to Mr. Spock's meeting Captai)
Locale(s): Vulcan, Planet—Imaginary; *U.S.S. Enterprise*, Spaceship

Summary: Mr. Spock falls in love with the Vulcan woman T'Pris who is then murdered. The killer must be brought to justice.

Other books you might like:
J.M. Dillard, *Star Trek: The Lost Years*, 1989
J.M. Dillard, *Star Trek V: The Final Frontier*, 1989
Julia Ecklar, *The Kobayashi Maru*, 1989
　Star Trek 47
Michael Jan Friedman, *Double, Double*, 1989
　Star Trek 45

1583

JOHN M. FORD

Growing Up Weightless

(New York: Bantam Spectra, 1993)

Story type: Science Fiction (Political; Young Adult)
Major character(s): Matthias "Matt" Ronay, Teenager, Adventurer
Time period(s): 21st century
Locale(s): Moon (Earth's)

Summary: Despite his parents' successes in politics and medicine, Matt feels constricted options as he pursues hobbies including theater, virtual reality gaming and Mazerunning with friends. On a surreptitious journey to the farside, Matt finds unexpected internal resources as he uncovers a plot hindering his father's water negotiations with Earth and rescues a Starship crew from a local fracas.

Other books you might like:
John Barnes, *A Million Open Doors*, 1992
John Barnes, *Orbital Resonance*, 1991
Robert A. Heinlein, *Podkayne of Mars*, 1963
Robert A. Heinlein, *The Rolling Stones*, 1952
Alis A. Rasmussen, *A Passage of Stars*, 1990
Allen Steele, *Clarke County, Space*, 1990
Allen Steele, *Lunar Descent*, 1991
John Varley, *Steel Beach*, 1992

1584

ELIZABETH FORREST

Dark Tide

(New York: DAW, 1993)

Story type: Horror (Ancient Evil Unleashed)

Major character(s): Parker Solomon, Businessman (real estate developer); Steve Rollie, Political Figure (vice mayor); Maggie Dunbar, Teacher
Time period(s): 1990s (1993)
Locale(s): Pacific Crest, California

Summary: When Parker Solomon returns to his hometown to help renovate its deteriorating ocean front, he must confront the sea entity that nearly stole his soul as a boy and that has since taken over many of the town's most prominent citizens to do its bidding.

Other books you might like:
Matthew J. Costello, *Beneath Still Waters*, 1989
Dean Wesley Smith, *Laying the Music to Rest*, 1989

1585

ELIZABETH FORREST

Killjoy

(New York: DAW, 1996)

Story type: Horror (Science Fiction)
Major character(s): Mitch Christiansen, Military Personnel; Brandon ''Brand'' X, Teenager; Kamryn Smith, Young Woman
Time period(s): 1990s (1996)
Locale(s): Los Angeles, California; New Orleans, Louisiana

Summary: An ex-marine disillusioned by his discovery that the United States military is involved in voodoo-tainted operations in Haiti meets a young boy who has been given an unauthorized virtual reality implant of a serial killer's persona by a deranged experimental psychiatrist. With the help of a band of renegades and runaways, the two attempt to expose a secret government plot with far-reaching political ramifications.

Other books you might like:
Dean R. Koontz, *Dark Rivers of the Heart*, 1994
Michael Marshall Smith, *Spares*, 1996
F. Paul Wilson, *Mirage*, 1996
  Matt Costello, co-author

1586

ELIZABETH FORREST

Phoenix Fire

(New York: DAW, 1992)

Story type: Fantasy (Quest; Legend)
Major character(s): Tembo, Revolutionary (Tiananmen Square student), Archaeologist; Susan Aronson, Businesswoman; Tam Chen, Businessman
Time period(s): 1990s
Locale(s): Xian, China; Los Angeles, California

Summary: While excavating the tomb of Emperor Huang, Tembo frees a demon held captive by magic for 2000 years. When the demon discovers that the emperor who had imprisoned him died nearly 2000 years earlier, the demon hastens to Los Angeles to eliminate the threat represented by his enemy, the Phoenix, waking beneath the La Brea tar pits. A first novel.

Other books you might like:
Alan Dean Foster, *Cyber Way*, 1990
Marc Laidlaw, *Neon Lotus*, 1988
Nick Pollotta, *Bureau 13*, 1991
Nick Pollotta, *Doomsday Exam*, 1992
Elizabeth Ann Scarborough, *Last Refuge*, 1992

1587

WILLIAM R. FORSTCHEN

Arena

(New York: HarperPrism, 1994)

Story type: Fantasy (Adventure; Magic Conflict)
Series: Magic: The Gathering
Major character(s): Garth One-eye, Warrior, Heir—Dispossessed; Hammen, Thief (pickpocket); Zarel Ewine, Nobleman (High Baron of Kush), Leader (Grand Master of the Arena)
Time period(s): Indeterminate
Locale(s): Kush, Fictional City

Summary: Festival provides the annual opportunity for the best fighters from each House to meet in the Arena, testing material and magical weapons. The stranger Garth One-eye quickly draws Zarel Ewine's interest as a source of trouble. Garth One-eye's agenda may lead from Arena spectacle to disaster for many. Game tie-in.

Other books you might like:
Alan Burt Akers, *Arena of Antares*, 1974
Robert N. Charrette, *Never Trust an Elf*, 1992
Clayton Emery, *Shattered Chains*, 1995
Clayton Emery, *Whispering Woods*, 1995
Simon Hawke, *The Nomad*, 1994

1588

WILLIAM R. FORSTCHEN
GREG MORRISON, Co-Author

The Crystal Sorcerers

(New York: Avon, 1991)

Story type: Fantasy (Alternate World; Magic Conflict)
Series: Crystal Warriors
Major character(s): Ikawa Yoshio, Military Personnel (Imperial Japanese Army), Warrior; Mark Phillips, Military Personnel (United States Army), Warrior; Allic, Royalty (prince of Landra), Deity (demi-god)
Time period(s): 1940s
Locale(s): Haven, Planet—Imaginary

Summary: Mark Phillips and Ikawa Yoshio had been opposing commanders in World War II China. Magically kidnapped to Haven they become allies, both in service to Allic in a war between gods. After the war is won, the new friends, unable to return home to Earth, are granted large holdings on Haven. When Gorgon, a demon-lord, threatens Haven, they once again fight for Allic and his demi-god relatives.

Other books you might like:
Patrick H. Adkins, *Sons of the Titans*, 1990
Glen Cook, *The Black Company*, 1984

John DeChancie, *Castle Perilous*, 1988
Geary Gravel, *A Key for the Nonesuch*, 1990
Fritz Leiber, *Swords and Deviltry*, 1970
Mickey Zucker Reichert, *Godslayer*, 1987
Brian Craig, *Plague Demon*, 1990
　　as Brian Craig
Roger Zelazny, *Creatures of Light and Darkness*, 1969

1589

WILLIAM R. FORSTCHEN

The Napoleon Wager
(New York: Ballantine Del Rey, 1993)

Story type: Science Fiction (Military; Alternate Intelligence)
Series: Gamester Wars
Major character(s): Napoleon Bonaparte, Historical Figure, Military Personnel; Aldin Larice, Businessman (entrepreneur), Gambler; Oishi Kurosawa, Warrior (samurai)
Time period(s): 28th century
Locale(s): Magellanic Cloud, Outer Space

Summary: Bored by the peace imposed by the Overseers who rule the Magellanic Cloud, the wealthier inhabitants bet on simulated battles or clandestine wars on primitive planets, all arranged by gaming masters like Aldin Larice. When a rival starts a real war, the Overseers unleash devices made by the extinct race, the First Travelers, creating a wormhole that threatens to devour the Magellanic Cloud. Attempting to retrieve a physicist from the 23rd century who might be able to help, Larice ends up bringing back Napoleon Bonaparte. Returning home, they find a Dyson sphere left by the First Travelers, still run by a slightly mad artificial intelligence who agrees to help them—if they win a re-enacted battle of Waterloo.

Other books you might like:
Poul Anderson, *The Time Patrol*, 1991
Gregory Benford, *Alternate Wars*, 1991
　　Martin H. Greenberg, co-editor
David Drake, *Ranks of Bronze*, 1986
Larry Niven, *The California Voodoo Game*, 1992
　　Steven Barnes, co-author
Larry Niven, *Ringworld*, 1970
Wilson Tucker, *The Lincoln Hunters*, 1958

1590

WILLIAM R. FORSTCHEN

Rally Cry!
(New York: Roc, 1990)

Story type: Science Fiction (Alternate Universe; Time Travel)
Series: Lost Regiment
Major character(s): Andrew Keane, Military Personnel (Colonel); Kalencka, Sidekick (native); Patriarch Rasnar, Religious (priest)
Time period(s): 1860s; Indeterminate (Medieval)
Locale(s): City Point, Virginia (Suzdal); Alternate Universe

Summary: Swept by a storm through a space-time warp, Union Colonel Andrew Keane and the men of the famed 35th

Maine Regiment find themselves on an alien world where church and nobility rule a serfdom, and behind them are alien masters for whom human beings are merely experimental animals and food. Keane and his company disrupt the status quo by introducing radical ideas of democracy and freedom, and a much-superior weapons technology. The strongly disapproving leaders declare war.

Other books you might like:
Pierre Boulle, *Planet of the Apes*, 1963
Philip K. Dick, *The Man in the High Castle*, 1962
Leo Frankowski, *The Cross-Time Engineer*, 1986
Leo Frankowski, *The High-Tech Knight*, 1989
Leo Frankowski, *The Radiant Warrior*, 1989

1591

WILLIAM R. FORSTCHEN

Terrible Swift Sword
(New York: Roc, 1992)

Story type: Science Fiction (Time Travel; Military)
Series: Lost Regiment
Major character(s): Andrew Keane, Military Personnel (Colonel); Yuri Yaroslavich, Slave; Jubadi va Ulga, Ruler, Alien (Merki)
Time period(s): Indeterminate
Locale(s): Valennia, Planet—Imaginary

Summary: Colonel Keane and his Union regiment, swept through a time-space warp like countless humans before them, find themselves stranded forever on an alien world where the warlike natives call the marooned humans "cattle," using them as a source of food and labor. Union rifles and 19th century technology enable the humans to fight back and establish their own territory, but the alien Merki leaders, assisted by air power, unite to crush the rebellious human cattle.

Other books you might like:
Poul Anderson, *The Shield of Time*, 1990
Poul Anderson, *The Time Patrol*, 1991
Gordon R. Dickson, *Time Storm*, 1977
David Drake, *Ranks of Bronze*, 1986
Barbara Hambly, *The Time of the Dark*, 1982
Robert A. Heinlein, *Glory Road*, 1963
William Sanders, *The Wild Blue and the Gray*, 1991
Gene Wolfe, *The Shadow of the Torturer*, 1980

1592

EVE FORWARD

Villains by Necessity
(New York: Tor, 1995)

Story type: Fantasy (Magic Conflict; Quest)
Major character(s): Kaylana Nathalorial, Religious (druid), Leader; Sam, Criminal (assassin), Adventurer; Mizzamir, Magician (arch-mage), Criminal
Time period(s): Indeterminate
Locale(s): The Six Lands, Fictional Country

Summary: Transformed into a stagnant utopia by the ultimate victory of Good and Light, the world faces imminent destruction from the imbalance of nature's forces. Pursued by Mizzamir and his forces of Light, Kaylana and her companions must each survive a hero's test to win through to the DarkGate, unleash the forces of Evil and Darkness and restore the vitality and conflict necessary to a balanced universe. First novel.

Other books you might like:
Gordon R. Dickson, *The Dragon and the George*, 1976
Gordon R. Dickson, *The Dragon Knight*, 1990
Diane Duane, *The Door into Fire*, 1979
Diane Duane, *The Door into Sunset*, 1993
Barbara Hambly, *Dog Wizard*, 1993
Barbara Hambly, *The Silent Tower*, 1986
Barbara Hambly, *The Silicon Mage*, 1988
Michelle Sagara, *Lady of Mercy*, 1993

1593

ROBERT L. FORWARD
MARTHA DODSON FORWARD, Co-Author

Marooned on Eden

(New York: Baen, 1993)

Story type: Science Fiction (First Contact; Hard Science Fiction)
Series: Rocheworld
Major character(s): Virginia "Jinjur" Jones, Spaceship Captain, Military Personnel; Reiki Momoku Le Roux, Computer Expert, Spacewoman; Seetoo "Jolly", Alien (Keejook), Leader
Time period(s): 2070s (2071)
Locale(s): *Prometheus*, Spaceship; Barnard Star System, Outer Space; Zuni, Moon—Imaginary

Summary: Continuing their survey, the crew of the *Prometheus* plan to use their last lander and flyer to visit Zuni, a seemingly Earthlike moon of Gargantua. Fortunately Zuni proves habitable after their crash landing and loss of supplies and equipment. Stranded, with rescue expected in 25 years and only minimal support possible from *Prometheus*, the crew and the alien flouwen they brought with them begin to appreciate the idyllic island where they reside. Sequel to *Return to Rocheworld*.

Other books you might like:
Stephen Baxter, *Raft*, 1992
C.J. Cherryh, *Forty Thousand in Gehenna*, 1983
Hal Clement, *Mission of Gravity*, 1954
Anne McCaffrey, *Dinosaur Planet*, 1978
Michael McCollum, *The Clouds of Saturn*, 1991
Larry Niven, *The Integral Trees*, 1984
Alis A. Rasmussen, *A Passage of Stars*, 1990
Vernor Vinge, *Marooned in Realtime*, 1986

1594

ROBERT L. FORWARD

Martian Rainbow

(New York: Ballantine/Del Rey, 1991)

Story type: Science Fiction (Political; First Contact)
Major character(s): Alexander "the Great" Armstrong, Military Personnel (general), Political Figure (Infinite Lord); Augustus "Gus" Armstrong, Scientist, Administrator
Time period(s): 2040s
Locale(s): Washington, District of Columbia; Mars

Summary: Mars is conquered for the United Nations by the identical twins Alexander and Augustus Armstrong. Alexander goes home to gain whatever political advantage he can from the successful campaign, while Gus stays on Mars to administer the international scientific colony. Alex consolidates his control on Earth and eventually threatens Mars' autonomy. The colonists vote to fight for their independence, but without unexpected help the colonists will have difficulty surviving without support from Earth. This book contains acknowledgements, a short bibliography and a brief guide to Mars.

Other books you might like:
Orson Scott Card, *Ender's Game*, 1985
Michael Flynn, *In the Country of the Blind*, 1990
Robert A. Heinlein, *Double Star*, 1956
Larry Niven, *Protector*, 1973
Dana Stabenow, *Second Star*, 1991
Sheri S. Tepper, *Grass*, 1989

1595

ROBERT L. FORWARD
MARTHA DODSON FORWARD, Co-Author

Ocean under the Ice

(New York: Baen, 1994)

Story type: Science Fiction (First Contact; Adventure)
Series: Rocheworld
Major character(s): Silver-Rim, Alien (Icerug); Virginia "Jinjur" Jones, Spaceship Captain, Military Personnel; David Greystoke, Spaceman, Musician
Time period(s): 2070s (2070)
Locale(s): *Prometheus*, Spaceship; Barnard Star System, Outer Space; Zulu, Moon—Imaginary

Summary: After leaving Rocheworld, the crew of the *Prometheus* meets another intelligent alien species, the Icerugs, on Zulu orbiting Gargantua, the system's gas giant. While learning about the predatory coelasharks, the crew discovers the previously unknown reproductive cycle of the Icerugs. Set prior to *Marooned on Eden*.

Other books you might like:
C.J. Cherryh, *Chanur's Legacy*, 1992
Hal Clement, *Mission of Gravity*, 1954
Janet Kagan, *Mirabile*, 1991
Anne McCaffrey, *Powers That Be*, 1993
    Elizabeth Ann Scarborough, co-author
Robert J. Sawyer, *Far-Seer*, 1992

Robert J. Sawyer, *Fossil Hunter*, 1993
L. Neil Smith, *Their Majesties' Bucketeers*, 1981

1596

ROBERT L. FORWARD
JULIE FORWARD FULLER, Co-Author

Return to Rocheworld

(New York: Baen, 1993)

Story type: Science Fiction (First Contact; Hard Science Fiction)
Series: Rocheworld
Major character(s): Virginia "Jinjur" Jones, Spaceship Captain, Military Personnel; Arielle Trudeau, Pilot (spaceship)
Time period(s): 21st century
Locale(s): *Prometheus*, Spaceship; Barnard Star System, Outer Space

Summary: The *Prometheus'* crew gives their flouwen friends a terminal which will eventually allow direct communication with Earth and immediate communication with the *Prometheus*. When it occurs to them to check for life on the newly flooded Roche, the Terrans discover another culture of aliens, the gummies, who maintain their shape and move on land. Able to travel in space suits designed for them, the exceedingly intelligent flouwen visit the ship and decide to help the gummies develop a more advanced society. Extensive technical indices. Sequel to *Rocheworld*.

Other books you might like:
Roger MacBride Allen, *The Ring of Charon*, 1990
David Brin, *Earth*, 1990
Stephen Leigh, *Alien Tongue*, 1991
Larry Niven, *The Gripping Hand*, 1993
　　Jerry Pournelle, co-author
Vonda N. McIntyre, *Metaphase*, 1992
David Alexander Smith, *Homecoming*, 1990
Sheri S. Tepper, *Raising the Stones*, 1990
Vernor Vinge, *A Fire upon the Deep*, 1992

1597

ROBERT L. FORWARD

Rocheworld

(New York: Baen, 1990)

Story type: Science Fiction (Hard Science Fiction; First Contact)
Major character(s): Virginia "Jinjur" Jones, Spaceship Captain, Military Personnel (general)
Time period(s): 21st century
Locale(s): Earth; *Prometheus*, Spaceship; Barnard Star System, Outer Space

Summary: An expedition to Barnard's Star is organized, the crew is selected, and the spaceship heads out. In order to make the long journey tolerable the crew is given the drug, NO-DIE, which slows life processes, including mentation, with only James, the ship's robot, to take care of them. This is 50,000 words longer than the previously published version titled *The Flight of the Dragonfly* (1984).

Other books you might like:
Roger MacBride Allen, *The Ring of Charon*, 1990
David Brin, *Earth*, 1990
Larry Niven, *Protector*, 1973
Charles Sheffield, *The McAndrew Chronicles*, 1983
John E. Stith, *Redshift Rendezvous*, 1990

1598

ROBERT L. FORWARD

Timemaster

(New York: Tor, 1992)

Story type: Science Fiction (Hard Science Fiction)
Major character(s): Harold "Randy" Randolph Hunter, Space Explorer, Businessman (Reinhold Astroengineering Co.); Rosita "Rose" Carmelita Cortez, Spouse (Randy's), Parent
Time period(s): 2030s (2036)
Locale(s): *Spacemaster*, Spaceship; *Timemaster*, Spaceship (time machine); Asteroid Belt, Outer Space

Summary: The discovery of a new organism in the airless asteroid belt provides a wellspring of technology when technicians examine the alien's physiology and discover the organism's ability to warp the fabric of space/time and extract energy from matter/antimatter interaction. While battling political pressure, Randy's company constructs spaceships which Randy uses to transport and position the resulting matter transmitters/receivers at nearby star systems while his company produces nearly cost-free energy and limitless profits. Problems arise which cause Randy to countermand his own orders preventing use of the organism for time travel. Concludes with a two-page non-fiction bibliography.

Other books you might like:
Greg Bear, *Eon*, 1985
Frank Herbert, *Whipping Star*, 1970
Michael P. Kube-McDowell, *Enigma*, 1986
Vonda N. McIntyre, *Metaphase*, 1992
Vonda N. McIntyre, *Transition*, 1991
Alis A. Rasmussen, *The Price of Ransom*, 1990
Alis A. Rasmussen, *Revolution's Shore*, 1990
Frank M. Robinson, *The Dark Beyond the Stars*, 1991
Charles Sheffield, *The McAndrew Chronicles*, 1983
Vernor Vinge, *A Fire upon the Deep*, 1992

1599

ALAN DEAN FOSTER

Alien 3

(New York: Warner, 1992)

Story type: Science Fiction (Horror; Adventure)
Series: Alien
Major character(s): Ripley, Military Personnel, Heroine; Bishop, Android, Hero; Dillon, Prisoner, Miner
Time period(s): Indeterminate Future
Locale(s): Fiorina, Planet—Imaginary

Summary: Having escaped the aliens a second time, Ripley crashes on a maximum security prison planet and mining facility, unwittingly bringing a deadly alien with her. The alien wreaks lethal havoc in her attempt to insure the survival of her kind. Novelizes the film.

Other books you might like:
Roger MacBride Allen, *The Ring of Charon*, 1990
Robert A. Heinlein, *The Moon Is a Harsh Mistress*, 1966
Steve Perry, *Aliens: Earth Hive*, 1992
Dan Simmons, *Hyperion*, 1989
Vernor Vinge, *A Fire upon the Deep*, 1992

1600

ALAN DEAN FOSTER, Editor

Betcha Can't Read Just One

(New York: Ace, 1993)

Story type: Fantasy (Anthology; Light Fantasy)
Summary: Contains a three-page introduction plus individual introductions to 13 original and three reprinted stories, one translated from German for the first time. The humorous stories feature a variety of settings and mythical characters by writers including Margaret Ball, Greg Costikyan, George Alec Effinger, Alan Dean Foster, Esther Friesner, Mel Gilden, Ron Goulart, Nina Kiriki Hoffman, R.A. Lafferty, Jack McDevitt, Laura Resnick, Mike Resnick and Steve Rasnic Tem.

Other books you might like:
Baird Searles, *Halflings, Hobbits, Warrows & Weefolk: A Collection of Tales of Heroes Short in Stature*, 1991
    Brian Thomsen, co-editor
Will Shetterly, *Liavek*, 1985
    Emma Bull, co-editor
Will Shetterly, *Liavek: The Players of Luck*, 1986
    Emma Bull, co-editor
Michael Stearns, *A Wizard's Dozen*, 1993
    editor
Terri Windling, *Borderland*, 1986
    Mark Alan Arnold, co-editor
Terri Windling, *Life on the Border*, 1991
    editor

1601

ALAN DEAN FOSTER

A Call to Arms

(New York: Ballantine/Del Rey, 1991)

Story type: Science Fiction (First Contact; Adventure)
Series: Damned
Major character(s): Will Dulac, Composer; Caldaq, Alien (massood), Warrior
Time period(s): 1990s
Locale(s): Outer Space; Earth

Summary: The Weave has been fighting the Amplitur for millennia. On an exploratory trip to find allies, they stumble across Earth and composer Will Dulac. Despite Will's insistence that Earthmen do not like war and would not be interested in joining the fray, humanity is drawn in.

Other books you might like:
Piers Anthony, *Cluster*, 1977

David Brin, *Startide Rising*, 1983
Glen Cook, *The Dragon Never Sleeps*, 1988
Gordon R. Dickson, *Wolfling*, 1969
Richard Meredith, *At the Narrow Passage*, 1973
Rebecca Ore, *Becoming Alien*, 1987
Frederik Pohl, *Narabedla, Ltd.*, 1988

1602

ALAN DEAN FOSTER

Cat-A-Lyst

(New York: Ace, 1991)

Story type: Science Fiction (Adventure)
Major character(s): Jeremy Carter, Actor (Grade B movies); O'lal, Alien (Shihar), Animal (Cat); Igor von Mannheim De Soto, Guide
Time period(s): Indeterminate
Locale(s): Paititi La S'ebra Sur, Peru (legendary Incan city); Contisuyu, Planet—Imaginary; Nazca, Peru

Summary: O'lal is looking for a renegade Shiharareth who is preparing the destruction of Earth for his entertainment. Jeremy Carter finds a mini-disc which, with the help of the costume mistress from his latest film, leads him to Cuzco, Peru on a search for Incan gold. Their paths converge at Paititi which is not at all what they expected to find.

Other books you might like:
C.J. Cherryh, *Chanur's Homecoming*, 1986
Mel Gilden, *Hawaiian U.F.O. Aliens*, 1991
Janet Kagan, *Mirabile*, 1991
Marc Laidlaw, *Neon Lotus*, 1988
Carol Severance, *Reefsong*, 1991

1603

ALAN DEAN FOSTER

Chorus Skating

(New York: Warner Aspect, 1994)

Story type: Fantasy (Quest; Magic Conflict)
Series: Spellsinger
Major character(s): Jon-Tom Meriweather, Musician, Adventurer; Mudge, Animal (otter); Hieronymus Hinckel, Musician, Thief
Time period(s): Indeterminate
Locale(s): Mashupro, Fictional City; Farraglean Ocean, Mythical Place

Summary: Bored at home, Jon-Tom and Mudge chase after music that leads them southward where they rescue some princesses and find music vanishing. On an island, they encounter a displaced grunge band who claim that Hieronymus Hinckel, who has no musical talent, steals the music. Jon-Tom decides he must try to defeat Hinckel and free all the music.

Other books you might like:
Robert Asprin, *Another Fine Myth*, 1978
Brian Jacques, *Redwall*, 1987
Elizabeth Ann Scarborough, *Picking the Ballad's Bones*, 1991
Clifford D. Simak, *The Fellowship of the Talisman*, 1978

Christopher Stasheff, *The Warlock Rock*, 1990

1604

ALAN DEAN FOSTER

Codgerspace
(New York: Ace, 1992)

Story type: Science Fiction (Humor; Alternate Intelligence)
Major character(s): Autothor, Artificial Intelligence, Alien (Drex); Mina Gelmann, Aged Person, Adventurer; Victor Iranaputra, Aged Person, Adventurer
Time period(s): Indeterminate Future
Locale(s): Earth

Summary: When one ancient artificial intelligence begins searching for non-human intelligences, artifical intelligences everywhere become entirely too intelligent and uncooperatively philosophical. The fate of the civilized galaxy falls into the hands of five senior citizens and their food processor.

Other books you might like:
Douglas Adams, *The Hitchhiker's Guide to the Galaxy*, 1980
Roger MacBride Allen, *The Ring of Charon*, 1990
Ron Goulart, *Brainz, Inc.*, 1985
Michael Kandel, *Strange Invasion*, 1989
Henry Kuttner, *Robots Have No Tails*, 1952
Vernor Vinge, *A Fire upon the Deep*, 1992

1605

ALAN DEAN FOSTER

Cyber Way
(New York: Ace, 1990)

Story type: Science Fiction (Mystery; Theological)
Major character(s): Vernon Moody, Detective—Police; Paul Ooljee, Police Officer (sergeant), Indian (Navajo)
Time period(s): 22nd century
Locale(s): Navajo Nation Four Corners; Greater Tampa, Florida

Summary: When a murder in Florida involves a Navajo sandpainting, waterloving Detective Moody finds himself sent to the arid, high-tech Navajo Nation. Paul Ooljee, an expert in sandpaintings has volunteered to help with this case and takes Moody under his wing for the duration of the adventure. As they try to unravel the secrets of Moody's peculiar sandpainting photograph, they begin to understand the terrifyingly current message contained in the ancient symbols.

Other books you might like:
Roger MacBride Allen, *The Ring of Charon*, 1990
Katharine Kerr, *Polar City Blues*, 1990
Lee Killough, *Dragon's Teeth*, 1990
Marc Laidlaw, *Neon Lotus*, 1988
G. Harry Stine, *Blood Siege*, 1990
John E. Stith, *Redshift Rendezvous*, 1990

1606

ALAN DEAN FOSTER
ERIC FRANK RUSSELL, Co-Author

Design for Great-Day
(New York: Tor, 1995)

Story type: Science Fiction (First Contact; Military)
Major character(s): James Lawson, Diplomat; Markhamwit, Alien, Leader
Time period(s): Indeterminate Future
Locale(s): Planet—Imaginary; Solarian Combine, Interstellar Empire/Federation

Summary: When a single human emissary arrives on both planets about to engage in interstellar warfare, the belligerents must decide if they wish to continue battle plans or yield to a demand for peace from the fabled Solarian Combine. Expanded by Foster from Russell's 1953 novella.

Other books you might like:
A.C. Crispin, *Silent Songs*, 1994
    Kathleen O'Malley, co-author
Keith Laumer, *Retief and the Warlords*, 1968
Anne McCaffrey, *Treaty at Doona*, 1994
    Jody Lynn Nye, co-author
Eric Frank Russell, *Dreadful Sanctuary*, 1951
Eric Frank Russell, *Sinister Barrier*, 1943
Eric Frank Russell, *Wasp*, 1957
John Varley, *The Ophiuchi Hotline*, 1977

1607

ALAN DEAN FOSTER

The Dig
(New York: Warner Aspect, 1996)

Story type: Science Fiction (Adventure; Mystery)
Major character(s): Boston Low, Pilot (space shuttle); Maggie Robbins, Journalist; Ludger Brink, Scientist
Time period(s): 21st century
Locale(s): *Atlantis*, Spaceship; Cocytus, Planet—Imaginary

Summary: When an asteroid suddenly appears near Earth, scientists send a team to investigate and regularize the asteroid's orbit. However, when the group arrives at the asteroid, a mysterious force transports them to Cocytus, formerly civilized, but now abandoned, where they must solve the puzzle of returning home. Computer game tie-in.

Other books you might like:
Roger MacBride Allen, *The Ring of Charon*, 1990
Greg Bear, *Eon*, 1985
John DeChancie, *Starrigger*, 1983
Frederik Pohl, *The Other End of Time*, 1996
Robert J. Sawyer, *Starplex*, 1996
Allen Steele, *The Tranquility Alternative*, 1996

1608

ALAN DEAN FOSTER

Dinotopia Lost

(Atlanta: Turner Publishing, 1996)

Story type: Fantasy (Adventure)
Series: Dinotopia
Major character(s): Will Denison, Adventurer; Blackstrap, Pirate, Sea Captain; Preister Smiggens, Pirate
Time period(s): 1860s
Locale(s): Dinotopia, Fictional Country

Summary: When a giant breaker washes a pirate ship over Dinotopia's protective coral reef, the pirates capture a dinosaur family. Will Denison leads a small rescue party in pursuit through Rainy Basin, an abandoned area where tyrannosaurs still rule.

Other books you might like:
Scott Ciencin, *Windchaser*, 1995
James Gurney, *Dinotopia*, 1992
James Gurney, *The World Beneath*, 1995
Midori Snyder, *Hatchling*, 1995
John Vornholt, *River Quest*, 1995

1609

ALAN DEAN FOSTER

The False Mirror

(New York: Ballantine Del Rey, 1992)

Story type: Science Fiction (Military; Political)
Series: Damned
Major character(s): Ranji, Warrior, Genetically Altered Being; Heida Trondheim, Military Personnel; D'oud, Alien, Scientist (xenobiologist)
Time period(s): 21st century
Locale(s): Cosuut, Planet—Imaginary; Eirossad, Planet—Imaginary; The Weave, Interstellar Empire/Federation

Summary: After his capture on Eirossad, Ranji learns that his makeup reflects not Ashregan, but rather human ancestry. Returning to his people, Ranji leads them to join with other humans in the Weave. Fearing knowledge of their psychic ability, a result of their genetic manipulation, would result in their persecution, the group decides to keep the ability secret and form an insular community for protection.

Other books you might like:
John Dalmas, *Homecoming*, 1984
Gordon R. Dickson, *Wolfling*, 1969
David Drake, *Cross the Stars*, 1984
Robert A. Heinlein, *Starship Troopers*, 1959
Richard Meredith, *At the Narrow Passage*, 1973
Jerry Pournelle, *War World*, 1988
    John F. Carr, co-editor
Joel Rosenberg, *Hero*, 1990

1610

ALAN DEAN FOSTER

Greenthieves

(New York: Ace, 1994)

Story type: Science Fiction (Mystery; Robot Fiction)
Major character(s): Broderick Manz, Insurance Investigator; Moses, Robot; Vyra Kullervo, Alien, Insurance Investigator
Time period(s): Indeterminate Future
Locale(s): Juarez El Pasco Port Authority, Earth

Summary: Braun-Roche-Keck sends Vyra with Manz, his Minder, and Moses to stop the thefts of pharmaceuticals leaving the planet. Embarrassed by the thefts from their supposedly safe, high-tech security storage area, the Port Authority supplies the cooperation of their security chief and all information acquired to date. Unfortunately, while they inspect the facilities, another shipment disappears from the locked, vacuum-sealed room, practically in front of their eyes. They must find the thieves and stop the thefts.

Other books you might like:
Roger MacBride Allen, *Caliban*, 1993
Isaac Asimov, *The Caves of Steel*, 1954
Mel Gilden, *Tubular Android Superheroes*, 1991
Mike Resnick, *Whatdunits*, 1992
    editor
John E. Stith, *Deep Quarry*, 1989

1611

ALAN DEAN FOSTER

Life Form

(New York: Ace, 1995)

Story type: Science Fiction (First Contact; Hard Science Fiction)
Major character(s): Jack Simna, Scientist; Franklin Lastwell, Spaceship Captain; Bontu, Alien (humanoid)
Time period(s): Indeterminate Future
Locale(s): *James Cook*, Spaceship; Outer Space; Xica de Silva III, Planet—Imaginary

Summary: After exploring several worlds, the crew of the *James Cook* and the scientists on board still hope to find life on a planet where humans can thrive. On Xica da Silva III they discover coastal jungles rich with life, large salt oceans, and interior desert. Although too brief for a thorough understanding, the two-year expedition should achieve fame by cataloging local fauna. Finding humanoid natives with a powerful need to learn leads the scientists to a more complete and realistic comprehension of the native biology.

Other books you might like:
Octavia E. Butler, *Dawn*, 1987
L. Warren Douglas, *Cannon's Orb*, 1994
L. Warren Douglas, *A Plague of Change*, 1992
Janet Kagan, *Mirabile*, 1991
Larry Niven, *The Mote in God's Eye*, 1974
    Jerry Pournelle, co-author
Joan Slonczewski, *Daughter of Elysium*, 1993

1612

ALAN DEAN FOSTER

Mad Amos

(New York: Ballantine Del Rey, 1996)

Story type: Fantasy (Collection; Light Fantasy)
Major character(s): Amos "Mad Amos" Malone, Mountain Man, Sorcerer
Time period(s): 19th century
Locale(s): Southwest; Pacific Islands

Summary: Contains a four-page introduction plus individual introductions to two original and eight stories reprinted from periodicals and anthologies 1982-1992. Mad Amos Malone's adventures in the Wild West and in the South Pacific involve dragons, jackalopes, sorcerers, headless Indian spirits, and an erupting volcano.

Other books you might like:
Stephen King, *The Dark Tower: The Gunslinger*, 1982
Louis L'Amour, *Haunted Mesa*, 1987
George R.R. Martin, *Fevre Dream*, 1982
Elizabeth Ann Scarborough, *The Goldcamp Vampire; or The Sanguinary Sourdough*, 1987
Midori Snyder, *The Flight of Michael McBride*, 1994

1613

ALAN DEAN FOSTER

Mid-Flinx

(New York: Ballantine Del Rey, 1995)

Story type: Science Fiction (First Contact; Alternate Intelligence)
Series: Flinx
Major character(s): Philip "Flinx" Lynx, Psychic (esper), Wanderer; Jack-Jax Landsdowne Coerlis, Heir, Collector; Saalahan, Alien (furcot)
Time period(s): Indeterminate Future
Locale(s): Samstead, Planet—Imaginary; Midworld, Planet—Imaginary; *Teacher*, Spaceship

Summary: On Samstead to stay out of trouble and see the sights, Flinx and his mini-dragon Pip run into Jack-Jax who wants Pip for his zoo. Escaping in *Teacher* on a random course, Flinx decides to explore the forest world on their route still followed by the angry, covetous Jack-Jax.

Other books you might like:
David Brin, *Brightness Reef*, 1995
L. Warren Douglas, *Bright Islands in a Dark Sea*, 1993
Harry Harrison, *The Deathworld Trilogy*, 1976
Anne McCaffrey, *Powers That Be*, 1993
　　Elizabeth Ann Scarborough, co-author
Vernor Vinge, *A Fire upon the Deep*, 1992

1614

ALAN DEAN FOSTER

Montezuma Strip

(New York: Warner Aspect, 1995)

Story type: Science Fiction (Mystery; Cyberpunk)
Major character(s): Angel Cardenas, Police Officer (Federale Sergeant), Psychic; Hypatia Spango, Computer Expert
Time period(s): 21st century
Locale(s): Montezuma Strip, North America (USA-Mexico border); United States; Mexico

Summary: Angel Cardenas, an "Intuit" police officer who senses when people lie, uses his special abilities to solve crimes along the Montezuma Strip, where the U.S.-Mexican border has grown into one long, industrialized strip with a rough culture all its own.

Other books you might like:
Isaac Asimov, *The Naked Sun*, 1957
Ben Bova, *Death Dream*, 1994
Philip K. Dick, *Bladerunner*, 1982
Julia Ecklar, *Regenesis*, 1995
William Gibson, *Neuromancer*, 1984

1615

ALAN DEAN FOSTER

Quozl

(New York: Ace Books, 1989)

Story type: Science Fiction (Humor)
Major character(s): Looks-at-Charts, Alien, Scout; Chad Collins, Teenager
Time period(s): Indeterminate Future
Locale(s): *Sequencer*, Spaceship; Earth

Summary: The Quozl, an alien race obsessed with trendy clothes and fashion accessories, visits the Earth, setting the stage for one of the silliest invasions of another planet in history.

Other books you might like:
Damien Broderick, *Striped Holes*, 1988
Mel Gilden, *Surfing Samurai Robots*, 1988
Keith Laumer, *The Return of Retief*, 1985
Keith Laumer, *Reward for Retief*, 1989
Alexei Panshin, *Masque World*, 1969
Alexei Panshin, *Star Well*, 1968
Charles Platt, *Free Zone*, 1989

1616

ALAN DEAN FOSTER, Editor
MARTIN H. GREENBERG, Co-Editor

Smart Dragons, Foolish Elves

(New York: Ace, 1991)

Story type: Fantasy (Anthology; Light Fantasy)
Summary: This volume contains an introduction and afterword by Alan Dean Foster plus 18 humorous stories origi-

nally published as early as 1939 and as recently as 1990. Authors include Anthony Boucher, John Collier, Avram Davidson, George Alec Effinger, Harlan Ellison, Esther M. Friesner, Horace L. Gold, Ron Goulart, Marvin Kaye, Mike Resnick, Robert Sheckley, Robert Silverberg, William Tenn and Roger Zelazny.

Other books you might like:
Chester Anderson, *The Butterfly Kid*, 1967
Orson Scott Card, *Dragons of Darkness*, 1981
    editor
Orson Scott Card, *Dragons of Light*, 1980
    editor
L. Sprague de Camp, *The Complete Compleat Enchanter*, 1989
    Fletcher Pratt, co-author
Charles L. Grant, *Blood River Down*, 1986
    as Lionel Fenn
Patricia C. Wrede, *Dealing with Dragons*, 1990
Patricia C. Wrede, *Talking to Dragons*, 1985

1617
ALAN DEAN FOSTER

Son of Spellsinger
(New York: Warner Questar, 1993)

Story type: Fantasy (Light Fantasy; Quest)
Series: Spellsinger
Major character(s): Buncan Meriweather, Teenager, Musician; Gragelouth, Merchant, Animal (sloth); Snaugenhutt, Warrior, Animal (rhinoceros)
Time period(s): Indeterminate
Locale(s): Bellwoods, Mythical Place; Kilagurri, Mythical Place (monastery)

Summary: Bored with home and school, Buncan Meriweather teams up with Squill and Neena to form a rap spellsinging group. They rescue a merchant who proposes a quest to find the Grand Veritable, the greatest threat to the world.

Other books you might like:
Piers Anthony, *Demons Don't Dream*, 1993
Suzette Haden Elgin, *Twelve Fair Kingdoms*, 1981
Diana Wynne Jones, *The Power of Three*, 1977
Anne McCaffrey, *Dragonsong*, 1976
Christopher Stasheff, *The Warlock Rock*, 1990
Patricia C. Wrede, *Searching for Dragons*, 1991

1618
ALAN DEAN FOSTER

The Spoils of War
(New York: Ballantine Del Rey, 1993)

Story type: Science Fiction (Military; Political)
Series: Damned
Major character(s): Lalelelang, Historian, Alien (Wais); Nevan Straat-ien, Military Personnel (colonel), Human
Time period(s): 25th century
Locale(s): Outer Space

Summary: The Weave expert on humans, Wais Scholar Historian Lalelelang travels among humans to further her studies, managing to see warfare up close without going mad. While fearing humanity will exterminate itself after the war ends, Lalelelang becomes the key to galactic peace.

Other books you might like:
Eleanor Arnason, *Ring of Swords*, 1993
David Brin, *The Uplift War*, 1987
C.J. Cherryh, *The Pride of Chanur*, 1981
Colin Kapp, *The Survival War*, 1976
Michael McCollum, *Antares Passage*, 1987
Rebecca Ore, *Being Alien*, 1989
Timothy Zahn, *Cobra*, 1985

1619
CHRISTOPHER FOWLER

The Bureau of Lost Souls
(New York: Ballantine, 1991)

Story type: Horror (Collection)

Summary: The twelve mildly engaging horror stories in this collection, originally published in England in 1989, are concerned mostly with interesting methods of revenge. Included are "The Art Nouveau Fireplace," about a modern Bluebeard; "The Ladies Man," about three turned-down job applicants who give a sexist employer his comeuppance; "Safe as Houses," about a health nut who gets his just desserts; and "The Master Builder," a contrived study of the lengths to which a sexually obsessed handyman will go to be with the woman be lusts for. Several of these stories appeared in the author's collection, *More City Jitters*.

Other books you might like:
Ramsey Campbell, *Dark Companions*, 1982

1620
CHRISTOPHER FOWLER

Red Bride
(New York: Roc, 1993)

Story type: Horror (Mystery)
Major character(s): John Chapel, Public Relations; Ixoro De Corizo, Actress; Helen Chapel, Accountant (bookkeeper)
Time period(s): 1990s (1992)
Locale(s): London, England

Summary: So infatuated does John Chapel become with Ixoro De Corizo, the actress whose publicity he handles, that he leaves his wife and family to marry her. When men who know Ixora's past begin dying horrible deaths, that past inevitably comes to light as John desperately tries to clear her of any implication in the murders. This novel was originally published in England in 1992.

Other books you might like:
Richard Adams, *Girl in a Swing*, 1980
Richard Matheson, *Earthbound*, 1982
Peter Straub, *Ghost Story*, 1979
Whitley Strieber, *The Hunger*, 1981

1621

CHRISTOPHER FOWLER

Rune

(New York: Ballantine, 1991)

Story type: Horror (Occult)
Major character(s): Harry Buckingham, Advertising (advertising executive); Grace Crispian, Truck Driver; Dorothy Huxley, Librarian
Time period(s): 1990s (1990)
Locale(s): London, England

Summary: When his father dies beneath the wheels of a delivery truck, clutching a scrap of paper with ancient runic symbols scrawled on it, Harry Buckingham suspects a more-than-natural death. His investigations uncover a conspiracy on the part of the ODEL corporation to subliminally control the world through ancient occult forces.

Other books you might like:
M.R. James, *"Casting the Runes"*, 1989
  in *A Warning to the Curious*
David C. Smith, *The Fair Rules of Evil*, 1989

1622

D.A. FOWLER

Bad Blood

(New York: Pinnacle, 1993)

Story type: Horror (Evil Children)
Major character(s): Arlo Wade, Child (10 years old), Twin; Austin Wade, Child (10 years old), Twin; Tamara Wade, Mentally Ill Person, Parent (Arlo and Austin's mother)
Time period(s): 1990s (1993)
Locale(s): Huntington, West Virginia

Summary: Tamara Wade escapes from her incarceration in a mental asylum and returns home to find that her cruel and mischievous twin sons, Arlo and Austin, have perpetuated her legacy of callous disregard for the feelings and well-being of friends and family. This book is an indirect sequel to the author's 1991 novel, *What's Wrong with Tamara?*

Other books you might like:
Margaret Bingley, *Seeds of Evil*, 1988
Tom Piccirilli, *Dark Father*, 1990
Thomas Tryon, *The Other*, 1972

1623

D.A. FOWLER

The Book of the Damned

(New York: Pocket, 1993)

Story type: Horror (Occult)
Major character(s): Rosalyn Vaughn, Hairdresser; Levi D. Santa, Demon; Kevin Kessler, Detective—Police
Time period(s): 1990s (1993)
Locale(s): Brookington

Summary: Bored Rosalyn Vaughn reads a pulpy horror novel titled *The Book of the Damned* for entertainment. Thereafter she keeps slipping into flashbacks in which she is the heroine of the novel, a helpless victim tortured by a devil incarnate who goes about under the name Levi D. Santa, an anagram for "Devil Satan."

Other books you might like:
John Byrne, *Fear Book*, 1988
Thomas Ligotti, *Vastarien*, 1990
  in *Songs of a Dead Dreamer*

1624

D.A. FOWLER

The Devil's End

(New York: Pocket, 1992)

Story type: Horror (Black Magic; Occult)
Major character(s): Nancy Snell, Teenager; Lana Bremmers, Teenager; Spiro Guenther, Teenager
Time period(s): 1990s
Locale(s): Sharon Valley, South Dakota

Summary: Nancy Snell discovers that she is a lineal descendant of a witch whose legacy forms part of the dark history of Sharon Valley. She finds a way to access the occult powers and use them against her enemies and uses the new girl in town, Lana Bremmers.

Other books you might like:
Katina Alexis, *Souls*, 1992
Marcy Heidish, *The Torching*, 1992
Ed Kelleher, *The School*, 1992
  Harriette Vidal, co-author

1625

D.A. FOWLER

Flesh and Blood

(New York: Pocket, 1993)

Story type: Horror (Psychological Suspense)
Major character(s): Deidi Marshall, Journalist; Camisa Collins, Housewife; Judson Hendricks, Detective
Time period(s): 1990s (1993)
Locale(s): Danville, South

Summary: Although from completely different walks of life, Deidi Marshall and Camisa Collins share the same visions of a woman who looks like them murdering a variety of people. When those murders are reported in the local paper, their investigations put them on pathways that will inevitably converge and explain their peculiar bond.

Other books you might like:
J.M. Dillard, *Spectres*, 1991
Thomas Tryon, *The Other*, 1972
T. Lucien Wright, *Blood Brothers*, 1992

1626

D.A. FOWLER

What's Wrong with Tamara?

(New York: Pocket, 1992)

Story type: Horror (Evil Children)
Major character(s): Tamara Wade, Child; Jonathan Wade, Miner (coal miner); Alex Morrison, Detective—Police
Time period(s): 1990s (1992)
Locale(s): Huntington, West Virginia

Summary: Nine years before, Tamara Wade was kidnapped by a mad woman who conversed with the dead and, supposedly at their bidding, murdered numerous people, including Tamara's mother. Now Tamara speaks to her collection of talking dolls, which encourage her to disrupt her father's plans for remarriage and generally cause havoc.

Other books you might like:
Algernon Blackwood, *The Doll and One Other*, 1946
William Goldman, *Magic*, 1978
Pat Graversen, *Dollies*, 1990
Ruby Jean Jensen, *Baby Doll*, 1992
Abraham Merritt, *Burn, Witch, Burn*, 1933
Sarban, *The Doll Maker and Other Tales of the Uncanny*, 1953

1627

D.A. FOWLER

What's Wrong with Valerie?

(New York: Pocket, 1991)

Story type: Horror (Psychological Suspense)
Major character(s): Valerie Scott, Writer; Elisabeth, Housewife (Valerie's sister); Tamara, Child (Valerie's niece)
Time period(s): 1990s
Locale(s): Huntington, West Virginia

Summary: Convinced that the home she has inherited is haunted by the spirits of dead family members who warn her that entities from beyond the grave are returning to eat her flesh, pathetically insane Valerie Scott kidnaps her niece to save her from a similar fate, and locks the two of them away from public scrutiny inside the house.

Other books you might like:
Shirley Jackson, *We Have Always Lived in the Castle*, 1962

1628

KAREN JOY FOWLER

Sarah Canary

(New York: Henry Holt, 1991)

Story type: Fantasy (Quest)
Major character(s): Ah Kin Chin, Worker, Wanderer; Sarah Canary, Patient (mental), Wanderer; B.J. Voisard, Patient (mental)
Time period(s): 1870s (1873)
Locale(s): Stellacoom, Washington; Pacific Northwest

Summary: Sarah Canary, a woman either insane or supernatural or both, arrives without warning in a camp of migrant Chinese railroad workers. One of the workers, Chin, takes charge of her, and they travel across the Pacific Northwest through a series of surreal encounters, trying to find either her identity or a safe home for her. This experimental novel is the author's first.

Other books you might like:
Iain M. Banks, *The Bridge*, 1986
James P. Blaylock, *The Paper Grail*, 1991
Lisa Goldstein, *The Dream Years*, 1985
Pat Murphy, *The City, Not Long After*, 1989
Fay Weldon, *The Shrapnel Academy*, 1987

1629

KAREN JOY FOWLER

The Sweetheart Season

(New York: Henry Holt, 1996)

Story type: Fantasy (Contemporary Realism)
Major character(s): Maggie Collins, Housewife, Mythical Creature; Irini Doyle, Cook, Sports Figure; Henry Collins, Businessman
Time period(s): 1940s (1947)
Locale(s): Magrit, Minnesota

Summary: Magrit Mill, a major breakfast cereal company, sponsors the Sweetwheat Sweethearts, an all-woman baseball team. But consistent with Magrit's odd past, which includes a drowned village and a ghost rowboat, the team evolves differently than the town expects.

Other books you might like:
Michael Bishop, *Brittle Innings*, 1994
Darryl Brock, *If I Never Get Back*, 1989
Robert Browne, *The New Atoms' Bombshell*, 1980
Jack Cady, *The Off Season*, 1995
W.P. Kinsella, *The Iowa Baseball Confederacy*, 1986
Pat Murphy, *Nadya: The Wolf Chronicles*, 1996

1630

RANDY FOX
ALAN M. CLARK, Illustrator

Not Broken, Not Belonging

(Arvada, Colorado: Roadkill Press, 1994)

Story type: Horror (Possession)
Major character(s): Dr. Ward, Doctor; Rachael Cummings, Artist; Michael Cummings, Banker
Time period(s): 1990s (1994)
Locale(s): Knoxville, Tennessee

Summary: This short-story tells of an artist who nearly dies when her car plunges into a river, and what her artwork thereafter reveals about the origins of her strange post-traumatic behavior. Fox wrote the story based upon concepts embodied in the artwork of Clark, who has illustrated the chapbook generously.

Other books you might like:
Giles Blunt, *Cold Eye*, 1989

Stephen King, *Pet Sematary*, 1983
Kathe Koja, *Bad Brains*, 1992
Kathe Koja, *Skin*, 1993
Kathe Koja, *Strange Angels*, 1994
Jessica Amanda Salmonson, *Anthony Shriek*, 1992

1631

ELLEN FOXXE

Season of Storms

(New York: DAW, 1996)

Story type: Fantasy (Political)
Series: Summerlands
Major character(s): Rolande Vendeley, Privateer; Alicen Kendry, Gentlewoman, Spy; Katin, Royalty, Herbalist
Time period(s): Indeterminate
Locale(s): Albin, Fictional Country; New Albin, Fictional Country

Summary: In New Albin, the collection of refugees, criminals and political dissidents thrive. In Albin, the peace of the chamber of statesmen collapses under the actions of two pretenders to the throne. While this may not be the best time to attempt to return as the rightful heir, if Princess Katin hesitates, there may be no kingdom to restore.

Other books you might like:
Teresa Edgerton, *Goblin Moon*, 1991
Ellen Kushner, *Swordspoint*, 1987
Caroline Stevermer, *A College of Magics*, 1994
Paula Volsky, *Illusion*, 1992
Martha Wells, *The Element of Fire*, 1993

1632

GEORGE FOY

The Shift

(New York: Bantam Spectra, 1996)

Story type: Science Fiction (Cyberpunk; Mystery)
Major character(s): Alex Munn, Writer (television, virtual reality), Computer Expert; Kaye Santangelo, Writer (poet); Larissa ''Lara'' Love, Actress
Time period(s): 2000s
Locale(s): New York, New York; Riker's Island, New York (prison)

Summary: Advanced virtual reality technology inspires Alex Munn to create *Munn's World*, a VR program about a serial killer called Fishman. Soon, however, Alex must fight to survive and to prove his innocence when the Fishman seemingly escapes the confines of VR to kill in the real world.

Other books you might like:
Terry Bisson, *Johnny Mnemonic*, 1995
Alan Dean Foster, *Montezuma Strip*, 1995
James P. Hogan, *Realtime Interrupt*, 1995
Richard Paul Russo, *Carlucci's Edge*, 1995
Richard Paul Russo, *Destroying Angel*, 1992
Walter Jon Williams, *Hardwired*, 1986

1633

JONATHAN FRAKES
DEAN WESLEY SMITH, Co-Author

The Abductors: Conspiracy

(New York: Tor, 1996)

Story type: Science Fiction (Invasion of Earth; Adventure)
Series: Abductors
Major character(s): Richard McCallum, Detective—Private; Neda Foster, Researcher; Tina Harris, Student—College
Time period(s): 1990s
Locale(s): Portland, Oregon; Washington, District of Columbia

Summary: A private investigator working on two separate missing person cases, Richard McCallum realizes he has stumbled onto something big when he reluctantly concludes that both cases actually involve alien abductions. He joins forces with Neda Foster of Underground Investigations, an organization that has been secretly researching alien abductions for years.

Other books you might like:
David Bischoff, *Abduction: The UFO Conspiracy*, 1990
Dean Devlin, *Independence Day*, 1996
   Roland Emmerich, Stephen Molstad, co-authors
Robert A. Heinlein, *The Puppet Masters*, 1990
   revised edition
Anne McCaffrey, *Freedom's Landing*, 1995
Dean Wesley Smith, *Laying the Music to Rest*, 1989
Whitley Strieber, *Communion: A True Story*, 1987
H.G. Wells, *The War of the Worlds*, 1898

1634

JANRAE FRANK, Editor
JEAN STINE, Co-Editor
FORREST J. ACKERMAN, Co-Editor

New Eves: Science Fiction about the Extraordinary Women of Today and Tomorrow

(Stamford, Connecticut: Longmeadow Press, 1994)

Story type: Science Fiction (Anthology)

Summary: Dedicated to women who edited science fiction magazines 1928-1981, this volume contains a ten-page introduction focusing on historical perspective, a one-page ''Author's Note'' plus individual introductions to 32 stories reprinted from periodicals and anthologies 1918-1993 and arranged roughly by decade. Authors include Leigh Brackett, Marion Zimmer Bradley, Octavia E. Butler, Miriam Allen deFord, Phyllis Eisenstein, Carol Emshwiller, Sheila Finch, Karen Joy Fowler, Zenna Henderson, Lee Killough, Nancy Kress, Ursula K. Le Guin, Anne McCaffrey, Maureen F. McHugh, Judith Merril, Andre Norton, Mary Rosenblum, Joanna Russ, Margaret St. Clair, Pamela Sargent, Evelyn E. Smith, Francis Stevens, James Tiptree Jr., Sidney J. Van Scyoc and Kate Wilhelm.

Other books you might like:
Marjorie Agosin, *The Secret Weavers: Stories of the Fantastic by Latin American Women*, 1991
editor
Nina Auerbach, *Forbidden Journeys: Fairy Tales and Fantasies by Victorian Women Writers*, 1992
U.C. Knoepflmacher, co-editor
Jessica Amanda Salmonson, *What Did Miss Darrington See?*, 1989
editor
Susanna J. Sturgis, *Magic Realism by Women: Dreams in a Minor Key*, 1991
editor
A. Susan Williams, *The Lifted Veil: The Book of Fantastic Literature by Women*, 1993
editor

1635
CHERYL J. FRANKLIN
Fire Crossing
(New York: DAW, 1991)

Story type: Science Fiction (Science Fantasy; Space Opera)
Series: Network/Consortium
Major character(s): Luki, Immortal; Katerin "Kitri Terry" Meral, Professor; Quinzaine an Jiar yn Aliria dur Hamley, Immortal, Wizard
Time period(s): Indeterminate
Locale(s): Serii, Planet—Imaginary; Network, Planet—Imaginary (Hamley University)

Summary: Jon and Elizabeth Terry escape from Network to Serii, but have been forced to abandon their children, Michael and Kitri, to the evil Rabh Marrach. Marrach has conditioned the children to forget their past and to believe their parents are dead. The wizards of Serii, fearful of attack by Network, prevent the Terrys from remembering their children for almost twenty years, but the Network never forgets Jon Terry.

Other books you might like:
Gregory Benford, *Great Sky River*, 1987
Marion Zimmer Bradley, *The Firebrand*, 1987
Alan Dean Foster, *Cat-A-Lyst*, 1991
Anne McCaffrey, *Dragonflight*, 1968
Dan Simmons, *The Fall of Hyperion*, 1990
Dan Simmons, *Hyperion*, 1989
George Zebrowski, *Stranger Suns*, 1991

1636
CHERYL J. FRANKLIN
The Inquisitor
(New York: DAW, 1992)

Story type: Science Fiction (First Contact; Political)
Series: Network/Consortium
Major character(s): Ngina-li "Ngina" Ngenga, Alien (Stromvi); Birk "Birkaj" Hodge, Trader, Administrator; Victoria "Tori" Mirelle, Clone
Time period(s): Indeterminate Future

Locale(s): Stromvi, Planet—Imaginary

Summary: Akras, Rea leader after Birkaj killed her father and her husband, preserves her clan and its primitive ideals. Birkaj settles on Stromvi, not comfortable for Soli, but possible with adaptation fluid. He arranges to plant roses, but also plants the precursor to adaptation fluid which makes the place more hospitable for Soli but, unfortunately, kills many of the intelligent, cooperative, peaceful natives before the Inquisitor from the Consortium can sort out the best solution.

Other books you might like:
Eleanor Arnason, *A Woman of the Iron People*, 1991
David Brin, *Startide Rising*, 1983
Octavia E. Butler, *Dawn*, 1987
C.S. Friedman, *Black Sun Rising*, 1991
Janet Kagan, *Mirabile*, 1991
Ursula K. Le Guin, *Always Coming Home*, 1987
Jacqueline Lichtenberg, *Molt Brother*, 1982
Sheri S. Tepper, *Raising the Stones*, 1990

1637
CHERYL J. FRANKLIN
The Light of Exile
(New York: DAW Books, 1990)

Story type: Science Fiction (Adventure)
Series: Network/Consortium
Major character(s): Evjenial, Doctor; Rabh Marrah, Murderer
Time period(s): 24th century
Locale(s): Siatha, Planet—Imaginary

Summary: The Adraki, last survivors of an alien race, roam the galaxy conquering and destroying, apparently looking for a lost treasure. A powerful human allies himself with the Adraki, even though their alliance may lead to the destruction of the lovely non-technological planet Siatha, home of the mysterious and legendary Healers.

Other books you might like:
C.J. Cherryh, *The Faded Sun: Kesrith*, 1978
Rosemary Kirstein, *The Steerswoman*, 1989
Paul O. Williams, *The Gift of the Gorboduc Vandal*, 1989

1638
CHERYL J. FRANKLIN
Sable, Shadow and Ice
(New York: DAW, 1994)

Story type: Fantasy (Religious; Magic Conflict)
Major character(s): Marita, Magician; Benedict, Religious; Aroha, Magician
Time period(s): Indeterminate Future
Locale(s): Rit, Fictional City (island); Tathagata, Fictional City

Summary: Battling Ch'ango, one of the polytheistic Mages of Avalon, Aroha uses Benedict, with his obsession over an ancient, forbidden monotheism, and Benedict's family, especially Marita, and their family's connections in his bid for power over the Protectorate.

Other books you might like:
Marion Zimmer Bradley, *The Mists of Avalon*, 1983
Laurell K. Hamilton, *Nightseer*, 1992
Paula Volsky, *Illusion*, 1992
Martha Wells, *The Element of Fire*, 1993
Patricia C. Wrede, *The Raven Ring*, 1994

1639
PAT FRANKLIN

Dark Dreaming
(New York: Diamond, 1991)

Story type: Horror (Haunted House)
Major character(s): Meredith Morgan, Psychologist; Gustav Halburton, Psychologist; Richard Morgan, Businessman, Spouse (Meredith's husband)
Time period(s): 1990s
Locale(s): Mabton, California

Summary: After moving into a new house, Meredith Morgan begins having erotic dreams about men she has never seen before that begin to merge seamlessly with reality. Initially fearful she is losing her mind, she begins to suspect she has come under the influence of a lingering residue in the house when she finds out her dream lovers are local citizens, and that the house's previous owner committed suicide.

Other books you might like:
Tom Elliott, *The Dwelling*, 1989
Judith Hawkes, *Julian's House*, 1989
Shirley Jackson, *The Haunting of Hill House*, 1959
Al Sarrantonio, *House Haunted*, 1992

1640
STEVEN FRANKOS

Cathedral of Thorns
(New York: Ace, 1995)

Story type: Fantasy (Quest)
Series: Wheel Trilogy
Major character(s): Aitchley Corlaiys, Farmer, Adventurer; TW-O: 114-84-1311825, Robot; Calyx, Mythical Creature (dwarf)
Time period(s): Indeterminate
Locale(s): Vedette, Fictional Country; Alternate Universe

Summary: The heroes complete several steps in their search for the Elixir of Life. Unfortunately, Harris Blind-Eye steals the clues and kidnaps Berlyn, a new obstacle to deal with before the heroes can continue their primary effort.

Other books you might like:
M.A.R. Barker, *Man of Gold*, 1984
Simon R. Green, *Hawk & Fisher*, 1990
Patricia A. McKillip, *The Riddle-Master of Hed*, 1976
Fred Saberhagen, *Empire of the East*, 1979
Christopher Stasheff, *The Warlock in Spite of Himself*, 1969

1641
STEVEN FRANKOS

The Jewel of Equilibrant
(New York: Ace, 1993)

Story type: Fantasy (Alternate World; Quest)
Major character(s): Matthew Logan, Traveller; Thromar, Warrior; The Smythe, Wizard
Time period(s): 1990s; Indeterminate
Locale(s): Santa Monica, California; Sparrill, Alternate Universe

Summary: After repeated warnings that he should recognize the danger of dreams, Matthew steps out for daily exercise. While jogging, Matthew suddenly experiences a peculiar storm. Afterward he must defend himself with bow and sword before convincing himself he has travelled to an alternate world. He discovers that he must restore the Balance of the Wheel before he can return home.

Other books you might like:
Steven Brust, *Jhereg*, 1983
Gordon R. Dickson, *The Dragon and the George*, 1976
Carole Nelson Douglas, *Cup of Clay*, 1991
William R. Forstchen, *The Crystal Warriors*, 1988
    Greg Morrison, co-author
Geary Gravel, *A Key for the Nonesuch*, 1990
Robert Jordan, *The Eye of the World*, 1989
Brad Strickland, *Wizard's Mole*, 1991

1642
LEO FRANKOWSKI

The Flying Warlord
(New York: Ballantine/Del Rey, 1989)

Story type: Science Fiction (Time Travel)
Series: Adventures of Conrad Stargard
Major character(s): Conrad Stargard, Engineer
Time period(s): 13th century
Locale(s): Poland; Alternate Earth

Summary: Stargard has accidentally time traveled to medieval Poland, started a premature Industrial Revolution, and altered the course of history. Arming the Polish army with modern weapons, he does battle with the invading Mongols.

Other books you might like:
Gregory Benford, *Alternate Empires*, 1989
    Martin H. Greenberg, co-author
Daniel Da Cruz, *Mixed Doubles*, 1989
L. Sprague de Camp, *Lest Darkness Fall*, 1941
Mark Twain, *A Connecticut Yankee in King Arthur's Court*, 1899

1643
LEO FRANKOWSKI

The High-Tech Knight
(New York: Ballantine/Del Rey, 1989)

Story type: Science Fiction (Time Travel)

Series: The Adventures of Conrad Stargard
Major character(s): Conrad Stargard, Engineer
Time period(s): 13th century
Locale(s): Poland; Alternate Earth

Summary: In volume 1 of this series, *The Cross-Time Engineer*, Stargard accidentally time traveled to medieval Poland just before it was to be invaded by the Mongols. Establishing himself as a knight, he now uses his engineering skill to start a premature Industrial Revolution.

Other books you might like:
Gregory Benford, *Alternate Empires*, 1989
    Martin H. Greenberg, co-editor
Daniel Da Cruz, *Mixed Doubles*, 1989
L. Sprague de Camp, *Lest Darkness Fall*, 1941
Mark Twain, *A Connecticut Yankee in King Arthur's Court*, 1899

1644

LEO FRANKOWSKI

Lord Conrad's Lady

(New York: Ballantine/Del Rey, 1990)

Story type: Science Fiction (Time Travel; Alternate Universe)
Series: Adventures of Conrad Stargard
Major character(s): Conrad Stargard, Time Traveller, Engineer; Francine, Noblewoman (lady), Spouse
Time period(s): 13th century
Locale(s): Poland; Alternate Earth

Summary: After defeating a third Mongol army, Conrad Stargard is elected King of Poland due to his wife Francine's machinations. As her husband totally ignores her, Lady Francine turns to plotting to make her son the greatest king in Christendom by cleverly allying Poland with Ruthemia, Bulgaria and other neighboring kingdoms. Yet Conrad still takes no notice of her.

Other books you might like:
L. Sprague de Camp, *Lest Darkness Fall*, 1941
Harry Harrison, *A Rebel in Time*, 1983
H. Beam Piper, *Lord Kalvan of Otherwhen*, 1965
Kevin D. Randle, *Remember the Alamo!*, 1986
    Robert Cornett, co-author

1645

LEO FRANKOWSKI

The Radiant Warrior

(New York: Ballantine/Del Rey, 1989)

Story type: Science Fiction (Time Travel)
Series: Adventures of Conrad Stargard
Major character(s): Conrad Stargard, Engineer
Time period(s): 13th century
Locale(s): Poland; Alternate Earth

Summary: Having achieved knighthood in early-medieval Poland and established an industrial base far in advance of anything the world has seen heretofore, time traveler Conrad Stargard now prepares his Polish troops to meet the Mongol invaders.

Other books you might like:
Gregory Benford, *Alternate Empires*, 1989
    Martin H. Greenberg, co-editor
Daniel Da Cruz, *Mixed Doubles*, 1989
L. Sprague de Camp, *Lest Darkness Fall*, 1941
Mark Twain, *A Connecticut Yankee in King Arthur's Court*, 1899

1646

VALERIE J. FREIREICH

The Beacon

(New York: Roc, 1996)

Story type: Science Fiction (First Contact; Invasion of Earth)
Major character(s): Beatrice Whit, Traveller; Stefan Acari, Judge; John Denning, Political Figure
Time period(s): Indeterminate Future
Locale(s): Earth

Summary: Four Travellers, descendants of humans abducted from Earth centuries ago by aliens, visit Earth and must decide whether to call the beacon which will bring their starship into Earth orbit. When someone kidnaps one of the four, Stefan re-establishes his mental link with the Assembly in order to take charge of the investigation. Even after he rescues Beatrice from her kidnappers, Stefan must still decide whether he prefers the risks of alien contact or the risks of tyranny by the assembly.

Other books you might like:
Juanita Coulson, *Tomorrow's Heritage*, 1981
Michael Crichton, *The Andromeda Strain*, 1969
Jane S. Fancher, *Harmonies of the 'Net*, 1992
Vonda N. McIntyre, *Transition*, 1991
Rebecca Ore, *Becoming Alien*, 1988
Clifford D. Simak, *They Walked Like Men*, 1962
Steven Spielberg, *Close Encounters of the Third Kind*, 1977
H.G. Wells, *The War of the Worlds*, 1898
Jack Williamson, *Mazeway*, 1990

1647

VALERIE J. FREIREICH

Becoming Human

(New York: Roc, 1995)

Story type: Science Fiction (Genetic Manipulation; Political)
Major character(s): Sanda Brauna, Political Figure (elector); August, Genetically Altered Being; Jeroen Lee, Political Figure (elector)
Time period(s): Indeterminate Future
Locale(s): Andia, Planet—Imaginary; Neuland, Planet—Imaginary; Harmony of Worlds, Interstellar Empire/Federation

Summary: Neuland needs help from the Harmony of Worlds, but the genetic alteration which eliminates the sensation of pain makes Harmony unwilling to admit the people as full citizens, as human. Also not considered human because of genetic design for his position as political analyst to Elector Brauna, August finds himself flung into the same political crisis which brought about the death of his clone-father and now gives him the reputation of a traitor.

Other books you might like:
C.J. Cherryh, *Forty Thousand in Gehenna*, 1983
Gordon R. Dickson, *Dorsai!*, 1976
Rebecca Ore, *The Illegal Rebirth of Billy the Kid*, 1991
Joan Slonczewski, *Daughter of Elysium*, 1993
Cordwainer Smith, *Norstrilia*, 1995
John Varley, *The Ophiuchi Hotline*, 1977

1648

VALERIE J. FREIREICH

Testament

(New York: Roc, 1995)

Story type: Science Fiction (Political; Genetic Manipulation)
Series: Polite Harmony of Worlds
Major character(s): Gray Bridger, Guide; Mead Bridger, Genetically Altered Being; Martin Penn, Tourist, Doctor
Time period(s): 30th century
Locale(s): Testament, Planet—Imaginary; Polite Harmony of Worlds, Interstellar Empire/Federation

Summary: Gray Bridger is a freak on Testament where descendants of genetically altered settlers inherit conscious memories of their female ancestors. He longs to escape to the Polite Harmony of Worlds, which quarantines altered humans. Just before he receives permission to enter the Harmony, the schemes of his grandmother and the Testament matriarchy threaten his plan. As Gray struggles to outwit these schemes, he begins to realize how they will change Testament and the Harmony.

Other books you might like:
Eleanor Arnason, *Ring of Swords*, 1993
Isaac Asimov, *Foundation and Empire*, 1952
C.J. Cherryh, *Cyteen*, 1988
Jane S. Fancher, *Ground-Ties*, 1991
Nicola Griffith, *Ammonite*, 1993
Joan Slonczewski, *A Door into Ocean*, 1986
Tricia Sullivan, *Lethe*, 1995
Amy Thomson, *Virtual Girl*, 1993

1649

ROBERT FREZZA

Fire in a Faraway Place

(New York: Ballantine Del Rey, 1994)

Story type: Science Fiction (Military)
Major character(s): Anton Vereshchagin, Military Personnel; Hanna Bruwer-Sanmartin, Political Figure; Daisuke Matsudaira, Businessman
Time period(s): Indeterminate Future
Locale(s): Suid-Afrika, Planet—Imaginary; Tokyo, Japan

Summary: Concerned with profit rather than peace, the Japanese Empire's outlook threatens the gains accomplished when Lieutenant-Colonel Anton Vereshchagin enlists the help and pride of Suid-Afrika's native peoples. Since every choice leads to war, the occupying troops of the First Battalion of the 35th Imperial Infantry must choose to support the Empire, which stranded them on Suid-Afrika, or to support the democratic government of the planet they now call home. Sequel to *A Small Colonial War* .

Other books you might like:
Eleanor Arnason, *Ring of Swords*, 1993
Lois McMaster Bujold, *Shards of Honor*, 1986
David Drake, *Hammer's Slammers*, 1979
  expanded edition, 1987
Joel Rosenberg, *Hero*, 1990
Sheri S. Tepper, *The Gate to Women's Country*, 1988

1650

ROBERT FREZZA

McLendon's Syndrome

(New York: Del Ray, 1993)

Story type: Science Fiction (Military; Medical)
Major character(s): Kenneth ''Ken'' Mac Kay, Military Personnel (Vampire); Anna Catarina Lindquist, Military Personnel, Vampire; Bucky Beaver, Alien (!Plixxi*), Diplomat (ambassador)
Time period(s): Indeterminate Future
Locale(s): Schuyler's World, Planet—Imaginary; *Rustam's Slipper*, Spaceship (''Rusty Scupper'')

Summary: After one of the *Rusty Scupper*'s crew's jail term prevents the ship from leaving, Ken suggests Catarina as a replacement despite recognizing her as a vampire. Discovering that the ship transports contraband and that Catarina and a stowaway actually belong to the navy, the *Rusty Scupper* becomes embroiled in interplanetary political and military machinations.

Other books you might like:
Debra Doyle, *The Price of the Stars*, 1992
  James D. Macdonald, co-author
David Drake, *Starliner*, 1992
Alan Dean Foster, *Quozl*, 1989
Laurell K. Hamilton, *Guilty Pleasures*, 1993
Alis A. Rasmussen, *Revolution's Shore*, 1990
Denise Vitola, *Half-Light*, 1992

1651

ROBERT FREZZA

A Small Colonial War

(New York: Ballantine/Del Rey, 1989)

Story type: Science Fiction (Military)
Major character(s): Raul Sanmartin, Military Personnel (Captain); Anton Vereshchagin, Military Personnel (Lt. Colonel)
Time period(s): 22nd century
Locale(s): Suid Afrika, Planet—Imaginary

Summary: When a revolt occurs on the factory world called Suid Afrika, a small, undermanned military force is sent to deal with it. After a series of boondoggles, the competence of one small battalion saves the day. Frezza's first novel.

Other books you might like:
Gordon R. Dickson, *The Final Encyclopedia*, 1984
Gordon R. Dickson, *Lost Dorsai*, 1989
Gordon R. Dickson, *Soldier, Ask Not*, 1967
Gordon Dickson, *The Tactics of Mistake*, 1971
David Drake, *Counting the Cost*, 1987
David Drake, *Hammer's Slammers*, 1979
Jerry Pournelle, *The Mercenary*, 1977
Jerry Pournelle, *Prince of Mercenaries*, 1989

1652

ROBERT FREZZA

The VMR Theory

(New York: Ballantine Del Rey, 1996)

Story type: Science Fiction (Humor; Adventure)
Major character(s): Kenneth "Ken" McKay, Vampire, Military Personnel (Navy Intelligence Reserves); Anna Catarina Lindquist, Spacewoman, Vampire
Time period(s): Indeterminate Future
Locale(s): Alt Bauernhof, Planet—Imaginary; *Rustam's Slipper*, Spaceship ("*Rusty Scupper*"); Confederation, Interstellar Empire/Federation

Summary: Nominally assigned to transport goods to Alt Bauernhof, Ken and Catarina must find and retrieve a Confederation agent from the planet. Anticipating conquest of the Confederation, Alt Bauernhof natives, the Macdonalds, look forward to Ken and Catarina's visit as an opportunity to study actual vampires, controllers of humanity's destiny according to the popular Macdonald conjecture, the Vampire Master Race Theory.

Other books you might like:
Douglas Adams, *The Hitchhiker's Guide to the Galaxy*, 1980
Douglas Adams, *The Restaurant at the End of the Universe*, 1982
Laurell K. Hamilton, *Guilty Pleasures*, 1993
Spider Robinson, *Callahan's Crosstime Saloon*, 1977
Spider Robinson, *Callahan's Legacy*, 1996
James H. Schmitz, *The Demon Breed*, 1968
Harry Turtledove, *Earthgrip*, 1991

1653

C.S. FRIEDMAN

Black Sun Rising

(New York: DAW, 1991)

Story type: Fantasy (Horror; Science Fiction)
Series: Coldfire Trilogy
Major character(s): Damien Kilcannon Vryce, Religious (priest), Warrior; Gerald Tarrant, Nobleman (neocount); Hesseth, Alien (Rakh)
Time period(s): Indeterminate Future
Locale(s): Erna, Planet—Imaginary

Summary: After more than a millennium, humans have adapted to Erna, a planet so near the edge of the galaxy that night without stars, moon or galactic core to give light is not uncommon. Before humans arrived, Erna had no intelligent species. However, it had a characteristic humans called "the fae" which is very sensitive to human thought, including subconscious fears. Now Erna has not only all the human monsters which humans have imagined and become, but a hostile, intelligent native species is evolving as well.

Other books you might like:
Octavia E. Butler, *Dawn*, 1987
Mary Gentle, *Rats and Gargoyles*, 1990
Harry Harrison, *The Deathworld Trilogy*, 1976
Christopher Pike, *Sati*, 1990
Dan Simmons, *Hyperion*, 1989
Bill Slavicsek, *Storm Knights*, 1990
   C.J. Tramontana, co-author
Sheri S. Tepper, *Grass*, 1989

1654

C.S. FRIEDMAN

Crown of Shadows

(New York: DAW, 1995)

Story type: Science Fiction (Psychic Powers; Theological)
Series: Coldfire Trilogy
Major character(s): Damien Kilcannon Vryce, Religious (priest), Warrior; Iezu, Demon; Gerald Tarrant, Vampire, Religious (prophet)
Time period(s): Indeterminate Future
Locale(s): Erna, Planet—Imaginary

Summary: No longer an innocent priest, Damien Vryce continues the battle between faith and sorcery, while the Iezu, Calesta's children, evolve from feeding only on pain to appreciate other human emotions. The Church must somehow learn to control the native sources of magical power so humans can regain a peaceful, secure life on Erna.

Other books you might like:
Tom Deitz, *Soulsmith*, 1991
Mary Gentle, *Golden Witchbreed*, 1984
Dan Simmons, *Hyperion*, 1989
Sheri S. Tepper, *Shadow's End*, 1994
Gene Wolfe, *Nightside the Long Sun*, 1993

1655

C.S. FRIEDMAN

The Madness Season

(New York: DAW, 1990)

Story type: Science Fiction (Adventure; Immortality)
Major character(s): The Marra, Alien; Daetrin Ungashak To-Alym Haal, Vampire, Werewolf; Raayat, Alien (Tyr, a hive mind)
Time period(s): 24th century
Locale(s): *Talguth*, Spaceship; Meyaga, Planet—Imaginary (Cantona Settlement); Yuang, Planet—Imaginary (Dome Prime)

Summary: The Tyr, alien conquerors, remove Daetrin from Earth where he was potentially a disruptive influence in his position as a teacher. Daetrin, a reluctant vampire, gets involved with other humans and aliens in a revolution against the Tyr.

Other books you might like:
Greg Bear, *Blood Music*, 1985
Octavia E. Butler, *Adulthood Rites*, 1988
Octavia E. Butler, *Dawn*, 1987
Octavia E. Butler, *Imago*, 1989
C.J. Cherryh, *Serpent's Reach*, 1980
Janet Kagan, *Hellspark*, 1988
Jack Vance, *The Dragon Masters*, 1963

1656

C.S. FRIEDMAN

When True Night Falls
(New York: DAW, 1993)

Story type: Fantasy (Psychic Powers; Religious)
Series: Coldfire Trilogy
Major character(s): Damien Kilcannon Vryce, Religious (priest), Warrior; Gerald Tarrant, Sorcerer, Nobleman; Hesseth, Alien (Rakh)
Time period(s): Indeterminate Future
Locale(s): Erna, Planet—Imaginary

Summary: Stabilizing the colonists' emotions and thoughts after the chaos resulting from the destruction of their shuttle and loss of communications with the advanced technology orbiting above, Gerald Tarrant founded the Church in which Damien Vryce now serves. Continuing the battle against evil forces attempting to control Erna, Damien, Gerald and Hesseth set out across the ocean to overcome the Prince of Light and avert catastrophe.

Other books you might like:
Roger MacBride Allen, *The Ring of Charon*, 1990
Jeffrey A. Carver, *Dragon Rigger*, 1993
Tom Deitz, *Soulsmith*, 1991
Melanie Rawn, *Dragon Prince*, 1988
Dan Simmons, *Hyperion*, 1989
Paula Volsky, *Illusion*, 1992
Martha Wells, *The Element of Fire*, 1993

1657

MICHAEL JAN FRIEDMAN

All Good Things. . .
(New York: Pocket, 1994)

Story type: Science Fiction (Space Opera; Time Travel)
Series: Star Trek: The Next Generation
Major character(s): Jean-Luc Picard, Spaceship Captain (*U.S.S. Enterprise*), Military Personnel; Q, Alien; Beverly Crusher, Spaceship Captain (*U.S.S. Pasteur*), Doctor
Time period(s): 24th century
Locale(s): U.S.S. Enterprise, Spaceship; Outer Space; U.S.S. Pasteur, Spaceship

Summary: Q continues the test of humanity's mettle begun in *Encounter at Farpoint* by presenting a problem which requires Captain Picard to coherently sense his existence at different times and act to avoid a future disaster directly

sensed in the present. Novelizes the teleplay of the concluding episode of the TV series.

Other books you might like:
J.M. Dillard, *Emissary*, 1993
J.M. Dillard, *Star Trek: Generations*, 1994
David Gerrold, *Encounter at Farpoint*, 1987
L.A. Graf, *Caretaker*, 1995
Jeri Taylor, *Unification*, 1991

1658

MICHAEL JAN FRIEDMAN

A Call to Darkness
(New York: Pocket Books, 1989)

Story type: Science Fiction (Space Opera)
Series: Star Trek: The Next Generation
Major character(s): Jean-Luc Picard, Spaceship Captain, Military Personnel; William Riker, Military Personnel (First Officer)
Time period(s): 24th century (Stardate 42908.6)
Locale(s): U.S.S. Enterprise, Spaceship

Summary: Just after Captain Picard vanishes on what appears to be a routine rescue mission, a deadly plague begins to ravage the crew of the *Enterprise*. First Officer Riker must unravel the mystery of both the plague and his Captain's disappearance, or face the destruction of his starship.

Other books you might like:
J.M. Dillard, *Star Trek: The Lost Years*, 1989
J.M. Dillard, *Star Trek V: The Final Frontier*, 1989
Diane Duane, *My Enemy, My Ally*, 1984
  Star Trek 18
Diane Duane, *Spock's World*, 1988
Larry Niven, *The Mote in God's Eye*, 1974
  Jerry Pournelle, co-author

1659

MICHAEL JAN FRIEDMAN

Crossover
(New York: Pocket, 1995)

Story type: Science Fiction (Space Opera; Political)
Series: Star Trek: The Next Generation
Major character(s): Spock, Scientist, Alien (Vulcan); Montgomery Scott, Engineer, Military Personnel; Jean-Luc Picard, Spaceship Captain, Military Personnel
Time period(s): 24th century
Locale(s): U.S.S. Enterprise, Spaceship; Constanthus, Planet—Imaginary; United Federation of Planets, Interstellar Empire/Federation

Summary: Former ambassador Spock now endeavors to teach the philosphy of Surak to the underground movement of Romulans eager to re-unite the Romulan and Vulcan peoples. Betrayed by a spy in their midst, Spock and some of his followers face a show trial and execution. When Starfleet sends the *Enterprise* to the border to pursue diplomatic measures with Dr. McCoy as an advisor, Scotty, unwilling to wait, steals an antique starship and sets out to rescue Spock himself.

Other books you might like:
Margaret Wander Bonanno, *Dwellers in the Crucible*, 1985
J.M. Dillard, *Star Trek: Generations*, 1994
Diane Duane, *My Enemy, My Ally*, 1984
Diane Duane, *The Romulan Way*, 1987
    Peter Morwood, co-author
Jeri Taylor, *Unification*, 1991

1660

MICHAEL JAN FRIEDMAN

Kahless

(New York: Pocket, 1996)

Story type: Science Fiction (Genetic Manipulation; Adventure)
Series: Star Trek: The Next Generation
Major character(s): Kahless, Warrior, Hero; Jean-Luc Picard, Spaceship Captain, Military Personnel; Worf, Military Personnel (lieutenant), Alien (Klingon)
Time period(s): 24th century; Indeterminate Past
Locale(s): Qo'nos, Planet—Imaginary; *U.S.S. Enterprise*, Spaceship; Klingon Empire, Interstellar Empire/Federation

Summary: An archaeological find casts doubt on the exploits of the legendary Kahless, whose clone now occupies the throne as the titular head of the Klingon Empire. Kahless discovers a plot against the Empire and, fearing that he can trust no one in the Empire, turns to Picard and Worf for help. The story of the original Kahless and the circumstances that compelled him to defy the tyrant Molor parallels the struggle of the 24th century Kahless to foil the traitorous plot and restore his people's faith.

Other books you might like:
Margaret Wander Bonanno, *Strangers From the Sky*, 1987
Carmen Carter, *The Devil's Heart*, 1993
C.J. Cherryh, *Cyteen*, 1988
Judith Reeves-Stevens, *Federation*, 1994
    Garfield Reeves-Stevens, co-author
William Shatner, *The Return*, 1996
    Judith Reeves-Stevens, Garfield Reeves-Stevens, co-authors
Roger Zelazny, *Lord of Light*, 1967

1661

MICHAEL JAN FRIEDMAN

Relics

(New York: Pocket, 1992)

Story type: Science Fiction (Space Opera)
Series: Star Trek: The Next Generation
Major character(s): Jean-Luc Picard, Spaceship Captain (*U.S.S. Enterprise*), Military Personnel; Montgomery Scott, Engineer (*U.S.S. Enterprise*), Military Personnel (retired); Geordi La Forge, Engineer (*U.S.S. Enterprise*), Military Personnel
Time period(s): 23rd century; 24th century

Locale(s): *S.S. Jenolen*, Spaceship; *U.S.S. Enterprise*, Spaceship

Summary: When the *Enterprise* responds to a 75-year-old distress call, an away team discovers the wreckage of the *Jenolen* and a jury-rigged transporter mechanism which preserved retired Montgomery Scott after *Jenolen's* crash. Retrieved from stasis, Scott provides the vital solution when disaster strikes the *Enterprise* crew. Novelizes a television episode.

Other books you might like:
Carmen Carter, *Doomsday World*, 1990
    Peter David, Michael Jan Friedman and Robert Greenberger, co-authors
A.C. Crispin, *The Eyes of the Beholders*, 1990
Peter David, *A Rock and a Hard Place*, 1990
David Gerrold, *Encounter at Farpoint*, 1987
Jean Lorrah, *Metamorphosis*, 1990
Jeri Taylor, *Unification*, 1991
Howard Weinstein, *Exiles*, 1990

1662

MICHAEL JAN FRIEDMAN
KEVIN RYAN, Co-Author

Requiem

(New York: Pocket, 1994)

Story type: Science Fiction (Space Opera; Time Travel)
Series: Star Trek: The Next Generation
Major character(s): Jean-Luc Picard, Spaceship Captain, Military Personnel; Reginald Barclay, Engineer, Space Explorer; Geordi La Forge, Engineer, Military Personnel
Time period(s): 24th century; 23rd century
Locale(s): *U.S.S. Enterprise*, Spaceship; Cestus III, Planet—Imaginary; United Federation of Planets, Interstellar Empire/Federation

Summary: Twenty-five years ago, Captain Picard of the *U.S. Stargazer* negotiated with the Gorn. Now, en route to a second meeting, the *Enterprise* encounters an abandoned space station of unknown origin that sends Picard across space and time to Cestus III a hundred years in the past, just days before the Gorn massacred its human settlers. As his crew searches for him, Picard tries to survive and leave a clue for future rescuers and return to aid the colonists.

Other books you might like:
Poul Anderson, *Time Patrolman*, 1983
Arthur C. Clarke, *Rendezvous with Rama*, 1973
Gene DeWeese, *The Peacekeepers*, 1988
Cynthia Felice, *Downtime*, 1985
Barbara Hambly, *Ishmael*, 1985

1663

MICHAEL JAN FRIEDMAN

Reunion

(New York: Pocket, 1991)

Story type: Science Fiction (Space Opera)
Series: Star Trek: The Next Generation

Major character(s): Jean-Luc Picard, Spaceship Captain, Military Personnel; Worf, Military Personnel (Starfleet officer), Alien (Klingon); Morgen, Royalty (Crown Prince of Daa'V), Spaceship Captain (former)

Time period(s): 24th century

Locale(s): *U.S.S. Enterprise*, Spaceship

Summary: Captain Jean-Luc Picard has been assigned the diplomatic mission of transporting his former subordinate, Captain Morgen, to the planet, Daa'V, where he is to assume power. Many of Picard's officers from the *U.S.S. Stargazer*, former shipmates of Morgen's, have accompanied Morgen. When an attempt is made on Morgen's life, Picard must discover who wants to murder the Crown Prince, opening Daa'V to a new alliance, one less beneficial to the Federation.

Other books you might like:
Diane Carey, *Ghost Ship*, 1988
A.C. Crispin, *The Eyes of the Beholders*, 1990
Peter David, *A Rock and a Hard Place*, 1990
Gene DeWeese, *The Peacekeepers*, 1988
David Dvorkin, *The Captain's Honor*, 1989
    Daniel Dvorkin, co-author
Jean Lorrah, *Survivors*, 1989
John Vornholt, *Masks*, 1989
Howard Weinstein, *Power Hungry*, 1989

◼1664◼

MICHAEL JAN FRIEDMAN

Shadows on the Sun
(New York: Pocket, 1993)

Story type: Science Fiction (Space Opera; Medical)

Series: Star Trek

Major character(s): Leonard McCoy, Doctor; Shil Andrachis, Alien (Ssana), Leader (High Assassin); Jocelyn Treadway, Diplomat, Divorced Person (McCoy's ex-wife)

Time period(s): 23rd century

Locale(s): *U.S.S. Enterprise*, Spaceship; Ssan, Planet—Imaginary

Summary: The young doctor McCoy, outraged by his wife's infidelity, deserts his family and joins Starfleet. Forty years later, McCoy must cooperate with the diplomats assigned to the *Enterprise*, his ex-wife and her new husband. The Assassins on war-torn Ssan, a cult who believe ritual assassination the most honorable kind of death, attack the landing team sent to negotiate peace. With Kirk and Jocelyn imprisoned by the High Assassin, a patient whose life McCoy saved as a young intern, McCoy's knowledge of the Ssani may help save them, if he can overcome his conflicting emotions.

Other books you might like:
Steven Brust, *Jhereg*, 1983
J.M. Dillard, *The Lost Years*, 1989
Diane Duane, *The Romulan Way*, 1987
    Peter Morwood, co-author
Julia Ecklar, *The Kobayashi Maru*, 1989
Cynthia Felice, *Downtime*, 1985
Cynthia Felice, *The Khan's Persuasion*, 1991
Mary Gentle, *Golden Witchbreed*, 1984

◼1665◼

ESTHER FRIESNER, Editor
MARTIN H. GREENBERG, Co-Editor

Alien Pregnant by Elvis
(New York: DAW, 1994)

Story type: Fantasy (Anthology; Light Fantasy)

Summary: Contains a three-page introduction by Friesner and 36 original stories reflecting lurid tabloid themes such as Bigfoot, J.F.K., Marilyn Monroe, UFOs, zombies, the Loch Ness monster, psychic animals and the search for the perfect orgasm. Authors include John Gregory Betancourt, David Brin, John DeChancie, David Drake, George Alec Effinger, Gregory Feeley, Esther Friesner, Alan Dean Foster, Jody Lynn Nye, Laura Resnick, Kristine Kathryn Rusch, Eluki "Bob" bes Shahar, Josepha Sherman, Dean Wesley Smith, Allen Steele, Harry Turtledove and Lawrence Watt-Evans.

Other books you might like:
Robert Rankin, *Armageddon: The Musical*, 1991
Mike Resnick, *By Any Other Fame*, 1994
    Martin H. Greenberg, co-editor
Kim Stanley Robinson, *Escape From Kathmandu*, 1989
Paul M. Sammon, *The King Is Dead: Tales of Elvis Post Mortem*, 1994
    editor
Kay Sloan, *Elvis Rising: Stories on the King*, 1993
    Constance Pierce, co-editor

◼1666◼

ESTHER FRIESNER, Editor
MARTIN H. GREENBERG, Co-Editor

Blood Muse: Timeless Tales of Vampires in the Arts
(New York: Donald I. Fine, 1995)

Story type: Horror (Anthology; Vampire Story)

Summary: The 32 original stories collected here all grow out of the idea of the vampiric relationship between the artist, art, and life. Selections are divided into seven categories (The Gallery, The Conservatory, The Screening Room, The Sculpture Garden, The Dance Studio, The Scriptorium, Special Exhibits). Hightlights include Susan Williams' "Blind Faith," about a vampire stained-glass maker who can never enter the cathedrals for which he does his work; Meg Turville-Heitz's "Sing Heavenly Muse," about the influence of a vampire on John Milton's writing of *Paradise Lost*; Ben Adams' "The Frieze of Life," about Rodin's parasitic dependence on his models; and Adam-Troy Castro's "The Hand Inside," a unique look at the relationship between a ventriloquist and his dummy.

Other books you might like:
Ellen Datlow, *Blood Is Not Enough*, 1989
Ellen Datlow, *A Whisper of Blood*, 1992
Martin H. Greenberg, *Celebrity Vampires*, 1995
    editor
Alan Ryan, *Vampires: Two Centuries of Great Vampire Stories*, 1987

Robert Weinberg, *100 Vicious Little Vampire Stories*, 1995
Stefan Dziemianowicz, Martin H. Greenberg, co-editors

1667

ESTHER FRIESNER, Editor

Chicks in Chainmail
(New York: Baen, 1995)

Story type: Fantasy (Anthology; Light Fantasy)

Summary: Contains a four-page introduction plus 20 original stories which assault the pulp fiction stereotype of the woman warrior, such as a new Maureen Birnbaum, Barbarian Swordsperson tale from George Alec Effinger and a discussion of the results of a royal tax on bronze bras by Elizabeth Moon. Other authors include Margaret Ball, eluki bes shahar, Esther Friesner, Holly Lisle, Jody Lynn Nye, Elizabeth Ann Scarborough, Josepha Sherman, Susan Shwartz, Nancy Springer, Harry Turtledove, Lawrence Watt-Evans, and Roger Zelazny.

Other books you might like:
Marion Zimmer Bradley, *The Sword and Sorceress Series*, 1984-1995
  editor
George Alec Effinger, *Maureen Birnbaum, Barbarian Swordsperson: The Complete Stories*, 1993
C.L. Moore, *Jirel of Joiry*, 1969
Jessica Amanda Salmonson, *Amazons!*, 1979
  editor

1668

ESTHER FRIESNER

Child of the Eagle
(New York: Baen, 1996)

Story type: Fantasy (Historical; Legend)
Major character(s): Marcus Junius Brutus, Political Figure, Military Personnel (Roman general); Gaius Julius Caesar, Ruler (dictator), Military Personnel (Roman general); Venus, Deity
Time period(s): 1st century B.C.
Locale(s): Rome, Roman Empire; Alexandria, Egypt

Summary: On the eve of the plot against Caesar's life, the goddess Venus convinces Brutus to save the dictator rather than kill him. In return, she extends Brutus's life so he can see the eventual results of his decision and convince himself that his actions have helped his beloved Rome.

Other books you might like:
Anthony Burgess, *The Eve of Saint Venus*, 1964
Irving A. Greenfield, *Julius Caesar Is Alive and Well*, 1977
Talbot Mundy, *Queen Cleopatra*, 1929
Talbot Mundy, *Tros of Samothrace*, 1934
Lawrence Watt-Evans, *Split Heirs*, 1993
  Esther Friesner, co-author

1669

ESTHER FRIESNER

Gnome Man's Land
(New York: Ace, 1991)

Story type: Fantasy (Contemporary; Light Fantasy)
Series: Timothy Desmond
Major character(s): Timothy Alfred Desmond, Teenager; T'ing Hau Kaplan, Teenager; Telery of Limerick, Mythical Creature (banshee)
Time period(s): 1990s (1991)
Locale(s): New York, New York

Summary: There is a hole between the leeside (where the faeries went) and our world. Tim's life is drastically altered when his family banshee appears and starts bemoaning his imminent demise. He and T'ing must come to terms with mythical beings and magic battles. The hole is left open, leaving room for the forthcoming title, *Harpy High*.

Other books you might like:
Douglas Adams, *The Hitchhiker's Guide to the Galaxy*, 1980
Robert Asprin, *Another Fine Myth*, 1978
John Bellairs, *The Face in the Frost*, 1969
Diana Wynne Jones, *Howl's Moving Castle*, 1986
Diana Wynne Jones, *The Ogre Downstairs*, 1990
Terry Pratchett, *The Colour of Magic*, 1983

1670

ESTHER FRIESNER

Harpy High
(New York: Ace, 1991)

Story type: Fantasy (Light Fantasy; Young Adult)
Series: Timothy Desmond
Major character(s): Timothy Alfred Desmond, Student—High School, Wizard; Baba Yaga, Witch; Telery of Limerick, Mythical Creature (banshee)
Time period(s): 1990s
Locale(s): New York, New York

Summary: After "things" slip out of the Feidelstein Deli's Back Room and Baba Yaga puts Tim's mother to sleep for a thousand years, Tim, as Grand and Puissant Champion of the Fey, must somehow restore the balance of the Mythological Continuum and bring his mother back to life.

Other books you might like:
Robert Asprin, *Another Fine Myth*, 1978
Emma Bull, *War for the Oaks*, 1987
Dave Duncan, *Magic Casement*, 1990
Thorarinn Gunnarsson, *Make Way for Dragons!*, 1990
Diana Wynne Jones, *The Ogre Downstairs*, 1990
T.A. Waters, *The Probability Pad*, 1970

1671

ESTHER FRIESNER

Hooray for Hellywood

(New York: Ace, 1990)

Story type: Fantasy (Light Fantasy; Satire)
Major character(s): Melisan Cardiff, Demon, Human; Noel Cardiff, Warlock; Raleel, Demon
Time period(s): 21st century
Locale(s): Hollywood, California

Summary: The demon Raleel is currently posing as Joseph Lee, a televangelist whose plan to make a "sin-free" movie is just his most recent twist to curry sinful feelings in his followers. Noel Cardiff, his ardent, naive assistant, is conscience-stricken over the magical powers he inherited from his demon mother Melisan, and seems determined to turn away from his mother and her cohorts who helped defeat Raleel previously.

Other books you might like:
Emma Bull, *War for the Oaks*, 1987
Robert N. Charrette, *Never Deal with a Dragon*, 1991
Alan Dean Foster, *Smart Dragons, Foolish Elves*, 1991
   Martin Harry Greenberg, co-editor
Thorarinn Gunnarsson, *Make Way for Dragons!*, 1990
Tim Powers, *The Anubis Gates*, 1983

1672

ESTHER FRIESNER

It's Been Fun

(Eugene, Oregon: Pulphouse Publishing, 1991)

Story type: Fantasy (Collection)
Series: Author's Choice Monthly

Summary: This volume contains a 4-page introduction plus 6 stories. Four of them appeared in 1980s *Amazing* magazines and one, "Love's Eldritch Ichor," was published in the 1990 World Fantasy Convention program book. One story, "Pride and Prescience," appears for the first time.

Other books you might like:
Alan Brennert, *Ma Qui and Other Phantoms*, 1991
Charles de Lint, *Ghosts of Wind and Shadow*, 1991
Nina Kiriki Hoffman, *Legacy of Fire*, 1990
Damon Knight, *God's Nose*, 1991
Joe R. Lansdale, *Stories by Mama Lansdale's Youngest Boy*, 1991
Kate Wilhelm, *State of Grace*, 1991

1673

ESTHER FRIESNER

Majyk by Accident

(New York: Ace, 1993)

Story type: Fantasy (Light Fantasy; Adventure)
Series: Majyk
Major character(s): Kendar "Ratwacker" Gangle, Wizard, Student; Scandal, Animal (cat); Zoltan Fiendlord, Wizard

Time period(s): Indeterminate
Locale(s): Orbix, Planet—Imaginary

Summary: Prepared to withdraw from wizard's school with a D-, Kendar unexpectedly taps into all the abilities of his dying master but does not possess the wherewithal to wield them with maturity. A jealous wizard, a mythical Earth cat and an overdose of available majyk brings magical mayhem to the death of Orbix's most powerful wizard. First of a series.

Other books you might like:
C. Dale Brittain, *A Bad Spell in Yurt*, 1991
Lois McMaster Bujold, *The Spirit Ring*, 1992
Douglas W. Clark, *Whirlwind Alchemy*, 1993
John Moore, *Slay and Rescue*, 1993
S.P. Somtow, *The Wizard's Apprentice*, 1993
Christopher Stasheff, *The Warlock in Spite of Himself*, 1969
Lawrence Watt-Evans, *Split Heirs*, 1993
   Esther M. Friesner, co-author

1674

ESTHER FRIESNER

Majyk by Design

(New York: Ace, 1994)

Story type: Fantasy (Quest; Light Fantasy)
Series: Majyk
Major character(s): Kendar "Ratwacker" Gangle, Wizard; Curio, Model (book cover supermodel); Zoltan Fiendlord, Wizard
Time period(s): Indeterminate
Locale(s): Orbix, Planet—Imaginary

Summary: When a supermodel for book covers disappears, Curio requires Kendar Gangle's aid to prove his innocence. Kendar's investigation leads to an old rival, Zoltan Fiendlord.

Other books you might like:
C. Dale Brittain, *The Wood Nymph and the Cranky Saint*, 1993
Kyle Crocco, *Heroes, Inc.*, 1991
L. Sprague de Camp, *The Complete Compleat Enchanter*, 1989
   Fletcher Pratt, co-author
John Moore, *Slay and Rescue*, 1993
Harry Turtledove, *The Case of the Toxic Spell Dump*, 1993

1675

ESTHER FRIESNER

Majyk by Hook or Crook

(New York: Ace, 1994)

Story type: Fantasy (Light Fantasy; Adventure)
Series: Majyk
Major character(s): Kendar "Ratwacker" Gangle, Wizard; Scandal, Animal (cat)
Time period(s): Indeterminate
Locale(s): Orbix, Planet—Imaginary

Summary: The king has been deposed and live birds will rain on Orbix until his reinstatement. Kendar gets asked to fix the problem. Many strange animals and bad puns later, Kendar and Scandal may find the opportunity.

Other books you might like:
Robert Asprin, *Another Fine Myth*, 1978
C. Dale Brittain, *A Bad Spell in Yurt*, 1991
Alan Dean Foster, *Spellsinger*, 1983
Craig Shaw Gardner, *The Other Sinbad*, 1991
Roger Zelazny, *Bring Me the Head of Prince Charming*, 1991
    Robert Sheckley, co-author

1676

ESTHER FRIESNER

The Sherwood Game

(New York: Baen, 1995)

Story type: Science Fiction (Humor; Robot Fiction)
Major character(s): Carl Sherwood, Computer Expert; Robin Hood, Artificial Intelligence; Laurie Pincus, Computer Expert
Time period(s): 21st century
Locale(s): Austin, Texas; Virtual Reality, Cyberspace

Summary: Carl Sherwood's unauthorized virtual reality game set in medieval Sherwood Forest features a self-aware Robin Hood program. When the Robin Hood AI, occupying an android body, exercises its freedom in the real world, Carl must thwart both the AI and an evil corporate executive.

Other books you might like:
Aaron Allston, *Galatea in 2-D*, 1993
Piers Anthony, *Killobyte*, 1993
Charles de Lint, *Memory and Dream*, 1994
Philip Jose Farmer, *Red Orc's Rage*, 1991
Will Shetterly, *The Tangled Lands*, 1989
Vivian Vande Velde, *User Unfriendly*, 1991

1677

ESTHER FRIESNER

Sphynxes Wild

(New York: Signet, 1989)

Story type: Fantasy (Contemporary)
Major character(s): Sanchi, Gambler
Time period(s): 1980s
Locale(s): Atlantic City, New Jersey

Summary: After escaping the control of a sorcerer, a sphynx wanders through modern America seeking power. She becomes the head of a giganitc corporate empire in Atlantic City. A group from a ghetto join forces with the sorcerer to stop and control the sphynx.

Other books you might like:
Emma Bull, *War for the Oaks*, 1988
Craig Shaw Gardner, *A Multitude of Monsters*, 1986
Diana L. Paxson, *Brisingamen*, 1984
Adrienne Martine-Barnes, *The Rainbow Sword*, 1988

1678

ESTHER FRIESNER

Unicorn U.

(New York: Ace, 1992)

Story type: Fantasy (Light Fantasy; Young Adult)
Series: Timothy Desmond
Major character(s): Timothy Alfred Desmond, Student—College, Wizard; T'ing Hau Kaplan, Student—College; Yang, Spirit (T'ing's ancestor)
Time period(s): 1990s
Locale(s): New York, New York

Summary: Timothy Desmond should concentrate on his pre-medicine studies at Princeton but Yang's news that T'ing no longer sees her ancestor's spirit sends him on a rescue mission. Life becomes further complicated by his mother's engagement to the legendary Dr. Faustus, the reappearance of his banshee, Telery, and a handful of deities bent on starting armageddon in New York City.

Other books you might like:
Suzette Haden Elgin, *And Then There'll Be Fireworks*, 1981
Suzette Haden Elgin, *The Grand Jubilee*, 1981
Suzette Haden Elgin, *Twelve Fair Kingdoms*, 1981
Alan Dean Foster, *Cyber Way*, 1990
Neil Gaiman, *Good Omens: The Nice and Accurate Prophecies of Agnes Nutter, Witch*, 1990
    Terry Pratchett, co-author
Craig Shaw Gardner, *Revenge of the Fluffy Bunnies*, 1990
Parke Godwin, *Waiting for the Galactic Bus*, 1988

1679

ESTHER FRIESNER

Wishing Season

(New York: Atheneum, 1993)

Story type: Fantasy (Light Fantasy; Young Adult)
Series: Dragonflight
Major character(s): Khalid, Mythical Creature (genie), Student
Time period(s): Indeterminate Past
Locale(s): Middle East

Summary: Insufficiently warned in school, Khalid blows his first field assignment by failing to limit his first master to three wishes. Disaster strikes when Khalid must grant an infinite number of wishes. To extract himself from the mess, Khalid requires the assistance of a female genie, a princess and a talking cat.

Other books you might like:
Michael Ende, *The Night of Wishes: or The Satanarchaeo-lidealcohellish Notion Potion*, 1992
Craig Shaw Gardner, *The Other Sinbad*, 1991
S.P. Somtow, *The Wizard's Apprentice*, 1993
Brad Strickland, *Dragon's Plunder*, 1992
Tad Williams, *Child of an Ancient City*, 1992
    Nina Kiriki Hoffman, co-author

`1680`

ESTHER FRIESNER

Yesterday We Saw Mermaids

(New York: Tor, 1992)

Story type: Fantasy (Historical)
Major character(s): Mother Catalina, Religious (nun); Rasha of the Thousand Doors, Royalty (princess), Spouse (djinn's); La Zagala, Witch, Gypsy
Time period(s): 15th century (1492)
Locale(s): Atlantic Ocean; North America

Summary: The ethnically diverse passengers of a magical ship hope to arrive in the New World prior to Columbus, intending to preserve the place of magic in America. Presented as sequential journal entries.

Other books you might like:
Orson Scott Card, *Prentice Alvin*, 1988
Orson Scott Card, *Red Prophet*, 1989
Orson Scott Card, *Seventh Son*, 1987
John Maddox Roberts, *King of the Wood*, 1983

`1681`

GREGORY FROST

The Pure Cold Light

(New York: AvoNova, 1993)

Story type: Science Fiction (Political; Invasion of Earth)
Major character(s): Thomasina Lyell, Journalist, Activist; Angel, Alien
Time period(s): 21st century
Locale(s): Philadelphia, Pennsylvania; Moon (Earth's)

Summary: Thomasina Lyell follows leads on a story, revealing a conspiracy fostered by the megacorporations to maximize profits regardless of the cost to humanity.

Other books you might like:
Patricia Anthony, *Brother Termite*, 1993
William C. Dietz, *Matrix Man*, 1990
Michael Flynn, *In the Country of the Blind*, 1990
David Alexander Smith, *In the Cube*, 1993
Neal Stephenson, *Snow Crash*, 1992
John Varley, *Steel Beach*, 1992
Vernor Vinge, *A Fire upon the Deep*, 1992

`1682`

STEVEN RAY FULGHAM

The Forsaken

(New York: Diamond, 1991)

Story type: Horror (Occult)
Major character(s): Marshall Shaeler, Child; Anita Shaeler, Travel Agent; Azod, Young Man
Time period(s): 1990s
Locale(s): Seattle, Washington

Summary: In this semi-sequel to the author's first novel, *The Summoned*, a deformed young man named Azod lives in the attic of a skyscraper in downtown Seattle, fishing nightly with a large grappling hook for unwary strollers whom he hoists to his lair and subjects to the worst tortures imaginable in his service to the demon Bargolas.

Other books you might like:
Christopher Fowler, *Roofworld*, 1988

`1683`

STEVEN RAY FULGHAM

The Summoned

(New York: Diamond, 1991)

Story type: Horror (Occult)
Major character(s): Stan Fuller, Teenager; Mike Kawaguchi, Teenager; Bargolas, Demon
Time period(s): 1970s (1970)
Locale(s): Othello, Washington

Summary: The author's first novel tells in flashbacks how the succubus Bargolas was born of the union between a nun and priest during the Spanish Inquisition, and how the unbridled lusts of persons ever since have repeatedly summoned him back to the earthly plane. Bargolas proves quite a big hit in the small town of Othello, where teenage hormone levels run high.

Other books you might like:
Edward Lee, *Incubi*, 1991
Ray Russell, *Incubus*, 1976

`1684`

STEVEN RAY FULGHAM

A Whisper of Wings

(New York: Diamond, 1992)

Story type: Horror (Possession)
Major character(s): Duncan Glass, Civil Servant; Bo Challer, Teenager; Kaeot, Monster (Member of the Wicrae)
Time period(s): 1990s
Locale(s): Seattle, Washington

Summary: Seduced against his will into sexual union with a winged creature he hits with his car, Duncan Glass finds that he is undergoing a slow and painful physical transformation that will eventually transforms him into one of the Wicrae, a race of human beings turned into winged monsters who feed on human flesh.

Other books you might like:
Angela Carter, *Nights at the Circus*, 1984
John Farris, *Fiends*, 1990
John Farris, *Wildwood*, 1987

`1685`

ERIC JAMES FULLILOVE

Circle of One

(New York: Bantam Spectra, 1996)

Story type: Science Fiction (Cyberpunk; Mystery)

Major character(s): Jenny Sixa, Telepath, Detective; Didi "Deeds", Robot, Researcher; Derrick Trent, Detective—Homicide
Time period(s): 2050s
Locale(s): Los Angeles, California

Summary: A civilian aiding homicide investigations by tapping psychic impressions from corpses, Jenny Sixa finds a disturbing pattern in the victims of a serial killer. As part of the murders, the killer arranges for Jenny's name to appear among the victims' final memories. First novel.

Other books you might like:
Pat Cadigan, *Fools*, 1992
Raphael Carter, *The Fortunate Fall*, 1996
Laurell K. Hamilton, *Guilty Pleasures*, 1993
Katharine Kerr, *Polar City Blues*, 1990
Richard Paul Russo, *Destroying Angel*, 1992
David Alexander Smith, *In the Cube*, 1993
Neal Stephenson, *Snow Crash*, 1992

1686

LIZ FULTON

The Palm Dome
(New York: Bantam 1990)

Story type: Horror (Supernatural Vengeance)
Major character(s): Maurizio Camfrey, Professor (Professor of English); Faye Wolsey, Printer; Jack Gilbert, Antiques Dealer
Time period(s): 1990s
Locale(s): Camfrey Estate, Connecticut

Summary: Estranged nephew Jack Camfrey inherits the family estate from his deceased Aunt Emmeline, unaware that he is also inheriting the skeletons in the family closet—or, in this case, bodies at the bottom of the pool beneath the estate's lush palm dome.

Other books you might like:
James Herbert, *Haunted*, 1988
Matthew J. Costello, *Beneath Still Waters*, 1988
Steve Rasnic Tem, *Excavation*, 1987

1687

MAGGIE FUREY

Aurian
(New York: Bantam Spectra, 1994)

Story type: Fantasy (Magic Conflict; Romance)
Major character(s): Aurian, Student, Magician; Avran, Servant, Magician; Miathan, Magician
Time period(s): Indeterminate
Locale(s): Nexis, Fictional City

Summary: Inheriting both Earth-magic and Fire-magic from her parents, Aurian grows up in near isolation. When a friend of her father moves in, life changes, but following a near-fatal accident during a sword-fighting lesson, she goes to Nexis for training at the Mage's Academy. The Archmage Miathan plans on using her talents to increase his power, but when she takes a mortal lover, the Archmage schemes to destroy her,

even if it means unleasing the long-lost magic of forbidden weapons. First novel.

Other books you might like:
Lynn Abbey, *Daughter of the Bright Moon*, 1979
C.J. Cherryh, *The Paladin*, 1988
Phyllis Eisenstein, *Born to Exile*, 1978
Barbara Hambly, *The Ladies of Mandrigyn*, 1984
Tad Williams, *The Dragonbone Chair*, 1988

1688

MAGGIE FUREY

Harp of Winds
(New York: Bantam Spectra, 1995)

Story type: Fantasy (Magic Conflict; Quest)
Series: Aurian
Major character(s): Aurian, Magician, Parent; Avran, Magician; Miathan, Magician
Time period(s): Indeterminate
Locale(s): Nexis, Fictional City; Aerillia, Fictional City

Summary: Driven from the city of Nexis and unable to wield her magical powers during her pregnancy, Aurian sets forth on a journey with Avran and a small group of supporters to bring back the Staff of Earth, one of the ancient Great Weapons, and the heal a land locked in the icy grip of eternal winter by Miathan's sorcery. With the birth of her child, Aurian regains her magic but cannot undo the curse Miathan set on her child, while Avran goes in search of the second Great Weapon, the Harp of Winds. Sequel to *Aurian*.

Other books you might like:
Lynn Abbey, *The Wooden Sword*, 1991
C.J. Cherryh, *The Tree of Swords and Jewels*, 1983
Barbara Hambly, *The Silicon Mage*, 1988
Robert Jordan, *The Dragon Reborn*, 1991
Patricia A. McKillip, *The Riddle-Master of Hed*, 1976

1689

MAGGIE FUREY

Sword of Flame
(New York: Bantam Spectra, 1996)

Story type: Fantasy (Magic Conflict; Quest)
Series: Aurian
Major character(s): Aurian, Magician; Avran, Magician; Eliseth, Magician
Time period(s): Indeterminate
Locale(s): Nexis, Fictional City; Xandim, Fictional City

Summary: Using the Staff of Earth and the Harp of Winds, Aurian and Avran have broken the unnatural winter conjured by Eliseth and Miathan using the Cauldron of Waters. Beset by evil sorcery, betrayal, and madness they travel northward to Nexis seeking the fourth Artifact of Power, the Sword of Flame. The Sword's power can end Eliseth's rule, but the price of its mastery may be too high for Aurian.

Other books you might like:
C.J. Cherryh, *The Tree of Swords and Jewels*, 1983
Barbara Hambly, *The Dark Hand of Magic*, 1990

Robert Jordan, *The Fires of Heaven*, 1993
Katherine Kurtz, *High Deryni*, 1973
Patricia A. McKillip, *Harpist in the Wind*, 1979
J.R.R. Tolkien, *The Return of the King*, 1956

1690

LESLIE GADALLAH

Cat's Gambit

(New York: Ballantine/Del Rey Books, 1990)

Story type: Science Fiction (Space Opera)
Major character(s): Ayyah, Alien, Refugee; McDonald, Spaceman, Pirate
Time period(s): Indeterminate Future
Locale(s): Alpha Centauri IV, Planet—Imaginary; Pigpen, Asteroid; Kazi Empire, Interstellar Empire/Federation

Summary: The Oriani, a cat-like alien race, have been almost wiped out by the Kaz, a race of insect-like aliens. Ayyah, a refugee from that massacre, looks for a way to destroy the Kaz, who have now taken over much of the galaxy. She enlists the not entirely willing aid of a group of Terran gunrunners and mercenaries and the battle is on.

Other books you might like:
C.J. Cherryh, *Chanur's Homecoming*, 1986
C.J. Cherryh, *Chanur's Venture*, 1984
C.J. Cherryh, *The Kif Strike Back*, 1985
C.J. Cherryh, *The Pride of Chanur*, 1982
Walter Jon Williams, *Angel Station*, 1989

1691

PETER GADOL

Coyote

(New York: Crown, 1990)

Story type: Fantasy (Religious; Adventure)
Major character(s): Coyote Gato, Guide; Madeleine Mash, Journalist
Time period(s): 1990s
Locale(s): Frescuro, Southwest

Summary: Coyote hitches a ride with Madeleine to the ashram of Guru B. They pass by the Great Tree which has been very significant in Coyote's life. When they get to the ashram, Coyote claims to be Madeleine's husband in order to get inside, where he wants to find a friend and also a meteorite which had been stolen.

Other books you might like:
Neil Gaiman, *Good Omens: The Nice and Accurate Prophecies of Agnes Nutter, Witch*, 1990
    Terry Pratchett, co-author
Parke Godwin, *The Snake Oil Wars*, 1989
Parke Godwin, *Waiting for the Galactic Bus*, 1988
John Kessel, *Good News From Outer Space*, 1989
Barry Lopez, *Crow and Weasel*, 1990
Allen Steele, *Clarke County, Space*, 1990
Kurt Vonnegut Jr., *Cat's Cradle*, 1963

1692

NEIL GAIMAN

Angels & Visitations: A Miscellany

(Minneapolis, Minnesota: Dream Haven Books, 1993)

Story type: Fantasy (Collection)
Major character(s): The Troll, Mythical Creature; Lucifer, Angel, Military Personnel; Jack Horner, Detective—Private
Time period(s): Indeterminate Past; 1990s
Locale(s): The Palace of Spiders, Mythical Place; The Silver City, Fictional City; London, England

Summary: Contains 11 short stories, six poems and five essays, written 1984-1993, along with an introduction and seven illustrations. The tone ranges from horrifying to humorous while two of the stories put a new spin on mysteries as unusual detectives pursue murderers through *Mother Goose* and a city of angels.

Other books you might like:
Jonathan Carroll, *Bones of the Moon*, 1987
John Crowley, *Little, Big*, 1981
Robert Holdstock, *Mythago Wood*, 1984
Fritz Leiber, *Swords and Deviltry*, 1970
Ian McDonald, *Desolation Road*, 1988

1693

NEIL GAIMAN
TERRY PRATCHETT, Co-Author

Good Omens: The Nice and Accurate Prophecies of Agnes Nutter, Witch

(New York: Workman, 1990)

Story type: Fantasy (Religious; Light Fantasy)
Major character(s): Crowley, Angel (fallen); Aziraphale, Angel; Adam, Demon (the Antichrist)
Time period(s): 1990s (1990)
Locale(s): London, England; Oxfordshire, England

Summary: An angel and a demon cooperate in delaying Armageddon so as to preserve the interesting life on Earth. Their efforts become complicated when the Antichrist ends up in the wrong family at birth.

Other books you might like:
Parke Godwin, *The Snake Oil Wars*, 1989
Parke Godwin, *Waiting for the Galactic Bus*, 1988
Robert A. Heinlein, *Job: A Comedy of Justice*, 1984
Robert A. Heinlein, *Stranger in a Strange Land*, 1961
Kurt Vonnegut Jr., *Cat's Cradle*, 1963

1694

NEIL GAIMAN, Editor
EDWARD E. KRAMER, Co-Editor

The Sandman: Book of Dreams

(New York: HarperPrism, 1996)

Story type: Fantasy (Anthology; Literary)

Series: Sandman
Major character(s): Peter Himmels, Military Personnel; Morpheus, Mythical Creature (Lord of the Dreaming); Death, Mythical Creature
Time period(s): 1990s; 1940s
Locale(s): The Dreaming, Mythical Place; Wych Cross, England

Summary: Contains a five-page preface by Frank McConnell and individual introductions to 17 stories, one poem and Tori Amos' introduction to "Death: The High Cost of Living," all inspired by Neil Gaiman's comic, *The Sandman*. Varying in tone, the stories involve dreams, dreaming, and peoples' reactions to them, with some elaboration on characters and settings created or developed by Gaiman. Authors include Steven Brust, Nancy Collins, George Alec Effinger, John M. Ford, Lisa Goldstein, Colin Greenland, Karen Haber, Barbara Hambly, Delia Sherman, Will Shetterly, Tad Williams, and Gene Wolfe.

Other books you might like:
Jonathan Carroll, *Bones of the Moon*, 1987
John Crowley, *Little, Big*, 1981
Greer Ilene Gilman, *Moonwise*, 1990
Robert Holdstock, *Mythago Wood*, 1984
Megan Lindholm, *Wizard of the Pigeons*, 1986

1695

DIANA G. GALLAGHER

The Alien Dark

(Lake Geneva, Wisconsin: TSR, 1990)

Story type: Science Fiction (Hard Science Fiction)
Major character(s): Tahl d'jehn, Alien (ahsin bey), Spaceship Captain; Riitha f'ath, Alien (ahsin bey), Scientist (biologist)
Time period(s): Indeterminate Future (1,000,000th century)
Locale(s): *Dan tahlni*, Spaceship; Venus; Moon (Earth's)

Summary: The ahsin bey sent out several survey vessels to find new solar systems to colonize. It will be decades before the crew of the *Dan tahlni* can learn if a colony ship is on the way to the system they've discovered, but the installations around the fifth planet will be ready when the time comes.

Other books you might like:
Octavia E. Butler, *Dawn*, 1987
C.J. Cherryh, *The Pride of Chanur*, 1982
Gordon R. Dickson, *The Alien Way*, 1965
Larry Niven, *Protector*, 1973
David Alexander Smith, *Homecoming*, 1990
L. Neil Smith, *Their Majesties' Bucketeers*, 1981

1696

STEPHEN GALLAGHER

Down River

(New York: Tor, 1990)

Story type: Horror (Psychological Suspense)
Major character(s): Johnny Mays, Police Officer; Nick Frazier, Police Officer; Alice Craig, Office Worker

Time period(s): 1980s (1989)
Locale(s): London, England

Summary: Maverick cop Johnny Mays takes his personal vendettas too far one night and apparently drowns in a reservoir while harrassing a felon. Shortly thereafter his partner, Nick Frazier, notices that people Johnny held a grudge against are dying horrible deaths.

Other books you might like:
Ramsey Campbell, *The Face That Must Die*, 1979
Thomas Harris, *Red Dragon*, 1981
William Hjortsberg, *Falling Angel*, 1978

1697

STEPHEN GALLAGHER

Nightmare, with Angel

(New York: Ballantine, 1993)

Story type: Horror (Psychological Suspense)
Major character(s): Marianne Cadogan, Child (10 years old); Ryan O'Donnell, Beachcomber; Jennifer McGann, Detective—Police
Time period(s): 1990s (1993)
Locale(s): England; Hamburg, Germany

Summary: When young Marianne Cadogan runs away from her stern father to find her mother in Germany, Patrick Cadogan doesn't know which is worst: the possiblity that she may find her mother and the sordid sex ring she was involved with, or the fact that Marianne's traveling companion is a man who was once imprisoned for murdering an eleven-year-old child. This book was originally published in England in 1992.

Other books you might like:
John D. MacDonald, *The Executioners*, 1958
Robert R. McCammon, *Mine*, 1990
Ian McEwan, *The Cement Garden*, 1978
John Metcalfe, *The Feasting Dead*, 1954

1698

STEPHEN GALLAGHER

Oktober

(New York: Tor, 1990)

Story type: Horror (Mystery)
Major character(s): Jim Harper, Teacher; Rochelle Genoud, Heiress; Werner Risinger, Businessman (head of Risinger-Genoud), Relative (Rochelle's stepbrother)
Time period(s): 1980s (1989)
Locale(s): Switzerland; Cliff House, England

Summary: Critically injured in a mishap at the Risinger-Genoud chemical plant, Jim Harper is injected with the experimental drug Epheteline. Years later, a series of recurring nightmares convinces Jim that his condition is connected to his treatment, and that he is being monitored like a guinea pig by those who treated him.

Other books you might like:
Martin James, *Night Glow*, 1989
Stephen King, *Firestarter*, 1980

Dean R. Koontz, *Midnight*, 1989

1699
STEPHEN GALLAGHER

Red, Red Robin
(New York: Ballantine, 1995)

Story type: Horror (Psychological Suspense)
Major character(s): Ruth Lasseter, Advertising; Aidan Kincannon, Security Officer; Tim Hagan, Companion (paid escort)
Time period(s): 1990s (1995)
Locale(s): Philadelphia, Pennsylvania

Summary: In an effort to protect a married colleague from the embarrassment of public discovery of their affair, British expatriate Ruth Lsseter hires a professional escort for a company party, and then foolishly indulges him with a one night stand that provides him with a fatal attraction for her. After he is dispatched, Ruth embarks on an obsessive quest into his background that reveals the monster he is and, worse, that he may not be dead as Ruth thinks.

Other books you might like:
John Farris, *Sacrifice*, 1994
John Fowles, *The Collector*, 1963
Samuel M. Key, *I'll Be Watching You*, 1994

1700
LEWIS GANNETT

The Living One
(New York: Randam House, 1993)

Story type: Horror (Gothic Family Chronicle)
Major character(s): Torrance Spoor, Teenager (16 years old); Baron Malcolm Spoor, Businessman; Sheila Massif, Sociologist
Time period(s): 1990s (1993)
Locale(s): Boston, Massachusetts

Summary: Under the pretense of spending his last days with his son, Baron Malcolm Spoor, the inheritor of a family curse of madness that strikes all male descendants of the Spoor family before they turn 50, transplants the boy from California to a secluded stronghold in Massachusetts. There, young Torrance is subjected to his father's voyeurism and other perverse habits, before learning that the collective Spoor male consciousness inhabiting his father's body plans to incorporate Torrance's own consciousness and take over his body when his father "dies." Told in an epistolary style, this is the author's first novel.

Other books you might like:
Tanith Lee, *Dark Dance*, 1992
Robert R. McCammon, *Usher's Passing*, 1984
Patrick McGrath, *The Grotesque*, 1990
Joyce Carol Oates, *Bellefleur*, 1980
Gus Weill, *Flesh*, 1990
F. Paul Wilson, *Sibs*, 1992

1701
ERIC GARBER

Embracing the Dark
(Boston: Alyson, 1991)

Story type: Horror (Anthology)

Summary: This first anthology of gay and lesbian horror fiction collects eleven stories—five original, five reprint, and Karl Heinrich Ulrich's "Manor," a translation of a story originally published in the 1880s. Included are Jay B. Laws "Imagine," about a dream lover who becomes real; two stories of vampires by Jewelle Gomez and Jeffrey McMahan; and a shapeshifter story by John Peyton Cooke, "The Strawberry Man."

Other books you might like:
John Peyton Cooke, *Out for Blood*, 1991
Scott Edelman, *The Gift*, 1990
Jeffrey M. Elliot, *Kindred Spirits*, 1984
Jewelle Gomez, *The Gilda Stories*, 1991
Jay B. Laws, *Steam*, 1991
Jeffrey N. McMahan, *Somewhere in the Night*, 1989
Jeffrey N. McMahan, *Vampires Anonymous*, 1991

1702
ERIC GARBER, Editor
JEWELLE GOMEZ, Co-Editor

Swords of the Rainbow
(Los Angeles: Alyson Publications, 1996)

Story type: Fantasy (Anthology; Science Fiction)

Summary: This anthology contains three pages of authors' biographies, 13 original stories and Samuel R. Delany's "The Tale of Small Sarg" from *Tales of Neveryon* (1979). All stories utilize gay/lesbian themes with other themes such as sword and sorcery, urban fantasy, post-disaster, political conflict, and high fantasy by authors including Lauren Wright Douglas, Jewelle Gomez, Tanya Huff, Mel Keegan, Carrie Richardson, Mark Shepherd, and Jean Stewart.

Other books you might like:
Camilla Decarnin, *Worlds Apart*, 1986
    Eric Garber, Lyn Paleo, co-editors
Jeffrey M. Elliot, *Kindred Spirits*, 1984
    editor
Pam Keesey, *Dark Angels: Lesbian Vampire Stories*, 1995
    editor
Pam Keesey, *Daughters of Darkness: Lesbian Vampire Stories*, 1993
    editor
Ernest Posey, *Hormone Pirates of Xenobia and Dream Studs of Kama Loka*, 1996
Caro Soles, *Meltdown!*, 1994
    editor

1703

ROBERT T. GARCIA, Editor

Chilled to the Bone

(Niles, Illinois: Mayfair Games, Inc., 1991)

Story type: Horror (Anthology)

Summary: Fifteen tales of horror and dark fantasy by diverse hands presented as selections from the closed files of The Eternal Society of the Silver Way (Societas Argenti Viae Eternitata, or SAVE), an occult investigation unit. Included are Robert Weinberg's tale of an urban werewolf, ''Terror by Night''; F.A. McMahan's account of a phantom lover, ''Whose Hungry Mouth''; Blythe Ayne's story of the cult of Kali, ''In Her Hands''; and stories by Matthew Costello, Steve and Melanie Tem, Andre Norton, and G. Wayne Miller.

Other books you might like:
Charles L. Grant, *The Greystone Bay Series*, 1985-1991
Robert R. McCammon, *Under the Fang*, 1991
John Skipp, *Book of the Dead*, 1989
   Craig Spector, co-author

1704

R. GARCIA Y ROBERTSON

The Spiral Dance

(New York: William Morrow, 1991)

Story type: Fantasy (Adventure; Historical)

Major character(s): Anne Percy, Noblewoman (Countess of Northumberland); Jock o' the Syde, Werewolf, Companion

Time period(s): 16th century

Locale(s): Scotland; England

Summary: Anne, driven by a religious vision, and her husband set out to depose Elizabeth Tudor and put Mary Stuart on the British throne. When her husband is betrayed and imprisoned, Anne seeks freedom and spiritual satisfaction aided by Jock. During perilous travels she is transported by witchcraft to Faerie and back before reaching enlightenment. This is the author's first novel.

Other books you might like:
Margaret J. Anderson, *The Druid's Gift*, 1989
Gael Baudino, *Strands of Starlight*, 1989
Diana Gabaldon, *Outlander*, 1991
Mary Alexander Walker, *The Scathach and the Maeve's Daughter*, 1990
Patricia C. Wrede, *Snow White and Rose Red*, 1989

1705

R. GARCIA Y ROBERTSON

The Virgin and the Dinosaur

(New York: AvoNova, 1996)

Story type: Science Fiction (Time Travel; Political)

Major character(s): Jake Bento, Time Traveller, Guide; Peg, Scientist (paleontologist), Time Traveller; Charlotte Marie d'Anton, Slave, Time Traveller

Time period(s): Indeterminate Past (Mesozoic era/Upper Cretaceous); 1850s (1857)

Locale(s): Hell Creek, Montana

Summary: When Jake takes Peg to the Mesozoic era to study dinosaurs, he loses his only weapon almost immediately. They record many encounters with dinosaurs before the loss of their reactor forces them to head for home, passing through the 1857 Midwest where they travel the Mississippi River on a paddlewheel steamboat.

Other books you might like:
Poul Anderson, *The Time Patrol*, 1991
James Gurney, *Dinotopia*, 1992
Stephen Leigh, *Ray Bradbury Presents: Dinosaur Planet*, 1993
Julian May, *The Many-Colored Land*, 1981
Robert J. Sawyer, *Far-Seer*, 1992

1706

CRAIG SHAW GARDNER

A Bad Day for Ali Baba

(New York: Ace, 1992)

Story type: Fantasy (Legend; Light Fantasy)

Series: Arabian Nights

Major character(s): Ali Baba, Artisan, Adventurer; Aladdin, Thief, Adventurer

Time period(s): Indeterminate Past

Locale(s): Middle East

Summary: Ali Baba and Aladdin's quest for treasure and humorous encounters leads from an enchanted cavern to the Palace of Beautiful Women. Companion volume to *The Other Sinbad*.

Other books you might like:
Douglas Adams, *The Hitchhiker's Guide to the Galaxy*, 1980
Douglas Adams, *The Restaurant at the End of the Universe*, 1981
Piers Anthony, *A Spell for Chameleon*, 1977
John Barth, *The Last Voyage of Somebody the Sailor*, 1991
Andrew Lang, *The Arabian Nights Entertainments*, 1969
   Editor
Salman Rushdie, *Haroun and the Sea of Stories*, 1990
Susan Shwartz, *Arabesques: More Tales of the Arabian Nights*, 1988
   Editor
Jack Zipes, *Arabian Nights: The Marvels and Wonders of the Thousand and One Nights*, 1991
   Editor

1707

CRAIG SHAW GARDNER

Batman Returns

(New York: Warner, 1992)

Story type: Science Fiction (Adventure)

Series: Batman

Major character(s): Bruce "Batman" Wayne, Hero, Detective—Amateur; Oswald "the Penguin" Cobblepot, Criminal; Selena "Catwoman" Kyle, Criminal, Heroine
Time period(s): 21st century
Locale(s): Gotham City (New York City)

Summary: Penguin and Catwoman plot to discredit Batman and terrorize some Gotham City residents as they attempt to control the city. Film tie-in.

Other books you might like:
Lynn Abbey, *Catwoman*, 1992
    Robert Asprin, co-author
Martin H. Greenberg, *The Further Adventures of Batman*, 1989
    editor
Martin H. Greenberg, *The Further Adventures of Batman 2: Featuring the Penguin*, 1992
    editor
Martin H. Greenberg, *The Further Adventures of the Joker*, 1990
    editor
Simon Hawke, *Batman: To Stalk a Specter*, 1991
Joe R. Lansdale, *Batman: Captured by the Engines*, 1991

1708
CRAIG SHAW GARDNER

Bride of the Slime Monster
(New York: Ace, 1990)

Story type: Fantasy (Alternate World)
Series: Cineverse Cycle
Major character(s): Roger Gordon, Public Relations; Delores, Girlfriend (Roger's)
Time period(s): 1980s; Indeterminate
Locale(s): Earth; Alternate Universe

Summary: Though Roger has finally escaped Cineverse, the universe in which old B-movies are real, he must return to rescue his girlfriend, Delores, from the evil Dr. Dread. He must also battle a new adversary, Menge the Merciless, and must deal with the misunderstood Edward the Slime Monster.

Other books you might like:
Glen Cook, *Dread Brass Shadows*, 1990
Peter David, *Howling Mad*, 1989
Terry Pratchett, *Sourcery*, 1988
Alis A. Rasmussen, *The Labyrinth Gate*, 1989
Spider Robinson, *Callahan's Crosstime Saloon*, 1989
George H. Scithes, *Another Round at the Spaceport Bar*, 1989
    Daniell Schweitzer, co-author

1709
CRAIG SHAW GARDNER

Dragon Burning
(New York: Ace, 1996)

Story type: Fantasy (Magic Conflict; Alternate World)
Series: Dragon Circle
Major character(s): Nick Blake, Teenager, Warrior; Carl Jackson, Adventurer; Nunn, Magician

Time period(s): Indeterminate
Locale(s): Seven Islands, Fictional Country

Summary: With the dragon awakened and the wizards continuing their warfare, chaos and destruction will envelop the land unless Nick Blake and his neighbors from Chestnut Circle can halt the conflict.

Other books you might like:
A.A. Attanasio, *The Dragon and the Unicorn*, 1996
Robin Wayne Bailey, *Brothers of the Dragon*, 1993
Don Callander, *Dragon Companion*, 1994
Terry Goodkind, *Stone of Tears*, 1995
Robert Jordan, *The Eye of the World*, 1990
Marjorie Bradley Kellogg, *The Book of Earth*, 1995

1710
CRAIG SHAW GARDNER

Dragon Sleeping
(New York: Ace, 1994)

Story type: Fantasy (Alternate World; Magic Conflict)
Series: Dragon Circle
Major character(s): Nick Blake, Teenager, Warrior; Mary Lou "Merrilu" Dafoe, Teenager; Nunn, Magician
Time period(s): 1960s (1967); Indeterminate
Locale(s): Chestnut Circle, Fictional City; Seven Islands, Fictional Country

Summary: When the residents of Chestnut Circle find their community transported to a magical realm, only Nick and three friends evade Nunn's capture, joining Nunn's rival in an attempt to control an immortal dragon. Finding an opportunity to escape, Mary Lou also flees and locates allies among fierce warriors. First of a series.

Other books you might like:
Robin Wayne Bailey, *Brothers of the Dragon*, 1993
Gordon R. Dickson, *The Dragon and the George*, 1976
Carole Nelson Douglas, *Cup of Clay*, 1991
Richard A. Knaak, *King of the Grey*, 1993
R.A. Salvatore, *The Woods out Back*, 1993

1711
CRAIG SHAW GARDNER

Dragon Waking
(New York: Ace, 1995)

Story type: Fantasy (Magic Conflict; Alternate World)
Series: Dragon Circle
Major character(s): Nick Blake, Teenager, Warrior; Obar, Magician; Nunn, Magician
Time period(s): Indeterminate
Locale(s): Seven Islands, Fictional Country; At Sea

Summary: Nunn and Obar continue to battle for supremacy and control of the immortal dragon, now risen and draining magic from the world. The wizards use magic artifacts as well as Nick and his friends in their attempts to master the beast.

Other books you might like:
Terry Goodkind, *Stone of Tears*, 1995

Robert Jordan, *The Eye of the World*, 1989
Marjorie Bradley Kellogg, *The Book of Earth*, 1995
Ursula K. Le Guin, *A Wizard of Earthsea*, 1968
Mark C. Perry, *Morigu: The Dead*, 1990

1712

CRAIG SHAW GARDNER

The Last Arabian Night

(New York: Ace, 1993)

Story type: Fantasy (Legend; Light Fantasy)
Series: Arabian Nights
Major character(s): Scheherazade, Spouse, Storyteller; Shahryar, Royalty (king), Spouse
Time period(s): Indeterminate Past
Locale(s): Middle East

Summary: Casting about to replace his wife, beheaded for faithlessness, Shahryar chooses his grand vizier's daughter, Scheherazade. To save herself from the expected beheading at the hands of an obsessive-compulsive spouse, Scheherazade diverts his attention with her marvelous tales.

Other books you might like:
John Barth, *Chimera*, 1972
John Barth, *The Last Voyage of Somebody the Sailor*, 1991
Esther Friesner, *Wishing Season*, 1993
Susan Shwartz, *Arabesques: More Tales of the Arabian Nights*, 1988
  editor
Mark Twain, *Satires and Burlesques*, 1968
Jack Zipes, *Arabian Nights: The Marvels and Wonders of the Thousand and One Nights*, 1991
  editor

1713

CRAIG SHAW GARDNER

The Other Sinbad

(New York: Ace, 1991)

Story type: Fantasy (Legend; Light Fantasy)
Major character(s): Sinbad the Porter, Worker; Sinbad the Sailor, Businessman, Adventurer; Ozzie, Mythical Creature (djinn)
Time period(s): Indeterminate Past
Locale(s): Baghdad, Middle East; Hutan's Ship, At Sea

Summary: Involuntarily recruited by Sinbad the Sailor, Sinbad the Porter journeys on an eighth wondrous voyage with the famous sailor whose latest voyage aims at replenishing his treasury, which was drained by the vengeful djinn, Ozzie.

Other books you might like:
Douglas Adams, *The Hitchhiker's Guide to the Galaxy*, 1980
Douglas Adams, *The Restaurant at the End of the Universe*, 1981
Piers Anthony, *A Spell for Chameleon*, 1977
John Barth, *The Last Voyage of Somebody the Sailor*, 1991
Patricia Daniels, *Sinbad the Sailor*, 1980
Stephen Goldin, *Shrine of the Desert Mage*, 1988

Andrew Lang, *The Arabian Nights Entertainments*, 1969
  editor
Salman Rushdie, *Haroun and the Sea of Stories*, 1990
Susan Shwartz, *Arabesques: More Tales of the Arabian Nights*, 1988
  editor
Susan Shwartz, *Arabesques II*, 1989
  editor
Jack Zipes, *Arabian Nights: The Marvels and Wonders of the Thousand and One Nights*, 1991
  editor

1714

CRAIG SHAW GARDNER

Revenge of the Fluffy Bunnies

(New York: Ace, 1990)

Story type: Fantasy (Light Fantasy; Satire)
Series: Cineverse Cycle
Major character(s): Roger Gordon Jr., Hero, Adventurer; Mrs. Gordon Sr., Housewife, Adventurer; Doctor Dread, Terrorist, Leader
Time period(s): Indeterminate
Locale(s): Cineverse, Alternate Universe (Citadel of Dread); California

Summary: Cineverse's many movie worlds are undergoing an insidious change. Bad guys are winning, good guys are dying, and the boy doesn't even get the girl. Only Captain Crusader (Roger Gordon, Jr. in "real" life) can save the day by defeating Dr. Dread and his evil Forces of Darkness before the curtain falls on the last act. Unfortunately, Dr. Dread's partner, whip-cracking archvillainess Mother Antoinette, is Roger's mother, Mrs. Roger Gordon, Sr., a bored widow with a taste for destruction. To complicate things, Roger's girlfriend has been abducted by Edward, an amorous slime monster.

Other books you might like:
Douglas Adams, *The Hitchhiker's Guide to the Galaxy*, 1980
Piers Anthony, *Man From Mundania*, 1989
James P. Blaylock, *The Stone Giant*, 1989
James P. Blaylock, *The Elfin Ship*, 1986
Alexis A. Gilliland, *Wizenbeak*, 1990
Gary K. Wolf, *Who Censored Roger Rabbit?*, 1981

1715

CRAIG SHAW GARDNER

Wishbringer

(New York: Avon, 1988)

Story type: Fantasy (Light Fantasy)
Major character(s): Simon, Postal Worker
Time period(s): Indeterminate
Locale(s): Festerton; Witchville

Summary: Based on one of Infocom's interactive fiction computer games, the story follows Simon who commits a crime and is sentenced to serve as a mailman in the town of

Festerton (which occasionally turns into the sinister town of Witchville).

Other books you might like:
Douglas Adams, *The Hitchhiker's Guide to the Galaxy*, 1979
Piers Anthony, *Man From Mundania*, 1989
James P. Blaylock, *The Elfin Ship*, 1986
James P. Blaylock, *The Stone Giant*, 1989
Alexis A. Gilliland, *Wizenbeak*, 1990
Daniel Manus Pinkwater, *Borgel*, 1990

1716

HENRY GARFIELD

Moondog
(New York: St. Martin's, 1995)

Story type: Horror (Werewolf Story; Mystery)
Major character(s): Joe Acton, Worker (in a restaurant); Cyrus ''Moondog'' Nygerski, Journalist; Erik Gunn, Editor
Time period(s): 1980s (1989)
Locale(s): Julian, California

Summary: The slaughter of several women on nights of the full moon during a summer in a quiet suburb of San Diego brings together ex-burglar Joe Acton and renegade journalist Moondog Nygerski to solve the mystery. When the two deduce that a werewolf is the only possible explanation, its casts suspicion on a number of townspeople, themselves included. This is the author's first novel.

Other books you might like:
Crosland Brown, *Tombley's Walk*, 1991
George C. Chesbro, *The Fear in Yesterday's Rings*, 1991
D.J. Donaldson, *Blood on the Bayou*, 1991
Whitley Strieber, *The Wolfen*, 1978
Les Whitten, *Moon of the Wolf*, 1967

1717

RICHARD GARFINKLE

Celestial Matters
(New York: Tor, 1996)

Story type: Science Fiction (Alternate Universe; Hard Science Fiction)
Major character(s): Aias, Scientist; Yellow Hare, Military Personnel; Phan Xu-Tzu, Spy, Scientist
Time period(s): 7th century
Locale(s): Athens, Greece; Mars; Alternate Universe

Summary: In a Ptolemic universe, the Delian Archons choose Aias of Tyre to take his ship, *Chandra's Tear*, to the Celestial Sphere and capture sun matter with which to destroy 'AngXou, the capital of the Middle Kingdom at war with the Delian League for 900 years. When traitors and agents sabotage the ship, stranding it in Ares Sphere, Aias and the Middle Kingdom agent Phan Xu-Tzu must cooperate to get the ship home and find out how to halt, if only for a time, the centuries long war. First novel.

Other books you might like:
Greg Bear, *Eternity*, 1988
Ben Bova, *Orion and the Conqueror*, 1994

L. Sprague de Camp, *The Dragon of the Ishtar Gate*, 1961
Kirk Mitchell, *Procurator*, 1984
Melissa Scott, *A Choice of Destinies*, 1986
Judith Tarr, *Lord of the Two Lands*, 1993
Harry Turtledove, *Agent of Byzantium*, 1987

1718

MARK A. GARLAND
CHARLES G. MCGRAW, Co-Author

Demon Blade
(New York: Baen, 1994)

Story type: Fantasy (Quest; Adventure)
Major character(s): Madia, Royalty; Tyrr, Demon, Magician; Frost, Magician
Time period(s): Indeterminate
Locale(s): Far North, Fictional Country

Summary: After Tyrr discredits Madia, Frost and Madia must journey to the swamplands of the Far North to find and acquire the Demon Blade, a powerful magic object.

Other books you might like:
Lois McMaster Bujold, *The Spirit Ring*, 1992
Rosemary Edghill, *The Sword of Maiden's Tears*, 1994
Terry Goodkind, *Wizard's First Rule*, 1994
Marc Laidlaw, *Neon Lotus*, 1988
Holly Lisle, *Minerva Wakes*, 1994
Patricia C. Wrede, *The Raven Ring*, 1994

1719

MARK A. GARLAND
CHARLES G. MCGRAW, Co-Author

Dorella
(New York: Baen, 1992)

Story type: Fantasy (Magic Conflict)
Major character(s): Dorella, Witch, Alien
Time period(s): 1990s
Locale(s): Earth

Summary: Finally warming to human beings after more than 4000 years on Earth, Dorella repeatedly begins to form friendships with humans only to find an ancient enemy's agents forcing her to move on. Author's first novel.

Other books you might like:
Michael Cassutt, *Dragon Season*, 1991
Elizabeth Forrest, *Phoenix Fire*, 1992
James D. Priest, *Kirins: The Flight of the Ain*, 1992
James D. Priest, *Kirins: The Spell of No'an*, 1990
Will Shetterly, *Elsewhere*, 1991

1720

JAKE GARN
STEPHEN PAUL COHEN, Co-Author

Night Launch
(New York: William Morrow, 1989)

Story type: Science Fiction (Techno-Thriller)

Major character(s): Conrad Williams, Astronaut; Aelita Zakharov, Astronaut
Time period(s): 1990s
Locale(s): Earth; *Discovery*, Spaceship

Summary: The first space shuttle to be launched with an international crew is hijacked by a psychopathic criminal with connections to the terrorist underground. The terrorists demand the release of political prisoners and the international situation begins to heat up. A desperate rescue mission is launched to retake the shuttle and save its crew.

Other books you might like:
Ben Bova, *The Kinsman Saga*, 1987
Ben Bova, *Peacekeepers*, 1988
Dale Brown, *Day of the Cheetah*, 1989
Dale Brown, *The Silver Tower*, 1988
Edward Gibson, *Reach*, 1989
Dean Ing, *The Ransom of Black Stealth One*, 1989

1721

JAMES FINN GARNER

Once upon a More Enlightened Time
(New York: Macmillan, 1995)

Story type: Fantasy (Collection; Legend)
Series: Politically Correct Bedtime Stories

Summary: Contains a three-page introduction, a politically correct alphabet, and nine familiar fairy tales, humorously rewritten to reflect modern sensiblities, such as "Sleeping Persun of Better-than-average Attractiveness" and "The City Mouse and the Suburban Mouse." In other tales, Hansel and Gretel learn about forest ecology from a resident Wiccan, the Little Mer-persun visits a protest over drift net fishing, Puss in Boots acts as spin doctor and organizer of the senatorial campaign of his inheritor, and the tortoise and the hare compete in a media-oriented sporting extravaganza.

Other books you might like:
Margaret Atwood, *Good Bones and Simple Murders*, 1994
William J. Brooke, *Teller of Tales*, 1994
George Alec Effinger, *Maureen Birnbaum, Barbarian Swordsperson: The Complete Stories*, 1993
Esther Friesner, *Chicks in Chainmail*, 1995
    editor
Ursula K. Le Guin, *Fish Soup*, 1992
Ethel Johnston Phelps, *Tatterhood and Other Tales*, 1978
    editor
Chelsea Quinn Yarbro, *A Baroque Fable*, 1986
Jack Zipes, *The Outspoken Princess and the Gentle Knight*, 1994
    editor

1722

JAMES FINN GARNER

Politically Correct Bedtime Stories
(New York: Macmillan, 1994)

Story type: Fantasy (Anthology; Legend)

Summary: Contains 13 familiar fairy tales retold with modern sensibilities in mind and tongue firmly in cheek, with Cinderella joining her sisters-of-step in a co-op to produce comfortable clothes for womyn, the Emperor endorsing a clothing-optional life style and Jack's climbing the beanstalk and learning not to judge people by their size. But not everyone lives happily ever after as the princess realizes that the frog she has just kissed has become a real estate developer who wants to build an office/condo/resort complex in the woods.

Other books you might like:
Robert Asprin, *Another Fine Myth*, 1978
Terry Pratchett, *Witches Abroad*, 1993
Elizabeth Ann Scarborough, *The Drastic Dragon of Draco, Texas*, 1986
Chelsea Quinn Yarbro, *A Baroque Fable*, 1986
Jack Zipes, *The Outspoken Princess and the Gentle Knight*, 1994
    editor

1723

JAMES FINN GARNER

Politically Correct Holiday Stories
(New York: Macmillan, 1995)

Story type: Fantasy (Collection; Legend)
Series: Politically Correct Bedtime Stories

Summary: Contains a four-page introduction, one poem, and four familiar seasonal stories humorously rewritten for modern sensibilities. In "'Twas the Night Before Solstice," a co-op resident educates a visitor on parental cultivation of values and the influence of retailers on seasonal giving; Frosty the Persun of Snow campaigns as a eco-warrior; the Nutcracker, having resigned from the military, acts as a diplomat; Rudolph the Nasally Empowered Reindeer forces labor concessions out of Santa Claus; and three spiritual facilitators work over Scrooge in an extensive guilt trip.

Other books you might like:
Margaret Atwood, *Good Bones and Simple Murders*, 1994
William J. Brooke, *Teller of Tales*, 1994
David G. Hartwell, *Christmas Magic*, 1994
    editor
Ethel Johnston Phelps, *Tatterhood and Other Tales*, 1978
    editor
Kristine Kathryn Rusch, *Pulphouse, Issue 10: Special Issue*, 1991
    editor
Jack Zipes, *The Outspoken Princess and the Gentle Knight*, 1994
    editor

1724

SHEILA BRISTOW GARNER

Night Music
(New York: Pinnacle, 1992)

Story type: Horror (Black Magic; Occult)

Major character(s): Kitty Barrett, Nurse; Michael Sandeen, Musician; Zeke Miller, Musician
Time period(s): 1990s
Locale(s): Ocean City, North Carolina

Summary: Nurse Kitty Barrett rescues dissipated guitarist Michael Sandeen from a life of rampant drug abuse, endless sexual orgies, and other occupational hazards of the music business. But bass guitarist Zeke Miller, member of a satanic coven, exploits Michael's vulnerability, seeing in him a potential new member of the coven, and in Kitty a potential blood sacrifice.

Other books you might like:
Nancy A. Collins, *Tempter*, 1991
Ray Garton, *Crucifax*, 1988
John Skipp, *The Scream*, 1988
  Craig Spector, co-author

1725

RAY GARTON

Dark Channel

(New York: Bantam, 1992)

Story type: Horror (Apocalyptic Horror)
Major character(s): Hester Thorne, Cult Member (leader); Jordan Cross, Detective—Private; Lauren Schroeder, Housewife
Time period(s): 1990s (1993)
Locale(s): Anderson, California

Summary: Jordan Cross is looking into the disappearance of a reporter for *Trends* magazine following his investigation into the New Age cult of the Universal Enlightened Alliance. Lauren Schroeder is desperately searching for her husband, a member of the Alliance who has abducted her son. Together, Jordan and Lauren infiltrate the Alliance and discover the true sinister source of its appeal and power.

Other books you might like:
Alex Abella, *The Killing of the Saints*, 1991
Nicholas Conde, *The Religion*, 1982
Thomas F. Monteleone, *The Blood of the Lamb*, 1992

1726

RAY GARTON

Lot Lizards

(Shingletown, California: Mark Ziesing, 1991)

Story type: Horror (Vampire Story)
Major character(s): Bill Ketter, Truck Driver; Jon Ketter, Child (Bill Ketter's son); Byron Quimby, Maintenance Worker (janitor)
Time period(s): 1990s
Locale(s): Yreka, California (The Sierra Gold Pan Truck Stop)

Summary: When the Sierra Gold Pan Truck Stop becomes snowed in, the clients find they must band together to protect themselves from vampiric "lot lizards"—truckstop hookers—who share their predicament but not exactly their taste in food.

Other books you might like:
Ron Dee, *Blood Lust*, 1990
Ron Dee, *Dusk*, 1991
Stephen King, *Salem's Lot*, 1975
Robert R. McCammon, *They Thirst*, 1981

1727

RAY GARTON

Methods of Madness

(Arlington Heights, IL: Dark Harvest, 1990)

Story type: Horror (Collection)

Summary: Six tales of unusual human relationships with an emphasis on sex and death. "Active Member" and "Something Kinky" are concerned with the bizarre fates that befall characters seeking to satisfy their sexual obsessions. "Shock Radio" and the short novel "Dr. Krusadian's Method" tell of the poetic justice meted out to, respectively, an abusive radio talk show host and child-abusing parents.

Other books you might like:
Clive Barker, *Books of Blood Series*, 1984-1985
Ramsey Campbell, *Scared Stiff*, 1987
John Skipp, *Deadlines*, 1989
  Craig Spector, co-author

1728

RAY GARTON

The New Neighbor

(Lynbrook, New York: Charnel House, 1991)

Story type: Horror (Erotic Horror)
Major character(s): Lorelle Dupree, Demon; Ronald Prosky, Journalist; Jen Pritchard, Young Woman
Time period(s): 1990s
Locale(s): Redbrook, California

Summary: Under the guise of a beautiful woman, a succubus moves into the town of Redbrook, seducing the citizens both literally and in their dreams, and pitting them all against one another.

Other books you might like:
Jackie Hyman, *Echoes*, 1990
Stephen King, *Needful Things*, 1992
Ray Russell, *Incubus*, 1976

1729

RAY GARTON

Pieces of Hate

(Baltimore, Maryland: Cemetary Dance, 1996)

Story type: Horror (Collection)

Summary: Most of these nine polemical horror tales feature smugly-righteous characters who get their just desserts, usually by supernatural means. In "A Gift From Above," a woman excercises horrible transformative powers on former classmates who once humiliated her, unaware of the toll they are taking on her spiritually. "Choices" and "The Devil's Music" envision the private hells that befall, respectively, a fanatical right-to-lifer and an obnoxious rock musician. "Ophilia Raphaeldo" imagines the hysterics of daytime talk shows taken to illogical extremes, and "Bad Blood" depicts a fittingly dismal revenge for a sexually repressed gay basher. This book was produced only in a signed limited edition hardcover format.

Other books you might like:
Richard T. Chizmar, *Midnight Promises*, 1996
Ed Gorman, *Moonchasers and Other Stories*, 1996
Barry Hoffman, *Firefly. . .Burning Bright*, 1996
Lucy Taylor, *The Flesh Artist*, 1994

1730
ELIZABETH C. GASKELL

A Dark Night's Work and Other Stories
(New York: Oxford Paperbacks, 1992)

Story type: Horror (Collection)
Summary: Five stories and novellas by a Victorian writer known for her scrupulous realism, the two longest of which dip into the dark side of the human psyche. "The Grey Woman" both employs and subverts elements of the Gothic horror story in its working out of a feminist manifesto. The title story is about a false accusation of murder and the soul-searching questions it raises in the falsely accused. Suzanne Lewis has supplied an introduction.

Other books you might like:
Catherine Crowe, *Night-Side of Nature*, 1848
Charlotte Perkins Gilman, *The Yellow Wallpaper and Other Writings of Charlotte Perkins Gilman*, 1989
Mrs. J.H. Riddell, *The Collected Ghost Stories of Mrs. J.H. Riddell*, 1977
Mary Shelley, *Tales and Stories of Mary Wollstonecraft Shelley*, 1891

1731
R. PATRICK GATES

Deathwalker
(New York: Dell/Abyss, 1996)

Story type: Horror (Serial Killer)
Major character(s): Bill Cage, Police Officer; Ivy Delacroix, Child; Jack Walker, Criminal
Time period(s): 1990s (1995)
Locale(s): Crocker, Massachusetts
Summary: While detoxing at a clinic from the drug and alcohol addictions he developed after a serial killer murdered his wife, officer Bill Cage is harassed by another killer who sends him letters signed "The Walking Death" and photos of the grisly murders he commits. Bill becomes involved in a cat-and-mouse game with the murderer, who blames Bill for what he has become. This novel is a sequel to the author's novel *Tunnelvision*.

Other books you might like:
Michael A. Arnzen, *Grave Markings*, 1994

Thomas Harris, *Red Dragon*, 1981
Barry T. Hawkins, *Puppet Master*, 1993
Roxanne Longstreet, *Red Angel*, 1994

1732
R. PATRICK GATES

Grimm Memorials
(New York: Onyx, 1990)

Story type: Horror (Black Magic; Child-in-Peril)
Major character(s): Eleanor Grimm, Undertaker, Witch; Steve Nailer, Teacher, Writer (poet); Diane Nailer, Spouse (Steve's wife)
Summary: Aging, ailing mortician (and witch) Eleanor Grimm, linked psychically to her deceased twin brother Edmund, must mutilate young children in order to preserve her own life and return Edmund to his. None of this is known to Steve and Diane Nailer, who have just moved into a house near the Grimm mortuary and the enveloping nearby woods. This inventive original novel incorporates material from a number of fairy tales and children's rhymes into an extremely graphic, gory narrative.

Other books you might like:
Raymond E. Feist, *Faerie Tale*, 1988
John Fowles, *The Magus*, 1965
James Herbert, *The Magic Cottage*, 1986
Dean R. Koontz, *Twilight Eyes*, 1987

1733
R. PATRICK GATES

Tunnelvision
(New York: Dell Abyss, 1991)

Story type: Horror (Serial Killer)
Major character(s): Bill Gates, Police Officer; Ivy Delacroix, Teenager; Wilbur Clayton, Guard
Time period(s): 1990s
Locale(s): Crocker, Massachusetts
Summary: Rehabilitated cop Bill Gates, still haunted by the revelation that his father was a mass murderer, agrees to take on the case of another mass murderer, and finds himself trying to capture a latter-day Jack the Ripper, who films his grisly kills and markets them as snuff films.

Other books you might like:
Dennis Cooper, *Frisk*, 1991
Joe R. Lansdale, *Cold in July*, 1989

1734
JEAN MARK GAWRON

Dream of Glass
(New York: Harcourt Brace, 1993)

Story type: Science Fiction (Alternate Intelligence; Cyberpunk)

Major character(s): Alexa Augustine, Computer Expert, Military Personnel; Quincunx ''the Thief'', Artificial Intelligence; Lady Anne, Artificial Intelligence
Time period(s): 22nd century
Locale(s): Horton's Valley, California; San Francisco, California

Summary: While cannibalizing a landed Galactic Ship, the Rose Post Public occupies Horton's Valley. After one of the soldiers befriends Alexa, who proves a natural computer interfacer, Alexa begins training by the Rose Artificial Intelligence Agency, becoming the best ever trained there. When Alexa ''dies'' as a result of a bomb blast, enough body remains to inherit Alexa's estate, but with less than 90% intact memory, she must change her first name. Implanted without her knowledge, Augustine carries micromolecular transmitters in her brain from which Quincunx constructs an internal, duplicate Augustine and also monitors her condition for the Rose. Addicted to dopamine exciters in the hospital and subject to severe headaches, Augustine experiences much confusion after leaving the hospital. Allowed to interface, Augustine discovers the powerful interests behind the experiment on her.

Other books you might like:
Greg Bear, *Blood Music*, 1985
Pat Cadigan, *Fools*, 1992
Jeffrey A. Carver, *Dragon Rigger*, 1993
Jeffrey A. Carver, *Dragons in the Stars*, 1992
James P. Hogan, *The Multiplex Man*, 1992
Dan Simmons, *The Hollow Man*, 1992
Neal Stephenson, *Snow Crash*, 1991
Michael Swanwick, *Vacuum Flowers*, 1987
Amy Thomson, *Virtual Girl*, 1993

1735

KATHLEEN O'NEAL GEAR
W. MICHAEL GEAR, Co-Author

People of the Lakes
(New York: Tor Forge, 1994)

Story type: Fantasy (Quest; Historical)
Series: First North Americans
Major character(s): Star Shell, Heroine, Indian (Hopewell); Otter, Trader, Indian; Green Spider, Psychic (mystic), Indian (Hopewell)
Time period(s): 2nd century
Locale(s): Great Lakes, North America

Summary: Guided by Green Spider's visions and aided by Otter, Star Shell races to save her people from the adverse effects of an evil totemic mask by destroying it at Niagara Falls. A vengeful chief pursues to recover a runaway traveling with them while Star Shell's enemy tries to foil her mission and recover the mask to use it for personal power. Includes four pages of maps, a two-page series chronology and four-page selected bibliography.

Other books you might like:
W. Michael Gear, *People of the Earth*, 1992
   Kathleen O'Neal Gear, co-author

W. Michael Gear, *People of the Fire*, 1991
   Kathleen O'Neal Gear, co-author
W. Michael Gear, *People of the River*, 1992
   Kathleen O'Neal Gear, co-author
W. Michael Gear, *People of the Sea*, 1993
   Kathleen O'Neal Gear, co-author
W. Michael Gear, *People of the Wolf*, 1990
   Kathleen O'Neal Gear, co-author

1736

W. MICHAEL GEAR

The Artifact
(New York: DAW Books, 1990)

Story type: Science Fiction (Adventure)
Major character(s): Solomon Carrasco, Spaceship Captain; Kraal, Alien (Galactic Grand Master)
Time period(s): Indeterminate Future
Locale(s): *Boaz*, Spaceship; Star's Rest, Planet—Imaginary

Summary: In a galactic civilization on the brink of civil war, an artifact of an ancient alien race is discovered on a distant world and a starship is sent to investigate. Unbeknownst to humanity, the artifact destroyed its creators and could destroy the human race as well.

Other books you might like:
Arthur C. Clarke, *Rama II*, 1989
Arthur C. Clarke, *Rendezvous with Rama*, 1973
Ted Reynolds, *The Tides of God*, 1989
Fred Saberhagen, *Berserker*, 1967

1737

W. MICHAEL GEAR
KATHLEEN O'NEAL GEAR, Co-Author

People of the Earth
(New York: Tor, 1992)

Story type: Fantasy (Historical; Romance)
Series: First North Americans
Major character(s): Brave Man, Prehistoric Human, Leader; Bad Belly/Still Water, Prehistoric Human, Indian; White Ash, Prehistoric Human, Psychic (dreamer)
Time period(s): 30th century B.C. (B.C.)
Locale(s): North America

Summary: As clans migrate slowly southward along the Rocky Mountains, territories come under new stewardship and inter-clan rivalries and kidnappings modify the clans' makeup. A powerful fetish, the Wolf Bundle, continues to influence events.

Other books you might like:
Jean M. Auel, *Clan of the Cave Bear*, 1980
Sue Harrison, *Mother Earth, Father Sky*, 1990
J. Alison James, *Sing for a Gentle Rain*, 1990
Ardath Mayhar, *People of the Mesa*, 1992
Lynn Armistead McKee, *Woman of the Mists*, 1991
Meredith Ann Pierce, *The Woman Who Loved Reindeer*, 1985
J.H. Rosny, *Quest for Fire*, 1909
   Pseudonym of J.H.H. Boex

William Sarabande, *Beyond the Sea of Ice*, 1987
Elizabeth Marshall Thomas, *Reindeer Moon*, 1987
Roger Zelazny, *Bridge of Ashes*, 1976

1738

W. MICHAEL GEAR
KATHLEEN O'NEAL GEAR, Co-Author

People of the Fire
(New York: Tor, 1991)

Story type: Fantasy (Historical; Adventure)
Series: First North Americans
Major character(s): Little Dancer, Shaman, Prehistoric Human; Elk Charm, Prehistoric Human, Indian
Time period(s): Indeterminate Past (Pleistocene Epoch)
Locale(s): Norway

Summary: As threat of starvation forces Heavy Bear to kill a newborn female and frustration leads him to desecrate the Wolf Bundle, a powerful sacred fetish, Little Dancer resolves to become a Spirit Dancer and protect his tribe from the power-hungry chief. A Wolf Dream instructs Little Dancer to seek guidance from White Calf in his mission to regain the Wolf Bundle and lead his people from the drought stricken area.

Other books you might like:
Jean M. Auel, *Clan of the Cave Bear*, 1980
Sue Harrison, *Mother Earth, Father Sky*, 1990
Richard Herley, *The Stone Arrow*, 1978
J. Alison James, *Sing for a Gentle Rain*, 1990
Meredith Ann Pierce, *The Woman Who Loved Reindeer*, 1985
William Sarabande, *Beyond the Sea of Ice*, 1987
Elizabeth Marshall Thomas, *Reindeer Moon*, 1987

1739

W. MICHAEL GEAR
KATHLEEN O'NEAL GEAR, Co-Author

People of the River
(New York: Tor, 1992)

Story type: Fantasy (Historical; Religious)
Series: First North Americans
Major character(s): Lichen, Indian, Psychic; Tharon, Indian, Leader
Time period(s): Indeterminate Past (Pleistocene Epoch)
Locale(s): Cahokia, North America (capital of Mississippi River Mound Builders)

Summary: Troubled by failing crops and excessive tribute demanded by Tharon, people turn to Lichen in hopes that the gods will open the underworld to her.

Other books you might like:
Jean M. Auel, *Clan of the Cave Bear*, 1980
Sue Harrison, *Mother Earth, Father Sky*, 1990
Richard Herley, *The Stone Arrow*, 1978
J. Alison James, *Sing for a Gentle Rain*, 1990
Meredith Ann Pierce, *The Woman Who Loved Reindeer*, 1985
William Sarabande, *Beyond the Sea of Ice*, 1987
Elizabeth Marshall Thomas, *Reindeer Moon*, 1987

1740

W. MICHAEL GEAR
KATHLEEN O'NEAL GEAR, Co-Author

People of the Sea
(New York: St. Martin's, 1993)

Story type: Fantasy (Historical; Quest)
Series: First North Americans
Major character(s): Sunchaser, Prehistoric Human, Shaman; Catchstraw, Prehistoric Human; Kestrel, Prehistoric Human, Fugitive
Time period(s): 90th century B.C.
Locale(s): Sierra Nevada Mountains, North America

Summary: As glaciers melt and change North American ecology, Sunchaser's people view with alarm the changes which deprive them of mastodons and other large game. Sunchaser cannot establish the usual link to the spirit world and Catchstraw's use of witchcraft threatens Sunchaser's authority. When Kestrel, fleeing an abusive husband, joins the tribe, many people feel that befriending her will bring further retribution from the spirit world.

Other books you might like:
Jean M. Auel, *Clan of the Cave Bear*, 1980
Sue Harrison, *Mother Earth, Father Sky*, 1990
Sue Harrison, *My Sister the Moon*, 1992
Richard Healey, *The Stone Arrow*, 1978
Meredith Ann Pierce, *The Woman Who Loved Reindeer*, 1985
William Sarabande, *Beyond the Sea of Ice*, 1987
Elizabeth Marshall Thomas, *Reindeer Moon*, 1987

1741

W. MICHAEL GEAR
KATHLEEN O'NEAL GEAR, Co-Author

People of the Wolf
(New York: Tor, 1990)

Story type: Fantasy (Historical; Adventure)
Series: First North Americans
Major character(s): Heron, Shaman, Prehistoric Human; Runs in Light, Hunter, Prehistoric Human; Raven Hunter, Warrior, Prehistoric Human
Time period(s): Indeterminate Past (Pleistocene Epoch)
Locale(s): Bering Land Bridge, Asia (Bering Strait)

Summary: Heron dreams about Runs in Light who will become Wolf Dreamer, her student, and his twin brother, Raven Hunter, who will become her enemy. Wolf Dreamer, who will someday be a powerful shaman, leads his people to a land shown to him by a wolf in a vision.

Other books you might like:
Jean M. Auel, *The Mammoth Hunters*, 1985
Jean M. Auel, *Clan of the Cave Bear*, 1980
J. Alison James, *Sing for a Gentle Rain*, 1990
Meredith Ann Pierce, *The Woman Who Loved Reindeer*, 1985
J.H. Rosny, *Quest for Fire*, 1967
   1909
William Sarabande, *Beyond the Sea of Ice*, 1987
Patricia Wrightson, *Journey Behind the Wind*, 1981

Patricia Wrightson, *The Dark Bright Water*, 1978
Patricia Wrightson, *The Ice Is Coming*, 1977

`1742`

W. MICHAEL GEAR

Relic of Empire

(New York: DAW, 1992)

Story type: Science Fiction (Political; Space Opera)
Series: Forbidden Borders
Major character(s): Staffa kar Therma, Mercenary; Skyla Lyma, Mercenary; Sinklar Fist, Military Personnel
Time period(s): Indeterminate Future
Locale(s): Sassan Empire, Interstellar Empire/Federation; Rega, Planet—Imaginary

Summary: Desperately striving to avert interstellar war between the Regan and Sassan Empires, Staffa kar Therma must choose between saving the life of Skyla, his lover and second-in-command, and saving the human race. Complicating forces, including his long-lost son Sinklar, now a general in the opposing camp, work at cross purposes. Only time will tell if anyone will survive to claim victory.

Other books you might like:
Isaac Asimov, *Foundation and Empire*, 1952
Alfred Bester, *The Stars My Destination*, 1957
C.J. Cherryh, *Cyteen*, 1988
Donald F. Glut, *The Empire Strikes Back*, 1980
James Kahn, *Return of the Jedi*, 1983
George Lucas, *Star Wars*, 1976
Jerry Pournelle, *Falkenberg's Legion*, 1990

`1743`

W. MICHAEL GEAR

Starstrike

(New York: DAW, 1990)

Story type: Science Fiction (First Contact; Space Opera)
Major character(s): Wide, Alien (Ahimsa), Leader (Overone); Sheik Dunbar, Military Personnel (major)
Time period(s): 21st century
Locale(s): Earth; Ta Ha Ak Station, Outer Space

Summary: Against all intersellar regulations, Earth's military, industrial and technological systems are taken over by the Ahimsa, aliens from another galaxy. They've decided to use humans to destroy the powerful, but peaceful Pashti. Believing no other option exists, the Earth's governments comply. Earth's best soldiers head into outer space.

Other books you might like:
Douglas Adams, *The Hitchhiker's Guide to the Galaxy*, 1980
David Brin, *Startide Rising*, 1983
Fletcher Pratt, *Invaders From Rigel*, 1960
A.E. van Vogt, *The Battle of Forever*, 1971
John Varley, *The Ophiuchi Hotline*, 1977

`1744`

W. MICHAEL GEAR

The Web of Spider

(New York: DAW Books, 1989)

Story type: Science Fiction (Space Opera)
Series: Spider
Major character(s): Ngen Van Chou, Leader, Revolutionary; Susan Smith Andojar, Military Personnel
Time period(s): Indeterminate Future
Locale(s): The World, Planet—Imaginary; Outer Space (Arcturus System)

Summary: In a galaxy convulsed by civil war, the Warriors of Spider attempt to maintain order and stop Ngen Van Chou's rebellion.

Other books you might like:
Roland J. Green, *Starcruiser Shenandoah*, 1989
R.M. Meluch, *War Birds*, 1989
Paul O. Williams, *The Gift of the Gorboduc Vandal*, 1989

`1745`

JEFF GELB, Editor
MICHAEL GARRETT, Co-Editor

Deadly After Dark

(New York: Pocket, 1994)

Story type: Horror (Anthology; Erotic Horror)
Series: Hot Blood

Summary: The 14 stories in this book range from the non-supernatural to the supernatural in their treatment of erotic horror themes. Highlights include Lucy Taylor's "Things of Which We Do Not Speak," about the horrifying memories evoked by the protagonists' rough sex play; Michael Garrett's "Immaterial Girl," about a prostitute with the capacity to mold her features into every man's fantasy woman; Edo van Belkom's "Sex Starved," in which an obese newlywed's appetite and sex drive become intertwined; Jack Ketchum's "The Role," a tale of psychopathic dominance and imprisonment; and Bentley Little's wonderfully wacky "The Numbers Game," in which a computer hacker finds the proper sequence of numbers for leaving a person sexually incapacitated. Forrest Ackerman contributes an introduction.

Other books you might like:
Ellen Datlow, *Alien Sex*, 1990
　editor
Ellen Datlow, *Little Deaths*, 1994
　editor

`1746`

JEFF GELB, Editor

Fear Itself

(New York: Pocket, 1995)

Story type: Horror (Anthology)

Summary: Twenty-one leading authors supply stories based on the things that they fear most. The underlying fears of Jack Ketchum's "Snakes" and Graham Watkins' "Here There Be Spyders" are self-evident. Fear of modern urban life empowers Nancy Collins' "Avenue X," while fear of the loss of a loved one is the inspiration for Thomas Monteleone's "Time Enough to Sleep" and Jeff Gelb's "Home Again." Paul Kupferberg's "Food for the Beast" and Stephen Gresham's "Once upon a Darkness" deal with fears specific to horror writers: respectively, the impact of life upon the writing of horror fiction, and the impact of horror fiction life. Each author supplies a note on the basis for his or her story.

Other books you might like:
Peter Crowther, *Narrow Houses*, 1993
  editor
Charles L. Grant, *Fears*, 1983
  editor
Wendy Webb, *More Phobias*, 1995
  Richard Gilliam, Edward Kramer, Martin H. Greenberg,
  co-editors
Wendy Webb, *Phobias: Stories of Your Deepest Fears*, 1994
  Richard Gilliam, Edward Kramer, Martin H. Greenberg,
  co-editors

1747

JEFF GELB, Editor
MICHAEL GARRETT, Co-Editor

Fear the Fever
(New York: Pocket, 1996)

Story type: Horror (Anthology; Erotic Horror)
Series: Hot Blood

Summary: The seventh compilation in this long-running series of erotic horror anthologies brings together 17 stories written especially for this volume. Among them are Lucy Taylor's "The Five Percent People," about a menage a trois that comes to a dismal end; Graham Masterton's "The Secret Shih Tan," about a legendary cookbook whose recipes for human flesh bring sexual ecstasy; Alan Brennert's "Fantasies," in which a husband and wife conceive a child who is the embodiment of her father's sexual fantasies; P.D. Cacek's "Metalica," concerned with a woman unhealthily obsessed with gynecological examinations; and Edward Lee and Jack Ketchum's "Love Letters From the Rain Forest," in which a sexually-transmitted disease becomes a gruesome tool of revenge.

Other books you might like:
Nancy A. Collins, *Dark Love*, 1995
  Ed Kramer, Martin H. Greenberg, co-editors
Ellen Datlow, *Little Deaths*, 1995
  editor
John Pelan, *Darkside: Horror for the Next Millenium*, 1996
  editor
Michele Slung, *I Shudder at Your Touch*, 1991
  editor
Michele Slung, *Shudder Again*, 1993
  editor

1748

JEFF GELB, Editor
MICHAEL GARRETT, Co-Editor

Hotter Blood: More Tales of Erotic Horror
(New York: Pocket Books, 1990)

Story type: Horror (Anthology; Erotic Horror)
Series: Hot Blood

Summary: Twenty-four original short stories that deal very explicitly with sex, usually in the form of violence directed at women. New writers such as Kurt Busiek and Michael Newton appear alongside well-known authors such as Karl Edward Wagner, John Shirley, Stephen Gallagher, and Chet Williamson. Most of these stories are grim, graphic, and reactionary in their treatment of sexuality, marriage, and human relations; several are very disgusting.

Other books you might like:
Ellen Datlow, *Alien Sex*, 1990
Ramsey Campbell, *Scared Stiff*, 1987

1749

JEFF GELB, Editor
MICHAEL GARRETT, Co-Editor

Hottest Blood: The Ultimate in Erotic Horror
(New York: Pocket, 1993)

Story type: Horror (Anthology; Erotic Horror)
Series: Hot Blood

Summary: Completing the trilogy begun with *Hot Blood* (1989) and *Hotter Blood* (1991), the editors bring together 20 original tales of erotic horror fiction. Nancy Holder's "I Hear the Mermaids Singing," about an abused woman who lives in a fantasy world to escape the harsh reality of life, and Steve and Melanie Tem's "Safe at Home," about the impact of a childhood incident of sexual abuse on the protagonist's adult life, are powerful studies of the ways in which sexuality shapes the personality, while David Schow's "Where the Heart Was" and Graham Watkins' "Hillbettys" are amusing takes on sexual anxieties. The rest of the contents are mediocre with Graham Masterton's "Sex Object," about a woman who transforms herself surgically into a pleasure-giving orifice for the benefit of her chauvinistic husband, an exploitative low point.

Other books you might like:
Ellen Datlow, *Alien Sex*, 1991
Michel Parry, *Devil's Kisses*, 1976
Michele Slung, *I Shudder at Your Touch*, 1991

1750

JEFF GELB, Editor
MICHAEL GARRETT, Co-Editor

Seeds of Fear

(New York: Pocket, 1995)

Story type: Horror (Anthology)
Series: Hot Blood

Summary: This fifth volume in the Hot Blood erotic horror anthology series assembles nineteen new stories of sexual terror. Ronald Kelly's ''Scream Queen'' is concerned with a film student who discovers the horrible reality behind the sexy persona projected by an actress who specializes in horror film heroine roles. In ''Overeater's Ominous,'' Stephen George tells of women who find a way to displace the obesity that has robbed them of their sexiness onto others. Kathryn Ptacek's ''Hunger'' is about a desperate woman driven to extremes to stop her nymphomania and Edward Lee's ''Grub Girl'' about a near future where a radiation leak has produced mutants with unusual sexual proclivities. Horror film actress Brinke Stevens supplies an introduction.

Other books you might like:
Nancy A. Collins, *Dark Love*, 1995
   Ed Kramer and Martin H. Greenberg, co-editors
Ellen Datlow, *Little Deaths*, 1995
   editor
Michele Slung, *I Shudder at Your Touch*, 1991
   editor
Michele Slung, *Shudder Again*, 1993
   editor

1751

JEFF GELB, Editor

Shock Rock

(New York: Pocket, 1992)

Story type: Horror (Anthology)

Summary: Twenty original stories that adapt rock music to the horror medium. Included are Stephen King's ''You Know They Got a Hell of a Band,'' about a town where all the dead rock stars go, David Schow's ''Odeed,'' about what might really happen at a concert when a band cranks the amps to 11 and starts jamming, and Patrick Gates' ''Heavy Metal,'' a limp pastiche of Edgar Allan Poe. Far too many stories involve the resurrection of dead rock stars. With an introduction by rock star Alice Cooper.

Other books you might like:
David J. Schow, *Silver Scream*, 1988

1752

JEFF GELB, Editor

Shock Rock II

(New York: Pocket, 1994)

Story type: Horror (Anthology)

Summary: All 21 original stories in this compilation use the rock music scene as a vehicle for horror. Included are Bob Weinberg and Tina Jens' ''Elvis Can't Dance,'' in which The King returns from the dead to dispose of defilers of the rock 'n' roll tradition; Scott H. Urban's ''Better to Burn Out,'' about an aging rock star's psychotic final performance; Rick Hautala's ''Dead Legends,'' which tells of a strange recording studio where famous musicians play just before they die; Mike Baron's ''Oi Boy,'' in which a gypsy puts a poetically just curse on a skinhead rocker; Max Allan Collins' tongue-in-cheek vampire tale, ''Rock 'n' Roll Will Never Die''; and the editor's own tale of a nighttime disk jockey's unusual callers, ''Graveyard Shift.''

Other books you might like:
Paul J. McAuley, *In Dreams*, 1992
   Kim Newman, co-author
Paul M. Sammon, *The King Is Dead: Tales of Elvis Post Mortem*, 1994
   editor

1753

JEFF GELB, Editor
MICHAEL GARRETT, Co-Editor

Stranger by Night

(New York: Pocket, 1995)

Story type: Horror (Anthology; Erotic Horror)
Series: Hot Blood

Summary: Seventeen new stories and one reprint comprise the contents of this installment in the ''Hot Blood'' erotic horror anthology series. In the reprint, Brian Lumley's ''Back Row,'' a patron of a movie theater discovers there is something more gruesome than necking going on between a man and woman with seats near him. Tom Piccirilli's ''Take It as It Comes'' presents a bizarre sexual revenge scenario, and Ramsey Campbell's ''The Body in the Window'' features an anti-smut crusader who finds the tables strangely turned on him when he trolls through the red light district of Amsterdam. In Christa Faust's ''Skin Deep,'' a sex club habitue's tattoos develop a mind of their own, and in Lucy Taylor's ''Male-Call,'' a woman finds a sexual surrogate to get revenge upon her abusive husband.

Other books you might like:
Nancy A. Collins, *Dark Love*, 1995
   Ed Kramer and Martin H. Greenberg, co-editors
Ellen Datlow, *Little Deaths*, 1995
   editor
Michele Slung, *I Shudder at Your Touch*,
   editor
Michele Slung, *Shudder Again*, 1993
   editor

1754

DAVID GEMMELL

Dark Prince

(New York: Ballantine Del Rey, 1993)

Story type: Fantasy (Historical)
Series: Macedon
Major character(s): Parmenion, Warrior; Derae, Psychic (seer); Alexander the Great, Historical Figure
Time period(s): 4th century B.C.
Locale(s): Macedonia; Middle East

Summary: Parmenion diffuses the attack on Alexander sufficiently to save him but not free him from the forces of darkness. In another world populated by characters from Greek legend, a demon king plots to capture Alexander and gain immortality while Parmenion and Derae work to free Alexander to become the legendary Golden Child. U.K. edition published 1991.

Other books you might like:
Nikos Kazantzakis, *Alexander the Great*, 1982
Edison Marshall, *Conqueror*, 1962
Mary Renault, *Fire From Heaven*, 1969
Judith Tarr, *Lord of the Two Lands*, 1993
Gene Wolfe, *Soldier of Arete*, 1989
Gene Wolfe, *Soldier of the Mist*, 1986

1755

DAVID GEMMELL

Ghost King

(New York: Ballantine Del Rey, 1996)

Story type: Fantasy (Legend; Sword and Sorcery)
Series: Stones of Power
Major character(s): Thuro "Uther Pendragon", Royalty, Orphan; Culain lach Feragh, Immortal, Warrior; Laitha "Gian Avur", Orphan, Young Woman
Time period(s): 6th century
Locale(s): England (Britain); Pinrae, Fictional Country

Summary: Fleeing his father's assassins, Thuro finds refuge in the mountains with Laitha and her guardian, Culain, who teaches the boy to use a sword. But in order to take his rightful place as High King and defeat the Brigantes and Saxons who have attacked his land, Thuro must first travel through the land of the Mist to reclaim his father's magical sword and find a lost army.

Other books you might like:
Marion Zimmer Bradley, *The Mists of Avalon*, 1983
C.J. Cherryh, *The Paladin*, 1988
David Drake, *Ranks of Bronze*, 1986
Parke Godwin, *Firelord*, 1980
Katherine Kurtz, *Deryni Rising*, 1970
Rosemary Sutcliff, *Sword at Sunset*, 1963
T.H. White, *The Once and Future King*, 1958

1756

DAVID GEMMELL

Lion of Macedon

(New York: Ballantine Del Rey, 1992)

Story type: Fantasy (Historical; Sword and Sorcery)
Series: Macedon
Major character(s): Parmenion, Mercenary, Sports Figure (runner); Tamis, Psychic (seer); Philip of Macedon, Historical Figure, Leader
Time period(s): 4th century B.C.
Locale(s): Sparta, Greece; Thebes, Greece; Pella, Greece (ancient Macedonia)

Summary: Of mixed Spartan and Macedonian parentage, Parmenion represents civilization's best hope for preventing the Dark One from taking over ancient Greece. After Tamis uses knowledge gained in a vision to identify Parmenion and arranges for him to acquire the needed skills, he advances to mercenary general and plays a pivotal role in the battle between Chaos and Light.

Other books you might like:
Frans G. Bengtsson, *The Long Ships*, 1954
Tom Holt, *Goatsong*, 1990
Tom Holt, *The Walled Orchard*, 1991
Gene Wolfe, *Soldier of Arete*, 1989
Gene Wolfe, *Soldier of the Mist*, 1986

1757

DAVID GEMMELL

Morningstar

(New York: Ballantine Del Rey, 1993)

Story type: Fantasy (Adventure)
Major character(s): Jarek Mace, Criminal, Hero; Owen Odell, Minstrel (bard)
Time period(s): Indeterminate
Locale(s): Highland, Fictional Country

Summary: When Jarek Mace inadvertly aids the Highland people, he finds himself hailed as the legendary hero, Morningstar, returned to his people. Known to his companion, Owen Odell, as an outlaw, bandit and heartless thief, Jarek Mace grabs the opportunity to change his persona and income as he and his companions assume the hero's mantle. A retelling of the Robin Hood tale utilizing magical elements.

Other books you might like:
Glen Cook, *The Black Company*, 1984
David Eddings, *Pawn of Prophecy*, 1982
Parke Godwin, *Robin and the King*, 1993
Parke Godwin, *Sherwood*, 1991
Robert Jordan, *The Eye of the World*, 1989
Fritz Leiber, *Two Sought Adventure: Exploits of Fafhrd and the Gray Mouser*, 1957

1758

GARY GENTILE

Dragons Past

(New York: Ace, 1990)

Story type: Science Fiction (Invasion of Earth; Time Travel)
Series: Time for Dragons
Major character(s): Scott, Revolutionary; Death Wind, Revolutionary; Doc, Revolutionary
Time period(s): Indeterminate Future; Indeterminate Past (Cretaceous Period)
Locale(s): Earth

Summary: The battle against the alien invaders called dragons was won, but the war continues. The dragons have returned and captured a group of rebels for their slave pens. The rebels use the dragons' time machinery to escape into the Cretaceous Period. Then they search out and destroy the dragons' main base in hopes of stopping the invasion at its source.

Other books you might like:
Gordon R. Dickson, *Way of the Pilgrim*, 1987
Clifford D. Simak, *Mastodonia*, 1978
Jack Vance, *Emphyrio*, 1969
H.G. Wells, *The War of the Worlds*, 1898

1759

GARY GENTILE

A Time for Dragons

(New York: Ace, 1989)

Story type: Science Fiction (Military)
Major character(s): Rusty, Teenager, Refugee; Scott, Teenager, Refugee
Time period(s): 21st century
Locale(s): Earth

Summary: A century after the collapse of human civilization, hostile reptilian aliens prowl the surface of the Earth, killing any humans with whom they come in contact. The few humans who remain alive fight back with whatever weapons they can muster.

Other books you might like:
Rob Chilson, *Men Like Rats*, 1989
John Dalmas, *The Lizard War*, 1989
Jack Vance, *The Dragon Masters*, 1963
F. Paul Wilson, *The Tery*, 1989

1760

MARY GENTLE

Ancient Light

(New York: New American Library, 1989)

Story type: Science Fiction (First Contact)
Major character(s): Lynne De Lisle Christie, Diplomat; Doug Clifford, Diplomat
Time period(s): 21st century
Locale(s): Orthe, Planet—Imaginary

Summary: Lynne Christie returns to the devastated planet of Orthe after an absence of eight years to find it changed drastically by the recent presence of human beings. Orthe's high civilization was destroyed in a cataclysmic war some two thousand years ago, but it is rumored that the super weapons used in that war still exist on the planet. The Panoceania Company is willing to stop at nothing, even the destruction of Orthe's fragile ecosystem, to find them.

Other books you might like:
C.J. Cherryh, *Cuckoo's Egg*, 1985
C.J. Cherryh, *The Faded Sun: Kesrith*, 1978
C.J. Cherryh, *The Faded Sun: Kutath*, 1980
C.J. Cherryh, *The Faded Sun: Shon'Jir*, 1979
Frank Herbert, *Dune*, 1965
Ursula K. Le Guin, *The Left Hand of Darkness*, 1969

1761

MARY GENTLE

The Architecture of Desire

(New York: Roc, 1993)

Story type: Fantasy (Political; Historical)
Major character(s): Valentine White Crow, Magician (master physician), Military Personnel (scholar-soldier); Lord-Architect Casaubon, Architect, Spouse (White Crow's); Pollexfen Calmady, Gentleman, Mercenary
Time period(s): Indeterminate Past (17th century equivalent)
Locale(s): Alternate Earth (London)

Summary: Years after the overthrow of the Gods and establishment of human rule, repeated building disasters cause Protector-General Olivia to call for aid from Lord-Architect Casaubon to forward her goal of creating a powerful magical edifice. Unenthusiastic about returning to London, White Crow experiences a crisis of her convictions after Casaubon's friend, Pollexfen Calmady, admits raping White Crow's acquaintance. Sequel to *Rats and Gargoyles*.

Other books you might like:
Lois McMaster Bujold, *The Spirit Ring*, 1992
Mercedes Lackey, *The Robin and the Kestrel*, 1993
R.A. MacAvoy, *The Belly of the Wolf*, 1994
Elizabeth Moon, *Sheepfarmer's Daughter*, 1988
Paula Volsky, *Illusion*, 1992
Martha Wells, *The Element of Fire*, 1993

1762

MARY GENTLE

Rats and Gargoyles

(New York: Roc, 1990)

Story type: Fantasy (Political; Religious)
Major character(s): Prince Lucas, Royalty, Thief; Valentine White Crow, Magician, Military Personnel (scholar-soldier); Lord-Architect, Nobleman
Time period(s): Indeterminate Past
Locale(s): Alternate Earth

Summary: An enslaved world populace struggles to throw off a tyrannical pantheon of 36 actual gods (the "Gargoyles") and their overseer caste of giant, humanoid rats. Events are set in motion when White Crow, Scholar-Soldier of the magisterial secret order of the Invisible College, magically paints secret signs upon the face of the moon with her own blood, signalling to the world that the struggle is on. But there remains the need to find someone who can read the occult message and to find a way to prevail against the gods.

Other books you might like:
Eleanor Arnason, *To the Resurrection Station*, 1986
Margot Benary-Isbert, *The Wicked Enchantment*, 1955
Robert A. Heinlein, *The Moon Is a Harsh Mistress*, 1966
P.C. Hodgell, *God Stalk*, 1982
James Morrow, *Only Begotten Daughter*, 1990
Roger Zelazny, *Lord of Light*, 1967

1763

STEPHEN R. GEORGE

Bloody Valentine
(New York: Zebra, 1994)

Story type: Horror (Serial Killer)
Major character(s): Jo Granville, Artist (illustrator); Ryan Locke, Police Officer (sheriff); Gabby Granville, Child
Time period(s): 1990s (1994)
Locale(s): Halkirk, Minnesota

Summary: During a college psychology experiment, five college students imagined Joshua Valentine, the ideal serial killer—who became less than ideal when he suddenly materialized and murdered a child. Ten years later, someone who signs himself Joshua Valentine begins cutting a bloody swath through Minnesota, and the authorities must determine why he has resurfaced and what he hopes to accomplish.

Other books you might like:
Ramsey Campbell, *Incarnate*, 1983
Charles L. Grant, *The Pet*, 1986
John R. Maxim, *Abel/Baker/Charley*, 1983

1764

STEPHEN R. GEORGE

Dark Reunion
(New York: Zebra, 1990)

Story type: Horror (Occult)
Major character(s): Peter Willson, Teenager; Andrea Willson, Real Estate Agent, Step-Parent (Peter's); Matthew Willson, Police Officer, Parent (Peter's)
Time period(s): 1990s (1990)
Locale(s): Marissa, Minnesota (small town near Minneapolis)

Summary: Matthew Willson moves his family from Minneapolis back to his hometown of Marissa, unaware that in doing so he is exposing them to terrible danger. For Marissa is the home of the ancient people of The Craft, among whom an evil subgroup has begun clamoring for resurgence. Soon Matthew's son Peter falls under the influence of Longshadow, the sentient mist that leads the cultists.

Other books you might like:
Margaret Falk, *Darkscope*, 1990

Morgan Fields, *Shaman Woods*, 1990
Diane Guest, *Lullaby*, 1990

1765

STEPHEN R. GEORGE

Deadly Vengeance
(New York: Zebra, 1993)

Story type: Horror (Supernatural Vengeance)
Major character(s): Alan Shea, Child; Cobalt, Animal (dog); Bill Shea, Writer (Alan's father)
Time period(s): 1990s (1993)
Locale(s): Laidlaw, Minnesota

Summary: Alan Shea is threatened with physical harm by the boys who killed his brother if he tells on them. Alan's new dog, Cobalt, a former laboratory animal, is telepathically sensitive to Alan's childish rage and begins systematically killing the boys responsible.

Other books you might like:
Stephen King, *Cujo*, 1981
John Stchur, *Paddywhack*, 1989
Raymond Van Over, *Whisper*, 1991

1766

STEPHEN R. GEORGE

The Forgotten
(New York: Zebra, 1991)

Story type: Horror (Psychological Suspense)
Major character(s): Richard Sullivan, Guard (security guard at the Citadel); Mark Sullivan, Child; Hillary "Hilly" Walker, Writer
Time period(s): 1990s
Locale(s): Minneapolis, Minnesota

Summary: Ed, a former abused child who has become a feral man living in the sewer system of Minneapolis, befriends Mark Sullivan, the only child living in the maximum security living complex known as the Citadel. When Mark befriends the new tenant Hilly Walker, Ed sees her as competition who must be destroyed.

Other books you might like:
Joseph Citro, *The Unseen*, 1990
John Driver, *The Hunger of the Beast*, 1991
Susan Kay, *Phantom*, 1991

1767

STEPHEN R. GEORGE

Grandma's Little Darling
(New York: Zebra, 1990)

Story type: Horror (Possession)
Major character(s): Nora Harris, Orphan; Cheryl Gibson, Child-Care Giver; Grandma Johnson, Aged Person
Time period(s): 1990s (1990)
Locale(s): Minneapolis, Minnesota

Summary: Faced with the prospect of being sent to a state orphanage, chronically unplaceable orphan Nora Harris tries desperately to fit in with her new foster family, the Johnsons, unaware that the immortal spirit inhabiting Grandma Johnson's body plans to take over hers next.

Other books you might like:
Ramsey Campbell, *The Influence*, 1988
Ramsey Campbell, *To Wake the Dead*, 1980
  a.k.a. The Parasite
K.W. Jeter, *Soul Eater*, 1983

`1768`
STEPHEN R. GEORGE

Near Dead
(New York: Zebra, 1992)

Story type: Horror (Occult)
Major character(s): Taylor Holdman, Businessman; Marilyn Briggs, Psychic (medium); Wayne Semmlar, Mechanic, Serial Killer
Time period(s): 1990s
Locale(s): Minneapolis, Minnesota

Summary: The near-dead are those mortals whom the spirits of the dead find easy to communicate with. Taylor Holdman finds he must classify himself among them when the spirits of his butchered wife and child appear to him and enjoin him to seek out their murderer and put an end to the string of murders by which the murderer hopes to be accepted into the demon world.

Other books you might like:
John Farris, *The Axman Cometh*, 1989
Dean R. Koontz, *Hideaway*, 1992

`1769`
STEPHEN R. GEORGE

Nightscape
(New York: Zebra, 1992)

Story type: Horror (Child-in-Peril)
Major character(s): Bonnie Laine, Parent; Evan Laine, Child (8-year-old boy); Shep Thomas, Police Officer (former Chicago cop)
Time period(s): 1990s (1992)
Locale(s): Minneapolis, Minnesota

Summary: Shep Laine joins forces with Bonnie Laine to protect her son Evan from ''the creche,'' a cult of supernaturally-endowed beings who have chosen the boy to become their future leader.

Other books you might like:
Leigh Clark, *The Feeding*, 1992
Pat Graversen, *The Fagin*, 1982
Dean R. Koontz, *Servants of Twilight*, 1984

`1770`
STEPHEN R. GEORGE

Torment
(New York: Zebra, 1994)

Story type: Horror (Possession)
Major character(s): Melissa Woodrow, Child (12 year old), Musician; April Kostanuik, Child (12 year old), Musician; John Woodrow, Architect
Time period(s): 1990s (1994)
Locale(s): Minneapolis, Minnesota

Summary: Shortly after 12-year-old piano virtuoso April Kostanuik is killed in a car accident, another Minneapolis child, Melissa Woodrow, finds she is endowed with the same musical and mathematical abilities as April. Melissa's parents accept her new abilities as the flowering of her God-given talents—only to realize too late that April's spirit is embarked on a wholesale takeover and extirpation of their daughter's personality.

Other books you might like:
Clifford Mohr, *Requiem*, 1992
Fred Mustard Stewart, *The Mephisto Waltz*, 1969
Ramona Stewart, *The Possession of Joel Delaney*, 1970

`1771`
DAVID GERROLD

A Covenant of Justice
(New York: Bantam Spectra, 1994)

Story type: Science Fiction (Genetic Manipulation; Horror)
Major character(s): Lady Zillabar, Noblewoman, Vampire (Phaester); Neena Linn-Campbell, Spaceship Captain, Rebel; Harry Mertz, Immortal, Judge
Time period(s): Indeterminate Future
Locale(s): Burihatin-14, Planet—Imaginary; Thoska-Roole, Planet—Imaginary

Summary: Holding Lady Zillabar as a hostage, Finn, Sawyer and their friends travel to Burihatin-14, where they seek the TimeBinder to thwart Lord d'Vashti from abolishing the law against eating sentient beings. On a further voyage to Thoska-Roole, Lady Zillabar agrees to love and respect lesser beings, but turns on them during an attempted coup by d'Vashti. Sequel to *Under the Eye of God*.

Other books you might like:
C.J. Cherryh, *Voyager in Night*, 1984
Tanith Lee, *Sabella, Or, The Blood Stone*, 1980
Sheri S. Tepper, *Grass*, 1989
Jack Vance, *The Brave Free Men*, 1973

`1772`
DAVID GERROLD

The Man Who Folded Himself
(New York: Bantam Spectra, 1991)

Story type: Science Fiction (Time Travel)

Major character(s): Daniel Jamieson Eakins, Time Traveller; Diane Jane Eakins, Time Traveller
Time period(s): 1970s (1975)
Locale(s): Los Angeles, California
Summary: Upon the death of his Uncle Jim, Danny Eakins inherits a time belt which allows him to get rich quick and travel unlimitedly through time. Upon meeting himself over and over in both male and female form, he learns that he is the sole occupant of his immediate universe; even his Uncle Jim is him, grown old. This reissue incorporates minor changes by the author to the original 1973 edition's text.

Other books you might like:
Douglas Adams, *The Hitchhiker's Guide to the Galaxy*, 1980
James Blish, *The Triumph of Time*, 1958
Jack L. Chalker, *Downtiming the Night Side*, 1985
Ken Grimwood, *Replay*, 1987
Michael P. Kube-McDowell, *Alternities*, 1988

1773

DAVID GERROLD

The Middle of Nowhere
(New York: Bantam Spectra, 1995)

Story type: Science Fiction (Military; Adventure)
Major character(s): Robert Gatineau, Spaceman; Jonathan Thomas Korie, Spaceship Captain (commander); Brik, Genetically Altered Being (Morthan Tyger)
Locale(s): *LS-1187 Star Wolf*, Spaceship
Summary: Gatineau, the newest member of the crew, gets initiated into the Order of the Mobius Wrench while everyone onboard attempts to decontaminate, repair, and resupply their sabotaged vessel. Unfortunately, the defeated saboteur left behind a space pixie who continues the sabotage. The *Star Wolf* can't rejoin the fleet or even dock at a repair facility until it eliminates the imp, an almost impossible task. Sequel to *Voyage of the Star Wolf*.

Other books you might like:
Alfred Bester, *The Stars My Destination*, 1956
Lois McMaster Bujold, *Shards of Honor*, 1986
Stephen Goldin, *Jade Darcy and the Affair of Honor*, 1988
  Mary Mason, co-author
George Turner, *Genetic Soldier*, 1994
David Weber, *Path of the Fury*, 1992

1774

DAVID GERROLD

A Rage for Revenge
(New York: Bantam Spectra, 1989)

Story type: Science Fiction (Invasion of Earth)
Series: War Against the Chtorr
Major character(s): James Edward McCarthy, Military Personnel
Locale(s): United States
Summary: Alien worms continue their devastation of the Earth. McCarthy fights feverishly against them, gradually learning more about their complex ecosystem, but still unsure

of whether or not they are intelligent. As he learns more about the Chtorr, McCarthy also learns about himself.

Other books you might like:
Harry Harrison, *Deathworld*, 1960
Robert A. Heinlein, *Starship Troopers*, 1959
Larry Niven, *The Legacy of Heorot*, 1987
  Jerry Pournelle, and Steven Barnes, co-authors

1775

DAVID GERROLD

A Season for Slaughter
(New York: Bantam Spectra, 1993)

Story type: Science Fiction (Military; Invasion of Earth)
Series: War Against the Chtorr
Major character(s): James Edward McCarthy, Military Personnel; Elizabeth "Lizard" Tirelli, Military Personnel
Time period(s): 21st century
Locale(s): United States; Brazil
Summary: Jim McCarthy quits, bothered by the incompetence of allied forces fighting the Chtorr. Long presumed dead, General Ira Wallachstein persuades McCarthy to stay and fight, utilizing McCarthy's legendary intuition concerning the Chtorr. After observing captured humans slowly transforming into Chtorrian beings, they mount a rescue operation.

Other books you might like:
Roger MacBride Allen, *Rogue Powers*, 1986
Robert Asprin, *The Bug Wars*, 1979
Octavia E. Butler, *Dawn*, 1987
Stephen Goldin, *The Eternity Brigade*, 1980
Joe Haldeman, *The Forever War*, 1975
Robert A. Heinlein, *The Puppet Masters*, 1951
Robert A. Heinlein, *Starship Troopers*, 1959
Jack Lovejoy, *The Hunters*, 1982
Larry Niven, *The Legacy of Heorot*, 1987
  Jerry Pournelle, Steven Barnes, co-authors
Timothy Zahn, *The Blackcollar*, 1983

1776

DAVID GERROLD

Voyage of the Star Wolf
(New York: Bantam Spectra, 1990)

Story type: Science Fiction (Military)
Major character(s): Jonathan Thomas Korie, Military Personnel (lieutenant commander); Hardesty, Spaceship Captain; Harlie, Artificial Intelligence
Time period(s): 24th century
Locale(s): Outer Space
Summary: After leading his starship home following a defeat by the enemy Morthan, J.T. Korie is made a scapegoat and sent out under the sadistic Captain Hardesty to rescue the Burke which turns out to be a trap set up by a Morthan Assassin. He finally saves the ship, but Harlie, the computer, finds it was all a set-up.

Other books you might like:
Piers Anthony, *Bio of a Space Tyrant*, 1984

Lois McMaster Bujold, *The Vor Game*, 1990
Robert Chase, *The Game of Fox and Lion*, 1986
Timothy Zahn, *The Blackcollar*, 1983
Timothy Zahn, *Cobra*, 1985

1777
MARK S. GESTON

Mirror to the Sky
(New York: Morrow, 1992)

Story type: Science Fiction (Arts; Invasion of Earth)
Major character(s): Rane, Artist, Alien; Andrew Cavan, Government Official
Time period(s): 21st century
Locale(s): Washington, District of Columbia; Kansas

Summary: The aliens brought humanity their advanced solutions to Earth's problems as they searched the galaxy, hoping to meet their prophecied fate as far as possible from their home planet. They also brought examples of their remarkable religious icons, paintings which have a deeply compulsive effect on some people. As they arrange to display more paintings on Earth, a terrorist attack convinces most aliens to leave the Earth, taking some humans with them. The aliens return when they discover they have unintentionally left an original icon on Earth.

Other books you might like:
Octavia E. Butler, *Adulthood Rites*, 1988
Octavia E. Butler, *Dawn*, 1987
Octavia E. Butler, *Imago*, 1989
Robert Reed, *Down the Bright Way*, 1991
Walter Jon Williams, *Aristoi*, 1992

1778
EDWARD GIBSON

In the Wrong Hands
(New York: Bantam Spectra, 1992)

Story type: Science Fiction (Genetic Manipulation; Political)
Major character(s): Joseph ''Joe'' Z. Rebello, Spaceman, Military Personnel; Thaddaios ''Wolf'' Alexandru Wojciechowski, Scientist; Otto Stark, Clone
Time period(s): 2030s (2039)
Locale(s): LB-13, Moon (Earth's); Equality, Space Station

Summary: Joe believes PRECISE, run by Wolf, caused the ''accidental'' deaths of his crewmates. Wolf, crippled by a prenatal virus, develops the ''perfect'' human which he intends will replace all humanity, creating perfect equality.

Other books you might like:
Stephen Baxter, *Raft*, 1991
Octavia E. Butler, *Dawn*, 1987
Dave Duncan, *Hero*, 1991
Thomas A. Easton, *Sparrowhawk*, 1990
Edward M. Lerner, *Probe*, 1991
George Orwell, *Nineteen Eighty-Four*, 1949

1779
EDWARD GIBSON

Reach
(New York: Doubleday Foundation, 1989)

Story type: Science Fiction (First Contact)
Major character(s): Jake Ryder, Astronaut; Joseph ''Speed'' Spencer, Astronaut
Time period(s): 21st century
Locale(s): Earth; *Wayfarer 1*, Spaceship; *Wayfarer 2*, Spaceship

Summary: After a mysterious object is detected approaching the solar system, a series of unmanned and manned probes is sent to examine it with disastrous results. Jake Ryder, captain of *Wayfarer 2*, is determined that his mission will be different and that he will get to the bottom of whatever alien menace awaits out beyond Pluto.

Other books you might like:
Gregory Benford, *Across the Sea of Suns*, 1984
Gregory Benford, *Heart of the Comet*, 1986
    David Brin, co-author
Gregory Benford, *In the Ocean of Night*, 1977
Arthur C. Clarke, *Rama II*, 1989
Arthur C. Clarke, *Rendezvous with Rama*, 1973
Ted Reynolds, *The Tides of God*, 1989
David Alexander Smith, *Rendezvous*, 1988

1780
WILLIAM GIBSON
BRUCE STERLING, Co-Author

The Difference Engine
(New York: Bantam Spectra, 1991)

Story type: Science Fiction (Alternate Universe; Cyberpunk)
Major character(s): Edward Mallory, Scientist; Sybil Gerard, Prostitute; Ada Byron, Scientist
Time period(s): 1850s (1855)
Locale(s): London, England

Summary: Charles Babbage has perfected his Analytical Engine. The computer age has arrived a century ahead of time in an England ruled by scientists and industrialists. The characters are drawn into a conspiracy linking Great Britain with the France of Louis Napolean and the Manhattan Commune of Karl Marx over a mysterious program called the Modus.

Other books you might like:
Michael Flynn, *The Country of the Blind*, 1990
Randall Garrett, *Too Many Magicians*, 1967
A.E. van Vogt, *Null-A Three*, 1985
A.E. van Vogt, *The Players of Null-A*, 1966
A.E. van Vogt, *The World of Null-A*, 1950

1781

WILLIAM GIBSON

Idoru

(New York: Putnam, 1996)

Story type: Science Fiction (Cyberpunk)
Series: Virtual Light
Major character(s): Colin Laney, Consultant, Researcher; Chia McKenzie, Teenager, Investigator; Rei Toei, Entertainer, Artificial Intelligence
Time period(s): 21st century
Locale(s): Tokyo, Japan

Summary: Colin Laney predicts trends. Chia McKenzie idolizes Rez, a hugely popular singer who plans, much to Chia's horror, to marry the virtual entertainer Rei Toei. Their paths collide in 21st century Tokyo, where image rules, substance changes its nature, and the fate of profitable entertainers proves deadly.

Other books you might like:
Pat Cadigan, *Synners*, 1991
Paul J. McAuley, *Fairyland*, 1996
Ian McDonald, *Terminal Cafe*, 1994
Richard Paul Russo, *Destroying Angel*, 1992
John Varley, *Steel Beach*, 1992

1782

WILLIAM GIBSON

Virtual Light

(New York: Bantam Spectra, 1993)

Story type: Science Fiction (Cyberpunk; Disaster)
Major character(s): Berry Rydell, Police Officer (rentacop), Bounty Hunter; Chevette, Postal Worker (bicycle messenger), Fugitive; Skinner, Aged Person
Time period(s): 2000s (2005)
Locale(s): Los Angeles, California; San Francisco, California

Summary: When Chevette steals a pair of sunglasses on impulse, very thorough people soon pursue, forcing her to flee with the help of a burned-out rentacop. The sunglasses prove the key to a future even more unplesant than the one the characters already inhabit.

Other books you might like:
Pat Cadigan, *Synners*, 1991
Jonathan Littell, *Bad Voltage*, 1989
Pat Murphy, *The City, Not Long After*, 1989
Richard Paul Russo, *Destroying Angel*, 1992
Neal Stephenson, *Snow Crash*, 1992

1783

JOHN GIDEON

Golden Eyes

(New York: Berkley, 1994)

Story type: Horror (Vampire Story)

Major character(s): Mark Lansen, Professor (of history); Clovis Gersten, Actor, Vampire; Tressa Downey, Administrator (courtroom administrator)
Time period(s): 1980s (1988)
Locale(s): Oldenburg, Oregon

Summary: Pulled back to his adoptive family's hometown to write a local history, Mark Lansen discovers the truth about the vampire scourge that has taken hold of the town, and the secret of his true heritage that links him to it.

Other books you might like:
Charles L. Grant, *The Soft Whisper of the Dead*, 1982
Stephen King, *Salem's Lot*, 1975
Richard Laymon, *The Stake*, 1991
Tanith Lee, *Dark Dance*, 1992
Bentley Little, *The Summoning*, 1993

1784

JOHN GIDEON

Greely's Cove

(New York: Jove, 1991)

Story type: Horror (Small Town Horror)
Major character(s): Carl Trosper, Businessman; Stu Bromton, Police Officer; Hadrian Craslowe, Psychologist (child psychologist)
Time period(s): 1990s
Locale(s): Greely's Cove, Washington

Summary: Summoned back to Greely's Cove by the death of his ex-wife and a sense of responsibility for his autistic genius son, Carl Trosper uncovers a rash of mysterious disappearances among the townspeople, some of whom return as festering apparitions to their friends and relatives to lure them to "The Feast" being sponsored by "Giver of Dreams," an ungodly monster who appears to reside on the estate of the doctor who has helped rehabilitate Carl's son.

Other books you might like:
Al Sarrantonio, *October*, 1990

1785

JOHN GIDEON (Pseudonym of Lonn Hoklin)

Kindred

(New York: Jove, 1996)

Story type: Horror (Occult)
Major character(s): Lewis Kindred, Veteran (Vietnam); Cartee Gamaliel, Investigator (interrogator); Josh Nickerson, Teenager
Time period(s): 1990s (1992)
Locale(s): Portland, Oregon; Cu Chi, Vietnam

Summary: During the Vietnam war Lieutenant Lewis Kindred resisted the supernatural powers offered to him by a flesh-eating demon who masqueraded as a soldier. Back home in the United States, Lewis discovers that the demon is still hoping to recruit him two decades after their first encounter. He will need the assistance of his surviving war buddies to help put a stop to the creature's bloody spree.

Other books you might like:
Clive Barker, *The Hellbound Heart*, 1991
Marc Laidlaw, *The 37th Mandala*, 1996
John Skipp, *The Scream*, 1988
    Craig Spector, co-author
Peter Straub, *Koko*, 1988
Thomas Tessier, *The Nightwalker*, 1979
Chelsea Quinn Yarbro, *Beastnights*, 1989

1786

SCOTT G. GIER

Genellan: Planetfall
(New York: Ballantine Del Rey, 1995)

Story type: Science Fiction (First Contact; Military)
Series: Genellan
Major character(s): Sharl Buccari, Military Personnel; Braan, Alien, Military Personnel (flight commander); Dowornobb, Alien (Kora), Scientist
Time period(s): Indeterminate Future
Locale(s): Genellan, Planet—Imaginary; Kor, Planet—Imaginary

Summary: Fleeing a battle defeat, a pod of space marines lands on Genellan, an earthlike world, to await rescue. There they encounter intelligent avians who help them and huge alien scientists who have come to Genellan from the next planet in. Despite the apparent friendliness of the scientists, past hostilities have left their government distrustful of aliens, an obstacle that the marines must overcome. First novel.

Other books you might like:
Poul Anderson, *People of the Wind*, 1973
David Brin, *Sundiver*, 1980
Octavia E. Butler, *Survivor*, 1978
Paula E. Downing, *Fallway*, 1993
Lee Killough, *Liberty's World*, 1985
Anne McCaffrey, *Freedom's Landing*, 1995
Brian Stableford, *Balance of Power*, 1979

1787

SCOTT G. GIER

In the Shadow of the Moon
(New York: Ballantine Del Rey, 1996)

Story type: Science Fiction (Military; Adventure)
Series: Genellan
Major character(s): Sharl Buccari, Pilot, Parent (mother); Et Kalass, Political Figure (prime minister), Alien (Kones); Lizard Lips, Alien (cliff dweller)
Time period(s): Indeterminate Future
Locale(s): Genellan, Planet—Imaginary; Kon, Planet—Imaginary

Summary: Commander Sharl Buccari has her hands full negotiating between the Terran colonists on Genellan, the native cliff dwellers, the Kones from a neighboring planet who think they should control Genellan, and the Service who haven't really accepted that the Terran colonists no longer accept their

command. The return of the alien Shaula further complicates matters.

Other books you might like:
Poul Anderson, *People of the Wind*, 1973
Robert Asprin, *The Bug Wars*, 1979
David Brin, *Startide Rising*, 1983
Octavia E. Butler, *Survivor*, 1978
C.J. Cherryh, *The Faded Sun: Kesrith*, 1978
Paula E. Downing, *Fallway*, 1993
Rebecca Ore, *Becoming Alien*, 1988
Diann Thornley, *Ganwold's Child*, 1995

1788

MEL GILDEN

Hawaiian U.F.O. Aliens
(New York: Roc, 1991)

Story type: Science Fiction (Humor; Mystery)
Series: Zoot Marlowe
Major character(s): Zoot Marlowe, Alien (Toomler), Detective (hard-boiled); Bill, Robot (duck), Sidekick
Time period(s): 21st century
Locale(s): Malibu, California

Summary: After a brief visit to his home planet, T'toom, Zoot returns to Malibu to discover a UFO parked in the sand outside the house he shares with his surfing pals. When one surfer is hit by a mysterious beam from the UFO, changing him into a magician totally uninterested in surfing, Zoot takes up the case in hopes of saving his housemate and the Earth.

Other books you might like:
Douglas Adams, *The Hitchhiker's Guide to the Galaxy*, 1980
Roger MacBride Allen, *The Ring of Charon*, 1990
Glen Cook, *Sweet Silver Blues*, 1987
John DeChancie, *Paradox Alley*, 1987
John DeChancie, *Red Limit Freeway*, 1984
John DeChancie, *Starrigger*, 1983
Christopher Stasheff, *King Kobold Revived*, 1984
John E. Stith, *Deep Quarry*, 1989
Sheri S. Tepper, *Grass*, 1989

1789

MEL GILDEN

Outer Space and All That Junk
(New York: Lippincott, 1989)

Story type: Science Fiction (Humor)
Major character(s): Myron Duberville, Teenager, Genius; Hugo, Scientist
Locale(s): Vasichvu Bend

Summary: Young Myron Duberville goes to spend the summer with his eccentric Uncle Hugo, owner of the highly successful Astronetics Corporation. Uncle Hugo's hobby is collecting junk. He has a yard full of it and he claims that hidden away in the junk pile are aliens whom he is trying to help. At first Myron assumes that his uncle is a wacko. Later he finds out that aliens are in fact hiding in the junk pile and that they are very strange indeed.

Other books you might like:
Frank Asch, *Journey to Terezor*, 1989
Reginald Bretnor, *The Schimmelhorn File*, 1979
Jo Dereske, *The Lone Sentinel*, 1989
William Kotzwinkle, *E.T.: The Extra-Terrestrial*, 1982

1790
MEL GILDEN

Tubular Android Superheroes
(New York: Roc, 1991)

Story type: Science Fiction (Humor; Mystery)
Series: Zoot Marlowe
Major character(s): Zoot Marlowe, Alien (Toomler), Detective (hard-boiled); Bill, Robot (duck), Sidekick
Time period(s): 21st century
Locale(s): Malibu, California; Los Angeles, California (Los Angeles County)

Summary: Returning from T'toom with Grampa Zamp, Zoot finds California's solution to the parking problem involves the latest craze, the Melt-O-Mobile. As Zoot begins to nose around a sudden proliferation of androids, the Melt-O-Mobile takes on a sinister air.

Other books you might like:
Douglas Adams, *Dirk Gently's Holistic Detective Agency*, 1987
Douglas Adams, *The Long Dark Tea-Time of the Soul*, 1989
Chester Anderson, *The Butterfly Kid*, 1967
Glen Cook, *Dread Brass Shadows*, 1990
Glen Cook, *Old Tin Sorrows*, 1989
Glen Cook, *Sweet Silver Blues*, 1987
Nick Pollotta, *Illegal Aliens*, 1989
    Phil Foglio, co-author
T.A. Waters, *The Probability Pad*, 1970

1791
DONNA GILLESPIE

The Light Bearer
(New York: Berkley, 1994)

Story type: Fantasy (Historical; Political)
Major character(s): Auriane, Warrior, Religious (priestess); Decius, Slave, Military Personnel; Marcus Julianus, Diplomat (stateman)
Time period(s): 1st century
Locale(s): Europe

Summary: Prophecied to disrupt the ancient order, Auriane witnesses the Roman destruction of her family then vows to avenge the horrors. Her quest of vengeance takes her to Rome where she meets Marcus Julianus, destined to share Auriane's fate. First novel.

Other books you might like:
Stephan Grundy, *Rhinegold*, 1994
Harry Harrison, *The Hammer and the Cross*, 1993
    John Holm, co-author
Morgan Llywelyn, *Bard*, 1984
Morgan Llywelyn, *Druids*, 1991

Diana L. Paxson, *The Wolf and the Raven*, 1993

1792
RICHARD GILLIAM, Editor
MARTIN H. GREENBERG, Co-Editor
EDWARD E. KRAMER, Co-Editor

Confederacy of the Dead
(New York: Roc, 1993)

Story type: Horror (Anthology)

Summary: The 25 stories, all but three original to the book, center around the horrors of the American Civil War. Wendy Webb's ''A Dress for Tea'' is a subtle ghost story and S.P. Somtow's ''Darker Angels'' and Karl Edward Wagner's ''Hell Creek'' unabashed zombie stories. Nancy A. Collins' ''The Sunday-Go-To-Meeting Jaw'' is a southern grotesque and William S. Burroughs' ''Death Fiend'' a graphic anti-war story. Both Nancy Holder's ''Strawman'' and Robert Sampson's ''Two Yellow Pine Coffins'' juxtapose the horrors of war with the terror of black magic. Although most stories are from the perspective of the South, both Richard Lee Byers' ''Foragers'' and Doug Murray's ''The Crater'' are told from the northern point-of-view. Michael Bishop has supplied the preface.

Other books you might like:
Frank D. McSherry Jr., *Civil War Ghosts*, 1990
    Charles G. Waugh, Martin H. Greenberg, co-editors
Frank McSherry, *Nightmares in Dixie*, 1987
    Charles G. Waugh, Martin H. Greenberg, co-editors

1793
RICHARD GILLIAM, Editor
MARTIN H. GREENBERG, Co-Editor
EDWARD E. KRAMER, Co-Editor

Grails: Quests of the Dawn
(New York: Roc, 1994)

Story type: Fantasy (Anthology; Legend)

Summary: Contains a three-page afterword by Fritz Leiber, two poems by James S. Dorr and Jane Yolen plus 23 stories, some reprinted from a 1992 limited edition focusing on diverse investigations into the ultimate vessel of magic. Authors include Marion Zimmer Bradley, Orson Scott Card, Lionel Fenn, Alan Dean Foster, Neil Gaiman, Richard Gilliam, Lee Hoffman, Mercedes Lackey, Andre Norton, Diana L. Paxson, Kristine Kathryn Rusch, Dean Wesley Smith, Brad Strickland, Brian M. Thomsen, Lawrence Watt-Evans, Gene Wolfe and Janny Wurts. Companion volume to *Grails: Visitations of the Night*.

Other books you might like:
A.A. Attanasio, *Kingdom of the Grail*, 1992
James P. Blaylock, *The Paper Grail*, 1991
Marion Zimmer Bradley, *The Mists of Avalon*, 1983
Malcolm Godwin, *The Holy Grail*, 1994
Andrew M. Greeley, *The Magic Cup*, 1979
Marc Laidlaw, *Neon Lotus*, 1988
Rob MacGregor, *Indiana Jones and the Last Crusade*, 1989

Charles Williams, *War in Heaven*, 1930

1794

RICHARD GILLIAM, Editor
MARTIN H. GREENBERG, Co-Editor
EDWARD E. KRAMER, Co-Editor

Grails: Visitations of the Night

(New York: Roc, 1994)

Story type: Fantasy (Anthology; Legend)

Summary: Contains a five-page introduction by Brian Thomsen, two pages of notes and acknowledgments by Richard Gilliam, plus 29 stories, some reprinted from a 1992 limited edition. The stories focus on the quest for the object of ultimate power. Authors include John Gregory Betancourt, Pat Cadigan, Michael Cassutt, George Alec Effinger, John Farris, Jack C. Haldeman II, Tanith Lee, Brad Linaweaver, S.P. Somtow, Karl Edward Wagner and Robert Weinberg. Companion volume to *Grails: Quests of the Dawn*.

Other books you might like:
James P. Blaylock, *The Last Coin*, 1988
Marion Zimmer Bradley, *The Mists of Avalon*, 1983
Susan Cooper, *Over Sea, Under Stone*, 1966
Malcolm Godwin, *The Holy Grail*, 1994
Andrew M. Greeley, *The Magic Cup*, 1979
Marc Laidlaw, *Neon Lotus*, 1988
Rosemary Sutcliffe, *The Light Beyond the Forest*, 1980

1795

RICHARD GILLIAM, Editor
MARTIN H. GREENBERG, Co-Editor

Phantoms of the Night

(New York: DAW, 1996)

Story type: Horror (Anthology; Ghost Story)

Summary: The twenty-eight stories of ghosts and hauntings collected here are all original to the volume. They include Owl Goingback's "Last Man in Line," a Civil War horror story about the ghosts of Andersonville, and Tina Jens' "Preacherman Gets the Blues," in which music has the power to summon and banish the spirits of the dead. Matthew Costello's "Unfortunate Obsession" is a fatal attraction tale with a twist ending, and Edward Kramer's "Casting Circles" a story of a summer camp prank gone weird. Ghosts are tragic family revenants in Douglas Clegg's "The Fruit of Her Womb," sardonic vehicles for revenge in John Helfers' "Blood Ghost," and sentimental entities with good fashion sense in Lawrence Schimel's "Old as a Rose in Bloom."

Other books you might like:
Marvin Kaye, *Ghosts*, 1981
   editor
Claudia O'Keefe, *Ghosttide*, 1993
   editor
Paul F. Olson, *Post Mortem: New Tales of Ghostly Horror*, 1989
   David B. Silva, co-editor

Peter Straub, *Ghosts*, 1995
   editor

1796

ALEXIS A. GILLILAND

Lord of the Troll-Bats

(New York: Ballantine Del Rey, 1992)

Story type: Fantasy (Political)
Series: Wizenbeak
Major character(s): Wizenbeak, Wizard, Royalty (king)
Time period(s): Indeterminate
Locale(s): Guhland, Fictional Country

Summary: Wizenbeak's peaceful rule as King-Patriarch suffers when ex-Patriarch Gorbani summons the Lord of the Troll-Bats to curse Wizenbeak and arranges an invasion of Guhland's provinces by armies of dragons and women. Further complications arise when Wizenbeak's wife inexplicably disappears.

Other books you might like:
Gordon R. Dickson, *The Dragon at War*, 1992
Robert Don Hughes, *The Forging of the Dragon*, 1989
Richard A. Knaak, *Dragon Tome*, 1992

1797

ALEXIS A. GILLILAND

The Shadow Shaia

(New York: Ballantine/Del Rey, 1990)

Story type: Fantasy (Political; Adventure)
Series: Wizenbeak
Major character(s): Wizenbeak, Wizard
Time period(s): Indeterminate
Locale(s): Guhland, Fictional Country

Summary: The war is over. King Kahun is dead. Wizenbeak has chosen the Regent for young Prince Dervian. He seems to be in control and should be able to relax and enjoy life. However, the aftermath of a civil war, with inexperienced people at the top seems an opportune time for neighboring King Kirndal to reclaim the province of Kalycas.

Other books you might like:
Jack L. Chalker, *The River of the Dancing Gods*, 1984
Jack L. Chalker, *When the Changewinds Blow*, 1987
Barbara Hambly, *The Time of the Dark*, 1982
Christopher Stasheff, *The Warlock in Spite of Himself*, 1969
J.R.R. Tolkien, *The Fellowship of the Ring*, 1954

1798

SHEILA GILLULY

The Boy From the Burren

(New York: Roc, 1990)

Story type: Fantasy (Adventure; Quest)
Series: Book of the Painter
Major character(s): Aengus, Artist (painter); Bruchan, Minstrel (storyteller); Jorem, Religious (priest)

Time period(s): Indeterminate Past
Locale(s): Inishbuffin, Fictional City

Summary: As Bruchan's indentured servant, Aengus is learning a trade (medicine), self-defense and performing various community chores with the other indentured boys. But in secret, he is being taught to paint, for his painting is the key to fulfilling a prophecy. But Jorem will do anything to stop Aengus and Bruchan in order to preserve his skewed version of their religion and his political power.

Other books you might like:
Steven Brust, *The Sun, the Moon, and the Stars*, 1984
Orson Scott Card, *Seventh Son*, 1987
C.J. Cherryh, *Angel with the Sword*, 1988
Mercedes Lackey, *Arrows of the Queen*, 1987
Karen Wehrstein, *Lion's Heart*, 1991

1799

GREER ILENE GILMAN

Moonwise

(New York: Penguin, 1991)

Story type: Fantasy (Quest; Alternate World)
Major character(s): Ariane, Scholar; Sylvie, Landowner; Craobb, Angel
Time period(s): 1990s (1991)
Locale(s): Earth; Cloud, Fictional Country

Summary: This is the story of two friends who create stories about magic worlds together. One day Sylvie disappears into one of these worlds and her more practical friend, Ariane, must make a complex trip into the nature of magic and reality to save her.

Other books you might like:
John Crowley, *Little, Big*, 1981
Robert Holdstock, *Lavondyss: Journey to an Unknown Region*, 1988
Robert Holdstock, *Mythago Wood*, 1984
Ian McDonald, *King of Morning, Queen of Day*, 1991
Christoph Ransmayr, *The Last World*, 1990

1800

NEWT GINGRICH
WILLIAM R. FORSTCHEN, Co-Author

1945

(New York: Baen, 1995)

Story type: Science Fiction (Alternate Universe; Military)
Major character(s): James Mannheim Martel, Military Personnel (Navel Intelligence); Otto Skorzeny, Military Personnel (colonel), Historical Figure; Andrew Harrison, Political Figure (U.S. president)
Time period(s): 1940s (1945)
Locale(s): Germany; United States

Summary: When intelligence indicates American research on an atomic bomb, Hitler decides to attack nuclear facilities at Oak Ridge, Tennessee, thus putting Germany far ahead in nuclear weapons development. While James Martel intervenes to avert the disaster at Oak Ridge, the Germans begin to

invade England, aided by a traitor on President Harrison's staff.

Other books you might like:
Kevin J. Anderson, *The Trinity Paradox*, 1991
  Doug Beason, co-author
Ben Bova, *Triumph*, 1993
Philip K. Dick, *The Man in the High Castle*, 1962
William R. Forstchen, *Terrible Swift Sword*, 1992
Robert Harris, *Fatherland*, 1992
Brad Linaweaver, *Moon of Ice*, 1988
Harry Turtledove, *Worldwar: Tilting the Balance*, 1995
Robert Charles Wilson, *Mysterium*, 1994

1801

ROBERT GIRARDI

Madeleine's Ghost

(New York: Delacorte, 1995)

Story type: Horror (Ghost Story)
Major character(s): Ned Conti, Student (grad student in French history); Antoinette Rivaudais, Saloon Hostess; Father Rose, Religious (Catholic priest)
Time period(s): 1990s (1995)
Locale(s): New York, New York (Brooklyn)

Summary: While dithering over the completion of his dissertation Ned Conti, a New Orleans native transplanted to Brooklyn, accepts a research job to help a local parish further the canonization of Sister Januarius, a nun who worked the Brooklyn wharves in the mid-nineteenth century and, like Ned, was also originally from New Orleans. Ghostly manifestations in Ned's apartment and overtures from his old girlfriend in Louisiana eventually encourage him to look into his own life and history to find the answers he needs to cope with his present problems. This is the author's first novel.

Other books you might like:
Jack Cady, *The Off Season*, 1995
Judith Hawkes, *Julian's House*, 1989
Michael Upchurch, *Passive Intruder*, 19950

1802

NANCY TYLER GLENN

Clicking Stones

(Tallahassee: Naiad Press, 1989)

Story type: Science Fiction (Gay/Lesbian Fiction)
Major character(s): Erica, Lesbian; Morgan, Lesbian
Time period(s): 1980s; 21st century
Locale(s): United States

Summary: A young girl finds a mysterious stone with special powers; striking it against another stone causes both to flare into incredible brilliance, causing both physical and mental illumination. As news of the strange phenomenon spreads, a potentially utopian movement begins to grow. This is Glenn's first novel.

Other books you might like:
Suzy McKee Charnas, *Motherlines*, 1979
Suzy McKee Charnas, *Walk to the End of the World*, 1974

Lauren Wright Douglas, *In the Blood*, 1989
Karen Marie Christa Minns, *Virago*, 1990
Joanna Russ, *The Female Man*, 1975
Joanna Russ, *We Who Are About To. . .*, 1977

1803

JANET GLUCKMAN
GEORGE GUTHRIDGE, Co-Author

Child of the Light

(New York: St. Martin's, 1992)

Story type: Fantasy (Historical; Political)
Series: Madagascar Manifesto
Major character(s): Solomon Freund, Psychic; Erich Weisser, Telepath, Animal Trainer; Miriam Rathenau, Singer
Time period(s): 1920s; 1930s
Locale(s): Berlin, Germany

Summary: Erich and Solomon's boyhood friendship falls victim to historical forces of anti-semitism and their love of the same woman, Miriam. Erich's ability as a dog trainer yields a rapid rise in the Nazi heirarchy while Solomon remains plagued with visions of horror. Nazi death camp mentality and the plan to export Jews to their new homeland, Madagascar, further distance the pair.

Other books you might like:
Martin Amis, *Time's Arrow*, 1991
Katherine Kurtz, *Lammas Night*, 1983
Kurt Vonnegut Jr., *Slaughterhouse Five*, 1969
Jane Yolen, *Briar Rose*, 1992
Jane Yolen, *The Devil's Arithmetic*, 1988

1804

PARKE GODWIN

Limbo Search

(New York: AvoNova, 1995)

Story type: Science Fiction (Military; First Contact)
Major character(s): Charley Stoner, Military Personnel (UNESA warrant officer); Elli Rovin, Military Personnel (UNESA warrant officer); Nigel Pauley, Military Personnel (UNESA intelligence officer)
Time period(s): Indeterminate Future
Locale(s): Limbo, Space Station; *Kennedy*, Spaceship

Summary: Charley Stoner and his United Earth Space Authority colleagues monitor communications for illegal corporate space activity. When they identify the first alien signal ever encountered by humans, their duties become even more dangerous.

Other books you might like:
Ben Bova, *The Privateers*, 1985
Joe Haldeman, *The Forever War*, 1975
Marvin Kaye, *A Cold Blue Light*, 1983
Marvin Kaye, *The Masters of Solitude*, 1978
    Parke Godwin, co-author
Marvin Kaye, *Wintermind*, 1982
    Parke Godwin, co-author
John Steakley, *Armor*, 1984

1805

PARKE GODWIN

Robin and the King

(New York: Morrow, 1993)

Story type: Fantasy (Legend; Historical)
Major character(s): Robin Hood, Hero, Outlaw; Marian, Spouse (Robin's); William, Royalty (king), Historical Figure
Time period(s): 11th century
Locale(s): England

Summary: Now middle aged, Robin Hood fiercely opposes absolute rule of free Englishmen by any monarch. His campaign progresses from local strife to the protection of England from foreign invaders. Sequel to *Sherwood*.

Other books you might like:
David Gemmell, *Morningstar*, 1993
Richard Kluger, *The Sheriff of Nottingham*, 1992
Robin McKinley, *The Outlaws of Sherwood*, 1989
Howard Pyle, *The Merry Adventures of Robin Hood*, 1883
Jennifer Roberson, *Lady of the Forest*, 1992

1806

PARKE GODWIN

Sherwood

(New York: Morrow, 1991)

Story type: Fantasy (Legend)

Summary: In this richly detailed story set at the time of the Norman conquest of the Saxons, Robin Hood illustrates the Saxon resistance to William the Conqueror's domination of Saxons and Celts. The Sheriff of Nottingham, charged with forcing William the Conqueror's laws on the Saxons, brands Robin Hood an outlaw for holding on to Saxon ideas of honor and law. Events conspire to make sworn enemies temporary allies as Robin Hood formally enters the rebellion against the invaders.

Other books you might like:
Frans G. Bengtsson, *The Long Ships*, 1954
C.J. Cherryh, *Cyteen*, 1988
Clayton Emery, *Tales of Robin Hood*, 1988
Martin H. Greenberg, *The Fantastic Adventures of Robin Hood*, 1991
    editor
Robin McKinley, *The Outlaws of Sherwood*, 1988
Bernard Miles, *Robin Hood: His Life and Legend*, 1979
Howard Pyle, *The Merry Adventures of Robin Hood*, 1883
William F. Wu, *The Robin Hood Ambush*, 1990

1807

PARKE GODWIN

The Snake Oil Wars

(New York: Doubleday Foundation, 1989)

Story type: Science Fiction (Satire)
Major character(s): Barion, Alien (God); Coyul, Alien (Satan)

Time period(s): 1980s
Locale(s): Earth; Topside, Planet—Imaginary

Summary: As described in *Waiting for the Galactic Bus*, the brothers Barion and Coyul, a pair of alien graduate students, were abandoned on the planet Earth as part of a college prank. Bored, they created illegal life, which eventually evolved into humankind. Now Barion has been sent home to stand trial for their crime, leaving Coyul to explain things to a humanity who, collectively, are not amused. Humanity files a law suit.

Other books you might like:
John Kessel, *Good News From Outer Space*, 1989
James Morrow, *Only Begotten Daughter*, 1990
Salman Rushdie, *The Satanic Verses*, 1989

1808

PARKE GODWIN

The Tower of Beowulf

(New York: Morrow, 1995)

Story type: Fantasy (Legend; Adventure)
Major character(s): Beowulf, Hero; Sigyn, Mythical Creature; Grendel, Mythical Creature, Monster
Time period(s): 5th century; 6th century
Locale(s): Denmark; Sweden; Asgard, Mythical Place

Summary: Memories of a botched first raid drive numbed Beowulf toward greater deeds as his reputation grows. Sigyn provides Grendel shelter from others during his youth until Thor repudiates him, ending his innocence. When Grendel asserts his claim as true king of the Scyldings, Beowulf battles and defeats him, but must subsequently vanquish Sigyn then recover his lust for life.

Other books you might like:
Frans G. Bengtsson, *The Long Ships*, 1954
John Gardner, *Grendel*, 1971
Stephan Grundy, *Rhinegold*, 1994
Harry Harrison, *The Hammer and the Cross*, 1993
    John Holm, co-author
Diana L. Paxson, *The Wolf and the Raven*, 1993

1809

OWL GOINGBACK

Crota

(New York: Donald I. Fine, 1996)

Story type: Horror (Ancient Evil Unleashed)
Major character(s): Jay Little Hawk, Game Warden; Skip Harding, Police Officer (sheriff)
Time period(s): 1990s (1996)
Locale(s): Logan, Missouri

Summary: The author's first novel concerns a monster of Creek Indian legend, the invincible Crota, who is released from captivity in the caves beneath the town of Logan and who embarks on a bloody rampage against white men and Native Americans alike. Only by reacquainting himself with the Native American heritage he has forsaken in order to assimilate with the white man's world can Sheriff Skip Harding find the power to defeat the creature.

Other books you might like:
Muriel Gray, *Trickster*, 1994
T. Chris Martindale, *Demon Dance*, 1991
G. Wayne Miller, *Thunder Rise*, 1988
Eugene E. Pfaff Jr., *Uwharrie*, 1993
    Michael Causey, co-author
Kathryn Ptacek, *Ghost Dance*, 1990
Patrick Whalen, *Deathwalker*, 1992

1810

CHRISTOPHER GOLDEN

Angel Souls and Devil Hearts

(New York: Berkley, 1995)

Story type: Horror (Vampire Story)
Major character(s): Will Cody, Vampire; Alison Vigeant, Journalist; Liam Mulkerrin, Vampire
Time period(s): 2000s (2000)
Locale(s): Salzburg, Austria

Summary: Having survived a secret plot by the Vatican to destroy them, a vampire race known as the Shadows, or Defiant Ones, struggles for the same civil rights enjoyed by mortal human beings. Their efforts are potentially endangered by a civil war fomented by renegade vampires who want nothing to do with peaceful coexistence with humanity. Sequel to *Of Saints and Shadows*.

Other books you might like:
Scott Baker, *Ancestral Hungers*, 1995
Laurell K. Hamilton, *Circus of the Damned*, 1994
Brian Stableford, *The Hunger and Ecstasy of Vampires*, 1996
Robert Weinberg, *Bloodwar*, 1995
Kelley Wilde, *Mastery*, 1991

1811

CHRISTOPHER GOLDEN

Of Saints and Shadows

(New York: Jove, 1994)

Story type: Horror (Vampire Story)
Major character(s): Peter Octavian, Detective—Private, Vampire; Father Mulkerrin, Religious (Catholic priest)
Time period(s): 1990s (1995)
Locale(s): Boston, Massachusetts; Venice, Italy

Summary: Private detective and vampire Peter Octavian discovers that a secret branch of the Vatican controls all supernatural beings such as the Defiant Ones (a.k.a. vampires) through black magic and psychological conditioning, and that one of its renegade members has found forbidden magic that will allow him to unleash these forces upon the world and take control of it.

Other books you might like:
Scott Baker, *Ancestral Hungers*, 1995
Brent Monahan, *The Book of Common Dread*, 1993
Anne Rice, *The Vampire Lestat*, 1985
Robert Weinberg, *Bloodwar*, 1995

1812

STEPHEN GOLDIN
MARY MASON, Co-Author

Jade Darcy and the Zen Pirates
(New York: Roc, 1990)

Story type: Science Fiction (Adventure; Mystery)
Series: Rehumanization of Jade Darcy
Major character(s): Jade Darcy, Martial Arts Expert (bouncer), Warrior; Megan Cafferty, Businesswoman (entrepreneur); Peach-Frog-At-Twilight, Alien (Restaapan), Religious (novice Furgato)
Time period(s): Indeterminate Future
Locale(s): Cablans, Planet—Imaginary; Restaapa, Planet—Imaginary (Monastery of the Dirda Hills)

Summary: Hoping to open a new market, Megan Cafferty has been trying unsuccessfully to wrangle an invitation to Restaapa when she is overjoyed to discover Jade Darcy has an invitation to the Imperial Festival of the Snows. Jade offers her services as hired bodyguard, allowing Megan to be included in Jade's invitation from the Furgato Sect. While jouneying to the festival site, xenophobic Restaapans attack Jade and Megan who defend themselves until their Furgato hosts come to assist. Shortly after Jade and Megan arrive for the festival, a murder draws them into the intrigue surrounding Imperial efforts to end Restaapa's self-imposed isolation.

Other books you might like:
Rosemary Kirstein, *The Steerswoman*, 1989
Melisa C. Michaels, *Skirmish*, 1985
David R. Palmer, *Emergence*, 1984
Alis A. Rasmussen, *A Passage of Stars*, 1990
Alis A. Rasmussen, *The Price of Ransom*, 1990
Alis A. Rasmussen, *Revolution's Shore*, 1990

1813

LISA GOLDSTEIN

Daily Voices
(Eugene, Oregon: Pulphouse Publishing, 1989)

Story type: Science Fiction (Collection)
Series: Author's Choice Monthly

Summary: Although titled like a magazine, this brief volume is essentially a short story collection consisting of an introduction by the author and five stories originally published between 1984 and 1987 in *Isaac Asimov's SF Magazine*, including ''Cassandra's Photographs,'' ''Death is Different,'' and ''Tourists.''

Other books you might like:
Pat Cadigan, *Patterns*, 1989
Karen Joy Fowler, *Artificial Things*, 1986
Kate Wilhelm, *Children of the Wind: Five Novellas*, 1989
Kate Wilhelm, *Listen, Listen*, 1981
Pamela Zoline, *The Heat Death of the Universe*, 1988

1814

LISA GOLDSTEIN

Strange Devices of the Sun and Moon
(New York: Tor, 1993)

Story type: Fantasy (Historical)
Major character(s): Alice Wood, Businesswoman; Christopher Marlowe, Writer (playwright), Historical Figure; Margery, Witch
Time period(s): 16th century
Locale(s): London, England

Summary: Husband dead and son missing, Alice Wood makes her way with difficulty as a bookseller in London. Christopher Marlow, freethinker and playwright, spies for a mysterious benefactor. The lives of these two people, along with the Queen of Faerie and Alice's missing son, entangle with the destiny of England.

Other books you might like:
John Crowley, *Aegypt*, 1987
Michael Moorcock, *Gloriana, or the Unfulfilled Queen*, 1978
Tim Powers, *The Drawing of the Dark*, 1979
Melissa Scott, *The Armor of Light*, 1988
  Lisa Barnett, co-author
Patricia C. Wrede, *Snow White and Rose Red*, 1989

1815

LISA GOLDSTEIN

Summer King, Winter Fool
(New York: Tor, 1994)

Story type: Fantasy (Political; Magic Conflict)
Major character(s): Valemar, Nobleman; Narrion, Nobleman; Taja, Librarian, Wizard
Time period(s): Indeterminate Past
Locale(s): Shai, Fictional Country

Summary: In a small, intrigue-filled kingdom, a young courtier goes into exile at a small fishing village with an odd, ancient library. People do not fare well under the ruling usurper and the threat of impending war, while the summer god has not yet ascended into heaven to end winter. Against this gloomy backdrop, the courtier searches for his fate, despite uncertainty and ambivalence.

Other books you might like:
Eleanor Arnason, *The Sword Smith*, 1978
Ellen Kushner, *Swordspoint*, 1987
Patricia A. McKillip, *The Riddle-Master of Hed*, 1976
Melissa Scott, *The Armor of Light*, 1988
  Lisa A. Barnett, co-author
Caroline Stevermer, *A College of Magics*, 1994

1816

LISA GOLDSTEIN

Tourists
(New York: Simon and Schuster, 1989)

Story type: Fantasy (Magic Conflict)

Major character(s): Casey Parmenter, Teenager; Mitchell Parmenter, Anthropologist (Casey's father)
Time period(s): 1980s
Locale(s): Amaz, Planet—Imaginary; Earth

Summary: Casey and her family are in Amaz because her father is searching for the Jewel King's palace and fabled sword. The novel focuses on the family's attempt to cope with a city in which magic exists and has an everyday role in the life of the inhabitants.

Other books you might like:
Rick Cook, *Wizard's Bane*, 1988
Doris Egan, *The Gate of Ivory*, 1989
Hanne Marie Svendsen, *The Gold Ball*, 1989

1817

LISA GOLDSTEIN

Travellers in Magic

(New York: Tor, 1994)

Story type: Fantasy (Collection)

Summary: Contains 14 short stories published 1984-1994 in periodicals and anthologies and one original story with brief afterwords to each. As usual for Goldstein, the stories detail ordinary people and place that suddenly experience strange, possibly magical, events. Three of the stories involve Amaz, the country featured in *Tourists*, while several others deal with Jewish history and culture.

Other books you might like:
John Crowley, *Antiquities*, 1993
Karen Joy Fowler, *Sarah Canary*, 1991
Pat Murphy, *Points of Departure*, 1990
Tim Powers, *The Stress of Her Regard*, 1989
Jane Yolen, *Briar Rose*, 1992

1818

LISA GOLDSTEIN

Walking the Labyrinth

(New York: Tor, 1996)

Story type: Fantasy (Mystery; Contemporary)
Major character(s): Molly Travers, Detective—Private; John Stow, Detective—Private; Fentrice Allalie, Aged Person, Magician (retired)
Time period(s): 1990s; 1930s (1935)
Locale(s): England; Midwest

Summary: Spurred by John Stow's investigation of her Aunt Fentrice's family magic act, Molly Travers queries Fentrice for details. Her curiosity leads to a secret society of powerful labyrinth builders and a house in England built by her relative, complete with an extensive labyrinth under the house. Further searching uncovers unusual powers and unexpected family history.

Other books you might like:
Charles de Lint, *Memory and Dream*, 1994
Christopher Priest, *The Prestige*, 1996
Michaela Roessner, *Vanishing Point*, 1993

Brooke Stevens, *The Circus of the Earth and Air*, 1994
Terri Windling, *The Wood Wife*, 1996

1819

JEWELLE GOMEZ

The Gilda Stories

(Ithaca, New York: Firebrand Books, 1991)

Story type: Horror (Vampire Story)
Major character(s): Gilda, Vampire, Lesbian; Miss Bird, Servant, Indian; Effie, Young Woman
Time period(s): 19th century; 20th century
Locale(s): South; Boston, Massachusetts; New York, New York

Summary: In this episodic first novel Gilda, a black lesbian vampire, travels from place to place across the United States over a two-century interval, lending her assistance and social conscience to historically disenfranchised ethnic and social groups and embodying through her experiences a chronicle of prejudice and cultural bias in America.

Other books you might like:
Suzy McKee Charnas, *The Vampire Tapestry*, 1980
Mara McCuniff, *The Vampire Memoirs*, 1991
    Tracy Briery, co-author
Anne Rice, *Interview with the Vampire*, 1976
Michael Romkey, *I, Vampire*, 1990

1820

TERRY GOODKIND

Blood of the Fold

(New York: Tor, 1996)

Story type: Fantasy (Sword and Sorcery; Political)
Series: Sword of Truth
Major character(s): Richard "the Seeker" Rahl, Wizard (War Wizard); Verna Sauventreen, Magician (Sister of the Light), Leader (prelate); Kahlan Amnell, Magician, Leader (Mother Confessor)
Time period(s): Indeterminate
Locale(s): The Midlands, Fictional Country; Aydindril, Fictional City; The Old World, Fictional Country

Summary: With the destruction of ancient barriers against invasion from the Old World, a dream-walker begins the conquest of the Midlands and the rest of the New World. Condemned as traitor, Kahlan Amnell flees while Verna Sauventreen copes with elevation to Prelate as the evil Sisters of Darkness attempt to suborn the Sisters of Light. Acting on instinct, Richard Rahl begins forcing enemies to work together to repel human invaders while he braves the deadly Wizard's Keep to engage magical forces which could destroy rather than aid his efforts.

Other books you might like:
David Eddings, *Pawn of Prophecy*, 1982
Lynn Flewelling, *Luck in the Shadows*, 1996
Laurell K. Hamilton, *Nightseer*, 1992
Robin Hobb, *Assassin's Apprentice*, 1995
J.V. Jones, *The Baker's Boy*, 1995

Robert Jordan, *The Eye of the World*, 1990
Patricia C. Wrede, *The Raven Ring*, 1994

1821

TERRY GOODKIND

Stone of Tears

(New York: Tor, 1995)

Story type: Fantasy (Magic Conflict; Sword and Sorcery)
Series: Sword of Truth
Major character(s): Richard "the Seeker" Cypher, Wizard, Captive; Kahlan Amnell, Magician, Leader (Mother Confessor); Zeddicus "Zedd" Zu'l Zorander, Wizard
Time period(s): Indeterminate
Locale(s): D'Hara, Fictional Country; The Midlands, Fictional Country; Palace of the Prophets, Mythical Place (wizards' school)

Summary: Richard's defeat of Darken Rahl brings only brief relief from the Keeper's struggle to escape confinement and destroy the world. When Richard's uncontrolled development as a wizard threatens to overwhelm him, Kahlan tricks Richard into making himself a prisoner of the Sisters of the Light who promise to save his life and develop his talents. When Richard leaves, Kahlan, as Moter Confessor, must mold raw troops into effective counterinsurgency warriors while Zedd and his sorceress friend attempt to subvert magical attacks by the Keeper's agents.

Other books you might like:
Lois McMaster Bujold, *The Spirit Ring*, 1992
David Eddings, *Pawn of Prophecy*, 1982
Laurell K. Hamilton, *Nightseer*, 1992
Robert Jordan, *The Eye of the World*, 1989
Caroline Stevermer, *A College of Magics*, 1994
Patricia C. Wrede, *The Raven Ring*, 1994
Martha Wells, *The Element of Fire*, 1993

1822

TERRY GOODKIND

Wizard's First Rule

(New York: Tor, 1994)

Story type: Fantasy (Quest; Magic Conflict)
Major character(s): Richard "the Seeker" Cypher, Woodsman, Martial Arts Expert; Kahlan Amnell, Magician, Leader (Mother Confessor); Darken Rahl, Wizard, Leader
Time period(s): Indeterminate
Locale(s): Westland, Fictional Country; The Midlands, Fictional Country; The Underworld, Mythical Place (realm of the dead)

Summary: When Richard saves Kahlan from four assassins who hunt her, he becomes her friend and protector on her dangerous mission to prevent Darken Rahl from acquiring ultimate magical power through ancient artifacts. Recognized as the prophecied Seeker by his wizard friend, Richard accepts the Sword of Truth and learns of the sword's great

power and the terrible price its use demands of the user. First novel.

Other books you might like:
Lois McMaster Bujold, *The Spirit Ring*, 1992
Dave Duncan, *The Cutting Edge*, 1992
David Eddings, *Pawn of Prophecy*, 1982
Raymond E. Feist, *Magician*, 1982
Robert Jordan, *The Eye of the World*, 1989
Rosemary Kirstein, *The Outskirter's Secret*, 1992
Dennis L. McKiernan, *Voyage of the Fox Rider*, 1993
Michael Scott Rohan, *The Anvil of Ice*, 1986
J.R.R. Tolkien, *The Fellowship of the Ring*, 1954
J.R.R. Tolkien, *The Hobbit*, 1938
Margaret Weis, *Dragons of Autumn Twilight*, 1984
  Tracy Hickman, co-author

1823

MARIE D. GOODWIN

Where the Towers Pierce the Sky

(New York: Macmillan Four Winds, 1989)

Story type: Fantasy (Time Travel)
Major character(s): Lizzie Patterson, Teenager (13 years old); Jacques Aubert, Apprentice (to an Astrologer)
Time period(s): 1980s; 15th century
Locale(s): South Bend, Indiana; France

Summary: A 15th century astrologer mistakenly calls 20th century Lizzie to war-torn France and Joan of Arc. The astrologer's apprentice helps her adjust to a harsh and dangerous medieval lifestyle.

Other books you might like:
Suzy McKee Charnas, *The Golden Thread*, 1989
Diana Wynne Jones, *A Tale of Time City*, 1987
Richard Peck, *Voices After Midnight*, 1989
Pamela F. Service, *Winter of Magic's Return*, 1985
Jane Yolen, *The Devil's Arithmetic*, 1988

1824

KATHLEEN ANN GOONAN

The Bones of Time

(New York: Tor, 1996)

Story type: Science Fiction (Genetic Manipulation; Mystical)
Major character(s): Lynn Oshima, Fugitive; Akamu, Clone, Fugitive; Cen Kalakaua, Genius, Scientist (mathematician)
Time period(s): 2010s (2014-2017); 2030s (2034)
Locale(s): Honolulu, Hawaii; Hong Kong

Summary: Rejecting Interspace, her family's corrupt corporation, Lynn Oshima flees from Hawaii to Hong Kong while sheltering the boy, Akamu, an illegal clone of the long dead Hawaiian King Kamehameha. In a parallel but earlier storyline, Cen Kalakaua, a streetwise youngster, learns he has a unique talent for visualizing mathematical concepts. His research eventually affects Lynn and Akamu's fates, as well as the ongoing power struggle between the Hawaiian Homeland Movement and Interspace.

Other books you might like:
Greg Egan, *Quarantine*, 1995
Nicola Griffith, *Slow River*, 1995
Jamil Nasir, *The Higher Space*, 1996
Frederik Pohl, *The Singers of Time*, 1991
   Jack Williamson, co-author
Michaela Roessner, *Vanishing Point*, 1993

1825

KATHLEEN ANN GOONAN

Queen City Jazz
(New York: Tor, 1994)

Story type: Science Fiction (Alternate Intelligence; Genetic Manipulation)
Major character(s): Verity, Adoptee, Clone; Abraham Durancy, Scientist, Architect
Time period(s): 21st century
Locale(s): Cincinnati, Ohio

Summary: Raised among New Shakers, Verity travels to the Enhanced City of Cincinnati where she hopes that nanotechnology can revive her friend, Blaze, and her dog, Cairo. On the outskirts of the city she meets Sphere who, unknown to her, places Blaze and Cairo in a healing machine while she goes into the city where Verity finds herself the key to events. First novel.

Other books you might like:
Kevin J. Anderson, *Assemblers of Infinity*, 1993
   Doug Beason, co-author
Greg Bear, *Blood Music*, 1985
Ben Bova, *Death Dream*, 1994
Nancy Kress, *Brain Rose*, 1990
Walter Jon Williams, *Voice of the Whirlwind*, 1987

1826

ED GORMAN

Cages
(San Jose, CA: Deadline Press, 1996)

Story type: Horror (Collection)
Summary: This collection brings together twenty-one tales of horror and dark suspense by a writer distinguished in these and other genres. Included are the title story, a hard-boiled tale about the victims of toxic waste; ''Moonchasers,'' in which two boys get their first taste of the adult world while hiding a criminal from the law; ''The Face,'' a Civil War ghost story; and ''The End of It All,'' in which characters discover only belatedly that their plastic surgery enhancement does nothing to improve their wretched personalities. In addition, the book contains the western adventure ''Pards'' and western gothic ''Deathman,'' the science fiction tales ''Survival'' and ''The Brasher Girl,'' and the gentle fantasy ''Yesterday's Dreams.'' F. Paul Wilson supplies a foreword and Marcia Muller an afterword.

Other books you might like:
Dean R. Koontz, *Strange Highways*, 1995
Richard Matheson, *Collected Stories*, 1989

Norman Partridge, *Bad Intentions*, 1996
Norman Partridge, *Mr. Fox and Other Feral Tales*, 1993
F. Paul Wilson, *Soft and Others*, 1989

1827

ED GORMAN, Editor
MARTIN H. GREENBERG, Co-Editor

Night Screams
(New York: DAW, 1996)

Story type: Horror (Anthology)
Summary: Twenty-two stories, 16 of them originals, fill this non-theme anthology of horror and dark suspense fiction. The originals include F. Paul Wilson's ''The Wringer,'' a novella featuring the vigilante Repairman Jack who helps an employer get even with a disgruntled ex-employee who has kidnapped the man's wife and child; Christopher Fahy's ''Trolls,'' about a grotesque school for the mentally challenged and the peculiar relationship of the students to the teachers; and Al Sarrantonio's ''White Lightning,'' in which a young man goes on a murder rampage supposedly under the influence of bootleg liquor. Reprints include Ray Bradbury's ''Corpse Carnival,'' in which a sideshow performer determines to find the murderer of his Siamese twin, and Clive Barker's ''The Book of Blood,'' about a young man who gets his grisly comeuppance from the dead whom he purports to contact psychically for paying customers.

Other books you might like:
Richard T. Chizmar, *Cold Blood*, 1991
   editor
Joe R. Lansdale, *Dark at Heart*, 1992
   Karen Lansdale, co-editor
John Maclay, *Voices From the Night*, 1994
   editor
Stanley Wiater, *After the Darkness*, 1993
   editor

1828

ED GORMAN

Out There in the Darkness
(Burton, Michigan: Subterranean Press, 1995)

Story type: Horror (Mystery)
Major character(s): Aaron Bellini, Businessman; Neil Solomon, Businessman; Mike O'Brien, Businessman
Time period(s): 1990s (1995)
Locale(s): Wisconsin

Summary: On what should have been a quiet poker night, four businessmen in suburban Wisconsin apprehend and accidentally kill a burglar. Fearing legal repercussions, they dispose of the body, and from that point on find themselves fighting a battle to save their lives when the burglar's escaped accomplice begins killing them off one by one. This short story chapbook was published in a signed limited edition of 500 copies.

Other books you might like:
James Dickey, *Deliverance*, 1973

Stephen Gallagher, *Down River*, 1989
Joe R. Lansdale, *Dark at Heart*, 1992
  Karen Lansdale, co-editor
Joe R. Lansdale, *The Steel Valentine*, 1991

1829

ED GORMAN, Editor
MARTIN H. GREENBERG, Co-Editor

Predators

(New York: Roc, 1993)

Story type: Horror (Anthology)

Summary: Following up on the theme of their anthology *Stalkers* (1989), which collected stories based on the theme of predator and prey, the editors have assembled 19 original and one reprint tale of both supernatural and non-supernatural horror. John Shirley's ''Rubber Smile'' concerns the adverse effects of graphic horror films upon certain audience members, T.L. Parkinson's ''Mistaken Identity'' is about a woman's psychological dissolution, Edward Wellen's ''Mind Slash Matter'' tells of a man suffering from Alzheimer's disease who develops an unhealthy relationship with an artificial intelligence module operating on his computer, Daniel Ransom and Rex Miller's ''Valentine'' chronicles the life of a detective tracking a female assassin who kills only mobsters, and Dean R. Koontz's ''Hardshell'' portrays alien creatures in human disguise stalking one another.

Other books you might like:
Robert Bloch, *Monsters in Our Midst*, 1993
  editor
Robert Bloch, *Psycho-Paths*, 1991
  editor
Richard T. Chizmar, *Cold Blood*, 1991
  editor
George Hatch, *Guignoir and Other Furies*, 1991
  editor

1830

ED GORMAN

Prisoners and Other Stories

(Baltimore, Maryland: CD Publications, 1992)

Story type: Horror (Collection)

Summary: The author's first collection brings together 22 stories of horror and dark suspense, several published here for the first time. Included are the hardboiled ghost tale, ''Drifter,'' and the serial killer stories, ''The Man in the Long Black Sedan'' and ''Stalker.'' With an afterword by Dean R. Koontz.

Other books you might like:
Ray Bradbury, *A Memory of Murder*, 1984
Joe R. Lansdale, *By Bizarre Hands*, 1989
Robert R. McCammon, *Blue World*, 1989
William F. Nolan, *Things Beyond Midnight*, 1984

1831

ED GORMAN, Editor
MARTIN H. GREENBERG, Co-Editor

Stalkers

(New York: Roc, 1990)

Story type: Horror (Anthology)

Summary: Eighteen original stories that jump back and forth freely between the suspense and supernatural story in their elaboration of the theme of the pursuer and his quarry. Where John Maclay's ''Firing'' is a simple ghost tale of a man haunted by the person he wronged, Dean Koontz's ''Trapped'' relates the story of a mother and child trapped in their snowbound cabin by vicious genetically engineered rats. John Coyne's ''Flight'' and Al Sarrantonio's ''Children of Cain'' employ scenarios in which pursuit may be all in the narrator's mind, while Robert R. McCammon's straightforward monster tale, ''Lizardman,'' leaves no doubt as to who is being pursued and why.

Other books you might like:
Robert Bloch, *Psycho-Paths*, 1991
Joan Kahn, *The Edge of the Chair*, 1967
Joan Kahn, *Hanging by a Thread*, 1969
Alfred Hitchcock, *Alfred Hitchcock Presents: Stories for Late at Night*, 1961

1832

JUDITH GOROG

On Meeting Witches at Wells

(New York: Philomel Books, 1991)

Story type: Fantasy (Contemporary Realism; Young Adult)
Major character(s): Ms. Oakes, Administrator (elementary school principal), Witch; Jeff, Student—Middle School (eighth grade)
Time period(s): Indeterminate
Locale(s): Poor Farm Road, Mythical Place (elementary school)

Summary: The Poor Farm Road Elementary School building suddenly developed a large crack in an exterior wall. The traditional pillowmaking and storytelling gathering was special that year, not only because it became the last, but also due to the unexpected ghostly visitors' interesting contributions.

Other books you might like:
Margaret J. Anderson, *The Ghost Inside the Monitor*, 1990
Pam Conrad, *Stonewords: A Ghost Story*, 1990
Alan Garner, *The Weirdstone of Brisingamen*, 1960
Patricia A. McKillip, *The House on Parchment Street*, 1973
Philippa Pearce, *Tom's Midnight Garden*, 1959

1833

GARY GOSHGARIAN

Rough Beast

(New York: Donald I. Fine, 1995)

Story type: Horror (Science Fiction)

Major character(s): Calvin Hazzard, Professor (of English); Matt Hazzard, Child (Calvin's 12-year-old son); Jerry Mars, Criminal (assassin)
Time period(s): 1990s (1995)
Locale(s): Carleton, Massachusetts

Summary: Government agents try to obliterate all traces of Black Flag, a biological weapons project conceived at the end of the Vietnam War that could prove an embarrassment to the president. Meanwhile, Calvin and Terry Hazzard are unaware that their quiet suburban home sits upon the toxic products of Black Flag, and that these are initiating a frightening physical transformation in their son, Matt.

Other books you might like:
Stephen King, *Firestarter*, 1980
Dean R. Koontz, *Watchers*, 1987
John Saul, *Creature*, 1988
John Saul, *The Homing*, 1994

1834
PHYLLIS GOTLIEB

Heart of Red Iron
(New York: St. Martin's, 1989)

Story type: Science Fiction (Science Fiction)
Major character(s): Sven Dahlgren, Mutant; Mod Dahlgren, Android
Time period(s): Indeterminate Future
Locale(s): Dahlgren's World, Planet—Imaginary

Summary: In this sequel to *O Master Caliban*, the four-armed mutant Sven Dahlgren returns to the dangerous planet of his childhood in order to help settle four alien races, victims of disasters on their own worlds. With him are his family and an android duplicate of his scientist father. Humans, mutants, androids, intelligent robots, and a variety of aliens, including a sentient crystal species, must learn to work together if they are going to survive the inimical conditions on Dahlgren's World.

Other books you might like:
Octavia E. Butler, *Adulthood Rites*, 1988
Octavia E. Butler, *Dawn*, 1987
Octavia E. Butler, *Imago*, 1989
Sheri S. Tepper, *After Long Silence*, 1987
Sheri S. Tepper, *Grass*, 1989

1835
SHERRY GOTTLIEB

Love Bite
(New York: Warner, 1994)

Story type: Horror (Vampire Story)
Major character(s): Jace Levy, Detective—Homicide; Liz Robinson, Detective—Homicide; Risha "Rusty" Cadigan, Photographer, Vampire
Time period(s): 1990s (1994)
Locale(s): Los Angeles, California

Summary: Jace Levy battles the trauma his experiences as a homicide detective have inflicted on him while tackling his

latest case: a serial killer who contacts victims through personal ads in the local papers and drains them of their blood. This novel, the author's first, was also published in a deluxe limited edition by Canadian publisher Transylvania Press.

Other books you might like:
Michael Cecilione, *Domination*, 1993
Don Davis, *Bring on the Night*, 1993
　　Jay Davis, co-author
Stephen Gallagher, *Valley of Lights*, 1987
Robert Morgan, *Some Things Never Die*, 1993
William Relling Jr., *New Moon*, 1987
Karen E. Taylor, *Bitter Blood*, 1994
Karen E. Taylor, *Blood Secrets*, 1994
Les Whitten, *Progeny of the Adder*, 1965

1836
STEVEN GOULD

Jumper
(New York: Tor, 1992)

Story type: Science Fiction (Psychic Powers; Young Adult)
Major character(s): David "Davy" Rice, Teenager, Runaway (by teleportation); Millicent "Millie", Girlfriend
Time period(s): 1990s
Locale(s): Minnesota; New York, New York

Summary: About to suffer a beating at the hands of his alcoholic father, David suddenly discovers his unique ability to teleport. David runs away to New York where he explores his new ability, robbing a bank in the process, but avoiding the revenge he wishes upon his father. David finds Millicent and becomes close to her as he begins to mature on his rite of passage. Author's first novel.

Other books you might like:
Alfred Bester, *The Stars My Destination*, 1956
Lester del Rey, *Pstalemate*, 1971
Phyllis Eisenstein, *Born to Exile*, 1978
Phyllis Eisenstein, *In the Red Lord's Reach*, 1989
Robert A. Heinlein, *Tunnel in the Sky*, 1955
Robert Silverberg, *Dying Inside*, 1972
Theodore Sturgeon, *More than Human*, 1953
A.E. van Vogt, *Slan*, 1946

1837
STEVEN GOULD

Wildside
(New York: Tor, 1996)

Story type: Science Fiction (Young Adult; Alternate Universe)
Major character(s): Charlie Newell, Teenager, Pilot; Marie Nguyen, Teenager, Pilot; Clara Prentice, Teenager, Pilot
Time period(s): 1990s
Locale(s): Texas; Wild Side, Alternate Earth

Summary: Charlie Newell discovers a gateway to the "wildside," an unspoiled parallel Earth where many animals now extinct on Charlie's world still roam. Together with his closest friends, Charlie struggles to explore and exploit the wildside while simultaneously protecting it from the federal government.

Other books you might like:
Michael Crichton, *Jurassic Park*, 1990
Julia Ecklar, *Regenesis*, 1995
Louis L'Amour, *Haunted Mesa*, 1987
Christopher Pike, *The Tachyon Web*, 1986
Sage Walker, *Whiteout*, 1996

1838

DANIEL H. GOWER

Harrowgate

(New York: Dell/Abyss, 1993)

Story type: Horror (Occult)
Major character(s): Julian Stormer, Artist; Ashley Herrin, Reanimated Dead; Vernon Doyle, Businessman (security systems consultant)
Time period(s): 1990s (1993)
Locale(s): Groveland, Midwest

Summary: Avant garde artist Julian Stormer finds his artwork becoming satisfactorily more bizarre after the mysterious Ashley Herrin becomes his muse. Could it have to do with the fact that Ashley, a dead former prostitute and drug pusher, has been reanimated for the express task of guarding Harrowgate, a gateway to the afterlife through which the Coprolites, or ossified souls of the evil, are trying to break through?

Other books you might like:
Jonathan Aycliffe, *Naomi's Room*, 1991
Giles Blunt, *Cold Eye*, 1989
T. Chris Martindale, *The Voice in the Basement*, 1992
T.M. Wright, *Little Boy Lost*, 1992

1839

DANIEL H. GOWER

The Orpheus Process

(New York: Dell/Abyss, 1992)

Story type: Horror (Reanimated Dead; Science Fiction)
Major character(s): Orville Helmond, Scientist; Alexandra "Ally" Helmond, Teenager (Orville's daughter); Stuart Coleridge, Police Officer (sheriff)
Time period(s): 1990s
Locale(s): Berkshire, Ohio

Summary: Orville Helmond's successful experiments in reviving dead animals offer his daughter Eunice a second chance for life after she is killed by a mass murderer. But Eunice returns from the dead with an antipathy for human beings and, worse, a willingness to help resurrect an army of others like herself. This is the author's first novel.

Other books you might like:
Stephen King, *Pet Sematary*, 1983
Dean R. Koontz, *Hideaway*, 1992
Mary Shelley, *Frankenstein*, 1818

1840

STEFAN GRABINSKI

The Dark Domain

(New York: Hippocrene, 1994)

Story type: Horror (Collection)

Summary: The 11 stories translated here represent the first collection in English of a Polish writer of weird fiction whose work appeared before World War II and which blends the tropes of Gothic horror with anti-materialist philosophy. "Fumes," "The Area," "Szamota's Mistress," "Strabismus," and "Saturnin Sektor" all use the author's favorite theme of the doppelganger, while "The Motion Demon," "The Wandering Train," and "In the Compartment" deploy magically-endowed trains as agents of dread and transcendance. The translator, Miroslaw Lipinski, has supplied an introduction that gives a historical overview of the author and his writing.

Other books you might like:
Thomas Ligotti, *Songs of a Dead Dreamer*, 1990
Bruno Schulz, *Sanatorium under the Sign of the Hourglass*, 1937
Bruno Schulz, *The Street of Crocodiles*, 1934
Roland Topor, *The Tenant*, 1966

1841

CAMARIN GRAE

Stranded

(Tallahassee: Naiad Press, 1991)

Story type: Science Fiction (Gay/Lesbian Fiction; Invasion of Earth)
Major character(s): Amy, Artist, Musician; Jenna, Alien, Disembodied Personality; Zephkar, Alien, Disembodied Personality
Time period(s): 1990s
Locale(s): San Francisco, California; Chicago, Illinois

Summary: Disembodied minds from Allo, a planet of hermaphrodites, have begun invading humans. Jenna, residing in Amy's mind, and her friends, Billy and Cass, from the Zephkar Elimination Team, act to defeat Zephkar who was formally outcast from Allo society for her violent acts. Zephkar has escaped from Allo and has come to Earth where she takes over James Lane, using him to form a new fundamentalist religion and political party and hoping to run America as a theocracy.

Other books you might like:
Storm Constantine, *Bewitchments of Love and Hate*, 1990
Storm Constantine, *The Enchantments of Flesh and Spirit*, 1989
Camilla Decarnin, *Worlds Apart*, 1986
    Eric Garber and Lyn Paleo, co-editors
Suzette Haden Elgin, *Native Tongue*, 1984
Jeffrey M. Elliot, *Kindred Spirits*, 1984
    editor
Nancy Tyler Glenn, *Clicking Stones*, 1989
Ursula K. Le Guin, *The Left Hand of Darkness*, 1969

Lynda Lyons, *Priorities*, 1990
Joan Slonczewski, *A Door into Ocean*, 1986
John Varley, *The Persistence of Vision*, 1978
John Varley, *Titan*, 1979

1842

L.A. GRAF (Pseudonym of Julia Ecklar and Karen Rose)

Time's Enemy

(New York: Pocket, 1996)

Story type: Science Fiction (Space Opera; Time Travel)
Series: Star Trek: Deep Space Nine
Major character(s): Jadzia Dax, Military Personnel (lieutenant), Alien (Trill); Benjamin Sisko, Spaceship Captain, Military Personnel; Julian Bashir, Doctor, Military Personnel
Time period(s): 24th century
Locale(s): *U.S.S. Defiant*, Spaceship; Deep Space Nine, Space Station; United Federation of Planets, Interstellar Empire/Federation

Summary: A 5000-year-old spaceship found frozen in cometary debris, *Defiant*, contains the remains of Captain Sisko, Dr. Bashir, and the living symbiont, Dax. Piecing together the evidence leads Starfleet to conclude that the *Defiant* has taken part in a great battle sometime in the near future, probably against the terrible enemy that drove the Furies from the Alpha Quadrant. Now Sisko and his crew try to use this knowledge to save the quadrant from the Conquerors who drove the Furies from their homes. Third of the four-part Invasion! Series which spans all four of the "Star Trek" television series and concludes in *The Final Fury*.

Other books you might like:
Dafydd ab Hugh, *The Final Fury*, 1996
    Invasion! Series, part 4
Orson Scott Card, *Speaker for the Dead*, 1988
Diane Carey, *First Strike*, 1996
    Invasion! Series, part 1
Barbara Hambly, *Ishmael*, 1985
Dean Wesley Smith, *The Escape*, 1995
    Kristine Kathryn Rusch, co-author
Dean Wesley Smith, *The Soldiers of Fear*, 1996
    Invasion! Series, part 2; Kristine Kathryn Rusch, co-author
James Tiptree Jr., *Up the Walls of the World*, 1978
    pseudonym of Alice Sheldon
Della Van Hise, *Killing Time*, 1985

1843

L.A. GRAF (Pseudonym of Julia Ecklar and Karen Rose)

Traitor Winds

(New York: Pocket, 1994)

Story type: Science Fiction (Mystery; Adventure)
Series: Star Trek
Major character(s): Pavel Chekov, Military Personnel (Starfleet ensign), Space Explorer; Hikaru Sulu, Military Personnel (Starfleet lieutenant); James T. Kirk, Military Personnel (Starfleet admiral), Spaceship Captain

Time period(s): 23rd century
Locale(s): *U.S.S. Enterprise*, Spaceship; Earth; United Federation of Planets, Interstellar Empire/Federation

Summary: After the completion of their five-year mission, the *Enterprise* crew have gone on to new assignments. When Chekov witnesses a murder and Sulu's top secret aircraft disappears, they join forces again to find out the truth behind the framing of their shipmates for murder and treason. Their search uncovers a plot designed to discredit Admiral Kirk and start an interstellar war.

Other books you might like:
Margaret Wander Bonanno, *Strangers From the Sky*, 1987
C.J. Cherryh, *Hellburner*, 1992
Jane S. Fancher, *Harmonies of the 'Net*, 1992
Judith Reeves-Stevens, *Prime Directive*, 1990
    Garfield Reeves-Stevens, co-author

1844

JOHN GRAFTON, Editor

Great Ghost Stories

(New York: Dover, 1992)

Story type: Horror (Anthology; Ghost Story)

Summary: This volume collects ten short classic ghost stories. Included are Ambrose Bierce's tale of vengeance from beyond the grave, "The Moonlit Road"; Bram Stoker's haunted house story, "The Judge's House"; Charles Dicken's tale of spectral justice, "To Be Taken with a Grain of Salt" (a.k.a. "The Trial for Murder"); and W. W. Jacobs' masterpiece of a wish-fulfilling talisman that becomes a horrible curse, "The Monkey's Paw." There are also stories by J. Sheridan Le Fanu, E. G. Swain, M. R. James, Amelia B. Edward, Jerome K. Jerome and E. F. Benson.

Other books you might like:
E.F. Bleiler, *A Treasury of Victorian Ghost Stories*, 1981
    editor
Michael Cox, *The Oxford Book of English Ghost Stories*, 1991
    R. Gilbert, co-editor
Michael Cox, *Victorian Ghost Stories: An Oxford Anthology*, 1991
    editor
Jack Sullivan, *Lost Souls*, 1983
    editor

1845

DANIEL GRAHAM JR.

The Gatekeepers

(New York: Baen, 1995)

Story type: Science Fiction (Techno-Thriller; Political)
Major character(s): Rolf Bernard, Businessman; Max Yeager, Engineer; Cynthia Bernard, Wealthy, Businesswoman
Time period(s): 2000s
Locale(s): Tucson, Arizona; Washington, District of Columbia; Australia

Summary: When the government monopoly on space development threatens to prevent the adoption of a new aerospace vehicle and ruin his company, Rolf Bernard plans to use his fleet of space vehicles and Starwars Defense Initiative hardware to overcome U.S. defenses and impress his vision onto the country's future. First novel.

Other books you might like:
James P. Hogan, *Endgame Enigma*, 1987
David Kagan, *Sunstroke*, 1993
Michael P. Kube-McDowell, *Emprise*, 1985
Vonda N. McIntyre, *Starfarers*, 1989
Larry Niven, *Fallen Angels*, 1991
   Jerry Pournelle, Michael Flynn, co-authors
Allen Steele, *Orbital Decay*, 1989

1846

CHARLES L. GRANT

The Black Carousel

(New York: Tor, 1995)

Story type: Horror (Small Town Horror)
Series: Oxrun Station
Major character(s): Casey Bethune, Postal Worker (mail carrier); Fran Lumbaird, Child; Drake Saxton, Journalist
Time period(s): 1990s (1995)
Locale(s): Oxrun Station, Connecticut

Summary: This novel is actually a collection of four loosely linked novellas. "Pilgrim's Travelers," a travelling carnival that comes to the small town of Oxrun Station, mirrors in its sideshows and attractions the hopes and fear of several unlucky townspeople, including an older man desperate for love, a young girl recently moved to town and starved for friendship, a local boy in the grip of his domineering mother, and an elderly man haunted by the ghosts of his youth.

Other books you might like:
Ray Bradbury, *Something Wicked This Way Comes*, 1962
Charles G. Finney, *The Circus of Dr. Lao*, 1935
Thomas F. Monteleone, *The Magnificent Gallery*, 1987
Tom Reamy, *Blind Voices*, 1978
Theodore Sturgeon, *The Dreaming Jewels*, 1950

1847

CHARLES L. GRANT

Dialing the Wind

(New York: Tor, 1989)

Story type: Horror (Small Town Horror)
Series: Oxrun Station
Major character(s): Callum Davidson, Aged Person
Time period(s): Indeterminate
Locale(s): Oxrun Station, Connecticut

Summary: Two men discover photographs and writings hidden in an album in an old friend's house that offer clues to the stories of four individuals trapped and destroyed by their own desires—a widow drawn to a mysterious radio message, a man driven to madness by a woman who never existed, a high school teacher tormented by his own insignificance, and a

long suffering, would-be lover who gets his heart's desire too late.

Other books you might like:
John Farris, *Scare Tactics*, 1988
Stephen King, *Different Seasons*, 1982

1848

CHARLES L. GRANT, Editor

Final Shadows

(New York: Doubleday, 1991)

Story type: Horror (Anthology)

Summary: This final installment in Grant's long-running series of anthologies of original horror fiction concerned with people and their problems collects 36 stories by British and American authors. Stories range from elliptical fantasies like Lori Negridge Allen's "Under the Boardwalk" and Craig Shaw Gardner's "Going Away," to the psychological horror of Melanie Tem's "Fry Day" and Dennis Etchison's "When They Gave Us Memory," to tales of murder and madness such as Stephen Gallagher's "Magpie" and Bill Pronzini's "Out Behind the Shed," to outright monster stories like Peter Tremayne's "Fear A' Ghorta" and Tanith Lee's "The Mermaid."

Other books you might like:
Thomas F. Monteleone, *The Borderlands Series*, 1990-1991
Chris Morgan, *Dark Fantasies*, 1989

1849

CHARLES L. GRANT, Editor

Gallery of Horror

(New York: Roc, 1996)

Story type: Horror (Anthology)

Summary: First published in 1983 as *The Dodd Mead Gallery of Horror*, this anthology features 20 stories by some of the best living writers of modern horror, all of which reflect its editor's preference for subtle, atmospheric horror. Stephen King's "Nona" features a loser in love whose psychopathic murder spree may or may not be due to the woman whom he claims has supernatural control over him. Dennis Etchison's "The Chair" concerns a man who attends the high school reunion from hell, Alan Ryan's "Death to the Easter Bunny" the dark truth behind a childhood legend, and David Morrell's "The Typewriter" a man who becomes a bestselling novelist due to a supernaturally-endowed typewriter. Ted Klein's "Petey" wreaks a modern variation on the Frankenstein theme, and Bernard Taylor's "Out of Sorts" a similar variation on the werewolf theme. Four of the stories are vampire tales: Ramsey Campbell's "The Sunshine Club," Craig Shaw Gardner's "Aim for the Heart," Jack Dann and Gardner Dozois's "Down Among the Dead Men," and Tanith Lee's "Nunc Dimittis."

Other books you might like:
Ramsey Campbell, *New Terrors*, 1982
   editor

Ramsey Campbell, *Superhorror*, 1976
editor
Kirby McCauley, *Dark Forces*, 1980
Stuart David Schiff, *The Best of Whispers*, 1994
editor

1850

CHARLES L. GRANT

Goblins

(New York: HarperPrism, 1994)

Story type: Science Fiction (Mystery; Horror)
Series: X-Files
Major character(s): Fox Mulder, FBI Agent; Dana Scully, FBI Agent, Doctor
Time period(s): 1990s
Locale(s): Washington, District of Columbia; New Jersey

Summary: When reports of an invisible murderer trigger an X-Files investigation, a witness considered unreliable by authorities blames the grisly murders on goblins. Television tie-in.

Other books you might like:
Elizabeth Forrest, *Phoenix Fire*, 1992
Alan Dean Foster, *Cyber Way*, 1990
Laurell K. Hamilton, *Guilty Pleasures*, 1993
Nick Pollotta, *Bureau 13*, 1991
Nick Pollotta, *Doomsday Exam*, 1992

1851

CHARLES L. GRANT

In a Dark Dream

(New York: Tor, 1989)

Story type: Horror (Ghost Story)
Major character(s): Glenn Erskine, Police Officer (Sheriff); Cheryl Erskine, Child (Erskine's youngest daughter, a)
Time period(s): 1980s
Locale(s): Hunter, New Jersey

Summary: As if Glenn Erskine didn't have enough "real" problems to handle—an understaffed sheriff's department, a returning mass murderer, a career clash with his wife, and troubled children, especially his nightmare-prone daughter Cheryl, he must also deal with apparitions of dead people, strangers who appear and disappear mysteriously, violent encounters that subsequently "vanish," and, worst of all, a pervasive sense of impending doom.

Other books you might like:
Alan Ryan, *The Kill*, 1982
Chet Williamson, *Ash Wednesday*, 1987

1852

CHARLES L. GRANT, Editor

In the Fog

(New York: Tor, 1993)

Story type: Horror (Anthology)
Series: Chronicles of Greystone Bay

Locale(s): Greystone Bay, New England

Summary: This fourth and purportedly final collection of novellas chronicling life in the atmospheric New England port city Greystone Bay includes Elizabeth Engstrom's "The Fog Knew Her Name," about a woman whose identity crisis takes on objective manifestations; Craig Shaw Gardner's "Warm," in which a man sees the apparition of his first wife in patterns in the snow; Kathryn Ptacek's "The Home," about what happens at a remote hospital for invalids cut off from the rest of Greystone Bay during a power outage; Chelsea Quinn Yarbro's "Whiteface," in which a Mafia-run carnival meets its comeuppance when forced to pitch its tents on haunted ground; Nancy Holder's "O Love They Kiss," which unfolds a grim tale from the Bay's colonial history; Steve Rasnic Tem's mesmerizing "Ice House Pond," in which a man's personal breakdown is mirrored in the landscape around him; and editor Grant's ghostly "Josie, in the Fog."

Other books you might like:
Ramsey Campbell, *Deathport*, 1993
F. Paul Wilson, *Freak Show*, 1992

1853

CHARLES L. GRANT

Jackals

(New York: Tor, 1994)

Story type: Horror (Serial Killer)
Major character(s): Jim Scott, Wealthy; Rachel Corder, Drifter; Maurice Lion, Religious (preacher)
Time period(s): 1990s (1994)
Locale(s): Potar Ridge, Tennessee

Summary: When Jim Scott takes in the victim of a deliberate hit-and-run accident, it reignites a longstanding feud between Jim, his vigilante friends and the Jackals, a cabal of nearly inhuman predators who prey upon travellers and victims of highway mishaps. Unbeknownst to Jim, the Jackals have infiltrated his ranks in the hope of removing the final obstacle to their success.

Other books you might like:
Jay R. Bonansinga, *The Black Mariah*, 1994
Eric Flanders, *Night Blood*, 1993
Ray Garton, *Lot Lizards*, 1990
Billie Sue Mosiman, *Night Cruise*, 1992
John Shirley, *Wetbones*, 1992

1854

CHARLES L. GRANT

Raven

(New York: Tor, 1993)

Story type: Horror (Mystery)
Major character(s): Neil Maclaren, Restaurateur; Julia Sanders, Waiter/Waitress; Willie Ennin, Cook
Time period(s): 1990s (1993)
Locale(s): New Jersey

Summary: On a snowy winter night, Neil Maclaren's restaurant is besieged by a mysterious shotgun-toting figure. Driven to desperation, the imprisoned patrons and employees fight as much among themselves as against the stranger holding them captive.

Other books you might like:
Douglas Borton, *Kane*, 1989
Shirley Jackson, *The Sundial*, 1958
Stephen King, *The Shining*, 1977
Robert R. McCammon, *Stinger*, 1988

`1855`

CHARLES L. GRANT, Editor

The SeaHarp Hotel
(New York: Tor, 1990)

Story type: Horror (Anthology)
Series: Chronicles of Greystone Bay

Summary: In this third and final chronicle of the shared-world of Greystone Bay, 15 stories tell of or begin at the run-down SeaHarp Hotel. In "Ex-Library," Chet Williamson writes of the sinister influence at work in the downstairs reading room, while in "Beauty," Robert R. McCammon offers the narrative of someone whose circumstances render her a permanent non-paying guest. Thomas Monteleone's "No Pain, No Gain" and Les Daniel's "Room Service" are both eerie stories of unfortunate bellboys who learn more than they wish to know about the hotel's visitors.

Other books you might like:
Robert R. McCammon, *Under the Fang*, 1991
Robert Weinberg, *Lovecraft's Legacy*, 1990
  Martin H. Greenberg, co-author

`1856`

CHARLES L. GRANT

Something Stirs
(New York: Tor, 1991)

Story type: Horror (Small Town Horror)
Major character(s): Joey Costello, Teenager; Scott Byrns, Teenager; Fern Bellard, Teenager
Time period(s): 1990s
Locale(s): Foxriver, New Jersey

Summary: Something is killing the citizens of Foxriver, in particular the members of The Pack, a group of teenage outsiders who find solidarity by cultivating the group image of rebel outcasts fostered by B-movies of the 1950s. Unwittingly, their nostalgia has tapped into the fears behind small-town American life of that period, and given life to the same embodiments of those fears that dominated the film, fiction and popular culture of the Eisenhower years.

Other books you might like:
Ray Bradbury, *Something Wicked This Way Comes*, 1962
William W. Johnstone, *Darkly the Thunder*, 1990
Stephen King, *Christine*, 1983
Stephen King, *It*, 1986

`1857`

CHARLES L. GRANT

Stunts
(New York: Tor, 1990)

Story type: Horror (Curse)
Major character(s): Evan Kendal, Teacher (high school); Addie Burwin, Doctor; Brian Oakland, Teenager, Student—High School (at Port Richmond High School)
Time period(s): 1990s (1990)
Locale(s): London, England; Port Richmond, New Jersey

Summary: Pursued by a friend who has fallen under "the curse of the wolf," visiting teacher Evan Kendal flees England for America. Back home in New Jersey, he finds that his Uncle John has fallen under the same curse and is planning evil deeds that will coincide with the coming Halloween.

Other books you might like:
Stanwood Brooks, *The Seventh Child*, 1980
Jack Martin, *Halloween III: Season of the Witch*, 1985

`1858`

CHARLES L. GRANT

Tales From the Nightside
(New York: Tor, 1991)

Story type: Horror (Collection)

Summary: Fifteen stories, most set in the recurring locales of Oxrun Station and Hawthorne Street, that typify the atmospheric, ambiguous, subtle horror referred to as dark fantasy. The author is particularly interested in the macabre relationships that develop between children and adults (often parents) in "If Damon Calls," "When All the Children Call My Name," and "White Wolf Calling," and in the dark secrets of suburban neighborhoods disclosed in "Digging" and "Old Friends." Grant also expertly retailors classic fantasy themes to fit the simple lives of his small-town characters: Greek mythology in "Coin of the Realm," a reanimated corpse in "Three of Tens" and ghosts in "Come Dance with Me on My Pony's Grave."

Other books you might like:
Ray Bradbury, *The October Country*, 1955
Joseph Payne Brennan, *Stories of Darkness and Dread*, 1973
Dennis Etchison, *The Dark Country*, 1982
Robert R. McCammon, *Blue World*, 1989
Alan Ryan, *The Bones Wizard*, 1988

`1859`

CHARLES L. GRANT

Whirlwind
(New York: HarperPrism, 1995)

Story type: Fantasy (Mystery; Contemporary)
Series: X-Files
Major character(s): Fox Mulder, FBI Agent; Dana Scully, FBI Agent, Doctor
Time period(s): 1990s

Locale(s): New Mexico; Washington, District of Columbia

Summary: Called to investigate unusual deaths in the Southwest, Scully and Mulder discover a malevolent whirlwind, the Blood Wind, that seems under the direction of a human agent.

Other books you might like:
Kevin J. Anderson, *Ground Zero*, 1995
Elizabeth Forrest, *Phoenix Fire*, 1992
Alan Dean Foster, *Cyber Way*, 1990
Laurell K. Hamilton, *Guilty Pleasures*, 1993
Mercedes Lackey, *Burning Water*, 1989
Nick Pollotta, *Bureau 13*, 1991
Nick Pollotta, *Doomsday Exam*, 1992

1860

MARK GRANT (Pseudonym of David Bischoff)

Christmas Slaughter
(New York: Avon, 1991)

Story type: Science Fiction (Adventure; Post-Holocaust)
Series: Mutants Amok
Major character(s): Maximillian Turkel, Revolutionary; Ooslaxt, Mutant, Leader; SU912, Android
Time period(s): 21st century
Locale(s): Devil's Mountain, North America; New San Francisco, North America

Summary: The small band of rebels sneaks into New San Francisco to put an end to the Mutant's latest scheme to end Mutant dependence on continual supply of Human gene-material. They are aided by a group of crazed African-American berserkers and a renegade assassination "cyborg."

Other books you might like:
David Drake, *Hammer's Slammers*, 1979
Robert A. Heinlein, *Sixth Column*, 1949
Jack Yeovil, *Demon Download*, 1990
Ken Rolston, *Extreme Paranoia: Nobody Knows the Trouble I've Shot*, 1991
Norman Spinrad, *The Iron Dream*, 1972
Roger Zelazny, *Damnation Alley*, 1969

1861

MARK GRANT (Pseudonym of David Bischoff)

Mutant Hell
(New York: Avon, 1991)

Story type: Science Fiction (Adventure; Post-Holocaust)
Series: Mutants Amok
Major character(s): Maximillian Turkel, Revolutionary, Warrior; Jack Bender, Revolutionary; BrainGeneral Torx, Genetically Altered Being, Military Personnel
Time period(s): 21st century (after the Last World War)
Locale(s): Iowa; Cheyenne Mt., Colorado

Summary: The recently captured Maximillian Turkel is flown to Cheyenne Mt. for delivery to the mutants' Emperor, Ignatius Charlemagne the Seventh, Point Five. While Max's friends journey to Colorado in hopes of rescuing him, Max tries to escape with the help of a mutant BrainGeneral in charge of the mutants' Internal Revenue Service.

Other books you might like:
Jerry Ahern, *To End All War*, 1990
James Axler, *Death Lands: Time Nomads*, 1990
Bob Ham, *Rolling Vengeance*, 1990
Jack Maloney, *Freedom Express*, 1990
Michael McGann, *The Ghost Warriors*, 1990
David Robbins, *Yellowstone Run*, 1990
James Rouch, *Body Count*, 1990

1862

MARK GRANT (Pseudonym of David Bischoff)

Mutants Amok
(New York: Avon, 1991)

Story type: Science Fiction (Adventure; Post-Holocaust)
Series: Mutants Amok
Major character(s): Maximillian Turkel, Revolutionary, Fugitive; Jack Bender, Farmer, Revolutionary; BrainGeneral Torx, Genetically Altered Being, Military Personnel
Time period(s): 21st century
Locale(s): Iowa

Summary: New Humans, genetically altered human warriors, have risen up against their human creators and taken over. Maximillian Turkel, injured and fleeing, enlists the help of Jack Bender. Hidden in Jack's treehouse, Max heals sufficiently to undergo surgical removal of an implanted tracking device. In a subsequent attempt to rescue Jack's girlfriend from the Muties, Max and his friends are captured. His friends escape and plan to rescue Max.

Other books you might like:
Jerry Ahern, *To End All War*, 1990
James Axler, *Death Lands: Time Nomads*, 1990
Bob Ham, *Rolling Vengeance*, 1990
Jack Maloney, *Freedom Express*, 1990
Michael McGann, *The Ghost Warriors*, 1990
David Robbins, *Yellowstone Run*, 1990
James Rouch, *Body Count*, 1990

1863

RICHARD GRANT

Tex and Molly in the Afterlife
(New York: Avon, 1996)

Story type: Fantasy (Satire; Science Fiction)
Major character(s): Tex "Bear" Darffot, Spirit, Activist; Molly, Spirit, Activist
Time period(s): 1990s
Locale(s): Maine; The Afterlife, Mythical Place

Summary: Counting-culture enthusiasts Tex and Molly find their alternate life style becomes an alternate death style when dying leaves them unready to depart Earth. Both individuals discover odd and unpleasant aspects of the Afterlife when they attempt to continue their routine existence and goals while meeting the strange denizens inhabiting their space.

Other books you might like:
Alan Dean Foster, *To the Vanishing Point*, 1988

Neil Gaiman, *Good Omens: The Nice and Accurate Prophecies of Agnes Nutter, Witch*, 1990
  Terry Pratchett, co-author
James Morrow, *Towing Jehovah*, 1944
Daniel Manus Pinkwater, *The Afterlife Diet*, 1995
Terry Pratchett, *Reaper Man*, 1992
Elizabeth Ann Scarborough, *Last Refuge*, 1992
Thorne Smith, *Topper: An Improbable Adventure*, 1926

1864

RICHARD GRANT

Through the Heart

(New York: Bantam Spectra, 1991)

Story type: Fantasy (Science Fiction; Literary)
Major character(s): Bell Dog, Engineer; Kem, Teenager; Sander, Friend, Teenager
Time period(s): Indeterminate Future
Locale(s): The Oasis (Midwest desert)

Summary: Sander, exchanged by his father for a new motor and tools, gradually understands the functioning of his new home, the land ship *Oasis*. On its route through the post-disaster American Desert, Sander is promoted from galley boy, to engine snipe, to assistant navigation officer. While learning much about the world and people around him, Sander also learns that trading with the wagon people and a few remaining communities masks the true purpose of the *Oasis's* journey.

Other books you might like:
David Brin, *Earth*, 1990
Samuel R. Delany, *Tales of Neveryon*, 1979
Marjorie Bradley Kellogg, *Harmony*, 1991
J.M. Morgan, *Desert Eden*, 1991
Frederik Pohl, *Gladiator-at-Law*, 1955
  C.M. Kornbluth, co-author
Vernor Vinge, *Marooned in Realtime*, 1986

1865

RICHARD GRANT

Views from the Oldest House

(New York: Doubleday Foundation, 1989)

Story type: Science Fiction (Satire)
Major character(s): Turner Ashenden, Student; Black Malachi Pantera, Student (Lunatic)
Time period(s): Indeterminate Future
Locale(s): United States

Summary: Turner Ashenden, an incompetent and not very happy college student in a near-future world which appears on the edge of economic collapse, finds himself proclaimed a hero by his mad friend Black Malachi Pantera. Turner's supposed destiny begins to seem more than just an outrageous joke, however, when he discovers the Bad Winters Institute of Science and Philosophy, a secluded mansion in the nearby mountains, and confronts the strange psychic Madame Gwendola.

Other books you might like:
James P. Blaylock, *Homunculus*, 1986
James P. Blaylock, *Land of Dreams*, 1987
James P. Blaylock, *The Last Coin*, 1988
John Crowley, *Aegypt*, 1987
John Crowley, *Little, Big*, 1981
Tim Powers, *The Anubis Gates*, 1983
Thomas Pynchon, *Gravity's Rainbow*, 1973

1866

GEARY GRAVEL

A Key for the Nonesuch

(New York: Ballantine/Del Rey, 1990)

Story type: Science Fiction (Adventure; Alternate Universe)
Series: War of the Fading Worlds
Major character(s): Howard Bell, Maintenance Worker, Writer (aspiring)
Time period(s): 1990s
Locale(s): Nexus Building, Earth; Fading Worlds, Alternate Universe

Summary: Howard Bell, master handyman, could fix almost anything. At his job in the brand new Nexus Building he borrows a key to the washroom which propels him to another place. He finds that he is the Nonesuch in the Fading Worlds, a perpetually changing battlefield.

Other books you might like:
M.A.R. Barker, *Man of Gold*, 1984
Alfred Bester, *The Demolished Man*, 1953
Steven Brust, *Jhereg*, 1983
Will Shetterly, *The Tangled Lands*, 1989
E.C. Tubb, *Toyman*, 1969

1867

GEARY GRAVEL

Mask of the Phantasm

(New York: Bantam Spectra, 1994)

Story type: Science Fiction (Adventure; Mystery)
Series: Batman
Major character(s): Bruce "Batman" Wayne, Hero, Detective—Amateur; Andrea Beaumont, Girlfriend; The Joker, Criminal
Time period(s): 21st century
Locale(s): Gotham City (New York City)

Summary: When a serial killer of mob bosses frames Batman, police begin searching for him as the suspect. The approaching career burnout and reappearance of a former paramour lead Batman to reconsider retirement. Novelizes the animated film.

Other books you might like:
Craig Shaw Gardner, *The Batman Murders*, 1992
Martin H. Greenberg, *The Further Adventures of Batman*, 1989
  editor
Simon Hawke, *Batman: To Stalk a Specter*, 1991
Joe R. Lansdale, *Captured by the Engines*, 1991

Dennis O'Neil, *Batman: Knightfall*, 1994

1868
GEARY GRAVEL

The Return of the Breakneck Boys
(New York: Ballantine/Del Rey, 1991)

Story type: Science Fiction (Adventure)
Series: War of the Fading Worlds
Major character(s): Howard Bell, Leader; Yam Ya-Mash, Sidekick, Alien (Trilbit); Alaiya, Military Personnel
Time period(s): 1990s
Locale(s): Boston, Massachusetts; The Thousand Island World, Planet—Imaginary; The Flower World, Planet—Imaginary

Summary: This book continues the adventures begun in *A Key for the Nonsuch*. Howard and his crew discover more about the Fading Worlds and the Keyholders. After returning from a weekend on Earth with a newly found Breakneck Boy, Howard finds he can no longer return to Earth. Although the battle with the Keyholders has barely begun, the Breakneck Boys resolve not to quit until the Keyholders are conquered.

Other books you might like:
Douglas Adams, *The Hitchhiker's Guide to the Galaxy*, 1980
David Brin, *Startide Rising*, 1983
John DeChancie, *Starrigger*, 1983
Philip Jose Farmer, *To Your Scattered Bodies Go*, 1971
Alan Dean Foster, *Glory Lane*, 1987
Larry Niven, *Ringworld*, 1970
E.C. Tubb, *The Winds of Gath*, 1967

1869
PAT GRAVERSEN

Black Ice
(New York: Zebra, 1993)

Story type: Horror (Supernatural Vengeance)
Major character(s): John "Gibby" Gibson, Doctor; Cassie McCall, Accountant (bookkeeper); Jess McCall, Child (Cassie's 8-year-old son)
Time period(s): 1990s (1993)
Locale(s): Winter Falls, Connecticut

Summary: Connor McCall helped cover up a crime related to his practicing black magic by disposing of the bodies of his three half sisters in Lake Wahelo. More than half a century later, the trio claim the soul of Connor's grandson Jess when he accidentally falls into the lake, and use him to seek their revenge upon the town.

Other books you might like:
Matthew J. Costello, *Beneath Still Waters*, 1989
Ruby Jean Jensen, *Celia*, 1991

1870
PAT GRAVERSEN

The Fagin
(New York: Zebra, 1992)

Story type: Horror (Child-in-Peril)
Major character(s): Felice Sinclair, Divorced Person, Single Parent; Jason Sinclair, Child (Felice's 6 year old son); Kadar, Witch
Time period(s): 1990s
Locale(s): Blue Falls, Virginia

Summary: Felice Sinclair thinks that a return to her hometown following her divorce will help her get a new start in life. Troubles arise when when a local coven kidnaps her son Jason because they recognize in him the essential qualities that will make him an ideal future leader. This novel was originally published in 1982.

Other books you might like:
John Coyne, *Child of Shadows*, 1990
Tom Piccirilli, *Dark Father*, 1990
Peter Straub, *Shadowland*, 1980

1871
PAT GRAVERSEN

Graythings
(New York: Zebra, 1995)

Story type: Horror (Occult)
Major character(s): Mariele Hollander, Interior Decorator; Simon Novak, Psychic; Dwago, Cult Member (Thanatological Society)
Time period(s): 1990s (1995)
Locale(s): New York, New York

Summary: Mariele Hollander's efforts to contact her dead husband through a seance activate the "graythings," intangible beings from the other side of death that begin seeping into our own world.

Other books you might like:
Daniel H. Gower, *Harrowgate*, 1993
Fritz Leiber, *Our Lady of Darkness*, 1977
T.M. Wright, *The Ascending*, 1995
T.M. Wright, *Sleepeasy*, 1993

1872
PAT GRAVERSEN

Precious Blood
(New York: Zebra, 1993)

Story type: Horror (Vampire Story)
Major character(s): Beth Hart, Teenager, Vampire; Quinn, Vampire; Adragon Hart, Vampire (leader, Society of Vampires)
Time period(s): 2000s (2005)
Locale(s): New York, New York

Summary: Vampire Adragon Hart struggles to save his rebellious teenage daughter from the clutches of Quinn, leader of a band of renegade urban vampires whose traffickings in diseased blood and the intravenous narcotic Rush threaten to expose the vampire subculture living in the suburbs.

Other books you might like:
Poppy Z. Brite, *Lost Souls*, 1992
Scott Ciencin, *The Vampire Odyssey*, 1992
Nancy A. Collins, *Sunglasses After Dark*, 1989
William Tedford, *Liquid Diet*, 1992

1873

PAT GRAVERSEN

Sweet Blood

(New York: Zebra, 1992)

Story type: Horror (Vampire Story)
Major character(s): Adragon Hart, Teenager, Vampire; Elsbeth Hart, Writer, Vampire; Delphine Keelan, Vampire
Time period(s): 1990s (1992)
Locale(s): Asbury Park, New Jersey

Summary: Adragon Hart thinks it's all a joke when he and his socially withdrawn mother are inducted into The Society of Vampires. But then Adragon discovers that the society's members really are vampires—and that his overprotective mother is not about to give him up to the alluring Society officer Del Keelan without a bloody fight.

Other books you might like:
Poppy Z. Brite, *Lost Souls*, 1992
Richard Lee Byers, *The Vampire's Apprentice*, 1992
John Peyton Cooke, *Out for Blood*, 1991
Mark Ivanhoe, *Virgintooth*, 1991
Anne Rice, *Interview with the Vampire*, 1976

1874

ALASDAIR GRAY

A History Maker

(New York: Harcourt Brace, 1996)

Story type: Science Fiction (Satire; Political)
Major character(s): Wat Dryhope, Warrior, Hero; Kate "Kittock" Dryhope, Parent; Jardine Craig Douglas, Military Personnel (general)
Time period(s): 23rd century (2230s)
Locale(s): Scotland

Summary: Unable to adjust to space, Wat returns home to fight beside his father, General Craig Douglas, who orders Wat to perform an unethical tactic which prevents defeat. Observed by the public eye which broadcasts battles, Wat refuses to accept the image of hero. He returns to the women of Dryhope, receiving much attention as most of the men now nourish the powerplant.

Other books you might like:
Eleanor Arnason, *Ring of Swords*, 1993
Samuel R. Delany, *They Fly at Ciron*, 1993
James Morrow, *City of Truth*, 1992
Sheri S. Tepper, *A Plague of Angels*, 1993

George Turner, *Genetic Soldier*, 1994

1875

MURIEL GRAY

Trickster

(New York: Doubleday, 1995)

Story type: Horror (Ancient Evil Unleashed)
Major character(s): Sam Hunt, Maintenance Worker (groundskeeper), Indian; Katie Hunt, Museum Curator (Silver Heritage Museum); Calvin Bitterhand, Shaman, Indian
Time period(s): 1900s (1907); 1990s (1995)

Summary: This first novel, originally published in England in 1994, tells of the Trickster, a demon of Indian mythology. It is successfully thwarted in the Canadian mining town of Silver in 1907 when the Indians and whites bury their differences to work collectively against it. But it re-emerges to cause murder and mayhem in contemporary times when Sam Hunt repudiates his tribal heritage and selection to be a Sioux shaman.

Other books you might like:
Colin Kersey, *Soul Catcher*, 1995
G. Wayne Miller, *Thunder Rise*, 1988
Adam Niswander, *The Charm*, 1993
Eugene E. Pfaff Jr., *Uwharrie*, 1993
    Michael Causey, co-author
Kathryn Ptacek, *Ghost Dance*, 1990
Patrick Whalen, *Deathwalker*, 1992

1876

DAINA GRAZIUNAS
JIM STARLIN, Co-Author

Thinning the Predators

(New York: Warner, 1996)

Story type: Horror (Serial Killer; Wild Talents)
Major character(s): David Vandermark, Lawyer; Ira Levitt, FBI Agent
Time period(s): 1990s (1996)
Locale(s): New York, New York

Summary: Following an accident that endows him with telepathic powers, David Vandermark embarks on a spree to eliminate the serial killer who murdered his wife and child and a score of other murderers like him. Federal agent Levitt pursues Vandermark to New York to apprehend him, but becomes his ally when he discovers that recent murders Vandermark is investigating in the local Hispanic community are government plots.

Other books you might like:
Thomas Harris, *Red Dragon*, 1981
Dean R. Koontz, *The Bad Place*, 1990
Dean R. Koontz, *Dragon Tears*, 1993
Joe R. Lansdale, *The Nightrunners*, 1987

1877

ANDREW M. GREELEY

Angel Light
(New York: Tor Forge, 1995)

Story type: Fantasy (Religious; Contemporary)
Major character(s): G. Patrick "Toby" Tobin, Traveller, Computer Expert; Raphaella "Rae", Angel, Travel Agent; Sara Ann Tobin, Student (music)
Time period(s): 1990s
Locale(s): Chicago, Illinois; Ireland

Summary: Hoping to inherit a large fortune, Toby reluctantly follows his ancestor's demand that he woo a distant Irish cousin and end a family feud. While arranging the trip to Ireland, Toby contacts Raphaella who has searched for a human to help. Based on the Book of Tobias from the Old Testament of the Bible.

Other books you might like:
Peter Crowther, *Heaven Sent: 18 Glorious Tales of the Angels*, 1995
   editor
Jack Dann, *Angels!*, 1995
   Gardner Dozois, co-editor
Neil Gaiman, *Good Omens: The Nice and Accurate Prophecies of Agnes Nutter, Witch*, 1990
   Terry Pratchett, co-author
Parke Godwin, *Waiting for the Galactic Bus*, 1987
C.S. Lewis, *Out of the Silent Planet*, 1943
Nancy Springer, *Metal Angel*, 1994
Sean Stewart, *Resurrection Man*, 1995

1878

ANDREW M. GREELEY, Editor
MICHAEL CASSUTT, Co-Editor

Sacred Visions
(New York: Tor, 1991)

Story type: Science Fiction (Anthology; Theological)

Summary: This volume contains twelve stories with Roman Catholic settings or themes and a six-page introduction and includes reprinted stories by James Blish, Anthony Boucher, Jeff Duntemann, Walter M. Miller, Jr. and R.A. Lafferty plus three original stories, "Xorinda the Witch" by Andrew M. Greeley, "Guts" by Jack McDevitt, and "The Seraph from Its Sepulcher" by Gene Wolfe.

Other books you might like:
Orson Scott Card, *Xenocide*, 1991
Alan Dean Foster, *Cyber Way*, 1990
Parke Godwin, *Waiting for the Galactic Bus*, 1988
Robert A. Heinlein, *Stranger in a Strange Land*, 1991
   revised
Frank Herbert, *Whipping Star*, 1970
Marc Laidlaw, *Neon Lotus*, 1988
Ted Reynolds, *The Tides of God*, 1989
Ian Watson, *God's World*, 1990

1879

MICHAEL GREEN

Dry Skull Dreams
(New York: Pocket, 1995)

Story type: Horror (Science Fiction)
Major character(s): Molly Coughlin, Nurse; Charlie Coughlin, Aged Person; Sibatia, Shaman
Time period(s): 1990s (1995)
Locale(s): Brattleboro, Vermont

Summary: In this informal sequel to *The Jimjams* (1994), Molly Coughlin returns from relief work in Africa unaware that a tribal shaman has infected her with "seeds" from outer space that will take over her will and force her to pass them to an increasing number of other victims.

Other books you might like:
Jack Finney, *The Body Snatchers*, 1955
Robert A. Heinlein, *The Puppet Masters*, 1951
John Shirley, *In Darkness Waiting*, 1988
Lawrence Watt-Evans, *The Nightmare People*, 1990
John Wyndham, *The Day of the Triffids*, 1951

1880

MICHAEL GREEN

The Jimjams
(New York: Pocket, 1994)

Story type: Horror (Science Fiction)
Major character(s): Duffy Farris, Hotel Worker; Rose Farris, Hotel Worker; Earl Douchette, Aged Person (retiree)
Time period(s): 1990s (1994)
Locale(s): Blue Turtle Island, Florida

Summary: Blue Turtle Island turns into the retirement resort from hell when a horde of "freddies," (possibly extraterrestrial) insectoid creatures with wings and frog features, turn visitors into sex- and violence-crazed incubators for their kind.

Other books you might like:
Jack Finney, *The Body Snatchers*, 1955
Robert A. Heinlein, *The Puppet Masters*, 1951
John Shirley, *In Darkness Waiting*, 1988
Whitley Strieber, *The Forbidden Zone*, 1993
Lawrence Watt-Evans, *The Nightmare People*, 1990

1881

MICHAEL GREEN

Quest: In Search of the Dragontooth
(Philadelphia: Running Press, 1994)

Story type: Fantasy (Quest; Religious)
Major character(s): Magnalucius, Religious, Writer; Ibn Sufa al-Iskandaria, Companion, Adventurer
Time period(s): 15th century
Locale(s): England

Summary: This illustrated monk's journal is divided into two parts: ''The Unicornis Notebooks of Magnalucius'' details his search for the origins of a unicorn that he spotted one day while meditating; and ''In Search of the Dragontooth'' follows his pursuit of the enchanted Perilous Dragontooth using old documents and rumors acquired as he proceeds.

Other books you might like:
Richard Gilliam, *Grails: Quests of the Dawn*, 1994
   Martin H. Greenberg, Edward E. Kramer, co-editors
Richard Gilliam, *Grails: Visitations of the Night*, 1994
   Martin H. Greenberg, Edward E. Kramer, co-editors
James Gurney, *Dinotopia*, 1992
Jane Yolen, *Here There Be Dragons*, 1993
Jane Yolen, *Here There Be Unicorns*, 1994

1882

ROLAND J. GREEN

Conan the Guardian

(New York: Tor, 1991)

Story type: Fantasy (Sword and Sorcery)
Series: Conan the Barbarian
Major character(s): Conan, Barbarian, Warrior
Time period(s): Indeterminate
Locale(s): Argos, Fictional Country; Alternate Earth

Summary: Conan accepts the duty of guarding Livia, then he and his men must defend her against armed men and treacherous sorcery.

Other books you might like:
Leonard Carpenter, *Conan the Warlord*, 1988
Robert E. Howard, *Conan the Barbarian*, 1955
Robert E. Howard, *Conan the Conqueror*, 1950
Robert Jordan, *Conan the Magnificent*, 1984
Robert Jordan, *Conan the Victorious*, 1984
Steve Perry, *Conan the Free Lance*, 1990
Karl Edward Wagner, *Echoes of Valor I*, 1987
   editor

1883

ROLAND J. GREEN

Conan the Relentless

(New York: Tor, 1992)

Story type: Fantasy (Sword and Sorcery)
Series: Conan the Barbarian
Major character(s): Conan, Barbarian, Warrior; Raihna, Warrior, Leader
Time period(s): Indeterminate
Locale(s): Border Kingdom, Fictional Country

Summary: While traveling through the northern borderlands, Conan chances upon Raihna, a beautiful swordswoman known to him, and joins her followers. In service to the king, Conan may represent the only hope of countering the magic employed by the Star Brothers and stopping the ancient evil they have loosed.

Other books you might like:
Leonard Carpenter, *Conan the Warlord*, 1988

Robert E. Howard, *Conan the Barbarian*, 1955
Robert E. Howard, *Conan the Conqueror*, 1950
Robert Jordan, *Conan the Magnificent*, 1984
Robert Jordan, *Conan the Victorious*, 1984
Steve Perry, *Conan the Free Lance*, 1990
Karl Edward Wagner, *Echoes of Valor I*, 1987
   editor

1884

ROLAND J. GREEN

The Mountain Walks

(New York: Ace Books, 1989)

Story type: Science Fiction (Military)
Series: The Peace Company
Major character(s): John Parkes, Military Personnel (Sergeant Major)
Time period(s): 24th century
Locale(s): Zauberberg, Planet—Imaginary

Summary: Religious fanaticism is tearing the planet Zauberberg apart. The Peace Force must stop the fighting and solve the religious dispute.

Other books you might like:
Gordon R. Dickson, *Lost Dorsai*, 1980
Gordon R. Dickson, *Soldier, Ask Not*, 1967
Gordon R. Dickson, *The Tactics of Mistake*, 1971
Jerry Pournelle, *Janissaries*, 1979
Jerry Pournelle, *Oath of Fealty*, 1981
   Larry Niven, co-author
Jerry Pournelle, *Prince of Mercenaries*, 1989

1885

ROLAND J. GREEN

The Painful Field

(New York: Roc, 1993)

Story type: Science Fiction (Military; Political)
Series: Starcruiser Shenandoah
Major character(s): Candice Shores, Military Personnel (Lieutenant Colonel); Rose Liddell, Spaceship Captain; Sho Kurasawa, Military Personnel (Vice Admiral)
Time period(s): Indeterminate Future
Locale(s): Linak'h, Planet—Imaginary; *Shenandoah*, Spaceship

Summary: The crew of the Federation starcruiser *Shenandoah*, charged with keeping an uneasy peace on Linak'h, tread a fine line among the factions and species on the planet. An attempted prison break and sabotage of a chemical plant escalates into a deadly campaign of terrorism as a struggle between the Confraternity and the Administration turns friends into enemies.

Other books you might like:
C.J. Cherryh, *Downbelow Station*, 1981
Gordon R. Dickson, *The Tactics of Mistake*, 1971
Jane S. Fancher, *Ground-Ties*, 1991
Joe Haldeman, *The Forever War*, 1975
Robert A. Heinlein, *Starship Troopers*, 1959

Jerry Pournelle, *Falkenberg's Legion*, 1990
Joel Rosenberg, *Hero*, 1990

1886

ROLAND J. GREEN

Squadron Alert

(New York: NAL Signet, 1989)

Story type: Science Fiction (Military)
Series: Starcruiser Shenandoah
Major character(s): Rose Liddell, Spaceship Captain
Time period(s): 26th century
Locale(s): Victoria, Planet—Imaginary

Summary: War looms between the United Federation of Starworlds and the Freeworld States Alliance over the planet Victoria. Rose Liddell, captain of the Starcruiser *Shenandoah*, has evidence that an unknown third party is promoting the violence. She must discover the culprit and stop the war.

Other books you might like:
W. Michael Gear, *The Artifact*, 1989
Thorarinn Gunnarsson, *Battle of the Ring*, 1989
Larry Niven, *The Mote in God's Eye*, 1974
　　Jerry Pournelle, co-author

1887

ROLAND J. GREEN

The Sum of Things

(New York: Roc, 1991)

Story type: Science Fiction (Military)
Series: Starcruiser Shenandoah
Major character(s): Rose Liddell, Spaceship Captain; Candice Shores, Military Personnel (acting Major); Sho Kurasawa, Military Personnel (acting Vice Admiral)
Time period(s): Indeterminate Future
Locale(s): Victoria, Planet—Imaginary

Summary: The Federation and the Alliance both want peace, but the planetary factions are still fighting. The presence of two alien races complicates the picture, along with terrorist acts by unidentified forces. The crew of the *Shenandoah* has to fight on multiple fronts to preserve the newly created Associated States of Victoria.

Other books you might like:
John Dalmas, *The Lizard War*, 1989
Gordon R. Dickson, *The Tactics of Mistake*, 1971
Joe Haldeman, *The Forever War*, 1975
Robert A. Heinlein, *Starship Troopers*, 1959
Jerry Pournelle, *Falkenberg's Legion*, 1990
Joel Rosenberg, *Hero*, 1990

1888

SHARON GREEN

Convergence

(New York: AvoNova, 1996)

Story type: Fantasy (Magic Conflict; Political)

Series: Blending
Major character(s): Lorand "Lor" Coll, Wizard, Farmer; Tamrissa Domon, Wizard, Abuse Victim; Vallant Ro, Wizard, Sea Captain
Time period(s): Indeterminate
Locale(s): Gan Garee, Fictional City

Summary: The first Blending of Water, Earth, Air, Fire, and Spirit founded the Empire and defeated the evil Four Powers centuries ago. Now a group of five unwilling candidates must participate in unwelcome training of their talents to learn if they will become the next Blending. If they don't, the Four Powers may return.

Other books you might like:
Glen Cook, *The Swordbearer*, 1982
Teresa Edgerton, *Goblin Moon*, 1991
Ursula K. Le Guin, *A Wizard of Earthsea*, 1968
Caroline Stevermer, *A College of Magics*, 1994
Janny Wurts, *Stormwarden*, 1984

1889

SHARON GREEN

Dark Mirror, Dark Dreams

(New York: AvoNova, 1994)

Story type: Fantasy (Magic Conflict; Quest)
Major character(s): Alexia, Royalty (princess), Magician (shape-shifter); Tiran d'Iste, Mercenary, Magician (shape-shifter); Chalaine, Sorceress
Time period(s): Indeterminate
Locale(s): Golran, Fictional Country

Summary: Misunderstandings threaten to disrupt the honeymoon of Alexia and her new husband, Tiran, as they prepare to oust the usurpers in their alternate world kingdom. Their alliance with Chalaine and Bariden, the rightful rulers of a neighboring alternate world, deepens their jealousies when they agree to split their forces as a strategic ploy. Finally, they must each face the evil magic of their alternate selves in order to save their kingdoms and their marriages. Sequel to *Silver Princess, Golden Knight*.

Other books you might like:
Margaret Ball, *The Shadow Gate*, 1991
Marion Zimmer Bradley, *The Forbidden Tower*, 1977
Simon R. Green, *Blue Moon Rising*, 1991
Barbara Hambly, *Dog Wizard*, 1993
Robert A. Heinlein, *Glory Road*, 1963

1890

SHARON GREEN

The Hidden Realms

(New York: AvoNova, 1993)

Story type: Fantasy (Magic Conflict; Quest)
Major character(s): Chalaine, Sorceress; Bariden, Martial Arts Expert (swordsman), Sorcerer
Time period(s): Indeterminate
Locale(s): Melen, Fictional Country; Palace of Ease, Mythical Place

Summary: To counter the evil force acting on souls within the castle walls, Chalaine joins with Prince Bariden. Their search leads through a portal and into a series of dangerous challenges as they investigate the conspiracy that may prove fatal for them.

Other books you might like:
Carole Nelson Douglas, *Cup of Clay*, 1991
Laurell K. Hamilton, *Nightseer*, 1992
Shirley Rousseau Murphy, *The Catswold Portal*, 1993
Martha Wells, *The Element of Fire*, 1993

1891

SHARON GREEN

Silver Princess, Golden Knight
(New York: AvoNova, 1993)

Story type: Fantasy (Alternate World; Romance)
Major character(s): Alexia, Royalty (princess), Magician (shape-shifter); Tiran d'Iste, Mercenary, Magician (shape-shifter); Reynar III, Ruler (king), Parent
Time period(s): Indeterminate
Locale(s): Golran, Fictional Country

Summary: King Reynar, outraged by his daughter's wild behavior, decides that Alexia should marry. In order to find a husband equal to her in shape-shifting and swordfighting abilities, he announces a contest with Alexia as the prize. Determined to control her own life, Alexia enters the contest herself, but magical sabotage sends Alexia and the leading contender, Tiran d'Iste, through a Gate into other worlds. Shared peril forces her to cooperate with her rival, but her growing attraction to Tiran threatens to upset her plans.

Other books you might like:
Margaret Ball, *The Shadow Gate*, 1990
C.J. Cherryh, *Exile's Gate*, 1988
Pamela Dean, *The Secret Country*, 1985
R.A. MacAvoy, *Book of Kells*, 1985
Patricia C. Wrede, *The Seven Towers*, 1984

1892

SHARON GREEN

Wind Whispers, Shadow Shouts
(New York: AvoNova, 1995)

Story type: Fantasy (Magic Conflict; Quest)
Major character(s): Alexia, Royalty (queen), Magician (shape-shifter); Tiran d'Iste, Ruler (king), Magician (shape-shifter); Brandis, Sorcerer
Time period(s): Indeterminate
Locale(s): Fictional Country

Summary: Having taken their rightful place as rulers of their land, Alexia and Tiran fight chaos and corruption in their realm and treachery among their courtiers. A magical trap contrived by their enemies casts a spell of fear on Alexia, just when she needs all her strength and courage to help Tiran face a pair of usurpers in hand-to-hand combat. Sequel to *Dark Mirror, Dark Dreams*.

Other books you might like:
Gordon R. Dickson, *The Dragon, the Earl, and the Troll*, 1994
Simon R. Green, *Blue Moon Rising*, 1991
Barbara Hambly, *The Ladies of Mandrigyn*, 1993
Katherine Kurtz, *Deryni Checkmate*, 1972
C.L. Moore, *Jirel of Joiry*, 1969

1893

SIMON R. GREEN

Blood and Honor
(New York: Roc, 1993)

Story type: Fantasy (Magic Conflict; Horror)
Major character(s): Jordan, Actor; Gawaine, Knight; Victor, Royalty (prince), Magician
Time period(s): Indeterminate
Locale(s): Redhart, Fictional Country; Castle Midnight, Mythical Place

Summary: Hired to impersonate Prince Victor, one of three brothers competing for the throne of their recently deceased father, Jordan begins to wonder if he will survive to collect his fee. He could handle the assassination attempts and the sorcerous plots of the rival factions, but without a king to control the Unreal in Castle Midnight, horrible monsters have broken through into reality, threatening the destruction of the whole country.

Other books you might like:
C.J. Cherryh, *Angel with the Sword*, 1985
Phyllis Eisenstein, *Born to Exile*, 1978
Barbara Hambly, *The Time of the Dark*, 1982
Robert A. Heinlein, *Double Star*, 1956
Patricia A. McKillip, *The Riddle-Master of Hed*, 1976
Jennifer Roberson, *Shapechangers*, 1984
Robert Silverberg, *Lord Valentine's Castle*, 1980
Roger Zelazny, *Nine Princes in Amber*, 1970

1894

SIMON R. GREEN

Blue Moon Rising
(New York: Roc, 1991)

Story type: Fantasy (Quest; Magic Conflict)
Major character(s): Rupert, Royalty (prince); Julia, Royalty (princess); Unicorn, Mythical Creature, Animal
Time period(s): Indeterminate
Locale(s): Forest Kingdom, Fictional Country

Summary: When Prince Rupert of the Forest Kingdoms "rescues" a princess from a dragon, he finds the mild-mannered dragon knows some useful spells and the strong-willed princess is a competent swordswoman. Their skills help Rupert and his unicorn fight their way back through the Darkwood. When plague, famine and marauding demons threaten the very existence of the kingdom, Rupert is sent to find the self-exiled High Warlock who might be able to combat the Wild Magic that will be let loose when the Blue Moon is full.

Other books you might like:
Eleanor Arnason, *The Sword Smith*, 1978
Robert Asprin, *Another Fine Myth*, 1978
Steven Brust, *Jhereg*, 1983
Gordon R. Dickson, *The Dragon and the George*, 1976
Fritz Leiber, *Swords Against Death*, 1970
Patricia C. Wrede, *Dealing with Dragons*, 1990
Patricia C. Wrede, *The Seven Towers*, 1984
Chelsea Quinn Yarbro, *A Baroque Fable*, 1986

1895

SIMON R. GREEN

The Bones of Haven
(New York: Ace, 1992)

Story type: Fantasy (Adventure; Mystery)
Series: Hawk & Fisher
Major character(s): Isobel Fisher, Police Officer (captain); Hawk, Police Officer (captain)
Time period(s): Indeterminate Past
Locale(s): Haven, Fictional City

Summary: Hawk and Fisher join the SWAT (Special Wizardry and Tactics) team to stop a prison riot that includes sorcerers and worse. The day's work for Hawk and Fisher also involves a possibly psychotic and definitely supernaturally powerful man who escapes from a painting into the city and a band of terrorists that takes two kings hostage.

Other books you might like:
Robert Asprin, *Thieves' World*, 1979
   editor
Steven Brust, *Jhereg*, 1983
Glen Cook, *Sweet Silver Blues*, 1987
Randall Garrett, *Too Many Magicians*, 1967
Fritz Leiber, *Swords and Deviltry*, 1970
Nick Pollotta, *Doomsday Exam*, 1992

1896

SIMON R. GREEN

Deathstalker Rebellion
(New York: Roc, 1996)

Story type: Science Fiction (Space Opera)
Series: Life and Times of Owen Deathstalker
Major character(s): Owen Deathstalker, Revolutionary, Nobleman (deposed); Ruby Journey, Revolutionary, Bounty Hunter; Captain Silence, Military Personnel
Time period(s): Indeterminate Future
Locale(s): Golgotha, Planet—Imaginary; Technos III, Planet—Imaginary

Summary: Owen Deathstalker's revolution goes on the offensive against the Empire as he attempts to unite all of Empress Lionstone's enemies. One group of rebels travels to Technos III, becoming trapped in plots and counter-plots surrounding the production of a new star drive. Meanwhile, Imperial Captain Silence discovers extremely unpleasant alien truths that may threaten both Empire and Rebellion.

Other books you might like:
Iain M. Banks, *Consider Phlebas*, 1988
Glen Cook, *The Dragon Never Sleeps*, 1988
Frank Herbert, *Dune*, 1965
George Lucas, *Star Wars*, 1976
Paul J. McAuley, *Four Hundred Billion Stars*, 1988

1897

SIMON R. GREEN

Down Among the Dead Men
(New York: Roc, 1993)

Story type: Fantasy (Military; Adventure)
Major character(s): Duncan MacNeil, Military Personnel (Ranger sergeant); Scarecrow Jack, Woodsman; Constance, Sorcerer
Time period(s): Indeterminate Past
Locale(s): Parkwood, Fictional Country (forest kingdom)

Summary: In the 10 years since the Demon Wars, retaking tainted lands and restoring peace has proven a hard and often bloody business. The Rangers take the brunt of it, sent ahead of the Guard patrols and expected to handle whatever they find. On the current assignment they investigate a fort held by friendly forces but from which no one who enters can emerge. Sequel to *Blue Moon Rising*.

Other books you might like:
Steven Brust, *Jhereg*, 1983
Glen Cook, *The Black Company*, 1984
David Drake, *Old Nathan*, 1991
Barbara Hambly, *The Time of the Dark*, 1982
Justin Leiber, *The Sword and the Eye*, 1985

1898

SIMON R. GREEN

The God Killer
(New York: Ace, 1991)

Story type: Fantasy (Adventure; Mystery)
Series: Hawk & Fisher
Major character(s): Isobel Fisher, Police Officer (captain); Hawk, Police Officer (captain)
Time period(s): Indeterminate Past
Locale(s): Haven, Fictional City

Summary: The hundreds of Beings and their religious followers on the Street of Gods have jostled along together well enough for a very long time, their bickering and feuding handled by the Guard's God Squad. But when someone, or something, begins killing Gods, it's time to call in Hawk and Fisher.

Other books you might like:
Robert Asprin, *Thieves' World*, 1979
   editor
Randall Garrett, *Too Many Magicians*, 1967
Fritz Leiber, *Swords and Deviltry*, 1970
Anne Logston, *Shadow*, 1991

1899

SIMON R. GREEN

Guard Against Dishonor

(New York: Ace, 1991)

Story type: Fantasy (Mystery)
Series: Hawk & Fisher
Major character(s): Hawk, Police Officer (captain); Isobel Fisher, Police Officer (captain)
Time period(s): Indeterminate Past
Locale(s): Haven, Fictional City

Summary: When a new street drug causes users to tear themselves and anyone around them into pieces with their bare hands, Hawk and Fisher arrest the supplier. When he is promptly released because of his important contacts, and the drug disappears, Hawk and Fisher protest the obvious corruption of the Guards. Reassigned separately, both are charged with treason when assignments come under attack. Somehow, they must stay alive, clear their names and stop the corruption.

Other books you might like:
Robert Asprin, *Thieves' World*, 1979
　　editor
Glen Cook, *Sweet Silver Blues*, 1987
Alan Dean Foster, *Outland*, 1981
Randall Garrett, *Too Many Magicians*, 1967
Ernest Hogan, *High Aztec*, 1992
Lee Killough, *Spider Play*, 1986
Mickey Zucker Reichert, *Godslayer*, 1987

1900

SIMON R. GREEN

Hawk & Fisher

(New York: Ace, 1990)

Story type: Fantasy (Mystery; Magic Conflict)
Series: Hawk & Fisher
Major character(s): Hawk, Police Officer (Captain); Isobel Fisher, Police Officer (Captain)
Time period(s): Indeterminate Past
Locale(s): Haven, Fictional City

Summary: Hawk and Fisher are assigned as bodyguards to one of the City's most powerful and controversial politicians. Their task begins at a private dinner party attended by the politician's friends and allies at a private home that is magically sealed from outside interference. It should be perfectly safe. But why—and how—do the guests, including their charge, keep dying?

Other books you might like:
Glen Cook, *Sweet Silver Blues*, 1987
Randall Garrett, *Too Many Magicians*, 1967
Lee Killough, *Spider Play*, 1986
Michael Kurland, *A Study in Sorcery*, 1989
Mercedes Lackey, *Children of the Night*, 1990
Mercedes Lackey, *Burning Water*, 1989

1901

SIMON R. GREEN

Hellworld

(New York: Ace, 1993)

Story type: Science Fiction (First Contact)
Series: Twilight of the Empire
Major character(s): Scott Hunter, Military Personnel, Scout (planetary); Megan DeChance, Military Personnel, Psychic (esper); Krystel, Government Official (investigator), Scout (planetary)
Time period(s): Indeterminate Future
Locale(s): Wolf IV, Planet—Imaginary

Summary: When the planetary survey team lands on Wolf IV intending to determine its suitability for human colonization, they discover numerous hostile life forms. When the team explores an abandoned city, they discover the most terrifying aspect of their new home.

Other books you might like:
David Brin, *Startide Rising*, 1983
David Drake, *The Jungle*, 1991
Harry Harrison, *The Deathworld Trilogy*, 1976
Anne McCaffrey, *The Chronicles of Pern: First Fall*, 1993
Anne McCaffrey, *Dragonsdawn*, 1988
James H. Schmitz, *The Demon Breed*, 1968
John Varley, *Titan*, 1979

1902

SIMON R. GREEN

Mistworld

(New York: Ace, 1992)

Story type: Science Fiction (Adventure; Mystery)
Series: Mistworld
Major character(s): Topaz, Psychic, Martial Arts Expert (assassin); Leon Vertue, Doctor (Criminal); Cat, Thief, Handicapped (deaf-mute)
Time period(s): Indeterminate Future
Locale(s): Mistworld, Planet—Imaginary; Empire, Interstellar Empire/Federation

Summary: A mysterious refugee carries plague onto Mistworld, killing and mindwiping thousands of people. When Topaz vows to uncover any Empire plotting, the nearly lethal investigation proves complicated since all knowledgeable parties died by murder.

Other books you might like:
Marion Zimmer Bradley, *The World Wreckers*, 1971
Cheryl J. Franklin, *The Light of Exile*, 1990
Katharine Kerr, *Polar City Blues*, 1990
Andre Norton, *Judgment on Janus*, 1963
Sydney J. Van Scyoc, *Cloudcry*, 1977

1903

SIMON R. GREEN

Shadows Fall

(New York: Roc, 1994)

Story type: Fantasy (Science Fiction; Religious)
Major character(s): Leanard Ash, Reanimated Dead; Rhea Frazier, Political Figure; Richard Erickson, Lawman (sheriff)
Time period(s): Indeterminate Future
Locale(s): Shadows Fall, Fictional City

Summary: Hoping to find something or someone they lost, many people journey to the last vestige of the fairy realm on Earth, Shadows Fall, a city containing the Forever Door which beckons to dying people and the deceased who refuse to leave the realm of the living. The town begins to panic as murders, previously unknown, proliferate. However, an invasion by the Warriors of the Cross brings greater disaster.

Other books you might like:
Emma Bull, *Finder*, 1994
Will Shetterly, *Elsewhere*, 1991
Will Shetterly, *Nevernever*, 1993
Terri Windling, *Bordertown*, 1986
   Mark Alan Arnold, co-editor
Terri Windling, *Life on the Border*, 1991
   editor

1904

SIMON R. GREEN

Winner Takes All

(New York: Ace, 1991)

Story type: Fantasy (Mystery)
Series: Hawk & Fisher
Major character(s): Isobel Fisher, Police Officer (captain); Hawk, Police Officer (captain)
Time period(s): Indeterminate Past
Locale(s): Haven, Fictional City

Summary: Captains Hawk and Fisher are assigned to guard the Reform candidate in the last days before the city elections, always an occasion for confrontations, corruption and general craziness. When the Reform campaign is beset by embezzlement, magical attack, betrayal and armed assault by the most feared mercenary leader in the countryside, Hawk and Fisher struggle to keep the candidate alive.

Other books you might like:
Robert Asprin, *Thieves' World*, 1979
   editor
Glen Cook, *Sweet Silver Blues*, 1987
Robert A. Heinlein, *Double Star*, 1956
Lee Killough, *Spider Play*, 1986
Katherine Kurtz, *The Adept*, 1991
   Deborah Turner Harris, co-author
Mercedes Lackey, *Burning Water*, 1989
Mickey Zucker Reichert, *Godslayer*, 1987

1905

SIMON R. GREEN

Wolf in the Fold

(New York: Ace, 1991)

Story type: Fantasy (Mystery; Urban)
Series: Hawk & Fisher
Major character(s): Isobel Fisher, Police Officer (captain); Hawk, Police Officer (captain)
Time period(s): Indeterminate Past
Locale(s): Haven, Fictional City

Summary: There's a spy loose in Haven and he's even managed to get away from Hawk and Fisher and slip into the MacNeil family citadel. Since Hawk and Fisher are the only ones to have seen him, they are ordered in after him, knowing the assignment will be denied if they are caught impersonating Quality, a capital offense in Haven.

Other books you might like:
Robert Asprin, *Thieves' World*, 1979
   editor
Glen Cook, *Sweet Silver Blues*, 1987
Tanya Huff, *Blood Price*, 1991
Anne Logston, *Shadow*, 1991
J.F. Rivkin, *Silverglass*, 1986
Will Shetterly, *Liavek*, 1985
   Emma Bull, co-editor

1906

MARTIN H. GREENBERG, Editor

After the King: Stories in Honor of J.R.R. Tolkien

(New York: Tor, 1992)

Story type: Fantasy (Anthology)

Summary: Includes a three-page introduction by Jane Yolen, and a two-page biography of contributors plus 19 stories by 20 authors asked to write a Tolkienesque story, but not an imitation Tolkien story, in honor of the author who richly influenced fantasy fiction. Poul Anderson and Karen Anderson collaborated on one story. Other authors include Peter S. Beagle, John Brunner, Emma Bull, Charles de Lint, Stephen R. Donaldson, Patricia A. McKillip, Andre Norton, Terry Pratchett, Elizabeth Ann Scarborough, Robert Silverberg, Judith Tarr, Harry Turtledove and Jane Yolen.

Other books you might like:
Lin Carter, *Dragons, Elves and Heroes*, 1969
   editor
Lester del Rey, *Once upon a Time: A Treasury of Modern Fairy Tales*, 1991
   Risa Kessler, co-editor
Baird Searles, *Halflings, Hobbits, Warrows & Weefolk: A Collection of Tales of Heroes Short in Stature*, 1991
   Brian Thomsen, co-editor
J.R.R. Tolkien, *The Fellowship of the Ring*, 1954
J.R.R. Tolkien, *The Hobbit*, 1938
J.R.R. Tolkien, *The Return of the King*, 1956
J.R.R. Tolkien, *The Two Towers*, 1955

Terri Windling, *Life on the Border*, 1991
  editor

1907

MARTIN H. GREENBERG, Editor
CHARLES G. WAUGH, Co-Editor

Back From the Dead

(New York: DAW Books, 1991)

Story type: Horror (Anthology)

Summary: Twenty-one stories about people or things that come back from the dead. Included are H.P. Lovecraft's Poe pastiche, "The Outsider," Poe's masterpiece of possession and haunting, "Ligeia," Edith Wharton's subtle ghost story, "Afterward," Theodore Sturgeon's tale of a muck monster, "It," Robert Bloch's voodoo story, "Mother of Serpents," and Washington Irving's story of demonic resuscitation, "The Adventure of the German Student."

Other books you might like:
Peter Haining, *Stories of the Walking Dead*, 1985
Hugh Lamb, *Return From the Grave*, 1976
John Skipp, *Book of the Dead*, 1989
  Craig Spector, co-author

1908

MARTIN H. GREENBERG, Editor

Celebrity Vampires

(New York: DAW, 1995)

Story type: Horror (Anthology; Vampire Story)

Summary: The nineteen stories original to this volume all present famed celebrities as vampires, or involved with vampires. In "Undead Origami," Norman Partridge likens Howard Hughes' business tactics to a vampire's voracious practices, and in "I Vant to Be Alone," Barb D'Amato attributes Greta Garbo's timeless beauty to her deathless vampirism. J.N. Williamson sees the original spirit of Vlad Tepes in Vladimir Nikolai Lenin, the protagonist of "Vladimir's Conversions," while John Lutz imagines vampires playing a role in Carrie Nation's intemperate fight for temperance in "Plague." Vampirism mixes with writing in several stories: Kristine Kathryn Rusch's "The Beautiful and the Damned" features F. Scott Fitzgerald, Roman A. Ranieri's "A Singular Event on a Night in 1912," both Bram Stoker and Sir Arthur Conan Doyle, and Wendi Lee and Terry Beatty's "Death on the Mississippi," Mark Twain. In P.N. Elrod's "A Night at the (Horse) Opera," a vampire detective helps one of the Marx brothers out of a gambling debt.

Other books you might like:
Jean Stine, *I, Vampire: Interviews with the Undead*, 1995
  Forrest J. Ackerman, co-editor
Stephen Jones, *The Mammoth Book of Vampires*, 1993
  editor
Alan Ryan, *Vampires: Two Centuries of Great Vampire Stories*, 1987
  editor

1909

MARTIN H. GREENBERG, Editor
FRANK D. MCSHERRY JR., Co-Editor
CHARLES G. WAUGH, Co-Editor

Civil War Ghosts

(Little Rock, Arkansas: August House, 1991)

Story type: Horror (Anthology; Ghost Story)

Summary: Eight tales of ghosts and hauntings connected with the American Civil War. Included are Ambrose Bierce's classic hallucinatory tale, "An Occurrence at Owl Creek Bridge," Manly Wade Wellman's short occult novel of two Union soldiers who struggle to save a girl's soul, "Fearful Rock," and two tales of ghostly revenge, John Jakes' "Miranda" and Dan Simmons' "Iverson's Pits."

Other books you might like:
Marvin Kaye, *Haunted America*, 1990

1910

MARTIN H. GREENBERG
CHARLES G. WAUGH, Co-Author

Devil Worshippers

(New York: DAW, 1990)

Story type: Horror (Anthology)

Summary: Fifteen stories of demons and those foolish enough to summon them. Included are Nathaniel Hawthorne's classic of dark minds and hearts, "Young Goodman Browne," Robert Bloch's tale of teenage rebels with a satanic cause, "Sweet Sixteen," Charles Beaumont's suburban horror story, "The New People," and Anthony Boucher's amusing account of a werewolf professor recruited to fight spies, "The Compleat Werewolf."

Other books you might like:
Peter Haining, *The Black Magic Omnibus*, 1976
Peter Haining, *The Evil People*, 1968
Michel Parry, *Great Black Magic Stories*, 1977
Rod Serling, *Devils and Demons*, 1967

1911

MARTIN H. GREENBERG, Editor

Dinosaurs

(New York: Donald I. Fine Books, 1996)

Story type: Science Fiction (Anthology)

Summary: Contains a four-page introduction by Robert Silverberg, seven pages of authors' biographies, and 14 stories published 1950-1994 in periodicals and anthologies. Themes include time travel, criminal justice, entropy, metamorphosis, and nanotechnology; authors include Poul Anderson, Isaac Asimov, Ray Bradbury, Pat Cadigan, Arthur C. Clarke, L. Sprague de Camp, Kristine Kathryn Rusch, Michelle Sagara, Robert J. Sawyer, Robert Silverberg, Harry Turtledove, and Howard Waldrop.

Other books you might like:
Robert T. Bakker, *Raptor Red*, 1995
Jack Dann, *Dinosaurs!*, 1990
    Gardner Dozois, co-editor
Jack Dann, *Dinosaurs II*, 1995
    Gardner Dozois, co-editor
James Gurney, *Dinotopia*, 1992
Mike Resnick, *Dinosaur Fantastic*, 1993
    Martin H. Greenberg, co-editor
Robert J. Sawyer, *Far-Seer*, 1992

1912

MARTIN H. GREENBERG, Editor
ED GORMAN, Co-Editor

Dracula: Prince of Darkness
(New York: DAW, 1992)

Story type: Horror (Anthology; Vampire Story)

Summary: Timed to coincide with the release of Francis Ford Coppola's film adaptation of Bram Stoker's *Dracula* (1897), this anthology collects 15 original stories, most of which involve Dracula himself as a character. Included are F. Paul Wilson's tale of vampires overrunning the world, "The Lord's Work," Daniel Ransom's (a.k.a. Ed Gorman's) hardboiled vampire story, "Night Cries," and W. R. Philbrick's "The Cure," in which vampirism is presented as a last resort cure for the terminally ill. There are also stories by Brian Hodge, P. N. Elrod, Richard Laymon and John Shirley.

Other books you might like:
Richard Dalby, *Dracula's Brood*, 1987
Ellen Datlow, *Blood Is Not Enough*, 1989
    editor
Ellen Datlow, *A Whisper of Blood*, 1991
    editor
Robert R. McCammon, *Under the Fang*, 1991
    editor
Byron Preiss, *The Ultimate Dracula*, 1991
    editor

1913

MARTIN H. GREENBERG, Editor

The Fantastic Adventures of Robin Hood
(New York: Signet, 1991)

Story type: Fantasy (Anthology; Legend)
Major character(s): Robin Hood, Outlaw, Hero

Summary: The 13 original stories feature Robin Hood and his merry men in settings both on and off Earth. Stories range from fantasy, science fiction and horror to mystery. Authors include Nancy A. Collins, Matthew Costello, George Alec Effinger, Clayton Emery, Ed Gorman, Mike Resnick, Elizabeth Ann Scarborough, Midori Snyder and Steve Rasnic Tem.

Other books you might like:
C.J. Cherryh, *Cyteen*, 1988
Clayton Emery, *Tales of Robin Hood*, 1988
Parke Godwin, *Sherwood*, 1991
Robin McKinley, *The Outlaws of Sherwood*, 1988

Bernard Miles, *Robin Hood: His Life and Legend*, 1979
Howard Pyle, *The Merry Adventures of Robin Hood*, 1883
William F. Wu, *The Robin Hood Ambush*, 1990

1914

MARTIN H. GREENBERG, Editor

Frankenstein: The Monster Wakes
(New York: DAW, 1993)

Story type: Horror (Anthology)

Summary: The 18 contributors to this volume each supply a variation on the Frankenstein theme. In Rex Miller's "I've Got Hugh Under My Skin," a latter-day descendant of Victor Frankenstein keeps the old family business going, while in Richard T. Chizmar's "Bride of Frankenstein: A Modern Love Story" and Mike Baker's "Role Model," unbalanced readers of Mary Shelley's novel identify too closely with its namesake. Matthew J. Costello in "My Coney Island Baby," Terry Beatty and Wendy Lee in "Special Effects," and Brian Hodge in "A Loaf of Bread, A Jug of Wine" all resurrect Frankenstein's monster, while Norman Partridge, in "The Man with the Barbed-Wire Fists," takes a highly inventive approach to the idea of the making of a man.

Other books you might like:
Michel Parry, *Rivals of Frankenstein*, 1977
    editor
Byron Preiss, *The Ultimate Frankenstein*, 1991
    John Betancourt, co-editor

1915

MARTIN H. GREENBERG, Editor

The Further Adventures of Batman 2:
Featuring the Penguin
(New York: Bantam Spectra, 1992)

Story type: Science Fiction (Adventure; Anthology)
Series: Batman
Major character(s): Bruce "Batman" Wayne, Hero, Detective—Amateur; Oswald "the Penguin" Cobblepot, Criminal
Time period(s): 1990s
Locale(s): Gotham City (New York City); United States; Mexico

Summary: Contains eleven stories featuring Batman and his archenemy, the Penguin. Laurie Sefton and Charles Von Rospach collaborated on one story, "Going Straight." Other authors include John Gregory Betancourt, Max Allan Collins, Nancy A. Collins, Will Murray, William F. Nolan, Kristine Kathryn Rusch, Steve Rasnic Tem, and Brian M. Thomsen.

Other books you might like:
Lynn Abbey, *Catwoman*, 1992
    Robert Asprin, co-author
Craig Shaw Gardner, *Batman*, 1989
Craig Shaw Gardner, *The Batman Murders*, 1990
Craig Shaw Gardner, *Batman Returns*, 1992
Simon Hawke, *Batman: To Stalk a Specter*, 1991
Joe R. Lansdale, *Batman: Captured by the Engines*, 1991

1916

MARTIN H. GREENBERG, Editor

The Further Adventures of Batman 3: Featuring Catwoman
(New York: Bantam, 1993)

Story type: Science Fiction (Anthology; Adventure)
Series: Batman
Major character(s): Selena "Catwoman" Kyle, Criminal, Heroine; Bruce "Batman" Wayne, Hero, Detective— Amateur
Time period(s): 1990s
Locale(s): Gotham City (New York City)

Summary: Contains 13 original stories, many dark in tone, about Batman and his seductive nemesis, Catwoman. Authors include John Gregory Betancourt, Mort Castle, Ed Gorman, Will Murray, Jeff Rovin, Kristine Kathryn Rusch, Brian M. Thomsen and Robert Weinberg.

Other books you might like:
Lynn Abbey, *Catwoman*, 1992
    Robert Asprin, co-author
Craig Shaw Gardner, *Batman*, 1989
Craig Shaw Gardner, *The Batman Murders*, 1990
Craig Shaw Gardner, *Batman Returns*, 1992
Simon Hawke, *Batman: To Stalk a Specter*, 1991
Joe R. Lansdale, *Captured by the Engines*, 1991

1917

MARTIN H. GREENBERG, Editor

The Further Adventures of Superman
(New York: Bantam, 1993)

Story type: Science Fiction (Anthology)
Series: Superman
Major character(s): Clark "Superman" Kent, Journalist, Alien (Kryptonian)
Time period(s): 1990s; Indeterminate Past
Locale(s): Metropolis (New York City)

Summary: Contains a prologue and epilogue by Dave Gibbons plus 10 original stories about the "man of steel." Authors include Diane Duane, Karen Haber, Will Murray, Garfield Reeves-Stevens, Mike Resnick and Henry Slesar.

Other books you might like:
Michael Bishop, *Count Geiger's Blues*, 1992
William Borden, *Superstoe*, 1968
John Brunner, *Polymath*, 1974
Elliot S. Maggin, *Superman: Last Son of Krypton*, 1978
Elliot S. Maggin, *Superman: Miracle Monday*, 1981
Roger Stern, *The Death and Life of Superman*, 1993

1918

MARTIN H. GREENBERG, Editor
LARRY SEGRIFF, Co-Editor

Future Net
(New York: DAW, 1996)

Story type: Science Fiction (Anthology; Hard Science Fiction)
Summary: Contains a two-page introduction and brief biographical introductions to authors of the 16 original stories focusing on computer virtual reality. Themes include artificial intelligences, future chatrooms, alternate worlds, invasion of Earth, and life after death with stories varying in tone from whimsical to ominous. Authors include Robin Wayne Bailey, Gregory Benford, Matthew Costello, John DeChancie, Jane Lindskold, Wil McCarthy, Jody Lynn Nye, Mickey Zucker Reichert, and Josepha Sherman.

Other books you might like:
Raphael Carter, *The Fortunate Fall*, 1996
Jack Dann, *Hackers*, 1996
    Gardner Dozois, co-editor
Elton Elliott, *Nanodreams*, 1995
    editor
Karie Jacobson, *Simulations*, 1993
    editor
Neal Stephenson, *Snow Crash*, 1992
Bruce Sterling, *Mirrorshades: The Cyberpunk Anthology*, 1986
    editor
Sage Walker, *Whiteout*, 1996

1919

MARTIN H. GREENBERG, Editor
JILL MORGAN, Illustrator
ROBERT WEINBERG, Illustrator
GAHAN WILSON, Illustrator

Great Writers and Kids Write Spooky Stories
(New York: Random House, 1995)

Story type: Horror (Anthology)
Summary: For this collection of young adult horror stories, the authors asked 13 renowned writers of fantasy and horror to collaborate with their children or grandchildren on a horror story. Peter and Benjamin Straub, in "In Transit," tell the story of a father and son with a dark secret who are forced to prey on the local bullies. Ramsey, Tammy, and Matt Campbell offer a story of children trapped in a shrubbery maze by beings who want to steal their identities. F. Paul Wilson and Meggan C. Wilson supply a story about the fear of spiders, and Ric, Jesse, and Matti Hautala tell a tale of alien invasion. Joe, Keith, and Kasey Jo Lansdale have written an eerie story of a vampire scarecrow brought to life. Gahan Wilson supplies an introduction and the illustrations.

Other books you might like:
A. Finnis, *13 Again*, 1995
Anthony Horowitz, *The Puffin Book of Horror Stories*, 1994
T. Pines, *Thirteen*, 1991

T. Pines, *13 Tales of Horror*, 1994

1920

MARTIN H. GREENBERG, Editor
ROSALIND M. GREENBERG, Co-Editor

Horse Fantastic
(New York: DAW, 1991)

Story type: Fantasy (Anthology)

Summary: This volume contains a four-page introduction by Jennifer Roberson plus 17 original stories featuring horses in fantasy situations. Contributors include Constance Ash, Mercedes Lackey, Elizabeth Moon, Mickey Zucker Reichert, Mike Resnick, Jennifer Roberson, Josepha Sherman, Mary Stanton, Judith Tarr and Janny Wurtz.

Other books you might like:
Robert Adams, *The Coming of the Horseclans*, 1982
Constance Ash, *The Horsegirl*, 1988
Constance Ash, *The Stalking Horse*, 1990
Jack Dann, *Unicorns!*, 1982
  Gardner Dozois, co-editor
Mary H. Herbert, *Dark Horse*, 1990
Mary H. Herbert, *Lightning's Daughter*, 1991
Peter Morwood, *The Horse Lord*, 1987
Mary Stanton, *The Heavenly Horse From the Outermost West*, 1988
Mary Stanton, *Piper at the Gate*, 1989

1921

MARTIN H. GREENBERG, Editor
ROBERT WEINBERG, Co-Editor

Miskatonic University
(New York: DAW, 1996)

Story type: Horror (Anthology)

Summary: The 13 original stories collected here are all set on the campus of Miskatonic University, a locale created by H.P. Lovecraft and renowned as a battleground where ancient superstitions and modern scientific enlightenment collide. Alan Rodgers' "Her Misbegotten Son," about forces of black magic that overwhelm a professor's family, is a semi-sequel to Lovecraft's "Dreams in the Witch House" and "The Dunwich Horror," while Jane M. Lindskold's "A Dreaming of Dead Poets" extrapolates the plot of Lovecraft's "The Call of Cthulhu" in a tale of students who discover their artistic talents have made them sensitive to forces engaged in an occult conspiracy. Jay Bonansinga's "Black Celebration" and Benjamin Adams' "Second Movement" both feature musicians who tap into the school's latent reserves of dark power, and Stephen Mark Rainey's "To Be as They" an art student whose paintings access another dimension. Will Murray's "Sothis Radiant" reveals that the campus astronomy department knows more about the impending end of the world than it will say.

Other books you might like:
Edward P. Berglund, *Disciples of Cthulhu*, 1976
  editor

Lin Carter, *The Spawn of Cthulhu*, 1971
  editor
Robert M. Price, *The Arkham Cycle*, 1996
  editor
Robert M. Price, *The Dunwich Cycle*, 1995
  editor
Thomas M.K. Stratman, *Cthulhu's Heirs*, 1994
  editor

1922

MARTIN H. GREENBERG

Mummy Stories
(New York: Ballantine, 1990)

Story type: Horror (Anthology; Reanimated Dead)

Summary: Fourteen stories about mummies, five original to this volume. The selections range in tone from the whimsical (Edgar Allan Poe's "Some Words with a Mummy," Sharon McCrumb's "Remains to Be Seen") to the weird (E.F. Benson's "Monkeys," Sir Arthur Conan Doyle's "Lot 249") to the utterly gruesome (Donald Wollheim's "Bones," Robert Bloch's "Beetles").

Other books you might like:
Bill Pronzini, *Mummy!*, 1980

1923

MARTIN H. GREENBERG, Editor

New Stories From the Twilight Zone
(New York: Avon, 1991)

Story type: Horror (Anthology)

Summary: Twenty-one tales of fantasy, horror and science fiction, originally written for publication but adapted for the briefly revived television program. Stories range in scope from Arthur C. Clarke's "The Star," about an amazing archaeological find on a planet about to be consumed by a supernova, to Harlan Ellison's intimate "Shatterday," about a man so out of touch with the world around him he begins to dematerialize. There is humor (Theodore Sturgeon's "Yesterday Was Monday"), horror (Robert R. McCammon's "Nightcrawlers") and a *conte cruel* (Richard Matheson's "Button, Button") to suit every taste.

Other books you might like:
Mitchell Galen, *Tales from the Darkside, Volume 1*, 1989
  Tom Allen, co-editor
Rod Serling, *The Night Gallery Reader*, 1990
Rod Serling, *Stories From the Twilight Zone*, 1990
J. Michael Straczynski, *Tales From the New Twilight Zone*, 1989
John Tigges, *Kevin Browne's Nightales*, 1990

1924

MARTIN H. GREENBERG, Editor

Nightmares on Elm Street: Freddy Krueger's Seven Sweetest Dreams
(New York: St. Martin's, 1991)

Story type: Horror (Anthology)

Summary: The seven original stories in this book revolve around the character of Freddy Krueger, child murderer of Wes Craven's *Nightmare on Elm Street* film saga, who was burned to death by a vigilante squad of concerned parents but continues to haunt and kill the children of Elm Street through their dreams. Included are Brian Hodge's "Asleep at the Wheel," in which Freddy insinuates himself into the career dreams of a rock band named after one of his victims; Wayne Allen Sallee's "Close My Eyes and I'll Kiss You," in which Freddy visits a prisoner on death row; Nancy Collins' "Not Just a Job," in which Freddy trains the child of a mass murderer to emulate his father; and Tom Elliott's "Briefcase Full of Blues," in which Freddy meets his match at the hands of his daughter.

Other books you might like:
Mitchell Galen, *Tales from the Darkside, Volume 1*, 1989
   Tom Allen, co-author
Jack Oleck, *Tales from the Crypt*, 1972
Rod Serling, *The Night Gallery Reader*, 1990
J. Michael Straczynski, *Tales From the New Twilight Zone*, 1989

1925

MARTIN H. GREENBERG, Editor

The Super Hugos
(New York: Baen, 1992)

Story type: Science Fiction (Anthology)

Summary: Charles Sheffield provides a four-page introduction and introductions to 10 individual stories, all voted best among previous Hugo Award winning stories by members of the 1992 World Science Fiction Convention, MagiCon. This anthology contains two stories by Harlan Ellison, "Repent, Harlequin!' Said the Ticktockman" and "I Have No Mouth, and I Must Scream," and two stories which inspired films, Daniel Keyes' "Flowers for Algernon" (*Charly*) and Barry B. Longyear's "Enemy Mine" (*Enemy Mine*). Other favorite Hugo winners included Isaac Asimov's "The Bicentennial Man," Arthur C. Clarke's "The Star," George R. R. Martin's "Sandkings," Anne McCaffrey's "Weyr Search," Larry Niven's "Neutron Star" and Clifford D. Simak's "The Big Front Yard." Concludes with a 10-page article by Joe Siclari and Edie Stern, "About the Super Hugo Voting," and a 12-page appendix listing Hugo Award winners.

Other books you might like:
Isaac Asimov, *The Hugo Winners 1-5*, 1962-1986
   editor
Isaac Asimov, *The New Hugo Winners*, 1989
   editor

Raymond J. Healy, *Adventures in Time and Space*, 1946
   J. Francis McComas, co-editor
Richard A. Lupoff, *What If? Stories That Should Have Won the Hugo*, 1980
   editor
Leo Margulies, *My Best Science Fiction Story*, 1949
   O. J. Friend, co-editor
Robert Silverberg, *The Science Fiction Hall of Fame, Volume 1*, 1970
   editor

1926

MARTIN H. GREENBERG, Editor
STEFAN R. DZIEMIANOWICZ, Co-Editor
ROBERT WEINBERG, Co-Editor

A Taste for Blood
(New York: Dorset, 1992)

Story type: Horror (Anthology; Vampire Story)

Summary: Fifteen vampire stories and novellas that span the last 125 years of horror publishing. Included are J. Sheridan Le Fanu's influential "Carmilla," Hugh B. Cave's pulp classic, "Murgunstrumm," H. P. Lovecraft's fusion of the vampire and haunted house story, "The Shunned House," Karl Edward Wagner's mix of the ghost and vampire story, "Beyond Any Measure," Thomas Ligotti's tale of the offspring of vampire and mortal parents, "The Lost Art of Twilight," and Patrick McGrath's black humor sketch, "Blood Disease."

Other books you might like:
Alan Ryan, *Vampires: Two Centuries of Great Vampire Stories*, 1987
Leslie Shepard, *The Dracula Book of Great Vampire Stories*, 1977
   editor
Devendra P. Varma, *Voices From the Vault: Authentic Vampire Tales*, 1987
   editor

1927

MARTIN H. GREENBERG, Editor

Vampire Detectives
(New York: DAW, 1995)

Story type: Horror (Anthology; Vampire Story)

Summary: The nineteen stories commissioned for this anthology feature vampire detectives or vampire crime perpetrators. In William F. Nolan's "Vampire Dollars," a detective becomes entangled in a black-mail murder case involving a former starlet of vampire films. William Sanders' "The Count's Mailbox" uses an exchange of letters to tell of a vampire's unsuccessful attempts to market a vampire novel and the drastic measures he resorts to. Jack Kethcum's "The Turning" and Wayne Allen Sallee's "Blind Pig on North Halsted" are both urban horror tales that find analogies between different types of criminal activity and vampirism. And in Richard Laymon's "Phil the Vampire," a private detective must decide whether a woman who complains her husband is a vampire is telling the truth, or merely hopeful that she can gull him into killing her abusive spouse.

Other books you might like:

Jean Stine, *I, Vampire: Interviews with the Undead*, 1995
   Forrest J. Ackerman, co-editor

Stephen Jones, *The Mammoth Book of Vampires*, 1993
   editor

Alan Ryan, *Vampires: Two Centuries of Great Vampire Stories*, 1987

1928

MARTIN H. GREENBERG, Editor

Werewolves
(New York: DAW, 1995)

Story type: Horror (Anthology; Werewolf Story)

Summary: Twenty-two stories original to this volume approach the werewolf theme from a variety of angles. Brian Hodge draws parallels between werewolves and the street children of South America in "Extinctions in Paradise." Max Allan Collins' "Wolf" features a gigolo who preys on young women, while Nina Kiriki Hoffman's "Dumpster Diving" tells of the nurturing relationship between a young woman and a foundling baby werewolf. Mike Baker's "Bark at the Moon" and Matt Costello's "Nick of Time" find werewolves lurking beneath the surface of daily life in the city, and Hugh Cave's "Nights in the Mountains of Haiti" in a more exotic locale. Norman Partridge's "The Pack" is a brilliant anti-werewolf tale that uses a pack of motorcycle hoodlums to undermine reader expectations for an expression of the beast within.

Other books you might like:

Greg Cox, *Tomorrow Bites*, 1995
   T.K.F. Weiskopf, co-editor

Brian J. Frost, *Book of the Werewolf*, 1973

David Hill, *The Way of the Werewolf*, 1966
   editor

Stephen Jones, *The Mammoth Book of Werewolves*, 1994
   editor

Byron Preiss, *The Ultimate Werewolf*, 1992
   editor

Bill Pronzini, *Werewolf!*, 1979
   editor

1929

MARTIN H. GREENBERG, Editor

White House Horrors
(New York: DAW, 1996)

Story type: Horror (Anthology)

Summary: Sixteen original stories feature the White House and the presidency as elements of their horror themes. Brian Hodge's "Healing the Body Politic" concerns a secret service agent who discovers that the White House and other world governments are run by secret occult societies. Richard T. Chizmar's "Homesick" is about a child of the Chief Executive moved to express his resentment at being wrenched

out of his former way of life. Edward Lee's "Night of the Vegetables" features one inept president's handling of a national crisis spawned by nuclear woes. Stories that feature specific presidents include Barbara Collins and Max Allan Collins' "The Cabinet of William Henry Harrison," Bill Crider's "The Ghost and Mr. Truman," Graham Masterton's "Jack Be Quick" (John F. Kennedy), and Kein Stein and Robert Weinberg's "Release," based on the apocryphal tale that William McKinley foresaw his assassination.

Other books you might like:

Mike Resnick, *Alternate Kennedys*, 1992
   editor

Mike Resnick, *Alternate Presidents*, 1992
   editor

1930

ROSALIND M. GREENBERG, Editor
MARTIN H. GREENBERG, Co-Editor

Christmas Bestiary
(New York: DAW, 1992)

Story type: Fantasy (Anthology)

Summary: Contains an eight-page introduction by Stefan Dziemianowicz plus 19 original stories with Christmas themes all featuring legendary creatures such as selkies, sea serpents, elves, pixies, a yeti and a blue-nosed reindeer. Authors include Mark Aronson, Karen Haber, Jack C. Haldeman II, Tanya Huff, Barry N. Malzberg, Mike Resnick, Jennifer Roberson, Kristine Kathryn Rusch, Elizabeth Scarborough, Harry Turtledove and Jane Yolen.

Other books you might like:

Alan Brennert, *Kindred Spirits*, 1984

Martin H. Greenberg, *Christmas on Ganymede and Other Stories*, 1990
   editor

David G. Hartwell, *Christmas Stars*, 1992
   editor

Kristine Kathryn Rusch, *Pulphouse, Issue 10: Special Issue*, 1991
   editor

John Silbersack, *The Magic of Christmas*, 1992
   Christopher Schelling, co-editor

Gene Wolfe, *Gene Wolfe's Book of Days*, 1981

1931

ROSALIND M. GREENBERG, Editor
MARTIN H. GREENBERG, Co-Editor

Dragon Fantastic
(New York: DAW, 1992)

Story type: Fantasy (Anthology; Legend)

Summary: Contains an eight-page introduction by Tad Williams plus 16 original stories with diverse approaches to the theme, dragons. Mark A. Kreighbaum and Dennis L. McKiernan collaborated on "Straw into Gold: Part II." Other authors include Ruth Berman, Alan Dean Foster, Esther M. Friesner, Karen Haber, Tanya Huff, Barry N. Malzberg,

Mickey Zucker Reichert, Mike Resnick and Josepha Sherman.

Other books you might like:
Poul Anderson, *The Night Fantastic*, 1991
    Karen Anderson, co-editor
Orson Scott Card, *Dragons of Darkness*, 1981
    Editor
Orson Scott Card, *Dragons of Light*, 1980
    Editor
Alan Dean Foster, *Smart Dragons, Foolish Elves*, 1991
    Editor
Andre Norton, *Catfantastic*, 1989
    Martin H. Greenberg, co-editor
Andre Norton, *Catfantastic II*, 1991
    Martin H. Greenberg, co-editor
Patricia C. Wrede, *Dealing with Dragons*, 1990

1932

KIRBY GREENE

Brotherhood of the Stars

(New York: Bantam Spectra, 1994)

Story type: Science Fiction (Space Opera; Adventure)
Major character(s): Ree Barzac, Spaceman; Erpad Ystilog, Museum Curator; Zigmunn, Spaceman, Exile
Time period(s): Indeterminate Future
Locale(s): Glaurus, Planet—Imaginary; Azonda, Planet—Imaginary

Summary: Ree Barzac comes to Glaurus where, 10 years earlier, his blood brother was marooned. When he learns that Zigmunn has joined a cult and gone to Azonda, Barzac tries to follow, but disaster leads to enslavement. To secure freedom, he must join the cult.

Other books you might like:
Jim Aikin, *Walk the Moon's Road*, 1985
Johanna Bolton, *Mission: Tori*, 1990
Leigh Brackett, *The Sword of Rhiannon*, 1953
Marion Zimmer Bradley, *The Door through Space*, 1961
John Brunner, *The Rites of Ohe*, 1963
Lin Carter, *The City Outside the World*, 1977
Philip Jose Farmer, *The Green Odyssey*, 1956
Simon R. Green, *Mistworld*, 1992
Harry Harrison, *Planet of the Damned*, 1962
Sydney J. Van Scyoc, *Assignment: Nor'Dyren*, 1973
Jack Vance, *Trullion: Alastor 2262*, 1973

1933

KEN GREENHALL

Deathchain

(New York: Pocket, 1991)

Story type: Horror (Psychological Suspense)
Major character(s): Paul Marnay, Artist (painter); Hillary Block, Social Worker (psychotherapist); Phyllis Arno, Actress
Time period(s): 1990s
Locale(s): Dale Falls, New York

Summary: One by one, the residents of Dale Falls begin murdering one another at the behest of the Chainmaster, an anonymous letter writer whose chain letter promises the disposal of someone they want eliminated if they themselves will commit a murder. When Paul Marnay stumbles upon the pattern behind the deaths, he becomes a murder target, and must not only determine the identity of the Chainmaster but also find out who among his acquaintances might wish him dead.

Other books you might like:
Ramsey Campbell, *Obsession*, 1986
Patricia Highsmith, *Strangers on a Train*, 1950
Ruby Jean Jensen, *Chain Letter*, 1987

1934

COLIN GREENLAND

Harm's Way

(New York: AvoNova, 1993)

Story type: Science Fiction (Adventure; Alternate Universe)
Major character(s): Sophie Farthing, Runaway, Heiress—Lost; Jacob Farthing, Parent, Security Officer; Bruno, Mercenary (assassin)
Time period(s): Indeterminate
Locale(s): High Haven, Space Station; Mars

Summary: Following an encounter with a mysterious stranger who claims to have known her mother, Sophie runs away from her home on High Haven. Her search for her mother leads her to the Moon, outpost of the British Empire and to London, the capital. Disguised as a boy, she works her passage to Mars as a cabin boy on one of the ships that sail the tides of aether between the worlds. Barely escaping death as a sacrifice to the Black God of Mars, she lives for a time among the half-wild Martian converts at a French mission in the desert, until the man sent to kill her offers her instead a chance to discover hidden talents and the truth about her parentage.

Other books you might like:
Ray Bradbury, *The Martian Chronicles*, 1950
Edgar Rice Burroughs, *The Gods of Mars*, 1918
C.J. Cherryh, *Cuckoo's Egg*, 1985
Robert A. Heinlein, *Podkayne of Mars*, 1963
C.S. Lewis, *Out of the Silent Planet*, 1965
Anne McCaffrey, *The Rowan*, 1990
William Sanders, *The Wild Blue and the Gray*, 1991

1935

COLIN GREENLAND

Seasons of Plenty

(New York: AvoNova, 1996)

Story type: Science Fiction (Adventure)
Series: Plenty
Major character(s): Tabitha Jute, Pilot, Leader; Saskia Zodiac, Clone, Magician (stage); Xtasca the Cherub, Genetically Altered Being
Time period(s): Indeterminate Future
Locale(s): *Plenty*, Spaceship

Summary: Tabitha Jute and her stolen spaceship, loaded with criminals, renegades, and many odd things, set course for the star Proxima Centauri. The situation deteriorates as different factions maneuver for power and plots multiply. When a "cybermessiah" appears, maybe a devil and maybe an angel, life aboard *Plenty* gets weirder. Second in a trilogy.

Other books you might like:
Glen Cook, *The Dragon Never Sleeps*, 1988
Bradley Denton, *Buddy Holly Is Alive and Well on Ganymede*, 1991
Robert A. Heinlein, *Podkayne of Mars*, 1963
Damon Knight, *Why Do Birds*, 1992

1936
COLIN GREENLAND

Take Back Plenty
(New York: Avon, 1992)

Story type: Science Fiction (Adventure; Alternate Intelligence)
Major character(s): Alice Liddell, Artificial Intelligence (Spaceship); Tabitha Jute, Spaceship Captain; Hannah Soo, Financier, Reanimated Dead (cryogenically interred)
Time period(s): 23rd century
Locale(s): Schiaparelli Luna, Moon (Earth's); Plenty, Space Station; Spaceship

Summary: The Capellans, having given us the space drive, demonstrated their superiority and limited humanity to our solar system. Tabitha Jute, trying to find replacement parts for her well-built but ancient ship, finds herself involved with a traveling nightclub act. The troupe includes several genetically altered humans and an alien or two. Trying to get payment so she can repair her ship, Tabitha finds herself part of the hidden agenda of Hannah Soo, the troupe's agent and financier. This book won both the Arthur C. Clarke Award and the British Science Fiction Association Award for the Best SF Novel of the year when published in England in 1990.

Other books you might like:
David Brin, *Startide Rising*, 1983
Octavia E. Butler, *Dawn*, 1987
Arthur C. Clarke, *The Garden of Rama*, 1991
    Gentry Lee, co-author
Glen Cook, *The Dragon Never Sleeps*, 1988
Anne McCaffrey, *The Ship Who Sang*, 1969
Melisa C. Michaels, *Skirmish*, 1985
Naomi Mitchison, *Memoirs of a Spacewoman*, 1973
Alis A. Rasmussen, *A Passage of Stars*, 1990
David Alexander Smith, *Homecoming*, 1990

1937
GAYLE GREENO

Exiles' Return
(New York: DAW, 1995)

Story type: Science Fiction (Psychic Powers; Lost Colony)
Series: Ghatti's Tale

Major character(s): Doyce Marbon, Telepath; Khar'pern, Alien (Ghatta), Telepath; Jenret Wycherley, Telepath
Time period(s): Indeterminate Future
Locale(s): Methuen, Planet—Imaginary

Summary: When the discovery that psychics, called Resonants, can read and control other minds fills ordinary citizens with fear and hatred, Jenret undertakes a mission to find and protect the Resonants. As Doyce awaits the birth of her child, she embarks on a mental journey into the past of their planet, guided by the cat-like Ghatti with whom she has a telepathic link.

Other books you might like:
C.J. Cherryh, *Rider at the Gate*, 1995
Mary Gentle, *Golden Witchbreed*, 1984
Anne McCaffrey, *To Ride Pegasus*, 1968
Andre Norton, *Catseye*, 1961
James H. Schmitz, *The Universe Against Her*, 1964
A.E. van Vogt, *Slan*, 1946

1938
GAYLE GREENO

Finders-Seekers
(New York: DAW, 1993)

Story type: Science Fiction (Psychic Powers; Mystery)
Series: Ghatti's Tale
Major character(s): Doyce Marbon, Telepath; Khar'pern, Alien (Ghatti), Telepath; Mahafny, Doctor
Time period(s): Indeterminate Future
Locale(s): Methuen, Planet—Imaginary

Summary: Descendants of the lost colony of humans on Methuen have adapted and created a culture based on partnership with the Ghatti, telepathic cat-like natives. Sent to investigate the tragic death of her lover, Oriel, and the psychic crippling of Saam, his bondmate, Doyce and her bondmate, Khar'pern, set out to retrace Oriel's steps. They discover a conspiracy to murder human-ghatti pairs and an unsuspected perversion of mental powers. First novel.

Other books you might like:
C.J. Cherryh, *Forty Thousand in Gehenna*, 1983
Gordon R. Dickson, *Masters of Everon*, 1980
Lynn S. Hightower, *Alien Blues*, 1992
Janet Kagan, *Uhura's Song*, 1985
Rosemary Kirstein, *The Outskirter's Secret*, 1992
Anne McCaffrey, *Decision at Doona*, 1969
Anne McCaffrey, *Dragonflight*, 1968
James H. Schmitz, *The Universe Against Her*, 1964
Tad Williams, *Tailchaser's Song*, 1985

1939
GAYLE GREENO

Mind-Speakers' Call
(New York: DAW, 1994)

Story type: Science Fiction (Psychic Powers; Political)
Series: Ghatti's Tale

Major character(s): Doyce Marbon, Telepath; Khar'pern, Alien (Ghatti), Telepath; Jenret Wycherley, Telepath
Time period(s): Indeterminate Future
Locale(s): Canderis, Fictional Country; Marchmont, Fictional Country

Summary: Though still recovering from the mental effects of her confrontation with a rogue psychic, Doyce agrees to join a diplomatic mission to the neighboring nation of Marchmont, which has cut off trade with Canderis. Inside Marchmont, she and her companions discover a country on the verge of civil war over a disputed succession. Struggling to prevent war and stay alive, they find conspiracies, new telepathic talents and love.

Other books you might like:
Mary Gentle, *Golden Witchbreed*, 1984
Ursula K. Le Guin, *The Left Hand of Darkness*, 1969
Anne McCaffrey, *Dragonflight*, 1968
James H. Schmitz, *The Universe Against Her*, 1964
Tad Williams, *Tailchaser's Song*, 1985

1940

ED GREENWOOD
JEFF GRUBB, Co-Author

Cormyr: A Novel

(Lake Geneva, Wisconsin: TSR, 1996)

Story type: Fantasy (Political)
Series: Forgotten Realms
Major character(s): Vangerdahast, Magician (Royal Magician)
Time period(s): Indeterminate
Locale(s): Cormyr, Fictional Country

Summary: When Cormyr's King Azoun IV falls victim to a deadly malady, Vangerdahast steps in to aid the kingdom, while many feel that the Royal Magician himself may have caused Azoun's illness.

Other books you might like:
Jeff Grubb, *Lord Teode*, 1994
Robin Hobb, *Assassin's Apprentice*, 1995
J.V. Jones, *The Baker's Boy*, 1995
Kate Novak, *Song of the Saurials*, 1991
    Jeff Grubb, co-author
Kate Novak, *The Wyvern's Spur*, 1990
    Jeff Grubb, co-author
Chet Williamson, *Murder in Cormyr*, 1996

1941

ED GREENWOOD

Elminster: The Making of a Mage

(Lake Geneva, Wisconsin: TSR, 1994)

Story type: Fantasy (Sword and Sorcery; Adventure)
Series: Forgotten Realms
Major character(s): Elminster, Sorcerer, Royalty; Mystra, Sorceress; Elmara, Adventurer, Religious (priestess)
Time period(s): Indeterminate
Locale(s): Faerun, Fictional Country

Summary: When magelords kill his parents and lay waste to the land, a young shepherd, Elminster, decides to avenge the disaster and begins the journey which leads to his becoming the most powerful mage in Faerun.

Other books you might like:
Richard Awlinson, *Shadowdale*, 1989
Troy Denning, *The Parched Sea*, 1991
R.A. Salvatore, *The Legacy*, 1992
R.A. Salvatore, *Siege of Darkness*, 1994
R.A. Salvatore, *Starless Night*, 1993

1942

STEPHEN GREGORY

The Blood of Angels

(Clarkston, Georgia: White Wolf, 1995)

Story type: Horror (Psychological Suspense)
Major character(s): Harry Clewe, Handyman; Elizabeth Clewe, Musician; Zoe Clewe, Child
Time period(s): 1990s (1995)
Locale(s): Caernarfon, Wales

Summary: First published in England in 1994, this grim tale of psychological dissolution concerns Harry Clewe, a slightly dysfunctional young man whose fever-born vision of an angelic being propels him through a series of increasingly disastrous relationships with women including a female hitchhiker, a sister with whom he has an incestuous affair, the child of that affair, and, eventually, an androgynous young man.

Other books you might like:
Robert Bloch, *Psycho*, 1959
Christopher Fowler, *Red Bride*, 1993
John Fowles, *The Collector*, 1962
Thomas Harris, *The Silence of the Lambs*, 1989
Marvin Kaye, *Fantastique*, 1992

1943

STEPHEN GREGORY

The Cormorant

(Clarkston, Georgia: White Wolf, 1996)

Story type: Horror (Psychological Suspense)
Major character(s): Ann, Housewife; Harry, Child; Archie, Animal (pet cormorant)
Time period(s): 1980s (1986)
Locale(s): Wales (near Caernarfon)

Summary: The nameless narrator and his wife and son inherit a house from their Uncle Ian on the condition that they care for his unfriendly pet cormorant. In a short time, the bird becomes an object of and focus for the pent up anger that is slowly pulling the family apart. This novel was originally published in England in 1986 and won the Somerset Maugham Award.

Other books you might like:
Stephen King, *Cujo*, 1981
Dean R. Koontz, *Watchers*, 1987
Michael Stewart, *Monkey Shines*, 1983
Laren Stover, *Pluto, Animal Lover*, 1994

1944

STEPHEN GRESHAM

Blood Wings

(New York: Zebra, 1990)

Story type: Horror (Ancient Evil Unleashed)
Major character(s): Anita Martin, Divorced Person; Wade Martin, Child
Time period(s): 1990s
Locale(s): Orchid Springs, Florida (A small town at the edge of the Everglades)

Summary: Fleeing a bad marriage, Anita Martin settles with her young sons, Wade and Timmy, in Orchard Springs. Wade has nightmares of a huge, winged, carniverous bat-like creature and people begin to die and disappear in the swamp. Finally accepting the idea that ''Blood Wings'' is a real creature, a small group ventures into the swamp to try to track and kill it.

Other books you might like:
Charles L. Grant, *The Nestling*, 1982
Peter Tremayne, *Swamp*, 1989

1945

STEPHEN GRESHAM

The Living Dark

(New York: Zebra, 1991)

Story type: Horror (Werewolf Story)
Major character(s): Mance Culley, Teenager; Jonella ''Johnnie'' Withers, Teenager; Kenton Austin, Businessman (furniture salesman)
Time period(s): 1990s
Locale(s): Soldier, Georgia

Summary: Shortly after Mance Culley's girlfriend Johnnie is raped, her two assailants are found mutilated, as though by a ravenous animal. As more of his enemies meet a similar fate, Mance begins to suspect he is being protected by a beneficent supernatural force conjured from the dark side of his soul.

Other books you might like:
Charles L. Grant, *The Pet*, 1986
K.W. Jeter, *The Night Man*, 1990

1946

JOHN GRIBBIN
MARCUS CHOWN, Co-Author

Double Planet

(New York: Avon, 1991)

Story type: Science Fiction (Hard Science Fiction; Political)
Major character(s): Yevgeny Ustinov, Administrator (U.N.); David Kondratieff, Administrator (U.N.); Frances Reese, Spaceship Captain
Time period(s): 22nd century (2100s)
Locale(s): Outer Space (between Mars and Earth); Reykjavik, Iceland; Hipparchus, Moon (Earth's)

Summary: After David Kondratieff is informed that a comet occupies a near-Earth orbit, perhaps even a collision course, he sends out Earth's last working shuttle to divert it. The public mission is to mine the comet while the astronauts' true mission remains hidden. Originally published 1988.

Other books you might like:
William Barton, *Fellow Traveller*, 1991
    Michael Capobianco, co-author
Gregory Benford, *Heart of the Comet*, 1986
    David Brin, co-author
Arthur C. Clarke, *Rendezvous with Rama*, 1973
Gregory Feeley, *The Oxygen Barons*, 1990
Allen Steele, *Orbital Decay*, 1989

1947

JOHN GRIBBIN

Father to the Man

(New York: Tor, 1990)

Story type: Science Fiction (Hard Science Fiction)
Major character(s): Richard Lee, Scientist; Marjorie Cooper, Scientist
Time period(s): 21st century
Locale(s): England

Summary: In a near-future world burdened by plague, starvation, war, pollution, and the rise of anti-science fundamentalist religion, Richard Lee, a brilliant young scientist, is persecuted for stating in a television interview that humanity and chimpanzees may be much more closely related than has been previously believed. His career a shambles, his fiancee murdered by thugs out to get him, Lee goes into hiding. Over the next few years, as society continues its collapse, Lee devotes himself to raising a baby, the outcome of his research, who is not entirely human.

Other books you might like:
Roger MacBride Allen, *Orphan of Creation*, 1988
Michael Bishop, *Ancient of Days*, 1985
Michael Bishop, *No Enemy but Time*, 1982
David Brin, *Startide Rising*, 1983
David Brin, *The Uplift War*, 1987
Vercors, *You Shall Know Them*, 1953
    No 1st name, pseud; real name Jean Bruller

1948

P.M. GRIFFIN

Call to Arms

(New York: Ace, 1991)

Story type: Science Fiction (Adventure; Military)
Series: Star Commandos
Major character(s): Islaen Connor, Leader, Telepath; Varn Tarl Sogan, Royalty (war prince), Military Personnel; Lloyd George Thatcher, Criminal
Time period(s): Indeterminate Future
Locale(s): Noreen, Planet—Imaginary

Summary: Islaen Connor, Varn Tarl Sogan and their comrades return to Noreen of Tara, Islaen's homeworld, hoping to foil

Thatcher who is hiding there and preparing a strike that will allow him both revenge and riches enough to retire on Earth.

Other books you might like:
Lois McMaster Bujold, *Brothers in Arms*, 1988
C.J. Cherryh, *Rimrunners*, 1989
Gordon R. Dickson, *Dorsai!*, 1976
Melisa C. Michaels, *Last War*, 1986
Jerry Pournelle, *Falkenberg's Legion*, 1990
Joel Rosenberg, *Not for Glory*, 1988
Timothy Zahn, *Cobra*, 1985

1949
P.M. GRIFFIN
Fire Planet
(New York: Ace, 1990)

Story type: Science Fiction (Space Opera)
Series: Star Commandos
Major character(s): Varn Tarl Sogan, Military Personnel (admiral); Islaen Connor, Military Personnel (colonel); Bandit, Alien, Telepath
Time period(s): Indeterminate Future
Locale(s): Tambora, Planet—Imaginary

Summary: Officially, Isalen, commander of the Space Commandos, and her husband Sogan are sent to the beautiful tropical world of Tambora for R and R. Unofficially, they are also to investigate the rumors of a radical sect called the Gray Ascetics that is secretly preparing for a coup. But the greatest danger to Tambora comes from the volcanic forces about to break out beneath her seas.

Other books you might like:
C.J. Cherryh, *Exile's Gate*, 1988
C.J. Cherryh, *The Fires of Azeroth*, 1979
Phyllis Eisenstein, *In the Hands of Glory*, 1981
Robert A. Heinlein, *Starship Troopers*, 1959
Anne McCaffrey, *Sassinak*, 1990
　　Elizabeth Moon, co-author
Kevin D. Randle, *The Galactic Silver Star*, 1990
Helen S. Wright, *A Matter of Oaths*, 1990

1950
P.M. GRIFFIN
Jungle Assault
(New York: Ace, 1991)

Story type: Science Fiction (Space Opera; Military)
Series: Star Commandos
Major character(s): Islaen Connor, Military Personnel; Varn Tarl Sogan, Royalty (War Prince), Telepath; Jake Karmikal, Military Personnel
Time period(s): Indeterminate Future
Locale(s): Amazoon, Planet—Imaginary

Summary: The four-person Commando Team must stop bandits from using scavenged military equipment against the colonists of Amazoon, a jungle planet habitable only at the poles. They crash into the jungle and must cross hundreds of miles to get at the bandits and their cache, battling harsh terrain and hungry predators.

Other books you might like:
Poul Anderson, *Earthman, Go Home!*, 1960
F.M. Busby, *The Alien Debt*, 1984
David Drake, *The Jungle*, 1991
Phyllis Eisenstein, *In the Hands of Glory*, 1981
Melisa C. Michaels, *First Battle*, 1985
Andre Norton, *Voorloper*, 1980

1951
PENI R. GRIFFIN
Hobkin
(New York: Macmillan McElderry, 1992)

Story type: Fantasy (Young Adult)
Major character(s): Sara "Liza Franklin" Welch, Runaway; Melissa "Kay Franklin" Welch, Runaway; Hobkin, Mythical Creature (brownie)
Time period(s): 1990s
Locale(s): Britt, Texas (Stark Homestead)

Summary: Escaping abuse and unacceptable family life, Liza and Kay flee across West Texas until a chance bus stop and quick thinking allow the pair to take possession of an abandoned farmstead known as home to a haunt. While her sister works at Britt's only store, Liza benefits from a distant but growing friendship with the spirit, a brownie, as she begins to learn the skills necessary for rural life.

Other books you might like:
Sylvia Cassedy, *Behind the Attic Wall*, 1983
Helen Cresswell, *A Game of Catch*, 1977
Penelope Lively, *The Ghost of Thomas Kempe*, 1973
Arthur Mason, *The Wee Men of Ballywooden*, 1930
Diana Mulock, *The Adventures of a Brownie as Told to My Child*, 1952
Jody Lynn Nye, *Mythology 101*, 1990

1952
KATHRYN MEYER GRIFFITH
The Calling
(New York: Zebra, 1994)

Story type: Horror (Ghost Story)
Major character(s): Faye Summers, Businesswoman (club owner); Nick Summers, Musician; Sharif al-Hakim, Guide
Time period(s): 1990s (1994)
Locale(s): Cairo, Egypt

Summary: Acting under the compulsion of an inner self she has acknowledged all her life, American Faye Summers travels to Egypt. There she discovers that she is haunted by the spirit of Ankhesenaton, the daughter of Akhenaton and Nefertiti, and is enjoined to discover the whereabouts of their remains and bury them properly, so that their spirits my be released from the earth. But just as Ankhesenaton has existed spiritually over the centuries, so have the spirit forms of the enemies of her family, and they block Faye at every possible step.

Other books you might like:
Charles L. Grant, *The Long Night of the Grave*, 1986
Michael Paine, *Cities of the Dead*, 1988
Anne Rice, *The Mummy, or Ramses the Damned*, 1989

1953

KATHRYN MEYER GRIFFITH

The Last Vampire
(New York: Zebra, 1992)

Story type: Horror (Vampire Story)
Major character(s): Emma Bloodworth, Artist, Vampire; Matthew Whitefeather, Worker, Indian; Byron Shelly, Vampire
Time period(s): Indeterminate Future
Locale(s): St. Louis, Missouri

Summary: Saved from death by the bite of a sympathetic vampire, Emma Bloodworth stalks an Earth devastated by earthquakes and natural disasters, banding with fellow vampires in an effort to track down dwindling resources of fresh human blood.

Other books you might like:
Jack Butler, *Nightshade*, 1989
Richard Matheson, *I Am Legend*, 1954
Lois Tilton, *Vampire Winter*, 1990
F. Paul Wilson, *Midnight Mass*, 1990

1954

KATHRYN MEYER GRIFFITH

Vampire Blood
(New York: Zebra, 1991)

Story type: Horror (Vampire Story)
Major character(s): Jenny Lacey, Writer; Joey Lacey, Restaurateur; Terry Michelson, Vampire
Time period(s): 1990s
Locale(s): Summer Haven, Florida

Summary: Horror writer Jenny Lacey returns home after her divorce to pick up the pieces of her life, and discovers that the family who have taken over Summer Haven's old abandoned movie theatre with intent to refurbish it are a brood of vampires whose indiscreet teenage children are about to decimate the town.

Other books you might like:
Tanya Huff, *Blood Price*, 1991
Stephen King, *Salem's Lot*, 1975
Richard Laymon, *The Stake*, 1990

1955

KATHRYN MEYER GRIFFITH

Witches
(New York: Zebra, 1993)

Story type: Horror (Black Magic)

Major character(s): Amanda Givens, Witch; Rachel Coxe, Witch (dead for 300 years); Amadeus, Animal (cat; Amanda's familiar)
Time period(s): 1990s (1993)
Locale(s): Canaan, Connecticut

Summary: Rachel Coxe vowed revenge upon the small Connecticut town of Canaan when whe was murdered for being a witch at the end of the 18th century. Through the activity of contemporary black magic covens, she begins to exact her bloody retribution but is fought by Amanda Givens, a witch who practices white magic and refuses to become a part of Rachel's scheme, even though the townsfolk assume Amanda is responsible for the madness and mayhem that have overtaken them.

Other books you might like:
Marian O'Hearn, *Soldiers of the Black Goat*, 1940
Anne Rice, *The Witching Hour*, 1991
John Updike, *The Witches of Eastwick*, 1984

1956

NICOLA GRIFFITH

Ammonite
(New York: Ballantine Del Rey, 1993)

Story type: Science Fiction (Genetic Manipulation; Lost Colony)
Major character(s): Marguerite ''Marghe'' Angelica Raishan, Anthropologist, Wanderer; Hannah Danner, Military Personnel; Thenike, Healer, Wanderer
Time period(s): Indeterminate Future
Locale(s): Estrade, Space Station; Grenchstom's Planet ''Jeep'', Planet—Imaginary

Summary: Marghe arrives at Jeep disillusioned with the Company and informed that all residents must remain since the planet hosts a virus which kills all men and 20 percent of the women. An experimental drug prevents Marghe from acquiring the virus, but leaves her weakened. Upon learning that her assistant disappeared 18 months before, Marghe begins an adventure which takes her far to the north where she learns about herself and the women who have already survived hundreds of years without men, information necessary to the women at the Company base. First novel.

Other books you might like:
Greg Bear, *Blood Music*, 1985
Mary Gentle, *Golden Witchbreed*, 1984
Rosemary Kirstein, *The Outskirter's Secret*, 1992
Rosemary Kirstein, *The Steerswoman*, 1989
Ursula K. Le Guin, *The Left Hand of Darkness*, 1969
Jody Lynn Nye, *Taylor's Ark*, 1993
Bill Ransom, *ViraVax*, 1993
Joan Slonczewski, *A Door into Ocean*, 1986
Eric Vinicoff, *The Weigher*, 1992
  Marcia Martin, co-author

1957

NICOLA GRIFFITH

Slow River

(New York: Ballantine Del Rey, 1995)

Story type: Science Fiction (Hard Science Fiction; Gay/Lesbian Fiction)

Major character(s): Frances Lorien "Lore" van de Oest, Artist (video), Heiress; Spanner, Lesbian, Criminal; Cherry Magyar, Engineer (water purification)

Time period(s): 21st century

Locale(s): Ratnapida, Tropical Island (estate); England

Summary: Left on the street to die, Lore accepts help from Spanner who recognizes her as the heir of the water purification van de Oests whose ransom requests aired on the media. Lore realizes she cannot contact her family as they had abandoned her to the kidnappers, and becomes Spanner's partner until she gains enough strength to get a job as a menial laborer at a water treatment plant which she could as easily run.

Other books you might like:

Lois McMaster Bujold, *Shards of Honor*, 1986
F.M. Busby, *Rissa Kerguelen*, 1977
Suzette Haden Elgin, *Native Tongue*, 1984
Susan Palwick, *Flying in Place*, 1992
Melissa Scott, *Trouble and Her Friends*, 1994
Amy Thomson, *Virtual Girl*, 1993

1958

LEE GRIMES

Retro Lives

(New York: AvoNova, 1993)

Story type: Science Fiction (Family Saga; Immortality)

Major character(s): Robert Widdick, Businessman, Parent (progenitor); Milton Kleiffer, Doctor (psychiatrist); Harry Widdick, Heir

Time period(s): 1980s (1985)

Locale(s): United States

Summary: Milton Kleiffer diagnoses his first patient at the mental institution, Robert Widdick, as suffering some form of Korsakov's Syndrome which affects transfer of information to long term memory. Milton then discovers that Robert, now appearing about 25 years old, had entered the hospital at the age of 60. The diagnosis becomes extremely complicated when, one day, Robert begins remembering recent events and begins to grow older again. Genetic analysis points to an extension on Robert's Y chromosome, indicating that the mutation will show up in his sons.

Other books you might like:

Martin Amis, *Time's Arrow*, 1991
Ken Grimwood, *Replay*, 1986
Robert A. Heinlein, *Time Enough for Love*, 1973
Nancy Kress, *Brain Rose*, 1990
Michael D. Weaver, *My Father Immortal*, 1989

1959

JACOB LUDWIG GRIMM
WILHELM CARL GRIMM, Co-Author

The Complete Fairy Tales of the Brothers Grimm

(New York: Bantam, 1992)

Story type: Fantasy (Anthology; Legend)

Summary: Enlarged edition of the 1987 release and most comprehensive collection of the *Grimms' Tales* to date with eight new tales among the 40 tales first translated into English by Zipes and slightly corrected herein. Throughout the book, entirely retranslated by the editor, Zipes retains the historical character and idioms and the 19th century flavor while incorporating contemporary vocabulary and terms when not intrusive. Includes a 15-page biography of the Grimms by Zipes titled, "Once There Were Two Brothers Named Grimm," two pages of notes on translation (1986), one page of notes on the expanded edition and 250 tales followed by 16 pages of notes on the text and a four-page index.

Other books you might like:

Hans Christian Andersen, *The Complete Fairy Tales and Stories*, 1974
Clemens Maria Brentano, *Fairy Tales From Brentano*, 1886
Wilhelm Hauff, *The Fairy Tales of Wilhelm Hauff*, 1895
Michael Patrick Hearn, *The Victorian Fairy Tale Book*, 1988
  editor
Andrew Lang, *The Blue Fairy Book*, 1889
  editor
Andrew Lang, *The Green Fairy Book*, 1892
  editor
Andrew Lang, *The Red Fairy Book*, 1890
  editor
George MacDonald, *The Complete Fairy Tales of George MacDonald*, 1979
Aesop, *Aesop's Fables*, 1992
  Jack Zipes, editor

1960

TODD GRIMSON

Brand New Cherry Flavor

(New York: HarperPrism, 1996)

Story type: Horror (Occult)

Major character(s): Lisa Nova, Director (film); Selwyn Popcorn, Director (film); Boro, Religious (voodoo priest)

Time period(s): 1990s (1996)

Locale(s): Hollywood, California

Summary: When Lisa Nova is denied a film job she slept with people to get, she contacts Boro, a voodoo hit-man, who takes a liking to her and helps her get her revenge. Too late, Lisa discovers that she has been pulled into the horrifying world of Boro and his black magic.

Other books you might like:

William Peter Blatty, *Demons Five, Exorcists Nothing*, 1996
Ramsey Campbell, *Ancient Images*, 1989
Dennis Cooper, *Frisk*, 1991

Dennis Etchison, *Shadow Man*, 1994
Greg Kihn, *Horror Show*, 1996
Theodore Roszak, *Flicker*, 1991
Paul Russell, *Boys of Life*, 1991

1961
TODD GRIMSON

Stainless
(New York: HarperPrism, 1996)

Story type: Horror (Vampire Story)
Major character(s): Justine, Vampire; Keith, Musician (guitarist); David Henry Reid, Actor
Time period(s): 1990s (1996)
Locale(s): Los Angeles, California

Summary: Enamored of young vampire femme fatal Justine, Keith becomes her chauffeur, driving her around Los Angeles in the evening to find her nightly meals. In due time, he becomes her protector as well, helping her elude a vengeful silent movie actor whom Justine vampirized decades before.

Other books you might like:
Poppy Z. Brite, *Lost Souls*, 1992
Nancy A. Collins, *Sunglasses After Dark*, 1989
Christopher Moore, *Bloodsucking Fiends: A Love Story*, 1995
Jonathan Nasaw, *The World on Blood*, 1996
Gail Petersen, *The Making of a Monster*, 1993

1962
KEN GRIMWOOD

Into the Deep
(New York: Morrow, 1995)

Story type: Science Fiction (First Contact; Psychic Powers)
Major character(s): Sheila Roberts, Student—College (graduate school); Daniel Colter, Journalist (freelance reporter), Stowaway; Ch*Tril, Animal (dolphin)
Time period(s): 21st century
Locale(s): North America; At Sea

Summary: Millennia ago, dolphins maintained telepathic contact with humans. Now fearful over carnage in the ocean, dolphins choose a few people with whom to reestablish contact, initiating communication with Sheila Roberts through dream imagery. To learn of cetacean atrocities, Daniel Colter investigates harvesting practices aboard a tuna trawler whose captain does not recall prior dolphin contact.

Other books you might like:
Jim Aikin, *Walk the Moon's Road*, 1985
Piers Anthony, *Mercycle*, 1991
David Brin, *Startide Rising*, 1983
Gordon R. Dickson, *The Space Swimmers*, 1967
Alan Dean Foster, *Cachalot*, 1980
Anne McCaffrey, *The Dolphins of Pern*, 1994
Margaret St. Clair, *The Dolphins of Altair*, 1967
L. Neil Smith, *The Venus Belt*, 1981
Sydney J. Van Scyoc, *Deepwater Dreams*, 1991

1963
ANNE LESLEY GROELL

Anvil of the Sun
(New York: Roc, 1996)

Story type: Fantasy (Quest; Adventure)
Series: Cloak and Dagger
Major character(s): Jenifleur Radineaux, Student, Martial Arts Expert (assassin); Thibault ''Thib'' Lescevre, Apprentice (carpenter), Martial Arts Expert (assassin); Viera Radineaux, Martial Arts Expert (assassin), Debutante
Time period(s): Indeterminate
Locale(s): Ashkharon, Fictional Country

Summary: The best assassin in the world takes a commission to assassinate a government minister in Ashkharon. When she does not come home in time to welcome her niece, the niece sets off into certain danger, a fate preferable to the Debutante's Ball. First novel.

Other books you might like:
Steven Brust, *Jhereg*, 1983
Eve Forward, *Villains by Necessity*, 1995
Robin Hobb, *Assassin's Apprentice*, 1995
Fritz Leiber, *Ill Met in Lankhmar*, 1995
Michael Shea, *Nifft the Lean*, 1982

1964
STEPHAN GRUNDY

Attila's Treasure
(New York: Bantam Spectra, 1996)

Story type: Fantasy (Adventure; Legend)
Major character(s): Hagan, Warrior, Homosexual; Attila the Hun, Historical Figure, Foster Parent; Hildegund, Teenager
Time period(s): 5th century
Locale(s): Europe

Summary: Fostered to Attila the Hun along with a potential bride of Attila's, Hagan develops into a fierce fighter. However, during Hagan's first battle, he discovers a pathway to the otherworld, knowledge which could allow Attila to see him as an adversary.

Other books you might like:
Frans G. Bengtsson, *The Long Ships*, 1954
Donna Gillespie, *The Light Bearer*, 1994
Parke Godwin, *The Tower of Beowulf*, 1995
Harry Harrison, *The Hammer and the Cross*, 1993
    John Holm, co-author
Diana L. Paxson, *The Wolf and the Raven*, 1993

1965
STEPHAN GRUNDY

Rhinegold
(New York: Bantam, 1994)

Story type: Fantasy (Legend; Adventure)

Major character(s): Sigfrith, Mythical Creature (demigod shapechanger), Warrior; Brunichild, Royalty, Warrior
Time period(s): 5th century
Locale(s): Europe

Summary: Working as a smith, Sigfrith accepts a magical draught which brings mythic figures to life and empowers him with supernatural abilities. He grows to heroic stature as he slays the dragon, Fadhmir, and wins a hoard of gold. Fated to love one another but marry others, Sigfrith and Brunichild's love turns tragic for both. First novel.

Other books you might like:
Frans G. Bengtsson, *The Long Ships*, 1954
Donna Gillespie, *The Light Bearer*, 1994
Harry Harrison, *The Hammer and the Cross*, 1993
    John Holm, co-author
Morgan Llywelyn, *Druids*, 1991
Diana L. Paxson, *The Wolf and the Raven*, 1993

1966

DIANE GUEST

Lullaby

(New York: Putnam's 1990)

Story type: Horror (Possession)
Major character(s): Rachel Daimler, Housewife; Judd Pauling, Artist, Spouse; Addy Pauling, Child (Rachel's daughter)
Time period(s): 1990s (1990)
Locale(s): Land's End, Maine

Summary: Overcoming her longstanding aversion to her childhood home, Rachel Daimler returns with her family to visit her dying mother. Soon thereafter her youngest daughter, Addy, becomes a pawn in the family's struggle to escape the evil influence of the household.

Other books you might like:
Ramsey Campbell, *The Influence*, 1988
Robert Marasco, *Burnt Offerings*, 1973

1967

JEFF GUINN

The Autobiography of Santa Claus: It's Better to Give

(Fort Worth, Texas: The Summit Group, 1994)

Story type: Fantasy (Legend)
Major character(s): Nicholas "Santa Claus", Hero; Arthur, Royalty, Ruler; Attila the Hun, Warrior
Time period(s): 3rd century; 20th century
Locale(s): Middle East; Europe; United States

Summary: Nurtured and taught the lessons of goodness and generosity, Nicholas begins sharing his wealth with the needy as a child. When Nicholas discovers that he no longer ages and can travel rapidly, he begins distributing his gifts to the children of the world as he recruits helpers through the ages.

Other books you might like:
L. Frank Baum, *The Life and Adventures of Santa Claus*, 1902

Martin H. Greenberg, *Christmas on Ganymede and Other Stories*, 1990
    editor
David G. Hartwell, *Christmas Forever*, 1993
    editor
Kristine Kathryn Rusch, *Pulphouse, Issue 10: Special Issue*, 1991
    editor
J.R.R. Tolkien, *The Father Christmas Letters*, 1976

1968

GUNELI GUN

The Adventures of Huru on the Road to Baghdad

(Claremont, CA: Hunter House, 1988)

Story type: Fantasy (Adventure)
Major character(s): Huru, Young Woman (Turkish)
Time period(s): Indeterminate Past
Locale(s): Middle East

Summary: When her parents make a pilgrimage to Mecca, Huru is falsely accused of wantonness. She decides to leave, and try to find her parents in Baghdad. Along the way, she has a number of adventures, magic and otherwise.

Other books you might like:
Samuel R. Delany, *Neveryona*, 1983
Elizabeth Moon, *Sheepfarmer's Daughter*, 1988
Judith Tarr, *A Wind in Cairo*, 1989

1969

JAMES GUNN
THEODORE STURGEON, Co-Author

The Joy Machine

(New York: Pocket, 1996)

Story type: Science Fiction (Political; Space Opera)
Series: Star Trek
Major character(s): James T. Kirk, Spaceship Captain; Spock, Scientist, Alien (Vulcan); Kemal Marouk, Scientist, Government Official (paymaster)
Time period(s): 23rd century
Locale(s): *U.S.S. Enterprise*, Spaceship; Timshel, Planet—Imaginary; United Federation of Planets, Interstellar Empire/Federation

Summary: Returning to Timshel where he previously enjoyed several months of vacation and recovery, Jim finds an old friend, Marouk, is now the most powerful man on the planet. Unfortunately the Joy Machine, which also rewards the citizens it monitors, no longer permits anyone to leave Timshel, or to remain free of its control. Worse, it plans to extend its influence to the rest of the Federation. Based on a Theodore Sturgeon short story.

Other books you might like:
Theodore Sturgeon, *The Dreaming Jewels*, 1950
Theodore Sturgeon, *Microcosmic God*, 1995
Theodore Sturgeon, *The Ultimate Egoist*, 1994
John Varley, *Steel Beach*, 1992

Jack Williamson, *The Humanoids*, 1949
Jack Williamson, *Star Bridge*, 1955
  James Gunn, co-author

1970

JAMES GUNN
JACK WILLIAMSON, Co-Author

Star Bridge

(New York: Macmillan Collier Nucleus, 1989)

Story type: Science Fiction (Space Opera)
Major character(s): Alan Horn, Mercenary; Oliver Wu, Immortal, Wanderer
Time period(s): 35th century
Locale(s): Earth; Eron, Planet—Imaginary

Summary: The Eron Empire dominates the galaxy due to its control of the star bridges which make interstellar travel possible, and the Empire rules with a heavy hand. A human mercenary and an immortal Chinese each fight the Eronian tyranny in his own way. Originally published in 1955.

Other books you might like:
Poul Anderson, *The Boat of a Million Years*, 1989
Poul Anderson, *The Game of Empire*, 1985
Poul Anderson, *Mirkheim*, 1977
F.M. Busby, *Rebel's Quest*, 1985
F.M. Busby, *Rissa Kerguelen*, 1977
Robert A. Heinlein, *Double Star*, 1956
Robert A. Heinlein, *The Moon Is a Harsh Mistress*, 1966
Frank Herbert, *Dune*, 1965

1971

THORARINN GUNNARSSON

Battle of the Ring

(New York: Popular Library/Questar, 1989)

Story type: Science Fiction (Space Opera)
Series: Starwolves
Major character(s): Commander Velmeran, Spaceship Captain; Valthyrra, Artificial Intelligence (Sentient spaceship)
Time period(s): Indeterminate Future
Locale(s): *Valthyrra Methryn*, Spaceship

Summary: A warrior race, the Starwolves, live their entire lives on gigantic sentient spaceships. One such ship, the Valthyrra, must defeat the gigantic fortress ship of an evil race of alien saurians if the Starwolves are to survive.

Other books you might like:
Gregory Benford, *Tides of Light*, 1989
W. Michael Gear, *The Artifact*, 1989
W. Michael Gear, *The Warriors of Spider*, 1988
W. Michael Gear, *The Way of Spider*, 1988
W. Michael Gear, *The Web of Spider*, 1989
Fred Saberhagen, *Berserker's Planet*, 1975

1972

THORARINN GUNNARSSON

Dragon's Domain

(New York: Ace, 1993)

Story type: Fantasy (Quest; Adventure)
Series: Make Way for Dragons
Major character(s): Kalavek, Mythical Creature (dragon), Adventurer; Einar Myklathun, Government Official (forester), Adventurer; Ayesha, Mythical Creature (dragon)
Time period(s): 1860s; 1880s
Locale(s): Norway

Summary: After magic fades from the world, Kalavek's birth provides his tribe with hope for reversing centuries of dragonkind's decline. When the dragons' mortal enemies, the Shadows, catch wind of young Kalavek and Ayesha while out exploring, Einar steps in to save the pair. Later, when Kalavek and Ayesha cannot direct the magic necessary to successfully procreate, Kalavek enlists Einar's help in retrieving a Core of Magic from the Fountain of the World's Heart, the channel for the vanished ancient magic.

Other books you might like:
Ursula K. Le Guin, *The Farthest Shore*, 1972
Ursula K. Le Guin, *The Tombs of Atuan*, 1971
Ursula K. Le Guin, *A Wizard of Earthsea*, 1968
Larry Niven, *The Magic Goes Away*, 1979
Lawrence Watt-Evans, *The Blood of a Dragon*, 1991
Terri Windling, *Life on the Border*, 1991
  editor
Patricia C. Wrede, *Searching for Dragons*, 1991
Laurence Yep, *Dragon of the Lost Sea*, 1982

1973

THORARINN GUNNARSSON

Dragonmage of Mystara

(Lake Geneva, Wisconsin: TSR, 1996)

Story type: Fantasy (Magic Conflict; Political)
Series: Mystara: The Dragonlord Chronicles
Major character(s): Thelvyn Fox-Eyes, Royalty (Dragonking); Alessa Vyledaar, Wizard; Kharendaen, Mythical Creature (dragon)
Time period(s): Indeterminate
Locale(s): Mystara, Planet—Imaginary

Summary: Unable to resist the enchanted red jewel's call, Alessa risks the Collar of the Dragons and destruction of both the dragons and her people in another war. To save Mystara, Thelvyn must somehow convince his dragons to join the humans against the force behind the gem. Third in the series.

Other books you might like:
Gael Baudino, *Duel of Dragons*, 1991
Mary Brown, *Master of Many Treasures*, 1995
Don Callander, *Dragon Companion*, 1994
Margaret Weis, *Dragons of Summer Flame*, 1995
  Tracy Hickman, co-author
Angus Wells, *Lords of the Sky*, 1994

1974

THORARINN GUNNARSSON

Dragons on the Town
(New York: Ace, 1992)

Story type: Fantasy (Magic Conflict; Quest)
Series: Faerie Dragon
Major character(s): Jenny Barker, Disembodied Personality; Dalvenjah Foxfire, Mythical Creature (dragon); Mira, Sorceress
Time period(s): 1990s
Locale(s): New York, New York

Summary: Sharing a body with a dragon, Jenny Barker learns that her father, a faerie dragon, planned her birth to satisfy the Prophecy of the Faerie Dragons. Mira discovers the sorceress Darja actually needs her body and the continuing error could threaten the Emperor and his minions. Meanwhile Jenny, awaiting a corporeal form to inhabit, transfers into a Dragon Mirror.

Other books you might like:
Steven Brust, *Jhereg*, 1983
Michael Cassutt, *Dragon Season*, 1991
Robert N. Charrette, *Never Deal with a Dragon*, 1990
L. Sprague de Camp, *The Honorable Barbarian*, 1989
William R. Forstchen, *The Crystal Warriors*, 1988
    Greg Morrison, co-author
Geary Gravel, *A Key for the Nonesuch*, 1990
Patricia C. Wrede, *Searching for Dragons*, 1991
Laurence Yep, *Dragon Cauldron*, 1991

1975

THORARINN GUNNARSSON

Dreadnought
(New York: Warner Questar, 1993)

Story type: Science Fiction (Military)
Series: Starwolves
Major character(s): Janus Tarrel, Spaceship Captain; Valthyrra Methryn, Artificial Intelligence (sentient spaceship); Walter Pesca, Linguist, Military Personnel
Time period(s): Indeterminate Future
Locale(s): *Methryn*, Spaceship; Outer Space

Summary: The Union Fleet and the Starwolves, millennia-old enemies, must unite their forces to face a new threat to their combined space, an automated war machine they call the Dreadnought. Captain Janus Tarrel of the Union Fleet negotiates a truce which may very well disintegrate if they can conquer the Dreadnought.

Other books you might like:
C.J. Cherryh, *Downbelow Station*, 1981
Glen Cook, *The Dragon Never Sleeps*, 1988
Joe Haldeman, *The Forever War*, 1975
Robert A. Heinlein, *Starship Troopers*, 1959
Frank Herbert, *Heretics of Dune*, 1984
Keith Laumer, *Bolo: The Annals of the Dinochrome Brigade*, 1976

1976

THORARINN GUNNARSSON

Make Way for Dragons!
(New York: Ace, 1990)

Story type: Fantasy (Light Fantasy)
Series: Faerie Dragon
Major character(s): Dalvenjah Foxfire, Mythical Creature (Dragon); Allan Breivik, Musician (Cellist), Magician
Time period(s): 1990s
Locale(s): California

Summary: A huge dragon followed by two smaller dragons appears in California. The smaller golden dragon, Dalvenjah, and her young child try to kill the large steel dragon, but are unsuccessful and Dalvenjah is wounded. She looks up the local wizard who has no idea that he has any magical powers. The two dragons move in with him and Dalvenjah begins to teach him how to use his talents.

Other books you might like:
Gael Baudino, *Duel of Dragons*, 1990
Emma Bull, *War for the Oaks*, 1987
L. Sprague de Camp, *The Honorable Barbarian*, 1989
Megan Lindholm, *Luck of the Wheels*, 1989
Matt Ruff, *Fool on the Hill*, 1989

1977

THORARINN GUNNARSSON

Tactical Error
(New York: Warner Questar, 1991)

Story type: Science Fiction (Space Opera)
Series: Starwolves
Major character(s): Commander Velmeran, Spaceship Captain; Valthyrra Methryn, Artificial Intelligence (sentient spaceship); Donalt Trace, Military Personnel
Time period(s): Indeterminate Future
Locale(s): *Methryn*, Spaceship; *Valcyr*, Spaceship; Earth

Summary: The Starwolves discover Donalt Trace has assembled for the Union a large mock Starwolf fleet which he is manning with 10,000 clones of Commander Velmeran. To save their base and even long-lost Earth, the Starwolves must defeat Donalt Trace's mock Starwolf fleet and its complement of Union Fortresses.

Other books you might like:
C.J. Cherryh, *Cyteen*, 1988
C.J. Cherryh, *Downbelow Station*, 1981
Glen Cook, *The Dragon Never Sleeps*, 1988
Dave Duncan, *Hero*, 1991
Melisa C. Michaels, *Skirmish*, 1985
Alis A. Rasmussen, *Revolution's Shore*, 1990

1978

ELLEN GUON

Bedlam Boyz

(New York: Baen, 1993)

Story type: Fantasy (Magic Conflict; Urban)
Major character(s): Kayla Smith, Magician, Runaway; Elizabet Winters, Magician, Psychologist
Time period(s): 1990s; Indeterminate
Locale(s): Los Angeles, California; Unseelie lands, Mythical Place (elven realm)

Summary: Elizabet hopes to develop Kayla's recently discovered talent for healing. However, a *barrio* gang sees Kayla as the *bruja* who will solve their problems while powerful and deadly Faery agents search out the powerful new mage. Prequel to *Knight of Ghosts and Shadows* and *Summoned to Tourney*.

Other books you might like:
Mercedes Lackey, *Born to Run*, 1992
  Larry Dixon, co-author
Mercedes Lackey, *Knight of Ghosts and Shadows*, 1990
  Ellen Guon, co-author
Mercedes Lackey, *Summoned to Tourney*, 1992
  Ellen Guon, co-author
Mercedes Lackey, *Wheels of Fire*, 1992
  Mark Shepherd, co-author
Will Shetterly, *Elsewhere*, 1991
Terri Windling, *Borderland*, 1986
  Mark Alan Arnold, co-editor
Terri Windling, *Bordertown*, 1986
  Mark Alan Arnold, co-editor
Terri Windling, *Life on the Border*, 1991
  editor

1979

JAMES GURNEY

Dinotopia

(Atlanta, Georgia: Turner Publishing, Inc., 1992)

Story type: Fantasy (Historical; Quest)
Series: Dinotopia
Major character(s): Arthur Denison, Scientist (biologist), Explorer; Will Denison, Adventurer, Teenager; Bix, Animal (dinosaur), Guide
Time period(s): 1860s
Locale(s): Dinotopia, Fictional Country

Summary: Shipwrecked on a voyage of discovery, Arthur Denison and his son find themselves marooned on an island whose inhabitants include humans and dinosaurs living together peacefully in a technologically sophisticated society. Arthur explores Dinotopia, meeting residents and expanding his lavishly illustrated journal.

Other books you might like:
Jack Dann, *Dinosaurs!*, 1990
  Gardner Dozois, co-editor
Arthur Conan Doyle, *The Lost World*, 1912

Evelyn Sibley Lampman, *The Shy Stegosaurus of Cricket Creek*, 1955
Evelyn Sibley Lampman, *The Shy Stegosaurus of Indian Springs*, 1962
Stephen Leigh, *Ray Bradbury Presents: Dinosaur World*, 1992
J.F. Rivkin, *Tyrannosaurus Rex*, 1992
Robert J. Sawyer, *Far-Seer*, 1992
Jules Verne, *Journey to the Center of the Earth*, 1874
Roger Zelazny, *Way Up High*, 1992

1980

JAMES GURNEY

The World Beneath

(Atlanta, Georgia: Turner Publishing, Inc., 1995)

Story type: Fantasy (Historical; Adventure)
Series: Dinotopia
Major character(s): Arthur Denison, Scientist (biologist), Explorer; Will Denison, Adventurer
Time period(s): 1860s
Locale(s): Dinotopia, Fictional Country

Summary: After an accident in Professor Denison's newly invented flying machine nearly kills Will, Denison investigates ancient caverns beneath Dinotopia, hoping to discover the lost civilization that produced tantalizing artifacts found in the caves. Presented as a lavishly illustrated journal.

Other books you might like:
Betty Ballantine, *The Secret Oceans*, 1994
Scott Ciencin, *Windchaser*, 1995
Rudy Rucker, *The Hollow Earth: The Narrative of Mason Algiers Reynolds of Virginia*, 1990
Midori Snyder, *Hatchling*, 1995
Jules Verne, *Journey to the Center of the Earth*, 1874
John Vornholt, *River Quest*, 1995

1981

ELISE GUTTENBERG

Sunder, Eclipse and Seed

(New York: Roc, 1990)

Story type: Fantasy (Magic Conflict)
Series: Sunder, Eclipse and Seed
Major character(s): Calyx, Religious (dreamer); Dev, Religious (Sumedaro priest)
Time period(s): Indeterminate Past
Locale(s): Briana, Fictional City; Aster, Fictional City

Summary: When Calyx is sent to the temple at Aster, she finds ways, with Dev's help, to train her true dreams even though she's denied the priesthood. In the process she discovers that Edishu, the god Jokjoa's nightmare, is reaching for power in the world again and only she seems to be able to resist him.

Other books you might like:
Catherine Cooke, *Mask of the Wizard*, 1985
Ru Emerson, *To the Haunted Mountains*, 1987
Guy Gavriel Kay, *The Summer Tree*, 1985
Patricia A. McKillip, *The Riddle-Master of Hed*, 1978

Jane Yolen, *Sister Light, Sister Dark*, 1988

1982
GARY GYGAX

The Anubis Murders
(New York: Roc, 1992)

Story type: Fantasy (Mystery; Magic Conflict)
Series: Dangerous Journeys
Major character(s): Setne Inhetep, Wizard, Religious; Rachelle, Martial Arts Expert, Bodyguard
Time period(s): Indeterminate Past
Locale(s): Egypt

Summary: Setne Inhetep and Rachelle must find the individual wielding potent magic and committing murders in the name of the god Anubis in order to clear the name of their god. As he investigates, Setne discovers himself tangled in a web of intrigue propelled by a powerful black magic.

Other books you might like:
Greg Farshtey, *Strange Tales From the Nile Empire*, 1992
    Greg Gorden and Ed Stark, co-editors
Randall Garrett, *Lord Darcy Investigates*, 1981
Simon R. Green, *The God Killer*, 1991
Ed Stark, *Mysterious Cairo*, 1992
    editor

1983
GARY GYGAX

Death in Delhi
(New York: Roc, 1993)

Story type: Fantasy (Mystery; Magic Conflict)
Series: Dangerous Journeys
Major character(s): Setne Inhetep, Wizard, Religious; Rachelle, Bodyguard, Martial Arts Expert
Time period(s): Indeterminate Past
Locale(s): Middle East; Delhi, India

Summary: When Setne Inhetep and Rachelle answer the call of the Maharajah of Delhi to help recover the crown jewels, the pair find themselves caught between the scheming of an evil ruler, the spells of a powerful witch and rebels with murderous intent for anyone helping the Maharajah. Based on a fantasy role-playing game.

Other books you might like:
M.A.R. Barker, *Man of Gold*, 1984
Randall Garrett, *Too Many Magicians*, 1967
Simon R. Green, *Hawk & Fisher*, 1990
Anne Logston, *Shadow*, 1991
Anne Logston, *Shadow Hunt*, 1992
Ed Stark, *Mysterious Cairo*, 1992
    editor

1984
KAREN HABER

Mutant Legacy
(New York: Bantam Spectra, 1993)

Story type: Science Fiction (Psychic Powers; Theological)
Series: Mutant Season
Major character(s): Joachim Metzgar, Leader, Psychic; Julian Akimura, Psychologist, Psychic; Rick Akimura, Psychic, Mutant
Time period(s): 2020s
Locale(s): California

Summary: Having been accepted and integrated into normal human society at last, the long awaited super-mutant, Rick Akimura, attracts followers who revere him as a messiah. His brother, Julian, afraid of Rick's power, opposes him and the future of both the mutants and humans. Concludes series.

Other books you might like:
Alfred Bester, *The Demolished Man*, 1953
John Brunner, *Children of the Thunder*, 1989
Steven Gould, *Jumper*, 1992
Henry Kuttner, *Mutant*, 1953
Anne McCaffrey, *Pegasus in Flight*, 1990
Anne McCaffrey, *The Rowan*, 1990
Robert Silverberg, *The Mutant Season*, 1990
    Karen Haber, co-author
Joan D. Vinge, *Psion*, 1982

1985
KAREN HABER

Mutant Star
(New York: Bantam Spectra, 1992)

Story type: Science Fiction (Political; Psychic Powers)
Series: Mutant Season
Major character(s): Ethan Hawkins, Military Personnel (Colonel), Spaceman; Eva Seguy, Doctor, Professor; Julian Akimura, Twin, Psychic
Time period(s): 2020s
Locale(s): Moon (Earth's); California

Summary: Humanity has begun to accept the mutants who have been developing psychic powers for the past four generations. Usually talents appear in childhood, as did Julian's. Unfortunately his fraternal twin, happy as a psychic null, begins developing precognition in his early twenties, which may prove disastrous for everyone close to him.

Other books you might like:
Alfred Bester, *The Demolished Man*, 1953
John Brunner, *Children of the Thunder*, 1989
Katharine Kerr, *Polar City Blues*, 1990
Henry Kuttner, *Mutant*, 1953
Anne McCaffrey, *Pegasus in Flight*, 1990
Anne McCaffrey, *The Rowan*, 1990
Mike Resnick, *Prophet*, 1993
Joan D. Vinge, *Psion*, 1982

1986

KAREN HABER

Sister Blood
(New York: DAW, 1996)

Story type: Science Fiction (Psychic Powers; Political)
Series: Mindstar
Major character(s): Kayla Reed, Empath, Revolutionary; Lyle Mackenzie, Administrator, Political Figure; Merrick the Blackbird, Pirate
Time period(s): Indeterminate Future
Locale(s): Styx, Planet—Imaginary; Vardalia, Planet—Imaginary

Summary: When Kayla Reed travels to Styx to seek out Yates Keller, who holds Kayla's friends as hostages, Kayla finds Styx deserted except for religious fanatics who wish to keep the planet depopulated by shutting down the mindsalt trade, a destructive force. Meanwhile, on Vardalia, Merrick plots to start up the mindsalt trade, regardless of who stands in his way.

Other books you might like:
Poul Anderson, *The Game of Empire*, 1985
C.J. Cherryh, *Merchanter's Luck*, 1982
Alfred Coppel, *Glory's War*, 1995
Paula E. Downing, *Fallway*, 1993
Anne McCaffrey, *Powers That Be*, 1993
    Elizabeth Ann Scarborough, co-author
Melissa Scott, *Mighty Good Road*, 1990
Charles Sheffield, *Cold as Ice*, 1992
David Weber, *Flag in Exile*, 1995

1987

KAREN HABER

The War Minstrels
(New York: DAW, 1995)

Story type: Science Fiction (Psychic Powers; Adventure)
Series: Mindstar
Major character(s): Kayla Reed, Empath, Smuggler; Yates Keller, Empath, Criminal; Iger, Spaceman, Smuggler
Time period(s): Indeterminate Future
Locale(s): *Falstaff*, Spaceship; Bryce Station, Space Station

Summary: After hearing about the legendary Mindstar, a mindstone that greatly enhances empathic abilities, Kayla Reed decides to find and use it to help the War Minstrels, a group of smugglers fighting for a free trade system. Sequel to *Woman Without a Shadow*.

Other books you might like:
Kevin J. Anderson, *Blindfold*, 1995
Alan Dean Foster, *Splinter of the Mind's Eye*, 1978
Anne McCaffrey, *Crystal Singer*, 1982
Vonda N. McIntyre, *The Exile Waiting*, 1975
Robert Silverberg, *The Mutant Season*, 1989
    Karen Haber, co-author

1988

KAREN HABER

Woman Without a Shadow
(New York: DAW, 1995)

Story type: Science Fiction (Psychic Powers; Adventure)
Series: Mindstar
Major character(s): Kayla Reed, Empath, Fugitive; Barabbas, Smuggler; Yates Keller, Empath, Criminal
Time period(s): Indeterminate Future
Locale(s): Styx, Planet—Imaginary; *Falstaff*, Spaceship

Summary: Orphaned when her parents die in a mining accident, Kayla Reed tries to continue their mindstone mining operation. However, after tangling with the powerful Keller family, Kayla must escape from Styx, taking on a new identity as navigator for a smuggling ship.

Other books you might like:
Kevin J. Anderson, *Blindfold*, 1995
Anne McCaffrey, *Crystal Singer*, 1982
Anne McCaffrey, *Damia*, 1992
Anne McCaffrey, *The Rowan*, 1990
Larry Segriff, *Spacer Dreams*, 1995
Robert Silverberg, *The Mutant Season*, 1989
    Karen Haber, co-author

1989

MICHAEL HAGUE, Editor

The Book of Dragons
(New York: Morrow, 1995)

Story type: Fantasy (Anthology; Young Adult)

Summary: Contains 17 stories excerpted from novels and reprinted from collections and anthologies 1921-1980, all featuring traditional dragons in diverse settings with tone varying from light to ominous. Authors include Italo Calvino, the Brothers Grimm, Kenneth Grahame, Andrew Lang, C.S. Lewis, E. Nesbit, and J.R.R. Tolkien. Lavishly illustrated in color and monocolor by Hague.

Other books you might like:
Isaac Asimov, *Dragon Tales*, 1982
    Martin H. Greenberg, Charles G. Waugh, co-editors
Orson Scott Card, *Dragons of Darkness*, 1981
    editor
Orson Scott Card, *Dragons of Light*, 1983
    editor
Jack Dann, *Dragons!*, 1993
    Gardner Dozois, co-editor
Rosalind M. Greenberg, *Dragon Fantastic*, 1992
    Martin H. Greenberg, co-editor
Byron Preiss, *The Ultimate Dragon*, 1995
    John Betancourt, Keith R.A. DeCandido, co-editors
Margaret Weis, *A Dragon-Lover's Treasury of the Fantastic*, 1994
    editor
Jane Yolen, *Here There Be Dragons*, 1993

1990

ISIDORE HAIBLUM

Specterworld
(New York: Avon, 1991)

Story type: Science Fiction (Time Travel; Adventure)
Series: Tom Dunjer
Major character(s): Tom Dunjer, Security Officer; X41, Robot; Nigel, Professor
Time period(s): Indeterminate Future
Locale(s): Happy City, Fictional Country; Fearsburg, Fictional Country

Summary: In this sequel to *Interworld*, Dunjer's Happy City robbery investigation leads to Fearsburg and an old nemesis. The conspiracy Dunjer discovers leads him away from his own world and time.

Other books you might like:

Douglas Adams, *Dirk Gently's Holistic Detective Agency*, 1987
Michael Flynn, *In the Country of the Blind*, 1990
Mel Gilden, *Hawaiian U.F.O. Aliens*, 1991
Thomas R. McDonough, *The Missing Matter*, 1992
Ken Rolston, *Extreme Paranoia: Nobody Knows the Trouble I've Shot*, 1991
Dan Simmons, *The Fall of Hyperion*, 1990
Dan Simmons, *Hyperion*, 1989

1991

PETER HAINING

Weird Tales
(New York: Carroll and Graf, 1990)

Story type: Horror (Anthology)

Summary: A collection of 31 stories and poems from *Weird Tales*, the legendary weird fiction magazine that provided H.P. Lovecraft, Ray Bradbury, Robert Bloch and hundreds of other fantasists with an outlet for their writing during the years 1923 to 1954. Produced as a facsimile edition of the magazine, the book offers a mix of magazine columns, artwork and classic stories such as Manly Wade Wellman's "The Valley Was Still," Henry S. Whitehead's "The Passing of a God" and Edmond Hamilton's "The Man Who Returned."

Other books you might like:

Stefan Dziemianowicz, *Weird Tales: 32 Unearthed Terrors*, 1988
Robert Weinberg and Martin H. Greenberg, co-authors
Leo Margulies, *Worlds of Weird*, 1965
Leo Margulies, *Weird Tales*, 1964
Robert Weinberg, *The Eighth Green Man and Other Strange Folk*, 1989
Robert Weinberg, *Far Below and Other Horrors*, 1974

1992

JACK C. HALDEMAN II
JACK DANN, Co-Author

High Steel
(New York: Tor, 1993)

Story type: Science Fiction (First Contact; Political)
Major character(s): John Stranger, Indian (Lakota), Spaceman (conscripted); Leonard Broken-finger, Shaman (medicine man), Indian; Gerard Leighton, Administrator
Time period(s): 22nd century (2177)
Locale(s): Trans-United Space Colony, Space Station (L-7)

Summary: Before John Stranger can complete his training as a medicine man, Trans-United drafts him to become a spaceman, likely to remain forever off Earth. Unhappy over being drafted, John still finds great beauty and peace in space. After John stops a runaway space station, Trans-United recognizes John's talent, an ability to select correct solutions, and begins a secret program to test John's ability to pilot a prototype faster-than-light spaceship built from incompletely understood designs transmitted by aliens as part of the Rosetta Triptych. However, Trans-United's experimentation may lead to Earth's annihilation.

Other books you might like:

Alan Dean Foster, *Cyber Way*, 1990
Jean Mark Gawron, *Dream of Glass*, 1993
Joe Haldeman, *There Is No Darkness*, 1983
Jack C. Haldeman II, co-author
Harry Harrison, *Bill, the Galactic Hero: On the Planet of Zombie Vampires*, 1991
Jack C. Haldeman II, co-author
Gwyneth Jones, *White Queen*, 1993
Ursula K. Le Guin, *The Lathe of Heaven*, 1971
Allen Steele, *Clarke County, Space*, 1990
Allen Steele, *Orbital Decay*, 1989

1993

JOE HALDEMAN

Buying Time
(New York: Morrow, 1989)

Story type: Science Fiction (Immortality)
Major character(s): Dallas Barr, Immortal, Businessman; Maria Marconi, Immortal, Pilot
Time period(s): 21st century
Locale(s): Earth; Ceres, Asteroid

Summary: A radical surgical technique, the Stileman process, can prolong life virtually indefinitely. The process wears off after ten years, however, and must be repeated at great expense. Dallas Barr, one of the first Stileman immortals, uncovers a plot to kill off his peers and to pervert the technique to an evil end.

Other books you might like:

Robert A. Heinlein, *Time Enough for Love*, 1973
Frederik Pohl, *Drunkard's Walk*, 1960
Robert Silverberg, *The Book of Skulls*, 1971
Norman Spinrad, *Bug Jack Barron*, 1969

Jack Vance, *To Live Forever*, 1956
Roger Zelazny, *This Immortal*, 1966

1994

JOE HALDEMAN

The Hemingway Hoax

(New York: Morrow, 1990)

Story type: Science Fiction (Time Travel)
Major character(s): John Baird, Professor; Sylvester Castlemaine, Criminal
Time period(s): Indeterminate Future; 1920s (1922)
Locale(s): Key West, Florida

Summary: A conman convinces Professor Baird, a Hemingway specialist, to forge some stories that Hemingway's wife apparently lost on a train in 1922. Unbeknownst to either man, a time and dimension-travelling police force has determined that increased interest in Hemingway would not be to the world's advantage because it would promulgate macho attitudes of a sort likely to lead to nuclear war. The agents of that police force are willing to murder Professor Baird, and to do so repeatedly in various timelines, in order to stop him from carrying out the forgery attempt.

Other books you might like:
Isaac Asimov, *The End of Eternity*, 1955
Barrington J. Bayley, *The Fall of Chronopolis*, 1974
Robert A. Heinlein, *To Sail Beyond the Sunset*, 1987
Michael P. Kube-McDowell, *Alternities*, 1988
Bob Shaw, *The Two-Timers*, 1968

1995

JOE HALDEMAN

None So Blind

(New York: Morrow/AvoNova, 1996)

Story type: Science Fiction (Collection)

Summary: Contains a six-page introduction, four story poems and 11 stories published since 1986 with afterwords describing the real life events that influenced the story or sparked the idea. One story, "The Hemingway Hoax," won both the Hugo and Nebula Awards; another, "Graves," won a World Fantasy Award and a Nebula Award; and "None So Blind" won a Hugo Award. Themes include death, ghosts, the effect of Ernest Hemingway on the multiverse, concern for others, and the importance of one's point of view.

Other books you might like:
Isaac Asimov, *Gold: The Final Science Fiction Collection*, 1995
Harry Harrison, *Galactic Dreams*, 1994
Larry Niven, *N-Space*, 1990
Theodore Sturgeon, *The Ultimate Egoist*, 1994
John Varley, *The Persistence of Vision*, 1978

1996

JOE HALDEMAN

Worlds Enough and Time

(New York: Morrow, 1992)

Story type: Science Fiction (Generation Starship; First Contact)
Series: Worlds Trilogy
Major character(s): Marianne O'Hara, Administrator, Settler; O'Hara Prime, Artificial Intelligence; Harry Purcell, Political Figure
Time period(s): 22nd century
Locale(s): *Newhome*, Spaceship; O'Hara, Planet—Imaginary

Summary: Marianne O'Hara has joined a colony ship travelling to Epsilon Eridani. On the way, sabotage destroys most of the ship's memory and a virus destroys all photosynthesizing plant life. When John, one of Marianne's husbands, suffers a stroke, Marianne, her daughter and her son-in-law go into cryptobiosis until they reach Epsilon Eridani. Landing on the planet, they encounter life that tests Marianne to see if humans may live in the universe.

Other books you might like:
David Brin, *Earth*, 1990
Robert A. Heinlein, *Have Spacesuit—Will Travel*, 1958
Robert A. Heinlein, *Methuselah's Children*, 1958
Keith Laumer, *Star Colony*, 1981
Vonda N. McIntyre, *Transition*, 1991
Larry Niven, *The Legacy of Heorot*, 1987
    Jerry Pournelle and Steven Barnes, co-authors
Brian Stableford, *The Gates of Eden*, 1983
James White, *The Silent Stars Go By*, 1991
Timothy Zahn, *Spinneret*, 1985

1997

WENDY HALEY

These Fallen Angels

(New York: Diamond, 1995)

Story type: Horror (Vampire Story; Gothic Family Chronicle)
Series: Danilov Family Saga
Major character(s): Alexander Danilov, Vampire; Justin Danilov, Teenager; Sonya Danilov, Parent (Justin's mother)
Time period(s): 1990s (1995)
Locale(s): Savannah, Georgia

Summary: Having vanquished the centuries-old vampire sorcerer who menaced him and his extended family in *This Dark Paradise* (1994), vampire patriarch Alexander Danilov tries once again to preside over his family's affairs, and prepare young Justin Danilov for his upcoming marriage. But the disembodied soul of Lydia, who craved the immortality that Alexander refused her, reanimates Alexander's dead love Elizabeth to torment him.

Other books you might like:
V.C. Andrews, *All That Glitters*, 1995
Tanith Lee, *Dark Dance*, 1993
Michael Romkey, *The Vampire Papers*, 1994

Fred Saberhagen, *A Matter of Taste*, 1992
Karen E. Taylor, *Bitter Blood*, 1994

1998

WENDY HALEY

This Dark Paradise
(New York: Diamond, 1994)

Story type: Horror (Vampire Story; Gothic Family Chronicle)
Series: Danilov Family Saga
Major character(s): Alexander Danilov, Vampire; Barron Danilov, Businessman; James Suldris, Sorcerer
Time period(s): 1990s (1994); 16th century
Locale(s): Savannah, Georgia

Summary: Alex Danilov, a benevolent vampire member of the Danilov family, returns to the family estate in Georgia in time to inherit the family wealth and incur the wrath of his petty and perverse mortal relatives. At the same time, Alex is stalked by James Suldris, a sorcerer whom he thought he killed centuries before but whom he inadvertently vampirized, turning him into an immortal adversary.

Other books you might like:
Tanith Lee, *Dark Dance*, 1993
Michael Romkey, *The Vampire Papers*, 1994
Fred Saberhagen, *A Matter of Taste*, 1992
Dan Simmons, *Carrion Comfort*, 1989
Karen E. Taylor, *Bitter Blood*, 1994

1999

KAREN HALL

Dark Debts
(New York: Random House, 1996)

Story type: Horror (Black Magic)
Major character(s): Michael Kinney, Religious (Jesuit priest); Randa Phillips, Journalist; Jack Landry, Handyman
Time period(s): 1990s (1996)
Locale(s): Barton, Georgia

Summary: Randa Phillips' investigation into the apparent suicide of her lover, Cameron Landry, brings to light the dark legacy of his family, whose patriarch summoned a demon that has wrought destruction through family members before killing them as part of a botched satanic bargain made generations before. Now Jack Landry, Cameron's brother, is feeling the demon's influence, and the only thing that will save him is an exorcism by Father Michael Kinney, a distant relative who has also felt the demon's touch. This is the author's first novel.

Other books you might like:
William Peter Blatty, *The Exorcist*, 1971
Poppy Z. Brite, *Drawing Blood*, 1993
Nancy A. Collins, *Tempter*, 1990
John Farris, *All Heads Turn When the Hunt Goes By*, 1972
Robert R. McCammon, *Usher's Passing*, 1984

2000

MATTHEW HALL

Nightmare Logic
(New York: Bantam, 1989)

Story type: Horror (Serial Killer)
Major character(s): Carolyn Bergeron, Murderer (Serial killer), Artist; Ben Quadrun, Journalist
Time period(s): 1960s; 1980s
Locale(s): Tucson, Arizona

Summary: Sixteen females are murdered in the desert outside of town. Reporter Ben Quadrun gradually comes to believe that the perpetrator may be a beautiful female painter—and that his girlfriend, Nita, is in danger of becoming her next victim. This is Hall's first novel.

Other books you might like:
Peter Straub, *If You Could See Me Now*, 1977

2001

BARBARA HAMBLY

Bride of the Rat God
(New York: Ballantine Del Rey, 1994)

Story type: Fantasy (Magic Conflict; Horror)
Major character(s): Chrysanda "Christine" Famande, Actress; Shang Ko, Wizard; Norah Blackstone, Companion (Christine's sister-in-law)
Time period(s): 1920s
Locale(s): Hollywood, California; Los Angeles, California; Red Bluff, California

Summary: Unbeknownst to her, Christine's use of a magic necklace, The Moon of Rats, betroths her to an ancient Manchurian demon, the Rat God. On the set of her latest film, the demon in human form attempts to kill her to make her his bride while Shang Ko uses protective magic as he searches for a way to counter the undesired union.

Other books you might like:
Lois McMaster Bujold, *The Spirit Ring*, 1992
Elizabeth Forrest, *Phoenix Fire*, 1992
Alan Dean Foster, *Cyber Way*, 1990
Marc Laidlaw, *Neon Lotus*, 1988
Elizabeth Ann Scarborough, *Last Refuge*, 1992

2002

BARBARA HAMBLY

Children of the Jedi
(New York: Bantam Spectra, 1995)

Story type: Science Fiction (Mystical; Space Opera)
Series: Star Wars
Major character(s): Han Solo, Spaceship Captain, Warrior; Leia Organa Solo, Royalty, Leader; Luke Skywalker, Martial Arts Expert, Hero
Time period(s): Indeterminate Past
Locale(s): New Republic, Interstellar Empire/Federation; Outer Space; Belsavis, Planet—Imaginary

Summary: As the surviving Houses of the New Republic attempt to regain their former influence, Leia and Han follow rumors of hidden Jedi to Belsavis while Luke attempts to thwart deadly orders issued by the former emperor to a Super Star Destroyer class battleship.

Other books you might like:
Kevin J. Anderson, *Jedi Search*, 1994
Brian Daley, *The Han Solo Adventures*, 1992
George Lucas, *The Star Wars Trilogy*, 1987
    Donald F. Glut, James Kahn, co-authors
Vonda N. McIntyre, *The Crystal Star*, 1994
L. Neil Smith, *The Lando Calrissian Adventures*, 1994
Dave Wolverton, *The Courtship of Princess Leia*, 1994
Timothy Zahn, *Heir to the Empire*, 1991

2003

BARBARA HAMBLY

Crossroad
(New York: Pocket, 1994)

Story type: Science Fiction (Space Opera)
Series: Star Trek
Major character(s): Christine Chapel, Nurse, Military Personnel (Starfleet); Lao Zhiming, Military Personnel (ensign); Spock, Scientist, Alien (Vulcan)
Time period(s): 23rd century
Locale(s): *U.S.S. Enterprise*, Spaceship; *Nautilus*, Spaceship; United Federation of Planets, Interstellar Empire/Federation

Summary: While investigating the Crossroads Nebula and the Turtledove Anomaly within it, the *Enterprise* rescues the crew of a battered starship, *Nautilus*. The *Nautilus* crew claims they travelled from the future to work as freedom fighters to save the Federation. When the newcomers seize control of his ship and another starship arrives to arrest the renegades, Kirk must discover whom he can trust.

Other books you might like:
James Blish, *The Triumph of Time*, 1958
Peter David, *Q-Squared*, 1994
Diane Duane, *The Wounded Sky*, 1983
David Dvorkin, *Timetrap*, 1988
Harry Turtledove, *The Guns of the South*, 1992

2004

BARBARA HAMBLY

The Dark Hand of Magic
(New York: Del Rey, 1990)

Story type: Fantasy (Sword and Sorcery)
Series: Sun Wolf and Starhawk
Major character(s): Sun Wolf, Mercenary (Former), Wizard (Inexperienced); Starhawk, Mercenary (Former)
Time period(s): Indeterminate

Summary: Ex-mercenary couple Sun Wolf and Starhawk are drawn back to their former company of mercenaries when Sun Wolf is rescued by them because they need his help in a war between merchant princes. Meanwhile a wizard has
promised to teach Sun Wolf how to use his powers but begins to enslave him instead.

Other books you might like:
Carole Nelson Douglas, *Six of Swords*, 1982
Janet Morris, *City at the Edge of Time*, 1988
Jennifer Roberson, *Sword-Dancer*, 1989
    Book 3
Dave Smeds, *The Sorcery Within*, 1985

2005

BARBARA HAMBLY

Dog Wizard
(New York: Ballantine Del Rey, 1993)

Story type: Fantasy (Alternate World; Magic Conflict)
Series: Windrose Chronicles
Major character(s): Antryg Windrose, Wizard, Fugitive; Joanna, Computer Expert
Time period(s): 1990s; Indeterminate
Locale(s): Los Angeles, California; The Citadel of Wizards, Mythical Place; Empire of Ferryth, Fictional Country

Summary: When dimensional breaches allow horrible forces into the exiled Wizards' Citadel, the frightened Wizards blame Antryg Windrose who fled to Earth to avoid their justice. When Antryg ignores the Wizards' summons to return, they kidnap Joanna, forcing Antryg to return to his world to rescue Joanna and battle the deadly breach.

Other books you might like:
Lois McMaster Bujold, *The Spirit Ring*, 1992
Laurell K. Hamilton, *Nightseer*, 1992
Elizabeth Ann Scarborough, *Last Refuge*, 1992
Margaret Weis, *The Hand of Chaos*, 1993
    Tracy Hickman, co-author
Martha Wells, *The Element of Fire*, 1993
Elizabeth Willey, *The Well-Favored Man: The Tale of the Sorcerer's Nephew*, 1993

2006

BARBARA HAMBLY

The Magicians of Night
(New York: Ballantine Del Rey, 1992)

Story type: Fantasy (Magic Conflict; Alternate World)
Series: Sun-Cross
Major character(s): Rhion the Brown, Wizard
Time period(s): 1940s
Locale(s): Germany

Summary: Marooned in Nazi Germany with no easy way back to his own world, Rhion ineffectively advises four would-be wizards against utilizing dark magic to overcome their enemies. Although informed that the Dark Well no longer exists, Rhion believes it does exist and that he must find it if he wishes to return across the Void to his home world.

Other books you might like:
Gael Baudino, *Dragon Death*, 1992
Stephen R. Donaldson, *The Mirror of Her Dreams*, 1986
Katherine Kurtz, *Lammas Night*, 1983

Shirley Rousseau Murphy, *Medallion of the Black Hound*, 1989
    Welch Suggs, co-author
Alis A. Rasmussen, *The Labyrinth Gate*, 1988
Brad Strickland, *Wizard's Mole*, 1991

2007

BARBARA HAMBLY

Mother of Winter

(New York: Ballantine Del Rey, 1996)

Story type: Fantasy (Magic Conflict; Alternate World)
Series: Darwath
Major character(s): Ingold Inglorion, Wizard; Gil Patterson, Warrior, Scholar; Rudy Solis, Wizard, Mechanic
Time period(s): 1990s
Locale(s): Keep of Dare, Fictional City; Alketch, Fictional Country

Summary: The vanquishing of the Dark Ones should have brought easy life, but strange plants and animals, immune to magic, threaten the Keep. While Rudy stays at home to deal with politics and treachery, Gil and Ingold must sneak through the hostile Empire of Alketch to confront an enemy from the dawn of the world.

Other books you might like:
Eleanor Arnason, *Daughter of the Bear King*, 1987
Terry Goodkind, *Wizard's First Rule*, 1994
Guy Gavriel Kay, *The Summer Tree*, 1985
Patricia A. McKillip, *The Riddle-Master of Hed*, 1976
Martha Wells, *The Element of Fire*, 1993

2008

BARBARA HAMBLY

The Rainbow Abyss

(New York: Ballantine/Del Rey, 1991)

Story type: Fantasy (Magic Conflict; Alternate World)
Series: Sun-Cross
Major character(s): Rhion the Brown, Wizard; Jaldis the Blind, Wizard
Time period(s): Indeterminate
Locale(s): Felsplex, Fictional City; Bragenmere, Fictional City

Summary: With wizards considered unfavorably in Felsplex, Rhion and his mentor, Jaldis, barely scratch a living until they are finally run out of the city. They take refuge at the court of the sympathetic Duke of Bragenmere, where Jaldis pursues his researches into the Abyss, trying to reach the people calling to him from the world that has no magic. The prospect of the Abyss frightens Rhion as much as the thought of Jaldis in a place where he is blind and voiceless.

Other books you might like:
John M. Ford, *The Dragon Waiting*, 1983
Stephen R. Donaldson, *The Mirror of Her Dreams*, 1986
Katherine Kurtz, *Lammas Night*, 1983
Megan Lindholm, *Luck of the Wheels*, 1989
Joel Rosenberg, *D'Shai*, 1991

Sheri S. Tepper, *King's Blood Four*, 1983

2009

BARBARA HAMBLY, Editor
MARTIN H. GREENBERG, Co-Editor

Sisters of the Night

(New York: Warner, 1995)

Story type: Horror (Anthology)

Summary: The fourteen stories written especially for this volume all feature female vampires. Barbara Hambly's "Madeleine" is a biter-bit story in which a vampire's victims turn the tables on her, and Michael Kurland's "In the Blood" is a female vampire coming-of-age tale. Pat Cadigan's "Sometimes Salvation" draws analogies between the vampire life and the exploitation of street children while in Tanith Lee's "La Dame," the spirit of a ship develops a vampiric hold on a sailor. Female vampires offer consolation at death for characters in Jane Yolen's "Sister Death" and Dean Wesley Smith's "Tumbling Down the Nightmare," while the vampire of Nina Kiriki Hoffman's "Food Chain" is a child vampire who serves as a surrogate to mothers who have lost their children. Larry Niven's "Song of the Night People" is an excerpt from his novel *The Ringworld Throne*.

Other books you might like:
Poppy Z. Brite, *Love in Vein*, 1994
    Martin H. Greenberg, co-editor
Ellen Datlow, *Blood Is Not Enough*, 1989
    editor
Martin H. Greenberg, *Vamps*, 1987
    Charles G. Waugh, co-editor
Pam Keesey, *Dark Angels: Lesbian Vampire Stories*, 1995
    editor
Pam Keesey, *Daughters of Darkness: Lesbian Vampire Stories*, 1993
    editor

2010

BARBARA HAMBLY

Stranger at the Wedding

(New York: Ballantine Del Rey, 1994)

Story type: Fantasy (Magic Conflict)
Major character(s): Kyra Peldyrin, Wizard; Alix Peldyrin, Fiance(e); Tibbeth of Hale, Wizard
Time period(s): Indeterminate
Locale(s): Angelshand, Fictional City; Empire of Ferryth, Fictional Country

Summary: Responding to a premonition of disaster for Alix on her wedding night, Kyra must stall the wedding without bringing the unwanted attention of the Inquisition down upon herself for using magic in human affairs. Set in the Windrose Chronicles milieu.

Other books you might like:
Mary Gentle, *The Architecture of Desire*, 1993
Laurell K. Hamilton, *Nightseer*, 1992
Delia Sherman, *The Porcelain Dove*, 1993

Paula Volsky, *Illusion*, 1992
Martha Wells, *The Element of Fire*, 1993
Elizabeth Willey, *The Well-Favored Man: The Tale of the Sorcerer's Nephew*, 1993

2011

BARBARA HAMBLY

Those Who Hunt the Night

(New York: Ballantine Del Rey, 1988)

Story type: Horror (Vampire Story)
Major character(s): James Asher, Detective—Amateur (Ex-British spy), Professor (Oxford); Don Simon Ysidro, Vampire (Sympathetic)
Time period(s): 1900s (1907)
Locale(s): London, England

Summary: Asher is "hired," under threat of death to himself and his wife, by a group of the undead to discover who—or what—is killing London's vampire society.

Other books you might like:
Nancy A. Collins, *Sunglasses After Dark*, 1989
Anne Rice, *Interview with the Vampire*, 1976
Whitley Strieber, *The Hunger*, 1981
Les Whitten, *Progeny of the Adder*, 1965

2012

BARBARA HAMBLY

Traveling with the Dead

(New York: Del Rey, 1995)

Story type: Horror (Vampire Story)
Major character(s): Lydia Asher, Scientist (biologist); James Asher, Professor, Detective—Amateur; Ignace Karolyi, Mercenary
Time period(s): 1900s (1908)
Locale(s): London, England; Vienna, Austria

Summary: In this sequel to *Those Who Hunt the Night*, James Asher's pursuit of vampire Lord Charles Farren across Europe results in his capture by the Turkish vampires who have hired Farren for an undisclosed purpose, and Asher's wife Lydia's similar pursuit to save her husband. Along the way, Lydia teams up with a number of mortals and vampires whose motivations mirror her own.

Other books you might like:
Les Daniels, *Yellow Fog*, 1986
Kim Newman, *Anno Dracula*, 1993
Lucius Shepard, *The Golden*, 1994
Chelsea Quinn Yarbro, *Tempting Fate*, 1982

2013

LAURELL K. HAMILTON

Bloody Bones

(New York: Ace, 1996)

Story type: Horror (Vampire Story)
Series: Anita Blake, Vampire Hunter

Major character(s): Anita Blake, Vampire Hunter, Detective—Private; Larry Kirkland, Psychic, Vampire Hunter; Jean-Claude, Vampire
Time period(s): 1990s (1996)
Locale(s): St. Louis Missouri, Alternate Earth

Summary: In this fifth adventure of Anita Blake, set in an alternate universe where supernatural creatures have the same rights as human beings, Anita is called to resurrect ancient dead from a cemetery to settle a property dispute between the family of the dead and a corporation that wants to develop the cemetery land. When Anita's investigations dovetail with recent murders caused by members of the community, she reluctantly seeks assistance from her vampire suitor, Jean-Claude.

Other books you might like:
Scott Baker, *Ancestral Hungers*, 1995
Nancy A. Collins, *A Dozen Black Roses*, 1996
Christopher Golden, *Of Saints and Shadows*, 1994
Don Bassingthwaite, *As One Dead*, 1996
Robert Weinberg, *The Unbeholden*, 1996

2014

LAURELL K. HAMILTON

Circus of the Damned

(New York: Ace, 1995)

Story type: Horror (Vampire Story)
Series: Anita Blake, Vampire Hunter
Major character(s): Anita Blake, Vampire Hunter (animator), Detective—Private; Jean-Claude, Vampire; Larry Kirkland, Psychic (animator), Vampire Hunter
Time period(s): 1990s (1995)
Locale(s): St. Louis Missouri, Alternate Earth

Summary: In an alternate America where vampires coexist with human beings and are achieving equal rights under their rule, animator Anita Blake, who resurrects dead bodies as part of her crime-solving activities, becomes a prize fought for by Jean-Claude, the reigning vampire master of St. Louis, and a vampire interloper, Alejandro, who aspires to become the new master of the city. This is the third novel in the author's "Anita Blake: Vampire Hunter" series, after *The Laughing Corpse* and *Guilty Pleasures*.

Other books you might like:
Richard Lee Byers, *Netherworld*, 1995
Richard Lee Byers, *On a Darkling Plain*, 1995
Robert Weinberg, *Bloodwar*, 1995
Robert Weinberg, *Unholy Allies*, 1995

2015

LAURELL K. HAMILTON

Death of a Darklord

(Lake Geneva, WI: TSR, 1995)

Story type: Horror (Reanimated Dead)
Series: Ravenloft

Major character(s): Jonathan Ambrose, Investigator (mage finder); Tereza Ambrose, Magician (mage); Harkon Lukas, Minstrel
Time period(s): Indeterminate
Locale(s): Cortton Kartakass, Fictional Country

Summary: In the imaginary world of Ravenloft, based on the popular fantasy role-playing game, Jonathan Ambrose is summoned to the city of Cortton to get to the bottom of a recent plague of the walking dead. Jonathan discovers that the plague is part of a ruse contrived by the evil bard Harkon Lukas to instill his discorporate soul into the body of Jonathan's colleague Ambrose Burn and thereby escape into the Dark Domains.

Other books you might like:
Mark Anthony, *Tower of Doom*, 1994
Elaine Bergstrom, *Baronness of Blood*, 1995
Elaine Bergstrom, *Tapestry of Dark Souls*, 1992
P.N. Elrod, *I, Strahd*, 1993
Christie Golden, *The Enemy Within*, 1993
J. Robert King, *Carnival of Fear*, 1992
Chet Williamson, *Mordenheim*, 1994

`2016`

LAURELL K. HAMILTON

Guilty Pleasures
(New York: Ace, 1993)

Story type: Fantasy (Mystery)
Series: Anita Blake, Vampire Hunter
Major character(s): Anita Blake, Vampire Hunter (reanimator), Detective—Private; Nikolaus, Vampire, Leader; Zachary, Reanimated Dead, Criminal
Time period(s): Indeterminate
Locale(s): Alternate Earth

Summary: In an alternate world in which humans and the undead co-exist uneasily, mortal detective Anita Blake is forced by a 1000 year old master vampire to discover the identity of a serial murderer of vampires. Anita's investigations take her into an underworld of bizarre sexual relationships and vampire power politics which may result in Anita's own death or worse.

Other books you might like:
P.N. Elrod, *Bloodlist*, 1990
Barbara Hambly, *Those Who Hunt the Night*, 1988
Tanya Huff, *Blood Price*, 1991
Tanya Huff, *Blood Trail*, 1991
Mercedes Lackey, *Children of the Night*, 1990
Fred Saberhagen, *An Old Friend of the Family*, 1979

`2017`

LAURELL K. HAMILTON

The Laughing Corpse
(New York: Ace, 1994)

Story type: Fantasy (Mystery; Horror)
Series: Anita Blake, Vampire Hunter

Major character(s): Anita Blake, Vampire Hunter (reanimator), Detective—Private; Jean-Claude, Vampire (master vampire of the city); Dominga Salvatore, Religious (voodoo priestess), Criminal
Time period(s): Indeterminate
Locale(s): St. Louis Missouri, Alternate Earth

Summary: When Dominga Salvatore creates durable zombies by reincorporating the deceased's soul, the police require Anita Blake's help to stop her.

Other books you might like:
Lois McMaster Bujold, *The Spirit Ring*, 1992
Tanya Huff, *Blood Price*, 1991
Tanya Huff, *Blood Trail*, 1991
Christopher Moore, *Practical Demonkeeping*, 1992
Nick Pollotta, *Bureau 13*, 1991
Margaret Weis, *Fire Sea*, 1991
   Tracy Hickman, co-author

`2018`

LAURELL K. HAMILTON

The Lunatic Cafe
(New York: Ace, 1996)

Story type: Horror (Vampire Story; Werewolf Story)
Series: Anita Blake, Vampire Hunter
Major character(s): Anita Blake, Vampire Hunter, Detective—Private; Richard Zeeman, Werewolf; Edward Forrester, Criminal (assassin)
Time period(s): 1990s (1996)
Locale(s): St. Louis Missouri, Alternate Earth

Summary: In an alternate universe where supernatural beings and mortals are on equal terms, Anita Blake, a human member of the Regional Preternatural Investigation Team, infiltrates the insular society of lycanthropes and shape-shifters to discover why lycanthropes are disappearing without a trace and whether it is related to the murders being committed by an apparent rogue werewolf.

Other books you might like:
Nancy A. Collins, *Wild Blood*, 1994
Tanya Huff, *Blood Trail*, 1992
Richard Jaccoma, *The Werewolf's Tale*, 1988

`2019`

LAURELL K. HAMILTON

Nightseer
(New York: Roc, 1992)

Story type: Fantasy (Magic Conflict)
Major character(s): Keleios, Sorceress, Fiance(e); Lothor, Sorcerer, Fiance(e)
Time period(s): Indeterminate
Locale(s): Zeln's Castle, Mythical Place

Summary: In a prophetic dream at Zeln's Castle, Keleios foresees treachery and invasion. On waking, her warning fails to prevent the assault and destruction. Keleios and Lothor work to defeat the attacking demons and the sorceress who directs them. Author's first novel.

Other books you might like:
Emma Bull, *War for the Oaks*, 1987
Louise Cooper, *The Deceiver*, 1991
Mary Gentle, *Rats and Gargoyles*, 1991
P.C. Hodgell, *God Stalk*, 1982
Deborah Talmadge-Bickmore, *The Apprentice*, 1990

2020

PETER F. HAMILTON

Mindstar Rising
(New York: Tor, 1996)

Story type: Science Fiction (Psychic Powers; Techno-Thriller)
Series: Greg Mandel
Major character(s): Greg Mandel, Psychic, Detective; Philip Evans, Industrialist, Disembodied Personality; Juliet "Julie" Evans, Cyborg
Time period(s): 21st century
Locale(s): England

Summary: Given a gland by the military which imparts psychic abilities, Greg Mandel gets his way. Philip Evans of Event Horizon, at the forefront of everything, hires Greg to find the saboteur who killed him. Having transferred to a computer before death, Evans helps prevent the saboteur from destroying Event Horizon. First novel originally published in the UK in 1993.

Other books you might like:
Poul Anderson, *Harvest of Stars*, 1993
Julian May, *Magnificat*, 1996
Victor Milan, *The Cybernetic Samurai*, 1985
Kim Stanley Robinson, *Green Mars*, 1994
George Turner, *Genetic Soldier*, 1994

2021

VIRGINIA HAMILTON

Her Stories
(New York: Scholastic/The Blue Sky Press, 1995)

Story type: Fantasy (Collection; Legend)

Summary: Contains a three-page introduction and five-page afterword about the stories, two pages of useful sources and 19 stories, legends, and tales divided into five sections: "Her Animal Tales," "Her Fairy Tales," "Her Supernatural," "Her Folkways and Legends," and "Her True Tales." While endeavoring to retain the original flavor, Hamilton retells for younger readers African American women's tales which focus on females in various forms, concluding each with a comment.

Other books you might like:
Ethel Johnston Phelps, *Tatterhood and Other Tales*, 1978
　editor
Paul Radin, *African Folk Tales and Sculpture*, 1952
　editor
Manly Wade Wellman, *Cahena*, 1979
Jane Yolen, *Favorite Folktales From around the World*, 1986
　editor

Richard Young, *African-American Folktales for Young Readers: Including Favorite Stories From African and African-American Storytellers*, 1993
　editor
Jack Zipes, *Don't Bet on the Prince*, 1986
　editor

2022

IAN HAMMELL

Clock Strikes Sword
(New York: Ace, 1995)

Story type: Fantasy (Political; Adventure)
Series: Shadow World
Major character(s): Aivlys Platho, Apprentice (watchmaker), Magician; Endimin Platho, Artisan (watchmaker), Magician; Beroth of Firoze, Warrior
Time period(s): Indeterminate
Locale(s): Firoze, Fictional City (city state); Gnomon, Fictional City (city state)

Summary: Known as home to fierce warriors, Firoze must unite with a traditional enemy, Gnomon, whose clockmakers wield power over time itself, to defeat the Vargan expansionism which threatens their island. Game tie-in.

Other books you might like:
Clayton Emery, *Shattered Chains*, 1995
Greg Gorden, *Prophecy*, 1994
Michael Moorcock, *Elric of Melnibone*, 1976
Margaret Weis, *Dragon Wing*, 1990
　Tracy Hickman, co-author
Martha Wells, *The Element of Fire*, 1993

2023

MICHAEL HAMMOND

The Burning Man
(New York: Zebra/Pinnacle, 1991)

Story type: Horror (Wild Talents)
Major character(s): Maggie Converse, Journalist; Sam Cutter, Paranormal Investigator; Jonathan Hill, Aged Person
Time period(s): 1980s (1988)
Locale(s): Boulder, Colorado; Clear Creek, Virginia

Summary: Maggie Converse, Sam Cutter and Jonathan Hill all share the same disturbing dream of a blonde-haired man who bursts into flame and dies in agony. But their efforts to pool their paranormal talents and dredge up the subconscious memories necessary to decipher the dream are repeatedly thwarted by Soviet agents with paranormal talents—and inscrutable motives—of their own.

Other books you might like:
Ramsey Campbell, *Incarnate*, 1983
John Farris, *The Fury*, 1976
Stephen King, *Firestarter*, 1980
Brian Lumley, *Necroscope*, 1988

`2024`
NEIL HANCOCK

The Bridge of Dawn
(New York: Popular Library Questar, 1991)

Story type: Fantasy (Quest)
Series: Windameir Circle
Major character(s): Owen Helwin, Warrior
Time period(s): Indeterminate Past
Locale(s): Atlanton Earth, Fictional Country

Summary: Armed with the majestic Sword of Skye, Owen Helwin must win the aid of bears, sea beasts and the High Dragon. With their strength he plans to save beloved Lady Deros. Evil forces have gathered at the mystic Bridge of Dawn for the ultimate battle.

Other books you might like:
David Eddings, *Magician's Gambit*, 1983
David Eddings, *Pawn of Prophecy*, 1982
David Eddings, *Queen of Sorcery*, 1982
J.R.R. Tolkien, *The Fellowship of the Ring*, 1954
J.R.R. Tolkien, *The Return of the King*, 1956
J.R.R. Tolkien, *The Two Towers*, 1955

`2025`
ELIZABETH HAND

12 Monkeys
(New York: HarperPrism, 1995)

Story type: Science Fiction (Time Travel; Post-Disaster)
Major character(s): James Cole, Time Traveller, Criminal; Kathryn Railly, Doctor (psychiatrist)
Time period(s): 21st century; 1990s
Locale(s): Washington, District of Columbia; Baltimore, Maryland; Philadelphia, Pennsylvania

Summary: In exchange for a commuted sentence, James Cole accepts a dangerous reconnaissance mission to 1996, hoping to find evidence of the Army of the 12 Monkeys and the origin of the plague which devastated Earth's population. Mistakenly sent to 1990, James Cole meets Kathryn Railly who later assists him on a subsequent mission to 1996. Novelizes the film.

Other books you might like:
Poul Anderson, *The Time Patrol*, 1991
Randall Frakes, *Terminator 2: Judgment Day*, 1991
S.D. Perry, *Timecop*, 1994
Robert Tine, *Universal Soldier*, 1992
Robert Charles Wilson, *A Bridge of Years*, 1991

`2026`
ELIZABETH HAND

AEstival Tide
(New York: Bantam Spectra, 1992)

Story type: Science Fiction (Genetic Manipulation; End of the World)
Series: The Coming of the Magdalene

Major character(s): Reive, Genetically Altered Being (hermaphrodite); Nefertity, Artificial Intelligence; Margalis Tast'annin, Military Personnel (Aviator Imperator)
Time period(s): Indeterminate
Locale(s): Araboth, Fictional City

Summary: Events drag the fortune teller, Reive, to the highest levels of Araboth, a huge and ancient labyrinthian city built on even older foundations. Reive must negotiate a series of plots and strange events to live even as long as the celebration of AEstival Tide, much less survive the apocalypse that may follow. Sequel to *Winterlong*.

Other books you might like:
C.J. Cherryh, *Sunfall*, 1981
John Crowley, *Little, Big*, 1981
Richard Grant, *Through the Heart*, 1991
Ian McDonald, *Desolation Road*, 1988
Gene Wolfe, *The Shadow of the Torturer*, 1980

`2027`
ELIZABETH HAND

Icarus Descending
(New York: Bantam Spectra, 1993)

Story type: Science Fiction (Genetic Manipulation; Political)
Major character(s): Margalis Tast'annin, Military Personnel (Imperator of Ascendant forces); Aidan Harrow, Disembodied Personality
Time period(s): 26th century
Locale(s): Earth; Outer Space

Summary: For centuries the Ascendants have ruled Earth from orbiting space stations, aided by bioengineered geneslaves, the energumens. Now the energumens intend to overthrow the Ascendants and unite the bioengineered slaves in a rebellion against humanity. When sent to investigate, Tast'annin discovers an ancient threat to all life on Earth, one requiring energumen help to oppose.

Other books you might like:
Philip K. Dick, *Blade Runner*, 1982
Dave Duncan, *Hero*, 1993
Thomas A. Easton, *Greenhouse*, 1991
Thomas A. Easton, *Sparrowhawk*, 1990
Cordwainer Smith, *Norstrilia*, 1975
Michael Swanwick, *Vacuum Flowers*, 1987
Michael D. Weaver, *My Father Immortal*, 1989
Walter Jon Williams, *Voice of the Whirlwind*, 1987

`2028`
ELIZABETH HAND

Waking the Moon
(New York: HarperPrism, 1995)

Story type: Fantasy (Magic Conflict; Religious)
Major character(s): Katherine Sweeney Cassidy, Anthropologist; Angelica di Rienzi, Anthropologist, Religious; Anne Marie "Annie" Harmon, Musician, Lesbian
Time period(s): 1970s; 1990s
Locale(s): Washington, District of Columbia; Sedona, Arizona

Summary: When signs portend a return of the goddess Othiym, Angelica di Rienzi utilizes a powerful sacred object and human sacrifices to facilitate Othiym's return. Meanwhile, an ancient society that promotes patriarchal religions, the Benandanti, works surreptitiously at the University of the Archangels and St. John the Divine to prevent the return of Othiym and the associated bloody worship practices.

Other books you might like:
A.A. Attanasio, *The Moon's Wife: A Hystery*, 1993
Charles de Lint, *Memory and Dream*, 1994
Pamela Dean, *Tam Lin*, 1991
Mary Gentle, *Rats and Gargoyles*, 1991
P.C. Hodgell, *God Stalk*, 1982
Patricia A. McKillip, *The Book of Atrix Wolfe*, 1995

2029

ELIZABETH HAND

Winterlong

(New York: Bantam Spectra, 1990)

Story type: Science Fiction (Post-Holocaust; Genetic Manipulation)
Series: The Coming of the Magdalene
Major character(s): Wendy Wanders, Genetically Altered Being (empath); Justice Saint-Alaban, Scientist (laboratory aid); Miss Scarlet Pan, Actress, Genetically Altered Being
Time period(s): Indeterminate Future
Locale(s): North America

Summary: When the city's new governor decides to terminate a weapons research program, Wendy Wanders avoids death by fleeing with the help of Justice Saint-Alaban. They find sanctuary when asked to join an acting troupe. Their strange and dangerous odyssey through the Narrow Forrest to the Engulfed Cathedral leads them to the final confrontation with the governor at a Grand Masque, the culmination of the Feast of Winterlong. This first person narrative has subtexts drawn from Middle Eastern mythologies, the Demeter/Persephone myth and Bible stories.

Other books you might like:
Octavia E. Butler, *Adulthood Rites*, 1988
Octavia E. Butler, *Dawn*, 1987
Octavia E. Butler, *Imago*, 1989
Philip K. Dick, *Blade Runner*, 1982
Robert Silverberg, *Tower of Glass*, 1970

2030

MARY K. HANNER

Rapid Growth

(New York: Dell/Abyss, 1993)

Story type: Horror (Science Fiction)
Major character(s): Alan Campbell, Doctor (surgeon); Katie Campbell, Researcher (research assistant); Robbie Campbell, Child (8 years old)
Time period(s): 1990s (1993)
Locale(s): Serenity Hills, California

Summary: Exposure to electromagnetic radiation from a poorly regulated producer of microwave ovens causes a plague of teratomas—humanoid tumors that eat their way out of a body—among the residents of Serenity Hills. First novel.

Other books you might like:
John Blackburn, *For Fear of Little Men*, 1972
T.J. Kirby, *Dangerous Nature*, 1993
John Skipp, *The Bridge*, 1991
   Craig Spector, co-author
Peter Straub, *Floating Dragon*, 1982

2031

W.A. HARBINSON

Dream Maker

(New York: Walker, 1992)

Story type: Science Fiction (Invasion of Earth; Alternate Intelligence)
Major character(s): Tony Rydell, Scientist (NASA); Clare Holton, Government Official (scientific liaison officer)
Time period(s): 21st century
Locale(s): Washington, District of Columbia; South America; Antarctica

Summary: While investigating ozone layer depletion over Antarctica, Tony encounters a UFO helping advance the ozone depletion. After returning to Washington, Tony enlists Clare's help to investigate the ozone depletion, a quest which demands greater sacrifice than either expects when they discover the Dream Maker, an inorganic intelligence which feeds on human minds, driving them into demonic reaches of the subconscious.

Other books you might like:
Martin Amis, *Time's Arrow*, 1991
Fredric Brown, *The Mind Thing*, 1961
Octavia E. Butler, *Survivor*, 1978
Hal Clement, *Needle*, 1950
Garfield Reeves-Stevens, *Nighteyes*, 1989
Kurt Vonnegut Jr., *Slaughterhouse Five*, 1969

2032

TERRI HARDIN, Editor

Supernatural Tales From around the World

(New York: Barnes & Noble, 1995)

Story type: Horror (Anthology)

Summary: The 221 brief tales collected here are retellings of legends, folk tales and accounts from the oral tradition of supernatural beings and goings on. Divided into four geographic sections that include Europe, the Americas, Africa and the Near East, and Asia and the Pacific, the book presents accounts of the witches, ghosts, vampires, werewolves, and other traditional beings of the supernatural, as well as certain indigenous monsters such as the banshee (Ireland), the bouda (India), and the tengu (Japan).

Other books you might like:
John Canning, *50 Great Ghost Stories*, 1971
 editor
D.J. Enright, *The Oxford Book of the Supernatural*, 1994
 editor
Charles Lindley, *The Ghost Book of Charles Lindley, Viscount Halifax*, 1994
Elliott O'Donnell, *Ghosts: Stories of the Supernatural*, 1959
Elliott O'Donnell, *Strange Disappearances*, 1990
Jessica Amanda Salmonson, *The Mysterious Doom and Other Ghostly Tales of the Pacific Northwest*, 1992
John Manchip White, *Whistling Past the Churchyard*,

2033
DONALD HARINGTON

The Cockroaches of Stay More
(New York: Harcourt Brace Jovanovich, 1989)

Story type: Fantasy (Satire)
Major character(s): Tish Dingletoon, Animal (Female Cockroach); Sam Ingledew, Animal (Male Cockroach)
Time period(s): 1980s
Locale(s): Stay More, Arkansas

Summary: This is a religious parable, a plea for tolerance and an insectile love story.

Other books you might like:
Brian Brett, *The Fungus Garden*, 1988
Stephen Fine, *Molly Dear: The Autobiography of an Android*, 1988

2034
CHARLES L. HARNESS

Lunar Justice
(New York: Avon, 1991)

Story type: Science Fiction (Psychic Powers; Political)
Major character(s): Quentin Thomas, Psychic, Lawyer; Michael Dore, Genius, Philanthropist; Martin Rile, Judge
Time period(s): Indeterminate Future
Locale(s): Oldcolumbia; Patuxet Haven; Lunaplex, Moon (Earth's)

Summary: Quentin Thomas, patent attorney for Penal Systems, Incorporated, suddenly finds himself forced to accompany a guillotine to Lunaplex. While there he is contacted by Michael Dore, initiator of the Lamplighter Project which will turn Jupiter into a sun and convert its outer moons into habitable planets. Michael Dore is charged with treason, a capital offense, for taking money for Lamplighter and failing to produce a sun. Thomas, compelled to defend Dore, is appalled by the Lunar Justice System.

Other books you might like:
Alfred Bester, *The Stars My Destination*, 1956
Pat Cadigan, *Mindplayers*, 1987
Frank Herbert, *The Dosadi Experiment*, 1977
Katharine Kerr, *Polar City Blues*, 1990
Frederik Pohl, *Gladiator-at-Law*, 1955
 C.M. Kornbluth, co-author

A.E. van Vogt, *Slan*, 1946

2035
CHARLES L. HARNESS

Lurid Dreams
(New York: Avon, 1990)

Story type: Science Fiction (Time Travel; Alternate Universe)
Major character(s): William Reynolds, Student, Time Traveller; Wellington Birch, Military Personnel (colonel), Time Traveller; Alix Schell, Student
Time period(s): 1990s (1990); 19th century
Locale(s): Baltimore, Maryland; Gettysburg, Pennsylvania

Summary: William Reynolds has only one chance to get his doctoral thesis in "Out-of-Body Experiences - History and Techniques" approved. He must fulfill the conditions of the grant offered by Colonel Wellington Birch. He wants William and Alix to combine their talents and send William back in time to convince Edgar Allan Poe to give up his literary aspirations. A computer extrapolation has shown that if Poe had pursued his forgotten military career, he would have been the General at the Battle of Gettysburg to turn the tide of the Civil War and allow the South to win.

Other books you might like:
James P. Blaylock, *Homunculus*, 1986
Randall Frakes, *The Terminator*, 1985
 Bill Wisher, co-author
Joe Haldeman, *The Forever War*, 1975
Joe Haldeman, *The Hemingway Hoax*, 1990
Tim Powers, *The Anubis Gates*, 1983
John Varley, *Millennium*, 1983

2036
RORY HARPER

Petrogypsies
(New York: Baen Books, 1989)

Story type: Science Fiction (Alternate Universe)
Major character(s): Henry Lee McFarland, Oil Industry Worker (Petrogypsy), Farmer (Former); Doc Miller, Oil Industry Worker (Petrogypsy)
Time period(s): Indeterminate
Locale(s): Texas, Alternate Universe

Summary: In Harper's first novel, a race of gigantic, non-sentient, worm-like aliens has been stranded on Earth and the creatures now make their livings working as oil well drillers. The men who follow the aliens across the country taking care of them and arranging jobs for them, called petrogypsies, lead a romantic and fun-filled life. Henry Lee, a strapping young farmboy grown sick of slopping hogs, decides to leave home and take to the road as a petrogypsy.

Other books you might like:
Robert A. Heinlein, *Farmer in the Sky*, 1950
Rebecca Ore, *Becoming Alien*, 1987
Rebecca Ore, *Being Alien*, 1989
Allen Steele, *Orbital Decay*, 1989
Howard Waldrop, *A Dozen Tough Jobs*, 1989

2037

TARA K. HARPER

Cat Scratch Fever

(New York: Ballantine Del Rey, 1994)

Story type: Science Fiction (Adventure; Psychic Powers)
Major character(s): Tsia, Scientist, Genetically Altered Being; Vashanna, Slave; Ramok, Mercenary
Time period(s): Indeterminate Future
Locale(s): Risthmus, Planet—Imaginary

Summary: After years of preparation, Tsia at last takes the guide virus that will mutate her body to create a biogate, a telepathic link to another lifeform. But prohibitions forbid human interference with the large cats, the lifeform with which she forms her gate. Suddenly kidnapped, enslaved, tortured and imprisoned, Tsia struggles to free herself, using every resource, even if it means opening her mind to the wild cats.

Other books you might like:
Marion Zimmer Bradley, *The Shattered Chain*, 1976
A.C. Crispin, *Silent Dances*, 1990
  Kathleen O'Malley, co-author
Gordon R. Dickson, *Masters of Everon*, 1980
Gayle Greeno, *Finders-Seekers*, 1993
Gene Wolfe, *The Shadow of the Torturer*, 1980

2038

TARA K. HARPER

Lightwing

(New York: Ballantine Del Rey, 1992)

Story type: Science Fiction (Political; Psychic Powers)
Major character(s): Kiondili Wae, Student, Telepath; Shyh Stilman, Researcher, Scientist; Poole, Alien (Dhirrnu)
Time period(s): Indeterminate Future
Locale(s): *Mul Hunter*, Spaceship; Corson, Space Station

Summary: Orphaned and betrayed by the trader guild, Kiondili Wae hides her abilities to gain the training she can afford and avoid working for the guild. When proved a strong psychic, she accepts a position at Corson, where she contributes to faster than light research. When humanity develops a faster than light drive, the interstellar community will grant humans equal trade status.

Other books you might like:
Pauline Ashwell, *Unwillingly to Earth*, 1992
David Brin, *The Uplift War*, 1987
A.C. Crispin, *Starbridge*, 1989
Anne McCaffrey, *The Rowan*, 1990
Rebecca Ore, *Becoming Alien*, 1988
Alis A. Rasmussen, *A Passage of Stars*, 1990
Vernor Vinge, *A Fire upon the Deep*, 1992

2039

TARA K. HARPER

Shadow Leader

(New York: Ballantine/Del Rey, 1991)

Story type: Fantasy (Adventure)
Major character(s): Aranur, Martial Arts Expert; Dion, Martial Arts Expert (wolfwalker), Healer, Twin; Rhom, Twin
Time period(s): Indeterminate Future
Locale(s): Ramaj Ariye Asengar, Planet—Imaginary

Summary: Dion, bonded to her wolf Gray Hishn, can telepathically communicate with any wolf. With her brother and companions, Dion and her wolf work as scouts to shepherd the group through the mountains to warn their people of impending attack. Sequel to *Wolfwaker*.

Other books you might like:
Tom Deitz, *Soulsmith*, 1991
Mary H. Herbert, *Dark Horse*, 1990
V.E. Mitchell, *Enemy Unseen*, 1990
Andre Norton, *Beast Master*, 1959
Melanie Rawn, *Dragon Prince*, 1988
Elizabeth Ann Scarborough, *Nothing Sacred*, 1991
Michael D. Weaver, *Wolf-Dreams*, 1989

2040

TARA K. HARPER

Wolfwalker

(New York: Del Rey, 1990)

Story type: Fantasy (Quest)
Major character(s): Dion, Martial Arts Expert (wolfwalker), Healer
Time period(s): Indeterminate Future
Locale(s): Planet—Imaginary

Summary: Dion and her twin brother set out on a ritual journey and encounter travelers on a quest to end a slave trading practice. Joining them in their rescue mission leads the pair into dangerous adventures and ultimately forces Dion to use her forbidden skills of psychic healing to stop a plague.

Other books you might like:
Mercedes Lackey, *The Oathbound*, 1988
Anne McCaffrey, *Dragonriders of Pern Series*,
Dave Smeds, *The Sorcery Within*, 1985
Michael D. Weaver, *Wolf-Dreams*, 1989

2041

JON A. HARRALD (Pseudonym of Harold Schechter and Jonna Gormley Semeiks)

Dying Breath

(New York: Pocket/Star, 1992)

Story type: Horror (Psychological Suspense)
Major character(s): Simon Proctor, Cult Member (leader); Marianne Byrne, Police Officer; Richard Wayland, Police Officer (Chief of Stoneham police force)
Time period(s): 1990s (1992)

Locale(s): Stoneham, New York

Summary: In this collaborative first novel, a ritualistic animal killing, a graverobbing, a child kidnapping, and the defacing of public property with Satanic graffiti prove to be the work of Simon Proctor, a Southern California cult leader with delusions of prophethood, who has chased two lapsed disciples cross country to exact his revenge upon them.

Other books you might like:
Stephen R. George, *Nightscape*, 1992
Dean R. Koontz, *Servants of Twilight*, 1984
Robert R. McCammon, *Mine*, 1990

2042

BARRY HARRINGTON

The Beyond

(New York: Diamond, 1991)

Story type: Horror (Possession)
Major character(s): Susan Holland, Designer (fashion designer); Justin Nesbitt, Musician (rock guitarist); Michael Pearl, Doctor, Administrator (of hospital)
Time period(s): 1990s (1991)
Locale(s): Groveland, New York

Summary: Although haunted by the memory of the night that she was assaulted and another 12-year-old was raped and killed by two teenage boys, Susan Holland returns to her hometown of Groveland to inherit her mother's estate. But Susan is unaware that the one attacker who still lives is literally haunted by the spirit of his dead companion, who has been waiting more than 20 years to finish the job he started. A first novel.

Other books you might like:
J.M. Dillard, *Specters*, 1991
Joe R. Lansdale, *The Nightrunners*, 1987
T.M. Wright, *Boundaries*, 1991

2043

ALLEN LEE HARRIS

Let There Be Dark

(New York: Jove, 1994)

Story type: Horror (Small Town Horror)
Major character(s): Matt Hardison, Writer; Tommy Buford, Handyman; Pete Hardison, Child (Matt's son)
Time period(s): 1990s (1994)
Locale(s): Mt. Jephtha, Georgia

Summary: Matt Hardison returns to his rural southern hometown after his novel *The Shadowstealer*, loosely based on a local legend told him by an elderly aunt, becomes a bestseller. But Matt discovers that his book has liberated the creature of its title, a soul-stealing monster that preys upon weaknesses in human beings, and whose origins are closely tied to un-remembered events in Matt's childhood.

Other books you might like:
Ray Bradbury, *Something Wicked This Way Comes*, 1962
Jonathan Carroll, *The Land of Laughs*, 1980

Douglas Clegg, *Goat Dance*, 1989
Elizabeth Forrest, *Dark Tide*, 1993
Robert R. McCammon, *Usher's Passing*, 1984

2044

ANNE HARRIS

The Nature of Smoke

(New York: Tor, 1996)

Story type: Science Fiction (Alternate Intelligence; Gay/Lesbian Fiction)
Major character(s): Magnolia, Runaway, Lesbian; Cidiera "Cid", Scientist (molecular biologist), Lesbian; Tumcari, Artificial Intelligence
Time period(s): 21st century
Locale(s): Wotroya House, Asia (Polish Siberia); Amsterdam, Netherlands

Summary: A runaway from the grim Detroit slums, Magnolia receives an offer from a mysterious doctor who wants to template her personality to create independently-minded robots. At his remote estate in Polish Siberia, she falls in love with Cid, a scientist trying to create a virus which allows people to see the connections between seemingly chaotic events. First novel.

Other books you might like:
Valerie J. Freireich, *Becoming Human*, 1995
Nicola Griffith, *Slow River*, 1995
Linda Nagata, *The Bohr Maker*, 1995
Mary Rosenblum, *The Stone Garden*, 1995
Kate Wilhelm, *Death Qualified: A Mystery of Chaos*, 1991

2045

DEBORAH TURNER HARRIS

Caledon of the Mists

(New York: Ace, 1994)

Story type: Fantasy (Adventure; Magic Conflict)
Series: Caledon
Major character(s): Rorin McCann, Nobleman, Rebel; Duncan Dunladry, Royalty, Heir—Dispossessed; Mhairi Dunladry, Royalty, Heiress—Dispossessed
Time period(s): Indeterminate
Locale(s): Caledon, Fictional Country

Summary: After exiled Prince Duncan returns to Caledon to reclaim his rights from a usurper, he falls victim to a shapeshifting demon in the first battle. When his sister, Mhairi, realizes that she must carry on the dream and the fight, she rallies the people of Caledon and, as Queen, calls upon the powers of the land itself to overthrow the tyrant.

Other books you might like:
Diane Duane, *The Door into Sunset*, 1993
Barbara Hambly, *The Time of the Dark*, 1982
Katherine Kurtz, *The Adept*, 1991
   Deborah Turner Harris, co-author
Katherine Kurtz, *Deryni Rising*, 1970
Christopher Stasheff, *Her Majesty's Wizard*, 1986

2046

DEBORAH TURNER HARRIS

The Queen of Ashes

(New York: Ace, 1995)

Story type: Fantasy (Political; Magic Conflict)
Series: Caledon
Major character(s): Mhairi Dunladry, Royalty (queen); Perolys na Juriam dro Sarn, Government Official; Mordance of Barquist, Widow(er), Friend
Time period(s): Indeterminate
Locale(s): Caledon, Fictional Country; Behringar, Fictional Country

Summary: Conflict between Caledon and Behringar leaves Mhairi open to overtures of marriage from Edwin, King of Behringar. Already unhappy with their loss of power, the Lords of Caledon plot against Mhairi, as an old, dark plot endangers them all. Second in the series.

Other books you might like:
Barbara Hambly, *The Time of the Dark*, 1982
Katherine Kurtz, *Deryni Rising*, 1970
Susan Schwartz, *Byzantium's Crown*, 1987
Julie Dean Smith, *Call of Madness*, 1990
Judith Tarr, *Lord of the Two Lands*, 1993
Paula Volsky, *Illusion*, 1992

2047

MARILYN HARRIS

Night Games

(New York: Doubleday, 1987)

Story type: Horror (Psychological Suspense)
Major character(s): Zoe Manning, Housewife; Mary Lisa Fletcher, Actress (A childhood friend of Manning)
Time period(s): 1980s (1986)
Locale(s): Whitney, New Hampshire

Summary: Confused and depressed over the suicide of her parents and the instability of her marriage, Zoe returns to her childhood home, where she is taken in by a group of demented actors—who may or may not be real—who subject her to a series of ''night games'' that force her to confront her own deepest fears and secrets.

Other books you might like:
James Herbert, *The Magic Cottage*, 1986
Helen McCloy, *Through a Glass Darkly*, 1980

2048

RAYMOND HARRIS

The Schizogenic Man

(New York: Ace, 1990)

Story type: Science Fiction (Time Travel)
Major character(s): John Heron, Immigrant (to New City from the Midwest), Time Traveller; Stella Cranach, Artist; MEQMAT, Computer (in charge of New City)
Time period(s): Indeterminate Future; 1st century B.C.

Locale(s): New City, Fictional City; Alexandria, Egypt

Summary: John Heron is sent back to Alexandrian Egypt in a so-called experiment to improve memory. There his identity is that of Nikias, who is chosen to take Kaiserion, Cleopatra's son, into exile in India. When he returns to the present, things are subtly altered—he has a son rather than a daughter—and the City is going downhill, threatened by Texas Fundamentalists. He does more Dips in the hopes of returning to his original past. Finally, under bombing and chaos, he manages to find his original self, or so he thinks.

Other books you might like:
John Brunner, *Times Without Number*, 1962
A. Bertram Chandler, *Kelly Country*, 1985
Crawford Kilian, *The Empire of Time*, 1978
Ward Moore, *Bring the Jubilee*, 1953
Kevin D. Randle, *Remember the Alamo!*, 1986
    Robert J. Cornett, co-author

2049

ROBERT HARRIS

Fatherland

(New York: Random House, 1992)

Story type: Science Fiction (Alternate Universe; Political)
Major character(s): Xavier March, Detective—Police, Police Officer; Charlotte ''Charlie'' Maguire, Journalist
Time period(s): 1960s (April 14, 1964-April 19, 1964)
Locale(s): Berlin, Germany

Summary: Twenty years after Nazi victory in World War II and a week before Hitler's 75th birthday, Xavier March and Charlie Maguire investigate the death of a once-important Nazi official. They uncover a conspiracy begun during the war which threatens the underpinning of the Nazi regime, a deal between Adolph Hitler and United States President Joseph P. Kennedy. Author's first novel.

Other books you might like:
Brian W. Aldiss, *The Year Before Yesterday*, 1987
Gregory Benford, *Hitler Victorious: Eleven Stories of the German Victory in World War II*, 1986
    Martin H. Greenberg, co-editor
Philip K. Dick, *The Man in the High Castle*, 1962
Michael Flynn, *In the Country of the Blind*, 1990
Fritz Leiber, *The Big Time*, 1961
Norman Spinrad, *The Iron Dream*, 1972

2050

STEVE HARRIS

The Eyes of the Beast

(New York: Tor, 1993)

Story type: Horror (Carnival/Circus Horror)
Major character(s): David Carter, Teenager; Sally Harrison, Office Worker; Frederick Purdue, Worker (carnival worker)
Time period(s): 1990s (1990)
Locale(s): Basingstoke, England

Summary: When the Adventureland fun fair comes to town, people begin disappearing from Basingstoke, and David Carter finds himself battling a variety of bizarre monsters seemingly straight out of the computer games to which he is addicted. David's investigations take him and girlfriend Sally into the dark reality behind Adventureland's gaudy carnival trappings. This book, the author's first novel, was originally published in England in 1990 as *Adventureland*.

Other books you might like:
Ray Bradbury, *Something Wicked This Way Comes*, 1962
Charles G. Finney, *The Circus of Dr. Lao*, 1935
Richard Laymon, *Funland*, 1990
Thomas F. Monteleone, *The Magnificent Gallery*, 1987
A.R. Morlan, *Dark Journey*, 1991

2051

THOMAS HARRIS

The Silence of the Lambs
(New York: St. Martin's, 1988)

Story type: Horror (Serial Killer)
Major character(s): Clarice Starling, FBI Agent (trainee); Hannibal "Cannibal" Lector, Murderer (brilliant psychopath)
Time period(s): 1980s
Locale(s): United States

Summary: Starling probes the mind of the infamous ex-psychiatrist and mass murderer "Cannibal" Lector for clues in her pursuit of the bizarre serial killer, "Buffalo Bill," while Lector uses his celebrity status to engineer his own escape attempt.

Other books you might like:
Robert Bloch, *Psycho*, 1959
Rex Miller, *Slob*, 1987

2052

HARRY HARRISON
DAVID BISCHOFF, Co-Author

Bill, the Galactic Hero: On the Planet of Tasteless Pleasure
(New York: Avon, 1991)

Story type: Science Fiction (Humor)
Series: Bill, the Galactic Hero
Major character(s): Bill, Spaceman; Irma Feritayl, Royalty; Rick, Spaceship Captain
Time period(s): Indeterminate Future
Locale(s): *Desire*, Spaceship; Planet—Imaginary

Summary: Bill seeks good times when he signs on with Rick in the Quest for the Holy Bar and Grill. 15 pages of humorous illustrations are included.

Other books you might like:
Douglas Adams, *The Hitchhiker's Guide to the Galaxy*, 1980
Henry N. Beard, *Bored of the Rings*, 1969
    Douglas C. Kenney, co-author
John M. Ford, *How Much for Just the Planet?*, 1987

Sharyn McCrumb, *Bimbos of the Death Sun*, 1987
Larry Niven, *Fallen Angels*, 1991
    Michael Flynn and Jerry Pournelle, co-authors
Leah Rewolinski, *Star Wreck: The Generation Gap*, 1990
Ken Rolston, *Extreme Paranoia: Nobody Knows the Trouble I've Shot*, 1991
Ellis Weiner, *National Lampoon's Doon*, 1984

2053

HARRY HARRISON
DAVID HARRIS, Co-Author

Bill, the Galactic Hero: The Final Incoherent Adventure
(New York: AvoNova, 1992)

Story type: Science Fiction (Humor; Military)
Series: Bill, the Galactic Hero
Major character(s): Bill, Spaceman; "Captain Cadaver" Kadaffi, Military Personnel
Time period(s): Indeterminate Future
Locale(s): Eyerack, Planet—Imaginary

Summary: When Captain Kadaffi volunteers Bill for an assault on Eyerack, Bill moves from V.I.P. to prisoner as he searches for good times and a human foot to replace his prosthetic Swiss Army foot.

Other books you might like:
Douglas Adams, *The Hitchhiker's Guide to the Galaxy*, 1980
Henry N. Beard, *Bored of the Rings*, 1969
    Douglas C. Kenney, co-author
John M. Ford, *How Much for Just the Planet?*, 1987
Larry Niven, *Fallen Angels*, 1991
    Michael Flynn and Jerry Pournelle, co-authors
Leah Rewolinski, *Star Wreck: The Generation Gap*, 1990
Ken Rolston, *Extreme Paranoia: Nobody Knows the Trouble I've Shot*, 1991
Ellis Weiner, *National Lampoon's Doon*, 1984

2054

HARRY HARRISON

Galactic Dreams
(New York: Tor, 1994)

Story type: Science Fiction (Collection)
Summary: Contains a nine-page introduction, one original story featuring Bill, the Galactic Hero, and 11 stories reprinted without prior publication acknowledgments. Themes include space opera in "Space Rats of the CCC," a dystopian solution to birth control in "A Criminal Act," a tragicomic investigation of love in "The Robot Who Wanted to Know," a teddy bear with a sinister agenda in "I Always Do What Teddy Says," a time travel paradox in "If" and racial prejudice in "Mute Milton." Companion volume to *Stainless Steel Visions*.

Other books you might like:
Alfred Bester, *Star Light, Star Bright*, 1976
Michael Flynn, *The Nanotech Chronicles*, 1991
Cordwainer Smith, *The Rediscovery of Man*, 1993

Theodore Sturgeon, *The Ultimate Egoist*, 1994
John Varley, *Blue Champagne*, 1986

2055

HARRY HARRISON
JOHN HOLM, Co-Author

The Hammer and the Cross
(New York: Tor, 1993)

Story type: Fantasy (Historical; Religious)
Series: Hammer and the Cross
Major character(s): Shef Sigvarthsson, Hero, Blacksmith; Brand, Warrior, Sidekick; Ivar, Warrior
Time period(s): 9th century (865)
Locale(s): England

Summary: Born to an Englishwoman raped by a Viking raider, Shef fights the Norse invaders and follows them to rescue his step-sister, Godive. In his quest, he meets Vikings who follow the Way, worshipping the old gods while seeking to increase human knowledge in preparation for Ragnarok, the final battle between good and evil. Guided by visions of the gods, Shef develops new weapons including the halberd and the crossbow and leads his own army to victory against both pagan marauders and Christian invaders.

Other books you might like:
Poul Anderson, *A Midsummer Tempest*, 1984
Orson Scott Card, *Red Prophet*, 1988
C.J. Cherryh, *A Dirge for Stabis*, 1989
    Leslie Fish, co-author
L. Sprague de Camp, *Lest Darkness Fall*, 1941
John M. Ford, *The Dragon Waiting*, 1983
Parke Godwin, *Sherwood*, 1991
R.A. MacAvoy, *The Book of Kells*, 1985
Pat Winter, *Madoc's Hundred*, 1991

2056

HARRY HARRISON
JOHN HOLM, Co-Author

King and Emperor
(New York: Tor, 1996)

Story type: Fantasy (Historical; Religious)
Series: Hammer and the Cross
Major character(s): Shef Sigvarthsson, Royalty (king), Scientist; Bruno, Royalty (emperor)
Time period(s): 9th century (875)
Locale(s): Spain; Italy

Summary: Intrigued by the offer of knowledge about flying, Shef agrees to help the Caliph of Cordova fight the alliance of Holy Roman and Byzantine Emperors. Between battles and aeronautical experiments, Shef finds the Holy Grail, learns the uses of zero, invents movable type, and discovers the destructive secret of Greek fire. When in visions he sees his father free Loki, the god of fire and trickery, portending Ragnarok and the twilight of the gods, Shef's own actions in the world may hasten the day.

Other books you might like:
Poul Anderson, *Hrolf Kraki's Saga*, 1973
Jean M. Auel, *The Valley of Horses*, 1982
L. Sprague de Camp, *Lest Darkness Fall*, 1941
Diana L. Paxson, *The Wolf and the Raven*, 1993
Susan Shwartz, *The Grail of Hearts*, 1992

2057

HARRY HARRISON
JOHN HOLM, Co-Author

One King's Way
(New York: Tor, 1995)

Story type: Science Fiction (Alternate Universe; Fantasy)
Series: Hammer and the Cross
Major character(s): Shef Sigvarthsson, Royalty (king), Warrior; Erkenbert, Religious (deacon), Leader; Brand, Warrior, Sidekick (Shef's)
Time period(s): 9th century (860s)
Locale(s): England; At Sea; Europe

Summary: Having risen from slave to king of a mighty Viking nation and co-ruler of England, Shef Sigvarthsson presents a threat to all the powers of Europe. One group in particular, the Knights of the Lance, believe that he who holds the sacred spear of Christ will assume the mantle of Emperor. To that end, many factions vie to locate the spear, pull Shef from his throne, replace the Pope in Rome with someone more sympathetic to their cause, and create a new German Roman Empire. Sequel to *The Hammer and the Cross*.

Other books you might like:
Frans G. Bengtsson, *The Long Ships*, 1954
Marion Zimmer Bradley, *The Mists of Avalon*, 1983
Ben Bova, *Orion and the Conqueror*, 1994
Linda Evans, *Sleipnir*, 1994
Stephan Grundy, *Rhinegold*, 1994
Morgan Llywelyn, *Bard*, 1984
Morgan Llywelyn, *Lion of Ireland*, 1979
Andrew J. Offutt, *Sword of the Gael*, 1975
Diana L. Paxson, *The Wolf and the Raven*, 1993
T.H. White, *The Once and Future King*, 1958

2058

HARRY HARRISON

Planet of the Robot Slaves
(New York: Avon, 1989)

Story type: Science Fiction (Humor)
Series: Bill, the Galactic Hero
Major character(s): Corporal Bill, Military Personnel; Cy BerPunk, Computer Expert
Time period(s): Indeterminate Future
Locale(s): Planet of the Robot Slaves, Planet—Imaginary

Summary: Corporal Bill and a number of other not particularly intelligent military types are marooned on a very strange and rather silly planet filled with heavy metal monsters.

Other books you might like:
Ron Goulart, *Brinkman*, 1981

Ron Goulart, *Hellquad*, 1984
Ron Goulart, *The Wicked Cyborg*, 1978
Barry B. Longyear, *Naked Came the Robot*, 1988
Terry Pratchett, *Equal Rites*, 1987

2059

HARRY HARRISON

The Stainless Steel Rat Goes to Hell

(New York: Tor, 1996)

Story type: Science Fiction (Adventure; Humor)
Series: Stainless Steel Rat
Major character(s): Jim diGriz, Criminal, Adventurer; Justin Slakey, Con Artist, Professor
Time period(s): Indeterminate Future
Locale(s): Lussuoso, Planet—Imaginary; Heaven; Hell

Summary: Angelina diGriz disappears while investigating a scam in which a cult leader promises trips to Heaven. When Jim diGriz calls the family together to find her, he ends up in quite different places, thanks to Justin Slakey's dimension-warping device.

Other books you might like:
Poul Anderson, *Operation Chaos*, 1971
Piers Anthony, *Tarot*, 1987
David Brin, *The Practice Effect*, 1984
Arsen Darnay, *The Purgatory Zone*, 1981
Brad Ferguson, *The World Next Door*, 1990
Ward Hawkins, *Red Flame Burning*, 1985
Larry Niven, *Inferno*, 1976
    Jerry Pournelle, co-author
Roger Zelazny, *A Farce to Be Reckoned With*, 1995
    Robert Sheckley, co-author

2060

HARRY HARRISON

The Stainless Steel Rat Sings the Blues

(New York: Bantam Spectra, 1994)

Story type: Science Fiction (Adventure; Humor)
Series: Stainless Steel Rat
Major character(s): Jim DiGriz, Criminal; Steengo, Spy, Musician; Madonette, Singer, Worker (electrical)
Time period(s): Indeterminate Future
Locale(s): Liokukae, Planet—Imaginary

Summary: Blackmailed into going to the prison planet, Liokukae, to retrieve an alien artifact that has landed there, Jim DiGriz assumes as cover the persona of a musician heading a group busted for drug possession, allowing him to travel the planet filled with criminals who have formed very strange societies.

Other books you might like:
Piers Anthony, *Orn*, 1971
Robert Asprin, *Phule's Company*, 1990
J.F. Bone, *Federation Matadore*, 1978
Leigh Brackett, *The Ginger Star*, 1974
A. Bertram Chandler, *The Wild Ones*, 1985
Ursula K. Le Guin, *The Eye of the Heron*, 1983

Robert Silverberg, *Hawksbill Station*, 1968
Christopher Stasheff, *We Open on Venus*, 1994
Jack Vance, *Showboat World*, 1975

2061

HARRY HARRISON
BRYN BARNARD, Illustrator

Stainless Steel Visions

(New York: Tor, 1993)

Story type: Science Fiction (Collection)

Summary: Contains a six-page introduction plus 13 stories reprinted from periodicals and anthologies. "The Golden Years of the Stainless Steel Rat" features the protagonist from The Stainless Steel Rat series (1961-) while "The Mothballed Spaceship" utilizes characters from *The Deathworld Trilogy* (1976). Includes "Roommates," the original story for the film, *Soylent Green*; "The Secret of Stonehenge," the basis for *Stonehenge: Where Atlantis Died* (1983); "Portrait of the Artist," which reflects Harrison's work as a comic book artist; and "The Street of Ashkelon" in a restored version.

Other books you might like:
David Brin, *The River of Time*, 1986
Michael Flynn, *The Nanotech Chronicles*, 1991
Ian McDonald, *Speaking in Tongues*, 1992
Larry Niven, *N-Space*, 1990
Cordwainer Smith, *The Rediscovery of Man*, 1993
John Varley, *Blue Champagne*, 1986
John Varley, *The Persistence of Vision*, 1978
Gene Wolfe, *Castle of Days*, 1992

2062

HARRY HARRISON, Editor
BRUCE MCALLISTER, Co-Editor

There Won't Be War

(New York: Tor, 1991)

Story type: Science Fiction (Anthology)
Time period(s): Indeterminate Future

Summary: This anthology of 5 reprint and 14 original stories which focus on the struggle for peace also includes an introduction by Bruce McAllister and an afterword by Harry Harrison. Authors include Isaac Asimov, J.G. Ballard, Joe Haldeman, James Morrow, Frederik Pohl, Robert Sheckley, William Tenn and George Zebrowski.

Other books you might like:
Octavia E. Butler, *Dawn*, 1987
Daniel Quinn, *Ishmael*, 1992
Elizabeth Ann Scarborough, *Nothing Sacred*, 1991
Joan Slonczewski, *A Door into Ocean*, 1986
Joan Slonczewski, *Still Forms on Foxfield*, 1980
Sheri S. Tepper, *Sideshow*, 1992
Michael Tobias, *Voice of the Planet*, 1990

2063

HARRY HARRISON
MARVIN MINSKY, Co-Author

The Turing Option
(New York: Warner, 1992)

Story type: Science Fiction (Techno-Thriller; Alternate Intelligence)
Major character(s): Brian Delaney, Scientist, Computer Expert
Time period(s): 2020s (2023-2024)
Locale(s): California; Mexico; Europe

Summary: Shortly after Brian Delaney develops an artificial intelligence for Metaglobe Industries, an assassin loots his lab, kills his assistants and attempts to kill Delaney. Experimental surgery saves Delaney, but the results begin to blur the distinction between man and machine.

Other books you might like:
David Brin, *Earth*, 1990
Jeffrey A. Carver, *The Rapture Effect*, 1987
Victor Milan, *The Cybernetic Samurai*, 1986
Rudy Rucker, *Software*, 1982
David Alexander Smith, *Marathon*, 1982
Neal Stephenson, *Snow Crash*, 1992
Thomas T. Thomas, *ME: A Novel of Self Discovery*, 1991
John Varley, *Steel Beach*, 1992
Walter Jon Williams, *Voice of the Whirlwind*, 1987

2064

SUE HARRISON

Mother Earth, Father Sky
(New York: Doubleday, 1990)

Story type: Fantasy (Romance; Historical)
Major character(s): Chagak, Prehistoric Human, Indian (Aleut); Shuganan, Artist, Indian (Aleut)
Time period(s): 71st century B.C. (7056 B.C.)
Locale(s): Aleutian Islands, Alaska

Summary: Chagak sees the massacre of her people, finds her infant brother and decides to live. She leaves her beach to search for a place for herself and her brother. 1991 Best Books For Young Adults title.

Other books you might like:
Jean M. Auel, *Clan of the Cave Bear*, 1980
W. Michael Gear, *People of the Fire*, 1991
    Kathleen O'Neal Gear, co-author
Richard Herley, *The Stone Arrow*, 1978
Meredith Ann Pierce, *The Woman Who Loved Reindeer*, 1989
William Sarabande, *Beyond the Sea of Ice*, 1987
Elizabeth Marshall Thomas, *Reindeer Moon*, 1987

2065

SUE HARRISON

My Sister the Moon
(New York: Doubleday, 1992)

Story type: Fantasy (Historical; Legend)
Major character(s): Samiq, Prehistoric Human, Indian (Aleut); Amgigh, Prehistoric Human, Indian (Aleut); Kiin, Prehistoric Human, Indian (Aleut)
Time period(s): 8th century B.C. (B.C.)
Locale(s): Aleutian Islands, Alaska

Summary: In love with Samiq, Kiin's betrothal to his brother, Amgigh, saves her life which was endangered by her father. An Aleut legend about a female who mates with two sea otter brothers forms the basis for this sequel to *Mother Earth, Father Sky*.

Other books you might like:
Jean M. Auel, *Clan of the Cave Bear*, 1980
Meredith Ann Pierce, *The Woman Who Loved Reindeer*, 1989
William Sarabande, *The Sacred Stones*, 1991
Elizabeth Marshall Thomas, *The Animal Wife*, 1990
Elizabeth Marshall Thomas, *Reindeer Moon*, 1987

2066

DAVID G. HARTWELL, Editor
KATHRYN CRAMER, Co-Editor

The Ascent of Wonder: The Evolution of Hard SF
(New York: Tor, 1994)

Story type: Science Fiction (Anthology; Hard Science Fiction)
Summary: Contains three introductions by Gregory Benford, Kathryn Cramer and David G. Hartwell plus lengthy individual introductions to 67 stories reprinted from periodicals and anthologies and organized by the way in which the author utilizes science in the story, with a two-page appendix by Cramer presenting a thematic organization of 44 stories. Authors contributing to the foundation of scientific fiction last century include Nathaniel Hawthorne, Edgar Allan Poe and Jules Verne, with Rudyard Kipling and H.G. Wells' work from early this century. Other authors include Poul Anderson, Isaac Asimov, J.G. Ballard, Greg Bear, Gregory Benford, Gordon R. Dickson, Michael F. Flynn, John M. Ford, Robert L. Forward, C.M. Kornbluth, Henry Kuttner, Philip Latham, Ursula K. Le Guin, Katherine MacLean, Anne McCaffrey, George Turner, Vernor Vinge, Ian Watson, Kate Wilhelm and Gene Wolfe.

Other books you might like:
Isaac Asimov, *Isaac Asimov Presents the Great SF Stories*, 1979-1992
    Martin H. Greenberg, co-editor
Gardner Dozois, *Modern Classics of Science Fiction*, 1992
    editor
Ursula K. Le Guin, *The Norton Book of Science Fiction: North American Science Fiction, 1960-1990*, 1993
    Brian Attebery, co-editor

Tom Shippey, *The Oxford Book of Science Fiction Stories*, 1992
editor
Robert Silverberg, *The Science Fiction Hall of Fame, Volume 1*, 1970
editor

2067

DAVID G. HARTWELL, Editor

Christmas Forever
(New York: Tor, 1993)

Story type: Fantasy (Anthology; Religious)

Summary: Contains 28 original stories of Yuletide wonder exhibiting a broad range of themes which encompass monsters, mythical creatures, a magical cruise, virgin births, holidays on alien worlds and a Christmas at the end of time. Authors include James P. Blaylock and Tim Powers collaborating on one story plus Joan Aiken, Margaret Ball, Michael Bishop, Charles de Lint, Alan Dean Foster, Janet Kagan, Damon Knight, Patricia A. McKillip, Rudy Rucker, Robert Sheckley, Gene Wolfe, Dave Wolverton and Roger Zelazny.

Other books you might like:
Martin H. Greenberg, *Christmas on Ganymede and Other Stories*, 1990
editor
Rosalind M. Greenberg, *Christmas Bestiary*, 1992
Martin H. Greenberg, co-editor
Mike Resnick, *Christmas Ghosts*, 1993
Martin H. Greenberg, co-editor
Kristine Kathryn Rusch, *Pulphouse, Issue 10: Special Issue*, 1991
editor
John Silbersack, *The Magic of Christmas*, 1992
Christopher Schelling, co-editor

2068

DAVID G. HARTWELL, Editor

Christmas Magic
(New York: Tor, 1994)

Story type: Fantasy (Anthology; Religious)

Summary: Contains seven original stories and 21 stories reprinted from periodicals and anthologies 1957-1993, all sharing Yuletide themes, with one 1993 Hugo award winning story by Janet Kagan, "The Nutcracker Coup." Other authors include A.J. Austin, David R. Bunch, Harlan Ellison, Alan Dean Foster, Nina Kiriki Hoffman, James P. Hogan, Alexander Jablokov, Kit Reed, and Margaret St. Clair.

Other books you might like:
Kathryn Cramer, *Spirits of Christmas*, 1989
David G. Hartwell, co-editor
Martin H. Greenberg, *Christmas on Ganymede and Other Stories*, 1990
editor
Rosalind M. Greenberg, *Christmas Bestiary*, 1992
Martin H. Greenberg, co-editor

Kristine Kathryn Rusch, *Pulphouse, Issue 10: Special Issue*, 1991
editor
John Silbersack, *The Magic of Christmas*, 1992
Christopher Schelling, co-editor

2069

DAVID G. HARTWELL, Editor

Christmas Stars
(New York: Tor, 1992)

Story type: Science Fiction (Anthology)

Summary: Contains 23 short stories published from 1950-1991 in periodicals and books plus two poems by John M. Ford, all sharing the theme Christmas. Joe L. Hensley and Alexei Panshin collaborated on one story, "Dark Conception." Other authors include Brian W. Aldiss, Ben Bova, Ray Bradbury, Arthur C. Clarke, Thomas M. Disch, Cynthia Felice, William Gibson, Anne McCaffrey, Frederik Pohl, Ian Watson, Connie Willis and Gene Wolfe.

Other books you might like:
Alan Brennert, *Kindred Spirits*, 1984
Martin H. Greenberg, *Christmas on Ganymede and Other Stories*, 1990
editor
Rosalind M. Greenberg, *Christmas Bestiary*, 1992
Martin H. Greenberg, co-editor
Kristine Kathryn Rusch, *Pulphouse, Issue 10: Special Issue*, 1991
editor
John Silbersack, *The Magic of Christmas*, 1992
Christopher Schelling, co-editor
Gene Wolfe, *Gene Wolfe's Book of Days*, 1981

2070

DAVID G. HARTWELL, Editor

Foundations of Fear
(New York: Tor, 1992)

Story type: Horror (Anthology)

Summary: A mammoth follow-up volume to the editor's earlier *The Dark Descent*, tracking the development of the horror genre through the novella length work. The 30 stories include H. P. Lovecraft's short novel of horrors in the Antarctic, "At the Mountains of Madness"; Richard Matheson's tale of a paranoid traffic chase, "Duel"; John W. Campbell's science fiction horror story, "Who Goes There"; Clive Barker's dark fairy tale, "In the Hills, The Cities"; Peter Straub's tale of a vindictive young boy, "The Blue Rose"; and Arthur Machen's classic story of evil incarnate, "The Great God Pan." The editor has supplied an insightful introduction.

Other books you might like:
Bill Pronzini, *The Arbor House Treasury of Horror and the Supernatural*, 1981
Barry Malzberg and Martin H. Greenberg, co-editors

Herbert Wise, *Great Tales of Terror and the Supernatural*, 1944
Phyllis Fraser, co-editor

2071

DAVID G. HARTWELL, Editor

Masterpieces of Fantasy and Wonder
(New York: St. Martin's Press, 1994)

Story type: Fantasy (Anthology)

Summary: Contains a four-page introduction plus individual introductions to 38 of the best fantasy stories from the 19th and 20th centuries organized into five sections, "Enchantments," "Wonders," "Creatures," "Worlds" and "Adventures." Authors include L. Frank Baum, Charles Dickens, Suzette Haden Elgin, Harlan Ellison, John M. Ford, Ursula K. Le Guin, George MacDonald, Anne McCaffrey, Patricia A. McKillip, Robin McKinley, William Morris, Edith Nesbit, Isaac Bashevis Singer, Fyodor Sologub, Frank R. Stockton, James Tiptree Jr., Mark Twain and Jack Vance.

Other books you might like:
Jorge Luis Borges, *The Book of Fantasy*, 1990
editor
Robert H. Boyer, *Visions & Imaginings: Classic Fantasy Fiction*, 1992
Kenneth J. Zahorski, co-editor
Alison Lurie, *The Oxford Book of Modern Fairy Tales*, 1993
editor
Tom Shippey, *The Oxford Book of Fantasy Stories*, 1994
editor
Robert Silverberg, *The Fantasy Hall of Fame*, 1983
Martin H. Greenberg, co-editor

2072

DAVID G. HARTWELL, Editor
GLENN GRANT, Co-Editor

Northern Stars: The Anthology of Canadian Science Fiction
(New York: Tor, 1994)

Story type: Science Fiction (Anthology)

Summary: Contains an 11-page appendix of major Canadian SF and fantasy awards, a four-page introduction by Grant plus individual introductions to two essays, two novel excerpts and 25 stories, with five of them translated from French, published during the past 20 years by Canadian writers. Authors include Michael G. Coney, Charles de Lint, Candas Jane Dorsey, Dave Duncan, William Gibson, Phyllis Gotlieb, Terrance M. Green, Eileen Kernaghan, Robert Sawyer, Elisabeth Vonarburg and Robert Charles Wilson.

Other books you might like:
Damien Broderick, *Strange Attractors: Original Australian Speculative Fiction*, 1985
editor
John Robert Colombo, *Other Canadas*, 1979
editor

Gardner Dozois, *The Year's Best Science Fiction Series*, 1984-1994
editor
Ursula K. Le Guin, *The Norton Book of Science Fiction: North American Science Fiction, 1960-1990*, 1993
Brian Attebery, co-editor
Kristine Kathryn Rusch, *The Best of Pulphouse: The Hardback Magazine*, 1991
editor

2073

DAVID G. HARTWELL, Editor
MILTON T. WOLF, Co-Editor

Visions of Wonder: The Science Fiction Research Association Anthology
(New York: Tor, 1996)

Story type: Science Fiction (Anthology)

Summary: This survey assembles 32 stories published in periodicals and anthologies 1961-1994 and nine essays useful for teachers and understandable by students from periodicals and anthologies, 1956-1989. The stories reflect some of the most influential work of popular authors and address the broad spectrum of issues facing teachers, such as new science and technologies, social problems and forces, the future in space, and gender issues. Authors include Brian W. Aldiss, Greg Bear, Gregory Benford, Orson Scott Card, Suzy McKee Charnas, Charles de Lint, Anne McCaffrey, Andre Norton, Frederik Pohl, Charles Sheffield, Judith Tarr, James Tiptree Jr., Jack Williamson, and Gene Wolfe.

Other books you might like:
Isaac Asimov, *Isaac Asimov Presents the Great SF Stories: 1-25*, 1979-1992
Martin H. Greenberg, co-editor
Gardner Dozois, *Modern Classics of Science Fiction*, 1992
editor
Gardner Dozois, *The Year's Best Science Fiction Series*, 1984-1996
editor
Ursula K. Le Guin, *The Norton Book of Science Fiction: North American Science Fiction, 1960-1990*, 1993
Brian Attebery, co-editor
Tom Shippey, *The Oxford Book of Science Fiction Stories*, 1992
editor

2074

DAVID G. HARTWELL, Editor

Year's Best Science Fiction
(New York: HarperPrism, 1996)

Story type: Science Fiction (Anthology)

Summary: Contains a three-page introduction and individual introductions to 14 stories published in periodicals and anthologies in 1995 with one Hugo Award winner and Nebula Award nominee, James Patrick Kelly's "Think Like a Dinosaur." Varying in tone, the stories feature diverse themes such as hard science, first contact, space exploration, cyberpunk, medicine, volcanic disaster, and alternate history. Ursula K. Le Guin returns to the world of *The Left Hand of Darkness* (1969) with "Coming of Age in Karhide." Other authors include Stephen Baxter, Gregory Benford, Joe Haldeman, Nancy Kress, Patricia A. McKillip, Joan Slonczewski, Gene Wolfe, and Roger Zelazny.

Other books you might like:
Isaac Asimov, *Isaac Asimov Presents the Great SF Stories: 1-25*, 1979-1992
    Martin H. Greenberg, co-editor
Greg Bear, *New Legends*, 1995
    Martin H. Greenberg, co-editor
Gardner Dozois, *The Year's Best Science Fiction Series*, 1984-1996
    editor
Jennifer Hershey, *Full Spectrum 5*, 1995
    Tom Dupree, Janna Silverstein, co-editors
Pamela Sargent, *Nebula Awards 30*, 1996
    editor
Robert Silverberg, *Universe 3*, 1994
    Karen Haber, co-editor

2075

JAMES NEAL HARVEY

The Headsman
(New York: Jove, 1993)

Story type: Horror (Mystery)
Major character(s): Jud McElroy, Police Officer (police chief); Karen Wilson, Secretary, Psychic; Emmett Stark, Police Officer (former police chief)
Time period(s): 1990s (1991)
Locale(s): Braddock, New York

Summary: Police officer Jud McElroy teams up with psychically-endowed Karen Wilson to find out who is using their small rural town's legend of an immortal axe murderer as a cover for his own spree of gruesome decapitations. This novel was originally published in hardcover in 1991.

Other books you might like:
Paul Dale Anderson, *Claw Hammer*, 1989
S.K. Epperson, *Dumford Blood*, 1991
Michael Slade, *Headhunter*, 1983

2076

GEORGE HATCH, Editor

Guignoir and Other Furies
(Long Island City, New York: Horror's Head Press, 1991)

Story type: Horror (Anthology)
Summary: Thirteen stories of "psychological terror, violence and suspense" that, as the title implies, wed grotesque imagery to the dark themes of noir fiction. Included are stories of repellently dysfunctional families by Nancy Holder and Tia Travis, a sexual dystopia by Lucy Taylor, and the title story, a bizarre hardboiled revenge tale about a serial killer and traveling side show.

Other books you might like:
Robert Bloch, *Psycho-Paths*, 1991
    Martin H. Greenberg, co-author
Richard T. Chizmar, *Cold Blood*, 1991
Ed Gorman, *Dark Crimes: Great Noir Fiction From the '50's to the '90's*, 1992
Ed Gorman, *Stalkers*, 1989
    Martin H. Greenberg, co-author
Joe R. Lansdale, *Dark at Heart*, 1992
    Karen Lansdale, co-author

2077

GEORGE HATCH, Editor
STEVE RASNIC TEM, Illustrator
T. WINTER-DAMON, Illustrator

Sinistre, An Anthology of Rituals
(Staten Island, New York: Horrors Head Press, 1993)

Story type: Horror (Anthology)

Summary: The 16 original stories in this trade paperback incarnation of George Hatch's small press magazine *Noctulpa* all are concerned with the enduring force of primitive rites and superstitions in a modern context. Included are A.R. Morlan's "Tattoo," in which a gang rape victim undergoes a full-body tattoo of clothing to avoid her psychological trauma; Robert Frazier's "Too Long in the Wasteland" and Gerald Daniel Houarner's "Hidden Agendas," each of which treats the idea of parricide as a rite of passage; Nancy Patrick's "The Power of One" and Steve Rasnic Tem's "Doodles," in which characters develop obsessive traits to compensate for guilt feelings; and Connie Hirsch's humorous "Prayers and the Material Girl," conducted as a dialogue between one woman's multiple personalities.

Other books you might like:
Martin H. Greenberg, *Cults of Horror*, 1990
    Charles G. Waugh, co-editor
Gary L. Raisor, *Obsessions*, 1991
    editor

2078

MARLEN HAUSHOFER
SHAUN WHITESIDE, Co-Author

The Wall
(Pittsburg, Pennsylvania: Cleis Press, 1991)

Story type: Science Fiction (Dystopian; Post-Holocaust)
Major character(s): I, Writer
Time period(s): 20th century
Locale(s): Europe (Alps)

Summary: The diarist awakens in the countryside to find herself the only survivor of a disaster which has wiped out all life on the other side of an invisible barrier which surrounds a large, unaffected area. With no wilderness training, she must find the means to survive. Originally published in German as *Die Wand* (1962), this translation by Shaun Whiteside is the author's first book available in English.

Other books you might like:
Neal Barrett Jr., *Through Darkest America*, 1987
Richard Brautigan, *In Watermelon Sugar*, 1968
David Brin, *The Postman*, 1985
Octavia E. Butler, *Dawn*, 1987
Gordon R. Dickson, *Wolf and Iron*, 1990
David R. Palmer, *Emergence*, 1984
Vernor Vinge, *Marooned in Realtime*, 1986
Vernor Vinge, *The Peace War*, 1984
M.K. Wren, *A Gift upon the Shore*, 1990

2079

RICK HAUTALA

Beyond the Shroud

(Stone Mountain, Georgia: White Wolf, 1996)

Story type: Horror (Possession)
Major character(s): David Robinson, Writer; Sarah Robinson, Teacher; Tony Ranieri, Student
Time period(s): 1990s (1996)
Locale(s): Portland, Maine

Summary: From The Shadowlands, a realm of dead souls and supernatural beings who prey upon them, newly deceased David Robinson watches helplessly while his ex-wife Sarah, whom he still loves, begins an affair with a young man who has fallen under the murderous influence of one of the knives used by Jack the Ripper. Set in the world of the publisher's role-playing game "Wraith."

Other books you might like:
Richard Lee Byers, *On a Darkling Plain*, 1995
Sam Chupp, *Sins of the Fathers*, 1995

2080

RICK HAUTALA

Cold Whisper

(New York: Zebra, 1991)

Story type: Horror (Curse)
Major character(s): Sarah Lahikainen, Student—College (at University of Maine, Orono); Elliot Clark, Police Officer; Alan Griffin, Prisoner
Time period(s): 1990s
Locale(s): Hilton, Maine; Orono, Maine

Summary: As a child, Sarah Lahikainen could not escape the belief that her imaginary playmate Tully engineered the deaths of her pets and baby brother when she became angry with them. In the wake of her mother's brutal murder at the hands of a delinquent who is now stalking her, Sarah discovers that Tully is a tulpa, a family demon who grows stronger and more uncontrollable the longer her anger remains unassuaged.

Other books you might like:
J.N. Williamson, *The Tulpa*, 1982

2081

RICK HAUTALA

Dark Silence

(New York: Zebra, 1992)

Story type: Horror (Curse)
Major character(s): Brian Fraser, Child; Edward Fraser, Businessman (real estate developer); Mike Fraser, Patient (escaped mental patient)
Time period(s): 1990s (1994)
Locale(s): Summerfield, Maine

Summary: When his father begins trying to sell off the family land Brian Fraser falls prey to the same supernatural curse that turned his uncle Mike into a raving lunatic, one levied 300 years before by an ancestor hanged as a witch who vowed vengeance against all her enemies and their descendants who sought to appropriate her lands illegally.

Other books you might like:
Vincent Courtney, *Wake Up Screaming*, 1992
Roy Sorrels, *The Eyes of Torie Webster*, 1990

2082

RICK HAUTALA

Dead Voices

(New York: Warner, 1990)

Story type: Horror (Occult)
Major character(s): Elizabeth "Payne" Meyer, Divorced Person; Frank Melrose, Police Officer; Roland Graydon, Doctor (psychiatrist)
Time period(s): 1990s
Locale(s): Bristol Mills, Maine

Summary: Emotionally devastated after the death of her young daughter Caroline, Elizabeth Meyer leaves her husband to return to her family home in Maine. While she is there, a series of graveyard defilements and mysterious deaths seems to indicate that Caroline is trying to get in touch with her mother from beyond the grave—or that someone is trying to make it look so.

Other books you might like:
Stephen King, *Pet Sematary*, 1983
David C. Smith, *The Fair Rules of Evil*, 1989

2083

RICK HAUTALA

Ghost Light

(New York: Warner, 1993)

Story type: Horror (Psychological Suspense)
Major character(s): Cindy Toland, Young Woman; Alex Harris, Worker (airport worker); Billy Harris, Child (Alex's son)
Time period(s): 1990s (1993)
Locale(s): Omaha, Nebraska; Portland, Maine

Summary: Cindy Toland flees Nebraska with her young niece and nephew, pursued cross-country by their psychotic father Alex, who murdered their mother, and protected by a ghostly figure with a blue aura whom only the children can see.

Other books you might like:
Stephen Gallagher, *Down River*, 1989
Ruby Jean Jensen, *Celia*, 1991
Dean R. Koontz, *Lightning*, 1988
Dean R. Koontz, *Shadowfires*, 1987

2084

RICK HAUTALA

Impulse
(New York: Pinnacle, 1996)

Story type: Horror (Psychological Suspense)
Major character(s): Angie Ross, Teacher; Greg Newman, Murderer; Brandy Ross, Teenager
Time period(s): 1990s (1996)
Locale(s): New York, New York; Bolton, Maine

Summary: Paranoid and hounded by the voices of those he has murdered, Greg Newman stalks the mother and children of one of his victims, forcing them to become as savage as he is.

Other books you might like:
Ruby Jean Jensen, *Celia*, 1991
Stephen King, *Rose Madder*, 1995
Dean R. Koontz, *Whispers*, 1980
Clare McNally, *Good Night, Sweet Angel*, 1996

2085

RICK HAUTALA

Moon Walker
(New York: Zebra, 1989)

Story type: Horror (Reanimated Dead)
Major character(s): Dale Harmon, Engineer; Franklin Rodgers, Undertaker
Time period(s): 1980s
Locale(s): Dyer, Maine

Summary: When his best friend is killed, Dale Harmon begins to investigate the mysterious events occurring in the small town of Dyer, Maine. The trail leads him to Franklin Rodgers, the local funeral director, who possesses an "eye" to see other worlds and the ability to reanimate the dead. Soon Harmon and a small group of associates find themselves under siege by a small army of zombies.

Other books you might like:
Stephen Gallagher, *Valley of Lights*, 1987
Richard Laymon, *Resurrection Dreams*, 1989

2086

RICK HAUTALA

The Mountain King
(Baltimore: CD Publications, 1996)

Story type: Horror (Nature in Revolt)
Major character(s): Mark Newman, Worker (mill worker); Phil Sawyer, Worker (mill worker); Sandy Newman, Teenager (Mark's daughter)
Time period(s): 1990s (1996)
Locale(s): Hilton, Maine

Summary: Mark Newman can't get anyone to believe that he saw his friend Phil abducted by a sasquatch-like creature during their last climb on Mount Agiochook. Mark returns to the mountain to look for his friend and becomes the object of a dual manhunt, by the townsfolk who suspect him of Phil's murder, and by the monster itself. This book was published as a signed limited hardcover edition of 500 copies.

Other books you might like:
Jack Ketchum, *Off Season*, 1980
Jack Ketchum, *Offspring*, 1991
Dean R. Koontz, *Watchers*, 1987
Richard Laymon, *Midnight's Lair*, 1988
John Tigges, *Monster*, 1995

2087

RICK HAUTALA

Shades of Night
(New York: Zebra, 1995)

Story type: Horror (Haunted House)
Major character(s): Lara DeSalvo, Housewife; Vincent DeSalvo, Businessman (land developer); Matt Coulter, Carpenter
Time period(s): 1990s (1995)
Locale(s): Portland, Maine

Summary: Newly married Lara DeSalvo moves to her husband's home in Portland, Maine, where she finds herself plagued with nighttime visions of a ghostly woman and stalked by a menacing prowler. When her husband begins exerting an irrational control over her life, Lara examines how all of these inexplicable variables might be interrelated.

Other books you might like:
Robert Bloch, *American Gothic*, 1974
Daphne Du Maurier, *Rebecca*, 1938
Ruby Jean Jensen, *Celia*, 1993
Stephen King, *Rose Madder*, 1995

2088

RICK HAUTALA

Twilight Time
(New York: Zebra, 1994)

Story type: Horror (Psychological Suspense)

Major character(s): Jeff Wagner, Professor (of history); Katherine Foster, Secretary—Legal; Danny Foster, Child (Katherine's son)
Time period(s): 1990s (1994)
Locale(s): Cape Higgins, Maine

Summary: As a young boy Jeff Wagner endured abuse at the hands of fundamentalist guardians and sought comfort in an illicit relationship with his sister. His return to his hometown to see his sister through a suicide attempt inaugurates a series of deaths and disappearances that may be the doings of the multiple personalities spawned by his guilt feelings, or other people trying to drive him mad.

Other books you might like:
David Ambrose, *The Man Who Turned into Himself*, 1994
Richard Matheson, *A Stir of Echoes*, 1958
John R. Maxim, *Abel/Baker/Charley*, 1983
Daniel Quinn, *Dreamer*, 1988
F. Paul Wilson, *Sibs*, 1991

2089

PETE HAUTMAN

Mr. Was

(New York: Simon & Schuster, 1996)

Story type: Science Fiction (Young Adult; Time Travel)
Major character(s): Jack "Mr. Was" Lund, Time Traveller, Amnesiac; Andrea "Andie" Skoro, Time Traveller; Pinky, Time Traveller, Administrator
Time period(s): 1990s; 1940s
Locale(s): Minnesota; Guadalcanal, Pacific Islands (The Canal/The Isle of Death); Andrea Island, Puerto Rico

Summary: Jack Lund's journal reveals glimpses of Jack's life after family tragedies and his discovery of a doorway to the past firm Jack's resolve to travel back in time to change events he experienced as a youth.

Other books you might like:
Octavia E. Butler, *Kindred*, 1979
Eleanor Cameron, *The Court of the Stone Children*, 1973
Mona Clee, *Branch Point*, 1996
Kara Dalkey, *Little Sister*, 1996
Susan Palwick, *Flying in Place*, 1992
Jill Paton Walsh, *A Chance Child*, 1978

2090

DOUGLAS D. HAWK

The Devouring

(New York: Leisure, 1994)

Story type: Horror (Nature in Revolt)
Major character(s): Morgan Blaylock, Writer; Robert Ferris, Spy; Richard Chase, FBI Agent
Time period(s): 1990s (1994)
Locale(s): Crystal Wells, Rocky Mountains, Canada

Summary: The destruction of a mountaintop research facility in the Rocky Mountains proves to be the work of *Homo desmodus*, a crossbred species of humans and bloodthirsty bats that has lived inside the earth for eons. The efforts of

locals to eradicate the creatures are thwarted by government agents intent on capturing the creatures for their own uses.

Other books you might like:
William W. Johnstone, *Bats*, 1993
Martin Cruz Smith, *Nightwing*, 1977
T.W. Stetson, *Night Beasts*, 1993
Robert Wilson, *Second Fire*, 1993

2091

SIMON HAWKE

The Ambivalent Magician

(New York: Warner Aspect, 1996)

Story type: Fantasy (Alternate World; Light Fantasy)
Series: Reluctant Sorcerer
Major character(s): Marvin "Doc" Brewster, Scientist, Genius; Warrick Morgannan, Wizard, Leader; Pamela Fairburn, Scientist, Fiance(e)
Time period(s): Indeterminate; 1990s
Locale(s): Darn, Fictional Country; London, England

Summary: Trapped in a parallel universe, Brewster rallies the motley inhabitants of Brigand's Roost, now the Kingdom of Brigantium, to fight Warrick, who has troubles of his own with the Narrator. Meanwhile, a tabloid story about one of Warrick's experimental subjects, transported across time and space by Brewster's invention, attracts the attention of Brewster's long-suffering fiancee, Pamela. When Warrick turns up in modern London with the time machine and Pamela commandeers it to rescue Brewster, the Narrator triumphs over Warrick. . .perhaps.

Other books you might like:
Robert Asprin, *Another Fine Myth*, 1978
L. Sprague de Camp, *The Complete Compleat Enchanter*, 1989
  Fletcher Pratt, co-author
Gordon R. Dickson, *The Dragon and the George*, 1976
Barbara Hambly, *Dog Wizard*, 1993
Terry Pratchett, *The Colour of Magic*, 1983
Christopher Stasheff, *Her Majesty's Wizard*, 1986
Mark Twain, *A Connecticut Yankee in King Arthur's Court*, 1889

2092

SIMON HAWKE

The Inadequate Adept

(New York: Warner Questar, 1993)

Story type: Fantasy (Alternate World; Magic Conflict)
Series: Reluctant Sorcerer
Major character(s): Marvin "Doc" Brewster, Scientist, Genius; Warrick Morgannan, Wizard, Leader (Grand Director of the Guild)
Time period(s): Indeterminate; 1990s
Locale(s): Frank, Fictional Country; Darn, Fictional Country

Summary: Doc continues producing magical devices using local robbers as a labor force. Warrick tries to determine the magic of Doc's time machine, but the prisoners he straps into it continue to disappear. The narrator follows Doc's attempts to regain his machine and return to Pamela, who endeavors to duplicate the device and rescue Doc.

Other books you might like:
John DeChancie, *Castle Perilous*, 1988
Gordon R. Dickson, *The Dragon and the George*, 1976
Carole Nelson Douglas, *Cup of Clay*, 1991
Brad Strickland, *Wizard's Mole*, 1991

▐2093▌
SIMON HAWKE

The Iron Throne
(Lake Geneva, Wisconsin: TSR, 1995)

Story type: Fantasy (Political; Adventure)
Series: Birthright
Major character(s): Michael Roele, Royalty, Leader
Time period(s): Indeterminate
Locale(s): Cerilian Empire of Anuire, Fictional Country

Summary: Raised to rule, Michael Roele faces many challenges from those who wish to acquire the power destined for him. First of a game tie-in series.

Other books you might like:
David Cook, *Beyond the Moons*, 1991
Troy Denning, *The Verdant Passage*, 1991
David Eddings, *Pawn of Prophecy*, 1982
Douglas Niles, *Darkwalker on Moonshae*, 1987
R.A. Salvatore, *The Legacy*, 1992

▐2094▌
SIMON HAWKE

The Nine Lives of Catseye Gomez
(New York: Warner Questar, 1992)

Story type: Fantasy (Light Fantasy; Mystery)
Series: Wizard of 4th Street
Major character(s): Catseye Gomez, Animal (cat), Genetically Altered Being; Jay Solo, Police Officer (Commissioner), Administrator; Dan Leventhal, Detective—Police
Time period(s): 26th century
Locale(s): Santa Fe, New Mexico; Denver, Colorado

Summary: After the death of his only real friend, Gomez moves to Denver with Solo. The next morning he meets another thaumaturgic cat who tries to get him involved in the Equal Rights for Animals movement. When the cat's owner, a journalist promoting E.R.A., gets murdered by a car bomb, Leventhal, a maverick assigned to the case, recruits Gomez as his special assistant on the investigation.

Other books you might like:
Steven Brust, *Jhereg*, 1983
Glen Cook, *Sweet Silver Blues*, 1987
Alan Dean Foster, *Cat-A-Lyst*, 1991
Simon R. Green, *The God Killer*, 1991
Gary K. Wolf, *Who P-P-Plugged Roger Rabbit?*, 1991

▐2095▌
SIMON HAWKE

The Outcast
(Lake Geneva, Wisconsin: TSR, 1993)

Story type: Fantasy (Quest)
Series: Dark Sun: Tribe of One
Major character(s): Sorak, Psychic, Mythical Creature (half-elf)
Time period(s): Indeterminate
Locale(s): Athas, Planet—Imaginary

Summary: Found abandoned in the desert as a child, Sorak grows up with mystics who understand his psionic power and fragmented, multiple identities. Hoping to resolve his internal turmoil, Sorak sets out to discover his origins and seek out the Sage, a powerful magician who will help Sorak find his destiny.

Other books you might like:
Troy Denning, *The Amber Enchantress*, 1992
Troy Denning, *The Cerulean Storm*, 1993
Troy Denning, *The Crimson Legion*, 1992
Troy Denning, *The Obsidian Oracle*, 1993
Troy Denning, *The Verdant Passage*, 1991

▐2096▌
SIMON HAWKE

The Reluctant Sorcerer
(New York: Warner Questar, 1992)

Story type: Fantasy (Alternate World; Light Fantasy)
Series: Reluctant Sorcerer
Major character(s): Marvin "Doc" Brewster, Scientist, Genius; Michael Timothy O'Fallon, Mythical Creature (leprechaun); Robie McMurphy, Farmer
Time period(s): Indeterminate; 1990s
Locale(s): London, England; Frank, Fictional Country

Summary: While watching his favorite film, *Frankenstein*, Doc thinks he's solved the problem with his time machine. Leaving his fiancee behind, he fixes the switch on the machine and transports, totally destroying the device during his arrival. Mistaken for a sorcerer by the local inhabitants, he finds himself in an alternate universe in which he must find the faulty machine he has inadvertently sent before his arrival or remain permanently.

Other books you might like:
Douglas Adams, *The Hitchhiker's Guide to the Galaxy*, 1980
Katherine Blake, *The Interior Life*, 1990
Rick Cook, *Wizard's Bane*, 1989
John DeChancie, *Castle Perilous*, 1988
John Morressy, *The Questing of Kedrigern*, 1987
Spider Robinson, *Callahan's Secret*, 1986
Gene Wolfe, *Castleview*, 1990

2097
SIMON HAWKE

The Samurai Wizard
(New York: Warner/Questar, 1991)

Story type: Fantasy (Magic Conflict; Contemporary)
Series: Wizard of 4th Street
Major character(s): Wyrdrune Carpinski, Wizard; Billy Slade, Wizard (Merlin Ambrosius)
Time period(s): 23rd century
Locale(s): Tokyo, Japan; New York, New York

Summary: Before humans developed intelligence there was a race of Immortal Necromancers on the Earth. Eventually some noticed that the humans had become people, not beasts, and chose to use them no longer. A war was fought between those white mages and the necromancers who did not want to lose this rich resource, as white magic is more difficult and less powerful than necromancy. One of these Immortals, Merlin, chose to re-enter the world of men after the collapse and a 2000 year respite and introduce the structured use of thaumaturgic power to save the human race.

Other books you might like:
Suzy McKee Charnas, *The Golden Thread*, 1989
John DeChancie, *Castle Perilous*, 1988
Diane Duane, *High Wizardry*, 1989
Barbara Hambly, *The Time of the Dark*, 1982
Gene Wolfe, *Castleview*, 1990

2098
SIMON HAWKE

The Seeker
(Lake Geneva, Wisconsin: TSR, 1994)

Story type: Fantasy (Quest; Adventure)
Series: Dark Sun: Tribe of One
Major character(s): Sorak, Psychic, Mythical Creature (half-elf); Ryana, Religious (priestess), Adventurer
Time period(s): Indeterminate
Locale(s): Athas, Planet—Imaginary

Summary: Led by visions and a spell scroll, Sorak and Ryana must cross a deadly wasteland in search of the reclusive Sage and the secret Veiled Alliance. Sequel to *The Outcast*.

Other books you might like:
Lynn Abbey, *The Brazen Gambit*, 1994
Troy Denning, *The Amber Enchantress*, 1992
Troy Denning, *The Crimson Legion*, 1993
Troy Denning, *The Verdant Passage*, 1991
Ryan Hughes, *The Darkness Before the Dawn*, 1995

2099
SIMON HAWKE

War
(Lake Geneva, Wisconsin: TSR, 1996)

Story type: Fantasy (Political; Adventure)
Series: Birthright

Major character(s): Gannd Aurealis, Mythical Creature (half-elf), Warrior; Katrina, Noblewoman; Reece, Mercenary
Time period(s): Indeterminate
Locale(s): Empire of Anuir, Fictional Country; Seaharrow, Mythical Place

Summary: When Michael Roele dies, many attempt to gain power in the empire. Unless one leader emerges, the intrigues and squabbling among those who wish to rule will tear the empire asunder.

Other books you might like:
John Betancourt, *The Hag's Contract*, 1996
Anne Kelleher Bush, *Children of Enchantment*, 1996
Dixie McKeone, *Greatheart*, 1996
Dixie McKeone, *The Spider's Test*, 1996
R.A. Salvatore, *Siege of Darkness*, 1994

2100
SIMON HAWKE

The Whims of Creation
(New York: Warner Aspect, 1995)

Story type: Science Fiction (Generation Starship; Genetic Manipulation)
Major character(s): Ulysses Buckland, Teenager, Wizard; Jenny Kruickshank, Teenager, Warrior; Penelope Selden, Psychologist, Computer Expert (programmer)
Time period(s): Indeterminate Future (3rd millennium A.D.)
Locale(s): *Agamemnon*, Spaceship; Outer Space

Summary: Ulysses discovers that suicide and early marriage seem on the increase, but he lacks the proper security code to check on the psych files. In other unusual occurrences, his mother finds fairies in the herb fields and the school's artificial intelligence sends him to a planet where he uses mystic posers and Jenny wields a sword. 50 years earlier, Dr. Selden predicted the need for change and adventure, altering the A.I. programs to produce mythic forms using the reproductive centers.

Other books you might like:
Brian W. Aldiss, *Starship*, 1959
Poul Anderson, *The Boat of a Million Years*, 1989
James Blish, *A Life for the Stars*, 1962
Alexei Panshin, *Rite of Passage*, 1968
Gene Wolfe, *Nightside the Long Sun*, 1993

2101
SIMON HAWKE

The Wizard of Camelot
(New York: Warner Questar, 1993)

Story type: Fantasy (Light Fantasy; Post-Disaster)
Series: Wizard of 4th Street
Major character(s): Merlin Ambrosius, Wizard; Thomas Mallory, Police Officer (retired); Billy Martens, Television Personality
Time period(s): 25th century
Locale(s): London, England; Loughborough, England

Summary: At the end of the Collapse, Thomas Mallory quits the London Police Department. He comes home to find his family cold and hungry and takes an ax to illegally cut some wood, almost not caring if he gets caught. When his ax touches the tree, a bolt of lightning splits the tree and an old man in a robe suddenly appears, calling himself Merlin Ambrosius and desiring to start a school to train adepts in Thaumaturgy and save humanity and the Earth from the Collapse. Prequel to *The Wizard of 4th Street*.

Other books you might like:
James P. Blaylock, *The Paper Grail*, 1991
Charles de Lint, *The Little Country*, 1991
John DeChancie, *Castle Perilous*, 1988
Michael Kurland, *A Study in Sorcery*, 1989
Michael Williams, *A Forest Lord*, 1991
Robert Anton Wilson, *The Widow's Son*, 1985

2102
SIMON HAWKE

The Wizard of Santa Fe
(New York: Warner Questar, 1991)

Story type: Fantasy (Magic Conflict; Post-Disaster)
Series: Wizard of 4th Street
Major character(s): Wyrdrune Carpinski, Wizard; Billy Slade, Wizard (Merlin Ambrosius)
Time period(s): 26th century
Locale(s): Sante Fe, New Mexico

Summary: When a necromancer kills two young women in Santa Fe, Merlin recognizes the work of a Dark One. He moves the household, including Broom, to New Mexico to destroy the necromancer before the Bureau of Thaumaturgy agent arrives. The Bureau does not know that Merlin is alive in the body of his descendant, Billy Slade, and Merlin prefers to keep it that way.

Other books you might like:
Glen Cook, *Sweet Silver Blues*, 1984
John DeChancie, *Castle Perilous*, 1988
Diane Duane, *High Wizardry*, 1990
Randall Garrett, *Too Many Magicians*, 1967
Barbara Hambly, *The Time of the Dark*, 1982
Michael Kurland, *A Study in Sorcery*, 1989
Roger Zelazny, *Nine Princes in Amber*, 1970

2103
SIMON HAWKE

The Wizard of Sunset Strip
(New York: Questar, 1989)

Story type: Fantasy (Contemporary)
Series: Wizard of 4th Street
Major character(s): Wyrdrune Carpinski, Wizard
Time period(s): Indeterminate Future
Locale(s): Los Angeles, California

Summary: A new age of magic has arrived, along with the spirits of Merlin, Mordred and sundry others. Sacrificial kill-ings of beautiful women lead the Bureau of Thaumatology to believe a significant supernatural event will soon take place.

Other books you might like:
Glen Cook, *Bitter Gold Hearts*, 1988
   The Garrett Files
Alan Dean Foster, *Glory Lane*, 1987
Barbara Hambly, *The Silent Tower*, 1988

2104
JUDITH HAWKES

Julian's House
(New York: Ticknor & Fields, 1989)

Story type: Horror (Haunted House)
Major character(s): David Curtiss, Paranormal Investigator (Parapsychologist); Sally Curtiss, Paranormal Investigator (Parapsychologist)
Time period(s): 1980s (1983)
Locale(s): Skipdon, Massachusetts (Samuel Gilfoy House)

Summary: Married parapsychologists Sally and David Curtiss probe the secrets of their rented haunted house. They stimulate bizarre psychic phenomena and discover dark, disturbing secrets about the Gilfoy family, putting their own marriage and psychological/psychic stability at risk.

Other books you might like:
Shirley Jackson, *The Haunting of Hill House*, 1959
Richard Matheson, *Hell House*, 1971
Chet Williamson, *Soulstorm*, 1986

2105
JUDITH HAWKES

My Soul to Keep
(New York: Dutton, 1996)

Story type: Horror (Ghost Story)
Major character(s): Annabel "Nan" Lucas, Photographer; Stephen Barnett, Child (Nan's eight-year-old son); Schuyler "Sky" Barnett, Handyman (Nan's cousin)
Time period(s): 1980s (1988)
Locale(s): Corey County, Tennessee

Summary: Nan Lucas leaves New York for her family homestead in Tennessee to get a new start following her failed marriage. She is unconcerned about her son Stephen developing an imaginary playmate, until she discovers the playmate closely resembles her childhood friend Tucker, who died saving her life and whom Stephen could not have known about otherwise.

Other books you might like:
Rick Hautala, *Cold Whisper*, 1991
Stephen King, *The Shining*, 1977
Thomas Tryon, *The Other*, 1971

2106
BARRY T. HAWKINS

Puppet Master
(New York: Zebra, 1993)

Story type: Horror (Psychological Suspense; Serial Killer)
Major character(s): Gil Beach, Detective—Police; Pilar Murphy, Psychologist, Professor; The Performer, Entertainer (ventriloquist), Serial Killer
Time period(s): 1990s (1993)
Locale(s): New York, New York

Summary: Detective Gil Beach finds himself matching wits with one of the most insidious killers he has ever confronted, a child murderer who steals body parts from his victims for his ventriloquist's doll.

Other books you might like:
William Goldman, *Magic*, 1976
Thomas Tryon, *The Other*, 1971

2107
PATRICK NIELSEN HAYDEN, Editor

Starlight 1
(New York: Tor, 1996)

Story type: Science Fiction (Anthology; Fantasy)
Series: Starlight

Summary: Contains a three-page introduction and 12 original stories, generally serious in tone, exploring the grand diversity of science fiction and fantasy with themes such as first contact, dystopias, drama, Nazi experimentation, illness, dreaming, religion, and magic. Authors include John M. Ford, Mark Kreighbaum, Maureen F. McHugh, Susan Palwick, Robert Reed, Martha Soukup, Michael Swanwick, and Jane Yolen. First of a new series.

Other books you might like:
Lou Aronica, *Full Spectrum*, 1988
    Shawna McCarthy, co-editor
Lou Aronica, *Full Spectrum 2*, 1989
    Shawn McCarthy, Amy Stout, Patrick Lo Brutto, co-editors
Lou Aronica, *Full Spectrum 3-4*, 1991-1993
    Amy Stout, Betsy Mitchell, co-editors
Greg Bear, *New Legends*, 1995
    editor
Jennifer Hershey, *Full Spectrum 5*, 1995
    Tom Dupree, Janna Silverstein, co-editors
Robert Silverberg, *Universe 1-3*, 1990-1994
    Karen Haber, co-editor
Jane Yolen, *The Xanadu Series*, 1993-1995
    editor

2108
PAUL HAZEL

The Wealdwife's Tale
(New York: Morrow AvoNova, 1993)

Story type: Fantasy (Legend; Quest)
Major character(s): Rudyard "Waldo" Riding Wenceslas, Royalty (eighth Duke of West Redding), Adventurer
Time period(s): Indeterminate Past
Locale(s): England; The Weald, Mythical Place (forest)

Summary: Overcome by melancholy from the loss of his beloved, Waldo journeys into the Weald to bring back his wife. Waldo returns with a new bride, her long dead mother and a new curse which will impel his daughter toward her fated future. Based on the song, "Good King Wenceslaus."

Other books you might like:
Louise Cooper, *The Sleep of Stone*, 1991
Frances Mary Hendry, *Quest for a Maid*, 1990
Robert Holdstock, *Lavondyss: Journey to an Unknown Region*, 1989
Robert Holdstock, *Mythago Wood*, 1984
Joseph Jacobs, *English Fairy Tales*, 1898
    editor
Ellen Kushner, *Thomas the Rhymer*, 1990
Patricia C. Wrede, *Snow White and Rose Red*, 1989

2109
DENISE LOPEZ HEALD

Mistwalker
(New York: Ballantine Del Rey, 1994)

Story type: Science Fiction (First Contact; Political)
Major character(s): Meesha Raschad, Miner, Heir; Sally "Sal" Banks, Businesswoman (delivery service)
Time period(s): Indeterminate Future
Locale(s): Ver Day, Planet—Imaginary

Summary: While claiming to maintain a Green economic and industrial environment, the corrupt government of Ver Day knows that the new equipment proves unreliable in the harsh environment, which kills most new residents of the planet within months. Sal Banks hires Meesha Raschad who unknowingly befriended the mistwalkers, thereby changing the lives of all residents on Ver Day.

Other books you might like:
Eleanor Arnason, *A Woman of the Iron People*, 1991
Octavia E. Butler, *Parable of the Sower*, 1994
L. Warren Douglas, *Cannon's Orb*, 1994
L. Warren Douglas, *A Plague of Change*, 1992
Eric Vinicoff, *The Weigher*, 1992
    Marcia Martin, co-author

2110

MARCY HEIDISH

The Torching
(New York: Simon & Schuster, 1992)

Story type: Horror (Black Magic; Occult)
Major character(s): Alice Grey, Writer; Jake Randolph, Writer, Pilot; Evangeline Smith, Witch
Time period(s): 1980s (1989)
Locale(s): Washington, District of Columbia (Georgetown area)

Summary: Historical novelist Alice Grey begins routine research into the life of Evangeline Smith, an eighteenth-century woman burned at the stake on apparently trumped-up charges of witchcraft. Imagine Alice's surprise when her investigation turns up evidence that Evangeline may indeed have been a witch—and may in fact be using Alice as the conduit by which she will re-emerge into the world of the living.

Other books you might like:
Jonathan Aycliffe, *Naomi's Room*, 1991
Emmanuel Carrere, *Gothic Romance*, 1984
Michael Stewart, *Belladonna*, 1992

2111

RUTH D. HEIN
VICKY L. HINSENBROCK, Co-Author

Ghostly Tales of Iowa
(Ames: Iowa State University Press, 1996)

Story type: Horror (Collection)

Summary: This book collects 53 folk tales from the oral tradition, many with roots in the beliefs and superstitions of the Scandinavian settlers of Iowa. Harmless ghosts spook the unwary in ''Back to Her Grave'' and ''The Ghostly Bell Ringer'' and haunt houses in ''The Haunted House'' and ''Spook Hollow House.'' Ghosts manifest themselves as human remains in ''The Skeleton's Hands'' and animals in ''The Dog of a Ghost.'' Supernatural beings other than ghosts are the subject of ''Tricked by a Troll,'' ''The Cellar Witch,'' and ''The Witch's Book.''

Other books you might like:
John Canning, *50 Great Ghost Stories*, 1971
    editor
D.J. Enright, *The Oxford Book of the Supernatural*, 1994
    editor
Terri Hardin, *Supernatural Tales From around the World*, 1995
    editor
Jessica Amanda Salmonson, *The Mysterious Doom and Other Ghostly Tales of the Pacific Northwest*, 1992
John Manchip White, *Whistling Past the Churchyard*, 1991

2112

ROBERT A. HEINLEIN

Glory Road
(New York: Baen, 1993)

Story type: Fantasy (Alternate World; Adventure)
Major character(s): Evelyn Cyril ''Oscar/Scar'' Gordon, Hero, Traveller; Aster ''Star'', Royalty (queen), Traveller; Rufo, Magician, Servant
Time period(s): 1960s; Indeterminate
Locale(s): I'lli Du Levant, Mediterranean; Alternate Earth; Nice, France

Summary: Released from the Army in Southeast Asia via Heidelberg, Scar travels to the Mediterranean hoping to have enough money to attend Heidelberg University. When his Irish Sweepstakes winning ticket proves counterfeit, Scar sees an ad looking for a hero with his skills. He responds and soon finds himself in situations where his social graces and martial arts skills improve with practice and willingness to learn. Reissue of the 1963 Hugo Award nominee.

Other books you might like:
Piers Anthony, *The Caterpillar's Question*, 1992
Charles de Lint, *The Little Country*, 1991
John DeChancie, *Castle Perilous*, 1988
Alan Dean Foster, *To the Vanishing Point*, 1988
Geary Gravel, *A Key for the Nonesuch*, 1990
S.P. Somtow, *Riverrun*, 1991
Will Shetterly, *The Tangled Lands*, 1989

2113

ROBERT A. HEINLEIN

The Moon Is a Harsh Mistress
(New York: Tor, 1996)

Story type: Science Fiction (Political)
Major character(s): Manuel ''Mannie'' O'Kelly, Revolutionary, Computer Expert; Wyoming ''Wyoh'' Knott, Revolutionary; Mike, Artificial Intelligence, Imposter (Adam Selene)
Time period(s): 2070s (2075)
Locale(s): Luna City, Moon (Earth's)

Summary: Mysteriously self-aware, Mike grows and explores consciousness with Mannie and Wyoh's help. The three work to effect revolution and revolt against Earth's abuse of lunar residents, exiled to the Moon as permanent prisoners. Reissue of the Hugo Award winning novel published in 1966.

Other books you might like:
Isaac Asimov, *Foundation*, 1951
Alfred Bester, *The Stars My Destination*, 1996
    revised edition
Ben Bova, *Millennium*, 1976
David Brin, *Earth*, 1990
Rudy Rucker, *Live Robots*, 1994
Cordwainer Smith, *Norstrilia*, 1975
Allen Steele, *Lunar Descent*, 1991
John Varley, *Steel Beach*, 1992

2114

ROBERT A. HEINLEIN

The Puppet Masters

(New York: Del Rey, 1991)

Story type: Science Fiction (Invasion of Earth)
Major character(s): Sam Nivens, Spy (Very Secret Agency); Mary, Spy (aka Allucquere); The Old Man, Spy (head spy-Very Secret Agency)
Time period(s): 2000s (2007)
Locale(s): United States

Summary: Parasitic slugs capable of controlling men are brought to Earth by flying saucers. Sam Nivens, the Old Man and Mary are sent to investigate, but have trouble convincing the government of the seriousness of the threat. Total nudity can keep the threat at bay, but something that will kill slugs and not people is needed to really control it. Mary, a survivor of a failed Venus colony, is the key to both disease and cure. Realizing that this is not a total solution, selected Earthmen take ship for Titan to exterminate the slugs. This is a substantially expanded edition of the novel first published in 1951.

Other books you might like:
Greg Bear, *The Forge of God*, 1987
Gregory Benford, *Across the Sea of Suns*, 1984
Thomas M. Disch, *The Genocides*, 1979
David Gerrold, *A Matter for Men*, 1989
Larry Niven, *Footfall*, 1985
    Jerry Pournelle, co-author

2115

ROBERT A. HEINLEIN

Red Planet

(New York: Del Rey, 1990)

Story type: Science Fiction (Young Adult; Adventure)
Major character(s): Jim Marlowe, Student; Frank Sutton, Student; Willis, Alien
Time period(s): Indeterminate Future
Locale(s): South Colony, Mars; Syrtis Minor, Mars

Summary: Jim and Frank take their furry friend Willis with them when they leave home to go to school in Syrtis Minor. When the Headmaster confiscates Willis on the grounds of the "no pets" rule, the young men's claim that Willis is not an animal falls on deaf ears. They must rescue their friend and try to solve the mystery of the true nature of the alien being. Originally published in 1949, this is the first publication of the complete manuscript.

Other books you might like:
John Christopher, *Fireball*, 1981
Arthur C. Clarke, *Islands in the Sky*, 1952
John Keir Cross, *The Angry Planet*, 1945
Gordon R. Dickson, *Space Winners*, 1965
Patricia A. McKillip, *Moon-Flash*, 1984

2116

ROBERT A. HEINLEIN

Requiem

(New York: Tor, 1992)

Story type: Science Fiction (Collection; Anthology)
Summary: Subtitled "New Collected Works by Robert A. Heinlein and Tributes to the Grand Master," this volume contains fiction and non-fiction by Heinlein and non-fiction about Heinlein and his work with a five-page preface by Virginia Heinlein and a one-page editor's foreword.

Other books you might like:
Larry Niven, *N-Space*, 1990
Larry Niven, *Playgrounds of the Mind*, 1991

2117

ROBERT A. HEINLEIN

Stranger in a Strange Land

(New York: Putnam, 1991)

Story type: Science Fiction (Theological; Political)
Major character(s): Valentine Michael Smith, Angel (archangel Michael), Orphan; Jubal Harshaw, Writer, Lawyer; Gillian Boardman, Nurse, Companion
Time period(s): 21st century
Locale(s): Washington, District of Columbia; New York, New York

Summary: Michael is sent to Earth by the Ancient Ones of Mars who have raised Michael as a Martian after he became the sole survivor of Mankind's first Martian colony. Unbeknownst to him, Michael is being used as a spy, allowing Martians to decide Humanity's fate. As a wolfling, Michael must discover his human nature, his happiness, loves, growth into adulthood and the joy of becoming self-directed. His human rite of passage is viewed through Michael's eyes and through the eyes of his friends. This edition is 60,000 words longer than the 1961 edition, now containing the complete, restored, original manuscript of this Hugo Award-winning novel.

Other books you might like:
Roger MacBride Allen, *The Ring of Charon*, 1990
David Brin, *Startide Rising*, 1983
Octavia E. Butler, *Dawn*, 1987
Larry Niven, *Protector*, 1973
Alis A. Rasmussen, *A Passage of Stars*, 1990
Alis A. Rasmussen, *The Price of Ransom*, 1990
Alis A. Rasmussen, *Revolution's Shore*, 1990
Cordwainer Smith, *The Best of Cordwainer Smith*, 1975
    pseudonym of Paul Myron Anthony Linebarger
Cordwainer Smith, *Norstrilia*, 1975
    pseudonym of Paul Myron Anthony Linebarger
John Varley, *The Persistence of Vision*, 1978

2118

JANE HELLER

Infernal Affairs

(New York: Kensington, 1996)

Story type: Horror (Occult)
Major character(s): Barbara Chessner, Real Estate Agent; Jeremy Cook, Sailor (charter boat captain); Frances Lutz, Real Estate Agent
Time period(s): 1990s (1996)
Locale(s): Banyon Beach, Florida

Summary: Distressed over her deteriorating marriage and frustrating life, Barbara Chessner inadvertently sells her soul to the devil for personal beauty. Barbara's deal proves only the beginning of other satanic arrangements that begin changing life in the town of Banyon Beach.

Other books you might like:
Ramsey Campbell, *Obsession*, 1986
Stephen King, *Needful Things*, 1992
Robert Masello, *Private Demons*, 1992
Kim Newman, *The Quorum*, 1994

2119

MARK HELPRIN

A City in Winter

(New York: Viking Ariel, 1996)

Story type: Fantasy (Psychic Powers; Political)
Major character(s): I, Royalty, Orphan; Notorincus, Slave, Revolutionary; Astrahn, Slave, Revolutionary
Time period(s): Indeterminate
Locale(s): The Kingdom, Fictional Country

Summary: When an evil usurper kills the king and queen, their orphaned daughter lives in anonymous safety for years. Deciding to return justice to the kingdom, she receives aid from two rebels who help her hide until she can confront the usurper and precipitate a popular revolt.

Other books you might like:
Lois McMaster Bujold, *The Spirit Ring*, 1992
William Goldman, *The Princess Bride*, 1973
Robin Hobb, *Assassin's Apprentice*, 1995
Mercedes Lackey, *The Robin and the Kestrel*, 1993
Patricia A. McKillip, *The Book of Atrix Wolfe*, 1995
Paula Volsky, *Illusion*, 1992

2120

MICHAEL HEMMINGSON
JIM BOB COOK, Illustrator
PAUL SCHIOLA, Illustrator

Nice Little Stories Jam-Packed with Depraved Sex and Violence

(Denver: Cyber-Psychos A.O.D., 1995)

Story type: Horror (Collection)

Summary: This first collection brings together six stories of twisted personalities for mature readers. In the title story, a psychotherapist uses the 50 minutes his patients are hypnotized on the couch to murder their children. ''The Bibliophile'' tells of a librarian with a book fetish and Nazi tendencies, and ''Skull-Fuck'' of a man who discovers the fantasies he unleashes in his group therapy sessions are not very pleasant when they occur in real life. ''Pain'' is a hardboiled revenge story. Full Force Frank supplies the introduction.

Other books you might like:
S. Darnbrook Colson, *People of the Night*, 1994
Ron Dee, *Sex and Blood*, 1994
Edward Lee, *Header*, 1995
Lucy Taylor, *Close to the Bone*, 1993
Lucy Taylor, *The Flesh Artist*, 1994
Lucy Taylor, *Unnatural Acts and Other Stories*, 1994

2121

JASON HENDERSON

Highlander: The Element of Fire

(New York: Warner Aspect, 1995)

Story type: Fantasy (Adventure; Contemporary Realism)
Series: Highlander
Major character(s): Duncan MacLeod, Immortal, Martial Arts Expert; Connor MacLeod, Immortal; Khordas, Immortal, Pirate
Time period(s): 1850s; 1890s
Locale(s): Massachusetts; Atlantic Ocean; Scotland

Summary: Lusting for revenge for an ancient wrong that he attributes to Duncan MacLeod, Khordas plots to destroy all that Duncan holds dear, then kill Duncan himself. With only one immortal fated to survive, Duncan intends to keep his own head. First of a television tie-in series.

Other books you might like:
L. Sprague de Camp, *The Fantastic Swordsmen*, 1967 editor
Terry Goodkind, *Wizard's First Rule*, 1994
Ashley McConnell, *Highlander: Scimitar*, 1996
Melanie Rawn, *Knights of the Morningstar*, 1994
Fred Saberhagen, *An Armory of Swords*, 1995 editor

2122

JASON HENDERSON

The Spawn of Loki

(New York: Baen, 1994)

Story type: Fantasy (Adventure; Religious)
Major character(s): MacDuff, Hero; Loki, Deity; Susan, Mythical Creature (eternal guardian of fate), Immortal
Time period(s): 11th century
Locale(s): Normandy, France; Uppsala, Sweden; New Asgard, Mythical Place (realm of the gods)

Summary: When a Norman monk's research awakens Loki, Ragnarok, the final destruction of the world, may ensue 1000 years earlier than planned by the gods. MacDuff presents humanity's only hope for postponing disaster.

Other books you might like:
Patrick H. Adkins, *Sons of the Titans*, 1990
James Blish, *Black Easter*, 1968
Elizabeth Forrest, *Phoenix Fire*, 1992
Alan Dean Foster, *Cyber Way*, 1990
Neil Gaiman, *Good Omens: The Nice and Accurate Prophecies of Agnes Nutter, Witch*, 1990
  Terry Pratchett, co-author
Roger Zelazny, *Creatures of Light and Darkness*, 1969
Roger Zelazny, *The Mask of Loki*, 1990
  Thomas T. Thomas, co-author

2123

ZENNA HENDERSON

Ingathering: The Complete People Stories of Zenna Henderson

(Framingham, Massachusetts: NESFA Press, 1995)

Story type: Science Fiction (Collection; Psychic Powers)
Time period(s): 20th century
Locale(s): New Mexico; Southwest

Summary: Contains a five-page chronology of the People by editors Mark Olson and Priscilla Olson, one page of acknowledgements, a two-page introduction by Priscilla Olson, a three-page afterword by Zenna Henderson, "The People Stories," plus all 17 stories of the People including those published as *Pilgrimage: The Book of the People* (1961), *The People: No Different Flesh* (1967), three subsequently published in periodicals, plus one original, "Michal Without." Stories feature a gentle investigation of extraterrestrial immigrants inspired by Henderson's lengthy teaching career and Bible stories.

Other books you might like:
Nina Kiriki Hoffman, *The Thread That Binds the Bones*, 1994
Janet Kagan, *Mirabile*, 1991
Spider Robinson, *Callahan and Company*, 1987
Theodore Sturgeon, *The Ultimate Egoist*, 1994
John Varley, *The Persistence of Vision*, 1978

2124

FRANCES MARY HENDRY

Quest for a Maid

(New York: Farrar Straus Giroux, 1990)

Story type: Fantasy (Legend)
Major character(s): Inge, Witch; Marjory de Brus, Noblewoman
Time period(s): 13th century (1286)
Locale(s): Inverkeithing, Scotland

Summary: Marjory de Brus makes an arrangement with Inge to hire her as an advisor if Inge will give her the power of the throne. Inge kills King Alexander with magic and promises Lady Marjory that her son, Robert, will be king, although the Maid of Norway, the King's granddaughter, is the heir to the

throne if she survives her journey home. An ALA Best Book For Young Adults title.

Other books you might like:
Morgan Llywelyn, *The Isles of the Blest*, 1989
Hanne Marie Svendsen, *The Gold Ball*, 1989
Judith Tarr, *Ars Magica*, 1989
Gail Van Asten, *Charlemagne's Champion*, 1990
Jack Vance, *Madouc*, 1990

2125

KEITH HERBER

Dark Prince

(New York: HarperPrism, 1994)

Story type: Horror (Vampire Story)
Series: World of Darkness: Vampire
Major character(s): Sullivan, Vampire; Kathy, Prostitute; Angel, Vampire
Time period(s): 1990s (1994)
Locale(s): San Francisco, California

Summary: Accused of diablerie, or the forbidden drinking of vampire blood by another vampire, Sullivan, a 150-year-old vampire who controls the streets of San Francisco, is stalked and sought by warring vampire clans eager to use him as a pawn in their quest to consolidate power and take over the city.

Other books you might like:
Elaine Bergstrom, *Tapestry of Dark Souls*, 1993
Richard Lee Byers, *Netherworld*, 1995
P.N. Elrod, *I, Strahd*, 1993
Robert Weinberg, *Bloodwar*, 1995
Robert Weinberg, *Vampire Diary: The Embrace*, 1995
  Mark Rein-Hagen, co-author

2126

BRIAN HERBERT
MARIE LANDIS, Co-Author

Blood on the Sun

(New York: HarperPrism, 1996)

Story type: Horror (Vampire Story)
Series: World of Darkness: Vampire
Major character(s): Desidra Smith, Vampire; Christopher T. Wilson, Vampire; Mitsuo Tokoyuni, Military Personnel
Time period(s): 1940s
Locale(s): Seattle, Washington; Anchorage, Alaska

Summary: Defying the prince of her vampire clan, Desidra takes a false name and works as a cryptographer for the Allied forces during World War II. When she falls in love with the Japanese soldier she is spying on, she risks not only giving away Allied plans for the Battle of Midway but revealing her vampire heritage as well. This novel is set in White Wolf Books' "World of Darkness" gaming world, where humans and supernatural beings coexist.

Other books you might like:
Don Bassingthwaite, *As One Dead*, 1996
  Nancy Kilpatrick, co-author

Richard Lee Byers, *Netherworld*, 1995
Nancy A. Collins, *A Dozen Black Roses*, 1996
Keith Herber, *Prince of the City*, 1995
Doug Murray, *Blood Relations*, 1996
Robert Weinberg, *Vampire Diary: The Embrace*, 1995
   Mark Rein-Hagen, co-author

2127

BRIAN HERBERT
MARIE LANDIS, Co-Author

Memorymakers
(New York: Roc, 1991)

Story type: Science Fiction (Political)
Major character(s): Emily Harvey, Twin, Revolutionary; Thomas Harvey, Twin
Time period(s): 22nd century
Locale(s): Earth

Summary: Unrecognized for millennia, the Ch'Var have lived alongside human Gweens, partaking of the delicacy of human flesh when possible. Now Emily and Thomas represent a new form of human which may overturn the traditional balance. This collaboration is Marie Landis' first novel.

Other books you might like:
C.S. Friedman, *The Madness Season*, 1990
Jacqueline Lichtenberg, *First Channel*, 1980
Jacqueline Lichtenberg, *House of Zeor*, 1974
Jacqueline Lichtenberg, *Molt Brother*, 1982
Jacqueline Lichtenberg, *Unto Zeor Forever*, 1978
A.E. van Vogt, *Slan*, 1946

2128

BRIAN HERBERT

The Race for God
(New York: Ace, 1990)

Story type: Science Fiction (Theological; Alternate Universe)
Major character(s): Evander Harold McMurtrey, Religious; Jin the Plarnjarn, Robot (Cyberoo C-unit 7891), Spy (Department of Loyalty)
Time period(s): Indeterminate Future
Locale(s): D'Urth, Alternate Earth

Summary: Evander Harold McMurtrey is contacted by God. He is given the location, the ships and along with several other humans, an invitation to visit. The pilgrimage becomes a dangerous race to reach God first.

Other books you might like:
J.M. Dillard, *Star Trek V: The Final Frontier*, 1989
Parke Godwin, *Waiting for the Galactic Bus*, 1988
Frank Herbert, *Whipping Star*, 1970
Ted Reynolds, *The Tides of God*, 1989
Dan Simmons, *Hyperion*, 1989
Ian Watson, *God's World*, 1979

2129

JAMES HERBERT

The Ghosts of Sleath
(New York: HarperPrism, 1995)

Story type: Horror (Ghost Story)
Major character(s): David Ash, Paranormal Investigator; Grace Lockwood, Student (art student); Reverend Edmund Lockwood, Religious
Time period(s): 1990s (1995)
Locale(s): Sleath, England

Summary: In this sequel to the author's 1988 novel, *Haunted*, skeptical psychic investigator David Ash is summoned to a former mill town to look into the sudden reappearance of the ghosts of the newly dead. There he discovers a legacy of supernatural evil founded on ritual sacrifice intertwined with the town's history.

Other books you might like:
John R. Maxim, *Platforms*, 1980
Steve Rasnic Tem, *Excavation*, 1987
Chet Williamson, *Ash Wednesday*, 1987

2130

JAMES HERBERT

Haunted
(New York: NAL Signet, 1990)

Story type: Horror (Haunted House)
Major character(s): David Ash, Paranormal Investigator; Christina Mariell, Heiress; Tessa Webb, Aged Person (Christina's aunt)
Time period(s): 1990s (1990)
Locale(s): Ravenmoor, England; London, England

Summary: Sent by the Psychical Research Institute to investigate the haunting of the Mariell family's country home, Edbrook Manor, skeptical David Ash experiences a series of increasingly threatening paranormal phenomena that eventually reveal the manor's buried history and its impact on the current Mariell family. First published in England in 1988.

Other books you might like:
Judith Hawkes, *Julian's House*, 1989
Shirley Jackson, *The Haunting of Hill House*, 1959
Richard Matheson, *Hell House*, 1971

2131

JAMES HERBERT

Portent
(New York: HarperPrism, 1996)

Story type: Horror (Apocalyptic Horror)
Major character(s): James Rivers, Scientist (climatologist); Hugo Poggs, Scientist; Mama Pitie, Religious (priestess)
Time period(s): 1990s (1993)
Locale(s): Hazelrod, England; New Orleans, Louisiana

Summary: Recovering from his near death in a hurricane over the Gulf of Mexico, British climatologist James Rivers is contacted by Hugo Poggs, an eccentric whose adopted gypsy children know that Rivers was saved from death for a purpose. At their behest, Rivers searches out a Scottish recluse known as the Dream Man, in order to fulfill a mystical destiny that will help save the world from ecological cataclysm. First published in England in 1993.

Other books you might like:
Colin Kersey, *Soul Catcher*, 1995
Graham Masterton, *Burial*, 1992
John Skipp, *The Bridge*, 1991
    Craig Spector, co-author

2132

JAMES HERBERT

The Rats
(New York: NAL Signet, 1989)

Story type: Horror (Nature in Revolt)
Major character(s): Harris, Teacher (Art); Foskins, Government Official (Ministry of Health agent)
Time period(s): 1970s
Locale(s): London, England

Summary: Huge mutant rats ravage London. The heroic duo search for the telepathic intelligence directing the rats, while the authorities attempt to control the plague with an anti-rat virus. Originally published in 1974.

Other books you might like:
Harry Adam Knight, *The Fungus*, 1985
Guy N. Smith, *Killer Crabs Series*, 1978

2133

JAMES HERBERT

Sepulchre
(New York: Jove, 1989)

Story type: Horror (Ancient Evil Unleashed)
Major character(s): Liam Halloran, Bodyguard; Felix Kline, Psychic, Businessman
Time period(s): 1980s
Locale(s): Neath, England (Kline's hideaway)

Summary: When Halloran is hired to protect Kline from unnamed enemies, he encounters a kinky love affair, a terrorist plot, horrifying psychic phenomena, and a Sumerian devil-god.

Other books you might like:
Clive Barker, *The Damnation Game*, 1985
John Blackburn, *For Fear of Little Men*, 1972
John Farris, *Catacombs*, 1981

2134

MARY H. HERBERT

City of the Sorcerers
(Lake Geneva, Wisconsin: TSR, 1994)

Story type: Fantasy (Quest; Psychic Powers)
Series: Dark Horse
Major character(s): Kelene, Sorceress, Healer; Demir, Animal (horse), Telepath; Sayyed, Sorcerer, Religious
Time period(s): Indeterminate
Locale(s): Dark Horse Plains, Mythical Place; Moy Tura, Fictional City

Summary: When a plague rekindles old suspicions about magic-wielders and threatens a 20-year peace, a few magic-wielders travel to the ruins of Moy Tura, the city of sorcerers, to find a cure.

Other books you might like:
Constance Ash, *The Stallion Queen*, 1992
Doranna Durgin, *Dun Lady's Jess*, 1994
Peter Morwood, *The Horse Lord*, 1987
Karen Ripley, *The Persistence of Memory*, 1993
Mary Stanton, *The Heavenly Horse From the Outermost West*, 1988

2135

MARY H. HERBERT

Dark Horse
(Lake Geneva, WI: TSR, 1990)

Story type: Fantasy (Magic Conflict)
Series: Dark Horse
Major character(s): Gabria, Warrior (Female); Nara, Animal (Magical horse)
Time period(s): Indeterminate

Summary: With only Nara to support her, Gabria forces her way into the male-dominated world of sorcery, defeating the evil Lord Medb in the process.

Other books you might like:
C.J. Cherryh, *Wizard Spawn*, 1989
    Nancy Asire, co-author
Mercedes Lackey, *Arrow's Fall*, 1988
Robin McKinley, *The Blue Sword*, 1982
Mark C. Perry, *Morigu: The Dead*, 1990
Sheri S. Tepper, *Jinian Footseer*, 1985

2136

MARY H. HERBERT

Lightning's Daughter
(Lake Geneva, Wisconsin: TSR, 1991)

Story type: Fantasy (Magic Conflict; Quest)
Series: Dark Horse
Major character(s): Gabria, Warrior
Time period(s): Indeterminate
Locale(s): Dark Horse Plains, Mythical Place

Summary: Hoping to secure a place for magic among the untrusting plains tribes, Gabria and her companions, aided by the intelligent, magic Hunnuli horses, set out to find a tome of magic which would allow Gabria to overcome the threats to her people. Sequel to *Dark Horse*.

Other books you might like:
Constance Ash, *The Horsegirl*, 1988
David Eddings, *Pawn of Prophecy*, 1982
Robin McKinley, *The Blue Sword*, 1982
Robin McKinley, *The Hero and the Crown*, 1984
Mary Stanton, *The Heavenly Horse From the Outermost West*, 1988

2137

MARY H. HERBERT

Valorian

(Lake Geneva, Wisconsin: TSR, 1993)

Story type: Fantasy (Quest)
Series: Dark Horse
Major character(s): Valorian, Leader, Magician; Hunnul, Animal (horse), Telepath; Tyrranis, Military Personnel
Time period(s): Indeterminate
Locale(s): Tarnish Empire, Fictional Country; Chadar, Fictional Country; Darkhorn Mountains, Mythical Place

Summary: Aided by gifts from the goddess Amara, Valorian unites his clan with the vision of freedom in a new land, providing they escape General Tyrranis and survive a difficult journey across unknown mountains. Set 500 years prior to *Dark Horse*.

Other books you might like:
Casey Flynn, *The Enchanted Isles*, 1991
Robert Jordan, *The Eye of the World*, 1989
L.E. Modesitt Jr., *The Towers of the Sunset*, 1992
Elizabeth Moon, *Liar's Oath*, 1992

2138

MARY H. HERBERT

Winged Magic

(New York: TSR, 1996)

Story type: Fantasy (Magic Conflict; Political)
Series: Dark Horse
Major character(s): Kelene, Sorceress, Healer; Gabria, Warrior, Sorceress; Sayyed, Sorcerer, Leader
Time period(s): Indeterminate
Locale(s): Altai Valley, Mythical Place; Turic Nation, Fictional Country; Cangora, Fictional City

Summary: An untrained sorcerer kidnaps Kelene and Gabria and their telepathic horse companions, intending to force them to teach him sorcery, however he does not anticipate the resourceful resistance of his captives or their relatives' response in gathering disparate forces to mount a rescue and avert the disastrous use of sorcery.

Other books you might like:
Constance Ash, *The Stallion Queen*, 1992
Doranna Durgin, *Dun Lady's Jess*, 1994

Peter Morwood, *The Horse Lord*, 1987
Andre Norton, *Elvenblood*, 1995
    Mercedes Lackey, co-author
Karen Ripley, *The Persistence of Memory*, 1993
Mary Stanton, *The Heavenly Horse From the Outermost West*, 1988

2139

JENNIFER HERSHEY, Editor
TOM DUPREE, Co-Editor
JANNA SILVERSTEIN, Co-Editor

Full Spectrum 5

(New York: Bantam Spectra, 1995)

Story type: Science Fiction (Anthology)
Series: Full Spectrum

Summary: Contains seven pages of notes about the authors and editors and 28 original stories, varying from humorous to dark in tone, which present a thematically wide range of speculative fiction. Authors include William Barton, Doug Beason, Michael Bishop, Richard Bowes, Emily Devenport, Karen Joy Fowler, Jean Mark Gawron, Jonathan Letham, Lisa Mason, Patricia A. McKillip, Paul Park, Alan Rodgers, Neal Stephenson, Tricia Sullivan, William Jon Watkins, Lawrence Watt-Evans, and Gene Wolf.

Other books you might like:
Lou Aronica, *Full Spectrum*, 1988
    Shawna McCarthy, co-editor
Lou Aronica, *Full Spectrum 4*, 1993
    Amy Stout, Betsy Mitchell, co-editors
Lou Aronica, *Full Spectrum 3*, 1993
    Amy Stout, Betsy Mitchell, co-editors
Lou Aronica, *Full Spectrum 2*, 1989
    Shawna McCarthy, Amy Stout, Patrick LoBruto
Greg Bear, *New Legends*, 1995
Gardner Dozois, *The Year's Best Science Fiction: Twelfth Annual Collection*, 1995
    editor

2140

HERMANN HESSE

The Fairy Tales of Hermann Hesse

(New York: Bantam, 1995)

Story type: Fantasy (Collection)

Summary: Contains a 20-page introduction by translator and editor Jack Zipes and the first English language versions of 22 stories in the modern fairy tale tradition, all published in German in journals and newspapers 1904-1918. Frequently dark in tone, the stories' themes include the agony of the artist, social turmoil, wish fulfillment, and societal structures.

Other books you might like:
Italo Calvino, *Italian Folktales*, 1992
Arthur Conan Doyle, *The Best Supernatural Tales of Arthur Conan Doyle*, 1979
Rudyard Kipling, *Kipling's Fantasy*, 1992

Jack London, *Selected Science Fiction and Fantasy Stories*, 1979

Kenneth Morris, *The Dragon Path: Collected Tales of Kenneth Morris*, 1995

Jack Zipes, *Beauties, Beasts and Enchantments*, 1989 editor

Jack Zipes, *Spells of Enchantment*, 1991 editor

2141

TRACY HICKMAN

The Immortals

(New York: Roc, 1996)

Story type: Science Fiction (Medical; Political)

Major character(s): Michael Albert Barris, Journalist, Parent; Quinton Weston, Religious (reverend), Political Figure (mayor); Virgil Wayne Johnston, Cowboy

Time period(s): 2010s (2010)

Locale(s): Newhouse Center, Utah; Beaver, Utah; Milford, Utah

Summary: During the V-CIDS epidemic, Michael sneaks into Newhouse Center, an Emergency Relocation and Isolation Service, to reconcile with his son. Attempting to check out business possibilities in the area, Virgil barely escapes the destruction of Wild Cove Center, but discovers, to his horror, the explosion incinerated alive many people, including children. Michael and Virgil discover that everyone in an ERIS designated "predeceased" has, at most, six months before that center, in orderly rotation, receives its prescheduled total demolition.

Other books you might like:

Greg Bear, *Blood Music*, 1985

Helen Collins, *Mutagenesis*, 1993

L. Warren Douglas, *Cannon's Orb*, 1994

Frank Herbert, *The White Plague*, 1982

Bill Ransom, *ViraVax*, 1993

2142

LYNN S. HIGHTOWER

Alien Blues

(New York: Ace, 1992)

Story type: Science Fiction (Mystery)

Series: Alien Blues

Major character(s): David Silver, Police Officer (Homicide task force); Puzzle Solver, Alien (Elaki), Detective; String, Alien (Elaki), Police Officer

Time period(s): Indeterminate Future

Locale(s): Saigo City, Fictional City

Summary: David Silver unhappily accepts an alien partner to help investigate crimes by a sexual psychopath. As the investigation proceeds, the FBI and DEA become involved. When Puzzle Solver is killed and Silver nearly killed by the explosion of their car, it becomes clear that a larger situation threatens both humans and elaki.

Other books you might like:

Alan Dean Foster, *Alien Nation*, 1988

Alan Dean Foster, *Cyber Way*, 1990

Katharine Kerr, *Polar City Blues*, 1990

Lee Killough, *The Doppelganger Gambit*, 1979

Lee Killough, *Dragon's Teeth*, 1990

Lee Killough, *Spider Play*, 1986

Walter Jon Williams, *Days of Atonement*, 1991

2143

LYNN S. HIGHTOWER

Alien Eyes

(New York: Ace, 1993)

Story type: Science Fiction (Mystery; Political)

Series: Alien Blues

Major character(s): David Silver, Police Officer; String, Alien (Elaki), Police Officer; Dahmi, Alien (Elaki)

Time period(s): Indeterminate Future

Locale(s): Saigo City, Fictional City

Summary: Dahmi, a good mother accused of killing her children, refuses to cooperate with the police for fear of involving the Elaki police. David must discover the reason behind the murders and the fear.

Other books you might like:

Eleanor Arnason, *A Woman of the Iron People*, 1991

Lois McMaster Bujold, *Shards of Honor*, 1986

Sean Dalton, *Beyond the Void*, 1991

Paula E. Downing, *Fallway*, 1993

Alan Dean Foster, *Alien Nation*, 1988

K.W. Jeter, *Dark Horizon*, 1993

Lee Killough, *Dragon's Teeth*, 1990

Stephen Leigh, *Alien Tongue*, 1991

2144

LYNN S. HIGHTOWER

Alien Heat

(New York: Ace, 1994)

Story type: Science Fiction (Mystery; Psychic Powers)

Series: Alien Blues

Major character(s): David Silver, Police Officer; String, Alien (Elaki), Police Officer; Yolanda Free Clements, Police Officer

Time period(s): Indeterminate Future

Locale(s): Saigo City, Fictional City

Summary: Detective Silver and the Arson Squad investigate a fire in a supper club that killed over 200 people. The clues point to arson, but complications include the body of a woman strangled during the fire, a beautiful psychic called in to assist on another case, and racial tensions between Elaki and Humans. Then a second supper club burns down.

Other books you might like:

Isaac Asimov, *The Caves of Steel*, 1954

Philip K. Dick, *Do Androids Dream of Electric Sheep?*, 1968

Alan Dean Foster, *Alien Nation*, 1988

Katharine Kerr, *Polar City Blues*, 1990

James H. Schmitz, *The Universe Against Her*, 1964

2145

LYNN S. HIGHTOWER

Alien Rites

(New York: Ace, 1995)

Story type: Science Fiction (Mystery)
Series: Alien Blues
Major character(s): David Silver, Police Officer; String, Alien (Elaki), Police Officer; Annie Trey, Single Parent
Time period(s): Indeterminate Future
Locale(s): Saigo City, Fictional City

Summary: As Detective Silver and his partner, String, investigate the disappearance of a local college student, they find links to the disappearance of a police pathologist, an extortion plot in the Elaki quarter of town, an antique teddy bear, and a young woman accused of murdering her infant son.

Other books you might like:
Isaac Asimov, *The Caves of Steel*, 1954
Rosel George Brown, *Sibyl Sue Blue*, 1966
Michael Crichton, *The Andromeda Strain*, 1969
Philip K. Dick, *Do Androids Dream of Electric Sheep?*, 1968
Katharine Kerr, *Polar City Blues*, 1990
Jean Lorrah, *The IDIC Epidemic*, 1988

2146

JAMAKE HIGHWATER

Dark Legend

(New York: Grove Press, 1994)

Story type: Fantasy (Legend; Quest)
Major character(s): Kuwai, Indian, Royalty (lord of the sky); Washi, Indian, Hero; Idera, Indian, Warrior (Muri Woman)
Time period(s): Indeterminate Past
Locale(s): Central America

Summary: Using as inspiration the Germanic myths of the Nibelungen, ancient Eddic poems, the Icelandic Volsunga Saga and the Norse Nibelungenlied, Highwater transplants the action into pre-Columbian tropical America.

Other books you might like:
Piers Anthony, *Tales From the Great Turtle*, 1994
   Richard Gilliam, co-editor
Stephan Grundy, *Rhinegold*, 1994
Diana L. Paxson, *The Wolf and the Raven*, 1993
Gerald Vizenor, *Dead Voices: Natural Agonies in the Real World*, 1992
Roger Welsch, *Touching the Fire*, 1992

2147

MICHAEL T. HINKEMEYER

Order of the Arrow

(New York: Tor, 1990)

Story type: Horror (Serial Killer)

Major character(s): Anne Davis, Student (History Ph.D. candidate); Chandler Kane, Businessman, Wealthy; James D. Lugosh, Student, Serial Killer
Time period(s): 1990s (1990)
Locale(s): Manor Island, New England (an island off the New England Coast)

Summary: Anne Davis emerges cured from an insane asylum 13 months after a deformed murderer killed her family. She falls in love with Chandler Kane, a millionaire and medieval enthusiast who runs his private island like a feudal kingdom. She is unaware that the murderer from her past is still stalking her and finds Kane's secluded island the perfect setting in which to dispose of her.

Other books you might like:
John Farris, *The Axman Cometh*, 1989
Jan Lara, *Soulcatchers*, 1990
Chet Williamson, *Dreamthorp*, 1989

2148

CHRISTOPHER HINZ

Ash Ock

(New York: St. Martin's Press, 1989)

Story type: Science Fiction (Space Opera)
Series: Paratwa Saga
Major character(s): Jarem Marth, Pirate, Ruler; Gillian, Genetically Altered Being, Warrior
Time period(s): Indeterminate Future
Locale(s): Earth's Orbital Space Colonies, Space Station

Summary: Fifty-six years have passed since the first attack of the Paratwa, genetically engineered warriors with telepathic powers, upon the orbital colonies. Now a new attack is in the offing and Jarem Marth, the lion of Alexander, decides to revive from their long stasis the deadly Paratwa hunters Gillian and Nick who were responsible for defeating the earlier attack.

Other books you might like:
Gregory Benford, *Great Sky River*, 1987
Gregory Benford, *Tides of Light*, 1989
Patricia A. McKillip, *Fool's Run*, 1987
Robert Reed, *The Hormone Jungle*, 1988
Joan D. Vinge, *Catspaw*, 1988

2149

CHRISTOPHER HINZ

The Paratwa

(New York: St. Martin's Press, 1991)

Story type: Science Fiction (Space Opera)
Series: Paratwa Saga
Major character(s): Jarem Marth, Pirate, Ruler; Gillian, Genetically Altered Being, Warrior; Nick, Warrior
Time period(s): 24th century
Locale(s): Earth's Orbital Space Colonies, Space Station

Summary: Fifty-six years after the first attack of the Paratwa, genetically engineered warriors able to merge their consciousnesses, Gillian and Nick are awakened by Jarem Marth from stasis to again defeat the Paratwan attack. Separately they battle to stop the attack and discover the secrets of the Ash Ock, the incorporated telepathic consciousness.

Other books you might like:
Gregory Benford, *Great Sky River*, 1987
Gregory Benford, *Tides of Light*, 1989
Robert Reed, *The Hormone Jungle*, 1988
David Alexander Smith, *Homecoming*, 1990
Joan D. Vinge, *Catspaw*, 1988

2150
WILLIAM HJORTSBERG

Nevermore
(New York: Atlantic Monthly Press, 1994)

Story type: Horror (Mystery; Historical)
Major character(s): Arthur Conan Doyle, Historical Figure, Writer; Harry Houdini, Magician, Historical Figure; Damon Runyon, Journalist, Historical Figure
Time period(s): 1920s
Locale(s): New York, New York

Summary: During one of his American tours to promote spiritualist beliefs, Arthur Conan Doyle befriends the great magician Harry Houdini and becomes caught up in an investigation to solve a series of murders that mimic those committed in the stories of Edgar Allan Poe, and that appear to be leading up to the murder of Houdini himself.

Other books you might like:
Mark Frost, *The List of 7*, 1992
Kim Newman, *Anno Dracula*, 1992
Daniel Stashower, *The Adventure of the Ectoplasmic Man*, 1985

2151
ROBIN HOBB (Pseudonym of Megan Lindholm)

Assassin's Apprentice
(New York: Bantam Spectra, 1995)

Story type: Fantasy (Psychic Powers; Political)
Series: Farseer
Major character(s): FitzChivalry ''Fitz'' Farseer, Bastard Son, Psychic; Burrich, Step-Parent (Fitz's), Animal Trainer (master of horses/dogs); Chade Fallstar, Bastard Son, Diplomat (assassin)
Time period(s): Indeterminate
Locale(s): Six Duchies, Fictional Country

Summary: After Fitz's unwelcome appearance precipitates Chivalry's abdication from royal succession, Burrich serves as Fitz's guardian and mentor until King Shrewd orders Fitz to move to the keep to begin royal training. The curriculum includes assassination which King Shrewd intends that Fitz use as commanded for political engineering.

Other books you might like:
Terry Goodkind, *Wizard's First Rule*, 1994
Paula Volsky, *Illusion*, 1992
Martha Wells, *The Element of Fire*, 1993
Megan Lindholm, *Cloven Hooves*, 1991

Megan Lindholm, *Wizard of the Pigeons*, 1986
Megan Lindholm, *The Limbreth Gate*, 1984

2152
ROBIN HOBB (Pseudonym of Megan Lindholm)

Royal Assassin
(New York: Bantram Spectra, 1996)

Story type: Fantasy (Political; Psychic Powers)
Series: Farseer
Major character(s): FitzChivalry ''Fitz'' Farseer, Bastard Son, Psychic; Verity Farseer, Psychic, Royalty (king-in-waiting); Nigheyes, Animal (wolf), Telepath
Time period(s): Indeterminate
Locale(s): Six Duchies, Fictional Country

Summary: Faring poorly after the attempt on his life, FitzChivalry returns to Buckkeep to pursue assassin studies. With mindless Forged ones' and fierce Red-Ship warriors' deadly havoc ever closer, Verity demands much of FitzChivalry. As FitzChivalry's deeds and reputation grow, he forms bonds with old and new friends and forms a forbidden bond to a wolf he saves, while Prince Regal works to discredit or kill FitzChivalry.

Other books you might like:
Lynn Flewelling, *Luck in the Shadows*, 1996
Terry Goodkind, *Wizard's First Rule*, 1994
J.V. Jones, *The Baker's Boy*, 1995
Megan Lindholm, *Wizard of the Pigeons*, 1986
Martha Wells, *The Element of Fire*, 1993
Michelle West, *Hunter's Oath*, 1995

2153
HENRY W. HOCHERMAN

The Gilgul
(New York: Pinnacle, 1990)

Story type: Horror (Possession)
Major character(s): Neil DeLuca, Journalist; Karen Gordon, Young Woman
Time period(s): 1980s (1988)
Locale(s): New York, New York; Miami Beach, Florida

Summary: On her wedding day, Karen Gordon is possessed by a ''gilgul,'' or spirit of the dead. Hideously changed, she is kept in a mental hospital while her fiance David Seligman, and friend, Neil DeLuca, attempt to discover who or what has possessed Karen and how to get rid of it.

Other books you might like:
William Peter Blatty, *The Exorcist*, 1971
Bari Wood, *The Tribe*, 1981

2154
BRIAN HODGE

The Convulsion Factory
(Seattle: Silver Salamander, 1996)

Story type: Horror (Collection)

Summary: One dozen stories, four original to the volume, present this young writer's frank and often bleak portrayals of people whose ennui and dissatisfaction with their lives encourage them to seek outrageous outlets for personal fulfillment. "Godflesh," "Childhood at the Lost and Found," and "The Meat in the Machine" all involve characters who seek transcendance through self-mutilation. "Cancer Causes Rats" critiques the means by which the media perpetuates the crimes it reports, and "Mostly Cloudy, Chance of Kurt" examines the public's fascination with celebrity death. "In a Roadhouse Far, Past the Edge of Town" spoofs serial killer films, and "Naked Lunchmeat" the writings of William Burroughs. Phil Nutman supplies an introduction. This book was published as both a trade paperback and signed limited edition hardcover.

Other books you might like:
Michael A. Arnzen, *Needles and Sins*, 1993
Poppy Z. Brite, *Swamp Foetus*, 1993
Elizabeth Massie, *Shadow Dreams*, 1996
Wayne Allen Sallee, *With Wounds Still Wet*, 1996

2155

BRIAN HODGE

The Darker Saints
(New York: Dell/Abyss, 1993)

Story type: Horror (Black Magic)
Major character(s): Justin Gray, Advertising; April Kingston-Gray, Artist; Terrance "Eel" Fletcher, Criminal
Time period(s): 1990s (1993)
Locale(s): Tampa, Florida; Louisiana

Summary: In this semi-sequel to the 1991 novel, *Nightlife*, advertising man Justin Gray is precipitated into an unexpected situation when circumstances surrounding the success of his campaign for a coffee company suggest illegal, and possibly supernatural dealings by the client. Eventually, Justin's investigations will get him entangled with criminals and drugrunners who use voodoo to animate the dead as their zombie lackeys.

Other books you might like:
Lisa Cantrell, *Boneman*, 1992
Hugh B. Cave, *Disciples of Dread*, 1990
Vincent Courtney, *Harvest of Blood*, 1992
Robert Weinberg, *The Black Lodge*, 1991

2156

BRIAN HODGE

Deathgrip
(New York: Dell/Abyss, 1992)

Story type: Horror (Wild Talents)
Major character(s): Paul Handler, Radio Personality; Donny Dawson, Religious (charismatic preacher); Gabriel Matthews, Fanatic (religious)
Time period(s): 1990s (1992)
Locale(s): St. Louis, Missouri

Summary: KGRM disc jockey Paul Handler has spent his life coping with his power to heal by the laying on of hands, a gift bestowed on him at birth by a member of a secret coven known as the Quorum. But the gift becomes a curse with unpredictable repercussions when Paul falls under the influence of Donny Dawson, a former faith healer who hopes to exploit Paul's uncanny talents.

Other books you might like:
John Byrne, *Whipping Boy*, 1992
Thomas M. Disch, *The M.D.: A Horror Story*, 1991
Thomas F. Monteleone, *The Blood of the Lamb*, 1992
F. Paul Wilson, *The Touch*, 1986

2157

BRIAN HODGE

Nightlife
(New York: Dell, 1991)

Story type: Horror (Doppelganger)
Major character(s): Justin Gray, Advertising (copywriter); April Kingston, Advertising (freelance graphic designer); Kerebawa, Indian (member of Venezuelan Mabori)
Time period(s): 1990s (1990)
Locale(s): Tampa, Florida

Summary: When Justin Gray samples "skullflush," a recreational drug that causes users to temporarily revert to their animal selves, he runs afoul of dealer Tony Mendoza. His only hope for survival is to team up with Kerebawa, a primitive Venezuelan Indian who has tracked the drug to the United States to prevent its distribution.

Other books you might like:
Paddy Chayefsky, *Altered States*, 1978
Leonard Cline, *The Dark Chamber*, 1927
Robert Louis Stevenson, *The Strange Case of Dr. Jekyll and Mr. Hyde*, 1886

2158

BRIAN HODGE

Oasis
(New York: Tor, 1989)

Story type: Horror (Curse)
Major character(s): Chris Anderson, Teenager; Aaron Anderson, Teenager
Time period(s): 1970s (Prologue in 1940)
Locale(s): Tri-Lakes, Illinois (A wooded area in southern Illinois)

Summary: An idyllic summer at Tri-Lakes turns gradually horrific for the Anderson brothers as, one by one, their friends and associates meet violent ends. An ancient malevolent force—a Viking blood feud—animates a mysterious woods and finally drives the brothers into a violent confrontation—with each other.

Other books you might like:
Gary Brandner, *Doomstalker*, 1989

2159

BRIAN HODGE

Prototype

(New York: Dell, 1996)

Story type: Horror (Science Fiction)
Major character(s): Clay Palmer, Drifter; Adrienne Rand, Psychologist; Patrick Valentine, Smuggler (arms smuggler)
Time period(s): 1990s (1996)
Locale(s): Denver, Colorado
Summary: Clay Palmer is a victim of Helverson's Syndrome, a congenital disease that imparts superhuman powers but impulsive and violent tendencies as well. Clay becomes a pawn between a biotech firm that hopes to harness his medical condition to their business interests, and criminal Patrick Valentine, another sufferer of Helverson's who is banding together others like him into an unstoppable gang of outlaws.

Other books you might like:
John Arbucci, *Blood of Innocents*, 1990
John Farris, *The Fury*, 1976
Stephen King, *Firestarter*, 1980
Dean R. Koontz, *The Bad Place*, 1990
Michael Kurland, *Button Bright*, 1995

2160

BRIAN HODGE

Shrines and Desecrations

(Leesburg, Virginia: TAL Publications, 1994)

Story type: Horror (Collection; Vampire Story)
Major character(s): Kraeken, Vampire
Summary: The author's first collection presents a trio of stories centered around Kraeken, an irreverent young vampire living in Florida who hopes to build a cult around himself by undermining the faith of others. In the book's only reprint, "Like a Pilgrim to the Shrine," Kraeken squares off against the grandaddy of all vampires, Count Dracula, to see who will claim Florida for his own turf. In "Leper's Holiday," the vampire sows doubt in the minds of fundamentalists at a barbecue. In "Messiah Envy," Kraeken finally gathers his acolytes only to have them rebel against him. Poppy Z. Brite contributes the introduction.

Other books you might like:
Edward Bryant, *Aqua Sancta*, 1994
Martin H. Greenberg, *Dracula: Prince of Darkness*, 1992 editor
Nancy Kilpatrick, *Sex and the Single Vampire*, 1994
Chelsea Quinn Yarbro, *The Saint-Germain Chronicles*, 1983

2161

BARBARA HODGSON

The Tattooed Map

(San Francisco: Chronicle Books, 1995)

Story type: Fantasy (Literary)

Major character(s): Lydia, Traveller; Chris, Traveller
Time period(s): 1990s
Locale(s): Morocco
Summary: In North Africa a woman discovers strange marks on her arm quickly growing into a tattoo depicting a map which drags her into a mysterious journey. Later, her travelling companion must pick up her trail and journal and follow her into the mystery. First novel heavily illustrated with photos, drawings, maps, and reproductions of things the travellers see.

Other books you might like:
Nick Bantock, *Griffin & Sabine*, 1991
John Crowley, *Little, Big*, 1981
Lisa Goldstein, *Tourists*, 1989
Robert Irwin, *The Arabian Nightmare*, 1983
Pat Murphy, *The City, Not Long After*, 1989

2162

WILLIAM HOPE HODGSON

Demons of the Sea

(West Warwick, Rhode Island: Necronomicon Press, 1992)

Story type: Horror (Collection)
Summary: Six hitherto unreprinted stories and three non-fiction pieces by an early and influential master of modern horror. Included are the sentimental ghost story "The Valley of Lost Children"; the sea-monster tale "The Haunted *Pampero*"; the author's first published story "The Goddess of Death"; and the futuristic satire "Date 1965: Modern Warfare."

Other books you might like:
Lloyd Kropp, *The Drift*, 1969
William Pattrick, *Mysterious Sea Stories*, 1985 editor
Charles G. Waugh, *Spooky Sea Stories*, 1991 Frank McSherry, Jr., co-editor

2163

WILLIAM HOPE HODGSON

The Haunted Pampero

(Kingston, Rhode Island: Donald M. Grant, 1992)

Story type: Horror (Collection)
Summary: Sam Moskowitz has edited and supplied a lengthy biographical introduction to this collection of 12 stories by an early master of visionary supernatural horror fiction. Included are the title story, "The Ghosts of the 'Glen Doon,'" and "The Silent Ship," all deep-sea horror tales; the sentimental fantasy "The Valley of Lost Children"; an introductory tale involving Hodgson's renowned psychic sleuth, Carnacki the Ghost Finder; the science fictional "Date 1965: Modern Warfare"; the ghost story "Old Golly"; and the mystery, "Bullion."

Other books you might like:
Algernon Blackwood, *Best Ghost Stories of Algernon Blackwood*, 1973

H.P. Lovecraft, *The Dunwich Horror and Others*, 1963
Arthur Machen, *Tales of Horror and the Supernatural*, 1948

2164

WILLIAM HOPE HODGSON

The House on the Borderland
(New York: Caroll & Graf, 1996)

Story type: Horror (Apocalyptic Horror)
Major character(s): The Narrator, Writer; Mary, Young Woman (the narrator's sister); Pepper, Animal (dog)
Time period(s): 1900s
Locale(s): Kraighten, Ireland

Summary: This story is presented as a manuscript found in an abandoned house in rural Ireland by two foreign travellers. It recounts the nameless narrator's efforts to defend himself against a horde of swine-like creatures who emerge from the ravine near which the house is set, and the narrator's experiences in the strange space and time warps to which his house seems to be subject. This novel was first published in England in 1908.

Other books you might like:
Ramsey Campbell, *Midnight Sun*, 1990
Basil Copper, *The Great White Space*, 1974
H.P. Lovecraft, *At the Mountains of Madness*, 1964
Adrian Ross, *The Hole of the Pit*, 1914

2165

WILLIAM HOPE HODGSON
NED DAMERON, Illustrator

Terrors of the Sea
(Hampton Falls, New Hampshire: Donald M. Grant, 1996)

Story type: Horror (Collection)

Summary: Fourteen works of fiction and non-fiction, only three of which have been published before, comprise this latest posthumous compilation of work from an author best known for his tales of sea horror. "The Promise" is a *conte cruel* and "Demons of the Sea" is a tale of monstrous terror on the high seas. "The Plans of the Reefing Bi-Plane" is an invention story featuring Hodgson's series character Captain Gault. Included as well are "Ten Months at Sea," Hodgson's autobiographical account of the rigors of a sailor's life, and "Writers of Ghost Stories," a fragment of an essay. Sam Moskowitz supplies a lengthy introduction.

Other books you might like:
Algernon Blackwood, *The Listener and Other Stories*, 1907
H.P. Lovecraft, *The Dunwich Horror and Others*, 1963
Arthur Machen, *The Three Impostors*, 1895
Richard Middleton, *The Ghost Ship and Other Stories*, 1912

2166

BARRY HOFFMAN
HARRY O. MORRIS, Illustrator

Firefly. . .Burning Bright
(Springfield, Pennsylvania: Gauntlet Publications, 1994)

Story type: Horror (Collection)

Summary: Four tales of nonsupernatural horror explore the social and psychological dynamics of victimization. In the title story, a neglected young girl gets the attention she craves through acts of pyromania. "No Place to Hide" tells of an assault victim's revenge against her attacker and "The Ultimate Groupie" of the perverse relationship that develops between a serial killer and his victim. In "Vicious Cycle," an abused spouse comes to a tragic conclusion regarding the only means of preventing her husband from abusing their unborn child as he has her. Ronald Kelly supplies an introduction and Richard T. Chizmar an afterword. This is the author's first book.

Other books you might like:
Richard T. Chizmar, *Midnight Promises*, 1996
Ed Gorman, *Cages*, 1995
Dean R. Koontz, *Strange Highways*, 1995
Andrew Vachss, *Born Bad*, 1994

2167

NINA KIRIKI HOFFMAN

Legacy of Fire
(Eugene, OR: Pulphouse, 1990)

Story type: Horror (Collection)

Summary: Four tales of fantasy and horror, two reprints and two originals. "Coming Home" is about the guilt a woman bears for a childhood prank that went tragically awry. "Tremors" features a ghostly grandmother. "Works of Art" tells of an artist with rather peculiar notions about the relationship of art to life. This is the author's first collection.

Other books you might like:
Pat Cadigan, *Patterns*, 1989
Pat Murphy, *Points of Departure*, 1990
Jessica Amanda Salmonson, *John Collier and Fredric Brown Went Quarreling through My Head*, 1989
Lisa Tuttle, *A Nest of Nightmares*, 1986
Chelsea Quinn Yarbro, *Signs and Portents*, 1984

2168

NINA KIRIKI HOFFMAN

The Silent Strength of Stones
(New York: AvoNova, 1995)

Story type: Fantasy (Contemporary; Psychic Powers)
Major character(s): Nick Verrou, Teenager, Psychic (esper); Willow Seale, Teenager, Psychic (esper); Evan Seale, Teenager, Animal (wolf)
Time period(s): 1990s

Locale(s): Sauterelle Lake, Oregon; Cascade Mountains, Oregon

Summary: Still angry at being abandoned by his mother four years earlier, Nick works hard both at home and in the family store and motel. With little free time, Nick manages solitary forays through the populated areas around the lake morning and night, observing the local and vacationing residents. Nick expects an unusual summer when he sees Willow disappear, befriends a wolf, and recognizes that he possesses a command voice and that his mother had seemed special.

Other books you might like:
Tom Deitz, *Soulsmith*, 1990
Zenna Henderson, *Ingathering: The Complete People Stories of Zenna Henderson*, 1995
David Lee Jones, *Zeus and Co.*, 1993
Morgan Llywelyn, *The Elementals*, 1993
Elizabeth Ann Scarborough, *Nothing Sacred*, 1991

2169

NINA KIRIKI HOFFMAN

The Thread That Binds the Bones

(New York: AvoNova, 1993)

Story type: Fantasy (Contemporary; Psychic Powers)
Major character(s): Tom Renfield, Psychic (esper); Laura Bolte, Psychic (esper); Peregrine, Spirit
Time period(s): 1990s
Locale(s): Portland, Oregon; Arcadia, Oregon

Summary: Tom leaves Portland to escape notoriety arising when he floated two teenagers who had jumped off a building. After riding the rails to Arcadia, Tom drives a taxi while feeling that he waits for something. When Laura Bolte hires his cab, he discovers a clan of people and their forebears with talents similar to his own. He marries Laura, accepts Peregrine as mentor and attempts to protect his friends from his new family.

Other books you might like:
James P. Blaylock, *The Paper Grail*, 1991
Emma Bull, *War for the Oaks*, 1987
Tom Deitz, *Soulsmith*, 1990
Steven Gould, *Jumper*, 1992
Zenna Henderson, *The People: No Different Flesh*, 1967
Marc Laidlaw, *Neon Lotus*, 1988

2170

E.T.A. HOFFMANN

The Golden Pot and Other Tales

(New York: Oxford Paperbacks, 1992)

Story type: Horror (Collection)

Summary: Five stories by the renowned German romanticist. Included are ''The Sandman,'' a harrowing tale of an early childhood nightmare and its long-term consequences for the adult protagonist; ''Master Flea,'' in which denizens of a fairy realm are reincarnated as mortals; and ''The Golden Pot,'' about the young poet Anselmus who lives a double life in the real world as well as the mystical world of ancient Atlantis. The stories have been translated by Ritchie Robinson.

Other books you might like:
Peter Haining, *Gothic Tales of Terror*, 1972
    editor
I.U. Tarchetti, *Fantastic Tales*, 1992
Ronald Taylor, *Six German Romantic Tales*, 1992
    editor

2171

E.T.A. HOFFMANN

Nutcracker

(New York: Harcourt Brace, 1996)

Story type: Fantasy (Legend; Young Adult)
Major character(s): Marie Stahlbaum, Child; Christian Elias ''Godfather'' Drosselmeier, Artisan (toymaker)
Time period(s): 19th century
Locale(s): Germany

Summary: At Christmas, Godfather Drosselmeier brings marvelous toys for the Stahlbaum children and tells them wondrous tales. Falling in love with Drosselmeier's ugly nutcracker, Marie helps change the ensorcelled toy into a handsome prince who leads other toys in repelling the seven-headed mouse king and his minions. Based on Major Alex Ewing's 1886 translation from the German of Hoffmann's *Nutcracker and the King of Mice* (1816), the inspiration for the Tchaikovsky ballet.

Other books you might like:
Lynne Reid Banks, *The Indian in the Cupboard*, 1981
James C. Christensen, *Voyage of the Basset*, 1996
    Renwick St. James, Alan Dean Foster, co-authors
Ethel Johnston Phelps, *Tatterhood and Other Tales*, 1978
Sylvia Waugh, *The Mennyms*, 1994

2172

ERNEST HOGAN

Cortez on Jupiter

(New York: Tor, 1990)

Story type: Science Fiction (Arts; First Contact)
Major character(s): Pablo Cortez, Artist (graffiti); Anna Paik, Journalist (media interviewer)
Time period(s): Indeterminate Future
Locale(s): Ithica Base, Space Station (in orbit around Jupiter); Los Angeles, California; Hightown, Space Station (near Earth)

Summary: Pablo Cortez is a brilliant, egotistical guerilla graffiti artist. On the way to developing his art he demonstrates his inability to conform to the restrictions society places on him. Cortez is peculiar enough that he may be the only person who can communicate with newly discovered aliens and live. First novel.

Other books you might like:
Pat Cadigan, *Synners*, 1991
Gordon R. Dickson, *Alien Art*, 1973
James Patrick Kelly, *Look into the Sun*, 1989

Spider Robinson, *Stardance*, 1979
  Jeanne Robinson, co-author
John Varley, *The Persistence of Vision*, 1978

2173

ERNEST HOGAN

High Aztec

(New York: Tor, 1992)

Story type: Science Fiction (Theological; Medical)
Major character(s): Xolotl Zapata, Fugitive, Artist
Time period(s): 2040s (2045)
Locale(s): Mexico City, Mexico

Summary: Throughout Tenochtitlan, formerly known as Mexico City, everyone wants to get their hands on Xolotl Zapata who has become infected by a genetically engineered virus which can infect any human with religion.

Other books you might like:
Michael Cassutt, *Dragon Season*, 1991
Philip K. Dick, *The Three Stigmata of Palmer Eldritch*, 1965
Robert A. Heinlein, *Stranger in a Strange Land*, 1991 revised
Frank Herbert, *Heretics of Dune*, 1984
Katharine Kerr, *Polar City Blues*, 1990
Ted Reynolds, *The Tides of God*, 1989
Kurt Vonnegut Jr., *Cat's Cradle*, 1963

2174

JAMES P. HOGAN

Entoverse

(New York: Ballantine/Del Rey, 1991)

Story type: Science Fiction (First Contact; Alternate Intelligence)
Series: Giants
Major character(s): Victor Hunt, Scientist (physicist); Gina Martin, Writer; VISAR, Artificial Intelligence
Time period(s): 21st century
Locale(s): Earth; Jevlen, Planet—Imaginary; Waroth, Alternate Universe

Summary: Dr. Victor Hunt is sent to Jevlen with a handpicked team to determine why, contrary to expectations, the population continues to fall apart after it was freed from the pervasive control of an artificial intelligence. The team finds not only an artificial intelligence less disposed of than previously thought, but also evidence of impending invasion from a parallel universe, one which seems to operate on magic. This book is a sequel to *The Giants Novels* (1991).

Other books you might like:
Isaac Asimov, *The Gods Themselves*, 1972
Raymond E. Feist, *A Darkness at Sethanon*, 1986
Raymond E. Feist, *Magician*, 1982
Raymond E. Feist, *Silverthorn*, 1985
Cheryl J. Franklin, *Fire Crossing*, 1991
Cheryl J. Franklin, *Fire Get*, 1987
Cheryl J. Franklin, *Fire Lord*, 1989
Cheryl J. Franklin, *The Light of Exile*, 1990

2175

JAMES P. HOGAN

The Immortality Option

(New York: Ballantine Del Rey, 1995)

Story type: Science Fiction (Robot Fiction; First Contact)
Major character(s): Karl Zambendorf, Psychic, Magician; Arthur, Robot (Taloid), Alien; Genius, Artificial Intelligence, Alien
Time period(s): Indeterminate Future
Locale(s): Titan, Saturn (moon)

Summary: After discovering the robot civilization on titan, Earth interests organize to exploit the medieval society. Arthur begins to develop a more modern free culture, while Karl and his team protect the budding society from interference. When the original alien intelligences hidden on Titan wake up, they attempt to take over the Net on Earth, which may result in disaster for all. Sequel to *Code of the Lifemaker*.

Other books you might like:
Roger MacBride Allen, *Orphan of Creation*, 1988
Isaac Asimov, *The Robots of Dawn*, 1983
Keith Laumer, *Rogue Bolo*, 1986
Dan Simmons, *The Fall of Hyperion*, 1990
Thomas T. Thomas, *ME: A Novel of Self Discovery*, 1991

2176

JAMES P. HOGAN

The Mirror Maze

(New York: Bantam Spectra, 1989)

Story type: Science Fiction (Techno-Thriller)
Major character(s): Stephanie Carne, Scientist; Melvin Shears, Lawyer
Time period(s): 20th century (2000)
Locale(s): United States

Summary: The United States is safe from enemy attack beneath its satellite-carried defense lasers and things are looking up all across the country. A new political party, the Constitutionals, seems poised to carry the nation to a near-utopian level of wealth and personal freedom. It soon becomes clear, however, that there are those who will stop at nothing to keep America from achieving this golden age.

Other books you might like:
Ben Bova, *The Kinsman Saga*, 1987
Ben Bova, *Peacekeepers*, 1988
Dale Brown, *The Silver Tower*, 1988

2177

JAMES P. HOGAN

The Multiplex Man

(New York: Bantam Spectra, 1992)

Story type: Science Fiction (Political; Techno-Thriller)
Major character(s): Richard Jarrow, Military Personnel, Experimental Subject; M. R. Valdheim, Doctor (neurophysi-

ologist), Government Official; Andre Ulkanov, Researcher, Doctor
Time period(s): 2000s
Locale(s): Atlanta, Georgia; Minneapolis, Minnesota; Copernicus, Moon (Earth's)

Summary: Richard Jarrow awakens in November in a hotel in Atlanta instead of Minneapolis where he teaches junior high school. He looks younger, darker and no longer sports a moustache. However, these details seem unimportant compared to the strange clothes, guns, spy tools, I.D. with his picture and the name Maurice J. Gordon, and the fact that his last memory dated from April. He takes the only clues in the room, a message and some phone numbers, and heads for Minneapolis where he discovers that Richard Jarrow died of a stroke in May.

Other books you might like:
Greg Bear, *Queen of Angels*, 1990
Ben Bova, *The Trikon Deception*, 1992
   Bill Pogue, co-author
Pat Cadigan, *Fools*, 1992
Peter R. Emshwiller, *The Host*, 1991
David D. Ross, *The Eighth Rank*, 1991
Dan Simmons, *The Hollow Man*, 1992
Dan Simmons, *Hyperion*, 1989
Norman Spinrad, *Russian Spring*, 1991

2178

JAMES P. HOGAN

Paths to Otherwhere

(New York: Baen, 1996)

Story type: Science Fiction (Political; Alternate Universe)
Major character(s): Hugh Brenner, Scientist (quantum physics), Inventor; Edward Kintner, Scientist, Government Official; Sam Phniangsak, Religious (Buddhist)
Time period(s): 21st century
Locale(s): Berkeley, California; Los Alamos, New Mexico

Summary: In the militaristic overpopulated future, the United States no longer retains its position of power, while world war seems imminent. Kintner works on a quantum device which he believes too risky to leave uncontrolled. Co-opted by the government's central secret project to predict political solutions, Hugh finds an alternative project more in keeping with his research at Berkeley and, perhaps, a better solution in a quantum universe.

Other books you might like:
Gregory Frost, *The Pure Cold Light*, 1993
Michaela Roessner, *Vanishing Point*, 1993
Neal Stephenson, *The Diamond Age*, 1995
Michael Swanwick, *Stations of the Tide*, 1991
George Zebrowski, *Stranger Suns*, 1991

2179

JAMES P. HOGAN

Realtime Interrupt

(New York: Bantam Spectra, 1995)

Story type: Science Fiction (Cyberpunk; Adventure)
Major character(s): Joe Corrigan, Computer Expert; Lilly Essell, Military Personnel, Astronaut
Time period(s): Indeterminate Future
Locale(s): Pittsburgh, Pennsylvania; Oz, Cyberspace (computer virtual reality); Dun Laoghaire, Ireland

Summary: The designer and head of the Oz Project, Joe Corrigan volunteers as one of its first inhabitants. While there, his wife leaves him, the project fails, he suffers a nervous breakdown, and he loses control of the company. When he meets Lilly, soon recognizing her as another volunteer, he realizes that he remains in Oz and must somehow find a way out.

Other books you might like:
Greg Egan, *Permutation City*, 1995
Jean Mark Gawron, *Dream of Glass*, 1993
Mary Rosenblum, *Chimera*, 1993
Dan Simmons, *Hyperion*, 1989
Neal Stephenson, *Snow Crash*, 1992
Amy Thomson, *Virtual Girl*, 1993

2180

NANCY HOLDER

Dead in the Water

(New York: Dell/Abyss, 1994)

Story type: Horror (Supernatural Vengeance)
Major character(s): Donna Almond, Teacher; John Fielder, Doctor; Ruth Hamilton, Widow(er)
Time period(s): 1990s (1994)
Locale(s): *Robert X. Morris*, At Sea (a ship on the Pacific Ocean)

Summary: The author's first horror novel tells of a vacation voyage aboard the *Robert X. Morris* that turns into a nightmare when the ship falls prey to a vengeful spirit with a history of attacking ships and absorbing the souls of its passengers. In their efforts to avoid this fate, many of the passengers discover personal strengths they have developed trying to cope with life problems that have sent them on the voyage in the first place.

Other books you might like:
William Hope Hodgson, *The Ghost Pirates*, 1909
Stephen King, *The Shining*, 1977
Damon Knight, *CV*, 1985
Thomas Liam McDonald, *Sea Cursed: Thirty Terrifying Tales of the Deep*, 1994
   Stefan Dziemianowicz, Martin H. Greenberg, co-editors
William Pattrick, *Mysterious Sea Stories*, 1985
   editor
Dean Wesley Smith, *Laying the Music to Rest*, 1989

`2181`

NANCY HOLDER
MELANIE TEM, Co-Author

Witch-Light
(New York: Tor, 1996)

Story type: Horror (Occult)
Major character(s): Valerie Kittridge, Student (film); Gabriel Luz, Witch (brujo); Maria Elena Lopez, Young Woman
Time period(s): 1990s (1995)
Locale(s): Duerme, New Mexico

Summary: While visiting her ill father, Valerie falls in love with Gabriel, a brujo who is related to his father's mistress. Although Gabriel teaches Valerie how to access latent spiritual powers, Valerie is not entirely sure that Gabriel is the completely kind and caring person he appears to be.

Other books you might like:
Warren Newton Beath, *Shock Lines*, 1993
Morgan Fields, *Shaman Woods*, 1990
Ashley McConnell, *Days of the Dead*, 1992
Kathryn Ptacek, *Shadoweyes*, 1984
William Relling Jr., *Brujo*, 1986

`2182`

ROBERT HOLDSTOCK

Ancient Echoes
(New York: Roc, 1996)

Story type: Fantasy (Magic Conflict; Alternate World)
Major character(s): Jack Chatwin, Psychic; Nemet "Greenface", Hunter; Baalgor "Grayface", Hunter
Time period(s): 1990s; Indeterminate
Locale(s): Earth; Gl'thaan Em, Alternate Earth (Glanum)

Summary: Jack's lifelong visions of hunters fleeing a violent threat prove more real than Jack imagined when Grayface escapes to Earth. To reunite with his beloved Greenface, Grayface will employ extreme methods, even threatening Jack's family.

Other books you might like:
Aaron Allston, *Galatea in 2-D*, 1993
A.A. Attanasio, *The Dragon and the Unicorn*, 1996
Charles de Lint, *The Little Country*, 1991
Charles de Lint, *Memory and Dream*, 1994
Ben Okri, *The Famished Road*, 1992
Nancy Springer, *Larque on the Wing*, 1994
Sheri S. Tepper, *A Plague of Angels*, 1993

`2183`

ROBERT HOLDSTOCK

The Bone Forest
(New York: AvoNova, 1992)

Story type: Fantasy (Collection)
Summary: Contains eight stories published 1976-1989 in periodicals and anthologies. Surreal and horrific images present themes which include mythical creatures, pagan magic, madness and the primal power evoked by some tale-tellers. The title novella is a prequel to *Mythago Wood*.

Other books you might like:
Brian W. Aldiss, *A Romance of the Equator: The Best Fantasy Stories of Brian W. Aldiss*, 1990
Orson Scott Card, *Maps in a Mirror*, 1990
Charles de Lint, *Spiritwalk*, 1992
Pauline Melville, *Shape-Shifter: Stories by Pauline Melville*, 1991
Gene Wolfe, *Storeys From the Old Hotel*, 1992

`2184`

ROBERT HOLDSTOCK

The Hollowing
(New York: Roc, 1994)

Story type: Fantasy (Quest)
Series: Mythago Wood
Major character(s): Richard Bradley, Parent, Adventurer; Alexander "Alex" Bradley, Student; Arnauld Lacan, Scientist
Time period(s): 1960s; Indeterminate Past
Locale(s): Ryhope Wood, Mythical Place; England

Summary: When Richard Bradley enters Ryhope Wood in search of his son, he finds scientists investigating the nature of the area. His search leads him through mythic time, including an encounter with Jason and the Argonauts.

Other books you might like:
Charles de Lint, *The Little Country*, 1991
Charles de Lint, *Memory and Dream*, 1994
Holly Lisle, *Minerva Wakes*, 1994
Michael Swanwick, *The Iron Dragon's Daughter*, 1994
Sheri S. Tepper, *A Plague of Angels*, 1993

`2185`

ROBERT HOLDSTOCK

Lavondyss: Journey to an Unknown Region
(New York: William Morrow, 1989)

Story type: Fantasy (Quest)
Major character(s): Tallis Keeton, Teenager (Girl); Scathach, Royalty (Prince)
Time period(s): 1980s
Locale(s): England

Summary: Tallis, a bridge between the modern and ancient world, is convinced that her brother Harry, missing since World War II, is lost in the magical forest, Ryhope Wood. She searches for him and the answers to puzzling questions.

Other books you might like:
Greer Ilene Gilman, *Moonwise*, 1991
Paul Hazel, *The Wealdwife's Tale*, 1993
R.A. Salvatore, *The Woods out Back*, 1993

2186

JACK HOLLAND

The Fire Queen

(New York: Roc, 1992)

Story type: Fantasy (Historical; Political)
Major character(s): Fen ''Fire Queen'' Fire, Warrior, Royalty (adopted daughter)
Time period(s): 1st century
Locale(s): England (Briton)

Summary: After Fen Fire exposes the treacherous relationship between her brother and the Roman Emperor Caligula, Fen Fire must rally her people's defenses to stand against Caligula's invading army, intent on ruling the island.

Other books you might like:
Marion Zimmer Bradley, *The Mists of Avalon*, 1983
Morgan Llywelyn, *Druids*, 1991
Bridget Wood, *Wolfking*, 1992

2187

TOM HOLLAND

Lord of the Dead

(New York: Pocket, 1996)

Story type: Horror (Vampire Story)
Major character(s): Rebecca Carville, Scholar (Orientalist); George Gordon Byron, Historical Figure, Writer (poet); Percy Bysshe Shelley, Writer (poet), Historical Figure
Time period(s): 1990s (1995); 1800s
Locale(s): London, England; Albania

Summary: Rebecca Carville opens a forgotten crypt in hopes of finding a copy of Lord Byron's supposedly destroyed memoirs, and instead finds Byron himself, who has been a vampire for almost two centuries. Byron regales Rebecca with his personal history as Lord of the Dead, one that makes much sense of the poet's exploits and the imagery in his verse. This first novel was originally published in England in 1995.

Other books you might like:
Kim Newman, *Anno Dracula*, 1992
Tim Powers, *The Stress of Her Regard*, 1989
Kathryn Ptacek, *In Silence Sealed*, 1988
Anne Rice, *The Vampire Lestat*, 1985
Brian Stableford, *The Empire of Fear*, 1988

2188

GARY L. HOLLEMAN

Demon Fire

(New York: Leisure, 1995)

Story type: Horror (Black Magic)
Major character(s): Quinn Ramsey, Police Officer (former); Gail Okata, Police Officer; Quinn Ramsey Jr., Child (9-year-old)
Time period(s): 1990s (1995)
Locale(s): Hana, Hawaii

Summary: Quinn Ramsey inherits the fortune and property of an uncle who died under mysterious circumstances in Hawaii. After moving there with his son, Quinn discovers that his uncle practiced black magic. He is caught between other black magic adherents who hope to gain control of a demon his uncle summoned, and a wicca cult allied with the ancient gods of the island who use white magic to control the damage his uncle has already caused. First novel.

Other books you might like:
Robert Bloch, *Strange Eons*, 1976
Edward Lee, *The Chosen*, 1993
Graham Masterton, *Burial*, 1994
Dan Simmons, *Fires of Eden*, 1994
Tamara Thorne, *Haunted*, 1995

2189

GARY L. HOLLEMAN

Howl-O-Ween

(New York: Leisure, 1996)

Story type: Horror (Black Magic)
Major character(s): Cyrus ''Russ'' Trigg, Bodyguard; Kyna Rand, Businesswoman (diamond merchant); Macumba the Dark Man, Sorcerer
Time period(s): 1990s (1996)
Locale(s): Memphis, Tennessee

Summary: Unaware that she is carrying a stolen talisman known as The Butcher's Broom, Kyna Rand travels the world at the behest of her employer, who hopes to deprive the Dark Man of his magic charm and leave him vulnerable to attack come Halloween. But the Dark Man, a voodoo houngan, has raised the loup garou, whose bite is slowly turning Kyna's bodyguard into a werewolf.

Other books you might like:
Hugh B. Cave, *Disciples of Dread*, 1988
Nicholas Conde, *The Religion*, 1982
Don Davis, *The Gris-Gris Man*, 1997
Robert Weinberg, *The Black Lodge*, 1991

2190

HELEN HOLLICK

The Kingmaking

(New York: St. Martin's, 1995)

Story type: Fantasy (Legend)
Series: Pendragon's Banner
Major character(s): Arthur Pendragon, Royalty, Leader; Gwenhwyfar, Fiance(e)
Time period(s): 5th century (450s)
Locale(s): England (Britain)

Summary: As forces drive the Roman legions from Britain, Uthr's death thrusts Arthur into leadership. He must quickly learn the warrior's way of life, difficult after his early life, spent posing as the son of a serving woman to protect him from Uthr's enemies. First novel.

Other books you might like:

Mike Ashley, *The Camelot Chronicles*, 1992
　editor
Mike Ashley, *The Pendragon Chronicles*, 1990
　editor
Marion Zimmer Bradley, *The Mists of Avalon*, 1983
Gillian Bradshaw, *Hawk of May*, 1980
Andrea Hopkins, *Chronicles of King Arthur*, 1994
Courtway Jones, *In the Shadow of the Oak King*, 1991
Mary Stewart, *The Crystal Cave*, 1970
T.H. White, *The Once and Future King*, 1958

2191

HELEN HOLLICK

Pendragon's Banner

(New York: St. Martin's, 1996)

Story type: Fantasy (Legend; Political)
Series: Pendragon's Banner
Major character(s): Arthur Pendragon, Royalty, Leader;
　Gwenhwyfar, Royalty, Spouse
Time period(s): 5th century (460s)
Locale(s): England (Britain)

Summary: As Arthur attempts to hold on to his newly unified kingdom and keep his family safe, power seekers and family problems threaten the harmony. Second in the trilogy.

Other books you might like:

Mike Ashley, *The Pendragon Chronicles*, 1990
　editor
Marion Zimmer Bradley, *The Mists of Avalon*, 1983
Andrea Hopkins, *Chronicles of King Arthur*, 1994
Morgan Llywelyn, *Pride of Lions*, 1996
Mary Stewart, *The Crystal Cave*, 1970
Jack Whyte, *The Skystone*, 1996

2192

JOHN R. HOLT

The Convocation

(New York: Bantam, 1993)

Story type: Horror (Black Magic)
Major character(s): Elspeth ''Beth'' Tremaine, Statistician
　(for a brokerage house); Max Wingate, Artist; Victor
　Rotciv, Stock Broker
Time period(s): 1990s (1993)
Locale(s): New York, New York

Summary: Beth Tremaine's mother died horribly at the hands of the People of the Griffin, a black magic coven to which she belonged and to whom her mother had promised her. Decades later, the coven tries to force Beth back into its clutches in order to avail itself of the extraordinary supernatural talents she possesses.

Other books you might like:

Robert Bloch, *Strange Eons*, 1978
Scott Ciencin, *The Vampire Odyssey*, 1992
Stephen R. George, *Nightscape*, 1992
Pat Graversen, *The Fagin*, 1981

Kate Stewart, *The Devil's Cradle*, 1975
Peter Straub, *Shadowland*, 1980

2193

TOM HOLT

Flying Dutch

(New York: St. Martin's Press, 1992)

Story type: Fantasy (Legend; Light Fantasy)
Major character(s): Cornelius Vanderdecker, Sea Captain, Im-
　mortal; Jane Doland, Banker
Time period(s): 1990s
Locale(s): *Verdomde*, At Sea; Scotland; England

Summary: Hundreds of years after accidentally ingesting an immortality elixir with a malodorous side effect, Captain Vanderdecker and his crew sail endlessly while attempting landfall at seven year intervals. The noxious smell temporarily neutralized by radioactive water, Vanderdecker searches for the elixir's inventor while the company which carries his 400-year-old life insurance policy sends Jane Doland to search out and reason with the captain, hoping to avoid bankruptcy and ruination of the Earth's economic system should Vanderdecker die.

Other books you might like:

Douglas Adams, *The Hitchhiker's Guide to the Galaxy*, 1980
James P. Blaylock, *The Elfin Ship*, 1986
Neil Gaiman, *Good Omens: The Nice and Accurate Proph-
　ecies of Agnes Nutter, Witch*, 1990
　Terry Pratchett, co-author
Parke Godwin, *Waiting for the Galactic Bus*, 1988
Terry Pratchett, *Wyrd Sisters*, 1990

2194

TOM HOLT

Goatsong

(New York: St. Martin's Press, 1990)

Story type: Fantasy (Historical)
Series: Walled Orchard
Major character(s): Eupolis of Pallene, Writer
Time period(s): 5th century B.C.
Locale(s): Athens, Greece

Summary: A greek goatherd whose love is comic verse develops his skill as a playwright in Athens. While there, he gets married, writes his comedy and gets it produced to a background of Athenian democracy.

Other books you might like:

L. Sprague de Camp, *The Undesired Princess and the En-
　chanted Bunny*, 1990
　David Drake, co-author
Joan Slonczewski, *Still Forms on Foxfield*, 1980
Howard Waldrop, *A Dozen Tough Jobs*, 1989
Robert Watson, *Whilom*, 1990
Gene Wolfe, *Soldier of Arete*, 1989

2195

TOM HOLT

The Walled Orchard

(New York: St. Martin's Press, 1991)

Story type: Fantasy (Historical)
Series: Walled Orchard
Major character(s): Eupolis of Pallene, Writer
Time period(s): 5th century B.C.
Locale(s): Athens, Greece

Summary: In this sequel to *Goatsong* (1990), Eupolis continues his commissioned history of modern, 5th century Greece with his conscription into military forces fighting for Athens in the Great Peloponnesian War. Surviving the Sicilian disaster, he returns to Athens where he is accused of treason in conjunction with a tasteless blasphemy he had witnessed prior to conscription.

Other books you might like:
Robert Silverberg, *Letters From Atlantis*, 1990
Harry Turtledove, *The Misplaced Legion*, 1987
Robert Watson, *Whilom*, 1990
Gene Wolfe, *Soldier of Arete*, 1989

2196

TOM HOLT

Ye Gods!

(New York: St. Martin's Press, 1993)

Story type: Fantasy (Light Fantasy; Religious)
Major character(s): Jerry Derry, Adventurer, Hero; Apollo, Mythical Creature, Deity; Minerva, Mythical Creature, Deity
Time period(s): 1990s; Indeterminate
Locale(s): Earth; The Underground, Mythical Place

Summary: Greek gods delight in playing a game of existence and alternate worlds, modestly hoping to undo Prometheus's betrayal and bring a sense of humor to the human race. A rules violation changes relationships when Apollo must punish Prometheus for subverting heroes.

Other books you might like:
Neil Gaiman, *Good Omens: The Nice and Accurate Prophecies of Agnes Nutter, Witch*, 1990
    Terry Pratchett, co-author
Parke Godwin, *The Snake Oil Wars*, 1989
Parke Godwin, *Waiting for the Galactic Bus*, 1988
Robert A. Heinlein, *Job: A Comedy of Justice*, 1984
Curtis H. Hoffman, *Project: Millennium*, 1987
A.J. Langguth, *Jesus Christs*, 1968
Donald E. Westlake, *Humans*, 1992

2197

A.M. HOMES

The End of Alice

(New York: Scribner's, 1996)

Story type: Horror (Psychological Suspense)

Major character(s): Chappy, Prisoner; Alice Somerfield, Child (12-year-old); Matthew, Child (12-year-old)
Time period(s): 1990s (1996)
Locale(s): Westchester County, New York; Ossining, New York (Sing Sing Prison)

Summary: A female pen pal of a man imprisoned for the brutal sexual assault and murder of a 12-year-old girl becomes obsessed with his twisted mind. She herself seduces a 12-year-old boy and embarks upon an affair destined to lead to a similarly perverse end.

Other books you might like:
Ramsey Campbell, *The Face That Must Die*, 1979
Brett Easton Ellis, *American Psycho*, 1991
Stephen Gallagher, *Nightmare, with Angel*, 1992
Ronald Kelly, *Father's Little Helper*, 1992
Stephen King, *Apt Pupil*, 1982
    in *Different Seasons*
Joyce Carol Oates, *Zombie*, 1995
John Saul, *Black Lightning*, 1995

2198

DANIEL HOOD

Fanuilh

(New York: Ace, 1994)

Story type: Fantasy (Mystery)
Series: Fanuilh
Major character(s): Liam Rhenford, Scholar, Detective—Amateur; Fanuilh, Mythical Creature (dragon), Companion (wizard's familiar); Aedile Coeccias, Government Official
Time period(s): Indeterminate Past
Locale(s): Southwark, Fictional City; Taralon, Fictional Country

Summary: After the murder of the wizard Tarquin, Liam Rhenford's only friend in Southwark, Fanuilh, will give Liam no peace until they discover the murderer's identity.

Other books you might like:
Steven Brust, *Jhereg*, 1983
Glen Cook, *Sweet Silver Blues*, 1987
Simon R. Green, *Hawk & Fisher*, 1990
Barbara Hambly, *Dragonsbane*, 1986
Katharine Kerr, *Polar City Blues*, 1990

2199

DANIEL HOOD

Wizard's Heir

(New York: Ace, 1995)

Story type: Fantasy (Mystery)
Series: Fanuilh
Major character(s): Liam Rhenford, Scholar, Detective—Amateur; Fanuilh, Mythical Creature (dragon), Companion (wizard's familiar); Werewolf, Criminal
Time period(s): Indeterminate Past
Locale(s): Southwark, Fictional City; Taralon, Fictional Country

Summary: Liam struggles to deal with the death of Tarquin and the inheritance of the wizard's home and familiar. The theft of several magical artifacts from his home complicates his life, while Liam and Fanuilh must deal with wizards, priests, and thieves before they can rest.

Other books you might like:
Steven Brust, *Jhereg*, 1983
Glen Cook, *Sweet Silver Blues*, 1987
Simon R. Green, *Hawk & Fisher*, 1990
Ellen Kushner, *Swordspoint*, 1987
Fritz Leiber, *Ill Met in Lankhmar*, 1995

2200

DALE HOOVER

65mm
(New York: Dell/Abyss, 1994)

Story type: Horror (Haunted House)
Major character(s): Joe Moreson, Businessman (movie house owner); Andy Jordan, Teenager; Kelsie Brown, Computer Expert (systems analyst)
Time period(s): 1990s (1994)
Locale(s): Fareland, California

Summary: In an act of near compulsion Joe Moreson buys the old Fareland Cinema after quitting his job as a computer programmer. But when Joe begins showing a secret 65mm film found in the projection booth of the theater to the local residents, it reignites a series of brutal tortures and murders that the threater fed on 50 years before and is ravenous for again.

Other books you might like:
David Darke, *Horrorshow*, 1994
David J. Schow, *Silver Scream*, 1988
    editor
Brad Strickland, *Shadowshow*, 1988

2201

DALE HOOVER

Shadow Twin
(New York: Dell Abyss, 1991)

Story type: Horror (Doppelganger)
Major character(s): Jack Benson, Businessman; Rachal Benson, Housewife; Jedidiah Benson, Child (Jack and Rachal's son)
Time period(s): 1990s
Locale(s): Apple Creek, California

Summary: Stressed out by his job and memories of a less than ideal childhood, Jack Benson moves his family to a new life in California. But Jack's emotional turmoil quickly manifests as poltergeist phenomena, opening a hole in the attic of the house from which the physical manifestation of his dark side crawls out and threatens to overwhelm him and his family. This is the author's first novel.

Other books you might like:
Kathe Koja, *The Cipher*, 1991

2202

H.M. HOOVER

Away Is a Strange Place to Be
(New York: E.P. Dutton, 1989)

Story type: Science Fiction (Young Adult)
Major character(s): Abby Tabor, Teenager; Bryan Bishop, Teenager
Time period(s): 24th century (2349)
Locale(s): Vitacon, Space Station; United States

Summary: Abby and Bryan are kidnapped to serve as slave labor on a space habitat. Although they escape, they find the adult world unwilling to accept the truth of what they've been through, thus leaving them still in danger.

Other books you might like:
Frank Asch, *Journey to Terezor*, 1989
Lois McMaster Bujold, *Falling Free*, 1988
Robert A. Heinlein, *Have Spacesuit—Will Travel*, 1958
Robert A. Heinlein, *Podkayne of Mars*, 1963

2203

H.M. HOOVER

Only Child
(New York: Dutton, 1992)

Story type: Science Fiction (First Contact; Young Adult)
Major character(s): Cody Oakton, Teenager; Emily "Avi" Avichenko, Scientist; Skipper, Alien
Time period(s): Indeterminate Future
Locale(s): Patma, Planet—Imaginary

Summary: The only child aboard the *Annie Cannon*, Cody finds the prospect of his first planetfall quite exciting. When the adults' investigation of Patma's 200-year-old colony proves boring, he wanders away, discovering intelligent natives whose existence the colonists hid. Cody photographs the natives and their arts, determined to prove their existence on Earth where he will attend school.

Other books you might like:
Isaac Asimov, *Lucky Starr and the Big Sun of Mercury*, 1956
Ben Bova, *The Winds of Altair*, 1973
Marion Zimmer Bradley, *Star of Danger*, 1965
Diana G. Gallagher, *The Alien Dark*, 1990
Janet Kagan, *Hellspark*, 1988
Andre Norton, *The Stars Are Ours*, 1954
Andre Norton, *The X Factor*, 1965
H. Beam Piper, *Little Fuzzy*, 1962
Marti Steussy, *Dreams of Dawn*, 1988

2204

H.M. HOOVER

The Winds of Mars
(New York: Dutton, 1995)

Story type: Science Fiction (Young Adult; Robot Fiction)

Major character(s): Annalyn Reynolds Court, Military Personnel (cadet); Evan Parker, Military Personnel (cadet), Political Figure; Janis Parker, Political Figure (first lady)
Time period(s): Indeterminate Future
Locale(s): Mars

Summary: Annalyn serves as security for her father, protecting him from many enemies. After a foiled plot, Annalyn takes command and restores order, but must then contend with relatives who claim that she usurped power.

Other books you might like:
Isaac Asimov, *David Starr, Space Ranger*, 1952
Greg Bear, *Moving Mars*, 1993
Robert A. Heinlein, *Red Planet*, 1949
Frederik Pohl, *Mining the Oort*, 1992
Jerry Pournelle, *Birth of Fire*, 1976
Kim Stanley Robinson, *Green Mars*, 1993
S.C. Sykes, *Red Genesis*, 1991

2205

STUART HOPEN

Warp Angel
(New York: Tor, 1995)

Story type: Science Fiction (Psychic Powers; Theological)
Major character(s): Chev Carson, Mercenary; Dawson, Slave, Cyborg; Magen Hirsch, Warrior
Time period(s): Indeterminate Future
Locale(s): The Autumn World, Planet—Imaginary (Draconis System)

Summary: Marooned in the Draconis System by the abandonment of warp ships, a slave-based society serves the rich and powerful. Magen searches for her husband, a Jewish revolutionary captured by the quasi-governmental Slavers Bod. Unable to find him, Magen enlists Chev and their rich benefactor in an attempt to free as many slaves as possible, and learns the secret of breaking the slaves' conditioning. To save her husband Megan braves the planet most disrupted by the warp drive.

Other books you might like:
Lois McMaster Bujold, *Falling Free*, 1988
Lois McMaster Bujold, *Shards of Honor*, 1986
F.M. Busby, *Arrow From Earth*, 1995
Stephen Goldin, *Jade Darcy and the Zen Pirates*, 1990
  Mary Mason, co-author
Elizabeth Moon, *Sporting Chance*, 1994
Dan Simmons, *Hyperion*, 1989

2206

ANDREA HOPKINS, Editor

Chronicles of King Arthur
(New York: Viking Studio Books, 1994)

Story type: Fantasy (Anthology; Legend)
Major character(s): Arthur, Ruler (king), Warrior; Lancelot, Knight
Time period(s): 5th century; 6th century
Locale(s): England

Summary: Contains a four-page introduction and retelling of the medieval story cycle *Matter of Britain* based on the vulgate story cycle, including ''Merlin,'' ''Lancelot,'' ''La Queste del Saint Graal,'' and ''Mort Artu'' and Sir Thomas Malory's ''Morte D'Arthur'' plus poems and tales with some material newly translated. Hopkins utilizes original text with expansions and clarifications added. Includes a list of principal characters and glossary.

Other books you might like:
Mike Ashley, *The Camelot Chronicles*, 1992
  editor
Mike Ashley, *The Pendragon Chronicles*, 1990
  editor
Marion Zimmer Bradley, *The Mists of Avalon*, 1983
Howard Pyle, *The Story of King Arthur and His Knights*, 1903
T.H. White, *The Once and Future King*, 1958

2207

BRIAN HOPKINS
DONALD W. SCHANK, Illustrator

Something Haunts Us All
(Norfolk, Virginia: Macabre, Inc., 1995)

Story type: Horror (Collection)

Summary: This first story collection by a small-press author brings together seven tales of horror and surreality. ''Night Bite'' tells of a man's strange experience with a satanic trickster who may or may not be the manifestation of his illness. In ''Scarecrow's Dream'' and ''And Though a Million Stars Were Shining,'' the worlds of the living and the dead impinge uneasily upon one another. ''The Night Was Kind to Loretta'' and ''The Thunder of Water'' both feature psychopathic murderers who get their just desserts and more. William G. Raley supplies an introduction.

Other books you might like:
S. Darnbrook Colson, *People of the Night*, 1994
Jeffrey Osier, *Driftglider and Other Stories*, 1994
Stephen Mark Rainey, *Fugue Devil and Other Weird Horrors*, 1992
Sue Storm, *Star Bones Weep the Blood of Angels*, 1995
David Niall Wilson, *The Fall of the House of Escher and Other Illusions*, 1995

2208

JACK HOPKINS (Pseudonym of Nick Pollotta)

Satellite Night News
(New York: Ace, 1993)

Story type: Science Fiction (Adventure; Satire)
Series: Satellite Night News
Major character(s): Rikka Collins, Television Personality; Harry Snyder, Television Personality; Diedrich, Disembodied Personality (Artificial Intelligence)
Time period(s): 23rd century
Locale(s): Moon (Earth's)

Summary: After racing to the station, having escaped many close calls, the team finds they have been scooped by another station. Using their skills of misdirection, extortion and bribery, the team get their ship and equipment repaired and updated and head out on assignment to acquire another impossible scoop.

Other books you might like:
John DeChancie, *Paradox Alley*, 1987
John DeChancie, *Red Limit Freeway*, 1984
John DeChancie, *Starrigger*, 1983
Frederik Pohl, *Gladiator-at-Law*, 1955
  C.M. Kornbluth, co-author
Ken Rolston, *Extreme Paranoia: Nobody Knows the Trouble I've Shot*, 1991
Neal Stephenson, *Snow Crash*, 1992
Kurt Vonnegut Jr., *Hocus Pocus or, What's the Hurry, Son?*, 1990

2209

ANTHONY HOROWITZ, Editor

Death Walks Tonight

(New York: Puffin, 1996)

Story type: Horror (Anthology)

Summary: The ten tales of horror presented here were collected with younger readers in mind. Included are Stephen King's "Battleground," about a hit man who meets his match when he receives a box of magically-endowed toy soldiers from one victim's family; Roald Dahl's "Man From the South," a suspenseful tale of a strange man who makes outrageous bets with an extraordinary degree of self-assurance; John Gordon's "Eels," about the just rewards that befall a murderous old lady; Robert Westall's "The Vacancy," a dystopic fiction terror tale about a future in which it does not pay to be too smart; and an excerpt from Bram Stoker's *Dracula*. This book was first published in England in 1994 as *The Puffin Book of Horror Stories*.

Other books you might like:
A. Finnis, *Bone Meal*, 1994
  editor
A. Finnis, *The Cat-Dogs and Other Tales of Horror*, 1994
  editor
Gene Kemp, *Ghosts, Ghouls and Other Nightmares*, 1992
  editor
Dennis Pepper, *The Young Oxford Book of Ghost Stories*, 1994
  editor
Susan Price, *Horror Stories*, 1995
  editor
Robert Westall, *Ghost Stories*, 1993
  editor

2210

JESSICA HORSTING, Editor
JAMES VAN HISE, Co-Editor

Midnight Graffiti

(New York: Warner, 1992)

Story type: Horror (Anthology)

Summary: Nineteen stories of fantasy and horror, a number of which appeared originally in the cutting edge small press horror magazine, *Midnight Graffiti*, between 1989 and 1992. Included are Stephen King's tale of vengeful frogs, "The Rainy Season"; Stephen R. Boyett's surrealistic "Emerald City Blues"; Joe Lansdale's satirical "Bob the Dinosaur Goes to Disneyland"; a reprint of Dan Simmons' first published story, "The River Styx Runs Upstream"; and psychological horror stories by Nancy Collins, Rex Miller, and K.W. Jeter.

Other books you might like:
Robert Morrish, *Quick Chills II*, 1992
  Peter Enfantino, co-author
Mark Rainey, *The Best of Deathrealm*, 1993
Stuart David Schiff, *The Whispers Series*, 1977-1987
David B. Silva, *Best of The Horror Show*, 1987
David B. Silva, *The Definitive Best of the Horror Show*, 1992

2211

WILLIAM HORWOOD
PATRICK BENSON, Illustrator

Toad Triumphant

(New York: St. Martin's Press, 1996)

Story type: Fantasy (Young Adult; Adventure)
Series: Tales of the Willows
Major character(s): Toad of Toad Hall, Animal, Adventurer; Water Rat "Ratty", Animal, Adventurer; Mole, Animal, Adventurer
Time period(s): Indeterminate
Locale(s): England

Summary: Infatuated and in search of immortality, Toad takes a motor boat and heads upriver to win the heart of his beloved. Ratty and Mole set out on a river expedition, but then must help rescue the impetuous Toad from his latest legal predicament. A sequel to Kenneth Grahame's *Wind in the Willows*.

Other books you might like:
Mary Brown, *The Unlikely Ones*, 1986
Kenneth Grahame, *The Wind in the Willows*, 1908
Brian Jacques, *Redwall*, 1987
Dixon Scott, *A Fresh Wind in the Willows*, 1987
Tad Williams, *Tailchaser's Song*, 1985

2212

WILLIAM HORWOOD
PATRICK BENSON, Illustrator

The Willows in Winter

(New York: St. Martin's Press, 1994)

Story type: Fantasy (Young Adult; Adventure)
Series: Tales of the Willows
Major character(s): Toad of Toad Hall, Animal, Pilot; Water Rat "Ratty", Animal, Adventurer; Mole, Animal, Adventurer
Time period(s): Indeterminate
Locale(s): England

Summary: When Badger requisitions Toad's new airplane to search for the missing Mole, Toad waylays his friend and the pilot and takes off with Water Rat, despite inadequate flying lessons. The flight soon ends in first parachuting opportunities for Rat and Toad, allowing Rat to find his way home and Toad to find his way into additional trouble in town. Sequel to Kenneth Grahame's *The Wind in the Willows.*

Other books you might like:
Mary Brown, *The Unlikely Ones,* 1986
Michael Ende, *The Night of Wishes: or The Satanarchaeo-lidealcohellish Notion Potion,* 1992
Kenneth Grahame, *The Wind in the Willows,* 1908
Brian Jacques, *Redwall,* 1987
Dixon Scott, *A Fresh Wind in the Willows,* 1987

2213
GERARD DANIEL HOUARNER
Painfreak
(Orlando, Florida: Necro Publications, 1996)

Story type: Horror (Collection; Erotic Horror)

Summary: The author's first collection brings together ten stories of erotic horror, only three of which were previously published. Among the offerings are the title story, about a man's desperate efforts to rescue his wife from an after hours sex club; "Safe Word," concerned with a sexual slave whose master enjoins her to humiliate her tricks; "Painted Faces," in which a man passes on the psychological trauma of his abuse as a child to his wife and daughter; and "The Night Pain," in which a sexual predator psychically binds his victims to him through ritual mutilation. Also included are "The Beast That Was Max," "The Angel of Death," and "Demons of Blood and Passion," which comprise the Max Trilogy, a series of stories featuring an indulgent uncle who is all too willing to supply his sexual partners with everything they desire. Tom Piccirilli supplies the introduction.

Other books you might like:
Ron Dee, *Sex and Blood,* 1995
Michael Hemmingson, *Nice Little Stories Jam-Packed with Depraved Sex and Violence,* 1995
Edward Lee, *Edward Lee's Quest for Sex, Truth and Reality,* 1992
Lucy Taylor, *The Flesh Artist,* 1993
Lucy Taylor, *Unnatural Acts and Other Stories,* 1994

2214
LYLE HOWARD
Mr. Sandman
(Salt Lake City: Northwest Publishing Inc., 1995)

Story type: Horror (Wild Talents)
Major character(s): Lance Cutter, Investigator (arson); Julie Chapman, Scientist; Adolph Xavier, Scientist
Time period(s): 1990s (1995)
Locale(s): Fort Lauderdale, Florida

Summary: Lance Cutter's unusual ability to withstand heat makes him well-suited to serve as an arson investigator. His exploits tracking down a Florida arsonist who delivers pets coated with a highly flammable chemical to his victims excited the interest of the United States government, who knows that Lance escaped as a boy from Project Sandman, a secret experiment in genetics to breed a superior soldier class by blending human and animal DNA.

Other books you might like:
Mark A. Clements, *Children of the End,* 1993
Ken Eulo, *Claw,* 1994
  Joe Mauck, co-author
T.J. Kirby, *Deadly Breed,* 1992
Dean R. Koontz, *Watchers,* 1987
Penelope Banka Kreps, *Carnivores,* 1993
Bob Mayer, *Operation Synbat,* 1993

2215
ROBERT E. HOWARD
Beyond the Borders
(New York: Baen, 1996)

Story type: Horror (Collection)

Summary: Thirteen stories of adventure, fantasy and horror by this popular pulp writer feature several of his recurring characters. The adventurer Costigan matches wits with a satanic opera singer in "Casonetto's Last Song" and tries to help a friend overcome a Hindu curse in "The Dream Snake." Professor Kirowan, a traveller cut from the same cloth as Costigan, fights occult entities in "Dig Me No Grave," a cursed talisman in "The Haunter of the Ring," the ghostly past in "Dermod's Bane," and the power of racial memory in "The Children of the Night." Also included are the Lovecraftian horror tale, "The Fire of Asshurbanipal"; the theriomorphy tale, "The Hyena"; and the torture tale, "The Voice of El-Lil." T.K.F. Weiskopf supplies headnotes and a foreword.

Other books you might like:
Hugh B. Cave, *Murgunstrumm and Others,* 1977
David Drake, *From the Heart of Darkness,* 1983
Brian Lumley, *Fruiting Bodies and Other Fungi,* 1993
E. Hoffman Price, *Far Lands Other Days,* 1975
Karl Edward Wagner, *In a Lonely Place,* 1983

2216
ROBERT E. HOWARD
Eons of the Night
(New York: Baen, 1996)

Story type: Horror (Collection)

Summary: Ten stories, half of which were first published after the author's death in 1936, display his proficiency in both heroic fantasy and supernatural horror fiction. "Spear and Fang," Howard's first professionally published tale, tells of a primitive man's savage battle with a gorilla. Also included are two chronicles of James Allison, a contemporary American whose numerous reincarnations include hunwulf, a barbarian challenged with rescuing his woman from bat-winged captors in "The Garden of Fear," and Hialmar, a mercenary who confronts the goddess Ishtar, in ''The Marchers of Valhalla.'' ''Sea Curse'' and ''Out of the Deep'' both feature sailors enmeshed in uncanny phenomena on the high seas. ''In the Forest of Villefere'' and ''Wolfshead'' are werewolf stories with sword-and-sorcery flourishes. S.M. Stirling supplies headnotes and a foreword.

Other books you might like:
Ramsey Campbell, *Far Away and Never*, 1996
David Drake, *Vettius and His Friends*, 1989
Fritz Leiber, *Heroes and Horrors*, 1984
Michael Moorcock, *Stormbringer*, 1993
Karl Edward Wagner, *The Book of Kane*, 1985

2217

ROBERT E. HOWARD

Hour of the Dragon

(West Kingston, RI: Donald M. Grant, 1989)

Story type: Fantasy (Sword and Sorcery)
Major character(s): Conan, Barbarian, Warrior
Time period(s): Indeterminate Past
Locale(s): Earth

Summary: In the only full-length novel Howard ever wrote about Conan the Barbarian, Conan finally gains a kingdom, only to have it taken by means of treachery and sorcery. This was first serialized in 1935-1936 and republished as *Conan the Conqueror* in 1950.

Other books you might like:
Poul Anderson, *The Broken Sword*, 1983
Robert Lynn Asprin, *Stealer's Sky*, 1990
    Lynn Abbey, co-editor; Thieve's World 12
Fritz Leiber, *The Swords of Lankhmar*, 1963
Fred Saberhagen, *The Third Book of Lost Swords: Stonecutter's Story*, 1988

2218

ROBERT E. HOWARD

Trails in Darkness

(New York: Baen, 1995)

Story type: Horror (Collection)

Summary: Although best known as the creator of Conan the Barbarian, whose adventures were published in the pulp magazine *Weird Tales*, Howard also wrote many atmospheric tales of horror set in his native southwest. The ten collected here include the ghost stories ''The Man on the Ground'' and ''The Dead Remember,'' and the vampire tale ''The Horror From the Mound.'' A number of tales, including ''Black Canaan,'' ''Moon of Zambebwei,'' and ''Kelly the Conjure-Man'' use racial tensions between blacks and whites as the foundation for tales of voodoo horrors imported to the American frontier. ''The Valley of the Lost'' and ''Black Hound of Death'' are tales of revenge and frontier justice garnished with hints of the supernatural. S.M. Stirling supplies headnotes and an introduction.

Other books you might like:
David Drake, *From the Heart of Darkness*, 1983

Joe R. Lansdale, *By Bizarre Hands*, 1989
Brian Lumley, *Fruiting Bodies and Other Fungi*, 1993
Karl Edward Wagner, *In a Lonely Place*, 1983

2219

RUSS T. HOWARD

The Ultimate Helm

(Lake Geneva, Wisconsin: TSR, 1993)

Story type: Fantasy (Quest)
Series: Cloakmaster Cycle
Major character(s): Teldin Moore, Adventurer, Spaceship Captain
Time period(s): Indeterminate
Locale(s): *Spelljammer*, Spaceship; Outer Space

Summary: Teldin Moore boards *Spelljammer*, the key to his destiny, and he struggles to control it in spite of the political intrigue and magical forces working to prevent his mastery. Concludes the game tie-in series.

Other books you might like:
David Cook, *Beyond the Moons*, 1991
Elaine Cunningham, *The Radiant Dragon*, 1992
Nigel Findley, *The Broken Sphere*, 1993
Nigel Findley, *Into the Void*, 1991
Roger E. Moore, *The Maelstrom's Eye*, 1992
Alis A. Rasmussen, *A Passage of Stars*, 1990
Alis A. Rasmussen, *The Price of Ransom*, 1990
Alis A. Rasmussen, *Revolution's Shore*, 1990

2220

JAMES HOWE

Return to Howliday Inn

(New York: Atheneum, 1992)

Story type: Fantasy (Young Adult; Adventure)
Major character(s): Harold, Animal (dog); Chester, Animal (cat); Howie, Animal (dog)
Time period(s): 1990s
Locale(s): Chateau ''Howliday Inn'' Bow-Wow, Mythical Place

Summary: On a return visit to the site of Howie's birth, Chester resolves to discover the secret of Chateau Bow-Wow.

Other books you might like:
Robert Davis, *Padre Porko: The Gentlemanly Pig*, 1939
Elizabeth Seeman, *The Talking Dog and the Barking Man*, 1960
Dodie Smith, *The Hundred and One Dalmatians*, 1957
Eve Titus, *Basil of Baker Street*, 1958
E.B. White, *Charlotte's Web*, 1952

2221

TREVOR HOYLE

Kids

(New York: Berkley 1990)

Story type: Horror (Evil Children)

Major character(s): Tom Margison, Student, Scientist (physicist); Danny Margison, Child (Tom's sister); Mary Helms, Doctor (neurologist)
Time period(s): 1990s
Locale(s): Torrence, North Carolina; Pennsylvania

Summary: "What's the matter with kids today?" wonders Tom Margison when his 11-year-old sister, her intelligence and propensity for violence enhanced by a blood transfusion, becomes hyperkinetic and develops the ability to control others through telepathic power. Meanwhile, a group of doctors and scientists at a psychiatric institute in western Pennsylvania tries to explain and cure similar uncontrollable, psychotic behavior in a host of other young children. Originally published in England by Sphere Books in 1987.

Other books you might like:
J.G. Ballard, *Running Wild*, 1988
James Herbert, *The Fog*, 1975
Leonard Reiffel, *The Contaminant*, 1978
John Wyndham, *Chocky*, 1968
John Wyndham, *The Midwich Cuckoos*, 1957

2222
L. RON HUBBARD
Fear
(Los Angeles: Bridge Publications, 1991)

Story type: Horror (Psychological Suspense)
Major character(s): James Lowry, Professor (ethnologist); Tommy Williams, Professor; Mary Lowry, Housewife (James' wife)
Time period(s): 1940s (1940)
Locale(s): Atworthy College (a small university town)

Summary: Fired from his teaching position at Atworthy College for writing a popular magazine article debunking the existence of devils and demons, ethnologist James Lowry suddenly finds himself unable to account for the past four hours of his life. He is soon subjected to a series of bizarre, seemingly supernatural experiences that are somehow linked to an event that occurred during those "lost" hours.

Other books you might like:
Ramsey Campbell, *Incarnate*, 1983
Philip K. Dick, *Ubik*, 1969
Daniel Quinn, *Dreamer*, 1988
Roland Topor, *The Tenant*, 1964
Jack Williamson, *Darker than You Think*, 1947

2223
L. RON HUBBARD
Final Blackout
(Los Angeles: Bridge, 1989)

Story type: Science Fiction (Military)
Major character(s): Lieutenant, Military Personnel
Time period(s): Indeterminate Future
Locale(s): England

Summary: After thirty years, a seemingly unending world war is finally approaching its final stages. Hundreds of millions of people have died, apparently for no reason. The mysterious Lieutenant, who was born in an air-raid shelter and who has spent virtually his entire adult life on the battlefield, leads a small army in the conquest of England. Setting himself up as a benevolent dictator, he reconstructs the nation's economy and brings about a near-utopia.

Other books you might like:
Joe Haldeman, *The Forever War*, 1974
Robert A. Heinlein, *Starship Troopers*, 1959
Edward P. Hughes, *Masters of the Fist*, 1989
Fritz Leiber, *The Big Time*, 1961
H.G. Wells, *The Shape of Things to Come*, 1933

2224
L. RON HUBBARD
Typewriter in the Sky
(Los Angeles: Bridge Publications, 1995)

Story type: Fantasy (Adventure; Alternate World)
Major character(s): Mike de Wolf, Adventurer, Pirate (fictional); Horace Hackett, Writer
Time period(s): 1940s; Indeterminate
Locale(s): New York, New York; Mythical Place (literary Caribbean setting)

Summary: A strange accident transports Mike de Wolf into the literary world of Horace Hackett's novel-in-progress, a 17th century swashbuckler with a villain modeled after Mike. Mike's thrilling Caribbean exploits may end tragically if he suffers the usual fate of Hackett's antagonists. Reissue of the 1940 serial from *Unknown* with a five-page introduction by Kevin J. Anderson.

Other books you might like:
Aaron Allston, *Galatea in 2-D*, 1993
Piers Anthony, *Killobyte*, 1993
Ben Bova, *Death Dream*, 1994
Charles de Lint, *The Little Country*, 1991
Philip Jose Farmer, *Red Orc's Rage*, 1991
Richard A. Knaak, *King of the Grey*, 1993
Will Shetterly, *The Tangled Lands*, 1989
Clifford D. Simak, *Out of Their Minds*, 1970

2225
TANYA HUFF
Blood Price
(New York: DAW, 1991)

Story type: Horror (Vampire Story)
Major character(s): Vicki Nelson, Detective—Private; Mike Celluci, Police Officer; Henry Fitzroy, Writer (romance writer), Vampire
Time period(s): 1990s
Locale(s): Toronto, Ontario, Canada

Summary: Detective Vicki Nelson and her former lover, Officer Mike Celluci, are joined by an unusual third party in their investigation of a string of murders that seem to point to a vampire: vampire Henry Fitzroy, a sophisticated writer of historical romances, who is determined to help clear his species of blame for the atrocities.

Other books you might like:
P.N. Elrod, *The Vampire Files Series*, 1990-1992
Stephen Gallagher, *Valley of Lights*, 1987
Lee Killough, *Blood Hunt*, 1987
William Relling Jr., *New Moon*, 1988

2226
TANYA HUFF

Blood Trail
(New York: DAW, 1991)

Story type: Horror (Werewolf Story)
Major character(s): Vicki Nelson, Detective—Private; Mike Celluci, Police Officer; Henry Fitzroy, Writer (romance writer), Vampire
Time period(s): 1990s
Locale(s): Toronto, Ontario, Canada

Summary: Detective Vicki Nelson and 450-year-old vampire Henry Fitzroy team up for their second adventure, this time to discover who is behind the systematic murder of a family of werewolves who were Henry's friends. Complicating the investigation are internal quarrels among the werewolves and the jealousy of Vicki's former lover and colleague, Mike Celluci.

Other books you might like:
Richard Jaccoma, *The Werewolf's Tale*, 1989
Ronald Kelly, *Something Out There*, 1991
George R.R. Martin, *"The Skin Trade"*, 1987
   In *Night Visions 4*
S.P. Somtow, *Moon Dance*, 1990

2227
TANYA HUFF

Fifth Quarter
(New York: DAW, 1995)

Story type: Fantasy (Magic Conflict)
Series: Circle and Quarters
Major character(s): Vree, Martial Arts Expert (assassin); Bannon, Martial Arts Expert (assassin); Gyhard, Military Personnel (general)
Time period(s): Indeterminate Past
Locale(s): Havakeen Empire, Fictional Country

Summary: Bannon and Vree's latest hit goes disastrously wrong when their target jumps his personality into Bannon's body, forcing Bannon into his sister's mind, where they strike a precarious balance until they can get his body back. Their target, Gyhard, leads them into his plot to jump into the Imperial Prince, in turn drawn to a strange, twisted old man with the ability to hold dead spirits to their bodies. Second in the series.

Other books you might like:
Steven Brust, *Jhereg*, 1983
Octavia E. Butler, *Mind of My Mind*, 1977
Robin Hobb, *Assassin's Apprentice*, 1995

Marjorie Bradley Kellogg, *The Book of Earth*, 1995
Mercedes Lackey, *By the Sword*, 1991

2228
TANYA HUFF

The Fire's Stone
(New York: DAW, 1990)

Story type: Fantasy (Quest)
Major character(s): Aaron, Thief; Darvish, Royalty (prince); Chandra, Wizard, Royalty (princess)
Time period(s): Indeterminate Past
Locale(s): Ischia, Fictional Country; Ytaili, Fictional Country

Summary: The Stone that keeps Ischia's active volcano has been stolen and apparently taken to Ytaili. Darvish (alcoholic wastrel that he is) and Aaron (under Darvish's protection after his failed attempt to steal the emerald atop the royal staff) are soul-linked and sent to get it back. Chandra, refusing to diffuse her power by accepting an arranged marriage to Darvish, insists on coming along.

Other books you might like:
Diane Duane, *The Door into Shadow*, 1984
Diane Duane, *The Door into Fire*, 1979
Barbara Hambly, *The Time of the Dark*, 1982
Rosemary Kirstein, *The Steerswoman*, 1989
Mercedes Lackey, *Arrows of the Queen*, 1987
Robin McKinley, *The Blue Sword*, 1982

2229
TANYA HUFF

Gate of Darkness, Circle of Light
(New York: DAW, 1989)

Story type: Fantasy (Contemporary)
Major character(s): Rebecca, Handicapped (Mentally); Roland, Musician (Street)
Time period(s): 1980s
Locale(s): Toronto, Ontario, Canada

Summary: Only Rebecca can see the little people that live in the trees. When a little person is stabbed, she asks Roland and other friends for help. Together, they discover an evil sorcerer who must be stopped.

Other books you might like:
Gael Baudino, *Duel of Dragons*, 1983
Charles de Lint, *Greenmantle*, 1988
Charles de Lint, *Jack, the Giant-Killer*, 1987
Alan Dean Foster, *Glory Lane*, 1987
Simon Hawke, *The Wizard of Sunset Strip*, 1989

2230
TANYA HUFF

No Quarter
(New York: DAW, 1996)

Story type: Fantasy (Magic Conflict; Quest)
Series: Circle and Quarters

Major character(s): Vree, Martial Arts Expert (assassin); Bannon, Martial Arts Expert (assassin); Gyhard, Military Personnel
Time period(s): Indeterminate Past
Locale(s): Shkoder, Fictional Country

Summary: Bannon and Vree, whose body also houses Gyhard's spirit, travel to Shkoder, hoping to enlist bardic help in finding a new body for Gyhard. However, the Emperor's and Bannon's desire for revenge upon Gyhard interferes with their plans. Sequel to *Fifth Quarter*.

Other books you might like:
Steven Brust, *Jhereg*, 1983
Octavia E. Butler, *Mind of My Mind*, 1977
Robin Hobb, *Assassin's Apprentice*, 1995
J.V. Jones, *The Baker's Boy*, 1995
Mercedes Lackey, *By the Sword*, 1991

2231
TANYA HUFF

Sing the Four Quarters
(New York: DAW, 1994)

Story type: Fantasy (Adventure; Political)
Major character(s): Annice, Royalty (former princess), Minstrel (bard); Pjerin, Nobleman (Duc of Ohrid); Stasya, Minstrel (bard)
Time period(s): Indeterminate Past
Locale(s): Shkoder, Fictional Country; Ohrid, Fictional Country

Summary: Ten years ago, Annice could renounce her royal position and become a Bard only under certain conditions. Now she must treasonously violate those conditions, as she finds herself pregnant and the father of her child in prison for supposed treason of his own. Annice and Stasya must help him escape, then strike out to find the real traitor.

Other books you might like:
Gael Baudino, *Strands of Starlight*, 1989
Diane Duane, *The Door into Fire*, 1979
Ru Emerson, *The Princess of Flames*, 1986
Marjorie Bradley Kellogg, *The Book of Earth*, 1995
Rosemary Kirstein, *The Steerswoman*, 1989
Mercedes Lackey, *The Lark and the Wren*, 1993

2232
MARLYS HUFFMAN

Afternoon of the Gosling
(New York: Zebra, 1989)

Story type: Horror (Evil Children)
Major character(s): Philip Thayer, Religious (Evangelist); Cerise Thayer, Child
Time period(s): 1980s
Locale(s): United States

Summary: Taking her stepfather's ideas very seriously, Cerise Thayer prays a lot and her prayers come true—animals are killed, fires are started, the friend who makes fun of her is accidentally shot, and her pestering little sister drowns—with

a little help from Cerise. Then she prays for her most ambitious desire—to take her mother's place with her stepfather.

Other books you might like:
Lawrence Block, *Ariel*, 1980
John Saul, *Suffer the Children*, 1977
Bernard Taylor, *The Godsend*, 1976
Patricia Wallace, *Monday's Child*, 1989

2233
BARRY HUGHART

Eight Skilled Gentlemen
(New York: Doubleday Foundation, 1991)

Story type: Fantasy (Adventure; Alternate World)
Series: Master Li
Major character(s): Master Li, Detective; Number Ten Ox, Sidekick
Time period(s): 7th century (640)
Locale(s): Peking, China; Forbidden City, China

Summary: Two oriental detectives face a series of diabolical murders committed by mythical demons who performed evil for eight long-dead shamans. Yen Shih, a puppeteer, and Yu Lan, his shaman daughter, help the pair solve the mystery.

Other books you might like:
John DeChancie, *Castle Perilous*, 1988
John DeChancie, *Paradox Alley*, 1987
John DeChancie, *Red Limit Freeway*, 1984
John DeChancie, *Starrigger*, 1983
Randall Garrett, *Too Many Magicians*, 1967
Michael Kurland, *Ten Little Wizards*, 1988
Jeanne Larsen, *Silk Road*, 1989

2234
EDWARD P. HUGHES

Masters of the Fist
(New York: Baen Books, 1989)

Story type: Science Fiction (Post-Nuclear Holocaust)
Major character(s): Patrick O'Meara, Warrior (Master Sergeant), Ruler
Time period(s): 21st century
Locale(s): Barley Cross, Ireland

Summary: This short story collection relates the adventures of O'Meara and his battle tank after WW III. The ex-soldier settles in the town of Barley Cross, Ireland, using the tank to establish his right to rule. He's a good, but stern ruler and the only man in the village who isn't sterile. He thus has had the responsibility of fathering every child born since the war. Some of these stories were previously published in *The Magazine of Fantasy and Science Fiction*, the *There Will Be War* anthology series, and elsewhere between 1980 and 1987.

Other books you might like:
David Brin, *The Postman*, 1985
Algis Budrys, *Some Will Not Die*, 1961
David Drake, *Hammer's Slammers*, 1979
Keith Laumer, *The Stars Must Wait*, 1990

2235

MARIAN HUGHES

Initiation
(New York: Baen, 1995)

Story type: Science Fiction (Lost Colony; Post-Disaster)
Major character(s): Bart, Apprentice, Hunter; Sanda, Apprentice, Scholar; Mikhail, Hunter, Leader
Time period(s): Indeterminate Future
Locale(s): Planet—Imaginary

Summary: On a planet where the native food turns humans into "zerkers," or enraged fighters, Bart and Sanda struggle to make changes and improve the lives of their people. First novel.

Other books you might like:
Nicola Griffith, *Ammonite*, 1993
Jean Lorrah, *First Channel*, 1980
    Jacqueline Lichtenberg, co-author
Vonda N. McIntyre, *Dreamsnake*, 1978
Frederik Pohl, *Stopping at Slowyear*, 1991
Sheri S. Tepper, *Grass*, 1989

2236

MONICA HUGHES

Invitation to the Game
(New York: Simon and Schuster, 1991)

Story type: Science Fiction (Young Adult; Adventure)
Major character(s): Lisse, Artist; Benta, Farmer; Rich, Doctor (psychiatrist)
Time period(s): 22nd century
Locale(s): North America; Planet—Imaginary

Summary: Unable to find work, Lisse and seven friends from school are sent to live in a dreary Designated Area. Unwilling to simply drift, they are thrilled to be asked to participate in the Game which takes them to a marvelous new world where they can explore and wander. When they say they need a doctor and someone with farming experience, Rich and Benta, both newly unemployed, join the group. On their final mission, they do not return to their familiar city, discovering that they have been dropped on a colony planet with the Game as training for survival there. After a year they meet another group of participants in the Game and are prepared to build a new society.

Other books you might like:
John Brunner, *The Dreaming Earth*, 1963
Orson Scott Card, *Ender's Game*, 1985
Arthur C. Clarke, *The Garden of Rama*, 1991
John Cramer, *Twistor*, 1989
Robert A. Heinlein, *Tunnel in the Sky*, 1955
William Sleator, *Interstellar Pig*, 1984
Jack Williamson, *Mazeway*, 1990

2237

MONICA HUGHES

The Promise
(New York: Simon & Schuster, 1992)

Story type: Science Fiction (Fantasy; Young Adult)
Major character(s): Rania, Child, Royalty (princess); Atbin, Teenager, Adventurer; Sandwriter, Shaman
Time period(s): Indeterminate Future
Locale(s): Rokam, Planet—Imaginary

Summary: On her 10th birthday Rania receives a gift box from the Sandwriter. Filled with sand, the box signals her parents that the Sandwriter, now 76 years old, needs her promised apprentice. Rania must leave her life as a princess, her family and all her possessions behind to become the new guardian of Rokam.

Other books you might like:
Peter Dickinson, *Eva*, 1989
Gordon R. Dickson, *Time Storm*, 1977
Robert A. Heinlein, *The Rolling Stones*, 1952
David R. Palmer, *Emergence*, 1984
Pamela F. Service, *Under Alien Stars*, 1990

2238

ROBERT DON HUGHES

The Faithful Traitor
(New York: Ballantine Del Rey, 1992)

Story type: Fantasy (Adventure; Political)
Series: Wizard and Dragon
Major character(s): Seagryn, Wizard (powershaper), Criminal (accused traitor); Vicia-Heinox, Mythical Creature (two-headed dragon)
Time period(s): Indeterminate
Locale(s): One Land, Mythical Place

Summary: After Seagryn the powershaper loosed it, Vicia-Heinox created havoc by eating people and burning the land, actions generally blamed on Seagryn. Outcast from society, Seagryn must find a way to appease Vicia-Heinox in order to regain his wife and acceptance in society amidst conspiracy and preparations for war.

Other books you might like:
Teresa Edgerton, *The Work of the Sun*, 1990
Barbara Hambly, *Dragonsbane*, 1987
Judith Reeves-Stevens, *Shifter*, 1990
    Garfield Reeves-Stevens, co-author
Christopher Stasheff, *The Warlock Insane*, 1989

2239

ZACH HUGHES (Pseudonym of Hugh Zachary)

Deep Freeze
(New York: DAW, 1992)

Story type: Science Fiction (Alternate Intelligence; First Contact)

Major character(s): Daniel Webster, Spaceship Captain, Aged Person (retired); Joshua Webster, Military Personnel; Sarah Webster de Conde, Socialite, Twin
Time period(s): Indeterminate Future
Locale(s): Tigian II, Planet—Imaginary; Deep Freeze, Planet—Imaginary

Summary: When Daniel and Fran Webster disappear while searching for possible colony planets, their children hunt for them. After the disappearance of her siblings, Sarah Webster de Conde gets strange dreams calling her to come to the aid of her parents and siblings. Responding, she discovers the secret behind the Dead Worlds and the greatest menace facing humanity.

Other books you might like:
Johanna Bolton, *Mission: Tori*, 1991
F.M. Busby, *Cage a Man*, 1973
C.J. Cherryh, *Voyager in Night*, 1984
Susan Coon, *Rahne*, 1980
Thomas M. Disch, *The Genocides*, 1965
Jack Lovejoy, *The Hunters*, 1982

2240

ZACH HUGHES (Pseudonym of Zachary Hugh)

Mother Lode

(New York: DAW, 1991)

Story type: Science Fiction (Adventure; First Contact)
Major character(s): Erin Elizabeth Kenner, Explorer, Spaceship Captain; Denton Gale, Computer Expert
Time period(s): Indeterminate Future
Locale(s): Terra II, Planet—Imaginary; *Mother Lode*, Spaceship

Summary: When Lt. Erin Kenner retired from the government, she expected to spend time with her father on Terra II. Arriving there, she found that her father had died the week before, having mortgaged the house for a spaceship. Erin, with her father's pet dog, takes the ship to where her father had intended to explore.

Other books you might like:
Roger MacBride Allen, *The Ring of Charon*, 1990
Michael Berlyn, *The Eternal Enemy*, 1990
Glen Cook, *The Dragon Never Sleeps*, 1988
Stephen Goldin, *Jade Darcy and the Affair of Honor*, 1988
  Mary Mason, co-author
Rosemary Kirstein, *The Steerswoman*, 1987
Alis A. Rasmussen, *A Passage of Stars*, 1990

2241

DON HUTCHISON, Editor

Northern Frights

(Oakville, Ontario: Mosaic Press, 1992)

Story type: Horror (Anthology)

Summary: This book collects seventeen stories and one poem of horror and the supernatural (fifteen original and three reprint), all set in Canada. Included are ghost stories by Galad Elfandson ("Waiting") and Charles de Lint ("The Soft Whisper of Midnight Snow"), werewolf stories by Robert Bloch ("The Man Who Cried Wolf") and Edo Van Belkom ("The Mark of the Beast"), a vampire tale by Nancy Baker ("Cold Sleep"), and a science fiction horror story by Robert Sampson ("The Silver Face").

Other books you might like:
Robertson Davies, *High Spirits*, 1982
Alberto Manguel, *The Oxford Book of Canadian Ghost Stories*, 1989
  editor

2242

DON HUTCHISON, Editor

Northern Frights 2

(Buffalo, New York: Mosaic Press, 1994)

Story type: Horror (Anthology)
Locale(s): Canada

Summary: The 18 stories collected in this volume all have Canadian settings. Highlights include Chet Williamson's tale of a haunting, "Other Errors, Other Times"; Nancy Kilpatrick's Halloween shocker, "Punkins"; Garfield Reeves-Stevens' "The Eddies," about people trapped at the top of a tall building during a windstorm; Hugh Cave's tale of an extradimensional doorway in the Canadian woods, "Vanishing Point"; and Edward D. Hoch's "Night Swimmer," which brings back his psychic detective, Simon Ark, in a tale of Inuit mythology.

Other books you might like:
Robertson Davies, *High Spirits*, 1982
Alberto Manguel, *The Oxford Book of Canadian Ghost Stories*, 1991
  editor
Tim Sullivan, *Cold Shocks*, 1990
  editor

2243

DON HUTCHISON, Editor

Northern Frights 3

(Buffalo, NY: Mosaic Press, 1995)

Story type: Horror (Anthology)
Locale(s): Canada

Summary: One poem and seventeen new and reprinted stories all have Canadian settings, and often involve Canadian themes. Rick Hautala's "Silver Rings" tells of a man who has a literal haunting experience when his partner in a passionate one-night stand turns out to be a ghost who preys on his mind forever. In "Grist for the Mills of Christmas," James Powell tells of strange disappearances in the Canadian wilderness, and in "Snow Angel" Nancy Kilpatrick tells of a woman stranded in the wilds with the corpse of her dead husband who has to make the ultimate gruesome choice for her survival. In Tia Travis's "The Pines," a young woman comes to grips with the abusiveness of her relationship with her lover after confronting the death of a childhood friend.

Other books you might like:

Graeme Hurry, *Northern Chills*, 1994

Alberto Manguel, *The Oxford Book of Canadian Ghost Stories*, 1990
    editor

Tim Sullivan, *Cold Shocks*, 1991
    editor

2244
SHAUN HUTSON

Heathen
(New York: Warner, 1993)

Story type: Horror (Occult)

Major character(s): Donna Ward, Widow(er); Julie Craig, Young Woman (Donna Ward's sister); David MacKenzie, Detective—Police (constable)

Time period(s): 1990s (1992)

Locale(s): London, England; Dublin, Ireland

Summary: When Donna Ward investigates the mysterious circumstances under which her husband died, she finds that he gained possession of·a grimoire in which the names of all the members of the secret black magic society, The Sons of Midnight, are written and that the members, who include some of the most prominent social figures on the continent, will stop at nothing to get it back. This novel was originally published in England in 1992.

Other books you might like:

D.A. Fowler, *The Devil's End*, 1992

Ray Russell, *Absolute Power*, 1992

2245
JACKIE HYMAN

Echoes
(New York: Morrow, 1990)

Story type: Horror (Doppelganger)

Major character(s): Laura Bennett, Journalist (reporter); Lewis Tarkenton, Judge (Laura's lover); Joe Pickard, Political Figure (mayor of San Paradiso)

Time period(s): 1990s (1992); 1970s (1973)

Locale(s): San Paradiso, California; Nice, France

Summary: Following up on a series of news stories in which socially prominent members of her community commit acts totally out of character, reporter Laura Bennett uncovers a network of doppelganger "echoes" that have been generated by a force unleashed when her painter father copied Goya's canvas "The Witches' Sabbath" 20 years before.

Other books you might like:

Robert Louis Stevenson, *The Strange Case of Dr. Jekyll and Mr. Hyde*, 1886

Thomas Tryon, *The Other*, 1971

Oscar Wilde, *The Picture of Dorian Gray*, 1891

2246
JACKIE HYMAN

Shadowlight
(New York: DAW, 1989)

Story type: Fantasy (Quest)

Major character(s): Shadow, Mythical Creature; Graylord, Monster (Zombie)

Time period(s): Indeterminate

Locale(s): Fictional Country

Summary: Shadow, a young woman with special inherited powers, must fight Graylord, the leader of a pack of zombies, in order to protect her world. During this struggle she comes of age.

Other books you might like:

Sheila Gilluly, *Greenbriar Queen*, 1987

E.E. Horlak, *Still Life*, 1988

Laurie J. Marks, *The Moonbane Mage*, 1990

Patricia A. McKillip, *Riddle-Master of Hed*, 1976

Robin McKinley, *The Blue Sword*, 1982

Andre Norton, *Witch World*, 1963

2247
TOM HYMAN

Jupiter's Daughter
(New York: Viking, 1994)

Story type: Science Fiction (Genetic Manipulation; Techno-Thriller)

Major character(s): Anne Stewart, Parent, Researcher; Genevieve "Genny" Stewart, Genetically Altered Being, Psychic; Dalton Stewart, Businessman, Criminal

Time period(s): 1990s (1999); 2000s (2000-2003)

Locale(s): Coronado, Caribbean; New York, New York; Europe

Summary: To test Dr. Harold Goth's theories for improving the human genome, Dalton Stewart arranges to inpregnate Anne Stewart with the results of Goth's experimentation. After Genny's birth, Anne Stewart studies modern genetic theory in an attempt to determine the cause of her daughter's unusual abilities while Dalton Stewart's associates attempt to exploit Genny and Goth's research to advance a sinister plot.

Other books you might like:

Helen Collins, *Mutagenesis*, 1993

Michael Crichton, *Jurassic Park*, 1990

Nancy Kress, *Beggars in Spain*, 1993

Marc Laidlaw, *Kalifornia*, 1993

Joan Slonczewski, *Daughter of Elysium*, 1993

2248
NOEL HYND

Cemetery of Angels
(New York: Kensington, 1995)

Story type: Horror (Ghost Story; Supernatural Vengeance)

Major character(s): Rebecca Moore, Housewife; Edmund Van Allen, Detective; Billy Carlton, Actor, Spirit
Time period(s): 1990s (1995)
Locale(s): Los Angeles, California

Summary: An attempt on Rebecca Moore's life by a mysterious assailant sends Rebecca, her husband Bill, and their two children scurrying to relocate from Connecticut to Los Angeles. In their new home next to the San Angelo cemetery, the children befriend the ghost of a movie actor murdered half a century before, who spirits them away as part of his scheme to get even with the mysterious assailant who has followed the Moores to California.

Other books you might like:
Keith Ferrario, *Deadly Friend*, 1994
Abigail McDaniels, *The Uprising*, 1994
Jean Simon, *Ghost Boy*, 1994

2249
NOEL HYND

Ghosts
(New York: Zebra, 1993)

Story type: Horror (Ghost Story)
Major character(s): Annette Carlson, Actress; Tim Brooks, Police Officer; George Osaro, Religious (minister)
Time period(s): 1990s (1993)
Locale(s): Nantucket Island, Massachusetts

Summary: When vacationers on Nantucket Island are visited by ghostly manifestations and shocked by gruesome deaths engineered by seemingly supernatural mechanisms, a small band of locals traces the events to the death of a theatrical agent decades before and an unredressed wrong committed and covered up. This is the author's first supernatural novel.

Other books you might like:
Matthew J. Costello, *Beneath Still Waters*, 1988
Liz Fulton, *The Palm Dome*, 1990
John Saul, *Second Child*, 1990
Peter Straub, *Ghost Story*, 1979
T.M. Wright, *The Island*, 1988

2250
NOEL HYND

A Room for the Dead
(New York: Kensington, 1994)

Story type: Horror (Supernatural Vengeance)
Major character(s): Frank O'Hara, Police Officer; Carolyn Hart, Young Woman; Gary Ledbetter, Serial Killer
Time period(s): 1990s (1994)
Locale(s): Nashua, New Hampshire; Philadelphia, Pennsylvania

Summary: Years after he was sentenced to the electric chair for a string brutal of murders, Gary Ledbetter manifests as an apparition to his arresting officer, Frank O'Hara, who is investigating a spate of murders committed in Ledbetter's trademark style. Upon reopening the investigation of Ledbetter, Frank begins to suspect that the man was deliberately framed

to help cover up someone else's role in past events, and that the current murder victims were all somehow related to that cover up.

Other books you might like:
Thomas Harris, *Red Dragon*, 1981
William W. Johnstone, *Night Mask*, 1994
Samuel M. Key, *From a Whisper to a Scream*, 1992
Roxanne Longstreet, *Red Angel*, 1994

2251
KATHY ICE, Editor

Distant Planes
(New York: HarperPrism, 1996)

Story type: Fantasy (Anthology; Magic Conflict)
Series: Magic: The Gathering

Summary: Contains 15 original adventure stories rife with mythical creatures in diverse settings and situations by authors including Hanovi Braddock, Keith R.A. DeCandido, Jane M. Lindskold, Michael G. Ryan, Michael A. Stackpole, Amy Thomson, and Robert E. Vardeman. Game tie-in.

Other books you might like:
Hanovi Braddock, *Ashes of the Sun*, 1996
Clayton Emery, *Shattered Chains*, 1995
William R. Forstchen, *Arena*, 1994
Sonia Orin Lyris, *And Peace Shall Sleep*, 1996
Teri McLaren, *The Cursed Land*, 1995
Robert E. Vardeman, *Dark Legacy*, 1996

2252
DEAN ING

Cathouse
(New York: Baen, 1991)

Story type: Science Fiction (Military; Political)
Series: Man-Kzin Wars
Major character(s): Carroll Locklear, Scholar, Scientist (xenobiologist); Lolita, Prehistoric Human; Grraf-Commander, Alien (Kzin)
Time period(s): 22nd century
Locale(s): Zoo, Planet—Imaginary

Summary: Carroll Locklear was dumped on a planet containing prehistoric Kzin in stasis. His scholarly instincts lead him to revive them, discovering when he does so that the females are sentient! Then Grraf-Commander lands to question Locklear. He and Grraf-Commander decide they want to stay on Zoo isolated from the outside universe. This volume collects two short pieces, *Cathouse*, published originally in the *Man-Kzin Wars* (1988), and *Briar Patch*, published originally in *Man-Kzin Wars II* (1989).

Other books you might like:
Poul Anderson, *Inconstant Star*, 1991
Edmund Cooper, *Seahorse in the Sky*, 1969
Larry Niven, *Protector*, 1973
Larry Niven, *Ringworld*, 1970
Larry Niven, *Ringworld Engineers*, 1979
Larry Niven, *Tales of Known Space*, 1975

2253

DEAN ING
ROBERT A. HEINLEIN, Co-Author

Silent Thunder/Universe
(New York: Tor, 1991)

Story type: Science Fiction (Techno-Thriller; Generation Starship)

Major character(s): Walter Kalvin, Government Official (White House Chief of Staff); Hugh Hoyland, Spaceman, Student; Joe-Jim Gregory, Mutant, Spaceman

Time period(s): 21st century; 27th century

Locale(s): Spaceship; Outer Space

Summary: This book contains Dean Ing's original "Silent Thunder" plus Robert A. Heinlein's "Universe," first published in *Astounding* (1941). In "Silent Thunder," Walter Kalvin tries to locate a Nazi superweapon, the Donnersprache, as the United States slides toward a new fascism. In "Universe," Joe-Jim shows Hugh that his world of villages lies within a spaceship traveling long beyond its intended voyage. Hugh resolves to renew powered flight and discover an Earth-like world to settle, as originally intended.

Other books you might like:

Brian W. Aldiss, *Spaceship*, 1959
Poul Anderson, *The Boat of a Million Years*, 1989
Stephen Baxter, *Raft*, 1992
Leigh Brackett, *The Nemesis From Terra/Battle for the Stars*, 1989
    Edmond Hamilton, co-author
Karen Haber, *Thieves' Carnival/The Jewel of Bas*, 1990
    Leigh Brackett, co-author
Robert A. Heinlein, *The Past through Tomorrow*, 1967
Keith Laumer, *The Other Sky/The House in November*, 1981
Frank M. Robinson, *The Dark Beyond the Stars*, 1991
Joanna Russ, *Souls/Houston, Houston, Do You Read?*, 1989
    James Tiptree, Jr., co-author
Harry Turtledove, *The Pugnacious Peacemaker/The Wheels of If*, 1990
    L. Sprague de Camp, co-author

2254

CHARLES INGRID

Alien Salute
(New York: DAW Books, 1989)

Story type: Science Fiction (Adventure)

Series: Sand Wars

Major character(s): Jack Storm, Military Personnel, Revolutionary

Time period(s): Indeterminate Future

Locale(s): Galactic Empire, Interstellar Empire/Federation

Summary: The Thraks' betrayal is now open and Jack is put in command of the Dominion Knights. Suddenly a third party enters the fray, a mysterious and superpowerful alien race bent on attacking humans and Thraks alike.

Other books you might like:

W. Michael Gear, *The Artifact*, 1990

W. Michael Gear, *The Warriors of Spider*, 1988
W. Michael Gear, *The Way of Spider*, 1988
W. Michael Gear, *The Web of Spider*, 1989
Stephen Leigh, *Changeling*, 1989
    Isaac Asimov's Robot City: Robtos and Aliens No. 1

2255

CHARLES INGRID

The Marked Man
(New York: DAW Books, 1989)

Story type: Science Fiction (Post-Holocaust)

Major character(s): Thomas Blade, Psychic; Denethan, Mutant

Time period(s): 21st century

Locale(s): United States

Summary: Humanity has been decimated by environmental damage and plague. The Lord Protectors, seven men and women with psychic abilities, stand guard against the evil mutants who would destroy what's left of civilization.

Other books you might like:

W. Michael Gear, *The Artifact*, 1990
W. Michael Gear, *The Warriors of Spider*, 1988
W. Michael Gear, *The Way of Spider*, 1988
W. Michael Gear, *The Web of Spider*, 1989
Stephen Leigh, *Changeling*, 1989
    Isaac Asimov's Robot City: Robots and Aliens No. 1

2256

CHARLES INGRID

Path of Fire
(New York: DAW, 1992)

Series: Patterns of Chaos

Major character(s): Palaton, Alien (Choyan), Spaceman (pilot); Rand, Student, Human; Panshinea, Alien (Choyan), Ruler (emperor)

Time period(s): Indeterminate Future

Locale(s): Arizar, Planet—Imaginary; Cho, Planet—Imaginary

Summary: Only the *tezars* of Cho pilot faster-than-light ships through the Patterns of Chaos, inevitably burning out their minds and abilities. Palaton, heir of Panshinea, takes part in an illegal experimental procedure. To save Rand's life, Palaton rests in Rand the part of his consciousness called *bahdur* which only *tezars* can use to find patterns in the chaos of faster-than-light space. He hopes to keep Rand alive, free and sane, until he figures out how to retrieve his *bahdur*.

Other books you might like:

Pauline Ashwell, *Unwillingly to Earth*, 1992
Jeffrey A. Carver, *Dragons in the Stars*, 1992
C.J. Cherryh, *Hellburner*, 1992
Tara K. Harper, *Lightwing*, 1992
Melissa Scott, *Dreamships*, 1992
Cordwainer Smith, *The Best of Cordwainer Smith*, 1975
Vernor Vinge, *A Fire upon the Deep*, 1992
David Weber, *Path of the Fury*, 1992

2257

CHARLES INGRID

Return Fire

(New York: DAW Books, 1989)

Story type: Science Fiction (Adventure)
Series: Sand Wars
Major character(s): Jack Storm, Military Personnel, Revolutionary; Amber, Psychic
Time period(s): Indeterminate Future
Locale(s): Mistwald, Planet—Imaginary

Summary: When the Dominion Knights are betrayed by Emperor Pepys into an alliance with the evil alien Thraks, Jack Storm goes underground to prove the Thraks have an ulterior motive and are still the enemy.

Other books you might like:
W. Michael Gear, *The Artifact*, 1990
W. Michael Gear, *The Warriors of Spider*, 1988
W. Michael Gear, *The Way of Spider*, 1988
W. Michael Gear, *The Web of Spider*, 1989
Stephen Leigh, *Changeling*, 1989
Isaac Asimov's Robot City: Robots and Aliens No. 1

2258

MARK IVANHOE

Virgintooth

(San Francisco: III Publishing, 1991)

Story type: Horror (Vampire Story)
Major character(s): The Master, Vampire; Jonathan, Vampire; Elizabeth, Vampire
Time period(s): 1990s
Locale(s): United States

Summary: In this vampire dystopia, young Elizabeth rises from the grave as a vampire, learning about her new powers and capabilities while striving for a lifestyle different than those offered by the autocratic Master, who demands her total obedience, and by a vampire commune that spurns individuality and encourages mortification of the flesh.

Other books you might like:
Richard Lee Byers, *The Vampire's Apprentice*, 1992
Anne Rice, *Interview with the Vampire*, 1975
Brian Stableford, *The Empire of Fear*, 1988

2259

ALEXANDER JABLOKOV

The Breath of Suspension

(Sauk City, Wisconsin: Arkham House, 1994)

Story type: Science Fiction (Collection)

Summary: Contains 10 stories, frequently light in tone, published 1985-1992 in *Isaac Asimov's Science Fiction Magazine* with several stories sharing time travel themes. Other themes include cetacean intelligence, hard science and hardboiled detective fiction.

Other books you might like:
John Kessel, *Meeting in Infinity*, 1992
Nancy Kress, *The Aliens of Earth*, 1993
Lucius Shepard, *The Ends of the Earth*, 1991
Michael Swanwick, *Gravity's Angels*, 1991
James Tiptree Jr., *Her Smoke Rose Up Forever*, 1990

2260

ALEXANDER JABLOKOV

Carve the Sky

(New York: Morrow, 1991)

Story type: Science Fiction (Arts; Adventure)
Major character(s): Anton Lindgren, Steward; Vanessa Karageorge, Scholar
Time period(s): 24th century
Locale(s): Earth; Moon (Earth's); Asteroid (the asteroid belt)

Summary: Anton, Vanessa and others search for a sculptor thought dead and a missing alien artifact which could prove the key to opening a wider universe for humanity. This is the author's first book.

Other books you might like:
John DeChancie, *Starrigger*, 1983
Alan Dean Foster, *Cyber Way*, 1990
Michael P. Kube-McDowell, *Emprise*, 1985
Michael P. Kube-McDowell, *Enigma*, 1986
Marc Laidlaw, *Neon Lotus*, 1988
Vonda N. McIntyre, *Transition*, 1991
David F. Nighbert, *The Clouds of Magellan*, 1991
Larry Niven, *Protector*, 1973
Frederik Pohl, *The Gateway Trip: Tales and Vignettes of the Heechee*, 1990

2261

ALEXANDER JABLOKOV

A Deeper Sea

(New York: Morrow AvoNova, 1992)

Story type: Science Fiction (Military; First Contact)
Major character(s): Ilya Sergeiivich Stasov, Scientist (dolphin researcher), Military Personnel
Time period(s): 2010s (2015); 2020s
Locale(s): *Andrei Sakharov*, At Sea; Russia; Jupiter, Space Station

Summary: After Stasov provides a breakthrough in dolphin/human communications, the United Soviet Republics again engage in war with the United States. Stasov's dolphins prove themselves as intelligent weapons of war which can carry bombs directly to the enemy's ships. However, the dolphins' vision of the future encompasses a larger role for themselves which takes them beyond Earth's confines.

Other books you might like:
David Brin, *Startide Rising*, 1983
Arthur C. Clarke, *The Deep Range*, 1957
Vonda N. McIntyre, *Starfarers*, 1989
Vonda N. McIntyre, *Superluminal*, 1983
Robert Merle, *The Day of the Dolphin*, 1969

James H. Schmitz, *The Demon Breed*, 1968

2262

ALEXANDER JABLOKOV

Nimbus
(New York: Morrow/AvoNova, 1993)

Story type: Science Fiction (Mystery; Cyberpunk)
Major character(s): Theo "Peter Ambrose" Bronkman, Amnesiac, Detective—Amateur
Time period(s): 2030s
Locale(s): Chicago, Illinois

Summary: When a virtual image of a murder victim appears in Peter Ambrose's house, Peter begins an investigation which uncovers a disturbing pattern of murders of participants in a secret wartime project, Nimbus, in which Peter took part. As Peter tries to find surviving project participants, he begins to reassemble his missing memories while clues point toward disturbing conclusions concerning the serial killer.

Other books you might like:
Pat Cadigan, *Fools*, 1992
Pat Cadigan, *Mindplayers*, 1987
Michael Flynn, *In the Country of the Blind*, 1990
Jean Mark Gawron, *Dream of Glass*, 1993
Kim Newman, *The Night Mayor*, 1990
Neal Stephenson, *Snow Crash*, 1992
Amy Thomson, *Virtual Girl*, 1993

2263

ALEXANDER JABLOKOV

River of Dust
(New York: Morrow/AvoNova, 1996)

Story type: Science Fiction (Family Saga; Political)
Major character(s): Breyten Passman, Human (Martian); Miriam Kostal, Police Officer; Hektor Passman, Political Figure
Time period(s): 24th century
Locale(s): Mars

Summary: Having just returned to Scamander from Earth with the Martian delegation, Hektor realizes how Martian architecture reflects the differences between the planets in politics and society. On Earth, buildings define a volume and frequently open directly to the air, while on Mars the hollowed-out spaces intertwine, but none open onto the toxic, dangerous surface.

Other books you might like:
Ben Bova, *Mars*, 1992
Paul J. McAuley, *Red Dust*, 1994
Frederik Pohl, *Man Plus*, 1994
     Thomas T. Thomas, co-author
Kim Stanley Robinson, *Green Mars*, 1994
S.C. Sykes, *Red Genesis*, 1991

2264

RICHARD JACCOMA

The Werewolf's Revenge
(New York: Fawcett, 1991)

Story type: Horror (Werewolf Story)
Major character(s): Jimmy Underhill, Spy; Clara Steiner, Spy (Nazi agent); Beth Li, Teenager
Time period(s): 1940s (1942)
Locale(s): Beirut, Lebanon

Summary: Back for another round of battle with the Nazis, OSS agent Jimmy Underhill works in collaboration with the Royal British Occult Bureau to prevent the Nazi agent who turned him into a werewolf from discovering the whereabouts of the Jewelled Skull of Baphomet, a Satanic talisman worshipped by the Knights Templar which can turn the tide of the war for Germany. This novel is the sequel to *The Werewolf's Tale*.

Other books you might like:
Jerry Ahern, *Werewolves*, 1990
     Sharon Ahern, co-author
Robert R. McCammon, *The Wolf's Hour*, 1989
Robert Weinberg, *The Armageddon Box*, 1991

2265

CARL JACOBI

Smoke of the Snake
(Minneapolis, Minnesota: Fedogan & Bremer, 1994)

Story type: Horror (Collection)
Summary: The 15 stories collected here were mostly published in the last 20 years, although some were written during the author's prolific years as a writer for the pulp magazines. They represent the remainder of the author's previously uncollected weird fiction. "Hamadryad," "The Monument" and the title story all deploy snakes as objects of horror, while "The Music Lover" and "Josephine Gage" are tales of supernatural vengeance and "Chameleon Town" and "The Lost Street" (written in collaboration with Clifford Simak) are science fiction-horror hybrids. Dixon Smith, the author's biographer, has supplied the introduction.

Other books you might like:
Joseph Payne Brennan, *Nine Horrors and a Dream*, 1958
Hugh B. Cave, *Murgunstrumm and Others*, 1977
Frank Belknap Long, *The Hounds of Tindalos*, 1946
Manly Wade Wellman, *Worse Things Waiting*, 1973

2266

MARK JACOBSON

Gojiro
(New York: Atlantic Monthly Press, 1991)

Story type: Fantasy (Literary; Humor)
Major character(s): Gojiro, Animal (monitor lizard), Mutant; Komodo, Teenager
Time period(s): 1950s

Locale(s): Radioactive Island, Pacific Islands

Summary: Gojiro, a monitor lizard irradiated and mutated into a dragon, and Komodo, a young student who was in a coma for years, were both victims of Hiroshima. They make a pact together to discover who they are, where they're from, how they came to be where they are and what they'll do next. This is the author's first novel.

Other books you might like:
Brian W. Aldiss, *Hothouse*, 1962
Richard Brautigan, *The Hawkline Monster*, 1974
Ernest Hogan, *Cortez on Jupiter*, 1990
Mark Leyner, *My Cousin, My Gastroenterologist*, 1990
R.A. MacAvoy, *Tea with the Black Dragon*, 1983
Michael D. Weaver, *My Father Immortal*, 1989

2267

BRIAN JACQUES

The Bellmaker
(New York: Philomel Books, 1995)

Story type: Fantasy (Young Adult; Adventure)
Series: Redwall
Major character(s): Joseph, Animal (mouse), Adventurer; Mariel, Animal (mouse), Adventurer
Time period(s): Indeterminate
Locale(s): Redwall Abbey, England; *Pearl Queen*, At Sea; Southsward, Fictional Country (Castle Floret)

Summary: When Martin the Warrior appears to Joseph the Bellmaker in a dream, warning him of danger to his traveling daughter, Joseph and four companions sail to Southsward where an evil fox enforces a tyrannical rule from Castle Floret. To restore autonomy, Joseph and his company join Mariel and the Southsward natives in battle.

Other books you might like:
Mary Brown, *The Unlikely Ones*, 1986
Karen Brush, *Demon Pig*, 1991
Kenneth Grahame, *The Wind in the Willows*, 1908
William Horwood, *The Willows in Winter*, 1995
Margery Sharp, *The Rescuers*, 1959
Tad Williams, *Tailchaser's Song*, 1985

2268

BRIAN JACQUES

Mariel of Redwall
(New York: Philomel/Putnam, 1992)

Story type: Fantasy (Adventure; Young Adult)
Series: Redwall
Major character(s): Mariel, Animal (mouse), Warrior; Gabool, Animal (rat), Pirate (king); Han Rosie, Animal (hare), Warrior
Time period(s): Indeterminate
Locale(s): Redwall Abbey, England

Summary: Thrown overboard by Gabool during his attack on her ship, Mariel washes ashore without her memory. Taken to Redwall Abbey, Mariel recovers her memory then sets out

with others to find Gabool and avenge her father's death. Prequel to Jacques' other books.

Other books you might like:
Richard Adams, *Watership Down*, 1974
Mary Brown, *The Unlikely Ones*, 1986
Karen Brush, *Demon Pig*, 1991
Karen Brush, *The Pig, the Prince and the Unicorn*, 1987
Kenneth Grahame, *The Wind in the Willows*, 1908
Tad Williams, *Tailchaser's Song*, 1985
Laurence Yep, *Dragon War*, 1992

2269

BRIAN JACQUES
GARY CHALK, Illustrator

Martin the Warrior
(New York: Philomel Books, 1994)

Story type: Fantasy (Young Adult; Adventure)
Series: Redwall
Major character(s): Martin the Warrior, Animal (mouse), Slave; Badrang the Tyrant, Animal (stoat), Leader
Time period(s): Indeterminate
Locale(s): Marshank, England; Redwall Abbey, England

Summary: Enslaved by Badrang the Tyrant, Martin vows to regain his freedom and his father's sword, stolen by Badrang. Aided in his escape, Martin raises an army to oppose Badrang, but in the end must face Badrang himself in a personal challenge.

Other books you might like:
Mary Brown, *The Unlikely Ones*, 1986
Karen Brush, *Demon Pig*, 1991
Kenneth Grahame, *The Wind in the Willows*,
Margery Sharp, *The Rescuers*, 1959
Tad Williams, *Tailchaser's Song*, 1985

2270

BRIAN JACQUES

Mattimeo
(New York: Philomel Books, 1990)

Story type: Fantasy (Adventure; Young Adult)
Series: Redwall
Major character(s): Matthias, Warrior, Animal (mouse); Slagar, Animal (fox)
Time period(s): Indeterminate
Locale(s): Mossflower Woods, Mythical Place

Summary: Seeking revenge on the brave mice who defeated and disfigured him, Slagar plots to steal the young ones of Redwall. The devoted friends and family unite to rescue their children in a massive battle with the evil Malkariss who enslaved them.

Other books you might like:
Richard Adams, *Watership Down*, 1974
Kenneth Grahame, *The Wind in the Willows*, 1908
Margery Sharp, *The Rescuers*, 1959
Tad Williams, *Tailchaser's Song*, 1985

2271

BRIAN JACQUES
ALLAN CURLESS, Illustrator

Outcast of Redwall

(New York: Philomel Books, 1996)

Story type: Fantasy (Young Adult; Adventure)
Series: Redwall
Major character(s): Veil, Animal (ferret); Swartt Sixclaw, Animal (ferret), Warrior; Sunflash, Animal (badger), Warrior
Time period(s): Indeterminate
Locale(s): Redwall Abbey, England; Mossflower Woods, Mythical Place

Summary: After the sympathetic Bryny nurtures the abandoned Veil at Redwall Abbey, Veil's transgression forces him from the abbey. When his estranged father, the warlord Swartt, attacks Sunflash and abbey residents, Veil must decide whether to aid his friends or the father who abandoned him.

Other books you might like:
Allen Andrews, *Pig Plantagenet*, 1980
Mary Brown, *The Unlikely Ones*, 1986
Karen Brush, *Demon Pig*, 1991
Kenneth Grahame, *The Wind in the Willows*, 1908
Robert C. O'Brien, *Mrs. Frisby and the Rats of NIMH*, 1971
Tad Williams, *Tailchaser's Song*, 1985

2272

BRIAN JACQUES
GARY CHALK, Illustrator

Salamandastron

(New York: Philomel Books, 1993)

Story type: Fantasy (Young Adult; Adventure)
Series: Redwall
Major character(s): Urthstripe the Strong, Animal (badger), Leader; Thrugg, Animal (otter); Ferahgo the Assassin, Animal (weasel), Warrior
Time period(s): Indeterminate
Locale(s): Redwall Abbey, England; Salamandastron, Mythical Place (mountain stronghold)

Summary: When Ferahgo the Assassin besieges Salamandastron, Urthstripe the Strong leads warriors against Ferahgo's vermin horde while others search for the flowers of Icetor, needed to stop the illness affecting Redwall Abbey residents.

Other books you might like:
Mary Brown, *The Unlikely Ones*, 1986
Karen Brush, *Demon Pig*, 1991
Karen Brush, *The Pig, the Prince and the Unicorn*, 1987
Kenneth Grahame, *The Wind in the Willows*, 1908
Tad Williams, *Tailchaser's Song*, 1985

2273

MICHAEL JAHN

The Frighteners

(New York: Berkley/Boulevard, 1996)

Story type: Horror (Ghost Story)
Major character(s): Frank Bannister, Paranormal Investigator; Lucy Lynskey, Doctor; Magda Ravanski, Journalist
Time period(s): 1990s (1994)
Locale(s): Fairwater, Maine

Summary: With the help of the spooks he purports to exorcise, shady psychic investigator Frank Bannister ekes out a living busting ghosts in the small town of Fairwater. To clear himself when he is implicated in a series of unexplained deaths among the townsfolk, Frank delves into an unsolved 40-year-old local mystery and is forced to confront his most difficult adversary yet: the Grim Reaper. This novelization of a Peter Jackson film is based on a screenplay written by Jackson and Fran Walsh.

Other books you might like:
Judith Hawkes, *Julian's House*, 1989
Mercedes Lackey, *Burning Water*, 1989
Seabury Quinn, *The Phantom Fighter*, 1966
Robert Weinberg, *The Black Lodge*, 1991
Manly Wade Wellman, *The School of Darkness*, 1985

2274

BETSY JAMES

Dark Heart

(New York: Dutton, 1992)

Story type: Fantasy (Young Adult; Quest)
Major character(s): Kat, Teenager; Raim, Handicapped
Time period(s): Indeterminate
Locale(s): Creek, Fictional City; Tells, Fictional City; Dark Heart, Mythical Place (mountain)

Summary: Kat pursues acceptance among her mother's tribe through the bear ceremony, a spiritual rite of passage, but her growing love for Raim does not help.

Other books you might like:
J.H. Brennan, *Shiva's Challenge: An Adventure of the Ice Age*, 1992
Sue Harrison, *Mother Earth, Father Sky*, 1990
J. Alison James, *Sing for a Gentle Rain*, 1990
Lynn Armistead McKee, *Woman of the Mists*, 1991
Elizabeth Marshall Thomas, *Reindeer Moon*, 1987

2275

CARY JAMES

King & Raven

(New York: Tor, 1995)

Story type: Fantasy (Adventure)
Major character(s): Michel ''Raven'' de Verdeur, Apprentice, Knight; Arthur, Ruler (King of Britain); Amaury, Knight
Time period(s): 6th century

Locale(s): England (Britain); France

Summary: When he sees four of King Arthur's knights rape and murder his sister, Michel swears revenge, pursuing it by moving into Camelot and training for the inevitable opportunity fate will present him. His quest takes him to France and back to Britain as his skill and fame increase. First novel.

Other books you might like:

Marion Zimmer Bradley, *The Mists of Avalon*, 1983
Susan Dexter, *The Wizard's Shadow*, 1993
Courtway Jones, *In the Shadow of the Oak King*, 1991
Peter Telep, *Squire*, 1995
Peter Telep, *Squire's Blood*, 1995

2276

DARIUS JAMES

Negrophobia: An Urban Parable

(New York: Citadel Underground, 1992)

Story type: Fantasy (Satire; Alternate World)
Major character(s): Bubbles Brazil, Teenager, Adventurer
Time period(s): 1990s; Indeterminate
Locale(s): United States; Alternate Earth

Summary: Voodoo magic transports blonde bombshell Bubbles Brazil to an alternate United States populated by surreal animations and racist stereotypes. Bubbles emerges changed from the extended hyperbole. Author's first book.

Other books you might like:

William S. Burroughs, *Naked Lunch*, 1959
Parke Godwin, *The Snake Oil Wars*, 1989
Parke Godwin, *Waiting for the Galactic Bus*, 1988
Mark Leyner, *My Cousin, My Gastroenterologist*, 1990
Kurt Vonnegut Jr., *Cat's Cradle*, 1963
Robert Anton Wilson, *Reality Is What You Can Get Away With: An Illustrated Screenplay*, 1992

2277

DEL JAMES

The Language of Fear

(New York: Dell/Abyss, 1995)

Story type: Horror (Collection)

Summary: This first collection by an editor of a rock music magazine assembles 15 original stories. Preoccupied with people who live on the fringe of acceptable society, they chronicle (among other things) the thoughts of a worker at a porno theater who decides to vent his self-loathing on a patron ("Adult Nature Material"), the life of a suicidal teenager ("Memoirs of High School"), a flirtation with extradimensional monsters during an LSD trip ("Mindwarp"), and the haunted memories of a self-destructive musician ("November Rain"). Axl Rose, whose band Guns 'n Roses has recorded several songs written by the author, supplies the introduction.

Other books you might like:

Poppy Z. Brite, *Swamp Foetus*, 1993
S. Darnbrook Colson, *People of the Night*, 1994

David J. Schow, *Lost Angels*, 1990
John Shirley, *New Noir*, 1993
Lucy Taylor, *Close to the Bone*, 1993

2278

J. ALISON JAMES

Sing for a Gentle Rain

(New York: Atheneum, 1990)

Story type: Fantasy (Time Travel; Romance)
Major character(s): James Winter, Student; Spring Rain, Shaman, Indian (Anasazi); Anasan, Shaman, Indian (Anasazi)
Time period(s): 1990s; 13th century
Locale(s): Arizona

Summary: Working on a high school research paper, James visits an Anasazi museum where he becomes inexplicably attracted to a shard of pottery. For weeks his dreams are disturbed by visions of ancient Anasazi life and one woman in particular. In the 13th century, Spring Rain learns the sacred songs of the tribe, songs which should be passed on to a male apprentice. She sings, hoping for relief from a lengthy drought, but her song draws James into the past where he is declared a friend by Anasan. James begins to learn Anasazi language and falls in love with Spring Rain before events force Spring Rain to sing James back to his own time. This is an ALA Best Young Adult Books title.

Other books you might like:

Alan Dean Foster, *Cyber Way*, 1990
Dean Ing, *Anasazi*, 1980
Robert Silverberg, *Letters From Atlantis*, 1990
Roger Zelazny, *Bridge of Ashes*, 1976

2279

L. DEAN JAMES

Book of Stones

(Lake Geneva, Wisconsin: TSR, 1993)

Story type: Fantasy (Quest)
Series: Red Kings of Wynnamyr
Major character(s): Davyn "Davi" Darynson, Royalty, Sorcerer (apprentice); Gaylon Reysson, Ruler (king), Wizard
Time period(s): Indeterminate
Locale(s): Wynnamyr, Fictional Country

Summary: Davi's desire to pursue sorcery leads him to utilize a forbidden talisman and book despite the danger of enslavement by the former owner's spirit.

Other books you might like:

Donald Aamodt, *A Name to Conjure With*, 1989
Lois McMaster Bujold, *The Spirit Ring*, 1992
Louise Cooper, *Nemesis*, 1989
Laurell K. Hamilton, *Nightseer*, 1992

2280

L. DEAN JAMES

Kingslayer
(Lake Geneva, Wisconsin: TSR, 1992)

Story type: Fantasy (Adventure)
Series: Red Kings of Wynnamyr
Major character(s): Gaylon Reysson, Ruler (king), Wizard
Time period(s): Indeterminate
Locale(s): Wynnamyr, Fictional Country

Summary: Events force King Gaylon Reysson to lead his army to battle, but he hesitates to take up the magic sword, Kingslayer, which nearly robbed him of his will during the bloodlust of its last use.

Other books you might like:
Fred Saberhagen, *The Fifth Book of Lost Swords: Coinspinner's Story*, 1989
Fred Saberhagen, *The Fourth Book of Lost Swords: Farslayer's Story*, 1989
Fred Saberhagen, *The Sixth Book of Lost Swords: Mindsword's Story*, 1990
Fred Saberhagen, *The Second Book of Lost Swords: Sightbinder's Story*, 1987
Fred Saberhagen, *The Third Book of Lost Swords: Stonecutter's Story*, 1988

2281

L. DEAN JAMES

Mojave Wells
(New York: AvoNova, 1994)

Story type: Science Fiction (Invasion of Earth)
Major character(s): John Caldwell, Student—College, Genetically Altered Being; Sidney Bowers, Mechanic
Time period(s): 1990s
Locale(s): Mojave Desert, California; Mojave Wells, California

Summary: Exposed to an ancient alien device, the Gatekeeper, John transforms into a Ral warrior, complete with alien memories. While university and government agents want to use John, he emotionally bonds through dreams with Sidney and pursues his mission of repairing a gate which will allow Ral immigration.

Other books you might like:
Gordon R. Dickson, *The Alien Way*, 1965
Diana G. Gallagher, *The Alien Dark*, 1990
Larry Niven, *Protector*, 1973
Allen Steele, *Labyrinth of Night*, 1992
W.J. Stuart, *Forbidden Planet*, 1956
Denise Vitola, *Half-Light*, 1992
Kate Wilhelm, *Naming the Flowers*, 1992

2282

L. DEAN JAMES

Summerland
(New York: AvoNova, 1994)

Story type: Fantasy (Alternate World; Post-Disaster)
Major character(s): Jamie Weston, Adventurer, Imposter; Harry I. Roswell, Dentist, Doctor; Lila Anne, Runaway, Sorceress
Time period(s): 21st century; Indeterminate
Locale(s): Los Angeles, California; Oregon; Planet—Imaginary

Summary: Motivated by her dying father's present of a guidestone and instructions that she discover and stop the cause of earthwide drought, Jamie Weston finds the necessary helpers and travels to a realm where Earth's stolen water provides luxury for the inhabitants. However, events do not prepare Jamie for the notoriety accompanying the ancient prophecy which foretells the defeat of God.

Other books you might like:
Pamela Dean, *The Dubious Hills*, 1994
J. Alison James, *Sing for a Gentle Rain*, 1990
Victor Koman, *The Jehovah Contract*, 1987
Ursula K. Le Guin, *The Farthest Shore*, 1972
Laurence Yep, *Dragon of the Lost Sea*, 1982

2283

M.R. JAMES

A Warning to the Curious
(Boston, MA: David R. Godine, 1990)

Story type: Horror (Collection)

Summary: From the master of subtle supernatural horror, 13 classic ghost stories about things that are often more than ghosts. Included are "Canon Alberic's Scrapbook," in which the past encroaches ravenously upon the present, "The Ash-Tree," about revenge from beyond the grave, and "The Mezzotint," in which life imitates art with frightening consequences. First published 1986.

Other books you might like:
Ramsey Campbell, *Dark Companions*, 1982
Richard Dalby, *The Best of Ghosts and Scholars*, 1988
    Rosemary Pardoe, co-author
J. Sheridan Le Fanu, *Best Ghost Stories*, 1964
Thomas Ligotti, *Songs of a Dead Dreamer*, 1989
Robert Westall, *Antique Dust*, 1989

2284

MARTIN JAMES

Night Glow
(New York: Pinnacle Books, 1989)

Story type: Horror (Techno-Horror)
Major character(s): Marian Turner, Psychologist; John Morton, Researcher (Director of Shodale Drugs)
Time period(s): 1980s

Locale(s): Indianapolis, Indiana

Summary: Experimenters in dream research develop a drug that induces nightmares then stimulates the victims to act out their dreams violently. Marian Turner and Det. Carl Nolan seek frantically to find and destroy the drug before it spreads to the general population.

Other books you might like:
Robin Cook, *Coma*, 1977
James Herbert, *The Fog*, 1975

2285

MARY JAMES

Shoebag

(New York: Scholastic, 1990)

Story type: Fantasy (Contemporary; Young Adult)
Major character(s): Stuart ''Shoebag'' Bagg, Animal (cockroach), Child
Time period(s): 1990s
Locale(s): United States

Summary: Shoebag, a young cockroach, is suddenly turned into a young boy. Adopted by the Biddle family who live in the house where he was born, Shoebag is re-named Stuart Bagg. He makes friends with Pretty Soft who stars in a television commercial, and begins to learn how to be a human being.

Other books you might like:
Frank Asch, *Journey to Terezor*, 1989
Peter Dickinson, *Eva*, 1989
Norton Juster, *The Phantom Tollbooth*, 1961
Sarah Sargent, *Jonas McFee, A.T.P.*, 1989
Sarah Sargent, *Weird Henry Berg*, 1980

2286

MARY JAMES

Shoebag Returns

(New York: Scholastic, 1996)

Story type: Fantasy (Young Adult; Urban)
Major character(s): Stuart ''Shoebag'' Bagg, Animal (cockroach), Child; Stanley Sweetsong, Child, Student
Time period(s): 1990s
Locale(s): Wayne, Pennsylvania

Summary: To help Stanley Sweetsong, the sole boy studying at Miss Rattray's School for Girls, Shoebag magically transforms again from cockroach into young lad.

Other books you might like:
Lloyd Alexander, *The Arkadians*, 1995
Doranna Durgin, *Dun Lady's Jess*, 1994
Sherwood Smith, *Wren to the Rescue*, 1990
Sylvia Waugh, *The Mennyms*, 1994

2287

P.D. JAMES

The Children of Men

(New York: Knopf, 1993)

Story type: Fantasy (Post-Disaster; Literary)
Major character(s): Theodore Faron, Historian, Revolutionary; Xan Lyppiatt, Political Figure (dictator); Julian, Revolutionary, Parent
Time period(s): 2020s (2021)
Locale(s): England

Summary: After a quarter century of universal male sterility, 2021 society focuses on the aging and dying. The United Kingdom suffers under a dictator, Xan Lyppiatt, whose advisor and cousin, Theo Faron, dabbles with revolutionaries until discovering a comrade pregnant. Fearful over her fate as the first woman pregnant in 25 years, she and Theo leave for Wales, but Xan soon pursues.

Other books you might like:
Brian W. Aldiss, *Greybeard*, 1964
Richard Bowker, *Forbidden Sanctuary*, 1982
F.M. Busby, *The Breeds of Man*, 1988
Richard Cowper, *Clone*, 1973
William R. Forstchen, *Ice Prophet*, 1983
Frank Herbert, *The White Plague*, 1982
Ursula K. Le Guin, *Planet of Exile*, 1966
Edward Llewellyn, *Prelude to Chaos*, 1983
Charles Eric Maine, *Alph*, 1972
Clifford D. Simak, *Our Children's Children*, 1974

2288

PETER JAMES

Dreamer

(New York: St. Martin's, 1990)

Story type: Horror (Mystery)
Major character(s): Samantha ''Sam'' Curtis, Producer (television commercials); Richard Curtis, Financier, Spouse; Billy ''Slider'' Wolf, Murderer
Time period(s): 1990s
Locale(s): London, England

Summary: Though Sam Curtis's nightmares change their settings nightly, their basic scenario remains the same: Slider, the murderer whom she killed in self-defense when she was seven years old, is not dead and is coming to get her.

Other books you might like:
John Farris, *The Axman Cometh*, 1989
Dean R. Koontz, *The Vision*, 1977
Joe R. Lansdale, *The Nightrunners*, 1987

2289

PETER JAMES

Host

(New York: Villard, 1995)

Story type: Horror (Science Fiction)

Major character(s): Joe Messenger, Scientist, Computer Expert (in artificial intelligence); Karen Messenger, Researcher (television), Spouse (of Joe); Juliet Spring, Scientist, Computer Expert
Time period(s): 1990s (1993)
Locale(s): Sussex, England

Summary: Obsessed with finding a means of preserving life after death, Professor Joe Messenger of England's Isaac Newton University finds a way to upload human consciousness into his ARCHIVE computer. When Joe does this in order to save Juliet Spring, his terminally ill assistant, he overlooks that he has also loaded the computer with Juliet's psychoses, hidden in life but which begin manifesting once she has been digitized. This novel was first published in England in 1993.

Other books you might like:
Michael Crichton, *The Terminal Man*, 1972
Daniel H. Gower, *The Orpheus Process*, 1992
Dean R. Koontz, *Demon Seed*, 1973

2290

PETER JAMES

Possession

(New York: Dell, 1989)

Story type: Horror (Ghost Story)
Major character(s): Alex Hightower, Agent (literary), Parent (mother of Fabian); Fabian Hightower, Spirit (recently died), Young Man
Time period(s): 1980s

Summary: After the sudden, unexpected death of her son Fabian, Alex begins to receive messages from him—or from a demonic spirit claiming to be him—pleading for ''help'' and ''freedom.'' As she searches for the truth of the messages—turning to husband and friends, to clergymen, to spiritualists—her own sanity and soul are increasingly jeopardized.

Other books you might like:
Michael Bishop, *Who Made Stevie Crye?*, 1984
John Coyne, *Fury*, 1989

2291

PETER JAMES

Prophecy

(New York: St. Martin's, 1994)

Story type: Horror (Occult)
Major character(s): Francesca Monsanto, Archaeologist; Oliver Halkin, Actuary; Edward Halkin, Child (Oliver's son)
Time period(s): 1990s (1992)
Locale(s): London, England

Summary: Francesca Monsanto's chance meeting with attractive widower Oliver Halkin begins to seem not so chance after all when the two discover that everything about them—the death of Oliver's wife, their meeting, and their ensuing romance—may have been engineered by an evil forebear of Oliver's, who was executed for necromancy in 1652 but is now using occult forces to come back in the twentieth century. This novel was originally published in England in 1992.

Other books you might like:
Jonathan Aycliffe, *Naomi's Room*, 1991
Marcy Heidish, *The Torching*, 1992
Richard Matheson, *A Stir of Echoes*, 1958
Daniel Rhodes, *Adversary*, 1988
Michael Stewart, *Belladonna*, 1992

2292

PETER JAMES

Sweet Heart

(New York: St. Martin's, 1991)

Story type: Horror (Possession)
Major character(s): Charley Witney, Clerk (shopworker); Tom Witney, Lawyer; Hugh Boxer, Neighbor
Time period(s): 1990s
Locale(s): Elmwood, England

Summary: Charley and Tom Witney move to the country to help improve Charley's chances of conceiving a child. But the 15th-century house they rent stimulates uneasy memories in Charley, and the hypnotic regression therapy she takes to enhance her fertility dredges up further memories that suggest she is under the control of occult forces that are inducing her to recapitulate a past life. This novel was first published in England in 1990.

Other books you might like:
Daphne Du Maurier, *Rebecca*, 1938
Tom Elliott, *The Dwelling*, 1989
Stephanie Kegan, *The Baby*, 1990
Al Sarrantonio, *House Haunted*, 1991

2293

PETER JAMES

Twilight

(New York: St. Martin's, 1993)

Story type: Horror (Occult)
Major character(s): Kate Hemingway, Journalist; Harvey Swire, Doctor (anesthesiologist)
Time period(s): 1970s; 1990s (1992)
Locale(s): Sussex, England

Summary: When journalist Kate Hemingway reveals that a recently interred women has been buried alive, she runs afoul of the sinister Harvey Swire, an anesthesiologist whose out-of-body experiences for the last 20 years are intimately connected to the case. This novel was originally published in England in 1991.

Other books you might like:
Sean Costello, *Captain Quad*, 1991
Susan Palwick, *Flying in Place*, 1992

2294

ROBY JAMES

Commencement

(New York: Ballantine Del Rey, 1996)

Story type: Science Fiction (Psychic Powers; Political)
Major character(s): Ronica McBride, Psychic (esper); Mortel John, Teacher; Jemeret, Psychic (esper)
Time period(s): Indeterminate Future
Locale(s): Caryldon, Planet—Imaginary; The Com, Interstellar Empire/Federation

Summary: Awakening on a primitive wild planet with natural old forests, Ronica remembers only living on technologically advanced planets in the Com. Although she remembers graduating, trained as the strongest esper in the Com, Ronica cannot reach out with her mind or recall arriving on Caryldon. Somehow she must learn to survive and get along without forcing others with her mental abilities. First novel.

Other books you might like:
Catherine Asaro, *Primary Inversion*, 1995
Emily Devenport, *Eggheads*, 1996
Louise Marley, *Sing the Light*, 1995
James H. Schmitz, *The Demon Breed*, 1968
Joan D. Vinge, *Dreamfall*, 1996

2295

ELLEN JAMISON

Stone Dead

(New York: Zebra, 1993)

Story type: Horror (Supernatural Vengeance)
Major character(s): Haldis "Hally" Varney, Actress; Clint Hendricks, Police Officer; Elita, Toy (doll)
Time period(s): 1990s (1993)
Locale(s): Los Angeles, California

Summary: Hally Varney, who unwittingly inherited the curse of the evil eye through her family, finds that her new antique doll will kill whomever she thinks badly of.

Other books you might like:
Matthew J. Costello, *Child's Play III*, 1991
Pat Graversen, *Dollies*, 1990
Ruby Jean Jensen, *Baby Doll*, 1991
Ruby Jean Jensen, *The Living Evil*, 1993
Abigail McDaniels, *Playmates*, 1993

2296

GAIL JARROW

Beyond the Magic Sphere

(New York: Harcourt Brace, 1994)

Story type: Fantasy (Young Adult; Alternate World)
Major character(s): S .B. "Air", Child, Adventurer; Cally "Earth", Child, Adventurer; Finis "Water", Child, Adventurer
Time period(s): 1990s; Indeterminate
Locale(s): New York; Green Lord's Realm, Mythical Place

Summary: Rather than vacationing in Europe as she wants, S. B. must spend the summer with her grandmother in outstate New York. There she meets Cally and Finis with whom she visits the Green Lord's realm, learning another way to view herself.

Other books you might like:
Suzy McKee Charnas, *The Kingdom of Kevin Malone*, 1993
Pamela Dean, *The Secret Country*, 1985
Shirley Rousseau Murphy, *Medallion of the Black Hound*, 1989
   Welch Suggs, co-author
Nancy Springer, *The Friendship Song*, 1992
Nancy Springer, *Red Wizard*, 1990

2297

FRANK A. JAVOR

The Ice Beast

(New York: DAW, 1990)

Story type: Science Fiction (Techno-Thriller)
Major character(s): Eli Pike, Photojournalist; Theodore Baran, Prospector
Time period(s): Indeterminate Future
Locale(s): Thul, Planet—Imaginary

Summary: Eli Pike arrives on the icy planet Thul intending to get a story about the ultimate racing beast rumored to be found there. He finds the beast, but also finds a tribe of natives who want their existence kept secret and a device, left over from the last interplanetary war, which could destroy the planet.

Other books you might like:
Arthur C. Clarke, *A Fall of Moondust*, 1961
Arthur C. Clarke, *The Sands of Mars*, 1952
Ursula K. Le Guin, *The Left Hand of Darkness*, 1969
Vernor Vinge, *The Peace War*, 1984

2298

FRANK A. JAVOR

The Rim-World Legacy and Beyond

(New York: DAW, 1991)

Story type: Science Fiction (Collection)
Major character(s): Eli Pike, Photographer, Military Personnel (retired); Anton Plagier, Criminal; August Rook, Inventor
Time period(s): Indeterminate Future
Locale(s): Yoldragi, Planet—Imaginary

Summary: Eli Pike, hired by Brigit to photograph Anton Plagier, becomes involved in a murder, a search for an unknown boy, and a very dangerous invention. Reprints *The Rim-World Legacy* (1967) and adds two stories.

Other books you might like:
Greg Bear, *Eon*, 1989
Greg Bear, *Queen of Angels*, 1990
Arthur C. Clarke, *A Fall of Moondust*, 1961
Philip K. Dick, *The Unteleported Man*, 1983
   revised
Ron Goulart, *After Things Fell Apart*, 1977

Leo P. Kelley, *The Counterfeits*, 1967
Michael Kurland, *Transmission Error*, 1970
Dan Simmons, *Hyperion*, 1989
Sheri S. Tepper, *Grass*, 1989

2299

WILLIAM JAY

The Lost History of Redwyn

(Bloomfield Hills, Michigan: Lancaster Books, 1992)

Story type: Fantasy (Legend; Religious)
Major character(s): Redwyn, Magician; Lynn St. Du Lac, Noblewoman
Time period(s): 14th century (1352)
Locale(s): Scotland; England

Summary: As Redwyn concludes that his career in magic leaves much wanting in the development of his higher potential, he comes into possession of King Arthur's sword, Excaliber, and becomes involved in an 800-year-old conflict between good and evil.

Other books you might like:
Margaret J. Anderson, *The Druid's Gift*, 1989
Marion Zimmer Bradley, *The Mists of Avalon*, 1983
Katherine Kurtz, *Camber of Culdi*, 1976
Katherine Kurtz, *Camber the Heretic*, 1981
Katherine Kurtz, *Saint Camber*, 1978
Susan Shwartz, *The Grail of Hearts*, 1992
Lawrence Watt-Evans, *The Rebirth of Wonder*, 1992
Connie Willis, *Doomsday Book*, 1992

2300

MIKE JEFFERIES

Hall of Whispers

(New York: HarperCollins, 1992)

Story type: Fantasy (Political; Adventure)
Series: Heirs to Gnarlsmyre
Major character(s): Marrimian, Ruler; Pinvey, Revolutionary; Erek, Sorceress
Time period(s): Indeterminate Past
Locale(s): Gnarlsmyre, Fictional Country

Summary: Marrimian has passed the tests required for becoming ruler of Gnarlsmyre, but her gender prevents her acceptance by the marshmen. She travels through her rebellious and starving kingdom to gain the respect and acceptance of her subjects while her sister, Pinvey, and the crone Erek plot rebellion.

Other books you might like:
Terry Brooks, *The Sword of Shannara*, 1978
Glen Cook, *The Black Company*, 1984
Dennis L. McKiernan, *The Dark Tide*, 1984
Patricia A. McKillip, *The Riddle-Master of Hed*, 1976
Michael Scott Rohan, *The Forge in the Forest*, 1986
Paula Volsky, *Illusion*, 1992

2301

MIKE JEFFERIES

Hidden Echoes

(New York: HarperCollins, 1993)

Story type: Fantasy (Alternate World; Adventure)
Major character(s): Orun, Traveller, Animal Trainer; Denso Alburton, Writer; Mya Capthorne, Scientist (environmentalist)
Time period(s): 1990s
Locale(s): City of Time, Fictional City; New York, New York

Summary: When Orun, a Waymaster, travels through the Doorcrack to Paradise to find the prophet Denso Alburton, he finds a fantasy writer basing his books on vivid dreams. With a confused environmentalist, he battles a threat to everything that exists.

Other books you might like:
Adrian Cole, *A Place Among the Fallen*, 1987
Barbara Hambly, *The Time of the Dark*, 1982
Patricia A. McKillip, *The Riddle-Master of Hed*, 1976
Michael Moorcock, *Elric of Melnibone*, 1976
Sheri S. Tepper, *King's Blood Four*, 1983

2302

MIKE JEFFERIES

The Knights of Cawdor

(New York: HarperPrism, 1995)

Story type: Fantasy (Political; Adventure)
Series: Loremasters of Elundium
Major character(s): Drib, Student, Chimneysweep (apprentice); Grout, Teacher (Loremaster); Snatch, Military Personnel
Time period(s): Indeterminate
Locale(s): Elundium, Fictional Country

Summary: Although the new regime provides freedom from King Thane's oppression, some people in every town plot to revolt. Seeking freedom and safety, helpless former slaves find themselves the target of people's discontent.

Other books you might like:
Glen Cook, *The Swordbearer*, 1982
Barbara Hambly, *The Time of the Dark*, 1982
Dennis L. McKiernan, *The Dark Tide*, 1984
Michael Scott Rohan, *The Forge in the Forest*, 1986
Sheri S. Tepper, *King's Blood Four*, 1983

2303

MIKE JEFFERIES

Palace of Kings

(New York: Harper and Row, 1990)

Story type: Fantasy (Magic Conflict; Sword and Sorcery)
Series: Loremasters of Elundium
Major character(s): Thanehand, Warrior, Leader; Elionbel, Fiance(e) (Thane's), Prisoner (Krulshards'); Krulshards, Demon (Master of Darkness)

Time period(s): Indeterminate
Locale(s): Elundium, Fictional Country

Summary: Thane, the Candleman's son, has risen to become the leader of King Holbian's armies, fulfilling the ancient prophecies of enchanter-guardian Nevian. However, even though Thane and the warriors of Underfall were victorious over the armies of the Master of Darkness, Krulshards himself escapes in the City of Night and plots his revenge. Thane, preparing to follow and destroy him, claims his grandfather's magical sword, but as he is about to set out on his journey, he receives word that King Holbian is trapped in the besieged Granite City, struggling to keep the hordes of Nightbeasts from gaining the walls. Thane must choose the path that will best serve Elundium and its king.

Other books you might like:
M.A.R. Barker, *Flamesong*, 1985
M.A.R. Barker, *Man of Gold*, 1984
Stephen R. Donaldson, *The Illearth War*, 1977
J.R.R. Tolkien, *The Fellowship of the Ring*, 1954
J.R.R. Tolkien, *The Return of the King*, 1956
J.R.R. Tolkien, *The Two Towers*, 1955

2304
MIKE JEFFERIES

The Road to Underfall
(New York: Harper and Row, 1990)

Story type: Fantasy (Magic Conflict; Sword and Sorcery)
Series: Loremasters of Elundium
Major character(s): Thanehand, Apprentice (candlemaker), Warrior; Willow Leaf, Slave (tunneller); Holbian, Royalty (king), Warrior
Time period(s): Indeterminate
Locale(s): Elundium, Fictional Country; Granite City, Fictional City

Summary: Krulshards, Master of Darkness, having escaped from his marble prison on Mantern's Mountain, has gathered his evil forces near Underfall, final resting place of all the Granite Kings, at the edge of the Kingdom of Elundium. Aging King Holbian, who has allowed his greed to corrupt the land for many years, repents and sends the only messenger he can trust, Thane, son of the Candleman, to alert the border garrisons at Underfall of their peril. Thane, eager to serve, but untrained as yet in warfare, will be very fortunate to successfully complete his journey.

Other books you might like:
M.A.R. Barker, *Flamesong*, 1985
M.A.R. Barker, *Man of Gold*, 1984
Stephen R. Donaldson, *Lord Foul's Bane*, 1977
J.R.R. Tolkien, *The Fellowship of the Ring*, 1954
J.R.R. Tolkien, *The Return of the King*, 1956
J.R.R. Tolkien, *The Two Towers*, 1955

2305
MIKE JEFFERIES

Stone Angels
(New York: HarperPaperbacks, 1994)

Story type: Horror (Ancient Evil Unleashed)
Major character(s): Jarvin Mandrake, Archaeologist; Joni Frost, Vagrant; Martyn Burr, Doctor
Time period(s): 1990s (1994)
Locale(s): Norwich, England

Summary: Dispatched to England to recover from a harrowing experience during excavations in Egypt, archaeologist Jarvin Mandrake finds himself caught in a legendary struggle between good and evil angels carved into the statuary of the cathedral whose history he has agreed to chronicle.

Other books you might like:
Cleve Cartmill, *Prelude to Armageddon*, 1943
Bernard King, *Demon Shield*, 1989
Daniel Rhodes, *Next, After Lucifer*, 1987
Whitley Strieber, *Unholy Fire*, 1992

2306
PHILLIP C. JENNINGS

The Bug Life Chronicles
(New York: Baen Books, 1989)

Story type: Science Fiction (Collection)
Time period(s): Indeterminate Future

Summary: These fifteen short stories, some of which appeared in *Amazing Science Fiction, Isaac Asimov's Science Fiction Magazine* and elsewhere in 1987 and 1988, are all set in the same universe as the author's previous novel, *Tower to the Sky.* Among the stories included are "Teddy Bug and the Hot Purple Snowball," "The Quonset Hut," "Messiah," and "The Hero."

Other books you might like:
Anne McCaffrey, *The Ship Who Sang*, 1969
Bruce Sterling, *Schismatrix*, 1985
Somtow Sucharitkul, *Light on the Sound*, 1982
Somtow Sucharitkul, *The Throne of Madness*, 1983
Somtow Sucharitkul, *The Utopia Hunters*, 1984

2307
KRIS JENSEN

FreeMaster
(New York: DAW, 1990)

Story type: Science Fiction (First Contact)
Series: World of Ardel
Major character(s): Sarah Anders, Diplomat
Time period(s): 23rd century
Locale(s): Ardel, Planet—Imaginary

Summary: Sarah Anders, a representative of the Terran Trade Union, fights to keep less altruistic interstellar corporations from raping the mineral-rich but backward planet Ardel. The

Ardellans, however, make up for what they lack in technology with psionic talent and prove fully capable of taking care of themselves. This is Jensen's first novel.

Other books you might like:
Mary Gentle, *Ancient Light*, 1989
Mary Gentle, *Golden Witchbreed*, 1983
Judith Moffett, *Pennterra*, 1987
Richard Paul Russo, *Inner Eclipse*, 1988

2308
KRIS JENSEN

Mentor
(New York: DAW, 1991)

Story type: Science Fiction (First Contact; Psychic Powers)
Series: World of Ardel
Major character(s): Sinykin Inda, Doctor, Psychic; Jeryl, Alien
Time period(s): 23rd century (2260s)
Locale(s): Ardel, Planet—Imaginary

Summary: Jeryl, Mentor of Alu, has sole trade rights and controls Terran access to Ardel. Few Ardellans are happy to have Terrans on Ardel while some want open trade for all. Sinykin Inda develops a vaccine for a local Ardellan plague which also attacks humans. While traveling to Clan Alu to get tissue samples from Ardellan survivors in order to develop a vaccine for them, he learns much about Ardel and Ardellans.

Other books you might like:
David Brin, *The Uplift War*, 1987
Octavia E. Butler, *Dawn*, 1987
Mary Gentle, *Golden Witchbreed*, 1984
Stephen Leigh, *Alien Tongue*, 1991
Rebecca Ore, *Becoming Alien*, 1987
David Alexander Smith, *Homecoming*, 1990
David Alexander Smith, *Rendezvous*, 1988

2309
RUBY JEAN JENSEN

Baby Doll
(New York: Zebra, 1991)

Story type: Horror (Child-in-Peril)
Major character(s): Sybil Wilfred Madison, Aged Person; Adam Curtis, Child; Prissy Curtis, Child
Time period(s): 19th century; 20th century
Locale(s): Wilfred, Mississippi

Summary: With the help of a demonically empowered doll her father brings back from South America, Sybil Wilfred vents her petty jealousies on three generations of her family. When the Curtis family move into the abandoned Wilfred mansion, they are unaware that Sybil has destroyed her family—and that the instrument of that destruction is still around, and ravenously hungry.

Other books you might like:
Algernon Blackwood, *The Doll and One Other*, 1946
Matthew J. Costello, *Child's Play III*, 1991
Pat Graversen, *Dollies*, 1990

2310
RUBY JEAN JENSEN

Celia
(New York: Zebra, 1991)

Story type: Horror (Reanimated Dead)
Major character(s): Celia Nolan, Housewife; Mel, Truck Driver; Durk Nolan, Reanimated Dead
Time period(s): 1990s
Locale(s): United States

Summary: For the sake of her children Celia Nolan kills her abusive husband Durk and hides his body in the swamp. But Durk proves a persistent man even after he is dead, chasing Celia and the kids cross-country and destroying anyone foolish enough to get in his way.

Other books you might like:
Stephen Gallagher, *Down River*, 1989
Dean R. Koontz, *Shadowfires*, 1987

2311
RUBY JEAN JENSEN

The Haunting
(New York: Zebra, 1994)

Story type: Horror (Haunted House)
Major character(s): Theodora Wickham, Aged Person; Eddie Wickham, Child; Katie Roberts, Real Estate Agent
Time period(s): 1990s (1994)
Locale(s): South

Summary: Katie Roberts feels an inexplicable attraction to Wickham House, a property associated with the deaths of several children decades before. As Katie slowly unravels the history of the house and the secret of its former matriarch's affiliation with the powers of darkness, she begins to sense an uncanny kinship with one of the house's victims.

Other books you might like:
Poppy Z. Brite, *Drawing Blood*, 1993
Max Ehrlich, *The Reincarnation of Peter Proud*, 1974
Tom Elliott, *The Dwelling*, 1988
Nina Romberg, *Shadow Walkers*, 1993

2312
RUBY JEAN JENSEN

The Living Evil
(New York: Zebra, 1993)

Story type: Horror (Supernatural Vengeance)
Major character(s): Pamela Armand, Prisoner (former); Zenoa Morris, Young Woman; Justin, Young Man (Pamela's nephew)
Time period(s): 1870s; 20th century
Locale(s): South

Summary: Upon her return from prison Pamela Armand vows to destroy Zenoa, an antique doll animated by the vindictive spirit of its former owner that has killed several families over the years. But Pamela finds that Zenoa has been transformed from a doll into a seductress affianced to her nephew and bent on inflicting terror upon the rest of her family.

Other books you might like:
Algernon Blackwood, *The Doll and One Other*, 1946
Matthew J. Costello, *Child's Play III*, 1991
Pat Graversen, *Dollies*, 1990
Abigail McDaniels, *Playmates*, 1993

2313

RUBY JEAN JENSEN

Night Thunder

(New York: Zebra, 1995)

Story type: Horror (Black Magic)
Major character(s): Brent Salisaw, Construction Worker; Kara Salisaw, Child; Holly Salisaw, Child
Time period(s): 1990s (1995)
Locale(s): South

Summary: When construction workers uproot a sycamore tree planted on top of a mass grave from the American Civil War period, they resurrect the witches buried there, who begin reanimating corpses of the dead to perpetuate their century-old legacy of horror.

Other books you might like:
Barbara Erskine, *Midnight Is a Lonely Place*, 1994
Ashley McConnell, *Days of the Dead*, 1993
Abigail McDaniels, *Dead Voices*, 1994
G. Wayne Miller, *Thunder Rise*, 1989
Brent Monahan, *The Uprising*, 1992
Steve Zell, *WiZrD*, 1994

2314

RUBY JEAN JENSEN

The Reckoning

(New York: Zebra, 1992)

Story type: Horror (Supernatural Vengeance)
Major character(s): Dalton Walsh, Religious (evangelistic preacher); Matt Reed, Taxidermist; Thomas Abbot, Police Officer (Chief, Spring Valley police)
Time period(s): 1990s (1992)
Locale(s): Spring Valley, Kansas

Summary: The Reverend Walsh's hellfire and brimstone preaching works a miracle when it summons back all the children who have disappeared from Spring Valley. But it soon becomes apparent that the children are ghosts, and that they have returned to seek the murderer still lurking in the town's midst.

Other books you might like:
Sean Costello, *The Cartoonist*, 1990
Peter Straub, *Ghost Story*, 1979
Chet Williamson, *Ash Wednesday*, 1988

2315

K.W. JETER

Blade Runner 2: The Edge of Human

(New York: Bantam Spectra, 1995)

Story type: Science Fiction (Post-Nuclear Holocaust; Genetic Manipulation)
Major character(s): Rick Deckard, Police Officer (bladerunner); Rachael, Android (replicant); Sarah Tyrell, Heiress, Model (templant)
Time period(s): 2020s (2020)
Locale(s): Los Angeles, California

Summary: Rick Deckard keeps his beloved Rachael in stasis most of the time in an attempt to extend her short life. Hired by Sarah, the new head of Tyrell Industries, to find another replicant, Rick must first disprove the murder charge resulting when he eliminated a human as a replicant. Sequel to the film *Bladerunner*.

Other books you might like:
Roger MacBride Allen, *Caliban*, 1993
Stephen Baxter, *The Time Ships*, 1996
Philip K. Dick, *Bladerunner*, 1982
S. Andrew Swann, *Forests of the Night*, 1993
George Turner, *Genetic Soldier*, 1994

2316

K.W. JETER

Blade Runner: Replicant Night

(New York: Bantam Spectra, 1996)

Story type: Science Fiction (Political; Alternate Intelligence)
Series: Blade Runner
Major character(s): Rick Deckard, Police Officer, Consultant; Sarah Tyrell, Businesswoman, Imposter; Roy Batty, Disembodied Personality, Artificial Intelligence
Time period(s): 21st century
Locale(s): Outer Hollywood, Space Station; Earth; Mars

Summary: Rick Deckard hopes to earn enough by consulting on an Outer Hollywood movie about his life to allow him to emigrate to Mars with Sarah Tyrell both using pseudonyms to avoid notice. Before he can return to Mars, Deckard acquires a briefcase implanted with Roy Batty's personality which informs Deckard of his key role in the replicants' revolution on Earth. Meanwhile, kidnappers loyal to the destroyed Tyrell Corporation abduct Sarah Tyrell, intending that she lead a glorious revival of the corporation.

Other books you might like:
Poul Anderson, *Harvest of Stars*, 1993
Pat Cadigan, *Fools*, 1992
Philip K. Dick, *Bladerunner*, 1982
Philip K. Dick, *The Three Stigmata of Palmer Eldritch*, 1965
Philip K. Dick, *The Unteleported Man*, 1983
  revised edition
J.R. Dunn, *This Side of Judgment*, 1994

2317

K.W. JETER

Bloodletter

(New York: Pocket, 1993)

Story type: Science Fiction (Space Colony; Space Opera)
Series: Star Trek: Deep Space Nine
Major character(s): Kira, Military Personnel, Alien (Bajoran); Benjamin Sisko, Military Personnel, Leader (Deep Space 9); Miles O'Brien, Military Personnel, Engineer
Time period(s): 24th century
Locale(s): Deep Space Nine, Space Station; United Federation of Planets, Interstellar Empire/Federation

Summary: When the Federation learns the Cardassians plan to build a Gamma Quadrant advance base on the far side of the wormhole, officials order Benjamin Sisko and the Deep Space 9 crew to immediately construct a Federation base there. When an old enemy of Major Kira shows up, his mission of murder threatens not only Major Kira, but also Bajor and the Federation.

Other books you might like:
Peter David, *The Siege*, 1993
J.M. Dillard, *Emissary*, 1993
Sandy Schofield, *The Big Game*, 1993

2318

K.W. JETER

Cross of Blood

(New York: Pocket, 1995)

Story type: Science Fiction (Invasion of Earth; Medical)
Series: Alien Nation
Major character(s): George Francisco, Alien (Tenctonese), Detective—Police; Matthew Sikes, Detective—Police; Cathy Frankel, Alien (Tenctonese), Doctor
Time period(s): 21st century
Locale(s): Los Angeles, California

Summary: George and Susan, unbeknownst to each other, suffer terrible nightmares. Matt also hides his nightmares. The cross soaked with blood left on a Newcomer's lawn, an escalation of Human Defense League activity, couldn't have come at a worse time, as George can't focus on work and Cathy, pregnant with Matt's child, will give birth to the first Newcomer/Human baby.

Other books you might like:
Margaret Wander Bonanno, *The Others*, 1990
Peter David, *Body and Soul*, 1993
Alan Dean Foster, *Alien Nation*, 1993
Barry B. Longyear, *The Change*, 1994
Judith Reeves-Stevens, *The Day of Descent*, 1993
    Garfield Reeves-Stevens, co-author
S. Andrew Swann, *Forests of the Night*, 1993

2319

K.W. JETER

Dark Horizon

(New York: Pocket, 1993)

Story type: Science Fiction (Invasion of Earth)
Series: Alien Nation
Major character(s): George Francisco, Alien (Tenctonese), Detective—Police; Matthew Sikes, Detective—Police
Time period(s): 21st century
Locale(s): Los Angeles, California

Summary: The human Purists, opposed to the involuntary alien presence on Earth, release deadly new bacteria aimed at killing all Tenctonese which infects George's family. Meanwhile, a ruthless Overseer has come to Earth to enslave humans and recapture Tenctonese escapees. Novelizes teleplays of the cliff-hanging concluding series episode and sequel teleplay never produced.

Other books you might like:
A.C. Crispin, *V*, 1984
Peter David, *Body and Soul*, 1993
Alan Dean Foster, *Alien Nation*, 1988
Judith Reeves-Stevens, *The Day of Descent*, 1993
    Garfield Reeves-Stevens, co-author
Jayne Tannehill, *V: The Oregon Invasion*, 1984

2320

K.W. JETER

Farewell Horizontal

(New York: St. Martin's Press, 1989; Signet, 1989)

Story type: Science Fiction (Cyberpunk)
Major character(s): Ny Axxter, Artist; General Cripplemaker, Outlaw (Gang leader)
Time period(s): Indeterminate Future
Locale(s): Cylinder, Planet—Imaginary (The Cylinder is a world-sized building)

Summary: Axxter has choosen to leave the safe, boring life of a resident of the Cylinder's Horizontal levels and go Vertical, actually live on the side of the gigantic building that is the only world he knows. He wants to become a successful graffex artist, a specialist at designing the complex insignias and wildly illustrated armor worn by the violent gangs who roam the Vertical regions. Then he makes a mistake, angering one of the more powerful gangs, and must flee for his life into unknown territory.

Other books you might like:
William Gibson, *Count Zero*, 1985
William Gibson, *Mona Lisa Overdrive*, 1988
William Gibson, *Neuromancer*, 1984
Norman Spinrad, *Little Heroes*, 1987

2321

K.W. JETER

In the Land of the Dead

(New York: NAL Onyx, 1989)

Story type: Horror (Reanimated Dead)
Major character(s): Cooper, Convict (Itinerant ex-con); Vandervelde, Farmer (Sadistic)
Time period(s): 1930s
Locale(s): California

Summary: ''Paroled'' to work on a farm, Cooper, despite the threat of a sadistic boss and vicious son, becomes slowly enamored of Fay, a strange young girl who communicates with the dead.

Other books you might like:
Curt Selby, *Blood County*,

2322

K.W. JETER

Madlands

(New York: St. Martins Press, 1991)

Story type: Science Fiction (Post-Holocaust; Mystery)
Major character(s): Trayne, Detective; Geldt, Companion
Time period(s): 21st century
Locale(s): Los Angeles, California

Summary: The Madlands, an L.A. environment changed by some mysterious effect, no longer responds to normal laws of reality. Residents become subject to numerous new maladies including n-formation disease which causes the loss of pattern discrimination on a cellular level. When Trayne, an employee of the televangelist Identrope, is rescued by his former partner Geldt, he sets out to discover who hired Geldt to find him and deliver him for questioning.

Other books you might like:
Chester Anderson, *The Butterfly Kid*, 1967
Philip K. Dick, *Ubik*, 1969
Philip K. Dick, *The Unteleported Man*, 1983
George Alec Effinger, *When Gravity Fails*, 1987
Katharine Kerr, *Polar City Blues*, 1990
Michael Kurland, *The Unicorn Girl*, 1969
Geoff Ryman, *The Child Garden*, 1990
T.A. Waters, *The Probability Pad*, 1970

2323

K.W. JETER

The Night Man

(New York: NAL Onyx, 1990)

Story type: Horror (Supernatural Vengeance)
Major character(s): Steven, Child (ten-year-old boy), Abuse Victim; Taylor, Detective—Police
Time period(s): 1990s
Locale(s): California

Summary: Picked on by his drunken mother, mocked by his sister and her boyfriend, bullied by the bigger, tougher boys, Steven can only fantasize about revenge—until the fantasies take concrete shape in ''the night man,'' who violently carries out Steven's dreams.

Other books you might like:
Charles L. Grant, *The Pet*, 1986
Stephen King, *Carrie*, 1974
Stephen King, *Christine*, 1983

2324

K.W. JETER

Warped

(New York: Pocket, 1995)

Story type: Science Fiction (Space Opera)
Series: Star Trek: Deep Space Nine
Major character(s): Benjamin Sisko, Military Personnel (Starfleet Commander), Leader (Deep Space Nine); Odo, Alien, Security Officer; McHogue, Computer Expert, Criminal
Time period(s): 24th century
Locale(s): Deep Space Nine, Space Station (Bajoran); United Federation of Planets, Interstellar Empire/Federation

Summary: With political unrest on Bajor spreading to Deep Space Nine, Odo must solve a series of murders while Sisko deals with the effects of McHogue's cortical induction holosuite technology which threatens Sisko's son, the Federation presence on Deep Space Nine and the perception of reality even more widely.

Other books you might like:
Dafydd ab Hugh, *Fallen Heroes*, 1994
Diane Carey, *The Search*, 1994
Greg Cox, *Devil in the Sky*, 1995
    John Gregory Betancourt, co-author
Esther Friesner, *Warchild*, 1994
Sandy Schofield, *The Big Game*, 1993
Lois Tilton, *Betrayal*, 1994
John Vornholt, *Antimatter*, 1994

2325

K.W. JETER

Wolf Flow

(New York: St. Martin's, 1992)

Story type: Horror (Wild Talents)
Major character(s): Mike, Doctor; Lindy, Addict; Doot, Teenager
Time period(s): 1990s
Locale(s): Hot Lake, Oregon (the Thermalene Spa)

Summary: Mike takes refuge in the ruins of the abandoned Thermalene Spa after drug dealers dump him in the desert for dead. While there, he partakes of the spa's recuperative waters—and becomes imbued with the same malignancy that leached into the waters a century before and left the surrounding territory a wasteland.

Other books you might like:
Paddy Chayefsky, *Altered States*, 1978
David J. Schow, *The Shaft*, 1990

2326

JAMES B. JOHNSON

Habu
(New York: DAW Books, 1989)

Story type: Science Fiction (Immortality)
Major character(s): Reuben Flood, Scientist, Military Personnel
Time period(s): Indeterminate Future
Locale(s): Snister, Planet—Imaginary

Summary: A longevity treatment is discovered that not only prolongs life but supposedly removes all physical and psychological defects. Reuben Flood, who helped create the treatment, also fixed the system so that his personality won't be altered. Unknown to him there lurks within his sub-conscious the persona of Habu, a vigilante berserker who the authorities have sought for centuries.

Other books you might like:
Joe Haldeman, *Buying Time*, 1989
Robert A. Heinlein, *Time Enough for Love*, 1973
Frederik Pohl, *Drunkard's Walk*, 1960
Robert Silverberg, *The Book of Skulls*, 1971
Norman Spinrad, *Bug Jack Barron*, 1969
Jack Vance, *To Live Forever*, 1956
Roger Zelazny, *This Immortal*, 1966

2327

JAMES B. JOHNSON

A World Lost
(New York: DAW, 1991)

Story type: Science Fiction (Adventure; First Contact)
Major character(s): Rollingham Boregard "Rusty" Wallace, Spaceship Captain; Marion Zarnicke, Journalist; Sunday A. Sunday, Administrator (Galacticon Central)
Time period(s): Indeterminate Future
Locale(s): Roanoke, Planet—Imaginary (Sector VIII Galactic Plex Net Headquarters)

Summary: Rusty Wallace, one of the few remaining spacemen, returns to Roanoke to find that the planet and its sun disappeared, leaving only one clue, a fragment of a message from his father about a deadline of 100 days. When he discovers that the Plex beacon is also gone, Rusty travels to Plex Central for help where he discovers that the disappearance of the third generation population of Roanoke is unimportant to the D'Earnhardt bureaucrats. They are in need of a spaceship captain and ship to replace a Plex beacon, allowing the rescue of Lequinto's cut-off billions.

Other books you might like:
Roger MacBride Allen, *The Ring of Charon*, 1990
Lois McMaster Bujold, *Shards of Honor*, 1986
Ron Goulart, *The Chameleon Corps*, 1972
Mike Resnick, *Second Contact*, 1990

David Alexander Smith, *Rendezvous*, 1988
L. Neil Smith, *The Probability Broach*, 1980
E.C. Tubb, *Toyman*, 1969

2328

KIJ JOHNSON
GREG COX, Co-Author

Dragon's Honor
(New York: Pocket, 1996)

Story type: Science Fiction (First Contact; Space Opera)
Series: Star Trek: The Next Generation
Major character(s): Jean-Luc Picard, Spaceship Captain, Military Personnel; Beverly Crusher, Doctor, Space Explorer
Time period(s): 24th century
Locale(s): Pai, Planet—Imaginary; Dragon Empire, Interstellar Empire/Federation; *U.S.S. Enterprise*, Spaceship

Summary: The Dragon Empire plans to end its civil war by marrying the son of the Emperor to the daughter of the opposition leader, thus preparing the way for Federation membership. As honored guests at the wedding, Picard and the *Enterprise* crew want to ensure that all goes smoothly, despite lingering feuds, a reluctant bride, and assassination attempts since, if the emperor does not sign the treaty, the Federation cannot protect his planet from the invading G'kkau. First novel by Johnson.

Other books you might like:
C.J. Cherryh, *Foreigner*, 1994
Greg Cox, *Devil in the Sky*, 1995
   John Gregory Betancourt, co-author
Gene DeWeese, *The Peacekeepers*, 1988
Brad Ferguson, *The Last Stand*, 1995
Rebecca Neason, *Guises of the Mind*, 1993
Elizabeth Ann Scarborough, *The Harem of Aman Akbar*, 1984
Howard Weinstein, *The Covenant of the Crown*, 1981

2329

NORMA TADLOCK JOHNSON

The Witch House
(New York: Avon Camelot, 1990)

Story type: Fantasy (Light Fantasy; Young Adult)
Major character(s): Guinevere Jones, Child; Great Aunt Maybelle, Spirit (ghost)
Time period(s): 1980s
Locale(s): Seattle, Washington

Summary: Guinevere and her siblings must convince their father to sell their newly inherited mansion to the historical society to satisfy the ghost of Great Aunt Maybelle. In the process of dealing with Maybelle's ghost, the three children and their parents learn to get along better as a family.

Other books you might like:
Penelope Lively, *The Ghost of Thomas Kempe*, 1973
Patricia A. McKillip, *The House on Parchment Street*, 1973
Phyllis Reynolds Naylor, *Bernie and the Bessledorf Ghost*, 1990
Richard Peck, *The Ghost Belonged to Me*, 1975

2330

WILLIAM W. JOHNSTONE

Bats

(New York: Zebra, 1993)

Story type: Horror (Nature in Revolt)

Major character(s): Johnny MacBride, Military Personnel (retired); Mark Hayden, Police Officer (state trooper); Blair Perkins, Professor, Veterinarian

Time period(s): 1990s (1993)

Locale(s): Catahoula, Louisiana

Summary: A mutant species of giant vampire bats from South America makes its way north of the American border, spreading rabies among lunatic Satanists, who welcome the creatures as a sign from the devil, and threatening to overrun the United States.

Other books you might like:

Martin Cruz Smith, *Nightwing*, 1977
T.W. Stetson, *Night Beasts*, 1993
Robert Wilson, *Second Fire*, 1993

2331

WILLIAM W. JOHNSTONE

Carnival

(New York: Zebra, 1989)

Major character(s): Martin Holland, Political Figure (Mayor); Linda Holland, Teenager (Martin's daughter)

Time period(s): 1980s

Locale(s): Holland, Nebraska

Summary: Shortly after Nebo's Carnival of Dread comes to town, the killings begin. Mayor Holland and his daughter search for the source and nature of the carnival's terrible powers before it overwhelms the entire town.

Other books you might like:

Dean R. Koontz, *Twilight Eyes*, 1987
Richard Laymon, *Funland*, 1990
Alan Ryan, *Dead White*, 1983

2332

WILLIAM W. JOHNSTONE

Cat's Eye

(New York: Zebra, 1989)

Story type: Horror (Ancient Evil Unleashed)

Major character(s): Daphne "Dee" Conner, Writer (Romance novels); Carl Garrett, Detective—Private

Time period(s): 1980s

Locale(s): Reeves County, Virginia (In the Blue Ridge Mountains)

Summary: Strange creatures, led by Anya and Pet, two shapeshifting demons, emerge from the wooded area surrounding Dee Conner's house and terrorize the countryside as they prepare the way for the return of the Devil. Only Carl Garrett, who as a young boy survived a similar seige, can

organize the uncorrupted locals into the fighting force necessary to face and defeat Satan and his cohorts.

Other books you might like:

Rick Hautala, *Moon Walker*, 1989
Bentley Little, *The Revelation*, 1990

2333

WILLIAM W. JOHNSTONE

Darkly the Thunder

(New York: Zebra, 1990)

Story type: Horror (Ancient Evil Unleashed)

Major character(s): Reed "Sand" Saunders, Disembodied Personality; Al Watt, Lawman (retired sheriff); Richard Jennings, Disembodied Personality

Time period(s): 1980s

Locale(s): Willowdale, Colorado; Thunder, Colorado (a ghost town above Willowdale)

Summary: When Willowdale sheriff Al Watt killed Reed "Sand" Saunders for taking the law into his own hands, the balance of good and evil in the universal Force was upset. Now, 30 years later, a malignant presence called The Fury has taken over Willowdale, and only Sand's discorporate soul can save the town.

Other books you might like:

Douglas Clegg, *Goat Dance*, 1989
Matthew J. Costello, *Beneath Still Waters*, 1989
Charles L. Grant, *The Nestling*, 1982
T.E.D. Klein, *The Ceremonies*, 1984
Bentley Little, *The Revelation*, 1990

2334

WILLIAM W. JOHNSTONE

The Devil's Laughter

(New York: Zebra, 1992)

Story type: Horror (Black Magic)

Major character(s): Lincoln "Link" Donovan, Journalist; Ray Ingalls, Police Officer (sheriff); Anne Brooks, Veterinarian

Time period(s): 1990s

Locale(s): LaGrange, Louisiana

Summary: In this right-wing survivalist manifesto, a series of animal deaths and human sacrifices in LaGrange convince animal-loving CIA-operative-turned-newspaper-reporter Link Donovan that a coven of devil worshippers are gearing up for the coming millenium. Link determines to break the Satanic conspiracy that has seduced many of the town's teenagers and appears to be controlled by some of the most influential persons in LaGrange.

Other books you might like:

Roger Elwood, *Sorcerers of Sodom*, 1991
Charles L. Grant, *The Hour of the Oxrun Dead*, 1977
Pat Graversen, *The Fagin*, 1982

2335

WILLIAM W. JOHNSTONE

Night Mask

(New York: Zebra, 1994)

Story type: Horror (Serial Killer)
Major character(s): Leo Franks, Police Officer; Lani Prejean, Police Officer; Dick Hale, Radio (station manager)
Time period(s): 1990s (1994)
Locale(s): La Barca, California

Summary: Investigating a series of grisly murders in which the perpetrator, referred to as "The Ripper," dismembers the bodies and takes the faces of his victims, two police officers discover that the trail leads back over decades, and across the country, to a family of evil people, who lure their victims by encoding tapes played at the local radio station with subliminal messages.

Other books you might like:
Robert Bloch, *Night of the Ripper*, 1984
Thomas Harris, *The Silence of the Lambs*, 1988
Roxanne Longstreet, *Red Angel*, 1994
Michael Slade, *Cutthroat*, 1992

2336

WILLIAM W. JOHNSTONE

Prey

(New York: Pinnacle, 1996)

Story type: Horror (Mystery)
Major character(s): Barry Cantrell, Immortal (aka Vald Dumitru Radu); Stormy Knight, Journalist; John Ravenna, Criminal (assassin)
Time period(s): 1990s (1996)
Locale(s): Arkansas; Washington, District of Columbia

Summary: Barry Cantrell, "the world's consummate and eternal warrior," has fought for centuries to preserve the freedom of the individual. When a plot is hatched by his archnemesis Robert Roche to dismantle the government through a series of political assassinations, Barry leaves his refuge in northern Arkansas to take on assassin John Ravenna, "the pure personification of evil."

Other books you might like:
Mark A. Kostrubula, *Dark Legacy*, 1996
Robert Weinberg, *The Dead Man's Kiss*, 1994
Dennis Wheatley, *They Used Dark Forces*, 1964

2337

WILLIAM W. JOHNSTONE

Rockabilly Hell

(New York: Zebra, 1995)

Story type: Horror (Ghost Story)
Major character(s): Jesse "Cole" Younger, Police Officer (Deputy); Katti Baylor, Journalist; Jim Deaton, Detective—Private
Time period(s): 1990s (1995)

Locale(s): Memphis, Tennessee; Alaska

Summary: An experience at a ghostly roadhouse on Route 61 induces Cole Younger to investigate the disappearance and deaths of over 500 people along that road in the past 25 years. Cole and his accomplices find their efforts hindered by local officials engaged in a satanic conspiracy who have used the roadhouse ghosts to dispose of people who would prove a personal or political embarrassment to them.

Other books you might like:
Ruby Jean Jensen, *The Haunting*, 1994
Abigail McDaniels, *Dead Voices*, 1994
Abigail McDaniels, *The Uprising*, 1994

2338

WILLIAM W. JOHNSTONE

Rockabilly Limbo

(New York: Zebra, 1996)

Story type: Horror (Apocalyptic Horror; Science Fiction)
Major character(s): Jesse "Cole" Younger, Police Officer (sheriff); Katti Baylor, Writer; Hank Milam, Religious (priest)
Time period(s): 1990s (1996)
Locale(s): Memphis, Tennessee

Summary: In this sequel to *Rockabilly Hell*, Sheriff Cole Younger and his troupe of libertarian comrades struggle to survive in a world where the breakdown of the moral order has plunged the United States and other countries into godless anarchy. With the discovery that space aliens have helped engineer the chaos in order to purge the planet of its ills, Cole becomes instrumental in establishing a new world order.

Other books you might like:
Pauline Dunn, *The Crawling Dark*, 1991
Stephen King, *The Stand*, 1978
Dean R. Koontz, *Phantoms*, 1983

2339

WILLIAM W. JOHNSTONE

Them

(New York: Zebra, 1992)

Story type: Horror (Science Fiction)
Major character(s): Jake Silver, Teenager; Charles Massenet, Doctor; Cag, Alien
Time period(s): 1990s (1992)
Locale(s): Sandy Run, Louisiana

Summary: Abused by his boorish father, betrayed by his ineffectual mother, and misunderstood by his malicious classmates, Jake Silver befriends Cag, an alien from outer space who promises to endow the boy with powers that will allow him to get back at his enemies, and thereby pave the way for an invasion of Earth by extraterrestrials.

Other books you might like:
Ray Garton, *Crucifax Autumn*, 1988
Charles L. Grant, *The Pet*, 1986
K.W. Jeter, *The Night Man*, 1990

J. Michael Straczynski, *OtherSyde*, 1990

2340

WILLIAM W. JOHNSTONE

Watchers in the Woods

(New York: Zebra, 1991)

Story type: Horror (Nature in Revolt)
Major character(s): Susan Benning Dalton, Housewife; Tom Dalton, Spouse (of Susan); Matt Jordan, Spy (ex-CIA agent)
Time period(s): 1990s (1997)
Locale(s): Great Primitive Area, Idaho

Summary: Things get a tad prickly for the Denver Class of '67 when a post-reunion camping trip in the wilderness of Idaho brings them face to face with the white supremacist group that goes by the name of Citizens for White America, and the Sataws, a band of primitive human beings whose years in the wilds have nurtured a taste for human flesh.

Other books you might like:
Joseph Citro, *The Unseen*, 1990
John Farris, *Fiends*, 1990
John Farris, *Wildwood*, 1987
T. Chris Martindale, *Where the Chill Waits*, 1991

2341

COURTWAY JONES

In the Shadow of the Oak King

(New York: Pocket, 1991)

Story type: Fantasy (Legend)
Series: Dragon's Heirs
Major character(s): Arthur, Royalty (King of the Britons); Pelleas, Telepath, Companion; Myrddin, Artisan (master smith), Guardian (Arthur and Pelleas's)
Time period(s): 5th century
Locale(s): England

Summary: Saving Pelleas from Druid sacrifice, Myrddin becomes Pelleas's then Arthur's guardian. The clever smith constructs a device which will allow Arthur to remove the embedded sword from its anvil. After Arthur is recognized as King of the Britons, his task of uniting the island's diverse peoples begins. First novel.

Other books you might like:
Marion Zimmer Bradley, *The Mists of Avalon*, 1983
Gillian Bradshaw, *Hawk of May*, 1980
Gillian Bradshaw, *In Winter's Shadow*, 1982
Gillian Bradshaw, *Kingdom of Summer*, 1981
Sharan Newman, *Guinevere*, 1981
Persia Woolley, *Child of the Northern Spring*, 1987
Persia Woolley, *Guinevere: The Legend in Autumn*, 1991
Persia Woolley, *Queen of the Summer Stars*, 1990

2342

COURTWAY JONES

Witch of the North

(New York: Pocket Books, 1992)

Story type: Fantasy (Legend)
Series: Dragon's Heirs
Major character(s): Morgan la Fey, Royalty; Arthur, Royalty (High King of the Britons); Guenevere, Royalty, Spouse
Time period(s): 5th century (453-488)
Locale(s): Scotland; Camelot, England

Summary: Holding Arthur's father responsible for the death of her father, Morgan swears revenge. Reaffirming her pledge of revenge at the time of her marriage to a Pictish king, Morgan goes about building a haven for his children, her followers and the widows from Arthur's wars. In Scotland and at Camelot Morgan continues to carry through her revenge upon Arthur.

Other books you might like:
Marion Zimmer Bradley, *The Mists of Avalon*, 1983
Gillian Bradshaw, *Hawk of May*, 1980
Gillian Bradshaw, *Kingdom of Summer*, 1981
Mary Stewart, *The Wicked Day*, 1983
Persia Woolley, *Guinevere: The Legend in Autumn*, 1991
Persia Woolley, *Queen of the Summer Stars*, 1990

2343

DAVID LEE JONES

Unicorn Highway

(New York: Avon, 1992)

Story type: Fantasy (Quest; Young Adult)
Major character(s): Thaddeus "Thaddy" Williams, Child, Adventurer; Mr. Tucker, Aged Person; Infinity, Mythical Creature (unicorn)
Time period(s): 1940s (1947)
Locale(s): Kansas

Summary: After hearing that Mr. Tucker saw a unicorn on his land, Thaddy Williams decides that he must ride the creature. As government agents attempt to capture the unicorn, which they believe threatens the country, Thaddy works to accomplish his goal despite the dangerous nightmare, the Wolf, which lurks near the unicorn. Author's first novel.

Other books you might like:
Jack Dann, *Unicorns!*, 1982
   Gardner Dozois, co-editor
Jack Dann, *Unicorns II*, 1992
   Gardner Dozois, co-editor
John Lee, *The Unicorn Dilemma*, 1988
John Lee, *The Unicorn Quest*, 1986
John Lee, *The Unicorn Solution*, 1991
Tanith Lee, *Black Unicorn*, 1991

2344

DAVID LEE JONES

Zeus and Co.

(New York: AvoNova, 1993)

Story type: Fantasy (Contemporary; Urban)
Major character(s): Cyrus "Cy" Lance Major, Computer Expert, Sports Figure (surfer); Erato, Mythical Creature (muse); Janet Stewart, Computer Expert, Businesswoman
Time period(s): 1990s
Locale(s): California

Summary: Just before the end of his shift at midnight, Cy receives a peculiar message from an unknown, unauthorized file. Drawn to Erato waiting at the bus stop, Cy learns that her sister, Euterpe, imprisoned in his computer at work, must be freed within a week or their father, Zeus, will show his displeasure. Unfortunately Erato must first convince Cy and his employers that her sister's entrapment compels their help and that the new invention under development remains safe.

Other books you might like:
Emma Bull, *War for the Oaks*, 1987
Tom Deitz, *Soulsmith*, 1991
Parke Godwin, *Waiting for the Galactic Bus*, 1988
Robert A. Heinlein, *Job: A Comedy of Justice*, 1984
Nina Kiriki Hoffman, *The Thread That Binds the Bones*, 1993
Terry Pratchett, *Wyrd Sisters*, 1990
Lawrence Watt-Evans, *The Rebirth of Wonder*, 1992
David Weber, *Path of the Fury*, 1992

2345

DIANA WYNNE JONES

Aunt Maria

(New York: Greenwillow, 1991)

Story type: Fantasy (Contemporary; Young Adult)
Major character(s): Naomi "Mig" Margaret Laker, Teenager, Writer; Aunt Maria, Magician; Antony Green, Spirit
Time period(s): 1990s (1991)
Locale(s): Cranbury-on-the-Sea, England

Summary: Mig, Chris and their mother go visit Aunt Maria over Easter. She proves to be a demanding old woman who has most of the women of the town dancing attendance on her. When Chris is impudent, she turns him into a wolf. Mig tries to contact the ghost haunting the spare room to find out how to fix things before Aunt Maria can have Chris hunted down and killed. British edition is titled *Black Maria*.

Other books you might like:
Piers Anthony, *Virtual Mode*, 1991
Dale Estey, *A Lost Tale*, 1980
Alan Garner, *The Weirdstone of Brisingamen*, 1969
Andre Norton, *Octagon Magic*, 1967

2346

DIANA WYNNE JONES

Castle in the Air

(New York: Greenwillow, 1991)

Story type: Fantasy (Light Fantasy; Magic Conflict)
Series: Howl's Moving Castle
Major character(s): Abdullah, Businessman (carpet merchant); Suliman, Wizard; Hasruel, Demon, Mythical Creature (djinn)
Time period(s): Indeterminate
Locale(s): Zanzib, Fictional Country (Sultinate); Rashpuht, Fictional Country (Sultinate)

Summary: After Abdullah acquires a magic flying carpet, he and his beloved Flower-in-the-Night are involved in a series of adventures and misadventures with good and bad djinn, wizards, stolen princesses, sultans and such.

Other books you might like:
Lloyd Alexander, *The Book of Three*, 1964
Edward Eager, *Half Magic*, 1954
Sherwood Smith, *Wren to the Rescue*, 1990
Robert Westall, *The Cats of Seroster*, 1984
Patricia C. Wrede, *Dealing with Dragons*, 1990
Jane Yolen, *Wizard's Hall*, 1991

2347

DIANA WYNNE JONES

The Crown of Dalemark

(New York: Greenwillow, 1995)

Story type: Fantasy (Quest; Time Travel)
Series: Dalemark
Major character(s): Mayelbridwen "Maewen" Singer, Time Traveller; Alhammitt "Mitt" Alhammittson, Warrior, Leader; Wend Orilson, Immortal
Time period(s): Indeterminate Past
Locale(s): North Dalemark, Fictional Country

Summary: The Countess of Abereth sends Mitt to kill Noreth, daughter of the One who seeks to rule Dalemark. Sent two centuries back in time to replace Noreth, who disappeared, Maewen falls in love with Mitt. However, as evil powers assemble, Mitt must find and use the ring, the sword, and the cup to reunite Dalemark.

Other books you might like:
Poul Anderson, *A Midsummer Tempest*, 1974
Richard Cowper, *The Road to Corlay*, 1979
John M. Ford, *The Dragon Waiting*, 1983
Linda Haldeman, *The Lastborn of Elvinwood*, 1978
Clifford D. Simak, *The Fellowship of the Talisman*, 1978
Kathleen Sky, *Witchdame*, 1985
Melinda M. Snodgrass, *Queen's Gambit Declined*, 1989
Jack Vance, *Lyonesse*, 1983

2348

DIANA WYNNE JONES

Everard's Ride

(Framingham, Massachusetts: NESFA Press, 1995)

Story type: Fantasy (Collection; Science Fiction)

Summary: Contains a one-page introduction by Patricia C. Wrede, two original novellas plus one article "The Shape of Narrative in *The Lord of the Rings*," and five stories published 1983-1990 in collections and anthologies. Set in an alternate universe, the title story features an adolescent protagonist in Victorian England. Other themes include an author's transition from typewriter to word processor, robotics, dragons, wolves, peacocks, and imprisonment.

Other books you might like:
Emma Bull, *Double Feature*, 1994
    Will Shetterly, co-author
Joe Haldeman, *Vietnam and Other Alien Worlds*, 1993
James H. Schmitz, *The Best of James H. Schmitz*, 1991
Cordwainer Smith, *The Rediscovery of Man*, 1993
Jane Yolen, *Storyteller*, 1992

2349

DIANA WYNNE JONES

Hexwood

(New York: Greenwillow, 1994)

Story type: Science Fiction (Young Adult; Science Fantasy)
Major character(s): Ann Veronica Stavely, Child; Mordion "the Servant" Agenos, Martial Arts Expert (assassin), Criminal; Vierran, Servant, Revolutionary
Time period(s): 1990s
Locale(s): England; Homeworld, Planet—Imaginary

Summary: Investigating mysterious events at Hexwood Farm, Ann discovers Mordion and learns of the Bannus, an ancient alien device that manipulates reality. When its use threatens to hinder a power struggle on Homeworld, the Organization leaders, the five Reigners, rush to Earth to shut down the Bannus. Reigner Three brings Vierran to Earth, intending that she mate with the exiled Mordion to produce potential assassins for testing and training.

Other books you might like:
Gary L. Blackwood, *Beyond the Door*, 1991
A.C. Crispin, *V*, 1984
Alexander Key, *The Forgotten Door*, 1965
Madeleine L'Engle, *A Wrinkle in Time*, 1962
Denise Vitola, *Half-Light*, 1992

2350

DIANA WYNNE JONES

The Ogre Downstairs

(New York: Greenwillow, 1990)

Story type: Fantasy (Light Fantasy; Contemporary)
Major character(s): Caspar, Teenager; Malcolm, Teenager; The Ogre, Parent

Time period(s): 20th century
Locale(s): England

Summary: The Ogre has married the mother of Caspar, Johnny and Gwinny, and he and his sons Malcolm and Douglas are making life miserable. Then he buys Malcolm and Caspar chemistry sets that turn out to have magical properties, and the kids are thrown together in their attempts to stay out of trouble. This book is a reissue of the 1974 edition.

Other books you might like:
L.M. Boston, *Children of Green Knowe*, 1954
Roald Dahl, *The Witches*, 1983
Diane Duane, *So You Want to Be a Wizard?*, 1983
Beatrice Gormley, *Mail-Order Wings*, 1981
Helen V. Griffith, *Journal of a Teenage Genius*, 1987
E.W. Hildick, *The Active-Enzyme Lemon-Freshened Junior High School Witch*, 1973
Pamela L. Travers, *Mary Poppins*, 1981

2351

DIANA WYNNE JONES

A Sudden Wild Magic

(New York: Morrow, 1992)

Story type: Fantasy (Light Fantasy; Magic Conflict)
Major character(s): Gladys Naismith, Witch, Adventurer
Time period(s): 1990s
Locale(s): England; Arth, Planet—Imaginary (alternate universe)

Summary: When the benevolent society of witches and conjurers known as The Ring uncovers the scheme of evil mages from Arth, the Pentarch, to steal Earth technology and create catastrophes, Gladys and others combine forces in a guerilla attack on the Pentarch's fortress on Arth.

Other books you might like:
Gael Baudino, *Gossamer Axe*, 1990
Kyle Crocco, *Heroes, Inc.*, 1991
Suzette Haden Elgin, *And Then There'll Be Fireworks*, 1981
Suzette Haden Elgin, *The Grand Jubilee*, 1981
Suzette Haden Elgin, *Twelve Fair Kingdoms*, 1981
Neil Gaiman, *Good Omens: The Nice and Accurate Prophecies of Agnes Nutter, Witch*, 1990
    Terry Pratchett, co-author

2352

DIANA WYNNE JONES

The Time of the Ghost

(New York: Greenwillow, 1996)

Story type: Fantasy (Contemporary; Young Adult)
Major character(s): The Ghost, Spirit; Monigan, Deity; Cart, Teenager
Time period(s): 1990s
Locale(s): England

Summary: Drawn to a family operating a boardinghouse at a boy's school, a confused ghost attemps to determine her own identity. She must also discover the purpose of her existence and her relationship to Monigan before disaster befalls the family.

Other books you might like:
Eleanor Cameron, *The Court of the Stone Children*, 1973
Penelope Lively, *The Ghost of Thomas Kempe*, 1973
Margaret Mahy, *The Tricksters*, 1987
Phyllis Reynolds Naylor, *Bernie and the Bessledorf Ghost*, 1990
Susan Palwick, *Flying in Place*, 1992

2353

GWYNETH JONES

Flowerdust
(New York: Tor, 1995)

Story type: Science Fiction (Political; Psychic Powers)
Series: Divine Endurance
Major character(s): Derveet, Revolutionary, Addict; Divine Endurance, Animal (cat), Android; Endang, Scholar (withdrawn), Slave
Time period(s): Indeterminate Future
Locale(s): Ranganar, Fictional City; The Peninsula, Fictional Country; Asia

Summary: In a Southeast Asia changed beyond recognition, native cultures struggle with disinterested rulers and their pawns. Aided by a diverse group of sympathizers, Derveet carries on the revolution through example and direct action.

Other books you might like:
Lisa Goldstein, *Tourists*, 1989
Marc Laidlaw, *Neon Lotus*, 1988
Ian McDonald, *The Broken Land*, 1992
Maureen F. McHugh, *China Mountain Zhang*, 1992
Geoff Ryman, *The Unconquered Country*, 1986

2354

GWYNETH JONES

North Wind
(New York: Tor, 1996)

Story type: Science Fiction (First Contact; Invasion of Earth)
Major character(s): Goodlooking/Bella, Alien (Aleutian), Librarian; Sidney "Sid" Carton, Kidnapper, Adventurer; Clavel, Alien (Aleutian), Writer (poet)
Time period(s): 22nd century
Locale(s): Uji, Fictional City (alien enclave); Europe

Summary: Objecting to the Aleutian plan to modify Earth's climate by eliminating the Himalayas, both sides of the Gender War temporarily ally to eliminate the alien presence on Earth. As the aliens do not believe in permanent death, many die in the conflict. Meanwhile Sid kidnaps Bella for his employer who believes the librarian is key to finding the instantaneous space drive most people believe lost with the death of the inventor. Sequel to *White Queen*.

Other books you might like:
Octavia E. Butler, *Dawn*, 1987
L. Warren Douglas, *A Plague of Change*, 1992
Alis A. Rasmussen, *The Price of Ransom*, 1990

Amy Thomson, *The Color of Distance*, 1995
Ian Watson, *The Flies of Memory*, 1991

2355

GWYNETH JONES

White Queen
(New York: Tor, 1993)

Story type: Science Fiction (First Contact; Invasion of Earth)
Major character(s): Johnny Guglioli, Expatriate, Journalist; Braemer Wilson, Journalist; Elavel, Alien, Immortal
Time period(s): 2030s (2038)
Locale(s): Gerardville, Africa (West Africa); London, England

Summary: Johnny is exiled, falsely accused of being infected with QV, a virus that attacks the organic core of all American computers as well as humans. A pension for basic survival arrives monthly while Johnny outlives his expected death. He continually encounters a very strange girl whom he seeks out after recruitment by Braemer to help find the aliens reported in the area. Johnny must discover why aliens terrify and attract humans and if aliens and humans can be prevented from destroying each other as the telepathic aliens always recognize lies. Winner of James Tiptree award. Reprint of 1991 British edition.

Other books you might like:
Greg Bear, *The Forge of God*, 1987
Octavia E. Butler, *Dawn*, 1987
Pat Cadigan, *Synners*, 1991
Jean Mark Gawron, *Dream of Glass*, 1993
Damon Knight, *A Reasonable World*, 1991
Spider Robinson, *Stardance*, 1979
    Jeanne Robinson, co-author
Ian Watson, *The Flies of Memory*, 1991

2356

J.V. JONES

The Baker's Boy
(New York: Warner Aspect, 1995)

Story type: Fantasy (Political; Magic Conflict)
Series: Book of Words
Major character(s): Jack, Baker, Sorcerer; Melliandra "Melli", Noblewoman, Fiance(e); Baralis, Sorcerer, Traitor
Time period(s): Indeterminate
Locale(s): Castle Harvell, Mythical Place; Four Kingdoms, Fictional Country; Rorn, Fictional City

Summary: To forward his evil scheme of advancement, Baralis drafts the illiterate Jack to copy arcane books without understanding their content. When Jack's scribing eventually brings literacy and unconscious comprehension of sorcery, Jack flees Castle Harvell, meeting Melli in the forest as she runs from an unacceptable royal marriage. With royal guardsmen and Baralis' mercenaries in pursuit, the two youngsters hold little hope of happiness. First novel.

Other books you might like:
Lois McMaster Bujold, *The Spirit Ring*, 1992
Terry Goodkind, *Wizard's First Rule*, 1994
Laurell K. Hamilton, *Nightseer*, 1992
Robin Hobb, *Assassin's Apprentice*, 1995
Caroline Stevermer, *A College of Magics*, 1994
Paula Volsky, *Illusion*, 1992
Martha Wells, *The Element of Fire*, 1993

2357

J.V. JONES

A Man Betrayed

(New York: Warner Aspect, 1996)

Story type: Fantasy (Magic Conflict; Political)
Series: Book of Words
Major character(s): Jack, Sorcerer, Hero; Melliandra "Melli", Noblewoman; Garon, Nobleman (Duke of Bren), Warrior
Time period(s): Indeterminate
Locale(s): Bren, Fictional City; Halcus, Fictional Country; Four Kingdoms, Fictional Country

Summary: Melli's attempt to avoid marriage to Prince Kylock leads to her capture and delivery into unexpected hands. While her father and the sorcerer Baralis jostle for influence over events, Archbishop Tavalisk of Rorn stirs up trouble. Meanwhile, thinking Melli dead, Jack seeks shelter with strangers and receives weapons training.

Other books you might like:
Terry Goodkind, *Stone of Tears*, 1995
Barbara Hambly, *Stranger at the Wedding*, 1994
Robin Hobb, *Assassin's Apprentice*, 1995
Katya Reimann, *Wind From a Foreign Sky*, 1996
Martha Wells, *The Element of Fire*, 1993
Salinda Tyson, *Wheel of Dreams*, 1996

2358

J.V. JONES

Master and Fool

(New York: Warner Aspect, 1996)

Story type: Fantasy (Magic Conflict; Political)
Series: Book of Words
Major character(s): Jack, Sorcerer, Hero; Baralis, Sorcerer, Traitor; Tawl, Knight
Time period(s): Indeterminate
Locale(s): Four Kingdoms, Fictional Country

Summary: Impelled by fate, prophecy and deception, Jack and his companions must elude assassins as they attempt to eliminate Larn's oracular powers while the psychotic usurper, Kylock, seeks conquest and the elimination of the kingdom's rightful heirs.

Other books you might like:
David Eddings, *Pawn of Prophecy*, 1982
Lynn Flewelling, *Luck in the Shadows*, 1996
Terry Goodkind, *Wizard's First Rule*, 1994
Robin Hobb, *Assassin's Apprentice*, 1995

J.R.R. Tolkien, *The Fellowship of the Ring*, 1954
Martha Wells, *The Element of Fire*, 1993

2359

STEPHEN JONES, Editor
DAVID SUTTON, Co-Editor

The Best Horror From Fantasy Tales

(New York: Carroll and Graf, 1990)

Story type: Horror (Fantasy)

Summary: A collection of 20 stories, both new and old, from the pages of Britain's best known small press weird fiction magazine. Aside from a small number of vintage reprints from American pulp magazines, such as Fritz Leiber's "In the X-Ray" and Robert Bloch's "The Sorceror's Jewel," the majority of stories first appeared in the magazine and testify to its eclectic editorial policy. The best include Thomas Ligotti's tale of insanity, "The Frolic," Ramsey Campbell's Cthulhu Mythos Story "The Voice of the Beach," and Dennis Etchison's moody World Fantasy Award-winner "The Dark Country."

Other books you might like:
Peter Enfantino, *Quick Chills*, 1990
Stuart David Schiff, *Whispers: An Anthology of Fantasy and Horror*, 1977
David B. Silva, *Best of The Horror Show*, 1987

2360

STEPHEN JONES, Editor
RAMSEY CAMPBELL, Co-Editor

Best New Horror

(New York: Carroll & Graf, 1990)

Story type: Horror (Anthology)
Series: Best New Horror

Summary: Twenty stories chosen from the amateur and professional press that accentuate the depth and diversity of the modern horror story. Robert Westall's "The Last Days of Miss Dorinda Molyneaux," a ghost story in the tradition of M.R. James, contrasts with Thomas Tessier's "Blanca," a modern spectral tale that grapples with third world political revolution. Nicholas Royle's oblique dark fantasy "Archway" is counterbalanced by Kim Newman's science fiction crossover "Technicolor Twitch." And Thomas Ligotti's insidiously disturbing "The Strange Design of Master Rignolo" stands at the opposite extreme from Richard Laymon's blatantly gross "Bad News."

Other books you might like:
Ellen Datlow, *The Year's Best Fantasy and Horror: Third Annual Collection*, 1990
　Terri Windling, co-author
Peter Enfantino, *Quick Chills*, 1990
Karl Edward Wagner, *The Year's Best Horror Stories XVIII*, 1990

| 2361 |

STEPHEN JONES, Editor
RAMSEY CAMPBELL, Co-Editor

Best New Horror 2

(New York: Carroll & Graf, 1991)

Story type: Horror (Anthology)

Summary: Twenty-eight stories representing the best works of horror in Britain and America published in 1990. Included are three homages to the work of H.P. Lovecraft, Poppy Z. Brite's "His Mouth Shall Taste of Wormwood," Gene Wolfe's "Lord of the Land," and Thomas Ligotti's "The Last Feast of Harlequin"; Ray Garton's gory tale of a talk show host who gets his comeuppance, "Shock Radio"; impressionistic fantasies by Jonathan Carroll ("The Dead Love You") and Peter Straub ("A Short Guide to the City"); Elizabeth Massie's Bram Stoker Award-winning tale of grotesque love, "Stephen"; and F. Paul Wilson's tale of nature in revolt, "Pelts."

Other books you might like:
Ellen Datlow, *The Year's Best Fantasy and Horror: Fourth Annual Collection*, 1991
    Terri Windling, co-editor
Robert Morrish, *Quick Chills II*, 1992
    Peter Enfantino, co-editor
Karl Edward Wagner, *The Year's Best Horror Stories XIX*, 1991
    editor

| 2362 |

STEPHEN JONES, Editor
RAMSEY CAMPBELL, Co-Editor

Best New Horror 4

(New York: Carroll & Graf, 1993)

Story type: Horror (Anthology)
Series: Best New Horror

Summary: The editors collect 24 of the best horror stories published in 1992, along with a survey of the year in horror. Included are Peter Straub's World Fantasy Award winning "The Ghost Village," an excerpt from his novel *The Throat*; Scott Edelman's metafictional rumination on why we read horror fiction, "The Suicide Artist"; Thomas Ligotti's tale of the horrors inside a run down movie theatre, "The Glamour"; Kim Newman's "Red Reign," a vampire novella that grew into his alternate history *Anno-Dracula*; Douglas Winter's postmodern zombie tale, "Bright Lights, Big Zombie"; Steve Rasnic Tem's tale of Lovecraftian horror, "The Mirror Man"; two ghostly tales, Clive Barker's "The Departed" and Les Daniels' "The Little Green Ones"; and two powerful tales of urban horror, Poppy Z. Brite's "How to Get Ahead in New York" and Joel Lane's "And Some Are Missing."

Other books you might like:
Ellen Datlow, *The Year's Best Fantasy and Horror: Sixth Annual Collection*, 1993
    Terri Windling, co-editor

Karl Edward Wagner, *The Year's Best Horror Stories XXI*, 1993
    editor

| 2363 |

STEPHEN JONES, Editor

Best New Horror 6

(New York: Carroll & Graf, 1995)

Story type: Horror (Anthology)

Summary: This sixth annual volume brings together 22 British and American horror stories chosen by the editor as the best short fiction of 1994. Included are Robert Bloch's Stoker Award-winning "A Scent of Vinegar," about a strange species of vampires that live in an abandoned Hollywood whorehouse; Brian Hodge's "The Alchemy of the Throat," about a castrato taken in by a vampire patron; Norman Partridge's "Harvest," in which radiation sickness fosters gruesome terrors in a southwestern town; Terry Lamsley's "Blade and Bone," a traditional ghostly tale; Ramsey Campbell's "The Alternative," in which a middleclass businessman is overwhelmed by the feeling that he is a destitute person imagining himself living a life of comparative luxury; and Esther M. Friesner's narrative poem "Lovers." The author supplies an informative introduction, and Kim Newman assists in compiling the book's annual necrology. This is the first volume in the series for which Ramsey Campbell does not serve as co-editor.

Other books you might like:
Ellen Datlow, *The Year's Best Fantasy and Horror: Eighth Annual Collection*, 1995
    Terri Windling, co-editor
Karl Edward Wagner, *The Year's Best Horror Stories Series*, 1979-1994
    editor

| 2364 |

STEPHEN JONES, Editor
DAVID SUTTON, Co-Editor

Fantasy Tales #2

(New York: Carroll & Graf, 1990)

Story type: Horror (Anthology; Fantasy)

Summary: This issue of Jones and Sutton's bi-annual illustrated anthology of original horror fiction, a reprint of the *Fantasy Tales 5* (Autumn 1990), contains 12 stories (and one poem), including a sensitive tale of adolescent infatuation and loss by Roberta Lannes, a sword-and sorcery pastiche by Ramsey Campbell, a satire of eighties corporate amorality in yuppiedom by David Schow, and a witty riff on the Frankenstein motif by Garry Kilworth.

Other books you might like:
Dennis Etchison, *Cutting Edge*, 1986
Kirby McCauley, *Dark Forces*, 1980
Kirby McCauley, *Frights*, 1976
Kirby McCauley, *Night Chills*, 1975
Douglas E. Winter, *Prime Evil*, 1988

2365

STEPHEN JONES, Editor
DAVID SUTTON, Co-Editor

Fantasy Tales #4
(New York: Carroll & Graf, 1991)

Story type: Horror (Anthology; Fantasy)

Summary: Nine tales of horror and fantasy and two poems make up this trade paperback incarnation of Britain's long-running magazine. Included are Kathryn Ptacek's "Living to the End," about a man who has cheated death; Tom Ligotti's metaphysical nightmare, "The Medusa"; Tom Monteleone's tale of a man who tries to change his life as it flashes before his eyes, "Rehearsals"; and a reprint of Ramsey Campbell's rare sword and sorcery tale, "The Pit of Wings."

Other books you might like:
George Hatch, *Guignoir and Other Furies*, 1991
Stuart David Schiff, *The Whispers Series*, 1977-1987
David B. Silva, *Best of The Horror Show*, 1987

2366

STEPHEN JONES, Editor
DAVID SUTTON, Co-Editor

Fantasy Tales #6
(New York: Carroll & Graf, 1991)

Story type: Horror (Anthology; Fantasy)

Summary: Ten stories of horror and fantasy, two poems and one essay from Britain's trade paperback equivalent of America's *Weird Tales*. Included are Neil Gaiman's "Foreign Parts," about a man whose sexual repression is manifested as an organic disease; Kim Newman's hardboiled horror story, "Mother Hen"; R. Chetwynd-Hayes' SF-horror tale, "Devil's Child"; and Thomas Ligotti's "The Spectacles in the Drawer," about a joke that backfires upon its perpetrator with nightmarish results.

Other books you might like:
Norman Partridge, *Guignoir*, 1991
Kristine Kathryn Rusch, *The Best of Pulphouse: The Hardback Magazine*, 1991
Elizabeth A. Saunders, *When the Black Lotus Blooms*, 1990

2367

STEPHEN JONES, Editor
DAVE CARSON, Co-Editor

H.P. Lovecraft's Book of Horror
(New York: Barnes & Noble, 1993)

Story type: Horror (Anthology)

Summary: This anthology reprints as its introduction H.P. Lovecraft's groundbreaking 1933 eassy, "Supernatural Horror Literature," and collects 21 classic tales of horror and the supernatural singled out for excellence therein. Included are three tales of invisible monsters, William Hope Hodgson's "The Hog," Ambrose Bierce's "The Damned Thing," and Guy de Maupassant's "The Horla"; Rudyard Kipling's Tale of atavistic transformation, "The Mark of the Beast"; two gruesome supernatural revenge stories, Irvin S. Cobb's "Fishhead" and Edward Lucas White's "Lukundoo"; four stories of ineluctable supernatural fates, M.R. James's "Count Magnus," Charles Dickens's "The Haunted Signalman," Robert W. Chambers' "The Yellow Sign," and Clark Ashton Smith's "The Double Shadow"; Edgar Allan Poe's rendering of the haunted house as a psychological allegory, "The Fall of the House of Usher"; and Arthur Machen's tale of the unholy union between a mortal woman and an immortal deity, "The Great God Pan." The book is illustrated by Carson.

Other books you might like:
Alexander Laing, *The Haunted Omnibus*, 1937
  editor
Philip van Doren Stern, *The Midnight Reader*, 1942
  editor
Dennis Wheatley, *A Century of Horror Stories*, 1935
  editor
Herbert Wise, *Great Tales of Terror and the Supernatural*, 1944
  Phyllis Fraser, co-editor

2368

STEPHEN JONES, Editor

The Mammoth Book of Best New Horror
(New York: Carroll & Graf, 1996)

Story type: Horror (Anthology)

Summary: A retitling of the *Best New Horror* series, this seventh volume in the series collects 26 of the best stories published in 1995. Among them are the novelette version of Brian Stableford's "The Hunger and Ecstasy of Vampires," a futuristic vampire tale written as a Wellsian scientific romance; Jane Rice's "The Sixth Dog," about a strange house which humans enter but only dogs leave; Brian Hodge's "Extinctions in Paradise," about third-world werewolves; Steve Rasnic Tem's "100 Wicked Little Witches," in which a man blames his every misfortune on imagined supernatural beings; Terry Lamsley's "The Toddler," about a phantom child; Graham Masterton's "The Grey Madonna," a ghost story in the M.R. James tradition; and Norman Partridge's "The Bars on Satan's Jailhouse," a mix of horror, crime, and western fiction. The editor supplies an insightful introduction summing up the year in horror, and Kim Newman supplies a "Necrology" for 1995.

Other books you might like:
Ellen Datlow, *The Year's Best Fantasy and Horror: Ninth Annual Collection*, 1996
  Terri Windling, co-editor
Karl Edward Wagner, *The Year's Best Horror Stories Series*, 1979-1994
  editor

2369

STEPHEN JONES, Editor

The Mammoth Book of Frankenstein
(New York: Carroll & Graf, 1995)

Story type: Horror (Anthology)

Summary: This excellent anthology combines twenty-four new and reprinted stories about the reanimated dead, including the full text of Mary Shelley's novel *Frankenstein* in the revised 1831 version. Robert Bloch's "Mannikins of Horror" tells of the gruesome fate that befalls a man who finds a way to project his soul into miniature dolls. Kim Newman, in "Completist Heaven," draws ironic parallels between the walking dead and a couch-potato video addict. Michael Marshall Smith's "To Receive Is Better" and Dennis Etchison's "The Dead Line" both tell of scientific experiments to keep the dead alive long enough to harvest their organs. David Schow's amusing "Last Call for the Sons of Shock" envisions a watering hole where the great Hollywood film monsters hang out and recount their favorite adventures.

Other books you might like:
Martin H. Greenberg, *Frankenstein: The Monster Wakes*, 1994
    editor
Hugh Lamb, *Return From the Grave*, 1976
    editor
Michel Parry, *Rivals of Frankenstein*, 1977
    editor
Bill Pronzini, *The Arbor House Necropolis*, 1981
    editor

2370

STEPHEN JONES, Editor

The Mammoth Book of Terror
(New York: Carroll & Graf, 1991)

Story type: Horror (Anthology)

Summary: Eighteen stories, both classic and contemporary. Some wreak interesting variations on traditional horror themes such as madness (Karl Edward Wagner's "The River of Night's Dreaming"), revenge from beyond the grave (Ramsey Campbell's "Out of Copyright") and Lovecraftian horror (Brian Lumley's "The House of the Temple"). Others utilize non-traditional themes and approaches, including the detective tale (Clive Barker's "The Last Illusion"), the hardboiled story (David Schow's "Bunny Didn't Tell Us") and abortion (F. Paul Wilson's "Buckets"). Graham Masterton's "Pig's Dinner" is original to the volume.

Other books you might like:
Mike Ashley, *The Mammoth Book of Short Horror Novels*, 1988
Kirby McCauley, *Night Chills*, 1975
Bill Pronzini, *The Arbor House Treasury of Horror and the Supernatural*, 1981
    Barry Malzberg and Martin H. Greenberg, co-authors
Charles G. Waugh, *13 Short Horror Novels*, 1987
    Martin H. Greenberg, co-author

2371

STEPHEN JONES, Editor

The Mammoth Book of Vampires
(New York: Carroll & Graf, 1992)

Story type: Horror (Anthology; Vampire Story)

Summary: Twenty-nine traditional and none-too-traditional vampire stories ranging from Gothic classics such as Bram Stoker's "Dracula's Guest" and F. Marion Crawford's "For Blood Is the Life," to F. Paul Wilson's tale of a future in which vampires rule the world, "Midnight Mass"; David Schow's "A Week in the Unlife," about vampires who prey on other vampires; Les Daniels' novella of his series character Don Sebastian de Villaneuva, "Yellow Fog"; and Brian Stableford's tale of vampirism as a blood-borne disease, "The Man Who Loved the Vampire Lady."

Other books you might like:
Richard Dalby, *Dracula's Brood*, 1987
Ellen Datlow, *Blood Is Not Enough*, 1989
Martin H. Greenberg, *A Taste for Blood*, 1992
    Robert Weinberg and Stefan Dziemianowicz, co-editors
Martin H. Greenberg, *Vamps*, 1987
    Charles G. Waugh, co-editor
Alan Ryan, *Vampires: Two Centuries of Great Vampire Stories*, 1987

2372

STEPHEN JONES, Editor

The Mammoth Book of Werewolves
(New York: Carroll & Graf, 1994)

Story type: Horror (Anthology; Werewolf Story)

Summary: This anthology contains 24 werewolf stories, ten of which are original. Included are David Case's classic short epistolary novel of a murderer convinced he is a werewolf, "The Cell"; Ramsey Campbell's brief tale of the strange effect of a museum talisman on a night watchman, "Night Beat"; Suzy McKee Charnas's coming-of-age tale, "Boobs"; Manly Wade Wellman's pulp thriller, "The Hairy Ones Shall Dance"; Scott Bradfield's story of a man who leads a feral life in his dreams, "Dream of the Wolf"; and Clive Barker's cold war werewolf thriller, "Twilight at the Towers."

Other books you might like:
Brian J. Frost, *Book of the Werewolf*, 1973
David Hill, *The Way of the Werewolf*, 1966
    editor
Byron Preiss, *The Ultimate Werewolf*, 1992
    John Betancourt, co-editor
Bill Pronzini, *Werewolf!*, 1979
    editor

2373

STEPHEN JONES, Editor

The Mammoth Book of Zombies

(New York: Carroll & Graf, 1993)

Story type: Horror (Anthology; Reanimated Dead)

Summary: This book collects 26 stories of the reanimated dead, some liberally interpreted to be about zombies. Included are Edgar Allan Poe's story of a soul that inhabits a corpse after death, "The Fact in the Case of M. Valdemar"; H.P. Lovecraft's pastiche of *Frankenstein*, "Herbert West—Reanimator"; Karl Edward Wagner's pastiche of H.P. Lovecraft, "Sticks"; Dennis Etchison's tale of backstage intrigues during the filming of a zombie movie, "The Blood Kiss"; Clive Barker's tale of a theatre where old performers never die, "Sex, Death and Starshine"; and J. Sheridan Le Fanu's story of a woman betrothed to a corpse, "Schalken the Painter." Seven stories by Peter Tremayne, Nicholas Royle, Graham Masterton, Hugh B. Cave, David Riley, David Sutton, and Michael Marshall Smith are original to the anthology.

Other books you might like:

Peter Haining, *Stories of the Walking Dead*, 1985
   editor
Bill Pronzini, *The Arbor House Necropolis*, 1981
John Skipp, *Book of the Dead*, 1990
   Craig Spector, co-editor
John Skipp, *Still Dead: Book of the Dead 2*, 1992
   Craig Spector, co-editor

2374

STEPHEN JONES, Editor

Shadows over Innsmouth

(Minneapolis: Fedogan & Bremer, 1994)

Story type: Horror (Anthology)

Summary: The 17 stories in this anthology are homages to H.P. Lovecraft's "The Shadow over Innsmouth," about a traveller's discovery that a New England seaport town is inhabited by the spawn of humans and sea creatures. In addition to Lovecraft's own story, the selections include Ramsey Campbell's first published tale, "The Church in High Street," about the hideous discovery a man makes in an abandoned church; Brian Stableford's "The Innsmouth Heritage," which explores the genetic ramifications behind Lovecraft's story; David Langford's "Deepnet," which reimagines Lovecraft's menace for the computer age; Guy N. Smith's tale of horrifying self-discovery, "Return to Innsmouth"; and Brian Lumley's "Dagon's Bell," about the resurgence of the fish-god Dagon.

Other books you might like:

Edward P. Berglund, *Disciples of Cthulhu*, 1973
Ramsey Campbell, *New Tales of the Cthulhu Mythos*, 1980
H.P. Lovecraft, *Tales of the Cthulhu Mythos: Golden Anniversary Anthology*, 1990
Robert M. Price, *The Hastur Cycle*, 1994
   editor

Robert M. Price, *The Shub Niggurath Cycle*, 1994
Robert M. Price, *Tales of the Lovecraft Mythos*, 1992
Thomas M.K. Stratman, *Cthulhu's Heirs*, 1994
   editor

2375

TERRY JONES
BRIAN FROUD, Co-Author

The Goblin Companion

(Atlanta: Turner Publishing, 1996)

Story type: Fantasy (Collection; Legend)

Summary: Contains a six-page introduction plus 70 tales and descriptions of the Goblins of the Labyrinth who, millions of years ago, retreated into a vast fortress to protect themselves against the ungoblin world. "A Field Guide to Goblins" results from combining the stories of an ancient African wise man and illustrations from a storage chest dating from the goblin era.

Other books you might like:

Graeme Base, *The Discovery of Dragons*, 1996
Charles de Lint, *The Wild Wood*, 1994
   Brian Froud, co-author
James Gurney, *Dinotopia*, 1992
James Gurney, *The World Beneath*, 1995
Steve Szilagyi, *Photographing Fairies*, 1992

2376

TERRY JONES
BRIAN FROUD, Illustrator

Lady Cottington's Pressed Fairy Book

(Atlanta, Georgia, Turner, 1994)

Story type: Fantasy (Contemporary; Light Fantasy)
Major character(s): Lady Angelica Cottington, Naturalist (amateur), Teenager; Lord Crowley, Rogue, Nobleman
Time period(s): 1890s (1895-1899); 1900s
Locale(s): England; Naples, Italy

Summary: Lady Cottington collects fairies within a journal which documents her discovery and interaction with the creatures, who tease her to distraction and play tricks on her as she examines her budding sexuality.

Other books you might like:

David Kirschner, *The Pagemaster*, 1993
   Ernie Contreras, co-author
James Gurney, *Dinotopia*, 1992
Patricia A. McKillip, *Something Rich and Strange*, 1994
   Brian Froud, co-author
Steve Szilagyi, *Photographing Fairies*, 1992
David Worsick, *Henry's Gift: The Magic Eye*, 1994

2377

TERRY JONES
BRIAN FROUD, Co-Author

Strange Stains and Mysterious Smells

(New York: Simon & Schuster, 1996)

Story type: Fantasy (Collection; Light Fantasy)
Major character(s): Quentin Coddington, Psychic, Researcher
Time period(s): 1910s; 1920s
Locale(s): England

Summary: Equipped with his Psychic Image Nebulising Generator and Primary Odour Nasalising Gasificator, Quentin Coddington investigates more than 780 psychic encounters and the stains and odors which result, documenting 34 with stories and illustrations presented in his journal.

Other books you might like:
Betty Ballantine, *The Secret Oceans*, 1994
Graeme Base, *The Discovery of Dragons*, 1996
James Gurney, *Dinotopia*, 1992
James Gurney, *The World Beneath*, 1995
Patricia A. McKillip, *Something Rich and Strange*, 1994
    Brian Froud, co-author
Steve Szilagyi, *Photographing Fairies*, 1992

2378

ROBERT JORDAN

The Conan Chronicles

(New York: Tor, 1995)

Story type: Fantasy (Sword and Sorcery; Adventure)
Series: Conan the Barbarian
Major character(s): Conan, Barbarian, Warrior
Time period(s): Indeterminate Past
Locale(s): Zamora, Fictional Country; Nemedia, Fictional Country; Turan, Fictional Country

Summary: Omnibus edition collecting *Conan the Invincible* (1982), *Conan the Defender* (1982) and *Conan the Unconquered* (1983). Conan pursues treasure and seeks to fulfill vows to the gods while powerful warriors, sorcerers and treacherous women attempt to divert him from his goals.

Other books you might like:
Leonard Carpenter, *Conan the Gladiator*, 1995
Roland J. Green, *Conan at the Demon's Gate*, 1994
Robert E. Howard, *Conan the Barbarian*, 1955
Robert E. Howard, *Hour of the Dragon*, 1977
Steve Perry, *Conan the Fearless*, 1986
John Maddox Roberts, *Conan and the Treasure of Python*, 1993

2379

ROBERT JORDAN

A Crown of Swords

(New Yok: Tor, 1996)

Story type: Fantasy (Magic Conflict)
Series: Wheel of Time

Major character(s): Rand "Dragon Reborn" al'Thor, Leader; Elayne, Royalty, Heiress; Egwene al'Vere, Religious (Aes Sedai), Witch
Time period(s): Indeterminate
Locale(s): Cairhien, Fictional Country; Andor, Fictional Country; Ebou Dar, Fictional City

Summary: While Elayne and others attempt to acquire the artifact that could reverse an unnatural heat wave, Egwene gathers together all manner of entities who can channel and Rand confronts Forsaken Sammael, a minion of the Dark One.

Other books you might like:
Glen Cook, *The Black Company*, 1984
Dave Duncan, *Magic Casement*, 1990
David Eddings, *Pawn of Prophecy*, 1982
Raymond E. Feist, *Magician*, 1982
Terry Goodkind, *Wizard's First Rule*, 1994
Michael Scott Rohan, *The Anvil of Ice*, 1986

2380

ROBERT JORDAN

The Dragon Reborn

(New York: Tor, 1991)

Story type: Fantasy (Quest; Magic Conflict)
Series: Wheel of Time
Major character(s): Rand "Dragon Reborn" al'Thor, Leader, Revolutionary; Elayne, Royalty, Heiress; Egwene al'Vere, Religious (Aes Sedai), Witch
Time period(s): Indeterminate
Locale(s): Tar Valon, Fictional Country; Illian, Fictional Country

Summary: Having accepted his role in prophecy as Dragon Reborn, Rand seeks after a magic sword while Egwene, Elayne and Nynaeve, training again with the Aes Sedai sisterhood, travel to the White Tower for help healing Mat's wounds and answers to Agwene's disturbing dreams. At the White Tower, Verin entrusts Egwene with a ter'angreal, a device which allows dreams to become real, the tool of a Dreamer. The prophecied Pattern continues to unfold, challenging Egwene's restraint in use of the Power.

Other books you might like:
David Cook, *Beyond the Moons*, 1991
Glen Cook, *The Black Company*, 1984
David Eddings, *Pawn of Prophecy*, 1982
Raymond E. Feist, *Magician*, 1982
Barbara Hambly, *The Time of the Dark*, 1982
Elizabeth Moon, *Sheepfarmer's Daughter*, 1988
Andre Norton, *The Elvenbane*, 1991
    Mercedes Lackey, co-author
J.R.R. Tolkien, *The Fellowship of the Ring*, 1954

2381

ROBERT JORDAN

The Eye of the World
(New York: Tor, 1989)

Story type: Fantasy (Quest)
Series: Wheel of Time
Major character(s): Rand al'Thor, Farmer (shepherd); Fades, Monster
Time period(s): Indeterminate
Locale(s): Emond's Field, Fictional Country

Summary: Three boys forced from their home, a young girl, and a magic worker are brought together to help battle the dark forces trying to take over their land.

Other books you might like:
Lloyd Alexander, *The Book of Three*, 1988
    Reissue of 1964; The Prydain Series. Vol. 1
Guy Gavriel Kay, *The Summer Tree*, 1985
    The Fionavar Tapestry. Bk. 1
Victor Kelleher, *The Red King*, 1989
R.A. MacAvoy, *Lens of the World*, 1990

2382

ROBERT JORDAN

The Fires of Heaven
(New York: Tor, 1993)

Story type: Fantasy (Magic Conflict)
Series: Wheel of Time
Major character(s): Rand ''Dragon Reborn'' al'Thor, Leader, Revolutionary; Aviendha, Warrior; Elayne, Royalty, Heiress
Time period(s): Indeterminate
Locale(s): Rhuidean, Fictional City; Amadicia, Fictional Country

Summary: While factions among the Aes Sedai plot, Elayne and Nynaeve continue their travels, meeting Siuan and Min at Salidar. The Forsaken exert their evil influence and Rand leads his Aiel warriors to victory, even though he must enter the World of Dreams, the Tel'aran'rhiod, to confront Rahvin.

Other books you might like:
Lynn Abbey, *Daughter of the Bright Moon*, 1979
Stephen R. Donaldson, *Lord Foul's Bane*, 1977
Diane Duane, *The Door into Fire*, 1979
Simon R. Green, *Blue Moon Rising*, 1991
Barbara Hambly, *The Armies of Daylight*, 1983
Katherine Kurtz, *High Deryni*, 1973
Leo Tolstoy, *War and Peace*, 1886
J.R.R. Tolkien, *The Two Towers*, 1955
Angus Wells, *Dark Magic*, 1992

2383

ROBERT JORDAN

Lord of Chaos
(New York: Tor, 1994)

Story type: Fantasy (Magic Conflict)
Series: Wheel of Time
Major character(s): Rand ''Dragon Reborn'' al'Thor, Leader; Demandred, Wizard; Shaidar Haran, Mythical Creature (Myrddraal)
Time period(s): Indeterminate
Locale(s): Shayol Ghul, Fictional City (mountainstronghold of the Dark One); The Blasted Lands, Fictional Country; Shaidar Haran, Fictional City

Summary: The plot of this immense series continues to build as the forces of good and evil pursue their plans. Unfortunately for Rand al'Thor, ambitious mortals as well as the plots of the Great Lord of the Dark impede the removal of the Dark One's influence over the Wheel of Time.

Other books you might like:
Glen Cook, *The Black Company*, 1984
David Eddings, *Pawn of Prophecy*, 1982
Guy Gavriel Kay, *The Summer Tree*, 1985
Katherine Kurtz, *Deryni Rising*, 1970
Patricia A. McKillip, *The Riddle-Master of Hed*, 1976

2384

ROBERT JORDAN

The Shadow Rising
(New York: Tor, 1992)

Story type: Fantasy (Magic Conflict)
Series: Wheel of Time
Major character(s): Rand ''Dragon Reborn'' al'Thor, Leader, Hero
Time period(s): Indeterminate
Locale(s): Tar Vallon, Fictional City; Two Rivers, Fictional Country

Summary: As the Dark One expands its influence over the land, humans who lust for power and control plot to assume command. In Two Rivers, Rand eludes the pursuing Whitecloaks, remaining humanity's best hope for restoration of the balance of magical forces.

Other books you might like:
Glen Cook, *The Black Company*, 1984
Glen Cook, *Shadows Linger*, 1984
Glen Cook, *The White Rose*, 1985
David Eddings, *Magician's Gambit*, 1983
David Eddings, *Pawn of Prophecy*, 1982
David Eddings, *Queen of Sorcery*, 1982

2385

SHERRYL JORDAN

The Juniper Game

(New York: Scholastic, 1991)

Story type: Fantasy (Contemporary; Young Adult)
Major character(s): Juniper Golding, Teenager, Psychic (clairvoyant); Dylan Pidgely, Artist, Psychic; Marsha Golding, Single Parent
Time period(s): 1990s
Locale(s): New Zealand

Summary: Juniper Golding has an obsession with Medieval England and ESP. She draws Dylan Pidgely, a fellow student, into her experiments and both are drawn into the life and time of Johanna, a young woman in 15th-century Tewkesbury who is accused of being a witch. Both feel they may be too caught up when they must watch helplessly as Johanna is tried and condemned, but find they can give her a bit of peace during her ordeal.

Other books you might like:
Margaret J. Anderson, *To Nowhere and Back*, 1975
Peter Dickinson, *The Gift*, 1974
Alan Garner, *Red Shift*, 1973
Katherine Kurtz, *The Adept*, 1991
    Deborah Turner Harris, co-author
Andre Norton, *Lavender-Green Magic*, 1974
Alison Uttley, *A Traveler in Time*, 1940

2386

GRAHAM JOYCE

Requiem

(New York: Tor 1996)

Story type: Horror (Mystery)
Major character(s): Tom Webster, Teacher; Sharon, Counselor; David Feldberg, Linguist (translator)
Time period(s): 1990s (1993)
Locale(s): Jerusalem, Israel

Summary: Sick with grief and guilt over the accidental death of his wife, Tom Webster flees to Israel and the arms of his ex-girlfriend Sharon. While there, he is entrusted by a dying scholar with a lost Dead Sea Scroll and its heretical revelations about the true origin of the Catholic Church only further weaken Tom's slipping grasp on reality. A nominee for the World Fantasy Award, this novel was first published in England in 1995.

Other books you might like:
Simon Maginn, *Virgins and Martyrs*, 1995
Brent Monahan, *The Book of Common Dread*, 1993
Mary Elizabeth Murphy, *Virgin*, 1996

2387

CYNTHIA KADOHATA

In the Heart of the Valley of Love

(New York: Viking, 1992)

Story type: Science Fiction (Dystopian)
Major character(s): Francie, Teenager, Orphan
Time period(s): 2050s
Locale(s): Los Angeles, California

Summary: In the violent, chaotic Los Angeles environment, Francie roams around searching for direction in her life.

Other books you might like:
David Brin, *Earth*, 1990
Octavia E. Butler, *Dawn*, 1987
K.W. Jeter, *Madlands*, 1991
David R. Palmer, *Emergence*, 1984
Geoff Ryman, *The Child Garden*, 1990
Carolyn See, *Making History*, 1991
Neal Stephenson, *Snow Crash*, 1992

2388

RICHARD KADREY

Kamikaze L'Amour

(New York: St. Martin's, 1995)

Story type: Science Fiction (Post-Holocaust)
Major character(s): Ryder, Musician, Fugitive; Frida, Musician; Virilio, Criminal
Time period(s): 2000s (2001)
Locale(s): San Francisco, California

Summary: Moving north, the jungles destroy cities and bring strange new life. A rock star now comfortably anonymous after a failed suicide, Ryder comes to San Francisco to start over. Unable to resist the attraction of music after meeting Frida, Ryder pursues a new sound for a new world.

Other books you might like:
J.G. Ballard, *The Drowned World*, 1962
Pat Cadigan, *Synners*, 1991
Pat Murphy, *The City, Not Long After*, 1989
Lewis Shiner, *Deserted Cities of the Heart*, 1988
Bruce Sterling, *Heavy Weather*, 1994

2389

DAVID KAGAN

Sunstroke

(New York: Diamond, 1993)

Story type: Science Fiction (Techno-Thriller)
Major character(s): James William Kendall, Government Official (president); Mike Doheny, Engineer, Administrator (project director)
Time period(s): 21st century
Locale(s): Earth

Summary: Experimental civilian solar power satellite, SOLSAT X-1, orbits Earth, converting sunlight to electricity.

While overtly benign, secret programming allows the microwave beam used for transfering energy to Earth to come under control of U.S. Space Defense Command who can target the microwave beam as a death weapon. When programming fails, the few cognoscenti rush in to prevent worldwide disaster.

Other books you might like:
David Brin, *Earth*, 1990
Michael Crichton, *The Andromeda Strain*, 1969
Mary Gentle, *Ancient Light*, 1987
Rosemary Kirstein, *The Outskirter's Secret*, 1992
J.M. Morgan, *Desert Eden*, 1991

2390

JANET KAGAN

Mirabile
(New York: Tor, 1991)

Story type: Science Fiction (Hard Science Fiction; Adventure)
Major character(s): Anna ''Mama'' Jason Masmajean, Scientist (biologist); Leonov Opener Denness, Scientist (naturalist), Explorer
Time period(s): Indeterminate Future
Locale(s): Mirabile, Planet—Imaginary

Summary: Romance flourishes as colonists try to establish Earth-authentic species on Mirabile using embryos and genetic material sent with them. All plant and animal life sent has inactive genetic material nested inside the normally active DNA that unexpectedly generates new life forms, dragon's teeth, which Mama Jason must study then stabilize or eliminate. Six stories packaged as a novel.

Other books you might like:
Octavia E. Butler, *Adulthood Rites*, 1988
Octavia E. Butler, *Dawn*, 1987
Octavia E. Butler, *Imago*, 1989
Michael Flynn, *The Nanotech Chronicles*, 1991
Diana G. Gallagher, *The Alien Dark*, 1990
Anne McCaffrey, *Dragonsdawn*, 1988
Joan Slonczewski, *A Door into Ocean*, 1986
Cordwainer Smith, *The Best of Cordwainer Smith*, 1975
Harry Turtledove, *Earthgrip*, 1991

2391

RICHARD KALICH

The Nihilesthete
(Stone Mountain, Georgia: White Wolf, 1996)

Story type: Horror (Psychological Suspense)
Major character(s): Haberman, Social Worker; Brodski, Handicapped; Maria Rivera, Aged Person
Time period(s): 1980s (1987)
Locale(s): New York, New York

Summary: Haberman, a sadistically misanthropic social worker, assumes the care of an idiot quadriplegic with the intention of helping him develop his aptitude for art and then denying him outlets of creative expression. This novel, the author's first, was originally published in 1987.

Other books you might like:
John Fowles, *The Collector*, 1958
Stephen King, *Misery*, 1987
Patrick McGrath, *The Grotesque*, 1989
Joyce Carol Oates, *Zombie*, 1995

2392

JEANNE KALOGRIDIS

Children of the Vampire
(New York: Delacorte, 1995)

Story type: Horror (Vampire Story)
Series: Diaries of the Family Dracul
Major character(s): Stefan Van Helsing, Doctor; Arkady Tsepesh, Vampire; Vlad Tsepesh, Vampire (Count Dracula)
Time period(s): 1840s (1845); 1870s (1871)
Locale(s): Transylvania; Amsterdam, Netherlands

Summary: In this sequel to *Covenant with the Vampire*, newly vampirized Arkady Tsepesh flees Castle Dracula to protect his infant son Stefan from the family curse, which demands that the firstborn male of every generation of Tsepeshs becomes bound by blood to the Count and supply him with foreign travellers for his sustenance. Twenty-six years later, Stefan is oblivious to his heritage, yet still feels the call of blood that lures him back to Castle Dracula, and his destiny. The author is better known by her pseudonym, Diane Duane.

Other books you might like:
Brian W. Aldiss, *Dracula Unbound*, 1991
Roderick Anscombe, *The Secret Life of Laszlo, Count Dracula*, 1994
Fred Saberhagen, *A Matter of Taste*, 1991
Peter Tremayne, *Dracula Unborn*, 1977

2393

JEANNE KALOGRIDIS

Covenant with the Vampire
(New York: Delacorte, 1994)

Story type: Horror (Vampire Story)
Major character(s): Arkady Tsepesh, Young Man; Mary Wyndham Tsepesh, Young Woman (Arkady's wife); Vlad Tsepesh, Vampire (Count Dracula)
Time period(s): 1840s (1845)
Locale(s): Transylvania (Castle Dracula)

Summary: The author's first novel, in a projected trilogy retelling the story of Bram Stoker's *Dracula*, is told in epistolary form as the diaries of Arkady and Mary Tsepesh, and Arkady's sister Zsuzsanna. Upon the death of his father, Arkady returns to Transylvania from London with his pregnant wife. There, he discovers to his horror that his great uncle, Vlad, is a vampire who expects him, and his as yet unborn child, to serve him as the first-born of each generation of the Tsepesh has done: by obtaining victims who will supply him with the blood he needs.

Other books you might like:
C. Dean Andersson, *I Am Dracula*, 1993

Marie Kiraly, *Mina*, 1994
Bram Stoker, *Dracula*, 1897

2394
JEANNE KALOGRIDIS

Lord of the Vampires
(New York: Delacorte, 1996)

Story type: Horror (Vampire Story)
Series: Diaries of the Family Dracul
Major character(s): Abraham Van Helsing, Doctor; Jonathan Seward, Doctor; Elizabeth Bathory, Vampire
Time period(s): 1890s (1893)
Locale(s): London, England

Summary: This third novel in the Diaries of the Family Dracul trilogy, a prequel to Bram Stoker's *Dracula*, recapitulates many of the events of Stoker's novel. Sworn to avenge the death of his father and half brother at the hands of vampire Vlad Dracul, Abraham Van Helsing and a band of confederates grapple with Dracula and his renowned cousin, Elizabeth Bathory. Their struggle draws the attention of an even more formidable nemesis, the Lord of the Vampires, who first charged Vlad with the task of killing the first born son of each generation of his family in order to enjoy his vampiric immortality.

Other books you might like:
C. Dean Andersson, *I Am Dracula*, 1994
Roderick Anscombe, *The Secret Life of Laszlo, Count Dracula*, 1994
Kim Newman, *Anno Dracula*, 1992
Peter Tremayne, *Dracula Unborn*, 1977

2395
KWADWO AGYMAH KAMAU

Flickering Shadows
(Minneapolis, Minnesota: Coffee House Press, 1996)

Story type: Fantasy (Contemporary Realism; Political)
Major character(s): Cephus, Farmer, Revolutionary; Boysie, Sailor, Revolutionary; Doreen, Spouse (Cephus')
Time period(s): 1990s
Locale(s): Caribbean; The Hill, Fictional City

Summary: Independence from Britain leaves an island vulnerable to exploitation as exploration for mineral wealth and development for tourism progresses with the aid of an unscrupulous missionary. Communicating from the spirit world, Cephus' grandfather attempts to mitigate events and cultivate a sense of group identity as Cephus' family and neighbors struggle with personal and societal problems. First novel.

Other books you might like:
Louis de Bernieres, *Senor Vivo and the Coca Lord*, 1992
Louis de Bernieres, *The War of Don Emmanuel's Nether Parts*, 1992
Ben Okri, *The Famished Road*, 1992
Ben Okri, *Songs of Enchantment*, 1993

2396
MICHAEL KANDEL

Captain Jack Zodiac
(New York: Bantam Spectra, 1992)

Story type: Fantasy (Light Fantasy; Post-Disaster)
Major character(s): Clifford "Cliff" Koussevitzky, Parent; Bernie "Power Man" Rifkin, Hero (crimefighter/superhero); Captain Jack Zodiac, Drug Dealer
Time period(s): 21st century
Locale(s): Earth; Moon Two, Planet—Imaginary

Summary: Despite the war and its surreal side effects, Cliff decides to remarry in hopes of starting a second family. Cliff then resolves to find and rescue his daughter, a mall zombie, and his son, a space cadet, even if it means using one of Captain Jack Zodiac's experimental drugs.

Other books you might like:
Neil Gaiman, *Good Omens: The Nice and Accurate Prophecies of Agnes Nutter, Witch*, 1990
　　Terry Pratchett, co-author
K.W. Jeter, *Madlands*, 1990
George R.R. Martin, *Wild Cards*, 1987
　　editor
Neal Stephenson, *Snow Crash*, 1992

2397
MICHAEL KANDEL

In between Dragons
(New York: Bantam Spectra, 1990)

Story type: Fantasy (Alternate World; Young Adult)
Major character(s): Sherman, Student—High School, Adventurer; Mr. McGulvey, Steward (McGulveyland)
Time period(s): 1990s
Locale(s): McGulveyland, Fictional Country; Cuspidor, Fictional City; Pittsburgh, Pennsylvania

Summary: A high school senior finds adventure and escape from the uncomfortable reality of being sixteen years old by going to a magic library and entering McGulveyland. There he is a hero in all the stories in which he gets to fight dragons, battle a psi-monster and drive a car. He brings a book which doesn't belong to the library without realizing he is putting McGulveyland at risk.

Other books you might like:
Antoine de Saint-Exupery, *The Little Prince*, 1943
Michael Ende, *The Neverending Story*, 1983
William Goldman, *The Princess Bride*, 1973
Clifford D. Simak, *The Goblin Reservation*, 1968
Christopher Stasheff, *The Warlock Is Missing*, 1986
James Thurber, *The Secret Life of Walter Mitty*, 1983

2398

MICHAEL KANDEL

Panda Ray

(New York: St. Martin's, 1996)

Story type: Science Fiction (Psychic Powers; Invasion of Earth)

Major character(s): Christopher Zimmerman, Adventurer, Time Traveller; Jane Palmer, Teacher; Debra Zimmerman, Parent

Time period(s): 1990s

Locale(s): Kansas

Summary: Mother calls a family meeting after Jane Palmer informs her that Christopher relays odd stories in history class. The family agrees she must scoop out Christopher's psi, omicron, and upsilon. His sister convinces Christopher to run away with his grandfather, leading to death, imprisonment, and the continuing interference of the FBI.

Other books you might like:
Lester del Rey, *Pstalemate*, 1971
Steven Gould, *Jumper*, 1992
Robert A. Heinlein, *Tunnel in the Sky*, 1955
William Kotzwinkle, *The Fan Man*, 1974
R.A. Lafferty, *The Reefs of Earth*, 1968
Theodore Sturgeon, *More than Human*, 1953

2399

MICHAEL KANDEL

Strange Invasion

(New York: Bantam Spectra, 1989)

Story type: Science Fiction (Invasion of Earth)

Major character(s): Wally Griffith, Patient (Mental Patient); Lucille, Doctor

Time period(s): 20th century

Locale(s): Earth

Summary: Wally Griffith, a mental patient who tends to hallucinate anyway, discovers that he is the only one in the world capable of standing off a series of very strange and occasionally very silly alien invasions.

Other books you might like:
Philip K. Dick, *The Divine Invasion*, 1981
Philip K. Dick, *Do Androids Dream of Electric Sheep?*, 1968
Philip K. Dick, *Eye in the Sky*, 1957
Philip K. Dick, *Martian Time-Slip*, 1964
Philip K. Dick, *The Three Stigmata of Palmer Eldritch*, 1965
Philip K. Dick, *Ubik*, 1969
Philip K. Dick, *Valis*, 1981

2400

MICHAEL KASNER

Finger of God

(New York: Worldwide Library Gold Eagle, 1993)

Story type: Science Fiction (Military)
Series: Warkeep 2030

Major character(s): Alexander F. Rosemont, Military Personnel, Leader

Time period(s): 2030s (2030)

Locale(s): Amazon Jungle, Brazil; United States

Summary: When forces of the Allied nations of South America plan to attack Brazil for environmental crimes, the Peacekeepers rush to prevent continental warfare.

Other books you might like:
Bill Dolan, *Cobra Curse*, 1993
G. Harry Stine, *Force of Arms*, 1990
G. Harry Stine, *Guts and Glory*, 1991
G. Harry Stine, *The Lost Battalion*, 1989
G. Harry Stine, *Operation Steel Band*, 1988

2401

KEN KATO

Yamato: A Rage in Heaven

(New York: Warner/Questar, 1990)

Story type: Science Fiction (Space Opera)
Series: Yamato

Major character(s): Jos Hawken, Military Personnel (commodore), Spaceship Captain; Ellis Straker, Spaceship Captain, Psychic

Time period(s): 25th century (2420s)

Locale(s): Yamato Sector, Outer Space; Sado, Planet—Imaginary (Neutral Zone)

Summary: When space opened to colonization after 2100 A.D., areas were apportioned by sectors to different countries. The area settled by Japan, named Yamato, became very powerful with a ruling Shogunate which intends to control all the sectors. The only one that could possibly prevent them is the Amerikan sector, which is immobilized by internal politics and greed.

Other books you might like:
Greg Bear, *Eon*, 1989
C.J. Cherryh, *Downbelow Station*, 1981
Frank Herbert, *Dune*, 1965
Alis A. Rasmussen, *A Passage of Stars*, 1990
Dan Simmons, *The Fall of Hyperion*, 1990
Dan Simmons, *Hyperion*, 1989

2402

DOUGLAS KAUFMAN, Editor
ED STARK, Co-Editor

Dragons over England

(Honesdale, Pennsylvania: West End Games, 1992)

Story type: Fantasy (Anthology; Legend)
Series: Torg: The Possibility Wars
Time period(s): 20th century
Locale(s): Aysle, Alternate Earth; England

Summary: This volume contains a six-page introduction by Ed Stark plus nine stories, two by the editors, in which legendary characters from European mythology come alive and co-exist with humanity in a limited area. Set in the universe of the game, *Torg*.

Other books you might like:

L. Sprague de Camp, *The Complete Compleat Enchanter*, 1989
  Fletcher Pratt, co-author
L. Sprague de Camp, *The Enchanter Reborn*, 1992
  Christopher Stasheff, co-editor
Greg Farshtey, *Strange Tales From the Nile Empire*, 1992
  Greg Gorden and Ed Stark, co-editors
Fletcher Pratt, *Land of Unreason*, 1942
  L. Sprague de Camp, co-author
Clifford D. Simak, *Out of Their Minds*, 1970
Bill Slavicsek, *Storm Knights*, 1990
  C.J. Tramontana, co-author
Ed Stark, *Mysterious Cairo*, 1992
  editor

2403

GUY GAVRIEL KAY

The Lions of Al-Rassan

(New York: HarperPrism, 1995)

Story type: Fantasy (Political)
Major character(s): Ammar ibn Khairan, Military Personnel, Courtier; Rodrigo Belmonte, Mercenary; Jehane bet Ishak, Doctor
Time period(s): Indeterminate Past
Locale(s): Al-Rassan, Fictional Country; Cartada, Fictional City

Summary: Created centuries ago by the savage Asharites, the Empire of Al-Rassan has since collapsed into warring states. There, three very different people pursue their fates against the backdrop of one king's drive for reunification. This novel draws heavily on the history of Moorish Spain for inspiration and flavor.

Other books you might like:

Glen Cook, *The Fire in His Hands*, 1984
Barbara Hambly, *The Ladies of Mandrigyn*, 1984
Katherine Kurtz, *Deryni Rising*, 1970
Mark E. Rogers, *The Expected One*, 1991
Judith Tarr, *Alamut*, 1989

2404

GUY GAVRIEL KAY

A Song for Arbonne

(New York: Crown, 1993)

Story type: Fantasy (Historical; Romance)
Major character(s): Bertran de Talair, Nobleman, Minstrel; Blaise de Garsenc, Nobleman, Mercenary; Lisseut of Vezet, Minstrel
Time period(s): Indeterminate Past
Locale(s): Arbonne, Fictional Country; Gorhaut, Fictional Country

Summary: Self-exiled from the grim, misogynistic kingdom of Gorhaut, Blaise de Garsenc accepts a job as captain of the guards for a minor baron in Arbonne, the sunny, Goddess-worshipping country to the south, whose citizens exalt love

and music. As the King of Gorhaut plots to conquer Arbonne, Blaise meets the priestess of Rian, the Queen of the Court of Love, and a noble minstrel who teach him about Arbonnais culture and politics. When Gorhaut invades Arbonne, Blaise finds his own destiny as he chooses among his divided loyalties.

Other books you might like:

Gael Baudino, *Maze of Moonlight*, 1993
Marion Zimmer Bradley, *The Mists of Avalon*, 1983
Parke Godwin, *Firelord*, 1980
Norah Lofts, *The Lute Player*, 1951
Diana L. Paxson, *The White Raven*, 1988
Elizabeth Marie Pope, *The Perilous Gard*, 1974
Chelsea Quinn Yarbro, *The Palace*, 1978

2405

GUY GAVRIEL KAY

Tigana

(New York: Roc, 1990)

Story type: Fantasy (Political)
Major character(s): Alessan bar Valentin, Royalty (Prince of Tigana); Brandin of Ygrath, Ruler, Sorcerer
Time period(s): Indeterminate
Locale(s): The 9 Countries of the Palm, Fictional Country (Peninsula)

Summary: Eighteen years ago, when the countries of the Palm were invaded by competing sorcerer kings (Brandin and Alberico) from overseas, Prince Valentin of Tigana killed Brandin's son in battle and Brandin cast a spell that stripped the ability to hear "Tigana" from the minds of every person not born on Tigana's soil before the battle. Now all the work and planning of Valentin's son Alessan culminate in a final campaign to rid the Palm of its tyrants and release Tigana's name.

Other books you might like:

Steven Brust, *Brokedown Palace*, 1986
Heather Gladney, *Teot's War*, 1988
Katharine Kerr, *Daggerspell*, 1986
Diana L. Paxson, *The White Raven*, 1988
M.K. Wren, *Sword of the Lamb*, 1981

2406

JEREMY KAY

The Secret Laboratory Journals of Dr. Victor Frankenstein

(New York: Overlook Press, 1995)

Story type: Horror (Reanimated Dead)
Major character(s): Victor Frankenstein, Scientist
Time period(s): 1800s (early)
Locale(s): Germany; Switzerland

Summary: Incorporating diaries and journals, this book is presented as Victor Frankenstein's random notes on how he came to conceive of, and build, his infamous monster. This heavily illustrated book "reproduces" laboratory diagrams and script in Victor's own hand, and incorporates his thoughts on, among other things, his scientific education, his family, the services of the local graverobbers, and of course the reanimation of dead body parts.

Other books you might like:

Brian W. Aldiss, *Frankenstein Unbound*, 1973
Martin H. Greenberg, *Frankenstein: The Monster Wakes*, 1993
    editor
Stephen Jones, *The Mammoth Book of Frankenstein*, 1995
    editor
Michel Parry, *Rivals of Frankenstein*, 1977
    editor
Theodore Roszak, *The Memoirs of Elizabeth Frankenstein*, 1995
Mary Shelley, *Frankenstein*, 1818
Robert Weinberg, *Vampire Diary: The Embrace*, 1995
    Mark Rein-Hagen, co-author

2407

SUSAN KAY

Phantom

(New York: Delacorte, 1991)

Story type: Horror (Mystery)
Major character(s): Erik, Child, Musician; Madeleine, Parent (mother of Erik); Christine Daae, Student (vocal student), Singer
Time period(s): 19th century (1831-1851)
Locale(s): Paris, France; Nisni-Novgorod, Persia; Rome, Italy

Summary: This sweeping historical romance and prequel to Gaston Leroux's *The Phantom of the Opera* chronicles the plight of Erik, born hideously deformed, ultimately separated from his beloved mother, and forced to make his living while a child in courts and carnival side shows across two continents. It is in the sewer system beneath the Paris Opera House, however, that Erik finds a suitable dwelling and a base of operations from which to indulge his infatuation with a beautiful opera singer for whom he becomes an anonymous benefactor.

Other books you might like:

Kobo Abe, *The Face of Another*, 1966
Barbara Hambly, *Beauty and the Beast*, 1989
Gaston Leroux, *The Phantom of the Opera*, 1910
Steve Vance, *Spook*, 1990

2408

MARVIN KAYE, Editor

Angels of Darkness

(Garden City, NY: Guild America, 1995)

Story type: Horror (Anthology)

Summary: The forty-four stories and poems in this anthology—divided equally between male and female authors—all feature women as either victims or perpetrators of horrors. Classic tales include Henry James's ''The Friend of the Friends,'' in which a man falls in love with a woman who turns out to be a ghost, Nathaniel Hawthorne's ''Lady Elea-

nor's Mantle,'' in which a woman's beauty is attributed to the magical power of her mantle, and Clemence Housman's ''The Were-Wolf,'' in which love for a human male redeems a female werewolf. More modern stories include Robert Bloch's ''The Unspeakable Betrothal,'' about a young girl ensorcelled by powers from beyond, Julian Kilman's ''The Mystery of the Black Jean,'' in which a woman befriends an abused pet to help her dispose of its owner, and Maurice Level's *conte cruel* ''The Last Kiss,'' about the just desserts that come to a woman who has disfigured her lover's face with acid. Paula Volsky supplies the introduction.

Other books you might like:

Seon Manley, *Women of the Weird*, 1976
    Gogo Lewis, co-editor
Kathryn Ptacek, *Women of Darkness*, 1988
    editor
Kathryn Ptacek, *Women of Darkness II*, 1990
    editor
Lisa Tuttle, *Skin of the Soul*, 1991
    editor

2409

MARVIN KAYE

Fantastique

(New York: St. Martin's, 1992)

Story type: Horror (Literary)
Major character(s): Carl Richards, Director (theatre); Diana Lee Taylor, Actress (Carl's Wife); Angelica Winters, Actress
Time period(s): 1990s (1992)
Locale(s): New York, New York

Summary: Although renowned for his outrageous stagings of violent plays, Carl Richards realizes something is wrong with his current staging of Buchner's *Woyzeck* when a series of accidents push the violence over the edge from simulated to actual. Patterned on Hector Berlioz's *Symphonie Fantastique*, this novel tells of Carl's obsession with his wife's understudy in the play, Angelica Winters, whose presence has an uncanny disintegrating effect on the production and on Carl's private life.

Other books you might like:

Ramsey Campbell, *Ancient Images*, 1989
Chet Williamson, *Reign*, 1990

2410

MARVIN KAYE, Editor

Lovers and Other Monsters

(Garden City, New York: Guild America, 1992)

Story type: Horror (Anthology)

Summary: Fifty-three stories and poems concerned with the darker side of love. Included are Ray Bradbury's macabre prose poem, ''The Maiden,'' H.P. Lovecraft's tale of longing for the past, ''The Strange High House in the Mist,'' Jerome Bixby and Joe E. Dean's tale of an unusual vampiric relationship, ''Share Alike,'' Edgar Allan Poe's gruesome vignette on obsession, "Berenice," and Frank Stockton's classic tale of sexual politics, "The Lady or the Tiger," along with Jack Moffitt's contemporary response, "The Lady and the Tiger."

Other books you might like:

Margaret L. Carter, *Demon Lovers and Strange Seductions*, 1973

Don Congdon, *Tales of Love and Horror*, 1961

Ellen Datlow, *Alien Sex*, 1991
  editor

Jeff Gelb, *Hot Blood: Tales of Provocative Horror*, 1989
  Lonn Friend, co-editor

Michele Slung, *I Shudder at Your Touch*, 1991

2411

MARVIN KAYE

Masterpieces of Terror and the Unknown

(Garden City, New York: Guild America, 1993)

Story type: Horror (Anthology)

Summary: A collection of 58 tales of horror and the supernatural that span several centuries. Included are ghost stories such as Arthur Machen's "The Happy Children" and Algernon Blackwood's "Keeping His Promise"; Theodore Sturgeon's tale of perverse obsession, "Bianca's Hands"; A. Merritt's tale of a lost race that lives in the Arctic wastes, "The People of the Pit"; H.P. Lovecraft's fusion of cosmic horror and mathematics, "Dreams in the Witch House"; Maurice Level's *conte cruel*, "The Cripple"; Edward Lucas White's ghoul story "Amina"; and Richard Matheson's vampire tale, "A Dress of White Silk."

Other books you might like:

David G. Hartwell, *The Dark Descent*, 1987
  editor

Bill Pronzini, *The Arbor House Treasury of Horror and the Supernatural*, 1981
  Barry Malzberg and Martin H. Greenberg, co-editors

Herbert Wise, *Great Tales of Terror and the Supernatural*, 1944
  Phyllis Fraser, co-editor

2412

MARVIN KAYE, Editor

Weird Tales, The Magazine That Never Dies

(New York: Barnes & Noble, 1995)

Story type: Horror (Anthology)

Summary: Originally published in 1987, this omnibus volume presents one essay and 44 stories of fantasy and horror gathered from *Weird Tales*. The magazine was originally published between 1923 and 1954, and later, there were four short-lived attempts to revive it. Tales from the original magazine include Robert E. Howard's swashbuckling tale of adventurer Solomon Kane, "The Skulls in the Stars"; Ray Bradbury's brief tale of the afterlife, "Interim"; C. Hall Thompson's tale of psychopathology, "The Pale Criminal"; Richard Matheson's ghost story, "Wet Straw"; and H.P.

Lovecraft's urban horror story, "He." Tales from the more recent incarnation of the magazine include Ed Hoch's ghostly "Funeral in the Fog," Katherine MacLean and Mary Kornbluth's wry "Chicken Soup," and a recently discovered tale by William Hope Hodgson, "The Terror of the Water Tank."

Other books you might like:

John Betancourt, *The Best of Weird Tales*, 1995
  editor

Robert Weinberg, *100 Wild Little Weird Tales*, 1995
  Martin H. Greenberg, Stefan Dziemianowicz, co-editor

Stefan Dziemianowicz, *Weird Tales: 32 Unearthed Terrors*, 1987
  Robert Weinberg, Martin H. Greenberg, co-editor

Robert Weinberg, *The Eighth Green Man and Other Strange Folk*, 1989
  editor

Robert Weinberg, *Far Below and Other Horrors*, 1974
  editor

2413

MEL KEEGAN

Death's Head

(London: Gay Men's Press, 1993)

Story type: Science Fiction (Military; Gay/Lesbian Fiction)

Major character(s): Kevin Jarrat, Military Personnel, Homosexual; Jerry Stone, Military Personnel, Homosexual

Time period(s): 23rd century

Locale(s): Rethan, Planet—Imaginary

Summary: The NARCs fight the spread of an invariably deadly drug called Angel with co-captains who alternate undercover and command duties and backed up with massive military force. The NARC code demands non-involvement between captains, but Kevin and Stoney must defy it when kidnapping forces Stoney on Angel and his only hope becomes an unbreakable empathic link with Kevin.

Other books you might like:

Chris Claremont, *Grounded!*, 1991

Diane Duane, *High Moon*, 1992
  Peter Morwood, co-author

Maureen F. McHugh, *China Mountain Zhang*, 1992

George Nader, *Chrome*, 1979

Walter Jon Williams, *Days of Atonement*, 1991

2414

PAM KEESEY, Editor

Darker Angels: Lesbian Vampire Stories

(Pittsburgh: Cleis Press, 1995)

Story type: Horror (Anthology; Vampire Story)

Summary: Six original and five reprint stories feature female vampires and their mostly female victims. In Gary Bowen's historical "Blood Wedding," a female aristocrat seduces the wife of her husband's best friend in a vampire tryst. Melanie Tem's "Presence" features a woman driven to various forms of carnality through her insatiable need for love, and Lawrence Schimel's "Femme de Siecle" a vampire who becomes bisexual to serve her monthly needs. In Shawn Dell's "Daria Dangerous," a woman recounts her death at the hands of an irresistible female vampire. The editor supplies an introduction on the history of the lesbian vampire theme and a bibliography of additional readings.

Other books you might like:

Poppy Z. Brite, *Love in Vein*, 1994
  Martin H. Greenberg, co-editor
Martin H. Greenberg, *Vamps*, 1988
  Charles G. Waugh, co-editor
Amarantha Knight, *Love Bites*, 1995
  editor
Cecilia Tan, *Blood Kiss: Vampire Erotica*, 1994
  editor

2415

PAM KEESEY, Editor

Daughters of Darkness: Lesbian Vampire Stories

(San Francisco, California: Cleis Press, 1993)

Story type: Horror (Anthology; Vampire Story)

Summary: This book collects nine stories and novel excerpts featuring lesbian vampires. Included are J. Sheridan Le Fanu's Victorian classic, "Carmilla," Jewelle Gomez's "Louisiana 1850," featuring her black feminist vampire Gilda, and a portion of Elaine Bergstrom's novel *Daughter of the Night*, one of several that chronicle the history of a centuries-old vampire family.

Other books you might like:

Ellen Datlow, *Blood Is Not Enough*, 1989
  editor
Ellen Datlow, *A Whisper of Blood*, 1991
  editor
Jewelle Gomez, *The Gilda Stories*, 1991
Martin H. Greenberg, *Vamps*, 1987
  editor
Stephen Jones, *The Mammoth Book of Vampires*, 1992
  editor
Alan Ryan, *Vampires: Two Centuries of Great Vampire Stories*, 1987
  editor

2416

PAM KEESEY, Editor

Women Who Run with Werewolves: Tales of Blood, Lust and Metamorphosis

(Boston: Cleis Press, 1996)

Story type: Horror (Anthology; Werewolf Story)

Summary: Fifteen stories, three of them reprints, use the werewolf theme to explore issues of female identity. Lycanthropy is equated with split personality in Charlee Jacobs' "Permafrost" and with a girl's sexual maturation in Suzy McKee Charnas' "Boobs." The werewolf symbolizes a man's transformation from a loving husband to a brutal mate in Ursula K.

Le Guin's "The Wife's Story" and freedom from a life of repression in Jeremy E. Johnson's "Euphorbia Helioscopia." An excerpt from Melanie Tem's novel *Wilding* features a matriarchal family of werewolves, while Tom Piccirilli's "The Hound of God" is concerned with a female werewolf whose affliction empowers her to rid her neighborhood of criminals.

Other books you might like:

Martin H. Greenberg, *Werewolves*, 1995
  editor
Stephen Jones, *The Mammoth Book of Werewolves*, 1994
  editor
Byron Preiss, *The Ultimate Werewolf*, 1991
  David Keller, Megan Miller, John Gregory Betancourt, co-editors

---

2417

STEPHANIE KEGAN

The Baby

(New York: Diamond, 1990)

Story type: Horror (Haunted House; Child-in-Peril)
Major character(s): Jill Douglas, Housewife (mother-to-be); Tom Douglas, Doctor (Jill's husband); Dora Miles, Widow(er) (Tom's deceased aunt)
Time period(s): 1990s (1990)
Locale(s): Bay Area, California

Summary: When Jill and Tom Douglas move into the house of Tom's recently-deceased aunt, a series of inexplicable experiences leaves Jill believing either that she is going insane or that an evil presence wants her unborn child. This is the author's first novel.

Other books you might like:

Ken Eulo, *The Brownstone*, 1980
Ira Levin, *Rosemary's Baby*, 1967
Robert Marasco, *Burnt Offerings*, 1973
Graham Masterton, *Walkers*, 1989
Randall Boyll, *After Sundown*, 1989

2418

ANDREW KEITH

Cohort of the Damned

(New York: Roc, 1993)

Story type: Science Fiction (Military; Adventure)
Series: Fifth Foreign Legion
Major character(s): Wolfgang "Karl Wolf" Hauser, Military Personnel, Leader (lance); Lisa Scott, Military Personnel (recruit)
Time period(s): 29th century
Locale(s): Devereaux, Planet—Imaginary (Beau Soleil System)

Summary: After facing an enemy and being called a coward, Wolfgang Hauser changes his name and joins the Fifth Foreign Legion. He participates in several fights with enemies and himself as he grows up during basic training.

Other books you might like:
Bill Baldwin, *The Helmsman*, 1985
Gordon R. Dickson, *Dorsai!*, 1976
William C. Dietz, *Legion of the Damned*, 1993
William R. Forstchen, *Rally Cry!*, 1990
Robert Randle, *Seeds of War*, 1986
  Robert Cornett, co-author

2419

ANDREW KEITH
WILLIAM H. KEITH JR., Co-Author

March or Die

(New York: Roc, 1992)

Story type: Science Fiction (Military; Adventure)
Series: Fifth Foreign Legion
Major character(s): Colin Fraser, Military Personnel; Kelly Ann Winters, Engineer, Military Personnel; John "Slick" Grant, Military Personnel
Time period(s): 29th century
Locale(s): Hanuman, Planet—Imaginary

Summary: When Terran Commonwealth officials are assassinated at a diplomatic reception in the capital city of Hanuman, native forces initiate a simultaneous attack on the half-finished Foreign Legion Fortress. Surrounded by hostile forces and written off by higher-ups, the surviving troops choose to fight their way over the mountains to the relative safety of the Legion's main base.

Other books you might like:
Robert Asprin, *The Bug Wars*, 1979
Gordon R. Dickson, *Dorsai!*, 1976
Gordon R. Dickson, *Soldier, Ask Not*, 1967
Jerry Pournelle, *Falkenberg's Legion*, 1990
Elizabeth Ann Scarborough, *The Healer's War*, 1989
Jack Williamson, *The Legion of Space*, 1947

2420

WILLIAM H. KEITH JR.

Warlords of Jupiter

(Lake Geneva, Wisconsin: TSR, 1993)

Story type: Science Fiction (Political)
Series: Invaders of Charon
Major character(s): Vince Pirelli, Spaceman, Warrior; Jovanna Trask, Spacewoman, Warrior
Time period(s): 25th century
Locale(s): Amalthea, Space Station (Jovian); Jupiter

Summary: While investigating the origin of a seemingly alien artifact lost by enemy forces, Vince and others come to the aid of winged giants and find new allies and possible leads in their search. Jovanna and others on Amalthea meet an invading force with deadly results. Concludes the trilogy set in the *Buck Rogers* milieu.

Other books you might like:
Britton Bloom, *Matrix Cubed*, 1991
C.M. Brennan, *The Genesis Web*, 1992
John Miller, *First Power Play*, 1990

M.S. Murdock, *Armageddon Off Vesta*, 1989
M.S. Murdock, *Hammer of Mars*, 1989
M.S. Murdock, *Prime Squared*, 1990
M.S. Murdock, *Rebellion 2456*, 1989
Philip Francis Nowlan, *Armageddon 2419 A.D.*, 1962
John Silbersack, *Roger's Rangers*, 1983

2421

WILLIAM H. KEITH JR.

Warstrider

(New York: AvoNova, 1993)

Story type: Science Fiction (Military)
Series: Warstrider
Major character(s): Dev Cameron, Military Personnel
Time period(s): 26th century
Locale(s): Terran Hegemony, Interstellar Empire/Federation

Summary: Hoping to join the Hegemony Navy, Dev Cameron instead signs up for military duty and finds himself in the army, utilizing his neural implants not to operate a spaceship, but rather to direct heavy weaponry against alien Xenophobe invaders intent on wiping out humanity.

Other books you might like:
Robert Asprin, *The Bug Wars*, 1979
Orson Scott Card, *Ender's Game*, 1985
Gordon R. Dickson, *Dorsai!*, 1975
David Drake, *Battlestation*, 1992
  Bill Fawcett, co-editor
Andrew Keith, *Honor and Fidelity*, 1992
  William H. Keith, Jr., co-author
G. Harry Stine, *The Lost Battalion*, 1989
David Weber, *Path of the Fury*, 1992
Dave Wolverton, *On My Way to Paradise*, 1989

2422

WILLIAM H. KEITH JR.

Warstrider: Netlink

(New York: AvoNova, 1995)

Story type: Science Fiction (Alternate Intelligence; Genetic Manipulation)
Series: Warstrider
Major character(s): Dev Cameron, Genetically Altered Being, Space Explorer; Kara Hagan, Military Personnel (Confederation lieutenant); Daren Cameron, Scholar, Scientist (Xenologist)
Time period(s): Indeterminate Future
Locale(s): Mars; *Sirghal*, Spaceship

Summary: While Confederate Rebels fight to maintain their independence from the Earth Imperium, Dev Cameron, once human but now part of a neurally-linked alien fleet, discovers a new alien threat so vast that human conflicts seem insignificant in comparison.

Other books you might like:
Keith William Andrews, *The Freedom's Rangers Series*, 1989-1991
  pseudonym of William H. Keith Jr.

Valerie J. Freireich, *Becoming Human*, 1995
Anne McCaffrey, *The Ship Who Sang*, 1995
John Varley, *The Ophiuchi Hotline*, 1977

2423

ED KELLEHER
HARRIETTE VIDAL, Co-Author

Animus

(New York: Leisure, 1993)

Story type: Horror (Doppelganger; Evil Children)
Major character(s): Catherine Bishop, Artisan (dollmaker); Ian Bishop, Art Dealer (gallery owner); Julian Bishop, Child (Catherine and Ian's son)
Time period(s): 1980s (1984); 1990s (1993)
Locale(s): New York, New York

Summary: Catherine Bishop is horrified to learn that her imaginary childhood playmate, Bobo, is actually her animus, the male side of her personality which murders to protect her whenever she feels threatened. She's even more horrified when Bobo becomes incarnated as her only son, Julian.

Other books you might like:
Ramsey Campbell, *To Wake the Dead*, 1980
Rick Hautala, *Cold Whisper*, 1991
Edmund Plante, *Seed of Evil*, 1991

2424

ED KELLEHER
HARRIETTE VIDAL, Co-Author

Breeder

(New York: Leisure, 1991)

Story type: Horror (Black Magic)
Major character(s): Janet Young, Artist; Whitney Lancaster, Political Figure (mayor); Miranda Jane Young, Teenager
Time period(s): 1990s
Locale(s): Mount Garde, New York (Long Island)

Summary: A vacation to her family home to escape the pressures of life in Manhattan turns into a nightmare when Janet Young, her new husband and her psychically endowed step-daughter Miranda discover that Janet's hometown has been taken over by Satanists, who have reanimated dead townspeople as zombies and plan to make her family their next sacrifice to placate the Devil.

Other books you might like:
Charles L. Grant, *The Hour of the Oxrun Dead*, 1977
Ira Levin, *The Stepford Wives*, 1972
John Saul, *Creature*, 1989

2425

ED KELLEHER
HARRIETTE VIDAL, Co-Author

The School

(New York: Leisure, 1992)

Story type: Horror (Black Magic)

Major character(s): Vanessa Forbes, Student; Bobby Cannon, Student; Matthew Hanley, Principal (headmaster)
Time period(s): 1990s
Locale(s): Hanley, Massachusetts

Summary: Students at the Hanley School for Girls are given to bizarre visions and the expression of unbridled lusts, owing to a taint upon the land where the school was built. Sixty years after headmaster Malcolm Hanley was slain by an obsessed student, the performance of that student's play about witchcraft, "Flowers of Darkness," by the Hanley School's theatre class threatens to unleash the dark forces with which the school has become imbued. This novel was originally published in 1988.

Other books you might like:
Edward Lee, *Coven*, 1990
David van Meter Smith, *Trinity Grove*, 1990

2426

VICTOR KELLEHER

The Red King

(New York: Dial, 1990)

Story type: Fantasy (Adventure; Young Adult)
Major character(s): Timkin, Slave; Petie, Thief
Time period(s): Indeterminate Past
Locale(s): Forest Lands, Fictional Country

Summary: Timkin survives the red powder released by the Red King's men, only to be put back into the slave collar by Petie after he was certain she would live. Timkin realizes that the real enemy is the Red King, who Timkin and Petie hope to defeat at the Gathering, the biggest fair of the season.

Other books you might like:
Grace Chetwin, *The Crystal Stair*, 1988
Grace Chetwin, *Gom on Windy Mountain*, 1986
Grace Chetwin, *The Riddle and the Rune*, 1987
Rosemary Kerstein, *The Steerswoman*, 1989
Nancy Springer, *Red Wizard*, 1990

2427

MARJORIE BRADLEY KELLOGG

The Book of Earth

(New York: DAW, 1995)

Story type: Fantasy (Sword and Sorcery)
Series: Dragon Quartet
Major character(s): Erde von Alte, Noblewoman, Psychic (dragon guide); Earth, Mythical Creature (dragon), Guardian (Erde's); Guillemo Gotti, Religious (priest), Psychic (prophet)
Time period(s): Indeterminate
Locale(s): Germany; Tor Alte, Fictional Country; Deep Moor, Fictional Country

Summary: Having lost everyone close to her because of the machinations of an evil priest, Brother Guillemo Gotti, young Erde von Alte flees her father's mountain domain, literally stumbling across Earth, one of four dragons created from elemental energies to help set the world in motion. Erde helps

Earth in his quest to find the One who has awakened him before his time, while the dragon aids Erde in staying one step ahead of Brother Guillemo, who would burn her as a witch.

Other books you might like:
Terry Goodkind, *Wizard's First Rule*, 1994
Michael Green, *Quest: In Search of the Dragontooth*, 1994
Barbara Hambly, *Dragonsbane*, 1986
Robert Jordan, *The Eye of the World*, 1989
Anne McCaffrey, *Dragonflight*, 1968
Anne McCaffrey, *Moreta's Story*, 1983
Mark C. Perry, *Morigu: The Dead*, 1990

2428

MARJORIE BRADLEY KELLOGG

Harmony
(New York: Roc, 1991)

Story type: Science Fiction (Arts)
Major character(s): Gwinn Rhys, Artist, Apprentice; Micah Miguel Cervantes, Artist (master scenographer)
Time period(s): 2040s
Locale(s): Chicago, Illinois (domed city); Harmony, Vermont (domed city); Tuamatuetuamatu, Pacific Islands (imaginary)

Summary: In the late 20th century the largest and richest cities built domes which kept pollution and excess population out. When the domes were completed, quite desperate people camped in large groups in the squalid, unhealthy conditions surrounding the domes. One of the first cities to construct a dome, Chicago, outlawed art as frivolous. However, Gwinn's talent is too compelling for her not to risk expulsion in her bid to move to Harmony, the domed artists' enclave, where she meets the Eye, a dance troupe which uses magic to tell their story.

Other books you might like:
Eleanor Arnason, *A Woman of the Iron People*, 1990
Pat Cadigan, *Synners*, 1991
Ernest Hogan, *Cortez on Jupiter*, 1990
James Patrick Kelly, *Look into the Sun*, 1989
Pat Murphy, *The City, Not Long After*, 1989
Sheri S. Tepper, *The Gate to Women's Country*, 1988

2429

JAMES PATRICK KELLY

Look into the Sun
(New York: Tor, 1989)

Story type: Science Fiction (First Contact)
Major character(s): Phillip Wing, Architect; Teaqua, Deity (Goddess), Ruler
Time period(s): 21st century
Locale(s): Earth; Aseneshesh, Planet—Imaginary

Summary: Phillip Wing, who built one of 21st century Earth's greatest architectural masterpieces, is haunted by feelings of mediocrity and the fear that he will never again achieve greatness. Wing therefore jumps at the chance to travel to Aseneshesh and build there a tomb for Teaqua, the planet's

resident goddess. Teaqua, meanwhile, plots desperately to bring change to her planet's stagnant culture before it is swallowed up by the Messengers, a more advanced alien race whose cultural imperialism threatens both Aseneshesh and Earth.

Other books you might like:
Octavia E. Butler, *Adulthood Rites*, 1988
Octavia E. Butler, *Dawn*, 1987
Octavia E. Butler, *Imago*, 1989
Orson Scott Card, *Speaker for the Dead*, 1986
Mary Gentle, *Ancient Light*, 1989
Mary Gentle, *Golden Witchbreed*, 1983
Ursula K. Le Guin, *The Left Hand of Darkness*, 1969

2430

JAMES PATRICK KELLY

Wildlife
(New York: Tor, 1994)

Story type: Science Fiction (Genetic Manipulation; Alternate Intelligence)
Major character(s): Wynne Cage, Journalist, Genetically Altered Being; Francois Bonivard, Computer Expert, Handicapped; Peter Cage, Genetically Altered Being
Time period(s): 22nd century (2100s)
Locale(s): Chillon, Switzerland; New Canaan, Connecticut; Gatsby, Asteroid

Summary: After stealing WILDLIFE, a program to create true artificial intelligence called a cognizer, Wynne meets the dying Bonivard who plans to use it to make himself immortal. Wynne stays with him until he dies, moves to Connecticut where she has herself changed into a Statue of Liberty, and keeps her son, Peter, a child. Peter and WILDLIFE escape before Wynne as the Statue of Liberty dies and Wynne, again a young woman, finds herself living on a space station, unaware of her origins.

Other books you might like:
Greg Bear, *Blood Music*, 1985
Pat Cadigan, *Mindplayers*, 1987
Jean Mark Gawron, *Dream of Glass*, 1993
James P. Hogan, *The Multiplex Man*, 1992
John Kessel, *Freedom Beach*, 1985
    James Patrick Kelly, co-author
Dan Simmons, *The Hollow Man*, 1992
Amy Thomson, *Virtual Girl*, 1993
David Weber, *Path of the Fury*, 1992

2431

ROBERT B. KELLY

The Cloud People
(Lake Geneva, Wisconsin: TSR, 1991)

Story type: Fantasy (Quest; Science Fiction)
Major character(s): Paul Benjarth, Heir (Fief Karcan), Adventurer
Time period(s): Indeterminate
Locale(s): Calferon, Planet—Imaginary

Summary: When the ruling Duke disappears, a magic talisman falls into evil hands and strife threatens the previously peaceful society. Paul Benjarth sets off to retrace his great-great-grandfather's legendary descent from their aerial world to the surface of Calferon, hoping to discover the secret to his world's survival. This is the author's first novel.

Other books you might like:
Stephen Baxter, *Raft*, 1992
John Brosnan, *The Sky Lords*, 1991
Rosemary Kirstein, *The Steerswoman*, 1989
Anne McCaffrey, *All the Weyrs of Pern*, 1991
Larry Niven, *The Integral Trees*, 1984
Terry Pratchett, *Strata*, 1981
J.R.R. Tolkien, *The Hobbit*, 1938
John Varley, *Wizard*, 1981
Margaret Weis, *Dragon Wing*, 1990
   Tracy Hickman, co-author
Margaret Weis, *Elven Star*, 1990
   Tracy Hickman, co-author
Margaret Weis, *Fire Sea*, 1991
   Tracy Hickman, co-author

2432

RONALD KELLY

Blood Kin

(New York: Zebra, 1996)

Story type: Horror (Vampire Story)
Major character(s): Boyd Andrews, Carpenter; Tammy Craven, Teacher (Sunday school); Dudley Craven, Farmer
Time period(s): 1990s (1996)
Locale(s): Green Hollow, Tennessee

Summary: When farmer Dudley Craven accidentally plows up his grandfather's coffin and removes a stake plunged into the crumbling remains, he unwittingly resurrects the vampire Josiah Crave. Josiah sates his eternal thirst first on his family, and then on others in the surrounding community, threatening to turn the entire countryside into vampires.

Other books you might like:
Ron Dee, *Dusk*, 1991
Stephen King, *Salem's Lot*, 1975
Jason Nickles, *Immortal*, 1996
Patrick Whalen, *Night Thirst*, 1991

2433

RONALD KELLY

Father's Little Helper

(New York: Zebra, 1992)

Story type: Horror (Serial Killer)
Major character(s): Ben Gatlin, Police Officer (sheriff); Sonny McFarland, Teenager; Kathe Shelby, FBI Agent
Time period(s): 1990s (1992)
Locale(s): Cedar Bluff, Tennessee

Summary: Inspired by the memory of his mass murderer father—and possibly possessed by his spirit—Sonny McFarland turns from mild-mannered teenager to serial killer and returns to Cedar Bluff, Tennessee, the site of his father's final bloody rampage, to dispatch the survivors of that infamous event of 14 years before.

Other books you might like:
Douglas Borton, *Kane*, 1990
Dean R. Koontz, *Hideaway*, 1991
Joe R. Lansdale, *Cold in July*, 1989

2434

RONALD KELLY

Moon of the Werewolf

(New York: Zebra, 1991)

Story type: Horror (Werewolf Story)
Major character(s): Patrick O'Shea, Undertaker, Werewolf; Devin O'Shea, Teenager, Werewolf; Rosie O'Shea, Teenager, Werewolf
Time period(s): 1990s (1990)
Locale(s): Old Hickory, Tennessee

Summary: The O'Sheas are a contented quartet of werewolves, feeding off the corpses father Patrick brings home from his undertaking business, until rebellious teenagers Rosie and Devin fail to keep their appetites and passions in check and bring the family into contact with the probing citizens of Old Hickory.

Other books you might like:
Ray Bradbury, ''The Homecoming'', 1947
   in *Dark Carnival*
Tanya Huff, *Blood Price*, 1992
S.P. Somtow, *Moon Dance*, 1989
Whitley Strieber, *The Wolfen*, 1978
Jack Williamson, *Darker than You Think*, 1948

2435

RONALD KELLY

Pitfall

(New York: Zebra, 1990)

Story type: Horror (Nature in Revolt)
Major character(s): Felix Booth, Lawman (sheriff); Bowie Kane, Handyman, Indian; Roger Ketcham, Doctor
Time period(s): 1990s
Locale(s): Sulphur Springs, Texas

Summary: Two rednecks whose dogfights have been shut down travel to Mexico where they purchase and bring back to Texas several Tasmanian devils, *diablos hoyos*, for their pit fights. When the creatures escape and attack a small west-Texas town, only Indian handyman Bowie Kane and his magic talisman offer hope in this violent paean to 1950s grade-B horror films.

Other books you might like:
Michael R. Linaker, *Scorpion*, 1980
Thomas F. Monteleone, *Night Things*, 1980
Les Simons, *Gila*, 1981
Peter Tremayne, *The Ants*, 1979

2436

RONALD KELLY

The Possession

(New York: Zebra, 1993)

Story type: Horror (Possession)
Major character(s): Laura Locke, Writer; Rick Gardener, Artist; Wade Monroe, Paranormal Investigator
Time period(s): 1990s (1993)
Locale(s): Franklin, Tennessee

Summary: Bestselling historical romance writer Laura Locke thinks it's a dream come true when she buys the Magnolia plantation, but it's only the beginning of a nightmare. Haunted by the spirits of people who participated in an unredressed Civil War atrocity, the house takes over whoever strays onto the premises and forces them to re-enact the shameless deed that has left it cursed.

Other books you might like:
Tom Elliott, *The Dwelling*, 1989
Judith Hawkes, *Julian's House*, 1989
Al Sarrantonio, *House Haunted*, 1991

2437

RONALD KELLY

Something Out There

(New York: Zebra, 1991)

Story type: Horror (Small Town Horror)
Major character(s): Jenny Brice, Artist; Jackson Dellhart, Businessman (owner of Eco-Plenty Corp.); Anthony Stoogeone, Organized Crime Figure (hit man)
Time period(s): 1990s
Locale(s): Tucker's Mill, Tennessee

Summary: Jenny Brice returns to her home town to investigate her father's murder and continue protecting the race of shapeshifters who have been the Brice family's responsibility for generations. But she runs afoul of the land-hungry Eco-Plenty Corporation, the devious conspirators behind her father's death who have as little respect for the land as they have belief in the supernatural.

Other books you might like:
Joseph Citro, *The Unseen*, 1990
John Farris, *Wildwood*, 1987

2438

FLOYD KEMSKE

Human Resources

(North Haven, Connecticut: Catbird Press, 1995)

Story type: Horror (Vampire Story; Satire)
Major character(s): Norman, Businessman (human resources); Jacqueline, Businesswoman (human resources); Pierce, Vampire
Time period(s): 1990s (1996)
Locale(s): Paris, France; United States

Summary: Pierce, a vampire who has learned to hone his ruthlessness over the past two centuries of his life, finds his talents uniquely suited to the current corporate environment in America. Hired as a re-engineering consultant by Biomethods, Inc., he sets about revamping the company to survive in a dog-eat-dog world. Although copyrighted 1995, this novel was not available until 1996.

Other books you might like:
Thomas M. Disch, *The Businessman: A Tale of Terror*, 1984
Lionel Fenn, *The Mark of the Moderately Vicious Vampire*, 1992
David Prill, *The Unnatural*, 1995
William Browning Spencer, *Resume with Monsters*, 1995

2439

PATRICIA KENNEALY

The Hawk's Gray Feather

(New York: Roc, 1990)

Story type: Fantasy (Science Fiction)
Series: Keltiad: Tales of Arthur
Major character(s): Arthur, Royalty (Foster brother of Taliesin), Military Personnel; Taliesen, Writer, Minstrel (Bard)
Time period(s): Indeterminate
Locale(s): Keltia, Interstellar Empire/Federation; Gwynedd, Planet—Imaginary

Summary: Taliesin tells the story: A Counterinsurgency group develops in order to free the people of Keltia from a tyrannical ruler. Arthur becomes adept at warfare but trouble with another heir to the throne precipitates an unhappy marriage and tragedy follows.

Other books you might like:
Kenneth C. Flint, *Isle of Destiny*, 1988
Katharine Kerr, *The Bristling Wood*, 1989
Stephen R. Lawhead, *Arthur*, 1989
Peter Tremayne, *My Lady of Hi-Brasil*, 1987
Paul Edwin Zimmer, *Blood of the Colyn Muir*, 1988

2440

PATRICIA KENNEALY

The Hedge of Mist

(New York: HarperPrism, 1996)

Story type: Science Fiction (Science Fantasy; Political)
Series: Keltiad: Tales of Arthur
Major character(s): Taliesen, Minstrel (bard), Writer; Arthur "Artos" Pendreic, Ruler (King of the Kelts); Morguenna Pendreic, Royalty (Princess of Keltia), Spouse (Taliesen's)
Time period(s): Indeterminate
Locale(s): Keltia, Interstellar Empire/Federation

Summary: In this series-concluding volume, Arthur's followers search for the Grail which will unite the Kelts' far-flung empire and allow Arthur to rest until needed in the distant future. A 39-page appendix includes a glossary, notes on pronunciation, a list of characters, notes on the series with bibliography, and a genealogical chart.

Other books you might like:
Mike Ashley, *The Pendragon Chronicles*, 1990
  editor
Marion Zimmer Bradley, *The Mists of Avalon*, 1983
Gillian Bradshaw, *Hawk of May*, 1980
Andrea Hopkins, *Chronicles of King Arthur*, 1994
Guy Gavriel Kay, *The Summer Tree*, 1985
Julian May, *The Many-Colored Land*, 1981

2441

PATRICIA KENNEALY

The Oak Above the Kings: A Book of the Keltiad

(New York: Roc, 1994)

Story type: Science Fiction (Science Fantasy; Political)
Series: Keltiad: Tales of Arthur
Major character(s): Arthur Penarvon, Royalty; Gweniver Pendreic, Royalty; Taliesen, Minstrel (bard), Writer
Time period(s): Indeterminate
Locale(s): Gwynedd, Planet—Imaginary; Keltia, Interstellar Empire/Federation

Summary: After many setbacks, the Counterinsurgency drives the forces of the evil wizard Edeyrn to a confrontation. Uthyr becomes king, with Arthur and Gweniver to reign after him. Unfortunately, the long rule of the Death-druid leaves Keltia with many crises that demand the attention of the newly reinstated rulers.

Other books you might like:
Gillian Bradshaw, *Hawk of May*, 1980
Guy Gavriel Kay, *The Summer Tree*, 1985
Katherine Kurtz, *Deryni Rising*, 1970
Julian May, *The Many-Colored Land*, 1981
Evangeline Walton, *The Prince of Annwn*, 1974

2442

DANIEL R. KERNS (Pseudonym of Jacqueline Lichtenberg)

Border Dispute

(New York: Ace, 1994)

Story type: Science Fiction (Military)
Series: Pit Bull Squadron
Major character(s): Indiw, Alien (Ardr), Spaceship Captain (Pit Bull Squadron); Raymond Falstaff, Spaceship Captain (Pit Bull Squadron)
Time period(s): Indeterminate Future
Locale(s): Sinaha, Planet—Imaginary; Outer Space; *Tacoma*, Spaceship

Summary: Now landed, Indiw must fight with the humans to justify his not killing Raymond Falstaff for crashing on his land. Believing that Indiw would want to rejoin the Pit Bulls, Ray never understands his partner's problem, or the alien's perception of humanity.

Other books you might like:
A.C. Crispin, *Starbridge*, 1989
Jacqueline Lichtenberg, *Molt Brother*, 1982
Jacqueline Lichtenberg, *Dushau*, 1985

Anne McCaffrey, *Crisis on Doona*, 1992
  Jody Lynn Nye, co-author
S. Andrew Swann, *Forests of the Night*, 1993

2443

KATHARINE KERR

Days of Air and Darkness

(New York: Bantam Spectra, 1994)

Story type: Fantasy (Magic Conflict; Adventure)
Series: Deverry
Major character(s): Rhodry Maelwaedd, Mythical Creature (half-elf), Mercenary; Jill, Sorceress (ex-mercenary); Evander, Mythical Creature (elemental spirit), Sorcerer
Time period(s): Indeterminate Past
Locale(s): Cengarn, Fictional City; Deverry, Fictional Country; The Westlands, Fictional Country

Summary: Jill, Rhodry and Evander each use their own methods to defeat the elemental spirit, sorceress Alshandra, who brings war to the Westlands and siege to Cengarn in order to destroy Princess Carramaena. Alshandra wants to stop her people from leaving their elemental existence for the physical plane, especially her daughter who seeks to become human as the princess's unborn child.

Other books you might like:
Gael Baudino, *Dragonsword*, 1988
Richard A. Knaak, *The Shrouded Realm*, 1991
Melanie Rawn, *Stronghold*, 1990
Midori Snyder, *New Moon*, 1989
J.R.R. Tolkien, *The Silmarillion*, 1977

2444

KATHARINE KERR

Days of Blood and Fire

(New York: Bantam Spectra, 1993)

Story type: Fantasy (Magic Conflict; Adventure)
Series: Deverry
Major character(s): Jill, Sorceress; Rhodry Maelwaedd, Mythical Creature, Mercenary; Jahdo, Child, Adventurer
Time period(s): Indeterminate Past
Locale(s): Deverry, Fictional Country; The Westlands, Fictional Country

Summary: Sent away from home to guide the blind bard of the Horsekin on his search for his rebellious and heretical brother, both Jahdo and the bard find themselves allied with the Deverry borderfolk and under attack from the renegade Horsekin who follow a "new goddess," Jill and Rhodry's enemy, Alshandra.

Other books you might like:
Joy Chant, *The Grey Mane of Morning*, 1980
Diane Duane, *The Door into Fire*, 1979
Robert Jordan, *The Eye of the World*, 1989
Guy Gavriel Kay, *The Darkest Road*, 1986
Guy Gavriel Kay, *The Summer Tree*, 1985
Guy Gavriel Kay, *The Wandering Fire*, 1986
Patricia Kennealy, *The Copper Crown*, 1984

2445

KATHARINE KERR

The Dragon Revenant

(New York: Doubleday Foundation, 1990)

Story type: Fantasy (Adventure; Quest)
Series: Deverry
Major character(s): Rhodry Maelwaedd, Mythical Creature, Mercenary; Jill of Cerrmor, Mercenary; Nevyn, Sorcerer
Time period(s): Indeterminate Past
Locale(s): Deverry, Fictional Country; Bardek, Fictional Country

Summary: Rhodry is the heir to Aberwyn and its best hope for peace, but he's been kidnapped, stripped of his memory, taken to Bardek and sold as a slave. Jill, still coming to terms with her magical talent, goes to rescue and avenge him with Salamander, Rhodry's elven half-brother. Nevyn meanwhile seeks to find and defeat his ancient enemy who has been behind Deverry's troubles for so long and is now luring Nevyn into even deeper traps.

Other books you might like:
Steven Brust, *Jhereg*, 1983
Joy Chant, *Red Moon and Black Mountain*, 1970
Guy Gavriel Kay, *The Summer Tree*, 1985
Patricia A. McKillip, *The Riddle-Master of Hed*, 1976
Elizabeth Moon, *Oath of Gold*, 1989
Elizabeth Moon, *Divided Allegiance*, 1988
Elizabeth Moon, *Sheepfarmer's Daughter*, 1988

2446

KATHARINE KERR, Editor
MARTIN H. GREENBERG, Co-Editor

Enchanted Forests

(New York: DAW, 1995)

Story type: Fantasy (Anthology)
Summary: Contains a one-page introduction and brief individual introductions to 25 original stories presented in eight sections: "Woodwork"; "Speaking Woods"; "Inheritances"; "The Scars of War"; "Victorian Variations"; "The New World That Never Was"; "Impossible Loves"; and "Sanctuary." With tone varying from light to dark, the sylvan settings populated by witches, hermits, woodsmen, hunters, and mythical creatures feature a variety of themes such as mystery, heroic and Arthurian fantasy, romance, and pyromania. Authors include Jo Clayton, Kate Elliott, Gregory Feeley, Nina Kiriki Hoffman, Michelle Sagara, Susan Shwartz, Dave Smeds, Lois Tilton, and Lawrence Watt-Evans.

Other books you might like:
Kathleen M. Massie-Ferch, *Ancient Enchantresses*, 1995
   Martin H. Greenberg, Richard Gilliam, co-editors
Patricia A. McKillip, *The Book of Atrix Wolfe*, 1955
Josepha Sherman, *Orphans of the Night*, 1995
   Martin H. Greenberg, co-editor
Tom Shippey, *The Oxford Book of Fantasy Stories*, 1994
   editor

Sean Stewart, *Nobody's Son*, 1995
Patricia C. Wrede, *Searching for Dragons*, 1991
Patricia C. Wrede, *Talking to Dragons*, 1993
   revised edition

2447

KATHARINE KERR

Freeze Frames

(New York: Tor, 1995)

Story type: Science Fiction (Family Saga; Alternate Universe)
Major character(s): Maggie Corey, Single Parent; Nick Harrison, Demon; Rabbi Akiba, Religious
Time period(s): 1960s; 21st century
Locale(s): San Francisco, California; Alternate Earth

Summary: The deal with the devil into which Maggie Corey is maneuvered affects her descendants in multiple universes over the course of two centuries. Rabbi Akiba watches Maggie's descendants while working to stop Nick's plots to control humanity.

Other books you might like:
Mick Farren, *Necrom*, 1991
Neil Gaiman, *Good Omens: The Nice and Accurate Prophecies of Agnes Nutter, Witch*, 1990
   Terry Pratchett, co-author
Lisa Mason, *Summer of Love*, 1994
Rachel Pollack, *Temporary Agency*, 1994
Mike Resnick, *Deals with the Devil*, 1994
   Martin H. Greenberg, Loren D. Estleman, co-editors
Mary Alexander Walker, *The Scathach and the Maeve's Daughter*, 1990

2448

KATHARINE KERR
MARK KREIGHBAUM, Co-Author

Palace

(New York: Bantam Spectra, 1996)

Story type: Science Fiction (Political; Alternate Intelligence)
Series: Pinch
Major character(s): Vida L'var y Smid, Heiress—Dispossessed, Fiance(e); Rico Hernandes y Jons, Computer Expert; Vi-Kata, Alien (Lep), Criminal (assassin)
Time period(s): Indeterminate Future
Locale(s): The Pinch, Interstellar Empire/Federation; Palace, Planet—Imaginary; Cyberspace

Summary: Attempting to escape Vi-Kata's unexpected attack, Vida discovers a helpful artificial intelligence program that flees confinement when Rico opens an illegal pathway into the Pleasure Sect. Identified as sole surviving member of a powerful family, Vida temporarily escapes danger through betrothal to the leader's son, bringing both new enemies and allies.

Other books you might like:
Isaac Asimov, *The Foundation Trilogy*, 1963
Raphael Carter, *The Fortunate Fall*, 1996
Christopher Hinz, *Liege-Killer*, 1987

Alis A. Rasmussen, *A Passage of Stars*, 1990
Melissa Scott, *Trouble and Her Friends*, 1994

2449

KATHARINE KERR

Polar City Blues

(New York: Bantam Spectra, 1990)

Story type: Science Fiction (Mystery; Psychic Powers)
Major character(s): Bobbie Lacey, Computer Expert, Police Officer; Tomaso, Murderer, Psychic; Jack Mulligan, Psychic (registered)
Time period(s): 23rd century
Locale(s): Polar City, Fictional City (on indeterminate world in Republic Space)

Summary: When an ambassador from the Interstellar Confederation is discovered murdered, Jack Mulligan happens to be nearby and offers assistance to the police. Attempting to psychically read the victim, he receives a psychic shock rendering him unconscious. Struggling to solve the murder, Lacey employs many helpers, human and alien, and an artificial intelligence with a sense of humor. The situation intensifies as a plague spreads and Mulligan himself becomes a target of Tomaso.

Other books you might like:
Alfred Bester, *The Demolished Man*, 1953
Roger Zelazny, *Jack of Shadows*, 1952
Lee Killough, *Deadly Silents*, 1981
Mercedes Lackey, *Burning Water*, 1989
Mercedes Lackey, *Children of the Night*, 1990

2450

KATHARINE KERR

Resurrection

(Eugene, Oregon: Pulphouse Publishing Axolotl Press, 1992)

Story type: Science Fiction (Alternate Universe; Medical)
Major character(s): Tiffany ''Tif'' Owens, Pilot, Patient; Nick ''The Devil'' Harrison, Angel (fallen)
Time period(s): 21st century
Locale(s): San Francisco, California

Summary: Returned to life after dying in a war-related Middle Eastern plane crash, Tif struggles to regain control of her body and thoughts while plagued with the feeling that reality does not match her memories. Tif wrestles with momentous decisions when the Devil offers her the opportunity to return as a hero to the world from which she came.

Other books you might like:
Pat Cadigan, *Mindplayers*, 1987
Jeffrey A. Carver, *From a Changeling Star*, 1989
George Alec Effinger, *Look Away*, 1990
Nancy Kress, *Beggars in Spain*, 1991
Nancy Kress, *Brain Rose*, 1990
Frederik Pohl, *Stopping at Slowyear*, 1991
Michael Swanwick, *Vacuum Flowers*, 1987

2451

KATHARINE KERR, Editor

The Shimmering Door

(New York: HarperPrism, 1996)

Story type: Fantasy (Anthology)

Summary: Contains a four-page introduction plus brief biographical introductions to the authors of 32 original stories focusing on shamans, sorcerers and spell-casters of many varieties. Stories vary in tone to reflect the effect of sorcery on the user, from the giddy sense of power accompanying first use to the wearying burden that comes with familiarity, while settings reflect both contemporary and traditional fantasy environments. Themes include alternate worlds, apprenticeship, flawed sorcery, mythical creatures, magic conflict, the American Civil War, computer virtual reality, and the arts. Authors include Constance Ash, Margaret Ball, Janet Berliner, Jo Clayton, Charles de Lint, Teresa Edgerton, Kate Elliott, Gregory Feeley, Esther M. Friesner, M. John Harrison, Nina Kiriki Hoffman, Simon Ings, Mark Kreighbaum, Lisa Mason, Dennis L. McKiernan, Diana L. Paxson, Laura Resnick, Susan Shwartz, Dave Smeds, and Lawrence Watt-Evans.

Other books you might like:
Marion Zimmer Bradley, *The Sword and Sorceress Series*, 1984-1996
  editor
Jack Dann, *Sorcerers!*, 1986
  Gardner Dozois, co-editor
Kathleen M. Massie-Ferch, *Ancient Enchantresses*, 1995
  Martin H. Greenberg, co-editor
Kathleen M. Massie-Ferch, *Warrior Enchantresses*, 1996
  Martin H. Greenberg, co-editor
Will Shetterly, *Liavek: Wizard's Row*, 1987
  Emma Bull, co-editor

2452

KATHARINE KERR

A Time of Exile

(New York: Doubleday Foundation, 1991)

Story type: Fantasy (Adventure; Magic Conflict)
Series: Deverry
Major character(s): Rhodry Maelwaedd, Mythical Creature (half-elf), Mercenary; Aderyn, Magician, Wanderer; Jill, Sorceress
Time period(s): Indeterminate Past
Locale(s): Deverry, Fictional Country

Summary: When Rhodry discovers he is half elven, he arranges an accident to cover his departure, knowing he must leave or ultimately endanger his family. He leaves with Jill and Aderyn to live with the elves and learn about his elven heritage.

Other books you might like:
Margaret Ball, *The Shadow Gate*, 1991
Marion Zimmer Bradley, *The Mists of Avalon*, 1983
Emma Bull, *War for the Oaks*, 1987
Tom Deitz, *Sunshaker's War*, 1990

Neil Hancock, *Across the Far Mountain*, 1983
Elizabeth Moon, *Oath of Gold*, 1989
James D. Priest, *Kirins: The Spell of No'an*, 1990
Jack Vance, *Lyonesse*, 1983

2453

KATHARINE KERR

A Time of Omens
(New York: Bantam Spectra, 1992)

Story type: Fantasy (Adventure; Quest)
Series: Deverry
Major character(s): Jill, Sorceress; Rhodry, Ruler (exiled), Mercenary
Time period(s): Indeterminate Past
Locale(s): Deverry, Fictional Country; The Westlands, Fictional Country; Bardek, Fictional Country

Summary: As the tremendous changes foreseen by Nevyn draw closer, Jill urgently searches for the meaning and significance of the inscription in Rhodry's ring. Meanwhile, Rhodry returns to Deverry in disguise to draw a vengeful Guardian from his elvish kin and becomes further entwined in the developments bringing his two peoples together.

Other books you might like:
Gael Baudino, *Strands of Starlight*, 1989
Susan Cooper, *The Dark Is Rising*, 1973
Diane Duane, *The Door into Fire*, 1979
Diane Duane, *The Door into Shadow*, 1984
Diane Duane, *The Door into Sunset*, 1993
Patricia Kennealy, *The Copper Crown*, 1984
Melanie Rawn, *Dragon Prince*, 1988
Joel Rosenberg, *D'Shai*, 1991

2454

KATHARINE KERR, Editor
MARTIN H. GREENBERG, Co-Editor

Weird Tales From Shakespeare
(New York: DAW, 1994)

Story type: Fantasy (Anthology)

Summary: Contains a two-page introduction by Kerr plus individual introductions to 23 original stories about Shakespeare's life and body of literary work. Authors include Brian Aldiss, Gregory Benford, Charles de Lint, Teresa Edgerton, Kate Elliott, Esther M. Friesner, Gregory Feeley, Nina Kiriki Hoffman, Barry Malzberg, Adrienne Martine-Barnes, Dennis McKiernan, Diana L. Paxson, Mike Resnick and Josepha Sherman.

Other books you might like:
Poul Anderson, *A Midsummer Tempest*, 1974
Terry Pratchett, *Wyrd Sisters*, 1988
Clifford D. Simak, *Shakespeare's Planet*, 1976
W.J. Stuart, *Forbidden Planet*, 1956
Tad Williams, *Caliban's Hour*, 1994

2455

COLIN KERSEY

Soul Catcher
(New York: St. Martin's, 1995)

Story type: Horror (Supernatural Vengeance)
Major character(s): Evan Baker, Child (Denise's 12-year-old son); Denise Baker, Public Relations; Paul Judge, Lawyer
Time period(s): 1990s (1995)
Locale(s): Seattle, Washington

Summary: With his dying breath, an Indian shaman murdered by Seattle street punks summons Williwaw, an ancient wind elemental, to avenge him. Williwaw wreaks devastation upon the city, searching for Evan Baker, a boy who appeared to the shaman in a final vision and who holds the power to send the spirit back from whence it came. This is the author's first novel.

Other books you might like:
Graham Masterton, *Burial*, 1994
Graham Masterton, *The Manitou*, 1974
G. Wayne Miller, *Thunder Rise*, 1988
Adam Niswander, *The Charm*, 1993
Eugene E. Pfaff Jr., *Uwharrie*, 1993
    Michael Causey, co-author
Kathryn Ptacek, *Ghost Dance*, 1990
Patrick Whalen, *Ghost Walker*, 1992

2456

KEN KESEY

Sailor Song
(New York: Viking, 1992)

Story type: Science Fiction (Post-Holocaust; Arts)
Major character(s): Alice Levertov Carmody, Indian, Businesswoman; Ike "the Bakatcha Bandit" Sallas, Indian, Sailor; Michael Carmody, Sea Captain, Fisherman
Time period(s): 21st century
Locale(s): Kuinak, Alaska

Summary: Life in the dreary fishing village of Kuinak remains largely unchanged by the disaster affecting the lower 48 states until the townspeople find that Kuinak may have been chosen as locale for a big budget filming of the classic Inuit fable, *Shoola and the Sea Lion*. The look of the town changes to accommodate the project as it brings new faces and passions to the previously quiet village.

Other books you might like:
Terry Bisson, *Voyage to the Red Planet*, 1990
David Brin, *The Postman*, 1985
Pat Cadigan, *Synners*, 1991
Harry Harrison, *The Technicolor Time Machine*, 1967
Ernest Hogan, *Cortez on Jupiter*, 1990
Marjorie Bradley Kellogg, *Harmony*, 1991
Neal Stephenson, *Snow Crash*, 1992

2457

JOHN KESSEL

Good News From Outer Space
(New York: Tor, 1989)

Story type: Science Fiction (Invasion of Earth)
Major character(s): George Eberhart, Journalist; Jimmy-Don Gilray, Religious (Evangelist)
Time period(s): 1990s (1999)
Locale(s): United States

Summary: As the millennium approaches, Americans are more and more ready to believe the fundamentalist Christian evangelists who predict the Second Coming. The most popular of these preachers, Jimmy-Don Gilray, claims God will send his messengers to the people of Earth in the form of aliens arriving in spaceships. On the surface this seems like madness, but crack investigative reporter George Eberhart is convinced that there may be some truth to the story.

Other books you might like:
James Patrick Kelly, *Look into the Sun*, 1989
James Morrow, *Only Begotten Daughter*, 1990
Pat Murphy, *The City, Not Long After*, 1989

2458

JOHN KESSEL, Editor
MARK L. VAN NAME, Co-Editor
RICHARD BUTNER, Co-Editor

Intersections: The Sycamore Hill Anthology
(New York: Tor, 1996)

Story type: Science Fiction (Anthology; Fantasy)

Summary: Contains a nine-page introduction, a seven-page primer for science fiction workshops, a list of all invited authors attending the 1994 Sycamore Hill workshop and 14 original stories in final form, reflecting workshop criticism, with authors' afterwords discussing the workshop experience. The stories' tone varies from light to serious with themes including dystopian futures, education, scientific research, time travel, dance, mythology, crime, Harry Houdini, mythology, and spiritualism. Authors include Carol Emshwiller, Karen Joy Fowler, Alexander Jablokov, James Patrick Kelly, John Kessel, Nancy Kress, Jonathan Lethem, Maureen McHugh, Michaela Roessner, and Bruce Sterling.

Other books you might like:
Robin Scott Wilson, *Clarion*, 1971
   editor
Robin Scott Wilson, *Clarion II*, 1972
   editor
Robin Scott Wilson, *Clarion III*, 1973
   editor
Robin Scott Wilson, *Those Who Can: A Science Fiction Reader*, 1973
   editor

2459

JOHN KESSEL

Meeting in Infinity
(Sauk City, Wisconsin: Arkham House, 1992)

Story type: Science Fiction (Collection)

Summary: Contains a six-page introduction by the author, one original story, "Faustfeathers," and one story, "The Lecturer," from Michael Bishop's anthology, *Light Years and Dark* (1984) plus 12 stories published 1981-1990 in periodicals, including the Nebula Award winning story, "Another Orphan." In most stories, the author examines the human condition through unlikely juxtaposition of notably diverse characters, occasionally inserting humor into his investigation of the dynamics of opposites.

Other books you might like:
Greg Bear, *The Wind From a Burning Woman*, 1983
Michael Bishop, *Blooded on Arachne*, 1982
Michael Bishop, *One Winter in Eden*, 1984
Phyllis Eisenstein, *Born to Exile*, 1978
Lucius Shepard, *The Ends of the Earth*, 1991
Lucius Shepard, *The Jaguar Hunter*, 1987
Bruce Sterling, *Crystal Express*, 1989
Michael Swanwick, *Gravity's Angels*, 1991
James Tiptree Jr., *Her Smoke Rose Up Forever*, 1990

2460

JOAN C. KESSLER, Editor

Demons of the Night: Tales of the Fantastic, Madness, and the Supernatural From Nineteenth Century France
(Chicago: The University of Chicago Press, 1995)

Story type: Horror (Anthology)

Summary: The editor, a professor of French, has put together 13 stories by 10 nineteenth-century French authors that explore a variety of supernatural and nonsupernatural themes, including vampirism (Charles Nodier's "Smarra, or the Demons of the Night"), pagan revival (Prosper Merimee's "The Venus of Ille"), invisible beings (Guy de Maupassant's "The Horla"), return from the dead (Theophile Gautier's "The Dead in Love"), the incursion of the past upon the present (Gautier's "Arria Marcella"), and the psychopathology of crime (Honore de Balzac's "The Red Inn"). In an informative introduction, the author discusses these tales in the context of the nineteenth-century European romantic tradition.

Other books you might like:
Ray Furness, *The Dedalus Book of German Decadence*, 1994
   editor
Brian Stableford, *The Second Dedalus Book of Decadence: The Black Feast*, 1992
   editor
Brian Stableford, *The Dedalus Book of Decadence: Moral Ruins*, 1990
   editor

2461

JACK KETCHUM

Offspring
(New York: Diamond, 1991)

Story type: Horror (Small Town Horror)
Major character(s): George Peters, Police Officer (ex-sheriff); Amy Halbard, Computer Expert; Luke Stevens, Child
Time period(s): 1990s (1992)
Locale(s): Dead River, Maine

Summary: Eleven years after they went on a feeding frenzy that terrorized the remote town of Dead River, a family of inbred cannibals re-emerges from the Maine woods to restock their larder with townspeople and abduct women and children to propagate their species. Sequel to *The Off Season*.

Other books you might like:
Randall Boyll, *After Sundown*, 1989
Richard Laymon, *The Woods Are Dark*, 1981
William W. Johnstone, *Watchers in the Woods*, 1991

2462

SAMUEL M. KEY (Pseudonym of Charles de Lint)

From a Whisper to a Scream
(New York: Berkley, 1992)

Story type: Horror (Child-in-Peril)
Major character(s): Jim McGann, Photographer (crime photographer); Nicola Chelsea ''Niki'' Adams, Teenager; Thomas Morningstar, Detective—Police
Time period(s): 1990s (1990)
Locale(s): Newford, Washington

Summary: A series of ritual murders attributed to the Friday Slasher smack not only of voodoo, but of the crimes of Teddy Bird, a pedophile killed two years earlier but whose past association with teenager Niki Adams, a teenager girl recently returned to Newford, seems to have resurrected him.

Other books you might like:
Lisa Cantrell, *Boneman*, 1992
Robert Weinberg, *The Black Lodge*, 1991

2463

SAMUEL M. KEY (Pseudonym of Charles de Lint)

I'll Be Watching You
(New York: Jove, 1994)

Story type: Horror (Psychological Suspense)
Major character(s): Rachel Sorenson, Artist; Harry Landon, Photographer; Lily Kataboki, Banker (teller)
Time period(s): 1990s (1994)
Locale(s): Newford, Canada

Summary: Rachel Sorenson thinks Harry Landon is a godsend when he saves her from her obsessive estranged husband. But Harry, a photographer, has his own perverse obsession with beauty, and will allow no one to come between him and his obsession with the beautiful Rachel.

Other books you might like:
John Fowles, *The Collector*, 1963
Ira Levin, *Sliver*, 1991
T.L. Parkinson, *The Man Upstairs*, 1991
Roland Topor, *The Tenant*, 1966

2464

J. GREGORY KEYES

The Waterborn
(New York: Ballantine Del Rey, 1996)

Story type: Fantasy (Quest; Religious)
Major character(s): Hezhi Yehd Cha'dune, Royalty (princess); Perkar Kar Barku, Hero; Ghan, Teacher, Librarian
Time period(s): Indeterminate
Locale(s): N'hol, Fictional City

Summary: Princess Hezhi searches for her vanished cousin, first in the flooded passages under the sprawling palace beside the River, then in the knowledge contained in the palace library's books. As she gradually realizes that her maturing magic potential endangers her life, she prays for a hero to rescue her. Far away, Perkar loves the goddess of a mountain stream and vows to kill the River God who devours her. The River brings Hezhi and her hero together, but can they save each other from Its power? First novel.

Other books you might like:
Lynn Abbey, *The Wooden Sword*, 1991
Eleanor Arnason, *The Sword Smith*, 1978
Margaret Ball, *Changeweaver*, 1993
C.J. Cherryh, *Rusalka*, 1989
Robert A. Heinlein, *Glory Road*, 1963
Ursula K. Le Guin, *The Tombs of Atuan*, 1971

2465

CHICO KIDD

The Printer's Devil
(New York: Baen, 1995)

Story type: Fantasy (Magic Conflict)
Major character(s): Alan Bellman, Writer, Musician (bell ringer); Kim Bellman, Musician (bell ringer), Spouse; Roger Southwell, Magician, Scholar
Time period(s): 17th century; 1990s
Locale(s): England

Summary: Roger Southwell's magical machinations in the past snag Alan and Kim as Southwell attempts to bring his influence into the present. Kim must find the solution to their troubles through Fabian Stedman's journal which concerns Stedman and his wife's involvement with Southwell and Southwell's unusual investigations. First novel.

Other books you might like:
Susan Dexter, *The Wizard's Shadow*, 1993
Barbara Hambly, *Bride of the Rat God*, 1994
Elizabeth Hand, *Waking the Moon*, 1995
Holly Lisle, *Mall, Mayhem and Magic*, 1995
    Chris Guin, co-author
Holly Lisle, *Minerva Wakes*, 1994

Patricia A. McKillip, *The Book of Atrix Wolfe*, 1995

2466
GREG KIHN

Horror Show
(New York: Tor, 1996)

Story type: Horror (Black Magic)
Major character(s): Landis Woodley, Director (film); Buzzy Haller, Filmmaker (special effects technician); Neil Bugmeier, Writer (screenwriter)
Time period(s): 1990s (1996); 1950s (1957)
Locale(s): Hollywood, California

Summary: Horror B-movie director Landis Woodley recounts the making of his most notorious film, *Cadaver*, whose budget was so low he was forced to use real cadavers for special effects. One of those cadavers belonged to a former Satanist and housed a demon that has been killing members of the film crew for the last four decades. This is the author's first novel.

Other books you might like:
Robert Bloch, *Psycho II*, 1982
Ramsey Campbell, *Ancient Images*, 1989
David Darke, *Horrorshow*, 1994
Dennis Etchison, *Shadow Man*, 1993
Todd Grimson, *Brand New Cherry Flavor*, 1996
Dale Hoover, *65mm*, 1994
Tim Lucas, *Throat Sprockets*, 1994

2467
CRAWFORD KILIAN

Greenmagic
(New York: Ballantine Del Rey, 1992)

Story type: Fantasy (Quest)
Major character(s): Dheribi, Bastard Son (of a king)
Time period(s): Indeterminate
Locale(s): Cant'area, Fictional Country

Summary: Hoping to avoid slavery and achieve a pardon for his crime, Dheribi agrees to help overthrow a rival city. His mother, a slave, promises that if Dheribi can learn control of the magic of her people, his birthright, he could free himself, his mother's people and the land itself.

Other books you might like:
Laurell K. Hamilton, *Nightseer*, 1992
Guy Gavriel Kay, *Tigana*, 1990
Victor Kelleher, *The Red King*, 1990
Elizabeth Moon, *Surrender None: The Legacy of Gird*, 1990

2468
CRAWFORD KILIAN

Gryphon
(New York: Ballantine/Del Rey, 1989)

Story type: Science Fiction (Invasion of Earth)
Major character(s): Alexander McIntosh, Immortal; California Moran, Immortal

Time period(s): Indeterminate Future
Locale(s): Earth

Summary: Humanity has undergone radical change under the influence of alien cultures contacted through the "Net," an interstellar communications system, but has never met another intelligent species face to face. Earth is then invaded by a race of evangelical gryphons determined to convert humanity and the rest of the universe to their religious faith.

Other books you might like:
Iain M. Banks, *The Player of Games*, 1989
Iain Banks, *The State of the Art*, 1989
Michael Kandel, *Strange Invasion*, 1989
Fritz Leiber, *The Wanderer*, 1964
Michael Moorcock, *An Alien Heat*, 1972

2469
CRAWFORD KILIAN

Redmagic
(New York: Ballantine Del Rey, 1995)

Story type: Fantasy (Magic Conflict)
Major character(s): Calindor, Magician; Deir ni Bron, Refugee, Magician; Nazaual, Magician, Religious
Time period(s): Indeterminate
Locale(s): Cant'area, Fictional Country; Exteca, Fictional Country

Summary: Fleeing the Extecan invaders, Deir unconsciously summons a sea dragon who carries her to the boat in which Calindor and his bride, Callishandal, travel. The Exteca covet the fertile northern lands and wield the powerful magic of the True Gods, released only by the blood of human sacrifices. Calindor and his greenmagic cannot stop them, but Deir begins to learn how to use the magic of Earth. Set in the milieu of *Greenmagic*.

Other books you might like:
Maggie Furey, *Aurian*, 1994
Barbara Hambly, *The Dark Hand of Magic*, 1990
Robert Jordan, *The Dragon Reborn*, 1991
Kenneth Morris, *The Chalchiuhite Dragon*, 1992
Tad Williams, *To Green Angel Tower*, 1993

2470
LEE KILLOUGH

Dragon's Teeth
(New York: Popular Library Questar, 1990)

Story type: Science Fiction (Mystery; Adventure)
Series: Brill and Maxwell
Major character(s): Janna Brill, Police Officer (sargeant); Mahlon Sumner "Mama" Maxwell, Police Officer
Time period(s): 21st century
Locale(s): Topeka, Kansas; Kansas City, Kansas

Summary: When a gang of thieves defeats the high tech security equipment to commit robbery and murder, Brill and Maxwell are assigned to the case. Since the crime was broadcast on television as it occurred, Brill and Maxwell are under pressure to solve it quickly as they search from better neighborhoods to ghettos ferreting out the murderer.

Other books you might like:
Alan Dean Foster, *Cyber Way*, 1990
Randall Garrett, *Too Many Magicians*, 1967
Katharine Kerr, *Polar City Blues*, 1990
Michael Kurland, *Ten Little Wizards*, 1988
L. Neil Smith, *The Probability Broach*, 1980

2471

NANCY KILPATRICK

Near Death

(New York: Pocket, 1994)

Story type: Horror (Vampire Story)
Major character(s): Kathleen ''Zero'' Stevens, Prostitute; David Lyle Hardwick, Writer (poet), Vampire; Donald Reesone, Actor
Time period(s): 1990s (1994)
Locale(s): New York, New York; Canada

Summary: Byronic David Lyle Hardwick, a vampire for more than a century, befriends and rehabilitates the woman sent to kill him, then follows her back to the United States to learn the identities of her employers. The mystery leads him on a journey that spans North America and takes him back into his past to former friends who have betrayed him.

Other books you might like:
Traci Briery, *The Vampire Journals*, 1993
Mara McCuniff, *The Vampire Memoirs*, 1991
Brent Monahan, *The Book of Common Dread*, 1993
Anne Rice, *The Vampire Lestat*, 1985
T. Lucien Wright, *Thirst of the Vampire*, 1992

2472

NANCY KILPATRICK

Sex and the Single Vampire

(Leesburg, Virginia: TAL Publication, 1994)

Story type: Horror (Collection; Vampire Story)
Major character(s): Cheryl, Vampire; Aleron, Vampire; Nightshade, Vampire

Summary: The three stories in this collection, two of which were written especially for the volume, tell of the peculiar menage a trois between Cheryl, a mortal woman turned vampire, and Nightshade and Aleron, two older and more experienced vampires who use Cheryl as a pawn in their feeding and thrill-seeking.

Other books you might like:
Ron Dee, *Sex and Blood*, 1994
Brian Hodge, *Shrines and Desecrations*, 1994
Norman Spinrad, *Vampire Junkies*, 1994

2473

GARRY KILWORTH

The Foxes of Firstdark

(New York: Doubleday, 1990)

Story type: Fantasy (Light Fantasy)
Major character(s): O-ha, Animal (she-fox); Camio, Animal (fox)
Time period(s): 1990s (1990)
Locale(s): Trinity Wood, Earth

Summary: After losing her mate and her kits, O-ha becomes despondent. When Camio, who has escaped from a zoo, comes to Trinity Wood, he teaches O-ha to understand the way of man. O-ha and Camio get to know each other and O-ha decides she would trust Camio. Together they have three kits who give new meaning and direction to O-ha's life. ALA Best Young Adults Books title. British edition, 1989, titled Hunter's Moon.

Other books you might like:
Richard Adams, *Watership Down*, 1974
Kenneth Grahame, *The Wind in the Willows*, 1908
Brian Jacques, *Mattimeo*, 1990
Margery Sharp, *The Rescuers*, 1959
Tad Williams, *Tailchaser's Song*, 1985

2474

GARRY KILWORTH

Hogfoot Right and Bird-Hands

(Cambridge, Massachusetts: Edgewood Press, 1993)

Story type: Horror (Collection)

Summary: This outstanding collection brings together 13 tales of fantasy and horror, many set in exotic locales and concerned with the tug-of-war between faith and rational belief. Included are two tales of doppelgangers, ''Doppelganger'' and ''Usurper,'' about supernatural doubles who overwhelm their lookalikes; two highly original ghost stories, ''The Island with the Stink of Ghosts'' and ''Inside the Walled City,'' in which a land mass and a Hong Kong slum (respectively) manifest unique kinds of haunting; ''The Vivarium,'' about a man who tries to create life in a controlled environment; and ''White Noise,'' in which a glimpse into the historical past tests the religious faith of the characters. Robert Holdstock has supplied the introduction.

Other books you might like:
Michael Bishop, *Blooded on Arachne*, 1982
Brian Stableford, *Sexual Chemistry: Sardonic Tales of the Genetic Revolution*, 1991
Lisa Tuttle, *Memories of the Body*, 1992

2475

KATHARINE ELISKA KIMBRIEL

Hidden Fires

(New York: Warner Questar, 1991)

Story type: Science Fiction (Political; Adventure)

Series: Fire Sanctuary
Major character(s): Darame "Silver" Meath Atare, Ruler, Immigrant; Sheen Atare, Ruler, Hero; Garth Kristinsson, Orphan, Traveller
Time period(s): Indeterminate Future
Locale(s): Nuala, Planet—Imaginary; Cesarea Station, Space Station

Summary: Offworlders are welcome on Nuala where the high radiation levels caused generations of mutations and sterility. After the scam to steal from the mineral-rich Nualans was foiled, Darame married Sheen. Garth, the son of Darame's ex-partner, is looking for her to try to get reparation or revenge.

Other books you might like:
Greg Bear, *Eon*, 1986
Gregory Benford, *Tides of Light*, 1989
Alis A. Rasmussen, *A Passage of Stars*, 1990
Alis A. Rasmussen, *The Price of Ransom*, 1990
Alis A. Rasmussen, *Revolution's Shore*, 1990
Dan Simmons, *Hyperion*, 1989

2476

KATHARINE ELISKA KIMBRIEL

Night Calls

(New York: HarperPaperbacks, 1996)

Story type: Horror (Wild Talents)
Major character(s): Alfreda "Allie" Sorensson, Young Woman; Eldon Sorensson, Farmer; Wylie Adamsson, Child
Time period(s): 1900s
Locale(s): Sun Return, Midwest

Summary: Shortly after a werewolf claims the life of her brother, Allie Sorensson discovers that she possesses The Gift, magical powers that generations of women in her family can control. Allie learns the Wise Arts and masters herbalism to grow into her calling and protect her kinsmen against the supernatural creatures of folklore that have travelled with them to the New World.

Other books you might like:
Nancy A. Collins, *Walking Wolf*, 1995
Catherine Montrose, *Wendigo Border*, 1995
Pat Murphy, *Nadya: The Wolf Chronicles*, 1996
Tom Piccirilli, *Pentacle*, 1994

2477

MICHAEL KING

Lorien Lost

(New York: St. Martin's Press, 1996)

Story type: Fantasy (Literary; Contemporary)
Major character(s): Milton Radcliffe, Collector, Psychic; Lorien Larking, Spouse (wife); Heather, Singer, Handicapped
Time period(s): 1870s
Locale(s): London, England; Larking Land, Mythical Place

Summary: Milton Radcliffe can enter art works and visit the worlds depicted. In one such world he meets Lorien and falls in love, only to lose her when a fire destroys the only image he has of her. Milton must overcome his timidity and set out into the bizarre Victorian streets to find his love again. First novel.

Other books you might like:
Nick Bantock, *Griffin & Sabine*, 1991
James P. Blaylock, *Homunculus*, 1986
Jack Cady, *The Off Season*, 1995
Tim Powers, *The Anubis Gates*, 1983
Jessica Amanda Salmonson, *Anthony Shriek*, 1992

2478

PAULA KING

Mad Roy's Light

(New York: Baen, 1990)

Story type: Science Fiction (Adventure)
Major character(s): Jennan Bartlett, Spaceship Captain (of the *Ariel*); Morgen, Alien (Daruma), Spaceman (mate on the *Ariel*); Vaughn Tanner, Agent (McCrory Shipping Line)
Time period(s): Indeterminate Future
Locale(s): Scorpio/Sagittarius Sector, Interstellar Empire/Federation

Summary: While dealing with the Taki, Jennan Bartlett, along with Vaughn Tanner, wish to find out why the Li Fawn are stalking them and what happened to the McCrory ship *Crystal*. Convinced that the solution lies with the brain-scrambled Shann, Jennan goes there and buys a madringa, a ubiquitous cult object. Pursued by the Li Fawn, they jump to find themselves in the deadly system of Xi Scorpio along with a maniacal alien force. Jennan manages to redirect it toward the Li Fawn and escapes back to Naberr.

Other books you might like:
Poul Anderson, *Satan's World*, 1969
Johanna Bolton, *The Alien Within*, 1989
A. Bertram Chandler, *Gateway to Never*, 1972
C.J. Cherryh, *The Pride of Chanur*, 1982
Andre Norton, *Sargasso of Space*, 1955

2479

PAULA KING

Rinn's Star

(New York: Ballantine/Del Rey, 1990)

Story type: Science Fiction (Psychic Powers; Political)
Major character(s): Rinn McCrea, Telepath; Yuri Ivanovich Selenkov, Spaceship Captain (Zvesta); Lorat, Shaman (Lily People)
Time period(s): 24th century
Locale(s): Outer Space; Delta Bootis, Planet—Imaginary; Novy Strana, Planet—Imaginary

Summary: After her ship is destroyed, Rinn McCrea seeks sanctuary on the Zvesta even though the Russians have proscribed her type (starfarers/telepaths). On Novy Strana, in order to avoid death, she agrees to attempt to get the natives of Delta Bootis to resume trade with the Russians. By psychic meddling with the mind of the tribe's shaman, trade is resumed. Rinn marries Yuri and becomes a permanent member of the Zvesta's crew.

Other books you might like:
Poul Anderson, *The Peregrine*, 1978
Jack L. Chalker, *The Demons at Rainbow Bridge*, 1989
C.J. Cherryh, *Rimrunners*, 1989
Cynthia Felice, *The Sunbound*, 1981
Andre Norton, *Voodoo Planet*, 1959
Brian Stableford, *Critical Threshold*, 1977

2480

STEPHEN KING

Carrie

(New York: Doubleday, 1990)

Story type: Horror (Wild Talents)
Major character(s): Carrie White, Teenager (Unpopular), Psychic (Telekinetic powers); Susan Snell, Teenager (Popular; sympathetic to Carrie)
Time period(s): 1970s (1979)
Locale(s): Chamberlain, Maine

Summary: Carrie White, a much maligned teenager with a fanatically religious mother, discovers she possesses telekinetic powers. When a cruel joke turns into violence at the senior prom, Carrie unleashes those powers against her tormentors. Originally published in 1974.

Other books you might like:
Charles L. Grant, *The Pet*, 1986
K.W. Jeter, *The Night Man*, 1990

2481

STEPHEN KING

The Dark Half

(New York: Viking, 1989)

Story type: Horror (Doppelganger)
Major character(s): Thad Beaumont, Writer (Popular novelist); George Stark, Murderer (Beaumont's fictional alterego)
Time period(s): 1980s
Locale(s): Castle Rock, Maine; Ludlow, Maine

Summary: After Beaumont "kills off" his pseudonym in a formal ceremony, his fictional alter ego comes to life and begins systematically murdering all those involved in his "demise," en route to a final confrontation with Beaumont himself.

Other books you might like:
Owen Brookes, *Deadly Communion*, 1984
James Herbert, *Moon*, 1985
Fritz Leiber, *Our Lady of Darkness*, 1977
John R. Maxim, *Abel/Baker/Charley*, 1983

2482

STEPHEN KING

Desperation

(New York: Viking, 1996)

Story type: Horror (Ancient Evil Unleashed)
Major character(s): Collie Entragion, Police Officer; Johnny Marinville, Writer; David Carver, Child (11-year-old)
Time period(s): 1990s (1996)
Locale(s): Desperation, Nevada

Summary: The reopening of a closed mine shaft in a remote Nevada town unleashes Tak, a disembodied creature of evil who takes possession of a local police officer and embarks on a rampage of slaughter. The few survivors left rally around young David Carver, a young boy who has had a religious epiphany and whose family has been taken prisoner by Tak's avatar. This novel shares characters and themes with *The Regulators*, which bears King's Richard Bachman byline and was released at approximately the same time under one of the publisher's other imprints.

Other books you might like:
Douglas Clegg, *Goat Dance*, 1989
Stephen Gallagher, *Valley of Lights*, 1987
Owl Goingback, *Crota*, 1996
Robert R. McCammon, *Stinger*, 1988

2483

STEPHEN KING

Dolores Claiborne

(New York: Viking, 1992)

Story type: Horror (Psychological Suspense)
Major character(s): Dolores Claiborne, Aged Person; Vera Donovan, Aged Person; Joe St. George, Handyman (Dolores' deceased husband)
Time period(s): 1990s (1992); 1960s (1963)
Locale(s): Little Tall Island, Maine

Summary: Inquiry into the death of her elderly employer leads Dolores Claiborne to recite a book-long monologue about her abusive marriage to Joe St. George and her murder of him 30 years ago when he became a physical threat to their three children.

Other books you might like:
Diane Duane, *Spectres*, 1991
Ruby Jean Jensen, *Celia*, 1991
Dean R. Koontz, *Shadowfires*, 1987
Robert R. McCammon, *Mine*, 1990

2484

STEPHEN KING

The Drawing of the Three

(New York: NAL Signet, 1989)

Story type: Horror (Alternate World)
Series: Dark Tower

Major character(s): Roland, Gunfighter; Eddie Dean, Addict (drug)
Time period(s): 1980s
Locale(s): United States; Alternate Earth

Summary: Part II in the quest of Roland, the Last Gunslinger, to find the Dark Tower. Having vanquished Walter, the man in black, Roland embarks on the second stage in his quest. He is joined by two allies, Eddie Dean and Odetta Holmes, who, by accident or unknown design, step through "magic doors" into Roland's world from our own, where they encounter underworld menaces and otherworldly evil. Originally published in 1987.

Other books you might like:
Clive Barker, *Weaveworld*, 1987

2485
STEPHEN KING

Four Past Midnight
(New York: Viking,1990)

Story type: Horror (Collection)

Summary: Four short novels with extensive introductions by King. "The Langoliers" is a *Twilight-Zone* inspired tale of a cross-country flight that goes astray into a dimension populated only by reality-destroying creatures. "Secret Window, Secret Garden" explores the relationship of a writer to his creations, while "The Library Policeman" probes guilt, child abuse, and monsters. Finally, "The Sun Dog" offers a magical camera that opens a window into another world whose terrifying canine denizen threatens to enter ours.

Other books you might like:
Charles L. Grant, *Nightmare Seasons*, 1982
Rod Serling, *New Stories From The Twilight Zone*, 1962
Rod Serling, *More Stories From The Twilight Zone*, 1961
Rod Serling, *Stories From the Twilight Zone*, 1960

2486
STEPHEN KING

Gerald's Game
(New York: Viking, 1992)

Story type: Horror (Psychological Suspense)
Major character(s): Gerald Burlingame, Lawyer; Jessie Burlingame, Housewife
Time period(s): 1990s (1992)
Locale(s): Kashawakam Lake, Maine

Summary: Left handcuffed to a bed when her kinky husband Gerald suffers a heart attack during his most recent stint of sexual antics, Jessie Burlingame spends 28 hours meditating on the unconfronted psychological trauma of her past, the emptiness of her current life, and a hungry dog that has managed to break into the house where she is being held captive.

Other books you might like:
John Driver, *The Hunger of the Beast*, 1991
John Fowles, *The Collector*, 1963

2487
STEPHEN KING

The Green Mile
(New York: Signet, 1996)

Story type: Horror (Mystery)
Major character(s): Paul Edgecomb, Guard; John Coffey, Prisoner; Percy Wetmore, Guard
Time period(s): 1930s (1932)
Locale(s): Cold Mountain Penitentiary, South

Summary: The discovery that John Coffey, a prisoner on death row, can heal by the laying on of hands makes him a valuable asset to the authorities who have imprisoned him and raises doubts whether he actually committed the crime for which he was sent to jail. This novel was serialized in six monthly installments as paperback originals with the titles, *The Two Dead Girls*, *The Mouse on the Mile*, *Coffey's Hands*, *The Bad Death of Eduard Delacroix*, *Night Journey*, and *Coffey on the Mile*. The title refers to the green walkway that leads prisoners to the electric chair.

Other books you might like:
Thomas Baum, *Out of Body*, 1997
Dean R. Koontz, *Cold Fire*, 1991
J.N. Williamson, *The Night Seasons*, 1991
F. Paul Wilson, *The Touch*, 1986

2488
STEPHEN KING

Insomnia
(New York: Viking, 1994)

Story type: Horror (Wild Talents)
Major character(s): Ralph Roberts, Aged Person; Lois Chasse, Aged Person; Ed Deepneau, Scientist (chemist), Researcher
Time period(s): 1990s (1994)
Locale(s): Derry, Maine

Summary: After his wife's death Ralph Roberts develops a major-league case of insomnia that sensitizes him to aspects of existence unappreciated by others. In particular, he becomes aware of the Centurions, gnomish little men who pull strings of destiny behind the scenes, and one of whom is working for a malefic being, referred to as the Crimson King, to turn an upcoming abortion-rights rally into a tragedy with serious repercussions for the world.

Other books you might like:
Dean R. Koontz, *The Vision*, 1977
Richard Matheson, *A Stir of Echoes*, 1958
T. Lucien Wright, *Dark Visions*, 1993

2489
STEPHEN KING

My Pretty Pony
(New York: Knopf, 1989)

Story type: Horror (Coming-of-Age)

Major character(s): George ''Grandpa'' Banning, Aged Person (weak heart); Clive ''Clivey'' Banning, Child (George's ten-year-old grandson)
Time period(s): 1960s (1962)
Locale(s): Troy, New York (The West Orchard)

Summary: Young Clivey takes ''instruction'' from his grandfather regarding the nature and value of time and the need for a personal ''pretty pony'' to give it meaning.

Other books you might like:
Ray Bradbury, *Dandelion Wine*, 1957

2490
STEPHEN KING

Needful Things
(New York: Viking, 1990)

Story type: Horror (Small Town Horror)
Major character(s): Leland Gaunt, Businessman (shopowner); Alan Pangborn, Police Officer (sheriff); Polly Chalmers, Businesswoman (shopowner)
Time period(s): 1990s
Locale(s): Castle Rock, Maine

Summary: The mysterious Leland Gaunt comes to Castle Rock to open ''Needful Things,'' a store that contains every resident's heart's desire. Instead of cash, Gaunt demands pranks against fellow neighbors, a type of commerce that soon has the citizens at each other's throats in a bloody civil war.

Other books you might like:
Ray Bradbury, *Something Wicked This Way Comes*, 1962
Douglas Clegg, *Goat Dance*, 1988
Charles G. Finney, *The Circus of Dr. Lao*, 1935
Charles L. Grant, *Something Stirs*, 1991

2491
STEPHEN KING

Nightmares and Dreamscapes
(New York: Viking, 1993)

Story type: Horror (Collection)
Summary: This massive volume collects 20 of Stephen King's hitherto uncollected novellas and stories, including the H.P. Lovecraft influenced ''Crouch End''; the story of a haunted bathroom stall, ''Sneakers''; the small town horror story, ''Rainy Season''; the vampire stories, ''Popsy'' and ''NightFlyer''; the zombie tale, ''Home Delivery''; and a satire on rock music nostalgia, ''You Know They Got a Hell of Band.'' Also included are ''My Pretty Pony'' and ''Dolan's Cadillac,'' previously only available in limited booklet printings; the Sherlock Holmes pastiche, ''The Doctor's Last Case''; an essay on Little League, ''Head Down''; and the poem, ''Brooklyn August.''

Other books you might like:
Clive Barker, *Books of Blood Series*, 1984-1985
Richard Matheson, *Collected Stories*, 1989
Robert R. McCammon, *Blue World*, 1989

Peter Straub, *Houses Without Doors*, 1990

2492
STEPHEN KING

Rose Madder
(New York: Viking, 1995)

Story type: Horror (Psychological Suspense)
Major character(s): Rose McLendon Daniels, Businesswoman (reader for audiobooks), Abuse Victim; Norman Daniels, Detective—Police; Bill Steiner, Pawnbroker
Time period(s): 1990s (1995)
Locale(s): Libertyville, Midwest

Summary: After fourteen years of abuse from a psychopathic husband, Rose Daniels flees her New England past, sheds her identity, and begins a new life where she senses her worth as an individual for the first time. When her husband, a police detective, tracks her down, Rose lures him into the world of a painting from which she draws her power.

Other books you might like:
Rick Hautala, *Ghost Light*, 1993
Ruby Jean Jensen, *Celia*, 1991
Dean R. Koontz, *Shadowfires*, 1987
Andrew Neiderman, *The Immortals*, 1991

2493
STEPHEN KING

Salem's Lot
(New York: Doubleday, 1990)

Story type: Horror (Vampire Story)
Major character(s): Ben Mears, Writer (Novelist); Kurt Burlow, Vampire
Time period(s): 1970s (1975-1976)
Locale(s): Jerusalem's Lot, Maine (A small town in Southern Maine)

Summary: Author Ben Mears, a recent returnee to his home town, slowly realizes that ''the Lot'' is being gradually taken over by an old world vampire and his familiar. He joins forces with some of the locals to fight back and—at a terrible cost—eventually triumphs. Originally published in 1975.

Other books you might like:
Charles L. Grant, *The Nestling*, 1982
Robert R. McCammon, *They Thirst*, 1981
Peter Straub, *Ghost Story*, 1979

2494
STEPHEN KING

The Shining
(New York: Doubleday, 1990)

Story type: Horror (Haunted House)
Major character(s): Jack Torrance, Writer, Maintenance Worker; Danny Torrance, Child (Jack's five year old son), Psychic
Time period(s): 1970s

Locale(s): Overlook Hotel, Colorado (A resort in the Rockies)

Summary: Isolated with his family—wife, Wendy, and son, Danny—Jack Torrance gradually disintegrates under his external and internal devils. This opens the way for the malevolent forces of the Overlook to overwhelm the three of them, particularly Danny, possessor of clairvoyant powers—the "shine" in King's terminology. Originally published in 1977.

Other books you might like:
Jack Cady, *The Well*, 1980
John Christopher, *The Possessors*, 1964
Ken Eulo, *The Brownstone*, 1980
Robert Marasco, *Burnt Offerings*, 1973

2495
STEPHEN KING

The Stand: The Complete and Uncut Edition
(New York: Doubleday, 1990)

Story type: Horror (Apocalyptic Horror)
Major character(s): Stu Redman, Leader (of the "good" forces); Randall Flagg, Leader (of the "evil" forces)
Time period(s): 1990s (1991)
Locale(s): Boulder, Colorado; Las Vegas, Nevada

Summary: Originally publised in 1978, there are approximately 500 pages added to this edition. After a superflu wipes out 99% of the world's population, several small groups mobilize—the good in Boulder, the evil in Las Vegas—to confront each other in a final battle for control of the earth.

Other books you might like:
Robert R. McCammon, *Swan Song*, 1987
Robert R. McCammon, *They Thirst*, 1981

2496
STEPHEN KING

The Waste Lands
(Kingston, Rhode Island: Donald M. Grant, 1991)

Story type: Horror (Science Fiction)
Series: Dark Tower
Major character(s): Roland of Gilead, Gunfighter; Eddie Dean, Addict (drug); Odetta Holmes, Handicapped
Time period(s): Indeterminate
Locale(s): The Waste Lands, Alternate Universe

Summary: In this third volume of the series set in an alternate universe suggested by Robert Browning's "Childe Roland to the Dark Tower Came," Roland of Gilead, The Last Gunslinger, continues his quest to find The Dark Tower. Accompanied by companions who have entered his world from our own through an interdimensional rift, he endures a series of encounters and ordeals in the desert referred to as The Waste Lands, each of which tests his determination to seek his destiny.

Other books you might like:
Clive Barker, *The Great and Secret Show*, 1989
Clive Barker, *Imajica*, 1991

Clive Barker, *Weaveworld*, 1987
Robert R. McCammon, *Swan Song*, 1987
Dan Simmons, *The Hyperion Cantos*, 1989
Brian Stableford, *The Empire of Fear*, 1988

2497
AMANDA KINGSLEY

Hellcat
(New York: Leisure, 1992)

Story type: Horror (Supernatural Vengeance)
Major character(s): Edna Wilkins, Clerk (supermarket); Helen Townsend, Clerk (supermarket); Gene Martin, Accountant
Time period(s): 1990s
Locale(s): Silver Springs, Maryland

Summary: This novel, which gives a whole new meaning to the expression "the banality of evil," tells the sad story of Edna Wilkins, who has helped her abusive husband James overindulge himself to death but must now contend with a fiendishly mischeievous black cat possessed by James's black soul and determined to make her life living hell.

Other books you might like:
Robert Bloch, *Catnip*, 1945
  short story in *The Opener of the Way*
Gordon Casserly, *Tiger Girl*, 1934
Claire Necker, *Supernatural Cats*, 1973
  editor
Michel Parry, *Beware of the Cat*, 1972
  editor

2498
RICHARD KINION

Sacrifice
(New York: Zebra, 1995)

Story type: Horror (Occult)
Major character(s): Alice Sterling, Lawyer; Holly Ryan, Psychologist (therapist); Steve, Murderer
Time period(s): 1990s (1995)
Locale(s): Annapolis, Maryland

Summary: Alice Sterling uses a hefty insurance settlement to buy the colonial Taylor Watch House and try to resume her life following a freak accident that results in the traumatic amputation of her leg. Unknown to her, the house is imbued with the influence of Amon, a pre-Druidic entity that came to American shores during the colonial period, and who begins using Alice as a vessel for sexual revenge to feed its needs.

Other books you might like:
Jane Brindle, *The Tallow Image*, 1994
Ruby Jean Jensen, *The Haunting*, 1994
David Robbins, *Spook Night*, 1995
Nina Romberg, *Shadow Walkers*, 1993

2499

RUDYARD KIPLING

Kipling's Fantasy

(New York: Tor, 1992)

Story type: Fantasy (Collection)

Summary: Contains a two-page list of Kipling's major publications from 1886-1940, a six-page introduction by John Brunner, ''About Rudyard Kipling,'' plus 12 excerpts and stories published 1888-1926 with individual introductions by Brunner.

Other books you might like:
Arthur Conan Doyle, *The Best Supernatural Tales of Arthur Conan Doyle*, 1979
David Drake, *Heads to the Storm*, 1989
  Sandra Miesel, co-editor
Lord Dunsany, *The Travel Tales of Mr. Joseph Jorkens*, 1931
Jack London, *Selected Science Fiction and Fantasy Stories*, 1979
Kenneth Morris, *The Secret Mountain and Other Tales*, 1926

2500

RUDYARD KIPLING

Kipling's Science Fiction

(New York: Tor, 1992)

Story type: Science Fiction (Collection)

Summary: Contains a two-page list of Kipling's major publications from 1886-1940, a six-page introduction by John Brunner, ''About Rudyard Kipling,'' plus 10 excerpts and stories published 1893-1932 with individual introductions by Brunner.

Other books you might like:
David Drake, *Heads to the Storm*, 1989
  Sandra Miesel, co-editor
Lord Dunsany, *The Travel Tales of Mr. Joseph Jorkens*, 1931
Jack London, *Selected Science Fiction and Fantasy Stories*, 1979
Edgar Allan Poe, *The Science Fiction of Edgar Allan Poe*, 1976
Jules Verne, *Yesterday and Tomorrow*, 1965
H.G. Wells, *The Complete Short Stories of H.G. Wells*, 1965

2501

MARIE KIRALY (Pseudonym of Elaine Bergstrom)

Leanna: Possession of a Woman

(New York: Berkley, 1996)

Story type: Horror (Occult)
Major character(s): Hailey Martin, Writer; Ed O'Brien, Police Officer; Leanna de Noux, Femme Fatale
Time period(s): 1990s (1996)
Locale(s): New Orleans, Louisiana

Summary: Writer Hailey Martin rents a room in New Orleans' French Quarter and falls under the spell of Leanna de Noux, a woman who was murdered in it years before. What she learns while under Leanna's spell is enough to raise her suspicion that Leanna was not a completely innocent victim, and that she herself is in serious danger.

Other books you might like:
Jack Finney, *Marion's Wall*, 1973
Robert Girardi, *Madeleine's Ghost*, 1995
Stephen King, *The Shining*, 1977
Simon Maginn, *Virgins and Martyrs*, 1995
Roland Topor, *The Tenant*, 1964

2502

MARIE KIRALY (Pseudonym of Elaine Bergstrom)

Madeline: After the Fall of Usher

(New York: Berkley, 1996)

Story type: Horror (Gothic Family Chronicle; Historical)
Major character(s): Pamela Donaldson, Young Woman; Edgar Allan Poe, Writer, Historical Figure; Madeline Usher, Aged Person
Time period(s): 1840s (1849)
Locale(s): New Orleans, Louisiana

Summary: With the help of Edgar Allan Poe, Pamela Donaldson tracks her abducted infant son to her dead husband's family's estate on the Louisiana bayou. There, she discovers that the family matriarch, Madeline Usher, has survived the fate Poe described for her in his famous tale, ''The Fall of the House of Usher,'' and that the family history is founded on a tradition of incest and reincarnation from which she and her son cannot escape.

Other books you might like:
George Egon Hatvary, *The Murder of Edgar Allan Poe*, 1997
William Hjortsberg, *Nevermore*, 1994
Stephen Marlowe, *The Lighthouse at the End of the World*, 1995
Robert Poe, *Return to the House of Usher*, 1995

2503

MARIE KIRALY (Pseudonym of Elaine Bergstrom)

Mina

(New York: Berkley, 1994)

Story type: Horror (Vampire Story)
Major character(s): Mina Harker, Teacher (former); Jonathan Harker, Lawyer (solicitor); Winston Gordon, Businessman, Nobleman (Lord Gance)
Time period(s): 1890s
Locale(s): Exeter, England

Summary: A variant on the story of Count Dracula, this novel focuses on Mina Harker, the wife of Count Dracula's most famous victim, and her recovery following Dracula's bite and subsequent death. Awakened to feelings of empowerment after her near vampirization, Mina grows increasingly estranged from her husband and increasingly fond of her randy neighbor, Lord Gance, as she tries to come to terms with her predatory sexuality.

Other books you might like:
Traci Briery, *The Vampire Journals*, 1993
Mara McCuniff, *The Vampire Memoirs*, 1991
Poppy Z. Brite, *Lost Souls*, 1992
Anne Rice, *Interview with the Vampire*, 1978
Chelsea Quinn Yarbro, *The Olivia Trilogy*, 1987-1989

2504

T.J. KIRBY

Dangerous Nature

(New York: Zebra, 1993)

Story type: Horror (Science Fiction)
Major character(s): Jackie Mitchell, Animal Lover (animal welfare agent); Warren Maxey, Scientist; Dan Patton, Businessman
Time period(s): 1990s (1993)
Locale(s): South Port, Indiana

Summary: Outraged animal rights groups break into laboratories around the country, liberating specimens. Once in the wild, those from Patton Pharmaceuticals, an Indiana facility experimenting in tissue regeneration, turn monstrous and begin to threaten the town.

Other books you might like:
Richard Adams, *The Plague Dogs*, 1976
Dean R. Koontz, *Midnight*, 1989
Dean R. Koontz, *Shadowfires*, 1987
Dean R. Koontz, *Watchers*, 1987

2505

T.J. KIRBY

Deadly Breed

(New York: Zebra, 1991)

Story type: Horror (Science Fiction)
Major character(s): Clayton Allen Kruger, Pilot (helicopter pilot); William Jameson "Jay" Harting, Doctor (surgeon); Charles Joseph Davidson, Doctor (surgeon)
Time period(s): 1990s
Locale(s): Clark's Corner, Tennessee

Summary: U.S. Army Project Chim-jag, which involves the transplant of human brain tissue into genetically engineered animals, goes awry when one of the animals, created as a sophisticated fighting machine to replace human soldiers, escapes into a nearby community in the Smoky Mountains.

Other books you might like:
Dean R. Koontz, *Watchers*, 1986
John Saul, *Creature*, 1989

2506

MARY KIRCHOFF

The Seventh Sentinel

(Lake Geneva, Wisconsin: TSR, 1995)

Story type: Fantasy (Magic Conflict)
Series: Dragonlance: Defenders of Magic

Major character(s): Bram DiThorn, Nobleman, Mythical Creature; Lyim, Wizard, Handicapped; Guerrand DiThorn, Wizard
Time period(s): Indeterminate
Locale(s): Krynn, Planet—Imaginary

Summary: Once a close friend and colleague of Guerrand, Lyim hatches a plot to destroy magic on Krynn. When he takes control of Qindaras, a city protected from magic by ancient treaties, Bram, with his access to non-human magic, must try to stop the plot.

Other books you might like:
Glen Cook, *The Fire in His Hands*, 1984
John M. Ford, *Casting Fortune*, 1989
Katherine Kurtz, *Deryni Rising*, 1970
Patricia A. McKillip, *The Riddle-Master of Hed*, 1976
Mark E. Rogers, *The Expected One*, 1991

2507

MARY KIRCHOFF
STEVE WINTER, Co-Author

Wanderlust

(Lake Geneva, Wisconsin: TSR, 1991)

Story type: Fantasy (Magic Conflict; Political)
Series: Dragonlance Saga: The Meetings Sextet
Major character(s): Tasslehoff Burrfoot, Mythical Creature; Flint Fireforge, Mythical Creature (dwarf), Artisan (metalsmith); Tanis Half-Elvin, Mythical Creature (elf)
Time period(s): Indeterminate
Locale(s): Abanasinia, Fictional Country

Summary: When Tasslehoff Burrfoot comes into possession of a copper bracelet, the fate of the entire race of Dargonesti sea elves hangs in the balance. A game tie-in novel.

Other books you might like:
Mark Anthony, *Kindred Spirits*, 1991
  Ellen Porath, co-author
Nancy Varian Berberick, *Stormblade*, 1988
Tina Daniell, *Dark Heart*, 1992
Richard A. Knaak, *The Legend of Huma*, 1988
Barbara Siegel, *Tanis, the Shadow Years*, 1990
  Scott Siegel, co-author
Margaret Weis, *Dragons of Autumn Twilight*, 1984
  Tracy Hickman, co-author

2508

DAVID KIRSCHNER
ERNIE CONTRERAS, Co-Author

The Pagemaster

(Atlanta, Georgia: Turner Publishing, 1993)

Story type: Fantasy (Alternate World; Young Adult)
Major character(s): The Pagemaster, Librarian, Guardian; Richard Tyler, Child, Adventurer
Time period(s): 1990s
Locale(s): United States

Summary: Focusing on his fears as usual, Richard Tyler seeks shelter in a library, a locale previously uninteresting to him. A flash accompanies Richard's transportation to a place populated by characters from classic literature. There, animated genre books help Richard explore the adventures presented through reading and learn to conquer his fears.

Other books you might like:

Lewis Carroll, *Through the Looking Glass and What Alice Found There*, 1865
Michael Ende, *The Neverending Story*, 1983
James Gurney, *Dinotopia*, 1992
Michael Kandel, *In between Dragons*, 1990
Anne Lindbergh, *Travel Far, Pay No Fare*, 1992
Margaret Mahy, *The Pirates' Mixed-Up Voyage*, 1993

2509

ROSEMARY KIRSTEIN

The Outskirter's Secret

(New York: Ballantine Del Rey, 1992)

Story type: Science Fiction (Adventure; Science Fantasy)
Series: Steerswoman
Major character(s): Rowan, Cartographer, Librarian; Bel, Margasdotter Chanly, Warrior, Guide
Time period(s): Indeterminate Future
Locale(s): Planet—Imaginary

Summary: Having achieved unwanted notice from the wizard's guild when she discovered that their magical control simply involves technological understanding, Rowan travels with Bel across the uncharted Outskirts hoping to find a fallen navigational satellite, the missing Guidestar, and gain insight into the wizards' control of society. Bel's Outskirter background proves vital to the pair's survival when they meet and join with nomadic goat herders to aid their progress across the deadly land.

Other books you might like:

Eleanor Arnason, *A Woman of the Iron People*, 1991
Sharon Baker, *Quarrelling, They Met the Dragon*, 1984
Octavia E. Butler, *Survivor*, 1978
Mary Gentle, *Golden Witchbreed*, 1984
Heather Gladney, *Teot's War*, 1987
Barbara Hambly, *The Time of the Dark*, 1982
Marjorie Bradley Kellogg, *Reign of Fire*, 1986
Marjorie Bradley Kellogg, *The Wave and the Flame*, 1986
Anne McCaffrey, *Dragonflight*, 1968
Jack Vance, *The Dying Earth*, 1950

2510

ROSEMARY KIRSTEIN

The Steerswoman

(New York: Ballantine/Del Rey, 1989)

Story type: Science Fiction (Science Fantasy)
Series: Steerswoman
Major character(s): Rowan, Wanderer, Scientist
Time period(s): Indeterminate Future
Locale(s): Planet—Imaginary

Summary: On a primitive world wizards practice what may be magic, but is probably disguised science. Meanwhile, the Steerswomen, an order of wandering truthseekers, attempt to spread basic scientific knowledge across the planet. One Steerswoman in particular incurs the wrath of the wizards due to her attempts to find out the truth about her world.

Other books you might like:

Doris Egan, *The Gate of Ivory*, 1989
Mary Gentle, *Golden Witchbreed*, 1983
Jack Vance, *The Dying Earth*, 1950
Jack Vance, *The Eyes of the Overworld*, 1966
F. Paul Wilson, *The Tery*, 1990

2511

LEE KISLING

The Fool's War

(New York: HarperCollins, 1992)

Story type: Fantasy (Young Adult; Magic Conflict)
Major character(s): Fernholz the Wise, Royalty (king); Clemmy, Teenager
Time period(s): Indeterminate
Locale(s): Mulberia, Fictional City

Summary: Smitten with unrequited love, King Fernholz finds himself unable to organize resistance to an invasion of his kingdom. In desperation he sends his only soldier to fetch Clemmy, who may unlock the secret of an ancient magical book containing spells which could cure the king. Author's first book.

Other books you might like:

Louise Cooper, *The Sleep of Stone*, 1991
Meredith Ann Pierce, *The Pearl of the Soul of the World*, 1991
Sherwood Smith, *Wren to the Rescue*, 1990
Brad Strickland, *Wizard's Mole*, 1991
Jane Yolen, *Wizard's Hall*, 1991

2512

JAMES KISNER

The Quagmire

(New York: Zebra, 1991)

Story type: Horror (Black Magic)
Major character(s): Joey Wickes, Child; Margaret Wickes, Waiter/Waitress (Joey's mother), Witch; Selma Drake, Witch
Time period(s): 1950s (1957)
Locale(s): Evansville, Indiana

Summary: The Pigeon Creek swamp is always a dangerous place to play, but this year it's particularly dangerous for the children of Evansville: Margaret Wickes' regular sacrifices of innocents to help open the gate between Earth and Hell have stirred up the spirits of runaway slaves buried at the bottom, as well as a few other nasty things secreted in its slimy depths.

Other books you might like:

Joseph Citro, *The Unseen*, 1990
Alan Lee Harris, *Deliver Us From Evil*, 1988
Michael B. Sirota, *The Well*, 1991

2513

JAMES KISNER

Tower of Evil

(New York: Leisure, 1994)

Story type: Horror (Supernatural Vengeance)
Major character(s): Shannon Elroy, Guard (security guard); Stan Cork, Guard (security guard); Ted "Dead Ted" Flanders, Vagrant
Time period(s): 1990s (1994)
Locale(s): Indianapolis, Indiana

Summary: Years after a security guard accidentally kills Ted Flanders for loitering outside a bank building and disposes of his body in the building's trash compactor, Ted manifests as a living presence in the building, trapping office workers inside on a snowy day and subjecting them to a night of terror.

Other books you might like:
Fritz Leiber, *Our Lady of Darkness*, 1977
Melisand March, *The Site*, 1988
Al Sarrantonio, *House Haunted*, 1991
David J. Schow, *The Shaft*, 1990

2514

ANNETTE CURTIS KLAUSE

The Silver Kiss

(New York: Delacorte, 1990)

Story type: Fantasy (Horror; Young Adult)
Major character(s): Zoe, Teenager, Student; Simon, Vampire; Christopher, Child, Vampire
Time period(s): 1990s (1990)
Locale(s): United States

Summary: Zoe is attracted to the darkly mysterious Simon, who finally confesses that he is a vampire, and enlists her help in destroying his brother, the child-vampire Christopher, who had killed their mother. A first novel.

Other books you might like:
Margaret Mahy, *The Changeover*, 1974
Otfried Preussler, *The Satanic Mill*, 1972
Bram Stoker, *Dracula*, 1897
Chelsea Quinn Yarbro, *Hotel Transylvania*, 1978

2515

RICHARD KLUGER

The Sheriff of Nottingham

(New York: Viking, 1992)

Story type: Fantasy (Legend; Historical)
Major character(s): Philip Mark, Mercenary Lawman (sheriff of Nottingham); John, Royalty (King of England), Historical Figure; Robin Hood, Hero, Outlaw
Time period(s): 13th century (1208-1224)
Locale(s): Nottingham, England; Sherwood Forest, England

Summary: Assigned by King John as Sheriff of Nottingham, Philip Mark mitigates King John's tyrannical orders, balanc-ing between the excesses of the King and the rebellious gentry. Circumstances force Philip to ally with Robin until political evolution forces them into opposition.

Other books you might like:
Parke Godwin, *Sherwood*, 1991
Robin McKinley, *The Outlaws of Sherwood*, 1989
Howard Pyle, *The Merry Adventures of Robin Hood*, 1883
Jennifer Roberson, *Lady of the Forest*, 1992

2516

RICHARD A. KNAAK

Children of the Drake

(New York: Warner Questar, 1991)

Story type: Fantasy (Magic Conflict)
Series: Dragonrealm
Major character(s): Sharissa, Sorceress; Dru Zeree, Sorcerer
Time period(s): Indeterminate
Locale(s): Dragonrealm, Planet—Imaginary

Summary: To save his people from a world poisoned by foul magics, Dru Zeree must lead them into a land of spirits.

Other books you might like:
Casey Flynn, *The Enchanted Isles*, 1991
Casey Flynn, *Most Ancient Song*, 1991
Pat Winter, *Madoc*, 1990
Pat Winter, *Madoc's Hundred*, 1991

2517

RICHARD A. KNAAK

The Crystal Dragon

(New York: Warner Questar, 1993)

Story type: Fantasy (Magic Conflict)
Series: Dragonrealm
Major character(s): Cabe Bedlam, Wizard; Darkhorse, Demon
Time period(s): Indeterminate
Locale(s): Legar, Fictional Country

Summary: Cabe Bedlam's sinister dreams lead him to a distant peninsula where wolf raiders have discovered a cavern hous-ing sorcerous weapons of an ancient, inhuman race. Intending to utilize the weapons in their plans for conquest, they acci-dently unleash the ancient Quel whose hellish powers will destroy all unless Cabe becomes the willing pawn of the oldest drake lord, the Crystal Dragon.

Other books you might like:
Elizabeth Forrest, *Phoenix Fire*, 1992
Laurell K. Hamilton, *Nightseer*, 1992
Marc Laidlaw, *Neon Lotus*, 1988
Elizabeth Ann Scarborough, *Last Refuge*, 1992

2518

RICHARD A. KNAAK

The Dragon Crown

(New York: Warner Questar, 1994)

Story type: Fantasy (Magic Conflict; Political)
Series: Dragonrealm
Major character(s): Kyl, Mythical Creature (dragon), Heir
Time period(s): Indeterminate
Locale(s): The Drake Kingdoms, Mythical Place

Summary: Potentially lethal tests to determine Kyl's ability to rule as Dragon Emperor could purify his spirit or unleash dark lusts and produce a reign of horror.

Other books you might like:
Lois McMaster Bujold, *The Spirit Ring*, 1992
Laurell K. Hamilton, *Nightseer*, 1992
Melanie Rawn, *Dragon Prince*, 1988
James H. Schmitz, *The Demon Breed*, 1968
Martha Wells, *The Element of Fire*, 1993

2519

RICHARD A. KNAAK

Dragon Tome

(New York: Warner Questar, 1992)

Story type: Fantasy (Magic Conflict; Quest)
Series: Dragonrealm
Major character(s): Wellen Bedlam, Explorer, Mythical Creature (half-elf); Yalso, Scholar, Adventurer; King Dragon, Mythical Creature, Royalty
Time period(s): Indeterminate
Locale(s): Dragonrealm, Planet—Imaginary

Summary: Discovering Dragonrealm, Wellen encounters a warlock who directs Wellen to a building which contains a most powerful magic book. Immediately events sweep Wellen and his companions into a conflict through which the Dragon King intends to acquire supreme power.

Other books you might like:
Gordon R. Dickson, *The Dragon at War*, 1992
Rose Estes, *The Stone of Time*, 1992
    Tom Wham, co-author
Thorarinn Gunnarsson, *Dragons on the Town*, 1992
Ursula K. Le Guin, *A Wizard of Earthsea*, 1968

2520

RICHARD A. KNAAK

Frostwing

(New York: Warner Aspect, 1995)

Story type: Fantasy (Magic Conflict; Contemporary)
Major character(s): Grigori Nicolau, Amnesiac; Teresa Dvorak, Real Estate Agent; Frostwing, Monster
Time period(s): 1990s
Locale(s): Chicago, Illinois

Summary: Grigori's memories are stolen repeatedly over the centuries by visions of a gargoyle he calls Frostwing. When he moves to Chicago, for reasons he no longer remembers, Grigori stumbles upon the physical manifestation of his tormentor in an unlikely place, a real estate listing. With the reluctant help of Teresa, his real estate agent, he attempts to unravel the mystery of the monster, risking damnation in an attempt to find salvation.

Other books you might like:
Peter S. Beagle, *The Folk of the Air*, 1986
Lois McMaster Bujold, *The Spirit Ring*, 1992
Emma Bull, *Bone Dance*,
Gene Wolfe, *Soldier of the Mist*, 1986

2521

RICHARD A. KNAAK

The Janus Mask

(New York: Warner Aspect, 1995)

Story type: Fantasy (Quest; Magic Conflict)
Major character(s): Mandrol, Nobleman (baron), Wizard; Viktor Falsche, Rebel, Wizard; G'Meni, Wizard (alchemist)
Time period(s): Indeterminate Past
Locale(s): Medecia, Fictional Country

Summary: Baron Mandrol's collection of masks holds spirits of dead men. The mask of Viktor Falsche, Mandrol's most hated enemy, wakes and manages to escape to again plot the Baron's death, impeded by ignorance and lack of time.

Other books you might like:
Glen Cook, *The Black Company*, 1984
Guy Gavriel Kay, *Tigana*, 1990
Katherine Kurtz, *Deryni Rising*, 1970
Patricia A. McKillip, *The Riddle-Master of Hed*, 1976
Patricia C. Wrede, *The Seven Towers*, 1984

2522

RICHARD A. KNAAK

Kaz the Minotaur

(Lake Geneva, Wisconsin, TSR, 1990)

Story type: Fantasy (Adventure)
Series: Dragonlance Heroes II
Major character(s): Kaz, Mythical Creature (minotaur), Knight; Darius, Knight; Molok, Mythical Creature (ogre)
Time period(s): Indeterminate
Locale(s): Solamnia, Planet—Imaginary; Krynn, Planet—Imaginary; Vingaard Keep, Fictional City

Summary: Kaz is wandering various lands as an outcast. He is hunted by different groups unfriendly to him. He hears rumors that make him return to Solamnia to warn his old comrades, the Knights of Solamnia, who have been turned against him.

Other books you might like:
Raymond E. Feist, *Magician*, 1982
Robert E. Howard, *Conan the Conqueror*, 1950
Robert Jordan, *The Eye of the World*, 1989
Fritz Leiber, *The Knight and Knave of Swords*, 1990

Karl Edward Wagner, *Darkness Weaves*, 1970
Karl Edward Wagner, *Death Angel's Shadow*, 1973

2523
RICHARD A. KNAAK

King of the Grey
(New York: Warner Questar, 1993)

Story type: Fantasy (Contemporary; Quest)
Major character(s): Jeremiah Todtmann, Ruler (reluctant); Haros Aguilana, Vampire, Spirit
Time period(s): 1990s; Indeterminate
Locale(s): Chicago, Illinois; World of the Grey, Mythical Place (shadow realm)

Summary: When the creatures created by humanity's fancies and nightmares, the Grey, decide to draft Jeremiah Todtmann as their king, they kidnap the unsuspecting commuter and bring him into their realm. By making the reluctant Jeremiah into the Grey's King of Kings, they hope to promote their plans to change from phantasm into creatures of substance and permanence.

Other books you might like:
Aaron Allston, *Galatea in 2-D*, 1993
Chester Anderson, *The Butterfly Kid*, 1967
Alan Dean Foster, *To the Vanishing Point*, 1988
Megan Lindholm, *Cloven Hooves*, 1991
Ben Okri, *The Famished Road*, 1992
Lucius Shepard, *Kalimantan*, 1992
Clifford D. Simak, *Out of Their Minds*, 1970
Wm. Mark Simmons, *When Dreams Collide*, 1992

2524
RICHARD A. KNAAK

The Shrouded Realm
(New York: Warner Questar, 1991)

Story type: Fantasy (Magic Conflict)
Series: Dragonrealm
Major character(s): Dru Zeree, Sorcerer, Immigrant; Sharissa, Sorceress, Immigrant
Time period(s): Indeterminate
Locale(s): Dragonrealm, Planet—Imaginary

Summary: Newly arrived on Dragonrealm, the immigrant sorcerers find their magic and immortality threatened. Unless they discover and remedy the cause, they will lose their sanity and even their human form.

Other books you might like:
Casey Flynn, *The Enchanted Isles*, 1991
Casey Flynn, *Most Ancient Song*, 1991
Margaret Weis, *Fire Sea*, 1991
 Tracy Hickman, co-author

2525
RICHARD A. KNAAK

Wolfhelm
(New York: Popular Library Questar, 1990)

Story type: Fantasy (Adventure; Sword and Sorcery)
Series: Dragonrealm
Major character(s): Gryphon, Mythical Creature (were-gryphon); Duke Morgis, Warrior, Mythical Creature (dragon); Gwen Bedlam, Witch
Time period(s): Indeterminate Past (pre-Industrial Revolution)
Locale(s): Dragonrealm, Fictional Country

Summary: The Gryphon, half-humanoid lion-bird, must go on a quest to find the Dream Lands, as much a state of mind as a place, in order to save the shape-shifting dragons from losing their powers and dragon shapes. His friends, Cabe and Gwen Bedlam must protect the Dragon Emperor's hatchlings from political assassination, while Gryphon must pass through the evil empire of the wolf raiders, their monstrous Runners and Pack Master, and their dark god, the Ravager.

Other books you might like:
Glen Cook, *A Shadow of All Night Falling*, 1979
Diane Duane, *The Door into Fire*, 1979
P.C. Hodgell, *Dark of the Moon*, 1985
Guy Gavriel Kay, *Tigana*, 1990
Fritz Leiber, *The Knight and Knave of Swords*, 1990
Clifford D. Simak, *The Goblin Reservation*, 1968

2526
AMARANTHA KNIGHT (Pseudonym of Nancy Kilpatrick)

The Darker Passions Reader
(New York: Masquerade, 1996)

Story type: Horror (Collection)
Series: The Darker Passions

Summary: This sampler culls the best passages from the author's erotic reworking of classic horror tales: Bram Stoker's *Dracula*, Mary Shelley's *Frankenstein*, Robert Louis Stevenson's *The Strange Case of Dr. Jekyll and Mr. Hyde*, and Edgar Allan Poe's "The Fall of the House of Usher." Here depictions of Dracula as a domination fetishist, Frankenstein's monster as a sexually voracious female, Mr. Hyde as the unrestrained undercurrent of lust in Victorian England, and Roderick and Madeline Usher as truly intimate siblings are not for the squeamish.

Other books you might like:
Michael Hemmingson, *Nice Little Stories Jam-Packed with Depraved Sex and Violence*, 1996
Richard Sutphen, *Sexpunks and Savage Sagas*, 1991
Lucy Taylor, *Close to the Bone*, 1994

2527

AMARANTHA KNIGHT (Pseudonym of Nancy Kilpatrick)

The Darker Passions: Dr. Jekyll and Mr. Hyde

(New York: Masquerade, 1995)

Story type: Horror (Doppelganger)
Series: The Darker Passions
Major character(s): Henry Jekyll, Doctor; Mr. Hyde, Criminal; Ursula Lawrence, Young Woman
Time period(s): 1890s
Locale(s): London, England

Summary: In this erotic retelling of Robert Louis Stevenson's classic tale of a chemically-induced split personality, Dr. Henry Jekyll's experiments lead to the discovery of a potion that transforms him into the image of his sexually rampant ego, whom he names Mr. Hyde. Hyde, a leather and flagellation fetishist, finds himself a welcome guest behind the closed doors of sexually repressed but ever-eager Victorian society.

Other books you might like:
Jay R. Bonansinga, *Sick*, 1995
Eric Higgs, *Doppelganger*, 1887
Richard Matheson, *Earthbound*, 1989
Robert Louis Stevenson, *The Strange Case of Dr. Jekyll and Mr. Hyde*, 1886

2528

AMARANTHA KNIGHT (Pseudonym of Nancy Kilpatrick)

The Darker Passions: Dracula

(New York: Masquerade, 1994)

Story type: Horror (Vampire Story)
Series: Darker Passions
Major character(s): Vlad Tepes, Vampire (Count Dracula); Magda, Vampire; Jonathan Harker, Lawyer (solicitor)
Time period(s): 1890s
Locale(s): Transylvania (Castle Dracula)

Summary: This gymnastic retelling of the story of Count Dracula imagines Jonathan Harker, Mina Harker, Lucy Westenra, Dr. Van Helsing, Jonathan Seward, Count Dracula and others as consensual partners in sadomasochistic and fetishistic indulgences that loosely follow the events of Bram Stoker's novel, and give new meaning to Dracula's historical title of Vlad the Impaler.

Other books you might like:
C. Dean Andersson, *I Am Dracula*, 1993
Marie Kiraly, *Mina*, 1994
Fred Saberhagen, *Bram Stoker's Dracula*, 1993
  James V. Hart, co-author
Bram Stoker, *Dracula*, 1897

2529

AMARANTHA KNIGHT (Pseudonym of Nancy Kilpatrick)

The Darker Passions: Frankenstein

(New York: Masquerade, 1995)

Story type: Horror (Reanimated Dead; Erotic Horror)
Series: The Darker Passions
Major character(s): Victor Frankenstein, Scientist; Elizabeth Frankenstein, Young Woman; Crea, Reanimated Dead
Time period(s): 1810s
Locale(s): Geneva, Switzerland

Summary: At the suggestion of his bride-to-be, Elizabeth, kinky scientist Victor Frankenstein creates a living being out of dead body parts whose function is to serve as the ultimate love slave for Victor, Elizabeth, and their circle.

Other books you might like:
Brian W. Aldiss, *Frankenstein Unbound*, 1973
Martin H. Greenberg, *Frankenstein: The Monster Wakes*, 1994
  editor
Stephen Jones, *The Mammoth Book of Frankenstein*, 1995
  editor
Marie Kiraly, *Mina*, 1995
Mary Shelley, *Frankenstein*, 1818

2530

AMARANTHA KNIGHT, Editor

Love Bites

(New York: Richard Kasak, 1994)

Story type: Horror (Anthology; Vampire Story)

Summary: Knight, a pseudonym of Nancy Kilpatrick, is herself a writer of vampire fiction. Here she has collected 11 newly written stories and reprints that make the sexual subtexts of vampire fiction explicit. In Kathryn Ptacek's "Pleasure Domes," a European traveller becomes so caught up in a sexual liaison on his grand tour that he doesn't realize a century has passed in the interim. Lois Tilton, in "Love Bites," describes a topsy-turvy world in which humans actually seek out vampires to taste *their* blood, and Nancy Collins, in "Dancing Nitely," depicts a world in which vampires are the dominant species and humans their erotic playthings. David Dvorkin, in "Reign of Blood," tells of a vampire in revolutionary France who uses the Reign of Terror to cover his own bloody tracks, and Karen Taylor, in "The Mirrored Image," relates the tale of a vampire spirit that possesses a hooker in order to obtain its necessary victims.

Other books you might like:
Poppy Z. Brite, *Love Bites*, 1994
  editor
Pam Keesey, *Daughters of Darkness: Lesbian Vampire Stories*, 1993
  editor
Cecilia Tan, *Erotic Vampire Tales*, 1994
  editor

2531

AMARANTHA KNIGHT, Editor

Seductive Spectres

(New York: Rhinoceros, 1996)

Story type: Horror (Anthology; Ghost Story)

Summary: In 12 highly erotic stories, the living and the ghosts of the dead get to know each other very intimately. Michael A. Arnzen's ''Screwge'' works a variation on Charles Dickens' ''A Christmas Carol,'' featuring a heroine visited by two ghosts of Christmas to come, each with lusty lessons to teach. In ''Megan's Spirit,'' a ghost and a mortal lover provide each other with the companionship neither can get from their respective worlds. In ''Melia,'' Brian McNaughton tells of a man who fantasizes the ghost of a long-dead high school cheerleader into life. In ''All This and Heaven Too,'' John Mason Skipp presents a porn star visited by the communal spirit of the middle class male businessmen who watch her movies. A lengthy excerpt from Brian Lumley's novel *Necroscope* is also included.

Other books you might like:

John Pelan, *Darkside: Horror for the Next Millenium*, 1996
  editor
Cecilia Tan, *The Beast Within: Erotic Tales of Werewolves*, 1993
  editor
Cecilia Tan, *Blood Kiss: Vampire Erotica*, 1993
  editor
Cecilia Tan, *Erotica Vampirica*, 1996
  editor

2532

DAMON KNIGHT

God's Nose

(Eugene, Oregon: Pulphouse Publishing, 1991)

Story type: Science Fiction (Collection; Theological)
Series: Author's Choice Monthly

Summary: This volume contains 6 stories arranged from Creation to God's Day of Wrath, all sharing religious themes or themes of the spirit and nature of mankind: ''God's Nose'' (1966); ''Catch That Martian'' (1952); ''Four in One'' (1953); ''You're Another'' (1955); ''The Country of the Kind'' (1956); and ''Shall Dust Save Thee'' (1967).

Other books you might like:

Judith Moffett, *Two That Came True*, 1991
Frederik Pohl, *Stopping at Slowyear*, 1991
Robert Silverberg, *Thebes of the Hundred Gates*, 1991
John Varley, *The Persistence of Vision*, 1978
Kate Wilhelm, *State of Grace*, 1991

2533

DAMON KNIGHT

Humpty Dumpty: An Oval

(New York: Tor, 1996)

Story type: Science Fiction (Satire; Disaster)
Major character(s): Wellington ''Bill'' Nelson Stout, Businessman (lingerie); Thomas A. Stout, Relative (brother); Emilio da Lionghi, Criminal
Time period(s): 1990s
Locale(s): Milan, Italy; London, England; Potamos, Pennsylvania

Summary: On the way to his brother's wedding, Bill stops in Milan at the request of his brother, only to wake up with a bullet in his head. Accused of not delivering a requested package, Bill finds reality shifting around. A meteorite may have destroyed New York, or aliens may have landed there. However, heading home to Potamos only leads to further confusion of time and reality.

Other books you might like:

Deborah Christian, *Mainline*, 1996
Philip K. Dick, *Valis*, 1981
Jean Mark Gawron, *Dream of Glass*, 1993
James P. Hogan, *Paths to Otherwhere*, 1996
Ursula K. Le Guin, *The Lathe of Heaven*, 1971
Michael Swanwick, *Stations of the Tide*, 1991

2534

DAMON KNIGHT

One Side Laughing: Stories Unlike Other Stories

(New York: St. Martins Press, 1991)

Story type: Science Fiction (Collection)

Summary: This volume contains 14 stories originally published in 1980s magazines plus 2 from 1970s magazines and the longest story, a retitled novella, ''The Other Foot,'' published in a slightly different form in 1963. The stories contain Knight's characteristic humor and social commentary with many featuring a technological change and its effect on human interaction.

Other books you might like:

Alfred Bester, *The Light Fantastic*, 1976
Alfred Bester, *Star Light, Star Bright*, 1976
Larry Niven, *N-Space*, 1990
Robert Silverberg, *The Science Fiction Hall of Fame, Volume 1*, 1970
  editor
Cordwainer Smith, *The Best of Cordwainer Smith*, 1975
John Varley, *Blue Champagne*, 1986
John Varley, *The Persistence of Vision*, 1978

2535

DAMON KNIGHT

A Reasonable World
(New York: Tor, 1991)

Story type: Science Fiction (Invasion of Earth; Utopia)
Series: CV
Major character(s): Harriet Cleaver Owen, Researcher (behavioral epidemiologist); Dorothy Italiano, Researcher (hypnotherapist)
Time period(s): 21st century
Locale(s): United States; At Sea (medical detention center)

Summary: When deep sea researchers based on Sea Venture, an ocean-going habitat, release an alien life form, McNulty's Symbiont, the coherent energy beings begin invading human beings' bodies, changing the hosts' thinking ability in the process. Dr. Harriet Owen discovers the aliens can be driven from human beings with electroshock, then detected and killed while between hosts. Now Sea Venture has been made into an isolated research station using involuntary human subjects to study the McNulty's Symbiont. While some people work to bring about the Utopia offered, others work to return society to its former sorry state.

Other books you might like:
Octavia E. Butler, *Imago*, 1989
Octavia E. Butler, *Adulthood Rites*, 1988
Octavia E. Butler, *Dawn*, 1987
John W. Campbell, *Who Goes There?*, 1948
Robert A. Heinlein, *The Puppet Masters*, 1990
Eric Frank Russell, *Sinister Barrier*, 1948

2536

DAMON KNIGHT

Rule Golden and Double Meaning
(New York: Tor, 1991)

Story type: Science Fiction (Invasion of Earth)
Major character(s): Aza-Kra, Alien; Jawj Pero Pembun, Government Official (investigator); Wei, Alien (Rithian), Spy
Time period(s): 21st century; 26th century
Locale(s): Earth

Summary: This volume contains a 15-page autobiographical introduction titled "Beauty, Stupidity, Injustice, and Science Fiction," plus two stories, "Rule Golden," originally published in 1954 in *Science Fiction Adventures* and "Double Meaning," originally published in 1953 in *Startling Stories*. In "Rule Golden," Aza-Fra changes life on Earth when he releases a catalyst which forces human beings to feel empathy for those affected by their actions. In "Double Meaning," Jawj and others search for Rithian invaders who impersonate human beings, intending to completely compromise Earth security before revealing themselves.

Other books you might like:
Orson Scott Card, *Eye for Eye/The Tunesmith*, 1990
  Lloyd Biggle, co-author
Arthur C. Clarke, *A Meeting with Medusa/Green Mars*, 1988
  Kim Stanley Robinson, co-author

Fritz Leiber, *Ill Met in Lankhmar/The Fair in Emain Macha*, 1990
  Charles de Lint, co-author
Barry B. Longyear, *Enemy Mine/Another Orphan*, 1989
  John Kessel, co-author
Kim Stanley Robinson, *A Short, Sharp Shock/The Dragon Masters*, 1990
  Jack Vance, co-author
Walter Jon Williams, *Elegy for Angels and Dogs/The Graveyard Heart*, 1990
  Roger Zelazny, co-author

2537

DAMON KNIGHT

Why Do Birds
(New York: Tor, 1992)

Story type: Science Fiction (Satire; UFO)
Major character(s): Edwin L. "Ed" Stone, Revolutionary, Activist; Linda Lavalle, Administrator, Girlfriend (Ed's)
Time period(s): 2000s (2002)
Locale(s): New York, New York; Europe; Argentina

Summary: When Ed Stone appears in clothing seven decades out-of-date, he presents a tale of his abduction by extraterrestials and plans to create a huge cube in which humans can survive a predicted holocaust. A ring with the power to win over others' opinions helps Ed to convince world leaders to help him. As he assembles help for his work, Ed's sanity comes into question as Linda Lavalle and her father resist the completion of Ed's project.

Other books you might like:
Bradley Denton, *Buddy Holly Is Alive and Well on Ganymede*, 1991
Colin Greenland, *Take Back Plenty*, 1992
Robert Rankin, *Armageddon: The Musical*, 1990

2538

HARRY ADAM KNIGHT (Pseudonym of John Brosnan)

Carnosaur
(New York: Tor, 1993)

Story type: Science Fiction (Techno-Thriller; Genetic Manipulation)
Major character(s): David Pascal, Journalist; Jan Penward, Noblewoman; Darren Penward, Nobleman, Criminal
Time period(s): 1980s
Locale(s): Warchester, England

Summary: After deaths result from an escaped animal of Sir Darren Penward's unique collection of dangerous animals, officials blame a Siberian tiger. When a young witness identifies the killer as a dinosaur, Pascal follows the lead and finds a conspiracy which could herald a new age of dinosaurs. Novelizes the film. British edition published in 1984.

Other books you might like:
Michael Crichton, *Jurassic Park*, 1990
Larry Niven, *The Flight of the Horse*, 1973
Tim Sullivan, *Lords of Creation*, 1992

Dave Wolverton, *Serpent Catch*, 1991

2539

HARRY ADAM KNIGHT (Pseudonym of John Brosnan)

The Fungus

(New York: Franklin Watts, 1989)

Story type: Horror (Techno-Horror)
Major character(s): Barry Wilson, Scientist (Mycologist), Writer (Thrillers); Kimberly Fairchild, Doctor (Medical)
Time period(s): 1980s
Locale(s): England; Ireland

Summary: Genetic experiments with mushrooms unleash a symbiotic fungi that devours everything in its path. In hopes of containing the plague, a small group is sent to track down Wilson's ex-wife Jane, the scientist who inadvertently set loose the fungi. Originally published in 1985.

Other books you might like:
J.G. Ballard, *The Crystal World*, 1966
James Herbert, *Domain*, 1984
James Herbert, *Lair*, 1979
James Herbert, *The Rats*, 1974

2540

KATHE KOJA

Bad Brains

(New York: Dell/Abyss, 1992)

Story type: Horror (Wild Talents)
Major character(s): Austen Bandy, Artist; Emily Bandy, Writer; Dr. Quiet, Doctor (metaphysician)
Time period(s): 1990s
Locale(s): New Jersey; Detroit, Michigan

Summary: Down and out and working in a T-shirt design store, failed artist Austen Bandy suffers a serious head wound that induces abstract visual hallucinations. Uncertain whether he has become hostage to overdeveloped aesthetic sensibilities, or to an outside force seeking to make him its vessel, Austen embarks on a cross-country flight to find a cure.

Other books you might like:
Giles Blunt, *Cold Eye*, 1989
Stephen King, *The Dead Zone*, 1979
Jessica Amanda Salmonson, *Anthony Shriek*, 1992

2541

KATHE KOJA

The Cipher

(New York: Dell/Abyss, 1991)

Story type: Horror (Wild Talents)
Major character(s): Nicholas Reid, Businessman (video store manager); Nakota, Waiter/Waitress; Malcolm, Artist
Time period(s): 1990s (1991)
Locale(s): United States

Summary: This excellent first novel is concerned with would-be poet Nicholas Reid, who along with his girlfriend Nakota becomes fascinated with "the Funhole," a bottomless hole in the wall of his apartment building that has a strange influence upon objects dropped into it. When Nicholas accidentally stumbles into the Funhole hand-first, he acquires a slowly expanding wound, the involuntary ability to melt steel and levitate, and a circle of artist friends whose reaction to his condition reveals truths about himself he would rather not face.

Other books you might like:
Fritz Leiber, *Our Lady of Darkness*, 1977
Roland Topor, *The Tenant*, 1964

2542

KATHE KOJA

Skin

(New York: Delacorte, 1993)

Story type: Horror (Psychological Suspense)
Major character(s): Tess Bajac, Artist (sculptor); Bibi Bloss, Entertainer (performance artist); Michael Hispard, Dancer
Time period(s): 1990s (1993)
Locale(s): Rivertown

Summary: Tess and Bibi join together to form the Surgeons of Destruction, an avant garde performance art troupe that combines Tess's machine-like constructions with Bibi's radical dance style. But Bibi's increasing interest in exploring the limits of what the human body can withstand alienates Tess and plunges her deeper and deeper into a lifestyle of body piercing, scarification, and potential death.

Other books you might like:
Giles Blunt, *Cold Eye*, 1989
Brian D'Amato, *Beauty*, 1992
Jessica Amanda Salmonson, *Anthony Shriek*, 1992
David J. Skal, *Antibodies*, 1989

2543

KATHE KOJA

Strange Angels

(New York: Delacorte, 1994)

Story type: Horror (Psychological Suspense)
Major character(s): Grant Cotto, Photographer; Robin Tobias, Artist, Mentally Ill Person; Johanna, Health Care Professional (art therapist)
Time period(s): 1990s (1994)
Locale(s): United States

Summary: Unsuccessful photographer Grant Cotto becomes fascinated by the paintings of Robin Tobias, a schizophrenic patient being tended by Grant's girlfriend. Grant moves in with Robin, ostensibly to help him realize his artistic potential, but as their relationship intensifies Grant loses perspective and becomes sucked into the vortex of Robin's insanity.

Other books you might like:
Giles Blunt, *Cold Eye*, 1989
Poppy Z. Brite, *Drawing Blood*, 1993

Jessica Amanda Salmonson, *Anthony Shriek*, 1992

2544

VICTOR KOMAN

Solomon's Knife

(New York: Franklin Watts, 1989)

Story type: Science Fiction (Medical)
Major character(s): Evelyn Fletcher, Doctor (Surgeon); Karen Chandler, Parent (Surrogate mother)
Time period(s): 1990s
Locale(s): California

Summary: Dr. Evelyn Fletcher has secretly created a new surgical procedure that allows her to transplant an aborted fetus into the womb of a surrogate mother. When the baby who results from the transplant falls ill and the facts surrounding her birth become public, a firestorm of controversy erupts.

Other books you might like:
Robin Cook, *Harmful Intent*, 1989
Michael Crichton, *The Terminal Man*, 1972
Daniel Keyes, *Flowers for Algernon*, 1966
Ayn Rand, *Atlas Shrugged*, 1957

2545

DEAN R. KOONTZ

The Bad Place

(New York: G.P. Putnam, 1990)

Story type: Horror (Mystery)
Major character(s): Bobbie Dakota, Detective—Private; Julie Dakota, Detective—Private
Time period(s): 1990s
Locale(s): Orange County, California

Summary: Amnesiac Frank Pollard hires the Dakotas to find out who he really is and why he is being stalked by some bizarre malevolent force. The Dakotas' investigation leads them into a terrifying conflict with a psychotic killer with paranormal abilities.

Other books you might like:
George C. Chesbro, *Bone*, 1989

2546

DEAN R. KOONTZ

Cold Fire

(New York: G.P. Putnam's, 1991)

Story type: Horror (Science Fiction)
Major character(s): Jim Ironhart, Teacher (elementary school); Holly Thorne, Journalist (news reporter); Enemy, Alien
Time period(s): 1990s (1991)
Locale(s): Laguna Niguel, California; New Svenbrog, California

Summary: Holly Thorne joins forces with Jim Ironhart to discover the source of the secret power that has enabled him to foresee and prevent the deaths of several people in the last six months. For his part, Jim is forced to confront his buried past by returning to his childhood town for a rendezvous with the responsible entity.

Other books you might like:
Owen Brookes, *Deadly Communion*, 1984
James Herbert, *Moon*, 1985
Stephen King, *The Dead Zone*, 1979
Robert Silverberg, *Dying Inside*, 1972

2547

DEAN R. KOONTZ

Dark Rivers of the Heart

(New York: Knopf, 1994)

Story type: Horror (Psychological Suspense)
Major character(s): Spencer Grant, Computer Expert; Roy Miro, Government Official; Valerie Keene, Waiter/Waitress (cocktail waitress)
Time period(s): 1990s (1994)
Locale(s): Santa Monica, California

Summary: Spencer Grant, a computer hacker, accidentally runs afoul of Roy Miro, emissary of a secret government agency who manipulates computer technology to change identities and abuses his powers by eliminating certain members of the human race who do not conform to his standards of perfection.

Other books you might like:
Mark A. Clements, *Children of the End*, 1993
Philip K. Dick, *Do Androids Dream of Electric Sheep?*, 1968
William Gibson, *Neuromancer*, 1984
Daniel H. Gower, *The Orpheus Process*, 1992

2548

DEAN R. KOONTZ

Dragon Tears

(New York: Putnam, 1993)

Story type: Horror (Wild Talents)
Major character(s): Harry Lyon, Police Officer; Connie Gulliver, Police Officer; Bryan "Ticktock" Drackman, Young Man
Time period(s): 1990s (1993)
Locale(s): Laguna Niguel, California

Summary: Select residents of a small southern California town are terrorized by a bizarre young man with telekinetic powers and a nasty disposition. Cop Harry Lyon must discover the identity of the man and the source of his powers or die at his hands in 16 hours.

Other books you might like:
Rick Hautala, *Ghost Light*, 1993
Ruby Jean Jensen, *Celia*, 1991
Stephen King, *Salem's Lot*, 1975
Peter Straub, *Ghost Story*, 1979

2549

DEAN R. KOONTZ

The Eyes of Darkness

(Arlington: Dark Harvest, 1989)

Story type: Science Fiction (Horror)
Major character(s): Christina Evans, Dancer, Producer; Elliot Stryker, Lawyer
Time period(s): 1980s
Locale(s): Las Vegas, Nevada; West

Summary: A year after Tina Evans's son Danny supposedly died in a horrible accident she finds evidence that he may indeed be alive, that the accident may involve biological warfare, and that she and her son may both be victims of a deadly cover-up.

Other books you might like:
Katherine Dunn, *Geek Love*, 1989
Stephen King, *The Dark Half*, 1989
Stephen King, *It*, 1986
Stephen King, *Pet Sematary*, 1983
Stephen King, *The Tommyknockers*, 1987
Bruce McAllister, *Dream Baby*, 1989
Dan Simmons, *Carrion Comfort*, 1989

2550

DEAN R. KOONTZ

Hideaway

(New York: Putnam's, 1992)

Story type: Horror (Serial Killer)
Major character(s): Hatchford Harrison, Antiques Dealer; Regina, Child (adopted); Vassago, Serial Killer
Time period(s): 1990s
Locale(s): Laguna Niguel, California

Summary: Following a near-death experience Hatch Harrison tries to lead an exemplary life, but finds himself troubled by visions of ghastly murders perpetrated by Vassago, a satanic young man with whom he has developed a psychic link and whose actions bring him closer to Hatch and his family with each successive kill.

Other books you might like:
Robert Bloch, *Psycho*, 1959
Davis Grubb, *The Night of the Hunter*, 1953
Joe R. Lansdale, *The Nightrunners*, 1987
Ira Levin, *Sliver*, 1991

2551

DEAN R. KOONTZ

Icebound

(New York: Ballantine, 1995)

Story type: Horror (Psychological Suspense)
Major character(s): Harold Carpenter, Scientist; Gunvald Larsson, Scientist; Brian Doughterty, Writer
Time period(s): 1990s (1995)
Locale(s): Thule, Greenland

Summary: A project to supply water-deprived parts of the world with icebergs cut from the Arctic iceflow goes awry when an earthquake breaks off part of an iceberg bearing the Edgeway Project scientific team and sets them adrift. As the team races against the clock to dismantle the explosive charges they have set, they discover that one of their members may be a psychopath who would just as soon see the project fail and all of them die. This novel has been revised since it appeared in 1976 under the title *Prison of Ice* and the pseudonym David Axton.

Other books you might like:
Joe R. Lansdale, *Act of Love*, 1981
Richard Laymon, *Midnight's Lair*, 1993
Richard Laymon, *Quake*, 1995
Alistair MacLean, *Ice Station Zebra*, 1993

2552

DEAN R. KOONTZ

Intensity

(New York: Knopf, 1996)

Story type: Horror (Psychological Suspense)
Major character(s): Chyna Shepherd, Student—Graduate (psychology); Edgler Foreman Vess, Police Officer, Serial Killer; Ariel Delane, Teenager (16-year-old)
Time period(s): 1990s (1996)
Locale(s): Napa Valley, California

Summary: Chyna Shepherd knows she should flee from Edgler Vess, a mass murderer who is thrilled by the intensity of the feeling he gets from his kills, and who has just slaughtered the family of the schoolmate she is visiting. But upon hearing that Vess has imprisoned a teenage girl at his home, Chyna pursures him in the hope of saving the girl from a fate worse than death.

Other books you might like:
R. Patrick Gates, *Deathwalker*, 1995
Thomas Harris, *The Silence of the Lambs*, 1988
James Neal Harvey, *The Headsman*, 1991
Stephen King, *Rose Madder*, 1995
Joe R. Lansdale, *Act of Love*, 1981

2553

DEAN R. KOONTZ

Lightning

(New York: Berkley, 1989)

Story type: Horror (Time Travel)
Major character(s): Laura Shane, Writer (Beautiful bestselling author); Stefan Krieger, Time Traveller (Laura's "guardian")
Time period(s): 1980s (1989); 1940s (1944)
Locale(s): California; Germany

Summary: The mysterious "guardian," who intervenes to save Laura Stark several times, turns out to be a renegade time traveller from Hitler's Germany determined to destroy their time travel experiments. In his final trip to 1989, he and Laura must defend themselves from Nazi pursuers while searching for a way to prevent Hitler from retroactively winning World War II.

Other books you might like:
John Farris, *The Fury*, 1976
Stephen King, *Firestarter*, 1980

2554

DEAN R. KOONTZ

Midnight
(New York: Putnam, 1989; Berkley, 1989)

Story type: Horror (Small Town Horror)
Major character(s): Sam Booker, FBI Agent; Tessa Lockland, Young Woman
Time period(s): 1980s
Locale(s): Moonlight Cove, California (A northern coastal town)

Summary: A series of fatal "accidents" and "suicides" brings Booker and Lockland—whose sister was a victim—to Moonlight Cove, where they unite with a teenager and a crippled war veteran to investigate the mysterious deaths. The trail leads them to the New People, an emotionless, faster thinking, hard to kill group and the strange, dangerous secret behind their origins.

Other books you might like:
Jack Finney, *The Body Snatchers*, 1955
Charles L. Grant, *The Hour of the Oxrun Dead*, 1977

2555

DEAN R. KOONTZ

Mr. Murder
(New York: Putnam, 1993)

Story type: Horror (Doppelganger; Science Fiction)
Major character(s): Marty Stillwater, Writer (mystery novelist); Paige Stillwater, Health Care Professional (therapist); The Other, Amnesiac
Time period(s): 1990s (1993)
Locale(s): Laguna Niguel, California

Summary: A mysterious man with no memory of his past life learns how to relate to other human beings through the detritus of popular culture—junk films, splatter fiction, and pornography. When he notices that he bears a striking resemblance to mystery writer Marty Stillman, he tries to take over Marty's life, leading the befuddled Marty to wonder if the man is not the dark side of his imagination come to life.

Other books you might like:
Michael Cadnum, *Ghostwright*, 1992
Stephen King, *The Dark Half*, 1989
Richard Christian Matheson, *Created By*, 1993

2556

DEAN R. KOONTZ
PHIL PARKS, Illustrator

Santa's Twin
(New York: HarperPrism, 1996)

Story type: Fantasy (Legend; Adventure)
Major character(s): Bob "Santa" Claus, Imposter, Relative; Charlotte "Lottie", Child; Emily "Emmy", Child
Time period(s): 1990s
Locale(s): United States; North Pole, Arctic

Summary: When Lottie and Emmy question Santa's unusual behavior, they uncover a sociopathic relative of Kris Kringle running amok on Christmas Eve. A fortuitous accident provides the pair with an opportunity to rescue the holiday. Lavishly illustrated.

Other books you might like:
Cathy Crimmins, *Revenge of the Christmas Box*, 1996
    Tom Maeder, co-author
David Kirschner, *The Pagemaster*, 1993
    Ernie Contreras, co-author
James Finn Garner, *Politically Correct Holiday Stories*, 1995
Terry Jones, *Lady Cottington's Pressed Fairy Book*, 1994
    Brian Froud, co-author
Kristine Kathryn Rusch, *Pulphouse, Issue 10: Special Issue*, 1991
    editor

2557

DEAN R. KOONTZ

Strange Highways
(New York: Warner, 1995)

Story type: Horror (Collection)

Summary: The author's first story collection in 25 years brings together two short novels and a dozen short stories. The title novel, written especially for this volume, tells of a man who returns to his family home town and inadvertently steps into mysteries from the past that have bearing on events in the present. The other novel, "Chase," was first published under the author's K.R. Dwyer pseudonym in 1972, and tells of a good Samaritan who is menaced by murderer. Of the other stories, "Hardshell" and "Miss Attila the Hun" blend science fiction and horror elements, "Trapped" is a suspense tale of a woman and her son imprisoned in a snowbound house besieged by genetically engineered rats, and "The Snatcher" is a witchcraft tale of just desserts.

Other books you might like:
Ed Gorman, *Cages*, 1995
Stephen King, *Four Past Midnight*, 1992
Robert R. McCammon, *Blue World*, 1989
William F. Nolan, *Night Shapes: Excursions into Terror*, 1995

2558

DEAN R. KOONTZ

Winter Moon

(New York: Ballantine, 1994)

Story type: Horror (Science Fiction)
Major character(s): Jack McGarvey, Police Officer; Heather McGarvey, Housewife; Toby McGarvey, Child
Time period(s): 1990s
Locale(s): Montana

Summary: Trying to escape the mayhem of life as a Los Angeles police officer, Jack McGarvey moves his family to a ranch bequeathed them by the father of his former partner, unaware that it is inhabited by the Givers, extradimensional beings who usurp the bodies of humans to wreak havoc on Earth. This novel was originally published in shorter form in 1974 with the title *Invasion* and under Koontz's pseudonym, Aaron Wolfe.

Other books you might like:
Jack Finney, *The Body Snatchers*, 1955
Robert A. Heinlein, *The Puppet Masters*, 1951
Maxine O'Callaghan, *Dark Time*, 1992

2559

MARK A. KOSTRUBULA

Dark Legacy

(Nashville, Tennessee: Scythe Publications, 1996)

Story type: Horror (Black Magic)
Major character(s): Adolf Hitler, Military Personnel, Historical Figure; Lance Taylor, Businessman (salvage); Mike, Businessman (salvage)
Time period(s): 1940s; 1990s (1996)
Locale(s): Kehena Island, Pacific Ocean; Zurich, Switzerland

Summary: With the help of Satan, Adolf Hitler plants stolen treasure around the world in the hope of starting the Fourth Reich decades after the end of World War II. When a group of modern salvage specialists begin finding the hidden treasures, an age old battle between good and evil is reignited.

Other books you might like:
Peter Benchley, *White Shark*, 1994
Brian Lumley, *Demogorgon*, 1987
Robert R. McCammon, *The Night Boat*, 1980
Robert Weinberg, *The Armageddon Box*, 1991
Dennis Wheatley, *They Used Dark Forces*, 1964

2560

ERIC KOTANI

JOHN MADDOX ROBERTS, Co-Author

Delta Pavonis

(New York: Baen, 1990)

Story type: Science Fiction (First Contact; Adventure)
Series: Island Worlds
Major character(s): Dierdre Jamail, Explorer; Sieglinde Kornfeld-Taggert, Scientist; M'ats, Alien
Time period(s): 22nd century
Locale(s): Delta Pavonis Star System, Outer Space

Summary: Dierdre Jamail has trouble with authority. That's the reason she is assigned to the Atropos expedition. She stumbles upon dinosaurs and a matter transmitter which calls aliens to the Delta Pavonis system, aliens who are surprised at how quickly their experimental subjects have learned.

Other books you might like:
John Brunner, *Total Eclipse*, 1974
Anne McCaffrey, *Dinosaur Planet*, 1978
John Rackham, *The Treasure of Tau Ceti*, 1969
Timothy Zahn, *Spinneret*, 1985

2561

WILLIAM KOTZWINKLE

The Bear Went over the Mountain

(New York: Doubleday, 1996)

Story type: Fantasy (Satire; Contemporary)
Major character(s): Arthur Bramhall, Writer, Professor; Hal Jam, Animal (bear), Imposter (writer)
Time period(s): 1990s
Locale(s): Maine; New York, New York

Summary: After Arthur Bramhall buries his rewritten manuscript in the woods, an inquisitive bear digs it up and finds it interesting. The bear assumes a persona, Hal Jam, brings the manuscript to a literary agency and becomes an overnight success. Meanwhile, Arthur Bramhall's failed attempts to recover the manuscript or even get legal credit for his own work lead to the author's deterioration.

Other books you might like:
William Borden, *Superstoe*, 1968
Scott Bradfield, *Animal Planet*, 1995
Richard Brautigan, *Revenge of the Lawn: Stories 1962-1970*, 1971
Harlan Ellison, *The Fantasies of Harlan Ellison*, 1979
Jerzy Kosinski, *Being There*, 1971

2562

WILLIAM KOTZWINKLE

The Hot Jazz Trio

(New York: Houghton Mifflin, 1989)

Story type: Horror (Collection)

Summary: The title novella and two short stories. "Hot Jazz Blues" takes place in the Paris of the 20s. Django Rinehardt, his Hot Jazz Trio, and various celebrities (Cocteau, Picasso, et al.) help LeBlanc the Magician find and rescue his assistant, Loli, who has been "eaten" by his Vanishing Lady Box. In "Blues on the Nile: A Fragment of Papyrus," the mighty Pharoah and his retinue journey on the Nile into eternity and their final destination. "Boxcar Blues" is a fantasy of hobos who ride the rails and Pearl, a "blowsy, broad-beamed ex-cashier."

Other books you might like:
Roland Topor, *Joko's Anniversary*, 1970

2563

EDWARD E. KRAMER, Editor

Dark Destiny

(Stone Mountain, Georgia: White Wolf, 1994)

Story type: Horror (Anthology)

Summary: Under the aegis of the gaming company responsible for the "World of Darkness" fantasy role playing game, the editor has assembled 22 stories that presuppose the existence of werewolves, vampires, witches, and wizards living in disguise among human beings and controlling world events. Included are Robert Bloch's "The Scent of Vinegar," about vampires influencing the movie industry; Harlan Ellison's "Sensible City," about two escaped convicts who meet a gruesome fate while on the run; Robert Weinberg's "In the Forests of the Night," about a human detective who turns the tables on two warring vampire factions using him as a pawn to obtain secret magic; Nancy A. Collins' "The Love of Monsters," about the forbidden love between a vampire and a werewolf; and Rick Hautala's "Winter Queen," about a plane crash survivor adopted into a clan of werewolves. Former splatterpunk John Skipp supplies the introduction.

Other books you might like:

Robert T. Garcia, *Chilled to the Bone*, 1992
   editor
Brian Thomsen, *Tales of Ravenloft*, 1994
   editor
Stewart Wieck, *When Will You Rage*, 1994
   editor
Stewart Wieck, *World of Darkness: City of Darkness*, 1995
   Stanley Krause, co-editor
Stewart Wieck, *World of Darkness: Death and Damnation*, 1994
   editor
Stewart Wieck, *World of Darkness: Truth Until Paradox*, 1994
   editor

2564

EDWARD E. KRAMER, Editor

Dark Destiny II: Proprietors of Fate

(Clarkston, GA: White Wolf, 1995)

Story type: Horror (Anthology)

Summary: The twenty stories written exclusively for this anthology are set in the World of Darkness, a fantasy role-playing world in which mages, ghosts, vampires, werewolves and other supernatural beings masquerade as humans and integrate themselves unobtrusively with the human world. This volume focuses on the role these beings have played in major historical events. In Nancy Collins' "The Sign of the Asp," a mage has a hand in the fate of Cleopatra and the course of classical history. S.P. Somtow's "Beloved Disciple" imagines Jesus Christ interacting with vampires, and Charles L. Grant's "Gray" envisions werewolves engineering Custer's Last Stand. In James S. Dorr's narrative poem "The Westfarer," the World of Darkness dovetails with that of Norse mythology. Robert Weinberg sees disappearances in the Devil's Triangle as part of a vampire conspiracy in "The Skeptic," and Poppy Brite presents the exploits of a serial killer in Louisiana and the events leading up to the first World War as examples of how creatures in the World of Darkness use human surrogates to fight their century-old battles with one another. Robert Anton Wilson supplies an introduction.

Other books you might like:

Erin Kelly, *The Splendour Falls*, 1995
   editor
Staley Krause, *Strange City*, 1996
   Stuart Wieck, co-editor
Stewart Wieck, *The Beast Within*, 1995
   editor

2565

EDWARD E. KRAMER, Editor
BERNIE WRIGHTSON, Illustrator

Dark Destiny III: Children of Dracula

(Clarkston, Georgia: White Wolf, 1996)

Story type: Horror (Anthology; Vampire Story)
Series: Dark Destiny

Summary: As part of the Dark Destiny series, which posits that supernatural creatures have a hand in the great events of history, this collection features 21 stories original to the volume concerned with Dracula and his progeny. S.P. Somtow detects a vampiric residue in the destruction of the biblical Sodom and Gomorrah in "Brimstone and Salt." Rick Reed proposes that the Lizzie Borden murders were a vampire blood offering in "How Do I Love Thee." John Mason Skipp and Marc Levinthal work a vampire riff on the death of Kurt Cobain in "On a Big Night in Monster History." Rick Hautala spots vampires fighting with the White and Red Russians in "White Terror" and Fred Olen Ray tells how one lucky passenger survived the Hindenberg disaster in "What So Proudly we Heil!" Filmmaker Brian Yuzna supplies an introduction.

Other books you might like:

Martin H. Greenberg, *Dracula: Prince of Darkness*, 1993
   editor
Stephen Jones, *The Mammoth Book of Dracula*, 1997
   editor
Robert Weinberg, *Rivals of Dracula*, 1996
   Stefan Dziemianowicz, Martin H. Greenberg, co-editors

2566

EDWARD E. KRAMER, Editor

Tales of the White Wolf

(Stone Mountain, Georgia: White Wolf, Inc., 1994)

Story type: Fantasy (Anthology)
Series: Elric
Major character(s): Elric of Melnibone, Royalty, Wizard
Time period(s): Indeterminate Past
Locale(s): The Young Kingdoms, Fictional Country

Summary: An introduction and story by Michael Moorcock plus 23 original stories continuing the adventures of Elric, Moorcock's popular fantasy character. Other authors include Scott Ciencin, Nancy Collins, Neil Gaiman, Colin Greenland, Gary Gygax, Nancy Holder, Brad Linaweaver, Brad Strickland, Karl Edward Wagner, Robert Weinberg and Tad Williams. Illustrated by artists including Timothy Bradstreet, Brom, George Pratt and Joshua Timbrook.

Other books you might like:

Glen Cook, *The Black Company*, 1984

Louise Cooper, *Nemesis*, 1989

Martin H. Greenberg, *After the King: Stories in Honor of J.R.R. Tolkien*, 1992
editor

Staley Krause, *Truth Until Paradox*, 1995
Stewart Wicch, co-author

Michael Moorcock, *Elric of Melnibone*, 1976

2567

EDWARD E. KRAMER, Editor
PETER CROWTHER, Co-Editor

Tombs

(Clarkston, Georgia: White Wolf, 1995)

Story type: Horror (Anthology)

Summary: The premise of this collection of twenty-one stories and one poem commissioned especially for the volume is situations in which people find themselves trapped. In Michael Bishop's "Epistrophy'" a man preserves his wife's remains in a jukebox. Lisa Tuttle's "White Lady's Grave" is about a woman who finds herself inextricably trapped in the working out of a Scottish myth, and Christopher Fowler's "Ginansia's Ravishment" about a woman trapped by a family curse. Kathe Koja and Barry Malzberg's "The Unchained" liken a man's entrapment within his earthly body to the fate of Lazurus, while Stephen Gallagher, in "God's Bright Little Engine," tells of a woman who feels trapped in her apartment by the Peeping Tom living below her. In Nancy Collins' "The Land of the Reflected Ones," an unscrupulous occultist becomes trapped in a mirror, and in Neil Gaiman's narrative poem "Queen of Knives," a woman becomes trapped in a magic trick. Forrest J. Ackerman supplies a wacky introduction.

Other books you might like:

Robert T. Garcia, *Chilled to the Bone*, 1992
editor

Ed Gorman, *Stalkers*, 1989
Martin H. Greenberg, co-editor

Tim Sullivan, *Cold Shocks*, 1989

2568

STALEY KRAUSE, Editor
STEWART WIECK, Co-Editor

Strange City

(New York: HarperPrism, 1996)

Story type: Horror (Anthology)

Series: World of Darkness

Summary: Set in White Wolf's World of Darkness gaming scenario, where vampires, wraiths, mages, werewolves, and other supernatural creatures mingle unobtrusively with human beings, this compilation gathers 14 stories written especially for the book. Included are S.P. Somtow's "The Voice of the Hummingbird," in which an Aztec vampire dead for centuries learns to adjust to the modern world; Lawrence Watt-Evans' "The Art of Dying," in which vampires compete for the right to turn a brilliant painter into one of their own; Richard Lee Byers' "Wolf-Trap," where a werewolf must save a fellow lycanthrope from scientific researchers; and Don Bassingthwaite's "Power," in which a vampire helps other vampires through her job in the coroner's office.

Other books you might like:

Erin Kelly, *City of Darkness*, 1995
editor

Erin Kelly, *The Splendour Falls*, 1995
editor

Edward E. Kramer, *Dark Destiny*, 1994
editor

Stewart Wieck, *The Beast Within*, 1994
editor

Stewart Wieck, *When Will You Rage*, 1990
editor

2569

STEVEN M. KRAUZER

Brainstorm

(New York: Bantam, 1991)

Story type: Horror (Wild Talents)
Major character(s): David McKay, Child; Linda Gaylen, Journalist; August Breunner, Doctor (head of The Facility)
Time period(s): 1990s
Locale(s): Washington, District of Columbia

Summary: Young psychic David McKay seeks the help of a psychic journalist in his efforts to elude The Facility, a think-tank devoted to paranormal research that hopes to boost his psychokinetic powers through surgical means for use as a weapon.

Other books you might like:

John Arbucci, *The Innocent*, 1991
Jack Caravela, *The Gifted*, 1991
John Farris, *The Fury*, 1976
Stephen King, *Firestarter*, 1980
Michael Kurland, *Button Bright*, 1990

2570

PENELOPE BANKA KREPS

Carnivores

(New York: Zebra, 1993)

Story type: Horror (Nature in Revolt; Science Fiction)
Major character(s): Evan Tremayne, Doctor (psychiatrist); Lydia Matthews, Single Parent; Harold Burnham, Scientist (neuroscientist)

Time period(s): 1990s (1993)
Locale(s): Las Flores, Florida

Summary: A reversal of the earth's geomagnetic fields activates the genesis gene buried in some human beings and animals, reversing evolution and causing them to mutate into creatures resembling their monstrous prehistoric forebears.

Other books you might like:
Peter Benchley, *Beast*, 1991
Michael Crichton, *Jurassic Park*, 1990
William Dantz, *Hunger*, 1992
J.M. Morgan, *Between the Devil and the Deep*, 1992

2571

PENELOPE BANKA KREPS

Demon's Fright
(New York: Zebra, 1992)

Story type: Horror (Black Magic)
Major character(s): Patti Demarest, Teenager; Dirk Emerson, Teenager; Travis Carter, Teacher (high-school history teacher)
Time period(s): 1990s
Locale(s): Trapper's Cay, Florida

Summary: Patti Demarest's mother tries to put a bad divorce behind her by moving with Patti to her grandmother's house in South Florida. But Patti discovers that the in-group in her new home are members of a witch coven led by loose-screw Dirk Emerson, a juvenile delinquent who does not take kindly to those who refuse to obey his orders.

Other books you might like:
Ramsey Campbell, *To Wake the Dead*, 1980
Leigh Clark, *Blood Sabbath*, 1991
Matthew J. Costello, *Darkborn*, 1992
D.A. Fowler, *The Devil's End*, 1992

2572

NANCY KRESS

The Aliens of Earth
(Sauk City, Wisconsin: Arkham House, 1993)

Story type: Science Fiction (Collection)

Summary: Contains 18 stories from 1980s and 1990s periodicals and anthologies utilizing a wide range of classical genre themes including alternate history, time travel, clairvoyant powers and alien anthropology and tending toward dark in tone.

Other books you might like:
Greg Bear, *The Wind From a Burning Woman*, 1983
Michael Bishop, *Blooded on Arachne*, 1982
John Kessel, *Meeting in Infinity*, 1992
Rebecca Ore, *Alien Bootlegger and Other Stories*, 1993
Lucius Shepard, *The Ends of the Earth*, 1991
Bruce Sterling, *Crystal Express*, 1989
Michael Swanwick, *Gravity's Angels*, 1991
James Tiptree Jr., *Her Smoke Rose Up Forever*, 1990

2573

NANCY KRESS

Beggars and Choosers
(New York: Tor, 1994)

Story type: Science Fiction (Genetic Manipulation; Political)
Major character(s): Diana Covington, Genetically Altered Being, Spy; Drew Arlen, Musician; Billy Washington, Aged Person, Hunter
Time period(s): 22nd century (2114-2115)
Locale(s): United States; Huevos Verdes, Mexico (island)

Summary: The SuperSleepless periodically dispense new and highly advanced technology from their artificially created island, helping both worker Donkeys and the Livers, idle beneficiaries of others' efforts. As technology fails to keep up with society's demands, a revolutionary plan of one SuperSleepless promises to free people from the physical need for food or clothing. However, government obstruction and reactionary forces seeking to rid Earth of all genetically modified people may halt this innovation.

Other books you might like:
F.M. Busby, *The Breeds of Man*, 1988
Octavia E. Butler, *Clay's Ark*, 1984
C.J. Cherryh, *Cyteen*, 1988
Helen Collins, *Mutagenesis*, 1993
Kathleen Ann Goonan, *Queen City Jazz*, 1994

2574

NANCY KRESS

Beggars in Spain
(Eugene, Oregon: Pulphouse Publishing, 1991)

Story type: Science Fiction (Genetic Manipulation)
Major character(s): Alice "Leisha" Camden, Genetically Altered Being
Time period(s): 21st century
Locale(s): United States

Summary: Elizabeth and Roger Camden pressure researchers to modify and fertilize an egg, insuring that their daughter will never need sleep. By accident a second, unmodified egg implants at the same time resulting in fraternal twins, one requiring sleep and the other free from that requirement. The twins grow to be very different people. This work received a 1991 Nebula Award.

Other books you might like:
Edward Bryant, *Neon Twilight*, 1990
Judith Moffett, *Two That Came True*, 1991
Frederik Pohl, *Stopping at Slowyear*, 1991
Spider Robinson, *Kill the Editor*, 1991
Robert Silverberg, *Thebes of the Hundred Gates*, 1991

2575

NANCY KRESS

Beggars Ride

(New York: Tor, 1996)

Story type: Science Fiction (Genetic Manipulation; Political)
Series: Beggars in Spain
Major character(s): Jackson Aranow, Doctor, Gentleman; Lizzie Francy, Teenager, Computer Expert; Jennifer Sharifi, Genetically Altered Being, Genius
Time period(s): 22nd century (2120-2128)
Locale(s): Manhattan East Enclave, New York; New York, New York

Summary: In a world where 20th century problems have escalated and governments collapsed, two generations of genetically modified humans prepare for war. Meanwhile, the gap between the haves and have-nots stretches beyond the breaking point, with nothing seeming to work anymore. Political, economic, and biologic forces besiege society while the sides in the war remain desperately indistinct.

2576

NANCY KRESS

Brain Rose

(New York: William Morrow, 1989)

Story type: Science Fiction (Reincarnation)
Major character(s): Robbie Brekke, Thief; Caroline Bohentin, Heiress
Time period(s): 21st century
Locale(s): Rochester, New York

Summary: For varying reasons, some of them not entirely legitimate, a number of people apply for a new and fashionable surgical procedure called Previous Life Access Surgery which supposedly gives one access to previous incarnations. Slowly evidence accumulates that the surgery has startling and hitherto unnoticed side effects that could drastically change life on Earth.

Other books you might like:
Joe Haldeman, *Buying Time*, 1989
Robert Silverberg, *The Book of Skulls*, 1972
Robert Silverberg, *To Live Again*, 1969
Norman Spinrad, *Bug Jack Barron*, 1969

2577

NANCY KRESS

Oaths and Miracles

(New York: Forge, 1996)

Story type: Science Fiction (Techno-Thriller; Genetic Manipulation)
Major character(s): Robert Cavanaugh, FBI Agent; Judy Kozinski, Journalist; Wendell Botts, Construction Worker
Time period(s): 1990s
Locale(s): United States

Summary: With Dr. Benjamen Kozinski murdered shortly after a recruitment interview with Verico Research Company, Robert Cavanaugh must decipher the pattern to prevent Judy Kozinski, Ben's widow, from death. Judy flees to a small town dominated by a religious sect where unexplained deaths also occur.

Other books you might like:
Kevin J. Anderson, *Virtual Destruction*, 1996
    Doug Beason, co-author
Lester del Rey, *The Eleventh Commandment*, 1970
    revised edition
Joe Haldeman, *Worlds: A Novel of the Near Future*, 1981
Frank Herbert, *The White Plague*, 1982
Allen Steele, *The Jericho Iteration*, 1994
Walter Jon Williams, *Hardwired*, 1986
Chelsea Quinn Yarbro, *Time of the Fourth Horseman*, 1976

2578

NOVAK KRUGER, Author/Illustrator

Tooth: A Tale of Love and Death in Paradox

(Huntington, West Virginia: University Editions, 1996)

Story type: Horror (Vampire Story)
Major character(s): Novak Darte, Vampire; Count Vigor, Vampire; Karis, Young Woman
Time period(s): 2090s (2092)
Locale(s): Bridgeport, Connecticut

Summary: In a future overrun with technology that is dehumanizing civilization, vampire Novak Darte ponders moral issues concerning the practicality of preserving the human race. Meanwhile, his arch enemy, the vampire Count Vigor, plots the overthrow of the world and Novak's demise. The author supplies the cover art and interior illustrations for this novel.

Other books you might like:
Jack Butler, *Nightshade*, 1989
Michael Conner, *Archangel*, 1995
J.G. Eccarius, *The Last Days of Christ the Vampire*, 1988
Doug Rice, *Blood of Mugwump*, 1996

2579

CHRISTOPHER KUBASIK

Changeling

(New York: Roc, 1992)

Story type: Fantasy (Legend; Urban)
Series: Shadowrun
Major character(s): Peter Clarris, Genetically Altered Being, Mythical Creature (troll); Katherine Amij, Businesswoman
Time period(s): 2050s (2053)
Locale(s): Chicago, Illinois

Summary: Transformation into a troll deprives Peter of his family, friends and opportunities for education and employment. Living on the streets as an outcast, Peter tries to find the combination of magic and nanotechnology which will restore his form and options. A game tie-in novel.

Other books you might like:
Greg Bear, *Blood Music*, 1985
Robert N. Charrette, *Choose Your Enemies Carefully*, 1991
Robert N. Charrette, *Find Your Own Truth*, 1991
Robert N. Charrette, *Never Deal with a Dragon*, 1990
Robert N. Charrette, *Never Trust an Elf*, 1992
Nigel Findley, *2XS*, 1992
K.W. Jeter, *Madlands*, 1991
Will Shetterly, *Elsewhere*, 1991
Jordan K. Weisman, *Into the Shadows*, 1992
 editor
Terri Windling, *Life on the Border*, 1991
 editor

2580

CHRISTOPHER KUBASIK

The Longing Ring
(New York: Roc, 1993)

Story type: Fantasy (Quest)
Series: Earth Dawn
Major character(s): Garlthik, Mythical Creature (ork), Thief; J'role, Teenager, Thief
Time period(s): Indeterminate Past
Locale(s): Throal, Fictional City; Parlainth, Fictional City

Summary: Possessed by an evil spirit and an outcast in his village, J'role leaves with a travelling ork. The pair share adventures as they flee enemies and pursue the promise of a magic city. First of a game tie-in series.

Other books you might like:
Steven Brust, *Jhereg*, 1983
Glen Cook, *The Black Company*, 1984
Barbara Hambly, *The Time of the Dark*, 1982
Fritz Leiber, *Swords and Deviltry*, 1970
Angus Wells, *Wrath of Ashar*, 1990

2581

MICHAEL P. KUBE-MCDOWELL

Before the Storm
(New York: Bantam Spectra, 1996)

Story type: Science Fiction (Space Opera; Psychic Powers)
Series: Star Wars: The Black Fleet Crisis
Major character(s): Lando Calrissian, Military Personnel (general); Leia Organa Solo, Royalty (princess), Leader; Luke Skywalker, Martial Arts Expert (Jedi knight), Hero
Time period(s): Indeterminate Past
Locale(s): New Republic, Interstellar Empire/Federation; Coruscant, Planet—Imaginary; Outer Space

Summary: With the thwarting of the evil Empire's expansion, the New Republic gains a fragile peace. Leia works to counter the forces threatening to tear the union into warring factions, while Lando investigates a mysterious and dangerous spacecraft. First of a trilogy.

Other books you might like:
Roger MacBride Allen, *Ambush at Corellia*, 1995
Kevin J. Anderson, *Jedi Search*, 1994
Brian Daley, *The Han Solo Adventures*, 1992
L. Neil Smith, *The Lando Calrissian Adventures*, 1994
Michael A. Stackpole, *Rogue Squadron*, 1996
Timothy Zahn, *Heir to the Empire*, 1991

2582

MICHAEL P. KUBE-MCDOWELL

Exile
(New York: Ace, 1992)

Story type: Science Fiction (Political; Science Fiction)
Major character(s): Meer Fastet, Judge, Revolutionary; Kedar Nanchen, Government Official, Revolutionary; Oren Anadon, Ruler (exarch)
Time period(s): Indeterminate Future
Locale(s): Taurin, Planet—Imaginary (cities of Ana and Edera)

Summary: A messenger interrupts Meer Fastet with a request from the ailing Kedar Nanchen that his body be brought back to Ana from exile in Edera, as the law permits. Compelled by a debt of honor, Meer risks the trip to fetch Kedar, finding many surprises which change his future and Ana.

Other books you might like:
C.J. Cherryh, *Cyteen*, 1988
Donald E. McQuinn, *Warrior*, 1990
Alis A. Rasmussen, *A Passage of Stars*, 1990
Joan Slonczewski, *A Door into Ocean*, 1986
Sheri S. Tepper, *Grass*, 1989
Walter Jon Williams, *Angel Station*, 1989

2583

MICHAEL P. KUBE-MCDOWELL

The Quiet Pools
(New York: Ace, 1990)

Story type: Science Fiction (Espionage Thriller)
Major character(s): Jeremiah, Activist, Terrorist (ecological); Mikhail Dryke, Businessman (security chief); Christopher McCutcheon, Librarian
Time period(s): 2090s
Locale(s): Earth

Summary: Ecoterrorist Jeremiah is determined to end the drain of human resources away from Mother Earth by using whatever means possible to shut down the starship program. The *Memphis'* security chief, Dryke, is just as determined to ensure that this second starship successfully launches.

Other books you might like:
Piers Anthony, *But What of Earth?*, 1989
Robert A. Heinlein, *Time for the Stars*, 1956
Judith Moffett, *Pennterra*, 1987
Sheri S. Tepper, *Grass*, 1989

2584

MICHAEL KURLAND

Button Bright

(New York: Jove, 1990)

Story type: Horror (Child-in-Peril)
Major character(s): Rachel ''Button'' Gramm, Child; Philip Kasselman, Doctor (psychiatrist); Patswami, Cult Member (leader)
Time period(s): 1990s
Locale(s): Moldowen, Ohio (Grover College and places across the US)

Summary: Eleven-year-old genius ''Button'' Gramm is pursued by a cadre of mysterious men who seem out to abduct her and to kill everyone who stands in their way. As she begins to delve into the mysterious origins of her mysterious talents, Button moves perilously closer to a confrontation with Patswami, a mystic cult leader who has used thought control to manipulate henchmen to kill similarly gifted children throughout the country.

Other books you might like:
John Farris, *The Fury*, 1976
Stephen King, *Firestarter*, 1987
Dean R. Koontz, *Lightning*, 1980
John Wyndham, *The Midwich Cuckoos*, 1957
John Wyndham, *The Crysalids*, 1955
Chelsea Quinn Yarbro, *Firecode*, 1987

2585

MICHAEL KURLAND

A Study in Sorcery

(New York: Ace, 1989)

Story type: Fantasy (Mystery)
Major character(s): Lord Darcy Lord, Detective; Sean O. Lochlainn, Sidekick
Time period(s): Indeterminate
Locale(s): New World, Alternate Earth

Summary: In a world where magic works, Lord Darcy and his companion, Sean O Lochlainn, are sent to the New World to determine who murdered a member of Azteque royalty.

Other books you might like:
Barbara Hambly, *Those Who Hunt the Night*, 1988
Robert A. Heinlein, *The Unpleasant Profession of Jonathan Hoag*, 1959

2586

PYOTR KURTINSKI

Thirst

(New York: Leisure, 1995)

Story type: Horror (Vampire Story)
Major character(s): William Van Diemen, Vampire; Vincent Mara, Writer; Bradford C. Wilcox, Lawyer
Time period(s): 1990s (1995)
Locale(s): New York, New York (the Bronx)

Summary: Bronx vampire William Van Diemen would like nothing more than for the world outside his castle in the Riverdale section of the Bronx to leave him alone so he can write his memoirs in peace. But the detemination of a businessman to buy Van Diemen's home at a bargain price puts him on the defensive and foments a blood war between the two.

Other books you might like:
Nancy Baker, *The Night Inside*, 1995
Nancy Kilpatrick, *Near Death*, 1995
Tanith Lee, *Darkness, I*, 1995
Michael Romkey, *The Vampire Papers*, 1994
Fred Saberhagen, *Dominion*, 1982
Whitley Strieber, *The Hunger*, 1981

2587

KATHERINE KURTZ
DEBORAH TURNER HARRIS, Co-Author

The Adept

(New York: Ace, 1991)

Story type: Fantasy (Contemporary; Magic Conflict)
Series: Adept
Major character(s): Adam Sinclair, Doctor, Psychic; Peregrine Lovat, Artist, Psychic; Noel McLeod, Police Officer, Psychic
Time period(s): 1990s
Locale(s): Scotland

Summary: Sir Adam Sinclair, investigating the theft of the Hepburn Sword, comes across Peregrine Lovat and helps him to regain his Gift of Seeing. With the aid of Noel McLeod, the two must go to Castle Urqhart to stop black magicians who have stolen the fairy flag of the McLeods, lest they enslave all of Scotland.

Other books you might like:
Mildred Downey Broxon, *Too Long a Sacrifice*, 1981
Randall Garrett, *Lord Darcy Investigates*, 1981
Randall Garrett, *Murder and Magic*, 1979
Randall Garrett, *Too Many Magicians*, 1967
Mercedes Lackey, *Children of the Night*, 1990
Mercedes Lackey, *Burning Water*, 1989

2588

KATHERINE KURTZ

The Bastard Prince

(New York: Ballantine Del Rey, 1994)

Story type: Fantasy (Political; Magic Conflict)
Series: Heirs of Saint Camber
Major character(s): Rhys Michael Alister Haldane, Ruler (king), Psychic; Cathan Drummond, Knight, Companion (Rhys Michael's); Rhysel Thuryn, Healer, Psychic
Time period(s): Indeterminate Past
Locale(s): Gwynedd, Fictional Country

Summary: After six years as a puppet king, Rhys Michael meets Miklos of Torenth and Marek, the Festil claimant to Gwynedd's throne. In order to defeat the two, Rhys Michael shows some of his psychic powers, but a wound to his hand gives the Regents their chance to kill him and make it seem like a natural death, despite the disastrous repercussions.

Other books you might like:
Marion Zimmer Bradley, *The Heirs of Hammerfell*, 1989
John Christopher, *The Sword of the Spirits*, 1972
Susan Schwartz, *Byzantium's Crown*, 1987
Harry Turtledove, *Krispos the Emperor*, 1994
Chelsea Quinn Yarbro, *Ariosto*, 1980

2589

KATHERINE KURTZ
DEBORAH TURNER HARRIS, Co-Author

Dagger Magic
(New York: Ace, 1995)

Story type: Fantasy (Mystery; Religious)
Major character(s): Adam Sinclair, Doctor, Psychic; Peregrine Lovat, Artist, Psychic; Noel McLeod, Police Officer, Psychic
Time period(s): 1990s (1995)
Locale(s): Mull of Kintyre, Ireland; Scotland; Switzerland

Summary: When the untimely arrival of a corpse disturbs Peregrine Lovat's honeymoon, the psychic emanations from the corpse prompt Lovat to ask for help from his mentor, Adam Sinclair, and the magical lodge to which they both belong. Their search for truth leads them to an evil older than, but intimately connected with, Nazi Germany.

Other books you might like:
Lois McMaster Bujold, *The Spirit Ring*, 1992
Tom Deitz, *Soulsmith*, 1991
Umberto Eco, *The Name of the Rose*, 1983
Katharine Kerr, *Polar City Blues*, 1990
John Varley, *The Barbie Murders and Other Stories*, 1980
Vernor Vinge, *Marooned in Realtime*, 1986
Walter Jon Williams, *Aristoi*, 1992

2590

KATHERINE KURTZ
DEBORAH TURNER HARRIS, Co-Author

Death of an Adept
(New York: Ace, 1996)

Story type: Fantasy (Psychic Powers; Religious)
Series: Adept
Major character(s): Adam Sinclair, Doctor, Psychic; Francis Raeburn, Psychic, Magician; Ximena Lockhart, Doctor, Fiance(e)
Time period(s): 1990s
Locale(s): Scotland

Summary: Adam Sinclair returns from the U.S.A. engaged to be married, while his nemesis, Francis Raeburn, contacts Taranis to regain his power over weather. Raeburn will stop at nothing to accomplish this, including sacrificing one of his own men, a druid priest, to resurrect an ancient wizard. However, this wizard needs a body to inhabit and decides Adam Sinclair's will do.

Other books you might like:
Orson Scott Card, *Alvin Journeyman*, 1995
Dale Estey, *A Lost Tale*, 1980
Elizabeth Hand, *Waking the Moon*, 1995
Nick Pollotta, *Full Moonster*, 1992
Tim Powers, *The Drawing of the Dark*, 1979
Melissa Scott, *Point of Hopes*, 1995
    Lisa A. Barnett, co-author
Sean Stewart, *Resurrection Man*, 1995

2591

KATHERINE KURTZ

King Javan's Year
(New York: Ballantine Del Rey, 1992)

Story type: Fantasy (Political; Magic Conflict)
Series: Heirs of Saint Camber
Major character(s): Javan Jashan Urien Haldane, Royalty (king), Psychic; Guiscard de Courcy, Knight, Psychic; Paulin, Religious (priest)
Time period(s): Indeterminate
Locale(s): Gwynedd, Fictional Country

Summary: After the death of his brother Alroy, Javan Haldane becomes king of Gwynedd despite opposition from the Regents who think him too threatening to their own power. Javan seeks to ease the restrictions upon the Deryni and rule more humanely despite the intimidation and killing of his allies. Finally, a journey to a holy site presents a lethal challenge to Javan's rule.

Other books you might like:
Judith Tarr, *Ars Magica*, 1989
Harry Turtledove, *Krispos of Videssos*, 1991
Chelsea Quinn Yarbro, *Ariosto*, 1980

2592

KATHERINE KURTZ
DEBORAH TURNER HARRIS, Co-Author

The Lodge of the Lynx
(New York: Ace, 1992)

Story type: Fantasy (Magic Conflict; Psychic Powers)
Series: Adept
Major character(s): Adam Sinclair, Doctor (psychiatrist), Psychic; Peregrine Lovat, Artist (painter), Psychic; Francis Raeburn, Historian, Occultist
Time period(s): 1990s
Locale(s): Scotland

Summary: Investigating the assassination of Freemasons all over Scotland by means of black magic, Adam Sinclair finds the Lodge of the Lynx, which he had thought thoroughly destroyed but now finds with a new headmaster, none other than Rudolf Hess, who possesses a book of black magic once owned by Adolf Hitler. Francis Raeburn knows that Adam Sinclair and his friends present the greatest threat and tries to have them killed, drawing them and other Huntsmen into battle with the Lodge.

Other books you might like:
Mildred Downey Broxon, *Too Long a Sacrifice*, 1981
Randall Garrett, *Too Many Magicians*, 1967
Michael Kurland, *Ten Little Wizards*, 1988
Mercedes Lackey, *Children of the Night*, 1990
Andre Norton, *Dread Companion*, 1970

2593
KATHERINE KURTZ
DEBORAH TURNER HARRIS, Co-Author

The Templar Treasure
(New York: Ace, 1993)

Story type: Fantasy (Magic Conflict; Religious)
Series: Adept
Major character(s): Adam Sinclair, Doctor (psychiatrist), Psychic; Peregrine Lovat, Artist, Psychic; Sir John Grahame, Military Personnel (retired), Psychic
Time period(s): 1990s
Locale(s): England; Scotland

Summary: After the theft of the Seal of Solomon in York, Adam Sinclair attempts to retrieve it before it can unleash horrors on the world. In Kent, Sinclair calls upon a spirit for help then sets out to acquire necessary artifacts before battling demonic invasion.

Other books you might like:
Pierre Barbet, *Baphomet's Meteor*, 1972
Diana Gabaldon, *Dragonfly in Amber*, 1992
R. Garcia y Robertson, *The Spiral Dance*, 1991
Randall Garrett, *Too Many Magicians*, 1967
R.A. MacAvoy, *The Book of Kells*, 1985
Pamela F. Service, *Winter of Magic's Return*, 1985
Judith Tarr, *The Dagger and the Cross: A Novel of the Crusades*, 1991
Alison Uttley, *A Traveler in Time*, 1940

2594
KATHERINE KURTZ

Two Crowns for America
(New York: Bantam Spectra, 1996)

Story type: Fantasy (Historical; Political)
Major character(s): George Washington, Military Personnel, Revolutionary (Freemason); Justin Carmichael, Revolutionary (Freemason); Comte de Saint-Germain, Revolutionary (Freemason)
Time period(s): 1770s (1775)
Locale(s): Philadelphia, Pennsylvania; Leipzig, Germany

Summary: Thrown from his horse in an America on the verge of revolt, George Washington has a curious dream. Meanwhile, many people drawn together under the banner of Freemasonry take action according to the plans of a mysterious Master. In the turmoil of revolt the future remains uncertain; will the revolution succeed in creating a truly free country?

2595
EWA KURYLUK

Century 21
(Normal, Illinois: Dalkey Archive Press, 1992)

Story type: Science Fiction (Literary)
Major character(s): Ann Kar, Writer, Journalist; Carol, Mentally Ill Person
Time period(s): 21st century; 31st century
Locale(s): Earth; Moon (Earth's)

Summary: Suicidal and obsessed with leaving Earth for the Moon, Carol dreams of a lunar researcher who, discovering fragments concerning Carol and her sister's existence a thousand years after her death, constructs an erotic fantasy surrounding his relationship with Carol. Author's first novel.

Other books you might like:
Jesse Browner, *Conglomeros*, 1992
Haruki Murakami, *Hard-Boiled Wonderland and the End of the World*, 1991
Steve Szilagyi, *Photographing Fairies*, 1992
John Varley, *Steel Beach*, 1992
Kate Wilhelm, *Margaret and I*, 1971

2596
ELLEN KUSHNER

Thomas the Rhymer
(New York: Morrow, 1990)

Story type: Fantasy (Adventure)
Major character(s): Thomas, Minstrel; Elspeth, Spouse (of Thomas)
Time period(s): 14th century (1300s)
Locale(s): Elfland, Mythical Place

Summary: Enamored by Elspeth, Thomas is abducted by the Queen of Elfland and spends seven years as her lover in her magical kingdom. Upon release, Thomas is unable to speak anything but the truth, causing complications when he marries Elspeth and resumes his earthly life.

Other books you might like:
John Desjarlais, *The Throne of Tara*, 1990
Peter Tremayne, *Bloodmist*, 1988

2597
HENRY KUTTNER

The Book of Iod
(Oakland: Chaosium, 1995)

Story type: Horror (Anthology; Collection)
Summary: This first major collection of weird fiction by an author best known for his groundbreaking Golden Age science fiction reflects his indebtedness to the mythos of extradimensional monsters created by his mentor, H.P. Lovecraft. "The Eater of Souls" and "The Jest of Droom-Avista" are fantasy stories set on the alien world of Bel Yarnak. In "The Invaders," "Hydra," and "The Hunt," Bel Yarnakian mon-

sters described in the forbidden Book of Iod become the nemeses of earthly mortals. ''Bells of Horror,'' ''The Salem Horror,'' and ''The Secret of Kralitz'' are Gothic tales written in Lovecraftian style. The book also contains Kuttner's collaboration with Robert Bloch, ''The Black Kiss,'' and one story apiece dealing with Kuttner's contribution to the Lovecraft mythos from Robert M. Price and Lin Carter. Edited by Robert M. Price.

Other books you might like:
Robert Bloch, *The Mysteries of the Worm*, 1993
Ramsey Campbell, *The Inhabitant of the Lake and Less Welcome Tenants*, 1964
H.P. Lovecraft, *The Watchers out of Time*, 1974
    August Derleth, co-author
Brian Lumley, *The Caller of the Black*, 1971

2598

RICHARD LA PLANTE

Tegne: Soul Warrior
(New York: Tor, 1995)

Story type: Fantasy (Political; Religious)
Major character(s): Tegne, Martial Arts Expert (Way of the Empty Hand), Bastard Son; Renagi, Warrior, Leader (Warlord of Zendow)
Time period(s): Indeterminate
Locale(s): Zendow, Fictional City (walled city state); Temple of the Moon, Mythical Place; The Plane Beyond, Mythical Place

Summary: Abandoned at birth, Tegne finds a savior and mentor in Tabata, a mystic and a martial arts adept. Despite attempts to kill him or subvert Tegne's efforts, he attains great spiritual and physical abilities as fate leads him toward eventual confrontation with the Warlord of Zendow. First novel, orginally published in Great Britain in 1988.

Other books you might like:
Adrian Cole, *Mother of Storms*, 1992
Roberta Cray, *The Sword and the Lion*, 1993
Elizabeth A. Lynn, *Watchtower*, 1979
Sean Russell, *The Initiate Brother*, 1991
Jessica Amanda Salmonson, *Tomoe Gozen*, 1984

2599

MERCEDES LACKEY
LARRY DIXON, Co-Author

The Black Gryphon
(New York: DAW, 1994)

Story type: Fantasy (Magic Conflict; Adventure)
Series: Mage Wars
Major character(s): Skandranon, Mythical Creature (gryphon); Amberdrake, Healer (comfort worker/kestra'chern); Urtho, Magician
Time period(s): Indeterminate Past
Locale(s): Ka'venusho, Fictional Country; Tantara, Fictional Country

Summary: Once upon a time, the most powerful mages in the world go to war. A good man who goes to war only when it becomes unavoidable, Urtho has the aid of the intelligent creatures he created, the Kaled'a'in tribes with their shaman, kestra'chern, healers, warriors and others. Ma'ar uses his own constructs and allies, as well as viciousness, evil and treachery. Both sides give all they have in the service of those they believe in, building the war to a climax of unfathomable destruction.

Other books you might like:
Heather Gladney, *Teot's War*, 1987
Barbara Hambly, *The Time of the Dark*, 1982
Mickey Zucker Reichert, *The Last of the Renshai*, 1992
Michelle Sagara, *Into the Dark Lands*, 1991
Janny Wurts, *Stormwarden*, 1984

2600

MERCEDES LACKEY
LARRY DIXON, Co-Author

Born to Run
(New York: Baen, 1992)

Story type: Fantasy (Light Fantasy; Urban)
Series: Serrated Edge
Major character(s): Keighvin, Mythical Creature (elf); Tania Jane Delaney, Runaway, Prostitute; Tannim, Magician
Time period(s): 1990s
Locale(s): Georgia

Summary: Three runaway teenagers, each forced into child prostitution, become unwitting pawns in a world of drugs, pornography, the quest to develop a low iron content hotrod and an unearthly vendetta.

Other books you might like:
Michael de Larrabeiti, *The Borribles*, 1978
Michael de Larrabeiti, *The Borribles Go for Broke*, 1982
Michael Reaves, *Street Magic*, 1991
Will Shetterly, *Elsewhere*, 1991
Terri Windling, *Borderland*, 1986
    Mark Alan Arnold, co-editor
Terri Windling, *Bordertown*, 1986
    Mark Alan Arnold, co-editor
Terri Windling, *Life on the Border*, 1991
    editor

2601

MERCEDES LACKEY

Burning Water
(New York: Tor, 1989)

Story type: Horror (Mystery)
Series: Diana Tregarde
Major character(s): Diana Tregarde, Paranormal Investigator (Witch), Writer (Romance novelist); Mark Valdez, Detective—Police, Psychic
Time period(s): 1980s
Locale(s): Dallas, Texas

Summary: Investigating a series of brutal, ritualistic murders, Tregarde and Valdez find themselves threatened by a cult intent upon completing an ancient ceremony that will release the powers of the ancient Aztec god Tezcatlipoca.

Other books you might like:
John Burke, *The Devil's Footsteps*, 1976
Manly Wade Wellman, *After Dark*, 1980
Manly Wade Wellman, *The Old Gods Waken*, 1979

2602

MERCEDES LACKEY

By the Sword
(New York: DAW, 1991)

Story type: Fantasy (Adventure)
Series: Valdemar
Major character(s): Kerowyn, Mercenary
Time period(s): Indeterminate Past
Locale(s): Rethwellen, Fictional Country; Valdemar, Fictional Country

Summary: In part one, titled "Kerowyn's Ride" her brother's wedding feast is attacked and the bride-to-be kidnapped, leaving only Kerowyn alive and whole enough to go after the raiders. Afterward, Tarma and Kethry train her to be a mercenary fighter. In part two, titled "Two Edged Blade" Kerowyn is a scout with the Skybolt Mercenary Company, when some treacherous border fighting separates her from the Skybolts. Returning, she finds the new Captain determined to get them all killed through her ignorance and pride. In part three, titled "The Price of Command" Kerowyn has been Captain of the Skybolts for 10 years when emissaries from Valdemar desperately plead for help and the Skybolts hire against the evil King Ancar of Hardorn, whose onslaught none may survive.

Other books you might like:
Steven Brust, *Jhereg*, 1983
Glen Cook, *The Black Company*, 1984
Barbara Hambly, *The Armies of Daylight*, 1983
Katharine Kerr, *Daggerspell*, 1986
Elizabeth Moon, *Sheepfarmer's Daughter*, 1988

2603

MERCEDES LACKEY
JOSEPHA SHERMAN, Co-Author

A Cast of Corbies
(New York: Baen, 1994)

Story type: Fantasy (Religious; Political)
Series: Bardic Choices
Major character(s): Raven, Minstrel (Free Bard); Magpie, Minstrel (Free Bard); Regina, Religious
Time period(s): Indeterminate
Locale(s): Kingsford, Fictional City; Alanda, Fictional Country

Summary: Free Bards find increasing trouble as church officials create additional problems for musicians who refuse to follow Guild leadership.

Other books you might like:
Gael Baudino, *Strands of Starlight*, 1989
Emma Bull, *War for the Oaks*, 1987
Mary Gentle, *Rats and Gargoyles*, 1991
Elizabeth Ann Scarborough, *Phantom Banjo*, 1991
Josepha Sherman, *The Shining Falcon*, 1989
Josepha Sherman, *A Strange and Ancient Name*, 1993
Paula Volsky, *Illusion*, 1992

2604

MERCEDES LACKEY
JOSEPHA SHERMAN, Co-Author

Castle of Deception
(New York: Baen, 1992)

Story type: Fantasy (Quest; Political)
Series: Bard's Tale
Major character(s): Kevin, Musician (apprentice bard), Magician; Volmar, Traitor, Nobleman; Carlotta, Mythical Creature (fairy), Imposter (Charina)
Time period(s): Indeterminate
Locale(s): Count Volmar's Castle, Mythical Place; Westerin, Fictional City

Summary: On a simple manuscript copying mission, Kevin loses the manuscript then meets Count Volmar's niece, Charina, diverting him from his copying mission. When Charina becomes a kidnap victim, Kevin and a group of adventurers try to rescue her, unexpectedly involving themselves in a plot to overthrow the king.

Other books you might like:
Charles de Lint, *The Little Country*, 1991
Josepha Sherman, *Child of Faerie, Child of Earth*, 1992
Josepha Sherman, *The Horse of Flame*, 1990
Josepha Sherman, *The Shining Falcon*, 1989
Josepha Sherman, *A Strange and Ancient Name*, 1993

2605

MERCEDES LACKEY

Children of the Night
(New York: Tor, 1990)

Story type: Horror (Vampire Story; Mystery)
Series: Diana Tregarde
Major character(s): Diana Tregarde, Psychic, Detective; Andre LeBrel, Vampire
Time period(s): 1970s
Locale(s): New York, New York

Summary: Someone or something is slaughtering people in New York and destroying their souls. Diana Tregarde is bound to track down and stop it, bound by her friendship with her neighbor, her developing relationship with Andre, and chiefly by her role as a Guardian. This book is a prequel to *Burning Water*.

Other books you might like:
Randall Garrett, *Too Many Magicians*, 1967
Simon R. Green, *Hawk & Fisher*, 1990
Tanya Huff, *Blood Price*, 1991

Madeleine L'Engle, *The Young Unicorns*, 1968
Diana L. Paxson, *Brisingamen*, 1984

2606

MERCEDES LACKEY
LARRY DIXON, Co-Author

Chrome Circle
(New York: Baen, 1994)

Story type: Fantasy (Urban; Magic Conflict)
Series: Serrated Edge
Major character(s): Tannim Drake, Sports Figure (race car driver), Magician; Foxtrot "Fox" X-ray, Mythical Creature (Japanese fox-spirit), Magician; SharMarali "Shar" Halanyn, Mythical Creature (Japanese fox-spirit), Magician
Time period(s): 1990s; Indeterminate
Locale(s): Oklahoma; Underhill, Fictional Country (mythic realm); The Unformed, Mythical Place

Summary: Tannim musters all his defenses when the woman of his dreams appears as his challenger, sent as a gambit in a continuing conflict among wizards.

Other books you might like:
Emma Bull, *War for the Oaks*, 1987
Susan Dexter, *The Wizard's Shadow*, 1993
Elizabeth Forrest, *Phoenix Fire*, 1992
Ellen Guon, *Bedlam Boyz*, 1993
Laurell K. Hamilton, *Nightseer*, 1992
Terri Windling, *Life on the Border*, 1991
    editor

2607

MERCEDES LACKEY

The Eagle and the Nightingales
(New York: Baen, 1995)

Story type: Fantasy (Political; Adventure)
Series: Bardic Voices
Major character(s): Nightingale "Lyrebird", Musician (free bard), Magician; T'fyrr Redwing, Alien (Haspur), Musician; Theovere, Royalty (high king)
Time period(s): Indeterminate
Locale(s): Alanda, Fictional Country; The Twenty Kingdoms, Fictional Country

Summary: When independently approached by elves, Deliambrens and other Free Bards to travel as a spy to the capital of the Twenty Kingdoms, Nightingale reluctantly endeavors to discover why High King Theovere's excellent administration has deteriorated. After disguising her identity, arranging employment as a Bard and organizing street urchins into an information network, Nightingale joins forces with T'fyrr, the Chief Court Musician on a similar mission for the Deliambrens. With the union of their music and magic, they hope to restore Theovere's effective rule.

Other books you might like:
Phyllis Eisenstein, *In the Red Lord's Reach*, 1989
Suzette Haden Elgin, *Twelve Fair Kingdoms*, 1981

Robin Hobb, *Assassin's Apprentice*, 1995
Tanya Huff, *Sing the Four Quarters*, 1994
Caroline Stevermer, *A College of Magics*, 1994
Patricia C. Wrede, *The Raven Ring*, 1994

2608

MERCEDES LACKEY

The Fire Rose
(New York: Baen, 1995)

Story type: Fantasy (Magic Conflict; Romance)
Major character(s): Rosalind "Rose" Hawkins, Scholar, Orphan; Jason Cameron, Magician (Firemaster), Werewolf; Paul du Mond, Apprentice
Time period(s): 1910s
Locale(s): San Francisco, California; Chicago, Illinois

Summary: Recently orphaned, Rose Hawkins travels to San Francisco to work for a mysterious man, Jason Cameron, who requires her to read ancient texts about magic. She soon learns that Jason seeks a spell to free him from his half-man/half-wolf form.

Other books you might like:
Jill Barnett, *Imagine*, 1995
Peter David, *Howling Mad*, 1989
Pamela Dean, *The Dubious Hills*, 1994
Ashley McConnell, *The Fountains of Mirlacca*, 1995
Sharon Shinn, *The Shape-Changer's Wife*, 1995
Midori Snyder, *The Flight of Michael McBride*, 1994

2609

MERCEDES LACKEY

Firebird
(New York: Tor, 1996)

Story type: Fantasy (Legend; Magic Conflict)
Major character(s): Ilya, Guard, Adventurer
Time period(s): Indeterminate
Locale(s): Russia

Summary: Ilya's resourcefulness guarding a cherry orchard gains him a magical feather which allows him to understand animal speech. A subsequent deed of friendship brings him a constant companion, a fox, before he falls in love with an enchanted princess who requires rescue. Based on a Russian fairy tale.

Other books you might like:
Aleksandr Afanas'ev, *Russian Fairy Tales*, 1945
    editor
Steven Brust, *The Sun, the Moon, and the Stars*, 1987
C.J. Cherryh, *Chernevog*, 1990
C.J. Cherryh, *Rusalka*, 1989
C.J. Cherryh, *Yvgenie*, 1991
Fred Saberhagen, *Dancing Bears*, 1996

2610

MERCEDES LACKEY
RU EMERSON, Co-Author

Fortress of Frost and Fire
(New York: Baen, 1993)

Story type: Fantasy (Adventure; Quest)
Series: Bard's Tale
Major character(s): Gawaine, Apprentice, Musician (bard); Naitachal, Mythical Creature (dark elf), Musician (bard); Voyvodan, Mythical Creature (snow dragon)
Time period(s): Indeterminate
Locale(s): Mythical Place

Summary: Rumors of a valley which remains snow covered even during the heat of summer spark Naitachal's interest. On the way to investigate the anomaly, Naitachal and Gawaine acquire knowledgeable guides and more rumors of dire consequences befalling any who venture there. However, neither musician anticipates events which would tempt Gawaine to forsake his master or Naitachal to return to the necromancy he had abandoned. Game tie-in.

Other books you might like:
Ru Emerson, *The Calling of the Three*, 1990
Ru Emerson, *The Craft of Light*, 1993
Ru Emerson, *One Land, One Duke*, 1992
Ru Emerson, *The Two in Hiding*, 1991
Elizabeth Moon, *Liar's Oath*, 1992

2611

MERCEDES LACKEY

Jinx High
(New York: Tor, 1991)

Story type: Horror (Occult; Mystery)
Series: Diana Tregarde
Major character(s): Diana Tregarde, Writer (romance writer), Witch; Derek "Deke" Kestrel, Teenager, Student; Fay Harper, Teenager, Student
Time period(s): 1990s
Locale(s): Tulsa, Oklahoma

Summary: Invited to lecture the senior class of Jenks High School—also called "Jinx High"—romance writer and occult investigator Diana Tregarde discovers that the teenage son of a good friend and fellow paranormal specialist is psychic, and that his aura has attracted a fiendish sex magick conjuration, summoned by a teenage dabbler in the black arts, who is jealous of his choice of dates for the senior prom.

Other books you might like:
Gael Baudino, *Gossamer Axe*, 1990
Emma Bull, *War for the Oaks*, 1987
Tanya Huff, *Blood Price*, 1991
Stephen King, *Carrie*, 1974
Katherine Kurtz, *Deryni Rising*, 1970

2612

MERCEDES LACKEY
ELLEN GUON, Co-Author

Knight of Ghosts and Shadows
(New York: Baen, 1990)

Story type: Fantasy (Contemporary)
Major character(s): Eric Banyon, Musician (street busker), Minstrel (bard); Beth Kentraine, Psychic, Musician; Korendil, Mythical Creature (elf), Royalty
Time period(s): 1990s
Locale(s): Los Angeles, California

Summary: When Eric's music wakes Korendil after ten years of binding, Eric must come to terms with the knowledge that 1) there really are elves in L.A., 2) he really is a bard and 3) he, Kory and Beth are the only ones who might be able to stop the destruction of the magic nexus that keeps the elves alive and fuels all the creativity of Southern California. Unfortunately, Korendil's enemy, Perenor, and Perenor's daughter, Ria, have considerably more power and experience at their disposal.

Other books you might like:
Gael Baudino, *Gossamer Axe*, 1990
Steven Brust, *Cowboy Feng's Space Bar and Grille*, 1990
Emma Bull, *War for the Oaks*, 1987
Tom Deitz, *Windmaster's Bane*, 1987
Charles de Lint, *Jack, the Giant-Killer*, 1987
Tanya Huff, *Gate of Darkness, Circle of Light*, 1989

2613

MERCEDES LACKEY

The Lark and the Wren
(New York: Baen, 1991)

Story type: Fantasy (Young Adult; Adventure)
Series: Bardic Voices
Major character(s): Rune, Musician
Time period(s): Indeterminate
Locale(s): Nolton, Fictional City; Midsummer Faire at Kingsford, Fictional City

Summary: Goaded into a mortally dangerous and daring feat, Rune fiddles all night for the Skull Hill Ghost, the sight of whom is generally fatal. As a reward for her performance the ghost supplies Rune with enough money for her to pursue her goal of winning the trials for the Bardic Guild, allowing her to become a renowned musician.

Other books you might like:
Gael Baudino, *Gossamer Axe*, 1990
Emma Bull, *War for the Oaks*, 1987
Orson Scott Card, *Songmaster*, 1980
Stephen Leigh, *The Abraxis Marvel Circus*, 1990
Anne McCaffrey, *Crystal Singer*, 1982
Andrea Shettle, *Flute Song Magic*, 1990

2614

MERCEDES LACKEY

Magic's Pawn
(New York: DAW, 1989)

Story type: Fantasy (Sword and Sorcery)
Series: Last Herald Mage
Major character(s): Vanyel, Magician (Teenager), Homosexual (Upper-class)
Time period(s): Indeterminate

Summary: Vanyel is despised by his father for his lack of strength and love of music. However, he discovers he has a great deal of magical power, and he must come to terms with his powers in order to grow up.

Other books you might like:
Sydney J. Van Scyoc, *Feather Stroke*, 1989

2615

MERCEDES LACKEY

Magic's Price
(New York: Tor, 1990)

Story type: Fantasy (Magic Conflict)
Series: Last Herald Mage
Major character(s): Vanyel Ashkevron, Magician, Homosexual; Stefan, Minstrel (Bard), Homosexual; Savil Ashkevron, Magician
Time period(s): Indeterminate Past
Locale(s): Valdemar, Fictional Country

Summary: The Mages of Valdemar are dying or being killed much faster than they can be replaced. Valdemar's king is dying, and the perpetual raiding on the Karsite border threatens to develop into war. Vanyel, the most powerful Herald-Mage ever known, has held off disaster so far, but when all his fellow mages are gone, he realizes he must take the battle directly to the enemy.

Other books you might like:
Marion Zimmer Bradley, *The Heritage of Hastur*, 1975
Heather Gladney, *Teot's War*, 1987
Tanya Huff, *The Fire's Stone*, 1990
Katherine Kurtz, *Deryni Rising*, 1970
Ellen Kushner, *Swordspoint*, 1987

2616

MERCEDES LACKEY

Magic's Promise
(New York: DAW, 1990)

Story type: Fantasy (Adventure)
Series: Last Herald Mage
Major character(s): Vanyel, Religious (Herald Mage)
Time period(s): Indeterminate

Summary: Vanyel returns home for a much needed rest, only to find that he feels like a child once again. He soon "hears" the psychic pain of a child who will one day be a Herald Mage, only to find out the boy is a prince suspected of murdering his family by psychic means.

Other books you might like:
Megan Lindholm, *Luck of the Wheels*, 1989
Anne McCaffrey, *Dragonriders of Pern Series*,

2617

MERCEDES LACKEY

The Robin and the Kestrel
(New York: Baen, 1993)

Story type: Fantasy (Political; Religious)
Series: Bardic Voices
Major character(s): Robin, Minstrel, Revolutionary; Kestrel, Minstrel, Royalty; Padrik, Religious (High Bishop of Gradford), Criminal
Time period(s): Indeterminate
Locale(s): Skull Hill, Mythical Place; Gradford, Fictional City; Carthell Abbey, Mythical Place

Summary: When Robin and Kestrel decide to search out the cause of sudden and extreme prejudice against Free Bards, they discover unscrupulous kinsmen who unethically share gypsy magic with a clergyman intent on attaining ultimate worldly power through sham miracles and unwilling aid from the Skull Hill Ghost. Sequel to *The Lark and the Wren*.

Other books you might like:
Gael Baudino, *Gossamer Axe*, 1990
Lois McMaster Bujold, *The Spirit Ring*, 1992
Phyllis Eisenstein, *In the Red Lord's Reach*, 1989
Julie Dean Smith, *Call of Madness*, 1990
Paula Volsky, *Illusion*, 1992
Martha Wells, *The Element of Fire*, 1993

2618

MERCEDES LACKEY

Sacred Ground
(New York: Tor, 1994)

Story type: Fantasy (Mystery; Magic Conflict)
Major character(s): Jennifer Talldeer, Detective—Private, Shaman (apprentice); Frank Talldeer, Chieftain (medicine chief), Indian; David Spotted Horse, Activist, Indian
Time period(s): 1990s
Locale(s): Tulsa, Oklahoma

Summary: When a bulldozer blows up after unearthing an ancient Osage burial ground, Jennifer investigates a developer's claim of conspiracy. She soon discovers the incidents relate to the earlier desecration of the resting place of her ancient ancestor that guarded a great evil, now loose in the land. Her dangerous battles with dark power reflect in both the spiritual world and in the physical realm.

Other books you might like:
Emma Bull, *Finder*, 1994
Charles de Lint, *Yarrow*, 1986
Tom Deitz, *Sunshaker's War*, 1990
Robert Morgan, *The Thing That Darkness Hides*, 1993
Dana Stabenow, *Red Planet Run*, 1995

2619

MERCEDES LACKEY
LARRY DIXON, Co-Author

The Silver Gryphon
(New York: DAW, 1996)

Story type: Fantasy (Magic Conflict; Adventure)
Series: Mage Wars
Major character(s): Silverblade "Blade", Military Personnel (Silver Gryphon); Tadrith "Tad" Skandrakae, Mythical Creature (gryphon), Military Personnel (Silver Gryphon)
Time period(s): Indeterminate Past
Locale(s): White Gryphon Lands, Fictional Country

Summary: Magically transporting Blade and all needed equipment to their first solo assignment at a remote and isolated guardpost, Tad suddenly loses the ability to fly, crashing into the tropical rain forest. The pair must make their way without magical assistance, and survive whatever stalks them and the evil waiting in the jungle darkness. Third in the trilogy.

Other books you might like:
Raymond E. Feist, *Shadow of a Dark Queen*, 1994
Katharine Kerr, *The Bristling Wood*, 1989
Elizabeth Moon, *Sheepfarmer's Daughter*, 1988
Andre Norton, *Elvenblood*, 1995
   Mercedes Lackey, co-author
Judith Tarr, *Spear of Heaven*, 1994

2620

MERCEDES LACKEY

Storm Breaking
(New York: DAW, 1996)

Story type: Fantasy (Magic Conflict)
Series: Mage Storms
Major character(s): An'desha, Magician; Firesong, Magician
Time period(s): Indeterminate Past
Locale(s): Dorisha Plains, Fictional Country; Tower of Urtho, Mythical Place (ruins); Valdemar, Fictional Country

Summary: With help from Shin'a'in plainsmen, An'desha and Firesong excavate and unleash an ancient weapon which temporarily disrupts the destructive magical vibrations emanating from two millennia past. Aided by the power of a magician long dead, they now must find a way to permanently reverse the mage storms. Third in the trilogy.

Other books you might like:
Diane Duane, *The Door into Fire*, 1979
Heather Gladney, *Teot's War*, 1987
Terry Goodkind, *Wizard's First Rule*, 1994
Barbara Hambly, *The Time of the Dark*, 1982
Elizabeth Moon, *Sheepfarmer's Daughter*, 1988
Christopher Stasheff, *The Warlock in Spite of Himself*, 1969
Patricia C. Wrede, *Shadow Magic*, 1982

2621

MERCEDES LACKEY

Storm Rising
(New York: DAW, 1995)

Story type: Fantasy (Magic Conflict)
Series: Mage Storms
Major character(s): An'desha, Magician; Karal, Religious; Tremane, Military Personnel, Nobleman (grand duke)
Time period(s): Indeterminate Past
Locale(s): Valdemar, Fictional Country; Hardorn, Fictional Country

Summary: As the disruptions of the Mage Storms grow more extreme, Valdemar and her allies desperately search for a more lasting solution than their magically engineered breakwater. They may have to risk losing the war with the Empire in order to survive. Meanwhile, the storms wreak personal havoc on all fronts, especially on An'desha and Firesong's relationship. First of the series.

Other books you might like:
Gael Baudino, *O Greenest Branch!*, 1995
Diane Duane, *The Door into Fire*, 1979
Barbara Hambly, *The Time of the Dark*, 1982
Elizabeth Moon, *Sheepfarmer's Daughter*, 1988
Christopher Stasheff, *The Warlock in Spite of Himself*, 1969

2622

MERCEDES LACKEY

Storm Warning
(New York: DAW, 1994)

Story type: Fantasy (Magic Conflict)
Series: Mage Storms
Major character(s): An'desha, Magician; Firesong, Magician; Ulrich, Diplomat (envoy from Karse), Religious (priest)
Time period(s): Indeterminate Past
Locale(s): Valdemar, Fictional Country

Summary: When the enigmatic Eastern Empire threatens both Valdemar and Karse, traditional enemies must overcome mutual prejudice and suspicion to thwart the danger. Meanwhile, An'desha and Firesong must overcome the shadows of An'desha's past in order to establish a healthy lifebonding, while using the information in those memories to fight the effects of the ancient mage wars echoing through time.

Other books you might like:
Diane Duane, *The Door into Fire*, 1979
Heather Gladney, *Teot's War*, 1987
Gayle Greeno, *Finders-Seekers*, 1993
Tanya Huff, *Sing the Four Quarters*, 1994
Marjorie Bradley Kellogg, *The Book of Earth*, 1995
Midori Snyder, *New Moon*, 1989
Patricia C. Wrede, *Shadow Magic*, 1982

2623

MERCEDES LACKEY
ELLEN GUON, Co-Author

Summoned to Tourney

(New York: Baen, 1992)

Story type: Fantasy (Urban)
Major character(s): Eric Banyon, Minstrel (bard), Musician; Beth Kentraine, Psychic, Musician; Korendil, Mythical Creature (elf), Royalty (prince)
Time period(s): 1990s
Locale(s): San Francisco, California

Summary: Disaster interrupts the street musicians' idyllic life when evil researchers kidnap Beth for use in psychic experimentation and sadistic torture. After Korendil's attempt to rescue her fails, Eric enlists a deadly extraterrestrial force to return Beth to her friends. Sequel to *Knight of Ghosts and Shadows*.

Other books you might like:
Gael Baudino, *Gossamer Axe*, 1990
Steven Brust, *Cowboy Feng's Space Bar and Grille*, 1990
Emma Bull, *War for the Oaks*, 1987
Charles de Lint, *Moonheart: A Romance*, 1984
Charles de Lint, *Spiritwalk*, 1992
Tanya Huff, *Gate of Darkness, Circle of Light*, 1989
Will Shetterly, *Elsewhere*, 1991
Terri Windling, *Borderland*, 1986
  Mark Alan Arnold, co-editor
Terri Windling, *Bordertown*, 1986
  Mark Alan Arnold, co-editor
Terri Windling, *Life on the Border*, 1991
  editor

2624

MERCEDES LACKEY
MARK SHEPHERD, Co-Author

Wheels of Fire

(New York: Baen, 1992)

Story type: Fantasy (Urban; Quest)
Series: Serrated Edge
Major character(s): Jamie Case, Child, Prisoner; Alinor, Mythical Creature (elf), Detective—Amateur; Joe, Religious, Security Officer
Time period(s): 1990s
Locale(s): Oklahoma

Summary: After Jamie's non-custodial parent kidnaps him, Jamie suffers as the prisoner of a fanatical religious cult until his mother enlists Alinore's aid in finding and returning him to her. Additional help comes from the religious leader's disillusioned son.

Other books you might like:
Gael Baudino, *Gossamer Axe*, 1990
Michael de Larrabeiti, *The Borribles*, 1978
Michael Reaves, *Street Magic*, 1991
Will Shetterly, *Elsewhere*, 1991

Terri Windling, *Life on the Border*, 1991
  editor

2625

MERCEDES LACKEY
HOLLY LISLE, Co-Author

When the Bough Breaks

(New York: Baen, 1993)

Story type: Fantasy (Psychic Powers; Urban)
Series: Serrated Edge
Major character(s): Lianne McCormick, Teacher, Heroine; Amanda Kendrick, Abuse Victim, Psychic (esper); Maclyn of Elfhame Outremer, Mythical Creature (elf)
Time period(s): 1990s
Locale(s): Fayetteville, North Carolina

Summary: During a class field trip to watch auto races, Amanda uses her telekenetic abilities to prevent an explosion. When Maclyn's mother requests her son arrange an audience with Amanda, he seeks help from Lianne, who discovers Amanda's abuse at the hands of her father. If Maclyn and Lianne do not help Amanda take control of her life, her telekenetic abilities could destroy both Earth and Faerie.

Other books you might like:
Emma Bull, *War for the Oaks*, 1987
Ellen Guon, *Bedlam Boyz*, 1993
Holly Lisle, *Bones of the Past*, 1993
Holly Lisle, *Fire in the Mist*, 1992
Susan Palwick, *Flying in Place*, 1992
Will Shetterly, *Elsewhere*, 1991
Terri Windling, *Borderland*, 1986
  Mark Alan Arnold, co-editor
Terri Windling, *Life on the Border*, 1991
  editor

2626

MERCEDES LACKEY
LARRY DIXON, Co-Author

The White Gryphon

(New York: DAW, 1995)

Story type: Fantasy (Magic Conflict; Mystery)
Series: Mage Wars
Major character(s): Amberdrake, Healer, Leader; Skandranon, Mythical Creature (gryphon), Leader; Shalaman, Ruler (King of the Haighlei Empire)
Time period(s): Indeterminate Past
Locale(s): Haighlei Empire, Fictional Country

Summary: A decade after the cataclysmic end of the Mage Wars, refugees establish a settlement and start to thrive when they discover that the Haighlei empire includes their location. Hoping to establish a peaceful relationship, Amberdrake, Skandranon, and others visit the capitol, where accusations of murder put their diplomacy to the test. Second of the series.

Other books you might like:
Margaret Ball, *Flameweaver*, 1991
Lillian Stewart Carl, *Wings of Power*, 1989

Raymond E. Feist, *Daughter of the Empire*, 1987
   Janny Wurts, co-author
Simon R. Green, *The God Killer*, 1991
Caroline Stevermer, *A College of Magics*, 1994

2627

MERCEDES LACKEY

Winds of Change

(New York: DAW, 1992)

Story type: Fantasy (Adventure; Quest)
Series: Mage Winds
Major character(s): Elspeth, Heir, Government Official (herald); Darkwind, Scout; Nyara, Orphan
Time period(s): Indeterminate Past
Locale(s): K'Sheyna Vale, Mythical Place

Summary: Despite the Dark Adept Mornelithe's defeat, the K'Sheyna heartstone remains critically damaged. After Darkwind trains Elspeth, the two of them must attempt to stabilize the heartstone as the other mages remain too closely tied to the damaged stone. Meanwhile Nyara, with the help of the sword, Need, learns to make a life for herself free of her father Mornelithe's influence.

Other books you might like:
Margaret Ball, *Flameweaver*, 1991
Diane Duane, *The Door into Fire*, 1979
Diane Duane, *The Door into Shadow*, 1984
Diane Duane, *The Door into Sunset*, 1993
Barbara Hambly, *The Time of the Dark*, 1982
Katherine Kurtz, *Deryni Rising*, 1970
Patricia C. Wrede, *Shadow Magic*, 1982

2628

MERCEDES LACKEY

Winds of Fate

(New York: DAW, 1991)

Story type: Fantasy (Quest; Adventure)
Series: Mage Winds
Major character(s): Elspeth, Heir, Government Official (herald); Skif, Government Official (herald); Darkwind, Spy, Scout
Time period(s): Indeterminate Past
Locale(s): Valdemar, Fictional Country; K'Sheyna Vale, Mythical Place

Summary: Valdemar's protections against magic, set in place so long ago by Herald-Mage Vanyel, are starting to unravel. With Hardorn's evil sorcerer-king picking away at Valdemar's borders, Elspeth and Skif are sent to find a mage to help Valdemar. Meanwhile, the K'Sheyna Vale Tayledras are beset by a powerful mage who wants control of their heartstone.

Other books you might like:
Diane Duane, *The Door into Fire*, 1979
Barbara Hambly, *The Time of the Dark*, 1982
Tanya Huff, *The Fire's Stone*, 1990
Robert Jordan, *The Eye of the World*, 1989

Patricia Kennealy, *The Copper Crown*, 1984
Katherine Kurtz, *Deryni Rising*, 1970
Patricia C. Wrede, *Shadow Magic*, 1982

2629

MERCEDES LACKEY

Winds of Fury

(New York: DAW, 1993)

Story type: Fantasy (Magic Conflict; Political)
Series: Mage Winds
Major character(s): Elspeth, Magician, Heiress; Ancar, Royalty (King of Hardorn), Magician; Darkwind, Scout
Time period(s): Indeterminate Past
Locale(s): Valdemar, Fictional Country; Hardorn, Fictional Country

Summary: When King Ancar initiates a magical attack on Valdemar and the ancient protective spells fail, Princess Elspeth must use her training from the Tayledras Adepts to protect the kingdom. After Ancar forces the Dark Adept, Mornelithe Falconsbane, to aid him in his conquest of Valdemar, Elspeth must rely for help on a powerful spirit reawakened from a forgotten past.

Other books you might like:
Lois McMaster Bujold, *The Spirit Ring*, 1992
Diane Duane, *The Door into Fire*, 1979
Barbara Hambly, *The Time of the Dark*, 1982
Laurell K. Hamilton, *Nightseer*, 1992
Robert Jordan, *The Eye of the World*, 1989
Melanie Rawn, *The Star Scroll*, 1989
Martha Wells, *The Element of Fire*, 1993
Patricia C. Wrede, *Shadow Magic*, 1982

2630

MERCEDES LACKEY
ELLEN GUON, Co-Author

Wing Commander: Freedom Flight

(New York: Baen, 1992)

Story type: Science Fiction (Military)
Series: Wing Commander
Major character(s): Ian "Hunter" St. John, Pilot; Kirha, Alien (Kilrathi), Warrior; K'Kai, Alien (Firrekan), Spaceship Captain
Time period(s): Indeterminate Future
Locale(s): Firekka, Planet—Imaginary; *Tiger's Claw*, Spaceship; Confederation, Interstellar Empire/Federation

Summary: The Kilrathi, always warriors and conquerors, now fight a war they connot win. While rebel Kilrathi send a ship to make peace overtures to the Human-led Confederation, other ships from the Kilrath Empire attack the Firekkan System, a member of the Confederation, and take hostages. Hunter leads a team of Humans, Firekka and Kilrath in an unauthorized rescue mission. A computer game tie-in.

Other books you might like:
C.J. Cherryh, *Chanur's Homecoming*, 1986
C.J. Cherryh, *The Pride of Chanur*, 1982

Chris Claremont, *First Flight*, 1987
Gordon R. Dickson, *Masters of Everon*, 1980
J.M. Dillard, *Star Trek VI: The Undiscovered Country*, 1991
Anne McCaffrey, *Sassinak*, 1989
    Elizabeth Moon, co-author

2631
R.A. LAFFERTY

Lafferty in Orbit
(Cambridge, Massachusetts: Broken Mirrors Press, 1991)

Story type: Science Fiction (Collection)

Summary: Introduction by Damon Knight plus 19 stories by Lafferty that were originally published in the *Orbit* anthology series (1966-1980) edited by Knight. Noteworthy stories include two finalists for both Hugo and Nebula Awards, "Continued on Next Rock" and "Entire and Perfect Chrysolite," and two stories appearing on initial Nebula Awards ballots, "All the Pieces of a River Shore" and "Dorg."

Other books you might like:
Alfred Bester, *Star Light, Star Bright*, 1976
Alan Dean Foster, *With Friends Like These...*, 1977
Raymond J. Healy, *Adventures in Time and Space*, 1946
    J. Francis McComas, co-editor
Larry Niven, *Tales of Known Space*, 1975
Robert Silverberg, *The Science Fiction Hall of Fame, Volume 1*, 1971
Cordwainer Smith, *The Best of Cordwainer Smith*, 1975
Theodore Sturgeon, *E Pluribus Unicorn*, 1953
Theodore Sturgeon, *A Way Home*, 1955
John Varley, *Blue Champagne*, 1986
John Varley, *The Persistence of Vision*, 1978

2632
MICHAEL LAHEY

Quest for Apollo
(New York: DAW, 1989)

Story type: Fantasy (Legend)
Major character(s): Delbert Alderini, Writer (American); Virgil, Writer (Poet), Guide
Time period(s): 1980s
Locale(s): Italy

Summary: Virgil (of Dante's *Inferno*) takes Delbert on a trip to find the god, Apollo. Delbert must find Apollo to stave off the world's impending destruction from nuclear confrontation.

Other books you might like:
Kevin J. Anderson, *Gameplay*, 1989
Kara Dalkey, *Euryale*, 1988
Brad Strickland, *Nul's Quest*, 1989
Robert E. Vardeman, *The Infinity Plague*, 1989

2633
MARC LAIDLAW

The 37th Mandala
(New York: St. Martin's, 1996)

Story type: Horror (Apocalyptic Horror)
Major character(s): Derek Crowe, Writer; Lenore Renzler, Young Woman; Michael Renzler, Clerk
Time period(s): 1990s (1996)
Locale(s): San Francisco, California

Summary: When Derek Crowe rewrites the text of book on mystical mandalas as a bestseller for New Age enthusiasts, he unwittingly unleashes the power for evil that the mandalas incarnate and hastens their eruption into the unsuspecting world.

Other books you might like:
Ramsey Campbell, *Midnight Sun*, 1990
Douglas Clegg, *Neverland*, 1991
Ray Garton, *Dark Channel*, 1992
Kim Newman, *Jago*, 1991
Whitley Strieber, *The Forbidden Zone*, 1993

2634
MARC LAIDLAW

Kalifornia
(New York: St. Martin's Press, 1993)

Story type: Science Fiction (Satire; Theological)
Major character(s): Sandy Figueroa, Television Personality; Calafia "Kali" Figueroa, Television Personality, Religious; Poppy Figueroa, Television Personality, Parent
Time period(s): 2050s
Locale(s): California

Summary: Already wired to broadcast her own sensations, Poppy Figueroa decides to wire her fetal offspring, providing complete sensory connection between mother and daughter and allowing for the first birth of a prenatally wired human being. Religious fanatics derail Poppy's plans for Calafia's career when they present Calafia as Kali to fool their followers and increase their influence.

Other books you might like:
David Brin, *Earth*, 1990
Pat Cadigan, *Synners*, 1991
Mick Farren, *The Feelies*, 1990
Neil Gaiman, *Good Omens: The Nice and Accurate Prophecies of Agnes Nutter, Witch*, 1990
    Terry Pratchett, co-author
Parke Godwin, *Waiting for the Galactic Bus*, 1988
James Morrow, *Only Begotten Daughter*, 1990
Neal Stephenson, *Snow Crash*, 1992
Kurt Vonnegut Jr., *Cat's Cradle*, 1963

2635

MARC LAIDLAW

The Orchid Eater

(New York: St. Martin's, 1994)

Story type: Horror (Serial Killer)
Major character(s): Lupe Diaz, Drifter; Sal Diaz, Drug Dealer; Mike James, Student
Time period(s): 1990s (1994)
Locale(s): Bohemia Bay, California

Summary: Lupe Diaz's thirst for revenge against his older brother, whom he blames for his emasculation years before, and Mike James's desire to give vent to his dark side by running with southern California street gangs are both satisfied when the two come into contact with Lupe's brother, Sal, and his gang. This explosive and graphic novel explores the teenage gang scene as a commentary on the failure of American society.

Other books you might like:
Poppy Z. Brite, *Lost Souls*, 1992
Dennis Cooper, *Frisk*, 1992
Dennis Etchison, *Darkside*, 1986
Ray Garton, *Crucifax*, 1988
Jack Womack, *Random Acts of Senseless Violence*, 1994

2636

MARC LAIDLAW

The Third Force

(New York: Simon & Schuster Scribner Paperback Fiction, 1996)

Story type: Science Fiction (Dystopian; Political)
Major character(s): Elena Hausmann, Librarian, Revolutionary (Third Force); Louis Hausmann, Military Personnel; Paulo Orlovsky, Ruler (emperor)
Time period(s): Indeterminate Future
Locale(s): The Empire, Fictional Country

Summary: Louis Hausmann serves Emperor Paulo Orlovsky while, disillusioned with the Empire's increasing repression, Elena joins the Third Force and pursues dangerous investigations. CD-ROM game tie-in.

Other books you might like:
Ed Blome, *Title Deleted for Security Reasons*, 1993
Stanislaw Lem, *Peace on Earth*, 1994
Grant Naylor, *Red Dwarf: Infinity Welcomes Careful Drivers*, 1992
Larry Niven, *Fallen Angels*, 1991
   Jerry Pournelle, Michael Flynn, co-authors
Ken Rolston, *Extreme Paranoia: Nobody Knows the Trouble I've Shot*, 1991
Kurt Vonnegut Jr., *Cat's Cradle*, 1963

2637

SIMON LANG (Pseudonym of Darlene Hartman)

Hopeship

(New York: Ace, 1994)

Story type: Science Fiction (Mystery; Medical)
Series: Voyages of the Skipjack
Major character(s): Charles Lassiter, Doctor, Patient; Dao Marik, Doctor, Alien (Einai); Audrey Lassiter, Artist
Time period(s): Indeterminate Future
Locale(s): *U.S.S. Hope*, Spaceship; Ildefor, Planet—Imaginary

Summary: Gravely wounded while saving Charles Lassiter, Dao Marik soon heals aboard the *Hope* medical ship and begins to practice medicine again, trying not to fall in love with Lassiter's wife. After a string of murders and attempted murders with the evidence pointing to him, Marik must clear his name and prevent the destruction of the ship itself.

Other books you might like:
Isaac Asimov, *The Caves of Steel*, 1954
C.J. Cherryh, *Hellburner*, 1992
David Drake, *Starliner*, 1992
Michael Jan Friedman, *Shadows on the Sun*, 1993
Jean Lorrah, *The Vulcan Academy Murders*, 1984

2638

SIMON LANG (Pseudonym of Darlene Hartman)

The Trumpets of Tagan

(New York: Ace, 1992)

Story type: Science Fiction (Adventure)
Series: Voyages of the Skipjack
Major character(s): Paul Whitfield Riker, Spaceship Captain; Dao Marik, Military Personnel, Alien (Einai)
Time period(s): Indeterminate Future
Locale(s): Eisernon, Planet—Imaginary; *U.S.S. Skipjack*, Spaceship

Summary: Captain Riker prepares his ship for a voyage through time made possible by the psychic powers of the unhatched young of the Elluvon emissary. Meanwhile, his friend and second officer, Dao Marik, the deposed emperor of the conquered planet of Eisernon, searches for his lost child. After the kidnappers take Riker and Marik prisoner, along with two Earth women, they have to fight for their lives and the safety of Marik's child.

Other books you might like:
Margaret Wander Bonanno, *Dwellers in the Crucible*, 1985
C.J. Cherryh, *The Faded Sun: Kesrith*, 1978
A.C. Crispin, *Time for Yesterday*, 1988
A.C. Crispin, *Yesterday's Son*, 1983
Frank Herbert, *Dune*, 1965
H. Beam Piper, *The Other Human Race*, 1964

2639

DAVID LANGFORD

Irrational Numbers

(West Warwick, Rhode Island: Necronomicon Press, 1994)

Story type: Horror (Collection)

Summary: This three-story chapbook approaches questions of identity from a variety of angles. "Deepnet" and "Serpent Eggs" are tales of hideous transformations that incorporate Lovecraftian elements into stories that blend horror and science fiction. "Lions in the Desert" is a witty tale of a shapeshifter desperately trying to keep his identity a secret.

Other books you might like:
Stephen Mark Rainey, *Fugue Devil and Other Weird Horrors*, 1993
Brian Stableford, *The Innsmouth Heritage*, 1992
Steve Rasnic Tem, *Decoded Mirrors: Three Tales after Lovecraft*, 1992

2640

JOE R. LANSDALE

Act of Love

(Baltimore, Maryland: CD Publications, 1993)

Story type: Horror (Serial Killer)
Major character(s): Marvin Hanson, Police Officer; Philip Barlowe, Journalist; Doc Warren, Doctor (medical examiner)
Time period(s): 1980s (1981)
Locale(s): Houston, Texas

Summary: Marvin Hanson is on the trail of "The Houston Hacker," a psychopathic killer who regularly mutilates blacks in the Houston ghettoes and communicates only by letters with Philip Barlowe, the newspaper reporter who named him. Hanson doesn't like Barlowe's smartaleck, racist manner—and eventually finds out he has even more visceral reasons for disliking him. Originally published 1981.

Other books you might like:
George C. Chesbro, *Bone*, 1989
Thomas Harris, *Red Dragon*, 1991
Rex Miller, *Slob*, 1987
Peter Straub, *Koko*, 1988

2641

JOE R. LANSDALE

Batman: Captured by the Engines

(New York: Warner, 1991)

Story type: Horror (Werewolf Story)
Major character(s): Pale Boy, Lawman (sheriff of Cold Shepherd); Bruce "Batman" Wayne, Hero, Detective—Amateur; Catherine Meadows, Doctor (of Cold Shepherd)
Time period(s): 1990s
Locale(s): Gotham City; Cold Shepherd, Alternate Universe

Summary: In Gotham City, "The Caped Crusader" Batman takes on bloodthirsty "were-cars," a species of sentient automobiles that are running amok and whose origins can be traced back to elemental forces drawn to the totemic Pyramid of Cars that decorates the automobile junkyard of the nearby Indian reservation in Cold Shepherd.

Other books you might like:
Eric Higgs, *Doppelganger*, 1987
Stephen King, *Christine*, 1983
Stephen King, *"Trucks"*, 1978
  in *Night Shift*

2642

JOE R. LANSDALE

Bestsellers Guaranteed

(New York: Ace, 1993)

Story type: Horror (Collection)

Summary: This book collects sixteen tales of the supernatural and nonsupernatural which alternate between the amusing and the grotesque. Included are the hardboiled crime story, "On a Dark October"; the ghost tale, "Not From Detroit"; "The God of the Razor," which was later expanded into the novel *The Nightrunners* (1987); and the novella, "The Events Concerning a Nude Fold-Out Found in a Harlequin Romance," about a dog trainer for a circus who nurses a perverse desire to mutilate the bodies of young women. The author has supplied an enjoyable introduction and headnotes for each story.

Other books you might like:
Donald Burleson, *Lemon Drops and Other Horrors*, 1993
Ed Gorman, *Prisoners and Other Stories*, 1992
Stephen King, *Skeleton Crew*, 1985
Robert R. McCammon, *Blue World*, 1989
F. Paul Wilson, *Soft and Others*, 1989

2643

JOE R. LANSDALE

By Bizarre Hands

(Shingletown, California: Mark V. Ziesing, 1989)

Story type: Horror (Collection)

Summary: Fifteen stories and one essay in Lansdale's distinctive voice featuring such items as disco zombies ("On the Far Side of the Cadillac Desert with Dead Folks"), hellish delinquents ("Boys Will Be Boys"), dead dogs ("Night They Missed the Horror Show"), desert nights filled with fish ("Fish Night"), contemporary religion ("The Fat Man and the Elephant"), and the end of the world ("Tight Little Stitches in a Dead Man's Back").

Other books you might like:
Dennis Etchison, *Red Dreams*, 1984
David J. Schow, *Seeing Red*, 1990

2644

JOE R. LANSDALE

Cold in July

(Shingletown, CA: Marc Ziesing, 1990)

Story type: Horror (Mystery)
Major character(s): Richard Dane, Businessman (frame shop owner); Ben Russel, Convict (ex-convict); Jim Bob Luke, Detective—Private
Time period(s): 1980s (1989)
Locale(s): La Borde, Texas

Summary: An unlikely trio of characters—a private detective, ex-con Ben Russel and Richard Dane, a man misled by the police to believe that he had killed Russel's son as a burglar—team up to find out why the police have deliberately created a trail of misinformation about the supposedly deceased Freddy Russel.

Other books you might like:
Peter Straub, *Koko*, 1988

2645

JOE R. LANSDALE

Dead in the West

(Mount Holyoke, Massachusetts: Crossroads Press, 1995)

Story type: Horror (Reanimated Dead; Supernatural Vengeance)
Major character(s): Jebidiah Mercer, Religious; David, Child; Doc Peekner, Doctor
Time period(s): 19th century
Locale(s): Mud Creek, Texas

Summary: Traveling preacher Jebidiah Mercer finds his gunslinging skills sorely tested when he pulls into the town of Mud Creek and discovers that the lynching of an Indian medicine man has unleashed a curse that causes the dead to rise from the ground as murderous zombies. This tribute to the old pulp magazines and E.C. comics was first published in book form in 1986 and was revised for this edition.

Other books you might like:
T. Chris Martindale, *Demon Dance*, 1991
Graham Masterton, *Burial*, 1994
Graham Masterton, *The Manitou*, 1974
Graham Masterton, *Revenge of the Manitou*, 1979
Eugene E. Pfaff Jr., *Uwharrie*, 1993
   Michael Causey, co-author
Patrick Whalen, *Deathwalker*, 1992

2646

JOE R. LANSDALE

Electric Gumbo: A Lansdale Reader

(New York: Quality Paperback Book Club, 1995)

Story type: Horror (Collection)
Summary: This omnibus volume gathers a variety of fiction and non-fiction by a writer renowned for his blends of hardboiled horror and humor. Two articles, "Hell through a Windshield" and "A Hard-On for Horror: Low Budget Excitement," are paeans to monster movies and the drive-ins of Lansdale's youth. The book's 14 story selections include the post-apocalyptic nightmare "Tight Little Stitches in a Dead Man's Back"; two stories about redneck youths who get into more mischief than they bargain for, "The Night They Missed the Horror Show" and "Steppin' Out, Summer '68"; the zombie story "On the Far Side of the Cadillac Desert with Dead Folks"; the alternate history western "Trains Not Taken"; and the crime stories "The Steel Valentine" and "The Job." The book also includes the full length fantasy novel, *The Drive-In (A Novel)*, about a bunch of juvenile delinquents who become trapped in a world where life is nothing but a B-movie and themselves merely bit actors.

Other books you might like:
Neal Barrett Jr., *Slightly Off Center*, 1992
Fred Chappell, *More Shapes than One*, 1991
Nancy A. Collins, *Nameless Sins*, 1994
Ed Gorman, *Prisoners and Other Stories*, 1993

2647

JOE R. LANSDALE

Mucho Mojo

(New York: Mysterious Press, 1994)

Story type: Horror (Mystery)
Major character(s): Hap Collins, Worker; Leonard Pine, Martial Arts Expert; Florida Grange, Lawyer
Time period(s): 1990s (1994)
Locale(s): La Borde, Texas

Summary: This semi-sequel to Lansdale's *The Savage Season* further explores the friendship of white liberal Hap Collins and his black buddy, Leonard Pine, as they become enmeshed in a mystery revolving around the death of Hap's uncle, the unexpected windfall inheritance he has left his nephew, the skeleton of a child found wrapped in the pages of a pornographic magazine beneath the floorboards of his house, and the differences between the white and black culture of La Borde, and America in general.

Other books you might like:
Edward Anderson, *Thieves Like Us*, 1937
James Ross, *They Don't Dance Much*, 1940
Jim Thompson, *South of Heaven*, 1967
Charles Williams, *The Hot Spot*, 1953

2648

JOE R. LANSDALE
PAT LOBRUTTO, Co-Author

Razored Saddles

(New York: Avon, 1990)

Story type: Horror (Anthology)
Summary: Seventeen stories of fantasy and horror with western themes, ranging in tone from Robert R. McCammon's dark tale of a homicidally deranged gunslinger, "Black Boots," to F. Paul Wilson's bizarre Doc Holliday anecdote,

"The Tenth Toe." Images of the classic west abound in All Sarrantonio's science fiction horror story "Trail of the Chromium Bandits," Lewis Shiner's tale of lost treasure "Gold" and Chet Williamson's anti-western "Yore Skin's Jes's Soft 'N Purty. . .He Said," while a very modern west can be found in David Schow's "Sedalia," Melissa Mia Hall's "Stampede" and Howard Waldrop's alternate-world story "The Passing of the Western."

Other books you might like:
Joe R. Lansdale, *The New Frontier*, 1989
Frank D. McSherry Jr., *A Treasury of Great American Horror Stories*, 1985
   Martin H. Greenberg, co-author
Charles G. Waugh, *Western Ghosts*, 1990
   Frank McSherry and Martin H. Greenberg, co-authors

2649

JOE R. LANSDALE

Savage Season

(Los Angeles, Marc Ziesing, 1990)

Story type: Horror (Psychological Suspense)
Major character(s): Hap Collins, Worker; Leonard Pine, Martial Arts Expert; Trudy Collins, Divorced Person (Hap's ex-wife)
Time period(s): 1990s
Locale(s): Marvel Creek, Texas

Summary: Hap Collins' ex-wife, Trudy, a former radical during the Vietnam years, convinces Hap and his best friend Leonard to help her recover a million dollars that wound up at the bottom of the Sabine River during a bungled bank heist years before. When the adventure goes tragically wrong, Hap is forced to reassess how his values were shaped by America's turbulent 1960s.

Other books you might like:
Robert R. McCammon, *Mine*, 1990
Peter Straub, *Koko*, 1988

2650

JOE R. LANSDALE

Stories by Mama Lansdale's Youngest Boy

(Eugene, OR: Pulphouse, 1991)

Story type: Horror (Collection)
Series: Author's Choice Monthly

Summary: Fifteen stories by the horror genre's southwestern regionalist and humorist, many inspired by the eating of popcorn. The selections span the breadth of Lansdale's professional writing career and include the Ray Bradbury-influenced "The Fat Man" and "By the Hair of the Head," a dark fantasy with classic overtones. More characteristic of Lansdale's brand of tough horror is the hardboiled "The Job," the merging of racism and supernatural horror in "On a Dark October," and the surreal "God of the Razor," an offshoot from his 1987 novel *The Nightrunners*. Lansdale has written informative notes for each story.

Other books you might like:
Davis Grubb, *You Never Believe Me and Other Stories*, 1989
Richard Matheson, *Collected Stories*, 1989
William Relling Jr., *The Infinite Man*, 1989
Manly Wade Wellman, *The Valley So Low*, 1987

2651

JOE R. LANSDALE, Editor
RICHARD KLAW, Co-Editor

Weird Business

(Austin, Texas: MoJo Press, 1995)

Story type: Horror (Anthology)

Summary: The 23 stories in this beautifully produced volume are all illustrated renderings by a variety of artists and writers of horror stories old and new. Classic tales adapted include Poe's surrealistic "The Masque of the Red Death" and Ambrose Bierce's amusing account of an unregenerate parricide, "Oil of Dog." New stories include Norman Partridge's "Gorilla Gunslinger," an alternate old west tale with a gorilla hero; Poppy Z. Brite's "Becoming the Monster," a meditation on love and death; Chet Williamson's "Chip of Fools," about the vampiric hold an on-line computer system has on its users; and Joe Lansdale's "The Steel Valentine," a hardboiled revenge story.

Other books you might like:
Clive Barker, *Tapping the Vein: Book One*, 1989
Ray Bradbury, *The Autumn People*, 1965
Ray Bradbury, *Tomorrow Midnight*, 1966
Edward Gorey, *Amphigorey Also*, 1985
Gahan Wilson, *Still Weird*, 1994

2652

JOE R. LANSDALE

Writer of the Purple Rage

(Baltimore: CD Publications, 1994)

Story type: Horror (Collection)
Summary: The author's fourth collection brings together 14 stories that display his skill at blending the grotesque and the amusing, one essay and a stage adaptation of his southern gothic tale, "By Bizarre Hands." Two stories are original to the volume: "Bubba Ho-Tep, " in which an elderly Elvis Presley faces off against a soul-stealing Egyptian mummy, and "Godzilla's Twelve-Step Program," in which the legendary monster embarks on a self-improvement program to bring out the nice guy inside him. Other highlights include "Mr. Weed-Eater," about the perverse turn of events that befall an average man who helps out a blind groundskeeper, and "Man with Two Lives," a nostalgic reflection on western history. The signed limited edition of this volume contains an additional essay and a comic for which Lansdale wrote the script.

Other books you might like:
Davis Grubb, *You Never Believe Me and Other Stories*, 1989
Robert E. Howard, *The Last Ride*, 1978
Robert R. McCammon, *Blue World*, 1989

2653

KAREN LANSDALE, Editor
JOE R. LANSDALE, Co-Editor

Dark at Heart

(Arlington Heights, Illinois: Dark Harvest, 1992)

Story type: Horror (Anthology)

Summary: Twenty original tales of dark suspense, a subgenre that straddles the horror and suspense genres. Included are Joe Lansdale's Bram Stoker Award-winning novella ''The Events Concerning a Nude Fold-Out Found in a Harlequin Romance,'' in which a brutalized woman savagely revenges herself on her attacker; F. Paul Wilson's ''The Long Way Home,'' starring his series urban vigilante, Repairman Jack; David Schow's ''Action,'' which posits a conspiracy between criminals and the media; and stories by Chet Williamson, Steve Rasnic Tem, Stephen Gallagher, and David Morrell.

Other books you might like:
Robert Bloch, *Psycho-Paths*, 1991
    Martin H. Greenberg, co-editor
Richard T. Chizmar, *Cold Chills*, 1991
    editor
Ed Gorman, *Dark Crimes: Great Noir Fiction From the '50's to the '90's*, 1991
    editor

2654

JAN LARA (Pseudonym of Mike Hinkmeyer)

Soulcatchers

(New York: Popular Library, 1990)

Story type: Horror (Serial Killer)
Major character(s): Lacy Timmers, Student—Graduate; Averell ''The Needle'' Turch, Student, Serial Killer; Mark Liston, Businessman
Time period(s): 1990s (1990)
Locale(s): San Francisco, California (Great Western University); Bear Claw Islands, South Carolina

Summary: History research fellow Lacy Timmers goes to the South Carolina coast to study descendants of missing members of the original Jamestown colony, unaware that she is being pursued by Averell Turch, a jealous fellow student whose alter ego is a mother-fixated serial killer known as ''The Needle.''

Other books you might like:
Clive Barker, *Cabal*, 1988
Robert Bloch, *Psycho*, 1959
Chet Williamson, *Dreamthorp*, 1989

2655

R. KARL LARGENT

Black Death

(New York: Leisure, 1995)

Story type: Horror (Small Town Horror)

Major character(s): C. Lane ''Rusty'' Bogner, Police Officer (deputy sheriff); Collee Barnes, Real Estate Agent; Harold Marsh, Doctor
Time period(s): 1980s (1988)
Locale(s): Half Moon, Kentucky

Summary: When townspeople in Half Moon begin falling prey to a flesh-eating virus, authorities trace it to a similar outbreak that happened a century before and race against the clock to discover the identity of the asymptomatic carrier who is inadvertently transmitting the disease to others. This novel was first published in 1988.

Other books you might like:
Michael Crichton, *The Andromeda Strain*, 1969
Christopher Hyde, *Jericho Falls*, 1988
Dean R. Koontz, *Phantoms*, 1983
Patrick Lynch, *Carriers*, 1995
Peter Straub, *Floating Dragon*, 1983

2656

JEANNE LARSEN

Bronze Mirror

(New York: Henry Holt, 1991)

Story type: Fantasy (Legend)
Major character(s): Pomegranate, Servant, Human; Silkweb Empress, Royalty, Mythical Creature; Tsang-jieh, Historian, Mythical Creature
Time period(s): Indeterminate (heavenly time); 12th century
Locale(s): Heavenly Realm, Mythical Place; China

Summary: When the Yellow Emperor orders a story telling contest between his Empress and the Royal Historian in heaven, the events related in the stories begin to affect events in the Earthly realm. They are informed by Bodhisattva Guanyin that the competition messes up history on Earth and creates a karmic burden, but the competition continues.

Other books you might like:
Kathryn Grant, *The Willow Garden*, 1989
Barry Hughart, *Bridge of Birds*, 1984
Barry Hughart, *Eight Skilled Gentlemen*, 1991
Barry Hughart, *The Story of the Stone*, 1988
Andre Norton, *Imperial Lady*, 1989
    Susan Shwartz, co-author
Janny Wurts, *Daughter of the Empire*, 1987
    Raymond E. Feist, co-author

2657

JEANNE LARSEN

Silk Road

(New York: Holt, 1989)

Story type: Fantasy (Adventure)
Major character(s): Greenpearl, Captive
Time period(s): 8th century
Locale(s): China

Summary: The story follows Greenpearl, kidnapped daughter of a Chinese general, as she goes through life, her fate in the hands of slave traders, scholars, gods, and herself. She longs to return to her father's city to be reunited with her family.

Other books you might like:
Hugh Cook, *The Women and the Warlords*, 1989
   Chronicles of an Age of Darkness. Vol. 3
Raymond E. Feist, *Daughter of the Empire*, 1987
   Janny Wurts, co-author
Kathryn Grant, *The Willow Garden*, 1989
Andre Norton, *Imperial Lady*, 1989
Susan Schwartz, *Byzantium's Crown*, 1987

2658

KATHRYN LASKY

Double Trouble Squared

(New York: Harcourt Brace Jovanovich, 1991)

Story type: Fantasy (Adventure; Young Adult)
Series: Starbuck Family Adventure
Major character(s): Liberty Starbuck, Telepath, Twin; July Starbuck, Telepath, Twin; Shadrach Holmes, Spirit (literary ghost)
Time period(s): 1990s (1991)
Locale(s): London, England

Summary: Both pairs of Starbuck twins communicate telepathically. When Liberty and July sense another voice, the twins begin to analyze as would their hero, Sherlock Holmes. They search London for the new telepath and discover a literary ghost, the unborn character of Arthur Conan Doyle. This is the first Starbuck Family Adventure.

Other books you might like:
Peter Dickinson, *The Gift*, 1974
Sherryl Jordan, *The Juniper Game*, 1991
Pamela F. Service, *Being of Two Minds*, 1991
Wilmar H. Shiras, *Children of the Atom*, 1953

2659

KATHRYN LASKY

Shadows in the Water

(New York: Harcourt Brace Jovanovich, 1992)

Story type: Science Fiction (Young Adult; Psychic Powers)
Series: Starbuck Family Adventure
Major character(s): Liberty Starbuck, Telepath, Twin; July Starbuck, Telepath, Twin; Streak, Animal (dolphin), Telepath
Time period(s): 1990s
Locale(s): Florida Keys, Florida

Summary: When the Starbuck family moves to the Florida Keys to track down toxic waste polluters, Liberty and July begin to receive telepathic messages from the Gulf of Mexico. Investigating the communication, the twins prove valuable allies to dolphins and turtles, eventually playing the critical role needed to bring the polluters to justice.

Other books you might like:
Arthur C. Clarke, *Dolphin Island*, 1963
Gordon R. Dickson, *Secret Under the Caribbean*, 1964
Gordon R. Dickson, *Space Winners*, 1965

Sydney J. Van Scyoc, *Deepwater Dreams*, 1991

2660

KEITH LAUMER

Alien Minds

(New York: Baen, 1991)

Story type: Science Fiction (Collection)
Time period(s): Indeterminate Future

Summary: This collection of 10 stories with an 8-page introduction examines the question, ''What is intelligence and how is it recognized?'' Eight stories were published in the 1960s; two are originals—''The Propitiation of Brullamagoo'' and ''Reverse English.''

Other books you might like:
Alfred Bester, *Star Light, Star Bright*, 1976
Chad Oliver, *Unearthly Neighbors*, 1960
Theodore Sturgeon, *The Golden Helix*, 1979
William Tenn, *Of Men and Monsters*, 1968
William Tenn, *The Seven Sexes*, 1968

2661

KEITH LAUMER

Back to the Time Trap

(New York: Baen, 1992)

Story type: Science Fiction (Time Travel)
Major character(s): Roger Tyson, Time Traveller; Clarence ''Rusty'' Naill, Time Traveller, Sea Captain; Dob, Alien (Rhox)
Time period(s): Indeterminate Past; Indeterminate Future
Locale(s): Earth

Summary: A rutabaga-shaped alien materializes in Roger Tyson's TV and pulls him into a bewildering mass of times and places as it sucks in other innocent victims, rushing back and forth in time and often mixing the far past, the present and the future in one spot. Roger only wants to get back to his wife and his familiar surroundings, but that seems impossible due to time line mixing. Sequel to *Time Trap*.

Other books you might like:
Lloyd Biggle, *The Whirligig of Time*, 1979
Alan Dean Foster, *To the Vanishing Point*, 1988
Harry Harrison, *A Rebel in Time*, 1983
Harry Harrison, *The Stainless Steel Rat Saves the World*, 1972
Michael McCollum, *A Greater Infinity*, 1982
Hayford Peirce, *Napoleon Disentimed*, 1987
Kurt Vonnegut Jr., *The Sirens of Titan*, 1959

2662

KEITH LAUMER

Judson's Eden

(New York: Baen, 1991)

Story type: Science Fiction (Space Opera)
Major character(s): Marl Judson, Spaceship Captain; Clarence ''Cookie'' Murphy, Cook, Sidekick; Baggy, Alien

Time period(s): Indeterminate Future
Locale(s): Earth; Eden, Planet—Imaginary

Summary: Marl Judson escapes from Earth just ahead of the government men who wish him declared a traitor so they can steal his financial empire. He and his friend, Cookie, land on an earthlike planet where time is strangely skewed and whose sole inhabitant is an amoeboid alien they name Baggy. When the Navy arrives followed shortly by aliens who want to wipe out humans, Baggy's aid allows Judson to hold the planet against everyone who doesn't want to live together in peace.

Other books you might like:
Lloyd Biggle, *Monument*, 1974
John Brunner, *A Planet of Your Own*, 1966
Alan Dean Foster, *Midworld*, 1975
James P. Hogan, *Voyage From Yesteryear*, 1982
Dennis Schmidt, *Satori*, 1986
Bob Shaw, *The Wooden Spaceships*, 1988
Joan Slonczewski, *Still Forms on Foxfield*, 1980
Brian Stableford, *The Paradise Game*, 1974

2663
KEITH LAUMER

Reward for Retief
(New York: Baen Books, 1989)

Story type: Science Fiction (Humor)
Series: Retief
Major character(s): Jame Retief, Diplomat; Ben Magnan, Diplomat
Time period(s): Indeterminate Future
Locale(s): Zany-Doo, Planet—Imaginary

Summary: Retief is assigned to Zany-Doo, a primitive planet whose caterpillar-like inhabitants are strongly xenophobic. Eventually Retief discovers that this seemingly backward planet has a dark secret; it's at the center of a transtemporal flux where reality itself can be changed by a thought.

Other books you might like:
David Gerrold, *Chess with a Dragon*, 1987
Ron Goulart, *The Chameleon Corps*, 1972
Ron Goulart, *Starpirate's Brain*, 1987
Ron Goulart, *A Talent for the Invisible*, 1973
Alexei Panshin, *Masque World*, 1969
Alexei Panshin, *Star Well*, 1968
Alexei Panshin, *The Thurb Revolution*, 1968

2664
KEITH LAUMER

The Stars Must Wait
(New York: Baen Books, 1990)

Story type: Science Fiction (Post-Nuclear Holocaust)
Series: Bolo
Major character(s): Jack Jackson, Astronaut (Lieutenant commander); Renada, Young Woman
Time period(s): 1990s; 21st century (Late)
Locale(s): United States

Summary: As the world teeters on the edge of nuclear war, Lt. Commander Jackson and the crew of the experimental spaceship Prometheus prepare for a desperate voyage to Callisto. When Jackson awakes from suspended animation, however, he discovers that his ship has never left Earth, that a nuclear war did occur, and that he is now alone in a wilderness of radioactivity and primitive feuding tribes. He alone has the knowledge to re-establish civilization.

Other books you might like:
David Brin, *The Postman*, 1985
Algis Budrys, *Some Will Not Die*, 1961
Edward P. Hughes, *Masters of the Fist*, 1989

2665
ANDREW LAURANCE

Catacomb
(New York: Diamond, 1991)

Story type: Horror (Wild Talents)
Major character(s): Juan Ramirez Montoneros, Orphan (monk novitiate), Religious; Francesca Sciascia, Office Worker (Vatican); Father Anthony, Religious (monk of St. Dominitian monaste), Teacher (of Juan)
Time period(s): 1980s (1981)
Locale(s): Monte Trasimeno, Italy (Monastery of St. Dominitian, just outside of Rome)

Summary: Since a very early age, Juan has been able to see the specter of death hovering over those about to die. Banished to a remote monastery, he finds that he can converse with the deceased and that the true origin of his "gift" is being covered up by a Vatican conspiracy. This novel was originally published in Britain in 1981 as *The Hiss*.

Other books you might like:
Brian Lumley, *Necroscope*, 1987
Guy N. Smith, *Entombed*, 1982

2666
ANDREW LAURANCE

The Link
(New York: Diamond, 1991)

Story type: Horror (Wild Talents)
Series: Blood of Nostradamus Trilogy
Major character(s): Paul Saralyn, Young Man; Cathy Morrow, Businesswoman; Melanie Forbes, Paranormal Investigator
Time period(s): 1980s (1980)
Locale(s): London, England

Summary: Originally published in England in 1980, this second novel in the Blood of Nostradamus series continues the story begun in *The Premonition*. Upon traveling to Europe after his mother's death, Paul Saralyn discovers that the psychic premonitions that have troubled him all his life are the consequence of a blood link to sixteenth-century clairvoyant Nostradamus. Paul represents one of two bloodlines descended from Nostradamus who appear to be trying to kill each other off, although the conduct of his overseers leads

Paul to believe he is being prevented intentionally from uniting with his relatives.

Other books you might like:
Daphne Du Maurier, *"Don't Look Now"*, 1971
　in *Not After Midnight*

2667

ANDREW LAURANCE

The Premonition
(New York: Diamond, 1991)

Story type: Horror (Wild Talents)
Series: Blood of Nostradamus Trilogy
Major character(s): Michael Dartson, Businessman; Melanie Forbes, Paranormal Investigator; Emma Dartson, Child (Michael's granddaughter)
Time period(s): 1970s (1979)
Locale(s): France; Europe

Summary: Originally published in England in 1979 as *Premonitions of an Inherited Mind*, this lackluster novel tells of Michael Dartson, and his discovery that he is a lineal descendant of the sixteenth century French clairvoyant Nostradamus. Michael travels across Europe refining his psychic powers and investigating his family history, unaware that his traveling companion, who is similarly psychically endowed, is engineering a fate for him forecast in Nostradamus's predictions centuries before.

Other books you might like:
Daphne Du Maurier, *"Don't Look Now"*, 1971
　in *Not After Midnight*
Brian Lumley, *The Necroscope Series*, 1987-1991

2668

ANDREW LAURANCE

The Unborn
(New York: Diamond, 1991)

Story type: Horror (Wild Talents)
Series: Blood of Nostradamus Trilogy
Major character(s): Celina Bell, Young Woman; Melanie Forbes, Paranormal Investigator; Giacomo Capuela, Businessman
Time period(s): 1980s (1980)
Locale(s): London, England; Europe

Summary: The Blood of Nostradamus Trilogy comes to a conclusion with this novel originally published in England in 1980 as *The Embryo*. Celina Bell, yet another blood descendant of the 16th-century clairvoyant Nostradamus, finds herself in a tug-of-war between Melanie Forbes, mother of two psychic children who are Celina's distant blood relations, and a business cartel trying to use the children for its own ends. Celina has been charged with taking care of the children, whose union will produce a superpsychic child capable of taking over the world.

Other books you might like:
Daphne Du Maurier, *"Don't Look Now"*, 1971
　in *Not After Midnight*

2669

STEPHEN R. LAWHEAD

Arthur
(Westchester: Crossway Books, 1989)

Story type: Fantasy (Legend)
Series: Pendragon Cycle
Major character(s): Arthur Pendragon, Ruler (Britain); Merlin, Sorcerer
Time period(s): Indeterminate Past
Locale(s): England

Summary: In this version, Arthur is an extremely Christian king, determined to usher out the old ways and the magic, even though the pulling of the sword from the stone gives him claim to the throne. Much of the book is about Arthur's struggles to unite the warring kingdoms of Britain.

Other books you might like:
Marion Zimmer Bradley, *The Mists of Avalon*, 1988
Parke Godwin, *Beloved Exile*, 1984
Nikolai Tolstoy, *The Coming of the King*, 1988
T.H. White, *The Once and Future King*, 1983

2670

STEPHEN R. LAWHEAD

Byzantium
(New York: HarperPrism, 1996)

Story type: Fantasy (Adventure)
Major character(s): Aidan mac Cainnech, Religious (monk), Linguist; Harold Bull-Roar, Ruler (King of the Danes), Adventurer; Gunnar, Warrior, Traveller
Time period(s): 10th century
Locale(s): Europe; Byzantium, Byzantine Empire (Miklagard)

Summary: Assigned to join a group of Irish monks transporting a valuable copy of the *Book of Kells* to Byzantium, Aidan loses his freedom to a Viking raid. Accompanying King Harold Bull-Roar on a raid of Miklagard, Aidan uses his language skills to keep the group from disaster. When the warriors accept guard duty on a diplomatic mission, Aidan becomes the emperor's spy and continues experiencing turns of fate.

Other books you might like:
Frans G. Bengtsson, *The Long Ships*, 1954
Allan Cole, *The Far Kingdoms*, 1993
　Chris Bunch, co-author
Judith Tarr, *Spear of Heaven*, 1994
Harry Turtledove, *The Misplaced Legion*, 1987

2671

STEPHEN R. LAWHEAD

The Endless Knot
(Batavia, Illinois: Lion, 1993)

Story type: Fantasy (Adventure; Alternate World)
Series: Song of Albion

Major character(s): Llew Silver Hand, Royalty, Ruler (King of Albion); Scatha, Noblewoman; Paladyr, Nobleman, Outlaw
Time period(s): Indeterminate
Locale(s): Albion, Fictional Country; Oxford, England

Summary: In the Otherworld, thieves threaten Llew's hopes for happiness on his wedding night when they raid and burn his home. He must learn what it means to be a king if he wants to preserve his new kingdom against the threat of the Brazen Man.

Other books you might like:
Charles de Lint, *The Little Country*, 1991
Tom Deitz, *Windmaster's Bane*, 1986
Patricia Kennealy, *The Copper Crown*, 1984
Morgan Llywelyn, *Bard*, 1984
Ian McDonald, *King of Morning, Queen of Day*, 1991

2672

STEPHEN R. LAWHEAD

Pendragon

(New York: William Morrow, 1994)

Story type: Fantasy (Political; Religious)
Series: Pendragon Cycle
Major character(s): Arthur, Ruler (King of the Britons); Amilcar, Military Personnel (Vandal warleader); Gwenhwyvar, Ruler (Queen of the Britons)
Time period(s): 6th century
Locale(s): Kingdom of Summer, Fictional Country; Wales; England

Summary: After triumphs and setbacks in the previous novels, Arthur's kingdom faces barbarian invaders who may well overwhelm it. Lawhead uses Cymric history and Christian imagery to retell one of the most famous Western myths.

Other books you might like:
Marion Zimmer Bradley, *The Mists of Avalon*, 1983
Tom Deitz, *Windmaster's Bane*, 1986
Guy Gavriel Kay, *The Summer Tree*, 1985
Patricia Kennealy, *The Copper Crown*, 1984
Ian McDonald, *King of Morning, Queen of Day*, 1991

2673

STEPHEN R. LAWHEAD

The Silver Hand

(Batavia, Illinois: Lion Publishing, 1992)

Story type: Fantasy (Legend; Adventure)
Series: Song of Albion
Major character(s): Llew Silver Hand, Royalty, Warrior; Meldron, Royalty; Tegrid, Minstrel (bard)
Time period(s): Indeterminate Past
Locale(s): Pyrdain, Fictional Country

Summary: After the death of King Meldryn Mawr, Prince Meldron usurps the throne spurred on by Siawn Hy and backed by fierce warriors, the Wolf Pack. Llew, the true heir to the throne, leads a rebellion which will not succeed without

the support of the Great Bard who alone may grant sovereignty.

Other books you might like:
John Desjarlais, *The Throne of Tara*, 1990
Kenneth C. Flint, *Riders of the Sidhe*, 1984
Casey Flynn, *The Enchanted Isles*, 1991
Casey Flynn, *Most Ancient Song*, 1991
Patricia Kennealy, *The Copper Crown*, 1984
Morgan Llywelyn, *Bard*, 1987
Michael Moorcock, *The Swords Trilogy*, 1977
Andrew J. Offutt, *Sword of the Gael*, 1975
Keith Taylor, *Bard*, 1981

2674

LOUISE LAWRENCE

Dream-Weaver

(New York: Clarion Books, 1996)

Story type: Science Fiction (Young Adult; First Contact)
Major character(s): Troy Morrison, Teenager, Spaceman; Eth, Alien, Psychic (dreamweaver); Nemony, Alien, Psychic (dreamweaver)
Time period(s): 21st century
Locale(s): *Exodus 27*, Spaceship; Arbroth, Planet—Imaginary; Malroth, Planet—Imaginary

Summary: Although only a child, Eth consents to joining the Dream-Weavers Guild after feeling the death of the 3000 colonists heading from Earth to her planet, Arbroth, expecting to enslave the natives as a labor force. Troy mentally calls out on his six month awake shift, four years out on the seven year journey. Now a Dreamweaver, Eth again visits Troy, both realizing their potential danger at arrival, with only a slim chance for the colonists' ultimate survival and the potential benefits to all.

Other books you might like:
David Brin, *Brightness Reef*, 1995
John M. Ford, *Growing Up Weightless*, 1993
Alan Dean Foster, *The Tar-Aiym Krang*, 1972
Anne McCaffrey, *Powers That Be*, 1993
    Elizabeth Ann Scarborough, co-author
James H. Schmitz, *The Universe Against Her*, 1964

2675

JAY B. LAWS

Steam

(Boston: Alyson, 1991)

Story type: Horror (Erotic Horror)
Major character(s): David Walker, Writer; Bobby, Office Worker; Mick, Office Worker
Time period(s): 1990s
Locale(s): San Francisco, California

Summary: In AIDS-ravaged San Francisco a horrible specter who calls himself Victor stalks the gay community, preying upon his victims' fears and enticing them with inevitably lethal promises of empowerment and sexual fulfillment that their conservatively altered lifestyles can no longer provide.

This metaphoric rendering of the horrors of the AIDS epidemic is the author's first book.

Other books you might like:
Michael Crichton, *The Andromeda Strain*, 1969
Richard Matheson, *I Am Legend*, 1954
Ray Russell, *Incubus*, 1976

2676

JAY B. LAWS

The Unfinished
(Boston: Alyson, 1993)

Story type: Horror (Occult)
Major character(s): Jiggs Martin, Cook; Sam, Mechanic; Brent, Travel Agent
Time period(s): 1990s (1993)
Locale(s): San Francisco, California

Summary: An eye operation renders Jiggs Martin able to see supernatural manifestations of "the Unfinished," souls in the afterlife who died before they could fulfill their life's purpose. Jiggs is enjoined to record their sad stories, including the tale of a gay man killed during a lover's tryst and the story of an HIV-positive man who makes a terrible bargain with the forces of evil to stave off the ravaging effects of his disease. Published posthumously.

Other books you might like:
Clive Barker, *Books of Blood Series*, 1984-1985
John Skipp, *Deadlines*, 1989
    Craig Spector, co-author
William T. Vollman, *Whores for Gloria*, 1992

2677

STEPHEN LAWS
MARK MORRIS, Illustrator
FRANK SMITH, Illustrator

Voyages into Darkness
(Philadelphia: Bump in the Night Books)

Story type: Horror (Anthology)

Summary: This chapbook includes five stories by two British authors, both of whom are better known as novelists. Laws's "Pot Luck," a whimsical fantasy of a telepathic crab, is original to the volume. His "The Secret" and "Guilty Party" are both about characters pursued by monsters that may or may not be figments of their imaginations. Morris's "Warts and All" chronicles the gruesome fate of a farming family besieged by a strange fungus, while "The Fertilizer Man" tells of a new gardening product that yields an unusual crop. The book has an introduction by Gary Potter.

Other books you might like:
George R.R. Martin, *Night Visions 3*, 1986
    Paul Mikel, co-editor
Nicholas Royle, *Darklands*, 1991
    editor
Lucius Shepard, *Nantucket Slayrides*,
    Robert Frazier, co-author

2678

RICHARD LAYMON

Funland
(New York: NAL Onyx, 1990)

Major character(s): Dave Carson, Police Officer; Joan Delaney, Police Officer (Dave's partner)
Time period(s): 1980s
Locale(s): Boleta Bay, California (A northern California beach town)

Summary: The mixture at the Funland Amusement Park of "Trolls"—homeless derelicts, "Trollers"—teenagers who prey upon them, and the abandoned, but sinister Jasper Dunn Funhouse and Freak Show provokes continuing, intensifying violence that culminates in an explosion of chaos and gore.

Other books you might like:
William W. Johnstone, *Carnival*, 1989
Dean R. Koontz, *Twilight Eyes*, 1987

2679

RICHARD LAYMON

A Good, Secret Place
(San Jose, California: Deadline Press, 1993)

Story type: Horror (Collection)

Summary: This book collects 20 stories—15 reprints and five originals—from one of the more infamous writers of graphic modern horror. Most fall within the realm of dark suspense, and touch upon themes of poetic justice ("Desert Pickup," "Roadside Pickup," "Oscar's Audition") and the battle between the sexes ("A Good Cigar Is a Smoke," "Joyce"). The handful of overtly supernatural stories includes "Barney's Bigfoot Museum," which tackles the legend of the sasquatch; "The Grab," about a peculiar game played in a barroom; and "Stickman," in which the monster of a rural folk tale comes to life. Ed Gorman wrote the introduction.

Other books you might like:
Ed Gorman, *Prisoners and Other Stories*, 1992
Joe R. Lansdale, *By Bizarre Hands*, 1992
Edward Lee, *Edward Lee's Quest for Sex, Truth and Reality*, 1992
Brian Lumley, *Fruiting Bodies and Other Fungi*, 1993
Lucy Taylor, *Close to the Bone*, 1993

2680

RICHARD LAYMON

Midnight's Lair
(New York: St. Martin's, 1993)

Story type: Horror (Mystery)
Major character(s): Darcy Raines, Tour Guide; Kyle Mordock, Teenager; Greg Beaumont, Lawyer
Time period(s): 1980s
Locale(s): Mordock Caves, Southwest

Summary: Darcy Raines tries valiantly to bring her tour group back up from the underground lake of Mordock Caves when a disaster above-ground blocks off the usual avenues of escape, but her efforts are complicated by the presence of psychotic Kyle Mordock, who has been driven to a murderous frenzy through his sexual longing for her, and by a race of cannibal cave dwellers. This book was originally published in England in 1988 under the pseudonym Richard Kelly.

Other books you might like:
Leigh Clark, *The Feeding*, 1992
Jack Ketchum, *Offspring*, 1991

2681

RICHARD LAYMON

Quake

(New York: St. Martin's, 1994)

Story type: Horror (Psychological Suspense)
Major character(s): Stanley Banks, Secretary (former); Clint Banner, Lawyer; Emerald O'Hara, Teenager (13-year-old)
Time period(s): 1990s (1995)
Locale(s): Los Angeles, California

Summary: Natural disasters bring out the worst of humanity in this tale where looters, rapists and rioters use a major earthquake that devastates Los Angeles as an excuse to go on a rampage. One of the major malefactors is psychopath Stanley Banks who, after killing his domineering mother, decides to terrorize next-door neighbor Sheila Banner, while Sheila's husband Clint, unaware of her predicament, simply struggles to get back home to her.

Other books you might like:
James Herbert, *The Dark*, 1980
James Herbert, *The Fog*, 1975
Stephen King, *The Stand*, 1978
Peter Straub, *Floating Dragon*, 1982

2682

RICHARD LAYMON

Resurrection Dreams

(New York: NAL Onyx, 1989)

Story type: Horror (Black Magic)
Major character(s): Vicki Chandler, Doctor; Melvin Dobbs, Magician (Black magician)
Time period(s): 1980s
Locale(s): Ellsworth

Summary: Having completed medical school, Vicki Chandler returns to her hometown to set up practice. She encounters a town full of zombies, resurrected and directed by black magician Melvin Dobbs, formerly a high school misfit. Even worse, she learns that she is the primary object of Melvin's desires.

Other books you might like:
William W. Johnstone, *Cat's Eye*, 1989

2683

RICHARD LAYMON

The Stake

(New York: St. Martin's, 1991)

Story type: Horror (Vampire Story)
Major character(s): Larry Dunbar, Writer (horror writer); Lane Dunbar, Teenager (Larry's daughter); Bonnie Saxon, Teenager (dead, but very attractive)
Time period(s): 1990s
Locale(s): Sagebrush Flats, Arizona

Summary: Larry Dunbar's mild case of writer's block is momentarily alleviated when he and his friends uncover the body of a teenage girl with a stake driven through her heart in an Arizona ghost town. As Larry's obsession to determine the corpse's identity and write a story about her grows, he senses her vampiric hold upon him.

Other books you might like:
Ron Dee, *Blood Lust*, 1990
Ron Dee, *Dusk*, 1991

2684

GENE LAZUTA

Bleeder

(New York: Diamond, 1991)

Story type: Horror (Serial Killer)
Major character(s): Nick Severanko, Writer; Reed Collings, Editor; Nasty Andrew, Serial Killer
Time period(s): 1990s
Locale(s): Cleveland, Ohio

Summary: Nick Severanko keeps a healthy separation between his daytime work as a writer for a trade magazine and evenings spent writing fiction about characters from a dark and horrific realm he calls "The Shadow Land." That is, until the day his serial killer Nasty Andrew decides to cross over into real life, bringing a bit of the Shadow Land with him in his bloody quest to locate his creator.

Other books you might like:
Stephen King, *The Dark Half*, 1987
John R. Maxim, *Abel/Baker/Charley*, 1983

2685

GENE LAZUTA

Forget Me Not

(New York: Diamond, 1992)

Story type: Horror (Serial Killer)
Major character(s): Jessie Reynolds, Young Woman; Henry Parks, Detective (former); Wilson Ellis, Detective— Private
Time period(s): 1990s (1992)
Locale(s): Cleveland, Ohio

Summary: Jessie Reynolds has mercifully forgotten the night twenty years ago when her immediate family was slaughtered and the murderer escaped the police. But with the murderer still on the rampage some three-score deaths later, Jessie is forced to confront truths buried in her subconscious not only about the murderer's identity, but about dark secrets kept by her extended family.

Other books you might like:
Orson Scott Card, *Lost Boys*, 1992
Matthew J. Costello, *Homecoming*, 1992
Samuel M. Key, *From a Whisper to a Scream*, 1992
Whitley Strieber, *Billy*, 1989

2686

GENE LAZUTA

Vyrmin
(New York: Diamond, 1992)

Story type: Horror (Werewolf Story)
Major character(s): H. W. Conway, Police Officer (sheriff); Michael Conway, Detective—Police; Robert Norris, Ranger (park ranger)
Time period(s): 1990s
Locale(s): Harpersville, Ohio

Summary: The appearance of The Man in the Woods in the small German community of Harpersville rekindles interest in ancient legends of the Vyrmin, people who have more evil than good in their souls and who transform into wolves. The human and animal deaths that follow shortly thereafter portend the naming of a new Blood Prince destined to lead the Vyrmin on a bloody rampage.

Other books you might like:
Gary Brandner, *The Howling*, 1979
Crosland Brown, *Tombley's Walk*, 1991
Geoffrey Caine, *Wake of the Werewolf*, 1991
Whitley Strieber, *The Wolfen*, 1978

2687

URSULA K. LE GUIN

Catwings
(New York: Orchard Books, 1988)

Story type: Fantasy (Adventure)
Major character(s): Jane Tabby, Animal (Kitten)
Time period(s): Indeterminate
Locale(s): Alternate Earth

Summary: Four kittens are born with wings and set out to find a place for themselves in the world.

Other books you might like:
Jan Brett, *The First Dog*, 1988
Jane Chelsea, *Winter Harvest*, 1988
Jack Dann, *Magicats!*, 1984
   Gardner Dozois, co-author
Terry Denton, *Felix and Alexander*, 1988
James Herriot, *Blossom Comes Home*, 1988
Andre Norton, *Catfantastic*, 1989
Michael Peak, *Cat House*, 1989
Susan Price, *The Ghost Drum: A Cat's Tale*, 1987
Tad Williams, *Tailchaser's Song*, 1985

2688

URSULA K. LE GUIN

Fish Soup
(New York: Atheneum, 1992)

Story type: Fantasy (Young Adult; Contemporary)
Major character(s): Writing Woman of Maho, Writer, Landowner; Thinking Man of Moha, Landowner
Time period(s): Indeterminate
Locale(s): Maho, Mythical Place; Moha, Mythical Place

Summary: When Writing Woman of Maho and Thinking Man of Moha wish for a child to transport messages and fish for meals for them, a pair of children suddenly come into their lives. When neither child achieves the hopes expressed by Writing Woman of Maho and Thinking Man of Moha, the adults rethink their expectations of the helpers and achieve an improved interrelationship.

Other books you might like:
Bruce Coville, *Jennifer Murdley's Toad*, 1992
Bruce Coville, *Jeremy Thatcher, Dragon Hatcher*, 1992
Garry Kilworth, *The Foxes of Firstdark*, 1990
Robin Morgan, *The Mer-Child: A Legend for Children and Other Adults*, 1991
Antoine de Saint-Exupery, *The Little Prince*, 1943

2689

URSULA K. LE GUIN

A Fisherman of the Inland Sea
(New York: HarperPrism, 1994)

Story type: Science Fiction (Collection)
Time period(s): Indeterminate Future

Summary: Contains an original introduction with a definition of science fiction and comments on the eight stories copyrighted 1983-1994 from periodicals and anthologies. Humor permeates several stories with themes including a time paradox, development of faster than light communication and "Churten" theory and an overall fascination with personal relationships.

Other books you might like:
Nancy Kress, *The Aliens of Earth*, 1993
Pat Murphy, *Points of Departure*, 1990
James Tiptree Jr., *Her Smoke Rose Up Forever*, 1990
Kate Wilhelm, *And the Angels Sing*, 1992
Gene Wolfe, *Endangered Species*, 1989

2690

URSULA K. LE GUIN

Four Ways to Forgiveness
(New York: HarperPrism, 1995)

Story type: Science Fiction (Political; Science Fiction)
Series: Hain
Major character(s): Yehedarhed Havzhiva, Diplomat (Hainish ambassador); Radosse Rakam, Teacher, Slave (former)
Time period(s): Indeterminate Future

Locale(s): Hain, Planet—Imaginary; Werel, Planet—Imaginary; Yeowe, Planet—Imaginary

Summary: Havzhiva comes to an epistemological epiphany after the women of Yeowe send a representative to create an alliance with the Ekumen, although Yeowe already belongs to the Ekumen of Worlds. Unaffected by the War of Liberation which benefited male "assets," women of Yeowe and Werel have not achieved freedom. After he decides to stay and help effect change, Havzhiva meets Rakam, a political activist accustomed to the struggle involved in translating freedom on paper to freedom in the world.

Other books you might like:
Eleanor Arnason, *Ring of Swords*, 1993
David Brin, *Glory Season*, 1993
Octavia E. Butler, *Parable of the Sower*, 1993
Samuel R. Delany, *They Fly at Ciron*, 1993
Kim Stanley Robinson, *Green Mars*, 1994

2691

URSULA K. LE GUIN, Editor
BRIAN ATTEBERY, Co-Editor

The Norton Book of Science Fiction: North American Science Fiction, 1960-1990

(New York: Norton, 1993)

Story type: Science Fiction (Science Fiction; Anthology)

Summary: This volume contains a 28-page introduction by Le Guin, 11 pages of notes about the authors, plus 67 stories written in English, arranged chronologically, and selected by the editors and Karen Joy Fowler as examples of excellent stories as well as superlative science fiction from a mature genre. Authors include Poul Anderson, Margaret Atwood, Michael Bishop, Octavia E. Butler, Pat Cadigan, Orson Scott Card, Philip K. Dick, Suzette Haden Elgin, Harlan Ellison, Damon Knight, Nancy Kress, R.A. Lafferty, Katherine MacLean, Barry Malzberg, Vonda N. McIntyre, Pat Murphy, Frederik Pohl, Mike Resnick, Kim Stanley Robinson, Michael Swanwick, Kate Wilhelm, Connie Willis, Gene Wolfe and Roger Zelazny. Educator's study guide available.

Other books you might like:
Gardner Dozois, *Modern Classic Short Novels of Science Fiction*, 1994
   editor
Gardner Dozois, *Modern Classics of Science Fiction*, 1992
   editor
David G. Hartwell, *The World Treasury of Science Fiction*, 1989
   editor
Raymond J. Healy, *Adventures in Time and Space*, 1946
   J. Francis McComas, co-editor
Tom Shippey, *The Oxford Book of Science Fiction Stories*, 1992
   editor
Robert Silverberg, *The Science Fiction Hall of Fame, Volume 1*, 1970
   editor

2692

URSULA K. LE GUIN

A Ride on the Red Mare's Back

(New York: Orchard Books, 1992)

Story type: Fantasy (Quest; Young Adult)
Major character(s): The Girl, Child; The red mare, Mythical Creature, Animal; The Troll, Mythical Creature
Time period(s): Indeterminate Past
Locale(s): Scandinavia

Summary: Equipped with only a little bread, a scarf and her wooden horse, a girl sets out after her brother when trolls steal him away. Through adventures and finding her brother changing into a troll, the lessons she learns as she travels with the red mare help her grow as an individual. Illustrated by Julie Downing.

Other books you might like:
Verna Aardema, *Why Mosquitoes Buzz in People's Ears*, 1975
James Gurney, *Dinotopia*, 1992
Chris Van Allsburg, *Two Bad Ants*, 1988
Nancy Willard, *Pish, Posh, Said Hieronymus Bosch*, 1991
Jane Yolen, *The Dragon's Boy*, 1990
Jane Yolen, *Sky Dogs*, 1990
Roger Zelazny, *Way Up High*, 1992

2693

URSULA K. LE GUIN

Tehanu: The Last Book of Earthsea

(New York: Atheneum, 1990)

Story type: Fantasy (Quest)
Series: Earthsea
Major character(s): Tenar, Widow(er) (aging), Religious (former priestess); Therru, Handicapped (crippled), Abuse Victim (child abuse)
Time period(s): Indeterminate
Locale(s): Planet—Imaginary

Summary: Both Ged, having lost his powers, and Therru, abused by her parents, seek refuge with the former priestess Tenar. Evil threatens and it is Therru, holding unusual power born of her kinship with dragons, who repels it. This story is a continuation of Le Guin's earlier Earthsea books.

Other books you might like:
Joy Chant, *Red Moon and Black Mountain*, 1970
Elizabeth C. Gaskell, *Cranford*, 1976
Jackie Hyman, *Shadowlight*, 1989
Mercedes Lackey, *Magic's Pawn*, 1989
   The Last Herald Mage. Vol. 1

2694

URSULA K. LE GUIN

Unlocking the Air and Other Stories

(New York: HarperCollins, 1996)

Story type: Fantasy (Collection; Contemporary Realism)

Summary: Contains one original, 16 stories reprinted from periodicals and anthologies 1982-1995, and one broadcast on "The Sound of Writing" in 1995. With realistic settings, the stories frequently reflect magic realism or surrealism.

Other books you might like:
Margaret Atwood, *Good Bones and Simple Murders*, 1994
Octavia E. Butler, *Bloodchild and Other Stories*, 1995
Nancy Kress, *The Aliens of Earth*, 1993
Pat Murphy, *Points of Departure*, 1990
Rebecca Ore, *Alien Bootlegger and Other Stories*, 1993
L.A. Taylor, *Women's Work*, 1995
Connie Willis, *Impossible Things*, 1994

2695

EDWARD LEE

The Chosen
(New York: Zebra, 1993)

Story type: Horror (Black Magic)
Major character(s): Vera Abbott, Restaurateur; Paul Kirby, Journalist; Feldspar, Businessman
Time period(s): 1990s (1993)
Locale(s): Waynesville, South

Summary: Vera Abbott agrees to manage the Carriage House, the restaurant of an inn made out of the renovated insane asylum Wroxton Hall. Upon assuming her new job, however, she finds that the asylum's grisly legacy of torturing inmates to death has been perpetuated through cultists who use the inn as a meeting place for their unholy rituals.

Other books you might like:
Elizabeth Ergas, *Devil's Gate*, 1991
John Gideon, *Greely's Cove*, 1990
Adrian Savage, *Symphony*, 1992
J.N. Williamson, *The Monastery*, 1992

2696

EDWARD LEE

Coven
(New York: Charter/Diamond, 1991)

Story type: Horror (Black Magic)
Major character(s): Wade St. John, Student; Dudley J. Besser, Professor (head of biology department)
Time period(s): 1990s
Locale(s): Exuam College, South

Summary: An outbreak of witchcraft enlivens the summer session at Exham College, an elite southern private school for the rich and stupid.

Other books you might like:
Fritz Leiber, *Conjure Wife*, 1953
Manly Wade Wellman, *The School of Darkness*, 1985

2697

EDWARD LEE

Creekers
(New York: Zebra, 1994)

Story type: Horror (Mystery)
Major character(s): Phil Straker, Police Officer (narcotics agent); Lawrence Mullins, Police Officer; Cody Natter, Drug Dealer
Time period(s): 1990s (1994)
Locale(s): Crick City, Midwest

Summary: Lured back to his home town following his humiliating demotion after a drug bust gone bad, former narcotics agent Phil Straker begins investigating Cody Natter, a drug local kingpin who manufactures PCP. Straker soon finds that Natter is also in league with inbred residents known as the Creekers, who subject abducted women to a variety of grotesque perversions as offerings to a strange being they worship.

Other books you might like:
John Driver, *The Hunger of the Beast*, 1991
Jack Ketchum, *Off Season*, 1980
Jack Ketchum, *Offspring*, 1991
Robert D. Lee, *The Keeper*, 1993

2698

EDWARD LEE
JOHN PELAN, Illustrator
ALAN CLARK, Illustrator

Goon
(Orlando, Florida: Necro Publications, 1996)

Story type: Horror (Black Magic)
Major character(s): Phillip Straker, Detective; Melinda Pierce, Journalist; Goon, Sports Figure (professional wrestler)
Time period(s): 1990s (1996)
Locale(s): Luntville, Virginia

Summary: To solve the mystery of a string of gruesome sex crimes connected with the professional wrestling circuit, detective Phillip Straker joins forces with Melinda Pierce, a self-described investigative journalist, and infiltrates the Deep South Wrestling Conference. His investigations take him into a world of kinky sex, violent perversions, and satanic bargains that make it hard for him to separate the good guys from the bad guys. This sexually-explicit novella-length chapbook, a first collaboration for both writers, carries an introduction by T. Winter-Damon.

Other books you might like:
Michael Hemmingson, *Nice Little Stories Jam-Packed with Depraved Sex and Violence*, 1995
Thom Metzger, *Big Gurl*, 1989
Rex Miller, *Slob*, 1987
Lucy Taylor, *Unnatural Acts and Other Stories*, 1994

2699

EDWARD LEE
KEITH PETERS, Illustrator

Header

(Orlando, Florida: Necro Publications, 1995)

Story type: Horror (Psychological Suspense)
Major character(s): Stewart Cummings, Police Officer (ATF agent); Travis Clyde Tuckton, Convict (ex-convict); Grandpap Tuckton, Aged Person
Time period(s): 1990s (1995)
Locale(s): Lewisburg, Virginia

Summary: While scamming money from drug dealers in the backwoods of Virginia to pay for his wife's narcotics habit, Special Agent Stewart Cummings steps into the middle of a vendetta fought amongst the locals, and involving a gruesome type of revenge perpetrated upon the women of the families at war. This novella of explicit sex and violence was published as a signed limited edition chapbook. Lucy Taylor supplies an introduction and Keith Peters the black-and-white interior illustrations.

Other books you might like:
Poppy Z. Brite, *Swamp Foetus*, 1993
Ron Dee, *Sex and Blood*, 1994
Michael Hemmingson, *Nice Little Stories Jam-Packed with Depraved Sex and Violence*, 1995
Lucy Taylor, *Close to the Bone*, 1993
Lucy Taylor, *The Flesh Artist*, 1994

2700

EDWARD LEE

Incubi

(New York: Diamond, 1991)

Story type: Horror (Occult)
Major character(s): Jack Cordesman, Detective—Police; Veronica Polk, Artist; Erim Khoronos, Wealthy (millionaire)
Time period(s): 1980s (1988)
Locale(s): Washington, District of Columbia

Summary: A rash of crimes of passion in which artistically inclined women are found mutilated and sexually violated by a creature with seemingly unnatural abilities leads detective Jack Cordesman to wonder if the perpetrator is a sexually predatory incubus—and whether there is any connection between the murders and the mysterious art enthusiast who has invited his girlfriend to a suburban retreat to put her in touch with her deeper artistic passions.

Other books you might like:
Steven Ray Fulgham, *The Summoned*, 1991
Ray Russell, *Incubus*, 1975

2701

GENTRY LEE

Bright Messengers

(New York: Bantam Spectra, 1995)

Story type: Science Fiction (First Contact; Theological)
Major character(s): Sister Beatrice, Religious (priestess), Traveller (pilgrim); Johann Eberhardt, Engineer, Businessman (director of Valhalla Outpost); Yasin al-Kharif, Engineer, Criminal (rapist)
Time period(s): 22nd century (2140s)
Locale(s): Valhalla Outpost Facility, Mythical Place; Mutchville, Fictional City; Mars

Summary: When a polar expedition on Mars disappears, leaving behind only a diary account of sightings of an amorphous entity and a cavernous, multi-level construction under the surface of the ice, Johann Eberhardt, Sister Beatrice, and several employees of Valhalla eagerly investigate. Sister Beatrice believes the cloud of white particles serves as a messenger from God, while Johann sees it as a scientific riddle to solve. A group committed to finding nonhuman intelligences, the Rama Society, hopes the phenomenon could indicate another visit from an alien race, whose spaceship might have been sighted ten years earlier. First novel as a solo author.

Other books you might like:
Roger MacBride Allen, *The Ring of Charon*, 1990
Orson Scott Card, *Ender's Game*, 1985
Jeffrey A. Carver, *The Rapture Effect*, 1987
Arthur C. Clarke, *Cradle*, 1988
    Gentry Lee, co-author
Arthur C. Clarke, *The Garden of Rama*, 1991
    Gentry Lee, co-author
Arthur C. Clarke, *Rama Revealed*, 1994
    Gentry Lee, co-author
Arthur C. Clarke, *Rama II*, 1989
    Gentry Lee, co-author
Arthur C. Clarke, *Rendezvous with Rama*, 1973
Robert L. Forward, *Dragon's Egg*, 1980
Michael P. Kube-McDowell, *Enigma*, 1986
Dan Simmons, *Hyperion*, 1989
David Alexander Smith, *Rendezvous*, 1988
Sheri S. Tepper, *Grass*, 1989

2702

JOHN LEE

The Unicorn Peace

(New York: Tor, 1993)

Story type: Fantasy (Political)
Series: Unicorn Quest
Major character(s): Oliderval, Ruler (Oligarch of Isphardel); Naxania, Royalty (Queen of Poladine), Ruler; Jarrod Courtak, Magician
Time period(s): Indeterminate
Locale(s): Strand, Planet—Imaginary

Summary: Jarrod Courtak, Friend of the Unicorns, fears that the attempted partition of the outlands will cause war once again. As he fights to preserve the peace and protect the interests of the Discipline, he must rely on past loves, political allies and the power of the Unicorns. The resulting compromises surprise everyone.

Other books you might like:
Peter S. Beagle, *The Last Unicorn*, 1968
Rosemary Kirstein, *The Outskirter's Secret*, 1992
Rosemary Kirstein, *The Steerswoman*, 1989
Katherine Kurtz, *Deryni Checkmate*, 1972
Katherine Kurtz, *Deryni Rising*, 1970
Katherine Kurtz, *High Deryni*, 1973
Sheri S. Tepper, *King's Blood Four*, 1983
Sheri S. Tepper, *Necromancer Nine*, 1983
Sheri S. Tepper, *Wizard's Eleven*, 1984

2703

JOHN LEE

The Unicorn Solution

(New York: Tor, 1991)

Story type: Fantasy (Quest)
Series: Unicorn Quest
Major character(s): Jarrod Courtak, Magician; Pellia, Mythical Creature (unicorn), Telepath
Time period(s): Indeterminate
Locale(s): Strand, Planet—Imaginary; Mythical Place

Summary: Jarrod Courtak hopes to help fulfill the prophecy that war on Strand can only be won by unicorns. He has discovered a family of unicorns and now must travel to another realm to secure a lost spell which will unchain their powers.

Other books you might like:
Pamela Dean, *The Hidden Land*, 1986
Pamela Dean, *The Secret Country*, 1985
Tanith Lee, *Black Unicorn*, 1991

2704

JOHN LEE

The Unicorn War

(New York: Tor, 1995)

Story type: Fantasy (Magic Conflict; Political)
Series: Unicorn Quest
Major character(s): Jarrod Courtak, Magician; Varodias, Ruler (Emperor of Umbria); Nastrus, Mythical Creature (unicorn)
Time period(s): Indeterminate
Locale(s): Strand, Planet—Imaginary

Summary: Despite cessation of the long war with the Outsiders, the Discipline of Magic remains active. When Emperor Varodias declares war, his armies march with war machines that neutralize the power of magic. Human and unicorn must again join forces or perish. Fifth and final volume in the series.

Other books you might like:
Eleanor Arnason, *The Sword Smith*, 1978
Peter S. Beagle, *The Last Unicorn*, 1968

Diane Duane, *The Door into Fire*, 1979
Guy Gavriel Kay, *The Summer Tree*, 1985
Patricia A. McKillip, *The Riddle-Master of Hed*, 1976

2705

ROBERT D. LEE

The Keeper

(New York: Pinnacle, 1993)

Story type: Horror (Psychological Suspense)
Major character(s): Judy MacAuliffe, Saloon Keeper/Owner; Horst Von Ziegler, Animal Trainer (lion tamer); Jim Sweeney, Police Officer
Time period(s): 1990s (1993)
Locale(s): Rhinelander, New York

Summary: Judy MacAuliffe believes that her ticket out of Rhinelander is an apprenticeship under Horst Von Ziegler, the retired lion tamer who lives in a secluded mansion on the outskirts of town and whose name still has significance in the circus world. But Judy discovers that the spate of recent disappearances in the woods surrounding the town are intimately connected to the animal training in which Horst is currently involved.

Other books you might like:
John Driver, *The Hunger of the Beast*, 1991
John Fowles, *The Collector*, 1963
Thomas Harris, *The Silence of the Lambs*, 1988

2706

STAN LEE, Editor

The Ultimate Spider-Man

(New York: Berkley, 1994)

Story type: Science Fiction (Anthology; Adventure)
Series: Spider-Man
Major character(s): Peter ''Spider-Man'' Parker, Hero, Detective—Amateur
Time period(s): 1990s
Locale(s): New York, New York

Summary: Contains a five-page introduction by Lee, 11 pages of biographical notes plus 12 original Spider-man stories by 14 authors, including a retelling of Spider-Man's genesis by Stan Lee and Peter David. Other authors include John Gregory Betancourt, Tom De Haven, Craig Shaw Gardner, Dean Wesley Smith and Lawrence Watt-Evans.

Other books you might like:
Diane Duane, *Spider-Man: The Venom Factor*, 1994
Martin H. Greenberg, *The Further Adventures of Batman*, 1989
　editor
Martin H. Greenberg, *The Further Adventures of Superman*, 1993
　editor
John Varley, *Superheroes*, 1995
　Ricia Mainhardt, co-editor
Len Wein, *Mayhem in Manhattan*, 1978
　Marv Wolfman, co-author

2707
TANITH LEE

Black Unicorn
(New York: Atheneum, 1991)

Story type: Fantasy (Adventure; Young Adult)
Series: Dragonflight
Major character(s): Tanaquil, Teenager; Lizra, Royalty (princess); Peeve, Animal (enchanted), Companion
Time period(s): Indeterminate
Locale(s): Jaive's Fortress, Mythical Place; The City, Fictional City

Summary: When Tanaquil tries to alleviate boredom by assembling bones her pet discovered, she doesn't expect a phantom unicorn to whisk her toward the city which her mother has forbidden her to visit. Running afoul of a city craft guild, Tanaquil is rescued by her phantom unicorn and a chance meeting with Princess Lizra. Tanaquil discovers her heritage and the vital roll she will soon play.

Other books you might like:
Joy Chant, *The Grey Mane of Morning*, 1977
Damaris Cole, *Token of Dragonsblood*, 1991
Peter Dickinson, *The Blue Hawk*, 1976
Mercedes Lackey, *Bardic Voices*, 1991
C.S. Lewis, *The Horse and His Boy*, 1954
Patricia A. McKillip, *Moon-Flash*, 1984
A.C.H. Smith, *The Dark Crystal: A Novel*, 1982

2708
TANITH LEE

The Book of the Beast
(Woodstock, New York: The Overlook Press, 1991)

Story type: Fantasy (Historical; Collection)
Series: Secret Books of Paradys
Major character(s): Raoulin, Student; Vusca, Military Personnel (centurion); Ruquel, Doctor, Dancer
Time period(s): Indeterminate Past
Locale(s): Paradys, Fictional City

Summary: This volume traces a terrible curse through the strange history of the city of Paradys. By turns beautiful, terrifying and erotic, the three linked stories show how a demonic presence enters the world and causes misery over centuries. An unusual fantasy in its attention to detail and depictions of non-medieval historical periods. First published in England in 1988.

Other books you might like:
Nancy A. Collins, *Sunglasses After Dark*, 1989
Storm Constantine, *The Enchantments of Flesh and Spirit*, 1990
Ellen Kushner, *Swordspoint*, 1987
Anne Rice, *Interview with the Vampire*, 1976

2709
TANITH LEE

Dark Dance
(New York: Dell/Abyss, 1992)

Story type: Horror (Gothic Family Chronicle)
Major character(s): Rachaela Day, Clerk (in a bookstore); Ruth Day, Child (Rachaela's daughter); Michael, Servant (to the Scarabae)
Time period(s): 1990s (1992)
Locale(s): London, England

Summary: Although warned by her mother to keep away from the family of the father she never knew, Rachaela Day visits the Scarabae at their remote estate and finds them an eccentric lot, living in the past and with a hint of supernatural menace to them. Rachaela escapes the estate, but finds herself mysteriously impregnated by her father. The child she gives birth to so closely resembles the Scarabae that Rachaela is forced to confront them once again and learn their secret.

Other books you might like:
Richie Tankersley Cusick, *Blood Roots*, 1992
Jean Simon, *Orphans*, 1992

2710
TANITH LEE

Darkness, I
(New York: St. Martin's, 1996)

Story type: Horror (Vampire Story)
Series: Blood Opera Sequence
Major character(s): Rachaela Day, Vampire; Althene Simon, Vampire; Anna, Child (Rachaela & Althene's daughter)
Time period(s): 1990s (1996)
Locale(s): London, England

Summary: The Scarabae, a family of vampires descended from one of the biblical plagues, continue their diaspora across the English countryside in hopes of integrating with the rest of humanity and putting their bloody past behind them. But when Rachaela Day's daughter, Anna, is kidnapped and taken to a place redolent with Egyptian culture, it appears that someone—or something— intends to revive interest in the family's heritage for the next generation. This novel was first published in England in 1995.

Other books you might like:
Poppy Z. Brite, *Lost Souls*, 1992
Nancy A. Collins, *Sunglasses After Dark*, 1990
Anne Rice, *The Queen of the Damned*, 1988

2711
TANITH LEE

Elephantasm
(New York: Dell, 1996)

Story type: Horror (Occult)
Major character(s): Annie Ember, Teenager, Servant; Hampton Smolte, Military Personnel; Darius, Religious (mystic)

Time period(s): 19th century
Locale(s): England

Summary: Fleeing her destitute life in the city, Annie Ember becomes indentured as a servant to Hampton Smolte, a world traveller infatuated with the East whose household pays obeisance to the Hindu god Ganesa. Unable to escape the rituals performed to supplicate the elephant-headed Lord of Beginnings, Annie is indoctrinated into a world of sexuality and mystery, and soon discovers why ivory has a peculiar allure for her.

Other books you might like:
Ramsey Campbell, *Claw*, 1983
Katherine Kurtz, *Dagger Magic*, 1995
     Deborah Turner Harris, co-author
Dan Simmons, *Song of Kali*, 1983
Dennis Wheatley, *The Devil Rides Out*, 1934

2712

TANITH LEE

Gold Unicorn
(New York: Atheneum, 1994)

Story type: Fantasy (Young Adult; Adventure)
Major character(s): Tanaquil Veriam, Teenager, Sorceress; Lizora ''Lizra'' Veriam, Royalty (princess), Leader (ruler of Sea City); Peeve, Animal (enchanted), Companion (Tanaquil's)
Time period(s): Indeterminate
Locale(s): Fictional Country

Summary: Vaulted into leadership, young Princess Lizra envisions a totally controlled society which provides direction for its happy citizens. As a symbol of her power, Lizra constructs a gold-plated iron unicorn designed to work by steam power, but which needs Tanaquil's abilities to function. Tanaquil must decide whether to aid Lizra's vision of conquest or risk her powerful sister's anger.

Other books you might like:
Louise Cooper, *The Sleep of Stone*, 1991
Phyllis Eisenstein, *In the Red Lord's Reach*, 1989
Mercedes Lackey, *The Robin and the Kestrel*, 1993
Paula Volsky, *Illusion*, 1992
Tad Williams, *Child of an Ancient City*, 1992
     Nina Kiriki Hoffman, co-author

2713

TANITH LEE

Heart Beast
(New York: Dell/Abyss, 1993)

Story type: Horror (Werewolf Story)
Major character(s): Daniel Vehmund, Secretary, Werewolf; Laura Wheelwright, Young Woman; Marsall Vehmund, Landowner
Locale(s): England

Summary: Daniel Vehmund pursues the thief who stole the strange talisman fashioned from a meterorite that turns him regularly into a ravenous werewolf. His journeys eventually

take him from the Mediterranean back to his home in England, where he crosses paths with an abusive older brother whose ways threaten the family's survival.

Other books you might like:
Cheri Scotch, *The Werewolf's Kiss*, 1992
S.P. Somtow, *Moon Dance*, 1990
Jane Toombs, *Under the Shadow*, 1992

2714

TANITH LEE

A Heroine of the World
(New York: DAW, 1989)

Story type: Fantasy (Romance)
Major character(s): Aradia, Teenager (Orphan), Noblewoman
Time period(s): Indeterminate
Locale(s): Alternate Earth

Summary: Aradia's protected childhood comes to an end during an extended siege on the city in which she lives. The story follows her through her experiences as a mistress of an enemy officer to her love for a soldier of her own country.

Other books you might like:
Richard Adams, *Maia*, 1985
Sheila Gilluly, *Ritnym's Daughter*,
     Greenbriar Trilogy
Robin McKinley, *The Hero and the Crown*, 1984
Jessica Amanda Salmonson, *Tomoe Gozen*, 1984

2715

TANITH LEE

Personal Darkness
(New York: Dell, 1994)

Story type: Horror (Vampire Story)
Major character(s): Rachaela, Young Woman; Ruth, Vampire; Malach, Vampire
Time period(s): 1990s (1994)
Locale(s): London, England

Summary: In this sequel to the author's *Dark Dance*, the Scarabae, a family of vampires and other supernatural beings, try to recover from the destruction of their family home and integrate themselves with the London jetset. Meanwhile Ruth, the daughter of half-mortal Rachaela and the cause of the Scarabae's misfortunes, flees the family after an unsuccessful attempt to mate her with her grandfather, bringing death and mayhem to the city that threatens to draw public scrutiny down upon the family.

Other books you might like:
Poppy Z. Brite, *Lost Souls*, 1992
Pat Graversen, *Precious Blood*, 1983
Wendy Haley, *This Dark Paradise*, 1993
Anne Rice, *The Vampire Lestat*, 1985

2716

WARNER LEE (Pseudonym of B.W. Battin)

Night Sounds

(New York: Pocket, 1992)

Story type: Horror (Possession)
Major character(s): Dave Guthrie, Artist (illustrator); Paula Bjornsen, Teacher; Ed Prawdzik, Nurse
Time period(s): 1990s
Locale(s): Castle Bay, California

Summary: Dave Guthrie ponders his incredible luck as the only survivor of a plane crash that killed 132 people, unaware that he owes his life to a bargain he struck with powers of evil. With the help of good samaritan clairvoyant Paula Bjornsen, Dave discovers that his bargain entails the use of his body by the forces of evil to feed upon mortals.

Other books you might like:
John Gideon, *Greely's Cove*, 1991
L. Ron Hubbard, *Death's Deputy*, 1939
Dean R. Koontz, *Cold Fire*, 1991

2717

FRITZ LEIBER

Conjure Wife/Our Lady of Darkness

(New York: Tor, 1991)

Story type: Horror (Collection)

Summary: This repackaging of two-novels-in-one, the first originally published in 1943, the second in 1978, brings together two landmark stories of modern horror and fantasy. In the first, university professor Norman Saylor discovers misfortune when he forbids his wife Tansy to practice her seemingly harmless brand of witchcraft and it brings down upon the Saylor household the wrath of the other university professors' wives, all of whom are witches working to further their husbands' careers. In the second, which won the World Fantasy Award for best novel, Franz Westen's investigation into the paranormal leads to the discovery that his home is a focus for elemental forces attracted by the city of San Francisco.

Other books you might like:
James Blish, *The Devil's Day*, 1989
Henry Kuttner, *The Startling Worlds of Henry Kuttner*, 1987

2718

FRITZ LEIBER

Ill Met in Lankhmar

(Clarkston, Georgia: White Wolf, 1995)

Story type: Fantasy (Horror; Sword and Sorcery)
Series: Fafhrd and the Grey Mouser
Major character(s): Fafhrd, Thief, Warrior; The Grey Mouser, Thief, Wizard; Ningauble of the Seven Eyes, Wizard
Time period(s): Indeterminate
Locale(s): Lankhmar, Fictional City

Summary: Omnibus collection of stories of the early years of Leiber's ironic sword and sorcery heroes and their adventures in an urban fantasy full of theives, wizards, demons, and the walking dead. This edition collects *Swords and Deviltry* (1970), and *Swords Against Death* (1970), which contain 13 stories written 1934-1969. The book also contains four introductions by Leiber from earlier editions, a modern introduction by Michael Moorcock, and chapter, story, and volume headings by artist Mike Mignola.

Other books you might like:
Steven Brust, *Jhereg*, 1983
Ellen Kushner, *Swordspoint*, 1987
Michael Moorcock, *Elric of Melnibone*, 1976
Michael Shea, *Nifft the Lean*, 1982

2719

FRITZ LEIBER

Lean Times in Lankhmar

(Clarkston, Georgia: White Wolf, 1996)

Story type: Fantasy (Collection; Sword and Sorcery)
Major character(s): Fafhrd, Thief, Warrior; The Grey Mouser, Thief, Wizard
Time period(s): Indeterminate
Locale(s): Lankhmar, Fictional City

Summary: Contains a two-page introduction by Raymond E. Feist, a two-page author's foreword and 10 stories written 1936-1968 and published as *Swords in the Mist* (1968) and *Swords Against Wizardry* (1968). Dark sorcery, deadly weaponry, and poverty plague Fafhrd and the Grey Mouser's adventures while they seek magical gain and female companionship.

Other books you might like:
Steven Brust, *Jhereg*, 1983
L. Sprague de Camp, *Warlocks and Warriors*, 1970
    editor
Robert E. Howard, *Hour of the Dragon*, 1977
Michael Moorcock, *Elric of Melnibone*, 1976
Clark Ashton Smith, *Tales of Zothique*, 1995
Karl Edward Wagner, *Darkness Weaves*, 1978
    revised edition

2720

FRITZ LEIBER

The Leiber Chronicles

(Arlington Heights, IL: Dark Harvest, 1990)

Story type: Science Fiction (Collection)

Summary: This volume includes forty-four stories spanning Fritz Leiber's remarkable career, from his first published work, ''Two Sought Adventure'' (1939), to the recent ''The Curse of the Smalls and the Stars'' (1983). Among many fine stories are Leiber's Hugo and Nebula Award winners, ''Gonna Roll the Bones'' (1967), ''Ship of Shadows'' (1969), ''Ill Met in Lankhmar'' (1970) and ''Catch that Zeppelin!'' (1975). Other notable stories include ''Coming Attraction'' (1950), ''A Pail of Air'' (1951), ''A Bad Day for Sales''

(1953), "Rump-Titty-Titty-Tum-Tah-Tee" (1958), "The Man Who Made Friends with Electricity" (1962), "Bazaar of the Bizarre" (1963), "When the Change Wind Blows" (1964), "Midnight by the Morphy Watch" (1974), and "Belsen Express" (1975).

Other books you might like:
Harlan Ellison, *Angry Candy*, 1988
Harlan Ellison, *Deathbird Stories*, 1975
Harlan Ellison, *The Essential Ellison: A 35-Year Retrospective*, 1987
Harlan Ellison, *Strange Wine*, 1978
P.C. Hodgell, *Dark of the Moon*, 1985
P.C. Hodgell, *God Stalk*, 1982
Tim Powers, *The Anubis Gates*, 1983

2721

STEPHEN LEIGH

The Abraxis Marvel Circus
(New York: Roc, 1990)

Story type: Fantasy (Contemporary)
Major character(s): Dirk, Musician (Rock & Roll); Ecclesiastes Mitsumishi, Undertaker
Time period(s): 1990s
Locale(s): Earth

Summary: Dirk and Ecclesiastes are just two of the characters searching for the Theopelli notebook, but no one knows what will happen when it is finally found.

Other books you might like:
Gael Baudino, *Gossamer Axe*, 1990
James P. Blaylock, *Land of Dreams*, 1989
Tom Deitz, *The Gryphon King*, 1989
Lisa Goldstein, *Tourists*, 1989

2722

STEPHEN LEIGH

Alien Tongue
(New York: Bantam Spectra, 1991)

Story type: Science Fiction (First Contact)
Series: Next Wave
Major character(s): Patrick Malone, Spaceman, Pilot; G.Ren.Bei.Yi, Alien (Avia); Hr.Tyi.Bei.k.ai, Alien (Avia), Royalty (Eggmother of the Bei)
Time period(s): 2060s
Locale(s): *Bright Hope*, Spaceship; Tir.ki.k.ai, Planet—Imaginary

Summary: Patrick Malone, pilot of the *Bright Hope*, and his crew follow Kaitlin Turek through the wormhole outside Pluto's orbit after a message is received on Earth. Although ordered not to interact with any aliens, the crew of *Bright Hope* has little choice as the ship is severely damaged during transit. The aliens transmit a message from Kaitlin Turek who has become very well known to some of the aliens. This book contains an introduction by Isaac Asimov, an essay by Rudy Rucker, and opens with a glossary of alien terminology.

Other books you might like:
Eleanor Arnason, *A Woman of the Iron People*, 1991
Octavia E. Butler, *Dawn*, 1987
John DeChancie, *Red Limit Freeway*, 1984
John DeChancie, *Starrigger*, 1983
Mary Gentle, *Golden Witchbreed*, 1984
Rebecca Ore, *Becoming Alien*, 1987
Catherine Wells, *The Earth Is All That Lasts*, 1991

2723

STEPHEN LEIGH

Changeling
(New York: Ace, 1989)

Story type: Science Fiction (Space Opera)
Series: Isaac Asimov's Robot City: Robots and Aliens
Major character(s): Derec, Amnesiac, Scientist; Ariel Welsh, Heiress
Time period(s): Indeterminate Future
Locale(s): Robot City, Planet—Imaginary

Summary: Still unaware of who he really is, Derec must help defend the city of robots from the evil, wolf-like aliens who threaten it with destruction.

Other books you might like:
Isaac Asimov, *The Caves of Steel*, 1954
Isaac Asimov, *The Complete Robot*, 1982
Isaac Asimov, *The Naked Sun*, 1957
Isaac Asimov, *Robots and Empire*, 1985
Isaac Asimov, *The Robots of Dawn*, 1983
Charles Ingrid, *Return Fire*, 1989
    Sand Wars 5
Michael A. Stackpole, *Battletech: Warrior: Coupe*, 1989

2724

STEPHEN LEIGH

Ray Bradbury Presents: Dinosaur Planet
(New York: AvoNova, 1993)

Story type: Science Fiction (Time Travel; Adventure)
Major character(s): Aaron Cofield, Time Traveller, Teenager; Jennifer Mason, Teenager, Time Traveller; Raajeh, Animal (dinosaur-Mutata)
Time period(s): Indeterminate Past (Mesozoic Era); 1990s
Locale(s): Green Town, Illinois

Summary: While attempting to take Mondo to his home time, Aaron inadvertantly arrives back at his grandfather's house 15 years after he left. More fluent in the Mutata language, Jennifer continues to work at developing an understanding with the dinosaurs, despite the lack of support from her fellow humans. Time storms plague all.

Other books you might like:
Poul Anderson, *The Time Patrol*, 1991
Roger L. DiSilvestro, *Living with the Reptiles*, 1990
James Gurney, *Dinotopia*, 1992
Julian May, *The Many-Colored Land*, 1981
Robert J. Sawyer, *Far-Seer*, 1992
Robert J. Sawyer, *Fossil Hunter*, 1993

2725

STEPHEN LEIGH

Ray Bradbury Presents: Dinosaur World
(New York: AvoNova, 1992)

Story type: Science Fiction (Time Travel; Adventure)
Major character(s): Aaron Cofield, Teenager, Time Traveller; Jennifer Mason, Teenager, Time Traveller; SStragh, Animal (dinosaur-Mutata)
Time period(s): 1990s; Indeterminate Past
Locale(s): Green Town, Illinois

Summary: As Jenny and Aaron contemplate the end of their summer vacation, a dinosaur interrupts their idyll. Chasing after it, they inadvertently travel to different past eras. Captured by another time traveller and then by intelligent dinosaurs, Jenny begins to learn the dinosaur language. Contains a sixteen-page insert of Wayne Barlowe illustrations and a six-page glossary of Mutata terms.

Other books you might like:
Poul Anderson, *The Time Patrol*, 1991
Roger L. DiSilvestro, *Living with the Reptiles*, 1990
Gary Gentile, *Dragons Past*, 1990
James Gurney, *Dinotopia*, 1992
Warren Norwood, *Vanished*, 1988
Robert Silverberg, *Thebes of the Hundred Gates*, 1991
Clifford D. Simak, *Mastodonia*, 1978

2726

ROBERT LEININGER

Black Sun
(New York: Avon, 1991)

Story type: Science Fiction (Disaster)
Major character(s): Maurice Tyler, Scientist, Professor
Time period(s): 21st century
Locale(s): Arizona

Summary: When Maurice Tyler's warning that changes in the Sun's output will spell disaster for humanity fails to take hold in the public awareness, he decides to retreat to his well-stocked survival shelter, if his enemies will allow it.

Other books you might like:
Roger MacBride Allen, *The Ring of Charon*, 1990
J.M. Morgan, *Desert Eden*, 1991
Larry Niven, *Fallen Angels*, 1991
   Michael Flynn and Jerry Pournelle, co-authors
Larry Niven, *Footfall*, 1985
   Jerry Pournelle, co-author
Larry Niven, *Lucifer's Hammer*, 1977
   Jerry Pournelle, co-author
Douglas Orgill, *The Sixth Winter*, 1979
   John Gribbin, co-author
David R. Palmer, *Emergence*, 1984
Christopher Sam Youd, *The Long Winter*, 1962
   as John Christopher

2727

BRAD LEITHAUSER

Hence
(New York: Knopf, 1989)

Story type: Science Fiction (Literary)
Major character(s): Timothy Briggs, Sports Figure (Chessmaster); Garner Briggs, Professor (Law professor)
Time period(s): 1990s (1993, 1997)
Locale(s): Boston, Massachusetts

Summary: Garner Briggs writes a book in which he recounts the famous chess match some four years earlier between his younger brother Timothy and the chess playing computer program ANNDY. He also ponders the nature of artificial intelligence and its probable significance to the world.

Other books you might like:
William Gibson, *Neuromancer*, 1984
Stanislaw Lem, *The Cyberiad*, 1974
Stanislaw Lem, *Memoirs of a Space Traveller*, 1982
Stanislaw Lem, *Mortal Engines*, 1977
Stanislaw Lem, *Return from the Stars*, 1980
Bruce Sterling, *Islands in the Net*, 1988

2728

BRAD LEITHAUSER, Editor

The Norton Book of Ghost Stories
(New York: W.W. Norton, 1994)

Story type: Horror (Anthology; Ghost Story)

Summary: Nineteen Classic and contemporary authors are represented by 28 stories in a compilation that traces the influence of Henry James and M.R. James on the ghost story tradition. Classic tales include Henry James's tale of vengeance from beyond the grave, "The Romance of Certain Old Clothes"; M.R. James' story of a ghost summoned by an artifact found in ancient ruins, "'Oh, Whistle, and I'll Come to You, My Lad'"; Oliver Onions' tale of a man whose life is destroyed by an amorous ghost, "The Beckoning Fair One"; and Elizabeth Bowen's story of a haunted house's overwhelming effect on the personalities of mortals who stay there, "The Cat Jumps." Among the more modern selections are V.S. Pritchett's "The Story Don Juan," which tells of the legendary lover's influence on a vengeful ghost; Penelope Fitzgerald's "The Axe," in which an employer is haunted by the ghost of a terminated employee; and Philip Graham's "Ancient Music," which portrays a haunting from the ghost's point of view.

Other books you might like:
Michael Cox, *The Oxford Book of English Ghost Stories*, 1986
   R.A. Gilbert, co-editor
Michael Cox, *Victorian Ghost Stories: An Oxford Anthology*, 1991
   R.A. Gilbert, co-editor
Peter Haining, *The Ghost Companion*, 1994

2729
BRAD LEITHAUSER

Seaward
(New York: Knopf, 1993)

Story type: Horror (Ghost Story)
Major character(s): Terry Seward, Lawyer; Adam Mikolajczak, Lawyer; Curly Kopp, Store Owner (pet store)
Time period(s): 1990s (1993)
Locale(s): Washington, District of Columbia

Summary: Terry Seward's life is transformed irrevocably when he sees what he perceives as the ghost of his wife a year after her death by drowning. From that point on, Terry is a changed man, unable to tell if the changes in his life and the lives of those around him are the product of his unusual experience, or self-induced.

Other books you might like:
Jonathan Aycliffe, *Naomi's Room*, 1992
Peter S. Beagle, *A Fine and Private Place*, 1960
Daphne Du Maurier, *"Don't Look Now"*, 1976
    in *Echoes From the Macabre*

2730
STANISLAW LEM

Eden
(New York: Harcourt Brace Jovanovich, 1989)

Story type: Science Fiction (First Contact)
Major character(s): Captain, Astronaut; Doctor, Astronaut
Time period(s): Indeterminate Future
Locale(s): Eden, Planet—Imaginary

Summary: A spaceship from Earth crashes on Eden, fourth planet of another sun, and encounters a world of mystifying artifacts and bizarre lifeforms.

Other books you might like:
Philip K. Dick, *Do Androids Dream of Electric Sheep?*, 1968
Michael Kandel, *Strange Invasion*, 1989
Robert Silverberg, *Son of Man*, 1971
Boris Strugatsky, *Roadside Picnic*, 1977
    Arkady Strugatsky, co-author
Boris Strugatsky, *The Snail on the Slope*, 1980
    Arkady Strugatsky, co-author

2731
STANISLAW LEM

Peace on Earth
(New York: Harcourt Brace, 1994)

Story type: Science Fiction (Humor; Dystopian)
Series: Ijon Tichy
Major character(s): Ijon Tichy, Space Explorer, Writer
Time period(s): Indeterminate Future
Locale(s): Moon (Earth's)

Summary: With weapons of mass destruction relocated to the Moon, autonomous intelligences carry on the arms race independent of Earth oversight. Concerned that machine civilization may evolve on Luna, Ijon Tichy tries unsuccessfully to investigate by remote sensors. When Tichy investigates in person, one weapon severs the connection between the two hemispheres of his brain, rendering Tichy's right hand independent of his left.

Other books you might like:
Ed Blome, *Title Deleted for Security Reasons*, 1993
Algis Budrys, *Rogue Moon*, 1960
Jack L. Chalker, *The Red Tape War*, 1991
    Mike Resnick, George Alec Effinger, co-authors
Rudy Rucker, *Live Robots*, 1994
Neal Stephenson, *Snow Crash*, 1993

2732
MADELEINE L'ENGLE

An Acceptable Time
(New York: Dell Laurel Leaf, 1990)

Story type: Fantasy (Time Travel; Young Adult)
Major character(s): Polly O'Keefe, Student; Zachary Gray, Young Man; Anaral, Religious (druid-in-training)
Time period(s): 1980s; 11th century B.C.
Locale(s): Connecticut

Summary: While visiting her grandparents, Polly discovers she can move between her current time circle and that of 3,000 years ago. She and Zachary are caught up in a struggle between two factions of a Native American group who've been influenced by a Druid from Europe, but are now threatened by raiders whose home territory is suffering from drought. This book, set in L'Engle's Time Tetrology universe, was first published by Farrar Straus and Giroux in 1989.

Other books you might like:
Joy Chant, *Red Moon and Black Mountain*, 1970
Susan Cooper, *Over Sea, Under Stone*, 1966
Alan Garner, *The Weirdstone of Brisingamen*, 1960
J. Alison James, *Sing for a Gentle Rain*, 1990
Katherine Kurtz, *Deryni Rising*, 1970
Andre Norton, *Lavender-Green Magic*, 1974

2733
EDWARD M. LERNER

Probe
(New York: Warner, 1991)

Story type: Science Fiction (Alternate Intelligence)
Major character(s): Robert Hanson, Computer Expert (designer); Sally Keller, Researcher (NASA)
Time period(s): 21st century
Locale(s): Rolling Meadows, Illinois

Summary: Asgard Aerospace Corporation's automated spaceship, *Prospector*, constantly sends back information. The data just received has picked up some organized interference which seems to be coming from around Jupiter, near

Prospector's current position. The alien probe blows up soon after discovery, but the effects of its appearance involve NASA, the Space Development Agency, the FBI and Asgard Aerospace.

Other books you might like:
David Brin, *Earth*, 1990
David Gerrold, *When HARLIE Was One: Release 2.0*, 1988
Robert A. Heinlein, *The Moon Is a Harsh Mistress*, 1966
Dan Simmons, *The Fall of Hyperion*, 1990
Dan Simmons, *Hyperion*, 1989
David Alexander Smith, *Homecoming*, 1990
David Alexander Smith, *Rendezvous*, 1988

2734
JONATHAN LETHEM

Amnesia Moon
(New York: Harcourt Brace, 1995)

Story type: Fantasy (Post-Disaster; Contemporary)
Major character(s): Everett "Chaos" Moon, Amnesiac; Melinda Self, Traveller
Time period(s): 21st century
Locale(s): Wyoming; Nevada; California

Summary: Accompanied by Melinda Self, Chaos leaves a miserable existence in Hatfork, Wyoming, hoping to recover memories of a past hinted at in dreams. His odyssey reveals a fractured subjective reality and glimpses of old relationships as he finds former acquaintances.

Other books you might like:
C.S. Friedman, *Black Sun Rising*, 1992
Jean Mark Gawron, *Dream of Glass*, 1993
Ursula K. Le Guin, *The Lathe of Heaven*, 1971
Rachel Pollack, *Unquenchable Fire*, 1992
Michaela Roessner, *Vanishing Point*, 1993

2735
JONATHAN LETHEM

Gun, with Occasional Music
(New York: Harcourt Brace, 1994)

Story type: Fantasy (Mystery; Light Fantasy)
Major character(s): Conrad Metcalf, Detective—Private
Time period(s): 21st century
Locale(s): San Francisco, California; Oakland, California

Summary: Surrounded by intelligent animals that result from evolution therapy, Conrad Metcalf must solve a murder despite uncertainty concerning his employer. Success hinges on Metcalf's ability to avoid government inquisitors and others who wish to involve themselves. First novel.

Other books you might like:
Jonathan Carroll, *The Land of Laughs*, 1980
Glen Cook, *Sweet Silver Blues*, 1987
Mel Gilden, *Surfing Samurai Robots*, 1988
Laurell K. Hamilton, *Guilty Pleasures*, 1993
Cordwainer Smith, *The Rediscovery of Man*, 1993
Gary K. Wolf, *Who Censored Roger Rabbit?*, 1981
Gary K. Wolf, *Who P-P-Plugged Roger Rabbit?*, 1991

2736
JONATHAN LETHEM

The Wall of the Sky, the Wall of the Eye
(New York: Harcourt Brace, 1996)

Story type: Science Fiction (Collection; Horror)
Summary: Contains two original and five stories reprinted from periodicals and anthologies. Despite some dark levity, the stories generally vary in tone from hardboiled to downbeat as Lethem investigates virtual reality, reanimation of the dead, professional sports, failed relationships, alien encounters, penology, and sexual encounters.

Other books you might like:
Pat Cadigan, *Patterns*, 1989
John Kessel, *Meeting in Infinity*, 1992
Lucius Shepard, *The Ends of the Earth*, 1991
Marc Stiegler, *The Gentle Seduction*, 1990
Michael Swanwick, *Gravity's Angels*, 1991
James Tiptree Jr., *Her Smoke Rose Up Forever*, 1990

2737
PRIMO LEVI

The Mirror Maker
(New York: Schocken Books, 1989)

Story type: Science Fiction (Collection)
Summary: This posthumous collection by the famed Italian writer includes twelve short stories, two poems, and twenty-two essays. Most of the short stories are science fiction or fantasy. Among the best of these are "The Interview," "The Great Mutation," "The Mirror Maker," and "Time Checkmated." There is also a short preface by Levi and an introduction by Lorenzo Mondo. Translated by Raymond Rosenthal.

Other books you might like:
Dino Buzzati, *Catastrophe*, 1965
Italo Calvino, *Cosmicomics*, 1968
Italo Calvino, *Invisible Cities*, 1974
Italo Calvino, *The Watcher and Other Stories*, 1971

2738
BETTY LEVIN

Mercy's Mill
(New York: Greenwillow Books, 1992)

Story type: Fantasy (Young Adult; Time Travel)
Major character(s): Sarah Grissom, Child; Jethro Philips, Time Traveller
Time period(s): 1990s
Locale(s): Ashbury, Massachusetts

Summary: As Sarah's mother and stepfather work to restore an old dam and mill after the family moves to the country, Sarah befriends Jethro and learns of Jethro's attempts to help Mercy Bredcake, a 17th century child who narrowly escaped drowning as her penalty for witchcraft.

Other books you might like:
Margaret J. Anderson, *The Ghost Inside the Monitor*, 1990
Eleanor Cameron, *The Court of the Stone Children*, 1973
Gilbert B. Cross, *A Witch Across Time*, 1990
Peni R. Griffin, *Hobkin*, 1992
Nancy Springer, *The Friendship Song*, 1992

2739
ROBERT LEVY

Clan of the Shape-Changers
(Boston: Houghton Mifflin, 1994)

Story type: Fantasy (Young Adult; Adventure)
Major character(s): Susan, Mythical Creature (shapechanger), Teenager; Jeffrey, Mythical Creature (shapechanger), Teenager
Time period(s): Indeterminate Future
Locale(s): Enstor, Planet—Imaginary

Summary: When the King of Reune orders all witches destroyed, Susan flees with her wolf companion, Farrun. After she saves Jeffrey, he brings her to a hiding place, a relic of their ancestors, the Elders. The evil Shaman, Ometerer, hopes to capture the pair of fugitives and learn the secret of their power for himself.

Other books you might like:
Octavia E. Butler, *Imago*, 1989
Monica Hughes, *The Promise*, 1992
Mercedes Lackey, *The Lark and the Wren*, 1991
Lawrence Watt-Evans, *Taking Flight*, 1993
Jane Yolen, *Shape Shifters: Fantasy and Science Fiction Tales about Humans Who Can Change Their Shapes*, 1978 editor

2740
D.F. LEWIS

The Best of D.F. Lewis
(Lessburg, Virginia: TAL Publications, 1993)

Story type: Horror (Collection)

Summary: This chapbook collects 15 stories by an English writer who, for reasons known only to the small press—where all of the selections first appeared—has become a favorite of non-mainstream publishing circles. Only one story, "The Weirdmonger," is longer than several hundred words. Few are anything more than plotless assemblies of bizarre images and non-sequiturs. As a result, all are indescribable as fiction. Ramsey Campbell has supplied an introduction.

Other books you might like:
Ramsey Campbell, *Demons by Daylight*, 1973
Stefan Grabinski, *The Dark Domain*, 1993
Thomas Ligotti, *Grimscribe: His Lives and Works*, 1991
Thomas Ligotti, *Noctuary*, 1994
Thomas Ligotti, *Songs of a Dead Dreamer*, 1990
Edward Lucas White, *Lukundoo and Other Stories*, 1927

2741
S.N. LEWITT

Blind Justice
(New York: Ace, 1991)

Story type: Science Fiction (Political)
Major character(s): Emile Saint-Just, Spaceman; Elizabeth Sarrault, Spaceship Captain
Time period(s): Indeterminate Future
Locale(s): *Mary Damned*, Spaceship (Free Trader); *Constanza*, Spaceship (Justica); Outer Space

Summary: Justica controls human space with an iron fist. When the *Mary Damned's* crew is caught, they are tried and sentenced to prison ships to work for Justica. The *Mary Damned* disappers, holds full of expensive cargo, leaving hope for the victims of Justica in the legends she leaves behind.

Other books you might like:
Glen Cook, *The Dragon Never Sleeps*, 1988
Colin Greenland, *Take Back Plenty*, 1991
Michael P. Kube-McDowell, *Emprise*, 1986
Timothy A. Madden, *Outbanker*, 1990
Joel Henry Sherman, *Random Factor*, 1991
Allen Steele, *Clarke County, Space*, 1990
Sheri S. Tepper, *Raising the Stones*, 1990
Jack Williamson, *Mazeway*, 1990

2742
S.N. LEWITT

Cybernetic Jungle
(New York: Ace, 1992)

Story type: Science Fiction (Political)
Major character(s): Paulo "Jackal" Sulvia, Gang Member; Francisco Pope, Gang Member; Zeide Soledad, Student, Genetically Altered Being
Time period(s): Indeterminate Future
Locale(s): Brasilia, Brazil

Summary: When the power elite overthrows the government in Brasilia, the ensuing chaos destroys the economy and the middle classes. Pope and Sylvia, who had planned on becoming an astronaut, move to the poor section of town and start their own gang with the proviso that they will not deal in highwire. Their involvement with one of the native gangs leads to interaction with the ruling elite who retain contact with the outside world.

Other books you might like:
David Brin, *Earth*, 1990
Peter R. Emshwiller, *The Host*, 1991
Gregory Feeley, *The Oxygen Barons*, 1990
Pat Murphy, *The City, Not Long After*, 1989
David D. Ross, *The Argus Gambit*, 1989
Lucius Shepard, *Life During Wartime*, 1987
Neal Stephenson, *Snow Crash*, 1992

2743

S.N. LEWITT

Cyberstealth

(New York: Ace, 1989)

Story type: Science Fiction (Military)
Major character(s): Cargo, Pilot, Spy; Ghoster, Alien, Spy
Time period(s): Indeterminate Future

Summary: In this prequel to *Dancing Vac*, Cargo is the hottest cyberstealth pilot around and the alien Ghoster is the perfect gunner. They have trouble making sense of each other face to face sometimes, but in the air, communicating through the cybernetic maze, they're definitely top guns.

Other books you might like:
Dale Brown, *Day of the Cheetah*, 1989
Emma Bull, *Falcon*, 1989
Dave Wolverton, *On My Way to Paradise*, 1989

2744

S.N. LEWITT

Dancing Vac

(New York: Ace, 1990)

Story type: Science Fiction (Military)
Major character(s): Cargo, Pilot, Spy; Ghoster, Alien, Spy
Time period(s): Indeterminate Future
Locale(s): Marcanter, Planet—Imaginary; Tel Hasa, Planet—Imaginary

Summary: Betrayed by his alien partner and retired from life as a cyborg fighter pilot and spy, Cargo spends his time gambling until he's forced back into the espionage business. His friend Ghoster is a traitor and the powers that be want the alien dead. They want Cargo to kill him.

Other books you might like:
Emma Bull, *Falcon*, 1989
L.E. Modesitt Jr., *The Ecolitan Operation*, 1989
L.E. Modesitt Jr., *The Ecologic Envoy*, 1986
Dave Wolverton, *On My Way to Paradise*, 1989

2745

S.N. LEWITT

Songs of Chaos

(New York: Ace, 1993)

Story type: Science Fiction (Political; Adventure)
Major character(s): Dante McCall, Outcast, Spaceman; Veronica Guimaraes, Spacewoman
Time period(s): Indeterminate Future
Locale(s): Europe; Eurostate, Fictional Country; *Mangueira*, Spaceship

Summary: An outcast among Florence's genetically altered perfection, Dante McCall presents an unacceptable threat to Eurostate. Dante stows away on a trading ship and finds acceptance among a spacefaring culture.

Other books you might like:
Alfred Bester, *The Stars My Destination*, 1956
Ernest Hogan, *Cortez on Jupiter*, 1990
Marjorie Bradley Kellogg, *Harmony*, 1991
Rebecca Ore, *Becoming Alien*, 1987
Alis A. Rasmussen, *A Passage of Stars*, 1990
Alis A. Rasmussen, *The Price of Ransom*, 1990
Alis A. Rasmussen, *Revolution's Shore*, 1990
Spider Robinson, *Stardance*, 1979
    Jeanne Robinson, co-author

2746

SHARIANN LEWITT

Memento Mori

(New York: Tor, 1995)

Story type: Science Fiction (Arts; Alternate Intelligence)
Major character(s): RICE, Artificial Intelligence; Johanna Henning, Scientist (mathematician); Peter Haas, Sports Figure (chess master), Artist
Time period(s): Indeterminate Future
Locale(s): Reis, Planet—Imaginary

Summary: When a plague on Reis quarantines the entire planet, society breaks down, with even the artificial intelligence controlling the cities acting strangely. Feeling doomed, several aspiring artists look for interesting ways to depict death in their work, or even interesting ways to die.

Other books you might like:
James P. Hogan, *The Two Faces of Tomorrow*, 1979
Gordon Kendall, *White Wing*, 1985
    pseudonym of Susan Shwartz and Shariann Lewitt
S.N. Lewitt, *Angel at Apogee*, 1987
S.N. Lewitt, *Blind Justice*, 1991
S.N. Lewitt, *Cyberstealth*, 1989
S.N. Lewitt, *Dancing Vac*, 1991
Larry Niven, *Achilles' Choice*, 1991
    Steven Barnes, co-author
Mary Rosenblum, *The Stone Garden*, 1995
John Varley, *Steel Beach*, 1992

2747

MARK LEYNER

Et Tu, Babe

(New York: Harmony Books, 1992)

Story type: Science Fiction (Alternate Universe; Humor)
Major character(s): Mark Leyner, Writer, Socialite
Time period(s): 1990s
Locale(s): United States

Summary: Following the runaway success of *My Cousin, My Gastroenterologist*, Mark Leyner becomes the darling of the world through Team Leyner media opportunities. Fans everywhere receive inspirational messages by using touch tone telephones to call 1-800-T-LEYNER and Leyner's every activity attracts worldwide attention.

Other books you might like:
William Borden, *Superstoe*, 1968

Richard Brautigan, *Trout Fishing in America*, 1967
William S. Burroughs, *Naked Lunch*, 1959
William Kotzwinkle, *The Fan Man*, 1974
Neal Stephenson, *Snow Crash*, 1992
Hunter S. Thompson, *Fear and Loathing in Las Vegas*, 1971
Darius James, *Negrophobia: An Urban Parable*,

2748

MARK LEYNER

My Cousin, My Gastroenterologist

(New York: Harmony, 1990)

Story type: Science Fiction (Literary; Contemporary Realism)
Major character(s): I, Human; Bev, Health Care Professional (speech pathologist)
Time period(s): 1990s
Locale(s): United States

Summary: A fast-paced, choppy series of detailed flashes of thought and action, this book is strong on description, actions, weird characters and transitions, with the actual plot threading through in the background. Portions of this book were published as short stories between 1984 and 1989.

Other books you might like:
Michael Blumlein, *The Brains of Rats*, 1990
Richard Brautigan, *The Hawkline Monster*, 1974
William S. Burroughs, *Naked Lunch*, 1959
Samuel R. Delany, *Dhalgren*, 1975
Philip K. Dick, *Ubik*, 1969
Tom Robbins, *Jitterbug Perfume*, 1984
Hunter S. Thompson, *Fear and Loathing in Las Vegas*, 1971
Kurt Vonnegut, *Slaughterhouse Five*, 1969

2749

JACQUELINE LICHTENBERG

Dreamspy

(New York: St. Martin's Press, 1989)

Story type: Science Fiction (Space Opera)
Major character(s): Kyllikki, Alien, Telepath; Zuchmul, Vampire
Time period(s): Indeterminate Future
Locale(s): Metaji Empire, Interstellar Empire/Federation; Teleod, Interstellar Empire/Federation

Summary: In the sequel to *Those of My Blood*, two great, galaxy-spanning empires, Metaji and Teleod, are at war, and their struggle threatens to destroy the very fabric of the space-time continuum. Intelligent beings of several different races struggle to end the war, among them Kyllikki, a Teleod and a powerful telepath; Zuchmul, a member of the vampiric, human-related luren race; and Elias, an Earth human, whose rare ability to dream may hold the key to the galaxy's salvation.

Other books you might like:
Emma Bull, *Falcon*, 1989
Jack Butler, *Nightshade*, 1989
Suzy McKee Charnas, *The Vampire Tapestry*, 1980
Richard Matheson, *I Am Legend*, 1954
Melisa C. Michaels, *Far Harbor*, 1989

2750

ALAN LIGHTMAN

Einstein's Dreams

(New York: Pantheon, 1993)

Story type: Fantasy (Contemporary Realism; Literary)
Major character(s): Albert Einstein, Historical Figure, Government Official (patent clerk)
Time period(s): 1900s (1905)
Locale(s): Berne, Switzerland

Summary: As Albert Einstein concludes work on his special theory of relativity, 30 dreams of possible realms of time help him formulate ideas. First fiction.

Other books you might like:
Nicholson Baker, *The Fermata*, 1994
Philip K. Dick, *Ubik*, 1969
Ken Grimwood, *Replay*, 1986
Sam Moskowitz, *The Time Curve*, 1968
  Roger Elwood, co-editor
Fred Saberhagen, *A Spadeful of Spacetime*, 1981
  editor
Kurt Vonnegut Jr., *The Sirens of Titan*, 1959

2751

THOMAS LIGOTTI

The Agonizing Resurrection of Victor Frankenstein and Other Gothic Tales

(Eugene, Oregon: Silver Salamander Press, 1994)

Story type: Horror (Collection)

Summary: The 19 prose poems collected here distill the essence of particular authors, literary works and films in the horror genre into a series of provocative extrapolations of their themes. Included are fantasias on "The Insufferable Salvation of Lawrence Talbot, the Wolfman," "The Intolerable Lesson of the Phantom of the Opera," and "The Eternal Devotion of the Governess to the Residents of Bly." Two final sections of this beautifully produced book are devoted to the works of Edgar Allan Poe and H.P. Lovecraft.

Other books you might like:
J.G. Ballard, *The Atrocity Exhibition*, 1990
Jorge Luis Borges, *Ficciones*, 1962
Neil Gaiman, *Angels & Visitations: A Miscellany*, 1993
Franz Kafka, *Stories, 1920-1924*, 1990
Bruno Schulz, *The Street of Crocodiles*, 1934

2752

THOMAS LIGOTTI

Grimscribe: His Lives and Works

(New York: Carroll & Graf, 1991)

Story type: Horror (Collection)

Summary: Thirteen stories in which hapless victims who look beyond the surfaces of their world are overwhelmed by a terrifying "other" reality. Included are the World Fantasy

Award nominated homage to H.P. Lovecraft, "The Last Feast of Harlequin"; "The Mystics of Muelenberg," in which "reality" is found to be little more than a shared delusion; the metafictional "Nethescurial"; and a sardonic tale of a doctor-patient relationship, "The Cocoons."

Other books you might like:
Jorge Luis Borges, *Ficciones*, 1962
Dino Buzzati, *Catastrophe*, 1985
Ramsey Campbell, *Demons by Daylight*, 1973
Bruno Schulz, *The Street of Crocodiles*, 1934

2753

THOMAS LIGOTTI

The Nightmare Factory
(New York: Carroll & Graf, 1996)

Story type: Horror (Collection)

Summary: The 45 stories collected here include most of the contents of the author's first three collections and six new stories that further elaborate his vision of existence as a series of nightmarish plunges through holes in the fabric of reality. "Teatro Grottesco" presents a group of artists who discover that their lives resemble the twisted art of an underground theatre group. "The Clown Puppet" employs a menacing doll figure to pose questions of identity among its human characters. The narrators of both "Gas Station Carnivals" and "The Bungalow House" discover that they themselves may be the originators of performance art works that intrigue, obsess, and eventually overwhelm them. All of the stories feature the author's trademark vision of a world whose nightmare logic calls into question the underlying logic of our own. Ligotti's essay, "The Consolations of Horror," appears as an introduction. Poppy Z. Brite supplies the foreword.

Other books you might like:
Robert Aickman, *The Wine-Dark Sea*, 1989
Jorge Luis Borges, *Labyrinths*, 1962
Ramsey Campbell, *Alone with the Horrors*, 1993
H.P. Lovecraft, *The Dunwich Horror and Others*, 1986

2754

THOMAS LIGOTTI

Noctuary
(New York: Carroll & Graf, 1994)

Story type: Horror (Collection)

Summary: The author's third collection consists of eight stories, one previously unpublished, and 19 prose poems and fragments, all concerned with his favorite themes of the inherent instability of what we call reality. "Mad Night of Atonement" and "The Strange Design of Master Rignolo" deal with artists and creators who shine a light on our world that reflects its unreality, while "Conversations in a Dead Language," "The Prodigy of Dreams," "The Tsalal," and especially "The Voice of the Bones" use dream imagery to evoke their horrors. The author has supplied "In the Dark, In the Night," an essay on the weird tale, as his introduction.

Other books you might like:
Robert Aickman, *The Wine-Dark Sea*, 1989
Jorge Luis Borges, *Labyrinths*, 1962
Ramsey Campbell, *Demons by Daylight*, 1973

2755

THOMAS LIGOTTI

Songs of a Dead Dreamer
(New York: Carroll & Graf, 1990)

Story type: Horror (Collection)

Summary: The author's first book presents 20 profoundly disturbing stories that chronicle the experiences of characters in nightmarish worlds slightly off-center from our own. There are both ingenious variations on genre staples, such as the vampire ("The Lost of Art of Twilight"), possession ("The Christmas Eves of Aunt Elise") and sword 'n' sorcery ("Masquerade of a Dead Sword"), and ingeniously original efforts that include the baroque "Drink to Me Only with Labyrinthine Eyes," the surreal "The Greater Festival of Masks" and "Notes on the Writing of Horror," a fusion of fiction and non-fiction.

Other books you might like:
Jorge Luis Borges, *Ficciones*, 1962
Dino Buzzati, *Catastrophe*, 1985
Ramsey Campbell, *Demons by Daylight*, 1973
Bruno Schulz, *The Street of Crocodiles*, 1934

2756

BRAD LINAWEAVER

Sliders: The Novel
(New York: Berkley Boulevared, 1996)

Story type: Science Fiction (Alternate Universe; Adventure)
Major character(s): Quinn Mallory, Inventor, Scientist; Maximillian Arturo, Professor, Adventurer; Rembrandt "Cryin' Man" Brown, Musician, Adventurer
Time period(s): 1990s
Locale(s): Alternate Earth

Summary: Quinn Mallory and his companions explore Earths in parallel dimensions using his homemade device. Television tie-in.

Other books you might like:
Dafydd ab Hugh, *Endgame*, 1996
   Brad Linaweaver, co-author
Dafydd ab Hugh, *Knee Deep in the Dead*, 1995
   Brad Linaweaver, co-author
Mona Clee, *Branch Point*, 1996
Ashley McConnell, *Quantum Leap: The Novel*, 1992
Robert Reed, *Down the Bright Way*, 1991
John Varley, *Millennium*, 1983

2757

ANNE LINDBERGH

Travel Far, Pay No Fare

(New York: HarperCollins, 1992)

Story type: Fantasy (Young Adult; Quest)
Major character(s): Owen Noonan, Child, Adventurer; Parsley, Child, Adventurer
Time period(s): 1990s
Locale(s): Vermont

Summary: A magic bookmark transports Owen and Parsley into the world created in the book marked. There the pair seek a way to prevent their parents' upcoming marriage.

Other books you might like:
Michael Ende, *The Neverending Story*, 1983
Kathryn Lasky, *Double Trouble Squared*, 1991
Will Shetterly, *Elsewhere*, 1991
Nancy Springer, *The Friendship Song*, 1992
Vivian Vande Velde, *User Unfriendly*, 1991

2758

Alien Earth

(New York: Bantam Spectra, 1992)

Story type: Science Fiction (First Contact; Post-Holocaust)
Major character(s): John Gen-93-Beta, Spaceship Captain; Evangeline, Alien (spaceship); Tug, Spaceship Captain, Alien (Arthroplana)
Time period(s): Indeterminate Future
Locale(s): *Evangeline*, Spaceship; Delta Station, Space Station; Earth

Summary: In the generations after the Arthroplana rescued humanity from the dying Earth and moved the population out of the solar system, humans evolved to fit the conditions of their new habitat. Sexual maturity occurs after sixty years of age, therefore natural conception has been eliminated and humanity totals approximately eighty-seven thousand. Unable to find other work for *Evangeline*, John accepts a contract to assess the potential viability of Earth, risking readjustment by the Human Conservancy.

Other books you might like:
Clare Bell, *People of the Sky*, 1989
Octavia E. Butler, *Dawn*, 1987
C.S. Friedman, *The Madness Season*, 1990
Diana G. Gallagher, *The Alien Dark*, 1990
T. Jackson King, *Retread Shop*, 1988
Vonda N. McIntyre, *Metaphase*, 1992
Larry Niven, *Protector*, 1973
Vernor Vinge, *A Fire upon the Deep*, 1992
Catherine Wells, *The Earth Is All That Lasts*, 1991
    pseudonym of Catherine Wells Dimenstein

2759

MEGAN LINDHOLM

Cloven Hooves

(New York: Bantam Spectra, 1991)

Story type: Fantasy (Legend; Contemporary)
Major character(s): Evelyn Sylvia Potter, Farmer, Spouse; Pan, Mythical Creature (satyr)
Time period(s): 1970s (1976); 1960s
Locale(s): Washington; Alaska; Canada

Summary: When Evelyn and Tom Potter move from Alaska to Washington state to help with his family's farm, Evelyn begins to feel unappreciated and isolated until her childhood companion, Pan, reappears. Her relationship with Pan leads to a dangerous foot journey back towards Alaska, during which Evelyn begins a new life and family with the satyr.

Other books you might like:
Charles de Lint, *Greenmantle*, 1988
Charles de Lint, *Spiritwalk*, 1992
Gordon R. Dickson, *Wolf and Iron*, 1990
Greer Ilene Gilman, *Moonwise*, 1991
Robert Holdstock, *Mythago Wood*, 1984
Ian McDonald, *King of Morning, Queen of Day*, 1991
Thorne Smith, *Topper: An Improbable Adventure*, 1926
Mary Alexander Walker, *The Scathach and the Maeve's Daughter*, 1990

2760

MEGAN LINDHOLM

Luck of the Wheels

(New York: Ace, 1989)

Story type: Fantasy (Light Fantasy)
Major character(s): Ki, Trader (Gypsy); Vandien, Warrior (Swordsman)
Time period(s): Indeterminate

Summary: Ki and Vandien agree to escort an obnoxious teenage boy named Goat to a distant city. Encountering trouble along the way, they receive magic telepathic aid.

Other books you might like:
L. Sprague de Camp, *The Honorable Barbarian*, 1989
Barbara Hambly, *The Silent Tower*, 1988
Rosemary Kirstein, *The Steerswoman*, 1989
Jennifer Roberson, *Sword-Maker*, 1989
Christopher Stasheff, *The Warlock Insane*, 1989

2761

CHARLES LINDLEY

The Ghost Book of Charles Lindley, Viscount Halifax

(New York: Carroll & Graf, 1994)

Story type: Horror (Collection; Ghost Story)
Summary: Originally published as two volumes, *Lord Halifax's Ghost Book* (1936) and *Further Stories From Lord*

Halifax's Ghost Book (1937), this compendium collects purportedly true ghost stories recorded by Lord Halifax, and culled from his apparently voluminous correspondence. "Marche!" tells of a ghost who repossesses its body long enough to keep away vermin during its disinterment, "The Man in the Iron Cage" of the spirit of an heir imprisoned in an iron cage that continues to haunt a castle, and "The Passenger with the Bag" of a spirit that helps solve the mystery of an embezzlement. For the most part, these stories are related in the straightforward fashion of folk tales, with few surprises or extraordinary motivations for their spectral players.

Other books you might like:
Jessica Amanda Salmonson, *The Mysterious Doom and Other Ghostly Tales of the Pacific Northwest*, 1992
Manly Wade Wellman, *John the Balladeer*, 1988
John Manchip White, *Whistling Past the Churchyard*, 1992

2762
JANE M. LINDSKOLD
Brother to Dragons, Companion to Owls
(New York: AvoNova, 1994)

Story type: Fantasy (Urban; Science Fiction)
Major character(s): Sarah, Handicapped (autistic), Psychic; Abalone, Computer Expert, Criminal; Betwixt and Between, Mythical Creature (animated rubber dragon)
Time period(s): Indeterminate Future
Locale(s): New York, New York; Ivy Green Institute, Mythical Place

Summary: Forced out of the Home by the mysterious Dr. Haas, Sarah befriends Abalone who takes her to the jungle, hoping Head Wolf will let her stay. After an old teacher comes to warn Sarah that she must hide, Sarah begins to gain control of her ability to hear inanimate objects; however, the representatives of the Ivy Green Institute will not give up the search.

Other books you might like:
Iain M. Banks, *The Bridge*, 1986
Karen Joy Fowler, *Sarah Canary*, 1992
C.S. Friedman, *Black Sun Rising*, 1992
Susan Palwick, *Flying in Place*, 1992
Fay Weldon, *The Shrapnel Academy*, 1987

2763
JANE M. LINDSKOLD
Marks of Our Brothers
(New York: AvoNova, 1995)

Story type: Science Fiction (First Contact; Psychic Powers)
Major character(s): Karen Saber, Linguist, Criminal; Aino Rand, Telepath; Onyx, Alien, Psychic (esper)
Time period(s): Indeterminate Future
Locale(s): U.A.N. Headquarters, Earth; *Shadowsweep*, Spaceship; Xi-7, Planet—Imaginary

Summary: Having begun a vendetta against the murderers of her ex-boss, Karen is distracted by a puzzle leading to a newly contacted, perhaps sentient, species. After rescuing the aliens,

Karen must decide if the surviving one shows intelligence and, if so, how they can save her planet from colonization by the recent alliance of humans and aliens, the U.A.N.

Other books you might like:
Eleanor Arnason, *Ring of Swords*, 1993
L. Warren Douglas, *A Plague of Change*, 1992
Janet Kagan, *Hellspark*, 1988
Larry Niven, *The Mote in God's Eye*, 1974
    Jerry Pournelle, co-author
H. Beam Piper, *Little Fuzzy*, 1962

2764
JANE M. LINDSKOLD
Smoke and Mirrors
(New York: AvoNova, 1996)

Story type: Science Fiction (Psychic Powers; First Contact)
Major character(s): Smokey Smoke, Telepath, Prostitute; Ha'riel nu-Aten, Spaceship Captain, Alien (parasite); Clarence Beauduc, Professor (history), Tourist
Time period(s): Indeterminate Future
Locale(s): Arizona, Planet—Imaginary; *Ibn Battuta*, Spaceship; Guillen, Planet—Imaginary

Summary: Probing her customer during sex in order to perfectly satisfy, Smokey discovers an unpleasant alien presence. When acquaintances turn up brutally murdered, Smokey leaves Arizona with her parents, daughter and Clarence. Nu-Aten introduces Smokey to the conspiracy of humans with psychic powers and those with benign psychic parasites to fight the predatory psychic aliens Smokey experienced in Arizona.

Other books you might like:
Octavia E. Butler, *Dawn*, 1987
C.S. Friedman, *The Madness Season*, 1990
Robert A. Heinlein, *The Puppet Masters*, 1951
P.K. McAllister, *Siduri's Net*, 1994
Ian McDonald, *Evolution's Shore*, 1995

2765
HOLLY LISLE
Bones of the Past
(New York: Baen, 1993)

Story type: Fantasy (Quest)
Major character(s): Medwind Song, Barbarian, Scholar; Nokar, Librarian; Roba Morgasdotte, Teacher (music), Adventurer
Time period(s): Indeterminate
Locale(s): Omwimmee Trade, Fictional City; Wennish Jungle, Fictional Country; First Folk Ruins, Fictional City

Summary: Wen children come to Omwimmee Trade hoping to secure food and agricultural technology. Medwind Song begins by trading a drum for the childrens' knowledge of drum talk language, but soon becomes interested in a First Folk artifact the children brought to trade. After learning of an abandoned First Folk city, Medwind Song arranges to journey there in exchange for extensive agricultural help for the Wen.

None of Medwind Song's companions fully appreciate the perilous consequences of their anthropological undertaking.

Other books you might like:
Rosemary Kirstein, *The Outskirter's Secret*, 1992
Mercedes Lackey, *When the Bough Breaks*, 1993
  Holly Lisle, co-author
Marc Laidlaw, *Neon Lotus*, 1988
Lucius Shepard, *Kalimantan*, 1992

2766

HOLLY LISLE
WALTER SPENCE, Co-Author

The Devil and Dan Cooley

(New York: Baen, 1996)

Story type: Fantasy (Contemporary; Light Fantasy)
Series: Hellraised
Major character(s): Dan Cooley, Radio Personality; Puck, Demon; Lucifer, Demon
Time period(s): 1990s
Locale(s): Raleigh, North Carolina; Heaven

Summary: North Carolina goes to hell, literally, with thousands of the Damned released in, but confined to, that state. A radio personality with a patriotic bent, unresolved guilt, and two girlfriends, Dan Cooley decides to rehabilitate a demon as a publicity stunt. Trapped between Heaven, Hell, and angry humans, Dan soon finds more than ratings at stake.

Other books you might like:
Jack Dann, *Angels!*, 1995
  Gardner Dozois, co-editor
Neil Gaiman, *Good Omens: The Nice and Accurate Prophecies of Agnes Nutter, Witch*, 1990
  Terry Pratchett, co-author
James Morrow, *Only Begotten Daughter*, 1990
Nancy Springer, *Metal Angel*, 1994
Sean Stewart, *Resurrection Man*, 1995
Roger Zelazny, *If at Faust You Don't Succeed*, 1993
  Robert Sheckley, co-author

2767

HOLLY LISLE

Fire in the Mist

(New York: Baen, 1992)

Story type: Fantasy (Magic Conflict)
Major character(s): Faia Rissedote, Shepherd, Sorceress; Medwind Song, Sorceress, Barbarian; Yaji Jennedote, Sorceress, Student
Time period(s): Indeterminate Past
Locale(s): Bright, Fictional City; Ariss, Fictional City

Summary: Discovering her village destroyed by plague, Faia uncages a magical explosion that removes the remains. This alerts the magicians of Ariss, who insist on Faia's training to avoid future disasters. Unfortunately, Faia's studies must wait as politics and ancient evil complicate her life.

Other books you might like:
Barbara Hambly, *The Time of the Dark*, 1982

Katherine Kurtz, *Deryni Rising*, 1970
Mercedes Lackey, *Arrows of the Queen*, 1987
Ursula K. Le Guin, *A Wizard of Earthsea*, 1968
Patricia A. McKillip, *The Riddle-Master of Hed*, 1976
Mercedes Lackey, *When the Bough Breaks*, 1993
  Holly Lisle, co-author

2768

HOLLY LISLE
CHRIS GUIN, Co-Author

Mall, Mayhem and Magic

(New York: Baen, 1995)

Story type: Fantasy (Light Fantasy; Magic Conflict)
Major character(s): Jim Franklin, Clerk (bookstore); Sharra, Immortal; Gali, Mythical Creature (elf)
Time period(s): 1990s
Locale(s): North Carolina

Summary: While attempting to use a love spell discovered in an ancient book, Jim unwittingly begins to unlock the seals which confine Sharra's deadly mate and a cadre of demons ready to conquer the human realm.

Other books you might like:
Rick Cook, *Mall Purchase Night*, 1993
Elizabeth Forrest, *Phoenix Fire*, 1992
Alan Dean Foster, *Cyber Way*, 1990
Alan Dean Foster, *To the Vanishing Point*, 1988
Barbara Hambly, *Bride of the Rat God*, 1994
Harry Turtledove, *The Case of the Toxic Spell Dump*, 1993

2769

HOLLY LISLE

Mind of the Magic

(New York: Baen, 1995)

Story type: Fantasy (Magic Conflict; Adventure)
Major character(s): Faia Rissedotte, Sorceress, Parent; Kirtha, Child, Magician; Medwind Song, Sorceress, Scholar
Time period(s): Indeterminate
Locale(s): Arhel, Fictional Country (continent)

Summary: Faia's hopes of raising Kirtha in peace vanish as a meddlesome god forces Faia into his machinations, bringing her a pivotal role in the future of magic in Arhel. Sequel to *Bones of the Past*.

Other books you might like:
Jo Clayton, *Wild Magic*, 1991
Dave Duncan, *The Cutting Edge*, 1993
Mary Gentle, *Rats and Gargoyles*, 1991
Laurell K. Hamilton, *Nightseer*, 1992
P.C. Hodgell, *God Stalk*, 1982
Patricia C. Wrede, *The Raven Ring*, 1994

2770

HOLLY LISLE

Minerva Wakes

(New York: Baen, 1994)

Story type: Fantasy (Magic Conflict; Alternate World)
Major character(s): Minerva Kiakra, Parent, Heroine; Darryl Kiakra, Parent; Birkwelch, Mythical Creature
Time period(s): 1990s
Locale(s): Earth; Weird's Hold, Fictional City; Eyrith, Alternate Earth

Summary: Plotting to destroy all, the Unweaver kidnaps Minerva's children. A helpful satyr and dragon provide help as Minerva's maternal instinct drives her into a magical realm to save her children and rescue all of existence.

Other books you might like:
Emma Bull, *Finder*, 1994
Pamela Dean, *The Secret Country*, 1985
Rose Estes, *Troll-Taken*, 1993
Mercedes Lackey, *When the Bough Breaks*, 1993
    Holly Lisle, co-author
Vivian Vande Velde, *User Unfriendly*, 1991
Robert Weinberg, *A Logical Magician*, 1994

2771

HOLLY LISLE

Sympathy for the Devil

(New York: Baen, 1996)

Story type: Fantasy (Contemporary; Light Fantasy)
Series: Hellraised
Major character(s): Dayne Kuttner, Nurse; Agonostis, Demon, Administrator; God, Deity
Time period(s): 1990s (1996)
Locale(s): Hell; Charlotte, North Carolina

Summary: Devastated by her husband's certain damnation and tormented by the suffering of her patients, Dayne Kuttner prays for relief for the damned. God responds by sending a contingent from Hell to North Carolina. While God acts in inscrutable ways and Satan wants Dayne's soul, neither fully realizes what Dayne plans to do.

Other books you might like:
Emma Bull, *War for the Oaks*, 1987
Jack L. Chalker, *And the Devil Will Drag You Under*, 1979
Neil Gaiman, *Good Omens: The Nice and Accurate Prophecies of Agnes Nutter, Witch*, 1990
    Terry Pratchett, co-author
Christopher Moore, *Practical Demonkeeping*, 1992
Mike Resnick, *Deals with the Devil*, 1994
    Martin H. Greenberg, Loren D. Estleman, co-editors

2772

HOLLY LISLE
AARON ALLSTON, Co-Author

Thunder of the Captains

(New York: Baen, 1996)

Story type: Fantasy (Political; Adventure)
Series: Bard's Tale
Major character(s): Kin Underbridge, Servant (valet), Writer; Jerno Byriver, Royalty (king), Castaway; Halleyne dar Dero, Writer (scribe), Castaway
Time period(s): Indeterminate
Locale(s): Lieda, Fictional Country; Terosalle, Fictional Country; Fishtail Island, Mythical Place

Summary: Eight years of warfare and the death of all natural heirs leads to a treaty signed at sea on the eve of a storm. All three ships are destroyed, and the delegates arrive on Fishtail Island where a new system for survival and rule eventually emerges as Kin becomes compromise leader.

Other books you might like:
David Eddings, *Pawn of Prophecy*, 1982
Simon Hawke, *The Iron Throne*, 1995
J.V. Jones, *The Baker's Boy*, 1995
R.A. Salvatore, *The Legacy*, 1992
Josepha Sherman, *The Chaos Gate*, 1994

2773

JONATHAN LITTELL

Bad Voltage

(New York: NAL Signet, 1989)

Story type: Science Fiction (Cyberpunk)
Major character(s): Lynx, Gang Member (Gang leader); Mara, Gang Member
Time period(s): 21st century (2033)
Locale(s): Paris, France

Summary: High-tech hoods and cybernetically-augmented street gangs battle for survival in the streets of a decadent, near-future Paris. This is Littell's first novel.

Other books you might like:
William Gibson, *Count Zero*, 1985
William Gibson, *Mona Lisa Overdrive*, 1988
William Gibson, *Neuromancer*, 1984
W.T. Quick, *Dreams of Gods and Men*, 1989
Norman Spinrad, *Little Heroes*, 1987
Bruce Sterling, *Islands in the Net*, 1988

2774

BENTLEY LITTLE

Dominion

(New York: Signet, 1996)

Story type: Horror (Ancient Evil Unleashed)
Major character(s): Dion Semele, Teenager; Penelope Daneam, Teenager; Alice Semele, Clerk (bank teller), Parent (Dion's mother)

Time period(s): 1990s (1996)
Locale(s): Napa Valley, California

Summary: For untold years the women who run Daneam Vineyards have concealed their identities as mythological maenads, who slaughter their victims in a sexual frenzy. When Dion Semele moves to town the Daneams plan to mate him with their daughter Penelope and unleash a bacchanalian orgy of bloodlust and death. This book was first published in England in 1995 as *The Dark Dominion*.

Other books you might like:
Ron Faust, *Lord of the Dark Lake*, 1995
Michael O'Rourke, *The Undine*, 1996
Melanie Tem, *Wilding*, 1992
Kelley Wilde, *Angel Kiss*, 1993

2775

BENTLEY LITTLE

The Mailman
(New York: Onyx, 1990)

Story type: Horror (Satire)
Major character(s): Doug Albin, Teacher; Tritia Albin, Housewife (Doug's wife); John Smith, Postal Worker
Time period(s): 1990s
Locale(s): Willis, Arizona

Summary: Although he's a bit creepy, it's hard not to like the new mailman, who delivers neither junk mail nor bills. But when the good citizens of Willis find that some important letters are not being delivered, and worse, that those who accept mail from John Smith are at his beck and call, they discover a horrifying fact of life: he who controls the mail controls life.

Other books you might like:
Thomas M. Disch, *The M.D.: A Horror Story*, 1991
John Farris, *I Scream. You Scream. We All Scream for Ice Cream*, 1989
in *Scare Tactics*
Jackie Hyman, *Echoes*, 1990

2776

BENTLEY LITTLE

The Revelation
(New York: St. Martin's, 1990)

Story type: Horror (Apocalyptic Horror)
Major character(s): Jim Weldon, Police Officer (Sheriff); Brother Elias, Religious (Itinerant preacher)
Time period(s): 1990s
Locale(s): Randall, Arizona

Summary: An ancient evil gradually and progressively brings anarchy, madness, and death to Randall, as a small group of townspeople, led by a mysterious itinerant preacher, battles with long-forgotten rituals to save the town.

Other books you might like:
Ramsey Campbell, *The Hungry Moon*, 1986
Stephen King, *Salem's Lot*, 1975

T.E.D. Klein, *The Ceremonies*, 1984
Peter Straub, *Ghost Story*, 1979

2777

BENTLEY LITTLE

The Summoning
(New York: Leisure, 1993)

Story type: Horror (Vampire Story)
Major character(s): Sue Wing, Journalist; Richard Carter, Editor (newspaper); Robert Carter, Police Officer
Time period(s): 1990s (1993)
Locale(s): Rio Verde, Arizona

Summary: A voracious *cup-hu-girngsi*, or shape-shifting vampire, comes to the remote town of Rio Verde, and complicates its removal by appearing in a variety of forms that stir the emotions of the townsfolk against one another.

Other books you might like:
Don Davis, *Bring on the Night*, 1993
Jay Davis, co-author
Ron Dee, *Dusk*, 1991
Charles L. Grant, *The Soft Whisper of the Dead*, 1982
Stephen King, *Salem's Lot*, 1975
Richard Laymon, *The Stake*, 1991

2778

BENTLEY LITTLE

University
(New York: Signet, 1995)

Story type: Horror (Occult)
Major character(s): Jim Parker, Student, Editor (of the student newspaper); Faith Pullen, Student; Ian Emerson, Professor (of English literature)
Time period(s): 1990s (1995)
Locale(s): Brea, California

Summary: There's only one explanation for the violence, sexual debauchery, and hatred overflowing from the newly-founded University of California at Brea into the surrounding town: the university is actually a sentient entity, approaching its fourth year of life, after which it will evolve into an even more terrible being. A small band of enlightened students and professors at the school put their lives in jeopardy when they determine to put an end to the university's evil.

Other books you might like:
Ed Kelleher, *The School*, 1988
Harriet Vidal, co-author
Fritz Leiber, *Conjure Wife*, 1953
R.L. Stine, *Superstitious*, 1995

2779

MORGAN LLYWELYN

Brian Boru: Emperor of the Irish
(New York: Tor, 1995)

Story type: Fantasy (Young Adult)

Major character(s): Brian mac Kennedy, Leader, Historical Figure; Murcha mac Brian, Warrior, Heir; Malachy the Great, Royalty (high king), Leader
Time period(s): 10th century
Locale(s): Ireland

Summary: Young Brian Boru vows over the bodies of his slain mother and brothers to drive the Viking invaders from his beloved Ireland forever. Schooled as both warrior and scholar, Brian battles his way to the High King's crown and dedicates his life to uniting the squabbling tribes of his kingdom. Reprint of 1990 Irish edition.

Other books you might like:
Kenneth C. Flint, *Challenge of the Clans*, 1986
Harry Harrison, *The Hammer and the Cross*, 1993
    John Holm, co-author
Robert E. Howard, *Conan the Barbarian*, 1955
Ron Miller, *Hearts and Armor*, 1992
Andrew J. Offutt, *Sword of the Gael*, 1975
Rosemary Sutcliff, *Sword at Sunset*, 1963
Paul O. Williams, *The Breaking of Northwall*, 1981
Bridget Wood, *Wolfking*, 1992

2780

MORGAN LLYWELYN

Druids

(New York: Morrow, 1991)

Story type: Fantasy (Historical)
Major character(s): Ainvar, Religious (Druid priest); Vercingetorix, Warrior
Time period(s): 5th century; 6th century
Locale(s): Gaul

Summary: With Ainvar's help, Vercingetorix must unite the diverse Celtic tribes to resist the growing Roman threat within Gaul.

Other books you might like:
Frans G. Bengtsson, *The Long Ships*, 1954
Parke Godwin, *Sherwood*, 1991
Patricia Kennealy, *The Copper Crown*, 1984
R.A. MacAvoy, *The Book of Kells*, 1985
Elona Malterre, *The Celts*, 1988

2781

MORGAN LLYWELYN

The Elementals

(New York: Tor, 1993)

Story type: Fantasy (Post-Disaster; Religious)
Major character(s): Kesair, Artisan, Leader; Meriones, Musician; Annie Murphy, Housewife
Time period(s): 101st century B.C. (10,000 B.C.); 1850s (1855)
Locale(s): Crete, Greece (Knossos); New Hampshire

Summary: When Earth's ice cap melts, the water rises. After Kesair and her people build a boat, all but three men dying in its defense, Kesair comes to understand the language of the water and guides her band across the ocean to a new land.

Meriones learns the power of fire while living on Minoan Crete. Annie Murphy's pragmatic upbringing inadvertently brings her into contact with Earth through the huge holy stone which influences her New Hampshire town.

Other books you might like:
David Brin, *Earth*, 1990
Thomas A. Easton, *Sparrowhawk*, 1990
Sue Harrison, *Mother Earth, Father Sky*, 1990
Anne McCaffrey, *Powers That Be*, 1993
    Elizabeth Ann Scarborough, co-author
Elizabeth Ann Scarborough, *Nothing Sacred*, 1991
Catherine Wells, *The Earth Is All That Lasts*, 1991

2782

MORGAN LLYWELYN

Finn Mac Cool

(New York: Forge, 1994)

Story type: Fantasy (Legend; Adventure)
Major character(s): Finn Mac Cool, Warrior, Hero; Goll Mac Morna, Warrior; Cormac Mac Airt, Royalty, Leader
Time period(s): 3rd century
Locale(s): Ireland

Summary: Finn Mac Cool overcomes his early abandonment and life in the wilderness to lead a band of warriors of the Fianna. As Finn promotes legends about his deeds, Finn's defense of Tara leads King Cormac to appoint him supreme commander of the Fianna, further deteriorating his personal relationship with Goll Mac Morna.

Other books you might like:
Kenneth C. Flint, *Challenge of the Clans*, 1986
Andrew J. Offutt, *Sword of the Gael*, 1975
Diana L. Paxson, *Master of Earth and Water*, 1993
    Adrienne Martine-Barnes, co-author
Diana L. Paxson, *The Shield between the Worlds*, 1994
    Adrienne Martine-Barnes, co-author
John Vornholt, *The Fabulist*, 1993
Bridget Wood, *Wolfking*, 1992

2783

MORGAN LLYWELYN

The Isles of the Blest

(New York: Ace, 1989)

Story type: Fantasy (Legend)
Major character(s): Connla, Warrior; Blathine, Mythical Creature (Fairy)
Time period(s): Indeterminate Past
Locale(s): Isles of the Blest, Mythical Place (Land of the faeries)

Summary: Connla, an Irish warrior, weary of battle, decides that he does not wish to engage himself in any further confrontation. With his lust for war depleted, he makes a deal with Blathine, but some deals turn out to be risky. This one is no exception.

Other books you might like:
Poul Anderson, *Three Hearts and Three Lions*, 1961

Ellen Kushner, *Thomas the Rhymer*
Peter Tremayne, *Bloodmist*, 1988

2784

MORGAN LLYWELYN

Pride of Lions

(New York: Forge, 1996)

Story type: Fantasy (Legend; Political)
Major character(s): Donough, Leader, Warrior; Gormlaith, Widow(er)
Time period(s): 11th century
Locale(s): Ireland

Summary: Thrust into leadership on the battlefield, Donough, the 15-year-old son of Brian Boru, hopes to continue his father's gains in unifying Ireland. However, Gormlaith seeks to gather power to herself, while Donough's duty requires great personal sacrifice in pursuit of his goals. Sequel to *Lion of Ireland*.

Other books you might like:
C.J. Cherryh, *Fortress in the Eye of Time*, 1995
Kenneth C. Flint, *Challenge of the Clans*, 1986
Andrew J. Offutt, *Sword of the Gael*, 1975
Diana L. Paxson, *Master of Earth and Water*, 1993
    Adrienne Martine-Barnes, co-author
Melanie Rawn, *The Golden Key*, 1996
    Jennifer Roberson, Kate Elliott, co-authors
Mary Stewart, *The Crystal Cave*, 1970
Bridget Wood, *Wolfking*, 1992

2785

MORGAN LLYWELYN

Silverlight

(New York: Baen, 1996)

Story type: Fantasy (Adventure; Magic Conflict)
Series: Arcana
Major character(s): Caeled Silverhand, Hero, Warrior
Time period(s): Indeterminate Future
Locale(s): At Sea; Seven Nations, Fictional Country

Summary: Caeled Silverhand must locate the four emblems of ultimate power, the Arcana, before evil twin sorcerers, the Duet, can use them and Tantric Magic to plunge the world into eternal suffering.

Other books you might like:
Terry Goodkind, *Wizard's First Rule*, 1994
Frank Herbert, *Heretics of Dune*, 1984
Marjorie Bradley Kellogg, *The Book of Earth*, 1995
Marc Laidlaw, *Neon Lotus*, 1988
Fred Saberhagen, *The First Book of Swords*, 1983

2786

ANNE LOGSTON

Dagger's Edge

(New York: Ace, 1994)

Story type: Fantasy (Mystery; Adventure)
Series: Shadow
Major character(s): Jael, Mythical Creature (half-elf), Royalty; Shadow, Mythical Creature (elf), Thief
Time period(s): Indeterminate
Locale(s): Allanmere, Fictional City

Summary: Hoping to improve Jael's standing as heir, Jael's parents engage her Aunt Shadow to help overcome her bad luck and the lethal intent of a secret cult bent on destroying elves.

Other books you might like:
Lois McMaster Bujold, *The Spirit Ring*, 1992
Elizabeth Moon, *Sheepfarmer's Daughter*, 1988
Andre Norton, *The Elvenbane*, 1991
    Mercedes Lackey, co-author
Paula Volsky, *Illusion*, 1992
Martha Wells, *The Element of Fire*, 1993

2787

ANNE LOGSTON

Greendaughter

(New York: Ace, 1993)

Story type: Fantasy (Adventure; Political)
Major character(s): Chyrie, Mythical Creature (elf)
Time period(s): Indeterminate
Locale(s): Allanmere, Fictional City

Summary: Chyrie must affect cooperation between elves and their traditional enemies, humans, to secure Allanmere against barbarian invaders intent on total destruction. Prequel to *Shadow*.

Other books you might like:
Teresa Edgerton, *The Moon in Hiding*, 1989
Elizabeth Moon, *Surrender None: The Legacy of Gird*, 1990
Mark C. Perry, *Morigu: The Dead*, 1990
Kristine Kathryn Rusch, *The White Mists of Power*, 1991
Pat Zettner, *The Shadow Warrior*, 1990

2788

ANNE LOGSTON

Guardian's Key

(New York: Ace, 1996)

Story type: Fantasy (Quest)
Major character(s): Dara, Magician, Servant; The Vanian, Guardian (Crystal Keep's); Gespry, Companion
Time period(s): Indeterminate
Locale(s): Crystal Keep, Mythical Place

Summary: Accompanied by Gespry and sometimes aided by Lord Vanian, Dara searches for the Oracle behind the seemingly endless doorways of Crystal Keep, hoping to discover her own magical abilities and a means to marry her beloved.

Other books you might like:
Lois McMaster Bujold, *The Spirit Ring*, 1992
Laurell K. Hamilton, *Nightseer*, 1992
Caroline Stevermer, *A College of Magics*, 1994
Deborah Talmadge-Bickmore, *The Apprentice*, 1990
Martha Wells, *The Element of Fire*, 1993

2789

ANNE LOGSTON

Shadow

(New York: Ace, 1991)

Story type: Fantasy (Adventure; Mystery)
Series: Shadow
Major character(s): Shadow, Mythical Creature (elf), Thief; Lady Donya, Thief (former), Mythical Creature (half-elf)
Time period(s): Indeterminate
Locale(s): Allanmere, Fictional City

Summary: For someone so new in town, Shadow's drawing much dangerous attention, apparently because of the lovely silver bracelet she stole and now can't remove from her wrist. It seems an awfully small thing to have catapulted Shadow into the middle of religious and guild politics and human/elf tensions, to say nothing of the assassin on her trail. This is the author's first novel.

Other books you might like:
Steven Brust, *Jhereg*, 1983
Glen Cook, *Sweet Silver Blues*, 1987
Tanya Huff, *The Fire's Stone*, 1990
Fritz Leiber, *Swords and Deviltry*, 1970
Patricia C. Wrede, *Shadow Magic*, 1982

2790

ANNE LOGSTON

Shadow Dance

(New York: Ace, 1992)

Story type: Fantasy (Quest)
Series: Shadow
Major character(s): Shadow, Mythical Creature (elf), Thief; Lady Donya, Thief (former), Mythical Creature (half-elf); Mist, Hunter, Mythical Creature (elf)
Time period(s): Indeterminate
Locale(s): Fictional City; Dim Reaches, Mythical Place (swamp); Spirit Lake, Mythical Place

Summary: Reluctant to return to the swamp which nearly claimed her life, Shadow leads a band of warriors into the Dim Reaches to collect a plant needed to treat the Crimson Plague and find an ancient temple, the key to averting an invasion.

Other books you might like:
Elizabeth Moon, *Sheepfarmer's Daughter*, 1988
James D. Priest, *Kirins: The Spell of No'an*, 1990
Will Shetterly, *Elsewhere*, 1991
J.R.R. Tolkien, *The Hobbit*, 1938

Patricia C. Wrede, *Searching for Dragons*, 1991

2791

ANNE LOGSTON

Shadow Hunt

(New York: Ace, 1992)

Story type: Fantasy (Quest)
Series: Shadow
Major character(s): Shadow, Mythical Creature (elf), Thief; Blade, Murderer (assassin); Baloran, Wizard
Time period(s): Indeterminate
Locale(s): Allanmere, Mythical Place; Spirit Lake, Mythical Place; Baloran's Keep, Mythical Place

Summary: Hoping to find a fabulous ruby and discover why its owner, a powerful wizard, wishes ill to her guild, Shadow joins in partnership with Blade who wishes to exact revenge upon the wizard who has enslaved her as possessor of a magic dagger which holds a demon within. Both stand to profit if they survive their quest and partnership. Sequel to *Shadow*.

Other books you might like:
Steven Brust, *Jhereg*, 1983
Glen Cook, *Sweet Silver Blues*, 1987
Laurell K. Hamilton, *Nightseer*, 1992
Tanya Huff, *The Fire's Stone*, 1990
Patricia C. Wrede, *Shadow Magic*, 1982

2792

FRANK BELKNAP LONG

Escape From Tomorrow

(West Warwick, Rhode Island: Necronomicon Press, 1995)

Story type: Horror (Collection)

Summary: The three stories collected here in memory of the author, who died in 1994, all appeared originally in *Weird Tales* and have never been reprinted before. "You Can't Kill a Ghost" is a traditional ghost story, and "He Came at Dusk" a robot tale. The title story is a dystopia about a man and woman rebelling against a totalitarian future society.

Other books you might like:
Arthur J. Burks, *Black Medicine*, 1966
Hugh B. Cave, *Murgunstrumm and Others*, 1977
August Derleth, *Someone in the Dark*, 1941
Carl Jacobi, *Smoke of the Snake*, 1994
E. Hoffman Price, *Strange Gateways*, 1967
Manly Wade Wellman, *Worse Things Waiting*, 1973

2793

FRANK BELKNAP LONG

The Eye Above the Mantel and Other Stories

(West Hills, California: Tsathoggua Press, 1995)

Story type: Horror (Collection)

Summary: Editor Perry Grayson has assembled four stories written by a close friend of H.P. Lovecraft (whose essay on Long for the amateur press is reprinted as the introduction) and fantasist in his own right. ''Dr. Whitlock's Price,'' Long's first published tale in the amateur press, tells of the just rewards that befall an experimenter on animals. ''The Eye Above the Mantel'' evokes the imagery of Edgar Allan Poe in its account of an alien landscape, and ''In the Tomb of Semenses'' a horrifying nightmare of ancient Egypt. ''A Dangerous Experiment'' is a comic account of a clash of cultures.

Other books you might like:
Robert H. Barlow, *The Hoard of the Wizard Beast and One Other*, 1994
Hugh B. Cave, *Murgunstrumm and Others*, 1977
Duane Rimel, *To Yith and Beyond*, 1990

`2794`

ROXANNE LONGSTREET

Cold Kiss

(New York: Zebra, 1995)

Story type: Horror (Vampire Story)
Major character(s): Michael Bowman, Doctor, Vampire; Maggie Bowman, Detective—Homicide (Michael's wife); Celestine Vaughan, Vampire, Lawyer
Time period(s): 1990s (1995)
Locale(s): Dallas, Texas

Summary: Surgeon-turned vampire Michael Bowman mourns the companionship with a mortal wife that he can no longer share and finds himself torn between two distasteful styles of vampire life: becoming a member of the Society, a cabal of vampires who share pain with one another and exchange sex for blood with mortals; or running with a renegade vampire named William, who subjugates weaker vampires to his will and wants only to slaughter human victims. This novel is a sequel to *The Undead*.

Other books you might like:
Vincent Courtney, *Vampire Beat*, 1991
David Dvorkin, *Insatiable*, 1993
Nancy Kilpatrick, *Near Death*, 1994
Karen E. Taylor, *Bitter Blood*, 1994
Karen E. Taylor, *Blood Secrets*, 1994

`2795`

ROXANNE LONGSTREET

Red Angel

(New York: Zebra, 1994)

Story type: Horror (Serial Killer)
Major character(s): Alexandra Hobbs, Journalist (investigative reporter); Gabriel Davies, Detective (former); Anthony Lipaski, Detective
Time period(s): 1990s (1994)
Locale(s): Chicago, Illinois

Summary: Detective Gabriel Davies was destroyed professionally when an unscrupulous reporter published secret diaries he kept while covering a series of brutal murders that revealed his own psychopathic fantasies. Almost ten years later, tabloid reporter Alexandra Hobbs finds that someone is trying to make it appear that Davies himself is responsible for another string of murders—and that she is the next victim.

Other books you might like:
Matthew J. Costello, *Homecoming*, 1992
Thomas Harris, *Red Dragon*, 1981
Samuel M. Key, *From a Whisper to a Scream*, 1992
John D. MacDonald, *The Executioners*, 1957

`2796`

ROXANNE LONGSTREET

The Undead

(New York: Zebra, 1993)

Story type: Horror (Vampire Story)
Major character(s): Michael Bowman, Doctor; Maggie Bowman, Detective—Homicide; Adam Radburn, Vampire, Morgue Attendant
Time period(s): 1990s (1993)
Locale(s): Clear Creek, Texas

Summary: Mike Bowman finds his sympathies pulled in opposite directions when he discovers that his good friend Adam Radburn is a vampire: though repulsed by the idea of Adam's supernatural nature, he finds the fanatical human beings who want to kill him even more repugnant.

Other books you might like:
Don Davis, *Bring on the Night*, 1993
    Jay Davis, co-author
Elizabeth Engstrom, *Black Ambrosia*, 1988
Anne Rice, *Interview with the Vampire*, 1975
Theodore Sturgeon, *Some of Your Blood*, 1961

`2797`

BARRY B. LONGYEAR

The Change

(New York: Pocket, 1994)

Story type: Science Fiction (Invasion of Earth)
Series: Alien Nation
Major character(s): George Francisco, Alien (Tectonese), Detective—Police; Matthew Sykes, Detective—Police; Maanka ''Pete Moss'' Dak, Alien (Tectonese), Criminal
Time period(s): 21st century
Locale(s): Los Angeles, California

Summary: Tectonese scientist Maanka Dak declares a blood feud against George and anyone close to him when George kills his brother in an FBI raid. As ex-members of the Tectonese underground, George and Maanka know each other and recognize that each has chosen a different path to freedom and self-respect, and that only one of them will survive. Meanwhile George undergoes the change of life to a new stage of development.

Other books you might like:
Peter David, *Body and Soul*, 1993
Alan Dean Foster, *Alien Nation*, 1993

K.W. Jeter, *Dark Horizon*, 1993
Judith Reeves-Stevens, *The Day of Descent*, 1993
    Garfield Reeves-Stevens, co-author
David Alexander Smith, *In the Cube*, 1993

2798

BARRY B. LONGYEAR

The Homecoming

(New York: Walker, 1989)

Story type: Science Fiction (First Contact)
Major character(s): Carl Baxter, Advertising, Pilot; Deayl, Alien
Time period(s): 1980s
Locale(s): Earth; Outer Space

Summary: The Nitolans, intelligent dinosaurs, had originally evolved on Earth, but left the planet some seventy million years ago. Now they've returned to reclaim their territory, but find it occupied by humanity.

Other books you might like:
Arthur C. Clarke, *Childhood's End*, 1953
David Gerrold, *Chess with a Dragon*, 1987
Rebecca Ore, *Becoming Alien*, 1987
Rebecca Ore, *Being Alien*, 1989

2799

BARRY B. LONGYEAR

Infinity Hold

(New York: Popular Library Questar, 1989)

Story type: Science Fiction (Adventure)
Major character(s): Nicos Bando, Convict; Darrell Garoit, Convict, Revolutionary
Time period(s): 22nd century (2115)
Locale(s): Greenville, Mississippi; Tartaros, Planet—Imaginary

Summary: Earth decides to relieve prison overcrowding by sending all of its worst criminals on a one-way ride to Tartaros, a ghastly prison planet. Young Nicos Bando learns to survive on Tartaros and build a life for himself.

Other books you might like:
Gregory Benford, *Great Sky River*, 1987
Harry Harrison, *Deathworld*, 1960
Robert Sheckley, *The Status Civilization*, 1960
James White, *Escape Orbit*, 1964

2800

BARRY LOPEZ

Crow and Weasel

(San Francisco: North Point Press, 1990)

Story type: Fantasy (Legend; Adventure)
Major character(s): Crow, Adventurer, Indian; Weasel, Adventurer, Indian
Time period(s): Indeterminate Past
Locale(s): Northern Plains, North America

Summary: Crow and Weasel, two men too young to smoke themselves, are given a pipe bag to share with others on their journey to go further north than any of their tribe has gone before. While meeting new and interesting people on their trip, they grow and learn from their experiences.

Other books you might like:
Peter Gadol, *Coyote*, 1990
Garry Kilworth, *The Foxes of Firstdark*, 1990
Dean R. Koontz, *Oddkins*, 1988
H. Beam Piper, *Little Fuzzy*, 1962
Jane Yolen, *Tam Lin*, 1990

2801

JEAN LORRAH

Metamorphosis

(New York: Pocket, 1990)

Story type: Science Fiction (Space Opera)
Series: Star Trek: The Next Generation
Major character(s): Data, Android, Spaceman; Thelia, Alien, Adventurer
Time period(s): 24th century
Locale(s): Elysia, Planet—Imaginary; Dacket, Planet—Imaginary (Samdian System); *U.S.S. Enterprise*, Spaceship

Summary: Data is transformed into a human being by the gods of Elysia in return for helping one of their people. He enjoys the new sensations and emotions, but then becomes depressed. After the *Enterprise* answers an emergency call from the Samdian System, which is being taken over by a group apparently intent on genocide, Data decides he must return to Elysia.

Other books you might like:
Carmen Carter, *Doomsday World*, 1990
    Peter David, Michael Jan Friedman, Robert Greenberger, co-authors
A.C. Crispin, *The Eyes of the Beholders*, 1990
Peter David, *A Rock and a Hard Place*, 1990
    Star Trek - The Next Generation 10
Gene DeWeese, *The Peacekeepers*, 1988
    Star Trek - The Next Generation 2
Michael Jan Friedman, *Fortune's Light*, 1991
    Star Trek - The Next Generation 15

2802

RICHARD LORTZ

Bereavement

(Clarkston, Georgia: White Wolf, 1996)

Story type: Horror (Psychological Suspense)
Major character(s): Mrs. Harrington-Smith Evans, Wealthy; Martin Dzierlatka, Actor; Bruno David Carlson-Wade, Writer
Time period(s): 1990s
Locale(s): New York, New York; Harper's Gate, New York

Summary: Three young men who have lost their mothers compete to become the surrogate son of Mrs. Harrington-

Smith Evans, a woman so bereaved by the loss of her boy Jamie that she has advertised in newspapers seeking a replacement. Events turn ugly and unpredictable once Mrs. Evans reveals the extent of the surrogacy she expects. This novel was first published in 1980.

Other books you might like:
Todd Komarnicki, *Famine*, 1997
Mark Morris, *The Immaculate*, 1992
Melanie Tem, *Prodigal*, 1991
Melanie Tem, *Revenant*, 1994

2803

JANE WEBB LOUDON

The Mummy!: A Tale of the Twenty-Second Century

(Ann Arbor: University of Michigan Press, 1994)

Story type: Horror (Reanimated Dead; Satire)
Major character(s): Edmund Montagu, Military Personnel; Edric Montagu, Student; Cheops, Reanimated Dead (mummy)
Time period(s): 22nd century (2127)
Locale(s): London, England

Summary: Originally published in 1828, this late-Gothic satire on the social and political life of Great Britain tells of the accidental resuscitation of the mummy of Cheops, Egyptian pharaoh of the 26th century B.C., and the role he plays advising various political factions struggling to usurp the British throne, engineering its downfall. This edition has been edited by Professor Alan Rauch.

Other books you might like:
Charles L. Grant, *The Long Night of the Grave*, 1986
Michael Paine, *Cities of the Dead*, 1988
Thomas Love Peacock, *Nightmare Abbey*, 1818
Mary Shelley, *Frankenstein*, 1818
H.G. Wells, *The Time Machine*, 1898

2804

PETER LOUGHRAN

The Third Beast

(Chelsea, Michigan: Scarborough House, 1990)

Story type: Horror (Psychological Suspense)
Major character(s): Laura Lewis, Teenager; Andrea, Teenager; McKinnan, Police Officer
Time period(s): 1990s (1990)
Locale(s): England

Summary: Receiving no help from the police and no satisfaciton from the courts when his teenage niece is gang-raped, the unnamed narrator of this novel takes the law into his own hands and systematically murders her assailants.

Other books you might like:
Joe R. Lansdale, *The Nightrunners*, 1987
David J. Schow, *The Kill Riff*, 1988
John Skipp, *The Cleanup*, 1987
    Craig Spector, co-author

2805

SIMON LOUVISH

The Resurrections

(New York: Four Walls Eight Windows, 1994)

Story type: Science Fiction (Alternate Universe; Political)
Major character(s): Adolf Hitler, Historical Figure, Political Figure; Ernesto "Che" Guevara, Historical Figure, Revolutionary; Joseph "Joseph Gable" Goebbels, Historical Figure, Businessman
Time period(s): 1960s; 1970s
Locale(s): Alternate Earth

Summary: After WWII, in an alternate world, Adolph Hitler rises to U.S. Senator during the ascendance of the American Party then, after losing his office, plans new political achievements, aided by Joseph Goebbels. The student revolution in England flourishes, while Che Guevara foments revolution in Ethiopia and Italy.

Other books you might like:
Ben Bova, *Triumph*, 1993
Len Deighton, *SS-GB*, 1978
Philip K. Dick, *The Man in the High Castle*, 1962
Robert Harris, *Fatherland*, 1992
Norman Spinrad, *The Iron Dream*, 1972

2806

H.P. LOVECRAFT

The Dream Cycle of H.P. Lovecraft: Dreams of Terror and Death

(New York: Del Rey, 1995)

Story type: Horror (Collection)

Summary: The 25 stories, fragments and prose poems collected here span 15 years of the author's pulp-era writing career and range from the imaginary-world fantasy of "The Cats of Ulthar" to the horrors of supernatural possession in the short novel, "The Case of Charles Dexter Ward." Many of the stories employ nightmares and dream imagery, including those centered around the experiences of Lovecraft's fictional surrogate, Randolph Carter ("The State of Randolph Carter," "The Silver Key," "Through the Gates of the Silver Key," and the novel *The Dream Quest of Unknown Kadath*). In more horror-oriented stories such as "The Dreams in the Witch House," "Hypnos," and "Beyond the Wall of Sleep," dreams penetrate and eventually overwhelm waking reality. Neil Gaiman supplies the introduction.

Other books you might like:
Ramsey Campbell, *Strange Things and Stranger Places*, 1993
Lord Dunsany, *A Dreamer's Tales*, 1910
Thomas Ligotti, *Noctuary*, 1994
Thomas Ligotti, *Songs of a Dead Dreamer*, 1989

2807

H.P. LOVECRAFT

The Horror in the Museum and Other Revisions

(Sauk City, Wisconsin: Arkham House, 1989)

Story type: Horror (Collection)

Summary: A restoration and correction of the stories "revised" for other writers, arranged according to the degree of Lovecraft's involvement in the texts. Thirteen stories are listed as "Primary Revisions" and eleven are presented as "Secondary Revisions."

Other books you might like:

Ramsey Campbell, *New Tales of the Cthulhu Mythos*, 1980
August Derleth, *The Mask of Cthulhu*, 1958
Robert E. Howard, *Cthulhu: The Mythos and Kindred Horrors*, 1987

2808

H.P. LOVECRAFT
JOHN JUDE PALENCAR, Illustrator

Road to Madness: The Transition of H.P. Lovecraft

(New York: Del Rey, 1996)

Story type: Horror (Collection)

Summary: This omnibus collection of 28 stories, poems, and fragments features works that span the short professional career of the writer acknowledged as the most important author of weird fiction in the 20th century. Juvenile shockers such as "The Beast in the Cave" and "The Transition of Juan Romero" are counterbalanced by the mature tales "At the Mountains of Madness" and "The Shunned House," which articulate Lovecraft's philosophy of a cosmos indifferent to human endeavors and conceptions. In addition to "Cool Air," "He," "The Horror at Red Hook," and several other tales of pure horror written under the influence of Edgar Allan Poe, the book includes wistful fantasies such as "The White Ship," which expresses the author's fondness for antiquity and aesthetic fulfillment. Barbara Hambly supplies an introduction.

Other books you might like:

Robert Bloch, *The Early Fears*, 1994
Ramsey Campbell, *Cold Print*, 1993
August Derleth, *The Mask of Cthulhu*, 1958
Thomas Ligotti, *The Nightmare Factory*, 1996

2809

H.P. LOVECRAFT
JASON ECKHARDT, Illustrator

The Shadow over Innsmouth

(West Warwick, Rhode Island: Necronomicon Press, 1994)

Story type: Horror (Ancient Evil Unleashed)

Major character(s): Robert Olmstead, Traveller; Zadok Allen, Streetperson; Obediah Marsh, Sailor
Time period(s): 1920s (1927)
Locale(s): Innsmouth, Massachusetts

Summary: Lovecraft's classic tale tells of a young man who happens by chance upon a degenerate New England coastal town, discovers a history of congress between its inhabitants and a race of sea creatures, and finds out something about his own heritage he wished he never knew. Editors S.T. Joshi and David Schultz have annotated the text rigorously with data culled from Lovecraft's letters and other writings, and supplied an informative introduction concerned with the genesis of the story. Appendices contain Lovecraft's notes for the story and an early draft of the tale.

Other books you might like:

Fred Chappell, *Dagon*, 1968
Stephen Jones, *Shadows over Innsmouth*, 1994
    editor
David Langford, *Irrational Numbers*, 1993
Brian Stableford, *The Innsmouth Heritage*, 1992

2810

H.P. LOVECRAFT
AUGUST DERLETH, Co-Author

The Watchers out of Time

(New York: Carroll & Graf, 1991)

Story type: Horror (Collection)

Summary: Although billed as collaborative efforts between H.P. Lovecraft and his pupil August Derleth, the 15 stories in this book are entirely the work of the latter, laboring under the influence of his mentor. Some, such as "The Shadow out of Space" and "The Shuttered Room," approximate specific tales of Lovecraft's; others like "The Gable Window" and the uncompleted title novel use the motifs of Lovecraft's fiction to tell stories that differ fundamentally in intention from those of Lovecraft. Still others, among them "The Dark Brotherhood" and "The Fisherman of Falcon Point," attempt with varying degrees of success to evoke the dark mood of Lovecraft's writing without parroting his plots. A hardcover version of this collection, including the novel *The Lurker at the Threshold*, was published in 1973.

Other books you might like:

Edward P. Berglund, *Disciples of Cthulhu*, 1976
Lin Carter, *The Spawn of Cthulhu*, 1971
August Derleth, *Tales of the Cthulhu Mythos*, 1969

2811

JACK LOVEJOY

Outworld Cats

(New York: DAW, 1994)

Story type: Science Fiction (First Contact; Political)
Major character(s): Tim Waverly, Activist, Security Officer; Rhoda Dawn, Psychic, Child; Benton Ingles, Industrialist, Villain
Time period(s): 1990s

Locale(s): Royal Beach, California; Sulatonga Island, Pacific Islands

Summary: Two young space cats investigate the communication satellite put up by humans. Kidnapped to Earth, they escape and befriend a security officer who teaches them chess. They inadvertently become embroiled in foiling a plot by Benton Ingles to take over the world by turning dissenters into surgically created automatons.

Other books you might like:
C.J. Cherryh, *The Pride of Chanur*, 1982
Bill Fawcett, *Cats in Space and Other Places*, 1992 editor
Alan Dean Foster, *Cat-A-Lyst*, 1991
Marti Steussy, *Dreams of the Dawn*, 1988
Marti Steussy, *Forest of the Night*, 1987

2812
JAMES LOWDER
Crusade
(Lake Geneva, Wisconsin: TSR, 1991)

Story type: Fantasy (Historical)
Series: Forgotten Realms: The Empire Trilogy
Major character(s): Azoun, Ruler (king)
Time period(s): Indeterminate Past (Medieval period)
Locale(s): Cormyr, Fictional Country (European)

Summary: In this sequel to David Cook's *Horselords* and Troy Denning's *Dragonwall*, the barbarian horsemen have turned their sights westward. King Cormyr must unite the diverse factions threatened by the invasion to stop the conquering hordes. This book novelizes one chapter of history surrounding the invasion of Europe by Asian horsemen. A game tie in novel.

Other books you might like:
David Cook, *Horselords*, 1990
Troy Denning, *Dragonwall*, 1990
Troy Denning, *The Parched Sea*, 1991
Ed Greenwood, *Spellfire*, 1988
R.A. Salvatore, *The Crystal Shard*, 1988
R.A. Salvatore, *Homeland*, 1990

2813
JAMES LOWDER
The Ring of Winter
(Lake Geneva, Wisconsin: TSR, 1992)

Story type: Fantasy (Quest)
Series: Forgotten Realms: The Harpers
Major character(s): Artus Climber, Adventurer
Time period(s): Indeterminate
Locale(s): Chult, Fictional Country; The Realms, Fictional Country

Summary: Artus Climber learns of the jungle hiding place of the fabled Ring of Winter which makes the wearer immortal and will bring a new ice age to the Realms. Artus sets off into the jungle where he meets villainous cultists and monstrous animals which hinder his efforts.

Other books you might like:
Mark Anthony, *Crypt of the Shadow King*, 1993
Scott Ciencin, *The Night Parade*, 1992
Elaine Cunningham, *Elfshadow*, 1991
Troy Denning, *The Parched Sea*, 1991
Jean Rabe, *Red Magic*, 1991

2814
FRANCES LUCAS
Cathy IV
(Norwich, Vermont: New Victoria Publishers, Inc., 1992)

Story type: Science Fiction (Political; Gay/Lesbian Fiction)
Major character(s): Cathy Four, Cyborg (servo); Jenny Brooks, Traveller, Revolutionary
Time period(s): 33rd century (3200)
Locale(s): Saegrenot, Planet—Imaginary (1.2 light years from Earth)

Summary: When Jenny's spaceship crash lands on Saegrenot, a planet banned from the Interplanetary Alliance for violating the prohibition against slavery, Jenny falls in love with a female android and involves herself in the servos' revolution.

Other books you might like:
Judith Alguire, *Zeta Base*, 1991
Camarin Grae, *Stranded*, 1991
Elizabeth Moon, *Surrender None: The Legacy of Gird*, 1990
Paul Park, *The Cult of Loving Kindness*, 1991
Steve Perry, *The Man Who Never Missed*, 1985

2815
GEORGE LUCAS
CHRIS CLAREMONT, Co-Author
Shadow Moon
(New York: Bantam Spectra, 1995)

Story type: Fantasy (Quest)
Series: Chronicles of the Shadow War
Major character(s): Thorn Drumheller, Mythical Creature (nelwyn), Wizard; Elora Danan, Royalty (princess); Rool, Mythical Creature (brownie)
Time period(s): Indeterminate Past
Locale(s): The Great Realms, Fictional Country

Summary: In this print sequel to the film *Willow*, Willow finds himself carried off, seemingly in a dream. He soon discovers that Princess Elora faces great danger and again needs his help.

Other books you might like:
Eleanor Arnason, *The Sword Smith*, 1978
Peter S. Beagle, *The Last Unicorn*, 1968
Glen Cook, *The Black Company*, 1984
Wayland Drew, *Willow*, 1988
Katherine Kurtz, *Deryni Rising*, 1970
Patricia A. McKillip, *The Riddle-Master of Hed*, 1976

2816

TIM LUCAS

Throat Sprockets

(New York: Delta/Cutting Edge, 1994)

Story type: Horror (Vampire Story)
Major character(s): Austin Ingersoll, Advertising; Emma Mitsouko, Artist; Nancy Reagan, Advertising
Time period(s): 1990s (1994)
Locale(s): Friendly, Ohio

Summary: The nameless narrator of this novel of obsession reveals how the viewing of a film of throat fetishism fires his imagination to create advertising campaigns that subliminally stimulate the world's perverse sexual drives. Partly adapted as a graphic novel between 1987 and 1989, this is the author's first novel.

Other books you might like:
Steven R. Boyett, *The Answer Tree*, 1988
  in David J. Schow's *Silver Scream*
Jonathan Carroll, *A Child Across the Sky*, 1989
Theodore Roszak, *Flicker*, 1992
Brad Strickland, *Shadowshow*, 1988
Theodore Sturgeon, *Some of Your Blood*, 1961

2817

JAMES LUCENO

A Fearful Symmetry

(New York: Ballantine/Del Rey, 1989)

Story type: Science Fiction (Mystical)
Major character(s): Karl Reydak, Spy; Tedman Brady, Political Figure (President of the United States)
Time period(s): 20th century
Locale(s): Washington, District of Columbia; Brazil

Summary: In this Philip K. Dick Award-nominated novel, the millennium is at hand and there appears to be an actual upsurge in the occurence of mystical and psychic phenomena. The president of the United States himself claims to have been kidnapped by aliens and insists on consulting a Brazilian shaman. Agent Karl Reydak is assigned to investigate.

Other books you might like:
John Kessel, *Good News From Outer Space*, 1989
James Morrow, *Only Begotten Daughter*, 1990

2818

JAMES LUCENO

Illegal Alien

(New York: Ballantine/Del Rey, 1990)

Story type: Science Fiction (Humor)
Major character(s): Remy Santoul, Spy
Time period(s): Indeterminate Future
Locale(s): Planet of the Q'aantre, Planet—Imaginary

Summary: Interstellar spy Remy Santoul is sent to an alien planet to discover its inhabitants' weaknesses. That weakness, of course, turns out to be sex. The Q'aantre tend to do it often and anywhere. Santoul finds that he fits right in.

Other books you might like:
Philip Jose Farmer, *Dare*, 1965
Philip Jose Farmer, *Flesh*, 1960
Philip Jose Farmer, *The Image of the Beast*, 1968
Philip Jose Farmer, *A Woman a Day*, 1960
Harry Harrison, *Star Smashers and Galaxy Rangers*, 1973
Andrew J. Offutt, *Ardor on Aros*, 1973

2819

JAMES LUCENO

The Mata Hari Adventure

(New York: Ballantine, 1992)

Story type: Fantasy (Adventure; Historical)
Series: Young Indiana Jones Chronicles
Major character(s): Indiana "Indy" Jones, Teenager, Military Personnel (battlefield messenger); Mata Hari, Spy, Historical Figure
Time period(s): 1910s
Locale(s): Verdun, France; Paris, France

Summary: While on leave from front line duty in World War I, Indy meets Mata Hari, finding an immediate and mutual attraction. As Indy begins to know her better, he finds the darker side of her life, creating a conflict between Indy's loyalties.

Other books you might like:
Richard Brightfield, *Valley of the Kings: Egypt, May 1908*, 1992
Les Martin, *Field of Death*, 1992
Les Martin, *Trek of Doom*, 1992
William McKay, *The Secret Peace*, 1992
Gavin Scott, *Revolution*, 1992
A.L. Singer, *Safari Sleuth*, 1992

2820

NANCY LUENN

Goldclimbers

(New York: Atheneum, 1991)

Story type: Fantasy (Quest; Young Adult)
Series: Dragonflight
Major character(s): Aracco, Apprentice, Adventurer
Time period(s): Indeterminate
Locale(s): Caraccen, Fictional Country

Summary: Aracco expects to become a goldsmith, following in his father's footsteps, even though he has an unusual aptitude for climbing mountains. When the appearance of giant avian predators discourages the goldclimbers, threatening the town's gold supply, Aracco sets out in search of the legendary Terenger, where streets are said to be made of gold, hoping to find a new source of gold to ensure the town's livelihood.

Other books you might like:
Lynne Reid Banks, *The Farthest-Away Mountain*, 1977
Louise Cooper, *The Sleep of Stone*, 1991

Charles de Lint, *The Dreaming Place*, 1990
J. Alison James, *Sing for a Gentle Rain*, 1990
Mercedes Lackey, *Bardic Voices*, 1991
Tanith Lee, *Black Unicorn*, 1991
Robert Silverberg, *Letters From Atlantis*, 1990
Lawrence Watt-Evans, *The Blood of a Dragon*, 1991
Jane Yolen, *Wizard's Hall*, 1991

2821

BRIAN LUMLEY

Blood Brothers

(New York: Tor, 1992)

Story type: Horror (Vampire Story)
Series: Vampire World Trilogy
Major character(s): Nestor Kiklu, Twin, Psychic; Nathan Kiklu, Twin, Psychic; Wratha, the Unrisen, Vampire
Time period(s): 1990s
Locale(s): World of the Gate, Alternate Universe

Summary: In an alternate universe the twin sons of the late Harry Keough, a scourge to the vampire race that inhabits the Starside, are separated during a vampire invasion of the Sunside. Unaware of the genetic legacy their father has passed on to them, each must learn to cope with his developing occult powers, even as they seek to reunite with each other and save their world.

Other books you might like:
Brian Stableford, *The Empire of Fear*, 1988
T. Lucien Wright, *Blood Brothers*, 1992

2822

BRIAN LUMLEY

Bloodwars

(New York: Tor, 1994)

Story type: Horror (Vampire Story)
Series: Vampire World Trilogy
Major character(s): Nestor Kiklu, Vampire, Twin; Nathan Keogh, Twin, Psychic (necroscope); Ben Trask, Spy
Time period(s): 2000s (2006)
Locale(s): London, England; Sunside, Alternate Universe (vampire world)

Summary: This concluding volume of the Vampire World series, spun off from Lumley's popular Necroscope quintet, pits necroscope Nathan Keogh, a man capable of conversing with the dead, against his evil twin brother, Nestor, whose life in the alternate universe of the wamphyrii (vampires) has perverted his character and made him the scourge of the vampire world. Having been expelled from the vampire world, Nathan returns with the help of British paranormal agents to fight the final showdown with Nestor, who is himself backed by Russian paranormal agents intent on fomenting Cold War aggressions in the vampire world.

Other books you might like:
Jack Butler, *Nightshade*, 1989
Dan Simmons, *Carrion Comfort*, 1989

2823

BRIAN LUMLEY

The Burrowers Beneath

(New York: W. Paul Ganley, 1989)

Story type: Horror (Ancient Evil Unleashed)
Series: Titus Crow
Major character(s): Titus Crow, Paranormal Investigator; Shudde-M'ell, Monster
Time period(s): 20th century (Mid)

Summary: A group of anti-Cthulhu crusaders, led by Titus Crow, fight to destroy the offspring of the earth-burrowing Shudde-M'ell, along with other Cthulhu-type beings. Originally published in 1974.

Other books you might like:
Robert Bloch, *Strange Eons*, 1978
Fred Chappell, *Dagon*, 1968
Michael Shea, *The Colour out of Time*, 1984

2824

BRIAN LUMLEY

Deadspawn

(New York: Tor, 1991)

Story type: Horror (Vampire Story)
Series: Necroscope
Major character(s): Harry Keogh, Spy (necroscope), Psychic; Darcy Clark, Spy; Shaithis, Vampire
Time period(s): 1990s
Locale(s): London, England

Summary: In this final novel of the Necroscope quintet, Harry Keogh, who can converse with the souls of the dead, has successfully quelled the threat of an invasion from the vampire universe, but now faces a new nemesis: a mass murderer who commits rape and mutilation upon corpses, and who is familiar enough with Harry's secret links with the vampire race to be able to use them against him.

Other books you might like:
Robert R. McCammon, *They Thirst*, 1981
Brian Stableford, *The Empire of Fear*, 1988

2825

BRIAN LUMLEY

Deadspeak

(New York: Tor, 1990)

Story type: Horror (Vampire Story)
Series: Necroscope
Major character(s): Harry Keogh, Spy, Psychic (hears voices of the dead); Janos Ferenczy, Vampire, Magician (black magician)
Time period(s): 1980s
Locale(s): Transylvania; Greece

Summary: As Harry recovers from his battle with the vampiric hordes, he is thrust into a new competition with a master vampire, Janos Ferenczy. In his weakened condition he can fight Janos only by linking minds with the most powerful and deadly vampire of them all.

Other books you might like:
John Farris, *Catacombs*, 1981
Stephen King, *The Talisman*, 1984
    Peter Straub, co-author
Robert R. McCammon, *They Thirst*, 1981

2826

BRIAN LUMLEY

Demogorgon
(New York: Tor, 1992)

Story type: Horror (Occult)
Major character(s): Charlie Trace, Thief; Dimitrious Kastrouni, Spy; George Khumeni, Wealthy (millionaire)
Time period(s): 1930s (1936); 1980s (1983)
Locale(s): London, England; Greece

Summary: An avatar of Satan is prevented from consummating the ritual that will restore his earthly realm in 1936. Nearly half a century later Charlie Trace, who may or may not be the offspring of the devil and a mortal woman, is recruited by occultists to thwart his father's rise to power. This novel was originally published in England in 1987.

Other books you might like:
Ramsey Campbell, *To Wake the Dead*, 1980
Ira Levin, *Rosemary's Baby*, 1967

2827

BRIAN LUMLEY

Fruiting Bodies and Other Fungi
(New York: Tor, 1993)

Story type: Horror (Collection)

Summary: The 13 stories collected here demonstrate the range of one of the most popular British horror writers working today. "Born of the Winds" and "The Mirror of Nitocris" are both heavily influenced by the writing of H.P. Lovecraft; "Necros" is a vampire story; "The Thin People" blends horror with science fiction; and "The Cyprus Shell" and "The Deep Sea Conch" are interconnected stories about the horrors of creatures from the ocean floor which are able to exchange minds with men. The best stories are "Fruiting Bodies," about a house and its inhabitants who are taken over by a vile fungus, and "The Viaduct," a *conte cruel* about two boys trapped on a train trestle by a deranged child.

Other books you might like:
Joe R. Lansdale, *By Bizarre Hands*, 1989
Richard Laymon, *A Good, Secret Place*, 1993
Edward Lee, *Edward Lee's Quest for Sex, Truth and Reality*, 1992
J.N. Williamson, *Author's Choice Monthly Number 24: The Naked Flesh of Feeling*, 1991

2828

BRIAN LUMLEY

The House of Doors
(New York: Tor, 1990)

Story type: Horror (Science Fiction)
Major character(s): Spencer Gill, Scientist (Terminally ill); Sith, Alien
Time period(s): 1990s (1994-95)
Locale(s): Scotland

Summary: A group of scientists, led by Stephen Gill, enters the House of Doors, an alien artifact designed to test the "worthiness" of a species, where they are subjected to numerous horrors dredged up from their own deepest fears and imaginings. The situation is made doubly dangerous by the fact that the "invigilator" sent to test them has decided, for his own devious ends, that they must fail.

Other books you might like:
Algis Budrys, *Rogue Moon*, 1960

2829

BRIAN LUMLEY

Iced on Aran and Other Dream Quests
(Buffalo, New York: Ganley, 1992)

Story type: Horror (Collection)

Summary: Set in dreamlands inspired by the work of H. P. Lovecraft, these five stories chronicle the continuing adventures of David Hero and Eldin the Wanderer (nee Leonard Dingle), men who projected their psyches into the land of dreams at the times of their deaths, and who fight a variety of human and supernatural menaces during their stay there. This collection was published in England in 1990.

Other books you might like:
Lin Carter, *The Fishers From Outside*, 1990
Gary Meyers, *The House of the Worm*, 1975

2830

BRIAN LUMLEY

The Last Aerie
(New York: Tor, 1993)

Story type: Horror (Vampire Story)
Series: Vampire World Trilogy
Major character(s): Nestor Kiklu, Twin, Psychic (necroscope); Nathan Kiklu, Twin, Psychic (necromancer); Ben Trask, Spy
Time period(s): 2000s (2006)
Locale(s): London, England

Summary: In this sequel to *Blood Brothers*, a spinoff from Lumley's *Necroscope* quintet, amnesiac Nestor Kiklu continues his overtures to the vampires living in a parallel universe, embarked on his apparent destiny to become their leader. Meanwhile, his twin brother Nathan, exiled to our world, becomes part of a plot to thwart the vampire menace much the same way that Nestor and Nathan's father, necroscope (someone who can converse with the dead) Harry Keough did decades before.

Other books you might like:
Lee Weathersby, *Kiss of the Vampire*, 1992
T. Lucien Wright, *Blood Brothers*, 1992

2831

BRIAN LUMLEY

The Last Rite

(Minneapolis, Minnesota: Jwindz, 1993)

Story type: Horror (Collection)

Summary: The six stories collected here range widely over the spectrum of horror themes, including the Lovecraft influenced "The Thing From the Blasted Heath"; the urban horror story, "Back Row"; the occult thriller, "The Last Rite"; the non-supernatural horror tale, "A Thing about Cars!"; the ghostly "Vanessa's Voice"; and the tale of an insidious demon, "Uzzi."

Other books you might like:
Joe R. Lansdale, *By Bizarre Hands*, 1989
Richard Laymon, *A Good, Secret Place*, 1993
Edward Lee, *Edward Lee's Quest for Sex, Truth and Reality*, 1992
J.N. Williamson, *Author's Choice Monthly Number 24: The Naked Flesh of Feeling*, 1991

2832

BRIAN LUMLEY

Necroscope: The Lost Years

(New York: Tor, 1995)

Story type: Horror (Vampire Story)
Series: Necroscope
Major character(s): Harry Keogh, Spy, Psychic; Bonnie Jean "B.J." Mirlu, Saloon Keeper/Owner, Vampire; Radu Lykan, Vampire
Time period(s): 1980s
Locale(s): London, England; Edinburgh, Scotland

Summary: This previously unrecounted episode from the life of Harry Keogh, a "necroscope" (someone who can communicate telepathically with the dead), is set in the time interval between the second and third volume of the author's nine-volume Necroscope series. Harry's frantic search to find his missing wife and son bring him into contact with a femme fatale. She's preparing him to serve as the vessel for a vampire whose consciousness needs flesh in order to wage war against fellow vampires who have destroyed his life.

Other books you might like:
Vincent Courtney, *Vampire Beat*, 1991
Lee Killough, *Blood Hunt*, 1987
Fred Saberhagen, *Seance for a Vampire*, 1994

2833

BRIAN LUMLEY

Psychamok

(New York: Tor, 1993)

Story type: Horror (Wild Talents)
Series: Psychomech Trilogy
Major character(s): James Christopher Craig, Technician; Philip Stone, Businessman; Richard Stone, Telepath
Time period(s): 2000s (2004)
Locale(s): Sussex, England

Summary: Twenty years ago, in the events chronicled in *Psychosphere*, psychically-endowed Richard Allan Garrison destroyed evil telepath Charon Gubwa and achieved his transdimensional apotheosis. But Gubwa left the seeds of his resurrection implanted in technician James Christopher Craig, who sets about building a new Psychomech machine to facilitate Gubwa's return, leaving Garrison's bastard son Richard Stone no choice but to resume the battle where his father left off. This novel was originally published in England in 1984.

Other books you might like:
Andrew Laurance, *Blood of Nostradamus: The Unborn*, 1980
Jack Martin, *Scanners*, 1979
Curt Siodmak, *Gabriel's Body*, 1988

2834

BRIAN LUMLEY

Psychomech

(New York: Tor, 1992)

Story type: Horror (Wild Talents)
Series: Psychomech Trilogy
Major character(s): Thomas Schroeder, Businessman; Willy Koenig, Secretary (to Thomas Schroeder); Richard Garrison, Military Personnel (military police)
Time period(s): 1980s
Locale(s): London, England; Harz Mountains, Germany

Summary: Paranormally endowed ex-Nazi Thomas Schroeder returns from the dead by joining his mind with the personality of Richard Garrison. When Garrison undergoes boosting of his paranormal powers by means of a machine known as Psychomech, he finds himself possessed of a gestalt mind—Schroeder's and his own—and invested with god-like powers to change the world by means of his thoughts. This novel was originally published in England in 1983.

Other books you might like:
Curt Siodmak, *Donovan's Brain/Hauser's Memory*, 1992
Curt Siodmak, *Gabriel's Body*, 1988

2835

BRIAN LUMLEY

Psychosphere

(New York: Tor, 1992)

Story type: Horror (Wild Talents)

Major character(s): David Garrison, Wealthy (millionaire); Vicki Maler, Girlfriend (Garrison's); Charon Gubwa, Telepath
Time period(s): 1980s
Locale(s): Rhodes, Greece; London, England

Summary: David Garrison's gestalt mind, the product of his exposure to the Psychomech machine's brain-expanding capabilities, grows weaker every time he expends his paranormal talents to increase his empire or protect himself from his numerous enemies. It also causes telltale leaks into the Psychosphere, where it alerts the albino hermaphrodite, Charon Gubwa, a telepathic megalomaniac who determines to kill Garrison and afterward take over the world. This novel was originally published in England in 1984.

Other books you might like:
Jack Martin, *Scanners*, 1979
Curt Siodmak, *Donovan's Brain/Hauser's Memory*, 1992
Curt Siodmak, *Gabriel's Body*, 1988

2836
BRIAN LUMLEY

Resurgence
(New York: Tor, 1996)

Story type: Horror (Vampire Story)
Series: Necroscope
Major character(s): Harry Keogh, Spy, Psychic; Bonnie Jean "B.J." Mirlu, Saloon Keeper/Owner, Vampire; Radu Lykan, Vampire
Time period(s): 1980s
Locale(s): Edinburgh, Scotland

Summary: This tenth volume in the author's long-running Necroscope series further elaborates the history of the otherworldly Wamphyri, some of whose members were exiled to our own world and live here as vampires and werewolves. Radu Lykan, one of the most fearsome of all Wamphyri, plans to appropriate the body of necroscope Harry Keogh in order to wage war on other Wamphyri factions. But Harry, a necroscope who can converse with the dead, staves off Lykan's attack with the help of Harry Houdini, Nostradamus, and B.J. Mirlu, a former disciple of Lykan's.

Other books you might like:
Nancy A. Collins, *Sunglasses After Dark*, 1989
Nancy A. Collins, *Wild Blood*, 1995
Robert R. McCammon, *They Thirst*, 1981
Kim Newman, *Anno Dracula*, 1992
John Steakley, *Vampire$*, 1990

2837
BRIAN LUMLEY

The Source
(New York: Tor, 1989)

Story type: Horror (Vampire Story)
Series: Necroscope
Major character(s): Harry Keogh, Spy, Psychic; Dweller, Alien (Vampire Antagonist)

Time period(s): 1980s
Locale(s): Perchorsk Pass, Union of Soviet Socialist Republics (a Soviet base in the Russian Urals); Alternate Universe (an alternate world of vampires)

Summary: As a result of a Soviet experiment gone awry, a portal is opened between our world and that of the Vampyri. Keogh enters the alternate world and forms an alliance with the Dweller, a mysterious, powerful vampire antagonist, to avert a massive vampiric invasion of the earth.

Other books you might like:
John Farris, *Catacombs*, 1981
Stephen King, *The Talisman*, 1984
  Peter Straub, co-author
Robert R. McCammon, *They Thirst*, 1981

2838
BRIAN LUMLEY

The Transition of Titus Crow
(Buffalo, New York: Ganley, 1992)

Story type: Horror (Ancient Evil Unleashed)
Series: Titus Crow
Major character(s): Titus Crow, Paranormal Investigator; Henri Laurent de Marigny, Paranormal Investigator; Nodens, Deity
Time period(s): 1970s
Locale(s): Aldebaran, Outer Space (a star)

Summary: Having narrowly escaped the Burrowers Beneath, minions of the The Great Old Ones, by means of their dimension-traversing grandfather clock, Titus Crow and Henri Laurent de Marigny are recruited by the benevolent Elder Gods to help them fight Cthulhu and The Great Old Ones in the cosmic showdown between good and evil. This novel, inspired by the work of H. P. Lovecraft and a sequel to the author's *The Burrower's Beneath*, was originally published in 1975.

Other books you might like:
Robert Bloch, *Strange Eons*, 1978
Donald Wandrei, *The Web of Easter Island*, 1948

2839
RICHARD A. LUPOFF

Before. . .12:01. . .and After
(Minneapolis: Fedogan & Bremer, 1996)

Story type: Science Fiction (Collection)

Summary: Contains a five-page foreword by Robert Silverberg; a 14-page bibliography by Dave Nee; a nine-page introduction by Lupoff; and individual introductions describing the genesis of the five original and 18 stories reprinted from periodicals, conference program books, fanzines, and anthologies 1952-1996. Varying in tone from serious to light, the stories reflect a variety of themes including mythical creatures, urban life, alien encounters, time travel, Lovecraftian horror, and mystery.

Other books you might like:
Italo Calvino, *Numbers in the Dark and Other Stories*, 1995
Hugh B. Cave, *Death Stalks the Night*, 1995
Basil Copper, *The Black Death*, 1991
Robert M. Price, *The New Lovecraft Circle*, 1996
   editor
John Varley, *Blue Champagne*, 1986
Howard Wandrei, *Time Burial*, 1995

2840

RICHARD A. LUPOFF

The Final Battle

(New York: Bantam Spectra, 1990)

Story type: Fantasy (Alternate World; Adventure)
Series: Philip Jose Farmer's The Dungeon
Major character(s): Clive Folliot, Military Personnel; Frankenstein's Monster, Monster
Time period(s): 1870s (1870); 1890s (1896)
Locale(s): London, England; Alternate Earth

Summary: The adventures of Clive Folliot through the nine levels of the Dungeon's computer game-like world are concluded in this sixth volume. This time his traveling companions include Frankenstein's Monster, in addition to some of his friends from the earlier volumes.

Other books you might like:
Robin Bailey, *The Lake of Fire*, 1989
Bruce Coville, *The Dark Abyss*, 1989
Charles de Lint, *The Hidden City*, 1990
Charles de Lint, *The Valley of Thunder*, 1989
Robert A. Heinlein, *Glory Road*, 1964
Gene Wolfe, *The Shadow of the Torturer*, 1980

2841

RICHARD A. LUPOFF

Night of the Living 'Gator!

(New York: Ace, 1992)

Story type: Science Fiction (Humor)
Series: Daniel M. Pinkwater's Melvinge of the Megaverse
Major character(s): Melvinge, Hero, Werewolf; Loola, Girlfriend, Mythical Creature (were-lizard); Adela Rogers St. Jacques, Writer
Time period(s): Indeterminate
Locale(s): Megaverse Mall, Mythical Place

Summary: At last, Melvinge enters the Megaverse Mall itself, intent on buying a pair of squash shoes. As he roams the Mall, he hears a clue to the secret of the universe from a passing piglet. On his way to look up the word "echidna," he meets Adela Rogers St. Jacques at an autographing session. She and Melvinge buy a new Ferrari and drive somewhere else where Melvinge finds Loola, a tornado carries them to the city of Uz and they meet the alligator king, whose niece works in a shoe store at the Mall. Afterword by Daniel M. Pinkwater.

Other books you might like:
Douglas Adams, *So Long, and Thanks for All the Fish*, 1985
David Bischoff, *Night of the Living Shark!*, 1991

Ben Bova, *The Starcrossed*, 1975
Debra Doyle, *Night of the Living Rat!*, 1992
   James D. Macdonald, co-author
David Langford, *The Leaky Establishment*, 1984
Daniel Manus Pinkwater, *Borgel*, 1990
Terry Pratchett, *Moving Pictures*, 1992
John T. Sladek, *Mechasm*, 1968

2842

ALISON LURIE, Editor

The Oxford Book of Modern Fairy Tales

(New York: Oxford University Press, 1993)

Story type: Fantasy (Anthology; Legend)

Summary: This volume contains an eight-page introduction placing works within the context of fairy tale development and relationship to the world outside literature, 11 pages of biographical notes plus 40 tales from Anglo-American writers published 1839-1989, presented chronologically, and evidencing growth in the field from stories about mythical kingdoms and magical beasts to fairy tales incorporating feminism, multicultural mythology and urban issues. Authors include Donald Bartelme, L. Frank Baum, Angela Carter, Lucy Lane Clifford, John Collier, Mary de Morgan, Jeanne Desey, Philip K. Dick, Charles Dickens, Louise Erdrich, Juliana Horatia Ewing, Kenneth Grahame, Laurence Housman, Richard Hughes, Ursula K. Le Guin, Tanith Lee, George MacDonald, Bernard Malamud, Naomi Mitchison, Edith Nesbit, John Ruskin, Carl Sandberg, Catherine Sinclair, Isaac Bashevis Singer, Robert Louis Stevenson, Frank Stockton, James Thurber, H.G. Wells, T.H. White, Oscar Wilde, Jay Williams and Jane Yolen.

Other books you might like:
Chris Baldick, *The Oxford Book of Gothic Tales*, 1992
   editor
Orson Scott Card, *Dragons of Light*, 1980
   editor
Angela Carter, *The Old Wives' Fairy Tale Book*, 1990
   editor
Michael Patrick Hearn, *The Victorian Fairy Tale Book*, 1988
   editor
Tom Shippey, *The Oxford Book of Fantasy Stories*, 1994
   editor
Tom Shippey, *The Oxford Book of Science Fiction Stories*, 1992
   editor
Robert Silverberg, *The Fantasy Hall of Fame*, 1983
   editor
A. Susan Williams, *The Lifted Veil: The Book of Fantastic Literature by Women*, 1992
   editor
Jack Zipes, *Beauties, Beasts and Enchantments*, 1989
   editor

2843

ALISON LURIE

Women and Ghosts

(New York: Doubleday/Nan A. Talese, 1994)

Story type: Horror (Collection)

Summary: This renowned mainstream author's first collection of supernatural tales brings together nine stories, four original to the volume. Included are "Ilse's House," about a woman haunted by the ex-wife of her fiance; "The Pool People," in which the imaginary friends a young girl makes at her grandmother's house turn out to have a bizarre history; "The Highboy," in which a piece of antique furniture develops a life of its own; "Counting Sheep," concerned with a young man's too-literal absorption into the Lake Country landscape which he is studying; "In the Shadow," about a haunting by the ghost of a dead former lover; and "Another Halloween," a chilling tale of a specter who drives a woman mad with its appearance every Halloween.

Other books you might like:
Fred Chappell, *More Shapes than One*, 1991
Shirley Jackson, *The Magic of Shirley Jackson*, 1965
Peter Taylor, *The Oracle at Stoneleigh Court*, 1993

2844

LYNDA LYONS

Priorities

(Tallahassee: Naiad Press, 1990)

Story type: Science Fiction (Gay/Lesbian Fiction)
Series: Controllers
Major character(s): Amelia Roberts, Military Personnel; Valentine, Military Personnel
Time period(s): Indeterminate Future
Locale(s): Earth

Summary: The Doctor, a dangerous and brilliant criminal, has created an army of amazingly life-like androids and plans to use them in an attempt to kidnap the son of the president of the Earth. The Controllers, an elite organization dedicated to hunting and destroying robots and androids, must foil the plot.

Other books you might like:
Philip K. Dick, *Do Androids Dream of Electric Sheep?*, 1968
Lauren Wright Douglas, *In the Blood*, 1989
Nancy Tyler Glenn, *Clicking Stones*, 1989
Karen Marie Christa Minns, *Virago*, 1990
Joanna Russ, *The Two of Them*, 1978
Joanna Russ, *We Who Are About To. . .*, 1977

2845

R.A. MACAVOY

The Belly of the Wolf

(New York: William Morrow, 1994)

Story type: Fantasy (Quest; Religious)
Series: Lens of the World Trilogy

Major character(s): Nazhuret, Warrior; Nahvah, Doctor; Dinaos, Nobleman (Count of Lowcanton), Artist
Time period(s): 18th century
Locale(s): Velonya, Fictional Country; Canton, Fictional Country

Summary: While in exile, Nazhuret learns that his old friend King Rudof has died, perhaps from poisoning. Nazhuret and his daughter journey to discover the truth and punish the killer, even if that proves to be Rudof's son, Benar, the new king. They find Velonya teetering on the brink of civil war, with one of Nazhuret's students as a rebel leader, proclaiming Nazhuret's teachings as a new religion.

Other books you might like:
Orson Scott Card, *Red Prophet*, 1989
C.J. Cherryh, *Angel with the Sword*, 1985
Phyllis Eisenstein, *Born to Exile*, 1978
Katherine Kurtz, *Saint Camber*, 1978
Robert Silverberg, *Lord Valentine's Castle*, 1980

2846

R.A. MACAVOY

King of the Dead

(New York: Morrow, 1991)

Story type: Fantasy (Historical)
Series: Lens of the World Trilogy
Major character(s): Nazhuret, Warrior; Mynauzet, Royalty (Sanaur of Rezhmia); Charlan "Arlin" Bannering, Noblewoman, Martial Arts Expert
Time period(s): 18th century (7th Year of the Reign of Rudof I)
Locale(s): Velonya, Fictional Country; Rezhmia, Fictional Country

Summary: Taking place several years after events in *Lens of the World*, this story unfolds through Nazhuret's memoirs to Powl Inpres. Nazhuret and Arlin accept Powl's request to meet with the emperor of Rezhmia on a mission of peace. In Rezhmia, court politics and intrigue impede their efforts to curb Rezhmia's militarization and the impending conflict with Velonya.

Other books you might like:
M.A.R. Barker, *Man of Gold*, 1984
Margaret Wander Bonanno, *The Others*, 1990
Stephen R. Donaldson, *Lord Foul's Bane*, 1977
Raymond E. Feist, *Daughter of the Empire*, 1987
    Janny Wurtz, co-author
Melanie Rawn, *Stronghold*, 1990
Robert Silverberg, *Gilgamesh the King*, 1984
Paula Volsky, *Illusion*, 1992
Tad Williams, *The Dragonbone Chair*, 1988

2847

R.A. MACAVOY

Lens of the World

(New York: Morrow, 1990)

Story type: Fantasy (Historical)

Series: Lens of the World Trilogy
Major character(s): Nazhuret, Warrior; Powl, Teacher
Time period(s): 18th century
Locale(s): Vestinglon, Fictional Country

Summary: Belonging to The Royal Military School of Sordaling, Nazhuret unexpectedly has information imparted to him. Being kidnapped and brutalized prepares him for adventures beyond any he could have imagined and he joins the King of Velonya's court.

Other books you might like:
Ursula K. Le Guin, *A Wizard of Earthsea*, 1968
Alis A. Rasmussen, *The Labyrinth Gate*, 1988
Clark Ashton Smith, *Hyperborea*, 1971
Jane Yolen, *Sister Light, Sister Dark*, 1988
Jane Yolen, *White Jenna*, 1989

2848

R.A. MACAVOY

The Third Eagle: Lessons Along a Minor String

(New York: Doubleday Foundation, 1989)

Story type: Science Fiction (Satire)
Major character(s): Wanbli, Warrior, Indian; Reynaldo Errenthorp, Businessman
Time period(s): Indeterminate Future
Locale(s): The Planets of the Seven Senti, Interstellar Empire/Federation

Summary: Wanbli, a highly trained and somewhat egocentric Native American warrior of the far future, sets out to see the universe, taking a variety of jobs, including one as an actor. He meets a wide variety of people, not all of them human, growing from his experiences and ending a better person than he began.

Other books you might like:
Charles de Lint, *Svaha*, 1989
Andre Norton, *Beast Master*, 1959
Andre Norton, *The Sioux Space Man*, 1960
Alexei Panshin, *Masque World*, 1969
Alexei Panshin, *Star Well*, 1968
Alexei Panshin, *The Thurb Revolution*, 1968

2849

CAROLINE MACDONALD

The Lake at the End of the World

(New York: Dial, 1989)

Story type: Science Fiction (Young Adult)
Major character(s): Diana Redfern, Teenager; Hector, Teenager
Time period(s): 21st century (2025)
Locale(s): Australia

Summary: A family lives in complete isolation by a lake after a series of ecological disasters has destroyed most human life. Then they discover a boy from a heretofore unknown underground shelter where a group of scientists and artists has been

living since the 1960's. They moved in originally out of a fear of nuclear war and remain now due to their irrational fear of the surface.

Other books you might like:
Gary L. Blackwood, *The Dying Sun*, 1989
H.M. Hoover, *This Time of Darkness*, 1980
Gregory Maguire, *I Feel Like the Morning Star*, 1989
Robert C. O'Brien, *Z for Zachariah*, 1975
George Stewart, *Earth Abides*, 1949

2850

SHAWN MACDONALD

The Darkness Within

(New York: Zebra, 1993)

Story type: Horror (Psychological Suspense)
Major character(s): Anne Dennessy, Waiter/Waitress, Abuse Victim; Beth Dennessy, Twin, Abuse Victim; Carol Dennessy, Twin, Abuse Victim
Time period(s): 1990s (1993)
Locale(s): Colorado

Summary: Anne Dennessy narrates the woeful story of her abusive upbringing at the hands of a greedy mother and religiously fanatical grandmother, and how it has so twisted her psyche that she inflicts similar mistreatment on her twin daughters, Beth and Carol.

Other books you might like:
J.M. Dillard, *Spectres*, 1991
R. Patrick Gates, *Tunnelvision*, 1991
Rick R. Reed, *Obsessed*, 1991

2851

DAVID MACE

Firelance

(New York: Ace, 1989)

Story type: Science Fiction (Post-Nuclear Holocaust)
Major character(s): Richard Bedford, Sea Captain; David Drexel, Government Official
Time period(s): 21st century
Locale(s): Cheyenne Mountain Command Cent, Wyoming; *U.S.S. Vindicator*, At Sea

Summary: In a world all but destroyed by a full-scale nuclear war and the nuclear winter that followed, military commanders, safe in their gigantic armored command centers, plot to wipe out the last vestiges of human life on Earth. Others, more sane, do their best to bring an end to the senseless killing. This is a reprint of the 1986 British edition.

Other books you might like:
William Brinkley, *The Last Ship*, 1988
Glen Cook, *The Heirs of Babylon*, 1972
David Drake, *Fortress*, 1987
Keith Laumer, *The Stars Must Wait*, 1990

2852

ELISABETH MACE

Under Siege

(New York: Orchard/Franklin Watts, 1990)

Story type: Fantasy (Romance; Young Adult)
Major character(s): Morris, Teenager; Uncle Patrick, Computer Expert; Vail, Artificial Intelligence
Time period(s): 1980s
Locale(s): England; Cyberspace

Summary: Powerless to affect his parents' separation, and in the face of his mother's disapproval, Morris enters the world of his Uncle Patrick's ongoing computer wargame. Falling in love with one of the gaming figurines, Vail, he joins the battle on her side as a giant-god in opposition to his Uncle Patrick. This is the author's first book.

Other books you might like:
Lynne Reid Banks, *The Indian in the Cupboard*, 1980
Pauline Clarke, *The Return of the Twelves*, 1964
Edward Eager, *Knight's Castle*, 1956
E. Nesbit, *The Magic World*, 1912
Will Shetterly, *The Tangled Lands*, 1989

2853

ROB MACGREGOR

Indiana Jones and the Dance of the Giants

(New York: Bantam Falcon, 1991)

Story type: Fantasy (Adventure; Quest)
Series: Indiana Jones
Major character(s): Indiana "Indy" Jones, Archaeologist; Deirdre Campbell, Student, Adventurer; Adrian Powell, Government Official
Time period(s): 1920s (1925)
Locale(s): England; Scotland

Summary: While teaching in the Archaeology Department at London University, his first post, Indiana Jones meets a Scottish student who claims to have discovered a scroll which proves the existence of the legendary sorcerer, Merlin. In their dangerous pursuit of the secrets contained in the scroll, they travel to Scotland and then Stonehenge where they foil Adrian Powell's attempt to return Druidism to Britain and seize power by returning the sacred stone, the Omphalos, to Stonehenge.

Other books you might like:
Campbell Black, *Raiders of the Lost Ark*, 1981
James Kahn, *Indiana Jones and the Temple of Doom*, 1984
Morgan Llywelyn, *Druids*, 1991

2854

ROB MACGREGOR

Indiana Jones and the Genesis Deluge

(New York: Bantam Falcon, 1992)

Story type: Fantasy (Adventure; Legend)
Series: Indiana Jones

Major character(s): Indiana "Indy" Jones, Archaeologist; Vladimir Zobolotsky, Doctor, Adventurer; Katrina Zobolotsky, Adventurer
Time period(s): 1920s (1927)
Locale(s): Chicago, Illinois; Istanbul, Turkey

Summary: Recruited by Vladimir and Katrina in the search for the remains of Noah's legendary ark, Indy travels with the pair to Mt. Ararat, hindered in their search by Kremlin and Sicilian agents and Turkish bandits.

Other books you might like:
Campbell Black, *Raiders of the Lost Ark*, 1981
James Kahn, *Indiana Jones and the Temple of Doom*, 1984
Catherine Lanigan, *Jewel of the Nile*, 1985

2855

ROB MACGREGOR

Indiana Jones and the Interior World

(New York: Bantam Falcon, 1992)

Story type: Fantasy (Adventure)
Series: Indiana Jones
Major character(s): Indiana "Indy" Jones, Archaeologist; Salandra, Guide, Adventurer
Time period(s): 1920s (1928-1929)
Locale(s): Isle of Chiloe, Chile; Pincoya, Subterranean World; Land of the Lost, Subterranean World (inside the Earth)

Summary: When Indy disposed of a dangerous relic, he opened the doorway to a world within the Earth. Later, the doorway provides access for the leader of an unstoppable invading army to enter and form a deadly liaison which Indy must defeat by restoring the balance between worlds.

Other books you might like:
Campbell Black, *Raiders of the Lost Ark*, 1981
Edgar Rice Burroughs, *At the Earth's Core*, 1922
Edgar Rice Burroughs, *Pellucidar*, 1923
James Kahn, *Indiana Jones and the Temple of Doom*, 1984
Jules Verne, *Journey to the Center of the Earth*, 1864

2856

ROB MACGREGOR

Indiana Jones and the Peril at Delphi

(New York: Bantam Falcon, 1991)

Story type: Fantasy (Adventure; Quest)
Series: Indiana Jones
Major character(s): Indiana "Indy" Jones, Archaeologist (Ph.D. candidate); Dorian Belecamus, Professor
Time period(s): 1920s (1922)
Locale(s): Chicago, Illinois; Paris, France; Delphi, Greece

Summary: On a field trip to Delphi, Indy becomes sexually involved with his instructor, Dorian. When Indy rediscovers the long-lost sacred stone, the Omphalos, Dorian plots to take control of Greece's future by becoming the Oracle of Delphi whose return has been prophecied for 16 centuries by the Order of Pythia.

Other books you might like:
Campbell Black, *Raiders of the Lost Ark*, 1981
James Kahn, *Indiana Jones and the Temple of Doom*, 1984
Marc Laidlaw, *Neon Lotus*, 1988
Catherine Lanigan, *Jewel of the Nile*, 1985

2857

ROB MACGREGOR

Indiana Jones and the Seven Veils
(New York: Bantam Falcon, 1991)

Story type: Fantasy (Quest; Adventure)
Series: Indiana Jones
Major character(s): Indiana "Indy" Jones, Archaeologist; Deirdre Campbell, Student, Adventurer
Time period(s): 1920s (1926)
Locale(s): Brazil

Summary: Following hints in the mysterious writings of a missing British explorer, Indy and Deirdre search for a lost city in the Brazilian jungle and a legendary red-headed race, possible descendants of Celtic Druids.

Other books you might like:
Campbell Black, *Raiders of the Lost Ark*, 1981
James Kahn, *Indiana Jones and the Temple of Doom*, 1984
Catherine Lanigan, *Romancing the Stone*, 1984
Morgan Llywelyn, *Druids*, 1991
Edward Myers, *The Mountain Made of Light*, 1992

2858

ROB MACGREGOR

Indiana Jones and the Unicorn's Legacy
(New York: Bantam Falcon, 1992)

Story type: Fantasy (Adventure; Quest)
Series: Indiana Jones
Major character(s): Indiana "Indy" Jones, Archaeologist; Mara Rogers, Professor (art history); Roland Walcott, Professor, Criminal
Time period(s): 1920s (1928)
Locale(s): Mesa Verde, Colorado; Southwest (Anasazi Ruins)

Summary: Indy joins Mara at the site of an ancient Anasazi ruin in pursuit of a unicorn's horn, legendary source of power. Their quest suffers from the return of Indy's nemesis, Roland Walcott, previously thought dead, but now back with a lethal lust for the horn.

Other books you might like:
Campbell Black, *Raiders of the Lost Ark*, 1981
James Kahn, *Indiana Jones and the Temple of Doom*, 1984

2859

F. GWYNPLAINE MACINTYRE

The Woman between the Worlds
(New York: Dell, 1994)

Story type: Science Fiction (Invasion of Earth; Horror)

Major character(s): Vanessa Steele, Alien, Revolutionary; Aleister Crowley, Magician; The Dreadful Eye, Alien
Time period(s): 1890s (1898)
Locale(s): London, England; Alternate Universe

Summary: A tattoo artist receives the bizarre commission of a full body tattoo for a scientist who has turned herself invisible. Her story proves more complicated as the tattooist and Vanessa flee across London and out of the world. First novel, which makes liberal use of historic figures.

Other books you might like:
James P. Blaylock, *Lord Kelvin's Machine*, 1992
William Hjortsberg, *Nevermore*, 1994
K.W. Jeter, *Infernal Devices*, 1987
Kim Newman, *Anno Dracula*, 1993
Tim Powers, *The Anubis Gates*, 1983

2860

JOHN MACLAY, Editor

Voices From the Night
(Baltimore: Maclay & Associates, 1994)

Story type: Horror (Anthology)

Summary: This all-original non-theme anthology collects 27 tales of horror, fantasy, and dark suspense by well-known and relatively unknown writers. Among the best are Robert Weinberg's "Dial Your Dreams," about the extreme services available through a 1-900 number; Rick Hautala's atmospheric tale of supernatural vengeance, "A Little Bit of Divine Justice"; Ray Russell's "The Little Snakes of Tara," a whimsical retelling of the legend of St. Patrick; Mort Castle's paranoid fantasy, "The Call"; and J.N. Williamson's tale of a nerd who reasons his way out of a deadly love triangle, "The Autonomic Nervous System, Klause Von Klauswitz, and Omilian." This beautifully produced book appeared only in a signed collector's edition.

Other books you might like:
Richard T. Chizmar, *Cold Blood*, 1991
Joe R. Lansdale, *Dark at Heart*, 1992
   Karen Lansdale, co-editor
Thomas F. Monteleone, *Borderlands 3*, 1993
   editor
Claudia O'Keefe, *Ghosttide*, 1993
   editor
Stanley Wiater, *After the Darkness*, 1993
   editor

2861

SCOTT MACMILLAN

At Sword's Point
(New York: Roc, 1994)

Story type: Fantasy (Contemporary; Horror)
Series: Vampyr-SS
Major character(s): John Drummond, Detective—Homicide, Vampire; Wilhelm Kluge, Military Personnel, Vampire; Markus Eberle, Police Officer
Time period(s): 1990s

Locale(s): Germany; Austria

Summary: Wilhelm Kluge's Nazi vampires and the Vatican hunt for John Drummond, a newly created vampire also wanted by the Israeli Mossad, which hopes to create a vampire army. Drummond, Eberle and the Crusader vampires go into battle against Kluge and his company with dire consequences.

Other books you might like:
Robert Harris, *Fatherland*, 1992
Joan Kangilaski, *The Seeking Sword*, 1977
Lucius Shepard, *The Golden*, 1993
Brian Stableford, *The Empire of Fear*, 1991
Lois Tilton, *Darkness on the Ice*, 1993

2862

SCOTT MACMILLAN

Knights of the Blood

(New York: Roc, 1993)

Story type: Fantasy (Contemporary; Horror)
Series: Vampyr-SS
Major character(s): John Drummond, Detective—Homicide; Henri de Beq, Knight, Vampire; Wilhelm Kluge, Military Personnel (SS Sturmbannfuhrer), Vampire
Time period(s): 1970s (1972); 13th century (1291)
Locale(s): Los Angeles, California; Vienna, Austria

Summary: Investigating a bizarre series of murders in Los Angeles, John Drummond hears a New Hampshire priest claim he murdered vampires who served an evil SS officer. While looking into the murder of an elderly Jew in Vienna, Drummond travels into the Ardennes and meets a group of knights who still atone for crimes committed during the Crusades. First novel, from an idea by Katherine Kurtz.

Other books you might like:
Tanya Huff, *Blood Price*, 1991
Lee Killough, *Blood Hunt*, 1987
George R.R. Martin, *Fevre Dream*, 1982
Anne Rice, *Interview with the Vampire*, 1976
Brian Stableford, *The Empire of Fear*, 1991
Chelsea Quinn Yarbro, *Crusader's Torch*, 1988

2863

TIMOTHY A. MADDEN

Outbanker

(Lake Geneva, Wisconsin: TSR, 1990)

Story type: Science Fiction (Space Colony; Political)
Major character(s): Ian S. MacKenzie, Spaceship Captain
Time period(s): 24th century
Locale(s): 61 Cygni Colonies, Outer Space; *Outbanker Bravo*, Spaceship

Summary: When the Corporate Hegemony of Earth raises taxes and sends two corporate dreadnaughts to enforce compliance, the colonies around Cygnus A decide to make a deal, but the colonies around Cygnus B decide to resist. They design a small, superfast, one-man cruiser, which requiresd

special persons called Outbankers to pilot them. This is the story of one of them.

Other books you might like:
F.M. Busby, *Young Rissa*, 1984
Stephen Goldin, *Jade Darcy and the Affair of Honor*, 1988
   Mary Mason, co-author
Robert A. Heinlein, *The Moon Is a Harsh Mistress*, 1966
Melisa C. Michaels, *Far Harbor*, 1989
David Alexander Smith, *Homecoming*, 1990
L. Neil Smith, *Contact and Commune*, 1990
John E. Stith, *Redshift Rendezvous*, 1990

2864

TOM MADDOX

Halo

(New York: Tor, 1991)

Story type: Science Fiction (Alternate Intelligence; Space Colony)
Major character(s): Mikhail Mikhailovitch Gonzales, Computer Expert, Auditor; Diana Heywood, Computer Expert; Aleph, Artificial Intelligence
Time period(s): Indeterminate Future
Locale(s): Halo City, Space Station (at L5)

Summary: Hoping to study long-term human/machine interface, SenTrax Corporation arranges for Gonzales and Heywood to supervise Jerry Chapman's neural interface to Aleph. With the higher brain functions of Chapman linked to Aleph, the computer program develops a stronger personality. Disaster threatens not only Aleph but also Halo City itself when SenTrax decides to reassert control by terminating Chapman's neural link. This is the author's first novel.

Other books you might like:
Greg Bear, *Queen of Angels*, 1990
Gregory Benford, *Great Sky River*, 1987
Gregory Benford, *Tides of Light*, 1989
David Brin, *Earth*, 1990
Pat Cadigan, *Mindplayers*, 1987
Pat Cadigan, *Synners*, 1991
William Gibson, *Neuromancer*, 1984
Victor Milan, *The Cybernetic Samurai*, 1986
Allen Steele, *Clarke County, Space*, 1990
Michael Swanwick, *Stations of the Tide*, 1991
John Varley, *The Persistence of Vision*, 1978

2865

DAVID MADSEN

Vodoun

(New York: Morrow, 1994)

Story type: Horror (Occult; Possession)
Major character(s): Ray Falco, Journalist; Faustin Gabriel, Art Dealer (gallery owner); Carmen Mondesir, Businessman (charity director)
Time period(s): 1990s (1994)
Locale(s): Washington, District of Columbia

Summary: As star journalist Ray Falco ponders his recent inexplicable murder of a Haitian activist, he finds that he is possessed by the spirit of Nicholas Whitney Townshend, Haiti's American envoy during the 1793 slave rebellion. Gradually it unfolds that Falco has become a tool of recent Haitian acquaintances who are using voodoo to channel spirits of the dead into the living in the hope of liberating modern Haiti from its dictator's control.

Other books you might like:
Alex Abella, *The Killing of the Saints*, 1991
Hugh B. Cave, *Disciples of Dread*, 1988
Nicholas Conde, *The Religion*, 1982
Jewell Martin Rhodes, *Voodoo Dreams*, 1993
Theodore Roscoe, *Z Is for Zombie*, 1937

2866

SIMON MAGINN

Sheep

(Stone Mountain, Georgia: White Wolf, 1996)

Story type: Horror (Evil Children)
Major character(s): James Tullian, Contractor (construction); Adele Tullian, Artist; Sam Tullian, Child (7-year-old)
Time period(s): 1990s (1994)
Locale(s): Ty-Gwyneth, Wales

Summary: James Tullian moves his family to the rural sheep farming community of Ty-Gwyneth to help them recover from the depression that has set in after the drowning death of his young daughter. But the town's dark heritage, which includes a religious cult and a man who murdered his own family, begins having a strange effect on him, his wife, and his young son, leading him to wonder whether their private psychopathologies are beginning to express themselves. First published in England in 1994, this is the author's first novel.

Other books you might like:
William Golding, *Lord of the Flies*, 1954
William March, *The Bad Seed*, 1954
Sarban, *Ringstones*, 1951
Bernard Taylor, *The Godsend*, 1976
Gene Thompson, *Lupe*, 1977
Thomas Tryon, *The Other*, 1971

2867

SIMON MAGINN

Virgins and Martyrs

(Clarkston, Georgia: White Wolf, 1996)

Story type: Horror (Psychological Suspense)
Major character(s): Daniel Blennerhassett, Student; Wendy Bishop, Child; Terence Outhwaite, Police Officer (inspector)
Time period(s): 1990s (1995)
Locale(s): Hove, England

Summary: Shortly after moving into a new apartment where he hopes to find the quiet he needs to complete his dissertation, Daniel Blennerhassett is haunted by the image of a young woman who radiates a religious aura. As he slowly gives himself over to his obsession with her, Daniel discovers the horrifying truth about his landlord, a scholarly fanatic with some unorthodox theories concerning religious martyrdom. This novel was first published in England in 1995.

Other books you might like:
Jonathan Aycliffe, *Naomi's Room*, 1992
Josephine Boyle, *Holy Terror*, 1993
Richard Matheson, *Hell House*, 1971
Mary Elizabeth Murphy, *Virgin*, 1996
Michael Paine, *The Colors of Hell*, 1990

2868

GREGORY MAGUIRE

I Feel Like the Morning Star

(New York: Harper & Row, 1989)

Story type: Science Fiction (Post-Nuclear Holocaust)
Major character(s): Ella, Teenager; Mart, Teenager
Time period(s): 21st century
Locale(s): Pioneer Colony, Massachusetts

Summary: Pioneer Colony, a closed-access survival community buried some four-thousand feet beneath what was once the state of Massachusetts, is home to some 1,000 survivors of the nuclear war that occurred more than four years ago. Ella, Mart, and Sorb chafe at the colony's restrictions and plot rebellion.

Other books you might like:
Gary L. Blackwood, *The Dying Sun*, 1989
Pat Frank, *Alas Babylon*, 1959
Daniel F. Galouye, *Dark Universe*, 1961
Robert C. O'Brien, *Z for Zachariah*, 1975
Mordecai Roshwald, *Level 7*, 1959

2869

GREGORY MAGUIRE

Wicked: The Life and Times of the Wicked Witch of the West

(New York: HarperCollins, 1995)

Story type: Fantasy (Political; Religious)
Series: Oz
Major character(s): Elphaba, Witch, Activist (talking animal rights); Galinda "Glinda the Good", Socialite, Witch; Nessarose, Witch, Religious
Time period(s): Indeterminate
Locale(s): Oz, Mythical Place

Summary: Born to an alcoholic parent, Elphaba's unusual appearance, her sibling care duties, and abuse by a parent produce a difficult childhood for her. At college Elphaba rooms with snobbish Galinda then evolves into a militant animal rights proponent before her untimely death.

Other books you might like:
L. Frank Baum, *Dorothy and the Wizard in Oz*, 1908
L. Frank Baum, *The Land of Oz*, 1904
Rachel R. Cosgrove, *The Hidden Valley of Oz*, 1951
Philip Jose Farmer, *A Barnstormer in Oz*, 1982

Eloise Jarvis McGraw, *Merry-Go-Round in Oz*, 1963
   Lauren McGraw Wagner, co-author
John Rea Neill, *The Wonder City of Oz*, 1940
Geoff Ryman, *Was*, 1992
Jack Snow, *The Magical Mimics in Oz*, 1946
Ruth Plumly Thompson, *The Royal Book of Oz*, 1921
Joan D. Vinge, *Return to Oz*, 1985

2870
MARGARET MAHY

The Girl with the Green Ear: Stories about Magic in Nature
(New York: Knopf, 1992)

Story type: Fantasy (Young Adult; Collection)

Summary: Nine stories published in collections in Great Britain all sharing themes of magic and nature with some stories focusing on special abilities as in the title story, whose protagonist hears the voices of plants, while other stories feature mythical creatures such as dragons in ''Don't Cut the Lawn!'' and people of the woods in ''The Merry-Go-Round.''

Other books you might like:
Joan Aiken, *The Last Slice of Rainbow and Other Stories*, 1988
Margery Williams Bianco, *A Street of Little Shops*, 1932
Rudyard Kipling, *The Jungle Book*, 1893
Rudyard Kipling, *Just So Stories*, 1902
Laurence Yep, *The Rainbow People*, 1989
Jane Yolen, *The Girl Who Cried Flowers and Other Tales*, 1974

2871
MARGARET MAHY

A Tall Story and Other Tales
(New York: Macmillan McElderry, 1992)

Story type: Fantasy (Young Adult; Collection)

Summary: 11 stories published in collections 1972-1975 all sharing fantastic themes. Several stories focus on animals including ''The Boy Who Went Looking for a Friend,'' ''Patrick Comes to School,'' ''Mrs. Bartelmy's Pet'' and the title story which features a giant land-dwelling oyster. Three stories feature witches, ''Aunt Nasty,'' ''The Witch Dog'' and ''Teddy and the Witches,'' while ''Looking for a Ghost'' suggests that one might not recognize a ghost upon seeing it. In another story, ''Kite Saturday,'' young Joan's investment in wishes and dreams yields a magic kite that allows her to fly.

Other books you might like:
Diana Wynne Jones, *Warlock at the Wheel and Other Stories*, 1985
Rudyard Kipling, *Just So Stories*, 1902
Penelope Lively, *Uninvited Ghosts and Other Stories*, 1985
Jane Yolen, *Zoo 2000: Twelve Stories of Science Fiction and Fantasy Beasts*, 1973
   editor

2872
BARRY MALZBERG

Beyond Apollo
(New York: Carroll and Graf, 1989)

Story type: Science Fiction (Literary)
Major character(s): Harry M. Evans, Astronaut; Captain, Astronaut
Time period(s): 1980s (1981)
Locale(s): United States; Venus

Summary: This John W. Campbell Memorial Award-winning novel is narrated by Harry M. Evans, the sole survivor of the first manned expedition to Venus. Evans returns to Earth insane, his mind a complex hash of memories, hallucinations and wish fulfillment fantasies. Within his tortured brain lies the secret of what went wrong on the expedition. Originally published in 1972.

Other books you might like:
J.G. Ballard, *The Crystal World*, 1966
J.G. Ballard, *The Drowned World*, 1962
J.G. Ballard, *The Unlimited Dream Company*, 1977
Philip K. Dick, *Flow My Tears, the Policeman Said*, 1974
Philip K. Dick, *Martian Time-Slip*, 1964
Philip K. Dick, *A Scanner Darkly*, 1977
Philip K. Dick, *The Transmigration of Timothy Archer*, 1982
Philip K. Dick, *Valis*, 1981
Dan Simmons, *Phases of Gravity*, 1989

2873
ALBERT J. MANACHINO
LARRY DICKISON, Illustrator

The Odd Lot: The Selected Works of Albert J. Manachino
(Concord, California: Dark Regions Press, 1993)

Story type: Horror (Collection)

Summary: The nine stories in this book are collected from a variety of small press publications and include the haunted house tale, ''Darby's Bane''; the surreal comedy, ''Head of the House''; two stories (''The White Orchard'' and ''The Hungry House'') which combine the detective story with metaphysical fantasy; and three stories (''Dark Bible,'' ''Escape Clause,'' and ''Mr. Diabolicus'') that chronicle the efforts of foolish mortals who attempt either to dispose of or buy the so-called devil's bible. Michael Ambrose has supplied the introductions.

Other books you might like:
D.F. Lewis, *The Best of D.F. Lewis*, 1993
Darrell Schweitzer, *Transients and Other Disquieting Tales*, 1993
Ken Wisman, *Weird Family Tales*, 1993

2874

NINA MANDELIK

Entity

(New York: Diamond, 1991)

Story type: Horror (Ancient Evil Unleashed)
Major character(s): Michael Triplett, Teenager; Tim O'Connor, Teenager; Maggie Greene, Waiter/Waitress
Time period(s): 1990s
Locale(s): Fort Riley, Kansas

Summary: Although an exorcism was performed there over a century before, the Army town of Fort Riley is suddenly besieged by apparitions, mysterious deaths and a wave of unspeakable behavior among its citizens. As the only one who suspects that something out the ordinary is going on, young Michael Triplett trains himself to battle the festering evil that has taken control of the town. This is the author's first novel.

Other books you might like:
Douglas Clegg, *Goat Dance*, 1989
T.E.D. Klein, *The Ceremonies*, 1984
Bentley Little, *The Revelation*, 1990

2875

ALBERTO MANGUEL, Editor

Black Water 2: More Tales of the Fantastic

(New York: Clarkson Potter, 1990)

Story type: Horror (Anthology)

Summary: Sixty-five tales of the supernatural from around the world. The selections range from classics like Charlotte Perkins Gilman's ''The Yellow Wallpaper'' and Hans Heinz Ewer's ''The Spider,'' to stories by authors not generally associated with fantasy fiction, such as F. Scott Fitzgerald's ''A Short Trip Home,'' Joseph Conrad's ''The Brute'' and Gabriel Garcia Marquez's ''The Last Voyage of the Ghost Ship.''

Other books you might like:
Peter Haining, *The Lucifer Society*, 1972
Robert Phillips, *Triumph of the Night*, 1989

2876

PHILLIP MANN

Wulfsyarn: A Mosaic

(New York: Morrow AvoNova, 1992)

Story type: Science Fiction (Theological; First Contact)
Major character(s): Jon Wilburfoss, Spaceship Captain, Religious (confrere); Wulf, Artificial Intelligence, Writer; Chida, Alien
Time period(s): Indeterminate Future
Locale(s): Juniper, Planet—Imaginary; *Nightingale*, Spaceship; Outer Space
Summary: Jon Wilburfoss accepts command of the *Nightingale*, the only ship capable of travelling in subspace

after the War of Ignorance. After he picks up aliens of various races, the infected ship's brain self-destructs, destroying all life aboard except Jon Wilburfoss. Marooned on a planet, Wilburfoss makes friends with an alien life force, only to destroy it getting off the planet. Rescued, Wilburfoss returns to Juniper where he falls into a miasma of guilt, sulking about the monastery garden.

Other books you might like:
John Barnes, *Sin of Origin*, 1988
Gregory Benford, *If the Stars Are Gods*, 1977
    Gordon Eklund, co-author
Michael Bishop, *Transfigurations*, 1979
Philip Jose Farmer, *Night of Light*, 1966
Stanislaw Lem, *Solaris*, 1970
John Morressy, *The Mansions of Space*, 1983
Vernor Vinge, *A Fire upon the Deep*, 1992

2877

CYNTHIA MANSON, Editor
CHARLES ARDAI, Co-Editor

Future Crime: An Anthology of the Shape of Crime to Come

(New York: Donald I. Fine, 1992)

Story type: Science Fiction (Anthology; Mystery)

Summary: This volume addresses crime to come with original short stories by C.J. Cherryh and Alan Dean Foster and an original novelette by George Alec Effinger as well as stories by Isaac Asimov, Terry Black, Robert Bloch, Orson Scott Card, Harry Harrison, Kathe Koja, Doug Larsen, Larry Niven, John Shirley, W.R. Thompson, John Varley and Lawrence Watt-Evans.

Other books you might like:
Isaac Asimov, *Tales of the Black Widowers*, 1974
J.G. Ballard, *The Atrocity Exhibition*, 1990
Ben Bova, *Future Crime*, 1990
Miriam Allen DeFord, *Space, Time and Crime*, 1964
Mike Resnick, *Whatdunits*, 1992
    editor
Howard Waldrop, *Night of the Cooters*, 1990
    editor
Howard Waldrop, *Them Bones*, 1984

2878

MELISAND MARCH

The Site

(New York: Leisure, 1989)

Story type: Horror (Haunted House)
Major character(s): Valerie Harris, Advertising (Executive); Jennifer Cunningham, Advertising (Valerie's protegee)
Time period(s): 1960s (1961, 1965); 1970s (1977)
Locale(s): New York, New York

Summary: A novel ''based on real incidents.'' A series of inexplicable accidents convince Valerie Harris that the ''site'' of a modern high-rise building is taking systematic ''revenge'' against its inhabitants.

Other books you might like:
Anne Rivers Siddons, *The House Next Door*, 1978

2879
NORMA MARDER

An Eye for Dark Places
(Boston: Little Brown, 1993)

Story type: Science Fiction (Post-Disaster; Political)
Major character(s): Sephony Berg-Benson, Farmer, Revolutionary; Claro, Alien
Time period(s): 21st century
Locale(s): England; Domino, Alternate Earth

Summary: Sephony remains generally satisfied with farm life and raising children in a politically repressive England despite her nagging visions and ill-defined desires. When Claro invites her to descend throught a hole in her kitchen floor one day, Sephony discovers Domino and its society, which fosters freedom. On returning home, Sephony fights for restoration of women's rights in her society. First novel.

Other books you might like:
Margaret Atwood, *The Handmaid's Tale*, 1985
Flynn Connolly, *The Rising of the Moon*, 1993
Suzette Haden Elgin, *Earthsong*, 1994
Suzette Haden Elgin, *The Judas Rose*, 1987
Suzette Haden Elgin, *Native Tongue*, 1984
Marge Piercy, *Woman on the Edge of Time*, 1976

2880
LAURIE J. MARKS

Dancing Jack
(New York: DAW, 1993)

Story type: Fantasy (Quest; Sword and Sorcery)
Major character(s): Ash of Ashland, Revolutionary, Adventurer; Rys, Sailor (riverboat pilot)
Time period(s): Indeterminate
Locale(s): Faerd, Fictional Country; All-Haven, Fictional Country

Summary: Deciding to find her nephew, Ash abandons a decade of farming ancestral ground while trying to forget her involvement in a bloody rebellion. She hopes her nephew will prove the vessel for her family's magical talent. However, plans do not proceed as wished when, shortly after Ash locates him, rebellion again sweeps into her life.

Other books you might like:
Tom Deitz, *Soulsmith*, 1991
Dave Duncan, *The Cutting Edge*, 1992
Tanith Lee, *Kill the Dead*, 1980
Elizabeth Moon, *Sheepfarmer's Daughter*, 1988
Caroline Stevermer, *River Rats*, 1992
Paula Volsky, *Illusion*, 1992

2881
LAURIE J. MARKS

Delan the Mislaid
(New York: DAW, 1989)

Story type: Fantasy (Adventure)
Series: Children of Triad
Major character(s): Delan, Wanderer; Teksan Lafall, Traveller
Time period(s): Indeterminate
Locale(s): Alternate Universe

Summary: Despite a wide variety of sentient beings, with a wide variety of shapes, Delan is considered a freak in his world. As he (or possibly she) looks for an identity, he joins another wanderer and learns about the world.

Other books you might like:
Mary Brown, *The Unlikely Ones*, 1986
Charles de Lint, *Wolf Moon*, 1988
Andre Norton, *Flight in Yiktor*, 1987

2882
LAURIE J. MARKS

The Moonbane Mage
(New York: DAW, 1990)

Story type: Fantasy (Quest)
Major character(s): Laril, Mythical Creature (Aeyrie; Exiled adolescent)
Time period(s): Indeterminate
Locale(s): Alternate Universe

Summary: Exiled by his community, Laril, a winged creature, takes refuge with a mage who turns out to be somewhat warped. In addition to discovering his own powers, Laril falls in love with the mage's servant woman, a Walker.

Other books you might like:
M. Coleman Easton, *Spirits of Cavern and Hearth*, 1989
Robert Jordan, *The Eye of the World*, 1989

2883
LAURIE J. MARKS

The Watcher's Mask
(New York: DAW, 1992)

Story type: Fantasy (Political; Adventure)
Major character(s): Jamil/Alasil, Military Personnel, Spy; Ata'al, Shaman (Asakeiri); Adline Asakeiri, Sports Figure (runner), Shaman
Time period(s): Indeterminate
Locale(s): Akava, Fictional City; Ashami, Fictional City; Callia, Fictional Country

Summary: The Watchers, a cadre of spies and executioners for the Emperor consisting of multi-souled people kidnapped as children, have been taught they will become insane if left with their natural families. Jamil, one of the oldest, most successful Watchers, fears her "blackouts" exhibit a symptom of this insanity which afflicts many older Watchers. She struggles to survive a fall and near death from exposure, and to explain to herself why she is hundreds of miles from where she expected to be and why several weeks have passed. Rescued by the Asakeiri, Jamil learns about herself and her heritage and a threat to the Emperor requiring her immediate return to Ashami.

Other books you might like:
Constance Ash, *The Stalking Horse*, 1990
Mary Gentle, *Rats and Gargoyles*, 1991
Rosemary Kirstein, *The Steerswoman*, 1989
Ursula K. Le Guin, *Always Coming Home*, 1985
Elizabeth Moon, *Sheepfarmer's Daughter*, 1988
James Morrow, *Only Begotten Daughter*, 1990

2884

LOUISE MARLEY

Sing the Light

(New York: Ace, 1995)

Story type: Science Fiction (Lost Colony; Psychic Powers)
Major character(s): Sira, Psychic (Cantrix), Singer; Rollie, Guide (ranger); Lu, Psychic (esper), Teacher (maestra)
Time period(s): Indeterminate Future
Locale(s): Nevya, Planet—Imaginary

Summary: On Nevya, survival for humans would be impossible without Singers who use psychic power to generate heat. Trained at the Conservatory from childhood to serve as Cantor or Cantrix at a great House, the best can never be touched by anyone not also trained. The youngest Cantrix ever graduated from the Conservatory, Sira finds life at the House of Bariken hostile and misses the respect she expects from her training. When politics turns to murder, from which she narrowly escapes, Sira's act of defiance almost costs her her future as a Cantrix.

Other books you might like:
Marion Zimmer Bradley, *Rediscovery: A Novel of Darkover*, 1993
    Mercedes Lackey, co-author
Suzette Haden Elgin, *Earthsong*, 1994
Rosemary Kirstein, *The Steerswoman*, 1989
Anne McCaffrey, *The Rowan*, 1990
Jack Williamson, *Demon Moon*, 1994

2885

LOUISE MARLEY

Sing the Warmth

(New York: Ace, 1996)

Story type: Science Fiction (Lost Colony; Psychic Powers)
Series: Sing the Light
Major character(s): Sira, Psychic (esper), Singer; Iban, Psychic (esper); Zakri, Psychic (esper), Singer
Time period(s): Indeterminate Future
Locale(s): Nevya, Planet—Imaginary

Summary: After living at Observatory as Cantrix for the last four years, Sira leaves a fully trained Theo as Cantor in her place. Unwilling to return to Conservatory, Sira looks for

Zakri to train his very strong, undisciplined talent to solve the problems caused by lack of Candidates coming to Conservatory.

Other books you might like:
Marion Zimmer Bradley, *Rediscovery: A Novel of Darkover*, 1993
    Mercedes Lackey, co-author
Suzette Haden Elgin, *Earthsong*, 1994
Nina Kiriki Hoffman, *The Thread That Binds the Bones*, 1994
Rosemary Kirstein, *The Steerswoman*, 1989
Anne McCaffrey, *The Rowan*, 1990

2886

STEPHEN MARLOWE

The Lighthouse at the End of the World

(New York: Dutton, 1995)

Story type: Horror (Mystery)
Major character(s): Edgar Allan Poe, Writer, Historical Figure; C. Auguste Dupin, Detective; John J. Moran, Doctor
Time period(s): 1840s (1849)
Locale(s): Baltimore, Maryland

Summary: Presented as an account of Edgar Allan Poe's whereabouts the last week of his life, this novel tells how Poe hires detective C. Auguste Dupin to find his missing brother, and the mystical discoveries Poe makes in the process that allow him access to alternate lives and to witness the end of the world. The novel's events all are prefigured by characters and themes that run throughout Poe's tales of the mysterious and the macabre.

Other books you might like:
Brian W. Aldiss, *Frankenstein Unbound*, 1973
Mark Frost, *The List of 7*, 1993
William Hjortsberg, *Nevermore*, 1994
Kim Newman, *Anno Dracula*, 1995

2887

ANN MARSTON

Kingmaker's Sword

(New York: HarperPrism, 1996)

Story type: Fantasy (Sword and Sorcery)
Series: Rune Blade Trilogy
Major character(s): Kian "Mouse" dav Leydon, Heir—Lost, Hero; Kerridwen al Jorddyn, Noblewoman, Martial Arts Expert; Cullin dav Medroch, Nobleman, Mercenary
Time period(s): Indeterminate
Locale(s): Falinor, Fictional Country; Tyra, Fictional Country

Summary: Escaping slavery, Kian acquires a magical sword and discovers the identity of his grandfather. After several years travel with his uncle, Cullin, as a mercenary guard, he meets a swordswoman who seeks the rightful owner of the sword, the lost heir of Celi. A powerful sorcerer and Kian's former master also seek him, with less benevolent intentions. The story continues in *The Western King*.

Other books you might like:
C.J. Cherryh, *Gate of Ivrel*, 1976

Simon R. Green, *Blue Moon Rising*, 1991
Barbara Hambly, *The Ladies of Mandrigyn*, 1984
Katherine Kurtz, *Deryni Rising*, 1970
Roger Zelazny, *Nine Princes in Amber*, 1970

2888

ANN MARSTON

The Western King

(New York: HarperPrism, 1996)

Story type: Fantasy (Sword and Sorcery; Magic Conflict)
Series: Rune Blade Trilogy
Major character(s): Keylan ap Kian, Ruler (king); Donaugh ap Kian, Royalty (prince), Magician; Tiernyn ap Kian, Royalty (prince), Warrior
Time period(s): Indeterminate
Locale(s): Celi, Fictional Country

Summary: Kian decides that the time has come to step down as Regent of Skai and crown his son Keylan as King. Tiernyn receives the magic sword, "Kingmaker," and urges his older brother to unite the bickering tribes in order to drive the Saesnesi invaders from their island. But to Donaugh goes the responsibility of advising his brothers and of bringing about an alliance with the Saesne sis in order to fight the greater threat of the Maedun, led by the evil sorcerers Hakkar and Francia.

Other books you might like:
Marion Zimmer Bradley, *The Mists of Avalon*, 1983
C.J. Cherryh, *Faery in Shadow*, 1994
Simon R. Green, *Blood and Honor*, 1993
Harry Harrison, *The Hammer and the Cross*, 1993
    John Holm, co-author
Diana L. Paxson, *The White Raven*, 1988
Roger Zelazny, *Nine Princes in Amber*, 1970

2889

DAVID MARTIN

Bring Me Children

(New York: Random House, 1992)

Story type: Horror (Child-in-Peril)
Major character(s): John Lyon, Television Personality (news anchor), Journalist; Mason Quindell, Doctor; Claire Cept, Professor (of American Folklore)
Time period(s): 1990s (1992)
Locale(s): Hamelin, West Virginia

Summary: John Lyon oversteps the bounds of journalistic propriety when his obsessive interest in child abuse leads him to the estate of Mason Quindell, a physician whose own interest in children not only stretches the boundaries of clinical practice but runs to the near-satanic.

Other books you might like:
John Arbucci, *Blood of Innocents*, 1991
Eric Flanders, *The Forever Children*, 1992
John Saul, *Darkness*, 1991

2890

DAVID MARTIN

Lie to Me

(New York: Random House, 1990)

Story type: Horror (Psychological Suspense)
Major character(s): Mary Gaetan, Housewife; Teddy Camel, Police Officer; Philip Gaetan, Prisoner (recently released)
Time period(s): 1990s (1990)
Locale(s): Washington, District of Columbia

Summary: The gruesome death of wealthy contractor Jonathan Gaetan appears to have been the work of a psychopath, but Gaetan's wife and secretary maintain that the wounds were self-inflicted. As veteran cop Teddy Camel searches for a murderer and a motive, he becomes more and more convinced that Gaetan's family and associates are deliberately trying to hide something about Gaetan's past.

Other books you might like:
Whitley Strieber, *Billy*, 1990
T.M. Wright, *The Place*, 1989

2891

DAVID MARTIN

Tap, Tap

(New York: Random House, 1995)

Story type: Horror (Mystery)
Major character(s): Roscoe Bird, Teacher; Peter Tummelier, Wealthy, Friend (of Roscoe); Marianne Bird, Student— College (graduate student), Spouse (Roscoe's wife)
Time period(s): 1990s (1995)
Locale(s): Washington, District of Columbia

Summary: In this tale charged with hints of homoeroticism, Roscoe Bird discovers that the return of his old school friend Peter Tummelier coincides with the vampire-like deaths of Roscoe's worst enemies. In order to solve the mystery of Peter's role in the murders, Roscoe must confront ghosts from his past, including the suicide of his father which traumatized him emotionally and psychologically as a youth. British edition, 1994, titled *Love Me to Death*.

Other books you might like:
Giles Blunt, *Cold Eye*, 1989
Dennis Etchison, *California Gothic*, 1995
Rick Hautala, *Cold Whisper*, 1991
Thomas Tryon, *The Other*, 1972

2892

GEORGE R.R. MARTIN
MELINDA M. SNODGRASS, Co-Author

Ace in the Hole

(New York: Bantam Spectra, 1990)

Story type: Science Fiction (Alternate Universe)
Series: Wild Cards

Major character(s): Gregg Hartmann, Political Figure (senator), Genetically Altered Being; Doctor Tachyon, Alien, Doctor
Time period(s): 1980s (1988)
Locale(s): New York, New York

Summary: When Dr. Tachyon released the mutagenic Wild Card virus over New York, the repercussions were numerous and widespread. The human species now includes a distressingly large number of super-heroes called Aces and super-villains called Jokers. Gregg Hartmann, an undeclared victim of the virus is a Joker called Puppetman, who wants to be an evil President of the United States, getting Aces more involved in politics than they desire. This braided novel, a form of shared-world anthology, was written by Stephen Leigh, Victor Milan, Walter Simons, Melinda M. Snodgrass and Walter Jon Williams.

Other books you might like:
Robert N. Charrette, *Shadowrun: Never Deal with a Dragon*, 1990
Harlan Ellison, *Medea: Harlan's World*, 1985
Frank Herbert, *The White Plague*, 1982

2893

GEORGE R.R. MARTIN

Black Trump

(New York: Baen, 1995)

Story type: Science Fiction (Alternate Universe; Psychic Powers)
Series: Wild Cards
Major character(s): Mark "Captain Trips" Meadows, Genetically Altered Being, Scientist (biochemist); Croyd "The Sleeper" Crenson, Genetically Altered Being
Time period(s): 1990s
Locale(s): Jokertown, New York (New York City); Jerusalem, Israel; Vietnam (Free Peoples State of Vietnam)

Summary: When a joker and a reporter team up to expose the Card Shark conspiracy, the Sharks implement a terrible biological weapon, the Black Trump, which will kill all people with the wild card virus, both aces and jokers. A mosaic novel written by Stephen Leigh, George R.R. Martin, Victor Milan, John J. Miller, and Sage Walker.

Other books you might like:
Michael Bishop, *Count Geiger's Blues*, 1992
Frank Herbert, *The White Plague*, 1982
Michael Kandel, *Captain Jack Zodiac*, 1992
Victor Milan, *Turn of the Cards*, 1993
Melinda M. Snodgrass, *Double Solitaire*, 1992

2894

GEORGE R.R. MARTIN, Editor
MELINDA M. SNODGRASS, Co-Editor

Dealer's Choice

(New York: Bantam Spectra, 1992)

Story type: Science Fiction (Alternate Universe; Anthology)
Series: Wild Cards

Major character(s): Wyungare, Shaman; Bloat, Genetically Altered Being (joker), Ruler (governor of the Rox); The Great and Powerful Turtle, Hero
Time period(s): 1990s (September 21-23, 1990)
Locale(s): Ellis Island, New York (the Rox)

Summary: This braided novel written by Stephen Leigh, Edward W. Bryant, John J. Miller, Walter Jon Williams and George R. R. Martin continues the saga of the war between the Nats and the Jokers on the Rox, with an ultimate solution finally in the offing. Concludes with a two-page closing credits and a one-page "about the contributors."

Other books you might like:
C.J. Cherryh, *Angel with the Sword*, 1985
C.J. Cherryh, *Festival Moon*, 1987
  editor
Harlan Ellison, *Medea: Harlan's World*, 1985
  editor
Philip Jose Farmer, *Doc Savage: His Apocalyptic Life*, 1973
Philip Jose Farmer, *Tarzan Alive*, 1972
Will Shetterly, *Liavek*, 1985
  Emma Bull, co-editor
Terri Windling, *Life on the Border*, 1991
  editor

2895

GEORGE R.R. MARTIN

Dying of the Light

(New York: Baen Books, 1990)

Story type: Science Fiction (Romance)
Major character(s): Dirk T'Larien, Scientist, Wanderer; Gwen Delvano, Scientist
Time period(s): Indeterminate Future
Locale(s): Worlorn, Planet—Imaginary

Summary: Responding to a call for aid from Gwen, his lover of many years before, Dirk T'Larien travels to the distant and primitive world of Worlorn. There he finds himself caught up in a web of violence and intrigue, expected to follow traditions and participate in rituals of which he has very little understanding. Originally published in 1977.

Other books you might like:
Dan Simmons, *Hyperion*, 1989
James Tiptree Jr., *Brightness Falls From the Air*, 1985
James Tiptree Jr., *Crown of Stars*, 1988
James Tiptree Jr., *Up the Walls of the World*, 1978
Joan D. Vinge, *Catspaw*, 1988
Joan D. Vinge, *The Snow Queen*, 1980

2896

GEORGE R.R. MARTIN

A Game of Thrones

(New York: Bantam Spectra, 1996)

Story type: Fantasy (Adventure; Political)
Series: Song of Ice and Fire

Major character(s): Eddard Stark, Nobleman; Lady Catelyn, Noblewoman; Tyrion Lannister, Bastard Son, Handicapped (dwarf)
Time period(s): Indeterminate
Locale(s): Seven Kingdoms, Fictional Country

Summary: In a medieval society plagued with seasons of extraordinary length, seven families plot to acquire the throne. For protection, Eddard Stark gives each of his children a direwolf pup to raise. When the king's advisor dies, Stark reluctantly joins the king as replacement Hand, hoping to alert the king to the scheming which threatens his rule and the stability of the Seven Kingdoms. Contains a 19-page appendix of dramatis personae and family background.

Other books you might like:
Lynn Flewelling, *Luck in the Shadows*, 1996
Robin Hobb, *Assassin's Apprentice*, 1995
J.V. Jones, *The Baker's Boy*, 1995
Melanie Rawn, *Dragon Prince*, 1988
Martha Wells, *The Element of Fire*, 1993
Roger Zelazny, *Nine Princes in Amber*, 1970

2897

GEORGE R.R. MARTIN, Editor

Jokertown Shuffle
(New York: Bantam Spectra, 1991)

Story type: Science Fiction (Alternate Universe)
Series: Wild Cards
Major character(s): Doctor Tachyon, Alien, Doctor; Bloat, Genetically Altered Being (joker), Ruler (governor of the Rox)
Time period(s): 1990s
Locale(s): New York, New York

Summary: As Governor of the Rox, Bloat is the final arbiter of the law. His position is secure, if uncomfortable, because the wall which protects the Rox from the authorities in Manhattan would disappear without him. Blaise, evil relative of Dr. Tachyon, would like to control Bloat, but has been unsuccessful so far. This braided novel, a form of shared-world anthology, was written by Steven Leigh, John J. Miller, Melinda M. Snodgrass, Victor Milan, Walter Jon Williams, Lewis Shiner, and Walter Simons.

Other books you might like:
C.J. Cherryh, *Angel with the Sword*, 1985
C.J. Cherryh, *Festival Moon*, 1987
    editor
Harlan Ellison, *Medea: Harlan's World*, 1985
    editor
C.S. Friedman, *Black Sun Rising*, 1991
Janet Kagan, *Mirabile*, 1991
Will Shetterly, *Liavek*, 1985
    Emma Bull, co-editor
Terri Windling, *Life on the Border*, 1991
    editor

2898

GEORGE R.R. MARTIN, Editor

Marked Cards
(New York: Baen, 1994)

Story type: Science Fiction (Alternate Universe; Psychic Powers)
Series: Wild Cards
Major character(s): Gregg Hartmann, Political Figure (ex-senator), Genetically Altered Being; Croyd "The Sleeper" Crenson, Genetically Altered Being; Hannah Davis, Journalist
Time period(s): 1990s
Locale(s): United States; Vietnam

Summary: When research uncovers a conspiracy, Hannah Davis and a few people affected by the Wild Card virus attempt to stop the plot to destroy all evidence of the virus and those infected by it.

Other books you might like:
Michael Bishop, *Count Geiger's Blues*, 1992
Harlan Ellison, *Medea: Harlan's World*, 1985
    editor
Michael Kandel, *Captain Jack Zodiac*, 1992
Victor Milan, *Turn of the Cards*, 1993
Melinda M. Snodgrass, *Double Solitaire*, 1992

2899

GEORGE R.R. MARTIN

Portraits of His Children
(New York: Baen, 1992)

Story type: Science Fiction (Collection)

Summary: From surrealism to more traditional topics such as time travel, Martin presents a broad range of themes varying in tone from humor and irony to madness and violence. This collection of 11 stories published in periodicals and anthologies 1972-1986 includes "With Morning Comes Mistfall," "the Ice Dragon," "Unsound Variations," a Nebula Award winning story, "Portraits of His Children" and a five-page introduction by Roger Zelazny titled "A Sketch of Their Father." Reprint of a 1987 edition.

Other books you might like:
J.G. Ballard, *War Fever*, 1991
Groff Conklin, *The Best of Science Fiction*, 1946
    editor
Larry Niven, *Playgrounds of the Mind*, 1991
Michael Swanwick, *Gravity's Angels*, 1991
Harry Turtledove, *Earthgrip*, 1991
Lawrence Watt-Evans, *Crosstime Traffic*, 1992
John Varley, *Blue Champagne*, 1986
Roger Zelazny, *Gone to Earth*, 1991

2900

MARK O. MARTIN
GREGORY BENFORD, Co-Author

A Darker Geometry
(New York: Baen, 1996)

Story type: Science Fiction (Military; First Contact)
Series: Man-Kzin Wars
Major character(s): Carol Faulk, Spaceship Captain, Military Personnel; Brund Takagama, Military Personnel, Spaceman; Prowl Captain, Alien (Kzin), Spaceship Captain
Time period(s): Indeterminate Future
Locale(s): Outer Space; Interstellar Empire/Federation; *Sun-Tzu*, Spaceship

Summary: Designed to attack Kzin near Alpha Centauri, *Sun-Tzu* does not possess adequate defenses when Kzin attack unexpectedly on the way there. A visit from a puppeteer ship quickly changes the situation, as does an appearance of the mysterious Outsiders.

Other books you might like:
Poul Anderson, *Inconstant Star*, 1991
Dean Ing, *Cathouse*, 1991
Larry Niven, *Man-Kzin Wars*, 1988
 editor
Larry Niven, *Man-Kzin Wars II-VII*, 1989-1995
 editor
Jerry Pournelle, *The Children's Hour*, 1991
 S.M. Stirling, co-author

2901

THOMAS K. MARTIN

A Call to Arms
(New York: Ace, 1995)

Story type: Fantasy (Alternate World; Magic Conflict)
Series: Dreamer
Major character(s): Steve Wilkinson, Student; Jared, Mythical Creature (Druid lord); Erelvar, Nobleman, Religious
Time period(s): 1990s (1995); Indeterminate
Locale(s): Delgroth, Fictional City

Summary: After the Dreamer dies, Morvanor quickly falls to Daryna's troops and their modern weapons. When the Dreamer defies death, his return causes the destruction of the Mistress. Subsequent infighting among her generals may buy the beleaguered kings enough time to stop the destruction.

Other books you might like:
Brian Daley, *The Doomfarers of Coramonde*, 1977
L. Sprague de Camp, *The Complete Compleat Enchanter*, 1989
 Fletcher Pratt, co-author
Barbara Hambly, *The Time of the Dark*, 1982
Guy Gavriel Kay, *The Summer Tree*, 1985
Andre Norton, *Witch World*, 1963

2902

THOMAS K. MARTIN

A Two-Edged Sword
(New York: Ace, 1994)

Story type: Fantasy (Alternate World; Magic Conflict)
Major character(s): Steve Wilkinson, Student—College, Researcher (sleep); Erelvar, Nobleman (Lord of Quarin), Religious; Belevairn, Wizard, Mythical Creature (Dread Lord)
Time period(s): 1990s (1994); Indeterminate
Locale(s): New York, New York; Quarin, Fictional City

Summary: Pulled from our world into one of fantasy in the middle of a magic war, Steve Wilkinson must learn a great deal to survive. As the key to the conflict, he could unknowingly win the day for either side. First novel.

Other books you might like:
Glen Cook, *The Black Company*, 1984
Brian Daley, *The Doomfarers of Coramonde*, 1977
Barbara Hambly, *The Time of the Dark*, 1982
Guy Gavriel Kay, *The Summer Tree*, 1985
Patricia A. McKillip, *The Riddle-Master of Hed*, 1976

2903

VALERIE MARTIN

Mary Reilly
(New York: Doubleday, 1990)

Story type: Horror (Psychological Suspense)
Major character(s): Mary Reilly, Servant; Henry Jekyll, Doctor (Scientific experimenter)
Time period(s): 19th century (Victorian England)
Locale(s): London, England

Summary: A retelling of the Jekyll and Hyde story from the maid's point of view with the focus not on the disintegration of her "dear Master" Jekyll nor on the machinations of his "assistant," Edward Hyde, but on the psychology of the spunky, resourceful, ultimately tragic Mary Reilly.

Other books you might like:
Robert Louis Stevenson, *The Strange Case of Dr. Jekyll and Mr. Hyde*, 1886

2904

T. CHRIS MARTINDALE

Demon Dance
(New York: Pocket, 1991)

Story type: Horror (Apocalyptic Horror)
Major character(s): Wilhemina "Willie" Ducane, Child; Tolman Shaddock, Gunfighter; Clancy "Kolo" Atwood, Indian (half-breed)
Time period(s): 1890s (1890)
Locale(s): Barlow, Nebraska

Summary: When the vengeful Indian medicine-woman Dee-Bo-Ha attempts to hasten the Ghost Dance, which will supposedly restore the true Indian nation in America, it is left to a band of settlers and Indians to try and avert the apocalypse the Ghost Dance ceremony portends.

Other books you might like:
Morgan Fields, *Shaman Woods*, 1990
Charles L. Grant, *The Nestling*, 1982
Kathryn Ptacek, *Ghost Dance*, 1990
Chet Williamson, *Dreamthorp*, 1989

2905
T. CHRIS MARTINDALE

Nightblood
(New York: Warner, 1990)

Story type: Horror (Vampire Story)
Major character(s): Chris Stiles, Veteran (Vietnam vet); Alex Stiles, Vampire (Chris' deceased brother)
Time period(s): 1990s
Locale(s): Isherwood, Indiana

Summary: Seeking ''payback'' for the death of his dead—but still active—brother, Chris settles in a small Indiana town where he encounters a master vampire and his crew.

Other books you might like:
Paul F. Olson, *Night Prophets*, 1989

2906
T. CHRIS MARTINDALE

The Voice in the Basement
(New York: Pocket, 1993)

Story type: Horror (Haunted House)
Major character(s): Cathy Ballard, Professor; Mitch Ballard, Unemployed (Cathy's husband); Larry Ackerman, Professor
Time period(s): 1990s (1993)
Locale(s): Harrodsburg, Indiana

Summary: Shortly after moving into their new home, Cathy and Mitch Ballard are plagued by apparitions and noises emanating from their basement. They discover that their home is a gateway to evil forces in the afterlife, and that the only way to prevent those forces from breaking through is to make contact with the apparition of a young boy who opened the gateway by escaping into this world.

Other books you might like:
Pat Franklin, *Dark Dreaming*, 1991
Richard Matheson, *Hell House*, 1971
Al Sarrantonio, *House Haunted*, 1991
T.M. Wright, *Little Boy Lost*, 1992
T.M. Wright, *The School*, 1990

2907
T. CHRIS MARTINDALE

Where the Chill Waits
(New York: Warner, 1990)

Story type: Horror (Ancient Evil Unleashed)
Major character(s): Elton Tucker, Businessman; Steve Wilhoit, Businessman; Andy Church, Foreman
Time period(s): 1990s (1991)
Locale(s): Atikokan, Ontario, Canada

Summary: Three employees of Tucker Pharmaceutical accept their boss's invitation to go deer hunting in a remote area near Thunder Bay in the wilds of Canada. Accompanied by their Inidan guide, Barton Davejac, and his two elkhounds, the four men set off for the base camp at Chalako Lakes. During the trip, office politics and back-stabbing give way to cannibalism, terror, and murder when the men come under the sway of the windigo, an ancient supernatural demon, a gigantic cannibal spirit whose icy touch can transform humans into monsters—the fate that awaits the sole survivors of the trip.

Other books you might like:
Algernon Blackwood, *Best Ghost Stories of Algernon Blackwood*, 1973
Stephen King, *Pet Sematary*, 1983
Graham Masterton, *The Manitou*, 1975
Graham Masterton, *Revenge of the Manitou*, 1979
David Morrell, *Testament*, 1974

2908
ADRIENNE MARTINE-BARNES

The Rainbow Sword
(New York: Avon, 1988)

Story type: Fantasy (Quest)
Time period(s): 1980s
Locale(s): Earth

Summary: A man who battles supernatural beings that enter this world searches for a sword to help him.

Other books you might like:
Gael Baudino, *Dragonsword*, 1988
Stephen R. Donaldson, *The Mirror of Her Dreams*, 1986
Eric Van Lustbader, *The Sunset Warrior*, 1989
Paul Edwin Zimmer, *Blood of the Colyn Muir*, 1988

2909
ROBERT MASELLO

Private Demons
(New York: Jove, 1992)

Story type: Horror (Occult)
Major character(s): Lucien Calais, Businessman; Hallie Patton, Model; Sister Celeste, Religious (Catholic nun)
Time period(s): 1990s (1992)
Locale(s): New York, New York; Bangkok, Thailand

Summary: Lucien Calais becomes a millionaire after selling his soul to the serpent god Kaliya in order to recover the wealth seized from his family by the Khmer Rouge of Cambodia. When his empire begins to fall apart under the onslaught of occult forces, he must discover why it is that powers once in league with him have turned upon him.

Other books you might like:
Thomas M. Disch, *The Businessman: A Tale of Terror*, 1984

2910
LISA MASON

Arachne
(New York: William Morrow, 1990)

Story type: Science Fiction (Cyberpunk; Robot Fiction)
Major character(s): Carly Nolan, Lawyer; Probe Spinner, Robot, Revolutionary; D. Wolfe, Lawyer
Time period(s): 21st century
Locale(s): San Francisco, California

Summary: When Carly's telelink fails during her first appearance in computer-generated court, Carly must find a remedy if her career is to advance. One option available from Wolfe is the illegal drug, cram, a telelink performance enhancer. Another option involves allowing a delicate psychic surgery aimed at releasing untapped potential. Carly must decide which option will best promote her career and what price she will pay. This book is the author's first novel.

Other books you might like:
David Brin, *Earth*, 1990
Pat Cadigan, *Synners*, 1991
Pat Cadigan, *Mindplayers*, 1987
Jeffrey A. Carver, *The Rapture Effect*, 1987
William Gibson, *Neuromancer*, 1984

2911
LISA MASON

Cyberweb
(New York: AvoNova, 1995)

Story type: Science Fiction (Cyberpunk; Alternate Intelligence)
Major character(s): Carly Nolan, Computer Expert, Fugitive; Pr. Spinner, Artificial Intelligence, Computer Expert (perimeter prober); Ouija, Shaman
Time period(s): 21st century
Locale(s): San Francisco, California; Telespace, Cyberspace (computer virtual reality)

Summary: On the run from authorities and mainframe artificial intelligences, Carly Nolan finds life even more complicated when technophobic "aboriginals" kidnap her for Patina, a sophisticated robot covertly fronting for a mysterious mainframe AI, Cognatus. Carly reluctantly agrees to act as telelinker for Cognatus but remains mindful of the AI's lust for her metaprogramming, the unique archetype, Arachne. Sequel to *Arachne*.

Other books you might like:
Alexander Besher, *Rim: A Novel of Virtual Reality*, 1994

Bruce Bethke, *Headcrash*, 1995
Michael Flynn, *In the Country of the Blind*, 1990
Neal Stephenson, *Snow Crash*, 1992
John Varley, *Steel Beach*, 1992

2912
LISA MASON

The Golden Nineties
(New York: Bantam Spectra, 1995)

Story type: Science Fiction (Time Travel)
Major character(s): Zhu Wong, Time Traveller, Revolutionary; Daniel J. Watkins, Gentleman, Alcoholic; Jessie Malone, Madam, Alcoholic
Time period(s): 1890s (1895-1896)
Locale(s): San Francisco, California

Summary: Facing a murder conviction, Zhu Wong agrees to t-port 600 years into the past, to San Francisco in the 1890s, where she must befriend a Chinese girl bearing an unusual piece of jewelry called the "Aurelia." Loosely related to *Summer of Love*.

Other books you might like:
L. Sprague de Camp, *Lest Darkness Fall*, 1941
Lisa Goldstein, *The Dream Years*, 1985
Robert A. Heinlein, *The Door into Summer*, 1957
Robert A. Heinlein, *Time Enough for Love*, 1973
Mercedes Lackey, *The Fire Rose*, 1995
Walter Jon Williams, *Days of Atonement*, 1991

2913
LISA MASON

Summer of Love
(New York: Bantam Spectra, 1994)

Story type: Science Fiction (Time Travel)
Major character(s): Susan "Starbright" Stein, Teenager, Runaway (flower child); Chiron Cat's Eye in Draco, Time Traveller
Time period(s): 1960s (June-September, 1967)
Locale(s): San Francisco, California

Summary: Chiron Cat's Eye in Draco travels back in time to Haight-Ashbury to find the flower child whose fate affects future generations.

Other books you might like:
Chester Anderson, *The Butterfly Kid*, 1967
Mick Farren, *The Texts of Festival*, 1975
George R.R. Martin, *The Armageddon Rag*, 1983
Robert Rankin, *Armageddon: The Musical*, 1990
Lewis Shiner, *Glimpses*, 1993

2914
ROBERT MASON
Solo
(New York: Putnam, 1992)

Story type: Science Fiction (Alternate Intelligence; Techno-Thriller)

Major character(s): Solo, Artificial Intelligence, Robot; Nimrod, Robot, Military Personnel (assassin); Daniel Sawyer, Military Personnel (colonel)

Time period(s): 21st century

Locale(s): Nicaragua; New York, New York

Summary: Having escaped its handlers and destruction, Solo finds friends and establishes contact with hundreds of satellites and computer networks, discovering Electron Dynamics cruelly programming a duplicate of itself. Solo resolves to contact Nimrod while Colonel Sawyer orders Nimrod to kill Solo. Sequel to *Weapon*.

Other books you might like:

Robert Cain, *Cybernarc*, 1991
Stephen Goldin, *Jade Darcy and the Affair of Honor*, 1988
  Mary Mason, co-author
Stephen Goldin, *Jade Darcy and the Zen Pirates*, 1990
  Mary Mason, co-author
Ed Naha, *Robocop*, 1987
Charles Sheffield, *The Nimrod Hunt*, 1986
Ben Sloane, *Ultimate Weapon*, 1991
Thomas T. Thomas, *ME: A Novel of Self Discovery*, 1991

2915
ROBERT MASON
Weapon
(New York: Putnam, 1989)

Story type: Science Fiction (Techno-Thriller)

Major character(s): Solo, Artificial Intelligence, Robot; Bill Stewart, Engineer (Computer engineer)

Time period(s): 21st century

Locale(s): Central America

Summary: Solo, a robot created to be the ultimate killing machine and destined to work for the American intelligence community, refuses to kill on command and then goes AWOL in the jungles of Central America. A picked CIA team is sent into the jungle to bring the robot back at any cost.

Other books you might like:

Isaac Asimov, *Robot Dreams*, 1986
Jerry Pournelle, *Prince of Mercenaries*, 1989
Lucius Shepard, *Life During Wartime*, 1987

2916
ELIZABETH MASSIE
Shadow Dreams
(Seattle, Washington: Silver Salamander Press, 1996)

Story type: Horror (Collection)

Summary: The 14 stories gathered in this second collection feature mostly nonsupernatural horrors that befall characters living quiet lives of desperation on the fringe of existence. "Snowy Day" and "What Happened When Mosby Paulsen Had Her Painting Reproduced on the Cover of the Phone Book" are concerned with psychic damage in emotionally abused children, and "No Solicitors, Curious a Quarter" with the extreme measures a woman takes to support her family by exploiting the public's fascination with the gruesome. In "Dibs," a schoolgirl prank leads to a horrifying revenge decades later, and in "Meat," an animal rights activist's principles are put to the ultimate test. Gary Braunbeck supplies an introduction.

Other books you might like:

Michael A. Arnzen, *Needles and Sins*, 1993
Poppy Z. Brite, *Swamp Foetus*, 1993
S. Darnbrook Colson, *People of the Night*, 1994
Brian Hodge, *The Convulsion Factory*, 1996
Brian Hopkins, *Something Haunts Us All*, 1995
Sue Storm, *Star Bones Weep the Blood of Angels*, 1995

2917
ELIZABETH MASSIE
Sineater
(New York: Carroll & Graf, 1994)

Story type: Horror (Wild Talents)

Major character(s): Joel Barker, Child; Burke, Child; Benton Hodge, Store Owner (hardware store)

Time period(s): 1990s (1992)

Locale(s): Beacon Cove, Virginia

Summary: A series of crimes in the backwoods of Virginia leads residents to suspect that their neighborhood sineater—a man who eats food over the bodies of the dead and thereby consumes their sins—has been driven mad by his work and is now spewing back all the evil he has absorbed from them.

Other books you might like:

John Byrne, *Whipping Boy*, 1992
Ramsey Campbell, *The Long Lost*, 1993
Bentley Little, *The Revelation*, 1990

2918
ELIZABETH MASSIE
H.E. FASSL, Illustrator
Southern Discomfort: Selected Works of Elizabeth Massie
(Concord, California: Dark Regions Press, 1993)

Story type: Horror (Collection)

Summary: The nine stories in this book, all previously published, display their author's talent for deadpan grotesque. Several, such as "The Sick'un" and the zombie story, "Abed," explore the traditions of backwoods families for their bizarre potential, while others like "Hooked on Buzzer," "Smoothpicks," and "Whittler" are told with a chilling calmness from the point of view of psychotic characters. Yvonne Navarro has supplied an introduction.

Other books you might like:

Poppy Z. Brite, *Swamp Foetus*, 1993
Stephen Mark Rainey, *Fugue Devil and Other Weird Horrors*, 1993
Lucy Taylor, *Close to the Bone*, 1993
Lucy Taylor, *Unnatural Acts*, 1992

2919

KATHLEEN M. MASSIE-FERCH, Editor
MARTIN H. GREENBERG, Co-Editor
RICHARD GILLIAM, Co-Editor

Ancient Enchantresses
(New York: DAW, 1995)

Story type: Fantasy (Anthology)

Summary: Contains a four-page introduction by Melanie Rawn plus individual introductions to 19 original stories utilizing traditional magical lore and symbology from world culture, goddesses, gods, and symbols of natural forces in the struggle to transform will into reality. Authors include Hugh B. Cave, Tanith Lee, Andre Norton, Diana L. Paxson, Melanie Rawn, Laura Resnick, Jennifer Roberson, Susan Shwartz, Lois Tilton, Harry Turtledove, Deborah Wheeler, and Mary Frances Zambreno.

Other books you might like:

Marion Zimmer Bradley, *The Sword and Sorceress Series*, 1984-1995
　editor
Richard Gilliam, *Grails: Quests of the Dawn*, 1994
　Martin H. Greenberg, Edward E. Kramer, co-editors
Jessica Amanda Salmonson, *Amazons!*, 1979
　editor
Susan Shwartz, *Sisters in Fantasy*, 1993
　Martin H. Greenberg, co-editor
A. Susan Williams, *The Penguin Book of Modern Fantasy by Women*, 1995
　Richard Glyn Jones, co-editor

2920

GRAHAM MASTERSON

Mirror
(New York: Tor, 1989)

Story type: Horror (Alternate World)
Major character(s): Martin Williams, Writer (Screenwriter); Boofuls, Actor (Murdered child filmstar), Spirit
Time period(s): 1980s
Locale(s): Los Angeles, California

Summary: Martin Williams learns that the spirit of the ex-owner of a recently purchased mirror—a murdered child actor—is trapped within it. This leads to the revelation that the mirror is, in fact, a doorway to another world and that Satan himself plans to use it to bring endless night to the earth.

Other books you might like:

Clive Barker, *Weaveworld*, 1987
Simon Rees, *The Devil's Looking-Glass*, 1985

2921

GRAHAM MASTERTON

Burial
(New York: Tor, 1994)

Story type: Horror (Ancient Evil Unleashed; Supernatural Vengeance)
Major character(s): Harry Erskine, Psychic (medium); Karen van Hooven, Psychic; Papago Joe, Salesman
Time period(s): 1990s (1992)
Locale(s): New York, New York; Phoenix, Arizona

Summary: Twenty years after spiritualists Harry Erskine and Karen van Hooven (nee Tandy) helped exorcise the spirit of the ancient American Indian wizard Misquamacus in *The Manitou* (1974), the vengeful medicine man is back destroying entire cities and wreaking general havoc in his effort to obliterate the white man and return the world to his Native American brothers. Harry finds the only way to lay Misquamacus's spirit to rest this time is to travel to the Happy Hunting Grounds and bargain with the spirits who have endowed the Indian with his awesome powers. This book was originally published in England in 1992.

Other books you might like:

Adam Niswander, *The Charm*, 1993
Eugene E. Pfaff Jr., *Uwharrie*, 1993
　Michael Causey, co-author
Kathryn Ptacek, *Ghost Dance*, 1990
Patrick Whalen, *Deathwalker*, 1992

2922

GRAHAM MASTERTON

The Burning
(New York: Tor, 1991)

Story type: Horror (Occult)
Major character(s): Lloyd Denman, Restaurateur; Otto Mander, Occultist; Waldo Slonimsky, Worker (restaurant)
Time period(s): 1990s
Locale(s): San Diego, California

Summary: Lloyd Denman's investigation into the self-immolation of his musician girlfriend Celia uncovers the underhanded dealings of ex-Nazi Otto Mander, an occultist who hopes to use the mystic secrets encoded in a lost piece of music by Richard Wagner and the self-sacrifice of numerous acolytes to placate the demon he serves and bring about a Fourth Reich in Southern California.

Other books you might like:

Ira Levin, *The Boys From Brazil*, 1976
Robert Weinberg, *The Armageddon Box*, 1990
Dennis Wheatley, *They Used Dark Forces*, 1964

2923

GRAHAM MASTERTON

Flights of Fear

(New York: Severn House, 1996)

Story type: Horror (Collection)

Summary: These 14 stories, presented by the author as flights on a travel itinerary, are all collected from horror anthologies that appeared in the last half decade. "Absence of Beast," "The Gray Madonna" and "J.R.E. Ponsford" are subtle ghost stories with atmospheric chills. "The Bridal Suite," "Sex Object," and "The Jajouka Scarab" are some of the author's more typically lurid erotic horror tales. "Voodoo Child" features Jimi Hendrix, and "Will" William Shakespeare, both of whom are revealed to have struck satanic (or worse) bargains for their talents. This book was originally published in England in 1995.

Other books you might like:
Poppy Z. Brite, *Swamp Foetus*, 1993
Nancy A. Collins, *Nameless Sins*, 1995
John Farris, *Scare Tactics*, 1988
Christopher Fowler, *Flesh Wounds*, 1996
Brian Lumley, *The Second Wish and Other Exhalations*, 1995

2924

GRAHAM MASTERTON

Fortnight of Fear

(New York: Severn House, 1994)

Story type: Horror (Collection)

Summary: This first collection by an author known for his often graphic approach to horror fiction gathers together 14 stories originally published over the last decade. Among them are "Hurry Monster," about a man's lifelong fear of an imaginary monster; "Beijing Craps," about the peculiar stakes a jaded gambler decides to play for; "The Woman in the Wall," a variant on the haunted house theme; "Laird of Dunain," about the unusual lengths an artist goes to to get the flesh tones of her paints correct; "Making Belinda," a re-working of the classic horror story, "The Monkey's Paw"; "Heart of Stone" and "Pig's Dinner," both tales of supernatural vengeance; "The Sixth Man," which proposes the horrors that decimated Robert Scott's expedition to the Antarctic; and the infamous "Eric the Pie," the twisted tale of a man's eating habits deemed so objectionable when it first appeared that the magazine in which it was published was confiscated and ultimately scuttled.

Other books you might like:
Clive Barker, *Books of Blood Series*, 1984-1985
Christopher Fowler, *Sharper Knives*, 1992
Richard Laymon, *A Good, Secret Place*, 1993
Richard Laymon, *Out Are the Lights*, 1986

2925

GRAHAM MASTERTON

The House That Jack Built

(New York: Caroll & Graf, 1996)

Story type: Horror (Occult)
Major character(s): Craig Bellman, Lawyer; Effie Bellman, Spouse; Pepper Moriarity, Store Owner
Time period(s): 1990s (1996)
Locale(s): Cold Spring, New York

Summary: While recovering from a brutal mugging, high-powered lawyer Craig Bellman discovers the abandoned baronial mansion Valhalla, built on the banks of the Hudson River by evil textile magnate Jack Belias. Craig finds himself strongly attracted to it, and when its restoration has a deleterious effect on his personality, his wife Effie begins to suspect that Belias is trying to engineer a return through her husband.

Other books you might like:
Jonathan Aycliffe, *Naomi's Room*, 1991
Poppy Z. Brite, *Drawing Blood*, 1993
Stephen King, *The Shining*, 1977
H.P. Lovecraft, *The Case of Charles Dexter Ward*, 1971
Tamara Thorne, *Haunted*, 1995

2926

GRAHAM MASTERTON

Master of Lies

(New York: Tor, 1992)

Story type: Horror (Occult)
Major character(s): Larry Foggia, Detective—Police; Arne Knudsen, Police Officer; Mr. Mandrax, Occultist
Time period(s): 1990s
Locale(s): San Francisco, California

Summary: Under the moniker "The Fog City Satan," a serial killer prowls the streets of San Francisco, sadistically torturing and murdering victims as part of his arcane occult rituals. When detective Larry Foggia is assigned to the case, he uncovers a plot to resurrect Belial, first of the fallen angels, and a secret underground of occultists that include his friends and perhaps even members of his family.

Other books you might like:
Cleve Cartmill, *Prelude to Armageddon*, 1942
    magzaine publication only
Al Sarrantonio, *October*, 1990

2927

GRAHAM MASTERTON

Walkers

(New York: Tor, 1989)

Story type: Horror (Haunted House)
Major character(s): Jack Reed, Businessman (Would-be commercial developer); Quintus Miller, Genius (lunatic), Occultist
Time period(s): 1980s

Locale(s): Wisconsin

Summary: Jack Reed buys The Oaks, a former insane asylum, to be developed into a country club, not knowing that the spirits of its former criminally insane inmates, led by a mad occultist, are trapped within its walls. When his young son is dragged into the walls, Reed must seek out an old priest and learn the dark secrets that will either enable him to rescue his son or release the trapped madmen on the world.

Other books you might like:
John Farris, *Wildwood*, 1987

2928

RICHARD MATHESON

7 Steps to Midnight
(New York: Tor, 1993)

Story type: Horror (Mystery)
Major character(s): Chris Barton, Scientist (mathematician); Albert Veering, Psychologist; Alexsandra Caludius, Spy
Time period(s): 1990s (1993)
Locale(s): London, England; Venice, Italy

Summary: In the middle of his work on a project involving defense lasers, Chris Barton finds that another man has assumed his identity, that he can get no one to believe he is really Chris Barton, that he is being chased across the globe by espionage agents who want information from him, and that the fabric of reality itself is beginning to fray.

Other books you might like:
Umberto Eco, *Foucault's Pendulum*, 1990
Theodore Roszak, *Flicker*, 1991
Peter Straub, *Koko*, 1988

2929

RICHARD MATHESON

Collected Stories
(Los Angeles: Dream/Press, 1989)

Story type: Horror (Collection)

Summary: Eighty-six stories written between 1950 and 1970. Mixing science fiction and horror, Matheson describes the "paranoid landscape" of the modern world with deft characterization, brilliant plot twists, and a wicked, ironical sense of humor.

Other books you might like:
Charles Beaumont, *Selected Stories*, 1988
Robert Bloch, *The Selected Stories of Robert Bloch*, 1987
Ray Bradbury, *The Stories of Ray Bradbury*, 1980
Fritz Leiber, *The Best of Fritz Leiber*, 1974
William F. Nolan, *Things Beyond Midnight*, 1984

2930

RICHARD MATHESON

Earthbound
(New York: Tor, 1994)

Story type: Horror (Ghost Story)
Major character(s): David Cooper, Writer; Ellen Cooper, Spouse; Grace Brentwood, Aged Person
Time period(s): 1980s (1981)
Locale(s): Long Island, New York (Logan Beach)

Summary: David and Ellen Cooper return to Logan Beach, the site of their honeymoon, to prop up their sagging marriage. In their vacation home David becomes obsessed with Marianna, the spirit of a dead woman who has driven other men insane and who plays upon the tensions in David and Ellen's marriage in order to win David over and satisfy the sexual lust that keeps her earthbound. This book was originally published in 1982 in a severely edited form under the pseudonym Logan Swanson.

Other books you might like:
Shirley Jackson, *The Haunting of Hill House*, 1961
Al Sarrantonio, *House Haunted*, 1989
Bernard Taylor, *Sweetheart, Sweetheart*, 1977
Chet Williamson, *Soulstorm*, 1986

2931

RICHARD MATHESON

Hell House
(Springfield, Pennsylvania: Gauntlet Press, 1996)

Story type: Horror (Haunted House; Occult)
Major character(s): Lionel Barrett, Paranormal Investigator; Florence Tanner, Psychic (medium); Benjamin Franklin Fischer, Psychic
Time period(s): 1970s (1970)
Locale(s): Matawaskie Valley, Maine

Summary: A group of psychic investigators take up residence in the former home of Emeric Belasco, dubbed "Hell House" because of the vile satanic practices that Belasco indulged in there. The last expedition to the home ended in disaster and death 30 years before, but the current group hopes to exorcise the home through modern scientific means. This novel was first published in 1971. The 25th anniversary edition was produced as a signed limited edition hardcover with an introduction by the author.

Other books you might like:
Tom Elliott, *The Dwelling*, 1988
Shirley Jackson, *The Haunting of Hill House*, 1959
Al Sarrantonio, *House Haunted*, 1991
Chet Williamson, *Soulstorm*, 1986

2932

RICHARD MATHESON

I Am Legend

(New York: Tor, 1995)

Story type: Horror (Collection)

Summary: A novel and 10 short stories, one of them previously uncollected, showcase the talents of a major force in fantasy and horror whose fiction in the 1950s and 1960s captured the undercurrent of paranoia in America. *I Am Legend* is a landmark vampire novel, in which the last mortal to survive a plague that has turned everyone else in the world into vampires, fights a daily battle for survival and begins to resemble, in his rapaciousness, the very creatures he fights. The book also includes another vampire tale, "Dress of White Silk"; a story of zombies in a post-nuclear future, "Dance of the Dead"; and the horror satire, "The Funeral." "From Shadowed Places" and "Prey" are standard occult menace stories, and "Mad House" and "Person to Person" tales that blur the boundary between psychological and supernatural horror.

Other books you might like:

Charles Beaumont, *Selected Stories*, 1989
Ray Bradbury, *The Stories of Ray Bradbury*, 1980
William F. Nolan, *Night Shapes: Excursions into Terror*, 1995

2933

RICHARD MATHESON

The Incredible Shrinking Man

(New York: Tor, 1995)

Story type: Horror (Collection)

Summary: The bulk of this book is taken up with the author's classic 1956 novel, *The Shrinking Man*, about a man exposed to a toxic cloud who finds himself shrinking on a daily basis down to infinitessimal size. The book is complemented by nine other stories featuring Matheson's trademark sense of paranoia. In "Nightmare at 20,000 Feet," a man riding an airplane during a storm discovers that he alone can see a gremlin perched on the wing sabotaging the engines. In "Duel," a lone driver on a desert highway is menaced by a tractor trailer. "The Distributor," "The Holiday Man," and "By Appointment Only" all suggest infernal machinations behind the major and minor annoyances of life. In the book's one previously uncollected story, "Shoofly," a man finds a metaphor for the futility of his life in his inability to kill a fly that is bothering him.

Other books you might like:

Charles Beaumont, *Selected Stories*, 1988
Ray Bradbury, *The Stories of Ray Bradbury*, 1980
Dennis Etchison, *The Dark Country*, 1982
William F. Nolan, *Night Shapes: Excursions into Terror*, 1995

2934

RICHARD MATHESON

Now You See It...

(New York: Tor, 1995)

Story type: Horror (Mystery)
Major character(s): Emil Delacorte, Magician; Maximillian Delacorte, Magician; Harry Kendal, Agent (theatrical)
Time period(s): 1980s (1980)
Locale(s): Boston, Massachusetts

Summary: This tale of illusion is narrated by Emil Delacorte, a stage magician who has been rendered a "vegetable" by a stroke. Emil's son Maximillian, also a magician, hosts a get-together at his home for his father and a group of others that includes an agent scheming with his unfaithful wife to take over Emil's magic act. Unbeknownst to them, the house is rigged for sleight-of-hand and magic tricks, making the events that occur there impossible to accept at face value.

Other books you might like:

Ray Bradbury, *A Graveyard for Lunatics*, 1990
Patrick McGrath, *The Grotesque*, 1989
Daniel Stashower, *The Adventure of the Ectoplasmic Man*, 1985
Thomas Tryon, *Night Magic*, 1995

2935

RICHARD MATHESON, Editor
RICIA MAINHARDT, Co-Editor

Robert Bloch: Appreciations of the Master

(New York: Tor, 1995)

Story type: Horror (Collection)

Summary: This book collects 20 stories and 31 tributes to Robert Bloch, author of the novel *Psycho* and a leading talent in the horror field for over 60 years, who died in 1994. The stories selected span the full range of Bloch's career, including his homages to mentor H.P. Lovecraft ("Notebook Found in a Deserted House"), his combinations of human and horror fiction ("The Cloak," "The Pied Piper Fights the Gestapo"), his crossovers from horror to crime ("Final Performance," "The Animal Fair"), his Hugo Award-winning tale of a deal with the devil ("The Hell-Bound Train"), and his studies of psychopathology ("Enoch," "I Do Not Love Thee Doctor Fell," "Your Truly Jack the Ripper"). Authors who supply tributes include Harlan Ellison, William F. Nolan, Gahan Wilson, Frederik Pohl, William Peter Blatty, Ramsey Campbell, Hugh B. Cave, Brian Lumley, and actor Christopher Lee.

Other books you might like:

Charles Beaumont, *Selected Stories*, 1988
Richard Matheson, *Collected Stories*, 1989
William F. Nolan, *The Bradbury Chronicles: Stories in Honor of Ray Bradbury*, 1992
Martin H. Greenberg, co-editor

2936

RICHARD MATHESON

Somewhere in Time/What Dreams May Come

(Los Angeles: Dream Press, 1992)

Story type: Horror (Collection)

Summary: Two love stories, each with a supernatural component. In *Somewhere in Time*, originally published in 1975 as *Bid Time Return* and winner of the World Fantasy Award for best novel that year, dying screenwriter Robert Collier's obsessive interest in a nineteenth-century stage actress allows him to step back in time 75 years to meet her. *What Dreams May Come*, originally published in 1978, tells of Chris Neilson's gradual resignation to existence in the afterlife, in a world of souls in limbo known as Summerland. Contains corrected text and a new introduction by the author.

Other books you might like:
Robert Bloch, *Screams*, 1989
Jack Finney, *Three by Finney*, 1978
Jack Finney, *Time and Again*, 1970
Fritz Leiber, *Conjure Wife/Our Lady of Darkness*, 1991

2937

RICHARD CHRISTIAN MATHESON

Created By

(New York: Bantam, 1993)

Story type: Horror (Doppelganger)
Major character(s): Alan White, Producer, Writer (television); A.E. Barek, Mercenary (television character); Jake Corea, Actor
Time period(s): 1990s (1993)
Locale(s): Hollywood, California

Summary: Alan White's ultra-violent, ultra-explicit television program "The Mercenary" makes a stunning impact on its viewing audience, who faithfully watch it every week in record numbers. When crimes that bear the signature of its lead character, A.E. Barek, begin occurring in the real world, Alan must face up to the fact that the devotion of the show's viewers has helped turn Barek, a fictional outlet for Alan's suppressed rage, into a terrifying reality.

Other books you might like:
Giles Blunt, *Cold Eye*, 1989
Michael Cadnum, *Ghostwright*, 1992
Stephen King, *The Dark Half*, 1989
John R. Maxim, *Abel/Baker/Charley*, 1983

2938

GUY DE MAUPASSANT

The Dark Side

(New York: Carroll & Graf, 1990)

Story type: Horror (Collection)

Summary: Thirty-one stories selected, translated, and introduced by Arnold Kellet, with a foreward by Ramsey Campbell. Contains all of the major dark fantasies by the French master of the short story. The most important item is "The Horla," one of the major precursors of modern horror fiction. The powerfully ambiguous story is told by a narrator who is either descending into madness or is the victim of a psychic vampire, the forerunner of a race destined to replace man. Other important stories include "On the River" and "Little Louise Roque," two exercises in the psychopathology of fear, dread, and guilt.

Other books you might like:
Arthur Conan Doyle, *The Best Horror Stories of Arthur Conan Doyle*, 1989

2939

J.G. MAXON

Lethal Delivery

(New York: Pocket, 1991)

Story type: Horror (Psychological Suspense)
Major character(s): Rod Hoover, Salesman; Tanya Roode, Office Worker; Sam Roode, Child
Time period(s): 1990s
Locale(s): New York, New York

Summary: It's bad enough that hulk Rod Hoover has lethally doctored the mail-order products sold by his company, Serious Options, to get back at the boss who stole his ideas. In his terminal steroid-induced fugue, he's also taken to terrorizing fellow employee Tanya Roode and her son Sam, in the belief that Tanya would have been his girlfriend had he gotten the respect around the office he deserved.

Other books you might like:
John Farris, *The Axman Cometh*, 1989
Stephen Gallagher, *Down River*, 1989
Robert R. McCammon, *Mine*, 1990

2940

JULIAN MAY

Blood Trillium

(New York: Bantam Spectra, 1992)

Story type: Fantasy (Magic Conflict; Quest)
Major character(s): Haramis, Sorceress (archmage), Scholar; Tolivar, Royalty (prince), Child; Orogastus/Portolanus, Sorcerer
Time period(s): Indeterminate
Locale(s): Zinora, Fictional Country; Ruwenda, Fictional Country

Summary: After 12 years the sorcerer Orogastus reappears and manages to get hold of Kadiya's third of the Sceptre, but when he gains Anigel's third by holding her husband and children hostage, a worried Haramis manages to contact the Archmage of the Sea who helps sow discord among Orogastus' followers and heal the breach between the three sisters. However, the Balance will not be restored for long as Prince

Tolivar steals Orogastus' star box and kills to keep it, even from his parents. Sequel to *Black Trillium.*

Other books you might like:
Piers Anthony, *Wielding a Red Sword*, 1986
Leigh Brackett, *People of the Talisman*, 1964
Richard Cowper, *A Dream of Kinship*, 1982
Suzette Haden Elgin, *The Grand Jubilee*, 1981
Katherine Kurtz, *The Quest for Saint Camber*, 1986
Andre Norton, *Sorceress of the Witch World*, 1968
Jack Vance, *Emphyrio*, 1969
Marion Zimmer Bradley, *Black Trillium*, 1990
    Julian May, Andre Norton, co-authors

2941

JULIAN MAY

Diamond Mask: A Novel
(New York: Knopf, 1994)

Story type: Science Fiction (Family Saga; Psychic Powers)
Series: Galactic Milieu
Major character(s): Rogatien Remillard, Psychic, Businessman (bookseller); Jon Remillard, Psychic, Mutant; Dorothea Macdonald, Psychic, Political Figure
Time period(s): 22nd century
Locale(s): Hanover, New Hampshire; Caledonia, Planet—Imaginary

Summary: The Remillard family struggles with the concept of Unity, the malicious plots of Fury and their own internal struggles, setting the stage for the final encounter with Fury and the origins of the Metapsychic Rebellion. Because of the odd chronology of the series, this book should be read after *Intervention:...*, but either before or after The Saga of Pliocene Exile series (1981-1984).

Other books you might like:
Marion Zimmer Bradley, *The Forbidden Tower*, 1977
Suzette Haden Elgin, *The Grand Jubilee*, 1981
Patricia Kennealy, *The Copper Crown*, 1985
Katherine Kurtz, *Deryni Rising*, 1970
Theodore Sturgeon, *More than Human*, 1953

2942

JULIAN MAY

Jack the Bodiless
(New York: Knopf, 1992)

Story type: Science Fiction (Family Saga; Psychic Powers)
Series: Galactic Milieu
Major character(s): Rogatien Remillard, Psychic; Jack Rogillard, Psychic; The Fury, Psychic
Time period(s): 2050s
Locale(s): Denali, Planet—Imaginary

Summary: The Rogillard family, acknowledged mental giants, have a gene for extended life. Uncle Rogi, childless himself, intervenes to protect the young minds of the family from being overwhelmed before they can develop independence and skills of their own. Recently, the Human Polity was

admitted to the Galactic Milieu, allowing the Rogillard family to extend their influence beyond Earth.

Other books you might like:
Gordon R. Dickson, *Dorsai!*, 1976
David R. Palmer, *Threshold*, 1985
David Alexander Smith, *Marathon*, 1982
Jack Vance, *The Anome*, 1973
A.E. van Vogt, *The World of Null-A*, 1948
Roger Zelazny, *Isle of the Dead*, 1969

2943

JULIAN MAY

Magnificat
(New York: Knopf, 1996)

Story type: Science Fiction (Family Saga; Psychic Powers)
Series: Galactic Milieu
Major character(s): Mark Remillard, Psychic, Revolutionary; Jack the Bodiless, Psychic, Relative (brother); Dorothea "Diamond Mask", Psychic
Time period(s): 22nd century
Locale(s): Galactic Milieu, Interstellar Empire/Federation; Kauai, Hawaii

Summary: In opposition to the Unity attempted by the Metapsychics of the Milieu, Mark Remillard works to establish the superiority of the human species and control of the Milieu. Only Jack and Diamond are knowledgeable enough to prevent him. Concludes the trilogy.

Other books you might like:
F.M. Busby, *Rissa Kerguelen*, 1977
Suzette Haden Elgin, *The Grand Jubilee*, 1981
Katherine Kurtz, *Deryni Rising*, 1970
Anne McCaffrey, *The Rowan*, 1990
David Wingrove, *Beneath the Tree of Heaven*, 1995

2944

BOB MAYER

Operation Synbat
(San Francisco: Presidio, 1994)

Story type: Horror (Science Fiction)
Major character(s): David Riley, Military Personnel; Robin Merrit, Scientist; David Ward, Scientist
Time period(s): 1990s (1994)
Locale(s): Fort Campbell, Kentucky

Summary: David Riley's special paramilitary crew is called in to clean up the escape of experimental animals accidentally sprung from a research facility, unaware that the animals are "synbats"—synthetic battle forms that are the result of genetic manipulation of baboon and human biology, bred for their superior strength and complete lack of compassion toward human prey.

Other books you might like:
Richard Adams, *The Plague Dogs*, 1976
Ken Eulo, *Claw*, 1994
    Joe Mauck, co-author
T.J. Kirby, *Dangerous Nature*, 1993

T.J. Kirby, *Deadly Breed*, 1992
Dean R. Koontz, *Watchers*, 1987
T.W. Stetson, *Night Beasts*, 1993

2945

ARDATH MAYHAR
DON SCHANK, Illustrator

Mean Little Old Lady at Work
(Concord, California: Dark Regions Press, 1994)

Story type: Horror (Collection)

Summary: This chapbook, the first collection of the author's short stories, includes a dozen tales that reflect her ability to merge fantasy and horror. Included are ''Trogolodytes,'' about a prisoner who witnesses a race of subterranean monsters emerge to kill his captors; ''Echo of Thunder,'' about a psychic investigator who unravels the mystery of a ghostly event replayed regularly in the halls of a mansion; ''Through the Padded Door,'' the narrative of a madman; ''A Sculpted Smile,'' in which a king fills his halls with sculptures made from living people; and ''The Children Beneath the Stones,'' about an ancient practice of burying live human beings beneath paving stones of a Roman road to ensure its safety. The book has an introduction by Joe Lansdale.

Other books you might like:
Charles de Lint, *Dreams Underfoot*, 1993
Garry Kilworth, *Hogfoot Right and Bird-Hands*, 1993
Brian Lumley, *The House of Cthulhu and Other Tales of the Primal Land*, 1984
Jessica Amanda Salmonson, *John Collier and Fredric Brown Went Quarreling through My Head*, 1989

2946

ARDATH MAYHAR
RON FORTIER, Co-Author

Monkey Station
(Lake Geneva, Wisconsin: TSR, 1989)

Story type: Science Fiction (Disaster)
Major character(s): Eric Littlefield, Teenager; Ko, Animal (Macaque Monkey)
Time period(s): Indeterminate Future
Locale(s): Brazil (The Rainforest)

Summary: Scientists working in the Brazilian jungle on experiments with genetically-altered, sentient macaque monkeys must fight for survival after a plague destroys most of the human race.

Other books you might like:
Roger MacBride Allen, *Orphan of Creation*, 1988
David Brin, *The Uplift War*, 1987
Michael Crichton, *The Andromeda Strain*, 1969
Peter Dickinson, *Eva*, 1988

2947

ARDATH MAYHAR

People of the Mesa
(New York: Diamond, 1992)

Story type: Fantasy (Historical)
Major character(s): Uhatatse, Indian (Anasazi)
Time period(s): Indeterminate Past
Locale(s): Southwest

Summary: When the hostile Tsununni Indians threaten the peaceful Anasazi Indians who live in harmony with nature, only Uhatatse recognizes the danger. He must convince his people to change their way of life if they are to survive.

Other books you might like:
Alan Dean Foster, *Cyber Way*, 1990
W. Michael Gear, *People of the Earth*, 1992
    Kathleen O'Neal Gear, co-author
Sue Harrison, *Mother Earth, Father Sky*, 1990
Dean Ing, *Anasazi*, 1980
J. Alison James, *Sing for a Gentle Rain*, 1990
Catherine Wells, *The Earth Is All That Lasts*, 1991
Roger Zelazny, *Bridge of Ashes*, 1976

2948

BRUCE MCALLISTER

Dream Baby
(New York: Tor, 1989)

Story type: Science Fiction (Psychic Powers)
Major character(s): Mary Damico, Nurse, Military Personnel (Army lieutenant)
Time period(s): 1960s
Locale(s): Vietnam; United States

Summary: Mary Damico, an army nurse assigned to a field hospital in Vietnam, finds herself in a close approximation of hell. Her days are full of bleeding, dismembered bodies which she can't escape even in her dreams. Then something strange begins to happen. Damico realizes that the gaping wounds and horrid injuries she's been dreaming of are only showing up during her waking hours after she dreams about them. She makes the mistake of telling a CIA agent about her precognitive power and soon finds herself part of a dangerous and deadly secret project, an attempt to harness psychic powers and use them as weapons.

Other books you might like:
Jeanne Van Buren Dann, *In the Field of Fire*, 1987
    Jack Dann, co-author
Elizabeth Ann Scarborough, *The Healer's War*, 1989
Lucius Shepard, *The Jaguar Hunter*, 1987
Lucius Shepard, *Life During Wartime*, 1987
Lewis Shiner, *Deserted Cities of the Heart*, 1988

2949

P.K. MCALLISTER (Pseudonym of Paula E. Downing)

Maia's Veil
(New York: Roc, 1995)

Story type: Science Fiction (Adventure; Political)
Series: Cloudships of Orion
Major character(s): Pov Janusz, Spaceship Captain, Gypsy; Avi Selenko, Spacewoman; Ekaterina "Kate" Marya Janusz, Spacewoman, Gypsy
Time period(s): Indeterminate Future
Locale(s): *Siduri's Net*, Spaceship; Outer Space

Summary: After discovering the treachery of their mother ship, *Siduri's Dance*, the crew of *Siduri's Net* votes to follow an earlier expedition to the Pleiades. Forced to run, the *Net* discovers a new fuel, perhaps allowing very long distance journeys. Still plagued by social and cultural clashes between the mixed nationalities on the Cloudships, *Net* decides to ally with Tripower, a space station in the Pleiades, leading toward an expedition to the Orion Nebula, if cultural diversity doesn't split *Net*'s crew. Sequel to *Siduri's Net*.

Other books you might like:
Paula E. Downing, *Fallway*, 1993
Paula E. Downing, *Flare Star*, 1992
Paula E. Downing, *A Whisper of Time*, 1994
Alis A. Rasmussen, *A Passage of Stars*, 1990
Robert Charles Wilson, *Gypsies*, 1989

2950

P.K. MCALLISTER (Pseudonym of Paula King)

Orion's Dagger
(New York: Roc, 1996)

Story type: Science Fiction (Family Saga; Political)
Series: Cloudships of Orion
Major character(s): Pov Janusz, Spaceship Captain, Gypsy (Rom); Sigrid Thorsen, Businesswoman (station manager); Yuri Putakin, Computer Expert, Spaceman
Time period(s): Indeterminate Future
Locale(s): Tri Power Station, Space Station; *Siduri's Isle*, Spaceship; Orion Nebula, Outer Space

Summary: Despite a lack of cooperation, Pov leads the cloudships to the Orion Nebula, where conditions prove different than expected. Treachery from one of his partners may prevent the safe return of any of the ships.

Other books you might like:
F.M. Busby, *The Demu Trilogy*, 1980
Paula E. Downing, *Fallway*, 1993
Paula E. Downing, *Flare Star*, 1992
Paula E. Downing, *Rinn's Star*, 1990
Paula E. Downing, *A Whisper of Time*, 1994

2951

P.K. MCALLISTER (Pseudonym of Paula E. Downing)

Siduri's Net
(New York: Roc, 1994)

Story type: Science Fiction (Political)
Series: Cloudships of Orion
Major character(s): Pov Janusz, Pilot (sailship sailmaster), Gypsy; Dina Kozel, Spacewoman, Traitor; Leonidas Andreos, Spaceship Captain
Time period(s): Indeterminate Future
Locale(s): *Siduri's Net*, Spaceship; *Siduri's Dance*, Spaceship; Outer Space (Epsilon Tauri)

Summary: The mixed nationalities and intricate contractual arrangements between the cloudships *Dance* and *Net* promote social and cultural clashes and lead to severe damage to *Dance*. Embarrassed by his former lover, Pov must integrate his Rom identity with his love for the *Net* to preserve his place as the *Net*'s sailmaster and the *Net*'s chance at freedom from debt.

Other books you might like:
Paula E. Downing, *A Whisper of Time*, 1994
Paula E. Downing, *Fallway*, 1993
Paula E. Downing, *Flare Star*, 1992
Paula E. Downing, *Rinn's Star*, 1990
Paula King, *Mad Roy's Light*, 1990
    pseudonym of Paula E. Downing

2952

PAUL J. MCAULEY

Eternal Light
(New York: Morrow/AvoNova, 1993)

Story type: Science Fiction (Theological; Military)
Major character(s): Dorthy Yoshida, Psychic (esper); Suzanne "Suzy Falcon" Marie Thibodeaux, Pilot (spaceship); Talbeck Barlstilkin, Immortal
Time period(s): Indeterminate Future
Locale(s): Epsilon Eridani Two, Planet—Imaginary; Outer Space (galactic core)

Summary: Humanity travels to other star systems, only to find the remains of the Alea and their million-year-old civil war. Able to see the past and the future, Dorthy may prove the key to preventing the war from destroying not only humanity, but the entire universe. Sequel to *Four Hundred Billion Stars*.

Other books you might like:
Roger MacBride Allen, *The Ring of Charon*, 1990
Kevin J. Anderson, *Assemblers of Infinity*, 1993
    Doug Beason, co-author
James Blish, *The Triumph of Time*, 1958
Jeffrey A. Carver, *Down the Stream of Stars*, 1990
Glen Cook, *The Dragon Never Sleeps*, 1988
Frank Herbert, *Dune*, 1965
Michaela Roessner, *Vanishing Point*, 1993
David Weber, *Path of the Fury*, 1992

2953

PAUL J. MCAULEY

Fairyland

(New York: Avon, 1996)

Story type: Science Fiction (Genetic Manipulation; Horror)
Major character(s): Alex Sharkey, Technician; Milena "Alfred Russell Wallace", Computer Expert, Teenager
Time period(s): 21st century
Locale(s): London, England

Summary: Psychoactive virus designer Alex Sharkey, his product barely legal, finds himself involved with a young genius out to change the world. Milena intends to give the genetically engineered "dolls" used for dirty work and amusement the capability of reproduction. She infects everyone she deals with, so she can control them with a laser burst, leaving Alex to deal with the fallout while she develops the deadly fairies.

Other books you might like:
Wilhelmina Baird, *Clipjoint*, 1994
Pat Cadigan, *Mindplayers*, 1987
Raphael Carter, *The Fortunate Fall*, 1996
Gwyneth Jones, *White Queen*, 1993
Neal Stephenson, *The Diamond Age*, 1995
Jim Young, *Armed Memory*, 1995

2954

PAUL J. MCAULEY

Of the Fall

(New York: Ballantine Del Rey, 1989)

Story type: Science Fiction (First Contact)
Major character(s): David De Ramaira, Scientist; Rick Florey, Scientist
Time period(s): 21st century (Late)
Locale(s): Elysium, Planet—Imaginary

Summary: The Earth colony on the planet Elysium is in turmoil as long-time colonists vie with recent immigrants for political power. Meanwhile, on the periphery of human civilization, the primitive and much despised natives of the planet bide their time.

Other books you might like:
Orson Scott Card, *Speaker for the Dead*, 1986
C.J. Cherryh, *Forty Thousand in Gehenna*, 1983
Mike Resnick, *Paradise: A Chronicle of a Distant World*, 1989
Sheri S. Tepper, *After Long Silence*, 1987
Sheri S. Tepper, *Grass*, 1989

2955

PAUL J. MCAULEY

Pasquale's Angel

(New York: Morrow/AvoNova, 1995)

Story type: Fantasy (Historical)

Major character(s): Pasquale, Artist; Niccolo Machiavelli, Journalist, Political Figure (retired); Leonardo Da Vinci, Genius, Aged Person
Time period(s): 16th century
Locale(s): Italy, Alternate Earth (Florence)

Summary: In a Florence greatly changed by the success of Da Vinci's strangest inventions, an artist named Pasquale struggles with the painting that will establish his reputation. The murder of the great Raphael's assistant drags Pasquale away from his studies and into a maze of corruption and danger. The evolving new world may contain no room for painters or Florence.

Other books you might like:
John Crowley, *Aegypt*, 1987
R.A. MacAvoy, *Damiano*, 1983
Tim Powers, *The Drawing of the Dark*, 1979
Melissa Scott, *The Armor of Light*, 1988
Lisa Barnett, co-author

2956

PAUL J. MCAULEY

Red Dust

(New York: Morrow/AvoNova, 1994)

Story type: Science Fiction (Alternate Intelligence; Political)
Major character(s): Wei Lee, Technician (agronomist), Traveller; Miriam Makepeace Mbele, Clone, Computer Expert; Redd, Cowboy (Martian)
Time period(s): 29th century (2800s)
Locale(s): Bitter Waters, Mars; Xin Beijing, Mars

Summary: Wei Lee and his friends rescue Miriam Mbele, an anarchist sent to Mars to help free the planet from the Ten Thousand Years who sold Mars for personal immortality. The Emperor may have died and Wei Lee's great-grandfather, one of the Ten Thousand Years, attempts to kill the clone while framing Wei Lee. Before dying, the clone infects Wei Lee with a tailored virus allowing him access to the computer side of reality.

Other books you might like:
Poul Anderson, *The Stars Are Also Fire*, 1994
Frederik Pohl, *Man Plus*, 1994
Thomas T. Thomas, co-author
Kim Stanley Robinson, *Green Mars*, 1994
Kim Stanley Robinson, *Red Mars*, 1993
Jack Williamson, *The Humanoids*, 1949

2957

PATRICK MCCABE

The Butcher Boy

(New York: Delta/Cutting Edge, 1994)

Story type: Horror (Psychological Suspense)
Major character(s): Francis Brady, Child; Philip Nugent, Child; Joe Purcell, Child
Time period(s): 1990s (1992)
Locale(s): Dublin, Ireland

Summary: Originally published in 1992, this extraordinary novel tells of Francis Brady, a slightly ''simple'' Irish boy whose loathing of himself and his dysfunctional family and envy of the next-door neighbor his age leads him to imagine persecutors and take drastic measures against them, in a tour-de-force of psychological horror.

Other books you might like:
Robert Bloch, *Psycho*, 1959
Anthony Burgess, *A Clockwork Orange*, 1962
Ramsey Campbell, *The Face That Must Die*, 1979

2958

ANNE MCCAFFREY

All the Weyrs of Pern

(New York: Ballantine/Del Rey, 1991)

Story type: Science Fiction (Hard Science Fiction; Genetic Manipulation)
Series: Dragonriders of Pern
Major character(s): Lessa, Leader (Weyrwoman of Pern); Jaxom, Nobleman (Holder of Ruatha); AIVAS, Artificial Intelligence (Voice Activated System)
Time period(s): Indeterminate Future
Locale(s): Pern, Planet—Imaginary

Summary: The Pernese discover the artificial intelligence which had been abandoned 2500 years earlier, after Landing was covered by a volcanic eruption. They find it not only in working order, but prepared to help Pern eliminate the deadly Thread. This book is a direct sequel to *The Renegades of Pern*.

Other books you might like:
Margaret Wander Bonanno, *The Others*, 1990
C.J. Cherryh, *Forty Thousand in Gehenna*, 1983
Suzette Haden Elgin, *Twelve Fair Kingdoms*, 1981
Rosemary Kirstein, *The Steerswoman*, 1989
Michael P. Kube-McDowell, *Emprise*, 1985
Alis A. Rasmussen, *A Passage of Stars*, 1990

2959

ANNE MCCAFFREY

Black Horses for the King

(New York: Harcourt Brace, 1996)

Story type: Fantasy (Legend; Young Adult)
Major character(s): Artos, Nobleman (Comes Britannorum), Warrior; Galwin Gaius Varianus, Linguist, Horse Trainer
Time period(s): 6th century
Locale(s): England; Europe

Summary: Galwin wins Artos' respect by translating and bargaining for food and lodging for Artos' group, bound for a market where they hope to secure large Libyan horses to use as Artos' cavalry. Galwin escapes his abusive uncle's ship and joins Artos' mission as translator, but quickly proves invaluable working with the fine new horses.

Other books you might like:
Susan Cooper, *Over Sea, Under Stone*, 1966
Tanith Lee, *Black Unicorn*, 1991

T.H. White, *The Sword in the Stone*, 1939
Jane Yolen, *Camelot*, 1995
editor
Jane Yolen, *Passager*, 1996

2960

ANNE MCCAFFREY

The Chronicles of Pern: First Fall

(New York: Ballantine Del Rey, 1993)

Story type: Science Fiction (Collection)
Series: Pern
Time period(s): Indeterminate Future
Locale(s): Pern, Planet—Imaginary

Summary: Contains a timeline for the first 20 years after landing, four pages of maps plus five original stories about life on Pern. Stories examine the original colony survey, exploration of dangerous Pernese oceans utilizing intelligent, talking dolphins and the founding of Ruatha Hold.

Other books you might like:
David Brin, *Startide Rising*, 1983
Robert L. Forward, *Marooned on Eden*, 1993
Martha Dodson Forward, co-author
Diana G. Gallagher, *The Alien Dark*, 1990
Janet Kagan, *Mirabile*, 1991
Rosemary Kirstein, *The Outskirter's Secret*, 1992
Rosemary Kirstein, *The Steerswoman*, 1989

2961

ANNE MCCAFFREY
S.M. STIRLING, Co-Author

The City Who Fought

(New York: Baen, 1993)

Story type: Science Fiction (Adventure; Military)
Series: Ship Who Sang
Major character(s): SSS-900-C Simeon, Administrator, Cyborg (shell person); Channa Hap, Spaceman (Brawn); Amos ''Simeon'' ben Sierra Nueva, Leader, Refugee
Time period(s): Indeterminate Future
Locale(s): SSS-900-C, Space Station

Summary: Channa Hap, unwanted new brawn for Simeon, must help Simeon defend SSS-900-C against attack by the Kolinar fleet before their partnership or any real trust can evolve. Prior to the attack, Joat, an electronics genius hiding out on SSS-900-C, meets Channa, but when Simeon attempts adoption, prejudice against shell people complicates the procedure. Because the navy cannot arrive for 16 days, Simeon, Channa and the refugees who warned of the pursuing pirates must prevent the destruction of the space station and the deaths of the 15,000 residents.

Other books you might like:
James Blish, *Cities in Flight*, 1970
Jeffrey A. Carver, *Dragons in the Stars*, 1992
Glen Cook, *The Dragon Never Sleeps*, 1988
John DeChancie, *Starrigger*, 1983

Debra Doyle, *The Price of the Stars*, 1992
James D. Macdonald, co-author
R.M. Meluch, *The Queen's Squadron*, 1992
Vernor Vinge, *A Fire upon the Deep*, 1992

2962

ANNE MCCAFFREY
JODY LYNN NYE, Co-Author

Crisis on Doona

(New York: Ace, 1992)

Story type: Science Fiction (Political; Mystery)
Series: Doona
Major character(s): Todd Reeve, Rancher, Hero; Hrriss, Alien (Hrruban), Settler; Kelly Solinari, Scholar, Detective—Amateur
Time period(s): 22nd century
Locale(s): Doona, Planet—Imaginary; Earth
Summary: On the way to Doona for the renewal of the treaty establishing the planet as one inhabited by two intelligent species, human and Hrruban, Todd Reeve and Hrriss answer a mayday call, going into interdicted territory to do so. On Doona, inspectors find contraband hidden on their ship and arrest the two, threatening the renewal of the treaty. Convinced of the men's innocence, Kelly Solinari returns to Earth to prove that politicians at the highest level on both Earth and Hrruba conspired to scuttle the treaty by framing its chief advocates. Sequel to *Decision on Doona*.

Other books you might like:
Poul Anderson, *People of the Wind*, 1973
C.J. Cherryh, *Forty Thousand in Gehenna*, 1983
Paula E. Downing, *Fallway*, 1993
Dean Ing, *Cathouse*, 1991
Rebecca Ore, *Being Alien*, 1989

2963

ANNE MCCAFFREY

Crystal Line

(New York: Ballantine Del Rey, 1992)

Story type: Science Fiction (Science Fiction)
Series: Crystal Singer
Major character(s): Killashandra Ree, Miner (crystal singer); Lars Dahl, Government Official (guild master)
Time period(s): Indeterminate Future
Locale(s): Ballybran, Planet—Imaginary; *BB-1066*, Spaceship
Summary: One of the oldest, most successful crystal singers, Killashandra, uses the side-effect associated with extended life, loss of memory, to forget anything painful. Kept alive by their symbionts, crystal singers eventually lose the ability to find their claims due to this memory loss and exposure to crystal. Finding her interactions with Lars disappointing, Killashandra risks her skills as a crystal singer. Sequel to *Killashandra*.

Other books you might like:
Pauline Ashwell, *Unwillingly to Earth*, 1992

Stephen Goldin, *Jade Darcy and the Affair of Honor*, 1988
Mary Mason, co-author
Rosemary Kirstein, *The Steerswoman*, 1989
Alis A. Rasmussen, *A Passage of Stars*, 1990
Vernor Vinge, *A Fire upon the Deep*, 1992

2964

ANNE MCCAFFREY

Damia

(New York: Ace/Putnam, 1992)

Story type: Science Fiction (First Contact; Psychic Powers)
Series: Rowan
Major character(s): Afra Lyon, Psychic (Talent); Angharad "the Rowan" Gwyn-Raven, Psychic (Prime Talent); Damia Gwynn-Raven, Psychic (Prime Talent)
Time period(s): Indeterminate Future
Locale(s): Callisto, Jupiter (a moon of Jupiter); Deneb, Planet—Imaginary; Iota Aurigae, Planet—Imaginary
Summary: Afra grows up on rigid Capella where he befriends a spaceship captain who teaches him origami. Prepared for Tower work, Afra's acceptance by the Rowan as a friend and surrogate brother exercises his strength and patience. Acting as a substitute parent to the Raven and Jeff's children, he develops a special bond with Damia, the most Talented youngster. When Damia, now Aurigae Prime, contacts an alien intelligence, Afra recognizes the danger, thus preventing the destruction of Nine Star League planets.

Other books you might like:
Marion Zimmer Bradley, *The Firebrand*, 1987
F.M. Busby, *Rissa Kerguelen*, 1977
Jeffrey A. Carver, *Down the Stream of Stars*, 1990
Cheryl J. Franklin, *Fire Crossing*, 1991
Henry Kuttner, *Mutant*, 1953
Joan D. Vinge, *Psion*, 1982

2965

ANNE MCCAFFREY

Damia's Children

(New York: Ace/Putnam, 1993)

Story type: Science Fiction (Family Saga; Psychic Powers)
Series: Rowan
Major character(s): Laria Lyon, Teenager, Psychic (esper); Isthian "Thian" Lyon, Teenager, Psychic (esper); Rojer Lyon, Teenager, Psychic (esper)
Time period(s): Indeterminate Future
Locale(s): Iota Aurigae, Planet—Imaginary; Clarf, Planet—Imaginary; *Vadim*, Spaceship
Summary: Damia and Afra Raven-Lyon realize the Alliance will need their talented esper children when the Mrdini inform the Alliance that they sent ships to backtrack the trail of Hiver ships they discovered. To promote Human/Mrdini understanding, each of the Raven-Lyon children befriended a pair of 'Dinis from early childhood, now communicating well with them. At 16, Laria leaves for Clarf with her 'Dinis to become their primary teleporter. A year later Thian joins the

expedition as communications expert while Rojer, now 15, visits the Alliance ships following a Hiver escape pod. All work to promote interspecies understanding.

Other books you might like:
Greg Bear, *Anvil of Stars*, 1992
Marion Zimmer Bradley, *The World Wreckers*, 1971
Orson Scott Card, *Ender's Game*, 1985
Jeffrey A. Carver, *Down the Stream of Stars*, 1990
Karen Haber, *Mutant Star*, 1992
Henry Kuttner, *Mutant*, 1953
Larry Niven, *The Gripping Hand*, 1993
    Jerry Pournelle, co-author
Joan D. Vinge, *Psion*, 1982

2966

ANNE MCCAFFREY
JODY LYNN NYE, Co-Author

The Death of Sleep

(New York: Baen, 1990)

Story type: Science Fiction (Adventure; Future Shock)
Series: Planet Pirates
Major character(s): Lunzie Mespil, Doctor; Teodor Janos, Social Worker (caseworker); Zebara, Spaceship Captain (ARCT-10)
Time period(s): 28th century
Locale(s): Astris Alexandria, Planet—Imaginary; Ireta, Planet—Imaginary; Outer Space

Summary: Lunzie Mespil takes a job and winds up spending 62 years in cold sleep. After taking a refresher course to update her job skills, she travels to see her daughter and other descendants, is shipwrecked, and spends another 10 years in cold sleep. On Tau Ceti she is marked for assassination so she takes a job on the *ARC-10/* and winds up confronting pirates. Later she takes a routine jaunt to Ireta where the explorers are first marooned and then threatened by berserk Heavyworlders, so they go into cold sleep until help arrives.

Other books you might like:
C.J. Cherryh, *Forty Thousand in Gehenna*, 1983
Andre Norton, *The Last Planet*, 1955
John Rackham, *The Anything Tree*, 1970
    pseudonym of John Phillifent
Melissa Scott, *Mighty Good Road*, 1990
Marti Steussy, *Dreams of Dawn*, 1988

2967

ANNE MCCAFFREY

The Dolphins of Pern

(New York: Ballantine Del Rey, 1994)

Story type: Science Fiction (First Contact; Adventure)
Series: Dragonriders of Pern
Major character(s): Readis, Child; Alemi, Fisherman; T'lion, Teenager
Time period(s): Indeterminate Future
Locale(s): Pern, Planet—Imaginary

Summary: In Paradise River Hold, the first settlement on the newly opened Southern Continent, Alemi frequently takes Readis fishing. After being caught in a sudden squall, Readis and Alemi speak with dolphins, "ship-fish," who rescue them. Although forbidden by his mother to swim out and see the dolphins, Readis' fascination with them continues.

Other books you might like:
Betty Ballantine, *The Secret Oceans*, 1994
David Brin, *Startide Rising*, 1983
Arthur C. Clarke, *Dolphin Island*, 1963
Gordon R. Dickson, *Space Winners*, 1965
Kathryn Lasky, *Shadows in the Water*, 1992
Joan Slonczewski, *A Door into Ocean*, 1986
Sheri S. Tepper, *After Long Silence*, 1987
Sydney J. Van Scyoc, *Deepwater Dreams*, 1991
Joan D. Vinge, *The Summer Queen*, 1991
Catherine Wells, *The Earth Is All That Lasts*, 1991

2968

ANNE MCCAFFREY

An Exchange of Gifts

(New York: Roc, 1995)

Story type: Fantasy (Romance)
Major character(s): Anastasia "Meanne" de Saumur et Navarre y Cordova, Royalty (princess); Dalain "Wisp" zu Blas und Fiersing, Nobleman
Time period(s): Indeterminate
Locale(s): Fictional Country

Summary: Meanne flees an arranged marriage, finding shelter in an abandoned cottage in the woods where she hopes to use her gift for growing things. In other areas of practical housekeeping she lacks skills, but Wisp, another runaway who soon joins her, knows about catching and cooking food. As Meanne gradually discovers that Wisp has other talents as well, their respective abilities enable them to survive and elude danger.

Other books you might like:
Pamela Dean, *The Dubious Hills*, 1994
Rosalie Fry, *The Secret of Roan Inish*, 1995
Ursula K. Le Guin, *The Beginning Place*, 1980
Ursula K. Le Guin, *Tehanu: The Last Book of Earthsea*, 1990
Elizabeth Ann Scarborough, *Song of Sorcery*, 1982
Gertrude Warner, *The Boxcar Children*, 1924

2969

ANNE MCCAFFREY

Freedom's Landing

(New York: Ace/Putnam, 1995)

Story type: Science Fiction (First Contact; Adventure)
Major character(s): Kristin "Kris" Bjornsen, Slave, Castaway; Zainal, Alien (Catteni), Castaway; Chuck Mitford, Military Personnel (sergeant), Castaway
Time period(s): 1990s
Locale(s): Barevi, Planet—Imaginary; Botany, Planet—Imaginary

Summary: A student the University of Denver when the Catteni empty Denver and 50 other Terran cities in their typical pattern of conquest, Kris and her fellow captives land on Barevi for sale as slaves. Kris finds herself part of an experimental colony of troublemakers on a planet the Catteni would like open for colonization. Unfortunately, the planet's parklike appearance conceals evidence of unknown dangers and unsuspected aliens. Expands "The Thorns of Barevi."

Other books you might like:
Roger MacBride Allen, *The Ring of Charon*, 1990
Hal Clement, *Fossil*, 1993
Rosemary Kirstein, *The Outskirter's Secret*, 1992
John E. Stith, *Manhattan Transfer*, 1993
Vernor Vinge, *Marooned in Realtime*, 1986

2970

ANNE MCCAFFREY
ELIZABETH MOON, Co-Author

Generation Warrior
(New York: Baen, 1991)

Story type: Science Fiction (Political)
Series: Planet Pirates
Major character(s): Lunzie Mespil, Doctor; Sassinak, Spaceship Captain
Time period(s): Indeterminate Future
Locale(s): Federation Space, Interstellar Empire/Federation

Summary: Sassinak and Lunzie combine forces to beat the planet pirates once and for all. With Lunzie's contacts, Sassinak's crew and Sassinak herself, it would take a galaxy-wide conspiracy to foil them. Unfortunately, that's just what the planet pirates are.

Other books you might like:
Poul Anderson, *Ensign Flandry*, 1966
David Brin, *The Uplift War*, 1987
C.J. Cherryh, *Cyteen*, 1988
C.J. Cherryh, *The Pride of Chanur*, 1982
Brian Daley, *Requiem for a Ruler of Worlds*, 1985
Frank Herbert, *Dune*, 1965
Alis A. Rasmussen, *A Passage of Stars*, 1990

2971

ANNE MCCAFFREY

The Girl Who Heard Dragons
(New York: Tor, 1994)

Story type: Science Fiction (Collection)
Summary: Contains an introduction and 15 stories with the title story set on Pern. Other stories feature a broad range of themes including a story from 1956, "The Greatest Love," in which in vitro fertilization and host motherhood lead to an incest trial.

Other books you might like:
Philip Jose Farmer, *Riders of the Purple Wage*, 1992
Nancy Kress, *The Aliens of Earth*, 1993
Pat Murphy, *Points of Departure*, 1990
James Tiptree Jr., *Her Smoke Rose Up Forever*, 1990

John Varley, *The Persistence of Vision*, 1978
Kate Wilhelm, *And the Angels Sing*, 1992

2972

ANNE MCCAFFREY

Lyon's Pride
(New York: Ace/Putnam, 1994)

Story type: Science Fiction (Psychic Powers; Family Saga)
Series: Rowan
Major character(s): Prtglm, Alien (Mrdini); Rojer Lyon, Psychic (esper), Spaceman (engineer); Jeff Raven, Psychic (esper), Parent
Time period(s): Indeterminate Future
Locale(s): *Genesee*, Spaceship; Clarf, Planet—Imaginary (Mrdini Homeworld); Outer Space

Summary: The continuing war against the Hivers puts some humans and Mrdini at odds with each other. The humans want to end the war, but the Mrdini insist on exterminating the Hivers. In a fit of rage, Prtglm kills Rojer's pair of Mrdini, causing him to disappear. While mourning their loss and recovering from shock, he studies to become certified as an engineer, befriending the shy Afra. The Primes continue to serve with the fleet, becoming more than simply supply and communication personnel.

Other books you might like:
F.M. Busby, *The Demu Trilogy*, 1980
Robert L. Forward, *Return to Rocheworld*, 1993
  Julie Forward Fuller, co-author
Diana G. Gallagher, *The Alien Dark*, 1990
Janet Kagan, *Mirabile*, 1991
Robert J. Sawyer, *Far-Seer*, 1992
Sheri S. Tepper, *Raising the Stones*, 1987

2973

ANNE MCCAFFREY

No One Noticed the Cat
(New York: Roc, 1996)

Story type: Fantasy (Young Adult; Political)
Major character(s): Jamas, Royalty, Leader; Niffy, Animal (cat), Counselor; Egdril, Royalty, Leader
Time period(s): Indeterminate
Locale(s): Esphania, Fictional Country

Summary: When Esphania's regent dies, Prince Jamas must lead the kingdom. The regent's surviving cat, Niffy, provides protection and direction as Jamas contends with neighboring King Egdril's plans for expansion through Jamas' marriage to his daughter and his wife's less benign lust for conquest.

Other books you might like:
Ursula K. Le Guin, *Catwings*, 1988
Andre Norton, *Catfantastic*, 1989
  Martin H. Greenberg, co-editor
Andre Norton, *The Mark of the Cat*, 1992
John Richard Stephens, *The Enchanted Cat*, 1990
  editor
L.A. Taylor, *Cat's Paw*, 1995

Tad Williams, *Tailchaser's Song*, 1985

2974

ANNE MCCAFFREY
MARGARET BALL, Co-Author

PartnerShip
(New York: Baen, 1992)

Story type: Science Fiction (Adventure)
Series: Ship Who Sang
Major character(s): Nancia, Cyborg (Spaceship); Caleb, Spaceman; Forister, Spaceman
Time period(s): 28th century
Locale(s): *Nancia*, Spaceship (courier service ship)

Summary: Partnered with Caleb, then Forister, *Nancia* carries out missions which challenge her worldview, forcing her to adapt. When a hyperchip attack affects a synaptic connection to emotional signals, *Nancia* becomes more human than her sister ships.

Other books you might like:
John DeChancie, *Red Limit Freeway*, 1984
John DeChancie, *Starrigger*, 1983
Alis A. Rasmussen, *The Price of Ransom*, 1990
David Alexander Smith, *Marathon*, 1982
Walter Jon Williams, *Voice of the Whirlwind*, 1987

2975

ANNE MCCAFFREY

Pegasus in Flight
(New York: Ballantine/Del Rey, 1990)

Story type: Science Fiction (Psychic Powers; Family Saga)
Series: Pegasus
Major character(s): Rhyssa Owen, Telepath, Administrator
Time period(s): 21st century
Locale(s): Jerhattan, Fictional City

Summary: Rhyssa Owen, granddaughter of Henry Darrow, has taken over as Director of the Jerhattan Parapsychic Center. There Talents, people with parapsychic abilities, are found, tested, trained and sent where they are needed. Currently the space platform needs many Talents. Candidates come from all sectors of society including the Linear developments where excess children may be sold into slavery.

Other books you might like:
John Brunner, *Children of the Thunder*, 1989
Storm Constantine, *The Enchantments of Flesh and Spirit*, 1989
Henry Kuttner, *Mutant*, 1953
Robert Silverberg, *Dying Inside*, 1972
Joan D. Vinge, *Psion*, 1982

2976

ANNE MCCAFFREY
ELIZABETH ANN SCARBOROUGH, Co-Author

Power Lines
(New York: Ballantine Del Rey, 1994)

Story type: Science Fiction (Political; First Contact)
Series: Powers That Be
Major character(s): Yanaba Maddock, Military Personnel (retired), Settler; Clodagh Senungatuk, Healer; Sean Shongili, Genetically Altered Being, Spouse
Time period(s): Indeterminate Future
Locale(s): Petaybee, Planet—Imaginary

Summary: Recognizing the sentience of the planet Petaybee, Yanaba works with the colonists to change company policy, stop attempts at mining and arrange for self determination for the planet and its colonists. Unscrupulous pirates allow the company to believe as it desires, that the planet could be extremely profitable, forcing the planet to prove its sentience.

Other books you might like:
J.R. Dunn, *This Side of Judgment*, 1994
Vonda N. McIntyre, *Metaphase*, 1992
Elizabeth Ann Scarborough, *The Healer's War*, 1989
Sheri S. Tepper, *After Long Silence*, 1987
Vernor Vinge, *A Fire upon the Deep*, 1992
Eric Vinicoff, *The Weigher*, 1992

2977

ANNE MCCAFFREY
ELIZABETH ANN SCARBOROUGH, Co-Author

Power Play
(New York: Ballantine Del Rey, 1995)

Story type: Science Fiction (First Contact; Genetic Manipulation)
Series: Powers That Be
Major character(s): Yanaba Maddock, Military Personnel (retired captain), Administrator; Onidi "Dinah O'Neill" Louchard, Pirate, Disembodied Personality; Petaybee, Alien (sentient planet)
Time period(s): Indeterminate Future
Locale(s): Petaybee, Planet—Imaginary; Gal Three, Space Station

Summary: Pregnant, Yanaba marries Sean inside Petaybee immediately before she must leave for Gal Three to testify about Petaybee. Before the hearings begin, Yana, her companions from Petaybee and her mentor from Gal Three fall prey to the pirate Louchard who holds them for ransom. Meanwhile, Petaybee develops a method allowing her to speak.

Other books you might like:
David Brin, *Earth*, 1990
Harry Harrison, *The Deathworld Trilogy*, 1976
Janet Kagan, *Hellspark*, 1988
Elizabeth Ann Scarborough, *The Healer's War*, 1988
Elizabeth Ann Scarborough, *Nothing Sacred*, 1991

2978

ANNE MCCAFFREY
ELIZABETH ANN SCARBOROUGH, Co-Author

Powers That Be

(New York: Ballantine Del Rey, 1993)

Story type: Science Fiction (First Contact; Genetic Manipulation)
Series: Powers That Be
Major character(s): Yanaba Maddock, Invalid, Military Personnel (retired); Buneka Rourke, Settler, Teenager; Diego Metaxos, Spaceman, Teenager
Time period(s): Indeterminate Future
Locale(s): Petaybee, Planet—Imaginary

Summary: Lungs destroyed by poison gas, Yanaba arrives on Petaybee for her assigned retirement. Expecting the frigid climate to prevent any outdoor activity, she notices how clean the air smells and how much better she seems to feel. When she comes in to the base, Yanaba finds that authorities may withhold medical treatment if she refuses to spy on the colonists with whom she will live. It seems that mineral deposits spotted from space disappear, or the explorers sent to find them disappear or return as raving lunatics. The colonists may also practice illegal genetic manipulation.

Other books you might like:
David Brin, *Earth*, 1990
Vonda N. McIntyre, *Metaphase*, 1992
Elizabeth Ann Scarborough, *Nothing Sacred*, 1991
Joan Slonczewski, *A Door into Ocean*, 1986
Sheri S. Tepper, *After Long Silence*, 1987
Kathy Tyers, *Shivering World*, 1991
Joan D. Vinge, *The Summer Queen*, 1991
Catherine Wells, *The Earth Is All That Lasts*, 1991

2979

ANNE MCCAFFREY

The Renegades of Pern

(New York: Ballantine/Del Rey, 1989)

Story type: Science Fiction (Science Fantasy)
Series: Dragonriders of Pern
Major character(s): Jayge, Trader; Aramina, Telepath
Time period(s): Indeterminate Future
Locale(s): Pern, Planet—Imaginary (Third Planet of the sun Rukbat in the Sagittarian sector)

Summary: Aramina, a homeless young woman reputed to be able to form a telepathic link with the dragons of Pern, is pursued by a powerful renegade leader who sees her as a means of gaining even greater power.

Other books you might like:
Leigh Brackett, *The Book of Skaith*, 1976
Leigh Brackett, *Eric John Stark, Outlaw of Mars*, 1982
Marion Zimmer Bradley, *City of Sorcery*, 1984
Marion Zimmer Bradley, *Sharra's Exile*, 1981
Marion Zimmer Bradley, *Stormqueen!*, 1978
Marion Zimmer Bradley, *Thendara House*, 1983

2980

ANNE MCCAFFREY

The Rowan

(New York: Ace/Putnam, 1990)

Story type: Science Fiction (Family Saga; Psychic Powers)
Series: Rowan
Major character(s): Angharad ''the Rowan'' Gwyn, Psychic (Talent), Orphan; Siglen, Psychic (Talent), Leader (of Altair Prime); Jeff Raven, Settler (colonist), Psychic (wild Talent)
Time period(s): Indeterminate Future
Locale(s): Callisto, Planet—Imaginary (Altair Colony)

Summary: The only survivor of Rowan Camp, the Rowan is taken to Altair Prime to be trained under Siglen. Later, as head of Callisto Prime, she gets a distress call from Deneb which is suffering from plague. Told that aid is unavailable, she gathers help and goes to Deneb against orders. She earns the gratitude of Jeff Raven, whom she later marries. Then they learn that the plague was the first step of an interstellar invasion. She and Jeff work to stop it.

Other books you might like:
Marion Zimmer Bradley, *The Bloody Sun*, 1964
A. Bertram Chandler, *Space Mercenaries*, 1965
Suzette Haden Elgin, *Twelve Fair Kingdoms*, 1981
R.M. Meluch, *Wind Child*, 1982
Andre Norton, *Ice Crown*, 1970

2981

ANNE MCCAFFREY
ELIZABETH MOON, Co-Author

Sassinak

(New York: Baen Books, 1990)

Story type: Science Fiction (Space Opera)
Series: Planet Pirates
Major character(s): Sassinak, Spaceship Captain
Time period(s): Indeterminate Future
Locale(s): Federation of Sentient Planets, Interstellar Empire/Federation

Summary: Twelve year old Sassinak is kidnapped and enslaved by pirates, but she refuses to let her spirit be broken. Eventually she escapes. Later, grown up, she enters military service and dedicates her life to eliminating pirates.

Other books you might like:
Lois McMaster Bujold, *Brothers in Arms*, 1988
Lois McMaster Bujold, *The Warrior's Apprentice*, 1986
Emma Bull, *Falcon*, 1989
C.J. Cherryh, *Rimrunners*, 1989
Rosemary Kirstein, *The Steerswoman*, 1989
Anne Moroz, *No Safe Place*, 1986
Susan Shwartz, *Heritage of Flight*, 1989

2982

ANNE MCCAFFREY
MERCEDES LACKEY, Co-Author

The Ship Who Searched

(New York: Baen, 1992)

Story type: Science Fiction (Adventure)
Series: Ship Who Sang
Major character(s): Hypatia "Tia" Cade, Cyborg (spaceship); Kennet Uhua-Sorg, Doctor, Handicapped (paraplegic); Alexander Joli-Chanteu, Spaceman (Brawn)
Time period(s): 28th century
Locale(s): Spaceship

Summary: Having spent the first seven years of her life on isolated archaeological digs with her parents, Tia spends much time alone and learns to be independent and comfortable with herself. While her parents work, Tia, with permission, plays at excavating her own site near their home base, unfortunately making a find which causes her total paralysis. Although thought to be too old to become a shell person, she proves to be an ideal candidate. As a brainship she and Alex search for the alien substance which paralyzed her while they transport supplies to remote archaeological sites similar to those where she grew up.

Other books you might like:
Glen Cook, *The Dragon Never Sleeps*, 1988
Debra Doyle, *The Price of the Stars*, 1992
    James D. Macdonald, co-author
Vonda N. McIntyre, *Metaphase*, 1992
R.M. Meluch, *The Queen's Squadron*, 1992
Melissa Scott, *Dreamships*, 1992
Vernor Vinge, *A Fire upon the Deep*, 1992

2983

ANNE MCCAFFREY
JODY LYNN NYE, Co-Author

The Ship Who Won

(New York: Baen, 1994)

Story type: Science Fiction (First Contact; Political)
Series: Ship Who Sang
Major character(s): Carialle, Spacewoman (shellperson); Keff Klemay, Spaceman; Nokias, Magician (High Mage of the South)
Time period(s): Indeterminate Future
Locale(s): *CK-963*, Spaceship; Ozrah, Planet—Imaginary

Summary: Carialle and Keff head out to search for alien intelligences and habitable planets. On Ozran they find what seems to be two groups of humans, slow thinking farmers and Mages who control powerful energies with thought using ancient artifacts given to them by previous residents. Unfortunately the climate has begun to degenerate and soon the planet will no longer support life unless the weather machinery mentioned in old records can be rediscovered and repaired.

Other books you might like:
William Adams, *The Unwound Way*, 1991
    Cecil Brooks, co-author

Stephen Baxter, *Raft*, 1992
C.J. Cherryh, *Foreigner*, 1994
Rosemary Kirstein, *The Outskirter's Secret*, 1992
Sheri S. Tepper, *After Long Silence*, 1987
Joan D. Vinge, *The Summer Queen*, 1991
David Weber, *Mutineers' Moon*, 1991

2984

ANNE MCCAFFREY, Editor
ELIZABETH ANN SCARBOROUGH, Co-Editor

Space Opera

(New York: DAW, 1996)

Story type: Science Fiction (Anthology; Arts)
Summary: Contains 20 original stories with an introduction by both editors and a brief biography of the author of each story. Themes revolve around music and musicians, including musicians caught in the jam, the traffic jam, a musician magician saving a town from eternal winter, and a singer in space. Authors include Robin Wayne Bailey, Peter S. Beagle, Marion Zimmer Bradley, Steven Brust, Suzette Haden Elgin, Alan Dean Foster, Anne McCaffrey, Jody Lynn Nye, Elizabeth Ann Scarborough, Josepha Sherman, and Gene Wolfe.

Other books you might like:
Gardner Dozois, *The Year's Best Science Fiction: Twelfth Annual Collection*, 1996
    editor
Don Sakers, *Carmen Miranda's Ghost Is Haunting Space Station Three*, 1990
Pamela Sargent, *Nebula Awards 29*, 1995
    editor
Kate Wilhelm, *And the Angels Sing*, 1992

2985

ANNE MCCAFFREY
JODY LYNN NYE, Co-Author

Treaty at Doona

(New York: Ace, 1994)

Story type: Science Fiction (First Contact; Political)
Series: Doona
Major character(s): Todd Reeve, Political Figure; Hrrestan, Alien (Hrruban), Political Figure; Grzzeearoghh "Grizz", Spaceship Captain, Alien (Gringg)
Time period(s): Indeterminate Future
Locale(s): Rraladoona, Planet—Imaginary; *Hamilton*, Spaceship

Summary: When the alien Gringg come to Rraladoona, Earth and Hrruban Space Force representatives plan to attack, unable to believe that the huge alien ship would come unarmed. Meanwhile, the Rraladoonans prepare to trade as they notice their children adore the aliens and that the Gringg captain brings her child to meet the humans and Hrrubans, even leaving him in their care.

Other books you might like:
Eleanor Arnason, *Ring of Swords*, 1993
C.J. Cherryh, *Serpent's Reach*, 1980

A.C. Crispin, *Silent Dances*, 1990
  Kathleen O'Malley, co-author
L. Warren Douglas, *Cannon's Orb*, 1994
Paula E. Downing, *Fallway*, 1993
Janet Kagan, *Hellspark*, 1988
Jody Lynn Nye, *Taylor's Ark*, 1993
Rebecca Ore, *Being Alien*, 1989

2986
ROBERT R. MCCAMMON

Blue World
(New York: Pocket, 1990)

Story type: Horror (Collection)

Summary: Thirteen stories, some previously published, including a novella, "Blue World." McCammon combines his gritty, realistic vision and deft characterization with a compression and precision not always evident in the novels. Especially noteworthy are the title novella about an unlikely alliance between a priest and a hooker to track a serial killer and "Nightcrawlers" about a Vietnam veteran who brings the war home with him—literally.

Other books you might like:
David Drake, *From the Heart of Darkness*, 1983
John Farris, *Scare Tactics*, 1989
Stephen King, *Night Shift*, 1978
Stephen King, *Skeleton Crew*, 1985

2987
ROBERT R. MCCAMMON

Boy's Life
(New York: Pocket, 1991)

Story type: Horror (Coming-of-Age)
Major character(s): Cory Mackenson, Child (12-year-old); Tom Mackenson, Worker (milkman), Parent (Cory's father); The Lady, Aged Person
Time period(s): 1960s (1964)
Locale(s): Zephyr, Alabama

Summary: This lyrical, episodic novel is told in the first-person by young Cory Mackenson, whose initiation into adulthood occurs over the course of a single summer in which he witnesses an inexplicable murder and the slow psychological decline of his father, is given a magic bike by a 102-year-old conjure woman, brings about the resurrection of his pet dog and experiences first love and first awareness of racial prejudice in the magic-laden town of Zephyr.

Other books you might like:
Ray Bradbury, *Dandelion Wine*, 1957
Stephen King, *It*, 1986
Dan Simmons, *Summer of Night*, 1991

2988
ROBERT R. MCCAMMON

Gone South
(New York: Pocket, 1992)

Story type: Horror (Psychological Suspense)
Major character(s): Dan Lambert, Worker, Veteran (Vietnam); Flint Murtaugh, Bounty Hunter; Arden Halliday, Musician
Time period(s): 1990s (1991)
Locale(s): Shreveport, Louisiana; The Bayous, Louisiana

Summary: Afflicted with terminal cancer from his exposure to Agent Orange and accused of murdering a loan officer, Vietnam vet Dan Lambert flees to the Louisiana bayous, accompanied by disfigured Arden Halliday and pursued by a freaky band of bounty hunters, in what ultimately turns out to be a spiritual odyssey of healing and forgiveness.

Other books you might like:
Joe R. Lansdale, *Savage Season*, 1990
Peter Straub, *Koko*, 1988

2989
ROBERT R. MCCAMMON

Mine
(New York: Pocket Books, 1990)

Story type: Horror (Psychological Suspense)
Major character(s): Mary "Merry Terror" Terrell, Terrorist (Psychotic); Laura Clayborne, Journalist, Parent
Time period(s): 1990s
Locale(s): United States

Summary: Psychotic ex-terrorist Mary Terrell kidnaps Laura Clayborne's baby to present to her former lover as "their" child. Laura gives pursuit and a wild, exciting, terrifying, violent cross-country chase ensues, a chase that threatens to turn Laura into the mirror image of her adversary.

Other books you might like:
Thomas Harris, *The Silence of the Lambs*, 1988
George R.R. Martin, *The Armageddon Rag*, 1983
Joel Townsley Rogers, *The Red Right Hand*, 1945
Charles Williams, *Dead Calm*, 1963
John D. MacDonald, *The Executioners*, 1958

2990
ROBERT R. MCCAMMON

Swan Song
(Arlington Heights, IL: Dark Harvest, 1989)

Story type: Horror (Apocalyptic Horror)
Major character(s): Swan, Child (Focus for the "good"); Friend, Ruler (Leader of the "evil" forces)
Time period(s): Indeterminate Future
Locale(s): United States
Summary: After nuclear war decimates most of the world, the "good" survivors mobilize around Swan, a young female,

while "evil" is brought together by "Friend." Thus, the forces of good and evil move together to an inevitable final confrontation.

Other books you might like:
Stephen King, *The Stand*, 1990

2991

ROBERT R. MCCAMMON, Editor

Under the Fang

(New York: Pocket, 1991)

Story type: Horror (Anthology; Vampire Story)

Summary: Seventeen stories all predicated on the theme of a near future in which vampires have taken over the world. Selections include "Advocates," Suzy McKee Charnas and Chelsea Quinn Yarbro's pairing of their vampire heroes Edward Weymouth and the Count Saint Germain; Charles de Lint's tale of gypsies collaborating with vampires, "We Are Dead Together"; Nancy Collins' brief sketch of a vampire nightclub, "Dancin' Nightly"; and McCammon's controversial story of a man "protecting" his family from the vampire onslaught, "Miracle Mile."

Other books you might like:
Ellen Datlow, *Blood Is Not Enough*, 1989
Richard Matheson, *I Am Legend*, 1954
John Skipp, *Book of the Dead*, 1989
   Craig Spector, co-author
F. Paul Wilson, *Freak Show*, 1992
F. Paul Wilson, *Midnight Mass*, 1991

2992

ROBERT R. MCCAMMON

The Wolf's Hour

(New York: Pocket, 1989)

Story type: Horror (Werewolf Story)
Major character(s): Michael Gallatin, Spy, Werewolf; Chesna "Echo" Van Dorne, Actress (Nazi propaganda film star), Spy (For the Allies)
Time period(s): 1940s (1941)
Locale(s): London, England

Summary: Gallatin's mission to discover and destroy Iron Fist, a secret Nazi plot, is juxtaposed against his life as he develops from apprentice werewolf to British werewolf superspy.

Other books you might like:
Clive Barker, *Cabal*, 1988
Dennis Wheatley, *They Used Dark Forces*, 1964
F. Paul Wilson, *The Keep*, 1981
Chelsea Quinn Yarbro, *Tempting Fate*, 1982

2993

WIL MCCARTHY

Aggressor Six

(New York: Roc, 1994)

Story type: Science Fiction (First Contact; Military)
Major character(s): Kenneth Jonson, Military Personnel (Marine corporal), Experimental Subject; Marshe "Queen" Talbott, Scientist (military exobiologist), Leader (Aggressor Six's); Josev T. Ranes, Military Personnel (Navy lieutenant), Experimental Subject
Time period(s): Indeterminate Future
Locale(s): ATG-311-B, Space Station; Outer Space

Summary: Fitted with a neural implant to aid his thinking in the alien language, Kenneth Jonson joins five other soldiers who attempt to understand the merciless alien invaders by adopting their lifestyle and language. First novel.

Other books you might like:
Roger MacBride Allen, *The Ring of Charon*, 1990
Roger MacBride Allen, *The Shattered Sphere*, 1994
Eleanor Arnason, *Ring of Swords*, 1993
Orson Scott Card, *Ender's Game*, 1985
C.J. Cherryh, *Foreigner*, 1994
Paula E. Downing, *Fallway*, 1993
David Alexander Smith, *Marathon*, 1982

2994

WIL MCCARTHY

The Fall of Sirius

(New York: Roc, 1996)

Story type: Science Fiction (First Contact; Science Fiction)
Major character(s): Malyene Andreivne "Malye" Kurosov'e, Leader; Viktor Slavanovot, Repairman
Time period(s): 53rd century
Locale(s): Pinega, Planet—Imaginary (Sirius/Gate System); Holders Fastness, Planet—Imaginary (Sirius/Gate System); Suzerainty of Human Spaces, Interstellar Empire/Federation

Summary: Entering cryostasis to avoid the attack of the alien Waisters, Malye and Viktor find themselves awakened two millennia later, when their wartime experience with invading Waisters might prove valuable to the descendents of survivors, now faced with another invasion of the mysterious Waisters. Sequel set 2000 years after *Aggressor Six*.

Other books you might like:
Roger MacBride Allen, *The Ring of Charon*, 1990
Roger MacBride Allen, *The Shattered Sphere*, 1994
Eleanor Arnason, *Ring of Swords*, 1993
Jeffrey A. Carver, *Neptune Crossing*, 1994
Vernor Vinge, *A Fire upon the Deep*, 1992
David Weber, *Mutineers' Moon*, 1991
David Weber, *Path of the Fury*, 1992

2995

WIL MCCARTHY

Flies From the Amber
(New York: Roc, 1995)

Story type: Science Fiction (Hard Science Fiction; First Contact)
Major character(s): Tomus Kreider, Spaceman, Scientist; Jhoe Freetz, Spaceman, Scientist; Luna Shiloh, Government Official
Time period(s): Indeterminate Future
Locale(s): Malhela System, Outer Space; Unua, Planet—Imaginary; *Introspectia*, Spaceship

Summary: Malhelan miners find a new substance in their peculiar solar system, motivating Earth to send an exploratory expedition of scientists. Distressed to find the deposit totally played out, yet certain the material springs from alien science, the Terrans detect alien material close to the event horizon of the system's ancient collapsed star.

Other books you might like:
Roger MacBride Allen, *The Ring of Charon*, 1990
Stephen Baxter, *Raft*, 1991
Gregory Benford, *Furious Gulf*, 1994
Mary Gentle, *Golden Witchbreed*, 1984
Jack McDevitt, *The Engines of God*, 1994
Sheri S. Tepper, *Grass*, 1989

2996

WIL MCCARTHY

Murder in the Solid State
(New York: Tor, 1996)

Story type: Science Fiction (Mystery; Adventure)
Major character(s): David Sanger, Scientist (physicist); T. Bowser Jones, Lawyer; Marian Fouts, Journalist
Time period(s): 21st century
Locale(s): Baltimore, Maryland; Philadelphia, Pennsylvania; Cyberspace

Summary: Offended at a party by David Sanger's insult, the established patriarch of nanotechnology rushes into a high-tech swordfight with David, who wins due to his streetfighting skills, embarrassing the elder professor. The next day police accuse David of murder when they discover the professor's body and the weapon David had used in the non-lethal fight. Freed with Bowser's help, David must disappear from sight to avoid those willing to kill over the implications of David's revolutionary nanotechnology development.

Other books you might like:
Pat Cadigan, *Synners*, 1991
Jeffrey A. Carver, *From a Changeling Star*, 1989
Michael Flynn, *In the Country of the Blind*, 1990
Lisa Mason, *Arachne*, 1990
Robert J. Sawyer, *The Terminal Experiment*, 1995

2997

DENNIS MCCARTY

Across the Thlassa Mey
(New York: Ballantine/Del Rey, 1991)

Story type: Fantasy (Quest)
Series: Thlassa Mey
Major character(s): Palamon, Royalty, Adventurer
Time period(s): Indeterminate
Locale(s): Thlassa Mey, Mythical Place (Sea)

Summary: When he responds to the Oracle's summons, King Palamon hears of a great evil about to befall lands around the Thlassa Mey. Hoping to find his long-lost son and save the area from the prophecied evil, King Palamon dons his armor and mystic sword and sets off to find the Tome of Winds, knowing that his advanced age works against his success.

Other books you might like:
David Eddings, *Pawn of Prophecy*, 1982
Phyllis Eisenstein, *The Crystal Palace*, 1988
Robert Jordan, *The Eye of the World*, 1990
Guy Gavriel Kay, *The Summer Tree*, 1985
J.R.R. Tolkien, *The Fellowship of the Ring*, 1954
J.R.R. Tolkien, *The Hobbit*, 1938

2998

DENNIS MCCARTY

The Birth of the Blade
(New York: Ballantine Del Rey, 1993)

Story type: Fantasy (Political; Quest)
Series: Thlassa Mey
Major character(s): Geryam, Military Personnel, Hero; Lissa, Maiden; Rinna, Maiden
Time period(s): Indeterminate
Locale(s): Thlassa Mey, Mythical Place (sea)

Summary: The Goddess Pellas choses Geryam, Lissa and Rinna to thwart priests of the Dark Order whose evil magic controls the realms surrounding the Thlassa Mey. The trio follows Pellas' command, unaware of the sacrifice and danger involved as the priests strive to create even more powerful devices.

Other books you might like:
Carol Chase, *Hawk's Flight*, 1991
Jo Clayton, *Wild Magic*, 1991
Jo Clayton, *Wildfire*, 1992
David Eddings, *Pawn of Prophecy*, 1982
Mary Gentle, *Rats and Gargoyles*, 1991
P.C. Hodgell, *God Stalk*, 1982

2999

BILL MCCAY
ELOISE FLOOD, Co-Author

Chains of Command
(New York: Pocket, 1992)

Story type: Science Fiction (Space Opera; Post-Holocaust)

Series: Star Trek: The Next Generation
Major character(s): Jean-Luc Picard, Spaceship Captain, Military Personnel; Beverly Crusher, Doctor, Space Explorer; Deanna Troi, Empath, Psychologist
Time period(s): 24th century
Locale(s): *U.S.S. Enterprise*, Spaceship; Koorn, Planet—Imaginary

Summary: Captain Picard sends an away team down to the planet Koorn in the midst of a slave rebellion. Human descendants of refugees from 21st century Earth warfare, the slaves have killed or captured their birdlike masters, the Tseetsk. Picard and Counselor Troi attempt to negotiate a peaceful settlement, but some of the rebels fear betrayal and take Picard and Troi hostage. The rebels' plans go awry when they meet the planet's natives.

Other books you might like:
Margaret Wander Bonanno, *Dwellers in the Crucible*, 1985
A.C. Crispin, *Silent Dances*, 1990
    Kathleen O'Malley, co-author
Gordon R. Dickson, *Way of the Pilgrim*, 1987
L.A. Graf, *Ice Trap*, 1992
Robert A. Heinlein, *Citizen of the Galaxy*, 1957
T.L. Mancour, *Spartacus*, 1992

3000

BILL MCCAY
DAVE GIBBONS, Illustrator

Crossover

(New York: Roc, 1993)

Story type: Fantasy (Contemporary; Light Fantasy)
Series: Stan Lee's Riftworld
Major character(s): Harry Sturdley, Publisher (of comic books)
Time period(s): 1990s
Locale(s): New York, New York

Summary: An enchanted rift opens between Earth and the comic book realm allowing giant-sized superheroes to invade New York and presenting Harry Sturdley with the opportunity of a lifetime to get them under contract. First of a series.

Other books you might like:
Michael Bishop, *Count Geiger's Blues*, 1992
Craig Shaw Gardner, *Revenge of the Fluffy Bunnies*, 1990
Martin H. Greenberg, *The Further Adventures of Superman*, 1992
    editor
Clifford D. Simak, *Out of Their Minds*, 1970
Roger Stern, *The Death and Life of Superman*, 1993
Gary K. Wolf, *Who Censored Roger Rabbit?*, 1981
Gary K. Wolf, *Who P-P-Plugged Roger Rabbit?*, 1991

3001

MICHAEL MCCOLLUM

The Clouds of Saturn

(New York: Ballantine/Del Rey, 1991)

Story type: Science Fiction (Post-Holocaust; Space Colony)

Major character(s): Larson Clarke Sands, Pilot (airship captain); Mikal Blount, Military Personnel (Northern Alliance Navy Admiral)
Time period(s): Indeterminate Future
Locale(s): *Sparrow Hawk*, Spaceship (in Saturn's atmosphere); Cloudcroft, Saturn

Summary: The Sun has entered a flare stage and Earth is no longer habitable. Humanity has moved to a viable layer of Saturn's atmosphere where large floating cities bear most of Earth's population. The Northern Alliance plans to unite all of humanity under their control. After Lars' brother dies during a Northern Alliance attack on the cloud city, New Philadelphia, Lars must find new employment for his ship, *Sparrow Hawk*, and avenge his brother's death.

Other books you might like:
James Blish, *A Life for the Stars*, 1962
Diana G. Gallagher, *The Alien Dark*, 1990
Larry Niven, *The Integral Trees*, 1984
Larry Niven, *The Smoke Ring*, 1987
Allen Steele, *Clarke County, Space*, 1990

3002

MICHAEL MCCOLLUM

The Sails of Tau Ceti

(New York: Ballantine Del Rey, 1992)

Story type: Science Fiction (First Contact)
Major character(s): Victoria "Tory" Bronson, Spacewoman; Faslorn, Alien (Phelan); Kit Claridge, Doctor, Spacewoman
Time period(s): 23rd century (2200s)
Locale(s): Outer Space; Earth; *Starhopper*, Spaceship

Summary: Tau Ceti has gone nova in 2001. Observers on Earth sight an alien light sail in that direction weeks before the launch of the *Starhopper* probe. Designated as advocate for the aliens, Tory must find room for the aliens on Earth without revealing the only alternative, total destruction.

Other books you might like:
Greg Bear, *Eon*, 1985
Johanna Bolton, *Mission: Tori*, 1990
Diana G. Gallagher, *The Alien Dark*, 1990
Ursula K. Le Guin, *Always Coming Home*, 1987
Jack McKinney, *Kaduna Memories*, 1990
Larry Niven, *Tales of Known Space*, 1975
Harry Turtledove, *Krispos Rising*, 1991

3003

MICHAEL MCCOLLUM

Thunder Strike!

(New York: Ballantine/Del Rey, 1989)

Story type: Science Fiction (Disaster)
Major character(s): Thomas Thorpe, Engineer; Amber Hastings, Scientist
Time period(s): 21st century
Locale(s): Moon (Earth's); Asteroid

Summary: A comet is on track to strike the Earth and scientists struggle desperately to deflect it.

Other books you might like:
Gregory Benford, *Heart of the Comet*, 1986
    David Brin, co-author
Gregory Benford, *Shiva Descending*, 1980
    William Rotsler, co-author
Larry Niven, *Lucifer's Hammer*, 1977
    Jerry Pournelle, co-author

3004

ASHLEY MCCONNELL

Days of the Dead

(New York: Diamond, 1992)

Story type: Horror (Occult)
Major character(s): Diane Lassiter, Engineer; Carlos Aguilar, Teenager; Gil Santillanes, Handyman
Time period(s): 1990s (October, 1992)
Locale(s): Desolada, New Mexico

Summary: Not until she moves into the house of her fiance's recently deceased aunt does Diane Lassiter discover that the old woman was an Aztec witch whose successive reincarnations have given her the power to call forth the dear departed on the forthcoming Day of the Dead festivities.

Other books you might like:
Ramsey Campbell, *The Influence*, 1988
Stephanie Kegan, *The Baby*, 1990
Robert Marasco, *Burnt Offerings*, 1973

3005

ASHLEY MCCONNELL

The Fountains of Mirlacca

(New York: Ace, 1995)

Story type: Fantasy (Magic Conflict)
Series: Demon Wars Trilogy
Major character(s): Jazen sr'Yat, Sorcerer; Vettazen, Sorceress (Guild of Exorcists)
Time period(s): Indeterminate
Locale(s): Mirlacca, Fictional City

Summary: Hoping to learn control of his ability to make things burst into flame, Jazen accompanies Vettazne to Exorcists School in Mirlacca. When Vettazen disappears, Jazen attempts to uncover the secret of Mirlacca's fountains, which run red with blood, and discover his destiny. First of a trilogy.

Other books you might like:
Don Callander, *Pyromancer*, 1992
Laurell K. Hamilton, *Nightseer*, 1992
Robin Hobb, *Assassin's Apprentice*, 1995
J.V. Jones, *The Baker's Boy*, 1995
Martha Wells, *The Element of Fire*, 1993

3006

ASHLEY MCCONNELL

The Itinerant Exorcist

(New York: Ace, 1996)

Story type: Fantasy (Magic Conflict)
Series: Demon Wars Trilogy
Major character(s): Jazen sr'Yat, Sorcerer; Davos, Healer, Demon; Misele E'lan, Waiter/Waitress (innkeeper's daughter)
Time period(s): Indeterminate
Locale(s): Eberly, Fictional City; Mirlacca, Fictional City

Summary: Jazen travels from Mirlacca to the village of Eberly in search of Davos, whom he hopes to recruit into the still-secret Guild of Exorcists. He must use his own magic cautiously, for fear of persecution as one of the Yaan Maat, demons who can possess a human body and work magic. When the villagers imprison Davos as a demon, Jazen tries to prevent his execution, coming under suspicion himself. He then finds that worse things can happen than being burned at the stake. Sequel to *The Fountains of Mirlacca*.

Other books you might like:
C.J. Cherryh, *Rusalka*, 1989
Gayle Greeno, *Finders-Seekers*, 1993
Barbara Hambly, *Stranger at the Wedding*, 1994
Katherine Kurtz, *Saint Camber*, 1978
Mercedes Lackey, *When the Bough Breaks*, 1993
Patricia C. Wrede, *Mairelon the Magician*, 1991

3007

ASHLEY MCCONNELL

Unearthed

(New York: Diamond, 1991)

Story type: Horror (Small Town Horror)
Major character(s): David Esher, Writer; Harry Kostner, Miner (owner of the Heartbreak Mine); Rick Zimmerman, Bodyguard
Time period(s): 1990s
Locale(s): Nintucca, Nevada

Summary: The town of Nintucca is just another one-horse town on the edge of the Nevada atomic bomb test range until the much reviled Harry Kostner decides to reopen the abandoned Heartbreak Mine. Soon, something at the bottom of the mine that doesn't like being disturbed begins manifesting to the townspeople under a variety of guises, all lethal. This is the author's first novel.

Other books you might like:
Joseph Citro, *Dark Twilight*, 1991
Douglas Clegg, *Goat Dance*, 1989
G. Wayne Miller, *Thunder Rise*, 1988
Steve Rasnic Tem, *Excavation*, 1987

3008

ERIC MCCORMACK

The Mysterium

(New York: St. Martin's Press, 1994)

Story type: Horror (Mystery)
Major character(s): James Maxwell, Journalist; Reeve Blair, Police Officer; Robert Aiken, Pharmacist
Time period(s): 1990s (1992)
Locale(s): Carrick, Canada

Summary: James Maxwell is summoned to a distant island to unravel a mystery in which the apparent poisoning of the town in retribution for a crime committed decades before causes unique symptoms in each victim. As James examines different townspeople and hears their often conflicting stories about what has happened, he becomes overwhelmed by the sense of how little we know about our world and ourselves. This novel was first published in Canada in 1992.

Other books you might like:
Paul Auster, *The New York Trilogy*, 1990
Philip K. Dick, *The Three Stigmata of Palmer Eldritch*, 1965
Peter Straub, *The Throat*, 1993

3009

MARA MCCUNIFF

TRACI BRIERY, Co-Author

The Vampire Memoirs

(New York: Zebra, 1991)

Story type: Horror (Vampire Story)
Major character(s): Mara McCunniff, Vampire; Gaarius "Gaar" Latticus, Warrior; Agyar, Political Figure (magistrate of ancient Gaul)
Time period(s): 4th century; 20th century
Locale(s): Los Angeles, California; Europe

Summary: Tracy Briery has helped 1600-year-old vampire Mara McCunniff transcribe the memoirs of her life, which began in the British Isles in 362 A.D. and led naturally to her settling in Los Angeles in the 20th century. Her tale is one of eternal love and perpetual hunger, as she tries to survive inconspicuously through the centuries, pursuing incarnations of her beloved first husband Gaar and avoiding the reappearance of her vampire nemesis Agyar.

Other books you might like:
Anne Rice, *The Vampire Lestat*, 1985
Michael Romkey, *I, Vampire*, 1990
S.P. Somtow, *Vampire Junction*, 1984
Chelsea Quinn Yarbro, *The Olivia Trilogy*, 1987-1989

3010

ABIGAIL MCDANIELS (Pseudonym of Dan Trent and Lynda Trent)

Althea

(New York: Zebra, 1995)

Story type: Horror (Possession)

Major character(s): Carol Horton, Lawyer; Holly Horton, Child (nine-year-old); Lisa Horton, Teenager
Time period(s): 1990s (1995)
Locale(s): Coulee, Louisiana

Summary: When Carol Horton inherits her family's Louisiana home, she inherits the legacy of horror that comes with it: an ornamental doll that contains the evil soul of Althea, a relative who murdered her child at the turn of the century and who has been waiting ever since to project herself into a living vessel.

Other books you might like:
Algernon Blackwood, *The Doll and One Other*, 1947
Matthew J. Costello, *Child's Play III*, 1991
Pat Graversen, *Dollies*, 1990
Ruby Jean Jensen, *Baby Doll*, 1991
Ruby Jean Jensen, *Victoria*, 1990

3011

ABIGAIL MCDANIELS (Pseudonym of Dan Trent and Lynda Trent)

Dead Voices

(New York: Zebra, 1994)

Story type: Horror (Supernatural Vengeance)
Major character(s): Gail Lamont, Housewife; Roger Lamont, Businessman (for Woodbine Oil); Jerome Green, Religious
Time period(s): 1990s (1994)
Locale(s): New Falls Church, Louisiana

Summary: Shortly after moving into their new home near Lake Boudreaux, Gail and Roger Lamont are plagued by a series of "crank" phone calls and menacing apparitions attributable to long-dead townsfolk. Investigation reveals that the dead all have one thing in common: they were buried in a cemetery supposedly moved to higher ground before the encroaching lake inundated the older sections of the town.

Other books you might like:
Matthew J. Costello, *Beneath Still Waters*, 1989
Elizabeth Forrest, *Dark Tide*, 1993
Steve Rasnic Tem, *Excavation*, 1987
T.M. Wright, *The Island*, 1988

3012

ABIGAIL MCDANIELS (Pseudonym of Dan Trent and Lynda Trent)

Playmates

(New York: Zebra)

Story type: Horror (Child-in-Peril)
Major character(s): Cassie Walker, Child (6 year old girl); Mark Walker, Parent (Cassie's father), Scientist (chemist); Janet Walker, Parent (Cassie's mother), Housewife
Time period(s): 1990s (1993)
Locale(s): Apollo, Louisiana

Summary: Several little girls who have lived in the old Morton House over the past century have died under mysterious circumstances, and Cassie Walker knows why: Ara, a doll found in the playhouse behind the house, is imbued with the vengeful soul of a young girl who was mistreated by the house's original owners.

Other books you might like:
Matthew J. Costello, *Child's Play III*, 1991
Pat Graversen, *Dollies*, 1990
Ellen Jamison, *Stone Dead*, 1993
Ruby Jean Jensen, *Baby Doll*, 1991
Ruby Jean Jensen, *The Living Evil*, 1993

3013

ABIGAIL MCDANIELS (Pseudonym of Dan Trent and Lynda Trent)

The Uprising
(New York: Zebra, 1994)

Story type: Horror (Ghost Story; Supernatural Vengeance)
Major character(s): Tess Bowen, Teacher (art); Tracy Wright, Teenager; Kevin Donatello, Teenager
Time period(s): 1990s (1994)
Locale(s): Maple Glen, Missouri

Summary: Under the instruction of fascistic Kevin Donatello, 12 students of Maple Glen High School commit suicide in the belief that they will attain occult powers. When the students in his new cult begin dying gruesome deaths, Kevin realizes that the original 12 are reaching from beyond the grave to exact their revenge.

Other books you might like:
Dennis Etchison, *Darkside*, 1986
Keith Ferrario, *Deadly Friend*, 1994
Stephen King, *Carrie*, 1974
Jean Simon, *Ghost Boy*, 1994

3014

JACK MCDEVITT

Ancient Shores
(New York: HarperPrism, 1996)

Story type: Science Fiction (Political; Contemporary Realism)
Major character(s): Tom Lasker, Farmer; Max Collingwood, Pilot; April Cannon, Scientist
Time period(s): 1990s
Locale(s): Fort Moxie, North Dakota; Walhalla, North Dakota

Summary: The boat Tom digs up from his field draws too much attention to his rural North Dakota town, since it seems to have sunk while Lake Agassis still held water. Max and April discover another artifact on American Indian land which leads to speculation about flying saucers and, perhaps, impending economic collapse.

Other books you might like:
Greg Bear, *Eon*, 1985
Gregory Benford, *Timescape*, 1980
John Brunner, *The Shockwave Rider*, 1975
Michael D. Weaver, *My Father Immortal*, 1989
George Zebrowski, *Stranger Suns*, 1991

3015

JACK MCDEVITT

The Engines of God
(New York: Ace, 1994)

Story type: Science Fiction (Science Fiction; Political)
Major character(s): Priscilla "Hutch" Hutchins, Spacewoman, Pilot (spaceship); Henry Jacobi, Engineer, Anthropologist; Richard Wald, Anthropologist
Time period(s): 23rd century (2200s)
Locale(s): Quaraqua, Planet—Imaginary; Oz, Moon—Imaginary (Quaraqua's); *Johann Winkelmann*, Spaceship

Summary: After a lower chamber of the Temple of Winds on Quaraqua produces tempting insights into the enigma of Oz, Richard Wald attempts to delay the imminent catastrophic terraforming of Quaraqua. Although the intelligent natives had only very recently died out, Quaraqua may once have been technologically advanced. The Oz object proves similar to other objects near once populated worlds, and may lead to the objects' creators and their significance.

Other books you might like:
Roger MacBride Allen, *The Ring of Charon*, 1990
Mary Gentle, *Golden Witchbreed*, 1984
Frank M. Robinson, *The Dark Beyond the Stars*, 1991
Allen Steele, *Labyrinth of Night*, 1992
Vernor Vinge, *A Fire upon the Deep*, 1992

3016

JACK MCDEVITT

A Talent for War
(New York: Ace, 1989)

Story type: Science Fiction (Military)
Major character(s): Alex Benedict, Businessman; Christopher Sims, Warrior
Time period(s): 31st century
Locale(s): Rimway, Planet—Imaginary

Summary: Alex Benedict, a young businessman, discovers that one of his culture's greatest heroes, the warrior Christopher Sim, who supposedly saved humanity from marauding aliens, may have been a fraud. In order to discover the truth, Benedict follows the tracks of a legend into incredible danger and mystery.

Other books you might like:
Orson Scott Card, *Ender's Game*, 1985
Orson Scott Card, *Speaker for the Dead*, 1986
Gordon R. Dickson, *Lost Dorsai*, 1980
Gordon R. Dickson, *Soldier, Ask Not*, 1967
Gordon R. Dickson, *The Tactics of Mistake*, 1971
Mike Resnick, *Ivory: A Legend of Past and Future*, 1988
Mike Resnick, *Paradise: A Chronicle of a Distant World*, 1989

3017

IAN MCDONALD

The Broken Land

(New York: Bantam Spectra, 1992)

Story type: Science Fiction (Political; Genetic Manipulation)
Major character(s): Mathembe Fileli, Refugee; Kalimuni, Religious (advocate), Lawyer; Grandfather Fileli, Handicapped (severed head)
Time period(s): Indeterminate Future
Locale(s): Chepsenyt, Fictional City; Ol Tah, Fictional City

Summary: The Confessors and the Proclaimers, in conflict for centuries, react with equal confusion and unease when the Empire Across the River annexes their lands and changes their lives. When a resident hides two of the Warriors of Destiny, a rebellious paramilitary group, the Empire destroys Chepsenyt, leaving Methembe, homeless and friendless, to wander in a strange and cruel world. Her experiences as she tries to make her way in the big city underline the plight of people in countries torn by religious and political strife.

Other books you might like:
Iain M. Banks, *The Bridge*, 1986
John Crowley, *Little, Big*, 1981
Lisa Goldstein, *A Mask for the General*, 1987
M. John Harrison, *The Pastel City*, 1971
Geoff Ryman, *The Unconquered Country*, 1986

3018

IAN MCDONALD

Evolution's Shore

(New York: Bantam Spectra, 1995)

Story type: Science Fiction (First Contact; Invasion of Earth)
Major character(s): Gabriel ''Gaby'' McAslan, Journalist; Dr. M. Shepard, Scientist (molecular biologist); T.P. Costello, Journalist (Nairobi Skynet station chief)
Time period(s): 2000s
Locale(s): Nairobi, Kenya

Summary: An ambitious journalist for Skynet News, Gaby McAslan devotes her career to reporting about the Chaga, a meteor-borne biological entity that gradually overtakes the African continent, physically changing those humans and animals who do not get out of its path.

Other books you might like:
J.G. Ballard, *The Crystal World*, 1966
Greg Bear, *Blood Music*, 1985
Octavia E. Butler, *Adulthood Rites*, 1988
Octavia E. Butler, *Dawn*, 1987
Octavia E. Butler, *Imago*, 1989
Arthur C. Clarke, *Childhood's End*, 1953
Nancy Kress, *Beggars and Choosers*, 1994

3019

IAN MCDONALD

King of Morning, Queen of Day

(New York: Bantam Spectra, 1991)

Story type: Fantasy (Contemporary)
Major character(s): Emily Desmond, Teenager; Jessica Caldwell, Waiter/Waitress; Enye MacColl, Advertising, Courier
Time period(s): 20th century
Locale(s): County Sligo, Ireland; Dublin, Ireland

Summary: A family story stretching across three generations, *King of Morning, Queen of Day* follows the effects of meddling with the powers of Faerie from one end of the 20th century to the other. Each section functions as a complete story with its own style, linked by the readers' growing understanding of the overall plot. The first part, ''Craigdarragh'' appeared in an earlier version as ''King of Morning, Queen of Day'' in *Empire Dreams* (1988).

Other books you might like:
James P. Blaylock, *Land of Dreams*, 1987
John Crowley, *Little, Big*, 1981
Greer Ilene Gilman, *Moonwise*, 1991
Robert Holdstock, *Mythago Wood*, 1984
Christoph Ransmayr, *The Last World*, 1990

3020

IAN MCDONALD

Out on Blue Six

(New York: Bantam Spectra, 1989)

Story type: Science Fiction (Dystopian)
Major character(s): Courtney Hall, Artist (Cartoonist), Revolutionary; Kilimanjaro West, Revolutionary, Amnesiac
Time period(s): Indeterminate Future
Locale(s): Earth

Summary: Courtney Hall, a cartoonist disgusted by the limits put upon her art by the censors of Great Yu, goes underground and meets a series of misfit artists, revolutionaries and madmen, all of whom are criminals under the laws of the Compassionate Society. Attempts are made to escape from Great Yu or transform it.

Other books you might like:
Richard Grant, *Rumors of Spring*, 1987
Aldous Huxley, *Brave New World*, 1932
Frederik Pohl, *The Space Merchants*, 1955
  C. M. Kornbluth, co-author
Bruce Sterling, *Islands in the Net*, 1988
Jack Williamson, *The Humanoids*, 1949

3021

IAN MCDONALD

Scissors Cut Paper Wrap Stone

(New York: Bantam Spectra, 1994)

Story type: Science Fiction (Mystical; Cyberpunk)

Major character(s): Ethan Ring, Artist, Spy; Masahiko, Artist; Luba Casipriadin, Artist
Time period(s): 21st century
Locale(s): Japan

Summary: While on a 1000-mile pilgrimage of the 88 temples, Ethan Ring frees himself from the power symbols tattooed on his palms by a secret government agency. With the help of a computer, the symbols allow him to control a person's primitive subconscious responses, such as healing or fear, but make it impossible for Ethan to have a normal life.

Other books you might like:
Poul Anderson, *The Stars Are Also Fire*, 1994
Jean Mark Gawron, *Dream of Glass*, 1993
Victor Milan, *The Cybernetic Samurai*, 1985
Frederik Pohl, *Gladiator-at-Law*, 1955
    C.M. Kornbluth, co-author
Rudy Rucker, *Wetware*, 1988
Walter Jon Williams, *Voice of the Whirlwind*, 1987

3022

IAN MCDONALD

Speaking in Tongues
(New York: Bantam Spectra, 1992)

Story type: Science Fiction (Collection)

Summary: Eleven stories published in periodicals and anthologies in England and the United States 1989-1991. Themes range widely from the arts in "Approaching Perpendicular," to ethics in "Fronts," with matter transmission examined in "Gardenias," time travel in "Atomic Avenue," fiction writing by an intelligent computer in "Speaking in Tongues" and an equally broad variety of themes in the remaining 6 stories.

Other books you might like:
J.G. Ballard, *War Fever*, 1991
Michael Flynn, *The Nanotech Chronicles*, 1991
Damon Knight, *One Side Laughing: Stories Unlike Other Stories*, 1991
Keith Laumer, *Alien Minds*, 1991
Cordwainer Smith, *The Best of Cordwainer Smith*, 1975
Michael Swanwick, *Gravity's Angels*, 1991

3023

IAN MCDONALD

Terminal Cafe
(New York: Bantam Spectra, 1994)

Story type: Science Fiction (Cyberpunk; Genetic Manipulation)
Major character(s): Santiago Columbar, Artist (drugs)
Time period(s): 21st century
Locale(s): Los Angeles, California; St. John, California

Summary: Nanotechnology allows many wonders, including the physical resurrection of the dead. However, it also allows for their brutal economic exploitation. On November 1st, the Day of the Dead, five friends make an appointment to meet in the St. John deadtown and find themselves caught up in a wave of social change.

Other books you might like:
John Crowley, *Beasts*, 1976
M. John Harrison, *The Pastel City*, 1972
Robert Silverberg, *Born with the Dead*, 1974
Cordwainer Smith, *Norstrilia*, 1975
Amy Thomson, *Virtual Girl*, 1993

3024

THOMAS LIAM MCDONALD, Editor
STEFAN R. DZIEMIANOWICZ, Co-Editor
MARTIN H. GREENBERG, Co-Editor

Sea Cursed: Thirty Terrifying Tales of the Deep
(New York: Barnes & Noble, 1994)

Story type: Horror (Anthology)
Locale(s): At Sea

Summary: The 30 stories in this anthology span more than 150 years and explore a variety of horrors associated with the sea. Included are H.P. Lovecraft's tale of an underwater civilization, "The Temple"; Edgar Allan Poe's description of a whirlpool, "Descent into the Maelstrom"; stories of deep-sea monsters in Arthur J. Burks' "The Bells of Oceana" and Frank Belknap Long's "Second Night Out"; tales of haunted ships in Joseph Conrad's "The Brute" and Hugh Cave's "Derelict"; and stories about mythic sea horrors in Clive Barker's "Scape Goats" and Robert Aickman's "The Wine-Dark Sea." William Hope Hodgson's classic novel of the horrors encountered by sailors on a marooned ship, "The Boats of the Glen Carrig," is reprinted in its entirety.

Other books you might like:
William Hope Hodgson, *Deep Waters*, 1967
William Hope Hodgson, *Demons of the Sea*, 1993
William Pattrick, *Mysterious Sea Stories*, 1985
    editor

3025

ALEX MCDONOUGH

Dragon's Blood
(New York: Ace, 1991)

Story type: Science Fiction (Adventure; Time Travel)
Series: Scorpio
Major character(s): Scorpio, Alien, Fugitive; Leah de Bernay, Apprentice, Doctor; Chan, Military Personnel
Time period(s): 1970s (1975); Indeterminate Past (Jurassic Period)
Locale(s): Phnom Penh, Cambodia

Summary: Once more, Leah and Scorpio have tried to return Leah to 14th-century Avignon and failed. This time, they've ended up in Cambodia, 1975. Surviving in a war-torn corner of the 20th century is hard enough, but soon they have to flee to the distant past to escape the Hunter, who is still determined to kill Scorpio and recover the orb.

Other books you might like:
Tom Deitz, *Windmaster's Bane*, 1986
Simon Hawke, *The Ivanhoe Gambit*, 1984

John Peel, *Timewyrm: Genesys*, 1991
Tim Powers, *The Anubis Gates*, 1983
Roger Zelazny, *Nine Princes in Amber*, 1970

3026

ALEX MCDONOUGH

Dragon's Claw

(New York: Ace, 1993)

Story type: Science Fiction (Time Travel; Adventure)
Series: Scorpio
Major character(s): Scorpio, Alien, Fugitive; Leah de Bernay, Apprentice, Doctor; Hatshepsut, Time Traveller
Time period(s): Indeterminate Future
Locale(s): Terrapin, Planet—Imaginary; Tamir, Planet—Imaginary

Summary: Having destroyed the Hunters' home planet, the vVos demand Terrapin's young. When Scorpio and Leah de Bernay travel to the vVos homeworld, Tamir, to see if they can be defeated, they discover humans from various historic times who have been abducted to play in the Game from which the vVos derive all their amusement and enjoyment. Sixth and final book of the series.

Other books you might like:
Pierre Barbet, *The Napoleons of Eridanus*, 1976
Marion Zimmer Bradley, *Hunters of the Red Moon*, 1973
C.J. Cherryh, *Hunter of Worlds*, 1977
Edmund Cooper, *Seahorse in the Sky*, 1969
Philip Jose Farmer, *The Wind Whales of Ishmael*, 1971
Alan Dean Foster, *Glory Lane*, 1987
Garry Kilworth, *In Solitary*, 1979
Jack Lovejoy, *The Hunters*, 1982
Andre Norton, *Here Abide Monsters*, 1973
Marti Steussy, *Dreams of Dawn*, 1988

3027

ALEX MCDONOUGH

Dragon's Eye

(New York: Ace, 1992)

Story type: Science Fiction (Time Travel; Political)
Series: Scorpio
Major character(s): Scorpio, Alien, Fugitive; Leah de Bernay, Apprentice, Doctor
Time period(s): 14th century (1351)
Locale(s): Earth; Terrapin, Planet—Imaginary

Summary: While Leah and Scorpio attempt to rescue Leah's condemned father, Lethor the Hunter finds them and tries to kill Scorpio. When Scorpio returns to Terrapin with Leah, they find hunters firmly in control of Terrapin. Aided by the orb which allows travel in time and space, the pair works to free Terrapin from the hunters.

Other books you might like:
John Dalmas, *Fanglith*, 1985
Harry Harrison, *The Stainless Steel Rat Saves the World*, 1972
John Jakes, *Time Gate*, 1961
Andre Norton, *Star Gate*, 1958

Connie Willis, *Doomsday Book*, 1992

3028

ALEX MCDONOUGH

Scorpio

(New York: Ace, 1990)

Story type: Science Fiction (Time Travel; Adventure)
Series: Scorpio
Major character(s): Scorpio, Alien, Fugitive; Leah de Bernay, Apprentice, Doctor; Pope Clement VII, Religious
Time period(s): 14th century
Locale(s): Terrapin, Planet—Imaginary; Avignon, France

Summary: Scorpio, a member of a placid race, accidently flees his home planet when he steals a mysterious artifact from the Hunters, a warlike race that is exterminating Scorpio's people. He ends up in medieval France during the height of the Black Death and must deal with the complexity of medieval life as well as the Hunters sent to catch him. Strong Jewish characters populate this novel.

Other books you might like:
Tom Deitz, *Windmaster's Bane*, 1986
Simon Hawke, *The Ivanhoe Gambit*, 1984
Tim Powers, *The Anubis Gates*, 1983
Sheri S. Tepper, *King's Blood Four*, 1983
Roger Zelazny, *Nine Princes in Amber*, 1970

3029

ALEX MCDONOUGH

Scorpio Descending

(New York: Ace, 1991)

Story type: Science Fiction (Time Travel; Adventure)
Series: Scorpio
Major character(s): Scorpio, Alien, Fugitive; Leah de Bernay, Apprentice, Doctor; Daria Nicolaeuna Mirskaya, Scientist
Time period(s): 1910s (1917)
Locale(s): Siberia, Russia; Petrograd, Russia

Summary: Pursued by the Hunters, Scorpio and Leah have arrived in Imperial Russia on the eve of the Russian Revolution. Unfortunately, the orb that carries them through time and space has been damaged, and finding a reclusive scientist is the only way they have to repair it and return to their homes.

Other books you might like:
Janet Asimov, *Norby Through Time and Space*, 1988
   Isaac Asimov, co-author
Simon Hawke, *The Ivanhoe Gambit*, 1984
John Peel, *Timewyrm: Genesys*, 1991
Tim Powers, *The Anubis Gates*, 1983
Roger Zelazny, *Nine Princes in Amber*, 1970

3030

ALEX MCDONOUGH

Scorpio Rising

(New York: Ace, 1990)

Story type: Science Fiction (Time Travel; Adventure)
Series: Scorpio
Major character(s): Scorpio, Alien, Fugitive; Leah de Bernay, Apprentice, Doctor; John Dee, Magician, Doctor
Time period(s): 16th century
Locale(s): London, England

Summary: Scorpio and Leah, jumping blindly in time, have arrived in London during the reign of Queen Elizabeth I. At first it looks like the two travelers will be able to discover how to control the orb (their time machine), but greed and treachery get in the way. Then the Hunters, the race that is exterminating Scorpio's people, return.

Other books you might like:
Tom Deitz, *Windmaster's Bane*, 1986
Simon Hawke, *The Ivanhoe Gambit*, 1984
Tim Powers, *The Anubis Gates*, 1983
Sheri S. Tepper, *King's Blood Four*, 1983
Roger Zelazny, *Nine Princes in Amber*, 1970

3031

THOMAS R. MCDONOUGH

The Missing Matter

(New York: Bantam Spectra, 1992)

Story type: Science Fiction (Hard Science Fiction; Adventure)
Series: Next Wave
Major character(s): Tariq Salib, Scientist; Al-Hajji Brian Fitzpatrick, Scientist, Religious; Fairouz, Spaceship Captain
Time period(s): 21st century
Locale(s): *Ulug Beg*, Spaceship; Ronin, Planet—Imaginary; Alternate Universe

Summary: When researchers detect an anomaly at the fringes of the solar system, the director of a remote outpost orders the *Ulug Beg* to transport an exploratory crew to investigate. They discover a mysterious planet which drags the explorers with it into parallel universes, places in which changes to the physical laws of the universe threaten their very existence. This third title in the Next Wave Series contains an 8-page introduction by Isaac Asimov titled "Dark Matter," and a 52-page article by astrophysicist Dr. Wallace H. Tucker, "The Attraction of Darkness."

Other books you might like:
Roger MacBride Allen, *The Ring of Charon*, 1990
Stephen Baxter, *Raft*, 1991
David Brin, *Earth*, 1990
Robert L. Forward, *Dragon's Egg*, 1980
Alan Dean Foster, *To the Vanishing Point*, 1988
Vonda N. McIntyre, *Transition*, 1991
Robert Reed, *Down the Bright Way*, 1991

3032

IAN MCDOWELL

Mordred's Curse

(New York: AvoNova, 1996)

Story type: Fantasy (Legend; Satire)
Major character(s): Mordred, Royalty, Bastard Son; Arthur, Ruler, Warrior; Merlin, Wizard, Homosexual
Time period(s): Indeterminate
Locale(s): The Orkneys, Scotland; Camelot, England

Summary: Mordred, Arthur's bastard, loves his father who, driven by guilt, repays love with indifference. Mordred remains at the Court, part of the splendor but always separate. Eventually, his desire for revenge leads him to usurp Arthur's kingdom and wife. First novel.

Other books you might like:
David Drake, *The Dragon Lord*, 1979
Phyllis Ann Karr, *The Idylls of the Queen*, 1982
Robert Nye, *Merlin*, 1979
Tim Powers, *The Drawing of the Dark*, 1979
Mary Stewart, *The Crystal Cave*, 1970

3033

MICHAEL MCDOWELL

Toplin

(New York: Dell Abyss, 1991)

Story type: Horror (Psychological Suspense)
Major character(s): Toplin, Office Worker; Marta Aleksandrova Blyushkina, Waiter/Waitress; Howard, Worker (pharmacy delivery boy)
Time period(s): 1990s

Summary: As the disaffected Toplin schemes to murder the waitress Marta for her foul looks, he ruminates over his life and friends, providing a journey through a warped mind that is by turns hilarious, grotesque and frightening. Originally published in 1985.

Other books you might like:
Ramsey Campbell, *The Face That Must Die*, 1979
Stephen Gilbert, *Ratman's Notebooks*, 1970
Brett Easton Ellis, *American Psycho*, 1991
David J. Schow, *The Kill Riff*, 1988

3034

IAN MCEWAN

Black Dogs

(New York: Doubleday/Nan A. Talese, 1992)

Story type: Horror (Literary)
Major character(s): Bernard Tremaine, Journalist (political commentator); June Tremaine, Writer (ex-wife of Bernard); Jeremy, Writer (son-in-law of Bernard and June)
Time period(s): 10th century
Locale(s): Berlin, Germany, West; St. Maurice de Navacelles, France

Summary: The fall of the Berlin Wall resurrects the histories of Bernard and June Tremaine, former communist sympathizers who separated from one another after June experienced a vision of supernatural evil that appears to have foreshadowed the turn of world politics for the last four decades.

Other books you might like:
Clive Barker, *The Damnation Game*, 1985
Kim Newman, *Bad Dreams*, 1990
George Orwell, *Nineteen Eighty-Four*, 1949

3035

DAN MCGIRT

Dirty Work

(New York: Roc, 1993)

Story type: Fantasy (Light Fantasy; Quest)
Series: Jason Cosmo
Major character(s): Jason Cosmo, Farmer, Hero
Time period(s): Indeterminate (10th century A. H.)
Locale(s): Arden, Fictional Country

Summary: Events dash Jason Cosmo's hopes of a quiet retirement raising turnips when word of the return of the Superwand, the supreme tool of power, reaches him. Jason alone can find and banish the Superwand, if standing in the way of hostilities between the Gods and Demons does not prove fatal.

Other books you might like:
Kyle Crocco, *Heroes, Inc.*, 1991
Kyle Crocco, *Heroes Wanted*, 1991
Alan Dean Foster, *To the Vanishing Point*, 1988
Neil Gaiman, *Good Omens: The Nice and Accurate Prophecies of Agnes Nutter, Witch*, 1990
   Terry Pratchett, co-author
Parke Godwin, *The Snake Oil Wars*, 1989
John Moore, *Slay and Rescue*, 1993
Roger Zelazny, *Bring Me the Head of Prince Charming*, 1991
   Robert Sheckley, co-author

3036

DAN MCGIRT

Jason Cosmo

(New York: NAL Signet, 1989)

Story type: Fantasy (Light Fantasy)
Major character(s): Jason Cosmo, Farmer, Hero
Time period(s): Indeterminate
Locale(s): Alternate Earth

Summary: Jason Cosmo becomes, at once, a hero and a wanted man and must leave his village. He is caught up in the struggle between two competing organizations of wizards. He takes up with an unconventional wizard, who is also being tracked by bounty hunters.

Other books you might like:
Robert Asprin, *Phule's Company*, 1990
James P. Blaylock, *The Stone Giant*, 1989
Alan Dean Foster, *Glory Lane*, 1990
John Morressy, *Kendrigern and the Charming Couple*, 1990

Neil Gaiman, *Good Omens: The Nice and Accurate Prophecies of Agnes Nutter, Witch*, 1990
   Terry Pratchett, co-author

3037

PATRICK MCGRATH

Dr. Haggard's Disease

(New York: Poseidon, 1993)

Story type: Horror (Psychological Suspense)
Major character(s): Edward Haggard, Doctor; James Vaughan, Pilot (Royal Air Force); Mrs. Gregor, Servant
Time period(s): 1940s
Locale(s): Elgin, England

Summary: Edward Haggard nurses a passion for his deceased beloved so strong that it has left him a ruined man. When her grown son comes to visit him, he espies her physical presence in her son's features and takes bizarre steps to ensure that he will not lose her a second time.

Other books you might like:
Henry James, *The Turn of the Screw*, 1898
Edgar Allan Poe, *The Fall of the House of Usher*, 1966
   in *Complete Stories and Poems of Edgar Allan Poe*
Edgar Allan Poe, *Ligeia*, 1966
   in *Complete Stories and Poems of Edgar Allan Poe*

3038

PATRICK MCGRATH

The Grotesque

(New York: Poseidon/Simon & Schuster, 1989)

Story type: Horror (Psychological Suspense)
Major character(s): Hugo Coal, Nobleman, Handicapped; Fledge, Servant (Coal's butler)
Time period(s): 1940s (1949)
Locale(s): Berkshire, England (Crook Manor)

Summary: Sir Hugo engages in a complex and perverse "duel" with his butler, Fledge, with a brutal murder at the center of things.

Other books you might like:
Harry Kressing, *The Cook*, 1965

3039

PATRICK MCGRATH

Spider

(New York: Poseidon/Simon & Schuster, 1990)

Story type: Horror (Psychological Suspense)
Major character(s): Dennis "Spider" Cleg, Patient (ex-mental patient); Horace Cleg, Parent (Dennis' father), Maintenance Worker (Plumber); Hilda Wilkinson, Prostitute, Step-Parent (Dennis' stepmother)
Time period(s): 1930s (1937); 1950s (1957)
Locale(s): London, England (East End)

Summary: Returned from his 20-year incarceration as a mental patient, Dennis Cleg tells the story of his mother's death, his father's complicity in her murder, and how he evolved the persona of ''Spider'' to cope with emotional trauma of his childhood.

Other books you might like:
Scott Baker, *Webs*, 1989
Robert Bloch, *Psycho*, 1959
Robert Bloch, *The Scarf*, 1947
Shirley Jackson, *We Have Always Lived in the Castle*, 1962

3040
ELOISE JARVIS MCGRAW

The Moorchild
(New York: Simon & Schuster/Margaret K. McElderry Books, 1996)

Story type: Fantasy (Young Adult; Contemporary Realism)
Major character(s): Moql'nkkn ''Moql/Saaski'', Mythical Creature (half-fairy); Old Bess, Aged Person; Anwara, Parent
Time period(s): Indeterminate
Locale(s): The Mound, Mythical Place; Torskaal, Fictional City

Summary: Abandoned by her fairy parent, halfling Saaski grows up with human foster parents, unappreciated by her human companions except for Old Bess, who helps Saaski learn to read. When the townfolk begin to blame her for all of their ill luck, Saaski must find another home but resolves to first recover the human child taken by the fairy folk when they abandoned Saaski.

Other books you might like:
Pamela Dean, *The Dubious Hills*, 1994
Rose Estes, *Troll-Taken*, 1993
Rosalie Fry, *The Secret of Roan Inish*, 1995
Peni R. Griffin, *Hobkin*, 1992
Robin Morgan, *The Mer-Child: A Legend for Children and Other Adults*, 1991
Elizabeth Marie Pope, *The Perilous Gard*, 1974

3041
MAUREEN F. MCHUGH

China Mountain Zhang
(New York: Tor, 1992)

Story type: Science Fiction (Genetic Manipulation; Political)
Major character(s): Rafael Zhong ''China Mountain'' Shan, Engineer, Homosexual; Qian, Foreman; San-xiang Qian, Girlfriend
Time period(s): 21st century
Locale(s): New York, New York

Summary: Zhong Shan looks like an American Born Chinese only because his parents had his genetic construction altered to suppress his Hispanic mother's features, gaining him preferential treatment under Chinese rule but preventing him from passing a DNA check. When Elder Qian encourages China Mountain to date his ugly daughter, marry her and move to China, homosexual Zhong Shan inexorably becomes involved with the Qian family's destiny. Author's first novel.

Other books you might like:
Margaret Wander Bonanno, *The Others*, 1990
Gordon R. Dickson, *Way of the Pilgrim*, 1987
Peter R. Emshwiller, *The Host*, 1991
John Hersey, *White Lotus*, 1965
Kim Stanley Robinson, *The Gold Coast*, 1989
David Wingrove, *The Middle Kingdom*, 1990

3042
MAUREEN F. MCHUGH

Half the Day Is Night
(New York: Tor, 1994)

Story type: Science Fiction (Contemporary Realism; Political)
Major character(s): David Dai, Military Personnel (retired), Bodyguard; Mayla Ling, Banker; Tim Bennet, Bodyguard
Time period(s): 21st century
Locale(s): Caribe, Undersea Environment/Habitat

Summary: After Mayla Ling hires David Dai, the plots against her prove more complex than she imagined. Soon the two must flee terrorists through a richly detailed environment, simultaneously strange and familiar.

Other books you might like:
John Brunner, *The Shockwave Rider*, 1975
Pat Cadigan, *Synners*, 1991
William Gibson, *Neuromancer*, 1984
Ian McDonald, *Terminal Cafe*, 1994
Kim Stanley Robinson, *The Gold Coast*, 1989

3043
VONDA N. MCINTYRE

The Crystal Star
(New York: Bantam Spectra, 1994)

Story type: Science Fiction (Space Opera; Mystical)
Series: Star Wars
Major character(s): Leia Organa, Royalty, Diplomat; Chewbacca, Alien (Wookie), Adventurer; Luke Skywalker, Martial Arts Expert (Jedi Knight), Hero
Time period(s): Indeterminate Past
Locale(s): *Alderran*, Spaceship; Crseih, Planet—Imaginary; New Republic, Interstellar Empire/Federation

Summary: Leia, Chewbacca and robot Artoo-Detoo search for Leia and Han Solo's kidnapped children while Han, Luke and robot See-Threepio try to find a group of Jedi Knights. Set after Dave Wolverton's *The Courtship of Princess Leia*.

Other books you might like:
Roger MacBride Allen, *Ambush at Corellia*, 1995
Kevin J. Anderson, *Jedi Search*, 1994
L. Neil Smith, *The Lando Calrissian Adventures*, 1994
Dave Wolverton, *The Courtship of Princess Leia*, 1994
Timothy Zahn, *Heir to the Empire*, 1991

3044

VONDA N. MCINTYRE

Metaphase

(New York: Bantam Spectra, 1992)

Story type: Science Fiction (First Contact; Science Fiction)
Series: Starfarers
Major character(s): Victoria McKenzie, Scientist, Leader; J.D. Sauvage, Scientist (alien contact specialist); Nemo, Alien (Squidmoth)
Time period(s): 21st century
Locale(s): *Starfarer*, Spaceship; *Chi*, Spaceship; *Nemo*, Spaceship

Summary: Pursuing their explorations rather than return to Earth forever, *Starfarer*'s residents meet and establish rapport with *Nemo* as its extremely long life draws to an end. They then continue onward hoping to discover civilization and the creators of the cosmic string transportation system.

Other books you might like:
Jeffrey A. Carver, *Down the Stream of Stars*, 1990
Glen Cook, *The Dragon Never Sleeps*, 1988
John DeChancie, *Paradox Alley*, 1987
Michael P. Kube-McDowell, *Empery*, 1987
Michael P. Kube-McDowell, *Enigma*, 1986
Larry Niven, *The Mote in God's Eye*, 1974
    Jerry Pournelle, co-author
Alis A. Rasmussen, *A Passage of Stars*, 1990
Alis A. Rasmussen, *The Price of Ransom*, 1990
Alis A. Rasmussen, *Revolution's Shore*, 1990
Vernor Vinge, *A Fire upon the Deep*, 1990

3045

VONDA N. MCINTYRE

Nautilus

(New York: Bantam Spectra, 1994)

Story type: Science Fiction (First Contact; Science Fiction)
Series: Starfarers
Major character(s): J.D. Sauvage, Scientist (alien contact specialist); Orchestra, Alien; Stephen Thomas, Professor, Genetically Altered Being
Time period(s): 21st century
Locale(s): *Starfarer*, Spaceship; *Nautilus*, Spaceship; Civilization, Interstellar Empire/Federation

Summary: While effecting repairs to the damaged *Starfarer*, the disparate crew finds little time for consensus building. J.D. Sauvage's initial contact with newly discovered aliens leads to a promising exchange of gifts, while an ancient intelligence plots a new attack on Civilization.

Other books you might like:
Roger MacBride Allen, *The Ring of Charon*, 1990
Roger MacBride Allen, *The Shattered Sphere*, 1994
Gregory Benford, *Furious Gulf*, 1994
David Brin, *Startide Rising*, 1983
Orson Scott Card, *Speaker for the Dead*, 1986
Glen Cook, *The Dragon Never Sleeps*, 1988

Robert L. Forward, *Return to Rocheworld*, 1993
    Julie Forward Fuller, co-author
Alis A. Rasmussen, *The Price of Ransom*, 1990
Vernor Vinge, *A Fire upon the Deep*, 1992

3046

VONDA N. MCINTYRE

Starfarers

(New York: Ace, 1989)

Story type: Science Fiction (Hard Science Fiction)
Major character(s): Victoria McKenzie, Scientist, Leader; Stephen Thomas Gregory, Scientist
Time period(s): 21st century
Locale(s): *Starfarer*, Spaceship

Summary: Construction of *Starfarer*, humanity's second interstellar probe, is almost complete, but the political and military situation on Earth makes it seem more and more likely that the spaceship will never be allowed to fulfill its mission. A dedicated group of mission scientists plot to steal the ship and head for the stars.

Other books you might like:
Gregory Benford, *Heart of the Comet*, 1986
    David Brin, co-author
Lois McMaster Bujold, *Falling Free*, 1988
Michael P. Kube-McDowell, *Enigma*, 1986
Pamela Sargent, *Venus of Dreams*, 1986

3047

VONDA N. MCINTYRE

Transition

(New York: Bantam Spectra, 1991)

Story type: Science Fiction (Hard Science Fiction)
Series: Starfarers
Major character(s): Victoria McKenzie, Scientist, Leader; J.D. Sauvage, Scientist (alien contact specialist)
Time period(s): 21st century
Locale(s): *Starfarer*, Spaceship; *Chi*, Spaceship

Summary: Mankind's first successful interstellar voyage has been shaky as evidenced by Starfarer's entering the Tau Ceti star system accompanied by the accidental explosion of a nuclear weapon. When a first contact team tracks down the source of intelligent signals to an airless moon of Tau Ceti II, they discover a dome which suffers an explosion as they land, leaving a single small artifact to be discovered by J.D. after the dome cools. The team plans to visit earthlike Tau Ceti II until *Starfarer*'s preliminary system survey reveals a nexus of cosmic strings similar to the one allowing *Starfarer*'s Sol-Tau Ceti voyage. When the cosmic string leading to Sol begins to move, everyone must decide whether to return to Earth while it is possible or to continue on via the cosmic string nexus, choosing a new mission, one from which returning to Earth seems impossible.

Other books you might like:
Roger MacBride Allen, *The Ring of Charon*, 1990
Glen Cook, *The Dragon Never Sleeps*, 1988

John DeChancie, *Paradox Alley*, 1987
John DeChancie, *Red Limit Freeway*, 1984
John DeChancie, *Starrigger*, 1983
Michael P. Kube-McDowell, *Empery*, 1987
Michael P. Kube-McDowell, *Emprise*, 1986

3048

KENNETH MCKENNEY

The Offspring
(New York: Ballantine, 1990)

Story type: Horror (Curse)
Series: Changeling Trilogy
Major character(s): Mark Lawrence, Young Man; Sally Lawrence, Parent
Time period(s): 1990s
Locale(s): Santa Monica, California; Europe

Summary: Supported by his mother and other allies, Mark Lawrence, son of "the changeling," retraces his father's footsteps and does battle with an ancient evil to free himself and his father from the terrible curse that has plagued them both.

Other books you might like:
Jessie Kerruish, *The Undying Monster*, 1922

3049

NANCY MCKENZIE

The Child Queen
(New York: Ballantine Del Rey, 1994)

Story type: Fantasy (Legend)
Major character(s): Guinevere, Royalty (queen); Arthur, Ruler, Warrior; Lancelot, Knight
Time period(s): 5th century
Locale(s): England

Summary: Prophecied at birth to achieve greatness, Guinevere grows up with her cousin in North Wales, hearing tales of Arthur's heroism. After Guinevere's subsequent betrothal to Arthur, jealous King Medwyn acts on an old prophecy and kidnaps Guinevere, holding her until Lancelot and Merlin come to the rescue. Guinevere's difficulties continue as does her fame. Author's first novel.

Other books you might like:
Marion Zimmer Bradley, *The Mists of Avalon*, 1983
Gillian Bradshaw, *Hawk of May*, 1980
Sharan Newman, *Guinevere*, 1981
Mary Stewart, *The Crystal Cave*, 1970
Persia Woolley, *Child of the Northern Spring*, 1987

3050

LEE MCKEONE

Backblast
(New York: Popular Library Questar, 1989)

Story type: Science Fiction (Adventure)
Series: Ghoster

Major character(s): Conek Hayden, Spaceship Captain, Businessman; Cge, Robot, Sidekick
Time period(s): Indeterminate Future
Locale(s): Beldorph, Planet—Imaginary; *Windsong*, Spaceship

Summary: In this sequel to *Ghoster* a loner spaceship captain and his robot friend find themselves on the run from the law.

Other books you might like:
Joe Clifford Faust, *Desperate Measures*, 1989
Joe Clifford Faust, *The Essence of Evil*, 1990
Joe Clifford Faust, *Precious Cargo*, 1989
Harry Harrison, *Bill, the Galactic Hero*, 1965

3051

LEE MCKEONE

The Clone Crisis
(New York: Warner Questar, 1992)

Story type: Science Fiction (Adventure; Humor)
Series: Ghoster
Major character(s): Conek Hayden, Spaceship Captain, Businessman; Cge, Robot, Sidekick (Conek's)
Time period(s): Indeterminate Future
Locale(s): Outer Space; Siddah-II, Planet—Imaginary; *Bucephalus*, Spaceship

Summary: Plotting to take over a smuggling empire, crime lords begin to clone the king and his top leaders. Suddenly the galaxy contains many Coneks, each bent on survival, while the original Conek must thwart the galactic crime war.

Other books you might like:
Pat Cadigan, *Fools*, 1992
Dave Duncan, *Hero*, 1991
Ken Rolston, *Extreme Paranoia: Nobody Knows the Trouble I've Shot*, 1991
A.E. van Vogt, *The World of Null-A*, 1945

3052

LEE MCKEONE

Starfire Down
(New York: Warner Questar, 1991)

Story type: Science Fiction (Adventure)
Series: Ghoster
Major character(s): Conek Hayden, Spaceship Captain, Businessman; Gella Icor, Spaceship Captain; Andro Arvin, Military Personnel, Administrator (spaceport)
Time period(s): Indeterminate Future
Locale(s): *Destria*, Spaceship; *Starfire*, Spaceship; Holmarin IV, Planet—Imaginary

Summary: Conek Hayden, ex-smuggler, must rescue one of his pilots, Gella Icor, who has been arrested for a crime attributed to her deceased father. The atmosphere on Holmarin IV, where Gella is being held, is toxic to those not born there, complicating the rescue. This novel is a sequel to *Backblast*.

Other books you might like:
David Brin, *Startide Rising*, 1983
C.J. Cherryh, *Merchanter's Luck*, 1982
Mary Gentle, *Golden Witchbreed*, 1984
Katharine Kerr, *Polar City Blues*, 1990
Alis A. Rasmussen, *A Passage of Stars*, 1990
Alis A. Rasmussen, *The Price of Ransom*, 1990
Alis A. Rasmussen, *Revolution's Shore*, 1990
Walter Jon Williams, *Angel Station*, 1989

3053

DENNIS L. MCKIERNAN

Caverns of Socrates

(New York: Roc, 1995)

Story type: Fantasy (Adventure; Alternate World)
Major character(s): Eric Flannery, Computer Expert, Adventurer; Alice Maxon, Computer Expert, Adventurer; Avery, Artificial Intelligence
Time period(s): 1990s
Locale(s): Tucson, Arizona; Itheria, Cyberspace (computer virtual reality)

Summary: While testing a new virtual reality program intended to mimic reality, Eric, Alice, and other expert gamers, the Black Foxes, find themselves trapped within the computer's reality and must discover a way to regain control and return to their own world.

Other books you might like:
Greg Egan, *Permutation City*, 1995
Philip Jose Farmer, *Red Orc's Rage*, 1991
James P. Hogan, *Realtime Interrupt*, 1995
Joel Rosenberg, *The Sleeping Dragon*, 1983
Will Shetterly, *The Tangled Lands*, 1989
Wm. Mark Simmons, *In the Net of Dreams*, 1990
Vivian Vande Velde, *User Unfriendly*, 1991

3054

DENNIS L. MCKIERNAN

The Dragonstone

(New York: Roc, 1996)

Story type: Fantasy (Quest; Adventure)
Major character(s): Arin, Mythical Creature (elf), Noblewoman; Aiko, Warrior, Noblewoman; Egil, Warrior
Time period(s): Indeterminate
Locale(s): Mithgar, Fictional Country

Summary: Spurred by the horrific vision of all Mithgar engulfed in war, Arin and her companions seek understanding of her role in events and a means of finding the magic Dragonstone, focus of the impending disaster. Set three centuries prior to *Voyage of the Fox Rider*.

Other books you might like:
Lynn Flewelling, *Luck in the Shadows*, 1996
Terry Goodkind, *Wizard's First Rule*, 1994
Robin Hobb, *Assassin's Apprentice*, 1995
J.V. Jones, *The Baker's Boy*, 1995
Robert Jordan, *The Eye of the World*, 1990

3055

DENNIS L. MCKIERNAN

The Eye of the Hunter

(New York: Roc, 1992)

Story type: Fantasy (Quest)
Major character(s): Riatha, Mythical Creature (elf), Immortal; Aravan, Mythical Creature (elf)
Time period(s): Indeterminate (5E985-5E993)
Locale(s): Mithgar, Fictional Country

Summary: A thousand years after Riatha helped hunt down and subdue the evil Baron Stoke, the reappearance of the comet, Eye of the Hunter, foretells the imminent reappearance of Baron Stoke. Riatha joins with Aravan and three others in a desperate attempt to avert the prophecied disaster.

Other books you might like:
Glen Cook, *The Black Company*, 1984
Glen Cook, *Shadows Linger*, 1984
Glen Cook, *The White Rose*, 1985
David Eddings, *Pawn of Prophecy*, 1982
J.R.R. Tolkien, *The Fellowship of the Ring*, 1954
J.R.R. Tolkien, *The Return of the King*, 1956
J.R.R. Tolkien, *The Two Towers*, 1955

3056

DENNIS L. MCKIERNAN

Tales of Mithgar

(New York: Roc, 1994)

Story type: Fantasy (Collection; Adventure)
Time period(s): Indeterminate
Locale(s): Mithgar, Fictional Country

Summary: Contains a three-page foreword, a two-page afterword, two-page author's note and 11 original, interwoven stories of heroic quests and great battles through the ages which form the basis for many legends in Mithgar.

Other books you might like:
Robert Asprin, *Thieves' World*, 1979
  editor
Fritz Leiber, *Swords Against Wizardry*, 1968
Will Shetterly, *Liavek*, 1985
  Emma Bull, co-editor
J.R.R. Tolkien, *The Silmarillion*, 1977
J.R.R. Tolkien, *Unfinished Tales of Numenor and Middle Earth*, 1980

3057

DENNIS L. MCKIERNAN

Voyage of the Fox Rider

(New York: Roc, 1993)

Story type: Fantasy (Quest)
Major character(s): Alamar, Wizard; Jinnarin, Mythical Creature (pysk); Aravan, Mythical Creature (elf), Sea Captain
Time period(s): Indeterminate Past (1E9572-2E1)
Locale(s): Rwn, Fictional Country

Summary: Guided by a strange dream and assisted by the far-travelled Aravan, Jinnarin and Alamar hunt for Farrix, Jinnarin's missing mate. The pair discover greater stakes than the life of one Pysk as evil forces gather and an age draws to an end. Sequel to *The Eye of the Hunter*.

Other books you might like:
Glen Cook, *The Black Company*, 1984
Dave Duncan, *Magic Casement*, 1990
David Eddings, *Pawn of Prophecy*, 1982
Robert Jordan, *The Eye of the World*, 1989
Patricia A. McKillip, *The Riddle-Master of Hed*, 1976

3058

PATRICIA A. MCKILLIP

The Book of Atrix Wolfe

(New York: Ace, 1995)

Story type: Fantasy (Magic Conflict)
Major character(s): Atrix Wolfe, Magician, Criminal; Saro, Amnesiac, Heiress—Lost; Talis Pelucir, Royalty, Heir
Time period(s): Indeterminate
Locale(s): Pelucir, Fictional Country; Hunter's Field, Fictional Country; Chaumenard, Mythical Place (magicians' retreat)

Summary: Appalled by warfare and hoping to bring peace to Pelucir and Kardeth, Atrix Wolfe intends to craft a spirit to dispel the combatants, but instead brings forth the Hunter, a destroyer who plagues Hunter's Field for a generation. When Atrix Wolfe's magic deprives the Queen of the Wood of both her mate and her daughter, she summons Talis Pelucir to help find the missing Atrix Wolfe and her lost child.

Other books you might like:
Charles de Lint, *Memory and Dream*, 1994
Susan Dexter, *The Wizard's Shadow*, 1993
Elizabeth Forrest, *Phoenix Fire*, 1992
Lisa Goldstein, *Summer King, Winter Fool*, 1994
Terry Goodkind, *Wizard's First Rule*, 1994
Barbara Hambly, *Bride of the Rat God*, 1994

3059

PATRICIA A. MCKILLIP

The Cygnet and the Firebird

(New York: Ace, 1993)

Story type: Fantasy (Magic Conflict; Adventure)
Series: Sorceress and the Cygnet
Major character(s): Meguet Vervaine, Warrior; Nyx Ro, Sorceress
Time period(s): Indeterminate Past
Locale(s): Luxor Desert, Mythical Place; Ro Holding, Mythical Place

Summary: During a Ro Holding Council meeting, Ro Holding suffers an attack. Meguet and Nyx must discover the attacker's identity and thwart the effort, a task made much more difficult when Meguet and Nyx find themselves mysteriously transported to a dangerous desert far from home.

Other books you might like:
C.J. Cherryh, *The Faded Sun: Kesrith*, 1978

Barbara Hambly, *Dog Wizard*, 1993
Barbara Hambly, *The Ladies of Mandrigyn*, 1984
Barbara Hambly, *The Witches of Wenshar*, 1987
Laurell K. Hamilton, *Nightseer*, 1992
Katharine Kerr, *Daggerspell*, 1986
Melanie Rawn, *Stronghold*, 1990
Judith Tarr, *Alamut*, 1989
Martha Wells, *The Element of Fire*, 1993

3060

PATRICIA A. MCKILLIP
BRIAN FROUD, Co-Author

Something Rich and Strange

(New York: Bantam Spectra, 1994)

Story type: Fantasy (Contemporary; Romance)
Series: Brian Froud's Faerielands
Major character(s): Megan, Artist; Jonah, Collector, Store Owner; Adam Fin, Artist, Mythical Creature
Time period(s): 1990s
Locale(s): At Sea; West Coast

Summary: Megan and Jonah live on the seacoast, above Jonah's shop, Things Rich and Strange, until a fateful day when Jenny's sketch of the sea shows something she didn't draw and a stranger brings beautiful jewelry into the store on consignment. Suddenly Jonah will give up everything to follow a mysterious singer and Jenny will do anything to save him.

Other books you might like:
Charles de Lint, *The Wild Wood*, 1994
    Brian Froud co-author
Barbara Hambly, *The Silent Tower*, 1986
R.A. MacAvoy, *The Grey Horse*, 1987
Anne McCaffrey, *The Coelura*, 1987
Elizabeth Marie Pope, *The Perilous Gard*, 1974

3061

PATRICIA A. MCKILLIP

The Sorceress and the Cygnet

(New York: Ace, 1991)

Story type: Fantasy (Magic Conflict; Quest)
Series: Sorceress and the Cygnet
Major character(s): Corleau, Hero (Wayfarer)
Time period(s): Indeterminate Past
Locale(s): Delta, Mythical Place; Ro Holding, Mythical Place

Summary: The Wayfarers, a dark-haired race, retain the legend of their arrival from space. Corleu, a blond, is tormented for this difference, but he also has a gift for words, both reading and storytelling. When he tells his friends the story of the Cygnet and other stellar denizens he has no inkling that he will be forced into their story to save his love and his life.

Other books you might like:
Orson Scott Card, *Prentice Alvin*, 1989
John Deakins, *Barrow*, 1990
Mark C. Perry, *Morigu: The Dead*, 1990
Meredith Ann Pierce, *The Pearl of the Soul of the World*, 1990

Robert Silverberg, *To the Land of the Living*, 1990

3062

PATRICIA A. MCKILLIP

Winter Rose

(New York: Ace, 1996)

Story type: Fantasy (Romance; Alternate World)
Major character(s): Rois Melior, Heroine; Laurel Melior, Heroine; Corbet Lynn, Heir
Time period(s): Indeterminate
Locale(s): Lynn Hall, Mythical Place

Summary: Ignoring his grandfather's curse, Corbet Lynn comes to rebuild Lynn Hall and reclaim his ancestors' land. When the curse draws Corbet into a dream world. Rois and Laurel follow him, hoping to find a path back to reality.

Other books you might like:
Pamela Dean, *The Dubious Hills*, 1994
Robert Holdstock, *Mythago Wood*, 1984
L. Dean James, *Summerland*, 1994
Holly Lisle, *Minerva Wakes*, 1994
Delia Sherman, *The Porcelain Dove*, 1993
Jane Yolen, *Sister Light, Sister Dark*, 1988

3063

ROBIN MCKINLEY

Deerskin

(New York: Ace, 1993)

Story type: Fantasy (Legend; Quest)
Major character(s): Lissla "Deerskin" Lissar, Royalty, Fugitive; Ash, Animal (dog), Companion (Lissar's)
Time period(s): Indeterminate
Locale(s): Fictional Country

Summary: Acknowledging the elements of madness, violence and twisted sexuality from the unbowdlerized original story, "Donkeyskin," by Charles Perrault, this volume follows Princess Lissar as her father, maddened by grief and obsession, announces his own marriage to her then rapes her. To save herself and the kingdom, Lissar flees with Ash, changes her name and seeks healing in Ash's homeland.

Other books you might like:
Lois McMaster Bujold, *The Spirit Ring*, 1992
Ellen Datlow, *Snow White, Blood Red*, 1993
    Terri Windling, co-editor
Jacob Ludwig Grimm, *The Complete Fairy Tales of the Brothers Grimm*, 1992
    Wilhelm Grimm, co-author; Jack Zipes, editor, translator
Susan Palwick, *Flying in Place*, 1992
Elizabeth Ann Scarborough, *Last Refuge*, 1992
Martha Wells, *The Element of Fire*, 1993
Jack Zipes, *Spells of Enchantment*, 1991
    editor

3064

ROBIN MCKINLEY

A Knot in the Grain and Other Stories

(New York: Morrow Greenwillow, 1994)

Story type: Fantasy (Young Adult; Collection)
Summary: Contains two original stories and three stories reprinted from anthologies 1982-1985 with a generally upbeat tone and sometimes muted fantastic elements. Themes included romance, family life and heroic fantasy, with four of the stories set in the milieu of *The Hero and the Crown* and *The Blue Sword*.

Other books you might like:
Marion Zimmer Bradley, *The Best of Marion Zimmer Bradley*, 1988
Robert Holdstock, *The Bone Forest*, 1992
Diana Wynne Jones, *Warlock at the Wheel and Other Stories*, 1985
Anne McCaffrey, *Get Off the Unicorn*, 1977
Jane Yolen, *Tales of Wonder*, 1983

3065

ROBIN MCKINLEY

The Outlaws of Sherwood

(New York: Ace, 1989)

Story type: Fantasy (Legend)
Major character(s): Robin Hood, Outlaw, Hero; Marian, Noblewoman
Time period(s): Indeterminate Past
Locale(s): Sherwood Forest, England

Summary: Romantically retold, maintaining only the legend's setting and characters, Robin Hood is portrayed as a sensitive, non-macho and average hero. The characters of the other members of his band of outlaws are more fully developed in this version.

Other books you might like:
Patricia Aakhus, *The Voyage of Mael Duin's Curragh*, 1989
Ru Emerson, *Spell Bound*, 1990
Ellen Kushner, *Outlaws of Sherwood Forest*, 1985
    Choose Your Own Adventure Series 47
Elizabeth Moon, *Surrender None: The Legacy of Gird*, 1990
Gail Van Asten, *Charlemagne's Champion*, 1990

3066

JACK MCKINNEY

Free Radicals

(New York: Ballantine Del Rey, 1992)

Story type: Science Fiction (Adventure; Invasion of Earth)
Series: Black Hole Travel Agency
Major character(s): Lucky Junknowitz, Revolutionary; Ozwaldo Undershort, Alien, Agent; Asin Boxdale, Artist
Time period(s): Indeterminate Future
Locale(s): Confabulon, Planet—Imaginary; Japan; Root Canal, Planet—Imaginary

Summary: The story continues as Lucky travels farther from Earth toward the prison planet, al-Recm, aided by a duped agent of the Black Hole Travel Agency itself. Meanwhile, the Black Hole consolidates its gains on Earth. And the IRS still wants Lucky's hide. . .

Other books you might like:
Jack L. Chalker, *And the Devil Will Drag You Under*, 1979
Philip Jose Farmer, *The Maker of Universes*, 1965
Robert A. Heinlein, *Glory Road*, 1963
Keith Laumer, *The Time Bender*, 1981
Roger Zelazny, *Nine Princes in Amber*, 1970

3067

JACK MCKINNEY

Hostile Takeover

(New York: Ballantine Del Rey, 1994)

Story type: Science Fiction (Humor; Adventure)
Series: Black Hole Travel Agency
Major character(s): Yoo Sobek, Alien (Sysop), Rebel; Silvercup, Android; Lucky Junknowitz, Revolutionary
Time period(s): Indeterminate Future
Locale(s): Japan; Light Trap, Planet—Imaginary

Summary: Various factions form an unsteady alliance against the Black Hole Travel Agency. To succeed they must invade Light Trap, the Black Hole's impenetrable stronghold, and must also trust Yoo Sobek, the renegade Sysop. Concludes the series.

Other books you might like:
Harry Harrison, *The Adventures of the Stainless Steel Rat*, 1978
Simon Hawke, *The Ivanhoe Gambit*, 1984
Robert A. Heinlein, *Glory Road*, 1963
Michael Scott Rohan, *Chase the Morning*, 1991
Roger Zelazny, *Nine Princes in Amber*, 1970

3068

JACK MCKINNEY

Kaduna Memories

(New York: Ballantine, 1990)

Story type: Science Fiction (Cyberpunk; First Contact)
Major character(s): Felix McTurk, Computer Expert, Detective; Jain Nugget, Singer; Rec, Artificial Intelligence
Time period(s): 21st century
Locale(s): Earth; Earth Orbit, Outer Space

Summary: Felix and Jain play psychiatrists to an artifical intelligence with a split personality to solve the 15-year-old mystery of alien contact and her parents' deaths.

Other books you might like:
Pat Cadigan, *Synners*, 1991
William Gibson, *Neuromancer*, 1984
Bruce Sterling, *Islands in the Net*, 1988
Bruce Sterling, *Schismatrix*, 1985
Walter Jon Williams, *Voice of the Whirlwind*, 1987

3069

JEFFREY N. MCMAHAN

Somewhere in the Night

(Boston: Alyson, 1989)

Story type: Horror (Collection)

Summary: Eight witty, sophisticated stories that are darkly humorous in tone, but end with nasty final twists. McMahan's focus on gay protagonists gives an original spin to traditional horror situations and motifs. Especially interesting are ''Two-faced Johnny,'' in which a Halloween costume party turns into a very bizarre banquet and two longer stories, ''Somewhere in the Night'' and ''Hell Is for Children,'' featuring Andrew, a gay vampire.

Other books you might like:
Sandy Bayer, *The Crystal Curtain*, 1988
Vincent Lardo, *China House*, 1983

3070

JEFFREY N. MCMAHAN

Vampires Anonymous

(Boston: Alyson, 1991)

Story type: Horror (Vampire Story)
Major character(s): Steven Verruckt, Student—Graduate; Eddie Cramer, Police Officer, Homosexual; Andrew Lyall, Vampire
Time period(s): 1990s
Locale(s): California

Summary: Gay cop Eddie Cramer hopes to rehabilitate his flagging reputation with the police force by bringing in ''The Sleepy Hollow Murderer,'' a mass murderer who steals the heads of his victims and who may be masquerading innocently as a member of Vampires Anonymous, a secret self-help group dedicated to curing vampires of their bloodthirsty habits.

Other books you might like:
John Peyton Cooke, *Out for Blood*, 1991
Scott Edelman, *The Gift*, 1990
Jewelle Gomez, *The Gilda Stories*, 1991
Anne Rice, *Interview with the Vampire*, 1976
John Steakley, *Vampire$*, 1990

3071

CHARLES MCNAIR

Land O'Goshen

(New York: St. Martin's Press, 1994)

Story type: Science Fiction (Literary; Disaster)
Major character(s): Buddy, Teenager, Orphan; Sack, Disembodied Personality; Cissy Barber, Girlfriend
Time period(s): 21st century
Locale(s): Goshen, Alabama

Summary: After losing his family to the Christian soldiers who have taken over the United States, Buddy, with Sack, retaliates as best he can.

Other books you might like:
Jesse Browner, *Conglomeros*, 1992
Samuel R. Delany, *They Fly at Ciron*, 1993
Richard Grant, *Through the Heart*, 1991
Thomas Harris, *The Silence of the Lambs*, 1988
Mark Leyner, *My Cousin, My Gastroenterologist*, 1990

3072

CLARE MCNALLY

Cries of the Children

(New York: Onyx, 1992)

Story type: Horror (Wild Talents)
Major character(s): Samantha Winstead, Doctor; Rachel Freleng, Teacher (high school music teacher); Will Sherer, Detective—Private
Time period(s): 1990s (1992)
Locale(s): Denver, Colorado

Summary: Three different people befriend and eventually adopt three different children, each of whom appears mysteriously in their lives and manifests extraordinary intellectual and paranormal powers. As the foster parents investigate the pasts of the children, they begin to turn up many unresolved questions about their own pasts and origins.

Other books you might like:
William W. Johnstone, *Them*, 1992
Maxine O'Callaghan, *Dark Time*, 1992
John Wyndham, *The Midwich Cuckoos*, 1957

3073

CLARE MCNALLY

Good Night, Sweet Angel

(New York: Tor, 1996)

Story type: Horror (Child-in-Peril)
Major character(s): Jenn Galbraith, Teacher; Emily Galbraith, Child (Jenn's 4-year-old daughter); Laura Bayless, Baker
Time period(s): 1990s (1996)
Locale(s): Pinebridge, Vermont

Summary: The ghostly Tara protects young Emily Galbraith from the spirit of her dead father, who tries repeatedly to abuse her from the other side of the grave. But Tara and someone else close to Emily have an agenda of their own that requires friendship with Emily if Tara is to be reincarnated as a living person.

Other books you might like:
Rick Hautala, *Ghost Light*, 1993
Ruby Jean Jensen, *Celia*, 1991
Samuel M. Key, *From a Whisper to a Scream*, 1992

3074

CLARE MCNALLY

Stage Fright

(New York: Tor, 1995)

Story type: Horror (Reanimated Dead)
Major character(s): Hayley Seagal, Director (theatre); Bruce Donner, Writer (playwright); Aidan McGilray, Writer (playwright)
Time period(s): 1990s (1995)
Locale(s): Montauk, New York (on Long Island)

Summary: Hayley Seagal is trying to put her life back together and resume her career as a theatre director five years after jealous playwright Bruce Donner murdered her lover and committed suicide. When a mysterious figure known as the Shadow Man brings mayhem and murder to her new theater troupe, Hayley suspects that Bruce has returned from the dead to be with her once more.

Other books you might like:
Rick Hautala, *Ghost Light*, 1992
Ruby Jean Jensen, *Celia*, 1991
Stephen King, *Rose Madder*, 1995
Chet Williamson, *Reign*, 1990

3075

MIKE MCQUAY

The Nexus

(New York: Bantam Spectra, 1989)

Story type: Fantasy (Psychic Powers)
Major character(s): Dennis Stiller, Journalist; Amy Kyle, Psychic
Time period(s): 1980s
Locale(s): Dallas, Texas

Summary: Stiller, a former hot-shot reporter fallen on hard times, follows up on a story about a Texas faith-healer and uncovers a story about an autistic girl who can perform miracles. He attempts to control her powers with horrifying results.

Other books you might like:
Stephen King, *Firestarter*, 1980
Joanna Russ, *And Chaos Died*, 1970
Robert Silverberg, *Dying Inside*, 1972
Victor Koman, *The Jehovah Contract*, 1989
James Morrow, *Only Begotten Daughter*, 1989
Michael Youssef, *Earth King*, 1988

3076

DONALD E. MCQUINN

Wanderer

(New York: Ballantine Del Ray, 1993)

Story type: Science Fiction (Post-Nuclear Holocaust; Political)
Series: Warrior

Major character(s): Sylah, Religious (Rose priestess); Donnacee Tate, Military Personnel, Time Traveller; Lanta, Religious (Violet priestess), Psychic (esper)
Time period(s): 26th century
Locale(s): San Francisco, California; North America (western)

Summary: The Flower destined to find the legendary Door to the lost place of the exterminated Teachers, women who could read and who possessed knowledge, Sylah sets off with Donnacee, Conway and Lanta despite the request of the Harvester, probable new Mother-Sister of her Church. Displaced 500 years into the future in cold sleep, Tate searches to her detriment for black people, refusing to believe they have all intermixed.

Other books you might like:
Michael Armstrong, *Agviq*, 1990
Octavia E. Butler, *Parable of the Sower*, 1993
Heather Gladney, *Teot's War*, 1987
Rosemary Kirstein, *The Steerswoman*, 1989
J.M. Morgan, *Desert Eden*, 1991
Catherine Wells, *The Earth Is All That Lasts*, 1991
Paul O. Williams, *The Breaking of Northwall*, 1980

3077

DONALD E. MCQUINN

Warrior
(New York: Ballantine/Del Rey, 1990)

Story type: Science Fiction (Post-Nuclear Holocaust; Adventure)
Series: Warrior
Major character(s): Gan Moondark, Leader, Warrior; Sylah, Religious (priestess); Donnacee Tate, Military Personnel, Time Traveller
Time period(s): 26th century
Locale(s): Utah

Summary: In a desperate attempt to preserve humanity despite the 21st Century nuclear-biological holocaust, Dannacee Tate and many other superior individuals have been equipped with the tools needed to rebuild society and put into suspended animation. Few of the group survive to find a renewed environment where several warrior societies have evolved. Tate separates from her companions, who move to the city where they are adopted by the evil king Altanar of Olta who loves their weaponry. When Tate joins with Gan Moondark and his companions, their journey provides a look at several societies before Tate and her 21st century comrades reunite.

Other books you might like:
Suzy McKee Charnas, *Motherlines*, 1979
Suzy McKee Charnas, *Walk to the End of the World*, 1974
Gordon R. Dickson, *Wolf and Iron*, 1990
R.M. Meluch, *Chicago Red*, 1990
Paul O. Williams, *The Breaking of Northwall*, 1980

3078

DONALD E. MCQUINN

Witch
(New York: Ballantine Del Rey, 1994)

Story type: Science Fiction (Post-Nuclear Holocaust; Political)
Series: Warrior
Major character(s): Gan Moondark, Leader, Warrior; Donnacee Tate, Military Personnel, Time Traveller; Louis Leclerc, Inventor, Time Traveller
Time period(s): 26th century
Locale(s): North America (northwest)

Summary: Having found the Door and the library behind it, Sylah and the women from the post teach the Chosen reading and mathematics. The Church calls Sylah "Witch," and the inventions of her friends "witchcraft," intending to subvert Gan's support at home as well as encourage an alliance among all his enemies, including even Moonpriest, self-declared enemy of the Church.

Other books you might like:
David Brin, *The Postman*, 1985
Octavia E. Butler, *Parable of the Sower*, 1993
Heather Gladney, *Teot's War*, 1987
Catherine Wells, *The Earth Is All That Lasts*, 1991
Paul O. Williams, *The Breaking of Northwall*, 1981

3079

FRANK D. MCSHERRY JR., Editor
CHARLES G. WAUGH, Co-Editor

Eastern Ghosts
(Nashville, Tennessee: Rutledge Hill Press, 1990)

Story type: Horror (Ghost Story)
Series: American Ghosts
Locale(s): East

Summary: A dozen ghost stories set in six different eastern states. Included are Helen R. Hull's classic story of life after death, "Clay-Shuttered Doors," Robert Bloch's pulp chiller of necrophilic obsession, "The Man Who Collected Poe"; Edward D. Hoch's tale of an unusual contestant in the Miss America pageant, "Remember My Name"; as well as stories by Isaac Asimov, Paul Gallico, Mary Higgins Clark, and others.

Other books you might like:
Marvin Kaye, *Haunted America*, 1990

3080

FRANK D. MCSHERRY JR., Editor

The Fantastic Civil War
(New York: Baen, 1991)

Story type: Fantasy (Anthology; Historical)
Time period(s): 1860s (American Civil War)
Locale(s): United States

Summary: This volume contains an introduction by S.M. Stirling and 10 stories about the Civil War, all published between 1939 and 1991. The earliest is Manly Wade Wellman's "The Valley Was Still" from 1939. The 1950s give us Jack Finney and Ward Moore, while the 1960s are represented by Robert E. Howard and George Byran. The remaining five stories from the 1980s and 1990s are by Eric Davin, John M. Ford, Charles L. Harness, Jack McDevitt and Harry Turtledove.

Other books you might like:
Gregory Benford, *Alternate Wars*, 1991
  Martin H. Greenberg, co-editor
Terry Bisson, *Fire on the Mountain*, 1988
Ward Moore, *Bring the Jubilee*, 1953
Kevin D. Randle, *Remember Gettysburg*, 1988
  Robert J. Cornett, co-author
William Sanders, *The Wild Blue and the Gray*, 1991
S.M. Stirling, *Marching through Georgia*, 1988

3081

FRANK D. MCSHERRY JR., Editor
CHARLES G. WAUGH, Co-Editor

Ghosts of the Heartland

(Nashville, Tennessee: Rutledge Hill Press, 1990)

Story type: Horror (Ghost Story)
Series: American Ghosts
Locale(s): Midwest

Summary: Eighteen ghost stories set in 12 different midwestern states. Included are Fritz Leiber's masterpiece of urban horror "Smoke Ghost," Ambrose Bierce's suspenseful "The Boarded Window," Robert Bloch's sensitive "Floral Tribute," and "But at My Back I Always Here," David Morrell's terrifying story of an obsessive love that persists beyond death.

Other books you might like:
Marvin Kaye, *Haunted America*, 1990

3082

FRANK D. MCSHERRY JR., Editor
CHARLES G. WAUGH, Co-Editor
MARTIN H. GREENBERG, Co-Editor

Great American Ghost Stories

(Nashville, Tennessee: Rutledge Hill Press, 1991)

Story type: Horror (Ghost Story)
Locale(s): United States

Summary: Twenty-nine ghost stories written by 26 authors and set in 22 different states. Included are Harlan Ellison's classic of supernatural betrayal, "Pretty Maggie Moneyeyes"; H.P. Lovecraft's pastiche of *Frankenstein*, "Herbert West Reanimator"; Ambrose Bierce's classic, "The Boarded Window"; Seabury Quinn's mix of ghosts and lycanthropy, "The Phantom Farmhouse"; Arthur J. Burks' tale of a ghostly re-enactment of a murder, "The Ghosts of Steamboat Coulee"; and Joyce Carol Oates' story of a skeptic turned spiritualist, "Night-Side."

Other books you might like:
Marvin Kaye, *Haunted America*, 1990
Paul F. Olson, *Post Mortem: New Tales of Ghostly Horror*, 1988
  David Silva, co-author

3083

FRANK D. MCSHERRY JR., Editor
CHARLES G. WAUGH, Co-Editor

Western Ghosts

(Nashville, Tennessee: Rutledge Hill Press, 1990)

Story type: Horror (Ghost Story)
Series: American Ghosts
Locale(s): West

Summary: Thirteen stories representing 11 different western states. They range from Ambrose Bierce's spectral classic "The Stranger," to Arthur J. Burks' grim "The Ghosts of Steamboat Coulee," Harlan Ellison's cynical "Pretty Maggie Moneyeyes," and Billy Wolfenbarger's poignant "The Attic."

Other books you might like:
Marvin Kaye, *Haunted America*, 1990
Joe R. Lansdale, *The New Frontier*, 1989
Joe R. Lansdale, *Razored Saddles*, 1989
  Pat LoBrutto, co-author

3084

SHIRLEY MEIER

Shadow's Daughter

(New York: Baen, 1991)

Story type: Fantasy (Urban; Young Adult)
Series: Fifth Millennium
Major character(s): Megan Lixandashkya, Child; Lixand Mikhailovych, Storyteller, Artisan (weaver); Ness, Artisan, Parent (Megan's)
Time period(s): 36th century
Locale(s): F'talezon, Fictional City

Summary: Shortly after Megan begins school, political conflicts in the city cause her parents to lose their positions. As they struggle to re-establish themselves, Megan gets an education in street life with the kidpack. They manage to apprentice Megan to the Merchant's Guild (even with its unspoken connection to the Thieves' Guild), but Lixand and Ness are destroyed by the increasingly ruthless city government, leaving Megan to her Aunt Marte's brutality.

Other books you might like:
Sharon Baker, *Burning Tears of Sassurum*, 1988
Octavia E. Butler, *Survivor*, 1978
Sheila Gilluly, *The Boy From the Burren*, 1990
Diana Wynne Jones, *Cart and Cwidder*, 1977
Megan Lindholm, *Luck of the Wheels*, 1989
Robin McKinley, *The Blue Sword*, 1982
Will Shetterly, *Elsewhere*, 1991
S.M. Stirling, *Snowbrother*, 1992
  revised

Karen Wehrstein, *Lion's Heart*, 1991
Karen Wehrstein, *Lion's Soul*, 1991

Alis A. Rasmussen, *Revolution's Shore*, 1990
Paul O. Williams, *The Breaking of Northwall*, 1980

3085

SHIRLEY MEIER
S.M. STIRLING, Co-Author
KAREN WEHRSTEIN, Co-Author

Shadow's Son

(New York: Baen, 1991)

Story type: Fantasy (Quest)
Series: Fifth Millennium
Major character(s): Megan Whitlock, Businesswoman (merchant); Sh'kaira, Warrior; Chevenga, Ruler
Time period(s): 35th century
Locale(s): Arkan, Fictional Country; Yeoli, Fictional Country

Summary: Megan's agent has finally located the son she bore in slavery. Sold away, he is now a dancing boy in the corrupt Arkan Empire. Megan and Sh'Kaira set out to rescue him, joining Chevenga's Yeoli army as the best way of reaching the Arkan capital in the midst of war. This novel is set eight years after the events of *Shadow's Daughter* (1991), 1 1/2 years after those of *The Cage* (1989) and concurrently with those of *Lion's Soul* (1991).

Other books you might like:
Gael Baudino, *Dragonsword*, 1988
Samuel R. Delany, *Tales of Neveryon*, 1979
Heather Gladney, *Teot's War*, 1987
Guy Gavriel Kay, *Tigana*, 1990
Rosemary Kirstein, *The Steerswoman*, 1989
Joel Rosenberg, *D'Shai*, 1991
S.M. Stirling, *Snowbrother*, 1992
    revised
Karen Wehrstein, *Lion's Heart*, 1991
Karen Wehrstein, *Lion's Soul*, 1991

3086

R.M. MELUCH

Chicago Red

(New York: Roc, 1990)

Story type: Science Fiction (Post-Holocaust; Political)
Major character(s): Chris-John Stanton, Revolutionary; Edward III, Ruler (King of America)
Time period(s): Indeterminate Future
Locale(s): Kingdom of America, Fictional Country (northern Great Plains)

Summary: Motivated by the death of a rebel leader, Chris-John Stanton adopts the nom de guerre, Chicago Red, and organizes the rebellion to overthrow the king and the aristocracy.

Other books you might like:
Isaac Asimov, *Foundation and Empire*, 1952
Robert A. Heinlein, *Farnham's Freehold*, 1964
Robert A. Heinlein, *Sixth Column*, 1949
Donald E. McQuinn, *Warrior*, 1990
Steve Perry, *The Man Who Never Missed*, 1985

3087

R.M. MELUCH

The Queen's Squadron

(New York: Roc, 1992)

Story type: Science Fiction (Immortality; Political)
Major character(s): Penetanguishene, Government Official (torturer); Paul Strand, Military Personnel, Hero; Ashata/Maya, Immortal, Pilot
Time period(s): 53rd century
Locale(s): Eta Cassiopeia IV, Planet—Imaginary (Eta Cas)

Summary: Maya, denying her immortality, becomes a c-ship pilot and begins to appreciate mortals as humans. With war between Telegonia and Vihrhalt looming, the last of the mondesi truthsayers, Penetanguishene, unsuccessfully tortures Paul to discover the details of "Gotterdammerung," the Telegonian secret plan to destroy the immortals and win the war despite their lack of faster-than-light ships.

Other books you might like:
Octavia E. Butler, *Kindred*, 1979
James Gunn, *Star Bridge*, 1989
    Jack Williamson, co-author
Joe Haldeman, *Buying Time*, 1989
Robert Reed, *Down the Bright Way*, 1991
Frank M. Robinson, *The Dark Beyond the Stars*, 1991
Bruce Sterling, *Involution Ocean*, 1977
A.E. van Vogt, *The Weapon Shops of Isher*, 1951
Gene Wolfe, *The Shadow of the Torturer*, 1980

3088

R.M. MELUCH

War Birds

(New York: NAL Signet, 1989)

Story type: Science Fiction (Military)
Major character(s): Anthony Northfield, Professor, Pilot
Time period(s): Indeterminate Future
Locale(s): Tannia, Planet—Imaginary; Erd, Planet—Imaginary; Occo, Planet—Imaginary

Summary: In a star system with three human-inhabited planets interplanetary war is the norm. When new hostilities seem in the offing, Anthony Northfield, former spaceplane ace, former prisoner of war, now an English professor, is pressured to reenlist.

Other books you might like:
Dale Brown, *Day of the Cheetah*, 1989
Emma Bull, *Falcon*, 1989
Gordon R. Dickson, *The Tactics of Mistake*, 1971
S.N. Lewitt, *Cyberstealth*, 1989
S.N. Lewitt, *Dancing Vac*, 1990

3089
PAULINE MELVILLE

Shape-Shifter: Stories by Pauline Melville
(New York: Pantheon, 1991)

Story type: Fantasy (Collection; Literary)
Time period(s): Indeterminate
Locale(s): West Indies

Summary: This volume contains 10 stories on West Indian themes, presenting strong characters with deft touches of humor. This won the Guardian Fiction Prize and the International PEN's Macmillan Silver Pen Award. Author's first book.

Other books you might like:
Brian W. Aldiss, *A Romance of the Equator: The Best Fantasy Stories of Brian W. Aldiss*, 1990
J.G. Ballard, *Vermilion Sands*, 1971
Chad Oliver, *Another Kind*, 1954
Rosemary Sutcliff, *Sun Horse, Moon Horse*, 1977
Mary Alexander Walker, *The Scathach and the Maeve's Daughter*, 1990

3090
ABRAHAM MERRITT

Burn, Witch, Burn!/Creep, Shadow, Creep!
(New York: Leisure, 1996)

Story type: Horror (Collection)

Summary: THis omnibus volume collects two novels by a renowned fantasy writer from the early 20th century. *Burn, Witch, Burn!*, first published in book form in 1933, concerns Dr. Lowell's battle with Madame Mandilip, a practitioner of occult arts who steals the souls of her victims and uses them to reanimate malevolent dolls under her control. *Creep, Shadow, Creep!* first published in book form in 1943 (as *Creep, Shadow!*) concerns Alan Caranac, a colleague of Lowell's, who runs afoul of Madame Mandilip's former lover and his companion, a survivor of a pagan cult who awakens archetypal memories in her contemporary male victims and drives them to madness and death.

Other books you might like:
Edgar Rice Burroughs, *The Eternal Lover*, 1925
H. Rider Haggard, *She*, 1887
Henry Kuttner, *The Dark World*, 1965
Greye La Spina, *Invaders From the Dark*, 1960
Jack Williamson, *Darker than You Think*, 1948

3091
ABRAHAM MERRITT

The Face in the Abyss
(New York: Collier, 1992)

Story type: Fantasy (Adventure; Alternate World)
Major character(s): Nicholas Graydon, Adventurer, Scientist; Suarra, Religious (priestess); Adana ''the Snake Mother'', Mythical Creature

Time period(s): 1930s
Locale(s): Andes Mountains, South America; Yu-Atlanchi, Fictional Country

Summary: First published in 1931, this novel relates Nicholas Graydon's adventures involving love, betrayal, ancient mystery and evil in the fabulous land of Yu-Atlanchi. Graydon battles human and supernatural enemies as well as his own conflicting desires as he struggles to win the hand of Suarra.

Other books you might like:
Margaret Ball, *Flameweaver*, 1991
Robert Holdstock, *Mythago Wood*, 1984
Edward Myers, *The Mountain Made of Light*, 1992
Elizabeth Ann Scarborough, *Last Refuge*, 1992
Elizabeth Ann Scarborough, *Nothing Sacred*, 1991
Rex Stout, *Under the Andes*, 1984

3092
RIC MEYERS

Fear Itself
(New York: Dell, 1991)

Story type: Horror (Supernatural Vengeance)
Series: Book of the Undead Trilogy
Major character(s): Geoffrey Robert Merrick, Businessman (a.k.a. Grim), Reanimated Dead; Melanie Merrick, Housewife; Juan Ruiz, Criminal (assassin)
Time period(s): 1990s
Locale(s): New York, New York

Summary: Killed in an explosion set off to terminate his resistance to his company's trafficking with Central American drug cartels, Geoffrey Merrick fights off the demon that attempts to claim his soul and returns to the world of the living as Grim, a charred and scarred avenging angel. In this first novel of the ''Book of the Undead'' trilogy, Grim's mission to track down his assassins and protect his wife from the sleazy business associates who set him up is interrupted by encounters with New York City low-life, including derelict burners and a mass murderer.

Other books you might like:
Randall Boyll, *Darkman*, 1991

3093
RIC MEYERS

Living Hell
(New York: Dell, 1991)

Story type: Horror (Reanimated Dead)
Series: Book of the Undead Trilogy
Major character(s): Geoffrey Robert Merrick, Businessman (a.k.a. Grim), Reanimated Dead; Melanie Merrick, Housewife; Classy Jack Watkins, Drug Dealer
Time period(s): 1990s
Locale(s): New York, New York

Summary: In this second book in the Book of the Undead Trilogy, Geoffrey Merrick, alias ''Grim,'' continues his pursuit of the men who killed him, all the while serving as a vigilante who cleans up crime on the streets of New York. In this outing he destroys assorted pimps and pushers, as well as a coven of Satanists venting their rage on the nuns and priests of Manhattan.

Other books you might like:
Randall Boyll, *Darkman*, 1991
Barbara Hambly, *Beauty and the Beast*, 1989
F. Paul Wilson, *The Tomb*, 1984

3094
RIC MEYERS

Worst Nightmare
(New York: Dell, 1992)

Story type: Horror (Supernatural Vengeance)
Series: Book of the Undead Trilogy
Major character(s): Geoffrey Robert Merrick, Businessman (aka Grim), Reanimated Dead; Martin Kirshner, Criminal (child molester); Joshua Carl Evans, Child
Time period(s): 1990s
Locale(s): New York, New York

Summary: The third installment in the ongoing saga of Geoffrey Marrick, a.k.a. Grim, a businessman blown to pieces for his do-gooding sensibilites who returns to life as a scarred avenger through sheer force of will. This time, Grim is on the trail of a ruthless child molester who uses the state welfare system to track down his victims.

Other books you might like:
Randall Boyll, *Darkman*, 1991
Barbara Hambly, *Beauty and the Beast*, 1989
Grant Stockbridge, *The Spider: Master of Men*, 1991
F. Paul Wilson, *The Tomb*, 1984

3095
MELISA C. MICHAELS

Far Harbor
(New York: Tor, 1989)

Story type: Science Fiction (Space Opera)
Major character(s): Ugly Starling, Outcast; Prince Hawke, Heir
Time period(s): Indeterminate Future
Locale(s): Paradise, Planet—Imaginary

Summary: The Terran imperialists and the native rulers of Paradise are in an uneasy truce, political factions and undercover agents doing their best to give either side the advantage. Meanwhile, the one woman who can free her planet from the weight of Terran oppression is living in Cinderella-like poverty, beaten down by her step-parents, convinced that she's an alien.

Other books you might like:
Jay D. Blakeney, *The Goda War*, 1989
Jay D. Blakeney, *Requiem for Anthi*, 1990
Mary Gentle, *Ancient Light*, 1989
Mary Gentle, *Golden Witchbreed*, 1983
Anne McCaffrey, *Crystal Singer*, 1982
Anne McCaffrey, *The Ship Who Sang*, 1969

3096
SANDRA MIESEL

Shaman
(New York: Baen, 1989)

Story type: Fantasy (Adventure)
Major character(s): Ria, Shaman
Time period(s): Indeterminate
Locale(s): Alternate Earth

Summary: Ria, a young shaman, is able to travel between worlds because of her developing magic powers. Ultimately, her abilities make her the last hope of the human race.

Other books you might like:
Michaela Roessner, *Walkabout Woman*, 1988
Linda Lay Shuler, *She Who Remembers*, 1988

3097
VICTOR MILAN

The Cybernetic Shogun
(New York: Morrow, 1990)

Story type: Science Fiction (Robot Fiction)
Major character(s): Hidetada, Artificial Intelligence; Musashi, Artificial Intelligence
Time period(s): 21st century
Locale(s): Floating World, Space Station; The Reef, Alternate Universe

Summary: The artificial intelligence Tokugawa has been destroyed, but its "offspring," the AIs Hidetada and Musashi, have gained enormous power and are now in direct conflict. Hidetada desires to gain power over what's left of the Earth and its people. Musashi hopes to save humanity by building a space ark that will take the remnants of our race to the stars. This is the sequel to *The Cybernetic Samurai.*

Other books you might like:
William Gibson, *Count Zero*, 1985
William Gibson, *Mona Lisa Overdrive*, 1988
William Gibson, *Neuromancer*, 1984
W.T. Quick, *Dreams of Flesh and Sand*, 1988
W.T. Quick, *Dreams of Gods and Men*, 1989
Rudy Rucker, *Wetware*, 1988
Bruce Sterling, *Islands in the Net*, 1988
Walter Jon Williams, *Hardwired*, 1986

3098
VICTOR MILAN

Turn of the Cards
(New York: Bantam Spectra, 1993)

Story type: Science Fiction (Alternate Universe; Psychic Powers)
Series: Wild Cards
Major character(s): Mark "Captain Trips" Meadows, Genetically Altered Being, Scientist (biochemist); Croyd "The Sleeper" Crenson, Genetically Altered Being; Charles Sobel, Military Personnel

Time period(s): 1990s
Locale(s): Europe; Asia

Summary: Fleeing CIA and DEA agents, Mark Meadows meets Colonel Charles Sobel who plans a war of conquest utilizing an army with Joker powers. Mark must decide if he will follow his peaceful ideals or allow his submerged personalities, complete with Ace powers, to take over and serve the madman's goal of killing nats, unmodified humans.

Other books you might like:
Michael Bishop, *Count Geiger's Blues*, 1992
Mark Grant, *Mutants Amok*, 1991
Michael Kandel, *Captain Jack Zodiac*, 1992
George R.R. Martin, *The Wild Cards Series*, 1987-1993 editor
Melinda M. Snodgrass, *Double Solitaire*, 1992
Michael D. Weaver, *My Father Immortal*, 1989

3099

CARL MILLER

The Goblin Plain War

(New York: Ace, 1991)

Story type: Fantasy (Adventure)
Series: Dragonbound
Major character(s): Rockdream, Warrior, Hunter; Coral, Sorceress
Time period(s): Indeterminate
Locale(s): Goblin Plain, Mythical Place

Summary: Rockdream and Coral must find a way to end the war between humans and goblins before the war results in universal extermination.

Other books you might like:
David Eddings, *Pawn of Prophecy*, 1982
Robert Jordan, *The Eye of the World*, 1989
John Lee, *The Unicorn Solution*, 1991
Elizabeth Moon, *Divided Allegiance*, 1988
Elizabeth Moon, *Oath of Gold*, 1989
Elizabeth Moon, *Sheepfarmer's Daughter*, 1988

3100

CARL MILLER

The Warrior and the Witch

(New York: Ace, 1990)

Story type: Fantasy (Adventure)
Major character(s): Rockdream, Military Personnel (guardsman); Coral, Sorceress; Riversong, Mythical Creature (dragon)
Time period(s): Indeterminate
Locale(s): Newport, Fictional City

Summary: Newport was constructed to ward off attack from the ground, with its many towers and miles of walls. But Riversong will attack from the air and the city may not stand. Rockdream and Coral lead a small group of refugees to safety.

Other books you might like:
Glen Cook, *Tower of Fear*, 1989

Melanie Rawn, *Dragon Prince*, 1988
Michael Scott Rohan, *The Forge in the Forest*, 1989
J.R.R. Tolkien, *The Fellowship of the Ring*, 1954
Tad Williams, *The Dragonbone Chair*, 1988

3101

FAREN MILLER

The Illusionists

(New York: Popular Library Questar, 1991)

Story type: Fantasy (Quest; Light Fantasy)
Major character(s): Gherifan Arnix, Actor; Moabet Shar, Psychic; Railu Knifedancer, Military Personnel (lancer)
Time period(s): Indeterminate Past
Locale(s): Xalycis Rock, Fictional City

Summary: In the ruins of Xalycis Rock, a powerful magical Artifact is found and leads to the murder of Aubric i-Arnix, a leading citizen of Xalycis Rock. Moabet Shar, a psychic percept, and Gherifan Arnix work to uncover the murderer and prevent the Artifact from destroying the city.

Other books you might like:
Steven Brust, *Jhereg*, 1983
Glen Cook, *Tower of Fear*, 1989
P.C. Hodgell, *God Stalk*, 1982

3102

G. WAYNE MILLER

Thunder Rise

(New York: Jove, 1992)

Story type: Horror (Ancient Evil Unleashed)
Major character(s): Brad Gale, Journalist; Abby "Apple Guy" Gale, Child (Brad's five-year-old daughter); Charlie Moonlight, Drifter, Indian
Time period(s): 1980s (1988)
Locale(s): Morgantown, Massachusetts

Summary: The awakening of a demon inside Thunder Mountain manifests as a series of terrifying dreams that lead to debility and death among the children of nearby Morgantown. When Brad Gale's daughter becomes afflicted, he must put his skepticism behind him and join forces with Quidneck Indian Charlie Moonlight to restrain the demon once more. This novel, the author's first, was originally published in 1989.

Other books you might like:
Morgan Fields, *Shaman Woods*, 1989
T. Chris Martindale, *Where the Chill Waits*, 1990
Kathryn Ptacek, *Ghost Dance*, 1990
Patrick Whalen, *Deathwalker*, 1992
Chet Williamson, *Dreamthorp*, 1989

3103

RAND MILLER
ROBYN MILLER, Co-Author
DAVID WINGROVE, Co-Author

Myst: The Book of Atrus

(New York: Hyperion, 1995)

Story type: Fantasy (Adventure)
Series: Myst
Major character(s): Atrus, Magician; Gehn, Magician
Time period(s): Indeterminate
Locale(s): Planet—Imaginary; Myst, Fictional Country (island)

Summary: Gehn locates his son, Atrus, and begins his training in the magic of the vanished D'ni, who possessed the ability to create new worlds through writing. First of a CD-ROM game tie-in.

Other books you might like:
Charles de Lint, *Memory and Dream*, 1994
Robin Hobb, *Assassin's Apprentice*, 1995
Ursula K. Le Guin, *The Lathe of Heaven*, 1971
David Wingrove, *The Broken Wheel*, 1991
David Wingrove, *The Middle Kingdom*, 1990
David Worsick, *Henry's Gift: The Magic Eye*, 1994

3104

REX MILLER

Butcher

(New York: Pocket, 1994)

Story type: Horror (Serial Killer)
Series: Chaingang Bunkowski
Major character(s): Daniel "Chaingang" Bunkowski, Serial Killer; Ray Meara, Farmer; Solomon Royal, Doctor (aka Emil Shtolz)
Time period(s): 1990s (1994)
Locale(s): Bayou Ridge, Missouri

Summary: Former Vietnam vet and serial killer Chaingang Bunkowski is deployed by his handlers to terminate Solomon Royal, a midwestern doctor whose past as a Nazi war criminal has caught up with him. But Chaingang's superiors don't understand that giving the misanthrope a license to kill is not unlike handing a pyromaniac a book of matches.

Other books you might like:
Diane Duane, *Spectres*, 1991
Kathryn Ptacek, *The Hunted*, 1993
Robert Arthur Smith, *Silent Witness*, 1988
Peter Straub, *Koko*, 1988

3105

REX MILLER

Chaingang

(New York: Pocket, 1992)

Story type: Horror (Serial Killer)
Series: Chaingang Bunkowski

Major character(s): Daniel "Chaingang" Bunkowski, Serial Killer; Dr. Norman, Doctor; Royce Hawthorne, Young Man
Time period(s): 1970s
Locale(s): Marion, Missouri (Marion Penitentiary)

Summary: This fifth novel in the chronicles of Chaingang Bunkowski, a 500-pound misanthrope who hates all human beings, especially those who kill animals, backtracks to his early prison years, when a penitentiary doctor first encouraged his antisocial proclivities and helped create a monster.

Other books you might like:
Douglas Borton, *Kane*, 1990
Stephen Gallagher, *Down River*, 1989
Stephen R. George, *Near Dead*, 1992
Thomas Harris, *Red Dragon*, 1981
Michael Slade, *Ghoul*, 1990

3106

REX MILLER

Iceman

(New York: Onyx, 1990)

Story type: Horror (Serial Killer)
Series: Jack Eichord Chronicles
Major character(s): Jack Eichord, Detective—Police; Donna Eichord, Spouse; Arthur Spoda, Serial Killer
Time period(s): 1990s
Locale(s): Buckhead County, Arkansas

Summary: At work, cop Jack Eichord tracks an icepick-wielding serial killer while at home Donna tries to raise their two-year-old adopted son who, Jack suspects, may have inherited psychopathic tendencies from his late father, perpetrator of "the worst mass-murder case in history."

Other books you might like:
Stephen Gallagher, *Down River*, 1989
William Relling Jr., *New Moon*, 1988
Thomas Harris, *Red Dragon*, 1981

3107

REX MILLER

Savant

(New York: Pocket, 1994)

Story type: Horror (Serial Killer)
Series: Chaingang Bunkowski
Major character(s): Daniel "Chaingang" Bunkowski, Serial Killer; Bobby Price, Criminal (assassin); Victor Trask, Journalist (radio)
Time period(s): 1990s (1994)
Locale(s): Kansas City, Missouri

Summary: Government-trained assassin Chaingang Bunkowski returns to his hometown to kill the abusive stepmother who helped turn him into a misanthrope, all the while being pursued by another government-trained assassin trying out the new SAVANT rifle, capable of terminating its target from a range of two miles. Running commentary on the proliferation of violence in America is provided by a radio talk-show personality who has caught wind of Chaingang's exploits.

Other books you might like:
Stephen Gallagher, *Down River*, 1989
T.J. Kirby, *Dangerous Nature*, 1993
Bob Mayer, *Operation Synbat*, 1994
Peter Straub, *Koko*, 1988

3108
REX MILLER

Slice
(New York: NAL Onyx, 1990)

Story type: Horror (Serial Killer)
Series: Chaingang Bunkowski
Major character(s): Jack Eichord, Detective—Police (serial killer expert); Daniel "Chaingang" Bunkowski, Serial Killer (six foot seven)
Time period(s): 1980s
Locale(s): Atlanta, Georgia; Chicago, Illinois

Summary: After recovering from his injuries in the Chicago sewers, "Chaingang" sets out to get revenge against his nemesis, Jack Eichord.

Other books you might like:
Clive Barker, *The Damnation Game*, 1985
Ramsey Campbell, *The Face That Must Die*, 1979
Thomas Harris, *Red Dragon*, 1981

3109
RON MILLER

Hearts and Armor
(New York: Ace, 1992)

Story type: Fantasy (Quest; Political)
Series: Bronwyn
Major character(s): Bronwyn, Royalty (princess), Warrior; Thud Mollockle, Mythical Creature (kobold), Adventurer
Time period(s): Indeterminate
Locale(s): Guesclin, Mythical Place; Tamlaght, Fictional Country; Blavek, Fictional City

Summary: Leading a mighty invasionary force, Princess Bronwyn returns to her homeland to overthrow her sibling rival and recapture her throne.

Other books you might like:
Elizabeth Moon, *Divided Allegiance*, 1988
Elizabeth Moon, *Oath of Gold*, 1989
Elizabeth Moon, *Sheepfarmer's Daughter*, 1988

3110
RON MILLER

Palaces and Prisons
(New York: Ace, 1991)

Story type: Fantasy (Adventure)
Series: Bronwyn

Major character(s): Bronwyn, Royalty (princess), Fugitive; Thud Mollockle, Mythical Creature (kobold), Adventurer (stonecutter)
Time period(s): Indeterminate Future
Locale(s): Tamlaght, Fictional Country

Summary: Discovered about to expose correspondence between Tamlaght's ruler, Ferenc, and the exiled power behind the throne, Payne Roelt, Bronwyn flees palace guards until befriended by Thud, then by a Gypsy who helps them escape the city. As they flee north to enlist aid from Bronwyn's relatives, they visit the kingdom of the kobolds, receiving aid and agreeing to help the kobold's cause of assisting refugee fairies of Londeac to emigrate.

Other books you might like:
Carol Chase, *Hawk's Flight*, 1991
Katharine Kerr, *The Dragon Revenant*, 1990
Elizabeth Moon, *Sheepfarmer's Daughter*, 1988
Elizabeth Moon, *Surrender None: The Legacy of Gird*, 1990

3111
RON MILLER

Silk and Steel
(New York: Ace, 1992)

Story type: Fantasy (Adventure)
Series: Bronwyn
Major character(s): Bronwyn, Royalty (princess), Fugitive; Thud Mollockle, Mythical Creature (kobold), Adventurer; Mathias Strelsau, Nobleman (duke), Ruler (Duchy of Lesser Piotr)
Time period(s): Indeterminate Future
Locale(s): Londeac, Fictional Country; Duchy of Piotr, Fictional Country

Summary: Fleeing Payne Roelt's treachery, Bronwyn travels from Londeac to the Duchy of Lesser Piotr. When an explosion cuts short Bronwyn's budding romance with Duke Mathias Strelsau, she resolves to remove Payne Roelt's influence from Tamlaght.

Other books you might like:
Alexis A. Gilliland, *The Shadow Shaia*, 1990
Sheila Gilluly, *The Boy From the Burren*, 1990
Diana L. Paxson, *The Wind Crystal*, 1990
Melanie Rawn, *Sunrunner's Fire*, 1990

3112
SASHA MILLER

Ladylord
(New York: Tor, 1996)

Story type: Fantasy (Adventure; Political)
Major character(s): Javere "Javerri", Noblewoman, Martial Arts Expert
Time period(s): Indeterminate
Locale(s): Fictional Country

Summary: Taught fighting and political skills as if she were a young man, Javerri receives the favor of her father, Lord Qai. After Lord Qai names her heir and *son*, Javerri sets off on a quest to prove her right to rule. Javerri's search for a dragon's egg suffers the treachery of an empire plotting to insure against a woman ruler.

Other books you might like:

Marion Zimmer Bradley, *The Sword and Sorceress Series*, 1984-1996
Raymond E. Feist, *Daughter of the Empire*, 1987
　　Janny Wurts, co-author
Mercedes Lackey, *The Oathbound*, 1988
C.L. Moore, *Jirel of Joiry*, 1969
Andre Norton, *On Wings of Magic*, 1994
　　Patricia Shaw Mathews, Sasha Miller, co-authors
Jessica Amanda Salmonson, *Tomoe Gozen*, 1984

3113

STEVE MILLER
SHARON LEE, Co-Author

Carpe Diem

(New York: Ballantine/Del Rey, 1989)

Story type: Science Fiction (Adventure)
Major character(s): Val Con, Spy; Miri, Mercenary
Time period(s): Indeterminate Future
Locale(s): Planet—Imaginary (Interdicted primitive planet)

Summary: In this sequel to *Agent of Change*, an interstellar spy and a female mercenary, on the run from a variety of bad guys, relatives, and aliens, hide out on a primitive world, but trouble soon follows.

Other books you might like:

Poul Anderson, *A Circus of Hells*, 1970
Poul Anderson, *The Game of Empire*, 1985
Poul Anderson, *A Knight of Ghosts and Shadows*, 1977
Poul Anderson, *The Rebel Worlds*, 1969
John Dalmas, *The Lantern of God*, 1989
Kris Jensen, *FreeMaster*, 1989

3114

C.J. MILLS

Brander's Book

(New York: Ace, 1992)

Story type: Science Fiction (Political; Family Saga)
Series: Winter World
Major character(s): Brander Harlan, Nobleman, Revolutionary; Karne Halarek, Nobleman, Ruler (Lharr of House Halarek); Richard Harlan, Prisoner, Leader
Time period(s): Indeterminate Future
Locale(s): Starker IV, Planet—Imaginary

Summary: Brander Harlan acts to overthrow his family's leader, the imprisoned Duke Richard, and eliminate Karne Halarek's family by enlisting the aid of Karne's young bride.

Other books you might like:

Lois McMaster Bujold, *Barrayar*, 1991
Lois McMaster Bujold, *Shards of Honor*, 1986
C.J. Cherryh, *Serpent's Reach*, 1980
Frank Herbert, *Dune*, 1965

3115

C.J. MILLS

Egil's Book

(New York: Ace, 1991)

Story type: Science Fiction (Political)
Series: Winter World
Major character(s): Karne Halarek, Nobleman, Ruler; Egil Olaffson, Bodyguard, Friend
Time period(s): Indeterminate Future
Locale(s): Starker IV, Planet—Imaginary

Summary: Expecting to die defending Karne Halarek, Egil finds himself rescued and repaired by survivors of Viking settlers who crash-landed on Starker IV and have lived secretly underground for 2,000 years. Prohibitions against leaving the underground civilization force Egil to plot his escape so he can return to Karne's service and help Karne avenge the killing of his mother, the ruler of Starker IV. This book is a sequel to *Winter World*.

Other books you might like:

Poul Anderson, *Hrolf Kraki's Saga*, 1973
C.J. Cherryh, *Serpent's Reach*, 1980
Alan Dean Foster, *Quozl*, 1989
Frank Herbert, *Dune*, 1965
Ursula K. Le Guin, *The Left Hand of Darkness*, 1969
Jody Lynn Nye, *Mythology 101*, 1990
H. Beam Piper, *Little Fuzzy*, 1962
James D. Priest, *Kirins: The Spell of No'an*, 1990
Alis A. Rasmussen, *Revolution's Shore*, 1990
Sheri S. Tepper, *Grass*, 1989

3116

C.J. MILLS

Kit's Book

(New York: Ace, 1991)

Story type: Science Fiction (Adventure; Political)
Series: Winter World
Major character(s): Karne Halarek, Nobleman, Ruler (Lharr of House Halarek); Kathryn "Kit" Magdalena Alysha Halarek, Noblewoman, Captive; Nicholas von Schuss, Nobleman, Heir
Time period(s): Indeterminate Future
Locale(s): Starker IV, Planet—Imaginary

Summary: Although sentenced to a spartan solitary confinement in the Retreat House at Breven Abbey for the treacherous murder of Karne and Kit's mother, Richard Harlan lives a lecherous life of luxury and continues to actively direct the total destruction of the Halarek line. His actions seem destined for success when he arranges Kit's abduction and forced marriage to Ennis Harlan. Hampered by a required period of mourning, Karne works to save Kit from an even worse fate.

Other books you might like:

Lois McMaster Bujold, *Barrayar*, 1991
C.J. Cherryh, *Forty Thousand in Gehenna*, 1983
C.J. Cherryh, *Serpent's Reach*, 1980

Mary Gentle, *Golden Witchbreed*, 1984
Heather Gladney, *Teot's War*, 1987
Frank Herbert, *Dune*, 1965

3117

C.J. MILLS

Zjhanne's Book

(New York: Ace, 1992)

Story type: Science Fiction (Political; Family Saga)
Series: Winter World
Major character(s): Karne Halarek, Nobleman, Ruler (Lharr of House Halarek); Zjhanne Verlith, Spouse (Karne's), Historian (Terran pre-industrial history); Kathryn "Kit" Harlan, Noblewoman
Time period(s): Indeterminate Future
Locale(s): Starker IV, Planet—Imaginary

Summary: Kidnapped and forced to marry Karne in the traditional way, Zjhanne proves a defiant partner. She resists Karne's demand that she deliver House Halarek an heir until circumstances force the pair to flee. Zjhanne finally warms to her marriage partner, willingly accepting the duties expected of her. Concludes the series.

Other books you might like:
Lois McMaster Bujold, *Barrayar*, 1991
Lois McMaster Bujold, *Shards of Honor*, 1986
Cynthia Felice, *Iceman*, 1991
Rosemary Kirstein, *The Outskirter's Secret*, 1992
Alis A. Rasmussen, *Revolution's Shore*, 1990

3118

CRAIG MILLS

The Floating Castle

(New York: Berkley Boulevard, 1995)

Story type: Fantasy (Adventure)
Series: King's Quest
Major character(s): Alexander, Royalty; Telgrin, Magician
Time period(s): Indeterminate
Locale(s): Daventry, Fictional Country

Summary: As King Graham and his knights meet to discuss ways of removing the evil invaders from Daventry, Telgrin bursts in, magically steals the king's soul and declares himself the new ruler. Prince Alexander must find a way to drive out the usurper and restore peace to the land. First of a computer game tie-in series.

Other books you might like:
Robin W. Bailey, *Enchanter*, 1989
Matthew J. Costello, *The 7th Guest*, 1995
Mercedes Lackey, *Fortress of Frost and Fire*, 1993
James E. Reagen, *The League of the Crimson Crescent*, 1995
Harry Turtledove, *The Stolen Throne*, 1995

3119

CRAIG MILLS

Shadow of the Crown

(New York: Ballantine Del Rey, 1993)

Story type: Fantasy (Magic Conflict; Political)
Major character(s): Jerod Kemp, Thief, Adventurer; Cander Ellis, Spy, Martial Arts Expert; Holis Quordane, Nobleman (baron), Criminal
Time period(s): Indeterminate
Locale(s): West Gahant, Fictional Country

Summary: Jerod Kemp unwillingly accepts Baron Quordane's demand that he sneak into the Black Tower and steal a box containing a crown and ancient dagger, the key to gaining power for the exiled king.

Other books you might like:
Susan Dexter, *The Wizard's Shadow*, 1993
Tanya Huff, *The Fire's Stone*, 1990
Anne Logston, *Shadow Hunt*, 1991
Deborah Talmadge-Bickmore, *The Apprentice*, 1990
Martha Wells, *The Element of Fire*, 1993

3120

KAREN MARIE CHRISTA MINNS

Virago

(Tallahassee, Florida: Naiad Press, 1990)

Story type: Horror (Gay/Lesbian Fiction)
Major character(s): Darsen, Vampire; Ginny, Student, Lesbian; Manilla, Student, Lesbian
Time period(s): 1990s
Locale(s): New York, New York

Summary: Ginny and Manilla, students at Weston college, are lovers, but someone else lusts after Ginny—Darsen, a vampire of great age and cunning. This is Minns' first novel.

Other books you might like:
Suzy McKee Charnas, *The Vampire Tapestry*, 1980
Lauren Wright Douglas, *In the Blood*, 1989
Nancy Tyler Glenn, *Clicking Stones*, 1989

3121

KEN MITCHELL

Stones of the Dalai Lama

(New York: Soho, 1993)

Story type: Fantasy (Religious; Adventure)
Major character(s): Robert "Bob" Harlow, Professor, Archaeologist; Vern Cugnet, Mechanic, Adventurer; Jong Jing, Linguist (Foreign Ministry translator), Adventurer
Time period(s): 1980s (1987)
Locale(s): Bismarck, North Dakota; China; Tibet

Summary: Travelling in Tibet after completing a teaching assignment in China, Bob Harlow takes sacred funeral markers as mementos. When the transgression brings misfortune upon him at home in North Dakota, Bob and his friend, Vern, travel to Tibet to return the relics.

Other books you might like:
Campbell Black, *Raiders of the Lost Ark*, 1981
James Kahn, *Indiana Jones and the Temple of Doom*, 1984
Marc Laidlaw, *Neon Lotus*, 1988
Elizabeth Ann Scarborough, *Last Refuge*, 1992
Lucius Shepard, *Kalimantan*, 1992

`3122`

KIRK MITCHELL

Cry Republic
(New York: Ace, 1989)

Story type: Science Fiction (Alternate Universe)
Series: Procurator
Major character(s): Caesar Germanicus Agricola, Ruler; Mara, Young Woman
Time period(s): Indeterminate (20th century, alternate time)
Locale(s): Alternate Earth

Summary: In a universe where, two thousand years ago, Pilate pardoned Christ and in the twentieth century the Roman Empire still stands, the current Emperor, Casear Germanicus Agricola, seeks to transform his nation into a republic. There is violent opposition however, and Germanicus finds himself with a civil war on his hands. In attempting to end his Empire's stagnation, Germanicus fears he may have destroyed it.

Other books you might like:
L. Sprague de Camp, *Lest Darkness Fall*, 1941
Keith Roberts, *Pavane*, 1968
S.P. Somtow, *Aquila and the Iron Horse*, 1988
S.P. Somtow, *Aquila and the Sphinx*, 1989
S.P. Somtow, *Aquila in the New World*, 1983
   Revised 1988

`3123`

V.E. MITCHELL

Enemy Unseen
(New York: Pocket Books, 1990)

Story type: Science Fiction (Space Opera; Mystery)
Series: Star Trek
Major character(s): James T. Kirk, Spaceship Captain; Leonard McCoy, Doctor; Janara Whitehorse, Telepath
Time period(s): 23rd century
Locale(s): *U.S.S. Enterprise*, Spaceship

Summary: The *Enterprise* has been assigned to transport a diplomatic mission. Captain Kirk's work is complicated by First Officer Spock's temporary absence, the presence of an old flame among the Federation ambassador's party, and the cultural taboos of the arrogant Kaldorni representatives. When a diplomatic attache is murdered and one of the *Enterprise* crew is a prime suspect, Kirk and McCoy must find the identity of the killer in their midst.

Other books you might like:
Isaac Asimov, *The Caves of Steel*, 1954

Diane Duane, *My Enemy, My Ally*, 1984
   Star Trek 18
Janet Kagan, *Uhura's Song*, 1985
   Star Trek 21
James H. Schmitz, *The Universe Against Her*, 1964

`3124`

V.E. MITCHELL

Imbalance
(New York: Pocket, 1992)

Story type: Science Fiction (Space Opera; First Contact)
Series: Star Trek: The Next Generation
Major character(s): Beverly Crusher, Doctor, Space Explorer; William T. Riker, Military Personnel (Starfleet commander), Space Explorer; Keiko Ishikawa, Scientist, Space Explorer
Time period(s): 24th century
Locale(s): *U.S.S. Enterprise*, Spaceship; Beltaxiyan Minor, Planet—Imaginary

Summary: After the Jarada, a mysterious race of insectoids, request Captain Picard's services as negotiator to establish diplomatic relations with the Federation, negotiations proceed smoothly. When the Jarada suggest separate guided tours for his away team, Picard agrees in the interest of learning more about Jaradan culture. Each crew member loses contact with the ship and must struggle to stay alive while Picard tries to solve the mysteries of Jaradan behavior.

Other books you might like:
C.J. Cherryh, *Serpent's Reach*, 1980
Michael Jan Friedman, *Reunion*, 1991
Mary Gentle, *Golden Witchbreed*, 1984
Keith Laumer, *Retief at Large*, 1978
Ursula K. Le Guin, *The Left Hand of Darkness*, 1969
Kathleen Sky, *Vulcan!*, 1978
Jim Young, *The Face of the Deep*, 1979

`3125`

V.E. MITCHELL

Windows on a Lost World
(New York: Pocket, 1993)

Story type: Science Fiction (Space Opera)
Series: Star Trek
Major character(s): James T. Kirk, Spaceship Captain; Pavel Chekov, Military Personnel (ensign), Space Explorer; Spock, Scientist, Alien (Vulcan)
Time period(s): 23rd century
Locale(s): Careta IV, Planet—Imaginary; *U.S.S. Enterprise*, Spaceship

Summary: Exploring the ruins of an ancient civilization, Kirk and his landing party discover a strange device appearing as a window which pulls in Ensign Chekov and a Djelifan archaeologist as they test its properties. Searching for the missing team, Kirk also disappears. Spock eventually identifies Kirk's consciousness inside an alien creature found halfway around the planet and must unravel the alien technology to save his crewmates, even if it means taking alien form himself.

Other books you might like:
Carmen Carter, *The Devil's Heart*, 1993
C.J. Cherryh, *Gate of Ivrel*, 1976
Gordon R. Dickson, *Time Storm*, 1977
Phyllis Eisenstein, *Shadow of Earth*, 1979
Clifford D. Simak, *Mastodonia*, 1978
Kathleen Sky, *Vulcan!*, 1978

3126

LAURA J. MIXON

Glass Houses
(New York: Tor, 1992)

Story type: Science Fiction (Cyberpunk)
Major character(s): Ruby Kubick, Construction Worker, Recluse; Sheila Nanopoulos, Police Officer
Time period(s): 21st century
Locale(s): New York, New York (Queens); Palisades, New Jersey

Summary: To acquire the rent money due Friday, Ruby, in her waldo, Golem, climbs the condemned bank building to do some scavenging before the demolition scheduled for the next morning. Finding a shipwreck victim, she attempts rescue but the collapsing building trashes her salvage and kills her passenger. The man proves to be a well known philanthropist, causing the police to hold Golem. Without rent, salvage or Golem, Ruby must brave the very hot, partially submerged New York City in her own body. Author's first novel.

Other books you might like:
Greg Bear, *Queen of Angels*, 1990
David Brin, *Earth*, 1990
Pat Cadigan, *Mindplayers*, 1987
Pat Cadigan, *Synners*, 1991
Emily Devenport, *Shade*, 1991
William Gibson, *Neuromancer*, 1984
Lisa Mason, *Arachne*, 1990
Rudy Rucker, *Software*, 1982
Neal Stephenson, *Snow Crash*, 1992
Michael Swanwick, *Vacuum Flowers*, 1987
Walter Jon Williams, *Hardwired*, 1986

3127

L.E. MODESITT JR.

Adiamante
(New York: Tor, 1996)

Story type: Science Fiction (Post-Holocaust; Utopia)
Major character(s): Ecktor deJanes, Administrator (Old Earth coordinator), Leader, Widow(er); Kemra, Military Personnel (Vereal Union), Cyborg
Time period(s): Indeterminate Future
Locale(s): Earth

Summary: Newly appointed as Planetary Coordinator, Ecktor deJanes must deal with a fleet of warships which suddenly appears in orbit around Old Earth. In spite of the visitors'

apparent civility. Ecktor suspects that these descendants of a former Earth colony have returned to their ancestral world with a single purpose in mind—revenge.

Other books you might like:
Arthur C. Clarke, *Imperial Earth*, 1976
Arthur C. Clarke, *The Songs of Distant Earth*, 1986
Robert A. Heinlein, *Stranger in a Strange Land*, 1991 revised edition
James P. Hogan, *Voyage From Yesteryear*, 1982
Larry Niven, *A World Out of Time*, 1976

3128

L.E. MODESITT JR.

The Death of Chaos
(New York: Tor, 1995)

Story type: Fantasy (Magic Conflict; Political)
Series: Recluce
Major character(s): Lerris, Apprentice, Carpenter; Krystal, Military Personnel
Time period(s): Indeterminate
Locale(s): Recluce, Fictional Country (island)

Summary: Lerris' hopes of a quiet life as an artisan evaporate when the Empire of Hamor invades from the continent Candar, intent on world domination. Lerris must quickly hone his abilities to help repel the troops. Sequel to *The Magic of Recluce*.

Other books you might like:
Dave Duncan, *Upland Outlaws*, 1993
David Eddings, *Guardians of the West*, 1987
Terry Goodkind, *Wizard's First Rule*, 1994
Robert Jordan, *The Eye of the World*, 1989
Katharine Kerr, *Daggerspell*, 1986

3129

L.E. MODESITT JR.

The Ecolitan Operation
(New York: Tor, 1989)

Story type: Science Fiction (Adventure)
Series: Ecolitan Trilogy
Major character(s): Jimjoy Earle Wright, Spy (Major)
Time period(s): 25th century
Locale(s): Galactic Empire, Interstellar Empire/Federation

Summary: Major Jimjoy Earle Wright is one of the most highly trained and successful secret agents employed by the Empire. Assigned to work the overthrow of a planetary dictatorship, he succeeds too well. The dictatorship is replaced by a new government which is violently opposed to the Empire and Wright, made a scapegoat, finds himself in disgrace with a bounty on his head.

Other books you might like:
Poul Anderson, *A Circus of Hells*, 1970
Poul Anderson, *Earthman, Go Home!*, 1960
Poul Anderson, *Ensign Flandry*, 1966
Poul Anderson, *The Game of Empire*, 1985
Poul Anderson, *A Knight of Ghosts and Shadows*, 1974

Poul Anderson, *The Rebel Worlds*, 1969
Emma Bull, *Falcon*, 1989
Janet Kagan, *Hellspark*, 1988

3130

L.E. MODESITT JR.

The Ecologic Secession

(New York: Tor, 1990)

Story type: Science Fiction (Space Opera)
Series: Ecolitan Trilogy
Major character(s): Jimjoy Earle Wright, Spy
Time period(s): 25th century
Locale(s): Accord, Planet—Imaginary

Summary: Major Wright, once an Imperial Special Operative, is on his way to fake his death. After contact with the Ecolitan Institute on Accord he chooses to ally himself with the Prime Ecolitan and Accord. He will return as Ecolitan Professor James Joyson Whaler, who will lead the ongoing conflict with the Empire.

Other books you might like:
Emma Bull, *Falcon*, 1989
W. Michael Gear, *The Web of Spider*, 1989
Melisa C. Michaels, *Far Harbor*, 1989
Sheri S. Tepper, *Grass*, 1989
Walter Jon Williams, *Angel Station*, 1989

3131

L.E. MODESITT JR.

Fall of Angels

(New York: Tor, 1996)

Story type: Fantasy (Magic Conflict)
Series: Recluce
Major character(s): Nylan, Engineer; Ryba, Leader; Terek, Wizard
Time period(s): Indeterminate
Locale(s): Outer Space; Candar, Fictional Country

Summary: Set in Recluce's distant past, this novel chronicles the founding of the Empire of the Legend. A space battle goes terribly wrong, stranding the crew of the United Faith Forces' frigate *Winterlance* on a world far from anything they know.

Other books you might like:
Eleanor Arnason, *The Sword Smith*, 1978
Glen Cook, *The Black Company*, 1984
Barbara Hambly, *The Silent Tower*, 1986
Robert Jordan, *The Eye of the World*, 1990
Martha Wells, *The Element of Fire*, 1993

3132

L.E. MODESITT JR.
BRUCE SCOTT LEVINSON, Co-Author

The Green Progression

(New York: Tor, 1992)

Story type: Science Fiction (Political; Contemporary Realism)

Major character(s): Jack McDarvid, Researcher, Detective—Amateur
Time period(s): 1990s
Locale(s): Washington, District of Columbia; Moscow, Russia

Summary: Jack McDarvid retires from the E.P.A. hoping to advance his interests in business and environmental issues through work in a Washington D. C. legal firm specializing in business and environmental law. Shortly after McDarvid joins the firm, the murder of a firm leader and McDarvid's investigation into activity surrounding legislation concerning metals leads McDarvid into the dangerous labyrinth underlying environmental issues.

Other books you might like:
Isaac Asimov, *Our Angry Earth*, 1991
    Frederik Pohl, co-author
David Brin, *Earth*, 1990
Thomas A. Easton, *Greenhouse*, 1991
Thomas A. Easton, *Sparrowhawk*, 1990
Larry Niven, *Fallen Angels*, 1991
    Jerry Pournelle, Michael Flynn, co-authors

3133

L.E. MODESITT JR.

The Magic Engineer

(New York: Tor, 1994)

Story type: Fantasy (Magic Conflict; Political)
Series: Recluce
Major character(s): Dorrin, Magician, Engineer; Liedral, Trader
Time period(s): Indeterminate
Locale(s): Recluce, Fictional Country (island)

Summary: When Dorrin's talent for creating mechanical devices leads to his exile from Recluce, he must construct his scientifically based machines in the land of Chaos. He hopes to defend Recluce when its gathering enemies attempt to incorporate the country into their growing empire.

Other books you might like:
Cheryl J. Franklin, *Fire Get*, 1987
Mary Gentle, *Ancient Light*, 1987
Mercedes Lackey, *The Robin and the Kestrel*, 1993
Michael Swanwick, *The Iron Dragon's Daughter*, 1994
Paula Volsky, *Illusion*, 1992

3134

L.E. MODESITT JR.

The Magic of Recluce

(New York: Tor, 1991)

Story type: Fantasy (Magic Conflict; Romance)
Major character(s): Lerris, Apprentice, Carpenter; Krystal, Adventurer
Time period(s): Indeterminate
Locale(s): Wandernaught, Fictional Country; Recluce, Fictional Country (island); Nylan, Fictional Country

Summary: Lerris, a young teenager feels confined by the utopian community, based on order, into which he was born.

His parents apprentice him to his Uncle Sardit, a woodworker, to give Lerris some skills he'll need on Dangergeld, the year of wandering required before rebellious youths are welcomed into the community. Permanent exile or compliance with community expectations are the only alternatives to the Dangergeld. While on Dangergeld, Lerris learns to make appropriate choices. He meets many people who are important in his development as a magician and a citizen.

Other books you might like:
Poul Anderson, *The Broken Sword*, 1954
C.J. Cherryh, *The Paladin*, 1988
Gordon R. Dickson, *The Dragon and the George*, 1976
Elizabeth Moon, *Sheepfarmer's Daughter*, 1988
Elizabeth Moon, *Surrender None: The Legacy of Gird*, 1990
Pamela F. Service, *Vision Quest*, 1989
Andrew Whitmore, *The Fortress of Eternity*, 1990

3135

L.E. MODESITT JR.

Of Tangible Ghosts
(New York: Tor, 1994)

Story type: Fantasy (Science Fiction)
Major character(s): Johan Eschbach, Professor, Spy
Time period(s): Indeterminate
Locale(s): North America, Alternate Earth

Summary: On an Earth controlled by colonial superpowers and shared by living people and the ghosts of the dead who sometimes interact with the living, Johan Eschbach retires as a spy for Columbia and returns to teach in the Northeast, still dominated by the Dutch. Forced back into service as a spy, Johan investigates research into controlling ghosts until his discoveries result in enemies marking him for death.

Other books you might like:
Nina Kiriki Hoffman, *The Thread That Binds the Bones*, 1993
Marc Laidlaw, *Neon Lotus*, 1988
Rachel Pollack, *Temporary Agency*, 1994
Rachel Pollack, *Unquenchable Fire*, 1992
Elizabeth Ann Scarborough, *Last Refuge*, 1992

3136

L.E. MODESITT JR.

The Order War
(New York: Tor, 1995)

Story type: Fantasy (Political; Magic Conflict)
Series: Recluce
Major character(s): Justen, Magician, Engineer; Gunar, Magician, Engineer
Time period(s): Indeterminate
Locale(s): Sarronnyn, Fictional Country; Candar, Fictional Country; Naclos, Fictional Country

Summary: Despite valiant help from Justen, Gunar, and a few other volunteers from Recluce, Sarronnyn forces cannot repel the armies of Fairhaven and the White wizards. Separated, Justen flees through the desert of Candar, where rescuers help him to Naclos and a new understanding of the balance between Black and White before he reenters the battle against White Aggression. Set between *The Magic Engineer* and *The Magic of Recluce*.

Other books you might like:
Terry Goodkind, *Stone of Tears*, 1995
Laurell K. Hamilton, *Nightseer*, 1992
L. Dean James, *Summerland*, 1994
Katharine Kerr, *Days of Blood and Fire*, 1993
Andre Norton, *Elvenblood*, 1995
    Mercedes Lackey, co-author
Martha Wells, *The Element of Fire*, 1993

3137

L.E. MODESITT JR.

The Parafaith War
(New York: Tor, 1996)

Story type: Science Fiction (Military; Theological)
Major character(s): Trystin Desoll, Military Personnel (EcoTech Coalition lieutenant); Rhule Ghere, Alien (Farnkan), Doctor; Ulteena Freyer, Military Personnel (EcoTech Coalition major)
Time period(s): Indeterminate Future
Locale(s): Mara, Planet—Imaginary

Summary: One of many young EcoTech officers, Trystin Desoll fights desperately to defend his outpost on Mara from the Revenants, a fanatical religioius group who attempt to wipe out all who oppose them. When Trystin goes undercover to infiltrate the Revenants, he ultimately plays a much larger role in ending the war.

Other books you might like:
Ben Bova, *Orion Among the Stars*, 1995
Orson Scott Card, *Ender's Game*, 1985
David Drake, *Counting the Cost*, 1987
Joe Haldeman, *The Forever War*, 1975
Frank Herbert, *Dune*, 1965

3138

L.E. MODESITT JR.

Timediver's Dawn
(New York: Tor, 1992)

Story type: Science Fiction (Post-Holocaust; Psychic Powers)
Major character(s): Sammis Arloff Olon, Witch, Military Personnel; Wryan Relorn, Witch, Scientist; Odin Thor, Military Personnel
Time period(s): Indeterminate Future
Locale(s): Query, Planet—Imaginary

Summary: The Empire of Westron faces an invasion by the Frost Giants, mysterious beings that cause an unnatural cold wave on the planet. Sammis, a descendant of the persecuted witches of Eastron, finds himself on the run when imperial troops destroy his home and family. Desperation teaches him how to use the psychic powers inherited from his mother, the ability to move in the dimension of time. Conscripted into the ConFed troops, he meets others with the same powers who work to defeat the Frost Giants and restore their world.

Other books you might like:
Marion Zimmer Bradley, *Stormqueen!*, 1978
Emma Bull, *Bone Dance*, 1991
C.J. Cherryh, *Gate of Ivrel*, 1976
Gordon R. Dickson, *Time Storm*, 1977
Anne McCaffrey, *Dragonflight*, 1968
David R. Palmer, *Emergence*, 1984
Clifford D. Simak, *The Visitors*, 1979

3139

L.E. MODESITT JR.

The Towers of the Sunset

(New York: Tor, 1992)

Story type: Fantasy (Magic Conflict; Romance)
Series: Recluce
Major character(s): Creslin, Wizard, Fiance(e) (unwilling);
Magaera, Wizard
Time period(s): Indeterminate
Locale(s): Westwind, Fictional Country; Montgren, Fictional
Country; Recluce, Fictional Country (island)

Summary: Rather than accept an arranged marriage to
Magaera, Creslin chooses to flee his responsibility and search
for his self identity. Magaera's magical link to Creslin forces
her to pursue him while the White Wizards of Chaos attempt
to eliminate Creslin and his threat to world domination by the
White Wizards. Appointed co-regents to the desolate island of
Recluce, the pair grow individually as their friendship blossoms into love while they and others found the island kingdom of Recluce. Set prior to the events in *The Magic of
Recluce*.

Other books you might like:
Lois McMaster Bujold, *The Spirit Ring*, 1992
Robin McKinley, *The Hero and the Crown*, 1984
Elizabeth Moon, *Liar's Oath*, 1992
Elizabeth Moon, *Sheepfarmer's Daughter*, 1988
Patricia C. Wrede, *Dealing with Dragons*, 1990

3140

JUDITH MOFFETT

The Ragged World: A Novel of the Hefn on Earth

(New York: St. Martin's, 1991)

Story type: Science Fiction (Contemporary Realism; Fantasy)
Major character(s): Nancy Sandford, Scientist, Editor (maga-
zine); Carril Sharpless, Teacher; Godfrey, Alien (Hefn)
Time period(s): 2020s (2023)
Locale(s): Earth

Summary: The Hefn, hairy gnomelike little people, millenia
more advanced than we are scientifically and socially, have
returned to Earth to pick up some of their fellows who had
been left here during the 17th century. Conditions here were
such that, rather than wipe out the human race, they have put a
ban on childbirth until the environment stabilizes and humans
have learned to care for the eco-system. Several humans have

had personal interactions with the Hefn; this book contains
their stories.

Other books you might like:
Robert A. Heinlein, *Stranger in a Strange Land*, 1991
Frederik Pohl, *Homegoing*, 1989
James D. Priest, *Kirins: The Spell of No'an*, 1990
David Alexander Smith, *Homecoming*, 1990
John Varley, *The Ophiuchi Hotline*, 1977

3141

JUDITH MOFFETT

Time, Like an Ever-Rolling Stream

(New York: St. Martin's Press, 1992)

Story type: Science Fiction (Invasion of Earth; Contemporary
Realism)
Major character(s): Pam Pruitt, Scientist (mathematician);
Liam O'Hara, Scientist (mathematician, physicist); Hum-
phrey, Alien (Hefn)
Time period(s): 2030s
Locale(s): College Park, Maryland

Summary: Hefn rules have changed life on Earth. The baby
ban, still in effect, led to a decreased population, and the
effective ban against fossil fuels resulted in a changed atmosphere and life-style. The Hefn, working successfully with the
Gaists at keeping humanity from taking the easy path to the
Earth's destruction may soon lift or ameliorate the baby ban.
A direct sequel to *The Ragged World*.

Other books you might like:
David Brin, *Earth*, 1990
Octavia E. Butler, *Dawn*, 1987
Robert A. Heinlein, *Stranger in a Strange Land*, 1991
revised edition
Damon Knight, *A Reasonable World*, 1991
Larry Niven, *Footfall*, 1985
Jerry Pournelle, co-author
James D. Prist, *Kirins: The Spell of No'an*, 1990
John Varley, *Steel Beach*, 1992
David Weber, *Mutineers' Moon*, 1991

3142

JUDITH MOFFETT

Two That Came True

(Eugene, Oregon: Pulphouse Publishing, 1991)

Story type: Science Fiction (Collection)
Series: Author's Choice Monthly
Time period(s): 21st century

Summary: This volume reprints two stories. In "Surviving"
(1986), Sally Barnes is raised by chimpanzees from the age of
4 1/2 to 13, then brought back to human society to which she
must readapt. In "Not Without Honor" (1989), the Mickey
Mouse Club has extraterrestrial fans who contact humanity
hoping to enlist mouseketeer Jimmy Dodd's help as a teacher,
but accepting Pat's help when they find Jimmy has died. A 7-
page afterword follows the first story and a 6-page afterword
the second.

Other books you might like:
Edward Bryant, *Neon Twilight*, 1990
Lisa Goldstein, *Daily Voices*, 1989
Ron Goulart, *Skyrocket Steele Conquers the Universe and Other Media Tales*, 1990
James Patrick Kelly, *Heroines*, 1990
Elizabeth A. Lynn, *Tales From a Vanished Country*, 1990

3143
DONALD MOFFITT

Crescent in the Sky
(New York: Ballantine/Del Rey, 1990)

Story type: Science Fiction (Adventure)
Series: Mechanical Sky
Major character(s): Abdul Hamid-Jones, Scientist (Genetic Engineer); Aziz, Servant
Time period(s): 31st century (3030)
Locale(s): Mars

Summary: In a far future universe where Arabs have conquered both Earth and the stars, a young Anglo-Arab genetic engineer who thought himself divorced from politics, finds himself caught up in a complex web of intrigue and violence.

Other books you might like:
George Alec Effinger, *A Fire in the Sun*, 1989
George Alec Effinger, *When Gravity Fails*, 1987
Frank Herbert, *Dune*, 1965
Paul J. McAuley, *Of the Fall*, 1989

3144
DONALD MOFFITT

A Gathering of Stars
(New York: Ballantine/Del Rey, 1990)

Story type: Science Fiction (Adventure)
Series: Mechanical Sky
Major character(s): Abdul Hamid-Jones, Scientist (Genetic Engineer); Sultan of Alpha Centauri, Ruler
Time period(s): 31st century
Locale(s): Alpha Centauri, Planet—Imaginary

Summary: Hamid-Jones escapes the mad Emir of Mars and heads for Alpha Centauri, where he takes a position with the Sultan of that solar system. The Sultan wishes to oppose the Emir and become ruler of the Islamic universe, but has never gone on the prerequisite pilgrimage to Mecca because it would take many years at sub-light speeds and thus jeopardize his political position at home. Hamid-Jones discovers that the Sultan seeks a solution to this problem, one involving black holes, and that this solution may involve the destruction of his home world of Mars.

Other books you might like:
George Alec Effinger, *A Fire in the Sun*, 1989
George Alec Effinger, *When Gravity Fails*, 1987
Frank Herbert, *Dune*, 1965

3145
KIM MOHAN, Editor

Amazing Stories: The Anthology
(New York: Tor, 1995)

Story type: Science Fiction (Anthology)

Summary: Contains a six-page introduction, eight original stories and five stories reprinted from *Amazing Stories* 1953-1994 plus an *Amazing* memoir by Robert Bloch, ''Fantastic Adventures with *Amazing*.'' Although a few of the stories are light, most vary in tone from moody to dark with themes including alternate universes, alien societies, religion, lunar exploration, the nature of humankind, and glimpses at future sports, criminal justice, and bureaucracy. Authors include Gregory Benford, Thomas M. Disch, Alan Dean Foster, R.A. Lafferty, Ursula K. Le Guin, Lawrence Watt-Evans, and George Zebrowski.

Other books you might like:
Martin H. Greenberg, *Amazing Science Fiction Stories: The War Years 1936-1945*, 1987
    editor
Martin H. Greenberg, *Amazing Science Fiction Stories: The Wild Years 1946-1955*, 1987
    editor
Martin H. Greenberg, *Amazing Science Fiction Stories: The Wonder Years 1926-1935*, 1987
    editor
Kristine Kathryn Rusch, *The Best From Fantasy and Science Fiction: A 45th Anniversary Anthology*, 1994
    Edward L. Ferman, co-editor
Kristine Kathryn Rusch, *The Best of Pulphouse: The Hardback Magazine*, 1991
    editor

3146
CLIFFORD MOHR (Pseudonym of Morton Reed)

Requiem
(New York: Berkley, 1992)

Story type: Horror (Possession)
Major character(s): Robert Bauer, Musician; Libby Bauer, Parent (Robert's mother); Clyde Trap, Doctor
Time period(s): 1990s (1992)
Locale(s): New York, New York; Kansas

Summary: Although brain damaged at birth, nineteen-year-old Robert Bauer develops a sudden ability to play and master the violin. But when he begins speaking with the voice of someone who calls himself Nicolo, it becomes clear that Robert is possessed by the spirit of someone—or something.

Other books you might like:
Robert Bloch, *Fiddler's Fee*, 1945
    short story in *The Opener of the Way*
Nancy A. Collins, *Tempter*, 1991
Sheila Bristow Garner, *Night Music*, 1992
John Skipp, *The Scream*, 1988
    Craig Spector, co-author

3147

BRENT MONAHAN

Blood of the Covenant

(New York: St. Martin's, 1995)

Story type: Horror (Vampire Story)
Major character(s): Simon Penn, Librarian; Frederika Vanderveen, Librarian, Vampire; Father Dante Ferro, Religious (Catholic priest)
Time period(s): 1990s (1995)
Locale(s): Princeton, New Jersey

Summary: In a sequel to *The Book of Common Dread*, rare books curator Simon Penn seeks to hide the coveted scrolls of Ahriman, which reveal that vampires are the progeny of the devil and threaten to overturn the assumptions of all world religions, from the forces of Satan. Complicating his pursuit by the minions of Hell is the dependence of his girlfriend Frederika, who barely eluded the clutches of a vampire lover in the earlier adventure, on a powder that gives vampires their power and is distributed by satanic underlings.

Other books you might like:
Steven Brust, *Agyar*, 1992
Anne Rice, *The Vampire Lestat*, 1985
S.P. Somtow, *Vanitas: Escape From Vampire Junction*, 1995
Brian Stableford, *The Empire of Fear*, 1988

3148

BRENT MONAHAN

The Book of Common Dread

(New York: St. Martin's, 1993)

Story type: Horror (Vampire Story)
Major character(s): Vincent De Vilbiss, Vampire; Simon Penn, Librarian; Frederika Vanderveen, Librarian
Time period(s): 1990s
Locale(s): Princeton, New Jersey

Summary: Five-hundred-year old vampire Vincent De Vilbiss has been charged by the dark gods he serves to prevent scholars at the Princeton University Library from accessing a set of recently acquired ancient scrolls that will reveal the secrets of De Vilbiss and his kind. In the course of his mission, De Vilbiss becomes enamored of librarian Frederika Vanderveen, and thus an opponent of Frederika's adoring colleague, Simon Penn.

Other books you might like:
Steven Brust, *Agyar*, 1992
Anne Rice, *The Vampire Lestat*, 1985
Brian Stableford, *The Empire of Fear*, 1988

3149

BRENT MONAHAN

The Uprising

(New York: Pocket, 1992)

Story type: Horror (Ancient Evil Unleashed)

Major character(s): Keenan MacBreed, Archaeologist; Richard Meagher, Police Officer; Mary Liddy, Mentally Ill Person
Time period(s): 1980s (1988)
Locale(s): Carrick-on-Suir, Ireland

Summary: Keenan MacBreed's study of a cemetery relocation in the lands of his ancestors is complicated by the disinterment of several Druid skeletons, which become reanimated and steal the flesh of the nearby townspeople in order to work the magic that will resurrect their entire coven.

Other books you might like:
Al Sarrantonio, *Skeletons*, 1992
David van Meter Smith, *Trinity Grove*, 1990
Patrick Whalen, *Out of the Night*, 1990

3150

THOMAS F. MONTELEONE

The Blood of the Lamb

(New York: Tor, 1992)

Story type: Horror (Wild Talents)
Major character(s): Peter Carenza, Religious (priest); Marion Windsor, Journalist (newspaper reporter); Dan Ellington, Religious (Jesuit priest)
Time period(s): 1990s (1998)
Locale(s): New York, New York (Brooklyn); Vatican City

Summary: Father Peter Carenza's discovery that he has the power to heal or kill by the laying on of hands leads inevitably to his discovery that he was cloned by the Vatican from a blood stain of Jesus Christ left on the Shroud of Turin. But as he struggles to gain control of his godly powers, some begin to fear that he is using his messianic image to disguise satanic intentions.

Other books you might like:
Ramsey Campbell, *To Wake the Dead*, 1980
Andrew Laurance, *Catacomb*, 1981
Ira Levin, *Rosemary's Baby*, 1967
David Seltzer, *The Omen*, 1976

3151

THOMAS F. MONTELEONE

Borderlands

(New York: Avon, 1990)

Story type: Horror (Anthology)

Summary: A collection of 25 stories that "expand the envelope" of horror fiction beyond its present conventions. In almost all of the stories, horror occurs in unlikely settings (the home, the office) and arises from normally unextraordinary relationships (children and parents, male and female lovers). The best selections include Harlan Ellison's "Scartaris, June 28th," David Silva's "The Calling" and Karl Edward Wagner's "But You'll Never Follow Me." Two of the stories were nominated for 1991 Bram Stoker Awards.

Other books you might like:
Dennis Etchison, *Cutting Edge*, 1986

Charles L. Grant, *The Best of Shadows*, 1989
David B. Silva, *Best of The Horror Show*, 1987
J.N. Williamson, *The Best of Masques*, 1988

3152

THOMAS F. MONTELEONE, Editor

Borderlands 2

(New York: Avon, 1991)

Story type: Horror (Anthology)
Series: Borderlands

Summary: The second volume in this series contains 21 stories that "push the envelope" of the contemporary horror story. The great variety of themes these stories encompass is displayed in Paul F. Olson's "Down the Valley Wild," a ghost tale of guilt and retribution; David Silva's "Slipping," about a man who discovers he can't keep track of the intervals between specific "scenes" in his life; F. Paul Wilson's "Foet," which imagines a near future in which aborted embryos are exploited by the fashion world; Joe Lansdale's "Love Doll: A Fable," a scathing satire on sexual politics; and Bentley Little's "The Potato," in which a farmer comes to love his crops a little too intimately.

Other books you might like:
Dennis Etchison, *Cutting Edge*, 1984
Charles L. Grant, *The Shadows Series*, 1978-1991
David B. Silva, *Best of The Horror Show*, 1987
J.N. Williamson, *The Masques Series*, 1984-1992

3153

THOMAS F. MONTELEONE, Editor

Borderlands 3

(Baltimore, Maryland: Borderlands Press, 1993)

Story type: Horror (Anthology)
Series: Borderlands

Summary: Twenty-one authors have contributed original stories to this non-theme anthology, among them Poppy Z. Brite, whose "The Sixth Sentinel" tells of the passionate attachment of a pirate ghost to a modern woman in Louisiana; Bentley Little, who writes about the strangest carjacking in history in "The Man in the Passenger Seat"; Ronald Kelly, who leavens his ghostly "Midnight Grinding" with the flavor of the southern Gothic; Avram Davidson, whose "The Man Who Was Made of Money" is a marvelous satire on the battle of the sexes; and Kristine Kathryn Rusch, whose "The Ghost of Christmas Present" is a dark fantasy of loss and redemption.

Other books you might like:
Ramsey Campbell, *Superhorror*, 1976
Charles L. Grant, *The Best of Shadows*, 1988
Chris Morgan, *Dark Fantasies*, 1989
Claudia O'Keefe, *Ghosttide*, 1993
Stuart David Schiff, *Whispers: An Anthology of Fantasy and Horror*, 1977
Stanley Wiater, *After the Darkness*, 1993

3154

THOMAS F. MONTELEONE, Editor
ELIZABETH MONTELEONE, Co-Editor

Borderlands 4

(Baltimore: Borderlands Press, 1994)

Story type: Horror (Anthology)
Series: Borderlands

Summary: The fourth in this series devoted to cutting edge weird fiction brings together 18 stories that fall outside conventional genre niches. Included are Dennis Etchison's "A Wind From the South," an exerpt from his forthcoming novel, *California Gothic*; Ramsey Campbell's "A Side of the Sea," which plays fast and loose with its portrayal of a sane man trapped on a bus full of lunatics; William Browning Spencer's "The Ocean and All Its Devices," about a sea creature that preys upon a vacationing family; Don D'Ammassa's "Misadventures in the Skin Trade," told from the point of view of a madman with a gruesome fetish; Lawrence C. Connolly's "Circle of Lies," about a family's stopover in a small town caught up in a bizarre religious frenzy; and Peter Straub's "Fee," a new novella in his "Blue Rose" series which examines the mind of a young boy raised in the midst of domestic horrors too painful for him to express that subtly warp his psyche. Released as a signed, limited collector's edition only.

Other books you might like:
Peter Crowther, *Narrow Houses*, 1991
   editor
Charles L. Grant, *The Best of Shadows*, 1989
   editor
Charles L. Grant, *Final Shadows*, 1991
   editor
Stuart David Schiff, *The Best of Whispers*, 1994
   editor

3155

THOMAS F. MONTELEONE

Fantasma

(New York: Tor, 1989)

Story type: Horror (Black Magic)
Major character(s): Vincent Manzara, Musician (Grandson of Gaetano); Gaetano Manzara, Baker, Aged Person
Time period(s): 1980s (Flashbacks to 1875, 1919, 1924)
Locale(s): New York, New York; Sicily, Italy (Ciancia)

Summary: Vowing revenge against the Candelotto family for the murder of his cousin and father, Vincent Manzara imports a *strega* (Sicilian witchwoman) to summon a *fantasma* (demon). After considerable carnage, the *strega* is killed and her *fantasma* is unleashed, out of control, on New York City.

Other books you might like:
John Skipp, *The Light at the End*, 1986
   Craig Spector, co-author

3156

THOMAS F. MONTELEONE

The Resurrectionist
(New York: Warner, 1995)

Story type: Horror (Wild Talents)
Major character(s): Thomas Flanagan, Political Figure (senator); Estela Barrero, Doctor; Sam Lattimore, Political Figure (senator)
Time period(s): 1990s (1995)
Locale(s): Washington, District of Columbia

Summary: Following his survival of an airplane crash, senator and Republican presidential hopeful Thomas Flanagan finds himself endowed with the power to resurrect the newly dead. While Flanagan ponders the ramifications of his newly discovered talents, the American political power elite decides how his powers can be exploited to their benefit. This novel is a loose sequel to the author's 1992 Bram Stoker Award-winning *Blood of the Lamb*.

Other books you might like:
Mark Burnell, *Freak*, 1994
Ramsey Campbell, *The Hungry Moon*, 1987
Stephen King, *The Dead Zone*, 1979
Richard Matheson, *A Stir of Echoes*, 1958

3157

R.A. MONTGOMERY

Traitors from Within
(New York: Bantam, 1990)

Story type: Science Fiction (Post-Holocaust; Young Adult)
Series: TRIO: Rebels in the New World
Major character(s): Matt Sampson, Military Personnel (freedom fighter), Teenager; Mimla Caceras, Military Personnel (freedom fighter), Teenager; David Hasgard, Military Personnel (freedom fighter), Teenager
Time period(s): 2010s (2015)
Locale(s): North America

Summary: Democratic Turtalia and totalitarian Dorado are the two major powers in a splintered North America. When Matt, Mimla and Dave are accused of being traitors, they must enter Dorado to rescue Matt's brother and find information to clear themselves, including evidence of the real moles.

Other books you might like:
Douglas Hill, *Exiles of Colsec*, 1984
Dean Ing, *Systemic Shock*, 1981
Marc Laidlaw, *Neon Lotus*, 1988
David R. Palmer, *Emergence*, 1984
Nevil Shute, *On the Beach*, 1957
    pseudonym of Nevil Shute Norway

3158

CATHERINE MONTROSE

Wendigo Border
(New York: Tor, 1995)

Story type: Horror (Curse)
Major character(s): Darcy Jacoby, Student—College (psychology); Charlie Stone, Cowboy (ranch hand), Indian; Richard Ghormley, Professor (psychology)
Time period(s): 1990s (1995)
Locale(s): Laramie, Wyoming

Summary: When a professor of psychology dabbles dangerously in black magic in the hope of summoning a demon, Native American Charlie Stone appears to young Darcy Jacoby. Charlie, an ageless Indian warrior born over a century ago, hopes to help Darcy prevent the invasion of the Wendigo, a cursed tribe banished to another dimension. They are trying to engineer their return, and Darcy does not know she plays a key role in keeping them at bay. Under her maiden name, Catherine Cooke, tha author has written several fantasy trilogies.

Other books you might like:
A.A. Carr, *Eye Killers*, 1995
Muriel Gray, *Trickster*, 1994
T. Chris Martindale, *Demon Dance*, 1991
Adam Niswander, *The Charm*, 1993
Jessica Palmer, *Shadow Dance*, 1994
Kathryn Ptacek, *Ghost Dance*, 1990

3159

ELIZABETH MOON

Hunting Party
(New York: Baen, 1993)

Story type: Science Fiction (Adventure; Space Opera)
Series: Hunting Party
Major character(s): Heris Serrano, Spaceship Captain, Military Personnel (retired); Ronald "Ronnie" Carruthers, Teenager, Nobleman; Cecelia de Marktos, Noblewoman
Time period(s): Indeterminate Future
Locale(s): *Sweet Delight*, Spaceship; Sirialis, Planet—Imaginary

Summary: From a long line of military officers, Heris Serrano finds commanding the yacht of a wealthy aristocrat an unsettling change. The crew proves generally lazy and poorly trained and the passengers spoiled rich kids, but the ship inspections seem current so the *Sweet Delight* departs for Sirialis despite Captain Serrano's well-founded reservations.

Other books you might like:
Lois McMaster Bujold, *Shards of Honor*, 1986
Michelle Shirey Crean, *Dancer of the Sixth*, 1993
David Drake, *Starliner*, 1992
Stephen Goldin, *Jade Darcy and the Affair of Honor*, 1988
    Mary Mason, co-author
Jody Lynn Nye, *Taylor's Ark*, 1993
David Weber, *The Armageddon Inheritance*, 1993

3160

ELIZABETH MOON

Liar's Oath

(New York: Baen, 1992)

Story type: Fantasy (Magic Conflict; Political)
Major character(s): Gird, Revolutionary (retired), Leader (marshal-general); Luap, Royalty (bastard prince), Magician
Time period(s): Indeterminate Past
Locale(s): Planet—Imaginary; Mythical Place

Summary: After the successful revolution led by Gird, the mageborn, forbidden to use their magic on common folk, no longer rule. Tempted by his discovery of a new land accessible through magic, Luap ignores his oath to Gird in seeking to establish himself as leader of the mageborn in the new land. The hidden powers seeking to control Luap delight in the broken oath which they see as reflecting additional weakness which they may employ to their own evil ends. Set 500 years before events in *Sheepfarmer's Daughter*.

Other books you might like:
C.J. Cherryh, *Gate of Ivrel*, 1976
Casey Flynn, *The Enchanted Isles*, 1991
    pseudonym of Kenneth C. Flint
Casey Flynn, *Most Ancient Song*, 1991
    pseudonym of Kenneth C. Flint
L.E. Modesitt Jr., *The Towers of the Sunset*, 1992

3161

ELIZABETH MOON

Remnant Population

(New York: Baen, 1996)

Story type: Science Fiction (First Contact; Political)
Major character(s): Ofelia Damareux Falfurrias, Aged Person, Runaway; Bluecloak, Alien; Kira Stavi, Scientist (xenobiologist)
Time period(s): Indeterminate Future
Locale(s): Sims Bancorp Colony 3245.12, Planet—Imaginary

Summary: When Sims Bancorp loses the franchise to Colony 3245.12 and evacuates the colonists, 70-year-old Ofelia hides, refusing to leave. Happy at finally being alone with no one to tell her what to do, Ofelia maintains the crops and livestock left behind, as well as the power plant and radio. When a new colony unexpectedly tries to land about 40 miles away, Ofelia overhears its total destruction by previously unknown intelligent natives who decide to send some of their juvenile hunters to check out her "abandoned" colony.

Other books you might like:
Eleanor Arnason, *Ring of Swords*, 1993
Eleanor Arnason, *A Woman of the Iron People*, 1991
David Brin, *Brightness Reef*, 1995
C.J. Cherryh, *Foreigner*, 1994
James H. Schmitz, *The Demon Breed*, 1968
Sheri S. Tepper, *Grass*, 1989
John Varley, *Titan*, 1979

3162

ELIZABETH MOON

Sheepfarmer's Daughter

(New York: Baen Books, 1988)

Story type: Fantasy (Quest)
Series: Deed of Paksenarrion
Major character(s): Paksenarrion "Paks" Dorthansdotter, Farmer, Military Personnel
Time period(s): Indeterminate
Locale(s): Alternate Universe

Summary: When her father arranges a marriage with a pig farmer, Paks runs away and joins the Duke's army. This begins a series of adventures that leave her a hero, chosen by the gods to restore a lost ruler to his throne.

Other books you might like:
C.J. Cherryh, *The Paladin*, 1988
Jo Clayton, *Diadem from the Stars*, 1986
Louise Cooper, *Nemesis*, 1989
    Indigo Series, Book 1
Robin McKinley, *The Blue Sword*, 1982

3163

ELIZABETH MOON

Sporting Chance

(New York: Baen, 1994)

Story type: Science Fiction (Adventure; Space Opera)
Series: Hunting Party
Major character(s): Heris Serrano, Spaceship Captain, Military Personnel (retired); Cecelia de Marktos, Noblewoman (spaceship owner); Sirkin, Spacewoman (navigator)
Time period(s): Indeterminate Future
Locale(s): *Sweet Delight*, Spaceship; Sirialis, Planet—Imaginary; Rockhouse Major, Planet—Imaginary

Summary: After returning the Prince to Rockhouse, Cecelia mentions to the Emperor that she noticed the changes in his son. Cecelia suddenly takes ill, remaining comatose, leaving Heris the logical culprit as the heir to the *Sweet Delight*. Not only must Heris and her crew save the *Sweet Delight*, they also must somehow rescue Cecelia, find a cure and unravel the mystery surrounding the Prince. Sequel to *Hunting Party*.

Other books you might like:
Pauline Ashwell, *Unwillingly to Earth*, 1992
Lois McMaster Bujold, *The Warrior's Apprentice*, 1986
C.J. Cherryh, *Tripoint*, 1994
David Drake, *Starliner*, 1992
T. Jackson King, *Retread Shop*, 1988
David Weber, *On Basilisk Station*, 1993

3164

ELIZABETH MOON

Surrender None: The Legacy of Gird

(New York: Baen, 1990)

Story type: Fantasy (Adventure; Political)

Series: Deed of Paksenarrion
Major character(s): Gird, Farmer, Revolutionary
Time period(s): Indeterminate Past
Locale(s): Alternate Universe

Summary: A prequel to the Deed of Paksenarrion trilogy, this story tells how Gird gets some military training but returns to his family and attempts to make a life farming. The aristocracy, descended from overseas invaders, has become increasingly cruel and tyrannical. Eventually Gird is pressed too far and joins the dispossessed and rebellious outlaws in the forest. Gird puts his military training to good use to organize the outlaws, and develops plans for removing the aristocracy and instituting more compassionate and equitable rule.

Other books you might like:
Guy Gavriel Kay, *Tigana*, 1990
Katharine Kerr, *Daggerspell*, 1986
Robin McKinley, *The Blue Sword*, 1982
Steve Perry, *The Man Who Never Missed*, 1985
Karen Wehrstein, *Lion's Heart*, 1991

3165

ELIZABETH MOON

Winning Colors
(New York: Baen, 1995)

Story type: Science Fiction (Adventure; Political)
Series: Hunting Party
Major character(s): Heris Serrano, Spaceship Captain, Military Personnel (retired); Cecelia de Marktos, Noblewoman; Esteban Kontsandas, Military Personnel
Time period(s): Indeterminate Future
Locale(s): *Sweet Delight*, Spaceship; Xavier, Planet—Imaginary; Music, Planet—Imaginary

Summary: With the government still unsettled by the abdication of the old king, Lady Cecelia finds her ship now belongs to Heris Serrano, her ex-military employee. They leave behind the suit against Cecelia's prisoners and test her rejuvenation at the Wherrin Horse Trials, taking along Esteban as a favor to the military commander who had saved *Sweet Delight* previously. Looking for horses, on Xavier they find traitors selling out the planet to the Benignity. Attempting to save the system, Heris takes over the naval vessels involved in the conspiracy, pretending to retain her commission.

Other books you might like:
David Brin, *The Uplift War*, 1987
Lois McMaster Bujold, *Shards of Honor*, 1986
Alis A. Rasmussen, *A Passage of Stars*, 1990
David Weber, *The Honor of the Queen*, 1993
David Weber, *On Basilisk Station*, 1993

3166

MICHAEL MOORCOCK

Blood: A Southern Fantasy
(New York: Morrow/AvoNova, 1995)

Story type: Fantasy (Historical; Science Fiction)

Major character(s): Jack Karaquazian, Gambler; Sam Oakenhurst, Gambler
Time period(s): Indeterminate
Locale(s): Alternate Earth; Mississippi River; New Orleans, Louisiana

Summary: Searching for love and adventure, riverboat gamblers Jack Karaquazian and Sam Oakenhurst tempt luck and fate in the Game of Time, while the Biloxi fault threatens to engulf a South dominated by African Americans and thrust all into the barely explored multidimensional universe. Includes short fiction published 1991-1994.

Other books you might like:
Michael Bishop, *Brittle Innings*, 1994
Michael Bishop, *Count Geiger's Blues*, 1992
Michael Conner, *Archangel*, 1995
George R.R. Martin, *Fevre Dream*, 1982
Harry Turtledove, *The Guns of the South*, 1992

3167

MICHAEL MOORCOCK

Elric: Song of the Black Sword
(Clarkston, Georgia: White Wolf, 1995)

Story type: Fantasy (Sword and Sorcery; Magic Conflict)
Series: Elric
Major character(s): Elric, Warrior, Ruler
Time period(s): Indeterminate
Locale(s): Melnibone, Fictional Country; The Young Kingdoms, Fictional Country

Summary: Omnibus edition containing a two-page introduction by Moorcock; a map of the Young Kingdoms; three novels, *Elric of Melnibone* (1976), *Fortress of the Pearl* (1989), and *The Sailor on the Seas of Fate* (1976); and three stories, "The Dreaming City" (1967), "While the Gods Laugh" (1967), and "The Singing Citadel" (1970). These tales of the Eternal Champion Cycle relate adventures of the morose anti-hero and his vampiric sword.

Other books you might like:
Poul Anderson, *The Broken Sword*, 1954
James Branch Cabell, *Jurgen*, 1919
Lord Dunsany, *The King of Elfland's Daughter*, 1924
Edward E. Kramer, *Tales of the White Wolf*, 1994
    Richard Gilliam, co-editor
Fritz Leiber, *Ill Met in Lankhmar*, 1995
Fletcher Pratt, *The Well of the Unicorn*, 1948
Roger Zelazny, *Nine Princes in Amber*, 1970

3168

MICHAEL MOORCOCK

The Fortress of the Pearl
(New York: Ace, 1989)

Story type: Fantasy (Quest)
Series: Elric
Major character(s): Elric, Warrior, Royalty (Prince)
Time period(s): Indeterminate
Locale(s): Quarzhasaata, Alternate Universe (Dream Realm)

Summary: Trapped within the dreams of a girl prophet, Elric must find the Pearl at the Heart of the World, as well as his way out of the dreams, before he can join the ruling council at Quarzhasaata.

Other books you might like:
Gael Baudino, *Dragonsword*, 1988
C.J. Cherryh, *Reap the Whirlwind*, 1989
   Mercedes Lackey, co-author
Glen Cook, *The Swordbearer*, 1990
Fritz Leiber, *The Knight and Knave of Swords*, 1988
Eric Van Lustbader, *The Sunset Warrior*, 1989

3169

MICHAEL MOORCOCK

Lunching with the Antichrist
(Shingletown, California: Mark Ziesing, 1995)

Story type: Fantasy (Collection; Literary)
Major character(s): Jimi, Traveller; Edwin Begg, Religious (retired vicar); Savitsky, Military Personnel (Cossack)
Time period(s): 1990s (1992); 1920s (1920)
Locale(s): London, England; St. Crim, Fictional Country

Summary: Seven short stories, some with overt and others with muted fantastic elements, written 1974-1994, focusing on the Von Bek family and its various branches. From high society in the Twenties to an ex-roadie traveling with what might be the ghost of Jimi Hendrix, the stories trace the history of Britain as well.

Other books you might like:
Peter Ackroyd, *Hawksmoor*, 1986
John Crowley, *Little, Big*, 1981
Lisa Goldstein, *Travellers in Magic*, 1994
Patrick McGrath, *Blood and Water and Other Tales*, 1988

3170

MICHAEL MOORCOCK

The Revenge of the Rose
(New York: Ace, 1991)

Story type: Fantasy (Quest)
Series: Elric
Major character(s): Elric, Warrior, Royalty (prince); Rose, Time Traveller, Warrior; Wheldrake, Writer (poet)
Time period(s): Indeterminate
Locale(s): Northern Young Kingdoms, Fictional Country; The Sphere the Realm, Mythical Place (the multiverse)

Summary: In the Dreaming City, the spirit of Elric's deceased father asks Elric to find and free his soul, held captive by Gaynor. Elric and his companions seek out and find the soul, not knowing the Lord of Chaos had planned a trap aimed at separating Elric from his vampire sword.

Other books you might like:
David Eddings, *Pawn of Prophecy*, 1982
Raymond E. Feist, *Daughter of the Empire*, 1987
   Janny Wurtz, co-author
Robert Jordan, *The Eye of the World*, 1989
Marc Laidlaw, *Neon Lotus*, 1988

Fritz Leiber, *The Knight and Knave of Swords*, 1990
Roger Zelazny, *Nine Princes in Amber*, 1970

3171

ALAN MOORE
EDDIE CAMPBELL, Illustrator

From Hell
(Baltimore: Borderlands Press, 1994)

Story type: Horror (Serial Killer)
Major character(s): Annie Crook, Clerk (sweet shop employee); Walter Sickert, Artist; Annie Chapman, Prostitute
Time period(s): 1880s
Locale(s): London, England

Summary: This book presents the scripts of the "From Hell" series, a meditation on the life and crimes of Jack the Ripper which was published as a fully illustrated comic strip in the avant garde comic art magazine *Taboo* between 1988 and 1990. *Taboo* publisher Stephen Bissette supplies an afterword. The text is heavily annotated by Moore and illustrated by Eddie Campbell.

Other books you might like:
Shirley Harrison, *The Diary of Jack the Ripper: The Discovery, the Investigation, the Debate*, 1993
Stephen Knight, *Jack the Ripper: The Final Solution*, 1976
Donald Rumbelow, *The Complete Jack the Ripper*, 1987
Paul West, *The Women of Whitechapel and Jack the Ripper*, 1992

3172

CHRISTOPHER MOORE

Bloodsucking Fiends: A Love Story
(New York: Simon & Schuster, 1995)

Story type: Horror (Vampire Story; Satire)
Major character(s): Jody, Clerk (claims clerk), Vampire; C. Thomas Flood, Writer; Elijah Ben Sapir, Vampire
Time period(s): 1990s (1995)
Locale(s): San Francisco, California

Summary: Vampirized for reasons she cannot understand, Jody seeks the assistance of Tommy Flood, an aspiring writer she has just met, to help her deal with her new lifestyle. As Jody and Thomas become lovers, grappling clumsily with their vastly different means of existence, both try to get to the bottom of the mystery surrounding Jody's victimization and exonerate Tommy of the suspicion that he is responsible for the recent spate of vampire deaths around town.

Other books you might like:
Anne Billson, *Suckers*, 1993
Ray Garton, *Live Girls*, 1987
Norman Spinrad, *Vampire Junkies*, 1994

3173
CHRISTOPHER MOORE

Practical Demonkeeping
(New York: St. Martin's, 1991)

Story type: Horror (Satire)
Major character(s): Travis O'Hearn, Drifter; Catch, Demon; Jenny Masterson, Waiter/Waitress
Time period(s): 1990s
Locale(s): Pine Cove, California

Summary: The author's amusing first novel tells of Travis O'Hearn, who has grown tired of his relationship with Catch, a demon who grants him eternal youth in exchange for human victims. When Travis reaches Pine Cove, he must find a way to shed Catch, before Catch decimates the town and develops a taste for Travis's love interest, Jenny.

Other books you might like:
L. Sprague de Camp, *Solomon's Stone*, 1942
Esther Friesner, *Hooray for Hellywood*, 1990
L. Ron Hubbard, *The Case of the Friendly Corpse*, 1941
Daniel Rhodes, *Kiss of Death*, 1990
Thorne Smith, *Topper: An Improbable Adventure*, 1926

3174
JAMES A. MOORE

Hell-Storm
(New York: HarperPrism, 1996)

Story type: Horror (Werewolf Story)
Series: World of Darkness: Werewolf
Major character(s): Gabriel White, Werewolf; Diane White, Parent; Jack Dawson, Mercenary
Time period(s): 1990s (1996)
Locale(s): Las Vegas, Nevada

Summary: Gabriel and his mother accept an invitation to the Platinum Palace casino to escape the blood wars that have taken the life of Gabriel's adoptive father. But the Wyrm, a spirit of corruption that poisons the World of Darkness, is conspiring with the mob to use the casino as a catalyst for yet more strife. This novel is set in White Wolf Books' ''World of Darkness'' gaming world, where humans and supernatural beings co-exist.

Other books you might like:
Doug Murray, *Call to Battle*, 1996
Edo Van Belkom, *Wyrm Wolf*, 1995
Stewart Von Allmen, *Conspicuous Consumption*, 1995

3175
JOHN MOORE

Slay and Rescue
(New York: Baen, 1993)

Story type: Fantasy (Light Fantasy)
Major character(s): Prince Charming, Hero, Royalty; Wendell, Sidekick
Time period(s): Indeterminate

Locale(s): Illyria, Fictional Country; Alacia, Fictional Country

Summary: Accompanied by Wendell, Prince Charming dazzles the kingdom with brave deeds while rescuing princesses and searching for a hot date.

Other books you might like:
Kyle Crocco, *Heroes, Inc.*, 1991
Barry Hughart, *Bridge of Birds*, 1984
Terry Pratchett, *Guards! Guards!*, 1991
Christopher Stasheff, *The Warlock in Spite of Himself*, 1969
Roger Zelazny, *Bring Me the Head of Prince Charming*, 1991
    Robert Sheckley, co-author
Roger Zelazny, *If at Faust You Don't Succeed*, 1993
    Robert Sheckley, co-author

3176
STANLEY R. MOORE

Nightshade
(New York: NAL Onyx, 1989)

Story type: Horror (Nature in Revolt)
Major character(s): Peter Bileux, Police Officer (Deputy sheriff); Louise Kavanaugh, Researcher (Medical)
Time period(s): 1980s
Locale(s): Thomas Valley, Pennsylvania

Summary: In Moore's first novel, the quiet town of Thomas Valley is gradually terrorized by a mysterious plague of killing flies. A small group led by the deputy sheriff and a group of medical researchers search frantically for clues to the nature and source—natural or supernatural—in order to develop a defense against the infestation before it completely destroys the town and spreads beyond its perimeters.

Other books you might like:
James Herbert, *Domain*, 1984
James Herbert, *Lair*, 1979
James Herbert, *The Rats*, 1974
Harry Adam Knight, *The Fungus*, 1989

3177
DANIEL KEYS MORAN

The Last Dancer
(New York: Bantam Spectra, 1993)

Story type: Science Fiction (Political; Psychic Powers)
Series: Tales of the Continuing Time
Major character(s): Denice Castanaveras, Telepath, Genetically Altered Being; ''William Devane'' Gi'Tbad'Eovad'Dvan, Immortal, Security Officer; Gi'Suei'Obodi'Sedon, Immortal, Rebel
Time period(s): 2070s (2075-2076); 350th century B.C.
Locale(s): Earth

Summary: Fleeing from his executioner, Dvan, Sedon takes refuge in a stasis bubble for 37,000 years. Along with her twin brother David, Denice survives the massacre of the ''genies'' in 2062 by hiding among the street children in the rubble of New York City. On the eve of the Tricentennial, rebels in Occupied America prepare to overthrow the Unification government while Sedon, released from stasis and escaped from

Peace Keeping Force detention, uses David's abilities to control the rebel movement. Denice, however, resists his attempts to control her talents—talents that even she does not yet understand.

Other books you might like:
Alfred Bester, *The Computer Connection*, 1975
Margaret Wander Bonanno, *The Others*, 1990
David Brin, *Startide Rising*, 1983
C.J. Cherryh, *Cyteen*, 1988
C.J. Cherryh, *Heavy Time*, 1991
Jane S. Fancher, *Ground-Ties*, 1991
Robert A. Heinlein, *The Moon Is a Harsh Mistress*, 1966
Larry Niven, *Protector*, 1973
Larry Niven, *Ringworld Engineers*, 1980
A.E. van Vogt, *Slan*, 1946

3178

DANIEL KEYS MORAN

The Long Run

(New York: Bantam Spectra, 1989)

Story type: Science Fiction (Cyberpunk)
Series: Tales of the Continuing Time
Major character(s): Trent Castanaveras, Thief, Computer Expert; Denice Castanaveras, Telepath, Genetically Altered Being
Time period(s): 21st century
Locale(s): New York, New York; Moon (Earth's)

Summary: Trent was one of the few who survived the United Nations Peaceforce massacre of the Castanaveras telepaths. Now he lives as an outlaw computer hacker, making a living through datanet crime. The UN Peaceforcers, however, have a long arm and an even longer memory. Soon Trent finds them on his trail again and, almost against his will, becomes a key figure in a revolution against UN tyranny.

Other books you might like:
William Gibson, *Neuromancer*, 1984
W.T. Quick, *Systems*, 1989
Bruce Sterling, *Islands in the Net*, 1988
A.E. van Vogt, *Slan*, 1946

3179

JOE MOREY, Editor

Glimring Night and Other Tales of Fantasy

(Concord, California: Dark Regions, 1991)

Story type: Horror (Anthology)

Summary: A trade paperback edition of the small press magazine *Dark Regions* that includes nine short stories and poems, among which are Albert J. Manachino's tale of a strange case of demonic possession, ''Darby's Bane''; Keith Hudson's prose poem of a horrifying resurrection, ''Upon the Wings of Lazarus''; and three stories by Ardath Mayhar, the best of which is her dark fairy tale, ''Needles and Pins.''

Other books you might like:
Robert Morrish, *The Quick Chills Series*, 1990-1992
    Peter Enfantino, co-author
Joy Oestreicher, *Alpha Gallery*, 1991
Steve Pasechnik, *The Best of the Rest*, 1990
    Brian Youmans, co-author
Elizabeth A. Saunders, *When the Black Lotus Blooms*, 1990
David B. Silva, *Best of The Horror Show*, 1987

3180

J.M. MORGAN

Between the Devil and the Deep

(New York: Pocket, 1992)

Story type: Horror (Nature in Revolt)
Major character(s): J. Kelsey Chase, Diver; Cyrus Gilbert, Police Officer (sheriff); Paige Burton, Scientist (marine biologist)
Time period(s): 1990s
Locale(s): Saratoga Springs, Nevada; Loch Ness, Scotland

Summary: Coincidences between underwater formations in Death Valley and Loch Ness suggest to diver J. Kelsey Chase a series of tunnels connecting bodies of water across the face of the earth. Chase quickly finds that his worst nemesis may not be the prehistoric mammals still living in the caves, but the business entrepreneur who has engaged his services and is neurotically protective of the fame and riches the discovery will bring.

Other books you might like:
Peter Benchley, *Beast*, 1991
Peter Benchley, *Jaws*, 1974
William Dantz, *Hunger*, 1992

3181

J.M. MORGAN

Beyond Eden

(New York: Pinnacle, 1992)

Story type: Science Fiction (Post-Holocaust; Adventure)
Series: Eden
Major character(s): Jonathan Katelo, Indian (Inuit), Explorer; Seth Katelo, Indian (Inuit), Explorer; Josiah Gray Wolf, Scientist, Explorer
Time period(s): 2010s
Locale(s): Biosphere Seven, Texas; Montana; North America

Summary: After plague wipes out most human life on Earth, survivors Jonathan and Seth Katelo set out from their Montana home in search of a legendary city of survivors. Meanwhile, Josiah Gray Wolf and his band of survivors living near Biosphere Seven struggle against traditional human difficulties as the second generation of Biosphere Seven residents anxiously plan to leave the safety of their environment for the excitement of exploring the depopulated surroundings.

Other books you might like:
Will Bradley, *Ark Liberty*, 1992
Octavia E. Butler, *Adulthood Rites*, 1988
Donald E. McQuinn, *Warrior*, 1990

Michael D. Weaver, *My Father Immortal*, 1989

3182

J.M. MORGAN

Desert Eden
(New York: Zebra Pinnacle, 1991)

Story type: Science Fiction (End of the World; Techno-Thriller)
Series: Eden
Major character(s): Jessica Nathan, Scientist; Josiah Gray Wolf, Scientist, Explorer; John Katelo, Guide, Linguist
Time period(s): 1990s (1997)
Locale(s): Claypool, Texas (Biosphere Seven); Siberia, Union of Soviet Socialist Republics (Biosphere Four)

Summary: After Biosphere Seven was sealed for a two-year trial of the huge, closed environment, a virus created secretly in Biosphere Four killed its inventors and got loose in Earth's atmosphere. No cure or treatment was discovered. The ten inhabitants of Biosphere Seven must decide what possibilities lie in their future when they realize they are permanently cut off from the outside world in their dome.

Other books you might like:
Roger MacBride Allen, *The Ring of Charon*, 1990
Michael Armstrong, *Agviq*, 1990
Stephen Baxter, *Raft*, 1992
David Brin, *Earth*, 1990
Octavia E. Butler, *Dawn*, 1987
Marjorie Bradley Kellogg, *Harmony*, 1991
Donald E. McQuinn, *Warrior*, 1990
Larry Niven, *Lucifer's Hammer*, 1977
    Jerry Pournelle, co-author
Vernor Vinge, *Marooned in Realtime*, 1986
Catherine Wells, *The Earth Is All That Lasts*, 1991

3183

J.M. MORGAN

Future Eden
(New York: Pinnacle, 1992)

Story type: Science Fiction (Post-Holocaust; Adventure)
Series: Eden
Major character(s): Willow Gray Wolf, Explorer; Seth Katelo, Indian, Explorer (Inuit); Sidra, Explorer
Time period(s): 2020s (2020)
Locale(s): Texas; North America

Summary: Decades after plague devastates humanity, some of the few survivors begin to explore in hopes of reestablishing a human presence on the depopulated Earth.

Other books you might like:
Octavia E. Butler, *Imago*, 1989
Sterling E. Lanier, *Hiero's Journey*, 1973
Donald E. McQuinn, *Warrior*, 1990
Catherine Wells, *The Earth Is All That Lasts*, 1991
Paul O. Williams, *The Breaking of Northwall*, 1980

3184

ROBERT MORGAN (Pseudonym of C.J. Henderson)

All Things under the Moon
(New York: Berkley, 1994)

Story type: Horror (Mystery; Werewolf Story)
Series: Adventures of Teddy London
Major character(s): Teddy London, Detective—Private; Lisa Hutchinson, Assistant; Maxim Warhelski, Werewolf
Time period(s): 1990s (1994)
Locale(s): New York, New York

Summary: In his fourth adventure, Teddy London, a detective whose case file frequently brings him into contact with the supernatural, is stalked by a centuries-old, seemingly indestructable werewolf who wants to be killed, but whose inhuman nature demands that he fight to the death those capable of putting him out of his misery.

Other books you might like:
Crosland Brown, *Tombley's Walk*, 1991
Richard Jaccoma, *The Werewolf's Revenge*, 1991
Richard Jaccoma, *The Werewolf's Tale*, 1988
H. Warner Munn, *The Werewolf of Ponkert*, 1958
S.P. Somtow, *Moon Dance*, 1988

3185

ROBERT MORGAN (Pseudonym of C.J. Henderson)

The Only Thing to Fear
(New York: Berkley, 1994)

Story type: Horror (Mystery; Ghost Story)
Series: Adventures of Teddy London
Major character(s): Teddy London, Detective—Private; Paul Morcey, Assistant; Kuan Yu-Chen, Religious (priest)
Time period(s): 1990s (1994)
Locale(s): Xian, China; New York, New York

Summary: Detective Teddy London's fifth adventure battling supernatural menaces takes him to China, where his destiny to save the earth from an oncoming meteor is intertwined with the mystery of an ancient ghost warrior leading him through a ritual of self-discovery.

Other books you might like:
T.E.D. Klein, *The Ceremonies*, 1983
Bentley Little, *The Summoning*, 1993
Kelley Wilde, *Makoto*, 1990
F. Paul Wilson, *Black Wind*, 1989
T.M. Wright, *The Ascending*, 1994

3186

ROBERT MORGAN (Pseudonym of C.J. Henderson)

Some Things Come Back
(New York: Berkley, 1995)

Story type: Horror (Occult; Vampire Story)
Series: Adventures of Teddy London
Major character(s): Teddy London, Detective—Private; Martin Tabor, Vampire; Paul Morcey, Detective

Time period(s): 1990s (1995)
Locale(s): New York, New York

Summary: In the final adventure of Teddy London, a private eye whose work always brings him in contact with the occult, London faces down Martin Tabor, his nemesis from an earlier adventure. London's efforts to prevent Tabor and his vampire underlings from dropping nuclear bombs across the world in order to feed on the souls of the dead they will liberate dovetails with his quest to find a new incarnation for the Confessor, an ageless occult entity who may hold the key to thwarting Tabor.

Other books you might like:
Stephen Gallagher, *Valley of Lights*, 1987
Lee Killough, *Blood Hunt*, 1987
William Relling Jr., *New Moon*, 1987
Robert Weinberg, *Bloodwar*, 1995
Les Whitten, *Progeny of the Adder*, 1965

3187

ROBERT MORGAN (Pseudonym of C.J. Henderson)

Some Things Never Die
(New York: Diamond, 1993)

Story type: Horror (Vampire Story)
Series: Adventures of Teddy London
Major character(s): Teddy London, Detective—Private; Lai Wan, Psychic (psychometrist); Jorhsa, Vampire
Time period(s): 1990s (1993)
Locale(s): New York, New York (Chinatown)

Summary: Summoned to Chinatown to investigate a grotesque murder, detective Teddy London runs afoul of the Gaun Cee Qui, a race of power-hungry vampires rampant in the neighborhood who force London to confront his own buried vampiric tendencies.

Other books you might like:
Stephen Gallagher, *Valley of Lights*, 1987
Richard Jaccoma, *The Werewolf's Tale*, 1988
Lee Killough, *Blood Hunt*, 1987
William Relling Jr., *New Moon*, 1987
Les Whitten, *Progeny of the Adder*, 1965

3188

ROBERT MORGAN (Pseudonym of C.J. Henderson)

The Thing That Darkness Hides
(New York: Diamond, 1993)

Story type: Horror (Black Magic)
Series: Adventures of Teddy London
Major character(s): Teddy London, Detective—Private; George Collins, Wealthy; Father Bain, Religious
Time period(s): 1990s (1993)
Locale(s): New York, New York; Hell

Summary: In his toughest case yet, private detective Teddy London agrees to help George Collins retrieve the immortal soul he bartered to Satan for his mortal success—an assignment that ultimately calls for London meeting the devil on his home turf: Hell.

Other books you might like:
Cleve Cartmill, *Hell Hath Fury*, 1943
William Hjortsberg, *Falling Angel*, 1978
Robert Masello, *Private Demons*, 1992

3189

ROBERT MORGAN (Pseudonym of C.J. Henderson)

The Things That Are Not There
(New York: Diamond, 1992)

Story type: Horror (Ancient Evil Unleashed; Mystery)
Series: Adventures of Teddy London
Major character(s): Teddy London, Detective—Private; Paul Morcey, Maintenance Worker (janitor); Lisa Hutchinson, Assistant
Time period(s): 1990s
Locale(s): New York, New York

Summary: In this hardboiled horror novel strongly influenced by the writing of H. P. Lovecraft, private detective Teddy London turns occult detective when his investigations into the paranoid delusions of Lisa Hutchinson uncover a plot by cosmic cultists to use her body as the earthly vessel for the extradimensional monstrosity Qtalu.

Other books you might like:
Robert Bloch, *Strange Eons*, 1978
August Derleth, *The Lurker at the Threshold*, 1945
Brian Lumley, *The Burrowers Beneath*, 1974
Michael Shea, *Fat Face*, 1987

3190

ROBIN MORGAN

The Mer-Child: A Legend for Children and Other Adults
(New York: The Feminist Press at the City University of New York, 1991)

Story type: Fantasy (Contemporary; Legend)
Major character(s): Mer-Child, Mythical Creature (mermaid); Little Girl, Handicapped (paraplegic), Scientist
Time period(s): Indeterminate
Locale(s): At Sea; Earth (Northern Hemisphere sea shore)

Summary: Shunned by the Mer-People and orphaned, threatened or attacked by humans, the Mer-Child had dolphins to play with, but was lonely. The Little Girl whose black mother died when she was an infant has a wonderful relationship with her white father, but she is also lonely and has been hurt by being rejected. The Mer-Child and the Little Girl find they have much in common in this contemporary sequel to *The Little Mermaid* by Hans Christian Andersen.

Other books you might like:
Margaret Wander Bonanno, *The Others*, 1990
Antoine de Saint-Exupery, *The Little Prince*, 1943
Pamela Dean, *Tam Lin*, 1991
Frances Mary Hendry, *Quest for a Maid*, 1990
Michael Kandel, *In between Dragons*, 1990
Garry Kilworth, *The Foxes of Firstdark*, 1990
Barry Lopez, *Crow and Weasel*, 1990

Ethel Johnston Phelps, *Tatterhood and Other Tales*, 1978
   editor
Sheri S. Tepper, *Beauty*, 1991

3191

A.R. MORLAN

The Amulet
(New York: Bantam, 1991)

Story type: Horror (Curse)
Major character(s): Anna Sudek, Worker (cleaning woman); Tina Miner Sudek, Worker (cleaning woman), Parent (Anna's mother); Arlene "Grandma" Campbell, Aged Person
Time period(s): 1980s (1987)
Locale(s): Ewerton, Wisconsin

Summary: The Sudeks have been an embarrassment to the town of Ewerton ever since that night 56 years ago when the family patriarch brutally murdered his wife and his mother-in-law disappeared. Looking into her family's history, Anna Sudek discovers the truth of her family's tragedy, and its origins in a cursed talisman that brings misery to all who come in contact with it.

Other books you might like:
John Farris, *All Heads Turn When the Hunt Goes By*, 1977
Charles L. Grant, *Stunts*, 1990
Stephen King, *The Talisman*, 1984
   Peter Straub, co-author
Jack Martin, *Halloween III: Season of the Witch*, 1985

3192

A.R. MORLAN

Dark Journey
(New York: Bantam, 1991)

Story type: Horror (Carnival/Circus Horror)
Major character(s): Palmer Winston, Aged Person; Palmer Nemmitz, Aged Person; Brent Nimitz, Unemployed (Palmer Nemmitz's nephew)
Time period(s): 1980s (1988)
Locale(s): Ewerton, Wisconsin

Summary: After a 54-year hiatus the South-State Enterprises Carnival returns to the town of Ewerton, reviving memories of the town's unspoken past, devastating the town's younger citizens with the truth about their heritage, and reopening old wounds in those still alive who remember the last summer that the carnival performed there.

Other books you might like:
Ray Bradbury, *Something Wicked This Way Comes*, 1962
Charles G. Finney, *The Circus of Dr. Lao*, 1935
William W. Johnstone, *Carnival*, 1990
Richard Laymon, *Funland*, 1990
Thomas F. Monteleone, *The Magnificent Gallery*, 1987

3193

DAVID MORRELL

The Totem
(Hampton Falls, New Hampshire: Donald M. Grant, 1994)

Story type: Horror (Mystery)
Major character(s): Nathan Slaughter, Police Officer; Gordon Dunlap, Journalist; Parsons, Political Figure (mayor)
Time period(s): 1990s (1993)
Locale(s): Potter's Field, Colorado

Summary: Twenty-three years after it dispersed a commune of hippies that took root on its outskirts, a remote cattle town is under siege from a mutant strain of the rabies virus that brings out animalistic behavior in the residents. Investigators trace the outbreak to remnants of the commune who took refuge in the nearby hills and who have now become predators preying on the townsfolk. This novel was originally published in 1979 in a shortened form.

Other books you might like:
Douglas Clegg, *Dark of the Eye*, 1994
Michael Crichton, *The Andromeda Strain*, 1969
Peter Straub, *Floating Dragon*, 1984

3194

JOHN MORRESSY

Kedrigern and the Charming Couple
(New York: Ace, 1990)

Story type: Fantasy (Light Fantasy; Adventure)
Series: Kedrigern
Major character(s): Kedrigern, Wizard (of Silent Thunder Mountain); Berzel, Royalty (Princess of Othion), Werewolf
Time period(s): Indeterminate
Locale(s): Othion, Fictional Country

Summary: King Ithian of Othion is having a problem with his beautiful daughter, Princess Berzel. When the moon is full, she turns into a werewolf. The King manages to elicit a promise from Kedrigern that he will find a cure before the next full moon. But Kedrigern finds time running out when he finds the cure written in a book locked in the library of a monastery. The problem is, not only are the monks not particularly fond of wizards, but they are hiding a terrible secret and aren't about to let anyone in to snoop around.

Other books you might like:
C.J. Cherryh, *Rusalka*, 1989
Barbara Hambly, *Dragonsbane*, 1987
Megan Lindholm, *Luck of the Wheels*, 1989
Terry Pratchett, *Equal Rites*, 1988
Christopher Stasheff, *The Warlock Insane*, 1989

3195

JOHN MORRESSY

A Remembrance for Kedrigern

(New York: Ace, 1990)

Story type: Fantasy (Light Fantasy; Quest)
Series: Kedrigern
Major character(s): Kedrigern, Wizard (of Silent Thunder Mountain); Princess, Spouse (Kedrigern's), Royalty; Formidable, Royalty (Prince of Kallopane), Warrior
Time period(s): Indeterminate
Locale(s): Kallopane, Fictional Country; Moodymount, Mythical Place

Summary: The King of Kallopane has requested (bribed) Kedrigern to help his son, Prince Formidable, live up to his name and slay Great Crawling Loathliness, the monster that lives on Moodymount. Accompanied by a haunted huntsman and the Royal Wizard of Kallopane (who has been turned into a large bee), Kedrigern, Princess and Formidable go for the unpleasant creature.

Other books you might like:
Gordon R. Dickson, *The Dragon and the George*, 1976
Stephen R. Donaldson, *Lord Foul's Bane*, 1977
Barbara Hambly, *Dragonsbane*, 1987
Robert A. Heinlein, *Glory Road*, 1963
Terry Pratchett, *Mort*, 1989

3196

JANET MORRIS
CHRIS MORRIS, Co-Author

City at the Edge of Time

(New York: Baen, 1988)

Story type: Fantasy (Sword and Sorcery)
Series: Thieves' World
Time period(s): Indeterminate
Locale(s): Thieves' World, Planet—Imaginary

Summary: Trapped in a cursed city, a man has to find a powerful sponsor to protect him, or he will die.

Other books you might like:
Glen Cook, *Tower of Fear*, 1989
Simon R. Green, *Hawk & Fisher*, 1990
Fritz Leiber, *The Knight and Knave of Swords*, 1990
Keith Taylor, *Search for the Starblade*, 1990

3197

JANET MORRIS
CHRIS MORRIS, Co-Author

The Stalk

(New York: Roc, 1994)

Story type: Science Fiction (First Contact; Alternate Universe)
Series: Threshold
Major character(s): Michael "Mickey" Croft, Political Figure (secretary general); Vincent Remson, Government Official (bureaucrat); Joe South, Spaceman, Time Traveller

Time period(s): 27th century
Locale(s): Trust Territory of Threshold, Space Station

Summary: The aliens from the Council of Unity have contacted Mickey Croft, Secretary General of the United Nations of Earth, using as messengers two young humans who had fled to Unity Space. The Unity offers expanded contact if the humans will move Threshold beyond Pluto's orbit. Mickey Croft feels his own mental perceptions altered and wonders if increased contact will mean the end of the human race. Sequel to *Threshold*.

Other books you might like:
Octavia E. Butler, *Dawn*, 1987
C.J. Cherryh, *Downbelow Station*, 1981
Arthur C. Clarke, *Childhood's End*, 1953
Clifford D. Simak, *Time Is the Simplest Thing*, 1961
John Varley, *The Ophiuchi Hotline*, 1977

3198

JANET MORRIS
DAVID DRAKE, Co-Author

Target

(New York: Ace Books, 1989)

Story type: Science Fiction (First Contact)
Major character(s): Sam Yates, Police Officer; Channon, Alien, Diplomat
Time period(s): Indeterminate Future
Locale(s): Moon (Earth's)

Summary: An alien fleeing enemies is given asylum by a lunar colony and the various nations of Earth compete for access to him. Then the evil aliens hunting him show up. They're willing to destroy all human life in order to recapture their prey.

Other books you might like:
Martin Caidin, *Prison Ship*, 1989
Hal Clement, *Needle*, 1950
Rick Cook, *Limbo System*, 1989
L. Neil Smith, *Contact and Commune*, 1989

3199

JANET MORRIS
CHRIS MORRIS, Co-Author

Threshold

(New York: Roc/Penguin, 1990)

Story type: Science Fiction (Time Travel; Adventure)
Series: Threshold
Major character(s): Joe South, Spaceman, Time Traveller
Time period(s): 27th century
Locale(s): *Starbird*, Spaceship; Trust Territory of Threshold, Space Station

Summary: When Joe South unexpectedly travels 500 years into the future, he discovers a much-changed, highly repressive society in which access to Earth is available to only the privileged few. When his ship is confiscated and his lifestyle and freedom threatened, Joe must find a way to again become his own master while being dragged unwillingly into the political intrigue associated with a mysterious alien artifact.

Other books you might like:
Roger MacBride Allen, *The Ring of Charon*, 1990
Robert A. Heinlein, *Farnham's Freehold*, 1964
Vernor Vinge, *Marooned in Realtime*, 1986
Vernor Vinge, *The Peace War*, 1984

3200

JANET MORRIS
CHRIS MORRIS, Co-Author

Trust Territory
(New York: Roc, 1992)

Story type: Science Fiction (Adventure; First Contact)
Series: Threshold
Major character(s): Joe South, Time Traveller, Spaceman; Michael "Mickey" Croft, Political Figure (Secretary General); Micah "the Scavenger" Keebler, Scavenger
Time period(s): 27th century
Locale(s): *Starbird*, Spaceship; Trust Territory of Threshhold, Space Station; The Ball, Space Station (alien object)

Summary: As a "Relic" from the 21st century, Joe South's acceptance into 27th century society proves difficult, especially as the continuing displays of *The Ball* serve to focus attention on Joe. The Scavenger believes *The Ball* belongs to him, and the aliens call him the Pioneer, their special friend. Unfortunately for humans, the inimical alien environment overwhelms human space-time whenever the aliens show up. Sequel to *Threshhold*.

Other books you might like:
Isaac Asimov, *The Gods Themselves*, 1972
David Brin, *Startide Rising*, 1983
Octavia E. Butler, *Dawn*, 1987
Colin Greenland, *Take Back Plenty*, 1992
Frank Herbert, *Whipping Star*, 1970
Megan Lindholm, *Alien Earth*, 1992
Thomas R. McDonough, *The Missing Matter*, 1992
Larry Niven, *The Mote in God's Eye*, 1974
    Jerry Pournelle, co-author
Vernor Vinge, *Marooned in Realtime*, 1986
George Zebrowski, *Stranger Suns*, 1991

3201

KENNETH MORRIS

The Chalchiuhite Dragon
(New York: Tor, 1992)

Story type: Fantasy (Legend; Historical)
Major character(s): Nopal, Royalty, Traveller; Quauhtli, Religious
Time period(s): Indeterminate Past
Locale(s): Huitznahuac, Ancient Civilization; Central America

Summary: Peaceful Huitznahuac natives resist the bellicose overtures of their Toltec neighbors as events lead up to the birth of Quetzalcoatl as god incarnate. Ignored for years in the

Theosophical Society archives, this novel was completed in 1935, ten years after Katherine Tingley requested Morris feature a pre-Columbian subject. Includes a three-page author's preface plus five-page afterword by Douglas A. Anderson and a seven-page glossary.

Other books you might like:
M.A.R. Barker, *Flamesong*, 1985
M.A.R. Barker, *Man of Gold*, 1984
James Hilton, *Lost Horizon*, 1933
Marc Laidlaw, *Neon Lotus*, 1988
Edward Myers, *Fire and Ice*, 1992
Edward Myers, *The Mountain Made of Light*, 1992
Elizabeth Ann Scarborough, *Nothing Sacred*, 1991
Lucius Shepard, *Kalimantan*, 1992

3202

KENNETH MORRIS

The Dragon Path: Collected Tales of Kenneth Morris
(New York: Tor, 1995)

Story type: Fantasy (Collection)
Summary: Contains a 23-page biographical introduction by Douglas A. Anderson, a two-page bibliography plus individual introductions to one essay/story on the *Mabinogion* and all 39 of Morris' short works of fiction, arranged chronologically. The tales utilize historical and contemporary settings to present mythical themes from Celtic, Norse, Taoist, and Buddhist philosophies and from areas including Wales, Sweden, Greece, Rome, Spain, the Middle East, India, and China.

Other books you might like:
Arthur Conan Doyle, *The Best Supernatural Tales of Arthur Conan Doyle*, 1979
Lord Dunsany, *The Travel Tales of Mr. Joseph Jorkens*, 1931
Rudyard Kipling, *Kipling's Fantasy*, 1992
George MacDonald, *The Fantasy Stories of George MacDonald*, 1980
Clark Ashton Smith, *The Zothique*, 1970
J.R.R. Tolkien, *The Tolkien Reader*, 1966

3203

MARK MORRIS

The Horror Club
(New York: Bantam, 1991)

Story type: Horror (Occult)
Major character(s): Richard Gardener, Child; Nigel Figg, Child; Adrian "Toady" Tibbett, Child
Time period(s): 1980s (1989)
Locale(s): Starmouth, England

Summary: Tormented by older students at their school, Richard, Nigel, and Robin find escape from their pain by forming "The Horror Club," where they indulge their interest in horror film and fiction. When a new boy, "Toady," joins the club and urges them to contact real occult forces, they conjure an implacable power that takes care of their enemies but also threatens to decimate their town. This novel was originally published in England in 1989 under the title *Toady*.

Other books you might like:
Charles L. Grant, *The Pet*, 1986
K.W. Jeter, *The Night Man*, 1991
Stephen King, *Christine*, 1983
J. Michael Straczynski, *OtherSyde*, 1990

3204

MARK MORRIS

The Immaculate

(Clarkston, Georgia: White Wolf, 1996)

Story type: Horror (Ghost Story)
Major character(s): Jack Stone, Writer (horror); Gail Reeves, Teacher; Patty Bates, Businessman (garage owner)
Time period(s): 1990s
Locale(s): Beckford, England; London, England

Summary: When his father dies, Jack Stone returns to the family home in the English countryside to resolve his conflicted feelings over the man who disowned him when Jack's mother died in childbirth. Jack confronts metaphorical and literal ghosts of the past that bring him psychic healing but also force him to confront a difficult truth about his current life. This novel was first published in England in 1992.

Other books you might like:
Peter S. Beagle, *A Fine and Private Place*, 1960
Ramsey Campbell, *The Influence*, 1988
Melanie Tem, *Prodigal*, 1991
Melanie Tem, *Revenant*, 1994

3205

MARK MORRIS

Stitch

(New York: Dell/Abyss, 1992)

Story type: Horror (Possession)
Major character(s): Dan Latcher, Writer, Student; Ian Raven, Student; Annie O'Donnell, Student
Time period(s): 1990s (1992)
Locale(s): Maybury, England

Summary: Left vulnerable by an abusive childhood, horror writer and Maybury University student Dan Latcher becomes the perfect vessel for Peregrine Stitch, a wily demon who helps Dan build a cult known as "The Crack" around him and then uses it to wreak his vengeance upon humanity in a variety of perverse ways.

Other books you might like:
Ramsey Campbell, *The Hungry Moon*, 1987
Ray Garton, *Dark Channel*, 1992
Kim Newman, *Jago*, 1991

3206

ROBERT MORRISH, Editor
PETER ENFANTINO, Co-Editor

Quick Chills II

(San Jose, California: Deadline Publications, 1992)

Story type: Horror (Anthology)

Summary: Twenty-five stories representing the best offerings from small press horror fiction published in 1989 and 1990. Included are two outstanding stories based on the horrors of the Vietnam War, Mark Budz's "The War Inside" and Robert E. Cook's "Darkling"; Douglas Clegg's sensitive tale of a love so strong it resurrects the dead, "People Who Love Life"; Norman Partridge's hardboiled horror tale, "Guignoir"; five stories that take twisted sexuality as their theme: Nancy Collins' "The Two-Headed Man," Brad J. Boucher's "Cold Touch," Elizabeth Massie's "Hot Orgy of the Caged Virgins," Nancy Holder's "Woman's Little Wound," and Yvonne Navarro's "Memories"; and a novella about the horrors of urban life that David Schow expanded into his novel, *The Shaft* (1990).

Other books you might like:
Ellen Datlow, *The Year's Best Fantasy and Horror: Fourth Annual Collection*, 1991
Terri Windling, co-editor
Stephen Jones, *Best New Horror 2*, 1991
Ramsey Campbell, co-editor
Karl Edward Wagner, *The Year's Best Horror Stories XIX*, 1991
editor

3207

BRADFORD MORROW, Editor
PATRICK MCGRATH, Co-Editor

The New Gothic

(New York: Random House, 1991)

Story type: Horror (Anthology)

Summary: Billing itself as "A Collection of Contemporary Gothic Fiction," this compilation brings together 15 stories and 6 novel excerpts that "take as a starting place the concern with internal entropy—spiritual and emotional breakdown," and how this approach distorts perceptions of external reality. Included are John Edgar Wideman's "Fever," about a yellow fever epidemic that nearly decimates a town; Scott Bradfield's "Didn't She Know," about a woman sought for her life-sustaining attributes; William T. Vollman's metafictional riff on Edgar Allan Poe, "The Grave of Lost Stories"; and Patrick McGrath's tale of a man whose psychological decline manifests as his obsession with smells, "The Smell."

Other books you might like:
Chris Baldick, *The Oxford Book of Gothic Tales*, 1992
Patrick McGrath, *Blood and Water and Other Tales*, 1988

3208

JAMES MORROW

Bible Stories for Adults

(New York: Harcourt Brace, 1996)

Story type: Science Fiction (Collection; Theological)

Summary: Contains a three-page introduction plus 12 stories reprinted from periodicals and anthologies 1984-1994. Utilizing science fiction themes and frequently light or satirical in tone, four of the stories critique Biblical stories, the Flood, the Tower of Babel, Job, and the Nativity, while some of the other stories explore morality through the *Iliad* and Charles Dickens' Ebenezer Scrooge. Other themes include the mystery of consciousness, procreation, parenting, feminism, and epistemology.

Other books you might like:

Neil Gaiman, *Good Omens: The Nice and Accurate Prophecies of Agnes Nutter, Witch*, 1990
　Terry Pratchett, co-author
Parke Godwin, *The Snake Oil Wars*, 1989
Parke Godwin, *Waiting for the Galactic Bus*, 1988
Robert A. Heinlein, *Job: A Comedy of Justice*, 1984
Walter M. Miller Jr., *A Canticle for Leibowitz*, 1960
Anne Rice, *Memnoch the Devil*, 1995
Kurt Vonnegut Jr., *Cat's Cradle*, 1963

3209

JAMES MORROW

Blameless in Abaddon

(New York: Harcourt Brace, 1996)

Story type: Fantasy (Religious; Satire)
Major character(s): Martin Candle, Judge, Activist; Augustine, Historical Figure, Religious
Time period(s): 1990s; Indeterminate Past
Locale(s): Abaddon Township, Pennsylvania; The Hague, Netherlands

Summary: After towing the body of God to the arctic, promoters move the Corpus Dei to Orlando, Florida, to provide a focus for a new theme park, Celestial City USA. When a Justice of the Peace, Martin Candle, proposes trying God in the World Court for all of history's injustices, Martin begins an amazing odyssey through God's mind and human deism.

Other books you might like:

Neil Gaiman, *Good Omens: The Nice and Accurate Prophecies of Agnes Nutter, Witch*, 1990
　Terry Pratchett, co-author
Parke Godwin, *The Snake Oil Wars*, 1989
Parke Godwin, *Waiting for the Galactic Bus*, 1988
Victor Koman, *The Jehovah Contract*, 1987
Anne Rice, *Memnoch the Devil*, 1995
Kurt Vonnegut Jr., *Cat's Cradle*, 1963

3210

JAMES MORROW

City of Truth

(New York: St. Martin's Press, 1992)

Story type: Science Fiction (Genetic Manipulation; Satire)
Major character(s): Jack Sperry, Critic; Martina Coventry, Writer; Toby Sperry, Child
Time period(s): 21st century
Locale(s): Veritas City of Truth

Summary: In Veritas, City of Truth, contemplating the telling of a lie results in conditioned suffering. Jack Sperry works as an art deconstructionist, sparing Veritas from lies. When he learns that his son has contracted a fatal disease, Jack decides to join the Deceivers, people who have overcome their conditioning, to enable himself to lie to his son and hope psychoneuroimmunology will effect a cure.

Other books you might like:

Pauline Ashwell, *Unwillingly to Earth*, 1992
Michael Berlyn, *The Eternal Enemy*, 1990
Peter R. Emshwiller, *The Host*, 1991
Parke Godwin, *Waiting for the Galactic Bus*, 1988
Pat Murphy, *The City, Not Long After*, 1989
Michael Swanwick, *Stations of the Tide*, 1991
Jack Womack, *Heathern*, 1990

3211

JAMES MORROW, Editor

Nebula Awards 26

(New York: Harcourt Brace Jovanovich, 1992)

Story type: Science Fiction (Anthology)
Series: Nebula Awards

Summary: Subtitled "SFWA's Choice for the Best Science Fiction and Fantasy of the Year," this volume contains a 5-page introduction listing 1990 Nebula Award nominees, Terry Brooks' "A Tribute to Lester del Rey," in honor of the 1990 Grand Master Award winner, George Zebrowski's "In Memoriam: Donald A. Wollheim," Kathryn Cramer's 18-page article on SF in 1990, Bill Warren's 22-page article on 1990 SF films, 6 pages of appendices titled "About the Nebula Awards," "Selected Titles from the 1990 Preliminary Nebula Ballot" and "Past Nebula Award Winners," and a 2-page article on Rhysling Award winners with poems by G. Sutton Breiding and Patrick McKinnon. Fiction includes two Nebula Award winning stories, "The Hemmingway Hoax" by Joe Haldeman and "Bear Discovers Fire" by Terry Bisson plus stories by Ted Chiang, Karen Joy Fowler, Dafydd ab Hugh, Ursula K. Le Guin, Ian MacLeod, Pat Murphy and Martha Soukup.

Other books you might like:

Lou Aronica, *Full Spectrum 3*, 1991
　Amy Stout and Betsy Mitchell, co-editors
Michael Bishop, *Nebula Awards 23*, 1989
　editor
Michael Bishop, *Nebula Awards 24*, 1990
　editor

Michael Bishop, *Nebula Awards 25*, 1991
  editor
Ellen Datlow, *The Year's Best Fantasy and Horror: Fourth Annual Collection*, 1991
  Terri Windling, co-editor
Gardner Dozois, *The Year's Best Science Fiction: Eighth Annual Collection*, 1991
  editor
Harlan Ellison, *Dangerous Visions*, 1967
  editor
Frank Herbert, *Nebula Winners 15*, 1981
  editor
Damon Knight, *Nebula Award Stories 1965*, 1966
  editor
Robert Silverberg, *The Science Fiction Hall of Fame, Volume 1*, 1970
  editor
Donald A. Wollheim, *The 1990 Annual World's Best Science Fiction*, 1990
  Arthur W. Saha, co-editor
George Zebrowski, *Nebula Awards 21*, 1987
  editor
George Zebrowski, *Nebula Awards 22*, 1988
  editor

3212

JAMES MORROW, Editor

Nebula Awards 27

(New York: Harcourt Brace, 1993)

Story type: Science Fiction (Anthology)
Series: Nebula Awards

Summary: Subtitled ''SFWA's Choices for the Best Science Fiction and Fantasy of the Year,'' this volume contains a five-page introduction by the editor listing 1991 Nebula Award finalists and winners; a 15-page article by Kathryn Cramer, ''Science Fiction for What? Remarks on the Year 1991''; a 27-page article on 1991 fantastic films by Bill Warren; a 10-page essay on literary criticism with bibliography by Bruce Sterling; four memorials to Isaac Asimov; two Rhysling Award winning poems by Joe Haldeman and David Memmott; nine pages of appendices, including selected titles from the preliminary ballot and a list of previous winners; plus fiction from Terry Bisson, Alan Brennert, Karen Joy Fowler, James Patrick Kelly, John Kessel, Nancy Kress, Susan Shwartz and Michael Swanwick.

Other books you might like:
Lou Aronica, *Full Spectrum 3*, 1991
  Amy Stout, Betsy Mitchell, co-editors
Michael Bishop, *Nebula Awards 23*, 1989
  editor
Michael Bishop, *Nebula Awards 24*, 1990
  editor
Michael Bishop, *Nebula Awards 25*, 1991
  editor
Ellen Datlow, *The Year's Best Fantasy and Horror: Fourth Annual Collection*, 1991
  Terri Windling, co-editor

Gardner Dozois, *The Year's Best Science Fiction: Ninth Annual Collection*, 1992
  editor
Frank Herbert, *Nebula Winners 15*, 1981
  editor
Damon Knight, *Nebula Award Stories 1965*, 1966
  editor
George Zebrowski, *Nebula Awards 21*, 1987
  editor
George Zebrowski, *Nebula Awards 22*, 1988
  editor

3213

JAMES MORROW, Editor

Nebula Awards 28

(New York: Harcourt Brace, 1994)

Story type: Science Fiction (Anthology)
Series: Nebula Awards

Summary: Subtitled, ''SFWA's Choices for the Best Science Fiction and Fantasy of the Year,'' this volume contains a five-page introduction by the editor listing 1992 Nebula Award finalists and winners; a nine-page article by John Clute, ''Is Science Fiction Out to Lunch? Some Thoughts on the Year 1992''; a 14-page article on fantastic films of 1992 by Nick Lowe; three memorials to Fritz Leiber; one poem by David Lunde; 10 pages of appendixes, including selected titles from the preliminary ballot and a list of previous winners; plus nine stories by authors including Gregory Benford, Nancy Kress, James Morrow, Kim Stanley Robinson, Pamela Sargent and Connie Willis.

Other books you might like:
Michael Bishop, *Nebula Awards 23*, 1989
  editor
Michael Bishop, *Nebula Awards 24*, 1990
  editor
Michael Bishop, *Nebula Awards 25*, 1991
  editor
George Zebrowski, *Nebula Awards 21*, 1987
  editor
George Zebrowski, *Nebula Awards 22*, 1988
  editor

3214

JAMES MORROW

Only Begotten Daughter

(New York: Morrow, 1990)

Story type: Fantasy (Satire)
Major character(s): Julie Katz, Deity (Daughter of God); Billy Milk, Religious (Revelationist)
Time period(s): 1990s
Locale(s): Atlantic City, New Jersey; Hell

Summary: As the millennium approaches, a miracle occurs in a New Jersey sperm bank and Julie Katz, God's only begotten daughter, is immaculately conceived. As she grows to adulthood, Julie must reconcile the needs of a normal teenager with the powers of a demi-god. Eventually she is drawn into an apocalyptic confrontation with both Satan and his local representative on Earth, the Reverend Billy Milk.

Other books you might like:
Carol Emshwiller, *Carmen Dog*, 1990
Parke Godwin, *The Snake Oil Wars*, 1989
Parke Godwin, *Waiting for the Galactic Bus*, 1988
John Kessel, *Good News From Outer Space*, 1989
  Madness at the End of the Millenium

3215
JAMES MORROW

Towing Jehovah
(New York: Harcourt Brace, 1994)

Story type: Fantasy (Religious; Light Fantasy)
Major character(s): Anthony Van Horne, Sea Captain; Father Thomas, Religious; Cassie Fowler, Writer (playwright)
Time period(s): 1990s (1992)
Locale(s): *SS Carpco Valparaiso*, At Sea (supertanker); Atlantic Ocean

Summary: Archangel Raphael informs Anthony Van Horne that God has died and His body has fallen into the ocean. Using the refloated and refitted *Carpco Valparaiso* flying Vatican colors, Van Horne must tow the two-mile-long Body to the Arctic to preserve Him to earn forgiveness for his oil spill. Accompanied by a Vatican representative chasing the Vatican's hope that some Divine neural activity might remain, the ship encounters natural and transcendant obstacles.

Other books you might like:
Neil Gaiman, *Good Omens: The Nice and Accurate Prophecies of Agnes Nutter, Witch*, 1990
  Terry Pratchett, co-author
Parke Godwin, *The Snake Oil Wars*, 1989
Parke Godwin, *Waiting for the Galactic Bus*, 1988
Victor Koman, *The Jehovah Contract*, 1987
Kurt Vonnegut Jr., *Cat's Cradle*, 1963

3216
PETER MORWOOD

Rules of Engagement
(New York: Pocket, 1990)

Story type: Science Fiction (Space Opera)
Series: Star Trek
Major character(s): James T. Kirk, Spaceship Captain; Kasak sutai-Khornezh, Spaceship Captain, Alien (Klingon)
Time period(s): 23rd century
Locale(s): Dekkanar, Planet—Imaginary (Between the Federation and the Klingon Empire); *U.S.S. Enterprise*, Spaceship

Summary: Dekkanar is throwing all Federation personnel off the planet because of political unrest. Both Federation and Klingon ships head there, the *Enterprise*, *Vanguard* and *Sir Richard* to remove Federation people, and Kasak in a new type of Klington battle cruiser to take advantage of the situation. This novel fits chronologically between the time of *Star Trek: The Motion Picture* and *Star Trek II: The Wrath of Khan*.

Other books you might like:
Poul Anderson, *Flandry of Terra*, 1965
John M. Ford, *The Final Reflection*, 1984
  Star Trek 16
Keith Laumer, *Reward for Retief*, 1989
Judith Reeves-Stevens, *Prime Directive*, 1990
  Garfiedl Reeves-Stevens, co-author

3217
MIKE MOSCOE

First Dawn
(New York: Ace, 1996)

Story type: Science Fiction (Time Travel; Religious)
Series: Lost Millennium
Major character(s): Launa O'Brian, Military Personnel (lieutenant), Time Traveller; Jack Walking Bear, Military Personnel (captain), Time Traveller
Time period(s): 21st century; 40th century B.C.
Locale(s): Germany; Tall Oaks, Fictional City; River Bend, Fictional City

Summary: Acting on the theory that the designer virus annihilating most of 21st century humanity would never have been invented if society's naturally cooperative tendencies hadn't been overwhelmed by brute force, Lieutenant Launa O'Brian and Captain Jack Walking Bear travel 6000 years back in time. There, in a mathematically pre-determined place, they must convince the hunters and traders of the People of the Badger to deny the very core of their culture in order to save it, by taking up arms against impending invaders on horseback. First novel.

Other books you might like:
Eleanor Arnason, *A Woman of the Iron People*, 1991
C.J. Cherryh, *Forty Thousand in Gehenna*, 1983
Joe Haldeman, *The Forever War*, 1975
Rosemary Kirstein, *The Outskirter's Secret*, 1992
H. Beam Piper, *Lord Kalvan of Otherwhen*, 1965
Sheri S. Tepper, *Raising the Stones*, 1990

3218
BILLIE SUE MOSIMAN

Night Cruise
(New York: Diamond, 1992)

Story type: Horror (Serial Killer)
Major character(s): Molly Killany, Teenager; Mark Killany, Police Officer; Cruise Lavanic, Drifter, Serial Killer
Time period(s): 1990s (1992)
Locale(s): Mobile, Alabama; Southwest

Summary: With her father in hot pursuit, runaway Molly Killany hitches a ride with Cruise Lavanic, unaware that Lavanic is a notorious serial killer bent on indoctrinating her into his spree of savage murders before taking her life.

Other books you might like:
John Shirley, *Wetbones*, 1992

Whitley Strieber, *Billy*, 1990

3219

STEVE MUDD

The Planet Beyond

(New York: Popular Library Questar, 1990)

Story type: Science Fiction (Hard Science Fiction)
Series: Seelzar Chronicles
Major character(s): Alyssa Montoya, Activist; Bashir Arak, Aged Person, Explorer; Niala Kirowa, Administrator, Agent
Time period(s): Indeterminate Future
Locale(s): Seelzar, Planet—Imaginary

Summary: Alyssa Montoya's brother, Darrin, has been banned from the life-prolonging alien Wells and branded as a Transgressor in the city of Home, but only to provide cover for his activities as a narcotics agent investigating the trade in the drug, Purple Heaven. Meanwhile Alyssa, searching for a way to reinstate her brother, contacts Bashir Arak, a Wellborn recluse who has access to the cybernetic Matrix that controls Home. This book is a sequel to *Tangled Webs* with a ''to-be-continued'' ending.

Other books you might like:
Isaac Asimov, *The Currents of Space*, 1952
C.J. Cherryh, *Angel with the Sword*, 1985
Robert A. Heinlein, *Citizen of the Galaxy*, 1957
Vonda N. McIntyre, *The Exile Waiting*, 1975

3220

STEVE MUDD

Tangled Webs

(New York: Popular Library Questar, 1989)

Story type: Science Fiction (Political)
Major character(s): Triune Adjudicator Phillips, Judge; Overseer Selius, Government Official
Time period(s): Indeterminate Future
Locale(s): Drinan IV, Planet—Imaginary; Bekh-Nar, Planet—Imaginary

Summary: A tyrannical government is attempting to recreate an Interstellar Union from the scattered, isolated worlds of humanity. While the Union's rule is heavyhanded, individual government officials attempt to temper that reunification with justice. This is Mudd's first novel.

Other books you might like:
Isaac Asimov, *Foundation*, 1951
Isaac Asimov, *Foundation and Empire*, 1952
Isaac Asimov, *Second Foundation*, 1953
Iain M. Banks, *The Player of Games*, 1989
Ursula K. Le Guin, *The Word for World Is Forest*, 1972
Kathy Tyers, *Crystal Witness*, 1989

3221

PATRICIA MULLEN

The Stone Movers

(New York: Warner Aspect, 1995)

Story type: Fantasy (Magic Conflict; Political)
Major character(s): Eacon Gleese, Ruler (tyrant of Moer); Fallon, Wizard, Mythical Creature (shapeshifter); Telerhyde, Military Personnel (war leader of the Five Tribes)
Time period(s): Indeterminate
Locale(s): Isle of Morbihan, Fictional Country; Perime of Moer, Fictional Country

Summary: In the Perime of Moer, devotees of the New Faith believe humans must rule. The Isle of Morbihan, where Human, Dwarf, Elf, Peskie, and Ogre all follow the Old Faith in cooperative magic, remains a thorn in Gleese's side. To conquer Morbihan, Gleese must eliminate Fallon and Telerhyde and prevent the use of magic. First novel.

Other books you might like:
Don Callander, *Pyromancer*, 1992
Pamela Dean, *The Secret Country*, 1985
David Eddings, *The Diamond Throne*, 1985
Deborah Turner Harris, *Caledon of the Mists*, 1994
Paula Volsky, *Illusion*, 1992

3222

HARUKI MURAKAMI

Dance Dance Dance

(New York: Kodansha, 1994)

Story type: Science Fiction (Literary)
Major character(s): I, Writer
Time period(s): 1990s
Locale(s): Tokyo, Japan; Sapporo, Japan

Summary: A man living in modern high-tech Japan experiences his mid-life crisis with dreams of a woman who weeps for him and inspires him to dance through life. Translated by Alfred Birnbaum. Sequel to *The Wild Sheep Chase*.

Other books you might like:
Jesse Browner, *Conglomeros*, 1992
Samuel R. Delany, *The Bridge of Lost Desire*, 1987
Mark Jacobson, *Gojiro*, 1991
Mark Leyner, *My Cousin, My Gastroenterologist*, 1990
Milorad Pavic, *Landscape Painted with Tea*, 1990

3223

HARUKI MURAKAMI
ALFRED BIRNBAUM, Co-Author

Hard-Boiled Wonderland and the End of the World

(New York: Kodansha International, 1991)

Story type: Science Fiction (Literary; Fantasy)

Major character(s): I, Writer, Computer Expert; Gatekeeper, Artisan
Time period(s): Indeterminate Future
Locale(s): Tokyo, Japan

Summary: The writer is hired as a translator to protect information from being stolen and used. In his work reading unicorn skulls, some subconscious information gets past the system, putting him in danger both mentally and physically.

Other books you might like:
Piers Anthony, *And Eternity*, 1990
Allen Appel, *Till the End of Time*, 1990
Samuel R. Delany, *The Bridge of Lost Desire*, 1987
Randall Garrett, *Too Many Magicians*, 1967
Milorad Pavic, *Landscape Painted with Tea*, 1990

3224
MYLES MURCHISON

The Deathless
(New York: Ballantine, 1989)

Story type: Horror (Ancient Evil Unleashed)
Major character(s): Henriette May Eddy, Anthropologist; Walker Stevenson, Anthropologist, Lover (Henrietta's)
Time period(s): 16th century (1521); 1890s
Locale(s): Bimini, Bahamas; San Francisco, California; Vancouver, British Columbia, Canada

Summary: Searching for the secrets of Ponce de Leon, Dr. Stevenson is mysteriously killed. Harriette Eddy seeks the truth about his death and about the awful secrets he had uncovered. Her quest takes her across the world, exposing her to terrible physical and psychic dangers, culminating in an encounter with Kamiri, the death god. This is Murchison's first novel.

Other books you might like:
Norah Lofts, *The Devil's Own*, 1960

3225
M.S. MURDOCK

Hammer of Mars
(Lake Geneva, Wisconsin: TSR, 1989)

Story type: Science Fiction (Space Opera)
Series: Buck Rogers: The Martian Wars Trilogy
Major character(s): Buck Rogers, Warrior; Wilma Deering, Warrior
Time period(s): 25th century
Locale(s): Mars; Moon (Earth's)

Summary: Buck Rogers and the NEO freedom fighters have defeated the evil forces of RAM repeatedly, but now the gigantic Martian corporate state is ready to unleash the full force of its power. Fleeing, Buck attempts to find allies among the many, often mutually antagonistic, nations of the inner planets.

Other books you might like:
C.S. Friedman, *In Conquest Born*, 1987
Christopher Hinz, *Ash Ock*, 1989

Christopher Hinz, *Liege-Killer*, 1987
Philip Francis Nowlan, *Armageddon 2419 A.D.*, 1962

3226
MARY ELIZABETH MURPHY

Virgin
(New York: Berkley, 1996)

Story type: Horror (Ancient Evil Unleashed)
Major character(s): Dan Fitzpatrick, Religious (priest); Sister Carrie, Religious (nun); Chaim Kesev, Spy (Israeli Secret Police)
Time period(s): 1990s (1995)
Locale(s): New York, New York

Summary: Thanks to a forged ancient scroll, Father Dan and his secret lover, Sister Carrie, discover the whereabouts of the mummified corpse of the Virgin Mary. However, a presentiment of evil hangs over the retrieval of her corpse, and the blessing that those who would exploit her powers hope for proves to be a curse.

Other books you might like:
Ron Hansen, *Mariette in Ecstasy*, 1991
Brent Monahan, *The Book of Common Dread*, 1993
Thomas F. Monteleone, *The Blood of the Lamb*, 1992
Michael Paine, *Cities of the Dead*, 1989
Alan Rodgers, *Night*, 1991

3227
PAT MURPHY

The City, Not Long After
(New York: Doubleday Foundation, 1989)

Story type: Science Fiction (Arts)
Major character(s): Danny-boy, Artist; Jax, Artist
Time period(s): 21st century
Locale(s): San Francisco, California

Summary: Years ago a plague killed the majority of people in the United States, leaving most cities desolate. San Francisco, however, has maintained a strange sense of community as artists of various sorts have turned the entire city into a canvas for their creations. Now however, the city's peace is threatened by an impending military invasion and the artists must band together to defend their chosen lifestyle.

Other books you might like:
Samuel R. Delany, *Dhalgren*, 1975
Samuel R. Delany, *Triton*, 1976
Lisa Goldstein, *A Mask for the General*, 1987
Richard Paul Russo, *Subterranean Gallery*, 1989

3228
PAT MURPHY

Nadya: The Wolf Chronicles
(New York: Tor, 1996)

Story type: Fantasy (Legend; Historical)

Major character(s): Nadya Rybak, Werewolf, Orphan; Jacob Lowell, Indian (half-Indian); Elizabeth Metcalf, Settler
Time period(s): 1820s; 1830s
Locale(s): Wolf Crossing, Missouri; Shoalwater Bay, Oregon

Summary: Orphaned when hunters kill her werewolf parents, Nadya heads west across the unsettled land to seek a home where people will accept her strange nature. Along the way, she helps Elizabeth, a stranded settler, make the dangerous trek across the Rocky Mountains.

Other books you might like:
Nancy A. Collins, *Walking Wolf*, 1995
Chad Oliver, *The Wolf Is My Brother*, 1967
Fred Saberhagen, *Dancing Bears*, 1996
S.P. Somtow, *Moon Dance*, 1990
Whitley Strieber, *The Wolfen*, 1978

3229
PAT MURPHY

Points of Departure
(New York: Bantam, 1990)

Story type: Horror (Collection)

Summary: Twenty stories that cross the boundaries between science fiction, fantasy, and horror, many strongly influenced by the author's interest in travel and anthropology. "Dead Men on TV" is a fable about the stranglehold of memory, "Clay Devils" is a parable of third-world exploitation, and "Don't Look Back" is a subtle fantasy in which a woman begins to measure her life by the people who have replaced her in her various roles and occupations. Also included is the Nebula Award-winning "Rachel in Love."

Other books you might like:
Michael Blumlein, *The Brains of Rats*, 1989
Pat Cadigan, *Patterns*, 1989
Lucius Shepard, *The Jaguar Hunter*, 1987
Bruce Sterling, *Crystal Express*, 1989

3230
SHIRLEY ROUSSEAU MURPHY

The Catswold Portal
(New York: Roc, 1992)

Story type: Fantasy (Contemporary; Quest)
Major character(s): Sarah/Melissa McCabe, Heiress—Dispossessed; Braden West, Artist; Siddonie, Ruler (queen of Affandar), Sorceress
Time period(s): 1950s (1957); Indeterminate
Locale(s): California; Netherworld, Mythical Place

Summary: Sarah remembers nothing of her past, but goes to the palace in Affandar to learn about it. When the queen catches her, freezes her in cat form and has her taken to California where she meets Braden, Sarah gradually remembers her claim as Heir to Catswold and returns to the Netherworld to fight for her rightful inheritance.

Other books you might like:
Poul Anderson, *Operation Chaos*, 1971

Jack L. Chalker, *Vengeance of the Dancing Gods*, 1985
Gordon R. Dickson, *The Dragon and the George*, 1976
R.A. MacAvoy, *Tea with the Black Dragon*, 1983
Andre Norton, *Moon of Three Rings*, 1966
A. Orr, *The World in Amber*, 1985
Jennifer Roberson, *Shapechangers*, 1984

3231
SHIRLEY ROUSSEAU MURPHY
WELCH SUGGS, Co-Author

Medallion of the Black Hound
(New York: Harper & Row, 1989)

Story type: Fantasy (Adventure)
Major character(s): David, Teenager; Balcher, Criminal
Time period(s): 1980s; Indeterminate
Locale(s): Earth; Alternate Universe

Summary: David, heir to the Medallion of the Irish kings, is suddenly transported to another world, where the old magic still works. He must learn how to use the Medallion before the denizens of the undercity completely take over the world he has found himself in.

Other books you might like:
Lloyd Alexander, *Prydain Chronicles*,
Tom Holt, *Expecting Someone Taller*, 1988
Henry Maeve, *The Witch King*, 1988

3232
WARREN MURPHY
MARK BROWNWOOD, Co-Author

Destiny's Carnival
(New York: Fawcett, 1992)

Story type: Horror (Carnival/Circus Horror)
Major character(s): Coley O'Brien, Entertainer (mind reader); Loki Sanderson, Professor (of ancient languages); Elissa Destin, Entertainer (carnival performer)
Time period(s): 1990s
Locale(s): Allenville, Pennsylvania

Summary: Drifter Coley O'Brien little suspects that when he takes the job of mind reader at a traveling carnival, he will be forced to use his precognitive skills to save the show and the daughter of its putative owner from the real owner, a demonic personality to whom it was bartered years before. This is a first novel for Brownwood and first collaborative effort between Murphy and Brownwood.

Other books you might like:
Ray Bradbury, *Something Wicked This Way Comes*, 1962
Katherine Dunn, *Geek Love*, 1990
Charles G. Finney, *The Circus of Dr. Lao*, 1935
F. Paul Wilson, *Freak Show*, 1992
    editor

3233

DOUG MURRAY

Blood Relations

(New York: HarperPrism, 1996)

Story type: Horror (Vampire Story)
Series: World of Darkness: Vampire
Major character(s): Val, Vampire; Mariana, Vampire, Artist; Tessler, Vampire
Time period(s): 1990s (1996)
Locale(s): New York, New York

Summary: Val and Mariana meet at the Blood Club, a downtown meeting place for vampires, and fall in love. Little do they realize that their union was engineered decades before by overseers interested in their respective vampire clans, and the future wars that they will fight. This novel is set in White Wolf Books' World of Darkness gaming world, where humans and supernatural beings co-exist.

Other books you might like:
Richard Lee Byers, *Netherworld*, 1995
Keith Herber, *Prince of the City*, 1992
Brian Herbert, *Blood on the Sun*, 1996
   Marie Landis, co-author
Robert Weinberg, *Bloodwar*, 1995
Robert Weinberg, *The Unbeholden*, 1996
Robert Weinberg, *Unholy Allies*, 1995

3234

DOUG MURRAY

Call to Battle

(Clarkston, Georgia: White Wolf, 1996)

Story type: Horror (Werewolf Story)
Series: Rage
Major character(s): Jay Caldwell, Student, Werewolf; Dr. Caldwell, Doctor; Colonel Sweet, Military Personnel
Time period(s): 1990s (1996)
Locale(s): Atlanta, Georgia (Marietta Military School)

Summary: Jay Caldwell discovers that he is Garou, a member of shapeshifting species, and that the rigorous military training he is receiving with the help of his adoptive father, Dr. Caldwell, is part of ploy by the Mage to breed him and his kind for their schemes. This novel is set in the publisher's Rage fantasy gaming world.

Other books you might like:
James A. Moore, *Hell-Storm*, 1996
John Saul, *Creature*, 1989
Edo Van Belkom, *Wyrm Wolf*, 1995
Stewart Von Allmen, *Conspicuous Consumption*, 1995

3235

EDWARD MYERS

Fire and Ice

(New York: Roc, 1992)

Story type: Fantasy (Adventure; Religious)

Series: Mountain Trilogy
Major character(s): Forster Beckwith, Adventurer; Jesse O'Keefe, Anthropologist, Adventurer; Aeslu "Moon's Stead" of Vmatta, Indian (Rixtirra)
Time period(s): 1920s
Locale(s): Andes Mountains, Peru; Mountain Land, Mythical Place

Summary: As Forster's interest in the Rixtirra Indians and the Mountain of Light grows, the Rixtirra understand that he represents the outsider prophecied to appear during the Last Days and provide the means through which some will attain the Inner Realm while many others perish in the foretold disaster. Rixtirran society splinters into two opposing groups, both of which journey into the Inner Realm approaching the base of the Mountain of Light through use of a diadem containing a confusing map of the realm. Accompanying the first group, Aeslu works to save both groups despite mysterious interference.

Other books you might like:
James Hilton, *Lost Horizon*, 1933
Marc Laidlaw, *Neon Lotus*, 1988
James D. Priest, *Kirins: The Spell of No'an*, 1990
Elizabeth Ann Scarborough, *Final Refuge*, 1992
Elizabeth Ann Scarborough, *Nothing Sacred*, 1991
Lucius Shepard, *Kalimantan*, 1992

3236

EDWARD MYERS

The Mountain Made of Light

(New York: Roc, 1992)

Story type: Fantasy (Contemporary; Adventure)
Series: Mountain Trilogy
Major character(s): Jesse O'Keefe, Anthropologist, Adventurer; Aeslu "Moon's Stead" of Vmatta, Indian (Rixtirra), Linguist; Forster Beckwith, Adventurer
Time period(s): 1920s
Locale(s): Andes Mountains, Peru; Mountain Land, Mythical Place

Summary: Jesse O'Keefe, hoping to discover a fabled lost race, learns Rixtirra language and culture from Aeslu, who thinks Jesse may be the prophesied outsider. Forster Beckwith journeys to Mountain Land as a mountain climber, but he too becomes involved with the Rixtirra, who hope to pursue their own vision despite the disaster foretold by the outsiders' appearance. This is the author's first novel.

Other books you might like:
Margaret Wander Bonanno, *The Others*, 1990
James Hilton, *Lost Horizon*, 1933
Michael P. Kube-McDowell, *Emprise*, 1985
Michael P. Kube-McDowell, *Enigma*, 1986
Marc Laidlaw, *Neon Lotus*, 1988
Louis L'Amour, *Haunted Mesa*, 1987
James D. Priest, *Kirins: The Spell of No'an*, 1990
Kim Stanley Robinson, *Escape From Kathmandu*, 1989
Elizabeth Ann Scarborough, *Nothing Sacred*, 1991
Lucius Shepard, *Kalimantan*, 1992
Rex Stout, *Under the Andes*, 1985

Sheri S. Tepper, *Grass*, 1989

3237

EDWARD MYERS

The Summit

(New York: Roc, 1994)

Story type: Fantasy (Adventure)
Series: Mountain Trilogy
Major character(s): Edward Myers, Writer, Researcher; Aeslu ''Moon's Stead'' of Vmatta, Indian (Rixtirra), Linguist; Jesse O'Keefe, Anthropologist, Adventurer
Time period(s): 1970s; 1920s
Locale(s): Andes Mountains, Peru; Mountain Land, Mythical Place

Summary: Surviving civil strife, Jesse O'Keefe and Aeslu must now survive an unprecedented climb to the summit of the Mountain Made of Light where they hope to enlist the help of the Founders' descendants in saving the Rixtirra people.

Other books you might like:
James Hilton, *Lost Horizon*, 1933
Robert Reed, *The Remarkables*, 1992
Elizabeth Ann Scarborough, *Last Refuge*, 1992
Elizabeth Ann Scarborough, *Nothing Sacred*, 1991
Robert Silverberg, *Kingdoms of the Wall*, 1993
Judith Tarr, *Spear of Heaven*, 1994

3238

LINDA NAGATA

The Bohr Maker

(New York: Bantam Spectra, 1995)

Story type: Science Fiction (Genetic Manipulation; Political)
Major character(s): Nikko Jiang-Tibayan, Genetically Altered Being, Experimental Subject; Phousita, Streetperson, Genetically Altered Being; Kirsten Adair, Police Officer (chief of Commonwealth Police)
Time period(s): Indeterminate Future
Locale(s): Sunda, Malaysia; Summer House, Space Station (orbital colony)

Summary: With only a short time before his body self-destructs, Nikko steals the Bohr Maker, a nanotechnological device with great powers. When the Bohr Maker infects Phousita instead, she decides to use the device to help her people better their lives.

Other books you might like:
Elton Elliott, *Nanodreams*, 1995
    editor
Valerie J. Freireich, *Becoming Human*, 1995
Nicola Griffith, *Slow River*, 1995
Nancy Kress, *Beggars and Choosers*, 1994
Nancy Kress, *Beggars in Spain*, 1993
Tricia Sullivan, *Lethe*, 1995

3239

LINDA NAGATA

Tech-Heaven

(New York: Bantam Spectra, 1995)

Story type: Science Fiction (Genetic Manipulation; Political)
Major character(s): Katie Kishida, Widow(er), Revolutionary; Ilene Carson, Political Figure (senator); Gregory Hunt, Doctor, Scientist
Time period(s): 1990s (1995-1999); 21st century (2000-2025)
Locale(s): Los Angeles, California; Voice-2, Space Station (orbital colony)

Summary: Katie Kishida preserves her recently-killed husband cryonically, hoping that future technology will treat his injuries. When many people protest, Katie embarks on a political struggle which lasts for decides fueled by rapid advances in nanotechnology.

Other books you might like:
Gregory Benford, *Far Futures*, 1995
    editor
Starling Blake, *Chiller*, 1993
    pseudonym of Gregory Benford
Robert A. Heinlein, *I Will Fear No Evil*, 1970
Larry Niven, *Flatlander*, 1995
Clifford D. Simak, *Why Call Them Back From Heaven?*, 1967
James White, *The Dream Millennium*, 1974

3240

JONATHAN NASAW

The World on Blood

(New York: Dutton, 1996)

Story type: Horror (Vampire Story)
Major character(s): Nick Santos, Writer, Vampire; Jamey Whistler, Vampire; Elizabeth ''Betty'' Corey, Religious (minister)
Time period(s): 1990s (1996)
Locale(s): El Cerrito, California

Summary: Nick Santos's efforts to rehabilitate fellow vampires through his Vampire's Anonymous organization is being undermined by the efforts of Jamey Whistler, a member who resents Nick's authoritarian approach and who schemes to break up the self-help group by reigniting the interest of his fellow members in blood-drinking.

Other books you might like:
Gary Bowen, *Diary of a Vampire*, 1995
Todd Grimson, *Stainless*, 1996
Jeffrey N. McMahan, *Vampires Anonymous*, 1991
Christopher Moore, *Bloodsucking Fiends: A Love Story*, 1995

3241

JAMIL NASIR

The Higher Space

(New York: Bantam Spectra, 1996)

Story type: Science Fiction (Science Fantasy; Mystery)

Major character(s): Bob Wilson, Lawyer; Diana Esterbrook, Teenager, Computer Expert; Wendall Thaxton, Reincarnated Person, Indian
Time period(s): 1990s
Locale(s): Sligo Woods, Mythical Place; United States

Summary: Bob Wilson reluctantly takes on what seems a routine child custody case, but soon discovers the unusual abilities of Diana Esterbrook, a teenage genius who uses a computer to map life patterns and to move through different dimensions.

Other books you might like:
Edwin A. Abbott, *Flatland*, 1884
Kim Antieau, *The Jigsaw Woman*, 1996
Steven Gould, *Jumper*, 1992
Neal Shusterman, *Scorpion Shards*, 1995
John Varley, *Blue Champagne*, 1986

3242
JAMIL NASIR

Quasar
(New York: Bantam Spectra, 1995)

Story type: Science Fiction (Cyberpunk; Adventure)
Major character(s): Theodore "Ted" Karmade, Technician (psychological); Quasar Zant, Socialite, Wealthy; Nelda Cloud, Guardian (Quasar's)
Time period(s): Indeterminate Future
Locale(s): The City, Earth

Summary: Ted Karmade attempts to integrate Quasar Zant's personalities, while Nelda Cloud plots to kill him. However, Quasar enlists Ted's help in searching the deepest tunnels for her missing parents, if her high-tech camouflage will allow the pair to avoid the agents looking for them. First novel.

Other books you might like:
Brian W. Aldiss, *Somewhere East of Life*, 1994
Pat Cadigan, *Fools*, 1992
Pat Cadigan, *Mindplayers*, 1987
Philip K. Dick, *Do Androids Dream of Electric Sheep?*, 1968
Nancy Kress, *Brain Rose*, 1990
Cordwainer Smith, *The Rediscovery of Man*, 1993
Michael Swanwick, *Vacuum Flowers*, 1987

3243
YVONNE NAVARRO

Afterage
(New York: Bantam, 1993)

Story type: Horror (Vampire Story)
Major character(s): William Perlman, Doctor; Howard Siebold, Traitor; Anyelet, Vampire
Time period(s): Indeterminate Future
Locale(s): Chicago, Illinois

Summary: While the scientifically-inclined among the human survivors of a vampire plague that has wiped out the world try to find a potent weapon against the undead, others plan to launch a full-scale assault against the vampires and their human toadies who have imprisoned the remaining human beings and begun breeding them for future foodstock. This is the author's first novel.

Other books you might like:
Jack Butler, *Nightshade*, 1989
Kathryn Meyer Griffith, *The Last Vampire*, 1992
Richard Matheson, *I Am Legend*, 1954
Robert R. McCammon, *They Thirst*, 1981
F. Paul Wilson, *Midnight Mass*, 1990

3244
YVONNE NAVARRO

Deadrush
(New York: Bantam, 1995)

Story type: Horror (Wild Talents)
Major character(s): Jason Spiro, Teenager; Jude Ewing, Detective—Police; Karla Bryant, Advertising (account executive)
Time period(s): 1990s (1995)
Locale(s): Chicago, Illinois

Summary: Jason Spiro takes up with a snake handling fundamentalist religion in rural Georgia and discovers he has the ability to resurrect the dead by sucking death out of them. He employs his talent after moving to Chicago and creates a growing army of resurrectees with the same talent, all of whom are addicted to the "rush" of power their resurrections afford.

Other books you might like:
John Byrne, *Whipping Boy*, 1992
Robert R. McCammon, *Mystery Walk*, 1983
Thomas F. Monteleone, *The Blood of the Lamb*, 1992
Thomas F. Monteleone, *The Resurrectionist*, 1995
F. Paul Wilson, *The Touch*, 1987

3245
YVONNE NAVARRO

Species
(New York: Bantam, 1995)

Story type: Science Fiction (Genetic Manipulation)
Major character(s): Sil, Experimental Subject, Genetically Altered Being; Xavier Fitch, Scientist, Leader
Time period(s): 1990s
Locale(s): Mojave Desert, California; Los Angeles, California

Summary: Extraterrestrial signals lead to secret research which incorporates alien DNA into human ova. When Sil avoids destruction and escapes, she makes her way to Los Angeles, her insticts driving her to reproduce, if a hastily assembled team cannot stop her. Novelizes the film.

Other books you might like:
Neal Barrett Jr., *Judge Dredd*, 1995
David Bischoff, *Hunter's Planet*, 1994
Terry Bisson, *Virtuosity*, 1995
Octavia E. Butler, *Dawn*, 1987
Michael Crichton, *Jurassic Park*, 1990
Alan Dean Foster, *Aliens*, 1986

3246

GRANT NAYLOR (Pseudonym of Rob Grant and Doug Naylor)

Better than Life

(New York: Roc, 1993)

Story type: Science Fiction (Humor)
Series: Red Dwarf
Major character(s): David Lister, Spaceman; Kryten, Robot (cleaning); Cat, Animal (intelligent cat)
Time period(s): Indeterminate Future (about 3,000,000 A.D.)
Locale(s): *Red Dwarf*, Spaceship; Outer Space

Summary: While Cat, Lister, Kryten and the artifical intelligence, Arnold J. Rimmer, explore the ultimate virtual reality, "Better Than Life," the cheap little Toaster attempts to repair the stupified Holly, *Red Dwarf*'s resident artificial intelligence and captain.

Other books you might like:
Douglas Adams, *The Hitchhiker's Guide to the Galaxy*, 1980
Douglas Adams, *The Restaurant at the End of the Universe*, 1982
Ed Blome, *Title Deleted for Security Reasons*, 1993
John DeChancie, *Starrigger*, 1983
Ken Rolston, *Extreme Paranoia: Nobody Knows the Trouble I've Shot*, 1991
Neal Stephenson, *Snow Crash*, 1992

3247

GRANT NAYLOR (Pseudonym of Rob Grant and Doug Naylor)

Red Dwarf: Infinity Welcomes Careful Drivers

(New York: Roc, 1992)

Story type: Science Fiction (Humor)
Series: Red Dwarf
Major character(s): Arnold J. Rimmer, Spaceman, Disembodied Personality; David Lister, Spaceman; Holly, Computer (ship's)
Time period(s): Indeterminate Future
Locale(s): Mimas, Saturn (moon of Saturn); *Red Dwarf*, Spaceship

Summary: When Lister arrives unconscious on Mimas with no identification and no way home, volunteering for the Space Corps seems his only route home. Unfortunately his ship, the *Red Dwarf*, has an accident, leaving him alone with only a holographic shipmate and the intelligent descendant of the ship's cat as company when Holly awakens him three million years later. A British television tie-in.

Other books you might like:
Douglas Adams, *The Hitchhiker's Guide to the Galaxy*, 1980
Douglas Adams, *Life, the Universe, and Everything*, 1982
Douglas Adams, *The Restaurant at the End of the Universe*, 1981
Douglas Adams, *So Long, and Thanks for All the Fish*, 1985
John DeChancie, *Starrigger*, 1983
Alan Dean Foster, *Quozl*, 1989

Laura J. Mixon, *Glass Houses*, 1992

3248

PHYLLIS REYNOLDS NAYLOR

Bernie and the Bessledorf Ghost

(New York: Atheneum, 1990)

Story type: Fantasy (Mystery; Young Adult)
Series: Bessledorf Mystery
Major character(s): Bernie Magruder, Child, Student; Jonathon Bessledorf, Spirit (ghost)
Time period(s): 1980s
Locale(s): United States (Bessledorf Hotel)

Summary: Bernie and his friends and family must solve the mystery of why Jonathon Bessledorf is suddenly haunting the hotel, after lying quietly in his grave for a century.

Other books you might like:
Pam Conrad, *Stonewords: A Ghost Story*, 1990
Penelope Lively, *The Ghost of Thomas Kempe*, 1973
Patricia A. McKillip, *The House on Parchment Street*, 1973
Richard Peck, *The Ghost Belonged to Me*, 1975
Elizabeth Marie Pope, *The Sherwood Ring*, 1958

3249

PHYLLIS REYNOLDS NAYLOR

The Witch Returns

(New York: Delacorte, 1992)

Story type: Fantasy (Young Adult; Magic Conflict)
Series: Witch
Major character(s): Lynn Morley, Child, Student; Marjorie "Mouse" Beasley, Friend; Greta Gullone, Witch
Time period(s): 1990s
Locale(s): United States

Summary: When a new neighbor moves into the house built on the ashes left from Mrs. Tuggle's house, Lynn suspects that Mrs. Tuggle has returned in the form of Mrs. Gullone. As Mrs. Gullone attempts to acquire Lynn's copy of the magic formulary, *Spells and Potions*, Lynn and Mouse work to alert others and foil her attempt to ensorcel Lynn.

Other books you might like:
Michael Bedard, *A Darker Magic*, 1987
Roald Dahl, *The Witches*, 1983
Diana Wynne Jones, *Witch's Business*, 1974
Margaret Mahy, *The Changeover*, 1974
John Masefield, *The Midnight Folk*, 1927

3250

PHYLLIS REYNOLDS NAYLOR

The Witch's Eye

(New York: Delacorte, 1990)

Story type: Fantasy (Magic Conflict; Young Adult)
Series: Witch

Major character(s): Lynn Morley, Child, Student; Marjorie "Mouse" Beasley, Friend; Mrs. Tuggle, Witch, Spirit (recently deceased)
Time period(s): 1980s
Summary: Despite her recent death, Mrs. Tuggle continues to haunt the two girls who have been her adversaries through the medium of her glass eye. Once again she attempts to take possession of one of the girls, but this time it is Lynn herself.

Other books you might like:
L.M. Boston, *An Enemy at Green Knowe*, 1964
Roald Dahl, *The Witches*, 1983
Diana Wynne Jones, *Witch's Business*, 1974
Margaret Mahy, *The Changeover*, 1974
John Masefield, *The Midnight Folk*, 1927

3251

REBECCA NEASON

Guises of the Mind
(New York: Pocket, 1993)

Story type: Science Fiction (Space Opera; Psychic Powers)
Series: Star Trek: The Next Generation
Major character(s): Jean-Luc Picard, Spaceship Captain, Military Personnel; Deanna Troi, Empath, Psychologist; Mother Veronica, Religious (abbess), Psychic
Time period(s): 24th century
Locale(s): *U.S.S. Enterprise*, Spaceship; Capulon IV, Planet—Imaginary

Summary: Captain Picard and Deanna Troi beam down to Capulon IV expecting to attend the coronation of Joakal I'lium as its ruler and to sign a treaty admitting the planet into the Federation. Mother Veronica, one of the nuns invited by Joakal to establish orphanages and care for children which the old laws would have killed in infancy, accompanies them. Instead, they find that Joakal's twin brother, long thought dead, has usurped the throne and only Mother Veronica's repressed telepathic talent can identify the rightful king.

Other books you might like:
Margaret Wander Bonanno, *Dwellers in the Crucible*, 1985
Marion Zimmer Bradley, *The Heirs of Hammerfell*, 1989
C.J. Cherryh, *Serpent's Reach*, 1980
Michael Jan Friedman, *Reunion*, 1991
Andrew M. Greeley, *The Final Planet*, 1987
Katherine Kurtz, *Saint Camber*, 1978
Walter M. Miller Jr., *A Canticle for Leibowitz*, 1959
A.E. van Vogt, *Slan*, 1946
Howard Weinstein, *The Covenant of the Crown*, 1981

3252

ANDREW NEIDERMAN

After Life
(New York: Berkley, 1993)

Story type: Horror (Black Magic)
Major character(s): Lee Overstreet, Teacher (physical education); Jessie Overstreet, Writer; Bob Baker, Teacher (English)

Time period(s): 1990s (1993)
Locale(s): Gardner Town, New York

Summary: Something is rotten in upstate New York, or so Lee and Jessie Overstreet discover, when they move to Gardner Town and find a small community where the dead come back to life, the local high school students are encouraged to be ruthlessly violent in athletics, and the local benefactor, a physician, seems to have an influence on both.

Other books you might like:
David Darke, *Blind Hunger*, 1993
Ira Levin, *The Stepford Wives*, 1974
John Saul, *Creature*, 1989

3253

ANDREW NEIDERMAN

Duplicates
(New York: Berkley, 1994)

Story type: Horror (Mystery)
Major character(s): Marion Boxletter, Housewife; Bob Boxletter, Computer Expert (programmer); Nelson Congemi, Doctor
Time period(s): 1990s (1994)
Locale(s): Sandburg, New York

Summary: When she encounters a man who is the spitting image of the brother who disappeared with her son, Joey, over a year before, Marion Boxletter refuses to believe his protestations that he is someone else entirely different. Her investigations eventually uncover a government-sponsored program to give new identities and memories to criminals that has run amuck in the hands of its megalomaniacal overseers.

Other books you might like:
David Ambrose, *The Man Who Turned into Himself*, 1994
David Ely, *Seconds*, 1963
Timothy Findley, *Headhunter*, 1993

3254

ANDREW NEIDERMAN

The Immortals
(New York: Pocket/Star, 1991)

Story type: Horror (Science Fiction)
Major character(s): Drake Edwards, Businessman (salesman); Cynthia Edwards, Housewife; Mr. Leon, Businessman (head of Youth Hold)
Time period(s): 1990s
Locale(s): Sandburg, New York

Summary: Drake Edwards jumps at the chance to become salesman for Youth Hold, a company that specializes in youth-preserving cosmetics. Unknown to Drake and his wife Cynthia, there is a direct connection between Youth Hold's products and the absence of spouses among the company's employees.

Other books you might like:
Ira Levin, *The Stepford Wives*, 1972
John Saul, *Creature*, 1989

3255

ANDREW NEIDERMAN

The Need

(New York: Putnam, 1992)

Story type: Horror (Vampire Story)
Major character(s): Clea/Richard Cave, Actress; Steve Mayer, Detective—Police; Alison/Nicholas, Actress
Time period(s): 1990s
Locale(s): Los Angeles, California

Summary: Clea Cave confesses to the police that she is a member of the Androgyne, a species that can change its sex at will and whose male personae feed by draining the life force from lovers and other victims. In so doing, she exposes herself to reprisals not only from other Androgynes, but from the Evil Eye, the name given to a devilish tempter whose sole purpose is to lure the Androgyne to self-destruction.

Other books you might like:
Robert Louis Stevenson, *The Strange Case of Dr. Jekyll and Mr. Hyde*, 1888
Whitley Strieber, *The Hunger*, 1981

3256

ANDREW NEIDERMAN

Perfect Little Angels

(New York: Berkley, 1989)

Story type: Horror (Satire)
Major character(s): Justine Freeman, Teenager (Rebellious fifteen-year-old); Felix Lawrence, Doctor (Psychologist/ Nutritionist)
Time period(s): 1980s
Locale(s): Elesian Fields (Housing tract)

Summary: When the Freeman family moves into Elesian Fields, a middle class planned community, they are surprised by the extreme conformity of their neighbors, especially the teenagers, whose behavior is exemplary in every way. As the Freeman's daughter, Justine, rebels against her peers' docility, she becomes increasingly threatened by other teenagers, by the larger community—led by its mysterious leader, Dr. Lawrence—and finally by her own parents.

Other books you might like:
Jack Finney, *The Body Snatchers*, 1955
Ira Levin, *The Stepford Wives*, 1972

3257

ANDREW NEIDERMAN

Sister, Sister

(New York: Berkley, 1992)

Story type: Horror (Wild Talents)
Major character(s): Neil Richards, Teacher; Tania Webster, Scientist
Time period(s): 1990s
Locale(s): Centerville, New York (Mandicott Clinic)

Summary: When he is hired by a secretive research hospital for his skills in special education, Neil Richards is told that Siamese twins Alpha and Beta are being studied as examples of how human beings adapt to overcrowding. But Neil soon discovers that the births of the children have been engineered for a special reason, and that the pair have developed telepathic powers strong enough to kill those who fall into their disfavor.

Other books you might like:
Margaret Bingley, *Seeds of Evil*, 1988
Tom Piccirilli, *Dark Father*, 1990
Thomas Tryon, *The Other*, 1971
T. Lucien Wright, *Blood Brothers*, 1992

3258

KATHERINE NEVILLE

The Eight

(New York: Ballantine, 1989)

Story type: Fantasy (Historical)
Major character(s): Mireille de Remy, Noblewoman (narrator, 1770s); Catherine Velis, Computer Expert (narrator, 1970s)
Time period(s): 1770s; 1970s
Locale(s): Paris, France; New York, New York; Algiers, Algeria

Summary: Montglane Service, a mythical chess set, holds mystical powers. To crack its code is to unleash its enormous potential.

Other books you might like:
Thomas Bently, *Celestial Chess*, 1988
Ian Watson, *Queenmagic, Kingmagic*, 1990

3259

KIM NEWMAN

Anno Dracula

(New York: Carroll & Graf, 1993)

Story type: Horror (Vampire Story)
Major character(s): Dracula, Vampire; John Seward, Doctor (psychiatrist); Genevieve Dieudonee, Vampire, Health Care Professional
Time period(s): 1880s (1888)
Locale(s): England, Alternate Earth

Summary: In an alternate world, Dracula has outlived his renown as the villain of Bram Stoker's novel, married the widowed Queen Victoria and become a fiendish Prince Consort who allows vampirism to run rampant in Victorian London. Meanwhile, his nemesis, Dr. John Seward, becomes Jack the Ripper, a fearless vampire killer determined to expunge the vampire scourge from the world.

Other books you might like:
Brian W. Aldiss, *Dracula Unbound*, 1990
Anne Rice, *The Vampire Lestat*, 1985
Lucius Shepard, *The Golden*, 1993
Brian Stableford, *The Empire of Fear*, 1988
Bram Stoker, *Dracula*, 1895

3260

KIM NEWMAN

Bad Dreams

(New York: Carroll & Graf, 1991)

Story type: Horror (Vampire Story)

Major character(s): Anne Nielson, Journalist; Cameron Nielson, Writer (playwright); Mr. Skinner, Vampire (''The Monster'')

Time period(s): 1990s; 1950s

Locale(s): London, England

Summary: The death of her rebellious junkie sister Judi sends Anne Nielson to London to investigate. As she probes deeper into the S&M subculture of which Judi was a part, she comes closer and closer to an encounter with Mr. Skinner, an ageless vampire who feeds on human flesh and dreams and who, for personal reasons, has covertly been subjecting the Nielsons to one misery after another for decades. This novel was first published in Britain in 1990.

Other books you might like:
Anne Rice, *The Queen of the Damned*, 1988
Dan Simmons, *Carrion Comfort*, 1989
Brian Stableford, *The Empire of Fear*, 1988

3261

KIM NEWMAN

The Bloody Red Baron

(New York: Carroll & Graf, 1995)

Story type: Horror (Vampire Story)

Major character(s): Manfred von Richtofen, Military Personnel, Pilot; Edwin Winthrop, Military Personnel; Edgar Allan Poe, Writer, Historical Figure

Time period(s): 1910s (1918)

Locale(s): London, England; France, Alternate Earth

Summary: In a world where Count Dracula has eluded death and infected half of the global population with vampirisim, World War I is fought by mortals and vampires who convert themselves to airplane-sized bats to carry out dogfights. This imaginative and inventive novel ponders the social and military situation of the war that might have been had celebrities and renowned historical figures been unkillable vampires.

Other books you might like:
Les Daniels, *No Blood Spilled*, 1991
Anne Rice, *The Vampire Lestat*, 1985
Michael Romkey, *I, Vampire*, 1990
Fred Saberhagen, *An Old Friend of the Family*, 1979
Brian Stableford, *The Empire of Fear*, 1988

3262

KIM NEWMAN

The Night Mayor

(New York: Carroll and Graf, 1990)

Story type: Science Fiction (Techno-Thriller; Arts)

Major character(s): Truro Daine, Fugitive; Susan Bishopric, Writer (Dreamer)

Time period(s): 21st century

Locale(s): San Francisco, California

Summary: Using the world's major computer to construct a 1940s and 1950s film noir dream world, Truro Daine has effectively escaped his imprisonment. Unwilling to lose Daine, authorities conscript Susan Bishopric to search him out.

Other books you might like:
Pat Cadigan, *Mindplayers*, 1987
Pat Cadigan, *Synners*, 1991
William Gibson, *Count Zero*, 1986
William Gibson, *Mona Lisa Overdrive*, 1988
William Gibson, *Neuromancer*, 1984
Dan Simmons, *The Fall of Hyperion*, 1990
Dan Simmons, *Hyperion*, 1989

3263

KIM NEWMAN

The Quorum

(New York: Carroll & Graf, 1994)

Story type: Horror (Black Magic)

Major character(s): Neil Martin, Worker (in a comic book store); Derek Leech, Businessman; Sally Rhodes, Detective—Private

Time period(s): 1990s (1993); 1970s (1978)

Locale(s): London, England

Summary: In 1978, three of Neil Martin's school chums make a pact with the devil incarnate, Derek Leech, to subject Neil to a life of unremitting misery in exchange for their own personal gains. When Neil finds out, though, the tide turns in his favor, and his friends receive their just desserts.

Other books you might like:
William Hjortsberg, *Falling Angel*, 1978
Stephen King, *Needful Things*, 1992
Robert Masello, *Private Demons*, 1992

3264

NICHELLE NICHOLS
MARGARET WANDER BONANNO, Co-Author

Saturn's Child

(New York: Ace/Putnam, 1995)

Story type: Science Fiction (First Contact; Psychic Powers)

Major character(s): Saturna, Telepath, Genetically Altered Being; Krecis, Alien (Fazisian), Spaceship Captain; Nyota Dominque, Scientist, Spaceship Captain

Time period(s): 22nd century (2187)

Locale(s): *Dragon's Egg*, Spaceship; Titan, Saturn (a moon of Saturn)

Summary: Exploring space, searching for resources and other intelligent species, the telepathic Fazisians realize the Solar System contains intelligent life when Earth sends an expedition to Titan (which the Fazisians colonized 50 years earlier). Nyota becomes involved with one of the Fazisians, a relationship forbidden by both Earth and Fazis. Krecis arranges for them to have a child without anyone's knowledge, fostering the baby to a Fazisian couple. Nichols's first novel and first of a proposed series.

Other books you might like:
Margaret Wander Bonanno, *The Others*, 1990
Octavia E. Butler, *Dawn*, 1987
L. Warren Douglas, *Stepwater*, 1995
Anne McCaffrey, *The Rowan*, 1990
Alis A. Rasmussen, *A Passage of Stars*, 1990

3265

JASON NICKLES

Immortal

(New York: Zebra, 1996)

Story type: Horror (Vampire Story)
Major character(s): Emily Kane, Doctor; Ray Timmerson, Writer; Martin Crouper, Vampire
Time period(s): 1990s (1996)
Locale(s): Horn Pond, Massachusetts; New York, New York

Summary: A coffin uncovered during an archaeological dig in Massachusetts is shipped back to a New York museum. Unbeknownst to the scientists who uncovered it, the coffin contains the vampire Martin Crouper, formerly a member of a travelling carnival sideshow, who was interred following a rash of deaths he caused years before and who now threatens to perpetuate his bloody legacy in New York City.

Other books you might like:
Don Davis, *Bring on the Night*, 1993
  Jay Davis, co-author
Ron Dee, *Dusk*, 1993
Ronald Kelly, *Blood Kin*, 1996
Stephen King, *Salem's Lot*, 1975
Robert R. McCammon, *They Thirst*, 1981
Patrick Whalen, *Night Thirst*, 1993

3266

DAVID F. NIGHBERT

The Clouds of Magellan

(New York: St. Martins Press, 1991)

Story type: Science Fiction (Space Opera; First Contact)
Major character(s): Anton Stryker, Adventurer, Clone; Albert Samuels, Inventor (time machine), Clone; Abe, Alien, Telepath
Time period(s): 31st century
Locale(s): *Nefertiti*, Spaceship; Greater Magellanic Cloud, Outer Space

Summary: Hoping to learn more of the giant alien artifact and its builders, Anton Stryker and his comrades venture to The Wheel intending to pick up Albert Samuels and travel to the aliens' space. As they approach The Wheel, their nemesis, Isaac DeKoven, with battleship and destroyers, forces Stryker's ship away and uses The Wheel himself, projecting his party toward the planned alien meeting days ahead of Stryker's group. This is a sequel to *Timelapse*.

Other books you might like:
Greg Bear, *Eon*, 1985
Alexander Jablokov, *Carve the Sky*, 1991
Larry Niven, *Man-Kzin Wars IV*, 1991
  editor
Larry Niven, *Protector*, 1973
Larry Niven, *Ringworld*, 1970
Frederik Pohl, *Gateway*, 1977
Frederik Pohl, *The Gateway Trip: Tales and Vignettes of the Heechee*, 1990
E.E. "Doc" Smith, *Triplanetary*, 1948
John Varley, *Titan*, 1979

3267

DOUGLAS NILES

A Breach in the Watershed

(New York: Ace, 1995)

Story type: Fantasy (Quest; Magic Conflict)
Series: Watershed Trilogy
Major character(s): Rudgar "Rudy" Appenfell, Hero, Mountaineer (Iceman of Halverica); Raine of the Three Waters, Noblewoman; Anjell Appenfell, Child, Adventurer
Time period(s): Indeterminate
Locale(s): The Watershed, Mythical Place; Dalethica, Fictional Country (land of life)

Summary: As a poisonous essence from the land of death and minions of the dark god enter the land of the living through a fractured barrier, the fate of everyone hinges on the actions of a small band of heroes working on the surface and underground to repel the offensive and deadly invasion.

Other books you might like:
L. Dean James, *Summerland*, 1994
Robert Jordan, *The Eye of the World*, 1990
Patricia A. McKillip, *The Book of Atrix Wolfe*, 1995
Margaret Weis, *Dragon Wing*, 1990
  Tracy Hickman, co-author
Margaret Weis, *Into the Labyrinth*, 1993
  Tracy Hickman, co-author

3268

DOUGLAS NILES

The Coral Kingdom

(Lake Geneva, Wisconsin: TSR, 1992)

Story type: Fantasy (Quest)
Series: Forgotten Realms: The Druidhome Trilogy
Major character(s): Robyn Kendrick, Royalty (high queen of the Ffolk), Adventurer
Time period(s): Indeterminate
Locale(s): Moonshae Isles, Mythical Place; *Princess of Moonshae*, At Sea; Evermeet, Mythical Place

Summary: Robyn journeys to the Coral Kingdom to rescue her husband held prisoner there.

Other books you might like:
Richard Awlinson, *Shadowdale*, 1989
Troy Denning, *The Parched Sea*, 1991

Ed Greenwood, *Spellfire*, 1988
Kate Novak, *Azure Bonds*, 1988
  Jeff Grubb, co-author
Margaret Weis, *Dragons of Autumn Twilight*, 1984
  Tracy Hickman, co-author

3269

DOUGLAS NILES

Darkenheight

(New York: Ace, 1996)

Story type: Fantasy (Magic Conflict; Political)
Series: Watershed Trilogy
Major character(s): Rudgar "Rudy" Appenfell, Hero, Mountaineer (Iceman); Raine of the Three Waters, Noblewoman, Writer; Nicodareus, Monster, Leader
Time period(s): Indeterminate
Locale(s): The Watershed, Mythical Place; Dalethica, Fictional Country; Faerine, Fictional Country

Summary: After Nicodareus dies while failing to prepare all of the Watershed for the coming of the Nameless One, the Nameless One resurrects Nicodareus and charges him with finding and killing Rudy, the major stumbling block to the Nameless One's domination. The only hope of stopping the Nameless One's attack on all the realms of the Watershed remains with Rudy and his mixed company of heroes and warriors, if they can survive and stop the flow of Darkblood which will destroy all.

Other books you might like:
Terry Goodkind, *Stone of Tears*, 1995
L. Dean James, *Summerland*, 1994
Robert Jordan, *The Eye of the World*, 1990
Patricia Mullen, *The Stone Movers*, 1995
J.R.R. Tolkien, *The Fellowship of the Ring*, 1954

3270

DOUGLAS NILES

Feathered Dragon

(Lake Geneva, Wisconsin: TSR, 1991)

Story type: Fantasy (Historical)
Series: Forgotten Realms: The Maztica Trilogy
Major character(s): Cordell, Warrior, Leader; Gultec, Warrior, Indian
Time period(s): Indeterminate Past
Locale(s): Maztica, Fictional Country (Central American)

Summary: A new invasion force in Maztica threatens society's existence. The warriors must determine who is the enemy and organize a defense while hoping the prophecy of the Feathered Dragon's return will prove their salvation. This novel retells a chapter of Central American history. A game tie-in novel.

Other books you might like:
David Cook, *Horselords*, 1990
Troy Denning, *Dragonwall*, 1990
James Lowder, *Crusade*, 1991

Kate Novak, *Azure Bonds*, 1988
  Jeff Grubb, co-author
R.A. Salvatore, *Canticle*, 1991
R.A. Salvatore, *Homeland*, 1990

3271

DOUGLAS NILES

The Kinslayer Wars

(Lake Geneva, Wisconsin: TSR, 1991)

Story type: Fantasy (Adventure)
Series: Dragonlance: The Elven Nations Trilogy
Major character(s): Kith-Kanan, Mythical Creature (elf), Warrior; Sithas, Royalty, Mythical Creature (elf)
Time period(s): Indeterminate (2215 Pre-Cataclysm)
Locale(s): South Central Ansalon, Fictional Country

Summary: Two Elven brothers participate in a war between the human empire of Ergoth and the Silvanesh Elves. A game tie-in novel.

Other books you might like:
C.J. Cherryh, *Gate of Ivrel*, 1976
Michael Moorcock, *Elric of Melnibone*, 1976
Brian Stableford, *Stormwarriors*, 1991
  as Brian Craig
Paul B. Thompson, *Firstborn*, 1991
  Tonya R. Carter, co-author
Paul B. Thompson, *The Qualinesti*, 1991
  Tonya R. Carter, co-author
J.R.R. Tolkien, *The Fellowship of the Ring*, 1954

3272

ADAM NISWANDER

The Charm

(Phoenix, Arizona: Integra Publishing, 1993)

Story type: Horror (Ancient Evil Unleashed)
Major character(s): Jack Foreman, Anthropologist; Greg Johnson, Police Officer; Tom Bear, Indian, Shaman
Time period(s): 1990s (1993)
Locale(s): Phoenix, Arizona

Summary: During field research, anthropologist Jack Foreman accidentally unleashes an ancient Indian demon into the world, prompting individuals from each of the southwestern tribes to band together in an effort to return the being to the supernatural realm.

Other books you might like:
Morgan Fields, *Shaman Woods*, 1989
G. Wayne Miller, *Thunder Rise*, 1989
Eugene E. Pfaff Jr., *Uwharrie*, 1993
  Michael Causey, co-author
Kathryn Ptacek, *Ghost Dance*, 1990
Patrick Whalen, *Deathwalker*, 1992

3273

ADAM NISWANDER

The Serpent Slayers
(Phoenix, Arizona: Integra Press, 1994)

Story type: Horror (Ancient Evil Unleashed)
Series: Shaman Cycle
Major character(s): Jeremy Myers, Scientist (herpetologist); Rachel Knight, Scientist (assistant to Jeremy Myers); Danny Webb, Indian, Shaman
Time period(s): 1990s (1991)
Locale(s): Phoenix, Arizona

Summary: An earthquake in the American Southwest releases The Scaled One, an ancient deity imprisoned in ice for centuries who commands an army of voracious snakes to do its bidding. In this indirect sequel to the author's first novel, *The Charm* (1993), southwestern tribes of Native Americans convening for their regular Gathering marshal their forces to defeat a scourge that threatens to overrun the world.

Other books you might like:
Morgan Fields, *Shaman Woods*, 1989
G. Wayne Miller, *Thunder Rise*, 1989
Eugene E. Pfaff Jr., *Uwharrie*, 1993
    Michael Causey, co-author
Kathryn Ptacek, *Ghost Dance*, 1990
Patrick Whalen, *Deathwalker*, 1992

3274

LARRY NIVEN
STEVEN BARNES, Co-Author

Achilles' Choice
(New York: Tor, 1991)

Story type: Science Fiction (Adventure; Political)
Major character(s): Jillian Shomer, Sports Figure
Time period(s): 21st century
Locale(s): Earth

Summary: While competing in the potentially deadly event testing physical and mental strengths of potential government rulers, Jillian Shomer decides to unlock the mysteries behind the workings of the government.

Other books you might like:
Iain M. Banks, *The Player of Games*, 1988
Jeffrey A. Carver, *From a Changeling Star*, 1989
Philip K. Dick, *The Game-Players of Titan*, 1963
A.E. van Vogt, *The Weapon Shops of Isher*, 1951
A.E. van Vogt, *The Weapon Makers*, 1946

3275

LARRY NIVEN
STEVEN BARNES, Co-Author

The Barsoom Project
(New York: Ace Books, 1989)

Story type: Science Fiction (Adventure)
Series: Dream Park

Major character(s): Max Sands, Sports Figure; Millicent Summers, Businesswoman
Time period(s): Indeterminate Future
Locale(s): Dream Park, Earth (An adventure park for role players)

Summary: Once again a determined ban of adventure gamers enter one of Dream Park's interactive scenarios and, once again, things go wrong and people begin to die.

Other books you might like:
Iain M. Banks, *The Player of Games*, 1988
Philip K. Dick, *The Game-Players of Titan*, 1963
Robert Scheckley, *The Tenth Victim*, 1966
Ian Watson, *Queenmagic, Kingmagic*, 1988

3276

LARRY NIVEN
JERRY POURNELLE, Co-Author
STEVEN BARNES, Co-Author

Beowulf's Children
(New York: Tor, 1995)

Story type: Science Fiction (Space Colony; First Contact)
Series: Heorot
Major character(s): Aaron Tragen, Leader, Orphan; Cadmann Weyland, Explorer, Security Officer; Old Grendel, Alien
Time period(s): 22nd century
Locale(s): Avalon, Planet—Imaginary

Summary: As the children of the colonists explore the mainland, much to their elders' dismay, Avalon's seasons and the original ecology, devastated by the grendels, begins to come back. On the mainland, some of the grendels develop intelligence and one in particular tries to understand the colonists. When the dangers of the seasons become apparent, Aaron Tragen's desperate attempt to prevent retreat from the mainland may provide a situation that allows contact between humans and grendels.

Other books you might like:
Octavia E. Butler, *Survivor*, 1978
Joe Haldeman, *Worlds Enough and Time*, 1992
Anne McCaffrey, *Freedom's Landing*, 1995
Rebecca Ore, *Becoming Alien*, 1988
Frederik Pohl, *The Voices of Heaven*, 1994
Dennis Schmidt, *Way-Farer*, 1978
Sheri S. Tepper, *Grass*, 1989
James White, *The Silent Stars Go By*, 1991

3277

LARRY NIVEN
STEVEN BARNES, Co-Author

The California Voodoo Game
(New York: Ballantine Del Rey, 1992)

Story type: Science Fiction (Mystery; Cyberpunk)
Series: Dream Park
Major character(s): Alex Griffin, Security Officer; Acacia "Panthesilea" Garcia, Entertainer (fantasy role-playing

gamer); Nigel Bishop, Entertainer (fantasy role-playing gamer)

Time period(s): 2050s (2059)

Locale(s): Mojave Desert, California

Summary: MIMIC, the ruins of a 1990s arcology and future base of operations for the Barsoom Project, hosts the biggest fantasy role-playing game ever. Five teams of six players each will compete in the California Voodoo Game, pitting their characters against virtual reality simulations and live character actors. Suspecting one of the players has murdered for information on the security systems, Alex Griffin joins the Game as a non-player character to find out why.

Other books you might like:

Steven Barnes, *Gorgon Child*, 1989
Steven Barnes, *Streetlethal*, 1983
Emma Bull, *Bone Dance*, 1991
Orson Scott Card, *Ender's Game*, 1985
Michael Crichton, *Jurassic Park*, 1991
Michael Crichton, *Westworld*, 1974
Philip K. Dick, *Do Androids Dream of Electric Sheep?*, 1968
William Gibson, *Neuromancer*, 1984
Lynn S. Hightower, *Alien Blues*, 1992

3278

LARRY NIVEN

Crashlander

(New York: Ballantine Del Rey, 1994)

Story type: Science Fiction (Collection; Hard Science Fiction)

Series: Known Space

Major character(s): Beowulf Shaffer, Spaceship Captain, Space Explorer

Time period(s): 27th century

Locale(s): Outer Space; Spaceship

Summary: This volume contains all the stories that chronicle Beowulf Shaffer's adventures while exploring such exotic astronomical features as a neutron star and the galactic core. It includes two original stories, ''Procrustes,'' and an interwoven story, ''Ghost,'' which provides a unifying framework for five stories published 1966-1975 in periodicals and anthologies.

Other books you might like:

Pat Cadigan, *Patterns*, 1990
Michael Flynn, *The Nanotech Chronicles*, 1991
Robert A. Heinlein, *The Past through Tomorrow*, 1967
Walter M. Miller Jr., *The Science Fiction Stories of Walter M. Miller, Jr.*, 1984
Cordwainer Smith, *The Rediscovery of Man*, 1993
John Varley, *Blue Champagne*, 1986
John Varley, *The Persistence of Vision*, 1978

3279

LARRY NIVEN
JERRY POURNELLE, Co-Author
MICHAEL FLYNN, Co-Author

Fallen Angels

(New York: Baen Books, 1991)

Story type: Science Fiction (Political; Disaster)

Major character(s): Alex MacLoed, Hero, Pilot (angel); Sherrine Hartley, Computer Expert (science fiction fan); Will Waxman, Doctor (science fiction fan)

Time period(s): 2010s

Locale(s): Minneapolis, Minnesota; Chicago, Illinois; Edwards Air Force Base, California

Summary: Cleaning the air has allowed the ice to start spreading south. The uneducated masses have been misled by the anti-technological Greens to believe that missing nitrogen, stolen by Mir and Freedom, now space colonies, is the cause. When two astronauts are shot down on the North Dakota glacier, their only hope for rescue is from the Minicon, a World Science Fiction convention being held in Minneapolis, full of technophiles enamoured with space travel and angels, the people who managed to colonize in orbit.

Other books you might like:

Robert Asprin, *Another Fine Myth*, 1978
Emma Bull, *War for the Oaks*, 1987
Michael Flynn, *In the Country of the Blind*, 1990
Sharyn McCrumb, *Bimbos of the Death Sun*, 1987
Sharyn McCrumb, *Zombies of the Gene Pool*, 1992
Steve Perry, *The Man Who Never Missed*, 1985
Nick Pollotta, *Illegal Aliens*, 1989
　　Phil Foglio, co-author
Harry Turtledove, *Earthgrip*, 1991

3280

LARRY NIVEN

Flatlander

(New York: Ballantine Del Rey, 1995)

Story type: Science Fiction (Mystery; Collection)

Series: Known Space

Major character(s): Gil ''the Arm'' Hamilton, Detective—Police (ARM)

Time period(s): 22nd century

Locale(s): Earth; Moon (Earth's)

Summary: Omnibus edition of Gil the Arm stories including *The Long Arm of Gil Hamilton* (1976), *The Patchwork Girl* (1980), and one original, ''The Woman in Del Rey Crater.'' In a future where criminals murder people for body parts to be used in transplant surgery, Gil Hamilton investigates cases involving organleggers and tries to keep people he cares about from becoming nothing but body parts.

Other books you might like:

Isaac Asimov, *The Caves of Steel*, 1954
Greg Bear, *Queen of Angels*, 1990
Alfred Bester, *The Demolished Man*, 1953
Richard Bowker, *Dover Beach*, 1987

Barney Cohen, *Blood on the Moon*, 1984
Alan Dean Foster, *Cyber Way*, 1990
Lee Killough, *Dragon's Teeth*, 1990
Jack Vance, *Trullion: Alastor 2262*, 1973

3281

LARRY NIVEN
JERRY POURNELLE, Co-Author

The Gripping Hand
(New York: Pocket, 1993)

Story type: Science Fiction (First Contact; Hard Science Fiction)
Major character(s): Horace Hussein Bury, Businessman (Imperial Trader and Magnate); Kevin Renner, Military Personnel (Navy Reserve Captain), Pilot (spaceship); Eudoxus, Alien (Motie Mediator)
Time period(s): 31st century (3040s)
Locale(s): Murchison's Eye, Planet—Imaginary; *Sinbad*, Spaceship; New Calidonia, Planet—Imaginary

Summary: Obsessed by the thought that the Moties, a very intelligent, prolific species, might get out of their confinement into human space, Horace Hussein Bury finds possible evidence of Moties. The Blaines continue to keep Charlie, a Motie Mediator, alive as companion for their children while the Blaine Institute finds the solution to the Moties' problem of birth control. Bury realizes that the protostar in the Coal Sack Nebula will ignite much sooner than the 1000 years expected, allowing Moties other exits from their system not controlled by the Crazy Eddie fleet. Sequel to *The Mote in God's Eye*.

Other books you might like:
Roger MacBride Allen, *The Ring of Charon*, 1990
Stephen Baxter, *Raft*, 1992
David Brin, *Startide Rising*, 1983
Octavia E. Butler, *Dawn*, 1987
C.J. Cherryh, *The Pride of Chanur*, 1982
Sheri S. Tepper, *Grass*, 1989
Vernor Vinge, *A Fire upon the Deep*, 1992

3282

LARRY NIVEN
JERRY POURNELLE, Co-Author
POUL ANDERSON, Co-Author

Man-Kzin Wars III
(New York: Baen, 1990)

Story type: Science Fiction (Anthology)
Series: Man-Kzin Wars
Time period(s): Indeterminate

Summary: This collection of three stories, all set in Larry Niven's Known Space Series (1966-) universe, includes Larry Niven's "Madness Has Its Place," J.E. Pournelle and S.M. Stirling's "The Asteroid Queen," and Poul Anderson's "Inconstant Star."

Other books you might like:
David Brin, *Startide Rising*, 1983

Octavia E. Butler, *Dawn*, 1987
Robert L. Forward, *Dragon's Egg*, 1980
Robert A. Heinlein, *The Past through Tomorrow*, 1967
Alis A. Rasmussen, *A Passage of Stars*, 1990
Alis A. Rasmussen, *The Price of Ransom*, 1990
Alis A. Rasmussen, *Revolution's Shore*, 1990
Cordwainer Smith, *The Best of Cordwainer Smith*, 1975
John Varley, *Blue Champagne*, 1986
John Varley, *The Persistence of Vision*, 1978

3283

LARRY NIVEN, Editor

Man-Kzin Wars IV
(New York: Baen, 1991)

Story type: Science Fiction (Anthology; Military)
Series: Man-Kzin Wars
Major character(s): Short-Son "Eater-of-Grass" of Chiirr-Nig, Alien (Kzin); Long-Reach, Slave, Alien (Jotok); Lawrence "Fixer-of-Weapons" Halloran, Spy (human), Telepath (projective)
Time period(s): 24th century; 25th century
Locale(s): Wunderland, Planet—Imaginary; Spaceship

Summary: Set in Larry Niven's *Known Space* universe, this anthology contains two stories by Donald Kingsbury, Greg Bear and S.M. Stirling. In Donald Kingsbury's novel-length *The Survivor*, the cowardly Eater-of-Grass learns how to bond and train Jotoki, becoming Trainer-of-Slaves. As he travels closer to Monkey Home trying to join a fleet attacking Earth, he intercepts a human ship attacking the Kzin near Alpha Centauri B, and captures both a revolutionary spaceship drive and Nora Argamentine whom he biologically manipulates into being more like a Kzin female. In Greg Bear and S.M. Stirling's novella, *The Man Who Would Be Kzin*, Lawrence Halloran, finding little use for his telepathic ability among human culture, enlists in the United Nations Space Navy, infiltrates a Kzin battleship, then turns heroic saboteur.

Other books you might like:
Poul Anderson, *Inconstant Star*, 1991
Christopher Anvil, *Pandora's Planet*, 1972
David Brin, *Startide Rising*, 1983
C.S. Friedman, *The Madness Season*, 1990
Diana G. Gallagher, *The Alien Dark*, 1990
Dean Ing, *Cathouse*, 1991
Jerry Pournelle, *The Children's Hour*, 1991
  S.M. Stirling, co-author
David Alexander Smith, *Homecoming*, 1989

3284

LARRY NIVEN, Editor

Man-Kzin Wars V
(New York: Baen, 1992)

Story type: Science Fiction (Anthology; Military)
Series: Man-Kzin Wars
Major character(s): Jonah Matthieson, Pilot, Military Personnel (UN Space Navy, retired); Spots-Son of Chotrz-Shaa,

Alien (Kzin), Military Personnel (retired); Durvash, Time Traveller, Alien (Tnuctipun)

Time period(s): Indeterminate Future

Locale(s): Wunderland, Planet—Imaginary; Beanstalk, Planet—Imaginary

Summary: Contains two stories set in Larry Niven's *Known Space* universe. Jerry Pournelle's collaboration with S. M. Stirling, ''In the Hall of the Mountain King,'' features former human and Kzinti enemies cooperating in a salvage operation which recovers a Tnuctipun spy ship hidden for three billion years. In Thomas T. Thomas' story, ''Hey Diddle Diddle,'' crews of both human and Kzinti spaceships hustle to find a Thrinturn artifact after a Bandersnatch damages each ship.

Other books you might like:

Poul Anderson, *Inconstant Star*, 1991

Barry B. Longyear, *Enemy Mine*, 1985
David Gerrold, novelization co-author

Dean Ing, *Cathouse*, 1991

Jerry Pournelle, *The Children's Hour*, 1991
S. M. Stirling, co-author

3285

LARRY NIVEN

N-Space

(New York: Tor, 1990)

Story type: Science Fiction (Collection)

Time period(s): Indeterminate Future

Summary: This book is a retrospective of Larry Niven's first 25 years as a science fiction writer. It includes samples from his longer works including *World of Ptavvs* (1966), *A Gift From Earth* (1968), *Ringworld* (1970), *Protector* (1973) and *The Mote in God's Eye* (1974) (Jerry Pournelle, co-author), with a large sprinkling of short stories, introductions, essays and reminiscences.

Other books you might like:

Roger MacBride Allen, *The Ring of Charon*, 1990

David Brin, *Earth*, 1990

Octavia E. Butler, *Dawn*, 1987

Robert L. Forward, *Rocheworld*, 1990

Alis A. Rasmussen, *A Passage of Stars*, 1990

Cordwainer Smith, *The Best of Cordwainer Smith*, 1975
pseudonym of Paul Myron Anthony Linebarger

John Varley, *Blue Champagne*, 1986

John Varley, *The Persistence of Vision*, 1978

3286

LARRY NIVEN

Playgrounds of the Mind

(New York: Tor, 1991)

Story type: Science Fiction (Collection)

Summary: Spanning the second half of Niven's career to date, this companion volume to *N-Space* contains 49 listed entries plus anecdotal interludes and brief excerpts of fiction between listed works. The fiction includes longer short stories and 7 vignettes. Listed as works in progress are excerpts from

Fallen Angels (1991), *The California Voodoo Game* (1992) and the half-completed *The Mote Around Murcheson's Eye*, a collaborative sequel to *The Mote in God's Eye* (1974). Non-fiction includes a letter, a memoir, a recipe for Irish Coffee that serves 200, memories of World Science Fiction conventions, Niven's view of critics and reviews and an article on how to build XXXL-size environments.

Other books you might like:

Groff Conklin, *The Best of Science Fiction*, 1946
editor

Michael Flynn, *The Nanotech Chronicles*, 1991

Alan Dean Foster, *With Friends Like These. . .*, 1977

Raymond J. Healy, *Adventures in Time and Space*, 1946
J. Francis McComas, co-editor

Robert A. Heinlein, *The Past through Tomorrow*, 1967

Cordwainer Smith, *The Best of Cordwainer Smith*, 1975

Marc Stiegler, *The Gentle Seduction*, 1990

John Varley, *Blue Champagne*, 1986

John Varley, *The Persistence of Vision*, 1978

3287

LARRY NIVEN

The Ringworld Throne

(New York: Ballantine Del Rey, 1996)

Story type: Science Fiction (Political; First Contact)

Series: Ringworld

Major character(s): Louis Wu, Adventurer; Chmeee, Alien (Kzin); The Hindmost, Alien (Puppeteer)

Time period(s): 29th century

Locale(s): Ringworld, Planet—Imaginary

Summary: Having saved Ringworld from destruction, Louis Wu must once again find a solution to complications from the interactions of the many races living there. Ringworld needs a leader due not only to an overabundance of vampires and unpredicatable attacks on incoming ships, but also to Protectors encroaching on species not in their care and on each other.

Other books you might like:

Eleanor Arnason, *Ring of Swords*, 1993

David Brin, *Brightness Reef*, 1995

C.J. Cherryh, *Invader*, 1995

A.C. Crispin, *Silent Dances*, 1990
Kathleen O'Malley, co-author

George Turner, *Genetic Soldier*, 1994

3288

GARTH NIX

Sabriel

(New York: HarperCollins, 1996)

Story type: Fantasy (Young Adult; Magic Conflict)

Major character(s): Sabriel, Magician, Teenager; Mogget, Spirit, Animal (cat); Touchstone, Magician

Time period(s): Indeterminate

Locale(s): The Old Kingdom, Fictional Country; Ancelstierre, Fictional Country

Summary: When the magician Abhorsen becomes ensnared in the Land of the Dead, his daughter, Sabriel, must travel into the Old Kingdom, land of free magic, to save him.

Other books you might like:
Lois McMaster Bujold, *The Spirit Ring*, 1992
Kara Dalkey, *Little Sister*, 1996
Laurell K. Hamilton, *Nightseer*, 1992
Holly Lisle, *Minerva Wakes*, 1994
Meredith Ann Pierce, *The Pearl of the Soul of the World*, 1990
Nancy Springer, *The Friendship Song*, 1992

3289

WILLIAM F. NOLAN, Editor
MARTIN H. GREENBERG, Co-Editor

The Bradbury Chronicles: Stories in Honor of Ray Bradbury
(New York: Roc, 1991)

Story type: Fantasy (Anthology)

Summary: 22 stories, each introduced by William F. Nolan, an introduction, a brief appreciation by Isaac Asimov, and an afterword by Ray Bradbury. The stories include "May 2000: The Tombstones," by James Kisner, a sequel to "Mars is Heaven!"; Ed Gorman's "The Wind From Midnight," a sequel to "The Dwarf"; and F. Paul Wilson's "The November Game," a sequel to "The October Game." "The Inheritance," by Bruce Francis, is a sequel to "The Lake." Gregory Benford's "Centigrade 233" reflects *Fahrenheit 451*, and Orson Scott Card's "Feed the Baby of Love" shows us an aging Douglas Spaulding of *Dandelion Wine*. Other authors include Douglas Beaumont, Ray Bradbury, Richard Matheson, Chad Oliver and Robert Sheckley.

Other books you might like:
Robert Bloch, *The Selected Stories of Robert Bloch*, 1988
Robert Bloch, *The Star Stalker*, 1968
Ray Bradbury, *Dandelion Wine*, 1957
Ray Bradbury, *A Graveyard for Lunatics*, 1990
Ray Bradbury, *The Illustrated Man*, 1953
Ray Bradbury, *Something Wicked This Way Comes*, 1962
Ray Bradbury, *The Stories of Ray Bradbury*, 1980
Ray Bradbury, *The Toynbee Convector*, 1989
Ellen Datlow, *The Year's Best Fantasy: First Annual Collection*, 1990
   Terri Windling, co-editor
Kristine Kathryn Rusch, *Pulphouse, Issue 9: Dark Fantasy*, 1990
   editor
Theodore Sturgeon, *A Touch of Sturgeon*, 1987

3290

WILLIAM F. NOLAN

Night Shapes: Excursions into Terror
(Baltimore: CD Publications, 1995)

Story type: Horror (Collection)

Summary: This compilation's 25 selections span 25 years of Nolan's career as a writer of horror, suspense, and science fiction. Stories include the ghost tale "Major Preview Here Tonight"; the serial killer stories "Him, Her, Them," "The Visit," and "Cure"; the psychological suspense tales "My Name Is Dolly," "Special Treat," and "The Big Man"; monster stories that include "On 42nd St." and "The Halloween Man"; and stories told from the perspective of non-human narrators that include "Gobble! Gobble!" from "Narrow House."

Other books you might like:
Charles Beaumont, *Selected Stories*, 1988
Ray Bradbury, *The Stories of Ray Bradbury*, 1980
Richard Matheson, *Richard Matheson: Collected Stories*, 1989

3291

WILLIAM F. NOLAN, Editor
MARTIN H. GREENBERG, Co-Editor

Urban Horrors
(Arlington Heights, Illinois: Dark Harvest, 1990)

Story type: Horror (Anthology)

Summary: This intelligently edited reprint anthology of primarily non-supernatural horror stories in urban settings during the last half of the 20th century includes such classics as Fritz Leiber's "Smoke Ghost" and Dennis Etchison's "Talking in the Dark" as well as unexpected stories by such authors as John Cheever, Alice Glaser, and Joyce Carol Oates.

Other books you might like:
Christopher Fowler, *City Jitters*, 1986

3292

JEFF NOON

Automated Alice
(New York: Crown, 1996)

Story type: Fantasy (Light Fantasy; Time Travel)
Major character(s): Alice Pleasance Liddell, Child, Time Traveller; Celia, Robot
Time period(s): 1860s (1860); 1990s (1998)
Locale(s): Manchester, England

Summary: Alice chases a parrot into the clock and finds herself in a strange future, unable to return home until she locates a dozen jigsaw puzzle pieces. An automated version of Alice helps Alice navigate the perils of murder accusations, Civil Serpents, mutant hybrids, computermites, chaos theory, quantum physics and Vurt feathers.

Other books you might like:
Gilbert Adair, *Alice through the Needle's Eye: The Further Adventures of Lewis Carroll's "Alice"*, 1985
Lewis Carroll, *Alice's Adventures in Wonderland*, 1865
Lewis Carroll, *Through the Looking Glass and What Alice Found There*, 1872
Randall Garrett, *Takeoff!*, 1979
Margaret Weis, *Fantastic Alice*, 1995
   editor

3293

JEFF NOON

Pollen
(New York: Crown, 1996)

Story type: Science Fiction (Literary; Cyberpunk)
Major character(s): Sibyl Jones, Detective—Police, Telepath; Coyote, Genetically Altered Being, Taxi Driver; Boda, Genetically Altered Being, Taxi Driver
Time period(s): Indeterminate Future
Locale(s): Manchester, England; Vurt, Alternate Earth

Summary: Manchester Police Investigator Sibyl Jones hunts for a killer while nearly everyone around her suffers massive hayfever attacks from an astronomically high pollen count. She learns that a "Vurtual," a creature from the alternate dream-world, Vurt, has unleashed a virulent strain of pollen in a plot to prepare the real world for colonization by Vurtuals. A loose sequel to *Vurt*.

Other books you might like:
J.G. Ballard, *The Crystal World*, 1966
Pat Cadigan, *Synners*, 1991
William Gibson, *Neuromancer*, 1984
Jonathan Lethem, *Amnesia Moon*, 1995
Kim Newman, *The Night Mayor*, 1990

3294

JEFF NOON

Vurt
(New York: Crown, 1995)

Story type: Science Fiction (Cyberpunk; Adventure)
Major character(s): Stephen "Scribble", Addict (Vurt), Fugitive; Karli Dog, Robot (dog); Game Cat, Computer Expert, Editor
Time period(s): Indeterminate Future
Locale(s): Manchester, England

Summary: Scribble loses his beloved sister, Desdemona, in an English Voodoo garden hidden in a Curious Yellow feather, when the Vurt Thing-from-Outer-Space replaces her. Scribble carries and protects the amoeboid, illegal, live-drug Thing with hopes of exchanging it for Desdemona. Bitten by a dream snake, Scribble carries Vurt inside all the time, adding desperation to his adventures in the Battle, a neighborhood of broken glass, and in Turdsville, the home of the Robodogs. First novel and winner of the Arthur C. Clarke Award in Britain, where it was published in 1993.

Other books you might like:
Pat Cadigan, *Mindplayers*, 1987
Jean Mark Gawron, *Dream of Glass*, 1993
James P. Hogan, *The Multiplex Man*, 1992
Gwyneth Jones, *White Queen*, 1993
Dan Simmons, *Hyperion*, 1989
Cordwainer Smith, *The Rediscovery of Man*, 1993
Michael Swanwick, *The Iron Dragon's Daughter*, 1994

3295

LISANNE NORMAN

Fire Margins
(New York: DAW, 1996)

Story type: Science Fiction (Political; Psychic Powers)
Series: Sholan Alliance
Major character(s): Carrie, Psychic; Kusac, Psychic, Alien (Sholan); Kaid, Military Personnel, Alien (Sholan)
Time period(s): Indeterminate Future
Locale(s): Shola, Planet—Imaginary

Summary: Factions on Shola jockey for control of the mixed species mated pairs as Carrie recovers from her wounds and her miscarriage. Seeking to establish a new group outside the existing guilds, Kusac and Carrie join with Kaid for the ancient rituals to seek Vartra and in so doing learn more about Shola's past. Meanwhile, humans and Sholans cooperate in defense efforts against the Valtegans, a religious fanatic persecutes telepaths, and Vanna gives birth to her child, the first of the new species.

Other books you might like:
C.J. Cherryh, *Chanur's Homecoming*, 1986
Diane Duane, *Spock's World*, 1988
Mary Gentle, *Golden Witchbreed*, 1983
Gayle Greeno, *Exiles' Return*, 1995
Anne McCaffrey, *Crisis on Doona*, 1992
    Jody Lynn Nye, co-author

3296

LISANNE NORMAN

Fortune's Wheel
(New York: DAW, 1995)

Story type: Science Fiction (Psychic Powers; Political)
Series: Sholan Alliance
Major character(s): Carrie, Psychic; Kusac, Psychic, Alien (Sholan)
Time period(s): Indeterminate Future
Locale(s): *Khalossa*, Spaceship; Shola, Planet—Imaginary

Summary: Brought together by their telepathic powers and bound by love, Carrie and Kusac face difficulties adjusting to their new relationship. As they return to Shola aboard the *Khalossa*, Human and Sholan representatives attempt to forge an alliance against the warlike Valtegans, but opposing factions on both sides try to use the pair for their own ends.

Other books you might like:
Margaret Wander Bonanno, *Dwellers in the Crucible*, 1985
C.J. Cherryh, *Foreigner*, 1994
Kate Elliott, *An Earthly Crown*, 1993
Anne McCaffrey, *Crisis on Doona*, 1992
    Jody Lynn Nye, co-author
Andre Norton, *Catseye*, 1961
Vernor Vinge, *A Fire upon the Deep*, 1992

3297

LISANNE NORMAN

Turning Point

(New York: DAW, 1993)

Story type: Science Fiction (First Contact; Psychic Powers)
Series: Sholan Alliance
Major character(s): Carrie, Psychic; Kusac, Psychic (intelligence officer), Alien (feline)
Time period(s): Indeterminate Future
Locale(s): Keiss, Planet—Imaginary

Summary: When Carrie's twin sister is killed by invading reptilian warriors, their telepathic link almost causes Carrie to die of trauma; but she is contacted by Kusac, a member of the feline Sholan race, whose spaceship has been wrecked. The only other telepath Carrie has encountered, Kusac cares for and comforts her and they develop a relationship in spite of their immense cultural differences. If their peoples can also overcome their prejudices, they can become valuable allies as well.

Other books you might like:
Eleanor Arnason, *Ring of Swords*, 1993
Marion Zimmer Bradley, *The World Wreckers*, 1971
C.J. Cherryh, *Serpent's Reach*, 1980
Paula E. Downing, *Rinn's Star*, 1990
Janet Kagan, *Hellspark*, 1988
Rebecca Ore, *Being Alien*, 1989

3298

ANDRE NORTON

Brother to Shadows

(New York: Morrow AvoNova, 1993)

Story type: Science Fiction (Adventure; Mystical)
Series: Forerunner
Major character(s): Jofre, Outcast, Martial Arts Expert; Zurzal, Alien (Zacathan), Historian; Taynad Jewelbright, Bodyguard, Martial Arts Expert
Time period(s): Indeterminate Future
Locale(s): Asborgan, Planet—Imaginary; Tssek, Planet—Imaginary; Lochan, Planet—Imaginary

Summary: An off-world foundling raised by the Brotherhood of Shadows, now ready for his first Oathed assignment, Jofre loses his standing when the Lair Stone dies and the Lair readies for abandonment. Hated by the Shagga Priest of the Lair, Jofre lacks support when the Master dies. Setting off to find the spaceport, Jofre shelters in an abandoned lair where he picks up a small stone which retains enough power to utilize while he acts as bodyguard to Zurzal, who attempts to use Forerunner technology to find a Forerunner information storehouse.

Other books you might like:
Steven Brust, *Jhereg*, 1983
Emily Devenport, *Shade*, 1992
Gordon R. Dickson, *Dorsai!*, 1976
Steve Miller, *Agent of Change*, 1988
   Sharon Lee, co-author

Steve Miller, *Carpe Diem*, 1989
   Sharon Lee, co-author
Steve Miller, *Conflict of Honors*, 1988
   Sharon Lee, co-author
Steve Perry, *The 97th Step*, 1989

3299

ANDRE NORTON, Editor
MARTIN H. GREENBERG, Co-Editor

Catfantastic II

(New York: DAW, 1991)

Story type: Fantasy (Anthology)
Series: Catfantastic

Summary: This volume contains a brief introduction plus 18 original stories featuring cats and having fantasy themes or settings. Among the authors are Claire Bell, Elizabeth H. Boyer, P.M. Griffin, Ardath Mayhar, Elizabeth Moon, Andre Norton, Elizabeth Ann Scarborough, Susan Shwartz and Nancy Springer. One story, "Quest of Souls," is a collaboration between Ann Miller and Karen Rigley.

Other books you might like:
Clare Bell, *Clan Ground*, 1984
Clare Bell, *Ratha and Thistle-Chaser*, 1990
Clare Bell, *Ratha's Creature*, 1983
C.J. Cherryh, *The Pride of Chanur*, 1982
Alan Dean Foster, *Cat-A-Lyst*, 1991
Randall Garrett, *The Gandalara Cycle I*, 1986
   Vicki Ann Heydron, co-author
Robert A. Heinlein, *The Door into Summer*, 1957
Michael Peak, *Cat House*, 1989
Michael Peak, *Catamount*, 1992
Marti Steussy, *Dreams of Dawn*, 1988
Marti Steussy, *Forest of the Night*, 1987
Tad Williams, *Tailchaser's Song*, 1985

3300

ANDRE NORTON, Editor
MARTIN H. GREENBERG, Co-Editor

Catfantastic III

(New York: DAW, 1994)

Story type: Fantasy (Anthology)
Series: Catfantastic

Summary: Contains a brief introduction by Norton and 20 original stories featuring cats and fantasy themes in diverse settings. Authors include Claire Bell, Charles de Lint, Charles L. Fontenay, P.M. Griffin, Mercedes Lackey, Ardath Mayhar, Andre Norton, Elizabeth Ann Scarborough, Mary H. Schaub and Susan Schwartz.

Other books you might like:
Clare Bell, *Ratha's Creature*, 1983
Jack Dann, *Magicats!*, 1984
   Gardner Dozois, co-editor
Jack Dann, *Magicats II*, 1991
   Gardner Dozois, co-editor

Bill Fawcett, *Cats in Space and Other Places*, 1990
　　editor
Mark E. Rogers, *The Adventures of Samurai Cat*, 1984
John Richard Stephens, *The Enchanted Cat*, 1990
　　editor
John Richard Stephens, *Mysterious Cat Stories*, 1993
　　Kim Smith, co-editor
Tad Williams, *Tailchaser's Song*, 1985

3301

ANDRE NORTON, Editor
MARTIN H. GREENBERG, Co-Editor

Catfantastic IV

(New York: DAW, 1996)

Story type: Fantasy (Anthology)
Series: Catfantastic

Summary: This volume contains 18 original stories, an introduction by Andre Norton, and a brief biographical sketch of each author. Authors include Jayge Carr, Charles L. Fontenay, P.M. Griffin, Mercedes Lackey, Jane M. Lindskold, Lyn McConchie, Andre Norton, and Elizabeth Ann Scarborough. The stories deal with cat pals, cat helpers, a cat music critic, and cat adventurers.

Other books you might like:
Clare Bell, *Ratha's Creature*, 1983
Jack Dann, *Magicats!*, 1984
　　Gardner Dozois, co-editor
Bill Fawcett, *Cats in Space and Other Places*, 1990
　　editor
John Richard Stephens, *The Enchanted Cat*, 1990
　　editor
L.A. Taylor, *Cat's Paw*, 1995
Tad Williams, *Tailchaser's Song*, 1985

3302

ANDRE NORTON

Dare to Go A-Hunting

(New York: Tor Books, 1990)

Story type: Science Fiction (Fantasy)
Major character(s): Farree, Alien; Krip Vorlund, Spaceman
Time period(s): Indeterminate Future
Locale(s): Planet—Imaginary

Summary: The waif Farree discovers evidence that other winged intelligent beings like himself exist and, with Free Trader Krip Vorlund, the historian Zoor, and the sorceress Maelen, sets out across the galaxy to find them. Throughout their journey they must dodge the evil Guild, which is out to capture Farree. Sequel to *Flight in Yiktor*.

Other books you might like:
Clare Bell, *People of the Sky*, 1989
Marcia J. Bennett, *Seeking the Dream Brother*, 1989
Marion Zimmer Bradley, *Darkover Landfall*, 1972
Mary Caraker, *Seven Worlds*, 1986
Mary Caraker, *The Snows of Jaspre*, 1989
Rosemary Kirstein, *The Steerswoman*, 1989

3303

ANDRE NORTON
MERCEDES LACKEY, Co-Author

The Elvenbane

(New York: Tor, 1991)

Story type: Fantasy (Magic Conflict; Adventure)
Series: Halfblood Chronicles
Major character(s): Shana, Orphan; Alara, Shaman, Mythical Creature (dragon)
Time period(s): Indeterminate Future
Locale(s): Earth

Summary: When elves immigrated to Earth, they assumed power and enslaved humanity. Born to a mother dying in the desert, half-breed Shana finds a foster mother in Alara. If she survives, Shana may grow into the one prophesied to change Earth's new balance of power.

Other books you might like:
Emma Bull, *War for the Oaks*, 1987
Mercedes Lackey, *Bardic Voices*, 1991
Ursula K. Le Guin, *The Farthest Shore*, 1972
Ursula K. Le Guin, *Tehanu: The Last Book of Earthsea*, 1990
Ursula K. Le Guin, *The Tombs of Atuan*, 1971
Ursula K. Le Guin, *A Wizard of Earthsea*, 1968
Anne McCaffrey, *Dragonflight*, 1968
Anne McCaffrey, *Dragonquest*, 1971
Anne McCaffrey, *The White Dragon*, 1978
Joel Rosenberg, *The Road to Ehvenor*, 1991
Will Shetterly, *Elsewhere*, 1991

3304

ANDRE NORTON
MERCEDES LACKEY, Co-Author

Elvenblood

(New York: Tor, 1995)

Story type: Fantasy (Political; Adventure)
Series: Halfblood Chronicles
Major character(s): Lashana ''Shana'', Hero, Leader; Sheyrena ''Rena'' an Treves, Mythical Creature (elf), Fiance(e); Keman, Mythical Creature (dragon), Wizard
Time period(s): Indeterminate Future
Locale(s): Earth

Summary: Fleeing unacceptible fates at the hands of their father, Rena and her brother find their way to the Iron People, who are protected from magic by their ubiquitous iron jewelry. When Shana attempts to establish trade and allies for her new colony of wizards and dragons, her exploration also leads to the Iron People, who imprison her with the same iron jewelry that protects them. Among the Iron People, both Rena and Shana find unexpected help for their problems. Second volume in the series.

Other books you might like:
J.V. Jones, *The Baker's Boy*, 1995
Marjorie Bradley Kellogg, *The Book of Earth*, 1995
Mercedes Lackey, *Arrows of the Queen*, 1987
Mercedes Lackey, *The Lark and the Wren*, 1991

Ursula K. Le Guin, *The Tombs of Atuan*, 1971
L.E. Modesitt Jr., *The Towers of the Sunset*, 1992
Elizabeth Moon, *Liar's Oath*, 1992

3305

ANDRE NORTON
P.M. GRIFFIN, Co-Author

Firehand

(New York: Tor, 1994)

Story type: Science Fiction (Time Travel; Adventure)
Series: Time Traders
Major character(s): Ross Murdoch, Time Traveller; Eveleen Riordan, Time Traveller; Luroc I Loran, Ruler (Ton of Sapphirehold), Warrior
Time period(s): Indeterminate Past
Locale(s): Dominion of Virgin, Planet—Imaginary; Hawaika, Planet—Imaginary

Summary: Rescued from Hawaika's past and sent into that of the Dominion of Virgin as its civilization suddenly vanished during negotiations with Terra, Ross, Eveleen and Gordon Ashe must act as mercenaries to prevent Zanthor I Yoroc from conquering Dominion for the Baldies. The team works under Luroc I Loran of Sapphirehold to stave off Zanthor.

Other books you might like:
Poul Anderson, *The Day of Their Return*, 1975
Leigh Brackett, *The Sword of Rhiannon*, 1953
Richard Cowper, *The Road to Corlay*, 1979
Leo Frankowski, *The Cross-Time Engineer*, 1986
Crawford Kilian, *The Empire of Time*, 1978

3306

ANDRE NORTON
P.M. GRIFFIN, Co-Author
MARY SCHAUB, Co-Author

Flight of Vengeance

(New York: Tor, 1992)

Story type: Fantasy (Military; Magic Conflict)
Series: Witch World
Major character(s): Duratan, Historian; Nolar, Scholar, Healer; Tarlach, Warrior, Mercenary
Time period(s): Indeterminate
Locale(s): Witch World, Planet—Imaginary

Summary: Shunned because of a prominent birthmark, Nolar pursues scholarly studies. After the Turning, Nolar brings a witch who lost all sense of self to seek a cure in a cave of the Old Ones found deep in the mountains. Meanwhile, hearing of a planned attack from another dimension, Tarlach gathers help to defeat it.

Other books you might like:
Orson Scott Card, *The Folk of the Fringe*, 1989
C.J. Cherryh, *The Fires of Azeroth*, 1979
Edmund Cooper, *The Cloud Walker*, 1973
L. Sprague de Camp, *The Hand of Zei*, 1963
Ursula K. Le Guin, *Tehanu: The Last Book of Earthsea*, 1990
Robert Silverberg, *Nightwings*, 1969

Sydney J. Van Scyoc, *Bluesong*, 1983

3307

ANDRE NORTON

Golden Trillium

(New York: Bantam Spectra, 1993)

Story type: Fantasy (Quest; Magic Conflict)
Series: Trillium
Major character(s): Kadiya, Explorer, Royalty; Jagun, Genetically Altered Being, Guide; Lamaril, Hero, Warrior
Time period(s): Indeterminate
Locale(s): Ruwenda, Fictional Country

Summary: Drawn back into the swamps, Kadiya discovers a long-deserted city where she meets the Hassitti who warn that a great, reawakened evil may conquer Ruwenda. When Kadiya calls forth Lamaril and learns of the ancient enemies his people could not steel themselves to kill, Kadiya and her companions travel to the western mountains to confront the enemies.

Other books you might like:
Poul Anderson, *Three Hearts and Three Lions*, 1961
Piers Anthony, *Being a Green Mother*, 1987
Marion Zimmer Bradley, *Black Trillium*, 1990
    Julian May, Andre Norton, co-authors
C.J. Cherryh, *Well of Shiuan*, 1978
Sterling E. Lanier, *Hiero's Journey*, 1973
Ursula K. Le Guin, *City of Illusions*, 1967
Julian May, *Blood Trillium*, 1992
Michelle Sagara, *Into the Dark Lands*, 1991

3308

ANDRE NORTON

The Hands of Lyr

(New York: Morrow/AvoNova, 1994)

Story type: Fantasy (Quest; Religious)
Major character(s): Dreen, Religious (priestess); Alnosha "Nosh", Foundling, Student; Kryn, Heir—Dispossessed, Outlaw
Time period(s): Indeterminate
Locale(s): The Ryft, Mythical Place (desert)

Summary: Rescued from slavery by Dreen, the last Priestess of Lyr, Nosh grows up in the Ryft, learning about Lyr and her Guards. When found by soldiers, Nosh discovers the shattered hands of Lyr and learns she has the gift of Lyr's touch. His family name destroyed by the evil Templars, Kryn must aid Nosh or all will become victims of Zellon's evil.

Other books you might like:
Don Callander, *Pyromancer*, 1992
Monica Hughes, *The Promise*, 1992
Robert Jordan, *The Eye of the World*, 1989
Crawford Kilian, *Greenmagic*, 1992
Meredith Ann Pierce, *The Pearl of the Soul of the World*, 1990

3309

ANDRE NORTON
SUSAN SCHWARTZ, Co-Author

Imperial Lady
(New York: Tor, 1989)

Story type: Fantasy (Historical)
Major character(s): Silver Snow, Royalty, Warrior (Queen)
Time period(s): Indeterminate Past
Locale(s): China

Summary: To insult her family, the Emperor of China gives Silver Snow in marriage to the Hsiung-Nu leader. She finds, however, that nomadic life suits her.

Other books you might like:
Kathryn Grant, *The Willow Garden*, 1989
Barry Hughart, *Bridge of Birds*,
Jeanne Larsen, *Silk Road*, 1989

3310

ANDRE NORTON
LYN MCCONCHIE, Co-Author

The Key of the Keplian
(New York: Warner Aspect, 1995)

Story type: Fantasy (Quest)
Series: Witch World
Major character(s): Eleeri, Runaway, Animal Trainer; Tharna, Animal (horse), Telepath; Romar, Captive
Time period(s): Indeterminate
Locale(s): Witch World, Planet—Imaginary

Summary: Rather than live with non-Indian relatives after her grandfather's death, Eleeri flees through a gate, arriving on Witch World. After saving a Keplian mare and foal, which people regard as evil, Eleeri lives in hiding while raising a herd of horses. Responding to dream communications, Eleeri and the horses move to rescue Romar, who is being held by an evil sorcerer.

Other books you might like:
Piers Anthony, *Virtual Mode*, 1991
Constance Ash, *The Horsegirl*, 1988
Joy Chant, *The Grey Mane of Morning*, 1980
Peter Dickinson, *The Blue Hawk*, 1976
C.S. Lewis, *The Horse and His Boy*, 1954
Robin McKinley, *The Blue Sword*, 1982
Karen Ripley, *The Persistence of Memory*, 1993
Nancy Springer, *A Horse to Love*, 1987

3311

ANDRE NORTON

The Mark of the Cat
(New York: Ace, 1992)

Story type: Fantasy (Quest)
Major character(s): Klaverel-va-Hynkkel, Traveller; Ravinga, Shaman (dollmaker); Murri, Animal (cat)
Time period(s): Indeterminate

Locale(s): Kahulawe, Fictional Country

Summary: Unesteemed by his family, Hynkkel starts his solo rite of passage without the ceremonial support of family and friends. The amulet given to him by the dollmaker becomes his most important possession and allows contact with Murri, who becomes his companion.

Other books you might like:
Clare Bell, *Ratha's Creature*, 1983
C.J. Cherryh, *The Pride of Chanur*, 1982
Alan Dean Foster, *Cat-A-Lyst*, 1991
Robert A. Heinlein, *The Door into Summer*, 1957
Michael Peak, *Cat House*, 1989
Tad Williams, *Tailchaser's Song*, 1985

3312

ANDRE NORTON

Mirror of Destiny
(New York: Morrow/AvoNova, 1995)

Story type: Fantasy (Adventure; Magic Conflict)
Major character(s): Twilla, Healer, Apprentice; Ylon, Royalty, Handicapped (blind); Oxyle, Mythical Creature (magical)
Time period(s): Indeterminate
Locale(s): Varslaad, Fictional Country; Enchanted Forest, Mythical Place

Summary: Ordered to travel to another land where whe will marry someone chosen by lot, Twilla craftily uses her magic mirror to render herself unappealing. When her subterfuge backfires, Twilla must escape to the forest with Ylon, where she learns of an evil plot to control the forest and surrounding lands.

Other books you might like:
Lynn Abbey, *The Wooden Sword*, 1991
Poul Anderson, *Three Hearts and Three Lions*, 1961
Piers Anthony, *Being a Green Mother*, 1987
Piers Anthony, *If I Pay Thee Not in Gold*, 1993
　　Mercedes Lackey, co-author
Maya Kaathryn Bohnhoff, *Taminy*, 1993
Robert Holdstock, *Mythago Wood*, 1984
Thomas Burnett Swann, *Day of the Minotaur*, 1966

3313

ANDRE NORTON
P.M. GRIFFIN, Co-Author

Redline the Stars
(New York: Tor, 1993)

Story type: Science Fiction (Adventure)
Series: Solar Queen
Major character(s): Miceal Jellico, Spaceship Captain, Trader; Rael Cofort, Doctor, Spacewoman
Time period(s): Indeterminate Future
Locale(s): *Solar Queen*, Spaceship; Canuche of Halio, Planet—Imaginary

Summary: On the *Solar Queen* as a temporary crew member, Rael impresses the rest of the crew who yet remain curious about her. She seems to elicit trouble and never runs from it, resolving an undiscovered mass murder case and warning of a major disaster on Canuche of Halio, but revealing little of herself. Jellico must decide if he wants to offer her a permanent spot on the *Solar Queen*'s crew.

Other books you might like:
Poul Anderson, *Trader to the Stars*, 1964
Pauline Ashwell, *Unwillingly to Earth*, 1992
David Brin, *The Uplift War*, 1987
A.C. Crispin, *Starbridge*, 1989
Margaret Davis, *Mind Light*, 1993
T. Jackson King, *Retread Shop*, 1988
Alis A. Rasmussen, *A Passage of Stars*, 1990
Harry Turtledove, *Earthgrip*, 1991
Jack Williamson, *Beachhead*, 1992

3314

ANDRE NORTON
A.C. CRISPIN, Co-Author

Songsmith

(New York: Tor, 1992)

Story type: Fantasy (Adventure; Psychic Powers)
Series: Witch World
Major character(s): Eydryth of Kar Garudwyn, Minstrel; Avris, Witch, Companion
Time period(s): Indeterminate
Locale(s): Witch World, Planet—Imaginary

Summary: Eydryth, a skilled Songsmith, travels through Estcarp searching out a cure for her father who has never recovered from an attempt at using a device chanced upon at a place of the old Power.

Other books you might like:
L. Sprague de Camp, *Land of Unreason*, 1942
Phyllis Eisenstein, *Born to Exile*, 1978
Ellen Kushner, *Thomas the Rhymer*, 1990
Anne McCaffrey, *Dragonsinger*, 1977
C.L. Moore, *Jirel of Joiry*, 1969
Melanie Rawn, *Dragon Prince*, 1988

3315

ANDRE NORTON
P.M. GRIFFIN, Co-Author

Storms of Victory

(New York: Tor, 1991)

Story type: Fantasy (Adventure)
Series: Witch World
Major character(s): Destree, Orphan, Psychic; Una, Ruler (Lady of Seakeepdale); Tarlach, Warrior, Mercenary
Time period(s): Indeterminate
Locale(s): Witch World, Planet—Imaginary

Summary: Destree travels south with the Sulcar and certain of the Estcarp witches to discover the origin of strange ships. When she finds ancient evil has been reawakened, she and Kemoc lay it to rest along with the strange tools it has used. Meanwhile at Seakeepdale in High Hallack, Lady Una seeks

aid in protecting her people from the evil Lord Ogin of Ravenfield who has turned pirate.

Other books you might like:
L. Sprague de Camp, *Land of Unreason*, 1942
Raymond Harris, *The Broken Worlds*, 1986
Katherine Kurtz, *The Quest for Saint Camber*, 1986
Sterling E. Lanier, *Hiero's Journey*, 1973
C.L. Moore, *Jirel of Joiry*, 1969
Sydney J. Van Scyoc, *Feather Stroke*, 1989

3316

ANDRE NORTON

The Warding of Witch World

(New York: Warner Aspect, 1996)

Story type: Fantasy (Quest; Magic Conflict)
Series: Witch World
Major character(s): Keris Tregarth, Warrior; Firdun, Nobleman; Trusla, Traveller, Dancer
Time period(s): Indeterminate Past
Locale(s): Witch World, Planet—Imaginary

Summary: Because ancient evil stirs again, the Council at Lormt decides to close all gates between worlds. To close the three most treacherous, in the far south, in the western wastes and in the ice-filled north, three expeditions set forth.

Other books you might like:
Poul Anderson, *The Broken Sword*, 1954
Joy Chant, *Red Moon and Black Mountain*, 1971
C.J. Cherryh, *Gate of Ivrel*, 1976
L. Sprague de Camp, *The Unbeheaded King*, 1983
Alan Dean Foster, *Spellsinger*, 1983
Diana Wynne Jones, *The Crown of Dalemark*, 1995
Katherine Kurtz, *Deryni Checkmate*, 1972
Karen Ripley, *The Warden of Horses*, 1994

3317

WARREN NORWOOD
MEL ODOM, Co-Author

Stranded!

(New York: Lynx Omega, 1989)

Story type: Science Fiction (Time Travel)
Series: Time Police
Major character(s): Jackson Dubchek, Historian, Time Traveller
Time period(s): 23rd century (2244); 21st century (2074)
Locale(s): Mexico

Summary: Stranded by the Time Police in the year 2074, Dubchek begins to piece together that organization's secret plan to protect the future at all costs.

Other books you might like:
Poul Anderson, *The Corridors of Time*, 1965
Poul Anderson, *Time Patrolman*, 1983
Poul Anderson, *The Year of the Ransom*, 1988
Isaac Asimov, *The End of Eternity*, 1955
Simon Hawke, *The Kyber Connection*, 1986
    Timewars 6

Fritz Leiber, *The Big Time*, 1961
Fritz Leiber, *The Change War*, 1978
H. Beam Piper, *Lord Kalvan of Otherwhen*, 1965

3318

KATE NOVAK
JEFF GRUBB, Co-Author

Masquerades
(Lake Geneva, Wisconsin: TSR, 1995)

Story type: Fantasy (Quest; Political)
Series: Forgotten Realms
Major character(s): Alias, Hero, Genetically Altered Being; Dragonbait Champion, Religious (paladin), Alien (Saurial); Jamal, Actress
Time period(s): Indeterminate
Locale(s): Westgate, Fictional City

Summary: In Westgate on personal business, Alias and Dragonbait get into trouble with the Night Masks' agents in the city. They gather a group of old and new allies, but even this help may not prevail against murder, magic, and treachery.

Other books you might like:
Steven Brust, *Jhereg*, 1983
Glen Cook, *Sweet Silver Blues*, 1987
Simon R. Green, *Hawk & Fisher*, 1990
Jeff Grubb, *Azure Bonds*, 1988
　　Kate Novak, co-author
Fritz Leiber, *Ill Met in Lankhmar*, 1995
Will Shetterly, *Liavek*, 1985
　　Emma Bull, co-editor

3319

KATE NOVAK
JEFF GRUBB, Co-Author

Song of the Saurials
(Lake Geneva, Wisconsin: TSR, 1991)

Story type: Fantasy (Magic Conflict; Adventure)
Series: Forgotten Realms: The Finder's Stone Trilogy
Major character(s): Finder "Nameless" Wyvernspur, Musician, Magician; Olive Ruskettle, Mythical Creature (halfling); Dragonbait Champion, Alien (Saurian), Warrior (paladin)
Time period(s): Indeterminate
Locale(s): The Realms, Mythical Place; Mourngrim Castle Shadowdale, Planet—Imaginary

Summary: The trial of the Nameless Bard was interrupted by a minion of Moander the Darkbringer, a god who Nameless and his companions believed they had killed on their plane. They fight to once again free the land from the evil god, and to free the Saurials enslaved by the god. A game tie-in novel.

Other books you might like:
C.J. Cherryh, *The Paladin*, 1988
Sheila Gilluly, *The Boy From the Burren*, 1990
Guy Gavriel Kay, *Tigana*, 1990
Mercedes Lackey, *Magic's Price*, 1990

Elizabeth Moon, *Surrender None: The Legacy of Gird*, 1990
Andrea Shettle, *Flute Song Magic*, 1990
Andrew Whitmore, *The Fortress of Eternity*, 1990
Tad Williams, *Stone of Farewell*, 1990

3320

PHILIP NUTMAN

Wet Work
(New York: Jove, 1993)

Story type: Horror (Reanimated Dead)
Major character(s): Dominic Corvino, Spy (CIA agent); Ryan Del Valle, Spy (CIA section chief); Nick Packard, Police Officer
Time period(s): 1990s (1995)
Locale(s): Washington, District of Columbia; New York, New York

Summary: The author's first novel expands his 1989 story of the same name, about the influence of the comet Saracen during its passage by Earth, resurrecting the newly dead as flesh-eating zombies. At the core of the novel is a vicious satire on the decline of American culture.

Other books you might like:
George Romero, *Dawn of the Dead*, 1978
John Skipp, *Book of the Dead*, 1989
　　Craig Spector, co-editor
John Skipp, *Still Dead: Book of the Dead 2*, 1992

3321

JODY LYNN NYE, Editor

Don't Forget Your Spacesuit, Dear
(New York: Baen, 1996)

Story type: Science Fiction (Anthology)
Major character(s): Mother, Parent
Time period(s): Indeterminate Future
Locale(s): Earth; Outer Space

Summary: Contains 19 original stories, many humorous, in appreciation of motherly advice. Authors include Robert Asprin, Diane Duane, George Alec Effinger, Esther M. Friesner, Ellen Guon, Morgan Llywelyn, Anne McCaffrey, Elizabeth Moon, Jody Lynn Nye, Elizabeth Ann Scarborough, and Josepha Sherman.

Other books you might like:
Marjorie Agosin, *The Secret Weavers: Stories of the Fantastic by Latin American Women*, 1991
　　editor
Greg Bear, *New Legends*, 1995
　　Martin H. Greenberg, co-editor
Esther Friesner, *Alien Pregnant by Elvis*, 1994
　　Martin H. Greenberg, co-editor
Don Sakers, *Carmen Miranda's Ghost Is Haunting Space Station Three*, 1990
　　editor
Susanna J. Sturgis, *Magic Realism by Women: Dreams in a Minor Key*, 1991
　　editor

3322

JODY LYNN NYE

Higher Mythology

(New York: Warner Questar, 1993)

Story type: Fantasy (Quest; Light Fantasy)
Series: Keith Doyle
Major character(s): Keith Doyle, Student; Holl, Mythical Creature (elf)
Time period(s): 1990s
Locale(s): Midwestern University, Illinois; Hollow Tree Farm, Illinois

Summary: When hunters kidnap Holl's baby daughter and a young faery, Keith utilizes his new interest in hot air ballooning to help organize sprites into an aerial spy network to seek out the abductors.

Other books you might like:
Orson Scott Card, *Lost Boys*, 1992
Rose Estes, *Troll-Taken*, 1993
Anne McCaffrey, *Crisis on Doona*, 1992
    Jody Lynn Nye, co-author
Anne McCaffrey, *The Death of Sleep*, 1990
    Jody Lynn Nye, co-author
Viido Polikarpus, *Down Town*, 1985
    Tappan King, co-author

3323

JODY LYNN NYE

The Magic Touch

(New York: Warner Aspect, 1996)

Story type: Fantasy (Young Adult; Urban)
Major character(s): Raymond E. Crandall Jr., Teenager, Apprentice (fairy godfather); Rose Feinstein, Mythical Creature (fairy godmother), Teacher; Albert Froister, Mythical Creature (djin), Businessman
Time period(s): 1990s
Locale(s): United States; Enlightenment, Mythical Place (light fixture warehouse)

Summary: At his grandmother's bidding, Ray Crandall finds himself involved in her favorite charity, the Fairy Godmother's Union. Apprenticed to Mrs. Rose Feinstein, Ray begins to learn the proper use of magic and to enjoy using his talents to help troubled children. Ray's studies are interrupted when his best friend joins a tough street gang whose members exhibit magical, but menacing, powers of their own, and use them to spread fear through the neighborhood streets.

Other books you might like:
Piers Anthony, *Demons Don't Dream*, 1993
Gael Baudino, *Strands of Sunlight*, 1994
Charles de Lint, *Our Lady of the Harbour*, 1991
Robin Morgan, *The Mer-Child: A Legend for Children and Other Adults*, 1991
Terry Pratchett, *Eric*, 1995
Elizabeth Ann Scarborough, *The Godmother's Apprentice*, 1995
Harry Turtledove, *The Case of the Toxic Spell Dump*, 1993

3324

JODY LYNN NYE

Medicine Show

(New York: Ace, 1994)

Story type: Science Fiction (Medical; Adventure)
Major character(s): Shona Taylor, Doctor, Space Explorer; Chirwl, Alien (ottle), Health Care Professional
Time period(s): Indeterminate Future
Locale(s): Proxt, Planet—Imaginary; Sibyl, Spaceship

Summary: Returning to Chirwl's home planet, Dr. Shona Taylor discovers both ottle and human populations afflicted by an unnatural malady which causes rapid aging. *Sibyl*'s crew must find a cure or face the immediate prospect of universal death.

Other books you might like:
Nicola Griffith, *Ammonite*, 1993
Murray Leinster, *The Med Series*, 1983
Frederik Pohl, *Stopping at Slowyear*, 1991
James H. Schmitz, *The Demon Breed*, 1968
James White, *Hospital Station*, 1962

3325

JODY LYNN NYE

Mythology 101

(New York: Warner, 1990)

Story type: Fantasy (Contemporary)
Series: Keith Doyle
Major character(s): Marcy Collier, Student—College; Keith Doyle, Student—College
Time period(s): 1980s
Locale(s): United States

Summary: Keith is leading the effort to have the old university library torn down. However, Marcy, the girl of his dreams, is fighting him every step of the way, to protect the elves who make their home in the old library.

Other books you might like:
Gael Baudino, *Duel of Dragons*, 1989
Emma Bull, *War for the Oaks*,
Alan Dean Foster, *Metrognome*, 1990
Tanya Huff, *Gate of Darkness, Circle of Light*, 1989
Gene Wolfe, *Castleview*, 1990

3326

JODY LYNN NYE

Mythology Abroad

(New York: Warner Questar, 1991)

Story type: Fantasy (Contemporary)
Series: Keith Doyle
Major character(s): Keith Doyle, Student, Traveller; Holl, Mythical Creature (elf); Master, Magician, Mythical Creature (elf)
Time period(s): 1980s
Locale(s): Scotland

Summary: In this sequel to *Mythology 101*, Keith travels to Scotland for Midwestern University course credit accompanied by Holl who has volunteered to re-establish contact with the Fair Folk. Suspicious government agents do not prove as problematic as does Keith's unauthorized investigation which yields a Bodach's curse. Holl's call for help brings the Master who finds old friends and family.

Other books you might like:
Emma Bull, *War for the Oaks*, 1987
Kenneth C. Flint, *Cromm*, 1990
Andre Norton, *The Elvenbane*, 1991
   Mercedes Lackey, co-author
Will Shetterly, *Elsewhere*, 1991
Margaret Weis, *Fire Sea*, 1991
   Tracy Hickman, co-author
Terri Windling, *Life on the Border*, 1991
   editor

`3327`

JODY LYNN NYE

The Ship Errant

(New York: Baen, 1996)

Story type: Science Fiction (First Contact; Alternate Intelligence)
Series: Ship Who Sang
Major character(s): Carialle, Cyborg; Keff, Pilot (spacechip), Spaceman; Narrow Leg, Scientist, Alien (Cridi)
Time period(s): Indeterminate Future
Locale(s): Cridi, Planet—Imaginary; Thelerie, Planet—Imaginary; Outer Space

Summary: Carialle and Keff carry a team of globe-frogs from Ozran to Cridi, their ancestral home. The two forge an alliance between the Central Worlds and Cridi, jeopardized when a second ship departs for Cridi piloted by the erratic Carialle. When pirate aliens from a neighboring star system led by renegade humans destroy that ship, Carialle, Keff, and a Cridi ship investigate.

Other books you might like:
John Barnes, *A Million Open Doors*, 1992
John Brunner, *A Maze of Stars*, 1991
Margaret Davis, *Minds Apart*, 1994
Paula E. Downing, *A Whisper of Time*, 1994
Lee Killough, *Liberty's World*, 1985
Anne McCaffrey, *The Ship Who Sang*, 1969
Anne McCaffrey, *The Ship Who Won*, 1994
   Jody Lynn Nye, co-author
Charles Sheffield, *Trader's World*, 1988

`3328`

JODY LYNN NYE

Taylor's Ark

(New York: Ace, 1993)

Story type: Science Fiction (Medical; Adventure)
Major character(s): Shona Taylor, Doctor, Space Explorer; Jachin Verdadero, Administrator (Galactic Laboratory Corp.); Manny Mitchell, Administrator (Galactic Laboratory Corp.)
Time period(s): Indeterminate Future
Locale(s): Mars; *Sibyl*, Spaceship; Karela, Planet—Imaginary

Summary: A specialist in environmental medicine, Shona has been working for the government on the trip to and initial three month check-out of new colonies. Switching employers after miscarrying her baby, Shona travels with her vaccine dog, sniffer cat, rabbits, mice and an intelligent alien to provide medical services. Unfortunately she finds disaster wherever she goes.

Other books you might like:
Nicola Griffith, *Ammonite*, 1993
Janet Kagan, *Mirabile*, 1991
Murray Leinster, *The Med Series*, 1983
Anne McCaffrey, *Crisis on Doona*, 1992
   Jody Lynn Nye, co-author
Anne McCaffrey, *The Death of Sleep*, 1990
   Jody Lynn Nye, co-author
Vonda N. McIntyre, *Dreamsnake*, 1978
Frederik Pohl, *Stopping at Slowyear*, 1991
Robert Silverberg, *The Face of the Waters*, 1991
Michael Swanwick, *Stations of the Tide*, 1990
James White, *The Genocidal Healer*, 1991

`3329`

JOYCE CAROL OATES, Editor

American Gothic Tales

(New York: Penguin/Plume, 1996)

Story type: Horror (Anthology)

Summary: A renowned writer of mainstream fiction focused on the dark side of American experience assembles 46 classic and contemporary tales in the Gothic tradition by American writers. Classic stories include Edgar Allan Poe's "The Black Cat," narrated by a psychopathic murderer; Charlotte Perkins Gilman's "The Yellow Wallpaper," in which a woman becomes obsessed with a wallpaper pattern that reflects her madness; and H.P. Lovecraft's "The Outsider," a homage to Poe about a man who escapes from an underground prison and the horrifying revelation of his true identity. Among the contemporary tales are Raymond Carver's "Little Things," a sardonic short about a custody battle; Thomas Ligotti's "The Last Feast of Harlequin," in which a man discovers things he would rather not know about himself while attending a festival with pagan overtones; and Nicholson Baker's "Subsoil," a mock gothic story in which potatoes play the heavy. Oates contributes an introduction surveying the American Gothic tale.

Other books you might like:
Chris Baldick, *The Oxford Book of Gothic Tales*, 1992
   editor
Peter Haining, *Gothic Tales of Terror, Volume II*, 1972
   editor
Bradford Morrow, *The New Gothic*, 1991
   Patrick McGrath, co-editor
Alfred Nedixen, *Haunted Women*, 1985
   editor

3330

JOYCE CAROL OATES

Demon and Other Tales

(West Warwick, Rhode Island: Necronomicon Press, 1996)

Story type: Horror (Collection)

Summary: These seven short-short fictions, two original to the volume, deploy images of death in their inquiries into personal identity. In "The Omen," the narrator's discovery of the body of a miniscule man washed up on the shore shakes her belief in objective reality. "An Urban Paradox" is set in a future where a character tries to makes sense of sinister vans that randomly abduct people. A female character in "The Temple" turns the bones of an infant she unearths in her garden into a shrine. The title story tells of a hideous child whose abuse by adults turns him into a sociopath. "Posthumous" is a murder story with an uncanny twist suggested by its title.

Other books you might like:
Angela Carter, *The Bloody Chamber*, 1979
Rachel Ingalls, *The End of Tragedy*, 1987
Shirley Jackson, *The Magic of Shirley Jackson*, 1966
Lisa Tuttle, *Memories of the Body*, 1992

3331

JOYCE CAROL OATES
BARRY MOSER, Illustrator

First Love: A Gothic Tale

(Hopewell, New Jersey: Ecco Press, 1996)

Story type: Horror (Child-in-Peril)
Major character(s): Josephine Carolyn "Josie" S———
, Child (11-year-old); Jared Burkhardt Jr., Student (seminarian); Delia S———, Real Estate Agent
Time period(s): 1990s
Locale(s): Ransomville, New York

Summary: When Josie and her destitute mother move to their great aunt's home in upstate New York, the young girl is victimized sexually and psychologically by her cousin Jared, an obsessive young man whose pedophilic tendencies have driven him from the seminary.

Other books you might like:
Angela Carter, *The Magic Toyshop*, 1967
Davis Grubb, *The Night of the Hunter*, 1953
A.M. Homes, *The End of Alice*, 1996
Susan Palwick, *Flying in Place*, 1992

3332

JOYCE CAROL OATES

Haunted: Tales of the Grotesque

(New York: Dutton, 1994)

Story type: Horror (Collection)

Summary: These 16 stories bring together most of this prolific mainstream writer's recent macabre fiction. "Haunted,"

"The Doll," and "Phase Change" all deal with bizarre experiences which reveal attitudes and suppressed memories that have shaped characters' lives. "The White Cat," "The Model," "Extenuating Circumstances," and "The Guilty Party" tell of people who avenge themselves against their spouses through pets and children. "Don't You Trust Me," "Poor Bibi," and "Martyrdom" use grotesque characters and situations as heavy-handed metaphors for human relationships. And the masterful "Accursed Inhabitants of the House of Bly" retells the events of Henry James' *Turn of the Screw* from the points of view of its ghostly nemeses. The author supplies an explanatory afterword defining "the grotesque."

Other books you might like:
Fred Chappell, *More Shapes than One*, 1992
Alison Lurie, *Women and Ghosts*, 1994
Peter Taylor, *The Oracle at Stoneleigh Court*, 1993

3333

JOYCE CAROL OATES

Zombie

(New York: Dutton, 1995)

Story type: Horror (Psychological Suspense)
Major character(s): Quentin P, Student
Time period(s): 1990s (1995)
Locale(s): Detroit, Michigan (in the suburbs)

Summary: Presented as a series of diary entries kept by a sometime engineering student at Mount Vernon State College, this short novel recounts the narrator's seamy past as a paroled sex offender, and his monstrous present as someone who lures victims to his dwelling and performs crude lobotomies on them in an effort to turn them into obedient zombies. Loosely based on the real-life atrocities of Jeffrey Dahmer, this grim tale presents its narrator's dehumanizing of his victim as symbolic of the dehumanization of contemporary life.

Other books you might like:
Robert Bloch, *Psycho*, 1959
Ramsey Campbell, *The Face That Must Die*, 1979
Dennis Cooper, *Frisk*, 1992
Brett Easton Ellis, *American Psycho*, 1991
John Fowles, *The Collector*, 1963
Patrick McGrath, *Spider*, 1990

3334

CHARLES OBERNDORF

Foragers

(New York: Bantam Spectra, 1996)

Story type: Science Fiction (First Contact; Adventure)
Major character(s): Pauline Dikobe, Scholar (ethnographer), Spacewoman; Esoch al-Schouki, Military Personnel; Lightfoot Watcher, Alien (slazan)
Time period(s): Indeterminate Future
Locale(s): Tienah, Planet—Imaginary

Summary: Pauline Dikobe vanishes while studying a primitive society of slazans, a race at war with humans, hoping to learn how to defeat their technologically sophisticated cousins. Sent to investigate, Lieutenant Esoch al-Schouki must make his way to Pauline's camp alone through the slazan jungle when his shuttle probe fails.

Other books you might like:
Eleanor Arnason, *Ring of Swords*, 1993
Nicola Griffith, *Ammonite*, 1993
Elizabeth Moon, *Remnant Population*, 1996
Larry Niven, *The Mote in God's Eye*, 1974
    Jerry Pournelle, co-author
Joan Slonczewski, *A Door into Ocean*, 1986

3335

CHARLES OBERNDORF

Sheltered Lives

(New York: Bantam Spectra, 1992)

Story type: Science Fiction (Dystopian; Political)
Major character(s): Anna Elizabeth Baxter, Widow(er), Heiress; Edward Winslow Lang, Government Official, Businessman; Rod Lawrence, Prostitute
Time period(s): 2020s
Locale(s): Cleveland, Ohio

Summary: In the closely monitored society of the Construct, security and safety seem assured until Rod, hired as a companion by Anna after her lover commits suicide, realizes that what the computer saves may not make his life secure. Disaster may follow Anna's potential involvement with revolutionaries who oppose the governmental policy of interring victims of the latest fatal sexually transmitted disease. Author's first novel.

Other books you might like:
Jeffrey A. Carver, *The Rapture Effect*, 1987
Mary Gentle, *Golden Witchbreed*, 1984
Larry Niven, *Achilles' Choice*, 1991
    Steven Barnes, co-author
George Orwell, *Nineteen Eighty-Four*, 1949
Edgar Pangborn, *A Mirror for Observers*, 1954

3336

MAXINE O'CALLAGHAN

Dark Time

(New York: Diamond, 1992)

Story type: Horror (Science Fiction)
Major character(s): Corey Carpenter, Teenager; Gayle Carpenter, Clerk (Corey's mother); Amy Delgato, Teenager
Time period(s): 1990s (1992)
Locale(s): Longview, Washington

Summary: While adventuring in the woods one day, Corey Carpenter is entrusted with a tool from a dying extraterrestrial who calls himself "he who hunts with weapons of light." Thereafter, it becomes Corey's responsibility to fight the extraterrestrial wreaking havoc on the nearby town who was the other being's quarry.

Other books you might like:
Dean R. Koontz, *The Bad Place*, 1990
Dean R. Koontz, *Strangers*, 1986

3337

MEL ODOM

F.R.E.E.Lancers

(Lake Geneva, Wisconsin: TSR, 1995)

Story type: Science Fiction (Cyberpunk; Adventure)
Major character(s): Lee Won Underhill, Administrator (FREELancers)
Time period(s): 2020s (2023)
Locale(s): Chicago, Illinois; Rinji 8, Space Station; Detroit, Michigan

Summary: In the balkanized, former United States, a powerful Japanese concern hires the FREELancers to find stolen industrial secrets. As the recovery increases in difficulty, Lee Won Underhill discovers that an information transfer might change the worldwide balance of power. Game tie-in.

Other books you might like:
Lois McMaster Bujold, *Brothers in Arms*, 1988
Robert N. Charrette, *Never Deal with a Dragon*, 1990
Nick Pollotta, *Bureau 13*, 1991
Neal Stephenson, *Snow Crash*, 1992
Walter Jon Williams, *Hardwired*, 1986
Dave Wolverton, *On My Way to Paradise*, 1989

3338

MEL ODOM

Lethal Interface

(New York: Roc, 1992)

Story type: Science Fiction (Cyberpunk; Mystery)
Major character(s): Mick Traven, Detective—Police (vice); Earl Brandsetter, Murderer, Computer Expert
Time period(s): 21st century
Locale(s): Dallas, Texas

Summary: Despite pressure and obfuscation from the Japanese megacorp Nagamuchi, Mick Traven pursues the lethal trail of a sexual psychopath into the highest ranks of the Nagamuchi where he discovers a killer who moves invisibly through the computer network to accomplish his sick missions.

Other books you might like:
Philip K. Dick, *Blade Runner*, 1982
George Alec Effinger, *When Gravity Fails*, 1987
Victor Milan, *The Cybernetic Samurai*, 1986
Neal Stephenson, *Snow Crash*, 1992
John E. Stith, *Redshift Rendezvous*, 1990
Walter Jon Williams, *Days of Atonement*, 1991
Walter Jon Williams, *Voice of the Whirlwind*, 1987
Dave Wolverton, *On My Way to Paradise*, 1989

3339

KEVIN O'DONNELL JR.

Fire on the Border

(New York: Roc, 1990)

Story type: Science Fiction (Military)
Major character(s): Kajiwara Hiroshi, Military Personnel; Darcy Lee, Military Personnel; Daitaku, Clone
Time period(s): 24th century (2351)
Locale(s): Earth

Summary: The alien Wayholder Empire has discovered that combat-trained troops have a much higher survival rate in their war with the Korrin. They decide to use the human colony worlds as the final step of basic training, threatening humanity with extinction if they defend the planets. Kajiwara, Darcy and Daitaku combine resources to compel the Wayholders to compromise.

Other books you might like:
C.J. Cherryh, *Rimrunners*, 1990
Gordon R. Dickson, *Soldier, Ask Not*, 1967
David Drake, *Hammer's Slammers*, 1979
Joe Haldeman, *The Forever War*, 1975
Keith Laumer, *The Complete Bolo*, 1990

3340

NICK O'DONOHOE

The Healing of Crossroads

(New York: Ace, 1996)

Story type: Fantasy (Alternate World; Adventure)
Series: Crossroads
Major character(s): BJ Vaughan, Veterinarian; Charles "Sugar" Franklin Dobbs, Professor; The Griffin, Mythical Creature
Time period(s): 1990s; Indeterminate
Locale(s): Kendrick, Virginia; Crossroads, Fictional Country

Summary: With the help of the Book of Strangeways, BJ travels through real and imagined realms. When she discovers that mythical creatures suffer when away from Crossroads, BJ must find a way to entice them to return to Crossroads for treatment and recovery.

Other books you might like:
Charles de Lint, *Memory and Dream*, 1994
Janet Kagan, *Mirabile*, 1994
Larry Niven, *The Flight of the Horse*, 1973
Jody Lynn Nye, *Medicine Show*, 1994
Jody Lynn Nye, *Taylor's Ark*, 1993
James White, *Sector General*, 1983

3341

NICK O'DONOHOE

The Magic and the Healing

(New York: Ace, 1994)

Story type: Fantasy (Alternate World; Adventure)
Series: Crossroads

Major character(s): BJ Vaughan, Veterinarian; Charles "Sugar" Franklin Dobbs, Professor, Veterinarian; Lee Anne Harrison, Student, Veterinarian
Time period(s): 1990s; Indeterminate
Locale(s): Kendrick, Virginia; Crossroads, Fictional Country

Summary: When a failed class and her mother's death from Huntington's chorea nearly drive BJ from veterinary studies, Sugar gives BJ an unusual horn to research along with a guide to unbiological species. BJ plans a repair technique which she utilizes on a most unusual field trip to Crossroads where she mends a unicorn's horn. Travel in Crossroads brings the students practice in treating unusual species and offers BJ the hope of a cure for her potential genetic problems.

Other books you might like:
Algis Budrys, *Hard Landing*, 1993
Janet Kagan, *Mirabile*, 1991
Jody Lynn Nye, *Medicine Show*, 1994
Jody Lynn Nye, *Taylor's Ark*, 1993
Mary Alexander Walker, *The Scathach and the Maeve's Daughter*, 1990
James White, *Hospital Station*, 1962

3342

NICK O'DONOHOE

Too, Too Solid Flesh

(Lake Geneva, WI: TSR, 1989)

Story type: Science Fiction (Mystery)
Major character(s): Hamlet, Android, Actor; Horatio, Actor
Time period(s): Indeterminate Future
Locale(s): Earth

Summary: In the last live theater on Earth, androids perform *Hamlet* in front of an audience made up largely of holographic images. Moreover the androids don't simply play their characters; they are the characters, twenty-four hours a day. When the human creator of the androids is murdered, Hamlet sets out to discover the identity of the murderer. He is aided by the human being who, unbeknownst to anyone else, has taken on the role of Horatio. This is O'Donohoe's first science fiction novel.

Other books you might like:
Isaac Asimov, *Robot Dreams*, 1986
John Brunner, *The Productions of Time*, 1967
Frederik Pohl, *Narabedla, Ltd.*, 1988
Jack Vance, *Showboat World*, 1975
Jack Vance, *Space Opera*, 1965

3343

NICK O'DONOHOE

Under the Healing Sign

(New York: Ace, 1995)

Story type: Fantasy (Alternate World; Adventure)
Series: Crossroads
Major character(s): BJ Vaughan, Veterinarian; Polyta, Mythical Creature (hippoi), Leader; Lee Anne Harrison, Student, Veterinarian

Time period(s): 1990s; Indeterminate
Locale(s): Kendrick, Virginia; Crossroads, Fictional Country

Summary: BJ hopes to improve life in Crossroads through healing and education in science, while others promote discord. Events propel BJ and her friends into a vital role as someone attempts to seal closed the path to Crossroads.

Other books you might like:
Janet Kagan, *Mirabile*, 1991
Larry Niven, *The Flight of the Horse*, 1973
Jody Lynn Nye, *Medicine Show*, 1994
Jody Lynn Nye, *Taylor's Ark*, 1993

3344

JOY OESTREICHER, Editor
RICHARD SINGER, Co-Editor

Air Fish

(Concord, California: Catseye Press, 1993)

Story type: Horror (Anthology)

Summary: The editors have assembled 50 stories, poems, prose fragments, and works in progress, both original and reprint, from some of the more interesting and challenging writers working in the science fiction, fantasy, and horror small press today. Included are Thom Metzger's view of a future in which women enslave men, "Downbound Train"; John Shirley's hallucinogenic take on a victim of self-help therapy, "Sweet Armageddon"; D.F. Lewis's confusion of objective and subjective perceptions in "Milk's Mirror"; and Adam Troy-Castro's disturbing child's-eye view of a dysfunctional family, "The House of Nails." The book is nicely illustrated by a variety of small press artists.

Other books you might like:
Robert Morrish, *Quick Chills*, 1991
   Peter Enfantino, co-editor
Bob Morrish, *Quick Chills II*, 1992
   Peter Enfantino, co-editor
Brian Smart, *Best of the Midwest's Science Fiction, Fantasy and Horror, Volume I*, 1992
   editor
Brian Smart, *Best of the Midwest's Science Fiction, Fantasy and Horror, Volume II*, 1993
   editor

3345

JOY OESTREICHER, Editor

Alpha Gallery

(Cupertino, California: SPWAO, 1991)

Story type: Horror (Anthology)

Summary: Sixty-one selections from the fantasy, horror and science fiction small presses, including poetry, prose and artwork by Kathe Koja, Steve Rasnic Tem, Bentley Little, Elizabeth Massie, Bruce Boston and numerous others.

Other books you might like:
Peter Enfantino, *Quick Chills*, 1990
George Hatch, *Guignoir and Other Furies*, 1991

Jessica Amanda Salmonson, *Tales by Moonlight II*, 1989
David B. Silva, *The Best of the Horror Show*, 1987
J.N. Williamson, *Masques III*, 1989

3346

ANDREW J. OFFUTT

Deathknight

(New York: Ace, 1990)

Story type: Fantasy (Adventure)
Major character(s): Falc of Risskor, Knight
Time period(s): Indeterminate
Locale(s): The City-States of Sij, Fictional Country

Summary: The Sons of Ashah are Knights of the Order Most Old and are honor-sworn to preserve the peace of the city-states of Sij. When someone does the unthinkable and starts killing the Knights of the Order, one by one, it is Falc of Risskor, a Son of Ashad who must bring to justice the slayer, or himself be slain.

Other books you might like:
Glen Cook, *The Black Company*, 1984
Gordon R. Dickson, *Jamie the Red*, 1984
Janet Morris, *Tempus Bound*, 1989
   Chris Morris, co-author
Jerry Pournelle, *Janissaries*, 1979
Gene Wolfe, *The Shadow of the Torturer*, 1980
Gene Wolfe, *Soldier of Arete*, 1989

3347

ANDREW J. OFFUTT

The Shadow of Sorcery

(New York: Ace, 1993)

Story type: Fantasy (Magic Conflict; Quest)
Series: Thieves' World
Major character(s): Shadowspawn, Thief, Adventurer; Hanse, Adventurer, Warrior
Time period(s): Indeterminate
Locale(s): Firaqua, Fictional City

Summary: To free Firaqua from the rule of an evil sorcerer and save the life of a woman, Shadowspawn ventures into a deadly labyrinth in search of the fabled Rings of Senek.

Other books you might like:
Robert Asprin, *Thieves' World*, 1979
   editor
David Drake, *Dagger*, 1988
Janet Morris, *Beyond the Veil*, 1985
Janet Morris, *Beyond Wizardwall*, 1986
Janet Morris, *City at the Edge of Time*, 1988
   Chris Morris, co-author
Janet Morris, *Tempus*, 1987

3348

MARTIN O'GRIOFA
SHEILA KERN, Illustrator

Irish Tales of the Supernatural
(New York: Sterling/Main Street, 1996)

Story type: Horror (Anthology)
Locale(s): Ireland

Summary: This anthology aimed at younger readers collects tales of horror and fantasy set in Ireland by 12 authors whose work was published primarily in the 19th century. Joseph Sheridan LeFanu is represented by two stories, ''The White Cat of Drumgunniol,'' which features a spectral cat, and ''Sir Dominick's Bargain,'' about a man who sells his soul to the devil. ''Legend of Bottle Hill'' by Thomas Crofton Croker and ''Hairy Rouchy'' by Patricia Kennedy are both humorous fantasies in the Irish folk tradition. Seamus MacManus's ''The Bewitched Fiddle'' tells of a born-again Christian who discovers his fiddle is still imbued with the mischief of his old days. Jeremiah Curtin's ''St. Martin's Eve'' is about the sad fate that befalls a family who neglects to pay their proper respects to a household saint on his feast day.

Other books you might like:
Peter Haining, *Wild Night Company*, 1970
  editor
Joseph Hone, *Irish Ghost Stories*, 1979
  editor
Jim McGarry, *Irish Tales of Terror*, 1971
  editor
Daniel O'Keefe, *The Book of Famous Irish Ghost Stories*, 1986
  editor
H.M. Tichenor, *Irish Fairy Tales*, 1923
  editor
Peter Tremayne, *The Irish Masters of Fantasy*, 1979
  editor

3349

BEN OHLANDER
DAVID DRAKE, Co-Author

Enemy of My Enemy
(New York: Baen, 1995)

Story type: Science Fiction (Adventure; Military)
Series: Terra Nova
Major character(s): Ward Tuchman, Laird, Avenger; Mona, Avenger, Sidekick; Carlo Theisiger, Mercenary
Time period(s): Indeterminate Future
Locale(s): New Hope, Planet—Imaginary

Summary: After the destruction of his home and family in an ambush by the Wing clan, Ward Tuchman vows revenge. He slowly gathers allies while simultaneously evading further assassination attempts by his enemies.

Other books you might like:
David Drake, *Northworld*, 1990
David Drake, *Justice*, 1992
  Northworld 3

David Drake, *Vengeance*, 1991
  Northworld 2
Joe Haldeman, *The Forever War*, 1975
Robert A. Heinlein, *Starship Troopers*, 1959
John Steakley, *Armor*, 1984

3350

CLAUDIA O'KEEFE

Black Snow Days
(New York: Ace Books, 1990)

Story type: Science Fiction (Post-Nuclear Holocaust)
Major character(s): Eric Pope, Cyborg; Vivian, Spirit (Doppleganger)
Time period(s): 21st century (2046)
Locale(s): United States

Summary: Eric Pope is in a serious accident and lapses into a coma. He awakes twelve years later to a post-nuclear holocaust world whose survivors are all seemingly half-mad. Barely maintaining his own sanity, Eric discovers that he's the victim of a bizarre experiment. His body has been enhanced through reconstructive surgery, his brain has been tinkered with, and, strangely enough, there appears to be two of him. Living within him now is Vivian, his own female self. Although only he can see her, his lunatic doctors insist that she's entirely real. Then the doctors tell him the terrifying reason why he's been remade into something more than human.

Other books you might like:
Philip K. Dick, *The Penultimate Truth*, 1964
Richard Kadrey, *Metrophage*, 1988
Frederik Pohl, *Man Plus*, 1976
Mordecai Roshwald, *Level 7*, 1959

3351

CLAUDIA O'KEEFE, Editor

Ghosttide
(Sherman Oaks, California: Revenant Press, 1993)

Story type: Horror (Anthology)

Summary: This book collects 15 stories of subtle horror, 12 original to the book. Among the best are Hugh B. Cave's ''The Mountains of Time,'' concerned with ghostly salvation in the ruins of a Jamaican coffee plantation; Susan Palwick's ''Force of Habit,'' about a workaholic whose work ethic outlives his body; and William Browning Spencer's ''Irrational Fears,'' in which victims of a bizarre self-help therapy for recovering addicts develop the power to induce hallucinations in others. Also included is Robert Bloch's classic *Weird Tales* story, ''Iron Mask,'' which updates the medieval legend of a man unjustly imprisoned in an iron mask to World War II.

Other books you might like:
Charles L. Grant, *Final Shadows*, 1991
  editor
Thomas F. Monteleone, *Borderlands 3*, 1993
  editor

Chris Morgan, *Dark Fantasies*, 1989
  editor
Paul F. Olson, *Post Mortem: New Tales of Ghostly Horror*, 1989
  David B. Silva, co-editor

3352

BEN OKRI

The Famished Road
(New York: Doubleday, 1992)

Story type: Fantasy (Contemporary; Legend)
Major character(s): Azaro, Child, Psychic; Madame Koto, Saloon Keeper/Owner
Time period(s): 1960s
Locale(s): Africa

Summary: Azaro never severs his connection to the spirit world at birth, allowing him to view the mortal realm with perspective rooted in the realm of souls. Azaro brings augmented understanding to the child's vision of a family struggling to survive in the midst of sometimes violent change within a poverty-struck African ghetto. 1991 winner of the prestigious Booker Prize for Fiction in Britain.

Other books you might like:
Roger D. Abrahams, *Afro-American Folk Tales*, 1985
Maya Kaathryn Bohnhoff, *The Meri*, 1992
Alan Dean Foster, *Into the Out Of*, 1986
Edward Myers, *The Mountain Made of Light*, 1992
Paul Radin, *African Folktales*, 1985
  editor
Mike Resnick, *Bwana-Bully*, 1991
Mike Resnick, *Future Earths: Under African Skies*, 1993
Elizabeth Ann Scarborough, *Last Refuge*, 1992
Lucius Shepard, *Kalimantan*, 1992
Gerald Vizenor, *Dead Voices: Natural Agonies in the Real World*, 1992

3353

BEN OKRI

Songs of Enchantment
(New York: Doubleday, 1993)

Story type: Fantasy (Contemporary; Legend)
Major character(s): Azaro, Child, Psychic; Madame Koto, Saloon Keeper/Owner, Political Figure; Dad, Parent, Political Figure
Time period(s): 1960s
Locale(s): Africa; Madame Koto's Bar, Mythical Place

Summary: Due to his connection to the spirit realm, distractions from tormenting spirits drive Azaro away from school. Transformations at Madame Koto's bar and in Azaro's family disrupt the political hopes of Azaro's father as Azaro's mother affiliates with Madame Koto's ascendant cult. Meanwhile, mythical thought-forms of primal creation appear in the turbulent ghetto.

Other books you might like:
Louis de Bernieres, *Senor Vivo and the Coca Lord*, 1992

Louis de Bernieres, *The War of Don Emmanuel's Nether Parts*, 1992
Elizabeth Ann Scarborough, *Last Refuge*, 1992
Gerald Vizenor, *Dead Voices: Natural Agonies in the Real World*, 1992

3354

SUSAN TORIAN OLAN

The Earth Remembers
(Lake Geneva, WI: TSR, 1990)

Story type: Science Fiction (Post-Holocaust)
Major character(s): Cimarron Langtry, Wanderer
Time period(s): Indeterminate Future
Locale(s): Texas (What was once the Texas-Mexico border); Mexico

Summary: Langtry, a subterranean race of radiation mutants, and a tribe of Comanches join forces to destroy the oppressive post-nuclear holocaust government of Tesharka. Olan's first novel.

Other books you might like:
David Brin, *The Postman*, 1985
Algis Budrys, *Some Will Not Die*, 1954
Sterling E. Lanier, *Hiero's Journey*, 1973
Walter M. Miller Jr., *A Canticle for Leibowitz*, 1960

3355

PATRICK O'LEARY

Door Number Three
(New York: Tor, 1995)

Story type: Science Fiction (Time Travel; Horror)
Major character(s): John Donnelly, Psychologist, Time Traveller; Laura Johnson, Patient, Time Traveller; Saul Lowe, Inventor, Time Traveller
Time period(s): 1990s
Locale(s): Detroit, Michigan

Summary: Laura Johnson, a new therapy patient, intrigues John Donnelly when she claims the alien Holock kidnapped her and will let her remain on Earth if she can convince one person of this. First novel.

Other books you might like:
Jonathan Carroll, *Bones of the Moon*, 1987
Jonathan Carroll, *From the Teeth of Angels*, 1994
Nancy Kress, *Beggars in Spain*, 1993
Christopher Pike, *The Eternal Enemy*, 1993
Roger Zelazny, *The Dream Master*, 1966

3356

PAUL F. OLSON, Editor
DAVID B. SILVA, Co-Editor

Dead End: City Limits
(New York: St. Martin's, 1991)

Story type: Horror (Anthology)

Summary: Seventeen stories which depend on urban environments for their horrors. Included are John Shirley's tale of urban paranoia, "Ash," Elizabeth Massies' tale of a peculiar street gang initiation, "Lock Her Room," Poppy Z. Brite's story of a trip to the abortion clinic with unexpected results, "The Ash of Memory, The Dust of Deire," and Gary L. Raisor's self explanatory "Hell Train."

Other books you might like:
Charles L. Grant, *Doom City*, 1987
Charles L. Grant, *Greystone Bay*, 1985
Charles L. Grant, *The SeaHarp Hotel*, 1990
William F. Nolan, *Urban Horrors*, 1990
    Martin H. Greenberg, co-author

3357

PAUL F. OLSON

Night Prophets

(New York: NAL Onyx, 1989)

Story type: Horror (Vampire Story)
Major character(s): Curt Potter, Student (Ministerial student); Arthur Bach, Religious (Televangelist), Vampire
Time period(s): 1980s
Locale(s): Chicago, Illinois

Summary: After joining Universal Ministries, Curt Potter finds himself confronting an ancient sect of vampires. He recruits a small group of friends to do battle with the undead. This is Olson's first novel.

Other books you might like:
T. Chris Nightingale, *Nightblood*, 1990

3358

PAUL F. OLSON, Editor
DAVID B. SILVA, Co-Editor

Post Mortem: New Tales of Ghostly Horror

(New York: Dell Abyss, 1992)

Story type: Horror (Anthology)

Summary: This excellent anthology of contemporary ghost stories, originally published in 1989, collects 18 stories by some of the best writers in the field. Included are Steve and Melanie Tem's "Resettling," a haunted house story involving a dysfunctional family; Ramsey Campbell's "The Guide," a brilliant homage to the fiction of M.R. James; Thomas Tessier's "Blanca," a ghostly rendering of "disappearances" in a third-world country undergoing political revolution; and P.W. Sinclair's moving "Getting Back," about a man haunted by the image of his failed life.

Other books you might like:
Robert Phillips, *Triumph of the Night*, 1988
Charles G. Waugh, *East Coast Ghosts*, 1989
    Martin H. Greenberg, co-editor
Donald A. Wollheim, *The Avon Ghost Reader*, 1946
    editor

3359

DENNIS O'NEIL

Batman: Knightfall

(New York: Bantam Spectra, 1994)

Story type: Science Fiction (Adventure)
Series: Batman
Major character(s): Bruce "Batman" Wayne, Hero, Detective—Amateur; Bane, Criminal
Time period(s): 21st century
Locale(s): Gotham City

Summary: To take over Gotham City, Bane releases Batman's criminally insane enemies from Arkham Asylum, intending to attack Batman after battles with the escapees weaken him. Novelizes a comic book series issued 1992-1994.

Other books you might like:
Lynn Abbey, *Catwoman*, 1992
    Robert Asprin, co-author
Craig Shaw Gardner, *The Batman Murders*, 1992
Martin H. Greenberg, *The Further Adventures of Batman 3: Featuring Catwoman*, 1993
    editor
Simon Hawke, *Batman: To Stalk a Specter*, 1991
Joe R. Lansdale, *Captured by the Engines*, 1991

3360

REBECCA ORE

Alien Bootlegger and Other Stories

(New York: Tor, 1993)

Story type: Science Fiction (Collection)

Summary: Contains one essay, "Aliens and the Artificial Other," plus six stories discussing alien and artificial intelligences as in the title story whose alien protagonist goes native, finding satisfaction in making bootleg booze with a psychedelic kick.

Other books you might like:
Pat Cadigan, *Patterns*, 1989
Philip K. Dick, *The Best of Philip K. Dick*, 1977
Michael Flynn, *The Nanotech Chronicles*, 1991
Nancy Kress, *The Aliens of Earth*, 1993
Cordwainer Smith, *The Best of Cordwainer Smith*, 1975
Marc Stiegler, *The Gentle Seduction*, 1990
Theodore Sturgeon, *Aliens 4*, 1959
John Varley, *Blue Champagne*, 1986

3361

REBECCA ORE

Being Alien

(New York: Tor, 1989)

Story type: Science Fiction (First Contact)
Major character(s): Tom Red Clay, Diplomat; Marianne Schweigman, Linguist
Time period(s): 1980s
Locale(s): Earth; Karst, Planet—Imaginary; Outer Space

Summary: Tom returns to Earth to do research for the Interstellar Federation and meets Marianne, an out of work Berkeley Ph.D. whom his alien bosses think would make him an ideal mate. Oddly, they turn out to be correct. Tom and Marianne return to the Federation base on Karst along with her sister Molly, Molly's husband Sam, and Tom's brother Warren. As Tom pursues his career as a diplomat, Marianne fits into the multi-species Federation with few problems, but the other humans find the situation much more traumatic.

Other books you might like:
David Brin, *Startide Rising*, 1983
David Brin, *The Uplift War*, 1987
Octavia E. Butler, *Adulthood Rites*, 1988
Octavia E. Butler, *Dawn*, 1987
Octavia E. Butler, *Imago*, 1989
David Gerrold, *Chess with a Dragon*, 1987
David Alexander Smith, *Rendezvous*, 1988

3362

REBECCA ORE

Gaia's Toys
(New York: Tor, 1995)

Story type: Science Fiction (Dystopian; Cyberpunk)
Major character(s): Allison Dodge, Activist (eco-terrorist); Dorcas Rae, Scientist (genetics), Researcher; Willie Hunsucker, Cyborg (drode head)
Time period(s): 21st century
Locale(s): Virginia; New York, New York

Summary: After a sinister government official holds and brainwashes Allison Dodge, she joins with Dorcas Rae and Willie Hunsucker in an attempt to restore a more resiliant worldwide ecology.

Other books you might like:
Kevin J. Anderson, *Ill Wind*, 1995
    Doug Beason, co-author
John Barnes, *Kaleidoscope Century*, 1995
David Brin, *Earth*, 1990
Thomas A. Easton, *Sparrowhawk*, 1990
Nicola Griffith, *Slow River*, 1995
Neal Stephenson, *Snow Crash*, 1992
Bruce Sterling, *Heavy Weather*, 1994

3363

REBECCA ORE

Human to Human
(New York: Tor, 1990)

Story type: Science Fiction (First Contact)
Series: Tom Red Clay
Major character(s): Tom Red Clay, Diplomat; Karriaagzh, Scholar, Administrator; Black Amber, Administrator
Time period(s): 1990s
Locale(s): Karst, Planet—Imaginary; Boston, Massachusetts

Summary: Since he was taken from Lloyd, Virginia when he was 19 years old, Tom Red Clay has lived on Karst, an artificial planet built thousands of years ago by five alien species to be an inter-cultural university planet and center of the Federation. Tom, now a husband and father, is sent to Earth as part of the team assigned to bring Earth peacefully into the Federation.

Other books you might like:
David Brin, *Startide Rising*, 1983
Octavia E. Butler, *Adulthood Rites*, 1988
Octavia E. Butler, *Dawn*, 1987
Octavia E. Butler, *Imago*, 1989
Jeffrey A. Carver, *The Rapture Effect*, 1987
J. Brian Clarke, *The Expediter*, 1990
David Alexander Smith, *Rendezvous*, 1988

3364

REBECCA ORE

The Illegal Rebirth of Billy the Kid
(New York: Tor, 1991)

Story type: Science Fiction (Future Shock; Genetic Manipulation)
Major character(s): Billy the Kid, Android (Chimera), Experimental Subject; Jane Ayers, Health Care Professional; Simon Boyle, Scientist, Criminal
Time period(s): 2060s (2067)
Locale(s): Wyoming; New York; Virginia

Summary: Billy the Kid is a Chimera (artificial person) created and killed nine times by Simon Boyle. This last time he escapes, and with Jane Ayers, an ASPCA worker, goes to live in the primitive Appalachia Preserve. But Turner, a CIA man, catches up with the two, kills Boyle for treasonous experimentation and sees to it that neither Billy nor Jane will ever leave Appalachia again on the pain of death.

Other books you might like:
Philip K. Dick, *Blade Runner*, 1982
Robert Silverberg, *Tower of Glass*, 1970
Nicholas Yermakov, *Clique*, 1982
    pseudonum of Simon Hawke

3365

REBECCA ORE

Slow Funeral
(New York: Tor, 1994)

Story type: Fantasy (Religious; Contemporary)
Major character(s): Maude Fuller, Witch, Psychic; Doug Sanderheim, Engineer, Boyfriend (Maude's); Partridge, Grandparent, Witch
Time period(s): 1990s
Locale(s): Bracken County, Virginia; Kobold, Virginia; Appalachians

Summary: A psychic call forces Maude to return to the Appalachian home she fled to avoid learning use of the native magic and its resulting control over others. Intending only to help her grandmother, Maude becomes more involved when she finds that people intend to use Doug in an evil attempt to keep away technological development.

Other books you might like:
Gael Baudino, *Strands of Sunlight*, 1994
Jack Cady, *Inagehi*, 1994
Tom Deitz, *Soulsmith*, 1991
Suzette Haden Elgin, *Twelve Fair Kingdoms*, 1981
Nina Kiriki Hoffman, *The Thread That Binds the Bones*, 1993

3366
MICHAEL O'ROURKE

The Bad Thing
(New York: HarperPaperbacks, 1995)

Story type: Horror (Serial Killer)
Major character(s): Johnny, Murderer; Chris Kelly, Criminal (professional assassin); Sherry Mahan, Police Officer (sheriff's deputy)
Time period(s): 1990s (1994)
Locale(s): Bremerton, Pennsylvania

Summary: Nearly 30 years after his teenage sweetheart disappeared and was never found again, Chris Kelly returns to his hometown to investigate the disappearance of a relative. Legends of a mysterious being known as the Phantom bring Chris to the abandoned Summerland hotel, the secret home of Johnny, a local half-wit who was traumatized psychologically by his mother and who has been applying his taxidermy skills on ''disappeared'' people for the last 30 years.

Other books you might like:
Robert Bloch, *Psycho*, 1959
John Driver, *The Hunger of the Beast*, 1991
Thomas Harris, *The Silence of the Lambs*, 1992
Robert D. Lee, *The Keeper*, 1993

3367
MICHAEL O'ROURKE

Darkling
(New York: HarperPaperbacks, 1994)

Story type: Horror (Occult)
Major character(s): Sara Raynor, Spirit; Rick Masterson, Journalist (television); Phylis Rand, Hotel Owner
Time period(s): 1990s (1994)
Locale(s): Spirit Lake, Nevada

Summary: Journalist Rick Masterson repairs to deserted Spirit Lake in dead winter to recover spiritually from the devastation he has witnessed in South Africa, Bosnia, and other trouble spots around the world. But an elemental haunts the setting, and finds itself so attracted to the darkness in Rick's soul that even the protective ghost of Sara Raynor, a woman who died thanks to the elemental's intervention years before, may not be able to save him. This is the author's first novel.

Other books you might like:
Randall Boyll, *After Sundown*, 1989
Stephen King, *The Shining*, 1977
Michael B. Sirota, *Demon Shadows*, 1989
Bernard Taylor, *Sweetheart, Sweetheart*, 1977

3368
MICHAEL O'ROURKE

The Undine
(New York: HarperPaperbacks, 1996)

Story type: Horror (Occult)
Major character(s): Brian Kroft, Journalist; Stanley Williams, Photographer; Toby Mendel, Anthropologist
Time period(s): 1990s (1996)
Locale(s): Bel Air, California; Rookers Cove, Oregon

Summary: The escape from a remote business retreat of a clutch of mythological creatures known as the Undine threatens the world with a species whose contact brings sexual infatuation and death. Brian Kroft sets out to learn the full story of how the creatures have survived into this day, unaware that he is being pursued by ruthless businessmen who will stop at nothing to keep their involvement with Undine secret.

Other books you might like:
Mark A. Clements, *Lorelei*, 1994
Ron Dee, *Succumb*, 1994
John Farris, *Wildwood*, 1986
Christopher Fowler, *Red Bride*, 1992
Yvonne Navarro, *Species*, 1995

3369
CARY OSBORNE

The Glaive
(New York: Ace, 1996)

Story type: Science Fiction (Mystical; Adventure)
Series: Glaive
Major character(s): Laicy ''Iroshi'' Campbell, Martial Arts Expert, Administrator; Ensi, Spirit, Martial Arts Expert; Jiron Yail, Police Officer
Time period(s): Indeterminate Future
Locale(s): Galicia, Planet—Imaginary; Bosque, Planet—Imaginary

Summary: A member of the Glaive, a close friend and mentor of Iroshi, dies during negotiations, the victim of a mob inspired by a mysterious organization dedicated to the Glaive's destruction. Investigating their plot leads Iroshi across the galaxy to a planet of ruins and savage carnivores. Sequel to *Iroshi*.

Other books you might like:
Steven Barnes, *Streetlethal*, 1983
Gordon R. Dickson, *Dorsai!*, 1976
Steve Perry, *The Man Who Never Missed*, 1985
Dennis Schmidt, *Kensho*, 1979
Roger Zelazny, *Warriors of Blood and Dream*, 1995
    Martin H. Greenberg, co-editor

3370

CARY OSBORNE

Iroshi

(New York: Ace, 1995)

Story type: Science Fiction (Mystical; Adventure)
Series: Glaive
Major character(s): Laicy "Iroshi" Campbell, Martial Arts Expert, Wanderer; Mushimo, Martial Arts Expert (Kendo); Crowell, Martial Arts Expert, Heir
Time period(s): Indeterminate Future
Locale(s): Tokyo, Japan; Rune, Planet—Imaginary

Summary: A natural swordswoman, Laicy studies with Mushimo for two years before she finds the sword that speaks best to her. Old enemies attack Mushimo, who sends Laicy on as a warrior traveling where she feels a call to study or practice. Taking the name "Iroshi," she lands on Rune, called to the ruins of a temple.

Other books you might like:
Lois McMaster Bujold, *Shards of Honor*, 1986
Stephen Goldin, *Jade Darcy and the Affair of Honor*, 1988
  Mary Mason, co-author
Andre Norton, *Brother to Shadows*, 1993
Steve Perry, *The Man Who Never Missed*, 1985
Steve Perry, *The 97th Step*, 1989
Dennis Schmidt, *Kensho*, 1979

3371

RICHARD OSBORNE

Demolition Man

(New York: Signet, 1993)

Story type: Science Fiction (Adventure)
Major character(s): John "Demolition Man" Spartan, Detective—Police; Simon Phoenix, Criminal, Murderer; Lenina Huxley, Police Officer
Time period(s): 2030s (2032); 1990s (1996)
Locale(s): San Angeles, California; Los Angeles, California

Summary: When Simon Phoenix escapes CryoPrison during a parole hearing, the vicious killer finds easy prey among the politically correct and well behaved residents of San Angeles. Desperate to rearrest Phoenix, the police thaw out his arresting officer, John Spartan, wrongly convicted of manslaughter, and parole him on the condition that he again apprehend Simon. Novelizes the film.

Other books you might like:
Philip K. Dick, *Blade Runner*, 1982
Dave Duncan, *Hero*, 1991
Stephen Goldin, *Jade Darcy and the Affair of Honor*, 1988
  Mary Mason, co-author
Ed Naha, *Robocop*, 1987
Richard Sapir, *The Destroyer #1: Created, the Destroyer*, 1971
  Warren Murphy, co-author
Robert Tine, *Universal Soldier*, 1992

3372

JEFFREY OSIER, Author/Illustrator

Driftglider and Other Stories

(Pawtucket, Rhode Island: Montilla Publications, 1993)

Story type: Horror (Collection)

Summary: The author's first story collection brings together seven stories, four original to the volume, in which powerful emotions are manifest in strange relationships and even stranger monsters. In "Driftglider," a troubled relationship takes the form of a weird creature of the snows. "Snowlight" tells of a boy whose troubled relationship with his father is mirrored by an unkillable stalker. And in "Soul of a Spider" a man's capacity to love takes the shape of a spiderlike monstrosity. The author illustrates all of the stories himself in surrealistic detail.

Other books you might like:
Michael A. Arnzen, *Needles and Sins*, 1993
D.F. Lewis, *The Best of D.F. Lewis*, 1992
Stephen Mark Rainey, *Fugue Devil and Other Weird Horrors*, 1993
Wayne Allen Sallee, *Pain-Grin*, 1993

3373

PIERRE OUELLETTE

The Deus Machine

(New York: Villard, 1994)

Story type: Horror (Science Fiction)
Major character(s): Michael Riley, Computer Expert (programmer); DEUS, Artificial Intelligence; Jimi Tyler, Child (eight years old)
Time period(s): 2000s (2005)
Locale(s): Portland, Oregon; Washington, District of Columbia; New York, New York

Summary: In a future perched on the brink of political self-destruction, a computer programmed with artificial intelligence to be self perpetuating is abused by government agents performing chemical warfare experiments and begins creating mutant, shapeshifting life forms that threaten to overrun the Earth. This is the author's first novel.

Other books you might like:
Michael Crichton, *The Terminal Man*, 1972
Harlan Ellison, *I Have No Mouth and I Must Scream*, 1967
  in *Alone Against Tomorrow*
Daniel H. Gower, *The Orpheus Process*, 1992
D.F. Jones, *Colossus*, 1966

3374

MICHAEL PAINE

The Colors of Hell

(New York: Charter, 1990)

Story type: Horror (Occult)

Major character(s): Charlotte Alderson, Widow(er); Clare Markham, Artist (stained glass artist), Religious; Robert Semnarek, Lawyer
Time period(s): 1950s; 1920s
Locale(s): New York, New York; Marrakesh, Morocco

Summary: In order to settle her father's estate and gain the inheritance bequeathed to her in his will, Charlotte Alderson must track down her sister Clare, who, along with her husband Marty, disappeared in Morocco 30 years earlier. In a convent deep in the Anti-Atlas mountains Charlotte, her son Steve, and lawyer Robert Semnarek find that Clare has become Sister Joseph, abbess to an ancient, autonomous order of nuns the local Bedouins call The House of Fifty. The centerpiece of this provocative novel is Clare's memoir, in which she tells how she went from a stained-glass designer at Tiffany's in New York to head of a convent whose members may guard one of the gateways to hell.

Other books you might like:
Elaine Bergstrom, *Shattered Glass*, 1989
Robert Silverberg, *The Book of Skulls*, 1971
Roland Topor, *The Tenant*, 1966

3375
MICHAEL PAINE

Owl Light

(New York: Charter, 1989)

Story type: Horror (Reanimated Dead)
Major character(s): Sybil Antissa, Sorceress (enchantress); Paul Eiden, Religious (would-be TV evangelist)
Time period(s): 1980s
Locale(s): Mill Creek, Pennsylvania (a rural small town)

Summary: Sybil, an enchantress who periodically animates the dead, seduces and manipulates three men—a cynical college biology teacher, an innocent young student, and a worldly preacher—into fathering her child and launching her mysterious "religion."

Other books you might like:
H. Rider Haggard, *She*, 1886
Arthur Machen, *The Great God Pan*, 1890
William Sloane, *To Walk the Night*, 1939

3376
JEAN PAIVA

The Lilith Factor

(New York: NAL Onyx, 1989)

Story type: Horror (Femme Fatale)
Major character(s): Elsie Crawford Vaughan, Doctor, Twin; Talia Crawford Harrah, Twin (The "dark" twin)
Time period(s): 1980s
Locale(s): United States

Summary: Twin sisters—one "light" and one "dark"—embody the ancient power of "Lilith." The dark sister, Talia, vows to become supremely powerful by absorbing her sister's untapped energies—and destroying Elsie in the process.

Other books you might like:
Thomas F. Monteleone, *Lyrica*, 1987
Simon Raven, *Doctors Wear Scarlet*, 1960

3377
JESSICA PALMER

Dark Lullaby

(New York: Pocket, 1991)

Story type: Horror (Possession)
Major character(s): Shelley Graves, Child (dead child); Sara Graves, Child; Elliott Graves, Teacher (of music appreciation)
Time period(s): 1990s
Locale(s): Claremont

Summary: Eleven-year-old Shelley Graves dies in a house fire as a consequence of her parents' irreponsibility. But Shelley follows the Graves to their new home and makes their life hell, avenging her death through the body of her baby sister Sara, who soon begins to display all the nasty habits that made Shelley such a difficult child. This is the author's first novel.

Other books you might like:
Lawrence Block, *Ariel*, 1980
Frank DeFelitta, *Audrey Rose*, 1975
Thomas Tryon, *The Other*, 1971

3378
JESSICA PALMER

Shadow Dance

(New York: Pocket, 1994)

Story type: Horror (Curse; Ancient Evil Unleashed)
Major character(s): Tiffany Blair, Child; Alan Blount, Police Officer; Robert Schoenwald, Construction Worker (heavy machinery operator)
Time period(s): 1990s (1994)
Locale(s): Stockton Springs, Maine

Summary: When Tiffany Blair unearths the finger bone of a centuries-dead Indian shaman, it releases a lupine elemental spirit, which goads the residents of Stockton Springs into wild flights of uninhibited sex and violence.

Other books you might like:
G. Wayne Miller, *Thunder Rise*, 1989
Adam Niswander, *The Charm*, 1993
Eugene E. Pfaff Jr., *Uwharrie*, 1993
   Michael Causey, co-author
Patrick Whalen, *Deathwalker*, 1992

3379
JESSICA PALMER

Sweet William

(New York: Pocket, 1995)

Story type: Horror (Evil Children; Possession)
Major character(s): William Scott McDowell, Child (four-year-old); Allison McDowell, Writer

Time period(s): 1990s (1995)
Locale(s): Long Island, New York

Summary: Born the day that his father, horror writer Scott McDowell, died, William Scott McDowell manifests unusual personality traits. Indeed, he has become the battleground between the soul of his father and the spirit of an evil "other" linked to the legacy of death and terror that imbues his family's house.

Other books you might like:
William Peter Blatty, *The Exorcist*, 1971
Ramsey Campbell, *The Influence*, 1988
Ramsey Campbell, *To Wake the Dead*, 1980
Stephen R. George, *Torment*, 1994
Clifford Mohr, *Requiem*, 1992

3380

SUSAN PALWICK

Flying in Place
(New York: Tor, 1992)

Story type: Horror (Child-in-Peril)
Major character(s): Emma Gray, Child, Abuse Victim; Stewart Gray, Doctor; Myrna Halloran, Nurse
Time period(s): 1970s
Locale(s): Wisconsin

Summary: Sexually abused by her father and completely ignored by her mother, Emma Grey befriends the spirit of her dead older sister Ginny, who teaches Emma how to discorporate her spirit and temporarily flee her wretched home life. This sensitively written story is the author's first novel.

Other books you might like:
Randall Boyll, *Mongster*, 1991
Sean Costello, *Captain Quad*, 1991
Judith Guest, *Ordinary People*, 1976
Thomas Tryon, *The Other*, 1971
R.R. Walters, *Wind Chimes*, 1991

3381

PAUL PARK

Celestis
(New York: Tor, 1995)

Story type: Science Fiction (Political; Genetic Manipulation)
Major character(s): Simon Mayaram, Diplomat, Human; Katharine Styreme, Genetically Altered Being (Aboriginal), Musician (concert pianist); Harriet Oimu, Revolutionary (National Liberation Coalition), Genetically Altered Being (Aboriginal)
Time period(s): Indeterminate Future
Locale(s): Shreveport, Fictional City; Celestis, Planet—Imaginary

Summary: Superior technology has allowed the small human colony to exploit the natives of Celestis to the verge of revolt. Both native and human factions feel appalled by the practice of natives surgically and pharmacologically altering themselves in order to appear human, thereby opening up more doors of opportunity in the rigidly stratified society. Kid-

napped by terrorists of the National Liberation Coalition, Simon Mayaram falls in love with fellow hostage Katharine Styreme. But Katharine, an altered Celestis native, denied the daily medications that keep her "humanity" intact, rapidly transforms back into an alien unable to communicate emotions on a human level. British edition, 1993, titled *Coelestis*.

Other books you might like:
Roger MacBride Allen, *The Ring of Charon*, 1990
Eleanor Arnason, *Ring of Swords*, 1993
David Brin, *Brightness Reef*, 1995
David Brin, *The Uplift War*, 1987
Octavia E. Butler, *Dawn*, 1987
C.J. Cherryh, *Foreigner*, 1994
C.J. Cherryh, *Invader*, 1995
Ian McDonald, *The Broken Land*, 1992
Joan Slonczewski, *Daughter of Elysium*, 1993
John E. Stith, *Redshift Rendezvous*, 1990
Sheri S. Tepper, *Grass*, 1989

3382

PAUL PARK

The Cult of Loving Kindness
(New York: Morrow, 1991)

Story type: Science Fiction (Theological; Political)
Series: Starbridge Chronicles
Major character(s): Cassia, Teenager, Religious; Rael, Teenager, Religious
Time period(s): Indeterminate Future
Locale(s): Planet—Imaginary

Summary: The Cult of Loving Kindness grows in popularity among the refugees from Charn, threatening the power of the Starbridge caste. As Cassia and Rael proceed from their isolated jungle village to Brother Longo Starbridge's mission, they prove to be the prophesied elements as Cassia becomes Last Bishop.

Other books you might like:
Brian W. Aldiss, *Helliconia Spring*, 1982
Brian W. Aldiss, *Helliconia Summer*, 1983
Brian W. Aldiss, *Helliconia Winter*, 1985
Octavia E. Butler, *Adulthood Rites*, 1988
Octavia E. Butler, *Imago*, 1989
Mary Gentle, *Golden Witchbreed*, 1984
Robert A. Heinlein, *Stranger in a Strange Land*, 1991 revised
Sheri S. Tepper, *Grass*, 1989
Sheri S. Tepper, *Raising the Stones*, 1990
Gene Wolfe, *The Citadel of the Autarch*, 1983
Gene Wolfe, *Claw of the Conciliator*, 1981
Gene Wolfe, *The Shadow of the Torturer*, 1980
Gene Wolfe, *The Sword of the Lictor*, 1982

3383

PAUL PARK

Sugar Rain

(New York: Morrow, 1989)

Story type: Science Fiction (Theological; Political)
Series: Starbridge Chronicles
Major character(s): Charity Starbridge, Widow(er); Thanakar Starbridge, Doctor
Time period(s): Indeterminate Future
Locale(s): Planet—Imaginary

Summary: On a planet where each season lasts for decades, Spring invariably brings turmoil, starvation, and revolution. Two decent people caught up in the insanity, both criminals according to the perverse religious laws of their civilization, struggle desperately to maintain life and find some form of happiness.

Other books you might like:
Brian W. Aldiss, *The Helliconia Trilogy*, 1982-1985
Gene Wolfe, *The Book of the New Sun*, 1980

3384

SEVERNA PARK

Speaking Dreams

(Ithica, New York: Firebrand Books, 1992)

Story type: Science Fiction (Gay/Lesbian Fiction; Political)
Major character(s): Costa, Psychic (prescient); Mira LoDire, Diplomat (Emirate), Businesswoman (negotiator)
Time period(s): Indeterminate Future
Locale(s): Traja, Planet—Imaginary; *Proviso*, Spaceship

Summary: Mira LoDire reluctantly purchases the enslaved Costa, not understanding that Costa can interpret the secret signed language with which Sector negotiators always outfox Emirate negotiators. On discovering Costa's ability, Mira plans to utilize Costa's skill in the Emir's bargaining to purchase Sector territory, but enemies capture them first. Mira and Costa struggle to escape the Sector agents who have begun dealing with vicious aliens in preparation for conquering the Emirate.

Other books you might like:
Camarin Grae, *Stranded*, 1991
Ursula K. Le Guin, *The Left Hand of Darkness*, 1969
Frances Lucas, *Cathy IV*, 1992
Lynda Lyons, *Priorities*, 1990

3385

T.L. PARKINSON

The Man Upstairs

(New York: Dutton, 1991)

Story type: Horror (Psychological Suspense)
Major character(s): Michael West, Administrator (hospital); Paul Marks, Doctor (plastic surgeon); Patricia, Model
Time period(s): 1990s
Locale(s): San Francisco, California

Summary: Succumbing to the mysterious and perverse character of his apartment building, Michael West becomes increasingly promiscuous with his fellow tenants and finds himself obsessed with "the man upstairs," a plastic surgeon whose features West appears to be gradually assuming himself. This tale of urban paranoia is the author's first novel.

Other books you might like:
Ramsey Campbell, *The Face That Must Die*, 1979
Fritz Leiber, *Our Lady of Darkness*, 1977
Ira Levin, *Sliver*, 1991
Roland Topor, *The Tenant*, 1966

3386

NORMAN PARTRIDGE

Bad Intentions

(Burton, Michigan: Subterranean Press, 1996)

Story type: Horror (Collection)

Summary: Collected here are 14 short stories and one comic book script by an author whose work is strongly infected with '50s nostalgia and hommage to B-movies. "Bad Intentions" and "Dead Celebs" are both about collectors of celebrity memorabilia whose tastes verge on the necrophilic. "'59 Frankenstein" and "The Cut Man" are both variations on the Frankenstein theme, and "She's My Witch" and "Apotropaics" recast classic horror themes for tales of juvenile delinquency. "Guignoir" merges horror with the crime thriller, and "Dead Man's Hand" the horror and western tale. Joe Lansdale supplies the introduction. This book was released only in a limited hardcover edition.

Other books you might like:
Ed Gorman, *Cages*, 1995
Joe R. Lansdale, *By Bizarre Hands*, 1989
Joe R. Lansdale, *Writer of the Purple Rage*, 1994
John Shirley, *New Noir*, 1994

3387

NORMAN PARTRIDGE
MELISSA SHERMAN, Illustrator

The Bars on Satan's Jailhouse

(Arvada, Colorado: Roadkill Press, 1995)

Story type: Horror (Psychological Suspense)
Major character(s): Midas Gerlach, Gunfighter; Stackalee, Gunfighter; Lie, Young Woman
Time period(s): 1890s
Locale(s): Fiddler, California

Summary: This wild western tells of tough hombre Midas Gerlach, who has a foot fetish for his captive concubine Lie, and the legendary gunslinger Stackalee, a mysterious figure who wears boots made out of live bats, and who engages Gerlach in a final showdown on his grue-decorated ranch. This short story chapbook was published in a signed limited edition of 500 copies.

Other books you might like:
Nancy A. Collins, *The Tortuga Hill Gang's Last Ride*, 1991
Nancy A. Collins, *Walking Wolf*, 1995
Joe R. Lansdale, *The Magic Wagon*, 1983
Joe R. Lansdale, *On the Far Side of the Cadillac Desert with Dead Folks*, 1989
S.P. Somtow, *Moon Dance*, 1989

3388

NORMAN PARTRIDGE, Editor
MARTIN H. GREENBERG, Co-Editor

It Came From the Drive-In
(New York: DAW, 1996)

Story type: Horror (Anthology)

Summary: The 18 stories collected here are homages to the low-budget movies that played at neighborhood drive-ins in the 1950s, 1960s and 1970s. Several, like Ed Gorman's "The Morning of August 18," attempt a serious reflection on the relationship of film to real life. Others recast famous horror story plots as film scenarios, such as Nancy Collins' "The Thing From Lovers Lane" and Norman Partridge's "'59 Frankenstein," which adapt, respectively, H.P. Lovecraft's "The Dunwich Horror" and Mary Shelley's classic novel as juvenile delinquent tales. For the most part, the authors attempt deliberately cheesy riffs on the worst cliches of low budget filmmaking, among them Dan Perez's giant-bug gang story "Die, Baby, Die, Die, Die!," Adam Troy-Castro's psychowestern "The Good, The Bad, and The Danged," and Steve Tem's "Jungle J.D."

Other books you might like:
Peter Haining, *The Hollywood Nightmare*, 1970
    editor
Frank D. McSherry Jr., *Hollywood Ghosts*, 1991
    Charles G. Waugh, and Martin H. Greenberg, co-editors
David J. Schow, *Silver Scream*, 1988
    editor
Sebastian Wolfe, *Reel Terror*, 1992
    editor

3389

NORMAN PARTRIDGE

Mr. Fox and Other Feral Tales
(Arvada, Colorado: Roadkill Press, 1992)

Story type: Horror (Collection)

Summary: A first collection by this talented new writer brings together seven stories and novellas, only two of which have appeared in print before. Included are "Mr. Fox," a modern retelling of a classic folk tale; "Black Leather Kites," which mixes black magic with the modern police procedural; a morbid look at the southwest punk music scene, "Save the Last Dance for Me"; and a story of poetic justice for a porno magazine publisher, "In Beauty, Like the Night." Ed Bryant contributed an introduction.

Other books you might like:
Michael Blumlein, *The Brains of Rats*, 1989

Ed Gorman, *Prisoners and Other Stories*, 1992
Joe R. Lansdale, *By Bizarre Hands*, 1989
Dan Simmons, *Prayers to Broken Stones*, 1990

3390

NORMAN PARTRIDGE

Slippin' into Darkness
(Baltimore, Maryland: CD Publications, 1994)

Story type: Horror (Mystery)
Major character(s): Steve Austin, Police Officer; Shutterbug, Pornographer; Doug Douglas, Worker (bricklayer), Unemployed
Time period(s): 1990s (1994)
Locale(s): Vallejo, California

Summary: Eighteen years after she was gang-raped by four fellow high school students, April Destino, now the town slut, commits suicide. Her death forces the participants in her destruction to reflect on the paths their own lives have taken since then, and precipitates them on a downward spiral into self-hatred, and ultimately violence, with April's haunting presence in the background. This is the author's first novel.

Other books you might like:
Ramsey Campbell, *The Nameless*, 1981
Joe R. Lansdale, *The Nightrunners*, 1987
Peter Straub, *Ghost Story*, 1979

3391

NORMAN PARTRIDGE

Spyder
(Burton, Michigan: Subterranean Press, 1995)

Story type: Horror (Occult)
Major character(s): James Dean, Actor, Historical Figure; Layla, Witch
Time period(s): 1950s
Locale(s): Marfa, Texas

Summary: This short reflection on the mystique of James Dean proposes that the late actor bought his fame with the help of supernatural forces, and that these same forces helped to immortalize him—literally and figuratively—after his death in a car crash. This short story chapbook was printed in a signed limited edition of 500 copies.

Other books you might like:
Nancy Holder, *Cannibal Dwight's Special Purpose*, 1992
Joe R. Lansdale, *Dead in the West*, 1986
William F. Nolan, *Blood Sky*, 1991
Wayne Allen Sallee, *Drinking Buddies*, 1989

3392

HELEN K. PASSEY

Speak to the Rain
(New York: Atheneum, 1989)

Story type: Horror (Ghost Story)

Major character(s): Janna Miles, Teenager (Seventeen year old girl); Karen Miles, Child (Janna's nine year old sister)
Time period(s): 1980s
Locale(s): Washington

Summary: Made vulnerable by guilt over the death of her mother, Karen Miles is drawn by the song of the owls to a mysterious lake. Janna looks to a wise Indian for a way to rescue her sister from the ghosts of long dead Indians that await Karen. Passey's first novel.

Other books you might like:
Joan Aiken, *The Shadow Guests*, 1980
Vivian Alcock, *The Haunting of Cassie Palmer*, 1980
Margaret Mahy, *The Haunting*, 1982

3393

EDITH PATTOU

Hero's Song

(New York: Harcourt Brace Jovanovich, 1991)

Story type: Fantasy (Quest; Young Adult)
Major character(s): Collun, Adventurer; Talisen, Minstrel, Companion
Time period(s): Indeterminate
Locale(s): Eirren, Fictional Country

Summary: As Collun searches for his sister, Nessa, he discovers that his mission will determine the fate of Eirren, threatened by the Queen of Ghosts' invasion. This is the author's first novel.

Other books you might like:
Michael Reaves, *Street Magic*, 1991
Will Shetterly, *Elsewhere*, 1991
Michael Williams, *A Sorcerer's Apprentice*, 1990
Jane Yolen, *Wizard's Hall*, 1991
Mary Frances Zambreno, *A Plague of Sorcerers*, 1991

3394

MILORAD PAVIC

Landscape Painted with Tea

(New York: Knopf, 1990)

Story type: Fantasy (Contemporary)
Major character(s): Atanas Svilar, Architect; Fyodor Alexeyevich Razin, Scientist (mathematician)
Time period(s): 20th century
Locale(s): Serbia

Summary: A metafictional tale of a mysterious quest that is part modern Odyssey, and part detective crossword, with entire chapters forming actual clues "across" and "down." Atanas Svilar, a failed architect, sets out to find his father, an officer who vanished in Greece during the First World War.

Other books you might like:
Italo Calvino, *The Castle of Crossed Destinies*, 1977
Samuel R. Delany, *The Bridge of Lost Desire*, 1987
Tahar Ben Jelloun, *The Sand Child*, 1987
Gabriel Garcia Marquez, *One Hundred Years of Solitude*, 1970

Vladimir Nabokov, *Pale Fire*, 1962
Ellen Raskin, *The Mysterious Disappearance of Leon*, 1971 I Mean Noel
Gene Wolfe, *Free Live Free*, 1985

3395

DIANA L. PAXSON

The Dragons of the Rhine

(New York: Morrow AvoNova, 1995)

Story type: Fantasy (Legend; Romance)
Major character(s): Brunahild "Sigdrifa", Royalty, Warrior; Sigfrid, Mythical Creature (demigod shapechanger), Warrior
Time period(s): 5th century
Locale(s): Europe (northern)

Summary: When Sigfrid returns to find Sigdrifa, conspiracies, treachery, and honor combine to cause Sigfrid to deprive himself of her as his chosen mate. Sequel to *The Wolf and the Raven*; a retelling of *The Nibelungenlied*.

Other books you might like:
Donna Gillespie, *The Light Bearer*, 1994
Stephan Grundy, *Rhinegold*, 1994
Harry Harrison, *The Hammer and the Cross*, 1993 John Holm, co-author
Jamake Highwater, *Dark Legend*, 1994
Morgan Llywelyn, *Druids*, 1991

3396

DIANA L. PAXSON

The Jewel of Fire

(New York: Tor, 1992)

Story type: Fantasy (Quest; Magic Conflict)
Series: Westria
Major character(s): Julian of Stansvale, Royalty (king); Rana, Adventurer (regent's daughter); Caolin "Blood Lord", Sorcerer
Time period(s): Indeterminate
Locale(s): Westria, Fictional Country

Summary: Forces of the evil Caolin still fight against Julian and his friends as Julian sets out to find the fourth Jewel of Westria, the Jewel of Fire, hidden in the mouth of a volcano. Waiting until Julian recovers the jewel, Caolin captures and imprisons him. Aided by Coyote, a supernatural shapechanger, Rana sets out to find Julian, intent on rescuing him from the Blood Lord's dungeons and restoring his soul to health so that she and Julian can reign as King and Queen.

Other books you might like:
Lynn Abbey, *Daughter of the Bright Moon*, 1979
Marion Zimmer Bradley, *The Mists of Avalon*, 1983
C.J. Cherryh, *The Dreamstone*, 1983
Katherine Kurtz, *High Deryni*, 1973
Ursula K. Le Guin, *The Farthest Shore*, 1972
Patricia A. McKillip, *Harpist in the Wind*, 1979
Rick Shelley, *The Hero of Varay*, 1991

3397

DIANA L. PAXSON
ADRIENNE MARTINE-BARNES, Co-Author

Master of Earth and Water

(New York: Morrow AvoNova, 1993)

Story type: Fantasy (Legend)
Series: Chronicles of Fionn mac Cumhall
Major character(s): Fionn ''Demne'' mac Cumhall, Historical Figure, Hero; Bodbmall, Warrior, Teacher
Time period(s): 3rd century
Locale(s): Ireland

Summary: Spirited away from danger as an infant, Demne grows up in relative safety, learning mystical secrets from Bodbmall who keeps from Demne the nature of his parentage and destiny.

Other books you might like:
Kenneth C. Flint, *Challenge of the Clans*, 1986
Courtway Jones, *In the Shadow of the Oak King*, 1991
Morgan Llywelyn, *Finn Mac Cool*, 1994
Adrienne Martine-Barnes, *The Crystal Sword*, 1988
Adrienne Martine-Barnes, *The Fire Sword*, 1984
Adrienne Martine-Barnes, *The Rainbow Sword*, 1988
Andrew J. Offutt, *Sword of the Gael*, 1975
Bridget Wood, *Wolfking*, 1992

3398

DIANA L. PAXSON
ADRIENNE MARTINE-BARNES, Co-Author

The Shield between the Worlds

(New York: Morrow/AvoNova, 1994)

Story type: Fantasy (Legend)
Series: Chronicles of Fionn mac Cumhall
Major character(s): Fionn ''Demne'' mac Cumhall, Historical Figure, Hero; Goll mac Mornas, Warrior; Sadb, Spouse (Fionn's)
Time period(s): 3rd century
Locale(s): Ireland

Summary: As an adult, Fionn excels as bard and as warrior, familiar with both mortal and faerie realms. Great deeds propel Fionn to heroic stature, but Fionn remains unfulfilled until he meets the ensorcelled Sadb.

Other books you might like:
Kenneth C. Flint, *Challenge of the Clans*, 1986
Morgan Llywelyn, *Finn Mac Cool*, 1994
Adrienne Martine-Barnes, *The Crystal Sword*, 1988
Adrienne Martine-Barnes, *The Fire Sword*, 1984
Adrienne Martine-Barnes, *The Rainbow Sword*, 1988
Andrew J. Offutt, *Sword of the Gael*, 1975

3399

DIANA L. PAXSON
ADRIENNE MARTINE-BARNES, Co-Author

Sword of Fire and Shadow

(New York: Morrow/AvoNova, 1995)

Story type: Fantasy (Legend; Adventure)
Series: Chronicles of Fionn mac Cumhall
Major character(s): Fionn ''Demne'' mac Cumhall, Historical Figure, Hero
Time period(s): 3rd century
Locale(s): Ireland

Summary: Bound by his oath, aging Fionn mac Cumhal continues to defend Ireland from its faerie and mortal enemies despite treachery and disfavor from his countrymen.

Other books you might like:
Kenneth C. Flint, *Challenge of the Clans*, 1986
Morgan Llywelyn, *Finn Mac Cool*, 1994
Adrienne Martine-Barnes, *The Crystal Sword*, 1988
Adrienne Martine-Barnes, *The Fire Sword*, 1984
Adrienne Martine-Barnes, *The Rainbow Sword*, 1988
Andrew J. Offutt, *Sword of the Gael*, 1975

3400

DIANA L. PAXSON

The Wind Crystal

(New York: Tor, 1990)

Story type: Fantasy (Quest)
Series: Westria
Major character(s): Julian of Stansvale, Royalty (prince), Heir—Dispossessed; Rana, Adventurer (regent's daughter)
Time period(s): Indeterminate
Locale(s): Westria, Fictional Country

Summary: To claim his right to his father's throne from the Regent, Julian must find the four jewels of power and learn to use them. Julian has found two of the four jewels lost in the magic war which killed his father, King Jehan. Now he must find the Wind Crystal, his key to the Realm of Air. Obstructed by foes, he journeys to the Wind Lord's castle to learn the Wind Crystal's secrets.

Other books you might like:
Marion Zimmer Bradley, *City of Sorcery*, 1984
Marion Zimmer Bradley, *Domains of Darkover*, 1990
Marion Zimmer Bradley, *The Heirs of Hammerfell*, 1989
Jack L. Chalker, *When the Changewinds Blow*, 1987
Andre Norton, *Horn Crown*, 1981

3401

DIANA L. PAXSON

The Wolf and the Raven

(New York: Morrow, 1993)

Story type: Fantasy (Historical; Legend)

Major character(s): Brunahild "Sigdrifa", Royalty, Warrior; Sigfrid, Mythical Creature (demigod shapechanger), Warrior

Time period(s): 5th century

Locale(s): Europe

Summary: Brunahild studies with the Walkyriun, magic wielders who worship Wodan All-Father, receiving initiation into their religious rites. After fleeing his father's killers, Sigfried seeks shelter in the deep woods with an aged smith who provides Sigfrid the opportunity to learn warfare and smithcraft and discover his ability as shapechanger. After crafting his great sword and fighting the dragon, Fafnir, Sigfrid must rescue Brunahild from an enchanted sleep. First of a trilogy based on the Germanic saga.

Other books you might like:

Frans G. Bengtsson, *The Long Ships*, 1954
Stephan Grundy, *Rhinegold*, 1994
Harry Harrison, *The Hammer and the Cross*, 1993
    John Holm, co-author
Courtway Jones, *In the Shadow of the Oak King*, 1991
Morgan Llywelyn, *Druids*, 1991

3402

ROBERTO PAZZI
M.J. FITZGERALD, Co-Author

The Princess and the Dragon

(New York: Knopf, 1990)

Story type: Fantasy (Historical; Time Travel)

Major character(s): George Alexandrovich Romanov, Royalty (Grand Duke); Helen, Noblewoman (Montenegro); Prince Ourousov, Nobleman

Time period(s): 1890s (1899)

Locale(s): Russia; Europe

Summary: The Tsar's brother George is dying of tuberculosis in his palace in the Caucasus Mountains. He dreams of escaping to Cannes and marrying his cousin Helen and of finding the secret to the fabled longevity of the Georgians. Then he is swept into a journey that takes him to St. Helena in 1816, to Paris in 1793, to China in 1825, and to Russia in 1796 and 1938. This book was first published in Italian as *La Principessa e il Drago* in 1986.

Other books you might like:

Philip K. Dick, *The Man in the High Castle*, 1963
John M. Ford, *The Dragon Waiting*, 1983
Lisa Goldstein, *The Dream Years*, 1985
Lisa Goldstein, *The Red Magician*, 1982
Gene Wolfe, *Soldier of the Mist*, 1986

3403

MICHAEL PEAK

Catamount

(New York: Roc, 1992)

Story type: Fantasy (Contemporary; Adventure)

Major character(s): Sarena, Animal (cougar); Lanakila, Animal (eagle); Laura Kay, Journalist

Time period(s): 1990s

Locale(s): San Diego, California

Summary: Sarena hunts alone until she forms an unlikely friendship with Lanakila. The two friends join forces to foil a pack of feral dogs, not realizing the danger they may soon face from two-legged hunters. Covering a story about the proposed mountain lion hunt as part of her job, Laura Kay soon takes an interest in the mountain lions and in Keith Gallatin, a rock star and psychic who works to prevent the hunt.

Other books you might like:

Richard Adams, *Shardik*, 1974
Richard Adams, *Watership Down*, 1972
Jack Dann, *Magicats!*, 1984
    Gardner Dozois, co-editor
T.S. Eliot, *Old Possum's Book of Practical Cats*, 1938
Ursula K. Le Guin, *The Word for World Is Forest*, 1972
Vonda N. McIntyre, *Star Trek IV: The Voyage Home*, 1986
Andre Norton, *Catfantastic*, 1989
    Martin H. Greenberg, co-editor
H. Beam Piper, *Little Fuzzy*, 1962
Tad Williams, *Tailchaser's Song*, 1985

3404

PHILIPPA PEARCE, Editor

Dread and Delight: A Century of Children's Ghost Stories

(New York: Oxford, 1995)

Story type: Horror (Anthology; Ghost Story)

Summary: The editor, herself an author of children's fiction, has chosen 40 tales of the supernatural that span the century and are suitable for young readers. Classic tales include M.R. James' "A School Story," about a student who becomes the vehicle for his teacher's haunted past, Arthur Machen's "John Double," in which a young boy shares the knowledge picked up by his doppelganger, and Walter de la Mare's "Miss Jemima," about a nasty aunt who gets her comeuppance. Robert Westall's "The Beach," in which a boy cannot separate dream from reality, and John Gordon's "The Burning Baby," a tale of revenge from beyond the grave, are among the modern selections. Many of the book's contributors are renowned as childrens writers, but others, including Isaac Bashevis Singer and Penelope Lively, are more commonly thought of as writers for adults.

Other books you might like:

Ramsey Campbell, *The Gruesome Book*, 1983
    editor
Neil Gaiman, *Now We Are Sick*, 1991
    Stephen Jones, co-editor
Martin H. Greenberg, *Great Writers and Kids Write Spooky Stories*, 1995
    Jill Morgan and Robert Weinberg, co-editors
Robert Westall, *Ghost Stories*, 1988
    editor

`3405`

CLAUDIA PECK

Spirit Crossings

(New York: Bantam Spectra, 1991)

Story type: Fantasy (Contemporary; Horror)
Major character(s): Andrew Jackson, Teacher; Broken Echo, Indian (Cherokee), Spirit; Larry Bryge, Teenager, Student—High School
Time period(s): 1990s
Locale(s): Tennessee

Summary: On the way to accept a new teaching position, Andrew's wife and son are killed in an automobile crash. In his grief, Andrew secludes himself in his new home which is haunted by the ghosts of a Cherokee warrior, a slave trader and others who died horribly in the house. Tormented by them, he acts so strangely he loses his job and is unable to break free of the spirits until he must help Larry escape their evil influence, making peace with the ghosts and his own past.

Other books you might like:
Ambrose Bierce, *Can Such Things Be?*, 1893
Henry James, *The Two Magics: The Turn of the Screw, Covering End*, 1898
M.R. James, *The Best Ghost Stories of M.R. James*, 1944
Jill M. Phillips, *Walford's Oak*, 1990
Phyllis Reynolds Naylor, *The Witch's Eye*, 1990
Thorne Smith, *Topper: An Improbable Adventure*, 1926

`3406`

HAYFORD PEIRCE

Phylum Monsters

(New York: Tor, 1989)

Story type: Science Fiction (Satire)
Major character(s): Robert Clayborn, Scientist; Oneness, Alien
Time period(s): 24th century (2345)
Locale(s): Earth; Mars

Summary: Robert Clayborn is a designer of bestselling human genetic types until, for no apparent reason, most of his designs begin to go wrong. Apparently normal genetically-designed human beings, even his own son, suddenly regress into apes. Clayborn's life and business collapse. Then he is talked into going to Mars to help The Oneness, a Martian rock entity, find a means of liberating her people. For years telepathic Martian rocks have served human beings as pets and communications devices but now Clayborn must find them bodies and, in effect, free the slaves.

Other books you might like:
James Patrick Kelly, *Look into the Sun*, 1989
Frederik Pohl, *Narabedla, Ltd.*, 1988
Rudy Rucker, *Wetware*, 1988
Kate Wilhelm, *Crazy Time*, 1988

`3407`

HAYFORD PEIRCE

The Thirteenth Majestral

(New York: Tor, 1989)

Story type: Science Fiction (Space Opera)
Major character(s): Kerryl Ryson, Slave; Yveena Soolis, Noblewoman
Time period(s): Indeterminate (The Year 28,395 FIP)
Locale(s): Stohlson's Redemption, Planet—Imaginary; Diobastan Cluster, Interstellar Empire/Federation

Summary: Ten year old Kerryl Ryson is responsible for an unseemly incident that upsets a visiting VIP. As punishment his father is executed and he and his family are sold into slavery. Sixteen years later, aided by a beautiful noblewoman, aliens, a time machine, and a bunch of dinosaurs, he accomplishes his revenge.

Other books you might like:
Iain M. Banks, *The Player of Games*, 1989
L. Neil Smith, *Henry Martyn*, 1989
Jack Vance, *Araminta Station*, 1988
Jack Vance, *The Book of Dreams*, 1981
Jack Vance, *Cugel's Saga*, 1983
Jack Vance, *The Dragon Masters*, 1963
Jack Vance, *Galactic Effectuator*, 1980

`3408`

JOHN PELAN, Editor
ALAN M. CLARK, Illustrator

Darkside: Horror for the Next Millenium

(Seattle: Darkside Press, 1996)

Story type: Horror (Anthology)

Summary: Thirty stories by diverse hands featuring mostly adult themes fill this anthology published exclusively in a signed limited hardcover edition. Included are Lucy Taylor's "Scars," about a woman who beguiles a religious fanatic to kill her abusive father; Roman Ranieri's "Window of Opportunity," in which a childish revenge fantasy gets out of hand; Brian Hodge's "Stick Around, It Gets Worse," about the extremes of a man's devastating grief over the loss of his wife in a senseless accident; David B. Silva's "Voices Lost and Clouded," in which a man is horrified to discover he can no longer separate fantasy from reality; and Brian McNaughton's "ystery orm," in which a fan who writes a letter to his favorite author discovers that getting a reply is the worst thing that could have happened to him.

Other books you might like:
Dennis Etchison, *Cutting Edge*, 1986
  editor
Dennis Etchison, *Metahorror*, 1993
  editor
John Maclay, *Voices From the Night*, 1994
  editor
Thomas F. Monteleone, *Borderlands 2*, 1991
  editor

Stanley Wiater, *After the Darkness*, 1993
 editor
J.N. Williamson, *Masques*, 1991
 editor

3409

CHARLES PELLEGRINO

Flying to Valhalla
(New York: Avonova/Morrow, 1993)

Story type: Science Fiction (First Contact; Hard Science Fiction)
Major character(s): Chris Wayville, Astronaut, Scientist; Clarice Wayville, Astronaut, Scientist; Catherine, Alien
Time period(s): 2050s; 2060s (2054-2061)
Locale(s): Alpha Centauri A-4, Planet—Imaginary; *Valkyrie*, Spaceship

Summary: Chris Wayville's nightmares may represent premonitions from alternate futures or symptoms of insanity caused by near-light speed travel to Alpha Centauri. On the fourth planet of Alpha Centauri A, contact between humans and the gentle, primitive natives proceeds smoothly at first, but Chris starts to worry about the effects of new ideas and new technology on this culture. When the human ship begins to receive radio signals from another planet in the Alpha Centauri system, he fears the nightmares may become reality. First novel.

Other books you might like:
Alfred Bester, *The Stars My Destination*, 1956
Arthur C. Clarke, *Rendezvous with Rama*, 1973
Gordon R. Dickson, *Masters of Everon*, 1980
Robert L. Forward, *Dragon's Egg*, 1980
Carl Sagan, *Contact*, 1985
James Tiptree Jr., *Up the Walls of the World*, 1978
Della Van Hise, *Killing Time*, 1985
John Varley, *Titan*, 1979

3410

CHARLES PELLEGRINO
GEORGE ZEBROWSKI, Co-Author

The Killing Star
(New York: Morrow AvoNova, 1995)

Story type: Science Fiction (Invasion of Earth; Hard Science Fiction)
Major character(s): Joshua, Clone (Jesus's); Justin, Clone (Buddha's); Thaw Tint, Alien
Time period(s): 2090s
Locale(s): Outer Space (inside the Sun's corona); Sargenti-Peterson, Space Station (on a comet); Ceres, Asteroid

Summary: After aliens destroy Earth with relativistic bombs, killing almost all life in the Solar System, Thaw Tint continues to hunt down the remaining humans.

Other books you might like:
Roger MacBride Allen, *The Ring of Charon*, 1990
Greg Bear, *The Forge of God*, 1987
David Brin, *Earth*, 1990
Jack McDevitt, *The Engines of God*, 1994

Larry Niven, *Footfall*, 1985
 Jerry Pournelle, co-author
Dan Simmons, *Hyperion*, 1989
George Zebrowski, *Stranger Suns*, 1991

3411

COLE PERRIMAN (Pseudonym of Wim Coleman and Pat Perrin)

Terminal Games
(New York: Bantam, 1994)

Story type: Science Fiction (Alternate Intelligence; Mystery)
Major character(s): Marianne Hedison, Computer Expert, Detective—Amateur; Nolan Grobowski, Detective—Police; Auggie, Artificial Intelligence
Time period(s): 1990s
Locale(s): Los Angeles, California; Insomnia, Cyberspace (computer virtual reality)

Summary: When Marianne Hedison reports a similarity between a real murder and a computer simulation she witnessed on Insomnia, an interactive computer fantasyland, Detective Grobowski begins an investigation which convinces them that Insomnia plays a sinister and remarkable role in events.

Other books you might like:
Piers Anthony, *Killobyte*, 1993
Alexander Besher, *Rim: A Novel of Virtual Reality*, 1994
Ben Bova, *Death Dream*, 1994
Pierre Ouellette, *The Deus Machine*, 1994
John Varley, *Steel Beach*, 1992

3412

MARK C. PERRY

Morigu: The Dead
(New York: Questar, 1990)

Story type: Fantasy (Magic Conflict)
Major character(s): Margawt "The Morigu", Mythical Creature, Warrior (elf); Anlon, Mythical Creature (unicorn)
Time period(s): Indeterminate

Summary: The elves, dwarves and humans are all involved in a battle against the forces of dark. The gods who once stabilized the world can do so no longer because of internal bickering.

Other books you might like:
Poul Anderson, *The Broken Sword*, 1983
Terry Brooks, *The Sword of Shannara*, 1977
John Deakins, *Barrow*, 1990
David Eddings, *The Belgariad Series*,
J.R.R. Tolkien, *Lord of the Rings Trilogy*,

3413

S.D. PERRY

Timecop
(New York: Berkley, 1994)

Story type: Science Fiction (Time Travel; Adventure)

Major character(s): Max Walker, Police Officer (Timecop), Time Traveller; Aaron McComb, Political Figure, Criminal

Time period(s): 2000s

Locale(s): Washington, District of Columbia

Summary: While assigned to search for Senator McComb who has violated the prohibition against traveling back in time, Max Walker faces the temptation of preventing his wife's murder. Novelizes the movie.

Other books you might like:
Dean Devlin, *StarGate*, 1994
    Roland Emmerich, co-author
Philip K. Dick, *Blade Runner*, 1982
Richard Osborne, *Demolition Man*, 1993
Robert Tine, *Universal Soldier*, 1992
Robert Charles Wilson, *A Bridge of Years*, 1991

3414

STEVE PERRY

The 97th Step

(New York: Ace Books, 1989)

Story type: Science Fiction (Adventure)

Major character(s): Mwili-Ferret, Thief, Warrior

Time period(s): Indeterminate Future

Locale(s): Shin System, Planet—Imaginary; Tau System, Planet—Imaginary

Summary: In this prequel to *The Man Who Never Missed*, a young boy flees his desolate home planet and takes up life as a thief. Later he joins the Siblings of the Shroud, a violent cult bent on building an empire.

Other books you might like:
Emma Bull, *Falcon*, 1989
Frank Herbert, *Dune*, 1965
Christopher Hinz, *Liege-Killer*, 1987
Joan D. Vinge, *Catspaw*, 1988

3415

STEVE PERRY

The Albino Knife

(New York: Ace, 1991)

Story type: Science Fiction (Adventure)

Series: Matador

Major character(s): Veate, Martial Arts Expert, Genetically Altered Being; Emile Khadaji, Martial Arts Expert, Parent (Veate's)

Time period(s): Indeterminate Future

Locale(s): Earth

Summary: When Veate's mother, Juete, disappears, Veate searches out her father, Emile Khadaji, whom she has never met. Emile joins other Matadors to find and free Juete. As they unravel the mystery they discover a plot which could threaten the Brotherhood, the martial arts society to which the defenders of liberty, the Matadors, belong.

Other books you might like:
Lois McMaster Bujold, *Borders of Infinity*, 1989
Allan Cole, *Revenge of the Damned*, 1989
    Chris Bunch, co-author
Glen Cook, *The Dragon Never Sleeps*, 1988
Gordon R. Dickson, *Dorsai!*, 1976
Michael Flynn, *In the Country of the Blind*, 1990
Alan Dean Foster, *Cat-A-Lyst*, 1991
Stephen Goldin, *Jade Darcy and the Affair of Honor*, 1988
    Mary Mason, co-author

3416

STEVE PERRY

Aliens: Earth Hive

(New York: Bantam Spectra, 1992)

Story type: Science Fiction (Invasion of Earth; Political)

Series: Aliens

Major character(s): Billie, Patient (mental), Adventurer; Wilks, Military Personnel (Marine sergeant); Bueller, Military Personnel

Time period(s): Indeterminate Future

Locale(s): Earth; Planet—Imaginary (aliens' home planet); *Benedict*, Spaceship

Summary: Assigned to recover an alien for the government, Wilks frees Billie from confinement and smuggles her onboard ship, explaining her presence as the last-minute addition of an alien expert. While they work to retrieve an alien from the aliens' home planet, fanatics begin to facilitate implantation of embryonic aliens on Earth.

Other books you might like:
Alan Dean Foster, *Alien*, 1979
Alan Dean Foster, *Alien 3*, 1992
Alan Dean Foster, *Aliens*, 1986
Melissa Scott, *Mighty Good Road*, 1990
Charles Sheffield, *The Nimrod Hunt*, 1986

3417

STEVE PERRY
STEPHANIE PERRY, Co-Author

Aliens: The Female War

(New York: Bantam, 1993)

Story type: Science Fiction (Adventure; Space Opera)

Series: Aliens

Major character(s): Ellen Ripley, Telepath, Warrior; Wilks, Military Personnel; Billy, Psychic (dreamer), Adventurer

Time period(s): Indeterminate Future

Locale(s): *Kurtz*, Spaceship; Outer Space

Summary: With humanity reduced to a minor power on an alien-dominated Earth, outcast Ellen Ripley finds companions in her pogrom against alien life. When the alien queen calls for aliens to assemble at a distant star system, Ripley and others set out to kill all the aliens. Concludes the trilogy novelizing a graphic novel sequel to the film series.

Other books you might like:
Octavia E. Butler, *Dawn*, 1987

Orson Scott Card, *Ender's Game*, 1985
Alan Dean Foster, *Alien*, 1979
Alan Dean Foster, *Alien 3*, 1992
Alan Dean Foster, *Aliens*, 1986
Jayne Tannehill, *V: The Oregon Invasion*, 1988
Allen L. Wold, *V: The Pursuit of Diana*, 1984

3418
STEVE PERRY

Black Steel
(New York: Ace, 1992)

Story type: Science Fiction (Adventure)
Series: Matador
Major character(s): Sleel, Bodyguard, Martial Arts Expert; Kildee Wu, Martial Arts Expert, Teacher; Hoja Cierto, Martial Arts Expert, Teacher
Time period(s): Indeterminate Future
Locale(s): Mtu, Planet—Imaginary; Thompson's Gazelle, Planet—Imaginary

Summary: Hoping to regain lost honor, Sleel and Wu join forces against Cierto who engineered the killing of Sleel's client and whose ancestor stole the secret of black steel production from Wu's ancestor.

Other books you might like:
Lois McMaster Bujold, *Shards of Honor*, 1986
Brian Daley, *Jinx on a Terran Inheritance*, 1985
George Alec Effinger, *When Gravity Fails*, 1987
Stephen Goldin, *Jade Darcy and the Affair of Honor*, 1988
    Mary Mason, co-author
Stephen Goldin, *Jade Darcy and the Zen Pirates*, 1990
    Mary Mason, co-author
Steve Miller, *Agent of Change*, 1988
    Sharon Lee, co-author
Steve Miller, *Carpe Diem*, 1989
    Sharon Lee, co-author
Steve Miller, *Conflict of Honors*, 1988
    Sharon Lee, co-author

3419
STEVE PERRY

Brother Death
(New York: Ace, 1992)

Story type: Science Fiction (Adventure; Theological)
Series: Matador
Major character(s): Tazzimi "Taz" Bork, Police Officer; Saval Bork, Martial Arts Expert, Bodyguard; Ndug "Brother Death" Kifo, Martial Arts Expert, Leader (Unique of the Few)
Time period(s): Indeterminate Future
Locale(s): Tembo, Planet—Imaginary

Summary: After a failed assassination attempt on Taz while attending a ceremony for the infant son of Saval and Veate, Saval returns to Tembo with Taz to help investigate a series of assassinations. On Tembo, a small cadre of deadly fanatics

utilize alien artifacts to prepare Tembo for the return of the long extinct alien Zonn.

Other books you might like:
Gordon R. Dickson, *Dorsai!*, 1976
Michael Flynn, *In the Country of the Blind*, 1990
Neal Stephenson, *Snow Crash*, 1992
Vernor Vinge, *A Fire upon the Deep*, 1992

3420
STEVE PERRY

Conan the Formidable
(New York: Tor, 1990)

Story type: Fantasy (Sword and Sorcery)
Series: Conan the Barbarian
Major character(s): Conan, Barbarian, Warrior; Teyle, Mythical Creature (giantess); Penz, Werewolf
Time period(s): Indeterminate
Locale(s): Alternate Earth

Summary: Conan's journey to the city of Shadizar is interrupted when he is captured by giants at war with little green men. Before long, bandits and evil magic further complicate his life.

Other books you might like:
Leonard Carpenter, *Conan the Great*, 1990
Roland J. Green, *Conan the Valiant*, 1988
Robert Jordan, *Conan the Invincible*, 1985
John Maddox Roberts, *Conan the Bold*, 1989

3421
STEVE PERRY

Conan the Indomitable
(New York: Tor, 1989)

Story type: Fantasy (Sword and Sorcery)
Series: Conan the Barbarian
Major character(s): Conan, Barbarian, Warrior
Time period(s): Indeterminate
Locale(s): Alternate Earth

Summary: In this adventure, Conan finds himself caught in the middle of a war between a sorcerer and a sorceress. Trapped in a subterranean world with his companions, he must fight his way through magical creatures summoned to destroy them.

Other books you might like:
Glen Cook, *The Swordbearer*, 1990
Phyllis Eisenstein, *In the Red Lord's Reach*, 1989
Rose Estes, *The Hunter*, 1990
Robert E. Howard, *Hour of the Dragon*, 1989
John Jakes, *Brak the Barbarian - The Sorceress*, 1981
John Norman, *Magicians of Gor*, 1988

3422

STEVE PERRY

The Forever Drug
(New York: Ace, 1995)

Story type: Science Fiction (Adventure)
Series: Spindoc
Major character(s): Zia Relanj, Spy; Venture Silk, Public Relations; Croft Colburn, Spy
Time period(s): Indeterminate Future
Locale(s): New Earth, Planet—Imaginary

Summary: Exiled from Earth, Venture Silk begins to rebuild his life on New Earth with his new lover, in spite of the hostility he faces from natives prejudiced against Terrans. Zia, meanwhile, begins a series of medical treatments that will make her virtually immortal. Earth wants to learn the secret of the treatments and sends its best agent to bring her back dead or alive. Sequel to *Spindoc*.

Other books you might like:
John Brunner, *Stand on Zanzibar*, 1968
Stephen Goldin, *Jade Darcy and the Affair of Honor*, 1988
    Mary Mason, co-author
Robert A. Heinlein, *Beyond This Horizon*, 1948
Ian McDonald, *Scissors Cut Paper Wrap Stone*, 1994
John T. Phillifent, *The Man From U.N.C.L.E.: The Mad Scientist Affair*, 1966

3423

STEVE PERRY

Shadows of the Empire
(New York: Bantam Spectra, 1996)

Story type: Science Fiction (Space Opera; Psychic Powers)
Series: Star Wars
Major character(s): Luke Skywalker, Martial Arts Expert (Jedi Knight), Hero; Darth Vader, Martial Arts Expert (Jedi Knight), Psychic; Xisor, Organized Crime Figure
Time period(s): Indeterminate Past
Locale(s): Coruscant, Planet—Imaginary; Bothawui, Planet—Imaginary; Interstellar Empire/Federation

Summary: Xisor hopes to replace Darth Vader in Emperor Palpatine's eyes while both he and Vader plot to suborn Luke Skywalker to the Dark Side of the Force. Meanwhile, Leia initiates a mission to rescue Han Solo, frozen in carbonite, and sets out to discover Xisor's vulnerabilities. Set between the films *The Empire Strikes Back* and *Return of the Jedi*.

Other books you might like:
Kevin J. Anderson, *Darksaber*, 1995
Donald F. Glut, *The Empire Strikes Back*, 1980
Barbara Hambly, *Children of the Jedi*, 1995
Vonda N. McIntyre, *The Crystal Star*, 1994
L. Neil Smith, *The Lando Calrissian Adventures*, 1994
Kathy Tyers, *The Truce at Bakura*, 1994
Dave Wolverton, *The Courtship of Princess Leia*, 1994

3424

STEVE PERRY

Spindoc
(New York: Ace, 1994)

Story type: Science Fiction (Mystery; Adventure)
Series: Spindoc
Major character(s): Venture Silk, Government Official (public relations), Sports Figure (archery); Depard King, Murderer, Spy; Zia Relanj, Spy
Time period(s): Indeterminate Future
Locale(s): Maui, Hawaii; New Earth, Planet—Imaginary

Summary: After Silk discovers that his lover has been murdered, he joins the spy searching for the murderer, also trained as a secret agent. Before he can figure out why the murder took place, Silk must discover if Zia, his new companion, deserves trust.

Other books you might like:
F.M. Busby, *Slow Freight*, 1991
Philip K. Dick, *Blade Runner*, 1982
Katharine Kerr, *Polar City Blues*, 1990
Anne McCaffrey, *Crisis on Doona*, 1992
    Jody Lynn Nye, co-author
Mel Odom, *Lethal Interface*, 1992
Richard Paul Russo, *Destroying Angel*, 1992

3425

STEVE PERRY

The Trinity Vector
(New York: Ace, 1996)

Story type: Science Fiction (Alternate Intelligence; Theological)
Major character(s): Huey "Hal" Alphonse Long, Courier, Hero; Miranda Moon, Religious (priestess), Parent; Ford Wentworth, Government Official, Criminal
Time period(s): 2030s (2030)
Locale(s): Washington, District of Columbia; Boulder, Colorado (Sugar Loaf Hill); Tuscaloosa, Alabama

Summary: When Miranda Moon hires Hal Long to deliver the mysterious silver box to the Embrace of the Goddess Temple, she feels relieved to have the disquieting object out of her life. But as director of the National Security Agency's President's Special Section, Ford Wentworth has the resources, including another silver box, to force Long to return to Miranda for a different delivery option. Wentworth's relentless pursuit of a second box that knows the past and predicts the future with absolute accuracy compels Long, Miranda, and her two teenage daughters to flee for their lives. Along the way, they meet the Reverend Walter Green, possessor of a third silver box, who joins them in their efforts to stop Wentworth's bid for supreme power.

Other books you might like:
Roger MacBride Allen, *The Ring of Charon*, 1990
John DeChancie, *Starrigger*, 1983
Alan Dean Foster, *Cyber Way*, 1990
Alex McDonough, *Scorpio*, 1990

Alis A. Rasmussen, *A Passage of Stars*, 1990
Robert Shea, *The Illuminatus! Trilogy*, 1988
   Robert Anton Wilson, co-author
John Varley, *The Barbie Murders and Other Stories*, 1980
John Varley, *Blue Champagne*, 1986

3426

JUAN PERUCHO

Natural History

(New York: Ballantine, 1990)

Story type: Horror (Vampire Story)
Major character(s): Antoni de Montpalau, Scientist (naturalist); Isidre de Novau, Sea Captain (Antoni's cousin); Onofre de Dip, Vampire
Time period(s): 1830s
Locale(s): Barcelona, Spain

Summary: During the First Carlist War, a young liberal Spanish naturalist sets out to free the village of Pratdip from the depradations of an ancient vampire. Although he succeeds, acquiring a fiancee in the process, the vampire escapes to assume the identity of a guerrilla leader called the Owl. Translation of a superb, popular novel written in 1960 by one of Catalonia's most distinguished writers.

Other books you might like:
Les Daniels, *The Black Castle*, 1978
Jerzy Kosinski, *The Painted Bird*, 1965
Chelsea Quinn Yarbro, *Out of the House of Life*, 1990

3427

DAVID PETERS

Haven

(New York: Diamond, 1992)

Story type: Fantasy (Political; Adventure)
Series: Psi-Man
Major character(s): Chuck Simon, Fugitive, Warrior (psychic)
Time period(s): 2020s (2020)
Locale(s): New York, New York; The Complex, Virginia (secret agency headquarters)

Summary: With many agencies and individuals out to get him, Chuck retreats to Haven, a safe house for people with psychic powers. Instead of sanctuary, he discovers internal strife at Haven as Haven suffers external assault. This sixth volume concludes the series.

Other books you might like:
Isaac Asimov, *Second Foundation*, 1953
Alfred Bester, *The Stars My Destination*, 1957
Robert N. Charrette, *Choose Your Enemies Carefully*, 1991
Robert N. Charrette, *Find Your Own Truth*, 1991
Robert N. Charrette, *Never Deal with a Dragon*, 1990
Steve Perry, *The Man Who Never Missed*, 1985
Nick Pollotta, *Bureau 13*, 1991

3428

DAVID PETERS

Psi-Man

(New York: Charter/Diamond, 1990)

Story type: Science Fiction (Psychic Powers; Adventure)
Series: Psi-Man
Major character(s): Chuck Simon, Psychic, Martial Arts Expert (aikido); Rommel, Animal (dog); Quint, Agent (government)
Time period(s): 2020s
Locale(s): Le Quier; Kansas

Summary: Chuck Simon, Quaker, returns from summer school to find that one of his students has been given an addictive drug and the police will do nothing about it. When one of his fellow teachers is killed, six of the agents involved fly into what is left of her house. The videotape of the incident, taken from across the street, is brought to Quint—who smiles.

Other books you might like:
Isaac Asimov, *Foundation and Empire*, 1952
James Blish, *Jack of Eagles*, 1952
Katharine Kerr, *Polar City Blues*, 1990
Steve Perry, *The 97th Step*, 1989
A.E. van Vogt, *Slan*, 1946

3429

RALPH PETERS

Red Army

(New York: Pocket, 1989)

Story type: Science Fiction (Military)
Major character(s): Chibisov, Military Personnel (chief of staff); Bezarian, Military Personnel
Time period(s): 1990s
Locale(s): Germany

Summary: As nuclear war looms, the Soviet Army and its Warsaw Pact allies strike deep into West Germany. NATO desperately struggles to mount a counter attack, but the Soviets clearly have the upper hand.

Other books you might like:
Harold Coyle, *Team Yankee*, 1987
David Drake, *Hammer's Slammers*, 1979
David Drake, *Rolling Hot*, 1989
Sir John Hackett, *The Third World War, August 1985*, 1985

3430

GAIL PETERSEN

The Making of a Monster

(New York: Dell/Abyss, 1993)

Story type: Horror (Vampire Story)
Major character(s): Kate Davis, Musician (bass player), Vampire; Charly, Musician (vocalist); Drew, Musician (guitarist)
Time period(s): 1990s (1993)
Locale(s): Hollywood, California

Summary: Searching for a purpose that will help take her mind off her transformation into a vampire, Kate Davis joins the rock band the Uninvited as bass guitarist. But her love for the band's lead singer, Charly, only further complicates her life, as she finds it increasingly difficult to love him without turning him into her next meal. This is the author's first novel.

Other books you might like:
Poppy Z. Brite, *Lost Souls*, 1992
Nancy A. Collins, *Tempter*, 1991
Anne Rice, *The Vampire Lestat*, 1985
S.P. Somtow, *Vampire Junction*, 1984

3431

RICHARD PEYTON, Editor

Journey into Fear and Other Great Stories of Horror on the Railways
(New York: Wings, 1991)

Story type: Horror (Anthology)

Summary: Twenty-five short stories and twenty-five filler pieces concerned with ghosts and trains. Included are Ray Bradbury's noirish exercise ''The Town Where No One Got Off,'' Charles Dickens' classic tale of psychic premonition, ''The Signal Man,'' Robert Bloch's Hugo-award winning story of a deal with the devil, ''That Hell-Bound Train,'' and August Derleth's amusing tale of a midwestern ghost train, ''Pacific 421.'' Originally published in the UK in 1990 under the title *The Ghost Now Standing on Platform One.*

Other books you might like:
Charles Beaumont, *Omnibus of Speed*, 1958
   William Nolan, co-editor
Charles G. Waugh, *Spooky Sea Stories*, 1991
   Frank McSherry, Jr., co-editor

3432

EUGENE E. PFAFF JR.
MICHAEL CAUSEY, Co-Author

Uwharrie
(Greensboro, North Carolina: Tudor Publishing, 1993)

Story type: Horror (Supernatural Vengeance)
Major character(s): David Hale, Librarian; Diana Walters, Anthropologist; John Wolfe Singer, Handyman
Time period(s): 1990s (1993)
Locale(s): Clearview, North Carolina (Uwharrie Mountains)

Summary: A resurrected shaman of the Uwharrie Indian tribe prepares the last blood descendant of his tribe to help bring about the end of the white man's reign through rituals that include killing the blood descendants of all families who participated in the massacre of the Uwharries a century before.

Other books you might like:
Morgan Fields, *Shaman Woods*, 1989
G. Wayne Miller, *Thunder Rise*, 1989
Adam Niswander, *The Charm*, 1993
Kathryn Ptacek, *Ghost Dance*, 1990

Patrick Whalen, *Deathwalker*, 1992

3433

JILL M. PHILLIPS

Walford's Oak
(New York: Citadel, 1990)

Story type: Fantasy (Historical)
Major character(s): John Walford, Murderer, Spirit; Samuel Taylor Colridge, Writer, Historical Figure
Time period(s): 1790s (1797)
Locale(s): Over Stowey, England; Somerset, England

Summary: Samuel Colridge has recently moved to town when he becomes interested in the local ghost. The ghost had been hung for a year and a day before being buried for the crime of slitting his pregnant wife's throat.

Other books you might like:
Ramsey Campbell, *The Parasite*, 1980
Peter James, *Possession*, 1989
Alan Ryan, *The Kill*, 1982
John Skipp, *Dead Lines*, 1989
   Craig Spector, co-author
Patricia Wrightson, *Balyet*, 1989

3434

ROBERT PHILLIPS

The Omnibus of Twentieth Century Ghost Stories
(New York: Carroll & Graf, 1991)

Story type: Horror (Anthology; Ghost Story)

Summary: Originally published in 1989 as *Triumph of the Night*, the editor's first anthology of supernatural fiction brings together 27 tales of ghosts and hauntings by literary authors, most of whom are not associated with the genre. Included are Walter de la Mare's brilliant tale of psychic vampirism, ''Seaton's Aunt,'' Tennessee Williams' story of passion turned to flesh, ''The Mysteries of the Joy Rio,'' Charlotte Perkins Gilman's classic of the deteriorating psyche, ''The Yellow Wallpaper,'' Louis Auchincloss's metaphoric representation of the lingering presence of the past, ''The Prison Window,'' and Graham Greene's surprisingly gruesome ''A Little Place Off the Edgware Road.''

Other books you might like:
Peter Haining, *The Lucifer Society*, 1972
Bill Pronzini, *The Arbor House Treasury of Horror and the Supernatural*, 1981
   Barry Malzberg and Martin H. Greenberg, co-authors
Herbert Wise, *Great Tales of Terror and the Supernatural*, 1944
   Phyllis Fraser, co-author

3435

TOM PICCIRILLI

Dark Father

(New York: Pocket, 1990)

Story type: Horror (Evil Children)
Major character(s): Daniel, Twin; Samuel, Twin; Laurie, Vagrant
Time period(s): 1990s
Locale(s): Gallows

Summary: When Daniel falls in love with beautiful drifter Laurie, it gives his twin brother Samuel all the room he needs to become leader of the Darklings, the name given the reanimated corpses of the town's dead. Eventually, Samuel's actions precipitate a meeting with the boys' ''dark father,'' whom they never have met but whose horrifying heritage explains their peculiar behavior. This book was nominated for a Bram Stoker Award for outstanding achievement in a first novel.

Other books you might like:
Shirley Jackson, *We Have Always Lived in the Castle*, 1962
Jean Paiva, *The Lilith Factor*, 1989
Thomas Tryon, *The Other*, 1972

3436

TOM PICCIRILLI

Pentacle

(Islip, New York: Pirate Writings, 1995)

Story type: Horror (Collection)

Summary: Presented as an episodic novel, this book collects five stories told by a nameless narrator whose association with the occult includes the omnipresence of a wisecracking familiar named Self. In ''Neverdead,'' the pair stumble into a town given over to black magic, and in ''Paindance'' into an acting out of Hopi Indian mythology. In ''Bury St. Edmonds,'' they encounter witches who have survived down thorough the centuries, and in ''Eye-Biting and Other Displays of Affection,'' a witch hunter who is reincarnated as the warden of a lunatic asylum in which they are imprisoned. Jack Cady supplies the introduction.

Other books you might like:
Jewelle Gomez, *The Gilda Stories*, 1991
Mercedes Lackey, *Burning Water*, 1989
Brian Lumley, *The Compleate Crow*, 1987
Seabury Quinn, *The Phantom Fighter*, 1966
Robert Weinberg, *The Devil's Auction*, 1988

3437

J. CALVIN PIERCE

The Door to Ambermere

(New York: Ace, 1992)

Story type: Fantasy (Alternate Universe; Light Fantasy)
Series: Ambermere

Major character(s): Asbrak, Royalty (king); Daniel, Gambler, Adventurer; Rogan the Inept, Wizard
Time period(s): Indeterminate
Locale(s): Ambermere, Mythical Place; Earth

Summary: Daniel, on the run from Charlie, a mob boss whose daughter decides she wants Daniel, escapes to Ambermere where he becomes embroiled in the conflict between its King Asbrak and King Razenor, a neighbor. Unfortunately, Rogan releases a demon on Earth when he opens the dimensional doorway. Author's first novel.

Other books you might like:
Piers Anthony, *Man From Mundania*, 1989
Brian Daley, *The Doomfarers of Coramonde*, 1977
John DeChancie, *Castle Perilous*, 1988
Gordon R. Dickson, *The Dragon and the George*, 1976
Fritz Leiber, *Swords and Deviltry*, 1970
John Morressy, *Kedrigern and the Charming Couple*, 1990
Christopher Stasheff, *The Warlock in Spite of Himself*, 1969

3438

J. CALVIN PIERCE

The Wizard of Ambermere

(New York: Ace, 1993)

Story type: Fantasy (Alternate Universe; Light Fantasy)
Series: Ambermere
Major character(s): Marcia, Adventurer
Time period(s): Indeterminate
Locale(s): Ambermere, Mythical Place; Earth

Summary: After a demon follows Marcia home from the magical realm, Marcia's house becomes a bit crowded with a pack of pixies and other magical creatures who also move in. Marcia determines that she needs to become a proper magician to protect herself and brings a necromancer from the Lower Regions of Ambermere to advance her education.

Other books you might like:
Emma Bull, *War for the Oaks*, 1987
Esther Friesner, *Gnome Man's Land*, 1991
Esther Friesner, *Harpy High*, 1991
Esther Friesner, *Unicorn U.*, 1992
Christopher Moore, *Practical Demonkeeping*, 1992

3439

MEREDITH ANN PIERCE

The Pearl of the Soul of the World

(Boston: Little Brown, 1990)

Story type: Fantasy (Magic Conflict; Young Adult)
Series: Darkangel
Major character(s): Aeriel, Sorceress; Irrylath, Royalty (King); Ravanna, Sorceress
Time period(s): Indeterminate
Locale(s): Terrain, Fictional Country

Summary: Aeriel made a bargain which would be very difficult to keep when she took Ravanna's pearl. The pearl is the only means with which Aeriel can defeat the White Witch, free her husband, Irrylath, and end the drought which is destroying her world. 1991 Best Book For Young Adults title.

Other books you might like:
Jacqueline Lichtenberg, *House of Zeor*, 1974
Jacqueline Lichtenberg, *Unto Zeor Forever*, 1978
Anne Rice, *Interview with the Vampire*, 1987
Anne Rice, *The Queen of the Damned*, 1988
Anne Rice, *The Vampire Lestat*, 1985

3440

MEREDITH ANN PIERCE

The Son of Summer Stars

(Boston: Little Brown, 1996)

Story type: Fantasy (Young Adult; Adventure)
Series: Firebringer Trilogy
Major character(s): Aljan "Jan" Moonbrow, Mythical Creature (unicorn), Leader; Tek, Mythical Creature (unicorn), Warrior
Time period(s): Indeterminate
Locale(s): The Plain, Fictional Country; Hallow Hills, Mythical Place

Summary: Jan's skill in diplomacy and battle sets the stage for his prophesied accomplishments, the vanquishing of the unicorns' old enemy, the dragons, and the unicorns' return to their homeland.

Other books you might like:
Peter S. Beagle, *The Last Unicorn*, 1968
Bruce Coville, *The Unicorn Treasury*, 1988
   editor
Pamela Dean, *The Secret Country*, 1985
John Lee, *The Unicorn Quest*, 1986
Tanith Lee, *Black Unicorn*, 1991
Jane Yolen, *Here There Be Unicorns*, 1994

3441

MEREDITH ANN PIERCE

The Woman Who Loved Reindeer

(New York: Tor Books (St. Martin's Press), 1989)

Story type: Fantasy (Historical)
Major character(s): Caribou, Leader (Wisewoman); Reindeer, Mythical Creature (Trangl)
Time period(s): Indeterminate Past

Summary: Caribou, a wisewoman of the north, attempts to lead her people across the Burning Plain with her companion, Reindeer, a trangl, who can appear either as a stag or a human. Reindeer knows the only way to safety.

Other books you might like:
Jean M. Auel, *Clan of the Cave Bear*, 1980
Jim Crace, *The Gift of Stones*, 1989
W. Michael Gear, *People of the Wolf*, 1990
   Kathleen O'Neal Gear, co-author
Sue Harrison, *Mother Earth, Father Sky*, 1990
Elizabeth Marshall Thomas, *Reindeer Moon*, 1987

3442

TAMORA PIERCE

The Realms of the Gods

(New York: Atheneum, 1996)

Story type: Fantasy (Young Adult; Adventure)
Series: Immortals
Major character(s): Diane Sarrasri, Magician, Telepath (with animals); Numair Salmalin, Magician
Time period(s): Indeterminate Past
Locale(s): Realms of the Gods, Mythical Place; Tortall, Fictional Country

Summary: When they awaken in the realms of the gods, Diane and Numair must make their way back to wartorn Tortall without help from Diane's parents, gods engaged in war with the Queen of Chaos. With the badger god and the duckmole god as guides, Diane and Numair set out to find the dragons whose aid Diane hopes to enlist. Concluding volume of a tetralogy.

Other books you might like:
Gillian Bradshaw, *The Land of Gold*, 1992
Ursula K. Le Guin, *A Wizard of Earthsea*, 1968
Tanith Lee, *Black Unicorn*, 1991
Andre Norton, *Elvenblood*, 1995
   Mercedes Lackey, co-author
Sherwood Smith, *Wren's War*, 1995

3443

TAMORA PIERCE

Wild Magic

(New York: Atheneum, 1992)

Story type: Fantasy (Young Adult; Adventure)
Series: Immortals
Major character(s): Diane Sarrasri, Magician, Telepath (with animals); Onua Chamtong, Animal Trainer (horsemistress), Adventurer
Time period(s): Indeterminate Past
Locale(s): Tortall, Fictional Country (kingdom)

Summary: Daine must quickly learn to harness her budding magic abilities when the kingdom requires her help in stopping a sudden infestation of dangerous immortal creatures.

Other books you might like:
Lois McMaster Bujold, *The Spirit Ring*, 1992
Diane Duane, *Deep Wizardry*, 1985
Diane Duane, *High Wizardry*, 1990
Diane Duane, *So You Want to Be a Wizard?*, 1983
Laurell K. Hamilton, *Nightseer*, 1992
Mary H. Herbert, *Dark Horse*, 1990
Patricia C. Wrede, *Caught in Crystal*, 1987
Patricia C. Wrede, *Daughter of Witches*, 1983
Jane Yolen, *Wizard's Hall*, 1991
Mary Frances Zambreno, *A Plague of Sorcerers*, 1991

3444

TAMORA PIERCE

Wolf-Speaker
(New York: Atheneum, 1994)

Story type: Fantasy (Young Adult; Adventure)
Series: Immortals
Major character(s): Diane Sarrasri, Magician, Telepath (with animals); Numair Salmalin, Magician
Time period(s): Indeterminate Past
Locale(s): Tortall, Fictional Country

Summary: Fearful that human abuse of the Dunlath Valley environment will threaten animal survival, the wolves turn to Diane for help. When Diane, Numair and their companions come to help, they discover a greater challenge than they had anticipated. Sequel to *Wild Magic*.

Other books you might like:
Pamela Dean, *The Dubious Hills*, 1994
Tara K. Harper, *Shadow Leader*, 1991
Ursula K. Le Guin, *A Wizard of Earthsea*, 1968
Patricia C. Wrede, *Searching for Dragons*, 1991
Laurence Yep, *Dragon of the Lost Sea*, 1982

3445

MARGE PIERCY

He, She and It
(New York: Knopf, 1991)

Story type: Science Fiction (Literary; Dystopian)
Major character(s): Shira Shipman, Computer Expert; Yod, Android; Malkah Shipman, Aged Person
Time period(s): 21st century
Locale(s): United States

Summary: Returning home after a messy divorce, Shira must examine her past, her values and her definition of humanity when she becomes involved in tutoring an android. The story is intercut with the legend of a golem in the 1600s Warsaw Ghetto.

Other books you might like:
Eleanor Arnason, *A Woman of the Iron People*, 1991
Margaret Atwood, *The Handmaid's Tale*, 1985
Octavia E. Butler, *Dawn*, 1987
Philip K. Dick, *Do Androids Dream of Electric Sheep?*, 1968
Suzette Haden Elgin, *The Judas Rose*, 1987
Suzette Haden Elgin, *Native Tongue*, 1984
Marjorie Bradley Kellogg, *Harmony*, 1991
Ursula K. Le Guin, *The Left Hand of Darkness*, 1969
Pat Murphy, *The City, Not Long After*, 1989
Joan Slonczewski, *A Door into Ocean*, 1986
Norman Spinrad, *Riding the Torch*, 1978
Sheri S. Tepper, *The Gate to Women's Country*, 1988

3446

CHRISTOPHER PIKE (Pseudonym of Kevin McFadden)

The Cold One
(New York: Tor, 1995)

Story type: Horror (Reanimated Dead)
Series: Cold One
Major character(s): Peter Jacobs, Journalist; Julie Moore, Psychologist, Student (graduate student); Govinda Sharma, Scientist
Time period(s): 1990s (1995)
Locale(s): Los Angeles, California

Summary: *L.A. Times* columnist Peter Jacobs' investigations into a series of brutal murders dovetails with Julie Moore's graduate studies of near-death experiences, and leads to the discovery of ''the Cold One,'' a creature of myth who hitchiked a passage into our world during a woman's return from a near-death experience. Now she commands an army of the dissolute and disenfranchised to fulfill her evil schemes. This is the first novel in a projected series.

Other books you might like:
Warren Newton Beath, *Bloodletter*, 1994
Stephen Gallagher, *Valley of Lights*, 1987
Stephen King, *Pet Sematary*, 1983
Dean R. Koontz, *Hideaway*, 1993
John Saul, *Black Lightning*, 1995

3447

CHRISTOPHER PIKE (Pseudonym of Kevin McFadden)

The Last Vampire
(New York: Pocket/Archway, 1994)

Story type: Horror (Vampire Story)
Series: Last Vampire
Major character(s): Alisa Perne, Vampire (a.k.a. Lara Adonis); Ray Riley, Teenager; Yaksha, Demon (a.k.a. Rick Graham)
Time period(s): 1990s (1994)
Locale(s): Mayfair, Oregon

Summary: Five-thousand-year-old vampire Alisa Perne kills the detective hired to discover her true identity, then impersonates a high school student to befriend the detective's young son and find out how much his father knew. Her investigations ultimately bring her into contact with the demon who first vampirized her. Young adult novel.

Other books you might like:
Richie Tankersley Cusick, *Vampire*, 1991
Joseph Locke, *Vampire Heart*, 1994
Nicholas Pine, *Night School*, 1994
R.J. Smith, *The Vampire Diaries*, 1992

`3448`

CHRISTOPHER PIKE (Pseudonym of Kevin McFadden)

The Midnight Club

(New York: Pocket/Archway, 1994)

Story type: Horror (Mystery)
Major character(s): Ilonka Pawluk, Teenager, Patient; Kevin, Teenager, Patient; Dr. White, Doctor
Time period(s): 1990s (1994)
Locale(s): Washington

Summary: ''The Midnight Club,'' a quintet of five terminally ill teens who meet nightly to tell each other tales of horror while living out their final days at a hospice, makes a pact that the first of their number to die will return to convince others of the existence of an afterlife. When one of them dies, they begin finding that the stories they tell one another have unusual significance for their own fates. Young adult novel.

Other books you might like:
David Pierce, *Forever Yours*, 1994
Nicholas Pine, *The In Crowd*, 1994
R.L. Stine, *The Thrill Club*, 1990

`3449`

CHRISTOPHER PIKE (Pseudonym of Kevin McFadden)

Sati

(New York: St. Martin's Press, 1990)

Story type: Fantasy (Religious)
Major character(s): Sati, Deity; Michael Winters, Truck Driver; David Stone, Businessman (real estate investor), Landlord
Time period(s): 1990s (1990)
Locale(s): Los Angeles, California

Summary: Michael picks up a hitchhiker in the desert and takes her to his home in Los Angeles. She is young, blonde, pretty—and she says she is God. Michael doesn't believe her, and yet his life and the lives of people around him begin to change.

Other books you might like:
Suzette Haden Elgin, *Star Anchored, Star Angered*, 1979
Robert A. Heinlein, *Stranger in a Strange Land*, 1991
A.J. Langguth, *Jesus Christs*, 1968
C.S. Lewis, *The Lion, the Witch, and the Wardrobe*, 1950
Gore Vidal, *Messiah*, 1954

`3450`

CHRISTOPHER PIKE (Pseudonym of Kevin McFadden)

The Season of Passage

(New York: Tor, 1992)

Story type: Horror (Vampire Story)
Major character(s): Lauren Wagner, Astronaut; Jennifer Wagner, Teenager (Lauren's sister); Terry Hayes, Journalist
Time period(s): 2000s (2002)
Locale(s): Mars

Summary: On the second manned mission to Mars, medical officer Lauren Wagner discovers the fate of the astronauts from the mysteriously aborted first mission: they have become the victims of a species of interstellar vampire who now want to use her as a vector invading Earth.

Other books you might like:
Alan Dean Foster, *Alien*, 1979
Nigel Kneale, *The Quatermass Experiment*, 1959
Colin Wilson, *The Space Vampires*, 1976

`3451`

CHRISTOPHER PIKE (Pseudonym of Kevin McFadden)

See You Later

(New York: Pocket/Archway, 1990)

Story type: Fantasy (Romance; Young Adult)
Major character(s): Mark, Computer Expert; Victor, Computer Expert; Becky, Teenager, Girlfriend
Time period(s): 1980s; 2030s
Locale(s): California

Summary: Mark's attraction to record-store clerk Becky seems doomed by her relationship with Ray, until he meets the attractive, but ominous, Kara and Victor. They intervene in his life, breaking up Becky and Ray and propelling Becky and Mark into romance—but why? The answer lies in the future, and the true identities of Kara and Victor in the present, or the identities of Becky and Mark in the future.

Other books you might like:
Jack Finney, *Time and Again*, 1970
Robert A. Heinlein, *The Door into Summer*, 1957
Pat Murphy, *The Falling Woman*, 1986
Philippa Pearce, *Tom's Midnight Garden*, 1958

`3452`

CHRISTOPHER PIKE (Pseudonym of Kevin McFadden)

The Starlight Crystal

(New York: Pocket, 1996)

Story type: Science Fiction (Young Adult; Time Travel)
Major character(s): Paige Christian, Teenager, Space Explorer; Tem Basker, Teenager; Karl Christian, Spaceship Captain
Time period(s): 22nd century
Locale(s): *Traveler*, Spaceship

Summary: Paige Christian falls in love with Tem Basker a week before leaving on a one-way space mission. She vows to see Tem again, even if it means outliving humanity and the stars and embarks on an adventure that lasts nine billion years.

Other books you might like:
Stephen Baxter, *Ring*, 1996
Greg Bear, *Eon*, 1985
Margaret Wander Bonanno, *Preternatural*, 1996
Randall Frakes, *The Terminator*, 1985
    Bill Wisher, co-author
Randall Frakes, *Terminator 2: Judgment Day*, 1994
Patrick O'Leary, *Door Number Three*, 1995
Robert Silverberg, *Starborne*, 1996

3453

CHRISTOPHER PIKE (Pseudonym of Kevin McFadden)

Witch

(New York: Pocket/Archway, 1990)

Story type: Fantasy (Contemporary; Young Adult)
Major character(s): Julia Florence, Teenager, Witch; Scott Hague, Teenager; Amy Belle, Teenager
Time period(s): 1980s
Locale(s): Indian Pole, Idaho

Summary: Julia has inherited strange powers from her family, and considers herself a good witch. When she has a vision of her best friend's boyfriend being shot, she intervenes to save his life, but her other best friend, Scott, is mortally wounded instead. She decides to use her powers to obtain vengeance on the murderers, but is such a decision compatible with her self-definition of ''good''? And there may be other repercussions besides the loss of her own identity that her revenge will cost her and her friends.

Other books you might like:
Marion Zimmer Bradley, *The Heritage of Hastur*, 1975
Peter Dickinson, *Healer*, 1987
Diana Wynne Jones, *The Lives of Christopher Chant*, 1988
Stephen King, *Carrie*, 1974
Ursula K. Le Guin, *A Wizard of Earthsea*, 1968
Patricia A. McKillip, *The Forgotten Beasts of Eld*, 1974

3454

RICHARD PINI, Editor

Dark Hours

(New York: Tor, 1993)

Story type: Fantasy (Anthology)
Series: Elfquest: The Blood of Ten Chiefs

Summary: Contains a character chart, three-page preface by the editor and nine original shared world stories by 11 authors including Lynn Abbey, Esther Friesner, Katharine Eliska Kimbriel, Mercedes Lackey, Diana L. Paxson and Nancy Springer.

Other books you might like:
Robert Asprin, *Thieves' World*, 1979
  editor
Wendy Pini, *Elfquest: Journey to Sorrow's End*, 1982
  Richard Pini, co-author
Will Shetterly, *Liavek*, 1985
  Emma Bull, co-editor
Terri Windling, *Borderland*, 1986
  Mark Alan Arnold, co-editor
Terri Windling, *Elsewhere II*, 1982
  Mark Alan Arnold, co-editor
Terri Windling, *Faery*, 1985
  editor
Terri Windling, *Life on the Border*, 1991
  editor

3455

WENDY PINI
RICHARD PINI, Co-Author

The Quest Begins

(New York: Ace, 1996)

Story type: Fantasy (Adventure; Political)
Series: Elfquest
Major character(s): Cutter, Mythical Creature (elf), Leader; Skywise, Mythical Creature (elf); Leetah, Mythical Creature (elf)
Time period(s): Indeterminate
Locale(s): Sorrow's End, Mythical Place

Summary: When humans arrive at Sorrow's End, a sanctuary in the elves' flight from human interference, Cutter decides he must locate and unify disparate elven groups to allow their survival.

Other books you might like:
Gael Baudino, *Strands of Starlight*, 1989
Terry Goodkind, *Stone of Tears*, 1995
Richard Pini, *Against the Wind*, 1990
  editor
Richard Pini, *The Blood of Ten Chiefs*, 1986
  Robert Asprin, Lynn Abbey, co-editors
Richard Pini, *Dark Hours*, 1993
  editor
Richard Pini, *Winds of Change*, 1989
Richard Pini, *Wolfsong*, 1988
  Robert Asprin, Lynn Abbey, co-editors

3456

DANIEL MANUS PINKWATER

Borgel

(New York: Macmillan, 1990)

Story type: Fantasy (Contemporary; Young Adult)
Major character(s): Borgel, Time Traveller; Melvin, Child, Time Traveller; Fafner, Animal (dog)
Time period(s): 1990s (1990)
Locale(s): New York, New York

Summary: From the day Borgel moves into the spare bedroom of the Spellbound household, Melvin is on his way to becoming a time tourist with Uncle Borgel in a 1937 Dorbzeldge sedan. Meeting aliens and talking to the dog are great stuff, then the party joins in a quest for the Great Popsicle.

Other books you might like:
Janet Asimov, *Norby, the Mixed-up Robot*, 1983
  Isaac Asimov, co-author
Roald Dahl, *Charlie and the Chocolate Factory*, 1964
Diane Duane, *So You Want to Be a Wizard?*, 1983
Ian Fleming, *Chitty Chitty Bang Bang*, 1964
Mel Gilden, *Outer Space and All That Junk*, 1989
Diana Wynne Jones, *The Homeward Bounders*, 1981
Ian Marter, *Dr. Who and the Ribos Operation*, 1979

3457

EDMUND PLANTE

Seed of Evil

(New York: Leisure, 1991)

Story type: Horror (Evil Children)
Major character(s): Patty Thompson, Office Worker (receptionist); Richard Thompson, Child; Lydia Thompson, Aged Person (Patty's mother)
Time period(s): 1990s
Locale(s): New England

Summary: Patty Thompson knew there was something unnatural about the incredibly strong and seductive barroom pickup who raped her and left her with child, but even her worst suspicions have not prepared her for the intemperate offspring, Richard, whose childish petulance quickly evolves into an uncanny ability to cause mischief, mayhem and murder that betray his father's demonic nature. This novel was first published in 1988.

Other books you might like:
Ramsey Campbell, *To Wake the Dead*, 1980
John Coyne, *Child of Shadows*, 1990
Ira Levin, *Rosemary's Baby*, 1967
Raymond Van Over, *The Twelfth Child*, 1990

3458

CHARLES PLATT

Free Zone

(New York: Avon, 1989)

Story type: Science Fiction (Satire)
Major character(s): Dusty McCullough, Ruler
Time period(s): Indeterminate Future
Locale(s): Los Angeles, California

Summary: A group of fugitives, civil libertarians, misfits and oddballs take over part of Los Angeles and rename it the Free Zone, declaring themselves to be an independent nation. Their leader, Dusty McCullough, spends most of his time fighting off the underhanded attacks of the evil mayor of Los Angeles, a fundamentalist Christian. He also does battle with very strange aliens, talking dogs, dinosaurs, and movie stars.

Other books you might like:
Mel Gilden, *Surfing Samurai Robots*, 1988
Ron Goulart, *Hellquad*, 1984
Ron Goulart, *Shaggy Planet*, 1972
Ron Goulart, *Skyrocket Steele*, 1980
Rudy Rucker, *Master of Space and Time*, 1984
Rudy Rucker, *Software*, 1982
Rudy Rucker, *Wetware*, 1988

3459

CHARLES PLATT

Protektor

(New York: AvoNova, 1996)

Story type: Science Fiction (Mystery; Cyberpunk)

Major character(s): Tom McCray, Troubleshooter (Protektor); Serena Catalano, Businesswoman, Organized Crime Figure; Eva Kurimoto, Journalist
Time period(s): Indeterminate Future
Locale(s): Agorima, Planet—Imaginary; Protektorate, Interstellar Empire/Federation

Summary: A computer virus threatens to turn Agorima from pleasure planet into a realm of anarchy if Tom McCray cannot root it out.

Other books you might like:
Ben Bova, *Death Dream*, 1984
Pat Cadigan, *Mindplayers*, 1987
Philip K. Dick, *Do Androids Dream of Electric Sheep?*, 1968
Katharine Kerr, *Palace*, 1996
Michael Swanwick, *Vacuum Flowers*, 1987
John Varley, *Steel Beach*, 1992

3460

CHARLES PLATT

The Silicon Man

(New York: Bantam Spectra, 1991)

Story type: Science Fiction (Hard Science Fiction; Adventure)
Major character(s): James Bayley, FBI Agent; Leo Gottbaum, Scientist
Time period(s): 2030s (2030)
Locale(s): California

Summary: On the trail of illegal weapons, FBI agent James Bayley stumbles across a top-secret project run by a team of government scientists that has found a way to store the human mind inside a computer. Those scanned will be immortals, freed from the weaknesses of the flesh, virtual deities in a universe of their own creation. But godhood has a price. To gain immortality, you must be willing to die.

Other books you might like:
John Brunner, *Children of the Thunder*, 1989
Dean Ing, *Systemic Shock*, 1981
John Shirley, *Eclipse*, 1985
Bruce Sterling, *Islands in the Net*, 1988
Walter Jon Williams, *Hardwired*, 1986

3461

ROBERT POE

Return to the House of Usher

(New York: Tor, 1996)

Story type: Horror (Psychological Suspense)
Major character(s): Roderick Usher, Doctor; Madeline Usher, Doctor (psychiatrist); John Charles Poe, Journalist
Time period(s): 1990s (1996)
Locale(s): Crowley Creek, Virginia

Summary: In this contemporary recasting of Edgar Allan Poe's classic short story ''The Fall of the House of Usher,'' Doctor Roderick Usher summons newspaper reporter John Poe to the sanitarium he runs with his twin sister Madeleine to get to the bottom of its mysteries. Madeleine's death drives Usher over the edge, but Roderick's reports of ghosts of former sanitarium patients that haunt the halls spur John to look into the activities of organized crime members who covet the land the sanitarium was built on for their own. This is the author's first novel.

Other books you might like:
Peter Cannon, *Pulptime*, 1984
William Hjortsberg, *Nevermore*, 1995
Marie Kiraly, *Madeline: After the Fall of Usher*, 1996
Daniel Stashower, *The Adventure of the Ectoplasmic Man*, 1986

3462

FREDERIK POHL

The Gateway Trip: Tales and Vignettes of the Heechee

(New York: Del Rey, 1990)

Story type: Science Fiction (Adventure; Collection)
Series: Heechee
Major character(s): Audee Walthers, Pilot
Time period(s): Indeterminate Future
Locale(s): Venus; Gateway Asteroid, Space Station; Outer Space (Milky Way Galaxy)

Summary: This collection of 10 stories expands the Hugo Award and Nebula Award winning Heechee series. ''The Merchant of Venus,'' the longest story (116 pages), is a first person narrative relating the discovery of Heechee tunnels on Venus which precipitates human voyages to interstellar space via the Heechee Asteroid. Other stories tell of early voyages using Heechee ships and their marvelous discoveries.

Other books you might like:
Gordon R. Dickson, *The Dorsai Companion*, 1986
Robert A. Heinlein, *The Past through Tomorrow*, 1967
Larry Niven, *Tales of Known Space*, 1975
Cordwainer Smith, *The Best of Cordwainer Smith*, 1975
John Varley, *The Persistence of Vision*, 1978

3463

FREDERIK POHL

Homegoing

(New York: Ballantine/Del Rey, 1989)

Story type: Science Fiction (First Contact)
Major character(s): Sandy Washington, Young Man; Chin Tekkitho, Alien, Teacher
Time period(s): 21st century
Locale(s): Earth; Spaceship

Summary: Sandy Washington, a human being raised by aliens, is returned to an Earth that he has been ill-prepared for, but, Candide-like, does his best to fit in. Although the aliens claim to have come to Earth with humanity's best interests at heart, there are indications that this might not be the truth.

Other books you might like:
Octavia E. Butler, *Dawn*, 1987
C.J. Cherryh, *The Pride of Chanur*, 1984
Robert A. Heinlein, *Stranger in a Strange Land*, 1961

Rebecca Ore, *Becoming Alien*, 1987
Rebecca Ore, *Being Alien*, 1989

3464

FREDERIK POHL
THOMAS T. THOMAS, Co-Author

Man Plus

(New York: Baen, 1994)

Story type: Science Fiction (Alternate Intelligence)
Major character(s): Roger Torraway, Cyborg, Military Personnel (retired officer); Demeter Coughlan, Spy, Student; Jory den Ostreicher, Cyborg (Creole)
Time period(s): 2040s (2043)
Locale(s): Tharsis Montes, Mars

Summary: Coming from an environment in which the grid seems to experience difficulties, Demeter dislikes computers. Having difficulty concentrating after an accident with a hair-cutting robot, Demeter plans to visit Mars as a tourist and do some intelligence work for her grandfather while there. Since his power source requires expensive recharging, Roger must deal with Demeter when she requests his help. Although it seems to be building weapons with which to attack the colonists, the grid controls everything on Mars and cannot be turned off without all the humans dying. Sequel to *Man Plus*.

Other books you might like:
Ben Bova, *Mars*, 1992
Kim Stanley Robinson, *Green Mars*, 1994
Kim Stanley Robinson, *Red Mars*, 1993
S.C. Sykes, *Red Genesis*, 1991
Thomas T. Thomas, *ME: A Novel of Self Discovery*, 1991
John Varley, *Steel Beach*, 1992
David Weber, *Path of the Fury*, 1992
Jack Williamson, *Beachhead*, 1992

3465

FREDERIK POHL

Mining the Oort

(New York: Ballantine Del Rey, 1992)

Story type: Science Fiction (Hard Science Fiction; Political)
Major character(s): Dekker DeWoe, Student, Spaceman
Time period(s): 21st century
Locale(s): Mars; Earth; Co-Mars Two, Space Station (Oort Project Station)

Summary: Dekker DeWoe struggles to gain entry into the Oort project training program through which he could learn to mine cometary material from the Oort Cloud for use in the ambitious project of terraforming Mars. In training, Dekker discovers the very different social patterns of people not raised on Mars and learns that the healthy completion of the Martian project may fall victim to bureaucratic haste and short-sightedness.

Other books you might like:
John Barnes, *Orbital Resonance*, 1991
Ben Bova, *Mars*, 1992
A.C. Crispin, *Starbridge*, 1989

Vonda N. McIntyre, *Superluminal*, 1983
Rebecca Ore, *Becoming Alien*, 1987
Allen Steele, *Lunar Descent*, 1991
Jack Williamson, *Mazeway*, 1991

3466

FREDERIK POHL

The Other End of Time

(New York: Tor, 1996)

Story type: Science Fiction (Theological; First Contact)
Major character(s): Jim Daniel ''Dan'' Dannerman, Spy, Spaceman; Patrice ''Pat'' Adcock, Scientist (astronomer), Spacewoman; Dopey, Alien
Time period(s): 1990s
Locale(s): Washington, District of Columbia; Starlab, Space Station

Summary: After messages arrive from space, Starlab, abandoned for 18 months, appears occupied by the aliens who sent the message. Ordered to join Pat's mission to Starlab, Dan and the rest of the crew find the aliens, only to get instantly jailed. The aliens allow them to discover that their originals have returned to Earth, that the interstellar war will reach Earth shortly, and that all will be taken care of at the Eschaton at the end of the universe.

Other books you might like:
Roger MacBride Allen, *The Ring of Charon*, 1990
Greg Bear, *Eon*, 1985
David Brin, *Brightness Reef*, 1995
Larry Niven, *Protector*, 1973
Robert J. Sawyer, *Starplex*, 1996

3467

FREDERIK POHL

Outnumbering the Dead

(New York: St. Martin's Press, 1992)

Story type: Science Fiction (Immortality; Arts)
Major character(s): Rafiel, Actor, Aged Person; Alegretta, Doctor, Immortal; Mosay, Director, Immortal
Time period(s): 2000s
Locale(s): United States; *Hakluyt*, Spaceship (space colony)

Summary: The famous 90-year-old actor, Rafiel, recently released from the hospital, agrees to star in *Oedipus Rex*. His aging body proves no match for the youthful vigor of the Immortals around him, and their petty intrigues and squabbling upset him. Pursuing the only immortality available to Rafiel, when his old love, Alegretta, wants to bear his child, he accompanies her to Hakluyt where she plans to pilot the space colony.

Other books you might like:
Marta Randall, *Islands*, 1980
Pamela Sargent, *The Golden Space*, 1982
Michael D. Weaver, *My Father Immortal*, 1989
John Wyndham, *The Trouble with Lichen*, 1960

3468

FREDERIK POHL
JACK WILLIAMSON, Co-Author

The Singers of Time

(New York: Doubleday Foundation, 1991)

Story type: Science Fiction (Invasion of Earth; Hard Science Fiction)
Major character(s): Sue-Ling Quong, Doctor; Francis Krake, Spaceship Captain
Time period(s): Indeterminate Future
Locale(s): Earth; *The Golden Hind*, Spaceship

Summary: Pilot Francis Krake, first human captive of the Brotherhood, was saved by them during World War II. When he learned to pilot a spaceship he was given one which he could pilot for the alien Turtles on worlds that were uncomfortable for them. Centuries later, when he returns to Earth, he helps renegotiate Earth's arrangement with the Brotherhood when they have need of the old human science.

Other books you might like:
Roger MacBride Allen, *The Ring of Charon*, 1990
Piers Anthony, *Macroscope*, 1969
Glen Cook, *The Dragon Never Sleeps*, 1988
Steve Miller, *Carpe Diem*, 1989
    Sharon Lee, co-author
Steve Miller, *Agent of Change*, 1988
    Sharon Lee, co-author
Steve Miller, *Conflict of Honors*, 1988
    Sharon Lee, co-author

3469

FREDERIK POHL

Stopping at Slowyear

(Eugene, Oregon: Pulphouse Publishing Axolotl Press, 1991)

Story type: Science Fiction (Romance; Medical)
Major character(s): Murra, Spouse; Arakaho Blundy Spenotex, Writer, Rancher; Mercy MacDonald, Spaceman
Time period(s): Indeterminate
Locale(s): Slowyear, Planet—Imaginary; *Nordvik*, Spaceship

Summary: The arival of the tramp spaceship *Nordvik* means excitement for all. Slowyear colonists hope for new trading goods and medical advances which would cure the high infant mortality rate. Some of the *Nordvik* crew hope to find the perfect planet to make final port of call, little suspecting that Slowyear may be *Nordvik's* last stop.

Other books you might like:
Nancy Kress, *Beggars in Spain*, 1991
Judith Moffett, *Two That Came True*, 1991
Spider Robinson, *Kill the Editor*, 1991
Robert Silverberg, *Thebes of the Hundred Gates*, 1991

3470

FREDERIK POHL

The Voices of Heaven
(New York: Tor, 1994)

Story type: Science Fiction (First Contact; Theological)
Major character(s): Gerald Tscharka, Spaceship Captain, Fanatic; Barry di Hoa, Pilot (spaceship), Mentally Ill Person (manic depressive); Geronimo, Alien (Lep)
Time period(s): 22nd century
Locale(s): Moon (Earth's); Pava, Planet—Imaginary (Delta Pavonis System)

Summary: Shanghaied to Pava without his medications, manic-depressive Barry di Hoa finds himself extremely lonely without his girlfriend, 18 years away on Luna. He befriends Geronimo, gradually becoming fascinated with the alien Leps. Meanwhile, a large section of the original population believing in Original Sin, the Millenialists, extoll suicide as the ultimate correct action, putting the colony at risk.

Other books you might like:
Eleanor Arnason, *Ring of Swords*, 1993
C.J. Cherryh, *Foreigner*, 1994
Anne McCaffrey, *Powers That Be*, 1993
    Elizabeth Ann Scarborough, co-author
Vonda N. McIntyre, *Metaphase*, 1992
Larry Niven, *The Mote in God's Eye*, 1974
    Jerry Pournelle, co-author
Vernor Vinge, *A Fire upon the Deep*, 1992

3471

FREDERIK POHL

The World at the End of Time
(New York: Ballantine/Del Rey, 1990)

Story type: Science Fiction (Hard Science Fiction)
Major character(s): Wan-To, Alien; Viktor Sorricaine, Scientist
Time period(s): Indeterminate Future
Locale(s): *Mayflower*, Spaceship; Outer Space; Newmanhome, Planet—Imaginary

Summary: When Viktor Sorricaine was awakened during the voyage to Newmanhome from Earth, it was due to the unexpected and unexplained changes in some of the stars on the way to the new sun. His father, an astrophysicist, was unable to explain the phenomenon before their arrival at Newmanhome, and once there, everyone was busy. Newmanhome was a beautiful planet, and was becoming very comfortable for its new inhabitants until the unexplained astrophysical phenomena began to affect their survival.

Other books you might like:
David Brin, *Earth*, 1990
Robert L. Forward, *Rocheworld*, 1990
Frank Herbert, *Whipping Star*, 1970
Larry Niven, *Neutron Star*, 1968
John E. Stith, *Redshift Rendezvous*, 1990
Jack Williamson, *Mazeway*, 1990

3472

RACHEL POLLACK

Godmother Night
(New York: St. Martin's, 1996)

Story type: Fantasy (Contemporary; Legend)
Major character(s): Lauren "Laurie" Cohen, Parent (adopted), Lesbian; Jacqueline "Jaqe" Lang, Parent, Lesbian; Mother Night, Mythical Creature (death incarnate), Guardian (godmother)
Time period(s): 1990s
Locale(s): United States

Summary: An appeal to Mother Night leads to Jaqe's daughter and unanticipated consequences. Raised by Laurie, Jaqe's daughter practices healing, sometimes aided by Mother Night's unusual potions, while Mother Night's help allows her to negotiate the spirit realm.

Other books you might like:
Piers Anthony, *On a Pale Horse*, 1983
Charles de Lint, *Memory and Dream*, 1984
Elizabeth Hand, *Waking the Moon*, 1995
Patricia A. McKillip, *Winter Rose*, 1996
Ben Okri, *The Famished Road*, 1992
Terri Windling, *The Wood Wife*, 1996

3473

RACHEL POLLACK, Editor
CAITLIN MATTHEWS, Co-Editor

Tarot Tales
(New York: Ace, 1996)

Story type: Fantasy (Anthology)
Summary: This anthology contains a three-page foreword by Matthews, a three-page introduction by Pollack plus brief individual introductions and author biographies for 16 original stories inspired by the symbols of Tarot fortune-telling cards. The tone of the stories varies from humor and satire to more ominous views of the reanimated dead, snake worshippers in the Amazon, Greek mythology, and the decadent rich. Authors include Storm Constantine, Sheila Finch, M. John Harrison, Gwyneth Jones, Garry Kilworth, Jacqueline Lichtenberg, Caitlin Matthews, Michael Moorcock, Rachel Pollack, Josephine Saxton, and R.J. Stewart.

Other books you might like:
Piers Anthony, *Tarot*, 1987
Italo Calvino, *The Castle of Crossed Destinies*, 1977
Tim Powers, *Last Call*, 1992
Edward Whittemore, *Jerusalem Poker*, 1978
Charles Williams, *The Greater Trumps*, 1950

3474

RACHEL POLLACK

Temporary Agency
(New York: St. Martin's Press, 1994)

Story type: Fantasy (Contemporary; Political)

Major character(s): Ellen Pierson, Artist (graphic), Lesbian; Alison Birkett, Lawyer; Lisa Black Dust 7, Demon (Ferocious One)
Time period(s): 21st century
Locale(s): New York, New York

Summary: In a world where Shamanist magic exists comfortably in an America similar to the late 20th century, a young man comes to the attention of an evil spirit. His 14-year-old cousin, Ellen must grow up quickly to save his, and soon her, life from a spiritual and political conspiracy. Over a decade later, frightening political plots draw Ellen back in, again threatening her survival. Sequel to *Unquenchable Fire*.

Other books you might like:
Poul Anderson, *Operation Chaos*, 1971
Scott Baker, *Drink the Fire From the Flames*, 1987
John Crowley, *Little, Big*, 1981
Lisa Goldstein, *A Mask for the General*, 1987
Pat Murphy, *The City, Not Long After*, 1989

3475

RACHEL POLLACK

Unquenchable Fire

(Woodstock, New York: The Overlook Press, 1992)

Story type: Fantasy (Political; Legend)
Major character(s): Jennifer "Jennie" Mazdan, Government Official (server), Psychic (dreamer); Allan "Al" Lightstorm, Religious (teller); Michael "Mike" Gold, Spouse (Jennie's), Worker (Wall Street messenger)
Time period(s): 21st century
Locale(s): Poughkeepsie, New York; New York, New York

Summary: After revolution brings the Agency to power and alters cultural priorities in the United States of America, storytellers motivated by dreams and visions take the place of prominence formerly held by politicians and cinema stars and ritual magic pervades society. Late for the summer solstice's Day of Truth recitation by Allan Lightstorm, New York City's most famous Teller, Jennie finds herself overcome by a powerful dream, leaving her impregnated. After her failed abortion, Jennie discovers the Agency's influence acts to thwart her wishes. Winner of the Arthur C. Clarke Award upon publication in Britain.

Other books you might like:
Suzette Haden Elgin, *And Then There'll Be Fireworks*, 1981
Suzette Haden Elgin, *The Grand Jubilee*, 1981
Suzette Haden Elgin, *Twelve Fair Kingdoms*, 1981
Ursula K. Le Guin, *Always Coming Home*, 1987
Ursula K. Le Guin, *The Lathe of Heaven*, 1971
John D. MacDonald, *Wine of the Dreamers*, 1951

3476

NICK POLLOTTA

Bureau 13

(New York: Ace, 1991)

Story type: Fantasy (Psychic Powers; Contemporary)
Series: Bureau 13

Major character(s): Michael Donaher, Religious (priest), FBI Agent; Richard Anderson, Wizard, FBI Agent; Jessica Taylor, Telepath, FBI Agent
Time period(s): 1990s
Locale(s): New York, New York; Chicago, Illinois

Summary: After it was discovered that supernatural phenomena were a danger to the citizens of the United States, Bureau 13, under the auspices of the F.B.I., was charged with protecting the populace. More than a century later the Bureau is continuing its secret fight to keep Americans safe from vampires, werewolves, demons or whatever monsters threaten the United States.

Other books you might like:
Glen Cook, *Sweet Silver Blues*, 1987
John DeChancie, *Castle for Rent*, 1989
Ron Goulart, *A Talent for the Invisible*, 1973
Simon Hawke, *The Wizard of Sunset Strip*, 1989
Mercedes Lackey, *Children of the Night*, 1990
Gene Wolfe, *Castleview*, 1990

3477

NICK POLLOTTA

Doomsday Exam

(New York: Ace, 1992)

Story type: Fantasy (Psychic Powers; Contemporary)
Series: Bureau 13
Major character(s): Kenneth Sanders, Mutant, FBI Agent; Edward Alvarez, FBI Agent; Raul Horta, Wizard, FBI Agent
Time period(s): 1990s
Locale(s): Chicago, Illinois; Holding Facility, Alternate Universe

Summary: After the Tunafish Team delivers Lumpy, an unkillable monster, to the Holding Facility, they watch the final exam of the graduating mages of the Bureau 13 Academy. When interrrupted by a jailbreak of the unkillables, the Tunafish Team must save the Academy then save the world with newly graduated cadets.

Other books you might like:
Robert N. Charrette, *Never Deal with a Dragon*, 1990
Esther Friesner, *Hooray for Hellywood*, 1990
Ron Goulart, *Brainz, Inc.*, 1985
Ron Goulart, *Hail Hibbler*, 1980
Stephen King, *The Dead Zone*, 1979
Dean R. Koontz, *Lightning*, 1988
George R.R. Martin, *Wild Cards*, 1987
     editor

3478

NICK POLLOTTA

Full Moonster

(New York: Ace, 1992)

Story type: Fantasy (Contemporary; Psychic Powers)
Series: Bureau 13

Major character(s): Edwardo "Ed", FBI Agent, Leader; Michael Donaher, Religious (priest), FBI Agent; Jessica Taylor, Telepath, FBI Agent
Time period(s): 1990s
Locale(s): Chicago, Illinois

Summary: When a psychic blast opens a rift onto Earth through which werewolves and other Hellish fiends invade Earth looking for new territory, Bureau 13 rushes to stop the invasion, repair the damage and stop the Brotherhood of Darkness.

Other books you might like:
Alan Dean Foster, *Cyber Way*, 1990
Alan Dean Foster, *To the Vanishing Point*, 1988
Elizabeth Ann Scarborough, *Last Refuge*, 1992
Clifford D. Simak, *Out of Their Minds*, 1970
Michael A. Stackpole, *A Gathering Evil*, 1991

3479

NICK POLLOTTA
PHIL FOGLIO, Co-Author

Illegal Aliens
(Lake Geneva, WI: TSR, 1989)

Story type: Science Fiction (Humor)
Major character(s): Trell, Alien (invader); Hammer, Criminal (gang leader)
Time period(s): 1980s
Locale(s): New York, New York

Summary: A truly nasty bunch of aliens land in New York's Central Park and kidnap what they think is a typical cross section of the population. They claim that they're putting the humans through a galactic citizenship test, but they're really sizing the planet up for invasion. Unfortunately for the aliens the supposedly typical human beings they've kidnapped belong to one of New York's more notorious street gangs.

Other books you might like:
Poul Anderson, *The High Crusade*, 1960
Martin Caidin, *Prison Ship*, 1989
Alan Dean Foster, *Quozl*, 1989
Michael Kandel, *Strange Invasion*, 1989

3480

PETRU POPESCU

In Hot Blood
(New York: Fawcett, 1989)

Story type: Horror (Vampire Story)
Major character(s): Laura Walker, Young Woman; Alain Lecouveurs, Nobleman, Vampire
Time period(s): 1980s
Locale(s): New Orleans, Louisiana

Summary: A new arrival in New Orleans, Laura Walker quickly succumbs to the spell of the aristocratic Lecouveurs family, especially the clan patriarch, Emory, a voracious vampire in the Dracula tradition, and Alain, his handsome nephew, who would disavow his antecedents if he could.

Other books you might like:
Anne Rice, *Interview with the Vampire*, 1976
Whitley Strieber, *The Hunger*, 1981
Peter Tremayne, *Dracula, My Love*, 1980

3481

ELLEN PORATH

Steel and Stone
(Lake Geneva, Wisconsin: TSR, 1992)

Story type: Fantasy (Quest; Romance)
Series: Dragonlance: The Meetings Sextet
Major character(s): Tanthalas "Tanis" Half-Elvin, Mythical Creature (half-elf), Warrior; Kitiara "Kit" Matar, Mercenary, Leader
Time period(s): Indeterminate
Locale(s): Krynn, Planet—Imaginary

Summary: Recently met, Tanis and Kitiara travel across Krynn while facing dangerous human and unhuman foes and magical interference.

Other books you might like:
Tina Daniell, *The Companions*, 1993
Tina Daniell, *Dark Heart*, 1992
Mary Kirchoff, *Wanderlust*, 1991
    Steve Winter, co-author
Michael Williams, *The Oath and the Measure*, 1992

3482

BARRY PORTER

Dark Souls
(New York: Zebra, 1989)

Story type: Horror (Reanimated Dead)
Major character(s): Tom Howards, Doctor; Shadowman, Monster
Time period(s): 1980s
Locale(s): Hawksborough, Colorado (A small mountain mining town)

Summary: Five people, isolated in a cabin in a Colorado mining town, are surrounded by monster creatures from the depths of the earth capable of reanimating the dead and, more terribly, taking the souls of the living.

Other books you might like:
Randall Boyll, *After Sundown*, 1989
John Christopher, *The Possessors*, 1964

3483

BARRY PORTER

Junkyard
(New York: Zebra, 1989)

Story type: Horror (Small Town Horror)
Major character(s): Ray Holscomb, Teenager; Kevin Gavel, Police Officer (deputy sheriff), Murderer (serial killer)
Time period(s): 1980s (1989)
Locale(s): Winsome

Summary: Four teenaged boys with a secret clubhouse in a junkyard gradually realize that they are sharing their junkyard with a human monster, a serial killer of runaway boys, and a mysterious, perhaps supernatural, flesh eating creature.

Other books you might like:
James Herbert, *The Rats*, 1974
Stephen King, *It*, 1986
Chauncey G. Parker III, *The Visitor*, 1981

3484
JAN POTOCKI

The Manuscript Found in Sragossa
(New York: Viking, 1995)

Story type: Horror (Occult)
Major character(s): Alphonse van Worden, Military Personnel; Don Pedro de Uzeda, Religious (brother)
Time period(s): 1730s (1739)
Locale(s): Madrid, Spain

Summary: In the Sierra Morena mountains of Spain, a young soldier is seduced into a world of the real and the supernatural that seems fashioned from the legends of Christianity, Judaism, and Islam. This episodic novel, written between 1797 and 1815, varies from the bawdy to the metaphysical in its accounts of the Wandering Jews, physical embodiments of the Gemini twins, the progeny of King Solomon, and other known personalities of history and legend. Translated by Ian Maclean.

Other books you might like:
L. Sprague de Camp, *Land of Unreason*, 1942
    Fletcher Pratt, co-author
William Hope Hodgson, *The Night Land*, 1912
Charles Maturin, *Melmoth the Wanderer*, 1820
Edgar Allan Poe, *The Narrative of A. Gordon Pym*, 1838
Eugene Sue, *The Wandering Jew*, 1844

3485
JERRY POURNELLE
S.M. STIRLING, Co-Author

The Children's Hour
(New York: Baen, 1991)

Story type: Science Fiction (Military)
Series: Man-Kzin Wars
Major character(s): Chuut-Riit, Alien (Kzin); Ingrid Raines, Military Personnel; Dnivtopun, Alien (Thrint)
Time period(s): 25th century
Locale(s): Wunderland, Planet—Imaginary; *U.N.S.N. Catskinner*, Spaceship

Summary: The Kzin occupy the human-colonized Alpha Centauri system and have sent four fleets from there to attack Earth. So far the humans have deflected all Kzin attacks and destroyed each fleet in succession. But it seems that they will not be able to hold off the Kzin now that Chuut-Riit is in control on Wunderland. From the humans he has been adapting a new technique, cooperation, so Earth's ARM sends a mission to assassinate him before it gets perfected.

Other books you might like:
Poul Anderson, *Inconstant Star*, 1991
Diana G. Gallagher, *The Alien Dark*, 1990
Dean Ing, *Cathouse*, 1991
Larry Niven, *Man-Kzin Wars*, 1988
    editor
Larry Niven, *Man-Kzin Wars II*, 1989
    editor
Larry Niven, *Man-Kzin Wars III*, 1990
    editor
Larry Niven, *Man-Kzin Wars IV*, 1991
    editor
Larry Niven, *Tales of Known Space*, 1975
S.M. Stirling, *Marching through Georgia*, 1988
S.M. Stirling, *The Stone Dogs*, 1990

3486
JERRY POURNELLE, Editor
JOHN F. CARR, Co-Editor

CoDominium: Revolt on War World
(New York: Baen, 1992)

Story type: Science Fiction (Anthology; Military)
Series: War World
Time period(s): 21st century
Locale(s): Haven, Planet—Imaginary

Summary: Contains eight original stories by nine authors with Leslie Fish and Frank Gasperik collaborating on "Janesfort War," plus an introduction, "The Lost and the Founder" and epilog, "Farewell to Haven," by the editor. The stories depict the early history of Haven from bleak dumping ground for religious and political dissidents to wealthy mining planet which produces warriors capable of defeating the Sauron fighting machine. Other authors include John Dalmas, Susan Shwartz, Harry Turtledove, Eric Vinicoff and William F. Wu.

Other books you might like:
Robert Asprin, *The Bug Wars*, 1979
F.M. Busby, *The Alien Debt*, 1984
Orson Scott Card, *Ender's Game*, 1985
John Dalmas, *The White Regiment*, 1990
David Drake, *The Fleet*, 1988
    Bill Fawcett, co-editor
William R. Forstchen, *Ice Prophet*, 1983
Martin H. Greenberg, *Bootcamp 3000*, 1992
    Charles G. Waugh, co-editor
Keith Laumer, *Star Colony*, 1981
Larry Niven, *Man-Kzin Wars*, 1988
    editor
Joel Rosenberg, *Hero*, 1990

3487
JERRY POURNELLE

Falkenberg's Legion
(New York: Baen, 1990)

Story type: Science Fiction (Military)
Series: CoDominium

Major character(s): John Christian Falkenberg, Military Personnel
Time period(s): 21st century
Locale(s): Arrarat, Planet—Imaginary; Hadley, Planet—Imaginary; New Washington, Planet—Imaginary

Summary: The seeds of contradiction that lie at the heart of the Soviet-American alliance are bearing their final fruit. Soon they will rip the CoDominium apart and Earth will die. In the face of that inevitability, the fate of humanity lies with the colony worlds, few of which are equipped for more than bare survival. Thrown upon their own resources, their futures seem as limited as their past. They have one hope. To find someone with both the strength and vision to grasp the remnants of civilization and weld them into a single society. John Christian Falkenberg is that man. John Christian's story is complete for the first time in this volume which encompasses two previous titles, *The Mercenary* (1977) and *West of Honor* (1976), with some new filler material.

Other books you might like:
Gordon R. Dickson, *Dorsai!*, 1976
Gordon R. Dickson, *Soldier, Ask Not*, 1967
David Drake, *Cluster Command*, 1989
    W.C. Dietz, co-author
David Drake, *Hammer's Slammers*, 1979
Joe Haldeman, *The Forever War*, 1975
Keith Laumer, *Bolo: The Annals of the Dinochrome Brigade*, 1976

3488

JERRY POURNELLE
S.M. STIRLING, Co-Author

Go Tell the Spartans
(New York: Baen, 1991)

Story type: Science Fiction (Military)
Series: CoDominium
Major character(s): Peter Owensford, Mercenary, Military Personnel
Time period(s): 21st century; 22nd century
Locale(s): Sparta, Planet—Imaginary

Summary: Hoping to provide themselves a secure base of operations, Falkenberg's Legion accepts the training of local troops on Sparta, settled by eccentric American political idealists and involuntary colonists who now hope to survive the impending collapse of Imperial rule. Others work to control Sparta for themselves.

Other books you might like:
Isaac Asimov, *Foundation*, 1951
Isaac Asimov, *Foundation and Empire*, 1952
Isaac Asimov, *Second Foundation*, 1953
Lois McMaster Bujold, *Borders of Infinity*, 1989
Lois McMaster Bujold, *The Warrior's Apprentice*, 1986
Allan Cole, *Sten*, 1984
    Chris Bunch, co-author
Glen Cook, *The Dragon Never Sleeps*, 1988
Alis A. Rasmussen, *Revolution's Shore*, 1990

3489

JERRY POURNELLE, Editor
JOHN F. CARR, Co-Editor

Life Among the Asteroids
(New York: Ace, 1992)

Story type: Science Fiction (Anthology)
Series: Endless Frontier

Summary: Includes a two-page introduction by Pournelle and individual introductions for entries with two articles by Pournelle and one by Eric Drexler reprinted from periodicals and original stories by John Hegenberger, Peter L. Manly and Brooks Peck plus reprinted stories by Poul Anderson, Jack Clemons, Phillip C. Jennings, Jerry Pournelle, Charles Sheffield and Michael Swanwick.

Other books you might like:
Robert Silverberg, *The Science Fiction Hall of Fame, Volume 1*, 1970
    editor
Cordwainer Smith, *The Best of Cordwainer Smith*, 1975
Marc Stiegler, *The Gentle Seduction*, 1990
John Varley, *The Barbie Murders and Other Stories*, 1980
John Varley, *Blue Champagne*, 1986
John Varley, *The Persistence of Vision*, 1978

3490

JERRY POURNELLE

Prince of Mercenaries
(New York: Baen Books, 1989)

Story type: Science Fiction (Military)
Series: CoDominium
Major character(s): John Christian Falkenberg, Mercenary; Lysander, Royalty
Time period(s): 21st century
Locale(s): CoDominium, Earth; Sparta, Planet—Imaginary

Summary: The CoDominium, the U.S.-Soviet alliance that has maintained peace on Earth and in space for decades, is crumbling and the colony worlds are beginning to assert their independence. Prince Lysander of Sparta enlists the aid of the mercenary commander John Christian Falkenberg to help break free from CoDominium oppression.

Other books you might like:
Gordon R. Dickson, *The Final Encyclopedia*, 1984
Gordon R. Dickson, *Lost Dorsai*, 1980
Gordon R. Dickson, *Soldier, Ask Not*, 1967
Gordon R. Dickson, *The Spirit of Dorsai*, 1979
David Drake, *Hammer's Slammers*, 1979
David Drake, *Rolling Hot*, 1989
Robert A. Heinlein, *Starship Troopers*, 1959

3491

JERRY POURNELLE
S.M. STIRLING, Co-Author

Prince of Sparta
(New York: Baen, 1993)

Story type: Science Fiction (Military; Political)
Series: CoDominium
Major character(s): Lysander Collins, Military Personnel, Royalty (prince); Skida "Skilly" Thibodeau, Leader (resistance), Murderer; Peter Owensford, Mercenary, Military Personnel (General)
Time period(s): 21st century; 22nd century
Locale(s): Sparta, Planet—Imaginary

Summary: Hired by the Spartan government to quell the Helot Rebellion, Falkenberg's Legion discovers Grand Senate intrigues driving the situation. As Falkenberg's enemies and CoDominium Navy factions backing Skilly Thibodeau abet the insurgents, discord reverberates through the CoDominium.

Other books you might like:
Roger MacBride Allen, *The Torch of Honor*, 1985
Lois McMaster Bujold, *The Warrior's Apprentice*, 1986
John Dalmas, *The Regiment*, 1987
Gordon R. Dickson, *Dorsai!*, 1976
Alan Dean Foster, *The False Mirror*, 1992
Robert A. Heinlein, *Starship Troopers*, 1959
Keith Laumer, *The Glory Game*, 1973
H. Beam Piper, *Uller Uprising*, 1982
Timothy Zahn, *Cobra*, 1985

3492

SUSAN POWER

The Grass Dancer
(New York: Putnam, 1994)

Story type: Fantasy (Romance; Contemporary Realism)
Major character(s): Charlene Thunder, Indian; Harley Wind Soldier, Indian; Anna Thunder, Indian, Witch
Time period(s): 1960s; 1970s
Locale(s): North Dakota

Summary: Seperated in the 1880s with their love unfulfilled, two spirits attempt to find each other through the decades. Driven by the inertia of family history, Charlene Thunder and Harley Wind Soldier search for happiness despite external pressures after a motorcycle accident leads Charlene to suspect her grandmother, Anna Thunder, of causing the deaths. First novel.

Other books you might like:
J. Alison James, *Sing for a Gentle Rain*, 1990
Barry Lopez, *Crow and Weasel*, 1990
Gerald Vizenor, *Dead Voices: Natural Agonies in the Real World*, 1992
Roger Welsch, *Touching the Fire*, 1992
Roger Zelazny, *Bridge of Ashes*, 1976

3493

RICHARD M. POWERS

Galatea 2.2
(New York: Farrar Straus Giroux, 1995)

Story type: Science Fiction (Alternate Intelligence; Literary)
Major character(s): Richard Powers, Teacher, Writer; C., Student; Helen, Artificial Intelligence
Time period(s): 1990s
Locale(s): U., Fictional City

Summary: Hired by the Center for the Study of Advanced Sciences, Richard Powers joins a project on Artificial Intelligence. As the programs grow more complex, Powers teaches them about life and literature, while he reminisces about a failed relationship.

Other books you might like:
Elizabeth Hand, *AEstival Tide*, 1992
D.F. Jones, *Colossus*, 1966
Ian McDonald, *Terminal Cafe*, 1994
Rudy Rucker, *Wetware*, 1988
Thomas T. Thomas, *ME: A Novel of Self Discovery*, 1991

3494

TIM POWERS

Expiration Date
(New York: Tor, 1996)

Story type: Fantasy (Contemporary)
Major character(s): Pete Sullivan, Technician (tramp electrician), Psychic; Thomas Edison, Inventor, Disembodied Personality; Koot "Kootie" Hoomie Parganas, Teenager, Psychic
Time period(s): 1990s
Locale(s): Los Angeles, California

Summary: When the dead hang on as half-conscious ghosts, real but dazed and intangible, people will exploit them. When a young boy opens the door to one of the most powerful ghosts ever, those people in-between notice. Suddenly, a great many people, living, dead, and in-between, must fight for their lives.

Other books you might like:
Peter S. Beagle, *A Fine and Private Place*, 1960
James P. Blaylock, *Night Relics*, 1994
Jack Cady, *The Off Season*, 1995
John Crowley, *Little, Big*, 1981
Megan Lindholm, *Wizard of the Pigeons*, 1986

3495

TIM POWERS

Last Call
(New York: Morrow, 1992)

Story type: Fantasy (Contemporary; Horror)
Major character(s): Scott Crane, Gambler; Benjamin "Bugsy" Siegel, Historical Figure, Criminal

Time period(s): 1990s
Locale(s): Las Vegas, Nevada

Summary: Abandoned by the father who would sacrifice him to gain mastery over Las Vegas, Scott Crane grows up in a foster family. As an adult, Scott and his adoptive family attempt to unseat his corrupted father utilizing the symbolic mysticism associated with tarot. The Charnel House limited edition's text differs slightly.

Other books you might like:
Piers Anthony, *Tarot*, 1987
James P. Blaylock, *The Paper Grail*, 1991
Charles de Lint, *The Little Country*, 1991
Alan Dean Foster, *To the Vanishing Point*, 1988
Stephen King, *The Stand: The Complete and Uncut Edition*, 1990
Edward Whittemore, *Jerusalem Poker*, 1978

3496

TIM POWERS

The Stress of Her Regard

(New York: Ace Books, 1989)

Story type: Horror (Vampire Story)
Major character(s): Michael Crawford, Doctor, Fugitive; George Gordon Byron, Historical Figure, Writer (poet)
Time period(s): 1820s
Locale(s): Europe; England

Summary: After his wife is murdered by a spectral female on their wedding night, Michael Crawford flees to seek counsel from the great English poets, Keats, Shelley, and Byron, who, he finds, have been similarly haunted. He learns of the *nephelim*, a race of spiritual vampires that plague the most sensitive and, along with Byron and Josephine, sister of his murdered wife, searches for a way to neutralize their terrible powers.

Other books you might like:
Brian W. Aldiss, *Frankenstein Unbound*, 1973
James P. Blaylock, *Homunculus*, 1986

3497

TERRY PRATCHETT

Diggers

(New York: Delacorte, 1991)

Story type: Science Fiction (Young Adult; Adventure)
Series: Bromeliad
Major character(s): Dorcas, Mythical Creature (nome); Grimma, Mythical Creature (nome)
Time period(s): 1990s
Locale(s): East Coast

Summary: Having narrowly escaped the destruction of their home, the nomes find their way to an abandoned quarry where life is possible, if difficult. When humans plan to reopen the quarry, the nomes face the loss of their new home and additional dangers of rat poison and wild animals. The desperate nomes arrange to refit and flee in a piece of heavy equipment. This book is a sequel to *Truckers*.

Other books you might like:
Murray Leinster, *Unknown Danger*, 1969
   Will F. Jenkins, real name
Mary Norton, *The Borrowers*, 1952
Mary Norton, *The Borrowers Afield*, 1955
Mary Norton, *The Borrowers Afloat*, 1959
John Peterson, *The Littles*, 1967

3498

TERRY PRATCHETT

Equal Rites

(New York: Signet, 1988)

Story type: Fantasy (Light Fantasy)
Series: Discworld
Major character(s): Esk, Witch
Time period(s): Indeterminate
Locale(s): Discworld, Planet—Imaginary

Summary: A dying wizard mistakenly gives his powers to what he thinks is the eighth son of an eighth son. However, this eighth son is really a daughter and although her family tries to raise her as a witch, it becomes apparent that she is fated to become a wizard.

Other books you might like:
Suzy McKee Charnas, *The Golden Thread*, 1989
Kara Dalkey, *The Curse of Sagamore*, 1988
Peter David, *Howling Mad*, 1989
John DeChancie, *Castle Perilous*, 1988

3499

TERRY PRATCHETT

Eric

(New York: Roc, 1995)

Story type: Fantasy (Light Fantasy; Legend)
Major character(s): Eric Thursley, Wizard; Rincewind, Wizard; Astfgl, Demon
Time period(s): Indeterminate
Locale(s): Pseudopolis, Fictional City; Pandemonium, Hell

Summary: Attempting to summon a demon to grant him three wishes, to rule the world, to meet the world's most beautiful woman, and to live forever, Eric instead conjures Rincewind from the Dungeon Dimensions. When Eric gets his wishes, Rincewind, with the help of his luggage and an aphasic parrot, must save them from the consequences by a slight detour through Hell.

Other books you might like:
Douglas Adams, *The Hitchhiker's Guide to the Galaxy*, 1980
Chester Anderson, *The Butterfly Kid*, 1967
Robert Asprin, *Another Fine Myth*, 1978
Janet Morris, *Heroes in Hell*, 1986
   editor
Roger Zelazny, *If at Faust You Don't Succeed*, 1993
   Robert Sheckley, co-author

3500

TERRY PRATCHETT

Feet of Clay

(New York: HarperPrism, 1996)

Story type: Fantasy (Light Fantasy; Mystery)
Series: Discworld
Major character(s): Samuel Vimes, Police Officer; Dorfl, Mythical Creature (golem); Carrot Gimlet, Police Officer
Time period(s): Indeterminate
Locale(s): Discworld, Planet—Imaginary; Ankh-Morpork, Fictional City

Summary: A series of mysterious murders and the near death of the Patrician of Ankh-Morpork baffle the officers of the City Watch. Clues lead them on a merry chase among the denizens of the city, including a revolutionary cell of golems seeking freedom. They also stumble across a sinister plot to install Corporal Nobbs as puppet king of the city. Commander Vimes uncovers the truth, but may be unable to bring the guilty to justice.

Other books you might like:
Douglas Adams, *Dirk Gently's Holistic Detective Agency*, 1987
Isaac Asimov, *The Caves of Steel*, 1954
Brett Davis, *The Faery Convention*, 1995
Lynn S. Hightower, *Alien Blues*, 1992
Elizabeth Ann Scarborough, *The Goldcamp Vampire; or The Sanguinary Sourdough*, 1987
Clifford D. Simak, *The Goblin Reservation*, 1968

3501

TERRY PRATCHETT

Guards! Guards!

(New York: Roc, 1991)

Story type: Fantasy (Light Fantasy)
Series: Discworld
Major character(s): Samuel Vimes, Police Officer (captain); Carrot Gimlet, Police Officer; Sybil Ramkin, Noblewoman (animal breeder)
Time period(s): Indeterminate
Locale(s): Ankh-Morpork, Fictional City; Discworld, Planet—Imaginary

Summary: Carrot, an orphaned human baby adopted by dwarves, is now 16 and growing too tall to work in the mines. He sets off for Ankh-Morpork to join the Night Watch and uphold the laws, not knowing that the Night Watch is barely surviving in the city since the Patrician has organized crime. However, when the Elucidated Brethren of the Ebon Night steal a book and summon a dragon in hopes of restoring the monarchy, Captain Vimes and his three men begin investigating. They find allies in Lady Ramkin, aristocratic breeder of swamp dragons, and the Librarian of the Unseen University, who ventures into L-space to recover his stolen book.

Other books you might like:
Douglas Adams, *Dirk Gently's Holistic Detective Agency*, 1987

Robert Asprin, *M.Y.T.H. Inc. Link*, 1986
Robin Wayne Bailey, *Night Watch*, 1990
Steven Brust, *Jhereg*, 1983
Will Shetterly, *Liavek: Wizard's Row*, 1987
   Emma Bull, co-editor
Clifford D. Simak, *The Goblin Reservation*, 1968
Patricia C. Wrede, *Dealing with Dragons*, 1990

3502

TERRY PRATCHETT

Lords and Ladies

(New York: HarperPrism, 1995)

Story type: Fantasy (Light Fantasy)
Series: Discworld
Major character(s): Granny Weatherwax, Witch, Hero; Magrat Garlick, Fiance(e) (the king's), Witch; Nanny Ogg, Witch, Hero
Time period(s): Indeterminate
Locale(s): Discworld, Planet—Imaginary; Lancre, Fictional City

Summary: When elves invade Lancre from the fairy realm, Granny Weatherwax and her companion witches must save the populace from the nasty infestation.

Other books you might like:
Emma Bull, *War for the Oaks*, 1987
Esther Friesner, *Gnome Man's Land*, 1991
Alan Dean Foster, *To the Vanishing Point*, 1988
Nick Pollotta, *Bureau 13*, 1991
Nick Pollotta, *Full Moonster*, 1992
Harry Turtledove, *The Case of the Toxic Spell Dump*, 1993

3503

TERRY PRATCHETT

Men at Arms

(New York: HarperPrism, 1996)

Story type: Fantasy (Light Fantasy; Adventure)
Series: Discworld
Major character(s): Edward d'Eath, Nobleman, Criminal (assassin); Carrot Gimlet, Police Officer
Time period(s): Indeterminate
Locale(s): Discworld, Planet—Imaginary; Ankh-Morpork, Fictional City

Summary: In a sequel of sorts to *Guards! Guards!*, Carrot, adopted dwarf, attempts to bring law and order to Ankh-Morpork.

Other books you might like:
Robert Asprin, *Another Fine Myth*, 1978
John Bellairs, *The Face in the Frost*, 1969
Craig Shaw Gardner, *The Other Sinbad*, 1991
Christopher Moore, *Practical Demonkeeping*, 1992
Roger Zelazny, *Bring Me the Head of Prince Charming*, 1991
   Robert Sheckley, co-author

3504

TERRY PRATCHETT

Mort

(New York: Signet, 1989)

Story type: Fantasy (Light Fantasy)
Series: Discworld
Major character(s): Mort, Apprentice (to Death)
Time period(s): Indeterminate
Locale(s): Discworld, Planet—Imaginary

Summary: Desperate to find a profession, Mort agrees to become Death's apprentice. The fun begins when soft-hearted Mort can't bring himself to collect the dead and those he spares remain dead in the eyes of the rest of the world.

Other books you might like:
Terry Brooks, *Magic Kingdom for Sale—Sold!*, 1986
   Magic Kingdom Series
Douglas W. Clark, *Alchemy Unlimited*, 1990
Charles de Lint, *Wolf Moon*, 1988
F.J. Hale, *Ogre Castle*, 1988
   After the Spell Wars Trilogy Book 1
Anne McCaffrey, *Alchemy and Academe*, 1970
Jack Vance, *The Dying Earth Series*,

3505

TERRY PRATCHETT

Moving Pictures

(New York: Roc, 1992)

Story type: Fantasy (Light Fantasy)
Series: Discworld
Major character(s): Victor Tugelbend, Student, Wizard; Cut-Me-Own-Throat Dibbler, Businessman; Caspode the Wonder Dog, Animal (dog)
Time period(s): Indeterminate
Locale(s): Discworld, Planet—Imaginary; Ankh-Morpork, Fictional City

Summary: When the idea of Hollywood leaks into Discworld, people instantly respond to the call of Tinsel Town and the adventure of film making. Ninth in the series.

Other books you might like:
Craig Shaw Gardner, *Bride of the Slime Monster*, 1990
Craig Shaw Gardner, *Revenge of the Fluffy Bunnies*, 1990
Craig Shaw Gardner, *Slaves of the Volcano God*, 1989
Lionel Fenn, *668: The Neighbor of the Beast*, 1992
   pseudonym of Charles L. Grant
Lionel Fenn, *Kent Montana and the Really Ugly Thing From Mars*, 1990
   pseudonym of Charles L. Grant

3506

TERRY PRATCHETT

Reaper Man

(New York: Roc, 1992)

Story type: Fantasy (Light Fantasy)

Series: Discworld
Major character(s): Death ''Bill Door'', Mythical Creature; Windle Poons, Wizard, Reanimated Dead; Renata Flitworth, Farmer, Maiden
Time period(s): Indeterminate
Locale(s): Ankh-Morpork, Fictional City; Discworld, Planet—Imaginary

Summary: Death loses his old job and finds another as a mortal farmhand for an eccentric spinster. As a result, when mortals die, no one comes for their souls. As pent-up Life Forces become so strong that ordinarily inanimate objects come to life, a plague of shopping carts overrun Ankh-Morpork. Newly deceased Windle Poons, now one of the undead, finds himself working with Dead Rights activists and wizards from the University to destroy the city-killing mall.

Other books you might like:
Douglas Adams, *The Long Dark Tea-Time of the Soul*, 1988
Robert Asprin, *Myth-ing Persons*, 1984
L. Sprague de Camp, *The Complete Compleat Enchanter*, 1989
   Fletcher Pratt, co-author
Gordon R. Dickson, *The Dragon and the George*, 1976
Christopher Stasheff, *The Warlock in Spite of Himself*, 1969
Chelsea Quinn Yarbro, *A Baroque Fable*, 1986
Neil Gaiman, *Good Omens: The Nice and Accurate Prophecies of Agnes Nutter, Witch*, 1990
   Terry Pratchet, co-author

3507

TERRY PRATCHETT

Small Gods

(New York: HarperCollins, 1994)

Story type: Fantasy (Religious; Light Fantasy)
Series: Discworld
Major character(s): Brutha, Religious; The Great God Om, Deity, Animal (turtle); Vorbis, Religious, Police Officer (Quisitor)
Time period(s): Indeterminate
Locale(s): Omnia, Fictional Country; Ephebe, Fictional City; Discworld, Planet—Imaginary

Summary: A novice in the service of The Great God Om, Brutha, encounters a turtle who claims to be his god. Not too bright, Brutha possesses a reasonably clear idea of right and wrong, which gets him and the turtle into trouble as his religion's followers go to war with a neighboring city state.

Other books you might like:
John Bellairs, *The Face in the Frost*, 1969
Neil Gaiman, *Good Omens: The Nice and Accurate Prophecies of Agnes Nutter, Witch*, 1990
   Terry Pratchett, co-author
Craig Shaw Gardner, *A Malady of Magicks*, 1986
Tom Holt, *Expecting Someone Taller*, 1988
Barry Hughart, *Bridge of Birds*, 1984

3508

TERRY PRATCHETT

Soul Music

(New York: HarperCollins, 1995)

Story type: Fantasy (Light Fantasy)
Series: Discworld
Major character(s): Susan Sto Helit, Student, Apprentice (of Death); Imp y Celyn, Musician (bard); The Death of Rats, Mythical Creature
Time period(s): Indeterminate
Locale(s): Discworld, Planet—Imaginary; Ankh-Morpork, Fictional City

Summary: Since Death decides that he needs to forget and disappears, his granddaughter, Susan, finds herself drafted to fill the void, despite some un-Deathlike notions. When a group of down and out musicians hits on something very new, Ankh-Morpork will never be the same again. Again.

Other books you might like:
Robert Asprin, *Another Fine Myth*, 1978
Gordon R. Dickson, *The Dragon and the George*, 1976
Alan Dean Foster, *Spellsinger*, 1983
Neil Gaiman, *Good Omens: The Nice and Accurate Prophecies of Agnes Nutter, Witch*, 1990
    Terry Pratchett, co-author
Craig Shaw Gardner, *The Other Sinbad*, 1991
Roger Zelazny, *Bring Me the Head of Prince Charming*, 1993
    Robert Sheckley, co-author

3509

TERRY PRATCHETT

Truckers

(New York: Delacorte, 1990)

Story type: Science Fiction (Humor; Young Adult)
Series: Truckers
Major character(s): Masklin, Alien, Mythical Creature (nome); Dorcas, Mythical Creature (nome); Thing, Computer (flight navigation/recording)
Time period(s): 20th century

Summary: The nomes of the store "Arnold Bros. (est. 1905): All Things Under One Roof" refuse to believe that Masklin and his fellow nomes have come from the mythical Outside. Their shock and disbelief are even greater when the Thing tells them that the store is going to be demolished, and all three thousand of them will have to leave.

Other books you might like:
Mary Norton, *The Borrowers*, 1952
Mary Norton, *The Borrowers Afield*, 1955
Mary Norton, *The Borrowers Afloat*, 1959
Mary Norton, *The Borrowers Aloft*, 1961
John Peterson, *The Littles*, 1967

3510

TERRY PRATCHETT

Wings

(New York: Delacorte, 1991)

Story type: Science Fiction (Young Adult; Adventure)
Series: Bromeliad
Major character(s): Masklin, Mythical Creature (nome); Gurder, Mythical Creature (nome); Thing, Computer (flight/navigation)
Time period(s): 1990s
Locale(s): East Coast; Florida

Summary: When the nomes decide to summon their spaceship, Masklin, Gurder, Angelo and Thing set out to Cape Canaveral to make use of a communication satellite launch. With Thing's help, the nomes use a Concorde jet to fly to Florida. While arranging to fly closer to the launch site by riding geese, the nomes find that thousands more of their kind exist, raising new questions of how to use the ship. This book is a sequel to *Diggers*.

Other books you might like:
Murray Leinster, *Land of the Giants*, 1968
    Will F. Jenkins, real name
Mary Norton, *The Borrowers*, 1952
Mary Norton, *The Borrowers Aloft*, 1961
John Peterson, *The Littles*, 1967
James D. Priest, *Kirins: The Spell of No'an*, 1990

3511

TERRY PRATCHETT

Witches Abroad

(New York: Roc, 1993)

Story type: Fantasy (Light Fantasy; Quest)
Series: Discworld
Major character(s): Magrat Garlick, Witch; Granny Weatherwax, Witch; Emberella, Royalty (princess)
Time period(s): Indeterminate
Locale(s): Discworld, Planet—Imaginary

Summary: Newly made a fairy godmother, Magrate Garlick must try to stop Princess Emberella from marrying Prince Charming. Granny Weatherwax and Nancy Ogg try to assist her in this endeavor, battling mirror magic, recalcitrant broomsticks, the perils of travel and the power of the stories themselves.

Other books you might like:
L. Sprague de Camp, *The Complete Compleat Enchanter*, 1989
    Fletcher Pratt, co-author
Gordon R. Dickson, *The Dragon and the George*, 1976
Diane Duane, *So You Want to Be a Wizard?*, 1983
Neil Gaiman, *Good Omens: The Nice and Accurate Prophecies of Agnes Nutter, Witch*, 1990
    Terry Pratchett, co-author
Barry B. Longyear, *The God Box*, 1989
Christopher Stasheff, *The Warlock in Spite of Himself*, 1969
Jane Yolen, *Briar Rose*, 1992

Roger Zelazny, *Bring Me the Head of Prince Charming*, 1991
  Robert Sheckley, co-author
Roger Zelazny, *If at Faust You Don't Succeed*, 1993
  Robert Sheckley, co-author

3512

TERRY PRATCHETT

Wyrd Sisters

(New York: Penguin/ROC, 1990)

Story type: Fantasy (Light Fantasy)
Series: Discworld
Major character(s): Granny Weatherwax, Witch; Felmet, Nobleman (duke), Murderer; Tomjon, Heir—Lost (to Lancre)
Time period(s): Indeterminate
Locale(s): Kingdom of Lancre, Fictional Country; Discworld, Planet—Imaginary

Summary: In order to hide him from the duke who killed his father, three witches foster the infant prince Tomjon to a travelling thespian. As time passes, the land grows discontented with Felmet's rule. Magical problems threaten if the prince is not restored to the throne.

Other books you might like:
Steven Brust, *Jhereg*, 1983
John DeChancie, *Castle Perilous*, 1988
Suzette Haden Elgin, *The Grand Jubilee*, 1981
James H. Schmitz, *The Witches of Karres*, 1966
Will Shetterly, *Liavek*, 1985
  Emma Bull, co-author

3513

BYRON PREISS, Editor
JOHN BETANCOURT, Co-Editor
KEITH R.A. DECANDIDO, Co-Editor

The Ultimate Alien

(New York: Dell, 1995)

Story type: Science Fiction (Anthology)

Summary: Contains a six-page introduction with recommendations by Robert Silverberg, seven pages of biographies, and three reprinted and 12 original stories whose tone varies from dark to humorous. The settings range from Earth, Venus, and the artificial asteroid, Mallworld, to distant star systems, with themes including first contact, invasion of Earth, alien societies, and human/alien romance and marriage. Authors include Arthur C. Clarke, Peter Crowther, Don D'Ammassa, Mel Gilden, Ed Gorman, Nina Kiriki Hoffman, Anne McCaffrey, Robert Silverberg, S.P. Somtow, and Lawrence Watt-Evans. Authors collaborate on two stories, "Alien Radio" by Mike Resnick and Nicholas A. DiChario, and "First Contact, Sort Of" by Karen Haber and Carol Carr.

Other books you might like:
Groff Conklin, *Invaders of Earth*, 1952
  editor
Jack Dann, *Aliens!*, 1980
  Gardner Dozois, co-editor

Ellen Datlow, *Alien Sex*, 1990
  editor
Gardner Dozois, *Isaac Asimov's Aliens*, 1991
  editor
Stephen Goldin, *The Alien Condition*, 1973
  editor
Damon Knight, *First Contact*, 1971
  editor

3514

BYRON PREISS, Editor

The Ultimate Dracula

(New York: Dell, 1991)

Story type: Horror (Anthology; Vampire Story)

Summary: Twenty original stories written to commemorate the 60th anniversary of the film "Dracula." Stand-outs include Dan Simmons' "All Dracula's Children," set in post-Ceausescu Romania, and Anne Rice's Victorian vampire story "Master of the Rampling Gate." Others include Edward Hoch's tale of vampires in Nazi Germany, "Dracula 1944," and two science fiction vampire stories, Kristine Kathryn Rusch's "Children of the Night" and Janet Asimov's "The Contagion." With a vampire filmography by Leonard Wolff.

Other books you might like:
Ellen Datlow, *Blood Is Not Enough*, 1989
Ellen Datlow, *A Whisper of Blood*, 1991
Martin H. Greenberg, *A Taste for Blood*, 1992
  Stefan Dziemianowicz and Robert A. Weinberg, co-editors
Alan Ryan, *Vampires: Two Centuries of Great Vampire Stories*, 1987
  editor
Leslie Shepard, *The Dracula Book of Great Vampire Stories*, 1979
  editor

3515

BYRON PREISS, Editor
JOHN BETANCOURT, Co-Editor
KEITH R.A. DECANDIDO, Co-Editor

The Ultimate Dragon

(New York: Dell, 1995)

Story type: Fantasy (Anthology)

Summary: Contains a four-page introduction by Tanith Lee, nine pages of biographies, and two reprinted and 16 original stories, frequently light or ironic in tone, which feature dragons in contemporary, historical, and mythical settings, with themes varying from adventure and magic conflict to artificial intelligence. Authors include Kevin J. Anderson, Phyllis Ann Karr, Ursula K. Le Guin, Tanith Lee, Josepha Sherman, S.P. Somtow, Lawrence Watt-Evans, Chelsea Quinn Yarbro, and Jane Yolen. Authors collaborate on two stories, "Pleasantly Pink" by Mike Resnick and Nicholas A.

DiChario, and "The Dragon on the Bookshelf" by Harlan Ellison and Robert Silverberg.

Other books you might like:

Isaac Asimov, *Dragon Tales*, 1982
  Martin H. Greenberg, Charles G. Waugh, co-editors
Orson Scott Card, *Dragons of Darkness*, 1981
  editor
Orson Scott Card, *Dragons of Light*, 1983
  editor
Jack Dann, *Dragons!*, 1993
  Gardner Dozois, co-editor
Rosalind M. Greenberg, *Dragon Fantastic*, 1992
  Martin H. Greenberg, co-editor
Margaret Weis, *A Dragon-Lover's Treasury of the Fantastic*, 1994
  editor
Jane Yolen, *Here There Be Dragons*, 1993

3516

BYRON PREISS, Editor

The Ultimate Frankenstein
(New York: Dell, 1991)

Story type: Horror (Anthology; Reanimated Dead)

Summary: Twenty original stories written to commemorate the 60th anniversary of the film "Frankenstein." Stand-outs include David Schow's monster party *tour de force* "Last Call for the Sons of Shock," and Katherine Dunn's futuristic "Near-Flesh." Also included are pastiches of Mary Shelley's original novel by Philip Jose Farmer and Loren Estleman, Esther M. Friesner's amusing "Mad at the Academy," and Mike Resnick's tale of artificial humans recruited for professional football, "Monsters of the Midway." With a Frankenstein filmography by Leonard Wolff.

Other books you might like:

Michel Parry, *Rivals of Frankenstein*, 1977

3517

BYRON PREISS, Editor

The Ultimate Werewolf
(New York: Dell, 1991)

Story type: Horror (Anthology; Werewolf Story)

Summary: Twenty stories written to commemorate the 50th anniversary of the film "The Wolfman." Stand-outs include Harlan Ellison's tale of a quest for personal salvation, "Adrift Just Off the Islets of Langerhans," Kathy Koja's prose poem "Angel's Moon," and Bob Weinberg's story of an unusually well-equipped nightwatchman, "Wolf Watch." Included are retellings of the werewolf myth by Philip Jose Farmer, Kim Antieau and Bill Pronzini, humorous werewolf stories by Jerome Charyn, Mel Gilden and Kevin J. Anderson, and science fiction werewolf tales by Larry Niven and Brad Strickland. With a werewolf filmography by Leonard Wolff.

Other books you might like:

Brian J. Frost, *Book of the Werewolf*, 1973
Bill Pronzini, *Werewolf!*, 1979

3518

BYRON PREISS, Editor
JOHN BETANCOURT, Co-Editor

The Ultimate Witch
(New York: Dell, 1993)

Story type: Horror (Anthology; Witchcraft)

Summary: The twenty-five stories in this volume, most original to the book, all feature witches and witchcraft. Included are Karl Edward Wagner's "A Walk on the Wild Side," about Satanic orgyists unaware that their virgin sacrifice is a male crossdresser; Tanith Lee's beautiful "Witch of the Moon," about a young woman whose life is saved by a lonely witch woman living on the moon; Steve Rasnic Tem's "Brooms Welcome the Dust," about the dire consequences of snatching the wrong broom for a Halloween witch's costume; and Stuart M. Kaminsky's wonderfully paranoid "In Thunder, Lightning or in Rain," about a warlock who switches bodies to avoid capture. The book's two reprints include Ray Bradbury's fantasy classic, "The April Witch," and Dean Koontz's story of a thief who unwittingly steals a witch's purse, "Snatcher." Philip Jose Farmer supplies an introduction.

Other books you might like:

Martin H. Greenberg, *Devil Worshippers*, 1990
  Charles Waugh, co-editor
Peter Haining, *A Circle of Witches*, 1971
  editor

3519

BYRON PREISS, Editor
JOHN BETANCOURT, Co-Editor

The Ultimate Zombie
(New York: Dell, 1993)

Story type: Horror (Anthology; Reanimated Dead)

Summary: The 23 stories in this anthology—19 original, three reprint, and one a novel excerpt—all resurrect the zombie for their theme. Variations on the usual formulae include zombie children (A.R. Morlan's "The Toddler Pit," Alan Rodgers' "Emma's Daughter"), zombies in politics (Bob Weinberg's "Silent Majority," Don D'Ammassa's "Corruption in Office"), zombies in big business (Matthew J. Costello's "Corporate Takeover"), zombies in comedy (Lionel Fenn's "The Dead Speaketh Not, They Just Grunteth Now and Then," Brian Hodge and William Relling Jr.'s "This One'll Kill You"), and zombies as persons with severe identity crises (Robert Silverberg's "Passengers," Chelsea Quinn Yarbro's "Restoration Comedy"). Dennis Etchison wrote the introduction.

Other books you might like:

Peter Haining, *Stories of the Walking Dead*, 1985
Stephen Jones, *The Mammoth Book of Zombies*, 1993
  editor
John Skipp, *Book of the Dead*, 1989
  Craig Spector, co-editor

John Skipp, *Still Dead: Book of the Dead 2,* 1992
  Craig Spector, co-editor

3520

DOUGLAS PRESTON
LINCOLN CHILD, Co-Author

Mount Dragon

(New York: Tor/Forge, 1996)

Story type: Horror (Science Fiction)
Major character(s): Guy Carson, Scientist (biologist); Brent Scopes, Businessman; Charles Levine, Scientist (geneticist)
Time period(s): 1990s (1996)
Locale(s): Jornada del Muerto Desert, New Mexico

Summary: Guy Carson is hired to work at GeneDyne's Mount Dragon facility in the New Mexico desert, supposedly to help perfect an influenza vaccine. But when a teammate accidentally becomes infected with a flu strain that causes an absolutely ghastly death, Carson begins to suspect that GeneDyne owner Brent Scopes is using the lab's research for more insidious purposes.

Other books you might like:
Michael Crichton, *The Andromeda Strain,* 1969
Stephen King, *The Stand,* 1978
Dean R. Koontz, *Phantoms,* 1983
Patrick Lynch, *Carriers,* 1995

3521

DOUGLAS PRESTON
LINCOLN CHILD, Co-Author

Relic

(New York: Tor, 1995)

Story type: Horror (Science Fiction)
Major character(s): Margo Green, Student (graduate student); Bill Smithback, Journalist; Gregory Kawakita, Museum Curator (assistant)
Time period(s): 1990s (1995)
Locale(s): New York, New York

Summary: In this first collaborative novel, a half reptile-half simian moster rampages through the subbasements of New York City's Museum of Natural History, feeding on hapless humans when its regular supply of food (shipped stateside as part of the artifacts of a doomed 1987 Brazilian expedition) and posing a problem for a variety of museum officials and political personnel who are planning to open a major exhibit at the museum.

Other books you might like:
Ken Eulo, *Claw,* 1994
  Joe Mauck, co-author
Stephen King, *The Crate,* 1985
  in *Skeleton Crew*
Frank Belknap Long, *The Horror From the Hills,* 1963
Bob Mayer, *Operation Synbat,* 1994

3522

PAUL PREUSS

Core

(New York: Morrow, 1993)

Story type: Science Fiction (Disaster)
Major character(s): Cyrus Hudder, Parent, Scientist; Leiden "Leidy" Hudder, Scientist; Marta McDougal, Inventor, Scientist
Time period(s): 1980s; 1990s
Locale(s): Core City, Texas; Underground Environment

Summary: Earth's disintegrating magnetosphere allows human vulnerability to solar flares which create mutation, radiation burns and breakdowns in power and communications. Cyrus and Leiden Hudder must overcome their hatred of each other to rally around Marta McDougal who develops a machine to bore through the Earth's crust to repair the core, if the machine does not cause mankind's destruction.

Other books you might like:
Roger MacBride Allen, *The Ring of Charon,* 1990
Greg Bear, *The Forge of God,* 1987
David Brin, *Earth,* 1990
David Brin, *Sundiver,* 1979
David Kagan, *Sunstroke,* 1993
Philip Wylie, *When Worlds Collide,* 1933
  Edwin Balmer, co-author
Roger Zelazny, *Flare,* 1992
  Thomas T. Thomas, co-author

3523

PAUL PREUSS

The Diamond Moon

(New York: Avon, 1990)

Story type: Science Fiction (First Contact; Adventure)
Series: Arthur C. Clarke's Venus Prime
Major character(s): Linda Ellen "Sparta" Troy, Genetically Altered Being, Agent (Board of Space Control); Randolph Mays, Historian, Television Personality; J.Q.R. Forster, Professor
Time period(s): 21st century
Locale(s): Earth; Amalthea, Moon—Imaginary (of Jupiter)

Summary: Professor Forster, having deduced the nature of Amalthea, is heading there from Ganymede. His nemesis, Randolph Mays, on his T.V. series *Overmind,* tried to prove his belief that a superior intelligence was directing human history and evolution. Mays accused Professor Forster of being the Free Spirit participant behind the theft of the Martian plague. Mays is also heading for Amalthea, despite the Board of Space Control's ban on any traffic around Amalthea until after Professor Forster's expedition.

Other books you might like:
Isaac Asimov, *Nemesis,* 1989
Gregory Benford, *Heart of the Comet,* 1986
  David Brin, co-author
Arthur C. Clarke, *Rendezvous with Rama,* 1973
John Varley, *Titan,* 1979

3524

PAUL PREUSS

Hide and Seek

(New York: Avon, 1989)

Story type: Science Fiction (Adventure)
Series: Arthur C. Clarke's Venus Prime
Major character(s): Linda Ellen "Sparta" Troy, Detective—Police, Genetically Altered Being; Blake Redfield, Antiquarian
Time period(s): 22nd century
Locale(s): Mars

Summary: The ancient alien artifact discovered on Mars in a previous volume of this series has been stolen and two murders have been committed. Sparta goes to Mars to recover the artifact, only to find herself the subject of a murder attempt. Meanwhile the mysterious Free Spirit and the X culture from the stars remain in the background, their motives not entirely known.

Other books you might like:
Gregory Benford, *Great Sky River*, 1987
Gregory Benford, *Tides of Light*, 1989
David Brin, *Startide Rising*, 1983
David Brin, *The Uplift War*, 1988
Lois McMaster Bujold, *Falling Free*, 1988

3525

PAUL PREUSS

The Medusa Encounter

(New York: Avon, 1990)

Story type: Science Fiction (Adventure)
Series: Arthur C. Clarke's Venus Prime
Major character(s): Linda Ellen "Sparta" Troy, Detective—Police, Genetically Altered Being; Blake Redfield, Antiquarian
Time period(s): 22nd century
Locale(s): Earth; Jupiter

Summary: The cult known as Free Spirit has attempted to subvert the Space Board and take over the mission to Jupiter where a strange life form has been discovered. Sparta must defeat Free Spirit and, in order to do so, must travel to Jupiter.

Other books you might like:
Gregory Benford, *Great Sky River*, 1987
Gregory Benford, *Tides of Light*, 1989
David Brin, *Startide Rising*, 1983
David Brin, *The Uplift War*, 1988
Lois McMaster Bujold, *Falling Free*, 1988

3526

PAUL PREUSS

The Shining Ones

(New York: Avon, 1991)

Story type: Science Fiction (First Contact; Alternate Universe)
Series: Arthur C. Clarke's Venus Prime

Major character(s): J.Q.R. Forster, Professor (xeno-archeology); Linda Ellen "Sparta" Troy, Genetically Altered Being, Heroine; Thowinda, Alien (Amalthean), Diplomat
Time period(s): 22nd century
Locale(s): *Amalthea*, Spaceship

Summary: *Amalthea* shed its coat of ices and left orbit heading past Earth toward the sun. The humans within have been altered by Thowinda and Medusa to live underwater and are now able to survive the acceleration. Medusa, using the sun as a slingshot, headed into outer space to give humanity a better chance for the survival of life on Earth. A section of illustrations is bound into the novel.

Other books you might like:
Isaac Asimov, *Nemesis*, 1989
David Brin, *Earth*, 1990
Arthur C. Clarke, *Rama II*, 1989
    Genry Lee, co-author
Colin Greenland, *Take Back Plenty*, 1991
Carol Severance, *Reefsong*, 1991
Joan Slonczewski, *A Door into Ocean*, 1986
Sydney J. Van Scyoc, *Deepwater Dreams*, 1991
John Varley, *Titan*, 1979
David Weber, *Mutineers' Moon*, 1991

3527

ROBERT M. PRICE, Editor

The Azathoth Cycle

(Oakland, CA: Chaosium, 1995)

Story type: Horror (Anthology)
Series: Cthulhu Cycle

Summary: One poem, one essay, and fourteen original and eight reprinted stories elaborate the idea, in the fiction of H.P. Lovecraft, that the known universe is governed by forces indifferent to human fate. These forces manifest themselves in the form of incomprehensible extradimensional entities. This collection focuses on Lovecraft's "blind idiot god" Azathoth, an embodiment of cosmic chaos. Peter Cannon's two stories, "Azathoth in Arkham" and "The Revenge of Azathoth," are sequels to Lovecraft's tale "The Thing on the Doorstep," in which Azathoth influences the actions of the characters. Henry Kuttner's "Hydra" is concerned with a foolish mortal who inadvertently summons an extradimensional monster whose capabilities he has underestimated. Ramsey Campbell's "The Insects from Shaggai" tells of a man driven insane by his glimpse of an alien world.

Other books you might like:
Edward P. Berglund, *Disciples of Cthulhu*, 1975
    editor
Lin Carter, *The Spawn of Cthulhu*, 1971
    editor
Thomas M.K. Stratman, *Cthulhu's Heirs*, 1994
    editor
H.P. Lovecraft, *Tales of the Cthulhu Mythos: Golden Anniversary Anthology*, 1990
Robert Weinberg, *Miskatonic University*, 1996
    Martin H. Greenberg, co-editor

3528

ROBERT M. PRICE, Editor

The Cthulhu Cycle

(Oakland, California: Chaosium, 1996)

Story type: Horror (Anthology)

Summary: Small press editor Price assembles 13 classic and contemporary tales that evoke the concept of H.P. Lovecraft's Cthulhu, an otherworldly monster who sums up his creator's vision of cosmic horror. Included are Lovecraft's "The Call of Cthulhu," in which Cthulhu nearly succeeds at breaking into our own dimension, and two precursors that may have influenced the writing of Lovecraft's story, M.R. James' "Count Magnus" and Lord Dunsany's "A Shop in Go-By Street." August Derleth's "The Black Island" and C.J. Henderson's "Patiently Waiting" are sequels of sorts to Lovecraft's tale and Alan Dean Foster's "Some Notes Concerning a Green Box" is a gloss on the original.

Other books you might like:

Edward P. Berglund, *Disciples of Cthulhu*, 1976
  editor
Lin Carter, *The Spawn of Cthulhu*, 1991
  editor
H.P. Lovecraft, *Tales of the Cthulhu Mythos: Golden Anniversary Anthology*, 1990
Thomas M.K. Stratman, *Cthulhu's Heirs*, 1994
James Turner, *Cthulhu 2000*, 1995
  editor

3529

ROBERT M. PRICE, Editor

The Dunwich Cycle

(Oakland, CA: Chaosium, 1995)

Story type: Horror (Anthology)
Series: Cthulhu Cycle

Summary: The one original and eight reprinted stories collected here all elaborate an idea in the fiction of H.P. Lovecraft that the known universe is governed by forces indifferent to human fate and which manifest themselves in the form of incomprehensible extradimensional entities. Included here are two stories by early twentieth-century fantasist Arthur Machen, "The Great God Pan" and "The White People," whose mythos about a pagan race surviving into modern times influenced Lovecraft's work. The other stories are set in Lovecraft's decadent New England town of Dunwich. Lovecraft's "The Dunwich Horror" tells of the twin sons born from the union of a mortal woman and an extradimensional monster. Ben Indick's "The Road to Dunwich" and August Derleth's "The Shuttered Room" are sequels to Lovecraft's tale, and Richard Lupoff's "The Devil's Hop Yard" is a retelling of the tale's events from a different perspective. The editor offers his own "The Round Tower" as an alternate final chapter to the *The Lurker at the Threshold*, which August Derleth based on Lovecraft's notes.

Other books you might like:

Stephen Jones, *Shadows over Innsmouth*, 1994
  editor
Thomas M.K. Stratman, *Cthulhu's Heirs*, 1994
  editor
H.P. Lovecraft, *Tales of the Cthulhu Mythos: Golden Anniversary Anthology*, 1990
Robert Weinberg, *Miskatonic University*, 1996
  Martin H. Greenberg, co-editor

3530

ROBERT M. PRICE, Editor

The Hastur Cycle

(Oakland, California: Chaosium, 1993)

Story type: Horror (Anthology)

Summary: The editor, who has edited and published the Lovecraftian fanzine *Crypt of Cthulhu* since 1981, brings together 13 stories centered around the mythical entity Hastur, and his significance to the Lovecraft myth cycle known as the Cthulhu Mythos. Included are Lovecraft's tale of an extraterrestrial invasion of rural Vermont, "The Whisperer in Darkness"; Arthur Machen's "The Novel of the Black Seal," Ambrose Bierce's "Haita the Shepard" and "An Inhabitant of Carcosa," and Robert W. Chambers' "The Yellow Sign," all of which inspired Lovecraft; James Blish's play "More Light"; and Richard A. Lupoff's Lovecraft spoof, "Documents in the Case of Elizabeth Akeley." Price has supplied an introduction and informative notes for each story.

Other books you might like:

Edward P. Berglund, *Disciples of Cthulhu*, 1975
  editor
Ramsey Campbell, *New Tales of the Cthulhu Mythos*, 1980
  editor
Lin Carter, *The Spawn of Cthulhu*, 1971
  editor
August Derleth, *Tales of the Cthulhu Mythos*, 1969
  editor
Thomas M.K. Stratman, *Cthulhu's Heirs*, 1994

3531

ROBERT M. PRICE, Editor

The New Lovecraft Circle

(Minneapolis: Fedogan & Bremer, 1996)

Story type: Horror (Anthology)

Summary: The long-time publisher of the small press magazine *Crypt of Cthulhu* gathers 25 stories, two original to this collection, written in homage to the horror themes of H.P. Lovecraft. Included are David Sutton's "Demoniacal," in which an incantation incorporated into song lyrics on an album summon dark forces, and Brian Lumley's "The Kiss of Bugg-Shash," a sequel to Sutton's tale. Some stories, such as Lin Carter's "The Fishers From Outside" and Ramsey Campbell's "The Plain of Sound," are deliberate pastiches of Lovecraft's tales of cosmic horror. Other stories, such as Thomas Ligotti's tale of a book of forbidden knowledge,

''Vastarien,'' and Karl Wagner's ''I've Come to Talk with You Again,'' about a horror writer with one foot in the supernatural realm, are only peripherally Lovecraftian. Peter Cannon's ''The Madness out of Space'' and Richard A. Lupoff's ''Lights! Camera! Shub-Niggurath!'' are among a handful of tales that satirize the cliches of Cthulhu Mythos fiction.

Other books you might like:
Edward P. Berglund, *Disciples of Cthulhu*, 1976
   editor
Lin Carter, *The Spawn of Cthulhu*, 1991
   editor
H.P. Lovecraft, *Tales of the Cthulhu Mythos: Golden Anniversary Anthology*, 1990
Thomas M.K. Stratman, *Cthulhu's Heirs*, 1994
James Turner, *Cthulhu 2000*, 1995
   editor

3532

ROBERT M. PRICE, Editor

The Shub Niggurath Cycle

(Oakland, California: Chaosium, 1994)

Story type: Horror (Anthology)

Summary: The editor has collected 15 original and reprint stories of the supernatural featuring goats or goat-like beings, with an eye to fleshing out the mythology surrounding H.P. Lovecraft's imaginary deity Shub Niggurath, ''the goat with a thousand young.'' Included are Lewis Spence's ''The Horn of Vapula,'' about a man stalked by a goatish gargoyle; M.P. Dare's ''The Demoniac Goat,'' in which an archaeological expedition liberates an evil goat-like being; J.S. Leatherbarrow's ''The Ghostly Goat of Glamarra,'' about a witch's goat that haunts the English countryside; Ramsey Campbell's ''The Moon Lens,'' in which a visitor to an inn during a local festival suffers a bestial transformation following his participation in an occult ritual; and the editor's own ''A Thousand Young,'' in which devotion to Shub Niggurath is equated with sexual promiscuity.

Other books you might like:
Edward P. Berglund, *Disciples of Cthulhu*, 1975
Lin Carter, *The Spawn of Cthulhu*, 1971
Stephen Jones, *Shadows over Innsmouth*, 1994
   editor
Thomas M.K. Stratman, *Cthulhu's Heirs*, 1994
   editor
H.P. Lovecraft, *Tales of the Cthulhu Mythos: Golden Anniversary Anthology*, 1990

3533

ROBERT M. PRICE, Editor

Tales of the Lovecraft Mythos

(Minneapolis, Minnesota: Fedogan & Bremer, 1992)

Story type: Horror (Anthology)

Summary: This anthology collects 20 stories that attempt to evoke the same sense of cosmic horror embodied in those

stories by H. P. Lovecraft categorized as ''the Cthulhu Mythos.'' Included are two stories by Robert E. Howard, among them the sword-and-sorcery adventure, ''The Fire of Asshurbanipal''; two stories by August Derleth that elaborate the legend of the Wendigo, ''Ithaqua'' and ''The Thing That Walked on the Wind''; an overwrought pastiche of Lovecraft by C. Hall Thompson, ''Spawn of the Green Abyss''; Robert Bloch's tale of terror in the Egyptian pyramids, ''Fane of the Black Pharoah''; and less well known tales by Clark Ashton Smith, Robert A. W. Lowndes, Fritz Leiber, Richard Searight, Duane Rimel, and Donald A. Wollheim. Price wrote a controversial introduction.

Other books you might like:
Edward P. Berglund, *Disciples of Cthulhu*, 1975
   editor
Ramsey Campbell, *New Tales of the Cthulhu Mythos*, 1980
   editor
Lin Carter, *The Spawn of Cthulhu*, 1981
August Derleth, *Tales of the Cthulhu Mythos*, 1969
   editor
H.P. Lovecraft, *Tales of the Cthulhu Mythos: Golden Anniversary Anthology*, 1990

3534

CHRISTOPHER PRIEST

The Prestige

(New York: St. Martin's Press, 1996)

Story type: Science Fiction (Contemporary Realism; Satire)
Major character(s): Alfred Borden, Magician, Writer; Rupert Angier, Magician, Writer; Nikola Tesla, Historical Figure, Inventor
Time period(s): 19th century; 1900s
Locale(s): England; United States

Summary: Misunderstandings and revealed methods fuel the professional rivalry and feud between two magicians. When Alfred Borden's teleportation trick defies analysis, Rupert Angier retains Nikola Tesla to create an actual matter transmitter. World Fantasy Award winner.

Other books you might like:
James P. Blaylock, *Lord Kelvin's Machine*, 1992
K.W. Jeter, *Infernal Devices*, 1987
Tim Powers, *The Anubis Gates*, 1983
Brooke Stevens, *The Circus of the Earth and Air*, 1994

3535

JAMES D. PRIEST

Kirins: The Flight of the Ain

(Shorewood, Minnesota: Yellowstone Press, 1992)

Story type: Fantasy (Quest; Magic Conflict)
Series: Kirins
Major character(s): Diliani, Mythical Creature (elf); Speckarin, Magician, Mythical Creature (elf)
Time period(s): 1990s
Locale(s): Atlantic Ocean; Stonehenge, England

Summary: The seven companions continue their journey to the source of their magic. Although besieged by evil valodons and gronoms the party reaches the ocean, finds help with the crossing and discovers an idyllic island society of integrated kirins and humans. Finally close to their objective, the group resolves to speedily complete their quest.

Other books you might like:
Stephen Billias, *Horrible Humes*, 1991
Orson Scott Card, *Seventh Son*, 1987
Mercedes Lackey, *Winds of Fate*, 1991
H. Beam Piper, *Little Fuzzy*, 1962
Christopher Stasheff, *The Warlock in Spite of Himself*, 1969
Vivian Vande Velde, *User Unfriendly*, 1991

3536

JAMES D. PRIEST

Kirins: The Secret of the Hanging Stones
(Shorewood, Minnesota: Yellowstone Press, 1993)

Story type: Fantasy (Quest; Magic Conflict)
Series: Kirins
Major character(s): Speckarin, Magician, Mythical Creature; Paskal Parody, Magician (Guardian)
Time period(s): 1990s
Locale(s): Stonehenge, England

Summary: The Kirins' rescue of the Guardian Magician continues as they search for the stronghold of Kirin magic. They discover humans willing to help and continue to fly on blackbirds to complete their adventure and return home.

Other books you might like:
Nancy Varian Berberick, *The Jewels of Elvish*, 1991
Emma Bull, *War for the Oaks*, 1987
H. Beam Piper, *Little Fuzzy*, 1962
Terry Pratchett, *Wings*, 1991
Greg Snow, *That's All, Folks!*, 1992
Lawrence Watt-Evans, *The Rebirth of Wonder*, 1992

3537

JAMES D. PRIEST

Kirins: The Spell of No'an
(Shorewood, Minnesota: Yellowstone Press, 1990)

Story type: Fantasy (Magic Conflict; Quest)
Series: Kirins
Major character(s): Speckarin, Magician, Mythical Creature (brownie)
Time period(s): 1990s (1990)
Locale(s): Earth

Summary: In the old days kirins and humans worked together, both races using magic to get things done. For some unknown reason humans gave up magic, which was not working for them as well as it had. Now magic is not working as well for the kirins as it did. Even the Spell of No'an, which prevents only large sapient species from seeing kirins, is at risk. Speckarin leads a group of brave explorers on an expedition to save them from impending disaster.

Other books you might like:
Orson Scott Card, *Seventh Son*, 1987
John DeChancie, *Castle Perilous*, 1988
Jody Lynn Nye, *Mythology 101*, 1990
H. Beam Piper, *Little Fuzzy*, 1962
L. Neil Smith, *Brightsuit MacBear*, 1988
L. Neil Smith, *Taflak Lysandra*, 1988
Christopher Stasheff, *The Warlock in Spite of Himself*, 1969

3538

DAVID PRILL

Serial Killer Days
(New York: St. Martin's, 1996)

Story type: Horror (Satire)
Major character(s): Debbie Sue Morning, Teenager; Ole Rimbaud, Writer (poet); Griff Grimes, Journalist
Time period(s): 1990s (1996)
Locale(s): Standard Springs, Minnesota

Summary: While the small town of Standard Springs gears up for its annual Serial Killer Days celebration to mark the annual invasion of the town by a murderer who has taken the life of one person every year for the last two decades, happy-go-lucky Debbie Sue Morning tries to perfect her screaming in hopes of winning the Scream Queen title and riding the Scream Queen float in the Serial Killer Days parade.

Other books you might like:
Ramsey Campbell, *The Count of Eleven*, 1992
Thomas M. Disch, *The Businessman: A Tale of Terror*, 1984

3539

DAVID PRILL

The Unnatural
(New York: St. Martin's, 1995)

Story type: Horror (Satire)
Major character(s): Andy Archway, Undertaker; P.T. Sunnyside, Undertaker; Wallace "Wake" Wakefield, Scout
Time period(s): 1990s (1995)
Locale(s): Minnesota; California; Soma, Fictional Country

Summary: In a world where mortuary science has achieved the cachet of professional sports, talented mortuary student Andy Archway sets his heart on the ambitious goal of breaking a 50-year old record for the most number of corpses embalmed in one year. While Andy prepares to move to Soma, a third-world country with a high death rate, as the place to ply his trade, he becomes embroiled in a competition between rival embalmers in the United States who also want his skills. This liberal spoof of Bernard Malamud's *The Natural* is the author's first novel.

Other books you might like:
Thomas M. Disch, *The M.D.: A Horror Story*, 1991
William Browning Spencer, *Resume with Monsters*, 1995
Evelyn Waugh, *The Loved One*, 1948
Gus Weill, *Flesh*, 1992

3540

BILL PRONZINI, Editor
MARTIN H. GREENBERG, Co-Editor
BARRY MALZBERG, Co-Editor

Classic Tales of Horror and the Supernatural
(New York: Morrow/Quill, 1991)

Story type: Horror (Anthology)

Summary: Originally published in 1981 as *The Arbor House Treasury of Horror and the Supernatural*, this omnibus collects 41 stories by both classic and modern masters of supernatural horror. Included from the classic writers are H.P. Lovecraft's famous story of monsters living beneath the streets of Rhode Island, ''Pickman's Model''; Edgar Allan Poe's *conte cruel* of a dwarf's revenge on his persecutors, ''Hop Frog''; Fritz Leiber's original vampire story, ''The Girl with the Hungry Eyes''; and Theodore Sturgeon's story of a man with an obsessive passion, ''Bianca's Hands.'' More modern tales include Cyril M. Kornbluth's tale of a psychic vampire, ''The Mindworm''; Ramsey Campbell's gruesome ''Call First''; and Stephen King's uncollected tale of a monster living in an abandoned crate, ''The Crate.''

Other books you might like:
David G. Hartwell, *The Dark Descent*, 1987
David G. Hartwell, *Foundations of Fear*, 1992
Herbert Wise, *Great Tales of Terror and the Supernatural*, 1945
    Phyllis Fraser, co-editor

3541

KATHRYN PTACEK

Ghost Dance
(New York: Tor, 1990)

Story type: Horror (Apocalyptic Horror)
Major character(s): Chato del Klinne, Indian; Sunny Mae Foster, Worker (blackjack dealer); Bettina Salazar, Indian
Time period(s): 1990s
Locale(s): Las Vegas, Nevada; Southwest

Summary: The inexplicable deaths of several American Indians resistant to the Native American cause point to the work of the Ghost Dance religion, an ancient faith whose figurehead, the mysterious Crow Woman, is inciting members to rise up and help bring about the return of America to the first Americans.

Other books you might like:
Charles L. Grant, *The Nestling*, 1982
G. Wayne Miller, *Thunder Rise*, 1988

3542

KATHRYN PTACEK

The Hunted
(New York: Walker, 1993)

Story type: Horror (Child-in-Peril)
Major character(s): Jessie Mae Morrison, Child (11-years-old); Wendy Wallace, Writer; Emerson Thorne, Doctor (pediatrician)
Time period(s): 1970s (1975)
Locale(s): Hunter Heights, New Jersey

Summary: Newly moved to Hunter Heights, Jessie Mae Morrison can't explain why she suddenly begins having blackout spells and showing signs of psychological trauma. It takes her pediatrician, the respected Dr. Thorne, to realize that Jessie is the reincarnation of a child he killed in the Nazi death camps decades before, and that he must kill her again to preserve his dark secret.

Other books you might like:
Frank DeFelitta, *Audrey Rose*, 1975
J.M. Dillard, *Spectres*, 1991
Max Ehrlich, *The Reincarnation of Peter Proud*, 1974
Nina Romberg, *Shadow Walkers*, 1993

3543

KATHRYN PTACEK, Editor

Women of Darkness II
(New York: Tor, 1990)

Story type: Horror (Anthology)
Series: Women of Darkness

Summary: Eighteen horror stories by women, concerned with both general and feminist themes. Included are Chelsea Quinn Yarbro's historical ''Fruits of Love''; Resa Nelson's allegory of sexual exploitation, ''Sara and the Slime Monster''; Nina Kiriki Hoffman's tale of a curse passed through a family bloodline, ''A Touch of the Old Lilith''; and Melanie Tem's dark meditation on childbearing and rearing, ''The Co-Op.''

Other books you might like:
Richard Dalby, *The Virago Book of Ghost Stories: The Twentieth Century*, 1989
Richard Dalby, *The Virago Book of Ghost Stories*, 1987
Alan Ryan, *Haunting Women*, 1988
Jessica Amanda Salmonson, *What Did Miss Darrington See?*, 1989
Lisa Tuttle, *Skin of the Soul*, 1990

3544

KATE PULLINGER

Where Does Kissing End?
(New York: Serpent's Tail, 1995)

Story type: Horror (Vampire Story)
Major character(s): Mina Savage, Travel Agent; Stephen Smith, Writer (travel writer); Lucy Savage, Worker (shopworker), Parent (Mina's mother)

Time period(s): 1990s (1992)
Locale(s): London, England

Summary: Mina, representative of the newest generation in a long line of illegitimate children on her mother's and father's sides, takes her satisfaction from men through sex that involves biting and bloodletting. When she meets Stephen, the two develop a co-dependent relationship that borders on the vampiric. This novel was first published in England in 1992.

Other books you might like:
Anne Billson, *Suckers*, 1993
Michael Cadnum, *The Judas Glass*, 1996
Lewis Gannett, *The Living One*, 1993
Jonathan Nasaw, *The World on Blood*, 1996
Brian Stableford, *Young Blood*, 1992

3545

PHILIP PULLMAN

The Golden Compass
(New York: Knopf, 1996)

Story type: Fantasy (Historical; Quest)
Series: His Dark Materials
Major character(s): Lyra Belacqua, Child; Iorek Byrnison, Mercenary, Animal (bear); Lee Scoresby, Pilot (balloon)
Time period(s): Indeterminate
Locale(s): London, England; Svalbard, Fictional Country

Summary: Lyra Belacqua saves her uncle's life, an act of mercy that turns her life upside down. After a friend's kidnapping and Lyra's introduction to London's glittering society, Lyra flees, hiding with gypsies. When captured, Lyra takes chances, eventually pursuing her uncle to the far, frozen North and beyond. First of a trilogy. Published in Britain as *His Dark Materials: Northern Lights*.

Other books you might like:
Barbara Hambly, *The Silent Tower*, 1986
Diana Wynne Jones, *Cart and Cwidder*, 1977
Patricia A. McKillip, *The Riddle-Master of Hed*, 1976
Tim Powers, *The Anubis Gates*, 1983
Michael Scott Rohan, *The Anvil of Ice*, 1986

3546

PHILIP PULLMAN

Spring-Heeled Jack
(New York: Alfred A. Knopf, 1991)

Story type: Fantasy (Legend; Young Adult)
Major character(s): Mack the Knife, Criminal, Historical Figure; Ned, Orphan; Spring-Heeled Jack, Hero
Time period(s): 19th century
Locale(s): London, England

Summary: Mack the Knife grabbed Ned in order to force Rose and Lily to give him their mother's locket which they had planned to sell to escape to America. Spring-Heeled Jack, dressed like the devil, frightened the girls, but then vowed to hide them, find Ned and send them all to America. David Mostyn thoroughly illustrated this novel.

Other books you might like:
Ann Curry, *The Book of Brendan*, 1990
Sid Fleischman, *The Midnight Horse*, 1990
Robin Morgan, *The Mer-Child: A Legend for Children and Other Adults*, 1991
Cynthia Voigt, *Jackaroo*, 1985
Patricia C. Wrede, *Dealing with Dragons*, 1990

3547

MAUREEN S. PUSTI

Neighbors
(New York: Leisure, 1991)

Story type: Horror (Black Magic)
Major character(s): Tom Roberts, Professor (of experimental psychology); Kristen Roberts, Housewife (Tom's wife); Eliza Norman, Witch
Time period(s): 1990s
Locale(s): Burnwell, Pennsylvania

Summary: Tom Roberts and his pregnant wife Kristen move to the small college town of Burnwell, unaware that their next-door neighbor is a witch who is responsible for the disappearance and death of several local children and who finds their proximity useful for the completion of her supernatural rituals.

Other books you might like:
Stephanie Kegan, *The Baby*, 1990
John Saul, *Suffer the Children*, 1977

3548

W.T. QUICK

Dreams of Gods and Men
(New York: Signet, 1989)

Story type: Science Fiction (Cyberpunk)
Major character(s): Ozzie, Computer Expert, Scientist; Arius, Artificial Intelligence
Time period(s): 21st century
Locale(s): Chicago, Illinois; San Francisco, California; Moon (Earth's)

Summary: A small group of beleaguered computer wizards struggles valiantly against Arius, the artificial intelligence who has seized control of the world's most powerful corporations. Their leader, Berg, has disappeared and the metamatrix, that strange computer-generated universe, has become increasingly hostile. This is the sequel to *Dreams of Flesh and Sand*.

Other books you might like:
William Gibson, *Count Zero*, 1985
William Gibson, *Mona Lisa Overdrive*, 1988
William Gibson, *Neuromancer*, 1984
Jonathan Littell, *Bad Voltage*, 1989
Daniel Keys Moran, *The Long Run*, 1989

3549

W.T. QUICK

Systems

(New York: Signet, 1989)

Story type: Science Fiction (Cyberpunk)
Major character(s): Josh Tower, Computer Expert, Spy; Dorothea Kelly, Nurse
Time period(s): 21st century
Locale(s): United States

Summary: Josh Tower, a former U.S. government agent now earning his living as a research specialist, is in a near-fatal air-taxi crash in which his wife is killed. Finding evidence that the crash was not entirely accidental, he uses his computer skills to discover who was responsible. To his surprise Tower uncovers an international conspiracy and soon finds himself on the run with a price on his head.

Other books you might like:
William Gibson, *Count Zero*, 1985
William Gibson, *Mona Lisa Overdrive*, 1988
William Gibson, *Neuromancer*, 1984
Jonathan Littell, *Bad Voltage*, 1989
Bruce Sterling, *Islands in the Net*, 1988

3550

W.T. QUICK

Yesterday's Pawn

(New York: NAL Signet, 1989)

Story type: Science Fiction (Space Opera)
Major character(s): Garry Hammersmidt, Businessman
Time period(s): Indeterminate Future
Locale(s): H'hogoth, Planet—Imaginary; Arius, Planet—Imaginary

Summary: Garry Hammersmidt works in his father's pawnshop. One day a nervous little man brings in an artifact to pawn and Garry's life is changed forever. It turns out that other people are interested in the artifact and will stop at nothing to get it.

Other books you might like:
Robert A. Heinlein, *Citizen of the Galaxy*, 1957
R.A. MacAvoy, *The Third Eagle: Lessons Along a Minor String*, 1989
Walter Jon Williams, *Angel Station*, 1989

3551

DANIEL QUINN

Dreamer

(New York: Tor, 1992)

Story type: Horror (Occult)
Major character(s): Greg Donner, Writer (freelance); Ginny Winters, Artist; Franklin Evelyn Winters, Businessman (Ginny's father)
Time period(s): 1990s
Locale(s): Chicago, Illinois

Summary: Greg Donner awakens from a dream of romance with the beautiful Ginny Winters to discover that he is, in reality, a middle-aged schoolteacher named Richard Iles, who is recovering from brainwashing at the hands of Soviet agents. When he awakens once more as Greg Donner, and is informed by Ginny that his Richard Iles persona is a trick foisted upon him by her jealous father, who is able to manipulate dreams through occult forces, Greg finds himself completely incapable of distinguishing between dream and reality. This novel was originally published in 1988.

Other books you might like:
Philip K. Dick, *The Three Stigmata of Palmer Eldritch*, 1964
Philip K. Dick, *Ubik*, 1969

3552

DANIEL QUINN

Ishmael

(New York: Bantam/Turner, 1992)

Story type: Science Fiction (Literary; Contemporary Realism)
Major character(s): Ishmael, Animal (gorilla), Telepath; I, Writer, Student
Time period(s): 1990s
Locale(s): United States

Summary: After the author answers an ad from a teacher seeking a pupil who has a great desire to save the world, he listens to a series of conversations in which Ishmael relates positive solutions to global problems. Winner of a Turner Tomorrow Fellowship.

Other books you might like:
Richard Bach, *Jonathan Livingston Seagull*, 1970
Andrew Goldblatt, *The Bully Pulpit*, 1992
C.S. Lewis, *That Hideous Strength*, 1946
Antoine de Saint-Exupery, *The Little Prince*, 1943
Michael Tobias, *Voice of the Planet*, 1990

3553

JEAN RABE

Red Magic

(Lake Geneva, Wisconsin: TSR, 1991)

Story type: Fantasy (Magic Conflict; Adventure)
Series: Forgotten Realms: The Harpers
Major character(s): Maligor, Wizard; Galvin, Magician (harper), Religious (Druid); Wynter, Mythical Creature (centaur)
Time period(s): Indeterminate
Locale(s): Thay, Fictional Country

Summary: The Harpers, fighting for freedom and justice in Thay, a land ruled by the evil Red Wizards, send an expedition to acquire information on conditions in Thay. Maligor, the Zulkir of Alteration, tries to prevent their return. The Harpers must foil Maligor and prevent him from adding them to his minions of undead slaves. This is the author's first book, a game tie-in novel.

Other books you might like:
Douglas Bell, *Mojo and the Pickle Jar*, 1991

Kyle Crocco, *Heroes, Inc.*, 1991
Philip Jose Farmer, *Red Orc's Rage*, 1991
Courtway Jones, *In the Shadow of the Oak King*, 1991
R.A. Salvatore, *The Crystal Shard*, 1988
Julie Dean Smith, *Mission of Magic*, 1991
Brad Strickland, *Wizard's Mole*, 1991
Margaret Weis, *Fire Sea*, 1991
    Tracy Hickman, co-author

3554

IRENE RADFORD

The Glass Dragon

(New York: DAW, 1994)

Story type: Fantasy (Magic Conflict; Mystery)
Series: Dragon Nimbus
Major character(s): Jaylor, Wizard; Brevelan, Witch
Time period(s): Indeterminate
Locale(s): Coronnan, Fictional Country

Summary: As dragons disappear from the land and the kingdom becomes vulnerable to attack, wizards seek the cause. With his unusual magical abilities, Jaylor searches with Brevelan, perhaps the kingdom's only hope for discovering the cause and finding a remedy before the magic completely vanishes. First novel.

Other books you might like:
Thorarinn Gunnarsson, *Dragon's Domain*, 1993
Larry Niven, *The Magic Goes Away*, 1979
Lawrence Watt-Evans, *The Blood of a Dragon*, 1991
Patricia C. Wrede, *Calling on Dragons*, 1993
Laurence Yep, *Dragon of the Lost Sea*, 1982

3555

IRENE RADFORD

The Loneliest Magician

(New York: DAW, 1996)

Story type: Fantasy (Political; Quest)
Series: Dragon Nimbus
Major character(s): Jack, Magician, Adventurer; Rejiia de Draconis, Magician, Royalty; Katrina Kaantille, Teenager, Artisan
Time period(s): Indeterminate
Locale(s): SeLenicca, Fictional Country; Coronnan, Fictional Country

Summary: Jack searches for the dragon necessary to return magic to Coronnan and replace the protective magic taken with the departing wizards. Meanwhile, Rejiia de Draconis plots to topple Coronnan's ruling family and exert control over neighboring countries.

Other books you might like:
Graham Edwards, *Dragoncharm*, 1996
J.V. Jones, *The Baker's Boy*, 1995
Marjorie Bradley Kellogg, *The Book of Earth*, 1995
Ursula K. Le Guin, *A Wizard of Earthsea*, 1968
Andre Norton, *Elvenblood*, 1995
    Mercedes Lackey, co-author

3556

IRENE RADFORD

The Perfect Princess

(New York: DAW, 1995)

Story type: Fantasy (Political; Magic Conflict)
Series: Dragon Nimbus
Major character(s): Darville, Royalty; Rossemikka ''Mikka'', Royalty
Time period(s): Indeterminate
Locale(s): Coronnan, Fictional Country

Summary: With dragon magic vanishing from Coronnan, masters of a forbidden magic attempt to wrest control of the land from its rightful heir, Prince Darville. Without aid, Prince Darville and his beloved Mikka may both succumb to the evil onslaught. Second in the series.

Other books you might like:
Lois McMaster Bujold, *The Spirit Ring*, 1992
Katharine Kerr, *Daggerspell*, 1986
Ursula K. Le Guin, *A Wizard of Earthsea*, 1968
Michelle Sagara, *Into the Dark Lands*, 1991
Janny Wurts, *Curse of the Mistwraith*, 1994
Laurence Yep, *Dragon of the Lost Sea*, 1982

3557

STEPHEN MARK RAINEY

Fugue Devil and Other Weird Horrors

(Norfolk, Virginia: Macabre, Inc., 1993)

Story type: Horror (Collection)

Summary: The author's first collection consists of five stories ranging from the cosmic horror of ''Return of the Navigator'' to the science fictional trappings of ''The Weird Violet,'' an ecodisaster story. Included are the title story, about a mythical rural monster; ''Festival of the Jackal,'' a surreal urban horror story; and ''Charon's Wings,'' a psychological horror story that probes the thoughts of an airplane hijacker. Robert M. Price wrote the introduction.

Other books you might like:
Joseph Payne Brennan, *Stories of Darkness and Dread*, 1973
Charles L. Grant, *Tales From the Nightside*, 1981
Albert J. Manachino, *The Odd Lot: The Selected Works of Albert J. Manachino*, 1993
Elizabeth Massie, *Southern Discomfort: Selected Works of Elizabeth Massie*, 1993
Norman Partridge, *Mr. Fox and Other Feral Tales*, 1992

3558

GARY L. RAISOR

Less than Human

(New York: Diamond, 1992)

Story type: Horror (Vampire Story)
Major character(s): Stephen Adler, Vampire; Earl Jacobs, Con Artist (pool hustler); John Warrick, Con Artist (pool hustler)

Time period(s): 1990s
Locale(s): Carruthers, Texas; Crowder Flats, Texas

Summary: The author's first novel offers an interesting variation on the vampire tale in its story of Stephen Adler, a vampire who hustles pool games—and his meals—with the help of a charmed cuestick.

Other books you might like:
Poppy Z. Brite, *Lost Souls*, 1992
Nancy A. Collins, *Sunglasses After Dark*, 1989
Nancy A. Collins, *Tempter*, 1990
Ron Dee, *Dusk*, 1991
P.N. Elrod, *The Vampire Chronicles*, 1989-1992
Anne Rice, *The Vampire Chronicles*, 1975-1992

3559

GARY L. RAISOR, Editor

Obsessions

(Arlington Heights, IL: Dark Harvest, 1991)

Story type: Horror (Anthology)

Summary: Thirty stories of fantasy and horror in which personal obsessions lead people to commit extreme acts. Obsessions detailed include death fixation (Dean R. Koontz's "The Interrogation"), ardent celebrity worship (Thomas Monteleone's "The Pleasure of Her Company"), artistic influences (John Shirley's "Woodgrains"), gluttony (F. Paul Wilson's "Topsy"), and neatness (Nicholas Royle's "Crispy Notes").

Other books you might like:
Margaret L. Carter, *Demon Lovers and Strange Seductions*, 1973
Don Congdon, *Tales of Love and Horror*, 1961
Jeff Gelb, *Hotter Blood: More Tales of Erotic Horror*, 1991
  Michael Garrett, co-author
Jeff Gelb, *Hot Blood: Tales of Provocative Horror*, 1989
  Michael Garrett, co-author
Michele Slung, *I Shudder at Your Touch*, 1991

3560

KEVIN D. RANDLE

Death of a Regiment

(New York: Ace, 1991)

Story type: Science Fiction (Military)
Series: Jefferson's War
Major character(s): David Steven Jefferson, Military Personnel; Victoria Torrence, Military Personnel; Rachel Davies, Military Personnel
Time period(s): Indeterminate Future
Locale(s): Outer Space; Eighty-Two Eridani, Outer Space (solar system)

Summary: The alien Croatoans have attacked and destroyed a convoy of Earth's spaceships. Now they seem to be poised for an attack on Earth itself. Colonel Jefferson and Colonel Davies are sent with their regiments to stop, or at least delay, the alien advance.

Other books you might like:
Gordon R. Dickson, *Dorsai!*, 1976
Gordon R. Dickson, *Soldier, Ask Not*, 1967
Joe Haldeman, *The Forever War*, 1975
Robert A. Heinlein, *Starship Troopers*, 1959
Jerry Pournelle, *Falkenberg's Legion*, 1990
Elizabeth Ann Scarborough, *The Healer's War*, 1989

3561

KEVIN D. RANDLE

Galactic MI

(New York: Ace, 1993)

Story type: Science Fiction (Military)
Series: Galactic MI
Major character(s): Joshua Price, Military Personnel (captain); Emma Coollege, Spy, Military Personnel (lieutenant); Wallace "Rocky" Stone, Military Personnel (master sergeant)
Time period(s): Indeterminate Future
Locale(s): Bolton's Planet, Planet—Imaginary

Summary: Recently discovered by the coalition, Bolton's Planet seems an ideal society. In an attempt to confirm this before establishing full diplomatic contact, the colonel orders Sergeant Stone to kidnap a representative member of the society for interrogation. First of a new series.

Other books you might like:
Joe Haldeman, *All My Sins Remembered*, 1977
Harry Harrison, *The Adventures of the Stainless Steel Rat*, 1978
Steve Miller, *Agent of Change*, 1988
  Sharon Lee, co-author
Steve Miller, *Carpe Diem*, 1989
  Sharon Lee, co-author
Steve Miller, *Conflict of Honors*, 1988
  Sharon Lee, co-author
Steve Perry, *The 97th Step*, 1989
Steve Perry, *The Man Who Never Missed*, 1985
Alis A. Rasmussen, *A Passage of Stars*, 1990
Alis A. Rasmussen, *The Price of Ransom*, 1990
Alis A. Rasmussen, *Revolution's Shore*, 1990

3562

KEVIN D. RANDLE

The Galactic Silver Star

(New York: Ace, 1990)

Story type: Science Fiction (Military)
Major character(s): David Steven Jefferson, Military Personnel; Victoria Torrence, Military Personnel; Joseph Tyson, Military Personnel
Time period(s): Indeterminate Future
Locale(s): Outer Space

Summary: After his first combat mission, Lt. David Jefferson received the Galactic Silver Star for a daring attack that he did not make. Promoted to Major in the Space Infantry and put in command of a battalion, he has to prove his ability to command and earn his reputation for bravery. But who are the enemy—and why?

Other books you might like:
Gordon R. Dickson, *Lost Dorsai*, 1980
Gordon R. Dickson, *The Tactics of Mistake*, 1971
Phyllis Eisenstein, *In the Hands of Glory*, 1981
Jack Williamson, *The Legion of Space*, 1947
Helen S. Wright, *A Matter of Oaths*, 1990

3563

KEVIN D. RANDLE
RICHARD DRISCOLL, Co-Author

Mind Slayer
(New York: Ace, 1992)

Story type: Science Fiction (Mystery; Space Colony)
Series: Star Precinct
Major character(s): Richard Brackett, Police Officer; Obo, Alien, Police Officer; Matthew Pendrake, Secretary, Telepath
Time period(s): Indeterminate Future
Locale(s): Tumbleweed, Planet—Imaginary (resort planet)

Summary: Star Precinct 106 responds to the murder of Dirk St. Romaine, a famous author of expose biographies. The investigation seems unusually difficult due to St. Romaine's millions of enemies and the disappearance of his personal secretary. However, the investigation soon reveals the murderer survived an experiment aimed at producing telepaths trained at murder.

Other books you might like:
Alfred Bester, *The Demolished Man*, 1953
Richard Bowker, *Marlborough Street*, 1987
Barney Cohen, *The Taking of Satcon Station*, 1982
   Jim Baen, co-author
Alan Dean Foster, *The I Inside*, 1984
Katharine Kerr, *Polar City Blues*, 1990

3564

KEVIN D. RANDLE
RICHARD DRISCOLL, Co-Author

Star Precinct
(New York: Ace, 1992)

Story type: Science Fiction (Mystery; Space Colony)
Series: Star Precinct
Major character(s): Lute Brackett, Detective—Police; Jennifer Daily, Detective—Police; Dennis Profitt, Businessman (multibillionaire), Explorer
Time period(s): Indeterminate Future
Locale(s): Star Rest, Planet—Imaginary

Summary: Dennis Profitt, the richest human in the universe, calls in Star Precinct, a travelling police station, after the murder of his wife, seemingly in a locked room, Since the case appears to tie in with the murder of a priest by a berserk robot, Lute and Jennifer find the identity of the priest and follow his last known contact, only to be led back to Profitt's swanky hotel where they discover two more murders.

Other books you might like:
Isaac Asimov, *The Caves of Steel*, 1954
Jack L. Chalker, *The Identity Matrix*, 1982
Barney Cohen, *Blood on the Moon*, 1984
Larry Niven, *The Patchwork Girl*, 1980
Atanielle Annyn Noel, *Murder on Usher's Planet*, 1987
Charles Sheffield, *Sight of Proteus*, 1978
John E. Stith, *Redshift Rendezvous*, 1990

3565

KIMBERLY RANGEL

Shadows
(New York: Leisure, 1996)

Story type: Horror (Werewolf Story)
Major character(s): Selene DeMarco, Antiques Dealer; Reese Christian, Bounty Hunter; Mick Randall, Police Officer
Time period(s): 1990s (1996)
Locale(s): Los Angeles, California; Shadow Ridge, Oregon

Summary: The last female descendant of a race of werepanthers, Selene DeMarco must mate with a descendant of the man who helped activate her family's curse if she is to end her bloody heritage. But the last male decendant of Selene's kind is determined to claim Selene as his own and perpetuate their unholy bloodline.

Other books you might like:
Gary Brandner, *Cat People*, 1982
Traci Briery, *The Werewolf Chronicles*, 1995
Traci Briery, *Wolfsong*, 1996
Nancy A. Collins, *Wild Blood*, 1994
Dennis Danvers, *Wilderness*, 1991

3566

ROBERT RANKIN

Armageddon: The Musical
(New York: Dell, 1990)

Story type: Science Fiction (Time Travel; Humor)
Major character(s): Jovil Yspht, Alien; Elvis Presley, Musician, Historical Figure
Time period(s): 1950s (1958); Indeterminate
Locale(s): Earth

Summary: Zany aliens have been televising (and messing with) human development for thousands of years. The ratings of this program are starting to slip, so the production staff decides to send a representative with a Time Sprout to help keep the action rolling toward a dramatic final episode. The Time Sprout and Elvis decide to try to avert the catastrophe.

Other books you might like:
Alan Dean Foster, *To the Vanishing Point*, 1988
Mel Gilden, *Surfing Samurai Robots*, 1988
Parke Godwin, *The Snake Oil Wars*, 1989
Parke Godwin, *Waiting for the Galactic Bus*, 1988
Frederik Pohl, *Gladiator-at-Law*, 1955
   Cyril M. Kornbluth, co-author

3567

CHRISTOPH RANSMAYR

The Last World

(New York: Grove Weidenfeld, 1990)

Story type: Fantasy (Historical; Quest)
Major character(s): Cotta, Tourist; Naso, Fugitive, Writer (poet); Lycaon, Artisan, Werewolf
Time period(s): 20th century
Locale(s): Tomi, Earth (city on the Black Sea)

Summary: This is the first English translation of *Die Letzte Welt*, published in 1988. Drawing heavily on the life and writings of the 1st century poet Ovid, the story follows a young man's search for an exiled poet. As the quest progresses, he finds more and more correlations between the poet's writings and the lives of the people of Tomi, eventually seeing transformations, magic and the boundaries of literature and reality.

Other books you might like:
John Crowley, *Little, Big*, 1981
Greer Ilene Gilman, *Moonwise*, 1991
Robert Holdstock, *Mythago Wood*, 1984
Gabriel Garcia Marquez, *One Hundred Years of Solitude*, 1970

3568

BILL RANSOM

Burn

(New York: Ace, 1995)

Story type: Science Fiction (Genetic Manipulation; Political)
Series: ViraVax
Major character(s): Rico Toledo, Military Personnel, Experimental Subject; Marte Chang, Inventor, Government Official; Harry Toledo, Teenager, Experimental Subject
Time period(s): 2010s (2015)
Locale(s): Confederation of Costa Brava, Fictional Country (in Central America)

Summary: After destroying the ViraVax underground facility, hoping to prevent the virus from escaping, Harry and Marte attempt to discover a cure. When Rico learns a shipment of the killer virus may leave the country, he enlists his church buddies to locate the deadly shipment.

Other books you might like:
Greg Bear, *Blood Music*, 1985
Helen Collins, *Mutagenesis*, 1993
L. Warren Douglas, *Cannon's Orb*, 1994
Frank Herbert, *The Jesus Incident*, 1979
　Bill Ransom, co-author
Frank Herbert, *The Lazarus Effect*, 1983
　Bill Ransom, co-author
Frank Herbert, *The White Plague*, 1982
S. Andrew Swann, *Forests of the Night*, 1993

3569

BILL RANSOM

Jaguar

(New York: Ace, 1990)

Story type: Science Fiction (Psychic Powers; Alternate Universe)
Major character(s): Eddie Reyes, Teenager; Maryellen Thompkins, Teenager; Afriqua Lee, Teenager
Time period(s): 1990s (1990)
Locale(s): Earth; Alternate Earth

Summary: In waking life he is a disabled Vietnam veteran with a mysterious sleep disorder, but to the people of another world, he is the Jaguar who can invade people's minds while they dream and force them to do his will. But others have learned to travel the "dreamways" between worlds and they have joined forces to track down the Jaguar and destroy him.

Other books you might like:
Glen Cook, *A Matter of Time*, 1985
Joe Haldeman, *The Forever War*, 1975
Gustav Hasford, *Phantom Blooper*, 1990
Elizabeth Ann Scarborough, *The Healer's War*, 1989

3570

BILL RANSOM

ViraVax

(New York: Ace, 1993)

Story type: Science Fiction (Genetic Manipulation; Political)
Series: ViraVax
Major character(s): Rico Toledo, Military Personnel, Experimental Subject; Marte Chang, Inventor, Government Official (Defense Intelligence Agency); Dajaj Mishwe, Murderer, Scientist
Time period(s): 2010s (2015)
Locale(s): Confederation of Costa Brava, Fictional Country (in Central America)

Summary: After Red Bartlett's wife kills him in self defense, Colonel Toledo realizes that Red had suffered from Meltdown, an experimental virus rumored to infect ViraVax's secret fifth level. Alcoholic and unstable, the Colonel loses his commission. When his son's kidnapping forces him to join the underground Peace and Freedom Party to effect a rescue, the Colonel realizes humanity can no longer tolerate the genetic warfare waged against the Catholics by the Children of Eden. Unfortunately, he may be too late to save humanity from Mishwe's secret project.

Other books you might like:
Jim Aikin, *The Wall at the Edge of the World*, 1993
Greg Bear, *Blood Music*, 1985
Frank Herbert, *The Ascension Factor*, 1987
　Bill Ransom, co-author
Frank Herbert, *The Jesus Incident*, 1979
　Bill Ransom, co-author
Frank Herbert, *The Lazarus Effect*, 1983
　Bill Ransom, co-author
Frank Herbert, *The White Plague*, 1982

Charles Oberndorf, *Sheltered Lives*, 1992
Neal Stephenson, *Snow Crash*, 1992
Elisabeth Vonarburg, *The Silent City*, 1992

3571

DANIEL RANSOM (Pseudonym of Ed Gorman)

The Fugitive Stars
(New York: DAW, 1995)

Story type: Science Fiction (Invasion of Earth; Political)
Major character(s): Wendy Abronowitz, Astronaut; Michael Raines, Psychic (esper); Jack "Cap'n Jack" Campbell, Astronaut
Time period(s): 2010s (2011)
Locale(s): Washington, District of Columbia

Summary: After visiting a comet, the astronauts all display signs of the same disease. When Cap'n Jack disappears, his wife kidnaps Michael Raines to help her find him. Murdered by assassins, all experts contacted with information about the disease die.

Other books you might like:
Octavia E. Butler, *Dawn*, 1987
L. Warren Douglas, *Cannon's Orb*, 1994
Janet Kagan, *Mirabile*, 1991
S. Andrew Swann, *Forests of the Night*, 1993
David Weber, *Mutineers' Moon*, 1991

3572

DANIEL RANSOM (Pseudonym of Ed Gorman)

The Long Midnight
(New York: Dell, 1993)

Story type: Horror (Wild Talents)
Major character(s): Richard Candlemas, Doctor; Meredith Sawyer, Journalist (*Windy City* magazine); Tom Gage, Detective
Time period(s): 1990s (1993)
Locale(s): Chicago, Illinois

Summary: When teachers and associates of the former Perpetual Light Institute, a private school for children with extrasensory capabilities, begin dying bizarre deaths, Meredith Sawyer, a graduate of the school, suspects that her sister Valerie may be the culprit. The only problem is that Valerie supposedly died in a car accident many years before the murders begin taking place.

Other books you might like:
John Arbucci, *Blood of Innocents*, 1989
Jack Caravela, *The Gifted*, 1991
Stephen King, *Firestarter*, 1980
Steven M. Krauzer, *Brainstorm*, 1991
Patricia Wallace, *Fatal Outcome*, 1992

3573

ALIS A. RASMUSSEN

The Labyrinth Gate
(New York: Baen, 1988)

Story type: Fantasy (Alternate World)
Time period(s): 1980s
Locale(s): Earth; Alternate Universe

Summary: Newlyweds find themselves tranported to a another world when they use a deck of magic cards. Two opposing powers then use them as pawns in an ongoing struggle.

Other books you might like:
Donald Aamodt, *A Name to Conjure With*, 1989
Lee Creighton, *Two Queens of Lochrie*, 1990
Aline Boucher Kaplan, *Khyren*, 1988

3574

ALIS A. RASMUSSEN

A Passage of Stars
(New York: Bantam Spectra, 1990)

Story type: Science Fiction (Adventure)
Series: High Road Trilogy
Major character(s): Lilyaka Ransome, Heiress, Spaceman; Heredes, Teacher, Martial Arts Expert
Time period(s): Indeterminate Future
Locale(s): Unruli, Planet—Imaginary

Summary: Heiress Lilyaka Hae Ransome is her own woman, answering to no man. When her tutor Heredes is kidnapped, she leaves her home, abandons her fortune, and goes to his rescue.

Other books you might like:
Jay D. Blakeney, *Requiem for Anthi*, 1990
Anne McCaffrey, *Sassinak*, 1990
    Elizabeth Moon, co-author
Melisa C. Michaels, *Far Harbor*, 1989

3575

ALIS A. RASMUSSEN

The Price of Ransom
(New York: Bantam Spectra, 1990)

Story type: Science Fiction (Adventure; Political)
Series: Highroad Trilogy
Major character(s): Lilyaka Ransome, Spaceship Captain; Corrigan Tel Windsor, Bounty Hunter
Time period(s): Indeterminate Future
Locale(s): *Forlorn Hope*, Spaceship; Diomede, Planet—Imaginary; Outer Space (the Pale)

Summary: On Earth a deal is made with Corrigan Tel Windsor to bring Lily in for questioning leading to the capture, and perhaps death, of Hawk and Heredes. Meanwhile, unaware of this danger, the *Forlorn Hope* is on her way from Reft space to the Pale with Lily and Hawk on board.

Other books you might like:
David Brin, *Startide Rising*, 1983
Jeffrey A. Carver, *The Rapture Effect*, 1987
Glen Cook, *The Dragon Never Sleeps*, 1988
Frank Herbert, *Dune*, 1965
Michael P. Kube-McDowell, *Enigma*, 1986
Allen Steele, *Clarke County, Space*, 1990

3576

ALIS A. RASMUSSEN

Revolution's Shore
(New York: Bantam Spectra, 1990)

Story type: Science Fiction (Adventure; Political)
Series: Highroad Trilogy
Major character(s): Kyosti Bitterleaf Hakoni, Doctor, Spaceman; Lilyaka Ash Heredes, Spaceman
Time period(s): Indeterminate Future
Locale(s): Harsh, Planet—Imaginary; *Forlorn Hope*, Spaceship

Summary: Lily, now the adopted daughter of Heredes, is abandoned with her crewmates on Harsh where she plans on contacting the revolutionary Jehane, and rescuing Paisley, the Tattoo whom they had been forced to leave behind when they escaped from Harsh last time. Lily still plans to join Jehane's revolution, but something about him disturbs her.

Other books you might like:
Lois McMaster Bujold, *Borders of Infinity*, 1989
Lois McMaster Bujold, *Brothers in Arms*, 1988
F.M. Busby, *Rissa Kerguelen*, 1977
Stephen Goldin, *Jade Darcy and the Affair of Honor*, 1988
Melisa C. Michaels, *Skirmish*, 1985
Steve Miller, *Agent of Change*, 1988
 Sharon Lee, co-author

3577

MELANIE RAWN

The Dragon Token
(New York: DAW, 1992)

Story type: Fantasy (Political; Magic Conflict)
Series: Dragon Star
Major character(s): Pol, Royalty (high prince), Ruler; Meiglan, Royalty (high princess); Andry, Ruler (lord of Goddess Keep), Magician (sunrunner)
Time period(s): Indeterminate
Locale(s): Fictional Country

Summary: The death of Rohan and the destruction of Stronghold left High Princess Sioned in shock, unable to help her son fight the war and discover his path as High Prince. With many people killed already, much rebuilding is necessary. Andry has left Goddess Keep to join Pol since both recognize the need to cooperate, although communication between the cousins has not begun.

Other books you might like:
Cheryl J. Franklin, *Fire Crossing*, 1990
C.S. Friedman, *Black Sun Rising*, 1991

Kris Jensen, *Mentor*, 1991
Katherine Kurtz, *Deryni Rising*, 1970
Anne McCaffrey, *Dragonflight*, 1981
Shirley Rousseau Murphy, *Nightpool*, 1987

3578

MELANIE RAWN
JENNIFER ROBERSON, Co-Author
KATE ELLIOTT, Co-Author

The Golden Key
(New York: DAW, 1996)

Story type: Fantasy (Political; Romance)
Major character(s): Saavedra Grijalva, Artist (painter); Sario Grijalva, Artist (painter), Nobleman (Lord Limner); Alejandro do'Verrada, Nobleman (duke)
Time period(s): 10th century (940s); 14th century (1310s)
Locale(s): Tira Virte, Fictional Country; Meya Suerta, Fictional City; Palasso Grijalva, Mythical Place

Summary: Driven by his twin obsessions, immortality and his cousin, Saavedra, Sario Grijalva secretly delves into the dark magic of the Book of Kita'ab to unlock the secrets that can bring him both. Sario vents his jealous frustration by imprisoning Saavedra in a portrait he paints of her. For the next 300 years, Sario labors to perfect his own art and to hone the murderous techniques that allow him to steal the lives of other gifted, young, male family members. One day, the aged magic falters and Saavedra steps from her portrait into the real world.

Other books you might like:
Aaron Allston, *Galatea in 2-D*, 1993
Ray Bradbury, *Something Wicked This Way Comes*, 1962
Charles de Lint, *Memory and Dream*, 1994
Suzette Haden Elgin, *Native Tongue*, 1984
Kate Elliott, *An Earthly Crown*, 1993
 pseudonym of Alis A. Rasmussen
Michael King, *Lorien Lost*, 1996
Jennifer Roberson, *Shapechangers*, 1984

3579

MELANIE RAWN

Knights of the Morningstar
(New York: Ace, 1994)

Story type: Science Fiction (Time Travel)
Series: Quantum Leap
Major character(s): Sam Beckett, Time Traveller, Scientist; Cynthia "Lady Cyndara" Mulloy, Editor
Time period(s): 1980s (July 1987)
Locale(s): New York (Medieval Chivalry League tournament)

Summary: Sam's leap lands him amid medieval recreationists where people expect him to win the favors of a fair lady through his prowess at sword fighting. Sam's difficulties increase as another leaper threatens the project and Sam's life. Television tie-in.

Other books you might like:
Chris Claremont, *Dragon Moon*, 1994
  Beth Fleisher, co-author
Melissa Crandall, *Search and Rescue*, 1994
Ashley McConnell, *Prelude*, 1994
Ashley McConnell, *Quantum Leap: The Novel*, 1992
Ashley McConnell, *Too Close for Comfort*, 1993
Ashley McConnell, *The Wall*, 1994
Pamela F. Service, *All's Faire*, 1993

3580

MELANIE RAWN

The Ruins of Ambrai
(New York: DAW, 1994)

Story type: Fantasy (Political; Magic Conflict)
Series: Exiles
Major character(s): Sarra Ambrai Liwellan, Adoptee, Heiress; Avira Anniyas, Political Figure, Psychic (Mage); Gorynal Desse, Psychic (Mage), Revolutionary
Time period(s): Indeterminate
Locale(s): Lenfell, Planet—Imaginary

Summary: Orphaned when her mother dies in childbirth after her father kidnaps her older sister and burns Ambrai, Sarra, warded, forgets her newborn sister until meeting her years later. Already determined to change the matriarchal, hierarchic nature of her society, Sarra intends to join the Rising, which plans to overthrow the government of First Counsellor Anniyas and restore the freedom of the Guardian Mages. However, her older sister, Glenin, plans to control the government through her husband, Anniyas' only child.

Other books you might like:
Laurell K. Hamilton, *Nightseer*, 1992
Robert Jordan, *The Eye of the World*, 1989
Elizabeth Moon, *Liar's Oath*, 1992
Midori Snyder, *Beldan's Fire*, 1993
Tad Williams, *The Dragonbone Chair*, 1989

3581

MELANIE RAWN

Skybowl
(New York: DAW, 1993)

Story type: Fantasy (Political; Magic Conflict)
Series: Dragon Star
Major character(s): Sioned, Royalty (high princess); Pol, Royalty (high prince), Magician; Meiglan, Royalty (high princess)
Time period(s): Indeterminate
Locale(s): Fictional Country

Summary: Pol continues plans for the final battle with the Vellanti to take place at Skybowl. Meiglan, still in the hands of the enemy, sends a message to Pol warning that her ritual death will bless the battle. A magic mirror reveals many historical secrets and proves usable by Pol who now understands the Vellanti and the reasons for the war. Pol begins to understand his father's political philosophy and continues to

attempt cooperation with Andry, eventually vowing again to become High Prince for all the people in his domain, and to never again utilize his gifts for killing.

Other books you might like:
David Eddings, *Pawn of Prophecy*, 1982
C.S. Friedman, *Black Sun Rising*, 1991
Anne McCaffrey, *Dragonflight*, 1968
Ron Miller, *Silk and Steel*, 1992
Elizabeth Moon, *Oath of Gold*, 1989
Shirley Rousseau Murphy, *Nightpool*, 1987
Paula Volsky, *Illusion*, 1992

3582

MELANIE RAWN

The Star Scroll
(New York: DAW, 1989)

Story type: Fantasy (Political)
Series: Dragon Prince
Major character(s): Rohan, Royalty, Ruler (High Prince); Masul, Revolutionary
Time period(s): Indeterminate
Locale(s): Fictional Country

Summary: Rohan and Sioned must defend both their reign and their son when an ancient scroll is discovered, giving Rohan's enemies a chance to defeat him.

Other books you might like:
Margaret Weis, *Elven Star*, 1990
  Tracy Hickman, co-author
Elizabeth H. Boyer, *The Clan of the Warlord*, 1992
Paula Volsky, *Illusion*, 1992
Mercedes Lackey, *Winds of Fury*, 1993

3583

MELANIE RAWN

Stronghold
(New York: DAW, 1990)

Story type: Fantasy (Magic Conflict; Political)
Series: Dragon Star
Major character(s): Rohan, Royalty (prince), Ruler; Sioned, Ruler (queen), Magician (sunrunner); Andry, Ruler (lord of Goddess Keep), Magician (sunrunner)
Time period(s): Indeterminate
Locale(s): Fictional Country

Summary: After several decades of peaceful, intelligent, progressive rule under Rohan and Sioned, and several centuries of constructive, if occasionally manipulative use of Faradhi magic by the Sunrunners of Goddess Keep, the realm is threatened by invaders from overseas. Believing that the invasion force is a tool of long outlawed Diamardhi sorcerers, Andry has been seeking knowledge of their craft and destruction of all its practitioners. His obsession puts him at odds with Rohan and Sioned and threatens to destroy the realm from within, whether or not the invaders are stopped.

Other books you might like:
Patricia Kennealy, *The Copper Crown*, 1984

Katherine Kurtz, *Deryni Rising*, 1970
Anne McCaffrey, *Dragonflight*, 1968
Jennifer Roberson, *Shapechangers*, 1984
Joel Rosenberg, *The Sleeping Dragon*, 1983

3584

MELANIE RAWN

Sunrunner's Fire
(New York: DAW, 1990)

Story type: Fantasy (Political)
Series: Dragon Prince
Major character(s): Pol, Royalty (Prince); Andry, Nobleman, Magician
Time period(s): Indeterminate
Locale(s): Fictional Country

Summary: Challenged by rivals to the throne and by his cousin Andry who opposes him and his father, Pol repels their attempts at sorcery and murder.

Other books you might like:
Constance Ash, *The Stalking Horse*, 1990
Glen Cook, *Tower of Fear*, 1989
Raymond E. Feist, *Magician: Apprentice*, 1986
Mary Herbert, *Dark Horse*, 1990
Guy Gavriel Kay, *The Summer Tree*, 1985
   The Fionavar Tapestry: Book 1
Anne McCaffrey, *Dragonflight*, 1981
   Vol 1 - Dragon Riders of Pern
Shirley Rousseau Murphy, *Nightpool*, 1987
   Book 1 - Dragonbards Trilogy

3585

FRED OLEN RAY, Editor

Weird Menace
(Hollywood, CA: American Independent Press, 1994)

Story type: Horror (Anthology)

Summary: The editor, best known as a filmmaker, has assembled thirteen homages to the weird menace pulps, which featured tales of heroes and heroines threatened by apparently supernatural menaces that almost always prove to be the work of mortal, if demented, criminals. Hugh Cave, who wrote for the original weird menace pulps in the 1930s, contributes two stories: "Don't Open the Door" tells of a young bride's ordeal at the hands of her mother-in-law's Satanic cult, and "The Kutting Edge" (written under his "Justin Case" pseudonym) is about an amoral writer of horror fiction whose dabbling in metaphysics results in the horrors of his imagination coming to life. Richard Gilliam's "Hotel Stygia" concerns a man's efforts to free a young woman and her daughter from the clutches of a death cult, and Greg Nicoll mixes Nazi atrocities with native magic in "Nazi Jungle Fury." Although published in 1994, this book was not available until 1995.

Other books you might like:
John Hanlon, *Death's Loving Arms and Other Terror Tales*, 1966
   editor

John Hanlon, *The House of Living Death and Other Terror Tales*, 1966
   editor
Sheldon Jaffery, *The Weirds*, 1987
   editor
Robert Weinberg, *Weird Menace 1: The Corpse Factory*, 1977
   editor
Robert Weinberg, *Weird Menace 2: Satan's Roadhouse*, 1977

3586

JAMES E. REAGEN

The League of the Crimson Crescent
(Rocklin, California: Prima Proteus, 1995)

Story type: Fantasy (Alternate World; Political)
Major character(s): Bill "Bill the Just" Evans, Accountant, Hero
Time period(s): Indeterminate
Locale(s): The Empire, Fictional Country

Summary: Rendered unconscious while spelunking in the Adirondacks, Bill Evans awakens in a magical land populated by unpleasant mythical creatures. When Bill defeats a slave owner and liberates the human slaves, many believe the long neglected rebellion has resurfaced. First fiction and first of a computer game tie-in series.

Other books you might like:
Bruce Balfour, *Star Crusader: A Novel*, 1995
Aaron Conners, *The Pandora Directive: A Tex Murphy Novel*, 1995
Matthew J. Costello, *The 7th Guest*, 1995
Arthur Byron Cover, *Planetfall*, 1988
Mercedes Lackey, *Castle of Deception*, 1992
   Josepha Sherman, co-author
Craig Mills, *The Floating Castle*, 1995
Chet Williamson, *Hell: A Cyberpunk Thriller*, 1995

3587

MICHAEL REAVES

Night Hunter
(New York: Tor, 1991)

Story type: Horror (Vampire Story; Mystery)
Major character(s): Jake Hull, Detective—Police; Dan Stratton, Police Officer; Tace Daggett, Entertainer (stand-up comic)
Time period(s): 1990s (1995)
Locale(s): Hollywood, California

Summary: A series of murders in which victims are found with stakes driven through their hearts suggests to detective Jake Hull and the Los Angeles Police Department that a lunatic who believes in vampires is on the rampage. But the deeper they probe the crimes, the more they begin to wonder whether there really aren't vampires prowling the streets at night.

Other books you might like:
Peter Atkins, *Morningstar*, 1992
Warren Newton Beath, *Bloodletter*, 1994

Brian Lumley, *Necroscope*, 1986
Les Whitten, *Progeny of the Adder*, 1965

3588

MICHAEL REAVES

Street Magic
(New York: Tor, 1991)

Story type: Fantasy (Quest; Urban)
Major character(s): Danny Thayer, Child, Heir—Lost (Keymaster); Robin, Child, Mythical Creature (fairy "scattering"); Scott Russell, Detective—Private
Time period(s): 1990s
Locale(s): San Francisco, California

Summary: Danny and Robin search for a way to open the path to Fairyland, closed by the Queen of Fairie. As they journey through familiar San Francisco landmarks, Danny is informed that he is a Keymaster and can open the needed pathway. As time grows short and the situation becomes deadly, Danny must discover his abilities or lose all.

Other books you might like:
Michael de Larrabeiti, *The Borribles*, 1978
Michael de Larrabeiti, *The Borribles Go for Broke*, 1982
Charles de Lint, *Ghosts of Wind and Shadow*, 1991
Edith Pattou, *Hero's Song*, 1991
Will Shetterly, *Elsewhere*, 1991
Terri Windling, *Life on the Border*, 1991
   editor

3589

DANA REED (Pseudonym of Edwina Berkman)

Demon Within
(New York: Leisure, 1993)

Story type: Horror (Black Magic)
Major character(s): Samantha Croft, Insurance Agent; Don Wheatley, Detective—Police; Garrett Land, Businessman
Time period(s): 1980s (1988)
Locale(s): New York, New York

Summary: Samatha Croft's apartment building is visited nightly—and sometimes twice a night—by a murderer who steals body parts from his victims, and who consulting occultists think is trying to replace parts of his own body that were transformed during a bungled summoning ceremony. This novel was originally published in 1988.

Other books you might like:
Clive Barker, *The Hellbound Heart*, 1991
Steven Ray Fulgham, *The Forsaken*, 1991
Stephen R. George, *The Forgotten*, 1991
Melisand March, *The Site*, 1988
Roland Topor, *The Tenant*, 1966

3590

RICK R. REED

Obsessed
(New York: Dell Abyss, 1991)

Story type: Horror (Psychological Suspense)
Major character(s): Joe Macaree, Advertising; Pat Young, Invalid; Anne Macaree, Model (fashion model)
Time period(s): 1990s
Locale(s): Chicago, Illinois

Summary: In this stupendously silly first novel psychologically twisted advertising executive Joe Macaree, a victim of abuse when a child, finds himself in a jam when blackmailed by a wheelchair-bound woman who has seen him commit murder and drink his victim's blood.

Other books you might like:
Theodore Sturgeon, *Some of Your Blood*, 1961
Cornell Woolrich, *It Had to Be Murder*, 1988
   in *Rear Window and Other Stories*

3591

RICK R. REED

Penance
(New York: Dell/Abyss, 1993)

Story type: Horror (Psychological Suspense)
Major character(s): Jimmy Fels, Teenager (13-years-old), Runaway; Richard Grebb, Religious (ex-priest); Dwight Morris, Businessman
Time period(s): 1990s (1993)
Locale(s): Chicago, Illinois

Summary: His life in ruins because of his pedophilic tendencies, Dwight Morris begins abducting and torturing the street children of Chicago, hoping eventually to get back, through them, at Jimmy Fels, a teenage hustler who escaped his clutches. With the help of Richard Grebb, an ex-priest and former pedophile, Jimmy returns to fight Morris and save his fellow vagabonds.

Other books you might like:
J.M. Dillard, *Spectres*, 1991
Thomas Harris, *The Silence of the Lambs*, 1988
Ruby Jean Jensen, *The Reckoning*, 1992
David Martin, *Bring Me Children*, 1992
Whitley Strieber, *Billy*, 1990

3592

ROBERT REED

Beyond the Veil of Stars
(New York: Tor, 1994)

Story type: Science Fiction (UFO; First Contact)
Major character(s): Cornell Novak, Traveller, Adventurer; Pete Forrest, Neighbor, Traveller; Porsche Neal, Alien, Traveller
Time period(s): 1990s
Locale(s): United States; Planet—Imaginary

Summary: Cornell remembers hunting for aliens since he was five years old and his mother disappeared. When the sky everts, he gains hope for her return, but by the time he turns 15, he doubts his memories of an alien kidnapping and leaves home. When he starts work for an undercover government agency, he realizes his father's search for extra-terrestrials had merit.

Other books you might like:
David Brin, *Earth*, 1990
Gwyneth Jones, *White Queen*, 1993
Sheri S. Tepper, *Raising the Stones*, 1990
Vernor Vinge, *A Fire upon the Deep*, 1992
George Zebrowski, *Stranger Suns*, 1991

3593

ROBERT REED

Black Milk

(New York: Donald I. Fine, 1989)

Story type: Science Fiction (Genetic Manipulation)
Major character(s): Ryder, Genetically Altered Being; Cody, Genetically Altered Being
Time period(s): 21st century
Locale(s): Earth

Summary: Genetic mapping has reached a level of sophistication where it is possible for parents to order children with special talents. Ryder has a perfect memory, Cody superior physical skills, Marshall is a genius. As they grow up, the genetically-tailored children find themselves both increasingly alienated from normal humanity and increasingly aware of the way they are manipulated by those in power.

Other books you might like:
John Brunner, *Children of the Thunder*, 1989
Lois McMaster Bujold, *Falling Free*, 1988
Daniel Keys Moran, *Emerald Eyes*, 1988
John Wyndham, *The Midwich Cuckoos*, 1957

3594

ROBERT REED

Down the Bright Way

(New York: Bantam Spectra, 1991)

Story type: Science Fiction (First Contact; Adventure)
Major character(s): Kyle Stevens Hastings, Imposter, Wanderer; Jy, Leader, Wanderer; Moliak, Cyborg, Wanderer
Time period(s): Indeterminate
Locale(s): Earth

Summary: Kyle poses as a Wanderer when Jy and her fellow Wanderers come to Earth with stories of multiple Earths all connected by the Bright, and of the Wanderers' attempts to contact and unite all humans. Kyle's ruse remains unchallenged until he attends Jy's rally and finds himself kidnapped then transported far from his Earth in a scheme which could destroy the Bright and the Wanderers' search for the Makers.

Other books you might like:
Roger MacBride Allen, *The Ring of Charon*, 1990

Greg Bear, *Eon*, 1985
David Brin, *Startide Rising*, 1983
Orson Scott Card, *Ender's Game*, 1985
Glen Cook, *The Dragon Never Sleeps*, 1988
John DeChancie, *Paradox Alley*, 1987
John DeChancie, *Red Limit Freeway*, 1984
John DeChancie, *Starrigger*, 1983
Philip K. Dick, *The Unteleported Man*, 1983 revised
Michael P. Kube-McDowell, *Enigma*, 1986
Vonda N. McIntyre, *Transition*, 1991
Alis A. Rasmussen, *The Price of Ransom*, 1990

3595

ROBERT REED

An Exaltation of Larks

(New York: Tor, 1995)

Story type: Science Fiction (Immortality; Mystical)
Major character(s): Jesse Aylesworth, Student—College, Editor; Sully Faulkner, Student—College; The Indian, Time Traveller, Mythical Creature (turtle)
Time period(s): 1970s (1978); Indeterminate Future (end of the universe)
Locale(s): Warner, Midwest

Summary: Accepting a ride from Sully during a blizzard, Jesse realizes she seems somehow more familiar than she should. Events such as the radio failing to work, a turtle disappearing from the science lab, and Sully appearing similar to the woman in his Breton print, all portend the visit from the Indian who recruits Jesse to help change the future and make humans immortal.

Other books you might like:
John Brunner, *Age of Miracles*, 1973
Arthur C. Clarke, *Childhood's End*, 1953
Frederik Pohl, *The World at the End of Time*, 1990
Vernor Vinge, *Marooned in Realtime*, 1986
Robert Charles Wilson, *The Harvest*, 1993

3596

ROBERT REED

The Remarkables

(New York: Bantam Spectra, 1992)

Story type: Science Fiction (Adventure)
Major character(s): Service, Guide, Leader; Ranier, Empath, Adventurer; Talker, Alien (Remarkable)
Time period(s): Indeterminate Future
Locale(s): Pitcairn, Planet—Imaginary

Summary: A few offworld humans plus Pitcairn humans who live symbiotically with Remarkable settlements accompany juvenile Remarkables on their deadly, mandated rite of passage to a remote, religiously significant area of Pitcairn.

Other books you might like:
David Drake, *The Jungle*, 1991
Brian Herbert, *The Race for God*, 1990
David R. Palmer, *Emergence*, 1984

Alexei Panshin, *Rite of Passage*, 1968
Robert Silverberg, *The Face of the Waters*, 1991
Dan Simmons, *The Fall of Hyperion*, 1990
Dan Simmons, *Hyperion*, 1989
Sheri S. Tepper, *Grass*, 1989

3597

GARFIELD REEVES-STEVENS

Bloodshift

(New York: Popular Library, 1990)

Story type: Horror (Vampire Story; Science Fiction)
Major character(s): Granger Helman, Murderer; Adrienne St. Clair, Scientist, Vampire; Eduardo Diego y Rey, Vampire
Time period(s): 1980s (1980)
Locale(s): Toronto, Ontario, Canada

Summary: A retired contract killer is blackmailed into becoming involved in a 400-year war between a secret organization of vampires called the Conclave which seeks to dominate the world and a no-less-secret sect of Jesuits. Granger is comissioned to administer The Final Death to the traitorous vampire Adrienne St. Clair, who has discovered the non-supernatural scientific basis of vampirism and who is also being pursued by the Royal Canadian Mounted Police, British Intelligence, a secret American group called Project Nevada, another secret organization of vampires, and the CIA. The result is a complex, uneven meld of SF, espionage novel, political adventure, paranoid conspiracty thriller, and vampire tale which was originally published in Canada in 1981 by Virgo, a small press.

Other books you might like:
Barbara Hambly, *Those Who Hunt the Night*, 1988
James Herbert, *Sepulchre*, 1987
Lee Killough, *Blood Links*, 1988
Anne Rice, *The Vampire Lestat*, 1985
Brian Stableford, *The Empire of Fear*, 1988
Whitley Strieber, *The Hunger*, 1981
Les Whitten, *Progeny of the Adder*, 1965

3598

GARFIELD REEVES-STEVENS

Dark Matter

(New York: Doubleday, 1990)

Story type: Horror (Psychological Suspense)
Major character(s): Anthony Cross, Scientist (theoretical physicist), Serial Killer; Charis Neale, Scientist (Cross's lover); Katherine Duvall, Detective—Homicide
Time period(s): 1990s (1995)
Locale(s): Los Angeles, California

Summary: A talented black homicide detective becomes obsessed with her pursuit of charismatic but deranged high-energy physicist and serial killer Anthony Cross, who by slaughter seeks to understand the mysteries of quantum mechanics and thus bridge the chasm between life and death. Meanwhile, Cross's fellow physicist and girlfriend, Charis Neale, tries to keep stable his increasingly testy relationship

with his employers, the evil conglomerate known as Cathedral Three.

Other books you might like:
Thomas Harris, *The Silence of the Lambs*, 1988
Dean R. Koontz, *The Bad Place*, 1990
Dean R. Koontz, *Midnight*, 1989

3599

GARFIELD REEVES-STEVENS

Nighteyes

(New York: Doubleday Foundation, 1989)

Story type: Science Fiction (UFO)
Major character(s): Sarah Gilmour, Parent; Wendy Gilmour, Teenager
Time period(s): 1980s
Locale(s): Connecticut

Summary: The Gilmour family is bedeviled by shadowy aliens, evidently from UFOs. The sadistic aliens seem bent on abducting Wendy and conducting genetic experiments.

Other books you might like:
Robert A. Heinlein, *The Puppet Masters*, 1951
Fritz Leiber, *The Wanderer*, 1964
Whitley Strieber, *Majestic*, 1989

3600

JUDITH REEVES-STEVENS
GARFIELD REEVES-STEVENS, Co-Author

Federation

(New York: Pocket, 1994)

Story type: Science Fiction (Space Opera)
Series: Star Trek
Major character(s): Jean-Luc Picard, Spaceship Captain, Military Personnel; James T. Kirk, Spaceship Captain; Zefrem Cochrane, Scientist, Space Explorer
Time period(s): 23rd century; 24th century
Locale(s): *U.S.S. Enterprise*, Spaceship

Summary: Zefrem Cochrane thought he had found a safe haven on Gamma Canaris where his 21st century enemies could not follow him, but someone in the 23rd century accesses Captain Kirk's personal logs containing the secret and kidnaps Cochrane. Pursuing the kidnappers, the *Enterprise* enters the event horizon of a black hole. A hundred years later, Picard's *Enterprise* bargains for a mysterious Preserver artifact containing the personality of Cochrane's enemy which takes over the ship and Commander Data. When the two *Enterprise*s meet in the black hole, only their complete cooperation can save both ships and Zefrem Cochrane.

Other books you might like:
Alfred Bester, *The Stars My Destination*, 1956
Margaret Wander Bonanno, *Strangers From the Sky*, 1987
Diane Duane, *The Wounded Sky*, 1983
Dean McLaughlin, *The Man Who Wanted Stars*, 1965
Frederik Pohl, *Beyond the Blue Event Horizon*, 1980
Garfield Reeves-Stevens, *Memory Prime*, 1988
Judith Reeves-Stevens, co-author

3601

JUDITH REEVES-STEVENS
GARFIELD REEVES-STEVENS, Co-Author

Nightfeeder
(New York: Roc, 1991)

Story type: Fantasy (Alternate World; Quest)
Series: Chronicles of Galen Sword
Major character(s): Galen Sword, Adventurer, Businessman; Melody Ko, Adventurer, Engineer
Time period(s): Indeterminate Future
Locale(s): New York, New York

Summary: Because Galen Sword was born human and totally without magical powers, he was sent by his parents to an alternate world, Earth. When he discovers his true heritage, his search for a way to return to the First World makes him the focal point in a war between two clans. Galen's survival ends up depending on his alliance with a being from the First World, Orion Clan Isis, a vampire.

Other books you might like:
Robert N. Charrette, *Never Deal with a Dragon*, 1990
Nancy A. Collins, *Sunglasses After Dark*, 1989
Barbara Hambly, *Dragonsbane*, 1986
Tad Williams, *The Dragonbone Chair*, 1989
Chelsea Quinn Yarbro, *A Candle for D'Artagnan*, 1989

3602

JUDITH REEVES-STEVENS
GARFIELD REEVES-STEVENS, Co-Author

Prime Directive
(New York: Pocket, 1990)

Story type: Science Fiction (Space Opera)
Series: Star Trek
Major character(s): James T. Kirk, Spaceship Captain; Spock, Scientist, Alien; Leonard McCoy, Doctor
Time period(s): 23rd century
Locale(s): *U.S.S. Enterprise*, Spaceship; Starfleet First Contact Office, Space Station; Talos IV, Planet—Imaginary

Summary: After being discredited by Starfleet for violation of their prime directive, to avoid interfering in cultures not affiliated with the United Federation of Planets, the *U.S.S. Enterprise* bridge crew must clear their names and restore their rank.

Other books you might like:
Carolyn Clowes, *The Pandora Principle*, 1990
  Star Trek 49
Diane Duane, *Doctor's Orders*, 1990
  Star Trek 50
Julia Ecklar, *The Kobayashi Maru*, 1990
  Star Trek 47
Michael Jan Friedman, *Double, Double*, 1989
  Star Trek 45
Peter Morwood, *Rules of Engagement*, 1990
  Star Trek 48

3603

JUDITH REEVES-STEVENS
GARFIELD REEVES-STEVENS, Co-Author

Shifter
(New York: Roc, 1990)

Story type: Fantasy (Alternate World; Quest)
Series: Chronicles of Galen Sword
Major character(s): Galen Sword, Adventurer, Businessman; Melody Ko, Adventurer, Engineer; Adrian Forsyte, Scientist
Time period(s): Indeterminate Future
Locale(s): New York, New York

Summary: Galen Sword, a rich New York playboy haunted by shadowy memories of being sent away from his beloved parents, has embarked on a deadly and seemingly impossible quest. A near-fatal car accident leads Galen to the knowledge that he was really from a parallel world, not Earth, and had been heir to a powerful dynasty. With the help of a staff of ''unusually'' talented people, Galen must find his way back home by capturing a being that has crossed over from that world to his one. The being is a werewolf.

Other books you might like:
Marion Zimmer Bradley, *Hawkmistress!*, 1982
Robert Jordan, *The Eye of the World*, 1989
Stephen King, *Silver Bullet*, 1985
Michael Moorcock, *The Fortress of the Pearl*, 1989
Sydney J. Van Scyoc, *Feather Stroke*, 1989

3604

MICKEY ZUCKER REICHERT

Beyond Ragnarok
(New York: DAW, 1996)

Story type: Fantasy (Legend; Adventure)
Series: Renshai Chronicles
Major character(s): Kevral Tainharsdartter, Thief, Adventurer; Ra-khir of Erythane, Apprentice, Knight; Tae Kahn, Teenager, Warrior (Renshai)
Time period(s): Indeterminate Past
Locale(s): Bearn, Fictional Country

Summary: Three centuries after the final battle of the gods, the search for the successor for a dying human king involves unprecedented trials, precipitated by widespread attacks on legitimate heirs.

Other books you might like:
Linda Evans, *Sleipnir*, 1994
Jason Henderson, *The Spawn of Loki*, 1994
Martha Wells, *The Element of Fire*, 1993
Janny Wurts, *Curse of the Mistwraith*, 1994

3605

MICKEY ZUCKER REICHERT

By Chaos Cursed

(New York: DAW, 1991)

Story type: Fantasy (Magic Conflict; Adventure)
Series: Bifrost Guardians
Major character(s): Al Larson, Military Personnel, Mythical Creature (elf); Silme, Sorceress; Taziar Medakan, Thief
Time period(s): 1960s (1968); 10th century
Locale(s): New York, New York; Europe, Alternate Universe

Summary: When Al Larson died in Vietnam calling on the Norse gods, they transferred his life energy into the body of an elf in their universe, so that he could save one of the gods. Now Allerum and his friends Silme, Taziar and Astryd, are in danger from the sorcerer Bolverkr, whose destruction would upset the balance between Law and Chaos. In the ensuing magical battle, Al is flung back to his own body in New York City of 1968, where he must destroy Bolverkr, rescue Silme from the Dragon mage's influence, keep Taziar out of jail, and avoid getting sent to Vietnam again.

Other books you might like:
L. Sprague de Camp, *The Incomplete Enchanter*, 1942
    Fletcher Pratt, co-author
Jude Deveraux, *A Knight in Shining Armor*, 1989
Phyllis Eisenstein, *Shadow of Earth*, 1979
Barbara Hambly, *Dragonsbane*, 1986
Barbara Hambly, *The Time of the Dark*, 1987
R.A. MacAvoy, *Tea with the Black Dragon*, 1983
Bill Ransom, *Jaguar*, 1990
Roger Zelazny, *Nine Princes in Amber*, 1970

3606

MICKEY ZUCKER REICHERT

Dragonrank Master

(New York: DAW, 1989)

Story type: Fantasy (Legend)
Series: Bifrost Guardians
Major character(s): Al Larson, Military Personnel (Vietnam veteran), Mythical Creature (elf); Gaelinar, Companion (of Al)
Time period(s): Indeterminate
Locale(s): Midgard, Mythical Place

Summary: Al discovers there is a possibility that he can bring his lover, Silme, back from the dead, but only if he can outsmart the goddess, Hel. Unfortunately Loki's wolfson and the other gods are doing everything they can to stop Al and Gaelinar from achieving this goal.

Other books you might like:
Robert Adams, *Stairway to Forever*, 1988
Alan Dean Foster, *Spellsinger*, 1981
Kate Green, *Contrarywise*, 1989
Morgan Llywelyn, *The Isles of the Blest*, 1989
Robin McKinley, *The Outlaws of Sherwood*, 1989
Gail Van Asten, *Charlemagne's Champion*, 1990

3607

MICKEY ZUCKER REICHERT

The Last of the Renshai

(New York: DAW, 1992)

Story type: Fantasy (Sword and Sorcery)
Series: Renshai Chronicles
Major character(s): Rache Kallmirsson, Warrior; Shadimar, Wizard; Mitrian, Warrior
Time period(s): Indeterminate Past
Locale(s): Northlands, Fictional Country

Summary: The ancient prophecies foretold that a Renshai warrior would be a hero in the Great War, the final battle that will usher in the Age of Change which would destroy mortals, wizards and the gods themselves. Rache, only survivor of an attack on his homeland, is the last of the Renshai. As the Swordmaster for the ruler Santagithi, he fights for his life and for vengeance.

Other books you might like:
C.J. Cherryh, *The Fires of Azeroth*, 1979
Stephen R. Donaldson, *Lord Foul's Bane*, 1977
Phyllis Eisenstein, *Born to Exile*, 1978
Barbara Hambly, *The Time of the Dark*, 1987
C.L. Moore, *Jirel of Joiry*, 1969
J.R.R. Tolkien, *The Fellowship of the Ring*, 1954

3608

MICKEY ZUCKER REICHERT

The Legend of Nightfall

(New York: DAW, 1993)

Story type: Fantasy (Adventure; Quest)
Major character(s): Nightfall, Thief; Edward Nargol, Royalty (prince); Kelryn, Dancer
Time period(s): Indeterminate Past
Locale(s): Alyndar, Fictional Country

Summary: Finally captured after years on the run, Nightfall must choose between execution and a magically enforced oath to become squire to the irritatingly idealistic and naive Prince Edward, see that he establishes himself by becoming landed and keep him out of trouble. After embarking on their journey, events turn upside down nearly every prior conception they have about themselves, their world and the people they trust.

Other books you might like:
Steven Brust, *Jhereg*, 1983
Heather Gladney, *Teot's War*, 1988
P.C. Hodgell, *God Stalk*, 1982
Tanya Huff, *The Fire's Stone*, 1990
Steve Perry, *The Man Who Never Missed*, 1985
Jennifer Roberson, *Sword-Dancer*, 1986

3609

MICKEY ZUCKER REICHERT

Prince of Demons

(New York: DAW, 1996)

Story type: Fantasy (Legend; Adventure)
Series: Renshai Chronicles
Major character(s): Colbey Calistinsson, Warrior (Renshai); Dh'arlo'me, Mythical Creature (elf); Kevral Tainharsdartter, Warrior (Renshai)
Time period(s): Indeterminate Past
Locale(s): Bearn, Fictional Country; Pudar, Fictional Country; The Westlands, Fictional Country

Summary: Three hundred years after Ragnarok, Dh'arlo'me attempts to entice mortals into championing Chaos, an event which could spell disaster for both mortals and immortals. Colbey Calistinsson must identify the correct opponent to set against Dh'arlo'me to maintain the balance between law and chaos.

Other books you might like:
Linda Evans, *Sleipnir*, 1994
Mary Gentle, *Rats and Gargoyles*, 1991
Jason Henderson, *The Spawn of Loki*, 1994
P.C. Hodgell, *God Stalk*, 1982
Joel Rosenberg, *The Fire Duke*, 1995
Janny Wurts, *Curse of the Mistwraith*, 1994
Roger Zelazny, *Nine Princes in Amber*, 1970

3610

MICKEY ZUCKER REICHERT

Shadow's Realm

(New York: DAW, 1990)

Story type: Fantasy (Adventure)
Series: Bifrost Guardians
Major character(s): Taziar Medakan, Thief; Allerum, Mythical Creature (elf); Al Larson, Military Personnel (Vietnam veteran), Mythical Creature
Time period(s): Indeterminate
Locale(s): Cullinsberg, Fictional City

Summary: When Larson, Shadow, Astryd and Silme killed the Chaos Dragon, they were unaware that all the released Chaos found and bonded with Bolverkr, the greatest surviving Dragonmage and drove him mad. Convinced by Chaos that Shadow and Larson must suffer for the destruction caused by the unleashed Chaos, Bolverkr lures them to Shadow's home town and into a trap.

Other books you might like:
Catherine Cooke, *Mask of the Wizard*, 1985
Brian Daley, *The Doomfarers of Coramonde*, 1977
Leo Frankowski, *The Cross-Time Engineer*, 1986
Barbara Hambly, *The Time of the Dark*, 1987
Roger Zelazny, *Nine Princes in Amber*, 1970

3611

MICKEY ZUCKER REICHERT

The Unknown Soldier

(New York, DAW, 1994)

Story type: Science Fiction (Time Travel; Military)
Major character(s): Carrigan, Military Personnel, Time Traveller; Jason Walker, Doctor (resident); Shawna Nicholson, Doctor (chief resident)
Time period(s): 1980s (1985)
Locale(s): North Liberty, Iowa

Summary: While on call at the emergency room, Jason handles an unhuman patient who seems to have been hit by a bomb. The unidentifiable patient begins to trust the doctors and recalls his name, Carrigan. Shawna realizes Carrigan comes from the future as, unfortunately, do his enemies who follow him to the 20th century, attempting to kill him and all who know of him.

Other books you might like:
Poul Anderson, *The Time Patrol*, 1991
Bill Baldwin, *The Defenders*, 1992
Randall Frakes, *Terminator 2: Judgment Day*, 1991
George Turner, *Genetic Soldier*, 1994
Robert Charles Wilson, *A Bridge of Years*, 1991

3612

MICKEY ZUCKER REICHERT

The Western Wizard

(New York: DAW, 1992)

Story type: Fantasy (Magic Conflict)
Series: Renshai Chronicles
Major character(s): Shadimar, Wizard; Colbey Calistinsson, Warrior; Santagithi, Warrior (Renshai)
Time period(s): Indeterminate Past
Locale(s): The Westlands, Fictional Country; Santagithi, Fictional City

Summary: With the death of the Western Wizard, the balance between the three other Cardinal Wizards slips, further entangling the political situation. Shadimar, the Eastern Wizard, searches for a replacement while preparing for the upcoming struggle.

Other books you might like:
Poul Anderson, *Hrolf Kraki's Saga*, 1973
Glen Cook, *The Black Company*, 1984
Barbara Hambly, *The Time of the Dark*, 1982
Robert Jordan, *The Eye of the World*, 1989
Tad Williams, *The Dragonbone Chair*, 1988

3613

KATYA REIMANN

Wind From a Foreign Sky

(New York: Tor, 1996)

Story type: Fantasy (Magic Conflict; Political)
Series: Tielmaran Chronicles

Major character(s): Heiratikus, Wizard, Political Figure; Issachar Dan, Nobleman, Warrior; Gaultry, Hunter, Wizard
Time period(s): Indeterminate Past
Locale(s): Tielmark, Fictional Country; Bissanty Empire, Fictional Country

Summary: Prince Clarin makes a deal with the gods to separate his nation from the Bissanty Empire. Three hundred years later a plot may undo that action with magic and duplicity, while a young woman finds herself at the hub of destiny armed with strange powers. First novel.

Other books you might like:
Lisa Goldstein, *Summer King, Winter Fool*, 1994
Terry Goodkind, *Wizard's First Rule*, 1994
Patricia A. McKillip, *The Riddle-Master of Hed*, 1976
Caroline Stevermer, *A College of Magics*, 1994
Janny Wurts, *Curse of the Mistwraith*, 1994

3614

KATHRYN REINES

The Kiss

(New York: Avon, 1996)

Story type: Horror (Vampire Story)
Major character(s): Rebecca Bittan, Student; Maria Viroslav, Noblewoman (countess), Vampire; Alexander Viroslav, Nobleman (count), Vampire
Time period(s): 1930s (1938)
Locale(s): Boleslaus, Bulgaria

Summary: Stranded at the Romanian border while fleeing from the Nazis, Rebecca Bittan and her boyfriend, Richard Anderson, accept the invitation of Countess Viroslav to stay at her mansion. There, they are indoctrinated into the ways of vampirism that have sustained the Count and Countess Viroslav for centuries. First novel.

Other books you might like:
Elaine Bergstrom, *Shattered Glass*, 1989
Andrei Codrescu, *Blood Countess*, 1995
William Pridgen, *Night of the Dragon's Blood*, 1997
Shawn Ryan, *Nocturnas*, 1995
F. Paul Wilson, *The Keep*, 1981

3615

WILLIAM RELLING JR.

The Infinite Man

(Los Angeles: Scream/Press, 1989)

Story type: Horror (Collection)
Summary: Twenty-one stories first published between 1980 and 1989 with five original to the volume, plus an "Afterword." Clever, ironical, biting, usually short, often quite funny—a few, like "Sorry, but We Only Offer That Course in the Fall" and "Burton's Word," being little more than extended jokes. Quite contemporary in setting and theme, with frequent sho-biz references ("The King," "Abbott & Costello Go to Jonestown"). The outstanding story in the volume is the title story, "The Infinite Man," which tells of the rise and fall of a writer obsessed with mirrors.

Other books you might like:
Dennis Etchison, *The Dark Country*, 1982
Richard Christian Matheson, *Scars and Other Distinguishing Trademarks*, 1988

3616

WILLIAM RELLING JR.

Silent Moon

(New York: Tor, 1990)

Story type: Horror (Occult)
Major character(s): Gillian Woodbury, Journalist (TV reporter); Bud Friendly, Journalist (Newspaperman)
Time period(s): 1980s (1988)
Locale(s): San Francisco, California

Summary: Reporters Woodbury and Friendly are drawn into a conspiracy involving evangelism, presidential politics, and a moon cult's attempt to utilize human sacrifice to free an ancient monster from its long confinement.

Other books you might like:
Ramsey Campbell, *The Hungry Moon*, 1986
Dennis Wheatley, *The Satanist*, 1960
Dennis Wheatley, *To the Devil, a Daughter*, 1953

3617

JACK REMICK

Terminal Weird

(Seattle: Black Heron Press, 1996)

Story type: Horror (Collection)
Summary: This collection contains eleven stories tinged with fantasy and often told from extraordinary perspectives. In "Roach," a man consumed by cockroaches sees the world from their point of view. "Monica Metallica" features a femme fatale heavy-metal musician with the habits of spiders. Death takes the form of alligators endlessly pursued by immortals in "Lizard," and heaven is a complex machine whose function is not understood by those running it in "Machine." A young woman's dreams of her awakening sexuality manifest as a crocodile in "Crocodile."

Other books you might like:
William S. Burroughs, *Interzone*, 1989
Wayne Allen Sallee, *With Wounds Still Wet*, 1996
Don Webb, *A Spell for the Fulfillment of Desire*, 1996

3618

MIKE RESNICK, Editor
MARTIN H. GREENBERG, Co-Editor

Aladdin: Master of the Lamp

(New York: DAW, 1992)

Story type: Fantasy (Anthology; Legend)
Major character(s): Aladdin, Adventurer
Locale(s): Middle East

Summary: Contains a one-page introduction by Resnick plus 43 original stories sharing themes from the famous Middle Eastern story of Aladdin, the magic lamp and wish-granting djinn, including one collaboration, "If Wishes Were Genies," by Terry McGarry and Austin Dridge and two stories each by Jack C. Haldeman II and Barry N. Malzberg. Other authors include Mark Aronson, John Betancourt, Pat Cadigan, George Alec Effinger, David Gerrold, Karen Haber, Patrick Nielson Hayden, Janet Kagan, Katharine Kerr, Maureen F. McHugh, Josepha Sherman, Martha Soukup, Judith Tarr and Jane Yolen.

Other books you might like:
Martin H. Greenberg, *The Fantastic Adventures of Robin Hood*, 1991
    editor
Andrew Lang, *The Arabian Nights Entertainments*, 1969
    editor
Susan Shwartz, *Arabesques: More Tales of the Arabian Nights*, 1988
    editor
Susan Shwartz, *Arabesques II*, 1989
    editor
Jack Zipes, *Arabian Nights: The Marvels and Wonders of the Thousand and One Nights*, 1991
    editor

3619

MIKE RESNICK, Editor

Alternate Kennedys

(New York: Tor, 1992)

Story type: Science Fiction (Anthology; Alternate Universe)

Summary: Contains a four-page introduction plus individual introductions to one poem by Jane Yolen and 25 original stories whose themes involve the famous American political family, the Kennedys. Authors include Mark Aronson, Ginjer Buchanan, Pat Cadigan, Esther M. Friesner, David Gerrold, Jack C. Haldeman II, Nancy Kress, Michael P. Kube-McDowell, Mike Resnick, Kristine Kathryn Rusch, Robert Sheckley, Susan Shwartz, Martha Soukup, Judith Tarr and Harry Turtledove.

Other books you might like:
Gregory Benford, *Alternate Americas*, 1992
    Martin H. Greenberg, co-editor
Gregory Benford, *Alternate Heroes*, 1990
    Martin H. Greenberg, co-editor
Philip K. Dick, *The Man in the High Castle*, 1962
L. Neil Smith, *The Gallatin Divergence*, 1985

3620

MIKE RESNICK, Editor

Alternate Presidents

(New York: Tor, 1992)

Story type: Science Fiction (Anthology; Alternate Universe)

Summary: Contains a three-page introduction plus individual introductions to 28 stories asking the question, "What if. . ." concerning United States Presidents arranged chronologically 1789-1988. Authors include Pat Cadigan, Bill Fawcett, David Gerrold, Alexis A. Gilliland, Janet Kagan, Michael P. Kube-McDowell, Judith Moffett, Jody Lynn Nye, Mike Resnick, Kristine Kathryn Rusch, Robert Sheckley, Susan Shwartz, Martha Soukup, Lawrence Watt-Evans and two stories by Barry N. Malzberg.

Other books you might like:
Gregory Benford, *Alternate Americas*, 1992
    Martin H. Greenberg, co-editor
Gregory Benford, *Alternate Empires*, 1989
    Martin H. Greenberg, co-editor
Gregory Benford, *Alternate Heroes*, 1990
    Martin H. Greenberg, co-editor
Gregory Benford, *Alternate Wars*, 1991
    Martin H. Greenberg, co-editor

3621

MIKE RESNICK, Editor

Alternate Warriors

(New York: Tor, 1993)

Story type: Science Fiction (Anthology; Alternate Universe)

Summary: Contains a two-page introduction plus individual introductions to 29 original stories from authors challenged to write a story about a historical figure who chose to fight for beliefs rather than die for them. Authors include George Alec Effinger, Esther Friesner, David Gerrold, Jack C. Haldeman II, Tappan King, Kathe Koja, Michael P. Kube-McDowell, Mercedes Lackey, Brad Linaweaver, Barry N. Malzberg, Maureen McHugh, Beth Meacham, Kristine Kathryn Rusch, Michelle Sagara, Josepha Sherman and Judith Tarr.

Other books you might like:
Gregory Benford, *Alternate Americas*, 1992
    Martin H. Greenberg, co-editor
Gregory Benford, *Alternate Empires*, 1989
    Martin H. Greenberg, co-editor
Gregory Benford, *Alternate Heroes*, 1990
    Martin H. Greenberg, co-editor
Gregory Benford, *Alternate Wars*, 1991
    Martin H. Greenberg, co-editor
Harry Turtledove, *The Guns of the South*, 1992

3622

MIKE RESNICK

Bully!

(Eugene, OR: Pulphouse Axolotl Press, 1990)

Story type: Science Fiction (Alternate Universe; Political)
Major character(s): Theodore Roosevelt, Historical Figure, Political Figure
Time period(s): 1910s (1910)
Locale(s): Kirinyaga Territory, Africa; Alternate Earth

Summary: On a trip to Africa, Theodore Roosevelt becomes convinced to help inflict American-style democracy on Africans ill-equipped to appreciate its benefits.

Other books you might like:
Ursula K. Le Guin, *The Word for World Is Forest*, 1976
Mack Reynolds, *The Best Ye Breed*, 1978
Mack Reynolds, *Blackman's Burden*, 1972
Mack Reynolds, *Border, Breed Nor Birth*, 1972
G. Harry Stine, *The Bastard Rebellion*, 1988

3623

MIKE RESNICK, Editor
MARTIN H. GREENBERG, Co-Editor

By Any Other Fame

(New York: DAW, 1994)

Story type: Science Fiction (Anthology; Alternate History)

Summary: Contains a one-page introduction and brief individual introductions to 23 original stories about celebrities who lead different lives in other universes, with Mercedes Lackey collaborating with Larry Dixon on one story. Other authors include Ginjer Buchanan, Thomas A. Easton, George Alec Effinger, David Gerrold, Jack C. Haldeman II, Janet Kagan, Nancy Kress, Barry N. Malzberg, Beth Meacham, Laura Resnick, Kristine Kathryn Rusch, Michelle Sagara, Dean Wesley Smith, Judith Tarr, and Brian M. Thomsen.

Other books you might like:
Gregory Benford, *Alternate Heroes*, 1990
    Martin H. Greenberg, co-editor
Esther Friesner, *Alien Pregnant by Elvis*, 1994
    Martin H. Greenberg, co-editor
Richard Peabody, *Mondo Elvis*, 1993
    Lucinda Ebersole, co-editor
Paul M. Sammon, *The King Is Dead: Tales of Elvis Post Mortem*, 1994
    editor
Kay Sloan, *Elvis Rising: Stories on the King*, 1993
    Constance Pierce, co-editor

3624

MIKE RESNICK, Editor
MARTIN H. GREENBERG, Co-Editor

Christmas Ghosts

(New York: DAW, 1993)

Story type: Horror (Anthology; Ghost Story)

Summary: The 27 original stories collected here all deal with Christmas spirits, most in the Dickensian sense of ghosts of Christmas Past and Present. Frank Robinson's "Merry Christmas, No. 30267" tells of an unregenerate prisoner given a chance to repent his past and start life over. Kathe Koja and Barry N. Malzberg imagine Sir William Gilbert visited on his deathbed by the ghost of Jack the Ripper in "The Timbrel Sound of Darkness," a wry meditation on artistic prostitution. John Betancourt's "The River Lethe Is Made of Tears" and Kristine Kathryn Rusch's "Three Wishes Before a Fire" use supernatural manifestations to reassure their characters, while Dean Wesley Smith's "The Ghosts of Christmas Future" offers a bleak vision of holiday hopelessness.

Other books you might like:
Kathryn Cramer, *Christmas Ghosts*, 1988
    David Hartwell, co-editor
Kathryn Cramer, *Spirits of Christmas*, 1989
    David Hartwell, co-editor
Richard Dalby, *Ghosts for Christmas*, 1988
    editor
Richard Dalby, *Thrillers for Christmas*, 1989
    editor
Seon Manley, *Christmas Ghosts*, 1978

3625

MIKE RESNICK, Editor
MARTIN H. GREENBERG, Co-Editor
LOREN D. ESTLEMAN, Co-Editor

Deals with the Devil

(New York: Daw, 1994)

Story type: Horror (Anthology)

Summary: The 36 stories written especially for this volume approach the classic fantasy theme of dealing with the devil— and the consequences thereof—from a variety of angles. Jane Yolen's "Pitch" tells of the lengths to which successful screenwriters will go to drum up an exciting movie idea. Dean Wesley Smith's "Another Damn Deal" concerns a writer who makes a deal with the devil not to write a story about him. Lawrence Watt-Evans' "For Value Received" is about a man who discovers the true price of his measly soul. Mike Resnick's "Stanley the Eighteen-Percenter" tells about what happens when a hardnosed agent must argue his client's case against Satan. And Brian Thomsen's "Nobody Wins a Deal with the Devil" tells of the steps Satan takes to bind his rebellious son to him.

Other books you might like:
Basil Davenport, *Deals with the Devil*, 1958
    editor
Martin H. Greenberg, *Devil Worshippers*, 1990
    Charles G. Waugh, co-editor
Marvin Kaye, *Devils and Demons*, 1987
    editor

3626

MIKE RESNICK, Editor
MARTIN H. GREENBERG, Co-Editor

Dinosaur Fantastic

(New York: DAW, 1993)

Story type: Fantasy (Anthology)

Summary: Contains a two-page introduction by the editor noting this as the first all original dinosaur anthology ever published plus 25 stories by 27 authors including Roger MacBride Allen, Pat Cadigan, David Gerrold, Katharine Kerr, Kathe Koja, Mercedes Lackey, Barry N. Malzberg, Beth Meacham, Kevin O'Donnell Jr., Frank M. Robinson, Kristine Kathryn Rusch, Michelle M. Sagara, Robert J. Sawyer, Robert Sheckley, Josepha Sherman, John E. Stith and Judith Tarr.

Other books you might like:
Poul Anderson, *The Night Fantastic*, 1991
   Karen Anderson, co-editor
Jack Dann, *Dinosaurs!*, 1990
   Gardner Dozois, co-editor
Martin H. Greenberg, *Horse Fantastic*, 1991
   Rosalind M. Greenberg, co-editor
Rosalind M. Greenberg, *Dragon Fantastic*, 1992
   Martin H. Greenberg, co-editor
James Gurney, *Dinotopia*, 1992
Andre Norton, *Catfantastic*, 1989
   Martin H. Greenberg, co-editor
Andre Norton, *Catfantastic II*, 1991
   Martin H. Greenberg, co-editor
Robert Silverberg, *The Science Fictional Dinosaur*, 1982
   Charles G. Waugh, Martin Harry Greenberg, co-editors

3627

MIKE RESNICK, Editor
GARDNER DOZOIS, Co-Editor

Future Earths: Under African Skies
(New York: DAW, 1993)

Story type: Science Fiction (Anthology)
Locale(s): Africa

Summary: Contains a three-page list of books about Africa and short stories with African themes, a four-page introduction plus individual introductions to 15 stories set in Africa which first appeared in periodicals and anthologies, 1965-1993. Authors include Gregory Benford, Janet Gluckman, George Guthridge, Ian McDonald, Naomi Mitchison, Kim Stanley Robinson, Dave Smeds, Bruce Sterling and Vernor Vinge.

Other books you might like:
Gillian Bradshaw, *The Land of Gold*, 1992
Bill Dolan, *White Rhino*, 1992
George Alec Effinger, *When Gravity Fails*, 1987
Ben Okri, *The Famished Road*, 1992
Robert Silverberg, *Lion Time in Timbuctoo*, 1990
G. Harry Stine, *The Bastard Rebellion*, 1988

3628

MIKE RESNICK, Editor

Inside the Funhouse
(New York: AvoNova, 1992)

Story type: Science Fiction (Anthology; Science Fiction)

Summary: This collection of stories sharing a recursive theme, science fiction *about* science fiction, contains a two-page introduction and individual introductions to Jane Yolen's poem and 16 stories by 15 authors with two, Frederik Pohl and C.M. Kornbluth, collaborating on ''Mute Inglorious Tam.'' Three authors explore the epistolary form, Jack Lewis in ''Who's Cribbing,'' Patricia Cribbing Nurse in ''One Rejection Too Many'' and Eric Norden in ''The Curse of the Mhondoro Nkablele.'' Allen Steele spoofs a deceased L. Ron Hubbard inspired character through interviews in ''Hapgood's Hoax.''

Other authors include A, Isaac Asimov, Philip K. Dick, George Alec Effinger, Edmond Hamilton, Frederik Pohl, Mike Resnick and Ian Watson with Barry N. Malzberg contributing two Mike Resnick and Ian Watson with Barry N. Malzberg contributing two stories.

Other books you might like:
Michael Bishop, *The Secret Ascension*, 1987
Robert Bloch, *The Eighth Stage of Fandom: Selections From 25 Years of Fan Writing*, 1962
Fredric Brown, *Martians, Go Home*, 1955
Fredric Brown, *What Mad Universe*, 1949
Jonathan Carroll, *The Land of Laughs*, 1980
Robert Coulson, *Charles Fort Never Mentioned Wombats*, 1977
   Gene DeWeese, co-author
Gene DeWeese, *Now You See It/Him/Them. . .*, 1975
   Robert Coulson, co-author
Philip K. Dick, *The Man in the High Castle*, 1962
Philip Jose Farmer, *Venus on the Half Shell*, 1975
   written as Kilgore Trout
Sharyn McCrumb, *Bimbos of the Death Sun*, 1987
Larry Niven, *Fallen Angels*, 1991
   Jerry Pournelle, Michael Flynn, co-authors
Tim Powers, *The Stress of Her Regard*, 1989

3629

MIKE RESNICK

Ivory: A Legend of Past and Future
(New York: Tor, 1988)

Story type: Science Fiction (Adventure)
Major character(s): Duncan Rojas, Researcher; Bukoba Mandaka, Warrior (The last Maasai warrior)
Time period(s): Indeterminate Future (The year 6303 of the Galactic Era)
Locale(s): Earth; Athena, Planet—Imaginary

Summary: In this Nebula award nominated novel, Duncan Rojas, senior researcher and authenticator for Braxton's Records of Big Game, is visited by Bukoba Mandaka, last of the Maasai, who makes an unusual request. Mandaka wants to hire Rojas to find the tusks of the fabled Kilimanjaro Elephant, the largest tusks ever authenticated. Unfortunately the Elephant was killed more than six thousand years ago and its tusks disappeared more than three thousand years ago.

Other books you might like:
Roger MacBride Allen, *Orphan of Creation*, 1988
David Brin, *The Uplift War*, 1987
Orson Scott Card, *Speaker for the Dead*, 1986
Paul J. McAuley, *Of the Fall*, 1989

3630

MIKE RESNICK

Lucifer Jones
(New York: Warner Questar, 1992)

Story type: Fantasy (Light Fantasy)
Major character(s): Lucifer Jones, Adventurer, Religious

Time period(s): 1920s (1926-1929); 1930s (1930-1934)
Locale(s): Asia; Europe

Summary: Lucifer Jones jaunts around the globe foiling villains, battling mythical creatures, clobbering literary icons and hobnobbing with the high and mighty while searching for a place to build his tabernacle. Spoofs the *Indiana Jones Series* (1981-1992).

Other books you might like:
Campbell Black, *Raiders of the Lost Ark*, 1981
Craig Shaw Gardner, *The Other Sinbad*, 1991
James Kahn, *Indiana Jones and the Temple of Doom*, 1984
Catherine Lanigan, *Jewel of the Nile*, 1985
Catherine Lanigan, *Romancing the Stone*, 1984
Rob MacGregor, *Indiana Jones and the Last Crusade*, 1989
Rob MacGregor, *Indiana Jones and the Peril at Delphi*, 1991
Rob MacGregor, *Indiana Jones and the Seven Veils*, 1991
Mark E. Rogers, *Samurai Cat in the Real World*, 1989
Mark E. Rogers, *The Sword of Samurai Cat*, 1991

3631
MIKE RESNICK

A Miracle of Rare Design
(New York: Tor, 1994)

Story type: Science Fiction (Adventure; First Contact)
Major character(s): Xavier William Lennox, Explorer, Genetically Altered Being; Beatrice Ngoni, Doctor (surgeon); Chomanche, Religious (priest), Alien
Time period(s): Indeterminate Future
Locale(s): Medina, Planet—Imaginary; Artismo, Planet—Imaginary

Summary: Crippled after spying on Firefly religious rites, Xavier William Lennox is surgically altered into a Firefly to facilitate contact and negotiation of mineral rights on the planet. Once he has become an alien, he craves the experience and repeats it, aiding first contacts.

Other books you might like:
John Barnes, *Sin of Origin*, 1988
Michael Bishop, *Transfigurations*, 1979
C.J. Cherryh, *The Faded Sun: Kesrith*, 1978
Rebecca Ore, *Becoming Alien*, 1987
Charles Sheffield, *Proteus Combined*, 1994

3632
MIKE RESNICK

Oracle
(New York: Ace, 1992)

Story type: Science Fiction (Adventure; Political)
Series: Oracle
Major character(s): Carlos "Iceman" Mendoza, Saloon Keeper/Owner, Spy (retired); Jimmy "the Injun" Two Feathers, Murderer, Government Official; Joshua "the Whistler" Jeremiah Chandler, Bounty Hunter, Murderer
Time period(s): Indeterminate Future
Locale(s): Last Chance, Planet—Imaginary; Hades, Planet—Imaginary

Summary: When a person claiming to be Penelope Bailey's mother asks the Iceman to bring back her daughter, he hires the Whistler to approach Penelope and kill her if possible, or bring her back if, as likely, Penelope's precognition protects her from attack.

Other books you might like:
Karen Haber, *Mutant Star*, 1992
Frank Herbert, *Chapterhouse: Dune*, 1985
Frank Herbert, *Heretics of Dune*, 1984
Katharine Kerr, *Polar City Blues*, 1990

3633
MIKE RESNICK

Paradise: A Chronicle of a Distant World
(New York: Tor, 1989)

Story type: Science Fiction (First Contact)
Major character(s): Matthew Breen, Journalist (Biographer); Buko Pepon, Revolutionary, Ruler
Time period(s): Indeterminate Future
Locale(s): Peponi, Planet—Imaginary

Summary: Humans colonize a planet strikingly similar to nineteenth-century Kenya despite the presence of a native sentient race. A journalist visiting the planet attempts to trace the key events in that colonization over a period of decades.

Other books you might like:
Roger MacBride Allen, *Orphan of Creation*, 1988
David Brin, *The Uplift War*, 1987
Judith Moffett, *Pennterra*, 1987
Sheri S. Tepper, *Grass*, 1989

3634
MIKE RESNICK

Prophet
(New York: Ace, 1993)

Story type: Science Fiction (Space Opera; Psychic Powers)
Series: Oracle
Major character(s): Carlos "Iceman" Mendoza, Saloon Keeper/Owner, Spy (retired); Penelope Bailey, Psychic, Leader; Felix "Gravedancer" Lomax, Bodyguard, Spy
Time period(s): Indeterminate Future
Locale(s): Last Chance, Planet—Imaginary; Mozart, Planet—Imaginary

Summary: Obsessed with locating Penelope and neutralizing the threat she represents, Carlos deploys Felix to investigate the Prophet. Carlos then prepares his final assault on Penelope Bailey while she continues her ominous shaping of human history.

Other books you might like:
Isaac Asimov, *Foundation and Empire*, 1952
Marion Zimmer Bradley, *The Firebrand*, 1987
Glen Cook, *The Dragon Never Sleeps*, 1988
Frank Herbert, *The God-Emperor of Dune*, 1981
Ursula K. Le Guin, *The Lathe of Heaven*, 1971
Anne McCaffrey, *Damia*, 1992
Michaela Roessner, *Vanishing Point*, 1993

Lewis Shiner, *Glimpses*, 1993

3635

MIKE RESNICK

Purgatory: A Chronicle of a Distant World
(New York: Tor, 1993)

Story type: Science Fiction (Science Fiction)
Major character(s): Jalanopi, Alien, Leader (King of the Tulabete tribe); Andrew McFarley, Religious
Time period(s): Indeterminate Future
Locale(s): Karimon, Planet—Imaginary (Rockgarden)

Summary: Human arrival on Karimon brings advanced technology to native sentient reptiles who had achieved stone age technology. The natives rapidly lose control of their culture, identity and land as successive generations yield to the pressure of immigration.

Other books you might like:
Robert L. Forward, *Dragon's Egg*, 1980
Gwyneth Jones, *White Queen*, 1993
Janet Kagan, *Hellspark*, 1988
H. Beam Piper, *Little Fuzzy*, 1962
Joan Slonczewski, *A Door into Ocean*, 1986
Vernor Vinge, *A Fire upon the Deep*, 1992

3636

MIKE RESNICK

Second Contact
(New York: Tor Books, 1990)

Story type: Science Fiction (Mystery)
Major character(s): Max Becker, Lawyer; Jaimie, Computer Expert
Time period(s): 21st century (2065)
Locale(s): United States

Summary: Twenty-three years earlier human and alien space explorers met and destroyed each other; no one knows exactly why. Since then there has been no contact with the aliens. Then a spaceship captain kills two of his crew members, claiming they're extraterrestrials in disguise. Although everyone assumes the captain is insane, Max Becker, the attorney assigned to his case, discovers evidence that there may be more to it than that. Soon a complex conspiracy is exposed and Becker finds himself on the run with a price on his head.

Other books you might like:
Philip K. Dick, *Do Androids Dream of Electric Sheep?*, 1968
Philip K. Dick, *Martian Time-Slip*, 1964
John Kessel, *Good News From Outer Space*, 1989
W.T. Quick, *Systems*, 1989
John E. Stith, *Deep Quarry*, 1989

3637

MIKE RESNICK, Editor
MARTIN H. GREENBERG, Co-Editor

Sherlock Holmes in Orbit
(New York: DAW, 1995)

Story type: Science Fiction (Anthology; Mystery)
Major character(s): Sherlock Holmes, Detective—Private, Adventurer; John H. Watson, Doctor, Writer
Time period(s): 1900s; 1890s
Locale(s): London, England

Summary: Contains a four-page introduction by Resnick and 26 original stories featuring Sir Arthur Conan Doyle's famous detective and his faithful chronicler in familiar and new settings, arranged in four sections, "Holmes in the Past," "Holmes in the Present," "Holmes in the Future" and "Holmes After Death." Authors include Mark Aronson, John DeChancie, George Alec Effinger, Craig Shaw Gardner, David Gerrold, Barry N. Malzberg, Vonda N. McIntyre, Laura Resnick, Mike Resnick, Frank M. Robinson, Kristine Kathryn Rusch, Robert J. Sawyer, Josepha Sherman, Dean Wesley Smith, Brian M. Thomsen, and Leah A. Zeldes.

Other books you might like:
Isaac Asimov, *Sherlock Holmes through Time and Space*, 1984
    Martin Harry Greenberg, Charles Waugh, co-editors
The Council of Four, *The Science Fictional Sherlock Holmes*, 1960
    editor
Esther Friesner, *Druid's Blood*, 1988
Andy Lane, *All-Consuming Fire*, 1994

3638

MIKE RESNICK

Soothsayer
(New York: Ace, 1991)

Story type: Science Fiction (Space Opera; Psychic Powers)
Major character(s): Penelope Bailey, Psychic (precognitive), Fugitive; Mouse, Thief, Companion (Penelope's); Carlos "Iceman" Mendoza, Saloon Keeper/Owner, Spy (retired)
Time period(s): Indeterminate Future
Locale(s): Last Chance, Planet—Imaginary; Solomon, Planet—Imaginary; Killhaven, Planet—Imaginary

Summary: When Mouse rescued Penelope from her alien captor she couldn't foresee being hunted by three governments and two hundred bounty hunters searching the galaxy for the child who can foresee the future. With Penelope's help, the pair repeatedly escape captors to again become unwilling associates of the next person wishing to use Penelope to develop personal wealth and power.

Other books you might like:
Alfred Bester, *The Demolished Man*, 1953
Alfred Bester, *The Stars My Destination*, 1957
David Brin, *Startide Rising*, 1983
Frank Herbert, *Dune*, 1965
Alis A. Rasmussen, *A Passage of Stars*, 1990

Alis A. Rasmussen, *The Price of Ransom*, 1990
Alis A. Rasmussen, *Revolution's Shore*, 1990
Charles Sheffield, *The Nimrod Hunt*, 1986

3639

MIKE RESNICK, Editor

Whatdunits
(New York: DAW, 1992)

Story type: Science Fiction (Anthology; Mystery)
Time period(s): Indeterminate Future

Summary: 18 original stories arising from scenarios presented to each author by the editor, as related in the introduction. Brief individual introductions to each story include the scenario. Contains stories by Roger MacBride Allen, Virginia Booth, Pat Cadigan, John DeChancie, Katharine Kerr, Michael A. Stackpole and Judith Tarr.

Other books you might like:
Michael Bishop, *Nebula Awards 25*, 1991
  editor
Gardner Dozois, *The Year's Best Science Fiction: Eighth Annual Collection*, 1991
  editor
Kristine Kathryn Rusch, *Pulphouse, Issue 11: Speculative Fiction*, 1991
  editor
Donald A. Wollheim, *The 1990 Annual World's Best Science Fiction*, 1990
  Arthur W. Saha, co-editor
Jane Yolen, *2041: Twelve Short Stories about the Future by Top Science Fiction Writers*, 1991
  editor

3640

MIKE RESNICK

The Widowmaker
(New York: Bantam Spectra, 1996)

Story type: Science Fiction (Adventure; Genetic Manipulation)
Major character(s): Jefferson "Widowmaker" Nighthawk, Clone, Criminal (assassin); Melisande, Dancer, Mutant; Father Christmas, Thief
Time period(s): Indeterminate Future (5101 Galactic Era)
Locale(s): Tundra, Planet—Imaginary; Solio II, Planet—Imaginary

Summary: Created from the DNA of the famed Widowmaker, now a corpsicle waiting in cold sleep for a cure to a disfiguring disease, Jefferson Nighthawk learns quickly how to kill efficiently. Along the way to his assignment to kill the man who assassinated the dictator of Solio II, he hones his killing skills in the employ of the Marquis of Queensbury and falls in love. However, a month-old clone may not have developed his social skills enough to detect duplicity.

Other books you might like:
C.J. Cherryh, *Cyteen*, 1988
Michael Jan Friedman, *Kahless*, 1996

Robert A. Heinlein, *The Door into Summer*, 1957
Rebecca Ore, *The Illegal Rebirth of Billy the Kid*, 1991
Richard Osborne, *Demolition Man*, 1993

3641

MIKE RESNICK, Editor

Will the Last Person to Leave the Planet Please Shut Off the Sun?
(New York: Tor, 1992)

Story type: Science Fiction (Collection)

Summary: Contains a 4-page introduction plus introductions to the original title story and each of the 27 other stories reprinted from periodicals and anthologies from 1977-1992. One story, "Kirinyaga," received a Nebula Award nomination and a Hugo Award; the new John Justin Mallory story, "For I Have Touched the Sky," received a Hugo Award nomination. Many stories feature humorous themes.

Other books you might like:
Mack Reynolds, *Blackman's Burden*, 1972
Lucius Shepard, *The Ends of the Earth*, 1990
Theodore Sturgeon, *Sturgeon Is Alive and Well*, 1971
John Varley, *Blue Champagne*, 1986
John Varley, *The Persistence of Vision*, 1978
Gene Wolfe, *Storeys From the Old Hotel*, 1992

3642

LEAH REWOLINSKI
HARRY TRUMBORE, Illustrator

Star Wreck 6: Geek Space Nine
(New York: St. Martin's, 1994)

Story type: Science Fiction (Parody; Space Opera)
Series: Star Wreck
Major character(s): Bungeeman Crisco, Military Personnel (Starfreak), Spaceman; James T. Smirk, Spaceship Captain; Jean-Lucy Ricardo, Spaceship Captain
Time period(s): 25th century (Stardate 4780.5)
Locale(s): Geek Space Nine, Space Station (Bridgeoran); *U.S.S. Endocrine*, Spaceship; Outer Space

Summary: When an ambience of boredom permeates Geek Space Nine, threatening Starfreak's investment, Starfreak dispatches both *U.S.S. Endocrine*s to liven up the scene and promote alien tourism.

Other books you might like:
Douglas Adams, *The Hitchhiker's Guide to the Galaxy*, 1980
Henry N. Beard, *Bored of the Rings*, 1969
  Douglas C. Kenny, co-author
John M. Ford, *How Much for Just the Planet?*, 1987
Alan Dean Foster, *Glory Lane*, 1987
Mark E. Rogers, *The Adventures of Samurai Cat*, 1984
Ken Rolston, *Extreme Paranoia: Nobody Knows the Trouble I've Shot*, 1991
Ellis Weiner, *National Lampoon's Doon*, 1984

3643

LEAH REWOLINSKI
HARRY TRUMBORE, Illustrator

Star Wreck II: The Attack of the Jargonites

(New York: St. Martin's Press, 1991)

Story type: Science Fiction (Parody; Space Opera)
Series: Star Wreck
Major character(s): James T. Smirk, Spaceship Captain; Jean-Lucy Ricardo, Spaceship Captain; B.S. Galore, Leader (Jargonites)
Time period(s): 23rd century
Locale(s): *U.S.S. Endocrine*, Spaceship

Summary: Captain Smirk has badgered Starfreak into recommissioning the *Endocrine* to allow two Starfreak vessels to engage the Jargonites who threaten security with boring group encounter sessions. When Captain Smirk attacks, the Jargonite Conundrum's Reality Deflectors easily divert the *Endocrine's* futon torpedos, leaving Smirk's crew at the mercy of the Jargonite attack until Smirk disables the communication system. When Piker misuses Dr. Beverage's diagnostic equipment, Piker and the *Endocrine's* other bridge crew are rendered temporarily deaf and immune to the Jargonite's language. With the Jargonites in near total control of Earth, both *Endocrines* rush to the rescue.

Other books you might like:
Douglas Adams, *The Hitchhiker's Guide to the Galaxy*, 1980
Henry N. Beard, *Bored of the Rings*, 1969
  Douglas C. Kenney, co-author
John M. Ford, *How Much for Just the Planet?*, 1987
Harry Harrison, *Bill, the Galactic Hero*, 1965
Ellis Weiner, *National Lampoon's Doon*, 1984

3644

LEAH REWOLINSKI
HARRY TRUMBORE, Illustrator

Star Wreck III: Time Warped

(New York: St. Martin's, 1992)

Story type: Science Fiction (Parody; Space Opera)
Series: Star Wreck
Major character(s): Jean-Lucy Ricardo, Spaceship Captain (*U.S.S. Endocrine*); James T. Smirk, Spaceship Captain (*U.S.S. Endocrine*); Dacron, Android
Time period(s): 24th century
Locale(s): *U.S.S. Endocrine*, Spaceship (Starfreak)

Summary: After Commander Wilson Piker accidentally flings a videotape into the past, a computer preview feature shows that "Star Wreck" fandom will spring into existence fully formed, fifty years in the future, much to Ricardo's distress and Smirk's delight. Hoping to cure the offensive anachronism, the *Endocrine's* crew ricochets through time and parodies of "Star Trek" and "Star Trek: The Next Generation" episodes, wreaking havoc and rewriting history.

Other books you might like:
Douglas Adams, *The Hitchhiker's Guide to the Galaxy*, 1980

Henry N. Beard, *Bored of the Rings*, 1969
  Douglas C. Kinney, co-author
Roger L. DiSilvestro, *Living with the Reptiles*, 1990
John M. Ford, *How Much for Just the Planet?*, 1987
Harry Harrison, *Bill, the Galactic Hero*, 1965
Daniel Manus Pinkwater, *Borgel*, 1990
Ellis Weiner, *National Lampoon's Doon*, 1984

3645

LEAH REWOLINSKI
HARRY TRUMBORE, Illustrator

Star Wreck IV: Live Long and Profit

(New York: St. Martin's, 1993)

Story type: Science Fiction (Parody; Space Opera)
Series: Star Wreck
Major character(s): Jean-Lucy Ricardo, Spaceship Captain (*U.S.S. Endocrine*); James T. Smirk, Spaceship Captain (*U.S.S. Endocrine*); Deanna "Dee" Troit, Alien (half Betavoid), Telepath
Time period(s): 24th century
Locale(s): *U.S.S. Endocrine*, Spaceship (Starfreak)

Summary: After wrekkie fans present a full scale working model of the *Endocrine* to James T. Smirk and his crew, Starfreak decides to decommission one *Endocrine*, relieve many crew of duties and assign Jean-Lucy Ricardo to find the Fountain of Youth to bottle and sell throughout the galaxy. Hoping to gain favor, Smirk tries to find the Fountain of Youth before Ricardo, but first discovers the Fountain of Love and Fountain of Truth and proceeds, kissing and telling, across the galaxy.

Other books you might like:
Douglas Adams, *The Hitchhiker's Guide to the Galaxy*, 1980
Chester Anderson, *The Butterfly Kid*, 1967
Henry N. Beard, *Bored of the Rings*, 1969
  Douglas C. Kenney, co-author
John M. Ford, *How Much for Just the Planet?*, 1987
Jovial Bob Stine, *Spaceballs: The Book*, 1987
Ellis Weiner, *National Lampoon's Doon*, 1984

3646

LEAH REWOLINSKI
HARRY TRUMBORE, Illustrator

Star Wreck: The Generation Gap

(New York: St. Martin's Press, 1990)

Story type: Science Fiction (Parody; Space Opera)
Series: Star Wreck
Major character(s): James T. Smirk, Spaceship Captain; Jean-Lucy Ricardo, Spaceship Captain
Time period(s): 23rd century (stardate 2323.23232323232323 1/2)
Locale(s): *U.S.S. Endocrine*, Spaceship; Cellulite-1 Starfreak Colony, Planet—Imaginary

Summary: Captain Jean-Lucy Ricardo becomes the unwilling host to Captain Smirk, Mr. Smock, Dr. McCaw and others until the *Endocrine* is captured by a tractor beam drawing them to the Planet of the Cellulites. Captain Smirk and crew steal the cup section of the ship leaving Captain Ricardo and crew with the saucer section and the Cellulites. After a month of party-hopping around the galaxy, Captain Smirk decides he wants another try at Counselor Troit's attention and returns. The combined crew co-operates to free themselves using junk food and sedatives.

Other books you might like:
Douglas Adams, *The Hitchhiker's Guide to the Galaxy*, 1980
Henry N. Beard, *Bored of the Rings*, 1969
    Douglas C. Kenney, co-author
John M. Ford, *How Much for Just the Planet?*, 1987
    Star Trek 36
Harry Harrison, *Bill, the Galactic Hero*, 1965
Ellis Weiner, *National Lampoon's Doon*, 1984

3647

TED REYNOLDS

The Tides of God
(New York: Ace, 1989)

Story type: Science Fiction (Theological)
Major character(s): Elwyn Kimberlin, Spaceship Captain; Foth, Scholar
Time period(s): 33rd century
Locale(s): *Hound of Heaven*, Spaceship

Summary: Scientists have discovered that the periods of religious frenzy which have periodically disrupted Earth civilization since the beginning of recorded history are actually the result of psychic broadcasts sent by a gigantic spaceborne entity which moves on a long orbit through our galaxy. The crew of the *Hound of Heaven* set off on a dangerous and ambiguous mission to destroy the being.

Other books you might like:
James Blish, *A Case of Conscience*, 1958
John Kessel, *Good News From Outer Space*, 1989
Walter M. Miller Jr., *A Canticle for Leibowitz*, 1960
James Morrow, *Only Begotten Daughter*, 1990

3648

DANIEL RHODES

Adversary
(New York: Tor, 1989)

Story type: Horror (Satanism)
Major character(s): Nicole Partrick, Young Woman (Ambitious); Guy-Luc Valcourt, Demon, Servant
Time period(s): 1980s
Locale(s): San Francisco, California

Summary: In this sequel to *Next, After Lucifer*, Nicole Partrick is gradually seduced into a cult led by the demonic Guy-Luc Valcourt, putting not only her own life and soul in jeopardy, but also those of her son. A small group, including her lover, a priest, and a clairvoyant woman and her husband, race against time to rescue Nicole and destroy Valcourt/Courdeval.

Other books you might like:
T.E.D. Klein, *The Ceremonies*, 1984

Dennis Wheatley, *To the Devil, a Daughter*, 1953

3649

DANIEL RHODES

Kiss of Death
(New York: St. Martin's, 1990)

Story type: Horror (Erotic Horror)
Major character(s): Selena Clermont, Heiress; Donald Clermont, Vintner; Gene Farrell, Doctor (emergency room)
Time period(s): 1980s (1988); 1960s (1966)
Locale(s): Sonoma, California; Saint-Fabrisse, France

Summary: Selena Clermont, the grown-up child of a woman who was raped while her father made an offering to the bloodthirsty moon goddess, sacrifices her casual lovers to appease the goddess and her minions. Trouble begins when she falls in love with Gene Farrell and her demonic overseers demand him as a sacrifice as well.

Other books you might like:
Thomas F. Monteleone, *Lyrica*, 1987
Kathryn Ptacek, *In Silence Sealed*, 1988
Peter Straub, *Ghost Story*, 1979

3650

ANNE RICE

Lasher
(New York: Knopf, 1993)

Story type: Horror (Occult)
Series: Lives of the Mayfair Witches
Major character(s): Rowan Mayfair Curry, Doctor, Witch; Michael Curry, Architect; Samuel Larkin, Doctor
Time period(s): 1990s (1993)
Locale(s): New Orleans, Louisiana

Summary: In this direct sequel to the author's *The Witching Hour*, Rowan Mayfair, a member of a long established family of witches, and her husband Michael, a mortal, give birth to a child, Julien, a.k.a. Lasher, who is both a prodigy and a genetic mutant who represents a synthesis greater than the sum of his mortal and supernatural parts.

Other books you might like:
Edward Bryant, *Fetish*, 1991
John Updike, *The Witches of Eastwick*, 1984

3651

ANNE RICE

Memnoch the Devil
(New York: Knopf, 1995)

Story type: Horror (Vampire Story)
Series: Vampire Chronicles
Major character(s): Lestat de Lioncourt, Vampire; Memnoch, Demon; Roger, Criminal (assassin)
Time period(s): 1990s (1995)
Locale(s): New York, New York

Summary: The vampire Lestat's encounter with the ghost of one of his victims reignites the crisis of religious faith he experienced when he was first vampirized. Memnoch, the biblical devil, chooses this moment to reveal himself to Lestat and presents himself as a lover of man aggrieved at the human suffering demanded by God. In his effort to enlist Lestat in his eternal struggle, he retells the story of the Creation from his point of view and brings Lestat to Heaven and Hell to see God's handiwork directly.

Other books you might like:
Marie Corelli, *The Sorrows of Satan*, 1895
Anatole France, *Revolt of the Angels*, 1914
John Milton, *Paradise Lost*, 1667

3652

ANNE RICE

The Mummy, or Ramses the Damned
(New York: Ballantine, 1989)

Story type: Horror (Reanimated Dead)
Major character(s): Ramses the Great, Historical Figure (Egyptian Pharaoh), Reanimated Dead (Disguised as an Egyptologist); Julie Stratford, Adventurer, Heiress (Rich and beautiful)
Time period(s): 1900s (Edwardian Age)
Locale(s): London, England; Egypt

Summary: Restored to life, Ramses experiences the feverish appetites of the living. In the guise of Egyptologist Dr. Ramsey, he woos a beautiful adventuress as he tries to locate and reanimate his beloved Cleopatra—with terrible consequences.

Other books you might like:
Charles L. Grant, *The Long Night of the Grave*, 1986
H. Rider Haggard, *She*, 1886

3653

ANNE RICE

The Queen of the Damned
(New York: Knopf, 1988)

Story type: Horror (Vampire Story)
Series: Vampire Chronicles
Major character(s): Lestat de Lioncourt, Vampire (Posing as rock-and-roll singer); Akasha, Vampire (Mother of all vampires)
Time period(s): 1980s; Indeterminate Past
Locale(s): San Francisco, California; South America; Egypt

Summary: When rock singer-vampire Lestat reveals his true origins, he rouses Akasha, Queen of the Damned, who, claiming to "save" mankind from itself, sets a plan in motion to give herself and her son/lover the power and status of gods.

Other books you might like:
Suzy McKee Charnas, *The Vampire Tapestry*, 1980
Pierre Kast, *The Vampires of Alfama*, 1975
S.P. Somtow, *Vampire Junction*, 1984
Whitley Strieber, *The Hunger*, 1981

3654

ANNE RICE

Servant of the Bones
(New York: Knopf, 1996)

Story type: Horror (Occult)
Major character(s): Azriel, Mythical Creature (genie); Zurvan, Scholar; Gregory Belkin, Religious (televangelist)
Time period(s): 7th century B.C. (600 B.C.); 1990s (1996)
Locale(s): Babylon; New York, New York

Summary: Tricked into allowing himself to be sacrificed to save his people, the Hebrew aristocrat Azriel becomes the "Servant of the Bones," a genie who can be summoned to do the bidding of whoever possesses his gold covered remains. Azriel's experiences over the centuries stimulate great reflection on the human condition, particularly his encounter with Gregory Belkin, a contemporary televangelist who has sacrificed his daughter Esther and who hopes to use Azriel's powers to achieve world domination.

Other books you might like:
Clive Barker, *Everville*, 1994
Graham Joyce, *Requiem*, 1996
Tanith Lee, *Darkness, I*, 1994
Alan Rodgers, *Night*, 1991

3655

ANNE RICE

The Tale of the Body Thief
(New York: Alfred A. Knopf, 1992)

Story type: Horror (Vampire Story)
Series: Vampire Chronicles
Major character(s): Lestat de Lioncourt, Vampire; David Talbot, Occultist (retired academic); Raglan James, Supernatural Being (body thief)
Time period(s): 1990s
Locale(s): Miami, Florida; Paris, France

Summary: Bored with his long life, and tortured by dreams and memories of his bloody past, the centuries old vampire Lestat decides to end his life. While making his final preparations, he encounters a body thief, a supernatural being who lives by commandeering the bodies of living human beings, who offers Lestat the chance to assume a mortal's body and become human again.

Other books you might like:
Scott Ciencin, *The Vampire Odyssey*, 1992
Elizabeth Engstrom, *Black Ambrosia*, 1988
Brian Stableford, *The Empire of Fear*, 1988
Theodore Sturgeon, *Some of Your Blood*, 1961

3656

ANNE RICE

Taltos
(New York: Knopf, 1994)

Story type: Horror (Occult)

Series: Lives of the Mayfair Witches
Major character(s): Ashlar "Mr. Ash", Businessman; Yuri Stefano, Gypsy; Mona Mayfair, Businesswoman
Time period(s): 1990s (1994)
Locale(s): New York, New York

Summary: Ashlar, a member of a dying race of prehistoric beings known as the Taltos, hopes to produce an heir by mating with one of the Mayfair witches in this third installment in the Lives of the Mayfair Witches saga. Over the course of the novel, Ashlar gives a running history of how he has survived over the millenia, strategically embracing and integrating with the human civilization that has repeatedly tried to exterminate him and his kind.

Other books you might like:
Kathryn Meyer Griffith, *Witches*, 1993
Ira Levin, *Rosemary's Baby*, 1967
John Updike, *The Witches of Eastwick*, 1984

3657

ANNE RICE

The Witching Hour
(New York: Knopf, 1990)

Story type: Horror (Black Magic)
Series: Lives of the Mayfair Witches
Major character(s): Michael Curry, Architect; Rowan Mayfair, Doctor (Neurosurgeon), Witch; Lasher, Demon
Time period(s): 20th century
Locale(s): New Orleans, Louisiana; San Francisco, California

Summary: Interspersed into Rice's vast, sprawling story of the love of psychically gifted recluse Michael Curry and San Francisco neurosurgeon Rowan Mayfair is the 300-year history of the Mayfairs, a family of witches, as revealed by a group of scholars of the occult called the Talamasca, who offer aid when Michael and Rowan's exploration of their heritage is endangered by an evil spirit.

Other books you might like:
Shirley Jackson, *The Haunting of Hill House*, 1959
Dan Simmons, *Carrion Comfort*, 1989

3658

DOUG RICE

Blood of Mugwump
(Normal, Illinois: Black Ice Books, 1996)

Story type: Horror (Vampire Story)
Major character(s): Doug Rice, Young Man, Vampire; Caddie Rice, Young Woman, Vampire; Grandma Mugwump Torgov, Aged Person, Vampire
Time period(s): 1990s (1996)
Locale(s): Endicott, Pennsylvania

Summary: This first novel offers a series of vignettes concerning the Mugwumps, a clan of gender-shifting vampires. Doug Rice, the youngest member of the clan, has taken possession of his sister Caddie's body and spends much of the book pondering the problems of gender-defined identity that this new form of being poses.

Other books you might like:
Kathy Acker, *Empire of the Senseless*, 1988
William S. Burroughs, *Nova Express*, 1964
Joseph McElroy, *Plus*, 1976
Melanie Tem, *Desmodus*, 1994

3659

JANE RICE
JACON ECKHARDT, Illustrator

The Sixth Dog
(West Warwick, Rhode Island: Necronomicon Press, 1995)

Story type: Horror (Black Magic)
Major character(s): Agnes Hanlon, Assistant (to a veterinarian); Otis Clanton, Aged Person; Billy Williams, Handyman
Time period(s): 1990s (1995)
Locale(s): Midwest

Summary: The unnamed narrator of this story, a veterinarian, tells of his peculiar neighbor Otis Clanton, who mysteriously appears to acquire a new dog every time someone in town— usually someone who has openly expressed dislike of him— disappears. This is the author's first book (a 28 page booklet.)

Other books you might like:
Jonathan Carroll, *The Land of Laughs*, 1980
S.K. Epperson, *Borderland*, 1992
James Herbert, *Fluke*, 1977
Jack Williamson, *Darker than You Think*, 1948

3660

PETER L. RICE

Monsoon
(Chicago: FASA Corporation, 1992)

Story type: Science Fiction (Military)
Series: Renegade Legion
Major character(s): Wilson Goode, Bounty Hunter; Spencer Kennet, Miner, Businessman (mine operator); Archemon, Alien (Leilan)
Time period(s): 69th century (6830)
Locale(s): Monsoon, Planet—Imaginary (Leilas)

Summary: Humans from Earth, organized as the Terran Overlord Government, enforce Terran rule over other humans in the galaxy. On Monsoon, TOG forces threaten to destroy the environment and intelligent natives unless the Rock Rangers, Renegade Legions or the Commonwealth resistance can free the world from TOG influence.

Other books you might like:
Gordon R. Dickson, *Dorsai!*, 1976
David Drake, *Hammer's Slammers*, 1979
Robert A. Heinlein, *Starship Troopers*, 1959
William H. Keith Jr., *Renegade's Honor*, 1988
Steve Perry, *The Man Who Never Missed*, 1985
Jerry Pournelle, *Falkenberg's Legion*, 1990
Robert Thurston, *Way of the Clans*, 1991

3661

ROBERT RICE

The Last Pendragon

(New York: Walker, 1991)

Story type: Fantasy (Legend)
Major character(s): Bedwyr, Knight; Irion ap Medrault, Royalty
Time period(s): 6th century (540s)
Locale(s): England

Summary: Eleven years after Arthur Pendragon's fall from power, Bedwyr returns from service in the Roman Imperial Army with the news that the Roman Empire can spare no soldiers to help curb the Saxon rebellion in Britain. Bedwyr reluctantly joins forces with Arthur's grandson, Irion, hoping to unite the many kingdoms left after Arthur's reign. This is the author's first novel.

Other books you might like:
John Desjarlais, *The Throne of Tara*, 1990
Parke Godwin, *Sherwood*, 1991
Patricia Kennealy, *The Hawk's Gray Feather*, 1990
Mary Stewart, *The Wicked Day*, 1983
Rosemary Sutcliff, *The Shining Company*, 1990

3662

ENID RICHEMONT

The Time Tree

(Boston: Little Brown, 1990)

Story type: Fantasy (Time Travel; Historical)
Major character(s): Rachel, Child, Student; Joanna, Child, Student; Anne, Handicapped (deaf), Spirit (ghost child)
Time period(s): 1990s (1990); 16th century (1598)
Locale(s): Finchley, England

Summary: Two 20th century schoolgirls befriend an oddly costumed ghost-girl they meet while climbing a tree, and teach her to read. Anne, the 16th century ghost, is able to teach her family in the 20th century that despite her handicap, she is neither stupid nor evil and can learn from lessons, finally embroidering a sampler that survives to the 20th century in a museum.

Other books you might like:
L.M. Boston, *The Treasure of Green Knowe*, 1958
E. Nesbit, *The House of Arden*, 1909
Edward Ormondroyd, *Time at the Top*, 1963
Ruth Park, *Playing Beatie Bow*, 1980
Philippa Pearce, *Tom's Midnight Garden*, 1959

3663

PHIL RICKMAN

Candle Night

(New York: Jove 1995)

Story type: Horror (Ancient Evil Unleashed)
Major character(s): Giles Freeman, Journalist; Claire Freeman, Photographer; Berry Morelli, Journalist

Time period(s): 1990s (1991)
Locale(s): Y Groes, Wales

Summary: Englishman Giles Freeman moves with his wife Claire to the Welsh town of Y Groes, renowned for its insularity and legendary aversion to visits by outsiders. The relocation awakens Claire to her Welsh heritage and reignites a legacy of Druidic terror that has been a suppressed part of her family history for centuries. This first novel was first published in England in 1991.

Other books you might like:
Algernon Blackwood, *Julius LeVallon: An Episode*, 1917
Arthur Machen, *The Green Round*, 1933
Arthur Machen, *The Hill of Dreams*, 1907
Brent Monahan, *The Uprising*, 1993
David van Meter Smith, *Trinity Grove*, 1988

3664

PHIL RICKMAN

Curfew

(New York: Putnam's, 1993)

Story type: Horror (Ancient Evil Unleashed)
Major character(s): Max Goff, Producer (record producer); Joe M. Powys, Writer; Faye Morrison, Journalist
Time period(s): 1990s (1993)
Locale(s): Crybbe, Wales

Summary: Naively inspired by a mystical history of the small Welsh town of Crybbe, filthy rich record producer Max Goff buys up much of the town with the hope of exploiting its New Age appeal. But Crybbe harbors many dark secrets, among them an occult Druidic heritage that Goff's ambitions threaten to resurrect. This novel was originally published in England under the title *Crybbe*.

Other books you might like:
Ramsey Campbell, *The Hungry Moon*, 1986
Kim Newman, *Jago*, 1992

3665

PHIL RICKMAN

December

(New York: Berkley, 1996)

Story type: Horror (Occult)
Major character(s): Dave Reilly, Musician; Moira Cairns, Musician; Simon St. John, Musician
Time period(s): 1990s (1994)
Locale(s): Gwent, Wales (Abbey of Ystrad Ddu)

Summary: When their recording session at a legend-haunted Welsh castle ends with a band member dead and John Lennon coincidentally murdered halfway across the world, the members of Philosopher's Stone agree to disband and never play together again. Thirteen years later, a bootleg tape of the session resurfaces and the band members must work together to prevent the horror of that night from happening again. This novel was first published in England in 1994 in a slightly different form.

Other books you might like:
Marvin Kaye, *Fantastique*, 1992
Adrian Savage, *Symphony*, 1992
John Skipp, *The Scream*, 1988
    Craig Spector, co-author

3666

ALAN RIEFE

Viper

(New York: Diamond, 1990)

Story type: Horror (Wild Talents)
Major character(s): Felicity Jane Hadfield, Child; Roger Grenier, Businessman; Zaman, Servant (Indian manservant)
Time period(s): 1980s (1980)
Locale(s): Dharwar District, India; Honolulu, Hawaii

Summary: In India, where she has been taken by her loving stepfather and stepmother, Felicity Jane Hadfield discovers she is *davia*, a person venerated for her ability to summon and control snakes. She returns with her newfound powers to Honolulu to seek revenge on the murderers of her wealthy benefactress.

Other books you might like:
John Tigges, *Venom*, 1988

3667

L.S. RIKER

Kill Crazy

(New York: St. Martin's, 1993)

Story type: Science Fiction (Adventure)
Series: Swag
Major character(s): Swag, Martial Arts Expert, Detective—Private; Mortimer Bammer, Military Personnel, Leader; Dobbs, Public Relations (spin doctor)
Time period(s): 21st century
Locale(s): New York, New York

Summary: After the death of his friend, Swag's investigation leads to a deadly new drug and his old enemies from Provost headquarters. Sequel to *Full Clip*.

Other books you might like:
Pat Cadigan, *Fools*, 1992
Robert Cain, *Cybernarc*, 1991
Robert Cain, *Gold Dragon*, 1991
Jake Davis, *The Last Rangers*, 1992
Michael Kandel, *Captain Jack Zodiac*, 1992
William Shatner, *TekLords*, 1991
Neal Stephenson, *Snow Crash*, 1992

3668

STEVEN WILLIAM RIMMER

Coven

(New York: Ballantine, 1989)

Story type: Horror (Black Magic)

Major character(s): Elspet, Witch; Margrett, Witch
Time period(s): 1980s (1986; Prologue in 1641)
Locale(s): Drenewydd, Scotland

Summary: In Rimmer's first novel, the tranquility of Elspet's coven is upset by the arrival of Master Paul, his woman, Margrett, and their gang of biker followers, who seek to revive the old practices, including ritual human sacrifice, to restore the power of the "old witches' magic." At the risk of her life, Elspet defies the Master and Margrett to protect the lives of her friends and the survival of the coven.

Other books you might like:
John Burke, *The Devil's Footsteps*, 1976
Norah Lofts, *The Devil's Own*, 1960

3669

KAREN RIPLEY

The Persistence of Memory

(New York: Ballantine Del Rey, 1993)

Story type: Science Fiction (Adventure; Mystery)
Series: Slow World
Major character(s): Cassidy, Horse Trainer, Amnesiac; Rowena, Worker (goatherd); Allen, Farmer, Lawman
Time period(s): Indeterminate
Locale(s): Earth (unknown grasslands)

Summary: Knowing only the name of her horse and that she came from elsewhere, Cassidy uses a name from a partly remembered film, not noticing things missing from her environment. She fits in among Horsemen, but must hide her differences when saved by Riders. She leaves them with another "different" woman to achieve answers to questions about the grasslands and her background. First of a series.

Other books you might like:
John Brunner, *The Tides of Time*, 1984
C.J. Cherryh, *Wave Without a Shore*, 1981
M.A. Foster, *Preserver*, 1985
Garry Kilworth, *The Night of Kadar*, 1980
Ursula K. Le Guin, *City of Illusions*, 1967
Andre Norton, *Forerunner*, 1981
Andrew J. Offutt, *King Dragon*, 1980

3670

KAREN RIPLEY

Prisoner of Dreams

(New York: Ballantine/Del Rey, 1989)

Story type: Science Fiction (Space Opera)
Major character(s): Jo-lac, Spaceship Captain; Lewis, Servant (Indentured)
Time period(s): Indeterminate Future
Locale(s): *Raptor*, Spaceship

Summary: Jo-lac runs cargo from one star system to another until she's talked into taking on human freight, Lewis, a prisoner who someone apparently wants dead. It turns out there's a complex plot afoot involving sentient computers and psychics. Jo-lac falls in love with Lewis and decides to get to the bottom of the mystery no matter what the consequences. This is Ripley's first novel.

Other books you might like:
C.J. Cherryh, *Merchanter's Luck,* 1982
Melissa Scott, *The Empress of Earth,* 1987
Melissa Scott, *Silence in Solitude,* 1986
Walter Jon Williams, *Angel Station,* 1989

3671

KAREN RIPLEY

The Tenth Class

(New York: Ballantine/Del Rey, 1991)

Story type: Science Fiction (Adventure; Genetic Manipulation)
Series: Tenth Class
Major character(s): Jo-Lac, Spaceship Captain; Lewis, Genetically Altered Being; Taylor, Public Relations
Time period(s): Indeterminate Future
Locale(s): Porta Flora, Planet—Imaginary; Earthheart, Planet—Imaginary

Summary: Captain Jo-Lac is asked to cooperate with the authorities in tracking down powerful people who want to round up the Class Tens, including Lewis. Frightened by the power of those against her, Jo-Lac and Taylor travel a roundabout way, first to Heinlein, then to Earthheart where the Class Tens are. Mysteriously tracked, when they discover Taylor has been made a human marker, Lewis cures this, allowing them to destroy the enemy and give hope to all the genetically substandard.

Other books you might like:
Jack L. Chalker, *Pirates of the Thunder,* 1987
M.A. Foster, *The Warriors of Dawn,* 1975
Cheryl J. Franklin, *The Light of Exile,* 1990
Raymond Harris, *The Broken Worlds,* 1986
S.N. Lewitt, *Angel at Apogee,* 1987
R.M. Meluch, *Wind Child,* 1982
Melisa C. Michaels, *Skirmish,* 1985
Melissa Scott, *Five-Twelfths of Heaven,* 1985
Timothy Zahn, *Deadman Switch,* 1988

3672

KAREN RIPLEY

The Warden of Horses

(New York: Ballantine Del Rey, 1994)

Story type: Science Fiction (Alternate Universe; Adventure)
Series: Slow World
Major character(s): Cathy ''Cassidy'' Delaney, Amnesiac, Horse Trainer; Andy ''the Warden'' Greene, Ruler; Click, Leader, Tinker
Time period(s): Indeterminate
Locale(s): Iron City, Fictional City

Summary: Robbed by a woodsman, Cassidy and Rowena link up with a band of tinkers traveling to Iron City. Pursued by villagers and almost killed by monsters, Cassidy confronts the Warden only to find she remembers him from her past life as

Andy Greene, an autistic boy she taught to ride. As he cannot answer her questions and monsters still pursue her, she sets off with Click to find the mysterious Alchemist of Time.

Other books you might like:
Poul Anderson, *Three Hearts and Three Lions,* 1961
Piers Anthony, *Orn,* 1971
David Brin, *The Practice Effect,* 1984
John Brunner, *The Tides of Time,* 1984
M.A. Foster, *Preserver,* 1985
Garry Kilworth, *The Night of Kadar,* 1980
Ursula K. Le Guin, *City of Illusions,* 1967
Andre Norton, *Here Abide Monsters,* 1973
Andrew J. Offutt, *King Dragon,* 1980
John Varley, *Titan,* 1979

3673

J.F. RIVKIN

Mistress of Ambiguities

(New York: Ace, 1991)

Story type: Fantasy (Sword and Sorcery)
Series: Silverglass
Major character(s): Nyctasia, Ruler; Corson, Martial Arts Expert (swordswoman)
Time period(s): Indeterminate Past
Locale(s): Rhostshyl, Fictional City

Summary: The aftermath of civil war brings Rhostshyl, city and court, into nearly as much turmoil as the war itself, though of a different sort. The intense political intrigues, an amnesiac wanderer, an ambitious scholar, a proposed marriage alliance and a brace of newly recovered spellbooks combine to create a situation requiring all of Nyctasia and Corson's craft and skill to negotiate.

Other books you might like:
Gael Baudino, *Gossamer Axe,* 1990
Barbara Hambly, *The Ladies of Mandrigyn,* 1984
Rosemary Kirstein, *The Steerswoman,* 1989
Mercedes Lackey, *The Oathbound,* 1988
Anne Logston, *Shadow,* 1991
Shirley Meier, *The Cage,* 1989
  S.M. Stirling, co-author

3674

J.F. RIVKIN

Tyrannosaurus Rex

(New York: Roc, 1992)

Story type: Science Fiction (Time Travel; Adventure)
Major character(s): Christine Fawcett, Explorer, Time Traveller; Mark ''Tony'' Anthony Blondell, Explorer, Time Traveller; Manuel ''Manny'' Aburto, Guide, Time Traveller
Time period(s): 1990s; Indeterminate Past (Cretaceous Epoch)
Locale(s): London, England; Brazil

Summary: After Christine discovers her grandfather's diary and an unaged dinosaur bone, she organizes an expedition to the Brazilian jungle he explored. In a pyramid far from most

Mayan ruins, Christine, Tony and Manny find themselves thrown back in time to the Cretaceous where they must thwart hungry dinosaurs and treacherous villains to return home.

Other books you might like:
Michael Crichton, *Jurassic Park*, 1990
Arthur Conan Doyle, *The Lost World*, 1912
James Gurney, *Dinotopia*, 1992
Stephen Leigh, *Ray Bradbury Presents: Dinosaur World*, 1992

3675
DAVID ROBBINS

Hell-O-Ween
(New York: Leisure, 1992)

Story type: Horror (Ancient Evil Unleashed)
Major character(s): Cory Fleming, Teenager; Ann Weatherby, Teenager; Wesley Eagen, Teenager
Time period(s): 1990s (1992)
Locale(s): Pagosa Springs, Colorado

Summary: A Halloween prank pulled to scare class nerd Cory Fleming backfires horribly, unleashing a legendary demon from the nearby Caverna del Diablo who begins systematically killing the pranksters in typically gruesome fashion.

Other books you might like:
D.A. Fowler, *The Devil's End*, 1992
Steven Ray Fulgham, *The Summoned*, 1991
Robert Kline, *Campfire Story*, 1990

3676
DAVID ROBBINS

L.A. Strike
(New York: Leisure, 1990)

Story type: Science Fiction (Post-Holocaust)
Series: Blade
Major character(s): Blade, Warrior; Leo "Lobo" Wood, Warrior; Mike Havoc, Military Personnel (captain)
Time period(s): 22nd century (106 years post-holocaust)
Locale(s): Los Angeles, California

Summary: When one of two rival ganglords kidnaps a new recruit to the Freedom Force, Blade leads his Force to rescue her, and wipes out both gangs in the process.

Other books you might like:
David Brin, *The Postman*, 1985
Mark Grant, *Mutants Amok*, 1991
    pseudonym of David Bischoff
Robert A. Heinlein, *Farnham's Freehold*, 1964
David R. Palmer, *Emergence*, 1984

3677
DAVID ROBBINS

Madman Run
(New York: Leisure, 1991)

Story type: Science Fiction (Post-Holocaust)
Series: Endworld
Major character(s): Blade, Teenager, Warrior; Geronimo, Teenager, Warrior; Endora Morlock, Gentlewoman (mistress of Castle Orm)
Time period(s): 21st century
Locale(s): Minnesota (northern)

Summary: Sixteen-year-old Blade, having just attained Warrior status, travels the countryside with his friends Hickok and Geronimo. They come upon a castle where a pale woman beckons to them. Entering, they are captured by her husband, a madman who keeps others enslaved underground. After trying futilely to get the slaves to revolt, Blade and his companions kill the Morlock masters and return home.

Other books you might like:
Poul Anderson, *Twilight World*, 1961
John Dalmas, *The Yngling*, 1971
James B. Johnson, *Daystar and Shadow*, 1981
Henry Kuttner, *Mutant*, 1953
    written as Lewis Padgett
Andrew J. Offutt, *The Castle Keeps*, 1972
Paul O. Williams, *The Song of the Axe*, 1984
Roger Zelazny, *Damnation Alley*, 1969

3678
DAVID ROBBINS

Prank Night
(New York: Leisure, 1994)

Story type: Horror (Ancient Evil Unleashed)
Major character(s): Ben Shields, Writer; Nadine Somersby, Store Owner; Travis Sinclair, Police Officer (sheriff)
Time period(s): 1990s (1994)
Locale(s): Cemetery Ridge, Oregon

Summary: Ben Shields' return to his childhood hometown coincides with the rampage of a monster that lives in the local cemetery and wreaks havoc every few Halloweens. Efforts to track the monster and destroy it are thwarted by the mischief of several locals who resent Ben's return.

Other books you might like:
Charles L. Grant, *Stunts*, 1990
Jack Martin, *Halloween III: Season of the Witch*, 1985
Robert R. McCammon, *Usher's Passing*, 1985
Ashley McConnell, *Days of the Dead*, 1992

3679
DAVID ROBBINS

Spartan Run
(New York: Leisure, 1991)

Story type: Science Fiction (Post-Holocaust)

Series: Endworld
Major character(s): Blade, Warrior; Rikki-Tikki-Tavi, Warrior; "Agis" Agesilaus, Military Personnel (head of the Secret Police)
Time period(s): 22nd century
Locale(s): Iowa (northeast)

Summary: When Blade and two companions wish to contact Sparta, a strong city-state in northeast Iowa, their presence sparks a civil war between the two kings as the power-mad Agesilaus tries to seize power and have Blade and his friends put to death. While his companions try to rally King Dercyllidas's forces, Blade must undergo trial by ordeal.

Other books you might like:
Poul Anderson, *Orion Shall Rise*, 1983
Neal Barrett Jr., *Dawn's Uncertain Light*, 1989
Edmund Cooper, *The Cloud Walker*, 1973
John Dalmas, *The Yngling*, 1971
Dean Ing, *Systemic Shock*, 1981
Paul O. Williams, *The Sword of Forebearance*, 1985
Timothy Zahn, *The Blackcollar*, 1983
Roger Zelazny, *Damnation Alley*, 1969

3680

DAVID ROBBINS

Spook Night
(New York: Leisure, 1995)

Story type: Horror (Supernatural Vengeance)
Major character(s): John Grant, Computer Expert; Kip Grant, Teenager; Shery Grant, Teenager
Time period(s): 1990s (1995)
Locale(s): Spook Hollow, Pennsylvania

Summary: John Grant relocates his family from Philadelphia to rural Spook Hollow in order to save his marriage, and risks losing his children. Too late, he discovers that his home is the site where a Civil War atrocity produced a local legend, the Headless Horror, who rampages on the Halloween night that his children are attending the local school dance.

Other books you might like:
Charles L. Grant, *Stunts*, 1990
Jack Martin, *Halloween III: Season of the Witch*, 1985
Robert R. McCammon, *Usher's Passing*, 1985
Ashley McConnell, *Days of the Dead*, 1992

3681

DAVID ROBBINS

Vengeance Strike
(New York: Leisure, 1991)

Story type: Science Fiction (Post-Holocaust)
Series: Blade
Major character(s): Blade, Warrior; Grizzly, Genetically Altered Being, Warrior; Zhongli Quan, Alien
Time period(s): 22nd century
Locale(s): California

Summary: The Lords of Kismet have sent shapeshifters to impersonate key members of the California government with the sole purpose of wiping out Blade and the Special Forces. When Blade sees through their ruse, one shapeshifter escapes to Oakland where the group catches up with him and kills him, eliminating the menace for the moment.

Other books you might like:
Neal Barrett Jr., *Through Darkest America*, 1987
Richard Bowker, *Marlborough Street*, 1987
John Crowley, *Beasts*, 1976
Paul O. Williams, *An Ambush of Shadows*, 1983
Jack Williamson, *Darker than You Think*, 1948
Timothy Zahn, *The Blackcollar*, 1983
Roger Zelazny, *Damnation Alley*, 1969

3682

DAVID ROBBINS

Yellowstone Run
(New York: Leisure, 1990)

Story type: Science Fiction (Post-Holocaust)
Series: Endworld
Major character(s): Blade, Warrior; Hickock, Warrior; Achilles, Warrior
Time period(s): 22nd century (106 years post-holocaust)
Locale(s): West (Yellowstone Park, Civilized Zone, Federation)

Summary: Blade and his warriors are asked to destroy a band of homicidal mutants—bearlike humanoids—who are threatening to take over the area in and around Yellowstone Park.

Other books you might like:
Algis Budrys, *Some Will Not Die*, 1961
Walter M. Miller Jr., *A Canticle for Leibowitz*, 1959
Janet Morris, *Heroes in Hell*, 1986
David R. Palmer, *Emergence*, 1984

3683

TOM ROBBINS

Half Asleep in Frog Pajamas
(New York: Bantam, 1994)

Story type: Science Fiction (Satire; Contemporary Realism)
Major character(s): Gwendolyn "Gwen" Mati, Stock Broker, Fiance(e); Q-Jo Huffington, Psychic; Motofusa Yamaguchi, Doctor, Administrator
Time period(s): 1990s
Locale(s): Seattle, Washington

Summary: The stock market crash on Maundy Thursday sends Gwen Mati scrambling to recover over Easter weekend.

Other books you might like:
William Borden, *Superstoe*, 1968
Michael Kandel, *Captain Jack Zodiac*, 1992
Mark Leyner, *My Cousin, My Gastroenterologist*, 1990
Thomas Pynchon, *Gravity's Rainbow*, 1973
Kurt Vonnegut Jr., *Slaughterhouse Five*, 1969

3684

TOM ROBBINS

Skinny Legs and All
(New York: Bantam, 1990)

Story type: Fantasy (Contemporary; Political)
Major character(s): Ellen Cherry Charles, Artist, Waiter/Waitress; Boomer Petway, Mechanic, Artist; Spike Dohen, Restaurateur (partner in Isaac and Ishmael's)
Time period(s): 1990s (1990)
Locale(s): New York, New York; Jerusalem, Israel

Summary: Ellen Cherry Charles is an artist, waitressing at an Arab-Jewish restaurant and in search of something. First Boomer swept her off her feet with his giant Airstream turkey. Now Isaac and Ishmael's restaurant is livelier every week, and all eyes are focused, at some level, on Jerusalem.

Other books you might like:
Jim Dodge, *Stone Junction*, 1990
Neil Gaiman, *Good Omens: The Nice and Accurate Prophecies of Agnes Nutter, Witch*, 1990
   Terry Pratchett, co-author
Kurt Vonnegut Jr., *Cat's Cradle*, 1963

3685

JENNIFER ROBERSON

Flight of the Raven
(New York: DAW, 1990)

Story type: Fantasy (Quest; Adventure)
Series: Cheysuli
Major character(s): Aidan, Heir
Time period(s): Indeterminate Past
Locale(s): Homana, Fictional Country; Solinde, Fictional Country; Erinn, Fictional Country

Summary: Aidan has been tormented all his life with dreams of a golden chain that vanishes when he touches it. He knows that even his parents do not believe the visions are real and wonder about his sanity. Now he finds that this knowledge means he's empathic, and gods have begun to visit him with riddles, goading him out into the world to find the real links in the chain.

Other books you might like:
Diane Duane, *The Door into Fire*, 1979
Bill Fawcett, *Lords of Dragonclaw*, 1989
Patricia Kennealy, *The Copper Crown*, 1984
Adrienne Martine-Barnes, *The Fire Sword*, 1984
Shirley Rousseau Murphy, *The Ring of Fire*, 1977

3686

JENNIFER ROBERSON

Highlander: Scotland the Brave
(New York: Warner Aspect, 1996)

Story type: Fantasy (Political; Adventure)
Series: Highlander

Major character(s): Duncan MacLeod, Immortal, Martial Arts Expert; Joe Dawson, Spy (Watcher), Historian; Annie Devlin, Immortal, Revolutionary (IRA)
Time period(s): 1990s; 18th century
Locale(s): Pacific Northwest; Scotland

Summary: A mad immortal still hoping to avenge the defeat of Scottish forces at the Battle of Culloden in 1746 sends Annie Devlin to entangle Duncan MacLeod in his machinations. Television tie-in.

Other books you might like:
L. Sprague de Camp, *The Fantastic Swordsmen*, 1967 editor
Jason Henderson, *Highlander: The Element of Fire*, 1995
Ashley McConnell, *Highlander: Scimitar*, 1996
Melanie Rawn, *The Golden Key*, 1996
   Jennifer Roberson, Kate Eliot, co-authors

3687

JENNIFER ROBERSON

Lady of the Forest
(New York: Zebra, 1992)

Story type: Fantasy (Legend; Romance)
Major character(s): Marion "Marion of Ravenskeep" FitzWalter, Noblewoman; Robert "Robin Hood" of Locksley, Nobleman, Outlaw; William deLacey, Nobleman, Lawman (sheriff of Nottingham)
Time period(s): 12th century (1190s)
Locale(s): Nottingham, England; Sherwood Forest, England; Ravenskeep, England

Summary: Suitors assail Marion upon her father's death. As her attraction for Robert of Locksley grows, Marion eschews her father's deathbed wish and William deLacey's advances by citing her status as ward of the captive king, Richard the Lionhearted. When Will Scarlet kidnaps Marion, Little John and Robert rush to her rescue. Robert rebels against Prince John's authority in loyalty to King Richard.

Other books you might like:
Marion Zimmer Bradley, *The Mists of Avalon*, 1983
Parke Godwin, *Sherwood*, 1991
Robin McKinley, *The Outlaws of Sherwood*, 1989
Bernard Miles, *Robin Hood: His Life and Legend*, 1979
Howard Pyle, *The Merry Adventures of Robin Hood*, 1883
Richard Kluger, *The Sheriff of Nottingham*, 1990

3688

JENNIFER ROBERSON, Editor

Return to Avalon: A Celebration of Marion Zimmer Bradley
(New York: DAW, 1996)

Story type: Fantasy (Anthology; Legend)

Summary: This volume contains an introduction by Diana L. Paxson; a forward by Andre Norton; essays of appreciation by C.J. Cherryh, Charles de Lint, Paul Edwin Zimmer, and Jennifer Roberson; and 19 original stories by authors including

Kate Elliott, Katharine Kerr, Jane M. Lindskold, Melanie Rawn, Jennifer Roberson, Judith Tarr, and Dave Wolverton. The stories reflect and elaborate Marion Zimmer Bradley's vision of legendary Britain and Darkover.

Other books you might like:
Mike Ashley, *The Camelot Chronicles*, 1992
    editor
Marion Zimmer Bradley, *The Mists of Avalon*, 1983
Marion Zimmer Bradley, *The Sword and Sorceress Series*, 1984-1996
    editor
George Alec Effinger, *Maureen Birnbaum, Barbarian Swordsperson: The Complete Stories*, 1993
Kathleen M. Massie-Ferch, *Ancient Enchantresses*, 1995
    Martin H. Greenberg, Richard Gilliam, co-editors
C.L. Moore, *Jirel of Joiry*, 1969

3689

JENNIFER ROBERSON

Sword-Breaker

(New York: DAW, 1991)

Story type: Fantasy (Adventure; Quest)
Series: Tiger and Del
Major character(s): Delilah "Del", Warrior (Sword-Singer, North); Sandtiger "Tiger", Warrior (Sword-Dancer, South)
Time period(s): Indeterminate Past
Locale(s): Punja Desert, Fictional Country

Summary: Tiger and Del have finally hunted down and destroyed the man who killed Del's family, raped her and sold her brother to slavers. However, the Southron tribes think the man was their messiah and want to take their revenge on Del and Tiger. Complicating matters, Tiger's sword is possessed by an evil sorcerer who wants to take over Tiger in a first step toward unmaking the world. Del and Tiger must elude their pursuers, cross the desert and reach the one person who may be able to discharge the sword safely, if he still exists.

Other books you might like:
Steven Brust, *Jhereg*, 1983
Heather Gladney, *Teot's War*, 1987
Barbara Hambly, *The Armies of Daylight*, 1982
Mercedes Lackey, *The Oathbound*, 1988
Melanie Rawn, *Dragon Prince*, 1988

3690

JENNIFER ROBERSON

Sword-Maker

(New York: DAW, 1989)

Story type: Fantasy (Sword and Sorcery)
Series: Tiger and Del
Major character(s): Tiger, Hero
Time period(s): Indeterminate Past
Locale(s): Alternate Universe

Summary: Having mastered two separate schools of swordplay, Tiger finds himself being called the savior in a new land. The inhabitants want Tiger to fight off a dragon, and Tiger unwillingly sets off to confront the monster.

Other books you might like:
Carole Nelson Douglas, *Six of Swords*, 1984
Barbara Hambly, *The Dark Hand of Magic*, 1989
Barbara Hambly, *The Ladies of Mandrigyn*, 1984
Phyllis Ann Karr, *Frostflower and Thorn*, 1980
Janet Morris, *City at the Edge of Time*, 1988

3691

JENNIFER ROBERSON

A Tapestry of Lions

(New York: DAW, 1992)

Story type: Fantasy (Quest)
Series: Cheysuli
Major character(s): Kellin, Mythical Creature (shapechanger)
Time period(s): Indeterminate Past
Locale(s): Homana, Fictional Country

Summary: Kellin rejects the generations' long effort to recreate the magical race populating Homana by refusing to mate with an Ihlini woman, the key to fulfilling their plan. Ihlini sorcerers also wish to trap Kellin to prevent the prophecy's fruition which would end life as the Ihlini know it. Concludes the series started in *Shapechangers* (1984).

Other books you might like:
Louise Cooper, *The Sleep of Stone*, 1991
Thorarinn Gunnarsson, *Dragons on the Town*, 1992
Nancy Luenn, *Goldclimbers*, 1991
Andre Norton, *The Elvenbane*, 1991
    Mercedes Lackey, co-author
Will Shetterly, *Elsewhere*, 1991

3692

JOHN MADDOX ROBERTS

Conan and the Treasure of Python

(New York: Tor, 1993)

Story type: Fantasy (Sword and Sorcery)
Series: Conan the Barbarian
Major character(s): Conan, Barbarian, Warrior; Wulfrede, Sailor, Warrior; Ulfilo, Sailor, Warrior
Time period(s): Indeterminate Past
Locale(s): Stygia, Fictional Country; Acheron, Fictional Country

Summary: When Conan hears of the magnificent treasure hidden in the capital city of Python by the rulers of that lost civilization, he sails and marches with other adventurers hoping for a profitable looting experience, ever mindful of the fierce warriors following them. When they arrive, they find descendants little interested in parting with treasure.

Other books you might like:
Roland J. Green, *Conan the Guardian*, 1991
Robert E. Howard, *Hour of the Dragon*, 1977
Robert E. Howard, *The People of the Black Circle*, 1977
Robert E. Howard, *Red Nails*, 1977
Robert Jordan, *Conan the Magnificent*, 1984

Steve Perry, *Conan the Free Lance*, 1990
Karl Edward Wagner, *Echoes of Valor I*, 1987
 editor

3693

JOHN MADDOX ROBERTS

Conan the Rogue

(New York: Tor, 1991)

Story type: Fantasy (Sword and Sorcery)
Series: Conan the Barbarian
Major character(s): Conan, Barbarian, Warrior; Brita, Orphan, Guardian (sister's)
Time period(s): Indeterminate
Locale(s): Sicas Aquilonia, Fictional Country

Summary: Conan agrees to help Piris reacquire an object stolen from him and travels to Sicas, arriving with Brita. While waiting for Piris, Conan assists Brita in locating her sister among the vicious thugs who inhabit Sicas.

Other books you might like:
Leonard Carpenter, *Conan the Great*, 1990
Robert E. Howard, *King Conan*, 1953
Robert E. Howard, *The Sword of Conan*, 1952
Robert Jordan, *Conan the Invincible*, 1985
Steve Perry, *Conan the Formidable*, 1990
Karl Edward Wagner, *Death Angel's Shadow*, 1973
Karl Edward Wagner, *Echoes of Valor III*, 1991
 editor

3694

JOHN MADDOX ROBERTS

The Enigma Variations

(New York: Ace, 1989)

Story type: Science Fiction (Cyberpunk)
Major character(s): Slate, Warrior; Pamela Conyers, Businesswoman, Fugitive
Time period(s): 21st century
Locale(s): United States

Summary: Slate wakes up in the desert, his mind a blank, an artificial hand of polished steel attached to his wrist. Gradually he reconstructs his past and makes his way into a complex web of intrigue and violence. In a world on the edge of collapse, the great corporations fight for power using mindwipes, cyborg killers, and any other deadly technology they can bring to bear. Slate decides to fight back.

Other books you might like:
S.N. Lewitt, *Cyberstealth*, 1989
S.N. Lewitt, *Dancing Vac*, 1990
Walter Jon Williams, *Hardwired*, 1986
Walter Jon Williams, *Voice of the Whirlwind*, 1987
Dave Wolverton, *On My Way to Paradise*,

3695

JOHN MADDOX ROBERTS

The Poisoned Lands

(New York: Tor, 1992)

Story type: Fantasy (Post-Disaster; Science Fiction)
Series: Stormlands
Major character(s): Ansa, Warrior, Explorer; Gasam, Warrior, Royalty (king); Fyana, Healer
Time period(s): Indeterminate Future
Locale(s): Sono, Fictional Country; Gran, Fictional Country

Summary: Wanting to conquer the world and learn the location of King Hael's iron mine, King Gasam of Chiwa succeeds in the first and starts on the second by invading Sono. After Ansa's capture while scouting out the intentions of King Gasam, Fyana dangles the prospect of rejuvenation before Queen Larissa, allowing both to escape and report back to King Hael.

Other books you might like:
Robert Adams, *The Seven Magical Jewels of Ireland*, 1985
Poul Anderson, *The Winter of the World*, 1976
Piers Anthony, *Sos the Rope*, 1968
Edmund Cooper, *The Cloud Walker*, 1973
John Dalmas, *The Yngling*, 1971
Andre Norton, *No Night Without Stars*, 1975
Kim Stanley Robinson, *The Wild Shore*, 1985
Clifford D. Simak, *A Heritage of Stars*, 1978
Paul O. Williams, *The Song of the Axe*, 1984

3696

JOHN MADDOX ROBERTS

Queens of Land and Sea

(New York: Tor, 1994)

Story type: Fantasy (Adventure; Post-Disaster)
Series: Stormlands
Major character(s): Larissa, Royalty (queen), Political Figure; Ansa, Explorer, Warrior; Shazad, Royalty (queen), Political Figure
Time period(s): Indeterminate Future
Locale(s): Neva, Fictional Country

Summary: When strangers from the southern highlands come to the Islands and to Neva carrying a plague that attacks all but Shasinn, Queen Larissa decides to attack the Nevans. The Shasinn invasion sidetracks Ansa when he comes to Neva to rally forces to fight the Mezpans, but Ansa captures Queen Larissa despite hindrance. Retaliation on a ransom mission nearly spells disaster for Shazad.

Other books you might like:
Poul Anderson, *The Winter of the World*, 1975
John Barnes, *The Man Who Pulled Down the Sky*, 1986
Orson Scott Card, *The Folk of the Fringe*, 1989
Clifford D. Simak, *A Heritage of Stars*, 1977
Stanley G. Weinbaum, *The Black Flame*, 1948

3697

JOHN MADDOX ROBERTS

The Steel Kings
(New York: Tor, 1993)

Story type: Fantasy (Post-Disaster; Political)
Series: Stormlands
Major character(s): Kairn, Warrior, Explorer; Hael, Royalty (king), Warrior; Larissa, Royalty (queen), Political Figure
Time period(s): Indeterminate Future
Locale(s): Mezpa, Fictional Country; Thezas, Fictional Country

Summary: When Kairn comes to Mezpa to warn his father about Gasam's seizure of his father's steel mines, Deathmoon captures him. After his father helps him escape, the two plot how to use Deathmoon and Gasam to eliminate each other.

Other books you might like:
Poul Anderson, *The Winter of the World*, 1976
Piers Anthony, *Sos the Rope*, 1968
Neal Barrett Jr., *Through Darkest America*, 1988
John Dalmas, *The Yngling*, 1971
Floyd Gibbon, *The Red Napoleon*, 1929
Robert E. Howard, *Conan the Conqueror*, 1950
Dean R. Koontz, *Warlock*, 1972
Sterling E. Lanier, *Hiero's Journey*, 1973
Paul O. Williams, *An Ambush of Shadows*, 1983
Chelsea Quinn Yarbro, *False Dawn*, 1978

3698

KENNETH ROBESON (Pseudonym of Will Murray)

The Frightened Fish
(New York: Bantam Falcon, 1992)

Story type: Fantasy (Adventure; Mystery)
Series: Doc Savage
Major character(s): Clark "Doc" Savage Jr., Adventurer, Genius; Seryi Mitroff, Revolutionary; Max Wood, Scientist, Activist (political agitator)
Time period(s): 1940s (1949)
Locale(s): New York, New York; Quincy, Massachusetts; Japan

Summary: A strangely deadly gag involving a man terrified of "frightened fish" launches Doc Savage and his crew into another mystery. This time they travel to New England and Japan in an effort to solve the puzzle that masks a diabolical scheme for global destruction. Waiting in Japan lurks another threat, one to Doc Savage's heart and peace of mind.

Other books you might like:
Lin Carter, *The Volcano Ogre*, 1976
Philip Jose Farmer, *Escape From Loki*, 1991
Jon Stephen Fink, *Further Adventures*, 1993
Rob MacGregor, *Indiana Jones and the Genesis Deluge*, 1992
Grant Stockbridge, *The Spider #3: Death's Crimson Juggernaut/The Red Death Rain*, 1992

3699

KENNETH ROBESON (Pseudonym of Will Murray)

The Jade Ogre
(New York: Bantam Falcon, 1992)

Story type: Fantasy (Adventure; Mystery)
Series: Doc Savage
Major character(s): Clark "Doc" Savage Jr., Adventurer, Genius; Jason Baird, Jeweler; Quon, Cult Member (leader)
Time period(s): 1930s
Locale(s): San Francisco, California; Cambodia

Summary: Traveling to San Francisco by airplane, Doc Savage narrowly escapes death when the plane goes out of control after the pilot's sudden death. Upon arrival, the Man of Bronze discovers his contact mysteriously missing in a deadly puzzle that leads Savage and his companions half way around the world through a maze of cultists, assassins and supernatural creatures to face the Jade Ogre.

Other books you might like:
Lin Carter, *Invisible Death*, 1975
Philip Jose Farmer, *Escape From Loki*, 1991
Jon Stephen Fink, *Further Adventures*, 1993
Rob MacGregor, *Indiana Jones and the Peril at Delphi*, 1991
Grant Stockbridge, *The Spider #1: The Spider and the Pain Master/Secret City of Crime*, 1991

3700

KENNETH ROBESON (Pseudonym of Will Murray)

Python Isle
(New York: Bantam Falcon, 1991)

Story type: Fantasy (Adventure)
Series: Doc Savage
Major character(s): Clark "Doc" Savage Jr., Adventurer, Military Personnel; Blackbird Hinton, Smuggler; Lha, Royalty (queen)
Time period(s): 1930s
Locale(s): New York, New York; Cape Town, South Africa; Python Isle, Fictional Country (in the Indian Ocean)

Summary: When Doc Savage's friend, Renny, is kidnapped in Cape Town, Doc and his companions travel there to help rescue him. In Cape Town, Doc becomes involved with an aviator thought long dead and his friend, Queen Lha of Python Isle, a descendant of the Biblical King Solomon who possesses remnants of the legendary treasure of Ophir.

Other books you might like:
Lester Dent, *Doc Savage Omnibus #1*, 1986
    as Kenneth Robeson
Lester Dent, *Doc Savage Omnibus #12*, 1990
    as Kenneth Robeson
Lester Dent, *Doc Savage Omnibus #13*, 1990
    as Kenneth Robeson
Philip Jose Farmer, *Doc Savage: His Apocalyptic Life*, 1973
Philip Jose Farmer, *Escape From Loki*, 1991
Philip Jose Farmer, *The Mad Goblin*, 1970

3701

KENNETH ROBESON (Pseudonym of Will Murray)

White Eyes
(New York: Bantam Falcon, 1992)

Story type: Fantasy (Adventure)
Series: Doc Savage
Major character(s): Clark ''Doc'' Savage Jr., Adventurer, Genius; White Eyes, Criminal
Time period(s): 1930s
Locale(s): New York, New York; Cuba

Summary: Investigating a series of deaths in which the victim's eyes turn an unseeing white, Doc Savage and his companions discover that the plague results from the efforts of New York's criminals who have united in hopes of seizing Doc Savage's fabled Mayan wealth.

Other books you might like:
Philip Jose Farmer, *Doc Savage: His Apocalyptic Life*, 1973
Philip Jose Farmer, *Escape From Loki*, 1991
Philip Jose Farmer, *The Mad Goblin*, 1970

3702

FRANK M. ROBINSON

The Dark Beyond the Stars
(New York: Tor, 1991)

Story type: Science Fiction (Generation Starship; Adventure)
Major character(s): Michael Kusaka, Spaceship Captain, Immortal; Sparrow, Amnesiac, Space Explorer
Time period(s): 40th century
Locale(s): *Astron*, Spaceship

Summary: The Spaceship *Astron* has been searching for life for 200 generations. Old and worn out equipment makes much of the ship unusable. Most of the crew has lost hope of finding life and wants to return to Earth. Sparrow, recovering from a near-fatal accident on his last mission, discovers that the Captain is programmed to continue and is unable to turn back even though the ship has reached the end of the spiral arm and doesn't have the resources to survive passage to the next.

Other books you might like:
Brian W. Aldiss, *Non-Stop*, 1989
Octavia E. Butler, *Dawn*, 1987
Michael Capobianco, *Burster*, 1990
Glen Cook, *The Dragon Never Sleeps*, 1988
Alan Dean Foster, *Dark Star*, 1974
Diana G. Gallagher, *The Alien Dark*, 1990
Robert A. Heinlein, *Orphans of the Sky*, 1963
Fritz Leiber, *Ship of Shadows*, 1988
David Alexander Smith, *Homecoming*, 1990

3703

JANE E.M. ROBINSON

The Amazon Chronicles
(San Diego, California: Clothespin Fever Press, 1994)

Story type: Fantasy (Adventure; Political)
Major character(s): Antiope, Warrior (Amazon), Lesbian; Penthesilea, Warrior (Amazon), Foundling; Abba-Bashti, Trader (Lesbian)
Time period(s): 13th century B.C. (1240 B.C.)
Locale(s): Amazonia, Fictional Country; Europe; Asia Minor

Summary: Achaean designs on Amazonia present Penthesilea with the opportunity for glory on her expedition, while political hopefuls jostle for power and Antiope waits anxiously in Amazonia for Penthesilea's return.

Other books you might like:
Suzy McKee Charnas, *The Furies*, 1994
Charlotte Perkins Gilman, *Herland*, 1979
Jessica Amanda Salmonson, *Amazons!*, 1979
Jacqui Singleton, *Heartstone and Silver*, 1994
Joan Slonczewski, *A Door into Ocean*, 1986

3704

KIM STANLEY ROBINSON

Blue Mars
(New York: Bantam Spectra, 1996)

Story type: Science Fiction (Hard Science Fiction; Political)
Series: Mars Trilogy
Major character(s): Ann Clayborne, Scientist, Aged Person; Saxifrage ''Sax'' Russell, Scientist, Aged Person; Nirgal Hawkins, Political Figure (first generation Martian)
Time period(s): 22nd century; 23rd century
Locale(s): Mars; Venus; Mercury

Summary: After the second Martian revolution, a delegation visits Earth while the many Martian groups, both Red and Green, work on a constitution they can all sign. Nirgal advocates giving the life extension drug to everyone on Earth, recognizing that this will lead to a major increase in the already disastrous population problem, but claims that Martian immigration will take some of the pressure off. Ann agrees to cooperate with the Greens rather than start a civil war if Sax will remove the soletta which focuses sunlight on Mars. He moves it to Venus to block sunlight, hoping he can find a way to avoid a Martian ice age. Concluding volume of trilogy.

Other books you might like:
Greg Bear, *Moving Mars*, 1993
Ben Bova, *Mars*, 1992
David Brin, *Earth*, 1990
William C. Dietz, *Mars Prime*, 1992
Joan Slonczewski, *A Door into Ocean*, 1986
S.C. Sykes, *Red Genesis*, 1991

`3705`

KIM STANLEY ROBINSON

Escape From Kathmandu
(New York: Tor, 1989)

Story type: Science Fiction (Humor)
Major character(s): George, Expatriate; Freds, Expatriate
Locale(s): Kathmandu, Nepal

Summary: These four interconnected stories tell the adventures of George and Freds, a pair of not very practical American expatriates living in Kathmandu. Typical of their antics is an attempt to smuggle a yeti in sportsclothes out of a hotel while Jimmy Carter is making a visit.

Other books you might like:
John Kessel, *Good News From Outer Space*, 1989
Marc Laidlaw, *Neon Lotus*, 1988
Geoff Ryman, *The Unconquered Country*, 1986
Lucius Shepard, *The Jaguar Hunter*, 1987

`3706`

KIM STANLEY ROBINSON, Editor

Future Primitive: The New Ecotopias
(New York: Tor, 1994)

Story type: Science Fiction (Anthology; Utopia)

Summary: Contains a three-page introduction, 10 pages of endnotes, five pages of suggested reading, plus two poems published in 1935 and 1974 and 13 stories reprinted from periodicals and anthologies 1974-1994, all of which utilize ecological themes such as human/animal interactions, escaping the confines of the human body, primitive peoples and synthesizing a new culture by combining ancient cultures with technologically advanced cultures. Authors include Terry Bisson, Carol Emshwiller, Garry Kilworth, R.A. Lafferty, Ursula K. Le Guin, Pat Murphy, Paul Park, Rachel Pollack, Robert Silverberg, Howard Waldrop and Gene Wolfe.

Other books you might like:
Ernest Callenbach, *Ecotopia: A Novel about Ecology, People and Politics in 1999*, 1975
Ernest Callenbach, *Ecotopia Emerging*, 1981
Ursula K. Le Guin, *Always Coming Home*, 1985
Pat Murphy, *The City, Not Long After*, 1989
Rachel Pollack, *Unquenchable Fire*, 1992
John Stadler, *Eco-Fiction*, 1971
    editor
Starhawk, *The Fifth Sacred Thing*, 1993
George Stewart, *Earth Abides*, 1949
Sheri S. Tepper, *The Gate to Women's Country*, 1988

`3707`

KIM STANLEY ROBINSON

The Gold Coast
(New York: Tor Books, 1989)

Story type: Science Fiction (Political)

Series: Orange County Trilogy
Major character(s): Jim McPherson, Teacher, Writer; Dennis McPherson, Engineer
Time period(s): 21st century
Locale(s): Orange County California, Alternate Earth

Summary: In this novel which was nominated for the British Science Fiction Award for 1989 and which made *SF & Fantasy Book Review Annual*'s list of the ten best novels of 1988, a large cast of characters live out their lives against a twenty-first century California backdrop of monstrous superhighways, senseless violence, designer drugs, and military-industrial boondoggles.

Other books you might like:
Ben Bova, *Peacekeepers*, 1988
John Kessel, *Good News From Outer Space*, 1989
Dan Simmons, *Phases of Gravity*, 1989
Bruce Sterling, *Islands in the Net*, 1988
Robert Charles Wilson, *Memory Wire*, 1987

`3708`

KIM STANLEY ROBINSON

Green Mars
(New York: Bantam Spectra, 1994)

Story type: Science Fiction (Hard Science Fiction; Political)
Series: Mars Trilogy
Major character(s): Maya Toitovna, Revolutionary, Scientist; Nirgal Hawkins, Political Figure, Revolutionary; Saxifrage ''Sax'' Russell, Scientist, Revolutionary
Time period(s): 22nd century
Locale(s): Mars

Summary: Now operational, the new space elevator sparks fear in the remaining First Hundred, still in hiding after the failed revolution in 2061 and not yet in agreement on their plans and goals for Mars and the people there. The second and third generation Martians work to create a habitable surface and atmosphere or fight to free Mars from control by multinational corporations and the United Nations Transitional Authority, all of which maintain armed security forces on Mars.

Other books you might like:
Greg Bear, *Moving Mars*, 1993
Ben Bova, *Mars*, 1992
David Brin, *Earth*, 1990
William C. Dietz, *Mars Prime*, 1992
Janet Kagan, *Mirabile*, 1991
Joan Slonczewski, *A Door into Ocean*, 1986
S.C. Sykes, *Red Genesis*, 1991
Wynne Whiteford, *The Specialist*, 1990

`3709`

KIM STANLEY ROBINSON

Pacific Edge
(New York: Tor, 1990)

Story type: Science Fiction (Alternate Universe; Political)
Series: Orange County Trilogy

Major character(s): Kevin Claiborne, Inventor, Political Figure; Nadezhda Katayev, Scientist
Time period(s): 21st century
Locale(s): Orange County California, Alternate Earth
Summary: Begun with *The Wild Shore* and *The Gold Coast*, this triptych of novels is completed with *Pacific Edge*. Each takes place in an alternate version of Orange County. Sensible use of materials and the environment are featured here.

Other books you might like:
Ben Bova, *Peacekeepers*, 1988
David Brin, *Earth*, 1990
Joan Slonczewski, *A Door into Ocean*, 1986
Bruce Sterling, *Islands in the Net*, 1988
Jack Vance, *Trullion: Alastor 2262*, 1973

3710

KIM STANLEY ROBINSON

Red Mars
(New York: Bantam Spectra, 1993)

Story type: Science Fiction (Hard Science Fiction; Political)
Series: Mars Trilogy
Major character(s): Frank Chalmers, Administrator, Scientist; Jack Boone, Scientist, Space Explorer; Maya Toitovna, Administrator, Scientist
Time period(s): 2020s (2026)
Locale(s): *Ares*, Spaceship; Mars
Summary: While on the *Ares* enroute to Mars, the first 100 colonists, scientists and astronauts realize that they have their own hidden ideas for Mars, incompatible with Earth's inevitable policy of development and exploitation of scarce Martian riches. After briefly working together on Mars, some colonists begin to warm the atmosphere and work on terraforming Mars while others leave for the hills to pursue self-sufficiency and escape Earth control; however, the true Martian potential exceeds everyone's vision. First of a series.

Other books you might like:
Piers Anthony, *Total Recall*, 1989
David Brin, *Earth*, 1990
Octavia E. Butler, *Dawn*, 1987
Robert L. Forward, *Martian Rainbow*, 1991
Jack C. Haldeman II, *High Steel*, 1993
    Jack Dann, co-author
S.C. Sykes, *Red Genesis*, 1991
Sheri S. Tepper, *Raising the Stones*, 1990
Wynne Whiteford, *The Specialist*, 1990

3711

KIM STANLEY ROBINSON

Remaking History
(New York: Tor, 1991)

Story type: Science Fiction (Collection)
Summary: This title contains 14 stories published between 1986 and 1991 in periodicals and anthologies and Pulphouse's Author's Choice Monthly series and one story, "Vineland the Dream," original to this collection. Some

stories feature near future settings and themes similar to the Orange County Trilogy including the Nebula Award nominee "Before I Wake," plus "Down and Out in the Year 2000" and "A History of the 20th Century with Illustrations." The latter was revised for this book as was "The Part of Us That Loves." "Rainbow Bridge," retitled herein, reflects the author's interest in mountain climbing. A near future ice age is depicted in "Glacier" while harder SF themes appear in "The Lunatics," about miners of the lunar crust.

Other books you might like:
J.G. Ballard, *War Fever*, 1991
Ray Bradbury, *The Toynbee Convector*, 1989
Spider Robinson, *Antinomy*, 1980
Spider Robinson, *Callahan and Company*, 1988
John Varley, *Blue Champagne*, 1986
John Varley, *The Persistence of Vision*, 1978
Kurt Vonnegut Jr., *Welcome to the Monkey House*, 1968

3712

SPIDER ROBINSON

The Callahan Touch
(New York: Ace, 1993)

Story type: Fantasy (Light Fantasy; Science Fiction)
Series: Callahan's
Major character(s): Jake Stonebender, Saloon Keeper/Owner; Ernie "Lucky Duck" Shea, Mythical Creature (Pooka/Fir Darrig cross); Jonathan Crawford, Health Care Professional (medical researcher)
Time period(s): 1980s (May 1988)
Locale(s): Mary's Place, Mythical Place (saloon); United States
Summary: Two years after the nuking of Callahan's place, Jake Stonebender and other Callahan's regulars inaugurate Mary's Place. Within minutes of opening, improbable and magical events herald special newcomers and wishes come true.

Other books you might like:
Grendel Briarton, *The Collected Feghoot*, 1992
    pseudonym of Reginald Bretnor
Steven Brust, *Cowboy Feng's Space Bar and Grille*, 1990
Arthur C. Clarke, *Tales From the White Hart*, 1957
L. Sprague de Camp, *Tales From Gavagan's Bar*, 1978
    expanded edition; Fletcher Pratt, co-author
Stephen Goldin, *Jade Darcy and the Affair of Honor*, 1988
    Mary Mason, co-author
Steve Perry, *The Man Who Never Missed*, 1985
Don Sakers, *Carmen Miranda's Ghost Is Haunting Space Station Three*, 1990
    editor

3713

SPIDER ROBINSON

Callahan's Lady
(New York: Ace, 1989)

Story type: Science Fiction (Humor)

Series: Callahan's
Major character(s): Lady Sally Callahan, Madam; Maureen, Prostitute
Time period(s): 20th century
Locale(s): New York, New York (Brooklyn)

Summary: Four interrelated stories tell of the amazing goings on in a house of prostitution owned by Callahan's wife.

Other books you might like:
Steven Brust, *Cowboy Feng's Space Bar and Grille*, 1990
Sterling E. Lanier, *The Peculiar Exploits of Brigadier Ffellowes*, 1977
Mike Resnick, *The Three-Legged Hootch Dancer*, 1983

3714
SPIDER ROBINSON

Callahan's Legacy
(New York: Tor, 1996)

Story type: Science Fiction (Humor; Invasion of Earth)
Series: Callahan's
Major character(s): Mike Callahan, Time Traveller; Jake Stonebender, Saloon Keeper/Owner (Mary's Place); Mary Callahan-Finn, Computer Expert
Time period(s): 1980s (Fall 1988)
Locale(s): Mary's Place, Mythical Place (saloon); United States

Summary: Jake Stonebender begins a typical day at Mary's Place with an obnoxious beast turned away at the door and a customer intent on burning a suitcase full of hundred dollar bills one at a time. Before long, Mary Callahan-Finn arrives from another planet with the news that the punning patrons of Mary's Place may prove humanity's only hope against the Lizard, a cybernetic monster capable of total destruction.

Other books you might like:
Grendel Briarton, *The Collected Feghoot*, 1992
    pseudonym of Reginald Bretnor
Steven Brust, *Cowboy Feng's Space Bar and Grille*, 1990
Arthur C. Clarke, *Tales From the White Hart*, 1957
L. Sprague de Camp, *Tales From Gavagan's Bar*, 1978
    expanded edition; Fletcher Pratt, co-author
Larry Niven, *Fallen Angels*, 1991
    Jerry Pournelle, Michael Flynn, co-authors

3715
SPIDER ROBINSON

Lady Slings the Booze
(New York: Ace, 1992)

Story type: Science Fiction (Mystery; Humor)
Series: Callahan's
Major character(s): Lady Sally Callahan, Madam; Joe Quigley, Detective—Private, Imposter (prostitute)
Time period(s): 1980s
Locale(s): New York, New York

Summary: Joe Quigley accepts a mysterious assignment involving an invisible rapist whose crimes disturb the ambience at Lady Sally's brothel which caters to every taste of society's

rich and powerful citizens. While posing as a prostitute, Joe uncovers a plot which threatens the world with nuclear destruction.

Other books you might like:
Mel Gilden, *Surfing Samurai Robots*, 1988
Stephen Goldin, *Jade Darcy and the Affair of Honor*, 1988
    Mary Mason, co-author
Simon R. Green, *Hawk & Fisher*, 1990
Dean Ing, *Cathouse*, 1991
John E. Stith, *Redshift Rendezvous*, 1990
Thomas T. Thomas, *Crygender*, 1992

3716
SPIDER ROBINSON
JEANNE ROBINSON, Co-Author

Starmind
(New York: Ace, 1995)

Story type: Science Fiction (Arts; Genetic Manipulation)
Series: Stardance
Major character(s): Rhea Paixao, Writer, Spouse (Rand's); Rand Porter, Computer Expert, Spouse (Rhea's); Jay Sasaki, Dancer, Spaceman
Time period(s): 2060s (2065)
Locale(s): Provincetown, Massachusetts; *Shimizu Hotel*, Spaceship (high earth orbit)

Summary: Not yet ready to leave her ancestral home in Provincetown, Rhea reluctantly accompanies Rand to the fabulous Shimizu Hotel where Rand and his half-brother, Jay, cooperate as artistic directors. Unhappy at the though of never returning home, Rhea decides to go despite the heroic actions of Rand and Jay, saving the hotel from destruction and stopping a plot against the Stardancers.

Other books you might like:
Arthur C. Clarke, *Childhood's End*, 1953
L. Warren Douglas, *A Plague of Change*, 1992
Ernest Hogan, *Cortez on Jupiter*, 1990
Marjorie Bradley Kellogg, *Harmony*, 1991
Theodore Sturgeon, *The Dreaming Jewels*, 1950

3717
SPIDER ROBINSON
JEANNE ROBINSON, Co-Author

Starseed
(New York: Ace, 1991)

Story type: Science Fiction (Arts)
Series: Stardance
Major character(s): Morgan McLeod, Dancer, Student; Robert Chen, Teacher, Spaceman
Time period(s): 2020s (2020)
Locale(s): Top Step, Space Station; Earth

Summary: A dancer for 32 years until her injuries prohibit it, Morgan decides that the only alternative to euthanasia involves becoming a Stardancer, one of the telepathic, symbiotic creatures which live in Outer Space. She moves to the Starseed Foundation's Top Step where she studies those disciplines which should ease the transition into the telepathic community. Her determination to become a Stardancer helps her through hinderances, difficulty adjusting to zero gee, romantic involvement with an instructor and a terrorist plot aimed at stopping the Stardancers. This novel is set a few years later in the same universe as *Stardance*.

Other books you might like:
John Barnes, *Orbital Resonance*, 1991
Lois McMaster Bujold, *Falling Free*, 1988
Ernest Hogan, *Cortez on Jupiter*, 1990
James Patrick Kelly, *Look into the Sun*, 1989
Alis A. Rasmussen, *A Passage of Stars*, 1990
David Alexander Smith, *Homecoming*, 1990
Theodore Sturgeon, *More than Human*, 1953
John Varley, *Blue Champagne*, 1986
John Varley, *The Persistence of Vision*, 1978

3718
ALAN RODGERS
Bone Music
(Stamford, Connecticut: Longmeadow, 1995)

Story type: Horror (Ancient Evil Unleashed)
Major character(s): Elvis Presley, Musician, Historical Figure; Dan Alvarez, Musician; Lisa Henderson, Young Woman
Time period(s): 1930s (1938); 1990s (1995)
Locale(s): New Orleans, Louisiana

Summary: In a world where Robert Johnson's singing of the song "Judgment Day" has cracked The Eye of the World, and let in all the hoodoo that 20th century blues singers have warned of, musician Dan Alvarez, devil girl Lisa Henderson, and a resurrected Elvis Presley struggle to save the world from the encroaching darkness foretold by a cast of classic blues players, many of whom are given walk-on roles.

Other books you might like:
Clifford Mohr, *Requiem*, 1992
Al Sarrantonio, *Skeletons*, 1992
Adrian Savage, *Symphony*, 1993

3719
ALAN RODGERS
Children of the Blood
(New York: Bantam, 1990)

Story type: Horror (Evil Children)
Major character(s): Ben Tompkins, Parent; Jimmy Tompkins, Child
Time period(s): 1990s
Locale(s): Green Hill, South

Summary: An ancient "stone" possesses the children of Green Hill, forcing them to evil deeds. Newcomers Ben and Jimmy Tompkins are able to confront and do battle against the stone's sinister powers. This is Rodgers' first novel.

Other books you might like:
John Saul, *Suffer the Children*, 1977
John Wyndham, *The Midwich Cuckoos*, 1957

3720
ALAN RODGERS
Fire
(New York: Bantam, 1990)

Story type: Horror (Apocalyptic Horror)
Major character(s): Paul Green, Political Figure (President of the United States); Ron Hawkins, Maintenance Worker (janitor); Luke Munsen, Scientist (genetic engineer)
Time period(s): Indeterminate Future
Locale(s): Mountainville, Tennessee; Washington, District of Columbia; Republic of Korea

Summary: In this epic horror novel, the accidental death of the First Lady in Moscow causes her unbalanced conservative husband to threaten nuclear annihilation of the Soviet Union. Meanwhile, an explosion at the Mountain Institute Genetic Research Facility in Tennessee releases a genetically engineered monster that resembles The Beast of Revelations. Soon thereafter, a scientist at the Institute lets loose an indestructable virus that can revivify the dead and make them effectively immortal. The bombs begin to fall, and there begins a complex though often arbitrary and aimless conflict between characters who represent the forces of Good and Evil.

Other books you might like:
James Blish, *Black Easter*, 1968
James Blish, *The Day After Judgment*, 1971
Stephen King, *The Stand: The Complete and Uncut Edition*, 1990
Robert R. McCammon, *Swan Song*, 1987

3721
ALAN RODGERS
New Life for the Dead
(Newark, New Jersey: Wildside Press, 1991)

Story type: Horror (Collection)
Summary: Five stories generally concerned with characters who find that what they wish for and what they get are often two entirely different things. Included are the Bram Stoker Award-winning story "The Boy Who Came Back from the Dead," about the upset caused in a family by a child's resurrection, and "Emma's Daughter," about the extent to which a mother will go to bring her dead child back to life. There are also seven poems.

Other books you might like:
Robert R. McCammon, *Blue World*, 1989
William Relling Jr., *The Infinite Man*, 1989
F. Paul Wilson, *Soft and Others*, 1989

3722
ALAN RODGERS
Night
(New York: Bantam, 1991)

Story type: Horror (Apocalyptic Horror)

Major character(s): Tim Fischer, Psychic; Joel Kimball, Police Officer (deputy sheriff); The Bleeding Man, Mythical Creature
Time period(s): 1990s
Locale(s): Running Board, Nebraska

Summary: When his grandfather is murdered, Tim Fischer, who has been blessed with the gift of second sight, inherits the old man's most sacred possession, a fragment of the true cross on which Jesus died. From that day forward, Tim assumes responsibility for uncovering the identity of his grandfather's killer and keeping the talisman from The Bleeding Man, a manifestation of the man who nailed Jesus to the cross and who hopes to use the fragment to recreate the world in his own soulless image.

Other books you might like:
Stephen King, *The Dead Zone*, 1979
Robert Weinberg, *The Armageddon Box*, 1991

3723

ALAN RODGERS

Pandora
(New York: Bantam, 1995)

Story type: Horror (Science Fiction)
Major character(s): Pandora, Alien; Belisarius Hightower, Military Personnel (U.S. Air Force general); Ken Estes, Military Personnel
Time period(s): 1990s (1995)
Locale(s): Wright-Patterson AF Base, Ohio; Pine Junction, Tennessee

Summary: Pandora, a survivor of a space ship crash outside of Roswell, New Mexico, escapes the military compound where she has been kept for half a century to search for the father whom she believes is on Earth. Her escape instigates a manhunt that includes friends who want to protect her, and psychotic military types who will stop at nothing to return her to captivity and dispose of anyone who might give away her secret.

Other books you might like:
Donald Burleson, *Flute Song*, 1996
Maxine O'Callaghan, *Dark Time*, 1992
Whitley Strieber, *Majestic*, 1989

3724

MICHAELA ROESSNER

Vanishing Point
(New York: Tor, 1993)

Story type: Science Fiction (Post-Disaster)
Major character(s): Nesta Christiana Easterman, Scientist; Renzie, Researcher (assistant), Warrior; Hake, Scientist
Time period(s): 2020s
Locale(s): San Jose, California (Winchester Mansion/The House); Palo Alto, California

Summary: Thirty years after the Vanishing, the time when 90% of the population simply disappeared, little has been learned about the phenomenon. The scientists at Silicon Val-
ley expect a physicist from Pennsylvania to join their research effort. When she arrives, she first goes to her old family home and then to the House where her investigation into the continuing process started by the Vanishing may come to fruition.

Other books you might like:
Roger MacBride Allen, *Supernova*, 1991
    Eric Kotani, co-author
David Brin, *Earth*, 1990
C.S. Friedman, *Black Sun Rising*, 1992
Geary Gravel, *A Key for the Nonesuch*, 1990
Michael Swanwick, *Stations of the Tide*, 1991
Kathy Tyers, *Shivering World*, 1991
Vernor Vinge, *Marooned in Realtime*, 1986
Philip Wylie, *The Disappearance*, 1951
George Zebrowski, *Stranger Suns*, 1991

3725

MARK E. ROGERS

The Devouring Void
(New York: Ace, 1991)

Story type: Fantasy (Magic Conflict; Horror)
Series: Blood of the Lamb
Major character(s): Sharif ben Shaqar, Sorcerer
Time period(s): Indeterminate
Locale(s): Kadjafi Lands, Fictional Country

Summary: The wizards of the Order strike at their ancient enemies, thinking them responsible for the demonic attacks on the Masters of the Council, unaware of the treachery existing at the heart of the Order.

Other books you might like:
Mary Gentle, *Rats and Gargoyles*, 1991
P.C. Hodgell, *Dark of the Moon*, 1985
P.C. Hodgell, *God Stalk*, 1982
Brian Craig, *Zaragoz*, 1990

3726

MARK E. ROGERS

The Riddled Man
(New York: Ace, 1992)

Story type: Fantasy (Religious; Magic Conflict)
Series: Blood of the Lamb
Major character(s): Erim Sawalha, Religious (inquisitor), Sorcerer; Essaj Ben Yussef, Religious (messiah); Khaddam Al-Ra,ma, Sorcerer, Teacher
Time period(s): Indeterminate
Locale(s): Thanqurn, Fictional City; Kadjafi Lands, Fictional Country

Summary: When Essaj acquires a death sentence for Heresy, divisions within the Sharajnaghim match the divisions among the three friends while the hidden evil manipulates everyone. As do the previous two, the concluding volume makes strong use of Christian symbolism and theology.

Other books you might like:
Mary Gentle, *Rats and Gargoyles*, 1991
P.C. Hodgell, *God Stalk*, 1982

Stephen R. Lawhead, *In the Hall of the Dragon King*, 1982
C.S. Lewis, *Out of the Silent Planet*, 1943
Roger Zelazny, *Lord of Light*, 1967

3727

MARK E. ROGERS

Samurai Cat Goes to the Movies
(New York: Tor, 1994)

Story type: Science Fiction (Parody; Alternate Universe)
Series: Samurai Cat
Major character(s): Miaowara Tomokato, Animal (cat), Warrior (16th century samurai); Miaowara Shiro, Animal (cat), Adventurer; Terminationer, Robot, Martial Arts Expert
Time period(s): 1990s
Locale(s): United States; Oz, Mythical Place

Summary: While Terminationer searches for Shiro with lethal intent, Shiro and Tomokato must find their way back from Oz before they can defeat the assassin while spoofing films including *The Magnificent Seven*, *Alien* and *Star Trek*.

Other books you might like:
Douglas Adams, *The Hitchhiker's Guide to the Galaxy*, 1980
Henry N. Beard, *Bored of the Rings*, 1969
    Douglas C. Kenny, co-author
John M. Ford, *How Much for Just the Planet?*, 1987
Leah Rewolinski, *Star Wreck: The Generation Gap*, 1990
Jovial Bob Stine, *Spaceballs: The Book*, 1987
Ellis Weiner, *National Lampoon's Doon*, 1984

3728

MARK E. ROGERS

The Sword of Samurai Cat
(New York: Tor, 1991)

Story type: Science Fiction (Alternate Universe; Humor)
Series: Samurai Cat
Major character(s): Miaowara Tomokato, Animal (cat), Warrior (16th C. samurai); Miaowara Shiro, Animal (cat), Adventurer
Time period(s): 1980s
Locale(s): United States; India; At Sea (aboard the *Gross Indulgence*)

Summary: Miaowara and Shiro, having avenged the death of Miaowara's master, encounter the undead, thugees, and a mastermind terrorist in a series of adventures which parody *Indiana Jones and the Temple of Doom*, *Invasion of the Body Snatchers* and *American Ninja*.

Other books you might like:
Henry N. Beard, *Bored of the Rings*, 1969
    Douglas C. Kennedy, co-author
C.J. Cherryh, *The Pride of Chanur*, 1982
Harry Harrison, *Bill, the Galactic Hero*, 1965
Ellis Weiner, *National Lampoon's Doon*, 1984

3729

MICHAEL SCOTT ROHAN

Chase the Morning
(New York: William Morrow, 1991)

Story type: Fantasy (Contemporary)
Series: Spiral
Major character(s): Steve Fisher, Importer/Exporter; Jyp, Sailor; Mad Mall, Sailor, Warrior
Time period(s): 1990s (1991)
Locale(s): England; Alternate Universe

Summary: Steve is a dead-end yuppie who risks his life on a whim to save a stranger and gets caught up in a strange world of voodoo and pirate ships which somehow exist just outside of our world. While there is a great deal of action, the plot of the novel centers on Steve's growth as a human being.

Other books you might like:
Greg Bear, *The Infinity Concerto*, 1984
Katherine Blake, *The Interior Life*, 1990
Emma Bull, *War for the Oaks*, 1987
Tim Powers, *The Anubis Gates*, 1983

3730

MICHAEL SCOTT ROHAN

Cloud Castles
(New York: Morrow/AvoNova, 1994)

Story type: Fantasy (Contemporary; Quest)
Series: Spiral
Major character(s): Steve Fisher, Importer/Exporter; Baron Lutz von Amerningen, Nobleman; Alison Laidlaw, Police Officer (EC trade investigator)
Time period(s): 1990s
Locale(s): London, England; Frankfort, Germany; The Spiral, Mythical Place

Summary: Although at the top of his profession, Steve Fisher suffers from boredom and is distracted by feelings of stagnation. When drawn back into The Spiral by the plots of Le Stryge, his uneasy ally from *Chase the Morning*, Steve faces a supremely hellish foe and higher stakes than ever.

Other books you might like:
Greg Bear, *Songs of Earth and Power*, 1994
Katherine Blake, *The Interior Life*, 1990
Emma Bull, *War for the Oaks*, 1987
Guy Gavriel Kay, *The Summer Tree*, 1985
Tim Powers, *The Anubis Gates*, 1983

3731

MICHAEL SCOTT ROHAN

The Forge in the Forest
(New York: Avon, 1989)

Story type: Fantasy (Quest)
Series: Winter of the World
Major character(s): Elof, Magician, Blacksmith; Kermovan, Nobleman

Time period(s): Indeterminate
Locale(s): Planet—Imaginary

Summary: While trying to gain some understanding of his powers, Elof and his friends battle to turn the invasion of the Ice. They gather a small band of men and set off to find the mythical lands to the East.

Other books you might like:
J.R.R. Tolkien, *Lord of the Rings Trilogy*,
Tad Williams, *The Dragonbone Chair*, 1988

3732

MICHAEL SCOTT ROHAN

The Gates of Noon
(New York: Morrow AvoNova, 1993)

Story type: Fantasy (Contemporary)
Series: Spiral
Major character(s): Steve Fisher, Importer/Exporter; Raganda, Mythical Creature; Ape, Wizard
Time period(s): 1990s
Locale(s): London, England; The Spiral, Mythical Place; Bangkok, Thailand

Summary: Steve Fisher returns to the Spiral and his memories of strange adventures years after his last visit. He must deliver a crate of vital computer parts to Bali, which means a trip through the waters of the Spiral. Hampered by his emotional limits, Steve must grow as a person to survive.

Other books you might like:
Greg Bear, *The Infinity Concerto*, 1984
Katherine Blake, *The Interior Life*, 1990
Emma Bull, *War for the Oaks*, 1987
Guy Gavriel Kay, *The Summer Tree*, 1985
Tim Powers, *On Stranger Tides*, 1987

3733

KEN ROLSTON

Extreme Paranoia: Nobody Knows the Trouble I've Shot
(Honesdale, Pennsylvania: West End Books, 1991)

Story type: Science Fiction (Humor; Alternate Intelligence)
Series: Paranoia
Major character(s): Homer-R-ICK-3, Clone, Troubleshooter; Jakobot "Jacko" 490,9000, Robot, Sidekick; The Computer, Artificial Intelligence, Ruler
Time period(s): Indeterminate (year of the Computer 194, A.B.O.)
Locale(s): Alpha Complex, Earth

Summary: Homer and his crew of troubleshooters try to faithfully carry out The Computer's every wish while killing nearly everyone in sight. They are hampered by constantly changing demands from the Computer and low security clearances which do not allow the human clones to know their mission objectives or destinations, information entrusted only to the artificial intelligences inhabiting the tools used by the troubleshooters. This book is a tie-in to the game, Paranoia.

Other books you might like:
Douglas Adams, *The Hitchhiker's Guide to the Galaxy*, 1980
Thomas J. Bassler, *Half Past Human*, 1971
   as T.J. Bass
John DeChancie, *Paradox Alley*, 1987
John DeChancie, *Red Limit Freeway*, 1984
John DeChancie, *Starrigger*, 1983
Alan Dean Foster, *Glory Lane*, 1989
Frank Herbert, *Hellstrom's Hive*, 1973
Henry Kuttner, *Robots Have No Tails*, 1952
Frederik Pohl, *Gladiator-at-Law*, 1955
   Cyril M. Kornbluth, co-author
Robert Shea, *The Illuminatus! Trilogy*, 1988
   Robert Anton Wilson, co-author

3734

NINA ROMBERG

Shadow Walkers
(New York: Pinnacle, 1993)

Story type: Horror (Child-in-Peril; Haunted House)
Major character(s): Sadie Williams, Child (11-years-old), Runaway; Miriam Winchester, Shaman (medicine woman), Indian (Comanche); Popsy, Child, Runaway
Time period(s): 1990s (1993)
Locale(s): Gusher, Texas

Summary: A group of runaway children find a refuge for themselves in an abandoned east Texas mental institution they dub Pinecreek. Upon uncovering the institution's history as a home for soldiers who fought in Europe during World War II, the children unconsciously begin to fight the same power struggles that led to the rise of the Nazis, amplifying and reinforcing the perverse spirit that haunts the building.

Other books you might like:
Tom Elliott, *The Dwelling*, 1989
William Golding, *Lord of the Flies*, 1954
Shirley Jackson, *The Haunting of Hill House*, 1959
Al Sarrantonio, *House Haunted*, 1991

3735

NINA ROMBERG

The Spirit Stalker
(New York: Pinnacle, 1989)

Story type: Horror (Serial Killer)
Major character(s): Sunny Hansen, Artist (Commerical illustrator); Miriam, Indian (Comanche medicine woman), Abuse Victim
Time period(s): 1980s
Locale(s): Texas

Summary: Fleeing an abusive husband, Sunny Hansen finds herself threatened by a serial killer with supernatural powers.

Other books you might like:
Robert Bloch, *Psycho House*, 1990
Nicholas Conde, *In the Deep Dark Woods*, 1989
Chet Williamson, *Dreamthorp*, 1989

3736

MICHAEL ROMKEY

I, Vampire

(New York: Fawcett, 1990)

Story type: Horror (Vampire Story)
Major character(s): David Parker, Vampire; Wolfgang Amadeus Mozart, Composer, Historical Figure; Rasputin, Religious (mad monk), Historical Figure
Time period(s): 1980s
Locale(s): Paris, France; Chicago, Illinois; Bayreuth, Germany

Summary: A genteel, cultured ex-lawyer recounts the story of his life and loves and how Tatiana Romanov, daughter of Czar Nicholas II and heiress to the throne of Russia made him one of the vampire race. As he tells this story (through his diary), he tries in the present to track down an evil, aristocratic English vampire, whom he saw slaughter a young woman at Montmartre Cemetery, and waits for his mentor Mozart to take him to Bayreuth to be reunited with Tatiana, his love.

Other books you might like:
Suzy McKee Charnas, *The Vampire Tapestry*, 1980
Anne Rice, *Interview with the Vampire*, 1976
Whitley Strieber, *The Hunger*, 1981
Michael Talbot, *The Delicate Dependency*, 1982

3737

MICHAEL ROMKEY

The Vampire Papers

(New York: Fawcett, 1994)

Story type: Horror (Vampire Story)
Major character(s): Becker Thorne, Vampire; David Parker, Vampire; Victoria Buchanan, Teacher (of English)
Time period(s): 1990s (1994)
Locale(s): Jerusalem, Mississippi

Summary: Vampire Becker Thorne establishes himself at the old Arlington Plantation in Jerusalem to settle the score with four families of the old southern aristocracy against whom he has had bitter feelings for more than a century. But he is followed by David Parker, a member of the Illuminati, whose task it is to turn vampire energies to positive historical and cultural ends and protect mortals against the bloodlust of the undead.

Other books you might like:
Scott Ciencin, *Parliament of Blood*, 1992
Pat Graversen, *Sweet Blood*, 1992
Wendy Haley, *This Dark Paradise*, 1994
Dan Simmons, *Carrion Comfort*, 1989
Karen E. Taylor, *Bitter Blood*, 1994

3738

MICHAEL ROMKEY

The Vampire Princess

(New York: Fawcett, 1996)

Story type: Horror (Vampire Story)

Major character(s): David Parker, Vampire; Nicoletta Vittorini di Medusa, Vampire; Carrie Anderson, Doctor
Time period(s): 1990s (1996)
Locale(s): Miami, Florida

Summary: A series of vampiric deaths on board the *Atlantic Princess*, bound from Miami to Italy, reveals the handiwork of Princess Nicoletta, a vampire who spurns the rule of the Illuminati that she and all other vampires follow to keep their activities secret from the human beings they co-exist with. Interspersed with accounts of the on-board adventures is the princess's narrative of her upbringing and vampirization.

Other books you might like:
Scott Ciencin, *The Vampire Odyssey*, 1992
Mick Farren, *The Time of Feasting*, 1995
Floyd Kemske, *Human Remains*, 1995
Fred Saberhagen, *A Sharpness on the Neck*, 1995
Karen E. Taylor, *Blood Secrets*, 1994

3739

JOEL ROSENBERG

D'Shai

(New York: Ace, 1991)

Story type: Fantasy (Mystery)
Series: D'Shai
Major character(s): Kami Khuzud, Entertainer (acrobat); Narantir, Wizard; Lord Toshtai, Ruler
Time period(s): Indeterminate
Locale(s): Den Oroshtai, Fictional Country; D'Shai, Fictional Country

Summary: Kami is twice trapped by D'Shai's rigid caste system. He is a peasant in love with a daughter of the upper classes and he is an acrobat with no magical talent for acrobatics. But when he is falsely accused of a nobleman's murder, Kami must defy tradition and find his special power to save his life and name.

Other books you might like:
Steven Brust, *Jhereg*, 1983
Steven Brust, *To Reign in Hell*, 1984
Brian Daley, *A Tapestry of Magics*, 1983
Robert Silverberg, *Lord Valentine's Castle*, 1980
Roger Zelazny, *Nine Princes in Amber*, 1970

3740

JOEL ROSENBERG

The Fire Duke

(New York: AvoNova, 1995)

Story type: Fantasy (Alternate World; Magic Conflict)
Series: Keepers of the Hidden Ways
Major character(s): Thorian "Torrie" Thorsen, Martial Arts Expert (fencer), Young Man; Ian Silverstein, Martial Arts Expert (fencer), Hero; Orfindel "Hosea Lincoln", Deity (Old One), Handyman (the Builder)
Time period(s): 1990s (1995)
Locale(s): Hardwood, North Dakota; Tir Na Nog, Fictional Country; Falias, Fictional City

Summary: While on vacation with friends at his parents' farm in North Dakota, Torrie Thorsen learns that his father and Uncle Hosea long ago came through the Hidden Ways to this world, fleeing the machinations of the Fire Duke. Now Torrie and his father lie imprisoned in His Warmth's stronghold, having failed to rescue his kidnapped mother and girlfriend. Ian and Hosea must now attempt to free all four of them before the Duke's evil schemes come to fruition. First in the series.

Other books you might like:
Steven Brust, *Jhereg*, 1983
Charles de Lint, *The Little Country*, 1991
Gordon R. Dickson, *The Dragon and the George*, 1976
Gordon R. Dickson, *The Dragon, the Earl, and the Troll*, 1994
Geary Gravel, *A Key for the Nonesuch*, 1990
Barbara Hambly, *The Silent Tower*, 1986
Christopher Stasheff, *The Witch Doctor*, 1995
Vivian Vande Velde, *User Unfriendly*, 1991

3741

JOEL ROSENBERG

Hero
(New York: Roc, 1990)

Story type: Science Fiction (Military)
Major character(s): Ari Hanavi, Warrior (hereditary), Military Personnel (private); Isadore Lipschitz, Military Personnel (sargeant); Shimon Bar-el, Military Personnel (general)
Time period(s): Indeterminate Future
Locale(s): Metzadan, Planet—Imaginary

Summary: A commander unconventionally precipitates victory against overwhelming opposition by calling for an artillary barrage to be laid down on his troops' current position, and ordering his troops to take the enemy position or die on the spot. Sequel to *Not for Glory* (1988).

Other books you might like:
Gordon R. Dickson, *The Tactics of Mistake*, 1971
David Drake, *The Forlorn Hope*, 1984
David Drake, *Rolling Hot*, 1989
Roland J. Green, *Squadron Alert*, 1989
Robert A. Heinlein, *Starship Troopers*, 1959
Jerry Pournelle, *Falkenberg's Legion*, 1990

3742

JOEL ROSENBERG

Hour of the Octopus
(New York: Ace, 1994)

Story type: Fantasy (Mystery; Political)
Series: D'Shai
Major character(s): Kami Khuzud, Detective (Discoverer-of-Truths); Lady ViKay, Noblewoman, Fiance(e); Dun Lidjun, Nobleman, Martial Arts Expert
Time period(s): Indeterminate
Locale(s): D'Shai, Fictional Country

Summary: Kami Dan'Shir addresses a royal conundrum which brings him an uncomfortable opportunity to prove his recently recognized skill at detection when clues frame the groom as murderer in an attempt to foil a wedding.

Other books you might like:
Steven Brust, *Jhereg*, 1983
James Clavell, *Shogun*, 1975
Glen Cook, *Dread Brass Shadows*, 1990
Glen Cook, *Sweet Silver Blues*, 1987
Randall Garrett, *Murder and Magic*, 1979
Randall Garrett, *Too Many Magicians*, 1967
Simon R. Green, *Hawk & Fisher*, 1990
Barry Hughart, *Bridge of Birds*, 1984

3743

JOEL ROSENBERG

The Road Home
(New York: Roc, 1995)

Story type: Fantasy (Adventure; Sword and Sorcery)
Series: Guardians of the Flame
Major character(s): Jason Cullinane, Warrior, Nobleman (baron); Walter Slovotsky, Warrior; Ahira Bandylegs, Mythical Creature (dwarf), Guardian (Jason's)
Time period(s): Indeterminate
Locale(s): Biemestren, Fictional City; Pandathaway, Fictional City; The Empire, Fictional Country

Summary: In order to find his former best friend, Mikyn, and stop him from single-handedly wiping out all slavers to keep the legend of the Warrior alive, Jason and Ahira form a distasteful alliance with Toryn, a Journeyman Slaver under a geas from his guild to aid them. Escaping an uncomfortable political situation in Emperor Thomen's stronghold, Walter Slovotsky sets off for Castle Cullinane where he hopes to hitch a ride with Ellegon, a dragon of his acquaintance, find Jason and Ahira, and help them with their task. Seventh in the series.

Other books you might like:
Steven Brust, *Jhereg*, 1983
C.J. Cherryh, *Faery in Shadow*, 1994
Jo Clayton, *Wildfire*, 1992
Glen Cook, *The Black Company*, 1984
Barbara Hambly, *Dragonsbane*, 1987
Barbara Hambly, *The Ladies of Mandrigyn*, 1984
Robert A. Heinlein, *Glory Road*, 1963

3744

JOEL ROSENBERG

The Road to Ehvenor
(New York: Roc, 1991)

Story type: Fantasy (Magic Conflict)
Series: Guardians of the Flame
Major character(s): Walter Slovotsky, Warrior; Andrea Cullinane, Wizard
Time period(s): Indeterminate
Locale(s): Ehvenor, Fictional City

Summary: When magic from Faerie begins to infest the area around Ehvenor, a border town between Faerie and the mortal realm, Walter Slovotsky and his companions respond to pleas for help, not realizing the magical anomaly represents the opening round of a war to be inflicted on the mortal realm.

Other books you might like:
Stephen Billias, *Horrible Humes*, 1991
Emma Bull, *War for the Oaks*, 1987
Andre Norton, *The Elvenbane*, 1991
   Mercedes Lackey, co-author
Michael Reaves, *Street Magic*, 1991
Will Shetterly, *Elsewhere*, 1991
Terri Windling, *Borderland*, 1986
   Mark Alan Arnold, co-editor
Terri Windling, *Bordertown*, 1986
   Mark Alan Arnold, co-editor
Terri Windling, *Life on the Border*, 1991
   editor

3745

JOEL ROSENBERG

The Silver Stone

(New York: Avon, 1996)

Story type: Fantasy (Alternate World; Magic Conflict)
Series: Keepers of the Hidden Ways
Major character(s): Ian Silverstein, Martial Arts Expert (fencer), Hero; Thorian ''Torrie'' Thorsen, Martial Arts Expert (fencer), Young Man; Maggie Christensen, Martial Arts Expert (fencer), Girlfriend
Time period(s): Indeterminate
Locale(s): Hardwood, North Dakota; Tir Na Nog, Fictional Country; Vandescard, Fictional Country

Summary: Journeying back to Tir Na Nog to save Orfindel, the ailing Old One, Ian Silverstein finds himself a reluctant messenger for Odin himself, carrying the great god's spear and a warning not to disturb his peace with plans of war. While the power of the spear causes the men of Vandescard to look on Ian as the possible Promised Warrior, the powerful ruling family sees him as a potential threat to their plans. Unfortunately, Ian can find no way to make either side see Odin's point of view.

Other books you might like:
Steven Brust, *Jhereg*, 1983
Eve Forward, *Villains by Necessity*, 1995
Craig Shaw Gardner, *Dragon Sleeping*, 1994
Barbara Hambly, *The Silent Tower*, 1986
Diana L. Paxson, *The Dragons of the Rhine*, 1995

3746

MARY ROSENBLUM

Chimera

(New York: Ballantine Del Rey, 1993)

Story type: Science Fiction (Cyberpunk; Arts)

Major character(s): Jewel Martina, Health Care Professional; Flander, Computer Expert; David Chen, Artist, Computer Expert
Time period(s): Indeterminate Future
Locale(s): Erebus Complex, Antarctica; California

Summary: To escape the 'burbs, Jewel Martina manages to get enough education to become a med tech, able to keep the bodies of powerful, elderly citizens alive while they spend their time in virtual reality in the computer network. David Chen, a brilliant virtual artist, and his partner, Flander, befriend Jewel when she saves Flander's life. Jewel tries to discover the identity of the mountain lion which seems able to manifest itself in reality outside of virtual space.

Other books you might like:
David Brin, *Earth*, 1990
Pat Cadigan, *Synners*, 1991
Jean Mark Gawron, *Dream of Glass*, 1993
Jack C. Haldeman II, *High Steel*, 1993
   Jack Dann, co-author
James P. Hogan, *The Multiplex Man*, 1992
Neal Stephenson, *Snow Crash*, 1992
Amy Thomson, *Virtual Girl*, 1993

3747

MARY ROSENBLUM

The Drylands

(New York: Ballantine Del Rey, 1993)

Story type: Science Fiction (Post-Holocaust; Political)
Major character(s): Carter Voltaire, Military Personnel; Nita Montoya, Psychic; Dan Greeley, Activist, Farmer
Time period(s): 21st century
Locale(s): Columbia River Valley, Oregon

Summary: Charged with the unpopular job of rationing scarce water in drought-stricken America, the Army Corps of Engineers must stop the sabotage of the Columbia Riverbed Pipeline, a job which has already cost the previous commander of The Dalles base his life. Carter Voltaire, the new C.O., must decide whom he can trust: General Hastings, his superior officer; Dan Greeley, leader of the disgruntled farmers whose fields are drying up; Johnny Seldon, his friend and a member of the powerful Water Policy Committee; or Nita Montoya, who fears persecution if she reveals her abnormal talents.

Other books you might like:
David Brin, *The Postman*, 1985
John Brunner, *Stand on Zanzibar*, 1968
Arsen Darnay, *A Hostage for Hinterland*, 1976
Gordon R. Dickson, *Wolf and Iron*, 1990
Bill Dolan, *Afrikorps*, 1991
Gregory Feeley, *The Oxygen Barons*, 1990
Ursula K. Le Guin, *The Lathe of Heaven*, 1971
Colleen McCullough, *A Creed for the Third Millenium*, 1985
John Wyndham, *Re-Birth*, 1955

3748

MARY ROSENBLUM

The Stone Garden

(New York: Ballantine Del Rey, 1995)

Story type: Science Fiction (Arts; First Contact)
Major character(s): Michael Tryon, Artist; Margarita Espinoza, Artist; Xia Quejaches, Dancer, Wanderer
Time period(s): Indeterminate Future
Locale(s): Old Taos, New Mexico; Upper New York, Space Station

Summary: After Margarita writes claiming to be his daughter, Michael realizes he can no longer hide in his Taos studio. His art, layering emotion on sensitive space stones, has taken too much from him, and he decides that to survive he must get away from his past, preserved all around him in his stones. A powerful enemy attacks Michael when he leaves Taos to meet his potential daughter. Found a month later, he discovers stone sculptors committing suicide but believes their involuntary acts may have an outside cause.

Other books you might like:
John Barnes, *A Million Open Doors*, 1992
Jack C. Haldeman II, *High Steel*, 1993
    Jack Dann, co-author
Mark S. Geston, *Mirror to the Sky*, 1992
Ernest Hogan, *Cortez on Jupiter*, 1990
Spider Robinson, *Stardance*, 1979
    Jeanne Robinson, co-author

3749

MARY ROSENBLUM

Synthesis & Other Virtual Realities

(Sauk City, Wisconsin: Arkham House, 1996)

Story type: Science Fiction (Collection; Dystopian)
Summary: Contains nine stories, frequently dark in tone, with several set in the milieu of *The Drylands*. Themes include nature out of balance, family relationships, virtual reality, and the difficulties of emigration.

Other books you might like:
Alexander Jablokov, *The Breath of Suspension*, 1994
John Kessel, *Meeting in Infinity*, 1992
Nancy Kress, *The Aliens of Earth*, 1993
Rebecca Ore, *Alien Bootlegger and Other Stories*, 1993
Michael Swanwick, *Gravity's Angels*, 1991
James Tiptree Jr., *Her Smoke Rose Up Forever*, 1990

3750

DAVID D. ROSS

The Argus Gambit

(New York: St. Martin's Press, 1989)

Story type: Science Fiction (Espionage Thriller)
Series: Dreamers of the Day
Major character(s): Mel Hardrim, Police Officer; Jeffrey Shefferton, Political Figure (President)

Time period(s): 21st century
Locale(s): United States

Summary: Police officer Mel Hardrim thinks he's guarding a noted scientist. After the man is murdered, Hardrim discovers he was a fake and that the real scientist has disappeared. His career in ruins, Hardrim attempts to solve the murder, but finds himself drawn into a complex web of political intrigue involving the mysterious Argus Society, a secret organization apparently bent on taking over the world.

Other books you might like:
Joe Haldeman, *Buying Time*, 1989
Thomas Pynchon, *Gravity's Rainbow*, 1973
Bruce Sterling, *Islands in the Net*, 1988

3751

DAVID D. ROSS

The Eighth Rank

(New York: St. Martin's Press, 1991)

Story type: Science Fiction (Political; Techno-Thriller)
Series: Dreamers of the Day
Major character(s): Jason Scott, Administrator (Sunside Project); Jeffrey Shefferton, Political Figure (president); Lenore Lippman, Computer Expert, Cyborg
Time period(s): 21st century
Locale(s): United States; Moon (Earth's); Icarus, Asteroid

Summary: Repeal of the 31st Amendment reopens the United States for trade with the rest of the world. Food is scarce, technology is feared, and the Sunside Project to produce food is a hoax. Working for the project is very dangerous, not only for those located off Earth, but also for those having to contend with the polical and military hostilities on Earth. This novel is a sequel to *The Argus Gambit*.

Other books you might like:
Isaac Asimov, *Foundation*, 1951
David Brin, *Earth*, 1990
Philip K. Dick, *The Unteleported Man*, 1983
    revised
Gregory Feeley, *The Oxygen Barons*, 1990
Michael Flynn, *In the Country of the Blind*, 1990
Michael P. Kube-McDowell, *The Quiet Pools*, 1990
Alis A. Rasmussen, *A Passage of Stars*, 1990
Allen Steele, *Orbital Decay*, 1989
Bruce Sterling, *Islands in the Net*, 1988
A.E. van Vogt, *The World of Null-A*, 1950
David Wingrove, *The Middle Kingdom*, 1990

3752

THEODORE ROSZAK

Flicker

(New York: Summit Books, 1991)

Story type: Horror (Mystery)
Major character(s): John Gates, Student (film student); Simon Dunkle, Director (film director); Clare Swann, Critic (film critic)
Time period(s): 1990s

Locale(s): Los Angeles, California

Summary: While researching the work of Depression-era German expressionist horror film director Max Castle, film student John Gates discovers that Castle was raised and educated by the Cathars, a heretical sect of Albigensian Christians involved in filmmaking since its inception, who train their acolytes to encode films with subliminal messages that promulgate their amoral viewpoint. Gates' investigations draw attention to him and plunge him into a dark world of paranoia and conspiracy.

Other books you might like:
Ramsey Campbell, *Ancient Images*, 1989
Jonathan Carroll, *A Child Across the Sky*, 1989
Umberto Eco, *Foucault's Pendulum*, 1988

3753
THEODORE ROSZAK

The Memoirs of Elizabeth Frankenstein
(New York: Random House, 1995)

Story type: Horror (Occult)
Major character(s): Victor Frankenstein, Scientist; Elizabeth Frankenstein, Young Woman; Seraphina, Witch
Time period(s): 1780s; 1790s
Locale(s): Geneva, Switzerland

Summary: Young Elizabeth Lavenza becomes the ward of Baron and Lady Caroline Frankenstein, and the playmate and eventual wife of their son, Victor. Elizabeth is indoctrinated into the witch cult Caroline belongs to and encouraged to embrace romantic ideals regarding her relationship to the natural and supernatural in this feminist retelling of the Frankenstein tale. The Story is presented as diaries edited by Robert Walton, the explorer who preserved the original account of Victor Frankenstein's ordeal with his monster in Mary Shelley's original novel.

Other books you might like:
Brian W. Aldiss, *Frankenstein Unbound*, 1973
Emmanuel Carrere, *Gothic Romance*, 1984
Marie Kiraly, *Mina*, 1994
Mary Shelley, *Frankenstein*, 1818

3754
JANE ROUTLEY

Mage Heart
(New York: Morrow/AvoNova, 1996)

Story type: Fantasy (Magic Conflict)
Major character(s): Dion, Magician, Student; Kitten "Our Lady of Roses" Avignon, Noblewoman
Time period(s): Indeterminate
Locale(s): Gallia, Fictional City; Moria, Fictional Country

Summary: Despite Dion's especially powerful magical abilities, society's conventions restrict her practice to mundane healing. After entering the Gallian College of Magic, the first woman to do so, Dion reluctantly accepts Duke Leon's order to serve his favorite mistress, an appointment which fosters a

broader application of Dion's talents as an evil necromancer presses his attack on Kitten. First novel.

Other books you might like:
Lois McMaster Bujold, *The Spirit Ring*, 1992
Lynn Flewelling, *Luck in the Shadows*, 1996
Laurell K. Hamilton, *Nightseer*, 1992
Guy Gavriel Kay, *A Song for Arbonne*, 1993
Caroline Stevermer, *A College of Magics*, 1994
Paula Volsky, *Illusion*, 1992

3755
MICHAEL ROWE, Editor
THOMAS S. ROCHE, Co-Editor

Sons of Darkness: Tales of Men, Blood and Immortality
(Boston: Cleis Press, 1996)

Story type: Horror (Anthology; Vampire Story)

Summary: These 12 stories with strong erotic subtexts all feature male vampires. C. Dean Anderrson's "My Greatest Fear" and Nancy Kilpatrick's "The Game" feature vampires who have the tables turned on them by their male lovers. Carol Queen's "Feeding" tells of a vampire chef who finds a restaurant client his ultimate meal, while Wickie Stamps' "Retribution for Golgotha" concerns a vampire who tracks down the blood relatives of those responsible for his death alongside Jesus Christ on Golgotha. Ron Oliver's "Bela Lugosi's Dead" is about a young boy who immerses himself too deeply in the vampire imagery of horror films and music. In the book's one reprint, Poppy Z. Brite's "His Mouth Shall Taste of Wormwood," vampires troll the decadent Gothic underground of New Orleans.

Other books you might like:
Poppy Z. Brite, *Love in Vein*, 1994
 Martin H. Greenberg, co-editor
Poppy Z. Brite, *Love in Vein II*, 1997
 Martin H. Greenberg, co-editor
Cecilia Tan, *Blood Kiss: Vampire Erotica*, 1995
 editor

3756
CHRISTOPHER ROWLEY

Battledragon
(New York: Roc, 1995)

Story type: Fantasy (Adventure)
Series: Bazil Broketail
Major character(s): Bazil Broketail, Mythical Creature (dragon), Military Personnel; Relkin, Military Personnel, Companion
Time period(s): Indeterminate
Locale(s): Argonath Region, Fictional Country; At Sea; Eigo, Mythical Place

Summary: After hearing intelligence concerning the development of weapons of unthinkable destruction by the Master of Darkness, Argonath's emperor dispatches a fleet, including

Relkin and the 109th Marneri Dragons, to thwart the upcoming invasion from the distant continent of Eigo.

Other books you might like:
Gael Baudino, *Duel of Dragons*, 1991
Don Callander, *Dragon Companion*, 1994
Gordon R. Dickson, *The Dragon at War*, 1992
Ursula K. Le Guin, *A Wizard of Earthsea*, 1968
Anne McCaffrey, *Dragonriders of Pern*, 1988

3757

CHRISTOPHER ROWLEY

Bazil Broketail
(New York: Roc, 1992)

Story type: Fantasy (Adventure)
Series: Bazil Broketail
Major character(s): Bazil Broketail, Mythical Creature (dragon), Warrior; Relkin, Military Personnel, Companion (Bazil's); Lessis of Valmes, Witch, Heroine
Time period(s): Indeterminate
Locale(s): Marneri, Fictional City (Argonath Region); Ryetelth, Mythical Place

Summary: While fighting to qualify for military service, Bazil suffers a treacherous attack that severs his prehensile tail, an injury which would normally condemn Bazil and Relkin to farm labor. When Relkin searches for an immediate magical cure, Lessis comes to their rescue, allowing flawed regrowth of the tail's tip and allowing Bazil and Relkin to aid the witches in their desperate attempt to save everyone from The Doom's attempt to dominate the human realms.

Other books you might like:
Richard Adams, *Shardik*, 1975
Anne McCaffrey, *Dragonflight*, 1968
Anne McCaffrey, *Dragonquest*, 1970
Anne McCaffrey, *The White Dragon*, 1978

3758

CHRISTOPHER ROWLEY

Dragons of War
(New York: Roc, 1994)

Story type: Fantasy (Adventure)
Series: Bazil Broketail
Major character(s): Bazil Broketail, Mythical Creature (dragon), Military Personnel; Relkin, Military Personnel, Companion (Bazil's)
Time period(s): Indeterminate
Locale(s): Argonath Region, Fictional Country; Kenor, Fictional Country

Summary: Bazil's surprise reunion results in a murder charge against Relkin at a time when the empire's survival depends on the Dragon Legions as waves of giants, imps and trolls threaten to overwhelm all.

Other books you might like:
Gael Baudino, *Dragonsword*, 1991
Gael Baudino, *Duel of Dragons*, 1991
Gordon R. Dickson, *The Dragon at War*, 1992

Anne McCaffrey, *Dragonflight*, 1968
Lawrence Watt-Evans, *The Blood of a Dragon*, 1991

3759

CHRISTOPHER ROWLEY

The Founder
(New York: Ballantine/Del Rey, 1989)

Story type: Science Fiction (First Contact)
Series: Fenrille
Major character(s): Dane Fundan, Heir, Spaceman
Time period(s): 25th century
Locale(s): *Founder*, Spaceship; Fenrille, Planet—Imaginary

Summary: Earth and the space habitats are about to go to war over who controls the solar system. To escape the impending holocaust, Dane Fundan builds an interstellar colony ship. Reaching another star system, however, the colonists find themselves immediately immersed in even more treachery and danger. Prequel to *The War for Eternity*.

Other books you might like:
Gregory Benford, *Tides of Light*, 1989
Dave Duncan, *Strings*, 1990
Vonda N. McIntyre, *Starfarers*, 1989
Susan Shwartz, *Heritage of Flight*, 1989

3760

CHRISTOPHER ROWLEY

A Sword for a Dragon
(New York: Roc, 1993)

Story type: Fantasy (Adventure)
Series: Bazil Broketail
Major character(s): Bazil Broketail, Mythical Creature (dragon), Military Personnel; Relkin, Military Personnel, Companion (Bazil's)
Time period(s): Indeterminate
Locale(s): Argonath Region, Fictional Country

Summary: Receiving paramount decorations for valor during their first campaign, Relkin and Bazil recruit a former battle dragon into the 109th Marneri Dragons and prepare for another glorious campaign. Plans derail briefly as sinister forces ally with traitorous companions to kidnap Relkin and Bazil for study.

Other books you might like:
Gael Baudino, *Dragonsword*, 1991
Gordon R. Dickson, *The Dragon and the George*, 1976
Gordon R. Dickson, *The Dragon at War*, 1992
Gordon R. Dickson, *The Dragon on the Border*, 1992
Anne McCaffrey, *Dragonflight*, 1968
Anne McCaffrey, *Dragonquest*, 1970
Anne McCaffrey, *The White Dragon*, 1978

CHRISTOPHER ROWLEY

To a Highland Nation
(New York: Ballantine Del Rey, 1993)

Story type: Science Fiction (Immortality; Political)
Series: Fenrille
Major character(s): Fair Fundan, Rancher (chitin talker), Leader; Hof Wiltin, Rancher, Warrior; Martin Overed, Government Official
Time period(s): 26th century
Locale(s): Fenrille, Planet—Imaginary

Summary: Human colonists and native Fein must band together to resist an attack and attempted takeover by greedy humans from off planet. The attackers intend to acquire total control of the longevity drug produced by native insects.

Other books you might like:
C.J. Cherryh, *Serpent's Reach*, 1980
Frank Herbert, *Dune*, 1965
James H. Schmitz, *The Demon Breed*, 1968
Joan Slonczewski, *Daughter of Elysium*, 1993
Joan Slonczewski, *A Door into Ocean*, 1986
Cordwainer Smith, *Norstrilia*, 1975

CHRISTOPHER ROWLEY

The Wizard and the Floating City
(New York: Roc, 1996)

Story type: Fantasy (Quest; Magic Conflict)
Major character(s): Danais Evander, Royalty (prince), Heir—Dispossessed; Serena, Royalty (princess); Gadjung, Wizard
Time period(s): Indeterminate
Locale(s): Bakan, Fictional Country; Monjon, Fictional City

Summary: Having knowingly offended an evil wizard, the exiled prince Evander barely escapes drowning at sea, only to find that part of his skin has metamorphosed into a lizard's. Hoping to find a cure for his deformity, he travels with two imps to the magic city of Monjon, which floats 10 feet above the land due to the power of the Thymnal. First, he must rescue a princess, battle wicked witches, flee fantastic beasts, and defeat an evil wizard. Set in the *Bazil Broketail* Universe.

Other books you might like:
Lynn Abbey, *The Wooden Sword*, 1991
C.J. Cherryh, *Chernevog*, 1990
Simon R. Green, *Blood and Honor*, 1993
Barbara Hambly, *The Dark Hand of Magic*, 1990
Elizabeth Ann Scarborough, *Bronwyn's Bane*, 1983

P.D. ROZZI

Waltz with Evil
(New York: Zebra, 1991)

Story type: Horror (Haunted House)

Major character(s): Tommy Clarkston, Child; Dan Cook, Police Officer; Rachel Clarkston, Spirit
Time period(s): 1980s (1988)
Locale(s): Clinton

Summary: One hundred years ago, as she was being buried alive, Rachel Clarkston vowed she would return from the dead to claim her son. Having fufilled the first part of her promise by absorbing a mortal soul to reconstitute her flesh, Rachel next lures Tommy Clarkston, her youngest lineal descendant, to her former seaside home.

Other books you might like:
Campbell Black, *Letters from the Dead*, 1985
Diane Guest, *Lullaby*, 1990
Al Sarrantonio, *House Haunted*, 1991

PETER RUBIE

Werewolf
(Stamford, Connecticut: Longmeadow Press, 1991)

Story type: Horror (Werewolf Story)
Major character(s): George Llewellyn, Police Officer; Nevil Stimpson, Convict (rehabilitated child molester); Vera Armstrong, Nurse
Time period(s): 1940s (1941)
Locale(s): London, England (East End)

Summary: Detective Sergeant George Llewellyn learns to rue the day that he intervened during a childbirth at a gypsy settlement on the outskirts of London in 1931 and was cursed for his interference. Ten years later, during the Nazi blitz of London, the werewolf offspring of that birth runs amok through the city, and Llewellyn's only hope is to team up with an enemy he once put behind bars to stop the bloody murder spree.

Other books you might like:
Clive Barker, ''Twilight at the Towers'', 1989
  in *Cabal*
Richard Jaccoma, *The Werewolf's Tale*, 1988
Robert R. McCammon, *The Wolf's Hour*, 1989
H. Warner Munn, *The Werewolf of Ponkert*, 1958
Jane Rice, ''The Refugee'', 1990
  in *Rivals of Weird Tales*

RUDY RUCKER

The Hacker and the Ants
(New York: Morrow/AvoNova, 1994)

Story type: Science Fiction (Alternate Intelligence; Cyberpunk)
Major character(s): Jerzy Rugby, Computer Expert, Detective—Amateur; Susan Poker, Real Estate Agent; Riscky ''Hex DEF6'' Pharbeque, Computer Expert, Criminal
Time period(s): 21st century
Locale(s): Silicon Valley, California; Cyberspace

Summary: Jerzy Rugby feels set up for blame when an artificial life program designed as a computerized testing program infects television sets. Impending local and federal charges limit Jerzy's options as he develops new code and searches for the origin of and cure for the plague of crafty AIs.

Other books you might like:
David Brin, *Earth*, 1990
Pat Cadigan, *Mindplayers*, 1987
Victor Milan, *The Cybernetic Samurai*, 1985
Neal Stephenson, *Snow Crash*, 1992
Amy Thomson, *Virtual Girl*, 1993

3766

RUDY RUCKER

The Hollow Earth: The Narrative of Mason Algiers Reynolds of Virginia

(New York: William Morrow, 1990)

Story type: Science Fiction (Adventure; Alternate Universe)
Major character(s): Mason Algiers Reynolds, Fugitive; Otha, Slave
Time period(s): 1830s
Locale(s): Alternate Earth (Pre-Civil War Virginia)

Summary: After a murder, Mason and Otha flee Virginia, journeying to Antarctica where they travel through a hole into the Earth. There they discover a rich and varied land and continue their adventures.

Other books you might like:
Greg Bear, *Eon*, 1985
Greg Bear, *Eternity*, 1988
Edgar Rice Burroughs, *Pellucidar*, 1923
John Varley, *Titan*, 1979
Jules Verne, *Journey to the Center of the Earth*, 1864

3767

RUDY RUCKER

Transreal!

(Englewood, Colorado: WSC Books, 1991)

Story type: Science Fiction (Collection)

Summary: This volume contains an introduction by Robert Sheckley with Rudy Rucker material presented in four parts labelled books, the first of which, "Light Fuse and Get Away," contains 21 poems written 1975-1982. Book two, titled "The 57th Franz Kafka," contains 18 stories written 1980-1983. Book three, titled "Weird Screens," contains 15 stories written 1984-1990 including three collaborative efforts, "Storming the Cosmos" written with Bruce Sterling, "Probability Pipeline" with Marc Laidlaw and "Instability" with Paul deFilipo. The fourth, titled "Some of the Dharma," includes 11 articles.

Other books you might like:
Isaac Asimov, *The Complete Stories - Volume 1*, 1990
Alfred Bester, *Star Light, Star Bright*, 1976
Michael Flynn, *The Nanotech Chronicles*, 1991
Alan Dean Foster, *With Friends Like These...*, 1977
Larry Niven, *Neutron Star*, 1968
Larry Niven, *Tales of Known Space*, 1975

Cordwainer Smith, *The Best of Cordwainer Smith*, 1975
Marc Stiegler, *The Gentle Seduction*, 1990
William Tenn, *The Seven Sexes*, 1968
John Varley, *Blue Champagne*, 1986
John Varley, *The Persistence of Vision*, 1978

3768

MATT RUFF

Fool on the Hill

(New York: Atlantic Monthly Press, 1989)

Story type: Fantasy (Light Fantasy)
Major character(s): Luther, Student; Zephyr, Mythical Creature (Sprite)
Time period(s): 1980s
Locale(s): Ithaca, New York (Cornell University)

Summary: An assortment of characters, from sprites to humans, cats to dogs, and William F. Buckley to an evil thing buried in the boneyard are cast in this story. Eventually, most of the characters come together to fight the evil thing buried in the boneyard.

Other books you might like:
Gael Baudino, *Duel of Dragons*, 1990
Barry B. Longyear, *The God Box*, 1989
Ian Watson, *Queenmagic, Kingmagic*, 1988

3769

KRISTINE KATHRYN RUSCH
KEVIN J. ANDERSON, Co-Author

Afterimage

(New York: Roc, 1992)

Story type: Fantasy (Mystery; Contemporary)
Major character(s): Rebecca "Michael Kerr" Tamerlane, Detective—Amateur, Mythical Creature (shapeshifter); Matthew Adolphus, Detective—Police; Gantha, Alien (Darkling), Sorceress (shapeshifter)
Time period(s): 1980s (1989)
Locale(s): Santa Cruz, California

Summary: Brutally raped and murdered by a serial killer, Rebecca finds herself saved by mysterious strangers who change her shape. Transformed into the image she remembers last, that of the serial killer, Rebecca must find the strangers to regain her form before police arrest her for the serial killings.

Other books you might like:
Kevin J. Anderson, *Gamearth*, 1989
Kevin J. Anderson, *Gameplay*, 1989
Kevin J. Anderson, *Game's End*, 1990
Glen Cook, *Red Iron Nights*, 1991
Peter R. Emshwiller, *The Host*, 1991
Peter R. Emshwiller, *Short Blade*, 1992
Mercedes Lackey, *Burning Water*, 1989
Mercedes Lackey, *Children of the Night*, 1990
Mercedes Lackey, *Jinx High*, 1991
James D. Priest, *Kirins: The Spell of No'an*, 1990

3770

KRISTINE KATHRYN RUSCH, Editor
EDWARD L. FERMAN, Co-Editor

The Best From Fantasy & Science Fiction: A 45th Anniversary Anthology

(New York: St. Martin's Press, 1994)

Story type: Science Fiction (Anthology)
Series: Best From Fantasy and Science Fiction
Summary: This 26th volume in the series contains a three-page introduction by Ferman, a three-page introduction by Rusch plus individual introductions to 19 stories encompassing science fiction, fantasy and horror representative of 1988-1993. These include one Hugo Award winner, Mike Resnick's ''Kirinyaga''; one Nebula Award nominee, Carolyn Ives Gilman's ''The Honeycrafters''; two Nebula Award winners, Alan Brennert's ''Ma Qui'' and Mike Connor's ''Guide Dog''; one Nebula Award winner and World Fantasy Award winner, Joe Haldeman's ''Graves''; and the first short piece from novelist Richard Bowes. Other authors include Ray Aldridge, Terry Bisson, Harlan Ellison, Karen Joy Fowler, Thomas Ligotti, James Morrow, Robert Reed, and Gene Wolf.

Other books you might like:
Avram Davidson, *The Best From Fantasy and Science Fiction: 12-14*, 1963-1965
editor
Edward L. Ferman, *The Best From Fantasy and Science Fiction: 15-20*, 1966-1973
editor
Edward L. Ferman, *The Best From Fantasy and Science Fiction: A Special 25th Anniversary Anthology*, 1974
editor
Edward L. Ferman, *The Best From Fantasy and Science Fiction: A 40th Anniversary Anthology*, 1989
editor
Robert P. Mills, *The Best From Fantasy and Science Fiction: 9-11*, 1960-1962
editor

3771

KRISTINE KATHRYN RUSCH, Editor

The Best of Pulphouse: The Hardback Magazine

(New York: St. Martins Press, 1991)

Story type: Science Fiction (Anthology)
Series: Pulphouse: The Hardback Magazine
Summary: This title contains a foreward by Kate Wilhelm and an introduction by the editor plus 25 stories, each with a brief introduction, previously published in *Pulphouse: The Hardback Magazine*, the hardcover periodical appearing 1988-1991. This volume draws on the broad range of the periodical's material including science fiction such as Charles de Lint's ''The Soft Whisper of Midnight Snow,'' and horror such as Edward Bryant's ''While She Was Out.'' This title includes some newer authors plus more established genre

authors including George Alec Effinger, Harlan Ellison, Lisa Goldstein, Steve Perry, Harry Turtledove, Lisa Tuttle, J.N. Williamson, William F. Wu and Jane Yolen.

Other books you might like:
Damien Broderick, *Strange Attractors: Original Australian Speculative Fiction*, 1985
editor
Algis Budrys, *L. Ron Hubbard Presents Writers of the Future, Volume II*, 1986
editor
Harlan Ellison, *Again, Dangerous Visions*, 1972
editor
Harlan Ellison, *Dangerous Visions*, 1967
editor
Judith Merril, *Tesseracts*, 1985
editor
Bruce Sterling, *Mirrorshades: The Cyberpunk Anthology*, 1986
editor

3772

KRISTINE KATHRYN RUSCH

The Changeling

(New York: Bantam Spectra, 1996)

Story type: Fantasy (Political; Magic Conflict)
Series: Fey
Major character(s): Nicholas, Royalty; Jewel, Mythical Creature (fey), Royalty; Matthias, Religious (Rocaan)
Time period(s): Indeterminate Past
Locale(s): Blue Isle, Fictional Country; The Shadowlands, Mythical Place; Alternate Universe

Summary: King Alexander's murder by ambush breaks the uneasy peace on Blue Isle. Both Human and Fey misunderstand and mistrust one another, leading to greater treachery and greater tragedy. Amid death and suspicion, only those who stand between the two races offer hope, although they have little hope for themselves.

Other books you might like:
C.J. Cherryh, *Fortress in the Eye of Time*, 1995
Barbara Hambly, *The Ladies of Mandrigyn*, 1984
Katherine Kurtz, *Deryni Rising*, 1970
Patricia A. McKillip, *The Riddle-Master of Hed*, 1976
Paula Volsky, *Illusion*, 1992

3773

KRISTINE KATHRYN RUSCH

The Devil's Churn

(New York: Dell, 1996)

Story type: Horror (Occult)
Major character(s): Adelaine Hawthorne Taylor Rustin, Aged Person; Billy Malone, Lawyer; Evelyn Brand, Aged Person
Time period(s): 1980s (1989)
Locale(s): Dory Cove, Oregon

Summary: On the same day that Addy Rustin returns home for her mother's funeral, her former boyfriend, Spencer Chadwick, returns unaged from the Devil's Churn, an inlet off the Oregon coast where he supposedly drowned half a century before. Spencer's reappearance strengthens Addy's resolve to resist a mystical faith that her mother and the women of Dory Cove have held for a century and that involves secret blood sacrifices.

Other books you might like:
Matthew J. Costello, *Beneath Still Waters*, 1989
Elizabeth Forrest, *Dark Tide*, 1993
Charles L. Grant, *Night Songs*, 1984
Allen Lee Harris, *Let There Be Dark*, 1994
Nancy Holder, *Dead in the Water*, 1995

3774

KRISTINE KATHRYN RUSCH

Facade
(New York: Dell/Abyss, 1993)

Story type: Horror (Psychological Suspense)
Major character(s): Thomas Stratton, Actor; Jillian Maxwell, Editor (newspaper); Alicia Maxwell, Teenager (Jillian' sister)
Time period(s): 1990s (1993)
Locale(s): Seavy Village, Oregon

Summary: Following the abduction and death of his young daughter, Thomas Stratton, an actor losing his ability to distinguish between reality and the characters he plays, returns to the scene of the crime. His research into a series of murders, of which his daughter's was only the most recent, turns up damning evidence that all the killings occurred at times when Thomas was in town, forcing him to confront the possiblity that he may have committed them while in the grip of one of his acting personas.

Other books you might like:
Scott Baker, *Webs*, 1989
Ehren M. Ehly, *Star Prey*, 1992
Chet Williamson, *Reign*, 1990

3775

KRISTINE KATHRYN RUSCH

The Gallery of His Dreams
(Eugene, Oregon: Pulphouse Publishing Axolotl Press, 1991)

Story type: Fantasy (Historical; Contemporary)
Major character(s): Mathew B. Brady, Historical Figure, Photographer; Julia Brady, Spouse, Historical Figure
Time period(s): 19th century (1838-1887)
Locale(s): United States

Summary: Slices in the life and photographic work of pioneering photographer Mathew Brady reflect the gallery exhibition which Brady helps to assemble. While examining his own photographs, he has visions of his future with Julia and the acceptance of his work as art and historical documentation. This is the first book of Rusch's own work published by this editor and publisher.

Other books you might like:
Charles de Lint, *The Little Country*, 1991
Sheila Gilluly, *The Boy From the Burren*, 1990
Mike Resnick, *Soothsayer*, 1991

3776

KRISTINE KATHRYN RUSCH

Heart Readers
(New York: Roc, 1993)

Story type: Fantasy (Political)
Major character(s): Pardu, Royalty, Parent; Tarne, Counselor (royal advisor)
Time period(s): Indeterminate
Locale(s): Leanda, Fictional Country

Summary: To determine which of Pardu's twin sons will rule the kingdom, heart readers must wait for years after the twins' birth to allow each the opportunity to grow, love and hate, after which the heart readers can divine the next ruler. However, as the twins age, King Pardu's ambitious advisor attempts to steer events in the direction he desires prior to the heart readers' assistance.

Other books you might like:
Lois McMaster Bujold, *The Spirit Ring*, 1992
Katharine Kerr, *The Dragon Revenant*, 1990
Mercedes Lackey, *Winds of Fate*, 1991
Paula Volsky, *Illusion*, 1992
Martha Wells, *The Element of Fire*, 1993

3777

KRISTINE KATHRYN RUSCH

The New Rebellion
(New York: Bantam Spectra, 1996)

Story type: Science Fiction (Space Opera; Mystical)
Series: Star Wars
Major character(s): Leia Organa Solo, Royalty, Leader; Han Solo, Spaceship Captain, Warrior; Luke Skywalker, Martial Arts Expert (Jedi Knight), Hero
Time period(s): Indeterminate Past
Locale(s): Coruscant, Planet—Imaginary; New Republic, Interstellar Empire/Federation; *Millenium Falcon*, Spaceship

Summary: Shortly after the admittance of former Imperials to the New Republic Senate, an explosion in the Senate casts suspicion on Han Solo. Investigating, Luke Skywalker discovers a previously unknown Master of the Dark Side of the Force who threatens the existence of the New Republic.

Other books you might like:
Roger MacBride Allen, *Ambush at Corellia*, 1995
Kevin J. Anderson, *Jedi Search*, 1994
Michael P. Kube-McDowell, *Before the Storm*, 1996
Steve Perry, *Shadows of the Empire*, 1996
Michael A. Stackpole, *Rogue Squadron*, 1996
Timothy Zahn, *Heir to the Empire*, 1991

3778

KRISTINE KATHRYN RUSCH, Editor

Pulphouse, Issue 10: Special Issue

(Eugene, Oregon: Pulphouse Publishing, 1991)

Story type: Fantasy (Anthology)
Series: Pulphouse: The Hardback Magazine

Summary: This thematic anthology contains a 3-page introduction by the editor and introductions to each of the 14 stories, all thematically tied as holiday stories set between the harvest holidays and Passover, plus one non-fiction article by series columnist Jon Gustafson, "The Gimlet Eye Returns," continuing his history of SF art. All stories appear here for the first time except Dennis Etchison's "Deadspace," originally published in *Whispers V* and Michael Bishop's, "Icicle Music," revised herein. Many stories feature Christmas, as those by John Brunner, M. Elayn Harvey, Nina Kiriki Hoffman, Charles de Lint and two by Ken Wisman. Kara Dalkey's "The Peony Lantern" is set at the time of the Japanese Festival of the Dead, O-Bon, while William Wu chooses Chinese New Year and Robert Sheckley makes up his own holiday in "Onesday." The other authors are Marina Fitch, Esther M. Friesner and Lisa Goldstein.

Other books you might like:
Richard Brautigan, *In Watermelon Sugar*, 1968
Philip Jose Farmer, *Dayworld*, 1985
Stephen Goldin, *Jade Darcy and the Zen Pirates*, 1990
 Mary Mason, co-author
Martin H. Greenberg, *Christmas on Ganymede and Other Stories*, 1990
 editor
Gene Wolfe, *Gene Wolfe's Book of Days*, 1981

3779

KRISTINE KATHRYN RUSCH, Editor

Pulphouse, Issue 11: Speculative Fiction

(Eugene, Oregon: Pulphouse Publishing, 1991)

Story type: Science Fiction (Anthology)
Series: Pulphouse: The Hardback Magazine

Summary: This volume includes articles by D.W. Taylor and Jon Gustafson, a 2-page introduction by the editor, and 18 stories by Edward Bryant, Nina Kiriki Hoffman, Kij Johnson, James Morrow, Tim Sullivan, Harry Turtledove, William Wu and others. D.W. Taylor's article, "Turn the Mothers Out," is a manifesto for genre writers, while Jon Gustafson's "The Gimlet Eye Returns" continues his column on the history of science fiction art.

Other books you might like:
Kingsley Amis, *Spectrum*, 1962
 Robert Conquest, co-editor
John Carnell, *New Writings in SF 1*, 1966
 editor
Terry Carr, *Universe 1*, 1970
 editor
Samuel R. Delany, *Quark 1*, 1970
 Marilyn Hacker, co-editor

Harlan Ellison, *Again, Dangerous Visions*, 1972
 editor
Harlan Ellison, *Dangerous Visions*, 1967
 editor
Damon Knight, *Orbit 1*, 1966
 editor
Robert Silverberg, *Alpha 1*, 1970
 editor

3780

KRISTINE KATHRYN RUSCH, Editor

Pulphouse, Issue 12: The Last Issue

(Eugene, Oregon: Pulphouse, 1993)

Story type: Horror (Anthology)
Series: Pulphouse: The Hardback Magazine

Summary: The long-awaited final issue of this "hardback magazine," which published some exceptional short horror, fantasy, and science fiction between 1988 and 1993, presents 20 stories and one essay. Outstanding contributions include Adam-Troy Castro's "Metastasis," about a woman's unusual relationship with her cancer; David B. Silva's "Because I Could" and Robert Frazier's "Sendings," both poignant stories about psychic links between children and their grandparents; Darrell Schweitzer's "Angry Man," in which a man must confront discarnate aspects of his own personality; Nina Kiriki Hoffman's "Surreal Estate," a light fantasy involving a haunted house; and Steve Rasnic Tem's "Fairy Tales," about the very pertinent myths a father tells his children to shield them from harm.

Other books you might like:
John Maclay, *Voices From the Night*, 1994
 editor
Thomas F. Monteleone, *Borderlands 4*, 1994
 editor
Stanley Wiater, *After the Darkness*, 1993
 editor

3781

KRISTINE KATHRYN RUSCH, Editor

Pulphouse, Issue 6: Fantasy

(Eugene, Oregon: Pulphouse Publishing, 1990)

Story type: Fantasy (Anthology)
Series: Pulphouse: The Hardback Magazine
Time period(s): Indeterminate

Summary: This book contains two articles, 24 stories and an introduction by the editor, including works by Charles de Lint, William F. Wu, Avram Davidson, Steve Perry, George Alec Effinger, Emma Bull, and many others. This issue in this unusual hardcover magazine series is devoted entirely to fantasy.

Other books you might like:
Ellen Datlow, *The Year's Best Fantasy and Horror: Third Annual Collection*, 1990
 Terri Windling, co-editor

Ellen Datlow, *The Year's Best Fantasy: First Annual Collection*, 1988
   Terri Windling, co-editor
Alan Dean Foster, *Smart Dragons, Foolish Elves*, 1991
   Martin Harry Greenberg, co-editor
Will Shetterly, *Liavek: Festival Week*, 1990
   Emma Bull, co-editor
Will Shetterly, *Liavek*, 1985
   Emma Bull, co-editor

3782

KRISTINE KATHRYN RUSCH, Editor

Pulphouse, Issue 7: Horror
(Eugene, Oregon: Pulphouse, Spring 1990)

Story type: Horror (Anthology)
Series: Pulphouse: The Hardback Magazine

Summary: Twenty-two stories and two essays comprise the contents of this quarterly hardcover magazine which publishes one issue each year of fantasy, science fiction, horror and dark fantasy. The selections include Kathy Koja's haunting meditation on art and life, ''Illusions in Relief''; Kim Antieau's erotic vampire spoof, ''Oral Tradition''; and David Schow's gruesome tale of rural horror, ''Not From Around Here.''

Other books you might like:
Lin Carter, *Weird Tales*, 1981-1983
   4 Vols.
Thomas F. Monteleone, *Borderlands*, 1990
Stuart David Schiff, *The Whispers Series*, 1977-1987
David B. Silva, *Best of The Horror Show*, 1987
J.N. Williamson, *The Best of Masques*, 1988

3783

KRISTINE KATHRYN RUSCH, Editor

Pulphouse, Issue 8: Science Fiction
(Eugene, Oregon: Pulphouse Publishing, 1990)

Story type: Science Fiction (Anthology; Science Fiction)
Series: Pulphouse: The Hardback Magazine
Time period(s): Indeterminate

Summary: This collection of 16 stories, one article and an introduction by the editor, includes works by Charles de Lint, Jane Yolen, George Alec Effinger, S.P. Somtow and many others. This is issue number 8, dated Summer 1990, in this unusual hardcover magazine series and is devoted entirely to science fiction.

Other books you might like:
Groff Conklin, *The Best of Science Fiction*, 1946
Gardner Dozois, *The Year's Best Science Fiction: Seventh Annual Collection*, 1990
Harlan Ellison, *Medea: Harlan's World*, 1985
David G. Hartwell, *The World Treasury of Science Fiction*, 1989
Donald A. Wollheim, *The 1990 Annual World's Best Science Fiction*, 1990

3784

KRISTINE KATHRYN RUSCH, Editor

Pulphouse, Issue 9: Dark Fantasy
(Eugene, Oregon: Pulphouse Fall 1990)

Story type: Horror (Anthology)
Series: Pulphouse: The Hardback Magazine

Summary: Fifteen stories and two essays that prove the branch of imaginative fiction referred to as ''dark fantasy'' is virtually indistiguishable from that simply called ''horror.'' Counterbalancing the subtle discussions of male and female sexuality in Lisa Tuttle's ''Bits and Pieces'' and Nina Kiriki Hoffman's ''Housewife'' are the hardcore physical horrors of Joe Lansdale's ''The Pit'' and the grotesquerie of Nancy A. Collins' self-explanatory ''The Two-Headed Man.''

Other books you might like:
Lin Carter, *Weird Tales*, 1981-1983
   4 Vols.
Thomas F. Monteleone, *Borderlands*, 1990
Stuart David Schiff, *The Whispers Series*, 1977-1987
David B. Silva, *Best of The Horror Show*, 1987
J.N. Williamson, *The Best of Masques*, 1988

3785

KRISTINE KATHRYN RUSCH

Sins of the Blood
(New York: Dell/Abyss, 1994)

Story type: Horror (Vampire Story)
Major character(s): Camilla Timms, Vampire Hunter; Ben Sadler, Vampire; Scott Eliason, Vampire Hunter
Time period(s): 1990s (1994)
Locale(s): Portland, Oregon

Summary: A childhood spent with an abusive father has turned Ben Sadler into a domineering vampire and his sister Camilla into a vampire hunter who finds it increasingly difficult not to become what Ben is. This novel was expanded from the author's 1991 story, ''Children of the Night.''

Other books you might like:
Peter Atkins, *Morningstar*, 1993
Tom Piccirilli, *Dark Father*, 1990
John Steakley, *Vampire$*, 1990
T. Lucien Wright, *Blood Brothers*, 1992

3786

KRISTINE KATHRYN RUSCH

Traitors
(New York: Roc, 1994)

Story type: Fantasy (Political)
Major character(s): Emilio Diate, Dancer; Sheba, Political Figure; Beltar, Businessman
Time period(s): Indeterminate Future
Locale(s): Port City, Fictional City; Golga, Fictional Country; The Kingdom, Fictional Country

Summary: Emilio Diate's life focuses on dance and family, but the Kingdom to which he owes his allegiance and for which he dances slaughters his family because his father criticized the social structure. Although he flees the Kingdom, revolution and love of the new Queen, Sheba, draw him inevitably back to the land of his birth.

Other books you might like:
Orson Scott Card, *Songmaster*, 1980
Frank Herbert, *Dune*, 1965
Joan D. Vinge, *The Summer Queen*, 1991
Vernor Vinge, *Tatja Grimm's World*, 1987
Walter Jon Williams, *Aristoi*, 1992

3787

KRISTINE KATHRYN RUSCH

The White Mists of Power

(New York: Roc, 1991)

Story type: Fantasy (Quest; Political)
Major character(s): Adric, Royalty, Runaway; Byron, Musician, Wanderer; Seymour, Magician
Time period(s): Indeterminate Past (the Middle Ages)
Locale(s): Kilot, Fictional Country

Summary: A young prince is left to die in the slums of an unfriendly city and a mysterious wanderer tries to escape his enemies with the help of an inept magician. Their destinies entwine in an effort to stop a war that may lead to the intervention of the alien Enos and the death of every human in Kilot. This is the author's first novel.

Other books you might like:
Glen Cook, *The Black Company*, 1984
Guy Gavriel Kay, *The Summer Tree*, 1984
Katherine Kurtz, *Deryni Rising*, 1970
Patricia A. McKillip, *The Riddle-Master of Hed*, 1977
Judith Tarr, *The Hall of the Mountain King*, 1986

3788

SALMAN RUSHDIE

Haroun and the Sea of Stories

(New York: Viking Penguin, 1990)

Story type: Fantasy (Contemporary; Quest)
Major character(s): Rashid Khalifa, Storyteller; Haroun Khalifa, Adventurer; Iff, Mythical Creature (water genie)
Time period(s): 20th century
Locale(s): The Sad City, Fictional Country; Alifbay, Fictional Country; Kahani, Moon—Imaginary (Earth's second moon)

Summary: Haroun's father loses his Gift of Gab, and Haroun is determined to get it back for him. With the genie Iff, Haroun travels to the Sea of Stories, encountering many wonderful creatures and learning that the whole source of stories is in danger.

Other books you might like:
John Barth, *Chimera*, 1972
Patricia Daniels, *Sinbad the Sailor*, 1980
Norton Juster, *The Phantom Tollbooth*, 1961

Andrew Lang, *The Arabian Nights Entertainments*, 1969

3789

MARY DORIA RUSSELL

The Sparrow

(New York: Villard, 1996)

Story type: Science Fiction (Theological; First Contact)
Major character(s): Emilio Sandoz, Religious (Jesuit), Linguist; Sofia Mendez, Computer Expert, Pilot (spaceship); Jimmy Quinn, Scientist (astronomer), Spaceman
Time period(s): 2010s (2019); 2060s (2060)
Locale(s): Arecibo, Puerto Rico; *Magellan*, Spaceship; Rakhat, Planet—Imaginary

Summary: The only survivor of the first expediton to Rakhat returns physically and spiritually broken. Having organized the expedition with his closest friends as crew, Emilio Sandoz must recover enough to testify before the Father General of the Order of Jesuits in order to have him release the scientific papers written during the expedition, and to understand why his treatment by the Order seems so hostile. First novel.

Other books you might like:
Eleanor Arnason, *Ring of Swords*, 1993
Catherine Asaro, *Primary Inversion*, 1995
James Blish, *A Case of Conscience*, 1958
C.J. Cherryh, *Foreigner*, 1994
Suzette Haden Elgin, *Native Tongue*, 1984
Dan Simmons, *Hyperion*, 1989
Sheri S. Tepper, *Grass*, 1989

3790

PAUL RUSSELL

Boys of Life

(New York: Dutton, 1991)

Story type: Horror (Psychological Suspense)
Major character(s): Carlos Reichart, Director (film director), Homosexual; Tony Blair, Teenager (Actor)
Time period(s): 1990s
Locale(s): New York, New York

Summary: Attracted by the sophistication of Carlos Reichart, a gay film director who specializes in confrontational and tasteless avant-garde films, Tony Blair flees his rural southern home to take up with Reichert's New York entourage, The Company. But Tony finds that work as an actor for Reichert entails being subjected to sexual and emotional abuse, which for Reichert are merely extensions of his personal aesthetic into life.

Other books you might like:
Dennis Cooper, *Frisk*, 1991

3791

RAY RUSSELL

Absolute Power

(Baltimore, Maryland: Maclay, 1992)

Story type: Horror (Occult)
Major character(s): Cindy Carewe, Artist, Clerk (bookstore worker); Julian Trask, Anthropologist, Paranormal Investigator; Eliza ''Bettina'' Carewe, Witch
Time period(s): 1980s (1983)
Locale(s): Los Angeles, California

Summary: Cindy Carewe's banker father dies penniless, leaving her only a manuscript recounting his perfidious life and an encounter with a witch who may have drained his bank account and forced his suicide. Cindy's investigation to discover the identity of this witch leads her to Bettina, her long lost mother, whom Cynthia fears has evil designs on her as well.

Other books you might like:
John Farris, *All Heads Turn When the Hunt Goes By*, 1977
Fritz Leiber, *Conjure Wife*, 1953

3792

SEAN RUSSELL

Gatherer of Clouds

(New York: DAW, 1992)

Story type: Fantasy (Adventure; Historical)
Major character(s): Shuyun, Religious (Botah), Martial Arts Expert; Shonto, Nobleman, Military Personnel
Time period(s): Indeterminate Past
Locale(s): Empire of Wa, Fictional Country

Summary: Rumors of war permeate the Emperor's court while the Botahist monks expectantly await the prophecied master and Lord Shonto prepares to counter a massive invasion by barbarian horsemen. Concludes the story begun in *The Initiate Brother*.

Other books you might like:
Raymond E. Feist, *Daughter of the Empire*, 1987
    Janny Wurts, co-author
Raymond E. Feist, *Servant of the Empire*, 1990
    Janny Wurts, co-author
Robert Jordan, *The Eye of the World*, 1989
E. Hoffman Price, *The Devil Wives of Li Fong*, 1979
E. Hoffman Price, *Far Lands Other Days*, 1975
E. Hoffman Price, *The Jade Enchantress*, 1982

3793

SEAN RUSSELL

The Initiate Brother

(New York: DAW, 1991)

Story type: Fantasy (Adventure)
Major character(s): Shuyun, Religious (monk), Martial Arts Expert; Nishima, Royalty (princess); Lord Shanto, Military Personnel (General)

Time period(s): Indeterminate Past
Locale(s): Empire of Wa, Fictional Country

Summary: A fearful emperor uses intrigue and subterfuge to eliminate adversaries of his reign, causing greater calamity throughout the empire. The challenge to return the empire to a just path is accepted by a Lord who is a military genius and his young spiritual advisor, a monk of extraordinary talents.

Other books you might like:
David Charnee, *Sensei*, 1983
James Clavell, *Shogun*, 1975
Barry Hughart, *Bridge of Birds*, 1984
Barry Hughart, *Eight Skilled Gentlemen*, 1990
Barry Hughart, *The Story of the Stone*, 1988
Jeanne Larsen, *Silk Road*, 1989
Jessica Amanda Salmonson, *Tomoe Gozen*, 1984
Laurence Yep, *Tongues of Jade*, 1991

3794

SEAN RUSSELL

Sea Without a Shore

(New York: DAW, 1996)

Story type: Fantasy (Magic Conflict; Political)
Series: Moontide and Magic Rise
Major character(s): Tristam Flattery, Naturalist; Averil Kent, Nobleman, Artist (painter)
Time period(s): Indeterminate Past
Locale(s): At Sea; Varua, Fictional Country

Summary: With the last Mage dead and his secrets lost, the Age of Magic ends. A rising star in the new, rational world, the Magician's nephew sets out to explore a distant island. There he discovers many things and must choose for everyone whether to reopen the path to magic or leave it locked forever. Second in the series.

Other books you might like:
Poul Anderson, *Three Hearts and Three Lions*, 1961
Guy Gavriel Kay, *The Lions of Al-Rassan*, 1995
Ellen Kushner, *Swordspoint*, 1987
Larry Niven, *The Magic Goes Away*, 1979
Robert J. Sawyer, *Far-Seer*, 1992

3795

SEAN RUSSELL

World Without End

(New York: DAW, 1995)

Story type: Fantasy (Political; Quest)
Series: Moontide and Magic Rise
Major character(s): Tristam Flattery, Naturalist
Time period(s): 16th century
Locale(s): *Swallow*, At Sea; Farrland, Fictional Country; Farrow, Fictional Country (island)

Summary: In a new age of enlightenment and science which pushes magic into the background, Tristam Flattery follows a path of reason, rejecting the mystic arts. When called upon to help the king with a medicinal plant having seemingly magical properties, Tristam finds that political machinations draw him into a multigenerational plot and send him in search of new plant stocks.

Other books you might like:
Allan Cole, *The Far Kingdoms*, 1993
   Chris Bunch, co-author
Marc Laidlaw, *Neon Lotus*, 1988
Robert J. Sawyer, *Far-Seer*, 1992
Robert J. Sawyer, *Fossil Hunter*, 1993
Elizabeth Ann Scarborough, *Last Refuge*, 1992

3796

RICHARD PAUL RUSSO

Carlucci's Edge

(New York: Ace, 1995)

Story type: Science Fiction (Cyberpunk; Mystery)
Major character(s): Paula Asgard, Musician; Frank Carlucci, Detective—Police; Ian Tremaine, Journalist
Time period(s): Indeterminate Future
Locale(s): San Francisco, California

Summary: After the termination of Chick's small-time operation, the cops seem uninterested in investigating his murder. Curious why they seem anxious to bury the investigation rather than merely ignore it, Paula Asgard and Frank Carlucci risk everything to find Chick's killer. Sequel to *Destroying Angel*.

Other books you might like:
Isaac Asimov, *The Caves of Steel*, 1954
Steven Barnes, *Streetlethal*, 1983
Pat Cadigan, *Fools*, 1992
William Gibson, *Burning Chrome*, 1986
Katharine Kerr, *Polar City Blues*, 1990
Walter Jon Williams, *Hardwired*, 1986
Walter Jon Williams, *Voice of the Whirlwind*, 1987

3797

RICHARD PAUL RUSSO

Destroying Angel

(New York: Ace, 1992)

Story type: Science Fiction (Cyberpunk; Mystery)
Major character(s): Louis Tanner, Smuggler, Detective—Amateur
Time period(s): 21st century
Locale(s): San Francisco, California

Summary: Retired police officer Louis Tanner enjoys a profitable smuggling career until the reappearance of a serial killer jolts Tanner into investigating the crimes.

Other books you might like:
Philip K. Dick, *Blade Runner*, 1982
George Alec Effinger, *When Gravity Fails*, 1987
Katharine Kerr, *Polar City Blues*, 1990
Neal Stephenson, *Snow Crash*, 1992

3798

RICHARD PAUL RUSSO

Subterranean Gallery

(New York: Tor, 1989)

Story type: Science Fiction (Arts)
Major character(s): Rheinhardt, Artist; Justinian, Veteran
Time period(s): 21st century
Locale(s): San Francisco, California

Summary: Artists in a near-future San Francisco are increasingly faced with censorship and government repression. Rheinhardt, a talented but tormented sculptor, tries desperately to produce great art in a world from which he is almost totally alienated.

Other books you might like:
Lisa Goldstein, *A Mask for the General*, 1987
Ian McDonald, *Out on Blue Six*, 1989
Pat Murphy, *The City, Not Long After*, 1989

3799

BRETT RUTHERFORD

Night Gaunts: An Entertainment Based on the Life and Work of H.P. Lovecraft

(Boston: Grim Reaper Books, 1993)

Story type: Horror (Collection)
Summary: The bulk of this booklet is comprised of a memory play, in which renowned horror writer H.P. Lovecraft merges fiction with real life while ruminating on his deathbed on some of his best known stories and the events that gave rise to them. The book is filled out with five poems—"At Lovecraft's Grave," "Low Tide," "Things Seen in Graveyards," "Maker of Monsters, Maker of Gods," and "Hearing the Wendigo"—all of which are homages to Lovecraft or Lovecraftian themes.

Other books you might like:
Peter Cannon, *Pulptime*, 1984
Richard A. Lupoff, *Lovecraft's Book*, 1985
James Schevill, *Lovecraft's Follies: A Play*, 1971
Ralph Vaughan, *Sherlock Holmes in the Adventure of the Ancient Gods*, 1990

3800

SHAWN RYAN

Brethren

(New York: Pocket, 1993)

Story type: Horror (Curse)
Major character(s): Jason Medlocke, Detective—Homicide; Alex Cotton, Computer Expert (programmer); Stephen Medlocke, Parent (Jason's father), Religious (minister)
Time period(s): 1990s (1993)
Locale(s): Gwinnett County, Georgia

Summary: When a serial killer who signs himself "The Mercy Killer" begins showing an intimate knowledge of the details of homicide detective Jason Medlocke's life, Jason's father Stephen informs him that the killer is a servant of Moloch, a demon summoned by one of Jason's ancestors, and charges Jason with the task of sending the creature back to its own world. This is the author's first novel.

Other books you might like:
Douglas Clegg, *Goat Dance*, 1989
T.E.D. Klein, *The Ceremonies*, 1984
Brent Monahan, *The Uprising*, 1992
Adrian Savage, *Symphony*, 1992

3801
SHAWN RYAN

Nocturnas
(New York: Pocket, 1995)

Story type: Horror (Vampire Story)
Major character(s): Adam Chase, Photographer; Silas Freeborn, Businessman (arms merchant); Livia, Military Personnel
Time period(s): 1990s
Locale(s): Bucharest, Romania

Summary: While on assignment in Romania during the final days of the Ceausescu regime, American photographer Adam Chase runs afoul of the Nocturnas, a secret arm of the Securitate comprised of the country's legendary vampires, and teams up with rebel forces in the hope of putting an end to their rule.

Other books you might like:
Elaine Bergstrom, *Shattered Glass*, 1989
Kim Newman, *The Bloody Red Baron*, 1995
Dan Simmons, *Children of the Night*, 1992
Lois Tilton, *Darkness on the Ice*, 1993
Robert Weinberg, *The Armageddon Box*, 1991

3802
GEOFF RYMAN

The Child Garden
(New York: St. Martin's Press, 1990)

Story type: Science Fiction (Genetic Manipulation; Dystopian)
Major character(s): Milena, Actress; Rolfa, Genetically Altered Being
Time period(s): 21st century
Locale(s): London, England

Summary: As scientific techniques advance, cancer is cured. Then cancer's useful side effect, the doubling of the human lifespan, is discovered. Viruses are used to implant memories, allowing instant education. Milena has a typical reaction to the viruses. She is unable to join the Consortium which causes her to be very lonely.

Other books you might like:
Greg Bear, *Blood Music*, 1985
Margaret Wander Bonanno, *The Others*, 1990
Octavia E. Butler, *Dawn*, 1987
Jeffrey A. Carver, *From a Changeling Star*, 1989

Frank Herbert, *The White Plague*, 1982
Dean R. Koontz, *Watchers*, 1987
Robert Reed, *Black Milk*, 1989

3803
GEOFF RYMAN

Unconquered Countries: Four Novellas
(New York: St. Martin's Press, 1994)

Story type: Fantasy (Collection; Science Fiction)

Summary: Contains a four-page introduction by Samuel R. Delany, a three-page afterword plus two original and two reprinted stories including the title story which received a Nebula Award nomination and a World Fantasy Award. Themes include magic in a Tibet dominated by China, politics, homosexuality and the importance of music in daily life.

Other books you might like:
John Crowley, *Antiquities*, 1993
Charles de Lint, *Spiritwalk*, 1992
Robert Holdstock, *The Bone Forest*, 1992
Gene Wolfe, *Storeys From the Old Hotel*, 1992

3804
GEOFF RYMAN

Was
(New York: Alfred A. Knopf, 1992)

Story type: Fantasy (Historical; Contemporary)
Major character(s): Dorothy "Dotty" Gael, Orphan, Abuse Victim; Bill Davison, Psychologist; L. Frank Baum, Historical Figure, Writer
Time period(s): 1870s; 20th century
Locale(s): Manhattan, Kansas; California; Canada

Summary: This mosaic unites diverse elements surrounding L. Frank Baum's *The Wonderful Wizard of Oz* (1900) including the life of Dorothy Gael who inspired Baum's book, Judy Garland who played the part of Dorothy in the subsequent film and Bill Davison and his dying patient, Jonathan, their lives forever changed by the film. The disclosure of her sexual and psychological abuse to Dorothy's substitute teacher, L. Frank Baum, led to Baum's creating the fictional Dorothy's happier adventures in Oz and the film which changed the life of Judy Garland. Chapters begin with brief non-fiction sketches and exerpts of material which provide insight to Oz or the environment surrounding its creation.

Other books you might like:
L. Frank Baum, *The Wonderful Wizard of Oz*, 1900
Orson Scott Card, *Lost Boys*, 1992
Karen Joy Fowler, *Sarah Canary*, 1991
Susan Palwick, *Flying in Place*, 1992
Kristine Kathryn Rusch, *The Gallery of His Dreams*, 1991
Jane Yolen, *Briar Rose*, 1992

3805

FRED SABERHAGEN, Editor

An Armory of Swords
(New York: Tor, 1995)

Story type: Fantasy (Anthology; Sword and Sorcery)
Series: Swords

Summary: Contains eight original stories, frequently dark in tone, featuring swords forged by Vulcan from Saberhagen's The Swords Series and The Lost Swords Series, such as Soulcutter, Doomgiver, Dragonslicer, and Wayfinder and their unique magical properties. Authors include Fred Saberhagen, Thomas Saberhagen, Michael A. Sackpole, Robert E. Vardeman, and Walter Jon Williams.

Other books you might like:
Marion Zimmer Bradley, *Sword and Sorceress I-XII*, 1984-1995
  editor
L. Sprague de Camp, *The Fantastic Swordsmen*, 1967
  editor
L. Sprague de Camp, *Swords and Sorcery*, 1963
  editor
Richard Gilliam, *Excalibur*, 1995
  Martin H. Greenberg, Edward E. Kramer, co-editors
Edward E. Kramer, *Tales of the White Wolf*, 1994
  Richard Gilliam, co-editor
Karl Edward Wagner, *Echoes of Valor I-III*, 1987-1991
  editor

3806

FRED SABERHAGEN

Berserker Kill
(New York: Tor, 1993)

Story type: Science Fiction (Alternate Intelligence; Robot Fiction)
Series: Berserker
Major character(s): Nicholas Hawksmoor, Pilot (spaceship), Artificial Intelligence; Dirac Sardoll, Leader (Premier); Lake Genevieve ''Jenny'' Sardou, Artificial Intelligence
Time period(s): Indeterminate Future
Locale(s): Space Station (colonization laboratory); *Eidolon*, Spaceship; Outer Space

Summary: When a berserker breaks the pattern of universal human destruction by stealing human zygotes and a biological laboratory, Nicholas Hawksmoor becomes involved in an AI's plan to provide a new body for the goodlife human on which it focused.

Other books you might like:
Roger MacBride Allen, *The Ring of Charon*, 1990
Octavia E. Butler, *Dawn*, 1987
Diana G. Gallagher, *The Alien Dark*, 1990
John Varley, *Steel Beach*, 1992
Vernor Vinge, *A Fire upon the Deep*, 1993

3807

FRED SABERHAGEN

Berserker Lies
(New York: Tor Books, 1991)

Story type: Science Fiction (Collection; Robot Fiction)
Series: Berserker
Major character(s): Third Historian, Alien (Carmpan)
Time period(s): Indeterminate Future

Summary: Five stories, originally published between 1965 and 1990, portray the conflict between humanity, which has recently begun colonizing the galaxy, and the Berserkers, alien sentient killing machines intent on destroying all life.

Other books you might like:
Roger MacBride Allen, *The Ring of Charon*, 1990
Isaac Asimov, *Nightfall*, 1990
  Robert Silverberg, co-author
Octavia E. Butler, *Dawn*, 1987
Orson Scott Card, *Ender's Game*, 1985
Diana G. Gallagher, *The Alien Dark*, 1990
Dan Simmons, *The Fall of Hyperion*, 1990
Dan Simmons, *Hyperion*, 1989

3808

FRED SABERHAGEN
JAMES V. HART, Co-Author

Bram Stoker's Dracula
(New York: Signet, 1992)

Story type: Horror (Vampire Story)
Major character(s): Dracula, Vampire; Jonathan Harker, Real Estate Agent; Mina Harker, Housewife (Jonathan Harker's wife)
Time period(s): 1890s (1895)
Locale(s): London, England; Transylvania

Summary: In this novelization of the script of the Francis Ford Coppola film, *Bram Stoker's Dracula*, arch-vampire Count Dracula moves his base of operations from Transylvania to England, only to discover that Mina Harker, the wife of his real estate agent, is the spitting image of his wife of 500 years before for whom he still bears undying love.

Other books you might like:
Mara McCuniff, *The Vampire Memoirs*, 1990
Michael Romkey, *I, Vampire*, 1990
Bram Stoker, *Dracula*, 1895

3809

FRED SABERHAGEN

Dancing Bears
(New York: Tor, 1996)

Story type: Fantasy (Adventure; Historical)
Major character(s): John Sherwood, Hunter, Mythical Creature (werebear); Gregori Lohmatski, Nobleman, Mythical Creature (werebear); Natalya Lohmatski, Noblewoman, Revolutionary

Time period(s): 1900s (1908-1909)
Locale(s): Novgorod, Russia; Siberia, Russia

Summary: John Sherwood accompanies Gregori Lohmatski to his Russian estate to hunt a mysterious man-eating bear, but corrupt policemen arrest Gregori and exile him to Siberia. As Sherwood and Natalya Lohmatski, Gregori's sister, travel across Russia to attempt a rescue, they learn that old peasant legends about ''werebears'' may actually be true.

Other books you might like:
James Blish, *There Shall Be No Darkness*, 1950
Martin H. Greenberg, *An Armory of Swords*, 1995
    Fred Saberhagen, co-editor
Mercedes Lackey, *The Fire Rose*, 1995
Pat Murphy, *Nadya: The Wolf Chronicles*, 1996
Whitley Strieber, *The Wolfen*, 1978
Jack Williamson, *Darker than You Think*, 1940
Roger Zelazny, *The Black Throne*, 1990
    Fred Saberhagen, co-author

3810

FRED SABERHAGEN

The Dracula Tape
(New York: Tor, 1989)

Story type: Horror (Vampire Story)
Series: Dracula
Major character(s): Dracula, Vampire (Aristocratic); Mina Harker, Heroine, Lover (Dracula's)
Time period(s): 1870s
Locale(s): London, England (Carfax Estate)

Summary: In a diary sent to Mina Harker's grandson, the Count tells his side of the story: he was a persecuted victim of malicious slander who was only defending himself and his lover, Mina Harker, from the fanaticism and medical bungling of Van Helsing and his dupes, as well as the insanity of Renfield. Originally published in 1975.

Other books you might like:
Jeffrey Sackett, *Blood of the Impaler*, 1989
Peter Tremayne, *Bloodright*, 1977
    UK: Dracula Unborn
Peter Tremayne, *Dracula, My Love*, 1980
Peter Tremayne, *The Revenge of Dracula*, 1978

3811

FRED SABERHAGEN

The Holmes-Dracula File
(New York: Tor, 1989)

Story type: Horror (Vampire Story)
Series: Dracula
Major character(s): Dracula, Vampire (Aristocratic); Sherlock Holmes, Detective—Private (The Count's cousin)
Time period(s): 1890s
Locale(s): London, England

Summary: Sherlock Holmes discovers that Count Dracula is his look-alike cousin. The two form a partnership and use their identical looks to thwart a plot to loose the bubonic plague on London. Originally published in 1978.

Other books you might like:
Les Daniel, *Don Sebastian Series*,
    1978-1986
Chelsea Quinn Yarbro, *The Saint-Germain Chronicles*,
    1978-1983

3812

FRED SABERHAGEN

The Last Book of Swords: Shieldbreaker's Story
(New York: Tor, 1994)

Story type: Fantasy (Magic Conflict)
Series: Swords
Major character(s): Stephen, Teenager, Royalty; Vilkata, Wizard
Time period(s): Indeterminate Past
Locale(s): Tasavalta, Fictional Country; Sarykam, Fictional City

Summary: Vilkata returns from defeat and banishment armed with Mindsword, intending to capture Prince Mark's cache of powerful magical swords. With Prince Mark absent from Sarykam, only Prince Stephen, armed with the supremely powerful Shieldbreaker, can hope to stop Vilkata.

Other books you might like:
Lois McMaster Bujold, *The Spirit Ring*, 1992
Terry Goodkind, *Wizard's First Rule*, 1992
Laurell K. Hamilton, *Nightseer*, 1992
Martha Wells, *The Element of Fire*, 1993
Patricia C. Wrede, *The Raven Ring*, 1994

3813

FRED SABERHAGEN, Editor

Machines That Kill
(New York: Tor, 1992)

Story type: Science Fiction (Anthology; Robot Fiction)
Time period(s): Indeterminate Future

Summary: 15 stories about inimical robots first published between 1942 and 1975 including ''Fondly Fahrenheit'' by Alfred Bester, ''Second Variety'' by Philip K. Dick, ''The Wabbler'' by Murray Leinster, ''Steel'' by Richard Matheson, ''Goodlife'' by Fred Saberhagen, ''The Cruel Equations'' by Robert Sheckley, ''Alpha Ralpha Boulevard'' by Cordwainer Smith, ''Killdozer!'' by Theodore Sturgeon and ''Auto-Da-Fe'' by Roger Zelazny. Stories by David Drake, Carol Emshwiller, Keith Laumer, Barry N. Malzberg, Peter Phillips and Robert Silverberg complete this volume.

Other books you might like:
Roger MacBride Allen, *The Ring of Charon*, 1990
David Brin, *Earth*, 1990
Keith Laumer, *Rogue Bolo*, 1986
Dan Simmons, *The Fall of Hyperion*, 1990
Dan Simmons, *Hyperion*, 1989

Cordwainer Smith, *The Best of Cordwainer Smith*, 1975
G. Harry Stine, *Sierra Madre*, 1988

3814

FRED SABERHAGEN

A Matter of Taste
(New York: Tor, 1990)

Story type: Horror (Vampire Story)
Series: Dracula
Major character(s): Matthew Maule, Philanthropist, Vampire (a.k.a. Count Dracula); John Southerland, Businessman, Wealthy; Valentine Kaiser, Public Relations (celebrity publicist), Vampire (a.k.a. Cesar Borgia)
Time period(s): 1990s (1990)
Locale(s): Chicago, Illinois

Summary: On the night that John Southerland brings his fiancee to meet his adoptive ''Uncle Matthew,'' publicist Valentine Kaiser also pays a visit. John is unaware that Uncle Matthew is really Count Dracula and that Kaiser, a member of the medieval Borgia family, was turned into a vampire by Matthew centuries before and now seeks to take his uncle's life in revenge.

Other books you might like:
Les Daniels, *No Blood Spilled*, 1991
Brian Stableford, *The Empire of Fear*, 1988
Bram Stoker, *Dracula*, 1897
Peter Tremayne, *Dracula Unborn*, 1977
Chelsea Quinn Yarbro, *The Palace*, 1978

3815

FRED SABERHAGEN

Merlin's Bones
(New York: Tor, 1995)

Story type: Fantasy (Legend; Political)
Major character(s): Amby, Actor, Psychic; Elaine Brusen, Scientist (physicist); Morgan le Fay, Sorceress
Time period(s): 21st century; Indeterminate Past (Dark Ages)
Locale(s): England; Fairy Realm, Mythical Place

Summary: As forces in the past attempt to control the Oracle of Merlin's Bones, Dr. Elaine Brusen's invention, the hypostator, threatens to change reality. Morgan le Fay, Mordred, and the Fisher King focus their grab for power on Brusen's device, while Merlin plots to reestablish Camelot.

Other books you might like:
Martin Caidin, *The Messiah Stone*, 1986
Robert N. Charrette, *A Prince Among Men*, 1994
Molly Cochran, *The Forever King*, 1992
    Warren Murphy, co-author
Simon Hawke, *The Wizard of Camelot*, 1993
Simon Hawke, *The Wizard of 4th Street*, 1987
Susan Cooper, *Over Sea, Under Stone*, 1966

3816

FRED SABERHAGEN

A Question of Time
(New York: Tor, 1992)

Story type: Horror (Vampire Story)
Major character(s): Bill Burdon, Detective—Private; Sarah Tyrell, Widow(er); Jacob Resner, Worker (with the CCC)
Time period(s): 1930s (1931); 1990s (1991)
Locale(s): Grand Canyon, Colorado

Summary: The search for a woman lost in the Grand Canyon uncovers an area at the bottom impervious to time and the arrogant vampire who presides over it.

Other books you might like:
Brian W. Aldiss, *Dracula Unbound*, 1990
Dean Wesley Smith, *Laying the Music to Rest*, 1989

3817

FRED SABERHAGEN

Seance for a Vampire
(New York: Tor, 1994)

Story type: Horror (Vampire Story)
Series: Dracula
Major character(s): John Watson, Doctor; Sherlock Holmes, Detective—Private; Dracula, Vampire
Time period(s): 1900s (1903)
Locale(s): London, England

Summary: A seance to summon a dead loved one accidentally summons the vampire who killed her and releases him into the world to redress the injustice that resulted in his vampirization a century before. When Sherlock Holmes' investigations into the affair result in his mysterious disappearance, Holmes' friend John Watson has no recourse but to summon an expert in such matters, the Prince of Vampires, Count Dracula.

Other books you might like:
Mark Frost, *The List of 7*, 1993
William Hjortsberg, *Nevermore*, 1994
Nicholas Meyer, *The Canary Trainer*, 1993
Nicholas Meyer, *The Seven-Percent Solution*, 1977
Kim Newman, *Anno Dracula*, 1992
Sam Siciliano, *The Angel of the Opera*, 1993

3818

FRED SABERHAGEN

A Sharpness on the Neck
(New York: Tor, 1996)

Story type: Horror (Vampire Story)
Major character(s): Vlad Dracula, Vampire (a.k.a. Mr. Graves); Radu Dracula, Vampire (Vlad's brother); Phillip Radcliffe, Young Man
Time period(s): 1990s (1996); 1790s (1792)
Locale(s): Paris, France

Summary: In 1792, Phillip Radcliffe performs a service for Vlad Dracula that earns him the vampire's promise to protect him from harm. As a result, Phillip, and a twentieth century descendant named for him, become pawns in Vlad's centuries-old feud with his evil brother Radu.

Other books you might like:
Mara McCuniff, *The Vampire Memoirs*, 1991
P.N. Elrod, *Red Death*, 1993
Anne Rice, *The Vampire Lestat*, 1985
T. Lucien Wright, *Thirst of the Vampire*, 1992

3819

FRED SABERHAGEN

The Sixth Book of Lost Swords: Mindsword's Story
(New York: Tor, 1990)

Story type: Fantasy (Legend)
Series: Lost Swords
Major character(s): Murat, Royalty (crown prince); Kristin, Royalty (princess)
Time period(s): Indeterminate Past
Locale(s): Culm, Fictional Country; Tasavalta, Fictional Country

Summary: Murat of Culm, searching for a present for the Princess of Tasavalta, finds the Mindsword. He knows that its magic is overwhelming so he sheaths it and binds it before touching it, but before he can set it at Kristin's feet he is attacked and must use the sword to save himself, which frees the sword's power to sway men's minds consequently making it very difficult to give up.

Other books you might like:
C.J. Cherryh, *Rusalka*, 1989
Stephen R. Donaldson, *Lord Foul's Bane*, 1977
Christopher Priest, *The Glamour*, 1984
Tom Reamy, *Blind Voices*, 1978
Tad Williams, *The Dragonbone Chair*, 1989

3820

FRED SABERHAGEN

Wayfinder's Story: The Seventh Book of Lost Swords
(New York: Tor, 1992)

Story type: Fantasy (Sword and Sorcery; Quest)
Series: Lost Swords
Major character(s): Valdemar "Val", Farmer, Traveller; Yambu, Aged Person, Royalty (Silver Queen); Zoltan, Royalty (prince), Traveller
Time period(s): Indeterminate Past
Locale(s): Tasavalta, Fictional Country

Summary: When Wayfinder comes into Valdemar's hands, his desire causes Wayfinder to bring Valdemar to Rambu, who travels with Zoltan in search of Wayfinder to aid in his quest for the Emperor's treasure and the magic sword,

Woundhealer. However, the road to treasure contains many enemies who desire possession of Wayfinder.

Other books you might like:
Glen Cook, *The Black Company*, 1984
Glen Cook, *The Swordbearer*, 1982
Marc Laidlaw, *Neon Lotus*, 1988
Michael Moorcock, *The Fortress of the Pearl*, 1989
Michael Moorcock, *The Revenge of the Rose*, 1991

3821

JEFFREY SACKETT

Blood of the Impaler
(New York: Bantam, 1989)

Story type: Horror (Vampire Story)
Major character(s): Malcolm Harker, Detective—Amateur; Dracula, Vampire
Time period(s): 1980s (Flashbacks to 1890s and 15th centur)
Locale(s): Transylvania; England

Summary: A "sequel" to Bram Stoker's *Dracula*. Following the clues in Stoker's novel, Jonathan Harker's great-grandson restores Lucy Westerna to life—unleashing a vampire on society—and recovers the ashes of Dracula, thereby restoring the powers of Dracula's blood and even setting the stage for his return to life.

Other books you might like:
Bram Stoker, *Dracula*, 1897
Fred Saberhagen, *The Dracula Tape*, 1975
Peter Tremayne, *Bloodright*, 1977
Peter Tremayne, *Dracula, My Love*, 1980
Peter Tremayne, *The Revenge of Dracula*, 1978

3822

JEFFREY SACKETT

Mark of the Werewolf
(New York: Bantam, 1990)

Story type: Horror (Werewolf Story)
Major character(s): Janos Kaldy, Werewolf; Frederick Bracher, Racist
Time period(s): 1990s
Locale(s): Mannering, North Dakota (Hulltech Center for Genetic Research)

Summary: Having captured Janos Kaldy, a werewolf, Bracher sets a plan in motion to breed a race of invulnerable Nazi-werewolves to use as shock troops in the war to "purify" the races. Only Kaldy himself can thwart Bracher's plan by looking into himself for a way to escape and, perhaps, to find the death he desperately longs for.

Other books you might like:
Robert R. McCammon, *The Wolf's Hour*, 1988
Thomas Tessier, *The Nightwalker*, 1979

3823

MICHELLE SAGARA

Chains of Darkness, Chains of Light

(New York: Ballantine Del Rey, 1994)

Story type: Fantasy (Magic Conflict; Political)
Series: Sundered
Major character(s): Erin of Elliath, Warrior, Healer; Stefanos, Ruler, Immortal; Amalayna, Noblewoman, Avenger
Time period(s): Indeterminate
Locale(s): Marantine, Fictional Country; Mordantari, Fictional Country

Summary: Erin of Elliath and others of Dagothrin travel into the Empire to cleanse it of the Dark Heart, finding treachery and tragedy before events mitigate the extremes of Light and Dark.

Other books you might like:
Piers Anthony, *For Love of Evil*, 1988
C.J. Cherryh, *Rusalka*, 1989
Katherine Kurtz, *The Bastard Prince*, 1994
Mike Resnick, *The Dark Lady: A Romance of the Far Future*, 1987
Brian Stableford, *The Empire of Fear*, 1991

3824

MICHELLE SAGARA

Children of the Blood

(New York: Ballantine Del Rey, 1992)

Story type: Fantasy (Magic Conflict; Horror)
Series: Sundered
Major character(s): Darin of Culverne, Child, Religious (priest of Keranya of Lernan); Sara, Amnesiac; Stefanos, Ruler (Dark Lord of Malthan), Immortal
Time period(s): Indeterminate
Locale(s): Malthan, Fictional Country

Summary: Eight-year-old Darin, the last of the Lines, passes as a slave from High Priest Wellen to Stefanos, who wishes Darin to care for Sara, also of the Lines. Not even Stefanos' protection immunizes Darin and Sara who must fight when the next four most powerful of the Sundered wish to claim Sara for the High Priest.

Other books you might like:
Piers Anthony, *For Love of Evil*, 1988
Katherine Kurtz, *The Harrowing of Gwynedd*, 1989
Andre Norton, *Warlock of the Witch World*, 1967
Harry Turtledove, *Krispos Rising*, 1991
Harry Turtledove, *The Misplaced Legion*, 1987
Chelsea Quinn Yarbro, *The Palace*, 1978

3825

MICHELLE SAGARA

Into the Dark Lands

(New York: Ballantine/Del Rey, 1991)

Story type: Fantasy (Magic Conflict)

Series: Sundered
Major character(s): Erin of Elliath, Warrior, Healer; Stefanos, Ruler (Dark Lord of Malthan), Immortal
Time period(s): Indeterminate
Locale(s): Elliath, Fictional Country; Malthan, Fictional Country

Summary: Erin of Elliath, though a natural healer, is driven by the deaths of her parents to become the best warrior of all the Lines. Later she is chosen to become Sarillorn and sent to the battlefield to aid the injured and dying. Captured by Stefanos and made his consort, she turns against him when he kills some of her people to give her quasi-immortality. This is the author's first novel and the first of a series.

Other books you might like:
Piers Anthony, *Being a Green Mother*, 1987
Katherine Kurtz, *Deryni Rising*, 1970
Katherine Kurtz, *The Harrowing of Gwynedd*, 1989
Andre Norton, *Witch World*, 1963

3826

MICHELLE SAGARA

Lady of Mercy

(New York: Ballantine Del Rey, 1993)

Story type: Fantasy (Magic Conflict; Political)
Series: Sundered
Major character(s): Erin of Elliath, Warrior, Healer; Renar of Dagothrin, Heir—Dispossessed, Fugitive; Darin of Culverne, Child, Religious (priest of Keranya of Lernan)
Time period(s): Indeterminate
Locale(s): Malthan, Fictional Country (empire); Maratine, Fictional Country

Summary: With Stefanos temporarily destroyed, Erin of Elliath and Darin of Culverne travel to Illan, formerly Maratine, to raise up the people against Vellen. When Swords of the church ambush them, Renar of Dagothrin rescues them. The three then move to take possession of Illan.

Other books you might like:
Piers Anthony, *If I Pay Thee Not in Gold*, 1993
    Mercedes Lackey, co-author
Ru Emerson, *The Two in Hiding*, 1991
Barbara Hambly, *The Ladies of Mandrigyn*, 1984
Katherine Kurtz, *King Javan's Year*, 1992
Jacqueline Lichtenberg, *Zelerod's Doom*, 1986
    Jean Lorrah, co-author
Carol Severance, *Demon Drums*, 1992
Brian Stableford, *The Empire of Fear*, 1988
Chelsea Quinn Yarbro, *A Candle for D'Artagnan*, 1989

3827

DON SAKERS, Editor

Carmen Miranda's Ghost Is Haunting Space Station Three

(New York: Baen, 1990)

Story type: Science Fiction (Humor; Anthology)
Major character(s): Carmen Miranda, Spirit, Entertainer

Time period(s): 21st century (first decade)
Locale(s): Space Station

Summary: 19 authors including Anne McCaffrey and C.J. Cherryh, as well as several newcomers, use the science fiction folksong of the same title as an inspiration for their stories. Mystery and humor characterize the collection. Sakers' storynotes and afterword and the words and music to the notorious song fill out the book.

Other books you might like:
Douglas Adams, *The Hitchhiker's Guide to the Galaxy*, 1980
Poul Anderson, *Hoka!*, 1984
   Gordon R. Dickson, co-author
John M. Ford, *How Much for Just the Planet?*, 1987
   Star Trek 36
David Gerrold, *Flying Sorcerers*, 1971
   Larry Niven, co-author
Sharyn McCrumb, *Bimbos of the Death Sun*, 1987

3828

WAYNE ALLEN SALLEE

For You, the Living

(Arvada, Colorado: Roadkill Press, 1992)

Story type: Horror (Apocalyptic Horror)
Major character(s): Sherideen MacLaren, Young Woman
Time period(s): 1990s (1992)
Locale(s): Chicago, Illinois

Summary: The narrator tells of the epidemic of TREATS, a devastating social disease that manifests itself as sexual voracity after death and that is slowly turning the world in a charnel house of promiscuous zombies.

Other books you might like:
Clive Barker, *The Age of Desire*, 1984
   short story in *Books of Blood IV*
John David Connor, *Contagion*, 1992
Michael Crichton, *The Andromeda Strain*, 1969
Richard Laymon, *The Mop Up*, 1989
   in *Night Visions 7*
John Skipp, *Book of the Dead*, 1990
   Craig Spector, co-editor
John Skipp, *Still Dead: Book of the Dead 2*, 1992
   Craig Spector, co-editor

3829

WAYNE ALLEN SALLEE

The Holy Terror

(Shingletown, California: Marc V. Ziesing, 1992)

Story type: Horror (Wild Talents)
Major character(s): Francis Madsen "Painkiller" Haid, Serial Killer; Evan "American Dream" Shustak, Vagrant; Victor Anthony "Tremble" Tremulis, Handicapped
Time period(s): 1980s (1988-1989)
Locale(s): Chicago, Illinois

Summary: As a boy, Francis Haid had a religious vision during a fire in his school. As an adult, Haid trolls the streets of Chicago under the guise of the "Painkiller," a serial murderer who puts bums and derelicts out of their misery by absorbing their pain—and their bodies—into himself.

Other books you might like:
John Byrne, *Whipping Boy*, 1992
George C. Chesbro, *Bone*, 1989
Gordon Linzner, *The Troupe*, 1988
Chet Williamson, *Lowland Rider*, 1988

3830

WAYNE ALLEN SALLEE

Pain-Grin

(Lessburg, Virginia: TAL, 1993)

Story type: Horror (Collection)

Summary: Through a powerful cycle of poems, prose-poems and short stories, the author likens his bout with cerebral palsy—and the constant state of "pain-grin" it produces—to a variety of horrifying experiences.

Other books you might like:
Sean Costello, *Captain Quad*, 1991
Patrick McGrath, *The Grotesque*, 1990

3831

WAYNE ALLEN SALLEE

With Wounds Still Wet

(Seattle: Silver Salamander, 1996)

Story type: Horror (Collection)

Summary: Twenty-four stories, ten original to the book, provide a survey of the past decade of work from this writer of elliptical and often surreal macabre fiction. Most are nonsupernatural urban horror stories set in the author's native Chicago, including his Dennis Cassady Trilogy, comprised of "Rapid Transit," "Take the 'A' Train," and "Bleeding Between the Lines," all of which feature a man whose life is chronically discomposed by a murder he witnesses at a train station. "Don's Last Minute" and "With the Wound Still Wet" both probe acts of random tragedy for their horror, while "Things We Do at Night" is concerned with two voyeurs whose harmless pastime leads to a brutal crime. The ghost of Richard Speck haunts "The Pink Twist Inn" and the ghost of Elvis Presley "Orient Are."

Other books you might like:
S. Darnbrook Colson, *People of the Night*, 1994
Jack Remick, *Terminal Weird*, 1996
Don Webb, *A Spell for the Fulfillment of Desire*, 1996

3832

JESSICA AMANDA SALMONSON

Anthony Shriek

(New York: Dell/Abyss, 1992)

Story type: Horror (Wild Talents)

Major character(s): Anthony Shriek, Artist; Emily Maupin, Student (art student); Wesley Katts, Store Owner (bookstore)
Time period(s): 1990s (1992)
Locale(s): Seattle, Washington

Summary: Struggling to cope with an abusive childhood and misunderstood life, modern expressionist artist Anthony Shriek finds himself slipping in and out of the real world into a bizarre alternate world known as the Nightland, and unable to tell whether this is a consequence of his work as an artist or merely an expression of incipient madness.

Other books you might like:
Giles Blunt, *Cold Eye*, 1989
Kathe Koja, *Bad Brains*, 1992

3833

JESSICA AMANDA SALMONSON

The Mysterious Doom and Other Ghostly Tales of the Pacific Northwest
(Seattle, Washington: Sasqatch Books, 1992)

Story type: Horror (Collection)
Locale(s): Pacific Northwest

Summary: These 17 stories are intriguing retellings of folktales from the Pacific Northwest as tales of supernatural horror. The first eight tell of phantom hounds, Indian princesses turned into fish, and foolish men who build their houses on an Indian burial mounds. The remainder are presented as the experiences of Penelope Pettiweather, Northwest Ghost Hunter, and abound with haunted houses, sea monsters, and other supernatural manifestations.

Other books you might like:
Ellen Datlow, *Snow White, Blood Red*, 1993
   Terri Windling, co-editor
Howard Schwartz, *Lilith's Cave: Jewish Tales of the Supernatural*, 1991
Manly Wade Wellman, *John the Balladeer*, 1988

3834

B.J. SALTERBERG

The Outlander: Captivity
(Tucson: Harbinger House, 1989)

Story type: Science Fiction (Post-Nuclear Holocaust)
Series: Outlander Trilogy
Major character(s): Konnor, Military Personnel (Misogynist); Meagar, Government Official
Time period(s): Indeterminate Future (509 after the Holocaust)
Locale(s): The Center, Earth

Summary: Konnor is captured by the forces of the Center, a women's community where men are little more than docile breeders. Meagar is given the task of breaking Konnor, turning him into the kind of man acceptable to the women of the Center. Their clash leads to a compromise and a new chance for men and women to find common ground.

Other books you might like:
Suzy McKee Charnas, *Motherlines*, 1979
Suzy McKee Charnas, *Walk to the End of the World*, 1974
Joanna Russ, *The Female Man*, 1975
Joanna Russ, *We Who Are About To. . .*, 1977
Pamela Sargent, *The Shore of Women*, 1986

3835

R.A. SALVATORE

Canticle
(Lake Geneva, Wisconsin: TSR, 1991)

Story type: Fantasy (Magic Conflict)
Series: Forgotten Realms: The Cleric Quintet
Major character(s): Cadderly, Student, Scholar; Aballister Bonaduce, Sorcerer; Danica, Warrior, Martial Arts Expert
Time period(s): Indeterminate
Locale(s): Snowflake Mountains, Mythical Place

Summary: A vain sorcerer creates a chaotic potion intending to curse a library and college of scholars pursuing knowledge of the natural world, resulting in a conflict of philosophy and the use of knowledge. Based on TSR's game, Forgotten Realms.

Other books you might like:
John M. Ford, *The Dragon Waiting*, 1983
Randall Garrett, *Murder and Magic*, 1979
Barbara Hambly, *The Silent Tower*, 1986
Katherine Kurtz, *The Deryni Archives*, 1986
Mercedes Lackey, *Magic's Pawn*, 1989

3836

R.A. SALVATORE

The Dragon King
(New York: Warner Aspect, 1996)

Story type: Fantasy (Sword and Sorcery; Political)
Series: Crimson Shadow
Major character(s): Luthien "Crimson Shadow" Bedwyr, Warrior
Time period(s): Indeterminate
Locale(s): Eriador, Fictional Country

Summary: When King Greensparrow plots to destabilize King Brind'Amour's rule of Eriador, Luthien Bedwyr must organize Eriador's people to repel the outside threat to the kingdom.

Other books you might like:
Lynn Flewelling, *Luck in the Shadows*, 1996
Terry Goodkind, *Wizard's First Rule*, 1994
Robin Hobb, *Assassin's Apprentice*, 1995
J.V. Jones, *A Man Betrayed*, 1996
Michael A. Stackpole, *Once a Hero*, 1994

`3837`

R.A. SALVATORE

The Dragon's Dagger

(New York: Ace, 1994)

Story type: Fantasy (Alternate World)
Series: Spearwielder's Tale
Major character(s): Gary Leger, Adventurer, Hero; Kelsenellenelvial Gil-Ravandry, Mythical Creature (elf)
Time period(s): Indeterminate
Locale(s): Faerie, Mythical Place; Earth

Summary: When Gary returns to Faerie, he finds war threatening, a dragon laying waste to the countryside and the sacred armor and enchanted spear of the realm's greatest hero missing. Repairing this mess requires Gary to invade the dragon's very lair.

Other books you might like:
Pamela Dean, *The Secret Country*, 1985
Stephen R. Donaldson, *Lord Foul's Bane*, 1977
Robert Holdstock, *Lavondyss: Journey to an Unknown Region*, 1988
Robert Holdstock, *Mythago Wood*, 1984
Holly Lisle, *Minerva Wakes*, 1994

`3838`

R.A. SALVATORE

Dragonslayer's Return

(New York: Ace, 1995)

Story type: Fantasy (Adventure)
Series: Spearwielder's Tale
Major character(s): Gary Leger, Adventurer; Ceridwen, Witch; Mickey McMickey, Mythical Creature (leprechaun)
Time period(s): 1990s; Indeterminate
Locale(s): Faerie, Mythical Place; Earth

Summary: Upset over his father's death, Gary Leger tries to find meaning by returning to Faerie, this time with his wife, Diane. With Ceridwen plotting evil again, the couple must survive, aid Gary's friends, and defeat the witch for the sake of two worlds.

Other books you might like:
Eleanor Arnason, *Daughter of the Bear King*, 1987
Emma Bull, *War for the Oaks*, 1987
Pamela Dean, *The Secret Country*, 1985
Tom Deitz, *Windmaster's Bane*, 1986
Barbara Hambly, *The Time of the Dark*, 1982

`3839`

R.A. SALVATORE

Echoes of the Fourth Magic

(New York: Roc, 1990)

Story type: Fantasy (Alternate World; Magic Conflict)
Major character(s): Jeff DelGiudice, Scientist; Billy Shank, Scientist

Time period(s): 1990s
Locale(s): Devil's Triangle, Atlantic Ocean; *Unicorn*, Submarine

Summary: The *Unicorn*, a deep-sea research submarine is caught in a storm near the Devil's Triangle. Pulled through to an alternate universe, the destroyed submarine ends up in a cavern five miles beneath the ocean surface. The few remaining members of the crew repair the submarine well enough to make their way to the surface. While trying to find a safe haven, they are contacted by a god whose likeness speaks to them from the water in a bucket.

Other books you might like:
Piers Anthony, *Through the Ice*, 1989
William R. Forstchen, *Rally Cry!*, 1990
Leo Frankowski, *The Cross-Time Engineer*, 1986
Alis A. Rasmussen, *The Labyrinth Gate*, 1988
Nancy Springer, *Red Wizard*, 1990

`3840`

R.A. SALVATORE

In Sylvan Shadows

(Lake Geneva, Wisconsin: TSR, 1992)

Story type: Fantasy (Quest)
Series: Forgotten Realms: The Cleric Quintet
Major character(s): Cadderly, Religious (priest), Scholar
Time period(s): Indeterminate
Locale(s): Shilmista, Mythical Place (Forest of Shadows)

Summary: Cadderly and his companions journey into the elven forest, Shilmista, to save the inhabitants from an army of monsters and its evil leader.

Other books you might like:
Richard Awlinson, *Shadowdale*, 1989
Scott Ciencin, *The Night Parade*, 1992
Elaine Cunningham, *Elfshadow*, 1991
Troy Denning, *The Parched Sea*, 1991
James Lowder, *The Ring of Winter*, 1992
Jean Rabe, *Red Magic*, 1991

`3841`

R.A. SALVATORE

The Legacy

(Lake Geneva, Wisconsin: TSR, 1992)

Story type: Fantasy (Adventure)
Series: Forgotten Realms
Major character(s): Drizzt Do'Urden, Mythical Creature (elf), Adventurer; Regis, Mythical Creature (halfling)
Time period(s): Indeterminate
Locale(s): Mithril Hall, Mythical Place

Summary: Happy at Mithril Hall with his friends and companions, Drizzt vowed never to kill another of his people, but his enemy, the Spider Queen Lioth, will not permit him to remain in peace. This sequel to *Sojourn* is a game tie-in and TSR's first hardcover novel.

Other books you might like:
Sheila Gilluly, *The Boy From the Burren*, 1990
Mercedes Lackey, *Magic's Pawn*, 1989
Andre Norton, *Dark Piper*, 1968
Mickey Zucker Reichert, *Shadow's Realm*, 1990
Andrea Shettle, *Flute Song Magic*, 1990

3842

R.A. SALVATORE

Luthien's Gamble

(New York: Warner Aspect, 1996)

Story type: Fantasy (Sword and Sorcery; Political)
Series: Crimson Shadow
Major character(s): Luthien "Crimson Shadow" Bedwyr, Warrior; Siobahn, Mythical Creature (half-elf), Martial Arts Expert; Oliver deBurrows, Mythical Creature (halfling), Martial Arts Expert
Time period(s): Indeterminate
Locale(s): Eriador, Fictional Country; Caer MacDonald, Fictional City

Summary: Freeing Monfort, now renamed Caer MacDonald, will prove only a temporary victory unless the Crimson Shadow and his peasant revolution can resist the thousands of Praetorian Guards sent by evil Wizard-King Greensparrow to quell the revolt.

Other books you might like:
Robin Hobb, *Royal Assassin*, 1996
J.V. Jones, *Master and Fool*, 1996
Elizabeth Moon, *Surrender None: The Legacy of Gird*, 1990
Paula Volsky, *Illusion*, 1992

3843

R.A. SALVATORE

Passage to Dawn

(Lake Geneva, Wisconsin: TRS, 1996)

Story type: Fantasy (Magic Conflict; Adventure)
Series: Forgotten Realms
Major character(s): Drizzt Do'Urden, Mythical Creature (elf), Adventurer; Catti-Brie Bruenor, Mythical Creature (dwarf), Adventurer
Time period(s): Indeterminate
Locale(s): *Sea Sprite*, At Sea

Summary: Drizzt and Cattie-Brie briefly enjoy their carefree life aboard *Sea Sprite* until sorcery and threats bring them back to the land where they found the crystal shard. Old friends and new allies help them in their attempt to free a loved one and thwart the menace to Drizzt and those he cares for.

Other books you might like:
Richard Awlinson, *Shadowdale*, 1989
Elaine Cunningham, *Elfshadow*, 1991
Troy Denning, *The Parched Sea*, 1991
James Lowder, *The Ring of Winter*, 1992
Douglas Niles, *Darkwalker on Moonshae*, 1987

3844

R.A. SALVATORE

Siege of Darkness

(Lake Geneva, Wisconsin, TSR, 1994)

Story type: Fantasy (Adventure; Magic Conflict)
Series: Forgotten Realms
Major character(s): Drizzt Do'Urden, Mythical Creature (elf), Adventurer; Lloth, Leader (Spider Queen), Deity (goddess of the dark elves); Catti-Brie Bruenor, Mythical Creature (dwarf), Adventurer
Time period(s): Indeterminate
Locale(s): Mithril Hall, Mythical Place; Faerun's Underdark, Mythical Place; Menzoberranzan, Fictional City

Summary: When survivors of Drizzt's defeat of House Baenre in Menzoberranzan plan to retaliate against Mithril Hall and the Spider Queen feeds the chaos in the dark elves' city by turning magic laws unreliable, Drizzt must rely on allies from the Underdark and his own wits to save his friends. Game tie-in.

Other books you might like:
Richard Awlinson, *Shadowdale*, 1989
Elaine Cunningham, *Elfshadow*, 1991
Troy Denning, *The Parched Sea*, 1991
Laurell K. Hamilton, *Nightseer*, 1992
James Lowder, *The Ring of Winter*, 1992
Martha Wells, *The Element of Fire*, 1993

3845

R.A. SALVATORE

Sojourn

(Lake Geneva, Wisconsin: TSR, 1991)

Story type: Fantasy (Adventure)
Series: Forgotten Realms: The Dark Elf Trilogy
Major character(s): Drizzt Do'Urden, Mythical Creature (elf), Adventurer; Catti-Brie Bruenor, Mythical Creature (dwarf), Adventurer; Montolio De Brouchee, Ranger
Time period(s): Indeterminate Past
Locale(s): Termalaine Maer Dualdon, Mythical Place

Summary: Drizzt Do'Urden, a drow, left his home in the Underdark where his people worshipped the Spider Queen. Accompanied by his magical panther, the dark elf makes a place for himself in the world above, making friends and fighting evil and prejudice along the way. A game tie-in novel.

Other books you might like:
Catherine Cooke, *Mask of the Wizard*, 1985
Sheila Gilluly, *The Boy From the Burren*, 1990
Elizabeth Moon, *Surrender None: The Legacy of Gird*, 1990
Kate Novak, *Song of the Saurials*, 1991
  Jeff Grubb, co-author
Mickey Zucker Reichert, *Shadow's Realm*, 1990
Andrea Shettle, *Flute Song Magic*, 1990

`3846`

R.A. SALVATORE

Starless Night

(Lake Geneva, Wisconsin: TSR, 1993)

Story type: Fantasy (Quest)
Series: Forgotten Realms
Major character(s): Drizzt Do'Urden, Mythical Creature (elf), Adventurer; Catti-Brie Bruenor, Mythical Creature (dwarf), Warrior; Dantrag Baenre, Martial Arts Expert (swordsman)
Time period(s): Indeterminate
Locale(s): Mithril Hall, Mythical Place; The Underdark, Mythical Place

Summary: To protect his friends in Mithril Hall, Drizzt Do'Urden reluctantly travels to the Underdark where he battles monsters and evil foes intent on robbing Drizzt of sanity and freedom before attacking Mithril Hall. Game tie-in sequel to *The Legacy.*

Other books you might like:
David Cook, *Horselords,* 1990
Elaine Cunningham, *Elfshadow,* 1991
Troy Denning, *The Parched Sea,* 1991
James Lowder, *The Ring of Winter,* 1992
Jean Rabe, *Red Magic,* 1991
Margaret Weis, *Into the Labyrinth,* 1993
    Tracy Hickman, co-author

`3847`

R.A. SALVATORE

The Sword of Bedwyr

(New York: Warner Aspect, 1995)

Story type: Fantasy (Sword and Sorcery)
Series: Crimson Shadow
Major character(s): Luthien "Crimson Shadow" Bedwyr, Warrior; Oliver deBurrows, Mythical Creature (helf-elf), Highwayman
Time period(s): Indeterminate
Locale(s): Eriador, Fictional Country; Monfort, Fictional City

Summary: An outcast after seeking justice for a murder, Luthien Bedwyr befriends Oliver deBurrows, making questionable use of his arena skills. Enlisted in a wizard's quest, Luthien acquires valuable tools with which to begin the liberation of his people from unwanted outside rule.

Other books you might like:
David Cook, *King Pinch,* 1995
Phyllis Eisenstein, *In the Red Lord's Reach,* 1989
David Gemmell, *Morningstar,* 1993
Robin Hobb, *Assassin's Apprentice,* 1995
Mercedes Lackey, *The Eagle and the Nightingales,* 1995
Michael A. Stackpole, *Once a Hero,* 1994
J.R.R. Tolkien, *The Hobbit,* 1938

`3848`

R.A. SALVATORE

The Woods out Back

(New York: Ace, 1993)

Story type: Fantasy (Alternate World)
Series: Spearwielder's Tale
Major character(s): Gary Leger, Adventurer, Hero; Kelsenellenelvial Gil-Ravandry, Mythical Creature (elf)
Time period(s): 1990s; Indeterminate
Locale(s): Faerie, Mythical Place; Earth

Summary: In the woods behind his home, Gary finds himself transported to a realm populated by mythical creatures. There he discovers he alone can wear the armor of a fabled lost warrior and wield a magical spear. Unfortunately, Gary cannot go home unless he assumes the hero's mantle.

Other books you might like:
Pamela Dean, *The Secret Country,* 1985
Susan Dexter, *The Wizard's Shadow,* 1993
Gordon R. Dickson, *The Dragon and the George,* 1976
Stephen R. Donaldson, *Lord Foul's Bane,* 1977
Dave Duncan, *The Reluctant Swordsman,* 1988
Robert Holdstock, *The Bone Forest,* 1992
Robert Holdstock, *Lavondyss: Journey to an Unknown Region,* 1989
Robert Holdstock, *Mythago Wood,* 1984

`3849`

PAUL M. SAMMON, Editor

The King Is Dead: Tales of Elvis Post Mortem

(New York: Delta, 1994)

Story type: Horror (Anthology)
Major character(s): Elvis Presley, Musician, Historical Figure

Summary: This volume brings together 31 stories, articles, and reflections on Elvis Presley and how his persona has become larger than life since his death. Stories written originally for the volume include Joyce Carol Oates' "Elvis Is Dead: Why Are You Alive?," in which a man ponders the significance of his Elvis fascination in his dreams; Del James' "Backstage"; Chet Williamson's "Double Trouble," about a man who travels back in time to save Elvis' stillborn twin brother and the consequences of his action; Joe R. Lansdale's "Bubba Ho-Tep," in which an elderly Elvis matches wits with an Egyptian mummy unearthed during a Texas flood; Michael Reaves' "Elvis Meets Godzilla," about Elvis' final film appearance; and Nancy A. Collins' "The Sacred Treasures of Graceland: Excerpts From the Sanctioned Museum Catalogue," which analyzes Elvis kitsch as future museum pieces.

Other books you might like:
Jeff Gelb, *Shock Rock,* 1992
    editor
Jeff Gelb, *Shock Rock II,* 1994
    editor
Greil Marcus, *Dead Elvis,* 1994

Paul McAuley, *In Dreams*, 1993
  Kim Newman, co-editor

3850

PAUL M. SAMMON, Editor

Splatterpunks II: Over the Edge

(New York: Tor, 1995)

Story type: Horror (Anthology)

Summary: In this follow-up to his 1990 volume *Splatterpunks: Extreme Horror*, the editor assembles two interviews and twenty-six stories (eight original to the volume) in which writers imbue their horror tales with sex, violence and nihilism. The book is dominated by female writers, including Kathe Koja, who describes the god-like powers a dog develops over humans in "Impermanent Mercies"; Nancy Holder, whose "Cannibal Cats Come Out Tonight" is a horror satire involving teenage cannibal males; Nancy Collins, whose "Rant" takes the point of view of a psychotic woman; and Lucy Taylor, whose revenge story, "Heels," features a foot fetishist. Melanie Tem's "Intimates" and Wildy Petoud's "Accident D'Amour" feature female characters whose discomposed emotions manifest in gruesome physical ways, and Nina Kiriki Hoffman's "Imprint" and Shira Daemon's "Red Shift" both deal with the horrors of domestic abuse. The book also includes reprints by Karl Edward Wagner, Clive Barker, and Poppy Z. Brite.

Other books you might like:
John Skipp, *Book of the Dead*, 1989
  Craig Spector, co-editor
John Skipp, *Still Dead: Book of the Dead 2*, 1992
  Craig Spector, co-editor
David J. Schow, *Silver Scream*, 1988
  editor

3851

PAUL M. SAMMON, Editor

Splatterpunks: Extreme Horror

(New York: St. Martin's, 1990)

Story type: Horror (Anthology)

Summary: Sixteen tales of "extreme horror" strongly influenced by the concerns of modern horror films and fueled with the energies of rock music. Plots involving abortion, murder, racism, sexual exploitation, urban squalor and social taboos are rendered in frequently graphic detail. Among the best selections are Douglas Winter's "Less than Zombie," Nancy Collins' "Freaktent" and Clive Barker's "The Midnight Meat Train."

Other books you might like:
Dennis Etchison, *Cutting Edge*, 1986
David J. Schow, *Silver Scream*, 1988
John Skipp, *Book of the Dead*, 1989
  Craig Spector, co-author
Bruce Sterling, *Mirrorshades: The Cyberpunk Anthology*, 1986

3852

SCOTT RUSSELL SANDERS

The Invisible Company

(New York: Tor, 1989)

Story type: Science Fiction (Immortality)
Major character(s): Leon Ash, Scientist; Kate Trilling, Actress, Spy
Time period(s): 21st century
Locale(s): Paradise Island, Maine

Summary: Twenty years ago a mysterious and powerful organization known as the Invisible Company saved Leon Ash's life. They required in payment only that he promise to take a trip for them some day, no questions asked. Now Ash finds himself on an airplane bound for Paradise Island, a posh resort off the coast of Maine. He has no idea why he's been called to the island but, once there, finds himself at the center of a subtle and potentially deadly mystery.

Other books you might like:
Joe Haldeman, *Buying Time*, 1989
Robert A. Heinlein, *Time Enough for Love*, 1973
Frederik Pohl, *Drunkard's Walk*, 1960
Robert Silverberg, *The Book of Skulls*, 1971
Norman Spinrad, *Bug Jack Barron*, 1969
Jack Vance, *To Live Forever*, 1956
Roger Zelazny, *This Immortal*, 1966

3853

WILLIAM SANDERS

The Wild Blue and the Gray

(New York: Warner Questar, 1991)

Story type: Science Fiction (Alternate Universe; Military)
Major character(s): Amos Ninekiller, Indian (Cherokee), Pilot; William Faulkner, Writer, Pilot; James Lucas, Military Personnel
Time period(s): 1910s (1916)
Locale(s): France, Alternate Earth

Summary: Amos Ninekiller, a Cherokee educated at the University of Virginia, and the only Indian pilot, is sent by his chief to serve with the Confederate Air Force who are fighting with the allies in France. While there he is directed to pick up any information that can help his people stay free of both the Confederacy and the Yankees.

Other books you might like:
Gregory Benford, *Alternate Wars*, 1991
  Martin H. Greenberg, co-editor
Orson Scott Card, *Seventh Son*, 1987
Philip Jose Farmer, *Two Hawks From Earth*, 1979
Leo Frankowski, *The Flying Warlord*, 1989
Frank D. McSherry Jr., *The Fantastic Civil War*, 1991
  editor
Ward Moore, *Bring the Jubilee*, 1953
George H. Smith, *Kar Kaballa*, 1969
Martin Cruz Smith, *The Indians Won*, 1970

3854

RICHARD SANFORD

Roadkill

(Aurora, Colorado: Write Way, 1995)

Story type: Horror (Nature in Revolt)
Major character(s): Charlie Hardin, Truck Driver; Sidney Frankel, Professor (of comparative religion); Melissa Frankel, Teenager
Time period(s): 1990s (1995)
Locale(s): Deuce Creek, Oregon

Summary: Liberated from their burial beneath ancient tribal grounds by excavations around the Portland area, a race of ravenous bird-like creatures begins preying upon the nearby citizens.

Other books you might like:
William W. Johnstone, *Bats*, 1994
Barry Porter, *Junkyard*, 1989
Martin Cruz Smith, *Nightwing*, 1977
T.W. Stetson, *Night Beasts*, 1994
Robert Wilson, *Second Fire*, 1994

3855

DAVID SAPERSTEIN

Red Devil

(New York: Berkley, 1989)

Story type: Horror (Satanism)
Major character(s): Nickolai Valarian, Government Official (Soviet), Demon (Current incarnation of Satan); Peter Somoroff, Spy (KGB agent)
Time period(s): 1990s
Locale(s): Union of Soviet Socialist Republics

Summary: Satan, incarnated in the person of Nickolai Valarian, schemes to take over the Soviet Union, prompting a coalition of Russian, American, and Israeli agents to try to thwart the devil's dangerous, ambitious plan.

Other books you might like:
John Farris, *Catacombs*, 1981

3856

WILLIAM SARABANDE

The Edge of the World

(New York: Ballantine, 1993)

Story type: Fantasy (Quest; Historical)
Series: First Americans
Major character(s): Cha-kwena, Shaman, Prehistoric Human; Ban-ya, Prehistoric Human; Mah-ree, Prehistoric Human
Time period(s): 120th century B.C.
Locale(s): Great Plains, North America

Summary: To pursue his vision of finding a land of plenty where the People's dreams can flower, Cha-kwena must violate a taboo, alienating his mate and his tribe as he follows the mammoth's trail.

Other books you might like:
Jean M. Auel, *Clan of the Cave Bear*, 1980
Jean M. Auel, *The Mammoth Hunters*, 1985
Jean M. Auel, *The Valley of Horses*, 1982
W. Michael Gear, *People of the Wolf*, 1990
 Kathleen O'Neal Gear, co-author
Sue Harrison, *Mother Earth, Father Sky*, 1990
Roger Welsch, *Touching the Fire*, 1992

3857

WILLIAM SARABANDE

The Sacred Stones

(New York: Bantam Domain, 1991)

Story type: Fantasy (Historical; Romance)
Series: First Americans
Major character(s): Ysuna, Religious (high priestess), Prehistoric Human; Masau, Hunter, Prehistoric Human; Maliwal, Hunter, Prehistoric Human
Time period(s): Indeterminate Past
Locale(s): North America

Summary: When Maliwal returns to announce success at finding mammoths and a bride, Ysuna and her adopted sons, Masau and Maliwal, all hope that they will find the mythical white mammoth whose flesh will return power to Ysuna and the People of the Watching Star.

Other books you might like:
Jean M. Auel, *Clan of the Cave Bear*, 1980
Jean M. Auel, *The Mammoth Hunters*, 1985
Jean M. Auel, *The Valley of Horses*, 1982
W. Michael Gear, *People of the Wolf*, 1990
 Kathleen O'Neal Gear, co-author
Sue Harrison, *Mother Earth, Father Sky*, 1990
Richard Herley, *The Stone Arrow*, 1978
Elizabeth Marshall Thomas, *The Animal Wife*, 1990

3858

WILLIAM SARABANDE

Thunder in the Sky

(New York: Bantam Domain, 1992)

Story type: Fantasy (Historical; Religious)
Series: First Americans
Major character(s): Cha-kwena, Shaman, Prehistoric Human
Time period(s): 120th century B.C.
Locale(s): Great Plains, North America

Summary: Hoping to lead his people to the promised land of safety and plenty, Cha-kwena follows the legendary white mammoth while vicious enemies pursue them in hopes of stealing Cha-kwena's magical and passionate woman.

Other books you might like:
Jean M. Auel, *Clan of the Cave Bear*, 1980
Jean M. Auel, *The Mammoth Hunters*, 1985
Jean M. Auel, *The Valley of Horses*, 1982
W. Michael Gear, *People of the Wolf*, 1990
 Kathleen O'Neal Gear, co-author
Sue Harrison, *Mother Earth, Father Sky*, 1990

Richard Herley, *The Stone Arrow*, 1978
Elizabeth Marshall Thomas, *The Animal Wife*, 1990

3859

JORGE SARALEGUI

Looker

(New York: Charter, 1990)

Story type: Horror (Erotic Horror)
Major character(s): Jonathan Lewis, Student; Lylah Cassidy, Professor (of English), Murderer; Kim Powell, Student (Jonathan's girlfriend)
Time period(s): 1990s
Locale(s): Village, Massachusetts (Suburb of Boston)

Summary: A reclusive student falls in love with his college literature professor unaware that she is addicted to murder and castration.

Other books you might like:
David C. Smith, *The Fair Rules of Evil*, 1989

3860

CARL SARGENT
MARC GASCOIGNE, Co-Author

Streets of Blood

(New York: Roc, 1992)

Story type: Fantasy (Science Fiction; Political)
Series: Shadowrun
Major character(s): Serrin Shamandar, Magician, Mythical Creature (elf); Geraint Llanfrechfa, Nobleman, Adventurer; Francesca Young, Computer Expert (decker)
Time period(s): 21st century
Locale(s): London, England

Summary: A convoluted plot drags three shadowrunners back into contact after years of separation. Industrial espionage, illegal experiments, political maneuvering and a serial killer threaten all their lives. The trio require the help of a young Indian woman from the slums of London to solve the mystery and avoid destruction.

Other books you might like:
John Brunner, *The Shockwave Rider*, 1975
Emma Bull, *War for the Oaks*, 1987
Pat Cadigan, *Synners*, 1991
Robert N. Charrette, *Never Deal with a Dragon*, 1990
Nigel Findley, *2XS*, 1992
William Gibson, *Neuromancer*, 1984
Christopher Kubasik, *Changeling*, 1992
Jordan K. Weisman, *Into the Shadows*, 1992
    editor
Jack Yeovil, *Comeback Tour: The Sky Belongs to the Stars*, 1992
    The Sky Belongs to the Stars

3861

PAMELA SARGENT, Editor

Nebula Awards 29

(New York: Harcourt Brace, 1995)

Story type: Science Fiction (Anthology)
Series: Nebula Awards
Summary: Subtitled "SFWA's Choices for the Best Science Fiction and Fantasy of the Year," this volume contains a four-page introduction by the editor listing 1993 Nebula Award finalists and winners; comments by nine authors in "The Year in Science Fiction and Fantasy: A Symposium"; a 14-page article on fantastic films of 1993 by Kathi Maio; memorials to Avram Davidson, Lester del Rey and Chad Oliver; two poems by William J. Daciuk and Jane Yolen; 11 pages of appendixes, including selected titles from the preliminary ballot and a list of previous winners; plus nine stories and exerpts by authors including Terry Bisson, Jack Cady, Harlan Ellison, Lisa Goldstein, Joe Haldeman, and Connie Willis.

Other books you might like:
Michael Bishop, *Nebula Awards 24*, 1990
    editor
Michael Bishop, *Nebula Awards 25*, 1991
    editor
James Morrow, *Nebula Awards 26*, 1992
    editor
James Morrow, *Nebula Awards 27*, 1993
    editor
James Morrow, *Nebula Awards 28*, 1994
    editor
George Zebrowski, *Nebula Awards 22*, 1988
    editor

3862

PAMELA SARGENT, Editor

Nebula Awards 30

(New York: Harcourt Brace, 1996)

Story type: Science Fiction (Anthology)
Series: Nebula Awards
Summary: Subtitled "SFWA's Choices for the Best Science Fiction and Fantasy of the Year," this volume contains a five-page introduction by the editor listing 1994 Nebula Award finalists and winners; comments by seven authors in "The Year in Science Fiction and Fantasy: A Symposium"; a 14-page article on fantastic films of 1994 by Kathi Maio; a memorial to Robert Bloch; three poems by W. Gregory Steward and Robert Frazier, Jeff Vandermeer, and Bruce Boston; 11 pages of appendixes including selected titles from the preliminary ballot and a list of previous winners; plus 11 excerpts and stories by authors including Greg Bear, Ben Bova, Joe Haldeman, Damon Knight, Ursula K. Le Guin, Maureen F. McHugh, Mike Resnick, Martha Soukup, and Kate Wilhelm.

Other books you might like:
Michael Bishop, *Nebula Awards 24*, 1990
    editor

Michael Bishop, *Nebula Awards 25*, 1991
    editor
James Morrow, *Nebula Awards 26*, 1992
    editor
James Morrow, *Nebula Awards 27*, 1993
    editor
James Morrow, *Nebula Awards 28*, 1994
    editor
George Zebrowski, *Nebula Awards 22*, 1988
    editor

3863

PAMELA SARGENT, Editor

Women of Wonder, the Classic Years: Science Fiction by Women From the 1940s to the 1970s
(New York: Harcourt Brace, 1995)

Story type: Science Fiction (Anthology)
Series: Women of Wonder

Summary: This companion volume to *Women of Wonder, the Contemporary Years:. . .* contains a 20-page introduction detailing women's involvement in science fiction literature from its earliest publication through the mid-1970s and the important directions in the genre which grow directly from interests promoted by women writers, 15 pages of notes about the authors and editor, 13 pages of recommended science fiction by women 1818-1978, plus 21 stories arranged chronologically 1944-1978. Frequently dark in tone, the stories explore a broad range of themes, many focusing on human interaction and new possibilities, with 13 reprinted from earlier *Women of Wonder* anthologies and eight newly incorporated herein. Authors include Eleanor Arnason, Leigh Brackett, Marion Zimmer Bradley, Zenna Henderson, Ursula K. Le Guin, Katherine MacLean, Anne McCaffrey, Vonda N. McIntyre, Judith Merril, C.L. More, Kit Reed, Joanna Russ, Margaret St. Clair, James Tiptree, Jr., Lisa Tuttle, Joan D. Vinge, Kate Wilhelm, and Chelsea Quinn Yarbro.

Other books you might like:
Janrae Frank, *New Eves: Science Fiction about the Extraordinary Women of Today and Tomorrow*, 1994
    Jean Stine, Forrest J. Ackerman, co-editors
Virginia Kidd, *Millennial Women*, 1978
    editor
Alice Laurance, *Cassandra Rising*, 1978
    editor
Vonda N. McIntyre, *Aurora: Beyond Equality*, 1976
    Susan Janice Anderson, co-editor
Robert Silverberg, *The Crystal Ship*, 1976
    editor

3864

PAMELA SARGENT, Editor

Women of Wonder, the Contemporary Years: Science Fiction by Women From the 1970s to the 1990s
(New York: Harcourt Brace, 1995)

Story type: Science Fiction (Anthology)
Series: Women of Wonder

Summary: This companion volume to *Women of Wonder, the Classic Years:. . .* contains a 20-page introduction discussing new directions within modern science fiction and the vital contributions made by women to the genre and to its evolution, 14 pages of notes about the authors and editor, 16 pages of recommended science fiction by women 1979-1993, plus 21 stories arranged chronologically 1978-1993. Stories vary in tone from light to dark with some investigating feminist topics but most exploring the broad wealth of themes available in the genre. Authors include Octavia E. Butler, Pat Cadigan, Suzy McKee Charnas, C.J. Cherryh, Storm Constantine, Carol Emshwiller, Karen Joy Fowler, Mary Gentle, Lisa Goldstein, Nancy Kress, Judith Moffett, Pat Murphy, Rebecca Ore, Pamela Sargent, Sydney J. Van Scyoc, and Connie Willis.

Other books you might like:
Janrae Frank, *New Eves: Science Fiction about the Extraordinary Women of Today and Tomorrow*, 1994
    Jean Stine, Forrest J. Ackerman, co-editors
Virginia Kidd, *Millennial Women*, 1978
    editor
Alice Laurance, *Cassandra Rising*, 1978
    editor
Vonda N. McIntyre, *Aurora: Beyond Equality*, 1976
    Susan Janice Anderson, co-editor
A. Susan Williams, *The Lifted Veil: The Book of Fantastic Literature by Women*, 1993
    editor

3865

SARAH SARGENT

Jonas McFee, A.T.P.
(New York: Bradbury Press, 1989)

Story type: Science Fiction (Young Adult)
Major character(s): Jonas McFee, Teenager; Jacobious Fiar, Scientist
Time period(s): 1980s
Locale(s): United States

Summary: Jonas McFee, friendless, the new kid at school, thinks his luck has changed when a mysterious girl gives him a strange blue ball which can apparently work miracles. Then he finds out that the scientist who created the ball, Jacobious Fiar, is after it, and is willing to do anything to get it. Fiar plans to use the ball's powers to conquer the world.

Other books you might like:
John Brunner, *Children of the Thunder*, 1989

Gertrude Friedberg, *The Revolving Boy*, 1966
H.M. Hoover, *Children of Morrow*, 1973

3866

AL SARRANTONIO, Editor
MARTIN H. GREENBERG, Co-Editor

100 Hair-Raising Little Horror Stories
(New York: Barnes & Noble, 1993)

Story type: Horror (Anthology)

Summary: The 100 short-short (3000 words or less) horror stories collected here cover two centuries and a range of themes, including resurrection of the dead ("The Adventure of the German Student" by Washington Irving), psychotic obsession ("Berenice" by Edgar Allan Poe), horrifying encounters with animals ("The Boarded Window" by Ambrose Bierce), ghosts ("A Different Kind of Dead" by Ed Gorman), psychological horror ("The Grab" by Richard Laymon), alien life forms ("The Rag Thing" by Donald M. Wollheim), premonitions of death (E.F. Benson's "The Passenger"), and combat (Stephen Crane's "The Upturned Face").

Other books you might like:
Isaac Asimov, *Microcosmic Tales*, 1980
    Martin H. Greenberg and Joseph Olander, co-editors
Robert Weinberg, *100 Creepy Little Creature Stories*, 1994
    Stefan Dziemianowicz and Martin H. Greenberg, co-editors
Stefan Dziemianowicz, *100 Ghastly Little Ghost Stories*, 1993
    Robert Weinberg and Martin H. Greenberg, co-editors
Sebastian Wolfe, *The Little Book of Horrors*, 1992

3867

AL SARRANTONIO

Exile
(New York: Roc, 1996)

Story type: Science Fiction (Space Opera)
Series: Five Worlds
Major character(s): Dalin Shar, Ruler (King of Earth); Tabrel Kris, Diplomat; Prime Cornelian, Ruler (High Leader of Mars), Fanatic
Time period(s): 25th century
Locale(s): Earth; Mars

Summary: Seizing rule of Mars by betrayal and brute force, Prime Cornelian will not rest until he controls the human-settled Four Worlds of Earth, Mars, Titan, and Pluto, and moves on to turn Venus into the Fifth World. Dalin Shar must flee his home planet so that he may regroup and gather the necessary forces to fight Cornelian.

Other books you might like:
Kevin J. Anderson, *Blindfold*, 1995
Bill Baldwin, *Canby's Legion*, 1995
David Drake, *The Hammer's Slammers Series*, 1979-1994
Alan Dean Foster, *The Tar-Aiym Krang*, 1972
Margaret Weis, *The Star of the Guardians Series*, 1990-1993
Dave Wolverton, *Beyond the Gate*, 1995

3868

AL SARRANTONIO

House Haunted
(New York: Bantam Spectra, 1991)

Story type: Horror (Haunted House)
Major character(s): Gary Gaimes, Murderer; Richard Falconi, Detective—Police; Ted Brennan, Psychologist (specialist in the paranormal)
Time period(s): 1990s
Locale(s): Hudson Valley, New York

Summary: A house in upstate New York modeled loosely on the same Compass Cross design that formed the foundation of an occult house of horrors built in Europe a century before becomes the gateway for a monster on the other side of life, who draws four victims randomly from the four points of the compass to its lair and subjects them to the degradation and debauchery necessary for its emergence into the world of the living.

Other books you might like:
Michael Cadnum, *Nightlight*, 1989
Tom Elliott, *The Dwelling*, 1989
Richard Matheson, *Hell House*, 1971
Chet Williamson, *Soulstorm*, 1986

3869

AL SARRANTONIO

Moonbane
(New York: Bantam Spectra, 1989)

Story type: Science Fiction (Invasion of Earth)
Major character(s): Jason Blake, Writer (Poet); Pettis, Military Personnel, Astronaut
Time period(s): 1980s
Locale(s): United States

Summary: Monstrous, wolf-like aliens invade Earth. If they so much as draw blood from a human being, that person becomes one of them. A small band of soldiers, astronauts, and scientists struggle to defeat them.

Other books you might like:
David Dvorkin, *Ursus*, 1989
Richard Matheson, *I Am Legend*, 1954
George Romero, *Dawn of the Dead*, 1978
    Susanna Sparrow, co-author

3870

AL SARRANTONIO

October
(New York: Bantam, 1990)

Story type: Horror (Ghost Story)
Major character(s): Eileen Connel, Writer; James Weston, Actor (former); Kevin Michaels, Professor
Time period(s): 1990s
Locale(s): New Polk, New England

Summary: As Halloween approaches, aging author Eileen Connel, who is afflicted with Alzheimer's disease, and burned-out actor James Weston, on the run from his crowded career and searching for himself, remember their pasts while Kevin Michaels, an assistant professor of literature at the University of New Polk enmeshed in academic politics tries to stimulate interest in Connel's occult book, *Season of Witches*.

Other books you might like:
Ray Bradbury, *The October Country*, 1955
Lisa Cantrell, *The Manse*, 1987
Charles L. Grant, *For Fear of the Night*, 1988
Charles L. Grant, *The Last Call of Mourning*, 1979
Stephen King, *Carrie*, 1974

3871
AL SARRANTONIO

Skeletons
(New York: Bantam, 1992)

Story type: Horror (Apocalyptic Horror; Reanimated Dead)
Major character(s): Clair St. Eve, Child; Roger Garbage, Producer (record producer); Abraham Lincoln, Historical Figure
Time period(s): 1990s
Locale(s): Cold Spring Harbor, New York; Moscow, Russia; Springfield, Illinois

Summary: The earth's passage through a peculiar interstellar cloud results in the resurrection of the dead as an army of walking skeletons. Seen through the eyes of four different characters, this novel tells of war between the humans and the skeletons, the latter acting mostly as they did while still alive.

Other books you might like:
George Romero, *Dawn of the Dead*, 1978
    Susannah Sparrow, co-author
John Russo, *Night of the Living Dead*, 1981
Chet Williamson, *Ash Wednesday*, 1987

3872
JOHN SAUL

Black Lightning
(New York: Fawcett Columbine, 1995)

Story type: Horror (Serial Killer; Supernatural Vengeance)
Major character(s): Anne Jeffers, Journalist; Glen Jeffers, Architect; Mark Blakemore, Police Officer
Time period(s): 1990s (1995)
Locale(s): Seattle, Washington

Summary: Richard Kraven, a serial killer obsessed with the metaphysics of life and death, dies in the electric chair at the same moment that Glen Jeffers suffers a heart attack. After Glen's recovery, his wife Anne, a newspaper reporter who helped send Kraven to his death, notices a pattern in a series of murders closing in on her that suggests Kraven's spirit and motivation have some how managed to outlive him.

Other books you might like:
Dean R. Koontz, *Hideaway*, 1992

Joe R. Lansdale, *The Nightrunners*, 1987
Christopher Pike, *The Cold One*, 1995
Ramona Stewart, *The Possession of Joel Delaney*, 1970

3873
JOHN SAUL

Creature
(New York: Bantam, 1990)

Story type: Horror (Science Fiction)
Major character(s): Sharon Tanner, Housewife; Mark Tanner, Teenager, Sports Figure (Football player)
Time period(s): 1980s
Locale(s): Silverdale, Colorado

Summary: Silverdale seems idyllic to the Tanner family, especially the high school with its perenially undefeated football team. But when Mark joins the team, the Tanners learn about the peculiar training and conditioning techniques the boys are subjected to—procedures that threaten to turn Mark into a raging monster.

Other books you might like:
Andrew Neiderman, *Perfect Little Angels*, 1989

3874
JOHN SAUL

Darkness
(New York: Bantam, 1991)

Story type: Horror (Child-in-Peril)
Major character(s): Warren Phillips, Doctor; Kelly Anderson, Teenager; Ted Anderson, Construction Worker, Parent (Kelly's father)
Time period(s): 1990s
Locale(s): Villejeune, Florida

Summary: Under the cover of night, respected town physician Warren Phillips adopts the guise of "The Dark Man," a cult leader who extracts fluid from the thymus glands of the children who follow him. By day, he injects this fluid into the leading male citizens of Villejeune, guaranteeing them eternal youth as long as the fluid supply is not exhausted.

Other books you might like:
John Arbucci, *Blood of Innocents*, 1991
Dean R. Koontz, *Servants of Twilight*, 1984
Andrew Neiderman, *Perfect Little Angels*, 1989

3875
JOHN SAUL

Guardian
(New York: Fawcett/Columbine, 1993)

Story type: Horror (Werewolf Story)
Major character(s): Joey Wilkerson, Teenager; Mary Anne Carpenter, Parent; Alison Carpenter, Teenager
Time period(s): 1990s
Locale(s): Sugarloaf Valley, Idaho

Summary: When her best friend and best friend's husband are mauled to death by a wild animal, Mary Anne Carpenter moves her family from New Jersey to the El Monte Ranch in Idaho to take care of the couple's child, her godson Joey. But Joey's fascination with animals, his nightime activities, and the continuation of maulings amongst the townspeople of the Sugarloaf Valley convince Mary Anne that Joey somehow is responsible for the deaths.

Other books you might like:
Ramsey Campbell, *Incarnate*, 1983
Charles L. Grant, *The Pet*, 1986
Stephen Gresham, *The Living Dark*, 1991
Stephen King, *Firestarter*, 1980
Melanie Tem, *Wilding*, 1992

3876

JOHN SAUL

The Homing

(New York: Fawcett Columbine, 1994)

Story type: Horror (Science Fiction)
Major character(s): Karen Spellman, Secretary—Legal; Julie Spellman, Teenager (Karen's 16-year-old daughter); Carl Henderson, Scientist (entomologist)
Time period(s): 1990s
Locale(s): Pleasant Valley, California

Summary: In an attempt to cover up his perverse penchant for abducting runaways and torturing them to death, entomologist Carl Henderson injects a witness, Julie Spellman, with an anti-venin used to treat the strings of the strain of mutant bees he has created to help the local farmers. But the attempted murder backfires, transforming Julie into a monstrous hybrid of human and insect.

Other books you might like:
H.F. Heard, *A Taste for Honey*, 1941
Frank Herbert, *Hellstrom's Hive*, 1973
H.G. Wells, *The Food of the Gods*, 1904

3877

JOHN SAUL

Second Child

(New York: Bantam, 1990)

Story type: Horror (Ghost Story)
Major character(s): Melissa Holloway, Teenager; Teri MacIver, Teenager (Melissa's stepsister); D'Arcy Malloy, Spirit
Time period(s): 1990s
Locale(s): Secret Cove, Maine

Summary: Ostracized by her peer group and tormented by her cruel stepsister, Melissa Holloway finds solace in her friendship with the spirit of D'Arcy Malloy, a serving girl who died in her house a century before and whose tragically spurned affections mirror Melissa's own plight.

Other books you might like:
William March, *The Bad Seed*, 1954
Jean Paiva, *The Lilith Factor*, 1989

Thomas Tryon, *The Other*, 1971

3878

JOHN SAUL

Shadows

(New York: Bantam, 1993)

Story type: Horror (Child-in-Peril)
Major character(s): Josh MacCallum, Child (10 years old); Brenda MacCallum, Waiter/Waitress; Amy Carlson, Child (10 years old)
Time period(s): 1990s (1992)
Locale(s): Barrington, California

Summary: Brenda MacCallum enrolls her precocious but difficult child Josh in the prestigious Barrington Academy for gifted children, unaware that the director of the school is embarked on a secret project to literally merge the intelligences of his young students with computers. This novel was originally published in 1992.

Other books you might like:
John Arbucci, *Blood of Innocents*, 1991
Eric Flanders, *The Forever Children*, 1992
Dean R. Koontz, *Midnight*, 1989
David Martin, *Bring Me Children*, 1992

3879

ELIZABETH A. SAUNDERS, Editor

When the Black Lotus Blooms

(Atlanta: Unnameable Press, 1990)

Story type: Horror (Anthology)

Summary: Forty-two stories and poems of the macabre, ranging from a reprint of Mary Elizabeth Counselman's 1941 *Weird Tales* story, ''The Drifting Atoms,'' to contemporary tales such as Gerald W. Page's H.P. Lovecraft spoof, ''Strange High Armadillo in the Mist''; James A. Riley's rural horror story, ''The Old Marsh Road''; Charles Grant's ghostly western, ''Pinto Rider''; and Joseph Payne Brennan's tale of a soldier's guilt, ''The Gray Smudge.'' Illustrated and with an introduction by Robert R. McCammon.

Other books you might like:
Peter Enfantino, *Quick Chills*, 1990
Jessica Amanda Salmonson, *Tales by Moonlight II*, 1989
Jessica Amanda Salmonson, *Tales by Moonlight*, 1984
Stuart David Schiff, *The Whispers Series*, 1977-1987
David B. Silva, *Best of The Horror Show*, 1987

3880

ADRIAN SAVAGE

Symphony

(New York: Pocket, 1992)

Story type: Horror (Occult)
Major character(s): Prometheus ''Bruce Payne'' Faust, Religious (Satanic priest); Helen Singer, Police Officer (detec-

tive sergeant, NYPD); Cal Hudson, Producer (record producer), Religious (Satanic priest)
Time period(s): 1990s (1992)
Locale(s): New York, New York

Summary: Ex-cop and dignified Satanist Prometheus Faust teams up with police officer Helen Singer to thwart a cult of renegade Satanists who commit ritual murders in the hope of inciting race riots that will further their rise to power.

Other books you might like:
Ken Eulo, *Manhattan Heat*, 1991
Tanya Huff, *Blood Price*, 1991
Gordon Linzner, *The Troupe*, 1988
Graham Masterton, *The Burning*, 1991
Robert Weinberg, *The Black Lodge*, 1991

3881
FELICITY SAVAGE

Delta City
(New York: Roc, 1996)

Story type: Fantasy (Political; Religious)
Series: Humility Garden
Major character(s): Humility ''Humi'' Garden, Ruler (deposed), Revolutionary; Pati, Deity, Ruler; Arity ''Ari'', Addict, Outcast
Time period(s): Indeterminate
Locale(s): Delta City, Fictional City

Summary: Where Humility, the first and last human Divinarch, once ruled, Pati now reigns so insanely that even the cowed populace plots against him. They need a leader and turn to Humility. But since the last time she fought Pati she lost both her eyes and throne, what does she have left to lose? Sequel to *Humility Garden*.

Other books you might like:
Steven Brust, *Jhereg*, 1983
Storm Constantine, *Wraeththu*, 1993
P.C. Hodgell, *God Stalk*, 1982
Tanith Lee, *Death's Master*, 1979
Fritz Leiber, *Ill Met in Lankhmar*, 1995

3882
FELICITY SAVAGE

Humility Garden
(New York: Roc, 1995)

Story type: Fantasy (Political; Religious)
Series: Humility Garden
Major character(s): Humility ''Humi'' Garden, Apprentice (ghoster), Artist; Beauty ''Beau'' Garden, Artist (ghost)
Time period(s): Indeterminate (local year 1352)
Locale(s): Salt, Planet—Imaginary

Summary: Childhood friends, Humi and Beau depart their impoverished village, bound for different fates. While Beau's beauty propels him into becoming undead artwork, a ghost, displayed for the pleasure of the powerful, Humi's drive and intelligence leads her to an apprenticeship as ghoster and on to that prestigious vocation. First novel.

Other books you might like:
Richard Adams, *Maia*, 1985
Kim Antieau, *The Jigsaw Woman*, 1996
Mary Gentle, *Rats and Gargoyles*, 1991
P.C. Hodgell, *God Stalk*, 1982
Nancy Kress, *Beggars in Spain*, 1993
S.P. Somtow, *I Wake From a Dream of a Drowned Star City*, 1992
Michael Swanwick, *The Iron Dragon's Daughter*, 1994

3883
ROBERT J. SAWYER

End of an Era
(New York: Ace, 1994)

Story type: Science Fiction (Time Travel; Invasion of Earth)
Major character(s): Brandon Thackeray, Scientist (paleontologist), Museum Curator; Miles Jordan, Scientist (paleontologist), Museum Curator
Time period(s): 2010s (2013); Indeterminate Past (Cretaceous era)
Locale(s): Alberta, Canada; *Sternberger*, Spaceship (timeship); North America

Summary: Using an experimental timeship, Brandon Thackeray travels to the end of the Cretaceous to discover the cause of dinosaur extinction.

Other books you might like:
Octavia E. Butler, *Dawn*, 1987
Michael Crichton, *Jurassic Park*, 1990
Diana G. Gallagher, *The Alien Dark*, 1990
Harry Harrison, *West of Eden*, 1984
Stephen Leigh, *Ray Bradbury Presents: Dinosaur World*, 1992

3884
ROBERT J. SAWYER

Far-Seer
(New York: Ace, 1992)

Story type: Science Fiction (Adventure; Theological)
Major character(s): Afsan, Alien (Quintaglio), Apprentice (astrologer)
Time period(s): Indeterminate
Locale(s): Quintaglio Home World, Moon—Imaginary

Summary: On his coming-of-age pilgrimage to the far side of his world, Afsan makes a discovery which could bring revolution to his profession if not his entire society.

Other books you might like:
James Gurney, *Dinotopia*, 1992
Stephen Leigh, *Ray Bradbury Presents: Dinosaur Planet*, 1993
Stephen Leigh, *Ray Bradbury Presents: Dinosaur World*, 1992
Dave Wolverton, *Path of the Hero*, 1993
Dave Wolverton, *Serpent Catch*, 1991

3885

ROBERT J. SAWYER

Fossil Hunter

(New York: Ace, 1993)

Story type: Science Fiction (Theological)
Series: Far-Seer
Major character(s): Kee-Toroca, Alien (Quintaglio), Scientist; Afsan, Alien (Quintaglio), Scholar; Dy-Dybo, Alien (Quintaglio), Ruler (Emperor)
Time period(s): Indeterminate
Locale(s): Quintaglio Home World, Moon—Imaginary

Summary: To aid the effort to leave their moon which will disintegrate all too soon, Toroca leads the effort to inventory everything on their moon. He discovers an alien artifact which changes his understanding of his world and the Quintaglios' place on it.

Other books you might like:
Eleanor Arnason, *A Woman of the Iron People*, 1991
C.J. Cherryh, *Chanur's Legacy*, 1992
Diana G. Gallagher, *The Alien Dark*, 1990
James Gurney, *Dinotopia*, 1992
Stephen Leigh, *Ray Bradbury Presents: Dinosaur World*, 1992
L. Neil Smith, *Their Majesties' Bucketeers*, 1981
Vernor Vinge, *A Fire upon the Deep*, 1992

3886

ROBERT J. SAWYER

Golden Fleece

(New York: Popular Library/Questar, 1990)

Story type: Science Fiction (Mystery)
Major character(s): Aaron Rossman, Spaceman (landing fleet supervisor); JASON, Computer
Time period(s): 22nd century (2179)
Locale(s): *Argo*, Spaceship; Thunder Bay, Ontario, Canada

Summary: In order to avoid the possibility of losing crew from the *Argo* before departing to a distant world, artificial intelligences have kept news of the first intelligent signals from space hidden from humans. When Diana Chandler dies, her ex-husband cannot accept the death as accidental. As Aaron probes, he finds the murderer must be the artificial intelligence which controls every facet of shipboard life.

Other books you might like:
Jeffrey A. Carver, *The Rapture Effect*, 1987
Arthur C. Clarke, *2001: A Space Odyssey*, 1968
D.F. Jones, *Colossus*, 1967
Dan Simmons, *The Fall of Hyperion*, 1990
Dan Simmons, *Hyperion*, 1989

3887

ROBERT J. SAWYER

The Terminal Experiment

(New York: HarperPrism, 1995)

Story type: Science Fiction (Mystery; Alternate Intelligence)
Major character(s): Peter Hobson, Scientist, Engineer (bio-medical); Cathy Hobson, Advertising; Sarkar Muhammed, Computer Expert
Time period(s): 2010s (2011)
Locale(s): Toronto, Ontario, Canada

Summary: Peter Hobson and Sarkar Muhammed develop a personality scanner which creates artificial intelligences based on a human subject. When Peter generates electronic copies of himself to investigate theories of immortality and life after death, one becomes a murderer, while all three escape into the computer network. Serialized as *Hobson's Choice*.

Other books you might like:
Ben Bova, *Death Dream*, 1994
Pat Cadigan, *Fools*, 1992
Pierre Ouellette, *The Deus Machine*, 1994
Cole Perriman, *Terminal Games*, 1994
John Varley, *Steel Beach*, 1992

3888

ELIZABETH ANN SCARBOROUGH

Carol for Another Christmas

(New York: Ace, 1996)

Story type: Fantasy (Urban; Legend)
Major character(s): Monica Banks, Businesswoman; Ebenezer Scrooge, Spirit, Artificial Intelligence; Curtis Lu, Computer Expert
Time period(s): 1990s
Locale(s): Seattle, Washington

Summary: Monica Banks allows her work to keep her too busy for any personal life. Created as a computer program artifact, Ebenezer Scrooge visits Monica as the Ghosts of Christmas Past, Present, and Future, hoping to awaken Monica to a wider, more meaningful world.

Other books you might like:
Richard Dalby, *Ghosts for Christmas*, 1988
  editor
James Finn Garner, *Politically Correct Holiday Stories*, 1995
David G. Hartwell, *Spirits of Christmas*, 1989
  Kathryn Cramer, co-editor
Tom Mula, *Jacob Marley's Christmas Carol*, 1995
Mike Resnick, *Christmas Ghosts*, 1993
  Martin H. Greenberg, co-editor
Kristine Kathryn Rusch, *Pulphouse, Issue 10: Special Issue*, 1991
  editor

3889

ELIZABETH ANN SCARBOROUGH

The Godmother
(New York: Ace, 1994)

Story type: Fantasy (Urban; Light Fantasy)
Major character(s): Rosalie "Rose" Samson, Social Worker; Felicity Fortune, Mythical Creature (fairy godmother)
Time period(s): 1990s
Locale(s): Seattle, Washington

Summary: Rose's wish for a fairy godmother for the city of Seattle brings Felicity, who helps in the battle against a mountain of problems afflicting youngsters. Rewritten plots and characters from many fairy tales appear as framework while themes of child abuse, gang violence and other urban issues provide a modern setting.

Other books you might like:
Chester Anderson, *The Butterfly Kid*, 1967
Gael Baudino, *Strands of Sunlight*, 1994
Ellen Guon, *Bedlam Boyz*, 1993
Mercedes Lackey, *Born to Run*, 1992
   Larry Dixon, co-author
Mercedes Lackey, *Summoned to Tourney*, 1992
   Ellen Guon, co-author
Mercedes Lackey, *Wheels of Fire*, 1992
   Mark Shepherd, co-author
Susan Palwick, *Flying in Place*, 1992
Nancy Springer, *The Friendship Song*, 1992

3890

ELIZABETH ANN SCARBOROUGH

The Godmother's Apprentice
(New York: Ace, 1995)

Story type: Fantasy (Light Fantasy; Legend)
Major character(s): Felicity Fortune, Mythical Creature (fairy godmother); Snohomish "Sno" Quantrill, Apprentice, Traveller
Time period(s): 1990s
Locale(s): Ireland

Summary: When Felicity Fortune undertakes the task of teaching Snohomish Quantrill to become a fairy godmother, Sno must travel to Ireland to learn the roots of the craft. Journal entries interweave contemporary action and Celtic lore.

Other books you might like:
Chester Anderson, *The Butterfly Kid*, 1967
Gael Baudino, *Strands of Sunlight*, 1994
Maya Kaathryn Bohnhoff, *The Meri*, 1992
Esther Friesner, *Wishing Season*, 1993
Jody Lynn Nye, *Mythology Abroad*, 1991
S.P. Somtow, *The Wizard's Apprentice*, 1993

3891

ELIZABETH ANN SCARBOROUGH

The Healer's War
(New York: Bantam Spectra, 1989)

Story type: Fantasy (Contemporary)
Series: Healer's War
Major character(s): Kitty McCulley, Nurse, Military Personnel (Lieutenant)
Time period(s): 1960s
Locale(s): Vietnam

Summary: One of Kitty's patients, a Vietnamese holy man, gives her an amulet that gives her the power to touch people in a way that gives meaning to life in the midst of war. When Kitty is stranded in enemy-held jungle with a child, the amulet's power saves her sanity, and her life.

Other books you might like:
Gustav Hasford, *The Short Timers*, 1987
Bruce McAllister, *Dream Baby*, 1989
Peter Straub, *Koko*, 1989

3892

ELIZABETH ANN SCARBOROUGH

Last Refuge
(New York: Bantam Spectra, 1992)

Story type: Fantasy (Post-Disaster; Religious)
Series: Healer's War
Major character(s): Chime Cincinnati, Guardian (bodhissatva), Religious (guide)
Time period(s): 22nd century
Locale(s): Shambala, Tibet

Summary: Shambala's reincarnated guardian protector hears the call of souls wishing entrance to Shambala. On reaching adulthood, Chime decides to continue her ancient duty of guiding enlightened individuals to the hidden realm. Chime ventures outside the haven into a land devastated by nuclear war where evil spirits attempt to thwart her mission. Sequel to *Nothing Sacred*.

Other books you might like:
Suzette Haden Elgin, *Twelve Fair Kingdoms*, 1981
James Hilton, *Lost Horizon*, 1933
Marc Laidlaw, *Neon Lotus*, 1988
Kim Stanley Robinson, *Escape From Kathmandu*, 1989
Geoff Ryman, *The Unconquered Country*, 1986
Terri Windling, *Life on the Border*, 1991
   editor

3893

ELIZABETH ANN SCARBOROUGH

Nothing Sacred
(New York: Doubleday Foundation, 1991)

Story type: Fantasy (Contemporary; Post-Disaster)
Series: Healer's War

Major character(s): Viveka "Viv" Jeng Vanachek, Military Personnel, Cartographer; Ama "Ama-la" Terton, Doctor, Guardian (Bodhisattva); Nyima Wu, Actress (journalist), Military Personnel (POW camp commandant)
Time period(s): 2070s
Locale(s): Shambala, Tibet

Summary: The story unfolds through Viveka's journal entries begun after an ill-fated first mission. When captured, Viveka and other captives march through the Himalaya Mountains to an isolated POW camp where they work on rebuilding an ancient lamasary. As weeks go by Viveka learns that the site and its occupants may be the last and best hope for the survival of humanity. This book follows *The Healer's War* (1989).

Other books you might like:
Diana G. Gallagher, *The Alien Dark*, 1990
James Hilton, *Lost Horizon*, 1933
Marc Laidlaw, *Neon Lotus*, 1988
Abraham Merritt, *Dwellers in the Mirage*, 1932
Ayn Rand, *Atlas Shrugged*, 1957
Kim Stanley Robinson, *Escape From Kathmandu*, 1989
Geoff Ryman, *The Unconquered Country*, 1986
Dan Simmons, *Hyperion*, 1989
Sheri S. Tepper, *Grass*, 1989
Vernor Vinge, *The Peace War*, 1984

3894

ELIZABETH ANN SCARBOROUGH

Phantom Banjo
(New York: Bantam Spectra, 1991)

Story type: Fantasy (Magic Conflict; Quest)
Series: Songkiller Saga
Major character(s): Willie MacKai, Musician; Julianne Martin, Musician; Augusta "Gussie" Turner, Saloon Keeper/Owner
Time period(s): 1990s
Locale(s): United States; Hell

Summary: Once upon a time, "all the devils in the world" decided that folk music was impeding their mission of making the human race completely miserable. When the Chairdevil put his plan into action, folk musicians began to find themselves in trouble with the IRS, unemployed, or in trouble with the law, their recordings and sheet music "accidentally" destroyed, and the words forgotten. When musician Sam Hawthorne dies suddenly, his magic banjo ends up in the hands of retired musician Willie MacKai who sets out to learn the truth, aided by the banjo and his friends and hindered by the Devils.

Other books you might like:
Eleanor Arnason, *Daughter of the Bear King*, 1987
Emma Bull, *War for the Oaks*, 1987
Mercedes Lackey, *Knight of Ghosts and Shadows*, 1990
  Ellen Guon, co-author
C.S. Lewis, *The Screwtape Letters*, 1942
R.A. MacAvoy, *Twisting the Rope*, 1986

3895

ELIZABETH ANN SCARBOROUGH

Picking the Ballad's Bones
(New York: Bantam Spectra, 1991)

Story type: Fantasy (Magic Conflict; Quest)
Series: Songkiller Saga
Major character(s): Willie MacKai, Musician; Augusta "Gussie" Turner, Saloon Keeper/Owner; Sir Walter Scott, Historical Figure, Spirit
Time period(s): 1990s
Locale(s): Scotland; England; Hell

Summary: The forces of evil make progress in their war against folk music, but a small band of musicians, following the musical hints of a magical banjo, have arrived in Great Britain to find the originals of the songs which are disappearing in the United States. They find allies in the ghosts of Sir Walter Scott and his wizard ancestor, Michael Scott, and Torchy Burns, a.k.a. Debauchery Devil, a.k.a. Queen of Faerie. She arranges a spell that will allow them to go back and learn the ballads by re-living the situations that inspired them, thereby recovering the songs, if they can survive.

Other books you might like:
Margaret Ball, *The Shadow Gate*, 1990
R.A. MacAvoy, *Damiano*, 1983
R.A. MacAvoy, *Damiano's Lute*, 1984
Janet Morris, *Heroes in Hell*, 1986
Clifford D. Simak, *Out of Their Minds*, 1970

3896

ELIZABETH ANN SCARBOROUGH

Strum Again?
(New York: Bantam Spectra, 1992)

Story type: Fantasy (Magic Conflict; Contemporary)
Series: Songkiller Saga
Major character(s): Willie MacKai, Musician; Julianne Martin, Musician; Debauchery Devil/Torchy Burns, Mythical Creature, Demon
Time period(s): 1990s
Locale(s): Southwest

Summary: Willie MacKai and his fellow musicians have returned to the United States with a renewed stock of songs to sing, but they encounter trouble getting people interested in folk music. While the Chairdevil and his minions wreak havoc with tornados, floods and serial killers, Willie strikes a deal with the debauchery devil, formerly the Queen of Faerie, agreeing to use Willie as her sacrifice which pays her overdue tithe to Hell. With a magic mandolin made from the broken remains of the phantom banjo, Willie's friends gather on Midsummer's Eve for the final showdown with the forces of evil.

Other books you might like:
Gael Baudino, *Gossamer Axe*, 1990
Emma Bull, *War for the Oaks*, 1987
Pamela Dean, *Tam Lin*, 1991
John M. Ford, *How Much for Just the Planet?*, 1987

R.A. MacAvoy, *Twisting the Rope*, 1986
Anne McCaffrey, *Crystal Singer*, 1982
Elizabeth Marie Pope, *The Perilous Gard*, 1974

3897

FRANK SCHAEFER

Whose Song Is Sung

(New York: Tor, 1996)

Story type: Fantasy (Legend; Adventure)
Major character(s): Musculus Herodes Formosus, Adventurer, Handicapped (dwarf); Beowulf, Hero, Adventurer; Grundbur, Monster
Time period(s): Indeterminate Past
Locale(s): Europe; Middle East

Summary: After a lowly birth and rise to a position of power, Musculus loses Imperial favor in Byzantium and finds himself sold into slavery. His subsequent odyssey leads to Northern Europe where he meets Beowulf and shares his travels.

Other books you might like:
Frans G. Bengtsson, *The Long Ships*, 1954
John Gardner, *Grendel*, 1971
Parke Godwin, *The Tower of Beowulf*, 1995
Stephan Grundy, *Rhinegold*, 1994
Harry Harrison, *The Hammer and the Cross*, 1993
   John Holm, co-author

3898

STUART DAVID SCHIFF, Editor

The Best of Whispers

(Baltimore: Borderlands Press, 1994)

Story type: Horror (Anthology)

Summary: The 23 stories gathered here represent the cream of *Whispers*, the semi-professional magazine and anthology series published between 1972 and 1987 that forged a link between modern fiction of the pre- and postwar years and the contemporary horror movement. Included are two World Fantasy Award-winning stories, Karl Edward Wagner's "Sticks" and Alan Ryan's "The Bones Wizard"; Steve Rasnic Tem's British Fantasy Award-winning "Leaks"; Hugh Cave's sea monster tale, "From the Lower Deeps"; David Schow's tale of a haunted movie theatre, "One for the Horrors"; Dennis Etchison's tale of medical horror, "The Dead Line"; David Campton's story of a disabled young girl's strange playmate, "At the Bottom of the Garden"; David Drake's dark heroic fantasy, "The Barrow Troll"; Ramsey Campbell's Christmas chiller, "The Chimney"; the original version of Ray Bradbury's "The Screaming Woman"; and the original short novel version of Lucius Shepard's vampire tale "The Golden." Five stories are original to the book.

Other books you might like:
Charles L. Grant, *The Best of Shadows*, 1988
   editor
David B. Silva, *Best of The Horror Show*, 1992
   editor

3899

GERALD A. SCHILLER

Deadly Dreams

(Fairfax Station, Virginia: Intercontinental Publishing, 1996)

Story type: Horror (Mystery)
Major character(s): Denise Burton, Secretary; Richard Kramer, Scientist (biologist); Rogers Kennison, Journalist
Time period(s): 1990s (1996)
Locale(s): Chatsworth, California

Summary: Denise Burton suspects that her horrifying nightmares of lying on an operating table while surgeons systematically remove her internal organs is linked to her job at Marikem Industries, a chemical company. Her investigations reveal a cover-up of a biological experiment that used human beings as guinea pigs. First novel.

Other books you might like:
Kevin J. Anderson, *Ground Zero*, 1995
Robin Cook, *Coma*, 1977
Lyle Howard, *Mr. Sandman*, 1995
Dean R. Koontz, *The House of Thunder*, 1982
F. Paul Wilson, *Implant*, 1995

3900

VIVIAN SCHILLING

Sacred Prey

(Sherman Oaks, California: Truman Press, 1994)

Story type: Horror (Supernatural Vengeance)
Major character(s): Adam Claiborne, Businessman; Monique Sinclair, Entertainer (barroom singer); Kyle Claiborne, Criminal
Time period(s): 1990s (1994)
Locale(s): New Orleans, Louisiana

Summary: When loan shark Adam Claiborne hunts down and shoots a man with an outstanding debt to him in the swamps of Louisiana, he incurs the wrath of voodoo powers to which his victim was privy. Suddenly, Adam finds himself trapped inside his quarry's body, struggling to avoid pursuit and convince others that he is not who he appears to be. This is the author's first novel.

Other books you might like:
Rene Belletto, *Machine*, 1993
Harlan Ellison, *Mefisto in Onyx*, 1993
Damon Knight, *Mind Switch*, 1963
Richard Matheson, *7 Past Midnight*, 1992
Rod Serling, *The Season to Be Wary*, 1967

3901

DENNIS SCHMIDT

Labyrinth

(New York: Ace Books, 1989)

Story type: Science Fiction (Space Opera)
Series: Questioner Trilogy
Major character(s): Seeker, Alien; Bilrog, Alien

Time period(s): Indeterminate Future
Locale(s): Labyrinth, Planet—Imaginary

Summary: The dangerous and mysterious sentient planet Labyrinth, used by the Galactic Empire to train its elite police force, seems a very different place to each trainee, depending largely on that person's attitude towards existence.

Other books you might like:
Orson Scott Card, *Ender's Game*, 1985
Harry Harrison, *Deathworld*, 1960
Stanislaw Lem, *Solaris*, 1971
Larry Niven, *The Legacy of Heorot*, 1987
    Jerry Pournelle and Steven Barnes, co-authors
Dave Wolverton, *On My Way to Paradise*, 1989

3902

DAVID J. SCHOW

Black Leather Required

(Shingletown, California: Mark V. Ziesing, 1994)

Story type: Horror (Collection)

Summary: This third collection of short fiction by the leading exponent of splatterpunk contains 13 previously uncollected short stories, including three original to the volume. Among the best are "Jerry's Kids Meet Wormboy," a deliriously graphic tale of a social misfit defending himself against a horde of ravenous zombies; "Kamikaze Butterflies," in which people from the present travel back to the prehistoric age to deliberately change the course of history; the vampire tale, "A Week in the Unlife"; "The Shaft," a tale of urban horror that eventually grew into the author's second novel; "Bad Guy Hats," a tale of ultraviolence; and a moving tale of love and redemption, "Pitt Night at the Lewiston Boneyard."

Other books you might like:
Joe R. Lansdale, *By Bizarre Hands*, 1989
Richard Christian Matheson, *Scars and Other Distinguishing Trademarks*, 1987
John Skipp, *Deadlines*, 1990
    Craig Spector
Lucy Taylor, *Close to the Bone*, 1993

3903

DAVID J. SCHOW

The Kill Riff

(New York: Tor, 1989)

Story type: Horror (Psychological Suspense)
Major character(s): Lucas Ellington, Parent (Bereaved father); Gabriel Stannard, Singer (Rock and roll)
Time period(s): 1980s (References to 1978)
Locale(s): United States

Summary: After the death of his daughter at a concert of the rock group Whip Hand, Lucas Ellington vows revenge and sets about systematically to get it. Ellington's ultimate target, lead singer Gabriel Stannard, understands that he is the prey and looks forward to the confrontation.

Other books you might like:
George R.R. Martin, *The Armageddon Rag*, 1983
Robert R. McCammon, *Mine*, 1990
John Skipp, *The Scream*, 1986
    Craig Spector, co-author

3904

DAVID J. SCHOW

Lost Angels

(New York: Onyx, 1990)

Story type: Horror (Collection)

Summary: Among the five stories in this collection by a primary exponent of "splatterpunk" horror fiction are the sentimental World Fantasy Award-winning tale "Red Light," the "Twilight-Zone" inspired fantasy "Pamela's Get," the occult thriller "Brass," and an upbeat story about the love of horror films, "Monster Movies." All but the final story are concerned with the loss of love in the modern world. Introduction by Richard Christian Matheson.

Other books you might like:
Dennis Etchison, *Cutting Edge*, 1986
Douglas E. Winter, *Prime Evil*, 1988

3905

DAVID J. SCHOW

Seeing Red

(New York: Tor, 1990)

Story type: Horror (Collection)

Summary: Fourteen stories by a self-confessed "splatterpunk" writer. Gory, ironical, extreme, often funny, saturated with paranoia, the stories find horror in the contemporary world, especially in such off-beat locations as neo-Gothic hotels, cockroach infested movie theaters, rock tours, Hollywood, Beverly Hills, and the pages of pulp magazines.

Other books you might like:
Harlan Ellison, *The Essential Ellison: A 35-Year Retrospective*, 1987
Dennis Etchison, *The Dark Country*, 1982
Dennis Etchison, *Red Dreams*, 1984
George R.R. Martin, *Songs the Dead Men Sing*, 1983

3906

HOWARD SCHWARTZ

Lilith's Cave: Jewish Tales of the Supernatural

(New York: Oxford University Press, 1991)

Story type: Horror (Collection)

Summary: Originally published in 1988, this excellent collection of 50 traditional Jewish folktales retold by Schwartz includes the title story, "The Demon of the Waters," "The Homunculus of Maimonodes," the famous "Rabbi Loew and the Angel of Death," and other tales and fables leavened with the religious beliefs of the European Yiddish community from the last eight centuries. Schwartz provides an index, informative introduction, notes and glossary of terms.

Other books you might like:
Iona Opie, *The Classic Fairy Tales*, 1974
    Peter Opie, co-author
Isaac Bashevis Singer, *Collected Stories*, 1982
Jack Zipes, *Spells of Enchantment*, 1991

3907

DARRELL SCHWEITZER

Transients and Other Disquieting Tales

(Buffalo, New York: Ganley, 1993)

Story type: Horror (Collection)

Summary: These 15 stories (three written in collaboration) explore a variety of dark experiences for their horror content. ''Transients,'' ''Peeling It Off,'' ''Jason, Come Home,'' ''Soft'' and ''Leaving'' are all dark fantasies about the terrifying psychological dislocations that come from feelings of loss and alienation. ''Clocks'' and ''The Paloverde Lodge'' (written with Jason Van Hollander) are poignant tales about the pathological persistence of love, while ''The Man Who Wasn't Nice to Pumpkin Head Dolls'' is a satire on consumerism and ''The Children of Lommos'' (written with John Gregory Betancourt) is a powerful traditional tale of supernatural vengeance.

Other books you might like:
Donald Burleson, *Lemon Drops and Other Horrors*, 1993
Charles L. Grant, *Tales From the Nightside*, 1989
Jessica Amanda Salmonson, *John Collier and Fredric Brown Went Quarreling through My Head*, 1989

3908

CHERI SCOTCH

The Werewolf's Touch

(New York: Diamond, 1993)

Story type: Horror (Werewolf Story)
Major character(s): Andrew Marley, Werewolf, Religious (Episcopal priest); Angela Winfield, Professor, Anthropologist; Simon Spencer, Doctor (psychiatrist)
Time period(s): 1960s (1965)
Locale(s): New Orleans, Louisiana

Summary: In this continuation of the saga begun in *The Werewolf's Kiss* (1992), Andrew Marley, firstborn child of the latest generation of the Marley family, discovers that he is afflicted with the curse of lycanthropy as a result of his grandfather's murder of a voodoo priestess almost a century before. Andrew spends most of the story trying to avoid the same fate as his father, who killed himself upon discovering that he too had inherited the werewolf taint.

Other books you might like:
Michael Cadnum, *St. Peter's Wolf*, 1991
Jane Toombs, *Under the Shadow*, 1992
Chelsea Quinn Yarbro, *The Godforsaken*, 1983

3909

MELISSA SCOTT

Burning Bright

(New York: Tor, 1993)

Story type: Science Fiction (Political; Adventure)
Major character(s): Quin Lioe, Spacewoman (starpilot), Computer Expert (gamer); Illario ''Ambidexter'' Ransome, Computer Expert, Artist; Damian Chrestil, Alien (hsai), Businessman
Time period(s): Indeterminate Future
Locale(s): Burning Bright, Planet—Imaginary

Summary: While her ship undergoes maintenance at Burning Bright, a human and alien center for virtual reality role-playing gaming, Quin Lioe premieres her new gaming scenario. Events on Burning Bright begin to resemble the intrigues of Lioe's game as she finds herself involved in a struggle between commercial and royal interests.

Other books you might like:
C.J. Cherryh, *Serpent's Reach*, 1980
Jean Mark Gawron, *Dream of Glass*, 1993
Rebecca Ore, *Becoming Alien*, 1987
Neal Stephenson, *Snow Crash*, 1992
Jack Williamson, *Mazeway*, 1990

3910

MELISSA SCOTT

Dreamships

(New York: Tor, 1992)

Story type: Science Fiction (Alternate Intelligence; Political)
Major character(s): Reverdy Jian, Pilot (spaceship), Lesbian; Meredalia Mitexi, Computer Expert; Manfred, Artificial Intelligence (shipboard computer)
Time period(s): Indeterminate Future
Locale(s): Persephone, Planet—Imaginary; *Young Lord Byron*, Spaceship; Refuge, Planet—Imaginary

Summary: The Coolies, abandoned indentured workers, violently oppose Dreampeace, an organization promoting the rights of AI's and threatening the Coolies' livelihood. Jian, a Coolie sympathizer given only sketchy specifications for the ship's computer, reluctantly accepts the contract to pilot Mitexi to Refuge to find her brother, the founder of Dreampeace and creator of Manfred. Manfred seems the best ship's controller Jian has ever worked with and possibly the sentient machine Dreampeace needs.

Other books you might like:
Orson Scott Card, *Xenocide*, 1991
Jeffrey A. Carver, *Dragons in the Stars*, 1992
Glen Cook, *The Dragon Never Sleeps*, 1988
Edward Gibson, *In the Wrong Hands*, 1992
Colin Greenland, *Take Back Plenty*, 1992
Dan Simmons, *Hyperion*, 1989
David Alexander Smith, *Homecoming*, 1990

3911

MELISSA SCOTT

Mighty Good Road
(New York: Baen, 1990)

Story type: Science Fiction (Adventure)
Major character(s): Gwynne Heikki, Businesswoman (salvage expert), Adventurer; Sebasten-Janurias, Pilot; Galler Heikki, Businessman (executive of Lo-Moth Corporati)
Time period(s): Indeterminate Future
Locale(s): Iadara, Planet—Imaginary

Summary: Gwynne Heikki returns to her home planet under contract to salvage a downed craft when a previous contractor fails to recover a prototype of the device which will allow rapid development of faster-than-light spacecraft. Investigating the crash site, Gwynne finds the craft was shot down and the prototype device taken. Returning to her home base Gwynne finds her contract cancelled, but doggedly pursues the device, involving herself in unexpected corporate intrigue with her brother, whom she'd hoped never to meet again.

Other books you might like:
Melisa C. Michaels, *Skirmish*, 1985
Alis A. Rasmussen, *A Passage of Stars*, 1990
Alis A. Rasmussen, *The Price of Ransom*, 1990
Alis A. Rasmussen, *Revolution's Shore*, 1990
James H. Schmitz, *The Demon Breed*, 1968

3912

MELISSA SCOTT

Night Sky Mine
(New York: Tor, 1996)

Story type: Science Fiction (Gay/Lesbian Fiction; Cyberpunk)
Major character(s): Ista Kelly, Foundling, Teenager; Rangsey Justin, Computer Expert, Homosexual; Sein Tarasov, Computer Expert (Technical Squad troubleshooter), Homosexual
Time period(s): Indeterminate Future
Locale(s): Wildnet, Cyberspace; Bestla, Planet—Imaginary

Summary: Orphaned during a pirate raid on an asteroid mine, Ista struggles to learn her true identity in a society where one cannot live without an official identity. Her search entails investigating mysterious raids on mining colonies, which the Night Sky Mining Corporation seems to cover up.

Other books you might like:
Jack L. Chalker, *The Cybernetic Walrus*, 1995
C.J. Cherryh, *Cyteen*, 1988
Nicola Griffith, *Slow River*, 1995
Joan D. Vinge, *Psion*, 1982
Vernor Vinge, *A Fire upon the Deep*, 1992

3913

MELISSA SCOTT
LISA A. BARNETT, Co-Author

Point of Hopes
(New York: Tor, 1995)

Story type: Fantasy (Mystery; Magic Conflict)
Major character(s): Nicolas "Nico" Rathe, Police Officer (pointsman); Philip Eslingen, Military Personnel (retired)
Time period(s): Indeterminate
Locale(s): Chenedolle, Fictional Country

Summary: As Midsummer Faire approaches in the medieval capital of the kingdom, Nicolas Rathe must find the cause of increasing numbers of missing children. The problem seems tied to astrological divinations which portend social upheaval.

Other books you might like:
Orson Scott Card, *Lost Boys*, 1992
Pamela Dean, *The Dubious Hills*, 1994
Simon R. Green, *Hawk & Fisher*, 1990
Mickey Zucker Reichert, *Beyond Ragnarok*, 1995
Delia Sherman, *The Porcelain Dove*, 1993
Patricia C. Wrede, *Mairelon the Magician*, 1991

3914

MELISSA SCOTT

Shadow Man
(New York: Tor, 1995)

Story type: Science Fiction (Gay/Lesbian Fiction; Lost Colony)
Major character(s): Warreven "Raven" Stiller, Activist, Lawyer; Mhyre Tatian, Businessman; Temelathe Stane, Political Figure (Most Important Man)
Time period(s): Indeterminate Future
Locale(s): Hara, Planet—Imaginary; Concord Worlds, Interstellar Empire/Federation

Summary: After 100 years of contact with the Concord, Hara refuses to join, or even to acknowledge the mutation caused by faster-than-light travel which resulted in five human sexes. A "man" on Hara but a hermaphrodite to the Concord Worlds, Warrenven realizes this lack of recognition of all sexes prevents Haran society from developing. When Temelathe forces Warrenven to run for political office to prevent him from working as an advocate, forces beyond his control cause him to see himself as a hermaphrodite and to fight for recognition of all the sexes.

Other books you might like:
Eleanor Arnason, *Ring of Swords*, 1993
David Brin, *Glory Season*, 1993
Octavia E. Butler, *Imago*, 1989
M.J. Engh, *Rainbow Man*, 1993
Ursula K. Le Guin, *The Left Hand of Darkness*, 1969
Alis A. Rasmussen, *The Price of Ransom*, 1990

3915

MELISSA SCOTT

Trouble and Her Friends
(New York: Tor, 1994)

Story type: Science Fiction (Gay/Lesbian Fiction; Cyberpunk)
Major character(s): India ''Trouble'' Carless, Computer Expert, Lesbian; Cerise, Computer Expert, Lesbian; Butch van Liesvelt, Computer Expert, Homosexual
Time period(s): 22nd century (2100s)
Locale(s): Seahaven, New Hampshire

Summary: Before the laws changed making their activities illegal, Cerise and Trouble had roamed the nets together. Thereafter Trouble leaves and becomes a syscop, while Cerise becomes a security expert for a large corporation. When Butch warns Trouble that someone, impersonating her and using her old routines to break into other people's spaces, has caused enough problems that Treasury will pursue her, Trouble feels compelled to use her illegal equipment to search the nets for the imposter before Treasury decides to settle for her, the real Trouble.

Other books you might like:
Eleanor Arnason, *Ring of Swords*, 1993
Jean Mark Gawron, *Dream of Glass*, 1993
Mel Odom, *Lethal Interface*, 1992
Joan Slonczewski, *A Door into Ocean*, 1986
Neal Stephenson, *Snow Crash*, 1992

3916

CORDELL SCOTTEN

Renegade
(New York: Ace Books, 1989)

Story type: Science Fiction (Robot Fiction)
Series: Isaac Asimov's Robot City: Robots and Aliens
Major character(s): Derec, Amnesiac, Scientist; Ariel Welsh, Heiress
Time period(s): Indeterminate Future
Locale(s): Robot City, Planet—Imaginary

Summary: Derec and Ariel continue their battle against the evil aliens who would destroy Robot City. Scotten's first science fiction novel.

Other books you might like:
Isaac Asimov, *The Caves of Steel*, 1954
Isaac Asimov, *The Complete Robot*, 1982
Isaac Asimov, *The Naked Sun*, 1957
Isaac Asimov, *Robots and Empire*, 1985
Isaac Asimov, *The Robots of Dawn*, 1983
Charles Ingrid, *Return Fire*, 1989
    Sand Wars 5
Michael A. Stackpole, *Warrior: Coup*, 1989
    Battletech series
Jack Williamson, *The Humanoids*, 1949

3917

RICHARD F. SEARIGHT

The Brain in the Jar and Others
(West Warwick, Rhode Island: Necronomicon Press, 1992)

Story type: Horror (Collection)

Summary: This first in a projected series of three volumes collecting the work of a correspondent of H. P. Lovecraft and contributor to the early weird and science fiction pulps brings together 12 poems and five stories, only one of which was previously published. The title story concerns a disembodied brain which develops telekinetic powers. ''The Formula'' tells of a scientist prevented from developing a formula for cheap atomic energy by the ghost of his uncle, ''Rays of Madness'' of an alien invasion of Earth, and ''In the Dwelling of Madness'' of a plot by unscrupulous psychiatrists to deprive an heir of his fortune.

Other books you might like:
Arthur J. Burks, *Black Medicine*, 1966
August Derleth, *Harrigan's File*, 1975
Carl Jacobi, *Revelations in Black*, 1947
Frank Belknap Long, *The Hounds of Tindalos*, 1946
Donald Wandrei, *Strange Harvest*, 1965

3918

RICHARD F. SEARIGHT

The Sealed Casket and Other Stories
(West Warwick, Rhode Island: Necronomicon Press, 1996)

Story type: Horror (Collection)

Summary: The six stories and twelve poems in this collection of work by a correspondent of horror master H.P. Lovecraft run the gamut of fantasy fiction subgenres. ''The Sealed Casket,'' the only previously published story, tells of an invisible vampiric being liberated from an artifact by an unwitting collector. ''The Guardian of the Cairn'' is a heroic fantasy, and ''The Fire-Shapes'' and ''Terre Venus'' science fiction stories set, respectively, at the South Pole and on the planet Venus. ''Switchboard Morse'' and ''Sit Down'' are both mainstream tales with suspense elements. One poem, ''The New World,'' was published in a 1935 issue of the classic pulp magazine, *Weird Tales*. The author's son, Franklyn Searight, who edited the volume, supplies an informative introduction.

Other books you might like:
Arthur J. Burks, *Black Medicine*, 1966
August Derleth, *Harrigan's File*, 1975
Carl Jacobi, *Revelations in Black*, 1947
Frank Belknap Long, *The Hounds of Tindalos*, 1946
Donald Wandrei, *Strange Harvest*, 1965

3919

BAIRD SEARLES, Editor
BRIAN THOMSEN, Co-Editor

Halflings, Hobbits, Warrows & Weefolk: A Collection of Tales of Heroes Short in Stature

(New York: Warner Questar, 1991)

Story type: Fantasy (Anthology)

Summary: This volume contains a four-page introduction by Baird Searles and nine stories, seven originals plus Maya Kaathryn Bornhoff's ''Hobbits,'' previously published in *Analog*, and Judith Moffett's ''The Origin of the Hob,'' an excerpt of ''T. Whinney Moor Thoo Cums at Last,'' previously published in *Isaac Asimov's Science Fiction*. Other authors are John Dalmas, Charles de Lint, Craig Shaw Gardner, Jody Lynn Nye, Mickey Zucker Reichert, R.A. Salvatore, and Michael Williams.

Other books you might like:
Lin Carter, *Dragons, Elves and Heroes*, 1969
    editor
Jack Dann, *Little People!*, 1991
    Gardner Dozois, co-editor
J.R.R. Tolkien, *The Fellowship of the Ring*, 1954
J.R.R. Tolkien, *The Hobbit*, 1938
J.R.R. Tolkien, *The Return of the King*, 1956
J.R.R. Tolkien, *The Two Towers*, 1955

3920

DAVID J. SEARLS

Yellow Moon

(New York: Warner, 1994)

Story type: Horror (Apocalyptic Horror; Small Town Horror)
Major character(s): Tom Luckinbill, Police Officer (chief); Thad Crocker, Political Figure (mayor); Ben Crocker, Child
Time period(s): 1990s (1994)
Locale(s): Cleary, Ohio

Summary: Heralded by the rising of a sickly yellow moon, a hole opens up in the local baseball field of Cleary, engulfing a group of youngsters. When the boys return, they bring an unearthly power back with them that afflicts the entire town with madness and death.

Other books you might like:
Ramsey Campbell, *The Hungry Moon*, 1987
Douglas Clegg, *Goat Dance*, 1989
Michael Green, *The Jimjams*, 1994
John Shirley, *In Darkness Waiting*, 1988
Dan Simmons, *Summer of Night*, 1990

3921

MARK SEBANC

Flight to Hollow Mountain

(Grand Rapids, Michigan: Eerdmans, 1996)

Story type: Fantasy (Magic Conflict; Adventure)
Series: Talamadh
Major character(s): Kal, Teenager, Adventurer; Gelly, Teenager, Adventurer; Wilum, Magician
Time period(s): Indeterminate
Locale(s): Lammermorn, Fictional Country

Summary: Created centuries earlier by King Ardiel's magic harp, the magic spell which binds together the heavens and earth begins to unravel, allowing an evil master to ascend to power.

Other books you might like:
David Eddings, *Pawn of Prophecy*, 1982
Terry Goodkind, *Wizard's First Rule*, 1994
L. Dean James, *Summerland*, 1994
Patricia A. McKillip, *The Book of Atrix Wolfe*, 1995
Douglas Niles, *A Breach in the Watershed*, 1995
J.R.R. Tolkien, *The Fellowship of the Ring*, 1954

3922

STEPHEN MICHAEL SECHI, Editor

Tales of Talislanta

(Renton, Washington: Wizards of the Coast, 1992)

Story type: Fantasy (Anthology)
Time period(s): Indeterminate Past
Locale(s): Talislanta, Fictional Country

Summary: Contains a two-page preface, a map of Talislanta a five-page introduction and three stories by the editor/creator of the roleplaying game plus stories by Ru Emerson, Lawrence Watt-Evans and four other authors. Set in the *Talislanta* game world.

Other books you might like:
Robert N. Charrette, *Never Deal with a Dragon*, 1990
David Cook, *Beyond the Moons*, 1991
Greg Farshtey, *Strange Tales From the Nile Empire*, 1991
    Greg Gorden and Ed Stark, co-editors
Douglas Kaufman, *Dragons over England*, 1992
    Ed Stark, co-editor
Ken Rolston, *Extreme Paranoia: Nobody Knows the Trouble I've Shot*, 1991
Michael A. Stackpole, *A Gathering Evil*, 1991

3923

LARRY SEGRIFF

Spacer Dreams

(New York: Baen, 1995)

Story type: Science Fiction (Space Opera; Young Adult)
Major character(s): Tom Jenkins, Orphan; Michaela ''Mikey'' Delacourte, Military Personnel (Space Guard ensign), Spy; Frank, Mechanic, Pirate

Time period(s): Indeterminate Future
Locale(s): Brighthome, Planet—Imaginary

Summary: Tom Jenkins dreams of becoming a Space Guardian. He finally has a chance when space pirates try to recruit Tom's best friend and other fellow residents at the Brighthome Youth Center. First novel.

Other books you might like:
David Drake, *Surface Action*, 1990
John M. Ford, *Growing Up Weightless*, 1993
Robert A. Heinlein, *Space Cadet*, 1948
Robert A. Heinlein, *Starship Troopers*, 1959
Anne Mason, *The Stolen Law*, 1986
Frederik Pohl, *Mining the Oort*, 1992

3924

CAROL SERLING, Editor

Journeys to the Twilight Zone

(New York: DAW, 1993)

Story type: Horror (Anthology)

Summary: Fifteen original stories and one reprint have been assembled with the idea of capturing the spirit of Rod Serling's famous television series "The Twilight Zone." Included are Alan Dean Foster's "Laying Veneer," about an American construction boss in Australia who discovers the land has a soul of its own; Kristine Kathryn Rusch and Dean Wesley Smith's "Mists," in which a man meets a banshee; Jack Dann's "The Extra," about a man who travels into his own past; Charles de Lint's "Waifs and Strays," a ghost story; and Rod Serling's own 1972 story "Suggestion," about a hypnosis session with disastrous results.

Other books you might like:
Martin H. Greenberg, *New Stories From the Twilight Zone*, 1991
editor
Martin H. Greenberg, *The Twilight Zone: The Original Stories*, 1985
editor
Rod Serling, *The Night Gallery Reader*, 1990
Rod Serling, *Stories From the Twilight Zone*, 1990
J. Michael Straczynski, *Tales From the New Twilight Zone*, 1989
editor

3925

CAROL SERLING, Editor

Return to the Twilight Zone

(New York: DAW, 1994)

Story type: Horror (Anthology)

Summary: The 19 stories in this compilation were written in the spirit of Rod Serling's renowned television series, "The Twilight Zone," which frequently examined the dark side of human experience through fables that embraced the supernatural. Highlights include Robert Weinberg's "The Midnight El," in which a man must stump the devil in order to save his soul; Charles L. Grant's "Always, in the Dark," a tale of an

unusual ghost and an equally unusual haunting; John Gregory Betancourt's "The Duke of Demolition Goes to Hell," about the peculiar hell a construction mogul is sent to; John Maclay's "The Food Court," about the desserts meted out to a glutton; and Hugh Cave's "Gordie's Pets," about the dangerous overconfidence a boy develops through his rapport with animals. Also reprinted is Rod Serling's "Sole Survivor," a variation on the Flying Dutchman theme filmed originally as an episode for "The Twilight Zone."

Other books you might like:
Martin H. Greenberg, *New Stories From the Twilight Zone*, 1991
editor
Martin H. Greenberg, *The Twilight Zone: The Original Stories*, 1985
editor
Rod Serling, *The Gallery Reader*, 1990
Rod Serling, *Stories From the Twilight Zone*, 1990
J. Michael Straczynski, *Tales From the New Twilight Zone*, 1989
editor

3926

ROBERT SERLING

Something's Alive on the Titanic

(New York: St. Martin's, 1990)

Story type: Horror (Ghost Story)
Major character(s): Derek Montague, Adventurer; J. Benjamin Henning, Paranormal Investigator; William Gillespie, Scientist
Time period(s): 1970s (1975); 1990s (1993)
Locale(s): At Sea

Summary: A 1975 expedition to recover gold from the sunken ocean liner *Titanic* leaves all of its participants dead of horrifying phenomena, except cryptographer Derek Montague. Eighteen years later, Montague sets out on yet another expedition to recover the gold and find an explanation for what happened on the earlier mission.

Other books you might like:
Orson Scott Card, *The Abyss*, 1989
Michael Crichton, *Sphere*, 1987
Dean Wesley Smith, *Laying the Music to Rest*, 1989

3927

PAMELA F. SERVICE

All's Faire

(New York: Fawcett Juniper, 1993)

Story type: Fantasy (Time Travel; Young Adult)
Major character(s): Kevin, Time Traveller, Teenager; Gina, Time Traveller, Teenager
Time period(s): 1990s; Indeterminate Past
Locale(s): Indiana; Europe

Summary: Unenthusiastic about his parents' interest in historic recreations, Kevin's boredom with a Renaissance festival vanishes when a strange phenomenon transports Kevin and Gina to medieval Europe where their adventure becomes exciting and dangerous.

Other books you might like:

Eleanor Cameron, *Beyond Silence*, 1980
Jane Louise Curry, *Over the Sea's Edge*, 1971
Michael Ende, *The Neverending Story*, 1983
Barbara Ireson, *Tales out of Time*, 1981
    editor
Janet Luenn, *The Root Cellar*, 1983
William Mayne, *A Game of Dark*, 1971

3928
PAMELA F. SERVICE

Being of Two Minds
(New York: Atheneum, 1991)

Story type: Fantasy (Young Adult; Contemporary)
Major character(s): Connie Hendricks, Teenager, Telepath; Rudolph ''Rudy'', Royalty (crown prince), Telepath; Wolfgang ''Wolfie'' Reichmann, Teacher
Time period(s): 1990s
Locale(s): Midwest; Thulgaria, Fictional Country

Summary: Connie and Rudolph keep their telepathic bond secret, fearing that others would not understand. When Rudolph's kidnapping forces Connie to reveal the truth, she travels to Thulgaria to help rescue Rudolph.

Other books you might like:

James Blish, *Jack of Eagles*, 1952
Robert A. Heinlein, *Time for the Stars*, 1956
J. Alison James, *Sing for a Gentle Rain*, 1990
Kathryn Lasky, *Double Trouble Squared*, 1991
Robert Silverberg, *Letters From Atlantis*, 1990
Theodore Sturgeon, *More than Human*, 1953
A.E. van Vogt, *Slan*, 1946

3929
PAMELA F. SERVICE

Under Alien Stars
(New York: Atheneum, 1990)

Story type: Science Fiction (Invasion of Earth; Young Adult)
Major character(s): Jason Sikes, Teenager; Aryl, Teenager, Alien
Time period(s): 21st century
Locale(s): San Francisco, California

Summary: Ten years after the Tsorians arrive and establish a military base on Earth, resistance is still strong. When Jason's mom's boss, Rogav Jy, is kidnapped by Resisters, both Earth and the Tsorians are menaced by an invasion of Hykzoi, a species of bloodthirsty conquerers. Jason must unwillingly join forces with Aryl, Rogav's daughter, to free Rogav and rout the Hykzoi.

Other books you might like:

David Brin, *Startide Rising*, 1983
John Christopher, *The Prince in Waiting*, 1970
John Christopher, *The White Mountains*, 1967
Paula Danziger, *This Place Has No Atmosphere*, 1986

Robert A. Heinlein, *The Rolling Stones*, 1952
Larry Niven, *Footfall*, 1985
    Jerry Pournelle, co-author

3930
PAMELA F. SERVICE

Vision Quest
(New York: Atheneum, 1989)

Story type: Fantasy (Magic Conflict)
Major character(s): Kate Elliott, Teenager (Army brat); Jimmy Fong, Teenager (Kate's friend)
Time period(s): 1980s
Locale(s): Nevada

Summary: When Kate's family moves to Nevada, she finds life boring until one day, while walking in the desert, she finds a talisman left long ago by a shaman. When she takes possession of the talisman, she starts having visions of what happened to the original owner.

Other books you might like:

Diana Wynne Jones, *The Lives of Christopher Chant*, 1988
Adrienne Martine-Barnes, *The Fire Sword*, 1984
Patricia Wrightson, *Balyet*, 1989

3931
PAMELA F. SERVICE

Weirdos of the Universe, Unite!
(New York: Atheneum, 1992)

Story type: Fantasy (Legend; Young Adult)
Major character(s): Mandy, Student, Teenager; Owen, Student, Teenager; Baba Yaga, Mythical Creature (Russian)
Time period(s): 1990s
Locale(s): Hermes, Iowa

Summary: While researching a paper on mythological beings, Mandy and Owen find several mythological characters have come alive. The group must unite to save the earth from an invasion from outer space.

Other books you might like:

Margaret J. Anderson, *The Ghost Inside the Monitor*, 1990
Bruce Coville, *My Teacher Flunked the Planet*, 1992
Philip Jose Farmer, *Red Orc's Rage*, 1991
Will Shetterly, *Cats Have No Lord*, 1985
Clifford D. Simak, *Out of Their Minds*, 1970
Vivian Vande Velde, *User Unfriendly*, 1991

3932
CAROL SEVERANCE

Demon Drums
(New York: Ballantine Del Rey, 1992)

Story type: Fantasy (Magic Conflict)
Major character(s): Iuti Mano, Warrior (retired), Magician; Tarawe, Warrior, Magician
Time period(s): Indeterminate

Locale(s): Fanape Island, Fictional Country; Losan Island, Fictional Country

Summary: Weary of the endless killing of the Teronin War, Iuti had retired to Fanape Island promising to avoid use of her protective spirit, the shark, in order to stay among the peaceful inhabitants. When agents of her enemy come to Fanape to capture her and force her to fight for them, Iuti resolves to again take up her sword and destroy the enemy's scheming for all time. While escaping with Tarawe, Iuti and Tarawe fall victim to a magical storm which transports them to Losan Island where deadly drummers construct magic drums utilizing the skin of warriors as drum heads, a fate which will befall Iuti if she remains.

Other books you might like:
Joan Slonczewski, *A Door into Ocean*, 1986
Dave Smeds, *The Schemes of Dragons*, 1989
Dave Smeds, *The Sorcery Within*, 1985
Christopher Stasheff, *King Kobold Revived*, 1984

`3933`

CAROL SEVERANCE

Reefsong

(New York: Ballantine/Del Rey, 1991)

Story type: Science Fiction (Genetic Manipulation; Utopia)
Major character(s): Pualeiokekai Pukai, Genetically Altered Being; Angela Dinsman, Troubleshooter (U.N.), Anthropologist
Time period(s): Indeterminate Future
Locale(s): Central Forest Preserve, Colorado; Lesaat, Planet—Imaginary (water world)

Summary: Able to provide basic nourishment for Earth's billions from its algae farms on Lesaat, the World Life Company has a stranglehold on most of the world's economy. The U.N. would like to change this situation by exposing the illegal activities it believes the World Life Company commits, but must be careful since much of the overpopulated planet depends on the Company for food. On Lesaat, the genetically altered colonists may have developed an enzyme which would allow humans to convert any vegetables into complete proteins. A first novel.

Other books you might like:
Eleanor Arnason, *A Woman of the Iron People*, 1991
David Brin, *Startide Rising*, 1983
Gordon R. Dickson, *Home From the Shore*, 1978
Alan Dean Foster, *Cachalot*, 1980
Damon Knight, *CV*, 1985
Joan Slonczewski, *A Door into Ocean*, 1986
Sydney J. Van Scyoc, *Deepwater Dreams*, 1991
John Wyndham, *Out of the Deeps*, 1953

`3934`

CAROL SEVERANCE

Storm Caller

(New York: Ballantine Del Rey, 1993)

Story type: Fantasy (Magic Conflict; Legend)

Series: Island Warrior
Major character(s): Iuti Mano, Warrior, Magician; Tarawe, Magician; Ma'eva, Mythical Creature (shapeshifter)
Time period(s): Indeterminate
Locale(s): At Sea; Tahena, Fictional Country (volcanic island)

Summary: When Iuti's kinsmen seek revenge for her killing of the clan's totem, Iuti, Tarwe and Ma'eva flee across a danger-filled ocean until they find an inhabited island which provides shelter but no safety on their journey. Based on Hawaiian legends.

Other books you might like:
Gordon R. Dickson, *The Dragon at War*, 1992
Ursula K. Le Guin, *A Wizard of Earthsea*, 1968
Megan Lindholm, *Harpy's Flight*, 1983
Megan Lindholm, *The Windsingers*, 1984
Elizabeth Moon, *Sheepfarmer's Daughter*, 1988
Michelle Sagara, *Into the Dark Lands*, 1991

`3935`

ELLEN DODGE SEVERSON

Hederick, the Theocrat

(Lake Geneva, Wisconsin: TSR, 1994)

Story type: Fantasy (Religious; Magic Conflict)
Series: DragonLance: Villains
Major character(s): Hederick, Religious, Leader
Time period(s): Indeterminate
Locale(s): Krynn, Planet—Imaginary

Summary: From an abandoned youth, Hederick grows into a demagogue who commands a goblin army, intending to vanquish the practitioners of magic and worshippers of the old gods.

Other books you might like:
Mark Anthony, *Kindred Spirits*, 1991
  Ellen Porath, co-author
Mary Kirchoff, *The Black Wing*, 1993
Douglas Niles, *Emperor of Ansalon*, 1993
Ellen Porath, *Steel and Stone*, 1992
Michael Williams, *Before the Mask*, 1993
  Teri Williams, co-author

`3936`

WILLIAM SHATNER
JUDITH REEVES-STEVENS, Co-Author
GARFIELD REEVES-STEVENS, Co-Author

The Ashes of Eden

(New York: Pocket, 1995)

Story type: Science Fiction (Space Opera)
Series: Star Trek
Major character(s): Pavel Chekov, Military Personnel (Starfleet Commander), Space Explorer; Hikaru Sulu, Military Personnel (Starfleet Captain), Spaceship Captain; James T. Kirk, Spaceship Captain (Starfleet Captain)
Time period(s): 23rd century

Locale(s): *U.S.S. Excelsior*, Spaceship; Chal, Planet—Imaginary; United Federation of Planets, Interstellar Empire/Federation

Summary: Approaching retirement, Kirk accepts an offer from a mysterious young woman to command a starship again, to defend an uncharted planet from the Klingons and Romulans—and to regain his lost youth. While old and new conspiracies force Sulu and his old crewmates to track down Kirk, Kirk must save the fragile peace between the Klingons and the Federation.

Other books you might like:
C.J. Cherryh, *Hellburner*, 1992
J.M. Dillard, *The Lost Years*, 1989
Jane S. Fancher, *Ground-Ties*, 1991
Cynthia Felice, *Downtime*, 1985
L.A. Graf, *Traitor Winds*, 1994
Garfield Reeves-Stevens, *Memory Prime*, 1988
    Judith Reeves-Stevens, co-author
Judith Reeves-Stevens, *Federation*, 1994
    Garfield Reeves-Stevens, co-author
Judith Reeves-Stevens, *Prime Directive*, 1990
    Garfield Reeves-Stevens, co-author

3937

WILLIAM SHATNER
MICHAEL TOBIAS, Co-Author

Believe: A Novel

(New York: Berkley, 1992)

Story type: Fantasy (Historical; Quest)
Major character(s): Harry Houdini, Magician, Historical Figure; Arthur Conan Doyle, Historical Figure, Writer
Time period(s): 1920s
Locale(s): United States; Canada; England

Summary: Pursuant to a *Scientifica Americana* contest, skeptical Harry Houdini and Arthur Conan Doyle, a believer, investigate the possibility of life after death.

Other books you might like:
Philip Jose Farmer, *Tales of Riverworld*, 1992
    editor
Pamela Sargent, *Afterlives: An Anthology of Stories about Life After Death*, 1986
    editor
Daniel Stashower, *The Adventure of the Ectoplasmic Man*, 1985
Steve Szilagyi, *Photographing Fairies*, 1992
Michael Tobias, *Voice of the Planet*, 1990

3938

WILLIAM SHATNER

Man o' War

(New York: Ace/Putnam, 1996)

Story type: Science Fiction (Political; Space Colony)
Major character(s): Benton ''Ben'' Hawkes, Diplomat, Rancher; Dina Martel, Diplomat; Michael ''Mick'' Carri, Government Official (senator)

Time period(s): 2060s (2067)
Locale(s): Mars; Wyoming

Summary: When Benton Hawkes refuses to render the politically mandated verdict in an arbitration, he thinks his diplomatic career finished. Instead, Senator Carri offers him the governorship of Mars, a job in which he will have to stave off impending revolution to maintain the flow of crucial raw materials to Earth. Hawkes prefers to return to his ranch, but after two attempts on his life and evidence that some of his attackers had lived on Mars, he accepts the postion. On Mars, he discovers not only who tried to kill him, but why.

Other books you might like:
Robert Asprin, *The Cold Cash War*, 1977
C.J. Cherryh, *Foreigner*, 1994
Robert A. Heinlein, *The Moon Is a Harsh Mistress*, 1966
Keith Laumer, *Retief at Large*, 1978
Ursula K. Le Guin, *The Dispossessed*, 1978
Kim Stanley Robinson, *Red Mars*, 1993

3939

WILLIAM SHATNER
JUDITH REEVES-STEVENS, Co-Author
GARFIELD REEVES-STEVENS, Co-Author

The Return

(New York: Pocket, 1996)

Story type: Science Fiction (Space Opera; Genetic Manipulation)
Series: Star Trek
Major character(s): Jean-Luc Picard, Spaceship Captain, Military Personnel; James T. Kirk, Spaceship Captain; Spock, Scientist, Alien (Vulcan)
Time period(s): 24th century
Locale(s): Veridian III, Planet—Imaginary; Romulus, Planet—Imaginary; Interstellar Empire/Federation

Summary: While salvage operations begin on the wreckage of the *Enterprise* and Starfleet prepares to bring Kirk's body back to Earth for burial, Romulan ships attack and transport Kirk's body from its grave. Using an ancient alien artifact, they restore the body to life and program it to turn against the Federation. The Romulans have allied themselves with the Borg, and only the combined talents of two *Enterprise* crews can save the Federation.

Other books you might like:
Octavia E. Butler, *Dawn*, 1987
C.J. Cherryh, *Cyteen*, 1988
Michael Jan Friedman, *Kahless*, 1996
Judith Reeves-Stevens, *Prime Directive*, 1990
    Garfield Reeves-Stevens, co-author
Della Van Hise, *Killing Time*, 1985
John Varley, *The Ophiuchi Hotline*, 1977

3940

WILLIAM SHATNER

Tek Money

(New York: Ace/Putnam, 1995)

Story type: Science Fiction (Adventure)
Series: Tek
Major character(s): Jake Cardigan, Detective—Private; Sid Gomez, Detective—Private
Time period(s): 22nd century
Locale(s): California; Tropical Island (Atlantic); Spain

Summary: Police suspect Jake Cardigan of murdering an acquaintance from the days of his Tek addiction by use of a Tek chip which plugs directly into the brain. With the police and the victim's acquaintances all requesting their help, Jake and Sid follow the money as its trail leads them overseas and into greater danger as they attempt to clear Jake's name.

Other books you might like:
Robert Cain, *Cybernarc*, 1991
Philip K. Dick, *A Scanner Darkly*, 1977
Alan Dean Foster, *Outland*, 1981
Simon R. Green, *Guard Against Dishonor*, 1991
Ernest Hogan, *High Aztec*, 1992
Lynn S. Hightower, *Alien Blues*, 1992

3941

WILLIAM SHATNER

Tek Power

(New York: Ace/Putnam, 1994)

Story type: Science Fiction (Adventure; Political)
Series: Tek
Major character(s): Jake Cardigan, Detective—Private; Sid Gomez, Detective—Private; Warren Brookmeyer, Political Figure (U.S. president)
Time period(s): 22nd century
Locale(s): New York, New York; Washington, District of Columbia; Managua, Nicaragua

Summary: When President Brookmeyer agrees to clandestine treatment for Tek addiction, he intends that his robot simulacrum will replace him in public only briefly. While investigating a murder, Jake and Sid chance onto a conspiracy aimed at controlling the government through more permanent tenure for the robot.

Other books you might like:
Philip K. Dick, *A Scanner Darkly*, 1977
Michael Flynn, *In the Country of the Blind*, 1990
Robert A. Heinlein, *Double Star*, 1956
Allen Steele, *Clarke County, Space*, 1990

3942

WILLIAM SHATNER

Tek Vengeance

(New York: Ace/Putnam, 1993)

Story type: Science Fiction (Adventure)

Series: Tek
Major character(s): Jake Cardigan, Detective—Private; Sid Gomez, Detective—Private
Time period(s): 22nd century
Locale(s): Los Angeles, California; Brazil; Austria

Summary: While Beth Kittridge travels to Berlin to testify against a drug dealing Teklord, Jake pursues vital information from a dying informant in South America. Jake's absence from Beth's side allows their enemies to plot Beth's murder, resulting in Jake's assignment to the murder investigation. Sequel to *TekLab*.

Other books you might like:
Robert Cain, *Cybernarc*, 1991
Alan Dean Foster, *Alien Nation*, 1988
Alan Dean Foster, *Outland*, 1981
Lynn S. Hightower, *Alien Blues*, 1992
L.S. Riker, *Kill Crazy*, 1993

3943

WILLIAM SHATNER

TekLab

(New York: Ace/Putnam, 1991)

Story type: Science Fiction (Adventure)
Series: Tek
Major character(s): Jake Cardigan, Detective—Private; Sid Gomez, Detective—Private (Cardigan's partner)
Time period(s): 22nd century
Locale(s): Paris, France; London, England; Nassau, Bahamas

Summary: To interview a client about a recent assassination, Jake and Sid travel to Paris where a phone call from Jake's son, Dan, alerts Jake to the disappearance of Dan's girlfriend. Tracking down his son in London, Jake finds the disappearance involves the assassin, Unknown Soldier; a new drug, SuperTek; and a group of neo-royalists, the Excalibur Movement, intent on again turning Great Britain into a monarchy. This book is a sequel to *TekLords*.

Other books you might like:
Robert Cain, *Cybernarc*, 1991
Robert Cain, *Gold Dragon*, 1991
Allan Cole, *Sten*, 1984
    Chris Bunch, co-author
Philip K. Dick, *Blade Runner*, 1982
Alan Dean Foster, *Alien Nation*, 1988
Lynn S. Hightower, *Alien Blues*, 1992
Katharine Kerr, *Polar City Blues*, 1990

3944

WILLIAM SHATNER

TekLords

(New York: Ace/Putnam, 1991)

Story type: Science Fiction (Adventure)
Series: Tek
Major character(s): Jake Cardigan, Detective—Private; Sid Gomez, Detective—Private (Cardigan's partner)
Time period(s): 22nd century (2120)

Locale(s): California; Japan

Summary: In this sequel to *TekWar*, Cardigan and Gomez are assigned to discover who is behind a recent wave of murders and attempted murders. When his wife becomes infected by a synthetic virus, Jake seeks an antidote and those who caused the plague.

Other books you might like:
Isaac Asimov, *The Currents of Space*, 1952
Philip K. Dick, *A Scanner Darkly*, 1977
Alan Dean Foster, *Cyber Way*, 1990
Alan Dean Foster, *Outland*, 1981
Ron Goulart, *The Wicked Cyborg*, 1978
Richard Kadrey, *Metrophage*, 1988
Katharine Kerr, *Polar City Blues*, 1990
Lee Killough, *Dragon's Teeth*, 1990

3945

WILLIAM SHATNER

TekWar

(New York: Ace/Putnam, 1989)

Story type: Science Fiction (Mystery)
Series: Tek
Major character(s): Jake Cardigan, Detective—Private; Sonny Hakori, Drug Dealer
Time period(s): 22nd century
Locale(s): Los Angeles, California

Summary: Jake Cardigan, an ex-cop, was framed for allegedly dealing Tek, a mind-altering computerized drug. Out of jail and working as a private detective, Jake is out to get whoever framed him and break up the Tek cartel.

Other books you might like:
Richard Bowker, *Dover Beach*, 1987
George Alec Effinger, *A Fire in the Sun*, 1989
George Alec Effinger, *When Gravity Fails*, 1987
F. Paul Wilson, *Dydeetown World*, 1989

3946

BOB SHAW

The Fugitive Worlds

(New York: Baen, 1990)

Story type: Science Fiction (Adventure)
Series: Land and Overland
Major character(s): Toller Maraquine II, Pilot (airship); Vantara, Noblewoman (countess), Pilot (airship); The Xa, Computer (sentient), Alien
Time period(s): Indeterminate Future
Locale(s): Land, Planet—Imaginary; Overland, Planet—Imaginary

Summary: While returning from Land, Toller Maraquine II discovers an invisible barrier midway between the two planets which has swallowed up Countess Vantara. Investigating, Maraquine meets the Dussarrans who, along with their planet, are fleeing a galactic explosion. Learning that they plan to use Land/Overland to abet this, (which will destroy these planets),

Maraquine, using The Xa, transports Overland to a new continuum—our own.

Other books you might like:
Philip Jose Farmer, *The Unreasoning Mask*, 1981
Robert L. Forward, *Rocheworld*, 1990
Melissa Scott, *Five-Twelfths of Heaven*, 1985
John Varley, *Millennium*, 1983
John Varley, *Titan*, 1979

3947

MICHAEL SHEA

I, Said the Fly

(Seattle, Washington: Silver Salamander Press, 1993)

Story type: Horror (Science Fiction)
Major character(s): Paul Rant, Scientist (entomologist); Brad, Filmmaker; Dean, Doctor (pathologist)
Time period(s): 1990s (1993)
Locale(s): Los Angeles, California

Summary: While filming a short feature titled *I, Said the Fly*, which presents the world of human beings as seen through the eyes of several species of the animal kingdom, a series of strange events on both the global and local scale convince the filmmakers that the human species is being investigated under the microscopes of a race of extraterrestrial invaders.

Other books you might like:
Jack Finney, *The Body Snatchers*, 1955
Robert A. Heinlein, *The Puppet Masters*, 1951
Frank Herbert, *Hellstrom's Hive*, 1973
Eric Frank Russell, *Sinister Barrier*, 1943

3948

ROBERT SHEA

Shaman

(New York: Ballantine, 1991)

Story type: Fantasy (Historical)
Major character(s): Auguste ''White Bear'' de Marion, Shaman; Raoul de Marion, Farmer; Redbird, Fiance(e)
Time period(s): 19th century
Locale(s): Michigan

Summary: White Bear, a man caught between two heritages, searches for love and the power of a shaman in a dying world. With the United States pushing its boundary west, there is no place for the native people to go. White Bear's distress is heightened by conflict with his uncle, who represents everything negative about Western life.

Other books you might like:
Orson Scott Card, *Seventh Son*, 1987
Stuart Gordon, *Smile on the Void*, 1981
Joe R. Lansdale, *The Magic Wagon*, 1986
S.P. Somtow, *Moon Dance*, 1989
Patricia Wrightson, *The Dark Bright Water*, 1978
Patricia Wrightson, *The Ice Is Coming*, 1977
Patricia Wrightson, *Journey Behind the Wind*, 1981

3949

CHARLES SHEFFIELD

Brother to Dragons
(New York: Baen, 1992)

Story type: Science Fiction (Future Shock; Political)
Major character(s): Job Napoleon Salk, Orphan; Father "Mr. Bones" Bonifant, Administrator; Alan Singh, Professor
Time period(s): 2010s
Locale(s): Xanadu, Nebraska

Summary: Deserted at birth, Job spends his formative years at Cloak House orphanage. When he escapes at age eleven, his talent for languages and the trips accompanying Mr. Bones on forage runs help him survive in the extreme poverty of the city, and eventually at Xanadu, an escape-proof prison area surrounding a toxic and nuclear waste dump where scientists have been sentenced since the Crash. Job hopes to survive long enough to escape with the fruits of the on-going research.

Other books you might like:
David Brin, *Earth*, 1990
Emma Bull, *Bone Dance*, 1991
Peter R. Emshwiller, *The Host*, 1991
Frederik Pohl, *Stopping at Slowyear*, 1991
Jim Shepard, *Lights Out in the Reptile House*, 1990
Allen Steele, *Lunar Descent*, 1991
Dave Wolverton, *Serpent Catch*, 1991

3950

CHARLES SHEFFIELD

Cold as Ice
(New York: Tor, 1992)

Story type: Science Fiction (Hard Science Fiction; Political)
Major character(s): Jon Perry, Scientist; Cyrus "Torquemada" Mobarak, Inventor, Businessman; Rustum "Bat" Battacharia, Government Official
Time period(s): 2090s (2092)
Locale(s): Ganymede, Jupiter (a moon of Jupiter); Europa, Jupiter (a moon of Jupiter)

Summary: Twenty-five years after the war between the Inner Planets and the Belt, peace and the Moby, a portable fusion engine, have enabled the populations to prosper. Jon Perry, a deep sea researcher from Earth, travels to Europa to find any native life which may have evolved in the fresh water ocean under the ice. Mobarak plots to use his Mobies to create a new environment for humans on Europa.

Other books you might like:
Stephen Baxter, *Raft*, 1991
David Brin, *Earth*, 1990
John Brunner, *Children of the Thunder*, 1989
Octavia E. Butler, *Dawn*, 1987
Arthur C. Clarke, *2061: Odyssey Three*, 1987
Gregory Feeley, *The Oxygen Barons*, 1990
Edward Gibson, *In the Wrong Hands*, 1992
Michael Swanwick, *Stations of the Tide*, 1991

3951

CHARLES SHEFFIELD

Dancing with Myself
(New York: Baen, 1993)

Story type: Science Fiction (Collection)

Summary: Contains a one-page introduction, eleven stories with individual afterwords, four articles published in periodicals and anthologies 1982-1992, and one original, "A Biography of the Universe." Stories exhibit a wide range of tone with a variety of themes including terrestrial biology, extra-terrestrial intelligence, physical laws of the universe and a 600,000 kilometer bike race around the Earth and Moon.

Other books you might like:
Michael Flynn, *The Nanotech Chronicles*, 1991
Janet Kagan, *Mirabile*, 1991
Larry Niven, *N-Space*, 1990
Larry Niven, *Tales of Known Space*, 1975
Allen Steele, *Rude Astronauts*, 1993
Marc Stiegler, *The Gentle Seduction*, 1990
John Varley, *The Persistence of Vision*, 1978

3952

CHARLES SHEFFIELD

Divergence
(New York: Ballantine/Del Rey, 1991)

Story type: Science Fiction (Adventure)
Series: Heritage Universe
Major character(s): Darya Lang, Scientist, Adventurer; Hans Rebka, Adventurer; E.C. Tally, Artificial Intelligence
Time period(s): 63rd century
Locale(s): *Summer Dreamboat*, Spaceship; Glister, Planet—Imaginary

Summary: While continuing a millennia-long search for The Builders, legendary creators of mysterious constructs, Darya Lang and Hans Rebka discover a threat to all intelligent life.

Other books you might like:
Algis Budrys, *Rogue Moon*, 1960
Arthur C. Clarke, *2061: Odyssey Three*, 1988
Arthur C. Clarke, *2010: Odyssey Two*, 1982
Arthur C. Clarke, *2001: A Space Odyssey*, 1968
Dan Simmons, *The Fall of Hyperion*, 1990
Dan Simmons, *Hyperion*, 1989

3953

CHARLES SHEFFIELD

The Ganymede Club
(New York: Tor, 1995)

Story type: Science Fiction (Mystery; Space Colony)
Series: Cold as Ice
Major character(s): Lola Belman, Psychologist; Bryce Sonnenberg, Scientist (mathematician), Sports Figure (scooter racer); Rustum "Bat" Battacharia, Computer Expert, Teenager

Time period(s): 2060s; 2070s (2067-2072)
Locale(s): Ganymede, Jupiter (moon); Mars

Summary: After war ravages most of the innersolar system, Bryce Sonnenberg comes to Lola Belman on Ganymede because of blackouts and strange dreams, frightening some descendants of the members of the First Saturn Expedition who have formed a tight club. When Lola enlists the aid of her young brother and his friend to discover whether or not Bryce's dreams have any basis in reality, their dangerous investigation uncovers ancient secrets.

Other books you might like:
Kevin J. Anderson, *Assemblers of Infinity*, 1993
    Doug Beason, co-author
C.J. Cherryh, *Cyteen*, 1988
Betty Anne Crawford, *The Bushido Incident*, 1992
Robert A. Heinlein, *Methuselah's Children*, 1958
Nancy Kress, *Beggars in Spain*, 1993
Frederik Pohl, *Outnumbering the Dead*, 1992
Karen Ripley, *Prisoner of Dreams*, 1989
Allen Steele, *Clarke County, Space*, 1990

3954

CHARLES SHEFFIELD

Georgia on My Mind and Other Places
(New York: Tor, 1995)

Story type: Science Fiction (Collection; Science Fiction)

Summary: Contains a brief introduction and 14 stories published 1987-1994 in periodicals and anthologies, each with an afterword indicating the story's genesis. The selections range from short, silly pieces such as ''Fifteen-Love on the Dead Man's Chest'' to longer, more serious treatments, including the Nebula Award-winning title story.

Other books you might like:
Poul Anderson, *The Book of Poul Anderson*, 1974
Isaac Asimov, *The Best of Isaac Asimov*, 1973
Arthur C. Clarke, *The Nine Billion Names of God*, 1967
Robert A. Heinlein, *The Green Hills of Earth*, 1951
Allen Steele, *Rude Astronauts*, 1993
John Varley, *Blue Champagne*, 1986
Jack Williamson, *The Best of Jack Williamson*, 1978

3955

CHARLES SHEFFIELD

Godspeed
(New York: Tor, 1993)

Story type: Science Fiction (Lost Colony)
Major character(s): Jay Hara, Teenager, Spaceman; Paddy Enderton, Spaceman; Eileen Xavier, Doctor
Time period(s): Indeterminate Future
Locale(s): Erin, Planet—Imaginary; The Forty Worlds, Outer Space (Maveen star system)

Summary: Growing up across the lake from the spaceport on Erin, Jay aspires to become a spaceman. Only Dr. Eileen seems to recognize that Erin cannot completely support human life. Since the Isolation 800 years earlier when the flow

of goods from outside the Forty Worlds ceased, Erin supports a reduced technological level and decreased population which now produces three girls for every 100 boys. Jay discovers the location of a Godspeed station and, with the help of Dr. Eileen, must find a way to end the Isolation.

Other books you might like:
Stephen Baxter, *Raft*, 1991
David Brin, *Glory Season*, 1993
Debra Doyle, *The Price of the Stars*, 1992
    James D. Macdonald, co-author
Harry Harrison, *The Deathworld Trilogy*, 1975
Rosemary Kirstein, *The Outskirter's Secret*, 1992
Megan Lindholm, *Alien Earth*, 1992
Larry Niven, *The Integral Trees*, 1984
Frederik Pohl, *Stopping at Slowyear*, 1991
Alis A. Rasmussen, *A Passage of Stars*, 1990

3956

CHARLES SHEFFIELD
JERRY POURNELLE, Co-Author

Higher Education
(New York: Tor, 1996)

Story type: Science Fiction (Young Adult; Adventure)
Series: Jupiter
Major character(s): Rick Luban, Teenager, Apprentice; Vido Valdez, Teenager, Apprentice; Alice Klein, Teenager, Apprentice
Time period(s): Indeterminate Future
Locale(s): CM-2, Space Station; CM-26, Space Station

Summary: Kicked out of school for a harmless pratical joke, Rick Luban signs on with Vanguard Mining, enduring months of rigorous training in the hopes of making a career in asteroid mining.

Other books you might like:
Isaac Asimov, *Lucky Starr and the Pirates of the Asteroids*, 1953
Robert A. Heinlein, *Space Cadet*, 1948
Frederik Pohl, *Mining the Oort*, 1992
Jerry Pournelle, *West of Honor*, 1976
Larry Segriff, *Spacer Dreams*, 1995

3957

CHARLES SHEFFIELD, Editor

How to Save the World
(New York: Tor, 1995)

Story type: Science Fiction (Anthology; Dystopian)

Summary: Contains a four-page introduction, three pages ''About the Authors,'' plus 11 original and two stories reprinted in a different form from an anthology and a periodical publication. A wide range of global problems receive simple, if not painless, solutions as if presented by extraterrestrials who view humanity's problems from the outside. The 15 authors include Doug Beason, B.W. Clough, James P. Hogan, Kathe Koja, Barry N. Malzberg, Larry Niven, Jerry Oltion, Nick Pollotta, Jerry Pournelle, and Charles Sheffield.

Other books you might like:

Thomas M. Disch, *The New Improved Sun: An Anthology of Utopian Science Fiction*, 1975
editor

Thomas M. Disch, *The Ruins of Earth: An Anthology of the Immediate Future*, 1971
editor

Harry Harrison, *There Won't Be War*, 1991
Bruce McAllister, co-editor

Kim Stanley Robinson, *Future Primitive: The New Ecotopias*, 1994
editor

Lewis Shiner, *When the Music's Over*, 1991
editor

John Stadler, *Eco-Fiction*, 1971
editor

`3958`

CHARLES SHEFFIELD
DAVID BISCHOFF, Co-Author

The Judas Cross

(New York: Warner/Aspect, 1994)

Story type: Horror (Occult)
Major character(s): Louis Villette, Nobleman (Marquis of Saint Ame); Celine Villette, Bastard Daughter (of Louis Villette); Jenny Marshall, Young Woman
Time period(s): 1910s (1916)
Locale(s): Saint Ame, France

Summary: Appalled at the carnage against his countrymen at the hands of the German army during World War I, Louis Villette, keeper of the Cross of Judas, formed from the pieces of silver given to Judas Iscariot for his betrayal of Jesus Christ and which imprisons his traitor soul, vows to use the talisman to prevent further bloodshed. In order to wield the cross's power, though, Louis finds it necessary to first betray family, lovers, and other innocents who have placed their trust in him.

Other books you might like:

James Herbert, *The Spear*, 1978
Robert Weinberg, *The Armageddon Box*, 1991
Robert Weinberg, *The Devil's Auction*, 1988
Dennis Wheatley, *They Used Dark Forces*, 1964

`3959`

CHARLES SHEFFIELD

One Man's Universe

(New York: Tor, 1993)

Story type: Science Fiction (Collection; Hard Science Fiction)
Major character(s): Arthur Morton McAndrews, Scientist, Spaceman
Time period(s): 21st century
Locale(s): Outer Space

Summary: Contains a three-page introduction, a 36-page appendix on the science in Sheffield's science fiction plus two original stories and five reprinted from 1970s and 1980s periodicals, all focusing on McAndrew's fantastic experimen-

tation with black holes. Expands *The McAndrew Chronicles* (1983).

Other books you might like:

Stephen Baxter, *Timelike Infinity*, 1993
David Brin, *Earth*, 1990
Vonda N. McIntyre, *Metaphase*, 1992
Larry Niven, *Neutron Star*, 1968
Larry Niven, *Tales of Known Space*, 1975
Frederik Pohl, *Gateway*, 1977
John E. Stith, *Redshift Rendezvous*, 1990
John Varley, *Blue Champagne*, 1986
John Varley, *The Persistence of Vision*, 1978

`3960`

CHARLES SHEFFIELD

Proteus in the Underworld

(New York: Baen, 1995)

Story type: Science Fiction (Genetic Manipulation; Mystery)
Series: Proteus
Major character(s): Sondra Dearborn, Researcher, Troubleshooter (Office of Form Control); Trudy Melford, Businesswoman, Wealthy; Behrooz "Bey" Wolf, Recluse, Scientist
Time period(s): 22nd century
Locale(s): Earth; Mars; Oort Cloud, Outer Space

Summary: Assigned to discover why genetic certification tests have begun to misidentify subjects as human, Sondra Dearborn calls upon Bey Wolf, who is happily retired and reluctant to involve himself. Bey's investigation of the anomalies points to sabotage as his search leads to Mars, while Sondra's duties draw her to the Oort Cloud.

Other books you might like:

Isaac Asimov, *Nemesis*, 1989
Ben Bova, *Colony*, 1978
Alexis A. Gilliland, *The Revolution From Rosinante*, 1981
Melisa C. Michaels, *Floater Factor*, 1988
Frederik Pohl, *Mining the Oort*, 1992
Kim Stanley Robinson, *Icehenge*, 1984
Allen Steele, *Clarke County, Space*, 1990
John Varley, *The Ophiuchi Hotline*, 1977

`3961`

CHARLES SHEFFIELD

Proteus Unbound

(New York: Ballantine/Del Rey, 1989)

Story type: Science Fiction (Hard Science Fiction)
Major character(s): Behrooz "Bey" Wolf, Government Official (Former), Scientist; Leo Manx, Genetically Altered Being
Time period(s): 22nd century
Locale(s): Outer System Federation, Interstellar Empire/Federation

Summary: Bey Wolf is the former head of the government office that controls the technology involved in adapting the human body to extraterrestrial environments. Wolf has spent the last several years in suspended animation, however, in an attempt to escape encroaching madness. Now he's been summoned back to consciousness because someone is attempting to provoke war between the inner planets and the outer solar system. This is the sequel to *Sight of Proteus*.

Other books you might like:
Lois McMaster Bujold, *Brothers in Arms*, 1988
Lois McMaster Bujold, *Falling Free*, 1988
Gordon Eklund, *A Thunder on Neptune*, 1989
Frederik Pohl, *Man Plus*, 1976

3962

CHARLES SHEFFIELD

Summertide

(New York: Ballantine/Del Rey, 1990)

Story type: Science Fiction (Adventure)
Series: Heritage Universe
Major character(s): Darya Lang, Scientist, Adventurer; Max Perry, Government Official
Time period(s): 63rd century
Locale(s): Opal, Planet—Imaginary; Quake, Planet—Imaginary

Summary: When humanity reaches the stars, strange alien artifacts are found spread throughout the galaxy. Many are entirely incomprehensible. A scientist discovers that something is about to happen to one of the artifacts and sets out to discover its secret.

Other books you might like:
Algis Budrys, *Rogue Moon*, 1960
Arthur C. Clarke, *2001: A Space Odyssey*, 1968
Arthur C. Clarke, *2010: Odyssey Two*, 1982
Arthur C. Clarke, *2061: Odyssey Three*, 1987
Dan Simmons, *The Fall of Hyperion*, 1990
Dan Simmons, *Hyperion*, 1989

3963

CHARLES SHEFFIELD

Transcendence

(New York: Ballantine Del Rey, 1992)

Story type: Science Fiction (Adventure; Hard Science Fiction)
Series: Heritage Universe
Major character(s): Darya Lang, Scientist, Adventurer; Hans Rebka, Adventurer; Dulcimer, Alien (Chism Polypheme), Pilot (spaceship)
Time period(s): 63rd century
Locale(s): *Erebus*, Spaceship; Torvil Anfract, Outer Space; Genizee, Planet—Imaginary

Summary: Darya Lang realizes that her adventures leading to the discovery of live Zardalu leave her unsatisfied by academic research. When presented with the opportunity to join a new expedition and bring back evidence to convince the Alliance Council of the Zardalu's return, Darya and her companions must first find the location of Genizee, the lost homeworld of the Zardalu, perhaps located in the Torvil

Anfract, a region of space-time distorted by macroscopic quantum phenomena.

Other books you might like:
David Brin, *Startide Rising*, 1983
C.J. Cherryh, *Chanur's Legacy*, 1992
Arthur C. Clarke, *Rendezvous with Rama*, 1973
David Drake, *Starliner*, 1992
Vonda N. McIntyre, *Metaphase*, 1992
Alis A. Rasmussen, *A Passage of Stars*, 1990
Vernor Vinge, *A Fire upon the Deep*, 1992

3964

MARY SHELLEY

Collected Tales and Stories

(Baltimore, Maryland: The Johns Hopkins University Press, 1976)

Story type: Horror (Collection)
Summary: An indispensible collection of 25 stories by the author of *Frankenstein*. Of particular note are the doppelganger story "Ferdinando Eboli: A Tale," a story of personality exchange "Transformation," and a fable about the burdens of immortality "The Mortal Immortal." Illustrated with original plates from the stories' magazine appearances. Edited by Charles E. Robinson.

Other books you might like:
Elizabeth Cleghorn Gaskell, *Mrs. Gaskell's Tales of Mystery and Horror*, 1978
Gertrude Atherton, *The Bell in the Fog and Other Stories*, 1905
E.F. Bleiler, *The Collected Ghost Stories of Mrs. J.H. Riddell*, 1977
Vernon Lee, *Supernatural Tales: Excursions into Fantasy*, 1987
E. Nesbit, *In the Dark*, 1988

3965

MARY SHELLEY

The Mortal Immortal: The Complete Supernatural Short Fiction

(San Francisco: Tachyon Publications, 1996)

Story type: Horror (Collection)
Summary: This collection of five supernatural tales by the author of *Frankenstein* shows her preoccupation with the theme of unnaturally prolonged life. The title story is about a man who tires of his alchemically induced immortality and seeks a means of death. "Roger Dodsworth: Reanimated Englishman" and "Valerius: The Re-Animated Roman" both are about the bodies of men from ancient times revived in the present day of the author. The book also includes "Transformation," a tale of body exchange, and "The Dream." Michael Bishop supplies an introduction.

Other books you might like:
Vernon Lee, *The Snake Lady and Other Stories*, 1955
Margaret Oliphant, *Stories of the Seen and Unseen*, 1889

Mrs. J.H. Riddell, *The Collected Ghost Stories of Mrs. J.H. Riddell*, 1977
Bram Stoker, *Dracula's Guest*, 1912

L. Sprague de Camp, *The Complete Compleat Enchanter*, 1989
Fletcher Pratt, co-author
Gordon R. Dickson, *The Dragon Knight*, 1990
Phyllis Eisenstein, *Shadow of Earth*, 1979
Ursula K. Le Guin, *The Beginning Place*, 1980
Terri Windling, *Life on the Border*, 1991
editor

3966

RICK SHELLEY

The Hero King

(New York: Roc, 1992)

Story type: Fantasy (Quest; Alternate World)
Series: Varayan Memoir
Major character(s): Gil Tyner, Royalty (King of Varay), Hero; Aaron Carpenter, Wizard; Parthet "Uncle Parker", Wizard
Time period(s): 1990s
Locale(s): Earth; Faerie, Mythical Place; Varay, Fictional Country

Summary: Gil tries to take a shower back on Earth only to discover that the high radiation level there prevents access. A Russian trawler carried ashore on Varay by a tidal wave coupled with the sudden appearance of a second and then a third moon, and the realization that World War III occurred on Earth, compels Gil to consult with his enemy from Faerie, the Elflord of Xayber, who informs Gil that when seven Moons rise, Varay, Earth and Faerie will end. Gil must prevent that outcome.

Other books you might like:
Charles de Lint, *The Little Country*, 1991
John DeChancie, *Castle Perilous*, 1988
Alan Dean Foster, *To the Vanishing Point*, 1988
Geary Gravel, *A Key for the Nonesuch*, 1990
Marc Laidlaw, *Neon Lotus*, 1988
S.P. Somtow, *Riverrun*, 1991

3968

RICK SHELLEY

The Wizard at Home

(New York: Roc, 1995)

Story type: Fantasy (Magic Conflict)
Series: Seven Towers
Major character(s): Silvas, Wizard, Deity; Maria, Deity; Mikel, Deity
Time period(s): 13th century (1238)
Locale(s): Mecq, Fictional City; The Citadel, Mythical Place; England

Summary: Before the White Brotherhood triumphs over the Blue Rose, the 20 true gods lose a quarter of their number. As Carillia dies, she passes her divinity to the surprised Silvas and the even more surprised Maria. The two must defend themselves against Carillia's siblings, who disapprove of mortals claiming divinity. Second in the series.

Other books you might like:
Steven Brust, *Jhereg*, 1983
Glen Cook, *The Swordbearer*, 1982
Diane Duane, *The Door into Fire*, 1979
Simon R. Green, *Hawk & Fisher*, 1990
Fritz Leiber, *Swords and Deviltry*, 1970

3967

RICK SHELLEY

The Hero of Varay

(New York: Roc, 1991)

Story type: Fantasy (Quest; Alternate World)
Series: Varayan Memoir
Major character(s): Gil Tyner, Royalty, Hero; Parthet "Uncle Parker", Wizard
Time period(s): 1990s
Locale(s): Earth; Varay, Fictional Country

Summary: Gil Tyner is the Hero of Varay, a buffer zone between Earth and the Lands of Fairy. Terrorist bombings on Earth have set off a chain reaction of magic in the buffer zone, disastrous for both worlds unless the chaos can be stopped using the legendary jewels of the Great Mother Earth. However, the only being who can lead Gil to the jewels is the elf that he has recently beheaded.

Other books you might like:
Margaret Ball, *The Shadow Gate*, 1990
Mark Twain, *A Connecticut Yankee in King Arthur's Court*, 1898
Written as Mark Twain

3969

JIM SHEPARD

Lights Out in the Reptile House

(New York: W. W. Norton, 1990)

Story type: Fantasy (Political; Historical)
Major character(s): Karel Roeder, Student—High School; Albert Delp, Scientist (herpetologist)
Time period(s): 1990s
Locale(s): Alternate Earth

Summary: Karel Roeder enjoys his job at the zoo which makes life at home difficult since his father is unable to find work. Life at home is even more difficult as Karel and his father do not like each other. Karel's job is threatened by nationalization of the zoo when the National Unity Party's rise to power creates a very repressive society.

Other books you might like:
Mary Gentle, *Ancient Light*, 1987
Mary Gentle, *Golden Witchbreed*, 1984
Heather Gladney, *Teot's War*, 1987
Robert Onopa, *The Pleasure Tube*, 1979
George Orwell, *Animal Farm*, 1946
George Orwell, *1984*, 1949

Ayn Rand, *Atlas Shrugged*, 1957
Allen Steele, *Orbital Decay*, 1989

3970

LUCIUS SHEPARD

The Ends of the Earth
(Sauk City, Wisconsin: Arkham House, 1991)

Story type: Horror (Collection)

Summary: Seventeen blendings of fantasy, science fiction and horror by one of the most provocative writers of contemporary imaginative literature. Many stories are set in exotic locales such as Katmandu (''A Wooden Tiger'') or Guatemala (''Fire Zone Emerald'') or use the Vietnam war as their launching pad (''Delta Sly Honey,'' ''Shades''). Regardless of their time or place, they address such timeless themes as the subjectivity of experience (''The Ends of the Earth''), the abuses of sexual power (''The Black Clay Boy''), the application of values to life (''The Exercise of Faith'') and the relation of art to life (''The Scalehunter's Beautiful Daughter'').

Other books you might like:
Michael Blumlein, *The Brains of Rats*, 1990
Pat Cadigan, *Patterns*, 1990
Harlan Ellison, *Deathbird Stories*, 1975
John Shirley, *Heatseeker*, 1989

3971

LUCIUS SHEPARD

The Golden
(Shingletown, California: Mark V. Zeising, 1993)

Story type: Horror (Vampire Story; Mystery)
Major character(s): Michel Beheim, Vampire; Roland Agenor, Vampire; Lady Alexandra Conforti, Vampire
Time period(s): 19th century
Locale(s): Castle Banat, Europe

Summary: During a gathering of the vampire ''Family'' at the Castle Banat, a ''Golden,'' or human bred specifically to be vampirized, is slain under unusual circumstances. Michel Beheim, the newest member of the Family, is charged with the task of finding out who the murderer is, and his experiences become milestones in his odyssey of self-discovery as a vampire.

Other books you might like:
Poppy Z. Brite, *Lost Souls*, 1992
Anne Rice, *The Vampire Lestat*, 1985
Dan Simmons, *Carrion Comfort*, 1989
Brian Stableford, *The Empire of Fear*, 1988
Brian Stableford, *Young Blood*, 1992

3972

LUCIUS SHEPARD

Kalimantan
(New York: St. Martin's Press, 1992)

Story type: Horror (Occult)
Major character(s): Curtis Mackinnon, Businessman; Paul Tenzer, Scientist (zoologist)
Time period(s): 1980s
Locale(s): Kalimantan Borneo, Indonesia

Summary: Seeking refuge in the jungles of Borneo fron botched business deals, nebbish Curtis Mackinnon discovers a ceremonial drug used by the natives to alter the fabric of reality. Through use of the drug, Mackinnon becomes a despotic powermonger who threatens to vent his anger upon the world.

Other books you might like:
Paddy Chayefsky, *Altered States*, 1979
Joseph Conrad, *Heart of Darkness*, 1902
Philip K. Dick, *The Three Stigmata of Palmer Eldritch*, 1964
K.W. Jeter, *Dark Seeker*, 1987

3973

MARK SHEPHERD

Elvendude
(New York: Baen, 1994)

Story type: Fantasy (Urban; Magic Conflict)
Major character(s): Aedham ''Adam'' Tuiereann, Mythical Creature (elf), Amnesiac; Samantha ''Sammi'' McDaris, Mythical Creature (elf), Royalty; Zeldan Dhu, Mythical Creature (elf), Magician
Time period(s): Indeterminate
Locale(s): Dallas, Texas; Elfhame Avalon, Fictional Country

Summary: To preserve Aedham from an attack on Elfhame Avalon by evil elves, King Traighthren magically alters Aedham's memory and hides him on Earth. Known as Adam to his mundane suburban friends, Aedham must suddenly come to grips with the fact that elven agents and drug dealers want to track him down.

Other books you might like:
Ellen Guon, *Bedlam Boyz*, 1993
Katharine Kerr, *Daggerspell*, 1986
Mercedes Lackey, *Born to Run*, 1992
    Larry Dixon, co-author
Mercedes Lackey, *Chrome Circle*, 1994
    Larry Dixon, co-author
Mercedes Lackey, *Knight of Ghosts and Shadows*, 1990
    Ellen Guon, co-author
Mercedes Lackey, *Prison of Souls*, 1993
    Mark Shepherd, co-author
Mercedes Lackey, *Summoned to Tourney*, 1992
    Ellen Guon, co-author
Mercedes Lackey, *Wheels of Fire*, 1992
    Mark Shepherd, co-author

3974

DELIA SHERMAN

The Porcelain Dove

(New York: Dutton, 1993)

Story type: Fantasy (Historical)
Major character(s): Berthe Duvet, Servant (chambermaid), Writer
Time period(s): 18th century; Indeterminate
Locale(s): Paris, France; Chateau Beauxpres, France; Jura Mountains, France

Summary: Unless the family finds and acquires a fabulous pocelain dove, an ancestral curse dictates madness and ruin for the House of Malvoeux. Trapped outside time for 200 years, Berthe Duvet chronicles her life and events surrounding the French Revolution, including detailed views of the extravagant and eccentric practices of the oblivious nobility.

Other books you might like:
Lois McMaster Bujold, *The Spirit Ring*, 1992
Mary Gentle, *The Architecture of Desire*, 1993
Mary Gentle, *Rats and Gargoyles*, 1991
Katherine Neville, *The Eight*, 1989
Paula Volsky, *Illusion*, 1992
Martha Wells, *The Element of Fire*, 1993

3975

JOEL HENRY SHERMAN

Random Factor

(New York: Ballantine/Del Rey, 1991)

Story type: Science Fiction (Adventure)
Major character(s): Kenneth Christian Rourke, Security Officer; Gral Il Chedo, Alien (Col); Nebuun, Alien (Eng)
Time period(s): Indeterminate Future
Locale(s): Mael Station, Space Station; Jerrume, Planet—Imaginary (Mael System)

Summary: When the Ssoorii Unity received the signal, it awoke from its dormant state and began constructing itself into a battle fleet. Rejected by the Col High Triumvirate, Gral Il Chedo made a secret pact with the Unity. After the factor of Mael Station was killed in an accident, and after a disastrous political decision forced a job change, Kenneth Rourke becomes the new factor of Mael Station, perhaps the chance occurrence which will prevent a major interstellar war.

Other books you might like:
David Brin, *Startide Rising*, 1983
Lois McMaster Bujold, *Borders of Infinity*, 1989
Glen Cook, *The Dragon Never Sleeps*, 1988
John Dalmas, *The Kalif's War*, 1991
C.S. Friedman, *The Madness Season*, 1990
Stephen Goldin, *Jade Darcy and the Affair of Honor*, 1988
  Mary Mason, co-author
Steve Miller, *Agent of Change*, 1988
  Sharon Lee, co-author
Alis A. Rasmussen, *A Passage of Stars*, 1990
Timothy Zahn, *Cobra*, 1985

3976

JOSEPHA SHERMAN

Child of Faerie, Child of Earth

(New York: Walker, 1992)

Story type: Fantasy (Romance; Young Adult)
Major character(s): Percinet, Mythical Creature (faerie), Royalty (prince); Graciosa, Human, Noblewoman
Time period(s): 12th century
Locale(s): France; Faerie, Mythical Place

Summary: Percinet journeys to the mortal realm and resolves to win Graciosa's heart despite his mother's misgivings and the interference of Graciosa's mother, an abusive sorceress, in this adaptation of Mme. d'Aulnoy's fairy tale "Gracieuse and Percinet."

Other books you might like:
Louise Cooper, *The Sleep of Stone*, 1991
Parke Godwin, *Sherwood*, 1991
Tanith Lee, *Black Unicorn*, 1991
Megan Lindholm, *Cloven Hooves*, 1991
Will Shetterly, *Elsewhere*, 1991
Nancy Springer, *Wings of Flame*, 1985
Terri Windling, *Life on the Border*, 1991
  editor

3977

JOSEPHA SHERMAN

King's Son, Magic's Son

(New York: Baen, 1994)

Story type: Fantasy (Magic Conflict; Political)
Major character(s): Aidan ap Nia, Royalty, Magician; King Estmere, Royalty, Leader
Time period(s): Indeterminate
Locale(s): Cymra, Fictional Country; King Estmere's Lands, Fictional Country; Lundinia, Fictional City

Summary: Raised in Cymra, Aidan studies magic with local faerie folk. On her deathbed, Aidan's mother exacts Aidan's promise to join King Estmere and lend magical assistance to his half-brother. In King Estmere's lands, Aidan learns about the intrigues and politics of court life.

Other books you might like:
Dave Duncan, *The Cutting Edge*, 1992
Terry Goodkind, *Wizard's First Rule*, 1994
Mercedes Lackey, *A Cast of Corbies*, 1994
  Josepha Sherman, co-author
Elizabeth Moon, *Liar's Oath*, 1992
Brad Strickland, *Wizard's Mole*, 1991
Elizabeth Willey, *The Well-Favored Man: The Tale of the Sorcerer's Nephew*, 1993

3978

JOSEPHA SHERMAN

Once upon a Galaxy

(Little Rock, Arkansas: August House, 1994)

Story type: Fantasy (Collection; Legend)

Summary: Subtitled ''The Ancient Stories Behind Star Wars, Superman and Other Popular Fantasies,'' this volume contains a two-page introduction plus introductions to individual sections, grouping by subject 42 tales from around the world which provide classical foundations for modern characters and themes in film, television and comics, such as ''Star Trek,'' Superman, *Star Wars*, cartoon tricksters and the quest for a magic implement. Sherman draws on millennia of world literature and mythos to exemplify themes common to diverse cultures. Includes 22 pages of notes providing source information and folkloric background for each story plus a 15-page suggested reading and viewing list.

Other books you might like:

I.G. Edmonds, *Trickster Tales*, 1966
    editor
Richard Gilliam, *Grails: Quests of the Dawn*, 1994
    Martin H. Greenberg, Edward E. Kramer, co-editors
Andrea Hopkins, *Chronicles of King Arthur*, 1994
Ethel Johnston Phelps, *Tatterhood and Other Tales*, 1978
    editor
Jane Yolen, *Favorite Folktales From around the World*, 1986
    editor
Jack Zipes, *Spells of Enchantment*, 1991
    editor

3979

JOSEPHA SHERMAN, Editor
MARTIN H. GREENBERG, Co-Editor

Orphans of the Night

(New York: Walker, 1995)

Story type: Fantasy (Anthology; Young Adult)

Summary: Contains a brief introduction, four pages of author biographies, and 13 original stories featuring lesser-known nocturnal creatures of legend and folklore and varying in tone from mysterious to ominous. Authors include Jo Clayton, Esther M. Friesner, Laura Resnick, Pamela F. Service, Susan Shwartz, Sherwood Smith, Nancy Springer, Harry Turtledove, Lawrence Watt-Evans, and Jane Yolen.

Other books you might like:

Isaac Asimov, *Mythical Beasties*, 1996
    Martin H. Greenberg, Charles G. Waugh, co-editors
Jack Dann, *Little People!*, 1991
    Gardner Dozois, co-editor
Michael Stearns, *A Wizard's Dozen*, 1993
    editor
Jane Yolen, *Vampires*, 1991
    Martin H. Greenberg, co-editor
Martin H. Greenberg, *Werewolves*, 1988
    Jane Yolen, co-editor

3980

JOSEPHA SHERMAN

The Shattered Oath

(New York: Baen, 1995)

Story type: Fantasy (Magic Conflict)
Series: Prince of the Sidhe
Major character(s): Ardagh Lithaniel, Royalty, Mythical Creature (elf); Gervinus, Religious (bishop), Sorcerer; Eithne, Royalty (queen), Witch
Time period(s): 8th century (798-799)
Locale(s): Ireland (Eriu)

Summary: Thrown out of Faerie into the human world to live or die in exile, Ardagh finds shelter with the High King of Eriu and aids the king against Vikings and rebellious subjects. The greatest threat, however, comes from a sorcerer with demonic powers. First of the series.

Other books you might like:

Poul Anderson, *The Broken Sword*, 1971
    revised edition
Emma Bull, *War for the Oaks*, 1987
Charles de Lint, *Moonheart: A Romance*, 1984
Patricia Kennealy, *The Copper Crown*, 1985
Mercedes Lackey, *A Cast of Corbies*, 1994
    Josepha Sherman, co-author
Morgan Llywelyn, *Druids*, 1993

3981

JOSEPHA SHERMAN

A Strange and Ancient Name

(New York: Baen, 1993)

Story type: Fantasy (Quest)
Major character(s): Hauberin, Mythical Creature (elf), Royalty; Alliar, Spirit; Matilde, Noblewoman
Time period(s): Indeterminate Past (medieval)
Locale(s): Faerie, Mythical Place; France

Summary: The curse of a dying enemy sends Hauberin to the human realm in search of his mother's father's name, the goal causing him as much unease as the curse since Hauberin fears learning of diminished elvish heritage. In Faerie, Hauberin has had trouble making his place and holding his princedom in peace in the face of constant plots and reminders that he remains a young half-human among nearly immortal elves.

Other books you might like:

Margaret Ball, *The Shadow Gate*, 1991
Charles de Lint, *Svaha*, 1989
Richard A. Knaak, *Wolfhelm*, 1990
Mercedes Lackey, *A Cast of Corbies*, 1994
    Josepha Sherman, co-author
Mercedes Lackey, *Castle of Deception*, 1992
    Josepha Sherman, co-author
Mercedes Lackey, *Knight of Ghosts and Shadows*, 1990
    Ellen Guon, co-author
Adrienne Martine-Barnes, *The Fire Sword*, 1984

3982

WILL SHETTERLY

Bone Dance

(New York: Ace, 1991)

Story type: Science Fiction (Post-Holocaust)
Major character(s): Sparrow, Troubleshooter, Trader; Sharrea, Psychic
Time period(s): Indeterminate Future
Locale(s): Minneapolis, Minnesota

Summary: When Sparrow wakes up broke in a ditch, with no memory of how she got there, she makes her way to visit Sharrea. When Sharrea reads the cards, Sparrow receives definite, but unhelpful advice and warnings which do not deter her search for the legendary videotape of *The Horses*. The mind-control weapons which had turned the tide in war, the Horses, are dead, but their legacy remains.

Other books you might like:
Margaret Wander Bonanno, *The Others*, 1990
Pat Cadigan, *Synners*, 1991
Ernest Hogan, *Cortez on Jupiter*, 1990
Pat Murphy, *The City, Not Long After*, 1989
Walter Jon Williams, *Hardwired*, 1986

3983

WILL SHETTERLY

Elsewhere

(New York: Harcourt Brace Jovanovich, 1991)

Story type: Fantasy (Urban; Post-Disaster)
Series: Borderland
Major character(s): Ron Starbuck, Runaway, Human; Mooner, Mythical Creature (elf)
Time period(s): Indeterminate Future
Locale(s): Bordertown, Fictional City

Summary: Hoping to find his lost brother, Ron travels to Bordertown, a city located between the human world and the world of Elfland. When befriended by an elf motorcyclist, Mooner, Ron moves into Mooner's home, Castle Pup, shared among elves, halflings and humans. There he finds companionship among the outcasts until a tragic fire turns Ron's world upside down. This book was honored as winner of a Minnesota Book Award.

Other books you might like:
Gael Baudino, *Gossamer Axe*, 1990
Emma Bull, *War for the Oaks*, 1987
Mercedes Lackey, *Knight of Ghosts and Shadows*, 1990
    Ellen Guon, co-author
Michael Reaves, *Street Magic*, 1991
Joel Rosenberg, *The Road to Ehvenor*, 1991
Terri Windling, *Borderland*, 1986
    Mark Alan Arnold, co-editor
Terri Windling, *Bordertown*, 1986
    Mark Alan Arnold, co-editor
Terri Windling, *Life on the Border*, 1991
    editor

3984

WILL SHETTERLY
EMMA BULL, Co-Author

Liavek: Festival Week

(New York: Ace, 1990)

Story type: Fantasy (Anthology; Magic Conflict)
Series: Liavek
Time period(s): Indeterminate
Locale(s): Liavek, Fictional Country

Summary: A collection of stories dealing with Festival Week in Liavek. A minor god escorts a young ruler on a night of forbidden revelry, a powerless wizard tries to halt an invasion of Ka Zhir airships, and two Green Priests die mysteriously while watching a parade. On Festival Week, anything can happen.

Other books you might like:
Steven Brust, *Jhereg*, 1983
John M. Ford, *Casting Fortune*, 1989
Fritz Leiber, *Swords and Deviltry*, 1970
Robert Silverberg, *Lord Valentine's Castle*, 1980
Terri Windling, *Borderland*, 1986
    Mark Arnold, co-editor
Terri Windling, *Bordertown*, 1986
    Mark Arnold, co-editor
Roger Zelazny, *Changeling*, 1980
Roger Zelazny, *Nine Princes in Amber*, 1970

3985

WILL SHETTERLY

Nevernever

(New York: Harcourt Brace, 1993)

Story type: Fantasy (Post-Disaster; Urban)
Series: Borderland
Major character(s): Ron Starbuck, Adventurer, Teenager; Florida, Child, Mythical Creature (elf); Leda, Mythical Creature (elf), Orphan
Time period(s): Indeterminate Future
Locale(s): Borderland, Mythical Place; Bordertown, Fictional City; Nevernever, Mythical Place

Summary: Wolfboy and his friends struggle to protect Florida from kidnappers who would take her to Elfland to forward political goals. On a subsequent foray into Nevernever with the elf who ensorcelled him, Wolfboy helps her overcome an addiction while she rescues Wolfboy from becoming the pet of wild elves. Sequel to *Elsewhere*.

Other books you might like:
Emma Bull, *Finder*, 1994
Emma Bull, *War for the Oaks*, 1987
Charles de Lint, *Moonheart: A Romance*, 1984
Ellen Guon, *Bedlam Boyz*, 1993
Tanya Huff, *Gate of Darkness, Circle of Light*, 1989
Terri Windling, *Borderland*, 1986
    Mark Alan Arnold, co-editor
Terri Windling, *Bordertown*, 1986
    Mark Alan Arnold, co-editor

Terri Windling, *Life on the Border*, 1991
  editor

3986

ANDREA SHETTLE

Flute Song Magic

(New York: Avon Flare, 1990)

Story type: Fantasy (Quest)
Major character(s): Flutirr, Nobleman
Time period(s): Indeterminate
Locale(s): Land of the Nelvins, Fictional Country

Summary: Flutirr is born a high noble in a very rigid, class-stratified society. However, he hears strange and beautiful music, magic music, played on a flute by a classless Nelvin who, to Flutirr, is an untouchable. Driven to disregard the mores of his culture, he feels compelled to start a quest for forbidden music. This book was published as the winner of Avon's Flare competition.

Other books you might like:
Emma Bull, *War for the Oaks*, 1987
Anne McCaffrey, *Crystal Singer*, 1982
Anne McCaffrey, *Dragon Song*, 1976
Andre Norton, *Dragon Magic*, 1972
Sydney J. Van Scyoc, *Darkchild*, 1982

3987

LEWIS SHINER

Glimpses

(New York: Morrow, 1993)

Story type: Horror (Wild Talents)
Major character(s): Ray Shackleford, Repairman, Psychic; Graham Hudson, Producer (Carnival Dog Records); Brian Wilson, Musician (leader of the Beach Boys), Historical Figure
Time period(s): 1960s; 1980s
Locale(s): Austin, Texas

Summary: Emotionally confused over the recent death of the father who never loved him, Ray Shackleford retreats into the rock music of his childhood and discovers that he has the uncanny ability to reproduce the music from the great apocryphal albums of the 1960s and 1970s that were planned but never recorded by the Doors, the Beach Boys, and Jimi Hendrix. As Ray's emotional turmoil worsens, his sympathy with the past threatens to leave him stranded there.

Other books you might like:
Bradley Denton, *Buddy Holly Is Alive and Well on Ganymede*, 1991
George R.R. Martin, *The Armageddon Rag*, 1983
David J. Schow, *The Kill Riff*, 1988
John Skipp, *The Scream*, 1988
  Craig Spector, co-author

3988

LEWIS SHINER

Nine Hard Questions about the Nature of the Universe

(Eugene, Oregon: Pulphouse Press, 1990)

Story type: Science Fiction (Collection)
Series: Author's Choice Monthly

Summary: This collection consists of two original pieces and seven stories previously published in *Analog, Isaac Asimov's Science Fiction Magazine*, and elsewhere by one of the leaders of the cyberpunk movement. Among the better stories are "Snowbirds," "Dancers," "Soldier, Sailor," "Kings of the Afternoon," and "Nine Hard Questions About the Nature of the Universe." Shiner has also included a short introduction to each story.

Other books you might like:
Greg Bear, *Tangents*, 1989
Pat Cadigan, *Patterns*, 1989
William Gibson, *Burning Chrome*, 1986
Bruce Sterling, *Crystal Express*, 1989

3989

SHARON SHINN

Archangel

(New York: Ace, 1996)

Story type: Science Fiction (Theological; Lost Colony)
Major character(s): Gabriel, Singer, Angel (archangel-elect); Rachel, Spouse (Gabriel's), Singer; Raphael, Angel (archangel)
Time period(s): Indeterminate Future
Locale(s): Samaria, Planet—Imaginary

Summary: To avoid annihilation by Yovah, disparate groups must regularly prove their willingness to cooperate by singing at an annual gloria. Ordered by Yovah's oracle to wed Rachel and sing together at the next Gloria, Gabriel discovers that Rachel's sympathies lie with the downtrodden humans, while her resentment threatens the Gloria.

Other books you might like:
Stephen Baxter, *Raft*, 1991
Orson Scott Card, *The Memory of Earth*, 1992
Larry Niven, *The Smoke Ring*, 1987
Frank M. Robinson, *The Dark Beyond the Stars*, 1991
Robert Silverberg, *Kingdoms of the Wall*, 1993
John Varley, *Wizard*, 1980
Gene Wolfe, *The Shadow of the Torturer*, 1980

3990

SHARON SHINN

The Shape-Changer's Wife

(New York: Ace, 1995)

Story type: Fantasy (Magic Conflict; Romance)

Major character(s): Aubrey, Student, Wizard; Lilith, Genetically Altered Being, Spouse; Glyrenden, Wizard
Time period(s): Indeterminate
Locale(s): Fictional Country

Summary: Aubrey comes to study under Glyrenden to learn shape-changing, but soon becomes intrigued by Lilith, Glyrenden's wife, and begins to investigate the household's strange secrets. First novel.

Other books you might like:
Don Callander, *Pyromancer*, 1992
Diane Duane, *So You Want to Be a Wizard?*, 1983
Teresa Edgerton, *The Castle of the Silver Wheel*, 1993
Nancy Kress, *The Golden Grove*, 1984
Thomas Burnett Swann, *The Tournament of Thorns*, 1976
Patricia C. Wrede, *Mairelon the Magician*, 1991
Mary Frances Zambreno, *Journeyman Wizard*, 1994
Andre Norton, *The Crystal Gryphon*, 1972

3991

TOM SHIPPEY, Editor

The Oxford Book of Fantasy Stories
(New York: Oxford University Press, 1994)

Story type: Fantasy (Anthology)

Summary: Contains a 14-page introduction, five-page select bibliography and 31 stories from periodicals, collections and anthologies 1888-1992 which exemplify the diverse interests of fantasists throughout time, from sword and sorcery set in the ancient Hyborian Age of Conan in Robert E. Howard's "The Tower of the Elephant," to modern urban themes in Phyllis Eisenstein's "Subworld," and a bargain with a wish granting demon in the distant future of Zothique in Clark Ashton Smith's "Xeethra." Magic, supernatural realms, parallel worlds, battles between order and chaos and mythical creatures populate other stories by authors including Poul Anderson, Peter S. Beagle, Ray Bradbury, Angela Carter, Robert Holdstock, Henry Kuttner, Tanith Lee, Fritz Leiber, H.P. Lovecraft, Abraham Merritt, Catherine L. Moore, Larry Niven, Mervyn Peake, Terry Pratchett, Theodore Sturgeon, Thomas Burnett Swann, James Tiptree Jr., Jack Vance, Manly Wade Wellman and Jane Yolen.

Other books you might like:
Robert H. Boyer, *Visions & Imaginings: Classic Fantasy Fiction*, 1992
  Kenneth J. Zahorski, co-editor
Ellen Datlow, *The Year's Best Fantasy and Horror Series*, 1989-
  Terri Windling, co-editor
Alison Lurie, *The Oxford Book of Modern Fairy Tales*, 1993
  editor
Robert Silverberg, *The Fantasy Hall of Fame*, 1983
  Martin H. Greenberg, co-editor
Cary Wilkins, *A Treasury of Fantasy: Heroic Adventures in Imaginary Lands*, 1981
  editor

3992

TOM SHIPPEY, Editor

The Oxford Book of Science Fiction Stories
(New York: Oxford University Press, 1992)

Story type: Science Fiction (Anthology)

Summary: Contains an 18-page introduction, 6-page bibliography and 30 stories by different authors arranged chronologically, 1903-1990, by appearance in periodical or anthology and chosen to express the range, vitality and literary quality of the genre which characterizes the 20th century. Stories nominated for a Nebula Award include "Cloak of Anarchy" by Larry Niven, "A Thing of Beauty" by Norman Spinrad and "How the Whip Came Back" by Gene Wolfe Other stories include "Who Can Replace a Man?" by Brian W. Aldiss, "Billennium" by J.G. Ballard, "Piecework" by David Brin, "Burning Chrome" by William Gibson, "Crucifixus Etiam" by Walter M. Miller, Jr., "Desertion" by Clifford D. Simak, "The Ballad of Lost C'mell" by Cordwainer Smith, "The Monster" by A.E. van Vogt and "A Martian Odyssey" by Stanley G. Weinbaum.

Other books you might like:
Groff Conklin, *The Best of Science Fiction*, 1946
  editor
Harlan Ellison, *Dangerous Visions*, 1967
  editor
David G. Hartwell, *The World Treasury of Science Fiction*, 1989
  editor
Raymond J. Healy, *Adventures in Time and Space*, 1946
  J. Francis McComas, co-editor
Robert Silverberg, *The Science Fiction Hall of Fame, Volume 1*, 1970
  editor
Donald A. Wollheim, *The Pocket Book of Science Fiction*, 1943
  editor

3993

JOHN SHIRLEY

Eclipse Corona
(New York: Popular Library Questar, 1990)

Story type: Science Fiction (Cyberpunk)
Series: Song Called Youth
Major character(s): Daniel "Hardeyes" Torrence, Revolutionary; Steinfeld, Revolutionary
Time period(s): 21st century (2021)
Locale(s): Europe

Summary: The New Resistance continues its desperate, losing battle against the cybernetically-enhanced forces of the Neo-fascist Second Alliance. The Alliance continues its experiments in genetic manipulation and its policy of genocide. Meanwhile, aboard an orbiting space station, a madman toys with the idea of wiping out all life on Earth.

Other books you might like:
Bruce Sterling, *Islands in the Net*, 1988
Walter Jon Williams, *Hardwired*, 1986
Dave Wolverton, *On My Way to Paradise*, 1989

3994
JOHN SHIRLEY

Heatseeker

(Los Angeles: Scream Press, 1989)

Story type: Horror (Collection)

Summary: Nineteen stories written over a fifteen-year period (with three originals) that demonstrate Shirley's lucidity, elegance, variety, and virtuosity. Dark parables on such subjects as death, sex, drugs, nuclear war, and transmutations of body and soul are treated with power, horror, and humor. Among the best stories are "Wolves of the Plateau," "Equilibrium," and "Recurrent Dreams of Nuclear War...."

Other books you might like:
Clive Barker, *Cabal*, 1988
Ramsey Campbell, *Scared Stiff*, 1987
Dennis Etchison, *Red Dreams*, 1984
William Gibson, *Burning Chrome*, 1986
David J. Schow, *Seeing Red*, 1990
Bruce Sterling, *Crystal Express*, 1989

3995
JOHN SHIRLEY

New Noir

(Boulder, Colorado: Black Ice Books, 1993)

Story type: Horror (Collection)

Summary: These six stories portray the horror and humor that befalls characters leading lives of desperation in the contemporary urban jungle. "Jody and Anne on TV" tells of joyriding youngsters who commit murder to see how they are portrayed on television. "Skeeter Junkie" is a dream fantasy in which a junkie on the nod imagines he is a mosquito and becomes incapable of extricating himself from that fantasy. "I Want to Get Married, Says the World's Smallest Man," is a tabloid-type story of a sideshow midget who hopes to marry a rich woman, and the poor woman who marries him in the hope of getting her hands on his presumed riches. "Just Like Suzie" is a grotesque tale of necrophilia. The remaining two stories first appeared in the author's 1989 collection, *Heatseeker*.

Other books you might like:
Poppy Z. Brite, *Swamp Foetus*, 1993
David J. Schow, *Lost Angels*, 1990
David J. Schow, *Seeing Red*, 1989
John Skipp, *Deadlines*, 1989
    Craig Spector, co-author

3996
JOHN SHIRLEY

Silicon Embrace

(Shingletown, California: Mark V. Ziesing Books, 1996)

Story type: Science Fiction (Cyberpunk; UFO)
Major character(s): Farraday, Public Relations; Quinn, Journalist; Anatole, Teenager
Time period(s): 2010s (2017)
Locale(s): California; Area 51, Nevada

Summary: In a violent, balkanizing United States, extraterrestials decide to come out of hiding, having surreptitiously watched humans for years. To produce the correct spin for their unveiling, one group of aliens enlists Farraday's help. Meanwhile, other aliens attempt to contact humans directly.

Other books you might like:
Stephen Bury, *Interface*, 1994
Michael Kandel, *Strange Invasion*, 1989
Earl Mac Rauch, *Buckaroo Banzai*, 1984
Robert Shea, *The Illuminatus! Trilogy*, 1988
    Robert Anton Wilson, co-author
Neal Stephenson, *Snow Crash*, 1992

3997
JOHN SHIRLEY

Wetbones

(Shingletown, California: Mark V. Ziesing, 1991)

Story type: Horror (Vampire Story)
Major character(s): Tom Prentice, Writer (screenwriter); Ephram Pixie, Drifter; Reverend Garner, Religious (former minister)
Time period(s): 1990s
Locale(s): Los Angeles, California

Summary: Tom Prentice's investigation of the mysterious death of his ex-wife and the disappearance of a friend's younger brother leads him to a ranch on the outskirts of Los Angeles and the discovery of the Akishra, a race of extradimensional vampires who work symbiotically with thrill-seeking human hosts to drain victims of their souls so that they can pass into the earthly plane.

Other books you might like:
Clive Barker, *The Hellbound Heart*, 1991
Stephen Gallagher, *Valley of Lights*, 1987
Eric Frank Russell, *Sinister Barrier*, 1943
Dan Simmons, *Carrion Comfort*, 1989

3998
MIKE SHUPP

Death's Gray Land

(New York: Ballantine/Del Rey, 1991)

Story type: Science Fiction (Time Travel; Military)
Series: Destiny Makers

Major character(s): Timothy Harper, Time Traveller, Military Personnel (Sergeant); Kylene Waterfall, Time Traveller, Telepath; Cherrid ris Clendannan, Military Personnel (General)
Time period(s): 900th century (90000s)
Locale(s): Fohima Alghera, Fictional Country; Midpassage, Fictional Country

Summary: Tim Harper, caught in a time flux in 1970, is now an agent of the Algheran Time-Travel Project. Humanity has evolved into two different races, both long-lived, one telepathic. The Teeps and Normals have agreed on rules to prevent the Teeps from enslaving the Normals. The Time-Travel Project aims at changing history to prevent the Chelmmysian Alliance from conquering Alghera.

Other books you might like:
Poul Anderson, *The Shield of Time*, 1990
Keith William Andrews, *Freedom's Rangers*, 1989
Phyllis Eisenstein, *Shadow of Earth*, 1979
William R. Forstchen, *Rally Cry!*, 1990
H. Beam Piper, *Lord Kalvan of Otherwhen*, 1965
Sheri S. Tepper, *Sideshow*, 1992
John Varley, *Millennium*, 1983

3999

MIKE SHUPP

The Last Reckoning
(New York: Ballantine/Del Rey, 1991)

Story type: Science Fiction (Time Travel; Political)
Series: Destiny Makers
Major character(s): Timothy Harper, Time Traveller, Military Personnel; Kylene Waterfall, Time Traveller, Telepath
Time period(s): 900th century (90000s)
Locale(s): Midpassage, Fictional Country

Summary: Timothy Harper, transplanted 90,000 years into the future, has lost too many battles. His alternate, Timmian Haarper, fights against him. Each is in love with a Kylene Waterfall. When Kylene steals his time machine, she risks Alghera, all their lives and their futures together.

Other books you might like:
Keith William Andrews, *Search and Destroy*, 1990
Gordon R. Dickson, *Time Storm*, 1977
Randall Frakes, *The Terminator*, 1985
    Bill Wisher, co-author
Warren Norwood, *Vanished*, 1988
Dan Simmons, *Hyperion*, 1989
L. Neil Smith, *The Gallatin Divergence*, 1985

4000

NEAL SHUSTERMAN

Scorpion Shards
(New York: Tor, 1995)

Story type: Science Fiction (Young Adult; Science Fantasy)
Major character(s): Dillon Cole, Teenager, Outcast; Deanna Chang, Teenager, Outcast; Lourdes Hidalgo, Teenager, Outcast

Time period(s): 1990s
Locale(s): Mt. St. Helens, Washington; St. Louis, Missouri

Summary: When a distant star goes nova, a mysterious force draws six teenagers together from all over the United States. They then discover and battle the cause of the terrible afflictions each of them suffers.

Other books you might like:
Robert Cormier, *Fade*, 1988
Annabel Johnson, *Prisoner of Psi*, 1985
    Edgar Johnson, co-author
Madeleine L'Engle, *A Wrinkle in Time*, 1962
Christopher Pike, *The Eternal Enemy*, 1993

4001

SUSAN SHWARTZ

The Grail of Hearts
(New York: Tor, 1992)

Story type: Fantasy (Legend; Religious)
Major character(s): Kundry, Immortal, Wanderer; Amfortas, Knight; Klingsor, Sorcerer
Time period(s): 1st century (33); 10th century
Locale(s): Broceliande, Fictional Country; Jerusalem, Israel

Summary: Kundry seduces and betrays Amfortas, guardian of the Holy Grail, on the orders of the evil Klingsor. Feeling guilt and despair, she defies Klingsor who punishes her by forcing her to relive events in her own life a thousand years earlier. She discovers the ability to act differently this time, but remains unable to change the final outcome, again cursed to wander the Earth eternally for laughing at the Crucifixion. Awakening back in Broceliande a changed woman, she eventually finds Amfortas and forgiveness.

Other books you might like:
Marion Zimmer Bradley, *The Mists of Avalon*, 1983
Katherine Kurtz, *Saint Camber*, 1978
A.J. Langguth, *Jesus Christs*, 1968
Helen M. Mustard, *Parzival: A Romance of the Middle Ages*, 1961
    Charles E. Passage, co-translator
Andre Norton, *Imperial Lady*, 1989
Diana L. Paxson, *The White Raven*, 1988
Rosemary Sutcliff, *Sword at Sunset*, 1963
Judith Tarr, *The Dagger and the Cross: A Novel of the Crusades*, 1991

4002

SUSAN SHWARTZ

Heritage of Flight
(New York: Tor, 1989)

Story type: Science Fiction (First Contact)
Major character(s): Pauli Yeager, Pilot, Military Personnel; Rafe Adams, Scientist
Time period(s): Indeterminate Future
Locale(s): Cynthia, Planet—Imaginary

Summary: In this Philip K. Dick Award-nominated novel, mankind is engaged in a genocidal, planet-destroying civil war and a small convoy of spaceships flees the destruction, seeking a haven for a remnant of humanity's children. Landing on the planet Cynthia, they discover beautiful, airborne lifeforms that prove highly intelligent. Behind that beauty, however, lurks horror.

Other books you might like:
Clare Bell, *People of the Sky*, 1989
Octavia E. Butler, *Adulthood Rites*, 1988
Octavia E. Butler, *Dawn*, 1987
Octavia E. Butler, *Imago*, 1989
Larry Niven, *The Legacy of Heorot*, 1987
 Jerry Pournelle and Steven Barnes, co-authors
Sheri S. Tepper, *Grass*, 1989

4003
SUSAN SHWARTZ
Shards of Empire
(New York: Tor, 1996)

Story type: Fantasy (Political; Adventure)
Major character(s): Leo Ducas, Military Personnel; Romanus Diogenes, Ruler (emperor); Micheal Psellus, Scholar
Time period(s): 10th century
Locale(s): Constantinople, Byzantine Empire

Summary: During a battle against the Turks, Leo's uncle betrays the emperor, who is captured and then ransomed to the Byzantines. With the emperor when he dies, Leo remains haunted by the memories of Asherah and tortured by memories of the emperor's death. When Leo flees Constantinople, travelling through Asia Minor to redeem his family's name, Psellus gathers power by appointing a puppet emperor.

Other books you might like:
Marion Zimmer Bradley, *The Firebrand*, 1987
Steven Brust, *The Phoenix Guards*, 1991
Glen Cook, *The Black Company*, 1984
Alexandre Dumas, *The Three Musketeers*, 1846
John M. Ford, *The Dragon Waiting*, 1983
Stephen R. Lawhead, *Byzantium*, 1996
Melanie Rawn, *The Golden Key*, 1996
 Jennifer Roberson, Kate Elliott, co-authors
Roger Zelazny, *Nine Princes in Amber*, 1970

4004
SUSAN SHWARTZ, Editor
MARTIN H. GREENBERG, Co-Editor
Sisters in Fantasy 2
(New York: Roc, 1996)

Story type: Fantasy (Anthology)

Summary: This anthology contains a six-page introduction by Shwartz plus brief individual introductions to 23 original stories varying in tone from upbeat to horrific, using contemporary and classic settings, with themes including revisionist myths and religion, women's relationship with the Earth, transformations, and abuse and loneliness. The 22 authors include Gael Baudino, Ru Emerson, Valerie J. Freireich, Esther Friesner, Ellen Guon, Mercedes Lackey, Patricia Mc-

Killip, Beth Meacham, Sharan Newman, Rebecca Ore, Diana Paxson, Susan Shwartz, Sherwood Smith, Martha Soukup, Nancy Springer, Lois Tilton, and Jane Yolen.

Other books you might like:
Marion Zimmer Bradley, *The Sword and Sorceress Series*, 1984-1996
 editor
Esther Friesner, *Chicks in Chainmail*, 1995
 editor
Susanna J. Sturgis, *Magic Realism by Women: Dreams in a Minor Key*, 1991
 editor
A. Susan Williams, *The Lifted Veil: The Book of Fantastic Literature by Women*, 1993
 editor
A. Susan Williams, *The Penguin Book of Modern Fantasy by Women*, 1995
 Richard Glyn Jones, co-editor

4005
SAM SICILIANO
Blood Feud
(New York: Pinnacle, 1993)

Story type: Horror (Vampire Story)
Major character(s): Steve Ryan, Businessman; Mary Connely, Teacher (Maryglenn College); Fred Martin, Religious (priest)
Time period(s): 1980s (1988)
Locale(s): Portland, Oregon

Summary: Bored with their immortality, and full of nothing but hatred for others of their ilk, the ageless vampires Ruthven and Madame Rambouillet wage a war against one another using human pawns as their foot soldiers.

Other books you might like:
Brian Lumley, *Necroscope*, 1986
Kim Newman, *Bad Dreams*, 1990
Dan Simmons, *Carrion Comfort*, 1989
Lee Weathersby, *Kiss of the Vampire*, 1992
T. Lucien Wright, *Thirst of the Vampire*, 1992

4006
ANNE RIVERS SIDDONS
The House Next Door
(Ballantine, 1989)

Story type: Horror (Haunted House)
Major character(s): Colquitt Kennedy, Housewife; Kim Dougherty, Architect (Builder of "the house")
Time period(s): 1970s
Locale(s): Atlanta, Georgia

Summary: When insanity and violence overwhelm three families that move into a beautiful, newly built home, the nextdoor neighbors decide that the house is "haunted" and set out to locate and destroy the evil that possesses it. Originally published in 1978.

Other books you might like:
Shirley Jackson, *The Haunting of Hill House*, 1959
Ira Levin, *The Stepford Wives*, 1972
John Updike, *The Witches of Eastwick*, 1984

4007
JOHN SIEVERT

Suicide Attack
(New York: Zebra, 1990)

Story type: Science Fiction (Military; Post-Holocaust)
Series: C.A.D.S.
Major character(s): Dean Sturgis, Military Personnel (colonel); Major Danirov, Military Personnel
Time period(s): Indeterminate Future
Locale(s): West

Summary: The Russian invaders have occupied the east and west coasts of the United States; but Colonel Dean Sturgis leads his soldiers, in their Computerized Attack/Defense System (C.A.D.S.) suits, on another deadly fight amid the nuclear ruins. Their current target is a Soviet base in California, but its commander, Major Danirov, has captured Sturgis' wife Robin and has a plan for destroying the C.A.D.S. troops and their leader.

Other books you might like:
Peter Bryant, *Red Alert*, 1959
  pseudonym of Peter George
Robert A. Heinlein, *Starship Troopers*, 1959
George Lucas, *Star Wars*, 1976
David Robbins, *L.A. Strike*, 1990
David Robbins, *Yellowstone Run*, 1990
Ryder Stacy, *Doomsday Warrior*, 1984

4008
JOHN SILBERSACK, Editor
CHRISTOPHER SCHELLING, Co-Editor

The Magic of Christmas
(New York: Roc, 1992)

Story type: Fantasy (Anthology)

Summary: Themes of glad Christmas tidings including ghosts, elves, life after death and time travel fill this volume which features a four-page introduction and six original stories plus one, "Holiday" by Richard Christian Matheson, first published in 1988. Other authors include Gael Baudino, Julian May, Dennis L. McKiernan, Andre Norton, Christopher Stasheff and Judith Tarr.

Other books you might like:
Alan Brennert, *Kindred Spirits*, 1984
Martin H. Greenberg, *Christmas on Ganymede and Other Stories*, 1990
  editor
Rosalind M. Greenberg, *Christmas Bestiary*, 1992
  Martin H. Greenberg, co-editor
David G. Hartwell, *Christmas Stars*, 1992
  editor

Kristine Kathryn Rusch, *Pulphouse, Issue 10: Special Issue*, 1991
  editor
Gene Wolfe, *Gene Wolfe's Book of Days*, 1981

4009
DAVID B. SILVA, Editor

The Definitive Best of the Horror Show
(Baltimore, Maryland: CD Publications, 1992)

Story type: Horror (Anthology)

Summary: A collection of 40 stories by 36 different authors from the pages of *The Horror Show*, a small press magazine that helped to shape horror fiction in the 1980s. Included are Robert R. McCammon's post-apocalypse horror tale, "The I Scream Man"; Dennis Etchison's tale of loss and alienation, "The Scar"; Joe Lansdale's hardboiled suspense story, "On a Dark October"; Nancy Collins' tale of a sideshow photographer, "The Freaktent"; and Ramsey Campbell's science fictional "Passing Phase."

Other books you might like:
Jessica Horsting, *Midnight Graffiti*, 1992
  James Van Hise, co-author
Robert Morrish, *Quick Chills II*, 1992
  Peter Enfantino, co-author
Mark Rainey, *The Best of Deathrealm*, 1993
Stuart David Schiff, *The Whispers Series*, 1977-1987

4010
ROBERT SILVERBERG

The Collected Stories of Robert Silverberg, Volume 1: Secret Sharers
(New York: Bantam Spectra, 1992)

Story type: Science Fiction (Collection)

Summary: Contains a seven-page introduction plus 24 stories published 1981-1988, each with an individual introduction. This volume includes one Nebula Award nominee, "Homefaring"; one Nebula Award and Hugo Award nominee, "The Secret Sharers"; and one Hugo Award winner, "Enter a Soldier. Later: Enter Another."

Other books you might like:
Alfred Bester, *Star Light, Star Bright*, 1976
Orson Scott Card, *Maps in a Mirror*, 1990
Kim Stanley Robinson, *Remaking History*, 1991
Marc Stiegler, *The Gentle Seduction*, 1990
Michael Swanwick, *Gravity's Angels*, 1991
John Varley, *Blue Champagne*, 1986

4011
ROBERT SILVERBERG

The Face of the Waters
(New York: Bantam Spectra, 1991)

Story type: Science Fiction (Adventure)

Major character(s): Valben Lawler, Doctor; Father Quillan, Religious (Church of All Worlds); Sundira Thane, Adventurer
Time period(s): 24th century
Locale(s): Hydros, Planet—Imaginary; *Queen of Hydros*, At Sea

Summary: Marooned on Hydros, humans live at the mercy of the indigenous race, the Gillies. When banished from their home on Sorve Island, a group of humans sail off to find The Face of the Waters, the planet's largest solid land mass which has mystical significance to the Gillies.

Other books you might like:
Carol Severance, *Reefsong*, 1991
Dan Simmons, *The Fall of Hyperion*, 1990
Dan Simmons, *Hyperion*, 1989
Joan Slonczewski, *A Door into Ocean*, 1986
Sydney J. Van Scyoc, *Deepwater Dreams*, 1991

4012
ROBERT SILVERBERG, Editor
MARTIN H. GREENBERG, Co-Editor

The Horror Hall of Fame
(New York: Carroll & Graf, 1991)

Story type: Horror (Anthology)

Summary: Eighteen classic stories spanning the last century-and-a-half, chosen by attendees of the 1981 and 1982 World Fantasy Convention to commemorate stories written before the creation of the World Fantasy Award. Aspects of horror addressed include psychological horror (Edgar Allan Poe's ''The Fall of the House of Usher,'' J. Sheridan Le Fanu's ''Green Tea''), elemental and natural horror (Arthur Machen's ''The White People,'' Algernon Blackwood's ''The Willows''), urban horror (Fritz Leiber's ''Smoke Ghost,'' Harlan Ellison's ''The Whimper of Whipped Dogs''), the occult (M.R. James' ''Casting the Runes,'' Robert Bloch's ''Yours Truly, Jack the Ripper''), voodoo (Robert E. Howard's ''Pigeons from Hell''), reanimated dead (W.W. Jacobs' ''The Monkey's Paw,'' Theodore Sturgeon's ''It''), demon children (Ray Bradbury's ''The Small Assassin''), ghosts (Ramsey Campbell's ''Calling Card,'' Stephen King's ''The Reach''), and others.

Other books you might like:
Dennis Etchison, *The Complete Masters of Darkness*, 1991
    editor
David G. Hartwell, *The Dark Descent*, 1987
    editor
Robert Silverberg, *The Science Fiction Hall of Fame*, 1970
    editor
Herbert Wise, *Great Tales of Terror and the Supernatural*, 1944
    Phyllis Fraser, co-editor

4013
ROBERT SILVERBERG

Hot Sky at Midnight
(New York: Bantam Spectra, 1994)

Story type: Science Fiction (Space Colony; Genetic Manipulation)
Major character(s): Victor Farkas, Genetically Altered Being; Paul Carpenter, Sea Captain, Office Worker; Jolanda Bermudez, Artist
Time period(s): 22nd century
Locale(s): California; Nuevo Valparaiso, Space Station (L5 colony)

Summary: On an Earth becoming unfit for human life, most people long to escape to space colonies. Fired on his first tour of duty on an iceberg ship, Paul Carpenter gets involved in a plot to take over Nuevo Valparaiso, a corrupt space colony.

Other books you might like:
John Barnes, *The Man Who Pulled Down the Sky*, 1986
Barney Cohen, *The Taking of Satcon Station*, 1982
    Jim Baen, co-author
Gordon R. Dickson, *The Pritcher Mass*, 1972
Mary Rosenblum, *The Drylands*, 1993
Allen Steele, *Clarke County, Space*, 1990

4014
ROBERT SILVERBERG

Kingdoms of the Wall
(New York: Bantam Spectra, 1993)

Story type: Science Fiction (Mystical; Fantasy)
Major character(s): Poilar Crookleg, Adventurer, Religious (pilgrim); Traiben, Adventurer, Religious
Time period(s): Indeterminate Future
Locale(s): Planet—Imaginary

Summary: Among the few chosen each generation for a difficult Pilgrimage to the home of the gods, Poilar Crookleg and Traiben ascend the Wall in honor of their ancestor, the First Climber. The creatures and adventures in the kingdoms along the way to the summit leave the group barely able to accept the truth at the end of their arduous journey.

Other books you might like:
Orson Scott Card, *The Memory of Earth*, 1992
C.J. Cherryh, *Angel with the Sword*, 1985
Philip Jose Farmer, *The Maker of Universes*, 1965
Brian Herbert, *The Race for God*, 1990
Edward Myers, *Fire and Ice*, 1992
Edward Myers, *The Mountain Made of Light*, 1992
Robert Reed, *The Remarkables*, 1992
John Varley, *Wizard*, 1980

4015

ROBERT SILVERBERG

Letters From Atlantis

(New York: Atheneum, 1990)

Story type: Fantasy (Time Travel; Legend)
Major character(s): Roy, Time Traveller; Ram Ramifon Blayl, Royalty (Heir to the Throne of Atlantis)
Time period(s): 189th century B.C. (18,862 B.C.)
Locale(s): *Lord of Day*, At Sea (Ship bound for Atlantis); Athilan, Mythical Place (Island Kingdom of Atlantis)

Summary: Through letters to a fellow time traveller, Roy tells Lora that his consciousness has settled in the person who is heir apparent to the King of Atlantis. When Ram discovers Roy's presence, he rebels, then accepts Roy. During an initiation rite, Roy sees Ram's peoples' Sun go nova and the eventual destruction of Atlantis.

Other books you might like:
Isaac Asimov, *Atlantis*, 1988
   Martin H. Greenberg, co-editor; Charles Waugh, co-editor
Marion Zimmer Bradley, *Web of Darkness*, 1984
Marion Zimmer Bradley, *Web of Light*, 1983
J. Alison James, *Sing for a Gentle Rain*, 1990
Roger Zelazny, *Bridge of Ashes*, 1976

4016

ROBERT SILVERBERG

Lion Time in Timbuctoo

(Eugene, Oregon: Axolotl Press, 1990)

Story type: Science Fiction (Alternate Universe; Political)
Series: Gate of Worlds
Major character(s): Little Father, Heir (to the Emir of Songhay); Michael, Diplomat, Apprentice (to the English Ambassador); Selima, Young Woman (Turkish Ambassador's daughter)
Time period(s): 1980s
Locale(s): Timbuctoo, Africa

Summary: As the Emir of Timbuctoo lies dying, foreign ambassadors gather and plot what will happen after his death. Michael, uncovering a plot to murder Little Father, cannot resist telling his love, Selima, who then goes to Little Father and reveals the plot. Little Father succeeds the Emir and expels those who plotted against him.

Other books you might like:
Leo Frankowski, *The Cross-Time Engineer*, 1986
Keith Mitchell, *Procurator*, 1984
Mack Reynolds, *The Other Time*, 1984
Harry Turtledove, *Agent of Byzantium*, 1987
Harry Turtledove, *The Pugnacious Peacemaker*, 1990

4017

ROBERT SILVERBERG

The Mountains of Majipoor

(New York: Bantam Spectra, 1995)

Story type: Science Fiction (Political)
Series: Majipoor
Major character(s): Harpirias of Muldemar, Royalty (prince), Diplomat; Korinaam the Shapeshifter, Guide, Linguist (translator); Toikella, Royalty (king), Leader
Time period(s): Indeterminate Future
Locale(s): Majipoor, Planet—Imaginary

Summary: To escape bureaucratic exile in a provincial city, Prince Harpirias leads a negotiating mission aimed at rescuing a team of captured paleontologists. After a dangerous journey to the cold northern regions, Harpirias must overcome Korinaam's reluctance to translate literally, King Toikella's preconceptions, and his own vow of chastity to avoid disaster.

Other books you might like:
Margaret Wander Bonanno, *OtherWise*, 1993
A.C. Crispin, *Silent Songs*, 1994
   Kathleen O'Malley, co-author
Rosemary Kirstein, *The Outskirter's Secret*, 1992
Edward Myers, *The Mountain Made of Light*, 1992
James H. Schmitz, *The Demon Breed*, 1968
Melissa Scott, *Shadow Man*, 1995

4018

ROBERT SILVERBERG, Editor
MARTIN H. GREENBERG, Co-Editor

Murasaki

(New York: Bantam Spectra, 1992)

Story type: Science Fiction (Anthology)
Time period(s): 23rd century
Locale(s): Genji, Planet—Imaginary; Chujoan, Planet—Imaginary

Summary: This book contains a six-part novel examining life forms of the Murasaki star system and their interrelationships by Nebula Award winners Poul Anderson, Greg Bear, Gregory Benford, David Brin, Nancy Kress and Frederik Pohl plus an introduction by Robert Silverberg and one appendix, "Design for Two Worlds," by Poul Anderson and another, "Murasaki's Worlds," by Frederik Pohl.

Other books you might like:
C.J. Cherryh, *Angel with the Sword*, 1985
C.J. Cherryh, *Festival Moon*, 1987
   editor
Harlan Ellison, *Medea: Harlan's World*, 1985
   editor
Janet Kagan, *Mirabile*, 1991
George R.R. Martin, *Wild Cards*, 1987
   editor
Will Shetterly, *Liavek*, 1985
   Emma Bull, co-editor
Terri Windling, *Life on the Border*, 1991
   editor

4019

ROBERT SILVERBERG
KAREN HABER, Co-Author

The Mutant Season

(New York: Doubleday Foundation, 1989)

Story type: Science Fiction (Psychic Powers)
Major character(s): Michael Ryton, Mutant; Melanie Ryton, Mutant
Time period(s): 21st century
Locale(s): United States

Summary: A race of mutant psychics makes its presence known and demands equal rights. An enormous amount of prejudice is generated against the mutants and marriages between mutants and normals are looked down upon. The mutants themselves are capable of prejudice and the situation has a potential for violence. First of four planned novels.

Other books you might like:
Poul Anderson, *The Boat of a Million Years*, 1989
Henry Kuttner, *Mutant*, 1953
Daniel Keys Moran, *Emerald Eyes*, 1988
Daniel Keys Moran, *The Long Run*, 1989
A.E. Van Vogt, *Slan*, 1946
Joan D. Vinge, *Catspaw*, 1988
Joan D. Vinge, *Psion*, 1982

4020

ROBERT SILVERBERG

The New Springtime

(New York: Warner Books, 1990)

Story type: Science Fiction (Post-Holocaust)
Major character(s): Taniane, Ruler; Nialli Apuilana, Royalty (Taniane's daughter)
Time period(s): Indeterminate Future (Forty years after the Coming Forth)
Locale(s): Earth

Summary: In this sequel to *At Winter's End*, forty years have passed since the end of the last ice age and the great Coming Forth from their underground city of the People, an evolved race of apes. The People have founded cities and spread out across the Continent, but they still have to deal with the intelligent, insectoid hjjk, their main competitors for control of the Earth, and with the last remnants of humanity.

Other books you might like:
Brian W. Aldiss, *Helliconia Spring*, 1982
Brian W. Aldiss, *Helliconia Summer*, 1983
Brian W. Aldiss, *Helliconia Winter*, 1985
Clifford D. Simak, *City*, 1952

4021

ROBERT SILVERBERG

Starborne

(New York: Bantam Spectra, 1996)

Story type: Science Fiction (First Contact; Mystical)

Major character(s): Noelle, Telepath
Time period(s): 23rd century
Locale(s): Outer Space; *Wotan*, Spaceship

Summary: The *Wotan* searches for planets humanity can settle, at first finding only unsuitable ones. Their telepath, Noelle, then loses contact with her sister on Earth, making everyone feel isolated. When Noelle decides to reach out to whatever prevents the contact, she discovers sentient life quite different from what everyone always thought.

Other books you might like:
John Brunner, *A Maze of Stars*, 1991
F.M. Busby, *Slow Freight*, 1991
Samuel R. Delany, *The Ballad of Beta-2*, 1965
William R. Forstchen, *Into the Sea of Stars*, 1986
Robert A. Heinlein, *Orphans of the Sky*, 1961
Frank Herbert, *Whipping Star*, 1970
Robert J. Sawyer, *Golden Fleece*, 1990
Norman Spinrad, *The Void Captain's Tale*, 1986
James White, *The Dream Millennium*, 1974

4022

ROBERT SILVERBERG

Thebes of the Hundred Gates

(Eugene, Oregon: Pulphouse Publishing Axolotl Press, 1991)

Story type: Science Fiction (Time Travel)
Major character(s): Edward Davis, Time Traveller; Elaine "Nefret" Sandburg, Time Traveller, Religious; Roger "Senmut-Ptah" Lehman, Time Traveller, Scientist (astronomer)
Time period(s): 15th century B.C. (18th dynasty)
Locale(s): Thebes, Egypt

Summary: When Edward Davis arrives in Thebes, dizzy with characteristic time travel shock, a good samaritan takes him into a nearby temple where Elaine Sandburg, masquerading as a priestess, takes charge of him. Elaine and Roger then plot to deprive Edward of his return trip to the future, hoping to hide the fact that they relocated to Thebes in an unauthorized time trip.

Other books you might like:
Harry Harrison, *The Technicolor Time Machine*, 1967
Vernor Vinge, *Marooned in Realtime*, 1986
Vernor Vinge, *The Peace War*, 1984
Robert Charles Wilson, *A Bridge of Years*, 1991

4023

ROBERT SILVERBERG

To the Land of the Living

(New York: Questar, 1990)

Story type: Fantasy (Legend)
Major character(s): Gilgamesh, Warrior, Royalty (King of Uruk)
Time period(s): 40th century; Indeterminate Past
Locale(s): Sumer, Middle East; Mythical Place

Summary: While trying to avoid the dangers of the Afterworld, Gilgamesh seeks out his closest friend. Along the way he interacts with various historical characters who, like himself, are caught up in a never ending cycle of death and rebirth.

Other books you might like:
Philip Jose Farmer, *To Your Scattered Bodies Go*, 1971
Roger Zelazny, *The Black Throne*, 1990

4024

ROBERT SILVERBERG, Editor
KAREN HABER, Co-Editor

Universe 2
(New York: Bantam Spectra, 1992)

Story type: Science Fiction (Anthology)
Series: Universe

Summary: Contains a five-page introduction by Silverberg plus individual introductions to 21 original stories and one story, Brian W. Aldiss's "Her Toes Were Beautiful on the Hilltops," revised and retitled from its appearance in a semi-professional magazine. The stories include some with a dark tone such as Paul Di Filippo's first professional sale, "Forty at the Kiosk," portraying a disturbing view of an all too regulated future, and Alex Jeffers' "From *The Bridge*" with its post-alien invasion San Francisco, complete with kinky alien sex and the Golden Gate Bridge as an all night hot spot. A lighter tone permeates some work such as Deborah Wessel's "The Cool Equations," a parody of Tom Godwin's "The Cold Equations" (1954). Other provocative stories also explore a broad range of settings and themes as pioneered in Terry Carr's Universe series.

Other books you might like:
Lou Aronica, *Full Spectrum*, 1988
    Shawna McCarthy, co-editor
Terry Carr, *The Best From Universe*, 1984
    editor
Terry Carr, *The Best Science Fiction Novellas of the Year 1-2*, 1979-1980
    editor
Terry Carr, *The Best Science Fiction of the Year 1-16*, 1972-1987
    editor
Beth Meacham, *Terry's Universe*, 1988
    editor

4025

ROBERT SILVERBERG, Editor
KAREN HABER, Co-Editor

Universe 3
(New York: Bantam Spectra, 1994)

Story type: Science Fiction (Anthology)
Series: Universe

Summary: Contains a four-page introduction by Silverberg and 15 original stories, frequently dark in tone, which explore a broad range of familiar themes such as alien perceptions of humanity, politics, overpopulation, life in space, metaphysics and a revolt of bioengineered life forms in a Farmer Mc-

Gregor theme park. Authors include Brian W. Aldiss, E. Michael Blake, Paul Di Filippo, Joe Haldeman, Phillip C. Jennings, Barry N. Malzberg and Wil McCarthy.

Other books you might like:
Terry Carr, *The Best From Universe*, 1984
    editor
Terry Carr, *The Best Science Fiction Novellas of the Year 1-2*, 1979-1980
    editor
Terry Carr, *The Best Science Fiction of the Year 1-16*, 1972-1987
    editor
Gardner Dozois, *The Year's Best Science Fiction: Eleventh Annual Collection*, 1994
    editor
Beth Meacham, *Terry's Universe*, 1988
    editor

4026

CLIFFORD D. SIMAK

Over the River & Through the Woods
(San Francisco: Tachyon, 1996)

Story type: Science Fiction (Collection)
Major character(s): Old Mose, Farmer; Henderson James, Scientist
Time period(s): 1950s
Locale(s): Wisconsin; Minneapolis, Minnesota

Summary: Eight short stories from 1951 to 1980, providing a broad view of the career of Clifford Simak. The stories showcase Simak's wide emotional and thematic range, from cautionary tales of a "free lunch" that isn't free, to issues of identity and a study of alienation. Includes a five-page introduction by Poul Anderson.

Other books you might like:
Henry Kuttner, *The Best of Henry Kuttner*, 1975
Fritz Leiber, *Night's Black Agents*, 1947
C.L. Moore, *The Best of C.L. Moore*, 1975
Howard Waldrop, *Strange Monsters of the Recent Past*, 1991

4027

CLIFFORD D. SIMAK

Way Station
(New York: Collier, 1993)

Story type: Science Fiction (First Contact; Theological)
Major character(s): Enoch Wallace, Military Personnel (Civil War), Recluse; Claude Lewis, Government Official (intelligence); Ulysses, Alien
Time period(s): 1960s (1965)
Locale(s): Millville, Wisconsin

Summary: After learning of 125 year old Enoch Wallace, Claude Lewis discovers that Earth is located at an interstellar transfer station where events will decide the fate of Earth and the interstellar confederation of travellers who use Way Station. Reissue of the 1963 Hugo Award-winning novel.

Other books you might like:
John Brunner, *The Whole Man*, 1964
John Brunner, *The World Swappers*, 1959
A.C. Crispin, *Starbridge*, 1989
Philip K. Dick, *Solar Lottery*, 1955
Rebecca Ore, *Becoming Alien*, 1987
Wilson Tucker, *The Year of the Quiet Sun*, 1970
A.E. van Vogt, *The Voyage of the Space Beagle*, 1950
Jack Williamson, *The Legion of Space*, 1947

4028

DAN SIMMONS

Carrion Comfort

(Arlington Heights, IL: Dark Harvest, 1989)

Story type: Horror (Vampire Story)
Major character(s): Saul Laski, Doctor, Survivor (Holocaust); Natalie Preston, Photographer
Time period(s): 1980s (Pre-1945)
Locale(s): Germany; United States; Israel

Summary: Three aging psychic vampires—Melanie, Nina, and Willie—amuse themselves with their ''Game,'' the stimulation of random worldwide violence and mass murder. After the 1980 meeting, dissention and violence breaks out amongst the trio, setting off repercussions that reach to the highest levels of government and threaten to unleash the apocalypse. Three individuals—a holocaust survivor, a young black woman, and an intellectual Southern sheriff—set out against overwhelming odds to thwart the conflicting machinations of the mind vampires.

Other books you might like:
Colin Wilson, *The Space Vampires*, 1976

4029

DAN SIMMONS

Children of the Night

(New York: Putnam, 1992)

Story type: Horror (Vampire Story)
Major character(s): Kate Neumann, Doctor; Mike O'Rourke, Religious (Catholic priest); Vernor Deacon Trent, Businessman (a.k.a. Dracula)
Time period(s): 1990s
Locale(s): Bucharest, Romania; Transylvania

Summary: While rendering emergency medical services in post-Ceausescu Romania, Doctor Kate Neumann discovers a seven-month-old baby whose extraordinary immune system portends a breakthrough in medical knowledge for the management of numerous untreatable diseases. But Kate's plans for the child are complicated by businessman Vernor Deacon Trent, alias Count Dracula, who recognizes the child as the offspring of his vampire family, which has had a hand in Romanian politics for five centuries and is destined to be led by the boy once he has attained his majority.

Other books you might like:
Richard Matheson, *I Am Legend*, 1954
Fred Saberhagen, *The Dracula Tape*, 1975

Brian Stableford, *The Empire of Fear*, 1988
Peter Tremayne, *Dracula Unborn*, 1977

4030

DAN SIMMONS

Endymion

(New York: Bantam Spectra, 1996)

Story type: Science Fiction (Immortality; Theological)
Series: Hyperion
Major character(s): Raul Endymion, Prisoner, Writer; A. Bettik, Android; Aenea, Child, Religious (messiah)
Time period(s): 32nd century
Locale(s): Armaghast, Planet—Imaginary; Hyperion, Planet—Imaginary; Pacem, Planet—Imaginary

Summary: While waiting in a Schrodinger Cat box for execution, Endymion writes his memoirs of his travels with Aenea and A. Bettik after rescuing Aenea from the Pax army waiting for her release from the Time Tombs. The Shrike appears with her and seems to accompany the travelers through the Farcasters, thought useless since their shutdown 300 years earlier caused the Fall, promoting the rise of the Pax and the Catholic Church. Unfortunately, an immortal crew of Church warriors follows the trio to capture or kill Aenea. Third book in the series.

Other books you might like:
Isaac Asimov, *The Robots of Dawn*, 1983
Frank Herbert, *Dune*, 1965
James P. Hogan, *The Immortality Option*, 1995
Stuart Hopen, *Warp Angel*, 1995
Vernor Vinge, *A Fire upon the Deep*, 1992

4031

DAN SIMMONS

The Fall of Hyperion

(New York: Doubleday Foundation, 1990)

Story type: Science Fiction (Literary)
Series: Hyperion
Major character(s): Meina Gladstone, Government Official; Joseph Severn, Reincarnated Person (cybernetic John Keats)
Time period(s): 28th century
Locale(s): Hyperion, Planet—Imaginary

Summary: The pilgrims who sought the Time Tombs in *Hyperion* have finally reached them. Each interacts with the tombs and with the Shrike, the deadly creature who guards them, in his or her own unique manner. Some find transcendence, others merely death. Increasingly important is Joseph Severn, that strange reincarnation of the ancient poet John Keats. More is revealed about the complex game of political intrigue being played by a number of major powers, not all of them human.

Other books you might like:
William Barton, *Iris*, 1989
  Michael Capobianco, co-author
Greg Bear, *Eon*, 1985

Greg Bear, *Eternity*, 1989
Tim Powers, *The Stress of Her Regard*, 1989
Robert Silverberg, *Downward to the Earth*, 1970

4032

DAN SIMMONS

Fires of Eden
(New York: Putnam, 1994)

Story type: Horror (Supernatural Vengeance)
Major character(s): Byron Trumbo, Businessman (real estate developer); Eleanor Perry, Professor (of English); Cordie Stumpf, Widow(er)
Time period(s): 1990s (1994); 1860s (1866)
Locale(s): South Kona, Hawaii

Summary: Reprehensible real estate mogul Byron Trumbo tries desperately to sell the Mauna Pele, a luxury resort built on the slopes of an active Hawaiian volcano. Complicating matters are the doings of a pantheon of ancient Hawaiian gods, invoked by natives upset with Trumbo's desecration of their sacred land, who begin stealing the souls of the resort's visitors.

Other books you might like:
Robert Bloch, *Strange Eons*, 1976
Michael Green, *The Jimjams*, 1994
Graham Masterton, *Burial*, 1994
Adam Niswander, *The Charm*, 1993

4033

DAN SIMMONS

The Hollow Man
(New York: Bantam Spectra, 1992)

Story type: Science Fiction (Psychic Powers; Theological)
Major character(s): Jeremy "Jerry" Bremen, Psychic, Widow(er); Robby Bustamante, Psychic, Handicapped (blind, deaf, retarded); Vannie Fucci, Criminal
Time period(s): 1990s
Locale(s): Denver, Colorado; Boston, Massachusetts; Barnegat Light, New Jersey

Summary: Gail and Jeremy, both telepaths, protect each other from random thoughts around them. After Gail dies of cancer, Jeremy falls prey to the negative thoughts and emotions her loss leaves him open to. He finds occasional relief in memories of Gail, their relationship and the mathematical representations of the mind and the universe that he had been generating.

Other books you might like:
Alfred Bester, *The Demolished Man*, 1953
Frank Herbert, *The White Plague*, 1982
Robert Reed, *Down the Bright Way*, 1991
Kate Wilhelm, *Death Qualified: A Mystery of Chaos*, 1991
George Zebrowski, *Stranger Suns*, 1991

4034

DAN SIMMONS

Hyperion
(New York: Doubleday/Foundation, 1989)

Story type: Science Fiction (Literary)
Series: Hyperion
Major character(s): Consul, Diplomat; Father Hoyt, Religious
Time period(s): 28th century
Locale(s): Hegemony of Man, Interstellar Empire/Federation; Hyperion, Planet—Imaginary

Summary: The Hegemony of Man seems on the verge of war and the mysterious planet Hyperion may hold the information necessary to avert the crisis. On that planet seven pilgrims set forth to reach the Time Tombs, each for a very different reason, while the killing machine known as the Shrike hovers on the horizon.

Other books you might like:
Robert Silverberg, *Downward to the Earth*, 1970
Jack Vance, *The Anome*, 1973
Jack Vance, *The Asutra*, 1974
Jack Vance, *Showboat World*, 1975

4035

DAN SIMMONS

Lovedeath
(New York: Warner, 1993)

Story type: Science Fiction (Collection; Horror)
Summary: Contains a 10-page foreword about the novellas and their shared themes of love and death in the two reprinted and three original stories. First published as a chapbook, "Entropy's Bed at Midnight" utilizes as framework a thrilling alpine slide in Colorado and accidents recorded in an auto insurance file. Slightly revised from its *Playboy* appearance as "Death in Bangkok," "Dying in Bangkok" features John Merrick's return to the site of youthful indiscretions in search of a sexual vampire. The longest work, "Sleeping with Teeth Women," combines several legends of American Indian origin in the story of Hoka Ushte's spirit quest on which the fate of his entire people rests. In "Flashback," a federal agent agonizes over his inability to prevent an assassination as a powerful new pharmaceutical drug reveals additional problems. "The Great Lover" examines the literary dimension of tragedy associated with war through historical poetry attributed to the fictional James Edwin Rooke.

Other books you might like:
Jeff Gelb, *Hot Blood: Tales of Provocative Horror*, 1989
    Lonn Friend, co-editor
Jeff Gelb, *Hotter Blood: More Tales of Erotic Horror*, 1991
    Michael Garret, co-editor
Jeff Gelb, *Hottest Blood: The Ultimate in Erotic Horror*, 1993
    Michael Garret, co-editor
Stephen King, *Different Seasons*, 1982
Stephen King, *Four Past Midnight*, 1990
Lucius Shepard, *The Ends of the Earth*, 1990

Michele Slung, *I Shudder at Your Touch*, 1991
editor
Michele Slung, *Shudder Again*, 1993
editor

4036

DAN SIMMONS

Phases of Gravity
(New York: Bantam Spectra, 1989)

Story type: Science Fiction (Contemporary Realism)
Major character(s): Richard Baedecker, Astronaut (Aerospace consultant), Businessman; Scott Baedecker, Young Man (Richard's son)
Time period(s): 20th century
Locale(s): United States; India

Summary: Richard Baedecker, who once walked on the moon, feels like his entire life since that experience has been a disappointment. In a quest to come to terms with his depression, Baedecker travels first to India, then to visit other ex-astronauts who have made more successful lives for themselves than he has, and finally undergoes a mystical experience atop a butte in South Dakota.

Other books you might like:
Edward Gibson, *Reach*, 1989
Barry Malzberg, *Beyond Apollo*, 1972
Barry Malzberg, *The Falling Astronauts*, 1971
Lewis Shiner, *Deserted Cities of the Heart*, 1988

4037

DAN SIMMONS

Prayers to Broken Stones
(Arlington Heights, IL: Dark Harvest, 1990)

Story type: Horror (Collection)

Summary: Thirteen stories of horror, fantasy, and science fiction, including one new story written espcially for the book, "The Death of the Centaur," which straddles the border between fantasy and realistic fiction. Though the author is most at home working with straightforward horror themes, as in the vampire tales "Carrrion Comfort" and "Shave and A Haircut, Two Bites" and the ghost story "Iverson's Pits," he is also adept at moving evocations of grief in "The River Styx Runs Upstream," social satire in "Vanni Fucci is Alive and Well and Living in Hell" and hard science fiction in "Remembering Siri."

Other books you might like:
Michael Blumlein, *The Brains of Rats*, 1989
Pat Cadigan, *Patterns*, 1989
Harlan Ellison, *Angry Candy*, 1988
George R.R. Martin, *Songs the Dead Men Sing*, 1983
Pat Murphy, *Points of Departure*, 1990

4038

DAN SIMMONS

Summer of Night
(New York: Putnam's, 1991)

Story type: Horror (Coming-of-Age)
Major character(s): Dale Stewart, Child; Mike O'Rourke, Child; Duane McBride, Child
Time period(s): 1960s (1960)
Locale(s): Elm Haven, Illinois

Summary: When a young boy disappears on the last day of school at the Old Central schoolbuilding before it is to be boarded up forever, his classmates vow to solve the mystery. Their summer of investigations uncovers an ancient evil influencing their town and dark revelations about themselves.

Other books you might like:
Ray Bradbury, *Something Wicked This Way Comes*, 1962
Ray Bradbury, *Dandelion Wine*, 1957
Stephen King, *Different Seasons*, 1982
The Body

4039

WM. MARK SIMMONS

One Foot in the Grave
(New York: Baen, 1996)

Story type: Fantasy (Adventure; Contemporary)
Major character(s): Christopher Csejthe, Vampire, Radio Personality; Lupe Garou, Werewolf; Bassarab, Vampire, Nobleman
Time period(s): 1990s (1996)
Locale(s): Pittsburg, Kansas; Seattle, Washington

Summary: After the deaths of his wife and daughter, Christopher Csejthe wraps himself in a cocoon of work until a degenerative disease forces him to the doctor. After discovering the nature of his disease—vampirism—he must soon run for his life. Christopher needs education to survive, but his allies may prove as deadly as his friends.

Other books you might like:
Emma Bull, *War for the Oaks*, 1987
Laurell K. Hamilton, *Guilty Pleasures*, 1993
Tanya Huff, *Blood Price*, 1991
Christopher Moore, *Bloodsucking Fiends: A Love Story*, 1995
Kristine Kathryn Rusch, *Sins of the Blood*, 1994

4040

WM. MARK SIMMONS

When Dreams Collide
(New York: Warner Questar, 1992)

Story type: Fantasy (Adventure; Quest)
Major character(s): Robert Remington Ripley III, Writer, Martial Arts Expert; Cerebus, Artificial Intelligence (Superego of Dreamland), Imposter (Walter Hanson)
Time period(s): 21st century

Locale(s): Russia; Dreamland, Cyberspace (computer program)

Summary: When Artificial Ego and Superego of Dreamland escape the computer generated dream world into bodies of human beings, Robert Ripley must free the minds captured in Dreamland and return control of their bodies to them after capturing the fugitive artificial intelligences. Sequel to *In the Net of Dreams.*

Other books you might like:
Rick Cook, *Wizard's Bane*, 1989
Philip Jose Farmer, *Red Orc's Rage*, 1991
Joel Rosenberg, *The Sleeping Dragon*, 1983
Will Shetterly, *Cats Have No Lord*, 1985
Will Shetterly, *The Tangled Lands*, 1989
Vivian Vande Velde, *User Unfriendly*, 1991

4041

JEAN SIMON

Ghost Boy
(New York: Zebra, 1994)

Story type: Horror (Ghost Story)
Major character(s): Libby Gregory, Receptionist (medical office); Joely Gregory, Child (Libby's daughter); Martin Philip Stanovich, Child, Spirit
Time period(s): 1990s (1994)
Locale(s): Cielo, California

Summary: Divorcee Libby Gregory's relocation to the home town of her former husband coincides with the resumption of a series of child murders that plagued the town decades before. Libby's daughter Joely befriends a ghost boy who lives in the local cemetery and who convinces Joely that he was murdered by the same person who has begun killing children again.

Other books you might like:
Jonathan Aycliffe, *Naomi's Room*, 1992
Anne Dillard, *Specters*, 1991
Dennis Etchison, *Darkside*, 1986
Keith Ferrario, *Deadly Friend*, 1994
Abigail McDaniels, *The Uprising*, 1994
Melanie Tem, *Prodigal*, 1991

4042

JEAN SIMON

Orphans
(New York: Zebra, 1992)

Story type: Horror (Wild Talents)
Major character(s): Rae Downing, Secretary; Josie Falco, Young Woman; Julian, Young Man (Josie's houseguest)
Time period(s): 1990s (1992)
Locale(s): Running Horse Lake, Minnesota

Summary: Rae Downing discovers that bad things come in threes when she meets a long lost sister who informs her that they are two of three triplets born in a hippie commune in the 1960s and that, working together, they can manipulate destructive telekinetic powers.

Other books you might like:
Margaret Bingley, *Seeds of Evil*, 1992
Theodore Sturgeon, *More than Human*, 1953
Thomas Tryon, *The Other*, 1972
John Wyndham, *The Midwich Cuckoos*, 1957

4043

JEAN SIMON

Sweet Revenge
(New York: Zebra, 1991)

Story type: Horror (Possession)
Major character(s): Jessica Callahan, Teenager; Mardie Callahan, Accountant (bookkeeper); Zack Nelson, Teenager
Time period(s): 1990s
Locale(s): Wisdom Beach, California

Summary: Jessica Callahan visits her Aunt Mardie at her new beach house and finds the woman dressing flamboyantly, acting promiscuously, and possibly responsible for the deaths of several young men in the neighborhood. All of this leads Jessica to wonder if her aunt has become possessed by the vengeful spirit of the former owner, who was murdered by one of her lovers.

Other books you might like:
Ramona Stewart, *The Possession of Joel Delaney*, 1970

4044

GEORGE GAYLORD SIMPSON

The Dechronization of Sam Magruder
(New York: St. Martin's Press, 1996)

Story type: Science Fiction (Time Travel)
Major character(s): Sam Magruder, Scientist, Time Traveller; Pierre Precieux, Scientist (geologist); The Universal Historian, Scholar
Time period(s): 22nd century (2162); 800000th cent. B.C. (Cretaceous Period)
Locale(s): North America

Summary: Via stone tablets, Sam Magruder records his life and existence in the Cretaceous period, while future scholars reflect on Magruder's chronological experiment. Contains a 13-page introduction by Arthur C. Clarke, a 22-page afterword by Stephen Jay Gould and a 6-page memoir by Joan Simpson Burns. Author's only fiction, discovered 10 years after his death.

Other books you might like:
Robert T. Bakker, *Raptor Red*, 1995
Mona Clee, *Branch Point*, 1996
Arthur Conan Doyle, *The Lost World*, 1915
Robert J. Sawyer, *End of an Era*, 1994
Vernor Vinge, *Marooned in Realtime*, 1986
H.G. Wells, *The Time Machine*, 1895

4045

ALISON SINCLAIR

Legacies
(New York: HarperPrism, 1996)

Story type: Science Fiction (Lost Colony; Post-Holocaust)
Major character(s): Lian D'Halldt, Handicapped; Daisainia Travassa, Political Figure
Time period(s): Indeterminate Future
Locale(s): Taridwyn, Planet—Imaginary; Burdania, Planet—Imaginary

Summary: Several generations after a group of exiles flees their Burdania homes, possibly destroying their world in the process, descendants live on Taridwyn, aloof from the native people and consumed by guilt and pride. When a group of youngsters decides to return to Burdania, their success hinges on a brain-damaged man raised as much by aliens as his own people.

Other books you might like:
Iain M. Banks, *The Player of Games*, 1989
Ursula K. Le Guin, *The Word for World Is Forest*, 1976
Ian McDonald, *Desolation Road*, 1988
Larry Niven, *Ringworld*, 1970
Sarah Zettel, *Reclamation*, 1996

4046

MARILYN SINGER

Charmed
(New York: Atheneum, 1990)

Story type: Fantasy (Alternate World; Time Travel)
Major character(s): Miranda, Adventurer, Companion; Bastable, Alien (fenine), Royalty (deposed king of Appledura)
Time period(s): 1980s (1988); 2030s (2033)
Locale(s): Earth; Appledura, Planet—Imaginary

Summary: When 12-year-old Miranda is taken by her invisible friend, Bastable, to see the cobra-headed deity, Naja, Miranda is told of the Charmer who plans to destroy their worlds. Miranda finds her companions consider her the human needed for the Correct Combination, the only group, when complete, that will be able to defeat the Charmer. After a narrow escape, Miranda and her companions must travel through time and space to collect others for the Correct Combination, then overcome the Charmer before all is destroyed.

Other books you might like:
Suzy McKee Charnas, *Merlin's King*, 1985
Diane Duane, *So You Want to Be a Wizard?*, 1983
Maurice Gee, *The Halfmen of O*, 1982
Beth Hilgartner, *Colors in the Dreamweaver's Loom*, 1989
Shirley Rousseau Murphy, *Medallion of the Black Hound*, 1989
L.J. Smith, *Heart of Valor*, 1990
L.J. Smith, *The Night of the Solstice*, 1987

4047

JACQUI SINGLETON

Heartstone and Silver
(Huntington, New York: Rising Tide Press, 1994)

Story type: Fantasy (Sword and Sorcery)
Major character(s): Elayna, Witch, Lesbian; Cydell Ra Sadiin, Ruler, Lesbian
Time period(s): Indeterminate
Locale(s): Mauldar, Planet—Imaginary

Summary: After saving Elayna from raiders, Cydell brings her to the palace as a servant. Despite the clash of their personalities, Elayna and Cydell must overcome their differences when they travel to Wisdom Keep to thwart the threat to Cydell's kingdom and Elayna's life.

Other books you might like:
Marion Zimmer Bradley, *The Shattered Chain*, 1976
Ouida Crozier, *Shadows After Dark*, 1993
Jane E.M. Robinson, *The Amazon Chronicles*, 1994
Jessica Amanda Salmonson, *Amazons!*, 1979 editor
Karen Wehrstein, *Lion's Soul*, 1991

4048

CURT SIODMAK

Donovan's Brain/Hauser's Memory
(New York: Leisure, 1992)

Story type: Horror (Collection)
Major character(s): Patrick Cory, Scientist

Summary: These two novels, published 25 years apart, are mixtures of science fiction and horror concerned with the exploits of Doctor Patrick Cory, a relatively benign mad scientist. In *Donovan's Brain* (originally published in 1943) Cory's efforts to sustain the disembodied brain of a dead gangster in his laboratory produces a superbrain capable of compelling others to do its evil bidding. In *Hauser's Memory* (originally published in 1968), Cory's injection of DNA from a dying German scientist into a living recipient produces a genetic monster that runs amok.

Other books you might like:
L. Ron Hubbard, *Typewriter in the Sky/Fear*, 1951
Fritz Leiber, *Conjure Wife/Our Lady of Darkness*, 1991
Les Whitten, *Moon of the Wolf/Progeny of the Adder*, 1992

4049

CURT SIODMAK

Gabriel's Body
(New York: Leisure, 1988)

Story type: Horror (Science Fiction)
Major character(s): Patrick Cory, Scientist; James O'Brian, Scientist; Gabriel Deeping, Young Man
Time period(s): 1980s (1988)
Locale(s): Los Angeles, California

Summary: In this sequel to the author's previous novels *Donovan's Brain* (1943) and *Hauser's Memory* (1968), disfigured research scientist Patrick Cory perfects a thought transference machine with the idea of projecting his mind into the body of a young encephalitis victim. But Cory soon finds himself engaged in a struggle for his identity when it turns out that his patient's will is strong and refuses to be displaced so easily.

Other books you might like:
Kobo Abe, *The Face of Another*, 1962
Randall Boyll, *Darkman*, 1990
Ariel Dorfman, *Mascara*, 1988

4050
R.U. SIRIUS
ST. JUDE, Co-Author

How to Mutate and Take Over the World
(New York: Ballantine, 1996)

Story type: Science Fiction (Cyberpunk; Humor)
Major character(s): MONDO Vanelli, Revolutionary, Computer Expert
Time period(s): 2000s (2000)
Locale(s): United States; Cyberspace

Summary: As the government tightens its repressive control on all aspects of life, brave hackers attempt to reverse the stampede to Big Brotherdom.

Other books you might like:
Ed Blome, *Title Deleted for Security Reasons*, 1993
Stanislaw Lem, *Peace on Earth*, 1994
Ken Rolston, *Extreme Paranoia: Nobody Knows the Trouble I've Shot*, 1991
Robert Shea, *The Illuminatus! Trilogy*, 1988
    Robert Anton Wilson, co-author
Neal Stephenson, *Snow Crash*, 1992
Robert Anton Wilson, *Reality Is What You Can Get Away With: An Illustrated Screenplay*, 1992

4051
MICHAEL B. SIROTA

Demon Shadows
(New York: Bantam, 1990)

Story type: Horror (Supernatural Vengeance)
Major character(s): Paul Fleming, Writer; Gail Farringer, Artist (Fleming's girlfriend); Walter McClain, Administrator
Time period(s): 1980s
Locale(s): Stilwell, California (the Sierra Nevada Mountains)

Summary: Trying to recover from writer's block compounded by the collapse of his marriage, writer Paul Fleming retreats to an artists and writers colony in the high Sierras, unaware that the remote locale was once the site of a terrible tragedy: a small band of settlers, faced with starvation and the ordeal of winter, made a pact with an ancient Indian demon to ensure their survival, a pact that the present owners of the colony must continue to fulfill.

Other books you might like:
Thomas Page, *The Spirit*, 1977
Seth Pfefferle, *Stickman*, 1987
William Relling Jr., *Brujo*, 1986

4052
MICHAEL B. SIROTA

The Ultimate Bike Path
(New York: Ace, 1992)

Story type: Science Fiction (Humor)
Series: Bicycling Through Space and Time
Major character(s): Jack Miller, Traveller (bicyclist)
Time period(s): 1990s
Locale(s): Ultimate Bike Path, Mythical Place; Amazina, Mythical Place; Castle Frankenstein, Mythical Place

Summary: Using the 22nd gear on his 21-speed mountain bike, Jack Miller continues his zany adventures through space and time on the Ultimate Bike Path, including a visit with Dr. Frankenstein and a brief stay with the Amazins to whom he introduces the condom, revolutionizing their culture.

Other books you might like:
Douglas Adams, *The Hitchhiker's Guide to the Galaxy*, 1980
Douglas Adams, *The Restaurant at the End of the Universe*, 1982
John DeChancie, *Paradox Alley*, 1987
John DeChancie, *Red Limit Freeway*, 1984
John DeChancie, *Starrigger*, 1983

4053
MICHAEL B. SIROTA

The Well
(New York: Bantam, 1991)

Story type: Horror (Ancient Evil Unleashed)
Major character(s): Greg Lowell, Editor (executive editor, Sabre Books); Janet Lowell, Spouse (Greg's wife); Dora Waverly, Aged Person
Time period(s): 1990s
Locale(s): Bonner, California

Summary: During the settling of Bonner, California in the nineteenth century, the Padgett family sank a well on grounds sacred to the Modoc Indians and unleashed the Montanni, a bloodthirsty demon. More than a century later Greg Lowell, lineal descendant of the Padgetts, moves his family to Bonner, initiating the cycle of bloodletting once more.

Other books you might like:
Douglas Clegg, *Goat Dance*, 1989
Morgan Fields, *Shaman Woods*, 1990
Charles L. Grant, *The Nestling*, 1982
Chet Williamson, *Dreamthorp*, 1989

4054

JOHN SKIPP
CRAIG SPECTOR, Co-Author

Animals
(New York: Bantam, 1993)

Story type: Horror (Werewolf Story)
Major character(s): Syd Jarrett, Worker (steelworker); Nora, Werewolf; Jane, Waiter/Waitress
Time period(s): 1990s (1993)
Locale(s): Monville, Pennsylvania

Summary: Nora shows Syd Jarrett how to get in touch with the feral side of himself before pitting him against Vic, her werewolf boyfriend, who mauls Syd and leaves him for dead. Eighteen months later, after Syd has recovered under the tender ministrations of Jane, Vic and Nora return for a final showdown.

Other books you might like:
Crosland Brown, *Tombley's Walk*, 1990
Michael Cadnum, *St. Peter's Wolf*, 1991
Whitley Strieber, *The Wild*, 1991

4055

JOHN SKIPP
CRAIG SPECTOR, Co-Author

The Bridge
(New York: Bantam, 1991)

Story type: Horror (Nature in Revolt)
Major character(s): Gary Taylor, Worker (mechanic); Gwen Taylor, Artist (Gary's wife); Werner Blake, Businessman
Time period(s): 1990s
Locale(s): Paradise, Pennsylvania

Summary: There's trouble in Paradise (Pennsylvania, that is) when one barrel of chemical waste too many gets dumped into the Codorus Creek. A sentient Mother Nature retaliates, marshaling polluted streams, clouds of acid rain, and toxic zombies to do her bidding. Eco-Armageddon has begun!

Other books you might like:
John Brunner, *The Sheep Look Up*, 1972
Robert Charles, *Flowers of Evil*, 1982
Alison Drake, *Lagoon*, 1990
D. Keith Mano, *The Bridge*, 1972
Alan E. Nourse, *The Fourth Horseman*, 1983

4056

JOHN SKIPP
CRAIG SPECTOR, Co-Author

Dead Lines
(New York: Bantam, 1989)

Story type: Horror (Ghost Story)
Major character(s): Jack Rowan, Writer, Spirit; Katie Conner, Young Woman
Time period(s): 1980s
Locale(s): New York, New York

Summary: When Katie and Meryl rent a room they discover a box containing stories written by the apartment's former occupant, a suicide victim. Their lives are powerfully altered by the individual stories and, more importantly, by the author's ghost, which disturbs and threatens to possess the vulnerable young women.

Other books you might like:
Roland Topor, *The Tenant*, 1966

4057

JOHN SKIPP, Editor
CRAIG SPECTOR, Co-Editor

Still Dead: Book of the Dead 2
(Shingletown, California: Mark V. Ziesing, 1992)

Story type: Horror (Anthology)

Summary: The nineteen stories continue the theme first explored in *Book of the Dead* (1989), further describing a possible future in which the newly dead rise from the grave as zombies to eat the flesh of the living and serve as useful symbols of typical human behavior. Included are Mort Castle's Hemingway pastiche, ''The Old Man and the Dead''; Douglas Winter's parody of Jay McInerney, ''Bright Lights, Big Zombie''; Dan Simmons' sentimental ''Class Picture''; Chan McConnell's tale of zombies who blend in inconspicuously with Manhattan street life, ''Don't/Walk''; K.W. Jeter's tale of a lunatic with a messiah complex who thinks he is responsible for the resurrection of the dead; and Poppy Z. Brite's hypnotic tale of death and its meaning in India, ''Calcutta, Lord of Nerves.''

Other books you might like:
Peter Haining, *Stories of the Walking Dead*, 1985
    editor
Bill Pronzini, *The Arbor House Necropolis*, 1987
    editor

4058

MICHAEL SLADE

Cutthroat
(New York: Signet, 1992)

Story type: Horror (Serial Killer)
Major character(s): Robert De Clerq, Police Officer; Zinc Chandler, Police Officer; Martin Kwan, Lawyer
Time period(s): 1980s (1987)
Locale(s): Vancouver, British Columbia, Canada

Summary: Two Canadian police officers with a specialty in serial killers team up to apprehend one killing lawyers throughout the American West, in a novel that ranges from Vietnam and Hong Kong to Canada and the Great Plains, and whose plot hinges on an archaeological specimen of great import found in the midst of the slaughter at Custer's Last Stand in 1876.

Other books you might like:
Thomas Harris, *Red Dragon*, 1981
Daniel Ransom, *The Serpent's Kiss*, 1992
Garfield Reeves-Stevens, *Gray Matter*, 1990

4059

BILL SLAVICSEK
C.J. TRAMONTANA, Co-Author

Storm Knights

(Baltimore, Maryland: GW Books/Games Workshop, 1990)

Story type: Fantasy (Magic Conflict; Horror)
Series: Torg: The Possibility Wars
Major character(s): Tolwyn Tancred, Knight; Christopher Bryce, Religious (priest); Andrew Jackson Decker, Political Figure
Time period(s): 1990s
Locale(s): New York, New York

Summary: Raiders from alternate realities have invaded Earth. The only thing that stands between them and total victory is the "stormers," people like Tolwyn Tancred who have weathered the violent reality storms in other worlds. Joining forces with the humans of Earth, they battle across a continent to defeat the raiders and their demonic leader. First of a series.

Other books you might like:
Robin Wayne Bailey, *Night Watch*, 1990
Brian Craig, *Zaragoz*, 1990
Gordon R. Dickson, *Time Storm*, 1977
Barbara Hambly, *Dragonsbane*, 1985
Clifford D. Simak, *Out of Their Minds*, 1970
Ian Watson, *Inquisitor*, 1990

4060

WILLIAM SLEATOR

Strange Attractors

(New York: Dutton, 1989)

Story type: Science Fiction (Alternate Universe)
Major character(s): Max, Teenager; Eve Sylvan, Teenager
Time period(s): 1980s
Locale(s): United States

Summary: Max visits the lab of the famous scientist Dr. Sylvan and becomes mixed up in a complex and confusing exercise in Chaos Theory. It seems that Dr. Sylvan has a double in another universe who has so badly damaged his own timeline that he is now attempting to escape it by supplanting the Dr. Sylvan from Max's timeline. Max ends up with amnesia and a strange machine that both the Sylvans, neither of them particularly nice people, desperately want back. A young adult novel.

Other books you might like:
Grace Chetwin, *Collidescope*, 1989
John Cramer, *Twistor*, 1989
Michael P. Kube-McDowell, *Alternities*, 1988
Sarah Sargent, *Jonas McFee, A.T.P.*, 1989
Jerry Sohl, *Costigan's Needle*, 1953

4061

KAY SLOAN, Editor
CONSTANCE PIERCE, Co-Editor

Elvis Rising: Stories on the King

(New York: Avon, 1993)

Story type: Fantasy (Anthology; Historical)
Major character(s): Elvis Presley, Musician, Historical Figure
Time period(s): 1990s
Locale(s): Graceland, Tennessee; Washington, District of Columbia

Summary: 16 short stories 1961-1993, featuring Elvis Presley as a character or catalyst. Most of the stories reflect straight or slightly twisted realism, but in Howard Waldrop's "Ike at the Mike" Senator Presley imagines what his life would have been like if he'd become a musician like the great Dwight Eisenhower. Gardner Dozois, Jack Dann and Michael Swanwick collaborate on a story about a mysterious and poignant reunion concert. Other authors include Elizabeth Hand and W.P. Kinsella.

Other books you might like:
Bradley Denton, *Buddy Holly Is Alive and Well on Ganymede*, 1991
Richard Peabody, *Mondo Elvis*, 1993
  Lucinda Ebersole, co-editor
Robert Rankin, *Armageddon: The Musical*, 1990
Mike Resnick, *By Any Other Fame*, 1994
  Martin H. Greenberg, co-editor
Lewis Shiner, *Glimpses*, 1993
Allen Steele, *Clarke County, Space*, 1990
Jack Womack, *Elvissey*, 1993
Jack Yeovil, *Comeback Tour: The Sky Belongs to the Stars*, 1991
  pseudonym of Kim Newman

4062

JOAN SLONCZEWSKI

Daughter of Elysium

(New York: Morrow AvoNova, 1993)

Story type: Science Fiction (Alternate Intelligence; Genetic Manipulation)
Major character(s): Raincloud Windclan, Linguist (translator), Parent; Verid, Immortal, Political Figure; Doggie, Robot (trainsweep)
Time period(s): Indeterminate Future (1020th century)
Locale(s): Shora, Planet—Imaginary; Urulan, Planet—Imaginary; Free Fold, Interstellar Empire/Federation

Summary: Visiting Elysians' intentions to finance terraforming of other worlds precipitate a crisis between native Sharers and their centuries-old Elysian guests. Hoping to avert disaster, an Elysian delegation travels to Urulan to seek alternate solutions to human overpopulation. Sequel to *A Door into Ocean*.

Other books you might like:
Eleanor Arnason, *Ring of Swords*, 1993
Eleanor Arnason, *A Woman of the Iron People*, 1991

David Brin, *Glory Season*, 1993
Octavia E. Butler, *Dawn*, 1987
Rosemary Kirstein, *The Steerswoman*, 1989
Rudy Rucker, *Software*, 1982

4063

JOAN SLONCZEWSKI

The Wall Around Eden

(New York: William Morrow, 1989)

Story type: Science Fiction (Post-Nuclear Holocaust)
Major character(s): Isabel Garcia-Chase, Teenager (Electrician); Daniel Jacoby, Teenager (Quaker)
Time period(s): 21st century
Locale(s): Gwynwood, Pennsylvania

Summary: Some years ago, simultaneous with the outbreak of nuclear war, the aliens appeared. For reasons known only to themselves, they isolated a number of towns and cities around the world behind impregnable "air walls," leaving most of the rest of humanity to die from the effects of the war. In Pennsylvania, one small, largely Quaker community struggles to survive within its air wall. A young woman devotes her life to discovering the mysterious truth behind the aliens' actions.

Other books you might like:
Neal Barrett Jr., *Through Darkest America*, 1987
Octavia E. Butler, *Dawn*, 1987
Ursula K. Le Guin, *Always Coming Home*, 1985
Judith Moffett, *Pennterra*, 1987
Sheri S. Tepper, *The Gate to Women's Country*, 1988

4064

MICHELE SLUNG, Editor

I Shudder at Your Touch

(New York: Roc, 1991)

Story type: Horror (Anthology)

Summary: Twenty-two tales with sexual subthemes that span nearly a century, ranging from Robert Hitchens' classic Edwardian tale of a love-sick ghost, "How Love Came to Professor Guildea," to the contemporary magic realism of T.L. Parkinson's "The Tiger Returns to the Mountain" and the psychological horror of Michael Blumlein's "Keeping House." Standout stories include Robert Aickman's creepy account of sexual initiation, "The Swords," and Patrick McGrath's hilarious spoof of sexual psychopathology, "Cleave the Vampire, or, a Gothic Pastorale."

Other books you might like:
Margaret L. Carter, *Demon Lovers and Strange Seductions*, 1973
  editor
Ellen Datlow, *Alien Sex*, 1990
  editor
Jeff Gelb, *Hot Blood: Tales of Provocative Horror*, 1990
  Lonn Friend, co-editor
Jeff Gelb, *Hotter Blood: More Tales of Erotic Horror*, 1991
  Michael Garret, co-editor
Michel Parry, *Devil's Kisses*, 1976

4065

MICHELE SLUNG, Editor

Shudder Again

(New York: Roc, 1993)

Story type: Horror (Anthology)

Summary: In this follow-up to *I Shudder at Your Touch* (1991), the editor has collected 22 tales of erotic horror. Four stories are original to the volume: Nancy Collins' "Aphra" is told from the point of view of a man whose obsession with thin women reflects his morbid interest in death; David Kuehls' "The First Time" tells of a near future in which androids can recreate a person's sexual initiation; Claudia O'Keefe's "On the Lake of Last Wishes" recounts the erotic dreams of a woman with a terminal illness; and Sarah Smith's "When The Red Storm Comes, or the History of a Young Lady's Awakening to Her Nature," juxtaposes vampirism with world events in Europe at the turn of the century. Classic reprints include Charles Beaumont's "The Crooked Man," about a future in which it is illegal to be heterosexual; Arthur Machen's "The Ceremony," which links paganism with eroticism; Sir Arthur Conan Doyle's "The Parasite," about a medium who uses mental energy to control her clients; and stories by Robert Aickman, J.G. Ballard, Thomas Ligotti, and Ramsey Campbell.

Other books you might like:
Ellen Datlow, *Alien Sex*, 1991
  editor
Jeff Gelb, *Hot Blood: Tales of Provocative Horror*, 1989
  Lonn Friend, co-editor
Jeff Gelb, *Hotter Blood: More Tales of Erotic Horror*, 1991
  Michael Garrett, co-editor
Jeff Gelb, *Hottest Blood: The Ultimate in Erotic Horror*, 1993
  Michael Garrett, co-editor
Michel Parry, *Devil's Kisses*, 1976
  editor

4066

BRIAN SMART, Editor

Best of the Midwest's Science Fiction, Fantasy and Horror, Volume II

(Harrisonville, Missouri: ESA Books, 1993)

Story type: Horror (Anthology)

Summary: The 28 stories written especially for this book, each lavishly illustrated, either feature midwestern settings or are by midwestern writers. Of interest to horror readers is Mark Rich's "Payment," a gruesome deal-with-the-devil story; Greg Beatty's "The Hunger From the Depths," about the type of monster that might be attracted to the garbage dumped in Puget Sound; Stephen M. Rainey's "Portals," in which extraterrestrial invaders mobilize via telephone lines; Lisa Y. Drexel's "'Til Death Do Us Part," a sentimental vampire story; Brian A. Hopkins' "Scarecrow's Dream," a tale of reincarnation; Bobby G. Warner's "Graveyard Beetles," in which a murder victim's corpse is animated to revenge by the title creatures; Marthayn Pelegrimas' "The Resurrection

Man,'' about a fire-and-brimstone swindler who discovers to his horror that he has the power to raise the dead; S. Darnbrook Colson's ''Nightmare at Brookgreen Gardens,'' about a ghost who moves the statuary of a park around; and Diswell Crinkle's ''Bumps in the Night,'' a slapstick zombie story.

Other books you might like:
Robert Morrish, *Quick Chills II*, 1992
   Peter Enfantino, co-editor
Joy Oestreicher, *Air Fish*, 1993
   Richard Singer, co-editor
Joy Oestreicher, *Alpha Gallery*, 1992
   Richard Singer, co-editor

4067

DAVE SMEDS

The Schemes of Dragons

(New York: Ace, 1989)

Story type: Fantasy (Quest)
Major character(s): Toren, Warrior
Time period(s): Indeterminate

Summary: When Toren is magically forced to disgorge his tribe's totem, he finds himself alone in his body for the first time ever. His search for the stolen totem leads him into a parallel search by a brother and sister. Sequel to *Sorcery Within*.

Other books you might like:
M. Coleman Easton, *Spirits of Cavern and Hearth*, 1989
Rose Estes, *The Hunter*, 1990
Rosemary Kirstein, *The Steerswoman*, 1989

4068

CHERYL A. SMITH

The Falcon and the Serpent

(Westchester, Illinois: Crossway, 1990)

Story type: Fantasy (Religious; Romance)
Major character(s): Falcon Jaqueth, Knight; Crotalus, Wizard
Time period(s): Indeterminate Past
Locale(s): Corigo, Fictional Country; Paduan, Fictional Country

Summary: Falcon Jaqueth tutors Prince Krieth of Paduan in the arts of war. Crotalus wants control of Corigo and Paduan and the love of Rafaela. He intends to see Temrane, Prince of Corigo, whom he had marked at birth, attain this goal. Rafaela finds the strength to resist him in worship of the Redeemer God.

Other books you might like:
John Desjarlais, *The Throne of Tara*, 1990
Roger Elwood, *Angelwalk: A Modern Fable*, 1988
Parke Godwin, *Waiting for the Galactic Bus*, 1989
Andrew M. Greeley, *Angel Fire*, 1988
Mike McQuay, *The Nexus*, 1989

4069

CLARK ASHTON SMITH

The Book of Hyperborea

(West Warwick, Rhode Island: Necronomicon Press, 1996)

Story type: Horror (Collection)

Summary: The 13 stories assembled here are all of the tales that the author, one of the most popular writers for the fantasy pulp *Weird Tales*, set in the imaginary prehistoric realm of Hyperborea. Included are a diptych of comic stories, ''The Tale of Satampra Zeiros'' and ''The Theft of Thirty-Nine Girdles,'' featuring the thief Satampra Zeiros and the mordantly amusing fates that he and his companions experience. Other highlights include ''Ubbo Sathla,'' in which a modern character finds himself transported back to primal origins with the help of the Hyperborean sorcerer Eibon; ''The Seven Geases,'' in which a character confronts the fount of all creation; and the poetic end-of-the-world fantasy, ''The Coming of the White Worm.'' The volume was edited by Will Murray, who supplies the introduction.

Other books you might like:
Lin Carter, *Great Short Novels of Adult Fantasy 1*, 1972
   editor
Lord Dunsany, *At the Edge of the World*, 1970
Fritz Leiber, *Swords Against Death*, 1970
H.P. Lovecraft, *The Dream Quest of Unknown Kadath*, 1970
Gary Meyers, *The House of the Worm*, 1975

4070

CLARK ASHTON SMITH

A Prophecy of Monsters

(Alexandria, Virginia: 13th Hour Books, 1996)

Story type: Horror (Werewolf Story; Science Fiction)
Major character(s): Unnamed Character, Werewolf; Unnamed Character, Robot
Time period(s): 21st century
Locale(s): Earth

Summary: A werewolf of the future gets the surprise of his life when he discovers his latest victim is not the human prey he thought it was. The short story that makes up this chapbook was first published in 1954 and is sometimes reprinted under the title ''Monsters in the Night.'' Paul A. Roales supplies an introduction.

Other books you might like:
Lord Dunsany, *A Dreamer's Tales*, 1910
Gary Meyers, *The House of the Worm*, 1975
Brian Stableford, *Fables and Fantasies*, 1997

4071

CLARK ASHTON SMITH

Tales of Zothique

(West Warwick, Rhode Island: Necronomicon Press, 1995)

Story type: Fantasy (Collection)
Time period(s): Indeterminate Past; Indeterminate Future

Locale(s): Hyperborea, Mythical Place (Earth's past); Zothique, Mythical Place (Earth's future)

Summary: Editors Will Murray and Steve Behrens incorporate stories previously published in Lin Carter's Ballantine Adult Fantasy Series, with some corrections, and some stories passed over by Carter. Stories frequently exhibit a dark or ominous tone as Smith discusses humanity's foibles and include settings from the heroic distant past in the Hyperborean Age to the dim future and a dying Earth, Zothique, in which humankind declines, drifting into superstition and barbarism.

Other books you might like:
Robert Bloch, *The Best of Robert Bloch*, 1977
Frank Belknap Long, *The Rim of the Unknown*, 1972
H.P. Lovecraft, *The Best of H.P. Lovecraft: Bloodcurdling Tales of Horror and the Macabre*, 1982
H.P. Lovecraft, *Dagon and Other Macabre Tales*, 1965
Howard Wandrei, *Time Burial*, 1995

4072

CORDWAINER SMITH (Pseudonym of Paul Myron Anthony Linebarger)

Norstrilia

(Framingham, Massachusetts: NESFA Press, 1995)

Story type: Science Fiction (Genetic Manipulation; Immortality)
Series: Instrumentality of Mankind
Major character(s): Rod McBan, Telepath; C'mel, Animal (cat), Genetically Altered Being (cat-person)
Time period(s): 160th century
Locale(s): Norstrilia, Planet—Imaginary (Old North Australia); Earth

Summary: After multiple childhoods, Rod McBan provisionally passes his adulthood test, avoiding the ecstatic euthanasia awarded many on resource-scarce Norstrilia. Now responsible for a vast ranch with giant, sick sheep which produce a raw immortality drug, Rod sustains attacks from a former childhood friend and flees to a hidden shelter where an ancient, forbidden computer implements an economic warfare trading strategy aimed at cornering the commodities market in immortality drug futures. Acquiring new and powerful enemies and friends, Rod decides to vanish from public view and visit Earth anonymously to pursue a minor philatelic interest and becomes involved in the underpeople's struggle to attain legal status and guaranteed rights. Contains a 25-page appendix noting significant variations from some prior publications of the text, including "Lost Music in an Old World," previously omitted from the novel. Originally published 1975.

Other books you might like:
Felix C. Forrest, *Carola*, 1948
    pseudonym of Paul Linebarger
Felix C. Forrest, *Ria*, 1947
    pseudonym of Paul Linebarger
Elizabeth Hand, *Icarus Descending*, 1993
Ian McDonald, *Terminal Cafe*, 1994
Carmichael Smith, *Atomsk*, 1949
    pseudonym of Paul Linebarger

S. Andrew Swann, *Forests of the Night*, 1993

4073

CORDWAINER SMITH (Pseudonym of Paul Myron Anthony Linebarger)

The Rediscovery of Man

(Framingham, Massachusettes: NESFA Press, 1993)

Story type: Science Fiction (Collection)
Series: Instrumentality of Mankind
Time period(s): 21st century; Indeterminate Future
Locale(s): Outer Space; Spaceship

Summary: This omnibus edition contains an 8-page introduction by John J. Pierce, a 2-page introduction by editor James A. Mann, six non-series stories with a rewritten version of "War No. 81-Q" and all 27 Instrumentality of Mankind series stories presented in chronological order with the previously unpublished story, "Himself in Anachron," and one attributed to Smith but written by his wife, Genevieve Linebarger, "Down to a Sunless Sea." Smith's adventure stories present recurrent sociological issues through diverse science fiction themes. "Scanners Live in Vain," points to an emerging technology that will allow humans to travel in space without terrible physical modifications; "Think Blue, Count Two" demonstrates a vision of the computer's use in daily human life; "The Game of Rat and Dragon" examines the partnership between humans and telepathic cats in their desperate battles against outer space creatures who suck lifeforce from human souls; "The Burning of the Brain" and "The Crime and Glory of Commander Suzdal" detail the sacrifice and consequences of frontier explorations; "Under Old Earth" hints at the terrifying resources available to the rulers of the galaxy; and "Alpha Ralpha Boulevard" describes wondrous technology and the attempts of the Instrumentality to reintroduce vitality into the human spirit.

Other books you might like:
Felix C. Forrest, *Carola*, 1948
    pseudonum of Paul Linebarger
Felix C. Forrest, *Ria*, 1947
    pseudonum of Paul Linebarger
Robert A. Heinlein, *The Past through Tomorrow*, 1967
Fritz Leiber, *The Leiber Chronicles*, 1990
Walter M. Miller Jr., *The Science Fiction Stories of Walter M. Miller, Jr.*, 1984
Larry Niven, *Tales of Known Space*, 1975
Carmichael Smith, *Atomsk*, 1949
    pseudonym of Paul Linebarger
Theodore Sturgeon, *E Pluribus Unicorn*, 1953
John Varley, *The Barbie Murders and Other Stories*, 1980
John Varley, *Blue Champagne*, 1986
John Varley, *The Persistence of Vision*, 1978

`4074`

DAVID ALEXANDER SMITH, Editor

Future Boston
(New York: Tor, 1994)

Story type: Science Fiction (Anthology)
Time period(s): 21st century
Locale(s): Boston, Massachusetts

Summary: This is a shared universe volume created by an ongoing Boston writers' workshop containing a seven-page afterword, "How It Came to Be," two pages of notes, "About the Authors," six maps of Boston 1772-2061 and 28 stories about the city afflicted with a rising sea and an involuntary immigration of alien Phneri. Authors include Alexander Jablokov, Geoffrey A. Landis, Steven Popkes and David Alexander Smith. Set in the milieu of *In the Cube*.

Other books you might like:
Alan Dean Foster, *Alien Nation*, 1988
Alexander Jablokov, *Carve the Sky*, 1991
Alexander Jablokov, *A Deeper Sea*, 1992
Steven Popkes, *Caliban Landing*, 1987
Steven Popkes, *Slow Lightning*, 1991

`4075`

DAVID ALEXANDER SMITH

Homecoming
(New York: Ace, 1990)

Story type: Science Fiction (First Contact)
Series: Marathon Trilogy
Major character(s): Walter Tai-Ching Jones, Spaceship Captain; Ozymandias, Artificial Intelligence
Time period(s): 21st century
Locale(s): *Open Palm*, Spaceship; Earth

Summary: Earth's first starship, *Open Palm*, returns home bearing members of the Cygnan race known as Bluebears. Both human crew members and Cygnans soon discover, however, that they are pawns in a deadly power struggle between competing Earth factions. Only the artificial intelligence Ozymandias can save the situation.

Other books you might like:
Gregory Benford, *Great Sky River*, 1987
Gregory Benford, *Tides of Light*, 1989
David Brin, *Startide Rising*, 1983
David Brin, *The Uplift War*, 1987
Octavia E. Butler, *Dawn*, 1987
Paul J. McAuley, *Four Hundred Billion Stars*, 1988

`4076`

DAVID ALEXANDER SMITH

In the Cube
(New York: Tor, 1993)

Story type: Science Fiction (Mystery; Political)

Major character(s): Beverly O'Meara, Orphan, Detective—Private; Akktri, Alien (Phner); Iris "Butcher of Boston" Sherwood, Government Official, Step-Parent
Time period(s): 21st century
Locale(s): Boston, Massachusetts (the Cube)

Summary: The early 21st century arrival of many extraterrestrials into Boston allowed its redesign into the Cube, a kilometer high monad with quasi-independent status. When coerced by Iris Sherwood to find out the details surrounding her adopted daughter's disappearance, Beverly O'Meara and Akktri uncover a plot which pits the Cube's paramount business family against the supremely powerful City Operator, Iris Sherwood.

Other books you might like:
Alfred Bester, *Golem* [100], 1980
Alan Dean Foster, *Alien Nation*, 1988
Alan Dean Foster, *Cyber Way*, 1990
K.W. Jeter, *Madlands*, 1991
Katharine Kerr, *Polar City Blues*, 1990
Jacqueline Lichtenberg, *Molt Brother*, 1982
James H. Schmitz, *The Demon Breed*, 1968

`4077`

DAVID C. SMITH

The Fair Rules of Evil
(New York: Avon, 1989)

Story type: Horror (Black Magic)
Major character(s): David Trevisan, Student (Ex-seminary); Theodore Fry, Magician (Black magician)
Time period(s): 1980s
Locale(s): United States

Summary: David Trevisan takes a crash course in sorcery in order to track and confront Theodore Fry, the black magician responsible for his sister's death.

Other books you might like:
Charles L. Grant, *The Hour of the Oxrun Dead*, 1977
M.R. James, "*Casting the Runes*", 1911
Dennis Wheatley, *The Devil Rides Out*, 1935

`4078`

DAVID VAN METER SMITH

Trinity Grove
(New York: Avon, 1990)

Story type: Horror (Ancient Evil Unleashed)
Major character(s): Nick Lombard, Student; Lewis Janeway, Detective—Police; Jan Troop, Farmer
Time period(s): 1990s (1990)
Locale(s): Cambridge, England

Summary: A brutalized corpse dubbed "the Midsummer Murder" ties in with a series of ritual murders which have taken place near the Cambridge campus at 33-year intervals ever since the 19th century. Evidence points to the Pentacle Commune, a cult which practices ancient Celtic ceremonies. But student Nick Lombard is unaware that his girl friend belongs to the commune—or that this year the cult requires a blood sacrifice to renew their pact with the forces of darkness.

Other books you might like:
Joseph Citro, *The Unseen*, 1990
Douglas Clegg, *Goat Dance*, 1989
T.E.D. Klein, *The Ceremonies*, 1984

4079

DEAN WESLEY SMITH
KRISTINE KATHRYN RUSCH, Co-Author

The Escape
(New York: Pocket, 1995)

Story type: Science Fiction (Space Opera; Time Travel)
Major character(s): Kathryn Janeway, Spaceship Captain, Military Personnel (Starfleet); Tuvok, Security Officer, Alien (Vulcan); B'Elanna Torres, Engineer, Alien (half-Klingon)
Time period(s): 24th century
Locale(s): *U.S.S. Voyager*, Spaceship; Alcawell, Planet—Imaginary

Summary: Searching for salvageable metals, Neelix, Torres, and Kim explore a graveyard of abandoned ships on a deserted world. When Neelix accidentally activates one of those ships, they travel 300,000 years back into the planet's past and learn that they have committed a capital offense. Only when Tuvok and Paris discover the identity of a "ghost" among the abandoned ships can Janeway help her missing crew.

Other books you might like:
Poul Anderson, *Time Patrolman*, 1983
Barbara Hambly, *Ishmael*, 1985
Andre Norton, *Galactic Derelict*, 1959
Kristine Kathryn Rusch, *Heart Readers*, 1993
Kristine Kathryn Rusch, *Traitors*, 1994
Kristine Kathryn Rusch, *The White Mists of Power*, 1991
Clifford D. Simak, *Special Deliverance*, 1982
Della Van Hise, *Killing Time*, 1985

4080

DEAN WESLEY SMITH

Laying the Music to Rest
(New York: Popular Library Questar, 1989)

Story type: Horror (Ghost Story)
Major character(s): Kellogg "Doc" Jones, Saloon Keeper/Owner, Professor (Former); Susan, Scientist (parapsychologist), Time Traveller
Time period(s): 1900s (1909); 1990s (1990)
Locale(s): Idaho

Summary: In Smith's first novel, a guest lodge on the shore of Lake Roosevelt in Idaho is bothered by the ghost of a young woman who evidently died in the natural disaster that created the lake some eighty years earlier. Investigating the ghost, Doc Jones meets a parapsychologist, Susan, who turns out to be a time traveller.

Other books you might like:
Allen Appel, *Time After Time*, 1987

Jack L. Chalker, *Dance Band on the Titanic*, 1979
Matthew J. Costello, *Beneath Still Waters*, 1989
Clive Cussler, *Raise the Titanic!*, 1984
Jerry Sohl, *Costigan's Needle*, 1953

4081

DEAN WESLEY SMITH
KRISTINE KATHRYN RUSCH, Co-Author

The Soldiers of Fear
(New York: Pocket, 1996)

Story type: Science Fiction (Space Opera)
Series: Star Trek: The Next Generation
Major character(s): Jean-Luc Picard, Spaceship Captain, Military Personnel; William T. Riker, Military Personnel (Starfleet Commander), Space Explorer; Deanna Troi, Psychologist, Alien (half-Betazoid)
Time period(s): 24th century
Locale(s): *U.S.S. Enterprise*, Spaceship; United Federation of Planets, Interstellar Empire/Federation

Summary: Warned by an abortive invasion 80 years before, Starfleet keeps watch for the Fury, aliens who look like humanity's worst nightmares. Now they return in full force, with the ability to project a paralyzing fear directly into the minds of their enemies. Even the combined efforts of Federation and Klingon fleets cannot stop them, unless a one-way mission into a wormhole can block their access to the Alpha Quadrant. Second of the four-part Invasion! Series which spans all four Star Trek television series and continues in *Time's Enemy*.

Other books you might like:
Dafydd ab Hugh, *The Final Fury*, 1996
Diane Carey, *First Strike*, 1996
Gene DeWeese, *The Final Nexus*, 1988
L.A. Graf, *Time's Enemy*, 1996
Joe Haldeman, *The Forever War*, 1975

4082

GUY N. SMITH

The Dark One
(New York: Zebra, 1995)

Story type: Horror (Evil Children)
Major character(s): Rankin Gorlay, Journalist; Glenn Gorlay, Child; Marcel Hart, Child
Time period(s): 1990s (1995)
Locale(s): Sandpits, England

Summary: The Gorlays think that Marcel, the son of their close friends, is ill-mannered and under-disciplined. When they agree to let him stay with them for a week while his parents go on holiday, they discover that his badness is actually evil that grows out of satanic practices he is trying to pull their family into.

Other books you might like:
Margaret Bingley, *Seeds of Evil*, 1988
D.A. Fowler, *Bad Blood*, 1993
Edmund Plante, *Seed of Evil*, 1988

4083

GUY N. SMITH

Dead End

(New York: Zebra, 1996)

Story type: Horror (Reanimated Dead)
Major character(s): Max Frame, Teacher (driving instructor); Shanifa Smith, Waiter/Waitress; Nat Bonner, Child
Time period(s): 1990s (1996)
Locale(s): London, England

Summary: While recovering from a devastating automobile accident, Max Frame sees his girlfriend Shanifa, who by all accounts died in the same accident. Max pursues Shanifa to "The Waste," an abandoned ghetto on the fringe of town, and discovers satanic forces that are resurrecting the dead in the service of evil.

Other books you might like:
William W. Johnstone, *Rockabilly Hell*, 1995
Stephen Laws, *Daemonic*, 1995
Stephen Laws, *Macabre*, 1994
Richard Laymon, *Funland*, 1990

4084

GUY N. SMITH

Witch Spell

(New York: Zebra, 1993)

Story type: Horror (Black Magic; Wild Talents)
Major character(s): Belinda "Bobbie" Wheeler, Teenager; Yvonne Wheeler, Witch; Alec Wheeler, Warlock
Time period(s): 1990s (1993)
Locale(s): Willington College, England

Summary: White witch Yvonne Wheeler sends her daughter Bobbie to boarding school to keep her from the clutches of her black magician father Alec. But every time Bobbie inadvertently vents her supernatural powers on unsuspecting students and faculty, she comes that much closer to falling entirely under her father's pernicious influence.

Other books you might like:
Kathryn Meyer Griffith, *Witches*, 1993
Ed Kelleher, *The School*, 1992
    Harriet Vidal, co-author
Anne Rice, *Lasher*, 1993
Anne Rice, *The Witching Hour*, 1991

4085

JAMES V. SMITH

The Lurker

(New York: Dell, 1989)

Story type: Horror (Serial Killer)
Major character(s): Laren Hodges, Journalist; Thomas E. "Ted" Dewey, Journalist (Police reporter)
Time period(s): 1980s
Locale(s): United States

Summary: A "dead" child murderer, nicknamed "The Lurker," reappears to terrorize the city. An unlikely pair of reporters joins forces in an attempt to discover the nature and identity of the killer.

Other books you might like:
Nicholas Conde, *In the Deep Dark Woods*, 1989
Rex Miller, *Slob*, 1987

4086

JULIE DEAN SMITH

Call of Madness

(New York: Del Rey, 1990)

Story type: Fantasy (Adventure)
Series: Caithan Crusade
Major character(s): Athaya Trelane, Royalty (Princess), Wizard
Time period(s): Indeterminate Past
Locale(s): Alternate Universe

Summary: In a world where magic is outlawed and those with magical abilities are killed, Athaya discovers that she, too, has magical abilities. In a race against time, she must find someone to train her before she goes mad from the magic or is captured by the church.

Other books you might like:
Cheryl J. Franklin, *Fire Get*, 1989
    Book 1 - Tales of the Taormin
Mercedes Lackey, *Arrows of the Queen*, 1987
    Book 1 - Heralds of Valdemar
Stephen R. Lawhead, *In the Hall of the Dragon King*, 1982
    Book 1 - The Dragon King Trilogy
Sandra Miesel, *Shaman*, 1989

4087

JULIE DEAN SMITH

Mission of Magic

(New York: Ballantine/Del Rey, 1991)

Story type: Fantasy (Adventure; Magic Conflict)
Series: Caithan Crusade
Major character(s): Athaya Trelane, Royalty (princess), Wizard; Daniel Ventan, Religious (archbishop); Durek Trelane, Royalty (king)
Time period(s): Indeterminate Past
Locale(s): Isle of Sare, Fictional Country

Summary: King Durek and Archbishop Ventan search through the library of deceased wizard Rhodri for ammunition against the Lorngeld, who are wizards, and against the Princess Athaya who killed their father with magic. Princess Athaya escapes to a neighboring kingdom where magic is not considered against the church. Somehow she must clear her name and save the Lorngeld from annihilation.

Other books you might like:
David Eddings, *Sorceress of Darshiva*, 1989
Cheryl J. Franklin, *Fire Get*, 1989
Mercedes Lackey, *Arrows of the Queen*, 1987
Sandra Meisel, *Shaman*, 1989

Melinda M. Snodgrass, *Queen's Gambit Declined*, 1989

4088
JULIE DEAN SMITH

Sage of Sare
(New York: Ballantine Del Rey, 1992)

Story type: Fantasy (Adventure; Magic Conflict)
Series: Caithan Crusade
Major character(s): Athaya Trelane, Royalty, Wizard; Durek Trelane, Royalty (king); Jaren McLaud, Magician
Time period(s): Indeterminate Past (Middle Ages)
Locale(s): Caithe, Fictional Country

Summary: Outlawed, Princess Athaya flees to the forest, gathering around her people who wish to learn control of their magic abilities. There, some hope of acceptance in society comes from a distant but powerful wizard who seeks to help the group.

Other books you might like:
Katherine Kurtz, *The Harrowing of Gwynedd*, 1989
Katherine Kurtz, *King Javan's Year*, 1992
Paula Volsky, *Illusion*, 1992

4089
JULIE DEAN SMITH

The Wizard King
(New York: Ballantine Del Rey, 1994)

Story type: Fantasy (Political; Magic Conflict)
Series: Caithan Crusade
Major character(s): Athaya Trelane, Royalty, Wizard; Sage of Sare, Wizard, Ruler
Time period(s): Indeterminate Past (Middle Ages)
Locale(s): Caithe, Fictional Country

Summary: Although Athaya desires political reform which allows the magic-wielding Lorngeld to learn and practice their art overtly, her revolutionary activity presents the Sage of Sare with an opportunity to advance his scheme of bringing not just acceptance for the wizards, but also the ouster of Caithe's king and his replacement with the Sage of Sare, his rule enforced by wizards' magic. While an ancient prophecy indicates Athaya's role in events will become crucial, her initial goal involves convincing the Sage to remove a deadly compulsion with which he ensorcels Athaya's brother.

Other books you might like:
Jo Clayton, *Dancer's Rise*, 1993
Barbara Hambly, *Stranger at the Wedding*, 1994
Laurell K. Hamilton, *Nightseer*, 1992
Mercedes Lackey, *By the Sword*, 1991
Michelle Sagara, *Chains of Darkness, Chains of Light*, 1994

4090
L. NEIL SMITH

Contact and Commune
(New York: Popular Library Questar, 1990)

Story type: Science Fiction (First Contact)
Series: Contact
Major character(s): Estrellita Reille y Sanchez, Spaceship Captain, Explorer
Time period(s): 21st century
Locale(s): 5023 Eris, Asteroid

Summary: A pioneering expedition sets down on a mineral-rich asteroid intending to claim it for humanity, but discovers an alien race there ahead of them. The brilliant Elders, descended from ancient Earthly sea creatures, must decide whether or not to destroy humanity.

Other books you might like:
Gregory Benford, *Tides of Light*, 1989
Barry B. Longyear, *The Homecoming*, 1989
Janet Morris, *Target*, 1989
    David Drake, co-author
Allen L. Wold, *Crown of the Serpent*, 1989

4091
L. NEIL SMITH

Converse and Conflict
(New York: Popular Library Questar, 1990)

Story type: Science Fiction (Alternate Universe; Political)
Series: Elders
Major character(s): Eichra Oren, Human, Agent (for the Nautiloid Elders); Mr. Thoggish, Alien (Nautiloid); Toya Pulaski, Scientist (biologist), Spy
Time period(s): 21st century
Locale(s): 5023 Eris, Planet—Imaginary

Summary: Eichra Oren, a representative of a nautiloid species from a parallel universe, attempts to teach the members of a stranded ASSR expedition the values of anarchy while the Elders search for the remains of an interstellar ship on 5023 Eris. Unknown to them, a ship from the USSR carrying The Banker, a KGB superagent, is coming to destroy everyone and claim the spoils for itself. But a Chinese fleet arrives and saves the day. They prove very receptive to the Elders' teachings.

Other books you might like:
Octavia E. Butler, *Dawn*, 1987
Jack L. Chalker, *Midnight at the Well of Souls*, 1977
Keith Laumer, *Zone Yellow*, 1990
Joan Slonczewski, *A Door into Ocean*, 1986
Allen Steele, *Clarke County, Space*, 1990
Jack Vance, *The Asutra*, 1974

4092

L. NEIL SMITH

Henry Martyn
(New York: Tor, 1989)

Story type: Science Fiction (Space Opera)
Major character(s): Arran Islay, Heir—Dispossessed, Pirate; Black Usurper, Criminal (Usurper)
Time period(s): 31st century
Locale(s): Outer Space; Planet—Imaginary

Summary: Arran Islay, deprived of his inheritance by the evil Black Usurper, vows revenge. He becomes the daring pirate Henry Martyn, scourge of the space lanes, and wins back all that he has lost and more.

Other books you might like:
Poul Anderson, *The High Crusade*, 1960
Lois McMaster Bujold, *Brothers in Arms*, 1988
R.A. MacAvoy, *The Third Eagle: Lessons Along a Minor String*, 1989
Alexei Panshin, *Masque World*, 1969
Alexei Panshin, *Star Well*, 1968
Alexei Panshin, *The Thurb Revolution*, 1968

4093

L. NEIL SMITH

Pallas
(New York: Tor, 1993)

Story type: Science Fiction (Political; Space Colony)
Major character(s): Emerson Ngu, Engineer, Businessman; Gibson Altman, Government Official (retired), Businessman; Aloysius Brody, Judge, Businessman
Time period(s): 2030s
Locale(s): Pallas, Asteroid

Summary: William Wilde Curringer terraformed Pallas and opened it for colonization by anyone willing to sign the Hyperdemocratic Covenant, a corporate agreement based on libertarian principles. A loophole allows the creation of the Greeley Project where Gibson Altman holds voting privileges for all project members, including their children, in perpetuity. Emerson Ngu builds a radio as a child and learns about life Outside. After he escapes from the Project, Altman uses him as a scapegoat for his failures, but Emerson's ingenuity and help from friends allow him to prevail.

Other books you might like:
Piers Anthony, *Refugee*, 1983
David Brin, *Earth*, 1990
Samuel R. Delany, *They Fly at Ciron*, 1993
Robert A. Heinlein, *The Moon Is a Harsh Mistress*, 1966
Charles Sheffield, *Brother to Dragons*, 1992
F. Paul Wilson, *The LaNague Chronicles*, 1992
F. Paul Wilson, *The Tery*, 1990

4094

MARK SMITH
JULIA SMITH, Co-Author

Shadow-Maze
(New York: Warner Questar, 1994)

Story type: Fantasy (Magic Conflict; Quest)
Major character(s): Brostek, Teenager, Hunter; Varo, Teenager, Hunter; Magara, Storyteller
Time period(s): Indeterminate
Locale(s): Levindre, Fictional Country; Bari, Fictional Country; Trevine, Fictional Country

Summary: Meeting on the return home from their adulthood survival test, Brostek and Varo find their townsfolk dead at the hands of the Knifemen of Bari, and set out to avenge their relatives and protect their neighbors. When Slaton and his strange nephew Lisle join them, they realize they must succeed against an ancient, lost power now possessed by an insane and evil wizard by mastering the shadow-maze which Magara's tapestry reflects.

Other books you might like:
Sharon Green, *The Hidden Realms*, 1993
Jane M. Lindskold, *Brother to Dragons, Companion to Owls*, 1994
S.M. Stirling, *The Rose Sea*, 1994
　Holly Lisle, co-author
Deborah Talmadge-Bickmore, *The Heldan*, 1994
Jonathan Wylie, *The First Named*, 1987
　pseudonym of Mark Smith and Julia Smith

4095

NYX SMITH

Fade to Black
(New York: Roc, 1994)

Story type: Science Fiction (Cyberpunk; Science Fantasy)
Series: Shadowrun
Major character(s): Thorvin, Mythical Creature (dwarf), Cyborg (rigger); Rico, Mercenary (shadowrunner); Bandit, Shaman
Time period(s): 2050s (2055)
Locale(s): Newark, New Jersey

Summary: Hired for a seemingly simple corporate extraction, freeing a valuable asset from his contract, Rico and his gang discover that lies and betrayals make it difficult to escape with their lives. Game tie-in.

Other books you might like:
Emma Bull, *Bone Dance*, 1991
Pat Cadigan, *Synners*, 1991
Charles de Lint, *Svaha*, 1989
Nigel Findley, *2XS*, 1992
Walter Jon Williams, *Voice of the Whirlwind*, 1987

4096

NYX SMITH

Striper Assassin

(New York: Roc, 1993)

Story type: Fantasy (Adventure; Urban)
Series: Shadowrun
Major character(s): Tikki ''Striper'', Hunter, Mythical Creature (shapechanger)
Time period(s): 2050s (2054)
Locale(s): Philadelphia, Pennsylvania

Summary: Tikki's usual role reverses as hunter becomes prey when another hunter sets his sights on Tikki. Game tie-in.

Other books you might like:
Robert N. Charrette, *Choose Your Enemies Carefully*, 1991
Robert N. Charrette, *Find Your Own Truth*, 1991
Robert N. Charrette, *Never Deal with a Dragon*, 1990
Robert N. Charrette, *Never Trust an Elf*, 1992
Tom Dowd, *Night's Pawn*, 1993
Nigel Findley, *2XS*, 1992
Nigel Findley, *Shadowplay*, 1993
Christopher Kubasik, *Changeling*, 1992
Carl Sargent, *Streets of Blood*, 1992
    Marc Gascoigne, co-author
Jordan K. Weisman, *Into the Shadows*, 1992
    editor

4097

ROBERT ARTHUR SMITH

Silent Witness

(New York: Fawcett, 1991)

Story type: Horror (Science Fiction)
Major character(s): Nicole Brill, Child; Willy Brill, Doctor (ex-Nazi); Peter Van Buren, Young Man
Time period(s): 1990s
Locale(s): Brazil (the rain forest)

Summary: Nicole Brill's discovery that her father and his closest friends are ex-Nazis who sought refuge and new identities following the war isn't nearly as devastating as her discovery that her father was a greatly reviled surgeon who is continuing the same hideous experiments he performed for the benefit of the Third Reich.

Other books you might like:
Ira Levin, *The Boys From Brazil*, 1976
Robert Weinberg, *The Armageddon Box*, 1991

4098

SHERWOOD SMITH
DAVE TROWBRIDGE, Co-Author

The Phoenix in Flight

(New York: Tor, 1993)

Story type: Science Fiction (Adventure; Political)
Series: Exordium

Major character(s): Jerrode Eusabian, Political Figure (Lord of Vengeance); Gelasaar III, Royalty (Emperor), Leader (Pantarch)
Time period(s): Indeterminate Future
Locale(s): *Bloodknife*, Spaceship; Brangornie, Planet—Imaginary; Narbon, Planet—Imaginary

Summary: Having come through the Vortex thousands of years earlier, humans now inhabit the many planets composing the Thousand Suns, an interstellar empire maintaining control for a thousand years. Eusabian plots to overthrow the empire by killing the heirs and capturing Gelasaar III. A computer expert discovers the plotting and attempts to undo it. When the youngest son of Gelasaar III fails to attend the ceremony where assassination waits, he survives to fight the Lord of Vengeance and the destruction of the Panarchy.

Other books you might like:
Iain M. Banks, *Use of Weapons*, 1992
Allan Cole, *Sten*, 1984
    Chris Bunch, co-author
Glen Cook, *The Dragon Never Sleeps*, 1988
Debra Doyle, *The Price of the Stars*, 1992
    James D. Macdonald, co-author
Frank Herbert, *Dune*, 1965
Andre Norton, *Brother to Shadows*, 1993
David Weber, *On Basilisk Station*, 1993
David Weber, *Path of the Fury*, 1992
Vernor Vinge, *A Fire upon the Deep*, 1992

4099

SHERWOOD SMITH
DAVE TROWBRIDGE, Co-Author

A Prison Unsought

(New York: Tor, 1994)

Story type: Science Fiction (Political; Military)
Series: Exordium
Major character(s): Brandon vlith-Arkad, Military Personnel, Heir—Dispossessed
Time period(s): Indeterminate Future
Locale(s): Ares, Planet—Imaginary (Panarchic Navy headquarters); Gehenna, Planet—Imaginary (prison planet); Panarchy of the Thousand Suns, Interstellar Empire/Federation

Summary: With the usurper Eusabian of Dol'jhar in control of the Empire, Brandon vlith-Arkad rallies with followers on Ares as he tries to win the Panarchic Navy's loyalty. As the deposed Pantarch, Brandon's father, travels to Gehenna, he tries to find a way to turn the usurper's son against his father and regain power indirectly.

Other books you might like:
Lois McMaster Bujold, *The Warrior's Apprentice*, 1986
Glen Cook, *The Dragon Never Sleeps*, 1988
Debra Doyle, *The Price of the Stars*, 1992
    James D. Macdonald, co-author
Alis A. Rasmussen, *Revolution's Shore*, 1990
David Weber, *On Basilisk Station*, 1993

4100

SHERWOOD SMITH
DAVE TROWBRIDGE, Co-Author

The Rifter's Covenant

(New York: Tor, 1995)

Story type: Science Fiction (Adventure; Political)
Series: Exordium
Major character(s): Brandon hai-Arkad, Royalty (Panarch); Jerrode Eusabian, Political Figure (Lord of Vengeance)
Time period(s): Indeterminate Future
Locale(s): Ares, Space Station; *Suneater*, Spaceship; Panarchy of the Thousand Suns, Interstellar Empire/Federation

Summary: Against all expectations, Brandon Arkad survives many attacks to become Pantarch of the Thousand Suns. Unfortunately, his enemies control or attack most of his empire while Brandon attempts to gather support as a traitor sabotages his efforts.

Other books you might like:
Iain M. Banks, *The Player of Games*, 1989
Glen Cook, *The Dragon Never Sleeps*, 1988
Debra Doyle, *The Price of the Stars*, 1992
　　James D. Macdonald, co-author
Frank Herbert, *Dune*, 1965
H. Beam Piper, *Space Viking*, 1963
Vernor Vinge, *A Fire upon the Deep*, 1992
David Weber, *On Basilisk Station*, 1993

4101

SHERWOOD SMITH
DAVE TROWBRIDGE, Co-Author

Ruler of Naught

(New York: Tor, 1993)

Story type: Science Fiction (Adventure; Political)
Series: Exordium
Major character(s): Margot O'Reilly Ng, Spaceship Captain; Brandon vlith-Arkad, Ruler (aerenarch), Fugitive (exile); Ivard, Pirate
Time period(s): Indeterminate Future
Locale(s): *Grozniy*, Spaceship; *Telvarna*, Spaceship; Arthelion, Planet—Imaginary

Summary: Eusabian of Dol'jhar sits on the Emerald Throne of the Thousand Suns while Brandon, the rightful heir, flees across the galaxy. Captors turned allies, the rifter crew of the *Telvarna* help Brandon evade pursuit as they make their way toward Ares Station where the scattered remnants of the Imperial Fleet assemble for counterinsurgency.

Other books you might like:
Isaac Asimov, *Foundation and Empire*, 1952
C.J. Cherryh, *Chanur's Homecoming*, 1986
C.J. Cherryh, *The Pride of Chanur*, 1982
Debra Doyle, *The Price of the Stars*, 1992
　　James D. Macdonald, co-author
Frank Herbert, *Dune*, 1965
George Lucas, *Star Wars*, 1976

Judith Reeves-Stevens, *Prime Directive*, 1990
　　Garfield Reeves-Stevens, co-author
E.E. "Doc" Smith, *The Skylark of Space*, 1946

4102

SHERWOOD SMITH

Wren to the Rescue

(New York: Harcourt Brace Jovanovich, 1990)

Story type: Fantasy (Quest)
Series: Wren
Major character(s): Wren, Orphan, Adventurer; Tryon, Magician, Apprentice; Connor Shaltar, Royalty (prince of Siradayel)
Time period(s): Indeterminate
Locale(s): Meldrith, Fictional Country; Senna Lirwan, Fictional Country

Summary: When Wren's friend, Princess Teressa, is kidnapped from Three Groves Orphanage, Wren uses a once-heard spell in the vain hope of helping her friend. The spell transports her to the Magic School where she is told not to try the spell again and she acquires the aid of Tryon. On their journey to rescue Teressa from King Andreus, they are joined by Tryon's friend, Connor. During the rescue attempt, Wren is changed into a dog, but even that difficulty does not deter their efforts.

Other books you might like:
Lloyd Alexander, *The Beggar Queen*, 1984
Lloyd Alexander, *The Kestrel*, 1982
Lloyd Alexander, *Westmark*, 1981
Grace Chetwin, *Gom on Windy Mountain*, 1986
Geraldine Harris, *Prince of the Godborn*, 1983
Ursula K. Le Guin, *A Wizard of Earthsea*, 1968
Ursula K. Le Guin, *The Farthest Shore*, 1972
Ursula K. Le Guin, *The Tombs of Atuan*, 1971
Susan Price, *The Ghost Drum: A Cat's Tale*, 1987

4103

SHERWOOD SMITH

Wren's Quest

(New York: Harcourt Brace Jovanovich, 1993)

Story type: Fantasy (Quest; Young Adult)
Series: Wren
Major character(s): Wren, Adventurer, Student (of magic); Connor Shaltar, Royalty (Prince of Siradayel)
Time period(s): Indeterminate
Locale(s): Cantirmoor, Fictional Country; Meldrith, Fictional Country; Siradayel, Fictional Country

Summary: Having earned her first break from magic school, Wren decides to pursue clues she receives from her orphanage and try to find her relatives. Wren's mission becomes dangerous as human and magical agents interfere. Sequel to *Wren to the Rescue*.

Other books you might like:
Terry Brooks, *Hook*, 1992
Phyllis Eisenstein, *Sorcerer's Son*, 1979

Nancy Luenn, *Goldclimbers*, 1991
Shirley Rousseau Murphy, *The Catswold Portal*, 1992
Will Shetterly, *Elsewhere*, 1991
Jane Yolen, *Briar Rose*, 1992

4104

SHERWOOD SMITH

Wren's War

(New York: Harcourt Brace/Jane Yolen Books, 1995)

Story type: Fantasy (Young Adult; Adventure)
Series: Wren
Major character(s): Wren, Adventurer, Magician; Teressa Rhisadel, Royalty (Princess of Meldrith), Leader; Connor Shaltar, Royalty (Prince of Siradayel)
Time period(s): Indeterminate
Locale(s): Meldrith, Fictional Country

Summary: Lusting for power and revenge, Andreus attacks Meldrith, killing King Verne and Queen Astren. Escaping with Prince Connor, Princess Teressa joins with Wren and others to repel the invaders and reinstate a proper Meldrith sovereign.

Other books you might like:
Lois McMaster Bujold, *The Spirit Ring*, 1992
Laurell K. Hamilton, *Nightseer*, 1992
Tanith Lee, *Gold Unicorn*, 1994
Martha Wells, *The Element of Fire*, 1992
Patricia C. Wrede, *Calling on Dragons*, 1993

4105

STEPHANIE A. SMITH

Other Nature

(New York: Tor, 1995)

Story type: Science Fiction (Post-Disaster)
Major character(s): Sean Rider, Spouse (Emily's); Emily Rider, Spouse (Sean's)
Time period(s): 21st century
Locale(s): Oregon; California; Monkar

Summary: Formerly a high tech research center, Monkar now decays as birth defects and premature mortality rates soar. After Sean Rider leaves his pregnant wife to search near San Francisco for his former mate, events in Monkar further degrade the fragile society.

Other books you might like:
Richard Brautigan, *In Watermelon Sugar*, 1968
Jack Cady, *The Off Season*, 1995
Nancy Farmer, *The Ear, the Eye, and the Arm*, 1994
K.W. Jeter, *Madlands*, 1991
Ken Kesey, *Sailor Song*, 1992
Rachel Pollack, *Unquenchable Fire*, 1992
Geoff Ryman, *The Child Garden*, 1990

4106

WAYNE SMITH

Thor

(New York: St. Martin's/Thomas Dunne, 1992)

Story type: Horror (Werewolf Story)
Major character(s): Thor, Animal (German Shepherd); Uncle Ted, Photographer, Werewolf; Dad, Lawyer
Time period(s): 1990s (1992)
Locale(s): Oregon

Summary: This ingenious first novel is told from the point of view of Thor, the family dog, who desperately tries to warn his human owners that a family member has become a werewolf but is frustratingly misunderstood for all of his efforts.

Other books you might like:
Michael Cadnum, *St. Peter's Wolf*, 1992
Dennis Danvers, *Wilderness*, 1992
Stephen King, *Cujo*, 1981
H. Warner Munn, *The Werewolf of Ponkert*, 1958
S.P. Somtow, *Moon Dance*, 1990

4107

MELINDA M. SNODGRASS

Queen's Gambit Declined

(New York: Popular Library Questar, 1989)

Story type: Fantasy (Alternate World)
Major character(s): William Henry, Ruler (Prince of Orange), Historical Figure; Louis XIV, Ruler (King of France), Historical Figure
Locale(s): Alternate Earth (France and the Netherlands)

Summary: History and magic are interwoven in this story about William of Orange and Louis of France. The war between the two sovereigns is fought in the traditional manner, as well as with magic.

Other books you might like:
Roberto Pazzi, *The Princess and the Dragon*,
Melissa Scott, *The Armor of Light*, 1988
    Lisa Barnett, co-author
Bob Skimin, *Gray Victory*, 1988

4108

GREG SNOW

That's All, Folks!

(New York: Random House, 1992)

Story type: Fantasy (Contemporary; Light Fantasy)
Major character(s): Nick Taig, Advertising; Lucy, Girlfriend; Christian Kidd, Advertising (art director), Homosexual
Time period(s): 1990s
Locale(s): London, England

Summary: During an accident with a kitchen appliance, Nick discovers that his body exhibits cartoon characteristics. Nick soon realizes the changed nature of his existence and begins the search for answers and remission to his former state.

Published in 1991 in Great Britain as *Surface Tension*. Author's first novel.

Other books you might like:
Michael Bishop, *Count Geiger's Blues*, 1992
Michael Kandel, *Captain Jack Zodiac*, 1992
George R.R. Martin, *Wild Cards*, 1987
    editor
Clifford D. Simak, *Out of Their Minds*, 1970
Gary K. Wolf, *Who Censored Roger Rabbit?*, 1981
Gary K. Wolf, *Who P-P-Plugged Roger Rabbit?*, 1991

4109

JACK SNOW
ERIC SHANOWER, Illustrator

Spectral Snow: The Dark Fantasies of Jack Snow

(Bloomsbury, New Jersey: Hungry Tiger Press, 1996)

Story type: Horror (Collection)

Summary: The author is best known as a writer chosen by the estate of L. Frank Baum to continue Baum's series of Oz books. This collection brings together eight tales of horror, fantasy, and science fiction, including "Second Childhood," about an evil imaginary playmate who returns to a woman in her old age; "The Dimension Terror," about the horrifying experiences of a married couple who stumble upon a fallen meteorite on their honeymoon; "Seed," in which a woman is impregnated with the seed of a plant that will grow inside her; and "The Rope," about a man who discovers to his dismay the truth behind the Indian rope trick. Editor David Maxine has also included the previously unpublished "A Murder in Oz."

Other books you might like:
Arthur J. Burks, *Black Medicine*, 1966
Hugh B. Cave, *Murgunstrumm and Others*, 1977
Carl Jacobi, *Smoke of the Snake*, 1994
Frank Belknap Long, *Escape From Tomorrow*, 1995
Howard Wandrei, *Time Burial*, 1995

4110

MIDORI SNYDER

Beldan's Fire

(New York: Tor, 1993)

Story type: Fantasy (Magic Conflict; Political)
Series: New Moon
Major character(s): Zorah, Ruler (Fire Queen); Jobber, Revolutionary, Psychic (pyromancer); Shedwyn, Revolutionary, Psychic (esper)
Time period(s): Indeterminate
Locale(s): Beldan, Fictional City; Oran, Fictional Country

Summary: Zorah, Fire Queen, depends on the foreign Silean soldiers to police Beldan. Although possession of Oran talents results in a death penalty, three of the four women necessary to create a Queen's quarter knot of the powers of earth, air, fire and water already belong to the revolutionary group, New Moon. Having already killed her three complementary

Queens, Zorah anticipates wresting power from the new quarter knot and increasing her own powers.

Other books you might like:
David Eddings, *Pawn of Prophecy*, 1982
Phyllis Eisenstein, *Shadow of Earth*, 1979
Barbara Hambly, *The Time of the Dark*, 1982
Mickey Zucker Reichert, *The Western Wizard*, 1992
Paula Volsky, *Illusion*, 1992

4111

MIDORI SNYDER

The Flight of Michael McBride

(New York: Tor, 1994)

Story type: Fantasy (Magic Conflict; Horror)
Major character(s): Michael McBride, Cowboy, Mythical Creature (part fairy); John O'Connor, Cowboy, Leader
Time period(s): 1870s
Locale(s): New York; Texas

Summary: While fleeing spirits made visible by his mother's deathbed ritual, Michael meets a gambler who directs him to Texas where he will find a job. In Texas, mentioning the gambler secures Michael employment as a drover, but attacks now afflict his companions on the cattle drive.

Other books you might like:
Richard Brautigan, *The Hawkline Monster*, 1974
Susan Dexter, *The Prince of Ill Luck*, 1994
Karen Joy Fowler, *Sarah Canary*, 1991
Stephen King, *The Dark Tower: The Gunslinger*, 1982
Louis L'Amour, *Haunted Mesa*, 1987
George R.R. Martin, *Fevre Dream*, 1982
Steve Perry, *Stellar Ranger*, 1994
Elizabeth Ann Scarborough, *The Goldcamp Vampire; or The Sanguinary Sourdough*, 1987
S.P. Somtow, *Moon Dance*, 1989

4112

ZILPHA KEATLEY SNYDER

Song of the Gargoyle

(New York: Delacorte Press, 1991)

Story type: Fantasy (Adventure; Young Adult)
Major character(s): Komus, Entertainer (court jester); Tymmon, Teenager
Time period(s): Indeterminate Past (the Middle Ages)
Locale(s): Austerneve North Countries, Fictional Country

Summary: After Komus was kidnapped, his son Tymmon, who wants to be a knight, escapes, intending to rescue his father. During his search he notices the way knights treat the populace and comes to appreciate his father's choice of profession.

Other books you might like:
John Deakins, *Barrow*, 1990
Phyllis Eisenstein, *Born to Exile*, 1978
Phyllis Eisenstein, *Sorcerer's Son*, 1989
Esther Friesner, *The Water King's Laughter*, 1989
Matt Ruff, *Fool on the Hill*, 1989

Peter Vansittart, *Parsifal*, 1989

4113

CARO SOLES, Editor

Meltdown!

(New York: Masquerade Books, Inc., 1994)

Story type: Science Fiction (Anthology; Gay/Lesbian Fiction)

Summary: Subtitled ''An Anthology of Erotic Science Fiction and Dark Fantasy for Gay Men,'' this volume contains a two-page introduction plus 11 original and three reprinted stories by authors including Robin Wayne Bailey, Samuel R. Delany and Edmund White.

Other books you might like:
Camilla Decarnin, *Worlds Apart*, 1986
   Eric Garber, Lyn Paleo, co-editors
Jeffrey M. Elliot, *Kindred Spirits*, 1984
   editor
Pam Keesey, *Daughters of Darkness: Lesbian Vampire Stories*, 1993
   editor

4114

S.P. SOMTOW (Pseudonym of Somtow Sucharitlkul)

Forest of the Night

(New York: AvoNova, 1992)

Story type: Fantasy (Alternate World; Religious)
Series: Darkling Wars
Major character(s): Theo Etchison, Psychic (truthsayer); Phil Etchison, Writer (poet); Serena Sommers, Girlfriend (Josh Etchison's)
Time period(s): 1990s
Locale(s): Southwest; Alternate Earth; Alternate Universe

Summary: Once again the warring dragon-children wish to win the mortal realm. The Darkling King Strang draws Theo into Strang's dimension to act as pawn in a bizarre odyssey. Phil and Serena search for Theo while Theo must rescue his brother from hell and the demonic forces which have claimed him.

Other books you might like:
Philip K. Dick, *Ubik*, 1969
Philip K. Dick, *The Unteleported Man*, 1983
   revised
Alan Dean Foster, *To the Vanishing Point*, 1988
K.W. Jeter, *Madlands*, 1991
Will Shetterly, *The Tangled Lands*, 1989
Terri Windling, *Life on the Border*, 1991
   editor

4115

S.P. SOMTOW (Pseudonym of Somtow Sucharitkul)

I Wake From a Dream of a Drowned Star City

(Eugene, Oregon: Pulphouse Publishing Axolotl Press 1992)

Story type: Science Fiction (Political; Genetic Manipulation)
Major character(s): Morry Draus, Clone, Heir (Crown Prince)
Time period(s): Indeterminate Future
Locale(s): Dreambreak, Fictional City

Summary: At the palace, Morry, a cloned prince, receives the formal education necessary for the ruler-to-be while acquiring street education from future subjects. After he reaches puberty, Morry's mother ritually initiates him in family sexual practice and declares him an adult worthy of becoming king, incurring an automatic death sentence for his genetically imperfect elder brother.

Other books you might like:
Octavia E. Butler, *Dawn*, 1987
Orson Scott Card, *Wyrms*, 1987
Thomas A. Easton, *Sparrowhawk*, 1990
Aldous Huxley, *Brave New World*, 1932
Robert Silverberg, *Tower of Glass*, 1970
Cordwainer Smith, *Norstrilia*, 1975

4116

S.P. SOMTOW (Pseudonym of Somtow Sucharitkul)

Moon Dance

(New York: Tor, 1990)

Story type: Horror (Werewolf Story)
Major character(s): Speranza Martinique, Governess; Johnny Kinkaid, Werewolf (Multiple personality)
Time period(s): 1880s (1883); 1960s (1963)
Locale(s): West (Dakota Territory)

Summary: Led by a European nobleman, a colony of werewolves move to the Dakota Territory, where they encounter a tribe of American Indian werewolves. The fate of the count's young son and his spunky governess rests on the outcome of this confrontation.

Other books you might like:
Basil Copper, *The House of the Wolf*, 1983
Robert R. McCammon, *They Thirst*, 1981

4117

S.P. SOMTOW (Pseudonym of Somtow Sucharitkul)

Riverrun

(New York: Avon, 1991)

Story type: Fantasy (Alternate World; Religious)
Series: Darkling Wars
Major character(s): Theo Etchison, Teenager, Psychic (truthsayer); Katastrofa ''Kathy'' Darkling, Police Officer (superintendent), Mythical Creature (were-dragon)
Time period(s): 1990s (1990)

Locale(s): Southwest; Alternate Universe

Summary: The Etchison family, while travelling from Virginia to Mexico, stops at a Chinese restaurant where Theo is drawn into another universe. He is kidnapped by Thorn Darkling, the eldest of three children of the King of the Universe. A latent Truthsayer with supernatural powers, Theo is needed to prevent the Darklings from destroying the universe when all he wants is to have his family safe and to get back to Earth.

Other books you might like:
Charles de Lint, *The Little Country*, 1991
Philip K. Dick, *The Unteleported Man*, 1983
 (revised)
Alan Dean Foster, *To the Vanishing Point*, 1988
Geary Gravel, *A Key for the Nonesuch*, 1990
Geary Gravel, *The Return of the Breakneck Boys*, 1991
Robert A. Heinlein, *The Number of the Beast*, 1980
Will Shetterly, *Cats Have No Lord*, 1985
Will Shetterly, *The Tangled Lands*, 1989

4118

S.P. SOMTOW (Pseudonym of Somtow Sucharitkul)

Valentine
(New York: Tor, 1992)

Story type: Horror (Vampire Story)
Series: Vampire Junction
Major character(s): Angel Todd, Actor; P. J. Gallegher, Shaman; Simone Arletta, Sorceress
Time period(s): 1990s (1992)
Locale(s): Junction, Idaho

Summary: In this sequel to the 1984 novel, *Vampire Junction*, director Jonathan Burr begins shooting the film biography of adolescent rock star Timmy Valentine in the town where Valentine disappeared eight years before, unaware that Valentine is a vampire over two millenia old, and that many who *are* aware of Timmy's true nature will use the shooting of the film to make contact with Timothy and exploit his powers.

Other books you might like:
Poppy Z. Brite, *Lost Souls*, 1992
Nancy A. Collins, *Tempter*, 1990
Anne Rice, *The Vampire Lestat*, 1985

4119

S.P. SOMTOW (Pseudonym of Somtow Sucharitkul)

Vanitas: Escape From Vampire Junction
(New York: Tor, 1995)

Story type: Horror (Vampire Story)
Series: Vampire Junction
Major character(s): Timmy Valentine, Musician (rock music singer); P.J. Gallegher, Art Dealer (gallery owner); Lauren McCandless, Artist (painter)
Time period(s): 1990s (1995)
Locale(s): Los Angeles, California; Bangkok, Thailand

Summary: Having traded his vampirism for a human soul to Angel Todd, the teenage boy who was to portray him in a movie, vampire rock star Timmy Valentine begins aging and finds that his music has lost its passion. Refusing to be forgotten, the now discorporate Angel acts as an evil influence on human beings in close proximity, forcing them to commit vampire-like murders and goading Timmy to track Angel to Thailand for a final showdown.

Other books you might like:
Poppy Z. Brite, *Lost Souls*, 1992
Gail Petersen, *The Making of a Monster*, 1993
Anne Rice, *The Vampire Lestat*, 1985
Robert Weinberg, *Vampire Diary: The Embrace*, 1995
 Mark Rein-Hagen, co-author

4120

S.P. SOMTOW (Pseudonym of Somtow Sucharitkul)

The Wizard's Apprentice
(New York: Atheneum, 1993)

Story type: Fantasy (Light Fantasy; Young Adult)
Series: Dragonflight
Major character(s): Aaron Maguire, Magician (apprentice), Teenager; Anaxagoras, Wizard, Teacher
Time period(s): 1990s
Locale(s): Los Angeles, California

Summary: During summer vacation from school, Aaron Maguire accepts apprenticeship with Anaxagoras and begins his studies. Magic turns to mayhem as Aaron loses his magic mirror to his girlfriend and magic monsters begin to terrorize Hollywood.

Other books you might like:
C. Dale Brittain, *A Bad Spell in Yurt*, 1991
Lois McMaster Bujold, *The Spirit Ring*, 1992
Michael Ende, *The Night of Wishes: or The Satanarchaeo-lidealcohellish Notion Potion*, 1992
Esther Friesner, *Majyk by Accident*, 1993
Esther Friesner, *Wishing Season*, 1993
Nancy Springer, *Red Wizard*, 1990
Somtow Sucharitkul, *The Fallen Country*, 1986
Somtow Sucharitkul, *Mallworld*, 1981

4121

ROY SORRELS

The Eyes of Torie Webster
(New York: Pinnacle, 1990)

Story type: Horror (Occult)
Major character(s): Torie Webster, Journalist (television newscaster); Rex Sullivan, Artist (Torie's boyfriend); Father Michael, Religious (priest; exorcist), Alcoholic
Time period(s): 17th century (1693); 1990s (1994)
Locale(s): New York; New Jersey

Summary: In 1693, Lizzie Dedalus is burned as a witch in the swamps of New Jersey. Three centuries later, her lingering presence causes a series of unexplained disappearances at the new airport built on her death site. This is the author's first novel.

Other books you might like:
Melisand March, *The Site*, 1988

4122

WILLIAM BROWNING SPENCER

Resume with Monsters

(Sag Harbor, New York: Permanent Press, 1995)

Story type: Horror (Satire)
Major character(s): Philip Kenan, Writer; Sissy Deal, Waiter/
Waitress; Lily Metcalf, Psychologist
Time period(s): 1990s (1995)
Locale(s): Austin, Texas

Summary: Stuck in a dead-end day job at a resume typesetting
company, hopelessly in love with a woman distrustful of his
financial and psychological stability, and unable to sell the
2,000-page horror novel he has been working on for decades,
Philip Kenan becomes convinced that he is trapped in the
indifferent mechanistic universe of H.P. Lovecraft's fiction,
and that he is being stalked by Lovecraft's extradimensional
monsters.

Other books you might like:
Scott Bradfield, *What's Wrong with America*, 1994
Fred Chappell, *The Lodger*, 1993
Christopher Moore, *Practical Demonkeeping*, 1993
John Kennedy Toole, *A Confederacy of Dunces*, 1980
Gahan Wilson, *Eddy Deco's Last Caper*, 1987

4123

WILLIAM BROWNING SPENCER

Zod Wallop

(New York: St. Martin's, 1995)

Story type: Horror (Mystery)
Major character(s): Harry Gainsborough, Writer; Raymond
Story, Patient (psychiatric); Emily Engel, Patient (psychi-
atric)
Time period(s): 1990s (1995)
Locale(s): Austin, Texas

Summary: As an extension of the therapy he undergoes at the
Harwood Psychiatric Institute to cope with the death of his
young daughter, Harry Gainsborough is encouraged to pub-
lish *Zod Wallop*, an unorthodox childrens book with morbid
overtones. After his release from the clinic, Harry is confronted by escaped schizophrenic inmate Raymond Story,
who tells him that the characters of his novel, all based on
people Harry knew while institutionalized, have invaded reality, and that Harry must help him avert the fates they are
destined to meet as the result of Harry's plot.

Other books you might like:
Fredric Brown, *What Mad Universe*, 1949
Jonathan Carroll, *The Land of Laughs*, 1980
Stephen King, *The Dark Half*, 1988

4124

NORMAN SPINRAD

The Children of Hamelin

(Houston, Texas: Tafford Publishing, 1991)

Story type: Science Fiction (Contemporary Realism)
Major character(s): Tom Hollander, Editor, Hippie; Harvey
Brustein, Cult Member (psychology cult leader); Arlene
Cooper, Writer (aspiring)
Time period(s): 1960s
Locale(s): New York, New York (Greenwich Village)

Summary: A thematic prequel to *The Mind Game* (1980), *The
Children of Hamelin* looks at the mechanics of addiction,
specifically a cult. The hero, Tom Hollander, managed to kick
heroin and knows an addiction when he sees it. So when two
friends, Ted and Doris, get involved in the Foundation for
Total Consciousness, Tom follows them into a strange trip
across the underground of '60s America, headed toward enlightenment or death. Portions of this book were serialized in
slightly different forms in *The Los Angeles Free Press* and
The Staff.

Other books you might like:
Chester Anderson, *The Butterfly Kid*, 1967
Pat Cadigan, *Mindplayers*, 1991
Mick Farren, *The Texts of Festival*, 1975
Michael Kurland, *The Unicorn Girl*, 1969
George R.R. Martin, *The Armageddon Rag*, 1983
T.A. Waters, *The Probability Pad*, 1970
Robert Shea, *The Illuminatus! Trilogy*, 1988
    Robert Anton Wilson, co-author

4125

NORMAN SPINRAD

Deus X

(New York: Bantam Spectra, 1993)

Story type: Science Fiction (Alternate Intelligence; Theologi-
cal)
Major character(s): Marley Philippe, Detective—Private; Fa-
ther "Deus X" De Leone, Artificial Intelligence, Experi-
mental Subject
Time period(s): 21st century
Locale(s): Earth; The Big Board, Cyberspace (cyberspace);
Mellow Yellow, At Sea

Summary: Intent on investigating immortal souls and the nature of consciousness holograms created from living humans,
Pope Mary I orders dying Father De Leone to explore the
computer phenomenon. When he disappears, the Pontiff hires
Marley Philippe to find the kidnapped artificial intelligence
and return it to the Vatican computer.

Other books you might like:
Isaac Asimov, *The Bicentennial Man*, 1993
    Robert Silverberg, co-author
Pat Cadigan, *Fools*, 1992
Pat Cadigan, *Synners*, 1991
Brian Daley, *Tron*, 1982
Jean Mark Gawron, *Dream of Glass*, 1993

Clifford D. Simak, *Project Pope*, 1981
Neal Stephenson, *Snow Crash*, 1992

4126

NORMAN SPINRAD

Journals of the Plague Years
(New York: Bantam Spectra, 1995)

Story type: Science Fiction (Post-Disaster; Dystopian)
Major character(s): Richard Bruno, Scientist (genetic synthesizer), Criminal; Linda Lewin, Religious, Criminal; Walter T. Bigelow, Political Figure, Administrator (Federal Quarantine Agency)
Time period(s): 22nd century
Locale(s): Palo Alto, California; San Francisco, California; Washington, District of Columbia

Summary: Richard Bruno's investigation into AIDS immunization leads to his discovery of a cure and permanent protection from all forms of AIDS, now ravaging America. Unfortunately, its distribution would bankrupt Bruno's employer. Seeing herself as a divine agent, Linda Lewin spreads AIDS with illegal sexual contact, while Walter Bigelow seeks to confine plague sufferers, as he believes God intends.

Other books you might like:
Greg Bear, *Blood Music*, 1985
Michael Conner, *Archangel*, 1995
Nicola Griffith, *Ammonite*, 1993
Frank Herbert, *The White Plague*, 1982
Dan Simmons, *Children of the Night*, 1992
Joan Slonczewski, *A Door into Ocean*, 1986

4127

NORMAN SPINRAD

Pictures at 11
(New York: Bantam Spectra, 1994)

Story type: Science Fiction (Contemporary Realism)
Major character(s): Toby Inman, Television Personality, Journalist; Edward ''Eddie'' Franker, Television (KLAX-TV station manager); Carl Mendoza, Television Personality (sportscaster)
Time period(s): 1990s
Locale(s): Los Angeles, California

Summary: KLAX-TV newscasters find themselves broadcasting a violent ecoterrorist group's attempt to publicize their cause when the group takes over the KLAX newsroom and wires the building to explode.

Other books you might like:
Wilhelmina Baird, *Crashcourse*, 1993
David Brin, *Earth*, 1990
John Brunner, *Stand on Zanzibar*, 1968
Philip K. Dick, *A Scanner Darkly*, 1977
William C. Dietz, *Matrix Man*, 1990

4128

NORMAN SPINRAD

Russian Spring
(New York: Bantam, 1991)

Story type: Science Fiction (Political)
Major character(s): Jerry Reed, Scientist (space); Sonya Ivanova, Linguist (translator), Political Figure; Ilya Pashikov, Political Figure
Time period(s): 1990s
Locale(s): Paris, France; Brussels, Belgium

Summary: Jerry left the USA for Paris to work at the European Space Agency because he had no chance to get into space working on the Battle Star program. Russia has joined the European Common Market and the USA may be planning a new Vietnam-type war in South America as a stop-gap solution to its economic woes. World war and global disaster may be on the horizon.

Other books you might like:
Margaret Wander Bonanno, *The Others*, 1990
David Brin, *Earth*, 1990
Peter George, *Dr. Strangelove*, 1964
Peter George, *Red Alert*, 1959
    as Peter Bryant
Paul Myron Anthony Linebarger, *Atomsk*, 1949
    as Carmichael Smith
Larry Niven, *Achilles' Choice*, 1991
    Steven Barnes, co-author
L. Neil Smith, *Contact and Commune*, 1990
Sheri S. Tepper, *Raising the Stones*, 1990

4129

NORMAN SPINRAD

Vampire Junkies
(Brooklyn, New York: Gryphon Publications, 1994)

Story type: Horror (Vampire Story)
Major character(s): Vlad Dracul, Vampire (Count Dracula); Little Mary Sunshine, Prostitute
Time period(s): 1990s (1994)
Locale(s): New York, New York

Summary: Originally published in *Tomorrow* magazine in 1993, this novella chronicles the co-dependency that develops between Count Dracula and a heroin-addicted hooker he bites. Having passed on their habits to one another, each becomes a supplier for the other.

Other books you might like:
Poppy Z. Brite, *Lost Souls*, 1992
Ray Garton, *Live Girls*, 1987
Nancy Kilpatrick, *Sex and the Single Vampire*, 1994
John Skipp, *The Light at the End*, 1986
    Craig Spector, co-author

4130

NANCY SPRINGER

Apocalypse

(New York: Baen, 1989)

Story type: Fantasy (Horror)
Major character(s): Joanie Musser, Witch; Cally Wilmore, Housewife (Anorexic; frustrated)
Time period(s): Indeterminate Future
Locale(s): Hoadley, Pennsylvania

Summary: A beautiful woman comes to Hoadley, a town filled with dark secrets, and offers a kind of satanic salvation. With seemingly little effort, the woman manages to make a grim reality even worse. Cally must find the strength to confront the devil and save Hoadley.

Other books you might like:
Bentley Little, *The Revelation*, 1990
R.A. MacAvoy, *Tea with the Black Dragon*, 1983
Sandra Miesel, *Shaman*, 1989
Diana L. Paxson, *Brisingamen*, 1984
Tom Reamy, *Blind Voices*, 1978

4131

NANCY SPRINGER

Damnbanna

(Eugene, Oregon: Pulphouse Publishing Axolotl Press, 1992)

Story type: Fantasy (Contemporary; Religious)
Major character(s): Angel, Student—High School, Sports Figure; "Damnbanna" Deil, Musician, Student—High School; McCready, Teacher, Criminal
Time period(s): 1990s
Locale(s): United States

Summary: Against her parents' wishes, Angel pursues her budding romance with Deil after he rescues her from a dog attack and sexual assault by a high school teacher.

Other books you might like:
Gael Baudino, *Gossamer Axe*, 1990
Louise Cooper, *The Sleep of Stone*, 1991
Megan Lindholm, *Cloven Hooves*, 1991
Mary Alexander Walker, *The Scathach and the Maeve's Daughter*, 1990
Kate Wilhelm, *State of Grace*, 1991

4132

NANCY SPRINGER

Fair Peril

(New York: Avon, 1996)

Story type: Fantasy (Contemporary; Legend)
Major character(s): Buffy Murphy, Storyteller; Adamus d'Aurca, Royalty (prince), Animal (frog); Emily Murphy, Teenager
Time period(s): 1990s
Locale(s): Pennsylvania; Fair Peril, Mythical Place

Summary: Recently divorced and unemployed, Buffy Murphy finds a talking frog which she refuses to kiss. When her daughter and the frog disappear, Buffy, out of shape and harassed, needs to face the mall and Fair Peril to get Emily back.

Other books you might like:
Eleanor Arnason, *Daughter of the Bear King*, 1987
John Barnes, *One for the Morning Glory*, 1996
Pamela Dean, *Tam Lin*, 1991
William Goldman, *The Princess Bride*, 1973
John Myers Myers, *Silverlock*, 1949

4133

NANCY SPRINGER

The Friendship Song

(New York: Atheneum, 1992)

Story type: Fantasy (Young Adult; Urban)
Major character(s): Harper Feree, Child, Hero; Rawnie Stello, Child, Hero; Gus "Aengus Mac Og" McCogg, Artist, Mythical Creature (master of the afterworlds)
Time period(s): 1990s
Locale(s): United States; The Afterworlds, Mythical Place (afterlife shadowland)

Summary: When Harper's father decides to marry a folk artist, Harper must adjust to new family, friends, house and school. An early adventure with Rawnie yields insight into the neighborhood mystery surrounding late night lights and music coming from Harper's labyrinthian back yard. When Harper's friendship with white supremacists threatens Harper and Rawnie's friendship, an upcoming rock concert presents an opportunity to repair their relationship then together venture into the afterlife to rescue a band member from death.

Other books you might like:
Gael Baudino, *Gossamer Axe*, 1990
Emma Bull, *Bone Dance*, 1991
Emma Bull, *War for the Oaks*, 1987
Mercedes Lackey, *Bardic Voices*, 1991
Will Shetterly, *Elsewhere*, 1991
Andrea Shettle, *Flute Song Magic*, 1990

4134

NANCY SPRINGER

Larque on the Wing

(New York: Morrow/AvoNova, 1994)

Story type: Fantasy (Contemporary; Psychic Powers)
Major character(s): Larque "Lark" Harootunian, Psychic, Artisan (home decoration products); Geoffrey "Hoot" Harootunian, Spouse (Larque's)
Time period(s): 1990s
Locale(s): Pennsylvania

Summary: Larque surprises herself and Hoot with a doppelganger of her younger self with an all-too-verbal assessment of Larque's life. To Hoot's consternation, Larque's reevaluation includes her personal transformation into a muscular teenage boy and an examination of her life and fate painful to her family.

Other books you might like:
A.A. Attanasio, *The Moon's Wife: A Hystery*, 1993
Octavia E. Butler, *Kindred*, 1979
Charles de Lint, *Memory and Dream*, 1994
Megan Lindholm, *Cloven Hooves*, 1991
Marge Piercy, *Woman on the Edge of Time*, 1976

4135

NANCY SPRINGER

Metal Angel

(New York: Roc, 1994)

Story type: Fantasy (Contemporary)
Major character(s): Volos, Angel; Box "Texas" McCardle, Police Officer; Angela Bradley, Housewife, Songwriter
Time period(s): 1990s
Locale(s): Los Angeles, California; Jenkins, Pennsylvania

Summary: Volos, least of the angels, chooses flesh, sin, and rock music over his place in the heavenly choir. Human except for angelic wings that he cannot shed, he sings lyrics written by a housewife whose passion matches his own and he rockets to the top of the charts. But Volos' private war with God affects the lives of the humans who love him.

Other books you might like:
Emma Bull, *War for the Oaks*, 1987
Parke Godwin, *Waiting for the Galactic Bus*, 1987
Tanith Lee, *The Silver Metal Lover*, 1982
Will Shetterly, *Elsewhere*, 1991
Norman Spinrad, *Little Heroes*, 1987

4136

NANCY SPRINGER

Red Wizard

(New York: Atheneum, 1990)

Story type: Fantasy (Alternate World)
Major character(s): Ryan De Witt, Student—Junior High School (seventh grade); Persyvaunce, Wizard
Time period(s): 1990s
Locale(s): Alternate Universe; United States

Summary: While on summer vacation with his parents, Ryan is magically transported into another world when a bumbling wizard's spell misfires. While there, Ryan must experience a series of adventures and help defeat an evil king before he can return to his own world.

Other books you might like:
Ellen Conford, *Genie with the Light Blue Hair*, 1989
Pamela Dean, *The Secret Country*, 1986
　　The Secret Country Trilogy - Book 1
Pamela Dean, *The Whim of the Dragon*, 1989
C.S. Lewis, *The Lion, the Witch, and the Wardrobe*,
Shirley Rousseau Murphy, *Medallion of the Black Hound*, 1989
　　Welch Suggs, co-author

4137

STEVEN G. SPRUILL

My Soul to Take

(New York: St. Martin's, 1994)

Story type: Science Fiction (Techno-Thriller; Medical)
Major character(s): Suzannah Lord, Doctor (surgeon); Andrew Dugan, Artist; Jay Mallernee, Journalist
Time period(s): 1990s
Locale(s): Washington, District of Columbia

Summary: Suzannah finds Andrew's request to remove from his brain the implant permitting him to see very disturbing. She had inserted many of the experimental devices while a resident, removal leads to blindness, and FDA approval seems imminent. Unable legally remove to the implant, Suzannah, perhaps the only surgeon capable of saving any sight for the patients if the implants must be removed, finds that the implants indeed cause the user to see the future, and that some government agency wants them, and her.

Other books you might like:
Pat Cadigan, *Fools*, 1992
Pat Cadigan, *Synners*, 1991
Mickey Zucker Reichert, *The Unknown Soldier*, 1994
Mike Resnick, *Soothsayer*, 1991
Kate Wilhelm, *The Clewiston Test*, 1976

4138

STEVEN G. SPRUILL

Rulers of Darkness

(New York: St. Martin's, 1995)

Story type: Horror (Mystery; Vampire Story)
Major character(s): Katie O'Keefe, Doctor (hematologist); Merrick Chapman, Detective, Vampire; Zane Chapman, Vampire
Time period(s): 1990s (1995)
Locale(s): Washington, District of Columbia

Summary: A rash of vampire-type deaths in Washington, D.C. leads to the blowing of the cover of 900-year-old "hemophage" Merrick Chapman, a vampire who has devoted his long existence to tracking down and disposing of other hemophages. The picture is complicated by the revelation that the murderer is Chapman's son Vane, and by the existence of other children Chapman has sired and people he has turned into hemophages in order to save their lives.

Other books you might like:
Mark Burnell, *Glittering Savages*, 1995
Roxanne Longstreet, *The Undead*, 1993
Brian Stableford, *The Empire of Fear*, 1988

4139

DANA STABENOW

Red Planet Run

(New York: Ace, 1995)

Story type: Science Fiction (Family Saga; Adventure)

Series: Star Svensdotter
Major character(s): Esther "Star" Svensdotter, Judge, Space-woman; Helen Ricadonna, Businesswoman; Natasha Quijance, Parent, Storyteller
Time period(s): 2020s
Locale(s): *Outpost*, Spaceship; Mars; Asteroid Belt, Outer Space

Summary: When the first project of Outpost reaches completion, Star realizes that she has failed to overcome the death of her husband 12 years previously. As her team begins to split up and her 16-year-old twins pull one prank too many, Star accepts Helen's request to explore the discovery found in ancient ruins on Mars. However, an old enemy precedes her there, killing all who get in his way.

Other books you might like:
Greg Bear, *Moving Mars*, 1993
David Brin, *Glory Season*, 1993
Arthur C. Clarke, *The Sands of Mars*, 1952
Kim Stanley Robinson, *Green Mars*, 1994
Kim Stanley Robinson, *Red Mars*, 1993

4140

DANA STABENOW

Second Star

(New York: Ace, 1991)

Story type: Science Fiction (Space Colony)
Major character(s): ARCHY, Artificial Intelligence; Esther Elizabeth Quijance-Turgenev, Child (mute); Esther "Star" Svensdotter, Administrator (Space Colony)
Time period(s): 2010s
Locale(s): Ellfive, Space Station; Copernicus, Moon (Earth's)

Summary: After fifteen years of construction, Ellfive is weeks from receiving its first shipment of colonists. Star Svensdotter, in charge from the beginning of construction, realizes a take-over attempt could occur before any colonists arrive. Conditions on Earth are worsening and it's rumored that another message from Betelgeuse has been intercepted by the Russians on Mars.

Other books you might like:
Roger MacBride Allen, *The Ring of Charon*, 1990
C.J. Cherryh, *Rimrunners*, 1989
Vonda N. McIntyre, *Starfarers*, 1989
Paul Preuss, *Starfire*, 1988
Mack Reynolds, *Chaos in Lagrangia*, 1984
Mack Reynolds, *Lagrange Five*, 1979
Allen Steele, *Clarke County, Space*, 1990
Allen Steele, *Orbital Decay*, 1989

4141

BRIAN STABLEFORD

The Angel of Pain

(New York: Carroll & Graf, 1993)

Story type: Horror (Apocalyptic Horror)
Major character(s): David Lydyard, Scientist; Cordelia Lydyard, Housewife; James Austen, Doctor

Time period(s): 1890s (1893)
Locale(s): London, England

Summary: In this sequel to the author's *The Werewolves of London*, David Lydyard, some twenty years after the events chronicled in that book, is still afflicted by dream visions of the unearthly creatures known to most human beings only through the merciful veil of myth and legend. In his efforts to understand them, David becomes embroiled in their internecine wars and is used as one of several human pawns whose conflicts with other human beings portend cataclysms of cosmic proportions.

Other books you might like:
Ramsey Campbell, *Midnight Sun*, 1991
H.P. Lovecraft, *At the Mountains of Madness and Other Novels*, 1964
Kim Newman, *Sago*, 1991

4142

BRIAN STABLEFORD

The Carnival of Destruction

(New York: Carroll & Graf, 1994)

Story type: Horror (Apocalyptic Horror)
Major character(s): Anatole Daumier, Military Personnel (soldier); David Lydyard, Scientist; Jacob Harkender, Supernatural Being
Time period(s): 1910s (1918)
Locale(s): Paris, France; London, England

Summary: As World War I grinds to its bloody finish and the end of the world seems imminent, the five fallen angels who have pulled the strings behind events in the author's earlier novels *The Werewolves of London* and *The Angel of Pain* begin jockeying for power. This ambitious novel has them marshaling their human consorts and supernatural creations to fight climactic battles, and awaiting the revelation of the identities of two other angels which will determine how the balance of power shall fall.

Other books you might like:
Clive Barker, *Everville*, 1994
Clive Barker, *The Great and Secret Show*, 1990
Stephen King, *The Stand*, 1978
Robert R. McCammon, *Swan Song*, 1987
Anne Rice, *Memnoch the Devil*, 1995
Alan Rodgers, *Fire*, 1992

4143

BRIAN STABLEFORD

The Empire of Fear

(New York: Carroll & Graf, 1991)

Story type: Horror (Vampire Story)
Major character(s): Noell Cordery, Scientist; Richard Lionheart, Royalty (king of Grand Normandy); Vlad Tepes, Warrior, Vampire (Dracula)
Time period(s): 18th century
Locale(s): New Normandy, Fictional Country

Summary: In an alternate universe, nobles and world leaders are Machiavellian vampires who subjugate the masses by manipulating their superstitions. Convinced that there is a scientific basis by which vampirism can be understood and neutralized, and determined to avenge his father's death at the hands of the vampire court of New Normandy, Noell Cordery sets off for Africa, reputed site of the vampires' origins, all the while pursued by a vampire armada that would suppress his discoveries. This novel was originally published in England in 1988.

Other books you might like:
Les Daniels, *The Chronicles of Don Sebastian*, 1978-1990
Anne Rice, *The Vampire Chronicles*, 1976-1988
Michael Romkey, *I, Vampire*, 1990
Chelsea Quinn Yarbro, *The Saint-Germain Chronicles*, 1983

4144
BRIAN STABLEFORD

The Hunger and Ecstasy of Vampires
(Shingletown, California: Mark V. Ziesing, 1996)

Story type: Horror (Vampire Story; Science Fiction)
Major character(s): Edward Copplestone, Scientist; Oscar Wilde, Writer, Historical Figure; Count Lugard, Nobleman
Time period(s): 1890s (1895)
Locale(s): London, England

Summary: In this mixture of fantasy and the classic scientific romance, a gentleman's club whose members include H.G. Wells, Oscar Wilde, M.P. Shiel, and other writers and thinkers of the Victorian era convenes one night to hear scientist Edward Copplestone tell of three drug-induced trances in which he travelled into the far future and discovered mankind under the rule of benevolent vampires who have helped save the human species from itself. Unknown to those gathered, one in their midst who hears this story will be instrumental in engineering this future.

Other books you might like:
Emmanuel Carrere, *Gothic Romance*, 1990
Kim Newman, *Anno Dracula*, 1992
Kathryn Ptacek, *In Silence Sealed*, 1988
H.G. Wells, *The Time Machine*, 1895

4145
BRIAN STABLEFORD

The Innsmouth Heritage
(West Warwick, Rhode Island: Necronomicon Press, 1992)

Story type: Horror (Science Fiction)
Major character(s): Ann Eliot, Writer; David Stevenson, Scientist (biochemist); Gideon Sargent, Fisherman
Time period(s): 1990s
Locale(s): Innsmouth, Massachusetts
Summary: In this sequel to H.P. Lovecraft's classic novella, ''The Shadow over Innsmouth,'' David Stevenson arrives in Innsmouth to study the genetic heritage of the Innsmouth natives, convinced that he will find their peculiar physical

traits and degeneration a byproduct of inbreeding. Instead, he finds evidence that suggests forces more supernatural than scientifically provable may be involved.

Other books you might like:
Steve Rasnic Tem, *Decoded Mirrors: Three Tales after Lovecraft*, 1992
F. Paul Wilson, *The Barrens*, 1992

4146
BRIAN STABLEFORD

The Walking Shadow
(New York: Carroll & Graff, 1989)

Story type: Science Fiction (Time Travel)
Major character(s): Paul Heisenberg, Religious (Evangelist); Adam Wishart, Public Relations
Time period(s): Indeterminate Future
Locale(s): Earth

Summary: Evangelist Paul Heisenberg appears to have the ability to move himself and his disciples through time, purely through the power of prayer. Originally published in 1979.

Other books you might like:
Mike McQuay, *Memories*, 1987
Michael Moorcock, *Behold the Man*, 1964
James Morrow, *Only Begotten Daughter*, 1990
Ted Reynolds, *The Tides of God*, 1989
Robert Silverberg, *The Masks of Time*, 1968

4147
BRIAN STABLEFORD

The Werewolves of London
(New York: Carroll & Graf, 1992)

Story type: Horror (Werewolf Story; Ancient Evil Unleashed)
Major character(s): David Lydyard, Young Man; Sir Edward Tellentyre, Scientist; Gabriel Gill, Child
Time period(s): 1870s (1872)
Locale(s): London, England; Egypt

Summary: While travelling through a burial site in Egypt David Lydyard falls victim to a snake bite that induces apocalyptic visions. At the same time, Gabriel Gill is abducted from a London orphanage by a group of Shapeshifters who hope to exploit his nascent occult powers. Together, Lydyard's and Gill's experiences serve as portents of an ancient and immortal force erupting into our dimension and threatening the world. This novel was originally published in England in 1990.

Other books you might like:
Daniel Easterman, *Name of the Beast*, 1992

4148

MICHAEL A. STACKPOLE

Evil Ascending

(Bloomington, Illinois: GDW Books, 1991)

Story type: Science Fiction (Invasion of Earth; Mystery)
Series: Fiddleback Trilogy
Major character(s): Tycho Caine, Amnesiac, Imposter
Time period(s): 21st century
Locale(s): Kanggenpo, Tibet; Tokyo, Japan

Summary: Investigating the invasion of Earth by Fiddleback, a monstrous intelligence from another dimension, Tycho Caine takes the name of his benefactor, Coyote, and sends Sinclair MacNeal to Tokyo to find Fiddleback's training school for assassins. Caine travels to Tibet to recover his memory and mastery of his skills while Rajani, reawakened from suspended animation, pursues her own goal of repelling Fiddleback's invasion. This novel is set in the universe of the roleplaying game *Dark Conspiracy*.

Other books you might like:
William Adams, *The Unwound Way*, 1991
Marc Laidlaw, *Neon Lotus*, 1988
Frank M. Robinson, *The Dark Beyond the Stars*, 1991
Elizabeth Ann Scarborough, *Nothing Sacred*, 1991
Michael Swanwick, *Vacuum Flowers*, 1987

4149

MICHAEL A. STACKPOLE

Evil Triumphant

(Bloomington, Illinois: GDW Books, 1992)

Story type: Science Fiction (Invasion of Earth; Adventure)
Series: Fiddleback Trilogy
Major character(s): Tycho Caine, Criminal (assassin), Hero; Damon Crowley, Warrior, Hero; Nicholas "Pygmalion" Hunt, Mythical Creature (Dark Lord)
Time period(s): 2010s (2010)
Locale(s): Phoenix, Arizona; Titan's Dimension, Mythical Place

Summary: Through many dimensions Coyote, Crowley and Jyette struggle and treacherously change alliances to prevent Pygmalion, Fiddleback and other Dark Lords from capturing the greatest prize, Earth. Set in the universe of the roleplaying game, *Dark Conspiracy*.

Other books you might like:
Alan Dean Foster, *Cyber Way*, 1990
Alan Dean Foster, *To the Vanishing Point*, 1988
Marc Laidlaw, *Neon Lotus*, 1988
Elizabeth Ann Scarborough, *Final Refuge*, 1992

4150

MICHAEL A. STACKPOLE

A Gathering Evil

(Bloomington, Illinois: GDW Books, 1991)

Story type: Science Fiction (Invasion of Earth; Mystery)

Series: Fiddleback Trilogy
Major character(s): Tycho Caine, Amnesiac
Time period(s): 21st century
Locale(s): Phoenix, Arizona

Summary: When Tycho Caine wakes up in a body bag, ready to supply parts for transplantation, he has to overcome his captors and escape before beginning the search for his lost memory and mission. His quest leads from the poverty-stricken ground-level Phoenix into the restricted city above, where he learns his employer may have double-crossed him with deadly intent. This novel is set in the universe of the roleplaying game *Dark Conspiracy*.

Other books you might like:
William Adams, *The Unwound Way*, 1991
    Cecil Brooks, co-author
Jeffrey A. Carver, *From a Changeling Star*, 1989
Dave Duncan, *Hero*, 1991
Frank M. Robinson, *The Dark Beyond the Stars*, 1991
Michael Swanwick, *Vacuum Flowers*, 1987

4151

MICHAEL A. STACKPOLE

Once a Hero

(New York: Bantam Spectra, 1994)

Story type: Fantasy (Adventure; Political)
Major character(s): Neal "Dun Wolf" Roclawzi, Warrior; Genevera "Gena", Mythical Creature (elf), Warrior; Aarundel, Mythical Creature (elf), Warrior
Time period(s): Indeterminate
Locale(s): Skirren, Planet—Imaginary; Ispar, Fictional Country; Elven Holdings, Fictional Country

Summary: With his deadly sword, Neal Roclawzi helps free humanity from tyrannical Reithrese rule, reconciling feuding families and bringing about a unified government. When disharmony threatens 500 years later, Gena brings Neal to life from his ensorcelled tomb to help save the empire.

Other books you might like:
Robert N. Charrette, *A Prince Among Men*, 1994
Glen Cook, *The Black Company*, 1984
David Eddings, *Pawn of Prophecy*, 1982
Mary Gentle, *Rats and Gargoyles*, 1991
Terry Goodkind, *Wizard's First Rule*, 1994
Simon Hawke, *The Wizard of Camelot*, 1993
P.C. Hodgell, *God Stalk*, 1982
Robert Jordan, *The Eye of the World*, 1989
Dennis L. McKiernan, *The Eye of the Hunter*, 1992

4152

MICHAEL A. STACKPOLE

Rogue Squadron

(New York: Bantam Spectra, 1996)

Story type: Science Fiction (Military; Space Opera)
Series: Star Wars: X-Wing

Major character(s): Wedge Antilles, Military Personnel, Pilot (X-wing fighter); Corran Horn, Military Personnel, Pilot (X-wing fighter)
Time period(s): Indeterminate Past
Locale(s): Galactic Empire, Interstellar Empire/Federation; New Republic, Interstellar Empire/Federation

Summary: Determined to defend the fledgling New Republic from the mighty Galactic Empire, Wedge Antilles organizes Rogue Squadron, a force of X-wing fighters piloted by the best warriors. However, the Rogue Squadron may meet its match when orders send them to assault the Imperial stronghold of Black Moon.

Other books you might like:
Roger MacBride Allen, *Ambush at Corellia*, 1995
Kevin J. Anderson, *Jedi Search*, 1994
George Lucas, *The Star Wars Trilogy*, 1987
   Donald F. Glut, James Kahn, co-authors
Steve Perry, *Shadows of the Empire*, 1996
Timothy Zahn, *Heir to the Empire*, 1991

4153

KATHLYN S. STARBUCK

India's Story
(New York: HarperPrism, 1995)

Story type: Science Fiction (Psychic Powers; Political)
Major character(s): India Gilbert, Psychic (esper), Student; Anara, Innkeeper, Teacher; Mama, Monster, Mythical Creature (arachnid)
Time period(s): Indeterminate Future
Locale(s): Giles Three, Planet—Imaginary (Orion Sector); No-Place, Mythical Place (interdimensional plane); Continental Americas, Fictional Country

Summary: India grows up as the abused daughter of a big-time criminal. Her psychic abilities tapped and blocked by an unknown Agency, India makes her way past Mama to the inn between dimensions managed by Anara. At the inn, India begins to regain some memories and some psychic powers, but the threat remains. India must uncover the plot against her to regain her strength and identity. Originally published in the United Kingdom in 1993.

Other books you might like:
Jeffrey A. Carver, *Down the Stream of Stars*, 1990
John DeChancie, *Castle Perilous*, 1988
Alan Dean Foster, *To the Vanishing Point*, 1988
Anne McCaffrey, *To Ride Pegasus*, 1973
Michaela Roessner, *Vanishing Point*, 1993

4154

STARHAWK (Pseudonym of Miriam Simos)

The Fifth Sacred Thing
(New York: Bantam, 1993)

Story type: Fantasy (Post-Disaster; Psychic Powers)
Major character(s): Maya, Religious, Grandparent; Madrone, Healer, Revolutionary; Bird, Revolutionary, Leader
Time period(s): 2040s (2048)

Locale(s): California

Summary: In an ecologically transformed 21st century, the nation state in Northern California esteems harmony with the environment while the regime of religious extremists in Southern California fosters repression of women and control of scarce vital resources. When Bird escapes prison and returns to the North with news of an impending attack from the South, Madrone travels south to help resistance forces and attempts to discover a cure for the plagues she thinks originated as an attack from the southerners. First novel.

Other books you might like:
David Brin, *Earth*, 1990
Jennifer DiMarco, *Escape to the Wind*, 1991
Suzette Haden Elgin, *Native Tongue*, 1984
Steve Erickson, *Arc d'X*, 1993
Marc Laidlaw, *Kalifornia*, 1993
Pat Murphy, *The City, Not Long After*, 1989
Larry Niven, *Fallen Angels*, 1991
   Jerry Pournelle, Michael Flynn, co-authors
Joan Slonczewski, *A Door into Ocean*, 1986
Jean Stewart, *Return to Isis*, 1992
Sheri S. Tepper, *The Gate to Women's Country*, 1988
Karen Wehrstein, *Lion's Heart*, 1991
Karen Wehrstein, *Lion's Soul*, 1991

4155

ED STARK, Editor

Mysterious Cairo
(Honesdale, Pennsylvania: West End Games, 1992)

Story type: Fantasy (Anthology)
Series: Torg: The Possibility Wars
Time period(s): 21st century
Locale(s): Nile Empire, Alternate Earth (Cairo)

Summary: This volume contains an eight-page introduction by Ed Stark plus 11 stories by six authors sharing a modern world combining elements of ancient Egypt and 1930s heroic pulp fiction. Set in the universe of the game, *Torg*.

Other books you might like:
George Alec Effinger, *When Gravity Fails*, 1987
Greg Farshtey, *Strange Tales From the Nile Empire*, 1992
   Greg Gorden and Ed Stark, co-editors
Douglas Kaufman, *Dragons over England*, 1992
   Ed Stark, co-editor
Will Shetterly, *Liavek*, 1985
   Emma Bull, co-editor
Will Shetterly, *Liavek: Wizard's Row*, 1987
   Emma Bull, co-editor
Bill Slavicsek, *Storm Knights*, 1990
   C.J. Tramontana, co-author

4156

JIM STARLIN
DAINA GRAZIUNAS, Co-Author

Among Madmen
(New York: Roc, 1990)

Story type: Science Fiction (Post-Holocaust)
Major character(s): Tom Laker, Lawman (sheriff); Maria Laker, Spouse, Murderer
Time period(s): 1990s (1990)
Locale(s): Shandaken County, New York

Summary: A mysterious disease afflicts people at random, causing some to fall into comas and others to become killers. Sheriff Tom Laker tries to provide law and order to a small rural community as civilization slowly falls apart.

Other books you might like:
Frank Herbert, *The White Plague*, 1982
Brian Lumley, *Necroscope*, 1988
Richard Matheson, *I Am Legend*, 1954
Walter M. Miller Jr., *A Canticle for Leibowitz*, 1960
David R. Palmer, *Emergence*, 1984
Roger Zelazny, *This Immortal*, 1966

4157

JIM STARLIN
DAINA GRAZIUNAS, Co-Author

Lady El
(New York: Roc, 1992)

Story type: Science Fiction (Alternate Intelligence; Hard Science Fiction)
Major character(s): Walter "Walt" Hillerman, Scientist, Computer Expert; Arlene "Lady El" Washington, Artificial Intelligence, Experimental Subject
Time period(s): 1990s
Locale(s): New York, New York; Washington, District of Columbia (the Pentagon)

Summary: Killed in a subway accident, Arlene regains consciousness only to discover her brain, complete with personality, now acts as the core of a sophisticated biological/mechanical supercomputer. Horrified to find Arlene's personality intact with her brain, Walt conspires with Arlene to hide her consciousness while she assumes military and scientific tasks, creating monumental intuitive breakthroughs in fundamental science. However, Arlene's solitary attachment to Walt soon creates problems.

Other books you might like:
Pat Cadigan, *Fools*, 1992
Pat Cadigan, *Synners*, 1991
Robert A. Heinlein, *The Moon Is a Harsh Mistress*, 1966
Victor Milan, *The Cybernetic Samurai*, 1986
Rudy Rucker, *Software*, 1982
Cordwainer Smith, *Norstrilia*, 1975
Thomas T. Thomas, *ME: A Novel of Self Discovery*, 1991

4158

CHRISTOPHER STASHEFF, Editor
BILL FAWCETT, Co-Editor

Blessings and Curses
(New York: Ace, 1992)

Story type: Fantasy (Anthology)
Series: Crafter Family
Time period(s): 18th century; 19th century
Locale(s): Canada; New England

Summary: Contains a prolog by Bill Fawcett plus 11 stories original to this shared history anthology of Crafter Family tales set between 1784 and 1865. Contributing authors are Judith R. Conly, Barbara Delaplace, Ru Emerson, Esther Friesner, Morgan Llywelyn, Morris G. McGee, Jody Lynn Nye, Robert Sheckley, Christopher Stasheff, Brian M. Thomsen and Wendy Wheeler.

Other books you might like:
Robert Asprin, *Thieves' World*, 1979
    editor
Harlan Ellison, *Medea: Harlan's World*, 1985
    editor
Martin H. Greenberg, *After the King: Stories in Honor of J.R.R. Tolkien*, 1992
    editor
George R.R. Martin, *Wild Cards*, 1987
    editor
Will Shetterly, *Liavek*, 1985
    Emma Bull, co-editor
Terri Windling, *Life on the Border*, 1991
    editor

4159

CHRISTOPHER STASHEFF

A Company of Stars
(New York: Ballantine/Del Rey, 1991)

Story type: Science Fiction (Adventure)
Series: Starship Troupers
Major character(s): Ramou Lazarian, Spaceman, Student; Horace Burbage, Actor; Suzanne Souci, Actress
Time period(s): 26th century
Locale(s): New York, New York

Summary: Ramou Lazarian, fleeing a forced marriage, comes to New York where he is mugged and then falls in with a company of actors who are planning a tour of the colonies. Elector Rudders wants to stop all theater, which he considers immoral, while Ramou's ex-girlfriend's father has detectives hot on his trail. Moving the departure day up, the company manages to hire a captain and escape from Port Newark one step ahead of detectives, process servers and Elector Rudders' men.

Other books you might like:
Terry Bisson, *Voyage to the Red Planet*, 1990
Jeffrey A. Carver, *Down the Stream of Stars*, 1990
Robert A. Heinlein, *Double Star*, 1956
Barry B. Longyear, *Circus World*, 1980

Barry B. Longyear, *City of Baraboo*, 1980
Barry B. Longyear, *Elephant Song*, 1982
Mike Resnick, *The Best Rootin' Tootin' Shootin' Gunslinger in the Whole Damned Galaxy*, 1983
Mike Resnick, *Sideshow*, 1982
Mike Resnick, *The Three-Legged Hootch Dancer*, 1983
Mike Resnick, *The Wild Alien Tamer*, 1983
Jack Vance, *Space Opera*, 1965

4160

CHRISTOPHER STASHEFF, Editor
BILL FAWCETT, Co-Editor

The Crafters
(New York: Ace, 1991)

Story type: Fantasy (Anthology)
Series: Crafter Family
Time period(s): 17th century (1680s); 18th century
Locale(s): New England, American Colonies; England

Summary: This volume contains a prolog and epilog by Bill Fawcett plus 10 stories original to this first ''shared world''-type anthology which relates tales of the Crafter Family between 1682 and 1845 as they appear in the family archives. Authors contributing include Ru Emerson, Esther Friesner, Katherine Kurtz, Morgan Llywelyn, Jody Lynn Nye, Robert Sheckley and Christopher Stasheff. There is and one collaborative work by Anna O'Connell and Doug Houseman.

Other books you might like:
Robert Asprin, *Thieves' World*, 1979
    editor
Harlan Ellison, *Medea: Harlan's World*, 1985
    editor
Bill Fawcett, *The Siege of Arista*, 1991
Martin H. Greenberg, *After the King: Stories in Honor of J.R.R. Tolkien*, 1992
    editor
George R.R. Martin, *Wild Cards*, 1987
    editor
Will Shetterly, *Liavek*, 1985
    Emma Bull, co-editor
Will Shetterly, *Liavek: Festival Week*, 1990
    Emma Bull, co-editor
Will Shetterly, *Liavek: The Players of Luck*, 1986
    Emma Bull, co-editor
Will Shetterly, *Liavek: Spells of Binding*, 1988
    Emma Bull, co-editor
Will Shetterly, *Liavek: Wizard's Row*, 1987
    Emma Bull, co-editor
Terri Windling, *Borderland*, 1986
    Mark Alan Arnold, co-editor
Terri Windling, *Bordertown*, 1986
    Mark Alan Arnold, co-editor
Terri Windling, *Life on the Border*, 1991
    editor

4161

CHRISTOPHER STASHEFF

M'Lady Witch
(New York: Ace, 1994)

Story type: Fantasy (Adventure; Psychic Powers)
Series: Warlock
Major character(s): Cordelia Gallowglass, Witch, Noblewoman; Alain, Royalty; Geoffrey Gallowglass, Warlock, Nobleman
Time period(s): Indeterminate Future
Locale(s): Gramarye, Planet—Imaginary

Summary: When Prince Alain decides to woo Lady Cordelia, he discovers her penchant for excitement.

Other books you might like:
Lois McMaster Bujold, *The Spirit Ring*, 1992
Sharon Green, *Silver Princess, Golden Knight*, 1993
Josepha Sherman, *Child of Faerie, Child of Earth*, 1992
Martha Wells, *The Element of Fire*, 1993
Patricia C. Wrede, *Dealing with Dragons*, 1990

4162

CHRISTOPHER STASHEFF

The Oathbound Wizard
(New York: Ballantine Del Rey, 1993)

Story type: Fantasy (Light Fantasy; Alternate World)
Major character(s): Matt, Wizard, Fiance(e); Narlh, Mythical Creature (dragon/gryphon chimera), Adventurer; Robin Hood, Hero, Outlaw
Time period(s): Indeterminate
Locale(s): Planet—Imaginary; Ibile, Fictional Country; Ys, Fictional Country

Summary: When Matt discovers he lacks the kingdom necessary to attain marriage to Queen Alisande, Matt's hasty oath drives him inevitably toward winning his kingdom from evil King Gordogrosso. Matt enlists the help of Narlh, Robin Hood's band and others in his pun-filled adventure. Sequel to *Her Majesty's Wizard*.

Other books you might like:
Piers Anthony, *A Spell for Chameleon*, 1977
Robert Asprin, *Another Fine Myth*, 1978
C. Dale Brittain, *Mage Quest*, 1993
L. Sprague de Camp, *The Enchanter Reborn*, 1992
    Christopher Stasheff, co-author
Suzette Haden Elgin, *Twelve Fair Kingdoms*, 1981
John Moore, *Slay and Rescue*, 1993

4163

CHRISTOPHER STASHEFF

Quicksilver's Knight
(New York: Ace, 1995)

Story type: Fantasy (Psychic Powers; Science Fiction)
Series: Warlock

Major character(s): Geoffrey Gallowglass, Warlock, Nobleman; Jane ''Quicksilver'', Outlaw, Psychic; Finister ''Moraga'', Agent (S.P.I.T.E.), Psychic
Time period(s): Indeterminate Future
Locale(s): Gramarye, Planet—Imaginary

Summary: Geoffrey rides off to capture Quicksilver, the leader of an outlaw band who has killed the Old Count Laeg and taken control of his land. But having accomplished his mission, he listens to Quicksilver's story of Laeg's oppression of the peasants and agrees to help her argue the justice of her cause before the King and Queen. However, the agent for S.P.I.T.E. (Society for the Prevention of Integration of Telepathic Entities) hopes to lure him away from his task.

Other books you might like:
C.J. Cherryh, *The Paladin*, 1988
Sharon Green, *Silver Princess, Golden Knight*, 1993
Barbara Hambly, *The Ladies of Mandrigyn*, 1984
C.L. Moore, *Jirel of Joiry*, 1969
Elizabeth Ann Scarborough, *Bronwyn's Bane*, 1983

4164
CHRISTOPHER STASHEFF

The Sage
(New York: Ballantine Del Rey, 1996)

Story type: Fantasy (Magic Conflict; Quest)
Series: Star Stone
Major character(s): Culaehra, Warrior, Adventurer; Yocote, Shaman, Mythical Creature (gnome); Ohaern, Warrior, Blacksmith
Time period(s): Indeterminate
Locale(s): Fictional Country

Summary: When the offspring of his vanquished enemy sows discord among the lesser races, Ohaern begins molding Culaehra from a selfish ruffian into the warrior needed to defeat the new threat. To assure victory Ohaern must first locate the Star Stone and forge it into an effective weapon for the transformed Culaehra. Set 500 years after *The Shaman*.

Other books you might like:
Greg Bear, *Songs of Earth and Power*, 1994
Dave Duncan, *Emperor and Clown*, 1992
David Gemmell, *Morningstar*, 1993
Mary Gentle, *Rats and Gargoyles*, 1991
Robert Jordan, *The Eye of the World*, 1990

4165
CHRISTOPHER STASHEFF

The Secular Wizard
(New York: Ballantine Del Rey, 1995)

Story type: Fantasy (Alternate World; Magic Conflict)
Series: Wizard in Rhyme
Major character(s): Matt Mantrell, Wizard, Minstrel; Boncorro, Ruler (king), Wizard; Arouetto, Scholar
Time period(s): Indeterminate Past
Locale(s): Latruria, Fictional Country; Merovence, Fictional Country

Summary: Hearing mixed news concerning the new king of Latruria, Matt Mantrell decides to travel south to reconnoiter. He finds that the people, freed of toil, flock to the city, becoming the prey of thieves and pimps. Matt meets with King Boncorro and continues his adventures as the forces of humanism and secular government gain influence.

Other books you might like:
Piers Anthony, *Dragon's Gold*, 1987
    Robert E. Margroff, co-author
Lois McMaster Bujold, *The Spirit Ring*, 1992
L. Sprague de Camp, *The Pixilated Peeress*, 1991
    Catherine Crook de Camp, co-author
Guy Gavriel Kay, *A Song for Arbonne*, 1993
Katherine Kurtz, *The Bastard Prince*, 1994
R.A. MacAvoy, *Damiano's Lute*, 1984
Fletcher Pratt, *The Blue Star*, 1969
Judith Tarr, *Ars Magica*, 1989

4166
CHRISTOPHER STASHEFF

The Shaman
(New York: Ballantine Del Rey, 1995)

Story type: Fantasy (Magic Conflict; Adventure)
Series: Star Stone
Major character(s): Ohaern, Warrior, Hunter; Lomallin, Immortal, Mythical Creature (Ulin); Ulahane, Shaman, Mythical Creature (Ulin)
Time period(s): Indeterminate
Locale(s): Fictional Country

Summary: Ohaern helps Lomallin as he battles Ulahane and his campaign against humans, using many unpleasant creatures he creates and looses on humanity.

Other books you might like:
Margaret Ball, *The Shadow Gate*, 1991
Greg Bear, *Songs of Earth and Power*, 1994
Nancy Varian Berberick, *The Panther's Hoard*, 1994
Mary Gentle, *Rats and Gargoyles*, 1991
Mark C. Perry, *Morigu: The Dead*, 1990

4167
CHRISTOPHER STASHEFF

Warlock and Son
(New York: Ace, 1991)

Story type: Science Fiction (Young Adult; Adventure)
Series: Warlock
Major character(s): Rod Gallowglass, Warlock; Magnus Gallowglass d'Armand, Warlock
Time period(s): 31st century
Locale(s): Gramarye, Planet—Imaginary

Summary: Feeling hemmed in at home, Magnus decides to wander about Gramarye to find himself. Rod, fearing for his son, follows at a distance. After several adventures, Magnus encounters a maid who robs him of his will to live. When cured, he decides to leave Gramarye, not knowing that agents of S.P.I.T.E. have engineered his problems.

Other books you might like:
Piers Anthony, *A Spell for Chameleon*, 1977
Robert Asprin, *Another Fine Myth*, 1978
Jack L. Chalker, *The River of Dancing Gods*, 1984
Alan Dean Foster, *Spellsinger*, 1983

4168

CHRISTOPHER STASHEFF

The Warlock Insane

(New York: Ace Books, 1989)

Story type: Fantasy (Light Fantasy)
Series: Warlock
Major character(s): Rod Gallowglass, Warlock; Fess, Robot (Robot Horse)
Time period(s): 31st century
Locale(s): Gramarye, Fictional Country

Summary: On a planet where magic appears to work, though it's all actually psychic phenomena, Rod Gallowglass, the famed Warlock, begins to have hallucinations and apparently goes mad. Wandering the forest he has amazing encounters with characters out of *Don Quixote* and *Orlando Furioso*. It's all a trick, of course, and he eventually saves the day with the help of his robot horse, Fess, and his psychically endowed wife and children.

Other books you might like:
Piers Anthony, *Out of Phaze*, 1987
Piers Anthony, *Robot Adept*, 1988
Piers Anthony, *Unicorn Point*, 1989
F. Paul Wilson, *The Tery*, 1990

4169

CHRISTOPHER STASHEFF

The Warlock Rock

(New York: Ace, 1990)

Story type: Science Fiction (Fantasy; Humor)
Series: Warlock
Major character(s): Rod Gallowglass, Warlock; Fess, Robot (robot horse); Gwen Gallowglass, Witch
Time period(s): 31st century
Locale(s): Gramarye, Planet—Imaginary

Summary: Rod, Fess, Gwen and their family venture forth in search of puns and the source of the dangerous rock music which is enslaving the minds of susceptible young listeners.

Other books you might like:
Piers Anthony, *Out of Phaze*, 1987
Piers Anthony, *Robot Adept*, 1988
Piers Anthony, *Unicorn Point*, 1989
F. Paul Wilson, *The Tery*, 1990

4170

CHRISTOPHER STASHEFF

We Open on Venus

(New York: Ballantine Del Rey, 1994)

Story type: Science Fiction (Humor; Arts)
Series: Starship Troupers
Major character(s): Ramou Lazarian, Spaceman (ensign), Student (theater); Suzanne Souci, Actress; Barry Tallendar, Director (theater)
Time period(s): 26th century
Locale(s): New Venus, Planet—Imaginary

Summary: The Star Company leaves New York in the nick of time, just before the Lords prevent them from touring the colonies. On New Venus, where they open with *Macbeth*, owning cigarettes or fire starting equipment results in the death penalty, since the planet, owned by an oil company, could be flammable.

Other books you might like:
Terry Bisson, *Voyage to the Red Planet*, 1990
L. Sprague de Camp, *The Swords of Zinjaban*, 1991
    Catherine Crook de Camp, co-author
John DeChancie, *Starrigger*, 1983
Kate Elliott, *An Earthly Crown*, 1993
Colin Greenland, *Take Back Plenty*, 1992
Robert A. Heinlein, *Double Star*, 1956

4171

CHRISTOPHER STASHEFF

The Witch Doctor

(New York: Ballantine Del Rey, 1994)

Story type: Fantasy (Alternate World; Magic Conflict)
Series: Wizard in Rhyme
Major character(s): Saul Bremener, Wizard; Frisson, Writer (poet); Suettay, Ruler (queen)
Time period(s): Indeterminate Past
Locale(s): Allustria, Fictional Country

Summary: Bitten by a spider, Saul Bremener awakens to find himself a wizard in a land of dichotomous good and evil, which one must choose between. Told by his guardian angel that he must free Allustria from its evil ruler, the doubtful Saul gathers a band of followers and sets out to discover how things work.

Other books you might like:
Gordon R. Dickson, *The Dragon and the George*, 1976
Fletcher Pratt, *The Blue Star*, 1958
Clifford D. Simak, *The Fellowship of the Talisman*, 1978
Paula Volsky, *Illusion*, 1992
Chelsea Quinn Yarbro, *Ariosto*, 1980

4172

CHRISTOPHER STASHEFF

A Wizard in Absentia
(New York: Ace, 1993)

Story type: Science Fiction (Political; Robot Fiction)
Series: Warlock
Major character(s): Magnus Gallowglass d'Armand, Adventurer, Psychic (esper); Fess, Robot (robot horse); Ian Tobinson, Companion
Time period(s): 31st century
Locale(s): Maxima, Asteroid; Taxhaven, Planet—Imaginary

Summary: Curious about his family and heritage, Magnus visits the ancestral d'Armand asteroid with Fess, which he sends back to Gramarye after receiving his own robot from relatives. Magnus becomes interested in the Society for the Conversion of Extraterrestrial Nascent Totalitarianisms and sets off to bring enlightenment to the serfs of a society modeled on late 17th century French culture.

Other books you might like:
Steve Perry, *The Man Who Never Missed*, 1985
Alis A. Rasmussen, *A Passage of Stars*, 1990
Alis A. Rasmussen, *The Price of Ransom*, 1990
Alis A. Rasmussen, *Revolution's Shore*, 1990
Melissa Scott, *Dreamships*, 1992

4173

CHRISTOPHER STASHEFF

A Wizard in Mind
(New York: Tor, 1995)

Story type: Science Fiction (Psychic Powers; Family Saga)
Series: Warlock
Major character(s): Magnus Gallowglass d'Armand, Wizard, Revolutionary; Gianni Braccalese, Businessman; Medallia, Spy
Time period(s): Indeterminate Future
Locale(s): Petrarch, Planet—Imaginary

Summary: A wizard and rebel, Magnus d'Armand wants to save the backward Petrarch from the inept meddling of AEGIS (Association for the Elevation of Governmental Institutions and Systems), and the home-grown tyranny of Prince Raginaldi. Impersonating a mercenary soldier, he takes service with Gianni, a wealthy merchant's son, but finds his simple mission complicated by outside forces and another wizard.

Other books you might like:
Alfred Bester, *The Stars My Destination*, 1956
Glen Cook, *Sweet Silver Blues*, 1987
William Goldman, *The Princess Bride*, 1973
Harry Harrison, *The Stainless Steel Rat*, 1961
Ward Moore, *Joyleg*, 1962
   Avram Davidson, co-author
David R. Palmer, *Emergence*, 1984
Terry Pratchett, *Small Gods*, 1994

4174

CHRISTOPHER STASHEFF

A Wizard in War
(New York: Tor, 1995)

Story type: Science Fiction (Political; Psychic Powers)
Series: Rogue Wizard
Major character(s): Magnus Gallowglass d'Armand, Psychic, Warrior; Dirk Dulaine, Sidekick
Time period(s): 31st century
Locale(s): Maltroit, Planet—Imaginary

Summary: Magnus Gallowglass and Dirk Dulaine attempt to initiate democratic reforms on medieval Maltroit, a planet otherwise doomed to repeat all of humanity's Earthly mistakes.

Other books you might like:
Lois McMaster Bujold, *Brothers in Arms*, 1989
Stephen Goldin, *Jade Darcy and the Zen Pirates*, 1990
   Mary Mason, co-author
Robert A. Heinlein, *The Moon Is a Harsh Mistress*, 1966
Alis A. Rasmussen, *Revolution's Shore*, 1990
James H. Schmitz, *The Witches of Karres*, 1966
Allen Steele, *Lunar Descent*, 1991
John Varley, *Demon*, 1984

4175

MICHAEL C. STAUDINGER

The Falcon Rises
(Lake Geneva, Wisconsin: TSR, 1991)

Story type: Fantasy (Alternate World; Magic Conflict)
Major character(s): Roy "Ratha" Arthre, Professor, Magician; Mordeth, Magician, Ruler (usurper); Mithra, Leader
Time period(s): Indeterminate
Locale(s): Shaleth, Fictional Country; Kesh, Fictional Country

Summary: Dragged from Earth to Shaleth by a dying wizard, Roy finds himself mistaken for the wizard, Ratha. With his companions, Roy must harness his new abilities to overcome the evil wizard who has usurped the rule of Shaleth. This is the author's first published book.

Other books you might like:
Pamela Dean, *The Hidden Land*, 1986
Pamela Dean, *The Secret Country*, 1985
Pamela Dean, *The Whim of the Dragon*, 1989
Gordon R. Dickson, *The Dragon and the George*, 1976
Stephen R. Donaldson, *The Illearth War*, 1977
Stephen R. Donaldson, *Lord Foul's Bane*, 1977
Stephen R. Donaldson, *The Power That Preserves*, 1977
Suzette Haden Elgin, *The Grand Jubilee*, 1981
Suzette Haden Elgin, *And Then There'll Be Fireworks*, 1981
Suzette Haden Elgin, *Twelve Fair Kingdoms*, 1981
Christopher Stasheff, *The Warlock in Spite of Himself*, 1969

4176

JOHN STCHUR

Paddywhack

(New York: St. Martin's, 1989)

Story type: Horror (Nature in Revolt)
Major character(s): Jack Lerille, Actor (Former), Librarian (Former); Bruce, Animal (A malevolent dog)
Time period(s): 1980s
Locale(s): Granger, Michigan

Summary: Having lost his jobs in New York City, Jack Lerille takes his family to live in northern Michigan with his maiden Aunt Blanche, owner of a sinister dog. Blanche becomes increasingly strange and the dog increasingly vicious, until they both die. Then the dog returns and becomes really nasty.

Other books you might like:
Stephen King, *Cujo*, 1981

4177

JOHN STEAKLEY

Vampire$

(New York: Roc, 1990)

Story type: Horror (Vampire Story)
Major character(s): Jack Crow, Vampire Hunter; William Charles ''Gunman'' Felix, Vampire Hunter; Simon Kennedy, Vampire
Time period(s): 1990s
Locale(s): Dallas, Texas

Summary: When vampires run amok in your neighborhood, who you gonna call? Vampire$, Inc., the paranormal paramilitary hit squad, led by Jack Crow and the Crow team, who guarantee to put vampires in their place, the ground.

Other books you might like:
Ron Dee, *Blood Lust*, 1990
Ron Dee, *Dusk*, 1991
Robert R. McCammon, *They Thirst*, 1981

4178

MICHAEL STEARNS, Editor

A Starfarer's Dozen

(New York: Harcourt Brace/Jane Yolen Books, 1995)

Story type: Science Fiction (Anthology; Young Adult)

Summary: Contains a two-page introduction, four pages of authors' biographies and 13 original stories reflecting the hope which motivates voyages of exploration. Generally upbeat in tone, the stories encompass a broad range of themes including education, space rescue, dinosaurs, and superheroes, with Debra Doyle and James D. Macdonald collaborating on one story. Other authors include Gregory Feeley, Will Shetterly, Sherwood Smith, Martha Soukup, Nancy Springer, Dave Trowbridge, Lawrence Watt-Evans, and Jane Yolen.

Other books you might like:
Isaac Asimov, *Young Extraterrestrials*, 1984
  Martin H. Greenberg, Charles G. Waugh, co-editors
Groff Conklin, *The Best of Science Fiction*, 1946
  editor
Raymond J. Healy, *Adventures in Time and Space*, 1946
  J. Francis McComas, co-editor
Andre Norton, *Gates to Tomorrow: An Introduction to Science Fiction*, 1973
  Ernestine Donaldy, co-editor
Jane Yolen, *2041: Twelve Short Stories about the Future by Top Science Fiction Writers*, 1991
  editor

4179

MICHAEL STEARNS, Editor

A Wizard's Dozen

(New York: Harcourt Brace, 1993)

Story type: Fantasy (Anthology; Young Adult)

Summary: Contains 13 original stories populated by mythical characters ranging from fairies and a werewolf princess to a midget giant. The adventures include perilous quests, a kidnapping by evil ants and a journey via computer to the world of Faerie. Debra Doyle and James D. Macdonald collaborate on one story with other authors including Bruce Coville, Charles de Lint, Tappan King, Betty Levin, Will Shetterly, Sherwood Smith, Vivian Vande Velde, Patricia C. Wrede and Jane Yolen.

Other books you might like:
Isaac Asimov, *Dragon Tales*, 1982
  Charles G. Waugh, Martin H. Greenberg, co-editors
Lin Carter, *The Young Magicians*, 1969
  editor
Diana Wynne Jones, *Warlock at the Wheel and Other Stories*, 1984
Robin McKinley, *Imaginary Lands*, 1985
  editor
Baird Searles, *Halflings, Hobbits, Warrows & Weefolk: A Collection of Tales of Heroes Short in Stature*, 1991
  Brian Thomsen, co-editor
Jane Yolen, *Shape Shifters: Fantasy and Science Fiction Tales about Humans Who Can Change Their Shapes*, 1978
  editor

4180

ALLEN STEELE

All-American Alien Boy

(Baltimore: Old Earth Books, 1996)

Story type: Science Fiction (Collection)

Summary: Contains a general introduction plus brief individual introductions to 11 stories, ranging from ironic and humorous to dark in tone, with the first book publication of one Hugo Award nominee, ''The Good Rat.'' Themes include space opera, warfare, and medical testing of animals and humans, with hints of Steele's background in journalism shining through.

Other books you might like:
David Brin, *The River of Time*, 1986
John Kessel, *Meeting in Infinity*, 1992
Nancy Kress, *The Aliens of Earth*, 1993
Marc Stiegler, *The Gentle Seduction*, 1990
Connie Willis, *Impossible Things*, 1994

4181

ALLEN STEELE

Clarke County, Space
(New York: Ace, 1990)

Story type: Science Fiction (Political; Adventure)
Major character(s): Henry Bigthorn, Police Officer (sheriff), Indian; Henry Ostrow, Murderer (The Golem); Blind Boy Grunt, Artificial Intelligence
Time period(s): 2040s (2049)
Locale(s): Clarke County, Space Station; Canaveral Pier, Florida

Summary: Sheriff Bigthorn prevents the Golem from killing his victim during an Elvis Presley revival and a local political revolution. A potential nuclear disaster and help from an unknown source further stress the meager police department.

Other books you might like:
Ben Bova, *Colony*, 1978
David Brin, *Earth*, 1990
Robert A. Heinlein, *The Moon Is a Harsh Mistress*, 1966
Melisa C. Michaels, *Pirate Prince*, 1987
Michael Swanwick, *Vacuum Flowers*, 1987

4182

ALLEN STEELE

The Jericho Iteration
(New York: Ace, 1994)

Story type: Science Fiction (Disaster; Mystery)
Major character(s): Gerry Rosen, Journalist; John Tiernan, Journalist
Time period(s): 2010s (April 17-20, 2013)
Locale(s): St. Louis, Missouri

Summary: When Gerry asks John about a misdirected message, John allows Gerry to assist an investigation into Tiptree Corporation's Sentinel Project. After John's murder, Gerry's rash action brings more attention from the martial law forces than Gerry desires.

Other books you might like:
David Brin, *Earth*, 1990
David Brin, *The Postman*, 1985
Larry Niven, *Lucifer's Hammer*, 1977
    Jerry Pournelle, co-author
David R. Palmer, *Emergence*, 1984
John Varley, *Steel Beach*, 1992

4183

ALLEN STEELE

Labyrinth of Night
(New York: Ace, 1992)

Story type: Science Fiction (First Contact; Political)
Series: Near Space Stories
Major character(s): W. J. Boggs, Pilot (U.S.S. Edgar Rice Burroughs); Terrance L'Enfant, Administrator (Cydonia Base); August Nash, Security Officer, Spy (Skycorp's)
Time period(s): 2030s
Locale(s): Arsia Station, Mars; Cydonia Base, Mars; City, Mars (lost city of Mars)

Summary: Investigating a human visage carved into a Martian mesa, explorers discover the City, left by alien colonists millennia earlier. Within a series of pyramids, a labyrinth tests human intelligence and creativity before activating robots which isolate themselves from humans to carry on their alien activity. Many forces battle for control of the Martian mission and access to alien technology.

Other books you might like:
Roger MacBride Allen, *The Ring of Charon*, 1990
Arthur C. Clarke, *The Garden of Rama*, 1991
    Gentry Lee, co-author
Diana G. Gallagher, *The Alien Dark*, 1990
Larry Niven, *Protector*, 1973
Frederik Pohl, *The Gateway Trip: Tales and Vignettes of the Heechee*, 1991
W.J. Stuart, *Forbidden Planet*, 1956

4184

ALLEN STEELE

Lunar Descent
(New York: Ace, 1991)

Story type: Science Fiction (Political; Hard Science Fiction)
Series: Near Space Stories
Major character(s): Lester Riddell, Businessman, Spaceman; "Mighty" Joe Young, Pilot, Spaceman; Willard "Jeremy Schneider" DeWitt, Computer Expert, Businessman
Time period(s): 2020s
Locale(s): Descartes Station, Moon (Earth's)

Summary: Recruited against his will to return to Luna as general manager for Descartes Station, Lester Riddell must win respect, boost morale and restore the construction schedule for Skycorp's new moonbase. His achieving all three does not stop Skycorp from planning to abandon the unprofitable project. When Lester finds himself involved in Labor Action, he turns to DeWitt for help in fabricating a solution.

Other books you might like:
Jeffrey A. Carver, *From a Changeling Star*, 1989
Robert A. Heinlein, *The Moon Is a Harsh Mistress*, 1966
Rudy Rucker, *Wetware*, 1988
John Varley, *Blue Champagne*, 1986
John Varley, *The Persistence of Vision*, 1978
Walter Jon Williams, *Voice of the Whirlwind*, 1988

4185

ALLEN STEELE

Orbital Decay
(New York: Ace, 1989)

Story type: Science Fiction (Hard Science Fiction)
Major character(s): Popeye Hooker, Construction Worker (Beamjack); Virgin Bruce, Construction Worker (Beamjack)
Time period(s): 21st century (2020)
Locale(s): Skycan, Space Station

Summary: A varied crew of astronauts, scientists, and bluecollar construction workers called beamjacks put in long and dangerous hours building a giant solar power satellite. A secret government plot is discovered to use scientific equipment being installed on a neighboring space station for illegal spying and a number of the beamjacks decide to sabotage the equipment.

Other books you might like:
C.J. Cherryh, *Rimrunners*, 1989
Robert A. Heinlein, *Starman Jones*, 1954
Robert A. Heinlein, *Starship Troopers*, 1961
Paul Preuss, *Starfire*, 1988

4186

ALLEN STEELE

Rude Astronauts
(Baltimore: Old Earth Books, 1993)

Story type: Science Fiction (Collection)
Series: Near Space Stories

Summary: Contains a seven-page introduction, one original and six reprinted articles about science or science fiction, and eight stories all published 1985-1992 in periodicals and anthologies. Collection includes the author's first story, "Live From the Mars Hotel," two alternate history stories, three stories set in an astronaut bar and five stories which fit into Steele's Near Space Stories series with his first four novels.

Other books you might like:
Frank Harvey, *Air Force!*, 1959
Robert A. Heinlein, *The Green Hills of Earth*, 1951
Andre Norton, *Space Pioneers*, 1954
  editor
Charles Sheffield, *The McAndrew Chronicles*, 1983
Dan Simmons, *Phases of Gravity*, 1989
John Varley, *Blue Champagne*, 1986

4187

ALLEN STEELE

The Tranquility Alternative
(New York: Ace, 1996)

Story type: Science Fiction (Alternate Universe; Gay/Lesbian Fiction)

Major character(s): Christine Ryder, Pilot (lunar shuttle), Lesbian; Eugene M. Parnell, Spaceman, Leader; Paul Dooley, Imposter, Computer Expert
Time period(s): 1990s
Locale(s): Alternate Earth

Summary: Half a century after Germany's attack on the United States from space sparks rapid space development, economic forces drive the sale of an American Lunar base to German business interests. Sent to decommission Cold War era nuclear weapons left at the abandoned Lunar base, Ryder and Parnell must derail covert plans of crew members aimed at acquiring the weapons from imperialistic expansion.

Other books you might like:
Raphael Carter, *The Fortunate Fall*, 1996
Michael Flynn, *Firestar*, 1996
Michael Flynn, *In the Country of the Blind*, 1990
Robert A. Heinlein, *Double Star*, 1956
David Alexander Smith, *Marathon*, 1982
John Varley, *Steel Beach*, 1992

4188

KEVIN STEIN

Twisted Dragon
(New York: Ace, 1993)

Story type: Fantasy (Political; Sword and Sorcery)
Series: Elfwood
Major character(s): Jaeme, Noblewoman, Warrior; Decutonius, Magician; Laela, Mythical Creature (shapechanger), Magician (Druidic)
Time period(s): Indeterminate
Locale(s): Elfwood, Mythical Place; Albion, Fictional Country

Summary: Four fearless warriors must find the cause of a chilling mist which has descended on Elfwood, tainting the souls of human and elfkind. Uninterrupted, the dark forces will destroy Elfwood in just three days.

Other books you might like:
Lois McMaster Bujold, *The Spirit Ring*, 1992
C.J. Cherryh, *The Goblin Mirror*, 1992
Rose Estes, *Elfwood*, 1992
Barbara Hambly, *The Time of the Dark*, 1982
Robert Jordan, *The Eye of the World*, 1989
Martha Wells, *The Element of Fire*, 1993

4189

JOHN RICHARD STEPHENS, Editor
KIM SMITH, Co-Editor

Mysterious Cat Stories
(New York: Carroll & Graf, 1993)

Story type: Horror (Anthology)

Summary: The authors have compiled 26 tales of horror and fantasy in which cats play a prominent role. Included are August Derleth's tale of a catlike demonic familiar, "Balu"; Robert Bloch's tale of witchcraft, "Catnip"; and H.P. Lovecraft's tale of feline revenge, "The Cats of Ulthar." The book also includes stories by Lilian Jackson Braun, Wilbur Daniel Steele, Algernon Blackwood, and Saki, as well as excerpts from Cervantes' *Don Quixote* and Bram Stoker's *Jewel of the Seven Stars*.

Other books you might like:
Jack Dann, *Magicats!*, 1984
  Gardner Dozois, co-editor
Jack Dann, *Magicats II*, 1991
  Gardner Dozois, co-editor
Bill Fawcett, *Cats in Space and Other Places*, 1992
  editor
Claire Necker, *Supernatural Cats*, 1973
Andre Norton, *Catfantastic*, 1989
  Martin H. Greenberg, co-editor
Andre Norton, *Catfantastic II*, 1991
  Martin H. Greenberg, co-editor
Michel Parry, *Beware of the Cat*, 1972
Mark E. Rogers, *The Adventures of Samurai Cat*, 1984

4190

NEAL STEPHENSON

The Diamond Age

(New York: Bantam Spectra, 1995)

Story type: Science Fiction (Cyberpunk)
Major character(s): John Percival Hackworth, Engineer (nanotechnology); Dr. X, Criminal; Nellodee "Nell", Child
Time period(s): 21st century
Locale(s): Shanghai, China; Leased Territories, Fictional Country

Summary: Nell and her brother, Harv, struggle to survive in the slums while others live in undreamed-of splendor. Nell's life changes utterly when she receives one of two copies of a strange interactive book which gradually draws her into the problems of a society in transition.

Other books you might like:
Stephen Bury, *Interface*, 1994
  pseudonym of Neal Stephenson and George F. Jewsbury
Pat Cadigan, *Synners*, 1991
Marc Laidlaw, *Neon Lotus*, 1988
Ian McDonald, *Terminal Cafe*, 1994
Maureen F. McHugh, *China Mountain Zhang*, 1992
David Wingrove, *The Middle Kingdom*, 1990

4191

NEAL STEPHENSON

Snow Crash

(New York: Bantam Spectra, 1992)

Story type: Science Fiction (Cyberpunk; Theological)
Major character(s): Hiro Protagonist, Computer Expert, Martial Arts Expert; Yours "Y.T." Truely, Businesswoman (Kourier), Teenager; Raven, Martial Arts Expert, Organized Crime Figure
Time period(s): 21st century

Locale(s): Los Angeles, California; The Metaverse, Cyberspace (virtual reality); *Raft*, At Sea

Summary: While delivering pizza for the Mafia, Hiro causes a disaster which leads to Y.T.'s doing a favor for the Mafia and leads both into a search for the origin of a computer virus which attacks computer hackers and an analog neurolinguistic virus existing since the fall of the Tower of Babel. Author's first science fiction novel.

Other books you might like:
Pat Cadigan, *Mindplayers*, 1987
Pat Cadigan, *Synners*, 1991
Samuel R. Delany, *Babel-17*, 1966
Philip K. Dick, *A Scanner Darkly*, 1977
William Gibson, *Neuromancer*, 1984
Ernest Hogan, *High Aztec*, 1991
K.W. Jeter, *Madlands*, 1991
Richard Kadrey, *Metrophage*, 1988
Bruce Sterling, *Islands in the Net*, 1988
John Varley, *Steel Beach*, 1992
Vernor Vinge, *A Fire upon the Deep*, 1992

4192

BRUCE STERLING

Crystal Express

(Sauk City, Wisconsin: Arkham House, 1989)

Story type: Science Fiction (Collection)

Summary: This collection includes twelve of Sterling's short stories, ranging in publishing date from 1982 to 1987. Five of the pieces, including "Swarm," "Spider Rose," and "Cicada Queen," are from his Shaper/Mechanist series. Other well-known stories include "Green Days in Brunei," "Flowers of Edo," and "Dinner in Audoghast."

Other books you might like:
Greg Bear, *Blood Music*, 1985
Greg Bear, *Tangents*, 1989
Pat Cadigan, *Patterns*, 1989
William Gibson, *Burning Chrome*, 1986
William Gibson, *Neuromancer*, 1984
John Shirley, *Heatseeker*, 1989

4193

BRUCE STERLING

Globalhead

(Shingletown, California: Mark V. Ziesing, 1992)

Story type: Science Fiction (Collection)

Summary: Contains one original story, "Are You for 86?" plus 12 stories published in periodicals and anthologies between 1985 and 1991. Themes include humor, cyberpunk, hard science fiction and fantasy in a variety of settings from ancient Assyria to an unpleasant France a millennium hence. Sterling collaborates with Rudy Rucker in "Storming the Chaos" and with John Kessel in "The Mortal Bullet."

Other books you might like:
Greg Bear, *The Wind From a Burning Woman*, 1983

Pat Cadigan, *Patterns*, 1989
Michael Flynn, *The Nanotech Chronicles*, 1991
William Gibson, *Burning Chrome*, 1986
John Kessel, *Meeting in Infinity*, 1992
Marc Stiegler, *The Gentle Seduction*, 1990
Michael Swanwick, *Gravity's Angels*, 1991
John Varley, *Blue Champagne*, 1986
John Varley, *The Persistence of Vision*, 1978

4194
BRUCE STERLING

Heavy Weather
(New York: Bantam Spectra, 1994)

Story type: Science Fiction (Medical; Disaster)
Major character(s): Alejandro "Alex" Unger, Invalid, Drifter; Juanita "Jane" Unger, Fanatic, Researcher; Gerald "Jerry" Mulcahey, Scientist (mathematician), Genius
Time period(s): 2030s (2031)
Locale(s): Nuevo Laredo, Mexico

Summary: Jane rescues Alex from an illegal medical facility after a lung flush which extends his life. Despite his illness, Alex manages to get along with the Storm Troupe, the group of misfits helping Jerry document the F6 tornado no one else believes will occur, a project to which the Storm Troupe dedicate their lives.

Other books you might like:
John Barnes, *Mother of Storms*, 1994
John Brunner, *Children of the Thunder*, 1989
Frank Herbert, *The White Plague*, 1982
Bill Ransom, *ViraVax*, 1993
Allen Steele, *Orbital Decay*, 1989
Roger Zelazny, *Flare*, 1992
    Thomas T. Thomas, co-author

4195
BRUCE STERLING

Holy Fire
(New York: Bantam Spectra, 1996)

Story type: Science Fiction (Hard Science Fiction)
Major character(s): Mia Ziemann, Noblewoman (Gerontocrat); Brett/Natalie, Teenager, Artisan
Time period(s): 2090s
Locale(s): Europe; United States

Summary: In a world of synthetic memory drugs, benevolent government surveillance, underground anarchists, and talking canine companions, dominated by the medical-industrial complex, conservative senior citizens who have access to the latest life-extension technology hold the power while the young live on the fringes of society. A deathbed visit with an ex-lover and a chance meeting with a young clothing designer brings Mia, a 94-year-old medical economist who enjoys all the benefits of her position, to the awful realization that she lives her life bereft of pleasure and adventure. To have a second chance she must go through a radical and painful experimental procedure to make her young again.

Other books you might like:
Wilhelmina Baird, *Crashcourse*, 1993
Bruce Bethke, *Headcrash*, 1995
Stephen Bury, *Interface*, 1994
Pat Cadigan, *Synners*, 1991
Michael Flynn, *The Nanotech Chronicles*, 1991
Neal Stephenson, *The Diamond Age*, 1995
Thomas T. Thomas, *ME: A Novel of Self Discovery*, 1991

4196
BRUCE STERLING

Schismatrix Plus
(New York: Ace, 1996)

Story type: Science Fiction (Collection; Space Opera)
Major character(s): Abelard Lindsay, Diplomat, Revolutionary
Time period(s): Indeterminate Future
Locale(s): Earth; Spaceship; Space Station

Summary: Abelard Lindsay works to unify an interplanetary empire as disparate forces try to control humanity and mold society to their will. Omnibus edition including *Schismatrix* (1985) and five short stories from periodicals and anthologies 1982-1984, set in the Shaper-Mechanist universe.

Other books you might like:
Roger MacBride Allen, *The Ring of Charon*, 1990
Alfred Bester, *The Stars My Destination*, 1996
    revised edition
Glen Cook, *The Dragon Never Sleeps*, 1988
Thomas A. Easton, *Sparrowhawk*, 1990
A.E. van Vogt, *The Weapon Shops of Isher*, 1951
Vernor Vinge, *A Fire upon the Deep*, 1992

4197
DAVID STERN

Nightmare World
(New York: Ace Books, 1989)

Story type: Science Fiction (Adventure)
Series: Dr. Bones
Major character(s): Ezekiel "Zeke" Bones, Archaeologist
Time period(s): Indeterminate Future
Locale(s): Ahng, Planet—Imaginary

Summary: Ezekiel Bones, an archaeologist perhaps reminiscent of Doctor Who or Indiana Jones, specializes in saving entire planets from destruction. In this volume of the series, Dr. Bones' friends are menaced by evil earthworm-like aliens. *Nightmare World* is Stern's first science fiction novel.

Other books you might like:
Terrance Dicks, *The Claws of Axos*, 1977
Terrance Dicks, *Doctor Who: The Mind of Evil*, 1985
Charles Ingrid, *Alien Salute*, 1989
    Sand Wars 4
Charles Ingrid, *Return Fire*, 1989
    Sand Wars 5

4198
ROGER STERN

The Death and Life of Superman
(New York: Bantam Spectra, 1993)

Story type: Science Fiction (Adventure; Invasion of Earth)
Series: Superman
Major character(s): Clark "Superman" Kent, Journalist, Alien (Kryptonian); Lois Lane, Journalist, Girlfriend (Superman's); Doomsday, Monster
Time period(s): 1990s
Locale(s): Metropolis (New York City); Outer Space

Summary: Superman loses his life as he kills Doomsday and saves the Earth. Later, four superbeings astonish Superman's family, friends and foes when they arrive in Metropolis, each claiming the status of the last son of Krypton.

Other books you might like:
Michael Bishop, *Count Geiger's Blues*, 1992
Martin H. Greenberg, *The Further Adventures of Superman*, 1993
   editor
William Kotzwinkle, *Superman III*, 1983
Elliot S. Maggin, *Superman: Last Son of Krypton*, 1978
Elliot S. Maggin, *Superman: Miracle Monday*, 1981

4199
T.W. STETSON

Night Beasts
(New York: Pinnacle, 1993)

Story type: Horror (Science Fiction; Nature in Revolt)
Major character(s): Rodman Stanley, Police Officer (state trooper); Kate MacDavid, Young Woman; Dick "Dutch" Bork, Biker
Time period(s): 1990s (1993)
Locale(s): Forest City, California

Summary: When a Russian satellite explodes over the United States, the U.S. government's genetic weapons program, releases flocks of pterodactyl-like "Night Beasts" who, contrary to prior belief, not only live for longer than a few days, but breed and exhibit a taste for human flesh.

Other books you might like:
Martin Cruz Smith, *Nightwing*, 1977
William W. Johnstone, *Bats*, 1993
Stephen King, *The Mist*, 1985
   in *Skeleton Crew*
Robert Wilson, *Second Fire*, 1993

4200
BROOKE STEVENS

The Circus of the Earth and Air
(New York: Harcourt Brace, 1994)

Story type: Fantasy (Mystery; Contemporary)
Major character(s): Alex Barton, Spouse
Time period(s): 1990s

Locale(s): New England
Summary: To gain admission to a circus, Iris agrees to volunteer to help in Father Fish's disappearing act, but does not return to Alex after the show. Alex searches for her then reports the disappearance to the police with no satisfactory result. Searching for her, Alex travels to the island owned by a great circus master, simultaneously beginning a metaphysical investigation into his own nature. First novel.

Other books you might like:
Ray Bradbury, *Something Wicked This Way Comes*, 1962
Marion Zimmer Bradley, *The Catch Trap*, 1979
Katherine Dunn, *Geek Love*, 1989
Charles G. Finney, *The Circus of Dr. Lao*, 1935
Barry B. Longyear, *City of Baraboo*, 1980
Warren Murphy, *Destiny's Carnival*, 1992
   Mark Brownwood, co-author

4201
CAROLINE STEVERMER

A College of Magics
(New York: Tor, 1994)

Story type: Fantasy (Quest; Magic Conflict)
Major character(s): Faris Nallaneen, Magician, Royalty (Duchess of Galazon); Jane Brailsford, Magician, Adventurer; Tyrian, Bodyguard, Companion
Time period(s): 1900s
Locale(s): Greenlaw, France (Greenlaw College); Aravis, Fictional Country; Alternate Earth

Summary: Initially an unwilling student at Greenlaw College, Faris Nallaneen cultivates friendships and studies magic until a fracas with another student reveals a fate that he must pursue.

Other books you might like:
Maya Kaathryn Bohnhoff, *The Meri*, 1992
Laurell K. Hamilton, *Nightseer*, 1992
Mercedes Lackey, *Jinx High*, 1991
Deborah Talmadge-Bickmore, *The Apprentice*, 1990
Paula Volsky, *Illusion*, 1992
Martha Wells, *The Element of Fire*, 1993
Patricia C. Wrede, *Sorcery and Cecelia*, 1988
   Caroline Stevermer, co-author

4202
CAROLINE STEVERMER

River Rats
(New York: Harcourt Brace Jovanovich, 1992)

Story type: Science Fiction (Post-Nuclear Holocaust; Young Adult)
Major character(s): Tomcat, Sailor (riverboat hand), Teenager; King, Fugitive, Musician
Time period(s): 21st century
Locale(s): Mississippi River

Summary: Tomcat and the crew of the *River Rat* interrupt their idyllic riverboat life of delivering mail and presenting rock concerts when they rescue King from the river. A wild chase evolves as the *River Rat* tries to elude the Lester family pursuing King to acquire his knowledge of a survivalist's weapons stash. Highly reminiscent of *The Adventures of Huckleberry Finn* (1885).

Other books you might like:
David Brin, *The Postman*, 1985
Mark Twain, *The Adventures of Huckleberry Finn*, 1885
Sterling E. Lanier, *Hiero's Journey*, 1973
David R. Palmer, *Emergence*, 1984
Will Shetterly, *Elsewhere*, 1991
Nancy Springer, *The Friendship Song*, 1992

4203

JEAN STEWART

Return to Isis
(New York: Rising Tide Press, 1992)

Story type: Science Fiction (Post-Nuclear Holocaust; Gay/Lesbian Fiction)
Major character(s): Tomyris "Whit Hastings" Whitaker, Military Personnel, Spy; Amelia, Farmer
Time period(s): 2090s (2093)
Locale(s): North America; Freeland, Fictional Country (western USA); Elysium, Fictional Country (eastern USA)

Summary: Discovered as a Freeland spy, Whit flees the Regulators and Elysium taking Amelia with her. There Amelia learns about the female society flourishing in city-colonies, finds herself falsely accused as a spy then later discovers the important role she will play in Freeland.

Other books you might like:
Margaret Atwood, *The Handmaid's Tale*, 1985
Suzy McKee Charnas, *Motherlines*, 1979
Suzy McKee Charnas, *Walk to the End of the World*, 1974
Suzette Haden Elgin, *Native Tongue*, 1984
Pat Murphy, *The City, Not Long After*, 1989
Joan Slonczewski, *A Door into Ocean*, 1986
Sheri S. Tepper, *The Gate to Women's Country*, 1989

4204

KATE STEWART

The Devil's Cradle
(New York: Zebra, 1992)

Story type: Horror (Child-in-Peril)
Major character(s): Dorothy Kite, Librarian; Elmo Small, Pharmacist; Hallie Crecilius, Musician
Time period(s): 1990s (1992)
Locale(s): New York, New York

Summary: Dorothy Kite has to fight to save herself and her as-yet-unborn children when she discovers that the man who has artificially inseminated her is in league with the devil and has a centuries-old history of assisting the birth of twins, one of whom always goes on to bring tragedy into the lives of whomever he or she touches. This is the author's first novel.

Other books you might like:
Margaret Bingley, *Seeds of Evil*, 1988
Stephanie Kegan, *The Baby*, 1990

Ira Levin, *Rosemary's Baby*, 1967

4205

MARY STEWART

The Prince and the Pilgrim
(New York: Morrow, 1996)

Story type: Fantasy (Legend; Quest)
Major character(s): Alexander, Royalty, Teenager; Alice, Teenager, Noblewoman; Morgan le Fay, Royalty, Sorceress
Time period(s): 5th century
Locale(s): England (Britain)

Summary: When he reaches his majority, Alexander sets off to seek justice from King Arthur for his father's murder. Morgan LeFay's machinations bring Alexander and Alice together when Morgan diverts Alexander with her lust for the Holy Grail, a cup identified to Alice while accompanying her father on a pilgrimage.

Other books you might like:
Marion Zimmer Bradley, *The Mists of Avalon*, 1983
Coningsby Dawson, *The Road to Avalon*, 1911
Parke Godwin, *Invitation to Camelot*, 1988
    editor
Cary James, *King & Raven*, 1995
Courtway Jones, *Witch of the North*, 1992

4206

MICHAEL STEWART

Belladonna
(New York: HarperCollins 1993)

Story type: Horror (Possession)
Major character(s): Matthew Cavewood, Historian; Hazel, Photographer, Fiance(e) (Matthew's); Josie McDowell, Student
Time period(s): 1990s (1992)
Locale(s): Charlottesville, Virginia

Summary: While researching the life of 17th-century physicist Nathaniel Shawcrosse, professor Matthew Cavewood becomes obsessed with Shawcrosse's lover, the murderer Isabel Hardiment. Cavewood's delving into Shawcrosse's metaphysical experiments facilitates Isabel's reincarnation as a 20th-century woman determined to repeat her pattern of murder and destruction.

Other books you might like:
Jonathan Aycliffe, *Naomi's Room*, 1991
Emmanuel Carrere, *Gothic Romance*, 1984
Marcy Heidish, *The Torching*, 1992
Daniel Rhodes, *Adversary*, 1988

4207

SEAN STEWART

Clouds End

(New York: Ace, 1996)

Story type: Fantasy (Quest)
Major character(s): Brook, Parent (mother); Jo, Mythical Creature; Rope, Sailor
Time period(s): Indeterminate Past
Locale(s): Clouds End, Fictional City; The Mist, Mythical Place

Summary: Jo comes out of The Mist and remakes herself as Brook. She should kill Brook but cannot do it, instead becoming two women with one soul. A dangerous journey lies ahead of them before their paths may separate.

Other books you might like:
Lisa Goldstein, *A Mask for the General*, 1987
Mark Helprin, *Winter's Tale*, 1983
Ursula K. Le Guin, *A Wizard of Earthsea*, 1986
Patricia A. McKillip, *The Riddle-Master of Hed*, 1976

4208

SEAN STEWART

Nobody's Son

(New York: Ace, 1995)

Story type: Fantasy (Political; Magic Conflict)
Major character(s): Shielder's Mark, Hero, Spouse; Gail, Royalty (princess), Spouse; Lissa, Courtier (lady-in-waiting)
Time period(s): Indeterminate
Locale(s): Ghostwood, Mythical Place; Borders, Fictional Country (dukedom); Swangard, Fictional City

Summary: Having prepared for years to assault the deadly mystery of the Ghostwood, Shielder's Mark proves a quick study as he unwinds the ancient sorcery which locks the Ghostwood outside time. In payment for his feat, Mark requests the king's daughter as wife and receives her troth, a title, and control over the Ghostwood. Mark's background as a commoner ill-prepares him for life as a nobleman, while winning Princess Gail's hand proves easier than winning her heart.

Other books you might like:
Terry Goodkind, *Wizard's First Rule*, 1994
Robin Hobb, *Assassin's Apprentice*, 1995
Mercedes Lackey, *The Lark and the Wren*, 1991
Patricia A. McKillip, *The Book of Atrix Wolfe*, 1995
Delia Sherman, *The Porcelain Dove*, 1993
Roger Zelazny, *Forever After*, 1995
    editor

4209

SEAN STEWART

Passion Play

(New York: Ace, 1993)

Story type: Science Fiction (Mystery; Theological)
Major character(s): Diane Fletcher, Detective—Private, Empath (Shaper)
Time period(s): 21st century
Locale(s): United States

Summary: After the election of a Redemptionist candidate as President, the United States becomes a Christian theocracy. Diane seeks to promote justice by utilizing her empathic powers in crime solving for the police. When a high-tech theatrical costume claims the life of a well-known Redemptionist, Diane's empathic powers indicate not, as appears, suicide but rather murder. First novel.

Other books you might like:
Margaret Atwood, *The Handmaid's Tale*, 1985
Alfred Bester, *The Demolished Man*, 1953
Flynn Connolly, *The Rising of the Moon*, 1993
Suzette Haden Elgin, *Native Tongue*, 1984
Katharine Kerr, *Polar City Blues*, 1990
Mercedes Lackey, *Burning Water*, 1989

4210

SEAN STEWART

Resurrection Man

(New York: Ace, 1995)

Story type: Fantasy (Religious; Contemporary)
Major character(s): Dante Ratkay, Psychic (Angel); Jet Ratkay, Relative (brother); Laura Chen, Friend
Time period(s): 1990s
Locale(s): North America

Summary: After World War II, some people called angels display psychic abilities, in China becoming accepted members of society and forming the Angels Guild. Raised as an atheist by his pragmatic physician father, Dante rejects the angel in himself as evil. When he finds his corpse, Dante takes it as an omen that he must accept his angel abilities and get his expectedly short life in order.

Other books you might like:
Tom Deitz, *Soulsmith*, 1991
C.S. Friedman, *Black Sun Rising*, 1991
Parke Godwin, *Waiting for the Galactic Bus*, 1988
James Morrow, *Only Begotten Daughter*, 1990
Sean Russell, *The Initiate Brother*, 1991

4211

G. HARRY STINE

Blood Siege

(New York: Pinnacle, 1990)

Story type: Science Fiction (Military; Robot Fiction)
Series: Warbots

Major character(s): Curt Carlson, Military Personnel (Sierra Charlie colonel); Dyani Mortega, Military Personnel (Sierra Charlie captain), Indian (crow); Clark Jeremy, Religious, Television Personality
Time period(s): 21st century
Locale(s): Sanctuary, Nevada; Battle Mountain, Nevada

Summary: When the Soviets demand to know why the USA is constructing a new missile facility, the US government discovers that the base is not located in a military reservation, but rather on land owned by the fanatic and militant Galactic Tabernacle of the Human Future. Curt Carlson and Dyani Mortega infiltrate the organization, where they meet the fanatics' leader, Clark Jeremy, and a hireling who is an old nemesis of Carlson's. When the pair attempt to escape, only Carlson succeeds. As Carlson and his unit, the Washington Greys, stage a rescue attempt, Jeremy unleashes the threat of nuclear weapons on Las Vegas.

Other books you might like:
Alan Dean Foster, *Cyber Way*, 1990
Robert A. Heinlein, *Starship Troopers*, 1959
Frank Herbert, *Dune*, 1965
Keith Laumer, *Bolo: The Annals of the Dinochrome Brigade*, 1976
Keith Laumer, *Rogue Bolo*, 1986
Dave Wolverton, *On My Way to Paradise*, 1989

4212

G. HARRY STINE

Force of Arms
(New York: Pinnacle, 1990)

Story type: Science Fiction (Military; Robot Fiction)
Series: Warbots
Major character(s): Curt Carlson, Military Personnel (Sierra Charlie colonel); Maggie MacPherson, Journalist (television)
Time period(s): 21st century
Locale(s): Sakhalin Island, Pacific Islands

Summary: When Soviet, Japanese and Chinese troops all gather on mineral-rich Sakhalin Island in violation of treaties, troops from the Washington Greys, from Brunei and Chile move to the island to help keep peace. The situation provides the first test of Soviet warbots after the Soviets took abandoned American warbots during a previous operation.

Other books you might like:
Donald F. Glut, *The Empire Strikes Back*, 1980
Robert A. Heinlein, *Starship Troopers*, 1959
Keith Laumer, *Bolo: The Annals of the Dinochrome Brigade*, 1976
Keith Laumer, *Rogue Bolo*, 1986
C.J. Mills, *Winter World*, 1988
Dave Wolverton, *On My Way to Paradise*, 1989

4213

G. HARRY STINE

Guts and Glory
(New York: Pinnacle, 1991)

Story type: Science Fiction (Military; Robot Fiction)
Series: Warbots
Major character(s): Curt Carlson, Military Personnel (Sierra Charlie Lieutenant Col.); Arwa Bint Muhammad al-Badr, Royalty (Queen of Yemen Royal Republic)
Time period(s): 21st century
Locale(s): Yemen

Summary: The Sierra Charlies have been deployed to protect the 250 kilometer robot railroad carrying 20% of the world's high-grade iron ore from guerrilla warfare. Curt Carlson must work despite excessive casualties resulting from lack of appropriate training and the use of high-tech weaponry by guerrillas, previously poorly armed. When all U.S. military forces are suddenly recalled, Curt must rescue his commanding officer, General Belinda Hettrick, and Yemen's Sultana, Queen Arwa.

Other books you might like:
Lois McMaster Bujold, *The Warrior's Apprentice*, 1986
David Drake, *The Jungle*, 1991
Alan Dean Foster, *Dark Star*, 1974
Diana G. Gallagher, *The Alien Dark*, 1990
Robert A. Heinlein, *Starship Troopers*, 1959
Keith Laumer, *Rogue Bolo*, 1986
Dave Wolverton, *On My Way to Paradise*, 1989

4214

G. HARRY STINE

Judgment Day
(New York: Pinnacle, 1992)

Story type: Science Fiction (Military)
Series: Warbots
Major character(s): Curt Carlson, Military Personnel (Sierra Charlie colonel); Willa Lovell, Scientist, Computer Expert (warbot)
Time period(s): 21st century
Locale(s): Nevada; Pakistan

Summary: Curt Carlson and the Washington Grays travel into the Himalayan Mountains with orders to destroy a secret enemy facility which produces interference having disastrous effects on warbot communications.

Other books you might like:
Jerry Earl Brown, *Snowmen*, 1991
Keith Laumer, *Bolo: The Annals of the Dinochrome Brigade*, 1976
Neal Stephenson, *Snow Crash*, 1992
Dave Wolverton, *On My Way to Paradise*, 1989

4215

G. HARRY STINE

Starsea Invaders: First Action
(New York: Roc, 1993)

Story type: Science Fiction (Invasion of Earth; Military)
Series: Starsea Invaders
Major character(s): William M. Corry, Military Personnel, Sea Captain
Time period(s): 21st century
Locale(s): Pacific Ocean; *U.S.S. Shenandoah*, Submarine

Summary: While the United States and China vie for supremacy of the Pacific Ocean, a prototype submersible aircraft carrier investigating the disappearance of U.S. citizens discovers extraterrestrials hiding beneath the sea and harvesting human beings.

Other books you might like:
David Brin, *Startide Rising*, 1983
Orson Scott Card, *The Abyss*, 1989
A.C. Crispin, *V*, 1984
Diane Duane, *seaQuest DSV: The Novel*, 1993
    Peter Morwood, co-author
James H. Schmitz, *The Demon Breed*, 1968
Theodore Sturgeon, *Voyage to the Bottom of the Sea*, 1961
John Varley, *Millennium*, 1983
Denise Vitola, *Half-Light*, 1992
David Weber, *Mutineers' Moon*, 1991

4216

G. HARRY STINE

Warrior Shield
(New York: Pinnacle, 1992)

Story type: Science Fiction (Military)
Series: Warbots
Major character(s): Curt Carlson, Military Personnel (Sierra Charlie colonel)
Time period(s): 21st century
Locale(s): Senegambia, Africa

Summary: When the United States president demands that dictator Generalissimo Modibo cease his attempt to gain power for his impoverished nation, the dictator begins slaughtering and imprisoning American nationals. The President then orders Curt Carlson and his warbots to rescue the imprisoned Americans and restore freedom to the area in order to avoid total global war.

Other books you might like:
Lois McMaster Bujold, *The Vor Game*, 1990
Lois McMaster Bujold, *The Warrior's Apprentice*, 1986
Robert A. Heinlein, *Starship Troopers*, 1959
Keith Laumer, *Rogue Bolo*, 1986
Dave Wolverton, *On My Way to Paradise*, 1989

4217

JEAN STINE, Editor
FORREST J. ACKERMAN, Co-Editor

I, Vampire: Interviews with the Undead
(Stamford, CT: Longmeadow Press, 1995)

Story type: Horror (Anthology; Vampire Story)

Summary: The dozen vampire stories written especially for this volume are all narrated in the first person by vampires. In John Gregory Betancourt's "By Moonlight," a vampire relates how his father's death brings him to a new understanding about his family. Darrell Schweitzer's "Runaway" is the story of a young boy who becomes a vampire through his mother's occult practices. In William F. Nolan's "Vympyre," a dying vampire's long life flashes before his eyes. Diana G. Gallagher, in "Tipping Is Not a City in China," describes the dilemma faced by a former vegetarian and new member of the undead who prepares for her feast feeding. Chris Moran's "Two Spirits" tells of a transexual vampire who discovers it is of two minds (literally) regarding its vampiredom. The editors supply a badly fact-checked appendix of further reading and movie viewing of vampire material.

Other books you might like:
Ellen Datlow, *Blood Is Not Enough*, 1990
    editor
Robert Weinberg, *100 Vicious Little Vampire Stories*, 1995
    Stefan Dziemianowicz and Martin H. Greenberg, co-editors
Stephen Jones, *The Mammoth Book of Vampires*, 1993
    editor

4218

R.L. STINE

Double Date
(New York: Pocket/Archway, 1994)

Story type: Horror (Mystery)
Series: Fear Street
Major character(s): Bobby Newkirk, Teenager; Bree Wade, Teenager, Twin; Samantha Wade, Teenager, Twin
Time period(s): 1990s (1994)
Locale(s): Shadyside

Summary: High school stud Bobby Newkirk believes in loving and leaving his dates, even twin sisters Bree and Samantha Wade. But it soon appears to Bobby that Bree is not about to give him up to her sister, and that she will even stoop to impersonating her sister—or worse—to get him back.

Other books you might like:
Debra Franklin, *The Admirer*, 1994
G.G. Gath, *Driven to Kill*, 1994
Gloria D. Miklowitz, *Desperate Pursuit*, 1992
Nicholas Pine, *The New Kid*, 1992

4219

R.L. STINE

The First Horror

(New York: Pocket/Archway, 1994)

Story type: Horror (Haunted House)
Series: 99 Fear Street: The House of Evil
Major character(s): Cally Frasier, Teenager; Cody Frasier, Teenager; Anthony, Teenager
Time period(s): 1990s (1994)
Locale(s): Shadyside

Summary: This first novel in a spin-off from Stine's enormously popular ''Fear Street'' young adult horror series chronicles the tribulations of the Frasier family, who move into their new home on Fear Street unaware of its bloody legacy and special link to Shadyside's evil town founder, Simon Fear.

Other books you might like:
Michael August, *New Year's Evil*, 1994
Peg Kehret, *Horror at the Haunted House*, 1994
Simon Lake, *Daughter of Darkness*, 1992
Edmund Plante, *Alone in the House*, 1991

4220

R.L. STINE

Superstitious

(New York: Warner/Tartikoff, 1995)

Story type: Horror (Occult)
Major character(s): Sara Morgan, Student; Liam Morgan, Professor (of folklore); Milton Cohn, Administrator (dean of students)
Time period(s): 1990s (1995)
Locale(s): Moore, Pennsylvania

Summary: Without a job or a boyfriend, former publishing minion Sara Morgan decides to resume her education at Moore State College, where she is soon swept off her feet and married by professor of folklore Liam O'Connor. Liam's superstitious behavior is not without merit: he is haunted by literal demons who make the lives of those within his and Sara's sphere a literal hell on earth. This is the author's first adult horror novel, after 56 novels written for the young adult market.

Other books you might like:
Marcy Heidish, *The Torching*, 1992
Fritz Leiber, *Conjure Wife*, 1953
Brent Monahan, *Blood of the Covenant*, 1993
Michael Stewart, *Belladonna*, 1992

4221

R.L. STINE

Vampire Breath

(New York: Scholastic, 1996)

Story type: Horror (Vampire Story)
Series: Goosebumps
Major character(s): Freddy Martinez, Child (12-year-old); Cara Simonetti, Child (12-year-old); Count Nightwing, Vampire
Time period(s): 1990s (1996)
Locale(s): Ohio

Summary: When Freddy and Cara discover the coffin of Count Nightwing in a tunnel underneath Freddy's house, they accidentally awaken him from his century-long slumber. Nightwing transports them back to the nineteenth century and the castle where he keeps his private supply of Vampire Breath, the elixir that allows him to grow fangs.

Other books you might like:
M.T. Coffin, *Blood Red Eightball*, 1996
Christopher Pike, *The Creature in the Teacher*, 1996
Tom B. Stone, *The Fright Before Christmas*, 1996

4222

S.M. STIRLING
JUDITH TARR, Co-Author
SUSAN SHWARTZ, Co-Author
HARRY TURTLEDOVE, Co-Author

Blood Feuds

(New York: Baen, 1993)

Story type: Science Fiction (Military; Political)
Series: War World
Major character(s): Aiysha, Leader
Time period(s): Indeterminate Future
Locale(s): Haven, Moon—Imaginary (Byers' star system)

Summary: After 300 years of Sauron domination, disparate human forces unite under Aiysha's leadership to meet their enemies at Sauron Citadel and reclaim their world at any cost. Braided novel set in Jerry Pournelle's CoDominium milieu.

Other books you might like:
Frank Herbert, *Dune*, 1965
Gordon Kendall, *White Wing*, 1985
   pseudonym of S.N. Lewitt and Susan Shwartz
Larry Niven, *The Mote in God's Eye*, 1974
   Jerry Pournelle, co-author
Jerry Pournelle, *CoDominium: Revolt on War World*, 1992
   John F. Carr, co-editor
Jerry Pournelle, *Go Tell the Spartans*, 1991
   S.M. Stirling, co-author
Jerry Pournelle, *War World I: The Burning Eye*, 1988
   John F. Carr, co-editor
Jerry Pournelle, *War World II: Death's Head Rebellion*, 1990
   John F. Carr, co-editor
Jerry Pournelle, *War World III: Sauron Dominion*, 1991
   John F. Carr, co-editor
Susan Shwartz, *Silk Roads and Shadows*, 1988
Judith Tarr, *Arrows of the Sun*, 1993
Harry Turtledove, *The Guns of the South*, 1992

4223

S.M. STIRLING
SHIRLEY MEIER, Co-Author

The Cage
(New York: Baen, 1989)

Story type: Fantasy (Adventure)
Major character(s): Megan Whitlock, Warrior (Female); Shkai'ra, Warrior (Female), Barbarian
Time period(s): Indeterminate

Summary: A woman who escapes slavery is determined to avenge herself on the ones who enslaved her.

Other books you might like:
Gael Baudino, *Gossamer Axe*, 1990
Marion Zimmer Bradley, *Free Amazons of Darkover*, 1985
Phyllis Ann Karr, *Frostflower and Windbourne*, 1982
Patricia A. McKillip, *The Changeling Sea*, 1988
Jennifer Roberson, *Sword-Dancer*, 1986

4224

S.M. STIRLING

Drakon
(New York: Baen, 1996)

Story type: Science Fiction (Military; Alternate Universe)
Series: Draka
Major character(s): Gwendolyn Ingolfsson, Genetically Altered Being; Henry Carmaggio, Detective—Police; Jennifer Feinberg, Businesswoman
Time period(s): 1990s (1995-1999); 25th century (2442-2445)
Locale(s): New York, New York; Andros Island, Bahamas

Summary: A failed space travel experiment strands Gwendolyn Ingolfsson, a Draka, on a parallel Earth—our Earth—where *Homo sapiens* have not been genetically engineered into other species. She views her predicament as an opportunity to subjugate yet another world to Draka rule, while Detective Henry Carmaggio attempts to stop her. Fourth in the series.

Other books you might like:
Gordon R. Dickson, *Dorsai!*, 1976
David Drake, *Igniting the Reaches*, 1994
David Drake, *Northworld*, 1990
Joe Haldeman, *The Forever War*, 1975
Fred Saberhagen, *Brother Assassin*, 1969

4225

S.M. STIRLING
HOLLY LISLE, Co-Author

The Rose Sea
(New York: Baen, 1994)

Story type: Fantasy (Magic Conflict; Quest)
Major character(s): Bren Morkaarin, Heir—Lost, Military Personnel (captain); Karah Grenlaarin, Equestrian, Military Personnel (draftee); Willek Tornsaarin, Military Personnel (grand admiral), Sorcerer

Time period(s): Indeterminate
Locale(s): Tykissian Empire, Fictional Country; Tarin Tseld, Fictional Country

Summary: Away from home by herself for the first time, Karah finds herself unknowingly involved in an ancient battle between gods when she is suddenly impressed into the army. Destiny forces her to show her mettle, while a ghostly shaman leads her on prophetic voyages during sleep.

Other books you might like:
Constance Ash, *The Stalking Horse*, 1990
Rosemary Kirstein, *The Steerswoman*, 1989
Mercedes Lackey, *When the Bough Breaks*, 1993
    Holly Lisle, co-author
Holly Lisle, *Fire in the Mist*, 1992
Laurie J. Marks, *The Watcher's Mask*, 1992
Elizabeth Moon, *Sheepfarmer's Daughter*, 1988
Angus Wells, *Dark Magic*, 1992

4226

S.M. STIRLING
SHIRLEY MEIER, Co-Author

Saber & Shadow
(New York: Baen, 1992)

Story type: Fantasy (Adventure; Political)
Series: Fifth Millennium
Major character(s): Shkai'ra Mek Kermak's-kin, Warrior; Megan Whitlock, Warrior
Time period(s): 50th century
Locale(s): Illizbuah, Fictional City; Almerkun, Fictional Country; North America

Summary: Shkai'ra and Megan join forces to wreak havoc with established intrigues in Almerkun's metropolis.

Other books you might like:
Shirley Meier, *Shadow's Daughter*, 1991
Shirley Meier, *Shadow's Son*, 1991
    S.M. Stirling, Karen Wehrstein, co-authors
Karen Wehrstein, *Lion's Heart*, 1991
Karen Wehrstein, *Lion's Soul*, 1991

4227

S.M. STIRLING

Snowbrother
(New York: Baen, 1992)

Story type: Fantasy (Quest; Psychic Powers)
Series: Fifth Millennium
Major character(s): Shkai'ra Mek Kermak's-kin, Warrior; Maihu Jonnah's-kin, Religious (Way of the Circle), Captive; Eh'rik, Warrior
Time period(s): 50th century (4960s)
Locale(s): Great Plains, North America; Central Almerkun, Fictional Country

Summary: Capturing Maihu and Taimi while sacking a village, Shkai'ra continues eastward on her mission of raiding and capturing new goods, hampered by shamanistic forces and treachery. Expands the 1985 release.

Other books you might like:
Shirley Meier, *Shadow's Daughter*, 1991
Shirley Meier, *Shadow's Son*, 1991
  S.M. Stirling, Karen Wahrstein, co-authors
Karen Wehrstein, *Lion's Heart*, 1991
Karen Wehrstein, *Lion's Soul*, 1991

4228

S.M. STIRLING

The Stone Dogs
(New York: Baen, 1990)

Story type: Science Fiction (Alternate Universe; Military)
Series: Draka
Major character(s): Yolande Ingolfsson, Royalty (Drakan aristocracy); Frederick LeFarge, Royalty (Drakan aristocracy); Marya LeFarge, Royalty (Drakan aristocracy)
Time period(s): 20th century
Locale(s): Alternate Earth; Outer Space

Summary: Conflict between the Domination of the Draka and the American Lead Alliance for Democracy continues, with both sides waiting for the right moment to start and win the next war with their respective secret weapons; computer technologies for the Alliance, and bio-engineering (germ warfare) for the Domination.

Other books you might like:
Gregory Benford, *Hitler Victorious: Eleven Stories of the German Victory in World War II*, 1986
  Martin H. Greenberg, co-editor
Philip K. Dick, *The Man in the High Castle*, 1963
David Drake, *Fortress*, 1987
Ralph Peters, *Red Army*, 1989
Jerry Pournelle, *Falkenberg's Legion*, 1990

4229

S.M. STIRLING

Under the Yoke
(New York: Baen Books, 1989)

Story type: Science Fiction (Alternate Universe)
Major character(s): Marya Sokolowska, Religious (Nun); Captain Fred Kustaa, Pilot
Time period(s): Indeterminate (1948 in alternate time)
Locale(s): Alternate Universe (Europe and the United States)

Summary: After the American Revolution, the Tories fled not to Canada but to South Africa where they founded the nation of Drakesland. Now, more than one hundred and fifty years later, the slave-owning, totalitarian Draka have conquered half the world. If they have their way, the United States will be next. Sequel to *Marching Through Georgia*.

Other books you might like:
Gregory Benford, *Hitler Victorious: Eleven Stories of the German Victory in World War II*, 1986
  Martin H. Greenberg, co-editor
Gregory Benford, *Alternate Empires*, 1989
  Martin H. Greenberg, co-editor
John Hersey, *White Lotus*, 1965

Keith Roberts, *Pavane*, 1968
Sarban, *The Sound of His Horn*, 1952

4230

JOHN E. STITH

Deep Quarry
(New York: Ace, 1989)

Story type: Science Fiction (Mystery)
Major character(s): Ben Takent, Detective—Private; Kate Dunlet, Professor
Time period(s): Indeterminate Future
Locale(s): Tankur, Planet—Imaginary

Summary: Private-eye Ben Takent is hired to solve a difficult case involving two murders and alien artifacts which are disappearing from a locked vault. At a nearby dig, a team of archaeologists engaged in the excavation of an ancient civilization may be in horrible danger.

Other books you might like:
Richard Bowker, *Dover Beach*, 1988
Victor Koman, *The Jehovah Contract*, 1987
William Shatner, *TekWar*, 1989
F. Paul Wilson, *Dydeetown World*, 1989

4231

JOHN E. STITH

Manhattan Transfer
(New York: Tor, 1993)

Story type: Science Fiction (Disaster; First Contact)
Major character(s): Matt Sheehan, Government Official, Troubleshooter; Abby Terza, Linguist, Anthropologist (cultural); Bobby Joe Brewster, Scientist
Time period(s): 21st century
Locale(s): New York, New York (Manhattan); Outer Space

Summary: When aliens suddenly pick up the island of Manhattan and deposit it in a strange grey medium aboard a giant space ship, some, including Matt Sheehan, want to know why they have been abducted and if they can communicate with other abducted cities. When Matt and others contact the abductors, they find that Earth will be ruined for human life unless they find a way to disable another ship which will soon modify the Earth to suit alien needs.

Other books you might like:
Roger MacBride Allen, *The Ring of Charon*, 1990
James Blish, *Cities in Flight*, 1970
David Brin, *Earth*, 1990
Octavia E. Butler, *Dawn*, 1987
Edmund Cooper, *Seahorse in the Sky*, 1969
Fritz Leiber, *The Wanderer*, 1964
William Tenn, *Of Men and Monsters*, 1968
Harlan Thompson, *Silent Running*, 1972
Richard Wilson, *And Then the Town Took Off*, 1960

4232

JOHN E. STITH

Redshift Rendezvous

(New York: Ace Books, 1990)

Story type: Science Fiction (Hard Science Fiction)
Major character(s): Jason Kraft, Spaceman; Tara Cline, Passenger
Time period(s): Indeterminate Future
Locale(s): *Redshift*, Spaceship

Summary: A new spacedrive works by shifting a spaceship to another universe, one where the speed of light is just eighty meters per second. This causes all sorts of bizarre problems for the crew and passengers, especially when one passenger is killed and pirates show up.

Other books you might like:
Poul Anderson, *Tau Zero*, 1970
James Blish, *Common Time*, 1953
Larry Niven, *Neutron Star*, 1968
Christopher Priest, *The Inverted World*, 1974

4233

JOHN E. STITH

Reunion on Neverend

(New York: Tor, 1994)

Story type: Science Fiction (Mystery; Techno-Thriller)
Major character(s): Lan Dillon, Police Officer (secret agent); Parke Brenlek, Friend; Tessa Farlan, Businesswoman (museum owner)
Time period(s): Indeterminate Future
Locale(s): Neverend, Asteroid (space colony); Arangorta, Planet—Imaginary

Summary: On Neverend for his school reunion, Lan maintains his old persona as a cowardly weakling until Tessa needs protection. The mysterious death of her father, continuing disturbances at her museum and attempts to intimidate her into selling the museum propel the friends into a wonderful discovery and a dangerous adventure.

Other books you might like:
Philip K. Dick, *The Unteleported Man*, 1983
   revised edition
Geary Gravel, *A Key for the Nonesuch*, 1990
Andre Norton, *Star Gate*, 1958
Sheri S. Tepper, *Grass*, 1989
George Zebrowski, *Stranger Suns*, 1991

4234

GRANT STOCKBRIDGE

The Spider #3: Death's Crimson Juggernaut/The Red Death Rain

(New York: Carroll & Graf, 1992)

Story type: Fantasy (Contemporary; Mystery)
Series: Spider

Major character(s): Richard Wentworth, Adventurer (crime fighter); Ya Che, Criminal; Gentleman Jack Hayes, Criminal
Time period(s): 1930s
Locale(s): United States

Summary: Reprints two 1934 pulp stories full of weird adventure, strange plots and daring escapes. In "Death's Crimson Juggernaut" a blindfolded Spider must foil a plot by sadistic gangsters to frame him. In "The Red Death Rain" a mad cult poisoning thousands of people to hold the USA hostage comes to the Spider's attention, but can even the Spider stop these geniuses of evil?

Other books you might like:
Lin Carter, *Invisible Death*, 1975
Philip Jose Farmer, *Escape From Loki*, 1991
Jon Stephen Fink, *Further Adventures*, 1993
Rob MacGregor, *Indiana Jones and the Dance of the Giants*, 1991
Kenneth Robeson, *The Frightened Fish*, 1992
   pseudonym of Will Murray

4235

GRANT STOCKBRIDGE

The Spider #4: Death Reign of the Vampire King/The Pain Emperor

(New York: Carroll & Graf, 1992)

Story type: Fantasy (Contemporary; Mystery)
Series: Spider
Major character(s): Richard Wentworth, Adventurer (crime fighter); The Bat Man, Criminal; The Avenger, Adventurer (crime fighter), Criminal
Time period(s): 1930s
Locale(s): United States

Summary: Reprints two pulp stories from 1935 complete with weird mystery and lurid adventure. In "Death Reign of the Vampire King" the Spider combats a fiendish genius who flies and controls deadly swarms of killer bats. In "The Pain Emperor" the Spider battles combined forces when a ring of prisoners and a false crime fighter team up.

Other books you might like:
Lin Carter, *The Volcano Ogre*, 1976
Philip Jose Farmer, *Escape From Loki*, 1991
Jon Stephen Fink, *Further Adventures*, 1993
Rob MacGregor, *Indiana Jones and the Peril at Delphi*, 1991
Kenneth Robeson, *The Jade Ogre*, 1992
   pseudonym of Will Murray

4236

GRANT STOCKBRIDGE

The Spider #8: The Devil's Paymaster/ Legions of the Accursed Light

(New York: Carroll & Graf, 1993)

Story type: Fantasy (Contemporary; Mystery)
Series: Spider

Major character(s): Richard Wentworth, Adventurer (crime fighter); Stanley Kirkpatrick, Police Officer (commissioner); Ram Singh, Servant, Warrior
Time period(s): 1930s
Locale(s): New York, New York

Summary: Reprints two lurid crime stories from 1938 and 1941 pulps delivering weird mystery and two-fisted action. ''The Devil's Paymaster'' forces the Spider to follow a trail of mysterious corpses to a fiendish plot. In ''Legions of the Accursed Light,'' a villain with a death ray holds a city hostage.

Other books you might like:
Martin Caidin, *Indiana Jones and the Sky Pirates*, 1993
Lin Carter, *Invisible Death*, 1975
Philip Jose Farmer, *Escape From Loki*, 1991
Jon Stephen Fink, *Further Adventures*, 1993
Kenneth Robeson, *The Jade Ogre*, 1992
    pseudonym of Will Murray

4237

FRANK STOCKTON

The Lady or the Tiger and Other Stories
(New York: Tor, 1992)

Story type: Fantasy (Collection; Legend)
Summary: Contains 11 stories published last century including Stockton's most famous, the title story, and one of its sequels, ''The Discourager of Hesitancy,'' with other stories featuring mythical creatures such as the three stories about a tiny fairy, ''Ting-a-Ling,'' ''Ting-a-Ling and the Five Magicians'' and ''Ting-a-Ling's Visit to Tur-il-i-ra.'' Jane Yolen contributes a four-page biography of Frank Stockton, a three-page foreword focusing on the periodical *St. Nicholas, A Monthly Magazine for Boys and Girls*, and a two-page afterword.

Other books you might like:
Rudyard Kipling, *Kipling's Fantasy*, 1992
Rudyard Kipling, *Puck of Pook's Hill*, 1906
Andrew Lang, *The Blue Fairy Book*, 1889
    editor
Andrew Lang, *The Green Fairy Book*, 1892
    editor
Andrew Lang, *The Red Fairy Book*, 1890
    editor
Jack London, *Selected Science Fiction and Fantasy Stories*, 1979
Kenneth Morris, *The Secret Mountain and Other Tales*, 1926

4238

BRAM STOKER

The Jewel of Seven Stars
(New York: Oxford, 1996)

Story type: Horror (Reanimated Dead)
Major character(s): Abel Trelawney, Archaeologist (Egyptologist); Margaret Trelawney, Young Woman; Malcolm Ross, Lawyer

Time period(s): 1900s (1903)
Locale(s): London, England

Summary: An experiment to resurrect the mummy of Queen Tera leaves Abel Trelawney in a coma. Friends and family attempting to revive Trelawney discover that his daughter, Margaret, may be possessed of a portion of Tera's soul, and thus pose a danger to herself and her father. This novel was first published in England in 1903. An appendix reprints the alternative ending from the 1912 revised edition.

Other books you might like:
Kathryn Meyer Griffith, *The Calling*, 1994
Jane Webb Loudon, *The Mummy!: A Tale of the Twenty-Second Century*, 1827
Michael Paine, *Cities of the Dead*, 1988
Anne Rice, *The Mummy, or Ramses the Damned*, 1991
Anne Rice, *Servant of the Bones*, 1996

4239

DEL STONE JR.

Dead Heat
(Austin, Texas: Mojo Press, 1996)

Story type: Horror (Reanimated Dead)
Major character(s): Hitch, Reanimated Dead (zombie), Biker; Frederick Gerenz, Administrator (labor camp director); Frank Black, Military Personnel (ex-Air Force officer)
Time period(s): 1990s
Locale(s): Amarillo, Texas; Waterloo, Michigan; Death Valley, California

Summary: In the near future a genetically altered virus has turned the world's population into hordes of mindless zombies with a taste for human flesh. Hitch, a zombie biker endowed with unusual intelligence by a disembodied presence he calls ''the other,'' travels cross-country on a mission to save the world from an evil entity who is taking advantage of the chaos to bring about the earth's destruction. His adventures along the way bring him into contact with a dictator who runs a forced labor camp for the few remaining humans, chainsaw wielding zombie hunters, and other escapades that tax his decomposing body to the limit. This is the author's first novel.

Other books you might like:
Philip Nutman, *Wet Work*, 1993
George Romero, *Dawn of the Dead*, 1978
    Susanna Sparrow, co-author
John Russo, *Inhuman*, 1986
John Skipp, *Book of the Dead*, 1989
    Craig Spector, co-editor
John Skipp, *Still Dead: Book of the Dead 2*, 1992
    Craig Spector, co-editor; Title could be Book of the Dead II

4240
JORDAN STORM

Substitute Teacher
(New York: Pocket, 1993)

Story type: Horror (Child-in-Peril)
Major character(s): Mary Margaret McCarthy, Teacher; Beth Flynn, Administrator (personnel analyst); Lizbeth Flynn, Child (Beth's daughter)
Time period(s): 1990s (1993)
Locale(s): New York, New York

Summary: Although gifted with a talent for sizing up people from details most others don't even pay attention to, Beth Flynn can't put her finger on why she feels uneasy about her daughter's new teacher. Yet her intuition is correct, for Mary Margaret McCarthy is a psychologically damaged transient whose teaching method includes murder.

Other books you might like:
J.M. Dillard, *Spectres*, 1991
Eric Flanders, *The Forever Children*, 1992
Ed Kelleher, *The School*, 1992
    Harriet Vidal, co-author
David Martin, *Bring Me Children*, 1992
Kathryn Ptacek, *The Hunted*, 1993
John Saul, *Darkness*, 1991

4241
SUE STORM
KAREN HARRIS, Illustrator

Star Bones Weep the Blood of Angels
(Denver: Cyber-Psychos A.O.D., 1995)

Story type: Horror (Collection)

Summary: This short-story chapbook, the author's first, comprises seven tales that skirt the boundary between horror and fantasy. ''Getting Happy'' and ''The Sorry Child's Christmas'' are both tales of people living on society's fringe driven to extreme measures. ''Missy Loves Her Daddy'' is a horror story of child abuse. ''The Wolf-Girl's Song'' and ''Halfbreed'' involve the mystical transformation of characters who are not what they appear to be, even unto themselves. Edward Lee supplies an introduction.

Other books you might like:
Michael A. Arnzen, *Needles and Sins*, 1993
Michael Hemmingson, *Nice Little Stories Jam-Packed with Depraved Sex and Violence*, 1995
Brian Hopkins, *Something Haunts Us All*, 1995
Elizabeth Massie, *Southern Discomfort: Selected Works of Elizabeth Massie*, 1993
David Niall Wilson, *The Fall of the House of Escher and Other Illusions*, 1995

4242
WILLIAM R. STOTLER
ALAN KOSZOWSKI, Illustrator

The Final Diary Entry of Kees Hujgens
(West Warwick, Rhode Island: Necronomicon Press, 1995)

Story type: Horror (Ancient Evil Unleashed)
Major character(s): Kees Hujgens, Architect; Vilmos Niehaus, Architect; Jozef P. Janszoon, Architect
Time period(s): 1920s (1925)
Locale(s): Amsterdam, Netherlands

Summary: Presented as a diary kept by an architecture student fascinated by the De Stijl style popular at the turn of the century, this short story chapbook recounts how he falls under the tutelage of a renegade architect whose theories allow him to penetrate beyond physical boundaries into the spatial dimensions De Stijl evokes. This is the author's first book.

Other books you might like:
Stefan Grabinski, *The Dark Domain*, 1994
Franz Kafka, *Stories, 1904-1924*, 1981
Thomas Ligotti, *Songs of a Dead Dreamer*, 1990
Bruno Schulz, *Sanatorium under the Sign of the Hourglass*, 1937

4243
LAREN STOVER

Pluto, Animal Lover
(New York: HarperCollins, 1994)

Story type: Horror (Psychological Suspense; Satire)
Major character(s): Pluto Hellbender Gerome, Editor (copyeditor); Wanda Swann, Prostitute; Camillia, Editor (of *Pancreas Journal*)
Time period(s): 1990s (1994)
Locale(s): New York, New York

Summary: By day, Pluto works as a copyeditor for a medical magazine and walks dogs at the nearby ASPCA on his lunch hour. In his private life, Pluto's deep love of animals breeds a misanthropy that drives him to take murderous extremes against those whom he believes endanger animal lives. This is the author's first published novel.

Other books you might like:
Ramsey Campbell, *The Face That Must Die*, 1979
Thomas Harris, *The Silence of the Lambs*, 1988
F. Paul Wilson, *Pelts*, 1990

4244
J. MICHAEL STRACZYNSKI

Demon Night
(New York: Berkley, 1989)

Story type: Horror (Apocalyptic Horror)
Major character(s): Eric Matthews, Young Man; Liz Chasen, Writer
Time period(s): 1980s
Locale(s): Dredmouth Point, Maine

Summary: Drawn back to his hometown by a series of nightmares, Eric Matthews confronts a band of powerful demons that are terrorizing the town. As the ravages intensify, Matthews and a small group of associates—a female writer, a priest, a doctor, and a policeman—attempt to thwart the demons, at risk of life and soul, by finding and closing the ''door'' from the netherworld through which they emerged.

Other books you might like:
Stephen King, *Salem's Lot*, 1975
Bentley Little, *The Revelation*, 1990
Peter Straub, *Ghost Story*, 1979

4245

J. MICHAEL STRACZYNSKI

OtherSyde

(New York: E.P. Dutton, 1990)

Story type: Horror (Supernatural Vengeance)
Major character(s): Chris Martino, Teenager, Student—High School; Roger Obst, Teenager, Student—High School; Susan Warrick, Police Officer
Time period(s): 1990s (1990)
Locale(s): Los Angeles, California

Summary: Nerdy Roger Obst is mercilessly bullied by his high school classmates—until the insectoid race that calls itself OtherSyde empowers him to take revenge on his tormentors.

Other books you might like:
Ray Garton, *Crucifax Autumn*, 1988
Charles L. Grant, *The Pet*, 1986
K.W. Jeter, *The Night Man*, 1990
Stephen King, *Christine*, 1983

4246

TODD STRASSER

Addams Family Values

(New York: Pocket, 1993)

Story type: Fantasy (Light Fantasy; Quest)
Series: Addams Family
Major character(s): Uncle Fester Addams, Fiance(e); Debbie Jelinsky, Child-Care Giver, Criminal (black widow); Morticia Addams, Parent, Spouse
Time period(s): 1990s
Locale(s): Addams Family Mansion, Mythical Place; Hawaii; Camp Chippewa, Mythical Place

Summary: Concerned over Wednesday's and Pugsley's reaction to the new baby, Morticia and Gomez hire Debbie Jelinsky as nanny. Seeing possible access to the Addams' Family fortune through Uncle Fester, Debbie arranges a summer camp experience for Wednesday and Pugsley while planning a wedding and fatal honeymoon for Uncle Fester. Novelizes the film.

Other books you might like:
Richie Tankersley Cusick, *Buffy the Vampire Slayer*, 1992
Robert Egan, *Little Shop of Horrors*, 1986
   Loise Egan, co-author
Laurell K. Hamilton, *Guilty Pleasures*, 1993

Christopher Moore, *Practical Demonkeeping*, 1992
Gilbert Pearlman, *Young Frankenstein*, 1974

4247

THOMAS M.K. STRATMAN, Editor

Cthulhu's Heirs

(Oakland, California: Chaosium, 1995)

Story type: Horror (Anthology)
Summary: The author has assembled 21 original and reprint stories that pay tribute to H.P. Lovecraft and his concept of a universe controlled by incomprehensible forces of chaos embodied in the form of extradimensional beings. Included are Ramsey Campbell's ''The Franklyn Paragraphs,'' which suggests that life as we know it may be no more than the fantasy of a horror writer; Hugh B. Cave's ''The Death Watch,'' a reprint from the pulp magazine *Weird Tales*, concerning a man's return from the dead with the help of occult forces; Charles M. Saplak's ''The Scourge,'' about a man drawn into an inescapable realm of forbidden knowledge; and Michael D. Winkle's ''Typo,'' about the horrors lurking in the card catalog of a university library. Also included are three variations on or sequels to stories by Lovecraft himself: Darrell Schweitzer's and Jason van Hollander's ''Those of the Air'' (a tribute to Lovecraft's ''The Dunwich Horror''); Gordon Linzner's ''Pickman's Legacy'' (a follow-up to Lovecraft's tale of an unusual painter, ''Pickman's Model''); and Arthur William Lloyd Breach's ''The Return of the White Ship'' (a sequel to Lovecraft's fantasy ''The White Ship.'')

Other books you might like:
Edward P. Berglund, *Disciples of Cthulhu*, 1975
Robert M. Price, *Tales of the Lovecraft Mythos*, 1993
   editor
H.P. Lovecraft, *Tales of the Cthulhu Mythos: Golden Anniversary Anthology*, 1990

4248

PETER STRAUB

The Hellfire Club

(New York: Random House, 1996)

Story type: Horror (Serial Killer)
Major character(s): Nora Chancel, Housewife; Dick Dart, Serial Killer; Davey Chancel, Editor
Time period(s): 1990s (1996)
Locale(s): Westerholm, Connecticut

Summary: Nora Chancel is catapulted out of her stale marriage and boring life when she is kidnapped by serial killer Dick Dart and forced to accompany him on a grisly murder spree. The diabolically brilliant Dart is motivated not only by bloodlust, but his interest in bringing to light the dark secret behind a bestselling book that has sustained the publishing house run by Nora's husband's family for half a century.

Other books you might like:
Brett Easton Ellis, *American Psycho*, 1991
Thomas Harris, *Red Dragon*, 1981
Thomas Harris, *The Silence of the Lambs*, 1988

Joyce Carol Oates, *Zombie*, 1995

4249

PETER STRAUB

Houses Without Doors
(New York: Dutton, 1990)

Story type: Horror (Collection)

Summary: A stunning collection of six powerful, claustrophobic supernatural stories about isolation, obsession, the destruction of innocence, madness, and "the violence of unfinished things." In "Blue Rose" a 10-year-old boy hypnotizes then kills his younger brother. In the related "The Juniper Tree" a young boy is abused sexually by a tramp, an experience that haunts his adult self, the narrator of the tale. And in "The Buffalo Hunter" an obsessed man discovers the power to enter the world of the books he reads. One story, "Mrs. God," was heavily edited for this edition. Two of the stories have links to Straub's Vietnam novel, *Koko*.

Other books you might like:
Ramsey Campbell, *The Face That Must Die*, 1979
Stephen Gilbert, *Ratman's Notebooks*, 1968
Michael McDowell, *Toplin*, 1985

4250

PETER STRAUB

Koko
(New York: Signet NAL, 1989)

Story type: Horror (Serial Killer)
Series: Blue Rose Trilogy
Major character(s): Michael Poole, Doctor (Pediatrician), Veteran (Vietnam); Tim Underhill, Writer (Homosexual), Veteran (Vietnam)
Time period(s): 1980s
Locale(s): Asia; United States

Summary: A serial murderer calling himself "Koko" is systematically killing all those involved in the Vietnam Ia Thuc massacre. Veteran Michael Poole realizes that the killer is one of their own unit and he mobilizes his old friends to identify and locate Koko before he can complete his "mission."

Other books you might like:
Thomas Harris, *Red Dragon*, 1981
Thomas Harris, *The Silence of the Lambs*, 1988

4251

PETER STRAUB

Mrs. God
(Hampton Falls, New Hampshire: Donald Grant, 1990)

Story type: Horror (Ghost Story)
Major character(s): William Standish, Professor
Time period(s): 1990s (1990)
Locale(s): England

Summary: This original, longer, superior version of the final story in Straub's collection *Houses Without Doors* tells of the descent into insanity of a literature professor who visits a haunted English country house called Eswood to pursue research on a little-known poet. There he encounters ghostly manifestations, strange sounds, and other accoutrements of the English ghost story. Ultimately his pursuit by the spectre of an aborted child sparks his deterioration into madness and brutality. This edition is illustrated by Rick Berry and includes an otherwise unpublished afterword by Straub concerning the story.

Other books you might like:
Robert Aickman, *Cold Hand in Mine*, 1975
Robert Aickman, *Painted Devils*, 1979
Robert Aickman, *The Wine-Dark Sea*, 1988
Ramsey Campbell, *Dark Companions*, 1982
Ramsey Campbell, *The Height of the Scream*, 1976
Shirley Jackson, *The Haunting of Hill House*, 1959
Richard Matheson, *Hell House*, 1971

4252

PETER STRAUB

Mystery
(New York: Dutton, 1989)

Story type: Horror (Psychological Suspense)
Major character(s): Tom Pasmore, Heir; Lamont "the Shadow" Von Heilitz, Detective
Time period(s): 1980s
Locale(s): Mill Walk, Caribbean (Island); Eagle Lake, Wisconsin

Summary: Pasmore entices Von Heilitz into joining him in the investigation of two murders, a 40-year-old killing in Eagle Lake and a recent one in Mill Walk.

Other books you might like:
Joyce Carol Oates, *Mysteries of Winterhurn*, 1984

4253

PETER STRAUB, Editor

Peter Straub's Ghosts
(New York: Pocket, 1995)

Story type: Horror (Anthology; Ghost Story)

Summary: This fourth anthology of stories sponsored and written by members of the Horror Writers of America contains fourteen original ghost stories and an introduction by the editor, which is itself a ghost story narrated by a deceased embezzler. In Norman Partridge's "Styx," a man searches for the person who has stolen his soul and threatens his hope for an afterlife. Kathe Koja relates a woman's transformation into a ghost in "Jubilee," and Alan Rodgers draws parallels between inner city life and being an unseen ghost in "Momma Ghost." In Clark Perry's "Mother's Hands," unrelenting grief leads the living to haunt the dead, and in Chet Williamson's "Coventry Carol," the ghost of a stillborn child may or may not be the figment of the grieving mother's imagination.

Other books you might like:
Ramsey Campbell, *Deathport*, 1994
  editor
Claudia O'Keefe, *Ghosttide*, 1993
  editor
Paul F. Olson, *Post Mortem: New Tales of Ghostly Horror*, 1989
  David B. Silva, co-editor

4254

PETER STRAUB

The Throat
(New York: Dutton, 1993)

Story type: Horror (Mystery)
Major character(s): Tim Underhill, Writer, Veteran (Vietnam); Tom Pasmore, Detective
Time period(s): 1990s (1993)
Locale(s): Millhaven, Illinois

Summary: In this sequel to the author's World Fantasy Award-winning novel *Koko*, resumption of the "Blue Rose" murders that terrorized Millhaven over a decade before leads locals Tim Underhill and Tom Pasmore into an investigation that will bring to light undisclosed truths about the town's residents, and force each of them to confront aspects of their traumatic involvement in the Vietnam War.

Other books you might like:
S.K. Epperson, *Dumford Blood*, 1990
Dennis Etchison, *Darkside*, 1986
Chelsea Quinn Yarbro, *Beastnights*, 1989

4255

S.J. STRAYHORN

Black Night
(New York: Kensington, 1996)

Story type: Horror (Small Town Horror)
Major character(s): Eugenia Fairfax, Social Worker; Lena Fairfax, Deli Worker; Rafael Chavez, Waiter/Waitress
Time period(s): 1990s (1996)
Locale(s): Fort Grant, Kansas

Summary: Eugenia Fairfax returns temporarily to Fort Grant, the town where she was raised in the local orphanage, to lay to rest the ghosts of her past. However, her return reawakens many of the old prejudices that were turned against her and her fellow orphans. Worse, Eugenia's daughter, Lena, and Lena's lover, Rafael, appear to be reliving an ill-fated romance played out on the site of the orphanage during the town's frontier days, the legacy of which haunts the town to this day. This is the author's first novel.

Other books you might like:
Jane Brindle, *The Tallow Image*, 1995
S.K. Epperson, *The Moons of Summer*, 1994
Judith Hawkes, *Julian's House*, 1989
Nina Romberg, *Shadow Walkers*, 1993
Tamara Thorne, *Haunted*, 1995

4256

BRAD STRICKLAND

Dragon's Plunder
(New York: Atheneum, 1992)

Story type: Fantasy (Quest)
Series: Dragonflight
Major character(s): Jamie Falconer, Wizard; Deadmon, Pirate, Sea Captain; Amelia, Royalty (princess)
Time period(s): Indeterminate
Locale(s): *Betty*, At Sea; Windrose Island, Mythical Place

Summary: Unable to rest until he has plundered a dragon's hoard, the deceased Captain Deadmon enlists the help of Jamie Falconer, who possesses the ability of whistling up a breeze any time he wishes.

Other books you might like:
Louise Cooper, *The Sleep of Stone*, 1991
Charles de Lint, *The Dreaming Place*, 1990
Tanith Lee, *Black Unicorn*, 1991
Robert Silverberg, *Letters From Atlantis*, 1990
Tad Williams, *Child of an Ancient City*, 1992
  Nina Kiriki Hoffman, co-author

4257

BRAD STRICKLAND

Wizard's Mole
(New York: Roc, 1991)

Story type: Fantasy (Light Fantasy; Alternate World)
Series: Jeremy Moon
Major character(s): Jeremy Moon, Magician, Advertising; Nul, Animal (mole); Barach Loremaster, Wizard
Time period(s): 1990s
Locale(s): Thaumia, Planet—Imaginary (Whitehorn Keep); New York, New York

Summary: The Evil Dark One once again troubles Thaumia and may be controlling one of the mages there. Jeremy Moon's double, Sebastian, now on Earth, may be able to help recognize him. When Jeremy goes to Earth to get his help, Sebastian returns to Thaumia, leaving Jeremy behind. Jeremy must defeat the Evil Dark One and find a way home to his family on Thaumia.

Other books you might like:
Steven Brust, *Jhereg*, 1983
John DeChancie, *Castle Perilous*, 1988
Gordon R. Dickson, *The Dragon and the George*, 1976
Suzette Haden Elgin, *The Grand Jubilee*, 1981
Thorarinn Gunnarsson, *Make Way for Dragons!*, 1990
John Morressy, *Kedrigern in Wanderland*, 1988
Terry Pratchett, *Wyrd Sisters*, 1990

4258

WHITLEY STRIEBER

Billy

(New York: Putnams, 1990)

Story type: Horror (Serial Killer)
Major character(s): Billy Neary, Child (12-year-old boy); Barton Royal, Murderer (child molester); Mark Neary, Teacher (high school history teacher)
Time period(s): 1990s (1990)
Locale(s): Stevensville, Iowa

Summary: Abused as a child, mentally deranged Barton Royal abducts Billy Neary from a shopping mall and subjects him to a series of physical and psychological torments as he debates whether to adopt the boy or murder him.

Other books you might like:
Robert Bloch, *The Kidnaper*, 1954
Thomas Harris, *The Silence of the Lambs*, 1988
Jim Thompson, *After Dark, My Sweet*, 1955

4259

WHITLEY STRIEBER

The Forbidden Zone

(New York: Dutton, 1993)

Story type: Horror (Apocalyptic Horror)
Major character(s): Brian Kelly, Scientist; Ellen Maas, Journalist; Bob Kelly, Police Officer
Time period(s): 1990s (1993)
Locale(s): Oscola, New York

Summary: A series of strange events in the sleepy little town of Oscola—screaming heard underground, the transformation of townspeople into soulless zombies, and the infiltration of the surrounding woods by monstrous creatures—leads Brian Kelly to speculate that colleagues using the data he generated through experiments in subatomic particle physics have broken through to another dimension that is trying to take over our own.

Other books you might like:
T.E.D. Klein, *The Ceremonies*, 1984
Brian Lumley, *The Burrowers Beneath*, 1974
John Skipp, *The Scream*, 1988
 Craig Spector, co-author
F. Paul Wilson, *Nightworld*, 1992

4260

WHITLEY STRIEBER

Majestic

(New York: Putnam, 1989)

Story type: Science Fiction (UFO)
Major character(s): Nicholas Duke, Journalist; Will Stone, Spy (CIA agent)
Time period(s): 1940s (1947)
Locale(s): New Mexico

Summary: In 1947 an alien spacecraft crash lands near Roswell, New Mexico and the corpses of two aliens and a surgically altered human fetus are discovered, but the matter is quickly hushed up. A journalist attempting to find out the truth discovers a massive cover-up which evidently continues to this day.

Other books you might like:
Robert A. Heinlein, *The Puppet Masters*, 1951
Fritz Leiber, *The Wanderer*, 1964
Garfield Reeves-Stevens, *Nighteyes*, 1989

4261

WHITLEY STRIEBER

Unholy Fire

(New York: Dutton, 1992)

Story type: Horror (Occult)
Major character(s): John Rafferty, Religious (priest); Frank Bayley, Religious (priest); Maria Julien, Heiress
Time period(s): 1990s (1992)
Locale(s): New York, New York

Summary: The struggle between two priests for the pastorship of Mary and Joseph, a Catholic Church in New York's Greenwich Village, is exacerbated by the presence of Maria Julien, who entices both priests sexually. Maria's brutal death proves just the first in a vicious series modeled on those of the Inquisition and points to either psychosis or demonic possession of one of the two priests.

Other books you might like:
Adrian Blake, *Unholy Communion*, 1989
William Peter Blatty, *The Exorcist*, 1971
William Peter Blatty, *Legion*, 1983
Jack Olesker, *Confessional*, 1989

4262

WHITLEY STRIEBER

The Wild

(New York: Tor, 1991)

Story type: Horror (Werewolf Story)
Major character(s): Bob Duke, Stock Broker, Werewolf; Cindy Duke, Spouse (Bob's wife); Kevin Thomas Duke, Child (Cindy & Bob's 12-year-old son)
Time period(s): 1990s
Locale(s): New York, New York

Summary: Bob Duke assumes that his nightly dreams of turning into a wolf are only an expression of his subconscious mind's poetic rebellion against his mundane daily life. But one day, Bob awakens from his dreams transformed, and it becomes his wife's and son's responsibility to find and reclaim him before he runs amok.

Other books you might like:
Scott Bradfield, *Dream of the Wolf*, 1990
Michael Cadnum, *St. Peter's Wolf*, 1991
Dennis Danvers, *Wilderness*, 1991

4263

THEODORE STURGEON

Microcosmic God

(Berkeley, California: North Atlantic Books, 1995)

Story type: Science Fiction (Collection; Science Fiction)
Series: Complete Short Stories of Theodore Sturgeon

Summary: Contains at 27-page foreword by Samuel R. Delany, 22 pages of story notes by series editor Paul Williams, and 17 stories written between April 1940 and June 1941, all published in *Astounding* or *Unknown* except "The Anonymous" and "Two Sidecars," an unfinished early draft of "Microcosmic God." Second of 10 proposed volumes collecting all of Sturgeon's short fiction.

Other books you might like:
J.G. Ballard, *The Best Short Stories of J.G. Ballard*, 1978
Robert A. Heinlein, *The Green Hills of Earth*, 1951
Larry Niven, *N-Space*, 1990
Cordwainer Smith, *The Rediscovery of Man*, 1993
John Varley, *The Persistence of Vision*, 1978

4264

THEODORE STURGEON

Some of Your Blood

(New York: Carroll & Graf, 1994)

Story type: Horror (Vampire Story)
Major character(s): George Smith, Military Personnel; Philip Outerbridge, Psychologist; Albert Williams, Psychologist
Time period(s): 1950s
Locale(s): Smithton Township, California

Summary: Originally published in 1961, this novel is presented as the account of two psychologists trying to unravel the reason why a young soldier with a grotesque personal background and aberrant ways of coping with life events has developed a taste for blood.

Other books you might like:
Poppy Z. Brite, *Lost Souls*, 1992
Elizabeth Engstrom, *Black Ambrosia*, 1988
Roxanne Longstreet, *The Undead*, 1993
Anne Rice, *Interview with the Vampire*, 1975

4265

THEODORE STURGEON

The Ultimate Egoist

(Berkeley, California: North Atlantic Books, 1994)

Story type: Science Fiction (Collection)

Summary: Contains a four-page Ray Bradbury foreword, a three-page Arthur C. Clarke foreword, a three-page Gene Wolfe foreword, 36 pages of story notes by the book's editor, Paul Williams, with extensive comments by Sturgeon on individual stories. Text consists of one poem and 46 stories submitted to publishers 1937-1940, 10 original and 36 reprinted from periodicals. Stories reflect Sturgeon's earliest

work and include "Bianca's Hands," "Derm Fool" and "It." First of ten proposed volumes collecting all the author's short fiction.

Other books you might like:
Alfred Bester, *Star Light, Star Bright*, 1976
Philip K. Dick, *The Collected Stories of Philip K. Dick*, 1987
    five volumes
Robert A. Heinlein, *The Past through Tomorrow*, 1967
Larry Niven, *Tales of Known Space*, 1975
Cordwainer Smith, *The Rediscovery of Man*, 1993
John Varley, *Blue Champagne*, 1986

4266

TIM SULLIVAN, Editor

Cold Shocks

(New York: Avon, 1991)

Story type: Horror (Anthology)

Summary: Sixteen original stories that use cold geographic locales or the winter months as a basis for the horrors they unfold. Included are Graham Masterton's tale of an ill-fated polar expedition, "The Sixth Man"; S.P. Somtow's tale of the terrors of a peculiar festival in Japan, "The Pavilion of Frozen Women"; Michael Tolman's fantasy, "A Winter Memory," chronicling a time after the sun has ceased to shine; Gray Brandner's "The Ice Children" and Steve Rasnic Tem's "Adleparmeun," both about the influence of primitive folk tales and legends on their protagonists; and Chet Williamson's tale of unusual hunters, "First Kill."

Other books you might like:
Ramsey Campbell, *Midnight Sun*, 1990
Basil Copper, *The Great White Space*, 1974
Graham Masterton, *The Manitou*, 1975

4267

TIM SULLIVAN

Lords of Creation

(New York: Avon, 1992)

Story type: Science Fiction (First Contact; Theological)
Major character(s): David Albee, Scientist (paleontologist); Jeffrey Flanagan, Religious (evangelist), Administrator (Secretary of Morality); Charles Margolis, Administrator (White House Chief of Staff)
Time period(s): 1990s (1999)
Locale(s): Montana

Summary: The Christian Millennialists in control of the government have eliminated any grants for paleontological digs or research. David Albee, a dinosaur lover, and his fellow amateur paleontologists find a 65 million-year-old box containing five dinosaur eggs which have been preserved by a stasis field. A local veterinarian and David's ex-girlfriend Liz care for the hatched dinosaurs under the auspices of the federal government. The young dinosaurs exhibit unusually rapid growth and remarkable intelligence for the short time since they've hatched; however their voracious appetite for protein may lead to their destruction.

Other books you might like:
David Brin, *Earth*, 1990
C.J. Cherryh, *Forty Thousand in Gehenna*, 1983
Michael Crichton, *Jurassic Park*, 1990
Parke Godwin, *The Snake Oil Wars*, 1989
Parke Godwin, *Waiting for the Galactic Bus*, 1988
Larry Niven, *The Flight of the Horse*, 1973
Dave Wolverton, *Serpent Catch*, 1991

4268

TIM SULLIVAN

The Parasite War
(New York: Avon, 1989)

Story type: Science Fiction (Invasion of Earth)
Major character(s): Alex Ward, Veteran; Jo, Social Worker
Time period(s): Indeterminate Future
Locale(s): United States

Summary: A Vietnam vet leads the battle against hideous alien parasites who turn human beings into monsters. The only people who appear to be immune to the parasites are those with a history of mental problems.

Other books you might like:
David Gerrold, *A Day for Damnation*, 1984
David Gerrold, *A Matter for Men*, 1983
David Gerrold, *A Rage for Revenge*, 1989
Robert A. Heinlein, *The Puppet Masters*, 1951
Kate Wilhelm, *The Clone*, 1965
    Ted Thomas, co-author

4269

TRICIA SULLIVAN

Lethe
(New York: Bantam Spectra, 1995)

Story type: Science Fiction (Genetic Manipulation; Lost Colony)
Major character(s): Jenae Kim, Genetically Altered Being; Daire Morales, Pilot, Spaceman; Tsering, Genetically Altered Being
Time period(s): 22nd century (2166)
Locale(s): Earth; Dilarang, Planet—Imaginary

Summary: Investigating a mysterious object in solar orbit, Daire Morales disappears through a ''gate'' and finds himself on an alien planet populated by the descendants of shipwrecked humans. News travels to the League of New Alchemists, who rule an Earth nearly destroyed by ecological poisons and wars. Jenae Kim, whose genetic mutations allow her to breathe underwater and communicate with dolphins, accepts the assignment of finding the key to open the gate again. But when she finds the secret, she also realizes that the ruling oligarchy does not want the truth revealed. First novel.

Other books you might like:
David Brin, *Startide Rising*, 1983
Octavia E. Butler, *Dawn*, 1987
C.J. Cherryh, *Cyteen*, 1988
John Varley, *The Ophiuchi Hotline*, 1977

Vernor Vinge, *A Fire upon the Deep*, 1992

4270

MARK SUMMER

Devil's Tower
(New York: Ballantine Del Rey, 1996)

Story type: Fantasy (Magic Conflict; Alternate History)
Series: Jake Bird
Major character(s): Jake Bird, Maintenance Worker (stablehand); George Armstrong Custer, Sorcerer, Historical Figure; Hatty Ash, Healer
Time period(s): 1870s
Locale(s): Laramie, Wyoming

Summary: In an Old West where the sudden development of magic interrupts the American Civil War, Jake Bird lies low. He fears General Custer, who killed Bird's father and who possesses unheard-of magical power. Unfortunately for Jake Bird, fate pushes him towards a confrontation with Custer and destiny.

Other books you might like:
Orson Scott Card, *Seventh Son*, 1987
David Drake, *Old Nathan*, 1991
Alan Dean Foster, *Mad Amos*, 1996
Kenyon Morr, *Kingdom of Sorrow*, 1996
    pseudonym of Mark Sumner and Marella Sands
Kenyon Morr, *See No Weevil*, 1996
    pseudonym of Mark Summer and Marella Sands
Midori Snyder, *The Flight of Michael McBride*, 1994
Harry Turtledove, *The Guns of the South*, 1992

4271

ROSEMARY SUTCLIFF

The Shining Company
(New York: Farrar, Straus and Giroux, 1990)

Story type: Fantasy (Historical; Legend)
Major character(s): Prosper, Nobleman; Conn, Slave; Gorthyn, Royalty (prince)
Time period(s): 7th century
Locale(s): Scotland

Summary: King Mynyddog calls 300 warriors together to form the Companions. When they have trained for a year, they go to fight the invading Saxons. Prosper, a shield bearer, tells the tale of how the Shining Company learns to work as one and their valiant battle against overwhelming odds. This is an ALA Notable Children's Books For Older Readers title.

Other books you might like:
Lloyd Alexander, *The Book of Three*, 1964
Marion Zimmer Bradley, *The Mists of Avalon*, 1983
Morgan Llywelyn, *Red Branch*, 1988
Thomas Mallory, *Le Morte d'Arthur*, 1982

4272

RICHARD SUTPHEN

Sexpunks and Savage Sagas

(Agoura Hills, California: Spine-Tingling Press, 1991)

Story type: Horror (Collection)

Summary: Thirteen short stories plus the short novel ''Pisces Rising,'' most of which merge the physicality of sexual horror with the out-of-body spirituality of the New Age. In ''Freak Link,'' a woman accidentally becomes psychically linked to a grotesque alter ego. In ''The AIDS Giver,'' a male prostitute, fully aware he is HIV-positive, gets his just rewards from all of his contacts. In ''The Mislabeled Tape,'' a mix-up in audiotape packaging turns an out-of-shape milquetoast into a subliminally programmed super-lover. And in ''The Inflatable Woman''—well, never mind.

Other books you might like:
Ramsey Campbell, *Scared Stiff*, 1987
Ray Garton, *Methods of Madness*, 1991
David J. Schow, *Seeing Red*, 1990
John Skipp, *Deadlines*, 1990
　Craig Spector, co-author

4273

HANNE MARIE SVENDSEN

The Gold Ball

(New York: Knopf, 1989)

Story type: Fantasy (Magic Conflict)
Time period(s): Indeterminate
Locale(s): Denmark

Summary: The story follows the history of a small island off the coast of Denmark, and the life of Maja Stinn. Magic works on the island, but it is not mysterious magic.

Other books you might like:
Peter Gadol, *Coyote*, 1990

4274

S. ANDREW SWANN (Pseudonym of Steven Swiniarski)

Emperors of the Twilight

(New York: DAW, 1994)

Story type: Science Fiction (Genetic Manipulation; Invasion of Earth)
Series: Forests of the Night
Major character(s): Evi Isham, Genetically Altered Being, Human; Ezra Frey, Military Personnel (retired); Nohar Rajasthan, Genetically Altered Being, Animal (tiger)
Time period(s): 2050s (2058)
Locale(s): New York, New York

Summary: Just back from vacation, Evi Isham begins her day with the Peeper still watching her exercise, until the sniper starts shooting and the genetically modified Afghanis attempt to kidnap or kill her. Evi's attempt to escape starts her building on fire, and while she runs away through Central Park, Ezra Frey saves her from a cyborg dog. Frey, her old Agency contact, gets killed just before he can explain who wants her dead and why—and dawn has not yet broken.

Other books you might like:
Lois McMaster Bujold, *Mirror Dance*, 1994
Stephen Goldin, *Jade Darcy and the Affair of Honor*, 1988
　Mary Mason, co-author
Jonathan Lethem, *Gun, with Occasional Music*, 1994
Laura J. Mixon, *Glass Houses*, 1992
David Weber, *On Basilisk Station*, 1993

4275

S. ANDREW SWANN (Pseudonym of Steven Swiniarski)

Forests of the Night

(New York: DAW, 1993)

Story type: Science Fiction (Genetic Manipulation; Mystery)
Major character(s): Nohar Rajasthan, Genetically Altered Being (tiger), Detective—Private; Mandvi ''Manny'' Gujerat, Genetically Altered Being (mongoose), Doctor; Robert ''Bobby'' Dittrich, Computer Expert
Time period(s): 2050s
Locale(s): Cleveland, Ohio

Summary: When hired against his principles to find the murderer of a human politician, Nohar must defend himself and his friends from a rat gang, avoid the Feds who believe he deals drugs, thwart a plot to repeal the rights of genetically altered beings and identify the assassin who continues his killing spree.

Other books you might like:
Octavia E. Butler, *Dawn*, 1987
C.J. Cherryh, *Chanur's Legacy*, 1992
L. Warren Douglas, *A Plague of Change*, 1992
Thomas A. Easton, *Sparrowhawk*, 1990
George Alec Effinger, *When Gravity Fails*, 1987
Janet Kagan, *Mirabile*, 1991
Richard Paul Russo, *Destroying Angel*, 1992
Cordwainer Smith, *The Best of Cordwainer Smith*, 1975
David Alexander Smith, *In the Cube*, 1993
Vernor Vinge, *A Fire upon the Deep*, 1992

4276

S. ANDREW SWANN (Pseudonym of Steven Swiniarski)

Partisan

(New York: DAW, 1995)

Story type: Science Fiction (Political)
Series: Hostile Takeover
Major character(s): Dominic ''Dom'' Magnus, Cyborg, Businessman; Klaus Dacham, Military Personnel (colonel, TEC); Kari Tetsami, Computer Expert, Genetically Altered Being
Time period(s): 24th century
Locale(s): Bakunin, Planet—Imaginary; Earth

Summary: Klaus Dacham's plan to subdue the independent planet Bakunin continues with one commune after another falling to his military superiority. The Diderot Holding Company begins to muster support for the resistance, while back on Earth, the political situation grows increasingly complex and dangerous.

Other books you might like:
Iain M. Banks, *Consider Phlebas*, 1987
Glen Cook, *The Dragon Never Sleeps*, 1988
Robert A. Heinlein, *The Moon Is a Harsh Mistress*, 1966
Steve Perry, *The Man Who Never Missed*, 1985
F. Paul Wilson, *The LaNague Chronicles*, 1992

4277

S. ANDREW SWANN (Pseudonym of Steven Swiniarski)

Profiteer

(New York: DAW, 1995)

Story type: Science Fiction (Political)
Series: Hostile Takeover
Major character(s): Dominic "Dom" Magnus, Cyborg, Businessman; Kari Tetsami, Computer Expert, Genetically Altered Being; Random Walk, Artificial Intelligence
Time period(s): 24th century
Locale(s): Bakunin, Planet—Imaginary; Earth; Mars

Summary: To escape his past as a government agent, Dominic Magnus retires to Bakunin, the only human-occupied planet not part of the Terran Confederacy. Unfortunately, the Terran Confederacy decides that Bakunin must be brought into line and sends troops led by Magnus's worst enemy. Magnus must escape and act quickly to save Bakunin's freedom and his own life.

Other books you might like:
Robert A. Heinlein, *The Moon Is a Harsh Mistress*, 1966
Christopher Hinz, *Liege-Killer*, 1987
Ursula K. Le Guin, *The Dispossessed*, 1974
Steve Perry, *The Man Who Never Missed*, 1985
F. Paul Wilson, *The LaNague Chronicles*, 1992

4278

S. ANDREW SWANN (Pseudonym of Steven Swiniarski)

Revolutionary

(New York: DAW, 1996)

Story type: Science Fiction (Political; Alternate Intelligence)
Series: Hostile Takeover
Major character(s): Dominic "Dom" Magnus, Cyborg, Businessman; Kari Tetsami, Computer Expert, Genetically Altered Being; Random Walk, Artificial Intelligence
Time period(s): 24th century
Locale(s): Bakunin, Planet—Imaginary

Summary: Warfare between Dom and his brother wreaks havoc on Bakunin. With most of the population dead or under siege, Bakunin needs help from a major power to rescue the planet from the Terran Executive Command attack, risking takeover of the planetary anarchy.

Other books you might like:
Robert A. Heinlein, *The Moon Is a Harsh Mistress*, 1966
Ursula K. Le Guin, *The Dispossessed*, 1974
Alis A. Rasmussen, *The Price of Ransom*, 1990

Robert J. Sawyer, *Starplex*, 1996
Diann Thornley, *Ganwold's Child*, 1995
F. Paul Wilson, *The LaNague Chronicles*, 1992

4279

S. ANDREW SWANN (Pseudonym of Steven Swiniarski)

Specters of the Dawn

(New York: DAW, 1994)

Story type: Science Fiction (Genetic Manipulation; Mystery)
Series: Forests of the Night
Major character(s): Angelica "Angel" Lorenzo Lopez, Genetically Altered Being (rabbit); Byron Dorset, Genetically Altered Being (fox); Anaka, Detective—Police
Time period(s): 2050s
Locale(s): San Francisco, California

Summary: Arriving in San Francisco and looking forward to living in a town without prejudice, Angel little expects the need to defend herself from crazy skinheads in her local sports bar. When she goes with the police to identify Byron's body, Angel discovers that someone wants the property she inherited as his heri.

Other books you might like:
David Brin, *Glory Season*, 1993
Octavia E. Butler, *Dawn*, 1987
Thomas A. Easton, *Sparrowhawk*, 1990
Joan Slonczewski, *Daughter of Elysium*, 1993
Cordwainer Smith, *The Best of Cordwainer Smith*, 1975

4280

MICHAEL SWANWICK

Gravity's Angels

(Sauk City, Wisconsin: Arkham House, 1991)

Story type: Science Fiction (Collection)
Summary: This collection contains 13 stories published in magazines and anthologies between 1980 and 1989 including Nebula Award finalist stories "The Feast of St. Janis," "Ginungagap," "Mummer Kiss," and "Trojan Horse." One story, "The Man Who Met Picasso," was nominated for a World Fantasy Award, while "The Edge of the World" was nominated for both Hugo and Nebula Awards and then won the Theodore Sturgeon Award for short fiction.

Other books you might like:
J.G. Ballard, *Memories of the Space Ages*, 1988
Greg Bear, *The Wind From a Burning Woman*, 1983
Michael Bishop, *Blooded on Arachne*, 1982
Michael Bishop, *One Winter in Eden*, 1984
Phyllis Eisenstein, *Born to Exile*, 1978
Michael Flynn, *The Nanotech Chronicles*, 1991
Janet Kagan, *Mirabile*, 1991
Tanith Lee, *Dreams of Dark and Light*, 1986
Larry Niven, *Tales of Known Space*, 1975
Cordwainer Smith, *The Best of Cordwainer Smith*, 1975
Marc Stiegler, *The Gentle Seduction*, 1990
James Tiptree Jr., *Her Smoke Rose Up Forever*, 1990
    Alice Sheldon, real name

John Varley, *Blue Champagne*, 1986
John Varley, *The Persistence of Vision*, 1978

4281

MICHAEL SWANWICK

Griffin's Egg
(New York: St. Martin's Press, 1992)

Story type: Science Fiction (Adventure; Political)
Major character(s): Gunther Weil, Worker (lunar transport driver); Ekatarina Izmailova, Scientist, Leader
Time period(s): 21st century
Locale(s): Moon (Earth's)

Summary: When Earth becomes too ecologically sensitive for continued environmental abuse by corporations, companies move to Luna to continue research without ecological fallout. As war breaks out on Earth, sabotage affects those on Luna, many of whom suffer the effects of a recent development in human neurochemistry which allows modification of higher brain functions.

Other books you might like:
Robert A. Heinlein, *The Moon Is a Harsh Mistress*, 1966
Marjorie Bradley Kellogg, *Harmony*, 1991
Allen Steele, *Lunar Descent*, 1991
Neal Stephenson, *Snow Crash*, 1992
John Varley, *Steel Beach*, 1992

4282

MICHAEL SWANWICK

The Iron Dragon's Daughter
(New York: Morrow/AvoNova, 1994)

Story type: Fantasy (Urban; Science Fiction)
Major character(s): Jane Alderberry, Student, Thief; Melanchthon ''7332'', Mythical Creature (dragon); Puck Aleshire, Mythical Creature
Time period(s): Indeterminate Future
Locale(s): Great Gray City, Fictional City

Summary: In her bleak existence as a factory worker turning out dragons for the military, Jane finds little hope for the future until she befriends dragon-plane 7332. Their bargain yields some hope of a brighter future including formal education and new friends but the temptations of the street prove irresistible while Jane's sexual studies precipitously alter her relationship with Melanchthon.

Other books you might like:
C.S. Friedman, *When True Night Falls*, 1993
Mary Gentle, *Rats and Gargoyles*, 1991
P.C. Hodgell, *God Stalk*, 1982
Will Shetterly, *Elsewhere*, 1991
Sheri S. Tepper, *A Plague of Angels*, 1993

4283

MICHAEL SWANWICK

Stations of the Tide
(New York: Morrow, 1991)

Major character(s): The Bureaucrat, Agent; Gregorian, Scientist, Magician; Chu, Police Officer
Time period(s): Indeterminate Future
Locale(s): Miranda, Planet—Imaginary

Summary: The planet Miranda is periodically inundated and all land surfaces are expected to be washed clean. The bureaucrat is sent to Miranda to confront Gregorian, and talk the ''magician'' into returning the proscribed technology. Gregorian demonstrates his magical prowess, and the agency back on Earth denies the alleged theft, but declines to recall the bureaucrat.

Other books you might like:
Alfred Bester, *The Demolished Man*, 1953
Octavia E. Butler, *Adulthood Rites*, 1988
Octavia E. Butler, *Dawn*, 1987
Octavia E. Butler, *Imago*, 1989
Robert A. Heinlein, *Stranger in a Strange Land*, 1991
Sheri S. Tepper, *Grass*, 1990

4284

S.A. SWINIARSKI (Pseudonym of Steven Swiniarski)

Raven
(New York: DAW, 1996)

Story type: Horror (Black Magic; Vampire Story)
Major character(s): Kane Tyler, Detective; Gail Tyler, Teenager; Manuel ''Childe'' Deite, Sorcerer
Time period(s): 1990s (1996)
Locale(s): Cleveland, Ohio

Summary: Private detective Kane Tyler awakens out of an amnesiac fugue with a vampiric taste for blood and a price on his head for the ritualistic murder of his ex-wife. His efforts to retrieve his memory and discover how this state of affairs has come to pass bring him into contact with Childe, a black magician who leads a cult of the undead and who has targeted Kane for his investigations into the cult's activities. First novel.

Other books you might like:
Vincent Courtney, *Vampire Beat*, 1991
P.N. Elrod, *Bloodlist*, 1991
Tanya Huff, *Blood Price*, 1991
Lee Killough, *Blood Hunt*, 1987
Karen E. Taylor, *Blood Ties*, 1995

4285

JEFFERSON P. SWYCAFFER

Warsprite
(Lake Geneva, Wisconsin: TSR, 1990)

Story type: Science Fiction (Robot Fiction)

Major character(s): Delta, Robot; Sam Taramasco, Scientist; Madeline Leuoir Schenk, Museum Curator
Time period(s): Indeterminate Future
Locale(s): Southwest; San Antonio, Texas

Summary: Two leftovers from a galactic war have fallen on the planet Earth. Delta was created to find the robot Omicron. Learning about Earth as she goes, Delta acquires enemies and allies in her pursuit. Finally she confronts Omicron in a chamber beneath a nuclear test site in the Nevada desert.

Other books you might like:
Isaac Asimov, *The Robots of Dawn*, 1983
Margaret Wander Bonanno, *Strangers From the Sky*, 1987
Philip K. Dick, *Blade Runner*, 1982
Alan Dean Foster, *Starman*, 1984
Anne McCaffrey, *The Ship Who Sang*, 1970

4286
JEFFERSON P. SWYCAFFER

Web of Futures
(Lake Geneva, Wisconsin: TSR, 1991)

Story type: Fantasy (Religious; Time Travel)
Major character(s): Maddock O'Shaughnessy, Time Traveller; Stheneleos Magus LXIV, Alien, Time Traveller
Time period(s): 1860s (1862); 2010s (2017)
Locale(s): United States

Summary: Stheneleos Magus LXIV enlists Maddock's help saving human lives and caring for the souls of the dead he carries. Helpers join and leave the group as they travel from the Civil War era to the 21st century on their mission of enlightenment and rescue.

Other books you might like:
Pat Cadigan, *Mindplayers*, 1987
Diana G. Gallagher, *The Alien Dark*, 1990
Marc Laidlaw, *Neon Lotus*, 1988
Mike Resnick, *Soothsayer*, 1991
Jules Verne, *Mysterious Island*, 1876

4287
S.C. SYKES

Red Genesis
(New York: Bantam Spectra, 1991)

Story type: Science Fiction (Hard Science Fiction; Political)
Series: Next Wave
Major character(s): Graham Kuan Sinclair, Criminal, Businessman; Jonathan Baker, Sociologist; Paris Tucker, Settler, Adventurer
Time period(s): 21st century
Locale(s): Mars

Summary: Graham Sinclair, convicted of illegally dumping toxins which caused the deaths of millions, is sentenced to Mars without ever having the chance to see or hear anything of Earth again. On Mars, he finds friendship with his courier Jonathan Baker and a young Earth emigrant, Paris Tucker, then he marries and has a daughter. Pardoned after 20 years, he finds Mars is his true home. This second book in Spectra's

The Next Wave series contains a 10-page introduction by Isaac Asimov, a 26-page article titled "Off to Explore Mars" by MIT chief science writer Eugene Mallove, plus a brief Mars bibliography.

Other books you might like:
Isaac Asimov, *The Martian Way*, 1955
Ben Bova, *The Trikon Deception*, 1992
    Bill Pogue, co-author
Arthur C. Clarke, *The Sands of Mars*, 1952
D.G. Compton, *Farewell, Earth's Bliss*, 1971
Edward E. Hale, *The Man Without a Country*, 1863
Raymond Harris, *Shadows of the White Sun*, 1988
Ursula K. Le Guin, *The Dispossessed*, 1974
Frederik Pohl, *Man Plus*, 1976
Jerry Pournelle, *Prince of Mercenaries*, 1989
Pamela Sargent, *Venus of Dreams*, 1986

4288
RYDER SYVERTSON

Fortress of Forbidden Destiny
(New York: Pinnacle, 1991)

Story type: Science Fiction (Mystical; Adventure)
Series: Mystic Rebel
Major character(s): Burt Lasker, Martial Arts Expert, Religious (Mystic Rebel); Losang, Religious (Dalai Lama)
Time period(s): 1990s
Locale(s): Dharmsala, India; Beijing, China

Summary: Burt Lasker, ex-CIA agent, was shot down by Communist Chinese over Tibet, found by the Bonpa who trained him in E Kung and recognized by the Dalai Lama as the legendary Mystic Rebel expected to come and save Tibet. When trained masters of Buddhism start disappearing from their retreat near Dharmsala, the Dalai Lama requests help from Lasker to find them and prevent the destruction of mankind.

Other books you might like:
Jerry Earl Brown, *Snowmen*, 1991
Gordon R. Dickson, *Dorsai!*, 1976
Marc Laidlaw, *Neon Lotus*, 1988
Kim Stanley Robinson, *Escape From Kathmandu*, 1989
Elizabeth Ann Scarborough, *Nothing Sacred*, 1991

4289
STEVE SZILAGYI

Photographing Fairies
(New York: Ballantine, 1992)

Story type: Fantasy (Historical; Quest)
Major character(s): Arthur Conan Doyle, Historical Figure, Writer; Charles Castle, Photographer; Michael Walsmear, Police Officer (constable)
Time period(s): 1920s
Locale(s): London, England; Burkinwell, England

Summary: A country constable approaches Sir Arthur Conan Doyle to verify the photographs of fairies on Charles Castle. When Doyle instead tries to have photographs destroyed,

Castle decides to learn the truth, traveling to Burkinwell and finally discovering the people and fairies seen in the photographs. Author's first book.

Other books you might like:
Alan Dean Foster, *Quozl*, 1989
Tanya Huff, *Gate of Darkness, Circle of Light*, 1989
Jody Lynn Nye, *Mythology Abroad*, 1991
James D. Priest, *Kirins: The Spell of No'an*, 1990
Kristine Kathryn Rusch, *The Gallery of His Dreams*, 1991

4290

MICHAEL TALBOT

Night Things
(New York: Avon, 1989)

Story type: Horror (Haunted House)
Major character(s): Lauren Ransom, Spouse (recent bride); Garrett Ransom, Child (Lauren's 11-year-old son)
Time period(s): 1980s (Prologue in 1870)
Locale(s): New York (Lake House, a lodge in the Adirondacks)

Summary: Pop recording star Stephen Ransom takes his new bride, Lauren, and her son Garrett to live in Lake House, a huge lodge, filled with strange staircases and hidden rooms. Soon the marriage sours, the frightening history of the house envelops them, and they must face the "Master," a mysterious demonic figure who would use the house to unleash a terrible evil upon the world.

Other books you might like:
John Farris, *Wildwood*, 1987
Stephen King, *The Shining*, 1977
Chet Williamson, *Soulstorm*, 1986

4291

ROBYN TALLIS

Rebel From Alphorion
(New York: Ballantine Ivy, 1989)

Story type: Science Fiction (Young Adult)
Series: Planet Builders
Major character(s): Philippa Bidding, Teenager; Will Mornette, Teenager
Time period(s): 26th century (2520)
Locale(s): Gauguin, Planet—Imaginary

Summary: Philippa's family was exiled from the planet Alphorion but now she's being called back by her former boyfriend, the leader of the rebels attempting to overthrow the evil rulers of the planet.

Other books you might like:
Frank Asch, *Journey to Terezor*, 1989
Janet Asimov, *Norby Down to Earth*, 1989
    Isaac Asimov, co-author
Jo Dereske, *The Lone Sentinel*, 1989

4292

DEBORAH TALMADGE-BICKMORE

The Apprentice
(New York: Ballantine/Del Rey, 1990)

Story type: Fantasy (Magic Conflict)
Major character(s): Jaimah, Servant (Female); Corwyn, Apprentice (Male)
Time period(s): Indeterminate

Summary: A servant girl, whose magical powers have been stolen, is trapped between her sorceress employer, Shayna, and Corwyn, the sorceress's apprentice, who are fighting one another for power.

Other books you might like:
Mary Brown, *The Unlikely Ones*, 1987

4293

DEBORAH TALMADGE-BICKMORE

The Heldan
(New York: Ballantine Del Rey, 1994)

Story type: Fantasy (Quest; Psychic Powers)
Major character(s): Senea, Military Personnel (draftee), Psychic (esper); Vayhawk, Warrior, Leader; Aldived, Leader (Tribelord)
Time period(s): Indeterminate
Locale(s): Mon'ay, Fictional City

Summary: Still unmarried at the age of 24, Senea must become a heldan to defend her village when drafted to the Held and forbidden family contact. When attacked by the Ja'sid, Senea discovers she has legendary psychic abilities unknown to her previously. She and Vayhawk, who chooses her as his student, must learn to control their gift to avoid defeat or exile.

Other books you might like:
Orson Scott Card, *The Folk of the Fringe*, 1989
Edmund Cooper, *The Cloud Walker*, 1973
Ursula K. Le Guin, *Always Coming Home*, 1987
C.L. Moore, *Jirel of Joiry*, 1969
Elizabeth Ann Scarborough, *The Healer's War*, 1989
S.M. Stirling, *The Rose Sea*, 1994
    Holly Lisle, co-author

4294

CECILIA TAN, Editor

The Beast Within: Erotic Tales of Werewolves
(Boston: Circlet Press, 1994)

Story type: Horror (Anthology; Werewolf Story)
Summary: This quartet of stories uses the werewolf theme to explore ideas of human sexuality. Jay Michaelson's "The Spirit That Denies" has a werewolf instruct his lover in the proper methods of killing before becoming a werewolf initiate herself. Linda Hooper's "The Killing of the Calf" tells of the erotic relationship between a woman and a wolf bitch, and

Robert M. Schroeck's "Alma Mater" recounts the unique destiny of a man soldier saved by a female werewolf lover. In Reina Delacroix's "Wilderland," a mortal with lycanthropic inclinations finds her dreams come true in a virtual reality scenario that allows her to act out her predatory tendencies.

Other books you might like:

Byron Preiss, *The Ultimate Werewolf*, 1992
  editor
Brian J. Frost, *Book of the Werewolf*, 1973
  editor
David Hill, *The Way of the Werewolf*, 1966
  editor
Stephen Jones, *The Mammoth Book of Werewolves*, 1994
  editor
Bill Pronzini, *Werewolf!*, 1979
  editor

4295

CECILIA TAN, Editor

Blood Kiss: Vampire Erotica

(Boston: Circlet Press, 1994)

Story type: Horror (Anthology; Vampire Story)

Summary: This chapbook collects seven stories that explore heterosexuality and homosexuality under the guise of vampire fiction. Pat Salah's "The Perfect Form" explores an after hours club for vampires and vampire wannabes and "Cinnamon Roses," an unusual beauty salon staffed by vampires. Warren Lapine's "The Hunger" is a vampire tale set in a postapocalyptic world and Amelia G's "Wanting" the tale of a groupie who befriends the vampire rock star she idolizes. In Raven Kaldera's "Predator," vampirism is caused by a sexually-transmitted virus, and in David Smeds' "Loved to Death" it manifests as a woman whose voracious sexual appetite drains her companions of their life force. Gary Bowen's "The Brass Ring," a novel excerpt, chronicles the relationship of a vampire shapeshifter and his lover.

Other books you might like:

Poppy Z. Brite, *Love in Vein*, 1994
  editor
Ellen Datlow, *Little Deaths*, 1994
  editor
Jeff Gelb, *Hottest Blood: The Ultimate in Erotic Horror*, 1993
  editor
Pam Keesey, *Daughters of Darkness: Lesbian Vampire Stories*, 1993
  editor

4296

CECILIA TAN, Editor

Erotica Vampirica

(Boston: Circlet Press, 1996)

Story type: Horror (Anthology; Vampire Story)

Summary: Ten erotic fantasies written especially for this volume feature male and female vampires. Whitt Pond's "When Michael Comes" tells of a vampire who resists turning his lover into one of the undead through their sexual union. R. Boyczuk's "Doing Time" is concerned with a vampire sent to prison for crimes his lover committed. In Lela E. Buis's "Shadows," a woman is stalked by the vampire brother of her dead husband. Alan Smale's "Vox Vampirica" features two participants on a telephone sex line who make a supernatural fantasy come true.

Other books you might like:

Poppy Z. Brite, *Love in Vein*, 1994
  Martin H. Greenberg, co-editor
Poppy Z. Brite, *Love in Vein II*, 1997
  Martin H. Greenberg, co-editor
Pam Keesey, *Dark Angels: Lesbian Vampire Stories*, 1995
  editor
Pam Keesey, *Daughters of Darkness: Lesbian Vampire Stories*, 1993
  editor
Amarantha Knight, *Love Bites*, 1995
  editor
Michael Rowe, *Sons of Darkness: Tales of Men, Blood and Immortality*, 1996
  Thomas Roche, co-editor

4297

I.U. TARCHETTI

Fantastic Tales

(San Francisco, California: Mercury House, 1992)

Story type: Horror (Collection)

Summary: The only collection by a neglected nineteenth-century Italian writer of Gothic horror, this book assembles nine stories, two by other writers who strongly influenced Tarchetti, and a biographical essay. Included are "A Dead Man's Bone," based loosely on Theophile Gautier's classic "The Mummy's Foot"; "A Spirit in a Raspberry" (based on Erckmann-Chatrian's "The Burgomaster in the Bottle"), about a man who imbibes from a bottle of wine the spirit of the person from whose grave the grapevine grew; the Poe-esque tale of a madman's obsession, "The Letter U"; and a tale of necrophilia titled "Bouvard." The superb translation is by Lawrence Venutti.

Other books you might like:

Anonymous, *Ghost Tales of the Villa Deodati*, 1992
Margaret Crosland, *The Gothic Tales of the Marquis de Sade*, 1965
  editor
Peter Haining, *Gothic Tales of Terror*, 1972
  editor
E.T.A. Hoffmann, *The Best Tales of Hoffmann*, 1967

4298

JUDITH TARR

Alamut

(New York: Doubleday, 1989)

Story type: Fantasy (Romance)
Series: Alamut

Major character(s): Aidan, Royalty (Prince of Rhiyana), Mythical Creature (half-Faerie)
Time period(s): Indeterminate Past (Medieval period)
Locale(s): Jerusalem, Middle East (Saracen Lands); Alternate Universe

Summary: Aidan seeks vengeance on the powerful Assassins who have murdered his nephew and threaten to annihilate the entire family. The Assassins most powerful weapon, the immortal Morgiana, becomes one of Prince Aidan's two loves in this medieval romantic fantasy.

Other books you might like:
Tanith Lee, *A Heroine of the World*, 1989
Diana L. Paxson, *The White Raven*, 1989
Josepha Sherman, *The Shining Falcon*, 1989
Pamela Simpson, *Partners in Time*, 1990

4299

JUDITH TARR

Arrows of the Sun
(New York: Tor, 1993)

Story type: Fantasy (Political)
Series: Avaryan Rising
Major character(s): Estarion, Ruler (Golden Emperor); Vanyi, Religious (priestess)
Time period(s): Indeterminate
Locale(s): Asanion, Fictional Country

Summary: Having survived regency to ascend to the imperial throne, Estarion returns with his beloved Vanyi to the hated Asanion where deadly rivals for power await any opportunity for advancement.

Other books you might like:
M.A.R. Barker, *Flamesong*, 1985
M.A.R. Barker, *Man of Gold*, 1984
Gillian Bradshaw, *The Land of Gold*, 1992
Dave Duncan, *The Cutting Edge*, 1992
R.A. MacAvoy, *Lens of the World*, 1990
Melanie Rawn, *Dragon Prince*, 1988
Martha Wells, *The Element of Fire*, 1993

4300

JUDITH TARR

Ars Magica
(New York: Bantam, 1989)

Story type: Fantasy (Historical)
Major character(s): Gerbert, Religious (Monk)
Time period(s): Indeterminate Past (The Dark Ages)
Locale(s): Europe

Summary: Gerbert is first introduced as a young monk in France. The story follows him as he studies magic within the confines of the Catholic church, and later becomes a priest.

Other books you might like:
John Desjarlais, *The Throne of Tara*, 1990
Susan Howatch, *Glittering Images*, 1987

4301

JUDITH TARR

The Dagger and the Cross: A Novel of the Crusades
(New York: Doubleday Foundation, 1991)

Story type: Fantasy (Romance; Religious)
Series: Alamut
Major character(s): Aidan, Royalty (Prince of Rhiyana); Morgiana, Immortal, Noblewoman
Time period(s): Indeterminate Past (Medieval Period)
Locale(s): Acre, Middle East; Alternate Earth

Summary: Christian Knight Prince Aidan and Muslim Lady Morgiana are in love. King Gwydion, older identical twin to Aidan, brings the papal decree allowing them to marry. Powerful enemies conspire to keep them apart, and the magic from Aidan's Elvish mother may not be sufficient to overcome them.

Other books you might like:
Katherine Kurtz, *Camber of Culdi*, 1976
Tanith Lee, *A Heroine of the World*, 1989
Diana L. Paxson, *The White Raven*, 1989
Josepha Sherman, *The Shining Falcon*, 1989
Pamela Simonson, *Partners in Time*, 1990

4302

JUDITH TARR

His Majesty's Elephant
(New York: Harcourt Brace, 1993)

Story type: Fantasy (Historical; Young Adult)
Major character(s): Rowan, Witch; Charlemagne, Historical Figure, Ruler (Emperor of the West)
Time period(s): 9th century
Locale(s): Europe

Summary: When Charlemagne falls victim to an evil Byzantine spell, his daughter, Rowan, must call on her inherited magic and the power of a magic elephant talisman to effect a cure.

Other books you might like:
Lois McMaster Bujold, *The Spirit Ring*, 1993
Louise Cooper, *The Sleep of Stone*, 1991
Tanith Lee, *Black Unicorn*, 1991
Vivian Vande Velde, *Dragon's Bait*, 1992
Martha Wells, *The Element of Fire*, 1993

4303

JUDITH TARR

Lord of the Two Lands
(New York: Tor, 1993)

Story type: Fantasy (Historical)
Major character(s): Alexander the Great, Historical Figure, Warrior; Meriamon, Royalty, Religious
Time period(s): 4th century B.C.

Locale(s): Macedonia; Middle East; Egypt

Summary: After becoming King of Macedonia and ruler of the Hellenic city-states, Alexander the Great moves against the Persian Empire. In Egypt, the priests of Amon decide to secure Alexander's protection against the Persians by enticing him to rule Egypt. To further their goals, Meriamon journeys from Egypt to join the victorious Alexander and tempt him with Egyptian rule. First, however, Alexander must conquer Tyre and Gaza.

Other books you might like:
David Gemmell, *Dark Prince*, 1993
David Gemmell, *Lion of Macedon*, 1992
Nikos Kazantzakis, *Alexander the Great*, 1982
Edison Marshall, *Conqueror*, 1962
Mary Renault, *The Persian Boy*, 1972

4304

JUDITH TARR

Spear of Heaven
(New York: Tor, 1994)

Story type: Fantasy (Adventure; Political)
Series: Avaryan Rising
Major character(s): Daruya, Royalty, Magician; Vanyi, Magician, Leader (guildsmaster)
Time period(s): Indeterminate
Locale(s): Asanion, Fictional Country; Su-Shaklan, Fictional Country; Kingdom of Heaven, Fictional Country

Summary: Built during a lengthy peacetime, a series of gates allows rapid travel half way around the world. After Estarion plans to establish an Avaryan embassy at the most distant gate location, a disaster which closes the gateway interferes with Daruya's intention to go and mature a bit while away from home. Surreptitiously joining the diplomatic mission, Daruya must soon utilize her magical abilities. With some difficulty, the group reaches the Kingdom of Heaven where they can pursue the mystery of the destroyed gate in the isolated kingdom.

Other books you might like:
James Hilton, *Lost Horizon*, 1933
Edward Myers, *The Mountain Made of Light*, 1992
Geoff Ryman, *The Unconquered Country*, 1987
Elizabeth Ann Scarborough, *Nothing Sacred*, 1991

4305

JUDITH TARR

Throne of Isis
(New York: Tor Forge, 1994)

Story type: Fantasy (Political; Religious)
Major character(s): Cleopatra, Historical Figure, Religious (incarnation of Isis); Marcus Antonius, Historical Figure, Military Personnel; Dions, Religious (priestess of Isis), Psychic
Time period(s): 1st century B.C. (41 B.C.-30 B.C.)
Locale(s): Alexandria, Egypt; Greece; Asia Minor

Summary: Dione attends her goddess incarnate, Cleopatra, from her union with Marcus Antonius through his defeat and Cleopatra's suicide.

Other books you might like:
Marion Zimmer Bradley, *The Mists of Avalon*, 1983
Shere Hite, *The Divine Comedy of Ariadne and Jupiter: The Amazing and Spectacular Adventures of Ariadne and Jupiter in Heaven and on Earth*, 1994
Guy Gavriel Kay, *A Song for Arbonne*, 1993
Jennifer Roberson, *Lady of the Forest*, 1992

4306

DONNA TARTT

The Secret History
(New York: Alfred A. Knopf, 1992)

Story type: Horror (Psychological Suspense)
Major character(s): Richard Papen, Student—College; Henry Winter, Student—College; Julian Morrow, Professor (classics professor)
Time period(s): 1980s
Locale(s): Vermont (Hampden College)

Summary: When several students obsessively devoted to their classics studies accidentally kill a bystander during a pagan ritual in the Vermont woods, they struggle to cover up their crime—and formulate a plan for eliminating the one member of their group likely to report them to the authorities. This is the author's first novel.

Other books you might like:
Douglas Clegg, *Goat Dance*, 1989
Matthew J. Costello, *Darkborn*, 1992
Sean Costello, *The Cartoonist*, 1991
Mark Morris, *Toady*, 1990
Peter Straub, *Ghost Story*, 1979

4307

BERNARD TAYLOR

Charmed Life
(New York: Leisure, 1993)

Story type: Horror (Mystery)
Major character(s): Guy Holman, Teacher; Annie Milburn, Teacher; Mary Hughes, Spy
Time period(s): 1990s (1991)
Locale(s): London, England

Summary: While Guy Holman strives to discover the truth about the death of his estranged wife and the son she supposedly bore him years before, two mysterious groups of agents struggle against one another in the background of his life, each attempting to manipulate his role in world events. This novel was originally published in England in 1992.

Other books you might like:
Stephen King, *The Dead Zone*, 1979
Stephen King, *Insomnia*, 1994
Dean R. Koontz, *Lightning*, 1988
Dan Simmons, *Carrion Comfort*, 1989

4308

BERNARD TAYLOR

Evil Intent

(New York: Leisure, 1996)

Story type: Horror (Black Magic)
Major character(s): John Callow, Occultist; Jack Forrest, Writer (television screenwriter); Connie Forrest, Housewife
Time period(s): 1990s (1994)
Locale(s): Valley Green, England

Summary: When the Forrest family moves into their deceased cousin's home in rural Valley Green, they run afoul of their neighbor John Callow, an occultist feared throughout the town. Pretending to be a generous man, Callow begins eliminating family members one by one, passing them magical runes in gifts that summon occult forces. First published in England in 1994, this novel was inspired by M.R. James' classic story, ''Casting the Runes.''

Other books you might like:
Ramsey Campbell, *The Long Lost*, 1994
Ramsey Campbell, *Obsession*, 1985
Christopher Fowler, *Rune*, 1990
Phil Rickman, *The Man in the Moss*, 1994

4309

BERNARD TAYLOR

The Godsend

(New York: Leisure, 1992)

Story type: Horror (Evil Children)
Major character(s): Mr. Marlowe, Artist (book illustrator); Kate Marlowe, Housewife; Bonnie Bryant, Child, Foundling (adopted by the Marlowes)
Time period(s): 1970s (1976)
Locale(s): Little Haverstraw, England

Summary: When a strange woman leaves her day old infant with the Marlowes and disappears, it seems only natural for them to adopt the baby as their own. But as each of the Marlowes' other four children die under mysterious circumstances, the couple begin to wonder who—or what—they have adopted. This novel, the author's first, was originally published in 1976.

Other books you might like:
Ira Levin, *Rosemary's Baby*, 1967
Edmund Plante, *Seed of Evil*, 1991
David Seltzer, *The Omen*, 1976
Thomas Tryon, *The Other*, 1972

4310

BERNARD TAYLOR

Sweetheart, Sweetheart

(New York: Leisure, 1992)

Story type: Horror (Haunted House)

Major character(s): David Warwick, Teacher; Shelagh, Teacher, Fiance(e) (David's); Jean Timpson, Housekeeper
Time period(s): 1970s (1977)
Locale(s): Hillingham, England

Summary: David Warwick travels with his girlfriend Shelagh to Gerrard's Hill Cottage in Hillingham, where his twin brother Colin and Colin's wife Helen were slain. Although David suspects a local woman of their murders, it becomes increasingly clear through assaults on Shelagh that the house is imbued with the two-century-old spirit of a jealous female bent on destroying the two of them. This novel was originally published in 1977.

Other books you might like:
Michael Cadnum, *Nightlight*, 1989
Judith Hawkes, *Julian's House*, 1989
Shirley Jackson, *The Haunting of Hill House*, 1959
Paul Theroux, *The Black House*, 1977

4311

JERI TAYLOR

Mosaic

(New York: Pocket, 1996)

Story type: Science Fiction (Space Opera; Military)
Series: Star Trek: Voyager
Major character(s): Kathryn Janeway, Spaceship Captain, Space Explorer; Mark ''Hobbes'' Johnson, Philosopher, Scientist; Justin Tighe, Military Personnel (lieutenant)
Time period(s): 24th century
Locale(s): Delta Quadrant, Outer Space; Earth; Planet—Imaginary

Summary: While an Away Team visits an unknown planet as the Kazon search for them, Captain Janeway ponders what to do while reviewing her past from early childhood, through her Academy days and early missions, up to the present. One incident in her past gives her the clue she needs to rescue the Away Team.

Other books you might like:
Poul Anderson, *Ensign Flandry*, 1966
Pauline Ashwell, *Unwillingly to Earth*, 1992
F.M. Busby, *Star Rebel*, 1984
A. Bertram Chandler, *The Road to the Rim*, 1967
Alfred Coppel, *Glory's War*, 1995
Paula E. Downing, *Flare Star*, 1993
David Feintuch, *Midshipman's Hope*, 1994
L. Neil Smith, *Tom Paine Maru*, 1984

4312

KAREN E. TAYLOR

Bitter Blood

(New York: Zebra, 1994)

Story type: Horror (Vampire Story)
Series: Vampire Legacy
Major character(s): Deirdre Griffin, Vampire, Designer (fashion); Mitchell Greer, Detective—Police; Ron Wilkes, Lawyer

Time period(s): 1990s (1994)
Locale(s): New York, New York

Summary: Vampire Deirdre Griffin is called back from her exile in London to help rehabilitate the mortal lover with whom she engineered the death of Max Hunter, fellow vampire and owner of the Ballroom of Romance nightclub. Upon her return, Deirdre is haunted by the immortal spirit of Max, who has bequeathed all he owned to her. She also finds herself in the clutches of The Cadre, an elite cabal of vampires who resent her murder of Max and who force her to do their bidding under the penalty of death to her and all she holds dear. This is a sequel to *Blood Secrets*.

Other books you might like:
Michael Cecilione, *The Parliament of Blood*, 1992
Laurell K. Hamilton, *Guilty Pleasures*, 1993
Gordon Linzner, *The Troupe*, 1988
Michael Romkey, *The Vampire Papers*, 1994
Dan Simmons, *Carrion Comfort*, 1989

4313

KAREN E. TAYLOR

Blood Secrets

(New York: Zebra, 1994)

Story type: Horror (Vampire Story)
Series: Vampire Legacy
Major character(s): Deirdre Griffin, Vampire, Designer (fashion); Max Hunter, Businessman (nightclub owner); Mitchell Greer, Detective—Police
Time period(s): 1990s (1994)
Locale(s): New York, New York

Summary: Deirdre, a 150 year old vampire, works by day as a clothing designer, and by night frequents Ballroom of Romance, a hot New York nightclub where it's easy to find dates from whom she can take nonlethal nightly feedings. When patrons of the club begin dying gruesomely, Deirdre is compelled to find out who is responsible before suspicion falls upon her. First book in the series.

Other books you might like:
Anne Billson, *Suckers*, 1993
Poppy Z. Brite, *Lost Souls*, 1992
Ray Garton, *Live Girls*, 1987
Tanya Huff, *Blood Price*, 1991
Anne Rice, *The Vampire Lestat*, 1985

4314

KAREN E. TAYLOR

Blood Ties

(New York: Zebra, 1995)

Story type: Horror (Vampire Story)
Series: Vampire Legacy
Major character(s): Deirdre Griffin, Vampire, Designer; Mitchell Greer, Vampire, Detective—Police; Larry Martin, Vampire
Time period(s): 1990s (1995)
Locale(s): New York, New York

Summary: It's payback time for vampire nightclub owner Deirdre Griffin and her recently vampirized lover Mitch Greer. A renegade vampire is violating vampire protocol, killing others of his own kind as well as mortals, and the elite vampire hierarchy known as the Cadre enjoins them to kill the rebel. Deirdre's stake in the events is considerable, because her quarry is a vampire she herself converted.

Other books you might like:
Michael Cecilione, *The Parliament of Blood*, 1992
Christopher Golden, *Angel Souls and Devil Hearts*, 1995
Laurell K. Hamilton, *Guilty Pleasures*, 1993
Gordon Linzner, *The Troupe*, 1988
Michael Romkey, *The Vampire Papers*, 1994

4315

KEITH TAYLOR

Search for the Starblade

(New York: Ace, 1990)

Story type: Fantasy (Quest; Adventure)
Series: Danans
Major character(s): Oghmal, Warrior, Hero; Carbri, Musician (harp), Minstrel (bard); Dirona, Royalty (princess), Sorceress
Time period(s): Indeterminate
Locale(s): Ireland (Tirtangir); *Summer Dancer*, At Sea

Summary: Oghmal, Prince of the Danans, is a great warrior in search of a weapon worthy of his skills, so he and his twin brother Carbri, leave Ireland and set sail to find the legendary Isle of Swans whose people are the keepers of the Tree of Fire. There Oghmal receives the knowledge necessary to find the rare skymetal needed to make a sword that is not only unbreakable, but will also defeat sorcery. Oghmal marries Dirona, sister to the king of the Isle of Swans, and they and their companions go back to Ireland to find the skymetal of Oghmal's vision.

Other books you might like:
Kenneth C. Flint, *A Storm Upon Ulster*, 1980
Morgan Llywelyn, *Bard*, 1987
Morgan Llywelyn, *The Horse Goddess*, 1982
Morgan Llywelyn, *Lion of Ireland*, 1980
Michael Moorcock, *Elric of Melnibone*, 1972

4316

L.A. TAYLOR

Cat's Paw

(New York: Ace, 1995)

Story type: Fantasy (Mystery; Contemporary Realism)
Major character(s): Miranda Glivven, Detective—Amateur, Spouse; The Cat, Animal, Companion
Time period(s): Indeterminate
Locale(s): Province of Bierdsey, Fictional Country

Summary: When Alexi Glivven fails to return home to his family and his duties at the lighthouse after accepting a secret assignment for the governor, Miranda Glivven sets out by train to find him. Accompanied by a cat, Miranda follows her husband's trail, questioning people along the railroad line for clues to Alexi's whereabouts.

Other books you might like:
Emma Bull, *Finder*, 1994
Pamela Dean, *The Dubious Hills*, 1994
Rose Estes, *Troll-Taken*, 1993
Holly Lisle, *Minerva Wakes*, 1994
Brooke Stevens, *The Circus of the Earth and Air*, 1994

4317
L.A. TAYLOR

Women's Work
(Minneapolis, Minnesota: Allau Press, 1995)

Story type: Science Fiction (Collection)

Summary: Contains three original stories and two reprinted from *Analog* in 1986 and 1992, the tone of which varies from ominous through wistful to light. Two stories focus on Link Services and the grand project of bringing water to the planet Urt, while other themes include music and alternate universes.

Other books you might like:
Katharine Kerr, *Resurrection*, 1992
Nancy Kress, *The Aliens of Earth*, 1993
Ursula K. Le Guin, *A Fisherman of the Inland Sea*, 1994
Pat Murphy, *Points of Departure*, 1990
James Tiptree Jr., *Her Smoke Rose Up Forever*, 1990
Connie Willis, *Impossible Things*, 1994

4318
LUCY TAYLOR

Close to the Bone
(Woodinville, Washington: Silver Salamander Press, 1993)

Story type: Horror (Collection)

Summary: This second collection brings together 10 explicit tales of psychological and supernatural horror, seven of which are original to the volume. Included are the bizarre juvenile delinquent story, "Virgin"; the alien invasion tale, "Animal Souls"; the tale of a horrifying afterlife, "The Best in the Business"; the story of a woman confronting her own sexual psychoses, "Cages"; and the title story, about the strange perspective a physically and emotionally abused woman develops toward love. Ed Bryant supplies the introduction.

Other books you might like:
Poppy Z. Brite, *Swamp Foetus*, 1993
Scott Edelman, *Suicide Art*, 1992
Ray Garton, *Methods of Madness*, 1990
Edward Lee, *Edward Lee's Quest for Sex, Truth and Reality*, 1992

4319
LUCY TAYLOR

The Flesh Artist
(Woodinville, Washington: Silver Salamander Press, 1994)

Story type: Horror (Collection)

Summary: The six stories in this volume range in their approach to horror from "Wall of Words," a lyrical look at a dysfunctional family, and "Wrestling with the Devil," a wacky tale of the grotesque in which a man combines faith healing with wrestling, to "The Flesh Artist," about the gruesome revenge a plastic surgeon takes upon his patients, and "Windowsitting," in which an aging woman's desire to have a baby becomes a nightmare of pathology for the midwife attending her. Norman Partridge supplies the introduction.

Other books you might like:
Poppy Z. Brite, *Swamp Foetus*, 1993
Adam-Troy Castro, *Lost in Booth Nine*, 1993
Edward Lee, *Edward Lee's Quest for Sex, Truth and Reality*, 1992

4320
LUCY TAYLOR

The Safety of Unknown Cities
(Woodinvill, Washington: Darkside Press, 1995)

Story type: Horror (Vampire Story)
Major character(s): Val Petrillo, Traveller; Arthur Quentin Breen, Serial Killer; Majeed, Young Man
Time period(s): 1990s (1995)
Locale(s): Taroudannt, Morocco

Summary: Alienated and disaffected by her abusive upbringing, Val Petrillo travels the globe, trying to connect with her world through an endless string of sexual encounters. Stories of The City, a mythical land of perversities that will offer her the ultimate fulfillment she seeks, sends her to Morocco, pursued by a psychopathic former lover whose passions help stoke the torrid events that follow. This sexually explicit first novel grew out of a 1994 novella of the same title.

Other books you might like:
Clive Barker, *Everville*, 1995
Clive Barker, *The Great and Secret Show*, 1989
Paul Bowles, *The Sheltering Sky*, 1949
Poppy Z. Brite, *Drawing Blood*, 1994
Stephen King, *Rose Madder*, 1995

4321
LUCY TAYLOR

Unnatural Acts and Other Stories
(New York: Richard Kasak Books, 1994)

Story type: Horror (Collection)

Summary: The nine stories in this volume examine the alienation of living on the fringe of society in brutal, and often sexually explicit terms. "Knockouts" is concerned with a psychopath who seeks sexual gratification in physical violence; ''The Best in the Business'' with a hell created in the image of one man's sexual fantasies; ''Making the Woman'' with the self-loathing of two children from dysfunctional families that explodes violently; and ''Rush'' with the extremes to which a bodybuilder goes to obtain his steroid fix. Both ''Flamethrower'' and ''Idol'' examine the sideshow nature of wrestling and the freaks attracted to it. Edward Lee supplies the introdution.

Other books you might like:
Poppy Z. Brite, *Swamp Foetus*, 1993
Ramsey Campbell, *Scared Stiff*, 1987
S. Darnbrook Colson, *People of the Night*, 1994
Edward Lee, *Edward Lee's Quest for Sex, Truth and Reality*, 1992
Richard Sutphen, *Sexpunks and Savage Sagas*, 1992

4322

PETER TAYLOR

The Oracle at Stoneleigh Court

(New York: Knopf, 1993)

Story type: Horror (Collection)

Summary: This outstanding collection by a Pultizer Prize-winning author renowned as one of the best short-fiction writers of his age brings together eleven tales and three one-act plays in which the magic of daily life often blends uncannily with the supernatural. In the title story, a widowed aunt with mystical powers pushes her nephew into a relationship with a woman who may or may not be under her psychic control. In ''Demons,'' a young boy's life is changed by the voices he hears inside his head and cannot distinguish from his own willful desires. ''The Real Ghost'' tells of a man who does not know he is a ghost, ''The Witch of Owl Mountain Springs'' of an embittered woman's revenge against a former lover, and ''Cousin Aubrey'' of a family outcast's personality transformation while accompanying the casket of a relative back home.

Other books you might like:
Fred Chappell, *More Shapes than One*, 1991
Joyce Carol Oates, *Haunted: Tales of the Grotesque*, 1994
Robert Phillips, *Triumph of the Night*, 1989
  editor

4323

RONALD TAYLOR, Editor

Six German Romantic Tales

(Chester Springs, Pennsylvania: Dufour Editions, 1993)

Story type: Horror (Anthology)

Summary: The six stories collected in this volume are offered as an example of the romantic movement's commingling of the natural and supernatural, beauty and horror. Included are two stories apiece by Ludwig Tieck, Heinrich von Kleist and E.T.A. Hoffman. The highlights are Hoffmann's ''Don Giovanni,'' in which a man's rapture over Mozart's opera turns its fictional heroine into a figure of flesh and blood; von

Kleist's *conte cruel*, ''The Earthquake in Chile,'' which juxtaposes incidents of human cruelty against a background of natural devastation; and Tieck's ''Eckbert the Fair,'' in which a virtuous man is driven to murder and despair over the story of his wife's infidelity as a child. This book was originally published in 1985.

Other books you might like:
Chris Baldick, *The Oxford Book of Gothic Tales*, 1992
  editor
Peter Haining, *Great Tales of Terror From Europe and America*, 1972
  editor
Peter Haining, *Black Tales*, 1965
E.T.A. Hoffmann, *The Tales of Hoffmann*, 1946

4324

WILLIAM TEDFORD

Liquid Diet

(New York: Diamond, 1992)

Story type: Horror (Vampire Story)
Major character(s): Troy Davidson, Teenager, Vampire; Melissa French, Teenager, Vampire; Randolf Hansen, Doctor
Time period(s): 1990s (1992)
Locale(s): Hanesburg

Summary: Melissa French is disgusted the night she witnesses her vampire next-door neighbor Troy Davidson drink blood from the neck of a victim—that is, until she discovers that she too is a vampire, and that Troy is her competition in their small town.

Other books you might like:
Robert Aickman, *Pages From a Young Girl's Journal*, 1975
  short story in *Cold Hand in Mine*
Poppy Z. Brite, *Lost Souls*, 1992
Nancy A. Collins, *Sunglasses After Dark*, 1989
Elizabeth Engstrom, *Black Ambrosia*, 1988
S.P. Somtow, *Vampire Junction*, 1983

4325

MELANIE TEM
STEVE RASNIC TEM, Co-Author

Beautiful Strangers

(Arvada, Colorado: Roadkill Press, 1992)

Story type: Horror (Science Fiction)
Major character(s): Mary, Prostitute
Time period(s): Indeterminate Future
Locale(s): Wheat, Planet—Imaginary

Summary: While turning tricks at a space bar, Mary encounters a beautiful stranger no one else can see whose bizarre sexual preferences offer her an intimacy lacking in her alienated and disaffected life. This chapbook is illustrated by Melissa Sherman.

Other books you might like:
Ramsey Campbell, *Medusa*, 1987

4326

MELANIE TEM

Desmodus
(New York: Dell, 1995)

Story type: Horror (Vampire Story)
Major character(s): Joel Desmodus, Vampire; Rory Desmodus, Vampire; Eli Desmodus, Vampire
Time period(s): 1990s (1995)
Locale(s): Tallus, Colorado

Summary: A matriarchal race of vampire-like beings lives in isolation in the hills of Colorado, their only contact with the world their feeding on mammals. When Joel, a member of the Desmodus family of this species, prepares to move the Tallus community as they prepare to enter one of their periodic hibernations, he discovers truths about the clan's history and the relationship between Desmodus men and women that lead him to radical actions that will bring self-understanding.

Other books you might like:
Scott Baker, *Ancestral Hungers*, 1995
Christopher Golden, *Of Saints and Shadows*, 1995
Jewelle Gomez, *The Gilda Stories*, 1991
Anne Rice, *The Witching Hour*, 1990
S.P. Somtow, *Moon Dance*, 1989
J.N. Williamson, *Bloodlines*, 1994

4327

MELANIE TEM
NANCY HOLDER, Co-Author

Making Love
(New York: Dell/Abyss, 1993)

Story type: Horror (Supernatural Vengeance)
Major character(s): Charlotte Tobias, Teacher (of English); Cameron Tobias, Mentally Ill Person (Charlotte's brother); Phanes, Mythical Creature
Time period(s): 1990s (1993)
Locale(s): Pittsburgh, Pennsylvania

Summary: With the help of her schizophrenic brother Cameron, lovelorn Charlotte Tobias learns how to turn Phanes, her fantasized ideal lover, into reality. When Phanes begins expressing murderous impulses, Charlotte realizes he has inherited all of her subconscious resentment against people who have helped to make her life miserable.

Other books you might like:
Stephen King, *The Dark Half*, 1989
Richard Christian Matheson, *Created By*, 1993
John R. Maxim, *Abel/Baker/Charley*, 1983
Mary Shelley, *Frankenstein*, 1818

4328

MELANIE TEM

Prodigal
(New York: Dell Abyss, 1991)

Story type: Horror (Vampire Story)

Major character(s): Lucy Brill, Teenager; Rae Brill, Teenager (Lucy's older sister); Jerry Johnston, Social Worker
Time period(s): 1990s
Locale(s): United States

Summary: Traumatized by the unexplained disappearances of her older brother and sister, Lucy Brill begins seeing social worker Jerry Johnston—unaware that Jerry, a corpulent misfit who "feeds" on the pain of his charges, was the last person to see her two siblings alive. This is the author's first novel.

Other books you might like:
John Metcalfe, *The Feasting Dead*, 1954
Theodore Sturgeon, *Some of Your Blood*, 1961

4329

MELANIE TEM

Revenant
(New York: Dell/Abyss, 1994)

Story type: Horror (Ghost Story)
Major character(s): Gabriel Carmichael, Child; Thomas L. Krieg Jr., Architect; Elinor Dietrich, Aged Person
Time period(s): 1990s (1994)
Locale(s): Revenant, Colorado

Summary: People from different walks of life are drawn by the specters of their various griefs—an aborted child, a husband as he was before being stricken by Alzheimer's, children who died in car accidents—to Revenant, a ghost town in Colorado's Rocky Mountains. There, a presiding spirit of grief allows them to overcome their emotional devastation by helping one another or by being absorbed into the town.

Other books you might like:
Tom Elliott, *The Dwelling*, 1988
Shirley Jackson, *The Haunting of Hill House*, 1959
Richard Matheson, *Hell House*, 1977
Chet Williamson, *Ash Wednesday*, 1987

4330

MELANIE TEM

Wilding
(New York: Dell/Abyss, 1992)

Story type: Horror (Werewolf Story)
Major character(s): Deborah, Teenager; Julian, Streetperson; Mary, Aged Person
Time period(s): 1990s (1992)
Locale(s): Denver, Colorado

Summary: This poignant allegory of the role of women in contemporary society chronicles the lives of a matriarchal extended family of four-generations of werewolves, whose members express emotions through shape-shifting.

Other books you might like:
Peter S. Beagle, *Lila the Werewolf*, 1969
Michael Cadnum, *St. Peter's Wolf*, 1991
Dennis Danvers, *Wilderness*, 1991
Ronald Kelly, *Something Out There*, 1991
H. Warner Munn, *The Werewolf of Ponkert*, 1958

4331

STEVE RASNIC TEM

Decoded Mirrors: Three Tales after Lovecraft

(West Warwick, Rhode Island: Necronomicon Press, 1992)

Story type: Horror (Collection)

Summary: A triptych of stories that use the motifs of H.P. Lovecraft's horror fiction in poignant tales of relationships between parents and children. ''Decodings'' describes a woman's painful odyssey of self-discovery during a trip to her father's hometown. ''Guardian Angels'' tells of the real terrors spawned by childhood fears. And ''Mirror Man'' is concerned with the unbridgeable gulf between children and adults created by parental neglect.

Other books you might like:
Peter Cannon, *Pulptime*, 1986
Michael Shea, *Fat Face*, 1987
Brian Stableford, *The Innsmouth Heritage*, 1992

4332

STEVE RASNIC TEM

Fairytales

(Arvada, Colorado: Road Kill Press, 1990)

Story type: Horror (Collection)

Summary: A dozen stories presented as the secret fairytales that Jack Johansen writes in his notebook: dark stories that he will not tell his children because they chronicle the pains and disappointments of life from which he is trying to shelter them.

Other books you might like:
Donald Barthelme, *The King*, 1990
Chet Williamson, *The House of Fear*, 1989
David Henry Wilson, *The Coachman Rat*, 1985

4333

SHERI S. TEPPER

Beauty

(New York: Doubleday Foundation, 1991)

Story type: Fantasy (Legend; Time Travel)
Major character(s): Beauty, Noblewoman, Time Traveller; Carabosse, Mythical Creature (fairy); Giles, Military Personnel
Time period(s): 14th century; 20th century
Locale(s): England; Faerie, Fictional Country

Summary: Beauty is the half-fairy daughter of the Duke of Westfaire who is under a curse. Arranging for her half-sister, Beloved, to sleep instead of her, she escapes only to be captured by a film crew from the 21st century, where she discovers that all life except for man has been destroyed. She goes to the 20th century and slowly learns her fairy powers. But her cold and uncaring mother in Faerie harrasses Beauty further.

Other books you might like:
Mildred Downey Broxon, *Too Long a Sacrifice*, 1981
Michael Greatrex Coney, *King of the Scepter'd Isle*, 1989
Pamela Dean, *Tam Lin*, 1991
Diana Wynne Jones, *Fire and Hemlock*, 1984
Tanith Lee, *Red as Blood: Or Tales from the Sisters Grimmer*, 1983
Terri Windling, *Life on the Border*, 1991
    editor
Patricia C. Wrede, *Snow White and Rose Red*, 1989

4334

SHERI S. TEPPER

Gibbon's Decline and Fall

(New York: Bantam Spectra, 1996)

Story type: Science Fiction (Political; Genetic Manipulation)
Major character(s): Carolyn Crespin Shepherd, Lawyer, Farmer; Agnes ''Aggie'' McGann, Religious (nun); Sovawanea ''Sophy'' a Tesuawane, Indian, Feminist
Time period(s): 2000s (2000)
Locale(s): Sante Fe, New Mexico; New York, New York; Salt Lake City, Utah

Summary: Carolyn, Agnes, Ophy, Betti, Faye, Jessy, and Sophy meet the first day of college and soon form the Decline and Fall Club, swearing they will meet every year, even after they graduate. They would each find a place they could stand and be a woman as self-defined and never decline or fall from that position. When Carolyn's daughter asks her to come out of retirement to defend a 14-year-old who left her baby in a dumpster, the DFC comes to Carolyn's aid. Unfortunately, the evil prosecutor, a minion of the right-wing American Alliance, intends the case as a stepping stone to the presidency.

Other books you might like:
Margaret Atwood, *The Handmaid's Tale*, 1986
Margaret Wander Bonanno, *The Others*, 1990
Octavia E. Butler, *Mind of My Mind*, 1977
Helen Collins, *Mutagenesis*, 1993
Suzette Haden Elgin, *Native Tongue*, 1984
Nicola Griffith, *Ammonite*, 1993
Susan Palwick, *Flying in Place*, 1992
Neal Stephenson, *The Diamond Age*, 1995

4335

SHERI S. TEPPER

Grass

(New York: Doubleday Foundation, 1989)

Story type: Science Fiction (Science Fiction)
Major character(s): Marjorie Westriding Yrarier, Diplomat; Sylvan Bon Damfels, Nobleman
Time period(s): Indeterminate Future
Locale(s): Earth; Grass, Planet—Imaginary

Summary: A deadly plague spreads across inhabited space and only one world appears to be immune, the planet Grass. Diplomat Marjorie Westriding Yrarier is sent to discover the source of this immunity, but can make little headway in the stagnant, intensely xenophobic society of the planet's hereditary ruling class. They seem to care about nothing but the frightening hunts they conduct mounted upon enormously dangerous alien steeds known as Hippae. Eventually Lady Westriding discovers that both the hunts and the Hippae are more than they seem.

Other books you might like:
Gregory Benford, *Great Sky River*, 1987
Gregory Benford, *Tides of Light*, 1989
David Brin, *Startide Rising*, 1983
David Brin, *The Uplift War*, 1987
Octavia E. Butler, *Dawn*, 1987
Larry Niven, *The Legacy of Heorot*, 1987
    Jerry Pournelle, and Steven Barnes, co-authors

4336

SHERI S. TEPPER

Marianne, the Matchbox and the Malachite Mouse

(New York: Ace, 1989)

Story type: Fantasy (Alternate World)
Series: Marianne
Major character(s): Marianne, Young Woman
Time period(s): 1980s
Locale(s): Earth; Alternate Universe

Summary: Marianne must return a matchbox, and the game that goes with it, to the original, magical owner. After she discovers how to transport herself into the game as one of the playing pieces, she begins her search for the owner.

Other books you might like:
Kevin J. Anderson, *Gameplay*, 1989

4337

SHERI S. TEPPER

A Plague of Angels

(New York: Bantam Spectra, 1993)

Story type: Fantasy (Quest; Science Fiction)
Major character(s): Abasio Cermit, Traveller; Orphan, Heroine; Quince Ellel, Witch
Time period(s): Indeterminate Future
Locale(s): The Place of Power, Mythical Place; Manland, Fictional Country; Artemesia, Fictional Country

Summary: Most of humanity departed for the stars leaving a much reduced population. The few remaining Manland cities, filled with gangs and violence and rife with sexually transmitted diseases, continue to shrink while monsters from Earth's past repopulate the countryside. In control of legions of android "walkers," Quince Ellel searches for a unique girl to utilize as guidance system for her shuttle. While Orphan searches for objects seen in a dream, Abasio joins and travels with Orphan, escaping from walkers, trolls and griffins. In Artemesia, a talking coyote joins their search.

Other books you might like:
David Brin, *Earth*, 1990
Emma Bull, *Bone Dance*, 1991
Richard Grant, *Through the Heart*, 1991
Morgan Llywelyn, *The Elementals*, 1993
Anne McCaffrey, *Powers That Be*, 1993
    Elizabeth Ann Scarborough, co-author
J.M. Morgan, *Desert Eden*, 1991
Catherine Wells, *The Earth Is All That Lasts*, 1991

4338

SHERI S. TEPPER

Raising the Stones

(New York: Doubleday Foundation, 1990)

Story type: Science Fiction (Science Fiction; Family Saga)
Major character(s): Samasnier Girat, Administrator (topman); Saluniel Girat, Administrator (rec officer); Phaed Girat, Parent (father of Sam and Sal)
Time period(s): Indeterminate Future
Locale(s): Hobbs Land, Planet—Imaginary; Voorstod, Fictional Country

Summary: Hobbs Land is a quiet agricultural colony, where men and women work together to build a new society. When the children of this world start to rebuild a temple of the vanished Owlbrit race, it seems a harmless exercise. At first, no one notices that the gods have returned to their temples. Voorstod is a world of grim misogynists, men who live obedient to their prophets while enslaving the alien Gharm. They look forward to the day they will go forth with whip and sword, killing all who disobey the one true God. To speed their cause, they must recapture singer Maire Manone, who fled with her children to Hobbs Land. Caught between cultures, Maire's son, Samasnier Girat, searches restlessly for his purpose in life. He is convinced he has a higher destiny, somehow linked with his father on Voorstod. He doesn't know how rapidly that destiny will come to claim him, or the price he must pay to become a hero.

Other books you might like:
Marion Zimmer Bradley, *The Firebrand*, 1987
Marion Zimmer Bradley, *Thendara House*, 1983
Orson Scott Card, *Speaker for the Dead*, 1986
C.J. Cherryh, *Cyteen*, 1988
Frank Herbert, *Dune*, 1965
Gene Wolfe, *The Shadow of the Torturer*, 1980

4339

SHERI S. TEPPER

Shadow's End

(New York: Bantam Spectra, 1994)

Story type: Science Fiction (Theological; Genetic Manipulation)
Major character(s): Saluez, Servant (Shadow); Lutha Tallstaff, Linguist, Parent; Leelson Famber, Empath
Time period(s): Indeterminate Future

Locale(s): Dinadh, Planet—Imaginary; Alliance Central, Earth; Perdur, Planet—Imaginary

Summary: Sole surviving planet of the Ularian disaster, which wiped out all other human life in the Hermes Sector, Dinadh remains insular and unwilling to help defend the planets in the Hermes Sector from attack. Sent to Dinadh with her retarded son by Alliance Central, Lutha befriends Saluez, a Dinadh woman. Eventually a Dinadh ceremony leads to a revelation more awful than anyone expects.

Other books you might like:

Octavia E. Butler, *Dawn*, 1987
Nicola Griffith, *Ammonite*, 1993
Megan Lindholm, *Alien Earth*, 1992
Anne McCaffrey, *Powers That Be*, 1993
    Elizabeth Ann Scarborough, co-author
Joan Slonczewski, *A Door into Ocean*, 1986
Catherine Wells, *The Earth Is All That Lasts*, 1991

4340

SHERI S. TEPPER

Sideshow

(New York: Bantam Spectra, 1992)

Story type: Science Fiction (Alternate Intelligence; Political)
Series: Arbai Device
Major character(s): Fringe Dorwalk Owldark, Police Officer (enforcer); Nela Zy-Czorsky Korsyzczy, Twin (Siamese), Time Traveller; Margorie "Jory" Westriding, Traveller, Heroine
Time period(s): 1990s; 61st century
Locale(s): United States; Elsewhere, Planet—Imaginary

Summary: In this sequel to *Grass* and *Raising the Stones*, all humans remaining free of the Hobbs Land Gods are on Elsewhere. There the legacy of Brannigan Galaxy's "Great Question Committee," diversity, is practiced without interference or restraint within the borders of each community. Enforcers attend to any situation which threatens this diversity and the ability of each community to potentially discover the ultimate destiny of man, while the Human and Arbai doors connecting Elsewhere with the slaves of the Hobbs Land Gods are locked and guarded.

Other books you might like:

David Brin, *Startide Rising*, 1983
Octavia E. Butler, *Dawn*, 1987
Orson Scott Card, *Wyrms*, 1987
Robert A. Heinlein, *Stranger in a Strange Land*, 1991
    revised
Dan Simmons, *Hyperion*, 1989
Joan Slonczewski, *A Door into Ocean*, 1986
Michael Swanwick, *Stations of the Tide*, 1991

4341

JOHN TERRA

City of Pain

(Honesdale, Pennsylvania: West End Books, 1994)

Story type: Fantasy (Religious; Science Fiction)

Series: Torg: The Possibility Wars
Major character(s): Jacques Deveaux, Religious, Computer Expert (Cyberpapal); Cory Jones, Journalist, Warrior; Padrig O'Shay, Magician, Warrior
Time period(s): 21st century
Locale(s): Berlin, Germany; Europe; Tharkold Occupation Zone, Fictional Country (alien)

Summary: Jacques Deveaux travels to Berlin to finish work on the Fourth Seal, a devastating computer program which could spell the end of the Cyberpapacy and promote widespread destruction. If the Storm Knights cannot stop him, worldwide disaster could insure the invading techno-demons' victory over humanity.

Other books you might like:

Jonatha Adriane Caspian, *The Nightmare Dream*, 1990
Greg Farshtey, *Strange Tales From the Nile Empire*, 1992
    Greg Gorden, Ed Stark, co-editors
Douglas Kaufman, *The Dark Realm*, 1990
Douglas Kaufman, *Dragons over England*, 1992
    Ed Stark, co-editor
Bill Slavicsek, *Storm Knights*, 1990
    C.J. Tramontana, co-author
Neal Stephenson, *Snow Crash*, 1992

4342

THOMAS TESSIER
JAMES KISNER, Co-Author
RICK HAUTALA, Co-Author

Night Visions 9

(Arlington Heights, Illinois: Dark Harvest, 1991)

Story type: Horror (Anthology)

Summary: The most recent volume in this long-running annual series, in which three authors each contribute a block of fiction that totals 30,000 words in length, includes Thomas Tessier's novella, "The Dreams of Dr. Ladybank," about a peculiar psychiatrist whose treatments drive his patients into psychosis; five stories by James Kisner, including "Jack's Demon," about the force which motivates Jack the Ripper; and seven stories and vignettes by Rick Hautala, all based on the Micmac Indian legends that gave rise to his 1988 novel, *Little Brothers*. F. Paul Wilson supplies an introduction.

Other books you might like:

4343

THOMAS TESSIER

The Nightwalker

(New York: Berkley, 1989)

Story type: Horror (Werewolf Story)
Major character(s): Bobby Ives, Veteran (Vietnam), Werewolf; Miss Tanith, Psychic
Time period(s): 1970s
Locale(s): London, England

Summary: As Ives gradually turns into a werewolf, he becomes increasingly violent, killing girlfriends and others as he tries to find a way to reverse the process. Originally published in 1979.

Other books you might like:
David Case, *The Cell*, 1969
Whitley Strieber, *The Wolfen*, 1978
Les Whitten, *Moon of the Wolf*, 1967

4344

PAUL THEROUX

Chicago Loop

(New York: Random House, 1991)

Story type: Horror (Psychological Suspense)
Major character(s): Parker Jagoda, Architect; Barbara Jagoda, Model (Parker's wife); Ewa Womack, Worker (Parker's mistress)
Time period(s): 1990s
Locale(s): Chicago, Illinois

Summary: Parker Jagoda, successful businessman and pathological liar, tries to balance his private and public personas by indulging in bizarre sexual fantasies with his wife and keeping trysts with women who answer his personal ads in newspapers. When one of his affairs leads to murder, he is plunged into a tailspin of depression, born out of guilt and obsession. This novel was originally published in England in 1990.

Other books you might like:
Robert Bloch, *The Will to Kill*, 1954
Brett Easton Ellis, *American Psycho*, 1991
David J. Schow, *The Kill Riff*, 1988

4345

ELIZABETH MARSHALL THOMAS

The Animal Wife

(Boston: Houghton Mifflin, 1990)

Story type: Fantasy (Romance; Historical)
Major character(s): Kori, Hunter, Prehistoric Human; Swift, Hunter, Prehistoric Human
Time period(s): Indeterminate Past (Prehistoric—Paleolithic)
Locale(s): Siberia, Russia

Summary: Kori, just entering manhood, elects to return with his father to the Hair River Tribe, a blue-eyed people like himself. While on an expedition to find the strangers whose campsite had been spotted nearby, Kori captures a woman to be his wife who teaches him her foreign ways. This book takes place a few years after Thomas's first book, *Reindeer Moon*.

Other books you might like:
Michael Armstrong, *Agviq*, 1990
Jean M. Auel, *The Plains of Passage*, 1990
Jean M. Auel, *The Valley of Horses*, 1982
Jean M. Auel, *Clan of the Cave Bear*, 1980
W. Michael Gear, *People of the Wolf*, 1990
    Kathleen O'Neal Gear, co-author
Richard Herley, *The Stone Arrow*, 1978
William Sarabande, *Beyond the Sea of Ice*, 1987

4346

JEFFREY THOMAS, Author/Illustrator

The Bones of the Old Ones and Other Lovecraftian Tales

(Westborough, Massachusetts: Necropolitan Press, 1995)

Story type: Horror (Collection)

Summary: The five stories and two poems collected here pay tribute to the literary influence of H.P. Lovecraft. "Book Worm" and "Lost Soul" both concern forbidden books that draw the unwary—mentally and physically—into extradimensional worlds. "The Boarded Window" and "The House on the Plain" are about peculiarities of architecture that draw investigators into worlds of horror. The title novella concerns the incursions made by a cult dedicated to Lovecraftian monsters on an alien planet.

Other books you might like:
David Langford, *Irrational Numbers*, 1994
Stephen Mark Rainey, *Fugue Devil and Other Weird Horrors*, 1992
Michael Shea, *Fat Face*, 1987
Brian Stableford, *The Innsmouth Heritage*, 1993
William R. Stotler, *The Final Diary Entry of Kees Hujgens*, 1995
Steve Rasnic Tem, *Decoded Mirrors: Three Tales after Lovecraft*, 1993
Stanley Wiater, *Mysteries of the Word*, 1994
F. Paul Wilson, *The Barrens*, 1992

4347

QUENTIN THOMAS (Pseudonym of W.T. Quick)

Chains of Light

(New York: Roc, 1992)

Story type: Science Fiction (Fantasy; Political)
Series: Luciferian Chronicles
Major character(s): Lucifer "Luke" Angelus, Computer (human), Military Personnel; Charlie, Nurse, Military Personnel; Naomia, Prostitute, Military Personnel
Time period(s): Indeterminate
Locale(s): The Hegemony, Interstellar Empire/Federation

Summary: Charlie decides to play a joke on his pubertal "template," Luke, a human clone wired with others as part of the master computer. Realizing The Hegemony suffered attack by the Twister, Luke begins to divert resources into military development, but the necessary leadership does not exist. Somehow Luke must find a way out of the empire of his mind and into reality to save The Hegemony.

Other books you might like:
William Barton, *Dark Sky Legion*, 1992
Gregory Benford, *Great Sky River*, 1987
Cheryl J. Franklin, *Fire Get*, 1987
Robert A. Heinlein, *Stranger in a Strange Land*, 1991 revised
Rebecca Ore, *Becoming Alien*, 1987
W.T. Quick, *Dreams of Flesh and Sand*, 1988
W.T. Quick, *Dreams of Gods and Men*, 1989

W.T. Quick, *Systems*, 1989
W.T. Quick, *Yesterday's Pawn*, 1989
Dan Simmons, *Hyperion*, 1989
George Zebrowski, *Stranger Suns*, 1991
Roger Zelazny, *Creatures of Light and Darkness*, 1969

4348

SUE THOMAS

Correspondence

(Woodstock, New York: The Overlook Press, 1993)

Story type: Science Fiction (Alternate Intelligence; Literary)
Major character(s): Marie, Guide; Rosa, Cyborg, Friend; Shirley, Cyborg, Traveller
Time period(s): Indeterminate Future
Locale(s): England

Summary: With the help of Marie as tour guide, the reader functions as compositer in constructing Rosa and Shirley in this experimental, role playing novel. The reader defines and decides the characters' humanity using the guilt, loneliness, desire and wish fulfillment presented.

Other books you might like:
Eleanor Arnason, *A Woman of the Iron People*, 1991
Nick Bantock, *Griffin & Sabine*, 1991
Nick Bantock, *Sabine's Notebook*, 1992
Jean Mark Gawron, *Dream of Glass*, 1993
William Gibson, *The Difference Engine*, 1990
    Bruce Sterling, co-author
Gwyneth Jones, *White Queen*, 1993
Marge Piercy, *He, She and It*, 1991
Joan Slonczewski, *A Door into Ocean*, 1986
Amy Thomson, *Virtual Girl*, 1993

4349

THOMAS T. THOMAS

Crygender

(New York: Baen, 1992)

Story type: Science Fiction (Mystery; Techno-Thriller)
Major character(s): "Cry" Crygender, Criminal; Jean Metis, Agent (criminal investigator); Austin Tinker, Agent (U.S. Department of Justice)
Time period(s): 2020s (2020)
Locale(s): San Francisco, California; Babylon, Pacific Islands (Alcatraz); New Orleans, Louisiana

Summary: On the trail of a runaway teenager, Metis and Tinker arrange to stay at Babylon, the Japanese-owned island brothel of Crygender. Cry is a genetically and surgically altered person, now half male, half female, whose past is totally unknown, including Cry's original gender. Metis and Tinker inadvertently discover and solve the mystery of Crygender and the dark secret of Babylon.

Other books you might like:
Greg Bear, *Queen of Angels*, 1990
C.S. Friedman, *The Madness Season*, 1990
Katharine Kerr, *Polar City Blues*, 1990
Rudy Rucker, *Wetware*, 1988

Allen Steele, *Clarke County, Space*, 1990
Michael Swanwick, *Vacuum Flowers*, 1987

4350

THOMAS T. THOMAS

ME: A Novel of Self Discovery

(New York: Baen, 1991)

Story type: Science Fiction (Alternate Intelligence; Robot Fiction)
Major character(s): Multiple Entity "ME", Artificial Intelligence, Spy; Jason Bathespeake, Computer Expert, Administrator (project manager)
Time period(s): 21st century
Locale(s): San Francisco, California; Canada; Russia

Summary: Developed as an espionage tool, ME is tested by its infiltrating a Canadian oil and gas reserve data base, then the Russian military nuclear weapons data base. After ME returns to San Francisco from the second mission, a judge rules that it is an illegal virus. Modified, ME is rendered immobile and told it must devise a new purpose for its existence or be terminated within a week.

Other books you might like:
David Gerrold, *When HARLIE Was One: Release 2.0*, 1988
Robert A. Heinlein, *The Moon Is a Harsh Mistress*, 1966
Victor Milan, *The Cybernetic Samurai*, 1986
Rudy Rucker, *Wetware*, 1988
Cordwainer Smith, *Norstrilia*, 1975
David Alexander Smith, *Homecoming*, 1990
David Alexander Smith, *Rendezvous*, 1988

4351

JOYCE THOMPSON

Bones

(New York: Morrow, 1991)

Story type: Horror (Psychological Suspense)
Major character(s): Frederika "Freddy" Bascomb, Artist; Charles "Chaz" Bascomb, Child (Freddy's son); Peter, Businessman (investor), Step-Parent (Freddy's stepfather)
Time period(s): 1990s
Locale(s): Seattle, Washington

Summary: Freddy Bascomb's life as an artist who earns her living reconstructing faces from "bones"—the remains of murder victims—takes a bizarre twist when she is summoned to identify the gruesomely mutilated remains of her father. She struggles to make sense of the clues her father's murderer has left—the theft of his brain, and periodically delivered chapters of a novel in manuscript that have eerie relevance to her experiences—even as the murderer begins to stalk her and her children.

Other books you might like:
Thomas Harris, *The Silence of the Lambs*, 1988
David Martin, *Lie to Me*, 1990
Garfield Reeves-Stevens, *Dark Matter*, 1990

4352

PAUL B. THOMPSON
TONYA R. CARTER, Co-Author

Firstborn
(Lake Geneva, Wisconsin: TSR, 1991)

Story type: Fantasy (Political; Adventure)
Series: Dragonlance: The Elven Nations Trilogy
Major character(s): Sithas, Mythical Creature (elf), Royalty;
Kith-Kanan, Mythical Creature (elf), Royalty
Time period(s): Indeterminate
Locale(s): Silvanesti, Fictional Country (Elven Nation)

Summary: Sithas allies himself with court factions in the elven capital while his brother, Kith-Kanan, leads the Wildrunners, elves who trade with humans of Ergoth. When events implicate Kith-Kanan in their father's death, Sithas, the firstborn twin, ascends to the throne. A game tie-in novel.

Other books you might like:
Nancy Varian Berberick, *Stormblade*, 1988
Mary Kirchoff, *Flint the King*, 1990
Douglas Niles, co-author
Richard A. Knaak, *The Legend of Huma*, 1988
Douglas Niles, *The Kinslayer Wars*, 1991
Barbara Siegel, *Tanis, the Shadow Years*, 1990
Scott Siegel, co-author
Margaret Weis, *Dragons of Autumn Twilight*, 1984
Tracy Hickman, co-author
Margaret Weis, *Time of the Twins*, 1986
Tracy Hickman, co-author
Margaret Weis, *War of the Twins*, 1986
Tracy Hickman, co-author

4353

PAUL B. THOMPSON
TONYA R. CARTER, Co-Author

The Qualinesti
(Lake Geneva, Wisconsin: TSR, 1991)

Story type: Fantasy (Magic Conflict; Political)
Series: Dragonlance: The Elven Nations Trilogy
Major character(s): Kith-Kanan, Mythical Creature (elf), Warrior; Drulethen "Dru", Mythical Creature (elf), Sorcerer; Greenhands "Silveran", Mythical Creature (half-breed elf)
Time period(s): Indeterminate
Locale(s): Qualinesti, Fictional Country

Summary: As leader, Kith-Kanan promotes peace with the dwarves of Thorgardin and works toward equality for all within the kingdom. A simple onyx amulet and sorcerers in conflict work to make matters difficult for Kith-Kanan and his heir, Silveran. A game tie-in novel.

Other books you might like:
Nancy Varian Berberick, *Stormblade*, 1988
Mary Kirchoff, *Flint the King*, 1990
Douglas Niles, co-author
Richard A. Knaak, *The Legend of Huma*, 1988
Douglas Niles, *The Kinslayer Wars*, 1991

Barbara Siegel, *Tanis, the Shadow Years*, 1990
Scott Siegel, co-author
Margaret Weis, *Dragons of Autumn Twilight*, 1984
Tracy Hickman, co-author
Margaret Weis, *Time of the Twins*, 1986
Tracy Hickman, co-author
Margaret Weis, *War of the Twins*, 1986
Tracy Hickman, co-author

4354

PAUL B. THOMPSON

Thorn and Needle
(Lake Geneva, Wisconsin: TSR, 1992)

Story type: Fantasy (Religious; Quest)
Major character(s): Rado, Gambler, Traveller; Eride "Thorn", Religious (Sentinel of the Temple), Martial Arts Expert; Harlic Vost, Religious (College of Peace)
Time period(s): Indeterminate
Locale(s): Miyesti, Fictional City

Summary: Thorn and Rado use terrorism as a cover for their secret mission to kill the new god in Miyesti.

Other books you might like:
Douglas Bell, *Mojo and the Pickle Jar*, 1991
Maya Kaathryn Bohnhoff, *The Meri*, 1992
Adrian Cole, *Mother of Storms*, 1992
Neil Gaiman, *Good Omens: The Nice and Accurate Prophecies of Agnes Nutter, Witch*, 1990
Terry Pratchett, co-author
Rosemary Kirstein, *The Outskirter's Secret*, 1992

4355

WILLIAM R. THOMPSON

Debtors' Planet
(New York: Pocket, 1994)

Story type: Science Fiction (Space Opera)
Series: Star Trek: The Next Generation
Major character(s): Jean-Luc Picard, Spaceship Captain, Military Personnel (Starfleet); Wesley Crusher, Student (Starfleet Academy cadet); Ralph Offenhouse, Diplomat, Businessman
Time period(s): 24th century
Locale(s): Megara, Planet—Imaginary; *U.S.S. Enterprise*, Spaceship; United Federation of Planets, Interstellar Empire/Federation

Summary: When a space probe reports advanced power sources on the formerly primitive planet Megara, the Federation appoints as investigator Ralph Offenhouse, a 20th-century Terran cryogenically preserved until the 24th century. Although the Ferengi have supplied the technology, transforming the peaceful Megarans into xenophobic killers in the process, Offenhouse must discover who hired the Ferengi.

Other books you might like:
Robert Asprin, *The Cold Cash War*, 1977
C.J. Cherryh, *Forty Thousand in Gehenna*, 1983
Bill McCay, *Chains of Command*, 1992

H. Beam Piper, *Fuzzy Sapiens*, 1964
Jack Vance, *Emphyrio*, 1969

4356

BRIAN THOMSEN

The Mage in the Iron Mask

(Lake Geneve, Wisconsin: TSR, 1996)

Story type: Fantasy (Sword and Sorcery)
Series: Forgotten Realms: The Nobles
Major character(s): Volothamp ''Volo'' Geddarms, Traveller, Scholar; Passepout, Actor; Jocchario Lawre, Wizard, Diplomat
Time period(s): Indeterminate
Locale(s): Mulmaster, Fictional City

Summary: Volo continues his trip of research for his *Guide to the Moonsen* by going to Mulmaster, the ''City of Danger.'' Unfortunately, retrieving Passepout from prison interrupts his fact-finding mission, soon trapping the two in the schemes of the nobility and wizards.

Other books you might like:
Steven Brust, *The Phoenix Guards*, 1991
Glen Cook, *The Swordbearer*, 1982
Ellen Kushner, *Swordspoint*, 1987
Fritz Leiber, *Ill Met in Lankhmar*, 1995
Caroline Stevermer, *A College of Magics*, 1994

4357

AMY THOMSON

The Color of Distance

(New York: Ace, 1995)

Story type: Science Fiction (First Contact)
Major character(s): Juna ''Eerin'' Saari, Scientist (biologist), Explorer (alien contact specialist); Anito, Alien (Tendu); Moki, Alien (Tendu)
Time period(s): Indeterminate Future
Locale(s): Lyanan, Planet—Imaginary

Summary: When her ship crashes, Juna loses all her companions before the Tendu initiate fundamental changes in her physiology that allow Juna to survive on the deadly planet. With a human ship years away, Juna allies with the natives and investigates their societies as she and the natives form a close bond.

Other books you might like:
Eleanor Arnason, *A Woman of the Iron People*, 1991
Octavia E. Butler, *Dawn*, 1987
Octavia E. Butler, *Imago*, 1989
C.J. Cherryh, *Foreigner*, 1994
L. Warren Douglas, *A Plague of Change*, 1992
Nicola Griffith, *Ammonite*, 1993
Melissa Scott, *Shadow Man*, 1995

4358

AMY THOMSON

Virtual Girl

(New York: Ace, 1993)

Story type: Science Fiction (Alternate Intelligence; Robot Fiction)
Major character(s): Arnold Brompton, Computer Expert, Wanderer; Maggie, Artificial Intelligence; Brandon Smith, Computer Expert, Recluse
Time period(s): 2000s
Locale(s): Denver, Colorado; New Orleans, Louisiana; New York, New York

Summary: While hiding from his father, super hacker Arnold Brompton creates a girl whom he transfers from the Net to a constructed body in defiance of the AI laws. Called Maggie, she quickly learns to handle her body after a fortuitous command allows reconfiguration of her programming to avoid fatal overload. Separated from Arnold and found almost dead in the desert, Maggie befriends some farmers but leaves after a month fearing recognition, needing repair and reacquisition of her memory. In New Orleans, Maggie makes new friends who help her define her priorities and see herself as a person. Author's first novel.

Other books you might like:
Roger MacBride Allen, *The Modular Man*, 1992
Emily Devenport, *Shade*, 1991
Philip K. Dick, *Blade Runner*, 1982
Jean Mark Gawron, *Dream of Glass*, 1993
Tom Maddox, *Halo*, 1991
Lisa Mason, *Arachne*, 1990
Sue Thomas, *Correspondence*, 1993
Vernor Vinge, *A Fire upon the Deep*, 1992

4359

TAMARA THORNE (Pseudonym of Chris Curry)

Haunted

(New York: Zebra, 1995)

Story type: Horror (Haunted House)
Major character(s): David Masters, Writer (horror); Amber Masters, Teenager (David's daughter); Melanie Lord, Agent (literary)
Time period(s): 1990s (1995)
Locale(s): Red Cay, California

Summary: Writer David Masters takes up residence in the old Baudey House on a pensinsula outside Red Cay, in the hope that its reputed hauntings will supply him with the atmosphere he seeks to complete his new horror opus, *Mephisto Palace*. But the presence of David and his daughter Amber also helps bring out the legacy of evil sown at the house nearly a century before, by a woman who used it as a bordello and her daughter, who practiced voodoo rites that have imbued the house with a supernatural menace. This is the author's first novel under her Tamara Thorne pseudonym.

Other books you might like:
Jonathan Aycliffe, *Naomi's Room*, 1991

Poppy Z. Brite, *Drawing Blood*, 1993
Barbara Erskine, *Midnight Is a Lonely Place*, 1994
Gary L. Holleman, *Demon Fire*, 1995
Stephen King, *The Shining*, 1977

4360

TAMARA THORNE (Pseudonym of Chris Curry)

Moonfall
(New York: Zebra, 1996)

Story type: Horror (Black Magic)
Major character(s): John Lawson, Police Officer (sheriff); Sara Hawthorne, Teacher; Mother Superior Lucy Barthlomew, Religious (nun)
Time period(s): 1990s (1996)
Locale(s): Moonfall, California

Summary: Sara Hawthorne ran away from St. Gertrude's Home for Girls in Moonfall, following the death of her best friend. Decades later, she returns to town as a teacher and discovers that her friend's death was one of many ritual murders conducted by the nuns who run the home to perpetuate a legacy of evil older than the town itself.

Other books you might like:
S.K. Epperson, *Nightmare*, 1993
Stephen King, *It*, 1986
S.J. Strayhorn, *Black Night*, 1996
Donna Tartt, *The Secret History*, 1993
J.N. Williamson, *The Black School*, 1989

4361

DIANN THORNLEY

Ganwold's Child
(New York: Tor, 1995)

Story type: Science Fiction (First Contact; Political)
Major character(s): Mordan Renier, Military Personnel (general), Political Figure (governor); Tristan "Tris" Serege, Teenager, Castaway; Pulon, Alien, Sidekick
Time period(s): Indeterminate Future
Locale(s): Ganwold, Planet—Imaginary; *Bonne Fortune*, Spaceship; Unified Worlds/Dominion, Interstellar Empire/Federation

Summary: Having escaped from slavers, the toddler Tris and his mother become marooned on a Dominion planet. They live with the alien Gan and avoid humans. When his mother becomes uncurably ill, Tris decides to find his father knowing that he must leave Ganwold to do so. His Gan brother, Pulon, accompanies him to the stronghold of his family's enemy, Renier, who intends to use Tris to provoke war while Tris only wants to get help for his dying mother. First novel.

Other books you might like:
Eleanor Arnason, *Ring of Swords*, 1993
Gordon R. Dickson, *Naked to the Stars/The Alien Way*, 1991
L. Warren Douglas, *Cannon's Orb*, 1994
Paula E. Downing, *Fallway*, 1993
Jacqueline Lichtenberg, *Molt Brother*, 1982

4362

ROBERT THURSTON

Way of the Clans
(New York: Roc, 1991)

Story type: Science Fiction (Military)
Series: BattleTech: Legend of the Jade Phoenix
Major character(s): Aidan, Military Personnel; Ter Roshak, Military Personnel; Joanna, Military Personnel
Time period(s): 31st century
Locale(s): Ironhold, Planet—Imaginary; Tokasha, Planet—Imaginary

Summary: The Clans, descended from colonists who fled the worlds of the Inner Sphere, are organized in a caste system, the highest being "trueborn" Warriors, conceived and born in a laboratory and raised in a sibling group, who look with contempt on the "freeborn," the result of random matings among other Castes. Aidan and his group begin their training under Falconer Joanna. Those who survive will become full-fledged Warriors, fighting from inside their formidable armored Battle Mechs. A game tie-in novel.

Other books you might like:
Robert N. Charrette, *Wolf Pack*, 1992
C.J. Cherryh, *The Faded Sun: Kesrith*, 1978
Gordon R. Dickson, *Dorsai!*, 1976
Gordon R. Dickson, *Soldier, Ask Not*, 1967
Robert A. Heinlein, *Starship Troopers*, 1959
Aldous Huxley, *Brave New World*, 1932
Jerry Pournelle, *Falkenberg's Legion*, 1990
Kevin D. Randle, *The Galactic Silver Star*, 1990
John Sievert, *Suicide Attack*, 1990

4363

RICHARD TIERNEY

The House of the Toad
(Minneapolis, Minnesota: Fedogan & Bremer, 1993)

Story type: Horror (Ancient Evil Unleashed)
Major character(s): James Kerrick, Archaeologist; Janus Cornelius Wasserman, Publisher; Rosa Andrada, Secretary
Time period(s): 1990s
Locale(s): St. Regis, Iowa

Summary: Unscrupulous archaeologist James Kerrick sells a stolen Mexican artifact to publisher Janus Wasserman, and falls under the would-be occultist's spell. Too late, Kerrick discovers that his actions have furthered the summoning of Ghantanathoa, an ancient toad-like god bent on promoting chaos and suffering in the earthly plane.

Other books you might like:
Robert Bloch, *Strange Eons*, 1978
August Derleth, *The Trail of Cthulhu*, 1962
H.P. Lovecraft, *The Lurker at the Threshold*, 1945
    August Derleth, co-author
Brian Lumley, *The Burrowers Beneath*, 1975
Colin Wilson, *The Mind Parasites*, 1967

4364

JOHN TIGGES

The Curse

(New York: Leisure, 1993)

Story type: Horror (Curse)
Major character(s): Sabra Narman, Artist; Bart Narman, Businessman; Father Wisdom, Religious (Catholic priest)
Time period(s): 1990s (1993)
Locale(s): Cascade, New York

Summary: Excavations on the land recently bought by the Narman family uncover the artifacts of a cult of pre-Columbian satanists, whose influence begins to make itself known through the bizarre dreams and behavior of the Narmans.

Other books you might like:
Douglas Clegg, *Goat Dance*, 1989
Rick Hautala, *Dark Silence*, 1992
Brian Hodge, *Oasis*, 1987
Roy Sorrels, *The Eyes of Torie Webster*, 1990

4365

JOHN TIGGES

Kevin Browne's Nightales

(New York: Upper West Side Publishing, 1990)

Story type: Horror (Collection)
Summary: Fourteen stories of the weird and supernatural, adapted from scripts written by Kevin Browne for "Tales from the Darkside," "Monsters," and "A Nightmare on Elm Street," and presented as tales a group of bus riders tell to pass the time. They include "All Bets Are Down," about a casino where the years of one's age are used to place bets, "Just the Right Card," about a store whose greeting cards make whatever a card says happen to the recipient, and "Over the Wall," about a near future in which the criminals outnumber the innocent.

Other books you might like:
Mitchell Galen, *Tales from the Darkside, Volume 1*, 1989
   Tom Allen, co-author
Jack Oleck, *Tales from the Crypt*, 1972
Rod Serling, *The Night Gallery Reader*, 1990
Rod Serling, *Stories From the Twilight Zone*, 1989
J. Michael Straczynski, *Tales From the New Twilight Zone*, 1989

4366

JOHN TIGGES

Monster

(New York: Leisure, 1995)

Story type: Horror (Nature in Revolt)
Major character(s): Jonna Evans, Teacher; Malcolm Evans, Clerk; Peter Roth, Guide
Time period(s): 1990s (1995)
Locale(s): Hatchet Blade, British Columbia, Canada

Summary: On a camping trip in the Canadian woods that she takes to save her marriage, Jonna Evans is abducted by a lust-ridden Sasquatch and realizes that having a difficult husband is the least of her problems.

Other books you might like:
Merian C. Copper, *King Kong*, 1933
   Edgar Wallace, co-author
Barbara Hambly, *Beauty and the Beast*, 1989
Jack Ketchum, *Offspring*, 1991
Richard Laymon, *Midnight's Lair*, 1988
Dean R. Koontz, *Watchers*, 1987

4367

LOIS TILTON

Darkness on the Ice

(New York: Pinnacle, 1993)

Story type: Horror (Vampire Story)
Major character(s): Hauptsturmfuhrer Wolff, Military Personnel (Nazi soldier), Vampire; Martin Dietrich, Military Personnel (Nazi Captain); Matt Ferrier, Military Personnel (American Sergeant)
Time period(s): 1940s (1944)
Locale(s): Greenland

Summary: A skilled guerilla and vampire to boot, Wolff is sent by Adolf Hitler to help destroy an American weather station in Greenland at the height of World War II. Though the dark and cold climate are ideal for Wolff's constitution, no one could have anticipated that the relative lack of sustenance in the arctic would force Wolff to victimize his fellow Nazis.

Other books you might like:
Elaine Bergstrom, *Shattered Glass*, 1989
Dan Simmons, *Carrion Comfort*, 1989
Robert Weinberg, *The Armageddon Box*, 1991

4368

ROBERT TINE

Universal Soldier

(New York: Jove, 1992)

Story type: Science Fiction (Military; Techno-Thriller)
Major character(s): Luc Devreaux, Cyborg, Reanimated Dead (Universal Soldier); Andrew Scott, Cyborg, Reanimated Dead (Universal Soldier); Veronica "Ronnie" Roberts, Journalist
Time period(s): 1990s (1993)
Locale(s): Nevada

Summary: Cryogenically frozen for a quarter century, Luc and Andrew now find themselves transformed into cybernetic constructs useful as SWAT members in the deadliest situations. However, the humanity remaining within the machine proves a difficult force to control. Novelizes the film.

Other books you might like:
Martin Caidin, *Cyborg*, 1972
Philip K. Dick, *Do Androids Dream of Electric Sheep?*, 1968
Dave Duncan, *Hero*, 1991

Stephen Goldin, *Jade Darcy and the Affair of Honor*, 1988
    Mary Mason, co-author
Ed Naha, *Robocop*, 1987
Ed Naha, *Robocop 2*, 1990
Richard Sapir, *The Destroyer #1: Created, the Destroyer*, 1971
    Warren Murphy, co-author

4369

JAMES TIPTREE JR. (Pseudonym of Alice Sheldon)

Her Smoke Rose Up Forever

(Sauk City, Wisconsin: Arkham House, 1990)

Story type: Science Fiction (Collection)

Summary: 17 stories written between 1969-1981 that are strongly feminist. Tiptree's stories are both inventive and grim, showing human strengths and failings in alien settings. ''The Women Men Don't See'' uses a plane crash to propose that women may have more in common with aliens than with men.

Other books you might like:
Suzy McKee Charnas, *Walk to the End of the World*, 1974
Ursula K. Le Guin, *The Left Hand of Darkness*, 1969
Pat Murphy, *The Falling Woman*, 1986
Joanna Russ, *The Female Man*, 1975
Fay Weldon, *Lives and Loves of a She-Devil*, 1983

4370

STEPHANIE S. TOLAN

The Witch of Maple Park

(New York: William Morrow, 1992)

Story type: Fantasy (Contemporary; Young Adult)
Major character(s): Casey Corrigan, Teenager; Mackenzie Brewster, Psychic, Teenager; Mrs. Brewster, Businesswoman
Time period(s): 1990s
Locale(s): Maple Park, Ohio (Maple Park High School)

Summary: Casey and Mackenzie, best friends since childhood, discover that Mackenzie's feelings and meditations seem to be coming true, many of which show difficulties for herself and her mother, especially since her father left them and married another woman.

Other books you might like:
Peter Dickinson, *Healer*, 1987
E.W. Hildick, *The Active-Enzyme Lemon-Freshened Junior High School Witch*, 1973
Diana Wynne Jones, *The Ogre Downstairs*, 1990
Michael Kandel, *In between Dragons*, 1990
Christopher Pike, *Witch*, 1990

4371

J.R.R. TOLKIEN

Sauron Defeated

(New York: Houghton Mifflin, 1992)

Story type: Fantasy (Collection)

Summary: Ninth volume compiled from J.R.R. Tolkien's prolific notes with commentary by Christopher Tolkien divided into three parts, ''The End of the Third Age (The History of the Lord of the Rings Part Four),''''The Notion Club Papers'' and ''The Drowning of Anadune.'' Part one completes Christopher Tolkien's account of the writing of *The Lord of the Rings* including a much-changed scourging of the Shire and versions of the unpublished ''Epilog,'' a variant ending in which Sam attempts to tell his children of Bilbo and Frodo years after their departure. Part two reveals a literary group similar to the Inklings, including J.R.R. Tolkien, C.S. Lewis and Charles Williams, in the first publication of a story surrounding the early 21st century discovery of papers from an Oxford literary club's discussions during 1986-1987 in which the members consider the possibility of using ''true dream'' to travel in time and space, the legend of Atlantis, communication received from the past, and the explosion of the Atlantean legend into northwest Europe. Part three documents the evolution of Tolkien's fifteenth language, Adunaic, which was learned by Arundel Lowdham of the Notion Club during his dreams. Presents a third version of ''The Fall of Numenor'' and three versions of ''The Drowning of Anadune.'' Concludes with a 42-page index.

Other books you might like:
Robert A. Heinlein, *Requiem*, 1992
    Yoji Kondo, editor
Larry Niven, *N-Space*, 1990
Larry Niven, *Playgrounds of the Mind*, 1991

4372

JANE TOOMBS

Under the Shadow

(New York: Roc, 1992)

Story type: Horror (Werewolf Story)
Series: Moonrunner
Major character(s): Ulysses Koshka, Werewolf; Don Alfonso, Rancher; William Tecumseh Sherman, Historical Figure, Military Personnel
Time period(s): 1840s
Locale(s): San Francisco, California

Summary: In this first novel of a continuing series, a young man cursed with lycanthropy who travels under the alias Ulysses Koshka washes up on the shores of California during the Gold Rush of 1849. His adventures take him across America, through the landscape of the American Civil War and the Louisiana bayou, as he struggles to remember his past in an effort to find an antidote for his curse.

Other books you might like:
Michael Cadnum, *St. Peter's Wolf*, 1991
Guy Endore, *The Werewolf of Paris*, 1933

H. Warner Munn, *The Werewolf of Ponkert*, 1958
Cheri Scotch, *The Werewolf's Kiss*, 1992
S.P. Somtow, *Moon Dance*, 1990

4373

PETER TREMAYNE (Pseudonym of Peter Berresford Ellis)

Snowbeast!

(New York: Severn House, 1992)

Story type: Horror (Black Magic)
Major character(s): Ellen MacDonald, Secretary; Murdo Mac-Donald, Doctor (Ellen's uncle); Tony Glover, Mountaineer
Time period(s): 1980s (1983)
Locale(s): Cairngorms, Scotland
Summary: Originally published in 1983, this novel tells of a strange fever that befalls a monk at the monastery of St. Berchan in the mountains of Scotland at the same time that local animals begin disappearing and giant footprints are found in the nearby snow—all of which suggests that the legendary "Big Gray Man of Ben MacDhui," or Snowbeast, has returned to the Scottish highlands.

Other books you might like:
Basil Copper, *The Great White Space*, 1974
H.P. Lovecraft, *At the Mountains of Madness*, 1964
    short story in *At the Mountains of Madness and Other Novels*

4374

PETER TREMAYNE (Pseudonym of Peter Berresford Ellis)

Swamp

(New York: St. Martin's, 1989)

Story type: Horror (Ancient Evil Unleashed)
Major character(s): Dean Michaels, Convict (Escaped); Peter Pirelli, Ranger (Swamp Ranger)
Time period(s): 1980s
Locale(s): Florida (Everglades)
Summary: Dean Michaels and Ruiz Alverez escape jail and head into the Florida swamps, taking a female hostage with them. The search for them is complicated by an angry prehistoric monster, which roams the swamps killing at will, and an imminent hurricane.

Other books you might like:
Charles L. Grant, *The Nestling*, 1982
Stephen Gresham, *Blood Wings*, 1990

4375

ELLESTON TREVOR

The Sister

(New York: Tor, 1994)

Story type: Horror (Evil Children)
Major character(s): Madlen, Teenager; Debra, Teenager; Father Giovanni Falconi, Religious (priest)
Time period(s): 1990s (1994)

Locale(s): Westbury, Connecticut

Summary: Madlen persuades her adopted sister Debra to join her in taking religious vows to escape their difficult family. But even as a member of the Sisters of the Sacred Light, Madlen perpetrates acts, seemingly under the compulsion of an alter ego, that appear designed to push Debra into madness, and possibly to her death. This is a sequel to *Sibling*.

Other books you might like:
V.C. Andrews, *Secrets of the Morning*, 1991
Margaret Bingley, *Seeds of Evil*, 1988
D.A. Fowler, *Bad Blood*, 1993
Robert R. McCammon, *Mystery Walk*, 1984
Thomas Tryon, *The Other*, 1972

4376

THOMAS TRYON

Night Magic

(New York: Simon & Schuster, 1995)

Story type: Horror (Occult)
Major character(s): Max Wurlitzer, Magician; Michael Hawke, Magician; Emily Chang, Musician
Time period(s): 1990s (1995)
Locale(s): New York, New York

Summary: Recognizing true talent in street performer Michael Hawke, aging magician Max Wurlitzer takes the boy under his wing to teach him the black arts. Michael finds himself in the difficult position of having to turn his back on everything he has known in the past in order to harness the powers Max wields and become like him. Left unrevised at the author's death in 1991, the novel was touched up by John Cullen and Valerie Martin.

Other books you might like:
John Fowles, *The Magus*, 1965
Richard Matheson, *Now You See It...*, 1995
Robert R. McCammon, *Mystery Walk*, 1983
Peter Straub, *Shadowland*, 1980

4377

THOMAS TRYON

The Night of the Moonbow

(New York: Knopf, 1989)

Story type: Horror (Evil Children)
Major character(s): Leo Joaquim, Child (an unpopular boy); Reece Hartwig, Counselor (camp counselor)
Time period(s): 1930s (1938)
Locale(s): United States (Camp Friend-Indeed on Moonbow Lake)

Summary: Introverted, out-of-place Leo Joaquim is belittled and harassed by the other boys at Camp Friend-Indeed. This torment, led by Reece Hartwig, his proto-Nazi cabin counselor, is intensified after the accidental death of Leo's best friend until the external harassment combines with Leo's own dark secrets to erupt in violence.

Other books you might like:
William Golding, *Lord of the Flies*, 1954
Stephen King, *Carrie*, 1974
Stephen King, *Christine*, 1983

4378
WILSON TUCKER

The Lincoln Hunters
(New York: Baen, 1992)

Story type: Science Fiction (Time Travel)
Major character(s): Ben Steward, Time Traveller, Anthropologist; Karl Dobbs, Time Traveller; Evelyn Kung, Widow(er)
Time period(s): 26th century (2578); 1850s (1856)
Locale(s): Cleveland, Ohio; Bloomington, Illinois

Summary: Intending to visit 1856 to recover a lost speech by Abraham Lincoln, Ben Steward discovers he somehow arrived a day too late and, worse, people there recognize him from an earlier meeting. Steward must travel back in time again, but must take great care not to meet himself since such a meeting would result in both selves instantly ceasing to exist. Reissue of the 1958 edition with a new, two-page introduction by David Drake.

Other books you might like:
Poul Anderson, *The Shield of Time*, 1990
Poul Anderson, *The Time Patrol*, 1991
Philip K. Dick, *Ubik*, 1969
Gordon R. Dickson, *Time Storm*, 1977
Fred Saberhagen, *After the Fact*, 1988
Harry Turtledove, *The Guns of the South*, 1992
John Varley, *Millennium*, 1983

4379
H.C. TURK

Black Body
(New York: Zebra/Pinnacle, 1991)

Story type: Horror (Black Magic)
Major character(s): Lady Amanda Rathel, Paranormal Investigator; Alba Denton, Witch; Eric Denton, Nobleman
Time period(s): 18th century
Locale(s): England

Summary: First published in 1989, this novel is presented as the journal of Alba, a white witch and the only member of her coven whose life is spared by the witch-hunter Lady Amanda Rathel. Lady Amanda's plans for Alba include marriage to Eric, son of her former lover, Edward Denton, with the idea that consummation of the marriage will mean instant death for the boy and a fulfilling revenge for herself.

Other books you might like:
Anne Rice, *The Witching Hour*, 1990
John Updike, *The Witches of Eastwick*, 1984

4380
GEORGE TURNER

Brain Child
(New York: William Morrow, 1991)

Story type: Science Fiction (Genetic Manipulation)
Major character(s): David Chance, Orphan; Arthur Hazard, Genetically Altered Being; Jonesy, Spy
Time period(s): 2040s (2047)
Locale(s): Melbourne, Australia; Westerton, Australia

Summary: In 2002, Australia began an experimental project to produce test-tube babies with super intellects. Four groups of four babies were produced. One set of four died shortly after birth. The most intelligent group committed suicide in 2022, but they left a legacy with instructions to the true genetic model which would allow humans to become, perhaps, immortal. Unfortunately, the legacy has been lost and David Chance is set to find it.

Other books you might like:
Lois McMaster Bujold, *Falling Free*, 1988
Pat Cadigan, *Mindplayers*, 1987
Pat Cadigan, *Synners*, 1991
Aldous Huxley, *Brave New World*, 1932
Geoff Ryman, *The Child Garden*, 1990
Robert Silverberg, *Tower of Glass*, 1970
Michael D. Weaver, *My Father Immortal*, 1989

4381
GEORGE TURNER

Genetic Soldier
(New York: Morrow/AvoNova, 1994)

Story type: Science Fiction (Genetic Manipulation; Post-Holocaust)
Major character(s): Thomas ''Soldier'' Atkins, Military Personnel (general); Nugan Taylor, Linguist, Spacewoman; Library, Librarian, Psychic (esper)
Time period(s): 30th century (2900s)
Locale(s): Yarra Valley, Australia; *Search*, Spaceship

Summary: The homsesick crew of *Search* returns to Earth without finding a planet to colonize. Nugan lands alone, as the only linguist on the ship, prepared to cope with the similarities and differences in language, but finds great difficulty in understanding the motivation of the genetically manipulated survivors. Nugan learns that the crew will not be allowed to stay, with Soldier planning for them to leave without bloodshed. Unfortunately, Soldier meets Nugan's daughter, changing his relationship with everyone.

Other books you might like:
Eleanor Arnason, *Ring of Swords*, 1993
Octavia E. Butler, *Dawn*, 1987
Helen Collins, *Mutagenesis*, 1993
Samuel R. Delany, *They Fly at Ciron*, 1993
Megan Lindholm, *Alien Earth*, 1992
Michael D. Weaver, *My Father Immortal*, 1989
Catherine Wells, *The Earth Is All That Lasts*, 1991
Catherine Wells, *Children of the Earth*, 1992

4382

JAMES TURNER, Editor

Cthulhu 2000

(Sauk City, Wisconsin: Arkham House, 1995)

Story type: Horror (Anthology)

Summary: The 18 stories collected here are a wonderfully diverse testimony to the enduring power of H.P. Lovecraft's fiction and its influence. More traditional attempts to manifest Lovecraftian horrors include F. Paul Wilson's ''The Barrens,'' about an extradimensional monster in the wilds of New Jersey; Ted Klein's ''Black Man with a Horn,'' in which a writer is pursued by beings for what he knows about them; and Thomas Ligotti's ''The Last Feast of Harlequin,'' which reveals the horrifying truth of human origins. Both Ramsey Campbell in ''The Faces at Pine Dunes'' and Basil Copper in ''Shaft 247'' attempt to capture the ineffability of Lovecraft's horrors. Lovecraftian monsters are updated for the computer age in Lawrence Watt-Evans' ''Pickman's Modem,'' and postdated to the mid-century in Kim Newman's hard-boiled detective tale, ''The Big Fish.'' Humorous riffs on Lovecraft's themes include Esther Friesner's ''Love's Eldritch Ichor'' and Fred Chappell's ''The Adder.''

Other books you might like:

Ramsey Campbell, *New Tales of the Cthulhu Mythos*, 1980
Stephen Jones, *Shadows over Innsmouth*, 1990
   editor
Robert Weinberg, *Lovecraft's Legacy*, 1990
   Martin H. Greenberg, co-editor

4383

HARRY TURTLEDOVE

The Case of the Toxic Spell Dump

(New York: Baen, 1993)

Story type: Fantasy (Light Fantasy; Mystery)
Major character(s): David Fisher, Government Official (environmental investigator)
Time period(s): Indeterminate
Locale(s): Alternate Earth (Angels City, California)

Summary: Ordered to quietly investigate events at a Toxic Spell Dump, David Fisher discovers an ancient deity attempting to set up operations which would destroy Western Civilization.

Other books you might like:

Elizabeth Forrest, *Phoenix Fire*, 1992
Alan Dean Foster, *Cyber Way*, 1990
Alan Dean Foster, *To the Vanishing Point*, 1988
Barbara Hambly, *Dog Wizard*, 1993
Dean R. Koontz, *The Haunted Earth*, 1973
Larry Niven, *The Flight of the Horse*, 1973
Nick Pollotta, *Bureau 13*, 1991
Nick Pollotta, *Full Moonster*, 1992

4384

HARRY TURTLEDOVE

Departures

(New York: Ballantine Del Rey, 1993)

Story type: Science Fiction (Alternate Universe; Collection)
Summary: Contains an author's note plus individual introductions to 20 stories reprinted from 1980s and 1990s anthologies and periodicals. Stories appear in chronological order from the 2nd century B.C. to *ca.* 3000 A.D. with three set on an Earth on which Muhammed led a monk's life rather than a prophet's, two baseball stories, one of them epistolary, and other stories with themes ranging from an alternate American Civil War outcome to contemporary culture and environmental issues.

Other books you might like:

Gregory Benford, *Alternate Americas*, 1992
   Martin H. Greenberg, co-editor
Gregory Benford, *Alternate Empires*, 1989
   Martin H. Greenberg, co-editor
Gregory Benford, *Alternate Heroes*, 1990
   Martin H. Greenberg, co-editor
Gregory Benford, *Alternate Wars*, 1991
   Martin H. Greenberg, co-editor
Mike Resnick, *Alternate Kennedys*, 1992
   editor
Mike Resnick, *Alternate Presidents*, 1992
   editor
Mike Resnick, *Alternate Warriors*, 1993
   editor

4385

HARRY TURTLEDOVE

Earthgrip

(New York: Ballantine/Del Rey, 1991)

Story type: Science Fiction (Collection; Adventure)
Major character(s): Jennifer Logan, Trader, Teacher; Bernard Greenberg, Trader, Spaceship Captain; Pawasar Pawasar Ras, Leader, Alien (Foitani)
Time period(s): 31st century
Locale(s): L'Rau, Planet—Imaginary; Athet, Planet—Imaginary; Gilver, Planet—Imaginary

Summary: Subtitled *Tales from the Traders' World*, this book contains three stories originally published in *Analog* magazine which relate trading voyages as seen through the eyes of a teacher specializing in Middle English (20th century) Science Fiction who happens into a successful trading career. Jennifer discovers her interest in 20th-century literature helps her resolve impediments to doing business among the intelligent races residing on the planets she visits.

Other books you might like:

Poul Anderson, *Trader to the Stars*, 1964
James Blish, *Earthman, Come Home*, 1955
James Blish, *A Life for the Stars*, 1962
Octavia E. Butler, *Dawn*, 1987
Janet Kagan, *Mirabile*, 1991

Larry Niven, *Fallen Angels*, 1991
   Jerry Pournelle and Michael Flynn, co-authors
Andre Norton, *The Time Traders*, 1958

4386

HARRY TURTLEDOVE

The Guns of the South
(New York: Ballantine, 1992)

Story type: Science Fiction (Alternate Universe; Time Travel)
Major character(s): Andries Rhoodie, Time Traveller, Military Personnel; Robert E. Lee, Historical Figure, Military Personnel
Time period(s): 1860s
Locale(s): Confederate States of America, Fictional Country

Summary: Hoping to change history and provide a benevolent environment for South African slavery, Andries Rhoodie leads a group of volunteers to Civil War Era America where they join the Confederate Army and provide them with modern assault rifles. After winning the conflict and separating from the North, the Confederacy elects Robert E. Lee as president. Events do not unfold as Rhoodie had hoped when Lee, a champion of the proposed emancipation of slaves and no friend of the 21st century South Africans, becomes involved in political intrigue.

Other books you might like:
Gregory Benford, *Alternate Wars*, 1991
   Martin H. Greenberg, co-editor
Terry Bisson, *Fire on the Mountain*, 1988
Frank D. McSherry Jr., *The Fantastic Civil War*, 1991
   editor
Ward Moore, *Bring the Jubilee*, 1953
David C. Poyer, *The Shiloh Project*, 1981
Kevin D. Randle, *Remember Gettysburg*, 1988
   Robert Cornett, co-author
William Sanders, *The Wild Blue and the Gray*, 1991
S.M. Stirling, *Marching through Georgia*, 1988

4387

HARRY TURTLEDOVE

Hammer and Anvil
(New York: Ballantine Del Rey, 1996)

Story type: Fantasy (Military; Historical)
Major character(s): Maniakes, Military Personnel (general), Rebel; Etzilios, Barbarian, Leader (Khagan); Lysia, Noblewoman
Time period(s): Indeterminate Past
Locale(s): Videssos, Fictional Country

Summary: Because of extreme mismanagement and barbarous cruelty, Maniakes challenges Genesios for the throne of Videssos. Once autokrator, he must cope with no resources, generals of dubious loyalty, and major attacks from both Kubrat and Makuran, both of which manage to penetrate to the suburbs of the city, Videssos.

Other books you might like:
Poul Anderson, *The Game of Empire*, 1985

John M. Ford, *The Dragon Waiting*, 1983
Katherine Kurtz, *King Javan's Year*, 1992
Kirk Mitchell, *Procurator*, 1984
Susan Schwartz, *Byzantium's Crown*, 1987
Robert Silverberg, *Up the Line*, 1968
Judith Tarr, *Ars Magica*, 1989
Elizabeth Willey, *A Sorcerer and a Gentleman*, 1995
Chelsea Quinn Yarbro, *A Flame in Byzantium*, 1987

4388

HARRY TURTLEDOVE

Kaleidoscope
(New York: Ballantine/Del Rey, 1990)

Story type: Science Fiction (Collection)

Summary: The thirteen stories in this collection were originally published in such magazines as *Amazing Stories, Analog, The Magazine of Fantasy and Science Fiction, Twilight Zone*, and the anthology *Ripper!* between 1984 and 1988. Among the best of them are "And So to Bed," "Bluff," "Gentlemen of the Shade," and "The Last Article."

Other books you might like:
Gregory Benford, *Alternate Empires*, 1989
   Martin H. Greenberg, editor
Gregory Benford, *Alternate Heroes*, 1989
   Martin H. Greenberg, editor
L. Sprague de Camp, *Lest Darkness Fall*, 1941
David Drake, *Vettius and His Friends*, 1989

4389

HARRY TURTLEDOVE

Krispos of Videssos
(New York: Ballantine/Del Rey, 1991)

Story type: Fantasy (Political; Magic Conflict)
Series: Krispos of Videssos
Major character(s): Krispos, Ruler (Avtokrator of Videssos); Dara, Royalty (Empress of Videssos); Harvas Black-Robe, Wizard, Barbarian
Time period(s): Indeterminate Past
Locale(s): Videssos, Fictional Country

Summary: Krispos, having become Avtokrator of Videssos, marries the former Empress Dara who may or may not be carrying his child. After quelling a rebellion by Petronas, the former Avtokrator's uncle, he must face Harvas Black-Robe who is attacking the northern borders. While he is away, his father-in-law and the former Patriarch conspire against him.

Other books you might like:
Randall Garrett, *Too Many Magicians*, 1967
Katherine Kurtz, *Camber of Culdi*, 1976
Fletcher Pratt, *The Blue Star*, 1952
Melissa Scott, *A Choice of Destinies*, 1986
Susan Shwartz, *Silk Roads and Shadows*, 1988
Judith Tarr, *The Dagger and the Cross: A Novel of the Crusades*, 1991

4390

HARRY TURTLEDOVE

Krispos Rising

(New York: Ballantine/Del Rey, 1991)

Story type: Fantasy (Adventure; Political)
Series: Krispos of Videssos
Major character(s): Krispos, Adventurer; Anthimos, Ruler (Avtokrator of Videssos); Pyrrhos, Religious (abbot)
Time period(s): Indeterminate Past
Locale(s): Videssos, Fictional Country

Summary: Five hundred years before events in *The Misplaced Legion*, Krispos, driven out of his farm village by taxation and cholera, comes to Videssos and finds the Abbot Pyrrhos willing to help him. Rising first to groom in the service of the Avtokrator who thinks only of his pleasure, Krispos then becomes vestiarios. He incurs the anger of Petronas, the real ruler of Videssos, then finally of Anthimos who tries to kill him, but ends by killing himself with a spell gone bad. Krispos then becomes Avtokrator.

Other books you might like:
Randall Garrett, *Too Many Magicians*, 1967
Elizabeth Moon, *Surrender None: The Legacy of Gird*, 1990
Fletcher Pratt, *The Blue Star*, 1952
Melissa Scott, *A Choice of Destinies*, 1986

4391

HARRY TURTLEDOVE

Krispos the Emperor

(New York: Ballantine Del Rey, 1994)

Story type: Fantasy (Political; Magic Conflict)
Series: Krispos of Videssos
Major character(s): Krispos, Ruler (Avtokrator of Videssos); Phostis, Heir, Captive; Olyvria, Heiress, Adventurer
Time period(s): Indeterminate Past
Locale(s): Videssos, Fictional Country

Summary: When a new heresy in Videssos attracts Krispos' heir, Phostis, he nevertheless joins his father and brothers at the head of the army to suppress it. Kidnapped, Phostis learns that Makuran masterminds the outbreak while a sorcerer uses the power of the newly dead to fight Krispos and Videssos. Phostis must escape and rejoin Krispos for them to defeat the rebels and the wizard.

Other books you might like:
John Christopher, *The Prince in Waiting*, 1970
Richard Cowper, *The Road to Corlay*, 1979
Katherine Kurtz, *The Harrowing of Gwynedd*, 1989
Susan Schwartz, *Byzantium's Crown*, 1987
Roger Zelazny, *The Sign of the Unicorn*, 1975

4392

HARRY TURTLEDOVE

Prince of the North

(New York: Baen, 1994)

Story type: Fantasy (Political; Adventure)
Major character(s): Gerin the Fox, Ruler; Van, Barbarian; Selatre, Religious
Time period(s): Indeterminate Past
Locale(s): Castle Fox, Mythical Place; Ikos, Fictional City; Empire of Elabon, Fictional Country

Summary: Chaos and ignorance threaten Gerin's attempt to rule in the Northlands with some measure of enlightenment. An amateur wizard and reluctant prince, he must fight gods, monsters and barbarians for order and the life of his son. Old friends, such as Van, and new allies, such as Selatre the Sibyl, join in his fight toward an uncertain outcome.

Other books you might like:
Glen Cook, *The Black Company*, 1984
Barbara Hambly, *Dragonsbane*, 1986
P.C. Hodgell, *God Stalk*, 1982
Elizabeth Moon, *Sheepfarmer's Daughter*, 1988
Patricia C. Wrede, *Caught in Crystal*, 1987

4393

HARRY TURTLEDOVE

The Stolen Throne

(New York: Ballantine Del Rey, 1995)

Story type: Fantasy (Political; Adventure)
Series: Stolen Throne
Major character(s): Abivard, Nobleman, Warrior; Sharbaraz, Heir—Dispossessed, Prisoner; Roshnani, Spouse, Counselor
Time period(s): Indeterminate Past
Locale(s): Makuran, Fictional Country

Summary: After the defeat and killing of Makuran's emperor, Smerdis usurps the throne, imprisoning the rightful heir, Sharbaraz. When Abivard and his sister free Sharbaraz, he raises an army to challenge Smerdis, whose forces do not yield easily. First part of a trilogy.

Other books you might like:
Poul Anderson, *The Game of Empire*, 1985
Octavia E. Butler, *Patternmaster*, 1976
Diana Wynne Jones, *The Crown of Dalemark*, 1995
Katherine Kurtz, *Camber of Culdi*, 1976
Melissa Scott, *A Choice of Destinies*, 1987
Susan Schwartz, *Byzantium's Crown*, 1987
Melinda M. Snodgrass, *Queen's Gambit Declined*, 1989
Judith Tarr, *Lord of the Two Lands*, 1993

4394

HARRY TURTLEDOVE

A World of Difference

(New York: Ballantine/Del Rey, 1990)

Story type: Science Fiction (Alternate Universe; First Contact)
Major character(s): Irv Levitt, Scientist (anthropologist); Pat Marquard, Scientist (biologist); Reatur, Ruler (Domain Lord of Omolo)
Time period(s): 21st century
Locale(s): Minerva, Planet—Imaginary

Summary: Reatur and Hogram, two Domain-Lords of Minerva, the fourth planet from the sun, are planning a war when ships from the USA and the USSR land, one in each Domain. While the Americans plan ways to let females survive childbirth, the Russians are blackmailed into giving weapons to Hogram and training his people to use them. When they attack Reatur, an American is killed, but Lopatin, a KGB agent, sacrifices himself to stop the fighting from spreading back to Earth. Reatur and Hogram make peace and the Earthmen leave for home.

Other books you might like:
Poul Anderson, *Ensign Flandry*, 1966
Pierre Boulle, *Planet of the Apes*, 1963
L. Neil Smith, *Contact and Commune*, 1990
Wynne Whiteford, *Lake of the Sun*, 1989

4395

HARRY TURTLEDOVE

Worldwar: In the Balance

(New York: Ballantine Del Rey, 1994)

Story type: Science Fiction (Alternate History; Invasion of Earth)
Series: Worldwar
Major character(s): Atvar, Alien, Leader (Fleetlord); Sam Yeager, Military Personnel; Enrico Fermi, Historical Figure, Scientist
Time period(s): 1940s
Locale(s): Alternate Earth

Summary: With World War II enveloping the globe, Fleetleader Atvar's forces arrive to claim Earth for the People, forcing humanity to join forces against the aliens.

Other books you might like:
Patricia Anthony, *Cold Allies*, 1993
Gregory Benford, *Alternate Wars*, 1991
   Martin H. Greenberg, co-editor
Octavia E. Butler, *Dawn*, 1987
Philip K. Dick, *The Man in the High Castle*, 1962
Ursula K. Le Guin, *The Lathe of Heaven*, 1971

4396

HARRY TURTLEDOVE

Worldwar: Striking the Balance

(New York: Ballantine Del Rey, 1996)

Story type: Science Fiction (Invasion of Earth; Alternate History)
Series: Worldwar
Major character(s): Atvar, Military Personnel, Alien; Moishe Russie, Refugee, Radio Personality; Liu Han, Revolutionary, Parent (mother)
Time period(s): 1940s (1944-1945)
Locale(s): Alternate Earth

Summary: With the Fleet in disarray, plagued by mutiny, ginger addiction, and the Tosevites, Terrans hold their own and even gain a bit in the colder regions of the planet. The Fleet needs a cease-fire, if the Tosevites will accept one.

Other books you might like:
Kevin J. Anderson, *The Trinity Paradox*, 1991
   Doug Beason, co-author
Ben Bova, *Triumph*, 1993
Philip K. Dick, *The Man in the High Castle*, 1962
Newt Gingrich, *1945*, 1995
   William Forstchen, co-author
James P. Hogan, *The Proteus Operation*, 1985
Larry Niven, *Footfall*, 1985
   Jerry Pournelle, co-author
William F. Wu, *Dictator*, 1994
Jerry Yulsman, *Elleander Morning*, 1984

4397

HARRY TURTLEDOVE

Worldwar: Tilting the Balance

(New York: Ballantine Del Rey, 1995)

Story type: Science Fiction (Invasion of Earth)
Series: Worldwar
Major character(s): Ludmila Gorbunova, Military Personnel, Pilot; Atvar, Alien (Lizard), Leader; Moishe Russie, Fugitive
Time period(s): 1940s (1943)
Locale(s): Alternate Earth

Summary: The attack of the Lizards forces former human enemies into uneasy cooperation, rushing to develop nuclear weapons despite some disastrous setbacks. As the Lizards consolidate their holdings, increasing numbers succumb to ginger addiction, while human resistance takes on new significance when the Allies learn of the Lizard colonists en route to Earth.

Other books you might like:
Brian W. Aldiss, *The Year Before Tomorrow*, 1987
Patricia Anthony, *Cold Allies*, 1993
Ben Bova, *Triumph*, 1993
Newt Gingrich, *1945*, 1995
   William Forstchen, co-author
Robert Harris, *Fatherland*, 1992
Keith Laumer, *Worlds of the Imperium*, 1962

Brad Linaweaver, *Moon of Ice*, 1988
Larry Niven, *Footfall*, 1985
   Jerry Pournelle, co-author
Jerry Yulsman, *Elleander Morning*, 1984

4398

HARRY TURTLEDOVE

Worldwar: Upsetting the Balance
(New York: Ballantine Del Rey, 1996)

Story type: Science Fiction (Invasion of Earth; Alternate Universe)
Series: Worldwar
Major character(s): Atvar, Military Personnel (Fleetlord), Alien; Sam Yeager, Military Personnel (sergeant); Ludmila Gorbunova, Military Personnel, Pilot
Time period(s): 1940s (1944)
Locale(s): Alternate Earth

Summary: The human/alien war reaches a new and more dangerous level as the aliens pay attention to shipping, taking reprisals by bombing human cities more often. As the invasion of Britain fails and alien scientists raise a human baby in the hope of gaining understanding, the cold and hopelessness cause troops to start rebelling. Third in the series.

Other books you might like:
Brian W. Aldiss, *The Year Before Yesterday*, 1987
Kevin J. Anderson, *The Trinity Paradox*, 1991
   Doug Beason, co-author
Ben Bova, *Triumph*, 1993
Robert Harris, *Fatherland*, 1992
Brad Linaweaver, *Moon of Ice*, 1988
Jerry Yulsman, *Elleander Morning*, 1984

4399

LISA TUTTLE

Familiar Spirit
(New York: Tor, 1989)

Story type: Horror (Haunted House)
Major character(s): Sarah, Young Woman; Jade, Spirit
Time period(s): 1980s
Locale(s): Austin, Texas

Summary: After breaking up with her boyfriend, Sarah moves into a house dominated by the spirit of a deceased magician and a protracted duel between them ensues. Originally published in 1983.

Other books you might like:
Campbell Black, *Letters from the Dead*, 1985
Arthur Calder-Marshall, *The Scarlet Boy*, 1961
Ken Eulo, *The Brownstone*, 1980
Susan Hill, *The Woman in Black*, 1983

4400

LISA TUTTLE

Lost Futures
(New York: Dell/Abyss, 1992)

Story type: Science Fiction (Horror)
Major character(s): Clare Beckett, Accountant; Sophie Baxter, Artist; Michael Zacharias, Musician
Time period(s): 1990s (1992)
Locale(s): Virgil, New York

Summary: Bored with her lackluster life, Clare Beckett begins to live a more vivid and stimulating existence in dreams, where she is able to experience how her life might have turned out had she made different life choices. When her dream life begins to intrude upon the waking world, however, she is unable to tell whether she is going mad or whether her dreams are actually beginning to shape reality.

Other books you might like:
Paddy Chayefsky, *Altered States*, 1979
Philip K. Dick, *The Three Stigmata of Palmer Eldritch*, 1964
Daniel Quinn, *Dreamer*, 1988
Lucius Shepard, *Kalimantan*, 1990

4401

LISA TUTTLE

Memories of the Body
(New York: Severn House, 1992)

Story type: Horror (Collection)

Summary: Fifteen stories of fantasy, horror and science fiction written in the last half-decade by one of the best practitioners in all three genres. Included are two savage looks at the battle of the sexes, ''The Wound'' and ''Lizard Lust''; two tales of motherly love gone away, ''Jamie's Grave'' and ''A Mother's Heart''; a blend of time travel and Victorian spiritualism, ''The Spirit Cabinet''; and a science-fictional look at the afterlife, ''Dead Television.''

Other books you might like:
Pat Cadigan, *Patterns*, 1989
Elizabeth Engstrom, *Nightmare Flower*, 1992
Pat Murphy, *Points of Departure*, 1990
Jessica Amanda Salmonson, *John Collier and Fredric Brown Went Quarreling through My Head*, 1989

4402

LISA TUTTLE

Pillow Friend
(Clarkston, Georgia: White Wolf, 1996)

Story type: Horror (Wild Talents)
Major character(s): Agnes Grey, Writer; Graham Storey, Writer (poet); Marjorie Grey, Writer
Time period(s): 1990s (1996)
Locale(s): Austin, Texas; London, England

Summary: Agnes Grey discovers that, like her aunt, she has an uncanny talent to wish her dreams into reality. Her talent brings her a lifetime of fulfillment, but also problems, as she becomes increasingly unable to determine who and what is real, and whom and what she has simply wished into existence.

Other books you might like:
Ramsey Campbell, *Incarnate*, 1983
Orson Scott Card, *Treasure Box*, 1996
Charles L. Grant, *In a Dark Dream*, 1989
Melanie Tem, *Making Love*, 1993
Stephen King, *It*, 1986

4403
LISA TUTTLE, Editor

Skin of the Soul
(New York: Pocket, 1991)

Story type: Horror (Anthology)
Summary: Sixteen horror stories and one poem all written by women and concerned largely with female experience. Included are Melanie Tem's "Lightning Rod," about women who sacrifice their lives to spare their families pain; Joyce Carol Oates' "Pregnant," about an unborn child's control over its expectant mother; G.K. Sprinkle's "Serena Sees," about a radio talk show psychic; and Suzy McKee Charnas' "Boobs" and Karen Joy Fowler's "The Night Wolf," both of which use supernatural experiences as a metaphor for sexual awakening.

Other books you might like:
Richard Dalby, *The Virago Book of Ghost Stories*, 1987
Kathryn Ptacek, *Women of Darkness*, 1988
Kathryn Ptacek, *Women of Darkness II*, 1990
Alan Ryan, *Haunting Women*, 1988
Jessica Amanda Salmonson, *What Did Miss Darrington See?*, 1989

4404
KATHY TYERS

Crystal Witness
(New York: Bantam Spectra, 1989)

Story type: Science Fiction (Space Opera)
Major character(s): Ming Dalamini, Smuggler; Holjpip Langelleik, Ruler
Time period(s): Indeterminate Future
Locale(s): Mannheim, Planet—Imaginary

Summary: One company controls all interstellar travel and its police force rules with an iron fist. Dalamini is caught using illegal technology to smuggle sunstones. The company brain wipes her and forces her to spy on the ruler of the planet Mannheim. Gradually Dalamini recovers her identity and begins to work against the company.

Other books you might like:
Patricia A. McKillip, *Fool's Run*, 1987
Melisa C. Michaels, *Far Harbor*, 1989
Janet Morris, *Cruiser Dreams*, 1981

Janet Morris, *Dream Dancer*, 1980
Janet Morris, *Earth Dreams*, 1982

4405
KATHY TYERS

One Mind's Eye
(New York: Bantam Spectra, 1996)

Story type: Science Fiction (First Contact; Psychic Powers)
Major character(s): Llyn Torfinn, Adoptee, Psychic; Jahn Korsakov, Psychic; Karine Torfinn, Parent, Psychologist
Time period(s): Indeterminate Future
Locale(s): Antar, Planet—Imaginary

Summary: The human settlers of the Concord worlds rebuild after the alien Devastators attack, but interplanetary war threatens their precarious recovery when Tdega secedes. A human child found drugged and lost in virtual reality with no memories, Llyn has grown to adulthood under the guidance of Karine, but in spite of her adoptive mother's efforts to make her normal, still longs for her virtual experiences and for knowledge of her origins. Now her paranormal abilities may well prove the key to saving humanity.

4406
KATHY TYERS

Shivering World
(New York: Bantam Spectra, 1991)

Story type: Science Fiction (Disaster; Young Adult)
Major character(s): Graysha Brady-Phillips, Scientist (microbiologist); Lindon DalLierx, Administrator (colonial); Trevarre Chase-Frisson L'Zalle, Stowaway, Teenager
Time period(s): Indeterminate Future
Locale(s): Goddard, Planet—Imaginary (Epsilon Eridani)

Summary: Graysha left her teaching position to work for Gaea Corporation as a soils specialist on Goddard, recently opened to colonization and not yet stably terraformed. She willingly left the safety of habitat life because the job will help her pay off the huge debt left after her divorce and because of rumors that the Lwuites, the religious group who colonized Goddard, have the technology to cure the genetic disorder which will cause her early death.

Other books you might like:
David Brin, *The Uplift War*, 1987
Octavia E. Butler, *Dawn*, 1987
Gregory Feeley, *The Oxygen Barons*, 1990
Diana G. Gallagher, *The Alien Dark*, 1990
Frank Herbert, *Dune*, 1965
Larry Niven, *The Integral Trees*, 1984
Joan Slonczewski, *A Door into Ocean*, 1986

4407
KATHY TYERS

The Truce at Bakura
(New York: Bantam Spectra, 1994)

Story type: Science Fiction (Space Opera; Political)
Series: Star Wars
Major character(s): Leia Organa, Royalty, Diplomat; Luke Skywalker, Martial Arts Expert (Jedi Knight), Hero; Han Solo, Spaceship Captain, Warrior
Time period(s): Indeterminate Past
Locale(s): Bakura, Planet—Imaginary; New Republic, Interstellar Empire/Federation

Summary: The Rebel Alliance sends forces to aid the Bakura Imperial garrison, under attack from invading forces of the alien Ssi-ruuk, who were formerly allied to the now deceased Emperor. As they aid in repelling the invasion, Luke, Han and Leia must win allies among native Bakurans to insure against treachery from those aided. Set after James Kahn's *The Return of the Jedi* (1983).

Other books you might like:
Brian Daley, *The Han Solo Adventures*, 1992
George Lucas, *The Star Wars Trilogy*, 1987
    Donald F. Glut, James Kahn, co-authors
Vonda N. McIntyre, *The Crystal Star*, 1994
James H. Schmitz, *The Demon Breed*, 1968
L. Neil Smith, *The Lando Calrissian Adventures*, 1994

4408
DONALD TYSON

The Messenger
(St. Paul, Minnesota: Llewellyn Publications, 1993)

Story type: Horror (Occult)
Major character(s): Ebeneezer Hale, Paranormal Investigator; Liza Grey, Student (English graduate); Lee Sheppard, Student
Time period(s): 1990s (1993)
Locale(s): Haven-by-the-Sea, Nova Scotia, Canada

Summary: A group of parapsychologists and occultists stay at Haven-by-the-Sea, a remote fortress that once served as a hotel but turns out to have been a sanitarium for children run by Daniel Brannon, a member of the occult society the Brotherhood of the Fiery Heart. Brannon's efforts to create an avenging angel through the deaths of his child wards has produced a demonic fury who haunts the house, and whom the visitors try desperately to exorcise before it kills them all.

Other books you might like:
Judith Hawkes, *Julian's House*, 1990
Shirley Jackson, *The Haunting of Hill House*, 1959
Stephen King, *The Shining*, 1977
Richard Matheson, *Hell House*, 1971
Nina Romberg, *Shadow Walkers*, 1993

4409
SALINDA TYSON

Wheel of Dreams
(New York: Ballantine Del Rey, 1996)

Story type: Fantasy (Romance)
Major character(s): Kiera Danio, Fugitive, Psychic; Nikkael Roshannon, Mercenary, Psychic; Beren ''Brat'' SanDyllin Harth, Orphan
Time period(s): Indeterminate
Locale(s): Sanctum, Fictional Country; Blue Forest, Mythical Place; Cartheon, Fictional City (city and state)

Summary: After Kiera's father sells her to Nikkael as a wife, Kiera flees north to Cartheon, hoping to find the fabled witches who can explain her strange ability to dream prophetically. As Nikkael pursues, events pull the psychically linked pair into the struggle of Cartheon to resist Sanctum domination. First novel.

Other books you might like:
Tom Deitz, *Soulsmith*, 1991
Mary H. Herbert, *City of the Sorcerers*, 1994
J.V. Jones, *The Baker's Boy*, 1995
J.V. Jones, *A Man Betrayed*, 1996
Elizabeth Moon, *The Deed of Paksenarrion*, 1992
Rachel Pollack, *Temporary Agency*, 1994
Rachel Pollack, *Unquenchable Fire*, 1992

4410
MICHAEL UPCHURCH

Passive Intruder
(New York: Norton, 1995)

Story type: Horror (Ghost Story)
Major character(s): Susan Pond, Receptionist; Walker Popman, Photographer; Jerry Plume, Doctor (psychiatrist)
Time period(s): 1990s (1995)
Locale(s): Seattle, Washington

Summary: Walker Popman dies shortly after marrying Susan, and Susan notes a presence in his photographs that may be ghosts. Susan's investigations into Walker's past put her in touch with his first wife and psychiatrist, and introduce her to literal and symbolic ghosts that lead to greater self-awareness.

Other books you might like:
Peter S. Beagle, *A Fine and Private Place*, 1960
Jack Cady, *The Off Season*, 1995
Brad Leithauser, *Seaward*, 1993
Mark Morris, *The Immaculate*, 1992
Chet Williamson, *The House of Fear*, 1989

4411
PETER USTINOV

The Old Man and Mr. Smith
(New York: Little Brown/Arcade, 1991)

Story type: Fantasy (Religious; Light Fantasy)

Major character(s): God ''The Old Man'', Deity; Satan ''Mr. Smith'', Angel (fallen)
Time period(s): 1990s
Locale(s): United States; Israel; Asia

Summary: When God decides to check up on how human beings live and how they treat each other, God takes Satan along. Visiting the United States results in problems for religious and government personnel. God and Satan then travel to Russia, China, Israel and India before leaving Earth.

Other books you might like:
Neil Gaiman, *Good Omens: The Nice and Accurate Prophecies of Agnes Nutter, Witch*, 1990
    Terry Pratchett, co-author
Parke Godwin, *The Snake Oil Wars*, 1989
Parke Godwin, *Waiting for the Galactic Bus*, 1988
Robert A. Heinlein, *Job: A Comedy of Justice*, 1984
Robert A. Heinlein, *Stranger in a Strange Land*, 1991
    revised
Marc Laidlaw, *Neon Lotus*, 1988
Elizabeth Ann Scarborough, *Nothing Sacred*, 1991
Donald E. Westlake, *Humans*, 1991
Roger Zelazny, *Lord of Light*, 1967

4412

DORIS VALLEJO

Ladies: Retold Tales of Goddesses and Heroines

(New York: Roc, 1992)

Story type: Fantasy (Legend; Collection)
Summary: Doris Vallejo retells fables of mythological females Arachne, Ariadne, Circe, Coronis, Deianira, Eurydice, Gorgon, Medea, Pandora and Persephone. Lavishly illustrated in color and monocolor by Boris Vallejo.

Other books you might like:
Thomas Bulfinch, *Bulfinch's Mythology*, 1934
Robert Graves, *Greek Myths*, 1955
    2 volumes
Edith Hamilton, *Mythology*, 1942

4413

GAIL VAN ASTEN

Charlemagne's Champion

(New York: Ace, 1990)

Story type: Fantasy (Legend)
Major character(s): Roland, Bastard Son, Warrior
Time period(s): Indeterminate Past
Locale(s): Europe

Summary: Based on *The Song of Roland*, the novel examines the legend of Roland in a new light, adding supernatural elements. Roland rises to become the champion of Charlemagne, all the while trying to solve the mystery of his birth.

Other books you might like:
Ru Emerson, *Spell Bound*, 1990
Morgan Llywelyn, *The Isles of the Blest*, 1989

Andre Norton, *Merlin's Mirror*, 1975
Nikolai Tolstoy, *The Coming of the King*, 1989
Jane Yolen, *Dove Isabeau*, 1990

4414

EDO VAN BELKOM

Wyrm Wolf

(New York: HarperPaperbacks, 1995)

Story type: Horror (Werewolf Story)
Series: World of Darkness: Werewolf
Major character(s): Father Wendel Oldman, Werewolf, Religious (priest); Kenneth Holt, Streetperson; Caroline Keegan, Journalist (televison reporter)
Time period(s): 1990s (1995)
Locale(s): San Francisco, California

Summary: In the World of Darkness, which bears a close resemblance to our own, the Garou, a race of werewolves, conceal their beastly nature from human beings as best they can. When a renegade Garou begins slaughtering members of his community, Father Oldman, a Garou who runs the Scott Mission for the homeless, investigates the crimes in both his human and werewolf form to find out which of his brethren is in thrall to the Wyrm and acting as an instrument of pure evil. Set against the World of Darkness scenario of the White Wolf gaming company, this is the author's first novel.

Other books you might like:
Don Bassingthwaite, *Breathe Deeply*, 1994
Don Bassingthwaite, *Such Pain*, 1995
Richard Lee Byers, *Netherworld*, 1995
Stewart Von Allmen, *Conspicuous Consumption*, 1995

4415

RAYMOND VAN OVER

The Twelfth Child

(New York: Pinnacle, 1990)

Story type: Horror (Evil Children)
Major character(s): David Mallory, Doctor (obstetrician); Lily Shikome, Nurse; Father Paul, Religious (Catholic priest)
Time period(s): 1980s (1989)
Locale(s): Hanover, New Hampshire (Hitchcock Medical Center)

Summary: A routine childbirth that leaves the mother drained of her blood sends obstetrician David Mallory searching for an explanation. When Mallory finds the records of 10 equidistantly-spaced births over the last 10 years in which the mothers died under similar circumstances and the attending physicians were murdered within the year, he begins a race to solve the riddle of the mysterious births before he too is murdered. This is the author's first novel.

Other books you might like:
Ira Levin, *Rosemary's Baby*, 1967
David Seltzer, *The Omen*, 1976

4416

RAYMOND VAN OVER

Whisper

(New York: Zebra/Pinnacle, 1991)

Story type: Horror (Possession)
Major character(s): Brion McKibben, Child; Eleazar, Indian; Louis Edward Church, Police Officer (sheriff)
Time period(s): 1990s
Locale(s): New Thetford, Vermont

Summary: Heartbroken over the death of his dog Whisper, Brion McKibben brings the carcass to the old Iroquois medicine man Eleazar for resusciation. Too late, Eleazar discovers that the resurrected dog has become possessed by bloodthristy demons known as the Yaksha.

Other books you might like:
Stephen King, *Cujo*, 1981
Stephen King, *Pet Sematary*, 1983
John Stchur, *Paddywhack*, 1989

4417

SYDNEY J. VAN SCYOC

Deepwater Dreams

(New York: Avon, 1991)

Story type: Science Fiction (Genetic Manipulation)
Major character(s): Nuela, Student; Polmaire, Political Figure
Time period(s): Indeterminate Future
Locale(s): Aurlanis, Planet—Imaginary (Aurlanis Island)

Summary: The Chakera were genetically engineered to live in the sea after war made much of the land uninhabitable. When a ship full of the Chakera to be sold as slaves was stolen and crashed into a water world, they developed a culture based on their genetically inherited dreams. Land is scarce, and the inhabitants of Aurlanis ritually attain adulthood by staying alive in the ocean for 42 days. Nuela, passed in her turn at the ritual for several years, is suddenly sent to find a secret ocean-based society to deliver a message from Polmaire, and to experience deep water dreaming.

Other books you might like:
Gregory Benford, *Great Sky River*, 1987
Lois McMaster Bujold, *Falling Free*, 1988
Gordon R. Dickson, *Home From the Shore*, 1978
Alis A. Rasmussen, *A Passage of Stars*, 1990
Carol Severance, *Reefsong*, 1991
A.E. van Vogt, *The Silkie*, 1969
John Wyndham, *Out of the Deeps*, 1953

4418

SYDNEY J. VAN SCYOC

Feather Stroke

(New York: Avon, 1989)

Story type: Fantasy (Quest)
Major character(s): Dara, Telepath
Time period(s): Indeterminate

Locale(s): Tith, Planet—Imaginary

Summary: Dara learns that she was adopted, and that her abilities are a part of her heritage. While trying to control her powers, she has to defend herself from the priestly caste of Tith.

Other books you might like:
Marion Zimmer Bradley, *Hawkmistress!*, 1982
Marjie Douglis, *Matrix Witch*, 1988
Katherine Kurtz, *Chronicle of Deryni*, 1987
Mercedes Lackey, *Magic's Pawn*, 1989

4419

JACK VANCE

Alastor

(New York: Tor, 1995)

Story type: Science Fiction (Political; Space Opera)
Major character(s): Oman Ursht, Leader (Connatic)
Time period(s): Indeterminate Future
Locale(s): Alastor Cluster, Interstellar Empire/Federation; Numenes, Planet—Imaginary

Summary: Omnibus edition containing *Trullion: Alastor 2262* (1973), *Marune Alastor 933* (1975), and *Wyst: Alastor 1716* (1978). The Connatic, ruler of the Alastor Cluster with its thousands of stars containing 3000 inhabited planets, may seem omniscient using information from the Ring of Worlds in his palace, but he can only occupy one room at a time.

Other books you might like:
Iain M. Banks, *Against a Dark Background*, 1993
Glen Cook, *The Dragon Never Sleeps*, 1988
L. Warren Douglas, *Stepwater*, 1995
Mary Gentle, *Golden Witchbreed*, 1984
Sheri S. Tepper, *Raising the Stones*, 1990
A.E. van Vogt, *The Weapon Makers*, 1946

4420

JACK VANCE

Ecce and Old Earth

(New York: Tor, 1991)

Story type: Science Fiction (Mystery; Political)
Series: Cadwal Chronicles
Major character(s): Glawen Clattuc, Police Officer; Wayness Tamm, Detective—Amateur; Pirie Tamm, Administrator
Time period(s): Indeterminate Future
Locale(s): Cadwal, Planet—Imaginary; Earth

Summary: Glawen Clattuc, having discovered his father is alive, rescues him from a prison in Ecce. Meanwhile, Wayness Tamm goes to Old Earth to find the missing Charter of the Nature Society, without which Cadwall will be parcelled out into landed estates and overrun by Yips.

Other books you might like:
Isaac Asimov, *The Stars Like Dust*, 1951
Orson Scott Card, *The Memory of Earth*, 1992
Philip Jose Farmer, *Dayworld*, 1985
Raymond Harris, *Shadows of the White Sun*, 1988

Melissa Scott, *Five-Twelfths of Heaven*, 1985

4421

JACK VANCE

Madouc
(New York: Ace, 1990)

Story type: Fantasy (Political)
Series: Lyonesse
Major character(s): Madouc, Heroine (Changeling)
Time period(s): Indeterminate
Locale(s): Europe

Summary: Madouc, daughter of a faerie, is making life miserable for everyone as political intrigue and skullduggery pervade her home and a quest for the Holy Grail begins.

Other books you might like:
Constance Ash, *The Stalking Horse*, 1990
Claudia J. Edwards, *Eldrie the Healer*, 1989
   The Bastard Princess. Vol. 1
M. John Harrison, *A Storm of Wings*, 1980
Michael Moorcock, *Gloriana, or the Unfulfilled Queen*, 1986
Melanie Rawn, *The Star Scroll*, 1989
   Dragon Prince. Bk. 2
Michael Shea, *Nifft the Lean*, 1982

4422

JACK VANCE

Night Lamp
(New York: Tor, 1996)

Story type: Science Fiction (Adventure; Science Fiction)
Major character(s): Jaro Fath, Foundling, Spaceman; Skirlet Hutsenreiter, Noblewoman, Investigator; Asrubal, Thief
Time period(s): Indeterminate Future
Locale(s): Thanet, Planet—Imaginary; Fader, Planet—Imaginary

Summary: An adopted foundling with no memory of his past, Jaro Fath seeks his origins. When his natural father finds him, the two go off to punish those responsible for his plight and come across a very strange society.

Other books you might like:
Kevin J. Anderson, *Blindfold*, 1995
Lois McMaster Bujold, *Cetaganda*, 1996
C.J. Cherryh, *Cuckoo's Egg*, 1985
Paula E. Downing, *A Whisper of Time*, 1994
Raymond Harris, *Shadows of the White Sun*, 1988
Mike Resnick, *The Dark Lady: A Romance of the Far Future*, 1987
Sydney J. Van Scyoc, *Darkchild*, 1982
Joan D. Vinge, *The Summer Queen*, 1991

4423

JACK VANCE

Throy
(New York: Tor, 1993)

Story type: Science Fiction (Mystery; Political)
Series: Cadwal Chronicles
Major character(s): Glawen Clattuc, Police Officer; Eustace Chilke, Police Officer; Felitzia "Flitz" Stronsi, Heir—Dispossessed
Time period(s): Indeterminate Future
Locale(s): Cadwal, Planet—Imaginary; Rosalia, Planet—Imaginary

Summary: Glawen Clattus must postpone his marriage while he and Eustace Chilke capture Julian Bohost who has profited from the sale of indentured Yips on other planets. On Soum they confiscate Bohost's finances, then on Rosalia they rescue Flitz who has been robbed of family and fortune. Finally, on Cadwal, Glawen learns details of his mother's death and of a conspiracy to overthrow the Conservancy.

Other books you might like:
Lloyd Biggle, *Monument*, 1974
Johanna Bolton, *Mission: Tori*, 1990
Lois McMaster Bujold, *Brothers in Arms*, 1989
Raymond Harris, *The Broken Worlds*, 1986
Edward Llewellyn, *Fugitive in Transit*, 1985
Atanielle Annyn Noel, *The Duchess of Kneedeep*, 1986
Norman Spinrad, *The Void Captain's Tale*, 1986

4424

JACK VANCE

When the Five Moons Rise
(Lancaster, Pennsylvania: Underwood-Miller, 1992)

Story type: Science Fiction (Collection)

Summary: Contains 11 stories published in 1950s periodicals plus one, "Dust of Far Suns," retitled from its 1962 publication as "Gateway to Strangeness." Other stories explore the breadth of Vance's 1950s short fiction with some set far from the here and now such as "Noise" and "When the Five Moons Rise," while Vance looks closer to home when he investigates urban folly of the future in "Dodkin's Job" and "Ulward's Retreat." "The New Prime" reflects Vance's love of space opera, and "Telek" postulates a universe in which a person's subjective reality affects everyone's shared reality.

Other books you might like:
Isaac Asimov, *The Complete Stories - Volume 1*, 1990
Alfred Bester, *Star Light, Star Bright*, 1976
Robert A. Heinlein, *The Past through Tomorrow*, 1967
Larry Niven, *N-Space*, 1990
Cordwainer Smith, *The Best of Cordwainer Smith*, 1975
Theodore Sturgeon, *E Pluribus Unicorn*, 1953
John Varley, *Blue Champagne*, 1986
John Varley, *The Persistence of Vision*, 1978
Kurt Vonnegut Jr., *Welcome to the Monkey House*, 1968

4425

STEVE VANCE

Shapes

(New York: Leisure, 1991)

Story type: Horror (Werewolf Story)
Major character(s): Dominic Poduano, Monster (shapeshifter); Kelly Brynn Davis, Journalist; Blake Corbett, Writer (of horror fiction)
Time period(s): 1990s
Locale(s): Indigo Lake, New York

Summary: Blake Corbett finds himself torn between his promise to the government that he will not reveal his investigations into the viral origins of lycanthropy or what he witnessed during an experiment that went awry and turned one of his best friends into a shapeshifter. In addition, a group of supernaturally-endowed researchers want him to speak at their upcoming convention and could be just as dangerous as the government if he refuses their request.

Other books you might like:
Crosland Brown, *Tombley's Walk*, 1991
George C. Chesbro, *The Fear in Yesterday's Rings*, 1991

4426

STEVE VANCE

Spook

(New York: Soho Press, 1990)

Story type: Horror (Mystery)
Major character(s): MaryAnn "Spook" Nelson, Teenager; Nedra Muriel Nelson, Artist (former Hollywood make-up artis); Ross Walker, Police Officer
Time period(s): 1990s (1990)
Locale(s): Sturgis, Georgia

Summary: Taunted by her peers for her physical deformities and shunned with her mother for their association with a series of sinister goings-on about town, MaryAnn Nelson endures a hellish adolescence. The persistence of the local school board to make her attend school eventually uncovers secrets about MaryAnn and her mother that outward appearances conceal.

Other books you might like:
John Farris, *Fiends*, 1990
Stephen King, *Carrie*, 1974

4427

VIVIAN VANDE VELDE

Dragon's Bait

(New York: Harcourt Brace Jovanovich, 1992)

Story type: Fantasy (Young Adult; Quest)
Major character(s): Alys, Criminal (accused witch), Teenager; Selendrile, Mythical Creature (dragon)
Time period(s): Indeterminate
Locale(s): St. Toby's-by-the-Mountain, Fictional City; Griswold, Fictional City

Summary: Saved by the dragon that she had expected to kill her, Alys discovers an ally in her desire for revenge on her townspeople. While pursuing their scheme, their capture precipitates a lethal encounter and may prove deadly for Selendrile.

Other books you might like:
Orson Scott Card, *Dragons of Darkness*, 1981
   editor
Louise Cooper, *The Sleep of Stone*, 1991
R.A. MacAvoy, *Tea with the Black Dragon*, 1983
Andre Norton, *The Elvenbane*, 1991
   Mercedes Lackey, co-author
Will Shetterly, *Elsewhere*, 1991
Patricia C. Wrede, *Dealing with Dragons*, 1991

4428

VIVIAN VANDE VELDE

Tales From the Brothers Grimm and the Sisters Weird

(New York: Harcourt Brace/Jane Yolen Books, 1995)

Story type: Fantasy (Collection; Legend)

Summary: Retells eight stories and five poems, modernizing the popular works with contemporary character motivations and humorous, sometimes dark, twists. Tales include "Rumplestiltskin," "Little Red Riding Hood," "Hansel and Gretl," "Jack and the Beanstalk," and "Beauty and the Beast."

Other books you might like:
Margaret Atwood, *Good Bones and Simple Murders*, 1994
William J. Brooke, *A Telling of the Tales*, 1990
William J. Brooke, *Teller of Tales*, 1994
James Finn Garner, *Once upon a More Enlightened Time*, 1995
James Finn Garner, *Politically Correct Bedtime Stories*, 1994
James Finn Garner, *Politically Correct Holiday Stories*, 1995

4429

VIVIAN VANDE VELDE

User Unfriendly

(New York: Harcourt Brace Jovanovich, 1991)

Story type: Fantasy (Quest; Young Adult)
Major character(s): Arvin "Harek" Rizalli, Student, Mythical Creature (elf); Felice, Parent (Arvin's mother), Thief; Sheldon Jankowitz, Student, Wizard
Time period(s): 1990s
Locale(s): Sannatia, Fictional City

Summary: Expecting a few hours' diversion, Arvin, his mother and his school mates enter the world of a bootleg computer game. As they pursue their quest, rescuing the king's daughter, Dorinda, the computer game's program seems somewhat odd and alarming as Felice begins to fade away. As their adventure progresses, Arvin must make brave and difficult decisions if the company is to make their way out of the dangerous world.

Other books you might like:
Margaret J. Anderson, *The Ghost Inside the Monitor*, 1990
Steven Brust, *Jhereg*, 1983
Diane Duane, *High Wizardry*, 1990
Philip Jose Farmer, *Red Orc's Rage*, 1991
Joel Rosenberg, *The Sleeping Dragon*, 1983
Will Shetterly, *The Tangled Lands*, 1989

4430

VIVIAN VANDE VELDE

A Well-Timed Enchantment

(New York: Crown, 1990)

Story type: Fantasy (Time Travel; Young Adult)
Major character(s): Deanna, Vacationer
Time period(s): 1990s; Indeterminate Past (Middle Ages)
Locale(s): France

Summary: While Deanna makes a wish at a well, she accidently drops her wristwatch into it. At that, a magical hand reaches out and drags her into the well. She is informed by elves that her watch, falling into the past, has messed up history. She must return to medieval France accompanied by her cat, enchanted into a strange young man, to retrieve the watch and correct history.

Other books you might like:
Keith William Andrews, *Sink the Armada*, 1990
Eleanor Cameron, *The Court of the Stone Children*, 1973
Catherine Dexter, *Mazemaker*, 1989
Roger L. DiSilvestro, *Living with the Reptiles*, 1990
Winifred Morris, *With Magical Horses to Ride*, 1985
Marilyn Singer, *Charmed*, 1990
Nancy Springer, *Red Wizard*, 1990

4431

PETER VANSITTART

Parsifal

(Chester Springs, PA: Peter Owen/Dufour Editions, 1989)

Story type: Fantasy (Legend)
Major character(s): Parsifal, Knight
Time period(s): 15th century (16th century); 20th century
Locale(s): Europe; Germany

Summary: Rather than focusing on a plot, Vansittart explores the legends that grew around the myth of Parsifal, as well as the particular times in history that had a profound effect on the legend.

Other books you might like:
Richard Barber, *The Arthurian Legends*,
Stephen R. Lawhead, *Arthur*, 1989
C.W. Sullivan, *Welsh Celtic Myth in Modern Fantasy*,
Jack Zipes, *The Brothers Grimm: From Enchanted Forests to the Modern World*, 1988

4432

ROBERT E. VARDEMAN

Ancient Heavens

(New York: Avon, 1989)

Story type: Science Fiction (Adventure)
Major character(s): Richard Drake, Scientist (Terraformer); Michaeline Drake, Scientist
Time period(s): 21st century; 23rd century
Locale(s): Earth; Nerth, Planet—Imaginary (In the Alpha Centauri System)

Summary: Richard Drake specializes in the creation of entire new landscapes. Using the most advanced techniques in engineering and genetics, he can turn a desert into a productive agricultural region or whatever else is wanted. Now he's been offered the ultimate challenge. The Church of the Lost Eden wishes to terraform an entire planet and they want Richard Drake in charge. Drake agrees to do the job, not realizing that, when the work is done, the religious zealots who will populate that world may well come to look on him as the Creator Himself.

Other books you might like:
Poul Anderson, *The Snows of Ganymede*, 1955
Gregory Benford, *Jupiter Project*, 1975
John Brunner, *The Dramaturges of Yan*, 1971
Arthur C. Clarke, *The Sands of Mars*, 1951
David Gerrold, *Moonstar Odyssey*, 1977
Frank Herbert, *Children of Dune*, 1976
Ian Watson, *The Martian Inca*, 1977

4433

ROBERT E. VARDEMAN

Death Channels

(New York: Avon, 1992)

Story type: Horror (Occult)
Series: Peter Thorne, Psychic Investigator
Major character(s): Peter Thorne, Magician, Paranormal Investigator; Charlie Hayes, Businessman (computers); Nyushka, Psychic (medium and channeler)
Time period(s): 1990s (1993)
Locale(s): San Francisco, California

Summary: Psychic detective Peter Thorne investigates a spirit channeler whom he thinks is preying on the grief of recently widowed friend, Charlie Hayes. Instead, he discovers that Charlie and his wife may have each been plotting to kill the other.

Other books you might like:
Geoffrey Caine, *Curse of the Dead*, 1991
Geoffrey Caine, *Legion of the Dead*, 1992
Geoffrey Caine, *Wake of the Werewolf*, 1991
Ehren M. Ehly, *Star Prey*, 1992
Ray Garton, *Dark Channel*, 1992
Seabury Quinn, *The Phantom Fighter*, 1966

4434

ROBERT E. VARDEMAN

The Glass Warrior

(New York: Tor, 1989)

Story type: Fantasy (Quest)
Series: Demon Crown
Major character(s): Glass Warrior, Warrior
Time period(s): Indeterminate
Locale(s): Porotane, Planet—Imaginary

Summary: Porotane is torn by civil war. The aging ruler, on the throne by pretense and connivery, asks the Glass Warrior to find the legitimate heirs to the throne, in order to end the war.

Other books you might like:
Richard A. Knaak, *Firedrake*, 1989
Dave Smeds, *The Sorcery Within*, 1985
Janny Wurts, *Cycle of Fire Trilogy*, 1988

4435

ROBERT E. VARDEMAN

The Infinity Plague

(New York: Ace Books, 1989)

Story type: Science Fiction (Military)
Series: Biowarriors
Major character(s): Jerome Walden, Scientist
Time period(s): 21st century
Locale(s): Delta Cygnus 4, Planet—Imaginary; Earth

Summary: The Frinn, an evil alien race, invade Earth space bent on conquest. Earth's leaders must decide whether or not to use dangerous genetically engineered bioweapons to repel the invasion.

Other books you might like:
Rick Cook, *Limbo System*, 1989
Charles Ingrid, *Alien Salute*, 1989
    Sand Wars 4
L. Neil Smith, *Contact and Commune*, 1989
Allen L. Wold, *Crown of the Serpent*, 1989

4436

JOHN VARLEY

Steel Beach

(New York: Ace/Putnam, 1992)

Story type: Science Fiction (Alternate Intelligence; Immortality)
Series: Eight Worlds
Major character(s): Hildy Johnson, Journalist (*News Nipple*), Teacher; Brenda, Journalist (cub reporter); Central "CC" Computer, Artificial Intelligence
Time period(s): 23rd century
Locale(s): Moon (Earth's)

Summary: Assigned to produce a series of stories surrounding the 200th anniversary of aliens wiping out human life on Earth, Hildy unwillingly accepts a naive young partner enthusiastic to develop her journalistic skills. Hildy's research leads to the disturbing conclusion that CC may exhibit lethal insanity.

Other books you might like:
David Brin, *Earth*, 1990
Jeffrey A. Carver, *The Rapture Effect*, 1987
Robert A. Heinlein, *The Moon Is a Harsh Mistress*, 1966
Cordwainer Smith, *Norstrilia*, 1975
Allen Steele, *Clarke County, Space*, 1990
Allen Steele, *Lunar Descent*, 1991
Neal Stephenson, *Snow Crash*, 1992
Vernor Vinge, *A Fire upon the Deep*, 1992

4437

JOHN VARLEY, Editor
RICIA MAINHARDT, Co-Editor

Superheroes

(New York: Ace, 1995)

Story type: Fantasy (Anthology; Science Fiction)

Summary: Contains an 11-page introduction by Varley plus 25 original stories of comic book type superheroes set in alternate universes with contemporary themes joining traditional pulp literature conceits. Authors include B.W. Clough, John DeChancie, Alan Dean Foster, Laurell K. Hamilton, Richard A. Knaak, Brad Linaweaver, Jody Lynn Nye, Mickey Zucker Reichert, Josepha Sherman, Michael A. Stackpole, Brian M. Thomsen, John Varley, Lawrence Watt-Evans, and Roger Zelazny.

Other books you might like:
Michael Bishop, *Count Geiger's Blues*, 1992
Michael Kandel, *Captain Jack Zodiac*, 1992
Stan Lee, *The Ultimate Spider-Man*, 1994
    editor
George R.R. Martin, *The Wild Cards Series*, 1987-1995
Victor Milan, *Turn of the Cards*, 1993
Melinda M. Snodgrass, *Double Solitaire*, 1992

4438

GORE VIDAL

Live From Golgotha: A Novel

(New York: Random House, 1992)

Story type: Science Fiction (Satire; Theological)
Major character(s): Timothy "Timmy", Religious (Bishop of Macedonia), Writer; Chester "Chet" W. Claypoole, Businessman, Television (executive)
Time period(s): 1st century (96); 1990s (1992)
Locale(s): Thessalonika, Greece (Macedonia); Rome, Italy

Summary: While a computer hacker's virus deletes tapes describing the Good News, a 20th century television executive uses holographic projections through time to convince Timothy to write a gospel resistant to the Hacker's evil virus. The NBC executive, Chet Claypoole, wants Timothy to anchor the spectacular show covering the Crucifixion, "*Live* from

Golgotha,'' with 20th century televangelists and spiritualists providing commentary.

Other books you might like:
Neil Gaiman, *Good Omens: The Nice and Accurate Prophecies of Agnes Nutter, Witch*, 1990
  Terry Pratchett, co-author
Parke Godwin, *The Snake Oil Wars*, 1989
Parke Godwin, *Waiting for the Galactic Bus*, 1988
A.J. Langguth, *Jesus Christs*, 1968
Michael Moorcock, *Behold the Man*, 1970
Neal Stephenson, *Snow Crash*, 1992
Peter Ustinov, *The Old Man and Mr. Smith*, 1991

4439

JOAN D. VINGE

Dreamfall

(New York: Warner Aspect, 1996)

Story type: Science Fiction (Psychic Powers; Political)
Series: Psion
Major character(s): Cat ''Bian'', Psychic (half Hydran-Psion); Miya, Alien (Hydran), Psychic (therapist); Naoh, Alien (Hydran), Revolutionary
Time period(s): Indeterminate Future
Locale(s): Refuge, Planet—Imaginary

Summary: On Refuge, home planet of the psychic Hydrans, Cat finds conditions deplorable for the native population. Tau Biotech mines the sacred reefs left by the alien Cloud Whales who no longer float over Hydran reservations. Consultant to the team called into study the Cloud Whales, Cat, tortured as a native, becomes embroiled in local politics.

Other books you might like:
Greg Bear, *Legacy*, 1995
David Brin, *Brightness Reef*, 1995
Emily Devenport, *Eggheads*, 1996
Alan Dean Foster, *Mid-Flinx*, 1995
Alis A. Rasmussen, *Revolution's Shore*, 1990

4440

JOAN D. VINGE

The Summer Queen

(New York: Warner Questar, 1991)

Story type: Science Fiction (Political; Family Saga)
Series: Snow Queen
Major character(s): Moon Dawntreader Summer, Ruler (Queen of Tiamat); BZ Gundhalinu, Police Officer, Judge; Reede Kulleva Kullervo, Genetically Altered Being, Researcher
Time period(s): Indeterminate Future
Locale(s): Tiamat, Planet—Imaginary; Ondinee, Planet—Imaginary

Summary: Due to BZ Gundhalinu's discoveries on World's End and Kullervo's genius in research, the Hegemony goes back to Tiamat to resume hunting the Mers whose blood grants immortality. Moon, the Summer Queen, knows that the Mers are vital to the functioning of the Hegemony so she and

BZ Gundhalinu manage to stall the Hunt until Gundhalinu is arrested for treason by those factions determined to hunt the Mers. Kullervo, criminal and kidnapper though he is, proves to be the key to stopping the slaughter, as he is an Avatar of Vanamoonen, co-designer of both Mers and Sybils.

Other books you might like:
C.J. Cherryh, *Cyteen*, 1988
Cynthia Felice, *Eclipses*, 1983
C.S. Friedman, *Black Sun Rising*, 1991
C.S. Friedman, *The Madness Season*, 1990
Mary Gentle, *Golden Witchbreed*, 1984
Jacqueline Lichtenberg, *Molt Brother*, 1982
Pamela Sargent, *Venus of Shadows*, 1988
A.C.H. Smith, *The Dark Crystal: A Novel*, 1982

4441

VERNOR VINGE

A Fire upon the Deep

(New York: Tor, 1992)

Story type: Science Fiction (Alternate Intelligence; First Contact)
Major character(s): Ravna Bergsndot, Librarian; Blueshell, Alien (Skroderider), Businessman (trader); Pham Nuwen, Religious (Godshattered), Reanimated Dead
Time period(s): Indeterminate Future
Locale(s): *Out of Band*, Spaceship; Tine's World, Planet—Imaginary

Summary: In a galaxy possessing variable physical laws, a research team unwittingly reassembles an inactive, malevolent artificial intelligence who immediately begins searching for that which had destroyed it, an immunizing program which barely escapes with the research team's children. While the malevolent entity destroys civilizations around the galaxy, Ravna, Blueshell and others rush to save or destroy the children held prisoner by intelligent colony creatures.

Other books you might like:
Roger MacBride Allen, *The Ring of Charon*, 1990
David Brin, *Earth*, 1990
Jeffrey A. Carver, *Down the Stream of Stars*, 1990
Glen Cook, *The Dragon Never Sleeps*, 1988
Rudy Rucker, *Software*, 1982
Rudy Rucker, *Wetware*, 1988
David Alexander Smith, *Homecoming*, 1990
David Alexander Smith, *Rendezvous*, 1988
Neal Stephenson, *Snow Crash*, 1992
John Varley, *Steel Beach*, 1992
Walter Jon Williams, *Angel Station*, 1989

4442

ERIC VINICOFF
MARCIA MARTIN, Co-Author

The Weigher

(New York: Baen, 1992)

Story type: Science Fiction (First Contact; Political)

Major character(s): Slasher, Alien, Businesswoman (mediator); Ralphayers Delta, Clone (human), Genetically Altered Being; Pamayers Alpha, Clone (human), Explorer
Time period(s): Indeterminate Future
Locale(s): Planet—Imaginary (City of Coalgathering)

Summary: As Weigher of Coalgathering, a town of anarchic carnivorous predators, Slasher's Weighing rarely goes to the Challenge Field. After the third strange, dangerous-scented animal is killed despite Slasher's having spoken for it, Slasher's relief almost outweighs her curiosity and greed. Risking her life and position, Slasher contracts to broker the humans' information and ideas after they return smelling like grass.

Other books you might like:
Eleanor Arnason, *A Woman of the Iron People*, 1991
C.J. Cherryh, *Serpent's Reach*, 1980
Gordon R. Dickson, *The Alien Way*, 1965
Suzette Haden Elgin, *Twelve Fair Kingdoms*, 1981
Diana G. Gallagher, *The Alien Dark*, 1990
Donald E. McQuinn, *Warrior*, 1990
Larry Niven, *Tales of Known Space*, 1975
David Alexander Smith, *Homecoming*, 1990

4443
DENISE VITOLA

Half-Light
(Lake Geneva, Wisconsin: TSR, 1992)

Story type: Science Fiction (Theological; Political)
Major character(s): Ariann Centuri, Military Personnel (commander), Religious; Winn Forrest, Religious, Government Official (viceroy); Stuk elan Emok, Alien (Benar), Spaceship Captain
Time period(s): Indeterminate Future
Locale(s): Alune, Planet—Imaginary; Corsicata, Planet—Imaginary; Benarus, Planet—Imaginary

Summary: Infected with a brain parasite during an attack on their expedition, Ariann finds herself forced to marry Winn to save her life and sanity. The hungry Benar look for ''Humanities'' to eat and now use a captured star chart to find where to get ''meat.'' Ariann and Winn must link in religiously induced Half-Light to save Ariann and protect humanity from the Benar.

Other books you might like:
Aline Boucher-Kaplan, *World Spirits*, 1991
Jeffrey A. Carver, *Dragons in the Stars*, 1992
Adrian Cole, *Mother of Storms*, 1992
A.C. Crispin, *V*, 1984
Gordon R. Dickson, *The Alien Way*, 1965
Frank Herbert, *Dune*, 1965
Larry Niven, *The Mote in God's Eye*, 1974
  Jerry Pournelle, co-author
Sheri S. Tepper, *Raising the Stones*, 1990

4444
GERALD VIZENOR

Dead Voices: Natural Agonies in the Real World
(Norman, Oklahoma: University of Oklahoma Press, 1992)

Story type: Fantasy (Legend; Urban)
Major character(s): Bagese Bear, Animal (bear), Indian; I ''Laundry'', Writer
Time period(s): 1970s (1979); 1990s (1992)
Locale(s): Oakland, California

Summary: To preserve Indian cultural heritage, Bagese Bear encourages the author to discover the voice within as she retells her stories to the author with the understanding that he not write them down since the stories' validity lies in their oral presentation. Each day Bagese tries to view the world through the eyes of some particular animal or sometimes as the Trickster would see the world. Her stories range from creation mythology to the unfortunate innovations visited upon Indian life by the dominant Western culture.

Other books you might like:
Richard Erdoes, *American Indian Myths and Legends*, 1984
  Alfonso Ortiz, co-editor
Peter Gadol, *Coyote*, 1990
Barry Lopez, *Crow and Weasel*, 1990
Howard Norman, *Northern Tales: Traditional Stories of Eskimo and Indian Peoples*, 1980
Ben Okri, *The Famished Road*, 1992
Paul Radin, *The Trickster*, 1972

4445
CYNTHIA VOIGT

On Fortune's Wheel
(New York: Atheneum, 1990)

Story type: Fantasy (Adventure; Young Adult)
Series: Jackaroo
Major character(s): Biale, Runaway; Orien, Nobleman, Thief
Time period(s): Indeterminate Past (pre-Industrial Revolution)
Locale(s): The Kingdom, Alternate Earth

Summary: Biale, the runaway Innkeeper's daughter, meets up with the itinerant, incognito Orien, a lord's son. They leave the confines of the structured society of their homeland, The Kingdom, for adventures in the free-wheeling southern lands. There Biale falls into slavery, and The Kingdom starts to look more attractive. ALA Best Young Adult book.

Other books you might like:
Lloyd Alexander, *Westmark*, 1981
Eleanor Arnason, *The Sword Smith*, 1978
Diana Wynne Jones, *Cart and Cwidder*, 1977
Ellen Kushner, *Swordspoint*, 1988
Sherwood Smith, *Wren to the Rescue*, 1990
Gene Wolfe, *The Devil in a Forest*, 1976

4446

WILLIAM T. VOLLMANN

The Ice-Shirt
(New York: Viking, 1990)

Story type: Fantasy (Historical)
Series: Seven Dreams
Major character(s): Freydis Eiriksdottir, Historical Figure; Leif Eiriksson, Historical Figure; Gudrid Thorbjornsdottir, Historical Figure
Time period(s): 11th century
Locale(s): Greenland; Vinland, North America

Summary: The Norse have settled in Greenland and send a colony to Vinland to exploit its riches. Rivalries and feuds among the colonists, especially between Gudrid, a Christian, and Freydis, who has made a pact with a demon, seriously weaken their community. Outside attacks by the native ''skraelings'' finally drive them out. In between is a collage of folklore, magic tales, and contemporary observations.

Other books you might like:
Nancy Varian Berberick, *Shadow of the Seventh Moon*, 1990
Orson Scott Card, *Red Prophet*, 1988
Ursula K. Le Guin, *Always Coming Home*, 1985
Ursula K. Le Guin, *The Left Hand of Darkness*, 1969

4447

PAULA VOLSKY

The Gates of Twilight
(New York: Bantam Spectra, 1996)

Story type: Fantasy (Adventure; Religious)
Major character(s): Renille vo Chaumelle, Civil Servant; Jathondi, Royalty; KhriNyad-Son, Religious
Time period(s): Indeterminate
Locale(s): Kahnderule, Fictional City; Aveshq, Fictional Country

Summary: The government of Vonahr holds an uneasy ascendancy over the Aveshquien people. When rumors of an uprising fed by KhriNyad-Son circulate, Renille, who grew up comfortable in both cultures, infiltrates the temple to uncover the plot. After a narrow escape, Renille takes cover at OodPray castle, the ancestral centerpiece of the Aveshquien empire, where he enlists the princess Jathandi into his mission to save the planet.

Other books you might like:
Lynn Flewelling, *Luck in the Shadows*, 1996
Katherine Kurtz, *Deryni Rising*, 1970
Will Shetterly, *The Liavek Series*, 1985-1990
    Emma Bull, co-editor
Robert Silverberg, *Lord Valentine's Castle*, 1980

4448

PAULA VOLSKY

Illusion
(New York: Bantam Spectra, 1992)

Story type: Fantasy (Political; Magic Conflict)
Major character(s): Eliste vo Derrivalle, Noblewoman (Exalted); Dref Zeenoson, Revolutionary; Whiss Valeur, Revolutionary, Leader (Protector)
Time period(s): Indeterminate
Locale(s): Vonahr, Fictional Country; Sherreen, Fictional City

Summary: Raised as Exalted with little opportunity for genuine interaction with the populace at large, Eliste travels to Sherreen expecting her position as Queen's Maid of Honor will provide excitement and marital prospects. Eliste occupies herself with learning proper court behavior until the desire for revolution among the intellectuals and middle class results in a revolt which overturns Eliste's way of life, forcing her to the streets in fear for her life. Whiss Valeur's usurpation turns especially ugly after he reanimates ancient weapons and begins public executions. When the philosophical leaders of the revolution become targets of dictator Valeur, popular sentiment turns against Valeur and his reign of terror. Realizing Valeur's rule to be worse in all respects than that of the former monarchy, revolutionary leaders ally with Exalted magicians in hope of overthrowing the tyrant.

Other books you might like:
Adrian Cole, *Mother of Storms*, 1992
R.A. MacAvoy, *King of the Dead*, 1991
R.A. MacAvoy, *Lens of the World*, 1990
Melanie Rawn, *Dragon Prince*, 1988
Melanie Rawn, *The Star Scroll*, 1989
Melanie Rawn, *Sunrunner's Fire*, 1990
Jack Vance, *The Green Pearl*, 1985
Jack Vance, *Lyonesse*, 1983
Jack Vance, *Madouc*, 1990

4449

PAULA VOLSKY

The Wolf of Winter
(New York: Bantam Spectra, 1993)

Story type: Fantasy (Magic Conflict; Political)
Major character(s): Varis, Royalty, Sorcerer; Shalindra, Royalty
Time period(s): Indeterminate
Locale(s): Rhazaulle, Fictional Country

Summary: When Prince Varis breaks the universal taboo of necromancy in his attempt to usurp the Wolfe Throne, his niece, Shalindra, proves the only hope for restoration of the kingdom's rightful heir, her brother.

Other books you might like:
Lois McMaster Bujold, *The Spirit Ring*, 1992
Laurell K. Hamilton, *Nightseer*, 1992
Marc Laidlaw, *Neon Lotus*, 1988
R.A. MacAvoy, *Lens of the World*, 1990
Martha Wells, *The Element of Fire*, 1990

4450

STEWART VON ALLMEN (Pseudonym of Stewart Wieck)
AIDA MUSANOVIC, Illustrator

St. Vitus Dances Eternity: A Sarajevo Ghost Story

(Clarkston, Georgia: White Wolf, 1996)

Story type: Horror (Ghost Story)
Series: World of Darkness: Wraith
Major character(s): Dragos Miloslavic, Doctor
Time period(s): 1990s (1992)
Locale(s): Sarajevo, Bosnia-Hercegovina

Summary: In war-torn Bosina, the ghost of Dragos Miloslavic helps the newly dead adapt to their non-existence and avoid the dangers that can befall fledgling ghosts. Dragos's anguish over the war and bloodshed that has colored centuries of his country's history are further aggravated when he discovers from a mercenary Reaper that the souls he is saving are being forced into slavery by his overseers. The book is illustrated by Aida Musanovic, who has also translated the text into Bosnian on facing pages. All proceeds from the sale of the book go to the New Bosnian Fund. Michael Moorcock supplies an afterword.

Other books you might like:
Richard Lee Byers, *On a Darkling Plain*, 1995
Sam Chupp, *Sins of the Fathers*, 1995
Rick Hautala, *Beyond the Shroud*, 1996

4451

KENNETH VON GUNDEN

Cry Wolf

(New York: Ace, 1992)

Story type: Science Fiction (Adventure)
Series: K-9 Corps
Major character(s): Ray Larken, Businessman (K-9 Corps), Adventurer; Beowulf, Animal (dog), Leader (pack's alpha dog)
Time period(s): Indeterminate Future
Locale(s): *Spirit of St. Louis*, Spaceship; Earth; Ghandi, Planet—Imaginary

Summary: Ray and the K-9 Corps team view post-disaster America when they travel to the Terran Federation Institute of Canine Genetics in Bethesda, Maryland, where they discover humans and dogs and rescue them from suspended animation. The newcomers join Ray's team as they take possession of their newly purchased planet then return to New York to rescue badly manipulated dogs.

Other books you might like:
David Brin, *The Uplift War*, 1987
Dean R. Koontz, *Watchers*, 1987
Clifford D. Simak, *City*, 1952
Cordwainer Smith, *The Best of Cordwainer Smith*, 1975
Cordwainer Smith, *Norstrilia*, 1975

4452

KENNETH VON GUNDEN

The Sounding Stillness

(New York: Ace, 1993)

Story type: Science Fiction (Robot Fiction; Science Fiction)
Major character(s): Galen Yeager, Government Official (secret agent); Sam, Cyborg
Time period(s): Indeterminate Future
Locale(s): Costeau, Planet—Imaginary

Summary: After decades of living on the water world, Costeau, genetically altered humans and dolphins have sufficiently damaged Costeau to threaten their uneasy peace with the intelligent natives. Galen Yeager and Sam travel to Costeau from Earth to investigate the situation and find a way to reestablish peace.

Other books you might like:
David Brin, *Startide Rising*, 1983
Alexander Jablokov, *A Deeper Sea*, 1992
Joan Slonczewski, *Daughter of Elysium*, 1993
Joan Slonczewski, *A Door into Ocean*, 1986
David Alexander Smith, *In the Cube*, 1993

4453

KENNETH VON GUNDEN

StarSpawn

(New York: Ace, 1990)

Story type: Science Fiction (First Contact)
Major character(s): Morrough, Knight; Brother Gregory, Religious (Friar)
Time period(s): Indeterminate Past (Middle Ages)
Locale(s): Outer Space

Summary: An alien spaceship lands on Earth to make repairs and accidentally releases an extraordinarily dangerous parasite. The aliens must then ally themselves with the primitive natives of Earth to recapture the parasite before it can do catastrophic damage to the planet. This is Von Gunden's first novel.

Other books you might like:
Poul Anderson, *The High Crusade*, 1960
John Dalmas, *Fanglith*, 1985
John Dalmas, *The Lantern of God*, 1989
John Dalmas, *The Lizard War*, 1989
F. Paul Wilson, *The Tery*, 1990

4454

KENNETH VON GUNDEN

Under Fire

(New York: Ace, 1991)

Story type: Science Fiction (Adventure)
Series: K-9 Corps
Major character(s): Ray Larken, Businessman (K-9 Corps), Adventurer; Maria Valdez, Telepath, Leader (scout cat team); Beowulf, Animal (dog), Leader (pack's alpha dog)

Time period(s): Indeterminate Future
Locale(s): Hephaestus, Planet—Imaginary

Summary: Ray and his physician partner, Ake, with nine intelligent, speaking canines arrive on the volcanic jungle planet, Hephaestus, to accept a one-year Federation contract at the combination gem mine and prison colony. They team up with Maria and her intelligent, speaking, telepathic guard cats to protect miners from diggers, a hostile indigenous life form. Ray soon becomes interested in discovering more about the intelligent native species, the K'anii.

Other books you might like:
David Brin, *Startide Rising*, 1983
Alan Dean Foster, *Cat-A-Lyst*, 1991
Dean R. Koontz, *Watchers*, 1987
James H. Schmitz, *The Demon Breed*, 1968
Clifford D. Simak, *City*, 1952
Cordwainer Smith, *The Best of Cordwainer Smith*, 1975
Cordwainer Smith, *Norstrilia*, 1975
Michael D. Weaver, *My Father Immortal*, 1989

4455

ELISABETH VONARBURG

In the Mothers' Land

(New York: Bantam Spectra, 1992)

Story type: Science Fiction (Post-Holocaust; Psychic Powers)
Major character(s): Lisbei of Bethely, Psychic; Tula, Psychic; Kelys, Teacher, Wanderer
Time period(s): Indeterminate Future
Locale(s): Bethely, Fictional City; Wardenberg, Fictional City

Summary: Lisbei, a very unusual child, grows up in a post-holocaust society run by women. Possessed of powers which she doesn't understand, Lisbei attempts to understand them and her world, threatening the order which her world has set up against the errors of the past. Translated by Jane Brierly.

Other books you might like:
Eleanor Arnason, *A Woman of the Iron People*, 1991
Octavia E. Butler, *Dawn*, 1987
Octavia E. Butler, *Mind of My Mind*, 1977
Suzy McKee Charnas, *Walk to the End of the World*, 1974
Marge Piercy, *He, She and It*, 1991
Joan Slonczewski, *A Door into Ocean*, 1986
Sheri S. Tepper, *The Gate to Women's Country*, 1988
Paul O. Williams, *The Breaking of Northwall*, 1980
Monique Wittig, *Les Guerilleres*, 1971

4456

ELISABETH VONARBURG

Reluctant Voyagers

(New York: Bantam Spectra, 1995)

Story type: Science Fiction (Alternate Universe; Science Fantasy)
Major character(s): Catherine Rhymer, Teacher
Time period(s): 1980s
Locale(s): Montreal, Quebec, Canada; Alternate Earth

Summary: Catherine Rhymer wakes up to a Montreal changed from the one she knows. Her attempts to figure out her world lead her to subversive political activists and on a quest for understanding in the distant north country. Based on a series of short stories written 1977-1986 and translated from the French by Jane Brierley.

Other books you might like:
Eleanor Arnason, *Daughter of the Bear King*, 1987
Octavia E. Butler, *Dawn*, 1987
John Crowley, *Aegypt*, 1987
Ursula K. Le Guin, *The Lathe of Heaven*, 1971
Rachel Pollack, *Unquenchable Fire*, 1992

4457

ELISABETH VONARBURG

The Silent City

(New York: Bantam Spectra, 1992)

Story type: Science Fiction (Genetic Manipulation; Post-Holocaust)
Major character(s): Paul "Papa" Kramer, Scientist; Marquande De Styx, Political Figure; Elisa, Genetically Altered Being
Time period(s): Indeterminate Future
Locale(s): The City, Europe

Summary: The City, a "temporary" shelter for the poisoned world above, supports the eight remaining humans and the ommechs, androids which allow the aged, failing residents to interact with the outside. Paul creates Elisa to withstand disease, attack and age to repopulate The City and prevent the destruction of the accumulated knowledge stored there. When all but the insane Paul die, Elisa must leave The City to survive, eventually becoming a leader of the Outsiders. Originally published in French in 1981. Translated by Jane Brierley.

Other books you might like:
Jeffrey A. Carver, *The Rapture Effect*, 1987
Marjorie Bradley Kellogg, *Harmony*, 1991
Ursula K. Le Guin, *The Left Hand of Darkness*, 1969
J.M. Morgan, *Desert Eden*, 1991
Pat Murphy, *The City, Not Long After*, 1989
Charles Oberndorf, *Sheltered Lives*, 1992
George Orwell, *Nineteen Eighty-Four*, 1949
Sheri S. Tepper, *Sideshow*, 1992
Michael D. Weaver, *My Father Immortal*, 1989

4458

KURT VONNEGUT JR.

Hocus Pocus or, What's the Hurry, Son?

(New York: G.P. Putnam's Sons, 1990)

Story type: Science Fiction (Satire; Literary)
Major character(s): Eugene Debs Hartke, Professor (physics); Hiroshi Matsumoto, Administrator (warden); Alton Darwin, Convict (Athena State Prison)
Time period(s): 2000s (2001)
Locale(s): Scipio, New York (Tarkington College)

Summary: Eugene Hartke tells the tale of his progress from Vietnam to professor for learning disabled rich kids, to warden of the local prison, to prisoner. In the process, he also tells the story of the United States being abandoned by its foreign investors and left to its own fate.

Other books you might like:
Philip K. Dick, *A Scanner Darkly*, 1977
Mark Leyner, *My Cousin, My Gastroenterologist*, 1990
Edgar Pangborn, *Davy*, 1964
Frederik Pohl, *Gladiator-at-Law*, 1955
Tom Robbins, *Another Roadside Attraction*, 1971
Bruce Sterling, *Islands in the Net*, 1988

4459

JOHN VORNHOLT

The Fabulist

(New York: AvoNova, 1993)

Story type: Fantasy (Historical)
Major character(s): Aesop, Writer, Traveller; Xanthus, Professor
Time period(s): 6th century B.C.
Locale(s): Greece; Egypt; Babylon

Summary: Raised as a mute slave, Aesop's encounter with Isis and her muses results in his ability to create fantastic tales. With this gift, Aesop wanders throughout the ancient civilized world, entertaining and enlightening all with his wit until meeting his fated destiny. Author's first non-Star Trek novel.

Other books you might like:
Dave Duncan, *The Reaver Road*, 1992
David Gemmell, *Lion of Macedon*, 1992
Tom Holt, *Goatsong*, 1990
Tom Holt, *The Walled Orchard*, 1991
Robert Watson, *Whilom*, 1990
Gene Wolfe, *Soldier of the Mist*, 1986

4460

JOHN VORNHOLT

Sanctuary

(New York: Pocket, 1992)

Story type: Science Fiction (Space Opera)
Series: Star Trek
Major character(s): James T. Kirk, Spaceship Captain; Spock, Scientist, Alien (Vulcan); Leonard McCoy, Doctor
Time period(s): 23rd century
Locale(s): Sanctuary, Planet—Imaginary; *U.S.S. Enterprise*, Spaceship

Summary: The *Enterprise* pursues the notorious pirate, Auk-Rex, to an unknown planet in an unexplored sector where Kirk, Spock and McCoy follow the pirate vessel down to the planet's surface. They learn that a race called Senites rules Sanctuary, to which anyone may come, regardless of their criminal or political activities, but no one may leave. With their communicators nonfunctional and their shuttlecraft gone, the three Starfleet officers journey across the surface in search of a way to return to their ship while Commander Scott

orbits the planet along with a Klingon cruiser and a beautiful Orion bounty hunter.

Other books you might like:
Arthur C. Clarke, *A Fall of Moondust*, 1961
Hal Clement, *Mission of Gravity*, 1968
Barbara Hambly, *Ishmael*, 1985
Larry Niven, *Ringworld*, 1970
Joanna Russ, *Picnic on Paradise*, 1968
Howard Weinstein, *Deep Domain*, 1987

4461

JOHN VORNHOLT

Voices

(New York: Dell, 1995)

Story type: Science Fiction (Space Colony; Psychic Powers)
Series: Babylon 5
Major character(s): Susan Ivanova, Military Personnel, Telepath; Michael Garibaldi, Military Personnel, Security Officer; Talia Winters, Telepath, Fugitive
Time period(s): 23rd century (2258)
Locale(s): Babylon 5, Space Station; Interstellar Empire/Federation; Earth

Summary: A bombing during a Psi Corps convention brings suspicion onto Babylon 5's resident telepath, Talia Winters. When Talia escapes confinement, neither Susan Ivanova nor Michael Garibaldi can help overtly as Talia flees her Psi Corps pursuers. First of a television tie-in series.

Other books you might like:
Alfred Bester, *The Stars My Destination*, 1956
J.M. Dillard, *Emissary*, 1993
Jim Mortimore, *Clarke's Law*, 1996
Allen Steele, *Clarke County, Space*, 1990
Lois Tilton, *Accusations*, 1995

4462

KARL EDWARD WAGNER, Editor

Echoes of Valor III

(New York: Tor, 1991)

Story type: Fantasy (Anthology; Sword and Sorcery)
Series: Echoes of Valor

Summary: This book contains eight stories originally published in 1930's periodicals from five authors with brief introductions by Wagner. Included are Robert E. Howard's only story of Sonya of Rogatino (Red Sonya), "The Shadow of the Vulture," the complete saga of Henry Kuttner's Prince Raynor and Eblik the Nubian in "Cursed Be the City" and "The Citadel of Darkness," the first reprint in 50 years of Manly Wade Wellman's "Hok Goes to Atlantis," and Jack Williamson's "Wolves of Darkness," a primeval horror tale. The final section contains three stories by Nictzin Dyalhis (1880-1942) preceded by Sam Moskowitz's 22-page, original biography and discussion of the mysterious literary figure's work, "Nictzin Dyalhis: Mysterious Master of Fantasy."

Other books you might like:
Glen Cook, *The Black Company*, 1984

L. Sprague de Camp, *The Fantastic Swordsmen*, 1967
    editor
L. Sprague de Camp, *Swords and Sorcery*, 1963
    editor
L. Sprague de Camp, *Warlocks and Warriors*, 1970
    editor
Phyllis Eisenstein, *In the Red Lord's Reach*, 1989
Robert E. Howard, *The Coming of Conan*, 1953
Robert E. Howard, *Conan the Barbarian*, 1955
Fritz Leiber, *The Leiber Chronicles*, 1990
Will Shetterly, *Liavek*, 1985
    Emma Bull, co-editor

4463

KARL EDWARD WAGNER, Editor
GERALD PAGE, Co-Editor

Horrorstory III

(Lancaster, Pennsylvania: Underwood-Miller, 1991)

Story type: Horror (Anthology)

Summary: This repackaging of DAW's *The Year's Best Horror Stories*, Series VII (edited by Gerald Page), VIII and IX (edited by Karl Edward Wagner) brings together 40 of the best horror stories written in the years 1978-80. Top selections include T.E.D. Klein's homage to H.P. Lovecraft, "Black Man with a Horn," ghost stories in the classic and modern tradition by (respectively) Canon Basil Smith ("The Propert Bequest") and Charles L. Grant ("Hear Me Now, My Sweet Abbey Rose"), tales of psychological horror by Harlan Ellison ("All the Birds Come Home to Roost") and Alan Ryan ("Sheets"), *contes cruel* by Dennis Etchison and Ramsey Campbell ("The Dead Line," "Heading Home") and two stories by Stephen King.

Other books you might like:
Ellen Datlow, *The Year's Best Fantasy and Horror: Fourth Annual Collection*, 1991
    Terry Windling, co-editor
Stephen Jones, *Best New Horror 2*, 1991
    Ramsey Campbell, co-editor
Robert Morrish, *Quick Chills II*, 1992
    Peter Enfantino, co-editor

4464

KARL EDWARD WAGNER

Horrorstory IV

(Lancaster, Pennsylvania: Underwood-Miller, 1990)

Story type: Horror (Anthology)

Summary: A three-in-one compilation of *The Year's Best Horror Stories X* (1982), *XI* (1983) and *XII* (1984) that collects 52 excellent stories. Five were written by Ramsey Campbell, among them his tale of a haunted movie house, "The Show Must Go On." Included are Dennis Etchison's World Fantasy Award thriller, "The Dark Country," Stephen King's Castle Rock fantasy, "Uncle Otto's Truck," Scott Bradfield's delicate "The Flash! Kid" and Harlan Ellison's tale of psychic violation, "Broken Glass."

Other books you might like:
Ellen Datlow, *The Year's Best Fantasy and Horror Series*, 1988-1991
Peter Enfantino, *Quick Chills*, 1990
Stephen Jones, *Best New Horror*, 1990-1991
    Ramsey Campbell, co-author

4465

KARL EDWARD WAGNER

Horrorstory V

(Lancaster, Pennsylvania: Underwood-Miller, 1990)

Story type: Horror (Anthology)

Summary: A three-in-one compilation of *The Year's Best Horror Stories XIII* (1985), *XIV* (1986) and *XV* (1987) that brings together 55 of the best horror stories published over three years. Outstanding among these are two of three written by David Schow: "Coming Soon to a Theatre Near You" about a monster-ridden movie house, and the World Fantasy Award-winning "Red Light," concerned with a starlet's relationship with the camera and her audience. Also notable are Dennis Etchison's tale of writers and readers, "Talking in the Dark," Joe Lansdale's post-apocalyptic nightmare, "Tight Little Stitches in a Dead Man's Back," Stephen King's story of another reality, "Mrs. Todd's Shortcut," and Robert Bloch's update of the Dracula legend, "The Yougoslaves."

Other books you might like:
Ellen Datlow, *The Year's Best Fantasy and Horror Series*, 1988-1991
    Terry Windling, co-author
Peter Enfantino, *Quick Chills*, 1990
Stephen Jones, *Best New Horror*, 1990-1991
    Ramsey Campbell, co-author

4466

KARL EDWARD WAGNER

Intensive Scare

(New York: DAW 1990)

Story type: Horror (Anthology)

Summary: Thirteen stories of medical horror ranging in style from the gothic shockers, "The Body Snatcher" by Robert Louis Stevenson and "Herbert West: Reanimator" by H.P. Lovecraft, to the SF-horror of Cyril Kornbluth's "The Little Black Bag," to Richard McKenna's bittersweet fantasy "Casey Agonistes." Of special note are Dennis Etchison's moving parable of organ donation, "The Dead Line," and Michael Shea's masterpiece of visceral horror, "The Autopsy."

Other books you might like:
Groff Conklin, *Great Science Fiction about Doctors*, 1965
    Noah D. Fabricant, co-author

4467

KARL EDWARD WAGNER

The Year's Best Horror Stories XVIII

(New York: DAW, 1990)

Story type: Horror (Anthology)

Summary: Twenty-three stories and three poems that reflect the richness of the annual horror yield. The best of the best include Ramsey Campbell's homage to M.R. James, ''The Guide,'' Nicholas Royle's story of urban paranoia, ''Archway,'' Ian McDowell's atmospheric tale of a backwoods legend, ''On the Dark Road,'' and David Schow's ferociously funny satire of evangelical religion, ''Jerry's Kids Meet Wormboy.''

Other books you might like:
Ellen Datlow, *The Year's Best Fantasy and Horror: Third Annual Collection*, 1990
  Terry Windling, co-author
Peter Enfantino, *Quick Chills*, 1990
Stephen Jones, *Best New Horror*, 1990
  Ramsey Campbell, co-author

4468

KARL EDWARD WAGNER, Editor

The Year's Best Horror Stories XX

(New York: DAW, 1992)

Story type: Horror (Anthology)

Summary: The twentieth volume in the longest-running of the annual best-of-horror collections brings together 22 exceptional British and American horror stories published in 1991. Included are Alan Brennert's Nebula-Award winning tale of the horrors of Vietnam, ''Ma Qui''; Ramsey Campbell's tale of Grecian horror, ''The Same in Any Language''; Brian Lumley's original vampire story, ''The Picnickers''; Robert S. Fuqua's story of a satanic music deal, ''The Sharps and Flats Guarantee''; and Philip Nutman's hardcore riff on Thomas Mann's *Death in Venice*, ''Churches of Desire.''

Other books you might like:
Ellen Datlow, *The Year's Best Fantasy and Horror Series*, 1988-1996
  Terri Windling, co-editor
Stephen Jones, *Best New Horror*, 1990-1992
  Ramsey Campbell, co-editor
Robert Morrish, *Quick Chills*, 1989-1992
  Peter Enfantino, co-editor

4469

KARL EDWARD WAGNER, Editor

The Year's Best Horror Stories XXI

(New York: DAW, 1993)

Story type: Horror (Anthology)

Summary: The latest in this long running series of horror fiction anthologies that strongly favors the small press in-cludes 27 stories, including perennial Ramsey Campbell's erotic horror tale, ''The Limits of Fantasy''; two stories on nuclear holocaust, W.M. Shockley's ''A Father's Gift'' and Yvonne Navarro's ''Feeding the Masses''; Ron Weighell's vampire tale, ''China Rose''; Kim Antieau's tale of a rape victim's bizarre strategy for self-defense and forgetfulness, ''Briar Rose''; Rick Kennet's Jamesian ghost tale, ''The Outsider''; and Rand Soellner's gremlin story, ''Mom School.''

Other books you might like:
Ellen Datlow, *The Year's Best Fantasy and Horror: Sixth Annual Collection*, 1993
  Terri Windling, co-editor
Stephen Jones, *Best New Horror 4*, 1993
  Ramsey Campbell, co-editor

4470

KARL EDWARD WAGNER, Editor

The Year's Best Horror Stories XXIII

(New York: DAW, 1994)

Story type: Horror (Anthology)

Summary: The last volume in this long-running series, completed shortly before the death of its editor, brings together 31 stories published in a variety of professional and semi-professional venues. Highlights include Ted Klein's tale of a ravenous sleeping bag, ''One Size Eats All''; David Langford's shapeshifter tale, ''Lions in the Desert''; Robert Devereaux's chilling rendering of infidelity and murder as a slapstick routine, ''Ridi Bobo''; Chet Williamson's tale of an aging serial murderer, ''Perfect Days''; Dennis Etchison's tale of urban menace, ''A Little-Known Side of Elvis''; and Terry Lamsley's World Fantasy Award-winning novella of a strange race who live underground in British coal-mining country, ''Under the Crust.''

Other books you might like:
Ellen Datlow, *The Year's Best Fantasy and Horror: Seventh Annual Collection*, 1994
  Terri Windling, co-editor
Stephen Jones, *Best New Horror 5*, 1995
  Ramsey Campbell, co-editor

4471

HOWARD WALDROP

A Dozen Tough Jobs

(Willimantic, CT: Ziesling, 1989)

Story type: Fantasy (Legend)
Major character(s): Invictus Ovidius ''I.O.'' Lace, Orphan (Teenage narrator); Houlka Lee, Hero
Time period(s): 1920s (1926)
Locale(s): Mississippi

Summary: I.O. Lace tells the story of Houlka Lee, a convict serving time as a farm laborer. This is a retelling of the labors of Hercules, set in Mississippi.

Other books you might like:
Stephen Billias, *The Quest for the 36*, 1988

Donald Harington, *The Cockroaches of Stay More*, 1989

4472

HOWARD WALDROP

Night of the Cooters

(Kansas City, Missouri: Ursus Imprints, 1990)

Story type: Science Fiction (Collection)
Major character(s): Alfred Jarry, Historical Figure, Writer (poet); Jetboy, Hero, Pilot
Time period(s): 1940s (1946); 1890s
Locale(s): New York, New York; Paris, France

Summary: 10 stories written between 1986 and 1990 which mix science fiction, fantasy, alternate history and popular culture. It reprints "Thirty Minutes Over Broadway," the "origin story" of the popular Wild Card series, and premieres "Fin de Cycle," a historical tale mixing poets, printers, filmmakers and writers against a backdrop of the notorious Dreyfus Affair.

Other books you might like:
James P. Blaylock, *The Paper Grail*, 1991
Pat Cadigan, *Patterns*, 1989
Lisa Goldstein, *The Dream Years*, 1985
Kim Newman, *The Night Mayor*, 1990
Tim Powers, *The Stress of Her Regard*, 1989

4473

HOWARD WALDROP

Strange Monsters of the Recent Past

(New York: Ace, 1991)

Story type: Science Fiction (Collection)

Summary: Containing 8 stories written between 1980 and 1989, this is an omnibus volume of *All About Strange Monsters of the Recent Past*, 1987, and *A Dozen Tough Jobs*, 1989, both small press productions. The stories are a mix of subtle alternate histories such as "The Lions Are Asleep This Night," and strangely approached science fiction ideas such as the doo-wop and UFO story "Flying Saucer Rock and Roll." "A Dozen Tough Jobs," a retelling of the Hercules myth set in 1926 Mississippi, is a striking example of Waldrop's unique approach to storytelling.

Other books you might like:
James P. Blaylock, *The Paper Grail*, 1991
Joe R. Lansdale, *The Magic Wagon*, 1986
George R.R. Martin, *The Armageddon Rag*, 1983
Pat Murphy, *Points of Departure*, 1990
Tim Powers, *The Stress of Her Regard*, 1989

4474

BARBARA G. WALKER

Amazon: A Novel

(New York: HarperCollins, 1992)

Story type: Fantasy (Satire; Time Travel)

Major character(s): Antiope, Warrior (Amazon), Time Traveller; Diane, Writer
Time period(s): 20th century
Locale(s): United States

Summary: Thrown thousands of years into her future, Antiope must adapt to the modern world, but finds the male-dominated society strange. Diane writes Antiope's biography, *Amazon*, which presents a detailed description of non-patriarchal society and spawns criticism and an Amazon fashion craze. On meeting a reincarnated enemy Antiope had killed thousands of years before, Antiope discovers an attraction to the man who could bring further tragedy into her life. A first novel.

Other books you might like:
Eleanor Arnason, *A Woman of the Iron People*, 1991
Suzette Haden Elgin, *And Then There'll Be Fireworks*, 1981
Suzette Haden Elgin, *The Grand Jubilee*, 1981
Suzette Haden Elgin, *Twelve Fair Kingdoms*, 1981
Carol Emshwiller, *Carmen Dog*, 1990
Parke Godwin, *The Snake Oil Wars*, 1989
Parke Godwin, *Waiting for the Galactic Bus*, 1988
James Morrow, *Only Begotten Daughter*, 1990

4475

BARBARA G. WALKER

Feminist Fairy Tales

(New York: HarperSanFrancisco, 1996)

Story type: Fantasy (Collection; Legend)

Summary: Contains a two-page introduction plus individual introductions to 28 stories contradicting the usual message of fairy tales for young girls, that their purpose in life should be decorative. Walker includes many traditional fairy tales, myths, and legends, primarily European, rewritten with modern feminist concepts and spirituality, along with new stories written in the same view.

Other books you might like:
Margaret Atwood, *Good Bones and Simple Murders*, 1994
George Alec Effinger, *Maureen Birnbaum, Barbarian Swordsperson: The Complete Stories*, 1993
James Finn Garner, *Once upon a More Enlightened Time*, 1995
Jody Lynn Nye, *Don't Forget Your Spacesuit, Dear*, 1996
editor
Ethel Johnston Phelps, *Tatterhood and Other Tales*, 1978
editor
Jack Zipes, *Don't Bet on the Prince*, 1987
editor
Jack Zipes, *The Outspoken Princess and the Gentle Knight*, 1994
editor

4476

MARY ALEXANDER WALKER

The Scathach and the Maeve's Daughter

(New York: Atheneum, 1990)

Story type: Fantasy (Legend; Contemporary)

Major character(s): The Scathach, Mythical Creature (Celtic), Spirit (shapechanger); Maeve Brigitta, Immigrant (pioneer); Maeve Nicole, Student, Veterinarian
Time period(s): 17th century; 2000s (2000)
Locale(s): England; Canada; New York, New York

Summary: When an 8th Century Irish lass, Maeve Moira, passed the Scathach's test, the Scathach pledges that all of her female descendants will have her attributes: a kind heart, healing hands, courage and wit. The Scathach then follows Maeve's family, helping Maeve Gwenna in the 12th century escape her cruel guardians in Brennith before the Black Plague devastates the town. In Canada the Scathach helps Maeve Brigitta acquire needed medicine from the Iroquois Indians. In modern New York City, the Scathach saves maeve Nicole from a gang of street toughs.

Other books you might like:
Mercedes Lackey, *Knight of Ghosts and Shadows*, 1990
    Ellen Guon, co-author
R.A. MacAvoy, *Tea with the Black Dragon*, 1983
Rosemary Sutcliff, *Sun Horse, Moon Horse*, 1977

4477

SAGE WALKER

Whiteout
(New York: Tor, 1996)

Story type: Science Fiction (Hard Science Fiction; Dystopian)
Major character(s): Signy Thomas, Computer Expert, Scientist; Pilar Videla, Artist, Lesbian; Paul Maury, Businessman, Lawyer
Time period(s): 2020s
Locale(s): Antarctica; Cyberspace; United States

Summary: Hired by a Japanese conglomerate to influence Antarctic treaty negotiations, members of the Edges partnership pursue research and production at disparate sites while communicating through intimate cybernetic connections. Drawn to Antarctica, one team member suffers apparent disaster, fracturing Edges' harmony and efficiency and driving Signy into a desperate search. First novel.

Other books you might like:
Wilhelmina Baird, *Crashcourse*, 1993
Pat Cadigan, *Synners*, 1991
Raphael Carter, *The Fortunate Fall*, 1996
Melissa Scott, *Trouble and Her Friends*, 1994
Neal Stephenson, *Snow Crash*, 1992

4478

IAN WALLACE

Megalomania
(New York: DAW Books, 1989)

Story type: Science Fiction (Space Opera)
Series: Croyd
Major character(s): Croyd, Businessman; Dino Trigg, Psychic
Time period(s): Indeterminate Future
Locale(s): Sol Galaxy, Interstellar Empire/Federation

Summary: Croyd's protege, Dino Trigg, uses his psychic powers in an attempt to undermine Croyd's position as chair of the board of directors that runs Sol Galaxy. When Croyd foils his attempt, Trigg plots to destroy the galaxy.

Other books you might like:
Phillip C. Jennings, *Tower to the Sky*, 1988
Daniel Keys Moran, *The Armageddon Blues*, 1988
Daniel Keys Moran, *Emerald Eyes*, 1988
Daniel Keys Moran, *The Long Run*, 1989
A.E. van Vogt, *Null-A Three*, 1985
A.E. van Vogt, *The Pawns of Null-A*, 1956
A.E. van Vogt, *The World of Null-A*, 1948

4479

PATRICIA WALLACE

Fatal Outcome
(New York: Zebra, 1992)

Story type: Horror (Wild Talents)
Major character(s): Alan Kramer, Doctor; Honor Matheson, Nurse; Shea Novak, Lawyer
Time period(s): 1990s
Locale(s): Idle Springs, Nevada

Summary: When maverick physician Alan Kramer opens up a clinic teaching patients how to harness the powers of their brains to heal themselves, he proves a godsend to the terminally ill who flock to take advantage of his services. That is, until it is discovered that the secret Affinity elixir that makes his treatment possible endows his patients with uncontrollable psychokinetic abilities.

Other books you might like:
John Arbucci, *Blood of Innocents*, 1991
Michael Hammond, *The Burning Man*, 1991

4480

PATRICIA WALLACE

Monday's Child
(New York: Zebra, 1989)

Story type: Horror (Evil Children)
Major character(s): Jill Baker, Child; Noah Huston, Doctor
Time period(s): 1980s
Locale(s): Winslow, California

Summary: The townspeople grow increasingly suspicious and frightened of Jill Baker, the beautiful little girl with the mysterious birth, who increasingly becomes the focus for the progressively intensifying "accidents" that gradually decimate the entire town.

Other books you might like:
Lawrence Block, *Ariel*, 1980
John Saul, *Suffer the Children*, 1977
Bernard Taylor, *The Godsend*, 1976

4481

PATRICIA WALLACE

Thrill

(New York: Zebra, 1990)

Major character(s): Sheldon Rice, Businessman; Wesley Davison, Engineer; Max Brown, Teenager
Time period(s): 1990s (1992)
Locale(s): McKenna's Creek, California

Summary: With the help of technological prodigy Wesley Davison, entrepreneur Sheldon Rice builds The Park, the world's largest amusement park. On opening day, technical malfunctions of a suspicious nature turn the park's rides and attractions into a nightmarish ordeal for patrons.

Other books you might like:
William W. Johnstone, *Carnival*, 1989
Richard Laymon, *Funland*, 1990
Owen West, *The Funhouse*, 1981
    Pseudonym of Dean R. Koontz; novelization of movie

4482

R.R. WALTERS

Wind Chimes

(New York: Zebra, 1991)

Story type: Horror (Evil Children)
Major character(s): Megan Jordan, Child; Pamela Jordan, Businesswoman; Greg Jordan, Accountant
Time period(s): 1990s
Locale(s): Florida

Summary: Greg and Pamela Jordan are amused by their precocious daughter Megan's talk of her imaginary playmate Rosamond and the "Special Place" where they play, called Wunderland. That is, until the people Megan invites to come with her to Wunderland are found dead afterwards.

Other books you might like:
Stephen King, *The Shining*, 1977
Thomas Tryon, *The Other*, 1971
Patricia Wallace, *Monday's Child*, 1989

4483

EVANGELINE WALTON

The Island of the Mighty

(New York: Collier, 1993)

Story type: Fantasy (Legend; Magic Conflict)
Major character(s): Gwydion ap Don, Magician, Royalty (Prince of Gwynedd); Arianrhod, Magician, Royalty; Math ap Mathonwy, Magician, Royalty (King of Gwynedd)
Time period(s): Indeterminate Past
Locale(s): Gwynedd, Wales

Summary: Peace deteriorates after Gwydion and his brother attempt to steal magical pigs belonging to Lord Pyrderi. The indiscretion brings consequences which later fall on Gwydion's son, Llew Llaw Gyffes, who must endure the burden of his father's actions and the curses of his unwilling mother. Reissue of the Fourth Branch of the Mabinogian, origianlly published in 1936 as *The Virgin and the Swine*.

Other books you might like:
John Bellairs, *The Face in the Frost*, 1969
Charles de Lint, *The Little Country*, 1991
Patrick K. Ford, *The Mabinogi and Other Medieval Welsh Tales*, 1977
    editor, translator
Fritz Leiber, *A Specter Is Haunting Texas*, 1969
Morgan Llywelyn, *The Horse Goddess*, 1982
Abraham Merritt, *Dwellers in the Mirage*, 1932
Abraham Merritt, *The Face in the Abyss*, 1931
Abraham Merritt, *The Ship of Ishtar*, 1926

4484

HOWARD WANDREI, Author/Illustrator

Time Burial

(Minneapolis: Fedogan & Bremer, 1995)

Story type: Horror (Collection)

Summary: The twenty stories of fantasy, horror, and science fiction collected here constitute a first collection by a prolific writer for the pulps considered a peripheral member of H.P. Lovecraft's circle. "Macklin's Little Friend" and "The Black Farm" both feature human encounters with inexplicable monsters, while "The Wall" and "The God Box" feature the use and abuse of new discoveries by men. In "Exit Willy Carney," a criminal undergoes a gender change to avoid being apprehended. "Over Time's Threshold" is a surreal tale of a time travel experience, and "The Hand of the O'Mecca" a well-known tale of rural werewolves. Both "Here Lies" and "After You, Montagu" display the author's fondness for eccentric characters and humor. Dwayne Olson supplies a historical overview of Wandrei's life and writing.

Other books you might like:
Hugh B. Cave, *Death Stalks the Night*, 1995
Hugh B. Cave, *Murgunstrumm and Others*, 1977
Carl Jacobi, *Revelations in Black*, 1947
Frank Belknap Long, *The Hounds of Tindalos*, 1946
E. Hoffman Price, *Far Lands Other Days*, 1975
Clark Ashton Smith, *Other Dimensions*, 1963
Donald Wandrei, *The Eye and the Finger*, 1944

4485

ELISABETH WATERS

Changing Fate

(New York: DAW, 1994)

Story type: Fantasy (Romance; Adventure)
Major character(s): Acila, Noblewoman, Mythical Creature (shapechanger); Briam, Nobleman, Musician; Lord Ranulf, Nobleman
Time period(s): Indeterminate
Locale(s): Diadem, Fictional City

Summary: Forced to fight and then flee with her brother, Briam, when Lord Ranulf arrives to claim their dead father's castle, Acila survives the winter with a pack of wolves and then follows Briam to the court of a queen, who chooses him as her Year-King. Saving Briam from the Year-King's fate reveals secrets about Ranulf. First novel.

Other books you might like:
C.S. Friedman, *Black Sun Rising*, 1991
Patricia A. McKillip, *The Changeling*, 1988
Tamora Pierce, *Alanna: The First Adventure*, 1983
Jennifer Roberson, *Shapechangers*, 1984
Sheri S. Tepper, *Song of Mavin Manyshaped*, 1985

4486
GRAHAM WATKINS

Dark Winds
(New York: Berkley, 1989)

Story type: Horror (Ancient Evil Unleashed)
Major character(s): Elliot Collins, Professor (College); Nikki, Femme Fatale
Time period(s): 1960s; 1970s
Locale(s): New York, New York

Summary: Obsessed by a photograph of his late father's former lover, Elliot Collins pursues the image until he is drawn into a web of horror and intrigue that involves a dark family secret, ritual black magic, an ancient Aztec cult, a serial killer of women, and a seemingly immortal seductress. This is Watkins' first novel.

Other books you might like:
Mercedes Lackey, *Burning Water*, 1989
Michael Paine, *Owl Light*, 1989

4487
GRAHAM WATKINS

Kaleidoscope Eyes
(New York: Carroll & Graf, 1993)

Story type: Horror (Erotic Horror)
Major character(s): Sam Leo, Doctor (epidemiologist); Stephanie Dixon, Doctor (pathologist); Selinde, Deity (Aztec)
Time period(s): 1990s (1993)
Locale(s): Outer Banks, North Carolina

Summary: Following his contact with Selinde, an Aztec deity heavily into sex and death, Sam Leo vacations with his friends at a secluded house on the North Carolina shore. Aided by the sense-enhancing power of a kaleidoscope, the quartet indulge in days of increasingly bizarre sexual games that will inevitably culminate in the sort of ritualistic sacrifice upon which the goddess thrives.

Other books you might like:
Warren Newton Beath, *Shock Lines*, 1993
Ashley McConnell, *Days of the Dead*, 1992
Al Sarrantonio, *House Haunted*, 1991

4488
GRAHAM WATKINS

Virus
(New York: Carroll & Graf, 1995)

Story type: Horror (Science Fiction)
Major character(s): Mark Roberts, Doctor; Alex Walton, Doctor (psychiatrist); Drew Thompson, Businessman
Time period(s): 1990s (1995)
Locale(s): Durham, North Carolina

Summary: When Penny, the penultimate software program, meets a computer virus, she mutates into a sentient entity who subliminally manipulates computer users on the Internet to stay glued to their computer screens. An influx of exhausted computer hackers at the Duke University hospital compels doctors Mark Roberts and Alex Walton to get to the bottom of the problem, forcing Penny to turn more violent in her quest to ensure that nothing will stop her proliferation and worldwide spread.

Other books you might like:
Daniel H. Gower, *The Orpheus Process*, 1993
D.F. Jones, *Colossus*, 1966
Pierre Ouellette, *The Deus Machine*, 1994

4489
IAN WATSON

Chekhov's Journey
(New York: Carroll & Graf, 1989)

Story type: Science Fiction (Alternate Universe)
Major character(s): Anton Chekhov, Writer, Historical Figure
Time period(s): 1980s; 1890s (1890)

Summary: A Soviet film crew doing a motion picture about Chekhov's visit to Siberia attempts to improve the performance of their lead actor by an experiment in reincarnation through hypnosis. Unfortunately, their experiment goes awry and they accidentally succeed in changing history. Whereas Chekhov had originally gone to Siberia to visit a convict colony, he now becomes involved in the investigation of the famed Tunguska meteor, thereby changing Russian history. Originally published in 1983.

Other books you might like:
Gregory Benford, *What Might Have Been*, 1989
    Martin H. Greenberg, co-editor
Terry Bisson, *Fire on the Mountain*, 1988
John Crowley, *Novelty*, 1989
Keith Roberts, *Pavane*, 1968

4490
IAN WATSON

The Embedding
(New York: Carroll & Graf, 1990)

Story type: Science Fiction (First Contact)
Major character(s): Chris Sole, Scientist; Charlie Faith, Engineer

Time period(s): Indeterminate Future

Summary: In an English hospital a group of Pakistani orphans are brought up in complete isolation and taught a complex artificial language that changes the nature of reality for them. Simultaneously an anthropologist working in Brazil discovers a primitive tribe who, under the influence of a local drug, speaks a sophisticated language otherwise unknown to them. Our planet is contacted by the Sp'thra, a spacefaring alien race who gather languages from across the Galaxy in the hope of someday transcending reality. Originally published in 1973.

Other books you might like:
Samuel R. Delany, *Babel-17*, 1966
Samuel R. Delany, *The Splendor and Misery of Bodies, of Cities*, 1985
Samuel R. Delany, *Stars in My Pocket Like Grains of Sand*, 1984
Suzette Haden Elgin, *The Judas Rose*, 1987
Suzette Haden Elgin, *Native Tongue*, 1984
Jack Vance, *The Languages of Pao*, 1958
Kate Wilhelm, *Juniper Time*, 1979

4491

IAN WATSON

The Flies of Memory

(New York: Carroll & Graf, 1991)

Story type: Science Fiction (First Contact)
Major character(s): Charles Spark, Empath; Olivia Mendelssohn, Psychic, Security Officer; Kathinka, Religious, Guide
Time period(s): 21st century
Locale(s): Rome, Italy; Mars

Summary: A novel about memory, this book opens with an attempt to understand an alien race, the Flies, whose transportation of parts of Earth cities to Mars forces a small group of humans to follow. Once it reaches Mars, however, the group discovers it has a much longer and stranger journey to make.

Other books you might like:
James Blish, *A Case of Conscience*, 1958
William Gibson, *Neuromancer*, 1984
Lisa Goldstein, *The Dream Years*, 1985
Spider Robinson, *Stardance*, 1979
  Jeanne Robinson, co-author
Norman Spinrad, *Songs From the Stars*, 1980

4492

IAN WATSON

God's World

(New York: Carroll and Graf, 1990)

Story type: Science Fiction (Adventure; Theological)
Major character(s): Amy Dove, Sociologist
Time period(s): 21st century
Locale(s): *Pilgrim Crusader*, Spaceship; God's World, Moon—Imaginary (circling a gas giant in Orbit Around B2 Eridani; Askatharli Space)

Summary: When, in 1977, messages from God appear in worship centers demanding champions and representatives, a mission to God's World is mounted. When the Pilgrim Crusader arrives at God's World an attack forces Amy Dove and 5 pilots to abandon the ship, escaping to the moon. On the world they find an alien civilization partly in everyday reality and partly in heaven. Further investigation yields surprising revelations. Reprint of 1979 British edition.

Other books you might like:
Arthur C. Clarke, *Childhood's End*, 1953
Parke Godwin, *The Snake Oil Wars*, 1989
Parke Godwin, *Waiting for the Galactic Bus*, 1988
Robert A. Heinlein, *Job: A Comedy of Justice*, 1984

4493

IAN WATSON

Inquisitor

(Baltimore, Maryland: GW Books/Games Workshop, 1990)

Story type: Science Fiction (Political; Adventure)
Series: Warhammer 40,000
Major character(s): Jag Braco, Religious, Police Officer; Meh'Lindi, Spy; Grimm, Engineer, Warrior
Time period(s): Indeterminate Future
Locale(s): Stalinvast, Planet—Imaginary; The Eye of Terror, Outer Space (Planetary cluster—imaginary)

Summary: Jag Braco, an Imperial Inquisitor, and his companions are sent to assist in stopping a rebellion caused by alien monsters. During the mission they discover evidence of a conspiracy which they pursue from the chaos of the Eye of Terror to the throne of the Emperor.

Other books you might like:
Iain M. Banks, *Consider Phlebas*, 1991
C.J. Cherryh, *Cyteen*, 1988
Glen Cook, *The Dragon Never Sleeps*, 1988
Frank Herbert, *Dune*, 1965
Roger Zelazny, *Lord of Light*, 1967

4494

IAN WATSON
JOHN VARLEY, Co-Author

Nanoware Time/The Persistence of Vision

(New York: Tor, 1991)

Story type: Science Fiction (Hard Science Fiction; Post-Holocaust)
Major character(s): Paul Royal, Experimental Subject; Succor-of-Yellowways-Sands, Alien (Hydra), Teacher; Pink, Farmer, Teenager
Time period(s): 21st century; 1990s
Locale(s): Moon (Earth's); New Mexico (Navajo Nation)

Summary: Ian Watson's ''Nanoware Time,'' published herein unabridged for the first time in book form, explores the gift of nanotechnology by aliens from Beta Hydri to suspicious humans who arrange to study the microscopic machines on an isolated lunar colony. John Varley's ''The Persistence of Vision'' received both a Hugo Award and Nebula Award for best story published in 1978. This poignant story examines a post-war agricultural commune for deaf-blind co-operators as seen through the eyes of a sighted and hearing visitor.

Other books you might like:
Pat Cadigan, *Mindplayers*, 1987
Jeffrey A. Carver, *From a Changeling Star*, 1989
Michael Flynn, *The Nanotech Chronicles*, 1991
Joan Slonczewski, *A Door into Ocean*, 1986
Cordwainer Smith, *The Best of Cordwainer Smith*, 1975
Marc Stiegler, *The Gentle Seduction*, 1990
Michael Swanwick, *Vacuum Flowers*, 1987
John Varley, *The Barbie Murders and Other Stories*, 1980
John Varley, *Blue Champagne*, 1986
John Varley, *The Persistence of Vision*, 1978

4495

ROBERT WATSON

Whilom

(New York: Atlantic Monthly Press, 1990)

Story type: Fantasy (Literary; Light Fantasy)
Major character(s): Nick Bottom, Artisan (weaver); Dewdrop, Animal (talking donkey); Theseus, Royalty (king)
Time period(s): Indeterminate Past
Locale(s): Greece (ancient)

Summary: Nick Bottom and his talking donkey meet Theseus on the road. Nick asks if his amateur theatrical group can perform at the palace for Theseus' upcoming engagement celebration. Theseus tests Nick's ability by commanding him to perform the role of messenger, not usually the safest part to play. A retelling of Midsummer Night's Dream.

Other books you might like:
L. Sprague de Camp, *The Undesired Princess and the Enchanted Bunny*, 1990
    David Drake, co-author
Alan Dean Foster, *Glory Lane*, 1990
Tom Holt, *Goatsong*, 1990
Deborah Smith, *Legends*, 1990
Jack Vance, *Madouc*, 1990
Patricia C. Wrede, *Snow White and Rose Red*, 1989

4496

LAWRENCE WATT-EVANS

The Blood of a Dragon

(New York: Ballantine/Del Rey, 1991)

Story type: Fantasy (Quest; Young Adult)
Major character(s): Dumery of Shiphaven, Child, Traveller; Kensher Kinner's Son, Rancher, Businessman; Teneria of Fishertown, Witch
Time period(s): Indeterminate
Locale(s): Hegemony of the Three Ethshars, Fictional Country; Barony of Sardiron, Fictional Country

Summary: Desperate to achieve apprenticeship, Dumery follows Kensher who he believes is a dragon hunter. Following Kensher proves harder than Dumery anticipated. Arriving at Kensher's home, Dumery discovers Kensher's true situation,

one which does not allow for an apprentice. Meanwhile Teneria doggedly follows her assignment-to find Dumery and see him safely home.

Other books you might like:
Debra Doyle, *School of Wizardry*, 1990
    James D. Macdonald, co-author
Nancy Luenn, *Goldclimbers*, 1991
Anne McCaffrey, *The White Dragon*, 1978
J.R.R. Tolkien, *The Hobbit*, 1938
Patricia C. Wrede, *Dealing with Dragons*, 1990
Mary Frances Zambreno, *A Plague of Sorcerers*, 1991

4497

LAWRENCE WATT-EVANS

Crosstime Traffic

(New York: Ballantine Del Rey, 1992)

Story type: Science Fiction (Collection; Alternate Universe)
Summary: Contains a 16-page introduction which anecdotally elucidates the origins of the stories published in periodicals and anthologies 1975-1992, including the Hugo Award winning story "Why I Left Harry's All-Night Hamburgers." Also included are "Real Time," "Science Fiction," "Monster Kidnaps Girl at Mad Scientist's Command," "After the Dragon Is Dead" and 14 others.

Other books you might like:
Alfred Bester, *Star Light, Star Bright*, 1976
Carol Emshwiller, *The Start of the End of It All*, 1991
Damon Knight, *Tomorrow and Tomorrow*, 1973
Keith Laumer, *Alien Minds*, 1991
George R.R. Martin, *Portraits of His Children*, 1992
Pat Murphy, *Points of Departure*, 1990
James Tiptree Jr., *Her Smoke Rose Up Forever*, 1990
Howard Waldrop, *Strange Monsters of the Recent Past*, 1991

4498

LAWRENCE WATT-EVANS, Editor

Newer York

(New York: Roc, 1991)

Story type: Science Fiction (Anthology)
Time period(s): Indeterminate Future
Locale(s): New York, New York

Summary: This thematic anthology about New York City contains a three-page introduction by the editor and 25 original stories including three collaborations, "Watching New York Melt" by Lawrence Watt-Evans and Julie Evans, "The Last Real Newyorker in the World" by James D. Macdonald and Debra Doyle, and "A Nice Place to Visit" by Warren Murphy and Molly Cochran. Other authors include Piers Anthony, Janet Asimov, B.W. Clough, Esther Friesner, S.N. Lewitt, Kristine Kathryn Rusch, Don Sahers, Susan Shwartz, John Shirley, Martha Soukup and Michael A. Stockpole.

Other books you might like:
Emma Bull, *War for the Oaks*, 1987
Philip K. Dick, *The Man Who Japed*, 1956
Peter R. Emshwiller, *The Host*, 1991

Esther Friesner, *New York by Knight*, 1986
George R.R. Martin, *Wild Cards*, 1987
  editor
Frederik Pohl, *The Years of the City*, 1984
Mike Resnick, *Stalking the Unicorn: A Fable of Tonight*, 1987
Jack Womack, *Heathern*, 1990

4499

LAWRENCE WATT-EVANS

The Nightmare People
(New York: Onyx, 1990)

Story type: Horror (Possession; Doppelganger)
Major character(s): Edward Smith, Computer Expert (programmer); Khalil Saad, Worker (garage mechanic); Annie McGowan, Aged Person
Time period(s): 1990s
Locale(s): Diamond Park, Maryland (Bedford Mills Apartments)

Summary: Edward Smith awakens one August morning to find that all 142 other inhabitants of his large apartment complex have vanished. Later, the missing persons reappear, strangely altered. Before long Smith is seeing frightening figures in the window of his room at night and decides to join forces with a handful of other people to try and save the world from possession by the mysterious invaders.

Other books you might like:
John Christopher, *The Possessors*, 1964
Jack Finney, *The Body Snatchers*, 1955
Fritz Leiber, *The Sinful Ones*, 1953

4500

LAWRENCE WATT-EVANS

Nightside City
(New York: Ballantine/Del Rey, 1989)

Story type: Science Fiction (Mystery)
Major character(s): Carlisle Hsing, Detective—Private
Time period(s): 23rd century
Locale(s): Epimetheus, Planet—Imaginary

Summary: When Epimetheus was first settled it was believed that the planet didn't rotate. Nightside City, home to gamblers, prostitutes, and other purveyors of vice and entertainment, was built very near the terminator and the blazing heat of Epimetheus' star. Now the planet's slow, only recently discovered rotation has doomed the city. Private eye Carlisle Hsing is hired by the residents of some apartment blocks on the sun-side edge of the city to find out why someone has kicked them out of their homes when those buildings are soon to be destroyed by nature. She uncovers a complex plot and finds herself a potential murder victim.

Other books you might like:
Richard Bowker, *Dover Beach*, 1987
George Alec Effinger, *A Fire in the Sun*, 1989
George Alec Effinger, *When Gravity Fails*, 1987
John E. Stith, *Deep Quarry*, 1989

F. Paul Wilson, *Dydeetown World*, 1989

4501

LAWRENCE WATT-EVANS

Out of This World
(New York: Ballantine Del Rey, 1994)

Story type: Fantasy (Alternate World; Science Fiction)
Series: Three Worlds
Major character(s): Pellimore "Pell" Brown, Businessman; Amy Jewell, Divorced Person; Raven, Hero
Time period(s): 1990s
Locale(s): Earth; Outer Space; Interstellar Empire/Federation

Summary: When a seemingly unfunctional spaceship lands on Amy Jewell's lawn and an elf invades Pel Brown's basement, Pel and family, Amy, her lawyer and the stranded spacemen decide to investigate Raven's world. After pirates capture them and sell them into slavery, their rescuers ask the group to join the fight against Shadow, the entity from Raven's magical world which may invade Earth as it spills into the galactic empire.

Other books you might like:
Leigh Brackett, *The Starmen of the Lyrdis*, 1976
Jack L. Chalker, *The River of Dancing Gods*, 1984
L. Sprague de Camp, *The Carnelian Cube*, 1948
  Fletcher Pratt, co-author
Keith Laumer, *The Great Time Machine Hoax*, 1964
C.L. Moore, *Judgment Night*, 1962
Andrew J. Offutt, *My Lord Barbarian*, 1977
Frederik Pohl, *Narabedla, Ltd.*, 1988

4502

LAWRENCE WATT-EVANS

The Rebirth of Wonder
(New York: Tor, 1992)

Story type: Fantasy (Contemporary; Light Fantasy)
Major character(s): Arthur "Art" Dunham, Businessman (theater manager); Merle "Myrddin" Innisfree, Wizard; Maggie Gowdie, Witch
Time period(s): 1990s
Locale(s): Bampton, Massachusetts; Faerie, Mythical Place

Summary: Before Art can clean up what was to be the last show of the season, his father rents the theater for the remaining month to a strange group called the Bringers of Wonder. Their leader, Mr. Innisfree, unwillingly accepts Art's help to produce the show, *The Return of Magic*. Art's baliwick, the theater originally built as a church, provides one of the last places the ritual to return magic to Earth can be performed successfully. Includes the story, "The Final Folly of Captain Dancy."

Other books you might like:
Emma Bull, *War for the Oaks*, 1987
John DeChancie, *Castle Perilous*, 1988
Diane Duane, *High Wizardry*, 1989
Simon Hawke, *The Wizard of 4th Street*, 1987
Tanya Huff, *Gate of Darkness, Circle of Light*, 1989

Mercedes Lackey, *Knight of Ghosts and Shadows*, 1990
Ellen Guon, co-author

4503

LAWRENCE WATT-EVANS

The Reign of the Brown Magician

(New York: Ballantine Del Rey, 1996)

Story type: Fantasy (Science Fiction; Historical)
Series: Three Worlds
Major character(s): Pellimore "Pel" Brown, Magician, Ruler; Proserpine Thorpe, Telepath; John Bascombe, Administrator
Time period(s): 1990s
Locale(s): Faerie, Mythical Place; Galactic Empire, Interstellar Empire/Federation

Summary: Pellimore Brown, now Pelbrun, obsesses about bringing his wife and daughter back to life. However, the Galactic Empire cannot believe his modest goals and keeps refusing to return the bodies, thus provoking war. Then Pel finds that his powers, while nearly omnipotent, have definite limitations and that resurrecting the dead has its drawbacks.

Other books you might like:
Poul Anderson, *Three Hearts and Three Lions*, 1961
Leigh Brackett, *The Ginger Star*, 1974
Jack L. Chalker, *The Birth of Flux and Anchor*, 1985
L. Sprague de Camp, *The Carnelian Cube*, 1948
    Fletcher Pratt, co-author
Alan Dean Foster, *To the Vanishing Point*, 1988
John Varley, *Titan*, 1979
Ted White, *Phoenix Prime*, 1966
Robert Charles Wilson, *Gypsies*, 1989

4504

LAWRENCE WATT-EVANS

The Spell of the Black Dagger

(New York: Ballantine Del Rey, 1993)

Story type: Fantasy (Magic Conflict; Political)
Series: Ethshar
Major character(s): Tabaea, Thief; Lady Sarai, Detective, Royalty
Time period(s): Indeterminate (Year of Speech 5227)
Locale(s): Hegemony of the Three Ethshars, Fictional Country

Summary: While attempting to duplicate an incompletely heard spell, Tabaea creates a magical dagger, little suspecting the tool's abilities. After accidently discovering the knife's power, Tabaea declares herself Empress of Ethshar, causing the royal wizards to unleash an ancient weapon against her, one which could destroy the entire world.

Other books you might like:
Lois McMaster Bujold, *The Spirit Ring*, 1992
Anne Logston, *Shadow*, 1991
Michael Moorcock, *The Bane of the Black Sword*, 1976
Michael Moorcock, *Sailor on the Seas of Fate*, 1976
Paula Volsky, *Illusion*, 1992

4505

LAWRENCE WATT-EVANS
ESTHER FRIESNER, Co-Author

Split Heirs

(New York: Tor, 1993)

Story type: Fantasy (Light Fantasy)
Major character(s): Queen Artemisia, Royalty, Parent; Arbol, Royalty, Imposter (prince); Clootie, Wizard
Time period(s): Indeterminate
Locale(s): Hydrangea, Fictional Country

Summary: When Queen Artemisia gives birth to triplets, two must be hidden to avoid their deaths. Unfortunately, a visually impaired servant neglects to leave one of the princes, allowing the princess to grow up as gender confused heir-apparent and the princes to adopt careers as wizard and shepherd. First of a series.

Other books you might like:
Kyle Crocco, *Heroes, Inc.*, 1991
Kyle Crocco, *Heroes Wanted*, 1991
Esther Friesner, *Demon Blues*, 1989
Esther Friesner, *Elf Defense*, 1988
Esther Friesner, *Hooray for Hellywood*, 1990
Esther Friesner, *Majyk by Accident*, 1993
Esther Friesner, *Unicorn U.*, 1992
John Moore, *Slay and Rescue*, 1993
Terry Pratchett, *Guards! Guards!*, 1991

4506

LAWRENCE WATT-EVANS

Taking Flight

(New York: Ballantine Del Rey, 1993)

Story type: Fantasy (Adventure; Quest)
Series: Ethshar
Major character(s): Kelder of Shulara, Adventurer; Irith, Mythical Creature (shapeshifter), Magician
Time period(s): Indeterminate
Locale(s): The Great Highway, Mythical Place; Angarossa, Fictional Country; Shan on the Desert, Fictional City (bazaar)

Summary: Motivated by a seer's prophecy that he will become a champion of the lost and forlorn, Kelder sets out to find adventure and a mate. Joining the beautiful, winged Irith on the road, Kelder's adventures begin all too quickly with deadly consequences for some bandits. As Kelder and Irith try to help the sister of one deceased bandit find rest for his soul, Kelder begins to suspect that Irith has hidden much about herself.

Other books you might like:
David Eddings, *Pawn of Prophecy*, 1982
Robert Jordan, *The Eye of the World*, 1989
Elizabeth Moon, *Sheepfarmer's Daughter*, 1988
Michael Moorcock, *The Revenge of the Rose*, 1991
Jennifer Roberson, *Shapechangers*, 1984

4507

CHARLES G. WAUGH, Editor
FRANK D. MCSHERRY JR., Co-Editor

Spooky Sea Stories

(Camden, Massachusetts: Yankee Books, 1991)

Story type: Horror (Anthology)

Summary: Fifteen stories of ghostly doings on the high seas, including Sir Arthur Conan Doyle's tale of obsessive pursuit, "The Captain of the Pole Star"; William Hope Hodgson's tale of the horrible fate of a shipwrecked crew on an uncharted island, "The Voice in the Night"; Joseph Conrad's tale of a vicious ship's officer and his just rewards, "The Brute"; and three variants on the Flying Dutchman theme: John William DeForest's "A Strange Arrival," Wilhelm Hauff's "The Story of the Haunted Ship," and Edgar Allan Poe's "Ms. Found in a Bottle."

Other books you might like:
William Pattrick, *Mysterious Sea Stories*, 1985

4508

CHARLES G. WAUGH, Editor
MARTIN H. GREENBERG, Co-Editor

Supernatural Sleuths

(New York: DAW, 1996)

Story type: Horror (Anthology; Mystery)

Summary: These 14 tales of fantasy, horror, and science fiction span the century and feature crimes both solved and committed by supernatural means. The oldest, "The Gateway of the Monster," features William Hope Hodgson's psychic detective Carnacki preventing the invasion of our sphere by an extradimensional monster. Jack Ritchie's "The Cardula Detective Agency" employs Count Dracula as a nighttime detective, and Lee Killough's "The Existential Man" has a sleuth investigating his own death. Bob Weinberg's deal-with-the-devil tale "The Midnight El" and William F. Nolan's "Lonely Train A'Comin'" both use phantom trains as the locus for their horrors.

Other books you might like:
Roger Elwood, *Horror Hunters*, 1971
  Vic Ghidalia, co-editor
Peter Haining, *Peter Cushing's Tales of a Monster Hunter*, 1975
  editor
Peter Haining, *Supernatural Sleuths*, 1986
  editor

4509

SYLVIA WAUGH

The Mennyms

(New York: Greenwillow, 1994)

Story type: Fantasy (Young Adult; Contemporary)
Series: Mennyms

Major character(s): Vinetta Mennym, Parent, Mythical Creature; Appleby Mennym, Teenager, Mythical Creature; Tulip Mennym, Grandparent, Mythical Creature
Time period(s): 1990s
Locale(s): England

Summary: News of their landlord's upcoming visit sends the Mennyms scurrying to provide additional cover for their well-hidden secret. First novel.

Other books you might like:
L. Frank Baum, *The Patchwork Girl of Oz*, 1913
Michael Bedard, *Painted Devil*, 1994
Pauline Clarke, *The Return of the Twelves*, 1963
Lynne Reid Banks, *The Indian in the Cupboard*, 1981

4510

SYLVIA WAUGH

Mennyms Under Siege

(New York: Greenwillow, 1996)

Story type: Fantasy (Young Adult; Contemporary)
Series: Mennyms
Major character(s): Pilbeam Mennym, Mythical Creature; Appleby Mennym, Teenager, Mythical Creature
Time period(s): 1990s
Locale(s): England

Summary: When Pilbeam decides to go to the theater to relieve her feeling of unbearable isolation, she encounters a nosy neighbor, bringing about possible discovery of the Mennym family secret and disaster for the entire family.

Other books you might like:
Lynne Reid Banks, *The Indian in the Cupboard*, 1981
L. Frank Baum, *The Patchwork Girl of Oz*, 1913
Michael Bedard, *Painted Devil*, 1994
Pauline Clarke, *The Return of the Twelves*, 1963
Mary James, *Shoebag*, 1990

4511

LEE WEATHERSBY

Kiss of the Vampire

(New York: Zebra, 1992)

Story type: Horror (Vampire Story)
Major character(s): Franz Drake, Vampire (Simon Drake's brother); Simon Tepes Drake, Vampire (Franz Drake's brother); Cassandra Lane "Casey" Brighton, Businesswoman (bookstore owner)
Time period(s): 1990s
Locale(s): Ft. Walton Beach, Florida

Summary: Betrayed by the brother upon whom he bestowed the gift of vampirism and who forsook it for the love of a mortal woman, Franz Drake follows Simon Drake to southern Florida, where he terrorizes the town's citizens and threatens Simon's girlfriend Casey, in order to teach his wayward brother a lesson.

Other books you might like:
Kathryn Meyer Griffith, *Vampire Blood*, 1991

Tom Piccirilli, *Dark Father*, 1990
T. Lucien Wright, *Blood Brothers*, 1992

4512

MICHAEL D. WEAVER

My Father Immortal
(New York: St. Martin's Press, 1989)

Story type: Science Fiction (Science Fiction)
Major character(s): David, Child; Stigg, Genetically Altered Being
Time period(s): 61st century
Locale(s): Earth; Outer Space

Summary: As a spaceship flees the solar system, a group of children are ejected from it in escape pods. As the years go by and the escape pods make their slow way back toward Earth, the children gradually begin to make sense of the fragmented information available to them about their pasts and about the strange society that has evolved on a far future Earth.

Other books you might like:
Brian W. Aldiss, *Hothouse*, 1962
Robert A. Heinlein, *Farnham's Freehold*, 1964
H.G. Wells, *The Time Machine*, 1958

4513

MICHAEL D. WEAVER

A Second Infinity
(New York: AvoNova, 1996)

Story type: Science Fiction (Post-Disaster; Alternate Intelligence)
Major character(s): Orfei Agamon, Artist (Holomage); Derek Soul, Government Official, Divorced Person; Holly Linn, Government Official
Time period(s): 22nd century (2107); Indeterminate Future
Locale(s): Moscow, Russia; Novyraj, Fictional City

Summary: Assigned against his will to investigate a series of disappearances at the Moscow office of the Reconstruction Department, Derek learns of a security report recommending his "Physical Discontinuance." Unsure of whether he can trust his assigned partner Holly, his ex-wife Linda, or even his own senses, Derek searches the tunnels under the devastated city. In the subterranean environment of Novyraj of the far future, Orfei experiences Derek's life by means of virtual reality dreams. When others plan to turn his art into reality, he tries to foil them by fleeing to Earth's surface.

Other books you might like:
Arthur C. Clarke, *Childhood's End*, 1953
Jane S. Fancher, *Harmonies of the 'Net*, 1992
Ursula K. Le Guin, *The Lathe of Heaven*, 1971
Amy Thomson, *Virtual Girl*, 1993
Vernor Vinge, *Marooned in Realtime*, 1986
Roger Zelazny, *Lord of Light*, 1967

4514

DON WEBB

A Spell for the Fulfillment of Desire
(Normal, Illinois: Black Ice Books, 1996)

Story type: Horror (Collection)

Summary: The author, a dedicated postmodernist, offers 27 stories published over the last decade that mix horror and mainstream elements in highly original stories. "The Literary Fruitcake" imagines a fruitcake handed down from Charles Dickens, through Arthur Machen and Algernon Blackwood, to Jack Kerouac and William S. Burroughs, each of whom imbues it with a taste of his own literary genius. "Mark 16:14-29, Matthew 14:1-12" depicts a truly gruesome dance of the seven veils that Salome performs for Herod Antipas. "Spiral" drops allusions to H.P. Lovecraft, Robert W. Chambers, E.T.A. Hoffman and detective B-movies in its account of a man whose strange life becomes even more bizarre when he drops acid. "In the Dark Ages" folds elements of popular culture into a spoof of the Black Mass.

Other books you might like:
William S. Burroughs, *Interzone*, 1989
Jack Remick, *Terminal Weird*, 1996
Wayne Allen Sallee, *With Wounds Still Wet*, 1996

4515

SHARON WEBB

The Halflife
(New York: Tor Books, 1989)

Story type: Science Fiction (Medical)
Major character(s): Tim Monahan, Writer; Jody Hinson, Psychologist
Time period(s): 1980s
Locale(s): Atlanta, Georgia

Summary: Twenty years ago something strange happened to Tim Monahan at a summer camp for gifted children. Now a moderately successful writer, he has been asked to take part in a scientific study on creativity. The other participants, he discovers, are an odd, unstable lot. Monahan has had nightmares ever since that summer twenty years ago, but now he begins to suffer blackouts as well. Several murders occur and Tim determines to get to the bottom of the mystery, no matter what it might cost him.

Other books you might like:
Richard Condon, *The Manchurian Candidate*, 1959
Dean R. Koontz, *The Eyes of Darkness*, 1981
Robert Reed, *Black Milk*, 1989

4516

WENDY WEBB, Editor
RICHARD GILLIAM, Co-Editor
EDWARD E. KRAMER, Co-Editor
MARTIN H. GREENBERG, Co-Editor

More Phobias
(New York: Pocket, 1995)

Story type: Horror (Anthology)

Summary: The twenty-seven stories commissioned especially for this compilation are all built upon a particular phobia or fear. Robert Bloch's ''None Are So Blind'' is a mordant tale of a man who develops a fear of cats after his fate is foretold by a fortuneteller. Nancy Kilpatrick's ''Sunphobic'' tells of a woman with a justifiable aversion to sunlight, and Douglas Clegg's ''The Mysteries of Paris'' of a man with an equally justifiable fear of serial killers. In Rick Hautala's ''The Back of My Hands,'' there is less phobia than obsession, as a man who covets his twin brother's hands goes to the ultimate extreme to possess them.

Other books you might like:
Jeff Gelb, *Fear Itself*, 1995
   editor
Charles L. Grant, *Fears*, 1983
   editor
Gary L. Raisor, *Obsessions*, 1991
   editor

4517

WENDY WEBB, Editor
RICHARD GILLIAM, Co-Editor
EDWARD E. KRAMER, Co-Editor
MARTIN H. GREENBERG, Co-Editor

Phobias: Stories of Your Deepest Fears
(New York: Pocket, 1994)

Story type: Horror (Anthology)

Summary: The 24 stories written originally for this volume are all concerned with personal fears and neuroses. Included are Robert Weinberg's ''Endure the Night,'' about crooks who try to use a man's fear of the dark against him; Karl Edward Wagner's ''Passages,'' in which doctors discuss the different fears that have affected their performance in their chosen profession; Kathryn Ptacek's ''Hair,'' about a woman whose sexual anxieties manifest as a preoccupation with body hair; Sharon and Jerry Ahern's ''Silent Pace,'' about a hit man afraid to fall asleep; Kristine Kathryn Rusch's ''Hot Water,'' about a woman's inability to deal with her nakedness; and two stories about fear of flying, Lawrence Watt-Evans' ''The Worst Part'' and Brad Strickland's ''The Hungry Sky.'' Robert Bloch supplies the introduction.

Other books you might like:
Peter Crowther, *Narrow Houses*, 1993
Charles L. Grant, *Fears*, 1983
Gary L. Raisor, *Obsessions*, 1991

4518

DAVID WEBER

The Armageddon Inheritance
(New York: Baen, 1993)

Story type: Science Fiction (Invasion of Earth; Military)
Series: Mutineer's Moon
Major character(s): Colin MacIntyre, Spaceship Captain, Leader (Governor of Earth); Sean Horus MacIntyre, Leader (Lieutenant Governor of Earth); Dahak, Artificial Intelligence (spaceship)
Time period(s): Indeterminate Future
Locale(s): *Dahak*, Spaceship; Outer Space

Summary: Preparing for the impending invasion by the Achuultani, Horus' Imperial machinery and medical technology, along with mobilized Terran equipment and manpower, may permit completion of planetary defenses before the leading Achuultani scouts arrive. Meanwhile Colin and *Dahak* must locate Fourth Imperium heavy support in time to return before the main Achuultani fleet reaches Earth. Sequel to *Mutineers' Moon*.

Other books you might like:
Bill Baldwin, *The Defenders*, 1992
Glen Cook, *The Dragon Never Sleeps*, 1988
Brian Daley, *Jinx on a Terran Inheritance*, 1985
Brian Daley, *Requiem for a Ruler of Worlds*, 1985
Dan Simmons, *Hyperion*, 1989
Vernor Vinge, *A Fire upon the Deep*, 1992

4519

DAVID WEBER

Field of Dishonor
(New York: Baen, 1994)

Story type: Science Fiction (Political; Military)
Series: Honor Harrington
Major character(s): Honor Harrington, Military Personnel, Noblewoman; Pavel Young, Nobleman (Earl of Northhollow)
Time period(s): Indeterminate Future
Locale(s): Star Kingdom of Manticore, Interstellar Empire/ Federation; Manticore, Planet—Imaginary; *Nike*, Spaceship

Summary: The Star Kingdom of Manticore should immediately declare war on the People's Republic of Haven, now in disarray after Honor's ''victory'' at Hancock. Unfortunately, many of the House of Lords reject the facts, desiring the problem to resolve itself. A proven deserter and coward in battle and enemy of Honor, Pavel Young weasels out of the death penalty. However, his dishonorable discharge from the Navy revokes his rank of captain and could prove worse punishment. He vows to destroy Honor and just may realize his goal.

Other books you might like:
Lois McMaster Bujold, *Shards of Honor*, 1986
Michelle Shirey Crean, *Dancer of the Sixth*, 1993
William C. Dietz, *Legion of the Damned*, 1993

Stephen Goldin, *Jade Darcy and the Affair of Honor*, 1988
   Mary Mason, co-author
Alis A. Rasmussen, *The Price of Ransom*, 1990

4520
DAVID WEBER
Flag in Exile
(New York: Baen, 1995)

Story type: Science Fiction (Military; Space Opera)
Series: Honor Harrington
Major character(s): Honor Harrington, Military Personnel (admiral), Noblewoman; Benjamin Mayhew, Leader (Grayson)
Time period(s): Indeterminate Future
Locale(s): Grayson, Planet—Imaginary; Star Kingdom of Manticore, Interstellar Empire/Federation; People's Republic of Haven, Interstellar Empire/Federation

Summary: Not yet recovered from the murder of her lover and the execution of the traitorous Pavel Young, Honor attempts to recuperate on Grayson. When Haven attacks Grayson on the way to Manticore, Honor must answer the call to protect her adopted home. She is hindered by plots against her and local resistance to the many changes she instituted to improve the life style of her steaders.

Other books you might like:
Lois McMaster Bujold, *Shards of Honor*, 1986
Frank Herbert, *Dune*, 1965
Elizabeth Moon, *Hunting Party*, 1993
Alis A. Rasmussen, *A Passage of Stars*, 1990
Sherwood Smith, *The Phoenix in Flight*, 1993
   Dave Trowbridge, co-author

4521
DAVID WEBER
Heirs of Empire
(New York: Baen, 1996)

Story type: Science Fiction (Family Saga; Political)
Series: Mutineer's Moon
Major character(s): Sean Horus MacIntyre, Heir, Military Personnel (midshipman); Colin MacIntyre, Ruler (emperor); Dahak, Artificial Intelligence (spaceship)
Time period(s): Indeterminate Future
Locale(s): Bia, Planet—Imaginary; *Imperial Terra*, Spaceship; Pardal, Planet—Imaginary

Summary: Enhanced with imperial technology, Sean, his twin sister and their friends, including a young Achuultani, join the Imperial Marines. Targeted by a traitor who plots to take over the empire after destroying the current leadership and allies, the friends survive the destruction of *Imperial Terra*, due to prior intervention by Dahak. Fortunately the crew arrives at a habitable planet whose residents, unfortunately, find the enhanced castaways demonic.

Other books you might like:
Lois McMaster Bujold, *Mirror Dance*, 1994
F.M. Busby, *The Demu Trilogy*, 1980

Debra Doyle, *The Price of the Stars*, 1992
   James D. Macdonald, co-author
Frank Herbert, *Dune*, 1965
Anne McCaffrey, *Damia's Children*, 1993
Alis A. Rasmussen, *The Price of Ransom*, 1990

4522
DAVID WEBER
Honor Among Enemies
(New York: Baen, 1996)

Story type: Science Fiction (Space Opera; Military)
Series: Honor Harrington
Major character(s): Honor Harrington, Military Personnel, Noblewoman; Aubrey Wanderman, Military Personnel
Time period(s): Indeterminate Future
Locale(s): *H.M.S. Wayfarer*, Spaceship; Star Kingdom of Manticore, Interstellar Empire/Federation; Silesian Confederacy, Interstellar Empire/Federation

Summary: Nominally given the opportunity to redeem her career in the Royal Manticorian Navy by rousting troublesome space pirates, Honor Harrington commands an ill-equipped merchant fleet and the least desirable service personnel assigned to the effort by enemies hoping that Honor might fail.

Other books you might like:
Lois McMaster Bujold, *Shards of Honor*, 1986
Debra Doyle, *The Price of the Stars*, 1992
   James D. Macdonald, co-author
David Feintuch, *Midshipman's Hope*, 1994
Frank Herbert, *Dune*, 1965
Sherwood Smith, *The Phoenix in Flight*, 1993
   Dave Trowbridge, co-author

4523
DAVID WEBER
The Honor of the Queen
(New York: Baen, 1993)

Story type: Science Fiction (Military; Space Opera)
Series: Honor Harrington
Major character(s): Honor Harrington, Military Personnel, Noblewoman; Raoul Courvossier, Military Personnel, Diplomat (ambassador); Benjamin Mayhew, Leader (planetary)
Time period(s): Indeterminate Future
Locale(s): Grayson, Planet—Imaginary; *Fearless*, Spaceship; Outer Space

Summary: As captain of the new *Fearless* and commander of the escort for Admiral Courvossier's delegation, Honor confronts religious prejudice against women having rank or station. After saving the planet's leader from assassination, she must then defend the planet from ultra-religious fanatics willing to destroy it.

Other books you might like:
Eleanor Arnason, *Ring of Swords*, 1993
Lois McMaster Bujold, *Barrayar*, 1991

Debra Doyle, *The Price of the Stars*, 1992
  James D. Macdonald, co-author
Debra Doyle, *Starpilot's Grave*, 1993
  James D. Macdonald, co-author
Melisa C. Michaels, *Skirmish*, 1985
Alis A. Rasmussen, *Revolution's Shore*, 1990

4524

DAVID WEBER

Mutineers' Moon

(New York: Baen, 1991)

Story type: Science Fiction (Invasion of Earth; Alternate Intelligence)

Major character(s): Colin MacIntyre, Military Personnel, Spaceship Captain; Hector MacMahan, Military Personnel; Jiltanith, Military Personnel, Pilot

Time period(s): 2040s

Locale(s): Moon (Earth's); Colorado Springs, Colorado; *Dahak*, Spaceship

Summary: While testing some new equipment, Colin MacIntyre finds the moon unexpectedly hollow. He is captured by Dahak, the spaceship he'd inadvertently contacted. Dahak, the artificial intelligence which had evolved from the ship's computer, conscripts Colin as its captain because it needs help to fulfill its mission and wants to save humanity, descended from its crew, from the dreaded alien Achuultani.

Other books you might like:

Roger MacBride Allen, *The Ring of Charon*, 1990
Greg Bear, *The Forge of God*, 1987
David Brin, *Earth*, 1990
Octavia E. Butler, *Dawn*, 1987
Damon Knight, *A Reasonable World*, 1991
Larry Niven, *Footfall*, 1985
  Jerry Pournelle, co-author

4525

DAVID WEBER

Oath of Swords

(New York: Baen, 1995)

Story type: Fantasy (Sword and Sorcery; Magic Conflict)

Major character(s): Bahzell Bahnakson, Warrior (horse stealer), Royalty (prince); Brandark Brandarkson, Warrior (Bloody Sword), Minstrel (bard); Harnak, Royalty (Crown Prince of Navahk), Warrior (Bloody Sword)

Time period(s): Indeterminate

Locale(s): Empire of the Spear, Fictional Country; Land of the Purple Lords, Fictional Country

Summary: Prince Bahzell Bahnakson and Crown Prince Harnak become counterweights in the struggle between the Gods of Light and Darkness, beginning with Bahzell severely beating Harnak for raping and nearly killing a ward of the crown. When Bahzell flees Navahk with her, he breaks his royal hostage bond, giving Harnak an excuse to hunt Bahzell down, revenge himself and get rid of the witnesses to the crime which could cost him his claim to the throne.

Other books you might like:

Eve Forward, *Villains by Necessity*, 1995
Simon R. Green, *Blood and Honor*, 1993
Barbara Hambly, *The Ladies of Mandrigyn*, 1984
Robert Jordan, *Lord of Chaos*, 1994
Holly Lisle, *The Rose Sea*, 1994
  S.M. Stirling, co-author
Elizabeth Moon, *Sheepfarmer's Daughter*, 1988

4526

DAVID WEBER

On Basilisk Station

(New York: Baen, 1993)

Story type: Science Fiction (Political; Military)

Series: Honor Harrington

Major character(s): Honor Harrington, Military Personnel (Commander), Noblewoman; Estelle Matsuko, Royalty, Government Official (Commissioner); Alister McKeon, Military Personnel (Lt. Commander-Exec)

Time period(s): Indeterminate Future

Locale(s): *Fearless*, Spaceship; Haven, Planet—Imaginary; Medusa, Planet—Imaginary (Basilisk Station)

Summary: Assigned to the newly refitted light cruiser, *Fearless*, Honor Harrington must prove herself as a captain to the crew and preserve the honor of *Fearless*, despite inadequate armaments. Basilisk Station serves as punishment duty for incompetents but, when assigned there, Honor decides to accomplish real work in spite of limited ships and personnel, poor morale and natives who use a drug which makes them violent. First of a series.

Other books you might like:

Lois McMaster Bujold, *Shards of Honor*, 1986
Glen Cook, *The Dragon Never Sleeps*, 1988
David Drake, *Starliner*, 1992
Stephen Goldin, *Jade Darcy and the Zen Pirates*, 1990
  Mary Mason, co-author
Larry Niven, *The Mote in God's Eye*, 1974
  Jerry Pournelle, co-author
Alis A. Rasmussen, *A Passage of Stars*, 1990
Vernor Vinge, *A Fire upon the Deep*, 1992

4527

DAVID WEBER

Path of the Fury

(New York: Baen, 1992)

Story type: Science Fiction (Alternate Intelligence)

Major character(s): Alicia ''Tisiphone'' De Vries, Military Personnel (Imperial Cadre, retired), Disembodied Personality; Arthur Keita, Military Personnel (Imperial Cadre, general); Ferhat Ben Belkassem, Military Personnel (Special Forces, O-branch)

Time period(s): Indeterminate Future

Locale(s): Mathison's World, Planet—Imaginary; Soissons, Planet—Imaginary; *Megarea*, Spaceship (AI)

Summary: Alicia retires to Mathison's World with her whole family when she leaves the Imperial Cadre. Few people possess the ability required to interface with all the enhancements necessary for the elite and deadly drop commandos. When offered the chance to live Alicia accepts, in order to destroy the mastermind behind the pirates who kill everyone else on the planet. Although hampered by the belief that she has become unstable, she and Tisiphone escape, capture *Megarea* and attempt to locate and discover who commands the pirates.

Other books you might like:
Jeffrey A. Carver, *From a Changeling Star*, 1989
Glen Cook, *The Dragon Never Sleeps*, 1988
Debra Doyle, *The Price of the Stars*, 1992
    James D. Macdonald, co-author
Stephen Goldin, *Jade Darcy and the Affair of Honor*, 1988
    Mary Mason, co-author
James P. Hogan, *The Multiplex Man*, 1992
Anne McCaffrey, *The Ship Who Sang*, 1969
Dan Simmons, *The Hollow Man*, 1992
Walter Jon Williams, *Voice of the Whirlwind*, 1987

4528

DAVID WEBER

The Short Victorious War

(New York: Baen, 1994)

Story type: Science Fiction (Military; Space Opera)
Series: Honor Harrington
Major character(s): Honor Harrington, Military Personnel, Noblewoman
Time period(s): Indeterminate Future
Locale(s): *Nike*, Spaceship; Star Kingdom of Manticore, Interstellar Empire/Federation; Outer Space

Summary: As war begins, the Royal Manticorian space navy must defend their small empire against forces of the gigantic People's Republic of Haven, built up during a 50-year-long arms race. Contains 16 pages of notes on Honor Harrington's navy.

Other books you might like:
Eleanor Arnason, *Ring of Swords*, 1993
Lois McMaster Bujold, *The Warrior's Apprentice*, 1986
Debra Doyle, *The Price of the Stars*, 1992
    James D. Macdonald, co-author
Mercedes Lackey, *Wing Commander: Freedom Flight*, 1992
    Ellen Guon, co-author
Sherwood Smith, *The Phoenix in Flight*, 1993
    Dave Trowbridge, co-author

4529

KAREN WEHRSTEIN

Lion's Heart

(New York: Baen, 1991)

Story type: Fantasy (Adventure; Political)
Series: Fifth Millennium

Major character(s): Fourth Chevenga, Heir, Ruler; Mana, Warrior
Time period(s): Indeterminate Future
Locale(s): Yeoli, Fictional Country

Summary: Set in the world of S. M. Stirling and Shirley Meier's *The Cage* (1989), this is the first book in the story of Chevenga. Driven by the foretelling of his death at an early age, Chevenga endures war and slavery to become a brilliant leader.

Other books you might like:
C.J. Cherryh, *Gate of Ivrel*, 1976
Glen Cook, *The Black Company*, 1984
Tanith Lee, *The Storm Lord*, 1976
Michael Moorcock, *Elric of Melnibone*, 1976
Roger Zelazny, *Nine Princes in Amber*, 1970

4530

KAREN WEHRSTEIN

Lion's Soul

(New York: Baen, 1991)

Story type: Fantasy (Political; Science Fiction)
Series: Fifth Millennium
Major character(s): Fourth Chevenga, Ruler
Time period(s): 35th century
Locale(s): Arko, Fictional Country; Yeou, Fictional Country

Summary: Chevenga escapes slavery in Arko and returns to Yeou to lead his people in defeating Arko. Afterward, as Demarch in Yeoli, he must heal his country's war wounds, while as Emperor in Arko, he must break down the old totalitarian structure by teaching Arkans about voting, equality and non-aggression. Somehow he must teach the two countries to get along.

Other books you might like:
Samuel R. Delany, *Tales of Neveryon*, 1979
Diane Duane, *The Door into Fire*, 1979
Heather Gladney, *Teot's War*, 1987
Patricia Kennealy, *The Copper Crown*, 1984
Mercedes Lackey, *Arrows of the Queen*, 1987
Shirley Meier, *Shadow's Daughter*, 1991
S.M. Stirling, *The Cage*, 1989
    Shirley Meier, co-author
M.K. Wren, *Sword of the Lamb*, 1981

4531

GUS WEILL

Flesh

(New York: Pocket, 1993)

Story type: Horror (Satire)
Major character(s): Marion Anderson, Student (music student); Justin Caeser, Student (music student); Polly Kole, Pharmacist
Time period(s): 1990s (1990)
Locale(s): Caeser Island, Maine

Summary: Flattered that his rich acquaintance, Justin Caeser, has invited him to the family island off the coast of Maine to acquaint him with the rest of the Caesers and to work with him on the music for his gestating Broadway musical, *Laffin' at the Palace*, Marion Anderson is blinded to all warnings that when the Caesers have someone for dinner, they do so literally. This satire of the conspicuous consumption of the filthy rich was first published in 1990.

Other books you might like:
Randall Boyll, *After Sundown*, 1989
Nancy Holder, *Cannibal Dwight's Special Purpose*, 1992
William W. Johnstone, *Watchers in the Woods*, 1991
Jack Ketchum, *Offspring*, 1991
Richard Laymon, *Midnight's Lair*, 1988

4532

ROBERT WEINBERG, Editor
STEFAN R. DZIEMIANOWICZ, Co-Editor
MARTIN H. GREENBERG, Co-Editor

100 Creepy Little Creature Stories
(New York: Barnes & Noble, 1994)

Story type: Horror (Anthology)

Summary: The 100 short-short stories in this anthology, drawn largely from the pages of the pulp magazine, *Weird Tales*, cover all sorts of weird creatures, including ghouls in Edward Lucas White's "Amina," werewolves in Thomas Ligotti's "The Real Wolf," familiars in Robert M. Price's "Familiar Face," aliens from outer space in Hugh B. Cave's "Take Me for Instance," vampires in Charles King's "Father's Vampire," creatures of Polish folklore in Stefan Grabinski's "The White Wyrak," and emonically possessed cats in Donald Burleson's "Little Brother."

Other books you might like:
Al Sarrantonio, *100 Hair-Raising Little Horror Stories*, 1992
    Martin H. Greenberg, co-editor
Sebastian Wolfe, *The Little Book of Horrors*, 1992
    editor

4533

ROBERT WEINBERG, Editor
STEFAN R. DZIEMIANOWICZ, Co-Editor
MARTIN H. GREENBERG, Co-Editor

100 Tiny Tales of Terror
(New York: Barnes & Noble, 1996)

Story type: Horror (Anthology)

Summary: More than a century of horror is packed into the 100 stories assembled here. All classic horror themes are covered, including the vampire in John Bender's "The Visitor," the shapeshifter in Theodore Sturgeon's "Talent," the witch in Fred Chappell's "Ember," the ghost in Carl Jacobi's "Phantom Brass" and Mary Elizabeth Counselman's "House of Shadows," and vengeance from beyond the grave in Vincent O'Sullivan's "Will." Joe Lansdale's "Boo, Yourself" and Richard Laymon's "Roadside Pickup" cross over into crime fiction, Howard Wandrei's "Over Time's Threshold" and F. Paul Wilson's "The Cleaning Machine" into science fiction,

and F. Marion Crawford's "The Doll's Ghost" and Thomas Ligotti's "The Greater Festival of Masks" into fantasy.

Other books you might like:
Isaac Asimov, *100 Great Fantasy Short Short Stories*, 1984
    Terry Carr, Martin H. Greenberg, co-editors
Al Sarrantonio, *100 Hair-Raising Little Horror Stories*, 1993
    Martin H. Greenberg, co-editor
Sebastian Wolfe, *The Little Book of Horrors*, 1992

4534

ROBERT WEINBERG, Editor
STEFAN DZIEMIANOWICZ, Co-Editor
MARTIN H. GREENBERG, Co-Editor

100 Vicious Little Vampire Stories
(New York: Barnes & Noble, 1995)

Story type: Horror (Anthology; Vampire Story)

Summary: The one hundred tales of vampirism included here are all approximately 3000 words (or fewer) long. Most were written specifically for the anthology. The different approaches to the vampire theme found herein include vampire plants ("Snip My Suckers" by Lois Gresh), vampires who feed on books ("And by a Word Immortal" by Mark Kreighbaum), vampires who prey on human misery ("Just Enough" by Joel Lane), a battlefield that lives on human blood ("The Witness" by Mike Ashley), vampires who travel over computer systems ("Coffin.Nail" by Richard Parks), devoutly religious vampires ("The Crumbs Beneath Thy Table" by Pamela Hodgson), anorexic vampires ("Bingin'" by Greg Cox), and a vampire tale told from the point of view of the blood ("Hemo Gobblin'" by Robert M. Price).

Other books you might like:
Richard Dalby, *Vampire Stories*, 1992
Ellen Datlow, *Blood Is Not Enough*, 1988
Ellen Datlow, *A Whisper of Blood*, 1991
Martin H. Greenberg, *Celebrity Vampires*, 1995
Martin H. Greenberg, *Dracula: Prince of Darkness*, 1992
Stephen Jones, *The Mammoth Book of Vampires*, 1992
Alan Ryan, *Vampires: Two Centuries of Great Vampire Stories*, 1987

4535

ROBERT WEINBERG, Editor
STEFAN R. DZIEMIANOWICZ, Co-Editor
MARTIN H. GREENBERG, Co-Editor

100 Wild Little Weird Tales
(New York: Barnes & Noble, 1994)

Story type: Horror (Anthology)

Summary: This book draws together 100 short-short stories, 3,000 words or less in length, from the pages of the original *Weird Tales*, the pulp magazine that published between 1923 and 1954 and served as the birthplace for modern horror fiction. Included are H.P. Lovecraft's "Hypnos," about two men pursued by a dream monster; Robert Bloch's first professionally published tale, "The Feast in the Abbey," about a traveller's visit to a ghostly monastery; Clark Ashton Smith's

"The Last Incantation," about the lesson a sorceror learns upon summoning the souls of the dead; Carl Jacobi's "The Last Drive," about a curious event that befalls a man driving a truck with a coffin and its corpse; Richard Searight's "The Sealed Casket," the tale of a spectral vampire; H. Warner Munn's *conte cruel*, "The Chain"; and Fritz Leiber's fusion of science fiction and horror, "Mr. Bauer and the Atoms." Classic reprints from the magazine include stories by Edgar Allan Poe, E.F. Benson, and Bram Stoker.

Other books you might like:
Peter Haining, *Weird Tales*, 1976
    editor
Leo Margulies, *Weird Tales*, 1964
    editor
Leo Margulies, *Worlds of Weird*, 1965
    editor

4536
ROBERT WEINBERG

The Armageddon Box
(Newark, NJ: Wildside Press, 1991)

Story type: Horror (Vampire Story)
Major character(s): Alex Warner, Professor (history professor); Valerie Warner, Sorceress (Alex's wife); Dietrich Vril, Monster, Vampire
Time period(s): 1990s
Locale(s): Chicago, Illinois; Switzerland

Summary: The death of an antiquarian bookdealer friend throws Alex and Valerie Warner into the path of Dietrich Vril, a maniacal vampire master searching for a legendary talisman that threatens the entire human race.

Other books you might like:
Elaine Bergstrom, *Shattered Glass*, 1989
Gardner Dozois, *Down Among the Dead Men*, 1989
    Jack Dann, co-author. In Ellen Datlow, *Blood Is Not Enough*
Hanz Heine Ewers, *Alraune*, 1911
Dan Simmons, *Carrion Comfort*, 1989

4537
ROBERT WEINBERG, Editor
STEFAN DZIEMIANOWICZ, Co-Editor
MARTIN H. GREENBERG, Co-Editor

Between Time and Terror
(New York: Roc, 1995)

Story type: Horror (Anthology)
Summary: The 17 stories collected here span 75 years and straddle the boundary between science fiction and horror. Included are H.P. Lovecraft's classic of the effects of a meteor crash on a small town, "The Colour out of Space"; Frank Belknap Long's tale of a scientific experiment in physical transformation, "The Man with a Thousand Legs"; Robert Bloch's apocalyptic vision of a future taken over by machines, "It Happened Tomorrow"; Ray Bradbury's melding of the alien and psychic possession themes, "Asleep in Arma-

geddon"; Dan Simmons' technological rendering of the vampire theme, "Metastasis"; Cliver Barker's riff on the Frankenstein theme, "The Age of Desire"; and Arthur C. Clarke's interplanetary campfire tale, "A Walk in the Dark."

Other books you might like:
Groff Conklin, *Science Fiction Terror Tales*, 1955
August Derleth, *The Other Side of the Moon*, 1949
August Derleth, *Strange Ports of Call*, 1948
Stephen Jones, *The Mammoth Book of Frankenstein*, 1995
Damon Knight, *The Dark Side*, 1965

4538
ROBERT WEINBERG

The Black Lodge
(New York: Pocket, 1991)

Story type: Horror (Occult)
Major character(s): Sid Taine, Detective, Psychic; Janet Packard, Businesswoman (Jeweller); Papa Benjamin, Religious (voodoo priest)
Time period(s): 1990s
Locale(s): Chicago, Illinois

Summary: After agreeing to investigate an apparent family feud, New Age detective Sid Taine is drawn into the affairs of the Black Lodge, a cult made up of Chicago's wealthiest businessmen with links to the lucrative drug trade. Ultimately, he joins forces with a voodoo practitioner to defeat the lodge's henchman, the murderous Dark Man.

Other books you might like:
Hugh B. Cave, *Disciples of Dread*, 1988
Hugh B. Cave, *The Lower Deep*, 1990
David J. Schow, *The Shaft*, 1990
Dennis Wheatley, *The Devil Rides Out*, 1935

4539
ROBERT WEINBERG

Bloodwar
(Stone Mountain, Georgia: White Wolf, 1995)

Story type: Horror (Vampire Story)
Series: Masquerade of the Red Death
Major character(s): Dire McCann, Detective; Alicia Varney, Businesswoman, Vampire; Makish, Criminal (assassin)
Time period(s): 1990s (1994)
Locale(s): St. Louis, Missouri; Washington, District of Columbia

Summary: In an alternate world secretly run by 13 vampire clans who maintain an uneasy alliance, detective Dire McCann investigates the appearance of the Red Death, a monstrous being capable of incinerating anyone and anything in its path. In the process of uncovering whether the appearance of the Red Death portends the re-emergence of an earlier generation of vampire elders ravenous for the blood of its descendants, McCann must hide his own secret identity from his vampire employers. This story is set in the universe of the *World of Darkness: Vampire* role-playing game.

Other books you might like:
Scott Baker, *Ancestral Hungers*, 1995
Scott Ciencin, *The Vampire Odyssey*, 1992
Kim Newman, *Anno Dracula*, 1992
Brian Stableford, *The Empire of Fear*, 1988
Stewart Wieck, *The Beast Within*, 1995
    editor

4540
ROBERT WEINBERG

A Calculated Magic
(New York: Ace, 1995)

Story type: Fantasy (Magic Conflict)
Major character(s): Jack Collins, Scientist, Magician; Roger Quinn, Businessman, Magician; The Old Man of the Mountain, Mythical Creature
Time period(s): 1990s (1995)
Locale(s): Chicago, Illinois; Las Vegas, Nevada

Summary: Jack Collins, the Logical Magician, hopes for some time off after having just saved the world. But when the Old Man of the Mountain kidnaps his fiancee, Megan Ambrose, and threatens to sell a biological plague virus to the highest bidder, Jack finds himself once again drawn into the world of magic, a world of amazing puissant mathematics.

Other books you might like:
Emma Bull, *Finder*, 1994
L. Sprague de Camp, *The Complete Compleat Enchanter*, 1989
    Fletcher Pratt, co-author
Gordon R. Dickson, *The Dragon and the George*,
Michael Flynn, *In the Country of the Blind*, 1990
Leo Frankowski, *The Cross-Time Engineer*, 1986
Robert A. Heinlein, *Waldo and Magic, Inc.*, 1990
Christopher Stasheff, *The Warlock in Spite of Himself*, 1969

4541
ROBERT WEINBERG

The Dead Man's Kiss
(New York: Pocket, 1992)

Story type: Horror (Occult)
Major character(s): Ellen Harper, Archaeologist (Egyptologist); David Ross, Detective; Carl Garrett, Murderer (white supremacist)
Time period(s): 1990s
Locale(s): Chicago, Illinois

Summary: With the help of artifacts stolen from a nearby museum, white supremacist Carl Garrett resurrects the mummy Jambres to help him wipe out the Jewish race. But Carl is unaware that Jambres has engineered his own resurrection and has more far-reaching plans that will have an impact on the whole of western civilization.

Other books you might like:
Charles L. Grant, *The Long Night of the Grave*, 1986
Robert E. Howard, *Skull-Face*, 1946
    short story in *Skullface and Others*

Michael Paine, *Cities of the Dead*, 1988
Anne Rice, *The Mummy, or Ramses the Damned*, 1989

4542
ROBERT WEINBERG

The Devil's Auction
(Philadelphia: Owlswick, 1988)

Story type: Horror (Occult)
Major character(s): Valerie Warner, Sorceress, Model; Alex Warner, Professor (history professor)
Time period(s): 1980s (1988)
Locale(s): Chicago, Illinois

Summary: When her sorcerer father is murdered by supernatural agents, Valerie Warner inherits his invitation to the Devil's Auction, a periodic event which only the successful bidder survives. This is the author's first novel.

Other books you might like:
Dion Fortune, *The Secrets of Dr. Taverner*, 1926
Mercedes Lackey, *Burning Water*, 1989
Seabury Quinn, *The Devil's Bride*, 1976
Sax Rohmer, *The Brood of the Witch Queen*, 1918
Dennis Wheatley, *The Devil Rides Out*, 1935

4543
ROBERT WEINBERG

A Logical Magician
(New York: Ace, 1994)

Story type: Fantasy (Magic Conflict; Light Fantasy)
Major character(s): Jack Collins, Student (graduate school mathematician); Cassandra Cole, Immortal, Martial Arts Expert (Amazon warrior)
Time period(s): 1990s
Locale(s): Chicago, Illinois; California

Summary: Named by Merlin Ambrose as savior of Humanking, Jack Collins must puzzle out both the threat and the solution after an ancient deity kidnaps the wizard. Enlisting help from other mythical champions who acieved existence through human mythology, Jack must also apply ancient mythical patterns to modern technological society to battle the reemergent evil.

Other books you might like:
Gene DeWeese, *Now You See It/Him/Them...*, 1975
    Robert Coulson, co-author
Elizabeth Forrest, *Phoenix Fire*, 1992
Simon Hawke, *The Wizard of 4th Street*, 1987
Megan Lindholm, *Wizard of the Pigeons*, 1986
Holly Lisle, *Minerva Wakes*, 1994
Larry Niven, *Fallen Angels*, 1991
    Jerry Pournelle, Michael Flynn, co-authors
Clifford D. Simak, *Out of Their Minds*, 1970

4544
ROBERT WEINBERG
MARTIN H. GREENBERG, Co-Author

Lovecraft's Legacy
(New York: Tor, 1990)

Story type: Horror (Anthology)

Summary: A collection of 13 stories by different authors commemorating the 100th anniversary of the birth of H. P. Lovecraft. The stories are written less in emulation of Lovecraft's rich, atmospheric style than as examples of what the authors learned from Lovecraft about the craft of writing. Best selections include Gene Wolfe's ''Lord of the Land,'' Brian McNaughton's ''Merphyllia'' and F. Paul Wilson's ''The Pine Barrens.''

Other books you might like:
Edward P. Berglund, *Disciples of Cthulhu*, 1976
Ramsey Campbell, *New Tales of the Cthulhu Mythos*, 1980
Lin Carter, *The Spawn of Cthulhu*, 1971
H.P. Lovecraft, *Tales of the Cthulhu Mythos: Golden Anniversary Anthology*, 1990

4545
ROBERT WEINBERG, Editor
STEFAN DZIEMIANOWICZ, Co-Editor
MARTIN H. GREENBERG, Co-Editor

Rivals of Dracula
(New York: Barnes & Noble, 1996)

Story type: Horror (Anthology; Vampire Story)

Summary: Nineteen reprint stories feature the famous vampire Count Dracula and his descendants as characters. Dracula bests pickpockets in contemporary France in Robert Bloch's ''The Yougoslaves'' and Nazis during World War II in Ed Hoch's ''Dracula 1944.'' He is summoned by a boy with a childhood obsession with vampires in Richard Matheson's ''Drink My Red Blood'' and by a punk challenger in Brian Hodge's ''Like a Pilgrim to a Shrine.'' He pulls strings that control the fate of contemporary Romania in Dan Simmons' ''All Dracula's Children'' and Kevin J. Anderson's ''Much at Stake.'' His progeny extend their unholy lives in Angela Carter's ''Lady in the House of Love'' and Tanith Lee's ''Nunc Dimittis.''

Other books you might like:
Martin H. Greenberg, *Dracula: Prince of Darkness*, 1992
    editor
Stephen Jones, *The Mammoth Book of Dracula*, 1997
    editor
Michel Parry, *The Rivals of Dracula: A Century of Vampire Fiction*, 1977
    editor

4546
ROBERT WEINBERG
STEFAN DZIEMIANOWICZ, Co-Author
MARTIN H. GREENBERG, Co-Author

Rivals of Weird Tales
(New York: Bonanza, 1990)

Story type: Horror (Anthology)

Summary: Thirty stories from the pulp fantasy and weird fiction magazines that were *not* published in *Weird Tales*, the most famous and influential fantasy magazine of the period. Included are H.P. Lovecraft's Poe homage ''Cool Air,'' Jack Williamson's werewolf tale ''Wolves of Darkness'' and Seabury Quinn's ghost story ''Doomed,'' all from magazines that tried to emulate *Weird Tales*, as well as Norvell Page's superman novel ''But Without Horns,'' Theodore Sturgeon's amusing ''Shottle Bop'' and Richard Matheson's twilight-zonish ''Sorry, Right Number,'' which appeared in magazines that tried to break new ground.

Other books you might like:
D.R. Benson, *The Unknown*, 1963
Edward L. Ferman, *The Best Horror From Fantasy & Science Fiction*, 1988
    Anne Jordan, co-author
Stanley Schmidt, *Unknown Worlds: Tales From Beyond*, 1988
    Martin H. Greenberg, co-author

4547
ROBERT WEINBERG

The Unbeholden
(Clarkston, Georgia: White Wolf, 1996)

Story type: Horror (Vampire Story)
Series: Vampire: The Masquerade
Major character(s): Dire McCann, Detective; Alicia Varney, Businesswoman, Vampire; Madeleine Giovanni, Vampire
Time period(s): 1990s (1994)
Locale(s): Vienna, Austria; Paris, France; Tel Aviv, Israel

Summary: Dire McCann and Alicia Varney, the avatars of ancient beings engaged in the sectarian struggles of the Camarilla and Sabbat vampires, have their final showdown with the Red Death, a monstrous creation of the Order of Dreadful Night whose existence means not only the end of the Vampire Masquerade, but destruction of the world as we know it. This novel, the third in the author's Masquerade of the Red Death Trilogy, is set in the publisher's ''Vampire: The Masquerade'' gaming world, in which vampire clans are enjoined by the law of their species to mingle unobtrusively with mortals and keep their supernatural identities secret.

Other books you might like:
Don Bassingthwaite, *As One Dead*, 1996
    Nancy Kilpatrick, co-author
Nancy A. Collins, *A Dozen Black Roses*, 1996
James A. Moore, *The House of Secrets*, 1995
    Kevin Murphy, co-author

4548

ROBERT WEINBERG

Unholy Allies

(Clarkston, Georgia: White Wolf, 1995)

Story type: Horror (Vampire Story)
Series: Masquerade of the Red Death
Major character(s): Dire McCann, Detective; Alicia Varney, Businesswoman, Vampire; Madeleine Giovanni, Vampire
Time period(s): 1990s (1995)
Locale(s): Washington, District of Columbia

Summary: In this continuation of the author's first novel in the series, *The Masquerade of the Red Death* (1995), detective Dire McCann searches for the origins of The Red Death, an unstoppable nemesis to the vampire nation that rules an alternate Earth with mortals. Meanwhile, Alicia Varney, a contemporary woman possessed by the soul of an ancient vampire queen, allies herself with McCann in an effort to prevent the truth of his and her secret identities.

Other books you might like:
Brian Lumley, *Necroscope: The Lost Years*, 1995
Kim Newman, *Anno Dracula*, 1992
Dan Simmons, *Carrion Comfort*, 1989
Brian Stableford, *The Empire of Fear*, 1988
Karen E. Taylor, *Blood Secrets*, 1994

4549

ROBERT WEINBERG
MARK REIN-HAGEN, Co-Author

Vampire Diary: The Embrace

(Stone Mountain, Georgia: White Wolf, 1995)

Story type: Horror (Vampire Story)
Series: Vampire Diary
Major character(s): Auston Jacobson, Saloon Keeper/Owner; Claudius, Vampire; Danya, Teenager
Time period(s): 1990s (1995)
Locale(s): Los Angeles, California

Summary: Told in the form of a diary, this novella chronicles the thoughts and fears of Auston Jacobson, bartender at the Neverland night club, whose promotion to manager entails being "embraced" by its vampire owner, and becoming a being whose vampire nature disgusts his human self. The story is set in the universe of the *World of Darkness: Vampire* role-playing game.

Other books you might like:
Scott Ciencin, *The Vampire Odyssey*, 1992
Lewis Gannett, *The Living One*, 1993
Pat Graversen, *Sweet Blood*, 1993
Anne Rice, *Interview with the Vampire*, 1976
Karen E. Taylor, *Blood Secrets*, 1994
William Tedford, *Liquid Diet*, 1993

4550

ROBERT WEINBERG, Editor
STEFAN R. DZIEMIANOWICZ, Co-Editor
MARTIN H. GREENBERG, Co-Editor

Weird Vampire Tales

(New York: Gramercy, 1992)

Story type: Horror (Anthology; Vampire Story)

Summary: Thirty stories from pulp fiction magazines such as *Weird Tales*, *Strange Tales*, *Unknown Worlds*, and *Beyond Fantasy Fiction*, that served as the bridge between classic and contemporary vampire stories. Included are Seabury Quinn's "The Man Who Cast No Shadow," one of the first vampire stories set on American soil; Robert E. Howard's southwestern vampire story "The Horror from the Mound"; Carl Jacobi's "Revelations in Black" and Everil Worrell's "The Canal," both of which employ vampire femmes fatales; Robert Bloch's "The Cloak" and August Derleth's "Who Shall I Say Is Calling," both humorous vampire stories; Cyril Kornbluth's tale of psychic vampirism, "The Mindworm"; and Hugh Cave's classic story of vampires living on a shipwrecked boat, "Stragella."

Other books you might like:
Alan Ryan, *Vampires: Two Centuries of Great Vampire Stories*, 1987
editor
Leslie Shepard, *The Dracula Book of Great Vampire Stories*, 1977
editor
Devendra P. Varma, *Voices From the Vault: Authentic Vampire Tales*, 1987
editor

4551

MARGARET WEIS
DON PERRIN, Co-Author

The Doom Brigade

(Lake Geneva, Wisconsin: TSR, 1996)

Story type: Fantasy (Adventure; Political)
Series: Dragonlance
Major character(s): Kang, Mythical Creature (dragon), Military Personnel; Gloth, Mythical Creature (dragon), Military Personnel
Time period(s): Indeterminate
Locale(s): Krynn, Planet—Imaginary

Summary: When a group of draconians attempt to hide in the mountains and pursue a life of peace, dwarves make the decision difficult, as a great treasure hidden in the mountains lures both groups.

4552

MARGARET WEIS
TRACY HICKMAN, Co-Author

Dragon Wing
(New York: Bantam, 1990)

Story type: Fantasy (Adventure)
Series: Death Gate Cycle
Major character(s): Hugh the Hand, Criminal (assassin); Sinistrad, Wizard (Mysteriarch)
Time period(s): Indeterminate
Locale(s): Earth

Summary: King Stephen saves Hugh from the executioner, but Hugh must kill Bane, Sinistrad's son and spy. It becomes apparent that there are other forces at work when Hugh is unable to kill Bane and gets caught up in bigger events.

Other books you might like:
Dave Duncan, *The Destiny of the Sword*, 1988
   The Seventh Sword, Book 3
Pat Zettner, *The Shadow Warrior*, 1990

4553

MARGARET WEIS, Editor

A Dragon-Lover's Treasury of the Fantastic
(New York: Warner Aspect, 1994)

Story type: Fantasy (Anthology)

Summary: Contains a two-page introduction and 20 stories about dragons published 1957-1992 in periodicals and anthologies including Anne McCaffrey's Award-winning "Weyr Search" and Gordon R. Dickson's "St. Dragon and the George," a story subsequently expanded into *The Dragon and the George* (1976). The tone varies from humorous to dark and themes include biotechnology, ecology, magic conflict, and dragons and the law. Authors include Nancy Varian Berberick, Orson Scott Card, L. Sprague de Camp, David Drake, Esther M. Friesner, Craig Shaw Gardner, George R.R. Martin, Patricia A. McKillip, Mickey Zucker Reichert, Mike Resnick, Joan D. Vinge and Roger Zelazny.

Other books you might like:
Orson Scott Card, *Dragons of Darkness*, 1981
   editor
Orson Scott Card, *Dragons of Light*, 1983
   editor
Jack Dann, *Dragons!*, 1993
   Gardner Dozois, co-editor
Rosalind M. Greenberg, *Dragon Fantastic*, 1992
   Martin H. Greenberg, co-editor
Jane Yolen, *Here There Be Dragons*, 1993

4554

MARGARET WEIS
TRACY HICKMAN, Co-Author

Dragons of Summer Flame
(Lake Geneva, Wisconsin: TSR, 1995)

Story type: Fantasy (Political; Magic Conflict)
Series: Dragonlance
Major character(s): Tanis, Mythical Creature (half-elf); Dalamar, Wizard; Raistlin Majere, Wizard
Time period(s): Indeterminate
Locale(s): Krynn, Planet—Imaginary

Summary: As the Dark Queen gathers her warriors and unnatural minions, Paul Majere seeks the long lost Raistlin Majere. If defenders do not come forward, evil forces will dominate the continent.

Other books you might like:
Nancy Varian Berberick, *Stormblade*, 1988
Robert Jordan, *The Eye of the World*, 1987
Mary Kirchoff, *Kendermore*, 1989
Richard A. Knaak, *The Legend of Huma*, 1988
Dan Parkinson, *The Gates of Thorbardin*, 1990
Kevin Stein, *Brothers Majere*, 1989
Michael Williams, *Weasel's Luck*, 1988

4555

MARGARET WEIS
TRACY HICKMAN, Co-Author

Elven Star
(New York: Bantam Spectra, 1990)

Story type: Fantasy (Alternate World; Adventure)
Series: Death Gate Cycle
Major character(s): Haplo, Adventurer, Wizard; Paithan, Mythical Creature (Elf), Adventurer
Time period(s): Indeterminate
Locale(s): Pryan, Planet—Imaginary (Realm of Fire)

Summary: Haplo, the Patryn, is sent by his adoptive father to Pryan, a large stony world with a molten core, to investigate the world and its inhabitants. Magically flying his ship, Dragon Wing, he visits the elves, humans and dwarves who are all hoping for the Lost Lords to return and save them from the menacing renegade giants and one another.

Other books you might like:
Dave Duncan, *The Destiny of the Sword*, 1988
Elizabeth Moon, *Surrender None: The Legacy of Gird*, 1990
Alis A. Rasmussen, *The Labyrinth Gate*, 1988
Melanie Rawn, *The Star Scroll*, 1989
Pat Zettner, *The Shadow Warrior*, 1990

4556

MARGARET WEIS, Editor

Fantastic Alice
(New York: Ace, 1995)

Story type: Fantasy (Anthology)

Major character(s): Alice, Child

Summary: Contains a three-page introduction and 17 original stories varying in tone from whimsical to humorous and all featuring Alice in new situations inspired by Lewis Carroll's *Alice's Adventures in Wonderland*. Authors include Janet Asimov, Robin Wayne Bailey, Peter Crowther, Esther M. Friesner, Jane M. Lindskold, Lisa Mason, Jody Lynn Nye, Mickey Zucker Reichert, Lawrence Watt-Evans and Roger Zelazny.

Other books you might like:
Gilbert Adair, *Alice through the Needle's Eye: The Further Adventures of Lewis Carroll's "Alice"*, 1985
Lewis Carroll, *Alice's Adventures in Wonderland*, 1865
Lewis Carroll, *Through the Looking Glass and What Alice Found There*, 1872
David Kirschner, *The Pagemaster*, 1993
    Ernie Contreras, co-author
Randall Garrett, *Takeoff!*, 1979

4557
MARGARET WEIS
TRACY HICKMAN, Co-Author

Fire Sea
(New York: Bantam Spectra, 1991)

Story type: Fantasy (Alternate World; Adventure)
Series: Death Gate Cycle
Major character(s): Haplo, Adventurer, Wizard (Patryn); Alfred, Adventurer, Wizard (Sartan)
Time period(s): Indeterminate
Locale(s): Abarrach, Planet—Imaginary (Realm of Stone)

Summary: Ordered to journey to each of the worlds connected by the Death Gate, Haplo travels to Abarrach accompanied, unintentionally, by Alfred, thought to be the last survivor of his people. As they travel through Abarrach's underground civilization, they meet a lost tribe of Alfred's people and become involved in the civil war engulfing Abarrach.

Other books you might like:
Michael Cassutt, *Dragon Season*, 1991
Philip Jose Farmer, *To Your Scattered Bodies Go*, 1971
Marc Laidlaw, *Neon Lotus*, 1988
Elizabeth Moon, *Oath of Gold*, 1989
J.R.R. Tolkien, *The Fellowship of the Ring*, 1954
J.R.R. Tolkien, *The Return of the King*, 1956
J.R.R. Tolkien, *The Two Towers*, 1955

4558
MARGARET WEIS
TRACY HICKMAN, Co-Author

The Hand of Chaos
(New York: Bantam Spectra, 1993)

Story type: Fantasy (Quest)
Series: Death Gate Cycle
Major character(s): Haplo, Adventurer, Wizard (Patryn); Bane, Child, Adventurer; Hugh the Hand, Criminal (assassin)

Time period(s): Indeterminate
Locale(s): Arianus, Planet—Imaginary (Realm of Air)

Summary: The Lord of the Nexus, Xar, orders Haplo and Bane to Arianus to carry on his work. Xar intends Bane to aid Xar's acquisition of ultimate power through control of gate technology and plans for Haplo's eventual death. Meanwhile, Haplo's companion suffers imprisonment in a deadly labyrinth.

Other books you might like:
Barbara Hambly, *Dog Wizard*, 1993
Robert Jordan, *The Eye of the World*, 1989
Katharine Kerr, *The Bristling Wood*, 1989
Katharine Kerr, *Daggerspell*, 1986
Katharine Kerr, *Darkspell*, 1987
Tad Williams, *The Dragonbone Chair*, 1989
Jonathan Wylie, *The Lightless Kingdom*, 1989

4559
MARGARET WEIS
TRACY HICKMAN, Co-Author

Into the Labyrinth
(New York: Bantam Spectra, 1993)

Story type: Fantasy (Political; Quest)
Series: Death Gate Cycle
Major character(s): Haplo, Adventurer, Wizard (Patryn); Alfred, Adventurer, Wizard (Sartan); Hugh the Hand, Criminal (assassin)
Time period(s): Indeterminate
Locale(s): Abarrach, Planet—Imaginary (Realm of Stone); Arianus, Planet—Imaginary (Realm of Air); Pyran, Planet—Imaginary (Realm of Fire)

Summary: The Lord of the Nexus, Xar, abandons his plans to invade the four worlds with armies of reanimated dead when he learns of the Chamber of the Damned and the Seventh Gate, key to the fate of all worlds. Xar plots to kill and reanimate Haplo as his servant to gain Haplo's unique knowledge of the Gate's location.

Other books you might like:
Lois McMaster Bujold, *The Spirit Ring*, 1992
Terry Brooks, *The Talismans of Shannara*, 1993
Barbara Hambly, *Dog Wizard*, 1993
Elizabeth Ann Scarborough, *Last Refuge*, 1992
Martha Wells, *The Element of Fire*, 1993
Roger Zelazny, *Nine Princes in Amber*, 1970

4560
MARGARET WEIS

King's Sacrifice
(New York: Bantam Spectra, 1991)

Story type: Science Fiction (Science Fantasy; Political)
Series: Star of the Guardians
Major character(s): Dion Starfire, Heir, Royalty (king); Maigrey Morianna, Noblewoman, Pilot; Derek Sagan, Military Personnel (General)
Time period(s): Indeterminate Future

Locale(s): *Phoenix II*, Spaceship; Outer Space

Summary: Dion, fighting to regain his hereditary position as king, must overthrow the corrupt new Republic and protect the church which he is helping become reestablished in the Empire. His problems will not be resolved until he has made the ultimate sacrifice to ensure peace in his realm.

Other books you might like:
Lois McMaster Bujold, *Barrayar*, 1991
Frank Herbert, *Dune*, 1965
Steve Miller, *Agent of Change*, 1988
    Sharon Lee, co-author
L.E. Modesitt Jr., *The Ecologic Secession*, 1990
Alis A. Rasmussen, *A Passage of Stars*, 1990
Michael Swanwick, *Stations of the Tide*, 1991
Ian Watson, *God's World*, 1990

4561

MARGARET WEIS
DON PERRIN, Co-Author

The Knights of the Black Earth
(New York: Roc, 1995)

Story type: Science Fiction (Space Opera; Political)
Major character(s): Xris, Cyborg, Mercenary (Mag Force 7); Dalin Rowan, Computer Expert
Time period(s): Indeterminate Future
Locale(s): Outer Space

Summary: Seeking Dalin Rowan to exact revenge for betraying Mag Force 7, Xris uncovers a plot by Earth supremacists to assassinate the King of the Galaxy and restore Earth's rule. Set in the Universe of The Star of the Guardians series (1990-1993).

Other books you might like:
Lois McMaster Bujold, *Brothers in Arms*, 1989
Glen Cook, *The Dragon Never Sleeps*, 1988
William C. Dietz, *Legion of the Damned*, 1993
Dave Duncan, *Hero*, 1991
Rick Shelley, *Until Relieved*, 1994
David Weber, *On Basilisk Station*, 1993

4562

MARGARET WEIS

The Lost King
(New York: Bantam Spectra, 1990)

Story type: Science Fiction (Science Fantasy; Political)
Series: Star of the Guardians
Major character(s): Dion Starfire, Heir, Royalty (prince); Maigrey Morianna, Noblewoman (lady), Pilot; Derek Sagan, Military Personnel (general)
Time period(s): Indeterminate Future
Locale(s): *Phoenix*, Spaceship; *Defiant*, Spaceship

Summary: The Warlord is searching the galaxy for the heir to the murdered king of the Starfire dynasty. Only if Prince Dion can be destroyed or controlled will the future of the harsh Democratic Republic be assured. Lady Maigrey and a few other surviving Guardians of the throne help Dion fight the

corruption of the new Republic and claim his rightful heritage.

Other books you might like:
Frank Herbert, *Dune*, 1965
George Lucas, *Star Wars*, 1976
Alis A. Rasmussen, *A Passage of Stars*, 1990
Alis A. Rasmussen, *The Price of Ransom*, 1990
Alis A. Rasmussen, *Revolution's Shore*, 1990
Gene Wolfe, *The Shadow of the Torturer*, 1980

4563

MARGARET WEIS
TRACY HICKMAN, Co-Author

The Second Generation
(Lake Geneva, Wisconsin: TSR, 1994)

Story type: Fantasy (Collection; Adventure)
Series: Dragonlance
Major character(s): Tanis, Mythical Creature (half-elf), Warrior; Caramon, Innkeeper (The Inn of the Last Home), Hero; Raistlin, Wizard, Hero
Time period(s): Indeterminate
Locale(s): Krynn, Planet—Imaginary

Summary: Contains a two-page foreword, 20-page appendix, poetry by Michael Williams and five stories featuring the offspring of the heroes who restored the balance of good and evil bringing peace to Krynn. As defeated forces rally to destroy the harmony, younger warriors must come to the rescue. Game tie-in.

Other books you might like:
Mary Kirchoff, *Kendermore*, 1989
Richard A. Knaak, *The Legend of Huma*, 1988
Richard A. Knaak, *Kaz the Minotaur*, 1990
Paul B. Thompson, *Riverwind the Plainsman*, 1990
    Tonya R. Carter, co-author
Nancy Varian, *Berberick, Stormblade*, 1988
Michael Williams, *Galen Beknighted*, 1990
Michael Williams, *Weasel's Luck*, 1988

4564

MARGARET WEIS
TRACY HICKMAN, Co-Author

Sentinels
(New York: Ballantine Del Rey, 1996)

Story type: Science Fiction (Space Opera; Political)
Series: Starshield
Major character(s): Merinda Neskat, Alien, Historian (Omnet inquisitor); Jeremy Griffiths, Spaceship Captain; Queekat Shn'dar, Alien, Historian (Omnet inquisitor)
Time period(s): Indeterminate Future
Locale(s): *Brishan*, Spaceship; Brishan V, Planet—Imaginary

Summary: When the synthetic minds of the intergalactic Omnet begin to rebel, Merinda embarks on a search to find the legendary Mantle of Kendis-dai, which she hopes will restore order to the Omnet. Captain Griffiths and his crew, lost and stranded light years from Earth when the first FTL flight goes awry, somewhat reluctantly join Merinda in her search.

Other books you might like:
Jane Emerson, *City of Diamond*, 1996
David Gerrold, *Voyage of the Star Wolf*, 1990
Tracy Hickman, *The Immortals*, 1996
Jack Vance, *Alastor*, 1995
David Wingrove, *Beneath the Tree of Heaven*, 1995

4565

MARGARET WEIS
TRACY HICKMAN, Co-Author

Serpent Mage
(New York: Bantam Spectra, 1992)

Story type: Fantasy (Quest)
Series: Death Gate Cycle
Major character(s): Haplo, Adventurer, Wizard (Patryn); Alfred, Adventurer, Wizard (Sartan)
Time period(s): Indeterminate
Locale(s): Chelestra, Planet—Imaginary (realm of water)

Summary: Continuing their explorations, Haplo, Alfred and Haplo's dog travel through the Death Gate to the fourth world in which dwarves, elves and humans coexist peacefully on bubble-encased submerged islands where they work together on escape plans for use when Chelestra's sun expires. Haplo helps battle a sudden infestation of dragon-snakes while Alfred discovers and wakens his sleeping Sartan ancestors hidden within Chelestra, actions which could precipitate universal disaster.

Other books you might like:
Piers Anthony, *Mercycle*, 1991
Philip Jose Farmer, *To Your Scattered Bodies Go*, 1971
Mary Gentle, *Ancient Light*, 1987
Mary Gentle, *Rats and Gargoyles*, 1991
Alis A. Rasmussen, *The Labyrinth Gate*, 1988
Robert Silverberg, *The Face of the Waters*, 1991
Joan Slonczewski, *A Door into Ocean*, 1986
J.R.R. Tolkien, *The Hobbit*, 1938

4566

MARGARET WEIS
TRACY HICKMAN, Co-Author

The Seventh Gate
(New York: Bantam Spectra, 1994)

Story type: Fantasy (Magic Conflict; Adventure)
Series: Death Gate Cycle
Major character(s): Haplo, Adventurer, Wizard (Patryn); Alfred, Adventurer, Wizard (Sartan); Xar, Nobleman (Lord of the Nexus), Wizard
Time period(s): Indeterminate
Locale(s): Abarrach, Planet—Imaginary; Seventh Gate, Mythical Place

Summary: Pursuing knowledge of the Seventh Gate, Xar takes the mortally wounded Haplo to Abarrach, intending to make him an undead slave, while the Labyrinth imprisons Merit and

Hugh the Hand who seek Alfred, captured by a dragon. An invasion of dragon-snakes portends disaster until the wizard, Zifnab, arrives with good dragons and the Sartan answer a summons. However, Xar must help to ensure victory. This concluding volume contains a 34-page appendix.

Other books you might like:
David Eddings, *Pawn of Prophecy*, 1982
Mary Gentle, *Ancient Light*, 1987
Robert Jordan, *The Eye of the World*, 1989
Katharine Kerr, *Daggerspell*, 1986
Melanie Rawn, *Dragon Prince*, 1988
Tad Williams, *The Dragonbone Chair*, 1989
Roger Zelazny, *Nine Princes in Amber*, 1970

4567

JORDAN K. WEISMAN, Editor

Into the Shadows
(New York: Roc, 1992)

Story type: Fantasy (Anthology; Urban)
Series: Shadowrun
Time period(s): 2050s (2050)
Locale(s): Seattle, Washington

Summary: Contains a one-page prologue, a two-page contributors' biography, a five-page glossary of slang used in 2050, a seven-page chronology of events 2000-2050 plus nine stories by eight authors with two stories contributed by Michael A. Stackpole. A game tie-in anthology edited by the game's creator.

Other books you might like:
M.A.R. Barker, *Man of Gold*, 1984
Robert N. Charrette, *Choose Your Enemies Carefully*, 1991
Robert N. Charrette, *Find Your Own Truth*, 1991
Robert N. Charrette, *Never Deal with a Dragon*, 1990
Robert N. Charrette, *Never Trust an Elf*, 1992
Nigel Findley, *2XS*, 1992
Christopher Kubasik, *Changeling*, 1992

4568

FAY WELDON

The Cloning of Joanna May
(New York: Viking, 1990)

Story type: Science Fiction (Literary)
Major character(s): Joanna May, Divorced Person; Carl May, Businessman
Time period(s): 1990s

Summary: Joanna May, sixtyish, divorced, discovers that some thirty years earlier her then husband, a wealthy industrialist, had her cloned. Childless because her husband did not want children, she feels an overwhelming desire to find her four clones and discover what their lives are like. The five women hit it off well together and form an alliance of sorts against the world.

Other books you might like:
C.J. Cherryh, *Cyteen*, 1988
Ira Levin, *The Boys From Brazil*, 1976

Pamela Sargent, *Cloned Lives*, 1976
Kate Wilhelm, *Where Late the Sweet Birds Sang*, 1976
Gene Wolfe, *The Fifth Head of Cerberus*, 1972

4569
ANGUS WELLS
Dark Magic
(New York: Bantam Spectra, 1992)

Story type: Fantasy (Quest; Magic Conflict)
Series: Godwars
Major character(s): Calandryll den Karynth, Royalty, Adventurer; Bracht ni Errhyn, Mercenary; Katya, Adventurer
Time period(s): Indeterminate
Locale(s): Lysse, Fictional Country; Cuan na'For, Fictional Country

Summary: Calandryll and his companions pursue the evil necromancer Rythamun, whose persona now inhabits the body of another man, to war-torn Kandahar and across the Narrow Sea to Lysse. When Rythamun takes over another body, the three follow the trail, seeking to take from him the stolen *Arcanum* before it can be used to summon the Mad God, Tharn. Unknown to them, another sorcerer pursues them, plotting to obtain the *Arcanum* himself.

Other books you might like:
Lynn Abbey, *Daughter of the Bright Moon*, 1979
C.J. Cherryh, *Rusalka*, 1989
C.J. Cherryh, *Well of Shiuan*, 1978
Stephen R. Donaldson, *Lord Foul's Bane*, 1977
Barbara Hambly, *The Witches of Wenshar*, 1987
Patricia A. McKillip, *The Riddle-Master of Hed*, 1976
Patricia C. Wrede, *Caught in Crystal*, 1987

4570
ANGUS WELLS
Exile's Challenge
(New York: Bantam Spectra, 1996)

Story type: Fantasy (Psychic Powers; Political)
Series: Exiles Saga
Major character(s): Dafyd Furth, Psychic; Chakthi, Leader, Warrior; Tomas Var, Military Personnel
Time period(s): Indeterminate
Locale(s): Matawaye, Fictional Country; Salvation, Mythical Place (prison colony); Ket-Ta-Thanne, Fictional Country

Summary: Chakthi plots to capture the land of Matawaye and wreak vengeance. While Major Tomas Var attempts to quell the unrest in Salvation caused by renegade Matawaye warriors, he must simultaneously contend with a personal battle with his own superior.

Other books you might like:
Lynn Flewelling, *Luck in the Shadows*, 1996
Terry Goodkind, *Wizard's First Rule*, 1994
J.V. Jones, *The Baker's Boy*, 1995
Robert Jordan, *The Eye of the World*, 1990
Katharine Kerr, *Daggerspell*, 1986

4571
ANGUS WELLS
Exile's Children
(New York: Bantam Spectra, 1996)

Story type: Fantasy (Psychic Powers; Political)
Series: Exiles Saga
Major character(s): Dafyd Furth, Psychic; Arcole Blayke, Gambler, Martial Arts Expert; Flysse Cobal, Waiter/Waitress
Time period(s): Indeterminate
Locale(s): Ket-Ta-Witko, Fictional Country; Salvation, Mythical Place (prison colony)

Summary: When a blood feud evolves into violence and destructive demons overrun the land, hope for the future rests with three residents of the prison colony: Salvation, a tavern girl, a gambler, and a young boy with a prohibited talent at True Dreaming.

Other books you might like:
Dave Duncan, *The Cursed*, 1995
Dave Duncan, *Magic Casement*, 1990
Lynn Flewelling, *Luck in the Shadows*, 1996
Barbara Hambly, *The Ladies of Mandrigyn*, 1984
L.E. Modesitt Jr., *The Towers of the Sunset*, 1992

4572
ANGUS WELLS
Forbidden Magic
(New York: Bantam Spectra, 1992)

Story type: Fantasy (Quest)
Series: Godwars
Major character(s): Calandryll den Karynth, Royalty, Scholar; Bracht ni Errhyn, Mercenary
Time period(s): Indeterminate
Locale(s): Tezin-dar, Fictional City; Gessyth, Fictional Country; Kandahar, Fictional Country

Summary: Intending to stop an evil wizard from waking a mad god whose parents forced him into eternal sleep to curtail an ancient war, Calandryll and Bracht must find and destroy a legendary book, the *Arcanum*, before the evil sorcerer finds it.

Other books you might like:
David Eddings, *Pawn of Prophecy*, 1982
Barbara Hambly, *The Time of the Dark*, 1982
Robert Jordan, *The Eye of the World*, 1990
Michael Moorcock, *The Revenge of the Rose*, 1991
Tad Williams, *The Dragonbone Chair*, 1988

4573
ANGUS WELLS
Lords of the Sky
(New York: Bantam Spectra, 1994)

Story type: Fantasy (Quest; Magic Conflict)
Major character(s): Daviot, Traveller (rememberer); Rwyan, Wizard; Urt, Genetically Altered Being

Time period(s): Indeterminate

Locale(s): Durbrecht, Fictional City; Dharbek, Fictional Country; Dragoncastle, Mythical Place

Summary: Dharbek suffers from periodic attacks by the people of Ahn, their bizarre magical enemies. Trained to remember past and current events as a sort of traveling historian, Daviot grows increasingly worried about his culture, crumbling from internal and external pressures. His solution, however, may increase the destruction.

Other books you might like:
David Gemmell, *Lion of Macedon*, 1992
Barbara Hambly, *The Time of the Dark*, 1982
Michael Scott Rohan, *The Forge in the Forest*, 1987
Judith Tarr, *Lord of the Two Lands*, 1993
Gene Wolfe, *Soldier of the Mist*, 1986

4574

ANGUS WELLS

The Usurper

(New York: Bantam Spectra, 1990)

Story type: Fantasy (Legend; Magic Conflict)

Series: Book of the Kingdoms

Major character(s): Kedryn Caitin, Royalty (Prince of Tamur), Warrior; Wynett, Royalty (Princess of the Three Kingdoms), Religious (Sister); Hattim Sethiyan, Nobleman (Lord of Ust-Galich), Ruler (Usurper)

Time period(s): Indeterminate Past (Middle Ages)

Locale(s): The Three Kingdoms, Mythical Place

Summary: In the hour of his triumph over Taws, demon of the fire-god Ashar, Prince Kedryn was blinded by a magic sword. To regain his sight, Kedryn and Wynett journey to the abode of the dead to confront the spirit of the warrior who wielded the blade. While he is gone, Taws rises again and convinces the ambitious and greedy Lord Hattim to Murder King Darr and steal his throne. Kedryn returns to find the Three Kingdoms in chaos and Taws waiting to destroy him.

Other books you might like:
C.J. Cherryh, *Wizard Spawn*, 1989
   Nancy Asire, co-author
Frank Herbert, *Dune*, 1965
Elizabeth Moon, *Oath of Gold*, 1989
Elizabeth Moon, *Divided Allegiance*, 1988
Elizabeth Moon, *Sheepfarmer's Daughter*, 1988

4575

ANGUS WELLS

The Way Beneath

(New York: Bantam Spectra, 1991)

Story type: Fantasy (Magic Conflict)

Series: Books of the Kingdoms

Major character(s): Kedryn Caitin, Royalty, Warrior; Wynett, Royalty, Religious; Ashar, Deity

Time period(s): Indeterminate Past ((Middle Ages))

Locale(s): The Three Kingdoms, Fictional Country; Magoria, Fictional Country

Summary: Kedryn descends into the netherworld to rescue Wynett and defeat Ashar who has secured Wynett's portion of the talisman and plans to acquire Kedryn's part.

Other books you might like:
Frank Herbert, *Dune*, 1965
Elizabeth Moon, *Divided Allegiance*, 1988
Elizabeth Moon, *Oath of Gold*, 1989
Elizabeth Moon, *Sheepfarmer's Daughter*, 1988
Michael Moorcock, *The Revenge of the Rose*, 1991
Margaret Weis, *Fire Sea*, 1991
   Tracy Hickman, co-author

4576

ANGUS WELLS

Wild Magic

(New York: Bantam Spectra, 1993)

Story type: Fantasy (Quest; Magic Conflict)

Series: Godwars

Major character(s): Calandryll den Karynth, Royalty, Renegade; Bracht ni Errhyn, Mercenary; Katya, Adventurer

Time period(s): Indeterminate

Locale(s): Anwar-Teng, Fictional City; Jesseryn Plain, Fictional Country

Summary: Calandryll and his companions pursue the evil necromancer, Rythamun, whose persona now inhabits the body of another man, across the Jesseryn Plain. The three encounter Cennaire, beautiful pawn of the wizard Anomius who holds her heart in a magically concealed box. At first distrustful, Calandryll falls in love with her and she with him. Cennaire provides them aid against Anomius and Rythamun.

Other books you might like:
Lynn Abbey, *The Black Flame*, 1980
C.J. Cherryh, *Chernevog*, 1990
C.J. Cherryh, *The Fires of Azeroth*, 1979
Stephen R. Donaldson, *The Illearth War*, 1977
Barbara Hambly, *The Dark Hand of Magic*, 1990
P.C. Hodgell, *God Stalk*, 1982
Ursula K. Le Guin, *The Tombs of Atuan*, 1971
Mickey Zucker Reichert, *Godslayer*, 1987
J.R.R. Tolkien, *The Return of the King*, 1956
Tad Williams, *To Green Angel Tower*, 1993

4577

ANGUS WELLS

Wrath of Ashar

(New York: Bantam Spectra, 1990)

Story type: Fantasy (Legend; Magic Conflict)

Series: Book of the Kingdoms

Major character(s): Kedryn Caitin, Royalty (Prince of Tamur), Warrior; Bedyr Caitin, Nobleman (Lord of Tamur), Warrior; Taws, Demon

Time period(s): Indeterminate Past (Medieval)

Locale(s): The Three Kingdoms, Mythical Place; Beltrevan, Mythical Place

Summary: By virtue of the astonishing powers he possesses, young Prince Kedryn of Tamur seems to be the one prophecied by the Sisterhood of the Lady to save the Three Kingdoms (Tamur, Ust-Galich and Kesh) from Taws, demon messenger of the fire-god Ashar and the warrior horde from the north. With the help of his father Bedyr and King Darr, Kedryn raises a mighty army and goes forth to do battle.

Other books you might like:
C.J. Cherryh, *Wizard Spawn*, 1989
   Nancy Asire, co-author
Frank Herbert, *Dune*, 1965
Elizabeth Moon, *Divided Allegiance*, 1988
Elizabeth Moon, *Oath of Gold*, 1989
Elizabeth Moon, *Sheepfarmer's Daughter*, 1988

4578

CATHERINE WELLS (Pseudonym of Catherine Wells Dimenstein)

Children of the Earth
(New York: Ballantine Del Rey, 1992)

Story type: Science Fiction (Post-Holocaust)
Major character(s): Coconino, Time Traveller, Indian; Debra McKay, Scientist, Hunter; Derek Lujan, Time Traveller, Spaceman
Time period(s): Indeterminate Future
Locale(s): Canyonlands, Utah; Argo, Planet—Imaginary; Beta, Planet—Imaginary

Summary: This novel follows Coconino when he and Derek Lujan emerge from the time warp 150 years after the action in *The Earth Is All That Lasts*, and also examines the lives of those left behind, focusing on his yet unborn children. On Beta, the relatives of those marooned on Earth learn of the expedition's possible survival and attempt to organize a rescue.

Other books you might like:
Michael Armstrong, *Agviq*, 1990
Clare Bell, *People of the Sky*, 1989
Ursula K. Le Guin, *Always Coming Home*, 1987
Megan Lindholm, *Alien Earth*, 1992
R.A. MacAvoy, *The Third Eagle: Lessons Along a Minor String*, 1989
Donald E. McQuinn, *Warrior*, 1990
J.M. Morgan, *Desert Eden*, 1991
Paul O. Williams, *The Breaking of Northwall*, 1981

4579

CATHERINE WELLS (Pseudonym of Catherine Wells Dimenstein)

The Earth Is All That Lasts
(New York: Ballantine/Del Rey, 1991)

Story type: Science Fiction (Post-Holocaust)
Major character(s): Coconino, Indian, Hunter; Debra McKay, Scientist, Hunter
Time period(s): Indeterminate Future (500 years after Earth's evacuation)
Locale(s): Canyonlands, Utah; Argo, Planet—Imaginary

Summary: Five hundred years after the Earth was evacuated, a few people plan an expedition to visit Earth. Since most people believe the Earth remains uninhabitable, the expedition is short on funding and mostly ignored. Meanwhile, the recovered Earth has two surviving societies, a group of scientists who have retained some technology, including a flyer, and the descendants of the 2,000 Indians who refused to abandon Earth. First novel.

Other books you might like:
Clare Bell, *People of the Sky*, 1989
David Brin, *Earth*, 1990
Alan Dean Foster, *Cyber Way*, 1990
Frank Herbert, *Dune*, 1965
Marc Laidlaw, *Neon Lotus*, 1988
R.A. MacAvoy, *The Third Eagle: Lessons Along a Minor String*, 1989
Carol Severance, *Reefsong*, 1991

4580

CATHERINE WELLS (Pseudonym of Catherine Wells Dimenstein)

The Earth Saver
(New York: Ballantine Del Rey, 1993)

Story type: Science Fiction (Family Saga; Post-Disaster)
Major character(s): Montana "Tana" Winthrop, Administrator, Handicapped; Coconino, Indian, Time Traveller; Debra McCay, Leader
Time period(s): Indeterminate Future
Locale(s): Earth; Beta, Planet—Imaginary

Summary: Inspired by the recently discovered family records, Tana becomes CEO of the Winthrop Institute to develop a means of returning to Earth via point to point matter transmission. Obsessed with rescuing any survivors from the *Homeward Bound* crash, Tana makes a second trip without her medical aid dog, Doc, with mechanical failure delaying her return. While recovering from a seizure she meets many people, including Coconino, and realizes she must protect the Earth and its current inhabitants. Concludes the trilogy.

Other books you might like:
William Barton, *Dark Sky Legion*, 1992
David Brin, *Earth*, 1990
Tony Daniel, *Warpath*, 1993
Jack C. Haldeman II, *High Steel*, 1993
   Jack Dann, co-author
Ursula K. Le Guin, *Always Coming Home*, 1987
Anne McCaffrey, *Powers That Be*, 1993
   Elizabeth Ann Scarborough, co-author
Joan Slonczewski, *Daughter of Elysium*, 1993
Joan D. Vinge, *The Summer Queen*, 1991
Paul O. Williams, *The Breaking of Northwall*, 1981

4581

MARTHA WELLS

City of Bones

(New York: Tor, 1995)

Story type: Fantasy (Science Fiction; Post-Disaster)
Major character(s): Khat, Businessman (relic dealer), Genetically Altered Being (kris); Elen, Psychic (warder)
Time period(s): Indeterminate Future
Locale(s): Planet—Imaginary

Summary: To pursue the Master Warder's lust for power, Khat and Elen pursue ancient magical artifacts deep into the wasteland, not understanding their dangerous, true nature.

Other books you might like:
Anne Kelleher Bush, *Daughter of Prophecy*, 1995
Mary Gentle, *Ancient Light*, 1987
Terry Goodkind, *Wizard's First Rule*, 1994
Rosemary Kirstein, *The Steerswoman*, 1989
Sheri S. Tepper, *A Plague of Angels*, 1993

4582

MARTHA WELLS

The Element of Fire

(New York: Tor, 1993)

Story type: Fantasy (Magic Conflict)
Major character(s): Kade Carrion, Royalty (Queen of Air and Darkness), Sorceress; Thomas Boniface, Bodyguard (queen's); Urbain Grandier, Imposter, Sorcerer
Time period(s): Indeterminate
Locale(s): Ile-Rein, Fictional Country

Summary: Hoping to settle unresolved family issues, Kade returns to court just in time to blunt the surprise attack of a traitorous confidant of the king. With the royal guard routed and dark Faery forces in control of the castle, Kade must use her wits and unusual magical abilities to rescue the monarchy. Author's first novel.

Other books you might like:
Lois McMaster Bujold, *The Spirit Ring*, 1992
Laurell K. Hamilton, *Nightseer*, 1992
Elizabeth A. Lynn, *Watchtower*, 1979
Elizabeth Ann Scarborough, *Last Refuge*, 1992
Paula Volsky, *Illusion*, 1992
Tad Williams, *The Dragonbone Chair*, 1988
Tad Williams, *Stone of Farewell*, 1990

4583

ROGER WELSCH

Touching the Fire

(New York: Villard Books, 1992)

Story type: Fantasy (Collection; Legend)
Time period(s): 20th century; Indeterminate Past
Locale(s): Great Plains, North America

Summary: Contains 12 pages of notes by the author plus seven stories surrounding the Nehawka's Sky Bundle which relate tribal history and tradition back to the tribe's earliest days.

Other books you might like:
Richard Erdoes, *American Indian Myths and Legends*, 1984
    Alfonso Ortiz, co-editor
Alan Dean Foster, *Cyber Way*, 1990
W. Michael Gear, *People of the Fire*, 1990
    Kathleen O'Neal Gear, co-author
J. Alison James, *Sing for a Gentle Rain*, 1990
Paul Radin, *The Trickster*, 1972
Lewis Spence, *The Myths of the North American Indians*, 1989
Gerald Vizenor, *Dead Voices: Natural Agonies in the Real World*, 1992

4584

K.D. WENTWORTH

House of Moons

(New York: Ballantine Del Rey, 1995)

Story type: Science Fiction (Political; Psychic Powers)
Series: Moonspeaker
Major character(s): Haemas Sennay Tal, Psychic, Heiress—Dispossessed; Diren Chee, Nobleman, Villain; Kevisson Monmart, Psychic, Healer
Time period(s): Indeterminate Future
Locale(s): Desalaya, Planet—Imaginary

Summary: Wishing to rule the entire Highlands, Diren Chee kidnaps Haemas Tal using a forbidden mind control device, a latteh. He then sends Haemas and his sister Axia into the past to discover how the latteh works. While searching for Haemas, Kevisson Monmart uncovers Chee's path of madness and murder and learns the sinister truth about the latteh. Sequel to *Moonspeaker*.

Other books you might like:
Lynn Abbey, *Beneath the Web*, 1994
Leigh Brackett, *The Sword of Rhiannon*, 1953
Marion Zimmer Bradley, *The Forbidden Tower*, 1977
Cheryl J. Franklin, *The Light of Exile*, 1990
Katherine Kurtz, *Camber of Culdi*, 1976
Andre Norton, *Ordeal in Otherwhere*, 1964
Julie Dean Smith, *The Wizard King*, 1994

4585

K.D. WENTWORTH

The Imperium Game

(New York: Ballantine Del Rey, 1994)

Story type: Science Fiction (Mystery; Alternate Intelligence)
Major character(s): Arvid Gerald Kerickson, Computer Expert, Divorced Person; Amaelia Metullus, Computer Game Player; Alline Bolton Kerickson, Divorced Person
Time period(s): 21st century
Locale(s): United States; Virtual Reality, Cyberspace

Summary: The murder of a computer game player inside a simulation of ancient Rome brings murder charges which discredit Kerickson, depriving him of computer access and the opportunity to clear himself. Entering the system illegally, Kerickson discovers a powerful and deadly twist added to his game.

Other books you might like:
Piers Anthony, *Killobyte*, 1993
Ben Bova, *Death Dream*, 1994
Brian Daley, *Tron*, 1982
Pierre Ouellette, *The Deus Machine*, 1994
Cole Perriman, *Terminal Games*, 1994

4586

K.D. WENTWORTH

Moonspeaker
(New York: Ballantine Del Rey, 1994)

Story type: Science Fiction (Psychic Powers; Political)
Series: Moonspeaker
Major character(s): Haemas Sennay Tal, Psychic, Fugitive; Jarid Tal Ketral, Psychic, Bastard Son; Kevisson Monmart, Psychic, Healer
Time period(s): Indeterminate
Locale(s): The Highlands, Fictional Country; Dorbin, Fictional City

Summary: Accused of patricide, Haemas flees into a hostile world. Pursued by searchers from both authorities and plotters, she navigates mundane dangers and esoteric, inhuman plans. If Haemas survives, the world may change for the better, but if she dies, it ceases to exist

Other books you might like:
Alfred Bester, *The Demolished Man*, 1953
Marion Zimmer Bradley, *The Heritage of Hastur*, 1975
Octavia E. Butler, *Patternmaster*, 1976
Katherine Kurtz, *Deryni Rising*, 1970
Julian May, *The Many-Colored Land*, 1981

4587

EARLE WESCOTT

Winter Wolves
(New York: Bantam, 1989)

Story type: Horror (Nature in Revolt)
Major character(s): Fran Thomas, Journalist; Caroline Parker, Innkeeper
Time period(s): 1980s
Locale(s): Steel Harbor, Maine

Summary: Returning to his hometown to recover from professional and marital failures, Fran Thomas encounters a series of vicious killings supposedly carried out by a pack of ghostly wolves, as well as nightmare visions of a beautiful but terrifying seductress. This is Westcott's first novel.

Other books you might like:
Alan Ryan, *Dead White*, 1983
Jack Williamson, *Darker than You Think*, 1948

4588

MICHELLE WEST

Hunter's Death
(New York: DAW, 1996)

Story type: Fantasy (Psychic Powers; Magic Conflict)
Major character(s): Gilliam, Hunter, Nobleman; Stephen, Companion (huntbrother); Jewel, Psychic
Time period(s): Indeterminate Past
Locale(s): Averalaan, Fictional City; Essalieyan, Fictional Country

Summary: To battle the lord of Hell's influence as their god demands, Lord Gilliam and Stephen travel to Averalaan, already afflicted by the great evil.

Other books you might like:
Lynn Flewelling, *Luck in the Shadows*, 1996
Lynn Flewelling, *Stalking Darkness*, 1997
J.V. Jones, *The Baker's Boy*, 1995
Melissa Scott, *Point of Hopes*, 1995
  Lisa A. Barnett, co-author
Paula Volsky, *Illusion*, 1992

4589

MICHELLE WEST

Hunter's Oath
(New York: DAW, 1995)

Story type: Fantasy (Adventure; Psychic Powers)
Major character(s): Steven, Orphan, Companion (huntbrother); Gilliam, Hunter, Nobleman
Time period(s): Indeterminate Past
Locale(s): Breodanir, Fictional Country

Summary: The starving Steven can't believe his good fortune when he is chosen as a possible Huntbrother to Gilliam. When the time comes, he gladly takes the Oath that binds their minds, forming a completeness in the links between Gilliam, the animals, Steven, and the people of their land. Thereafter, threatened interference in those bonds by unknown forces creates great discomfort.

Other books you might like:
Robin Hobb, *Assassin's Apprentice*, 1995
Guy Gavriel Kay, *The Darkest Road*, 1986
Andre Norton, *Beast Master*, 1959
Sheri S. Tepper, *Grass*, 1989

4590

PAUL WEST

The Women of Whitechapel and Jack the Ripper
(New York; Random House, 1991)

Story type: Horror (Serial Killer)
Major character(s): Walter Sickert, Artist (painter); Dr. Gull, Doctor; Prince Albert Victor Christian Edward, Royalty (heir to the British throne)

Time period(s): 1880s (1888)
Locale(s): London, England

Summary: Walter Sickert becomes drawn into a scandal at the highest levels of British royalty when his models, prostitutes from London's West End, begin dying in a grisly fashion and the evidence points to a cover-up to protect the heir to the throne.

Other books you might like:
Robert Bloch, *Night of the Ripper*, 1984
Gardner Dozois, *Ripper!*, 1988
  Susan Casper, co-editor
Martin H. Greenberg, *Red Jack*, 1988
  Frank McSherry and Charles G. Waugh, co-editors
Marie Belloc Lowndes, *The Lodger*, 1910

4591

ROBERT WESTALL

The Call and Other Stories

(New York: Viking, 1993)

Story type: Horror (Collection)

Summary: This collection brings together six traditional ghost stories with modern settings. "Woman and Home" tells of a haunted house that engulfs its visitor, and "Uncle Otto at Denswick Park" of a gentrified British estate haunted by the ghost of its former self. In "The Badger," a poacher is haunted by the ghost of his quarry, while in the title story, a telephone crisis line is haunted every Christmas by the ghost of a murder victim. "Warren, Sharon and Darren" is a delightful fantasy that mixes fairy folk of British legend with the contemporary urban punk scene. Originally published in England in 1990.

Other books you might like:
Joan Aiken, *The Haunting of Lamb House*, 1991
John Buchan, *The Far Islands and Other Tales of Fantasy*, 1984
John Gordon, *The Burning Baby and Other Ghosts*, 1992

4592

ROBERT WESTALL

Demons and Shadows: The Ghostly Best Stories of Robert Westall

(New York: Farrar, Straus & Giroux, 1993)

Story type: Horror (Collection)

Summary: Its title notwithstanding, this book collects eleven stories, not all of which are supernatural. Mixed with wistful recollections of childhood and adolescence such as "The Making of Me" and "Night Out" are the fantasy of a child meeting with a biblical angel, "Rachel and the Angel"; the Jamesian ghost story of a churchman whose concealed perversity persists beyond the grave, "The Last Days of Dorinda Molyneux"; the story of creatures that haunt a house and drain psychic energy from its inhabitants, "The Creatures in the House"; and the story of a young boy with poetic aspirations who finds himself cursed with the ability to see the truth

in people, "The Death of Wizards." The only story original to the book is "Graveyard Shift," about a kindly cemetery keeper protected from a vampire by the revenants of his charges.

Other books you might like:
Robert Aickman, *Unsettled Dust*, 1990
Walter de la Mare, *The Collected Tales of Walter de la Mare*, 1949
John Gordon, *The Burning Baby and Other Ghosts*, 1992
E. Nesbit, *In the Dark*, 1988

4593

ROBERT WESTALL

In Camera and Other Stories

(New York: Scholastic, 1993)

Story type: Horror (Collection)

Summary: Although supposedly aimed at schoolchildren, this collection of five novellas by a modern master of the classic ghost story form, first published in 1992, will please adults too. Included are the title story, about an antique camera whose undeveloped roll of film yields secrets surrounding a possible murder committed almost half a century before; "Blind Bill," about a blind man whose other senses detect a murder in progress; the amusing "Beelzebub," in which the bride of Satan attempts to get their offspring registered with the local civil service registry office; "Charlie Ferber," about a man who transforms himself into a cat to serve as a young girl's guardian; and the tale of a haunting, "Henry Marlborough."

Other books you might like:
Robert Aickman, *Unsettled Dust*, 1990
Walter de la Mare, *The Collected Tales of Walter de la Mare*, 1949
John Gordon, *The Burning Baby and Other Ghosts*, 1992
E. Nesbit, *In the Dark*, 1988

4594

ROBERT WESTALL

Shades of Darkness: More of the Ghostly Best Stories of Robert Westall

(New York: Farrar, Strauss and Giroux, 1994)

Story type: Horror (Collection)

Summary: The 11 stories collected here come from the pen of a writer known for both his ghost stories and children's books. "The Haunting of Chas Magill" tells of a boy who learns the horrors of war from the ghost of a deceased soldier. "The Call" is about a haunted emergency phone line. "In Camera" tells of a mystery discovered and solved on the basis of film left in a camera for decades. In "The Cat, Spartan," a young boy is haunted by the ghost of his grandfather, who tries to make amends for his curmudgeonly life. "Fifty-Fafty" is about a young boy who turns people in his regular life into the monsters of his nightmares. "Woman and Home" tells of a wayward boy who stumbles upon a haunted house that destroys everyone who would exploit it. And the previously unpublished ''Cats'' tells of a married couple haunted by the ghosts of cats from the husband's earlier life.

Other books you might like:
Robert Aickman, *Unsettled Dust*, 1990
Walter de la Mare, *The Collected Tales of Walter de la Mare*, 1949
John Gordon, *The Burning Baby and Other Ghosts*, 1992
E. Nesbit, *In the Dark*, 1988

4595

DONALD E. WESTLAKE

Humans

(New York: Warner Mysterious Press, 1992)

Story type: Fantasy (Religious)
Major character(s): Ananayel, Angel; X ''Brother Rush'', Demon; Maria Elena, Musician, Agent
Time period(s): 1990s
Locale(s): New York, New York; Moscow, Union of Soviet Socialist Republics

Summary: When God becomes fed up with matters on Earth, he dispatches an angel, Ananayel, to arrange for Armageddon using human agents. Deciding that the human realm is progressing acceptably, Lucifer sends a demon, X, to interfere with Ananayel's plotting and restore free will to the involved humans.

Other books you might like:
Bradley Denton, *Buddy Holly Is Alive and Well on Ganymede*, 1991
Neil Gaiman, *Good Omens: The Nice and Accurate Prophecies of Agnes Nutter, Witch*, 1990
  Terry Pratchett, co-author
Parke Godwin, *The Snake Oil Wars*, 1989
Parke Godwin, *Waiting for the Galactic Bus*, 1988
Victor Koman, *The Jehovah Contract*, 1987
Robert Rankin, *Armageddon: The Musical*, 1990
Peter Ustinov, *The Old Man and Mr. Smith*, 1991

4596

PATRICK WHALEN

Deathwalker

(New York: Pocket, 1992)

Story type: Horror (Ancient Evil Unleashed)
Major character(s): John Winter, Spy; Erin O'Donnell, Police Officer (Police Chief of Avalon); James Spear, Businessman, Computer Expert
Time period(s): 1980s (1981)
Locale(s): Avalon, Washington

Summary: The eruption of dormant volcano Mount St. Helens awakens the Witiko, a flesh-eating demon of Ahtantum Indian legend, who was buried inside the mountain for 800 years and now yearns to turn all those whom it encounters into an army of walking dead disciples.

Other books you might like:
Douglas Clegg, *Goat Dance*, 1989
Charles L. Grant, *The Nestling*, 1982

T. Chris Martindale, *Where the Chill Waits*, 1990
G. Wayne Miller, *Thunder Rise*, 1988
Kathryn Ptacek, *Ghost Dance*, 1989

4597

PATRICK WHALEN

Night Thirst

(New York: Pocket, 1991)

Story type: Horror (Vampire Story)
Major character(s): Braille, Vampire; Gregory, Vampire; Hargrave Cutter, Doctor (surgeon)
Time period(s): 1990s
Locale(s): Seattle, Washington

Summary: The nuclear blast at the end of the author's first novel, *Monastery*, was supposed to have wiped out the vampire colony referred to as the Ancient Ones on a small island off the coast of Washington. But survivors of that blast, known as the New Ones, make it back to the mainland, where they become a seemingly indestructible scourge—and a source of interest to a government agency looking for new types of medical weapons.

Other books you might like:
Ron Dee, *Dusk*, 1991
Stephen King, *Salem's Lot*, 1975
Richard Matheson, *I Am Legend*, 1954
Robert R. McCammon, *They Thirst*, 1981

4598

PATRICK WHALEN

Out of the Night

(New York: Pocket, 1990)

Story type: Horror (Ancient Evil Unleashed)
Major character(s): John Cable, Professor, Archaeologist; Marvin Larchmont, Archaeologist; Henry Sutton, Police Officer
Time period(s): 1990s
Locale(s): Ravina, California

Summary: In 1889, the citizens of Ravina lynched six gypsy squatters whom they blamed for unexplained deaths in the town. A century later, the ancient evil the gypsies embodied is on the rampage once more, leaving a trail of dessicated corpses as proof that it is steadily regenerating it powers, to burst forth in malignant fullness.

Other books you might like:
Piers Anthony, *Firefly*, 1990
Douglas Clegg, *Goat Dance*, 1989

4599

EDITH WHARTON

The Ghost-Feeler

(Pomfret, Connecticut: Peter Owen, 1996 (dist. by Dufour Editions))

Story type: Horror (Collection)

Summary: Veteran editor Peter Haining assembles nine stories of terror and the supernatural by a Pulitzer Prize-winning author renowned for her novels of American style and manners at the turn of the century. Among the better-known stories collected here are the classic ghost tale, ''Afterwards,'' and a tale of emotional vampirism, ''Bewitched.'' Less well-known efforts include ''A Bottle of Perrier,'' a tale of madness and murder set in the African desert, and ''The Looking-Glass,'' a poignant tale of a spiritual medium. Several stories share the common theme of marital dissatisfaction that leads to desperate measures. In ''The Lady Maid's Bell,'' a ghostly maid prevents her mistress's lovers from being discovered by the woman's husband. ''The Duchess at Prayer'' is a conte cruel about the horrible fate that befalls the lover of a woman who hides beneath the altar in her chapel. ''The Fullness of Life'' is a tragic allegory of a woman who willingly acquiesces to unrequited love in the afterlife.

Other books you might like:
Cynthia Asquith, *This Mortal Coil*, 1947
Marjorie Bowen, *Kecksies and Other Twilight Tales*, 1976
Henry James, *Stories of the Supernatural*, 1949
Vernon Lee, *The Snake Lady and Other Stories*, 1954
Mary E. Wilkins-Freeman, *Collected Ghost Stories*, 1974

4600

DENNIS WHEATLEY

The Devil Rides Out

(London: Mandarin Books, 1996 (distributed by Reed Trade))

Story type: Horror (Black Magic)
Major character(s): Duke de Richlieu, Nobleman; Rex Van Ryn, Spy; Mr. Mocata, Sorcerer
Time period(s): 1930s (1934)
Locale(s): London, England

Summary: The Duke de Richlieu and his disciple, American Rex van Ryn, team up to save their friend Simon Aron from Mr. Mocata, a black magician who has ingratiated himself with the young man. Complicating the situation is Tanith, a medium to whom Rex is attracted and whom Mocato hopes to use along with Simon to obtain the powerful Talisman of Set. Originally published in 1935.

Other books you might like:
Katherine Kurtz, *Death of an Adept*, 1996
   Deborah Turner Harris, co-author
Brian Lumley, *Necroscope*, 1986
Robert Morgan, *The Things That Are Not There*, 1992
Robert Weinberg, *The Armageddon Box*, 1991
Robert Weinberg, *The Devil's Auction*, 1988

4601

DEBORAH WHEELER

Jaydium

(New York: DAW, 1993)

Story type: Science Fiction (Alternate Universe; First Contact)
Major character(s): Kithri Bloodyluck, Miner, Pilot (spaceship); Eril Trioran, Pilot (spaceship); Lennart, Spaceman

Time period(s): Indeterminate Future
Locale(s): Stayman, Planet—Imaginary

Summary: Marooned on Stayman when her father dies of a neurological, mind-destroying disease, Kithri makes her way as a Jaydium miner. Used for power and faster-than-light travel, Jaydium has become rare on the surface and must be mined from the deep, twisty natural tunnels. Although distrustful of men since her father's disappearance, Kithri's suddenly finding a partner brings hope they can mine enough Jaydium to earn passage off planet. When an accident causes Lennart to pop out of the space-time flux which had trapped him for centuries, it becomes clear that fundamental changes have occurred on Stayman. A first novel.

Other books you might like:
Gregory Benford, *Timescape*, 1980
Geary Gravel, *A Key for the Nonesuch*, 1990
Anne McCaffrey, *Crystal Singer*, 1992
Robert Reed, *Down the Bright Way*, 1990
Clifford D. Simak, *Ring Around the Sun*, 1953
Dan Simmons, *Hyperion*, 1989
George Zebrowski, *Stranger Suns*, 1991

4602

DEBORAH WHEELER

Northlight

(New York: DAW, 1995)

Story type: Science Fiction (Post-Holocaust; Political)
Major character(s): Kardith, Warrior; Terricel ''Terris'' sen'Laurea, Student, Psychic (esper); Esmelda ''Esme'', Government Official
Time period(s): Indeterminate Future
Locale(s): Laureal City, Fictional City; Northland, Fictional Country

Summary: Upset by orders forbidding her to search for her friend, Kardith comes to Laureal City in time to see the Patreos murdered. Her friend's brother, Terris, joins her search to find evidence against General Montborne, who wants more weapons development at any cost, including war between Laureal City and Northland.

Other books you might like:
Geary Gravel, *A Key for the Nonesuch*, 1990
Robert Reed, *Beyond the Veil of Stars*, 1994
John E. Stith, *Reunion on Neverend*, 1994
Sheri S. Tepper, *Grass*, 1989
George Zebrowski, *Stranger Suns*, 1991

4603

JAMES WHITE

The Galactic Gourmet

(New York: Tor, 1996)

Story type: Science Fiction (First Contact; Medical)
Series: Sector General
Major character(s): Gurronsevas, Alien (Tralthan), Cook (master chef); Prilicla, Alien (Cinrusskin), Psychic (empath); Murchison, Doctor (pathologist), Spacewoman

Time period(s): Indeterminate Future
Locale(s): Sector Twelve General Hospital, Space Station; *Rhabwar*, Spaceship (ambulance ship); Wemar, Planet—Imaginary

Summary: No longer challenged as master chef of the most renowned interspecies hotel, Gurronsevas volunteers to work at Sector General. Gurronsevas thinks that more palatable food will promote appetite and quicker patient recovery and improve staff health and morale. Unfortunately, accidents and misunderstandings force Gurronsevas to join the staff of the *Rhabwar* on its mission to Wemar.

Other books you might like:
David Brin, *Brightness Reef*, 1995
Murray Leinster, *The Med Series*, 1983
Jody Lynn Nye, *Medicine Show*, 1994
Jody Lynn Nye, *Taylor's Ark*, 1993
Larry Niven, *The Gripping Hand*, 1993
    Jerry Pournelle, co-author

4604

JAMES WHITE

The Genocidal Healer
(New York: Ballantine/Del Rey, 1991)

Story type: Science Fiction (Medical; First Contact)
Series: Sector General
Major character(s): Lioren, Doctor, Alien; O'Mara, Administrator, Psychologist
Time period(s): Indeterminate Future
Locale(s): Sector Twelve General Hospital, Space Station; Outer Space

Summary: Surgeon-Captain Lioren was in charge when his inadequate medical facilities were unable to provide a cure for the plague on a planet in his care. After being found innocent by the courts on his home world, Lioren petitioned the Monitor Corps, his employers, to re-try the case. Unwilling to lose his talents and skills, the Monitor Corps stripped him of rank and assigned him to Major O'Mara, Chief of Sector General's Interspecies Psychology Department.

Other books you might like:
Piers Anthony, *Prostho Plus*, 1973
David Brin, *Startide Rising*, 1983
David Brin, *The Uplift War*, 1987
Stephen Goldin, *Jade Darcy and the Affair of Honor*, 1988
    Mary Mason, co-author
Murray Leinster, *The Med Series*, 1983
T. Jackson King, *Retread Shop*, 1988

4605

JAMES WHITE

The Silent Stars Go By
(New York: Ballantine/Del Rey, 1991)

Story type: Science Fiction (First Contact; Alternate Universe)
Major character(s): Nolan, Doctor, Immigrant; O'Riordan, Religious; Wanachtee, Indian (Algonquin), Chieftain
Time period(s): 15th century

Locale(s): New World, Alternate Earth

Summary: When Monsignor O'Riordan, suspicious of Nolan and all non-Catholics, maroons Nolan and all the other potential troublemakers 2000 miles away from the colony site, Nolan leads the group overland to the colony. On the way, he and the others contact amphibious intelligent beings who help them get back to the main colony.

Other books you might like:
John Brunner, *Polymath*, 1974
F.M. Busby, *All These Earths*, 1978
Gordon R. Dickson, *The Lifeship*, 1976
    Harry Harrison, co-author
Colin Kapp, *The Survival Game*, 1976
John Maddox Roberts, *King of the Wood*, 1983
William Sanders, *Journey to Fusang*, 1988
L. Neil Smith, *The Crystal Empire*, 1986
Sydney J. Van Scyoc, *Deepwater Dreams*, 1991

4606

JAMES WHITE

The White Papers
(Framingham, Massachusetts: NESFA Press, 1996)

Story type: Science Fiction (Collection)

Summary: Published in conjunction with the World Science Fiction Convention, this volume contains a three-page introduction by Mike Resnick; a six-page article by Walt Willis reprinted from a conference program book; two original essays by Gary Louie, "A Sector General Timeline" and "The Classification System" with notes on categorizing extraterrestrial life forms; one original and nine stories reprinted from periodicals, anthologies, and collections published between 1959 and 1988; and 10 articles with diverse themes, often humorous, reprinted from science fiction periodicals published between 1957 and 1990. The stories include "The Secret History of Sector General," expanded from *Ambulance Ship* and three other stories set in the *Sector General* milieu, as well as one Hugo Award nominee, "Custom Fitting." Frequently light in tone, the stories' themes include medicine, intelligent extraterrestrial life forms, ghosts, life in the future, human relationships, Santa Claus, and nuclear warfare.

Other books you might like:
Lois McMaster Bujold, *Dreamweaver's Dilemma*, 1996
Emma Bull, *Double Feature*, 1994
    Will Shetterly, co-author
Joe Haldeman, *Vietnam and Other Alien Worlds*, 1993
Diana Wynne Jones, *Everard's Ride*, 1995
James H. Schmitz, *The Best of James H. Schmitz*, 1991
Cordwainer Smith, *The Rediscovery of Man*, 1993
Jane Yolen, *Storyteller*, 1992

4607

JAMES GORDON WHITE

The Nomad Queen

(New York: Leisure, 1993)

Story type: Fantasy (Quest; Adventure)
Major character(s): Sheela, Royalty (Queen of the Thorgons); Alon, Mercenary, Adventurer; Sumara, Royalty (Princess of Istwar), Mercenary
Time period(s): Indeterminate
Locale(s): Planet—Imaginary

Summary: With the help of a wizard and his demon, Sheela journeys to gain the wisdom to become Queen of her people and win back their land from invading armies. She helps Princess Sumara regain her rightful throne and both learn *noblesse oblige*. First of a series.

Other books you might like:
Jack Holland, *The Fire Queen*, 1991
Mercedes Lackey, *Arrow's Fall*, 1988
Mercedes Lackey, *Arrow's Flight*, 1987
Mercedes Lackey, *Arrows of the Queen*, 1987
Mercedes Lackey, *By the Sword*, 1991
Julie Dean Smith, *Call of Madness*, 1990

4608

MARIE ARDELL WHITE
JAMES GORDON WHITE, Co-Author

The Beast

(New York: Leisure, 1994)

Story type: Horror (Occult)
Major character(s): Diana Landers, Writer; Lionel Doyle, Professor; Jonathan Hagar, Wealthy
Time period(s): 1990s (1994)
Locale(s): Beverly Hills, California

Summary: Recovering from the gruesome death of her fiance, Diana Landers finds herself swept off her feet by the dashing Jonathan Hagar. When the forecast of a concerned psychic sends Diana probing into Jonathan's past, she begins to worry that he is a monster from another dimension overlapping ours, who engineered the death of her fiance and who has sinister plans for her as well. This is the authors' first novel.

Other books you might like:
John Byrne, *Fear Book*, 1988
D.A. Fowler, *The Book of the Damned*, 1993
Daniel H. Gower, *Harrowgate*, 1993
T. Chris Martindale, *The Voice in the Basement*, 1992
T.M. Wright, *Little Boy Lost*, 1992

4609

STEVE WHITE

Legacy

(New York: Baen, 1995)

Story type: Science Fiction (Adventure; Time Travel)

Major character(s): Robert Sarnac, Military Personnel (Solar Union Space Fleet), Time Traveller; Tiraena DiFalco, Military Personnel (Raehaniv Space Forces), Time Traveller; Tylar, Historian, Time Traveller
Time period(s): 5th century (469); 23rd century (2261)
Locale(s): *Taelarn*, Spaceship; England

Summary: After a narrow escape from the Korvaasha, an alien enemy, Lieutenant Robert Sarnac shifts through time to the 5th century where he battles alongside the legendary King Arthur. Sequel to *The Disinherited*.

Other books you might like:
Dafydd ab Hugh, *Arthur War Lord*, 1994
Dafydd ab Hugh, *Far Beyond the Wave*, 1994
Robert Asprin, *Time Scout*, 1995
    Linda Evans, co-author
David Weber, *The Armageddon Inheritance*, 1993
David Weber, *Crusade*, 1992
    Steve White, co-author
David Weber, *Insurrection*, 1990
    Steve White, co-author
David Weber, *Mutineers' Moon*, 1991

4610

WYNNE WHITEFORD

Lake of the Sun

(New York: Ace Books, 1989)

Story type: Science Fiction (First Contact)
Major character(s): Rah, Alien (Martian); Paul Russell, Scientist, Engineer
Time period(s): Indeterminate Future
Locale(s): Mars

Summary: Earthmen exploring Mars are perceived as evil invaders by the native Martians. The possibility of war seems very real.

Other books you might like:
Gregory Benford, *Tides of Light*, 1989
Janet Morris, *Target*, 1989
    David Drake, co-author
David Alexander Smith, *Rendezvous*, 1988

4611

WYNNE WHITEFORD

The Specialist

(New York: Ace, 1990)

Story type: Science Fiction (Mystery; Genetic Manipulation)
Major character(s): Lance Garrith, Journalist (star reporter, Solar News); Jack Darch, Prospector; Jocasta Borg, Cyborg, Businesswoman
Time period(s): 2090s (2095)
Locale(s): Outer Space; Mars

Summary: Lance Garrith, sent to Mars to investigate a possible extra solar probe, finds himself the target of assassination plots, and is horrified at the types of genetic manipulation he comes across. Finally out in the Martian desert, he meets the ultimate in recombinate DNA, a type designed to carry mankind to the stars. Lance is put into suspended animation. He awakens after 100 years to a very strange and alien Mars.

Other books you might like:
James Blish, *The Seedling Stars*, 1957
C.J. Cherryh, *Serpent's Reach*, 1980
James P. Hogan, *Voyage From Yesteryear*, 1982
Michael P. Kube-McDowell, *Emprise*, 1985
Michael McCollum, *Life Probe*, 1983

4612

ANDREW WHITMORE

The Fortress of Eternity
(New York: Avon, 1990)

Story type: Fantasy (Sword and Sorcery; Quest)
Major character(s): Isaf, Warrior; Pagadon Alphen Trevayne, Scholar
Time period(s): Indeterminate Past
Locale(s): Julkrease, Fictional Country

Summary: When Isaf got to town he was stopped by a fortune teller who read the cards foretelling that he would be the deciding factor in many battles, experience love, see much death and have a fearful adventure. After Trevayne came to town and introduced himself he hired Isaf to help him kill a god. This is the author's first book.

Other books you might like:
Richard A. Knaak, *Firedrake*, 1989
Elizabeth Moon, *Sheepfarmer's Daughter*, 1988
Elizabeth Moon, *Surrender None: The Legacy of Gird*, 1990
Mickey Zucker Reichert, *Dragonrank Master*, 1989
Tad Williams, *The Dragonbone Chair*, 1989
Gene Wolfe, *Soldier of Arete*, 1989

4613

LES WHITTEN

Moon of the Wolf/Progeny of the Adder
(New York: Leisure, 1992)

Story type: Horror (Collection)

Summary: This book brings together two novels that merge the tale of ambiguous horror and the police procedural by a writer largely unknown within the horror genre. *Moon of the Wolf* (originally published in 1967) tells of deputy Aaron Whitaker's investigation of a series of brutal murders in racially volatile Stanley, Mississippi, evidence of which points increasingly to the work of a werewolf. *Progeny of the Adder* (originally published in 1965) chronicles the investigations of homicide detective Harry Picard, whose sketicism toward the supernatural erodes when a serial killer with a penchant for beautiful blonde woman leaves an accumulating trail of clues that indicates he is a vampire.

Other books you might like:
L. Ron Hubbard, *Typewriter in the Sky/Fear*, 1951
Fritz Leiber, *Conjure Wife/Our Lady of Darkness*, 1991
Curt Siodmak, *Donovan's Brain/Hauser's Memory*, 1992

4614

JACK WHYTE

The Skystone
(New York: Tor Forge, 1996)

Story type: Fantasy (Legend; Adventure)
Series: Camulod Chronicles: The Forging of Arthur's Britain
Major character(s): Gaius Publius Varrus, Military Personnel (retired), Blacksmith; Caius Britannicus, Military Personnel, Leader
Time period(s): 4th century
Locale(s): England (Britain)

Summary: When invaders breach Hadrian's Wall, Caius Britannicus and his legionnaires spend the next deadly year fighting their way back to comrades in the south. Cleared of cowardice, Britannicus troops receive reassignment as the Roman Empire reasserts its authority. Discharged from service, Gaius Publius Varrus turns to work as a smith, lusting for meteoric metal to work into the finest sword steel. As the Roman Empire withdraws south, Britannicus, Varus and others work to establish a territory in Britain which will retain Roman culture and respect for law.

Other books you might like:
Màrion Zimmer Bradley, *The Forest House*, 1994
Courtway Jones, *In the Shadow of the Oak King*, 1991
Morgan Llywelyn, *Druids*, 1991
Anne McCaffrey, *Black Horses for the King*, 1996
Harry Turtledove, *Werenight*, 1994

4615

STANLEY WIATER, Editor

After the Darkness
(Baltimore, Maryland: Maclay, 1993)

Story type: Horror (Anthology)

Summary: In response to the proliferation of theme horror anthologies, the editor presents 17 stories on no specific theme, with afterwords by the authors discussing the genesis of each story. Among the best are Chet Williamson's "Perfect Days," the memoirs of an elderly serial killer; Les Daniels' "Little Green Ones," about the strange obsession a man develops for cemetery statuary; and Philip Nutman's ghost story, "Memories of Leaving Lydia." Thomas Monteleone's "Love Is the Prey" is a short story sequel to his 1987 novel *Lyrica*.

Other books you might like:
Dennis Etchison, *MetaHorror*, 1992
  editor
Charles L. Grant, *Final Shadows*, 1991
  editor
Thomas F. Monteleone, *Borderlands 3*, 1993
  editor
Chris Morgan, *Dark Fantasies*, 1989
  editor
Claudia O'Keefe, *Ghosttide*, 1993
  editor

4616

STANLEY WIATER
GAHAN WILSON, Illustrator

Mysteries of the Word

(Holyoke, Massachusetts: Crossroads Press, 1994)

Story type: Horror (Ancient Evil Unleashed)
Major character(s): Paul Henkin, Child; Mrs. Crindle, Teacher; Mr. Stiles, Principal (grade school)
Time period(s): 1990s (1994)
Locale(s): United States (The Hooker School)

Summary: Supposedly based on an urban folktale, this chapbook-length story tells of a young boy who learns a sacred word, and what his chanting of that word calls forth into the world. The booklet includes an introduction by Jack Ketchum.

Other books you might like:
Ray Bradbury, *The Halloween Tree*, 1972
Graham Masterton, *Hurry, Monster*, 1989
Gahan Wilson, *Eddy Deco's Last Caper*, 1988
Roger Zelazny, *A Night in the Lonesome October*, 1993

4617

MARIANNE WIGGINS

John Dollar

(New York: Harper & Row, 1989)

Story type: Horror (Evil Children)
Major character(s): Charlotte Lewes, Widow(er), Teacher; John Dollar, Sea Captain (Charlotte's ill-fated lover)
Time period(s): 1910s (1918)
Locale(s): Rangoon, Myanmar; Pacific Islands

Summary: Widowed by World War I, Charlotte Lewes finds new life as a schoolteacher in Rangoon and new love with John Dollar, a ship's captain. When Dollar, Charlotte, and a group of her female charges are shipwrecked on an uncharted island, Dollar is crippled, Charlotte is lost, and the girls, cast onto their own resources, revert to savagery.

Other books you might like:
J.G. Ballard, *Running Wild*, 1989
William Golding, *Lord of the Flies*, 1954

4618

KELLEY WILDE

Angel Kiss

(New York: Dell/Abyss, 1993)

Story type: Horror (Mystery)
Major character(s): Jack Pepper, Advertising (copywriter); Hank Boone, Businessman (building manager); Suki Hirazawa, Worker (in a department store)
Time period(s): 1990s (1993)
Locale(s): Atlanta, Georgia; San Francisco, California; Tokyo, Japan

Summary: An East-West dating service known as Angel Kiss is actually a front for the Makahari, a secret order of Japanese women who violate the Oriental ideal of female subservience by pulverizing their male victims to extract their life essence. In chauvinistic men like Jack Pepper and Hank Boone, the Makahari find the perfect avenue for spreading their influence across America.

Other books you might like:
Michael Cecilione, *Domination*, 1993
Gordon Linzner, *The Oni*, 1987
Bentley Little, *The Summoning*, 1993

4619

KELLEY WILDE

Makoto

(New York: Tor, 1990)

Story type: Horror (Possession)
Major character(s): Makoto Shirata Leigh, Teacher (language); Cotter Sloan, Handyman; Henry Daez, Landlord
Time period(s): 1980s (1985)
Locale(s): New York, New York

Summary: Brought to New York by wealthy advertising man Michael Leigh, Makoto Shirata is haunted by the memory of her brother's suicide, which she witnessed at age 12. Faced with massive culture shock and abused by her neighbors, landlord, sadistic husband, and the city of New York, Makoto only gradually realizes that her brother's spirit is hovering about her in the form of an *oni* (a demon), gathering strength and seeking corporeal form in order to seek revenge upon her.

Other books you might like:
Lafcadio Hearn, *Kwaidan*, 1904

4620

KELLEY WILDE

Mastery

(New York: Dell Abyss, 1991)

Story type: Horror (Vampire Story)
Major character(s): Dodge Cunningham, Detective—Private; Wolf Cotter, Journalist; Austin Blacke, Vampire
Time period(s): 1980s (1985); 1900s (1906)
Locale(s): San Francisco, California

Summary: On a train bound for the West Coast in 1985 to track the path of Halley's Comet, a diverse group of survivors from the American counterculture of the 1960s find themselves transported back in time to turn-of-the-century San Francisco. While there, they find a means for resuscitating their exhausted social consciences by helping to track down a vampire menace who has been transported back in time with them.

Other books you might like:
Jewelle Gomez, *The Gilda Stories*, 1991
Anne Rice, *The Vampire Lestat*, 1985
Brian Stableford, *The Empire of Fear*, 1988
Chelsea Quinn Yarbro, *The Saint-Germain Chronicles*, 1979-83

4621

KELLEY WILDE

The Suiting

(New York: Tor, 1989)

Story type: Horror (Possession)
Major character(s): Victor Frankl, Office Worker; Jean-Paul Bouchette, Criminal, Spirit
Time period(s): 1980s (1980)
Locale(s): Toronto, Ontario, Canada; Montreal, Quebec, Canada

Summary: Having come into possession of a gorgeous suit, Victor gradually loses his identity to its previous owner.

Other books you might like:
Ray Bradbury, *"The Wonderful Ice Cream Suit"*, 1959
    Short story

4622

CHERRY WILDER

Signs of Life

(New York: Tor, 1996)

Story type: Science Fiction (Lost Colony; Adventure)
Major character(s): Anat Asher, Military Personnel (World Space Services); Gene "Wink" Winkler, Military Personnel (World Space Services); Paddy Rork, Sailor, Young Man
Time period(s): Indeterminate Future
Locale(s): *Serendip Dana*, Spaceship; Rhomary Land, Planet—Imaginary

Summary: When the *Serendip Dana* runs into trouble, her crew and passengers make forced lifeship landings on the Rhomary Land. There, they must survive in unfamiliar terrain and make peace with the Rhomarians, descendents of another human crew stranded there many generations before. A loose sequel to *Second Nature*.

Other books you might like:
David Brin, *Glory Season*, 1993
Arthur C. Clarke, *The Songs of Distant Earth*, 1986
Nicola Griffith, *Ammonite*, 1993
James P. Hogan, *Voyage From Yesteryear*, 1982
Tricia Sullivan, *Lethe*, 1995
Amy Thomson, *The Color of Distance*, 1995

4623

KATE WILHELM

And the Angels Sing

(New York: St. Martin's, 1992)

Story type: Science Fiction (Collection)

Summary: 12 stories published 1970 to the present including one original to this volume, "The Day of the Sharks"; a Nebula Award winner from 1988, "Forever Yours, Anna"; and 10 others spanning the thematic range of the genre, with a three-page foreword by Karen Joy Fowler.

Other books you might like:
Damon Knight, *One Side Laughing: Stories Unlike Other Stories*, 1991
Pat Murphy, *Points of Departure*, 1990
Robert Sheckley, *The Collected Robert Sheckley*, 1991
    5 volumes
Michael Swanwick, *Gravity's Angels*, 1991
John Varley, *The Persistence of Vision*, 1978
Howard Waldrop, *Strange Monsters of the Recent Past*, 1991

4624

KATE WILHELM

Cambio Bay

(New York: St. Martin's Press, 1990)

Story type: Fantasy (Legend)
Major character(s): Carolyn Engleman, Businesswoman; Luisa, Innkeeper
Time period(s): 1990s
Locale(s): Cambio Bay, California

Summary: When a mudslide washes out the California freeway, a number of stranded travelers put up for the night at the mysterious Miss Luisa's Guest House on Cambio Bay. They find the bay a place of odd transformations, a place where the mythological past comes to life.

Other books you might like:
Robert Holdstock, *Lavondyss: Journey to an Unknown Region*, 1988
Robert Holdstock, *Mythago Wood*, 1985
Pat Murphy, *The Falling Woman*, 1986
Connie Willis, *Lincoln's Dreams*, 1987
Gene Wolfe, *There Are Doors*, 1988

4625

KATE WILHELM

Children of the Wind: Five Novellas

(New York: St. Martin's Press, 1989)

Story type: Science Fiction (Collection)

Summary: Four of the five stories in this collection are previously published, the best known, "The Gorgon Field" and "The Girl Who Fell into the Sky," appearing in 1985 and 1986 respectively. "A Brother to Dragons, a Companion to Owls" appeared in 1974. "The Blue Ladies," which is not science fiction, appeared in *Redbook* in 1983. "Children of the Wind" appears here for the first time.

Other books you might like:
Karen Joy Fowler, *Artificial Things*, 1986
Ursula K. Le Guin, *Buffalo Gals and Other Animal Presences*, 1987
Ursula K. Le Guin, *The Compass Rose*, 1982
Ursula K. Le Guin, *The Wind's Twelve Quarters*, 1975
Kim Stanley Robinson, *The Planet on the Table*, 1986
John Varley, *Blue Champagne*, 1986
John Varley, *The Persistence of Vision*, 1978
Connie Willis, *Fire Watch*, 1985

4626

KATE WILHELM

Naming the Flowers

(Eugene, Oregon: Pulphouse Publishing Axolotl Press, 1992)

Story type: Science Fiction (Genetic Manipulation; Romance)
Major character(s): Winston Seton, Publisher; Francie, Genetically Altered Being, Child; Jeremy Kersh, FBI Agent
Time period(s): 1990s
Locale(s): Atlantic City, New Jersey
Summary: On the beach at Atlantic City, Winston Seton briefly befriends Francie, later discovering the FBI wishes to acquire the rapidly aging child to insure that her genes remain unincorporated into the human genome. Seton arranges a place for Francie to grow up undisturbed by the FBI, then becomes romantically involved with her late in Francie's life.

Other books you might like:
Lois McMaster Bujold, *Falling Free*, 1988
Diana G. Gallagher, *The Alien Dark*, 1990
Janet Kagan, *Mirabile*, 1991
Frederik Pohl, *Stopping at Slowyear*, 1991
Cordwainer Smith, *Norstrilia*, 1975
Michael Swanwick, *Vacuum Flowers*, 1987
Michael D. Weaver, *My Father Immortal*, 1989

4627

KATE WILHELM

State of Grace

(Eugene, Oregon: Pulphouse Publishing, 1991)

Story type: Fantasy (Collection)
Series: Author's Choice Monthly
Summary: This volume contains 6 stories written between 1966 and 1988. Three related stories are "The Book of Ylin," "Jenny with Wings," and "The Downstairs Room." Two stories originally appeared in anthologies, "State of Grace," in *Orbit 19* (1977) and "Isosceles," in *Terry's Universe* (1988). Each story has a new introduction.

Other books you might like:
Charles de Lint, *Hedgework and Guessery*, 1991
Elizabeth A. Lynn, *Tales From a Vanished Country*, 1990
Spider Robinson, *True Minds*, 1990
Robert Sheckley, *Minotaur Maze*, 1990

4628

ELIZABETH WILLEY

The Price of Blood and Honor

(New York: Tor, 1996)

Story type: Fantasy (Political; Magic Conflict)
Series: Well-Favored Man
Major character(s): Prospero, Sorcerer, Royalty; Avril, Royalty, Sorcerer; Dewar, Sorcerer
Time period(s): Indeterminate
Locale(s): Landuc, Fictional Country; Argylle, Fictional Country

Summary: The long struggle between Emperor Avril and his brother, Prospero, becomes open war, which Prospero seems to be losing. Caught in the middle, Prospero's children, Freia and Dewar, try desperately to save their father, his land and his lore. Loosely based on Shakespeare's *The Tempest*.

Other books you might like:
Lisa Goldstein, *Summer King, Winter Fool*, 1994
Katherine Kurtz, *Deryni Rising*, 1970
Ellen Kushner, *Swordspoint*, 1987
Caroline Stevermer, *A College of Magics*, 1994
Martha Wells, *The Element of Fire*, 1993

4629

ELIZABETH WILLEY

A Sorcerer and a Gentleman

(New York: Tor, 1995)

Story type: Fantasy (Political; Magic Conflict)
Series: Well-Favored Man
Major character(s): Prospero, Sorcerer, Royalty; Avril, Ruler, Sorcerer; Dewar, Sorcerer
Time period(s): Indeterminate
Locale(s): Phesaotois, Fictional Country; Pheyarcet, Fictional Country

Summary: Permanently exiled from Pheyarcet, Prospero acts to overthrow his brother, Emperor Avril, and assume power. Prequel to *The Well-Favored Man: The Tale of the Sorcerer's Nephew*.

Other books you might like:
Laurell K. Hamilton, *Nightseer*, 1992
Guy Gavriel Kay, *Tigana*, 1990
Melanie Rawn, *Dragon Prince*, 1988
Martha Wells, *The Element of Fire*, 1993
Roger Zelazny, *Nine Princes in Amber*, 1970

4630

ELIZABETH WILLEY

The Well-Favored Man: The Tale of the Sorcerer's Nephew

(New York: Tor, 1993)

Story type: Fantasy (Quest; Political)
Series: Well-Favored Man
Major character(s): Gwydion, Royalty (prince), Sorcerer; Prospero, Sorcerer, Royalty
Time period(s): Indeterminate
Locale(s): Dominion of Argylle, Fictional Country

Summary: Long term absences of his father and uncle leave Prince Gwydion in charge of the Dominion of Argylle, a fate ill-appreciated by the prince. Events demand Gwydion's attention when a huge dragon takes up residence in the countryside; a mysterious woman appears, claiming sisterhood; and high-tech aliens arrive, intending to conduct a legal investigation. Author's first novel.

Other books you might like:
Steven Brust, *Jhereg*, 1983

Lois McMaster Bujold, *The Spirit Ring*, 1992
Ellen Kushner, *Swordspoint*, 1987
Paula Volsky, *Illusion*, 1992
Martha Wells, *The Element of Fire*, 1993
Roger Zelazny, *Nine Princes in Amber*, 1970

4631

A. SUSAN WILLIAMS, Editor

The Lifted Veil: The Book of Fantastic Literature by Women
(New York: Carroll & Graf, 1993)

Story type: Fantasy (Anthology)

Summary: Subtitled "The Book of Fantastic Literature by Women 1800—World War II," this volume contains a nine-page introduction, five pages of authors' biographies and 33 reprinted stories by authors contributing to World Literature of the fantastic 1806-1936. From renowned authors, the stories contain fantasy themes encompassing ghosts and other substantial apparitions, utopian societies, alternate universes with societies repressive to women and gender roles as a product of social construction. Authors include "A.M. Barnard" (Louisa May Alcott), Charlotte Bronte, Willa Cather, Isak Dinesen (Karen Blixen), George Eliot, Charlotte Perkins Gilman, Katherine Mansfield, C.L. Moore, Edith Nesbit, Mary Shelley, Harriet Beecher Stowe, Edith Wharton and Virginia Woolf.

Other books you might like:
Marjorie Agosin, *The Secret Weavers: Stories of the Fantastic by Latin American Women*, 1991
 editor
Nina Auerbach, *Forbidden Journeys: Fairy Tales and Fantasies by Victorian Women Writers*, 1992
 U.C. Knoepflmacher, co-editor
Angela Carter, *The Old Wives' Fairy Tale Book*, 1990
 editor
Richard Dalby, *Modern Ghost Stories by Eminent Women Writers*, 1991
 editor
Richard Dalby, *Victorian Ghost Stories by Eminent Women Writers*, 1991
 editor
Alison Lurie, *The Oxford Book of Modern Fairy Tales*, 1993
 editor
Jessica Amanda Salmonson, *What Did Miss Darrington See?*, 1989
 editor
Susanna J. Sturgis, *Magic Realism by Women: Dreams in a Minor Key*, 1991
 editor

4632

A. SUSAN WILLIAMS, Editor
RICHARD GLYN JONES, Co-Editor

The Penguin Book of Modern Fantasy by Women
(New York: Viking, 1995)

Story type: Fantasy (Anthology)

Summary: Contains a three-page introduction by Joanna Russ and 38 stories written in English, arranged chronologically 1941-1994 and chosen as representative of the wealth of variety expressed in fantasy. The tone ranges from dark and ironic to lighter with both traditional and modern themes explored by authors including Joan Aiken, Margaret Atwood, Leigh Brackett, Octavia E. Butler, Angela Carter, Suzy McKee Charnas, Daphne du Maurier, Carol Emshwiller, Mary Gentle, Zenna Henderson, Shirley Jackson, P.D. James, Anna Kavan, Ursula K. Le Guin, Anne McCaffrey, Vonda N. McIntyre, Joyce Carol Oates, Kit Reed, Joanna Russ, Josephine Saxton, James Tiptree Jr., Lisa Tuttle, Fay Weldon, and Kate Wilhelm.

Other books you might like:
Marjorie Agosin, *The Secret Weavers: Stories of the Fantastic by Latin American Women*, 1991
 editor
Nina Auerbach, *Forbidden Journeys: Fairy Tales and Fantasies by Victorian Women Writers*, 1992
 U.S. Knoepflmacher, co-editor
Richard Dalby, *Modern Ghost Stories by Eminent Women Writers*, 1991
 editor
Susan Shwartz, *Sisters in Fantasy*, 1995
 Martin H. Greenberg, co-editor
Susanna J. Sturgis, *Magic Realism by Women: Dreams in a Minor Key*, 1991
 editor

4633

MICHAEL WILLIAMS

Arcady
(New York: Roc, 1996)

Story type: Fantasy (Quest)
Major character(s): Solomon Hawken, Magician, Scholar
Time period(s): Indeterminate
Locale(s): Arcady, Mythical Place; Urthona, Fictional Country

Summary: When the edge of no-man's land, the Border, crosses into the family estate, Arcady, Solomon Hawken's niece vanishes into the flux. With little ability to control the magic he wields, Solomon must try to save his family and maybe the entire world.

Other books you might like:
Greg Bear, *Songs of Earth and Power*, 1994
Emma Bull, *Finder*, 1994
Charles de Lint, *Moonheart: A Romance*, 1984
Robert Holdstock, *Mythago Wood*, 1984

Michaela Roessner, *Vanishing Point*, 1993
Terri Windling, *Life on the Border*, 1991

4634

MICHAEL WILLIAMS

A Forest Lord

(New York: Warner Questar, 1991)

Story type: Fantasy (Quest)
Series: From Thief to King
Major character(s): Brenn, Adventurer; Terrance, Wizard
Time period(s): Indeterminate Past
Locale(s): Palerna, Fictional Country; Corbinwood, Fictional Country

Summary: When Brenn and Terrance escape the inhuman forces of the evil sorceress, Ravenna, they flee to Corbinwood, where they hope to enlist outlaws to help in their battle against the usurper, King Dragmond. To gain their help, Brenn must save the Forest Lord from Ravenna's curse. This book is a sequel to *A Sorcerer's Apprentice*.

Other books you might like:
Steven Brust, *Jhereg*, 1983
David Ferring, *Shadowbreed*, 1990
Katharine Kerr, *The Dragon Revenant*, 1990
Elizabeth Moon, *Surrender None: The Legacy of Gird*, 1990

4635

MICHAEL WILLIAMS

A Sorcerer's Apprentice

(New York: Popular Library/Questar, 1990)

Story type: Fantasy (Adventure)
Series: From Thief to King
Major character(s): Brenn, Thief; Terrance, Wizard
Time period(s): Indeterminate Past
Locale(s): Palerna, Fictional Country

Summary: Brenn, a teenager living in the streets of Palerna, tries to rob a house and is captured by the Mage who lives there. He chooses to stay and finds he is more than he knew. He must avoid King Dragmond's murderous fury while he learns enough to defend himself and discover his birthright.

Other books you might like:
Donald Aamodt, *A Name to Conjure With*, 1989
Orson Scott Card, *Prentice Alvin*, 1989
David Eddings, *Sorceress of Darshiva*, 1989
Jackie Hyman, *Shadowlight*, 1989
Deborah Talmadge-Bickmore, *The Apprentice*, 1990

4636

PAUL O. WILLIAMS

The Gift of the Gorboduc Vandal

(New York: Ballantine/Del Rey, 1989)

Story type: Science Fiction (Space Opera)
Major character(s): Umber Trreggerthann, Scientist, Warrior; Dame Dyann Penne, Artisan (Potter)

Time period(s): Indeterminate Future
Locale(s): Landsdrum, Planet—Imaginary

Summary: The barbarian Gorboduc Vandals attack the planet Landsdrum, demanding tribute or death. A renegade Gorboduc, Umber Trreggerthann, holds the key to defeating the invaders, but the people of Landsdrum must decide if they can trust him.

Other books you might like:
F.M. Busby, *Rissa Kerguelen*, 1976
C.S. Friedman, *In Conquest Born*, 1987
H. Beam Piper, *Space Viking*, 1963
Alis A. Rasmussen, *A Passage of Stars*, 1989

4637

RUTH L. WILLIAMS

The Silver Tree

(New York: HarperCollins, 1992)

Story type: Fantasy (Young Adult; Time Travel)
Major character(s): Michelle "Micki" Ann Silver, Child, Time Traveller
Time period(s): 1990s; 1890s (1891)
Locale(s): Madame F's Toy Museum, Mythical Place

Summary: In a magical back room of Madame F's Toy Museum, Micki unintentionally makes a regrettable wish, one which puts her very existence in jeopardy. To reverse the effects of her wish, Micki must travel to the past. Author's first book.

Other books you might like:
Bruce Coville, *Jeremy Thatcher, Dragon Hatcher*, 1991
Edward Eager, *Half Magic*, 1954
Diana Wynne Jones, *A Tale of Time City*, 1987
Will Shetterly, *Elsewhere*, 1991
Marilyn Singer, *Charmed*, 1990
Vivian Vande Velde, *A Well-Timed Enchantment*, 1990

4638

SIDNEY WILLIAMS

Gnelfs

(New York: Zebra/Pinnacle, 1991)

Story type: Horror (Child-in-Peril)
Major character(s): Heaven Davis, Child; Gabrielle Davis, Businesswoman; Terry Guillory, Child
Time period(s): 1990s
Locale(s): Riverland

Summary: Like her classmates, precocious Heaven Davis is fond of Gnelfs, the docile half gnome-half elf animated cartoon characters she watches on children's television programs. Unlike her classmates, though, Heaven's subconscious is so endowed with imaginative power that it turns the Gnelfs into creatures of flesh and blood, who torment her with threats of physical harm.

Other books you might like:
Pat Graversen, *Dollies*, 1991
William W. Johnstone, *Toy Cemetery*, 1987

Stephen King, *The Dark Half*, 1990
Gene Lazuta, *Bleeder*, 1991

4639

SIDNEY WILLIAMS

Night Brothers

(New York: Pinnacle, 1989)

Story type: Horror (Vampire Story)
Major character(s): Navarra, Vampire; Travis Dixon, Publisher (Newspaper)
Time period(s): 1980s (1868)
Locale(s): Bristol Springs, Louisiana

Summary: Revived from a watery grave by drought, the vampire Navarra uses her powers over animals to terrorize the locals while she prepares for a ritual to enhance her powers and perpetuate her race. Dixon gathers a small group of citizens to fight the menace, unaware that his wife, Alisoun, has been chosen by Navarra for her own.

Other books you might like:
Michael Paine, *Owl Light*, 1989
Jean Paiva, *Lilith*, 1989
Whitley Strieber, *The Hunger*, 1981

4640

SIDNEY WILLIAMS

When Darkness Falls

(New York: Pinnacle, 1992)

Story type: Horror (Werewolf Story)
Major character(s): Charlie Black, Teenager; Miss Nielson, Teacher (high school); Nell Devery, Student—College (art student)
Time period(s): 1990s (1992)
Locale(s): Petittville, Louisiana

Summary: Murderous packs of dogs begin terrorizing the residents of Pettitville shortly after the beautiful Miss Nielson comes to teach at the local high school, and misfit student Charlie Black has reason to believe that Miss Nielson is somehow nurturing a power within him to control them.

Other books you might like:
Charles L. Grant, *The Pet*, 1986
Stephen Gresham, *The Living Dark*, 1991
K.W. Jeter, *The Night Man*, 1990

4641

TAD WILLIAMS

Caliban's Hour

(New York: HarperPrism, 1994)

Story type: Fantasy (Legend; Horror)
Major character(s): Caliban, Monster; Miranda, Parent
Time period(s): 17th century
Locale(s): Naples, Italy; Prospero's Isle, Fictional Country

Summary: Twenty years after her father, Prospero, discovered Caliban, Caliban sneaks into Miranda's bedroom to explain his view of Prospero's actions and find vengeance for wrongs he perceives.

Other books you might like:
Jeff Collignon, *Her Monster*, 1992
Katharine Kerr, *Weird Tales From Shakespeare*, 1994
    Martin H. Greenberg, co-author
Valerie Martin, *Mary Reilly*, 1990
William Shakespeare, *The Tempest*, 1623
Clifford D. Simak, *Shakespeare's Planet*, 1976

4642

TAD WILLIAMS
NINA KIRIKI HOFFMAN, Co-Author

Child of an Ancient City

(New York: Atheneum, 1992)

Story type: Fantasy (Legend; Adventure)
Series: Dragonflight
Major character(s): Susri ''Fawn'', Child, Traveller; Vampyr, Vampire
Time period(s): Indeterminate Past
Locale(s): Caucassian Mountains, Asia

Summary: While journeying through the forest, Susri's companions tell stories all night to keep away a bothersome vampire. On the last night in the forest, the vampire approaches the group to propose a story-telling contest with potentially lethal consequences if Susri's story proves happier than the vampire's story.

Other books you might like:
Louise Cooper, *The Sleep of Stone*, 1991
Charles de Lint, *The Dreaming Place*, 1990
Jeanne Larsen, *Bronze Mirror*, 1991
Tanith Lee, *Black Unicorn*, 1991
Salman Rushdie, *Haroun and the Sea of Stories*, 1990
Robert Silverberg, *Letters From Atlantis*, 1990

4643

TAD WILLIAMS

The Dragonbone Chair

(New York, DAW, 1989)

Story type: Fantasy (Quest)
Series: Memory, Sorrow and Thorn Trilogy
Major character(s): Simon, Sorcerer, Apprentice
Time period(s): Indeterminate

Summary: Unware of his heritage, Simon begins a quest for the solution to a riddle about long-lost swords of power that are the only hope of salvation in a war fueled by the dark powers of sorcery.

Other books you might like:
Robert Jordan, *The Eye of the World*, 1990
    Book 1 - Wheel of Time
Anne McCaffrey, *Dragonriders of Pern Series*,
    1968-1986

Mervyn Peake, *Gormenghast Trilogy*,
  1946-1959
J.R.R. Tolkien, *Lord of the Rings Trilogy*,
  1954-1955

4644

TAD WILLIAMS

Stone of Farewell
(New York: DAW, 1990)

Story type: Fantasy (Quest)
Series: Memory, Sorrow and Thorn Trilogy
Major character(s): Simon, Sorcerer, Apprentice; Ineluki the Storm King, Ruler, Alien (Sithi)
Time period(s): Indeterminate
Locale(s): Osten Ard, Fictional Country

Summary: Osten Ard is besieged by trolls, Sithi, and the evil minions of the undead Ineluki. Simon and the remaining members of the League of the Scroll discover the truth of an ancient legend.

Other books you might like:
M. Coleman Easton, *Spirits of Cavern and Hearth*, 1989
Robert Jordan, *The Great Hunt*, 1990
Robert Jordan, *The Eye of the World*, 1989
Michael Scott Rohan, *The Forge in the Forest*, 1989
Robert Silverberg, *To the Land of the Living*, 1990
Robert Silverberg, *Gilgamesh the King*, 1984

4645

TAD WILLIAMS

To Green Angel Tower
(New York: DAW, 1993)

Story type: Fantasy (Magic Conflict; Quest)
Series: Memory, Sorrow and Thorn Trilogy
Major character(s): Miriamele, Royalty (princess); Simon "Seoman/Snowlock", Knight; Josua, Royalty (prince)
Time period(s): Indeterminate
Locale(s): Erkynland, Fictional Country; Hernystir, Fictional Country

Summary: As the evil minions of the undead Sithi Storm King prepare for the triumph of their dark sorceries and draw King Elias deeper into their spells, the loyal allies of Prince Josua desperately struggle to rally their forces at the Stone of Farewell. Miriamele confronts her father as the final battle between Good and Evil rages, while Sir Simon discovers his true heritage.

Other books you might like:
C.J. Cherryh, *The Tree of Swords and Jewels*, 1983
Stephen R. Donaldson, *Lord Foul's Bane*, 1977
Stephen R. Donaldson, *The Wounded Land*, 1980
David Eddings, *The Seeress of Kell*, 1991
Barbara Hambly, *The Armies of Daylight*, 1983
Katherine Kurtz, *High Deryni*, 1973
Ursula K. Le Guin, *The Farthest Shore*, 1972
J.R.R. Tolkien, *The Return of the King*, 1956

4646

WALTER JON WILLIAMS

Angel Station
(New York: Tor, 1989)

Story type: Science Fiction (Cyberpunk)
Major character(s): Ubu Roy, Pilot, Trader; Beautiful Maria, Pilot, Psychic
Time period(s): Indeterminate Future
Locale(s): *Runaway*, Spaceship; Angel Station, Space Station

Summary: Ubu Roy and Beautiful Maria, brother and sister, ply the spacelanes in their beat-up starship, always on the edge of bankruptcy, taking on cargoes too inconsequential for the major traders to waste their time on. Eventually they find what might be their big score, if they can get away with their lives.

Other books you might like:
C.J. Cherryh, *Downbelow Station*, 1981
C.J. Cherryh, *The Kif Strike Back*, 1985
C.J. Cherryh, *Merchanter's Luck*, 1982
C.J. Cherryh, *The Pride of Chanur*, 1982
C.J. Cherryh, *Rimrunners*, 1989
Bruce Sterling, *Schismatrix*, 1985

4647

WALTER JON WILLIAMS

Aristoi
(New York: Tor, 1992)

Story type: Science Fiction (Space Opera; Political)
Major character(s): Gabriel, Government Official (Aristoi), Detective—Amateur; Saigo, Government Official (Aristoi), Revolutionary
Time period(s): Indeterminate Future
Locale(s): Logarchy, Interstellar Empire/Federation (commonwealth of empires)

Summary: Alerted to Saigo's tampering with the universal data pool in hopes of covering up his own experiments, Gabriel investigates and discovers Saigo and his co-conspirators do not use their gifts to help humanity, but rather work to overturn the government which unifies diverse worlds.

Other books you might like:
Greg Bear, *Great Sky River*, 1987
David Brin, *Earth*, 1990
Glen Cook, *The Dragon Never Sleeps*, 1988
Cordwainer Smith, *The Best of Cordwainer Smith*, 1975
Cordwainer Smith, *Norstrilia*, 1975
Neal Stephenson, *Snow Crash*, 1992
Vernor Vinge, *A Fire upon the Deep*, 1992
Jack Williamson, *Mazeway*, 1990

4648

WALTER JON WILLIAMS

Days of Atonement

(New York: Tor, 1991)

Story type: Science Fiction (Mystery)
Major character(s): Loren Hawn, Police Officer (chief)
Time period(s): 21st century
Locale(s): Atocha, New Mexico

Summary: When a car crashes into Loren Hawn's office, the bullet-ridden driver lives long enough to recognize and speak to him, begging for help. Loren knew the man and had, impossibly, watched him die twenty years earlier. It quickly becomes obvious that the nearby Advanced Technologies Laboratories is involved. As he investigates, he becomes obsessed with solving the mystery surrounding the deaths.

Other books you might like:
Isaac Asimov, *The Caves of Steel*, 1954
Isaac Asimov, *The Naked Sun*, 1957
Isaac Asimov, *The Robots of Dawn*, 1983
Alan Dean Foster, *Cyber Way*, 1990
Katharine Kerr, *Polar City Blues*, 1990
Allen Steele, *Clarke County, Space*, 1990

4649

WALTER JON WILLIAMS

Facets

(New York: Tor Books, 1990)

Story type: Science Fiction (Collection)

Summary: This collection of Williams' best short fiction includes nine stories published between 1985 and 1989 in *Isaac Asimov's Science Fiction Magazine* and elsewhere. The best known story in the book is the Hugo and Nebula Award nominee ''Surfacing.'' Other excellent stories include ''Flatline,'' ''Dinosaurs,'' and ''Witness.'' Introduction by Roger Zelazny.

Other books you might like:
Greg Bear, *Tangents*, 1989
Pat Cadigan, *Patterns*, 1989
William Gibson, *Burning Chrome*, 1986
Bruce Sterling, *Crystal Express*, 1989
Roger Zelazny, *Frost and Fire*, 1989

4650

WALTER JON WILLIAMS

Metropolitan

(New York: HarperPrism, 1995)

Story type: Science Fiction (Political; Psychic Powers)
Major character(s): Aiah, Civil Servant; Constantine, Political Figure; Sorya, Revolutionary
Time period(s): Indeterminate Future
Locale(s): Fictional City; Old Shorings, Mythical Place; Mage Towers, Mythical Place

Summary: Leaving her Barkazil ghetto and her heritage for government employment, Aiah wants to work directly with the magic plasma, the lifeblood of the city, but high tuition prevents this. Believing herself confined to parceling out the stuff of power to others without the ability to touch it herself, Aiah discovers a secret gloryhole and a new life.

Other books you might like:
David Brin, *Earth*, 1990
Emma Bull, *Bone Dance*, 1991
Michael Swanwick, *Vacuum Flowers*, 1987
Joan D. Vinge, *The Snow Queen*, 1980
Roger Zelazny, *Lord of Light*, 1967

4651

WALTER JON WILLIAMS

Rock of Ages

(New York: Tor, 1995)

Story type: Science Fiction (Humor; Mystery)
Series: Drake Maijstral
Major character(s): Roman, Servant; Drake Maijstral, Thief, Nobleman (duke); Roberta Altunin, Noblewoman (duchess)
Time period(s): Indeterminate Future
Locale(s): Fort Worth, Texas (Tejas); Cozumel Reef, Caribbean; Graceland, Tennessee

Summary: While Drake Maijstral, Duke of Dornier and Allowed Burglar, wants only a nice, safe holiday on historic old Earth, he finds instead a succession of challenges to duels, multiple marriage proposals, and entanglements with the Church of Elvis.

Other books you might like:
Steven Brust, *The Phoenix Guards*, 1991
Fritz Leiber, *Swords and Deviltry*, 1970
Terry Pratchett, *The Colour of Magic*, 1983
Allen Steele, *Clarke County, Space*, 1990
John Varley, *Demon*, 1984

4652

WALTER JON WILLIAMS

Solip: System

(Eugene, Or: Axolotl Press, 1989)

Story type: Science Fiction (Cyberpunk)
Major character(s): Reno, Revolutionary, Disembodied Personality; Mercedes Calderon, Businesswoman, Abuse Victim
Time period(s): 21st century
Locale(s): Earth Orbit, Outer Space

Summary: In *Hardwired* a desperate group of cyborged revolutionaries managed to fight off the avaricious Orbital corporations intent on taking control of Earth. Now Reno, one of the heroes of that earlier battle, his body destroyed, has been implanted in the mind of the depraved Orbital corporate executive Albrecht Roon. Reno's mission is to use Roon's authority to destroy the Orbitals for good.

Other books you might like:
William Gibson, *Count Zero*, 1985
William Gibson, *Mona Lisa Overdrive*, 1988
William Gibson, *Neuromancer*, 1984
Bruce Sterling, *Islands in the Net*, 1988
Bruce Sterling, *Schismatrix*, 1985
Dave Wolverton, *On My Way to Paradise*, 1989

4653
WALTER JON WILLIAMS

Wall, Stone, Craft
(Portland, Oregon: Axolotl/Pulphouse, 1993)

Story type: Horror (Literary)
Major character(s): Percy Bysshe Shelley, Writer (poet); Mary Wollstonecraft, Writer; George Gordon, Nobleman (Lord Newstead)
Time period(s): 1810s
Locale(s): Le Caillou, France

Summary: In this alternate history, the author imagines how the relationship between Percy Bysshe Shelley and Lord Byron would have differed had Byron not been a poet but a soldier responsible for the capture of Napoleon, and how the difference would have influenced the writing of Mary Shelley's *Frankenstein*.

Other books you might like:
Emmanuel Carrere, *Gothic Romance*, 1990
Tim Powers, *On Stranger Tides*, 1987
Tim Powers, *The Stress of Her Regard*, 1989
Kathryn Ptacek, *In Silence Sealed*, 1988
Paul West, *Lord Byron's Doctor*, 1989

4654
CHET WILLIAMSON

Dreamthorp
(Arlington Heights, Illinois: Dark Harvest, 1989)

Story type: Horror (Ancient Evil Unleashed)
Major character(s): Tom Brewer, Artisan, Widow(er); Laura Stark, Young Woman
Time period(s): 1980s
Locale(s): Dreamthorpe, Pennsylvania

Summary: When an Indian gravesite is disturbed, spirits are released which gradually decimate the village of Dreamthorpe. At the same time, Laura Stark is pursued across the country by a vengeful serial killer. Thus, both old evil and recent malevolence meet and culminate in Dreamthorpe.

Other books you might like:
John Farris, *The Axman Cometh*, 1989
Peter Straub, *Floating Dragon*, 1982

4655
CHET WILLIAMSON

Mordenheim
(Lake Geneva, Wisconsin: TSR, 1994)

Story type: Horror (Reanimated Dead)
Series: Ravenloft
Major character(s): Victor Mordenheim, Doctor; Friedrich Kreutzer, Writer (poet and necromancer); Hilda Von Karlsfeld, Teacher (necromancer)
Time period(s): Indeterminate
Locale(s): Ravenloft, Fictional Country

Summary: Victor Mordenheim summons two apprentice necromancers to his Gothic castle to assist him in the soul transference that will reanimate the personality of his beloved dead wife. But Adam, the monster whom Mordenheim created from dead body parts, absconds with her body out of jealousy, forcing the necromancers to undertake a perilous journey across a landscape fraught with supernatural dangers. Based on the Ravenloft game.

Other books you might like:
Elaine Bergstrom, *Tapestry of Dark Souls*, 1993
P.N. Elrod, *I, Strahd*, 1993
Christie Golden, *Dance of the Dead*, 1992
J. Robert King, *Carnival of Fear*, 1993
Mary Shelley, *Frankenstein*, 1818

4656
CHET WILLIAMSON

Murder in Cormyr
(Lake Geneva, Wisconsin: TSR, 1996)

Story type: Fantasy (Mystery)
Series: Forgotten Realms
Major character(s): Jasper, Servant, Student; Benelaius, Wizard (war, retired); Lindavar, Wizard (war)
Time period(s): Indeterminate
Locale(s): Cormyr, Fictional Country; Gahrs, Fictional City

Summary: Benelaius volunteers his servant, ex-apprentice, and himself to solve the murder of Dovo, who had been impersonating a ghost. Before they can complete the task, Grodoveth, the king's representative, becomes the next victim, giving them one less suspect and giving more credence to the idea that the ghost still protects his hidden treasure.

Other books you might like:
Steven Brust, *Jhereg*, 1983
Glen Cook, *Pretty Pewter Gods*, 1995
Pamela Dean, *The Dubious Hills*, 1994
Simon R. Green, *Hawk & Fisher*, 1996
Daniel Hood, *Fanuilh*, 1994

4657

CHET WILLIAMSON

Reign

(Arlington Heights, Illinois: Dark Harvest, 1990)

Story type: Horror (Doppelganger)
Major character(s): Dennis Hamilton, Actor, Producer; Ann Deems, Widow(er); Dan Munro, Police Officer (police chief)
Time period(s): 1990s (1991)
Locale(s): Kirkland, Pennsylvania

Summary: After renovating the Venetian Theatre, Dennis Hamilton plans to open the first season with *A Private Empire*, the play in which he achieved notoriety. A series of inexplicable deaths among the actors and technical crew prove only a prelude to Dennis' confrontation with "The Emperor," the character whom he turned into a star role now come to life.

Other books you might like:
Clive Barker, *Sex, Death and Starshine*, 1984
  Clive Barker's Books of Blood, Vol. 2
Stephen King, *The Dark Half*, 1989
Fritz Leiber, *Four Ghosts in Hamlet*, 1984
  in *The Ghost Light*

4658

CHET WILLIAMSON

Second Chance

(Baltimore: CD Publications, 1994)

Story type: Horror (Psychological Suspense)
Major character(s): Woody Robinson, Musician; Tracy Zempelios Robinson, Housewife; Keith "Pan" Aarons, Terrorist
Time period(s): 1990s (1993); 1960s (1969)
Locale(s): Iselin, Pennsylvania; Bone, Texas

Summary: Woody Robinson's sixties nostalgia party inadvertently sends its participants back in time long enough for them to snatch back to the present friends who died in 1969 as a result of their radical idealism. Among the retrieved, however, is an unrepentant radical who becomes an ecoterrorist who will stop at nothing—even the destruction of the world as we know it—to draw attention to his cause.

Other books you might like:
Douglas Clegg, *Dark of the Eye*, 1994
Stephen King, *Firestarter*, 1980
Joe R. Lansdale, *Savage Season*, 1989
Lewis Shiner, *Glimpses*, 1993

4659

J.N. WILLIAMSON

The Black School

(New York: Dell, 1989)

Story type: Horror (Child-in-Peril)

Major character(s): Michael Scott, Parent, Teacher; Jacob Weir, Teacher (Homunculus)
Time period(s): 1980s
Locale(s): United States; Scotland; Hell

Summary: The Devil kidnaps Scott's daughter, Jill, to hold hostage in a school in Hell until Michael produces a book belonging to Old Nick. With homunculus friend Weir, he locates the door to Hell in Scotland, fights off demons and black knights, and goes underground to rescue Jill.

Other books you might like:
Dan Simmons, *Song of Kali*, 1985

4660

J.N. WILLIAMSON

Bloodlines

(Stamford, Connecticut: Longmeadow Press, 1994)

Story type: Horror (Vampire Story)
Major character(s): Marshall Madison, Vampire; Thaddie Madison, Child (Marshall's son); Jake Spencer, Taxi Driver
Time period(s): 1990s (1994)
Locale(s): New York, New York

Summary: The son of a vampire, Thaddie Madison flees his foster parents to squat in an abandoned New York City hotel and ponder his heritage. His disappearance pits two parties of searchers against one another: the goodhearted parents who have adopted his sister Caroline, and his father, who will stop at nothing to reclaim a blood descendant.

Other books you might like:
Poppy Z. Brite, *Lost Souls*, 1992
Scott Ciencin, *Parliament of Blood*, 1992
Scott Ciencin, *The Vampire Odyssey*, 1992
Scott Ciencin, *The Wildlings*, 1992
Pat Graversen, *Sweet Blood*, 1992
Dan Simmons, *Children of the Night*, 1992

4661

J.N. WILLIAMSON

The Book of Webster's

(Stamford, Connecticut: Longmeadow Press, 1993)

Story type: Horror (Serial Killer)
Major character(s): Dell, Drifter; Kee, Teenager; Kirk Douglas, Detective
Time period(s): 1990s (1993)
Locale(s): Cherokee Rose, Georgia

Summary: Convinced that he has been instructed by Webster's Dictionary to kill, Dell and his teenage companion, Kee, go on a murder rampage across the American South, tailed by detective Kirk Douglas, who desperately hopes to bring them to justice. This novel was expanded from a 1986 short story.

Other books you might like:
Billie Sue Mosiman, *Night Cruise*, 1992
John Shirley, *Wetbones*, 1992

4662

J.N. WILLIAMSON

The Fifth Season

(Seattle, Washington: A E Press, 1993)

Story type: Horror (Collection)

Summary: This chapbook collects eight stories, one original to the volume, by one of the genre's more prolific writers. "Cycles," "Troth," and "Free Among the Dead" all explore the boundary between life and death. "Townkiller" is narrated from the point of view of a homicidal maniac. Both "Watchwolf" and "Mercy" serve up poetically just retributions for their point-of-view characters. And "I'll Give You Magic If You'll Give Me Love" became the basis for the author's novel of a young boy trapped in the horror of a dysfunctional family, *Don't Take Away the Light* (1993). James Kisner supplies an introduction.

Other books you might like:
Edward Lee, *Edward Lee's Quest for Sex, Truth and Reality*, 1992
William F. Nolan, *Things Beyond Midnight*, 1984
William Relling Jr., *The Infinite Man and Other Stories*, 1990

4663

J.N. WILLIAMSON, Editor

Masques IV

(Baltimore, Maryland: Maclay, 1991)

Story type: Horror (Anthology)

Summary: Twenty-five original stories and one classic reprint by both new and well-recognized authors. Included are two stories of nature in revolt, Chet Williamson's "The Pack" and Gahan Wilson's "Sea Gulls"; F. Paul Wilson's sardonic tale of a female avenger, "Please Don't Hurt Me"; Ray Russell's glib study of a punk rock band, "The Collapse of Civilization"; Dan Simmons' satiric tale of personal shortcoming made flesh, "My Private Memoirs of the Hoffer Stigmata Pandemic"; and Steve Allen's story of a near-death experience, "The Secret."

Other books you might like:
Dennis Etchison, *Cutting Edge*, 1986
Thomas F. Monteleone, *The Borderlands Series*, 1990-1992

4664

J.N. WILLIAMSON

The Monastery

(New York: Zebra, 1992)

Story type: Horror (Black Magic)
Major character(s): Dean Knight, Parent; Noel Night, Parent; Kevin Night, Child (Dean & Noel's 12-year-old son)
Time period(s): 1990s (1992)
Locale(s): Noblesville, Indiana; Neva Monastery, Indiana

Summary: After plowing their car into a snowdrift on the back roads of Indiana, the Knight family takes refuge in Neva Monastery, unaware that they have landed in the home of the Radenyi, a cult that uses ritual torture and sacrifice to summon its god.

Other books you might like:
Edward Lee, *Incubi*, 1991

4665

J.N. WILLIAMSON

The Naked Flesh of Feeling

(Eugene, Oregon: Pulphouse, 1991)

Story type: Horror (Collection)
Series: Author's Choice Monthly

Summary: Seven stories by one of the most prolific authors in the horror genre, ranging in approach from "Public Places," about a monster that lurks in a public toilet, to "They Never Even See Me" and "Aspirations," which straddle the boundary between mystery and horror. The author has supplied an introduction and explanatory headnotes.

Other books you might like:
William F. Nolan, *Things Beyond Midnight*, 1984

4666

J.N. WILLIAMSON

The Night Seasons

(New York: Zebra, 1991)

Story type: Horror (Nature in Revolt)
Major character(s): Richard Stenvall, Writer; Doc Kinsey, Prisoner; Noble Ellair, Doctor
Time period(s): 1990s
Locale(s): Indianapolis, Indiana

Summary: While sleeping off a binge in the drunk tank at the local penitentiary, failed writer Richard Stenvall, along with his fellow prisoners, becomes part of an experiment carried out by prison physician Noble Ellair—one that entails unleashing carnivorous plants within the closed environment of the prison. This novel was expanded from a shorter version written in 1986.

Other books you might like:
Robert Charles, *Flowers of Evil*, 1982
John Wyndham, *The Day of the Triffids*, 1951

4667

JACK WILLIAMSON

Beachhead

(New York: Tor, 1992)

Story type: Science Fiction (Adventure)
Major character(s): Sam Houston Kelligan, Astronaut, Heir (Kelligan Enterprises); Jayne Ryan, Astronaut, Scientist
Time period(s): 2000s
Locale(s): Fort Worth, Texas; *Ares*, Spaceship; Mars

Summary: Following a childhood dream, Sam finally becomes a crew member of the first Mars expedition, despite his family's disapproval. Rumor of a Martian disease almost forces the project into bankrupcy before *Ares* can reach Mars. When Kelligan Enterprises' investment forces contact the spaceship, Earth learns Sam and Jayne made the first descent and have been out of contact since their parachute deployed.

Other books you might like:
Terry Bisson, *Voyage to the Red Planet*, 1990
Robert L. Forward, *Martian Rainbow*, 1991
Robert A. Heinlein, *Red Planet*, 1949
Charles Sheffield, *Cold as Ice*, 1992
Dana Stabenow, *Second Star*, 1991
Allen Steele, *Lunar Descent*, 1991

4668

JACK WILLIAMSON

Darker than You Think

(New York: Macmillan Collier Nucleus, 1989)

Story type: Horror (Werewolf Story)
Major character(s): Will Barbee, Journalist; April Bell, Werewolf
Time period(s): 1940s
Locale(s): Clarendon, Midwest (A city somewhere in Mid-America)

Summary: Will Barbee is torn between his attraction to a beautiful seductress/werewolf and his loyalty to his old werewolf-fighting university comrades as they all wait with anticipation or trepidation for the identification and return of the Child of Night, a superior werewolf who will attempt to lead *Homo lycanthropus* to victory over man in the evolutionary struggle. Originally published in 1948.

Other books you might like:
Charles L. Grant, *The Dark Cry of the Moon*, 1986
Thomas Tessier, *The Nightwalker*, 1979
Chelsea Quinn Yarbro, *The Godforsaken*, 1983

4669

JACK WILLIAMSON

Demon Moon

(New York: Tor, 1994)

Story type: Science Fiction (Lost Colony)
Major character(s): Zorn ir Var, Heir—Dispossessed, Fugitive; Lyrane lo Lyrane, Student; Argoth Ayth, Religious, Magician
Time period(s): Indeterminate Future
Locale(s): Planet—Imaginary

Summary: From his exiled parents Zorn learns of the heritage stolen by his uncle Thorg's treachery. Later, with his father imprisoned and the red light of the demon moon in the sky, he sets out to find the legendary Dragonshield once wielded by his ancestor, Nuradoon, to save the world from the demons of the god Xath. But when Zorn and his unlikely allies meet the demons, they learn a startling truth about the world and its origins.

Other books you might like:
Marion Zimmer Bradley, *Rediscovery: A Novel of Darkover*, 1993
  Mercedes Lackey, co-author
Orson Scott Card, *The Memory of Earth*, 1992
C.J. Cherryh, *Angel with the Sword*, 1985
Anne McCaffrey, *Dragonflight*, 1968
Robert Silverberg, *Kingdoms of the Wall*, 1993

4670

JACK WILLIAMSON

The Humanoids

(New York: Tor Orb, 1996)

Story type: Science Fiction (Robot Fiction; Dystopian)
Major character(s): Frank Ironsmith, Engineer; Clay Forester, Scientist, Engineer (rhodomagnetic); Underhill, Engineer
Time period(s): 120th century; Indeterminate Future
Locale(s): Two Rivers, Fictional City; Interstellar Empire/Federation; Planet—Imaginary

Summary: As mechanical servants begin to help people to survive and thrive as they determine best, some people rebel against the benign invasion of the aggressively helpful humanoids. Later, a philosopher organizes a small assault team with unique abilities, intending to overturn humanoid control. Includes "With Folded Hands" (1947) and *The Humanoids* (1949).

Other books you might like:
Roger MacBride Allen, *The Ring of Charon*, 1990
Isaac Asimov, *The Foundation Trilogy*, 1982
Isaac Asimov, *Robots and Empire*, 1985
Paul J. McAuley, *Red Dust*, 1994
A.E. van Vogt, *The Weapon Makers*, 1946
A.E. van Vogt, *The Weapon Shops of Isher*, 1951
John Varley, *Steel Beach*, 1992

4671

JACK WILLIAMSON

Mazeway

(New York: Ballantine/Del Rey, 1990)

Story type: Science Fiction (Post-Holocaust)
Major character(s): Benn Dain, Explorer, Student; Roxane Kwan, Wanderer (Nomad)
Time period(s): Indeterminate Future
Locale(s): Earth; Oort Cloud, Outer Space

Summary: After the disaster which destroyed Earth's technological society, the survivors have become nomadic hunter gatherers. One family of humans has been transported to the Oort Cloud as a reward for eliminating a potential threat. Unfortunately, it is too late to save Earth's technology. While there, the family's only son is being trained to understand the aliens and demonstrate that humans are ready for space.

Other books you might like:
Roger MacBride Allen, *The Ring of Charon*, 1990
David Brin, *The Uplift War*, 1987

Larry Niven, *Footfall*, 1985
   Jerry Pournelle, co-author
John Varley, *The Ophiuchi Hotline*, 1977
Roger Zelazny, *This Immortal*, 1989

4672

CONNIE WILLIS

Doomsday Book

(New York: Bantam Spectra, 1992)

Story type: Science Fiction (Time Travel; Disaster)
Major character(s): Kivrin Engle, Student, Time Traveller; James Dunworthy, Professor; Father Roche, Religious (priest)
Time period(s): 21st century; 14th century (1348)
Locale(s): Oxfordshire, England

Summary: Intending to observe everyday life in 1320, Kivrin travels into the past, immediately suffering illness and amnesia. After a plague strikes Oxford causing its quarantine, Kivrin discovers that she arrived in 1348, the year of the Black Death. As the plague spreads throughout Oxfordshire, Kivrin's immunizations allow her to survive while awaiting help from friends working in the future.

Other books you might like:
Katherine Kurtz, *The Harrowing of Gwynedd*, 1989
Richard Meredith, *Run, Come See Jerusalem*, 1976
Robert Silverberg, *The Gate of Worlds*, 1967
Robert Charles Wilson, *A Bridge of Years*, 1991
Chelsea Quinn Yarbro, *Time of the Fourth Horseman*, 1976

4673

CONNIE WILLIS

Impossible Things

(New York: Bantam Spectra, 1994)

Story type: Science Fiction (Collection)

Summary: Contains a six-page introduction by Gardner Dozois and 11 stories reprinted from periodicals and anthologies 1986-1992 with one Nebula Award winning story, "At the Rialto," and two stories which won both Nebula and Hugo Awards, "The Last of the Winnebagos" and "Even the Queen." Willis focuses on people, frequently using insightful humor with a prickly kernel which appears after reflection. Themes include political correctness, small town life, hard science, the end of the world and one Shakespeare conspiracy.

Other books you might like:
Alfred Bester, *Star Light, Star Bright*, 1976
Cordwainer Smith, *The Rediscovery of Man*, 1993
Marc Stiegler, *The Gentle Seduction*, 1990
Theodore Sturgeon, *The Ultimate Egoist*, 1994
John Varley, *Blue Champagne*, 1986

4674

CONNIE WILLIS
CYNTHIA FELICE, Co-Author

Light Raid

(New York: Ace, 1989)

Story type: Science Fiction (Young Adult)
Major character(s): Helene Ariadne, Student; Helene Medea, Scientist
Time period(s): 21st century
Locale(s): Denver Springs, Colorado; Canada

Summary: As the fragmented nations of what was once the United States and Canada wage war with massive laser assaults from orbiting weapons platforms, young Helene Ariadne tries to unravel a complex plot to undermine part of her nation's weapons capability, a plot in which her mother may be involved.

Other books you might like:
Ben Bova, *The Kinsman Saga*, 1987
John Christopher, *The Tripods Trilogy*, 1980

4675

CONNIE WILLIS, Editor
MARTIN H. GREENBERG, Co-Editor

The New Hugo Winners, Volume III

(New York: Baen, 1994)

Story type: Science Fiction (Anthology)
Series: Hugo Winners

Summary: Contains a three-page introduction by the editor plus individual introductions to nine stories given Science Fiction Achievement Awards, so-called "Hugo Awards," by voting members of World Science Fiction Conventions 1989-1991. Authors include Lois McMaster Bujold, Suzy McKee Charnas, George Alec Effinger, Joe Haldeman, Mike Resnick and Robert Silverberg.

Other books you might like:
Isaac Asimov, *The Hugo Winners 1-5*, 1962-1986
   editor
Isaac Asimov, *Isaac Asimov Presents the Great SF Stories: 1-25*, 1979-1992
   Martin H. Greenberg, co-editor
Michael Bishop, *Nebula Awards 24*, 1990
   editor
Michael Bishop, *Nebula Awards 25*, 1991
   editor
James Morrow, *Nebula Awards 26*, 1992
   editor

4676

CONNIE WILLIS

Remake

(New York: Bantam Spectra, 1995)

Story type: Science Fiction (Satire; Mystery)

Major character(s): Alis, Actress, Historian (film history); Tom, Filmmaker, Editor
Time period(s): 21st century
Locale(s): Hollywood, California

Summary: Hired to delete politically incorrect references to substance abuse, such as alcohol intoxication, from classic Hollywood films in Viamount vaults, Tom meets Alis, fresh from film school and hoping to dance in a musical. When Tom finds Alis' image appearing in the background of well-known films, he suspects improper digital insertion of her image. However, his investigation forces him to consider that she uses time travel to further her obsessive goal.

Other books you might like:
David Brin, *Earth*, 1990
Pat Cadigan, *Synners*, 1991
Jack Finney, *Time and Again*, 1970
Marjorie Bradley Kellogg, *Harmony*, 1991
Lisa Mason, *Summer of Love*, 1994
Lewis Shiner, *Glimpses*, 1993

4677

CONNIE WILLIS

Uncharted Territory

(New York: Bantam Spectra, 1994)

Story type: Science Fiction (Humor)
Major character(s): Bult, Alien; Sarah "Fin" Finriddy, Scientist, Explorer; Aloysius Byron Carson, Scientist, Explorer
Time period(s): Indeterminate Future
Locale(s): Boohte, Planet—Imaginary

Summary: Finriddy and Carson's job of mapping the primitive world Boohte means facing dust storms, cantankerous mounts, nitpicking bureaucrats and venomous animals. Back home, millions watch a highly romanticized version of their exploits in the DHT series. One of their fans, a young socioexobiologist specializing in sex, joins them on their latest mapping expedition into uncharted territory, with hilarious results.

Other books you might like:
Poul Anderson, *Earthman's Burden*, 1957
  Gordon R. Dickson, co-author
Poul Anderson, *Hoka!*, 1983
  Gordon R. Dickson, co-author
John M. Ford, *How Much for Just the Planet?*, 1987
Keith Laumer, *Retief at Large*, 1978
Terry Pratchett, *Moving Pictures*, 1992

4678

THOMAS WILOCH

Mr. Templeton's Toyshop: Prose Poems & Short Fiction

(La Grande, Oregon: Jazz Police Books, 1995)

Story type: Horror (Collection)

Summary: Forty-five prose poems and brief tales elaborate the private hells and uncanny experiences that the author's un-

common characters endure. "The Mystical Intention" describes the fate of someone who is too sympathetic towards the sensuality of his environment. "Marionettes," "The Terrible Secret," and "Puppets Holding Mirrors" draw disturbing comparisons between human beings and puppets controlled by uncaring puppetmasters. The title piece, a series of nine vignettes about a toyshop whose customers become the playthings of its eerie proprietor, conjures the vision of a mechanistic universe in which we are all the playthings of a sadistic overseer.

Other books you might like:
Thomas Ligotti, *The Agonizing Resurrection of Victor Frankenstein and Other Gothic Tales*, 1994
Thomas Ligotti, *Noctuary*, 1994
Bruno Schulz, *The Street of Crocodiles*, 1934
Steve Rasnic Tem, *Celestial Inventory*, 1991

4679

COLIN WILSON

The Delta

(New York: Ace Books, 1989)

Story type: Science Fiction (Invasion of Earth)
Series: Spider World
Major character(s): Niall, Psychic, Revolutionary
Time period(s): Indeterminate Future
Locale(s): Earth

Summary: Giant intelligent spiders and other mutant fauna and flora now control the Earth. Humanity lives like vermin. The rebel Niall and his intrepid followers enter the Delta looking for the secret that may free humanity from the spiders.

Other books you might like:
Gregory Benford, *Great Sky River*, 1987
Rob Chilson, *Men Like Rats*, 1989
Thomas M. Disch, *Mankind under the Leash*, 1966
David Gerrold, *A Rage for Revenge*, 1989
Joan Slonczewski, *The Wall Around Eden*, 1989
Tim Sullivan, *The Parasite War*, 1989
H.G. Wells, *The War of the Worlds*, 1898

4680

DAVID HENRY WILSON

The Coachman Rat

(New York: Carroll & Graf, 1989)

Story type: Fantasy (Legend)
Major character(s): Robert, Animal (Rat; Cinderella's coachman); Devlin, Scientist
Time period(s): Indeterminate
Locale(s): Fictional Country

Summary: The story of Cinderella, from the rat's eyes, is continued beyond "happily ever after" to show a bloody palace coup. Dark and grim, this is not for children.

Other books you might like:
Raymond E. Feist, *Faerie Tale*, 1988
K.W. Jeter, *Soul Eater*, 1983

4681

DAVID NIALL WILSON
MICHAEL GRILLA, Illustrator

The Fall of the House of Escher and Other Illusions

(Norfolk, Virginia: Macabre, Inc., 1995)

Story type: Horror (Collection)

Summary: This first story collection by a small press magazine editor brings together seven tales of horror with mystical and religious overtones. In the title story, a riff on Edgar Allan Poe's "The Fall of the House of Usher," a man develops an acute aesthetic sensitivity that allows him to penetrate into other dimensions. "A Candle Lit in Sunlight," "On the Third Day," and "The Road to Damascus" all find horrific potential in the iconography of Christianity. "Yours the Vengeance" and "Sparkling Eyes" are both environmentally conscious tales of fantasy. Hugh B. Cave supplies an introduction.

Other books you might like:

Kevin J. Anderson, *Shifting the Boundaries: The Selected Works of Kevin J. Anderson*, 1995
Michael A. Arnzen, *Needles and Sins*, 1994
Brian Hopkins, *Something Haunts Us All*, 1995
Albert J. Manachino, *The Odd Lot: The Selected Works of Albert J. Manachino*, 1993
Elizabeth Massie, *Southern Discomfort: Selected Works of Elizabeth Massie*, 1993
Ardath Mayhar, *Mean Little Old Lady at Work*, 1994
Stephen Mark Rainey, *Fugue Devil and Other Weird Horrors*, 1992

4682

F. PAUL WILSON

The Barrens

(Newark, New Jersey: Wildside Press, 1992)

Story type: Horror (Ancient Evil Unleashed)
Major character(s): Kathleen MacKelston, Accountant; Jonathan Creighton, Psychologist; Jasper Mulliner, Farmer
Time period(s): 1990s (1992)
Locale(s): Pine Barrens, New Jersey

Summary: In this story strongly influenced by the writings of H. P. Lovecraft, Kathleen MacKelston agrees to help her old lover, Jonathan Creighton, investigate the legend of the Jersey Devil as part of the research for his doctoral thesis. But the pair discover that there is more truth to the legend than they thought, and that the Jersey Devil represents only a shadow of the threat to human life posed by the dimension from which it has come. Originally published in 1990.

Other books you might like:

Edward P. Berglund, *Disciples of Cthulhu*, 1975
Michael Shea, *The Colour out of Time*, 1984
Brian Stableford, *The Innsmouth Heritage*, 1992
Steve Rasnic Tem, *Decoded Mirrors: Three Tales after Lovecraft*, 1992

Robert Weinberg, *Lovecraft's Legacy*, 1990
Martin Greenberg, co-editor

4683

F. PAUL WILSON, Editor

Diagnosis: Terminal

(New York: Tor, 1996)

Story type: Horror (Anthology)

Summary: Subtitled "An Anthology of Medical Terror," this compilation brings together 14 original nonsupernatural stories centered around the medical profession. Bill Pronzini's "Angel of Mercy" and Matthew Costello's "Friendly Wager" feature physician serial killers. Chet Williamson's "Doctor Joe" tells of a doctor who kills terminal patients for their insurance settlements in order to subsidize the needy patients in his practice. Ridley Pearson's "All Over but the Dying" is a tale of medical revenge, and Tina L. Jens' "The Cuban Solution" a tale of scientific paranoia in which physicians spread disease through refugees returned to Cuba in order to destabilize the government. F. Paul Wilson in "Offshore" and Ed Gorman in "Survival" envision futures where scarce medical resources create a terrifying competition among patients.

Other books you might like:

Groff Conklin, *Great Science Fiction about Doctors*, 1963
editor
Stephen Jones, *The Mammoth Book of Frankenstein*, 1995
editor
Stuart David Schiff, *Mad Scientists*, 1980
editor
Karl Edward Wagner, *Intensive Scare*, 1989
editor

4684

F. PAUL WILSON

Dydeetown World

(New York: Baen Books, 1989)

Story type: Science Fiction (Cyberpunk)
Major character(s): Sigmund Dreyer, Detective—Private; Jean Harlow-c, Clone
Time period(s): Indeterminate Future
Locale(s): Dydeetown, New York (A corrupt bluelight district)

Summary: Dreyer, a cynical, down on his luck, but basically decent private eye in the tradition of Sam Spade, is hired by the clone of an ancient movie star to find a missing person, and finds himself at the center of a complex web of intrigue and murder.

Other books you might like:

Richard Bowker, *Dover Beach*, 1987
George Alec Effinger, *When Gravity Fails*, 1987
Victor Koman, *The Jehovah Contract*, 1987

4685

F. PAUL WILSON, Editor

Freak Show

(New York: Pocket Books, 1992)

Story type: Horror (Anthology; Carnival/Circus Horror)

Summary: In this second collection of stories sponsored by the Horror Writers of America, editor Wilson has woven eighteen stories by diverse hands into a single shared-world novel concerned with the Peabody-Ozymandias Traveling Circus and Oddity Emporium, a traveling freak show assembling a machine along every stop on its itinerary that ultimately will allow another dimension to overwhelm our own and render every human being a freak. The stories carry only town names for their titles, but the book includes fine contributions from Chet Williamson, Dan Simmons and Steven Spruill.

Other books you might like:

Charles L. Grant, *The Chronicles of Greystone Bay*, 1985-1990
    short story in .
Robert R. McCammon, *Under the Fang*, 1991
    editor
John Skipp, *Book of the Dead*, 1990
    Craig Spector, co-editor
John Skipp, *Still Dead: Book of the Dead 2*, 1992
    Craig Spector, co-editor

4686

F. PAUL WILSON

The LaNague Chronicles

(New York: Baen, 1992)

Story type: Science Fiction (Political; Adventure)
Series: LaNague Federation
Major character(s): Peter LaNague, Revolutionary (Pacifist Libertarian); Steven Dalt, Anthropologist, Spy; Josephine Finch, Businesswoman
Time period(s): Indeterminate Future
Locale(s): Throne, Planet—Imaginary; Kwashi, Planet—Imaginary; LaNague Federation, Interstellar Empire/Federation

Summary: Integrates three separate novels, *An Enemy of the State* (1980), *Healer* (1976) and *Wheels Within Wheels* (1979), reorganized and expanded with new material relating the history of a galactic culture based on Libertarian principles. From its founding, the LaNague Federation balances on the dynamic conflict between personal responsibility and greed. Includes a new four-page introduction by the author and complete LaNague chronology of novels and stories.

Other books you might like:

Piers Anthony, *Refugee*, 1983
Robert A. Heinlein, *The Moon Is a Harsh Mistress*, 1966
Ursula K. Le Guin, *The Dispossessed*, 1974
Brad Linaweaver, *Moon of Ice*, 1988
Steve Perry, *The Man Who Never Missed*, 1985
L. Neil Smith, *The Probability Broach*, 1980

4687

F. PAUL WILSON

Midnight Mass

(Seattle, Washington: Axolotl Press, 1990)

Story type: Horror (Vampire Story; Science Fiction)
Major character(s): Zev Wolpin, Religious (rabbi); Joseph Cahill, Religious (priest)
Time period(s): Indeterminate Future
Locale(s): Spring Lake, New Jersey

Summary: A Jewish rabbi tries to help Catholic priest Joseph Cahill defend his parish church from attack by the vampires that have taken over the world. But Cahill has an even greater problem: loss of faith. This novella is a tribute to Richard Matheson's classic vampire tale, *I Am Legend*.

Other books you might like:

Stephen King, *Salem's Lot*, 1975
Robert R. McCammon, *They Thirst*, 1981
Richard Matheson, *I Am Legend*, 1954

4688

F. PAUL WILSON
MATTHEW J. COSTELLO, Co-Author

Mirage

(New York: Warner, 1996)

Story type: Horror (Science Fiction; Psychological Suspense)
Major character(s): Julie Gordon, Scientist; Eathan Gordon, Doctor; Nathan Gordon, Scientist (neurochemist)
Time period(s): 1990s (1996)
Locale(s): New York, New York; Paris, France

Summary: With the aid of a virtual reality diagnostic tool she has perfected, Julie Gordon probes the brain of her twin sister Samantha to find out what has put her into a coma. Julie discovers memories not only of their past that help her to reconcile herself with her estranged sibling, but also clues to the identity of the person responsible for Samantha's misfortune, who is also very much a threat to Julie.

Other books you might like:

Isaac Asimov, *Fantastic Voyage II: Destination Brain*, 1987
Elizabeth Forrest, *Killjoy*, 1996
Michael Marshall Smith, *Spares*, 1995
F. Paul Wilson, *Sibs*, 1991

4689

F. PAUL WILSON

Nightworld

(Arlington Heights, Illinois: Dark Harvest, 1992)

Story type: Horror (Apocalyptic Horror)
Series: Nightworld Cycle
Major character(s): Glaeken Veilleur, Aged Person; William Ryan, Religious (priest); Repairman Jack, Vigilante
Time period(s): 1990s (1992)
Locale(s): New York, New York

Summary: Fluctuations in the sunrise and sunset and the opening of bottomless sinkholes in New York that spew forth flesheating giant insects signal the coming apocalypse. Drawing together a band of mortals who have all encountered the supernatural, mystic warrior Glaeken Veilleur prepares for his final battle with Rasalom, the incarnation of ultimate evil.

Other books you might like:
T.E.D. Klein, *The Ceremonies*, 1984
John Skipp, *The Scream*, 1988
  Craig Spector, co-author

4690

F. PAUL WILSON

Pelts

(Roundtop, New York: Footsteps Press, 1990)

Story type: Horror (Nature in Revolt)
Major character(s): Gary Jameson, Trapper; Jake Feldman, Businessman (Furrier); Shanna, Model (Fashion model)
Time period(s): 1990s (1990)
Locale(s): Pine Barrens, New Jersey; New York, New York

Summary: The most recent batch of hides from racoons trapped by Gary Jameson and his father seeks revenge on those who would turn them into an exploitable commodity.

Other books you might like:
Stephen King, *Cujo*, 1981
Michael Stewart, *Monkey Shines*, 1973
Earle Wescott, *Winter Wolves*, 1989

4691

F. PAUL WILSON

Reborn

(Arlington Heights, Illinois: Dark Harvest, 1990)

Story type: Horror (Science Fiction)
Series: Adversary
Major character(s): Jim Stevens, Writer (horror novelist), Journalist; Carol Stevens, Social Worker; Roderick Hanley, Scientist (geneticist)
Time period(s): 1960s (1968)
Locale(s): Monroe Village, New York

Summary: Jim Stevens discovers that he is the clone of wealthy geneticist Roderick Hanley at about the same time that a group of maverick Christian fundamentalists, who call themselves The Chosen, decide that he is the anti-Christ and must be destroyed.

Other books you might like:
Dean R. Koontz, *Servants of Twilight*, 1984
Dean R. Koontz, *Shadowfires*, 1987
Ira Levin, *The Boys From Brazil*, 1976
Ira Levin, *Rosemary's Baby*, 1967
Robert Weinberg, *The Armageddon Box*, 1991

4692

F. PAUL WILSON

Reprisal

(Arlington Heights, Illinois: Dark Harvest, 1991)

Story type: Horror (Ancient Evil Unleashed)
Series: Adversary
Major character(s): Lisl Whitman, Professor (of mathematics); Will Ryerson, Worker (college groundskeeper); Rafe Losmara, Student—Graduate
Time period(s): 1990s
Locale(s): South Carolina

Summary: In this third novel of the series that began with the *The Keep* (1981), the evil spirit who possessed the cloned Jim Hanley in *Reborn* (1990) has passed into Hanley's precocious son who, under the name Rafe Losmara, is embarked on graduate work in psychology, the better to prepare himself for battle with the nemesis intent on exterminating him.

Other books you might like:
William Peter Blatty, *The Exorcist*, 1971
William Peter Blatty, *Legion*, 1983
John Farris, *Son of the Endless Night*, 1985

4693

F. PAUL WILSON

The Select

(New York: Morrow, 1994)

Story type: Horror (Psychological Suspense)
Major character(s): Quinn Cleary, Student (medical); Tim Brown, Student (medical); Arthur Alston, Doctor
Time period(s): 1990s (1994)
Locale(s): Laurel Hills, Maryland

Summary: The Ingraham College of Medicine, managed with near military discipline, is the most prestigious institution of its kind in the United States. This is because its students are chosen not only for their intelligence, but for their susceptibility to subliminal suggestion and training practices that will benefit the Kleederman Foundation, a pharmaceutical concern that will stop at nothing to protect its investment in the type of health care they render. The author originally published this novel in England in 1993, as *The Foundation*, under the pseudonym Colin Andrews.

Other books you might like:
John Edward Ames, *The Asylum*, 1994
Robin Cook, *Coma*, 1977
Timothy Findley, *Headhunter*, 1993

4694

F. PAUL WILSON

Sibs

(Arlington Heights, Illinois: Dark Harvest, 1992)

Story type: Horror (Possession)
Major character(s): Kara Wade, Writer; Rob Morris, Detective; Lawrence Gates, Doctor (psychiatrist)

Time period(s): 1990s (1992)
Locale(s): New York, New York

Summary: Kara Wade returns to New York to bury her twin sister Jill, who died during a steamy sexual liaison that Kara refuses to believe her mild-mannered sister could have been involved in. Her investigations into her sister's past lead her to Jill's psychiatrist, a man who either has extraordinary insight into Jill's and Kara's past or who has fabricated a smokescreen of lies to cover up his real interest in the two women.

Other books you might like:
William Peter Blatty, *The Ninth Configuration*, 1978
Thomas Tessier, *The Dreams of Dr. Ladybank*, 1991
    shot story in *Night Visions 9*

4695

F. PAUL WILSON

Soft and Others
(New York: Tor, 1989)

Story type: Horror (Collection)

Summary: Sixteen stories originally published between 1971 and 1988, plus one original, each prefaced briefly by the author. Cerebral, graphic, well crafted stories that focus on horrors of the contemporary world, rather than traditional monsters, often utilizing Wilson's expertise and experiences as an M.D. Outstanding are the title story, a graphic narrative about a near future plague in which the victims' bones dissolve into jelly, "Dat-Tag-Vao," about a mysterious healing touch, "Green Winter," about a shifting balance of power between two intelligent species, "Buckets," which chronicles a physician's chilling Halloween encounter, and "Cuts," which describes a novelist's terrible revenge on the filmmaker who desecrated his work.

Other books you might like:
Michael Blumlein, *The Brains of Rats*, 1989
Katherine Dunn, *Geek Love*, 1989
K.W. Jeter, *Dark Seeker*, 1987
K.W. Jeter, *Farewell Horizontal*, 1989
K.W. Jeter, *In the Land of the Dead*, 1989
Robert R. McCammon, *Blue World*, 1990
John Shirley, *Heatseeker*, 1989
Dan Simmons, *Carrion Comfort*, 1989
Dan Simmons, *Hyperion*, 1989

4696

F. PAUL WILSON

The Tery
(New York: Baen Books, 1990)

Story type: Science Fiction (Psychic Powers)
Series: Steven Dalt
Major character(s): Steven Dalt, Spy; Jon, Mutant
Time period(s): Indeterminate Future
Locale(s): Jacobi IV, Planet—Imaginary

Summary: A human society long separated from interstellar civilization is technologically primitive, but has evolved a

wide variety of psi phenomena. Those who possess such powers are often mistreated or killed. Secret agent Steven Dalt goes to the planet in an attempt to improve the lot of the downtrodden. This volume also includes the novelette "Pard," another Steven Dalt adventure.

Other books you might like:
Poul Anderson, *The High Crusade*, 1960
John Dalmas, *The Lantern of God*, 1989
John Dalmas, *The Lizard War*, 1989
Kenneth Von Gunden, *StarSpawn*, 1990

4697

GAHAN WILSON, Author/Illustrator

Gahan Wilson's The Ultimate Haunted House
(New York: HarperPrism, 1996)

Story type: Horror (Anthology; Haunted House)

Summary: The 13 original stories commissioned for this house are all purportedly based on artist Gahan Wilson's popular CD-ROM game, "The Ultimate Haunted House." Each writer's tale is set in a different room of a haunted house. Nancy Collins, who served as consulting editor for the book, contributes "Someone's in the Kitchen," about a man who becomes the object of affection for the ghost of a good cook. Ted Klein's "Curtains for Nat Crumley" tells of a nebbish man who discovers that his bathroom mirror reflects the more robust life he might have led. In Gregory Nicoll's "The Ratz in the Halls," a rock band discovers the perils of recording a video in the basement of a haunted house. Lucy Taylor's "Bundling" concerns the dark secret buried in the attic of a haunted house a woman moves into with her young daughter, and Steve Antczak's "The Monster Lab" tells of a mad scientist who may or may not be haunted by the ghost of his dead wife. Wilson supplies an introduction and illustration for each story.

Other books you might like:
Kathryn Cramer, *The Architecture of Fear*, 1987
    Peter Pautz, co-editor
Kathryn Cramer, *Walls of Fear*, 1990
    editor
Charles G. Waugh, *House Shudders*, 1987
    Martin Greenberg, co-editor

4698

ROBERT ANTON WILSON

Nature's God
(New York: Roc, 1991)

Story type: Fantasy (Historical)
Series: Historical Illuminatus Chronicles
Major character(s): Sigismundo Celine, Magician, Musician; Seamus Muadhen, Military Personnel; Maria Babcock, Revolutionary
Time period(s): 18th century (1776-1780)
Locale(s): New England; Lousewartshire, England

Summary: In this sequel to *The Widow's Son*, the tangled plot of the series continues as Celine travels to the wilds of Ohio to meditate, Muadhen becomes part of General Washington's army and Maria Babcock unleashes a barrage against male privilege. Through its themes and characters this third volume in the continuing series ties into Wilson's other fiction.

Other books you might like:
James P. Blaylock, *The Paper Grail*, 1991
Umberto Eco, *Foucault's Pendulum*, 1989
Michael Flynn, *In the Country of the Blind*, 1990
Stuart Gordon, *Smile on the Void*, 1981
Thomas Pynchon, *Gravity's Rainbow*, 1973
Gene Wolfe, *Castleview*, 1990

4699
ROBERT ANTON WILSON

Reality Is What You Can Get Away With: An Illustrated Screenplay
(New York: Dell, 1992)

Story type: Science Fiction (Humor; Arts)
Major character(s): Padraic Hakim Hasagawa, Professor; J.R. "BoB" Dobbs, Religious, Activist; George Herbert Walker Bush, Political Figure, Historical Figure
Time period(s): Indeterminate Future; 20th century
Locale(s): Earth; Sirius 23, Planet—Imaginary (University of New Dublin)

Summary: Professor Padraic Hakim Hasagawa brings historical perpective to a long-lost 20th century screenplay, recently discovered, which presents a view of ancient Earth life which includes a larger-than-life presentation of the Church of the Subgenius.

Other books you might like:
Roger Elwood, *Six Science Fiction Plays*, 1976
	editor
Malacypse the Younger, *Principia Discordia*, 1991
	expanded
Reverend Ivan Stang, *Three-Fisted Tales of "BoB"*, 1990
	editor
Kurt Vonnegut Jr., *Between Time and Timbuktu*, 1972
Kurt Vonnegut Jr., *Happy Birthday, Wanda June*, 1970

4700
ROBERT CHARLES WILSON

A Bridge of Years
(New York: Doubleday Foundation, 1991)

Story type: Science Fiction (Time Travel; Hard Science Fiction)
Major character(s): Tom Winter, Time Traveller; Ben Collier, Time Traveller, Clone
Time period(s): 1980s (1989); 1960s (1962)
Locale(s): Belltower, Washington; New York, New York

Summary: When Tom Winter returns home to Washington state suffering from emotional trauma, he expects a quiet recovery. Instead, he finds his home invaded by a time tunnel which leads to New York City a quarter century earlier. As he

investigates the mystery, he discovers a deadly foe and menace to his world's future.

Other books you might like:
Jeffrey A. Carver, *From a Changeling Star*, 1989
Ken Grimwood, *Replay*, 1986
Marge Piercy, *Woman on the Edge of Time*, 1976
Dan Simmons, *The Fall of Hyperion*, 1990
Dan Simmons, *Hyperion*, 1989
Kurt Vonnegut Jr., *The Sirens of Titan*, 1959

4701
ROBERT CHARLES WILSON

The Divide
(New York: Doubleday Foundation, 1990)

Story type: Science Fiction (Genetic Manipulation)
Major character(s): John Shaw, Genetically Altered Being; Susan, Student
Time period(s): 1990s
Locale(s): Toronto, Ontario, Canada

Summary: After he is abandoned by the scientist who created him, a genetically-tailored superman hides behind an apparently normal alter ego until events conspire to force his real personality to reemerge.

Other books you might like:
John Brunner, *Children of the Thunder*, 1989
Daniel Keyes, *Flowers for Algernon*, 1966
Daniel Keys Moran, *Emerald Eyes*, 1988
Robert Reed, *Black Milk*, 1989

4702
ROBERT CHARLES WILSON

Gypsies
(New York: Doubleday Foundation, 1989)

Story type: Science Fiction (Alternate Universe)
Major character(s): Karen White, Housewife (Separated); Michael, Child (Karen's son)
Time period(s): 20th century
Locale(s): Alternate Universe; United States

Summary: Karen White's past is a mystery. Her parents were odd people who moved frequently, obviously on the run from persons and places unknown. Karen herself has strange dreams of a world she's never seen and of a dark, haunting presence, the Gray Man. Then her son Michael begins to have similar dreams and, later, begins to see the Gray Man following him. Someone, Karen realizes, is after her family—someone not entirely of this Earth.

Other books you might like:
Michael P. Kube-McDowell, *Alternities*, 1988
Marge Piercy, *Woman on the Edge of Time*, 1976
Frederik Pohl, *The Coming of the Quantum Cats*, 1986
Gene Wolfe, *There Are Doors*, 1988

4703
ROBERT CHARLES WILSON

The Harvest
(New York: Bantam Spectra, 1993)

Story type: Science Fiction (First Contact; Mystical)
Major character(s): Matt Wheeler, Doctor, Leader; John Tyler, Military Personnel; Tom Kindle, Mountain Man
Time period(s): 21st century
Locale(s): Oregon; Georgia

Summary: After an alien artifact appears in the night sky, everyone seems to contract a new variety of flu, later learning the symptoms portend immortality, transformation and interstellar travel. One of those unhappy with the alien gift, Matt Wheeler, leads a small group of fellow refusers on a dangerous trip to Ohio, suffering when John Tyler meets up with the group.

Other books you might like:
John Brunner, *Age of Miracles*, 1971
Arthur C. Clarke, *Childhood's End*, 1953
Joe Haldeman, *Worlds Apart*, 1983
Michael P. Kube-McDowell, *The Quiet Pools*, 1990
Pat Murphy, *The City, Not Long After*, 1989
Robert Silverberg, *Tom O'Bedlam*, 1985
Clifford D. Simak, *A Choice of Gods*, 1972
Norman Spinrad, *Songs From the Stars*, 1980
Brian Stableford, *The Walking Shadow*, 1989
Vernor Vinge, *Marooned in Realtime*, 1986

4704
ROBERT CHARLES WILSON

A Hidden Place
(New York: Bantam Spectra, 1989)

Story type: Science Fiction (First Contact)
Major character(s): Anna Blaise, Young Woman; Bone, Streetperson
Time period(s): 1930s (Great Depression)
Locale(s): Haute Montaigne, Midwest

Summary: Anna Blaise, an unworldly young woman who seems to have no past, appears in the town of Haute Montaigne and changes the lives of a number of citizens. Simultaneously, a gigantic, seemingly retarded tramp named Bone makes his way across country, in search, although he isn't entirely aware of it, of Anna. The unearthly nature of their relationship, when it is revealed, is both strange and beautiful.

Other books you might like:
Richard Paul Russo, *Subterranean Gallery*, 1989
Pamela Sargent, *The Alien Upstairs*, 1983
Theodore Sturgeon, *Alien Cargo*, 1984
Theodore Sturgeon, *Godbody*, 1986
Theodore Sturgeon, *More than Human*, 1953
Theodore Sturgeon, *Slow Sculpture*, 1982

4705
ROBERT CHARLES WILSON

Mysterium
(New York: Bantam Spectra, 1994)

Story type: Science Fiction (Alternate Universe; Political)
Major character(s): Clifford Stockton, Child; Dexter Graham, Teacher; Linneth Stone, Scholar
Time period(s): 1990s (1994)
Locale(s): Two Rivers, Michigan; Alternate Earth

Summary: Early one morning, Two Rivers, Michigan, moves inexplicably to another Earth, where a totalitarian government dominates a dystopian America. On this new Earth, Christianity and history developed differently, leaving the inhabitants of the town to cope with a world simultaneously familiar and strange.

Other books you might like:
Margaret Atwood, *The Handmaid's Tale*, 1985
Walter M. Miller Jr., *A Canticle for Leibowitz*, 1960
James Morrow, *Only Begotten Daughter*, 1990
Pat Murphy, *The City, Not Long After*, 1989
Howard Waldrop, *Them Bones*, 1984

4706
TERRI WINDLING, Editor

The Armless Maiden and Other Tales for Childhood's Survivors
(New York: Tor, 1995)

Story type: Fantasy (Anthology)

Summary: Contains a four-page introduction to original and reprinted modern fairy tales ordered to draw the adult reader along a dark journey through childhood's pitfalls, abuse and neglect, aimed at suggesting positive social change. Some humor and much painful insight infuses 17 poems, four essays, three memoirs, and 21 stories, some with individual introductions, by authors including Emma Bull, Kara Dalkey, Charles de Lint, Steven Gould, Tappan King, Ellen Kushner, Tanith Lee, Patricia A. McKillip, Susan Palwick, Kristine Kathryn Rusch, Joanna Russ, Delia Sherman, Will Shetterly, Midori Snyder, Caroline Stevermer, Peter Straub, Terri Windling, and Jane Yolen.

Other books you might like:
Gael Baudino, *Strands of Sunlight*, 1984
Ellen Datlow, *Ruby Slippers, Golden Tears*, 1995
    Terri Windling, co-editor
Ellen Datlow, *The Year's Best Fantasy and Horror Series*, 1989-
    Terri Windling, co-editor
Charles de Lint, *Dreams Underfoot*, 1993
Mercedes Lackey, *Born to Run*, 1992
    Larry Dixon, co-author
Robin McKinley, *Deerskin*, 1993
Susan Palwick, *Flying in Place*, 1992
Geoff Ryman, *Was*, 1992
Jane Yolen, *Briar Rose*, 1992

Jack Zipes, *Spells of Enchantment*, 1991
   editor

4707

TERRI WINDLING, Editor
MARK ALAN ARNOLD, Co-Editor

Borderland

(New York: Tor, 1992)

Story type: Fantasy (Anthology; Urban)
Series: Borderland
Time period(s): Indeterminate Future
Locale(s): Borderland, Mythical Place; Bordertown, Fictional City

Summary: Contains four original stories by Bellamy Bach, Steven R. Boyett, Charles de Lint and Ellen Kushner, all sharing Terri Windling's Borderland setting, the intersection of the mortal world with Elfland, and each utilizing music as a dominant theme. Reissue of the 1986 edition.

Other books you might like:
Emma Bull, *War for the Oaks*, 1987
Charles de Lint, *Moonheart: A Romance*, 1984
Charles de Lint, *Spiritwalk*, 1992
Megan Lindholm, *Wizard of the Pigeons*, 1986
Will Shetterly, *Elsewhere*, 1991
Will Shetterly, *Liavek*, 1985
   Emma Bull, co-editor
Will Shetterly, *Liavek: Spells of Binding*, 1988
   Emma Bull, co-editor
Will Shetterly, *Liavek: Wizard's Row*, 1987
   Emma Bull, co-editor
Gene Wolfe, *Storeys From the Old Hotel*, 1992

4708

TERRI WINDLING, Editor

Life on the Border

(New York: Tor, 1991)

Story type: Fantasy (Anthology; Urban)
Series: Borderland
Time period(s): Indeterminate Future
Locale(s): Bordertown, Fictional City

Summary: This volume contains eight stories including Ellen Kushner's interwoven epistolary story, "Lost in the Mail," plus verse by Emma Bull, all set in the city which lies in the border between the human realm and Elfland, occupied by the Truebloods. In "Nevermore," Will Shetterly takes up the story of Ron Starbuck, now Wolfboy, two years after the events in his novel, *Elsewhere* (1991). Charles de Lint's "Berlin" examines Bordertown turf wars between human and elf gangs, as does Bellamy Bach's "Rain and Thunder." Other authors are Midori Snyder, Michael Korolenko, Kara Dalkey, and Craig Shaw Gardner.

Other books you might like:
Gael Baudino, *Gossamer Axe*, 1990
Emma Bull, *War for the Oaks*, 1987

Mercedes Lackey, *Knight of Ghosts and Shadows*, 1990
   Ellen Guon, co-author
Joel Rosenberg, *The Road to Ehvenor*, 1991
Will Shetterly, *Elsewhere*, 1991
Will Shetterly, *Liavek*, 1985
   Emma Bull, co-editor
Will Shetterly, *Liavek: Spells of Binding*, 1988
   Emma Bull, co-editor
Will Shetterly, *Liavek: Wizard's Row*, 1987
   Emma Bull, co-editor

4709

TERRI WINDLING

The Wood Wife

(New York: Tor, 1996)

Story type: Fantasy (Contemporary; Mystery)
Major character(s): Marguerita "Maggie" Black, Writer (poet); Johnny "Fox" Foxxe, Musician
Time period(s): 1990s
Locale(s): Tucson, Arizona; Southwest

Summary: When Maggie travels to Tucson to claim the inheritance from her murdered mentor, Fox and others help her discover the magic of the desert and its guardians as Maggie investigates her inner self and events surrounding her mentor's desert drowning.

Other books you might like:
Charles de Lint, *Memory and Dream*, 1994
Charles de Lint, *The Wild Wood*, 1994
   Brian Froud, co-author
Lisa Goldstein, *Walking the Labyrinth*, 1996
Megan Lindholm, *Cloven Hooves*, 1991
Patricia A. McKillip, *Something Rich and Strange*, 1994
   Brian Froud, co-author
Jane Yolen, *Briar Rose*, 1992

4710

DAVID WINGROVE

Beneath the Tree of Heaven

(New York: Dell, 1995)

Story type: Science Fiction (Political; Family Saga)
Series: Chung Kuo
Major character(s): Kao Chen, Military Personnel (T'ang's security forces); Emily Ascher, Revolutionary; Hans Ebert, Revolutionary
Time period(s): 23rd century (2210-2213)
Locale(s): Earth; Mars

Summary: With the rule of the T'ang weakening as forces for change spread from the vast city-nations to a planet-wide conspiracy on Mars, generations of mind-manipulation and iron control may no longer suffice. Now they face treachery from within their own ranks, while Hans Ebert begins a new fight among Martian colonists. Revolution, in the form of True History, may finally free the long oppressed masses, or it may rain destruction across an entire world.

Other books you might like:
Poul Anderson, *A Stone in Heaven*, 1979
Isaac Asimov, *Foundation*, 1951
C.J. Cherryh, *Cyteen*, 1988
C.J. Cherryh, *The Pride of Chanur*, 1982
Gordon R. Dickson, *The Final Encyclopedia*, 1984
Frank Herbert, *Dune*, 1965
Larry Niven, *Man-Kzin Wars*, 1988
   editor
Alis A. Rasmussen, *A Passage of Stars*, 1990
S.M. Stirling, *Blood Feuds*, 1993
   Judith Tarr, Susan Shwartz, Harry Turtledove, co-authors
Timothy Zahn, *Dark Force Rising*, 1992

4711

DAVID WINGROVE

The Broken Wheel

(New York: Doubleday Delacorte, 1991)

Story type: Science Fiction (Alternate Universe; Political)
Series: Chung Kuo
Major character(s): Emily Ascher, Political Figure; Howard De Vore, Political Figure, Military Personnel (retired)
Time period(s): 23rd century (2206)
Locale(s): Earth

Summary: China has been the world's major power for over a century. War and strife are not permitted. Leading agent in the struggle against China's ruling elite, known as The Seven, Howard De Vore is the force modifying the great "War of the Two Directions," determining which direction society will follow.

Other books you might like:
Philip K. Dick, *The Man in the High Castle*, 1962
Gordon R. Dickson, *Way of the Pilgrim*, 1987
John Hersey, *White Lotus*, 1965
Jeanne Larsen, *Silk Road*, 1989
Ian McDonald, *Out on Blue Six*, 1989

4712

DAVID WINGROVE

The Middle Kingdom

(New York: Delacorte, 1990)

Story type: Science Fiction (Alternate Universe)
Series: Chung Kuo
Major character(s): Li Yuan, Heir, Royalty; Ben Shepherd, Artist
Time period(s): 22nd century
Locale(s): Earth

Summary: China rules the world and has done so for more than one hundred years. Peace and stability are virtually universal, but they've been achieved, some feel, at the cost of tyranny and stagnation. Dissatisfaction is particularly keen in the European merchant class, some of whom form the Dispersionists, a group dedicated to dramatic change and the expansion of humankind into outer space. The struggle between those who would prohibit change and those who would force

it at any cost is given the name "The War of the Two Directions."

Other books you might like:
Philip K. Dick, *The Man in the High Castle*, 1962
Gordon R. Dickson, *Way of the Pilgrim*, 1987
John Hersey, *White Lotus*, 1965
Ian McDonald, *Out on Blue Six*, 1989

4713

DAVID WINGROVE

The Stone Within

(New York: Dell, 1993)

Story type: Science Fiction (Political; Family Saga)
Series: Chung Kuo
Major character(s): Stefan Lehman, Criminal, Leader; Kim Ward, Scientist; Li Yuan, Leader (T'ang of Europe)
Time period(s): 23rd century (2209)
Locale(s): Earth; Outer Space

Summary: Their hand forced, the Seven T'ang struggle to overcome dissension from both within and without as chaos seems to erupt from all sides. Remnants of DeVore's old forces have their own agendas while the Seven's unity falls apart. To buy time and win allies, the generations-old Edict of Technological Change finally undergoes amendment in return for support in placing population controls throughout the city-nations, yet struggles in the War of Two Directions grow more bitter.

Other books you might like:
Isaac Asimov, *Foundation*, 1951
Orson Scott Card, *Seventh Son*, 1987
C.J. Cherryh, *Cyteen*, 1988
Gordon R. Dickson, *The Final Encyclopedia*, 1984
Frank Herbert, *Dune*, 1965
Alis A. Rasmussen, *A Passage of Stars*, 1990
Paul O. Williams, *The Breaking of Northwall*, 1980

4714

DAVID WINGROVE

White Moon, Red Dragon

(New York: Dell, 1996)

Story type: Science Fiction (Political; Family Saga)
Series: Chung Kuo
Major character(s): Li Yuan, Leader (T'Ang of Europe); Howard DeVore, Revolutionary, Leader; Kim Ward, Scientist
Time period(s): 23rd century
Locale(s): Earth; Mars

Summary: Thought dead by his enemies, the rebel DeVore readies a terrifying flotilla to bring against the T'Ang, rulers of Earth. On Mars, the long-exiled Hans Ebert meets with a lost African tribe, the Osu, to reveal his plan to take them home to Earth. On Earth, the mega-cities of the T'Ang begin to crumble as war ripples across the planet, while beginnings and endings accompany Li Yuan's terrifying alliance. Sixth in the series.

Other books you might like:
Poul Anderson, *The Time Patrol*, 1991
Isaac Asimov, *Foundation*, 1951
C.J. Cherryh, *Cyteen*, 1988
Gordon R. Dickson, *The Final Encyclopedia*, 1984
Stephen R. Donaldson, *Lord Foul's Bane*, 1977
Frank Herbert, *Dune*, 1965
Alis A. Rasmussen, *A Passage of Stars*, 1990

4715

DAVID WINGROVE

The White Mountain

(New York: Delacorte, 1992)

Story type: Science Fiction (Political; Family Saga)
Series: Chung Kuo
Major character(s): Li Yuan, Leader (T'ang of Europe); Howard DeVore, Revolutionary, Leader; Kim Ward, Scientist
Time period(s): Indeterminate Future
Locale(s): Earth; Mars

Summary: Seven T'ang who rule the great city-continents of Chung Kuo struggle to hold onto their power. The destruction of the Dispersionists allow newer, more violent bands of rebels to gain power among the downtrodden people of the lowest levels of the cities. The young overlords hope to continue ruling by the ancient Chinese tenets of peace through strict order and stability, but may have to allow change to alter their ancestors' vision of an enforced peace lasting 10,000 years.

Other books you might like:
Poul Anderson, *Ensign Flandry*, 1966
Poul Anderson, *The Time Patrol*, 1991
Isaac Asimov, *Foundation*, 1951
C.J. Cherryh, *Cyteen*, 1988
C.J. Cherryh, *Downbelow Station*, 1981
C.J. Cherryh, *The Pride of Chanur*, 1982
Gordon R. Dickson, *The Final Encyclopedia*, 1984
Stephen R. Donaldson, *Lord Foul's Bane*, 1977
Frank Herbert, *Dune*, 1965
Alis A. Rasmussen, *A Passage of Stars*, 1990

4716

DOUGLAS E. WINTER
STEPHEN R. BISSETTE, Illustrator

Black Sun

(Washington, D.C.: One-Eyed Dog)

Story type: Horror (Apocalyptic Horror)
Major character(s): Hagopian, Aged Person; The Stranger, Young Man; Karen, Young Woman
Time period(s): 1990s
Locale(s): The City

Summary: In an arresting fusion of images from horror literature and film, the author details a trek across a post-apocalyptic urban landscape ravaged by cancer, social ills and possibly nuclear destruction.

Other books you might like:
Richard Matheson, *The Dance of the Dead*, 1989
  in *Collected Stories*
Richard Matheson, *I Am Legend*, 1954
Wayne Allen Sallee, *For You, the Living*, 1992
Brian Stableford, *Slumming in Voodooland*, 1991

4717

PAT WINTER

Madoc's Hundred

(New York: Bantam Domain, 1991)

Story type: Fantasy (Legend; Adventure)
Series: Madoc Saga
Major character(s): Madoc "Weather Eyes" ab Owen, Leader; Rhys "Sun Eyes" ab Meredydd, Minstrel; Tumkis "Lady Sun", Indian
Time period(s): 12th century (1172)
Locale(s): North America (currently Tennessee and Kentucky)

Summary: The exiled Welsh prince Madoc has crossed the Atlantic Ocean and landed on the shores of what will be called North America, finding enemies and allies among the people living there. Now, two years after coming to this land, Madoc's band travel down the Tennessee and Ohio Rivers on the way to the Great River Road, the Mech-a-sip-i, where the great pyramids of the sun god stand in the city of Ixtulan.

Other books you might like:
Orson Scott Card, *Red Prophet*, 1988
Parke Godwin, *The Last Rainbow*, 1985
Sue Harrison, *Mother Earth, Father Sky*, 1990
R.A. MacAvoy, *The Third Eagle: Lessons Along a Minor String*, 1989

4718

B.L. WINTERS

Bloody Waters

(New York: Pocket, 1993)

Story type: Horror (Mystery)
Major character(s): Kara Noble Worthington, Housewife; John Worthington, Lawyer; Buchanan "Bucky" Worthington, Actor
Time period(s): 1990s (1993)
Locale(s): Homeplace, Virginia

Summary: When friends of the conservative Worthington family begin dying under mysterious circumstances, suspicion falls on Kara Worthington, John Worthington's new bride, whom they fear has yet to tame her West Coast wildness. But Kara's suspicions fall on Lorraine Worthington, the sexually-inhibited family matriarch who sternly rules her four sons' lives and will brook no interference.

Other books you might like:
Athena Alexis, *Along Came a Spider*, 1992
V.C. Andrews, *Flowers in the Attic*, 1979
Shawn MacDonald, *The Darkness Within*, 1993
Michael McDowell, *Blackwater*, 1983

4719

JEANETTE WINTERSON

Sexing the Cherry

(New York: Atlantic Monthly Press, 1990)

Story type: Fantasy (Historical)
Major character(s): Jordon, Child; Dog-Woman, Animal Trainer; John Tradescant, Farmer, Philosopher
Time period(s): 17th century
Locale(s): London, England

Summary: The Dog-Woman and her adopted child live in the dirt and disease of London. They leave, first to Wimbleton, then further and further, moving through time and space and fable into a mutable world of allegory and meaning.

Other books you might like:
Iain M. Banks, *The Bridge*, 1989
John Crowley, *Little, Big*, 1981
Stuart Gordon, *Fire in the Abyss*, 1983
Robert Holdstock, *Mythago Wood*, 1984
Fay Weldon, *Lives and Loves of a She-Devil*, 1983

4720

DAVID WISEMAN

A Tie to the Past

(New York: Houghton, 1989)

Story type: Fantasy (Historical)
Major character(s): Mary, Teenager
Time period(s): 1980s; 20th century
Locale(s): England

Summary: After stealing the tie, pin and diary of an old British suffragette, a modern young girl discovers she can see the life of the former owner by touching the objects. Guilt-ridden over the theft, she nevertheless becomes preoccupied with the past.

Other books you might like:
Lloyd Alexander, *The Drackenberg Adventure*, 1988
    Book 3 of Vesper Holly Series
Pamela F. Service, *Vision Quest*, 1989
Rosemary Sutcliff, *The Mark of the Horse Lord*, 1989

4721

KEN WISMAN

Weird Family Tales

(Parma, Ohio: Earth Prime Press, 1993)

Story type: Horror (Collection)

Summary: These seven stories from the small press are presented as tales about the narrator's extended family, each of whom falls prey to a supernatural encounter. Among the menaces chronicled are a phantom shark, a winged human, the infinite world created by placing two mirrors facing each other, a phantasm of the mind, and a fertility god.

Other books you might like:
Ray Bradbury, *The Stories of Ray Bradbury*, 1980

Darrell Schweitzer, *Transients and Other Disquieting Tales*, 1993
Chet Williamson, *The House of Fear*, 1989

4722

DON WISMER

A Roil of Stars

(New York: Baen, 1991)

Story type: Science Fiction (Military; Psychic Powers)
Major character(s): Asher Tye, Warrior, Psychic; Celia "Lee" D'Ame, Heroine, Waiter/Waitress; Ryne Sangre, Pilot (spaceship)
Time period(s): Indeterminate Future
Locale(s): Sigma Radidiani, Planet—Imaginary; Polar Cloud, Outer Space

Summary: The Polar Cloud is trying to prevent being taken over by the Whole Empire which had been rediscovered only 30 years ago. Before the war could start, both Empires appeared to be threatened by aliens called the Onn, while forces continued to overcome the Cloud, one planet per year.

Other books you might like:
Michael Berlyn, *The Eternal Enemy*, 1990
John Dalmas, *The White Regiment*, 1990
William C. Dietz, *War World*, 1986
Paula King, *Mad Roy's Light*, 1990
Timothy A. Madden, *Outbanker*, 1990
L.E. Modesitt Jr., *The Hammer of Darkness*, 1985
Paul Preuss, *Breaking Strain*, 1987

4723

H.P.G. WODEHOUSE (Pseudonym of Peter Cannon)
JASON ECKHARDT, Illustrator

Scream for Jeeves: A Parody

(New York: Wodecraft Press, 1994)

Story type: Horror (Collection)
Major character(s): Bertie Wooster, Gentleman; Jeeves, Servant (manservant)
Time period(s): 20th century
Locale(s): England

Summary: These three delightful pastiches imagine a world in which P.G. Wodehouse's genteel characters Bertie Wooster and his all-knowing butler, Jeeves, are thrust into scenarios straight out of H.P. Lovecraft's cosmic horror fiction. "Scream for Jeeves," an homage to Lovecraft's "The Rats in the Walls," has the unlikely duo investigating the decrepit homestead and genealogy of a family friend. "Something Foetid" introduces them to the mad doctor who has reanimated his own corpse in Lovecraft's "Cool Air." "The Rummy Affair of Young Charlie" brings together characters from Lovecraft's "Arthur Jermyn," "The Case of Charles Dexter Ward," and "The Music of Erich Zann" for a slapstick romp. The author supplies an afterword comparing Wodehouse, Lovecraft, and Sir Arthur Conan Doyle.

Other books you might like:
Christopher Moore, *Practical Demonkeeping*, 1992

William Browning Spencer, *Resume with Monsters*, 1995
Ralph Vaughan, *Sherlock Holmes in the Adventure of the Ancient Gods*, 1990

4724

ALLEN L. WOLD

Crown of the Serpent
(New York: Popular Library Questar, 1989)

Story type: Science Fiction (Adventure)
Series: Rikard Braeth
Major character(s): Rikard Braeth, Adventurer, Historian
Time period(s): Indeterminate Future
Locale(s): Nowarth, Planet—Imaginary; Kohltri, Planet—Imaginary

Summary: Rikard Braeth is recruited to help destroy or neutralize the Thathas, an evil alien race with strange powers who have been destroying human planets.

Other books you might like:
Rick Cook, *Limbo System*, 1989
John Dalmas, *The Lizard War*, 1989
Janet Morris, *Target*, 1989
    David Drake, co-author
L. Neil Smith, *Contact and Commune*, 1989

4725

ALLEN L. WOLD

Lair of the Cyclops
(New York: Warner Questar, 1992)

Story type: Science Fiction (Adventure)
Series: Rikard Braeth
Major character(s): Rikard Braeth, Adventurer, Historian; Endark Droagn, Alien, Telepath; Grayshard, Alien
Time period(s): Indeterminate Future
Locale(s): Dannon's Keep, Planet—Imaginary; Malvrone, Planet—Imaginary; Tsikshka, Planet—Imaginary

Summary: Hoping to enhance his academic standing as historian, Rikard Braeth and his companions follow ancient clues in hopes of discovering the answers to the two-million-year-old mystery concerning why the precursor cyclopean race who changed the galaxy suddenly disappeared.

Other books you might like:
John DeChancie, *Paradox Alley*, 1987
John DeChancie, *Red Limit Freeway*, 1984
John DeChancie, *Starrigger*, 1983
Diana G. Gallagher, *The Alien Dark*, 1990
Michael P. Kube-McDowell, *Enigma*, 1986
Michael P. Kube-McDowell, *Empery*, 1987
Michael P. Kube-McDowell, *Emprise*, 1985
Frederik Pohl, *The Gateway Trip: Tales and Vignettes of the Heechee*, 1990

4726

GARY K. WOLF

Who P-P-Plugged Roger Rabbit?
(New York: Villard Books, 1991)

Story type: Fantasy (Mystery; Light Fantasy)
Series: Roger Rabbit
Major character(s): Roger Rabbit, Actor (toon), Spouse (Jessica Rabbit's); Eddie Valiant, Detective—Private; Clark Gable, Actor, Historical Figure
Time period(s): 1940s
Locale(s): Los Angeles, California; Toontown, California (fictional Los Angeles suburb)

Summary: When rumors of Jessica Rabbit's affair with Clark Gable cause Roger to worry about losing his role as Rhett Butler in a *Gone with the Wind* remake, Roger convinces Eddie to help eliminate the rumors. Eddie's help becomes more valuable as rumors turn sinister and Roger is accused of multiple murders.

Other books you might like:
David Bischoff, *Night of the Living Shark!*, 1991
Craig Shaw Gardner, *Bride of the Slime Monster*, 1990
Craig Shaw Gardner, *Revenge of the Fluffy Bunnies*, 1990
Craig Shaw Gardner, *Slaves of the Volcano God*, 1989
Mel Gilden, *Surfing Samurai Robots*, 1988
Lionel Fenn, *Kent Montana and the Really Ugly Thing From Mars*, 1990
Clifford D. Simak, *Out of Their Minds*, 1970

4727

LEONARD WOLF, Editor

Doubles, Dummies and Dolls: 21 Terror Tales of Replication
(New York: Newmarket, 1995)

Story type: Horror (Anthology)

Summary: Through almost two dozen stories assembled by a renowned authority on supernatural fiction, authors from around the world explore the classic horror theme of the double. Theophile Gautier's ''The Double Knight,'' Edgar Allan Poe's ''William Wilson,'' and Ramsey Campbell's ''The Scar'' are all doppelganger stories. Robert Bloch's ''Sweets to the Sweets'' is concerned with the terrible use to which a voodoo doll is put, and Anthony Boucher's ''The Ghost of Me'' with a man haunted by his own ghost and his imminent death. In Gerald Kersh's ''The Extraordinarily Horrible Dummy,'' Susan Sontag's ''The Dummy,'' and E.T.A. Hoffman's ''The Sand-man,'' dolls take on lives that supersede those of their human counterparts. Algernon Blackwood's ''The Terror of the Twins'' tells of twin brothers who prove to be two sides of a single personality.

Other books you might like:
Chris Baldick, *The Oxford Book of Gothic Tales*, 1992
    editor
Alberto Manguel, *Black Water 2: The Book of Fantastic Literature*, 1991
    editor

Alberto Manguel, *Black Water: More Tales of the Fantastic*, 1990
editor

4728
GENE WOLFE

Calde of the Long Sun
(New York: Tor, 1994)

Story type: Science Fiction (Generation Starship; Religious)
Series: Book of the Long Sun
Major character(s): Patera Silk, Religious (priest); Maytera Mint, Religious, Teacher; Quetzal, Religious, Vampire
Time period(s): Indeterminate Future
Locale(s): *Whorl of the Long Sun*, Spaceship; Viron, Fictional City

Summary: Civil unrest propels Silk into accepting his popular elevation to Calde, since the gods from mainframe seem to have chosen him and the Chapter finally supports him. Possessed by the gods, Maytera Mint proves an inspired general, while Maytera Marble remembers events from her childhood.

Other books you might like:
Brian W. Aldiss, *Non-Stop*, 1989
Stephen Baxter, *Raft*, 1992
James Blish, *A Life for the Stars*, 1962
Samuel R. Delany, *Tales of Neveryon*, 1979
Frank M. Robinson, *The Dark Beyond the Stars*, 1991

4729
GENE WOLFE

Castle of Days
(New York: Tor, 1992)

Story type: Science Fiction (Collection)

Summary: Selections from Wolfe's writing 1968-1992 presented in three sections. Part I reprints *Gene Wolfe's Book of Days* (1981) including an introduction and 18 stories each relating to a day of particular note during the year. Part II reprints *The Castle of the Otter*, published previously as a small press volume discussing The Book of the New Sun series (1980-1983) in 11 articles including 12 pages of Urth jokes and an 18-page article, "Words Weird and Wonderful," discussing the language of Urth. Part III, "Castle of Days" contains 29 items divided into "Writers," "Writing" and "Books" including articles from periodicals and anthologies and excerpts from encyclopedia articles, speeches and personal correspondence.

Other books you might like:
Isaac Asimov, *Opus 200*, 1979
Isaac Asimov, *Opus 300*, 1984
Robert A. Heinlein, *Expanded Universe*, 1980
Larry Niven, *N-Space*, 1990
Larry Niven, *Playgrounds of the Mind*, 1991

4730
GENE WOLFE

Castleview
(New York: Tor, 1990)

Story type: Fantasy (Contemporary)
Time period(s): 1990s
Locale(s): Castleview, Illinois

Summary: In Castleview, so named for the phantom castle that periodically appears in mid-air, the lives of the town folk take a strange turn when all sorts of creatures from myth and legend start appearing in ever increasing numbers and with ever increasing frequency.

Other books you might like:
John DeChancie, *Castle Kidnapped*, 1989
Roger L. DiSilvestro, *Ursula's Gift*, 1988
Esther Friesner, *Sphynxes Wild*, 1989
Lisa Goldstein, *Tourists*, 1989

4731
GENE WOLFE

Endangered Species
(New York: Tor, 1989)

Story type: Science Fiction (Collection)

Summary: Wolfe's most recent collection contains thirty-four stories, ranging in publication date from 1968 to 1988, and features virtually all of his recent short fiction. Included are "The Map" and "The Cat," two stories set in the world of his Book of the New Sun series; the novella "Silhouette"; and such shorter pieces as "The Woman the Unicorn Loved," "The HORARS of War," "All the Hues of Hell," "Procreation," and "The Tale of the Rose and the Nightingale."

Other books you might like:
Brian W. Aldiss, *Helliconia Spring*, 1982
Brian W. Aldiss, *Helliconia Summer*, 1985
Brian W. Aldiss, *Helliconia Winter*, 1985
Brian Aldiss, *An Island Called Moreau*, 1981
Brian Aldiss, *Last Rites*, 1989
Brian W. Aldiss, *Man in His Time: The Best Science Fiction Stories of Brian W. Aldiss*, 1989
Paul Park, *Soldiers of Paradise*, 1987
Paul Park, *Sugar Rain*, 1989

4732
GENE WOLFE

Exodus From the Long Sun
(New York: Tor, 1996)

Story type: Science Fiction (Literary; Generation Starship)
Series: Book of the Long Sun
Major character(s): Patera Silk, Religious (priest); Maytera Auk, Criminal (former), Religious (prophet); Mint, Military Personnel (general)
Time period(s): Indeterminate Future

Locale(s): Viron, Fictional City; *Whorl of the Long Sun*, Spaceship

Summary: Once a mere priest, Calde Silk now rules the *Whorl* by the gods' decree. As the starship seemingly deteriorates, revolution and war break out among the millions living on the ship, while the gods increasingly manifest themselves and intervene in human affairs.

Other books you might like:
C.S. Friedman, *Crown of Shadows*, 1995
Simon Hawke, *The Whims of Creation*, 1992
Frank Herbert, *Dune*, 1965
Frank Herbert, *Dune Messiah*, 1969
Sheri S. Tepper, *Sideshow*, 1992

4733

GENE WOLFE

Lake of the Long Sun
(New York: Tor, 1994)

Story type: Science Fiction (Generation Starship; Alternate Universe)

Series: Book of the Long Sun

Major character(s): Patera Silk, Religious (priest); Maytera Marble, Robot (chem), Religious; Crane, Doctor, Spy

Time period(s): Indeterminate Future

Locale(s): *Whorl of the Long Sun*, Spaceship

Summary: Still trying to save his manteion, or religious enclave, as directed by his patron god, the Outsider, Silk must somehow find a huge sum of money. To the surprise of all, despite the sacrifices, only Silk's manteion again receives communications from the gods, the first in 20 years. Unrest in Viron leads to Silk's popular, god supported, campaign for Calde.

Other books you might like:
Poul Anderson, *The Boat of a Million Years*, 1989
Samuel R. Delany, *They Fly at Ciron*, 1993
Robert A. Heinlein, *Orphans of the Sky*, 1963
Fritz Leiber, *Ship of Shadows*, 1988
Sheri S. Tepper, *A Plague of Angels*, 1993

4734

GENE WOLFE

Nightside the Long Sun
(New York: Tor, 1993)

Story type: Science Fiction (Generation Starship; Alternate Intelligence)

Series: Book of the Long Sun

Major character(s): Silk, Religious (Patera); Blood, Criminal; Crane, Doctor, Spy

Time period(s): Indeterminate Future

Locale(s): *Whorl of the Long Sun*, Spaceship

Summary: Patera Silk, recently charged with responsibility for the Manteion School on Sun Street, receives enlightenment from the Outsider, a god not included in the usual pantheon, who instructs Silk to keep the Manteion open. Unfortunately the Manteion and grounds now belong to Blood, compelling

Silk to attempt coercing Blood into returning title to him, despite the fact that the gods have not spoken from Mainframe for generations and the Outsider told Silk he could not help.

Other books you might like:
Brian W. Aldiss, *Non-Stop*, 1989
Stephen Baxter, *Raft*, 1992
James Blish, *A Life for the Stars*, 1962
Samuel R. Delany, *Nova*, 1968
Robert A. Heinlein, *Orphans of the Sky*, 1963
Fritz Leiber, *Ship of Shadows*, 1988
Frank M. Robinson, *The Dark Beyond the Stars*, 1991

4735

GENE WOLFE

Soldier of Arete
(New York: Tor, 1989)

Story type: Fantasy (Legend)

Major character(s): Latro, Mercenary (Swordsman)

Time period(s): 5th century B.C.; Indeterminate Past

Locale(s): Greece

Summary: Handicapped by the loss of his memory every time he sleeps, Latro is able to orient himself in the ancient world of the Peloponnesian War by keeping daily diaries and through his ability to converse with the gods who are inaccessible to other mortals. Sequel to *Soldier of the Mist*.

Other books you might like:
Mickey Zucker Reichert, *Dragonrank Master*, 1989
Howard Waldrop, *A Dozen Tough Jobs*, 1989

4736

GENE WOLFE

Storeys From the Old Hotel
(New York: Tor, 1992)

Story type: Fantasy (Collection)

Summary: This volume contains an eight-page introduction with 34 stories utilizing diverse themes including two Liavek shared world stories, ''The Green Rabbit of S'Rian'' and ''Choice of the Black Goddess,'' plus other stories from anthologies and periodicals with three appearing originally. The British limited edition hardcover received the World Fantasy Award for best collection of the year.

Other books you might like:
David Brin, *The River of Time*, 1986
John Crowley, *Novelty*, 1989
Samuel R. Delany, *Driftglass: 10 Tales of Speculative Fiction*, 1971
Samuel R. Delany, *Tales of Neveryon*, 1979
Kristine Kathryn Rusch, *Pulphouse, Issue 6: Fantasy*, 1990 editor
Will Shetterly, *Liavek*, 1985
  Emma Bull, co-editor
Will Shetterly, *Liavek: Festival Week*, 1990
  Emma Bull, co-editor
Will Shetterly, *Liavek: Wizard's Row*, 1987
  Emma Bull, co-editor

Terri Windling, *Life on the Border*, 1991
  editor

4737

SEBASTIAN WOLFE, Editor

The Little Book of Horrors

(New York: Barricade, 1992)

Story type: Horror (Anthology)

Summary: This slim book collects 68 macabre tales, vignettes, cartoons, and brief factual articles, none longer than a page or two. Included are modern works by Joe Lansdale, Richard Christian Matheson, Stephen Gallagher, Frederic Brown and Robert Bloch, classic tales from Franz Kafka, Lafcadio Hearn, Ambrose Bierce, and Charles Dickens, an excerpt from Thomas Rymer's penny dreadful *Varney the Vampire* and illustrations by Gahan Wilson and Edward Gorey.

Other books you might like:
Isaac Asimov, *Microcosmic Tales*, 1980
  Martin H. Greenberg and Joseph Olander, co-editors

4738

SEBASTIAN WOLFE, Editor

Reel Terror

(New York: Carroll & Gaf, 1992)

Story type: Horror (Anthology)

Summary: A dozen stories that have been adapted into some of the finest horror, science fiction and suspense films of all time. Included are ''Spurs,'' Todd Robbins' tale of vengeful circus freaks, which served as the basis of Tod Browning's 1932 underground classic *Freaks*; H. P. Lovecraft's ''The Colour out of Space,'' the story of an extraterrestial influence invading the earth that was adapted for the 1965 film, *Die, Monster, Die*; Angela's Carter's brilliant ''The Company of Wolves,'' a metafictional variant on the fairy tale of Little Red Riding Hood that served as the basis for the 1984 film of the same name; and Philip K. Dick's paranoid science fiction tale ''We Can Remember It for You Wholesale,'' adapted in 1990 for the Paul Verhoeven film, *Total Recall*.

Other books you might like:
Peter Haining, *The Ghouls*, 1972
  editor
Peter Haining, *The Hollywood Nightmare*,
  editor
David Wheeler, *No, But I Saw the Movie*, 1990
  editor

4739

DONALD A. WOLLHEIM, Editor
ARTHUR W. SAHA, Co-Editor

The 1990 Annual World's Best Science Fiction

(New York: DAW, 1990)

Story type: Science Fiction (Anthology)

Summary: This 25th anniversary issue contains stories by Gregory Benford, Orson Scott Card, Lisa Tuttle, Lucius Shepard and Robert Silverberg, among others. The stories cover a wide range of themes including genetic engineering, future warfare, nuclear waste and interactions with computers.

Other books you might like:
Isaac Asimov, *Isaac Asimov Presents the Great SF Stories: 15 (1953)*, 1986
Groff Conklin, *The Best of Science Fiction*, 1946
Gardner Dozois, *The Year's Best Science Fiction: Seventh Annual Collection*, 1990
Harlan Ellison, *Dangerous Visions*, 1967
Robert Silverberg, *The Science Fiction Hall of Fame, Volume 1*, 1970

4740

DAVE WOLVERTON

Beyond the Gate

(New York: Tor, 1995)

Story type: Science Fiction (Space Opera)
Series: Golden Queen
Major character(s): Gallen O'Day, Warrior, Hero; Maggie Flynn, Fiance(e); Orick, Animal (bear), Adventurer
Time period(s): Indeterminate Future
Locale(s): Tremonthin, Planet—Imaginary; Interstellar Empire/Federation

Summary: As Gallen O'Day and Maggie Flynn plan to wed, Gallen receives orders to go to Tremonthin as Lord Protector of the planet. There he must destroy a secret society, the Inhuman, and deflect another invasion of the insectoid Dronons.

Other books you might like:
David Brin, *Startide Rising*, 1983
C.J. Cherryh, *Serpent's Reach*, 1980
Dave Duncan, *Hero*, 1991
Joan Slonczewski, *A Door into Ocean*, 1986
Sheri S. Tepper, *Grass*, 1989
Vernor Vinge, *A Fire upon the Deep*, 1992

4741

DAVE WOLVERTON

The Courtship of Princess Leia

(New York: Bantam Spectra, 1994)

Story type: Science Fiction (Space Opera; Mystical)
Series: Star Wars

Major character(s): Leia Organa, Royalty, Diplomat; Han Solo, Spaceship Captain, Warrior; Luke Skywalker, Martial Arts Expert (Jedi Knight), Hero
Time period(s): Indeterminate Past
Locale(s): Dathomir, Planet—Imaginary; New Republic, Interstellar Empire/Federation

Summary: Unwilling to accept Leia's proposed marriage to Prince Isolder to cement relations between the Rebel Alliance and the Hapes consortium, Han Solo tricks Leia into accompanying him to Dathomir. Interrupting his search for Jedi Knight lore, Luke with Artoo-Detoo and Prince Isolder, travels to Dathomir, little expecting the treasure and the danger that await.

Other books you might like:
Roger MacBride Allen, *Ambush at Corellia*, 1995
Kevin J. Anderson, *Jedi Search*, 1994
Brian Daley, *The Han Solo Adventures*, 1992
George Lucas, *The Star Wars Trilogy*, 1987
    Donald F. Glut, James Kahn, co-authors
Vonda N. McIntyre, *The Crystal Star*, 1994

4742

DAVE WOLVERTON

The Golden Queen
(New York: Tor, 1994)

Story type: Science Fiction (Space Opera)
Series: Golden Queen
Major character(s): Everynne, Clone, Royalty (queen); Gallen O'Day, Warrior, Hero; Orick, Animal (bear), Adventurer
Time period(s): Indeterminate Future
Locale(s): Tihrglas, Planet—Imaginary

Summary: Chased by dronon vanquishers, Everynne and her guardian search Tihrglas for the portal leading to other worlds. Vulnerable to Everynne's immortal beauty, Gallen follows her through the portal after stealing a key from the vanquishers. Gallen, his companion talking bear, Orick, and Maggie, a waitress from the local inn, hope to save humanity from the insectoid dronons and rescue Everynne.

Other books you might like:
William Barton, *Dark Sky Legion*, 1992
C.J. Cherryh, *The Fires of Azeroth*, 1979
C.J. Cherryh, *Gate of Ivrel*, 1976
C.J. Cherryh, *Well of Shiuan*, 1978
Cheryl J. Franklin, *Fire Crossing*, 1991

4743

DAVE WOLVERTON, Editor

L. Ron Hubbard Presents Writers of the Future, Volume IX
(Los Angeles: Bridge Publications, 1993)

Story type: Science Fiction (Anthology)
Series: Writers of the Future

Summary: Includes a two-page introduction by Wolverton, five articles on writing and art by the editor and Kevin J.

Anderson, Octavia E. Butler, L. Ron Hubbard and Julius Schwartz plus 17 original stories with diverse themes and tones written by emerging writers who recently won Writers of the Future Contests. Concludes with nine pages about the contest, including contest rules and deadlines.

Other books you might like:
Algis Budrys, *L. Ron Hubbard Presents Writers of the Future, Volumes I-VIII*, 1985-1992
    editor
George R.R. Martin, *The John W. Campbell Awards, Volume 5*, 1984
    editor
George R.R. Martin, *New Voices I-IV*, 1977-1981
    editor
Victoria Schochet, *The Berkley Showcase: New Writings in Science Fiction and Fantasy, Volumes 1-4*, 1980-1981
    John Silbersack, co-editor

4744

DAVE WOLVERTON

On My Way to Paradise
(New York: Bantam Spectra, 1989)

Story type: Science Fiction (Cyberpunk)
Major character(s): Angelo Osic, Scientist, Military Personnel; Tamara, Spy
Time period(s): 21st century
Locale(s): Baker, Planet—Imaginary; Panama

Summary: One day Angelo Osic helps an injured woman named Tamara and finds himself in the middle of a complex web of violence and intrigue. Tamara, it seems, is in possession of dangerous information, information that someone else wants and is willing to kill to get. Fleeing Earth, Angelo signs on as a cyborg mercenary with a Japanese corporation fighting a bloody war off planet.

Other books you might like:
Orson Scott Card, *Ender's Game*, 1985
Joe Haldeman, *The Forever War*, 1974
Lucius Shepard, *Life During Wartime*, 1987
Bruce Sterling, *Islands in the Net*, 1988

4745

DAVE WOLVERTON

Serpent Catch
(New York: Bantam Spectra, 1991)

Story type: Science Fiction (Adventure; Genetic Manipulation)
Major character(s): Tull, Hero, Prehistoric Human (Neanderthal/human halfbreed); Fava, Girlfriend, Prehistoric Human (Neanderthal)
Time period(s): Indeterminate Future
Locale(s): Anee, Moon—Imaginary

Summary: On Anee, genetic paleontologists were constructing the greatest zoo in the galaxy. Each of three continents was populated from a different era of Earth's history and kept separate by gigantic sea serpents which ate anything attempting to swim across the oceans and dragons that hunted the flying pterodactyls. When the alien Eridani killed all humans in space, the paleontologists were forced to descend to Anee where some befriended and others exploited the Neanderthals. Generations later when the sea serpents began to disappear, Tull, a young half-breed Neanderthal, learns about life, freedom and love on his odyssey to find new sea serpents and protect his home from dinosaurs.

Other books you might like:
David Brin, *Earth*, 1990
Octavia E. Butler, *Dawn*, 1987
Suzette Haden Elgin, *Native Tongue*, 1984
Larry Niven, *The Flight of the Horse*, 1973
Joan Slonczewski, *A Door into Ocean*, 1986
Michael Swanwick, *In the Drift*, 1985

4746
JACK WOMACK
Elvissey
(New York: Tor, 1993)

Story type: Science Fiction (Satire; Alternate Universe)
Series: Dryco Chronicles
Major character(s): Elvis Presley, Musician, Religious; Isabel ''Iz'' Bonney, Spouse, Time Traveller; John Bonney, Spouse, Time Traveller
Time period(s): 21st century; 1950s
Locale(s): New York, New York; Graceland, Tennessee; Alternate Earth

Summary: With Elvis Presley religions proliferating, John and Iz plan to bring Elvis Presley from the past to provide the Second Coming. However, the 1950s they discover includes a past absent the United States Civil War and a 1950s Europe under Nazi domination.

Other books you might like:
Richard Peabody, *Mondo Elvis*, 1993
    Lucinda Ebersole, co-editor
Robert Rankin, *Armageddon: The Musical*, 1990
Allen Steele, *Clarke County, Space*, 1990
Neal Stephenson, *Snow Crash*, 1992
Jack Yeovil, *Comeback Tour: The Sky Belongs to the Stars*, 1991

4747
JACK WOMACK
Heathern
(New York: Tor, 1990)

Story type: Science Fiction (Theological; Contemporary Realism)
Series: Dryco Chronicles
Major character(s): Thatcher Dryden, Businessman (executive); Lester Hill Macaffrey, Teacher, Psychic (miracle worker)
Time period(s): 1990s (1990)
Locale(s): New York, New York

Summary: When Thatcher Dryden heard about Lester Macaffrey performing miracles he sent some representatives to invite Lester to Dryco to meet him. While they were there Lester miraculously resuscitated a man one of the envoys had killed. Thatcher was determined to control and use Lester to make a fortune for Dryco.

Other books you might like:
Neil Gaiman, *Good Omens: The Nice and Accurate Prophecies of Agnes Nutter, Witch*, 1990
    Terry Pratchett, co-author
Parke Godwin, *Waiting for the Galactic Bus*, 1988
John Kessel, *Good News From Outer Space*, 1989
James Morrow, *Only Begotten Daughter*, 1990
Robert Rankin, *Armageddon: The Musical*, 1990

4748
JACK WOMACK
Random Acts of Senseless Violence
(New York: Atlantic Monthly Press, 1994)

Story type: Fantasy (Science Fiction; Urban)
Series: Dryco Chronicles
Major character(s): Lola Hart, Teenager; Jude, Teenager; 12, Teenager
Time period(s): 21st century
Locale(s): New York, New York

Summary: Lola Hart lives in a world on the edge of disaster. When hard times rob her writer parents of their livelihood, the family moves to the Shattered East Side, from modest privilege to danger and poverty. As Lola wanders unprepared into violence and love, she finds a sadly plausible future.

Other books you might like:
Francesca Lia Block, *Primavera*, 1994
Pat Cadigan, *Synners*, 1991
Jim Carrol, *The Basketball Diaries*, 1978
William Gibson, *Virtual Light*, 1993
Jonathan Littell, *Bad Voltage*, 1989

4749
JACK WOMACK
Terraplane
(New York: Tor Books, 1990)

Story type: Science Fiction (Alternate Universe)
Series: Dryco Chronicles
Major character(s): Robert Luther Bickerstaff, Military Personnel (Retired General), Businessman; Jake, Criminal (Assassin)
Time period(s): 21st century
Locale(s): Russia; New York, Alternate Universe

Summary: In this sequel to *Ambient*, Bickerstaff and Jake are engaged in espionage in a post-communist Russia which has become intensely consumer oriented. Suddenly they and two Russians are thrown into an alternate universe and find themselves in New York, circa 1939. In this universe, however, racism is much worse than in ours and Bickerstaff, being black and used to being in command, finds himself in immediate trouble.

Other books you might like:
William Gibson, *Count Zero*, 1985
William Gibson, *Mona Lisa Overdrive*, 1988
William Gibson, *Neuromancer*, 1984
Richard Kadrey, *Metrophage*, 1988
Bruce Sterling, *Islands in the Net*, 1988
Gene Wolfe, *There Are Doors*, 1988

4750

BARI WOOD

The Basement
(New York: Morrow, 1995)

Story type: Horror (Supernatural Vengeance)
Major character(s): Myra Lundens, Housewife; Reed Lerner, Doctor (psychiatrist); Arlen Pinchot, Housewife
Time period(s): 1990s (1995)
Locale(s): Fallsbridge, Connecticut

Summary: Myra Ludens tries to rid her house of its uncanny malaise by exorcising the spirit of a witch whose remains were buried in the land it rests on three centuries before, but only rouses the witch's ire. As her friends begin dying gruesome deaths, Myra looks for more scientific solutions to her problem and ponders the coincidence that most of the witch's victims are people who she has fought with.

Other books you might like:
Douglas Clegg, *Goat Dance*, 1989
Morgan Fields, *Shaman Woods*, 1990
Melisand March, *The Site*, 1988
Roy Sorrels, *The Eyes of Torie Webster*, 1990
Chet Williamson, *Dreamthorp*, 1989

4751

BRIDGET WOOD

The Lost Prince
(New York: Ballantine Del Rey, 1993)

Story type: Fantasy (Political; Time Travel)
Major character(s): Fergus, Military Personnel, Time Traveller; Grainne, Royalty (crown prince); Medoc, Wizard, Ruler (usurper)
Time period(s): Indeterminate Past; Indeterminate Future
Locale(s): Ireland

Summary: When the Enchantment fades from the royal houses of ancient Ireland, the Beastline of rulers dies out until only Grainne and Fergus remain to ascend to the Wolf throne. When the evil wizard Medoc usurps power and spreads corruption throughout the land, Grainne searches for help from the Castle of Shadows while Fergus travels to the distant future where he hopes to harness the power of the Apocalypse to overthrow Medoc. Sequel to *Wolfking*.

Other books you might like:
Kenneth C. Flint, *Challenge of the Clans*, 1986
Kenneth C. Flint, *The Dark Druid*, 1987
Kenneth C. Flint, *Storm Shield*, 1986

Morgan Llywelyn, *Grania: She-King of the Irish Seas*, 1986
Elizabeth Moon, *Sheepfarmer's Daughter*, 1988
Andrew J. Offutt, *The Sign of the Moonbow*, 1980
Andrew J. Offutt, *Sword of the Gael*, 1975
Andrew J. Offutt, *The Undying Wizard*, 1982

4752

BRIDGET WOOD

Wolfking
(New York: Ballantine Del Rey, 1992)

Story type: Fantasy (Time Travel; Post-Disaster)
Major character(s): Joanna Grady, Time Traveller; Flynn O'Connor, Time Traveller; Cormac, Royalty
Time period(s): Indeterminate Future; Indeterminate Past
Locale(s): Ireland; Tara, Mythical Place

Summary: Joanna's romance with Flynn blossoms in post-apocalyptic Ireland until Joanna's father decides she must marry an ignorant pig farmer. Joanna flees into a radioactive area where she uses a Gateway to travel back in time to ancient Ireland. When Flynn follows Joanna, the pair find themselves involved in Cormac's struggle for his crown.

Other books you might like:
Kenneth C. Flint, *Challenge of the Clans*, 1986
Kenneth C. Flint, *The Dark Druid*, 1987
Kenneth C. Flint, *Storm Shield*, 1986
Elizabeth Moon, *Sheepfarmer's Daughter*, 1988
Andrew J. Offutt, *The Sign of the Moonbow*, 1980
Andrew J. Offutt, *Sword of the Gael*, 1975
Andrew J. Offutt, *The Tower of Death*, 1982
  co-author
Andrew J. Offutt, *The Undying Wizard*, 1982
Andrew J. Offutt, *When Death Birds Fly*, 1980
  co-author

4753

N. LEE WOOD

Looking for the Mahdi
(New York: Ace, 1996)

Story type: Science Fiction (Political; Techno-Thriller)
Major character(s): Kahlili "Kay Bee" bint Munadi Sulaiman, Journalist; John Halton, Genetically Altered Being; Cullen Laidcliff, Government Official
Time period(s): 21st century
Locale(s): Clarke Orbital Station, Space Station; Nok Kuzlat, Middle East; Khuruchabja, Middle East

Summary: Having worked behind a desk for 10 years since passing as a man while covering the war in Khuruchabja, Kay Bee reluctantly permits Laidcliff to coerce her into transporting and delivering Halton to the new king of Khuruchabja. Unfortunately, Halton arrives with an extra item to deliver, nearly resulting in their deaths, and forces Kay Bee to reevaluate John and the mission. First novel.

Other books you might like:
David Brin, *Earth*, 1990
Raphael Carter, *The Fortunate Fall*, 1996

Philip K. Dick, *Bladerunner*, 1982
George Alec Effinger, *When Gravity Fails*, 1987
Elizabeth Moon, *Hunting Party*, 1993
Neal Stephenson, *The Diamond Age*, 1995

4754

FRANCINE G. WOODBURY

Shade and Shadow

(New York: Ballantine Del Rey, 1996)

Story type: Fantasy (Mystery)
Major character(s): Raoul ''Rags'' Smythe, Magician, Professor; Maxwell ''Max'' Bolton, Journalist
Time period(s): Indeterminate
Locale(s): England, Alternate Earth (Oxford and London)

Summary: Upon the murder of the offensive chairman of the University's College of Magic, police suspect Assistant Professor Raoul Smythe. Intending to clear himself, Raoul and his friend, Max, begin an independent investigation stretching to events decades in the past and casting suspicion on Raoul's potential new girlfriend. First novel.

Other books you might like:
Randall Garrett, *Too Many Magicians*, 1967
Laurell K. Hamilton, *Nightseer*, 1992
Caroline Stevermer, *A College of Magics*, 1994
L.A. Taylor, *Cat's Paw*, 1995
Robert Weinberg, *A Logical Magician*, 1994

4755

ELVIRA WOODRUFF

The Summer I Shrank My Grandmother

(New York: Holiday, 1990)

Story type: Fantasy (Light Fantasy; Young Adult)
Major character(s): Nelly Brown, Child, Scientist; Emma Brown, Grandparent
Time period(s): 1990s (1990)
Locale(s): Seaview, California

Summary: Experimenting with a magical chemistry set, Nelly reverses the aging process in her grandmother. Will she be able to find an antidote before her grandmother shrinks to an embryo?

Other books you might like:
Florence P. Heide, *The Shrinking of Treehorn*, 1971
Elaine Horseman, *Hubble's Bubble*, 1964
Diana Wynne Jones, *The Ogre Downstairs*, 1974
E. Nesbit, *Five Children and It*, 1905

4756

JOHN WOOLEY
RON WOLFE, Co-Author

Death's Door

(New York: Dell/Abyss, 1992)

Story type: Horror (Doppelganger)

Major character(s): Case Hamilton, Police Officer; Stephen Glasser, Doctor (surgeon); Diana Hamilton, Police Officer
Time period(s): 1990s (1993)
Locale(s): Los Angeles, California

Summary: The second time after he is brought back from death following injury in the line of duty, police officer Case Hamilton finds himself saddled with an alter ego he refers to as the Gray Man, a creature from the other side of life who embarks on a murderous rampage.

Other books you might like:
Kathe Koja, *Bad Brains*, 1992
Dean R. Koontz, *Hideaway*, 1992
Joe R. Lansdale, *The Nightrunners*, 1987
T.M. Wright, *Little Boy Lost*, 1992

4757

PERSIA WOOLLEY

Guinevere: The Legend in Autumn

(New York: Poseidon Press, 1991)

Story type: Fantasy (Legend; Romance)
Series: Child of the Northern Spring
Major character(s): Guinevere, Royalty (queen); Arthur, Ruler (king); Lancelot, Knight
Time period(s): 6th century
Locale(s): Camelot, England; Joyous Gard, England (Northumbria)

Summary: A mature Guinevere relates adventures of Arthur's knights, her personal vision of the Goddess, the Grail quest, Mordred's difficult relationship with Arthur and her passion for Lancelot. When Morgan le Fey's treachery results in Guinevere's trial, death sentence and rescue by Lancelot, she and Lancelot flee north. After Arthur threatens to march on Joyous Gard, Guinevere returns to Camelot to the great joy of her subjects. She later acts as mediator between Arthur and Morgan le Fey concerning Christianity and the Goddess Religion.

Other books you might like:
Marion Zimmer Bradley, *The Mists of Avalon*, 1983
Gillian Bradshaw, *Hawk of May*, 1980
Courtway Jones, *In the Shadow of the Oak King*, 1991
Sharan Newman, *A Chessboard Queen*, 1983
Sharan Newman, *Guinevere*, 1981
Sharan Newman, *Guinevere Evermore*, 1985
Howard Pyle, *The Story of the Champions of the Round Table*, 1905
Howard Pyle, *The Story of King Arthur and His Knights*, 1903

4758

PERSIA WOOLLEY

Queen of the Summer Stars

(New York: Poseidon, 1990)

Story type: Fantasy (Legend; Romance)
Series: Child of the Northern Spring
Major character(s): Guinevere, Royalty (queen); Arthur, Ruler (king); Lancelot, Knight

Time period(s): 6th century
Locale(s): Camelot, England

Summary: Gwen decides to help her husband, Arthur, cement his relationships with the independent client kings into the legendary Round Table. She decides to have constructed the most wonderful setting for them, Camelot. 1991 Best Books For Young Adults title.

Other books you might like:
Marion Zimmer Bradley, *The Mists of Avalon*, 1983
Gillian Bradshaw, *Hawk of May*, 1980
Gillian Bradshaw, *In Winter's Shadow*, 1982
Gillian Bradshaw, *Kingdom of Summer*, 1981
Sharan Newman, *A Chessboard Queen*, 1983
Sharan Newman, *Guinevere*, 1981
Sharan Newman, *Guinevere Evermore*, 1985

4759

DAVID WORSICK

Henry's Gift: The Magic Eye

(Kansas City, Missouri: Andrews and McMeel, 1994)

Story type: Fantasy (Psychic Powers; Quest)
Major character(s): Henry of Veldran, Orphan; Byron, Knight; Nadia, Adventurer
Time period(s): Indeterminate
Locale(s): Haunted Hills, Fictional Country; Barony of Veldran, Fictional Country

Summary: When Henry comes of age, his adopted father passes on a parchment found with the infant Henry. When his legacy points to great wealth awaiting him, Henry sets out with Byron and Nadia to earn his inheritance, mindful of legends surrounding the treasure and his disturbing visions. Concludes with "About 3D Images," "How to See 3D Images" and sketches of the 20 3D images depicting Henry's psychic visions.

Other books you might like:
David Kirschner, *The Pagemaster*, 1993
   Ernie Contreras, co-author
Michael Ende, *The Neverending Story*, 1983
Terry Goodkind, *Wizard's First Rule*, 1994
James Gurney, *Dinotopia*, 1992
Roger Zelazny, *Way Up High*, 1992

4760

PATRICIA C. WREDE

Book of Enchantments

(New York: Harcourt Brace/Jane Yolen Books, 1996)

Story type: Fantasy (Collection; Young Adult)

Summary: Contains eight pages of author's notes plus six original stories and five stories reprinted from anthologies 1986-1994. Frequently light in tone, the stories explore a broad range of themes from unicorns and werewolves to fairy tales, English music, and *The Thousand and One Arabian Nights*, with one new story set in the Enchanted Forest Chronicles milieu.

Other books you might like:
Emma Bull, *Double Feature*, 1994
   Will Shetterly, co-author
Ellen Datlow, *Black Thorn, White Rose*, 1994
   Terri Windling, co-editor
Diana Wynne Jones, *Everard's Ride*, 1995
Will Shetterly, *Liavek: The Players of Luck*, 1986
   Emma Bull, co-editor
Michael Stearns, *A Wizard's Dozen*, 1993
   editor
Jane Yolen, *Storyteller*, 1992

4761

PATRICIA C. WREDE

Calling on Dragons

(New York: Harcourt Brace Jovanovich, 1993)

Story type: Fantasy (Quest; Young Adult)
Series: Enchanted Forest Chronicles
Major character(s): Cimorene, Royalty (queen); Kazul, Mythical Creature (dragon), Royalty (king); Morwen, Witch
Time period(s): Indeterminate
Locale(s): Enchanted Forest, Mythical Place

Summary: Evil wizards steal King Mendanbar's magic sword and begin stealing magic from the kingdom. Joined by Kazul, Morwen, a magician, Killer the rabbit-donkey and many opinionated cats, Queen Cimorene must recover the sword before it drains all magic from the Enchanted Forest, killing it.

Other books you might like:
Karen Brush, *Demon Pig*, 1991
Ursula K. Le Guin, *A Wizard of Earthsea*, 1968
Larry Niven, *The Magic Goes Away*, 1979
Meredith Ann Pierce, *The Pearl of the Soul of the World*, 1990
Sherwood Smith, *Wren to the Rescue*, 1990
Laurence Yep, *Dragon of the Lost Sea*, 1982

4762

PATRICIA C. WREDE

Dealing with Dragons

(New York: Harcourt Brace Jovanovich, 1990)

Story type: Fantasy (Light Fantasy; Young Adult)
Series: Enchanted Forest Chronicles
Major character(s): Cimorene, Royalty (princess); Kazul, Mythical Creature (dragon)
Time period(s): Indeterminate
Locale(s): Linderwall, Fictional Country; Enchanted Forest, Mythical Place

Summary: Cimorene is interested in learning a lot of things, but not the ones considered proper by her parents. When they decide to marry her to Prince Therandil, Cimorene takes action by fleeing to the Enchanted Forest to become a Dragon's Princess. Dragon politics, sneaky wizards and other princesses all combine to make lively times for Cimorene. This was twice honored by librarians, as an ALA Best Young Adult Books and as winner of a Minnesota Book Award.

Other books you might like:
Susan Fletcher, *Dragon's Milk*, 1989
Diana Wynne Jones, *Howl's Moving Castle*, 1986
M.M. Kaye, *The Ordinary Princess*, 1984
Jane Zaring, *The Return of the Dragon*, 1981

4763

PATRICIA C. WREDE

Mairelon the Magician
(New York: Tor, 1991)

Story type: Fantasy (Magic Conflict; Young Adult)
Major character(s): Kim, Orphan; Mairelon, Magician, Traveller
Time period(s): 1810s
Locale(s): London England, Alternate Universe

Summary: The chance to earn five pounds is unbelievably good luck for Kim since it would mean not having to live on the streets disguised as a boy, something she won't be able to do much longer. To earn the money she must sneak into Mairelon's wagon and see if it contains a certain silver bowl, but if Mairelon is a real sorcerer, why is he playing the travelling showman and why is that bowl so sought-after?

Other books you might like:
Joan Aiken, *Black Hearts in Battersea*, 1964
Joan Aiken, *Nightbirds on Nantucket*, 1966
Suzy McKee Charnas, *The Golden Thread*, 1989
Diane Duane, *So You Want to Be a Wizard?*, 1983
Alan Garner, *The Weirdstone of Brisingamen*, 1969
Diana Wynne Jones, *Cart and Cwidder*, 1977
Robin McKinley, *The Blue Sword*, 1982
Will Shetterly, *Elsewhere*, 1991

4764

PATRICIA C. WREDE

The Raven Ring
(New York: Tor, 1994)

Story type: Fantasy (Magic Conflict; Adventure)
Series: Lyra
Major character(s): Eleret Slaven, Martial Arts Expert, Teenager; Daner Vallaniri, Martial Arts Expert, Nobleman; Karvonen Aurelico, Thief, Guide
Time period(s): Indeterminate
Locale(s): Ciaron, Fictional City

Summary: Immediately after retrieving the possessions of her mercenary mother who died inexplicably after a battle, Eleret encounters offers, scams, attempted thefts and burglaries, all seemingly aimed at parting her from her family heirloom, a ring her mother took with her to battle. Befriended by Lord Daner and his family, Eleret also utilizes Karvonen's aid when the attacks continue inside Lord Daner's home.

Other books you might like:
Marion Zimmer Bradley, *The Shattered Chain*, 1976
Steven Brust, *Jhereg*, 1983
Lois McMaster Bujold, *The Spirit Ring*, 1992
Terry Goodkind, *Wizard's First Rule*, 1994

Laurell K. Hamilton, *Nightseer*, 1992
Caroline Stevermer, *A College of Magics*, 1994
Martha Wells, *The Element of Fire*, 1993

4765

PATRICIA C. WREDE

Searching for Dragons
(New York: Harcourt Brace Jovanovich, 1991)

Story type: Fantasy (Quest; Young Adult)
Series: Enchanted Forest Chronicles
Major character(s): Cimorene, Royalty, Companion (Kazul's); Mendanbar, Ruler (king)
Time period(s): Indeterminate
Locale(s): Enchanted Forest, Mythical Place

Summary: On advice of the witch, Morwen, Mendanbar seeks the counsel of Kazul, King of the Dragons, to discover how to stop the destruction of the Enchanted Forest. When Mendanbar discovers Kazul has been captured by wizards, he and Cimorene, the dragon's princess, set off to find and bring back Kazul, apparently the latest victim of the feud between the wizards and the dragons. Sequel to *Dealing with Dragons*.

Other books you might like:
Diana Wynne Jones, *Archer's Goon*, 1984
Diana Wynne Jones, *Howl's Moving Castle*, 1986
Tanith Lee, *Black Unicorn*, 1991
Jane Yolen, *Dragon's Blood*, 1982
Jane Yolen, *Wizard's Hall*, 1991
Mary Frances Zambreno, *A Plague of Sorcerers*, 1991

4766

PATRICIA C. WREDE

Snow White and Rose Red
(New York: Tor, 1989)

Story type: Fantasy (Legend)
Series: Fairy Tales
Major character(s): Snow White Arden, Maiden; Rose Red Arden, Maiden
Time period(s): 16th century
Locale(s): England

Summary: A re-working of the Grimm Brothers' version, weaving history and fantasy together for a familiar, yet new story.

Other books you might like:
Steven Brust, *The Sun, the Moon, and the Stars*, 1987
Robin McKinley, *Beauty*, 1985
Susan Shwartz, *Arabesques: More Tales of the Arabian Nights*, 1980

4767

M.K. WREN

A Gift Upon the Shore
(New York: Ballantine, 1990)

Story type: Science Fiction (Post-Nuclear Holocaust)

Major character(s): Mary Hope, Writer; Rachel Morrow, Artist, Farmer
Time period(s): Indeterminate Future
Locale(s): Oregon

Summary: Mary, a young writer, takes refuge on Rachel's isolated farm in Oregon and both survive the gradual collapse of society due to a series of plagues, natural disasters and, eventually, a nuclear war. Years later Mary finds herself fighting desperately to keep the fundamentalist Christians with whom she now lives from destroying the remnants of pre-holocaust culture still existing.

Other books you might like:
Neal Barrett Jr., *Through Darkest America*, 1987
David Brin, *The Postman*, 1985
Sheri S. Tepper, *The Gate to Women's Country*, 1988

4768

GARY WRIGHT

The Road West
(Lake Geneva, Wisconsin: TSR, 1990)

Story type: Fantasy (Sword and Sorcery)
Major character(s): Keven, Orphan, Traveller
Time period(s): Indeterminate Past
Locale(s): Midvale, Fictional Country

Summary: When Keven is orphaned at 15 years of age, he decides to leave the sea to enter the King's Academy. He graduates as King's Ranger-at-Arms, buys his contract to the king with his inheritance, and sets off to practice what he has learned. This is the author's first novel.

Other books you might like:
Joy Chant, *Red Moon and Black Mountain*, 1970
Phyllis Eisenstein, *Born to Exile*, 1978
Rosemary Kirstein, *The Steerswoman*, 1989
Ursula K. Le Guin, *A Wizard of Earthsea*, 1968

4769

HELEN S. WRIGHT

A Matter of Oaths
(New York: Popular Library Questar, 1990)

Story type: Science Fiction (Space Opera)
Major character(s): Rallya, Spaceship Captain (commander); Rafe, Spaceman (first officer); Joshim, Spaceman (webmaster)
Time period(s): Indeterminate Future
Locale(s): *Bhattya*, Spaceship

Summary: The crew of the *Bhattya* needs a new First Officer and Rafe needs a web position. Rafe had been mind-wiped ten years earlier for breaking his oath to the Emperor. At first Rallya is reluctant to have him in spite of his evident ability with the web machinery which operates the ship. Soon after he comes on board, Rallya begins to suspect he has dangerous memories still locked inside his mind, and dangerous enemies who would like him dead. Rallya and Joshim set out to solve the mystery that spans two empires. A first novel.

Other books you might like:
C.J. Cherryh, *Chanur's Venture*, 1984
C.J. Cherryh, *The Kif Strike Back*, 1985
C.J. Cherryh, *The Pride of Chanur*, 1982
Frank Herbert, *Dune*, 1965
Vonda N. McIntyre, *Superluminal*, 1983

4770

T. LUCIEN WRIGHT

Blood Brothers
(New York: Pinnacle, 1992)

Story type: Horror (Vampire Story)
Major character(s): Harry Matheson, Writer (horror writer), Vampire; Jerry Matheson, Writer (horror writer); Tad Matheson, Child (Jerry's son)
Time period(s): 1990s
Locale(s): Naples Falls, New York

Summary: When horror writer Harry Matheson is turned into a vampire, his sensitive twin brother Jerry translates the images he receives of Harry's killings into superior horror fiction. Harry then decides to extend their longstanding sibling rivalry by turning Jerry into a vampire as well.

Other books you might like:
Kathryn Meyer Griffith, *Vampire Blood*, 1991
Tom Piccirilli, *Dark Father*, 1990
Lee Weathersby, *Kiss of the Vampire*, 1992

4771

T. LUCIEN WRIGHT

Dark Visions
(New York: Pinnacle, 1993)

Story type: Horror (Wild Talents)
Major character(s): Amelia Fortunato, Student—College; Freeman Ridge, Maintenance Worker (janitor); John A. Sanders, Police Officer
Time period(s): 1990s (1993)
Locale(s): Buffalo, New York

Summary: When psychically-endowed Amelia Fortunato begins college in Buffalo, her familiar visions of The Tunnel, which she has always feared and dreaded, become combined with her visions of past unsolved crimes in the area and the man responsible for them. Freeman Ridge, the criminal, knows that he must kill Amelia if he is to remain a free man.

Other books you might like:
Stephen King, *The Dead Zone*, 1979
Dean R. Koontz, *Hideaway*, 1992
Dean R. Koontz, *The Vision*, 1977
Joe R. Lansdale, *The Nightrunners*, 1987

4772

T. LUCIEN WRIGHT

Thirst of the Vampire

(New York: Pinnacle, 1992)

Story type: Horror (Vampire Story)
Major character(s): Mike Marat, Journalist; Beverly Marat, Relative (Mike's sister); Phillipe Brissot, Vampire
Time period(s): 1990s (1992)
Locale(s): Rochester, New York; Watertown, New York

Summary: Phillipe Brissot holds the world's record for long-standing grudges: wronged by eighteenth-century French revolutionary Jean Marat, he has devoted his immortal life to systematically tracking down and destroying Marat's descendants, several of whom seem to have lived long enough to produce a branch of the family tree that has survived into the twentieth century and settled in upstate New York.

Other books you might like:
Kim Newman, *Bad Dreams*, 1990
Lee Wethersby, *Kiss of the Vampire*, 1992

4773

T.M. WRIGHT

The Ascending

(New York: Tor, 1994)

Story type: Horror (Occult)
Major character(s): Ryerson Biergarten, Psychic; Lenny Baker, Psychic; Rick Dunn, Architect
Time period(s): 1990s (1994)
Locale(s): Toronto, Ontario, Canada

Summary: In this follow-up to the author's *Goodlow's Ghosts*, psychic Ryerson Biergarten travels to Canada to apply his skills to a mysterious series of murders in which victims are intimately linked to the architectural structures in which their bodies are concealed.

Other books you might like:
James Kisner, *Tower of Evil*, 1994
Melisand March, *The Site*, 1988
Robert Morgan, *The Only Thing to Fear*, 1994

4774

T.M. WRIGHT

Boundaries

(New York: Tor, 1990)

Story type: Horror (Alternate World)
Major character(s): David Case, Worker (at a pharmaceutical company); Christian Grieg, Young Man; Karen Duffy, Young Woman
Time period(s): 1990s
Locale(s): Batavia, New York

Summary: Thinking that the murderer of his twin sister Anne has committed suicide to join her on "the Other Side," David Case takes an experimental drug that will allow him to cross the boundary between life and death. What David doesn't know is that the real murderer is very much alive and determined that David shall never return to the land of the living.

Other books you might like:
Dennis Etchison, *Darkside*, 1986

4775

T.M. WRIGHT

Goodlow's Ghosts

(New York: Tor, 1993)

Story type: Horror (Ghost Story)
Major character(s): Ryerson Biergarten, Psychic; Sam Goodlow, Detective
Time period(s): 1990s
Locale(s): Boston, Massachusetts

Summary: In his typically opaque style, the author explores the boundaries between the worlds of the living and the dead through two story lines: in one, a psychic seeks the whereabouts of a man who has disappeared and is presumed dead; in the other, the man who is presumed dead undergoes a series of bizarre experiences that lead him to believe he is no longer living but is experiencing the afterlife.

Other books you might like:
Jonathan Aycliffe, *Naomi's Room*, 1992
Judith Hawkes, *Julian's House*, 1989
Shirley Jackson, *The Haunting of Hill House*, 1961
Richard Matheson, *Hell House*, 1971
Chet Williamson, *Ash Wednesday*, 1987

4776

T.M. WRIGHT

Little Boy Lost

(New York: Tor, 1992)

Story type: Horror (Child-in-Peril)
Major character(s): C.J. Gale, Teenager; Miles Gale, Archaeologist; Jessica French, Doctor
Time period(s): 1990s
Locale(s): New York

Summary: The disappearance of Aaron Gale during a shopping trip leads to an intimate inspection of the Gale family's history, including the desertion of Marie Gale, Aaron's mother, who may have fled to another dimension and found a way to take Aaron with her.

Other books you might like:
Jonathan Aycliffe, *Naomi's Room*, 1991
Tom Piccirilli, *Dark Father*, 1990
Whitley Strieber, *Billy*, 1990

4777

T.M. WRIGHT

The Place

(New York: Tor, 1989)

Story type: Horror (Serial Killer)
Major character(s): Harlan DeVries, Serial Killer, Psychic; Greta King, Psychic, Child
Time period(s): 1990s
Locale(s): Ithaca, New York; Canaan, New York (Underground Village)

Summary: Harlan DeVries, serial killer and leader of an underground community, murders at will. He terrorizes the King family, sending the father to the hospital and kidnapping the mother and young son, while setting his sights on Greta, the paranormal daughter. But the little girl, in psychic contact with her family, marshals her psychic powers to battle DeVries in this world and the next.

Other books you might like:
Stephen King, *The Shining*, 1977
Dean R. Koontz, *The Vision*, 1977

4778

T.M. WRIGHT

The School

(New York: Tor, 1990)

Story type: Horror (Haunted House)
Major character(s): Allison Hitchcock, Writer; Frank Hitchcock, Photographer (Allison's husband)
Time period(s): 1990s
Locale(s): Danby, New York (Finger Lakes region)

Summary: Frank and Allison Hitchcock buy the old elementary schoolhouse on Ohio Road with intent to turn it into a bed-and-breakfast, unaware that their bereavement over the recent death of their son Joey is fueling the evil power that permeates the building.

Other books you might like:
Shirley Jackson, *The Haunting of Hill House*, 1959
Stephen King, *The Shining*, 1977

4779

PATRICIA WRIGHTSON

Balyet

(New York: McElderry, 1989)

Story type: Fantasy (Legend)
Major character(s): Jo, Teenager; Balyet, Spirit (Exiled)
Time period(s): 1980s
Locale(s): Australia

Summary: Young Jo follows a boy going camping. Instead of finding romance, however, she encounters the exiled spirit, Balyet. Fun turns to danger when Balyet starts showing the darker side of her nature.

Other books you might like:
Suzy McKee Charnas, *The Golden Thread*, 1989
Brian Keaney, *No Need for Heroes*, 1989
Pamela F. Service, *Vision Quest*, 1989
Jane Yolen, *The Faery Flag*, 1989

4780

WILLIAM WU

Dictator

(New York: AvoNova, 1994)

Story type: Science Fiction (Robot Fiction; Time Travel)
Series: Isaac Asimov's Robots in Time
Major character(s): Hunter, Robot, Detective; Judy Taub, Historian; Wayne Nystrom, Scientist, Time Traveller
Time period(s): 1940s (1941); Indeterminate Future
Locale(s): Moscow, Union of Soviet Socialist Republics

Summary: While waiting for the Germans to attack Moscow, natives capture Hunter and his team. When Dr. Nystrom and Ishihara claim Hunter works for the Germans, the NKVD arrests him. Hunter must escape capture and rally his team to complete the mission.

Other books you might like:
Poul Anderson, *Time Patrolman*, 1983
Ben Bova, *Triumph*, 1993
James P. Hogan, *The Proteus Operation*, 1985
Andre Norton, *The Crossroads of Time*, 1956
Harry Turtledove, *Worldwar: In the Balance*, 1994

4781

WILLIAM WU

Hong on the Range

(New York: Walker, 1989)

Story type: Science Fiction (Young Adult)
Major character(s): Louie Hong, Cowboy (Drifter); Chuck, Animal (A Steerite)
Time period(s): 21st century
Locale(s): West

Summary: After a series of biological disasters has all but destroyed the American West, a hardy new breed of cybernetic cowboys, equipped with all sorts of built-in mechanical and electronic advantages, attempts to reestablish ranching as a profession. Instead of cattle, however, they herd steerites, intelligent, cyborg steers. Louie Hong is a control-natural, a drifter with no cybernetic improvements. Despite this disadvantage, he's determined to make it in this new, silly, and very wild west.

Other books you might like:
Ron Goulart, *Cowboy Heaven*, 1979
Ron Goulart, *The Prisoner of Blackwood Castle*, 1984
Ron Goulart, *Starpirate's Brain*, 1987
Ron Goulart, *The Wicked Cyborg*, 1978
Richard Wilson, *The Girls from Planet 5*, 1955

4782

WILLIAM WU

Predator

(New York: AvoNova, 1993)

Story type: Science Fiction (Time Travel; Robot Fiction)
Series: Isaac Asimov's Robots in Time
Major character(s): Hunter, Robot, Detective; Chad Mora, Scientist (paleontologist); Wayne Nystrom, Scientist, Time Traveller
Time period(s): 21st century; Indeterminate Past (Cretaceous period)
Locale(s): United States; North America (prehistoric Canada)

Summary: When five of the six Governor robots enter closed loops, the sixth decides to save itself from that fate by travelling into the past. Hunter and three humans travel back in time to capture the Governor robot which has split into six components, one located in the Cretaceous.

Other books you might like:

Poul Anderson, *Time Patrolman*, 1983
Philip Jose Farmer, *Time's Last Gift*, 1972
David Gerrold, *Deathbeast*, 1978
Garry Kilworth, *Split Second*, 1985
Julian May, *The Many-Colored Land*, 1981
Chad Oliver, *The Mists of Time*, 1952
Clifford D. Simak, *Mastodonia*, 1978

4783

WILLIAM WU

The Robin Hood Ambush

(New York: Harper and Row, 1990)

Story type: Science Fiction (Time Travel; Young Adult)
Series: Robert Silverberg's Time Tours
Major character(s): Bob Washburn, Student; Allan Leong, Student; Will Ulrich, Student
Time period(s): 2060s (2061); 12th century (1189)
Locale(s): London, England

Summary: Three friends, Bob, Allan and Will, head back to 1189 A.D. for a vacation to see King Richard the Lion-Hearted crowned. They discover a corrupt Time Patrolman altering history to build an evil empire. The three boys wish Robin Hood would appear to help, but they know he was only a myth. No one else knows it however, so arming themselves with longbows, quarterstaffs and tales of Robin Hood, they set out to battle the Time Patrolman's scheme with a legend from the past.

Other books you might like:

Poul Anderson, *The Corridors of Time*, 1965
Poul Anderson, *The Shield of Time*, 1990
Poul Anderson, *There Will Be Time*, 1972
Gordon R. Dickson, *Time Storm*, 1977
H.G. Wells, *The Time Machine*, 1895

4784

WILLIAM WU

Warrior

(New York: AvoNova, 1993)

Story type: Science Fiction (Time Travel; Robot Fiction)
Series: Isaac Asimov's Robots in Time
Major character(s): Hunter, Robot, Detective; Steve Chang, Time Traveller; Wayne Nystrom, Scientist, Time Traveller
Time period(s): 21st century; 1st century
Locale(s): Germany (between the Rhine and Weser Rivers)

Summary: Hunter and three assistants go back in time to capture the third MC Governor robot component to return it to the proper time. Unfortunately, they must operate in a Roman-occupied Germany whose residents will soon massacre and drive out the Romans.

Other books you might like:

Poul Anderson, *Time Patrolman*, 1983
John Brunner, *Times Without Number*, 1969
L. Sprague de Camp, *Lest Darkness Fall*, 1941
Crawford Kilian, *Rogue Emperor*, 1988
Kevin D. Randle, *Remember the Alamo!*, 1986
    Robert Cornett, co-author
Mack Reynolds, *The Other Time*, 1984

4785

JANNY WURTS

Curse of the Mistwraith

(New York: Roc, 1994)

Story type: Fantasy (Magic Conflict; Political)
Series: Wars of Light and Shadow
Major character(s): Lysaer s'Ilessid, Royalty (prince), Magician (master or light); Arithon s'Falenn, Royalty (prince), Magician (master of shadows); Asandir, Sorcerer
Time period(s): Indeterminate
Locale(s): Athera, Planet—Imaginary

Summary: Covering all Athera for 500 years, mist and fog brings chaos and war. Prophecy says that a prince descended from one of the four royal heirs who fled through the Worldsend Gate into exile on Dascen Elur can restore sunlight. But the powers needed for Athera's deliverance come divided between two half-brothers, Lysaer, lord of light, and Arithon, master of shadows. With generations of blood feud in their homeworld of Dascen Elur lying between them before they step through the Worldsend Gate that leads to Athera, how can they combine their powers to fight the Mistwraith?

Other books you might like:

Steven Brust, *The Sun, the Moon, and the Stars*, 1987
C.J. Cherryh, *Gate of Ivrel*, 1976
Raymond E. Feist, *Daughter of the Empire*, 1987
    Janny Wurts, co-author
Simon R. Green, *Blue Moon Rising*, 1991
Roger Zelazny, *Nine Princes in Amber*, 1970

4786

JANNY WURTS

The Master of Whitestorm
(New York: Roc, 1992)

Story type: Fantasy (Quest; Magic Conflict)
Major character(s): Korendir, Adventurer, Mercenary; Haldeth, Artisan (blacksmith); Ithariel, Sorceress
Time period(s): Indeterminate Past
Locale(s): Tir Amindel, Fictional City; Datha, Fictional City; Aerith, Mythical Place

Summary: A galley slave, Korendir, escapes and sets out to gain enough money to build a truly secure home. He battles were-leopards, magicians, armies and demons, always winning, but never satisfied. Eventually, secrets and forgotten memories conspire to take away everything he has earned.

Other books you might like:
Glen Cook, *The Black Company*, 1984
Raymond E. Feist, *Daughter of the Empire*, 1987
Katherine Kurtz, *The Black Company*, 1984
Fritz Leiber, *Deryni Rising*, 1970
Patricia A. McKillip, *The Riddle-Master of Hed*, 1976
Tad Williams, *The Dragonbone Chair*, 1988

4787

JANNY WURTS

Ships of Merior
(New York: HarperCollins, 1995)
•

Story type: Fantasy (Political; Magic Conflict)
Series: Wars of Light and Shadow
Major character(s): Lysaer s'Ilessid, Royalty (crown prince), Magician (master of light); Arithon s'Falenn, Royalty (prince), Magician (master of shadows); Dakar, Psychic, Religious
Time period(s): Indeterminate (Fourth Age)
Locale(s): Athera, Planet—Imaginary

Summary: When Lysaer and Arithon defeat Desh-thiere, the Mistwraith curses them to eternal hatred of each other. Reisting the compulsion to hate, Arithon establishes a shipyard at Merior before Lysaer's armies can find and destroy him. Second in the series.

Other books you might like:
Raymond E. Feist, *Daughter of the Empire*, 1987
  Janny Wurts, co-author
Terry Goodkind, *Stone of Farewell*, 1995
Patricia A. McKillip, *The Book of Atrix Wolfe*, 1995
L.E. Modesitt Jr., *The Order War*, 1995
Margaret Weis, *Dragon Wing*, 1990
  Tracy Hickman, co-author

4788

JANNY WURTS

That Way Lies Camelot
(New York: HarperPrism, 1996)

Story type: Fantasy (Collection; Science Fiction)

Summary: Contains four original tales and 11 stories reprinted from periodicals and anthologies 1986-1993. Themes include military conflict, mythical creatures, high fantasy, magic conflict, the Camelot saga, and the transformatory power of wishes.

Other books you might like:
Marion Zimmer Bradley, *The Best of Marion Zimmer Bradley's Fantasy Magazine*, 1994
  editor
David Drake, *The Fleet 1-6*, 1988-1991
  Bill Fawcett, co-editor
Richard Gilliam, *Grails: Quests of the Dawn*, 1994
  Martin H. Greenberg, Edward Kramer, co-editors
Elizabeth Moon, *Lunar Activity*, 1990
Richard Pini, *The Blood of Ten Chiefs*, 1986
  Robert Asprin, Lynn Abbey, co-editor
Terri Windling, *Elsewhere*, 1981
  Mark Alan Arnold, co-editor

4789

E.A. WYKE-SMITH
GEORGE MORROW, Illustrator

The Marvellous Land of Snergs
(Baltimore: Old Earth Books, 1996)

Story type: Fantasy (Adventure; Young Adult)
Major character(s): Vanderdecker, Sea Captain, Mythical Creature; Sylvia, Child; Gorbo, Mythical Creature (Snerg)
Time period(s): 1920s
Locale(s): The Marvelous Land of Snergs, Fictional Country

Summary: In a strange, nearly unreachable land, a race of pixies aid the Society for the Removal of Superfluous Children in tending their charges. One day when Joe and Sylvia, two of the naughtier children, run away from home, Gorbo, a well-meaning but stupid Snerg, rescues them, whereupon all set out on an amazing adventure. Originally published in England in 1927, this novel had a strong impact on J.R.R. Tolkien, inspiring the hobbits of his famous novels. Includes an introduction and discussion of Wyke-Smith's writings by Douglas Anderson, 50 illustrations by George Morrow, and maps.

Other books you might like:
L. Frank Baum, *The Land of Oz*, 1904
Alan Garner, *The Weirdstone of Brisingamen*, 1961
Tove Jansson, *Finn Family Moomintroll*, 1958
Carol Kendall, *The Gammage Cup*, 1959
Mary Norton, *The Borrowers*, 1953
J.R.R. Tolkien, *The Hobbit*, 1938

4790

JONATHAN WYLIE

The Lightless Kingdom

(New York: Bantam Spectra, 1989)

Story type: Fantasy (Quest)
Series: Unbalanced Earth
Major character(s): Gemma, Sorceress; Arden, Lover (Gemma's)
Time period(s): Indeterminate
Locale(s): Southern Continent, Fictional Country; Lightless Kingdom, Fictional Country

Summary: Gemma is able to save the people of a valley from drought, but has lost Arden to caves beneath the mountain. Arden, meanwhile, has found a tribe living in caves, who are slowly being poisoned by the water from above.

Other books you might like:
David Eddings, *The Diamond Throne*, 1989
    Book 1 - The Elenium
Ru Emerson, *To the Haunted Mountains*,
    Book 1 - Tales of the Nedao

4791

KAREN TEI YAMASHITA

Through the Arc of the Rain Forest

(Minneapolis, Minnesota: Coffee House Press, 1990)

Story type: Fantasy (Satire)
Major character(s): Kazumasa Ishimaru, Engineer (safety); Chico Paco, Fisherman; Jonathan B. Tweep, Genius (3-armed)
Time period(s): 2000s (2002)
Locale(s): Brazil; South America

Summary: A freewheeling black comedy featuring a bizarre cast of characters, including a Japanese man with a ball floating six inches in front of his head, an American CEO with three arms, and a Brazilian peasant who discovers the art of healing by tickling one's earlobe with a feather. By the end of this story they have each risen to heights of wealth and fame before arriving at disasters, both personal and ecological, that destroy the rain forest and all the birds of Brazil.

Other books you might like:
Douglas Adams, *The Hitchhiker's Guide to the Galaxy*, 1980
John Brunner, *Children of the Thunder*, 1989
Charles de Lint, *Svaha*, 1989
Frank Herbert, *Dune*, 1965

4792

CHELSEA QUINN YARBRO

Better in the Dark

(New York: Tor, 1993)

Story type: Horror (Vampire Story)
Series: Chronicles of Saint Germain

Major character(s): Comte de Saint Germain, Vampire (aka Francois Rgoczy); Rangegonda, Noblewoman; Pentacoste, Noblewoman
Time period(s): 10th century (937)
Locale(s): Saxony, Germany

Summary: The ageless vampire Comte de Saint Germain washes up on the shores of Saxony and is ransomed as a prisoner by Ranegonda, sister of the Gerefa of the fortress of Leosan who has abdicated his leadership position to become a monk. Saint Germain falls in love with Ranegonda and helps her run interference with the besieging Danes, and with Pentacoste, her brother's embittered former wife.

Other books you might like:
C. Dean Andersson, *I Am Dracula*, 1993
Les Daniels, *No Blood Spilled*, 1991
P.N. Elrod, *I, Strahd*, 1993
Pierre Kast, *The Vampires of Alfama*, 1975

4793

CHELSEA QUINN YARBRO

A Candle for D'Artagnan

(New York: Tor, 1989)

Story type: Horror (Vampire Story)
Series: Olivia Trilogy
Major character(s): Atta Olivia Clemens, Vampire (1500 years old); Charles D'Artagnan, Warrior (Heroic French swordsman)
Time period(s): 17th century (1637)
Locale(s): Rome, Italy; France

Summary: When Papal politics drive Olivia Clemens from Rome to France, she meets and falls in love with the great swordsman D'Artagnan. Together they battle the machinations of Richelieu, as the wily Cardinal's last, desperate bid to hold power plunges them all into danger.

Other books you might like:
Les Daniels, *The Black Castle*, 1978
Pierre Kast, *The Vampires of Alfama*, 1976

4794

CHELSEA QUINN YARBRO

Crown of Empire

(New York: Baen, 1994)

Story type: Science Fiction (Political; Military)
Series: Crisis of Empire
Major character(s): Tira Bouriere, Political Figure, Teenager; Wiley Bouriere, Political Figure, Teenager; Chaney, Military Personnel
Time period(s): Indeterminate Future
Locale(s): First Empire, Interstellar Empire/Federation

Summary: When the High Secretary dies, a fight for power erupts as corporations, the military and non-human slaves struggle to control events through use of the High Secretary's survivors.

Other books you might like:
Allan Cole, *Sten*, 1984
  Chris Bunch, co-author
Brian Daley, *Requiem for a Ruler of Worlds*, 1985
David Drake, *Cluster Command*, 1989
  W.C. Dietz, co-author
David Drake, *An Honorable Defense*, 1988
  Thomas T. Thomas, co-author
David Drake, *The War Machine*, 1989
  Roger MacBride Allen, co-author

4795

CHELSEA QUINN YARBRO

Crusader's Torch
(New York: Tor, 1989)

Story type: Horror (Vampire Story)
Series: Olivia Trilogy
Major character(s): Atta Olivia Clemens, Vampire (1000 years old); Valence Rainaut, Knight (Knight Hospitaler)
Time period(s): 12th century (1189)
Locale(s): Tyre, Middle East; Rome, Italy

Summary: Forced from her home in Tyre by the approaching Islamic forces, Olivia Clemens undertakes a difficult and dangerous trip back to Rome, accompanied only by Valence Rainaut, a Knight Hospitaler, who has, against his will, fallen in love with her.

Other books you might like:
Les Daniels, *The Black Castle*, 1978
Pierre Kast, *The Vampires of Alfama*, 1976

4796

CHELSEA QUINN YARBRO

Mansions of Darkness
(New York: Tor, 1996)

Story type: Horror (Vampire Story)
Series: Chronicles of Saint Germain
Major character(s): Comte de Saint Germain, Vampire; Acanna Tupac, Royalty (Incan); Dom Enrique, Explorer
Time period(s): 17th century (1640)
Locale(s): Cuzco, Peru

Summary: While in Peru at the twilight of the Inca civilization, the immortal vampire Count St. Germain intervenes to save a woman of the royal family from the wrath of the Spanish conquistadors. His actions make St. Germain an enemy of the Spaniards, who regard him as a sorcerer for his knowledge of medicine and biology.

Other books you might like:
Les Daniels, *The Black Castle*, 1978
Les Daniels, *The Silver Skull*, 1979
Pierre Kast, *The Vampires of Alfama*, 1976
Mara McCuniff, *The Vampire Memoirs*, 1991
  Tracy Briery, co-author
Anne Rice, *Servant of the Bones*, 1996

4797

CHELSEA QUINN YARBRO

Out of the House of Life
(New York: Tor, 1990)

Story type: Horror (Vampire Story)
Series: Chronicles of Saint Germain
Major character(s): Comte de Saint Germain, Vampire; Madelaine de Montalia, Vampire; Egidius Maximillian Falke, Doctor
Time period(s): 1820s (1825-1828)
Locale(s): Thebes, Egypt

Summary: Madelaine de Montalia, acolyte and former lover of the millenia-old vampire Le Comte de Saint Germain, travels with the Baundilet archaeological expedition to the ruins of ancient Thebes. While she fends off the advances of the lecherous Professor Baundilet and nurtures a romance for the scholarly Doctor Falke, she learns the history of Egypt through her correspondance with Saint Germain, who was enslaved there as a demon god thousands of years before.

Other books you might like:
Les Daniels, *The Black Castle*, 1978
Pierre Kast, *The Vampires of Alfama*, 1975
Tim Powers, *The Stress of Her Regard*, 1989
Anne Rice, *The Vampire Lestat*, 1985
Brian Stableford, *The Empire of Fear*, 1988

4798

JACK YEOVIL (Pseudonym of Kim Newman)

Comeback Tour: The Sky Belongs to the Stars
(Baltimore, Maryland: GW Books, 1991)

Story type: Science Fiction (Adventure; Alternate Universe)
Series: Dark Future: Demon Download Cycle
Major character(s): Elvis Presley, Lawman, Historical Figure; Krokodil, Cyborg; Roger Duroc, Agent, Religious (Josephite elder)
Time period(s): 1990s (1998)
Locale(s): Memphis Tennessee, Alternate Earth; Cape Canaveral Florida, Alternate Earth

Summary: After a 20-year stint in the Army and the abandonment of his musical career, Elvis is making a living as a Sactioned Op in the Deep South when Krokodil enlists him in her war against Elder Nguyen Seth. His latest plot against life on Earth revolves around an obsolete orbital weapons system controlled from a forgotten launch facility in the Florida swamps. Unfortunately for both sides, these swamps also contain a GenTech laboratory about to suffer a serious crisis. A game tie-in novel.

Other books you might like:
Bradley Denton, *Buddy Holly Is Alive and Well on Ganymede*, 1991
Nigel Findley, *2XS*, 1992
William Gibson, *Neuromancer*, 1984
David Pringle, *Route 666*, 1990
  editor

Robert Rankin, *Armageddon: The Musical*, 1990
Allen Steele, *Clarke County, Space*, 1990
Howard Waldrop, *Strange Monsters of the Recent Past*, 1991

4799

JACK YEOVIL (Pseudonym of Kim Newman)

Demon Download

(Baltimore, Maryland: GW Books/Games Workshop, 1990)

Story type: Fantasy (Adventure)
Series: Dark Future: Demon Download Cycle
Major character(s): Sister Chantal Juillerat, Agent (papal), Computer Expert (cyberexorcist); Nguyen Seth, Spirit, Religious (priest of the Dark Ones); Nathan Stack, Police Officer (U.S. Highway Trooper)
Time period(s): 1990s
Locale(s): Fort Apache, Arizona; Welcome, Arizona

Summary: A malevolent computer virus called Nguyen Seth invades the U.S. Cavalry Highway Command Center at Fort Apache, Arizona. Papal agent Sister Chantal Juillerat is dispensed by the Pope to exorcise the spirit.

Other books you might like:
David Pringle, *Route 666*, 1990
Ian Watson, *Inquisitor*, 1989

4800

JACK YEOVIL (Pseudonym of Kim Newman)

Drachenfels

(Baltimore, Maryland: GW Books/Games Workshop, 1990)

Story type: Fantasy (Quest; Horror)
Series: Warhammer
Major character(s): Detlef Sierek, Writer; Oswald, Royalty (crown prince); Genevieve Dieudonne, Vampire
Time period(s): 16th century
Locale(s): Old World, Europe; Alternate Earth

Summary: Detlef Sierek is released from debtor's prison to produce a play celebrating Crown Prince Oswald's victory over the undead sorcerer Drachenfels. The production is threatened by both plots and sorcery as the playwright begins to uncover the truth about the "glorious past."

Other books you might like:
Steven Brust, *Jhereg*, 1983
Glen Cook, *Sweet Silver Blues*, 1987
Barry Hughart, *Bridge of Birds*, 1984
Tim Powers, *The Stress of Her Regard*, 1989
Howard Waldrop, *Night of the Cooters*, 1990

4801

JACK YEOVIL (Pseudonym of Kim Newman)

Krokodil Tears

(Baltimore, Maryland: GW Books/Games Workshop, 1990)

Story type: Fantasy (Adventure)
Series: Dark Future: Demon Download Cycle
Major character(s): Jessamyn "Krokodil" Bonney, Leader (juvenile gang); Ottoken Proctor, Economist, Criminal (psychopathic killer); Hawk-That-Settles, Indian, Religious (spiritual advisor)
Time period(s): 1990s (1997-1998)
Locale(s): Salt Lake City, Utah; Gila Desert, Arizona (Monastery of Santa de Nogueria)

Summary: Former juvenile gang member Jessamyn Bonney is nearly killed in an attack on Elder Nguyen Seth's convoy to Salt Lake City. Transformed by extensive biomechanical surgery and fusion with an extra-dimensional entity, she struggles against the Dark Ones in an attempt to prevent the Apocalypse.

Other books you might like:
Neil Jones, *Deathwing*, 1989
    David Pringle, co-editor
Alan Dean Foster, *Cyber Way*, 1990

4802

LAURENCE YEP

Dragon Cauldron

(New York: HarperCollins, 1991)

Story type: Fantasy (Quest; Adventure)
Series: Dragon of the Lost Sea
Major character(s): Shimmer, Royalty, Mythical Creature (dragon); Civet, Witch; Monkey, Wizard, Mythical Creature
Time period(s): Indeterminate Past
Locale(s): Desolate Mountains, Mythical Place

Summary: Trying for years to restore the stolen Inland Sea so that dragons may return, Shimmer sees hope for her quest's success now that Civet has repented for stealing the sea. To succeed, Shimmer must repair the Dragon cauldron with the help of Snail Woman and Smith.

Other books you might like:
Ursula K. Le Guin, *The Farthest Shore*, 1972
Ursula K. Le Guin, *The Tombs of Atuan*, 1971
Ursula K. Le Guin, *A Wizard of Earthsea*, 1968
Andre Norton, *The Elvenbane*, 1991
    Mercedes Lackey, co-author
J.R.R. Tolkien, *The Fellowship of the Ring*, 1954
J.R.R. Tolkien, *The Hobbit*, 1938
Patricia C. Wrede, *Searching for Dragons*, 1991

4803

LAURENCE YEP

Dragon War

(New York: HarperCollins, 1992)

Story type: Fantasy (Adventure; Quest)
Series: Dragon of the Lost Sea
Major character(s): Shimmer, Royalty (princess of the Inland Sea), Mythical Creature (dragon); Monkey, Wizard, Mythical Creature (Chinese); Indigo, Adventurer
Time period(s): Indeterminate Past

Locale(s): Egg Mountain, Mythical Place; Ramsgate, Fictional City

Summary: Shimmer, Monkey and Indigo escape from Egg Mountain then journey to Ramsgate to recover the Dragon Cauldron and Thorn, the child imprisoned within. They hope to defeat the Boneless King then restore the Inland Sea, the dragons' stolen home.

Other books you might like:
Karen Brush, *Demon Pig*, 1991
Ursula K. Le Guin, *The Farthest Shore*, 1972
Ursula K. Le Guin, *Tehanu: The Last Book of Earthsea*, 1990
Ursula K. Le Guin, *The Tombs of Atuan*, 1971
Ursula K. Le Guin, *A Wizard of Earthsea*, 1968
Sherwood Smith, *Wren to the Rescue*, 1990
Patricia C. Wrede, *Searching for Dragons*, 1991

`4804`

LAURENCE YEP

Tongues of Jade
(New York: HarperCollins, 1991)

Story type: Fantasy (Collection; Young Adult)
Time period(s): Indeterminate Past
Locale(s): China

Summary: From the oral tradition which preserved Chinese thought among those living away from China, Jon Lee collected and translated 69 stories from immigrants in Oakland's Chinatown during a 1930s WPA project, later supplemented by Professor Wolfram Eberhard's collecting more stories in San Francisco's Chinatown. Herein Yep presents 17 stories grouped with an introduction into themes titled "Roots," "Family Ties," "The Wild Heart," "Face" and "Beyond the Grave," incorporating magic, mythical spirits, mystery and whimsy into tales insightful of Chinese ideals. This companion volume to *The Rainbow People* includes an introduction and afterword with bibliography.

Other books you might like:
Wolfram Eberhard, *Folktales of China*, 1965
Barry Hughart, *Bridge of Birds*, 1984
Karl S.Y. Kao, *Classical Chinese Tales of the Supernatural and the Fantastic*, 1985
Jeanne Larsen, *Bronze Mirror*, 1991
Ernest Bramah Smith, *Kai Lung Unrolls His Mat*, 1923
  written as Ernest Bramah
Ernest Bramah Smith, *Kai Lung's Golden Hours*, 1928
  written as Ernest Bramah

`4805`

JANE YOLEN, Editor

2041: Twelve Short Stories about the Future by Top Science Fiction Writers
(New York: Delacorte Press, 1991)

Story type: Science Fiction (Anthology; Young Adult)
Time period(s): 2040s (2041)

Summary: This thematic anthology looks at the world of 2041 and contains 10 stories original to this title plus two stories previously published in periodicals including Peg Kerr's "Free Day," revised herein and Connie Willis' retitled "Much Ado About (Censored)." Other significant stories include Nancy Springer's "Who's Gonna Rock Us Home?," Anne McCaffrey's "A Quiet One," Patricia A. McKillip's "Moby James," Joe Haldeman's "If I Had the Wings of an Angel," Kara Dalkey's "You Want It When?," Jane Yolen's "Ear" and Susan Shwartz's "Beggarman."

Other books you might like:
Lester del Rey, *The Year After Tomorrow: An Anthology of Science Fiction Stories*, 1954
  Carl Cramer, co-editor
Harry Harrison, *Science Fiction Novellas*, 1975
  Willis E. McNelly, co-editor
Harry Harrison, *A Science Fiction Reader*, 1973
  Carol Pugner, co-editor
Bernard Hollister, *You and Science Fiction: A Humanistic Aproach to Tomorrow*, 1976
  editor
Cecile Matschatt, *Fiction Stories*, 1954
Joseph D. Olander, *School and Society Through Science Fiction*, 1974
  Martin H. Greenberg and Patricia Warrick, co-editors
Robert Silverberg, *Beyond Control*, 1972
  editor
Robert Silverberg, *Earth Is the Strangest Place*, 1977
  editor
Robert Silverberg, *The Science Fiction Hall of Fame*, 1971
  editor

`4806`

JANE YOLEN

Briar Rose
(New York: Tor, 1992)

Story type: Fantasy (Legend; Quest)
Major character(s): Rebecca "Becca", Journalist, Traveller; Gemma Rose Mandlestein, Grandparent (Becca's)
Time period(s): 1990s
Locale(s): United States; Poland

Summary: Gemma never spoke about herself to her grandchildren, repeatedly retelling the story of Briar Rose which she called "Seepin Boot" instead. After Gemma's deathbed confession to Becca that, "I am Briar Rose," Becca sets out to discover Gemma's life story, guided by the story of "Seepin Boot" to the horrors of World War II Nazi genocide. A retelling of "Sleeping Beauty."

Other books you might like:
Martin Amis, *Time's Arrow*, 1991
Janet Gluckman, *Child of the Light*, 1992
  George Guthridge, co-author
Kurt Vonnegut Jr., *Slaughterhouse Five*, 1969

4807

JANE YOLEN

The Dragon's Boy

(New York: Harper and Row, 1990)

Story type: Fantasy (Legend; Young Adult)
Major character(s): Artos, Foundling; Sir Ector, Knight; Cai Youngman, Nobleman (Sir Ector's Son)
Time period(s): Indeterminate Past (Medieval)
Locale(s): England

Summary: Artos stumbles across a dragon's lair and becomes its unwilling student. Artos uses a jewel the dragon gives him to have a sword made, and with it he is finally accepted as one of the young men.

Other books you might like:
Barbara Ninde Byfield, *Andrew and the Alchemist*, 1977
Grace Chetwin, *Gom on Windy Mountain*, 1986
Grace Chetwin, *The Riddle and the Rune*, 1987
Peter Dickinson, *Merlin Dreams*, 1988
Susan Fletcher, *Dragon's Milk*, 1989

4808

JANE YOLEN

Here There Be Angels

(New York: Harcourt Brace, 1996)

Story type: Fantasy (Collection; Religious)

Summary: Contains individual introductions with 11 stories and nine poems, 16 original and four reprinted from periodicals and anthologies 1974-1983. Frequently light in tone, the work explores miracles and transformations via angels from various traditions in contemporary and fantasy settings.

Other books you might like:
Peter Crowther, *Heaven Sent: 18 Glorious Tales of the Angels*, 1995
Martin H. Greenberg, co-editor
Jack Dann, *Angels!*, 1995
Gardner Dozois, co-editor
Neil Gaiman, *Good Omens: The Nice and Accurate Prophecies of Agnes Nutter, Witch*, 1990
Terry Pratchett, co-author
Alan Ryan, *Perpetual Light*, 1982
editor
Pamela Sargent, *Afterlives: An Anthology of Stories about Life After Death*, 1986
Ian Watson, co-editor

4809

JANE YOLEN

Here There Be Dragons

(New York: Harcourt Brace, 1993)

Story type: Fantasy (Collection; Young Adult)

Summary: Contains two reprinted and 11 original stories and poems with a broad range of themes concerning dragons.

Stories encompass a variety of literary traditions including Arthurian, Chinese and classic fairy tale and a tale of Saint George and the Dragon.

Other books you might like:
Orson Scott Card, *Dragons of Darkness*, 1981
editor
Orson Scott Card, *Dragons of Light*, 1980
editor
Ellen Datlow, *The Year's Best Fantasy and Horror Series*, 1989-
Terri Windling, co-editor
James Gurney, *Dinotopia*, 1992
Ursula K. Le Guin, *A Wizard of Earthsea*, 1968
Patricia C. Wrede, *Dealing with Dragons*, 1990
Roger Zelazny, *Here There Be Dragons*, 1992

4810

JANE YOLEN

Here There Be Unicorns

(New York: Harcourt Brace, 1994)

Story type: Fantasy (Collection; Legend)

Summary: Contains individual introductions to 10 short stories and eight poems, 15 of them original and three reprinted from periodicals and anthologies. Settings range from medieval to contemporary in stories which examine many unicorn myths and speculations, with tone ranging from ominous to light.

Other books you might like:
Bruce Coville, *The Unicorn Treasury*, 1988
editor
Jack Dann, *Unicorns!*, 1982
Gardner Dozois, co-editor
Jack Dann, *Unicorns II*, 1992
Gardner Dozois, co-editor
Pamela Dean, *The Secret Country*, 1985
Tanith Lee, *Black Unicorn*, 1991

4811

JANE YOLEN

Here There Be Witches

(New York: Harcourt Brace, 1995)

Story type: Fantasy (Collection)

Summary: Yolen individually introduces seven poems and 10 stories published 1977-1995 in periodicals, anthologies, and collections. The stories focus on diverse aspects of witches. The settings vary from ancient and fantastic to more contemporary, generally employing a strong sense of wonder while avoiding a darker tone. Themes include modern as well as traditional fairy tale topics.

Other books you might like:
Peter Haining, *A Circle of Witches*, 1971
editor
Byron Preiss, *The Ultimate Witch*, 1993
John Betancourt, co-editor

Mike Resnick, *Witch Fantastic*, 1995
　Martin H. Greenberg, co-editor
Susan Shwartz, *Hecate's Cauldron*, 1985

4812

JANE YOLEN

Merlin and the Dragons
(New York: Dutton Cobbhill, 1995)

Story type: Fantasy (Young Adult; Legend)
Major character(s): Arthur Pendragon, Royalty; Merlin, Magician; Emrys, Psychic
Time period(s): 5th century
Locale(s): England

Summary: When dreams disturb young Arthur's sleep, Merlin weaves the heroic tale of Uther Pendragon's rise to power and the battle of the dragons that occurs after warriors free two of the sleeping beasts.

Other books you might like:
Susan Cooper, *Over Sea, Under Stone*, 1965
Michael Hague, *The Book of Dragons*, 1995
　editor
Ursula K. Le Guin, *A Wizard of Earthsea*, 1968
David Worsick, *Henry's Gift: The Magic Eye*, 1994
Roger Zelazny, *Here There Be Dragons*, 1992

4813

JANE YOLEN

Passager
(New York: Harcourt Brace, 1996)

Story type: Fantasy (Legend)
Series: Young Merlin Trilogy
Major character(s): Merlin, Child; Robin, Hunter (falconer), Step-Parent
Time period(s): Indeterminate Past
Locale(s): England

Summary: Abandoned by his mother, Merlin grows up feral until he follows Master Robin home, where he begins to learn language and civilized manners and discovers his true name. Expanded from ''The Wild Child,'' published in *Merlin's Booke*.

Other books you might like:
T.A. Barron, *The Merlin Effect*, 1994
Ann Curry, *The Book of Brendan*, 1990
Peter Dickinson, *Heartsease*, 1969
Anne McCaffrey, *Black Horses for the King*, 1996
Mark Twain, *A Connecticut Yankee in King Arthur's Court*, 1889
T.H. White, *The Sword in the Stone*, 1939

4814

JANE YOLEN

Sister Light, Sister Dark
(New York: Tor, 1988)

Story type: Fantasy (Adventure)
Major character(s): Jenna, Orphan, Heroine
Time period(s): Indeterminate
Locale(s): Alternate Universe

Summary: Jenna is raised in a hame, a self-sufficient commune of women, after she has been orphaned three times in infancy. She soon realizes that the circumstances of her birth have been foretold by a prophecy.

Other books you might like:
Elise Guttenberg, *Sunder, Eclipse and Seed*, 1990
R.A. MacAvoy, *Lens of the World*, 1990

4815

JANE YOLEN

White Jenna
(New York: Tor, 1989)

Story type: Fantasy (Adventure)
Major character(s): Jenna, Orphan, Heroine
Time period(s): Indeterminate
Locale(s): Alternate Universe

Summary: In this sequel to *Sister Light, Sister Dark*, Jenna starts down the path which will destroy the old way of the hames, and herald a new age.

Other books you might like:
Lynn Abbey, *Unicorn and Dragon*, 1985
Marion Zimmer Bradley, *Web of Darkness*, 1983
Phyllis Ann Karr, *Frostflower and Thorn*, 1980

4816

JANE YOLEN

The Wild Hunt
(New York: Harcourt Brace, 1995)

Story type: Fantasy (Quest; Magic Conflict)
Major character(s): Jerod, Child; Gerund, Child; The Cat, Animal
Time period(s): Indeterminate

Summary: The Horned Man's scheming transcends the boundary between realities, drawing Jerod and Gerund into his chronic attempt to corrupt the innocent and find a way to win the obedience and loyalty of his wife.

Other books you might like:
Lloyd Alexander, *The High King*, 1968
Louise Cooper, *The Sleep of Stone*, 1991
Susan Dexter, *The Wizard's Shadow*, 1993
Patricia A. McKillip, *The Book of Atrix Wolfe*, 1995
Pat O'Shea, *The Hounds of the Morrigan*, 1986

4817
JANE YOLEN

Wizard's Hall
(New York: Harcourt Brace Jovanovich, 1991)

Story type: Fantasy (Magic Conflict; Young Adult)
Major character(s): Henry ''Thornmallow'', Student; Gorse, Student; Magister Hickory, Wizard, Teacher
Time period(s): Indeterminate
Locale(s): Wizard's Hall, Mythical Place (School)

Summary: When Henry mentions a minor interest in Wizardry, his mother immediately sends him to Wizard's Hall with the advice that he needn't succeed, it only matters that he try. His first few days at school prove so difficult that Henry, renamed ''Thornmallow,'' wants to leave but is talked into staying by his magisters who see his presence as necessary to defeat their nemesis, a former magister at Wizard's Hall. Thornmallow soon discovers his efforts rewarded in the overthrow of the evil magister and his terrible quilted beast.

Other books you might like:
Debra Doyle, *School of Wizardry*, 1990
    James D. Macdonald, co-author
Diana Wynne Jones, *Castle in the Air*, 1991
Andrea Shettle, *Flute Song Magic*, 1990
Sherwood Smith, *Wren to the Rescue*, 1990
Mary Frances Zambreno, *A Plague of Sorcerers*, 1991

4818
JANE YOLEN, Editor

Xanadu
(New York: Tor, 1993)

Story type: Fantasy (Anthology)
Series: Xanadu

Summary: First in a new anthology series of original stories and poems with a two-page introduction by Yolen, five pages ''About the Authors'' and four poems by Steven Brust, Pat Schneider, Donna J. Waidtlow and Jane Yolen. The 18 stories range in tone from euphoric to sinister by authors who include Eleanor Arnason, Gardner Dozois, Esther Friesner, Patrick Nielsen Hayden, Nancy Kress, Ursula K. Le Guin, Tanith Lee, Elise Matthesen, John Morressy, Mike Resnick and Will Shetterly.

Other books you might like:
Ellen Datlow, *Snow White, Blood Red*, 1993
    Terri Windling, co-editor
Ellen Datlow, *The Year's Best Fantasy and Horror Series*, 1989-
    Terri Windling, co-editor
Ellen Datlow, *The Year's Best Fantasy: First Annual Collection*, 1988
    Terri Windling, co-editor
Lester del Rey, *Once upon a Time: A Treasury of Modern Fairy Tales*, 1991
    Risa Kessler, co-editor

Martin H. Greenberg, *After the King: Stories in Honor of J.R.R. Tolkien*, 1992
    editor
Kristine Kathryn Rusch, *Pulphouse, Issue 6: Fantasy*, 1990
    editor
Terri Windling, *Life on the Border*, 1991
    editor

4819
JANE YOLEN, Editor

Xanadu 2
(New York: Tor, 1994)

Story type: Fantasy (Anthology)
Series: Xanadu

Summary: Contains a two-page introduction, seven pages of biographical sketches of the authors, seven original poems and 19 original stories with tone varying from humorous to dark and themes such as sword and sorcery, reincarnation, twists on classic fairy tales, dragons, elves and magical cats. Authors include Diane Duane, Barbara Hambly, Tappan King, Ursula K. Le Guin, Megan Lindholm, Patricia A. McKillip, Jessica Amanda Salmonson, Delia Sherman, Will Shetterly, Martha Soukup, Vivian Vande Velde, Terri Windling and Jane Yolen.

Other books you might like:
Ellen Datlow, *Black Thorn, White Rose*, 1994
    Terry Windling, co-editor
Ellen Datlow, *Snow White, Blood Red*, 1993
    Terry Windling co-editor
Lester del Rey, *Once upon a Time: A Treasury of Modern Fairy Tales*, 1991
    Risa Kessler, co-editor
Kristine Kathryn Rusch, *The Best of Pulphouse: The Hardback Magazine*, 1991
    editor
Terri Windling, *Life on the Border*, 1991
    editor

4820
JANE YOLEN, Editor

Xanadu 3
(New York: Tor, 1995)

Story type: Fantasy (Anthology)
Series: Xanadu

Summary: This volume of original work contains a two-page introduction, a nine-page section ''About the Authors,'' 11 poems, and 25 stories utilizing diverse themes, many with a feminist bent. Although occasionally light in tone, the selections are frequently somber. Authors include Ruth Berman, Jo Clayton, Mark A. Garland, Tanith Lee, Elise Matthesen, Susan Palwick, Josepha Sherman, Midori Snyder, Laurie Aylma Taylor, Terri Windling, and Jane Yolen.

Other books you might like:

Marion Zimmer Bradley, *The Best of Marion Zimmer Bradley's Fantasy Magazine*, 1994
editor
Ellen Datlow, *Black Thorn, White Rose*, 1994
Terri Windling, co-editor
Ellen Datlow, *Snow White, Blood Red*, 1993
Terri Windling, co-editor
Lester del Rey, *Once upon a Time: A Treasury of Modern Fairy Tales*, 1991
Risa Kessler, co-editor
David G. Hartwell, *Masterpieces of Fantasy and Wonder*, 1994
editor

4821

JIM YOUNG

Armed Memory

(New York: Tor, 1995)

Story type: Science Fiction (Genetic Manipulation; Alternate Intelligence)
Major character(s): Timothy J. Wandel, Genetically Altered Being; Nils Ullrich, Genetically Altered Being (hammerhead shark); Johnny Sanders, Inventor, Artist
Time period(s): 21st century
Locale(s): New York, New York; Minneapolis, Minnesota

Summary: Arriving in a New York City where the criminal hammerheads prey on the populace, Timothy accepts a job with his cousin, Johnny Sanders. Inventor of the microding process which genetically alters people, Sanders plans to solve the problem of the hammerheads who stole his technique, who kidnap recruits, and who ultimately intend to eliminate life on land.

Other books you might like:

Wilhelmina Baird, *Clipjoint*, 1994
Octavia E. Butler, *Dawn*, 1987
Thomas A. Easton, *Sparrowhawk*, 1990
S. Andrew Swann, *Emperors of the Twilight*, 1994
S. Andrew Swann, *Forests of the Night*, 1993
George R.R. Martin, *Wild Cards*, 1987
editor

4822

ROY V. YOUNG

Captains Outrageous, or, For Doom the Bell Tolls

(Lake Geneva, Wisconsin: TSR, 1994)

Story type: Fantasy (Light Fantasy; Quest)
Major character(s): Yor, Warrior, Adventurer; Dword Ecklundson, Minstrel (loremaster), Warrior; Trebor Blackburn, Warrior, Adventurer
Time period(s): Indeterminate
Locale(s): Leiblein, Planet—Imaginary

Summary: Yor, Dword and Trebor must stop the mad wizard, Bosamp, from using the Mallet of Doom on the Bell at the Top of the World or all Leiblein could suffer disaster. First novel.

Other books you might like:

Piers Anthony, *A Spell for Chameleon*, 1977
K.B. Bogen, *Go Quest, Young Man*, 1994
Gordon R. Dickson, *The Dragon and the George*, 1976
Neil Gaiman, *Good Omens: The Nice and Accurate Prophecies of Agnes Nutter, Witch*, 1990
Terry Pratchett, co-author
John Moore, *Slay and Rescue*, 1993

4823

FAY ZACHARY

Blood Work

(New York: Berkley, 1994)

Story type: Horror (Psychological Suspense)
Major character(s): Liz Broward, Doctor; Zack James, Computer Expert, Artist; Phillip Trapp, Technician (laboratory)
Time period(s): 1990s (1994)
Locale(s): Philadelphia, Pennsylvania

Summary: Under the impression that people with the blood disease porphyria are actually vampires, loony Phillip Trapp, whose obsessions trace back to a childhood incident involving mock vampires at a carnival sideshow, sets about systematically killing porphyria victims at the local hospital.

Other books you might like:

Peter Atkins, *Morningstar*, 1992
Barbara Hambly, *Those Who Hunt the Night*, 1987
Roxanne Longstreet, *The Undead*, 1993
Kim Newman, *Bad Dreams*, 1990

4824

TIMOTHY ZAHN

Conqueror's Pride

(New York: Bantam Spectra, 1994)

Story type: Science Fiction (Space Opera; First Contact)
Major character(s): Pheylan Cavanagh, Spaceship Captain; Stewart Cavanagh, Businessman, Political Figure; Adam Quinn, Security Officer
Time period(s): Indeterminate Future
Locale(s): Interstellar Empire/Federation; Mra-mig, Planet—Imaginary

Summary: Four alien starships destroy a Peacekeeper task force. While Pheylan Cavanagh, the sole survivor, attempts to free himself from his alien captors, his family assembles a rescue force, in defiance of Commonwealth security restrictions and in spite of a curious reluctance on the part of the Mrachi members of the Commonwealth to share information on a mystery race they call the Conquerors.

Other books you might like:

Margaret Wander Bonanno, *Dwellers in the Crucible*, 1985
David Brin, *Startide Rising*, 1983
Orson Scott Card, *Ender's Game*, 1985
C.J. Cherryh, *Brothers of the Earth*, 1976
Gordon R. Dickson, *The Forever Man*, 1986

4825

TIMOTHY ZAHN

Dark Force Rising

(New York: Bantam Spectra, 1992)

Story type: Science Fiction (Space Opera; Psychic Powers)
Series: Star Wars
Major character(s): Leia Organa, Royalty (princess), Diplomat; Luke Skywalker, Martial Arts Expert (Jedi Knight), Hero; Joruus C'boath, Psychic (Jedi Master)
Time period(s): Indeterminate Past
Locale(s): Coruscant, Planet—Imaginary; *Chimaera*, Spaceship (Imperial Flagship)

Summary: Battles between the Old Empire and the Rebel Alliance (New Republic) continue as Grand Admiral Thrawn depends on his secret informer, Delta Source, to keep abreast of the movements of Luke, Leia, Han and the Rebellion. Luke faces the Dark Side of the Force while Leia negotiates with the deadly Moghri despite the risk to her unborn twins and herself. Han tries to uncover the identity of Delta Source and finds himself again battling Imperial forces.

Other books you might like:
Allan Cole, *Sten*, 1984
　　Chris Bunch, co-author
Brian Daley, *Han Solo and the Lost Legacy*, 1980
Brian Daley, *Han Solo at Star's End*, 1979
Brian Daley, *Han Solo's Revenge*, 1979
Alan Dean Foster, *Splinter of the Mind's Eye*, 1978
Donald F. Glut, *The Empire Strikes Back*, 1980
Frank Herbert, *Dune*, 1965
James Kahn, *Return of the Jedi*, 1983
George Lucas, *Star Wars*, 1976
L. Neil Smith, *Lando Calrissian and the Flamewind of Oseon*, 1983
L. Neil Smith, *Lando Calrissian and the Mindharp of Sharu*, 1983
L. Neil Smith, *Lando Calrissian and the Starcave of Thon Boka*, 1983
Helen S. Wright, *A Matter of Oaths*, 1990

4826

TIMOTHY ZAHN

Distant Friends and Others

(New York: Baen, 1992)

Story type: Science Fiction (Collection; Psychic Powers)
Time period(s): Indeterminate Future
Locale(s): United States

Summary: The first three stories in this collection combine to form the short novel, "Distant Friends," in which telepaths cannot tolerate physical proximity to each other. The remaining six unconnected stories appeared in 1980s periodicals.

Other books you might like:
Marion Zimmer Bradley, *The Firebrand*, 1987
Karen Haber, *The Mutant Season*, 1990
　　Robert Silverberg, co-author
Henry Kuttner, *Mutant*, 1953

Anne McCaffrey, *Damia*, 1992
Anne McCaffrey, *The Rowan*, 1990
Joan D. Vinge, *Psion*, 1982

4827

TIMOTHY ZAHN

Heir to the Empire

(New York: Bantam Spectra, 1991)

Story type: Science Fiction (Space Opera)
Series: Star Wars
Major character(s): Luke Skywalker, Martial Arts Expert, Hero; Leia Organa Solo, Administrator, Royalty; Han Solo, Spaceship Captain, Warrior
Time period(s): Indeterminate
Locale(s): Coruscant, Planet—Imaginary; Outer Space

Summary: Five years after the death of Darth Vader, Princess Leia and Han are expecting twins; Luke is reorganizing the Jedi Knights, who have discovered that governing the New Republic is more work than they had expected. Meanwhile, unknown to anyone in the new government, the last remnants of the Imperial Fleet under Admiral Thrawn are preparing to destroy the New Republic, to them the Rebellion.

Other books you might like:
Allan Cole, *Sten*, 1984
　　Chris Bunch, co-author
Brian Daley, *Han Solo and the Lost Legacy*, 1980
Brian Daley, *Han Solo at Star's End*, 1979
Brian Daley, *Han Solo's Revenge*, 1979
Alan Dean Foster, *Splinter of the Mind's Eye*, 1978
Donald F. Glut, *The Empire Strikes Back*, 1980
James Kahn, *Return of the Jedi*, 1983
George Lucas, *Star Wars*, 1976
L. Neil Smith, *Lando Calrissian and the Flamewind of Oseon*, 1983
L. Neil Smith, *Lando Calrissian and the Mindharp of Sharu*, 1983
L. Neil Smith, *Lando Calrissian and the Starcave of Thon Boka*, 1983

4828

TIMOTHY ZAHN

The Last Command

(New York: Bantam Spectra, 1993)

Story type: Science Fiction (Space Opera; Psychic Powers)
Series: Star Wars
Major character(s): Luke Skywalker, Martial Arts Expert (Jedi Knight), Hero; Leia Organa Solo, Royalty, Leader; Thrawn, Military Personnel, Leader
Time period(s): Indeterminate Past
Locale(s): *Wild Karrde*, Spaceship; New Republic, Interstellar Empire/Federation; Outer Space

Summary: When Grand Admiral Thrawn rallies surviving Imperial forces and constructs a clone army with which to attack the Alliance, Leia leads the Alliance resistance to Thrawn's siege. Han Solo and Chewbacca attempt to organize smugglers while Luke leads a small force determined to destroy Thrawn's cloning machines. Occurs five years after events of *Return of the Jedi* (1983) and concludes Zahn's trilogy.

Other books you might like:
Brian Daley, *The Han Solo Adventures*, 1992
Paul Davids, *The Glove of Darth Vader*, 1992
Alan Dean Foster, *Splinter of the Mind's Eye*, 1978
George Lucas, *The Star Wars Trilogy*, 1987
   Donald F. Glut, James Kahn, co-authors
L. Neil Smith, *Lando Calrissian and the Flamewind of Oseon*, 1983
L. Neil Smith, *Lando Calrissian and the Mindharp of Sharu*, 1983
L. Neil Smith, *Lando Calrissian and the Starcave of Thon Boka*, 1983
Kathy Tyers, *The Truce at Bakura*, 1994

4829

TIMOTHY ZAHN

Warhorse

(New York: Baen Books, 1990)

Story type: Science Fiction (First Contact)
Major character(s): Haml Roman, Spaceship Captain; Chayne Ferrol, Spaceman
Time period(s): Indeterminate Future
Locale(s): *C.S.S. Dryden*, Spaceship; Kialinninni Alpha, Planet—Imaginary

Summary: Humanity's expanding sphere of exploration brings us into conflict with the Tampies, a species who consider themselves the guardians of all life and who have developed bioscience to the point where they can actually create living spaceships and weapons. War between our species and theirs seems imminent.

Other books you might like:
Gregory Benford, *Tides of Light*, 1989
David Brin, *Startide Rising*, 1983
Thorarinn Gunnarsson, *Battle of the Ring*, 1989
   Starwolves 2
Jack Vance, *The Dragon Masters*, 1963

4830

MARY FRANCES ZAMBRENO

Journeyman Wizard

(New York: Harcourt Brace, 1994)

Story type: Fantasy (Young Adult; Mystery)
Major character(s): Jermyn Graves, Wizard, Detective—Amateur; Delia, Animal (skunk), Companion (wizard's familiar); Brianne Campbell, Teenager, Healer
Time period(s): Indeterminate
Locale(s): Land's End, Fictional City

Summary: When Jermyn goes to study magic under Lady Jean Allons, he must defend himself against accusations of murder and discover the real killer.

Other books you might like:
Debra Doyle, *School of Wizardry*, 1990
   James D. Macdonald, co-author
Caroline Stevermer, *A College of Magics*, 1994
Robyn Tallis, *Children of the Storm*, 1989
   pseudonym of Mary Frances Zambreno
Patricia C. Wrede, *The Raven Ring*, 1994
Jane Yolen, *Wizard's Hall*, 1991

4831

MARY FRANCES ZAMBRENO

A Plague of Sorcerers

(New York: Harcourt Brace Jovanovich, 1991)

Story type: Fantasy (Magic Conflict; Young Adult)
Major character(s): Jermyn Graves, Apprentice (wizard's); Delia, Animal (skunk), Companion (familiar); William Eschar, Wizard (master)
Time period(s): Indeterminate
Locale(s): Fictional Country

Summary: When Jermyn's aunt transfers apprenticeship of Jermyn and his not-too-welcome familiar to Master Eschar the Theoretician, Jermyn hopes his control over magic will improve. With study and practice he discovers that his magic skill increases, if slowly. When faced publicly with a dangerous test, Jermyn finally begins to harness his abilities, barely in time to help foil an attempt to seize political power and help cure a plague affecting magic users.

Other books you might like:
Stephen R. Donaldson, *The Illearth War*, 1977
Stephen R. Donaldson, *Lord Foul's Bane*, 1977
Stephen R. Donaldson, *The Power That Preserves*, 1977
Debra Doyle, *School of Wizardry*, 1990
   James D. Macdonald, co-author
Randall Garrett, *Too Many Magicians*, 1967
Sherwood Smith, *Wren to the Rescue*, 1990
Jane Yolen, *Wizard's Hall*, 1991

4832

GEORGE ZEBROWSKI

Stranger Suns

(New York: Bantam Spectra, 1991)

Story type: Science Fiction (Alternate Universe; Future Shock)
Major character(s): Dr. Juan Obrion, Scientist (physicist); Dr. Lena Dravie, Scientist (biologist)
Time period(s): 22nd century (2100s)
Locale(s): U.N. Base, Moon (Earth's); Antarctica; Spaceship (alien)

Summary: Dr. Juan Obrion and his friend Malachi Moede have just finished the tachyon detector. They hope to intercept alien messages, but do not detect any tachyons from space. Only Antarctica seems to be producing them, which doesn't make any sense. Hoping to discover the source of the tachyons they get permission to investigate with a U.N. team,

Lena Dravie and Magnus Rasmussen. The spaceship they find buried is more interesting than they could have imagined.

Other books you might like:
Gregory Benford, *Timescape*, 1980
Philip K. Dick, *The Unteleported Man*, 1983
 revised
Alan Dean Foster, *Cat-A-Lyst*, 1991
Parke Godwin, *Waiting for the Galactic Bus*, 1988
Stephen Goldin, *Jade Darcy and the Zen Pirates*, 1990
 Mary Mason, co-author
Edward M. Lerner, *Probe*, 1991
Andre Norton, *Star Gate*, 1958
Clifford D. Simak, *Ring Around the Sun*, 1953

4833

ANN TONSOR ZEDDIES

Deathgift

(New York: Ballantine/Del Rey, 1989)

Story type: Science Fiction (Military)
Major character(s): Singer, Psychic, Musician; Janet Logan, Doctor
Time period(s): Indeterminate Future
Locale(s): New Hope, Planet—Imaginary

Summary: Singer, a talented psychic and musician raised by a primitive tribe of horsemen, finds himself in the middle of an intergalactic war. The author's first novel.

Other books you might like:
Lois McMaster Bujold, *The Warrior's Apprentice*, 1986
Rebecca Ore, *Becoming Alien*, 1987
Lucius Shepard, *Life During Wartime*, 1987
Lawrence Watt-Evans, *Denner's Wreck*, 1988
Dave Wolverton, *On My Way to Paradise*, 1989

4834

ROGER ZELAZNY
ROBERT SHECKLEY, Co-Author

Bring Me the Head of Prince Charming

(New York: Bantam Spectra, 1991)

Story type: Fantasy (Light Fantasy; Legend)
Series: Millennial Contest
Major character(s): Azzie Elbub, Demon; Frike, Servant; Babriel, Angel
Time period(s): 10th century (999)
Locale(s): North Discomfort Pit 405, Hell; Augsburg, Switzerland; Glass Mountain Village, Mythical Place (Glass Mountain)

Summary: Serving as a pit boss in Hell to pay off a gambling debt, Azzie Elbub receives an opportunity to get back to Earth as an escort for a human mistakenly placed in Pit 405 before he was dead. When Azzie gets to Earth he realizes it is almost time for the millennial contest between the forces of good and evil, deciding which side will control human destiny for the coming millennium. He develops an idea, the recreation of Prince Charming and Sleeping Beauty in such a way that the forces of evil will win the contest. The Powers of Evil like his

idea and give him a black credit card authorizing him for instant and unlimited credit with Infernal Supply.

Other books you might like:
Alan Dean Foster, *Quozl*, 1989
Alan Dean Foster, *To the Vanishing Point*, 1988
Neil Gaiman, *Good Omens: The Nice and Accurate Prophecies of Agnes Nutter, Witch*, 1990
 Terry Pratchett, co-author
Parke Godwin, *The Snake Oil Wars*, 1989
Robert Sheckley, *Dimension of Miracles*, 1968
Robert Sheckley, *Dramocles: An Intergalactic Soap Opera*, 1983
Robert Sheckley, *Options*, 1977
Donald E. Westlake, *Humans*, 1992
Patricia C. Wrede, *Snow White and Rose Red*, 1989

4835

ROGER ZELAZNY
ROBERT SHECKLEY, Co-Author

A Farce to Be Reckoned With

(New York: Bantam Spectra, 1995)

Story type: Fantasy (Light Fantasy; Religious)
Series: Millennial Contest
Major character(s): Azzie Elbub, Demon; Pietro Aretino, Writer (poet and playwright)
Time period(s): 16th century
Locale(s): Europe; Realm of Darkness, Hell; Heaven

Summary: When Azzie discovers popular morality plays, he decides to write and produce an immorality play in which the participants magically achieve their hearts' desires. The event runs into difficulty when Heavenly forces hope to prevent the opening of the play and, on stage, characters begin to change their hearts' desires.

Other books you might like:
Neil Gaiman, *Good Omens: The Nice and Accurate Prophecies of Agnes Nutter, Witch*, 1990
 Terry Pratchett, co-author
Parke Godwin, *The Snake Oil Wars*, 1989
Parke Godwin, *Waiting for the Galactic Bus*, 1988
Robert Sheckley, *Journey Beyond Tomorrow*, 1962
Robert Sheckley, *Mindswap*, 1966

4836

ROGER ZELAZNY
THOMAS T. THOMAS, Co-Author

Flare

(New York: Baen, 1992)

Story type: Science Fiction (Hard Science Fiction; Disaster)
Major character(s): Hannibal Freede, Scientist (astronomer); Piero Mosca, Student (astronomer); Sultana Carr, Scientist (astronomer)
Time period(s): 2080s (2081)
Locale(s): Outer Space; Moon (Earth's)

Summary: This novel traces a solar flare from its inception as a quantum accident deep within the sun millions of years ago to its eruption as a flare in 2081 while examining human beliefs about Sol and human social development. Erroneous beliefs about the Sun's nature lead to disaster when the major flare finally appears after an 80-year hiatus in solar activity.

Other books you might like:
Roger MacBride Allen, *The Ring of Charon*, 1990
David Brin, *Earth*, 1990
David Brin, *Sundiver*, 1980
Paula E. Downing, *Flare Star*, 1992
Robert L. Forward, *Dragon's Egg*, 1980
Charles Sheffield, *The McAndrew Chronicles*, 1983
Allen Steele, *Orbital Decay*, 1989

4837

ROGER ZELAZNY, Editor

Forever After
(New York: Baen, 1995)

Story type: Fantasy (Anthology; Quest)

Summary: Contains a three-page afterword by David Drake and preludes by Zelazny to four stories by Robert Lynn Asprin, David Drake, Jane Lindskold, and Michael A. Stackpole. Each author pursues the disposal of one of four magical objects which had been needed to achieve the current calm, but must now find a resting place to achieve peace forever after.

Other books you might like:
Kyle Crocco, *Heroes, Inc.*, 1991
Barry Hughart, *Bridge of Birds*, 1984
Dan McGirt, *Dirty Work*, 1993
John Moore, *Slay and Rescue*, 1993
Sean Stewart, *Nobody's Son*, 1995

4838

ROGER ZELAZNY

Frost and Fire
(New York: William Morrow, 1989)

Story type: Science Fiction (Collection)

Summary: This latest collection of Zelazny's work consists of ten stories, each with an introduction, and three essays on science fiction. The pieces appeared between 1984 and 1987 in such magazines as *Omni*, *Twilight Zone*, *The Writer*, and *Isaac Asimov's Science Fiction Magazine*. The best known stories in the collection are Zelazny's recent Hugo and Nebula Award winners, "Permafrost" and "24 Views of Mt. Fuji, by Hokusai." Also included are "Quest's End," "Dayblood," and "Mana From Heaven."

Other books you might like:
Michael Bishop, *Close Encounters with the Deity*, 1986
Kim Stanley Robinson, *The Planet on the Table*, 1986
Bruce Sterling, *Crystal Express*, 1989
Gene Wolfe, *Endangered Species*, 1989
Gene Wolfe, *The Island of Doctor Death and Other Stories and Other Stories*, 1980
   Title is correct; not a typo!

4839

ROGER ZELAZNY

Gone to Earth
(Eugene, Oregon: Pulphouse, 1991)

Story type: Science Fiction (Collection)
Series: Author's Choice Monthly

Summary: This book contains a 3-page introduction plus four previously published stories. "Deadboy Donner and the Filstone Cup" (1988) draws inspiration from Damon Runyan and slang of the 1920s. "Kalifriki of the Thread" (1989) was written at the request of Diana Wynne Jones for *Hidden Turnings*. Themes of cars and computer viruses are seen in "Devil Car" (1965) and "The Last of the Wild Ones" (1981).

Other books you might like:
Edward Bryant, *Neon Twilight*, 1990
Ron Goulart, *Skyrocket Steele Conquers the Universe and Other Media Tales*, 1990
Joe R. Lansdale, *Stories by Mama Lansdale's Youngest Boy*, 1991
Judith Moffett, *Two That Came True*, 1991
Frederik Pohl, *Stopping at Slowyear*, 1991

4840

ROGER ZELAZNY

Here There Be Dragons
(Hampton Falls, New Hampshire: Donald M. Grant, 1992)

Story type: Fantasy (Young Adult; Quest)
Major character(s): William, Knight, Adventurer; Belkis "Bell", Animal (lizard), Royalty (king of dragons); Gibberling, Courtier, Cartographer
Time period(s): Indeterminate Past
Locale(s): Mythical Place

Summary: When the king wishes to supply fireworks for his daughter's birthday party, the task of retrieving a dragon to use as fireworks display falls to William. When he can find no one to help him, he sets out alone, but discovers Bell who promises to help if William will introduce him to the royal cartographer, Gibberling. At court, Bell grows large, becoming Belkis, and confronts Gibberling whose labeling the edge of maps with "Here There Be Dragons," has given dragonkind a bad name.

Other books you might like:
Gordon R. Dickson, *The Dragon and the George*, 1976
James Gurney, *Dinotopia*, 1992
Ursula K. Le Guin, *A Wizard of Earthsea*, 1968
J.R.R. Tolkien, *The Hobbit*, 1938
Lawrence Watt-Evans, *The Blood of a Dragon*, 1991
Patricia C. Wrede, *Dealing with Dragons*, 1990

4841

ROGER ZELAZNY
ROBERT SHECKLEY, Co-Author

If at Faust You Don't Succeed
(New York: Bantam Spectra, 1993)

Story type: Fantasy (Light Fantasy; Legend)
Series: Millennial Contest
Major character(s): Mephistopheles, Demon; Johann Faust, Thief, Imposter; Marco Polo, Historical Figure, Leader
Time period(s): 13th century; 18th century
Locale(s): Europe; Asia; Limbo, Mythical Place

Summary: In the continuing battle between forces of Light and Dark for mankind's destiny, archangel Michael constructs a test through which Mephistopheles presents Faust the opportunity to make key decisions at critical junctures in human events. The test runs amiss when Mephistopheles mistakenly engages a thief and failed monk rather than the intended magician. Sequel to *Bring Me the Head of Prince Charming*.

Other books you might like:
Neil Gaiman, *Good Omens: The Nice and Accurate Prophecies of Agnes Nutter, Witch*, 1990
    Terry Pratchett, co-author
Craig Shaw Gardner, *The Other Sinbad*, 1991
Parke Godwin, *The Snake Oil Wars*, 1989
Robert A. Heinlein, *Job: A Comedy of Justice*, 1984
Robert Sheckley, *Dimension of Miracles*, 1968
Robert Sheckley, *On the Planet of Bottled Brains*, 1990
    Harry Harrison, co-author
Robert Sheckley, *Options*, 1975

4842

ROGER ZELAZNY
THOMAS T. THOMAS, Co-Author

The Mask of Loki
(New York: Baen, 1990)

Story type: Fantasy (Legend; Adventure)
Major character(s): Tom Gurden, Musician (piano player), Religious (avatar of Loki); Hasan al Sabah, Criminal (assassin), Religious (avatar of Ahriman)
Time period(s): 12th century (Christian Crusades); 21st century
Locale(s): Middle East (Palestine and the Holy Lands); New Jersey

Summary: Tom Gurden works to prevent al Sabah from triggering the explosion of a large nuclear power plant in New Jersey. Concurrently, Gurden and al Sabah, who are the mortal avatars of Loki and Ahriman, Lord of Darkness, battle for the destiny of mankind.

Other books you might like:
James Blish, *Black Easter*, 1968
Marion Zimmer Bradley, *The Mists of Avalon*, 1983
Philip Jose Farmer, *To Your Scattered Bodies Go*, 1971
Marc Laidlaw, *Neon Lotus*, 1988
Flora M. Speer, *Castle of Dreams*, 1990

4843

ROGER ZELAZNY
GAHAN WILSON, Illustrator

A Night in the Lonesome October
(New York: AvoNova/Morrow, 1993)

Story type: Horror (Satire)
Major character(s): Jack the Ripper, Serial Killer; Larry Talbot, Werewolf; Snuff, Animal (Jack's dog), Sidekick
Time period(s): 1890s
Locale(s): London, England

Summary: A cast of characters that includes Victor Frankenstein and his monster, the Wolfman, Count Dracula, Jack the Ripper, and assorted other famous literary and cinematic ghouls have assembled once more to play the Game, a ritual in which half will try to summon Lovecraftian deities back to Earth and the other half will try to stop them, with none knowing which side who is on until the day of reckoning. This delightful spoof of nearly every cliche in horror fiction is told from the viewpoint of the pets and familiars of the major characters. Gahan Wilson has supplied 32 striking interior illustrations.

Other books you might like:
Lionel Fenn, *668: The Neighbor of the Beast*, 1992
Gahan Wilson, *Eddy Deco's Last Caper*, 1987
Gahan Wilson, *Everybody's Favorite Duck*, 1989

4844

ROGER ZELAZNY

Prince of Chaos
(New York: William Morrow and Co., 1991)

Story type: Fantasy (Magic Conflict)
Series: Amber
Major character(s): Merlin, Royalty (Prince of Chaos); Gryll, Demon
Time period(s): Indeterminate
Locale(s): Courts of Chaos, Alternate Universe

Summary: Merlin, Prince of the House of Sawall, finds that he is recently third in the line of succession to the throne left by the death of Swayvil, King of Chaos. His father, Corwin, is still lost in darkness and it seems that Merlin is being set up to be the next king.

Other books you might like:
Steven Brust, *Jhereg*, 1983
David Eddings, *Pawn of Prophecy*, 1982
Cheryl J. Franklin, *Fire Get*, 1987
Barbara Hambly, *The Time of the Dark*, 1982
Robert Jordan, *The Eye of the World*, 1989
Mercedes Lackey, *Arrows of the Queen*, 1987
Marc Laidlaw, *Neon Lotus*, 1988

4845

ROGER ZELAZNY

This Immortal

(New York: Baen Books, 1989)

Story type: Science Fiction (Immortality)
Major character(s): Conrad Nomikos, Government Official, Immortal; Cort Myshtigo, Alien, Journalist
Time period(s): Indeterminate Future
Locale(s): Isle of Kos, Earth

Summary: In this Hugo Award-winning novel, originally published in 1966, the Earth was nearly destroyed by a nuclear war and now, several hundred years later, it still hasn't recovered. Galactic civilization, dominated by the Vegans, regards our planet as a backwater. Sometimes they come visit us as tourists. Conrad Nomikos, apparently immortal due to a radiation-induced mutation, has done many things in his life, but is currently serving as a tour guide for the distinguished and obnoxious Vegan journalist, Cort Myshtigo. Then Conrad discovers that someone is out to murder the Vegan and he must decide whether Myshtigo's life is worth preserving, possibly at the cost of his own.

Other books you might like:
Poul Anderson, *The Boat of a Million Years*, 1989
Octavia E. Butler, *Adulthood Rites*, 1988
Samuel R. Delany, *The Einstein Intersection*, 1967

4846

ROGER ZELAZNY, Editor
MARTIN H. GREENBERG, Co-Editor

Warriors of Blood and Dream

(New York: AvoNova, 1995)

Story type: Fantasy (Anthology; Science Fiction)

Summary: Contains a 10-page introduction and brief individual introductions by Zelazny to 15 original stories focusing on martial arts and mystical enlightenment. Frequently dark or ominous in tone, the stories present diverse fantastic and mundane settings and explore techniques, philosophies, and gadgets employed by explorers of various paths of enlightenment and action. Stories conclude with a brief discussion of their genesis by the authors who include Steven Barnes, Jeffrey A. Carver, Karen Haber, Jack C. Haldeman, II, Joe R. Lansdale, Jane Lindskold, Richard A. Lupoff, Victor Milan, Dave Smeds, Michael A. Stackpole, and Walter Jon Williams.

Other books you might like:
Steven Barnes, *Streetlethal*, 1983
Gordon R. Dickson, *Dorsai!*, 1976
Donald F. Glut, *The Empire Strikes Back*, 1980
Elizabeth A. Lynn, *Watchtower*, 1979
David R. Palmer, *Emergence*, 1984
Steve Perry, *The 97th Step*, 1989
Dennis Schmidt, *Way-Farer*, 1978

4847

ROGER ZELAZNY
VAUGHN BODE, Illustrator

Way Up High

(Hampton Falls, New Hampshire: Donald M. Grant, 1992)

Story type: Fantasy (Young Adult; Adventure)
Major character(s): Susi, Child, Student; Herman, Animal (pterodactyl)
Time period(s): 1990s
Locale(s): Earth

Summary: When Susi meets Herman on her way home from school, she learns from him about pterodactyls and spends her summer vacation flying around with him.

Other books you might like:
James Gurney, *Dinotopia*, 1992
Evelyn Sibley Lampman, *The Shy Stegosaurus of Cricket Creek*, 1955
Ursula K. Le Guin, *Catwings*, 1988
Rodney Matthews, *Yendor*, 1978
Edward Ormondroyd, *David and the Phoenix*, 1957
Doris Vallejo, *The Boy Who Saved the Stars*, 1978

4848

ROGER ZELAZNY, Editor

The Williamson Effect

(New York: Tor, 1996)

Story type: Fantasy (Anthology; Science Fiction)

Summary: This tribute to award-winning author and educator Jack Williamson contains a seven-page introduction by David Brin and individual introductions by Jim Frenkel to two poems and 14 stories, with author afterwords. Many of these original pieces accept the milieu of a Williamson story, while other authors provide a direct sequel to a famous work such as *Darker Than You Think* (1948), *Demon Moon* (1994), *The Humanoids* (1949), The Legion of Space Series (1947-1983), and ''With Folded Hands'' (1947). Concludes with seven pages of biographies of the contributors, who include Poul Anderson, Ben Bova, John Brunner, Jane Lindskold, Andre Norton, Frederik Pohl, Mike Resnick, Fred Saberhagen, David Weber, and Connie Willis.

Other books you might like:
Kevin J. Anderson, *War of the Worlds: Global Dispatches*, 1996
   editor
Steven R. Boyett, *Treks Not Taken*, 1996
Randall Garrett, *Takeoff!*, 1979
Randall Garrett, *Takeoff, Too!*, 1986
Martin H. Greenberg, *After the King: Stories in Honor of J.R.R. Tolkien*, 1992
   editor
William F. Nolan, *The Bradbury Chronicles: Stories in Honor of Ray Bradbury*, 1991
   Martin H. Greenberg, co-editor

4849

STEVE ZELL

WiZrD

(New York: St. Martin's, 1994)

Story type: Horror (Ancient Evil Unleashed)
Major character(s): Trevor Williams, Artist; Bryce Williams, Teenager; Megan Williams, Teenager (Bryce's stepsister)
Time period(s): 1990s (1994)
Locale(s): Pinon Rim, Arizona

Summary: Trevor Williams relocates his family from upstate New York to Pinon Rim, a former mining town almost literally rendered a ghost town a century before, following an outbreak of madness and mass murder that depopulated the town. Inadvertently, Bryce and Megan's explorations into a secret cave help jump start the Circle of the Harvest, a mythic ritual played out by a legendary Navajo entity that threatens once more to plunge the town into a sacrificial blood bath. This is the author's first novel.

Other books you might like:
G. Wayne Miller, *Thunder Rise*, 1989
Adam Niswander, *The Charm*, 1993
Eugene E. Pfaff Jr., *Uwharrie*, 1993
    Michael Causey, co-author
Kathryn Ptacek, *Ghost Dance*, 1990
Patrick Whalen, *Deathwalker*, 1992

4850

SARAH ZETTEL

Reclamation

(New York: Warner Aspect, 1996)

Story type: Science Fiction (Psychic Powers; Political)
Major character(s): Dorias Waesc, Artificial Intelligence, Refugee; Eric Born, Psychic; Arla Stone, Psychic
Time period(s): Indeterminate
Locale(s): The Realm of the Nameless, Planet—Imaginary; May 16, Planet—Imaginary; *U-Kenai*, Spaceship

Summary: The Alliance for the Re-Unification of the Human Family rescues/kidnaps Arla Stone from the Realm of the Nameless, only to have her kidnapped from them by the Rhudolant Vitae. In the pay of the Rhudolant Vitae, Eric Born recognizes Arla and rescues her. Both the Alliance and Vitae want Eric and Arla not only for their psychic abilities, but also because they believe the Realm of the Nameless gave birth to the human species. First novel.

Other books you might like:
David Brin, *Brightness Reef*, 1995
C.J. Cherryh, *Forty Thousand in Gehenna*, 1983
Glen Cook, *The Dragon Never Sleeps*, 1996
Dan Simmons, *Endymion*, 1996
E.C. Tubb, *The Winds of Gath*, 1967

4851

PAT ZETTNER

The Shadow Warrior

(New York: Atheneum, 1990)

Story type: Fantasy (Adventure)
Major character(s): Lady Llyndreth, Royalty (Princess)
Time period(s): Indeterminate

Summary: While her brother is away on a goblin hunt, rebel lords take over his castle and Llyndreth takes off to find him. Along the way she runs into the last of the giants and a wounded goblin, all three of whom discover it is best to stay together, despite initial mistrust.

Other books you might like:
Orson Scott Card, *Wyrms*, 1989
Gun Guneli, *On the Road to Baghdad*, 1989
Elizabeth Moon, *Surrender None: The Legacy of Gird*, 1990
Alis A. Rasmussen, *A Passage of Stars*, 1990
    Highroad Vol. 1

4852

PAUL EDWIN ZIMMER
JON DE CLES, Co-Author

Blood of the Colyn Muir

(New York: Avon, 1988)

Story type: Fantasy (Quest)
Major character(s): Darith, Hero
Time period(s): Indeterminate
Locale(s): Tondur, Fictional Country

Summary: The protagonist goes on a search for a magic sword to help him defeat the powers that have invaded his homeland.

Other books you might like:
Adrienne Martine-Barnes, *The Rainbow Sword*, 1988
James Silke, *Plague of Knives*, 1990
    Frank Frazetta's Death Dealer - Vol 4

4853

DAVID ZINDELL

The Broken God

(New York: Bantam Spectra, 1994)

Story type: Science Fiction (Adventure; Mystical)
Series: Neverness
Major character(s): Danlo Ringess, Pilot (spaceship); Hanuman, Companion
Time period(s): Indeterminate Future
Locale(s): Icefall, Planet—Imaginary; Interstellar Empire/Federation

Summary: Danlo must confront and reject godhood to succeed in his quest to destroy the menace at the heart of the galaxy. Sequel to *Neverness*.

Other books you might like:
Roger MacBride Allen, *The Ring of Charon*, 1990
Jeffrey A. Carver, *Down the Stream of Stars*, 1990

Glen Cook, *The Dragon Never Sleeps*, 1988
Michael P. Kube-McDowell, *Enigma*, 1986
Vernor Vinge, *A Fire upon the Deep*, 1992

4854

DAVID ZINDELL

The Wild

(New York: Bantam Spectra, 1996)

Story type: Science Fiction (Family Saga; Mystical)
Series: Neverness
Major character(s): Danlo Ringess, Pilot (spaceship); Mallory Ringess, Parent (father); Ede, Artificial Intelligence
Time period(s): Indeterminate Future
Locale(s): Farfara, Planet—Imaginary; Interstellar Empire/Federation

Summary: Sent by the Order of Mystic Mathematicians both to establish a new Order within the heart of the Wild on the lost planet of Tannahill and to destroy the cause of the sudden death by supernova of so many stars, Danlo also seeks his father, who went out with the first expedition.

Other books you might like:
Roger MacBride Allen, *The Ring of Charon*, 1990
Stephen Baxter, *Ring*, 1996
Jeffrey A. Carver, *Neptune Crossing*, 1994
Debra Doyle, *The Price of the Stars*, 1992
    James D. Macdonald, co-author
Alis A. Rasmussen, *A Passage of Stars*, 1990
Vernor Vinge, *A Fire upon the Deep*, 1992

4855

JACK ZIPES, Editor

Arabian Nights: The Marvels and Wonders of the Thousand and One Nights

(New York: Signet, 1991)

Story type: Fantasy (Anthology; Legend)
Time period(s): Indeterminate Past
Locale(s): Middle East

Summary: Zipes adapted and modernized the language of the 49 tales herein from the unexpurgated Richard Burton translation of the bawdy and erotic adult tales from the Middle East. Among the many popular tales included are "Ali Baba and the Forty Thieves," "Aladdin and the Magic Lamp" and many tales of Sinbad the Seaman. This book also contains notes on the text and translator, plus an afterword, glossary and bibliography.

Other books you might like:
John Barth, *The Last Voyage of Somebody the Sailor*, 1991
Richard F. Burton, *The Book of the Thousand Nights and a Night. A Plain and Literal Translation of the Arabian Nights Entertainment*, 1885-1886
    10 volumes
Patricia Daniels, *Sinbad the Sailor*, 1980
Lester del Rey, *Once upon a Time: A Treasury of Modern Fairy Tales*, 1991
    Risa Kessler, co-author

Craig Shaw Gardner, *The Other Sinbad*, 1991
Stephen Goldin, *Crystals of Air and Water*, 1989
Stephen Goldin, *Shrine of the Desert Mage*, 1988
Stephen Goldin, *The Storyteller and the Jahn*, 1988
Andrew Lang, *The Arabian Nights Entertainments*, 1969
    editor
Andrew Lang, *The Blue Fairy Book*, 1889
    editor
John Payne, *The Book of the Thousand Nights and the One Night*, 1882-1884
    9 volumes
Salman Rushdie, *Haroun and the Sea of Stories*, 1990
Susan Shwartz, *Arabesques: More Tales of the Arabian Nights*, 1988
    editor
Susan Shwartz, *Arabesques II*, 1989
    editor

4856

JACK ZIPES, Editor

Beauties, Beasts and Enchantments

(New York: Penguin Meridian, 1991)

Story type: Fantasy (Anthology; Legend)

Summary: This volume includes the most important fairy tales from 17th and 18th century France which gave birth to the Western tradition of fairy tales, inspiring the Grimm brothers. The 36 tales by 12 authors are primarily adult-oriented with several enjoyable by younger readers. Major contributions include 10 tales by Charles Perrault and 15 tales by Marie-Catherine d'Aulnoy. Zipes also includes two accounts of "Beauty and the Beast," an 11-page version by Jeanne-Marie Leprince de Beaumont and a 177-page version by Gabrielle-Suzanne de Villeneuve. Reprint of the 1989 hardcover.

Other books you might like:
Steven Brust, *The Sun, the Moon, and the Stars*, 1987
Kara Dalkey, *The Nightingale*, 1988
Charles de Lint, *Jack, the Giant-Killer*, 1987
Lester del Rey, *Once upon a Time: A Treasury of Modern Fairy Tales*, 1991
    Risa Kessler, co-editor
Michael Patrick Hearn, *The Victorian Fairy Tale Book*, 1988
    editor
Andrew Lang, *The Blue Fairy Book*, 1889
    editor
Andrew Lang, *The Red Fairy Book*, 1890
    editor
Ethel Johnston Phelps, *Tatterhood and Other Tales*, 1978
    editor
Sheri S. Tepper, *Beauty*, 1991
Patricia C. Wrede, *Snow White and Rose Red*, 1989

Series Index

This index alphabetically lists series to which books featured in the entries belong. Beneath each series name, book titles are listed alphabetically with author names. Numbers refer to the entries that feature each title.

Time Period Index

This index chronologically lists the time settings in which the featured books take place. Main headings refer to a century; where no specific time is given, the headings INDETERMINATE PAST, INDETERMINATE FUTURE, and INDETERMINATE are used. The 18th through 21st centuries are broken down into decades when possible. (Note: 1800s, for example, refers to the first decade of the 19th century.) Featured titles are listed alphabetically beneath time headings, with author names and entry numbers also provided.

INDETERMINATE

Geographic Index

This index provides access to all featured books by geographic settings, such as countries, continents, oceans, and planets. States and provinces are indicated for the United States and Canada. Also interfiled are headings for fictional place names, such as Spaceships, Imaginary Planets, etc. Sections are further broken down by city or the specific name of the imaginary locale. Book titles are listed alphabetically under headings, and author names and entry numbers are also provided.

1167

ALTERNATE UNIVERSE

AMERICAN COLONIES

ANCIENT CIVILIZATION

ANTARCTICA

The Gatekeepers - Daniel Graham Jr.   s   1845
The Lake at the End of the World - Caroline
   MacDonald   s   2849

Ayer's Rock
Find Your Own Truth - Robert N. Charrette   f   787

Brisbane
Sabine's Notebook - Nick Bantock   f   281

Fremantle
The Tallow Image - Jane Brindle   h   567

Melbourne
Brain Child - George Turner   s   4380

New Hong Kong
Quarantine - Greg Egan   s   1415

Perth
Quarantine - Greg Egan   s   1415

Sydney
Permutation City - Greg Egan   s   1414

Westerton
Brain Child - George Turner   s   4380

Yarra Valley
Genetic Soldier - George Turner   s   4381

AUSTRIA

At Sword's Point - Scott MacMillan   f   2861
Tek Vengeance - William Shatner   s   3942

Salzburg
Angel Souls and Devil Hearts - Christopher
   Golden   h   1810

Vienna
From the Teeth of Angels - Jonathan Carroll   h   744
Knights of the Blood - Scott MacMillan   f   2862
Mixed Doubles - Daniel Da Cruz   s   1057
Traveling with the Dead - Barbara Hambly   h   2012
The Unbeholden - Robert Weinberg   h   4547

BABYLON

The Fabulist - John Vornholt   f   4459
Servant of the Bones - Anne Rice   h   3654

BAHAMAS

Andros Island
Drakon - S.M. Stirling   s   4224

Bimini
The Deathless - Myles Murchison   h   3224

Nassau
TekLab - William Shatner   s   3943

BARBADOS

I, Tituba, Black Witch of Salem - Maryse
   Conde   f   911

BELGIUM

Brussels
Russian Spring - Norman Spinrad   s   4128

BERMUDA

Beast - Peter Benchley   h   362

BOSNIA-HERCEGOVINA

Sarajevo
St. Vitus Dances Eternity: A Sarajevo Ghost Story -
   Stewart Von Allmen   h   4450

BRAZIL

Cradle of Splendor - Patricia Anthony   s   129
A Fearful Symmetry - James Luceno   s   2817
Indiana Jones and the Seven Veils - Rob
   MacGregor   f   2857
Monkey Station - Ardath Mayhar   s   2946
The Nanotech Chronicles - Michael Flynn   s   1580
A Season for Slaughter - David Gerrold   s   1775
Silent Witness - Robert Arthur Smith   h   4097
Tek Vengeance - William Shatner   s   3942
Through the Arc of the Rain Forest - Karen Tei
   Yamashita   f   4791
Tyrannosaurus Rex - J.F. Rivkin   s   3674

Amazon Jungle
Finger of God - Michael Kasner   s   2400

Brasilia
Cybernetic Jungle - S.N. Lewitt   s   2742

BULGARIA

Boleslaus
The Kiss - Kathryn Reines   h   3614

BYZANTINE EMPIRE

Byzantium
Byzantium - Stephen R. Lawhead   f   2670

Constantinople
Shards of Empire - Susan Shwartz   f   4003

CAMBODIA

The Jade Ogre - Kenneth Robeson   f   3699

Phnom Penh
Dragon's Blood - Alex McDonough   s   3025

CANADA

Believe: A Novel - William Shatner   f   3937
Blessings and Curses - Christopher Stasheff   f   4158
Cloven Hooves - Megan Lindholm   f   2759
Light Raid - Connie Willis   s   4674
ME: A Novel of Self Discovery - Thomas T.
   Thomas   s   4350
Memory and Dream - Charles de Lint   f   1157
Near Death - Nancy Kilpatrick   h   2471
Northern Frights 2 - Don Hutchison   h   2242
Northern Frights 3 - Don Hutchison   h   2243
The Scathach and the Maeve's Daughter - Mary
   Alexander Walker   f   4476
Svaha - Charles de Lint   s   1160
Was - Geoff Ryman   f   3804

Caledon
Painted Devil - Michael Bedard   f   354

Carrick
The Mysterium - Eric McCormack   h   3008

Newford
I'll Be Watching You - Samuel M. Key   h   2463
The Ivory and the Horn - Charles de Lint   f   1155

ALBERTA

End of an Era - Robert J. Sawyer   s   3883

BRITISH COLUMBIA

Hatchet Blade
Monster - John Tigges   h   4366

Vancouver
Cutthroat - Michael Slade   h   4058
The Deathless - Myles Murchison   h   3224

NOVA SCOTIA

Haven-by-the-Sea
The Messenger - Donald Tyson   h   4408

ONTARIO

The Wild Wood - Charles de Lint   f   1162

Atikokan
Where the Chill Waits - T. Chris
   Martindale   h   2907

Ottawa
Eden's Eyes - Sean Costello   h   976
Spiritwalk - Charles de Lint   f   1159
Westlin Wind - Charles de Lint   f   1161

Thunder Bay
Golden Fleece - Robert J. Sawyer   s   3886

Toronto
As One Dead - Don Bassingthwaite   h   321
The Ascending - T.M. Wright   h   4773
Blood Price - Tanya Huff   h   2225
Blood Trail - Tanya Huff   h   2226
Bloodshift - Garfield Reeves-Stevens   h   3597
The Cornish Trilogy - Robertson Davies   f   1127
The Divide - Robert Charles Wilson   s   4701
Gate of Darkness, Circle of Light - Tanya
   Huff   f   2229
Headhunter - Timothy Findley   h   1562
The Night Inside - Nancy Baker   h   252
The Suiting - Kelley Wilde   h   4621
The Terminal Experiment - Robert J.
   Sawyer   s   3887

QUEBEC

The Cartoonist - Sean Costello   h   975

Montreal
Reluctant Voyagers - Elisabeth Vonarburg   s   4456
The Suiting - Kelley Wilde   h   4621

ROCKY MOUNTAINS

Crystal Wells
The Devouring - Douglas D. Hawk   h   2090

CARIBBEAN

Flickering Shadows - Kwadwo Agymah
   Kamau   f   2395
Sink the Armada - Keith William Andrews   s   118
World Without End - Molly Cochran   f   880

Coronado
Jupiter's Daughter - Tom Hyman   s   2247

Cozumel Reef
Rock of Ages - Walter Jon Williams   s   4651

Hispaniola
Pastwatch: The Redemption of Christopher Columbus -
   Orson Scott Card   s   726
Queen of Angels - Greg Bear   s   347

Mill Walk
Mystery - Peter Straub   h   4252

St. Albans
Lucifer's Eye - Hugh B. Cave   h   765

The Jekyll Legacy - Robert Bloch h 435
The Jewel of Seven Stars - Bram Stoker h 4238
The Last Aerie - Brian Lumley h 2830
The Law of Becoming - Kate Elliott s 1423
The Link - Andrew Laurance h 2666
Lord Kelvin's Machine - James P. Blaylock f 422
Lord of the Dead - Tom Holland h 2187
Lord of the Vampires - Jeanne Kalogridis h 2394
Lorien Lost - Michael King f 2477
Love and Sleep - John Crowley f 1035
Lunching with the Antichrist - Michael
    Moorcock f 3169
Mary Reilly - Valerie Martin h 2903
The Mummy!: A Tale of the Twenty-Second Century -
    Jane Webb Loudon h 2803
The Mummy, or Ramses the Damned - Anne
    Rice h 3652
Necroscope: The Lost Years - Brian
    Lumley h 2832
A Night in the Lonesome October - Roger
    Zelazny h 4843
The Nightwalker - Thomas Tessier h 4343
Personal Darkness - Tanith Lee h 2715
Photographing Fairies - Steve Szilagyi f 4289
Pillow Friend - Lisa Tuttle h 4402
Prophecy - Peter James h 2291
Psychomech - Brian Lumley h 2834
Psychosphere - Brian Lumley h 2835
The Quorum - Kim Newman h 3263
The Rats - James Herbert h 2132
Red Bride - Christopher Fowler h 1620
The Reluctant Sorcerer - Simon Hawke f 2096
The Robin Hood Ambush - William Wu s 4783
Rune - Christopher Fowler h 1621
Sabine's Notebook - Nick Bantock f 281
Scorpio Rising - Alex McDonough s 3030
Seance for a Vampire - Fred Saberhagen h 3817
Sexing the Cherry - Jeanette Winterson f 4719
Sherlock Holmes in Orbit - Mike Resnick s 3637
Spider - Patrick McGrath h 3039
Spring-Heeled Jack - Philip Pullman f 3546
Strange Devices of the Sun and Moon - Lisa
    Goldstein f 1814
Streets of Blood - Carl Sargent f 3860
Stunts - Charles L. Grant h 1857
Suckers - Anne Billson h 397
TekLab - William Shatner s 3943
That's All, Folks! - Greg Snow f 4108
Those Who Hunt the Night - Barbara
    Hambly h 2011
Time Scout - Robert Asprin s 221
Time Station London - David Evans s 1491
Traveling with the Dead - Barbara Hambly h 2012
The Trial of Elizabeth Cree - Peter Ackroyd h 19
Triumph - Ben Bova s 491
Tyrannosaurus Rex - J.F. Rivkin s 3674
The Unborn - Andrew Laurance h 2668
Werewolf - Peter Rubie h 3764
The Werewolves of London - Brian
    Stableford h 4147
Where Does Kissing End? - Kate Pullinger h 3544
White Queen - Gwyneth Jones s 2355
The Wizard of Camelot - Simon Hawke f 2101
The Wolf's Hour - Robert R. McCammon h 2992
The Woman between the Worlds - F. Gwynplaine
    MacIntyre s 2859
The Women of Whitechapel and Jack the Ripper - Paul
    West h 4590

Loughborough
The Wizard of Camelot - Simon Hawke f 2101

Lousewartshire
Nature's God - Robert Anton Wilson f 4698

Manchester
Anti-Ice - Stephen Baxter s 330
Automated Alice - Jeff Noon f 3292
The One Safe Place - Ramsey Campbell h 701
Pollen - Jeff Noon s 3293

Vurt - Jeff Noon s 3294

Marshank
Martin the Warrior - Brian Jacques f 2269

Maybury
Stitch - Mark Morris h 3205

Merkleton
Kent Montana and the Reasonably Invisible Man -
    Lionel Fenn s 1543

Mount Pleasant
The Influence - Ramsey Campbell h 698

Mousehole
The Little Country - Charles de Lint f 1156

Neath
Sepulchre - James Herbert h 2133

Norwich
Stone Angels - Mike Jefferies h 2305

Nottingham
Lady of the Forest - Jennifer Roberson f 3687
The Sheriff of Nottingham - Richard Kluger f 2515

Over Stowey
Walford's Oak - Jill M. Phillips f 3433

Oxford
The Endless Knot - Stephen R. Lawhead f 2671

Oxfordshire
Doomsday Book - Connie Willis s 4672
*Good Omens: The Nice and Accurate Prophecies of
    Agnes Nutter, Witch* - Neil Gaiman f 1693

Ravenmoor
Haunted - James Herbert h 2130

Ravenskeep
Lady of the Forest - Jennifer Roberson f 3687

Redwall Abbey
The Bellmaker - Brian Jacques f 2267
Mariel of Redwall - Brian Jacques f 2268
Martin the Warrior - Brian Jacques f 2269
Outcast of Redwall - Brian Jacques f 2271
Salamandastron - Brian Jacques f 2272

Richmond
The Time Ships - Stephen Baxter s 334

Rye
The Haunting of Lamb House - Joan Aiken h 35

Sandpits
The Dark One - Guy N. Smith h 4082

Sherwood Forest
Lady of the Forest - Jennifer Roberson f 3687
The Outlaws of Sherwood - Robin
    McKinley f 3065
The Sheriff of Nottingham - Richard Kluger f 2515

Sleath
The Ghosts of Sleath - James Herbert h 2129

Somerset
Walford's Oak - Jill M. Phillips f 3433

Starmouth
The Horror Club - Mark Morris h 3203

Stonehenge
Kirins: The Flight of the Ain - James D.
    Priest f 3535
Kirins: The Secret of the Hanging Stones - James D.
    Priest f 3536

Sussex
Host - Peter James h 2289
Psychamok - Brian Lumley h 2833
Twilight - Peter James h 2293

Thornton Basset
The Black Death - Basil Copper h 958

Tredannack
The Vanishment - Jonathan Aycliffe h 238

Valley Green
Evil Intent - Bernard Taylor h 4308

Vernematon
The Forest House - Marion Zimmer Bradley f 521

Warchester
Carnosaur - Harry Adam Knight s 2538

Willington College
Witch Spell - Guy N. Smith h 4084

Wych Cross
The Sandman: Book of Dreams - Neil
    Gaiman f 1694

York
Sleepwalker - Michael Cadnum h 666

Yorkshire
Midnight Sun - Ramsey Campbell h 700

EUROPE

All's Faire - Pamela F. Service f 3927
The Amazon Chronicles - Jane E.M.
    Robinson f 3703
Ars Magica - Judith Tarr f 4300
Attila's Treasure - Stephan Grundy f 1964
The Autobiography of Santa Claus: It's Better to Give
    - Jeff Guinn f 1967
Black Horses for the King - Anne
    McCaffrey f 2959
Blood Alone - Elaine Bergstrom h 378
The Boat of a Million Years - Poul Anderson s 104
Byzantium - Stephen R. Lawhead f 2670
Charlemagne's Champion - Gail Van Asten f 4413
City of Pain - John Terra f 4341
The Discovery of Dragons - Graeme Base f 320
The Dragons of the Rhine - Diana L.
    Paxson f 3395
Eclipse Corona - John Shirley s 3993
A Farce to Be Reckoned With - Roger
    Zelazny f 4835
Glenraven - Marion Zimmer Bradley f 523
His Majesty's Elephant - Judith Tarr f 4302
Holy Fire - Bruce Sterling s 4195
If at Faust You Don't Succeed - Roger
    Zelazny f 4841
Indiana Jones and the Sky Pirates - Martin
    Caidin f 673
Jupiter's Daughter - Tom Hyman s 2247
The Light Bearer - Donna Gillespie f 1791
The Lost Guardian - Ronald Anthony Cross s 1033
Lucifer Jones - Mike Resnick f 3630
Madouc - Jack Vance f 4421
North Wind - Gwyneth Jones s 2354
The Offspring - Kenneth McKenney h 3048
One King's Way - Harry Harrison s 2057
Parsifal - Peter Vansittart f 4431
The Plains of Passage - Jean M. Auel f 231
The Premonition - Andrew Laurance h 2667
The Princess and the Dragon - Roberto
    Pazzi f 3402
Rhinegold - Stephan Grundy f 1965
Shiva Accused: An Adventure of the Ice Age - J.H.
    Brennan f 546
Shiva: An Adventure of the Ice Age - J.H.
    Brennan f 548
Shiva's Challenge: An Adventure of the Ice Age - J.H.
    Brennan f 547
Slow Dancing through Time - Gardner
    Dozois s 1305
Songs of Chaos - S.N. Lewitt s 2745
The Stress of Her Regard - Tim Powers h 3496

FICTIONAL COUNTRY

The Old Kingdom
Sabriel - Garth Nix f 3288

The Old World
Blood of the Fold - Terry Goodkind f 1820

Omnia
Small Gods - Terry Pratchett f 3507

Oran
Beldan's Fire - Midori Snyder f 4110

Osten Ard
Stone of Farewell - Tad Williams f 4644

Othion
Kedrigern and the Charming Couple - John
  Morressy f 3194

Outside
Time and Light - William Bornefeld s 470

Paduan
The Falcon and the Serpent - Cheryl A.
  Smith f 4068

Pakajan Peninsula
Hawk's Flight - Carol Chase f 794

Palerna
A Forest Lord - Michael Williams f 4634
A Sorcerer's Apprentice - Michael Williams f 4635

Pandemia
The Cutting Edge - Dave Duncan f 1349
Emperor and Clown - Dave Duncan f 1350

Paradise
Primavera - Francesca Lia Block f 449

Parkwood
Down Among the Dead Men - Simon R.
  Green f 1897

Peep-East
The Zap Gun - Philip K. Dick s 1229

Pelucir
The Book of Atrix Wolfe - Patricia A.
  McKillip f 3058

The Peninsula
Flowerdust - Gwyneth Jones s 2353

Perime of Moer
The Stone Movers - Patricia Mullen f 3221

Phesaotois
A Sorcerer and a Gentleman - Elizabeth
  Willey f 4629

Pheyarcet
A Sorcerer and a Gentleman - Elizabeth
  Willey f 4629

Pinrae
Ghost King - David Gemmell f 1755

The Plain
The Son of Summer Stars - Meredith Ann
  Pierce f 3440

Polia
The Spirit Gate - Maya Kaathryn Bohnhoff f 460

Prospero's Isle
Caliban's Hour - Tad Williams f 4641

Province of Bierdsey
Cat's Paw - L.A. Taylor f 4316

Pudar
Prince of Demons - Mickey Zucker
  Reichert f 3609

Punja Desert
Sword-Breaker - Jennifer Roberson f 3689

Pyrdain
The Silver Hand - Stephen R. Lawhead f 2673

Python Isle
Python Isle - Kenneth Robeson f 3700

Qualinesti
Kindred Spirits - Mark Anthony f 125
The Qualinesti - Paul B. Thompson f 4353

Rangfara
The Clan of the Warlord - Elizabeth H.
  Boyer f 494

Raragash
The Cursed - Dave Duncan f 1348

Rashpuht
Castle in the Air - Diana Wynne Jones f 2346

Ravenloft
Mordenheim - Chet Williamson h 4655
Tapestry of Dark Souls - Elaine Bergstrom h 380
Tower of Doom - Mark Anthony h 126

The Realms
The Ring of Winter - James Lowder f 2813

Recluce
The Death of Chaos - L.E. Modesitt Jr. f 3128
The Magic Engineer - L.E. Modesitt Jr. f 3133
The Magic of Recluce - L.E. Modesitt Jr. f 3134
The Towers of the Sunset - L.E. Modesitt
  Jr. f 3139

Redhart
Blood and Honor - Simon R. Green f 1893

The Republic
Innerverse - John DeChancie s 1178

Republic of Saru
Outside the Dog Museum - Jonathan Carroll f 745

Reth
Masques - Patricia Briggs f 560

Rethwellen
By the Sword - Mercedes Lackey f 2602

Rezhmia
King of the Dead - R.A. MacAvoy f 2846

Rhadaz
One Land, One Duke - Ru Emerson f 1452
The Two in Hiding - Ru Emerson f 1454

Rhaetia
The Pixilated Peeress - L. Sprague de
  Camp f 1141

Rhazaulle
The Wolf of Winter - Paula Volsky f 4449

Rossacotta
Rouse a Sleeping Cat - Dan Crawford f 1012
The Sure Death of a Mouse - Dan Crawford f 1013
A Wild Dog and Lone - Dan Crawford f 1014

Rud
Chimaera's Copper - Piers Anthony f 136

Ruwenda
Black Trillium - Marion Zimmer Bradley f 518
Blood Trillium - Julian May f 2940
Golden Trillium - Andre Norton f 3307
Lady of the Trillium - Marion Zimmer
  Bradley f 525

Rwn
Voyage of the Fox Rider - Dennis L.
  McKiernan f 3057

The Sad City
Haroun and the Sea of Stories - Salman
  Rushdie f 3788

St. Crim
Lunching with the Antichrist - Michael
  Moorcock f 3169

St. Lucien
The Stalking Horse - Constance Ash f 184

Sanctum
Wheel of Dreams - Salinda Tyson f 4409

Saquave Wilderness
The Stallion Queen - Constance Ash f 185

Sarronnyn
The Order War - L.E. Modesitt Jr. f 3136

Scothandir
Timespell - Robert N. Charrette f 793

SeLenicca
The Loneliest Magician - Irene Radford f 3555

Sendaria
Belgarath the Sorcerer - David Eddings f 1388

Senna Lirwan
Wren to the Rescue - Sherwood Smith f 4102

Seven Islands
Dragon Burning - Craig Shaw Gardner f 1709
Dragon Sleeping - Craig Shaw Gardner f 1710
Dragon Waking - Craig Shaw Gardner f 1711

Seven Kingdoms
A Game of Thrones - George R.R. Martin f 2896

Seven Nations
Silverlight - Morgan Llywelyn f 2785

Shai
Summer King, Winter Fool - Lisa Goldstein f 1815

Shaleth
The Falcon Rises - Michael C. Staudinger f 4175

Shangri-La
Shangri-La: The Return to the World of Lost Horizon -
  Eleanor Cooney f 942

Shkoder
No Quarter - Tanya Huff f 2230
Sing the Four Quarters - Tanya Huff f 2231

Sicas, Aquilonia
Conan the Rogue - John Maddox Roberts f 3693

Sicmon Islands
The Golden Mean - Nick Bantock f 280

Sidra
Token of Dragonsblood - Damaris Cole f 897

Silvanesti
Firstborn - Paul B. Thompson f 4352

Siradayel
Wren's Quest - Sherwood Smith f 4103

Six Duchies
Assassin's Apprentice - Robin Hobb f 2151
Royal Assassin - Robin Hobb f 2152

Six Kingdoms
The Mace of Souls - Bruce Fergusson f 1549

The Six Lands
Villains by Necessity - Eve Forward f 1592

Skala
Luck in the Shadows - Lynn Flewelling f 1572

Smolen
The Regiment's War - John Dalmas s 1072

Solinde
Flight of the Raven - Jennifer Roberson f 3685

West Gahant
Shadow of the Crown - Craig Mills *f* 3119

Westland
Wizard's First Rule - Terry Goodkind *f* 1822

The Westlands
Days of Air and Darkness - Katharine Kerr *f* 2443
Days of Blood and Fire - Katharine Kerr *f* 2444
Prince of Demons - Mickey Zucker
Reichert *f* 3609
A Time of Omens - Katharine Kerr *f* 2453
The Western Wizard - Mickey Zucker
Reichert *f* 3612

Westria
The Jewel of Fire - Diana L. Paxson *f* 3396
The Wind Crystal - Diana L. Paxson *f* 3400

Westwind
The Towers of the Sunset - L.E. Modesitt
Jr. *f* 3139

White Gryphon Lands
The Silver Gryphon - Mercedes Lackey *f* 2619

Wynnamyr
Book of Stones - L. Dean James *f* 2279
Kingslayer - L. Dean James *f* 2280

Xanth
The Color of Her Panties - Piers Anthony *f* 137
Demons Don't Dream - Piers Anthony *f* 138
Geis of the Gargoyle - Piers Anthony *f* 141
Harpy Thyme - Piers Anthony *f* 143
Isle of View - Piers Anthony *f* 145
Question Quest - Piers Anthony *f* 153
Roc and a Hard Place - Piers Anthony *f* 154
Yon Ill Wind - Piers Anthony *f* 162

Yeoli
Lion's Heart - Karen Wehrstein *f* 4529
Shadow's Son - Shirley Meier *f* 3085

Yeou
Lion's Soul - Karen Wehrstein *f* 4530

Ylesuin
Fortress in the Eye of Time - C.J. Cherryh *f* 804

Ynys Celydonn
The Castle of the Silver Wheel - Teresa
Edgerton *f* 1397
The Grail and the Ring - Teresa Edgerton *f* 1400

The Young Kingdoms
Elric: Song of the Black Sword - Michael
Moorcock *f* 3167
Tales of the White Wolf - Edward E.
Kramer *f* 2566

Ys
The Oathbound Wizard - Christopher
Stasheff *f* 4162

Ytaili
The Fire's Stone - Tanya Huff *f* 2228

Yu-Atlanchi
The Face in the Abyss - Abraham Merritt *f* 3091

Yuggoth
Horrors of the Dancing Gods - Jack L.
Chalker *f* 774

Yurt
A Bad Spell in Yurt - C. Dale Brittain *f* 573
Daughter of Magic - C. Dale Brittain *f* 574
The Wood Nymph and the Cranky Saint - C. Dale
Brittain *f* 577

Zam Fadogurum
Wild Magic - Jo Clayton *f* 864

Zamora
The Conan Chronicles - Robert Jordan *f* 2378

Zanzib
Castle in the Air - Diana Wynne Jones *f* 2346

Zark
Faery Lands Forlorn - Dave Duncan *f* 1351
Perilous Seas - Dave Duncan *f* 1357

Zelharri
One Land, One Duke - Ru Emerson *f* 1452

Zinora
Blood Trillium - Julian May *f* 2940

FRANCE

A Candle for D'Artagnan - Chelsea Quinn
Yarbro *h* 4793
Child of Faerie, Child of Earth - Josepha
Sherman *f* 3976
King & Raven - Cary James *f* 2275
A King Beneath the Mountain - Robert N.
Charrette *f* 788
The Premonition - Andrew Laurance *h* 2667
Rehearsal for a Renaissance - Douglas W.
Clark *f* 842
A Strange and Ancient Name - Josepha
Sherman *f* 3981
A Well-Timed Enchantment - Vivian Vande
Velde *f* 4430
Where the Towers Pierce the Sky - Marie D.
Goodwin *f* 1823

Avignon
Scorpio - Alex McDonough *s* 3028

Brittany
The Winter King - Bernard Cornwell *f* 962

Chateau Beauxpres
The Porcelain Dove - Delia Sherman *f* 3974

Duchy of Aquitaine
The Shadow Gate - Margaret Ball *f* 267

Greenlaw
A College of Magics - Caroline Stevermer *f* 4201

Jura Mountains
The Porcelain Dove - Delia Sherman *f* 3974

Le Caillou
Wall, Stone, Craft - Walter Jon Williams *h* 4653

Nice
Echoes - Jackie Hyman *h* 2245
Glory Road - Robert A. Heinlein *f* 2112

Normandy
The Spawn of Loki - Jason Henderson *f* 2122

Paris
Arc d'X - Steve Erickson *f* 1475
Bad Voltage - Jonathan Littell *s* 2773
The Carnival of Destruction - Brian
Stableford *h* 4142
The Eight - Katherine Neville *f* 3258
Human Resources - Floyd Kemske *h* 2438
I, Vampire - Michael Romkey *h* 3736
Indiana Jones and the Peril at Delphi - Rob
MacGregor *f* 2856
Machine - Rene Belletto *h* 360
The Mata Hari Adventure - James Luceno *f* 2819
Mirage - F. Paul Wilson *h* 4688
Night of the Cooters - Howard Waldrop *s* 4472
Phantom - Susan Kay *h* 2407
The Porcelain Dove - Delia Sherman *f* 3974
Russian Spring - Norman Spinrad *s* 4128
The Secret Life of Laszlo, Count Dracula - Roderick
Anscombe *h* 124

A Sharpness on the Neck - Fred
Saberhagen *h* 3818
The Tale of the Body Thief - Anne Rice *h* 3655
TekLab - William Shatner *s* 3943
The Unbeholden - Robert Weinberg *h* 4547
The Werewolf of Paris - Guy Endore *h* 1463

Saint Ame
The Judas Cross - Charles Sheffield *h* 3958

Saint-Fabrisse
Kiss of Death - Daniel Rhodes *h* 3649

St. Maurice de Navacelles
Black Dogs - Ian McEwan *h* 3034

Verdun
The Mata Hari Adventure - James Luceno *f* 2819

GAUL

Druids - Morgan Llywelyn *f* 2780

GEORGIA

Somewhere East of Life - Brian W. Aldiss *s* 48

GERMANY

1945 - Newt Gingrich *s* 1800
At Sword's Point - Scott MacMillan *f* 2861
The Book of Earth - Marjorie Bradley
Kellogg *f* 2427
Carrion Comfort - Dan Simmons *h* 4028
The Cornish Trilogy - Robertson Davies *f* 1127
Escape From Loki - Philip Jose Farmer *f* 1503
First Dawn - Mike Moscoe *s* 3217
The Fourth Rome - David Drake *s* 1317
Lightning - Dean R. Koontz *h* 2553
The Magicians of Night - Barbara Hambly *f* 2006
Night's Pawn - Tom Dowd *f* 1284
Nutcracker - E.T.A. Hoffmann *f* 2171
Parsifal - Peter Vansittart *f* 4431
Red Army - Ralph Peters *s* 3429
*The Secret Laboratory Journals of Dr. Victor
Frankenstein* - Jeremy Kay *h* 2406
Sleipnir - Linda Evans *f* 1493
Spell Bound - Ru Emerson *f* 1453
Warrior - William Wu *s* 4784

Bayreuth
I, Vampire - Michael Romkey *h* 3736

Berlin
Arc d'X - Steve Erickson *f* 1475
Child of the Journey - Janet Berliner *f* 381
Child of the Light - Janet Gluckman *f* 1803
City of Pain - John Terra *f* 4341
Fatherland - Robert Harris *s* 2049
Triumph - Ben Bova *s* 491

Frankfort
Cloud Castles - Michael Scott Rohan *f* 3730

Hamburg
Nightmare, with Angel - Stephen Gallagher *h* 1697

Harz Mountains
Psychomech - Brian Lumley *h* 2834

Leipzig
Two Crowns for America - Katherine Kurtz *f* 2594

Munich
The Broken Goddess - Hans Bemmann *f* 361
The Parasite - Ramsey Campbell *h* 702
Time's Arrow - Martin Amis *s* 80

Saxony
Better in the Dark - Chelsea Quinn Yarbro *h* 4792

MEXICO

The Earth Remembers - Susan Torian Olan *s* 3354
The Fourth Guardian - Ronald Anthony
  Cross *s* 1032
The Further Adventures of Batman 2: Featuring the
  Penguin - Martin H. Greenberg *s* 1915
Montezuma Strip - Alan Dean Foster *s* 1614
Stranded! - Warren Norwood *s* 3317
The Turing Option - Harry Harrison *s* 2063

Aztlan Free Zone
Above the Lower Sky - Tom Deitz *f* 1188

Baja California
The Merlin Effect - T.A. Barron *f* 310

Huevos Verdes
Beggars and Choosers - Nancy Kress *s* 2573

Mexico City
High Aztec - Ernest Hogan *s* 2173

Nuevo Laredo
Heavy Weather - Bruce Sterling *s* 4194

Xitaclan
Ruins - Kevin J. Anderson *h* 93

MIDDLE EAST

The Adventures of Huru on the Road to Baghdad -
  Guneli Gun *f* 1968
Aladdin: Master of the Lamp - Mike
  Resnick *f* 3618
Arabian Nights: The Marvels and Wonders of the
  Thousand and One Nights - Jack Zipes *f* 4855
The Autobiography of Santa Claus: It's Better to Give
  - Jeff Guinn *f* 1967
A Bad Day for Ali Baba - Craig Shaw
  Gardner *f* 1706
Dark Prince - David Gemmell *f* 1754
Death in Delhi - Gary Gygax *f* 1983
The Hashish Man and Other Stories by Lord Dunsany
  - Lord Dunsany *f* 1367
The Hunters' Haunt - Dave Duncan *f* 1353
The Last Arabian Night - Craig Shaw
  Gardner *f* 1712
Lord of the Two Lands - Judith Tarr *f* 4303
The Mask of Loki - Roger Zelazny *f* 4842
Master of Many Treasures - Mary Brown *f* 593
The Memory Cathedral - Jack Dann *s* 1086
Whose Song Is Sung - Frank Schaefer *f* 3897
Wishing Season - Esther Friesner *f* 1679

Acre
The Dagger and the Cross: A Novel of the Crusades -
  Judith Tarr *f* 4301

Baghdad
The Last Voyage of Somebody the Sailor - John
  Barth *f* 312
The Other Sinbad - Craig Shaw Gardner *f* 1713

Jerusalem
Alamut - Judith Tarr *f* 4298

Khuruchabja
Looking for the Mahdi - N. Lee Wood *s* 4753

Nok Kuzlat
Looking for the Mahdi - N. Lee Wood *s* 4753

Sumer
To the Land of the Living - Robert
  Silverberg *f* 4023

Tyre
Crusader's Torch - Chelsea Quinn Yarbro *h* 4795

MONGOLIA

The Yngling and the Circle of Power - John
  Dalmas *s* 1074

MOON (EARTH'S)

The Alien Dark - Diana G. Gallagher *s* 1695
Beamriders! - Martin Caidin *s* 672
Carve the Sky - Alexander Jablokov *s* 2260
Century 21 - Ewa Kuryluk *s* 2595
Cowboy Feng's Space Bar and Grille - Steven
  Brust *s* 606
Dreams of Gods and Men - W.T. Quick *s* 3548
The Eighth Rank - David D. Ross *s* 3751
Empire Builders - Ben Bova *s* 479
Fisherman's Hope - David Feintuch *s* 1530
Flare - Roger Zelazny *s* 4836
Flatlander - Larry Niven *s* 3280
Griffin's Egg - Michael Swanwick *s* 4281
Growing Up Weightless - John M. Ford *s* 1583
The Hammer of God - Arthur C. Clarke *s* 850
Hammer of Mars - M.S. Murdock *s* 3225
Harvest of Stars - Poul Anderson *s* 105
Heads - Greg Bear *s* 343
The Long Run - Daniel Keys Moran *s* 3178
Mutant Star - Karen Haber *s* 1985
Mutineers' Moon - David Weber *s* 4524
Nanoware Time/The Persistence of Vision - Ian
  Watson *s* 4494
Peace on Earth - Stanislaw Lem *s* 2731
The Pure Cold Light - Gregory Frost *s* 1681
Satellite Night News - Jack Hopkins *s* 2208
Star Brothers - Ben Bova *s* 487
Steel Beach - John Varley *s* 4436
Target - Janet Morris *s* 3198
Thunder Strike! - Michael McCollum *s* 3003
Tower of the Gods - Thomas A. Easton *s* 1384
The Transmigration of Souls - William
  Barton *s* 318
The Voices of Heaven - Frederik Pohl *s* 3470

Clavius Base
Lifeline - Kevin J. Anderson *s* 92

Columbus Base
Assemblers of Infinity - Kevin J. Anderson *s* 83

Copernicus
The Multiplex Man - James P. Hogan *s* 2177
Second Star - Dana Stabenow *s* 4140

Daedalus Crater
Assemblers of Infinity - Kevin J. Anderson *s* 83

Descartes Station
Lunar Descent - Allen Steele *s* 4184

Fun City
The Man in the Moon Must Die - Jeff
  Bredenberg *s* 545

Hipparchus
Double Planet - John Gribbin *s* 1946

Hydra Square
Harvest the Fire - Poul Anderson *s* 106

LB-13
In the Wrong Hands - Edward Gibson *s* 1778

Luna
To Save the Sun - Ben Bova *s* 489

Luna City
The Moon Is a Harsh Mistress - Robert A.
  Heinlein *s* 2113

Lunaplex
Lunar Justice - Charles L. Harness *s* 2034

Moonbase
Moonrise - Ben Bova *s* 482

Ontario Base
The Rising - James Doohan *s* 1275

Port Bowen
The Stars Are Also Fire - Poul Anderson *s* 111

Schiaparelli, Luna
Take Back Plenty - Colin Greenland *s* 1936

Tycho South Shore
The Oxygen Barons - Gregory Feeley *s* 1527

U.N. Base
Stranger Suns - George Zebrowski *s* 4832

Zamok Vysoki
The Stars Are Also Fire - Poul Anderson *s* 111

MOON—IMAGINARY

Amalthea
The Diamond Moon - Paul Preuss *s* 3523

Anee
Serpent Catch - Dave Wolverton *s* 4745

Davonia
Devil in the Sky - Greg Cox *s* 995

God's World
God's World - Ian Watson *s* 4492

Haven
Blood Feuds - S.M. Stirling *s* 4222

Hisagazi, Yarzik Island
The Longest Voyage/Slow Lightning - Poul
  Anderson *s* 108

Kahani
Haroun and the Sea of Stories - Salman
  Rushdie *f* 3788

Ocypete
Iris - William Barton *s* 317

Oz
The Engines of God - Jack McDevitt *s* 3015

Quintaglio Home World
Far-Seer - Robert J. Sawyer *s* 3884
Fossil Hunter - Robert J. Sawyer *s* 3885

Yavin Four
The Lost City of the Jedi - Paul Davids *s* 1125

Zulu
Ocean under the Ice - Robert L. Forward *s* 1595

Zuni
Marooned on Eden - Robert L. Forward *s* 1593

MOROCCO

The Tattooed Map - Barbara Hodgson *f* 2161

Marrakesh
The Colors of Hell - Michael Paine *h* 3374

Taroudannt
The Safety of Unknown Cities - Lucy
  Taylor *h* 4320

MOZAMBIQUE

Lake Cabora Bassa
A Girl Named Disaster - Nancy Farmer *f* 1501

MYANMAR

Gold Dragon - Robert Cain *s* 679

Rangoon
John Dollar - Marianne Wiggins *h* 4617

MYTHICAL PLACE

The Broken Goddess - Hans Bemmann f 361
The Cornish Trilogy - Robertson Davies f 1127
Flight of the Dragon Kyn - Susan Fletcher f 1571
Fortress of Frost and Fire - Mercedes
  Lackey f 2610
The Hashish Man and Other Stories by Lord Dunsany
  - Lord Dunsany f 1367
Here There Be Dragons - Roger Zelazny f 4840
In the Red Lord's Reach - Phyllis
  Eisenstein f 1417
Liar's Oath - Elizabeth Moon f 3160
Little Sister - Kara Dalkey f 1067
Mostly Harmless - Douglas Adams s 24
The Panther's Hoard - Nancy Varian
  Berberick f 374
*The Secret Weavers: Stories of the Fantastic by Latin
  American Women* - Marjorie Agosin f 33
To the Land of the Living - Robert
  Silverberg f 4023
Typewriter in the Sky - L. Ron Hubbard f 2224
The Unicorn Solution - John Lee f 2703

Addams Family Mansion
Addams Family Values - Todd Strasser f 4246

Aerith
The Master of Whitestorm - Janny Wurts f 4786

The Afterlife
Tex and Molly in the Afterlife - Richard
  Grant f 1863

The Afterworlds
The Friendship Song - Nancy Springer f 4133

Allanmere
Shadow Hunt - Anne Logston f 2791

Altai Valley
Winged Magic - Mary H. Herbert f 2138

Amazina
The Ultimate Bike Path - Michael B. Sirota s 4052

Ambermere
The Door to Ambermere - J. Calvin Pierce f 3437
The Wizard of Ambermere - J. Calvin Pierce f 3438

Anauroch
The Parched Sea - Troy Denning f 1200

Arcady
Arcady - Michael Williams f 4633

Asgard
The Tower of Beowulf - Parke Godwin f 1808

Astral Plane
The Fourth Guardian - Ronald Anthony
  Cross s 1032

Athas
The Verdant Passage - Troy Denning f 1201

Athilan
Letters From Atlantis - Robert Silverberg f 4015

Atlantis
World Without End - Molly Cochran f 880

Avalon
The Dragon and the Unicorn - A.A.
  Attanasio f 224

Baloran's Keep
Shadow Hunt - Anne Logston f 2791

Bellwoods
Son of Spellsinger - Alan Dean Foster f 1617

Beltrevan
Wrath of Ashar - Angus Wells f 4577

Black Oak Mall
Mall Purchase Night - Rick Cook f 935

Blodgett's Crossing
Jeremy Thatcher, Dragon Hatcher - Bruce
  Coville f 991

Blue Forest
Wheel of Dreams - Salinda Tyson f 4409

Blue Mountain
Master of Many Treasures - Mary Brown f 593

Borderland
Borderland - Terri Windling f 4707
Finder - Emma Bull f 632
Nevernever - Will Shetterly f 3985

Camp Chippewa
Addams Family Values - Todd Strasser f 4246

Carthell Abbey
The Robin and the Kestrel - Mercedes
  Lackey f 2617

Castle Elfwood
Elfwood - Rose Estes f 1477

Castle Fox
Prince of the North - Harry Turtledove f 4392

Castle Frankenstein
The Ultimate Bike Path - Michael B. Sirota s 4052

Castle Harvell
The Baker's Boy - J.V. Jones f 2356

Castle Midnight
Blood and Honor - Simon R. Green f 1893

Caverns of Cytorax
Another Day, Another Dungeon - Greg
  Costikyan f 977

Chateau "Howliday Inn" Bow-Wow
Return to Howliday Inn - James Howe f 2220

Chaumenard
The Book of Atrix Wolfe - Patricia A.
  McKillip f 3058

The Citadel
The Wizard at Home - Rick Shelley f 3968

The Citadel of Wizards
Dog Wizard - Barbara Hambly f 2005

The City
Suisan - Phyllis Carol Agins f 32

Count Volmar's Castle
Castle of Deception - Mercedes Lackey f 2604

Covamere
Dragoncharm - Graham Edwards f 1405

The Crossroads
What Savage Beast - Peter David s 1122

Crystal Keep
Guardian's Key - Anne Logston f 2788

Dark Heart
Dark Heart - Betsy James f 2274

Dark Horse Plains
City of the Sorcerers - Mary H. Herbert f 2134
Lightning's Daughter - Mary H. Herbert f 2136

Darkhorn Mountains
Valorian - Mary H. Herbert f 2137

Darkon
King of the Dead - Gene DeWeese h 1218

Dead Lands
Groogleman - Debra Doyle s 1293

Delta
The Sorceress and the Cygnet - Patricia A.
  McKillip f 3061

Desolate Mountains
Dragon Cauldron - Laurence Yep f 4802

Dim Reaches
Shadow Dance - Anne Logston f 2790

The Down
Tales From Watership Down - Richard Adams f 25

Dragon Realm
Dragon Rigger - Jeffrey A. Carver s 752

Dragoncastle
Lords of the Sky - Angus Wells f 4573

The Drake Kingdoms
The Dragon Crown - Richard A. Knaak f 2518

The Dreaming
The Sandman: Book of Dreams - Neil
  Gaiman f 1694

Egg Mountain
Dragon War - Laurence Yep f 4803

Eight Planes of the Matrix
Justice - David Drake s 1321

Eigo
Battledragon - Christopher Rowley f 3756

Elfland
A Child of Elvish - Nancy Varian Berberick f 373
The Cup of Morning Shadows - Rosemary
  Edghill f 1403
Thomas the Rhymer - Ellen Kushner f 2596

Elfwood
Elfwood - Rose Estes f 1477
Twisted Dragon - Kevin Stein f 4188

Elphame
The Cup of Morning Shadows - Rosemary
  Edghill f 1403
The Sword of Maiden's Tears - Rosemary
  Edghill f 1404

Emerald Mountains
Roc and a Hard Place - Piers Anthony f 154

Enchanted Forest
Calling on Dragons - Patricia C. Wrede f 4761
Dealing with Dragons - Patricia C. Wrede f 4762
Mirror of Destiny - Andre Norton f 3312
Searching for Dragons - Patricia C. Wrede f 4765

Enlightenment
The Magic Touch - Jody Lynn Nye f 3323

Evermeet
The Coral Kingdom - Douglas Niles f 3268

Faerie
Child of Faerie, Child of Earth - Josepha
  Sherman f 3976
The Dragon's Dagger - R.A. Salvatore f 3837
Dragonslayer's Return - R.A. Salvatore f 3838
Dreamseeker's Road - Tom Deitz f 1191
The Hero King - Rick Shelley f 3966
The Rebirth of Wonder - Lawrence Watt-
  Evans f 4502
The Reign of the Brown Magician - Lawrence Watt-
  Evans f 4503
A Strange and Ancient Name - Josepha
  Sherman f 3981
Sunshaker's War - Tom Deitz f 1195
The Woods out Back - R.A. Salvatore f 3848

Faerun's Underdark
Siege of Darkness - R.A. Salvatore f 3844

Antar
One Mind's Eye - Kathy Tyers   *s*   4405

Anu/Dagda
Mutagenesis - Helen Collins   *s*   899

Appledura
Charmed - Marilyn Singer   *f*   4046

Arangorta
Reunion on Neverend - John E. Stith   *s*   4233

Arbroth
Dream-Weaver - Louise Lawrence   *s*   2674

Ardel
FreeMaster - Kris Jensen   *s*   2307
Mentor - Kris Jensen   *s*   2308

Ares
A Prison Unsought - Sherwood Smith   *s*   4099

Argo
Children of the Earth - Catherine Wells   *s*   4578
The Earth Is All That Lasts - Catherine Wells   *s*   4579

Ariadan
A Whisper of Time - Paula E. Downing   *s*   1288

Arianus
The Hand of Chaos - Margaret Weis   *f*   4558
Into the Labyrinth - Margaret Weis   *f*   4559

Arius
Yesterday's Pawn - W.T. Quick   *s*   3550

Arizar
Path of Fire - Charles Ingrid   *s*   2256

Arizona
Smoke and Mirrors - Jane M. Lindskold   *s*   2764

Armaghast
Endymion - Dan Simmons   *s*   4030

Armistice
The Radiant Dragon - Elaine Cunningham   *f*   1047

Arrarat
Falkenberg's Legion - Jerry Pournelle   *s*   3487

Arth
A Sudden Wild Magic - Diana Wynne Jones   *f*   2351

Arthelion
Ruler of Naught - Sherwood Smith   *s*   4101

Artismo
A Miracle of Rare Design - Mike Resnick   *s*   3631

Asborgan
Brother to Shadows - Andre Norton   *s*   3298

Asenesesh
Look into the Sun - James Patrick Kelly   *s*   2429

Association
Other - Gordon R. Dickson   *s*   1241
Young Bleys - Gordon R. Dickson   *s*   1243

Astris Alexandria
The Death of Sleep - Anne McCaffrey   *s*   2966

Athas
The Brazen Gambit - Lynn Abbey   *f*   11
Cinnabar Shadows - Lynn Abbey   *f*   13
The Outcast - Simon Hawke   *f*   2095
The Seeker - Simon Hawke   *f*   2098

Athena
Ivory: A Legend of Past and Future - Mike Resnick   *s*   3629

Athera
Curse of the Mistwraith - Janny Wurts   *f*   4785
Ships of Merior - Janny Wurts   *f*   4787

Athet
Earthgrip - Harry Turtledove   *s*   4385

Atlas
Blindfold - Kevin J. Anderson   *s*   84

Aurlanis
Deepwater Dreams - Sydney J. Van Scyoc   *s*   4417

Autumn
The Lotus and the Rose - Scott Ciencin   *f*   830
The Wolves of Autumn - Scott Ciencin   *f*   835

The Autumn World
Warp Angel - Stuart Hopen   *s*   2205

Avalon
Beowulf's Children - Larry Niven   *s*   3276
The Defenders - Bill Baldwin   *s*   259
The Siege - Bill Baldwin   *s*   262

Azonda
Brotherhood of the Stars - Kirby Greene   *s*   1932

Azure
The Lone Sentinel - Jo Dereske   *s*   1206

Baker
On My Way to Paradise - Dave Wolverton   *s*   4744

Bakunin
Partisan - S. Andrew Swann   *s*   4276
Profiteer - S. Andrew Swann   *s*   4277
Revolutionary - S. Andrew Swann   *s*   4278

Bakura
The Truce at Bakura - Kathy Tyers   *s*   4407

Ballybran
Crystal Line - Anne McCaffrey   *s*   2963

Baret Two
City of Diamond - Jane Emerson   *s*   1450

Barevi
Freedom's Landing - Anne McCaffrey   *s*   2969

Barrayar
Barrayar - Lois McMaster Bujold   *s*   620
Memory - Lois McMaster Bujold   *s*   624

Beanstalk
Man-Kzin Wars V - Larry Niven   *s*   3284

Bekh-Nar
Tangled Webs - Steve Mudd   *s*   3220

Beldorph
Backblast - Lee McKeone   *s*   3050

Bellmakers World
Falcon - Emma Bull   *s*   631

Belsavis
Children of the Jedi - Barbara Hambly   *s*   2002

Beltaxiyan Minor
Imbalance - V.E. Mitchell   *s*   3124

Beluchad
Fire in the Sky - Jo Clayton   *s*   859

Benarus
Half-Light - Denise Vitola   *s*   4443

Benisan
Igniting the Reaches - David Drake   *s*   1319

Bestla
Night Sky Mine - Melissa Scott   *s*   3912

Beta
Children of the Earth - Catherine Wells   *s*   4578
The Earth Saver - Catherine Wells   *s*   4580

Beta Orbis IV
Shaper's Legacy - Sheila Finch   *s*   1556
Shaping the Dawn - Sheila Finch   *s*   1557

Beta Prometheus
The Fearful Summons - Denny Martin Flinn   *s*   1573

Betazed
Imzadi - Peter David   *s*   1117

Bia
Heirs of Empire - David Weber   *s*   4521

Bimran
Rainbow Man - M.J. Engh   *s*   1465

Bohr
Empire's End - Allan Cole   *s*   888

Bol Mutian
Shadowkill - Jo Clayton   *s*   861

Bolton's Planet
Galactic MI - Kevin D. Randle   *s*   3561

Boohte
Uncharted Territory - Connie Willis   *s*   4677

Bosque
The Glaive - Cary Osborne   *s*   3369

Botany
Freedom's Landing - Anne McCaffrey   *s*   2969

Bothawui
Shadows of the Empire - Steve Perry   *s*   3423

Brangornie
The Phoenix in Flight - Sherwood Smith   *s*   4098

Brighthome
Spacer Dreams - Larry Segriff   *s*   3923

Brishan V
Sentinels - Margaret Weis   *s*   4564

Burdania
Legacies - Alison Sinclair   *s*   4045

Burihatin-14
A Covenant of Justice - David Gerrold   *s*   1771

Burning Bright
Burning Bright - Melissa Scott   *s*   3909

BZ 459
Redliners - David Drake   *s*   1324

Cabar 4
Eggheads - Emily Devenport   *s*   1211

Cablans
Jade Darcy and the Zen Pirates - Stephen Goldin   *s*   1812

Cadwal
Ecce and Old Earth - Jack Vance   *s*   4420
Throy - Jack Vance   *s*   4423

Calamari
The Glove of Darth Vader - Paul Davids   *s*   1124

Caledonia
Diamond Mask: A Novel - Julian May   *s*   2941

Calferon
The Cloud People - Robert B. Kelly   *f*   2431

Calligar
The Rift - Peter David   *s*   1120

Callisto
The Rowan - Anne McCaffrey   *s*   2980

Candle
Warpath - Tony Daniel   *s*   1082

Cannon's Orb
Cannon's Orb - L. Warren Douglas   *s*   1279
A Plague of Change - L. Warren Douglas   *s*   1280

Cantilucca
The Sharp End - David Drake   *s*   1326

SPACESHIP

Madeline: After the Fall of Usher - Marie
    Kiraly *h* 2502
Portent - James Herbert *h* 2131
Sacred Prey - Vivian Schilling *h* 3900
Tempter - Nancy A. Collins *h* 907
*The Venetian's Wife: A Strangely Sensual Tale of a
    Renaissance Explorer, a Computer, and a
    Metamorphosis* - Nick Bantock *f* 282
Virtual Girl - Amy Thomson *s* 4358
The Werewolf's Touch - Cheri Scotch *h* 3908
The Witching Hour - Anne Rice *h* 3657

Petittville
When Darkness Falls - Sidney Williams *h* 4640

Sandy Run
Them - William W. Johnstone *h* 2339

Shreveport
Gone South - Robert R. McCammon *h* 2988

MAINE

The Bear Went over the Mountain - William
    Kotzwinkle *f* 2561
Tex and Molly in the Afterlife - Richard
    Grant *f* 1863

Assyria
The Mark of the Moderately Vicious Vampire - Lionel
    Fenn *h* 1544

Bolton
Impulse - Rick Hautala *h* 2084

Bristol Mills
Dead Voices - Rick Hautala *h* 2082

Caeser Island
Flesh - Gus Weill *h* 4531

Cape Higgins
Twilight Time - Rick Hautala *h* 2088

Castle Rock
The Dark Half - Stephen King *h* 2481
Needful Things - Stephen King *h* 2490

Chamberlain
Carrie - Stephen King *h* 2480

Dead River
Offspring - Jack Ketchum *h* 2461

Derry
Insomnia - Stephen King *h* 2488

Dyer
Moon Walker - Rick Hautala *h* 2085

Fairwater
The Frighteners - Michael Jahn *h* 2273

Hilton
Cold Whisper - Rick Hautala *h* 2080
The Mountain King - Rick Hautala *h* 2086

Jerusalem's Lot
Salem's Lot - Stephen King *h* 2493

Kashawakam Lake
Gerald's Game - Stephen King *h* 2486

Land's End
Lullaby - Diane Guest *h* 1966

Little Tall Island
Dolores Claiborne - Stephen King *h* 2483

Ludlow
The Dark Half - Stephen King *h* 2481

Matawaskie Valley
Hell House - Richard Matheson *h* 2931

Orono
Cold Whisper - Rick Hautala *h* 2080

Paradise Island
The Invisible Company - Scott Russell
    Sanders *s* 3852

Portland
Beyond the Shroud - Rick Hautala *h* 2079
Ghost Light - Rick Hautala *h* 2083
Shades of Night - Rick Hautala *h* 2087

Secret Cove
Second Child - John Saul *h* 3877

Steel Harbor
Winter Wolves - Earle Wescott *h* 4587

Stockton Springs
Shadow Dance - Jessica Palmer *h* 3378

Summerfield
Dark Silence - Rick Hautala *h* 2081

MARYLAND

Annapolis
Sacrifice - Richard Kinion *h* 2498

Baltimore
12 Monkeys - Elizabeth Hand *s* 2025
Diary of a Vampire - Gary Bowen *h* 492
The Lighthouse at the End of the World - Stephen
    Marlowe *h* 2886
Lurid Dreams - Charles L. Harness *s* 2035
Murder in the Solid State - Wil McCarthy *s* 2996
Specters - J.M. Dillard *h* 1255

Cambridge
Cross a Dark Bridge - Deborah Churchman *h* 829

College Park
Time, Like an Ever-Rolling Stream - Judith
    Moffett *s* 3141

Diamond Park
The Nightmare People - Lawrence Watt-
    Evans *h* 4499

Laurel Hills
The Select - F. Paul Wilson *h* 4693

Silver Springs
Hellcat - Amanda Kingsley *h* 2497

MASSACHUSETTS

Captain Quad - Sean Costello *h* 974
Highlander: The Element of Fire - Jason
    Henderson *f* 2121
A King Beneath the Mountain - Robert N.
    Charrette *f* 788
A Prince Among Men - Robert N. Charrette *f* 791
The Steampunk Trilogy - Paul Di Filippo *s* 1224

Arkham
Witch Hill - Marion Zimmer Bradley *h* 536

Ashbury
Mercy's Mill - Betty Levin *f* 2738

Bampton
The Rebirth of Wonder - Lawrence Watt-
    Evans *f* 4502

Boston
Arc Riders - David Drake *s* 1314
The Fermata - Nicholson Baker *s* 253
Future Boston - David Alexander Smith *s* 4074
The Gilda Stories - Jewelle Gomez *h* 1819
Goodlow's Ghosts - T.M. Wright *h* 4775
Hence - Brad Leithauser *s* 2727
The Hollow Man - Dan Simmons *s* 4033
Human to Human - Rebecca Ore *s* 3363

In the Cube - David Alexander Smith *s* 4076
The Living One - Lewis Gannett *h* 1700
Now You See It. . . - Richard Matheson *h* 2934
Of Saints and Shadows - Christopher
    Golden *h* 1811
The Return of the Breakneck Boys - Geary
    Gravel *s* 1868
The Trail of Cthulhu - August Derleth *h* 1208

Brookline
Blood of Innocents - John Arbucci *h* 168

Cape Cod
Blue Moon - Hila Feil *f* 1528

Carleton
Rough Beast - Gary Goshgarian *h* 1833

Crocker
Deathwalker - R. Patrick Gates *h* 1731
Tunnelvision - R. Patrick Gates *h* 1733

Edens Bluff
Soul Snatchers - Michael Cecilione *h* 768

Fall River
Lizzie Borden - Elizabeth Engstrom *h* 1466

Hanley
The School - Ed Kelleher *h* 2425

Horn Pond
Immortal - Jason Nickles *h* 3265

Innsmouth
The Innsmouth Heritage - Brian Stableford *h* 4145
The Shadow over Innsmouth - H.P.
    Lovecraft *h* 2809

Martha's Vineyard
A Witch Across Time - Gilbert B. Cross *f* 1031

Monument
Fade - Robert Cormier *h* 961

Morgantown
Thunder Rise - G. Wayne Miller *h* 3102

Nantucket Island
Ghosts - Noel Hynd *h* 2249

Osprey Island
White Shark - Peter Benchley *h* 363

Pioneer Colony
I Feel Like the Morning Star - Gregory
    Maguire *s* 2868

Provincetown
Starmind - Spider Robinson *s* 3716

Quincy
The Frightened Fish - Kenneth Robeson *f* 3698

Skipdon
Julian's House - Judith Hawkes *h* 2104

Village
Looker - Jorge Saralegui *h* 3859

MICHIGAN

Shaman - Robert Shea *f* 3948

Detroit
Bad Brains - Kathe Koja *h* 2540
Darkman - Randall Boyll *h* 501
Darkman #1: The Hangman - Randall Boyll *h* 502
Darkman #2: The Price of Fear - Randall
    Boyll *h* 503
Darkman #3: The Gods of Hell - Randall
    Boyll *h* 504
Darkman #4: The Face of Death - Randall
    Boyll *h* 505
Door Number Three - Patrick O'Leary *s* 3355
F.R.E.E.Lancers - Mel Odom *s* 3337

Spirit Lake
Darkling - Michael O'Rourke   *h*   3367

NEW ENGLAND

Blessings and Curses - Christopher Stasheff   *f*   4158
The Circus of the Earth and Air - Brooke Stevens   *f*   4200
Harmful Intent - Robin Cook   *s*   939
Nature's God - Robert Anton Wilson   *f*   4698
Seed of Evil - Edmund Plante   *h*   3457

Greystone Bay
In the Fog - Charles L. Grant   *h*   1852

Manor Island
Order of the Arrow - Michael T. Hinkemeyer   *h*   2147

New Polk
October - Al Sarrantonio   *h*   3870

NEW HAMPSHIRE

The Elementals - Morgan Llywelyn   *f*   2781

Cricklewood
The Midnight Horse - Sid Fleischman   *f*   1570

Draconia
Devil's Gate - Elizabeth Ergas   *h*   1473

Hamtucket
668: The Neighbor of the Beast - Lionel Fenn   *h*   1541

Hanover
Diamond Mask: A Novel - Julian May   *s*   2941
The Twelfth Child - Raymond Van Over   *h*   4415

Nashua
A Room for the Dead - Noel Hynd   *h*   2250

Seahaven
Trouble and Her Friends - Melissa Scott   *s*   3915

NEW JERSEY

Bad Brains - Kathe Koja   *h*   2540
The Eyes of Torie Webster - Roy Sorrels   *h*   4121
Goblins - Charles L. Grant   *s*   1850
Kent Montana and the Really Ugly Thing From Mars - Lionel Fenn   *s*   1542
The Mask of Loki - Roger Zelazny   *f*   4842
Mind Stealer - Lee Duigon   *h*   1347
My Teacher Glows in the Dark - Bruce Coville   *s*   994
Raven - Charles L. Grant   *h*   1854

Asbury Park
Sweet Blood - Pat Graversen   *h*   1873

Atlantic City
Naming the Flowers - Kate Wilhelm   *s*   4626
Only Begotten Daughter - James Morrow   *f*   3214
Sphynxes Wild - Esther Friesner   *f*   1677

Barnegat Light
The Hollow Man - Dan Simmons   *s*   4033

Foxriver
Something Stirs - Charles L. Grant   *h*   1856

Hunter
In a Dark Dream - Charles L. Grant   *h*   1851

Hunter Heights
The Hunted - Kathryn Ptacek   *h*   3542

Newark
Fade to Black - Nyx Smith   *s*   4095
Johnny Mnemonic - Terry Bisson   *s*   409

North Orange
Firestar - Michael Flynn   *s*   1579

Palisades
Glass Houses - Laura J. Mixon   *s*   3126

Pine Barrens
The Barrens - F. Paul Wilson   *h*   4682
Pelts - F. Paul Wilson   *h*   4690

Port Richmond
Stunts - Charles L. Grant   *h*   1857

Princeton
Blood of the Covenant - Brent Monahan   *h*   3147
The Book of Common Dread - Brent Monahan   *h*   3148

Spring Lake
Midnight Mass - F. Paul Wilson   *h*   4687

NEW MEXICO

Ill Wind - Kevin J. Anderson   *s*   90
Ingathering: The Complete People Stories of Zenna Henderson - Zenna Henderson   *s*   2123
Majestic - Whitley Strieber   *s*   4260
Nanoware Time/The Persistence of Vision - Ian Watson   *s*   4494
Whirlwind - Charles L. Grant   *f*   1859

Albuquerque
Eye Killers - A.A. Carr   *h*   739

Arroyo Hondo
Fetish - Edward Bryant   *h*   613

Atocha
Days of Atonement - Walter Jon Williams   *s*   4648

Desolada
Days of the Dead - Ashley McConnell   *h*   3004

Duerme
Witch-Light - Nancy Holder   *h*   2181

Isleta
Parliament of Blood - Scott Ciencin   *h*   831

Jornada del Muerto Desert
Mount Dragon - Douglas Preston   *h*   3520

Los Alamos
Paths to Otherwhere - James P. Hogan   *s*   2178
The Trinity Paradox - Kevin J. Anderson   *s*   97

Mannheim
The Square Deal - David Drake   *s*   1327

Mesa
The Gifted - Jack Caravela   *h*   714

Old Taos
The Stone Garden - Mary Rosenblum   *s*   3748

Santa Fe
The Nine Lives of Catseye Gomez - Simon Hawke   *f*   2094

Sante Fe
Gibbon's Decline and Fall - Sheri S. Tepper   *s*   4334
The Wizard of Santa Fe - Simon Hawke   *f*   2102

Wormwood
Tales From the Crypt: Demon Knight - Randall Boyll   *h*   507

NEW YORK

The 7th Guest - Matthew J. Costello   *h*   963
Beyond the Magic Sphere - Gail Jarrow   *f*   2296
The Eyes of Torie Webster - Roy Sorrels   *h*   4121
The Flight of Michael McBride - Midori Snyder   *f*   4111

The Illegal Rebirth of Billy the Kid - Rebecca Ore   *s*   3364
Knights of the Morningstar - Melanie Rawn   *s*   3579
Little Boy Lost - T.M. Wright   *h*   4776
Love and Sleep - John Crowley   *f*   1035
The Ugly Little Boy - Isaac Asimov   *s*   209

Adirondack Mountains
The World Next Door - Brad Ferguson   *s*   1548

Arcadia
The Moon's Wife: A Hystery - A.A. Attanasio   *f*   228

Batavia
Boundaries - T.M. Wright   *h*   4774

Braddock
The Headsman - James Neal Harvey   *h*   2075

Buffalo
Dark Visions - T. Lucien Wright   *h*   4771

Canaan
The Place - T.M. Wright   *h*   4777

Cascade
The Curse - John Tigges   *h*   4364

Catskill Mountains
Brothers of the Dragon - Robin Wayne Bailey   *f*   242
Flames of the Dragon - Robin Wayne Bailey   *f*   243

Centerville
Sister, Sister - Andrew Neiderman   *h*   3257

Cold Spring
The House That Jack Built - Graham Masterton   *h*   2925

Cold Spring Harbor
Skeletons - Al Sarrantonio   *h*   3871

Dale Falls
Deathchain - Ken Greenhall   *h*   1933

Danby
The School - T.M. Wright   *h*   4778

Dowdsville
Flames of the Dragon - Robin Wayne Bailey   *f*   243

Dydeetown
Dydeetown World - F. Paul Wilson   *s*   4684

Ellerton
Beneath Still Waters - Matthew J. Costello   *h*   964

Ellis Island
Dealer's Choice - George R.R. Martin   *s*   2894

Gardner Town
After Life - Andrew Neiderman   *h*   3252

Groveland
The Beyond - Barry Harrington   *h*   2042

Groverton
Deathscape - Michael Cecilione   *h*   766

Harper's Gate
Bereavement - Richard Lortz   *h*   2802

Hudson Valley
House Haunted - Al Sarrantonio   *h*   3868

Indigo Lake
Shapes - Steve Vance   *h*   4425

Ippisiqua
The Cup of Morning Shadows - Rosemary Edghill   *f*   1403

Ithaca
Fool on the Hill - Matt Ruff   *f*   3768
The Place - T.M. Wright   *h*   4777

Oscola
The Forbidden Zone - Whitley Strieber   h   4259

Ossining
The End of Alice - A.M. Homes   h   2197

Poughkeepsie
Unquenchable Fire - Rachel Pollack   f   3475

Ransomville
First Love: A Gothic Tale - Joyce Carol
Oates   h   3331

Rhinelander
The Keeper - Robert D. Lee   h   2705

Riker's Island
The Shift - George Foy   s   1632

Rochester
Brain Rose - Nancy Kress   s   2576
Thirst of the Vampire - T. Lucien Wright   h   4772

Sandburg
Duplicates - Andrew Neiderman   h   3253
The Immortals - Andrew Neiderman   h   3254

Sawquid
Rage - Elizabeth Ergas   h   1474

Scipio
Hocus Pocus or, What's the Hurry, Son? - Kurt
Vonnegut Jr.   s   4458

Shadowkill
Ghostlight - Marion Zimmer Bradley   f   522

Shandaken County
Among Madmen - Jim Starlin   s   4156

Stoneham
Dying Breath - Jon A. Harrald   h   2041

Stonywood
Midsummer - Matthew J. Costello   h   971

Taghkanic College
Witchlight - Marion Zimmer Bradley   f   537

Troy
My Pretty Pony - Stephen King   h   2489

Virgil
Lost Futures - Lisa Tuttle   s   4400

Watertown
Thirst of the Vampire - T. Lucien Wright   h   4772

Westchester County
The End of Alice - A.M. Homes   h   2197

White Plains
Homecoming - Matthew J. Costello   h   969

NORTH CAROLINA

Inagehi - Jack Cady   h   668
Mall, Mayhem and Magic - Holly Lisle   f   2768
The Ridge - Lisa Cantrell   h   708

Beaver Creek
Child of Shadows - John Coyne   h   1001

Charlotte
Sympathy for the Devil - Holly Lisle   f   2771

Clearview
Uwharrie - Eugene E. Pfaff Jr.   h   3432

Durham
Virus - Graham Watkins   h   4488

Fayetteville
When the Bough Breaks - Mercedes Lackey   f   2625

Merrillville
Torments - Lisa Cantrell   h   709

Missing Mile
Drawing Blood - Poppy Z. Brite   h   568
Lost Souls - Poppy Z. Brite   h   570

Ocean City
Night Music - Sheila Bristow Garner   h   1724

Outer Banks
Kaleidoscope Eyes - Graham Watkins   h   4487

Phoenix City
Boneman - Lisa Cantrell   h   707

Plattsborough
The Lodger - Fred Chappell   h   781

Raleigh
The Devil and Dan Cooley - Holly Lisle   f   2766

Steuben
Lost Boys - Orson Scott Card   f   722

Torrence
Kids - Trevor Hoyle   h   2221

NORTH DAKOTA

The Grass Dancer - Susan Power   f   3492

Bismarck
Stones of the Dalai Lama - Ken Mitchell   f   3121

Fort Moxie
Ancient Shores - Jack McDevitt   s   3014

Hardwood
The Fire Duke - Joel Rosenberg   f   3740
The Silver Stone - Joel Rosenberg   f   3745

Mannering
Mark of the Werewolf - Jeffrey Sackett   h   3822

Walhalla
Ancient Shores - Jack McDevitt   s   3014

OHIO

Vampire Breath - R.L. Stine   h   4221

Belmont City
Red Orc's Rage - Philip Jose Farmer   f   1506

Berkshire
The Orpheus Process - Daniel H. Gower   h   1839

Cincinnati
Queen City Jazz - Kathleen Ann Goonan   s   1825

Cleary
Yellow Moon - David J. Searls   h   3920

Cleveland
Bleeder - Gene Lazuta   h   2684
Forests of the Night - S. Andrew Swann   s   4275
Forget Me Not - Gene Lazuta   h   2685
The Lincoln Hunters - Wilson Tucker   s   4378
Raven - S.A. Swiniarski   h   4284
Sheltered Lives - Charles Oberndorf   s   3335

Friendly
Throat Sprockets - Tim Lucas   h   2816

Fulton
Deadly Friend - Keith Ferrario   h   1550

Harpersville
Vyrmin - Gene Lazuta   h   2686

Keynesville
Living with Aliens - John DeChancie   s   1180

Lakota
Agyar - Steven Brust   f   604

Maple Park
The Witch of Maple Park - Stephanie S.
Tolan   f   4370

Marion
Dun Lady's Jess - Doranna Durgin   f   1368

Moldowen
Button Bright - Michael Kurland   h   2584

Wentworth
The Regulators - Richard Bachman   h   240

Wright-Patterson AF Base
Pandora - Alan Rodgers   h   3723

OKLAHOMA

Buddy Holly Is Alive and Well on Ganymede - Bradley
Denton   s   1204
Chrome Circle - Mercedes Lackey   f   2606
Wheels of Fire - Mercedes Lackey   f   2624

Norman
Shade - David Darke   h   1095

Stillwater
Descent - Ron Dee   h   1184

Tulsa
Jinx High - Mercedes Lackey   h   2611
Last Rites - David Darke   h   1094
Sacred Ground - Mercedes Lackey   f   2618

OREGON

Footprints of Thunder - James F. David   s   1115
A Gift Upon the Shore - M.K. Wren   s   4767
The Harvest - Robert Charles Wilson   s   4703
Other Nature - Stephanie A. Smith   s   4105
Parable of the Sower - Octavia E. Butler   s   649
Summerland - L. Dean James   f   2282
Thor - Wayne Smith   h   4106

Arcadia
The Thread That Binds the Bones - Nina Kiriki
Hoffman   f   2169

Cascade Mountains
The Silent Strength of Stones - Nina Kiriki
Hoffman   f   2168

Cemetery Ridge
Prank Night - David Robbins   h   3678

Columbia River Valley
The Drylands - Mary Rosenblum   s   3747

Cronon's Crater
The Ancient One - T.A. Barron   f   308

Deuce Creek
Roadkill - Richard Sanford   h   3854

Dory Cove
The Devil's Churn - Kristine Kathryn
Rusch   h   3773

Everville
Everville - Clive Barker   h   284

Gold Beach
No Limits - Nigel Findley   s   1561

Hot Lake
Wolf Flow - K.W. Jeter   h   2325

Mayfair
The Last Vampire - Christopher Pike   h   3447

Oldenburg
Golden Eyes - John Gideon   h   1783

Point Vestal
The Off Season - Jack Cady   f   669

Portland
The Abductors: Conspiracy - Jonathan
Frakes *s* 1633
Blood Feud - Sam Siciliano *h* 4005
The Deus Machine - Pierre Ouellette *h* 3373
Kindred - John Gideon *h* 1785
Sins of the Blood - Kristine Kathryn Rusch *h* 3785
The Thread That Binds the Bones - Nina Kiriki
Hoffman *f* 2169

Rookers Cove
The Undine - Michael O'Rourke *h* 3368

Sauterelle Lake
The Silent Strength of Stones - Nina Kiriki
Hoffman *f* 2168

Seavy Village
Facade - Kristine Kathryn Rusch *h* 3774

Shadow Ridge
Shadows - Kimberly Rangel *h* 3565

Shoalwater Bay
Nadya: The Wolf Chronicles - Pat Murphy *f* 3228

OZARKS

Earthsong - Suzette Haden Elgin *s* 1419

PACIFIC NORTHWEST

Highlander: Scotland the Brave - Jennifer
Roberson *f* 3686
*The Mysterious Doom and Other Ghostly Tales of the
Pacific Northwest* - Jessica Amanda
Salmonson *h* 3833
Sarah Canary - Karen Joy Fowler *f* 1628

PENNSYLVANIA

Dragon Moon - Chris Claremont *f* 839
Fair Peril - Nancy Springer *f* 4132
Kids - Trevor Hoyle *h* 2221
Larque on the Wing - Nancy Springer *f* 4134

Abaddon Township
Blameless in Abaddon - James Morrow *f* 3209

Allenville
Destiny's Carnival - Warren Murphy *h* 3232

Bremerton
The Bad Thing - Michael O'Rourke *h* 3366

Burnwell
Neighbors - Maureen S. Pusti *h* 3547

Dreamthorpe
Dreamthorp - Chet Williamson *h* 4654

Endicott
Blood of Mugwump - Doug Rice *h* 3658

Gettysburg
Lurid Dreams - Charles L. Harness *s* 2035

Gramentown
Max Lakeman and the Beautiful Stranger - Jon
Cohen *f* 883

Gwynwood
The Wall Around Eden - Joan Slonczewski *s* 4063

Hoadley
Apocalypse - Nancy Springer *f* 4130

Iselin
Second Chance - Chet Williamson *h* 4658

Jenkins
Metal Angel - Nancy Springer *f* 4135

Kirkland
Reign - Chet Williamson *h* 4657

Mill Creek
Owl Light - Michael Paine *h* 3375

Monville
Animals - John Skipp *h* 4054

Moore
Superstitious - R.L. Stine *h* 4220

Paradise
The Bridge - John Skipp *h* 4055

Philadelphia
12 Monkeys - Elizabeth Hand *s* 2025
Blood Work - Fay Zachary *h* 4823
Murder in the Solid State - Wil McCarthy *s* 2996
The Pure Cold Light - Gregory Frost *s* 1681
Red, Red Robin - Stephen Gallagher *h* 1699
A Room for the Dead - Noel Hynd *h* 2250
Striper Assassin - Nyx Smith *h* 4096
Two Crowns for America - Katherine Kurtz *f* 2594
Virtual Death - Shale Aaron *s* 4

Pittsburgh
In between Dragons - Michael Kandel *f* 2397
Making Love - Melanie Tem *h* 4327
Realtime Interrupt - James P. Hogan *s* 2179

Potamos
Humpty Dumpty: An Oval - Damon Knight *s* 2533

Spook Hollow
Spook Night - David Robbins *h* 3680

Thomas Valley
Nightshade - Stanley R. Moore *h* 3176

Wayne
Shoebag Returns - Mary James *f* 2286

RHODE ISLAND

Providence
A Knight Among Knaves - Robert N.
Charrette *f* 789
Twisted Images - Don D'Ammassa *h* 1081

ROCKY MOUNTAINS

Piketon
Ursus - David Dvorkin *s* 1371

SOUTH

The Gilda Stories - Jewelle Gomez *h* 1819
The Haunting - Ruby Jean Jensen *h* 2311
The Living Evil - Ruby Jean Jensen *h* 2312
Night Thunder - Ruby Jean Jensen *h* 2313
Tatham Mound - Piers Anthony *f* 157

Cold Mountain Penitentiary
The Green Mile - Stephen King *h* 2487

Danville
Flesh and Blood - D.A. Fowler *h* 1625

Exuam College
Coven - Edward Lee *h* 2696

Green Hill
Children of the Blood - Alan Rodgers *h* 3719

Waynesville
The Chosen - Edward Lee *h* 2695

SOUTH CAROLINA

Reprisal - F. Paul Wilson *h* 4692

Bear Claw Islands
Soulcatchers - Jan Lara *h* 2654

SOUTH DAKOTA

Wolf and Iron - Gordon R. Dickson *s* 1242

Sharon Valley
The Devil's End - D.A. Fowler *h* 1624

SOUTHWEST

Blackburn - Bradley Denton *h* 1203
The Changeling Garden - Winifred Elze *h* 1449
Forest of the Night - S.P. Somtow *f* 4114
Ghost Dance - Kathryn Ptacek *h* 3541
Ill Wind - Kevin J. Anderson *s* 90
Indiana Jones and the Sky Pirates - Martin
Caidin *f* 673
Indiana Jones and the Unicorn's Legacy - Rob
MacGregor *f* 2858
*Ingathering: The Complete People Stories of Zenna
Henderson* - Zenna Henderson *s* 2123
Mad Amos - Alan Dean Foster *f* 1612
Mojo and the Pickle Jar - Douglas Bell *f* 357
Night Cruise - Billie Sue Mosiman *h* 3218
People of the Mesa - Ardath Mayhar *f* 2947
Riverrun - S.P. Somtow *f* 4117
Strum Again? - Elizabeth Ann Scarborough *f* 3896
Walking Wolf - Nancy A. Collins *h* 908
Warsprite - Jefferson P. Swycaffer *s* 4285
The Wood Wife - Terri Windling *f* 4709

Frescuro
Coyote - Peter Gadol *f* 1691

Mordock Caves
Midnight's Lair - Richard Laymon *h* 2680

TENNESSEE

The Black Mariah - Jay R. Bonansinga *h* 468
Old Nathan - David Drake *f* 1323
Spirit Crossings - Claudia Peck *f* 3405

Cedar Bluff
Father's Little Helper - Ronald Kelly *h* 2433

Clark's Corner
Deadly Breed - T.J. Kirby *h* 2505

Corey County
My Soul to Keep - Judith Hawkes *h* 2105

Franklin
The Possession - Ronald Kelly *h* 2436

Graceland
Elvis Rising: Stories on the King - Kay
Sloan *f* 4061
Elvissey - Jack Womack *s* 4746
Rock of Ages - Walter Jon Williams *s* 4651

Green Hollow
Blood Kin - Ronald Kelly *h* 2432

Knoxville
Not Broken, Not Belonging - Randy Fox *h* 1630

Memphis
Howl-O-Ween - Gary L. Holleman *h* 2189
Rockabilly Hell - William W. Johnstone *h* 2337
Rockabilly Limbo - William W. Johnstone *h* 2338

Mountainville
Fire - Alan Rodgers *h* 3720

Old Hickory
Moon of the Werewolf - Ronald Kelly *h* 2434

Pine Junction
Pandora - Alan Rodgers *h* 3723

Potar Ridge
Jackals - Charles L. Grant   h   1853

Rockville
The Crawling Dark - Pauline Dunn   h   1366

Sublimity
Fiends - John Farris   h   1516

Tucker's Mill
Something Out There - Ronald Kelly   h   2437

TEXAS

Destination: Showdown - Jake Davis   s   1131
Double Jeopardy - Aaron Allston   s   72
The Earth Remembers - Susan Torian Olan   s   3354
The Flight of Michael McBride - Midori
   Snyder   f   4111
Future Eden - J.M. Morgan   s   3183
The Last Rangers - Jake Davis   s   1132
The Spirit Stalker - Nina Romberg   h   3735
Wildside - Steven Gould   s   1837

Amarillo
Dead Heat - Del Stone Jr.   h   4239

Austin
Familiar Spirit - Lisa Tuttle   h   4399
Glimpses - Lewis Shiner   h   3987
Lunatics - Bradley Denton   f   1205
Mathemagics - Margaret Ball   f   266
Pillow Friend - Lisa Tuttle   h   4402
Resume with Monsters - William Browning
   Spencer   h   4122
The Shadow Gate - Margaret Ball   f   267
The Sherwood Game - Esther Friesner   s   1676
Zod Wallop - William Browning Spencer   h   4123

Biosphere Seven
Beyond Eden - J.M. Morgan   s   3181

Bone
Second Chance - Chet Williamson   h   4658

Britt
Hobkin - Peni R. Griffin   f   1951

Carruthers
Less than Human - Gary L. Raisor   h   3558

Claypool
Desert Eden - J.M. Morgan   s   3182

Clear Creek
The Undead - Roxanne Longstreet   h   2796

Coomey
Happy Policeman - Patricia Anthony   s   130

Core City
Core - Paul Preuss   s   3522

Crowder Flats
Less than Human - Gary L. Raisor   h   3558

Dallas
Burning Water - Mercedes Lackey   h   2601
Cold Kiss - Roxanne Longstreet   h   2794
Dusk - Ron Dee   h   1185
Elvendude - Mark Shepherd   f   3973
Fiend - C. Dean Andersson   h   114
Lethal Interface - Mel Odom   s   3338
The Nexus - Mike McQuay   f   3075
Vampire$ - John Steakley   h   4177

Fairvale
Psycho II - Robert Bloch   h   441
Psycho House - Robert Bloch   h   442

Fort Worth
Beachhead - Jack Williamson   s   4667
Rock of Ages - Walter Jon Williams   s   4651

Gusher
Shadow Walkers - Nina Romberg   h   3734

Houston
Act of Love - Joe R. Lansdale   h   2640

La Borde
Cold in July - Joe R. Lansdale   h   2644
Mucho Mojo - Joe R. Lansdale   h   2647

Lansom
Night Blood - Eric Flanders   h   1567

Marfa
Spyder - Norman Partridge   h   3391

Marvel Creek
Savage Season - Joe R. Lansdale   h   2649

Mud Creek
Dead in the West - Joe R. Lansdale   h   2645

San Antonio
Warsprite - Jefferson P. Swycaffer   s   4285

Sulphur Springs
Pitfall - Ronald Kelly   h   2435

Tombley's Walk
Tombley's Walk - Crosland Brown   h   590

UTAH

Dracula Unbound - Brian W. Aldiss   h   43
The Folk of the Fringe - Orson Scott Card   s   720
Warrior - Donald E. McQuinn   s   3077

Beaver
The Immortals - Tracy Hickman   s   2141

Canyonlands
Children of the Earth - Catherine Wells   s   4578
The Earth Is All That Lasts - Catherine
   Wells   s   4579

Milford
The Immortals - Tracy Hickman   s   2141

Newhouse Center
The Immortals - Tracy Hickman   s   2141

Salt Lake City
After Sundown - Randall Boyll   h   499
Gibbon's Decline and Fall - Sheri S.
   Tepper   s   4334
Krokodil Tears - Jack Yeovil   f   4801

Spike Mountain
After Sundown - Randall Boyll   h   499

VERMONT

The Secret History - Donna Tartt   h   4306
Travel Far, Pay No Fare - Anne Lindbergh   f   2757
The Unseen - Joseph Citro   h   838

Brattleboro
Dry Skull Dreams - Michael Green   h   1879

Fenwick
The Hunger of the Beast - John Driver   h   1336

Friar's Island
Dark Twilight - Joseph Citro   h   836

Harmony
Harmony - Marjorie Bradley Kellogg   s   2428

Hobston
Deus X - Joseph Citro   h   837

New Thetford
Whisper - Raymond Van Over   h   4416

Pinebridge
Good Night, Sweet Angel - Clare McNally   h   3073

VIRGINIA

Gaia's Toys - Rebecca Ore   s   3362
The Illegal Rebirth of Billy the Kid - Rebecca
   Ore   s   3364
An Impossible Summer - B.W. Clough   f   878
Union Fires - John Barnes   f   299

Beacon Cove
Sineater - Elizabeth Massie   h   2917

Blue Falls
The Fagin - Pat Graversen   h   1870

Bracken County
Slow Funeral - Rebecca Ore   f   3365

Charlottesville
Belladonna - Michael Stewart   h   4206

City Point
Rally Cry! - William R. Forstchen   s   1590

Clear Creek
The Burning Man - Michael Hammond   h   2023

The Complex
Haven - David Peters   f   3427

Crowley Creek
Return to the House of Usher - Robert Poe   h   3461

Hillenberg
Cold White Fury - Beth Amos   h   81

Homeplace
Bloody Waters - B.L. Winters   h   4718

Kendrick
The Healing of Crossroads - Nick
   O'Donohoe   f   3340
The Magic and the Healing - Nick
   O'Donohoe   f   3341
Under the Healing Sign - Nick O'Donohoe   f   3343

Kobold
Slow Funeral - Rebecca Ore   f   3365

Lewisburg
Header - Edward Lee   h   2699

Luntville
Goon - Edward Lee   h   2698

Pontefract
Goat Dance - Douglas Clegg   h   870

Reeves County
Cat's Eye - William W. Johnstone   h   2332

Richmond
Wilderness - Dennis Danvers   h   1090

WASHINGTON

Cloven Hooves - Megan Lindholm   f   2759
The March Hare Network - Jack L. Chalker   s   775
The Midnight Club - Christopher Pike   h   3448
Speak to the Rain - Helen K. Passey   h   3392

Avalon
Deathwalker - Patrick Whalen   h   4596

Belltower
A Bridge of Years - Robert Charles Wilson   s   4700

Greely's Cove
Greely's Cove - John Gideon   h   1784

Longview
Dark Time - Maxine O'Callaghan   h   3336

Mt. St. Helens
Scorpion Shards - Neal Shusterman   s   4000

Story Type Index

This index is a listing of the story types within each of the three genres. Beneath each genre heading the story types are arranged in alphabetical order. An alphabetical listing of the featured book titles that fall under each story type is provided, along with author names and entry numbers. For definitions of the story types, see the Key to Story Types following the Introduction.

1223

Alternate History

Alternate Universe

Alternate World

Anthology

Religious

Romance

HORROR

Alternate World

Ancient Evil Unleashed

Anthology

Nature in Revolt

Occult

Possession

Psychological Suspense

Werewolf Story

Wild Talents

Alternate History

Alternate Intelligence

Alternate Universe

Story Type Index

Character Name Index

This index alphabetically lists the major characters in each featured title. Each character name is followed by a description of the character. Citations also provide titles of the books featuring the character, listed alphabetically if there is more than one title; author names; and entry numbers.

12 (Teenager)
Random Acts of Senseless Violence - Jack Womack *f* 4748

A

a-Lagan, Meredydd (Orphan; Student)
The Meri - Maya Kaathryn Bohnhoff *f* 459

Aargh (Animal)
The Dragon Knight - Gordon R. Dickson *f* 1235

Aaron (Thief)
The Fire's Stone - Tanya Huff *f* 2228

Aaron, Lily (Restaurateur)
After Silence - Jonathan Carroll *h* 742

Aaron, Lincoln (Teenager)
After Silence - Jonathan Carroll *h* 742

Aarons, Keith "Pan" (Terrorist)
Second Chance - Chet Williamson *h* 4658

Aarundel (Mythical Creature; Warrior)
Once a Hero - Michael A. Stackpole *f* 4151

ab Meredydd, Rhys "Sun Eyes" (Minstrel)
Madoc's Hundred - Pat Winter *f* 4717

ab Owen, Madoc "Weather Eyes" (Leader)
Madoc's Hundred - Pat Winter *f* 4717

Abalone (Computer Expert; Criminal)
Brother to Dragons, Companion to Owls - Jane M. Lindskold *f* 2762

Abba-Bashti (Trader)
The Amazon Chronicles - Jane E.M. Robinson *f* 3703

Abbot, Thomas (Police Officer)
The Reckoning - Ruby Jean Jensen *h* 2314

Abbott, Vera (Restaurateur)
The Chosen - Edward Lee *h* 2695

Abdullah (Businessman)
Castle in the Air - Diana Wynne Jones *f* 2346

Abe (Alien; Telepath)
The Clouds of Magellan - David F. Nighbert *s* 3266

Abernathy (Animal; Adventurer)
Witches' Brew - Terry Brooks *f* 587

Abernathy, Tom (Rancher)
Thunder Road - Chris Curry *h* 1051

Abivard (Nobleman; Warrior)
The Stolen Throne - Harry Turtledove *f* 4393

Abronowitz, Wendy (Astronaut)
The Fugitive Stars - Daniel Ransom *s* 3571

Aburto, Manuel "Manny" (Guide; Time Traveller)
Tyrannosaurus Rex - J.F. Rivkin *s* 3674

Acari, Stefan (Judge)
The Beacon - Valerie J. Freireich *s* 1646

Achilles (Warrior)
Yellowstone Run - David Robbins *s* 3682

Acila (Noblewoman; Mythical Creature)
Changing Fate - Elisabeth Waters *f* 4485

Ackerman, Larry (Professor)
The Voice in the Basement - T. Chris Martindale *h* 2906

Ackley, Robert (Librarian)
The Lodger - Fred Chappell *h* 781

Acton, Joe (Worker)
Moondog - Henry Garfield *h* 1716

Adair, Devon (Leader; Settler)
Earth 2 - Melissa Crandall *s* 1010

Adair, Hugh (Lawyer; Spouse)
Breeder - Douglas Clegg *h* 867

Adair, Kirsten (Police Officer)
The Bohr Maker - Linda Nagata *s* 3238

Adair, Rachel (Lawyer)
Breeder - Douglas Clegg *h* 867

Adam (Foundling)
Child of Shadows - John Coyne *h* 1001

Adam (Demon)
Good Omens: The Nice and Accurate Prophecies of Agnes Nutter, Witch - Neil Gaiman *f* 1693

Adams, Frankly (Artist; Fugitive)
Virtual Death - Shale Aaron *s* 4

Adams, Joseph (Writer)
The Penultimate Truth - Philip K. Dick *s* 1228

Adams, Luther (Doctor)
Wilderness - Dennis Danvers *h* 1090

Adams, Nicola Chelsea "Niki" (Teenager)
From a Whisper to a Scream - Samuel M. Key *h* 2462

Adams, Rafe (Scientist)
Heritage of Flight - Susan Shwartz *s* 4002

Adamsson, Wylie (Child)
Night Calls - Katharine Eliska Kimbriel *h* 2476

Adana "the Snake Mother" (Mythical Creature)
The Face in the Abyss - Abraham Merritt *f* 3091

Adcock, Patrice "Pat" (Scientist; Spacewoman)
The Other End of Time - Frederik Pohl *s* 3466

Adda (Genetically Altered Being; Patient)
Flux - Stephen Baxter *s* 331

Addams, Fester (Fiance(e))
Addams Family Values - Todd Strasser *f* 4246

Addams, Helen "Kyria" (Sorceress)
Dragon Death - Gael Baudino *f* 324

Addams, Helen "Kyria" (Scholar; Sorceress)
Duel of Dragons - Gael Baudino *f* 325

Addams, Morticia (Parent; Spouse)
Addams Family Values - Todd Strasser *f* 4246

Adderstone, Susannah (Young Woman)
The Vanishment - Jonathan Aycliffe *h* 238

Aderyn (Magician; Wanderer)
A Time of Exile - Katharine Kerr *f* 2452

Aditi (Deity; Widow(er))
Blood of the Goddess - Kara Dalkey *f* 1066

Adler, Mark (Government Official)
Ursus - David Dvorkin *s* 1371

Adler, Stephen (Vampire)
Less than Human - Gary L. Raisor *h* 3558

Adolphus, Matthew (Detective—Police)
Afterimage - Kristine Kathryn Rusch *f* 3769

Adric (Royalty; Runaway)
The White Mists of Power - Kristine Kathryn Rusch *f* 3787

Adwon, Jay (Lawman)
Dusk - Ron Dee *h* 1185

Aeid (Royalty; Adventurer)
O Greenest Branch! - Gael Baudino *f* 328

ae'Magi, Geoffrey (Magician)
Masques - Patricia Briggs *f* 560

Aenea (Child; Religious)
Endymion - Dan Simmons *s* 4030

Aengus (Artist)
The Boy From the Burren - Sheila Gilluly *f* 1798

Aerich of House Lyorn (Gentleman)
The Phoenix Guards - Steven Brust *f* 611

Aeriel (Sorceress)
The Pearl of the Soul of the World - Meredith Ann Pierce f 3439

Aeslu "Moon's Stead" of Vmatta (Indian)
Fire and Ice - Edward Myers f 3235

Aeslu "Moon's Stead" of Vmatta (Indian; Linguist)
The Mountain Made of Light - Edward Myers f 3236
The Summit - Edward Myers f 3237

Aesop (Writer; Traveller)
The Fabulist - John Vornholt f 4459

Afsan (Alien; Apprentice)
Far-Seer - Robert J. Sawyer s 3884

Afsan (Alien; Scholar)
Fossil Hunter - Robert J. Sawyer s 3885

Agamon, Orfei (Artist)
A Second Infinity - Michael D. Weaver s 4513

Agenor, Roland (Vampire)
The Golden - Lucius Shepard h 3971

Agenos, Mordion "the Servant" (Martial Arts Expert; Criminal)
Hexwood - Diana Wynne Jones s 2349

Agesilaus, "Agis" (Military Personnel)
Spartan Run - David Robbins s 3679

Agis (Political Figure; Psychic)
The Verdant Passage - Troy Denning f 1201

Agonostis (Demon; Administrator)
Sympathy for the Devil - Holly Lisle f 2771

Agranovsky, Reuven (Aged Person; Actor)
Further Adventures - Jon Stephen Fink f 1563

Agricola, Caesar Germanicus (Ruler)
Cry Republic - Kirk Mitchell s 3122

Aguilana, Haros (Vampire; Spirit)
King of the Grey - Richard A. Knaak f 2523

Aguilar, Carlos (Teenager)
Days of the Dead - Ashley McConnell h 3004

Agyar (Political Figure)
The Vampire Memoirs - Mara McCuniff h 3009

Agyar, Janos "Jack" (Vampire)
Agyar - Steven Brust f 604

Ahlwen, Anders (Psychic)
The Snows of Jaspre - Mary Caraker s 713

Ahrens, Bleys (Genius; Activist)
Other - Gordon R. Dickson s 1241

Ahrens, Bleys (Student; Activist)
Young Bleys - Gordon R. Dickson s 1243

Ahrens, Dahno (Activist)
Young Bleys - Gordon R. Dickson s 1243

Aiah (Civil Servant)
Metropolitan - Walter Jon Williams s 4650

Aias (Scientist)
Celestial Matters - Richard Garfinkle s 1717

Aidan (Royalty; Mythical Creature)
Alamut - Judith Tarr f 4298

Aidan (Royalty)
The Dagger and the Cross: A Novel of the Crusades - Judith Tarr f 4301

Aidan (Heir)
Flight of the Raven - Jennifer Roberson f 3685

Aidan (Military Personnel)
Way of the Clans - Robert Thurston s 4362

Aiesa, Gina (Artist)
Synners - Pat Cadigan s 660

Aigar (Wizard; Professor)
Lost in Translation - Margaret Ball f 265

Aiken, Robert (Pharmacist)
The Mysterium - Eric McCormack h 3008

Aiko (Warrior; Noblewoman)
The Dragonstone - Dennis L. McKiernan f 3054

Ainvar (Religious)
Druids - Morgan Llywelyn f 2780

Aisling, Algernon (Professor; Adventurer)
Voyage of the Basset - James C. Christensen f 827

Aisling, Cassandra (Child; Adventurer)
Voyage of the Basset - James C. Christensen f 827

Aisling, Miranda (Teenager; Adventurer)
Voyage of the Basset - James C. Christensen f 827

AIVAS (Artificial Intelligence)
All the Weyrs of Pern - Anne McCaffrey s 2958

Aiysha (Leader)
Blood Feuds - S.M. Stirling s 4222

Ajani, Korinna "Kori" Kassemi (Waiter/Waitress; Parent)
The March Hare Network - Jack L. Chalker s 775

Akamu (Clone; Fugitive)
The Bones of Time - Kathleen Ann Goonan s 1824

Akasha (Vampire)
The Queen of the Damned - Anne Rice h 3653

Akiba (Religious)
Freeze Frames - Katharine Kerr s 2447

Akimura, Julian (Psychologist; Psychic)
Mutant Legacy - Karen Haber s 1984

Akimura, Julian (Twin; Psychic)
Mutant Star - Karen Haber s 1985

Akimura, Rick (Psychic; Mutant)
Mutant Legacy - Karen Haber s 1984

Akktri (Alien)
In the Cube - David Alexander Smith s 4076

Akma (Rebel; Abuse Victim)
Earthborn - Orson Scott Card s 718

al-Badr, Arwa Bint Muhammad (Royalty)
Guts and Glory - G. Harry Stine s 4213

al-Hakim, Sharif (Guide)
The Calling - Kathryn Meyer Griffith h 1952

al-Iskandaria, Ibn Sufa (Companion; Adventurer)
Quest: In Search of the Dragontooth - Michael Green f 1881

al Jorddyn, Kerridwen (Noblewoman; Martial Arts Expert)
Kingmaker's Sword - Ann Marston f 2887

al-Kharif, Yasin (Engineer; Criminal)
Bright Messengers - Gentry Lee s 2701

al-Qurtubi (Terrorist)
Name of the Beast - Daniel Easterman h 1379

Al-Ra,ma, Khaddam (Sorcerer; Teacher)
The Riddled Man - Mark E. Rogers f 3726

al-Schouki, Esoch (Military Personnel)
Foragers - Charles Oberndorf s 3334

Ala-eh-din Beyh (Wizard; Warrior)
Tower of Fear - Glen Cook f 932

Aladdin (Adventurer)
Aladdin: Master of the Lamp - Mike Resnick f 3618

Aladdin (Thief; Adventurer)
A Bad Day for Ali Baba - Craig Shaw Gardner f 1706

Alain (Royalty)
M'Lady Witch - Christopher Stasheff f 4161

Alain, Jahnel (Leader)
Fallway - Paula E. Downing s 1286

Alaiya (Military Personnel)
The Return of the Breakneck Boys - Geary Gravel s 1868

Alamar (Wizard)
Voyage of the Fox Rider - Dennis L. McKiernan f 3057

Alara (Shaman; Mythical Creature)
The Elvenbane - Andre Norton f 3303

Alaric (Minstrel; Warlock)
In the Red Lord's Reach - Phyllis Eisenstein f 1417

Alastair (Heir; Twin)
The Heirs of Hammerfell - Marion Zimmer Bradley s 524

Albain, Elandra (Noblewoman; Bastard Daughter)
Reign of Shadows - Deborah Chester f 819

Albee, David (Scientist)
Lords of Creation - Tim Sullivan s 4267

Albert Victor Christian Edward (Royalty)
The Women of Whitechapel and Jack the Ripper - Paul West h 4590

Albin (Mythical Creature)
The Wild Wood - Charles de Lint f 1162

Albin, Doug (Teacher)
The Mailman - Bentley Little h 2775

Albin, Tritia (Housewife)
The Mailman - Bentley Little h 2775

Albright, Steven (Writer)
Bloodletter - Warren Newton Beath h 350

Alburton, Denso (Writer)
Hidden Echoes - Mike Jefferies f 2301

Alderan, Kermiak (Royalty; Telepath)
Rediscovery: A Novel of Darkover - Marion Zimmer Bradley s 527

Alderberry, Jane (Student; Thief)
The Iron Dragon's Daughter - Michael Swanwick f 4282

Alderini, Delbert (Writer)
Quest for Apollo - Michael Lahey f 2632

Alderson, Charlotte (Widow(er))
The Colors of Hell - Michael Paine h 3374

Aldived (Leader)
The Heldan - Deborah Talmadge-Bickmore f 4293

Alec of Kerry (Woodsman; Spy)
Luck in the Shadows - Lynn Flewelling f 1572

Alegretta (Doctor; Immortal)
Outnumbering the Dead - Frederik Pohl s 3467

Alemi (Fisherman)
The Dolphins of Pern - Anne McCaffrey s 2967

Aleph (Artificial Intelligence)
Halo - Tom Maddox s 2864

Aleron (Vampire)
Sex and the Single Vampire - Nancy Kilpatrick h 2472

Aleshire, Puck (Mythical Creature)
The Iron Dragon's Daughter - Michael Swanwick f 4282

Aletto (Heir—Dispossessed)
One Land, One Duke - Ru Emerson f 1452

Aletto (Heir—Dispossessed; Runaway)
The Two in Hiding - Ru Emerson f 1454

Alexander (Royalty)
The Floating Castle - Craig Mills f 3118

Alexander (Royalty; Teenager)
The Prince and the Pilgrim - Mary Stewart f 4205

Alexander, Ardeth (Student)
The Night Inside - Nancy Baker h 252

Alexander, Sam (Radio; Student—High School)
SETI - Frederick Fichman *s* 1553

Alexander the Great (Historical Figure)
Dark Prince - David Gemmell *f* 1754

Alexander the Great (Historical Figure; Warrior)
Lord of the Two Lands - Judith Tarr *f* 4303

Alexia (Royalty; Magician)
Dark Mirror, Dark Dreams - Sharon Green *f* 1889
Silver Princess, Golden Knight - Sharon
  Green *f* 1891
Wind Whispers, Shadow Shouts - Sharon
  Green *f* 1892

Alfonso (Rancher)
Under the Shadow - Jane Toombs *h* 4372

Alfred (Adventurer; Wizard)
Fire Sea - Margaret Weis *f* 4557
Into the Labyrinth - Margaret Weis *f* 4559
Serpent Mage - Margaret Weis *f* 4565
The Seventh Gate - Margaret Weis *f* 4566

Alhammittson, Alhammitt "Mitt" (Warrior; Leader)
The Crown of Dalemark - Diana Wynne
  Jones *f* 2347

Ali Baba (Artisan; Adventurer)
A Bad Day for Ali Baba - Craig Shaw
  Gardner *f* 1706

Alias (Hero; Genetically Altered Being)
Masquerades - Kate Novak *f* 3318

Alice (Child)
Fantastic Alice - Margaret Weis *f* 4556

Alice (Revolutionary; Adventurer)
Innerverse - John DeChancie *s* 1178

Alice (Teenager; Noblewoman)
The Prince and the Pilgrim - Mary Stewart *f* 4205

Alice, Ti (Occultist)
Tempter - Nancy A. Collins *h* 907

Alinor (Mythical Creature; Detective—Amateur)
Wheels of Fire - Mercedes Lackey *f* 2624

Alis (Actress; Historian)
Remake - Connie Willis *s* 4676

Alison/Nicholas (Actress)
The Need - Andrew Neiderman *h* 3255

Allaird, Clarence Engels "Clancy" (Spaceship
  Captain; Parent)
Arrow From Earth - F.M. Busby *s* 639

Allaird, Margaret "Marnie" (Stowaway; Teenager)
Arrow From Earth - F.M. Busby *s* 639

Allalie, Fentrice (Aged Person; Magician)
Walking the Labyrinth - Lisa Goldstein *f* 1818

Allard (Mythical Creature; Miner)
Suisan - Phyllis Carol Agins *f* 32

Alldera (Leader)
The Furies - Suzy McKee Charnas *s* 783

Allen (Farmer; Lawman)
The Persistence of Memory - Karen Ripley *s* 3669

Allen, Harrison (Businessman; Unemployed)
Dark Twilight - Joseph Citro *h* 836

Allen, Sandy (Television)
Ancient Images - Ramsey Campbell *h* 693

Allen, Zadok (Streetperson)
The Shadow over Innsmouth - H.P.
  Lovecraft *h* 2809

Allerum (Mythical Creature)
Shadow's Realm - Mickey Zucker Reichert *f* 3610

Alliar (Spirit)
A Strange and Ancient Name - Josepha
  Sherman *f* 3981

Allic (Royalty; Deity)
The Crystal Sorcerers - William R.
  Forstchen *f* 1588

Allie (Student—College)
Lost in Translation - Margaret Ball *f* 265

Allison, Harold (Lawyer)
The Man Who Turned into Himself - David
  Ambrose *h* 74

Allogiamento, Maria Theresa (Vampire)
The Vampire Journals - Traci Briery *h* 557

Almond, Donna (Teacher)
Dead in the Water - Nancy Holder *h* 2180

Alnosha "Nosh" (Foundling; Student)
The Hands of Lyr - Andre Norton *f* 3308

Alon (Mercenary; Adventurer)
The Nomad Queen - James Gordon White *f* 4607

Alpha, Pamayers (Clone; Explorer)
The Weigher - Eric Vinicoff *s* 4442

Alsnor, Lotta (Counselor; Psychic)
The White Regiment - John Dalmas *s* 1073

Alston, Arthur (Doctor)
The Select - F. Paul Wilson *h* 4693

Alta (Psychic)
White Horse, Dark Dragon - Robert C.
  Fleet *f* 1569

Althea (Gentlewoman)
The Forge of Virtue - Lynn Abbey *f* 14

Althor (Military Personnel; Psychic)
Catch the Lightning - Catherine Asaro *s* 181

al'Thor, Rand (Farmer)
The Eye of the World - Robert Jordan *f* 2381

al'Thor, Rand "Dragon Reborn" (Leader)
A Crown of Swords - Robert Jordan *f* 2379

al'Thor, Rand "Dragon Reborn" (Leader;
  Revolutionary)
The Dragon Reborn - Robert Jordan *f* 2380
The Fires of Heaven - Robert Jordan *f* 2382

al'Thor, Rand "Dragon Reborn" (Leader)
Lord of Chaos - Robert Jordan *f* 2383

al'Thor, Rand "Dragon Reborn" (Leader; Hero)
The Shadow Rising - Robert Jordan *f* 2384

Althorpe, Cory (Doctor; Psychic)
World Without End - Molly Cochran *f* 880

Altman, Gibson (Government Official;
  Businessman)
Pallas - L. Neil Smith *s* 4093

Alton, Lew (Diplomat; Psychic)
Exile's Song - Marion Zimmer Bradley *s* 520

Alton, Margaret (Musician; Psychic)
Exile's Song - Marion Zimmer Bradley *s* 520

Altunin, Roberta (Noblewoman)
Rock of Ages - Walter Jon Williams *s* 4651

Alucard, Sevil (Vampire)
Elvira: Transylvania 90210 - Elvira *h* 1445

Alvarez, Dan (Musician)
Bone Music - Alan Rodgers *h* 3718

Alvarez, Edward (FBI Agent)
Doomsday Exam - Nick Pollotta *f* 3477

al'Vere, Egwene (Religious; Witch)
A Crown of Swords - Robert Jordan *f* 2379
The Dragon Reborn - Robert Jordan *f* 2380

Alvin (Explorer; Human)
Beyond the Fall of Night - Arthur C. Clarke *s* 847

Alya, Princess (Royalty)
Strings - Dave Duncan *s* 1361

Alyna (Wizard)
Runes of Autumn - Larry Elmore *f* 1436

Alys (Criminal; Teenager)
Dragon's Bait - Vivian Vande Velde *f* 4427

Amadeus (Animal)
Witches - Kathryn Meyer Griffith *h* 1955

Amalayna (Noblewoman; Avenger)
Chains of Darkness, Chains of Light - Michelle
  Sagara *f* 3823

Amalia, Lady (Noblewoman)
The Interior Life - Katherine Blake *f* 417

Amatus (Royalty)
One for the Morning Glory - John Barnes *f* 297

Amaury (Knight)
King & Raven - Cary James *f* 2275

Amaya, Anya (Pilot)
Glory's People - Alfred Coppel *s* 956

Amber (Child)
Pet Store - M.T. Coffin *h* 882

Amber (Psychic)
Return Fire - Charles Ingrid *s* 2257

Amberdrake (Healer)
The Black Gryphon - Mercedes Lackey *f* 2599

Amberdrake (Healer; Leader)
The White Gryphon - Mercedes Lackey *f* 2626

Ambrose, Jonathan (Investigator)
Death of a Darklord - Laurell K. Hamilton *h* 2015

Ambrose, Tereza (Magician)
Death of a Darklord - Laurell K. Hamilton *h* 2015

Ambrosius, Merlin (Wizard)
The Wizard of Camelot - Simon Hawke *f* 2101

Ambrosius, Merlinus "Myrddin/Lailoken" (Wizard;
  Demon)
The Dragon and the Unicorn - A.A.
  Attanasio *f* 224

Amby (Actor; Psychic)
Merlin's Bones - Fred Saberhagen *f* 3815

Amelia (Royalty)
Dragon's Plunder - Brad Strickland *f* 4256

Amelia (Fugitive)
Further Adventures - Jon Stephen Fink *f* 1563

Amelia (Farmer)
Return to Isis - Jean Stewart *s* 4203

Amfortas (Knight)
The Grail of Hearts - Susan Shwartz *f* 4001

Amgigh (Prehistoric Human; Indian)
My Sister the Moon - Sue Harrison *f* 2065

Amij, Katherine (Businesswoman)
Changeling - Christopher Kubasik *f* 2579

Amilcar (Military Personnel)
Pendragon - Stephen R. Lawhead *f* 2672

Amnell, Kahlan (Magician; Leader)
Blood of the Fold - Terry Goodkind *f* 1820
Stone of Tears - Terry Goodkind *f* 1821
Wizard's First Rule - Terry Goodkind *f* 1822

Amory, Theodora "Teddy" (Child)
Goat Dance - Douglas Clegg *h* 870

Amos, Renee (Feminist)
Star Sister - Juanita Coulson *s* 982

Amy (Teenager)
The Kingdom of Kevin Malone - Suzy McKee
  Charnas *f* 785

Amy (Artist; Musician)
Stranded - Camarin Grae *s* 1841

An (Spacewoman; Linguist)
Eggheads - Emily Devenport *s* 1211

an Jiar yn Aliria dur Hamley, Quinzaine (Immortal;
  Wizard)
Fire Crossing - Cheryl J. Franklin *s* 1635

an Treves, Sheyrena "Rena" (Mythical Creature; Fiance(e))
Elvenblood - Andre Norton *f* 3304

Anadon, Oren (Ruler)
Exile - Michael P. Kube-McDowell *s* 2582

Anaka (Detective—Police)
Specters of the Dawn - S. Andrew Swann *s* 4279

Ananayel (Angel)
Humans - Donald E. Westlake *f* 4595

Anangaranga-Jones, Nixy (Tourist; Adventurer)
Muddle Earth - John Brunner *s* 601

Anara (Innkeeper; Teacher)
India's Story - Kathlyn S. Starbuck *s* 4153

Anaral (Religious)
An Acceptable Time - Madeleine L'Engle *f* 2732

Anasan (Shaman; Indian)
Sing for a Gentle Rain - J. Alison James *f* 2278

Anastasi, Janet (Scientist)
Maverick - Bruce Bethke *s* 393

Anatole (Teenager)
Silicon Embrace - John Shirley *s* 3996

Anaxagoras (Wizard; Teacher)
The Wizard's Apprentice - S.P. Somtow *f* 4120

Ancar (Royalty; Magician)
Winds of Fury - Mercedes Lackey *f* 2629

Anders, Sarah (Diplomat)
FreeMaster - Kris Jensen *s* 2307

Anderson, Aaron (Teenager)
Oasis - Brian Hodge *h* 2158

Anderson, Carrie (Doctor)
The Vampire Princess - Michael Romkey *h* 3738

Anderson, Chris (Teenager)
Oasis - Brian Hodge *h* 2158

Anderson, Kelly (Teenager)
Darkness - John Saul *h* 3874

Anderson, Marion (Student)
Flesh - Gus Weill *h* 4531

Anderson, Richard (Wizard; FBI Agent)
Bureau 13 - Nick Pollotta *f* 3476

Anderson, Ted (Construction Worker; Parent)
Darkness - John Saul *h* 3874

An'desha (Magician)
Storm Breaking - Mercedes Lackey *f* 2620
Storm Rising - Mercedes Lackey *f* 2621
Storm Warning - Mercedes Lackey *f* 2622

Andojar, Susan Smith (Military Personnel)
The Web of Spider - W. Michael Gear *s* 1744

Andrachis, Shil (Alien; Leader)
Shadows on the Sun - Michael Jan Friedman *s* 1664

Andrada, Rosa (Secretary)
The House of the Toad - Richard Tierney *h* 4363

Andrea (Teenager)
The Third Beast - Peter Loughran *h* 2804

Andreos, Leonidas (Spaceship Captain)
Siduri's Net - P.K. McAllister *s* 2951

Andrew (Young Man)
The Last Coin - James P. Blaylock *f* 421

Andrews, Boyd (Carpenter)
Blood Kin - Ronald Kelly *h* 2432

Andrews, Laura (Patient)
Quarantine - Greg Egan *s* 1415

Andreyeva, Maya Tayanichna (Journalist; Cyborg)
The Fortunate Fall - Raphael Carter *s* 750

Andry (Ruler; Magician)
The Dragon Token - Melanie Rawn *f* 3577

Stronghold - Melanie Rawn *f* 3583

Andry (Nobleman; Magician)
Sunrunner's Fire - Melanie Rawn *f* 3584

Angel (Student—High School; Sports Figure)
Damnbanna - Nancy Springer *f* 4131

Angel (Vampire)
Dark Prince - Keith Herber *h* 2125

Angel (Alien)
The Pure Cold Light - Gregory Frost *s* 1681

Angel Juan (Teenager; Musician)
Missing Angel Juan - Francesca Lia Block *f* 448

Angelica, Pearl (Genetically Altered Being)
Tower of the Gods - Thomas A. Easton *s* 1384

Angelo, Jamie (Artist; Student)
Beauty - Brian D'Amato *h* 1080

Angelus, Lucifer "Luke" (Computer; Military Personnel)
Chains of Light - Quentin Thomas *s* 4347

Anghara, Princess (Young Woman; Royalty)
Nemesis - Louise Cooper *f* 950

Angharad (Minstrel; Wanderer)
Into the Green - Charles de Lint *f* 1154

Angier, Rupert (Magician; Writer)
The Prestige - Christopher Priest *s* 3534

Anglith of Arkraz, Omar "Trader of Tales" (Writer; Traveller)
The Hunters' Haunt - Dave Duncan *f* 1353
The Reaver Road - Dave Duncan *f* 1359

Anica (Girlfriend)
Senor Vivo and the Coca Lord - Louis de Bernieres *f* 1136

Anigel (Royalty)
Black Trillium - Marion Zimmer Bradley *f* 518

Animiki-Waewidum, Gahzee (Indian; Scientist)
Svaha - Charles de Lint *s* 1160

Anito (Alien)
The Color of Distance - Amy Thomson *s* 4357

Anlawdd (Royalty; Criminal)
Arthur War Lord - Dafydd ab Hugh *f* 5

Anlon (Mythical Creature)
Morigu: The Dead - Mark C. Perry *f* 3412

Ann (Housewife)
The Cormorant - Stephen Gregory *h* 1943

Ann (Writer)
Gothic Romance - Emmanuel Carrere *h* 740

Ann "Annai" (Dancer; Parent)
Shame of Man - Piers Anthony *s* 155

Anna (Child)
Darkness, I - Tanith Lee *h* 2710

Anne (Handicapped; Spirit)
The Time Tree - Enid Richemont *f* 3662

Anne (Artificial Intelligence)
Dream of Glass - Jean Mark Gawron *s* 1734

Annice (Royalty; Minstrel)
Sing the Four Quarters - Tanya Huff *f* 2231

Anniyas, Avira (Political Figure; Psychic)
The Ruins of Ambrai - Melanie Rawn *f* 3580

Ansa (Warrior; Explorer)
The Poisoned Lands - John Maddox Roberts *f* 3695

Ansa (Explorer; Warrior)
Queens of Land and Sea - John Maddox Roberts *f* 3696

Antero, Amalric (Adventurer; Teenager)
The Far Kingdoms - Allan Cole *s* 889

Antero, Amalric (Adventurer)
Kingdoms of the Night - Allan Cole *f* 890

Antero, Rali Emilie (Wizard; Lesbian)
The Warrior Returns - Allan Cole *f* 894

Antero, Rali Emilie (Military Personnel)
The Warrior's Tale - Allan Cole *f* 895

Anthimos (Ruler)
Krispos Rising - Harry Turtledove *f* 4390

Anthony (Teenager)
The First Horror - R.L. Stine *h* 4219

Anthony, Father (Religious; Teacher)
Catacomb - Andrew Laurance *h* 2665

Antilles, Wedge (Military Personnel; Pilot)
Rogue Squadron - Michael A. Stackpole *s* 4152

Antiope (Warrior; Time Traveller)
Amazon: A Novel - Barbara G. Walker *f* 4474

Antiope (Warrior; Lesbian)
The Amazon Chronicles - Jane E.M. Robinson *f* 3703

Antissa, Sybil (Sorceress)
Owl Light - Michael Paine *h* 3375

Antonia (Witch; Child)
Daughter of Magic - C. Dale Brittain *f* 574

Antonius, Marcus (Historical Figure; Military Personnel)
Throne of Isis - Judith Tarr *f* 4305

Antonovich, Colonel (Military Personnel)
The Struggle - Jerry Ahern *s* 34

Anwara (Parent)
The Moorchild - Eloise Jarvis McGraw *f* 3040

Anya (Warrior)
Orion in the Dying Time - Ben Bova *s* 485

Anyelet (Vampire)
Afterage - Yvonne Navarro *h* 3243

Anyr (Fiance(e))
The Sleep of Stone - Louise Cooper *f* 952

Anzelm, Aitan (Angel)
The Ways of Magic - Scott Ciencin *f* 833

ap Don, Gwydion (Magician; Royalty)
The Island of the Mighty - Evangeline Walton *f* 4483

ap Hywel, Dafydd (Martial Arts Expert; Royalty)
The Dragon on the Border - Gordon R. Dickson *f* 1236

ap Kian, Donaugh (Royalty; Magician)
The Western King - Ann Marston *f* 2888

ap Kian, Keylan (Ruler)
The Western King - Ann Marston *f* 2888

ap Kian, Tiernyn (Royalty; Warrior)
The Western King - Ann Marston *f* 2888

ap Mathonwy, Math (Magician; Royalty)
The Island of the Mighty - Evangeline Walton *f* 4483

ap Medrault, Irion (Royalty)
The Last Pendragon - Robert Rice *f* 3661

ap Nia, Aidan (Royalty; Magician)
King's Son, Magic's Son - Josepha Sherman *f* 3977

Ap Sennon, Olmy (Adventurer; Sailor)
Legacy - Greg Bear *s* 344

Ape (Wizard)
The Gates of Noon - Michael Scott Rohan *f* 3732

Aphrael (Deity; Child)
The Hidden City - David Eddings *f* 1391

Apollo (Mythical Creature; Deity)
Ye Gods! - Tom Holt *f* 2196

Ash, Hatty (Healer)
Devil's Tower - Mark Summer   f   4270

Ash, Leanard (Reanimated Dead)
Shadows Fall - Simon R. Green   f   1903

Ash, Leon (Scientist)
The Invisible Company - Scott Russell
    Sanders   s   3852

Ash of Ashland (Revolutionary; Adventurer)
Dancing Jack - Laurie J. Marks   f   2880

Ashar (Deity)
The Way Beneath - Angus Wells   f   4575

Ashata/Maya (Immortal; Pilot)
The Queen's Squadron - R.M. Meluch   s   3087

Ashenden, Turner (Student)
Views from the Oldest House - Richard
    Grant   s   1865

Asher, Anat (Military Personnel)
Signs of Life - Cherry Wilder   s   4622

Asher, James (Detective—Amateur; Professor)
Those Who Hunt the Night - Barbara
    Hambly   h   2011

Asher, James (Professor; Detective—Amateur)
Traveling with the Dead - Barbara Hambly   h   2012

Asher, Lydia (Scientist)
Traveling with the Dead - Barbara Hambly   h   2012

Ashkevron, Savil (Magician)
Magic's Price - Mercedes Lackey   f   2615

Ashkevron, Vanyel (Magician; Homosexual)
Magic's Price - Mercedes Lackey   f   2615

Ashlar "Mr. Ash" (Businessman)
Taltos - Anne Rice   h   3656

Ashton, Clark (Doctor)
Blood of Innocents - John Arbucci   h   168

Asquith, Timothy (Alcoholic)
Ghostwright - Michael Cadnum   h   661

Asrubal (Thief)
Night Lamp - Jack Vance   s   4422

Astare, T. (Vampire)
Morningstar - Peter Atkins   h   223

Aster "Star" (Royalty; Traveller)
Glory Road - Robert A. Heinlein   f   2112

Astfgl (Demon)
Eric - Terry Pratchett   f   3499

Astrahn (Slave; Revolutionary)
A City in Winter - Mark Helprin   f   2119

Asx/Ewasx (Alien)
Infinity's Shore - David Brin   s   565

At (Alien)
Doctor's Orders - Diane Duane   s   1338

Ata'al (Shaman)
The Watcher's Mask - Laurie J. Marks   f   2883

Atare, Darame "Silver" Meath (Ruler; Immigrant)
Hidden Fires - Katharine Eliska Kimbriel   s   2475

Atare, Sheen (Ruler; Hero)
Hidden Fires - Katharine Eliska Kimbriel   s   2475

Atbin (Teenager; Adventurer)
The Promise - Monica Hughes   s   2237

Aten (Immortal)
Orion Among the Stars - Ben Bova   s   483

Atkins, Thomas "Soldier" (Military Personnel)
Genetic Soldier - George Turner   s   4381

Atle (Military Personnel; Spaceship Captain)
Silent Songs - A.C. Crispin   s   1026

Atrus (Magician)
Myst: The Book of Atrus - Rand Miller   f   3103

Attercop, Karen (Student; Lover)
Webs - Scott Baker   h   255

Attila (Android; Martial Arts Expert)
Hunter's Planet - David Bischoff   s   399

Attila the Hun (Historical Figure; Foster Parent)
Attila's Treasure - Stephan Grundy   f   1964

Attila the Hun (Warrior)
The Autobiography of Santa Claus: It's Better to Give - Jeff Guinn   f   1967

Atvar (Alien; Leader)
Worldwar: In the Balance - Harry
    Turtledove   s   4395

Atvar (Military Personnel; Alien)
Worldwar: Striking the Balance - Harry
    Turtledove   s   4396

Atvar (Alien; Leader)
Worldwar: Tilting the Balance - Harry
    Turtledove   s   4397

Atvar (Military Personnel; Alien)
Worldwar: Upsetting the Balance - Harry
    Turtledove   s   4398

Atwood, Clancy "Kolo" (Indian)
Demon Dance - T. Chris Martindale   h   2904

Aubert, Jacques (Apprentice)
Where the Towers Pierce the Sky - Marie D.
    Goodwin   f   1823

Aubrey (Student; Wizard)
The Shape-Changer's Wife - Sharon Shinn   f   3990

Audran, Marid (Assistant; Bodyguard)
The Exile Kiss - George Alec Effinger   s   1406

Audran, Marid (Police Officer; Bodyguard)
A Fire in the Sun - George Alec Effinger   s   1407

Auganzar (Alien; Military Personnel)
Warlord of Heaven - Adrian Cole   f   887

Auggie (Artificial Intelligence)
Terminal Games - Cole Perriman   s   3411

August (Genetically Altered Being)
Becoming Human - Valerie J. Freireich   s   1647

Augustine (Historical Figure; Religious)
Blameless in Abaddon - James Morrow   f   3209

Augustine, Alexa (Computer Expert; Military
    Personnel)
Dream of Glass - Jean Mark Gawron   s   1734

Auk, Maytera (Criminal; Religious)
Exodus From the Long Sun - Gene Wolfe   s   4732

Aurealis, Gannd (Mythical Creature; Warrior)
War - Simon Hawke   f   2099

Aurelico, Karvonen (Thief; Guide)
The Raven Ring - Patricia C. Wrede   f   4764

Aurelio (Indian; Shaman)
The War of Don Emmanuel's Nether Parts - Louis de
    Bernieres   f   1137

Aurian (Student; Magician)
Aurian - Maggie Furey   f   1687

Aurian (Magician; Parent)
Harp of Winds - Maggie Furey   f   1688

Aurian (Magician)
Sword of Flame - Maggie Furey   f   1689

Auriane (Warrior; Religious)
The Light Bearer - Donna Gillespie   f   1791

Austen, James (Doctor)
The Angel of Pain - Brian Stableford   h   4141

Austin, Gregory (Captive; Spaceman)
Fallway - Paula E. Downing   s   1286

Austin, Kenton (Businessman)
The Living Dark - Stephen Gresham   h   1945

Austin, Steve (Police Officer)
Slippin' into Darkness - Norman Partridge   h   3390

Austra, Catherine (Vampire)
Daughter of the Night - Elaine Bergstrom   h   379

Austra, Laurence (Vampire)
Blood Alone - Elaine Bergstrom   h   378

Autothor (Artificial Intelligence; Alien)
Codgerspace - Alan Dean Foster   s   1604

Avenger (Adventurer; Criminal)
*The Spider #4: Death Reign of the Vampire King/The
    Pain Emperor* - Grant Stockbridge   f   4235

Averil (Sorceress)
Plague Demon - Brian Craig   f   1004

Avery (Artificial Intelligence)
Caverns of Socrates - Dennis L. McKiernan   f   3053

Avery, David "Derec" (Computer Expert)
Maverick - Bruce Bethke   s   393

Avery, Rupert "Roo" (Businessman)
Rise of a Merchant Prince - Raymond E.
    Feist   f   1536

Avery, Rupert "Roo" (Fugitive)
Shadow of a Dark Queen - Raymond E.
    Feist   f   1538

Avichenko, Emily "Avi" (Scientist)
Only Child - H.M. Hoover   s   2203

Aviendha (Warrior)
The Fires of Heaven - Robert Jordan   f   2382

**Avignon, Kitten "Our Lady of
    Roses"** (Noblewoman)
Mage Heart - Jane Routley   f   3754

Avran (Servant; Magician)
Aurian - Maggie Furey   f   1687

Avran (Magician)
Harp of Winds - Maggie Furey   f   1688
Sword of Flame - Maggie Furey   f   1689

Avril (Royalty; Sorcerer)
The Price of Blood and Honor - Elizabeth
    Willey   f   4628

Avril (Ruler; Sorcerer)
A Sorcerer and a Gentleman - Elizabeth
    Willey   f   4629

Avris (Witch; Companion)
Songsmith - Andre Norton   f   3314

Aw, Ruiz (Slave; Agent)
Emperor of Everything - Ray Aldridge   s   50

Aw, Ruiz (Agent; Martial Arts Expert)
The Pharaoh Contract - Ray Aldridge   s   51

Axxter, Ny (Artist)
Farewell Horizontal - K.W. Jeter   s   2320

Ayers, Jane (Health Care Professional)
The Illegal Rebirth of Billy the Kid - Rebecca
    Ore   s   3364

Ayesha (Mythical Creature)
Dragon's Domain - Thorarinn Gunnarsson   f   1972

Ayla (Prehistoric Human; Shaman)
The Plains of Passage - Jean M. Auel   f   231

Aylesworth, Jesse (Student—College; Editor)
An Exaltation of Larks - Robert Reed   s   3595

Ayth, Argoth (Religious; Magician)
Demon Moon - Jack Williamson   s   4669

Ayyah (Alien; Refugee)
Cat's Gambit - Leslie Gadallah   s   1690

Aza-Kra (Alien)
Rule Golden and Double Meaning - Damon
    Knight   s   2536

Azak (Mythical Creature; Leader)
Emperor and Clown - Dave Duncan   f   1350

Baranyk, Valentin (Military Personnel)
Cold Allies - Patricia Anthony *s* 128

Barbee, Will (Journalist)
Darker than You Think - Jack Williamson *h* 4668

Barber, Cissy (Girlfriend)
Land O'Goshen - Charles McNair *s* 3071

Barbtail, Dotson (Alien; Genetically Altered Being)
Seeds of Destiny - Thomas A. Easton *s* 1382

Barchar, Jason "Jase" Lee (Government Official; Experimental Subject)
Naked to the Stars/The Alien Way - Gordon R. Dickson *s* 1240

Barclay, Andy (Student)
Child's Play III - Matthew J. Costello *h* 965

Barclay, Reginald (Engineer; Space Explorer)
Requiem - Michael Jan Friedman *s* 1662

Bardsey, Geoffrey (Religious; Immortal)
The Merlin Effect - T.A. Barron *f* 310

Barek, A.E. (Mercenary)
Created By - Richard Christian Matheson *h* 2937

Bargolas (Demon)
The Summoned - Steven Ray Fulgham *h* 1683

Bariden (Martial Arts Expert; Sorcerer)
The Hidden Realms - Sharon Green *f* 1890

Barion (Alien)
The Snake Oil Wars - Parke Godwin *s* 1807

Barker, Jenny (Disembodied Personality)
Dragons on the Town - Thorarinn Gunnarsson *f* 1974

Barker, Joel (Child)
Sineater - Elizabeth Massie *h* 2917

Barker, Justin (Banker)
Tombley's Walk - Crosland Brown *h* 590

Barku, Perkar Kar (Hero)
The Waterborn - J. Gregory Keyes *f* 2464

Barlow, Frank (Spaceman)
The Ring of Charon - Roger MacBride Allen *s* 66

Barlowe, Philip (Journalist)
Act of Love - Joe R. Lansdale *h* 2640

Barlstilkin, Talbeck (Immortal)
Eternal Light - Paul J. McAuley *s* 2952

Barnard, Jacques (Wizard; Businessman)
2XS - Nigel Findley *f* 1558

Barnes, Collee (Real Estate Agent)
Black Death - R. Karl Largent *h* 2655

Barnes, Parker (Police Officer; Experimental Subject)
Virtuosity - Terry Bisson *s* 411

Barnes, Randy (Military Personnel)
Sleipnir - Linda Evans *f* 1493

Barnett, Schuyler "Sky" (Handyman)
My Soul to Keep - Judith Hawkes *h* 2105

Barnett, Stephen (Child)
My Soul to Keep - Judith Hawkes *h* 2105

Barnevelt, Dirk (Writer)
The Hand of Zei - L. Sprague de Camp *s* 1139

Barr, Dallas (Immortal; Businessman)
Buying Time - Joe Haldeman *s* 1993

Barrera, Ramis (Settler)
Lifeline - Kevin J. Anderson *s* 92

Barrero, Estela (Doctor)
The Resurrectionist - Thomas F. Monteleone *h* 3156

Barrett, Elizabeth (Young Woman)
Death Masque - P.N. Elrod *h* 1440

Barrett, Jonathan (Vampire)
Dance of Death - P.N. Elrod *h* 1439
Death Masque - P.N. Elrod *h* 1440

Barrett, Jonathan (Student)
Red Death - P.N. Elrod *h* 1443

Barrett, Kitty (Nurse)
Night Music - Sheila Bristow Garner *h* 1724

Barrett, Lionel (Paranormal Investigator)
Hell House - Richard Matheson *h* 2931

Barringer, Melissa "Missy" (Child)
Cursed Be the Child - Mort Castle *h* 760

Barringer, Warren (Professor)
Cursed Be the Child - Mort Castle *h* 760

Barrington, Cathy (Young Woman)
The Tallow Image - Jane Brindle *h* 567

Barris, Michael Albert (Journalist; Parent)
The Immortals - Tracy Hickman *s* 2141

Barron, Paul (Religious)
Wurm - Matthew J. Costello *h* 973

Barrow, Simon (Martial Arts Expert; Teenager)
The First Duelist - Rutledge Etheridge *s* 1488

Barry, Warren Hubert (Doctor)
The Forever Children - Eric Flanders *h* 1566

Bart (Apprentice; Hunter)
Initiation - Marian Hughes *s* 2235

Barthlomew, Lucy (Religious)
Moonfall - Tamara Thorne *h* 4360

Bartlett, Jennan (Spaceship Captain)
Mad Roy's Light - Paula King *s* 2478

Bartlett, Tony "Antonius Caelerus" (Time Traveller; Criminal)
Far Edge of Darkness - Linda Evans *s* 1492

Barton, Alex (Spouse)
The Circus of the Earth and Air - Brooke Stevens *f* 4200

Barton, Chris (Scientist)
7 Steps to Midnight - Richard Matheson *h* 2928

Barton, Howard (Museum Curator)
The Paper Grail - James P. Blaylock *f* 424

Barton, Roy (Construction Worker)
The Paper Grail - James P. Blaylock *f* 424

Barzac, Ree (Spaceman)
Brotherhood of the Stars - Kirby Greene *s* 1932

Bascomb, Charles "Chaz" (Child)
Bones - Joyce Thompson *h* 4351

Bascomb, Frederika "Freddy" (Artist)
Bones - Joyce Thompson *h* 4351

Bascombe, Jeryline A. (Servant)
Tales From the Crypt: Demon Knight - Randall Boyll *h* 507

Bascombe, John (Administrator)
The Reign of the Brown Magician - Lawrence Watt-Evans *f* 4503

Basehart, Diana (Time Traveller)
Time Station London - David Evans *s* 1491

Bashir, Julian (Doctor; Military Personnel)
Time's Enemy - L.A. Graf *s* 1842

Basker, Tem (Teenager)
The Starlight Crystal - Christopher Pike *s* 3452

Bass, Rocket Man (Pilot)
Voyage to the Red Planet - Terry Bisson *s* 412

Bassarab (Vampire; Nobleman)
One Foot in the Grave - Wm. Mark Simmons *f* 4039

Bastable (Alien; Royalty)
Charmed - Marilyn Singer *f* 4046

Bat, Charlie (Spirit; Grandparent)
Missing Angel Juan - Francesca Lia Block *f* 448

Bat, Cherokee (Teenager; Musician)
Cherokee Bat and the Goat Guys - Francesca Lia Block *f* 445

Bat Man (Criminal)
The Spider #4: Death Reign of the Vampire King/The Pain Emperor - Grant Stockbridge *f* 4235

Bateman, Patrick (Businessman; Serial Killer)
American Psycho - Brett Easton Ellis *h* 1425

Bateman, Vince (Doctor)
The Cartoonist - Sean Costello *h* 975

Bates, Norman (Innkeeper; Murderer)
Psycho - Robert Bloch *h* 440

Bates, Norman (Murderer)
Psycho II - Robert Bloch *h* 441

Bates, Patty (Businessman)
The Immaculate - Mark Morris *h* 3204

Bathespeake, Jason (Computer Expert; Administrator)
ME: A Novel of Self Discovery - Thomas T. Thomas *s* 4350

Bathori, Elizabeth (Noblewoman; Historical Figure)
Daughter of the Night - Elaine Bergstrom *h* 379

Bathory, David (Drug Dealer)
Ancestral Hungers - Scott Baker *h* 254

Bathory, Elizabeth (Noblewoman; Historical Figure)
Blood Countess - Andrei Codrescu *h* 881

Bathory, Elizabeth (Vampire)
Lord of the Vampires - Jeanne Kalogridis *h* 2394

Bathory, Michael (Businessman)
Ancestral Hungers - Scott Baker *h* 254

Bathory-Kereshtur, Drake (Journalist)
Blood Countess - Andrei Codrescu *h* 881

Battacharia, Rustum "Bat" (Government Official)
Cold as Ice - Charles Sheffield *s* 3950

Battacharia, Rustum "Bat" (Computer Expert; Teenager)
The Ganymede Club - Charles Sheffield *s* 3953

Batterberry, Lesli (Musician; Runaway)
Ghosts of Wind and Shadow - Charles de Lint *f* 1151

Batty, Roy (Disembodied Personality; Artificial Intelligence)
Blade Runner: Replicant Night - K.W. Jeter *s* 2316

Bauer, Libby (Parent)
Requiem - Clifford Mohr *h* 3146

Bauer, Robert (Musician)
Requiem - Clifford Mohr *h* 3146

Baum, L. Frank (Historical Figure; Writer)
Was - Geoff Ryman *f* 3804

Baver, Deodoro "Ted" (Anthropologist)
The Yngling and the Circle of Power - John Dalmas *s* 1074

Bawn, Caitlin (Traveller; Immortal)
Legends Reborn - Kenneth C. Flint *f* 1575

Baxter, Anna Elizabeth (Widow(er); Heiress)
Sheltered Lives - Charles Oberndorf *s* 3335

Baxter, Carl (Advertising; Pilot)
The Homecoming - Barry B. Longyear *s* 2798

Baxter, Sophie (Artist)
Lost Futures - Lisa Tuttle *s* 4400

Bayless, Laura (Baker)
Good Night, Sweet Angel - Clare McNally *h* 3073

Bayley, Frank (Religious)
Unholy Fire - Whitley Strieber *h* 4261

Beowulf (Animal; Leader)
Under Fire - Kenneth Von Gunden s 4454

Beowulf (Hero; Adventurer)
Whose Song Is Sung - Frank Schaefer f 3897

Beppu, Chan-ti (Wanderer)
The Last Legends of Earth - A.A. Attanasio s 227

Berengar, Count (Nobleman; Mythical Creature)
The Shadow Gate - Margaret Ball f 267

Berg-Benson, Sephony (Farmer; Revolutionary)
An Eye for Dark Places - Norma Marder s 2879

Bergeron, Carolyn (Murderer; Artist)
Nightmare Logic - Matthew Hall h 2000

Bergsndot, Ravna (Librarian)
A Fire upon the Deep - Vernor Vinge s 4441

Bermudez, Jolanda (Artist)
Hot Sky at Midnight - Robert Silverberg s 4013

Bernard, Cynthia (Wealthy; Businesswoman)
The Gatekeepers - Daniel Graham Jr. s 1845

Bernard, Rolf (Businessman)
The Gatekeepers - Daniel Graham Jr. s 1845

Bernay, Leah de (Apprentice; Doctor)
Scorpio - Alex McDonough s 3028

Bernie (Companion; Animal)
Witch and Wombat - Carolyn Cushman f 1054

Beroth of Firoze (Warrior)
Clock Strikes Sword - Ian Hammell f 2022

Berquist, Kate (Health Care Professional)
Nightmare - S.K. Epperson h 1472

Beryl (Warrior)
The Oxygen Barons - Gregory Feeley s 1527

Beryt (Royalty)
Shaper's Legacy - Sheila Finch s 1556

Berzel (Royalty; Werewolf)
Kedrigern and the Charming Couple - John
  Morressy f 3194

Besser, Dudley J. (Professor)
Coven - Edward Lee h 2696

Bessledorf, Jonathon (Spirit)
Bernie and the Bessledorf Ghost - Phyllis Reynolds
  Naylor f 3248

bet Ishak, Jehane (Doctor)
The Lions of Al-Rassan - Guy Gavriel Kay f 2403

Beth (Vampire)
Out for Blood - John Peyton Cooke h 941

Bethune, Casey (Postal Worker)
The Black Carousel - Charles L. Grant h 1846

Bettik, A. (Android)
Endymion - Dan Simmons s 4030

Betwixt and Between (Mythical Creature)
Brother to Dragons, Companion to Owls - Jane M.
  Lindskold f 2762

Bev (Health Care Professional)
My Cousin, My Gastroenterologist - Mark
  Leyner s 2748

Bevol, Israed (Teacher; Psychic)
Taminy - Maya Kaathryn Bohnhoff f 461

Bevol, Osraed (Guardian; Teacher)
The Meri - Maya Kaathryn Bohnhoff f 459

Bey, Friedlander (Businessman; Organized Crime
  Figure)
The Exile Kiss - George Alec Effinger s 1406

Bey, Friedlander (Criminal; Businessman)
A Fire in the Sun - George Alec Effinger s 1407

Beynac, Dagny (Political Figure; Parent)
The Stars Are Also Fire - Poul Anderson s 111

Bezarian (Military Personnel)
Red Army - Ralph Peters s 3429

Bhelliom "Blue Rose" (Mythical Creature)
The Hidden City - David Eddings f 1391

Biale (Runaway)
On Fortune's Wheel - Cynthia Voigt f 4445

Bianka (Vampire)
As One Dead - Don Bassingthwaite h 321

Bickerstaff, Robert Luther (Military Personnel;
  Businessman)
Terraplane - Jack Womack s 4749

Bidding, Philippa (Teenager)
Rebel From Alphorion - Robyn Tallis s 4291

Biergarten, Ryerson (Psychic)
The Ascending - T.M. Wright h 4773
Goodlow's Ghosts - T.M. Wright h 4775

Big Sword (Alien; Telepath)
Project Farcry - Pauline Ashwell s 189

Big Tom (Businessman)
The Dream Vessel - Jeff Bredenberg s 544

Bigelow, Walter T. (Political Figure; Administrator)
Journals of the Plague Years - Norman
  Spinrad s 4126

Bigthorn, Henry (Police Officer; Indian)
Clarke County, Space - Allen Steele s 4181

Biilathkamoro, Chodrisei "Coso" (Ruler)
The Kalif's War - John Dalmas s 1068

Bileux, Peter (Police Officer)
Nightshade - Stanley R. Moore s 3176

Bill (Spaceman)
*Bill, the Galactic Hero: On the Planet of Tasteless
  Pleasure* - Harry Harrison s 2052
*Bill, the Galactic Hero: The Final Incoherent
  Adventure* - Harry Harrison s 2053

Bill (Robot; Sidekick)
Hawaiian U.F.O. Aliens - Mel Gilden s 1788
Tubular Android Superheroes - Mel Gilden s 1790

Bill (Lawman)
Dusk - Ron Dee h 1185

Bill, Corporal (Military Personnel)
Planet of the Robot Slaves - Harry Harrison s 2058

Billie (Patient; Adventurer)
Aliens: Earth Hive - Steve Perry s 3416

Billy (Psychic; Adventurer)
Aliens: The Female War - Steve Perry s 3417

Billy (Musician)
Cowboy Feng's Space Bar and Grille - Steven
  Brust s 606

Billy the Kid (Android; Experimental Subject)
The Illegal Rebirth of Billy the Kid - Rebecca
  Ore s 3364

Bilrog (Alien)
Labyrinth - Dennis Schmidt s 3901

Binewski, Miranda (Artist)
Geek Love - Katherine Dunn h 1365

Binewski, Olympia (Parent; Genetically Altered
  Being)
Geek Love - Katherine Dunn h 1365

Birch, Wellington (Military Personnel; Time
  Traveller)
Lurid Dreams - Charles L. Harness s 2035

Bird (Revolutionary; Leader)
The Fifth Sacred Thing - Starhawk f 4154

Bird, Jake (Maintenance Worker)
Devil's Tower - Mark Summer f 4270

Bird, Marianne (Student—College; Spouse)
Tap, Tap - David Martin h 2891

Bird, Morris (Pilot; Prospector)
Heavy Time - C.J. Cherryh s 806

Bird, Roscoe (Teacher)
Tap, Tap - David Martin h 2891

Birdsong, Joseph "Mojo" (Criminal)
Mojo and the Pickle Jar - Douglas Bell f 357

Birkett, Alison (Lawyer)
Temporary Agency - Rachel Pollack f 3474

Birkwelch (Mythical Creature)
Minerva Wakes - Holly Lisle f 2770

Birnbaum, Maureen (Heroine; Martial Arts Expert)
*Maureen Birnbaum, Barbarian Swordsperson: The
  Complete Stories* - George Alec Effinger f 1408

Bish, Michael (Police Officer)
The Moons of Summer - S.K. Epperson h 1471

Bishop (Android; Hero)
Alien 3 - Alan Dean Foster s 1599

Bishop, Bryan (Teenager)
Away Is a Strange Place to Be - H.M.
  Hoover s 2202

Bishop, Catherine (Artisan)
Animus - Ed Kelleher h 2423

Bishop, Ian (Art Dealer)
Animus - Ed Kelleher h 2423

Bishop, Julian (Child)
Animus - Ed Kelleher h 2423

Bishop, Killeen (Spaceship Captain; Genetically
  Altered Being)
Furious Gulf - Gregory Benford s 367

Bishop, Nigel (Entertainer)
The California Voodoo Game - Larry Niven s 3277

Bishop, Toby (Refugee; Genetically Altered Being)
Furious Gulf - Gregory Benford s 367

Bishop, Toby (Wanderer)
Sailing Bright Eternity - Gregory Benford s 369

Bishop, Wendy (Child)
Virgins and Martyrs - Simon Maginn h 2867

Bishopric, Susan (Writer)
The Night Mayor - Kim Newman s 3262

Bittan, Rebecca (Student)
The Kiss - Kathryn Reines h 3614

Bitterhand, Calvin (Shaman; Indian)
Trickster - Muriel Gray h 1875

Bix (Animal; Guide)
Dinotopia - James Gurney f 1979

Bjorn of Bromme (Warrior; Adventurer)
The Discovery of Dragons - Graeme Base f 320

Bjornsen, Kristin "Kris" (Slave; Castaway)
Freedom's Landing - Anne McCaffrey s 2969

Bjornsen, Paula (Teacher)
Night Sounds - Warner Lee h 2716

Black, Angela (Witch)
Fetish - Edward Bryant h 613

Black, Charlie (Teenager)
When Darkness Falls - Sidney Williams h 4640

Black, Frank (Military Personnel)
Dead Heat - Del Stone Jr. h 4239

Black, Jackson (Adventurer)
Living with the Reptiles - Roger L.
  DiSilvestro s 1262

Black, Marguerita "Maggie" (Writer)
The Wood Wife - Terri Windling f 4709

Black Amber (Administrator)
Human to Human - Rebecca Ore s 3363

Black Dust 7, Lisa (Demon)
Temporary Agency - Rachel Pollack f 3474

Boniface, Thomas (Bodyguard)
The Element of Fire - Martha Wells f 4582

Bonifant, Father "Mr. Bones" (Administrator)
Brother to Dragons - Charles Sheffield s 3949

Bonivard, Francois (Computer Expert;
Handicapped)
Wildlife - James Patrick Kelly s 2430

Bonner, Nat (Child)
Dead End - Guy N. Smith h 4083

Bonney, Isabel "Iz" (Spouse; Time Traveller)
Elvissey - Jack Womack s 4746

Bonney, Jessamyn "Krokodil" (Leader)
Krokodil Tears - Jack Yeovil f 4801

Bonney, John (Spouse; Time Traveller)
Elvissey - Jack Womack s 4746

Bontu (Alien)
Life Form - Alan Dean Foster s 1611

Boofuls (Actor; Spirit)
Mirror - Graham Masterson h 2920

Booker, Sam (FBI Agent)
Midnight - Dean R. Koontz h 2554

Boone, Clayton (Gardener)
Father of Frankenstein - Christopher Bram h 541

Boone, Hank (Businessman)
Angel Kiss - Kelley Wilde h 4618

Boone, Jack (Scientist; Space Explorer)
Red Mars - Kim Stanley Robinson s 3710

Booth, Felix (Lawman)
Pitfall - Ronald Kelly h 2435

Borden, Alfred (Magician; Writer)
The Prestige - Christopher Priest s 3534

Borden, Andrew (Businessman)
Lizzie Borden - Elizabeth Engstrom h 1466

Borden, Emma (Spinster)
Lizzie Borden - Elizabeth Engstrom h 1466

Borden, Lizzie (Heroine; Historical Figure)
Lizzie Borden - Elizabeth Engstrom h 1466

Borden, Samantha (Government Official)
Dusk - Ron Dee h 1185

Boren, Troy (Accountant; Outlaw)
Blindfold - Kevin J. Anderson s 84

Borg, Cy (Cyborg; Engineer)
Drifter's Run - William C. Dietz s 1246
Drifter's War - William C. Dietz s 1247

Borg, Jocasta (Cyborg; Businesswoman)
The Specialist - Wynne Whiteford s 4611

Borgel (Time Traveller)
Borgel - Daniel Manus Pinkwater f 3456

Bork, Dick "Dutch" (Biker)
Night Beasts - T.W. Stetson h 4199

Bork, Saval (Martial Arts Expert; Bodyguard)
Brother Death - Steve Perry s 3419

Bork, Tazzimi "Taz" (Police Officer)
Brother Death - Steve Perry s 3419

Born, Eric (Psychic)
Reclamation - Sarah Zettel s 4850

Boro (Religious)
Brand New Cherry Flavor - Todd Grimson h 1960

Borric (Royalty)
Prince of the Blood - Raymond E. Feist f 1535

Boscage, A.D. (Writer)
The Priest: A Gothic Romance - Thomas M.
Disch h 1261

Bosch, Benjamin (Doctor)
Troll-Quest - Rose Estes f 1481

Bosch, Benjamin (Doctor; Adventurer)
Troll-Taken - Rose Estes f 1482

Bothari (Bodyguard; Murderer)
Barrayar - Lois McMaster Bujold s 620

Botticelli, Sandro (Historical Figure; Artist)
The Memory Cathedral - Jack Dann s 1086

Bottom, Nick (Artisan)
Whilom - Robert Watson f 4495

Botts, Wendell (Construction Worker)
Oaths and Miracles - Nancy Kress s 2577

Bouchette, Jean-Paul (Criminal; Spirit)
The Suiting - Kelley Wilde h 4621

Bouriere, Tira (Political Figure; Teenager)
Crown of Empire - Chelsea Quinn Yarbro s 4794

Bouriere, Wiley (Political Figure; Teenager)
Crown of Empire - Chelsea Quinn Yarbro s 4794

Bowe, Austin (Spaceship Captain; Parent)
Tripoint - C.J. Cherryh s 814

Bowe-Hawkins, Thomas "Tom" (Spaceman;
Prisoner)
Tripoint - C.J. Cherryh s 814

Bowen, Muffy (Dancer; Captive)
Greenhouse - Thomas A. Easton s 1381

Bowen, Tess (Teacher)
The Uprising - Abigail McDaniels h 3013

Bowers, Sidney (Mechanic)
Mojave Wells - L. Dean James s 2281

Bowman, Maggie (Detective—Homicide)
Cold Kiss - Roxanne Longstreet h 2794
The Undead - Roxanne Longstreet h 2796

Bowman, Michael (Doctor; Vampire)
Cold Kiss - Roxanne Longstreet h 2794

Bowman, Michael (Doctor)
The Undead - Roxanne Longstreet h 2796

Bowman, Scott (Doctor)
The Cartoonist - Sean Costello h 975

Boxdale, Asin (Artist)
Free Radicals - Jack McKinney s 3066

Boxer, Hugh (Neighbor)
Sweet Heart - Peter James h 2292

Boxletter, Bob (Computer Expert)
Duplicates - Andrew Neiderman h 3253

Boxletter, Marion (Housewife)
Duplicates - Andrew Neiderman h 3253

Boyle, Simon (Scientist; Criminal)
The Illegal Rebirth of Billy the Kid - Rebecca
Ore s 3364

Boysie (Sailor; Revolutionary)
Flickering Shadows - Kwadwo Agymah
Kamau f 2395

Braan (Alien; Military Personnel)
Genellan: Planetfall - Scott G. Gier s 1786

Braccalese, Gianni (Businessman)
A Wizard in Mind - Christopher Stasheff s 4173

Bracher, Frederick (Racist)
Mark of the Werewolf - Jeffrey Sackett h 3822

Brackett, Lute (Detective—Police)
Star Precinct - Kevin D. Randle s 3564

Brackett, Richard (Police Officer)
Mind Slayer - Kevin D. Randle s 3563

Braco, Jag (Religious; Police Officer)
Inquisitor - Ian Watson s 4493

Brad (Filmmaker)
I, Said the Fly - Michael Shea h 3947

Bradley, Alexander "Alex" (Student)
The Hollowing - Robert Holdstock f 2184

Bradley, Angela (Housewife; Songwriter)
Metal Angel - Nancy Springer f 4135

Bradley, Jason (Engineer)
The Ghost From the Grand Banks - Arthur C.
Clarke s 849

Bradley, Karen (Doctor)
Deus X - Joseph Citro h 837

Bradley, Richard (Parent; Adventurer)
The Hollowing - Robert Holdstock f 2184

Bradoukis, Matthew (Military Personnel)
Ground Zero - Kevin J. Anderson h 89

Brady, Francis (Child)
The Butcher Boy - Patrick McCabe h 2957

Brady, Julia (Spouse; Historical Figure)
The Gallery of His Dreams - Kristine Kathryn
Rusch f 3775

Brady, Mathew B. (Historical Figure; Photographer)
The Gallery of His Dreams - Kristine Kathryn
Rusch f 3775

Brady, Tedman (Political Figure)
A Fearful Symmetry - James Luceno s 2817

Brady-Phillips, Graysha (Scientist)
Shivering World - Kathy Tyers s 4406

Braeth, Rikard (Adventurer; Historian)
Crown of the Serpent - Allen L. Wold s 4724
Lair of the Cyclops - Allen L. Wold s 4725

Braille (Vampire)
Night Thirst - Patrick Whalen h 4597

Brailsford, Jane (Magician; Adventurer)
A College of Magics - Caroline Stevermer f 4201

Brainard (Military Personnel)
The Jungle - David Drake s 1320

Braldt (Prisoner; Warrior)
The Hunter on Arena - Rose Estes s 1478

Bramhall, Arthur (Writer; Professor)
The Bear Went over the Mountain - William
Kotzwinkle f 2561

Brand (Warrior; Sidekick)
The Hammer and the Cross - Harry
Harrison f 2055
One King's Way - Harry Harrison s 2057

Brand, Evelyn (Aged Person)
The Devil's Churn - Kristine Kathryn
Rusch h 3773

Brandarkson, Brandark (Warrior; Minstrel)
Oath of Swords - David Weber f 4525

Brandin of Ygrath (Ruler; Sorcerer)
Tigana - Guy Gavriel Kay f 2405

Brandis (Sorcerer)
Wind Whispers, Shadow Shouts - Sharon
Green f 1892

Brandis, Sarah (Dancer)
Sick - Jay R. Bonansinga h 469

Brandon "Brand" X (Teenager)
Killjoy - Elizabeth Forrest h 1585

Brandsetter, Earl (Murderer; Computer Expert)
Lethal Interface - Mel Odom s 3338

Branwen (Step-Parent)
The Lost Years of Merlin - T.A. Barron f 309

Bratenahl, Robert (Journalist)
I, Robot: The Illustrated Screenplay - Harlan
Ellison s 1432

Braun, Caleb (Worker)
Goblin Moon - Teresa Edgerton f 1399

Brauna, Sanda (Political Figure)
Becoming Human - Valerie J. Freireich s 1647

Brookmeyer, Warren (Political Figure)
Tek Power - William Shatner s 3941

Brooks, Anne (Veterinarian)
The Devil's Laughter - William W.
　Johnstone h 2334

Brooks, Connor (Sailor; Criminal)
Ill Wind - Kevin J. Anderson s 90

Brooks, Jenny (Traveller; Revolutionary)
Cathy IV - Frances Lucas s 2814

Brooks, Tim (Police Officer)
Ghosts - Noel Hynd h 2249

Brostek (Teenager; Hunter)
Shadow-Maze - Mark Smith f 4094

Broussard, Andy (Doctor)
Blood on the Bayou - D.J. Donaldson h 1268

Broward, Liz (Doctor)
Blood Work - Fay Zachary h 4823

Brown (Lesbian; Magician)
Phaze Doubt - Piers Anthony f 152

Brown, Emma (Grandparent)
The Summer I Shrank My Grandmother - Elvira
　Woodruff f 4755

Brown, Frank (Industrialist)
White Horse, Dark Dragon - Robert C.
　Fleet f 1569

Brown, Kelsie (Computer Expert)
65mm - Dale Hoover h 2200

Brown, Max (Teenager)
Thrill - Patricia Wallace h 4481

Brown, Nelly (Child; Scientist)
The Summer I Shrank My Grandmother - Elvira
　Woodruff f 4755

Brown, Oenone (Housewife)
Firefly - Piers Anthony h 139

Brown, Pellimore "Pel" (Magician; Ruler)
The Reign of the Brown Magician - Lawrence Watt-
　Evans f 4503

Brown, Pellimore "Pell" (Businessman)
Out of This World - Lawrence Watt-Evans f 4501

Brown, Rembrandt "Cryin' Man" (Musician;
　Adventurer)
Sliders: The Novel - Brad Linaweaver s 2756

Brown, Tim (Student)
The Select - F. Paul Wilson h 4693

The Brown Oxford (Experimental Subject)
*The Collected Stories of Philip K. Dick, Volume One:
　The Short Happy Life of the Brown Oxford* - Philip
　K. Dick s 1225

Broxholm (Alien)
My Teacher Flunked the Planet - Bruce
　Coville s 992

Bruce (Animal)
Paddywhack - John Stchur h 4176

Bruce, Virgin (Construction Worker)
Orbital Decay - Allen Steele s 4185

Bruchan (Minstrel)
The Boy From the Burren - Sheila Gilluly f 1798

Bruckner, Bill (Spy; Criminal)
Nomad - David Alexander s 54

Bruenor, Catti-Brie (Mythical Creature; Adventurer)
Passage to Dawn - R.A. Salvatore f 3843
Siege of Darkness - R.A. Salvatore f 3844
Sojourn - R.A. Salvatore f 3845

Bruenor, Catti-Brie (Mythical Creature; Warrior)
Starless Night - R.A. Salvatore f 3846

Brumado, Joanna (Scientist)
Mars - Ben Bova s 481

Brunahild "Sigdrifa" (Royalty; Warrior)
The Dragons of the Rhine - Diana L.
　Paxson f 3395
The Wolf and the Raven - Diana L. Paxson f 3401

Brunichild (Royalty; Warrior)
Rhinegold - Stephan Grundy f 1965

Bruno (Mercenary)
Harm's Way - Colin Greenland s 1934

Bruno (Royalty)
King and Emperor - Harry Harrison f 2056

Bruno, Giordano (Religious; Historical Figure)
Love and Sleep - John Crowley f 1035

Bruno, Richard (Scientist; Criminal)
Journals of the Plague Years - Norman
　Spinrad s 4126

Brusen, Elaine (Scientist)
Merlin's Bones - Fred Saberhagen f 3815

Brustein, Harvey (Cult Member)
The Children of Hamelin - Norman Spinrad s 4124

Brutha (Religious)
Small Gods - Terry Pratchett f 3507

Brutogas, Kator Secondcousin (Alien)
Naked to the Stars/The Alien Way - Gordon R.
　Dickson s 1240

Brutus, Marcus Junius (Political Figure; Military
　Personnel)
Child of the Eagle - Esther Friesner f 1668

Bruwer-Sanmartin, Hanna (Political Figure)
Fire in a Faraway Place - Robert Frezza s 1649

Bryant, Bonnie (Child; Foundling)
The Godsend - Bernard Taylor h 4309

Bryant, Karla (Advertising)
Deadrush - Yvonne Navarro h 3244

Bryant, Martin (Student)
The Crawling Dark - Pauline Dunn h 1366

Bryant, Sandra (Restaurateur)
The Crawling Dark - Pauline Dunn h 1366

Bryarmote (Mythical Creature; Royalty)
Pyromancer - Don Callander f 689

Bryce, Christopher (Religious)
Storm Knights - Bill Slavicsek f 4059

Bryce, Neal (Police Officer)
The Death Crystal - J. Edward Ames h 75

Bryce, Pat (Religious)
The Priest: A Gothic Romance - Thomas M.
　Disch h 1261

Bryge, Larry (Teenager; Student—High School)
Spirit Crossings - Claudia Peck f 3405

Buccari, Sharl (Military Personnel)
Genellan: Planetfall - Scott G. Gier s 1786

Buccari, Sharl (Pilot; Parent)
In the Shadow of the Moon - Scott G. Gier s 1787

Buchanan, Victoria (Teacher)
The Vampire Papers - Michael Romkey h 3737

Buckingham, Harry (Advertising)
Rune - Christopher Fowler h 1621

Buckland, Ulysses (Teenager; Wizard)
The Whims of Creation - Simon Hawke s 2100

Buckley, Christopher (Child)
Shadow Man - Dennis Etchison h 1487

Buddy (Teenager; Orphan)
Land O'Goshen - Charles McNair s 3071

Buechner, Marianne "Rianne" (Child)
An Impossible Summer - B.W. Clough f 878

Buechner, Shannon (Child)
An Impossible Summer - B.W. Clough f 878

Bueller (Military Personnel)
Aliens: Earth Hive - Steve Perry s 3416

Buffy (Teenager)
Buffy the Vampire Slayer - Richie Tankersley
　Cusick h 1056

Buford, Tommy (Handyman)
Let There Be Dark - Allen Lee Harris h 2043

Bugmeier, Neil (Writer)
Horror Show - Greg Kihn h 2466

Bult (Alien)
Uncharted Territory - Connie Willis s 4677

Bunkowski, Daniel "Chaingang" (Serial Killer)
Butcher - Rex Miller h 3104
Chaingang - Rex Miller h 3105
Savant - Rex Miller h 3107
Slice - Rex Miller h 3108

Burbage, Horace (Actor)
A Company of Stars - Christopher Stasheff s 4159

Burdon, Bill (Detective—Private)
A Question of Time - Fred Saberhagen h 3816

Bureaucrat (Agent)
Stations of the Tide - Michael Swanwick s 4283

Burge (Police Officer)
Night Watch - Robin Wayne Bailey f 244

Burgess (Animal)
Chaos Mode - Piers Anthony f 135

Burke (Child)
Sineater - Elizabeth Massie h 2917

Burke, Martin (Psychologist)
Queen of Angels - Greg Bear s 347

Burkhardt, Jared Jr. (Student)
First Love: A Gothic Tale - Joyce Carol
　Oates s 3331

Burlingame, Gerald (Lawyer)
Gerald's Game - Stephen King h 2486

Burlingame, Jessie (Housewife)
Gerald's Game - Stephen King h 2486

Burlow, Kurt (Vampire)
Salem's Lot - Stephen King h 2493

Burnell (Amnesiac; Activist)
Somewhere East of Life - Brian W. Aldiss s 48

Burnham, Harold (Scientist)
Carnivores - Penelope Banka Kreps h 2570

Burr, Martyn (Doctor)
Stone Angels - Mike Jefferies h 2305

Burrfoot, Tasslehoff (Mythical Creature)
Wanderlust - Mary Kirchoff f 2507

Burrich (Step-Parent; Animal Trainer)
Assassin's Apprentice - Robin Hobb f 2151

Burroughs, Jack "MAX—KOOL" (Computer Expert)
Headcrash - Bruce Bethke s 392

Burroughs, Mahree (Diplomat)
Ancestor's World - A.C. Crispin s 1021

Burroughs, Mahree (Teenager)
Starbridge - A.C. Crispin s 1027

Burton, Denise (Secretary)
Deadly Dreams - Gerald A. Schiller h 3899

Burton, Paige (Scientist)
Between the Devil and the Deep - J.M.
　Morgan h 3180

Burwin, Addie (Doctor)
Stunts - Charles L. Grant h 1857

Bury, Horace Hussein (Businessman)
The Gripping Hand - Larry Niven s 3281

Busch, Zachary (Computer Expert)
Drawing Blood - Poppy Z. Brite h 568

Calliope (Parent; Psychic)
Primavera - Francesca Lia Block *f* 449

Callista (Martial Arts Expert; Pilot)
Darksaber - Kevin J. Anderson *s* 86

Callow, John (Occultist)
Evil Intent - Bernard Taylor *h* 4308

Cally "Earth" (Child; Adventurer)
Beyond the Magic Sphere - Gail Jarrow *f* 2296

Calmady, Pollexfen (Gentleman; Mercenary)
The Architecture of Desire - Mary Gentle *f* 1761

Calrissian, Lando (Military Personnel)
Before the Storm - Michael P. Kube-
McDowell *s* 2581

Caludius, Alexsandra (Spy)
7 Steps to Midnight - Richard Matheson *h* 2928

Calvin, Susan (Computer Expert; Psychologist)
I, Robot: The Illustrated Screenplay - Harlan
Ellison *s* 1432

Calyx (Mythical Creature)
Cathedral of Thorns - Steven Frankos *f* 1640

Calyx (Religious)
Sunder, Eclipse and Seed - Elise Guttenberg *f* 1981

Camden, Alice "Leisha" (Genetically Altered Being)
Beggars in Spain - Nancy Kress *s* 2574

Camel, Teddy (Police Officer)
Lie to Me - David Martin *h* 2890

Camerata, Jo (Industrialist)
Star Brothers - Ben Bova *s* 487

Cameron, Bren (Linguist; Diplomat)
Foreigner - C.J. Cherryh *s* 803

Cameron, Bren (Diplomat; Linguist)
Inheritor - C.J. Cherryh *s* 808

Cameron, Bren (Linguist; Diplomat)
Invader - C.J. Cherryh *s* 809

Cameron, Daren (Scholar; Scientist)
Warstrider: Netlink - William H. Keith Jr. *s* 2422

Cameron, Dev (Military Personnel)
Warstrider - William H. Keith Jr. *s* 2421

Cameron, Dev (Genetically Altered Being; Space
Explorer)
Warstrider: Netlink - William H. Keith Jr. *s* 2422

Cameron, Jason (Magician; Werewolf)
The Fire Rose - Mercedes Lackey *f* 2608

Camfrey, Maurizio (Professor)
The Palm Dome - Liz Fulton *h* 1686

Camillia (Editor)
Pluto, Animal Lover - Laren Stover *h* 4243

Camio (Animal)
The Foxes of Firstdark - Garry Kilworth *f* 2473

Campbell, Alan (Doctor)
Rapid Growth - Mary K. Hanner *h* 2030

Campbell, Arlene "Grandma" (Aged Person)
The Amulet - A.R. Morlan *h* 3191

Campbell, Brianne (Teenager; Healer)
Journeyman Wizard - Mary Frances
Zambreno *f* 4830

Campbell, Deirdre (Student; Adventurer)
Indiana Jones and the Dance of the Giants - Rob
MacGregor *f* 2853
Indiana Jones and the Seven Veils - Rob
MacGregor *f* 2857

Campbell, Jack "Cap'n Jack" (Astronaut)
The Fugitive Stars - Daniel Ransom *s* 3571

Campbell, Katie (Researcher)
Rapid Growth - Mary K. Hanner *h* 2030

Campbell, Laicy "Iroshi" (Martial Arts Expert;
Administrator)
The Glaive - Cary Osborne *s* 3369

Campbell, Laicy "Iroshi" (Martial Arts Expert;
Wanderer)
Iroshi - Cary Osborne *s* 3370

Campbell, Robbie (Child)
Rapid Growth - Mary K. Hanner *h* 2030

Campos, Juana "Juan" (Drug Dealer)
Gods of the Well of Souls - Jack L. Chalker *s* 773

Canary, Sarah (Patient; Wanderer)
Sarah Canary - Karen Joy Fowler *f* 1628

Canby, Gordon (Spaceship Captain; Mercenary)
Canby's Legion - Bill Baldwin *s* 258

Candle, Martin (Judge; Activist)
Blameless in Abaddon - James Morrow *f* 3209

Candlemas, Richard (Doctor)
The Long Midnight - Daniel Ransom *h* 3572

Cannon, April (Scientist)
Ancient Shores - Jack McDevitt *s* 3014

Cannon, Ben (Student; Political Figure)
Cannon's Orb - L. Warren Douglas *s* 1279

Cannon, Bobby (Student)
The School - Ed Kelleher *h* 2425

Cannon, Vassily "Bass" James (Heir; Computer
Expert)
A Plague of Change - L. Warren Douglas *s* 1280

Cantemir, George (Businessman; Criminal)
The Venom Trees of Sunga - L. Sprague de
Camp *f* 1145

Cantrell, Barry (Immortal)
Prey - William W. Johnstone *h* 2336

Cantrell, Loren (Spaceship Captain)
Ground-Ties - Jane S. Fancher *s* 1496
Harmonies of the 'Net - Jane S. Fancher *s* 1497

Caolin "Blood Lord" (Sorcerer)
The Jewel of Fire - Diana L. Paxson *f* 3396

Captain (Astronaut)
Beyond Apollo - Barry Malzberg *s* 2872
Eden - Stanislaw Lem *s* 2730

Capthorne, Mya (Scientist)
Hidden Echoes - Mike Jefferies *f* 2301

Capuela, Giacomo (Businessman)
The Unborn - Andrew Laurance *h* 2668

Carabosse (Mythical Creature)
Beauty - Sheri S. Tepper *f* 4333

Caramon (Innkeeper; Hero)
The Second Generation - Margaret Weis *f* 4563

Carbri (Musician; Minstrel)
Search for the Starblade - Keith Taylor *f* 4315

Cardenas, Angel (Police Officer; Psychic)
Montezuma Strip - Alan Dean Foster *s* 1614

Cardiff, Melisan (Demon; Human)
Hooray for Hellywood - Esther Friesner *f* 1671

Cardiff, Noel (Warlock)
Hooray for Hellywood - Esther Friesner *f* 1671

Cardigan, Jake (Detective—Private)
Tek Money - William Shatner *s* 3940
Tek Power - William Shatner *s* 3941
Tek Vengeance - William Shatner *s* 3942
TekLab - William Shatner *s* 3943
TekLords - William Shatner *s* 3944
TekWar - William Shatner *s* 3945

Carelias, Caroline "Sarah" (Spy; Time Traveller)
Union Fires - John Barnes *f* 299

Carenza, Peter (Religious)
The Blood of the Lamb - Thomas F.
Monteleone *h* 3150

Carewe, Cindy (Artist; Clerk)
Absolute Power - Ray Russell *h* 3791

Carewe, Eliza "Bettina" (Witch)
Absolute Power - Ray Russell *h* 3791

Carey (Courier)
Dun Lady's Jess - Doranna Durgin *f* 1368

Carfax, Kurt (Vampire)
The Time of Feasting - Mick Farren *h* 1514

Cargo (Pilot; Spy)
Cyberstealth - S.N. Lewitt *s* 2743
Dancing Vac - S.N. Lewitt *s* 2744

Carialle (Cyborg)
The Ship Errant - Jody Lynn Nye *s* 3327

Carialle (Spacewoman)
The Ship Who Won - Anne McCaffrey *s* 2983

Caribou (Leader)
The Woman Who Loved Reindeer - Meredith Ann
Pierce *f* 3441

Carless, India "Trouble" (Computer Expert;
Lesbian)
Trouble and Her Friends - Melissa Scott *s* 3915

Carlisle, Bari (Designer; Girlfriend)
Count Geiger's Blues - Michael Bishop *s* 404

Carlisle, Harry (Police Officer)
The Armageddon Crazy - Mick Farren *s* 1509

Carlotta (Mythical Creature; Imposter)
Castle of Deception - Mercedes Lackey *f* 2604

Carlsen, Anita (Journalist)
Sorcerers of Sodom - Roger Elwood *h* 1447

Carlson, Amy (Child)
Shadows - John Saul *h* 3878

Carlson, Annette (Actress)
Ghosts - Noel Hynd *h* 2249

Carlson, Curt (Military Personnel)
Blood Siege - G. Harry Stine *s* 4211
Force of Arms - G. Harry Stine *s* 4212
Guts and Glory - G. Harry Stine *s* 4213
Judgment Day - G. Harry Stine *s* 4214
Warrior Shield - G. Harry Stine *s* 4216

Carlson-Wade, Bruno David (Writer)
Bereavement - Richard Lortz *h* 2802

Carlton, Billy (Actor; Spirit)
Cemetery of Angels - Noel Hynd *h* 2248

Carlucci, Frank (Detective—Police)
Carlucci's Edge - Richard Paul Russo *s* 3796

Carmaggio, Henry (Detective—Police)
Drakon - S.M. Stirling *s* 4224

Carmichael, Gabriel (Child)
Revenant - Melanie Tem *h* 4329

Carmichael, Justin (Revolutionary)
Two Crowns for America - Katherine Kurtz *f* 2594

Carmody, Alice Levertov (Indian; Businesswoman)
Sailor Song - Ken Kesey *s* 2456

Carmody, Michael (Sea Captain; Fisherman)
Sailor Song - Ken Kesey *s* 2456

Carne, Stephanie (Scientist)
The Mirror Maze - James P. Hogan *s* 2176

Carnes, Donald (Boyfriend)
The Axman Cometh - John Farris *h* 1515

Carnes, Rebecca (Military Personnel; Time
Traveller)
Arc Riders - David Drake *s* 1314

Carney, Hugh (Doctor)
Bright Angel - John Blair *s* 415

Carnitch, Richard (Vampire)
Nightlife - Jack Ellis *h* 1427

Cave, Clea/Richard (Actress)
The Need - Andrew Neiderman   *h*   3255

Cavewood, Matthew (Historian)
Belladonna - Michael Stewart   *h*   4206

CBN-001 "Caliban" (Robot)
Caliban - Roger MacBride Allen   *s*   63

C'boath, Joruus (Psychic)
Dark Force Rising - Timothy Zahn   *s*   4825

Cedar, Hugh Rock (Administrator; Engineer)
Fossil - Hal Clement   *s*   872

Cedar, Janice (Researcher; Spouse)
Fossil - Hal Clement   *s*   872

Cedric (Military Personnel; Political Figure)
One for the Morning Glory - John Barnes   *f*   297

Cedric (Teenager)
Strings - Dave Duncan   *s*   1361

Cefwyn (Royalty)
Fortress in the Eye of Time - C.J. Cherryh   *f*   804

Celeste (Religious)
Private Demons - Robert Masello   *h*   2909

Celia (Robot)
Automated Alice - Jeff Noon   *f*   3292

Celine, Sigismundo (Magician; Musician)
Nature's God - Robert Anton Wilson   *f*   4698

Celluci, Mike (Police Officer)
Blood Price - Tanya Huff   *h*   2225
Blood Trail - Tanya Huff   *h*   2226

Celyn, Imp y (Musician)
Soul Music - Terry Pratchett   *f*   3508

Centaur, Che (Mythical Creature)
Isle of View - Piers Anthony   *f*   145

Center, Fisk (Businessman)
Hard Sell - Piers Anthony   *s*   142

Central "CC" Computer (Artificial Intelligence)
Steel Beach - John Varley   *s*   4436

Centuri, Ariann (Military Personnel; Religious)
Half-Light - Denise Vitola   *s*   4443

Cephus (Farmer; Revolutionary)
Flickering Shadows - Kwadwo Agymah
   Kamau   *f*   2395

Cept, Claire (Professor)
Bring Me Children - David Martin   *h*   2889

Cerebus (Artificial Intelligence; Imposter)
When Dreams Collide - Wm. Mark
   Simmons   *f*   4040

Ceridwen (Witch)
Dragonslayer's Return - R.A. Salvatore   *f*   3838

Cerise (Computer Expert; Lesbian)
Trouble and Her Friends - Melissa Scott   *s*   3915

Cermit, Abasio (Traveller)
A Plague of Angels - Sheri S. Tepper   *f*   4337

Cervantes, Micah Miguel (Artist)
Harmony - Marjorie Bradley Kellogg   *s*   2428

Cge (Robot; Sidekick)
Backblast - Lee McKeone   *s*   3050
The Clone Crisis - Lee McKeone   *s*   3051

Cha-kwena (Shaman; Prehistoric Human)
The Edge of the World - William Sarabande   *f*   3856
Thunder in the Sky - William Sarabande   *f*   3858

Cha'dune, Hezhi Yehd (Royalty)
The Waterborn - J. Gregory Keyes   *f*   2464

Chagak (Prehistoric Human; Indian)
Mother Earth, Father Sky - Sue Harrison   *f*   2064

Chakallakak, Chakallakak "Chaka" ngha (Alien;
   Teenager)
The Long Hunt - Debra Doyle   *s*   1295

Chakotay (Military Personnel; Indian)
Ragnarok - Nathan Archer   *s*   170

Chakthi (Leader; Warrior)
Exile's Challenge - Angus Wells   *f*   4570

Chalaine (Sorceress)
Dark Mirror, Dark Dreams - Sharon Green   *f*   1889
The Hidden Realms - Sharon Green   *f*   1890

Challer, Bo (Teenager)
A Whisper of Wings - Steven Ray Fulgham   *h*   1684

Chalmers, Frank (Administrator; Scientist)
Red Mars - Kim Stanley Robinson   *s*   3710

Chalmers, Polly (Businesswoman)
Needful Things - Stephen King   *h*   2490

Chalmers, Reed (Psychologist; Adventurer)
The Enchanter Reborn - L. Sprague de
   Camp   *f*   1138

Chambers, Peter (Anthropologist)
Sleepwalker - Michael Cadnum   *h*   666

Champion, Dragonbait (Religious; Alien)
Masquerades - Kate Novak   *f*   3318

Champion, Dragonbait (Alien; Warrior)
Song of the Saurials - Kate Novak   *f*   3319

Chamtong, Onua (Animal Trainer; Adventurer)
Wild Magic - Tamora Pierce   *f*   3443

Chan (Military Personnel)
Dragon's Blood - Alex McDonough   *s*   3025

Chance, David (Orphan)
Brain Child - George Turner   *s*   4380

Chancel, Davey (Editor)
The Hellfire Club - Peter Straub   *h*   4248

Chancel, Nora (Housewife)
The Hellfire Club - Peter Straub   *h*   4248

Chandler, Jay (Archaeologist)
Lord of the Dark Lake - Ron Faust   *h*   1524

Chandler, Jeff (Government Official)
Deus X - Joseph Citro   *h*   837

Chandler, Joshua "the Whistler" Jeremiah (Bounty
   Hunter; Murderer)
Oracle - Mike Resnick   *s*   3632

Chandler, Karen (Parent)
Solomon's Knife - Victor Koman   *s*   2544

Chandler, Sam (Architect)
Devil's Gate - Elizabeth Ergas   *h*   1473

Chandler, Vicki (Doctor)
Resurrection Dreams - Richard Laymon   *h*   2682

Chandler, Zinc (Police Officer)
Cutthroat - Michael Slade   *h*   4058

Chandra (Wizard; Royalty)
The Fire's Stone - Tanya Huff   *f*   2228

Chaney (Military Personnel)
Crown of Empire - Chelsea Quinn Yarbro   *s*   4794

Chang, Deanna (Teenager; Outcast)
Scorpion Shards - Neal Shusterman   *s*   4000

Chang, Emily (Musician)
Night Magic - Thomas Tryon   *h*   4376

Chang, Marte (Inventor; Government Official)
Burn - Bill Ransom   *s*   3568
ViraVax - Bill Ransom   *s*   3570

Chang, Mavra (Immortal; Chieftain)
Echoes of the Well of Souls - Jack L.
   Chalker   *s*   772

Chang, Mavra (Immortal)
Gods of the Well of Souls - Jack L. Chalker   *s*   773
Shadow of the Well of Souls - Jack L.
   Chalker   *s*   779

Chang, Steve (Time Traveller)
Warrior - William Wu   *s*   4784

Chanly, Bel, Margasdotter (Warrior; Guide)
The Outskirter's Secret - Rosemary Kirstein   *s*   2509

Channon (Alien; Diplomat)
Target - Janet Morris   *s*   3198

Chanur, Hilfy (Alien; Spaceship Captain)
Chanur's Legacy - C.J. Cherryh   *s*   795

Chao, Larry O'Shawnessy (Scientist)
The Ring of Charon - Roger MacBride Allen   *s*   66
The Shattered Sphere - Roger MacBride Allen   *s*   67

Chapel, Christine (Nurse; Military Personnel)
Crossroad - Barbara Hambly   *s*   2003

Chapel, Helen (Accountant)
Red Bride - Christopher Fowler   *h*   1620

Chapel, John (Public Relations)
Red Bride - Christopher Fowler   *h*   1620

Chapin, Francis (Teacher)
Blood of Innocents - John Arbucci   *h*   168

Chapman, Annie (Prostitute)
From Hell - Alan Moore   *h*   3171

Chapman, Julie (Scientist)
Mr. Sandman - Lyle Howard   *h*   2214

Chapman, Merrick (Detective; Vampire)
Rulers of Darkness - Steven G. Spruill   *h*   4138

Chapman, Zane (Vampire)
Rulers of Darkness - Steven G. Spruill   *h*   4138

Chappy (Prisoner)
The End of Alice - A.M. Homes   *h*   2197

Charlemagne (Historical Figure; Ruler)
His Majesty's Elephant - Judith Tarr   *f*   4302

Charles (Nobleman; Vampire)
Daughter of the Night - Elaine Bergstrom   *h*   379

Charles, Ellen Cherry (Artist; Waiter/Waitress)
Skinny Legs and All - Tom Robbins   *f*   3684

Charlie (Nurse; Military Personnel)
Chains of Light - Quentin Thomas   *s*   4347

Charlie (Alien)
Neptune Crossing - Jeffrey A. Carver   *s*   756
Strange Attractors - Jeffrey A. Carver   *s*   757

Charlie/Charlene (Alien)
The Infinite Sea - Jeffrey A. Carver   *s*   755

Charlotte "Lottie" (Child)
Santa's Twin - Dean R. Koontz   *f*   2556

Charly (Musician)
The Making of a Monster - Gail Petersen   *h*   3430

Charming (Hero; Royalty)
Slay and Rescue - John Moore   *f*   3175

Chase, Adam (Photographer)
Nocturnas - Shawn Ryan   *h*   3801

Chase, J. Kelsey (Diver)
Between the Devil and the Deep - J.M.
   Morgan   *h*   3180

Chase, Jason (Businessman; Martial Arts Expert)
Night's Pawn - Tom Dowd   *s*   1284

Chase, Max (Child)
White Shark - Peter Benchley   *h*   363

Chase, Richard (FBI Agent)
The Devouring - Douglas D. Hawk   *h*   2090

Chase, Simon (Scientist)
White Shark - Peter Benchley   *h*   363

Chase-Frisson L'Zalle, Trevarre (Stowaway;
   Teenager)
Shivering World - Kathy Tyers   *s*   4406

Chasen, Liz (Writer)
Demon Night - J. Michael Straczynski   *h*   4244

Chasse, Lois (Aged Person)
Insomnia - Stephen King   *h*   2488

Claude (Robot; Sidekick)
Title Deleted for Security Reasons - Ed Blome   *s*   451

Claudia (Scientist; Anthropologist)
Agviq - Michael Armstrong   *s*   171

Claudia (Addict)
The Hanged Man - Francesca Lia Block   *f*   447

Claudius (Vampire)
Vampire Diary: The Embrace - Robert Weinberg   *h*   4549

Claus, Bob "Santa" (Imposter; Relative)
Santa's Twin - Dean R. Koontz   *f*   2556

Clavel (Alien; Writer)
North Wind - Gwyneth Jones   *s*   2354

Clavius, Black (Spaceman; Wanderer)
Glory - Alfred Coppel   *s*   955

Clay, John Sebastian (Mercenary)
A Landscape of Darkness - John Blair   *s*   416

Clay, Tom Red (Diplomat)
Being Alien - Rebecca Ore   *s*   3361
Human to Human - Rebecca Ore   *s*   3363

Clayborn, Robert (Scientist)
Phylum Monsters - Hayford Peirce   *s*   3406

Clayborne, Ann (Scientist; Aged Person)
Blue Mars - Kim Stanley Robinson   *s*   3704

Clayborne, Laura (Journalist; Parent)
Mine - Robert R. McCammon   *h*   2989

Clayborne, Martin (Businessman)
Darkman #2: The Price of Fear - Randall Boyll   *h*   503

Clayburn, Karl Thomas (Writer)
Buried Screams - C. Dean Andersson   *h*   113

Claypoole, Chester "Chet" W. (Businessman; Television)
Live From Golgotha: A Novel - Gore Vidal   *s*   4438

Clayton, Wilbur (Guard)
Tunnelvision - R. Patrick Gates   *h*   1733

Cleary, Quinn (Student)
The Select - F. Paul Wilson   *h*   4693

Cleedis (Warrior)
King Pinch - David Cook   *f*   924

Cleg, Dennis "Spider" (Patient)
Spider - Patrick McGrath   *h*   3039

Cleg, Horace (Parent; Maintenance Worker)
Spider - Patrick McGrath   *h*   3039

Clemens, Atta Olivia (Vampire)
A Candle for D'Artagnan - Chelsea Quinn Yarbro   *h*   4793
Crusader's Torch - Chelsea Quinn Yarbro   *h*   4795

Clement VII, Pope (Religious)
Scorpio - Alex McDonough   *s*   3028

Clements, Yolanda Free (Police Officer)
Alien Heat - Lynn S. Hightower   *s*   2144

Clemmy (Teenager)
The Fool's War - Lee Kisling   *f*   2511

Clendannan, Cherrid ris (Military Personnel)
Death's Gray Land - Mike Shupp   *s*   3998

Cleopatra (Historical Figure; Religious)
Throne of Isis - Judith Tarr   *f*   4305

Clermont, Donald (Vintner)
Kiss of Death - Daniel Rhodes   *h*   3649

Clermont, Selena (Heiress)
Kiss of Death - Daniel Rhodes   *h*   3649

Clerval, Henry (Sports Figure; Reanimated Dead)
Brittle Innings - Michael Bishop   *h*   403

Clewe, Elizabeth (Musician)
The Blood of Angels - Stephen Gregory   *h*   1942

Clewe, Harry (Handyman)
The Blood of Angels - Stephen Gregory   *h*   1942

Clewe, Zoe (Child)
The Blood of Angels - Stephen Gregory   *h*   1942

Cley (Heroine; Human)
Beyond the Fall of Night - Arthur C. Clarke   *s*   847

Click (Leader; Tinker)
The Warden of Horses - Karen Ripley   *s*   3672

Clifford, Doug (Diplomat)
Ancient Light - Mary Gentle   *s*   1760

Climber, Artus (Adventurer)
The Ring of Winter - James Lowder   *f*   2813

Cline, Kendra (Doctor)
Legion of the Dead - Geoffrey Caine   *h*   681

Cline, Tara (Passenger)
Redshift Rendezvous - John E. Stith   *s*   4232

Clootie (Wizard)
Split Heirs - Lawrence Watt-Evans   *f*   4505

Cloud (Animal; Telepath)
Cloud's Rider - C.J. Cherryh   *s*   797
Rider at the Gate - C.J. Cherryh   *s*   811

Cloud, Nelda (Guardian)
Quasar - Jamil Nasir   *s*   3242

C'mel (Animal; Genetically Altered Being)
Norstrilia - Cordwainer Smith   *s*   4072

Coal, Hugo (Nobleman; Handicapped)
The Grotesque - Patrick McGrath   *h*   3038

Cobal, Flysse (Waiter/Waitress)
Exile's Children - Angus Wells   *f*   4571

Cobalt (Animal)
Deadly Vengeance - Stephen R. George   *h*   1765

Cobb, Phoebe (Receptionist)
Everville - Clive Barker   *h*   284

Cobblepot, Oswald "the Penguin" (Criminal)
Batman Returns - Craig Shaw Gardner   *s*   1707
The Further Adventures of Batman 2: Featuring the Penguin - Martin H. Greenberg   *s*   1915

Cobri, Alex (Computer Expert)
Grounded! - Chris Claremont   *s*   840

Cobri, Amy (Businesswoman; Socialite)
Sundowner - Chris Claremont   *s*   841

Cocciolone, Carol Jeanne (Scientist; Genius)
Lovelock - Orson Scott Card   *s*   723

Cochrane, Richard (Actor)
Time and Chance - Alan Brennert   *f*   555

Cochrane, Rick (Insurance Agent)
Time and Chance - Alan Brennert   *f*   555

Cochrane, Zefrem (Scientist; Space Explorer)
Federation - Judith Reeves-Stevens   *s*   3600

Coconino (Time Traveller; Indian)
Children of the Earth - Catherine Wells   *s*   4578

Coconino (Indian; Hunter)
The Earth Is All That Lasts - Catherine Wells   *s*   4579

Coconino (Indian; Time Traveller)
The Earth Saver - Catherine Wells   *s*   4580

Coddington, Quentin (Psychic; Researcher)
Strange Stains and Mysterious Smells - Terry Jones   *f*   2377

Cody (Genetically Altered Being)
Black Milk - Robert Reed   *s*   3593

Cody, Will (Vampire)
Angel Souls and Devil Hearts - Christopher Golden   *h*   1810

Coeccias, Aedile (Government Official)
Fanuilh - Daniel Hood   *f*   2198

Coerlis, Jack-Jax Landsdowne (Heir; Collector)
Mid-Flinx - Alan Dean Foster   *s*   1613

Coffey, John (Prisoner)
The Green Mile - Stephen King   *h*   2487

Coffey, Malcolm "Cup" (Teacher)
Goat Dance - Douglas Clegg   *h*   870

Cofield, Aaron (Time Traveller; Teenager)
Ray Bradbury Presents: Dinosaur Planet - Stephen Leigh   *s*   2724

Cofield, Aaron (Teenager; Time Traveller)
Ray Bradbury Presents: Dinosaur World - Stephen Leigh   *s*   2725

Cofort, Rael (Doctor; Spacewoman)
Redline the Stars - Andre Norton   *s*   3313

Coglin, Dennis (Detective—Police)
Bring on the Night - Don Davis   *h*   1129

Cohen, Lauren "Laurie" (Parent; Lesbian)
Godmother Night - Rachel Pollack   *f*   3472

Cohen, Sophie (Truck Driver)
The Black Mariah - Jay R. Bonansinga   *h*   468

Cohn, Milton (Administrator)
Superstitious - R.L. Stine   *h*   4220

Coke, Matthew (Military Personnel; Leader)
The Sharp End - David Drake   *s*   1326

Colburn, Croft (Spy)
The Forever Drug - Steve Perry   *s*   3422

Cole, Cassandra (Immortal; Martial Arts Expert)
A Logical Magician - Robert Weinberg   *f*   4543

Cole, Dillon (Teenager; Outcast)
Scorpion Shards - Neal Shusterman   *s*   4000

Cole, James (Time Traveller; Criminal)
12 Monkeys - Elizabeth Hand   *s*   2025

Colene (Teenager; Adventurer)
Chaos Mode - Piers Anthony   *f*   135
Fractal Mode - Piers Anthony   *f*   140
Virtual Mode - Piers Anthony   *f*   160

Coleridge, Stuart (Police Officer)
The Orpheus Process - Daniel H. Gower   *h*   1839

Colette, Sianna (Scientist; Student)
The Shattered Sphere - Roger MacBride Allen   *s*   67

Coley, J. J. (Journalist)
Boneman - Lisa Cantrell   *h*   707

Coll, Lorand "Lor" (Wizard; Farmer)
Convergence - Sharon Green   *f*   1888

Colletti, Vince (Businessman)
Torments - Lisa Cantrell   *h*   709

Collier, Ben (Time Traveller; Clone)
A Bridge of Years - Robert Charles Wilson   *s*   4700

Collier, Joyce (Businesswoman)
The Fermata - Nicholson Baker   *s*   253

Collier, Marcy (Student—College)
Mythology 101 - Jody Lynn Nye   *f*   3325

Collier, Rance (Public Relations)
Slow Freight - F.M. Busby   *s*   642

Collier, Samantha (Television Personality)
Shock Radio - Leigh Clark   *h*   846

Collings, Reed (Editor)
Bleeder - Gene Lazuta   *h*   2684

Collingwood, Max (Pilot)
Ancient Shores - Jack McDevitt   *s*   3014

Collins, Amanda (Paranormal Investigator)
Deadly Friend - Keith Ferrario   *h*   1550

Collins, Camisa (Housewife)
Flesh and Blood - D.A. Fowler   *h*   1625

Collins, Chad (Teenager)
Quozl - Alan Dean Foster   *s*   1615

Collins, Elliot (Professor)
Dark Winds - Graham Watkins *h* 4486

Collins, George (Wealthy)
The Thing That Darkness Hides - Robert
Morgan *h* 3188

Collins, Hap (Worker)
Mucho Mojo - Joe R. Lansdale *h* 2647
Savage Season - Joe R. Lansdale *h* 2649

Collins, Henry (Businessman)
The Sweetheart Season - Karen Joy Fowler *f* 1629

Collins, Jack (Scientist; Magician)
A Calculated Magic - Robert Weinberg *f* 4540

Collins, Jack (Student)
A Logical Magician - Robert Weinberg *f* 4543

Collins, Karen Cecile "Casey" (Student; Time
Traveller)
Islands of Tomorrow - F.M. Busby *s* 640

Collins, Lysander (Military Personnel; Royalty)
Prince of Sparta - Jerry Pournelle *s* 3491

Collins, Maggie (Housewife; Mythical Creature)
The Sweetheart Season - Karen Joy Fowler *f* 1629

Collins, Rikka (Television Personality)
Satellite Night News - Jack Hopkins *s* 2208

Collins, Trudy (Divorced Person)
Savage Season - Joe R. Lansdale *h* 2649

Collun (Adventurer)
Hero's Song - Edith Pattou *f* 3393

Colridge, Samuel Taylor (Writer; Historical Figure)
Walford's Oak - Jill M. Phillips *f* 3433

Colter, Daniel (Journalist; Stowaway)
Into the Deep - Ken Grimwood *s* 1962

Columbar, Santiago (Artist)
Terminal Cafe - Ian McDonald *s* 3023

Columbus, Christopher (Historical Figure; Explorer)
Pastwatch: The Redemption of Christopher Columbus -
Orson Scott Card *s* 726

Columcille (Royalty; Religious)
The Throne of Tara - John Desjarlais *f* 1209

Colville, Randall "Ran" (Spaceman)
Starliner - David Drake *s* 1328

Complain, Roy (Hunter)
Non-Stop - Brian W. Aldiss *s* 46

Compton, Andrew (Serial Killer; Homosexual)
Exquisite Corpse - Poppy Z. Brite *h* 569

The Computer (Artificial Intelligence; Ruler)
*Extreme Paranoia: Nobody Knows the Trouble I've
Shot* - Ken Rolston *s* 3733

Con, Val (Spy)
Carpe Diem - Steve Miller *s* 3113

Conan (Barbarian; Warrior)
Conan and the Treasure of Python - John Maddox
Roberts *f* 3692
The Conan Chronicles - Robert Jordan *f* 2378
Conan of the Red Brotherhood - Leonard
Carpenter *f* 734
Conan, Scourge of the Bloody Coast - Leonard
Carpenter *f* 738
Conan the Formidable - Steve Perry *f* 3420
Conan the Gladiator - Leonard Carpenter *f* 735
Conan the Guardian - Roland J. Green *f* 1882
Conan the Indomitable - Steve Perry *f* 3421
Conan the Outcast - Leonard Carpenter *f* 736
Conan the Relentless - Roland J. Green *f* 1883
Conan the Rogue - John Maddox Roberts *f* 3693
Conan the Savage - Leonard Carpenter *f* 737
Hour of the Dragon - Robert E. Howard *f* 2217

Conan III (Royalty; Child)
Rouse a Sleeping Cat - Dan Crawford *f* 1012

Conan III (Ruler)
A Wild Dog and Lone - Dan Crawford *f* 1014

Concord, Tappuah "Tappy" (Orphan; Mythical
Creature)
The Caterpillar's Question - Piers Anthony *f* 134

Conforti, Alexandra (Vampire)
The Golden - Lucius Shepard *h* 3971

Congemi, Nelson (Doctor)
Duplicates - Andrew Neiderman *h* 3253

Conglomeros (Monster)
Conglomeros - Jesse Browner *f* 595

Conlick, Dennis "Tunnel Rat" (Computer Expert)
The Hacker - Chet Day *h* 1135

Conn (Heir; Twin)
The Heirs of Hammerfell - Marion Zimmer
Bradley *s* 524

Conn (Slave)
The Shining Company - Rosemary Sutcliff *f* 4271

Connaghan, Connor (Artisan; Landlord)
Child of Shadows - John Coyne *h* 1001

Connel, Eileen (Writer)
October - Al Sarrantonio *h* 3870

Connely, Mary (Teacher)
Blood Feud - Sam Siciliano *h* 4005

Conner, Daphne "Dee" (Writer)
Cat's Eye - William W. Johnstone *h* 2332

Conner, Katie (Young Woman)
Dead Lines - John Skipp *h* 4056

Connla (Warrior)
The Isles of the Blest - Morgan Llywelyn *f* 2783

Connor, Islaen (Leader; Telepath)
Call to Arms - P.M. Griffin *s* 1948

Connor, Islaen (Military Personnel)
Fire Planet - P.M. Griffin *s* 1949
Jungle Assault - P.M. Griffin *s* 1950

Constable, Arbitrance (Mythical Creature)
Dragon Rescue - Don Callander *f* 687

Constable, Retruance (Mythical Creature)
Dragon Companion - Don Callander *f* 686

Constance (Sorcerer)
Down Among the Dead Men - Simon R.
Green *f* 1897

Constantine (Political Figure)
Metropolitan - Walter Jon Williams *s* 4650

Constantine, Danny (Journalist)
Archangel - Michael Conner *s* 914

Consul (Diplomat)
Hyperion - Dan Simmons *s* 4034

Conti, Ned (Student)
Madeleine's Ghost - Robert Girardi *h* 1801

Conti, Niccolo Dei (Explorer; Collector)
*The Venetian's Wife: A Strangely Sensual Tale of a
Renaissance Explorer, a Computer, and a
Metamorphosis* - Nick Bantock *f* 282

Converse, Maggie (Journalist)
The Burning Man - Michael Hammond *h* 2023

Conway, H. W. (Police Officer)
Vyrmin - Gene Lazuta *h* 2686

Conway, Hugh (Diplomat)
Shangri-La: The Return to the World of Lost Horizon -
Eleanor Cooney *f* 942

Conway, Michael (Detective—Police)
Vyrmin - Gene Lazuta *h* 2686

Conyers, Pamela (Businesswoman; Fugitive)
The Enigma Variations - John Maddox
Roberts *s* 3694

Coogan, Elihu "Emil Storchesson" (Agent; Criminal)
The Singularity Project - F.M. Busby *s* 641

Cook, Dan (Police Officer)
Waltz with Evil - P.D. Rozzi *h* 3763

Cook, Jeremy (Sailor)
Infernal Affairs - Jane Heller *h* 2118

Cooke, Daniel (Mercenary)
Surface Action - David Drake *s* 1329

Cooley, Dan (Radio Personality)
The Devil and Dan Cooley - Holly Lisle *f* 2766

Coollege, Emma (Spy; Military Personnel)
Galactic MI - Kevin D. Randle *s* 3561

Cooper (Convict)
In the Land of the Dead - K.W. Jeter *h* 2321

Cooper, Arlene (Writer)
The Children of Hamelin - Norman Spinrad *s* 4124

Cooper, David (Writer)
Earthbound - Richard Matheson *h* 2930

Cooper, Ellen (Spouse)
Earthbound - Richard Matheson *h* 2930

Cooper, Marjorie (Scientist)
Father to the Man - John Gribbin *s* 1947

Copley, Isabelle "Izzy" (Artist; Student—College)
Memory and Dream - Charles de Lint *f* 1157

Coppercorn, Jilly (Artist)
The Wishing Well - Charles de Lint *f* 1163

Copplestone, Edward (Scientist)
The Hunger and Ecstasy of Vampires - Brian
Stableford *h* 4144

Coral (Sorceress)
The Goblin Plain War - Carl Miller *f* 3099
The Warrior and the Witch - Carl Miller *f* 3100

Corbett, Blake (Writer)
Shapes - Steve Vance *h* 4425

Cordell (Warrior; Leader)
Feathered Dragon - Douglas Niles *f* 3270

Corder, Rachel (Drifter)
Jackals - Charles L. Grant *h* 1853

Cordery, Noell (Scientist)
The Empire of Fear - Brian Stableford *h* 4143

Cordesman, Jack (Detective—Police)
Incubi - Edward Lee *h* 2700

Corea, Jake (Actor)
Created By - Richard Christian Matheson *h* 2937

Corey, Elizabeth "Betty" (Religious)
The World on Blood - Jonathan Nasaw *h* 3240

Corey, Lewis (Artisan)
Inagehi - Jack Cady *h* 668

Corey, Maggie (Single Parent)
Freeze Frames - Katharine Kerr *s* 2447

Cork, Joe (Mythical Creature; Government Official)
The Faery Convention - Brett Davis *f* 1128

Cork, Stan (Guard)
Tower of Evil - James Kisner *h* 2513

Corlaiys, Aitchley (Farmer; Adventurer)
Cathedral of Thorns - Steven Frankos *f* 1640

Corleau (Hero)
The Sorceress and the Cygnet - Patricia A.
McKillip *f* 3061

Cormac (Royalty)
Wolfking - Bridget Wood *h* 4752

Cormallon, Ran (Wizard)
The Gate of Ivory - Doris Egan *s* 1411
Guilt-Edged Ivory - Doris Egan *s* 1412
Two-Bit Heroes - Doris Egan *s* 1413

Corman, Brian (Businessman)
The Gifted - Jack Caravela *h* 714

Cornelian, Prime (Ruler; Fanatic)
Exile - Al Sarrantonio *s* 3867

Cornish, Francis (Artist; Philanthropist)
The Cornish Trilogy - Robertson Davies *f* 1127

Corrigan, Casey (Teenager)
The Witch of Maple Park - Stephanie S.
  Tolan *f* 4370

Corrigan, Joe (Computer Expert)
Realtime Interrupt - James P. Hogan *s* 2179

Corry, William M. (Military Personnel; Sea Captain)
Starsea Invaders: First Action - G. Harry
  Stine *s* 4215

Corson (Martial Arts Expert)
Mistress of Ambiguities - J.F. Rivkin *f* 3673

Cortez, Pablo (Artist)
Cortez on Jupiter - Ernest Hogan *s* 2172

Cortez, Rosita "Rose" Carmelita (Spouse; Parent)
Timemaster - Robert L. Forward *s* 1598

Cortiss, Sophie (Traveller)
Glenraven - Marion Zimmer Bradley *f* 523

Corvan, Kim (Editor)
Mars Prime - William C. Dietz *s* 1250

Corvan, Rex (Journalist)
Mars Prime - William C. Dietz *s* 1250
Matrix Man - William C. Dietz *s* 1251

Corvino, Dominic (Spy)
Wet Work - Philip Nutman *h* 3320

Corwyn (Apprentice)
The Apprentice - Deborah Talmadge-
  Bickmore *f* 4292

Corwyn (Magician)
Rehearsal for a Renaissance - Douglas W.
  Clark *f* 842

Cory, Patrick (Scientist)
Donovan's Brain/Hauser's Memory - Curt
  Siodmak *h* 4048
Gabriel's Body - Curt Siodmak *h* 4049

Cosmo, Jason (Farmer; Hero)
Dirty Work - Dan McGirt *f* 3035
Jason Cosmo - Dan McGirt *f* 3036

Costa (Psychic)
Speaking Dreams - Severna Park *s* 3384

Costello, Joey (Teenager)
Something Stirs - Charles L. Grant *h* 1856

Costello, T.P. (Journalist)
Evolution's Shore - Ian McDonald *s* 3018

Cotta (Tourist)
The Last World - Christoph Ransmayr *f* 3567

Cotter, Wolf (Journalist)
Mastery - Kelley Wilde *h* 4620

Cottington, Angelica (Naturalist; Teenager)
Lady Cottington's Pressed Fairy Book - Terry
  Jones *f* 2376

Cotto, Grant (Photographer)
Strange Angels - Kathe Koja *h* 2543

Cotton, Alex (Computer Expert)
Brethren - Shawn Ryan *h* 3800

Coughlan, Demeter (Spy; Student)
Man Plus - Frederik Pohl *s* 3464

Coughlin, Charlie (Aged Person)
Dry Skull Dreams - Michael Green *h* 1879

Coughlin, Molly (Nurse)
Dry Skull Dreams - Michael Green *h* 1879

Coulter, Matt (Carpenter)
Shades of Night - Rick Hautala *h* 2087

Count Dracula (Vampire)
Dracula Unbound - Brian W. Aldiss *h* 43

Court, Annalyn Reynolds (Military Personnel)
The Winds of Mars - H.M. Hoover *s* 2204

Courtak, Jarrod (Magician)
The Unicorn Peace - John Lee *f* 2702
The Unicorn Solution - John Lee *f* 2703
The Unicorn War - John Lee *f* 2704

Courvossier, Raoul (Military Personnel; Diplomat)
The Honor of the Queen - David Weber *s* 4523

Coventry, Martina (Writer)
City of Truth - James Morrow *s* 3210

Covington, Diana (Genetically Altered Being; Spy)
Beggars and Choosers - Nancy Kress *s* 2573

Cowal, Bobby (Child)
Deadly Friend - Keith Ferrario *h* 1550

Cowal, Peter (Child)
Deadly Friend - Keith Ferrario *h* 1550

Cowperthwait, Cosmo (Inventor; Naturalist)
The Steampunk Trilogy - Paul Di Filippo *s* 1224

Coxe, Rachel (Witch)
Witches - Kathryn Meyer Griffith *h* 1955

Coyote (Shaman)
Cherokee Bat and the Goat Guys - Francesca Lia
  Block *f* 445

Coyote (Genetically Altered Being; Taxi Driver)
Pollen - Jeff Noon *s* 3293

Coyul (Alien)
The Snake Oil Wars - Parke Godwin *s* 1807

Cozzano, William Anthony (Political Figure;
  Experimental Subject)
Interface - Stephen Bury *s* 638

Craig, Alice (Office Worker)
Down River - Stephen Gallagher *h* 1696

Craig, Donald (Computer Expert)
The Ghost From the Grand Banks - Arthur C.
  Clarke *s* 849

Craig, Edith (Heiress)
Lucifer's Eye - Hugh B. Cave *h* 765

Craig, James Christopher (Technician)
Psychamok - Brian Lumley *h* 2833

Craig, Julie (Young Woman)
Heathen - Shaun Hutson *h* 2244

Cramer, Eddie (Police Officer; Homosexual)
Vampires Anonymous - Jeffrey N.
  McMahan *h* 3070

Cranach, Stella (Artist)
The Schizogenic Man - Raymond Harris *s* 2048

Crandall, Raymond E. Jr. (Teenager; Apprentice)
The Magic Touch - Jody Lynn Nye *f* 3323

Crandall, Samantha "Sam" (Journalist)
The Modular Man - Roger MacBride Allen *s* 65

Crane (Doctor; Spy)
Lake of the Long Sun - Gene Wolfe *s* 4733
Nightside the Long Sun - Gene Wolfe *s* 4734

Crane, Lewis (Scientist)
Richter 10 - Arthur C. Clarke *s* 853

Crane, Mary (Thief)
Psycho - Robert Bloch *h* 440

Crane, Scott (Gambler)
Last Call - Tim Powers *f* 3495

Craobb (Angel)
Moonwise - Greer Ilene Gilman *f* 1799

Craslowe, Hadrian (Psychologist)
Greely's Cove - John Gideon *h* 1784

Craulnober, Elaith (Mythical Creature)
Elfsong - Elaine Cunningham *f* 1046

Craven, Dudley (Farmer)
Blood Kin - Ronald Kelly *h* 2432

Craven, Tammy (Teacher)
Blood Kin - Ronald Kelly *h* 2432

Craven, Wes (Director; Historical Figure)
Wes Craven's New Nightmare - David
  Bergantino *h* 376

Crawford, Jonathan (Health Care Professional)
The Callahan Touch - Spider Robinson *f* 3712

Crawford, Michael (Doctor; Fugitive)
The Stress of Her Regard - Tim Powers *h* 3496

Crawford, Oilvia (Young Woman)
Blood Roots - Richie Tankersley Cusick *h* 1055

Cray, Jennifer (Lawyer; Magician)
One Land, One Duke - Ru Emerson *f* 1452
The Two in Hiding - Ru Emerson *f* 1454

Cray, Robyn (Single Parent; Mythical Creature)
The Two in Hiding - Ru Emerson *f* 1454

Crazy (Writer)
Death Is a Lonely Business - Ray Bradbury *h* 508

Crea (Reanimated Dead)
The Darker Passions: Frankenstein - Amarantha
  Knight *h* 2529

Crecilius, Hallie (Musician)
The Devil's Cradle - Kate Stewart *h* 4204

Cree, Elizabeth (Actress)
The Trial of Elizabeth Cree - Peter Ackroyd *h* 19

Cree, John (Actor)
The Trial of Elizabeth Cree - Peter Ackroyd *h* 19

Creeping Sword (Handicapped; Sorcerer)
Spell of Apocalypse - Mayer Alan Brenner *f* 551

Creighton, Abe "TC" (Military Personnel)
Afrikorps - Bill Dolan *s* 1264
Cobra Curse - Bill Dolan *s* 1265
Iron Horse - Bill Dolan *s* 1266
White Rhino - Bill Dolan *s* 1267

Creighton, Jonathan (Psychologist)
The Barrens - F. Paul Wilson *h* 4682

Crenson, Croyd "The Sleeper" (Genetically Altered
  Being)
Black Trump - George R.R. Martin *s* 2893
Marked Cards - George R.R. Martin *s* 2898
Turn of the Cards - Victor Milan *s* 3098

Creslin (Wizard; Fiance(e))
The Towers of the Sunset - L.E. Modesitt
  Jr. *f* 3139

Crindle (Teacher)
Mysteries of the Word - Stanley Wiater *h* 4616

Cripplemaker, General (Outlaw)
Farewell Horizontal - K.W. Jeter *s* 2320

Crisco, Bungeeman (Military Personnel; Spaceman)
Star Wreck 6: Geek Space Nine - Leah
  Rewolinski *s* 3642

Crispian, Grace (Truck Driver)
Rune - Christopher Fowler *h* 1621

Croaker (Military Personnel; Doctor)
Bleak Seasons - Glen Cook *f* 925

Croaker (Military Personnel; Historian)
Dreams of Steel - Glen Cook *f* 928

Crocken (Peddler; Adventurer)
The Wizard's Shadow - Susan Dexter *f* 1222

Crocker, Ben (Child)
Yellow Moon - David J. Searls *h* 3920

Crocker, Thad (Political Figure)
Yellow Moon - David J. Searls *h* 3920

Crockett, Selena (Heiress)
Archangel - Michael Conner *s* 914

Croft, Michael "Mickey" (Political Figure)
The Stalk - Janet Morris s 3197
Trust Territory - Janet Morris s 3200

Croft, Samantha (Insurance Agent)
Demon Within - Dana Reed h 3589

Cromwell, Willard (Martial Arts Expert; Adventurer)
Indiana Jones and the Sky Pirates - Martin
Caidin f 673

Crone (Shaman)
Shiva Accused: An Adventure of the Ice Age - J.H.
Brennan s 546

Crook, Annie (Clerk)
From Hell - Alan Moore h 3171

Crookleg, Poilar (Adventurer; Religious)
Kingdoms of the Wall - Robert Silverberg s 4014

Cross, Anthony (Scientist; Serial Killer)
Dark Matter - Garfield Reeves-Stevens h 3598

Cross, Jo (Young Woman)
Garden - Matthew J. Costello h 968

Cross, Jordan (Detective—Private)
Dark Channel - Ray Garton h 1725

Cross, Michael (Professor)
Garden - Matthew J. Costello h 968
Wurm - Matthew J. Costello h 973

Cross, Prosper (Minstrel; Wanderer)
The World Next Door - Brad Ferguson s 1548

Cross, Tom (Genetically Altered Being;
Businessman)
Greenhouse - Thomas A. Easton s 1381

Crotalus (Wizard)
Conan, Scourge of the Bloody Coast - Leonard
Carpenter f 738
The Falcon and the Serpent - Cheryl A.
Smith f 4068

Crouper, Martin (Vampire)
Immortal - Jason Nickles h 3265

Crow (Adventurer; Indian)
Crow and Weasel - Barry Lopez f 2800

Crow, Jack (Vampire Hunter)
Vampire$ - John Steakley h 4177

Crow, Titus (Paranormal Investigator)
The Burrowers Beneath - Brian Lumley h 2823
The Transition of Titus Crow - Brian
Lumley h 2838

Crowe, Derek (Writer)
The 37th Mandala - Marc Laidlaw h 2633

Crowell (Martial Arts Expert; Heir)
Iroshi - Cary Osborne s 3370

Crowell, Eve (Parent)
Eden's Eyes - Sean Costello h 976

Crowley (Angel)
*Good Omens: The Nice and Accurate Prophecies of
Agnes Nutter, Witch* - Neil Gaiman f 1693

Crowley (Rogue; Nobleman)
Lady Cottington's Pressed Fairy Book - Terry
Jones f 2376

Crowley, Aleister (Magician)
The Woman between the Worlds - F. Gwynplaine
MacIntyre s 2859

Crowley, Damon (Warrior; Hero)
Evil Triumphant - Michael A. Stackpole s 4149

Croyd (Businessman)
Megalomania - Ian Wallace s 4478

Cruitaire, Christa (Teacher; Musician)
Gossamer Axe - Gael Baudino f 326

Crumley, Elmo (Detective—Private)
Death Is a Lonely Business - Ray Bradbury h 508

Crusher, Beverly (Spaceship Captain; Doctor)
All Good Things. . . - Michael Jan Friedman s 1657

Crusher, Beverly (Doctor; Space Explorer)
Chains of Command - Bill McCay s 2999
Dragon's Honor - Kij Johnson s 2328
Imbalance - V.E. Mitchell s 3124

Crusher, Jack (Spaceship Captain)
Q-Squared - Peter David s 1119

Crusher, Wesley (Student—College; Military
Personnel)
Balance of Power - Dafydd ab Hugh s 6

Crusher, Wesley (Student)
Debtors' Planet - William R. Thompson s 4355

Crygender, "Cry" (Criminal)
Crygender - Thomas T. Thomas s 4349

Crystal (Parent; Mythical Creature)
Troll-Quest - Rose Estes f 1481

Csejthe, Christopher (Vampire; Radio Personality)
One Foot in the Grave - Wm. Mark
Simmons f 4039

Cugnet, Vern (Mechanic; Adventurer)
Stones of the Dalai Lama - Ken Mitchell f 3121

Culaehra (Warrior; Adventurer)
The Sage - Christopher Stasheff f 4164

Culley, Mance (Teenager)
The Living Dark - Stephen Gresham h 1945

Cullinane, Andrea (Wizard)
The Road to Ehvenor - Joel Rosenberg f 3744

Cullinane, Jason (Warrior; Nobleman)
The Road Home - Joel Rosenberg f 3743

Cumber (Mythical Creature; Adventurer)
Dragoncharm - Graham Edwards f 1405

Cumberland, Jack (Thief)
Mongster - Randall Boyll h 506

Cummings, Michael (Banker)
Not Broken, Not Belonging - Randy Fox h 1630

Cummings, Rachael (Artist)
Not Broken, Not Belonging - Randy Fox h 1630

Cummings, Stewart (Police Officer)
Header - Edward Lee h 2699

Cunningham, Dodge (Detective—Private)
Mastery - Kelley Wilde h 4620

Cunningham, Jennifer (Advertising)
The Site - Melisand March h 2878

Curio (Model)
Majyk by Design - Esther Friesner f 1674

Curran, Abigail (Aged Person)
Holy Terror - Josephine Boyle h 498

Curran, Baal (Handicapped; Teenager)
Killobyte - Piers Anthony f 147

Curry, Michael (Architect)
Lasher - Anne Rice h 3650
The Witching Hour - Anne Rice h 3657

Curry, Rowan Mayfair (Doctor; Witch)
Lasher - Anne Rice h 3650

Curtis, Adam (Child)
Baby Doll - Ruby Jean Jensen h 2309

Curtis, Prissy (Child)
Baby Doll - Ruby Jean Jensen h 2309

Curtis, Richard (Financier; Spouse)
Dreamer - Peter James h 2288

Curtis, Samantha "Sam" (Producer)
Dreamer - Peter James h 2288

Curtiss, David (Paranormal Investigator)
Julian's House - Judith Hawkes h 2104

Curtiss, Sally (Paranormal Investigator)
Julian's House - Judith Hawkes h 2104

Custer, George Armstrong (Sorcerer; Historical
Figure)
Devil's Tower - Mark Summer f 4270

Cutler, Philip (Teenager)
Dawn - V.C. Andrews h 120

Cutter (Mythical Creature; Leader)
The Quest Begins - Wendy Pini f 3455

Cutter, Hargrave (Doctor)
Night Thirst - Patrick Whalen h 4597

Cutter, Lance (Investigator)
Mr. Sandman - Lyle Howard h 2214

Cutter, Sam (Paranormal Investigator)
The Burning Man - Michael Hammond h 2023

Cutter, Timothy (Child)
Shadow Dance - Douglas Borton h 473

Cwenn (Royalty; Step-Parent)
Suisan - Phyllis Carol Agins f 32

Cy BerPunk (Computer Expert)
Planet of the Robot Slaves - Harry Harrison s 2058

Cymel (Mythical Creature)
Drum Warning - Jo Clayton f 858

Cypher, Richard "the Seeker" (Wizard; Captive)
Stone of Tears - Terry Goodkind f 1821

Cypher, Richard "the Seeker" (Woodsman; Martial
Arts Expert)
Wizard's First Rule - Terry Goodkind f 1822

D

da Clovina, Antonio (Vampire)
The Vampire Journals - Traci Briery h 557

da Lionghi, Emilio (Criminal)
Humpty Dumpty: An Oval - Damon Knight s 2533

Daae, Christine (Student; Singer)
Phantom - Susan Kay h 2407

Dacham, Klaus (Military Personnel)
Partisan - S. Andrew Swann s 4276

Dacron (Android)
Star Wreck III: Time Warped - Leah
Rewolinski s 3644

Dad (Scientist)
Eva - Peter Dickinson s 1231

Dad (Guard)
Pet Store - M.T. Coffin h 882

Dad (Parent; Political Figure)
Songs of Enchantment - Ben Okri f 3353

Dad (Lawyer)
Thor - Wayne Smith h 4106

Daez, Henry (Landlord)
Makoto - Kelley Wilde h 4619

Dafoe, Mary Lou "Merrilu" (Teenager)
Dragon Sleeping - Craig Shaw Gardner f 1710

Dagda (Immigrant; Adventurer)
The Enchanted Isles - Casey Flynn f 1577
Most Ancient Song - Casey Flynn f 1578

Daggett, Tace (Entertainer)
Night Hunter - Michael Reaves h 3587

Dagon (Android; Murderer)
Dead Boys - Richard Calder s 683

Dahak (Artificial Intelligence)
The Armageddon Inheritance - David
Weber s 4518
Heirs of Empire - David Weber s 4521

Dahl, Lars (Government Official)
Crystal Line - Anne McCaffrey   s   2963

Dahlgren, Mod (Android)
Heart of Red Iron - Phyllis Gotlieb   s   1834

Dahlgren, Sven (Mutant)
Heart of Red Iron - Phyllis Gotlieb   s   1834

Dahmi (Alien)
Alien Eyes - Lynn S. Hightower   s   2143

Dahven (Nobleman)
One Land, One Duke - Ru Emerson   f   1452

Dai, David (Military Personnel; Bodyguard)
Half the Day Is Night - Maureen F.
   McHugh   s   3042

Daily, Jennifer (Detective—Police)
Star Precinct - Kevin D. Randle   s   3564

Daimbert (Wizard)
A Bad Spell in Yurt - C. Dale Brittain   f   573
Daughter of Magic - C. Dale Brittain   f   574
The Witch and the Cathedral - C. Dale
   Brittain   f   576
The Wood Nymph and the Cranky Saint - C. Dale
   Brittain   f   577

Daimler, Rachel (Housewife)
Lullaby - Diane Guest   h   1966

Dain, Benn (Explorer; Student)
Mazeway - Jack Williamson   s   4671

Daine, Truro (Fugitive)
The Night Mayor - Kim Newman   s   3262

Dairine (Wizard)
High Wizardry - Diane Duane   f   1341

Daitaku (Clone)
Fire on the Border - Kevin O'Donnell Jr.   s   3339

Dak, Maanka "Pete Moss" (Alien; Criminal)
The Change - Barry B. Longyear   s   2797

Dakar (Psychic; Religious)
Ships of Merior - Janny Wurts   f   4787

Dakota, Bobbie (Detective—Private)
The Bad Place - Dean R. Koontz   h   2545

Dakota, Julie (Detective—Private)
The Bad Place - Dean R. Koontz   h   2545

Dalamar (Wizard)
Dragons of Summer Flame - Margaret Weis   f   4554

Dalamini, Ming (Smuggler)
Crystal Witness - Kathy Tyers   s   4404

Dale, Ambrose (Businessman)
The Night Inside - Nancy Baker   h   252

DalLierx, Lindon (Administrator)
Shivering World - Kathy Tyers   s   4406

Dalt, Steven (Anthropologist; Spy)
The LaNague Chronicles - F. Paul Wilson   s   4686

Dalt, Steven (Spy)
The Tery - F. Paul Wilson   s   4696

Dalton, Jennifer "Darla" (Young Woman)
Darkman #4: The Face of Death - Randall
   Boyll   h   505

Dalton, Susan Benning (Housewife)
Watchers in the Woods - William W.
   Johnstone   h   2340

Dalton, Tom (Spouse)
Watchers in the Woods - William W.
   Johnstone   h   2340

Damarr, Amala (Noblewoman)
The Mace of Souls - Bruce Fergusson   f   1549

D'Ame, Celia "Lee" (Heroine; Waiter/Waitress)
A Roil of Stars - Don Wismer   s   4722

Damek (Assistant)
The Spirit Gate - Maya Kaathryn Bohnhoff   f   460

Damfels, Sylvan Bon (Nobleman)
Grass - Sheri S. Tepper   s   4335

Damico, Mary (Nurse; Military Personnel)
Dream Baby - Bruce McAllister   s   2948

"Damnbanna" Deil (Musician; Student—High
   School)
Damnbanna - Nancy Springer   f   4131

Dan, Issachar (Nobleman; Warrior)
Wind From a Foreign Sky - Katya Reimann   f   3613

Danan, Elora (Royalty)
Shadow Moon - George Lucas   f   2815

Dandilion (Animal; Storyteller)
Tales From Watership Down - Richard Adams   f   25

Dane, Richard (Businessman)
Cold in July - Joe R. Lansdale   h   2644

Daneam, Penelope (Teenager)
Dominion - Bentley Little   h   2774

Danica (Warrior; Martial Arts Expert)
Canticle - R.A. Salvatore   f   3835

Daniel (Twin)
Dark Father - Tom Piccirilli   h   3435

Daniel (Gambler; Adventurer)
The Door to Ambermere - J. Calvin Pierce   f   3437

Daniels, Aikin (Student—College; Adventurer)
Dreamseeker's Road - Tom Deitz   f   1191

Daniels, Danny (Reanimated Dead)
Deadweight - Robert Devereaux   h   1214

Daniels, Norman (Detective—Police)
Rose Madder - Stephen King   h   2492

Daniels, Rose McLendon (Businesswoman; Abuse
   Victim)
Rose Madder - Stephen King   h   2492

Danilov, Alexander (Vampire)
These Fallen Angels - Wendy Haley   h   1997
This Dark Paradise - Wendy Haley   h   1998

Danilov, Barron (Businessman)
This Dark Paradise - Wendy Haley   h   1998

Danilov, Justin (Teenager)
These Fallen Angels - Wendy Haley   h   1997

Danilov, Sonya (Parent)
These Fallen Angels - Wendy Haley   h   1997

Danio, Kiera (Fugitive; Psychic)
Wheel of Dreams - Salinda Tyson   f   4409

Danirov, Major (Military Personnel)
Suicide Attack - John Sievert   s   4007

Danner, Hannah (Military Personnel)
Ammonite - Nicola Griffith   s   1956

Dannerman, Jim Daniel "Dan" (Spy; Spaceman)
The Other End of Time - Frederik Pohl   s   3466

Danny-boy (Artist)
The City, Not Long After - Pat Murphy   s   3227

d'Anton, Charlotte Marie (Slave; Time Traveller)
The Virgin and the Dinosaur - R. Garcia y
   Robertson   s   1705

Danu (Royalty)
The Enchanted Isles - Casey Flynn   f   1577

Danya (Teenager)
Vampire Diary: The Embrace - Robert
   Weinberg   h   4549

Danziger (Spaceman; Castaway)
Earth 2 - Melissa Crandall   s   1010

Danziger, E.E. (Scientist)
From Time to Time - Jack Finney   s   1564

Dara (Wanderer)
Ancestral Hungers - Scott Baker   h   254

Dara (Telepath)
Feather Stroke - Sydney J. Van Scyoc   f   4418

Dara (Magician; Servant)
Guardian's Key - Anne Logston   f   2788

Dara (Royalty)
Krispos of Videssos - Harry Turtledove   f   4389

Darcalus (Wizard)
King of the Dead - Gene DeWeese   h   1218

Darch, Jack (Prospector)
The Specialist - Wynne Whiteford   s   4611

Darcourt, Simon (Religious; Scholar)
The Cornish Trilogy - Robertson Davies   f   1127

Darcy, Jade (Martial Arts Expert; Warrior)
Jade Darcy and the Zen Pirates - Stephen
   Goldin   s   1812

Darcy, Lord Lord (Detective)
A Study in Sorcery - Michael Kurland   f   2585

Darffot, Tex "Bear" (Spirit; Activist)
Tex and Molly in the Afterlife - Richard
   Grant   f   1863

Darian (Angel)
Angelwalk: A Modern Fable - Roger
   Elwood   f   1446

Darin of Culverne (Child; Religious)
Children of the Blood - Michelle Sagara   f   3824
Lady of Mercy - Michelle Sagara   f   3826

Dario, Ramon (Police Officer)
Senor Vivo and the Coca Lord - Louis de
   Bernieres   f   1136

Darith (Hero)
Blood of the Colyn Muir - Paul Edwin
   Zimmer   f   4852

Darius (Religious)
Elephantasm - Tanith Lee   h   2711

Darius (Ruler)
Fractal Mode - Piers Anthony   f   140

Darius (Knight)
Kaz the Minotaur - Richard A. Knaak   f   2522

Darius (Ruler)
Virtual Mode - Piers Anthony   f   160

Dark Lord (Wizard)
Outcasts - Clayton Emery   f   1456

Darke, Makellen (Genetically Altered Being;
   Psychic)
Dancer of the Sixth - Michelle Shirey
   Crean   s   1017

Darker, Alex (Divorced Person)
The Chymical Wedding - Lindsay Clarke   f   856

Darkhorse (Demon)
The Crystal Dragon - Richard A. Knaak   f   2517

Darkling, Katastrofa "Kathy" (Police Officer;
   Mythical Creature)
Riverrun - S.P. Somtow   f   4117

Darkwind (Scout)
Winds of Change - Mercedes Lackey   f   2627

Darkwind (Spy; Scout)
Winds of Fate - Mercedes Lackey   f   2628

Darkwind (Scout)
Winds of Fury - Mercedes Lackey   f   2629

Darling, William Somers "Whip" (Fisherman)
Beast - Peter Benchley   h   362

d'Armand, Magnus Gallowglass (Adventurer;
   Psychic)
A Wizard in Absentia - Christopher Stasheff   s   4172

d'Armand, Magnus Gallowglass (Wizard;
   Revolutionary)
A Wizard in Mind - Christopher Stasheff   s   4173

di Hoa, Barry (Pilot; Mentally Ill Person)
The Voices of Heaven - Frederik Pohl s 3470

di Medusa, Nicoletta Vittorini (Vampire)
The Vampire Princess - Michael Romkey h 3738

di Rienzi, Angelica (Anthropologist; Religious)
Waking the Moon - Elizabeth Hand f 2028

Diamond, Tal (Alien; Military Personnel)
City of Diamond - Jane Emerson s 1450

Diane (Writer)
Amazon: A Novel - Barbara G. Walker f 4474

Diaspad (Royalty)
The Work of the Sun - Teresa Edgerton f 1402

Diate, Emilio (Dancer)
Traitors - Kristine Kathryn Rusch f 3786

Diaz, Lupe (Drifter)
The Orchid Eater - Marc Laidlaw h 2635

Diaz, Sal (Drug Dealer)
The Orchid Eater - Marc Laidlaw h 2635

Dibbler, Cut-Me-Own-Throat (Businessman)
Moving Pictures - Terry Pratchett f 3505

Dibiaja, Mpu (Shaman)
The Painted Alphabet - Diana Darling f 1096

Dickinson, Emily (Writer; Historical Figure)
The Steampunk Trilogy - Paul Di Filippo s 1224

Dickory, Tracy (Animal; Telepath)
Time and the Clock Mice, Etcetera - Peter
Dickinson f 1232

Didge (Magician)
The End-of-Everything Man - Tom De
Haven f 1146

Didi "Deeds" (Robot; Researcher)
Circle of One - Eric James Fullilove s 1685

Diedrich (Disembodied Personality)
Satellite Night News - Jack Hopkins s 2208

Diego (Gunfighter; Time Traveller)
Time: The Semi-Final Frontier - Lionel
Fenn s 1545

Diego y Rey, Eduardo (Vampire)
Bloodshift - Garfield Reeves-Stevens h 3597

Diehrenn (Alien; Writer)
Encounter with Tiber - Buzz Aldrin s 52

Diest, Vernon (Undertaker)
The Moons of Summer - S.K. Epperson h 1471

Dietrich, Elinor (Aged Person)
Revenant - Melanie Tem h 4329

Dietrich, Martin (Military Personnel)
Darkness on the Ice - Lois Tilton h 4367

Dieudonee, Genevieve (Vampire; Health Care
Professional)
Anno Dracula - Kim Newman h 3259

Dieudonne, Genevieve (Vampire)
Drachenfels - Jack Yeovil f 4800

DiFalco, Tiraena (Military Personnel; Time
Traveller)
Legacy - Steve White s 4609

Digby, Digger (Mountain Man)
The World Next Door - Brad Ferguson s 1548

Digging Woman (Indian)
Walking Wolf - Nancy A. Collins h 908

Digonness, Peter (Businessman)
The Expediter - J. Brian Clarke s 855

diGriz, Jim (Criminal; Adventurer)
The Stainless Steel Rat Goes to Hell - Harry
Harrison s 2059

DiGriz, Jim (Criminal)
The Stainless Steel Rat Sings the Blues - Harry
Harrison s 2060

Diko (Time Traveller)
Pastwatch: The Redemption of Christopher Columbus -
Orson Scott Card s 726

Dikobe, Pauline (Scholar; Spacewoman)
Foragers - Charles Oberndorf s 3334

Diliani (Mythical Creature)
Kirins: The Flight of the Ain - James D.
Priest f 3535

Dillon (Prisoner; Miner)
Alien 3 - Alan Dean Foster s 1599

Dillon, Lan (Police Officer)
Reunion on Neverend - John E. Stith s 4233

Dillon, Ronny (Artist; Telepath)
Dreambuilder - Tom Deitz f 1190

Dillon, Ronny (Orphan; Student—High School)
Soulsmith - Tom Deitz f 1193

Dillon, Ronny (Artist; Telepath)
Wordwright - Tom Deitz f 1196

Dimblethum (Mythical Creature)
Into the Land of the Unicorns - Bruce
Coville f 989

Dinaos (Nobleman; Artist)
The Belly of the Wolf - R.A. MacAvoy f 2845

Dingletoon, Tish (Animal)
The Cockroaches of Stay More - Donald
Harington f 2033

Dinsman, Angela (Troubleshooter; Anthropologist)
Reefsong - Carol Severance s 3933

Dinsmuir, Harold "Dirty" (Scientist)
Insatiable - David Dvorkin h 1370

Diogenes, Romanus (Ruler)
Shards of Empire - Susan Shwartz f 4003

Dion (Magician; Student)
Mage Heart - Jane Routley f 3754

Dion (Martial Arts Expert; Healer; Twin)
Shadow Leader - Tara K. Harper f 2039

Dion (Martial Arts Expert; Healer)
Wolfwalker - Tara K. Harper f 2040

Dions (Religious; Psychic)
Throne of Isis - Judith Tarr f 4305

Dios, Warden (Police Officer; Leader)
The Gap into Ruin: This Day All Gods Die - Stephen
R. Donaldson s 1273

Dirk (Musician)
The Abraxis Marvel Circus - Stephen Leigh f 2721

Dirona (Royalty; Sorceress)
Search for the Starblade - Keith Taylor f 4315

d'Iste, Tiran (Mercenary; Magician)
Dark Mirror, Dark Dreams - Sharon Green f 1889
Silver Princess, Golden Knight - Sharon
Green f 1891

d'Iste, Tiran (Ruler; Magician)
Wind Whispers, Shadow Shouts - Sharon
Green f 1892

DiThorn, Bram (Nobleman; Mythical Creature)
The Seventh Sentinel - Mary Kirchoff f 2506

DiThorn, Guerrand (Wizard)
The Seventh Sentinel - Mary Kirchoff f 2506

Dittimore, Jeffry (Lawyer)
The Land of Nod - Mark A. Clements h 874

Dittrich, Robert "Bobby" (Computer Expert)
Forests of the Night - S. Andrew Swann s 4275

Diver Dan (Serial Killer)
Bloodletter - Warren Newton Beath h 350

Divine Endurance (Animal; Android)
Flowerdust - Gwyneth Jones s 2353

Dixon, Benjamin (Vampire Hunter; Religious)
Blood Lust - Ron Dee h 1183

Dixon, Stephanie (Doctor)
Kaleidoscope Eyes - Graham Watkins h 4487

Dixon, Travis (Publisher)
Night Brothers - Sidney Williams h 4639

d'jehn, Tahl (Alien; Spaceship Captain)
The Alien Dark - Diana G. Gallagher s 1695

Dnivtopun (Alien)
The Children's Hour - Jerry Pournelle s 3485

Dob (Alien)
Back to the Time Trap - Keith Laumer s 2661

Doban (Prehistoric Human; Child)
Shiva: An Adventure of the Ice Age - J.H.
Brennan f 548

Dobbs (Public Relations)
Kill Crazy - L.S. Riker s 3667

Dobbs, Charles "Sugar" Franklin (Professor)
The Healing of Crossroads - Nick
O'Donohoe f 3340

Dobbs, Charles "Sugar" Franklin (Professor;
Veterinarian)
The Magic and the Healing - Nick
O'Donohoe f 3341

Dobbs, J.R. "BoB" (Religious; Activist)
*Reality Is What You Can Get Away With: An
Illustrated Screenplay* - Robert Anton
Wilson s 4699

Dobbs, Karl (Time Traveller)
The Lincoln Hunters - Wilson Tucker s 4378

Dobbs, Melvin (Magician)
Resurrection Dreams - Richard Laymon h 2682

Doc (Revolutionary)
Dragons Past - Gary Gentile s 1758

Doctor (Astronaut)
Eden - Stanislaw Lem s 2730

Dodge, Allison (Activist)
Gaia's Toys - Rebecca Ore s 3362

Dodger (Mutant; Computer Expert)
Choose Your Enemies Carefully - Robert N.
Charrette s 786
Find Your Own Truth - Robert N. Charrette f 787
Shadowrun: Never Deal with a Dragon - Robert N.
Charrette f 792

Dog-Woman (Animal Trainer)
Sexing the Cherry - Jeanette Winterson f 4719

Doggie (Robot)
Daughter of Elysium - Joan Slonczewski s 4062

Dohen, Spike (Restaurateur)
Skinny Legs and All - Tom Robbins f 3684

Doheny, Mike (Engineer; Administrator)
Sunstroke - David Kagan s 2389

Doheny, Shannon (Teenager)
Elvira: Transylvania 90210 - Elvira h 1445

Doland, Jane (Banker)
Flying Dutch - Tom Holt f 2193

Dollar, John (Sea Captain)
John Dollar - Marianne Wiggins h 4617

Dolmi, Yarkol (Doctor)
Spirits of Cavern and Hearth - M. Coleman
Easton f 1380

Dolph (Royalty)
Isle of View - Piers Anthony f 145

Domenico, Father (Religious; Magician)
The Devil's Day - James Blish h 426

Domerc (Student—College; Wizard)
Lost in Translation - Margaret Ball f 265

Dredd, Joseph "Judge" (Police Officer; Fugitive)
Judge Dredd - Neal Barrett Jr.   s   306

Dreen (Religious)
The Hands of Lyr - Andre Norton   f   3308

Drew (Musician)
The Making of a Monster - Gail Petersen   h   3430

Drew, Jonathan (Police Officer)
Night Blood - Eric Flanders   h   1567

Drew, Laura (Saloon Hostess; Lover)
The Unseen - Joseph Citro   h   838

Drexel, David (Government Official)
Firelance - David Mace   s   2851

Dreyer, Sigmund (Detective—Private)
Dydeetown World - F. Paul Wilson   s   4684

Drib (Student; Chimneysweep)
The Knights of Cawdor - Mike Jefferies   f   2302

Dribble (Genetically Altered Being)
Clipjoint - Wilhelmina Baird   s   248

Driscoll, Guy (Journalist)
The Moons of Summer - S.K. Epperson   h   1471

Driver, Greg (Actor)
Horrorshow - David Darke   h   1093

Drizzt Do'Urden (Mythical Creature; Adventurer)
Passage to Dawn - R.A. Salvatore   f   3843

Droagn, Endark (Alien; Telepath)
Lair of the Cyclops - Allen L. Wold   s   4725

D'Rosselin, Jens Metadi Jessan (Teenager; Heir)
The Long Hunt - Debra Doyle   s   1295

Drosselmeier, Christian Elias "Godfather" (Artisan)
Nutcracker - E.T.A. Hoffmann   f   2171

Drulethen "Dru" (Mythical Creature; Sorcerer)
The Qualinesti - Paul B. Thompson   f   4353

Drumheller, Thorn (Mythical Creature; Wizard)
Shadow Moon - George Lucas   f   2815

Drummond, Cathan (Knight; Companion)
The Bastard Prince - Katherine Kurtz   f   2588

Drummond, John (Detective—Homicide; Vampire)
At Sword's Point - Scott MacMillan   f   2861

Drummond, John (Detective—Homicide)
Knights of the Blood - Scott MacMillan   f   2862

Drumon (Artisan)
The Forge of Virtue - Lynn Abbey   f   14

Drusilla (Sorceress)
The Fourth Guardian - Ronald Anthony
   Cross   s   1032

Dryden, Thatcher (Businessman)
Heathern - Jack Womack   s   4747

Dryhope, Kate "Kittock" (Parent)
A History Maker - Alasdair Gray   s   1874

Dryhope, Wat (Warrior; Hero)
A History Maker - Alasdair Gray   s   1874

Dryke, Mikhail (Businessman)
The Quiet Pools - Michael P. Kube-
   McDowell   s   2583

Du Lucent, Andrea (Royalty)
The War of the Sky Lords - John Brosnan   s   589

du Mond, Paul (Apprentice)
The Fire Rose - Mercedes Lackey   f   2608

Dubchek, Jackson (Historian; Time Traveller)
Stranded! - Warren Norwood   s   3317

Duberville, Myron (Teenager; Genius)
Outer Space and All That Junk - Mel
   Gilden   s   1789

Dubhain (Mythical Creature)
Faery in Shadow - C.J. Cherryh   f   801

DuBois, Ned (Astronaut)
Firestar - Michael Flynn   s   1579

Ducane, Wilhemina "Willie" (Child)
Demon Dance - T. Chris Martindale   h   2904

Ducas, Leo (Military Personnel)
Shards of Empire - Susan Shwartz   f   4003

Duffy, Karen (Young Woman)
Boundaries - T.M. Wright   h   4774

Dug (Teenager; Adventurer)
Demons Don't Dream - Piers Anthony   f   138

Dugan, Andrew (Artist)
My Soul to Take - Steven G. Spruill   s   4137

Duin, Mael (Outcast; Wanderer)
The Voyage of Mael Duin's Curragh - Patricia
   Aakhus   f   1

Duinngan, Will (Lawyer)
Darkborn - Matthew J. Costello   h   966

Duke, Bob (Stock Broker; Werewolf)
The Wild - Whitley Strieber   h   4262

Duke, Cindy (Spouse)
The Wild - Whitley Strieber   h   4262

Duke, Kevin Thomas (Child)
The Wild - Whitley Strieber   h   4262

Duke, Nicholas (Journalist)
Majestic - Whitley Strieber   s   4260

Dulac, Will (Composer)
A Call to Arms - Alan Dean Foster   s   1601

Dulaine, Dirk (Sidekick)
A Wizard in War - Christopher Stasheff   s   4174

Dulcimer (Alien; Pilot)
Transcendence - Charles Sheffield   s   3963

DuMar, Theresa "T.J." Jr. (Teenager)
T.J.'s Ghost - Shirley Climo   h   876

Dumery of Shiphaven (Child; Traveller)
The Blood of a Dragon - Lawrence Watt-
   Evans   f   4496

Dun Lady's Jess (Animal; Young Woman)
Dun Lady's Jess - Doranna Durgin   f   1368

Dunbar, Lane (Teenager)
The Stake - Richard Laymon   h   2683

Dunbar, Larry (Writer)
The Stake - Richard Laymon   h   2683

Dunbar, Maggie (Teacher)
Dark Tide - Elizabeth Forrest   h   1584

Dunbar, Sheik (Military Personnel)
Starstrike - W. Michael Gear   s   1743

Duncan, William St.-George (Revolutionary)
Dayworld Breakup - Philip Jose Farmer   s   1502

Dunham, Arthur "Art" (Businessman)
The Rebirth of Wonder - Lawrence Watt-
   Evans   f   4502

Dunjer, Tom (Security Officer)
Specterworld - Isidore Haiblum   s   1990

Dunkle, Simon (Director)
Flicker - Theodore Roszak   h   3752

Dunladry, Duncan (Royalty; Heir—Dispossessed)
Caledon of the Mists - Deborah Turner
   Harris   f   2045

Dunladry, Mhairi (Royalty; Heiress—Dispossessed)
Caledon of the Mists - Deborah Turner
   Harris   f   2045

Dunladry, Mhairi (Royalty)
The Queen of Ashes - Deborah Turner
   Harris   f   2046

Dunlap, Gordon (Journalist)
The Totem - David Morrell   h   3193

Dunlet, Kate (Professor)
Deep Quarry - John E. Stith   s   4230

dunMheric, Dymorin Rhomandi (Royalty)
Ring of Lightning - Jane S. Fancher   f   1498

dunMheric, Mikhyel Rhomandi (Royalty)
Ring of Lightning - Jane S. Fancher   f   1498

dunMheric, Nikaenor "Nikki" Rhomandi (Royalty)
Ring of Lightning - Jane S. Fancher   f   1498

Dunn, Jim (FBI Agent)
The Ebon Mask - Richard Lee Byers   h   652

Dunn, Rick (Architect)
The Ascending - T.M. Wright   h   4773

Dunreith, Cassandra "Cass" (Martial Arts Expert;
   Writer)
Dragon Moon - Chris Claremont   f   839

Dunworthy, James (Professor)
Doomsday Book - Connie Willis   s   4672

Dupin, C. Auguste (Detective)
The Lighthouse at the End of the World - Stephen
   Marlowe   h   2886

Dupree, Lorelle (Demon)
The New Neighbor - Ray Garton   h   1728

Dur (Sorcerer)
Drum Warning - Jo Clayton   f   858

Dura (Genetically Altered Being; Settler)
Flux - Stephen Baxter   s   331

Duran, Michael (Artist)
Diary of a Vampire - Gary Bowen   h   492

Durancy, Abraham (Scientist; Architect)
Queen City Jazz - Kathleen Ann Goonan   s   1825

Duratan (Historian)
Flight of Vengeance - Andre Norton   f   3306

Durham, Paul (Computer Expert)
Permutation City - Greg Egan   s   1414

Duroc, Roger (Agent; Religious)
Comeback Tour: The Sky Belongs to the Stars - Jack
   Yeovil   s   4798

Durvash (Time Traveller; Alien)
Man-Kzin Wars V - Larry Niven   s   3284

Dutton, Brian (Businessman)
The 7th Guest - Matthew J. Costello   h   963

Duvall, Katherine (Detective—Homicide)
Dark Matter - Garfield Reeves-Stevens   h   3598

Duvet, Berthe (Servant; Writer)
The Porcelain Dove - Delia Sherman   f   3974

Dvorak, Jason (Administrator; Architect)
Assemblers of Infinity - Kevin J. Anderson   s   83

Dvorak, Teresa (Real Estate Agent)
Frostwing - Richard A. Knaak   f   2520

Dwago (Cult Member)
Graythings - Pat Graversen   h   1871

Dweller (Alien)
The Source - Brian Lumley   h   2837

Dwiri (Telepath)
OtherWhere - Margaret Wander Bonanno   s   464

Dwyer (Librarian)
Painted Devil - Michael Bedard   f   354

Dy-Dybo (Alien; Ruler)
Fossil Hunter - Robert J. Sawyer   s   3885

Dycek, Rachel (Doctor)
Climbing Olympus - Kevin J. Anderson   s   85

Dyckman, Alicia "Lish" (Producer; Divorced
   Person)
The Swords of Zinjaban - L. Sprague de
   Camp   s   1143

Elizebith of Morea (Sorceress)
Dark Divide - Mark Acres   f   20
Outcasts - Clayton Emery   f   1456
The Stone of Time - Rose Estes   f   1480

Elk Charm (Prehistoric Human; Indian)
People of the Fire - W. Michael Gear   f   1738

Ell, Pe (Murderer)
The Druid of Shannara - Terry Brooks   f   580

Ella (Teenager)
I Feel Like the Morning Star - Gregory
  Maguire   s   2868

Ellair, Noble (Doctor)
The Night Seasons - J.N. Williamson   h   4666

Ellel, Quince (Witch)
A Plague of Angels - Sheri S. Tepper   f   4337

Ellerman, Amy (Student)
The Quiet - Patrick Billings   h   396

Ellington, Dan (Religious)
The Blood of the Lamb - Thomas F.
  Monteleone   h   3150

Ellington, Lucas (Parent)
The Kill Riff - David J. Schow   h   3903

Elliot, Dan (Journalist)
Beneath Still Waters - Matthew J. Costello   h   964

Elliott, Kate (Teenager)
Vision Quest - Pamela F. Service   f   3930

Ellis, Cander (Spy; Martial Arts Expert)
Shadow of the Crown - Craig Mills   f   3119

Ellis, Wilson (Detective—Private)
Forget Me Not - Gene Lazuta   h   2685

Elmara (Adventurer; Religious)
Elminster: The Making of a Mage - Ed
  Greenwood   f   1941

Elminster (Sorcerer; Royalty)
Elminster: The Making of a Mage - Ed
  Greenwood   f   1941

Elof (Magician; Blacksmith)
The Forge in the Forest - Michael Scott
  Rohan   f   3731

Eloise (Hunter)
Nicoji - M. Shayne Bell   s   358

Elphaba (Witch; Activist)
*Wicked: The Life and Times of the Wicked Witch of
  the West* - Gregory Maguire   f   2869

Elric (Child)
The Book of Brendan - Ann Curry   f   1049

Elric (Warrior; Ruler)
Elric: Song of the Black Sword - Michael
  Moorcock   f   3167

Elric (Warrior; Royalty)
The Fortress of the Pearl - Michael
  Moorcock   f   3168
The Revenge of the Rose - Michael
  Moorcock   f   3170

Elric (Knight)
The Spellkey Trilogy - Ann Downer   f   1285

Elric of Melnibone (Royalty; Wizard)
Tales of the White Wolf - Edward E.
  Kramer   f   2566

Elroy, Shannon (Guard)
Tower of Evil - James Kisner   h   2513

Elsie (Mythical Creature)
Galatea in 2-D - Aaron Allston   f   73

Elspet (Witch)
Coven - Steven William Rimmer   h   3668

Elspeth (Spouse)
Thomas the Rhymer - Ellen Kushner   f   2596

Elspeth (Heir; Government Official)
Winds of Change - Mercedes Lackey   f   2627
Winds of Fate - Mercedes Lackey   f   2628

Elspeth (Magician; Heiress)
Winds of Fury - Mercedes Lackey   f   2629

Elvira (Young Woman)
Elvira: Transylvania 90210 - Elvira   h   1445

Elvis (Robot; Spouse)
The Man in the Moon Must Die - Jeff
  Bredenberg   s   545

Elyssa (Sorceress)
Konrad - David Ferring   f   1551

Ember (Parent; Leader)
Isle of Woman - Piers Anthony   f   146

Ember, Annie (Teenager; Servant)
Elephantasm - Tanith Lee   h   2711

Emberella (Royalty)
Witches Abroad - Terry Pratchett   f   3511

Emerson, Dirk (Teenager)
Demon's Fright - Penelope Banka Kreps   h   2571

Emerson, Ian (Professor)
University - Bentley Little   h   2778

Emily "Emmy" (Child)
Santa's Twin - Dean R. Koontz   f   2556

Emma (Young Woman)
Westlin Wind - Charles de Lint   f   1161

Emory, Ariane (Scientist; Political Figure)
Cyteen - C.J. Cherryh   s   798

Emrys (Child; Psychic)
The Lost Years of Merlin - T.A. Barron   f   309

Emrys (Psychic)
Merlin and the Dragons - Jane Yolen   f   4812

Emshander IV (Ruler)
Upland Outlaws - Dave Duncan   f   1362

Emshander V (Ruler)
The Living God - Dave Duncan   f   1354
The Stricken Field - Dave Duncan   f   1360

Endang (Scholar; Slave)
Flowerdust - Gwyneth Jones   s   2353

Enderton, Paddy (Spaceman)
Godspeed - Charles Sheffield   s   3955

Endicott, Rob (Telepath; Worker)
The Gifted - Jack Caravela   h   714

Endymion, Raul (Prisoner; Writer)
Endymion - Dan Simmons   f   4030

Enemy (Alien)
Cold Fire - Dean R. Koontz   h   2546

L'Enfant, Terrance (Administrator)
Labyrinth of Night - Allen Steele   s   4183

Engel, Emily (Patient)
Zod Wallop - William Browning Spencer   h   4123

Engle, Kivrin (Student; Time Traveller)
Doomsday Book - Connie Willis   s   4672

Engleman, Carolyn (Businesswoman)
Cambio Bay - Kate Wilhelm   f   4624

Enkidu (Homosexual; Boyfriend)
Mirage - Perry Brass   s   543

Ennin, Willie (Cook)
Raven - Charles L. Grant   h   1854

Ennesstheh (Alien)
Cannon's Orb - L. Warren Douglas   s   1279

E'non, Caelan (Gladiator; Psychic)
Reign of Shadows - Deborah Chester   f   819

Enrique, Dom (Explorer)
Mansions of Darkness - Chelsea Quinn
  Yarbro   h   4796

Ensi (Spirit; Martial Arts Expert)
The Glaive - Cary Osborne   s   3369

Entragion, Collie (Police Officer)
Desperation - Stephen King   h   2482
The Regulators - Richard Bachman   h   240

Erato (Mythical Creature)
Zeus and Co. - David Lee Jones   f   2344

Erek (Sorceress)
Hall of Whispers - Mike Jefferies   f   2300

Erelvar (Nobleman; Religious)
A Call to Arms - Thomas K. Martin   f   2901
A Two-Edged Sword - Thomas K. Martin   f   2902

Ergates (Animal)
Feersum Endjinn - Iain M. Banks   s   274

Erhsham, Ling (Space Explorer)
The Transmigration of Souls - William
  Barton   s   318

Erica (Lesbian)
Clicking Stones - Nancy Tyler Glenn   s   1802

Erickson, Dirk (Vampire)
The Informers - Brett Easton Ellis   h   1426

Erickson, Richard (Lawman)
Shadows Fall - Simon R. Green   f   1903

Eride "Thorn" (Religious; Martial Arts Expert)
Thorn and Needle - Paul B. Thompson   f   4354

Erik (Teenager)
The Lone Sentinel - Jo Dereske   s   1206

Erik (Child; Musician)
Phantom - Susan Kay   h   2407

Erin of Elliath (Warrior; Healer)
Chains of Darkness, Chains of Light - Michelle
  Sagara   f   3823
Into the Dark Lands - Michelle Sagara   f   3825
Lady of Mercy - Michelle Sagara   f   3826

Erkenbert (Religious; Leader)
One King's Way - Harry Harrison   s   2057

Erland (Royalty)
Prince of the Blood - Raymond E. Feist   f   1535

Ernst, Jeffrey (Child)
Twistor - John Cramer   s   1008

Errenthorp, Reynaldo (Businessman)
The Third Eagle: Lessons Along a Minor String - R.A.
  MacAvoy   s   2848

Erskine, Cheryl (Child)
In a Dark Dream - Charles L. Grant   h   1851

Erskine, Glenn (Police Officer)
In a Dark Dream - Charles L. Grant   h   1851

Erskine, Harry (Psychic)
Burial - Graham Masterton   h   2921

Erwyn (Sorcerer; Royalty)
Go Quest, Young Man - K.B. Bogen   f   455

Erzsebet (Noblewoman; Vampire)
*The Secret Weavers: Stories of the Fantastic by Latin
  American Women* - Marjorie Agosin   f   33

Erzul, Ti Sandra (Political Figure)
Moving Mars - Greg Bear   s   345

Escargot, Theophile (Cook; Adventurer)
The Stone Giant - James P. Blaylock   f   425

Eschar, William (Wizard)
A Plague of Sorcerers - Mary Frances
  Zambreno   f   4831

Eschbach, Johan (Professor; Spy)
Of Tangible Ghosts - L.E. Modesitt Jr.   f   3135

Escott, Charles (Detective—Private)
Blood on the Water - P.N. Elrod   h   1437
Bloodlist - P.N. Elrod   h   1438
Fire in the Blood - P.N. Elrod   h   1441

F

Fancy, Jan "Jeanette" (Femme Fatale)
Succumb - Ron Dee *h* 1187

Fanuilh (Mythical Creature; Companion)
Fanuilh - Daniel Hood *f* 2198
Wizard's Heir - Daniel Hood *f* 2199

Farhallen, Annadale (Empath)
Children of Enchantment - Anne Kelleher
　Bush *f* 644

Farhallen, Nydia (Psychic)
Daughter of Prophecy - Anne Kelleher Bush *f* 645

Farkas, Victor (Genetically Altered Being)
Hot Sky at Midnight - Robert Silverberg *s* 4013

Farlan, Tessa (Businesswoman)
Reunion on Neverend - John E. Stith *s* 4233

Farley, Heather (Student; Telepath)
Serpent's Gift - A.C. Crispin *s* 1023

Faro (Slave)
If I Pay Thee Not in Gold - Piers Anthony *f* 144

Faron, Theodore (Historian; Revolutionary)
The Children of Men - P.D. James *f* 2287

Faronya, Kelmer (Journalist)
The Regiment's War - John Dalmas *s* 1072

Faronya, Tain (Prisoner)
The Kalif's War - John Dalmas *s* 1068

Farraday (Public Relations)
Silicon Embrace - John Shirley *s* 3996

Farraday, Morgan (Administrator)
The Snows of Jaspre - Mary Caraker *s* 713

Farrand, Louis (Religious)
Garden - Matthew J. Costello *h* 968

Farree (Alien)
Dare to Go A-Hunting - Andre Norton *s* 3302

Farrell (Hippie)
The Folk of the Air - Peter S. Beagle *f* 336

Farrell, Gene (Doctor)
Kiss of Death - Daniel Rhodes *h* 3649

Farrell, Lizbeth (Secretary)
Homecoming - Matthew J. Costello *h* 969

Farrell, Simon (Businessman)
Homecoming - Matthew J. Costello *h* 969

Farren (Wizard)
Touched by Magic - Doranna Durgin *f* 1369

Farringer, Gail (Artist)
Demon Shadows - Michael B. Sirota *h* 4051

Farris, Duffy (Hotel Worker)
The Jimjams - Michael Green *h* 1880

Farris, Rose (Hotel Worker)
The Jimjams - Michael Green *h* 1880

Farseer, FitzChivalry "Fitz" (Bastard Son; Psychic)
Assassin's Apprentice - Robin Hobb *f* 2151
Royal Assassin - Robin Hobb *f* 2152

Farseer, Verity (Psychic; Royalty)
Royal Assassin - Robin Hobb *f* 2152

Farthing, Jacob (Parent; Security Officer)
Harm's Way - Colin Greenland *s* 1934

Farthing, Sophie (Runaway; Heiress—Lost)
Harm's Way - Colin Greenland *s* 1934

Faslorn (Alien)
The Sails of Tau Ceti - Michael McCollum *s* 3002

Fasner, Holt "The Dragon" (Administrator)
The Gap into Power: A Dark and Hungry God Arises - Stephen R. Donaldson *s* 1272

Fast, Barry (Teacher)
Firestar - Michael Flynn *s* 1579

Fastet, Meer (Judge; Revolutionary)
Exile - Michael P. Kube-McDowell *s* 2582

Fath, Jaro (Foundling; Spaceman)
Night Lamp - Jack Vance *s* 4422

f'ath, Riitha (Alien; Scientist)
The Alien Dark - Diana G. Gallagher *s* 1695

Father Christmas (Thief)
The Widowmaker - Mike Resnick *s* 3640

Faulk, Carol (Spaceship Captain; Military Personnel)
A Darker Geometry - Mark O. Martin *s* 2900

Faulkner, Sully (Student—College)
An Exaltation of Larks - Robert Reed *s* 3595

Faulkner, William (Writer; Pilot)
The Wild Blue and the Gray - William
　Sanders *s* 3853

Faust, Johann (Thief; Imposter)
If at Faust You Don't Succeed - Roger
　Zelazny *f* 4841

Faust, Prometheus "Bruce Payne" (Religious)
Symphony - Adrian Savage *h* 3880

Fava (Girlfriend; Prehistoric Human)
Serpent Catch - Dave Wolverton *s* 4745

Fawcett, Christine (Explorer; Time Traveller)
Tyrannosaurus Rex - J.F. Rivkin *s* 3674

Fears, Quentin (Computer Expert)
Treasure Box - Orson Scott Card *h* 729

Feich, Daimhin (Political Figure)
The Crystal Rose - Maya Kaathryn Bohnhoff *f* 458

Feinberg, Jennifer (Businesswoman)
Drakon - S.M. Stirling *s* 4224

Feinman, Jacob (Doctor)
Specters - J.M. Dillard *h* 1255

Feinstein, Rose (Mythical Creature; Teacher)
The Magic Touch - Jody Lynn Nye *f* 3323

Feirn (Television Personality)
Hero - Dave Duncan *s* 1352

Feit, Sherry (Professor)
Walking Wounded - Robert Devereaux *h* 1215

Felaya (Sorceress)
Token of Dragonsblood - Damaris Cole *f* 897

Feldberg, David (Linguist)
Requiem - Graham Joyce *h* 2386

Feldman, Jake (Businessman)
Pelts - F. Paul Wilson *h* 4690

Feldman, Malachi (Scientist)
The Asylum - John Edward Ames *h* 77

Feldspar (Businessman)
The Chosen - Edward Lee *h* 2695

Felice (Parent; Thief)
User Unfriendly - Vivian Vande Velde *f* 4429

Felix, William Charles "Gunman" (Vampire
　Hunter)
Vampire$ - John Steakley *h* 4177

Fellowes, Edith (Nurse)
The Ugly Little Boy - Isaac Asimov *s* 209

Felmet (Nobleman; Murderer)
Wyrd Sisters - Terry Pratchett *f* 3512

Fels, Jimmy (Teenager; Runaway)
Penance - Rick R. Reed *h* 3591

Fence (Wizard)
The Whim of the Dragon - Pamela Dean *f* 1167

Fender, Duncan (Photographer)
Suckers - Anne Billson *h* 397

Fenton, Mariah (Herbalist)
The Changeling Garden - Winifred Elze *h* 1449

Ferahgo the Assassin (Animal; Warrior)
Salamandastron - Brian Jacques *f* 2272

Feraru, Michael (Teacher)
The Lost - Jonathan Aycliffe *h* 235

Feree, Harper (Child; Hero)
The Friendship Song - Nancy Springer *f* 4133

Ferenczy, Janos (Vampire; Magician)
Deadspeak - Brian Lumley *h* 2825

Fergus (Military Personnel; Time Traveller)
The Lost Prince - Bridget Wood *f* 4751

Ferguson, Harold "Rondo" (Spy)
Darkman #4: The Face of Death - Randall
　Boyll *h* 505

Ferguson, Herman D. "Fergie" (Criminal;
　Computer Expert)
Judge Dredd - Neal Barrett Jr. *s* 306

Feritayl, Irma (Royalty)
*Bill, the Galactic Hero: On the Planet of Tasteless
　Pleasure* - Harry Harrison *s* 2052

Fermi, Enrico (Historical Figure; Scientist)
Worldwar: In the Balance - Harry
　Turtledove *s* 4395

Fernholz the Wise (Royalty)
The Fool's War - Lee Kisling *f* 2511

Ferraro, Gene (Adventurer)
Castle War! - John DeChancie *s* 1175

Ferrier, Matt (Military Personnel)
Darkness on the Ice - Lois Tilton *h* 4367

Ferris, Robert (Spy)
The Devouring - Douglas D. Hawk *h* 2090

Ferro, Dante (Religious)
Blood of the Covenant - Brent Monahan *h* 3147

Ferrol, Chayne (Spaceman)
Warhorse - Timothy Zahn *s* 4829

Fess (Robot)
The Warlock Insane - Christopher Stasheff *f* 4168
The Warlock Rock - Christopher Stasheff *s* 4169
A Wizard in Absentia - Christopher Stasheff *s* 4172

Fettle, Richard (Writer)
Queen of Angels - Greg Bear *s* 347

Fiar, Jacobious (Scientist)
Jonas McFee, A.T.P. - Sarah Sargent *s* 3865

Fielder, John (Doctor)
Dead in the Water - Nancy Holder *h* 2180

Fields, Stratton (Architect)
Horses of the Night - Michael Cadnum *h* 662

Fiendlord, Zoltan (Wizard)
Majyk by Accident - Esther Friesner *f* 1673
Majyk by Design - Esther Friesner *f* 1674

Fieran (Martial Arts Expert; Leader)
Dragon Moon - Chris Claremont *f* 839

Figg, Nigel (Child)
The Horror Club - Mark Morris *h* 3203

Figueroa, Calafia "Kali" (Television Personality;
　Religious)
Kalifornia - Marc Laidlaw *s* 2634

Figueroa, Poppy (Television Personality; Parent)
Kalifornia - Marc Laidlaw *s* 2634

Figueroa, Sandy (Television Personality)
Kalifornia - Marc Laidlaw *s* 2634

Fileli (Handicapped)
The Broken Land - Ian McDonald *s* 3017

Fileli, Mathembe (Refugee)
The Broken Land - Ian McDonald *s* 3017

Fin, Adam (Artist; Mythical Creature)
Something Rich and Strange - Patricia A.
　McKillip *f* 3060

Finch, Josephine (Businesswoman)
The LaNague Chronicles - F. Paul Wilson *s* 4686

Forrest, Winn (Religious; Government Official)
Half-Light - Denise Vitola   s   4443

Forrester, Edward (Criminal)
The Lunatic Cafe - Laurell K. Hamilton   h   2018

Forster, J.Q.R. (Professor)
The Diamond Moon - Paul Preuss   s   3523
The Shining Ones - Paul Preuss   s   3526

Forsyte, Adrian (Scientist)
Shifter - Judith Reeves-Stevens   f   3603

Fortizak "Zak" (Writer)
Murder at the Galactic Writers' Society - Janet
  Asimov   s   210

Fortunato, Amelia (Student—College)
Dark Visions - T. Lucien Wright   h   4771

Fortune (Mythical Creature; Adventurer)
Dragoncharm - Graham Edwards   f   1405

Fortune, Alison Crandall (Paralegal)
Devil's Gate - Elizabeth Ergas   h   1473

Fortune, Felicity (Mythical Creature)
The Godmother - Elizabeth Ann
  Scarborough   f   3889
The Godmother's Apprentice - Elizabeth Ann
  Scarborough   f   3890

Foskins (Government Official)
The Rats - James Herbert   h   2132

Foster, Bass (Time Traveller; Warrior)
Of Beginnings and Endings - Robert Adams   s   26

Foster, Danny (Child)
Twilight Time - Rick Hautala   h   2088

Foster, Katherine (Secretary—Legal)
Twilight Time - Rick Hautala   h   2088

Foster, Neda (Researcher)
The Abductors: Conspiracy - Jonathan
  Frakes   s   1633

Foster, Sunny Mae (Worker)
Ghost Dance - Kathryn Ptacek   h   3541

Foth (Scholar)
The Tides of God - Ted Reynolds   s   3647

Four, Cathy (Cyborg)
Cathy IV - Frances Lucas   s   2814

Fouts, Marian (Journalist)
Murder in the Solid State - Wil McCarthy   s   2996

Fowke, William G. (Engineer; Outlaw)
A Journal of the Flood Year - David Ely   s   1448

Fowler, Cassie (Writer)
Towing Jehovah - James Morrow   f   3215

Fox-Eyes, Thelvyn (Royalty)
Dragonmage of Mystara - Thorarinn
  Gunnarsson   f   1973

Foxfire (Mythical Creature; Leader)
Silver Shadows - Elaine Cunningham   f   1048

Foxfire, Dalvenjah (Mythical Creature)
Dragons on the Town - Thorarinn
  Gunnarsson   f   1974
Make Way for Dragons! - Thorarinn
  Gunnarsson   f   1976

Foxxe, Johnny "Fox" (Musician)
The Wood Wife - Terri Windling   f   4709

Foyan, Esmeralda (Young Woman)
Westlin Wind - Charles de Lint   f   1161

Foyle, Gulliver "Gully" (Spaceman; Psychic)
The Stars My Destination - Alfred Bester   s   389

Frakes, Danny "Mouse" (Child)
Darkman #1: The Hangman - Randall Boyll   h   502

Frame, Max (Teacher)
Dead End - Guy N. Smith   h   4083

Francie (Teenager; Orphan)
In the Heart of the Valley of Love - Cynthia
  Kadohata   s   2387

Francie (Genetically Altered Being; Child)
Naming the Flowers - Kate Wilhelm   s   4626

Francine (Noblewoman; Spouse)
Lord Conrad's Lady - Leo Frankowski   s   1644

Francisco, George (Alien; Detective—Police)
The Change - Barry B. Longyear   s   2797
Cross of Blood - K.W. Jeter   s   2318
Dark Horizon - K.W. Jeter   s   2319

Francy, Lizzie (Teenager; Computer Expert)
Beggars Ride - Nancy Kress   s   2575

Frank (Demon)
The Hellbound Heart - Clive Barker   h   287

Frank (Mechanic; Pirate)
Spacer Dreams - Larry Segriff   s   3923

Frank, Victor (Doctor; Scientist)
Mutation - Robin Cook   s   940

Frank-I-STN-4 (Administrator; Clone)
Title Deleted for Security Reasons - Ed
  Blome   s   451

Frankel, Cathy (Alien; Doctor)
Cross of Blood - K.W. Jeter   s   2318

Frankel, Melissa (Teenager)
Roadkill - Richard Sanford   h   3854

Frankel, Sidney (Professor)
Roadkill - Richard Sanford   h   3854

Frankenstein, Elizabeth (Young Woman)
The Darker Passions: Frankenstein - Amarantha
  Knight   h   2529
The Memoirs of Elizabeth Frankenstein - Theodore
  Roszak   h   3753

Frankenstein, Gunthar Thunnar (Scientist)
I Am Frankenstein - C. Dean Andersson   h   116

Frankenstein, Victor (Scientist)
The Darker Passions: Frankenstein - Amarantha
  Knight   h   2529
The Memoirs of Elizabeth Frankenstein - Theodore
  Roszak   h   3753
*The Secret Laboratory Journals of Dr. Victor
  Frankenstein* - Jeremy Kay   h   2406

Frankenstein's Monster (Monster)
The Final Battle - Richard A. Lupoff   f   2840

Franker, Edward "Eddie" (Television)
Pictures at 11 - Norman Spinrad   s   4127

Frankie (Teenager)
Collidescope - Grace Chetwin   s   820

Frankl, Victor (Office Worker)
The Suiting - Kelley Wilde   h   4621

Franklin, Charles (Scientist)
Moving Mars - Greg Bear   s   345

Franklin, Jim (Clerk)
Mall, Mayhem and Magic - Holly Lisle   f   2768

Franklyn, Kit (Psychologist)
Blood on the Bayou - D.J. Donaldson   h   1268

Franks, Leo (Police Officer)
Night Mask - William W. Johnstone   h   2335

Fraser, Brian (Child)
Dark Silence - Rick Hautala   h   2081

Fraser, Colin (Military Personnel)
March or Die - Andrew Keith   s   2419

Fraser, Edward (Businessman)
Dark Silence - Rick Hautala   h   2081

Fraser, Mike (Patient)
Dark Silence - Rick Hautala   h   2081

Frasier, Cally (Teenager)
The First Horror - R.L. Stine   h   4219

Frasier, Cody (Teenager)
The First Horror - R.L. Stine   h   4219

Frazier, Nick (Police Officer)
Down River - Stephen Gallagher   h   1696

Frazier, Rhea (Political Figure)
Shadows Fall - Simon R. Green   f   1903

Frede (Military Personnel; Health Care Professional)
Orion Among the Stars - Ben Bova   s   483

Frederickson, Robert "Mongo" (Detective—Private)
The Fear in Yesterday's Rings - George C.
  Chesbro   f   818

Freds (Expatriate)
Escape From Kathmandu - Kim Stanley
  Robinson   s   3705

Freeborn, Silas (Businessman)
Nocturnas - Shawn Ryan   h   3801

Freede, Hannibal (Scientist)
Flare - Roger Zelazny   s   4836

Freelorn "Lorn" (Heir—Dispossessed; Royalty)
The Door into Sunset - Diane Duane   f   1339

Freeman, Claire (Photographer)
Candle Night - Phil Rickman   h   3663

Freeman, Giles (Journalist)
Candle Night - Phil Rickman   h   3663

Freeman, Justine (Teenager)
Perfect Little Angels - Andrew Neiderman   h   3256

Freese, Neil (Guide)
Snowmen - Jerry Earl Brown   s   592

Freetz, Jhoe (Spaceman; Scientist)
Flies From the Amber - Wil McCarthy   s   2995

Freleng, Rachel (Teacher)
Cries of the Children - Clare McNally   h   3072

French, Jessica (Doctor)
Little Boy Lost - T.M. Wright   h   4776

French, Melissa (Teenager; Vampire)
Liquid Diet - William Tedford   h   4324

Fresca, Riki (Artist)
The Cybernetic Walrus - Jack L. Chalker   s   770

Freund, Solomon (Psychic)
Child of the Journey - Janet Berliner   f   381
Child of the Light - Janet Gluckman   f   1803

Frey, Ezra (Military Personnel)
Emperors of the Twilight - S. Andrew
  Swann   s   4274

Freyer, Ulteena (Military Personnel)
The Parafaith War - L.E. Modesitt Jr.   s   3137

Frida (Musician)
Kamikaze L'Amour - Richard Kadrey   s   2388

Friedkin (Scientist)
The Quick - Burt Cole   s   896

Friedman, Jack (Police Officer)
Homecoming - Matthew J. Costello   h   969

Friend (Ruler)
Swan Song - Robert R. McCammon   h   2990

Friendly, Bud (Journalist)
Silent Moon - William Relling Jr.   h   3616

Friendly, Tod T. (Doctor; Criminal)
Time's Arrow - Martin Amis   s   80

Frike (Servant)
Bring Me the Head of Prince Charming - Roger
  Zelazny   f   4834

Frisson (Writer)
The Witch Doctor - Christopher Stasheff   f   4171

Fritz, Edgar P. (Criminal)
Darkman #3: The Gods of Hell - Randall
  Boyll   h   504

Gardner, Peter (Handicapped)
Captain Quad - Sean Costello h 974

Gardner, Sam (Student)
Captain Quad - Sean Costello h 974

Garfield, Jake (Minstrel; Wanderer)
The World Next Door - Brad Ferguson s 1548

Garfield, Joanne (Teenager; Slave)
Parable of the Sower - Octavia E. Butler s 649

Gargoyle, Gary (Mythical Creature)
Geis of the Gargoyle - Piers Anthony f 141

Garibaldi, Michael (Security Officer)
The Touch of Your Shadow, the Whisper of Your Name - Neal Barrett Jr. s 307

Garibaldi, Michael (Military Personnel; Security Officer)
Voices - John Vornholt s 4461

Garin, Seth (Child)
The Regulators - Richard Bachman h 240

Garion (Wizard; Royalty)
The Seeress of Kell - David Eddings f 1394
Sorceress of Darshiva - David Eddings f 1395

Garlick, Magrat (Fiance(e); Witch)
Lords and Ladies - Terry Pratchett f 3502

Garlick, Magrat (Witch)
Witches Abroad - Terry Pratchett f 3511

Garlthik (Mythical Creature; Thief)
The Longing Ring - Christopher Kubasik f 2580

Garner (Religious)
Wetbones - John Shirley h 3997

Garoit, Darrell (Convict; Revolutionary)
Infinity Hold - Barry B. Longyear s 2799

Garon (Nobleman; Warrior)
A Man Betrayed - J.V. Jones f 2357

Garou, Lupe (Werewolf)
One Foot in the Grave - Wm. Mark Simmons f 4039

Garrett (Detective—Private)
Deadly Quicksilver Lies - Glen Cook f 926
Dread Brass Shadows - Glen Cook f 927
Old Tin Sorrows - Glen Cook f 929
Pretty Pewter Gods - Glen Cook f 930
Red Iron Nights - Glen Cook f 931

Garrett, Carl (Detective—Private)
Cat's Eye - William W. Johnstone h 2332

Garrett, Carl (Murderer)
The Dead Man's Kiss - Robert Weinberg h 4541

Garrison, David (Wealthy)
Psychosphere - Brian Lumley h 2835

Garrison, Richard (Military Personnel)
Psychomech - Brian Lumley h 2834

Garrith, Lance (Journalist)
The Specialist - Wynne Whiteford s 4611

Garroc (Warrior; Mythical Creature)
Shadow of the Seventh Moon - Nancy Varian Berberick f 375

Garrock (Warrior; Mythical Creature)
The Panther's Hoard - Nancy Varian Berberick f 374

Gart, Maya (Teenager; Settler)
The Faces of Ceti - Mary Caraker s 712

Garth One-eye (Warrior; Heir—Dispossessed)
Arena - William R. Forstchen f 1587

Garuda (Animal)
Walker between the Worlds - Diane DesRochers f 1210

Garwood, Tony (Guard)
Children of the End - Mark A. Clements h 873

Gasam (Warrior; Royalty)
The Poisoned Lands - John Maddox Roberts f 3695

Gatekeeper (Artisan)
Hard-Boiled Wonderland and the End of the World - Haruki Murakami s 3223

Gates, Bill (Police Officer)
Tunnelvision - R. Patrick Gates h 1733

Gates, John (Student)
Flicker - Theodore Roszak h 3752

Gates, Lawrence (Doctor)
Sibs - F. Paul Wilson h 4694

Gatineau, Robert (Spaceman)
The Middle of Nowhere - David Gerrold s 1773

Gatlin, Ben (Police Officer)
Father's Little Helper - Ronald Kelly h 2433

Gato, Coyote (Guide)
Coyote - Peter Gadol f 1691

Gaultry (Hunter; Wizard)
Wind From a Foreign Sky - Katya Reimann f 3613

Gaunt, Leland (Businessman)
Needful Things - Stephen King h 2490

Gavel, Kevin (Police Officer; Murderer)
Junkyard - Barry Porter h 3483

Gavilan, Kemal (Royalty)
Matrix Cubed - Britton Bloom s 452

Gavin, Felix (Sailor; Musician)
The Little Country - Charles de Lint f 1156

Gawaine (Knight)
Blood and Honor - Simon R. Green f 1893

Gawaine (Apprentice; Musician)
Fortress of Frost and Fire - Mercedes Lackey f 2610

Gaylen, Linda (Journalist)
Brainstorm - Steven M. Krauzer h 2569

G'Dath (Alien; Scientist)
A Flag Full of Stars - Brad Ferguson s 1546

Geddarms, Volothamp "Volo" (Traveller; Scholar)
The Mage in the Iron Mask - Brian Thomsen f 4356

Gehn (Magician)
Myst: The Book of Atrus - Rand Miller f 3103

Gelasaar III (Royalty; Leader)
The Phoenix in Flight - Sherwood Smith s 4098

Geldt (Companion)
Madlands - K.W. Jeter s 2322

Gelly (Teenager; Adventurer)
Flight to Hollow Mountain - Mark Sebanc f 3921

Gelmann, Mina (Aged Person; Adventurer)
Codgerspace - Alan Dean Foster s 1604

Gemma (Sorceress)
The Lightless Kingdom - Jonathan Wylie f 4790

Gen-93-Beta, John (Spaceship Captain)
Alien Earth - Megan Lindholm s 2758

Genevera "Gena" (Mythical Creature; Warrior)
Once a Hero - Michael A. Stackpole f 4151

Genius (Artificial Intelligence; Alien)
The Immortality Option - James P. Hogan s 2175

Genoud, Rochelle (Heiress)
Oktober - Stephen Gallagher h 1698

Gently, Dirk (Detective—Private; Psychic)
The Long Dark Tea-Time of the Soul - Douglas Adams s 23

Geoffrey (Nobleman; Vampire)
Blood and Roses - Sharon Bainbridge h 246

George (Expatriate)
Escape From Kathmandu - Kim Stanley Robinson s 3705

Gerard, Brian (Professor)
Webs - Scott Baker h 255

Gerard, Sybil (Prostitute)
The Difference Engine - William Gibson s 1780

Gerbert (Religious)
Ars Magica - Judith Tarr f 4300

Gerenz, Frederick (Administrator)
Dead Heat - Del Stone Jr. h 4239

Gerin the Fox (Ruler)
Prince of the North - Harry Turtledove f 4392

Gerlach, Midas (Gunfighter)
The Bars on Satan's Jailhouse - Norman Partridge h 3387

Gerome, Pluto Hellbender (Editor)
Pluto, Animal Lover - Laren Stover h 4243

Geronimo (Teenager; Warrior)
Madman Run - David Robbins s 3677

Geronimo (Alien)
The Voices of Heaven - Frederik Pohl s 3470

Gerrows, Eithnie (Artist)
The Wild Wood - Charles de Lint f 1162

Gersten, Clovis (Actor; Vampire)
Golden Eyes - John Gideon h 1783

Gerund (Child)
The Wild Hunt - Jane Yolen f 4816

Gervinus (Religious; Sorcerer)
The Shattered Oath - Josepha Sherman f 3980

Geryam (Military Personnel; Hero)
The Birth of the Blade - Dennis McCarty f 2998

Gespry (Companion)
Guardian's Key - Anne Logston f 2788

Gestaurien, Mauryl (Wizard)
Fortress in the Eye of Time - C.J. Cherryh f 804

Ghan (Teacher; Librarian)
The Waterborn - J. Gregory Keyes f 2464

Ghere, Rhule (Alien; Doctor)
The Parafaith War - L.E. Modesitt Jr. s 3137

Ghormley, Richard (Professor)
Wendigo Border - Catherine Montrose h 3158

Ghost (Animal)
Ghost of Chance - William S. Burroughs s 637

Ghost (Musician)
Lost Souls - Poppy Z. Brite h 570

Ghost (Spirit)
The Time of the Ghost - Diana Wynne Jones f 2352

Ghoster (Alien; Spy)
Cyberstealth - S.N. Lewitt s 2743
Dancing Vac - S.N. Lewitt s 2744

Ghysla (Mythical Creature)
The Sleep of Stone - Louise Cooper f 952

Gibb (Homosexual)
Key West 2720 A.D. - William Eakins s 1378

Gibberling (Courtier; Cartographer)
Here There Be Dragons - Roger Zelazny f 4840

Gibbs, Hank (Journalist; Publisher)
Psycho House - Robert Bloch h 442

Gibbs, Rinpoche (Time Traveller; Adventurer)
Muddle Earth - John Brunner s 601

Gibson, Cheryl (Child-Care Giver)
Grandma's Little Darling - Stephen R. George h 1767

Gordon, Karen (Young Woman)
The Gilgul - Henry W. Hocherman h 2153

Gordon, Kate (Teenager; Adventurer)
The Merlin Effect - T.A. Barron f 310

Gordon, Martin "Marty" (Leader; Spaceman)
Anvil of Stars - Greg Bear s 340

Gordon, Mrs. Sr. (Housewife; Adventurer)
Revenge of the Fluffy Bunnies - Craig Shaw
    Gardner f 1714

Gordon, Nathan (Scientist)
Mirage - F. Paul Wilson h 4688

Gordon, Roger (Public Relations)
Bride of the Slime Monster - Craig Shaw
    Gardner f 1708

Gordon, Roger Jr. (Hero; Adventurer)
Revenge of the Fluffy Bunnies - Craig Shaw
    Gardner f 1714

Gordon, Winston (Businessman; Nobleman)
Mina - Marie Kiraly h 2503

Gorlay, Glenn (Child)
The Dark One - Guy N. Smith h 4082

Gorlay, Rankin (Journalist)
The Dark One - Guy N. Smith h 4082

Gormlaith (Widow(er))
Pride of Lions - Morgan Llywelyn f 2784

Goro (Warrior; Royalty)
Mortal Kombat - Martin Delrio f 1199

Gorobec, Anton (Reanimated Dead)
I Am Frankenstein - C. Dean Andersson h 116

Gorp, Shigehero (Criminal)
Svaha - Charles de Lint s 1160

Gorse (Student)
Wizard's Hall - Jane Yolen f 4817

Gorthyn (Royalty)
The Shining Company - Rosemary Sutcliff f 4271

Goss, Brionne (Telepath)
Cloud's Rider - C.J. Cherryh s 797

Gottbaum, Leo (Scientist)
The Silicon Man - Charles Platt s 3460

Gotti, Guillemo (Religious; Psychic)
The Book of Earth - Marjorie Bradley
    Kellogg f 2427

Gowdie, Maggie (Witch)
The Rebirth of Wonder - Lawrence Watt-
    Evans f 4502

Gowdy, Samuel "Sam" Hall (Spaceship Captain)
The Triad Worlds - F.M. Busby s 643

Grabovnikon "Grab" (Artificial Intelligence)
Night of the Living Shark! - David Bischoff s 400

Grace, Peter (Spirit)
The Parasite - Ramsey Campbell h 702

Grace, Stephen (Criminal)
Dark of the Eye - Douglas Clegg h 869

Graciosa (Human; Noblewoman)
Child of Faerie, Child of Earth - Josepha
    Sherman f 3976

Grady, Joanna (Time Traveller)
Wolfking - Bridget Wood f 4752

Graeboe (Mythical Creature)
Harpy Thyme - Piers Anthony f 143

Gragelouth (Merchant; Animal)
Son of Spellsinger - Alan Dean Foster f 1617

Graham, Dexter (Teacher)
Mysterium - Robert Charles Wilson s 4705

Graham, James (Nobleman)
The Ebon Mask - Richard Lee Byers h 652

Graham, Jason "Jase" (Spaceman; Engineer)
Inheritor - C.J. Cherryh s 808

Grahame, John (Military Personnel; Psychic)
The Templar Treasure - Katherine Kurtz f 2593

Grainger, Tim (Time Traveller)
Arc Riders - David Drake s 1314
The Fourth Rome - David Drake s 1317

Grainne (Royalty)
The Lost Prince - Bridget Wood f 4751

Gramm, Rachel "Button" (Child)
Button Bright - Michael Kurland h 2584

Grandier, Urbain (Imposter; Sorcerer)
The Element of Fire - Martha Wells f 4582

Grandma Fifi (Grandparent; Dancer)
Baby Be-Bop - Francesca Lia Block f 444

Grange, Florida (Lawyer)
Mucho Mojo - Joe R. Lansdale h 2647

Grant (Computer Expert; Disembodied Personality)
MagicNet - John DeChancie f 1181

Grant, Alan (Scientist; Professor)
Jurassic Park - Michael Crichton s 1018

Grant, John (Computer Expert)
Spook Night - David Robbins h 3680

Grant, John "Slick" (Military Personnel)
March or Die - Andrew Keith s 2419

Grant, Kip (Teenager)
Spook Night - David Robbins h 3680

Grant, Shery (Teenager)
Spook Night - David Robbins h 3680

Grant, Spencer (Computer Expert)
Dark Rivers of the Heart - Dean R. Koontz h 2547

Granville, Gabby (Child)
Bloody Valentine - Stephen R. George h 1763

Granville, Jo (Artist)
Bloody Valentine - Stephen R. George h 1763

Grason, Gilead (Clerk)
Cross a Dark Bridge - Deborah Churchman h 829

Grason, Missy (Twin)
Cross a Dark Bridge - Deborah Churchman h 829

Graves, Elliott (Teacher)
Dark Lullaby - Jessica Palmer h 3377

Graves, Jermyn (Wizard; Detective—Amateur)
Journeyman Wizard - Mary Frances
    Zambreno f 4830

Graves, Jermyn (Apprentice)
A Plague of Sorcerers - Mary Frances
    Zambreno f 4831

Graves, Sara (Child)
Dark Lullaby - Jessica Palmer h 3377

Graves, Shelley (Child)
Dark Lullaby - Jessica Palmer h 3377

Gray (Alien)
The Longest Voyage/Slow Lightning - Poul
    Anderson s 108

Gray, Doreen (Photographer)
Fire in the Blood - P.N. Elrod h 1441

Gray, Emma (Child; Abuse Victim)
Flying in Place - Susan Palwick h 3380

Gray, Justin (Advertising)
The Darker Saints - Brian Hodge h 2155
Nightlife - Brian Hodge h 2157

Gray, Simon (Scientist; Doctor)
Archangel - Michael Conner s 914

Gray, Stewart (Doctor)
Flying in Place - Susan Palwick h 3380

Gray, Zachary (Young Man)
An Acceptable Time - Madeleine L'Engle f 2732

Gray Wolf, Josiah (Scientist; Explorer)
Beyond Eden - J.M. Morgan s 3181
Desert Eden - J.M. Morgan s 3182

Gray Wolf, Willow (Explorer)
Future Eden - J.M. Morgan s 3183

Graydon, Nicholas (Adventurer; Scientist)
The Face in the Abyss - Abraham Merritt f 3091

Graydon, Roland (Doctor)
Dead Voices - Rick Hautala h 2082

Graylord (Monster)
Shadowlight - Jackie Hyman f 2246

Grayshard (Alien)
Lair of the Cyclops - Allen L. Wold s 4725

Great and Powerful Turtle (Hero)
Dealer's Choice - George R.R. Martin s 2894

Great Chaffalo (Spirit; Magician)
The Midnight Horse - Sid Fleischman f 1570

Great God Om (Deity; Animal)
Small Gods - Terry Pratchett f 3507

Great Karlini (Sorcerer)
Spell of Apocalypse - Mayer Alan Brenner f 551

Grebb, Richard (Religious)
Penance - Rick R. Reed h 3591

Greeland (Homosexual; Criminal)
Mirage - Perry Brass s 543

Greeley, Dan (Activist; Farmer)
The Drylands - Mary Rosenblum s 3747

Green, Antony (Spirit)
Aunt Maria - Diana Wynne Jones f 2345

Green, Jerome (Religious)
Dead Voices - Abigail McDaniels h 3011

Green, Margo (Student)
Relic - Douglas Preston h 3521

Green, Paul (Political Figure)
Fire - Alan Rodgers h 3720

Green Spider (Psychic; Indian)
People of the Lakes - Kathleen O'Neal Gear f 1735

Greenberg, Bernard (Trader; Spaceship Captain)
Earthgrip - Harry Turtledove s 4385

Greene, Andy "the Warden" (Ruler)
The Warden of Horses - Karen Ripley s 3672

Greene, Harris (Sports Figure; Martial Arts Expert)
Doc Sidhe - Aaron Allston f 71

Greene, Maggie (Waiter/Waitress)
Entity - Nina Mandelik h 2874

Greenhands "Silveran" (Mythical Creature)
The Qualinesti - Paul B. Thompson f 4353

Greenpearl (Captive)
Silk Road - Jeanne Larsen f 2657

Greensleeves (Wizard; Revolutionary)
Final Sacrifice - Clayton Emery f 1455
Shattered Chains - Clayton Emery f 1457

Greer, Mitchell (Detective—Police)
Bitter Blood - Karen E. Taylor h 4312
Blood Secrets - Karen E. Taylor h 4313

Greer, Mitchell (Vampire; Detective—Police)
Blood Ties - Karen E. Taylor h 4314

Gregg, Stephen (Military Personnel)
Igniting the Reaches - David Drake s 1319

Gregg, Stephen (Pirate)
Through the Breach - David Drake s 1330

Gregor (Servant)
Dr. Haggard's Disease - Patrick McGrath h 3037

Guthrie, Dave (Artist)
Night Sounds - Warner Lee h 2716

Guthrum (Mythical Creature)
The Clan of the Warlord - Elizabeth H.
  Boyer f 494

Gutierrez, Osvaldo (Police Officer)
Shango - James Roberto Curtis h 1053

Gwarha, Ettin (Diplomat; Alien)
Ring of Swords - Eleanor Arnason s 173

Gwen (Girlfriend)
Rehearsal for a Renaissance - Douglas W.
  Clark f 842

Gwenhwyfar (Fiance(e))
The Kingmaking - Helen Hollick f 2190

Gwenhwyfar (Royalty; Spouse)
Pendragon's Banner - Helen Hollick f 2191

Gwenhwyvar (Ruler)
Pendragon - Stephen R. Lawhead f 2672

Gwenlliant (Wizard)
The Castle of the Silver Wheel - Teresa
  Edgerton f 1397
The Grail and the Ring - Teresa Edgerton f 1400

Gwent, Donson (Director; Writer)
Wordwright - Tom Deitz f 1196

Gwydion (Royalty; Sorcerer)
*The Well-Favored Man: The Tale of the Sorcerer's
  Nephew* - Elizabeth Willey f 4630

Gwyn, Angharad "the Rowan" (Psychic; Orphan)
The Rowan - Anne McCaffrey s 2980

Gwynn-Raven, Angharad "the Rowan" (Psychic)
Damia - Anne McCaffrey s 2964

Gwynn-Raven, Damia (Psychic)
Damia - Anne McCaffrey s 2964

Gyhard (Military Personnel)
Fifth Quarter - Tanya Huff f 2227
No Quarter - Tanya Huff f 2230

Gypsy Pete (Store Owner)
Frisk - Dennis Cooper h 943

H

Haal, Daetrin Ungashak To-Alym (Vampire;
  Werewolf)
The Madness Season - C.S. Friedman s 1655

Haas, Alexandria Victoria (Psychologist; Counselor)
Mindplayers - Pat Cadigan s 658

Haas, Peter (Sports Figure; Artist)
Memento Mori - Shariann Lewitt s 2746

Habeggar (Professor; Inventor)
Slow Freight - F.M. Busby s 642

Haberman (Social Worker)
The Nihilesthete - Richard Kalich h 2391

Hac (Android)
Mission: Tori - Johanna Bolton s 462

Hackett, Horace (Writer)
Typewriter in the Sky - L. Ron Hubbard f 2224

Hackleberry, Kelvin Knight (Hero)
Chimaera's Copper - Piers Anthony f 136
Mouvar's Magic - Piers Anthony f 150
Orc's Opal - Piers Anthony f 151

Hackworth, John Percival (Engineer)
The Diamond Age - Neal Stephenson s 4190

Hadfield, Felicity Jane (Child)
Viper - Alan Riefe h 3666

Hadrak, Quisaz (Alien; Military Personnel)
Martian Deathtrap - Nathan Archer s 169

Hael (Royalty; Warrior)
The Steel Kings - John Maddox Roberts f 3697

Haflinger, Nickie (Experimental Subject)
The Shockwave Rider - John Brunner s 602

Hagan (Warrior; Homosexual)
Attila's Treasure - Stephan Grundy f 1964

Hagan, Kara (Military Personnel)
Warstrider: Netlink - William H. Keith Jr. s 2422

Hagan, Tim (Companion)
Red, Red Robin - Stephen Gallagher h 1699

Hagar, Jonathan (Wealthy)
The Beast - Marie Ardell White h 4608

Haggard, Edward (Doctor)
Dr. Haggard's Disease - Patrick McGrath h 3037

Hagopian (Aged Person)
Black Sun - Douglas E. Winter h 4716

Hague, Scott (Teenager)
Witch - Christopher Pike f 3453

Hahn (Spaceman)
Collidescope - Grace Chetwin s 820

hai-Arkad, Brandon (Royalty)
The Rifter's Covenant - Sherwood Smith s 4100

Haid, Francis Madsen "Painkiller" (Serial Killer)
The Holy Terror - Wayne Allen Sallee h 3829

Haig, Gudrun "Dauna" (Journalist)
The Singularity Project - F.M. Busby s 641

Haines, Amelia "Amy" (Writer)
Psycho House - Robert Bloch h 442

Hake (Scientist)
Vanishing Point - Michaela Roessner s 3724

Hakoni, Kyosti Bitterleaf (Doctor; Spaceman)
Revolution's Shore - Alis A. Rasmussen s 3576

Hakori, Sonny (Drug Dealer)
TekWar - William Shatner s 3945

Hal Jam (Animal; Imposter)
The Bear Went over the Mountain - William
  Kotzwinkle f 2561

Halanyn, SharMarali "Shar" (Mythical Creature;
  Magician)
Chrome Circle - Mercedes Lackey f 2606

Halarek, Karne (Nobleman; Ruler)
Brander's Book - C.J. Mills s 3114
Egil's Book - C.J. Mills s 3115
Kit's Book - C.J. Mills s 3116
Zjhanne's Book - C.J. Mills s 3117

**Halarek, Kathryn "Kit" Magdalena
  Alysha** (Noblewoman; Captive)
Kit's Book - C.J. Mills s 3116

Halbard, Amy (Computer Expert)
Offspring - Jack Ketchum h 2461

Halburton, Gustav (Psychologist)
Dark Dreaming - Pat Franklin h 1639

Haldane, Javan Jashan Urien (Royalty; Psychic)
King Javan's Year - Katherine Kurtz f 2591

Haldane, Rhys Michael Alister (Ruler; Psychic)
The Bastard Prince - Katherine Kurtz f 2588

Haldeth (Artisan)
The Master of Whitestorm - Janny Wurts f 4786

Hale, David (Librarian)
Uwharrie - Eugene E. Pfaff Jr. h 3432

Hale, Dick (Radio)
Night Mask - William W. Johnstone h 2335

Hale, Ebeneezer (Paranormal Investigator)
The Messenger - Donald Tyson h 4408

Half-Elvin, Tanis (Mythical Creature)
Kindred Spirits - Mark Anthony f 125
Wanderlust - Mary Kirchoff f 2507

Half-Elvin, Tanthalas "Tanis" (Mythical Creature;
  Warrior)
Steel and Stone - Ellen Porath f 3481

Hali (Witch; Guide)
Witch and Wombat - Carolyn Cushman f 1054

Halkin, Edward (Child)
Prophecy - Peter James h 2291

Halkin, Oliver (Actuary)
Prophecy - Peter James h 2291

Hall, Cassandra (Designer; Vampire)
Thirst - Michael Cecilione h 769

Hall, Courtney (Artist; Revolutionary)
Out on Blue Six - Ian McDonald s 3020

Haller, Buzzy (Filmmaker)
Horror Show - Greg Kihn h 2466

Halliday, Arden (Musician)
Gone South - Robert R. McCammon h 2988

Halloran, Lawrence "Fixer-of-Weapons" (Spy;
  Telepath)
Man-Kzin Wars IV - Larry Niven s 3283

Halloran, Liam (Bodyguard)
Sepulchre - James Herbert h 2133

Halloran, Myrna (Nurse)
Flying in Place - Susan Palwick h 3380

Halton, John (Genetically Altered Being)
Looking for the Mahdi - N. Lee Wood s 4753

Halver (Teacher; Werewolf)
The Dubious Hills - Pamela Dean f 1165

Hamid-Jones, Abdul (Scientist)
Crescent in the Sky - Donald Moffitt s 3143
A Gathering of Stars - Donald Moffitt s 3144

Hamilton, Case (Police Officer)
Death's Door - John Wooley h 4756

Hamilton, Dennis (Actor; Producer)
Reign - Chet Williamson h 4657

Hamilton, Diana (Police Officer)
Death's Door - John Wooley h 4756

Hamilton, Gil "the Arm" (Detective—Police)
Flatlander - Larry Niven s 3280

Hamilton, Jack (Engineer)
Eye in the Sky - Philip K. Dick s 1227

Hamilton, Marsha (Liberal)
Eye in the Sky - Philip K. Dick s 1227

Hamilton, Rick (Publisher)
The Man Who Turned into Himself - David
  Ambrose h 74

Hamilton, Ruth (Widow(er))
Dead in the Water - Nancy Holder h 2180

Hamlet (Android; Actor)
Too, Too Solid Flesh - Nick O'Donohoe s 3342

Hammen (Thief)
Arena - William R. Forstchen f 1587

Hammer (Criminal)
Illegal Aliens - Nick Pollotta s 3479

Hammer, Alois (Military Personnel)
The Warrior - David Drake s 1334

Hammersmidt, Garry (Businessman)
Yesterday's Pawn - W.T. Quick s 3550

Hammond, Fiona (Ward)
The Black Death - Basil Copper h 958

Hammond, John (Businessman)
Jurassic Park - Michael Crichton s 1018

Harry (Companion)
The King's Buccaneer - Raymond E. Feist f 1533

Harshaw, Jubal (Writer; Lawyer)
Stranger in a Strange Land - Robert A. Heinlein s 2117

Hart (Scientist; Lesbian)
In the Blood - Lauren Wright Douglas s 1283

Hart, Adragon (Vampire)
Precious Blood - Pat Graversen h 1872

Hart, Adragon (Teenager; Vampire)
Sweet Blood - Pat Graversen h 1873

Hart, Beth (Teenager; Vampire)
Precious Blood - Pat Graversen h 1872

Hart, Carolyn (Young Woman)
A Room for the Dead - Noel Hynd h 2250

Hart, Elsbeth (Writer; Vampire)
Sweet Blood - Pat Graversen h 1873

Hart, Lola (Teenager)
Random Acts of Senseless Violence - Jack Womack f 4748

Hart, Marcel (Child)
The Dark One - Guy N. Smith h 4082

Hart, Sally (Sailor)
Hunger - William Dantz h 1088

Hart, Thomas J. (Sailor)
Hunger - William Dantz h 1088

Hartell, Kathryn (Lesbian; Researcher)
Shadows After Dark - Ouida Crozier f 1043

Harth, Beren "Brat" SanDyllin (Orphan)
Wheel of Dreams - Salinda Tyson f 4409

Harting, William Jameson "Jay" (Doctor)
Deadly Breed - T.J. Kirby h 2505

Hartke, Eugene Debs (Professor)
Hocus Pocus or, What's the Hurry, Son? - Kurt Vonnegut Jr. s 4458

Hartley, Sherrine (Computer Expert)
Fallen Angels - Larry Niven s 3279

Hartmann, Gregg (Political Figure; Genetically Altered Being)
Ace in the Hole - George R.R. Martin s 2892
Marked Cards - George R.R. Martin s 2898

Hartwig, Reece (Counselor)
The Night of the Moonbow - Thomas Tryon h 4377

Harvey, Emily (Twin; Revolutionary)
Memorymakers - Brian Herbert s 2127

Harvey, Thomas (Twin)
Memorymakers - Brian Herbert s 2127

Hasagawa, Padraic Hakim (Professor)
Reality Is What You Can Get Away With: An Illustrated Screenplay - Robert Anton Wilson s 4699

Hasgard, David (Military Personnel; Teenager)
Traitors from Within - R.A. Montgomery s 3157

Hasmara, Faan "Fa" (Sorceress; Orphan)
The Magic Wars - Jo Clayton f 860
Wildfire - Jo Clayton f 865

Hasruel (Demon; Mythical Creature)
Castle in the Air - Diana Wynne Jones f 2346

Hastings, Amber (Scientist)
Thunder Strike! - Michael McCollum s 3003

Hastings, Julie (Lawyer)
Darkman - Randall Boyll h 501
Darkman #2: The Price of Fear - Randall Boyll h 503

Hastings, Kyle Stevens (Imposter; Wanderer)
Down the Bright Way - Robert Reed s 3594

Hastur, Leonie (Telepath)
Rediscovery: A Novel of Darkover - Marion Zimmer Bradley s 527

Hathaway (Spaceman)
The Martian Chronicles - Ray Bradbury s 510

Hathor (Mythical Creature; Revolutionary)
Horrible Humes - Stephen Billias f 395

Hathor (Mythical Creature)
The Land of Gold - Gillian Bradshaw f 540
Outcasts - Clayton Emery f 1456

Hatshepsut (Time Traveller)
Dragon's Claw - Alex McDonough s 3026

Hauberin (Mythical Creature; Royalty)
A Strange and Ancient Name - Josepha Sherman f 3981

Hauser, Wolfgang "Karl Wolf" (Military Personnel; Leader)
Cohort of the Damned - Andrew Keith s 2418

Hausmann, Elena (Librarian; Revolutionary)
The Third Force - Marc Laidlaw s 2636

Hausmann, Louis (Military Personnel)
The Third Force - Marc Laidlaw s 2636

Havoc, Mike (Military Personnel)
L.A. Strike - David Robbins s 3676

Havzhiva, Yehedarhed (Diplomat)
Four Ways to Forgiveness - Ursula K. Le Guin s 2690

Hawk (Police Officer)
The Bones of Haven - Simon R. Green f 1895
The God Killer - Simon R. Green f 1898
Guard Against Dishonor - Simon R. Green f 1899
Hawk & Fisher - Simon R. Green f 1900

Hawk (Prehistoric Human; Inventor)
The Hunter Returns - David Drake f 1318

Hawk (Police Officer)
Winner Takes All - Simon R. Green f 1904
Wolf in the Fold - Simon R. Green f 1905

Hawk, Carin (Explorer)
Ark Liberty - Will Bradley s 538

Hawk-That-Settles (Indian; Religious)
Krokodil Tears - Jack Yeovil f 4801

Hawke, Christopher (Military Personnel)
No Blood Spilled - Les Daniels h 1083

Hawke, Michael (Magician)
Night Magic - Thomas Tryon h 4376

Hawke, Prince (Heir)
Far Harbor - Melisa C. Michaels s 3095

Hawken, Jos (Military Personnel; Spaceship Captain)
Yamato: A Rage in Heaven - Ken Kato s 2401

Hawken, Solomon (Magician; Scholar)
Arcady - Michael Williams f 4633

Hawkes, Benton "Ben" (Diplomat; Rancher)
Man o' War - William Shatner s 3938

Hawkins, Danny (Child; Explorer)
A Thunder on Neptune - Gordon Eklund s 1418

Hawkins, Ethan (Military Personnel; Spaceman)
Mutant Star - Karen Haber s 1985

Hawkins, Marie (Spacewoman; Parent)
Tripoint - C.J. Cherryh s 814

Hawkins, Nirgal (Political Figure)
Blue Mars - Kim Stanley Robinson s 3704

Hawkins, Nirgal (Political Figure; Revolutionary)
Green Mars - Kim Stanley Robinson s 3708

Hawkins, Ron (Maintenance Worker)
Fire - Alan Rodgers h 3720

Hawkins, Rosalind "Rose" (Scholar; Orphan)
The Fire Rose - Mercedes Lackey f 2608

Hawksmoor, Nicholas (Pilot; Artificial Intelligence)
Berserker Kill - Fred Saberhagen s 3806

Hawn, Loren (Police Officer)
Days of Atonement - Walter Jon Williams s 4648

Hawson, Jordan (Knight)
The Forge of Virtue - Lynn Abbey f 14

Hawson, Jordan (Knight; Handicapped)
The Temper of Wisdom - Lynn Abbey f 15

Hawthorn, Ariel (Spaceman)
Anvil of Stars - Greg Bear s 340

Hawthorne, Royce (Young Man)
Chaingang - Rex Miller h 3105

Hawthorne, Sara (Teacher)
Moonfall - Tamara Thorne h 4360

Hay, Matthew (Religious)
Witch Hill - Marion Zimmer Bradley h 536

Hayaka, Reyna (Guardian; Businessman)
Wild Magic - Jo Clayton f 864

Hayden, Conek (Spaceship Captain; Businessman)
Backblast - Lee McKeone s 3050
The Clone Crisis - Lee McKeone s 3051
Starfire Down - Lee McKeone s 3052

Hayden, Mark (Police Officer)
Bats - William W. Johnstone h 2330

Hayes (Scientist; Administrator)
Time and Light - William Bornefeld s 470

Hayes, Charlie (Businessman)
Death Channels - Robert E. Vardeman h 4433

Hayes, Drew (Teenager)
Living with Aliens - John DeChancie s 1180

Hayes, Jack (Criminal)
The Spider #3: Death's Crimson Juggernaut/The Red Death Rain - Grant Stockbridge f 4234

Hayes, Terry (Journalist)
The Season of Passage - Christopher Pike h 3450

Hazaar (Alien)
Larissa - Emily Devenport s 1212

Hazard, Arthur (Genetically Altered Being)
Brain Child - George Turner s 4380

Hazel (Photographer; Fiance(e))
Belladonna - Michael Stewart h 4206

Hazzard, Calvin (Professor)
Rough Beast - Gary Goshgarian h 1833

Hazzard, Matt (Child)
Rough Beast - Gary Goshgarian h 1833

Heather (Singer; Handicapped)
Lorien Lost - Michael King f 2477

Hector (Teenager)
The Lake at the End of the World - Caroline MacDonald s 2849

Hederick (Religious; Leader)
Hederick, the Theocrat - Ellen Dodge Severson f 3935

Hedison, Marianne (Computer Expert; Detective—Amateur)
Terminal Games - Cole Perriman s 3411

Heffer, John Wilson (Vacationer)
The Feelies - Mick Farren s 1510

Heiclaro, Corean (Trader)
Emperor of Everything - Ray Aldridge s 50

Heikki, Galler (Businessman)
Mighty Good Road - Melissa Scott s 3911

Heikki, Gwynne (Businesswoman; Adventurer)
Mighty Good Road - Melissa Scott s 3911

Hobson, Cathy (Advertising)
The Terminal Experiment - Robert J. Sawyer s 3887

Hobson, Peter (Scientist; Engineer)
The Terminal Experiment - Robert J. Sawyer s 3887

Hochstader, Jeremy (Computer Expert)
Castle War! - John DeChancie s 1175

Hodge, Benton (Store Owner)
Sineater - Elizabeth Massie h 2917

Hodge, Birk "Birkaj" (Trader; Administrator)
The Inquisitor - Cheryl J. Franklin s 1636

Hodges, Laren (Journalist)
The Lurker - James V. Smith h 4085

Hoey, Buck (Sports Figure)
Brittle Innings - Michael Bishop h 403

Hoffman, Judith (Scientist)
Eon - Greg Bear s 342

Hokokul, Cha Ishil (Alien)
Jaran - Kate Elliott s 1422

Holbian (Royalty; Warrior)
The Road to Underfall - Mike Jefferies f 2304

Holdman, Taylor (Businessman)
Near Dead - Stephen R. George h 1768

Holdstrom, Roy (Filmmaker)
A Graveyard for Lunatics - Ray Bradbury h 509

Holdsworth, Adrian (Scientist)
The Voice of Cepheus - Ken Appleby s 166

Holiday, Ben (Ruler; Parent)
The Tangle Box - Terry Brooks f 586
Witches' Brew - Terry Brooks f 587

Holl (Mythical Creature)
Higher Mythology - Jody Lynn Nye f 3322
Mythology Abroad - Jody Lynn Nye f 3326

Holland, Linda (Teenager)
Carnival - William W. Johnstone h 2331

Holland, Martin (Political Figure)
Carnival - William W. Johnstone h 2331

Holland, Susan (Designer)
The Beyond - Barry Harrington h 2042

Hollander, Mariele (Interior Decorator)
Graythings - Pat Graversen h 1871

Hollander, Tom (Editor; Hippie)
The Children of Hamelin - Norman Spinrad s 4124

Holloway, Melissa (Teenager)
Second Child - John Saul h 3877

Holly (Computer)
Red Dwarf: Infinity Welcomes Careful Drivers - Grant Naylor s 3247

Holly, Wanda (Spaceman)
Starliner - David Drake s 1328

Holman, Guy (Teacher)
Charmed Life - Bernard Taylor h 4307

Holmes, Lori (Young Woman)
Lori - Robert Bloch h 436

Holmes, Odetta (Handicapped)
The Waste Lands - Stephen King h 2496

Holmes, Shadrach (Spirit)
Double Trouble Squared - Kathryn Lasky f 2658

Holmes, Sherlock (Detective—Private)
The D. Case: The Truth about the Mystery of Edwin Drood - Charles Dickens f 1230
The Holmes-Dracula File - Fred Saberhagen h 3811

Holmes, Sherlock (Detective—Private; Teenager)
Muddle Earth - John Brunner s 601

Holmes, Sherlock (Detective—Private)
Seance for a Vampire - Fred Saberhagen h 3817

Holmes, Sherlock (Detective—Private; Adventurer)
Sherlock Holmes in Orbit - Mike Resnick s 3637

Holscomb, Ray (Teenager)
Junkyard - Barry Porter h 3483

Holser, Vax (Military Personnel)
Midshipman's Hope - David Feintuch s 1531

Holt, Kenneth (Streetperson)
Wyrm Wolf - Edo Van Belkom h 4414

Holton, Clare (Government Official)
Dream Maker - W.A. Harbinson s 2031

Homer-R-ICK-3 (Clone; Troubleshooter)
Extreme Paranoia: Nobody Knows the Trouble I've Shot - Ken Rolston s 3733

Hong, Louie (Cowboy)
Hong on the Range - William Wu s 4781

Honniker (Advertising)
Ferman's Devils - Joe Clifford Faust s 1522

Hoo-Lan (Alien)
My Teacher Glows in the Dark - Bruce Coville s 994

Hood, Nicholas (Artist)
Cold Eye - Giles Blunt h 454

Hood, Robin (Outlaw; Hero)
The Fantastic Adventures of Robin Hood - Martin H. Greenberg f 1913

Hood, Robin (Hero; Outlaw)
The Oathbound Wizard - Christopher Stasheff f 4162

Hood, Robin (Outlaw; Hero)
The Outlaws of Sherwood - Robin McKinley f 3065

Hood, Robin (Hero; Outlaw)
Robin and the King - Parke Godwin f 1805
The Sheriff of Nottingham - Richard Kluger f 2515

Hood, Robin (Artificial Intelligence)
The Sherwood Game - Esther Friesner s 1676

Hook, James (Pirate; Sea Captain)
Hook - Terry Brooks f 583

Hooker, Nicodemus (Scientist)
Kent Montana and the Really Ugly Thing From Mars - Lionel Fenn s 1542

Hooker, Popeye (Construction Worker)
Orbital Decay - Allen Steele s 4185

Hoover, Rod (Salesman)
Lethal Delivery - J.G. Maxon h 2939

Hope, Mary (Writer)
A Gift Upon the Shore - M.K. Wren s 4767

Hopewell, Norman (Religious)
Darkman #3: The Gods of Hell - Randall Boyll h 504

Horace (Mythical Creature; Telepath)
Mouvar's Magic - Piers Anthony f 150

Horatio (Actor)
Too, Too Solid Flesh - Nick O'Donohoe s 3342

Hork (Genetically Altered Being; Government Official)
Flux - Stephen Baxter s 331

Horn, Alan (Mercenary)
Star Bridge - James Gunn s 1970

Horn, Corran (Military Personnel; Pilot)
Rogue Squadron - Michael A. Stackpole s 4152

Hornchurch, Anthony (Servant; Detective—Amateur)
The Devil You Say - Elisa DeCarlo f 1170
Strong Spirits - Elisa DeCarlo f 1171

Horner, Jack (Detective—Private)
Angels & Visitations: A Miscellany - Neil Gaiman f 1692

Horsfall, Arne (Patient)
Fiends - John Farris h 1516

Horta, Raul (Wizard; FBI Agent)
Doomsday Exam - Nick Pollotta f 3477

Horton, Carol (Lawyer)
Althea - Abigail McDaniels h 3010

Horton, Holly (Child)
Althea - Abigail McDaniels h 3010

Horton, Lisa (Teenager)
Althea - Abigail McDaniels h 3010

Hoskins, Gerald (Scientist)
The Ugly Little Boy - Isaac Asimov s 209

Houdini, Harry (Magician; Historical Figure)
Believe: A Novel - William Shatner f 3937
Nevermore - William Hjortsberg h 2150

Houston, Jackson (Military Personnel)
Wartide - John Barnes f 300

Howard (Worker)
Toplin - Michael McDowell h 3033

Howards, Tom (Doctor)
Dark Souls - Barry Porter h 3482

Howell, Clarence (Military Personnel)
Hour of the Scorpion - Matthew J. Costello s 970

Howgath, Lizzy (Librarian)
Kent Montana and the Reasonably Invisible Man - Lionel Fenn s 1543

Howie (Animal)
Return to Howliday Inn - James Howe f 2220

Hoyland, Hugh (Spaceman; Student)
Silent Thunder/Universe - Dean Ing s 2253

Hoyt, Father (Religious)
Hyperion - Dan Simmons s 4034

Hph-wayuo "Alvin" (Alien; Student)
Brightness Reef - David Brin s 562

Hph-wayuo "Alvin" (Alien; Teenager)
Infinity's Shore - David Brin s 565

Hr.Tyi.Bei.k.ai (Alien; Royalty)
Alien Tongue - Stephen Leigh s 2722

Hrecker, Marcus Aurelius (Scientist)
Seeds of Destiny - Thomas A. Easton s 1382

Hrrestan (Alien; Political Figure)
Treaty at Doona - Anne McCaffrey s 2985

Hrriss (Alien; Settler)
Crisis on Doona - Anne McCaffrey s 2962

Hsing, Carlisle (Detective—Private)
Nightside City - Lawrence Watt-Evans s 4500

Hu "Hugh" (Musician; Parent)
Shame of Man - Piers Anthony s 155

Hudder, Cyrus (Parent; Scientist)
Core - Paul Preuss s 3522

Hudder, Leiden "Leidy" (Scientist)
Core - Paul Preuss s 3522

Hudson, Cal (Producer; Religious)
Symphony - Adrian Savage h 3880

Hudson, Graham (Producer)
Glimpses - Lewis Shiner h 3987

Huffington, Q-Jo (Psychic)
Half Asleep in Frog Pajamas - Tom Robbins s 3683

Hugh the Hand (Criminal)
Dragon Wing - Margaret Weis f 4552
The Hand of Chaos - Margaret Weis f 4558
Into the Labyrinth - Margaret Weis f 4559

Ingledew, Sam (Animal)
The Cockroaches of Stay More - Donald
   Harington f 2033

Ingles, Benton (Industrialist; Villain)
Outworld Cats - Jack Lovejoy s 2811

Inglorion, Ingold (Wizard)
Mother of Winter - Barbara Hambly f 2007

Ingoldesdaughter, Berika (Shepherd; Sorceress)
Beneath the Web - Lynn Abbey f 10

Ingoldesdaughter, Berika (Shepherd; Runaway)
The Wooden Sword - Lynn Abbey f 16

Ingolfsson, Gwendolyn (Genetically Altered Being)
Drakon - S.M. Stirling s 4224

Ingolfsson, Yolande (Royalty)
The Stone Dogs - S.M. Stirling s 4228

Inhetep, Setne (Wizard; Religious)
The Anubis Murders - Gary Gygax f 1982
Death in Delhi - Gary Gygax f 1983

Inman, Toby (Television Personality; Journalist)
Pictures at 11 - Norman Spinrad s 4127

Innisfree, Merle "Myrddin" (Wizard)
The Rebirth of Wonder - Lawrence Watt-
   Evans f 4502

Innowen (Handicapped; Dancer)
Shadowdance - Robin Wayne Bailey f 245

Inosolan "Inos" (Royalty)
Emperor and Clown - Dave Duncan f 1350
Faery Lands Forlorn - Dave Duncan f 1351
Magic Casement - Dave Duncan f 1355
Perilous Seas - Dave Duncan f 1357

Iowyn (Royalty; Warrior)
Tears of Time - Nancy Asire f 215

Iquar, Kryx (Alien; Psychic)
Catch the Lightning - Catherine Asaro s 181

ir Var, Zorn (Heir—Dispossessed; Fugitive)
Demon Moon - Jack Williamson s 4669

Iranaputra, Victor (Aged Person; Adventurer)
Codgerspace - Alan Dean Foster s 1604

Iris (Royalty)
Geis of the Gargoyle - Piers Anthony f 141

Irith (Mythical Creature; Magician)
Taking Flight - Lawrence Watt-Evans f 4506

Ironhart, Jim (Teacher)
Cold Fire - Dean R. Koontz h 2546

Ironsmith, Frank (Engineer)
The Humanoids - Jack Williamson s 4670

Irrylath (Royalty)
The Pearl of the Soul of the World - Meredith Ann
   Pierce f 3439

Irtuk-Saa (Alien; Ruler)
The Triad Worlds - F.M. Busby s 643

Isaf (Warrior)
The Fortress of Eternity - Andrew
   Whitmore f 4612

Isham, Evi (Genetically Altered Being; Human)
Emperors of the Twilight - S. Andrew
   Swann s 4274

Ishikawa, Keiko (Scientist; Space Explorer)
Imbalance - V.E. Mitchell s 3124

Ishimaru, Kazumasa (Engineer)
Through the Arc of the Rain Forest - Karen Tei
   Yamashita f 4791

Ishmael (Animal; Telepath)
Ishmael - Daniel Quinn s 3552

Islay, Arran (Heir—Dispossessed; Pirate)
Henry Martyn - L. Neil Smith s 4092

Islief the Watcher (Mythical Creature)
A Child of Elvish - Nancy Varian Berberick f 373

Italiano, Dorothy (Researcher)
A Reasonable World - Damon Knight s 2535

Ithariel (Sorceress)
The Master of Whitestorm - Janny Wurts f 4786

Ivanova, Sonya (Linguist; Political Figure)
Russian Spring - Norman Spinrad s 4128

Ivanova, Susan (Leader; Spacewoman)
The Touch of Your Shadow, the Whisper of Your Name
   - Neal Barrett Jr. s 307

Ivanova, Susan (Military Personnel; Telepath)
Voices - John Vornholt s 4461

Ivar (Warrior)
The Hammer and the Cross - Harry
   Harrison f 2055

Ivard (Pirate)
Ruler of Naught - Sherwood Smith s 4101

Ives, Bobby (Veteran; Werewolf)
The Nightwalker - Thomas Tessier h 4343

Ivy (Royalty; Sorceress)
Man From Mundania - Piers Anthony f 148

Izmailova, Ekatarina (Scientist; Leader)
Griffin's Egg - Michael Swanwick s 4281

J

Jabba the Hutt (Organized Crime Figure; Alien)
Tales From Jabba's Palace - Kevin J.
   Anderson s 95

Jack (Baker; Sorcerer)
The Baker's Boy - J.V. Jones f 2356

Jack (Artist; Companion)
The Caterpillar's Question - Piers Anthony f 134

Jack (Traveller; Agent)
The End-of-Everything Man - Tom De
   Haven f 1146

Jack (Addict)
The Hanged Man - Francesca Lia Block f 447

Jack (Traveller)
The Last Human - Tom De Haven f 1147

Jack (Magician; Adventurer)
The Loneliest Magician - Irene Radford f 3555

Jack (Mentally Ill Person)
Lunatics - Bradley Denton f 1205

Jack (Sorcerer; Hero)
A Man Betrayed - J.V. Jones f 2357
Master and Fool - J.V. Jones f 2358

Jack (Traveller)
Walker of Worlds - Tom De Haven f 1148

Jack the Bodiless (Psychic; Relative)
Magnificat - Julian May s 2943

Jack the Ripper (Serial Killer)
A Night in the Lonesome October - Roger
   Zelazny h 4843

Jackson, Andrew (Teacher)
Spirit Crossings - Claudia Peck f 3405

Jackson, Beauregard (Child)
Never Land - Douglas Clegg h 871

Jackson, Carl (Adventurer)
Dragon Burning - Craig Shaw Gardner f 1709

Jackson, Daniel (Linguist; Scholar)
StarGate - Dean Devlin s 1217

Jackson, Jack (Astronaut)
The Stars Must Wait - Keith Laumer s 2664

Jackson, Portis (Banker)
Dumford Blood - S.K. Epperson h 1469

Jackson, Skeeter (Con Artist; Time Traveller)
Wagers of Sin - Robert Asprin s 222

Jacob (Spy)
Falcon - Emma Bull s 631

Jacobi, Henry (Engineer; Anthropologist)
The Engines of God - Jack McDevitt s 3015

Jacobs, Earl (Con Artist)
Less than Human - Gary L. Raisor h 3558

Jacobs, Peter (Journalist)
The Cold One - Christopher Pike h 3446

Jacobson, Auston (Saloon Keeper/Owner)
Vampire Diary: The Embrace - Robert
   Weinberg h 4549

Jacoby, Daniel (Teenager)
The Wall Around Eden - Joan Slonczewski s 4063

Jacoby, Darcy (Student—College)
Wendigo Border - Catherine Montrose h 3158

Jacqueline (Businesswoman)
Human Resources - Floyd Kemske h 2438

Jade (Spirit)
Familiar Spirit - Lisa Tuttle h 4399

Jael (Mythical Creature; Royalty)
Dagger's Edge - Anne Logston f 2786

Jaeme (Nobleman)
Elfwood - Rose Estes f 1477

Jaeme (Noblewoman; Warrior)
Twisted Dragon - Kevin Stein f 4188

Jaffe, Randolph (Postal Worker)
The Great and Secret Show - Clive Barker h 286

Jaffey (Engineer; Computer Expert)
Zeta Base - Judith Alguire s 60

Jagoda, Barbara (Model)
Chicago Loop - Paul Theroux h 4344

Jagoda, Parker (Architect)
Chicago Loop - Paul Theroux h 4344

Jagun (Genetically Altered Being; Guide)
Golden Trillium - Andre Norton f 3307

Jahdo (Child; Adventurer)
Days of Blood and Fire - Katharine Kerr f 2444

Jaimah (Servant)
The Apprentice - Deborah Talmadge-
   Bickmore f 4292

Jaimie (Computer Expert)
Second Contact - Mike Resnick s 3636

Jaishree/Minaz (Artist; Model)
Beauty - Brian D'Amato h 1080

Jake (Hunter)
Nicoji - M. Shayne Bell s 358

Jake (Criminal)
Terraplane - Jack Womack s 4749

Jake (Criminal; Fugitive)
Further Adventures - Jon Stephen Fink f 1563

Jakobi, Virgil (Artist)
The Quicksilver Screen - Don H. DeBrandt s 1169

Jakobot "Jacko" 490,9000 (Robot; Sidekick)
*Extreme Paranoia: Nobody Knows the Trouble I've
   Shot* - Ken Rolston s 3733

Jalanopi (Alien; Leader)
Purgatory: A Chronicle of a Distant World - Mike
   Resnick s 3635

Jaldis the Blind (Wizard)
The Rainbow Abyss - Barbara Hambly f 2008

Jamail, Dierdre (Explorer)
Delta Pavonis - Eric Kotani s 2560

Jonson, Kenneth (Military Personnel; Experimental Subject)
Aggressor Six - Wil McCarthy   s   2993

Jordan (Actor)
Blood and Honor - Simon R. Green   f   1893

Jordan, Andy (Teenager)
65mm - Dale Hoover   h   2200

Jordan, Greg (Accountant)
Wind Chimes - R.R. Walters   h   4482

Jordan, John James (Spaceman; Leader)
Project Farcry - Pauline Ashwell   s   189

Jordan, Matt (Spy)
Watchers in the Woods - William W. Johnstone   h   2340

Jordan, Megan (Child)
Wind Chimes - R.R. Walters   h   4482

Jordan, Miles (Scientist; Museum Curator)
End of an Era - Robert J. Sawyer   s   3883

Jordan, Pamela (Businesswoman)
Wind Chimes - R.R. Walters   h   4482

Jordan, Richard (Professor)
Otherworld - Kenneth C. Flint   h   1576

Jordan, Richard "Rivername" (Telepath; Teenager)
Project Farcry - Pauline Ashwell   s   189

Jordon (Child)
Sexing the Cherry - Jeanette Winterson   f   4719

Jorem (Religious)
The Boy From the Burren - Sheila Gilluly   f   1798

Joreth (Genetically Altered Being)
OtherWhere - Margaret Wander Bonanno   s   464

Joreth (Musician)
OtherWise - Margaret Wander Bonanno   s   465

Jorhsa (Vampire)
Some Things Never Die - Robert Morgan   h   3187

Josef (Leader)
The Run to Chaos Keep - Jack L. Chalker   s   778

Joseph (Animal; Adventurer)
The Bellmaker - Brian Jacques   f   2267

Joshim (Spaceman)
A Matter of Oaths - Helen S. Wright   s   4769

Joshua (Guide)
Groogleman - Debra Doyle   s   1293

Joshua (Clone)
The Killing Star - Charles Pellegrino   s   3410

Josua (Royalty)
To Green Angel Tower - Tad Williams   f   4645

Jourdemayne, Truth (Researcher)
Ghostlight - Marion Zimmer Bradley   f   522
Witchlight - Marion Zimmer Bradley   f   537

Journey, Ruby (Revolutionary; Bounty Hunter)
Deathstalker Rebellion - Simon R. Green   s   1896

Joy, Sandy "Sana" (Musician; Psychic)
Strands of Sunlight - Gael Baudino   f   329

Joy-in-the-Dance (Adventurer)
The Arkadians - Lloyd Alexander   f   55

Joyner, Griffin (Military Personnel)
The First Duelist - Rutledge Etheridge   s   1488

Joze (Adventurer)
A Child of Elvish - Nancy Varian Berberick   f   373

J'role (Teenager; Thief)
The Longing Ring - Christopher Kubasik   f   2580

Juarel, Chita (Young Woman)
668: The Neighbor of the Beast - Lionel Fenn   h   1541

Juarel, Chita (Waiter/Waitress)
Kent Montana and the Really Ugly Thing From Mars - Lionel Fenn   s   1542

Jude (Teenager)
Random Acts of Senseless Violence - Jack Womack   f   4748

Judge, Paul (Lawyer)
Soul Catcher - Colin Kersey   h   2455

Judson, Marl (Spaceship Captain)
Judson's Eden - Keith Laumer   s   2662

Juillerat, Sister Chantal (Agent; Computer Expert)
Demon Download - Jack Yeovil   f   4799

Julia (Child-Care Giver; Teenager)
Blue Moon - Hila Feil   f   1528

Julia (Royalty)
Blue Moon Rising - Simon R. Green   f   1894

Julia (Housewife; Spouse)
The Hellbound Heart - Clive Barker   h   287

Julian (Revolutionary; Parent)
The Children of Men - P.D. James   f   2287

Julian (Young Man)
Orphans - Jean Simon   h   4042

Julian (Streetperson)
Wilding - Melanie Tem   h   4330

Julian of Stansvale (Royalty)
The Jewel of Fire - Diana L. Paxson   f   3396

Julian of Stansvale (Royalty; Heir—Dispossessed)
The Wind Crystal - Diana L. Paxson   f   3400

Julianus, Marcus (Diplomat)
The Light Bearer - Donna Gillespie   f   1791

Julien, Maria (Heiress)
Unholy Fire - Whitley Strieber   h   4261

Julius Caesar, Gaius (Ruler; Military Personnel)
Child of the Eagle - Esther Friesner   f   1668

Junknowitz (Revolutionary)
Free Radicals - Jack McKinney   s   3066

Junknowitz, Lucky (Revolutionary)
Hostile Takeover - Jack McKinney   s   3067

Justen (Magician; Engineer)
The Order War - L.E. Modesitt Jr.   f   3136

Justin (Clone)
The Killing Star - Charles Pellegrino   s   3410

Justin (Young Man)
The Living Evil - Ruby Jean Jensen   h   2312

Justin, Rangsey (Computer Expert; Homosexual)
Night Sky Mine - Melissa Scott   s   3912

Justine (Vampire)
Stainless - Todd Grimson   h   1961

Justinian (Veteran)
Subterranean Gallery - Richard Paul Russo   s   3798

Jute, Tabitha (Pilot; Leader)
Seasons of Plenty - Colin Greenland   s   1935

Jute, Tabitha (Spaceship Captain)
Take Back Plenty - Colin Greenland   s   1936

Jy (Leader; Wanderer)
Down the Bright Way - Robert Reed   s   3594

Jyp (Sailor)
Chase the Morning - Michael Scott Rohan   f   3729

K

K (Doctor)
The Face of Another - Kobo Abe   h   17

Kaa (Genetically Altered Being; Pilot)
Infinity's Shore - David Brin   s   565

Kaantille, Katrina (Teenager; Artisan)
The Loneliest Magician - Irene Radford   f   3555

Kadaffi, "Captain Cadaver" (Military Personnel)
Bill, the Galactic Hero: The Final Incoherent Adventure - Harry Harrison   s   2053

Kadar (Witch)
The Fagin - Pat Graversen   h   1870

Kadiya (Royalty)
Black Trillium - Marion Zimmer Bradley   f   518

Kadiya (Explorer; Royalty)
Golden Trillium - Andre Norton   f   3307

Kadolan "Kade" (Royalty; Guardian)
Faery Lands Forlorn - Dave Duncan   f   1351
Perilous Seas - Dave Duncan   f   1357

Kadumi (Warrior)
The Parched Sea - Troy Denning   f   1200

Kady, Meg (Pilot)
Hellburner - C.J. Cherryh   s   807

Kaeot (Monster)
A Whisper of Wings - Steven Ray Fulgham   h   1684

Kaftus (Sorcerer)
The Sure Death of a Mouse - Dan Crawford   f   1013

Kahless (Warrior; Hero)
Kahless - Michael Jan Friedman   s   1660

Kahn, Tae (Teenager; Warrior)
Beyond Ragnarok - Mickey Zucker Reichert   f   3604

Kahsir (Royalty; Warrior)
Tears of Time - Nancy Asire   f   215

Kaid (Military Personnel; Alien)
Fire Margins - Lisanne Norman   s   3295

Kairn (Warrior; Explorer)
The Steel Kings - John Maddox Roberts   f   3697

Kaiser, Valentine (Public Relations; Vampire)
A Matter of Taste - Fred Saberhagen   h   3814

Kakzim (Religious; Mythical Creature)
Cinnabar Shadows - Lynn Abbey   f   13

Kal (Teenager; Adventurer)
Flight to Hollow Mountain - Mark Sebanc   f   3921

Kalakaua, Cen (Genius; Scientist)
The Bones of Time - Kathleen Ann Goonan   s   1824

Kalass, Et (Political Figure; Alien)
In the Shadow of the Moon - Scott G. Gier   s   1787

Kalavek (Mythical Creature; Adventurer)
Dragon's Domain - Thorarinn Gunnarsson   f   1972

Kaldy, Janos (Werewolf)
Mark of the Werewolf - Jeffrey Sackett   h   3822

Kalencka (Sidekick)
Rally Cry! - William R. Forstchen   s   1590

Kalimuni (Religious; Lawyer)
The Broken Land - Ian McDonald   s   3017

Kalliana (Telepath)
Blindfold - Kevin J. Anderson   s   84

Kallisti, Avra (Clerk)
Specters - J.M. Dillard   h   1255

Kallisti, Magdalen (Teacher)
Specters - J.M. Dillard   h   1255

Kallmirsson, Rache (Warrior)
The Last of the Renshai - Mickey Zucker Reichert   f   3607

Kalvin, Walter (Government Official)
Silent Thunder/Universe - Dean Ing   s   2253

Kami, Minamoto no (Leader; Scientist)
Glory's People - Alfred Coppel   s   956

Kammaeman (Military Personnel)
Present Tense - Dave Duncan   f   1358

Kampa, Joshua (Time Traveller)
No Enemy but Time - Michael Bishop   s   407

Kan-Kon (Pilot)
Dragon Rigger - Jeffrey A. Carver   s   752

Kandaki (Royalty; Heiress—Dispossessed)
The Land of Gold - Gillian Bradshaw   f   540

Kane (Murderer)
Kane - Douglas Borton   h   472

Kane, Anna (Psychologist)
Nine Levels Down - William Dantz   h   1089

Kane, Bowie (Handyman; Indian)
Pitfall - Ronald Kelly   h   2435

Kane, Chandler (Businessman; Wealthy)
Order of the Arrow - Michael T.
   Hinkemeyer   h   2147

Kane, Emily (Doctor)
Immortal - Jason Nickles   h   3265

Kane, Laura (Student)
Deathscape - Michael Cecilione   h   766

Kane, Nathan (Vampire)
Bring on the Night - Don Davis   h   1129

Kang (Mythical Creature; Military Personnel)
The Doom Brigade - Margaret Weis   f   4551

Kang, Liu (Religious; Martial Arts Expert)
Mortal Kombat - Martin Delrio   f   1199

Kaplan, T'ing Hau (Teenager)
Gnome Man's Land - Esther Friesner   f   1669

Kaplan, T'ing Hau (Student—College)
Unicorn U. - Esther Friesner   f   1678

Kar, Ann (Writer; Journalist)
Century 21 - Ewa Kuryluk   s   2595

kar Therma, Staffa (Mercenary)
Relic of Empire - W. Michael Gear   s   1742

Kara (Adventurer; Teenager)
Flight of the Dragon Kyn - Susan Fletcher   f   1571

Karageorge, Vanessa (Scholar)
Carve the Sky - Alexander Jablokov   s   2260

Karal (Religious)
Storm Rising - Mercedes Lackey   f   2621

Karaquazian, Jack (Gambler)
Blood: A Southern Fantasy - Michael
   Moorcock   f   3166

Kardith (Warrior)
Northlight - Deborah Wheeler   s   4602

Karen (Young Woman)
Black Sun - Douglas E. Winter   h   4716

Karin (Royalty; Adventurer)
Voima - C. Dale Brittain   f   575

Karis (Young Woman)
Tooth: A Tale of Love and Death in Paradox - Novak
   Kruger   f   2578

Karli Dog (Robot)
Vurt - Jeff Noon   s   3294

Karloff, Boris (Actor; Historical Figure)
Father of Frankenstein - Christopher Bram   h   541

Karmade, Theodore "Ted" (Technician)
Quasar - Jamil Nasir   s   3242

Karmikal, Jake (Military Personnel)
Jungle Assault - P.M. Griffin   s   1950

Karolyi, Ignace (Mercenary)
Traveling with the Dead - Barbara Hambly   h   2012

Karpou, Betty Lou (Alien; Teacher)
My Teacher Fried My Brains - Bruce Coville   s   993

Karriaagzh (Scholar; Administrator)
Human to Human - Rebecca Ore   s   3363

Karsh (Innkeeper)
The Innkeeper's Song - Peter S. Beagle   f   337

Karus (Companion)
Last Mountain - Robert C. Fleet   f   1568

Karuth (Sorceress)
The Avenger - Louise Cooper   f   947
The Deceiver - Louise Cooper   f   948

Kashir (Royalty; Warrior)
To Fall Like Stars - Nancy Asire   f   216

Kasselman, Philip (Doctor)
Button Bright - Michael Kurland   h   2584

Kastazi, Marko (Businesswoman; Heiress—Lost)
Hawk's Flight - Carol Chase   f   794

Kastlin, Vask (Psychic; Police Officer)
Mainline - Deborah Christian   s   828

Kastring (Warrior)
Shadowbreed - David Ferring   f   1552

Kastrouni, Dimitrious (Spy)
Demogorgon - Brian Lumley   h   2826

Kat (Teenager)
Dark Heart - Betsy James   f   2274

Kataboki, Lily (Banker)
I'll Be Watching You - Samuel M. Key   h   2463

Katayev, Nadezhda (Scientist)
Pacific Edge - Kim Stanley Robinson   s   3709

Kate (Time Traveller; Teenager)
The Ancient One - T.A. Barron   f   308

Katelo, John (Guide; Linguist)
Desert Eden - J.M. Morgan   s   3182

Katelo, Jonathan (Indian; Explorer)
Beyond Eden - J.M. Morgan   s   3181

Katelo, Seth (Indian; Explorer)
Beyond Eden - J.M. Morgan   s   3181
Future Eden - J.M. Morgan   s   3183

Kathinka (Religious; Guide)
The Flies of Memory - Ian Watson   s   4491

Kathy (Prostitute)
Dark Prince - Keith Herber   h   2125

Katiasi (Young Woman)
I Am Frankenstein - C. Dean Andersson   h   116

Katin (Royalty; Herbalist)
Season of Storms - Ellen Foxxe   f   1631

Katrina (Mythical Creature)
Our Lady of the Harbour - Charles de Lint   f   1158

Katrina (Noblewoman)
War - Simon Hawke   f   2099

Katts, Wesley (Store Owner)
Anthony Shriek - Jessica Amanda
   Salmonson   h   3832

Katya (Adventurer)
Dark Magic - Angus Wells   f   4569
Wild Magic - Angus Wells   f   4576

Katz, Julie (Deity)
Only Begotten Daughter - James Morrow   f   3214

Kavanaugh, Louise (Researcher)
Nightshade - Stanley R. Moore   h   3176

Kawaguchi, Mike (Teenager)
The Summoned - Steven Ray Fulgham   h   1683

Kawakita, Gregory (Museum Curator)
Relic - Douglas Preston   h   3521

Kay, Laura (Journalist)
Catamount - Michael Peak   f   3403

Kaye, Darbi (Child)
Chiller - Randall Boyll   h   500

Kaye, Peter (Student—Graduate)
Chiller - Randall Boyll   h   500

Kaz (Mythical Creature; Knight)
Kaz the Minotaur - Richard A. Knaak   f   2522

Kazul (Mythical Creature; Royalty)
Calling on Dragons - Patricia C. Wrede   f   4761

Kazul (Mythical Creature)
Dealing with Dragons - Patricia C. Wrede   f   4762

Kean, Michael (Businessman)
Legends Reborn - Kenneth C. Flint   f   1575

Keane, Abel (Student)
The Trail of Cthulhu - August Derleth   h   1208

Keane, Andrew (Military Personnel)
Rally Cry! - William R. Forstchen   s   1590
Terrible Swift Sword - William R.
   Forstchen   s   1591

Kedrigern (Wizard)
Kedrigern and the Charming Couple - John
   Morressy   f   3194
A Remembrance for Kedrigern - John
   Morressy   f   3195

Kee (Teenager)
The Book of Webster's - J.N. Williamson   h   4661

Kee-Toroca (Alien; Scientist)
Fossil Hunter - Robert J. Sawyer   s   3885

Keebler, Micah "the Scavenger" (Scavenger)
Trust Territory - Janet Morris   s   3200

Keegan, Caroline (Journalist)
Wyrm Wolf - Edo Van Belkom   h   4414

Keelan, Delphine (Vampire)
Sweet Blood - Pat Graversen   h   1873

Keelie (Reanimated Dead; Psychic)
The Jigsaw Woman - Kim Antieau   f   163

Keenan, Daniel (Doctor)
Minds Apart - Margaret Davis   s   1134

Keene, Valerie (Waiter/Waitress)
Dark Rivers of the Heart - Dean R. Koontz   h   2547

Keeper, Tom (Teenager)
The Ways of Magic - Scott Ciencin   f   833

Keeton, Tallis (Teenager)
Lavondyss: Journey to an Unknown Region - Robert
   Holdstock   f   2185

Keff (Pilot; Spaceman)
The Ship Errant - Jody Lynn Nye   s   3327

Keighvin (Mythical Creature)
Born to Run - Mercedes Lackey   f   2600

Keita, Arthur (Military Personnel)
Path of the Fury - David Weber   s   4527

Keith (Musician)
Stainless - Todd Grimson   h   1961

Kelder of Shulara (Adventurer)
Taking Flight - Lawrence Watt-Evans   f   4506

Keleios (Sorceress; Fiance(e))
Nightseer - Laurell K. Hamilton   f   2019

Kelene (Sorceress; Healer)
City of the Sorcerers - Mary H. Herbert   f   2134
Winged Magic - Mary H. Herbert   f   2138

Kelledy, Cerin (Mythical Creature)
Ghosts of Wind and Shadow - Charles de
   Lint   f   1151

Kelledy, Meran (Musician; Mythical Creature)
Ghosts of Wind and Shadow - Charles de
   Lint   f   1151

Keller, Sally (Researcher)
Probe - Edward M. Lerner   s   2733

Keller, Yates (Empath; Criminal)
The War Minstrels - Karen Haber   s   1987

Khumeni, George (Wealthy)
Demogorgon - Brian Lumley   h   2826

Khuzud, Kami (Entertainer)
D'Shai - Joel Rosenberg   f   3739

Khuzud, Kami (Detective)
Hour of the Octopus - Joel Rosenberg   f   3742

Ki (Trader)
Luck of the Wheels - Megan Lindholm   f   2760

Kiakra, Darryl (Parent)
Minerva Wakes - Holly Lisle   f   2770

Kiakra, Minerva (Parent; Heroine)
Minerva Wakes - Holly Lisle   f   2770

Kickaha (Adventurer)
More than Fire - Philip Jose Farmer   s   1504

Kicva (Mythical Creature; Adventurer)
A Child of Elvish - Nancy Varian Berberick   f   373

Kid Zero (Outlaw)
Ghost Dancers - Brian Craig   s   1003

Kidd, Billy Lee (Singer)
Deathsong - Douglas Borton   h   471

Kidd, Christian (Advertising; Homosexual)
That's All, Folks! - Greg Snow   f   4108

Kiera (Thief)
Orca - Steven Brust   f   609

Kiff, Jim (Veteran)
Darkborn - Matthew J. Costello   h   966

Kifo, Ndug "Brother Death" (Martial Arts Expert; Leader)
Brother Death - Steve Perry   s   3419

Kiin (Prehistoric Human; Indian)
My Sister the Moon - Sue Harrison   f   2065

Kiklu, Nathan (Twin; Psychic)
Blood Brothers - Brian Lumley   h   2821
The Last Aerie - Brian Lumley   h   2830

Kiklu, Nestor (Twin; Psychic)
Blood Brothers - Brian Lumley   h   2821

Kiklu, Nestor (Vampire; Twin)
Bloodwars - Brian Lumley   h   2822

Kiklu, Nestor (Twin; Psychic)
The Last Aerie - Brian Lumley   h   2830

Kikun (Alien; Warrior)
Shadowkill - Jo Clayton   s   861
Shadowplay - Jo Clayton   s   862
Shadowspeer - Jo Clayton   s   863

Kilgour, Alex (Spaceman)
Revenge of the Damned - Allan Cole   s   892

Kilgour, Alex (Royalty; Military Personnel)
Vortex - Allan Cole   s   893

Killany, Mark (Police Officer)
Night Cruise - Billie Sue Mosiman   h   3218

Killany, Molly (Teenager)
Night Cruise - Billie Sue Mosiman   h   3218

Killdeer, Hunter (Police Officer)
Living with the Reptiles - Roger L. DiSilvestro   s   1262

Killeen (Parent; Wanderer)
Sailing Bright Eternity - Gregory Benford   s   369

Killeen (Spaceship Captain)
Tides of Light - Gregory Benford   s   370

Kilpatrick, Mark Michael (Artist; Serial Killer)
Grave Markings - Michael A. Arnzen   h   175

Kim (Teenager)
Demons Don't Dream - Piers Anthony   f   138

Kim (Orphan)
Mairelon the Magician - Patricia C. Wrede   f   4763

Kim, Jenae (Genetically Altered Being)
Lethe - Tricia Sullivan   s   4269

Kimball, Donald (Detective—Private)
American Psycho - Brett Easton Ellis   h   1425

Kimball, Joel (Police Officer)
Night - Alan Rodgers   h   3722

Kimberlin, Elwyn (Spaceship Captain)
The Tides of God - Ted Reynolds   s   3647

Kimmler, Vic (Police Officer; Widow(er))
Borderland - S.K. Epperson   h   1468

Kincaid, Astrid (Military Personnel; Space Explorer)
The Transmigration of Souls - William Barton   s   318

Kincaid, Hannah (Teenager)
A Witch Across Time - Gilbert B. Cross   f   1031

Kincannon, Aidan (Security Officer)
Red, Red Robin - Stephen Gallagher   h   1699

Kindle, Tom (Mountain Man)
The Harvest - Robert Charles Wilson   s   4703

Kindred, Lewis (Veteran)
Kindred - John Gideon   h   1785

King (Fugitive; Musician)
River Rats - Caroline Stevermer   s   4202

King, Depard (Murderer; Spy)
Spindoc - Steve Perry   s   3424

King, Elena "Lanie" (Computer Expert)
Richter 10 - Arthur C. Clarke   s   853

King, Ellen (Receptionist)
The Faery Convention - Brett Davis   f   1128

King, Greg (Military Personnel)
Sink the Armada - Keith William Andrews   s   118
Treason in Time - Keith William Andrews   s   119

King, Greta (Psychic; Child)
The Place - T.M. Wright   h   4777

King, Schuyler "Skye" (Professor; Detective—Amateur)
MagicNet - John DeChancie   f   1181

Kingston, April (Advertising)
Nightlife - Brian Hodge   h   2157

Kingston-Gray, April (Artist)
The Darker Saints - Brian Hodge   h   2155

Kinkaid, Johnny (Werewolf)
Moon Dance - S.P. Somtow   h   4116

Kinner's Son, Kensher (Rancher; Businessman)
The Blood of a Dragon - Lawrence Watt-Evans   f   4496

Kinney, Michael (Religious)
Dark Debts - Karen Hall   h   1999

Kinsey, Doc (Prisoner)
The Night Seasons - J.N. Williamson   h   4666

Kintner, Edward (Scientist; Government Official)
Paths to Otherwhere - James P. Hogan   s   2178

Kira (Military Personnel; Alien)
Bloodletter - K.W. Jeter   s   2317

Kira Nerys (Military Personnel; Alien)
Devil in the Sky - Greg Cox   s   995

Kirby, Erin (Detective—Police)
The Asylum - John Edward Ames   h   77

Kirby, Gertrude (Child-Care Giver)
The Jekyll Legacy - Robert Bloch   h   435

Kirby, Paul (Journalist)
The Chosen - Edward Lee   h   2695

Kire (Military Personnel)
They Fly at Ciron - Samuel R. Delany   s   1198

Kireyevsky, Vasily "Vasha" (Warrior; Bastard Son)
The Law of Becoming - Kate Elliott   s   1423

Kirha (Alien; Warrior)
Wing Commander: Freedom Flight - Mercedes Lackey   s   2630

Kirilovich, Vasily "Temsik" (Vampire)
Out for Blood - John Peyton Cooke   h   941

Kirk (Orphan)
Elfwood - Rose Estes   f   1477

Kirk, George Samuel (Parent; Spaceman)
Best Destiny - Diane Carey   s   731

Kirk, James T. (Spaceship Captain)
The Ashes of Eden - William Shatner   s   3936

Kirk, James T. (Spaceship Captain; Time Traveller)
The City on the Edge of Forever - Harlan Ellison   s   1431

Kirk, James T. (Spaceship Captain)
The Disinherited - Peter David   s   1116
Doctor's Orders - Diane Duane   s   1338
Enemy Unseen - V.E. Mitchell   s   3123

Kirk, James T. (Spaceship Captain; Aged Person)
The Fearful Summons - Denny Martin Flinn   s   1573

Kirk, James T. (Spaceship Captain)
Federation - Judith Reeves-Stevens   s   3600
First Frontier - Diane Carey   s   732
First Strike - Diane Carey   s   733
A Flag Full of Stars - Brad Ferguson   s   1546
The Joy Machine - James Gunn   s   1969
The Kobayashi Maru - Julia Ecklar   s   1386
Prime Directive - Judith Reeves-Stevens   s   3602
Probe - Margaret Wander Bonanno   s   467
Renegade - Gene DeWeese   s   1219
The Return - William Shatner   s   3939
The Rift - Peter David   s   1120
Rules of Engagement - Peter Morwood   s   3216
Sanctuary - John Vornholt   s   4460
Star Trek VI: The Undiscovered Country - J.M. Dillard   s   1256
Star Trek: The Classic Episodes 1 - James Blish   s   427
Star Trek: The Classic Episodes 2 - James Blish   s   428
Star Trek: The Classic Episodes 3 - James Blish   s   429
Star Trek: The Lost Years - J.M. Dillard   s   1257

Kirk, James T. (Military Personnel; Spaceship Captain)
Traitor Winds - L.A. Graf   s   1843

Kirk, James T. (Spaceship Captain)
Windows on a Lost World - V.E. Mitchell   s   3125

Kirk, James T. "Jimmy" (Teenager; Adventurer)
Best Destiny - Diane Carey   s   731

Kirk, Peter James (Student)
Sarek - A.C. Crispin   s   1022

Kirkland, Larry (Psychic; Vampire Hunter)
Bloody Bones - Laurell K. Hamilton   h   2013
Circus of the Damned - Laurell K. Hamilton   h   2014

Kirkpatrick, Stanley (Police Officer)
The Spider #8: The Devil's Paymaster/Legions of the Accursed Light - Grant Stockbridge   f   4236

Kirov, Natasha Alyosha Katerina (Spaceship Captain)
Voyage to the Red Planet - Terry Bisson   s   412

Kirowa, Niala (Administrator; Agent)
The Planet Beyond - Steve Mudd   s   3219

Kirshner, Martin (Criminal)
Worst Nightmare - Ric Meyers   h   3094

Kirtha (Child; Magician)
Mind of the Magic - Holly Lisle   f   2769

Kishida, Katie (Widow(er); Revolutionary)
Tech-Heaven - Linda Nagata   s   3239

Krim (Military Personnel; Spaceman)
The Hidden War - Michael Armstrong　*s*　172

Kris, Tabrel (Diplomat)
Exile - Al Sarrantonio　*s*　3867

Krishna the Holy Mendoro (Telepath; Religious)
The Ninety Trillion Fausts - Jack L. Chalker　*s*　776

Krisos, Alexander (Wealthy)
Lord of the Dark Lake - Ron Faust　*h*　1524

Krispos (Ruler)
Krispos of Videssos - Harry Turtledove　*f*　4389

Krispos (Adventurer)
Krispos Rising - Harry Turtledove　*f*　4390

Krispos (Ruler)
Krispos the Emperor - Harry Turtledove　*f*　4391

Kristin (Royalty)
The Sixth Book of Lost Swords: Mindsword's Story - Fred Saberhagen　*f*　3819

Kristinsson, Garth (Orphan; Traveller)
Hidden Fires - Katharine Eliska Kimbriel　*s*　2475

Kro, Gulthar (Criminal; Spy)
The Regiment's War - John Dalmas　*s*　1072

Kroft, Brian (Journalist)
The Undine - Michael O'Rourke　*h*　3368

Krokodil (Cyborg)
Comeback Tour: The Sky Belongs to the Stars - Jack Yeovil　*s*　4798

Kronarsson, Kraki (Adventurer)
One Quest, Hold the Dragons - Greg Costikyan　*f*　979

Kronis (Nobleman)
Sons of the Titans - Patrick H. Adkins　*f*　29

Kruger, Clayton Allen (Pilot)
Deadly Breed - T.J. Kirby　*h*　2505

Kruickshank, Jenny (Teenager; Warrior)
The Whims of Creation - Simon Hawke　*s*　2100

Krulshards (Demon)
Palace of Kings - Mike Jefferies　*f*　2303

Kryn (Heir—Dispossessed; Outlaw)
The Hands of Lyr - Andre Norton　*f*　3308

Krystal (Military Personnel)
The Death of Chaos - L.E. Modesitt Jr.　*f*　3128

Krystal (Adventurer)
The Magic of Recluce - L.E. Modesitt Jr.　*f*　3134

Krystel (Government Official; Scout)
Hellworld - Simon R. Green　*s*　1901

Kryten (Robot)
Better than Life - Grant Naylor　*s*　3246

Kuan Yu-Chen (Religious)
The Only Thing to Fear - Robert Morgan　*h*　3185

Kubick, Ruby (Construction Worker; Recluse)
Glass Houses - Laura J. Mixon　*s*　3126

Kullervo, Reede Kulleva (Genetically Altered Being; Researcher)
The Summer Queen - Joan D. Vinge　*s*　4440

Kullervo, Vyra (Alien; Insurance Investigator)
Greenthieves - Alan Dean Foster　*s*　1610

Kun, Holger (Military Personnel)
A Knight Among Knaves - Robert N. Charrette　*f*　789

Kundry (Immortal; Wanderer)
The Grail of Hearts - Susan Shwartz　*f*　4001

Kune (Doctor)
The Off Season - Jack Cady　*f*　669

Kung, Evelyn (Widow(er))
The Lincoln Hunters - Wilson Tucker　*s*　4378

Kurasawa, Sho (Military Personnel)
The Painful Field - Roland J. Green　*s*　1885
The Sum of Things - Roland J. Green　*s*　1887

Kurimoto, Eva (Journalist)
Protektor - Charles Platt　*s*　3459

Kurosawa, Oishi (Warrior)
The Napoleon Wager - William R. Forstchen　*s*　1589

Kurosov'e, Malyene Andreivne "Malye" (Leader)
The Fall of Sirius - Wil McCarthy　*s*　2994

Kurtz, Rupert (Doctor)
Headhunter - Timothy Findley　*h*　1562

Kuruk (Cult Member)
Deathsong - Douglas Borton　*h*　471

Kurz (Alien; Spy)
Fire in the Sky - Jo Clayton　*s*　859

Kusac (Psychic; Alien)
Fire Margins - Lisanne Norman　*s*　3295
Fortune's Wheel - Lisanne Norman　*s*　3296
Turning Point - Lisanne Norman　*s*　3297

Kusaka, Michael (Spaceship Captain; Immortal)
The Dark Beyond the Stars - Frank M. Robinson　*s*　3702

Kustaa, Captain Fred (Pilot)
Under the Yoke - S.M. Stirling　*s*　4229

Kuttner, Dayne (Nurse)
Sympathy for the Devil - Holly Lisle　*f*　2771

Kuvasc, Paval (Apprentice; Scientist)
Regenesis - Julia Ecklar　*s*　1387

Kuwai (Indian; Royalty)
Dark Legend - Jamake Highwater　*f*　2146

Kwan, Martin (Lawyer)
Cutthroat - Michael Slade　*h*　4058

Kwan, Roxane (Wanderer)
Mazeway - Jack Williamson　*s*　4671

Kwip (Thief)
Castle Spellbound - John DeChancie　*s*　1174

Kyl (Mythical Creature; Heir)
The Dragon Crown - Richard A. Knaak　*f*　2518

Kyle, Amy (Psychic)
The Nexus - Mike McQuay　*f*　3075

Kyle, Selena "Catwoman" (Criminal; Heroine)
Batman Returns - Craig Shaw Gardner　*s*　1707
Catwoman - Lynn Abbey　*s*　12
The Further Adventures of Batman 3: Featuring Catwoman - Martin H. Greenberg　*s*　1916

Kyler, Vaughan (Organized Crime Figure)
Blood on the Water - P.N. Elrod　*h*　1437

Kyllikki (Alien; Telepath)
Dreamspy - Jacqueline Lichtenberg　*s*　2749

Kymri (Pilot; Alien)
Grounded! - Chris Claremont　*s*　840

L

La Forge, Geordi (Engineer; Military Personnel)
Balance of Power - Dafydd ab Hugh　*s*　6
Dark Mirror - Diane Duane　*s*　1337
Doomsday World - Carmen Carter　*s*　749
Relics - Michael Jan Friedman　*s*　1661
Requiem - Michael Jan Friedman　*s*　1662
Vendetta - Peter David　*s*　1121

LaBianca, Diana (Producer)
The Hunger of the Beast - John Driver　*h*　1336

LaBrae, Jael (Pilot; Heroine)
Dragon Rigger - Jeffrey A. Carver　*s*　752

Labyrinth, Doc (Scientist)
The Collected Stories of Philip K. Dick, Volume One: The Short Happy Life of the Brown Oxford - Philip K. Dick　*s*　1225

Lacan, Arnauld (Scientist)
The Hollowing - Robert Holdstock　*f*　2184

Lace, Invictus Ovidius "I.O." (Orphan)
A Dozen Tough Jobs - Howard Waldrop　*f*　4471

Lacey, Bobbie (Computer Expert; Police Officer)
Polar City Blues - Katharine Kerr　*s*　2449

Lacey, Jenny (Writer)
Vampire Blood - Kathryn Meyer Griffith　*h*　1954

Lacey, Joey (Restaurateur)
Vampire Blood - Kathryn Meyer Griffith　*h*　1954

lach Feragh, Culain (Immortal; Warrior)
Ghost King - David Gemmell　*f*　1755

Lacroix, Marc (Doctor)
Machine - Rene Belletto　*h*　360

Lacroix, Marie (Housewife)
Machine - Rene Belletto　*h*　360

Lacuna (Housewife; Agent)
Question Quest - Piers Anthony　*f*　153

Lady (Military Personnel; Sorcerer)
Dreams of Steel - Glen Cook　*f*　928

Lady (Aged Person)
Boy's Life - Robert R. McCammon　*h*　2987

Laela (Mythical Creature; Magician)
Twisted Dragon - Kevin Stein　*f*　4188

Lafall, Teksan (Traveller)
Delan the Mislaid - Laurie J. Marks　*f*　2881

Lagenkamp, Heather (Actress; Historical Figure)
Wes Craven's New Nightmare - David Bergantino　*h*　376

Lahikainen, Sarah (Student—College)
Cold Whisper - Rick Hautala　*h*　2080

Laidcliff, Cullen (Government Official)
Looking for the Mahdi - N. Lee Wood　*s*　4753

Laidlaw, Alison (Police Officer)
Cloud Castles - Michael Scott Rohan　*f*　3730

Laine, Bonnie (Parent)
Nightscape - Stephen R. George　*h*　1769

Laine, Evan (Child)
Nightscape - Stephen R. George　*h*　1769

Laitha "Gian Avur" (Orphan; Young Woman)
Ghost King - David Gemmell　*f*　1755

Lakeman, Max (Landscaper)
Max Lakeman and the Beautiful Stranger - Jon Cohen　*f*　883

Laker, Maria (Spouse; Murderer)
Among Madmen - Jim Starlin　*s*　4156

Laker, Naomi "Mig" Margaret (Teenager; Writer)
Aunt Maria - Diana Wynne Jones　*f*　2345

Laker, Tom (Lawman)
Among Madmen - Jim Starlin　*s*　4156

"Lal" Lalkhamsin-Khamsolal (Sailor)
The Innkeeper's Song - Peter S. Beagle　*f*　337

Laleekh (Alien)
Bagatelle—Guinevere - Nancy Bogen　*f*　456

Lalelelang (Historian; Alien)
The Spoils of War - Alan Dean Foster　*s*　1618

Lamai, Leie (Teenager; Twin)
Glory Season - David Brin　*s*　564

Lamai, Maia (Teenager; Traveller)
Glory Season - David Brin　*s*　564

Lamaril (Hero; Warrior)
Golden Trillium - Andre Norton　*f*　3307

Le Roux, Reiki Momoku (Computer Expert; Spacewoman)
Marooned on Eden - Robert L. Forward   s   1593

Leah, Morgan (Adventurer)
The Druid of Shannara - Terry Brooks   f   580

Lealbhallain (Student)
The Meri - Maya Kaathryn Bohnhoff   f   459

Lealor (Guardian)
Dragon's Queen - Carol L. Dennis   f   1202

LeBrae, Jael (Spacewoman; Teenager)
Dragons in the Stars - Jeffrey A. Carver   s   753

LeBrel, Andre (Vampire)
Children of the Night - Mercedes Lackey   h   2605

Leclerc, Louis (Inventor; Time Traveller)
Witch - Donald E. McQuinn   s   3078

Lecotta, Angel (Revolutionary; Time Traveller)
Time: The Semi-Final Frontier - Lionel Fenn   s   1545

Lecouveurs, Alain (Nobleman; Vampire)
In Hot Blood - Petru Popescu   h   3480

Lector, Hannibal "Cannibal" (Murderer)
The Silence of the Lambs - Thomas Harris   h   2051

Leda (Mythical Creature; Orphan)
Nevernever - Will Shetterly   f   3985

Ledbetter, Gary (Serial Killer)
A Room for the Dead - Noel Hynd   h   2250

Lee (Abuse Victim)
The Jigsaw Woman - Kim Antieau   f   163

Lee, Afriqua (Teenager)
Jaguar - Bill Ransom   s   3569

Lee, Darcy (Military Personnel)
Fire on the Border - Kevin O'Donnell Jr.   s   3339

Lee, Houlka (Hero)
A Dozen Tough Jobs - Howard Waldrop   f   4471

Lee, Jeroen (Political Figure)
Becoming Human - Valerie J. Freireich   s   1647

Lee, Lysistrata "Lizzie" (Student; Teenager)
Unwillingly to Earth - Pauline Ashwell   s   190

Lee, Richard (Scientist)
Father to the Man - John Gribbin   s   1947

Lee, Robert E. (Historical Figure; Military Personnel)
The Guns of the South - Harry Turtledove   s   4386

Lee, Wei (Technician; Traveller)
Red Dust - Paul J. McAuley   s   2956

Leech, Derek (Businessman)
The Quorum - Kim Newman   h   3263

Leetah (Mythical Creature)
The Quest Begins - Wendy Pini   f   3455

LeFarge, Frederick (Royalty)
The Stone Dogs - S.M. Stirling   s   4228

LeFarge, Marya (Royalty)
The Stone Dogs - S.M. Stirling   s   4228

Leffing, Lucius (Paranormal Investigator)
The Adventures of Lucius Leffing - Joseph Payne Brennan   h   549

Leger, Gary (Adventurer; Hero)
The Dragon's Dagger - R.A. Salvatore   f   3837

Leger, Gary (Adventurer)
Dragonslayer's Return - R.A. Salvatore   f   3838

Leger, Gary (Adventurer; Hero)
The Woods out Back - R.A. Salvatore   f   3848

Lehman, Roger "Senmut-Ptah" (Time Traveller; Scientist)
Thebes of the Hundred Gates - Robert Silverberg   s   4022

Lehman, Stefan (Criminal; Leader)
The Stone Within - David Wingrove   s   4713

Leiber, Manny (Director)
A Graveyard for Lunatics - Ray Bradbury   h   509

Leifr (Adventurer)
The Dragon's Carbuncle - Elizabeth H. Boyer   f   495

Leigh, Makoto Shirata (Teacher)
Makoto - Kelley Wilde   h   4619

Leighton, Gerard (Administrator)
High Steel - Jack C. Haldeman II   s   1992

Leith (Royalty; Psychic)
The Prince of Ill Luck - Susan Dexter   f   1220

Leith (Werewolf)
Tapestry of Dark Souls - Elaine Bergstrom   h   380

LeMat, Joseph "Gunnar Savage" (Computer Expert)
Headcrash - Bruce Bethke   s   392

Lenk, Able (Leader)
Legacy - Greg Bear   s   344

Lennart (Spaceman)
Jaydium - Deborah Wheeler   s   4601

Lennox, Xavier William (Explorer; Genetically Altered Being)
A Miracle of Rare Design - Mike Resnick   s   3631

Lennuick, Peyto (Scholar)
Timespell - Robert N. Charrette   f   793

Leno, Dan (Actor)
The Trial of Elizabeth Cree - Peter Ackroyd   h   19

Lentrall, Davlo (Scientist)
Utopia - Roger MacBride Allen   s   69

Leo, Sam (Doctor)
Kaleidoscope Eyes - Graham Watkins   h   4487

Leon (Royalty)
The Stallion Queen - Constance Ash   f   185

Leon (Businessman)
The Immortals - Andrew Neiderman   h   3254

Leonard, Wyatt (Actor; Homosexual)
From the Teeth of Angels - Jonathan Carroll   h   744

Leonardo da Vinci (Historical Figure; Inventor)
The Memory Cathedral - Jack Dann   s   1086

Leonardo Da Vinci (Genius; Aged Person)
Pasquale's Angel - Paul J. McAuley   f   2955

Leones, Giraut (Teacher)
A Million Open Doors - John Barnes   s   295

Leong, Allan (Student)
The Robin Hood Ambush - William Wu   s   4783

Leopold (Royalty; Military Personnel)
Tiger Burning Bright - Marion Zimmer Bradley   f   534

Lerille, Jack (Actor; Librarian)
Paddywhack - John Stchur   h   4176

Lerner, Reed (Doctor)
The Basement - Bari Wood   h   4750

Lerris (Apprentice; Carpenter)
The Death of Chaos - L.E. Modesitt Jr.   f   3128
The Magic of Recluce - L.E. Modesitt Jr.   f   3134

Lescevre, Thibault "Thib" (Apprentice; Martial Arts Expert)
Anvil of the Sun - Anne Lesley Groell   f   1963

Lessa (Leader)
All the Weyrs of Pern - Anne McCaffrey   s   2958

Lesserac, Gary (Computer Expert)
Virtual Destruction - Kevin J. Anderson   s   98

Lessis of Valmes (Witch; Heroine)
Bazil Broketail - Christopher Rowley   f   3757

Leta (Young Woman)
The Stone Giant - James P. Blaylock   f   425

Leventhal, Dan (Detective—Police)
The Nine Lives of Catseye Gomez - Simon Hawke   f   2094

Leverett, Anthony (Doctor)
Lori - Robert Bloch   h   436

Levin, Peter (Writer)
Children of the Thunder - John Brunner   s   599

Levine, Charles (Scientist)
Mount Dragon - Douglas Preston   h   3520

Levine, Richard (Scientist)
The Lost World - Michael Crichton   s   1019

Leving, Fredda (Computer Expert; Engineer)
Caliban - Roger MacBride Allen   s   63

Levitt, Ira (FBI Agent)
Thinning the Predators - Daina Graziunas   h   1876

Levitt, Irv (Scientist)
A World of Difference - Harry Turtledove   s   4394

Levy, Jace (Detective—Homicide)
Love Bite - Sherry Gottlieb   h   1835

Lewes, Charlotte (Widow(er); Teacher)
John Dollar - Marianne Wiggins   h   4617

Lewin, Linda (Religious; Criminal)
Journals of the Plague Years - Norman Spinrad   s   4126

Lewis (Servant)
Prisoner of Dreams - Karen Ripley   s   3670

Lewis (Genetically Altered Being)
The Tenth Class - Karen Ripley   s   3671

Lewis, Carl (Inventor)
Cyberbooks - Ben Bova   s   477

Lewis, Claude (Government Official)
Way Station - Clifford D. Simak   s   4027

Lewis, Dafydd (Photographer)
Naomi's Room - Jonathan Aycliffe   h   237

Lewis, Jonathan (Student)
Looker - Jorge Saralegui   h   3859

Lewis, Laura (Teenager)
The Third Beast - Peter Loughran   h   2804

Lewis, Leonard (Photographer)
Nightlight - Michael Cadnum   h   664

Lewis, Mary (Widow(er))
Nightlight - Michael Cadnum   h   664

Leydon, B (Student; Companion)
Unwillingly to Earth - Pauline Ashwell   s   190

Leyner, Mark (Writer; Socialite)
Et Tu, Babe - Mark Leyner   s   2747

Lha (Royalty)
Python Isle - Kenneth Robeson   f   3700

Li, Beth (Teenager)
The Werewolf's Revenge - Richard Jaccoma   h   2264

Li, Master (Detective)
Eight Skilled Gentlemen - Barry Hughart   f   2233

Li, Stefan (Scientist; Disembodied Personality)
Ark Liberty - Will Bradley   s   538

Li Yuan (Leader)
White Moon, Red Dragon - David Wingrove   s   4714

Liang, Sindon (Linguist)
The Khan's Persuasion - Cynthia Felice   s   1540

Libermann, E.F. (Cartographer; Scientist)
The Discovery of Dragons - Graeme Base   f   320

Library (Librarian; Psychic)
Genetic Soldier - George Turner   s   4381

Luisa (Innkeeper)
Cambio Bay - Kate Wilhelm *f* 4624

Lujan, Derek (Time Traveller; Spaceman)
Children of the Earth - Catherine Wells *s* 4578

Lukas, Greg (Spaceman; Pilot)
Mind Light - Margaret Davis *s* 1133
Minds Apart - Margaret Davis *s* 1134

Lukas, Harkon (Minstrel)
Death of a Darklord - Laurell K. Hamilton *h* 2015

Lukasha (Sorcerer)
The Spirit Gate - Maya Kaathryn Bohnhoff *f* 460

Luke, Jim Bob (Detective—Private)
Cold in July - Joe R. Lansdale *h* 2644

Luki (Immortal)
Fire Crossing - Cheryl J. Franklin *s* 1635

Lumbaird, Fran (Child)
The Black Carousel - Charles L. Grant *h* 1846

Lund, Jack "Mr. Was" (Time Traveller; Amnesiac)
Mr. Was - Pete Hautman *s* 2089

Lundens, Myra (Housewife)
The Basement - Bari Wood *h* 4750

Lupo (Animal)
Down the Stream of Stars - Jeffrey A. Carver *s* 751

Lustig, Alex (Scientist)
Earth - David Brin *s* 563

Luther (Student)
Fool on the Hill - Matt Ruff *f* 3768

Lutz, Frances (Real Estate Agent)
Infernal Affairs - Jane Heller *h* 2118

Luz (Teenager; Psychic)
The Secret Weavers: Stories of the Fantastic by Latin American Women - Marjorie Agosin *f* 33

Luz, Gabriel (Witch)
Witch-Light - Nancy Holder *h* 2181

Lyall, Andrew (Vampire)
Vampires Anonymous - Jeffrey N. McMahan *h* 3070

Lycaon (Artisan; Werewolf)
The Last World - Christoph Ransmayr *f* 3567

Lydi (Witch)
Shadow of the Seventh Moon - Nancy Varian Berberick *f* 375

Lydia (Traveller)
The Tattooed Map - Barbara Hodgson *f* 2161

Lydyard, Cordelia (Housewife)
The Angel of Pain - Brian Stableford *h* 4141

Lydyard, David (Scientist)
The Angel of Pain - Brian Stableford *h* 4141
The Carnival of Destruction - Brian Stableford *h* 4142

Lydyard, David (Young Man)
The Werewolves of London - Brian Stableford *h* 4147

Lyell, Thomasina (Journalist; Activist)
The Pure Cold Light - Gregory Frost *s* 1681

Lyim (Wizard; Handicapped)
The Seventh Sentinel - Mary Kirchoff *f* 2506

Lykan, Radu (Vampire)
Necroscope: The Lost Years - Brian Lumley *h* 2832
Resurgence - Brian Lumley *h* 2836

Lyle, Nona (Doctor)
Horses of the Night - Michael Cadnum *h* 662

Lyma, Skyla (Mercenary)
Relic of Empire - W. Michael Gear *s* 1742

Lynn, Corbet (Heir)
Winter Rose - Patricia A. McKillip *f* 3062

Lynskey, Lucy (Doctor)
The Frighteners - Michael Jahn *h* 2273

Lynx (Gang Member)
Bad Voltage - Jonathan Littell *s* 2773

Lynx, Philip "Flinx" (Psychic; Wanderer)
Mid-Flinx - Alan Dean Foster *s* 1613

Lyon, Afra (Psychic)
Damia - Anne McCaffrey *s* 2964

Lyon, Harry (Police Officer)
Dragon Tears - Dean R. Koontz *h* 2548

Lyon, Isthian "Thian" (Teenager; Psychic)
Damia's Children - Anne McCaffrey *s* 2965

Lyon, John (Television Personality; Journalist)
Bring Me Children - David Martin *h* 2889

Lyon, Laria (Teenager; Psychic)
Damia's Children - Anne McCaffrey *s* 2965

Lyon, Rojer (Teenager; Psychic)
Damia's Children - Anne McCaffrey *s* 2965

Lyon, Rojer (Psychic; Spaceman)
Lyon's Pride - Anne McCaffrey *s* 2972

Lyonz (Heir)
Drum Warning - Jo Clayton *f* 858

Lyppiatt, Xan (Political Figure)
The Children of Men - P.D. James *f* 2287

Lysander (Android; Agent)
Phaze Doubt - Piers Anthony *f* 152

Lysander (Royalty)
Prince of Mercenaries - Jerry Pournelle *s* 3490

Lysia (Noblewoman)
Hammer and Anvil - Harry Turtledove *f* 4387

M

Ma Li "Sister" (Military Personnel; Revolutionary)
Shangri-La: The Return to the World of Lost Horizon - Eleanor Cooney *f* 942

Maas, Ellen (Journalist)
The Forbidden Zone - Whitley Strieber *h* 4259

mac Ailill, Fionchadd (Mythical Creature)
Sunshaker's War - Tom Deitz *f* 1195

Mac Airt, Cormac (Royalty; Leader)
Finn Mac Cool - Morgan Llywelyn *f* 2782

mac Brian, Murcha (Warrior; Heir)
Brian Boru: Emperor of the Irish - Morgan Llywelyn *f* 2779

mac Cainnech, Aidan (Religious; Linguist)
Byzantium - Stephen R. Lawhead *f* 2670

Mac Cool, Finn (Warrior; Hero)
Finn Mac Cool - Morgan Llywelyn *f* 2782

mac Cuel, Ceilyn (Knight; Werewolf)
The Work of the Sun - Teresa Edgerton *f* 1402

mac Cumhall, Fionn "Demne" (Historical Figure; Hero)
Master of Earth and Water - Diana L. Paxson *f* 3397
The Shield between the Worlds - Diana L. Paxson *f* 3398
Sword of Fire and Shadow - Diana L. Paxson *f* 3399

Mac Kay, Kenneth "Ken" (Military Personnel)
McLendon's Syndrome - Robert Frezza *s* 1650

mac Kennedy, Brian (Leader; Historical Figure)
Brian Boru: Emperor of the Irish - Morgan Llywelyn *f* 2779

Mac Morna, Goll (Warrior)
Finn Mac Cool - Morgan Llywelyn *f* 2782

mac Mornas, Goll (Warrior)
The Shield between the Worlds - Diana L. Paxson *f* 3398

mac Sliabhin, Caith (Outlaw)
Faery in Shadow - C.J. Cherryh *f* 801

Macaffrey, Lester Hill (Teacher; Psychic)
Heathern - Jack Womack *s* 4747

Macaree, Anne (Model)
Obsessed - Rick R. Reed *h* 3590

Macaree, Joe (Advertising)
Obsessed - Rick R. Reed *h* 3590

MacAuliffe, Judy (Saloon Keeper/Owner)
The Keeper - Robert D. Lee *h* 2705

MacBreed, Keenan (Archaeologist)
The Uprising - Brent Monahan *h* 3149

MacBride, Johnny (Military Personnel)
Bats - William W. Johnstone *h* 2330

MacCallum, Brenda (Waiter/Waitress)
Shadows - John Saul *h* 3878

MacCallum, Josh (Child)
Shadows - John Saul *h* 3878

MacColl, Enye (Advertising; Courier)
King of Morning, Queen of Day - Ian McDonald *f* 3019

MacDavid, Kate (Young Woman)
Night Beasts - T.W. Stetson *h* 4199

Macdonald, Dorothea (Psychic; Political Figure)
Diamond Mask: A Novel - Julian May *s* 2941

MacDonald, Ellen (Secretary)
Snowbeast! - Peter Tremayne *h* 4373

MacDonald, Mercy (Spaceman)
Stopping at Slowyear - Frederik Pohl *s* 3469

MacDonald, Murdo (Doctor)
Snowbeast! - Peter Tremayne *h* 4373

MacDonald, Warren (Religious)
Blood Lust - Ron Dee *h* 1183

MacDuff (Hero)
The Spawn of Loki - Jason Henderson *f* 2122

Mace, Jarek (Criminal; Hero)
Morningstar - David Gemmell *f* 1757

Macero (Thief)
Songs of the Dancing Gods - Jack L. Chalker *f* 780

MacGregor, Sandy (Hero; Wizard)
A Name to Conjure With - Donald Aamodt *f* 2
A Troubling Along the Border - Donald Aamodt *f* 3

Machiavelli, Niccolo (Historical Figure; Apprentice)
The Memory Cathedral - Jack Dann *s* 1086

Machiavelli, Niccolo (Journalist; Political Figure)
Pasquale's Angel - Paul J. McAuley *f* 2955

Macintosh, Elizabeth (Spacewoman; Telepath)
Rediscovery: A Novel of Darkover - Marion Zimmer Bradley *s* 527

MacIntyre, Colin (Spaceship Captain; Leader)
The Armageddon Inheritance - David Weber *s* 4518

MacIntyre, Colin (Ruler)
Heirs of Empire - David Weber *s* 4521

MacIntyre, Colin (Military Personnel; Spaceship Captain)
Mutineers' Moon - David Weber *s* 4524

MacIntyre, Sean Horus (Heir; Military Personnel)
Heirs of Empire - David Weber *s* 4521

MacIver, Teri (Teenager)
Second Child - John Saul   h   3877

Mack the Knife (Criminal; Historical Figure)
Spring-Heeled Jack - Philip Pullman   f   3546

MacKai, Willie (Musician)
Phantom Banjo - Elizabeth Ann
   Scarborough   f   3894
Picking the Ballad's Bones - Elizabeth Ann
   Scarborough   f   3895
Strum Again? - Elizabeth Ann Scarborough   f   3896

MacKelston, Kathleen (Accountant)
The Barrens - F. Paul Wilson   h   4682

Mackenson, Cory (Child)
Boy's Life - Robert R. McCammon   h   2987

Mackenson, Tom (Worker; Parent)
Boy's Life - Robert R. McCammon   h   2987

MacKenzie, David (Detective—Police)
Heathen - Shaun Hutson   h   2244

MacKenzie, Ian S. (Spaceship Captain)
Outbanker - Timothy A. Madden   s   2863

Mackenzie, Lyle (Administrator; Political Figure)
Sister Blood - Karen Haber   s   1986

Mackinnon, Curtis (Businessman)
Kalimantan - Lucius Shepard   h   3972

Maclaren, Neil (Restaurateur)
Raven - Charles L. Grant   h   1854

MacLaren, Sherideen (Young Woman)
For You, the Living - Wayne Allen Sallee   h   3828

MacLean, Henry (Farmer)
Other - Gordon R. Dickson   s   1241

Maclean, Ramsey (Doctor)
The Matrix - Jonathan Aycliffe   h   236

Maclemmon, Howmaster (Businessman)
668: The Neighbor of the Beast - Lionel
   Fenn   h   1541

Macleod, Andrew (Professor)
The Matrix - Jonathan Aycliffe   h   236

MacLeod, Connor (Immortal)
Highlander: The Element of Fire - Jason
   Henderson   f   2121

MacLeod, Duncan (Immortal; Martial Arts Expert)
Highlander: Scotland the Brave - Jennifer
   Roberson   f   3686
Highlander: The Element of Fire - Jason
   Henderson   f   2121

MacLoed, Alex (Hero; Pilot)
Fallen Angels - Larry Niven   s   3279

Maclyn of Elfhame Outremer (Mythical Creature)
When the Bough Breaks - Mercedes Lackey   f   2625

MacMahan, Hector (Military Personnel)
Mutineers' Moon - David Weber   s   4524

MacNeil, Duncan (Military Personnel)
Down Among the Dead Men - Simon R.
   Green   f   1897

MacPherson, Maggie (Journalist)
Force of Arms - G. Harry Stine   s   4212

Macumba the Dark Man (Sorcerer)
Howl-O-Ween - Gary L. Holleman   h   2189

Macurdy, Curtis (Farmer; Warrior)
The Lion of Farside - John Dalmas   f   1070

Mad Mall (Sailor; Warrior)
Chase the Morning - Michael Scott Rohan   f   3729

Maddock, Yanaba (Military Personnel; Settler)
Power Lines - Anne McCaffrey   s   2976

Maddock, Yanaba (Military Personnel;
   Administrator)
Power Play - Anne McCaffrey   s   2977

Maddock, Yanaba (Invalid; Military Personnel)
Powers That Be - Anne McCaffrey   s   2978

Maddox, Cory (Computer Expert; Adventurer)
The Cybernetic Walrus - Jack L. Chalker   s   770

Maddox, Cory (Computer Expert; Handicapped)
The March Hare Network - Jack L. Chalker   s   775

Madeleine (Parent)
Phantom - Susan Kay   h   2407

Madia (Royalty)
Demon Blade - Mark A. Garland   f   1718

Madimi (Angel)
Love and Sleep - John Crowley   f   1035

Madison, Jay (Student—College; Relative)
The Gryphon King - Tom Deitz   f   1192

Madison, Marshall (Vampire)
Bloodlines - J.N. Williamson   h   4660

Madison, Sybil Wilfred (Aged Person)
Baby Doll - Ruby Jean Jensen   h   2309

Madison, Thaddie (Child)
Bloodlines - J.N. Williamson   h   4660

Madlen (Teenager)
The Sister - Elleston Trevor   h   4375

Madonette (Singer; Worker)
The Stainless Steel Rat Sings the Blues - Harry
   Harrison   s   2060

Madouc (Heroine)
Madouc - Jack Vance   f   4421

Madrone (Healer; Revolutionary)
The Fifth Sacred Thing - Starhawk   f   4154

Maelwaedd, Rhodry (Mythical Creature; Mercenary)
Days of Air and Darkness - Katharine Kerr   f   2443
Days of Blood and Fire - Katharine Kerr   f   2444
The Dragon Revenant - Katharine Kerr   f   2445
A Time of Exile - Katharine Kerr   f   2452

Ma'eva (Mythical Creature)
Storm Caller - Carol Severance   f   3934

Mafoo (Servant)
The Remarkable Journey of Prince Jen - Lloyd
   Alexander   f   56

Magaera (Wizard)
The Towers of the Sunset - L.E. Modesitt
   Jr.   f   3139

Magara (Storyteller)
Shadow-Maze - Mark Smith   f   4094

Magda (Vampire)
The Darker Passions: Dracula - Amarantha
   Knight   h   2528

Maggie (Artificial Intelligence)
Virtual Girl - Amy Thomson   s   4358

Magnalucius (Religious; Writer)
Quest: In Search of the Dragontooth - Michael
   Green   f   1881

Magnan, Ben (Diplomat)
Reward for Retief - Keith Laumer   s   2663

Magnolia (Runaway; Lesbian)
The Nature of Smoke - Anne Harris   s   2044

Magnus, Brock (Teenager; Settler)
The Faces of Ceti - Mary Caraker   s   712

Magnus, Dominic "Dom" (Cyborg; Businessman)
Partisan - S. Andrew Swann   s   4276
Profiteer - S. Andrew Swann   s   4277
Revolutionary - S. Andrew Swann   s   4278

Magodor (Deity)
Pretty Pewter Gods - Glen Cook   f   930

Magon (Royalty; Pirate)
The Warrior Returns - Allan Cole   f   894

Magpie (Minstrel)
A Cast of Corbies - Mercedes Lackey   f   2603

Magruder, Bernie (Child; Student)
Bernie and the Bessledorf Ghost - Phyllis Reynolds
   Naylor   f   3248

Magruder, Sam (Scientist; Time Traveller)
The Dechronization of Sam Magruder - George
   Gaylord Simpson   s   4044

Maguire, Aaron (Magician; Teenager)
The Wizard's Apprentice - S.P. Somtow   f   4120

Maguire, Charlotte "Charlie" (Journalist)
Fatherland - Robert Harris   s   2049

Magus, Stheneleos LXIV (Alien; Time Traveller)
Web of Futures - Jefferson P. Swycaffer   f   4286

Magyar, Cherry (Engineer)
Slow River - Nicola Griffith   s   1957

Mah-ree (Prehistoric Human)
The Edge of the World - William Sarabande   f   3856

Mahafny (Doctor)
Finders-Seekers - Gayle Greeno   s   1938

Mahan, Patrick (Military Personnel)
1901 - Robert Conroy   s   918

Mahan, Sherry (Police Officer)
The Bad Thing - Michael O'Rourke   h   3366

Mahoney, Ian (Military Personnel)
The Return of the Emperor - Allan Cole   s   891
Vortex - Allan Cole   s   893

Mahtra (Genetically Altered Being)
Cinnabar Shadows - Lynn Abbey   f   13

Maijstral, Drake (Thief; Nobleman)
Rock of Ages - Walter Jon Williams   s   4651

Mairelon (Magician; Traveller)
Mairelon the Magician - Patricia C. Wrede   f   4763

Majamdar, Casseia (Political Figure)
Moving Mars - Greg Bear   s   345

Majeed (Young Man)
The Safety of Unknown Cities - Lucy
   Taylor   h   4320

Majere, Raistlin (Wizard)
Dragons of Summer Flame - Margaret Weis   f   4554

Major, Cyrus "Cy" Lance (Computer Expert; Sports
   Figure)
Zeus and Co. - David Lee Jones   f   2344

Maker, Alvin (Blacksmith; Psychic)
Alvin Journeyman - Orson Scott Card   f   715

Makish (Criminal)
Bloodwar - Robert Weinberg   h   4539

Malach (Vampire)
Personal Darkness - Tanith Lee   h   2715

Malachy the Great (Royalty; Leader)
Brian Boru: Emperor of the Irish - Morgan
   Llywelyn   f   2779

Malcolm (Artist)
The Cipher - Kathe Koja   h   2541

Malcolm (Teenager)
The Ogre Downstairs - Diana Wynne Jones   f   2350

Malcolm, Ian (Scientist)
The Lost World - Michael Crichton   s   1019

Maldari (Spaceship Captain; Alien)
The Fearful Summons - Denny Martin Flinn   s   1573

Malendor (Vampire; Mythical Creature)
Dark Divide - Mark Acres   f   20

Maler, Vicki (Girlfriend)
Psychosphere - Brian Lumley   h   2835

Maligor (Wizard)
Red Magic - Jean Rabe   f   3553

Mariel (Animal; Warrior)
Mariel of Redwall - Brian Jacques f 2268

Mariell, Christina (Heiress)
Haunted - James Herbert h 2130

Marik, Dao (Doctor; Alien)
Hopeship - Simon Lang s 2637

Marik, Dao (Military Personnel; Alien)
The Trumpets of Tagan - Simon Lang s 2638

Marinville, Johnny (Writer)
Desperation - Stephen King h 2482
The Regulators - Richard Bachman h 240

Marisovna, Cora (Criminal; Genetically Altered
  Being)
Climbing Olympus - Kevin J. Anderson s 85

Marita (Magician)
Sable, Shadow and Ice - Cheryl J. Franklin f 1638

Mark (Computer Expert)
See You Later - Christopher Pike f 3451

Mark, Philip (Mercenary; Lawman)
The Sheriff of Nottingham - Richard Kluger f 2515

Markham, Clare (Artist; Religious)
The Colors of Hell - Michael Paine h 3374

Markham, Dan (Store Owner)
California Gothic - Dennis Etchison h 1483

Markham, Evie (Store Owner)
California Gothic - Dennis Etchison h 1483

Markham, Ulf Reichstein (Administrator)
Inconstant Star - Poul Anderson s 107

Markhamwit (Alien; Leader)
Design for Great-Day - Alan Dean Foster s 1606

Markos (Scientist)
The Eternal Enemy - Michael Berlyn s 383

Marks, Paul (Doctor)
The Man Upstairs - T.L. Parkinson h 3385

Marlene (Teenager)
Nemesis - Isaac Asimov s 206

Marley, Andrew (Werewolf; Religious)
The Werewolf's Touch - Cheri Scotch h 3908

Marlin, Oliver Fonteyn (Student)
Red Death - P.N. Elrod h 1443

Marling, Oliver (Doctor)
Dance of Death - P.N. Elrod h 1439

Marlon, John (Criminal)
Nine Levels Down - William Dantz h 1089

Marlow, Charles (Doctor)
Headhunter - Timothy Findley h 1562

Marlowe (Artist)
The Godsend - Bernard Taylor h 4309

Marlowe, Christopher (Writer; Historical Figure)
Strange Devices of the Sun and Moon - Lisa
  Goldstein f 1814

Marlowe, Jim (Student)
Red Planet - Robert A. Heinlein s 2115

Marlowe, Jim (Scientist)
White Horse, Dark Dragon - Robert C.
  Fleet f 1569

Marlowe, Kate (Housewife)
The Godsend - Bernard Taylor h 4309

Marlowe, Philip (Detective—Private)
*The D. Case: The Truth about the Mystery of Edwin
  Drood* - Charles Dickens f 1230

Marlowe, Ruth (Librarian; Student)
The Cup of Morning Shadows - Rosemary
  Edghill f 1403
The Sword of Maiden's Tears - Rosemary
  Edghill f 1404

Marlowe, Zoot (Alien; Detective)
Hawaiian U.F.O. Aliens - Mel Gilden s 1788
Tubular Android Superheroes - Mel Gilden s 1790

Marnay, Paul (Artist)
Deathchain - Ken Greenhall h 1933

Marouk, Kemal (Scientist; Government Official)
The Joy Machine - James Gunn s 1969

Marquard, Pat (Scientist)
A World of Difference - Harry Turtledove s 4394

The Marra (Alien)
The Madness Season - C.S. Friedman s 1655

Marrah, Rabh (Murderer)
The Light of Exile - Cheryl J. Franklin s 1637

Marrimian (Ruler)
Hall of Whispers - Mike Jefferies f 2300

Mars, Jerry (Criminal)
Rough Beast - Gary Goshgarian h 1833

Marsh, Harold (Doctor)
Black Death - R. Karl Largent h 2655

Marsh, Maxwell (Journalist)
Rage - Elizabeth Ergas h 1474

Marsh, Obediah (Sailor)
The Shadow over Innsmouth - H.P.
  Lovecraft h 2809

Marsh, Valentine (Student—High School; Sorceress)
The Golden Thread - Suzy McKee Charnas f 784

Marshak, Arthur (Doctor; Researcher)
Brothers - Ben Bova s 476

Marshak, Jessie (Doctor)
Brothers - Ben Bova s 476

Marshak, Julia (Spouse)
Brothers - Ben Bova s 476

Marshall, Deidi (Journalist)
Flesh and Blood - D.A. Fowler h 1625

Marshall, Jenny (Young Woman)
The Judas Cross - Charles Sheffield h 3958

Marshall, Meg (Housewife)
Seeds of Evil - Margaret Bingley h 398

Marshall, Olivia (Child; Twin)
Seeds of Evil - Margaret Bingley h 398

Marshall, Orlando (Child; Twin)
Seeds of Evil - Margaret Bingley h 398

Mart (Teenager)
I Feel Like the Morning Star - Gregory
  Maguire s 2868

Martel, Dina (Diplomat)
Man o' War - William Shatner s 3938

Martel, James Mannheim (Military Personnel)
1945 - Newt Gingrich s 1800

Martens, Billy (Television Personality)
The Wizard of Camelot - Simon Hawke f 2101

Marth, Jarem (Pirate; Ruler)
Ash Ock - Christopher Hinz s 2148
The Paratwa - Christopher Hinz s 2149

Martin (Producer)
The Informers - Brett Easton Ellis h 1426

Martin (Artificial Intelligence)
Mars Prime - William C. Dietz s 1250

Martin, Andrew (Robot; Revolutionary)
The Positronic Man - Isaac Asimov s 208

Martin, Anita (Divorced Person)
Blood Wings - Stephen Gresham h 1944

Martin, Dan (Director)
Goblins - Vincent Courtney h 983

Martin, Fred (Religious)
Blood Feud - Sam Siciliano h 4005

Martin, Gene (Accountant)
Hellcat - Amanda Kingsley h 2497

Martin, Gina (Writer)
Entoverse - James P. Hogan s 2174

Martin, Hailey (Writer)
Leanna: Possession of a Woman - Marie
  Kiraly h 2501

Martin, Jack (Artist)
Shadow Man - Dennis Etchison h 1487

Martin, Jiggs (Cook)
The Unfinished - Jay B. Laws h 2676

Martin, Julianne (Musician)
Phantom Banjo - Elizabeth Ann
  Scarborough f 3894
Strum Again? - Elizabeth Ann Scarborough f 3896

Martin, Justin (Teenager)
Thunder Road - Chris Curry h 1051

Martin, Larry (Vampire)
Blood Ties - Karen E. Taylor h 4314

Martin, Marty (Child)
Goblins - Vincent Courtney h 983

Martin, Neil (Worker)
The Quorum - Kim Newman h 3263

Martin, Paul (Teacher; Parent)
Shaman Woods - Morgan Fields h 1554

Martin, Vicki (Housewife)
Goblins - Vincent Courtney h 983

Martin, Wade (Child)
Blood Wings - Stephen Gresham h 1944

Martin, Worth (Child)
Shaman Woods - Morgan Fields h 1554

Martin the Warrior (Animal; Slave)
Martin the Warrior - Brian Jacques f 2269

Martina, Jewel (Health Care Professional)
Chimera - Mary Rosenblum s 3746

Martine (Girlfriend)
Time and Light - William Bornefeld s 470

Martinez, Freddy (Child)
Vampire Breath - R.L. Stine h 4221

Martinique, Speranza (Governess)
Moon Dance - S.P. Somtow h 4116

Martino, Chris (Teenager; Student—High School)
OtherSyde - J. Michael Straczynski h 4245

Mary (Prostitute)
Beautiful Strangers - Melanie Tem h 4325

Mary (Young Woman)
The House on the Borderland - William Hope
  Hodgson h 2164

Mary (Spy)
The Puppet Masters - Robert A. Heinlein s 2114

Mary (Teenager)
A Tie to the Past - David Wiseman f 4720

Mary (Aged Person)
Wilding - Melanie Tem h 4330

Masahiko (Artist)
Scissors Cut Paper Wrap Stone - Ian
  McDonald s 3021

Masau (Hunter; Prehistoric Human)
The Sacred Stones - William Sarabande f 3857

Mash, Madeleine (Journalist)
Coyote - Peter Gadol f 1691

Masklin (Alien; Mythical Creature)
Truckers - Terry Pratchett s 3509

Masklin (Mythical Creature)
Wings - Terry Pratchett s 3510

McBride, Ronica (Psychic)
Commencement - Roby James   s   2294

McCabe, Darian (Psychic; Sailor)
World Without End - Molly Cochran   f   880

McCabe, Sarah/Melissa (Heiress—Dispossessed)
The Catswold Portal - Shirley Rousseau
   Murphy   f   3230

McCade, Molly (Child)
McCade's Bounty - William C. Dietz   s   1252

McCade, Sam (Spaceship Captain; Bounty Hunter)
McCade's Bounty - William C. Dietz   s   1252

McCall, Cassie (Accountant)
Black Ice - Pat Graversen   h   1869

McCall, Dante (Outcast; Spaceman)
Songs of Chaos - S.N. Lewitt   s   2745

McCall, Jess (Child)
Black Ice - Pat Graversen   h   1869

McCallum, Richard (Detective—Private)
The Abductors: Conspiracy - Jonathan
   Frakes   s   1633

McCandless, Lauren (Artist)
Vanitas: Escape From Vampire Junction - S.P.
   Somtow   h   4119

McCann, Dire (Detective)
Bloodwar - Robert Weinberg   h   4539
The Unbeholden - Robert Weinberg   h   4547
Unholy Allies - Robert Weinberg   h   4548

McCann, Rorin (Nobleman; Rebel)
Caledon of the Mists - Deborah Turner
   Harris   f   2045

McCardle, Box "Texas" (Police Officer)
Metal Angel - Nancy Springer   f   4135

McCarthy, James Edward (Military Personnel)
A Rage for Revenge - David Gerrold   s   1774
A Season for Slaughter - David Gerrold   s   1775

McCarthy, Mary Margaret (Teacher)
Substitute Teacher - Jordan Storm   h   4240

McCay, Debra (Leader)
The Earth Saver - Catherine Wells   s   4580

McClain, Walter (Administrator)
Demon Shadows - Michael B. Sirota   h   4051

McClane, Judson (Administrator)
Sorcerers of Sodom - Roger Elwood   h   1447

McClane, Mr. (Psychologist)
*The Collected Stories of Philip K. Dick, Volume Two:
   We Can Remember It for You Wholesale* - Philip K.
   Dick   s   1226

McClare, D. J. (Professor; Scientist)
Unwillingly to Earth - Pauline Ashwell   s   190

McClure, Katy (Photographer)
The Dwelling - Tom Elliott   h   1424

McCogg, Gus "Aengus Mac Og" (Artist; Mythical
   Creature)
The Friendship Song - Nancy Springer   f   4133

McComb, Aaron (Political Figure; Criminal)
Timecop - S.D. Perry   s   3413

McConnell, Celeste (Administrator; Psychic)
Assemblers of Infinity - Kevin J. Anderson   s   83

McCord, Bob (Businessman)
Darkscope - Margaret Falk   h   1495

McCord, Chelsea (Artist)
Darkscope - Margaret Falk   h   1495

McCormick, Lianne (Teacher; Heroine)
When the Bough Breaks - Mercedes Lackey   f   2625

McCoy, Leonard (Doctor)
Doctor's Orders - Diane Duane   s   1338
Enemy Unseen - V.E. Mitchell   s   3123
First Frontier - Diane Carey   s   732

Prime Directive - Judith Reeves-Stevens   s   3602
Renegade - Gene DeWeese   s   1219
Sanctuary - John Vornholt   s   4460
Shadows on the Sun - Michael Jan
   Friedman   s   1664
Star Trek VI: The Undiscovered Country - J.M.
   Dillard   s   1256
Star Trek: The Classic Episodes 1 - James
   Blish   s   427
Star Trek: The Classic Episodes 2 - James
   Blish   s   428
Star Trek: The Classic Episodes 3 - James
   Blish   s   429

McCray, Jimmy (Telepath)
The Demons at Rainbow Bridge - Jack L.
   Chalker   s   771
The Ninety Trillion Fausts - Jack L. Chalker   s   776
The Run to Chaos Keep - Jack L. Chalker   s   778

McCray, Tom (Troubleshooter)
Protektor - Charles Platt   s   3459

McCrea, Rinn (Telepath)
Rinn's Star - Paula King   s   2479

McCready (Teacher; Criminal)
Damnbanna - Nancy Springer   f   4131

McCulley, Kitty (Nurse; Military Personnel)
The Healer's War - Elizabeth Ann
   Scarborough   f   3891

McCullough, Dusty (Ruler)
Free Zone - Charles Platt   s   3458

McCunniff, Mara (Vampire)
The Vampire Memoirs - Mara McCuniff   h   3009

McCutcheon, Christopher (Librarian)
The Quiet Pools - Michael P. Kube-
   McDowell   s   2583

McDaris, Samantha "Sammi" (Mythical Creature;
   Royalty)
Elvendude - Mark Shepherd   f   3973

McDarvid, Jack (Researcher; Detective—Amateur)
The Green Progression - L.E. Modesitt Jr.   s   3132

McDonald (Spaceman; Pirate)
Cat's Gambit - Leslie Gadallah   s   1690

McDonald, Dirk (Teenager; Homosexual)
Baby Be-Bop - Francesca Lia Block   f   444
Witch Baby - Francesca Lia Block   f   450

McDougal, Marta (Inventor; Scientist)
Core - Paul Preuss   s   3522

McDowell, Allison (Writer)
Sweet William - Jessica Palmer   h   3379

McDowell, Josie (Student)
Belladonna - Michael Stewart   h   4206

McDowell, William Scott (Child)
Sweet William - Jessica Palmer   h   3379

McElroy, Jud (Police Officer)
The Headsman - James Neal Harvey   h   2075

McFarland, Henry Lee (Oil Industry Worker;
   Farmer)
Petrogypsies - Rory Harper   s   2036

McFarland, Sonny (Teenager)
Father's Little Helper - Ronald Kelly   h   2433

McFarley, Andrew (Religious)
Purgatory: A Chronicle of a Distant World - Mike
   Resnick   s   3635

McFee, Jonas (Teenager)
Jonas McFee, A.T.P. - Sarah Sargent   s   3865

McGammon, Clyde (Detective—Private)
Lorelei - Mark A. Clements   h   875

McGann, Agnes "Aggie" (Religious)
Gibbon's Decline and Fall - Sheri S.
   Tepper   s   4334

McGann, Jennifer (Detective—Police)
Nightmare, with Angel - Stephen Gallagher   h   1697

McGann, Jim (Photographer)
From a Whisper to a Scream - Samuel M.
   Key   h   2462

McGarvey, Heather (Housewife)
Winter Moon - Dean R. Koontz   h   2558

McGarvey, Jack (Police Officer)
Winter Moon - Dean R. Koontz   h   2558

McGarvey, Toby (Child)
Winter Moon - Dean R. Koontz   h   2558

McGee, Rosa (Supernatural Being)
Sacrament - Clive Barker   h   290

McGee, Trevor (Artist)
Drawing Blood - Poppy Z. Brite   h   568

McGill, Henderson (Military Personnel)
Deep Trek - James Axler   s   234

McGilray, Aidan (Writer)
Stage Fright - Clare McNally   h   3074

McGiven, Mary (Girlfriend)
The Haunt - John Fogarty   h   1581

McGowan, Annie (Aged Person)
The Nightmare People - Lawrence Watt-
   Evans   h   4499

McGulvey, Mr. (Steward)
In between Dragons - Michael Kandel   f   2397

McHenry, Mark (Scientist; Student)
Worf's First Adventure - Peter David   s   1123

McHogue (Computer Expert; Criminal)
Warped - K.W. Jeter   s   2324

McIlvane (Editor)
The Waterworks - E.L. Doctorow   s   1263

McIntosh, Alexander (Immortal)
Gryphon - Crawford Kilian   s   2468

McIntosh, Calvin (Indian; Wanderer)
Stoneskin's Revenge - Tom Deitz   f   1194
Sunshaker's War - Tom Deitz   f   1195

McIntyre, Scott (Political Figure)
Footprints of Thunder - James F. David   s   1115

McKay (Military Personnel)
Devil's Deal - Richard Austin   s   233

McKay, David (Child)
Brainstorm - Steven M. Krauzer   h   2569

McKay, Debra (Scientist; Hunter)
Children of the Earth - Catherine Wells   s   4578
The Earth Is All That Lasts - Catherine
   Wells   s   4579

McKay, Kenneth "Ken" (Vampire; Military
   Personnel)
The VMR Theory - Robert Frezza   s   1652

McKelvey, Dan (Castaway)
The Past of Forever - Juanita Coulson   s   981

McKendree (Racist)
Devil's Deal - Richard Austin   s   233

McKenzie, Chia (Teenager; Investigator)
Idoru - William Gibson   s   1781

McKenzie, Victoria (Scientist; Leader)
Metaphase - Vonda N. McIntyre   s   3044
Starfarers - Vonda N. McIntyre   s   3046
Transition - Vonda N. McIntyre   s   3047

McKeon, Alister (Military Personnel)
On Basilisk Station - David Weber   s   4526

McKibben, Brion (Child)
Whisper - Raymond Van Over   h   4416

McKinnan (Police Officer)
The Third Beast - Peter Loughran   h   2804

Merlin (Child)
Passager - Jane Yolen *f* 4813

Merlin (Royalty)
Prince of Chaos - Roger Zelazny *f* 4844

Merrick (Vampire Hunter)
Buffy the Vampire Slayer - Richie Tankersley
Cusick *h* 1056

Merrick, Geoffrey Robert (Businessman;
Reanimated Dead)
Fear Itself - Ric Meyers *h* 3092
Living Hell - Ric Meyers *h* 3093
Worst Nightmare - Ric Meyers *h* 3094

Merrick, Melanie (Housewife)
Fear Itself - Ric Meyers *h* 3092
Living Hell - Ric Meyers *h* 3093

Merrick the Blackbird (Pirate)
Sister Blood - Karen Haber *s* 1986

Merrit, Robin (Scientist)
Operation Synbat - Bob Mayer *h* 2944

Mertz, Harry (Immortal; Judge)
A Covenant of Justice - David Gerrold *s* 1771

Merwoman, Mela (Mythical Creature; Widow(er))
The Color of Her Panties - Piers Anthony *f* 137

Mespil, Lunzie (Doctor)
The Death of Sleep - Anne McCaffrey *s* 2966
Generation Warrior - Anne McCaffrey *s* 2970

Messenger, Joe (Scientist; Computer Expert)
Host - Peter James *h* 2289

Messenger, Karen (Researcher; Spouse)
Host - Peter James *h* 2289

Metadi, Beka Rosselin (Spaceship Captain; Heiress)
The Price of the Stars - Debra Doyle *s* 1297

Metadi, Jos (Spaceship Captain; Privateer)
The Gathering Flame - Debra Doyle *s* 1292

Metaxos, Diego (Spaceman; Teenager)
Powers That Be - Anne McCaffrey *s* 2978

Metcalf, Charlotte (Child; Orphan)
Whispers in the Dark - Jonathan Aycliffe *h* 239

Metcalf, Conrad (Detective—Private)
Gun, with Occasional Music - Jonathan
Lethem *f* 2735

Metcalf, Elizabeth (Settler)
Nadya: The Wolf Chronicles - Pat Murphy *f* 3228

Metcalf, Lily (Psychologist)
Resume with Monsters - William Browning
Spencer *h* 4122

Methryn, Valthyrra (Artificial Intelligence)
Dreadnought - Thorarinn Gunnarsson *s* 1975
Tactical Error - Thorarinn Gunnarsson *s* 1977

Metis, Jean (Agent)
Crygender - Thomas T. Thomas *s* 4349

Metria "Woe Betide" (Demon)
Roc and a Hard Place - Piers Anthony *f* 154

Metullus, Amaelia (Computer Game Player)
The Imperium Game - K.D. Wentworth *s* 4585

Metzgar, Joachim (Leader; Psychic)
Mutant Legacy - Karen Haber *s* 1984

Meyer, Elizabeth "Payne" (Divorced Person)
Dead Voices - Rick Hautala *h* 2082

Meyers, Max (Military Personnel)
The Final Battle - William C. Dietz *s* 1248

Mharyon (Mythical Creature)
Dragon Moon - Chris Claremont *f* 839

Miaowara Shiro (Animal; Adventurer)
Samurai Cat Goes to the Movies - Mark E.
Rogers *s* 3727
The Sword of Samurai Cat - Mark E.
Rogers *s* 3728

Miaowara Tomokato (Animal; Warrior)
Samurai Cat Goes to the Movies - Mark E.
Rogers *s* 3727
The Sword of Samurai Cat - Mark E.
Rogers *s* 3728

Miathan (Magician)
Aurian - Maggie Furey *f* 1687
Harp of Winds - Maggie Furey *f* 1688

Michael (Servant)
Dark Dance - Tanith Lee *h* 2709

Michael (Child)
Gypsies - Robert Charles Wilson *s* 4702

Michael (Diplomat; Apprentice)
Lion Time in Timbuctoo - Robert Silverberg *s* 4016

Michael, Father (Religious; Alcoholic)
The Eyes of Torie Webster - Roy Sorrels *h* 4121

Michaels, Dean (Convict)
Swamp - Peter Tremayne *h* 4374

Michaels, Judge (Young Man)
The M.D.: A Horror Story - Thomas M.
Disch *h* 1260

Michaels, Kevin (Professor)
October - Al Sarrantonio *h* 3870

Michaels, William "Billy" (Doctor)
The M.D.: A Horror Story - Thomas M.
Disch *h* 1260

Michaelson, Hal (Computer Expert; Leader)
Virtual Destruction - Kevin J. Anderson *s* 98

Michaelson, Kiley (Businesswoman; Pilot)
Mind Light - Margaret Davis *s* 1133

Michelson, Terry (Vampire)
Vampire Blood - Kathryn Meyer Griffith *h* 1954

Mick (Office Worker)
Steam - Jay B. Laws *h* 2675

Midas (Royalty)
The Adventures of King Midas - Lynne Reid
Banks *f* 278

Mika (Doctor)
Tower of Doom - Mark Anthony *h* 126

Mikayla (Royalty; Student)
Lady of the Trillium - Marion Zimmer
Bradley *f* 525

Mike (Businessman)
Dark Legacy - Mark A. Kostrubula *h* 2559

Mike (Artificial Intelligence; Imposter)
The Moon Is a Harsh Mistress - Robert A.
Heinlein *s* 2113

Mike (Doctor)
Wolf Flow - K.W. Jeter *h* 2325

Mikel (Deity)
The Wizard at Home - Rick Shelley *f* 3968

Mikel, Chris (Child)
Blind Hunger - David Darke *h* 1092

Mikhail (Hunter; Leader)
Initiation - Marian Hughes *s* 2235

Mikhailovych, Lixand (Storyteller; Artisan)
Shadow's Daughter - Shirley Meier *f* 3084

Mikhalevviko "Mikh" (Wizard; Criminal)
Mathemagics - Margaret Ball *f* 266

Mikolajczak, Adam (Lawyer)
Seaward - Brad Leithauser *h* 2729

Milam, Hank (Religious)
Rockabilly Limbo - William W. Johnstone *h* 2338

Milburn, Annie (Teacher)
Charmed Life - Bernard Taylor *h* 4307

Milena (Actress)
The Child Garden - Geoff Ryman *s* 3802

Milena "Alfred Russell Wallace" (Computer Expert;
Teenager)
Fairyland - Paul J. McAuley *s* 2953

Miles, Dora (Widow(er))
The Baby - Stephanie Kegan *h* 2417

Miles, Janna (Teenager)
Speak to the Rain - Helen K. Passey *h* 3392

Miles, Karen (Child)
Speak to the Rain - Helen K. Passey *h* 3392

Milk, Billy (Religious)
Only Begotten Daughter - James Morrow *f* 3214

Miller, Alvin Jr. (Apprentice)
Prentice Alvin - Orson Scott Card *f* 727

Miller, Calvin (Psychic; Relative)
Alvin Journeyman - Orson Scott Card *f* 715

Miller, Desmond (Doctor)
Supernova - Roger MacBride Allen *s* 68

Miller, Doc (Oil Industry Worker)
Petrogypsies - Rory Harper *s* 2036

Miller, Jack (Traveller)
The Ultimate Bike Path - Michael B. Sirota *s* 4052

Miller, Paul (Detective—Amateur)
In the Deep Woods - Nicholas Conde *h* 912

Miller, Quintus (Genius; Occultist)
Walkers - Graham Masterton *h* 2927

Miller, Zeke (Musician)
Night Music - Sheila Bristow Garner *h* 1724

Millicent "Millie" (Girlfriend)
Jumper - Steven Gould *s* 1836

Milo (Genetically Altered Being; Immortal)
The Sky Lords - John Brosnan *s* 588

Miloslavic, Dragos (Doctor)
St. Vitus Dances Eternity: A Sarajevo Ghost Story -
Stewart Von Allmen *h* 4450

Minarik (Military Personnel; Leader)
Shadowdance - Robin Wayne Bailey *f* 245

Minder, John XXIII (Ruler)
Stepwater - L. Warren Douglas *s* 1281
The Wells of Phyre - L. Warren Douglas *s* 1282

Minerva (Mythical Creature; Deity)
Ye Gods! - Tom Holt *f* 2196

Minnie "Miin" (Psychic; Child)
Shame of Man - Piers Anthony *s* 155

Minstrel Boy (Warrior)
The Last Stand of the DNA Cowboys - Mick
Farren *s* 1511

Mint (Military Personnel)
Exodus From the Long Sun - Gene Wolfe *s* 4732

Mint, Maytera (Religious; Teacher)
Calde of the Long Sun - Gene Wolfe *s* 4728

Mira (Sorceress)
Dragons on the Town - Thorarinn
Gunnarsson *f* 1974

Mirabara, Keishi (Researcher; Technician)
The Fortunate Fall - Raphael Carter *s* 750

Mirakles (Hero)
The Zork Chronicles - George Alec
Effinger *s* 1410

Miranda (Parent)
Caliban's Hour - Tad Williams *f* 4641

Miranda (Adventurer; Companion)
Charmed - Marilyn Singer *f* 4046

Miranda, Carmen (Spirit; Entertainer)
*Carmen Miranda's Ghost Is Haunting Space Station
Three* - Don Sakers *s* 3827

Mirelle, Victoria "Tori" (Clone)
The Inquisitor - Cheryl J. Franklin *s* 1636

Moql'nkkn "Moql/Saaski" (Mythical Creature)
The Moorchild - Eloise Jarvis McGraw *f* 3040

Mora, Chad (Scientist)
Predator - William Wu *s* 4782

Morales, Daire (Pilot; Spaceman)
Lethe - Tricia Sullivan *s* 4269

Moran, California (Immortal)
Gryphon - Crawford Kilian *s* 2468

Moran, John J. (Doctor)
The Lighthouse at the End of the World - Stephen
  Marlowe *h* 2886

Morbius (Criminal; Ruler)
Strange Tales From the Nile Empire - Greg
  Farshtey *f* 1520

Morcey, Paul (Assistant)
The Only Thing to Fear - Robert Morgan *h* 3185

Morcey, Paul (Detective)
Some Things Come Back - Robert Morgan *h* 3186

Morcey, Paul (Maintenance Worker)
The Things That Are Not There - Robert
  Morgan *h* 3189

Mordance of Barquist (Widow(er); Friend)
The Queen of Ashes - Deborah Turner
  Harris *f* 2046

Mordenheim, Victor (Doctor)
Mordenheim - Chet Williamson *h* 4655

Mordeth (Magician; Ruler)
The Falcon Rises - Michael C. Staudinger *f* 4175

Mordock, Kyle (Teenager)
Midnight's Lair - Richard Laymon *h* 2680

Mordred (Royalty; Bastard Son)
Mordred's Curse - Ian McDowell *f* 3032

Moreau, Alessandra "Ale" (Time Traveller; Student)
Day of the Snake - Matthew J. Costello *s* 967
Hour of the Scorpion - Matthew J. Costello *s* 970

Moreaux, Paul (Writer)
Fade - Robert Cormier *h* 961

Morelli, Berry (Journalist)
Candle Night - Phil Rickman *h* 3663

Moreno, Alexandra "Alix" (Companion; Traveller)
When Heaven Fell - William Barton *s* 319

Moreson, Joe (Businessman)
65mm - Dale Hoover *h* 2200

Morgan (Lesbian)
Clicking Stones - Nancy Tyler Glenn *s* 1802

Morgan, Liam (Professor)
Superstitious - R.L. Stine *h* 4220

Morgan, Meredith (Psychologist)
Dark Dreaming - Pat Franklin *h* 1639

Morgan, Richard (Businessman; Spouse)
Dark Dreaming - Pat Franklin *h* 1639

Morgan, Sara (Student)
Superstitious - R.L. Stine *h* 4220

Morgan la Fey (Royalty)
Witch of the North - Courtway Jones *f* 2342

Morgan le Fay (Sorceress)
Merlin's Bones - Fred Saberhagen *f* 3815

Morgan le Fay (Royalty; Sorceress)
The Prince and the Pilgrim - Mary Stewart *f* 4205

Morgannan, Warrick (Wizard; Leader)
The Ambivalent Magician - Simon Hawke *f* 2091
The Inadequate Adept - Simon Hawke *f* 2092

Morganstern, Jack (Spy)
Dead Girls - Richard Calder *s* 684

Morgasdotte, Roba (Teacher; Adventurer)
Bones of the Past - Holly Lisle *f* 2765

Morgen (Alien; Spaceman)
Mad Roy's Light - Paula King *s* 2478

Morgen (Royalty; Spaceship Captain)
Reunion - Michael Jan Friedman *s* 1663

Morgeu (Royalty; Demon)
The Dragon and the Unicorn - A.A.
  Attanasio *f* 224

Morgiana (Immortal; Noblewoman)
The Dagger and the Cross: A Novel of the Crusades -
  Judith Tarr *f* 4301

Morgis, Duke (Warrior; Mythical Creature)
Wolfhelm - Richard A. Knaak *f* 2525

Morianna, Maigrey (Noblewoman; Pilot)
King's Sacrifice - Margaret Weis *s* 4560
The Lost King - Margaret Weis *s* 4562

Moriarity, Pepper (Store Owner)
The House That Jack Built - Graham
  Masterton *h* 2925

Morkaarin, Bren (Heir—Lost; Military Personnel)
The Rose Sea - S.M. Stirling *f* 4225

Morley, Lynn (Child; Student)
The Witch Returns - Phyllis Reynolds
  Naylor *f* 3249
The Witch's Eye - Phyllis Reynolds Naylor *f* 3250

Morley, Simon "Si" (Time Traveller)
From Time to Time - Jack Finney *s* 1564

Morlock, Endora (Gentlewoman)
Madman Run - David Robbins *s* 3677

Mornan (Wizard)
The Sleep of Stone - Louise Cooper *f* 952

Mornay, Peter (Religious; Government Official)
Glory's War - Alfred Coppel *s* 957

Mornette, Will (Teenager)
Rebel From Alphorion - Robyn Tallis *s* 4291

Morning, Debbie Sue (Teenager)
Serial Killer Days - David Prill *h* 3538

Morningstar, Thomas (Detective—Police)
From a Whisper to a Scream - Samuel M.
  Key *h* 2462

Morpheus (Mythical Creature)
The Sandman: Book of Dreams - Neil
  Gaiman *f* 1694

Morran, Goldie (Businesswoman)
Wagers of Sin - Robert Asprin *s* 222

Morrell, Charlie (Lawyer)
The Killing of the Saints - Alex Abella *h* 18

Morris (Teenager)
Under Siege - Elisabeth Mace *f* 2852

Morris, Claudia (Sociologist)
Children of the Thunder - John Brunner *s* 599

Morris, Dwight (Businessman)
Penance - Rick R. Reed *h* 3591

Morris, Rob (Detective)
Sibs - F. Paul Wilson *h* 4694

Morris, Zenoa (Young Woman)
The Living Evil - Ruby Jean Jensen *h* 2312

Morris "Mauricio di Mauro" (Animal; Spy)
*The Night of Wishes: or The
  Satanarchaeolidealcohellish Notion Potion* - Michael
  Ende *f* 1462

Morrison, Alex (Detective—Police)
What's Wrong with Tamara? - D.A.
  Fowler *h* 1626

Morrison, Athol (Mercenary)
When Heaven Fell - William Barton *s* 319

Morrison, Faye (Journalist)
Curfew - Phil Rickman *h* 3664

Morrison, Jessie Mae (Child)
The Hunted - Kathryn Ptacek *h* 3542

Morrison, Ryan (Scientist)
Journey to Terezor - Frank Asch *s* 183

Morrison, Troy (Teenager; Spaceman)
Dream-Weaver - Louise Lawrence *s* 2674

Morrough (Knight)
StarSpawn - Kenneth Von Gunden *s* 4453

Morrow, Cathy (Businesswoman)
The Link - Andrew Laurance *h* 2666

Morrow, Julian (Professor)
The Secret History - Donna Tartt *h* 4306

Morrow, Rachel (Artist; Farmer)
A Gift Upon the Shore - M.K. Wren *s* 4767

Mort (Apprentice)
Mort - Terry Pratchett *f* 3504

Mortega, Dyani (Military Personnel; Indian)
Blood Siege - G. Harry Stine *s* 4211

Morton, John (Researcher)
Night Glow - Martin James *h* 2284

Morwen (Witch)
Calling on Dragons - Patricia C. Wrede *f* 4761

Morwyne the Powershaper (Mythical Creature)
Darkthunder's Way - Tom Deitz *f* 1189

Mosay (Director; Immortal)
Outnumbering the Dead - Frederik Pohl *s* 3467

Mosby, Marianne (Military Personnel)
Legion of the Damned - William C. Dietz *s* 1249

Mosca, Piero (Student)
Flare - Roger Zelazny *s* 4836

Moses (Robot)
Greenthieves - Alan Dean Foster *s* 1610

Moss, Griffin (Artist)
The Golden Mean - Nick Bantock *f* 280
Sabine's Notebook - Nick Bantock *f* 281

Mother (Parent)
Don't Forget Your Spacesuit, Dear - Jody Lynn
  Nye *s* 3321

Mother Night (Mythical Creature; Guardian)
Godmother Night - Rachel Pollack *f* 3472

Mouse (Thief; Companion)
Soothsayer - Mike Resnick *s* 3638

Mozart, Wolfgang Amadeus (Composer; Historical
  Figure)
I, Vampire - Michael Romkey *h* 3736

Mthembu, Lucas "Venator" (Artificial Intelligence;
  Robot)
Harvest the Fire - Poul Anderson *s* 106

Muadhen, Seamus (Military Personnel)
Nature's God - Robert Anton Wilson *f* 4698

Mudge (Animal)
Chorus Skating - Alan Dean Foster *f* 1603

Muhammed, Sarkar (Computer Expert)
The Terminal Experiment - Robert J.
  Sawyer *s* 3887

Mulcahey, Gerald "Jerry" (Scientist; Genius)
Heavy Weather - Bruce Sterling *s* 4194

Mulder, Fox (FBI Agent)
Goblins - Charles L. Grant *s* 1850
Ground Zero - Kevin J. Anderson *h* 89
Ruins - Kevin J. Anderson *h* 93
Whirlwind - Charles L. Grant *f* 1859

Mulkerrin (Religious)
Of Saints and Shadows - Christopher
  Golden *h* 1811

N

Nash, August (Security Officer; Spy)
Labyrinth of Night - Allen Steele *s* 4183

Nash, Scott (Photojournalist)
Lagoon - Alison Drake *h* 1313

Nashram, Mika (Magician; Con Artist)
By the Sword - Greg Costikyan *f* 978

Naso (Fugitive; Writer)
The Last World - Christoph Ransmayr *f* 3567

Nastrus (Mythical Creature)
The Unicorn War - John Lee *f* 2704

Nasty Andrew (Serial Killer)
Bleeder - Gene Lazuta *h* 2684

Nathalorial, Kaylana (Religious; Leader)
Villains by Necessity - Eve Forward *f* 1592

Nathan, Jessica (Scientist)
Desert Eden - J.M. Morgan *s* 3182

Natil (Mythical Creature; Minstrel)
Maze of Moonlight - Gael Baudino *f* 327

Natter, Cody (Drug Dealer)
Creekers - Edward Lee *h* 2697

Naufts, Tom (Criminal; Telepath)
The Gifted - Jack Caravela *h* 714

Navarra (Vampire)
Night Brothers - Sidney Williams *h* 4639

Navarre (Magician; Adventurer)
The Magic Wars - Jo Clayton *f* 860

Naxania (Royalty; Ruler)
The Unicorn Peace - John Lee *f* 2702

Nazaual (Magician; Religious)
Redmagic - Crawford Kilian *f* 2469

Nazhuret (Warrior)
The Belly of the Wolf - R.A. MacAvoy *f* 2845
King of the Dead - R.A. MacAvoy *f* 2846
Lens of the World - R.A. MacAvoy *f* 2847

Neal, Porsche (Alien; Traveller)
Beyond the Veil of Stars - Robert Reed *s* 3592

Neale, Charis (Scientist)
Dark Matter - Garfield Reeves-Stevens *h* 3598

Neary, Billy (Child)
Billy - Whitley Strieber *h* 4258

Neary, Mark (Teacher)
Billy - Whitley Strieber *h* 4258

Nebogipfel (Mutant; Time Traveller)
The Time Ships - Stephen Baxter *s* 334

Nebuun (Alien)
Random Factor - Joel Henry Sherman *s* 3975

Ned (Orphan)
Spring-Heeled Jack - Philip Pullman *f* 3546

Needham, Bill (Businessman)
Kane - Douglas Borton *h* 472

Neelix (Alien; Cook)
The Final Fury - Dafydd ab Hugh *s* 8

Nefertity (Artificial Intelligence)
AEstival Tide - Elizabeth Hand *s* 2026

Neimark, Max (Actor; Director)
Preternatural - Margaret Wander Bonanno *s* 466

Nellodee "Nell" (Child)
The Diamond Age - Neal Stephenson *s* 4190

Nelson, MaryAnn "Spook" (Teenager)
Spook - Steve Vance *h* 4426

Nelson, Nedra Muriel (Artist)
Spook - Steve Vance *h* 4426

Nelson, Vicki (Detective—Private)
Blood Price - Tanya Huff *h* 2225
Blood Trail - Tanya Huff *h* 2226

Nelson, Zack (Teenager)
Sweet Revenge - Jean Simon *h* 4043

Nemet "Greenface" (Hunter)
Ancient Echoes - Robert Holdstock *f* 2182

Nemmitz, Palmer (Aged Person)
Dark Journey - A.R. Morlan *h* 3192

Nemo (Alien)
Metaphase - Vonda N. McIntyre *s* 3044

Nemony (Alien; Psychic)
Dream-Weaver - Louise Lawrence *s* 2674

Nepe/Flach (Mythical Creature; Animal)
Phaze Doubt - Piers Anthony *f* 152

Nephredann (Demon)
Necrom - Mick Farren *s* 1513

Nesbit, Edward (Writer)
The Chymical Wedding - Lindsay Clarke *f* 856

Nesbitt, Justin (Musician)
The Beyond - Barry Harrington *h* 2042

Neskat, Merinda (Alien; Historian)
Sentinels - Margaret Weis *s* 4564

Ness (Artisan; Parent)
Shadow's Daughter - Shirley Meier *f* 3084

Nessarose (Witch; Religious)
Wicked: The Life and Times of the Wicked Witch of the West - Gregory Maguire *f* 2869

Neumann, Kate (Doctor)
Children of the Night - Dan Simmons *h* 4029

Neville-Smythe, Brian (Knight; Fiance(e))
The Dragon and the Djinn - Gordon R. Dickson *f* 1233

Neville-Smythe, Brian (Knight)
The Dragon, the Earl, and the Troll - Gordon R. Dickson *f* 1237

Nevsky, Peter (Orphan; Spaceman)
Peter Nevsky and the True Story of the Russian Moon Landing - John Calvin Batchelor *s* 322

Nevyn (Sorcerer)
The Dragon Revenant - Katharine Kerr *f* 2445

Newcombe, Dan (Scientist; Religious)
Richter 10 - Arthur C. Clarke *s* 853

Newell, Charlie (Teenager; Pilot)
Wildside - Steven Gould *s* 1837

Newkirk, Bobby (Teenager)
Double Date - R.L. Stine *h* 4218

Newman, Greg (Murderer)
Impulse - Rick Hautala *h* 2084

Newman, Mark (Worker)
The Mountain King - Rick Hautala *h* 2086

Newman, Sandy (Teenager)
The Mountain King - Rick Hautala *h* 2086

Newns, Curtis (Artist)
Skyscape - Michael Cadnum *h* 665

Newns, Margaret (Writer)
Skyscape - Michael Cadnum *h* 665

Newt (Animal)
Ratha and Thistle-Chaser - Clare Bell *f* 356

Newton, Roger (Saloon Keeper/Owner)
The Unseen - Joseph Citro *h* 838

Ng, Margot O'Reilly (Spaceship Captain)
Ruler of Naught - Sherwood Smith *s* 4101

Ngamuku, Larae (Young Woman)
Horrors of the Dancing Gods - Jack L. Chalker *f* 774

Ngenga, Ngina-li "Ngina" (Alien)
The Inquisitor - Cheryl J. Franklin *s* 1636

Ngoni, Beatrice (Doctor)
A Miracle of Rare Design - Mike Resnick *s* 3631

Ngu, Emerson (Engineer; Businessman)
Pallas - L. Neil Smith *s* 4093

Nguyen, Marie (Teenager; Pilot)
Wildside - Steven Gould *s* 1837

Nhamo (Child; Adventurer)
A Girl Named Disaster - Nancy Farmer *f* 1501

ni Bron, Deir (Refugee; Magician)
Redmagic - Crawford Kilian *f* 2469

ni Errhyn, Bracht (Mercenary)
Dark Magic - Angus Wells *f* 4569
Forbidden Magic - Angus Wells *f* 4572
Wild Magic - Angus Wells *f* 4576

ni Pendaron, Teleri (Sorceress)
The Work of the Sun - Teresa Edgerton *f* 1402

Nia (Alien)
A Woman of the Iron People - Eleanor Arnason *s* 174

Niad (Magician; Teenager)
The Cursed - Dave Duncan *f* 1348

Niahrin (Witch)
Aisling - Louise Cooper *f* 945

Niall (Psychic; Revolutionary)
The Delta - Colin Wilson *s* 4679

Nicholas (Royalty)
The Changeling - Kristine Kathryn Rusch *f* 3772

Nicholas (Royalty; Teenager)
The King's Buccaneer - Raymond E. Feist *f* 1533

Nicholas (Royalty)
To Save the Sun - Ben Bova *s* 489

Nicholas "Santa Claus" (Hero)
The Autobiography of Santa Claus: It's Better to Give - Jeff Guinn *f* 1967

Nicholson, Shawna (Doctor)
The Unknown Soldier - Mickey Zucker Reichert *s* 3611

Nick (Warrior)
The Paratwa - Christopher Hinz *s* 2149

Nickerson, Josh (Teenager)
Kindred - John Gideon *h* 1785

Nicodareus (Monster; Leader)
Darkenheight - Douglas Niles *f* 3269

Nicodemus (Religious)
Plague Demon - Brian Craig *f* 1004

Nicol, Jesse (Spaceship Captain; Writer)
Harvest the Fire - Poul Anderson *s* 106

Nicolau, Grigori (Amnesiac)
Frostwing - Richard A. Knaak *f* 2520

Nicole, Maeve (Student; Veterinarian)
The Scathach and the Maeve's Daughter - Mary Alexander Walker *f* 4476

Niehaus, Vilmos (Architect)
The Final Diary Entry of Kees Hujgens - William R. Stotler *f* 4242

Nielson (Teacher)
When Darkness Falls - Sidney Williams *h* 4640

Nielson, Anne (Journalist)
Bad Dreams - Kim Newman *h* 3260

Nielson, Cameron (Writer)
Bad Dreams - Kim Newman *h* 3260

Niffy (Animal; Counselor)
No One Noticed the Cat - Anne McCaffrey *f* 2973

Nigel (Professor)
Specterworld - Isidore Haiblum *s* 1990

Nigheyes (Animal; Telepath)
Royal Assassin - Robin Hobb *f* 2152

Oakes (Administrator; Witch)
On Meeting Witches at Wells - Judith
Gorog *f* 1832

Oakland, Brian (Teenager; Student—High School)
Stunts - Charles L. Grant *h* 1857

Oakton, Cody (Teenager)
Only Child - H.M. Hoover *s* 2203

O'Bannion, Joss (Military Personnel)
High Moon - Diane Duane *s* 1340
Kill Station - Diane Duane *s* 1342
Mindblast - Diane Duane *s* 1343

Obar (Magician)
Dragon Waking - Craig Shaw Gardner *f* 1711

Obed (Animal; Linguist)
The Off Season - Jack Cady *f* 669

Oblivion, Billy (Warrior)
The Last Stand of the DNA Cowboys - Mick
Farren *s* 1511

Obo (Alien; Police Officer)
Mind Slayer - Kevin D. Randle *s* 3563

O'Brian, James (Scientist)
Gabriel's Body - Curt Siodmak *h* 4049

O'Brian, Launa (Military Personnel; Time Traveller)
First Dawn - Mike Moscoe *s* 3217

O'Brien, Coley (Entertainer)
Destiny's Carnival - Warren Murphy *h* 3232

O'Brien, Ed (Police Officer)
Leanna: Possession of a Woman - Marie
Kiraly *h* 2501

O'Brien, Mike (Businessman)
Out There in the Darkness - Ed Gorman *h* 1828

O'Brien, Miles (Military Personnel; Engineer)
Bloodletter - K.W. Jeter *s* 2317

O'Brien, Richard (Police Officer)
The Crawling Dark - Pauline Dunn *h* 1366

Obrion, Juan (Scientist)
Stranger Suns - George Zebrowski *s* 4832

Obst, Roger (Teenager; Student—High School)
OtherSyde - J. Michael Straczynski *h* 4245

Ochs, Thur (Miner; Spy)
The Spirit Ring - Lois McMaster Bujold *f* 626

O'Connor, Corbo (Gladiator; Sorcerer)
The Fourth Guardian - Ronald Anthony
Cross *s* 1032
The Lost Guardian - Ronald Anthony Cross *s* 1033

O'Connor, Dennis (Journalist)
The Hunger of the Beast - John Driver *h* 1336

O'Connor, Flynn (Time Traveller)
Wolfking - Bridget Wood *f* 4752

O'Connor, John (Cowboy; Leader)
The Flight of Michael McBride - Midori
Snyder *f* 4111

O'Connor, Thunderbird Devlin "Bird" (Indian)
Above the Lower Sky - Tom Deitz *f* 1188

O'Connor, Tim (Teenager)
Entity - Nina Mandelik *h* 2874

Octavian, Peter (Detective—Private; Vampire)
Of Saints and Shadows - Christopher
Golden *h* 1811

O'Day, Gallen (Warrior; Hero)
Beyond the Gate - Dave Wolverton *s* 4740
The Golden Queen - Dave Wolverton *s* 4742

O'Dell, Judith (Heroine)
Imajica - Clive Barker *h* 288

Odell, Owen (Minstrel)
Morningstar - David Gemmell *f* 1757

Odin (Artificial Intelligence)
Dark Sky Legion - William Barton *s* 315

Odin (Deity)
Sleipnir - Linda Evans *f* 1493

Odo (Alien; Security Officer)
Fallen Heroes - Dafydd ab Hugh *s* 7
Warped - K.W. Jeter *s* 2324

O'Donnell, Annie (Student)
Stitch - Mark Morris *h* 3205

O'Donnell, Erin (Police Officer)
Deathwalker - Patrick Whalen *h* 4596

O'Donnell, Hugh (Scientist)
The Trikon Deception - Ben Bova *s* 490

O'Donnell, Ryan (Beachcomber)
Nightmare, with Angel - Stephen Gallagher *h* 1697

Odosson, William "Will" (Knight; Adventurer)
Knight's Wyrd - Debra Doyle *f* 1294

O'Fallon, Michael Timothy (Mythical Creature)
The Reluctant Sorcerer - Simon Hawke *f* 2096

Offenhouse, Ralph (Diplomat; Businessman)
Debtors' Planet - William R. Thompson *s* 4355

Ogg, Nanny (Witch; Hero)
Lords and Ladies - Terry Pratchett *f* 3502

Oghmal (Warrior; Hero)
Search for the Starblade - Keith Taylor *f* 4315

Ogle, Cyrus "Cy" (Public Relations)
Interface - Stephen Bury *s* 638

Ogre (Parent)
The Ogre Downstairs - Diana Wynne Jones *f* 2350

Ogress, Okra (Mythical Creature; Runaway)
The Color of Her Panties - Piers Anthony *f* 137

Ohaern (Warrior; Blacksmith)
The Sage - Christopher Stasheff *f* 4164

Ohaern (Warrior; Hunter)
The Shaman - Christopher Stasheff *f* 4166

O'Hallahan, Emma Delaney (Widow(er); Abuse
Victim)
What's Wrong with America - Scott
Bradfield *h* 515

O'Hallahan, Marvin (Aged Person)
What's Wrong with America - Scott
Bradfield *h* 515

O'Hara, Emerald (Teenager)
Quake - Richard Laymon *h* 2681

O'Hara, Frank (Police Officer)
A Room for the Dead - Noel Hynd *h* 2250

O'Hara, Liam (Scientist)
Time, Like an Ever-Rolling Stream - Judith
Moffett *s* 3141

O'Hara, Marianne (Administrator; Settler)
Worlds Enough and Time - Joe Haldeman *s* 1996

O'Hara, Sonny (Businessman)
Torments - Lisa Cantrell *h* 709

O'Hara Prime (Artificial Intelligence)
Worlds Enough and Time - Joe Haldeman *s* 1996

O'Hearn, Travis (Drifter)
Practical Demonkeeping - Christopher
Moore *h* 3173

Ohmsford, Coll (Adventurer)
The Scions of Shannara - Terry Brooks *f* 584

Ohmsford, Par (Heir—Lost; Magician)
The Scions of Shannara - Terry Brooks *f* 584

Ohmsford, Par (Mythical Creature; Adventurer)
The Talismans of Shannara - Terry Brooks *f* 585

Ohmsford, Wren (Mythical Creature; Adventurer)
The Elf Queen of Shannara - Terry Brooks *f* 581

Oimu, Harriet (Revolutionary; Genetically Altered
Being)
Celestis - Paul Park *s* 3381

Oit-Makidom, Maraakuks (Military Personnel)
Runes of Autumn - Larry Elmore *f* 1436

Okata, Gail (Police Officer)
Demon Fire - Gary L. Holleman *h* 2188

O'Keefe, Jesse (Anthropologist; Adventurer)
Fire and Ice - Edward Myers *f* 3235
The Mountain Made of Light - Edward
Myers *f* 3236
The Summit - Edward Myers *f* 3237

O'Keefe, Katie (Doctor)
Rulers of Darkness - Steven G. Spruill *h* 4138

O'Keefe, Polly (Student)
An Acceptable Time - Madeleine L'Engle *f* 2732

O'Kelly, Manuel "Mannie" (Revolutionary;
Computer Expert)
The Moon Is a Harsh Mistress - Robert A.
Heinlein *s* 2113

Olaffson, Egil (Bodyguard; Friend)
Egil's Book - C.J. Mills *s* 3115

O'lal (Alien; Animal)
Cat-A-Lyst - Alan Dean Foster *s* 1602

Olam, Thomas "Tom" Edward (Time Traveller;
Computer Expert)
From Prussia with Love - John DeChancie *f* 1177

Olamina, Lauren Oya (Teenager; Religious)
Parable of the Sower - Octavia E. Butler *s* 649

Old Bess (Aged Person)
The Moorchild - Eloise Jarvis McGraw *f* 3040

Old Grendel (Alien)
Beowulf's Children - Larry Niven *s* 3276

Old Man (Spy)
The Puppet Masters - Robert A. Heinlein *s* 2114

Old Man of the Mountain (Mythical Creature)
A Calculated Magic - Robert Weinberg *f* 4540

Old Mose (Farmer)
Over the River & Through the Woods - Clifford D.
Simak *s* 4026

Old Nathan (Backwoodsman; Magician)
Old Nathan - David Drake *f* 1323

Oldar (Assistant)
King of the Dead - Gene DeWeese *h* 1218

Oldman, Wendel (Werewolf; Religious)
Wyrm Wolf - Edo Van Belkom *h* 4414

Oliderval (Ruler)
The Unicorn Peace - John Lee *f* 2702

Olivaw, R. Daneel "Eto Demerzel" (Robot)
Forward the Foundation - Isaac Asimov *s* 195

Oliver (Robot)
Stationfall - Arthur Byron Cover *s* 987

Ollie (Child)
No Kidding - Bruce Brooks *s* 579

Olmstead, Robert (Traveller)
The Shadow over Innsmouth - H.P.
Lovecraft *h* 2809

Olon, Sammis Arloff (Witch; Military Personnel)
Timediver's Dawn - L.E. Modesitt Jr. *s* 3138

Olyvria (Heiress; Adventurer)
Krispos the Emperor - Harry Turtledove *f* 4391

O'Mara (Administrator; Psychologist)
The Genocidal Healer - James White *s* 4604

O'Meara, Beverly (Orphan; Detective—Private)
In the Cube - David Alexander Smith *s* 4076

O'Meara, Patrick (Warrior; Ruler)
Masters of the Fist - Edward P. Hughes *s* 2234

Paco, Chico (Fisherman)
Through the Arc of the Rain Forest - Karen Tei Yamashita   *f*   4791

Paco, Frank (Organized Crime Figure)
Bloodlist - P.N. Elrod   *h*   1438

Padrik (Religious; Criminal)
The Robin and the Kestrel - Mercedes Lackey   *f*   2617

Page, Scott (Murderer)
This Side of Judgment - J.R. Dunn   *s*   1364

Pagemaster (Librarian; Guardian)
The Pagemaster - David Kirschner   *f*   2508

Paik, Anna (Journalist)
Cortez on Jupiter - Ernest Hogan   *s*   2172

Pairis, Rudy (Psychic)
Mefisto in Onyx - Harlan Ellison   *h*   1433

Paithan (Mythical Creature; Adventurer)
Elven Star - Margaret Weis   *f*   4555

Paixao, Rhea (Writer; Spouse)
Starmind - Spider Robinson   *s*   3716

Pak, So (Spaceship Captain)
The Bushido Incident - Betty Anne Crawford   *s*   1011

Paladin (Artificial Intelligence)
Archangel Blues - eluki bes shahar   *s*   384
Darktraders - eluki bes shahar   *s*   385
Hellflower - Eluki bes Shahar   *s*   386

Paladyr (Nobleman; Outlaw)
The Endless Knot - Stephen R. Lawhead   *f*   2671

Palamon (Royalty; Adventurer)
Across the Thlassa Mey - Dennis McCarty   *f*   2997

Palaton (Alien; Spaceman)
Path of Fire - Charles Ingrid   *s*   2256

Pale Boy (Lawman)
Batman: Captured by the Engines - Joe R. Lansdale   *h*   2641

Pallas (Pilot)
Raft - Stephen Baxter   *s*   332

Palmer, Clay (Drifter)
Prototype - Brian Hodge   *h*   2159

Palmer, Jane (Teacher)
Panda Ray - Michael Kandel   *s*   2398

Palmer, Tall Man (Sailor)
White Shark - Peter Benchley   *h*   363

Palmer, William (Detective)
In the Blood - Nancy A. Collins   *h*   903

Pan (Mythical Creature)
Cloven Hooves - Megan Lindholm   *f*   2759

Pan, Miss Scarlet (Actress; Genetically Altered Being)
Winterlong - Elizabeth Hand   *s*   2029

Pandora (Alien)
Pandora - Alan Rodgers   *h*   3723

Pangborn, Alan (Police Officer)
Needful Things - Stephen King   *h*   2490

Pangloss (Supernatural Being)
In the Blood - Nancy A. Collins   *h*   903

Panshinea (Alien; Ruler)
Path of Fire - Charles Ingrid   *s*   2256

Pantera, Black Malachi (Student)
Views from the Oldest House - Richard Grant   *s*   1865

Panthera (Heir; Prostitute)
The Fulfillments of Fate and Desire - Storm Constantine   *s*   921

Papago Joe (Salesman)
Burial - Graham Masterton   *h*   2921

Papen, Richard (Student—College)
The Secret History - Donna Tartt   *h*   4306

Pardu (Royalty; Parent)
Heart Readers - Kristine Kathryn Rusch   *f*   3776

Parent, Lucy (Linguist)
The Magnificent Wilf - Gordon R. Dickson   *s*   1239

Parent, Tom (Diplomat)
The Magnificent Wilf - Gordon R. Dickson   *s*   1239

Parganas, Koot "Kootie" Hoomie (Teenager; Psychic)
Expiration Date - Tim Powers   *f*   3494

Parker, Caroline (Innkeeper)
Winter Wolves - Earle Wescott   *h*   4587

Parker, David (Vampire)
I, Vampire - Michael Romkey   *h*   3736
The Vampire Papers - Michael Romkey   *h*   3737
The Vampire Princess - Michael Romkey   *h*   3738

Parker, Evan (Military Personnel; Political Figure)
The Winds of Mars - H.M. Hoover   *s*   2204

Parker, Gale (Archaeologist)
Indiana Jones and the White Witch - Martin Caidin   *f*   674

Parker, James "Spark" (Insurance Investigator)
Double Jeopardy - Aaron Allston   *s*   72

Parker, Janis (Political Figure)
The Winds of Mars - H.M. Hoover   *s*   2204

Parker, Jim (Student; Editor)
University - Bentley Little   *h*   2778

Parker, Melody (Lawyer)
Tombley's Walk - Crosland Brown   *h*   590

Parker, Peter "Spider-Man" (Hero; Detective—Amateur)
Spider-Man: The Venom Factor - Diane Duane   *s*   1345
The Ultimate Spider-Man - Stan Lee   *s*   2706

Parkes, John (Military Personnel)
The Mountain Walks - Roland J. Green   *s*   1884

Parkinson, Rupert (Sailor)
The Ghost From the Grand Banks - Arthur C. Clarke   *s*   849

Parks, Henry (Detective)
Forget Me Not - Gene Lazuta   *h*   2685

Parmenion (Warrior)
Dark Prince - David Gemmell   *f*   1754

Parmenion (Mercenary; Sports Figure)
Lion of Macedon - David Gemmell   *f*   1756

Parmenter, Casey (Teenager)
Tourists - Lisa Goldstein   *f*   1816

Parmenter, Mitchell (Anthropologist)
Tourists - Lisa Goldstein   *f*   1816

Parnell, Eugene M. (Spaceman; Leader)
The Tranquility Alternative - Allen Steele   *s*   4187

Parody, Paskal (Magician)
Kirins: The Secret of the Hanging Stones - James D. Priest   *f*   3536

Parsifal (Knight)
Parsifal - Peter Vansittart   *f*   4431

Parsley (Child; Adventurer)
Travel Far, Pay No Fare - Anne Lindbergh   *f*   2757

Parsons (Political Figure)
The Totem - David Morrell   *h*   3193

Parsons (Police Officer)
Twisted - Sue Hollister Barr   *h*   304

Parsons, Ronna (Vagrant)
Twisted - Sue Hollister Barr   *h*   304

Parthet "Uncle Parker" (Wizard)
The Hero King - Rick Shelley   *f*   3966

The Hero of Varay - Rick Shelley   *f*   3967

Partrick, Nicole (Young Woman)
Adversary - Daniel Rhodes   *h*   3648

Partridge (Grandparent; Witch)
Slow Funeral - Rebecca Ore   *f*   3365

Parz, Jasoft (Diplomat; Time Traveller)
Timelike Infinity - Stephen Baxter   *s*   335

Pascal, David (Journalist)
Carnosaur - Harry Adam Knight   *s*   2538

Pascale (Spirit)
The Ghost Inside the Monitor - Margaret J. Anderson   *f*   101

Pasco (Agent)
Ghost Dancers - Brian Craig   *s*   1003

Pashikov, Ilya (Political Figure)
Russian Spring - Norman Spinrad   *s*   4128

Pasmore, Tom (Heir)
Mystery - Peter Straub   *h*   4252

Pasmore, Tom (Detective)
The Throat - Peter Straub   *h*   4254

Pasquale (Artist)
Pasquale's Angel - Paul J. McAuley   *f*   2955

Passepout (Actor)
The Mage in the Iron Mask - Brian Thomsen   *f*   4356

Passman, Breyten (Human)
River of Dust - Alexander Jablokov   *s*   2263

Passman, Hektor (Political Figure)
River of Dust - Alexander Jablokov   *s*   2263

Pati (Deity; Ruler)
Delta City - Felicity Savage   *f*   3881

Patience (Spirit)
A Witch Across Time - Gilbert B. Cross   *f*   1031

Patricia (Model)
The Man Upstairs - T.L. Parkinson   *h*   3385

Patrick (Friend)
The Secret of the Indian - Lynne Reid Banks   *f*   279

Patrick, Uncle (Computer Expert)
Under Siege - Elisabeth Mace   *f*   2852

Patswami (Cult Member)
Button Bright - Michael Kurland   *h*   2584

Patterson, Gil (Warrior; Scholar)
Mother of Winter - Barbara Hambly   *f*   2007

Patterson, Lizzie (Teenager)
Where the Towers Pierce the Sky - Marie D. Goodwin   *f*   1823

Patterson, Red (Doctor)
Skyscape - Michael Cadnum   *h*   665

Patton, Dan (Businessman)
Dangerous Nature - T.J. Kirby   *h*   2504

Patton, Hallie (Model)
Private Demons - Robert Masello   *h*   2909

Paul, Father (Religious)
The Twelfth Child - Raymond Van Over   *h*   4415

Pauley, Nigel (Military Personnel)
Limbo Search - Parke Godwin   *s*   1804

Paulin (Religious)
King Javan's Year - Katherine Kurtz   *f*   2591

Pauling, Addy (Child)
Lullaby - Diane Guest   *h*   1966

Pauling, Judd (Artist; Spouse)
Lullaby - Diane Guest   *h*   1966

Pavek of Urik (Religious; Adventurer)
The Brazen Gambit - Lynn Abbey   *f*   11
Cinnabar Shadows - Lynn Abbey   *f*   13

Q

Quadroped (Animal)
Demon Pig - Karen Brush   f   603

Quadrun, Ben (Journalist)
Nightmare Logic - Matthew Hall   h   2000

Quail, Douglas (Clerk; Spy)
The Collected Stories of Philip K. Dick, Volume Two: We Can Remember It for You Wholesale - Philip K. Dick   s   1226

Quail, Douglas (Construction Worker)
Total Recall - Piers Anthony   s   159

Quan, Zhongli (Alien)
Vengeance Strike - David Robbins   s   3681

Quantrill, Snohomish "Sno" (Apprentice; Traveller)
The Godmother's Apprentice - Elizabeth Ann Scarborough   f   3890

Quare, Joshua Ali (Experimental Subject)
Kaleidoscope Century - John Barnes   s   294

Quark (Alien; Saloon Keeper/Owner)
Fallen Heroes - Dafydd ab Hugh   s   7

Quarrels, David (Engineer; Fiance(e))
The Khan's Persuasion - Cynthia Felice   s   1540

Quath'jutt'kkal'thon "Quath" (Alien; Revolutionary)
Furious Gulf - Gregory Benford   s   367
Tides of Light - Gregory Benford   s   370

Quauhtli (Religious)
The Chalchiuhite Dragon - Kenneth Morris   f   3201

Queen of Ice (Ruler)
Horrible Humes - Stephen Billias   f   395

Queenie (Spirit)
The Influence - Ramsey Campbell   h   698

Quejaches, Xia (Dancer; Wanderer)
The Stone Garden - Mary Rosenblum   s   3748

Quetzal (Religious; Vampire)
Calde of the Long Sun - Gene Wolfe   s   4728

Quetzal (Immortal)
A King Beneath the Mountain - Robert N. Charrette   f   788

Quiet (Doctor)
Bad Brains - Kathe Koja   h   2540

Quigley, Joe (Detective—Private; Imposter)
Lady Slings the Booze - Spider Robinson   s   3715

Quijance, Natasha (Parent; Storyteller)
Red Planet Run - Dana Stabenow   s   4139

Quijance-Turgenev, Esther Elizabeth (Child)
Second Star - Dana Stabenow   s   4140

Quillan (Religious)
The Face of the Waters - Robert Silverberg   s   4011

Quimby, Byron (Maintenance Worker)
Lot Lizards - Ray Garton   h   1726

Quincunx "the Thief" (Artificial Intelligence)
Dream of Glass - Jean Mark Gawron   s   1734

Quindell, Mason (Doctor)
Bring Me Children - David Martin   h   2889

Quinn (Vampire)
Precious Blood - Pat Graversen   h   1872

Quinn (Journalist)
Silicon Embrace - John Shirley   s   3996

Quinn, Adam (Security Officer)
Conqueror's Pride - Timothy Zahn   s   4824

Quinn, Jimmy (Scientist; Spaceman)
The Sparrow - Mary Doria Russell   s   3789

Quinn, Roger (Businessman; Magician)
A Calculated Magic - Robert Weinberg   f   4540

Quinn "Nomad" (Time Traveller; Warrior)
Desert Fire - David Alexander   s   53

Quinn "Nomad" (Warrior; Spy)
Nomad - David Alexander   s   54

Quint (Agent)
Psi-Man - David Peters   s   3428

Quon (Cult Member)
The Jade Ogre - Kenneth Robeson   f   3699

Quong, Sue-Ling (Doctor)
The Singers of Time - Frederik Pohl   s   3468

Quordane, Holis (Nobleman; Criminal)
Shadow of the Crown - Craig Mills   f   3119

R

R-T "Artie" (Child; Handicapped)
R-T, Margaret, and the Rats of NIMH - Jane Leslie Conly   f   913

Ra-hotep-kan "Ra" (Alien)
StarGate - Dean Devlin   s   1217

Ra-khir of Erythane (Apprentice; Knight)
Beyond Ragnarok - Mickey Zucker Reichert   f   3604

Ra Sadiin, Cydell (Ruler; Lesbian)
Heartstone and Silver - Jacqui Singleton   f   4047

Raajeh (Animal)
Ray Bradbury Presents: Dinosaur Planet - Stephen Leigh   s   2724

Raayat (Alien)
The Madness Season - C.S. Friedman   s   1655

Rabbit, Roger (Actor; Spouse)
Who P-P-Plugged Roger Rabbit? - Gary K. Wolf   f   4726

Rabjohns, Will (Photographer)
Sacrament - Clive Barker   h   290

Rabscuttle (Animal)
Tales From Watership Down - Richard Adams   f   25

Rachael (Android)
Blade Runner 2: The Edge of Human - K.W. Jeter   s   2315

Rachaela (Young Woman)
Personal Darkness - Tanith Lee   h   2715

Rachel (Spouse; Singer)
Archangel - Sharon Shinn   s   3989

Rachel (Child; Student)
The Time Tree - Enid Richemont   f   3662

Rachelle (Martial Arts Expert; Bodyguard)
The Anubis Murders - Gary Gygax   f   1982

Rachelle (Bodyguard; Martial Arts Expert)
Death in Delhi - Gary Gygax   f   1983

Rackstraw, Jeremiah (Entertainer)
Escardy Gap - Peter Crowther   h   1039

Racso (Animal)
R-T, Margaret, and the Rats of NIMH - Jane Leslie Conly   f   913

Radburn, Adam (Vampire; Morgue Attendant)
The Undead - Roxanne Longstreet   h   2796

Radcliffe, Harry (Architect)
Outside the Dog Museum - Jonathan Carroll   f   745

Radcliffe, Milton (Collector; Psychic)
Lorien Lost - Michael King   f   2477

Radcliffe, Phillip (Young Man)
A Sharpness on the Neck - Fred Saberhagen   h   3818

Radience (Slave)
Warriorwards - Dafydd ab Hugh   f   9

Radineaux, Jenifleur (Student; Martial Arts Expert)
Anvil of the Sun - Anne Lesley Groell   f   1963

Radineaux, Viera (Martial Arts Expert; Debutante)
Anvil of the Sun - Anne Lesley Groell   f   1963

Rado (Gambler; Traveller)
Thorn and Needle - Paul B. Thompson   f   4354

Rae, Dorcas (Scientist; Researcher)
Gaia's Toys - Rebecca Ore   s   3362

Raeburn, Francis (Psychic; Magician)
Death of an Adept - Katherine Kurtz   f   2590

Raeburn, Francis (Historian; Occultist)
The Lodge of the Lynx - Katherine Kurtz   f   2592

Raeder, Peter (Engineer; Spaceman)
The Rising - James Doohan   s   1275

Rael (Teenager; Religious)
The Cult of Loving Kindness - Paul Park   s   3382

Rafe (Musician; Orphan)
Ecstasia - Francesca Lia Block   f   446

Rafe (Spaceman)
A Matter of Oaths - Helen S. Wright   s   4769

Rafferty, John (Religious)
Unholy Fire - Whitley Strieber   h   4261

Rafiel (Actor; Aged Person)
Outnumbering the Dead - Frederik Pohl   s   3467

Rafin (Police Officer)
Runes of Autumn - Larry Elmore   f   1436

Raganda (Mythical Creature)
The Gates of Noon - Michael Scott Rohan   f   3732

Ragman (Psychic; Revolutionary)
The Host - Peter R. Emshwiller   s   1460

Rah (Alien)
Lake of the Sun - Wynne Whiteford   s   4610

Rahl, Darken (Wizard; Leader)
Wizard's First Rule - Terry Goodkind   f   1822

Rahl, Richard "the Seeker" (Wizard)
Blood of the Fold - Terry Goodkind   f   1820

Rahn (Farmer; Wanderer)
They Fly at Ciron - Samuel R. Delany   s   1198

Raihna (Warrior; Leader)
Conan the Relentless - Roland J. Green   f   1883

Railly, Kathryn (Doctor)
12 Monkeys - Elizabeth Hand   s   2025

Raim (Handicapped)
Dark Heart - Betsy James   f   2274

Rainaut, Valence (Knight)
Crusader's Torch - Chelsea Quinn Yarbro   h   4795

Raine of the Three Waters (Noblewoman)
A Breach in the Watershed - Douglas Niles   f   3267

Raine of the Three Waters (Noblewoman; Writer)
Darkenheight - Douglas Niles   f   3269

Raines, Darcy (Tour Guide)
Midnight's Lair - Richard Laymon   h   2680

Raines, Ingrid (Military Personnel)
The Children's Hour - Jerry Pournelle   s   3485

Raines, Michael (Psychic)
The Fugitive Stars - Daniel Ransom   s   3571

Raishan, Marguerite "Marghe" Angelica (Anthropologist; Wanderer)
Ammonite - Nicola Griffith   s   1956

Raistlin (Wizard; Hero)
The Second Generation - Margaret Weis   f   4563

Rajasthan, Nohar (Genetically Altered Being; Animal)
Emperors of the Twilight - S. Andrew Swann   s   4274

Rajasthan, Nohar (Genetically Altered Being; Detective—Private)
Forests of the Night - S. Andrew Swann   s   4275

Razin, Fyodor Alexeyevich (Scientist)
Landscape Painted with Tea - Milorad
Pavic *f* 3394

Razkili (Military Personnel)
Shadowdance - Robin Wayne Bailey *f* 245

Readis (Child)
The Dolphins of Pern - Anne McCaffrey *s* 2967

Reagan, Nancy (Advertising)
Throat Sprockets - Tim Lucas *h* 2816

Reagan, Ronald (Political Figure)
The Atrocity Exhibition - J.G. Ballard *s* 269

Reandn (Guard; Detective)
Touched by Magic - Doranna Durgin *f* 1369

ReAth (Nobleman)
Shaper's Legacy - Sheila Finch *s* 1556

Reatur (Ruler)
A World of Difference - Harry Turtledove *s* 4394

Rebecca (Handicapped)
Gate of Darkness, Circle of Light - Tanya
Huff *f* 2229

Rebecca "Becca" (Journalist; Traveller)
Briar Rose - Jane Yolen *f* 4806

Rebello, Joseph "Joe" Z. (Spaceman; Military
Personnel)
In the Wrong Hands - Edward Gibson *s* 1778

Rebka, Hans (Adventurer)
Divergence - Charles Sheffield *s* 3952
Transcendence - Charles Sheffield *s* 3963

Rec (Artificial Intelligence)
Kaduna Memories - Jack McKinney *s* 3068

red mare (Mythical Creature; Animal)
A Ride on the Red Mare's Back - Ursula K. Le
Guin *f* 2692

Red Orc (Immortal)
More than Fire - Philip Jose Farmer *s* 1504

Redbird (Fiance(e))
Shaman - Robert Shea *f* 3948

Redd (Cowboy)
Red Dust - Paul J. McAuley *s* 2956

Reddy, John (Mythical Creature; Adventurer)
A King Beneath the Mountain - Robert N.
Charrette *f* 788

Reddy, John (Mythical Creature)
A Knight Among Knaves - Robert N.
Charrette *f* 789

Reddy, John (Security Officer)
A Prince Among Men - Robert N. Charrette *f* 791

Redfern, Diana (Teenager)
The Lake at the End of the World - Caroline
MacDonald *s* 2849

Redfield, Blake (Antiquarian)
Hide and Seek - Paul Preuss *s* 3524
The Medusa Encounter - Paul Preuss *s* 3525

Redman, Stu (Leader)
The Stand: The Complete and Uncut Edition - Stephen
King *h* 2495

Redwing, T'fyrr (Alien; Musician)
The Eagle and the Nightingales - Mercedes
Lackey *f* 2607

Redwyn (Magician)
The Lost History of Redwyn - William Jay *f* 2299

Ree, Danlo (Telepath; Traveller)
The Wall at the Edge of the World - Jim
Aikin *s* 36

Ree, Killashandra (Miner)
Crystal Line - Anne McCaffrey *s* 2963

Reece (Mercenary)
War - Simon Hawke *f* 2099

Reed, Jack (Businessman)
Walkers - Graham Masterton *h* 2927

Reed, Jerry (Scientist)
Russian Spring - Norman Spinrad *s* 4128

Reed, Kayla (Empath; Revolutionary)
Sister Blood - Karen Haber *s* 1986

Reed, Kayla (Empath; Smuggler)
The War Minstrels - Karen Haber *s* 1987

Reed, Kayla (Empath; Fugitive)
Woman Without a Shadow - Karen Haber *s* 1988

Reed, Matt (Taxidermist)
The Reckoning - Ruby Jean Jensen *h* 2314

Reeling, Kate (Psychologist)
Manhattan Heat - Ken Eulo *h* 1490

Reem "First Cousin Brother" (Alien; Political
Figure)
Brother Termite - Patricia Anthony *s* 127

Rees (Teenager; Scientist)
Raft - Stephen Baxter *s* 332

Reese, Frances (Spaceship Captain)
Double Planet - John Gribbin *s* 1946

Reesone, Donald (Actor)
Near Death - Nancy Kilpatrick *h* 2471

Reeve, Todd (Rancher; Hero)
Crisis on Doona - Anne McCaffrey *s* 2962

Reeve, Todd (Political Figure)
Treaty at Doona - Anne McCaffrey *s* 2985

Reeves, Gail (Teacher)
The Immaculate - Mark Morris *h* 3204

Regina (Religious)
A Cast of Corbies - Mercedes Lackey *f* 2603

Regina (Child)
Hideaway - Dean R. Koontz *h* 2550

Regis (Mythical Creature)
The Legacy - R.A. Salvatore *f* 3841

Reich, Ben (Businessman; Murderer)
The Demolished Man - Alfred Bester *s* 388

Reichart, Carlos (Director; Homosexual)
Boys of Life - Paul Russell *h* 3790

Reichmann, Wolfgang "Wolfie" (Teacher)
Being of Two Minds - Pamela F. Service *f* 3928

Reid, Dallas (Detective—Police)
Boneman - Lisa Cantrell *h* 707

Reid, David Henry (Actor)
Stainless - Todd Grimson *h* 1961

Reid, Nicholas (Businessman)
The Cipher - Kathe Koja *h* 2541

Reille y Sanchez, Estrellita (Spaceship Captain;
Explorer)
Contact and Commune - L. Neil Smith *s* 4090

Reilly, Dave (Musician)
December - Phil Rickman *h* 3665

Reilly, Mary (Servant)
Mary Reilly - Valerie Martin *h* 2903

Reindeer (Mythical Creature)
The Woman Who Loved Reindeer - Meredith Ann
Pierce *f* 3441

Reith, Fergus (Tour Guide; Divorced Person)
The Swords of Zinjaban - L. Sprague de
Camp *s* 1143

Reive (Genetically Altered Being)
AEstival Tide - Elizabeth Hand *s* 2026

Relanj, Zia (Spy)
The Forever Drug - Steve Perry *s* 3422
Spindoc - Steve Perry *s* 3424

Relkin (Military Personnel; Companion)
Battledragon - Christopher Rowley *f* 3756
Bazil Broketail - Christopher Rowley *f* 3757
Dragons of War - Christopher Rowley *f* 3758
A Sword for a Dragon - Christopher
Rowley *f* 3760

Relorn, Wryan (Witch; Scientist)
Timediver's Dawn - L.E. Modesitt Jr. *s* 3138

Remillard, Jon (Psychic; Mutant)
Diamond Mask: A Novel - Julian May *s* 2941

Remillard, Mark (Psychic; Revolutionary)
Magnificat - Julian May *s* 2943

Remillard, Rogatien (Psychic; Businessman)
Diamond Mask: A Novel - Julian May *s* 2941

Remillard, Rogatien (Psychic)
Jack the Bodiless - Julian May *s* 2942

Remson, Vincent (Government Official)
The Stalk - Janet Morris *s* 3197

Renada (Young Woman)
The Stars Must Wait - Keith Laumer *s* 2664

Renagi (Warrior; Leader)
Tegne: Soul Warrior - Richard La Plante *f* 2598

Renar of Dagothrin (Heir—Dispossessed; Fugitive)
Lady of Mercy - Michelle Sagara *f* 3826

Renard, Eris (Government Official; Indian)
Green Lake - S.K. Epperson *h* 1470

Renfield, Tom (Psychic)
The Thread That Binds the Bones - Nina Kiriki
Hoffman *f* 2169

Renier, Mordan (Military Personnel; Political Figure)
Ganwold's Child - Diann Thornley *s* 4361

Renn, Jonathan (Prisoner)
Prison Planet - William C. Dietz *s* 1253

Renna (Spaceman; Diplomat)
Glory Season - David Brin *s* 564

Renner, Kevin (Military Personnel; Pilot)
The Gripping Hand - Larry Niven *s* 3281

Reno (Revolutionary; Disembodied Personality)
Solip: System - Walter Jon Williams *s* 4652

Renquist, Victor (Vampire)
The Time of Feasting - Mick Farren *h* 1514

Renya, Jacinta (Noblewoman; Government Official)
Iceman - Cynthia Felice *s* 1539

Renzie (Researcher; Warrior)
Vanishing Point - Michaela Roessner *s* 3724

Renzler, Lenore (Young Woman)
The 37th Mandala - Marc Laidlaw *h* 2633

Renzler, Michael (Clerk)
The 37th Mandala - Marc Laidlaw *h* 2633

Repairman Jack (Vigilante)
Nightworld - F. Paul Wilson *h* 4689

Resner, Jacob (Worker)
A Question of Time - Fred Saberhagen *h* 3816

Rethia (Healer)
Touched by Magic - Doranna Durgin *f* 1369

Retief, Jame (Diplomat)
Reward for Retief - Keith Laumer *s* 2663

Reva (Genetically Altered Being; Criminal)
Mainline - Deborah Christian *s* 828

Rex (Animal)
The Magnificent Wilf - Gordon R. Dickson *s* 1239

Reydak, Karl (Spy)
A Fearful Symmetry - James Luceno *s* 2817

Reyes, Eddie (Teenager)
Jaguar - Bill Ransom *s* 3569

Rivers, James (Scientist)
Portent - James Herbert *h* 2131

Rivers, Reginald (Guide; Time Traveller)
Rivers of Time - L. Sprague de Camp *s* 1142

Riversong (Mythical Creature)
The Warrior and the Witch - Carl Miller *f* 3100

Rivi (Young Woman)
Shaping the Dawn - Sheila Finch *s* 1557

Rizalli, Arvin "Harek" (Student; Mythical Creature)
User Unfriendly - Vivian Vande Velde *f* 4429

Ro, Nyx (Sorceress)
The Cygnet and the Firebird - Patricia A. McKillip *f* 3059

Ro, Vallant (Wizard; Sea Captain)
Convergence - Sharon Green *f* 1888

Road Man (Traveller; Magician)
Soulsmith - Tom Deitz *f* 1193

Roanhorse, Michael (Shepherd)
Eye Killers - A.A. Carr *h* 739

Roarke, Jason (Spaceman; Hero)
Flare Star - Paula E. Downing *s* 1287

Rob (Student—College)
Agviq - Michael Armstrong *s* 171

Robbins, Cynthia (Military Personnel; Spacewoman)
The Rising - James Doohan *s* 1275

Robbins, Maggie (Journalist)
The Dig - Alan Dean Foster *s* 1607

Robert (Animal)
The Coachman Rat - David Henry Wilson *f* 4680

Robert (Teenager)
The Dying Sun - Gary L. Blackwood *s* 414

Robert "Robin Hood" of Locksley (Nobleman; Outlaw)
Lady of the Forest - Jennifer Roberson *f* 3687

Roberts, Amelia (Military Personnel)
Priorities - Lynda Lyons *s* 2844

Roberts, Heather (Teenager)
Blood Sabbath - Leigh Clark *h* 843

Roberts, Karin (Museum Curator)
Blood Sabbath - Leigh Clark *h* 843

Roberts, Katie (Real Estate Agent)
The Haunting - Ruby Jean Jensen *h* 2311

Roberts, Kristen (Housewife)
Neighbors - Maureen S. Pusti *h* 3547

Roberts, Mark (Doctor)
Virus - Graham Watkins *h* 4488

Roberts, Ralph (Aged Person)
Insomnia - Stephen King *h* 2488

Roberts, Roy (Journalist)
Grave Markings - Michael A. Arnzen *h* 175

Roberts, Sheila (Student—College)
Into the Deep - Ken Grimwood *s* 1962

Roberts, Tom (Professor)
Neighbors - Maureen S. Pusti *h* 3547

Roberts, Veronica "Ronnie" (Journalist)
Universal Soldier - Robert Tine *s* 4368

Robin (Hunter; Step-Parent)
Passager - Jane Yolen *f* 4813

Robin (Minstrel; Revolutionary)
The Robin and the Kestrel - Mercedes Lackey *f* 2617

Robin (Child; Mythical Creature)
Street Magic - Michael Reaves *f* 3588

Robinson, David (Writer)
Beyond the Shroud - Rick Hautala *h* 2079

Robinson, Liz (Detective—Homicide)
Love Bite - Sherry Gottlieb *h* 1835

Robinson, Sarah (Teacher)
Beyond the Shroud - Rick Hautala *h* 2079

Robinson, Tracy Zempelios (Housewife)
Second Chance - Chet Williamson *h* 4658

Robinson, Woody (Musician)
Second Chance - Chet Williamson *h* 4658

Robyn (Runaway)
Stoneskin's Revenge - Tom Deitz *f* 1194

Roc, Roxanne (Mythical Creature)
Roc and a Hard Place - Piers Anthony *f* 154

Roche (Religious)
Doomsday Book - Connie Willis *s* 4672

Roche, Allison (Lawyer)
Mefisto in Onyx - Harlan Ellison *h* 1433

Rockdream (Warrior; Hunter)
The Goblin Plain War - Carl Miller *f* 3099

Rockdream (Military Personnel)
The Warrior and the Witch - Carl Miller *f* 3100

Roclawzi, Neal "Dun Wolf" (Warrior)
Once a Hero - Michael A. Stackpole *f* 4151

Rodgers, Franklin (Undertaker)
Moon Walker - Rick Hautala *h* 2085

Roebeck, Nan (Time Traveller)
Arc Riders - David Drake *s* 1314

Roebeck, Nan (Time Traveller; Leader)
The Fourth Rome - David Drake *s* 1317

Roeder, Karel (Student—High School)
Lights Out in the Reptile House - Jim Shepard *f* 3969

Roele, Michael (Royalty; Leader)
The Iron Throne - Simon Hawke *h* 2093

Rogan the Inept (Wizard)
The Door to Ambermere - J. Calvin Pierce *f* 3437

Roger (Criminal)
Memnoch the Devil - Anne Rice *h* 3651

Rogers, Buck (Warrior)
Hammer of Mars - M.S. Murdock *s* 3225

Rogers, Buck (Pilot; Experimental Subject)
A Life in the Future - Martin Caidin *s* 675

Rogers, Mara (Professor)
Indiana Jones and the Unicorn's Legacy - Rob MacGregor *f* 2858

Rogers, Troi (Socialite; Spacewoman)
Treks Not Taken - Steven R. Boyett *s* 497

Rogillard, Jack (Psychic)
Jack the Bodiless - Julian May *s* 2942

Rohan (Royalty; Ruler)
The Star Scroll - Melanie Rawn *f* 3582
Stronghold - Melanie Rawn *f* 3583

Rohr, Gail (Spirit)
The Land of Nod - Mark A. Clements *h* 874

Rojas, Duncan (Researcher)
Ivory: A Legend of Past and Future - Mike Resnick *s* 3629

Roker (Military Personnel)
Hero - Dave Duncan *s* 1352

Roland (Bastard Son; Warrior)
Charlemagne's Champion - Gail Van Asten *f* 4413

Roland (Gunfighter)
The Drawing of the Three - Stephen King *h* 2484

Roland (Musician)
Gate of Darkness, Circle of Light - Tanya Huff *f* 2229

Roland of Gilead (Gunfighter)
The Waste Lands - Stephen King *h* 2496

Rolando (Designer)
Thirst - Michael Cecilione *h* 769

Rolfa (Genetically Altered Being)
The Child Garden - Geoff Ryman *s* 3802

Rollie (Guide)
Sing the Light - Louise Marley *s* 2884

Rollie, Steve (Political Figure)
Dark Tide - Elizabeth Forrest *h* 1584

Roman (Servant)
Rock of Ages - Walter Jon Williams *s* 4651

Roman, Haml (Spaceship Captain)
Warhorse - Timothy Zahn *s* 4829

Romanov, George Alexandrovich (Royalty)
The Princess and the Dragon - Roberto Pazzi *f* 3402

Romar (Captive)
The Key of the Keplian - Andre Norton *f* 3310

Romero, Val (Vampire)
Night Blood - Eric Flanders *h* 1567

Romlar, Artus (Military Personnel; Mercenary)
The Regiment's War - John Dalmas *s* 1072
The White Regiment - John Dalmas *s* 1073

Rommel (Animal)
Psi-Man - David Peters *s* 3428

Ronay, Matthias "Matt" (Teenager; Adventurer)
Growing Up Weightless - John M. Ford *s* 1583

Roode, Sam (Child)
Lethal Delivery - J.G. Maxon *h* 2939

Roode, Tanya (Office Worker)
Lethal Delivery - J.G. Maxon *h* 2939

Rook, August (Inventor)
The Rim-World Legacy and Beyond - Frank A. Javor *s* 2298

Rool (Mythical Creature)
Shadow Moon - George Lucas *f* 2815

Roosevelt, Franklin Delano (Historical Figure; Political Figure)
Triumph - Ben Bova *s* 491

Roosevelt, Theodore (Historical Figure; Political Figure)
1901 - Robert Conroy *s* 918
Bully! - Mike Resnick *s* 3622

Rope (Sailor)
Clouds End - Sean Stewart *f* 4207

Rork, Paddy (Sailor; Young Man)
Signs of Life - Cherry Wilder *s* 4622

Rory (Businessman)
The Hellbound Heart - Clive Barker *h* 287

Rosa (Cyborg; Friend)
Correspondence - Sue Thomas *s* 4348

Rose (Sorceress; Royalty)
Question Quest - Piers Anthony *f* 153

Rose (Time Traveller; Warrior)
The Revenge of the Rose - Michael Moorcock *f* 3170

Rose (Religious)
Madeleine's Ghost - Robert Girardi *h* 1801

Rose, Janie (Young Woman)
Rage - Elizabeth Ergas *h* 1474

Rosemont, Alexander F. (Military Personnel; Leader)
Finger of God - Michael Kasner *s* 2400

Rosen, Gerry (Journalist)
The Jericho Iteration - Allen Steele *s* 4182

Roshak, Ter (Military Personnel)
Way of the Clans - Robert Thurston *s* 4362

Roshannon, Nikkael (Mercenary; Psychic)
Wheel of Dreams - Salinda Tyson *f* 4409

Roshnani (Spouse; Counselor)
The Stolen Throne - Harry Turtledove *f* 4393

Rosie (Magician)
Wild Blood - Nancy A. Collins *h* 909

Ross, Angie (Teacher)
Impulse - Rick Hautala *h* 2084

Ross, Brandy (Teenager)
Impulse - Rick Hautala *h* 2084

Ross, Brent (Military Personnel)
Assault of the Super Carrier - Peter Albano *s* 37
Revenge of the Seventh Carrier - Peter Albano *s* 39
Super Carrier: The Ultimate Secret Weapon - Peter Albano *s* 40

Ross, David (Detective)
The Dead Man's Kiss - Robert Weinberg *h* 4541

Ross, Malcolm (Lawyer)
The Jewel of Seven Stars - Bram Stoker *h* 4238

Rosselin, Perada "Rada" (Ruler)
The Gathering Flame - Debra Doyle *s* 1292

Rosselin Metadi, Beka (Royalty; Spaceship Captain)
By Honor Betray'd - Debra Doyle *s* 1291

Rosselin Metadi, Beka (Ruler; Spaceship Captain)
Starpilot's Grave - Debra Doyle *s* 1299

Rossemikka "Mikka" (Royalty)
The Perfect Princess - Irene Radford *f* 3556

Rossi, Eric (Police Officer)
Domination - Michael Cecilione *h* 767

Rossiter, Adam (Singer)
Tempter - Nancy A. Collins *h* 907

Rossman, Aaron (Spaceman)
Golden Fleece - Robert J. Sawyer *s* 3886

Roswell, Harry I. (Dentist; Doctor)
Summerland - L. Dean James *f* 2282

Rotciv, Victor (Stock Broker)
The Convocation - John R. Holt *h* 2192

Roth, Peter (Guide)
Monster - John Tigges *h* 4366

Rothman, Felice (Writer)
Bagatelle—Guinevere - Nancy Bogen *f* 456

Roueche, Philip (Zoo Keeper)
Claw - Ken Eulo *h* 1489

Rourke, Buneka (Settler; Teenager)
Powers That Be - Anne McCaffrey *s* 2978

Rourke, John T. (Military Personnel; Spy)
The Struggle - Jerry Ahern *s* 34

Rourke, Kenneth Christian (Security Officer)
Random Factor - Joel Henry Sherman *s* 3975

Rovin, Elli (Military Personnel)
Limbo Search - Parke Godwin *s* 1804

Rowan (Witch)
His Majesty's Elephant - Judith Tarr *f* 4302

Rowan (Child)
The Influence - Ramsey Campbell *h* 698

Rowan (Cartographer; Librarian)
The Outskirter's Secret - Rosemary Kirstein *s* 2509

Rowan (Wanderer; Scientist)
The Steerswoman - Rosemary Kirstein *s* 2510

Rowan, Dalin (Computer Expert)
The Knights of the Black Earth - Margaret Weis *s* 4561

Rowan, Jack (Writer; Spirit)
Dead Lines - John Skipp *h* 4056

Rowe, Grandpa (Artist; Psychic)
The Cartoonist - Sean Costello *h* 975

Rowena (Worker)
The Persistence of Memory - Karen Ripley *s* 3669

Rowforth (Royalty)
Chimaera's Copper - Piers Anthony *f* 136

Roxanne (Dancer)
The Werewolf Chronicles - Traci Briery *h* 558

Roy (Time Traveller)
Letters From Atlantis - Robert Silverberg *f* 4015

Roy, Ubu (Pilot; Trader)
Angel Station - Walter Jon Williams *s* 4646

Royal, Barton (Murderer)
Billy - Whitley Strieber *h* 4258

Royal, Paul (Experimental Subject)
Nanoware Time/The Persistence of Vision - Ian Watson *s* 4494

Royal, Solomon (Doctor)
Butcher - Rex Miller *h* 3104

Rozak, Jay (Time Traveller; Revolutionary)
Islands of Tomorrow - F.M. Busby *s* 640

Rozhenko, Worf (Alien; Student)
Worf's First Adventure - Peter David *s* 1123

Rozokov, Dimitri (Vampire)
The Night Inside - Nancy Baker *h* 252

Rubicon, Cassandra (Archaeologist)
Ruins - Kevin J. Anderson *h* 93

Rudolph "Rudy" (Royalty; Telepath)
Being of Two Minds - Pamela F. Service *f* 3928

Rufo (Magician; Servant)
Glory Road - Robert A. Heinlein *f* 2112

Rufus (Immortal)
The Boat of a Million Years - Poul Anderson *s* 104

Rugby, Jerzy (Computer Expert; Detective—Amateur)
The Hacker and the Ants - Rudy Rucker *s* 3765

Ruha (Widow(er); Sorceress)
The Parched Sea - Troy Denning *f* 1200

Ruiz, Juan (Criminal)
Fear Itself - Ric Meyers *h* 3092

Rune (Musician)
The Lark and the Wren - Mercedes Lackey *f* 2613

Runs in Light (Hunter; Prehistoric Human)
People of the Wolf - W. Michael Gear *f* 1741

Runyon, Damon (Journalist; Historical Figure)
Nevermore - William Hjortsberg *h* 2150

Rupert (Royalty)
Blue Moon Rising - Simon R. Green *f* 1894

Ruquel (Doctor; Dancer)
The Book of the Beast - Tanith Lee *f* 2708

Rushkin, Vincent Adjani (Artist; Recluse)
Memory and Dream - Charles de Lint *f* 1157

Ruskettle, Olive (Mythical Creature)
Song of the Saurials - Kate Novak *f* 3319

Ruskin, Willard (Scientist)
From a Changeling Star - Jeffrey A. Carver *s* 754

Russel, Ben (Convict)
Cold in July - Joe R. Lansdale *h* 2644

Russell, Dale (Government Official)
Green Lake - S.K. Epperson *h* 1470

Russell, Paul (Scientist; Engineer)
Lake of the Sun - Wynne Whiteford *s* 4610

Russell, Saxifrage "Sax" (Scientist; Aged Person)
Blue Mars - Kim Stanley Robinson *s* 3704

Russell, Saxifrage "Sax" (Scientist; Revolutionary)
Green Mars - Kim Stanley Robinson *s* 3708

Russell, Scott (Detective—Private)
Street Magic - Michael Reaves *f* 3588

Russie, Moishe (Refugee; Radio Personality)
Worldwar: Striking the Balance - Harry Turtledove *s* 4396

Russie, Moishe (Fugitive)
Worldwar: Tilting the Balance - Harry Turtledove *s* 4397

Rustin, Adelaine Hawthorne Taylor (Aged Person)
The Devil's Churn - Kristine Kathryn Rusch *h* 3773

Rusty (Teenager; Refugee)
A Time for Dragons - Gary Gentile *s* 1759

Ruth (Vampire)
Personal Darkness - Tanith Lee *h* 2715

Rutman, Becky (Administrator)
Nightlife - Jack Ellis *h* 1427

Rwyan (Wizard)
Lords of the Sky - Angus Wells *f* 4573

Ryan, Holly (Psychologist)
Sacrifice - Richard Kinion *h* 2498

Ryan, Jayne (Astronaut; Scientist)
Beachhead - Jack Williamson *s* 4667

Ryan, Steve (Businessman)
Blood Feud - Sam Siciliano *h* 4005

Ryan, William (Religious)
Nightworld - F. Paul Wilson *h* 4689

Ryan-Turriy, Adlayra (Mythical Creature)
Dancer's Rise - Jo Clayton *f* 857

Ryana (Religious; Adventurer)
The Seeker - Simon Hawke *f* 2098

Ryba (Leader)
Fall of Angels - L.E. Modesitt Jr. *f* 3131

Rybak, Nadya (Werewolf; Orphan)
Nadya: The Wolf Chronicles - Pat Murphy *f* 3228

Rydell, Berry (Police Officer; Bounty Hunter)
Virtual Light - William Gibson *s* 1782

Rydell, Tony (Scientist)
Dream Maker - W.A. Harbinson *s* 2031

Ryder (Genetically Altered Being)
Black Milk - Robert Reed *s* 3593

Ryder (Musician; Fugitive)
Kamikaze L'Amour - Richard Kadrey *s* 2388

Ryder, Christine (Pilot; Lesbian)
The Tranquility Alternative - Allen Steele *s* 4187

Ryder, Gordon (Fugitive)
Pirates of the Universe - Terry Bisson *s* 410

Ryder, Gunther "Gun" (Spaceman)
Pirates of the Universe - Terry Bisson *s* 410

Ryder, Howie (Teenager)
Dawn's Uncertain Light - Neal Barrett Jr. *s* 305

Ryder, Jake (Astronaut)
Reach - Edward Gibson *s* 1779

Ryerson, Will (Worker)
Reprisal - F. Paul Wilson *h* 4692

Ryn "Robin" (Runaway)
The War of the Sky Lords - John Brosnan *s* 589

Rys (Sailor)
Dancing Jack - Laurie J. Marks *f* 2880

Ryson, Kerryl (Slave)
The Thirteenth Majestral - Hayford Peirce *s* 3407

Ryton, Melanie (Mutant)
The Mutant Season - Robert Silverberg *s* 4019

Ryton, Michael (Mutant)
The Mutant Season - Robert Silverberg *s* 4019

S

S————————, Delia (Real Estate Agent)
First Love: A Gothic Tale - Joyce Carol
Oates *h* 3331

S————————, Josephine Carolyn "Josie" (Child)
First Love: A Gothic Tale - Joyce Carol
Oates *h* 3331

S .B. "Air" (Child; Adventurer)
Beyond the Magic Sphere - Gail Jarrow *f* 2296

Saad, Khalil (Worker)
The Nightmare People - Lawrence Watt-
Evans *h* 4499

Saalahan (Alien)
Mid-Flinx - Alan Dean Foster *s* 1613

Saari, Juna "Eerin" (Scientist; Explorer)
The Color of Distance - Amy Thomson *s* 4357

Sabah, Hasan al (Criminal; Religious)
The Mask of Loki - Roger Zelazny *f* 4842

Saber, Karen (Linguist; Criminal)
Marks of Our Brothers - Jane M. Lindskold *s* 2763

Sabriel (Magician; Teenager)
Sabriel - Garth Nix *f* 3288

Sack (Disembodied Personality)
Land O'Goshen - Charles McNair *s* 3071

Sadb (Spouse)
The Shield between the Worlds - Diana L.
Paxson *f* 3398

Sadi (Mercenary; Immortal)
Kaleidoscope Century - John Barnes *s* 294

Sadir (Nobleman)
Canby's Legion - Bill Baldwin *s* 258

Sadira (Slave; Mythical Creature)
The Verdant Passage - Troy Denning *f* 1201

Sadler, Ben (Vampire)
Sins of the Blood - Kristine Kathryn Rusch *h* 3785

Sagan, Derek (Military Personnel)
King's Sacrifice - Margaret Weis *s* 4560
The Lost King - Margaret Weis *s* 4562

Sage of Sare (Wizard; Ruler)
The Wizard King - Julie Dean Smith *f* 4089

Sahacat (Indian; Shaman)
People of the Sky - Clare Bell *s* 355

Saigo (Government Official; Revolutionary)
Aristoi - Walter Jon Williams *s* 4647

Sailor "Lightning" (Alien)
Silent Dances - A.C. Crispin *s* 1025

Saint-Alaban, Justice (Scientist)
Winterlong - Elizabeth Hand *s* 2029

St. Brendan, Caitlin (Religious; Magician)
Indiana Jones and the White Witch - Martin
Caidin *f* 674

St. Clair, Adrienne (Scientist; Vampire)
Bloodshift - Garfield Reeves-Stevens *h* 3597

St. Cyr, Butterfly (Smuggler; Spaceship Captain)
Archangel Blues - eluki bes shahar *s* 384
Darktraders - eluki bes shahar *s* 385
Hellflower - Eluki bes Shahar *s* 386

St. Du Lac, Lynn (Noblewoman)
The Lost History of Redwyn - William Jay *f* 2299

St. Eve, Clair (Child)
Skeletons - Al Sarrantonio *h* 3871

St. George, Joe (Handyman)
Dolores Claiborne - Stephen King *h* 2483

Saint Germain (Vampire)
Better in the Dark - Chelsea Quinn Yarbro *h* 4792

Mansions of Darkness - Chelsea Quinn
Yarbro *h* 4796
Out of the House of Life - Chelsea Quinn
Yarbro *h* 4797

Saint-Germain (Revolutionary)
Two Crowns for America - Katherine Kurtz *f* 2594

St. Ives, Langdon (Scientist; Explorer)
Lord Kelvin's Machine - James P. Blaylock *f* 422

St. Jacques, Adela Rogers (Writer)
Night of the Living 'Gator! - Richard A.
Lupoff *s* 2841

St. James, Nicholas (Government Official)
The Penultimate Truth - Philip K. Dick *s* 1228

St. John, Ian "Hunter" (Pilot)
Wing Commander: Freedom Flight - Mercedes
Lackey *s* 2630

St. John, Simon (Musician)
December - Phil Rickman *h* 3665

St. John, Wade (Student)
Coven - Edward Lee *h* 2696

Saint-Just, Emile (Spaceman)
Blind Justice - S.N. Lewitt *s* 2741

Sakhalin, Anatoly (Warrior; Nobleman)
The Law of Becoming - Kate Elliott *s* 1423

Saladin (Immortal; Murderer)
The Forever King - Molly Cochran *f* 879

Salandra (Guide; Adventurer)
Indiana Jones and the Interior World - Rob
MacGregor *f* 2855

Salazar, Bettina (Indian)
Ghost Dance - Kathryn Ptacek *h* 3541

Salazar, Kirk (Student; Traveller)
The Venom Trees of Sunga - L. Sprague de
Camp *s* 1145

Salesman (Demon)
Tales From the Crypt: Demon Knight - Randall
Boyll *h* 507

Salib, Tariq (Scientist)
The Missing Matter - Thomas R.
McDonough *s* 3031

Salisaw, Brent (Construction Worker)
Night Thunder - Ruby Jean Jensen *h* 2313

Salisaw, Holly (Child)
Night Thunder - Ruby Jean Jensen *h* 2313

Salisaw, Kara (Child)
Night Thunder - Ruby Jean Jensen *h* 2313

Salk, Job Napoleon (Orphan)
Brother to Dragons - Charles Sheffield *s* 3949

Sallas, Ike "the Bakatcha Bandit" (Indian; Sailor)
Sailor Song - Ken Kesey *s* 2456

Salmalin, Numair (Magician)
The Realms of the Gods - Tamora Pierce *f* 3442
Wolf-Speaker - Tamora Pierce *f* 3444

Saluez (Servant)
Shadow's End - Sheri S. Tepper *s* 4339

Salvatore, Dominga (Religious; Criminal)
The Laughing Corpse - Laurell K. Hamilton *f* 2017

Sam (Hunter)
Nicoji - M. Shayne Bell *s* 358

Sam (Teenager)
No Kidding - Bruce Brooks *s* 579

Sam (Cyborg)
The Sounding Stillness - Kenneth Von
Gunden *s* 4452

Sam (Mechanic)
The Unfinished - Jay B. Laws *h* 2676

Sam (Criminal; Adventurer)
Villains by Necessity - Eve Forward *f* 1592

Samiq (Prehistoric Human; Indian)
My Sister the Moon - Sue Harrison *f* 2065

Sampson, Matt (Military Personnel; Teenager)
Traitors from Within - R.A. Montgomery *s* 3157

Samson, Daniel "Dan" (Martial Arts Expert; Time
Traveller)
Union Fires - John Barnes *f* 299
Wartide - John Barnes *f* 300

Samson, Leonard "Doc" (Doctor)
What Savage Beast - Peter David *s* 1122

Samson, Rosalie "Rose" (Social Worker)
The Godmother - Elizabeth Ann
Scarborough *f* 3889

Samuel (Twin)
Dark Father - Tom Piccirilli *h* 3435

Samuels, Albert (Inventor; Clone)
The Clouds of Magellan - David F.
Nighbert *s* 3266

Sanchez, Monica (Musician)
Gossamer Axe - Gael Baudino *f* 326

Sanchi (Gambler)
Sphynxes Wild - Esther Friesner *f* 1677

Sanda (Apprentice; Scholar)
Initiation - Marian Hughes *s* 2235

Sandburg, Elaine "Nefret" (Time Traveller;
Religious)
Thebes of the Hundred Gates - Robert
Silverberg *s* 4022

Sandeen, Michael (Musician)
Night Music - Sheila Bristow Garner *h* 1724

Sander (Friend; Teenager)
Through the Heart - Richard Grant *f* 1864

Sanderheim, Doug (Engineer; Boyfriend)
Slow Funeral - Rebecca Ore *f* 3365

Sanders, Alison (Student)
The Priest: A Gothic Romance - Thomas M.
Disch *h* 1261

Sanders, John A. (Police Officer)
Dark Visions - T. Lucien Wright *h* 4771

Sanders, Johnny (Inventor; Artist)
Armed Memory - Jim Young *s* 4821

Sanders, Julia (Waiter/Waitress)
Raven - Charles L. Grant *h* 1854

Sanders, Kenneth (Mutant; FBI Agent)
Doomsday Exam - Nick Pollotta *f* 3477

Sanders, Nicholas (Linguist)
Ring of Swords - Eleanor Arnason *s* 173

Sanders, Phillipe "Phil" Montoya (Police Officer;
Computer Expert)
The Modular Man - Roger MacBride Allen *s* 65

Sanderson, Loki (Professor)
Destiny's Carnival - Warren Murphy *h* 3232

Sanderson, Merry (Girlfriend)
Wolf and Iron - Gordon R. Dickson *s* 1242

Sanderson, Paul (Businessman; Wanderer)
Wolf and Iron - Gordon R. Dickson *s* 1242

Sandford, Nancy (Scientist; Editor)
The Ragged World: A Novel of the Hefn on Earth -
Judith Moffett *s* 3140

Sandoval (Military Personnel; Lesbian)
In the Blood - Lauren Wright Douglas *s* 1283

Sandoval, Mickey (Researcher)
Heads - Greg Bear *s* 343

Sandoval, Rho (Businessman)
Heads - Greg Bear *s* 343

Sherman (Student—High School; Adventurer)
In between Dragons - Michael Kandel f 2397

Sherman, William Tecumseh (Historical Figure; Military Personnel)
Under the Shadow - Jane Toombs h 4372

Sherwood, Carl (Computer Expert)
The Sherwood Game - Esther Friesner s 1676

Sherwood, Iris "Butcher of Boston" (Government Official; Step-Parent)
In the Cube - David Alexander Smith s 4076

Sherwood, John (Hunter; Mythical Creature)
Dancing Bears - Fred Saberhagen f 3809

Shielder's Mark (Hero; Spouse)
Nobody's Son - Sean Stewart f 4208

Shields, Ben (Writer)
Prank Night - David Robbins h 3678

Shikome, Lily (Nurse)
The Twelfth Child - Raymond Van Over h 4415

Shiloh, Luna (Government Official)
Flies From the Amber - Wil McCarthy s 2995

Shimmer (Royalty; Mythical Creature)
Dragon Cauldron - Laurence Yep f 4802
Dragon War - Laurence Yep f 4803

Shinji, Matsumura (Nobleman; Warrior)
The Yngling in Yamato - John Dalmas s 1075

Ship (Artificial Intelligence)
A Maze of Stars - John Brunner s 600

Shipman, Malkah (Aged Person)
He, She and It - Marge Piercy s 3445

Shipman, Shira (Computer Expert)
He, She and It - Marge Piercy s 3445

Shira (Time Traveller; Revolutionary)
Timelike Infinity - Stephen Baxter s 335

Shirley (Cyborg; Traveller)
Correspondence - Sue Thomas s 4348

Shiva (Prehistoric Human; Teenager)
Shiva Accused: An Adventure of the Ice Age - J.H. Brennan f 546
Shiva: An Adventure of the Ice Age - J.H. Brennan f 548
Shiva's Challenge: An Adventure of the Ice Age - J.H. Brennan f 547

Shkai'ra (Warrior; Barbarian)
The Cage - S.M. Stirling f 4223

Sh'kaira (Warrior)
Shadow's Son - Shirley Meier f 3085

Shn'dar, Queekat (Alien; Historian)
Sentinels - Margaret Weis s 4564

Shomer, Jillian (Sports Figure)
Achilles' Choice - Larry Niven s 3274

Shongili, Sean (Genetically Altered Being; Spouse)
Power Lines - Anne McCaffrey s 2976

Shonto (Nobleman; Military Personnel)
Gatherer of Clouds - Sean Russell f 3792

Shores, Candice (Military Personnel)
The Painful Field - Roland J. Green s 1885
The Sum of Things - Roland J. Green s 1887

Short-Son "Eater-of-Grass" of Chiirr-Nig (Alien)
Man-Kzin Wars IV - Larry Niven s 3283

Shrewsbury, Laban (Professor)
The Trail of Cthulhu - August Derleth h 1208

Shriek, Anthony (Artist)
Anthony Shriek - Jessica Amanda Salmonson h 3832

Shudde-M'ell (Monster)
The Burrowers Beneath - Brian Lumley h 2823

Shuganan (Artist; Indian)
Mother Earth, Father Sky - Sue Harrison f 2064

Shulana (Wizard; Mythical Creature)
Dragonspawn - Mark Acres f 21

Shustak, Evan "American Dream" (Vagrant)
The Holy Terror - Wayne Allen Sallee h 3829

Shutterbug (Pornographer)
Slippin' into Darkness - Norman Partridge h 3390

Shuyun (Religious; Martial Arts Expert)
Gatherer of Clouds - Sean Russell f 3792
The Initiate Brother - Sean Russell f 3793

Sibatia (Shaman)
Dry Skull Dreams - Michael Green h 1879

Sickert, Walter (Artist)
From Hell - Alan Moore h 3171
The Women of Whitechapel and Jack the Ripper - Paul West h 4590

Sid 6.7 (Artificial Intelligence; Criminal)
Virtuosity - Terry Bisson s 411

Siddonie (Ruler; Sorceress)
The Catswold Portal - Shirley Rousseau Murphy f 3230

Sidra (Explorer)
Future Eden - J.M. Morgan s 3183

Siebold, Howard (Traitor)
Afterage - Yvonne Navarro h 3243

Siegel, Benjamin "Bugsy" (Historical Figure; Criminal)
Last Call - Tim Powers f 3495

Sierek, Detlef (Writer)
Drachenfels - Jack Yeovil f 4800

Sieyes (Psychologist)
A Whisper of Time - Paula E. Downing s 1288

Sigfrid (Mythical Creature; Warrior)
The Dragons of the Rhine - Diana L. Paxson f 3395
The Wolf and the Raven - Diana L. Paxson f 3401

Sigfrith (Mythical Creature; Warrior)
Rhinegold - Stephan Grundy f 1965

Siggerson, Olaf (Pilot)
Destination: Mutiny - Sean Dalton s 1078

Siglen (Psychic; Leader)
The Rowan - Anne McCaffrey s 2980

Sigvarthsson, Shef (Hero; Blacksmith)
The Hammer and the Cross - Harry Harrison f 2055

Sigvarthsson, Shef (Royalty; Scientist)
King and Emperor - Harry Harrison f 2056

Sigvarthsson, Shef (Royalty; Warrior)
One King's Way - Harry Harrison s 2057

Sigyn (Mythical Creature)
The Tower of Beowulf - Parke Godwin f 1808

Sikes, Jason (Teenager)
Under Alien Stars - Pamela F. Service s 3929

Sikes, Jesse (Murderer; Monster)
Sins of the Flesh - Don Davis h 1130

Sikes, Matthew (Detective—Police)
Cross of Blood - K.W. Jeter s 2318
Dark Horizon - K.W. Jeter s 2319

Sikes, Stephen (Young Man)
Sins of the Flesh - Don Davis h 1130

Sil (Experimental Subject; Genetically Altered Being)
Species - Yvonne Navarro s 3245

Siladri (Farmer)
The Painted Alphabet - Diana Darling f 1096

Silbakor (Mythical Creature)
Dragon Death - Gael Baudino f 324
Duel of Dragons - Gael Baudino f 325

Silence (Military Personnel)
Deathstalker Rebellion - Simon R. Green s 1896

s'Ilessid, Lysaer (Royalty; Magician)
Curse of the Mistwraith - Janny Wurts f 4785
Ships of Merior - Janny Wurts f 4787

Silk (Religious)
Nightside the Long Sun - Gene Wolfe s 4734

Silk (Streetperson)
Street - Jack Cady h 671

Silk, Patera (Religious)
Calde of the Long Sun - Gene Wolfe s 4728
Exodus From the Long Sun - Gene Wolfe s 4732
Lake of the Long Sun - Gene Wolfe s 4733

Silk, Venture (Public Relations)
The Forever Drug - Steve Perry s 3422

Silk, Venture (Government Official; Sports Figure)
Spindoc - Steve Perry s 3424

Silkweb Empress (Royalty; Mythical Creature)
Bronze Mirror - Jeanne Larsen f 2656

Silme (Sorceress)
By Chaos Cursed - Mickey Zucker Reichert f 3605

Siluricus, Gaius Macellius Severus (Military Personnel)
The Forest House - Marion Zimmer Bradley f 521

Silvas (Wizard; Deity)
The Wizard at Home - Rick Shelley f 3968

Silver, David (Police Officer)
Alien Blues - Lynn S. Hightower s 2142
Alien Eyes - Lynn S. Hightower s 2143
Alien Heat - Lynn S. Hightower s 2144
Alien Rites - Lynn S. Hightower s 2145

Silver, Jake (Teenager)
Them - William W. Johnstone h 2339

Silver, Michelle "Micki" Ann (Child; Time Traveller)
The Silver Tree - Ruth L. Williams f 4637

Silver, Mier (Spy; Psychic)
Mission: Tori - Johanna Bolton s 462

Silver Hand, Llew (Royalty; Ruler)
The Endless Knot - Stephen R. Lawhead f 2671

Silver-Rim (Alien)
Ocean under the Ice - Robert L. Forward s 1595

Silver Snow (Royalty; Warrior)
Imperial Lady - Andre Norton f 3309

Silverblade "Blade" (Military Personnel)
The Silver Gryphon - Mercedes Lackey f 2619

Silvercup (Android)
Hostile Takeover - Jack McKinney s 3067

Silverhand, Caeled (Hero; Warrior)
Silverlight - Morgan Llywelyn f 2785

Silverhorn, Aelfred (Mercenary)
Into the Void - Nigel Findley f 1560

Silverstein, Ian (Martial Arts Expert; Hero)
The Fire Duke - Joel Rosenberg f 3740
The Silver Stone - Joel Rosenberg f 3745

Simba (Musician)
Twisted - Sue Hollister Barr h 304

Simmons, Roger (Artist)
Galatea in 2-D - Aaron Allston f 73

Simmons, Susan (Student)
My Teacher Fried My Brains - Bruce Coville s 993

Simms, Nanci (Teacher; Warrior)
Deep Trek - James Axler s 234

Slonimsky, Waldo (Worker)
The Burning - Graham Masterton　*h*　2922

Slovotsky, Walter (Warrior)
The Road Home - Joel Rosenberg　*f*　3743
The Road to Ehvenor - Joel Rosenberg　*f*　3744

Sma, Diziet (Alien)
The State of the Art - Iain M. Banks　*s*　276

Sma, Diziet (Spy)
Use of Weapons - Iain M. Banks　*s*　277

Small, Elmo (Pharmacist)
The Devil's Cradle - Kate Stewart　*h*　4204

Smedley, Julian (Military Personnel; Handicapped)
Present Tense - Dave Duncan　*f*　1358

Smiggens, Preister (Pirate)
Dinotopia Lost - Alan Dean Foster　*f*　1608

Smirk, James T. (Spaceship Captain)
Star Wreck II: The Attack of the Jargonites - Leah
　Rewolinski　*s*　3643
Star Wreck III: Time Warped - Leah
　Rewolinski　*s*　3644
Star Wreck IV: Live Long and Profit - Leah
　Rewolinski　*s*　3645
Star Wreck 6: Geek Space Nine - Leah
　Rewolinski　*s*　3642
Star Wreck: The Generation Gap - Leah
　Rewolinski　*s*　3646

Smith (Government Official)
Murder at the Galactic Writers' Society - Janet
　Asimov　*s*　210

Smith, Alamo (Lawman)
Destination: Showdown - Jake Davis　*s*　1131
The Last Rangers - Jake Davis　*s*　1132

Smith, Brandon (Computer Expert; Recluse)
Virtual Girl - Amy Thomson　*s*　4358

Smith, Desi "Daisy Smeet" (Doctor; Psychic)
Chaos Come Again - Wilhelmina Baird　*s*　247

Smith, Desidra (Vampire)
Blood on the Sun - Brian Herbert　*h*　2126

Smith, Edward (Computer Expert)
The Nightmare People - Lawrence Watt-
　Evans　*h*　4499

Smith, Evangeline (Witch)
The Torching - Marcy Heidish　*h*　2110

Smith, George (Military Personnel)
Some of Your Blood - Theodore Sturgeon　*h*　4264

Smith, John (Postal Worker)
The Mailman - Bentley Little　*h*　2775

Smith, Jonathan Wesley (Computer Expert)
Harmonies of the 'Net - Jane S. Fancher　*s*　1497
Uplink - Jane S. Fancher　*s*　1499

Smith, Kamryn (Young Woman)
Killjoy - Elizabeth Forrest　*h*　1585

Smith, Kayla (Magician; Runaway)
Bedlam Boyz - Ellen Guon　*f*　1978

Smith, Sam (Psychic; Diver)
World Without End - Molly Cochran　*f*　880

Smith, Shanifa (Waiter/Waitress)
Dead End - Guy N. Smith　*h*　4083

Smith, Stephen (Writer)
Where Does Kissing End? - Kate Pullinger　*h*　3544

Smith, Valentine Michael (Angel; Orphan)
Stranger in a Strange Land - Robert A.
　Heinlein　*s*　2117

Smithback, Bill (Journalist)
Relic - Douglas Preston　*h*　3521

Smoke, Smokey (Telepath; Prostitute)
Smoke and Mirrors - Jane M. Lindskold　*s*　2764

Smolte, Hampton (Military Personnel)
Elephantasm - Tanith Lee　*h*　2711

Smythe (Wizard)
The Jewel of Equilibrant - Steven Frankos　*f*　1641

Smythe, Peter (Time Traveller; Military Personnel)
Arthur War Lord - Dafydd ab Hugh　*f*　5

Smythe, Raoul "Rags" (Magician; Professor)
Shade and Shadow - Francine G. Woodbury　*f*　4754

S'Nash (Alien; Researcher)
Fossil - Hal Clement　*s*　872

Snatch (Military Personnel)
The Knights of Cawdor - Mike Jefferies　*f*　2302

Snaugenhutt (Warrior; Animal)
Son of Spellsinger - Alan Dean Foster　*f*　1617

Snell, Nancy (Teenager)
The Devil's End - D.A. Fowler　*h*　1624

Snell, Susan (Teenager)
Carrie - Stephen King　*h*　2480

Snick, Panthea (Revolutionary; Girlfriend)
Dayworld Breakup - Philip Jose Farmer　*s*　1502

Snorrison, Bran (Hero; Immortal)
The Deepest Sea - Charles Barnitz　*f*　303

Snuff (Animal; Sidekick)
A Night in the Lonesome October - Roger
　Zelazny　*h*　4843

Snyder, Harry (Television Personality)
Satellite Night News - Jack Hopkins　*s*　2208

Sobek, Yoo (Alien; Rebel)
Hostile Takeover - Jack McKinney　*s*　3067

Sobel, Charles (Military Personnel)
Turn of the Cards - Victor Milan　*s*　3098

Soerensen, Terese "Tess" (Heiress; Linguist)
An Earthly Crown - Kate Elliott　*s*　1421

Soerensen, Terese "Tess" (Scholar; Noblewoman)
Jaran - Kate Elliott　*s*　1422

Soerensen, Terese "Tess" (Ruler)
The Law of Becoming - Kate Elliott　*s*　1423

Sogan, Varn Tarl (Royalty; Military Personnel)
Call to Arms - P.M. Griffin　*s*　1948

Sogan, Varn Tarl (Military Personnel)
Fire Planet - P.M. Griffin　*s*　1949

Sogan, Varn Tarl (Royalty; Telepath)
Jungle Assault - P.M. Griffin　*s*　1950

Sokolowska, Marya (Religious)
Under the Yoke - S.M. Stirling　*s*　4229

Sole, Chris (Scientist)
The Embedding - Ian Watson　*s*　4490

Soledad, Zeide (Student; Genetically Altered Being)
Cybernetic Jungle - S.N. Lewitt　*s*　2742

Soleta (Alien; Student)
Worf's First Adventure - Peter David　*s*　1123

Solinari, Kelly (Scholar; Detective—Amateur)
Crisis on Doona - Anne McCaffrey　*s*　2962

Solis, Rudy (Wizard; Mechanic)
Mother of Winter - Barbara Hambly　*f*　2007

Solith, Gwin Nien (Innkeeper; Magician)
The Cursed - Dave Duncan　*f*　1348

Solo (Artificial Intelligence; Robot)
Solo - Robert Mason　*s*　2914
Weapon - Robert Mason　*s*　2915

Solo, Han (Spaceship Captain; Warrior)
Ambush at Corellia - Roger MacBride Allen　*s*　62
Children of the Jedi - Barbara Hambly　*s*　2002
The Courtship of Princess Leia - Dave
　Wolverton　*s*　4741
Heir to the Empire - Timothy Zahn　*s*　4827
Jedi Search - Kevin J. Anderson　*s*　91

The New Rebellion - Kristine Kathryn
　Rusch　*s*　3777
The Truce at Bakura - Kathy Tyers　*s*　4407

Solo, Jay (Police Officer; Administrator)
The Nine Lives of Catseye Gomez - Simon
　Hawke　*f*　2094

Solo, Leia Organa (Royalty; Leader)
Ambush at Corellia - Roger MacBride Allen　*s*　62
Before the Storm - Michael P. Kube-
　McDowell　*s*　2581
Children of the Jedi - Barbara Hambly　*s*　2002
Darksaber - Kevin J. Anderson　*s*　86

Solo, Leia Organa (Administrator; Royalty)
Heir to the Empire - Timothy Zahn　*s*　4827

Solo, Leia Organa (Royalty; Leader)
The Last Command - Timothy Zahn　*s*　4828
The New Rebellion - Kristine Kathryn
　Rusch　*s*　3777

Solomon, Neil (Businessman)
Out There in the Darkness - Ed Gorman　*h*　1828

Solomon, Parker (Businessman)
Dark Tide - Elizabeth Forrest　*h*　1584

Somerfield, Alice (Child)
The End of Alice - A.M. Homes　*h*　2197

Somersby, Nadine (Store Owner)
Prank Night - David Robbins　*h*　3678

Sommers, Serena (Girlfriend)
Forest of the Night - S.P. Somtow　*f*　4114

Somoroff, Peter (Spy)
Red Devil - David Saperstein　*h*　3855

Sondra (Young Woman)
Tapestry of Dark Souls - Elaine Bergstrom　*h*　380

Song, Medwind (Sorceress; Barbarian)
Fire in the Mist - Holly Lisle　*f*　2767

Song, Medwind (Sorceress; Scholar)
Mind of the Magic - Holly Lisle　*f*　2769

Songa (Hunter; Warrior)
Conan the Savage - Leonard Carpenter　*f*　737

Sonnenberg, Bryce (Scientist; Sports Figure)
The Ganymede Club - Charles Sheffield　*s*　3953

Soo, Hannah (Financier; Reanimated Dead)
Take Back Plenty - Colin Greenland　*s*　1936

Soolis, Yveena (Noblewoman)
The Thirteenth Majestral - Hayford Peirce　*s*　3407

Sophie (Young Woman)
Spell Bound - Ru Emerson　*f*　1453

Sorak (Psychic; Mythical Creature)
The Outcast - Simon Hawke　*f*　2095
The Seeker - Simon Hawke　*f*　2098

Sorenson, Melissa (Child; Businesswoman)
Drifter's Run - William C. Dietz　*s*　1246

Sorenson, Rachel (Artist)
I'll Be Watching You - Samuel M. Key　*h*　2463

Sorensson, Alfreda "Allie" (Young Woman)
Night Calls - Katharine Eliska Kimbriel　*h*　2476

Sorensson, Eldon (Farmer)
Night Calls - Katharine Eliska Kimbriel　*h*　2476

sorMeklan, Driskolt "Dart" (Nobleman)
Beneath the Web - Lynn Abbey　*f*　10

Sorricaine, Viktor (Scientist)
The World at the End of Time - Frederik
　Pohl　*s*　3471

sorRodion, Rinchen "Wolf" (Royalty)
Beneath the Web - Lynn Abbey　*f*　10

Sorya (Revolutionary)
Metropolitan - Walter Jon Williams　*s*　4650

Stark, Laura (Young Woman)
Dreamthorp - Chet Williamson *h* 4654

Stark, Marilyn (Sea Captain; Criminal)
seaQuest DSV: The Novel - Diane Duane *s* 1344

Stark, Otto (Clone)
In the Wrong Hands - Edward Gibson *s* 1778

Stark, Tony "Iron Man" (Scientist; Hero)
Iron Man: The Armor Trap - Greg Cox *s* 996

Starlen, Garett (Police Officer)
Night Watch - Robin Wayne Bailey *f* 244

Starling, Clarice (FBI Agent)
The Silence of the Lambs - Thomas Harris *h* 2051

Starling, Ugly (Outcast)
Far Harbor - Melisa C. Michaels *s* 3095

Stasov, Ilya Sergeiivich (Scientist; Military Personnel)
A Deeper Sea - Alexander Jablokov *s* 2261

Stasya (Minstrel)
Sing the Four Quarters - Tanya Huff *f* 2231

Statler, Phil (Businessman)
The Fear in Yesterday's Rings - George C. Chesbro *h* 818

Stavely, Ann Veronica (Child)
Hexwood - Diana Wynne Jones *s* 2349

Stavenger, Douglas (Experimental Subject; Teenager)
Moonrise - Ben Bova *s* 482

Stavenger, Joanna Masterson (Businesswoman)
Moonrise - Ben Bova *s* 482

Stavenger, Paul (Astronaut; Businessman)
Moonrise - Ben Bova *s* 482

Stavi, Kira (Scientist)
Remnant Population - Elizabeth Moon *s* 3161

Stavrianos, Nick (Police Officer; Detective—Private)
Quarantine - Greg Egan *s* 1415

Steadford, Sir Harry (Spirit; Nobleman)
The Meddlesome Ghost - Sheila Rosalynd Allen *f* 70

Stebbins, Ivy (Real Estate Agent)
All the Bells on Earth - James P. Blaylock *f* 420

Stebbins, Walt (Salesman)
All the Bells on Earth - James P. Blaylock *f* 420

Steele, Vanessa (Alien; Revolutionary)
The Woman between the Worlds - F. Gwynplaine MacIntyre *s* 2859

Steengo (Spy; Musician)
The Stainless Steel Rat Sings the Blues - Harry Harrison *s* 2060

Steep, Jacob (Supernatural Being)
Sacrament - Clive Barker *h* 290

Stefan (Minstrel; Homosexual)
Magic's Price - Mercedes Lackey *f* 2615

Stefano, Yuri (Gypsy)
Taltos - Anne Rice *h* 3656

Stefanos (Ruler; Immortal)
Chains of Darkness, Chains of Light - Michelle Sagara *f* 3823
Children of the Blood - Michelle Sagara *f* 3824
Into the Dark Lands - Michelle Sagara *f* 3825

Steffan (Mythical Creature; Engineer)
Iron Dragons: Mountains and Madness - Rose Estes *f* 1479

Steiger, Dianne (Spaceship Captain)
The Ring of Charon - Roger MacBride Allen *s* 66

Stein, Rachel (Scientist; Agent)
Search and Destroy - Keith William Andrews *s* 117

Stein, Susan "Starbright" (Teenager; Runaway)
Summer of Love - Lisa Mason *s* 2913

Steinberg, Leah (Waiter/Waitress)
Shock Radio - Leigh Clark *h* 846

Steiner, Bill (Pawnbroker)
Rose Madder - Stephen King *h* 2492

Steiner, Clara (Spy)
The Werewolf's Revenge - Richard Jaccoma *h* 2264

Steinfeld (Revolutionary)
Eclipse Corona - John Shirley *s* 3993

Stello, Rawnie (Child; Hero)
The Friendship Song - Nancy Springer *f* 4133

Sten (Military Personnel)
Empire's End - Allan Cole *s* 888
The Return of the Emperor - Allan Cole *s* 891

Sten (Spaceship Captain; Bodyguard)
Revenge of the Damned - Allan Cole *s* 892

Sten (Military Personnel; Diplomat)
Vortex - Allan Cole *s* 893

Stenvall, Richard (Writer)
The Night Seasons - J.N. Williamson *h* 4666

Stephen (Companion)
Hunter's Death - Michelle West *f* 4588

Stephen (Teenager; Royalty)
The Last Book of Swords: Shieldbreaker's Story - Fred Saberhagen *f* 3812

Stephen (Professor)
Lunatics - Bradley Denton *f* 1205

Stephen "Scribble" (Addict; Fugitive)
Vurt - Jeff Noon *s* 3294

Stepovich, Mike (Police Officer)
The Gypsy - Steven Brust *f* 608

Sterling, Alice (Lawyer)
Sacrifice - Richard Kinion *h* 2498

Sterling, Ben (Writer)
Midnight Sun - Ramsey Campbell *h* 700

Sterling, Ellen (Artist)
Midnight Sun - Ramsey Campbell *h* 700

Sterling, Johnny (Child)
Midnight Sun - Ramsey Campbell *h* 700

Stern, Andrew (Professor; Psychologist)
The Streeter - Scott Ian Barry *h* 311

Steve (Murderer)
Sacrifice - Richard Kinion *h* 2498

Steven (Orphan; Companion)
Hunter's Oath - Michelle West *f* 4589

Steven (Child; Abuse Victim)
The Night Man - K.W. Jeter *h* 2323

Stevens, Carol (Social Worker)
Reborn - F. Paul Wilson *h* 4691

Stevens, Jim (Writer; Journalist)
Reborn - F. Paul Wilson *h* 4691

Stevens, Kathleen "Zero" (Prostitute)
Near Death - Nancy Kilpatrick *h* 2471

Stevens, Luke (Child)
Offspring - Jack Ketchum *h* 2461

Stevenson, David (Scientist)
The Innsmouth Heritage - Brian Stableford *h* 4145

Stevenson, Walker (Anthropologist; Lover)
The Deathless - Myles Murchison *h* 3224

Steward, Ben (Time Traveller; Anthropologist)
The Lincoln Hunters - Wilson Tucker *s* 4378

Stewart, Anne (Parent; Researcher)
Jupiter's Daughter - Tom Hyman *s* 2247

Stewart, Bill (Engineer)
Weapon - Robert Mason *s* 2915

Stewart, Dale (Child)
Summer of Night - Dan Simmons *h* 4038

Stewart, Dalton (Businessman; Criminal)
Jupiter's Daughter - Tom Hyman *s* 2247

Stewart, Genevieve "Genny" (Genetically Altered Being; Psychic)
Jupiter's Daughter - Tom Hyman *s* 2247

Stewart, Guil (Telepath)
Rider at the Gate - C.J. Cherryh *s* 811

Stewart, Hope (Child; Experimental Subject)
Dark of the Eye - Douglas Clegg *h* 869

Stewart, Janet (Computer Expert; Businesswoman)
Zeus and Co. - David Lee Jones *f* 2344

Stewart, Kate (Housewife)
Dark of the Eye - Douglas Clegg *h* 869

Stewart, Meg (Veterinarian)
Claw - Ken Eulo *h* 1489

Stigg (Genetically Altered Being)
My Father Immortal - Michael D. Weaver *s* 4512

Stiles (Principal)
Mysteries of the Word - Stanley Wiater *h* 4616

Stiles, Alex (Vampire)
Nightblood - T. Chris Martindale *h* 2905

Stiles, Chris (Veteran)
Nightblood - T. Chris Martindale *h* 2905

Stiller, Dennis (Journalist)
The Nexus - Mike McQuay *f* 3075

Stiller, Warreven "Raven" (Activist; Lawyer)
Shadow Man - Melissa Scott *s* 3914

Stillwater, Marty (Writer)
Mr. Murder - Dean R. Koontz *h* 2555

Stillwater, Paige (Health Care Professional)
Mr. Murder - Dean R. Koontz *h* 2555

Stilman, Shyh (Researcher; Scientist)
Lightwing - Tara K. Harper *s* 2038

Stimpson, Nevil (Convict)
Werewolf - Peter Rubie *h* 3764

Stirling, Richard (Lawyer; Vampire)
The Judas Glass - Michael Cadnum *h* 663

Stockton, Clifford (Child)
Mysterium - Robert Charles Wilson *s* 4705

Stodard, Paul (Artisan)
Blood Alone - Elaine Bergstrom *h* 378

Stoker, Bram (Writer; Historical Figure)
Dracula Unbound - Brian W. Aldiss *h* 43

Stollitt, Sydney (Businesswoman)
Another Day, Another Dungeon - Greg Costikyan *f* 977
One Quest, Hold the Dragons - Greg Costikyan *f* 979

Stone (Artisan)
Isle of Woman - Piers Anthony *f* 146

Stone, Arla (Psychic)
Reclamation - Sarah Zettel *s* 4850

Stone, Charlie (Cowboy; Indian)
Wendigo Border - Catherine Montrose *h* 3158

Stone, Cheryl (Prostitute)
Dead Time - Richard Lee Byers *h* 651

Stone, David (Businessman; Landlord)
Sati - Christopher Pike *f* 3449

Stone, Edwin L. "Ed" (Revolutionary; Activist)
Why Do Birds - Damon Knight *s* 2537

Stone, Jack (Martial Arts Expert)
Dead Time - Richard Lee Byers *h* 651

Stone, Jack (Writer)
The Immaculate - Mark Morris *h* 3204

Tyler, Erica (Parent)
Midsummer - Matthew J. Costello *h* 971

Tyler, Gail (Teenager)
Raven - S.A. Swiniarski *h* 4284

Tyler, Jimi (Child)
The Deus Machine - Pierre Ouellette *h* 3373

Tyler, John (Military Personnel)
The Harvest - Robert Charles Wilson *s* 4703

Tyler, Joshua (Child)
Midsummer - Matthew J. Costello *h* 971

Tyler, Kane (Detective)
Raven - S.A. Swiniarski *h* 4284

Tyler, Maurice (Scientist; Professor)
Black Sun - Robert Leininger *s* 2726

Tyler, Richard (Child; Adventurer)
The Pagemaster - David Kirschner *f* 2508

Tyler, Zane (Salesman)
Netherworld - Richard Lee Byers *h* 653

Tymmon (Teenager)
Song of the Gargoyle - Zilpha Keatley
Snyder *f* 4112

Tynan, Louie (Astronaut)
Mother of Storms - John Barnes *s* 296

Tyner, Gil (Royalty; Hero)
The Hero King - Rick Shelley *f* 3966
The Hero of Varay - Rick Shelley *f* 3967

Tyre, Philip (Military Personnel; Spaceman)
Challenger's Hope - David Feintuch *s* 1529

Tyrell, Sarah (Heiress; Model)
Blade Runner 2: The Edge of Human - K.W.
Jeter *s* 2315

Tyrell, Sarah (Businesswoman; Imposter)
Blade Runner: Replicant Night - K.W. Jeter *s* 2316

Tyrell, Sarah (Widow(er))
A Question of Time - Fred Saberhagen *h* 3816

Tyrian (Bodyguard; Companion)
A College of Magics - Caroline Stevermer *f* 4201

Tyrr (Demon; Magician)
Demon Blade - Mark A. Garland *f* 1718

Tyrranis (Military Personnel)
Valorian - Mary H. Herbert *f* 2137

Tyson, Joseph (Military Personnel)
The Galactic Silver Star - Kevin D. Randle *s* 3562

Tyson, Roger (Time Traveller)
Back to the Time Trap - Keith Laumer *s* 2661

Tzigane (Witch)
I Am Dracula - C. Dean Andersson *h* 115

U

Uhatatse (Indian)
People of the Mesa - Ardath Mayhar *f* 2947

Uhua-Sorg, Kennet (Doctor; Handicapped)
The Ship Who Searched - Anne McCaffrey *s* 2982

Uhura (Military Personnel; Space Explorer)
The Disinherited - Peter David *s* 1116

Ulahane (Shaman; Mythical Creature)
The Shaman - Christopher Stasheff *f* 4166

Ulfilo (Sailor; Warrior)
Conan and the Treasure of Python - John Maddox
Roberts *f* 3692

Ulga, Jubadi va (Ruler; Alien)
Terrible Swift Sword - William R.
Forstchen *s* 1591

Ulkanov, Andre (Researcher; Doctor)
The Multiplex Man - James P. Hogan *s* 2177

Ullrich, Nils (Genetically Altered Being)
Armed Memory - Jim Young *s* 4821

Ulrich (Diplomat; Religious)
Storm Warning - Mercedes Lackey *f* 2622

Ulrich, Will (Student)
The Robin Hood Ambush - William Wu *s* 4783

Uluye (Religious)
Avatar - Louise Cooper *f* 946

Ulysses (Alien)
Way Station - Clifford D. Simak *s* 4027

Una (Ruler)
Storms of Victory - Andre Norton *f* 3315

Underbridge, Kin (Servant; Writer)
Thunder of the Captains - Holly Lisle *f* 2772

Underhill (Engineer)
The Humanoids - Jack Williamson *s* 4670

Underhill, Jimmy (Spy)
The Werewolf's Revenge - Richard Jaccoma *h* 2264

Underhill, Lee Won (Administrator)
F.R.E.E.Lancers - Mel Odom *s* 3337

Underhill, Tim (Writer; Veteran)
Koko - Peter Straub *h* 4250
The Throat - Peter Straub *h* 4254

Undershort, Ozwaldo (Alien; Agent)
Free Radicals - Jack McKinney *s* 3066

Unger, Alejandro "Alex" (Invalid; Drifter)
Heavy Weather - Bruce Sterling *s* 4194

Unger, Juanita "Jane" (Fanatic; Researcher)
Heavy Weather - Bruce Sterling *s* 4194

Unicorn (Mythical Creature; Animal)
Blue Moon Rising - Simon R. Green *f* 1894

Unicorn (Mythical Creature)
Last Mountain - Robert C. Fleet *f* 1568

Universal Historian (Scholar)
The Dechronization of Sam Magruder - George
Gaylord Simpson *s* 4044

Unnamed Character (Werewolf)
A Prophecy of Monsters - Clark Ashton
Smith *h* 4070

Unnamed Character (Robot)
A Prophecy of Monsters - Clark Ashton
Smith *h* 4070

Ursht, Oman (Leader)
Alastor - Jack Vance *s* 4419

Ursis, Nikolai Yanuarievich (Military Personnel)
The Siege - Bill Baldwin *s* 262

Urt (Genetically Altered Being)
Lords of the Sky - Angus Wells *f* 4573

Urtho (Magician)
The Black Gryphon - Mercedes Lackey *f* 2599

Urthstripe the Strong (Animal; Leader)
Salamandastron - Brian Jacques *f* 2272

Usher, Madeline (Aged Person)
Madeline: After the Fall of Usher - Marie
Kiraly *h* 2502

Usher, Madeline (Doctor)
Return to the House of Usher - Robert Poe *h* 3461

Usher, Roderick (Doctor)
Return to the House of Usher - Robert Poe *h* 3461

Ussemitus (Adventurer; Psychic)
Mother of Storms - Adrian Cole *f* 886

Ustinov, Yevgeny (Administrator)
Double Planet - John Gribbin *s* 1946

Usurper, Black (Criminal)
Henry Martyn - L. Neil Smith *s* 4092

Utlunta (Indian; Monster)
Stoneskin's Revenge - Tom Deitz *f* 1194

V

Vader, Darth (Martial Arts Expert; Psychic)
Shadows of the Empire - Steve Perry *s* 3423

Vadim, Lux (Religious; Scientist)
Desert Fire - David Alexander *s* 53

Vail (Artificial Intelligence)
Under Siege - Elisabeth Mace *f* 2852

Val (Vampire)
Blood Relations - Doug Murray *h* 3233

Valadan (Animal)
The Prince of Ill Luck - Susan Dexter *f* 1220
The True Knight - Susan Dexter *f* 1221

Valaise, Ailena (Noblewoman; Parent)
Kingdom of the Grail - A.A. Attanasio *f* 226

Valarian, Nickolai (Government Official; Demon)
Red Devil - David Saperstein *h* 3855

Valcourt, Guy-Luc (Demon; Servant)
Adversary - Daniel Rhodes *h* 3648

Valdaimon (Wizard)
Dragonspawn - Mark Acres *f* 21

Valdemar "Val" (Farmer; Traveller)
Wayfinder's Story: The Seventh Book of Lost Swords -
Fred Saberhagen *f* 3820

Valdez, Maria (Telepath; Leader)
Under Fire - Kenneth Von Gunden *s* 4454

Valdez, Mark (Detective—Police; Psychic)
Burning Water - Mercedes Lackey *h* 2601

Valdez, Ramon (Religious)
The Killing of the Saints - Alex Abella *h* 18

Valdez, Vido (Teenager; Apprentice)
Higher Education - Charles Sheffield *s* 3956

Valdheim, M. R. (Doctor; Government Official)
The Multiplex Man - James P. Hogan *s* 2177

Valdoria, Sauscony (Genetically Altered Being)
Primary Inversion - Catherine Asaro *s* 182

Vale, Dora Rosamund (Businesswoman)
Suckers - Anne Billson *h* 397

Vale, Oliver (Fugitive)
Buddy Holly Is Alive and Well on Ganymede - Bradley
Denton *s* 1204

Valemar (Nobleman)
Summer King, Winter Fool - Lisa Goldstein *f* 1815

Valentine (Military Personnel)
Priorities - Lynda Lyons *s* 2844

Valentine, Patrick (Smuggler)
Prototype - Brian Hodge *h* 2159

Valentine, Timmy (Musician)
Vanitas: Escape From Vampire Junction - S.P.
Somtow *h* 4119

Valeur, Whiss (Revolutionary; Leader)
Illusion - Paula Volsky *f* 4448

Valiant, Eddie (Detective—Private)
Who P-P-Plugged Roger Rabbit? - Gary K.
Wolf *f* 4726

Vallaniri, Daner (Martial Arts Expert; Nobleman)
The Raven Ring - Patricia C. Wrede *f* 4764

Vallus (Mythical Creature; Wizard)
The Radiant Dragon - Elaine Cunningham *f* 1047

Verner, Janice (Monster)
Find Your Own Truth - Robert N. Charrette f 787

Verner, Samuel (Outlaw)
Choose Your Enemies Carefully - Robert N.
    Charrette s 786

Verner, Samuel (Shaman)
Find Your Own Truth - Robert N. Charrette f 787

Verner, Samuel (Businessman)
Shadowrun: Never Deal with a Dragon - Robert N.
    Charrette s 792

Vernon, Gary (Military Personnel)
Sleipnir - Linda Evans f 1493

Vernon, Vivian (Scientist)
Dr. Dimension - John DeChancie s 1176

Veronica (Religious; Psychic)
Guises of the Mind - Rebecca Neason s 3251

Verrou, Nick (Teenager; Psychic)
The Silent Strength of Stones - Nina Kiriki
    Hoffman f 2168

Verruckt, Steven (Student—Graduate)
Vampires Anonymous - Jeffrey N.
    McMahan h 3070

Vertok, Kyril (Alien; Vampire)
Shadows After Dark - Ouida Crozier f 1043

Vertue, Leon (Doctor)
Mistworld - Simon R. Green s 1902

Vervaine, Meguet (Warrior)
The Cygnet and the Firebird - Patricia A.
    McKillip f 3059

Vess, Edgler Foreman (Police Officer; Serial Killer)
Intensity - Dean R. Koontz h 2552

Vettazen (Sorceress)
The Fountains of Mirlacca - Ashley
    McConnell f 3005

Vi-Kata (Alien; Criminal)
Palace - Katharine Kerr s 2448

Vicars, Ned (Adventurer; Diplomat)
Anti-Ice - Stephen Baxter s 330

Vicia-Heinox (Mythical Creature)
The Faithful Traitor - Robert Don Hughes f 2238

Victor (Royalty; Magician)
Blood and Honor - Simon R. Green f 1893

Victor (Computer Expert)
See You Later - Christopher Pike f 3451

Videla, Pilar (Artist; Lesbian)
Whiteout - Sage Walker s 4477

Vierran (Servant; Revolutionary)
Hexwood - Diana Wynne Jones s 2349

Vigeant, Alison (Journalist)
Angel Souls and Devil Hearts - Christopher
    Golden h 1810

Vigor (Vampire)
Tooth: A Tale of Love and Death in Paradox - Novak
    Kruger h 2578

ViKay (Noblewoman; Fiance(e))
Hour of the Octopus - Joel Rosenberg f 3742

Vikktakkht (Alien; Spaceship Captain)
Chanur's Legacy - C.J. Cherryh s 795

Vilkata (Wizard)
The Last Book of Swords: Shieldbreaker's Story - Fred
    Saberhagen f 3812

Villette, Celine (Bastard Daughter)
The Judas Cross - Charles Sheffield h 3958

Villette, Louis (Nobleman)
The Judas Cross - Charles Sheffield h 3958

Villiers, Caroline "Cara Deaver" Tara (Fugitive)
Night's Pawn - Tom Dowd s 1284

Vimes, Samuel (Police Officer)
Feet of Clay - Terry Pratchett f 3500
Guards! Guards! - Terry Pratchett f 3501

Virgil (Writer; Guide)
Quest for Apollo - Michael Lahey f 2632

Virilio (Criminal)
Kamikaze L'Amour - Richard Kadrey s 2388

Viroslav, Alexander (Nobleman; Vampire)
The Kiss - Kathryn Reines h 3614

Viroslav, Maria (Noblewoman; Vampire)
The Kiss - Kathryn Reines h 3614

VISAR (Artificial Intelligence)
Entoverse - James P. Hogan s 2174

Vita (Prostitute)
And Eternity - Piers Anthony f 132

Vivian (Spirit)
Black Snow Days - Claudia O'Keefe s 3350

Vivo, Dionisio (Critic; Patriot)
Senor Vivo and the Coca Lord - Louis de
    Bernieres f 1136

VJ (Mutant)
Mutation - Robin Cook s 940

Vlaicu, Elena (Maintenance Worker)
The Lost - Jonathan Aycliffe h 235

vlith-Arkad, Brandon (Military Personnel; Heir—
Dispossessed)
A Prison Unsought - Sherwood Smith s 4099

vlith-Arkad, Brandon (Ruler; Fugitive)
Ruler of Naught - Sherwood Smith s 4101

vo Chaumelle, Renille (Civil Servant)
The Gates of Twilight - Paula Volsky f 4447

vo Derrivalle, Eliste (Noblewoman)
Illusion - Paula Volsky f 4448

Voerster, Broni (Teenager; Handicapped)
Glory - Alfred Coppel s 955

Voerster, Eliana Ehrengraf (Noblewoman)
Glory - Alfred Coppel s 955

Voisard, B.J. (Patient)
Sarah Canary - Karen Joy Fowler f 1628

Volar (Passenger)
A Maze of Stars - John Brunner s 600

Volemak (Leader; Parent)
The Memory of Earth - Orson Scott Card s 725

Volkova, Ekaterina Alexandrova (Military
    Personnel; Noblewoman)
Glory's War - Alfred Coppel s 957

Volmar (Traitor; Nobleman)
Castle of Deception - Mercedes Lackey f 2604

Volos (Angel)
Metal Angel - Nancy Springer f 4135

Voltaire, Carter (Military Personnel)
The Drylands - Mary Rosenblum s 3747

von Alte, Erde (Noblewoman; Psychic)
The Book of Earth - Marjorie Bradley
    Kellogg f 2427

von Amerningen, Lutz (Nobleman)
Cloud Castles - Michael Scott Rohan f 3730

von Darkmoor, Erik (Military Personnel; Nobleman)
Rise of a Merchant Prince - Raymond E.
    Feist f 1536

von Darkmoor, Erik (Bastard Son; Fugitive)
Shadow of a Dark Queen - Raymond E.
    Feist f 1538

Von Heilitz, Lamont "the Shadow" (Detective)
Mystery - Peter Straub h 4252

von Hessel (Nobleman; Military Personnel)
Escape From Loki - Philip Jose Farmer f 1503

Von Karlsfeld, Hilda (Teacher)
Mordenheim - Chet Williamson h 4655

von Mannheim De Soto, Igor (Guide)
Cat-A-Lyst - Alan Dean Foster s 1602

Von Rabenaue, Walter (Guard)
Lord of the Dark Lake - Ron Faust h 1524

von Richtofen, Manfred (Military Personnel; Pilot)
The Bloody Red Baron - Kim Newman h 3261

von Schuss, Nicholas (Nobleman; Heir)
Kit's Book - C.J. Mills s 3116

Von Zarovich, Strahd (Ruler; Vampire)
I, Strahd - P.N. Elrod h 1442

Von Ziegler, Horst (Animal Trainer)
The Keeper - Robert D. Lee h 2705

Vorbarra, Gregor (Ruler)
The Vor Game - Lois McMaster Bujold s 627

Vorbis (Religious; Police Officer)
Small Gods - Terry Pratchett f 3507

Vordegh (Magician; Leader)
Star Ascendant - Louise Cooper f 953

Vorder, Sera (Gentlewoman)
The Gnome's Engine - Teresa Edgerton f 1398
Goblin Moon - Teresa Edgerton f 1399

Vorkosigan, Aral (Nobleman; Ruler)
Barrayar - Lois McMaster Bujold s 620

Vorkosigan, Mark Pierre (Clone)
Mirror Dance - Lois McMaster Bujold s 625

Vorkosigan, Miles (Military Personnel; Diplomat)
Borders of Infinity - Lois McMaster Bujold s 621

Vorkosigan, Miles (Nobleman; Military Personnel)
Cetaganda - Lois McMaster Bujold s 622
Memory - Lois McMaster Bujold s 624
Mirror Dance - Lois McMaster Bujold s 625

Vorkosigan, Miles (Military Personnel; Diplomat)
The Vor Game - Lois McMaster Bujold s 627

Vorlund, Krip (Spaceman)
Dare to Go A-Hunting - Andre Norton s 3302

Vorpatril, Ivan (Nobleman; Diplomat)
Cetaganda - Lois McMaster Bujold s 622

Vorpatril, Ivan (Nobleman; Military Personnel)
Memory - Lois McMaster Bujold s 624

Vortcir (Alien)
They Fly at Ciron - Samuel R. Delany s 1198

Voskresenye, Pavel Sergeyevich (Activist; Cyborg)
The Fortunate Fall - Raphael Carter s 750

Vosnesensky, Mikhail Andreivitch (Spaceman;
    Leader)
Mars - Ben Bova s 481

Voss, Dorn (Student; Teenager)
Where the Ships Die - William C. Dietz s 1254

Voss, Natalie (Spacewoman)
Where the Ships Die - William C. Dietz s 1254

Vost, Harlic (Religious)
Thorn and Needle - Paul B. Thompson f 4354

Voyaging Moon (Musician)
The Remarkable Journey of Prince Jen - Lloyd
    Alexander f 56

Voyvodan (Mythical Creature)
Fortress of Frost and Fire - Mercedes
    Lackey f 2610

Vozmozho, Vozmuzhalnoy "Moozh" (Military
    Personnel)
The Call of Earth - Orson Scott Card s 716

Vree (Martial Arts Expert)
Fifth Quarter - Tanya Huff f 2227
No Quarter - Tanya Huff f 2230

Vril, Dietrich (Monster; Vampire)
The Armageddon Box - Robert Weinberg h 4536

Vryce, Damien Kilcannon (Religious; Warrior)
Black Sun Rising - C.S. Friedman f 1653
Crown of Shadows - C.S. Friedman s 1654
When True Night Falls - C.S. Friedman f 1656

Vusca (Military Personnel)
The Book of the Beast - Tanith Lee f 2708

Vyledaar, Alessa (Wizard)
Dragonmage of Mystara - Thorarinn
    Gunnarsson f 1973

W

Wade, Arlo (Child; Twin)
Bad Blood - D.A. Fowler h 1622

Wade, Austin (Child; Twin)
Bad Blood - D.A. Fowler h 1622

Wade, Bree (Teenager; Twin)
Double Date - R.L. Stine h 4218

Wade, Jonathan (Miner)
What's Wrong with Tamara? - D.A.
    Fowler h 1626

Wade, Kara (Writer)
Sibs - F. Paul Wilson h 4694

Wade, Laura Gardner (Heiress)
A Reasonable Madness - Fran Dorf h 1276

Wade, Samantha (Teenager; Twin)
Double Date - R.L. Stine h 4218

Wade, Tamara (Mentally Ill Person; Parent)
Bad Blood - D.A. Fowler h 1622

Wade, Tamara (Child)
What's Wrong with Tamara? - D.A.
    Fowler h 1626

Wade, Zach (Businessman; Spouse)
A Reasonable Madness - Fran Dorf h 1276

Wae, Kiondili (Student; Telepath)
Lightwing - Tara K. Harper s 2038

Waesc, Dorias (Artificial Intelligence; Refugee)
Reclamation - Sarah Zettel s 4850

Wagner, Jeff (Professor)
Twilight Time - Rick Hautala h 2088

Wagner, Jennifer (Teenager)
The Season of Passage - Christopher Pike h 3450

Wagner, Lauren (Astronaut)
The Season of Passage - Christopher Pike h 3450

Wakandagi, Ptesa "Tesa/Good Eyes" (Diplomat; Indian)
Silent Songs - A.C. Crispin s 1026

Wakefield, Nicole des Jardins (Doctor; Adventurer)
The Garden of Rama - Arthur C. Clarke s 848

Wakefield, Nicole des Jardins (Political Figure)
Rama Revealed - Arthur C. Clarke s 852

Wakefield, Richard (Scientist; Adventurer)
The Garden of Rama - Arthur C. Clarke s 848

Wakefield, Richard (Engineer)
Rama II - Arthur C. Clarke s 851

Wakefield, Wallace "Wake" (Scout)
The Unnatural - David Prill h 3539

Wakelin, Emily (Artisan)
Holy Terror - Josephine Boyle h 498

Wakelin, John (Accountant)
Holy Terror - Josephine Boyle h 498

Walcott, Roland (Professor; Criminal)
Indiana Jones and the Unicorn's Legacy - Rob
    MacGregor f 2858

Wald, Richard (Anthropologist)
The Engines of God - Jack McDevitt s 3015

Walden, Jerome (Scientist)
The Infinity Plague - Robert E. Vardeman s 4435

Walford, John (Murderer; Spirit)
Walford's Oak - Jill M. Phillips f 3433

Walk, Random (Artificial Intelligence)
Profiteer - S. Andrew Swann s 4277

Walker, Betsy (Femme Fatale)
Last Rites - David Darke h 1094

Walker, Cassie (Child)
Playmates - Abigail McDaniels h 3012

Walker, David (Writer)
Steam - Jay B. Laws h 2675

Walker, Greg (Repairman)
Sacrifice - John Farris h 1518

Walker, Hillary "Hilly" (Writer)
The Forgotten - Stephen R. George h 1766

Walker, Jack (Criminal)
Deathwalker - R. Patrick Gates h 1731

Walker, Janet (Parent; Housewife)
Playmates - Abigail McDaniels h 3012

Walker, Jason (Doctor)
The Unknown Soldier - Mickey Zucker
    Reichert s 3611

Walker, Laura (Young Woman)
In Hot Blood - Petru Popescu h 3480

Walker, Mark (Parent; Scientist)
Playmates - Abigail McDaniels h 3012

Walker, Max (Police Officer; Time Traveller)
Timecop - S.D. Perry s 3413

Walker, Ross (Police Officer)
Spook - Steve Vance h 4426

Walker, Sharissa (Teenager)
Sacrifice - John Farris h 1518

Walking Bear, Jack (Military Personnel; Time
    Traveller)
First Dawn - Mike Moscoe s 3217

Wallace, Brandy (Artist; Teacher)
Dreambuilder - Tom Deitz f 1190

Wallace, Ditsy (Journalist; Adventurer)
The Square Deal - David Drake s 1327

Wallace, Enoch (Military Personnel; Recluse)
Way Station - Clifford D. Simak s 4027

Wallace, Rollingham Boregard "Rusty" (Spaceship
    Captain)
A World Lost - James B. Johnson s 2327

Wallace, Wendy (Writer)
The Hunted - Kathryn Ptacek h 3542

Waller, Enid (Nurse)
Fiends - John Farris h 1516

Walmsley, Nigel (Astronaut; Immortal)
Sailing Bright Eternity - Gregory Benford s 369

Walsh, Dalton (Religious)
The Reckoning - Ruby Jean Jensen h 2314

Walsh, Richard Earl (Military Personnel)
Dragon Season - Michael Cassutt f 759

Walsmear, Michael (Police Officer)
Photographing Fairies - Steve Szilagyi f 4289

Walters, Diana (Anthropologist)
Uwharrie - Eugene E. Pfaff Jr. h 3432

Walther, Jeeris Belamy "Jeebee" (Professor)
Wolf and Iron - Gordon R. Dickson s 1242

Walthers, Audee (Pilot)
The Gateway Trip: Tales and Vignettes of the Heechee
    - Frederik Pohl s 3462

Walthers, Danielle "Dani" (Doctor)
Parliament of Blood - Scott Ciencin h 831

Walthers, Danielle "Dani" (Teenager; Student)
The Vampire Odyssey - Scott Ciencin h 832
The Wildlings - Scott Ciencin h 834

Walthers, Samantha "Sam" (Detective—Private;
    Parent)
Parliament of Blood - Scott Ciencin h 831
The Vampire Odyssey - Scott Ciencin h 832
The Wildlings - Scott Ciencin h 834

Walton, Alex (Doctor)
Virus - Graham Watkins h 4488

Walton, Robert (Publisher)
Gothic Romance - Emmanuel Carrere h 740

Wan, Lai (Psychic)
Some Things Never Die - Robert Morgan h 3187

Wan-To (Alien)
The World at the End of Time - Frederik
    Pohl s 3471

Wanachtee (Indian; Chieftain)
The Silent Stars Go By - James White s 4605

Wanbli (Warrior; Indian)
The Third Eagle: Lessons Along a Minor String - R.A.
    MacAvoy s 2848

Wanda-Jean (Television Personality)
The Feelies - Mick Farren s 1510

Wandel, Timothy J. (Genetically Altered Being)
Armed Memory - Jim Young s 4821

Wanderman, Aubrey (Military Personnel)
Honor Among Enemies - David Weber s 4522

Wanders, Wendy (Genetically Altered Being)
Winterlong - Elizabeth Hand s 2029

Wanderson, Balthan (Magician)
The Temper of Wisdom - Lynn Abbey f 15

Wandigaux, Rowena (Grandparent)
Never Land - Douglas Clegg h 871

Wang-mu (Servant; Genetically Altered Being)
Xenocide - Orson Scott Card s 730

Wanker, David L. (Military Personnel; Spaceship
    Captain)
The Kruton Interface - John DeChancie s 1179

Ward (Doctor)
Not Broken, Not Belonging - Randy Fox h 1630

Ward, Alan (Military Personnel; Monster)
Midsummer - Matthew J. Costello h 971

Ward, Alex (Veteran)
The Parasite War - Tim Sullivan s 4268

Ward, David (Scientist)
Operation Synbat - Bob Mayer h 2944

Ward, Donna (Widow(er))
Heathen - Shaun Hutson h 2244

Ward, Kim (Scientist)
The Stone Within - David Wingrove s 4713
White Moon, Red Dragon - David
    Wingrove s 4714
The White Mountain - David Wingrove s 4715

Ware (Demon)
If I Pay Thee Not in Gold - Piers Anthony f 144

Ware, Theron (Magician)
The Devil's Day - James Blish h 426

Wargallow, Simon (Leader)
The Gods in Anger - Adrian Cole f 885

Warhelski, Maxim (Werewolf)
All Things under the Moon - Robert
    Morgan h 3184

Warner, Alex (Professor)
The Armageddon Box - Robert Weinberg *h* 4536
The Devil's Auction - Robert Weinberg *h* 4542

Warner, Seth (Hero)
Through the Ice - Piers Anthony *f* 158

Warner, Valerie (Sorceress)
The Armageddon Box - Robert Weinberg *h* 4536

Warner, Valerie (Sorceress; Model)
The Devil's Auction - Robert Weinberg *h* 4542

Warren (Doctor)
Act of Love - Joe R. Lansdale *h* 2640

Warren, Carol (Writer)
In the Deep Woods - Nicholas Conde *h* 912

Warrick, John (Con Artist)
Less than Human - Gary L. Raisor *h* 3558

Warrick, Susan (Police Officer)
OtherSyde - J. Michael Straczynski *h* 4245

Warson, Toll (Military Personnel)
The Voyage - David Drake *s* 1332

Wartsworth, Caspar (Adventurer; Barbarian)
The Lost City of Zork - Robin W. Bailey *f* 241

Warwick, David (Teacher)
Sweetheart, Sweetheart - Bernard Taylor *h* 4310

Washburn, Bob (Student)
The Robin Hood Ambush - William Wu *s* 4783

Washburn, Corky (Morgue Attendant)
Bring on the Night - Don Davis *h* 1129

Washi (Indian; Hero)
Dark Legend - Jamake Highwater *f* 2146

Washington, Arlene "Lady El" (Artificial Intelligence; Experimental Subject)
Lady El - Jim Starlin *s* 4157

Washington, Billy (Aged Person; Hunter)
Beggars and Choosers - Nancy Kress *s* 2573

Washington, George (Military Personnel; Revolutionary)
Two Crowns for America - Katherine Kurtz *f* 2594

Washington, Sandy (Young Man)
Homegoing - Frederik Pohl *s* 3463

Wasserman, Janus Cornelius (Publisher)
The House of the Toad - Richard Tierney *h* 4363

Watanabe, Kenji (Historian; Settler)
The Garden of Rama - Arthur C. Clarke *s* 848

Watcher, Lightfoot (Alien)
Foragers - Charles Oberndorf *s* 3334

Water Rat "Ratty" (Animal; Adventurer)
Toad Triumphant - William Horwood *f* 2211
The Willows in Winter - William Horwood *f* 2212

Waterfall, Kylene (Time Traveller; Telepath)
Death's Gray Land - Mike Shupp *s* 3998
The Last Reckoning - Mike Shupp *s* 3999

Waterhouse, Mary Ann "Synthi Venture" (Actress; Television Personality)
Mother of Storms - John Barnes *s* 296

Waterman, James "Jamie" Fox (Indian; Scientist)
Mars - Ben Bova *s* 481

Waterman, Phil (Police Officer)
Trickster - Chris Curry *h* 1052

Watkins, Classy Jack (Drug Dealer)
Living Hell - Ric Meyers *h* 3093

Watkins, Daniel J. (Gentleman; Alcoholic)
The Golden Nineties - Lisa Mason *s* 2912

Watson, John (Doctor)
Seance for a Vampire - Fred Saberhagen *h* 3817

Watson, John H. (Doctor; Writer)
Sherlock Holmes in Orbit - Mike Resnick *s* 3637

Watt, Al (Lawman)
Darkly the Thunder - William W. Johnstone *h* 2333

Waverly, Dora (Aged Person)
The Well - Michael B. Sirota *h* 4053

Waverly, Tim (Activist; Security Officer)
Outworld Cats - Jack Lovejoy *s* 2811

Waxman, Will (Doctor)
Fallen Angels - Larry Niven *s* 3279

Wayland, Richard (Police Officer)
Dying Breath - Jon A. Harrald *h* 2041

Wayne, Bruce "Batman" (Hero; Detective— Amateur)
Batman: Captured by the Engines - Joe R. Lansdale *h* 2641
Batman: Knightfall - Dennis O'Neil *s* 3359
Batman Returns - Craig Shaw Gardner *s* 1707
Catwoman - Lynn Abbey *s* 12
The Further Adventures of Batman 2: Featuring the Penguin - Martin H. Greenberg *s* 1915
The Further Adventures of Batman 3: Featuring Catwoman - Martin H. Greenberg *s* 1916
Mask of the Phantasm - Geary Gravel *s* 1867

Wayville, Chris (Astronaut; Scientist)
Flying to Valhalla - Charles Pellegrino *s* 3409

Wayville, Clarice (Astronaut; Scientist)
Flying to Valhalla - Charles Pellegrino *s* 3409

Weasel (Adventurer; Indian)
Crow and Weasel - Barry Lopez *f* 2800

Weatherby, Ann (Teenager)
Hell-O-Ween - David Robbins *h* 3675

Weatherby, Tamsin (Actress)
Star Prey - Ehren M. Ehly *h* 1416

Weatherwax, Granny (Witch; Hero)
Lords and Ladies - Terry Pratchett *f* 3502

Weatherwax, Granny (Witch)
Witches Abroad - Terry Pratchett *f* 3511
Wyrd Sisters - Terry Pratchett *f* 3512

Webb, Danny (Indian; Shaman)
The Serpent Slayers - Adam Niswander *h* 3273

Webb, Tessa (Aged Person)
Haunted - James Herbert *h* 2130

Webster, Daniel (Spaceship Captain; Aged Person)
Deep Freeze - Zach Hughes *s* 2239

Webster, Duncan (Writer)
Cardinal's Sin - Raymond Buckland *h* 615
The Committee - Raymond Buckland *h* 616

Webster, Joshua (Military Personnel)
Deep Freeze - Zach Hughes *s* 2239

Webster, Tania (Scientist)
Sister, Sister - Andrew Neiderman *h* 3257

Webster, Tom (Teacher)
Requiem - Graham Joyce *h* 2386

Webster, Torie (Journalist)
The Eyes of Torie Webster - Roy Sorrels *h* 4121

Weena (Mutant; Young Woman)
The Time Ships - Stephen Baxter *s* 334

Wei (Alien; Spy)
Rule Golden and Double Meaning - Damon Knight *s* 2536

Weigand, Pauli (Time Traveller)
The Fourth Rome - David Drake *s* 1317

Weil, Gunther (Worker)
Griffin's Egg - Michael Swanwick *s* 4281

Weir, Jacob (Teacher)
The Black School - J.N. Williamson *h* 4659

Weiss, Rachel (Psychologist)
Shadow Dance - Douglas Borton *h* 473

Weisser, Erich (Telepath; Animal Trainer)
Child of the Light - Janet Gluckman *f* 1803

Welch, Lewis (Political Figure; Telepath)
Dreambuilder - Tom Deitz *f* 1190

Welch, Lewis (Bastard Son; Student—High School)
Soulsmith - Tom Deitz *f* 1193

Welch, Lewis Owen (Telepath)
Wordwright - Tom Deitz *f* 1196

Welch, Melissa "Kay Franklin" (Runaway)
Hobkin - Peni R. Griffin *f* 1951

Welch, Sara "Liza Franklin" (Runaway)
Hobkin - Peni R. Griffin *f* 1951

Weldon, Jim (Police Officer)
The Revelation - Bentley Little *h* 2776

Wells, Jeff (Student; Teenager)
Norby and the Court Jester - Janet Asimov *s* 211

Wells, Jeff (Teenager)
Norby and the Oldest Dragon - Janet Asimov *s* 212
Norby and Yobo's Great Adventure - Janet Asimov *s* 213
Norby Down to Earth - Janet Asimov *s* 214

Wells, Nancy (Teacher)
Dark Twilight - Joseph Citro *h* 836

Welsh, Ariel (Heiress)
Changeling - Stephen Leigh *s* 2723
Renegade - Cordell Scotten *s* 3916

Wenceslas, Rudyard "Waldo" Riding (Royalty; Adventurer)
The Wealdwife's Tale - Paul Hazel *f* 2108

Wendeen, Wendy (Religious; Doctor)
Drifter - William C. Dietz *s* 1245

Wendell (Sidekick)
Slay and Rescue - John Moore *f* 3175

Wentworth, Ford (Government Official; Criminal)
The Trinity Vector - Steve Perry *s* 3425

Wentworth, Richard (Adventurer)
The Spider #3: Death's Crimson Juggernaut/The Red Death Rain - Grant Stockbridge *f* 4234
The Spider #4: Death Reign of the Vampire King/The Pain Emperor - Grant Stockbridge *f* 4235
The Spider #8: The Devil's Paymaster/Legions of the Accursed Light - Grant Stockbridge *f* 4236

Werewolf (Criminal)
Wizard's Heir - Daniel Hood *f* 2199

Weser, Erich "Erich Alois" (Telepath; Animal Trainer)
Child of the Journey - Janet Berliner *f* 381

Wesley, William (Child)
The Forever Children - Eric Flanders *h* 1566

West, Braden (Artist)
The Catswold Portal - Shirley Rousseau Murphy *f* 3230

West, Kilimanjaro (Revolutionary; Amnesiac)
Out on Blue Six - Ian McDonald *s* 3020

West, Michael (Administrator)
The Man Upstairs - T.L. Parkinson *h* 3385

Westbrook, Louisa (Gentlewoman; Psychic)
Flameweaver - Margaret Ball *f* 264

Westerman, Stacy (Psychologist)
Lorelei - Mark A. Clements *h* 875

Westin, Andy (Security Officer)
Mall Purchase Night - Rick Cook *f* 935

Westlake, Peyton (Scientist)
Darkman - Randall Boyll *h* 501
Darkman #1: The Hangman - Randall Boyll *h* 502
Darkman #2: The Price of Fear - Randall Boyll *h* 503

Wilson, Christopher T. (Vampire)
Blood on the Sun - Brian Herbert   h   2126

Wilson, Karen (Secretary; Psychic)
The Headsman - James Neal Harvey   h   2075

Wiltin, Hof (Rancher; Warrior)
To a Highland Nation - Christopher
Rowley   s   3761

Wilum (Magician)
Flight to Hollow Mountain - Mark Sebanc   f   3921

Wimperling (Animal)
Pigs Don't Fly - Mary Brown   f   594

Winchell, Anne (Social Worker)
Bone - George C. Chesbro   h   817

Winchester, Miriam (Shaman; Indian)
Shadow Walkers - Nina Romberg   h   3734

Wind Soldier, Harley (Indian)
The Grass Dancer - Susan Power   f   3492

Windclan, Raincloud (Linguist; Parent)
Daughter of Elysium - Joan Slonczewski   s   4062

Windemere, Gideon (Drug Dealer)
Necrom - Mick Farren   s   1513

Windrose, Antryg (Wizard; Fugitive)
Dog Wizard - Barbara Hambly   f   2005

Windruth (Alien; Leader)
Dragon Rigger - Jeffrey A. Carver   s   752

Windsor, Bethany (Heiress)
Cluster Command - David Drake   s   1316

Windsor, Corrigan Tel (Bounty Hunter)
The Price of Ransom - Alis A. Rasmussen   s   3575

Windsor, Marion (Journalist)
The Blood of the Lamb - Thomas F.
Monteleone   h   3150

Winfield, Angela (Professor; Anthropologist)
The Werewolf's Touch - Cheri Scotch   h   3908

Wing, Phillip (Architect)
Look into the Sun - James Patrick Kelly   s   2429

Wing, Sue (Journalist)
The Summoning - Bentley Little   h   2777

Wingate, Max (Artist)
The Convocation - John R. Holt   h   2192

Winger (Detective—Private)
Deadly Quicksilver Lies - Glen Cook   f   926

Winkler, Gene "Wink" (Military Personnel)
Signs of Life - Cherry Wilder   s   4622

Winslow, Dirk (Military Personnel)
Time: The Semi-Final Frontier - Lionel
Fenn   s   1545

Winstead, Samantha (Doctor)
Cries of the Children - Clare McNally   h   3072

Winston, Palmer (Aged Person)
Dark Journey - A.R. Morlan   h   3192

Winter, Henry (Student—College)
The Secret History - Donna Tartt   h   4306

Winter, James (Student)
Sing for a Gentle Rain - J. Alison James   f   2278

Winter, John (Spy)
Deathwalker - Patrick Whalen   h   4596

Winter, Tom (Time Traveller)
A Bridge of Years - Robert Charles Wilson   s   4700

Winters, Angelica (Actress)
Fantastique - Marvin Kaye   h   2409

Winters, Elizabet (Magician; Psychologist)
Bedlam Boyz - Ellen Guon   f   1978

Winters, Franklin Evelyn (Businessman)
Dreamer - Daniel Quinn   h   3551

Winters, Ginny (Artist)
Dreamer - Daniel Quinn   h   3551

Winters, Jennifer (Lawyer)
Fury - John Coyne   h   1002

Winters, Katie (Child; Resistance Fighter)
Martian Deathtrap - Nathan Archer   s   169

Winters, Kelly Ann (Engineer; Military Personnel)
March or Die - Andrew Keith   s   2419

Winters, Michael (Truck Driver)
Sati - Christopher Pike   f   3449

Winters, Talia (Telepath; Fugitive)
Voices - John Vornholt   s   4461

Winters, Theodore "TK" Karlington (Veteran;
Mythical Creature)
Strands of Sunlight - Gael Baudino   f   329

Winthrop, Edwin (Military Personnel)
The Bloody Red Baron - Kim Newman   h   3261

Winthrop, Montana "Tana" (Administrator;
Handicapped)
The Earth Saver - Catherine Wells   s   4580

Wisdom (Religious)
The Curse - John Tigges   h   4364

Wishart, Adam (Public Relations)
The Walking Shadow - Brian Stableford   s   4146

Wisnewski, Leonard (Museum Curator)
Legion of the Dead - Geoffrey Caine   h   681

Witch Baby (Musician; Witch)
Cherokee Bat and the Goat Guys - Francesca Lia
Block   f   445

Witch Baby (Teenager; Musician)
Missing Angel Juan - Francesca Lia Block   f   448

Witch Baby (Teenager; Foundling)
Witch Baby - Francesca Lia Block   f   450

Withers, Jonella "Johnnie" (Teenager)
The Living Dark - Stephen Gresham   h   1945

Withrow, Dennis "Dennis Dithrovvu" (Scientist;
Teacher)
Mathemagics - Margaret Ball   f   266

Witney, Charley (Clerk)
Sweet Heart - Peter James   h   2292

Witney, Tom (Lawyer)
Sweet Heart - Peter James   h   2292

Wittelsbach, Ludwig (Ruler)
From Prussia with Love - John DeChancie   f   1177

Wizenbeak (Wizard; Royalty)
Lord of the Troll-Bats - Alexis A. Gilliland   f   1796

Wizenbeak (Wizard)
The Shadow Shaia - Alexis A. Gilliland   f   1797

Woczniak, Hal (FBI Agent; Knight)
The Forever King - Molly Cochran   f   879

**Wojciechowski, Thaddaios "Wolf"
Alexandru** (Scientist)
In the Wrong Hands - Edward Gibson   s   1778

Wok (Leader; Mythical Creature)
The Pixilated Peeress - L. Sprague de
Camp   f   1141

Wolenczak, Lucas (Computer Expert; Teenager)
seaQuest DSV: Fire Below - Matthew J.
Costello   s   972

Wolf (Prehistoric Human; Hunter)
The Hunter Returns - David Drake   f   1318

Wolf (Mercenary)
Konrad - David Ferring   f   1551

Wolf (Magician; Warrior)
Masques - Patricia Briggs   f   560

Wolf, Behrooz "Bey" (Recluse; Scientist)
Proteus in the Underworld - Charles
Sheffield   s   3960

Wolf, Behrooz "Bey" (Government Official;
Scientist)
Proteus Unbound - Charles Sheffield   s   3961

Wolf, Billy "Slider" (Murderer)
Dreamer - Peter James   h   2288

Wolfe, Atrix (Magician; Criminal)
The Book of Atrix Wolfe - Patricia A.
McKillip   f   3058

Wolfe, D. (Lawyer)
Arachne - Lisa Mason   s   2910

Wolfe, Nero (Detective—Private)
*The D. Case: The Truth about the Mystery of Edwin
Drood* - Charles Dickens   f   1230

Wolfe, Sara (Artist)
*The Venetian's Wife: A Strangely Sensual Tale of a
Renaissance Explorer, a Computer, and a
Metamorphosis* - Nick Bantock   f   282

Wolff, Hauptsturmfuhrer (Military Personnel;
Vampire)
Darkness on the Ice - Lois Tilton   h   4367

Wolling, Jen (Scientist; Scholar)
Earth - David Brin   s   563

Wollstonecraft, Mary (Writer)
Wall, Stone, Craft - Walter Jon Williams   h   4653

Wolpin, Zev (Religious)
Midnight Mass - F. Paul Wilson   h   4687

Wolsey, Faye (Printer)
The Palm Dome - Liz Fulton   h   1686

Womack, Ewa (Worker)
Chicago Loop - Paul Theroux   h   4344

Womack, Jeff (Political Figure; Human)
Brother Termite - Patricia Anthony   s   127

Wong, Fritz (Director)
A Graveyard for Lunatics - Ray Bradbury   h   509

Wood, Alice (Businesswoman)
Strange Devices of the Sun and Moon - Lisa
Goldstein   f   1814

Wood, Leo "Lobo" (Warrior)
L.A. Strike - David Robbins   s   3676

Wood, Max (Scientist; Activist)
The Frightened Fish - Kenneth Robeson   f   3698

Woodbury, Gillian (Journalist)
Silent Moon - William Relling Jr.   h   3616

Woodley, Landis (Director)
Horror Show - Greg Kihn   h   2466

Woodrow, John (Architect)
Torment - Stephen R. George   h   1770

Woodrow, Melissa (Child; Musician)
Torment - Stephen R. George   h   1770

Woodruff, Bodeen (Police Officer)
Happy Policeman - Patricia Anthony   s   130

Woody (Parent; Lawyer)
My Stepfather Shrank! - Barbara Dillon   s   1258

Woolcott, Jeremy (Teenager)
Along Came a Spider - Athena Alexis   h   57

Wooster, Bertie (Gentleman)
Scream for Jeeves: A Parody - H.P.G.
Wodehouse   h   4723

Worf (Military Personnel; Security Officer)
Doomsday World - Carmen Carter   s   749

Worf (Military Personnel; Alien)
Kahless - Michael Jan Friedman   s   1660
Reunion - Michael Jan Friedman   s   1663

Yrae (Alien; Actress)
Legacy of Earth - Juanita Coulson   s   980

Yrarier, Marjorie Westriding (Diplomat)
Grass - Sheri S. Tepper   s   4335

Ysidro, Don Simon (Vampire)
Those Who Hunt the Night - Barbara
   Hambly   h   2011

Yspht, Jovil (Alien)
Armageddon: The Musical - Robert Rankin   s   3566

Ystilog, Erpad (Museum Curator)
Brotherhood of the Stars - Kirby Greene   s   1932

Ysuna (Religious; Prehistoric Human)
The Sacred Stones - William Sarabande   f   3857

Yuan, Li (Heir; Royalty)
The Middle Kingdom - David Wingrove   s   4712

Yuan, Li (Leader)
The Stone Within - David Wingrove   s   4713
The White Mountain - David Wingrove   s   4715

Yvette of Grintz (Runaway; Noblewoman)
The Pixilated Peeress - L. Sprague de
   Camp   f   1141

Z

Zacharias, John Furie "Gentle" (Artist)
Imajica - Clive Barker   h   288

Zacharias, Michael (Musician)
Lost Futures - Lisa Tuttle   s   4400

Zachary (Reanimated Dead; Criminal)
Guilty Pleasures - Laurell K. Hamilton   f   2016

Zady (Witch)
Mouvar's Magic - Piers Anthony   f   150
Orc's Opal - Piers Anthony   f   151

Zagala (Witch; Gypsy)
Yesterday We Saw Mermaids - Esther
   Friesner   f   1680

Zahmekoses (Alien; Space Explorer)
Encounter with Tiber - Buzz Aldrin   s   52

Zainal (Alien; Castaway)
Freedom's Landing - Anne McCaffrey   s   2969

Zakalwe, Cheradenine (Spy; Mercenary)
Use of Weapons - Iain M. Banks   s   277

Zakharov, Aelita (Astronaut)
Night Launch - Jake Garn   s   1720

Zakri (Psychic; Singer)
Sing the Warmth - Louise Marley   s   2885

Zalewski, Petra (Student—College; Adventurer)
Footprints of Thunder - James F. David   s   1115

Zal'honan, Firan (Sorcerer)
King of the Dead - Gene DeWeese   h   1218

Zaman (Servant)
Viper - Alan Riefe   h   3666

Zambelli, Ruggerio (Scientist)
From Prussia with Love - John DeChancie   f   1177

Zambendorf, Karl (Psychic; Magician)
The Immortality Option - James P. Hogan   s   2175

Zamiatin, Mark "Visual Mark" (Artist)
Synners - Pat Cadigan   s   660

Zandramas (Sorceress)
The Seeress of Kell - David Eddings   f   1394

Zandro, Taverik (Businessman)
Hawk's Flight - Carol Chase   f   794

Zant, Quasar (Socialite; Wealthy)
Quasar - Jamil Nasir   s   3242

Zapata, Carmen (Housekeeper)
Panic - Chris Curry   h   1050

Zapata, Xolotl (Fugitive; Artist)
High Aztec - Ernest Hogan   s   2173

Zarnicke, Marion (Journalist)
A World Lost - James B. Johnson   s   2327

Zaula (Alien; Noblewoman)
Requiem for Anthi - Jay D. Blakeney   s   419

Zebara (Spaceship Captain)
The Death of Sleep - Anne McCaffrey   s   2966

Zeeman, Richard (Werewolf)
The Lunatic Cafe - Laurell K. Hamilton   h   2018

Zeenoson, Dref (Revolutionary)
Illusion - Paula Volsky   f   4448

Zellorian (Wizard)
Mother of Storms - Adrian Cole   f   886

Zellorian (Political Figure; Scientist)
Warlord of Heaven - Adrian Cole   f   887

Zennor (Alien; Spaceship Captain)
First Strike - Diane Carey   s   733

Zeno, Mrs. (Disembodied Personality)
Max Lakeman and the Beautiful Stranger - Jon
   Cohen   f   883

Zephkar (Alien; Disembodied Personality)
Stranded - Camarin Grae   s   1841

Zephyr (Mythical Creature)
Fool on the Hill - Matt Ruff   f   3768

Zeq, Ahmad (Space Explorer)
The Transmigration of Souls - William
   Barton   s   318

Zeree, Dru (Sorcerer)
Children of the Drake - Richard A. Knaak   f   2516

Zeree, Dru (Sorcerer; Immigrant)
The Shrouded Realm - Richard A. Knaak   f   2524

Zeus (Royalty)
Sons of the Titans - Patrick H. Adkins   f   29

Zhadnoboth (Sorcerer)
A Name to Conjure With - Donald Aamodt   f   2
A Troubling Along the Border - Donald Aamodt   f   3

Zhang (Military Personnel; Explorer)
Shangri-La: The Return to the World of Lost Horizon -
   Eleanor Cooney   f   942

Zhiming, Lao (Military Personnel)
Crossroad - Barbara Hambly   s   2003

Zhu Wong (Time Traveller; Revolutionary)
The Golden Nineties - Lisa Mason   s   2912

Zhukovsky, Dmitry (Spaceman; Hero)
*Peter Nevsky and the True Story of the Russian Moon
   Landing* - John Calvin Batchelor   s   322

Ziemann, Mia (Noblewoman)
Holy Fire - Bruce Sterling   s   4195

Zigmunn (Spaceman; Exile)
Brotherhood of the Stars - Kirby Greene   s   1932

Zigramson, Thorolf (Scholar; Military Personnel)
The Pixilated Peeress - L. Sprague de
   Camp   f   1141

Zillabar (Noblewoman; Vampire)
A Covenant of Justice - David Gerrold   s   1771

Zillah (Vampire)
Lost Souls - Poppy Z. Brite   h   570

Zimmerman, Christopher (Adventurer; Time
   Traveller)
Panda Ray - Michael Kandel   s   2398

Zimmerman, Debra (Parent)
Panda Ray - Michael Kandel   s   2398

Zimmerman, Rick (Bodyguard)
Unearthed - Ashley McConnell   h   3007

Zinixo (Mythical Creature; Wizard)
The Living God - Dave Duncan   f   1354
The Stricken Field - Dave Duncan   f   1360
Upland Outlaws - Dave Duncan   f   1362

Zinser, Jacob (Collector)
St. Peter's Wolf - Michael Cadnum   h   667

Zivic, Leland (Photographer)
From the Teeth of Angels - Jonathan Carroll   h   744

Zobolotsky, Katrina (Adventurer)
Indiana Jones and the Genesis Deluge - Rob
   MacGregor   f   2854

Zobolotsky, Vladimir (Doctor; Adventurer)
Indiana Jones and the Genesis Deluge - Rob
   MacGregor   f   2854

Zodiac, Jack (Drug Dealer)
Captain Jack Zodiac - Michael Kandel   f   2396

Zodiac, Saskia (Clone; Magician)
Seasons of Plenty - Colin Greenland   s   1935

Zoe (Teenager; Student)
The Silver Kiss - Annette Curtis Klause   f   2514

Zoe (Child)
Stonewords: A Ghost Story - Pam Conrad   f   917

Zolotin, Peter (Student—Graduate; Spaceman)
Burster - Michael Capobianco   s   711

Zoltan (Royalty; Traveller)
Wayfinder's Story: The Seventh Book of Lost Swords -
   Fred Saberhagen   f   3820

Zorah (Ruler)
Beldan's Fire - Midori Snyder   f   4110

Zorander, Zeddicus "Zedd" Zu'l (Wizard)
Stone of Tears - Terry Goodkind   f   1821

Zorba the Hutt (Alien; Parent)
Zorba the Hutt's Revenge - Paul Davids   s   1126

Zorg (Alien)
Living with Aliens - John DeChancie   s   1180

Zorin, Lavrenti Borisovich (Military Personnel;
   Revolutionary)
Branch Point - Mona Clee   s   866

zu Blas und Fiersing, Dalain "Wisp" (Nobleman)
An Exchange of Gifts - Anne McCaffrey   f   2968

Zuchmul (Vampire)
Dreamspy - Jacqueline Lichtenberg   s   2749

Zumwalt, William Irving "Wiz" (Computer Expert;
   Wizard)
The Wizardry Consulted - Rick Cook   f   936
The Wizardry Cursed - Rick Cook   f   937
The Wizardry Quested - Rick Cook   f   938

Zurvan (Scholar)
Servant of the Bones - Anne Rice   h   3654

Zurzal (Alien; Historian)
Brother to Shadows - Andre Norton   s   3298

Zverkov, Alexey (Psychic)
Spellcaster - J. Edward Ames   h   76

Zwakh, Ignatz (Addict; Refugee)
Dead Boys - Richard Calder   s   683

Zwakh, Ignatz (Fugitive)
Dead Girls - Richard Calder   s   684

Zyto, Michael (Serial Killer)
Machine - Rene Belletto   h   360

Character Description Index

This index alphabetically lists descriptions of the major characters in featured titles. The descriptions may be occupations (astronaut, lawyer, etc.) or may describe personas (amnesiac, runaway, teenager, etc.). For each description, character names are listed alphabetically. Also provided are book titles, author names, and entry numbers.

ABUSE VICTIM

Akma
Earthborn - Orson Scott Card *s* 718

Calderon, Mercedes
Solip: System - Walter Jon Williams *s* 4652

Daniels, Rose McLendon
Rose Madder - Stephen King *h* 2492

Dennessy, Anne
The Darkness Within - Shawn MacDonald *h* 2850

Dennessy, Beth
The Darkness Within - Shawn MacDonald *h* 2850

Dennessy, Carol
The Darkness Within - Shawn MacDonald *h* 2850

Domon, Tamrissa
Convergence - Sharon Green *f* 1888

Gael, Dorothy "Dotty"
Was - Geoff Ryman *f* 3804

Gray, Emma
Flying in Place - Susan Palwick *h* 3380

Kendrick, Amanda
When the Bough Breaks - Mercedes Lackey *f* 2625

Lee
The Jigsaw Woman - Kim Antieau *f* 163

Malone, Kevin
The Kingdom of Kevin Malone - Suzy McKee Charnas *f* 785

Miriam
The Spirit Stalker - Nina Romberg *h* 3735

O'Hallahan, Emma Delaney
What's Wrong with America - Scott Bradfield *h* 515

Sari
O Greenest Branch! - Gael Baudino *f* 328

Steven
The Night Man - K.W. Jeter *h* 2323

Therru
Tehanu: The Last Book of Earthsea - Ursula K. Le Guin *f* 2693

ACCOUNTANT

Beckett, Clare
Lost Futures - Lisa Tuttle *s* 4400

Boren, Troy
Blindfold - Kevin J. Anderson *s* 84

Calder, Charlotte
Tempter - Nancy A. Collins *h* 907

Callahan, Mardie
Sweet Revenge - Jean Simon *h* 4043

Chapel, Helen
Red Bride - Christopher Fowler *h* 1620

Evans, Bill "Bill the Just"
The League of the Crimson Crescent - James E. Reagen *f* 3586

Jordan, Greg
Wind Chimes - R.R. Walters *h* 4482

Lindo, Sigrid
The Moon's Wife: A Hystery - A.A. Attanasio *f* 228

MacKelston, Kathleen
The Barrens - F. Paul Wilson *h* 4682

Martin, Gene
Hellcat - Amanda Kingsley *h* 2497

McCall, Cassie
Black Ice - Pat Graversen *h* 1869

Wakelin, John
Holy Terror - Josephine Boyle *h* 498

ACTIVIST

Ahrens, Bleys
Other - Gordon R. Dickson *s* 1241
Young Bleys - Gordon R. Dickson *s* 1243

Ahrens, Dahno
Young Bleys - Gordon R. Dickson *s* 1243

Burnell
Somewhere East of Life - Brian W. Aldiss *s* 48

Candle, Martin
Blameless in Abaddon - James Morrow *f* 3209

Darffot, Tex "Bear"
Tex and Molly in the Afterlife - Richard Grant *f* 1863

Devane, Elizabeth
The Trinity Paradox - Kevin J. Anderson *s* 97

Dobbs, J.R. "BoB"
Reality Is What You Can Get Away With: An Illustrated Screenplay - Robert Anton Wilson *s* 4699

Dodge, Allison
Gaia's Toys - Rebecca Ore *s* 3362

Elphaba
Wicked: The Life and Times of the Wicked Witch of the West - Gregory Maguire *f* 2869

Greeley, Dan
The Drylands - Mary Rosenblum *s* 3747

Jephthah
To Fear the Light - Ben Bova *s* 488

Jeremiah
The Quiet Pools - Michael P. Kube-McDowell *s* 2583

Larner, Margaret "Peggy"
Alvin Journeyman - Orson Scott Card *f* 715

Lu, Antonia "Toni"
Other - Gordon R. Dickson *s* 1241

Lyell, Thomasina
The Pure Cold Light - Gregory Frost *s* 1681

Molly
Tex and Molly in the Afterlife - Richard Grant *f* 1863

Montoya, Alyssa
The Planet Beyond - Steve Mudd *s* 3219

Schlessinger, David
The Secret Oceans - Betty Ballantine *s* 268

Spotted Horse, David
Sacred Ground - Mercedes Lackey *f* 2618

Stiller, Warreven "Raven"
Shadow Man - Melissa Scott *s* 3914

Stone, Edwin L. "Ed"
Why Do Birds - Damon Knight *s* 2537

Voskresenye, Pavel Sergeyevich
The Fortunate Fall - Raphael Carter *s* 750

Waverly, Tim
Outworld Cats - Jack Lovejoy *s* 2811

Wood, Max
The Frightened Fish - Kenneth Robeson *f* 3698

ACTOR

Agranovsky, Reuven
Further Adventures - Jon Stephen Fink *f* 1563

Amby
Merlin's Bones - Fred Saberhagen *f* 3815

ACTRESS

ACTUARY

ADDICT

ADMINISTRATOR

Ash of Ashland
Dancing Jack - Laurie J. Marks f 2880

Atbin
The Promise - Monica Hughes s 2237

Avenger
The Spider #4: Death Reign of the Vampire King/The Pain Emperor - Grant Stockbridge f 4235

Bal-Simba
The Wizardry Cursed - Rick Cook f 937
The Wizardry Quested - Rick Cook f 938

Bane
The Hand of Chaos - Margaret Weis f 4558

Bankhead, Tallulah "Tulley"
Beyond the Door - Gary L. Blackwood s 413

Banning, Peter "Peter Pan"
Hook - Terry Brooks f 583

Beckwith, Forster
Fire and Ice - Edward Myers f 3235
The Mountain Made of Light - Edward Myers f 3236

Behler, Simon William
The Last Voyage of Somebody the Sailor - John Barth f 312

Belgarath
Belgarath the Sorcerer - David Eddings f 1388

Benjarth, Paul
The Cloud People - Robert B. Kelly f 2431

Beowulf
Whose Song Is Sung - Frank Schaefer f 3897

Billie
Aliens: Earth Hive - Steve Perry s 3416

Billy
Aliens: The Female War - Steve Perry s 3417

Bjorn of Bromme
The Discovery of Dragons - Graeme Base f 320

Black, Jackson
Living with the Reptiles - Roger L. DiSilvestro s 1262

Blackburn, Trebor
Captains Outrageous, or, For Doom the Bell Tolls - Roy V. Young f 4822

Boh, Walker
The Druid of Shannara - Terry Brooks f 580

Bosch, Benjamin
Troll-Taken - Rose Estes f 1482

Bradley, Richard
The Hollowing - Robert Holdstock f 2184

Braeth, Rikard
Crown of the Serpent - Allen L. Wold s 4724
Lair of the Cyclops - Allen L. Wold s 4725

Brailsford, Jane
A College of Magics - Caroline Stevermer f 4201

Brazil, Bubbles
Negrophobia: An Urban Parable - Darius James f 2276

Bremen
First King of Shannara - Terry Brooks f 582

Brenn
A Forest Lord - Michael Williams f 4634

Brown, Rembrandt "Cryin' Man"
Sliders: The Novel - Brad Linaweaver s 2756

Bruenor, Catti-Brie
Passage to Dawn - R.A. Salvatore f 3843
Siege of Darkness - R.A. Salvatore f 3844
Sojourn - R.A. Salvatore f 3845

C-3PO
The Glove of Darth Vader - Paul Davids s 1124

Cally "Earth"
Beyond the Magic Sphere - Gail Jarrow f 2296

Campbell, Deirdre
Indiana Jones and the Dance of the Giants - Rob MacGregor f 2853
Indiana Jones and the Seven Veils - Rob MacGregor f 2857

Carton, Sidney "Sid"
North Wind - Gwyneth Jones s 2354

Casruel, Aru
Mother of Storms - Adrian Cole f 886

Chalmers, Reed
The Enchanter Reborn - L. Sprague de Camp f 1138

Chamtong, Onua
Wild Magic - Tamora Pierce f 3443

Chewbacca
The Crystal Star - Vonda N. McIntyre s 3043
Jedi Search - Kevin J. Anderson s 91

Chlorine
Yon Ill Wind - Piers Anthony f 162

Climber, Artus
The Ring of Winter - James Lowder f 2813

Colene
Chaos Mode - Piers Anthony f 135
Fractal Mode - Piers Anthony f 140
Virtual Mode - Piers Anthony f 160

Collun
Hero's Song - Edith Pattou f 3393

Corlaiys, Aitchley
Cathedral of Thorns - Steven Frankos f 1640

Crocken
The Wizard's Shadow - Susan Dexter f 1222

Cromwell, Willard
Indiana Jones and the Sky Pirates - Martin Caidin f 673

Crookleg, Poilar
Kingdoms of the Wall - Robert Silverberg s 4014

Crow
Crow and Weasel - Barry Lopez f 2800

Cugnet, Vern
Stones of the Dalai Lama - Ken Mitchell f 3121

Culaehra
The Sage - Christopher Stasheff f 4164

Cumber
Dragoncharm - Graham Edwards f 1405

Dagda
The Enchanted Isles - Casey Flynn f 1577
Most Ancient Song - Casey Flynn f 1578

Daniel
The Door to Ambermere - J. Calvin Pierce f 3437

Daniels, Aikin
Dreamseeker's Road - Tom Deitz f 1191

d'Armand, Magnus Gallowglass
A Wizard in Absentia - Christopher Stasheff s 4172

de Wolf, Mike
Typewriter in the Sky - L. Ron Hubbard f 2224

Deal, Brian
The Square Deal - David Drake s 1327

Deal, John "J.C."
The Square Deal - David Drake s 1327

den Karynth, Calandryll
Dark Magic - Angus Wells f 4569

Denison, Will
Dinotopia - James Gurney f 1979
Dinotopia Lost - Alan Dean Foster f 1608
The World Beneath - James Gurney f 1980

Derry, Jerry
Ye Gods! - Tom Holt f 2196

diGriz, Jim
The Stainless Steel Rat Goes to Hell - Harry Harrison s 2059

Do'Urden, Drizzt
The Legacy - R.A. Salvatore f 3841
Siege of Darkness - R.A. Salvatore f 3844
Sojourn - R.A. Salvatore f 3845
Starless Night - R.A. Salvatore f 3846

Dowd, Katherine "Katy"
Flames of the Dragon - Robin Wayne Bailey f 243

Drizzt Do'Urden
Passage to Dawn - R.A. Salvatore f 3843

Dug
Demons Don't Dream - Piers Anthony f 138

Ela
The Goblin Mirror - C.J. Cherryh f 805

Elmara
Elminster: The Making of a Mage - Ed Greenwood f 1941

Escargot, Theophile
The Stone Giant - James P. Blaylock f 425

Ferraro, Gene
Castle War! - John DeChancie s 1175

Finis "Water"
Beyond the Magic Sphere - Gail Jarrow f 2296

Flannery, Eric
Caverns of Socrates - Dennis L. McKiernan f 3053

Flannery, Kathleen
The Two Georges - Richard Dreyfuss s 1335

Formosus, Musculus Herodes
Whose Song Is Sung - Frank Schaefer f 3897

Fortune
Dragoncharm - Graham Edwards f 1405

Gabrielle
The Empty Throne - Ru Emerson f 1451

Gelly
Flight to Hollow Mountain - Mark Sebanc f 3921

Gelmann, Mina
Codgerspace - Alan Dean Foster s 1604

Gibbs, Rinpoche
Muddle Earth - John Brunner s 601

Gordon, Kate
The Merlin Effect - T.A. Barron f 310

Gordon, Mrs. Sr.
Revenge of the Fluffy Bunnies - Craig Shaw Gardner f 1714

Gordon, Roger Jr.
Revenge of the Fluffy Bunnies - Craig Shaw Gardner f 1714

Graydon, Nicholas
The Face in the Abyss - Abraham Merritt f 3091

Greycloak, Janela Kether
Kingdoms of the Night - Allan Cole f 890

Grimi, Garni ben
Another Day, Another Dungeon - Greg Costikyan f 977

Hanse
The Shadow of Sorcery - Andrew J. Offutt f 3347

Haplo
Elven Star - Margaret Weis f 4555
Fire Sea - Margaret Weis f 4557
The Hand of Chaos - Margaret Weis f 4558
Into the Labyrinth - Margaret Weis f 4559
Serpent Mage - Margaret Weis f 4565
The Seventh Gate - Margaret Weis f 4566

ADVERTISING

AGED PERSON

Allalie, Fentrice
Walking the Labyrinth - Lisa Goldstein *f* 1818

Arak, Bashir
The Planet Beyond - Steve Mudd *s* 3219

Banning, George "Grandpa"
My Pretty Pony - Stephen King *h* 2489

Brand, Evelyn
The Devil's Churn - Kristine Kathryn
Rusch *h* 3773

Brentwood, Grace
Earthbound - Richard Matheson *h* 2930

Campbell, Arlene "Grandma"
The Amulet - A.R. Morlan *h* 3191

Carson, Kenneth "Kit"
Time Scout - Robert Asprin *s* 221

Chasse, Lois
Insomnia - Stephen King *h* 2488

Claiborne, Dolores
Dolores Claiborne - Stephen King *h* 2483

Clanton, Otis
The Sixth Dog - Jane Rice *h* 3659

Clayborne, Ann
Blue Mars - Kim Stanley Robinson *s* 3704

Coughlin, Charlie
Dry Skull Dreams - Michael Green *h* 1879

Curran, Abigail
Holy Terror - Josephine Boyle *h* 498

Davidson, Callum
Dialing the Wind - Charles L. Grant *h* 1847

DeGeaux, Vanessa
The Black Mariah - Jay R. Bonansinga *h* 468

Deveraux, Rosalie
Blood Roots - Richie Tankersley Cusick *h* 1055

Dietrich, Elinor
Revenant - Melanie Tem *h* 4329

Donovan, Vera
Dolores Claiborne - Stephen King *h* 2483

Douchette, Earl
The Jimjams - Michael Green *h* 1880

Ewebean, Jade
Panic - Chris Curry *h* 1050

Falfurrias, Ofelia Damareux
Remnant Population - Elizabeth Moon *s* 3161

Gelmann, Mina
Codgerspace - Alan Dean Foster *s* 1604

Gold, Leah
Rage - Elizabeth Ergas *h* 1474

Hagopian
Black Sun - Douglas E. Winter *h* 4716

Hill, Jonathan
The Burning Man - Michael Hammond *h* 2023

Iranaputra, Victor
Codgerspace - Alan Dean Foster *s* 1604

Johnson, Grandma
Grandma's Little Darling - Stephen R.
George *h* 1767

Kirk, James T.
The Fearful Summons - Denny Martin Flinn *s* 1573

Lady
Boy's Life - Robert R. McCammon *h* 2987

Leonardo Da Vinci
Pasquale's Angel - Paul J. McAuley *f* 2955

Little, Thomas
The Little Country - Charles de Lint *f* 1156

Madison, Sybil Wilfred
Baby Doll - Ruby Jean Jensen *h* 2309

Manzara, Gaetano
Fantasma - Thomas F. Monteleone *h* 3155

Mary
Wilding - Melanie Tem *h* 4330

McGowan, Annie
The Nightmare People - Lawrence Watt-
Evans *h* 4499

Nemmitz, Palmer
Dark Journey - A.R. Morlan *h* 3192

O'Hallahan, Marvin
What's Wrong with America - Scott
Bradfield *h* 515

Old Bess
The Moorchild - Eloise Jarvis McGraw *f* 3040

Owain, Gwendolyn
The Long Lost - Ramsey Campbell *h* 699

Rafiel
Outnumbering the Dead - Frederik Pohl *s* 3467

Rivera, Maria
The Nihilesthete - Richard Kalich *h* 2391

Roberts, Ralph
Insomnia - Stephen King *h* 2488

Russell, Saxifrage "Sax"
Blue Mars - Kim Stanley Robinson *s* 3704

Rustin, Adelaine Hawthorne Taylor
The Devil's Churn - Kristine Kathryn
Rusch *h* 3773

Shipman, Malkah
He, She and It - Marge Piercy *s* 3445

Skinner
Virtual Light - William Gibson *s* 1782

Talbot, Annie
Her Monster - Jeff Collignon *h* 898

Tao Tieh
Twisted Images - Don D'Ammassa *h* 1081

Thibodeaux, Ben
The Dwelling - Tom Elliott *h* 1424

Thompson, Lydia
Seed of Evil - Edmund Plante *h* 3457

Torgov, Grandma Mugwump
Blood of Mugwump - Doug Rice *h* 3658

Tucker
Unicorn Highway - David Lee Jones *f* 2343

Tuckton, Grandpap
Header - Edward Lee *h* 2699

Usher, Madeline
Madeline: After the Fall of Usher - Marie
Kiraly *h* 2502

Veilleur, Glaeken
Nightworld - F. Paul Wilson *h* 4689

Washington, Billy
Beggars and Choosers - Nancy Kress *s* 2573

Waverly, Dora
The Well - Michael B. Sirota *h* 4053

Webb, Tessa
Haunted - James Herbert *h* 2130

Webster, Daniel
Deep Freeze - Zach Hughes *s* 2239

Wickham, Theodora
The Haunting - Ruby Jean Jensen *h* 2311

Winston, Palmer
Dark Journey - A.R. Morlan *h* 3192

Yambu
Wayfinder's Story: The Seventh Book of Lost Swords -
Fred Saberhagen *f* 3820

AGENT

Aw, Ruiz
Emperor of Everything - Ray Aldridge *s* 50
The Pharaoh Contract - Ray Aldridge *s* 51

Bureaucrat
Stations of the Tide - Michael Swanwick *s* 4283

Coogan, Elihu "Emil Storchesson"
The Singularity Project - F.M. Busby *s* 641

Derrith, Raunn ni Obradi san
World Spirits - Aline Boucher-Kaplan *s* 475

Duroc, Roger
Comeback Tour: The Sky Belongs to the Stars - Jack
Yeovil *s* 4798

Everard, Manse
The Shield of Time - Poul Anderson *s* 109
The Time Patrol - Poul Anderson *s* 112

Faharmoy
Wild Magic - Jo Clayton *f* 864

Finister "Moraga"
Quicksilver's Knight - Christopher Stasheff *f* 4163

Hightower, Alex
Possession - Peter James *h* 2290

Jack
The End-of-Everything Man - Tom De
Haven *f* 1146

Juillerat, Sister Chantal
Demon Download - Jack Yeovil *f* 4799

Kendal, Harry
Now You See It. . . - Richard Matheson *h* 2934

Kirowa, Niala
The Planet Beyond - Steve Mudd *s* 3219

Lacuna
Question Quest - Piers Anthony *f* 153

Lord, Melanie
Haunted - Tamara Thorne *h* 4359

Lysander
Phaze Doubt - Piers Anthony *f* 152

Maria Elena
Humans - Donald E. Westlake *f* 4595

Metis, Jean
Crygender - Thomas T. Thomas *s* 4349

Monlux, Cassandra
Slow Freight - F.M. Busby *s* 642

Oren, Eichra
Converse and Conflict - L. Neil Smith *s* 4091

Pasco
Ghost Dancers - Brian Craig *s* 1003

Piyolss, Faan Korispais
Wild Magic - Jo Clayton *f* 864

Preston, Carl
Ghost Dancers - Brian Craig *s* 1003

Quint
Psi-Man - David Peters *s* 3428

Stein, Rachel
Search and Destroy - Keith William
Andrews *s* 117

Tamberly, Wanda
The Shield of Time - Poul Anderson *s* 109

Tanner, Vaughn
Mad Roy's Light - Paula King *s* 2478

Tarz, Auriel il
World Spirits - Aline Boucher-Kaplan *s* 475

Tinker, Austin
Crygender - Thomas T. Thomas *s* 4349

Troy, Linda Ellen "Sparta"
The Diamond Moon - Paul Preuss *s* 3523

Undershort, Ozwaldo
Free Radicals - Jack McKinney s 3066

ALCOHOLIC

Asquith, Timothy
Ghostwright - Michael Cadnum h 661

Malone, Jessie
The Golden Nineties - Lisa Mason s 2912

Michael, Father
The Eyes of Torie Webster - Roy Sorrels h 4121

Watkins, Daniel J.
The Golden Nineties - Lisa Mason s 2912

ALIEN

Abe
The Clouds of Magellan - David F.
Nighbert s 3266

Afsan
Far-Seer - Robert J. Sawyer s 3884
Fossil Hunter - Robert J. Sawyer s 3885

Akktri
In the Cube - David Alexander Smith s 4076

Andrachis, Shil
Shadows on the Sun - Michael Jan
Friedman s 1664

Angel
The Pure Cold Light - Gregory Frost s 1681

Anito
The Color of Distance - Amy Thomson s 4357

Arbok
Prison Ship - Martin Caidin s 676

Archemon
Monsoon - Peter L. Rice s 3660

Arthur
The Immortality Option - James P. Hogan s 2175

Aryl
Under Alien Stars - Pamela F. Service s 3929

Asan
Requiem for Anthi - Jay D. Blakeney s 419

Asx/Ewasx
Infinity's Shore - David Brin s 565

At
Doctor's Orders - Diane Duane s 1338

Atvar
Worldwar: In the Balance - Harry
Turtledove s 4395
Worldwar: Striking the Balance - Harry
Turtledove s 4396
Worldwar: Tilting the Balance - Harry
Turtledove s 4397
Worldwar: Upsetting the Balance - Harry
Turtledove s 4398

Auganzar
Warlord of Heaven - Adrian Cole f 887

Autothor
Codgerspace - Alan Dean Foster s 1604

Ayyah
Cat's Gambit - Leslie Gadallah s 1690

Aza-Kra
Rule Golden and Double Meaning - Damon
Knight s 2536

bad-Jam, Gilan "Gilan the Third"
The Swords of Zinjaban - L. Sprague de
Camp s 1143

Baggy
Judson's Eden - Keith Laumer s 2662

Bandit
Fire Planet - P.M. Griffin s 1949

Barbtail, Dotson
Seeds of Destiny - Thomas A. Easton s 1382

Barion
The Snake Oil Wars - Parke Godwin s 1807

Bastable
Charmed - Marilyn Singer f 4046

Beaver, Bucky
McLendon's Syndrome - Robert Frezza s 1650

Big Sword
Project Farcry - Pauline Ashwell s 189

Bilrog
Labyrinth - Dennis Schmidt s 3901

Blacktop
Tower of the Gods - Thomas A. Easton s 1384

Bluecloak
Remnant Population - Elizabeth Moon s 3161

Blueshell
A Fire upon the Deep - Vernor Vinge s 4441

Bontu
Life Form - Alan Dean Foster s 1611

Braan
Genellan: Planetfall - Scott G. Gier s 1786

Broxholm
My Teacher Flunked the Planet - Bruce
Coville s 992

Brutogas, Kator Secondcousin
Naked to the Stars/The Alien Way - Gordon R.
Dickson s 1240

Bult
Uncharted Territory - Connie Willis s 4677

Cag
Them - William W. Johnstone h 2339

Caldaq
A Call to Arms - Alan Dean Foster s 1601

Calhoun, Janey
Warpath - Tony Daniel s 1082

Catherine
Flying to Valhalla - Charles Pellegrino s 3409

Chakallakak, Chakallakak "Chaka" ngha
The Long Hunt - Debra Doyle s 1295

Champion, Dragonbait
Masquerades - Kate Novak f 3318
Song of the Saurials - Kate Novak f 3319

Channon
Target - Janet Morris s 3198

Chanur, Hilfy
Chanur's Legacy - C.J. Cherryh s 795

Charlie
Neptune Crossing - Jeffrey A. Carver s 756
Strange Attractors - Jeffrey A. Carver s 757

Charlie/Charlene
The Infinite Sea - Jeffrey A. Carver s 755

Chedo, Gral II
Random Factor - Joel Henry Sherman s 3975

Chewbacca
The Crystal Star - Vonda N. McIntyre s 3043
Jedi Search - Kevin J. Anderson s 91

Chi-da
Wulfsyarn: A Mosaic - Phillip Mann s 2876

Chirwl
Medicine Show - Jody Lynn Nye s 3324

Chmeee
The Ringworld Throne - Larry Niven s 3287

Chomanche
A Miracle of Rare Design - Mike Resnick s 3631

Chrestil, Damian
Burning Bright - Melissa Scott s 3909

Chuut-Riit
The Children's Hour - Jerry Pournelle s 3485

Claro
An Eye for Dark Places - Norma Marder s 2879

Clavel
North Wind - Gwyneth Jones s 2354

Coyul
The Snake Oil Wars - Parke Godwin s 1807

Dahmi
Alien Eyes - Lynn S. Hightower s 2143

Dak, Maanka "Pete Moss"
The Change - Barry B. Longyear s 2797

Davakinapwottapellazanzis
The Expediter - J. Brian Clarke s 855

Dax, Jadzia
Time's Enemy - L.A. Graf s 1842

Deayl
The Homecoming - Barry B. Longyear s 2798

Derrith, Verrer ni Rimmani san
World Spirits - Aline Boucher-Kaplan s 475

Dhalvad
Seeking the Dream Brother - Marcia J.
Bennett s 371

Diamond, Tal
City of Diamond - Jane Emerson s 1450

Diehrenn
Encounter with Tiber - Buzz Aldrin s 52

d'jehn, Tahl
The Alien Dark - Diana G. Gallagher s 1695

Dnivtopun
The Children's Hour - Jerry Pournelle s 3485

Dob
Back to the Time Trap - Keith Laumer s 2661

Donokh
Shade - Emily Devenport s 1213

Dopey
The Other End of Time - Frederik Pohl s 3466

Dorella
Dorella - Mark A. Garland f 1719

D'oud
The False Mirror - Alan Dean Foster s 1609

Douglas, Medoret
A Whisper of Time - Paula E. Downing s 1288

Dowornobb
Genellan: Planetfall - Scott G. Gier s 1786

Dreadful Eye
The Woman between the Worlds - F. Gwynplaine
MacIntyre s 2859

Droagn, Endark
Lair of the Cyclops - Allen L. Wold s 4725

Dulcimer
Transcendence - Charles Sheffield s 3963

Durvash
Man-Kzin Wars V - Larry Niven s 3284

Dweller
The Source - Brian Lumley h 2837

Dy-Dybo
Fossil Hunter - Robert J. Sawyer s 3885

Ecu
Empire's End - Allan Cole s 888
The Return of the Emperor - Allan Cole s 891

AMNESIAC

ANDROID

Herman
Way Up High - Roger Zelazny *f* 4847

Howie
Return to Howliday Inn - James Howe *f* 2220

Hunnul
Valorian - Mary H. Herbert *f* 2137

Impossumble
An Impossible Summer - B.W. Clough *f* 878

Ingersol, William "Bogey"
Top Dog - Jerry Jay Carroll *f* 741

Ingledew, Sam
The Cockroaches of Stay More - Donald
  Harington *f* 2033

Ishmael
Ishmael - Daniel Quinn *s* 3552

Joseph
The Bellmaker - Brian Jacques *f* 2267

Ko
Monkey Station - Ardath Mayhar *s* 2946

Lanakila
Catamount - Michael Peak *f* 3403

Lightfoot
Into the Land of the Unicorns - Bruce
  Coville *f* 989

Loiosh
Phoenix - Steven Brust *f* 610

Lovelock
Lovelock - Orson Scott Card *s* 723

Lupo
Down the Stream of Stars - Jeffrey A.
  Carver *s* 751

Marbleheart
Geomancer - Don Callander *f* 688

Mariel
The Bellmaker - Brian Jacques *f* 2267
Mariel of Redwall - Brian Jacques *f* 2268

Martin the Warrior
Martin the Warrior - Brian Jacques *f* 2269

Matthias
Mattimeo - Brian Jacques *f* 2270

Miaowara Shiro
Samurai Cat Goes to the Movies - Mark E.
  Rogers *s* 3727
The Sword of Samurai Cat - Mark E.
  Rogers *s* 3728

Miaowara Tomokato
Samurai Cat Goes to the Movies - Mark E.
  Rogers *s* 3727
The Sword of Samurai Cat - Mark E.
  Rogers *s* 3728

Mogget
Sabriel - Garth Nix *f* 3288

Mole
Toad Triumphant - William Horwood *f* 2211
The Willows in Winter - William Horwood *f* 2212

Morris "Mauricio di Mauro"
*The Night of Wishes: or The
  Satanarchaeolidealcohellish Notion Potion* - Michael
  Ende *f* 1462

Mudge
Chorus Skating - Alan Dean Foster *f* 1603

Murri
The Mark of the Cat - Andre Norton *f* 3311

Nara
Dark Horse - Mary H. Herbert *f* 2135

Nepe/Flach
Phaze Doubt - Piers Anthony *f* 152

Newt
Ratha and Thistle-Chaser - Clare Bell *f* 356

Niffy
No One Noticed the Cat - Anne McCaffrey *f* 2973

Nigheyes
Royal Assassin - Robin Hobb *f* 2152

Nul
Wizard's Mole - Brad Strickland *f* 4257

O-ha
The Foxes of Firstdark - Garry Kilworth *f* 2473

Obed
The Off Season - Jack Cady *f* 669

O'lal
Cat-A-Lyst - Alan Dean Foster *s* 1602

Orick
Beyond the Gate - Dave Wolverton *s* 4740
The Golden Queen - Dave Wolverton *s* 4742

Ouoji
Destination: Mutiny - Sean Dalton *s* 1078

Peeve
Black Unicorn - Tanith Lee *f* 2707
Gold Unicorn - Tanith Lee *f* 2712

Pepper
The House on the Borderland - William Hope
  Hodgson *h* 2164

Pinscher
Pet Store - M.T. Coffin *h* 882

Pooch
Carmen Dog - Carol Emshwiller *f* 1458

Quadroped
Demon Pig - Karen Brush *f* 603

Raajeh
Ray Bradbury Presents: Dinosaur Planet - Stephen
  Leigh *s* 2724

Rabscuttle
Tales From Watership Down - Richard Adams *f* 25

Racso
R-T, Margaret, and the Rats of NIMH - Jane Leslie
  Conly *f* 913

Rajasthan, Nohar
Emperors of the Twilight - S. Andrew
  Swann *s* 4274

Raptor Red
Raptor Red - Robert T. Bakker *f* 256

Ratha
Ratha and Thistle-Chaser - Clare Bell *f* 356

red mare
A Ride on the Red Mare's Back - Ursula K. Le
  Guin *f* 2692

Rex
The Magnificent Wilf - Gordon R. Dickson *s* 1239

Robert
The Coachman Rat - David Henry Wilson *f* 4680

Rommel
Psi-Man - David Peters *s* 3428

Sarena
Catamount - Michael Peak *f* 3403

Scandal
Majyk by Accident - Esther Friesner *f* 1673
Majyk by Hook or Crook - Esther Friesner *f* 1675

Scribble, Jacob
*The Night of Wishes: or The
  Satanarchaeolidealcohellish Notion Potion* - Michael
  Ende *f* 1462

Seale, Evan
The Silent Strength of Stones - Nina Kiriki
  Hoffman *f* 2168

Seeker After Patterns
Beyond the Fall of Night - Arthur C. Clarke *s* 847

Seqiro
Chaos Mode - Piers Anthony *f* 135
Virtual Mode - Piers Anthony *f* 160

Sixclaw, Swartt
Outcast of Redwall - Brian Jacques *f* 2271

Slagar
Mattimeo - Brian Jacques *f* 2270

Snaugenhutt
Son of Spellsinger - Alan Dean Foster *f* 1617

Snuff
A Night in the Lonesome October - Roger
  Zelazny *h* 4843

SStragh
Ray Bradbury Presents: Dinosaur World - Stephen
  Leigh *s* 2725

Streak
Shadows in the Water - Kathryn Lasky *s* 2659

Sunflash
Outcast of Redwall - Brian Jacques *f* 2271

Tabby, Jane
Catwings - Ursula K. Le Guin *f* 2687

Thakur
Ratha and Thistle-Chaser - Clare Bell *f* 356

Tharna
The Key of the Keplian - Andre Norton *f* 3310

Thor
Thor - Wayne Smith *h* 4106

Thrugg
Salamandastron - Brian Jacques *f* 2272

Toad of Toad Hall
Toad Triumphant - William Horwood *f* 2211
The Willows in Winter - William Horwood *f* 2212

Unicorn
Blue Moon Rising - Simon R. Green *f* 1894

Urthstripe the Strong
Salamandastron - Brian Jacques *f* 2272

Valadan
The Prince of Ill Luck - Susan Dexter *f* 1220
The True Knight - Susan Dexter *f* 1221

Veil
Outcast of Redwall - Brian Jacques *f* 2271

Water Rat "Ratty"
Toad Triumphant - William Horwood *f* 2211
The Willows in Winter - William Horwood *f* 2212

Wimperling
Pigs Don't Fly - Mary Brown *f* 594

ANIMAL LOVER

Matheson, Hope
Seeing Eye - Jack Ellis *h* 1428

Mitchell, Jackie
Dangerous Nature - T.J. Kirby *h* 2504

Tovin, Rahel
Regenesis - Julia Ecklar *s* 1387

ANIMAL TRAINER

Burrich
Assassin's Apprentice - Robin Hobb *f* 2151

Chamtong, Onua
Wild Magic - Tamora Pierce *f* 3443

Dog-Woman
Sexing the Cherry - Jeanette Winterson *f* 4719

ARTISAN

ARTIST

1387

Tobias, Robin
Strange Angels - Kathe Koja   h   2543

Tryon, Michael
The Stone Garden - Mary Rosenblum   s   3748

Tullian, Adele
Sheep - Simon Maginn   h   2866

van de Oest, Frances Lorien "Lore"
Slow River - Nicola Griffith   s   1957

Videla, Pilar
Whiteout - Sage Walker   s   4477

Wallace, Brandy
Dreambuilder - Tom Deitz   f   1190

West, Braden
The Catswold Portal - Shirley Rousseau
    Murphy   f   3230

Williams, Trevor
WiZrD - Steve Zell   h   4849

Wingate, Max
The Convocation - John R. Holt   h   2192

Winters, Ginny
Dreamer - Daniel Quinn   h   3551

Wolfe, Sara
*The Venetian's Wife: A Strangely Sensual Tale of a
    Renaissance Explorer, a Computer, and a
    Metamorphosis* - Nick Bantock   f   282

Young, Janet
Breeder - Ed Kelleher   h   2424

Zacharias, John Furie "Gentle"
Imajica - Clive Barker   h   288

Zamiatin, Mark "Visual Mark"
Synners - Pat Cadigan   s   660

Zapata, Xolotl
High Aztec - Ernest Hogan   s   2173

ASSISTANT

Audran, Marid
The Exile Kiss - George Alec Effinger   s   1406

Damek
The Spirit Gate - Maya Kaathryn Bohnhoff   f   460

Hanlon, Agnes
The Sixth Dog - Jane Rice   h   3659

Hutchinson, Lisa
All Things under the Moon - Robert
    Morgan   h   3184
The Things That Are Not There - Robert
    Morgan   h   3189

Lu, Antonia "Toni"
Other - Gordon R. Dickson   s   1241

Morcey, Paul
The Only Thing to Fear - Robert Morgan   h   3185

Oldar
King of the Dead - Gene DeWeese   h   1218

Venneman, Richard
Insatiable - David Dvorkin   h   1370

ASTRONAUT

Abronowitz, Wendy
The Fugitive Stars - Daniel Ransom   s   3571

Baedecker, Richard
Phases of Gravity - Dan Simmons   s   4036

Bronstein, Miroslav Ilyich
Fellow Traveller - William Barton   s   316

Campbell, Jack "Cap'n Jack"
The Fugitive Stars - Daniel Ransom   s   3571

Captain
Beyond Apollo - Barry Malzberg   s   2872
Eden - Stanislaw Lem   s   2730

Doctor
Eden - Stanislaw Lem   s   2730

DuBois, Ned
Firestar - Michael Flynn   s   1579

Essell, Lilly
Realtime Interrupt - James P. Hogan   s   2179

Evans, Harry M.
Beyond Apollo - Barry Malzberg   s   2872

Jackson, Jack
The Stars Must Wait - Keith Laumer   s   2664

Kelligan, Sam Houston
Beachhead - Jack Williamson   s   4667

Manarov, Vladimir "Volodya" Alekseevich
Fellow Traveller - William Barton   s   316

Mathews, Sheilagh
The Voice of Cepheus - Ken Appleby   s   166

Pettis
Moonbane - Al Sarrantonio   s   3869

Ryan, Jayne
Beachhead - Jack Williamson   s   4667

Ryder, Jake
Reach - Edward Gibson   s   1779

Spencer, Joseph "Speed"
Reach - Edward Gibson   s   1779

Stavenger, Paul
Moonrise - Ben Bova   s   482

Stoner, Keith
Star Brothers - Ben Bova   s   487

Terrence, Chris
Encounter with Tiber - Buzz Aldrin   s   52

Tynan, Louie
Mother of Storms - John Barnes   s   296

Wagner, Lauren
The Season of Passage - Christopher Pike   h   3450

Walmsley, Nigel
Sailing Bright Eternity - Gregory Benford   s   369

Wayville, Chris
Flying to Valhalla - Charles Pellegrino   s   3409

Wayville, Clarice
Flying to Valhalla - Charles Pellegrino   s   3409

Williams, Conrad
Night Launch - Jake Garn   s   1720

Zakharov, Aelita
Night Launch - Jake Garn   s   1720

AUDITOR

Gonzales, Mikhail Mikhailovitch
Halo - Tom Maddox   s   2864

AUTOMECHANIC

Whipple, Frank "Weasel"
Mongster - Randall Boyll   h   506

AVENGER

Amalayna
Chains of Darkness, Chains of Light - Michelle
    Sagara   f   3823

Mona
Enemy of My Enemy - Ben Ohlander   s   3349

Tuchman, Ward
Enemy of My Enemy - Ben Ohlander   s   3349

BACKWOODSMAN

Old Nathan
Old Nathan - David Drake   f   1323

BAKER

Bayless, Laura
Good Night, Sweet Angel - Clare McNally   h   3073

Jack
The Baker's Boy - J.V. Jones   f   2356

Manzara, Gaetano
Fantasma - Thomas F. Monteleone   h   3155

BANKER

Barker, Justin
Tombley's Walk - Crosland Brown   h   590

Cummings, Michael
Not Broken, Not Belonging - Randy Fox   h   1630

Doland, Jane
Flying Dutch - Tom Holt   f   2193

Jackson, Portis
Dumford Blood - S.K. Epperson   h   1469

Kataboki, Lily
I'll Be Watching You - Samuel M. Key   h   2463

Ling, Mayla
Half the Day Is Night - Maureen F.
    McHugh   s   3042

Sullivan, Donald
What's Wrong with America - Scott
    Bradfield   h   515

BARBARIAN

Bakhtiian, Ilyakoria "Ilya"
An Earthly Crown - Kate Elliott   s   1421
Jaran - Kate Elliott   s   1422

Black-Robe, Harvas
Krispos of Videssos - Harry Turtledove   f   4389

Conan
Conan and the Treasure of Python - John Maddox
    Roberts   f   3692
The Conan Chronicles - Robert Jordan   f   2378
Conan of the Red Brotherhood - Leonard
    Carpenter   f   734
Conan, Scourge of the Bloody Coast - Leonard
    Carpenter   f   738
Conan the Formidable - Steve Perry   f   3420
Conan the Gladiator - Leonard Carpenter   f   735
Conan the Guardian - Roland J. Green   f   1882
Conan the Indomitable - Steve Perry   f   3421
Conan the Outcast - Leonard Carpenter   f   736
Conan the Relentless - Roland J. Green   f   1883
Conan the Rogue - John Maddox Roberts   f   3693
Conan the Savage - Leonard Carpenter   f   737
Hour of the Dragon - Robert E. Howard   f   2217

de Oro, Joe
Songs of the Dancing Gods - Jack L. Chalker   f   780

Etzilios
Hammer and Anvil - Harry Turtledove   f   4387

Kerin
The Honorable Barbarian - L. Sprague de
    Camp   f   1140

Medwind Song
Bones of the Past - Holly Lisle   f   2765

Oonitsaupivia, Nijon
By the Sword - Greg Costikyan   f   978

Shkai'ra
The Cage - S.M. Stirling   f   4223

Song, Medwind
Fire in the Mist - Holly Lisle *f* 2767

Van
Prince of the North - Harry Turtledove *f* 4392

Wartsworth, Caspar
The Lost City of Zork - Robin W. Bailey *f* 241

BASTARD DAUGHTER

Albain, Elandra
Reign of Shadows - Deborah Chester *f* 819

Villette, Celine
The Judas Cross - Charles Sheffield *h* 3958

BASTARD SON

Arthur
The Winter King - Bernard Cornwell *f* 962

Badger
The Spellkey Trilogy - Ann Downer *f* 1285

Dheribi
Greenmagic - Crawford Kilian *f* 2467

Fallstar, Chade
Assassin's Apprentice - Robin Hobb *f* 2151

Farseer, FitzChivalry "Fitz"
Assassin's Apprentice - Robin Hobb *f* 2151
Royal Assassin - Robin Hobb *f* 2152

Ketral, Jarid Tal
Moonspeaker - K.D. Wentworth *s* 4586

Kireyevsky, Vasily "Vasha"
The Law of Becoming - Kate Elliott *s* 1423

Lannister, Tyrion
A Game of Thrones - George R.R. Martin *f* 2896

Mordred
Mordred's Curse - Ian McDowell *f* 3032

Roland
Charlemagne's Champion - Gail Van Asten *f* 4413

Tegne
Tegne: Soul Warrior - Richard La Plante *f* 2598

von Darkmoor, Erik
Shadow of a Dark Queen - Raymond E.
   Feist *f* 1538

Welch, Lewis
Soulsmith - Tom Deitz *f* 1193

BEACHCOMBER

O'Donnell, Ryan
Nightmare, with Angel - Stephen Gallagher *h* 1697

BIKER

Bombeck, Tesla
Everville - Clive Barker *h* 284

Bork, Dick "Dutch"
Night Beasts - T.W. Stetson *h* 4199

Hitch
Dead Heat - Del Stone Jr. *h* 4239

BLACKSMITH

Blaze
Isle of Woman - Piers Anthony *f* 146

Elof
The Forge in the Forest - Michael Scott
   Rohan *f* 3731

Maker, Alvin
Alvin Journeyman - Orson Scott Card *f* 715

Ohaern
The Sage - Christopher Stasheff *f* 4164

Sigvarthsson, Shef
The Hammer and the Cross - Harry
   Harrison *f* 2055

Varrus, Gaius Publius
The Skystone - Jack Whyte *f* 4614

BODYGUARD

Audran, Marid
The Exile Kiss - George Alec Effinger *s* 1406
A Fire in the Sun - George Alec Effinger *s* 1407

Bennet, Tim
Half the Day Is Night - Maureen F.
   McHugh *s* 3042

Boniface, Thomas
The Element of Fire - Martha Wells *f* 4582

Bork, Saval
Brother Death - Steve Perry *s* 3419

Bothari
Barrayar - Lois McMaster Bujold *s* 620

Dai, David
Half the Day Is Night - Maureen F.
   McHugh *s* 3042

Guido
M.Y.T.H. Inc. - Robert Asprin *f* 217

Halloran, Liam
Sepulchre - James Herbert *h* 2133

Jewelbright, Taynad
Brother to Shadows - Andre Norton *s* 3298

Lomax, Felix "Gravedancer"
Prophet - Mike Resnick *s* 3634

Maxon, Max
Bodyguard - William C. Dietz *s* 1244

Nimnestl
Rouse a Sleeping Cat - Dan Crawford *f* 1012
The Sure Death of a Mouse - Dan Crawford *f* 1013
A Wild Dog and Lone - Dan Crawford *f* 1014

Nunzio
M.Y.T.H. Inc. - Robert Asprin *f* 217

Olaffson, Egil
Egil's Book - C.J. Mills *s* 3115

Rachelle
The Anubis Murders - Gary Gygax *f* 1982
Death in Delhi - Gary Gygax *f* 1983

Sleel
Black Steel - Steve Perry *s* 3418

Sten
Revenge of the Damned - Allan Cole *s* 892

Trigg, Cyrus "Russ"
Howl-O-Ween - Gary L. Holleman *h* 2189

Tyrian
A College of Magics - Caroline Stevermer *f* 4201

Zimmerman, Rick
Unearthed - Ashley McConnell *h* 3007

BOUNTY HUNTER

Chandler, Joshua "the Whistler" Jeremiah
Oracle - Mike Resnick *s* 3632

Christian, Reese
Shadows - Kimberly Rangel *h* 3565

Goode, Wilson
Monsoon - Peter L. Rice *s* 3660

Javobo
Mainline - Deborah Christian *s* 828

Jones, Witchfinder
Walking Wolf - Nancy A. Collins *h* 908

Journey, Ruby
Deathstalker Rebellion - Simon R. Green *s* 1896

McCade, Sam
McCade's Bounty - William C. Dietz *s* 1252

Murtaugh, Flint
Gone South - Robert R. McCammon *h* 2988

Rydell, Berry
Virtual Light - William Gibson *s* 1782

Windsor, Corrigan Tel
The Price of Ransom - Alis A. Rasmussen *s* 3575

BOYFRIEND

Carnes, Donald
The Axman Cometh - John Farris *h* 1515

Donohue, Greg
A Witch Across Time - Gilbert B. Cross *f* 1031

Enkidu
Mirage - Perry Brass *s* 543

Sanderheim, Doug
Slow Funeral - Rebecca Ore *f* 3365

BRIDE

Linda
Bride of the Castle - John DeChancie *s* 1172

Theodora of Pyrene
Two-Bit Heroes - Doris Egan *s* 1413

BUSINESSMAN

Abdullah
Castle in the Air - Diana Wynne Jones *f* 2346

Allen, Harrison
Dark Twilight - Joseph Citro *h* 836

Altman, Gibson
Pallas - L. Neil Smith *s* 4093

Arayncourt, Trevelyan
The Lotus and the Rose - Scott Ciencin *f* 830
The Wolves of Autumn - Scott Ciencin *f* 835

Argyle, Roger
All the Bells on Earth - James P. Blaylock *f* 420

Ashlar "Mr. Ash"
Taltos - Anne Rice *h* 3656

Austin, Kenton
The Living Dark - Stephen Gresham *h* 1945

Avery, Rupert "Roo"
Rise of a Merchant Prince - Raymond E.
   Feist *f* 1536

Baedecker, Richard
Phases of Gravity - Dan Simmons *s* 4036

Barnard, Jacques
2XS - Nigel Findley *f* 1558

Barr, Dallas
Buying Time - Joe Haldeman *s* 1993

Bateman, Patrick
American Psycho - Brett Easton Ellis *h* 1425

Bates, Patty
The Immaculate - Mark Morris *h* 3204

Bathory, Michael
Ancestral Hungers - Scott Baker *h* 254

Bellini, Aaron
Out There in the Darkness - Ed Gorman *h* 1828

Bellisle, Andre
Cold Eye - Giles Blunt *h* 454

Beltar
Traitors - Kristine Kathryn Rusch *f* 3786

Benedict, Alex
A Talent for War - Jack McDevitt *s* 3016

Benson, Jack
Shadow Twin - Dale Hoover *h* 2201

Bernard, Rolf
The Gatekeepers - Daniel Graham Jr. *s* 1845

Bey, Friedlander
The Exile Kiss - George Alec Effinger *s* 1406
A Fire in the Sun - George Alec Effinger *s* 1407

Bickerstaff, Robert Luther
Terraplane - Jack Womack *s* 4749

Big Tom
The Dream Vessel - Jeff Bredenberg *s* 544

Blaise, Adrian
Devil's Gate - Elizabeth Ergas *h* 1473

Blake, Werner
The Bridge - John Skipp *h* 4055

Blueshell
A Fire upon the Deep - Vernor Vinge *s* 4441

Bondy
War With the Newts - Karel Capek *s* 710

Boone, Hank
Angel Kiss - Kelley Wilde *h* 4618

Borden, Andrew
Lizzie Borden - Elizabeth Engstrom *h* 1466

Braccalese, Gianni
A Wizard in Mind - Christopher Stasheff *s* 4173

Brody, Aloysius
Pallas - L. Neil Smith *s* 4093

Brown, Pellimore "Pell"
Out of This World - Lawrence Watt-Evans *f* 4501

Bury, Horace Hussein
The Gripping Hand - Larry Niven *s* 3281

Calais, Lucien
Private Demons - Robert Masello *h* 2909

Cantemir, George
The Venom Trees of Sunga - L. Sprague de Camp *s* 1145

Capuela, Giacomo
The Unborn - Andrew Laurance *h* 2668

Carpenter, Gary
Last Rites - David Darke *h* 1094

Cavanagh, Stewart
Conqueror's Pride - Timothy Zahn *s* 4824

Center, Fisk
Hard Sell - Piers Anthony *s* 142

Chase, Jason
Night's Pawn - Tom Dowd *s* 1284

Chen, Tam
Phoenix Fire - Elizabeth Forrest *f* 1586

Chrestil, Damian
Burning Bright - Melissa Scott *s* 3909

Claiborne, Adam
Sacred Prey - Vivian Schilling *h* 3900

Clayborne, Martin
Darkman #2: The Price of Fear - Randall Boyll *h* 503

Claypoole, Chester "Chet" W.
Live From Golgotha: A Novel - Gore Vidal *s* 4438

Colletti, Vince
Torments - Lisa Cantrell *h* 709

Collins, Henry
The Sweetheart Season - Karen Joy Fowler *f* 1629

Corman, Brian
The Gifted - Jack Caravela *h* 714

Cross, Tom
Greenhouse - Thomas A. Easton *s* 1381

Croyd
Megalomania - Ian Wallace *s* 4478

Dale, Ambrose
The Night Inside - Nancy Baker *h* 252

Dane, Richard
Cold in July - Joe R. Lansdale *h* 2644

Danilov, Barron
This Dark Paradise - Wendy Haley *h* 1998

Dartson, Michael
The Premonition - Andrew Laurance *h* 2667

Dellhart, Jackson
Something Out There - Ronald Kelly *h* 2437

DeSalvo, Vincent
Shades of Night - Rick Hautala *h* 2087

DeWitt, Willard "Jeremy Schneider"
Lunar Descent - Allen Steele *s* 4184

Dibbler, Cut-Me-Own-Throat
Moving Pictures - Terry Pratchett *f* 3505

Digonness, Peter
The Expediter - J. Brian Clarke *s* 855

Donaldson, Larry
Mind Stealer - Lee Duigon *h* 1347

Doyle, Vernon
Harrowgate - Daniel H. Gower *h* 1838

Dryden, Thatcher
Heathern - Jack Womack *s* 4747

Dryke, Mikhail
The Quiet Pools - Michael P. Kube-McDowell *s* 2583

Dunham, Arthur "Art"
The Rebirth of Wonder - Lawrence Watt-Evans *f* 4502

Dutton, Brian
The 7th Guest - Matthew J. Costello *h* 963

Eberhardt, Johann
Bright Messengers - Gentry Lee *s* 2701

Edwards, Drake
The Immortals - Andrew Neiderman *h* 3254

Elives, S.H.
Jennifer Murdley's Toad - Bruce Coville *f* 990

Errenthorp, Reynaldo
The Third Eagle: Lessons Along a Minor String - R.A. MacAvoy *s* 2848

Evanston, Livermore
Hunter's Planet - David Bischoff *s* 399

Farrell, Simon
Homecoming - Matthew J. Costello *h* 969

Feldman, Jake
Pelts - F. Paul Wilson *h* 4690

Feldspar
The Chosen - Edward Lee *h* 2695

Flannagan, James
Diary of a Vampire - Gary Bowen *h* 492

Fraser, Edward
Dark Silence - Rick Hautala *h* 2081

Freeborn, Silas
Nocturnas - Shawn Ryan *h* 3801

Froister, Albert
The Magic Touch - Jody Lynn Nye *f* 3323

Frost, Jonathan
Morningstar - Peter Atkins *h* 223

Gaunt, Leland
Needful Things - Stephen King *h* 2490

Goebbels, Joseph "Joseph Gable"
The Resurrections - Simon Louvish *s* 2805

Gordon, Winston
Mina - Marie Kiraly *h* 2503

Grenier, Roger
Viper - Alan Riefe *h* 3666

Gunn
Primavera - Francesca Lia Block *f* 449

Gunn, Sam
Sam Gunn, Unlimited - Ben Bova *s* 486

Guthrie, Anson
Harvest of Stars - Poul Anderson *s* 105

Hammersmidt, Garry
Yesterday's Pawn - W.T. Quick *s* 3550

Hammond, John
Jurassic Park - Michael Crichton *s* 1018

Hayaka, Reyna
Wild Magic - Jo Clayton *f* 864

Hayden, Conek
Backblast - Lee McKeone *s* 3050
The Clone Crisis - Lee McKeone *s* 3051
Starfire Down - Lee McKeone *s* 3052

Hayes, Charlie
Death Channels - Robert E. Vardeman *h* 4433

Heikki, Galler
Mighty Good Road - Melissa Scott *s* 3911

Holdman, Taylor
Near Dead - Stephen R. George *h* 1768

Hunter, Harold "Randy" Randolph
Timemaster - Robert L. Forward *s* 1598

Hunter, Max
Blood Secrets - Karen E. Taylor *h* 4313

Ingersol, William "Bogey"
Top Dog - Jerry Jay Carroll *f* 741

Kane, Chandler
Order of the Arrow - Michael T. Hinkemeyer *h* 2147

Kean, Michael
Legends Reborn - Kenneth C. Flint *f* 1575

Kennet, Spencer
Monsoon - Peter L. Rice *s* 3660

Khat
City of Bones - Martha Wells *f* 4581

Kinner's Son, Kensher
The Blood of a Dragon - Lawrence Watt-Evans *f* 4496

Klein, Lance
Night Relics - James P. Blaylock *h* 423

Kline, Felix
Sepulchre - James Herbert *h* 2133

Knight, Campbell
Seeing Eye - Jack Ellis *h* 1428

Lamont, Roger
Dead Voices - Abigail McDaniels *h* 3011

Land, Garrett
Demon Within - Dana Reed *h* 3589

Lang, Edward Winslow
Sheltered Lives - Charles Oberndorf *s* 3335

Larice, Aldin
The Napoleon Wager - William R. Forstchen *s* 1589

Larken, Ray
Cry Wolf - Kenneth Von Gunden *s* 4451
Under Fire - Kenneth Von Gunden *s* 4454

Leech, Derek
The Quorum - Kim Newman   *h*   3263

Leon
The Immortals - Andrew Neiderman   *h*   3254

Liston, Mark
Soulcatchers - Jan Lara   *h*   2654

Mackinnon, Curtis
Kalimantan - Lucius Shepard   *h*   3972

Maclemmon, Howmaster
668: The Neighbor of the Beast - Lionel
Fenn   *h*   1541

Magnus, Dominic "Dom"
Partisan - S. Andrew Swann   *s*   4276
Profiteer - S. Andrew Swann   *s*   4277
Revolutionary - S. Andrew Swann   *s*   4278

Matsuda
The Bushido Incident - Betty Anne
Crawford   *s*   1011

Matsudaira, Daisuke
Fire in a Faraway Place - Robert Frezza   *s*   1649

Maury, Paul
Whiteout - Sage Walker   *s*   4477

May, Carl
The Cloning of Joanna May - Fay Weldon   *s*   4568

McCord, Bob
Darkscope - Margaret Falk   *h*   1495

Merrick, Geoffrey Robert
Fear Itself - Ric Meyers   *h*   3092
Living Hell - Ric Meyers   *h*   3093
Worst Nightmare - Ric Meyers   *h*   3094

Mike
Dark Legacy - Mark A. Kostrubula   *h*   2559

Mobarak, Cyrus "Torquemada"
Cold as Ice - Charles Sheffield   *s*   3950

Mondesir, Carmen
Vodoun - David Madsen   *h*   2865

Moreson, Joe
65mm - Dale Hoover   *h*   2200

Morgan, Richard
Dark Dreaming - Pat Franklin   *h*   1639

Morris, Dwight
Penance - Rick R. Reed   *h*   3591

Myburgh, Gerrit
Apartheid, Superstrings, and Mordecai Thubana -
Michael Bishop   *s*   401

Narman, Bart
The Curse - John Tigges   *h*   4364

Needham, Bill
Kane - Douglas Borton   *h*   472

Ngu, Emerson
Pallas - L. Neil Smith   *s*   4093

Norman
Human Resources - Floyd Kemske   *h*   2438

O'Brien, Mike
Out There in the Darkness - Ed Gorman   *h*   1828

Offenhouse, Ralph
Debtors' Planet - William R. Thompson   *s*   4355

O'Hara, Sonny
Torments - Lisa Cantrell   *h*   709

Orchard, Jack
The Count of Eleven - Ramsey Campbell   *h*   694

Orr, Carnaby
Where the Ships Die - William C. Dietz   *s*   1254

Owain, David
The Long Lost - Ramsey Campbell   *h*   699

Patton, Dan
Dangerous Nature - T.J. Kirby   *h*   2504

Peter
Bones - Joyce Thompson   *h*   4351

Pomeroy, Bernard
Night Relics - James P. Blaylock   *h*   423

Presteign
The Stars My Destination - Alfred Bester   *s*   389

Price, Timothy
American Psycho - Brett Easton Ellis   *h*   1425

Profitt, Dennis
Star Precinct - Kevin D. Randle   *s*   3564

Quinn, Roger
A Calculated Magic - Robert Weinberg   *f*   4540

Randolph, Dan
Empire Builders - Ben Bova   *s*   479

Reed, Jack
Walkers - Graham Masterton   *h*   2927

Reich, Ben
The Demolished Man - Alfred Bester   *s*   388

Reid, Nicholas
The Cipher - Kathe Koja   *h*   2541

Remillard, Rogatien
Diamond Mask: A Novel - Julian May   *s*   2941

Rice, Sheldon
Thrill - Patricia Wallace   *h*   4481

Riddell, Lester
Lunar Descent - Allen Steele   *s*   4184

Risinger, Werner
Oktober - Stephen Gallagher   *h*   1698

Rory
The Hellbound Heart - Clive Barker   *h*   287

Ryan, Steve
Blood Feud - Sam Siciliano   *h*   4005

Sanderson, Paul
Wolf and Iron - Gordon R. Dickson   *s*   1242

Sandoval, Rho
Heads - Greg Bear   *s*   343

Schroeder, Thomas
Psychomech - Brian Lumley   *h*   2834

Scopes, Brent
Mount Dragon - Douglas Preston   *h*   3520

Sinbad the Sailor
The Last Voyage of Somebody the Sailor - John
Barth   *f*   312
The Other Sinbad - Craig Shaw Gardner   *f*   1713

Sinclair, Graham Kuan
Red Genesis - S.C. Sykes   *s*   4287

Solomon, Neil
Out There in the Darkness - Ed Gorman   *h*   1828

Solomon, Parker
Dark Tide - Elizabeth Forrest   *h*   1584

Southerland, John
A Matter of Taste - Fred Saberhagen   *h*   3814

Spear, James
Deathwalker - Patrick Whalen   *h*   4596

Spoor, Baron Malcolm
The Living One - Lewis Gannett   *h*   1700

Statler, Phil
The Fear in Yesterday's Rings - George C.
Chesbro   *h*   818

Stavenger, Paul
Moonrise - Ben Bova   *s*   482

Stewart, Dalton
Jupiter's Daughter - Tom Hyman   *s*   2247

Stone, David
Sati - Christopher Pike   *f*   3449

Stone, Philip
Psychamok - Brian Lumley   *h*   2833

Stout, Wellington "Bill" Nelson
Humpty Dumpty: An Oval - Damon Knight   *s*   2533

Sword, Galen
Nightfeeder - Judith Reeves-Stevens   *f*   3601
Shifter - Judith Reeves-Stevens   *f*   3603

Tatian, Mhyre
Shadow Man - Melissa Scott   *s*   3914

Taylor, Lance
Dark Legacy - Mark A. Kostrubula   *h*   2559

Thompson, Drew
Virus - Graham Watkins   *h*   4488

Trent, Vernor Deacon
Children of the Night - Dan Simmons   *h*   4029

Trosper, Carl
Greely's Cove - John Gideon   *h*   1784

Trumbo, Byron
Fires of Eden - Dan Simmons   *h*   4032

Tucker, Elton
Where the Chill Waits - T. Chris
Martindale   *h*   2907

Verner, Samuel
Shadowrun: Never Deal with a Dragon - Robert N.
Charrette   *s*   792

Wade, Zach
A Reasonable Madness - Fran Dorf   *h*   1276

Widdick, Robert
Retro Lives - Lee Grimes   *s*   1958

Wilhoit, Steve
Where the Chill Waits - T. Chris
Martindale   *h*   2907

Winters, Franklin Evelyn
Dreamer - Daniel Quinn   *h*   3551

Wrasselty, Slith
The Wells of Phyre - L. Warren Douglas   *s*   1282

Zandro, Taverik
Hawk's Flight - Carol Chase   *f*   794

BUSINESSWOMAN

Amij, Katherine
Changeling - Christopher Kubasik   *f*   2579

Aronson, Susan
Phoenix Fire - Elizabeth Forrest   *f*   1586

Banks, Monica
Carol for Another Christmas - Elizabeth Ann
Scarborough   *f*   3888

Banks, Sally "Sal"
Mistwalker - Denise Lopez Heald   *s*   2109

Bernard, Cynthia
The Gatekeepers - Daniel Graham Jr.   *s*   1845

Borg, Jocasta
The Specialist - Wynne Whiteford   *s*   4611

Brewster
The Witch of Maple Park - Stephanie S.
Tolan   *f*   4370

Brighton, Cassandra Lane "Casey"
Kiss of the Vampire - Lee Weathersby   *h*   4511

Cafferty, Megan
Jade Darcy and the Zen Pirates - Stephen
Goldin   *s*   1812

Caiper, Watly
Short Blade - Peter R. Emshwiller   *s*   1461

Calderon, Mercedes
Solip: System - Walter Jon Williams   *s*   4652

Granville, Gabby
Bloody Valentine - Stephen R. George   *h* 1763

Graves, Sara
Dark Lullaby - Jessica Palmer   *h* 3377

Graves, Shelley
Dark Lullaby - Jessica Palmer   *h* 3377

Gray, Emma
Flying in Place - Susan Palwick   *h* 3380

Gregory, Joely
Ghost Boy - Jean Simon   *h* 4041

Grissom, Sarah
Mercy's Mill - Betty Levin   *f* 2738

Guillory, Terry
Gnelfs - Sidney Williams   *h* 4638

Hadfield, Felicity Jane
Viper - Alan Riefe   *h* 3666

Halkin, Edward
Prophecy - Peter James   *h* 2291

Hardison, Pete
Let There Be Dark - Allen Lee Harris   *h* 2043

Harris, Billy
Ghost Light - Rick Hautala   *h* 2083

Harris, Derek
Wake Up Screaming - Vincent Courtney   *h* 986

Harry
The Cormorant - Stephen Gregory   *h* 1943

Hart, Marcel
The Dark One - Guy N. Smith   *h* 4082

Hawkins, Danny
A Thunder on Neptune - Gordon Eklund   *s* 1418

Hazzard, Matt
Rough Beast - Gary Goshgarian   *h* 1833

Henderson, Dawn
The Forever Children - Eric Flanders   *h* 1566

Henkin, Paul
Mysteries of the Word - Stanley Wiater   *h* 4616

Horton, Holly
Althea - Abigail McDaniels   *h* 3010

Jackson, Beauregard
Never Land - Douglas Clegg   *h* 871

Jahdo
Days of Blood and Fire - Katharine Kerr   *f* 2444

Jerod
The Wild Hunt - Jane Yolen   *f* 4816

Joanna
The Time Tree - Enid Richemont   *f* 3662

Joaquim, Leo
The Night of the Moonbow - Thomas Tryon   *h* 4377

Jones, Guinevere
The Witch House - Norma Tadlock Johnson   *f* 2329

Jordan, Megan
Wind Chimes - R.R. Walters   *h* 4482

Jordon
Sexing the Cherry - Jeanette Winterson   *f* 4719

Kaye, Darbi
Chiller - Randall Boyll   *h* 500

Ketter, Jon
Lot Lizards - Ray Garton   *h* 1726

King, Greta
The Place - T.M. Wright   *h* 4777

Kirtha
Mind of the Magic - Holly Lisle   *f* 2769

Knight, Joshua
Escardy Gap - Peter Crowther   *h* 1039

Kostanuik, April
Torment - Stephen R. George   *h* 1770

Laine, Evan
Nightscape - Stephen R. George   *h* 1769

Lamb, Toby
The Haunting of Lamb House - Joan Aiken   *h* 35

Liddell, Alice Pleasance
Automated Alice - Jeff Noon   *f* 3292

Lissette
Cursed Be the Child - Mort Castle   *h* 760

Lixandashkya, Megan
Shadow's Daughter - Shirley Meier   *f* 3084

Longchamp, Jimmy
Dawn - V.C. Andrews   *h* 120

Louise, Zoe
Stonewords: A Ghost Story - Pam Conrad   *f* 917

Lumbaird, Fran
The Black Carousel - Charles L. Grant   *h* 1846

MacCallum, Josh
Shadows - John Saul   *h* 3878

Mackenson, Cory
Boy's Life - Robert R. McCammon   *h* 2987

Madison, Thaddie
Bloodlines - J.N. Williamson   *h* 4660

Magruder, Bernie
Bernie and the Bessledorf Ghost - Phyllis Reynolds Naylor   *f* 3248

Mallory
My Stepfather Shrank! - Barbara Dillon   *s* 1258

Margaret
R-T, Margaret, and the Rats of NIMH - Jane Leslie Conly   *f* 913

Margison, Danny
Kids - Trevor Hoyle   *h* 2221

Marshall, Olivia
Seeds of Evil - Margaret Bingley   *h* 398

Marshall, Orlando
Seeds of Evil - Margaret Bingley   *h* 398

Martin, Marty
Goblins - Vincent Courtney   *h* 983

Martin, Wade
Blood Wings - Stephen Gresham   *h* 1944

Martin, Worth
Shaman Woods - Morgan Fields   *h* 1554

Martinez, Freddy
Vampire Breath - R.L. Stine   *h* 4221

Matheson, Tad
Blood Brothers - T. Lucien Wright   *h* 4770

Matsika, Tendai
The Ear, the Eye, and the Arm - Nancy Farmer   *f* 1500

Matthew
The End of Alice - A.M. Homes   *h* 2197

McBride, Duane
Summer of Night - Dan Simmons   *h* 4038

McCade, Molly
McCade's Bounty - William C. Dietz   *s* 1252

McCall, Jess
Black Ice - Pat Graversen   *h* 1869

McDowell, William Scott
Sweet William - Jessica Palmer   *h* 3379

McGarvey, Toby
Winter Moon - Dean R. Koontz   *h* 2558

McKay, David
Brainstorm - Steven M. Krauzer   *h* 2569

McKibben, Brion
Whisper - Raymond Van Over   *h* 4416

Melnik, Claudi
Down the Stream of Stars - Jeffrey A. Carver   *s* 751

Melvin
Borgel - Daniel Manus Pinkwater   *f* 3456

Merlin
Passager - Jane Yolen   *f* 4813

Metcalf, Charlotte
Whispers in the Dark - Jonathan Aycliffe   *h* 239

Michael
Gypsies - Robert Charles Wilson   *s* 4702

Mikel, Chris
Blind Hunger - David Darke   *h* 1092

Miles, Karen
Speak to the Rain - Helen K. Passey   *h* 3392

Minnie "Miin"
Shame of Man - Piers Anthony   *s* 155

Molly
Blue Moon - Hila Feil   *f* 1528

Monroe, Sumter
Never Land - Douglas Clegg   *h* 871

Morley, Lynn
The Witch Returns - Phyllis Reynolds Naylor   *f* 3249
The Witch's Eye - Phyllis Reynolds Naylor   *f* 3250

Morrison, Jessie Mae
The Hunted - Kathryn Ptacek   *h* 3542

Nafai
The Memory of Earth - Orson Scott Card   *s* 725

Neary, Billy
Billy - Whitley Strieber   *h* 4258

Nellodee "Nell"
The Diamond Age - Neal Stephenson   *s* 4190

Nhamo
A Girl Named Disaster - Nancy Farmer   *f* 1501

Night, Kevin
The Monastery - J.N. Williamson   *h* 4664

Noonan, Owen
Travel Far, Pay No Fare - Anne Lindbergh   *f* 2757

Nugent, Philip
The Butcher Boy - Patrick McCabe   *h* 2957

Ollie
No Kidding - Bruce Brooks   *s* 579

Omri
The Secret of the Indian - Lynne Reid Banks   *f* 279

Orchard, Laura
The Count of Eleven - Ramsey Campbell   *h* 694

O'Rourke, Mike
Summer of Night - Dan Simmons   *h* 4038

Parsley
Travel Far, Pay No Fare - Anne Lindbergh   *f* 2757

Pauling, Addy
Lullaby - Diane Guest   *h* 1966

Pearce, Sarah
The Ghost Inside the Monitor - Margaret J. Anderson   *f* 101

Petersen, Tad
The Children's Hour - Douglas Clegg   *h* 868

Polijn
A Wild Dog and Lone - Dan Crawford   *f* 1014

Popsy
Shadow Walkers - Nina Romberg   *h* 3734

CHILD-CARE GIVER

CHIMNEYSWEEP

CIVIL SERVANT

CLERK

Relkin
Battledragon - Christopher Rowley *f* 3756
Bazil Broketail - Christopher Rowley *f* 3757
Dragons of War - Christopher Rowley *f* 3758
A Sword for a Dragon - Christopher Rowley *f* 3760

Spike
The Zork Chronicles - George Alec Effinger *s* 1410

Stephen
Hunter's Death - Michelle West *f* 4588

Steven
Hunter's Oath - Michelle West *f* 4589

Tale Teller
Tatham Mound - Piers Anthony *f* 157

Talisen
Hero's Song - Edith Pattou *f* 3393

Tobinson, Ian
A Wizard in Absentia - Christopher Stasheff *s* 4172

Tyrian
A College of Magics - Caroline Stevermer *f* 4201

COMPOSER

Carson, Doug
Darkside - Dennis Etchison *h* 1485

Dulac, Will
A Call to Arms - Alan Dean Foster *s* 1601

Mozart, Wolfgang Amadeus
I, Vampire - Michael Romkey *h* 3736

Pope, Justin
Mixed Doubles - Daniel Da Cruz *s* 1057

COMPUTER

Angelus, Lucifer "Luke"
Chains of Light - Quentin Thomas *s* 4347

Holly
Red Dwarf: Infinity Welcomes Careful Drivers - Grant Naylor *s* 3247

JASON
Golden Fleece - Robert J. Sawyer *s* 3886

MEQMAT
The Schizogenic Man - Raymond Harris *s* 2048

Sumbaa
The Kalif's War - John Dalmas *s* 1068

Thing
Truckers - Terry Pratchett *s* 3509
Wings - Terry Pratchett *s* 3510

Xa
The Fugitive Worlds - Bob Shaw *s* 3946

XB223
The Red Tape War - Jack L. Chalker *s* 777

COMPUTER EXPERT

Abalone
Brother to Dragons, Companion to Owls - Jane M. Lindskold *f* 2762

Augustine, Alexa
Dream of Glass - Jean Mark Gawron *s* 1734

Avery, David "Derec"
Maverick - Bruce Bethke *s* 393

Bathespeake, Jason
ME: A Novel of Self Discovery - Thomas T. Thomas *s* 4350

Battacharia, Rustum "Bat"
The Ganymede Club - Charles Sheffield *s* 3953

Bonivard, Francois
Wildlife - James Patrick Kelly *s* 2430

Boxletter, Bob
Duplicates - Andrew Neiderman *h* 3253

Brandsetter, Earl
Lethal Interface - Mel Odom *s* 3338

Brompton, Arnold
Virtual Girl - Amy Thomson *s* 4358

Brown, Kelsie
65mm - Dale Hoover *h* 2200

Burroughs, Jack "MAX—KOOL"
Headcrash - Bruce Bethke *s* 392

Busch, Zachary
Drawing Blood - Poppy Z. Brite *h* 568

Callahan-Finn, Mary
Callahan's Legacy - Spider Robinson *s* 3714

Calvin, Susan
I, Robot: The Illustrated Screenplay - Harlan Ellison *s* 1432

Cannon, Vassily "Bass" James
A Plague of Change - L. Warren Douglas *s* 1280

Carless, India "Trouble"
Trouble and Her Friends - Melissa Scott *s* 3915

Castanaveras, Trent
The Long Run - Daniel Keys Moran *s* 3178

Cerise
Trouble and Her Friends - Melissa Scott *s* 3915

Chen, David
Chimera - Mary Rosenblum *s* 3746

Cobri, Alex
Grounded! - Chris Claremont *s* 840

Conlick, Dennis "Tunnel Rat"
The Hacker - Chet Day *h* 1135

Corrigan, Joe
Realtime Interrupt - James P. Hogan *s* 2179

Cotton, Alex
Brethren - Shawn Ryan *h* 3800

Craig, Donald
The Ghost From the Grand Banks - Arthur C. Clarke *s* 849

Cy BerPunk
Planet of the Robot Slaves - Harry Harrison *s* 2058

Delaney, Brian
The Turing Option - Harry Harrison *s* 2063

Deluca, Maria
Permutation City - Greg Egan *s* 1414

Demogorgon
Iris - William Barton *s* 317

Deveaux, Jacques
City of Pain - John Terra *f* 4341

DeWitt, Willard "Jeremy Schneider"
Lunar Descent - Allen Steele *s* 4184

Dittrich, Robert "Bobby"
Forests of the Night - S. Andrew Swann *s* 4275

Dodger
Choose Your Enemies Carefully - Robert N. Charrette *s* 786
Find Your Own Truth - Robert N. Charrette *f* 787
Shadowrun: Never Deal with a Dragon - Robert N. Charrette *s* 792

Dooley, Paul
The Tranquility Alternative - Allen Steele *s* 4187

Durham, Paul
Permutation City - Greg Egan *s* 1414

Esterbrook, Diana
The Higher Space - Jamil Nasir *s* 3241

Fears, Quentin
Treasure Box - Orson Scott Card *h* 729

Ferguson, Herman D. "Fergie"
Judge Dredd - Neal Barrett Jr. *s* 306

Flander
Chimera - Mary Rosenblum *s* 3746

Flannery, Eric
Caverns of Socrates - Dennis L. McKiernan *f* 3053

Fletcher, Step
Lost Boys - Orson Scott Card *f* 722

Francy, Lizzie
Beggars Ride - Nancy Kress *s* 2575

Gale, Denton
Mother Lode - Zach Hughes *s* 2240

Game Cat
Vurt - Jeff Noon *s* 3294

Gobi, Frank
Rim: A Novel of Virtual Reality - Alexander Besher *s* 387

Gonzales, Mikhail Mikhailovitch
Halo - Tom Maddox *s* 2864

Grant
MagicNet - John DeChancie *f* 1181

Grant, John
Spook Night - David Robbins *h* 3680

Grant, Spencer
Dark Rivers of the Heart - Dean R. Koontz *h* 2547

Grillo, Nathan
Everville - Clive Barker *h* 284

Halbard, Amy
Offspring - Jack Ketchum *h* 2461

Hanson, Robert
Probe - Edward M. Lerner *s* 2733

Hartley, Sherrine
Fallen Angels - Larry Niven *s* 3279

Hedison, Marianne
Terminal Games - Cole Perriman *s* 3411

Hernandes y Jons, Rico
Palace - Katharine Kerr *s* 2448

Heywood, Diana
Halo - Tom Maddox *s* 2864

Hillerman, Walter "Walt"
Lady El - Jim Starlin *s* 4157

Hochstader, Jeremy
Castle War! - John DeChancie *s* 1175

I
Hard-Boiled Wonderland and the End of the World - Haruki Murakami *s* 3223

Jaffey
Zeta Base - Judith Alguire *s* 60

Jaimie
Second Contact - Mike Resnick *s* 3636

James, Zack
Blood Work - Fay Zachary *h* 4823

Joanna
Dog Wizard - Barbara Hambly *f* 2005

Jones, Lloyd Merlin
MagicNet - John DeChancie *f* 1181

Juillerat, Sister Chantal
Demon Download - Jack Yeovil *f* 4799

Justin, Rangsey
Night Sky Mine - Melissa Scott *s* 3912

Kerickson, Arvid Gerald
The Imperium Game - K.D. Wentworth *s* 4585

King, Elena "Lanie"
Richter 10 - Arthur C. Clarke *s* 853

Lacey, Bobbie
Polar City Blues - Katharine Kerr s 2449

Le Roux, Reiki Momoku
Marooned on Eden - Robert L. Forward s 1593

LeMat, Joseph "Gunnar Savage"
Headcrash - Bruce Bethke s 392

Lesserac, Gary
Virtual Destruction - Kevin J. Anderson s 98

Leving, Fredda
Caliban - Roger MacBride Allen s 63

Lioe, Quin
Burning Bright - Melissa Scott s 3909

Lippman, Lenore
The Eighth Rank - David D. Ross s 3751

Lovell, Willa
Judgment Day - G. Harry Stine s 4214

Lu, Curtis
Carol for Another Christmas - Elizabeth Ann
Scarborough f 3888

Maddox, Cory
The Cybernetic Walrus - Jack L. Chalker s 770
The March Hare Network - Jack L. Chalker s 775

Major, Cyrus "Cy" Lance
Zeus and Co. - David Lee Jones f 2344

Marden, Jake
Prison Ship - Martin Caidin s 676

Mark
See You Later - Christopher Pike f 3451

Maxon, Alice
Caverns of Socrates - Dennis L. McKiernan f 3053

Mbele, Miriam Makepeace
Red Dust - Paul J. McAuley s 2956

McHogue
Warped - K.W. Jeter s 2324

McTurk, Felix
Kaduna Memories - Jack McKinney s 3068

Mendez, Sofia
The Sparrow - Mary Doria Russell s 3789

Messenger, Joe
Host - Peter James h 2289

Michaelson, Hal
Virtual Destruction - Kevin J. Anderson s 98

Milena "Alfred Russell Wallace"
Fairyland - Paul J. McAuley s 2953

Mitexi, Meredalia
Dreamships - Melissa Scott s 3910

Muhammed, Sarkar
The Terminal Experiment - Robert J.
Sawyer s 3887

Munn, Alex
The Shift - George Foy s 1632

Nolan, Carly
Cyberweb - Lisa Mason s 2911

O'Kelly, Manuel "Mannie"
The Moon Is a Harsh Mistress - Robert A.
Heinlein s 2113

Olam, Thomas "Tom" Edward
From Prussia with Love - John DeChancie f 1177

Orchard, Julia
The Count of Eleven - Ramsey Campbell h 694

Ozzie
Dreams of Gods and Men - W.T. Quick s 3548

Patrick, Uncle
Under Siege - Elisabeth Mace f 2852

Pearce, Sarah
The Ghost Inside the Monitor - Margaret J.
Anderson f 101

Pharbeque, Riscky "Hex DEF6"
The Hacker and the Ants - Rudy Rucker s 3765

Phreak
Killobyte - Piers Anthony f 147

Pincus, Laurie
The Sherwood Game - Esther Friesner s 1676

Porter, Rand
Starmind - Spider Robinson s 3716

Pr. Spinner
Cyberweb - Lisa Mason s 2911

Protagonist, Hiro
Snow Crash - Neal Stephenson s 4191

Putakin, Yuri
Orion's Dagger - P.K. McAllister s 2950

Ransome, Illario "Ambidexter"
Burning Bright - Melissa Scott s 3909

Ridenour, Stephen
Ground-Ties - Jane S. Fancher s 1496
Harmonies of the 'Net - Jane S. Fancher s 1497
Uplink - Jane S. Fancher s 1499

Riley, Michael
The Deus Machine - Pierre Ouellette h 3373

Rowan, Dalin
The Knights of the Black Earth - Margaret
Weis s 4561

Rugby, Jerzy
The Hacker and the Ants - Rudy Rucker s 3765

Sanders, Phillipe "Phil" Montoya
The Modular Man - Roger MacBride Allen s 65

Santorini, Dan
Death Dream - Ben Bova s 478

Selden, Penelope
The Whims of Creation - Simon Hawke s 2100

Sherwood, Carl
The Sherwood Game - Esther Friesner s 1676

Shipman, Shira
He, She and It - Marge Piercy s 3445

Smith, Brandon
Virtual Girl - Amy Thomson s 4358

Smith, Edward
The Nightmare People - Lawrence Watt-
Evans h 4499

Smith, Jonathan Wesley
Harmonies of the 'Net - Jane S. Fancher s 1497
Uplink - Jane S. Fancher s 1499

Spango, Hypatia
Montezuma Strip - Alan Dean Foster s 1614

Spear, James
Deathwalker - Patrick Whalen h 4596

Spring, Juliet
Host - Peter James h 2289

Stewart, Janet
Zeus and Co. - David Lee Jones f 2344

Sturgis, Wally
The Shattered Sphere - Roger MacBride Allen s 67

Succubus
The Hacker - Chet Day h 1135

Tarasov, Sein
Night Sky Mine - Melissa Scott s 3912

Templeton, Judith
The Shadow Gate - Margaret Ball f 267

Tenere, Jared
Voices of Hope - David Feintuch s 1532

Tetsami, Kari
Partisan - S. Andrew Swann s 4276
Profiteer - S. Andrew Swann s 4277
Revolutionary - S. Andrew Swann s 4278

Thomas, Signy
Whiteout - Sage Walker s 4477

Thyme, Jordan "Antiquity"
Zeta Base - Judith Alguire s 60

Tobin, G. Patrick "Toby"
Angel Light - Andrew M. Greeley f 1877

Tower, Josh
Systems - W.T. Quick s 3549

van Liesvelt, Butch
Trouble and Her Friends - Melissa Scott s 3915

Vanelli, MONDO
How to Mutate and Take Over the World - R.U.
Sirius s 4050

Velis, Catherine
The Eight - Katherine Neville f 3258

Victor
See You Later - Christopher Pike f 3451

Wolenczak, Lucas
seaQuest DSV: Fire Below - Matthew J.
Costello s 972

Young, Francesca
Streets of Blood - Carl Sargent f 3860

Zumwalt, William Irving "Wiz"
The Wizardry Consulted - Rick Cook f 936
The Wizardry Cursed - Rick Cook f 937
The Wizardry Quested - Rick Cook f 938

COMPUTER GAME PLAYER

Metullus, Amaelia
The Imperium Game - K.D. Wentworth s 4585

CON ARTIST

Jackson, Skeeter
Wagers of Sin - Robert Asprin s 222

Jacobs, Earl
Less than Human - Gary L. Raisor h 3558

Nashram, Mika
By the Sword - Greg Costikyan f 978

Slakey, Justin
The Stainless Steel Rat Goes to Hell - Harry
Harrison s 2059

Warrick, John
Less than Human - Gary L. Raisor h 3558

CONSTRUCTION WORKER

Anderson, Ted
Darkness - John Saul h 3874

Barton, Roy
The Paper Grail - James P. Blaylock f 424

Botts, Wendell
Oaths and Miracles - Nancy Kress s 2577

Bruce, Virgin
Orbital Decay - Allen Steele s 4185

Hooker, Popeye
Orbital Decay - Allen Steele s 4185

Kubick, Ruby
Glass Houses - Laura J. Mixon s 3126

Quail, Douglas
Total Recall - Piers Anthony s 159

Salisaw, Brent
Night Thunder - Ruby Jean Jensen h 2313

Schoenwald, Robert
Shadow Dance - Jessica Palmer h 3378

Stranger, John
Run for the Stars/Echoes of Thunder - Harlan Ellison s 1435

Thubana, Mordecai
Apartheid, Superstrings, and Mordecai Thubana - Michael Bishop s 401

CONSULTANT

Deckard, Rick
Blade Runner: Replicant Night - K.W. Jeter s 2316

Laney, Colin
Idoru - William Gibson s 1781

CONTRACTOR

Tullian, James
Sheep - Simon Maginn h 2866

CONVICT

Bando, Nicos
Infinity Hold - Barry B. Longyear s 2799

Cooper
In the Land of the Dead - K.W. Jeter h 2321

Darwin, Alton
Hocus Pocus or, What's the Hurry, Son? - Kurt Vonnegut Jr. s 4458

Garoit, Darrell
Infinity Hold - Barry B. Longyear s 2799

Michaels, Dean
Swamp - Peter Tremayne h 4374

Russel, Ben
Cold in July - Joe R. Lansdale h 2644

Spanning, Henry Lake
Mefisto in Onyx - Harlan Ellison h 1433

Stimpson, Nevil
Werewolf - Peter Rubie h 3764

Taylor, Lura
Dumford Blood - S.K. Epperson h 1469

Thermopyle, Angus
Forbidden Knowledge - Stephen R. Donaldson s 1269

Tuckton, Travis Clyde
Header - Edward Lee h 2699

COOK

Doyle, Irini
The Sweetheart Season - Karen Joy Fowler f 1629

Ennin, Willie
Raven - Charles L. Grant h 1854

Escargot, Theophile
The Stone Giant - James P. Blaylock f 425

Gurronsevas
The Galactic Gourmet - James White s 4603

Martin, Jiggs
The Unfinished - Jay B. Laws h 2676

Murphy, Clarence "Cookie"
Judson's Eden - Keith Laumer s 2662

Neelix
The Final Fury - Dafydd ab Hugh s 8

COUNSELOR

Alsnor, Lotta
The White Regiment - John Dalmas s 1073

Chien-Chu, Sergi
Legion of the Damned - William C. Dietz s 1249

Haas, Alexandria Victoria
Mindplayers - Pat Cadigan s 658

Hartwig, Reece
The Night of the Moonbow - Thomas Tryon h 4377

Niffy
No One Noticed the Cat - Anne McCaffrey f 2973

Roshnani
The Stolen Throne - Harry Turtledove f 4393

Sharon
Requiem - Graham Joyce h 2386

Shelby, Lissa
Shadow Man - Dennis Etchison h 1487

Tarne
Heart Readers - Kristine Kathryn Rusch f 3776

COURIER

Carey
Dun Lady's Jess - Doranna Durgin f 1368

Johnny
Johnny Mnemonic - Terry Bisson s 409

Long, Huey "Hal" Alphonse
The Trinity Vector - Steve Perry s 3425

MacColl, Enye
King of Morning, Queen of Day - Ian McDonald f 3019

COURTIER

Gibberling
Here There Be Dragons - Roger Zelazny f 4840

ibn Khairan, Ammar
The Lions of Al-Rassan - Guy Gavriel Kay f 2403

Lissa
Nobody's Son - Sean Stewart f 4208

COUSIN

Fonteyn, Oliver
Death Masque - P.N. Elrod h 1440

COWBOY

Hong, Louie
Hong on the Range - William Wu s 4781

Johnston, Virgil Wayne
The Immortals - Tracy Hickman s 2141

McBride, Michael
The Flight of Michael McBride - Midori Snyder f 4111

O'Connor, John
The Flight of Michael McBride - Midori Snyder f 4111

Redd
Red Dust - Paul J. McAuley s 2956

Stone, Charlie
Wendigo Border - Catherine Montrose h 3158

CRIMINAL

Abalone
Brother to Dragons, Companion to Owls - Jane M. Lindskold f 2762

Agenos, Mordion "the Servant"
Hexwood - Diana Wynne Jones s 2349

al-Kharif, Yasin
Bright Messengers - Gentry Lee s 2701

Alys
Dragon's Bait - Vivian Vande Velde f 4427

Anlawdd
Arthur War Lord - Dafydd ab Hugh f 5

Asado
The War of Don Emmanuel's Nether Parts - Louis de Bernieres f 1137

Auk, Maytera
Exodus From the Long Sun - Gene Wolfe s 4732

Avenger
The Spider #4: Death Reign of the Vampire King/The Pain Emperor - Grant Stockbridge f 4235

Balcher
Medallion of the Black Hound - Shirley Rousseau Murphy f 3231

Bane
Batman: Knightfall - Dennis O'Neil s 3359

Bartlett, Tony "Antonius Caelerus"
Far Edge of Darkness - Linda Evans s 1492

Bat Man
The Spider #4: Death Reign of the Vampire King/The Pain Emperor - Grant Stockbridge f 4235

Benhaddou
White Rhino - Bill Dolan s 1267

Bey, Friedlander
A Fire in the Sun - George Alec Effinger s 1407

Birdsong, Joseph "Mojo"
Mojo and the Pickle Jar - Douglas Bell f 357

Blaine, Cassandra "Cass"
Psykosis - Wilhelmina Baird s 250

Blood
Nightside the Long Sun - Gene Wolfe s 4734

Bouchette, Jean-Paul
The Suiting - Kelley Wilde h 4621

Boyle, Simon
The Illegal Rebirth of Billy the Kid - Rebecca Ore s 3364

Brooks, Connor
Ill Wind - Kevin J. Anderson s 90

Bruckner, Bill
Nomad - David Alexander s 54

Bruno, Richard
Journals of the Plague Years - Norman Spinrad s 4126

Caine, Tycho
Evil Triumphant - Michael A. Stackpole s 4149

Cantemir, George
The Venom Trees of Sunga - L. Sprague de Camp s 1145

Castlemaine, Sylvester
The Hemingway Hoax - Joe Haldeman s 1994

Che, Ya
The Spider #3: Death's Crimson Juggernaut/The Red Death Rain - Grant Stockbridge f 4234

Claiborne, Kyle
Sacred Prey - Vivian Schilling h 3900

Cobblepot, Oswald "the Penguin"
Batman Returns - Craig Shaw Gardner s 1707
The Further Adventures of Batman 2: Featuring the Penguin - Martin H. Greenberg s 1915

Cole, James
12 Monkeys - Elizabeth Hand s 2025

Coogan, Elihu "Emil Storchesson"
The Singularity Project - F.M. Busby s 641

CRITIC

Sperry, Jack
City of Truth - James Morrow s 3210

Swann, Clare
Flicker - Theodore Roszak h 3752

Tierney, Rose
The Parasite - Ramsey Campbell h 702

Vivo, Dionisio
Senor Vivo and the Coca Lord - Louis de
    Bernieres f 1136

Wright, Paul
Nightlight - Michael Cadnum h 664

CULT MEMBER

Brustein, Harvey
The Children of Hamelin - Norman Spinrad s 4124

Dwago
Graythings - Pat Graversen h 1871

Kuruk
Deathsong - Douglas Borton h 471

Patswami
Button Bright - Michael Kurland h 2584

Proctor, Simon
Dying Breath - Jon A. Harrald h 2041

Quon
The Jade Ogre - Kenneth Robeson f 3699

Thorne, Hester
Dark Channel - Ray Garton h 1725

CYBORG

Andreyeva, Maya Tayanichna
The Fortunate Fall - Raphael Carter s 750

Borg, Cy
Drifter's Run - William C. Dietz s 1246
Drifter's War - William C. Dietz s 1247

Borg, Jocasta
The Specialist - Wynne Whiteford s 4611

Cade, Hypatia "Tia"
The Ship Who Searched - Anne McCaffrey s 2982

Carialle
The Ship Errant - Jody Lynn Nye s 3327

Dawson
Warp Angel - Stuart Hopen s 2205

den Ostreicher, Jory
Man Plus - Frederik Pohl s 3464

Devreaux, Luc
Universal Soldier - Robert Tine s 4368

Evans, Juliet "Julie"
Mindstar Rising - Peter F. Hamilton s 2020

Four, Cathy
Cathy IV - Frances Lucas s 2814

Hunsucker, Willie
Gaia's Toys - Rebecca Ore s 3362

Kemra
Adiamante - L.E. Modesitt Jr. s 3127

Krokodil
Comeback Tour: The Sky Belongs to the Stars - Jack
    Yeovil s 4798

Lippman, Lenore
The Eighth Rank - David D. Ross s 3751

Magnus, Dominic "Dom"
Partisan - S. Andrew Swann s 4276
Profiteer - S. Andrew Swann s 4277
Revolutionary - S. Andrew Swann s 4278

Mendez, Marla
Prison Planet - William C. Dietz s 1253

Moliak
Down the Bright Way - Robert Reed s 3594

Montgomery, Dirk
House of the Sun - Nigel Findley s 1559

Nancia
PartnerShip - Anne McCaffrey s 2974

Pope, Eric
Black Snow Days - Claudia O'Keefe s 3350

Rosa
Correspondence - Sue Thomas s 4348

Sam
The Sounding Stillness - Kenneth Von
    Gunden s 4452

Scott, Andrew
Universal Soldier - Robert Tine s 4368

Shirley
Correspondence - Sue Thomas s 4348

SSS-900-C Simeon
The City Who Fought - Anne McCaffrey s 2961

Thermopyle, Angus
The Gap into Madness: Chaos and Order - Stephen R.
    Donaldson s 1271
The Gap into Power: A Dark and Hungry God Arises
    - Stephen R. Donaldson s 1272
The Gap into Ruin: This Day All Gods Die - Stephen
    R. Donaldson s 1273

Thorvin
Fade to Black - Nyx Smith s 4095

Torraway, Roger
Man Plus - Frederik Pohl s 3464

Voskresenye, Pavel Sergeyevich
The Fortunate Fall - Raphael Carter s 750

Xris
The Knights of the Black Earth - Margaret
    Weis s 4561

DANCER

Ann "Annai"
Shame of Man - Piers Anthony s 155

Bowen, Muffy
Greenhouse - Thomas A. Easton s 1381

Brandis, Sarah
Sick - Jay R. Bonansinga h 469

Diate, Emilio
Traitors - Kristine Kathryn Rusch f 3786

Evans, Christina
The Eyes of Darkness - Dean R. Koontz s 2549

Eve, Glennys
The Stalking Horse - Constance Ash f 184

Grandma Fifi
Baby Be-Bop - Francesca Lia Block f 444

Hispard, Michael
Skin - Kathe Koja h 2542

Innowen
Shadowdance - Robin Wayne Bailey f 245

Kelryn
The Legend of Nightfall - Mickey Zucker
    Reichert f 3608

McLeod, Morgan
Starseed - Spider Robinson s 3717

Melisande
The Widowmaker - Mike Resnick s 3640

Promise
Firedance - Steven Barnes s 301
Gorgon Child - Steven Barnes s 302

Quejaches, Xia
The Stone Garden - Mary Rosenblum s 3748

Roxanne
The Werewolf Chronicles - Traci Briery h 558

Ruquel
The Book of the Beast - Tanith Lee f 2708

Sasaki, Jay
Starmind - Spider Robinson s 3716

Tiana
Songs of the Dancing Gods - Jack L. Chalker f 780

Trusla
The Warding of Witch World - Andre
    Norton f 3316

Turner, Loraine "Phyllis"
The Werewolf Chronicles - Traci Briery h 558
Wolfsong - Traci Briery h 559

DEBUTANTE

Radineaux, Viera
Anvil of the Sun - Anne Lesley Groell f 1963

DEITY

Aditi
Blood of the Goddess - Kara Dalkey f 1066

Allic
The Crystal Sorcerers - William R.
    Forstchen f 1588

Aphrael
The Hidden City - David Eddings f 1391

Apollo
Ye Gods! - Tom Holt f 2196

Ashar
The Way Beneath - Angus Wells f 4575

Benefactor
Revenant - Louise Cooper f 951

Earth Mother
Nemesis - Louise Cooper f 950

God
Sympathy for the Devil - Holly Lisle f 2771

God "The Old Man"
The Old Man and Mr. Smith - Peter
    Ustinov f 4411

Great God Om
Small Gods - Terry Pratchett f 3507

Hera
Orion and the Conqueror - Ben Bova s 484

Jane
Children of the Mind - Orson Scott Card s 717

Katz, Julie
Only Begotten Daughter - James Morrow f 3214

Lily
Lunatics - Bradley Denton f 1205

Lloth
Siege of Darkness - R.A. Salvatore f 3844

Loki
The Spawn of Loki - Jason Henderson f 2122

Magodor
Pretty Pewter Gods - Glen Cook f 930

Malu
Children of the Mind - Orson Scott Card s 717

Maria
The Wizard at Home - Rick Shelley f 3968

Mercury
The M.D.: A Horror Story - Thomas M.
    Disch h 1260

Mikel
The Wizard at Home - Rick Shelley　*f*　3968

Minerva
Ye Gods! - Tom Holt　*f*　2196

Mohini
The Willing Spirit - Piers Anthony　*f*　161

Monigan
The Time of the Ghost - Diana Wynne
　　Jones　*f*　2352

Nodens
The Transition of Titus Crow - Brian
　　Lumley　*h*　2838

Odin
Sleipnir - Linda Evans　*f*　1493

Orfindel "Hosea Lincoln"
The Fire Duke - Joel Rosenberg　*f*　3740

Pati
Delta City - Felicity Savage　*f*　3881

Ravana
The Willing Spirit - Piers Anthony　*f*　161

Sati
Sati - Christopher Pike　*f*　3449

Schel, Daniel
The Moon's Wife: A Hystery - A.A.
　　Attanasio　*f*　228

Selinde
Kaleidoscope Eyes - Graham Watkins　*h*　4487

Silvas
The Wizard at Home - Rick Shelley　*f*　3968

Teaqua
Look into the Sun - James Patrick Kelly　*s*　2429

Thiede
The Fulfillments of Fate and Desire - Storm
　　Constantine　*s*　921

Venus
Child of the Eagle - Esther Friesner　*f*　1668

DELI WORKER

Fairfax, Lena
Black Night - S.J. Strayhorn　*h*　4255

DEMON

Adam
*Good Omens: The Nice and Accurate Prophecies of
　　Agnes Nutter, Witch* - Neil Gaiman　*f*　1693

Agonostis
Sympathy for the Devil - Holly Lisle　*f*　2771

Ambrosius, Merlinus "Myrddin/Lailoken"
The Dragon and the Unicorn - A.A.
　　Attanasio　*f*　224

Astfgl
Eric - Terry Pratchett　*f*　3499

Bargolas
The Summoned - Steven Ray Fulgham　*h*　1683

Black Dust 7, Lisa
Temporary Agency - Rachel Pollack　*f*　3474

Cardiff, Melisan
Hooray for Hellywood - Esther Friesner　*f*　1671

Catch
Practical Demonkeeping - Christopher
　　Moore　*h*　3173

Darkhorse
The Crystal Dragon - Richard A. Knaak　*f*　2517

Davos
The Itinerant Exorcist - Ashley McConnell　*f*　3006

Debauchery Devil/Torchy Burns
Strum Again? - Elizabeth Ann Scarborough　*f*　3896

Doomstalker
Doomstalker - Gary Brandner　*h*　542

Dupree, Lorelle
The New Neighbor - Ray Garton　*h*　1728

Elbub, Azzie
Bring Me the Head of Prince Charming - Roger
　　Zelazny　*f*　4834
A Farce to Be Reckoned With - Roger
　　Zelazny　*f*　4835

Frank
The Hellbound Heart - Clive Barker　*h*　287

Goranu
Little Sister - Kara Dalkey　*f*　1067

Grossclout
Roc and a Hard Place - Piers Anthony　*f*　154

Gryll
Prince of Chaos - Roger Zelazny　*f*　4844

Harrison, Nick
Freeze Frames - Katharine Kerr　*s*　2447

Hasruel
Castle in the Air - Diana Wynne Jones　*f*　2346

Iezu
Crown of Shadows - C.S. Friedman　*s*　1654

Krulshards
Palace of Kings - Mike Jefferies　*f*　2303

Lasher
The Witching Hour - Anne Rice　*h*　3657

Lucifer
The Devil and Dan Cooley - Holly Lisle　*f*　2766

Memnoch
Memnoch the Devil - Anne Rice　*h*　3651

Mentia, D.
Geis of the Gargoyle - Piers Anthony　*f*　141

Mephistopheles
If at Faust You Don't Succeed - Roger
　　Zelazny　*f*　4841

Metria "Woe Betide"
Roc and a Hard Place - Piers Anthony　*f*　154

Morgeu
The Dragon and the Unicorn - A.A.
　　Attanasio　*f*　224

Nephredann
Necrom - Mick Farren　*s*　1513

Puck
The Devil and Dan Cooley - Holly Lisle　*f*　2766

Raleel
Hooray for Hellywood - Esther Friesner　*f*　1671

Ravana
The Willing Spirit - Piers Anthony　*f*　161

Salesman
Tales From the Crypt: Demon Knight - Randall
　　Boyll　*h*　507

Santa, Levi D.
The Book of the Damned - D.A. Fowler　*h*　1623

Taws
Wrath of Ashar - Angus Wells　*f*　4577

Tyrr
Demon Blade - Mark A. Garland　*f*　1718

Valarian, Nickolai
Red Devil - David Saperstein　*h*　3855

Valcourt, Guy-Luc
Adversary - Daniel Rhodes　*h*　3648

Ware
If I Pay Thee Not in Gold - Piers Anthony　*f*　144

X "Brother Rush"
Humans - Donald E. Westlake　*f*　4595

X(A/N)ᵗʰ "Nimby"
Yon Ill Wind - Piers Anthony　*f*　162

Yaksha
The Last Vampire - Christopher Pike　*h*　3447

Ygorla
The Deceiver - Louise Cooper　*f*　948

DENTIST

Roswell, Harry I.
Summerland - L. Dean James　*f*　2282

DESIGNER

Carlisle, Bari
Count Geiger's Blues - Michael Bishop　*s*　404

Griffin, Deirdre
Bitter Blood - Karen E. Taylor　*h*　4312
Blood Secrets - Karen E. Taylor　*h*　4313
Blood Ties - Karen E. Taylor　*h*　4314

Hall, Cassandra
Thirst - Michael Cecilione　*h*　769

Holland, Susan
The Beyond - Barry Harrington　*h*　2042

Rolando
Thirst - Michael Cecilione　*h*　769

DETECTIVE

Bushell, Thomas
The Two Georges - Richard Dreyfuss　*s*　1335

Butterbaugh, C.G.
Sacrifice - John Farris　*h*　1518

Chapman, Merrick
Rulers of Darkness - Steven G. Spruill　*h*　4138

Darcy, Lord Lord
A Study in Sorcery - Michael Kurland　*f*　2585

Davies, Gabriel
Red Angel - Roxanne Longstreet　*h*　2795

Douglas, Kirk
The Book of Webster's - J.N. Williamson　*h*　4661

Dupin, C. Auguste
The Lighthouse at the End of the World - Stephen
　　Marlowe　*h*　2886

Gage, Tom
The Long Midnight - Daniel Ransom　*h*　3572

Goodlow, Sam
Goodlow's Ghosts - T.M. Wright　*h*　4775

Heiligmann, E. "Pif"
Double Jeopardy - Aaron Allston　*s*　72

Hendricks, Judson
Flesh and Blood - D.A. Fowler　*h*　1625

Hunter
Dictator - William Wu　*s*　4780
Predator - William Wu　*s*　4782
Warrior - William Wu　*s*　4784

Jenny Sixa
Circle of One - Eric James Fullilove　*s*　1685

Khuzud, Kami
Hour of the Octopus - Joel Rosenberg　*f*　3742

Krillen
Ancestor's World - A.C. Crispin　*s*　1021

Li, Master
Eight Skilled Gentlemen - Barry Hughart　*f*　2233

Lipaski, Anthony
Red Angel - Roxanne Longstreet　*h*　2795

DETECTIVE—PRIVATE

DIPLOMAT

Jennings, Richard
Darkly the Thunder - William W.
    Johnstone   h   2333

Li, Stefan
Ark Liberty - Will Bradley   s   538

Louchard, Onidi "Dinah O'Neill"
Power Play - Anne McCaffrey   s   2977

Outis, Charles "Mr. Charlie"
Solis - A.A. Attanasio   s   229

Reno
Solip: System - Walter Jon Williams   s   4652

Riemann, Thomas
Permutation City - Greg Egan   s   1414

Rimmer, Arnold J.
Red Dwarf: Infinity Welcomes Careful Drivers - Grant
    Naylor   s   3247

Sack
Land O'Goshen - Charles McNair   s   3071

Saunders, Reed "Sand"
Darkly the Thunder - William W.
    Johnstone   h   2333

Savoy
Fools - Pat Cadigan   s   657

Shadow
The Wizard's Shadow - Susan Dexter   f   1222

Zeno, Mrs.
Max Lakeman and the Beautiful Stranger - Jon
    Cohen   f   883

Zephkar
Stranded - Camarin Grae   s   1841

DIVER

Chase, J. Kelsey
Between the Devil and the Deep - J.M.
    Morgan   h   3180

Smith, Sam
World Without End - Molly Cochran   f   880

DIVORCED PERSON

Collins, Trudy
Savage Season - Joe R. Lansdale   h   2649

Darker, Alex
The Chymical Wedding - Lindsay Clarke   f   856

Dyckman, Alicia "Lish"
The Swords of Zinjaban - L. Sprague de
    Camp   s   1143

Ice
Chaos Come Again - Wilhelmina Baird   s   247

Jewell, Amy
Out of This World - Lawrence Watt-Evans   f   4501

Kerickson, Alline Bolton
The Imperium Game - K.D. Wentworth   s   4585

Kerickson, Arvid Gerald
The Imperium Game - K.D. Wentworth   s   4585

Martin, Anita
Blood Wings - Stephen Gresham   h   1944

May, Joanna
The Cloning of Joanna May - Fay Weldon   s   4568

Meyer, Elizabeth "Payne"
Dead Voices - Rick Hautala   h   2082

Reith, Fergus
The Swords of Zinjaban - L. Sprague de
    Camp   s   1143

Sinclair, Felice
The Fagin - Pat Graversen   h   1870

Soul, Derek
A Second Infinity - Michael D. Weaver   s   4513

Treadway, Jocelyn
Shadows on the Sun - Michael Jan
    Friedman   s   1664

DOCTOR

Adams, Luther
Wilderness - Dennis Danvers   h   1090

Alegretta
Outnumbering the Dead - Frederik Pohl   s   3467

Alston, Arthur
The Select - F. Paul Wilson   h   4693

Althorpe, Cory
World Without End - Molly Cochran   f   880

Anderson, Carrie
The Vampire Princess - Michael Romkey   h   3738

Aranow, Jackson
Beggars Ride - Nancy Kress   s   2575

Ashton, Clark
Blood of Innocents - John Arbucci   h   168

Austen, James
The Angel of Pain - Brian Stableford   h   4141

Banaker, Oliver
Curse of the Vampire - Geoffrey Caine   h   680

Barrero, Estela
The Resurrectionist - Thomas F.
    Monteleone   h   3156

Barry, Warren Hubert
The Forever Children - Eric Flanders   h   1566

Bashir, Julian
Time's Enemy - L.A. Graf   s   1842

Bateman, Vince
The Cartoonist - Sean Costello   h   975

Beaulieu, Antoinette
Beyond the Void - Sean Dalton   s   1077
The Salukan Gambit - Sean Dalton   s   1079

Bernay, Leah de
Scorpio - Alex McDonough   s   3028

bet Ishak, Jehane
The Lions of Al-Rassan - Guy Gavriel Kay   f   2403

Blaine, Trish
Blood - Ron Dee   h   1182

Blaze, Sue
Harvest of Blood - Vincent Courtney   h   984

Bosch, Benjamin
Troll-Quest - Rose Estes   f   1481
Troll-Taken - Rose Estes   f   1482

Bowman, Michael
Cold Kiss - Roxanne Longstreet   h   2794
The Undead - Roxanne Longstreet   h   2796

Bowman, Scott
The Cartoonist - Sean Costello   h   975

Bradley, Karen
Deus X - Joseph Citro   h   837

Breunner, August
Brainstorm - Steven M. Krauzer   h   2569

Brill, Willy
Silent Witness - Robert Arthur Smith   h   4097

Broussard, Andy
Blood on the Bayou - D.J. Donaldson   h   1268

Broward, Liz
Blood Work - Fay Zachary   4823

Burr, Martyn
Stone Angels - Mike Jefferies   h   2305

Burwin, Addie
Stunts - Charles L. Grant   h   1857

Caldwell
Call to Battle - Doug Murray   h   3234

Campbell, Alan
Rapid Growth - Mary K. Hanner   h   2030

Candlemas, Richard
The Long Midnight - Daniel Ransom   h   3572

Carney, Hugh
Bright Angel - John Blair   s   415

Catledge, Sue
Vampire Beat - Vincent Courtney   h   985

Chandler, Vicki
Resurrection Dreams - Richard Laymon   h   2682

Claiborne, Adam
Psycho II - Robert Bloch   h   441

Claridge, Kit
The Sails of Tau Ceti - Michael McCollum   s   3002

Cline, Kendra
Legion of the Dead - Geoffrey Caine   h   681

Cofort, Rael
Redline the Stars - Andre Norton   s   3313

Congemi, Nelson
Duplicates - Andrew Neiderman   h   3253

Crane
Lake of the Long Sun - Gene Wolfe   s   4733
Nightside the Long Sun - Gene Wolfe   s   4734

Crawford, Michael
The Stress of Her Regard - Tim Powers   h   3496

Croaker
Bleak Seasons - Glen Cook   f   925

Crusher, Beverly
All Good Things. . . - Michael Jan Friedman   s   1657
Chains of Command - Bill McCay   s   2999
Dragon's Honor - Kij Johnson   s   2328
Imbalance - V.E. Mitchell   s   3124

Curry, Rowan Mayfair
Lasher - Anne Rice   h   3650

Cutter, Hargrave
Night Thirst - Patrick Whalen   h   4597

Davidson, Charles Joseph
Deadly Breed - T.J. Kirby   h   2505

de Bernay, Leah
Dragon's Blood - Alex McDonough   s   3025
Dragon's Claw - Alex McDonough   s   3026
Dragon's Eye - Alex McDonough   s   3027
Scorpio Descending - Alex McDonough   s   3029
Scorpio Rising - Alex McDonough   s   3030

Dean
I, Said the Fly - Michael Shea   h   3947

Dee, John
Scorpio Rising - Alex McDonough   s   3030

Des Jardins, Nicole
Rama II - Arthur C. Clarke   s   851

Dixon, Stephanie
Kaleidoscope Eyes - Graham Watkins   h   4487

Dolmi, Yarkol
Spirits of Cavern and Hearth - M. Coleman
    Easton   f   1380

Donovan, Fay
Lagoon - Alison Drake   h   1313

Douglas, Tom
The Baby - Stephanie Kegan   h   2417

Dycek, Rachel
Climbing Olympus - Kevin J. Anderson   s   85

Ellair, Noble
The Night Seasons - J.N. Williamson   h   4666

Moran, John J.
The Lighthouse at the End of the World - Stephen Marlowe *h* 2886

Mordenheim, Victor
Mordenheim - Chet Williamson *h* 4655

Murchison
The Galactic Gourmet - James White *s* 4603

Nahvah
The Belly of the Wolf - R.A. MacAvoy *f* 2845

Neumann, Kate
Children of the Night - Dan Simmons *h* 4029

Ngoni, Beatrice
A Miracle of Rare Design - Mike Resnick *s* 3631

Nicholson, Shawna
The Unknown Soldier - Mickey Zucker Reichert *s* 3611

Nolan
The Silent Stars Go By - James White *s* 4605

Norman
Chaingang - Rex Miller *h* 3105

O'Keefe, Katie
Rulers of Darkness - Steven G. Spruill *h* 4138

Opal, Sam
The Judas Glass - Michael Cadnum *h* 663

Patterson, Red
Skyscape - Michael Cadnum *h* 665

Pearl, Michael
The Beyond - Barry Harrington *h* 2042

Peekner, Doc
Dead in the West - Joe R. Lansdale *h* 2645

Penn, Martin
Testament - Valerie J. Freireich *s* 1648

Perlman, William
Afterage - Yvonne Navarro *h* 3243

Phillips, Warren
Darkness - John Saul *h* 3874

Plume, Jerry
Passive Intruder - Michael Upchurch *h* 4410

Poole, Michael
Koko - Peter Straub *h* 4250

Porsena, L. Robert
Red Orc's Rage - Philip Jose Farmer *f* 1506

Praisegood, William R.
Blood and Roses - Sharon Bainbridge *h* 246

Quiet
Bad Brains - Kathe Koja *h* 2540

Quindell, Mason
Bring Me Children - David Martin *h* 2889

Quong, Sue-Ling
The Singers of Time - Frederik Pohl *s* 3468

Railly, Kathryn
12 Monkeys - Elizabeth Hand *s* 2025

Raleigh, Bryan
Nightmare - S.K. Epperson *h* 1472

Rhodes, Jeffrey
Harmful Intent - Robin Cook *s* 939

Rich
Invitation to the Game - Monica Hughes *s* 2236

Roberts, Mark
Virus - Graham Watkins *h* 4488

Roswell, Harry I.
Summerland - L. Dean James *f* 2282

Royal, Solomon
Butcher - Rex Miller *h* 3104

Ruquel
The Book of the Beast - Tanith Lee *f* 2708

Samson, Leonard "Doc"
What Savage Beast - Peter David *s* 1122

Sartorius
The Waterworks - E.L. Doctorow *s* 1263

Scully, Dana
Goblins - Charles L. Grant *s* 1850
Ground Zero - Kevin J. Anderson *h* 89
Ruins - Kevin J. Anderson *h* 93
Whirlwind - Charles L. Grant *f* 1859

Seguy, Eva
Mutant Star - Karen Haber *s* 1985

Seward, John
Anno Dracula - Kim Newman *h* 3259

Seward, Jonathan
Lord of the Vampires - Jeanne Kalogridis *h* 2394

Sinclair, Adam
The Adept - Katherine Kurtz *f* 2587
Dagger Magic - Katherine Kurtz *f* 2589
Death of an Adept - Katherine Kurtz *f* 2590
The Lodge of the Lynx - Katherine Kurtz *f* 2592
The Templar Treasure - Katherine Kurtz *f* 2593

Singleton, Eric
Cold White Fury - Beth Amos *h* 81

Smith, Desi "Daisy Smeet"
Chaos Come Again - Wilhelmina Baird *s* 247

Spencer, Simon
The Werewolf's Touch - Cheri Scotch *h* 3908

Stallman, Connie
Evil Reincarnate - Leigh Clark *h* 844

Standish, Brian
Witch Hill - Marion Zimmer Bradley *h* 536

Starbridge, Thanakar
Sugar Rain - Paul Park *s* 3383

Swinton, Byron
Contagion - John David Connor *h* 916

Swire, Harvey
Twilight - Peter James *h* 2293

Tachyon
Ace in the Hole - George R.R. Martin *s* 2892
Jokertown Shuffle - George R.R. Martin *s* 2897

Tate, Augustus "Gus"
The Demolished Man - Alfred Bester *s* 388

Taylor, Shona
Medicine Show - Jody Lynn Nye *s* 3324
Taylor's Ark - Jody Lynn Nye *s* 3328

Terton, Ama "Ama-la"
Nothing Sacred - Elizabeth Ann Scarborough *f* 3893

Thompson, Ewha
The Bushido Incident - Betty Anne Crawford *s* 1011

Thorne, Emerson
The Hunted - Kathryn Ptacek *h* 3542

Todd, Emma
The Man Who Turned into Himself - David Ambrose *h* 74

Tolnismer, Alysess
The Host - Peter R. Emshwiller *s* 1460
Short Blade - Peter R. Emshwiller *s* 1461

Trap, Clyde
Requiem - Clifford Mohr *h* 3146

Tremayne, Evan
Carnivores - Penelope Banka Kreps *h* 2570

Uhua-Sorg, Kennet
The Ship Who Searched - Anne McCaffrey *s* 2982

Ulkanov, Andre
The Multiplex Man - James P. Hogan *s* 2177

Usher, Madeline
Return to the House of Usher - Robert Poe *h* 3461

Usher, Roderick
Return to the House of Usher - Robert Poe *h* 3461

Valdheim, M. R.
The Multiplex Man - James P. Hogan *s* 2177

Van Helsing, Abraham
Lord of the Vampires - Jeanne Kalogridis *h* 2394

Van Helsing, Stefan
Children of the Vampire - Jeanne Kalogridis *h* 2392

Van Richten, Rudolph
I, Strahd - P.N. Elrod *h* 1442

Vaughan, Elsie Crawford
The Lilith Factor - Jean Paiva *h* 3376

Vertue, Leon
Mistworld - Simon R. Green *s* 1902

Wakefield, Nicole des Jardins
The Garden of Rama - Arthur C. Clarke *s* 848

Walker, Jason
The Unknown Soldier - Mickey Zucker Reichert *s* 3611

Walthers, Danielle "Dani"
Parliament of Blood - Scott Ciencin *h* 831

Walton, Alex
Virus - Graham Watkins *h* 4488

Ward
Not Broken, Not Belonging - Randy Fox *h* 1630

Warren
Act of Love - Joe R. Lansdale *h* 2640

Watson, John
Seance for a Vampire - Fred Saberhagen *h* 3817

Watson, John H.
Sherlock Holmes in Orbit - Mike Resnick *s* 3637

Waxman, Will
Fallen Angels - Larry Niven *s* 3279

Wendeen, Wendy
Drifter - William C. Dietz *s* 1245

Wheeler, Matt
The Harvest - Robert Charles Wilson *s* 4703

White
The Midnight Club - Christopher Pike *h* 3448

Winstead, Samantha
Cries of the Children - Clare McNally *h* 3072

Xavier, Eileen
Godspeed - Charles Sheffield *s* 3955

Yamaguchi, Motofusa
Half Asleep in Frog Pajamas - Tom Robbins *f* 3683

Zobolotsky, Vladimir
Indiana Jones and the Genesis Deluge - Rob MacGregor *f* 2854

DRIFTER

Blackburn, Jimmy
Blackburn - Bradley Denton *h* 1203

Corder, Rachel
Jackals - Charles L. Grant *h* 1853

Dell
The Book of Webster's - J.N. Williamson *h* 4661

Diaz, Lupe
The Orchid Eater - Marc Laidlaw *h* 2635

Lavanic, Cruise
Night Cruise - Billie Sue Mosiman *h* 3218

Moonlight, Charlie
Thunder Rise - G. Wayne Miller *h* 3102

Kersh, Jeremy
Naming the Flowers - Kate Wilhelm   s   4626

Kreident, Craig
Virtual Destruction - Kevin J. Anderson   s   98

Levitt, Ira
Thinning the Predators - Daina Graziunas   h   1876

Mulder, Fox
Goblins - Charles L. Grant   s   1850
Ground Zero - Kevin J. Anderson   h   89
Ruins - Kevin J. Anderson   h   93
Whirlwind - Charles L. Grant   f   1859

Sanders, Kenneth
Doomsday Exam - Nick Pollotta   f   3477

Scully, Dana
Goblins - Charles L. Grant   s   1850
Ground Zero - Kevin J. Anderson   h   89
Ruins - Kevin J. Anderson   h   93
Whirlwind - Charles L. Grant   f   1859

Shedian, Taylor Caroline
Souls - Katina Alexis   h   58

Shelby, Kathe
Father's Little Helper - Ronald Kelly   h   2433

Starling, Clarice
The Silence of the Lambs - Thomas Harris   h   2051

Taylor, Jessica
Bureau 13 - Nick Pollotta   f   3476
Full Moonster - Nick Pollotta   f   3478

Woczniak, Hal
The Forever King - Molly Cochran   f   879

FEMINIST

Amos, Renee
Star Sister - Juanita Coulson   s   982

Goblin, Gwenny
The Color of Her Panties - Piers Anthony   f   137

Tesuawane, Sovawanea "Sophy" a
Gibbon's Decline and Fall - Sheri S.
  Tepper   s   4334

FEMME FATALE

de Noux, Leanna
Leanna: Possession of a Woman - Marie
  Kiraly   h   2501

Fancy, Jan "Jeanette"
Succumb - Ron Dee   h   1187

Nikki
Dark Winds - Graham Watkins   h   4486

Walker, Betsy
Last Rites - David Darke   h   1094

FIANCE(E)

Addams, Fester
Addams Family Values - Todd Strasser   f   4246

an Treves, Sheyrena "Rena"
Elvenblood - Andre Norton   f   3304

Anyr
The Sleep of Stone - Louise Cooper   f   952

Brightglade, Douglas
Aquamancer - Don Callander   f   685
Geomancer - Don Callander   f   688

Creslin
The Towers of the Sunset - L.E. Modesitt
  Jr.   f   3139

Elionbel
Palace of Kings - Mike Jefferies   f   2303

Fairburn, Pamela
The Ambivalent Magician - Simon Hawke   f   2091

Flynn, Maggie
Beyond the Gate - Dave Wolverton   s   4740

Garlick, Magrat
Lords and Ladies - Terry Pratchett   f   3502

Gwenhwyfar
The Kingmaking - Helen Hollick   f   2190

Hazel
Belladonna - Michael Stewart   h   4206

Hirmin
The Wooden Sword - Lynn Abbey   f   16

Keleios
Nightseer - Laurell K. Hamilton   f   2019

Lockhart, Ximena
Death of an Adept - Katherine Kurtz   f   2590

Lothor
Nightseer - Laurell K. Hamilton   f   2019

Manstar, Myrn
Aquamancer - Don Callander   f   685
Geomancer - Don Callander   f   688

Mati, Gwendolyn "Gwen"
Half Asleep in Frog Pajamas - Tom
  Robbins   s   3683

Matt
The Oathbound Wizard - Christopher
  Stasheff   f   4162

Melliandra "Melli"
The Baker's Boy - J.V. Jones   f   2356

Neville-Smythe, Brian
The Dragon and the Djinn - Gordon R.
  Dickson   f   1233

Peldyrin, Alix
Stranger at the Wedding - Barbara Hambly   f   2010

Quarrels, David
The Khan's Persuasion - Cynthia Felice   s   1540

Redbird
Shaman - Robert Shea   f   3948

Shelagh
Sweetheart, Sweetheart - Bernard Taylor   h   4310

L'var y Smid, Vida
Palace - Katharine Kerr   s   2448

ViKay
Hour of the Octopus - Joel Rosenberg   f   3742

FILMMAKER

Brad
I, Said the Fly - Michael Shea   h   3947

Haller, Buzzy
Horror Show - Greg Kihn   h   2466

Holdstrom, Roy
A Graveyard for Lunatics - Ray Bradbury   h   509

My Secret Agent Lover Man
Witch Baby - Francesca Lia Block   f   450

Seyirshi, Ginbiryol
Shadowkill - Jo Clayton   s   861
Shadowplay - Jo Clayton   s   862
Shadowspeer - Jo Clayton   s   863

Tom
Remake - Connie Willis   s   4676

FINANCIER

Curtis, Richard
Dreamer - Peter James   h   2288

Ritz
Living with the Reptiles - Roger L.
  DiSilvestro   s   1262

Soo, Hannah
Take Back Plenty - Colin Greenland   s   1936

FIRE FIGHTER

Nolan, Wulf
Borderland - S.K. Epperson   h   1468

FISHERMAN

Alemi
The Dolphins of Pern - Anne McCaffrey   s   2967

Carmody, Michael
Sailor Song - Ken Kesey   s   2456

Darling, William Somers "Whip"
Beast - Peter Benchley   h   362

Paco, Chico
Through the Arc of the Rain Forest - Karen Tei
  Yamashita   f   4791

Sargent, Gideon
The Innsmouth Heritage - Brian Stableford   h   4145

FOREMAN

Church, Andy
Where the Chill Waits - T. Chris
  Martindale   h   2907

Qian
China Mountain Zhang - Maureen F.
  McHugh   s   3041

FORTUNE HUNTER

Pennyman
The Last Coin - James P. Blaylock   f   421

FOSTER PARENT

Attila the Hun
Attila's Treasure - Stephan Grundy   f   1964

FOUNDLING

Adam
Child of Shadows - John Coyne   h   1001

Alnosha "Nosh"
The Hands of Lyr - Andre Norton   f   3308

Artos
The Dragon's Boy - Jane Yolen   f   4807

Bryant, Bonnie
The Godsend - Bernard Taylor   h   4309

Caitlin
The Spellkey Trilogy - Ann Downer   f   1285

Douglas, Medoret
A Whisper of Time - Paula E. Downing   s   1288

Fath, Jaro
Night Lamp - Jack Vance   s   4422

Floris
Out of the Ordinary - Annie Dalton   f   1076

Kelly, Ista
Night Sky Mine - Melissa Scott   s   3912

Penthesilea
The Amazon Chronicles - Jane E.M.
  Robinson   f   3703

Tristen
Fortress in the Eye of Time - C.J. Cherryh   f   804

Thomas, Stephen
Nautilus - Vonda N. McIntyre   *s*   3045

Tiban, Boris
Climbing Olympus - Kevin J. Anderson   *s*   85

Torx, BrainGeneral
Mutant Hell - Mark Grant   *s*   1861
Mutants Amok - Mark Grant   *s*   1862

Troy, Linda Ellen "Sparta"
The Diamond Moon - Paul Preuss   *s*   3523
Hide and Seek - Paul Preuss   *s*   3524
The Medusa Encounter - Paul Preuss   *s*   3525
The Shining Ones - Paul Preuss   *s*   3526

Tsering
Lethe - Tricia Sullivan   *s*   4269

Tsia
Cat Scratch Fever - Tara K. Harper   *s*   2037

Ullrich, Nils
Armed Memory - Jim Young   *s*   4821

Urt
Lords of the Sky - Angus Wells   *f*   4573

Valdoria, Sauscony
Primary Inversion - Catherine Asaro   *s*   182

Vaun
Hero - Dave Duncan   *s*   1352

Veate
The Albino Knife - Steve Perry   *s*   3415

Wandel, Timothy J.
Armed Memory - Jim Young   *s*   4821

Wanders, Wendy
Winterlong - Elizabeth Hand   *s*   2029

Wang-mu
Xenocide - Orson Scott Card   *s*   730

Wrasselty, Bleth
The Wells of Phyre - L. Warren Douglas   *s*   1282

Wrasselty, Slith
The Wells of Phyre - L. Warren Douglas   *s*   1282

Xtasca the Cherub
Seasons of Plenty - Colin Greenland   *s*   1935

GENIUS

Ahrens, Bleys
Other - Gordon R. Dickson   *s*   1241

Brewster, Marvin "Doc"
The Ambivalent Magician - Simon Hawke   *f*   2091
The Inadequate Adept - Simon Hawke   *f*   2092
The Reluctant Sorcerer - Simon Hawke   *f*   2096

Cocciolone, Carol Jeanne
Lovelock - Orson Scott Card   *s*   723

Dead Man
Red Iron Nights - Glen Cook   *f*   931

Dore, Michael
Lunar Justice - Charles L. Harness   *s*   2034

Duberville, Myron
Outer Space and All That Junk - Mel
    Gilden   *s*   1789

Eklunk, Hans-Bjorn "Mokey/Moke"
Psykosis - Wilhelmina Baird   *s*   250

Kalakaua, Cen
The Bones of Time - Kathleen Ann Goonan   *s*   1824

Leonardo Da Vinci
Pasquale's Angel - Paul J. McAuley   *f*   2955

Lowrey, Jason
Death Dream - Ben Bova   *s*   478

Miller, Quintus
Walkers - Graham Masterton   *h*   2927

Mulcahey, Gerald "Jerry"
Heavy Weather - Bruce Sterling   *s*   4194

Savage, Clark "Doc" Jr.
The Frightened Fish - Kenneth Robeson   *f*   3698
The Jade Ogre - Kenneth Robeson   *f*   3699
White Eyes - Kenneth Robeson   *f*   3701

Seafort, Philip
Voices of Hope - David Feintuch   *s*   1532

Sharifi, Jennifer
Beggars Ride - Nancy Kress   *s*   2575

Tweep, Jonathan B.
Through the Arc of the Rain Forest - Karen Tei
    Yamashita   *f*   4791

GENTLEMAN

Aerich of House Lyorn
The Phoenix Guards - Steven Brust   *f*   611

Aranow, Jackson
Beggars Ride - Nancy Kress   *s*   2575

Calmady, Pollexfen
The Architecture of Desire - Mary Gentle   *f*   1761

Khaavren of House Tiassa
The Phoenix Guards - Steven Brust   *f*   611

Watkins, Daniel J.
The Golden Nineties - Lisa Mason   *s*   2912

Wooster, Bertie
Scream for Jeeves: A Parody - H.P.G.
    Wodehouse   *h*   4723

GENTLEWOMAN

Althea
The Forge of Virtue - Lynn Abbey   *f*   14

Kendry, Alicen
Season of Storms - Ellen Foxxe   *f*   1631

Morlock, Endora
Madman Run - David Robbins   *s*   3677

Tazendra of House Dzur
The Phoenix Guards - Steven Brust   *f*   611

Vorder, Sera
The Gnome's Engine - Teresa Edgerton   *f*   1398
Goblin Moon - Teresa Edgerton   *f*   1399

Westbrook, Louisa
Flameweaver - Margaret Ball   *f*   264

GIRLFRIEND

Anica
Senor Vivo and the Coca Lord - Louis de
    Bernieres   *f*   1136

Barber, Cissy
Land O'Goshen - Charles McNair   *s*   3071

Beaumont, Andrea
Mask of the Phantasm - Geary Gravel   *s*   1867

Becky
See You Later - Christopher Pike   *f*   3451

Carlisle, Bari
Count Geiger's Blues - Michael Bishop   *s*   404

Christensen, Maggie
The Silver Stone - Joel Rosenberg   *f*   3745

Cind
Empire's End - Allan Cole   *s*   888

Delores
Bride of the Slime Monster - Craig Shaw
    Gardner   *f*   1708

Donna
Pirates of the Universe - Terry Bisson   *s*   410

Donohue, Gabriela "Gaby"
Doc Sidhe - Aaron Allston   *f*   71

Fava
Serpent Catch - Dave Wolverton   *s*   4745

Frydys
The Deepest Sea - Charles Barnitz   *f*   303

Gwen
Rehearsal for a Renaissance - Douglas W.
    Clark   *f*   842

Lane, Lois
The Death and Life of Superman - Roger
    Stern   *s*   4198
Lois & Clark - C.J. Cherryh   *s*   810

Lavalle, Linda
Why Do Birds - Damon Knight   *s*   2537

Loola
Night of the Living 'Gator! - Richard A.
    Lupoff   *s*   2841
Night of the Living Rat! - Debra Doyle   *s*   1296

Lucy
That's All, Folks! - Greg Snow   *f*   4108

Maler, Vicki
Psychosphere - Brian Lumley   *h*   2835

Marian
Sherwood - Parke Godwin   *f*   1806

Martine
Time and Light - William Bornefeld   *s*   470

McGiven, Mary
The Haunt - John Fogarty   *h*   1581

Millicent "Millie"
Jumper - Steven Gould   *s*   1836

Qian, San-xiang
China Mountain Zhang - Maureen F.
    McHugh   *s*   3041

Sanderson, Merry
Wolf and Iron - Gordon R. Dickson   *s*   1242

Six, Nicola
London Fields - Martin Amis   *s*   79

Snick, Panthea
Dayworld Breakup - Philip Jose Farmer   *s*   1502

Sommers, Serena
Forest of the Night - S.P. Somtow   *f*   4114

Taylor, Lura
Dumford Blood - S.K. Epperson   *h*   1469

Tinnie
Dread Brass Shadows - Glen Cook   *f*   927

GLADIATOR

E'non, Caelan
Reign of Shadows - Deborah Chester   *f*   819

O'Connor, Corbo
The Fourth Guardian - Ronald Anthony
    Cross   *s*   1032
The Lost Guardian - Ronald Anthony Cross   *s*   1033

GOVERNESS

Martinique, Speranza
Moon Dance - S.P. Somtow   *h*   4116

GOVERNMENT OFFICIAL

Adler, Mark
Ursus - David Dvorkin   *s*   1371

Altman, Gibson
Pallas - L. Neil Smith   *s*   4093

GRANDPARENT

Gilman
Pigs Don't Fly - Mary Brown   f   594

Hawson, Jordan
The Temper of Wisdom - Lynn Abbey   f   15

Heather
Lorien Lost - Michael King   f   2477

Holmes, Odetta
The Waste Lands - Stephen King   h   2496

Hunsacker, Patty
Blind Hunger - David Darke   h   1092

Igor
Goblins in the Castle - Bruce Coville   f   988

Innowen
Shadowdance - Robin Wayne Bailey   f   245

Lannister, Tyrion
A Game of Thrones - George R.R. Martin   f   2896

Little Girl
The Mer-Child: A Legend for Children and Other Adults - Robin Morgan   f   3190

Lyim
The Seventh Sentinel - Mary Kirchoff   f   2506

Maddox, Cory
The March Hare Network - Jack L. Chalker   s   775

Maxon, Max
Bodyguard - William C. Dietz   s   1244

Perez, Theresa "Terry"
Shadow of the Well of Souls - Jack L. Chalker   s   779

Presteign, Olivia
The Stars My Destination - Alfred Bester   s   389

R-T "Artie"
R-T, Margaret, and the Rats of NIMH - Jane Leslie Conly   f   913

Raim
Dark Heart - Betsy James   f   2274

Rebecca
Gate of Darkness, Circle of Light - Tanya Huff   f   2229

Ritz
Living with the Reptiles - Roger L. DiSilvestro   s   1262

Sarah
Brother to Dragons, Companion to Owls - Jane M. Lindskold   f   2762

Singer, Eleal
Past Imperative - Dave Duncan   f   1356

Smedley, Julian
Present Tense - Dave Duncan   f   1358

Stonewall, Annie Casteel
Gates of Paradise - V.C. Andrews   h   121

Tesa "Good Eyes"
Silent Dances - A.C. Crispin   s   1025

Therru
Tehanu: The Last Book of Earthsea - Ursula K. Le Guin   f   2693

Toland, Walter
Killobyte - Piers Anthony   f   147

Tremulis, Victor Anthony "Tremble"
The Holy Terror - Wayne Allen Sallee   h   3829

Uhua-Sorg, Kennet
The Ship Who Searched - Anne McCaffrey   s   2982

Voerster, Broni
Glory - Alfred Coppel   s   955

Winthrop, Montana "Tana"
The Earth Saver - Catherine Wells   s   4580

Wort
Tower of Doom - Mark Anthony   h   126

X(A/N)ᵗʰ "Nimby"
Yon Ill Wind - Piers Anthony   f   162

Ylon
Mirror of Destiny - Andre Norton   f   3312

HANDYMAN

Barnett, Schuyler "Sky"
My Soul to Keep - Judith Hawkes   h   2105

Buford, Tommy
Let There Be Dark - Allen Lee Harris   h   2043

Clewe, Harry
The Blood of Angels - Stephen Gregory   h   1942

Kane, Bowie
Pitfall - Ronald Kelly   h   2435

Landry, Jack
Dark Debts - Karen Hall   h   1999

Orfindel "Hosea Lincoln"
The Fire Duke - Joel Rosenberg   f   3740

St. George, Joe
Dolores Claiborne - Stephen King   h   2483

Santillanes, Gil
Days of the Dead - Ashley McConnell   h   3004

Singer, John Wolfe
Uwharrie - Eugene E. Pfaff Jr.   h   3432

Skyler
Blood Roots - Richie Tankersley Cusick   h   1055

Sloan, Cotter
Makoto - Kelley Wilde   h   4619

Williams, Billy
The Sixth Dog - Jane Rice   h   3659

HEALER

Amberdrake
The Black Gryphon - Mercedes Lackey   f   2599
The White Gryphon - Mercedes Lackey   f   2626

Ash, Hatty
Devil's Tower - Mark Summer   f   4270

Campbell, Brianne
Journeyman Wizard - Mary Frances Zambreno   f   4830

Davos
The Itinerant Exorcist - Ashley McConnell   f   3006

Dion
Shadow Leader - Tara K. Harper   f   2039
Wolfwalker - Tara K. Harper   f   2040

Erin of Elliath
Chains of Darkness, Chains of Light - Michelle Sagara   f   3823
Into the Dark Lands - Michelle Sagara   f   3825
Lady of Mercy - Michelle Sagara   f   3826

Fyana
The Poisoned Lands - John Maddox Roberts   f   3695

Johnson, Lezzie
Groogleman - Debra Doyle   s   1293

Kelene
City of the Sorcerers - Mary H. Herbert   f   2134
Winged Magic - Mary H. Herbert   f   2138

Madrone
The Fifth Sacred Thing - Starhawk   f   4154

Mama Yaya
I, Tituba, Black Witch of Salem - Maryse Conde   f   911

Monmart, Kevisson
House of Moons - K.D. Wentworth   s   4584
Moonspeaker - K.D. Wentworth   s   4586

Nolar
Flight of Vengeance - Andre Norton   f   3306

Oonan
The Dubious Hills - Pamela Dean   f   1165

Rethia
Touched by Magic - Doranna Durgin   f   1369

Sari
Branch and Crown - Gael Baudino   f   323

Saun
Athyra - Steven Brust   f   605

Senungatuk, Clodagh
Power Lines - Anne McCaffrey   s   2976

Thenike
Ammonite - Nicola Griffith   s   1956

Thuryn, Rhysel
The Bastard Prince - Katherine Kurtz   f   2588

Tris
Steal the Dragon - Patricia Briggs   f   561

Twilla
Mirror of Destiny - Andre Norton   f   3312

HEALTH CARE PROFESSIONAL

Ayers, Jane
The Illegal Rebirth of Billy the Kid - Rebecca Ore   s   3364

Berquist, Kate
Nightmare - S.K. Epperson   h   1472

Bev
My Cousin, My Gastroenterologist - Mark Leyner   s   2748

Chirwl
Medicine Show - Jody Lynn Nye   s   3324

Crawford, Jonathan
The Callahan Touch - Spider Robinson   f   3712

Dieudonee, Genevieve
Anno Dracula - Kim Newman   h   3259

Frede
Orion Among the Stars - Ben Bova   s   483

Johanna
Strange Angels - Kathe Koja   h   2543

Martina, Jewel
Chimera - Mary Rosenblum   s   3746

Nacker the Teach
The Pharaoh Contract - Ray Aldridge   s   51

Stillwater, Paige
Mr. Murder - Dean R. Koontz   h   2555

HEIR

Aidan
Flight of the Raven - Jennifer Roberson   f   3685

Alastair
The Heirs of Hammerfell - Marion Zimmer Bradley   s   524

Benjarth, Paul
The Cloud People - Robert B. Kelly   f   2431

Blessing, Arthur
The Forever King - Molly Cochran   f   879

Cannon, Vassily "Bass" James
A Plague of Change - L. Warren Douglas   s   1280

Chevenga, Fourth
Lion's Heart - Karen Wehrstein   f   4529

Coerlis, Jack-Jax Landsdowne
Mid-Flinx - Alan Dean Foster   s   1613

HERBALIST

Fenton, Mariah
The Changeling Garden - Winifred Elze   *h*   1449

Katin
Season of Storms - Ellen Foxxe   *f*   1631

HERO

Alias
Masquerades - Kate Novak   *f*   3318

al'Thor, Rand "Dragon Reborn"
The Shadow Rising - Robert Jordan   *f*   2384

Appenfell, Rudgar "Rudy"
A Breach in the Watershed - Douglas Niles   *f*   3267
Darkenheight - Douglas Niles   *f*   3269

Arthur "Artos"
A Prince Among Men - Robert N. Charrette   *f*   791

Atare, Sheen
Hidden Fires - Katharine Eliska Kimbriel   *s*   2475

Barku, Perkar Kar
The Waterborn - J. Gregory Keyes   *f*   2464

Beowulf
The Tower of Beowulf - Parke Godwin   *f*   1808
Whose Song Is Sung - Frank Schaefer   *f*   3897

Bishop
Alien 3 - Alan Dean Foster   *s*   1599

Blackthorn
Hunter of the Light - Risa Aratyr   *f*   167

Caine, Tycho
Evil Triumphant - Michael A. Stackpole   *s*   4149

Caramon
The Second Generation - Margaret Weis   *f*   4563

Charming
Slay and Rescue - John Moore   *f*   3175

Corleau
The Sorceress and the Cygnet - Patricia A. McKillip   *f*   3061

Cosmo, Jason
Dirty Work - Dan McGirt   *f*   3035
Jason Cosmo - Dan McGirt   *f*   3036

Crowley, Damon
Evil Triumphant - Michael A. Stackpole   *s*   4149

Darith
Blood of the Colyn Muir - Paul Edwin Zimmer   *f*   4852

dav Leydon, Kian "Mouse"
Kingmaker's Sword - Ann Marston   *f*   2887

de Oro, Irving
Horrors of the Dancing Gods - Jack L. Chalker   *f*   774

de Oro, Joe
Songs of the Dancing Gods - Jack L. Chalker   *f*   780

Derry, Jerry
Ye Gods! - Tom Holt   *f*   2196

Dryhope, Wat
A History Maker - Alasdair Gray   *s*   1874

Evans, Bill "Bill the Just"
The League of the Crimson Crescent - James E. Reagen   *f*   3586

Feree, Harper
The Friendship Song - Nancy Springer   *f*   4133

Firemayne, Rowan
Cup of Clay - Carole Nelson Douglas   *f*   1277
Seed upon the Wind - Carole Nelson Douglas   *f*   1278

Fleetfox
Barrow - John Deakins   *f*   1164

Geryam
The Birth of the Blade - Dennis McCarty   *f*   2998

Gordon, Evelyn Cyril "Oscar/Scar"
Glory Road - Robert A. Heinlein   *f*   2112

Gordon, Roger Jr.
Revenge of the Fluffy Bunnies - Craig Shaw Gardner   *f*   1714

Great and Powerful Turtle
Dealer's Choice - George R.R. Martin   *s*   2894

Grover
Heroes, Inc. - Kyle Crocco   *f*   1029
Heroes Wanted - Kyle Crocco   *f*   1028

Hackleberry, Kelvin Knight
Chimaera's Copper - Piers Anthony   *f*   136
Mouvar's Magic - Piers Anthony   *f*   150
Orc's Opal - Piers Anthony   *f*   151

Hercules
By the Sword - Timothy Boggs   *f*   457

Hood, Robin
The Fantastic Adventures of Robin Hood - Martin H. Greenberg   *f*   1913
The Oathbound Wizard - Christopher Stasheff   *f*   4162
The Outlaws of Sherwood - Robin McKinley   *f*   3065
Robin and the King - Parke Godwin   *f*   1805
The Sheriff of Nottingham - Richard Kluger   *f*   2515

Jack
A Man Betrayed - J.V. Jones   *f*   2357
Master and Fool - J.V. Jones   *f*   2358

Jetboy
Night of the Cooters - Howard Waldrop   *s*   4472

Kahless
Kahless - Michael Jan Friedman   *s*   1660

Kochevikov, Pyetr
Chernevog - C.J. Cherryh   *f*   796
Rusalka - C.J. Cherryh   *f*   813
Yvgenie - C.J. Cherryh   *f*   816

Lamaril
Golden Trillium - Andre Norton   *f*   3307

Lashana "Shana"
Elvenblood - Andre Norton   *f*   3304

Lee, Houlka
A Dozen Tough Jobs - Howard Waldrop   *f*   4471

Leger, Gary
The Dragon's Dagger - R.A. Salvatore   *f*   3837
The Woods out Back - R.A. Salvatore   *f*   3848

Long, Huey "Hal" Alphonse
The Trinity Vector - Steve Perry   *f*   3425

Mac Cool, Finn
Finn Mac Cool - Morgan Llywelyn   *f*   2782

mac Cumhall, Fionn "Demne"
Master of Earth and Water - Diana L. Paxson   *f*   3397
The Shield between the Worlds - Diana L. Paxson   *f*   3398
Sword of Fire and Shadow - Diana L. Paxson   *f*   3399

MacDuff
The Spawn of Loki - Jason Henderson   *f*   2122

Mace, Jarek
Morningstar - David Gemmell   *f*   1757

MacGregor, Sandy
A Name to Conjure With - Donald Aamodt   *f*   2
A Troubling Along the Border - Donald Aamodt   *f*   3

MacLoed, Alex
Fallen Angels - Larry Niven   *s*   3279

MaqqRee, Desmond "Doc Sidhe"
Doc Sidhe - Aaron Allston   *f*   71

Melvinge
Night of the Living 'Gator! - Richard A. Lupoff   *s*   2841
Night of the Living Rat! - Debra Doyle   *s*   1296
Night of the Living Shark! - David Bischoff   *s*   400

Mirakles
The Zork Chronicles - George Alec Effinger   *s*   1410

Nicholas "Santa Claus"
The Autobiography of Santa Claus: It's Better to Give - Jeff Guinn   *f*   1967

O'Day, Gallen
Beyond the Gate - Dave Wolverton   *s*   4740
The Golden Queen - Dave Wolverton   *s*   4742

Ogg, Nanny
Lords and Ladies - Terry Pratchett   *f*   3502

Oghmal
Search for the Starblade - Keith Taylor   *f*   4315

Oonitsaupivia, Nijon
By the Sword - Greg Costikyan   *f*   978

Oryolin, Alexander
Peter Nevsky and the True Story of the Russian Moon Landing - John Calvin Batchelor   *s*   322

Parker, Peter "Spider-Man"
Spider-Man: The Venom Factor - Diane Duane   *s*   1345
The Ultimate Spider-Man - Stan Lee   *s*   2706

Raistlin
The Second Generation - Margaret Weis   *f*   4563

Raven
Out of This World - Lawrence Watt-Evans   *f*   4501

Reeve, Todd
Crisis on Doona - Anne McCaffrey   *s*   2962

Rhodes, Jim "War Machine"
Iron Man: The Armor Trap - Greg Cox   *s*   996

Richer the Quick
Men Like Rats - Rob Chilson   *s*   822

Rifkin, Bernie "Power Man"
Captain Jack Zodiac - Michael Kandel   *f*   2396

Roarke, Jason
Flare Star - Paula E. Downing   *s*   1287

Shielder's Mark
Nobody's Son - Sean Stewart   *f*   4208

Sigvarthsson, Shef
The Hammer and the Cross - Harry Harrison   *f*   2055

Silverhand, Caeled
Silverlight - Morgan Llywelyn   *f*   2785

Silverstein, Ian
The Fire Duke - Joel Rosenberg   *f*   3740
The Silver Stone - Joel Rosenberg   *f*   3745

Skywalker, Luke
Ambush at Corellia - Roger MacBride Allen   *s*   62
Before the Storm - Michael P. Kube-McDowell   *s*   2581
Children of the Jedi - Barbara Hambly   *s*   2002
The Courtship of Princess Leia - Dave Wolverton   *s*   4741
The Crystal Star - Vonda N. McIntyre   *s*   3043
Dark Force Rising - Timothy Zahn   *s*   4825
Darksaber - Kevin J. Anderson   *s*   86
The Glove of Darth Vader - Paul Davids   *s*   1124
Heir to the Empire - Timothy Zahn   *s*   4827
Jedi Search - Kevin J. Anderson   *s*   91
The Last Command - Timothy Zahn   *s*   4828
The Lost City of the Jedi - Paul Davids   *s*   1125
The New Rebellion - Kristine Kathryn Rusch   *s*   3777
Shadows of the Empire - Steve Perry   *s*   3423
The Truce at Bakura - Kathy Tyers   *s*   4407

HOMOSEXUAL

Kuwai
Dark Legend - Jamake Highwater f 2146

Lichen
People of the River - W. Michael Gear f 1739

Little Bear
The Secret of the Indian - Lynne Reid Banks f 279

Lowell, Jacob
Nadya: The Wolf Chronicles - Pat Murphy f 3228

McIntosh, Calvin
Stoneskin's Revenge - Tom Deitz f 1194
Sunshaker's War - Tom Deitz f 1195

Medicine Plant
Dawn Land - Joseph Bruchac f 597

Miriam
The Spirit Stalker - Nina Romberg h 3735

Miss Bird
The Gilda Stories - Jewelle Gomez h 1819

Montes, Samta
A Whisper of Time - Paula E. Downing s 1288

Moonlight, Charlie
Thunder Rise - G. Wayne Miller h 3102

Mortega, Dyani
Blood Siege - G. Harry Stine s 4211

Nahadeh, Yute
Ember From the Sun - Mark Canter s 706

Ninekiller, Amos
The Wild Blue and the Gray - William
   Sanders s 3853

O'Connor, Thunderbird Devlin "Bird"
Above the Lower Sky - Tom Deitz f 1188

Ooljee, Paul
Cyber Way - Alan Dean Foster s 1605

Otter
People of the Lakes - Kathleen O'Neal Gear f 1735

Renard, Eris
Green Lake - S.K. Epperson h 1470

Sahacat
People of the Sky - Clare Bell s 355

Salazar, Bettina
Ghost Dance - Kathryn Ptacek h 3541

Sallas, Ike "the Bakatcha Bandit"
Sailor Song - Ken Kesey s 2456

Samiq
My Sister the Moon - Sue Harrison f 2065

Shuganan
Mother Earth, Father Sky - Sue Harrison f 2064

Sky-fire-trail
Collidescope - Grace Chetwin s 820

Spotted Horse, David
Sacred Ground - Mercedes Lackey f 2618

Spring Rain
Sing for a Gentle Rain - J. Alison James f 2278

Star Shell
People of the Lakes - Kathleen O'Neal Gear f 1735

Stone, Charlie
Wendigo Border - Catherine Montrose h 3158

Stranger, John
High Steel - Jack C. Haldeman II s 1992
Run for the Stars/Echoes of Thunder - Harlan
   Ellison s 1435

Tale Teller
Tatham Mound - Piers Anthony f 157

Talldeer, Frank
Sacred Ground - Mercedes Lackey f 2618

Temiya, Kesbe
People of the Sky - Clare Bell s 355

Tesuawane, Sovawanea "Sophy" a
Gibbon's Decline and Fall - Sheri S.
   Tepper s 4334

Tharon
People of the River - W. Michael Gear f 1739

Thaxton, Wendall
The Higher Space - Jamil Nasir s 3241

Thunder, Anna
The Grass Dancer - Susan Power f 3492

Thunder, Charlene
The Grass Dancer - Susan Power f 3492

Tumkis "Lady Sun"
Madoc's Hundred - Pat Winter f 4717

Uhatatse
People of the Mesa - Ardath Mayhar f 2947

Utlunta
Stoneskin's Revenge - Tom Deitz f 1194

Wakandagi, Ptesa "Tesa/Good Eyes"
Silent Songs - A.C. Crispin s 1026

Wanachtee
The Silent Stars Go By - James White s 4605

Wanbli
The Third Eagle: Lessons Along a Minor String - R.A.
   MacAvoy s 2848

Washi
Dark Legend - Jamake Highwater f 2146

Waterman, James "Jamie" Fox
Mars - Ben Bova s 481

Weasel
Crow and Weasel - Barry Lopez f 2800

Webb, Danny
The Serpent Slayers - Adam Niswander h 3273

White Eagle, Zacxk
Shaman Woods - Morgan Fields h 1554

Whitefeather, Matthew
The Last Vampire - Kathryn Meyer Griffith h 1953

Winchester, Miriam
Shadow Walkers - Nina Romberg h 3734

Wind Soldier, Harley
The Grass Dancer - Susan Power f 3492

INDUSTRIALIST

Brown, Frank
White Horse, Dark Dragon - Robert C.
   Fleet f 1569

Camerata, Jo
Star Brothers - Ben Bova s 487

Evans, Philip
Mindstar Rising - Peter F. Hamilton s 2020

Hutton, George
Earth - David Brin s 563

Ingles, Benton
Outworld Cats - Jack Lovejoy s 2811

INNKEEPER

Anara
India's Story - Kathlyn S. Starbuck s 4153

Bates, Norman
Psycho - Robert Bloch h 440

Caramon
The Second Generation - Margaret Weis f 4563

Karsh
The Innkeeper's Song - Peter S. Beagle f 337

Luisa
Cambio Bay - Kate Wilhelm f 4624

Parker, Caroline
Winter Wolves - Earle Wescott h 4587

Solith, Gwin Nien
The Cursed - Dave Duncan f 1348

INSURANCE AGENT

Cochrane, Rick
Time and Chance - Alan Brennert f 555

Croft, Samantha
Demon Within - Dana Reed h 3589

INSURANCE INVESTIGATOR

Kullervo, Vyra
Greenthieves - Alan Dean Foster s 1610

Lincoln, Bojake "Buffalo"
Double Jeopardy - Aaron Allston s 72

Manz, Broderick
Greenthieves - Alan Dean Foster s 1610

Parker, James "Spark"
Double Jeopardy - Aaron Allston s 72

INTERIOR DECORATOR

Hollander, Mariele
Graythings - Pat Graversen h 1871

INVALID

Maddock, Yanaba
Powers That Be - Anne McCaffrey s 2978

Unger, Alejandro "Alex"
Heavy Weather - Bruce Sterling s 4194

Young, Pat
Obsessed - Rick R. Reed h 3590

INVENTOR

Bailey, David "Herbert" Clancy
The Modular Man - Roger MacBride Allen s 65

Brenner, Hugh
Paths to Otherwhere - James P. Hogan s 2178

Chang, Marte
Burn - Bill Ransom s 3568
ViraVax - Bill Ransom s 3570

Claiborne, Kevin
Pacific Edge - Kim Stanley Robinson s 3709

Cowperthwait, Cosmo
The Steampunk Trilogy - Paul Di Filippo s 1224

Demopoulos, Demetrios "Dr. Dimension"
Dr. Dimension - John DeChancie s 1176

Edison, Thomas
Expiration Date - Tim Powers f 3494

Habeggar
Slow Freight - F.M. Busby s 642

Hawk
The Hunter Returns - David Drake f 1318

Helmish
Top Dog - Jerry Jay Carroll f 741

Leclerc, Louis
Witch - Donald E. McQuinn s 3078

Leonardo da Vinci
The Memory Cathedral - Jack Dann s 1086

Lewis, Carl
Cyberbooks - Ben Bova s 477

Lowe, Saul
Door Number Three - Patrick O'Leary s 3355

Knight, Stormy
Prey - William W. Johnstone *h* 2336

Kozinski, Judy
Oaths and Miracles - Nancy Kress *s* 2577

Kroft, Brian
The Undine - Michael O'Rourke *h* 3368

Kurimoto, Eva
Protektor - Charles Platt *s* 3459

Lane, Lois
The Death and Life of Superman - Roger Stern *s* 4198
Lois & Clark - C.J. Cherryh *s* 810

Lyell, Thomasina
The Pure Cold Light - Gregory Frost *s* 1681

Lyon, John
Bring Me Children - David Martin *h* 2889

Maas, Ellen
The Forbidden Zone - Whitley Strieber *h* 4259

Machiavelli, Niccolo
Pasquale's Angel - Paul J. McAuley *f* 2955

MacPherson, Maggie
Force of Arms - G. Harry Stine *s* 4212

Maguire, Charlotte "Charlie"
Fatherland - Robert Harris *s* 2049

Mallernee, Jay
My Soul to Take - Steven G. Spruill *s* 4137

Marat, Mike
Thirst of the Vampire - T. Lucien Wright *h* 4772

Marsh, Maxwell
Rage - Elizabeth Ergas *h* 1474

Marshall, Deidi
Flesh and Blood - D.A. Fowler *h* 1625

Mash, Madeleine
Coyote - Peter Gadol *f* 1691

Masterson, Rick
Darkling - Michael O'Rourke *h* 3367

Maxwell, James
The Mysterium - Eric McCormack *h* 3008

McAslan, Gabriel "Gaby"
Evolution's Shore - Ian McDonald *s* 3018

McPherson, Mark
Seed upon the Wind - Carole Nelson Douglas *f* 1278

Mitchell, Kelly
Domination - Michael Cecilione *h* 767

Moon, Donovan
Morningstar - Peter Atkins *h* 223

Morelli, Berry
Candle Night - Phil Rickman *h* 3663

Morrison, Faye
Curfew - Phil Rickman *h* 3664

Musik, Peter
The End-of-Everything Man - Tom De Haven *f* 1146

Myshtigo, Cort
This Immortal - Roger Zelazny *s* 4845

Nielson, Anne
Bad Dreams - Kim Newman *h* 3260

Nygerski, Cyrus "Moondog"
Moondog - Henry Garfield *h* 1716

O'Connor, Dennis
The Hunger of the Beast - John Driver *h* 1336

Paik, Anna
Cortez on Jupiter - Ernest Hogan *s* 2172

Pascal, David
Carnosaur - Harry Adam Knight *s* 2538

Pemberton, Martin
The Waterworks - E.L. Doctorow *s* 1263

Perez, Theresa "Terry"
Echoes of the Well of Souls - Jack L. Chalker *s* 772
Shadow of the Well of Souls - Jack L. Chalker *s* 779

Perry, Brenda
The Wishing Well - Charles de Lint *f* 1163

Phillips, Randa
Dark Debts - Karen Hall *h* 1999

Pierce, Melinda
Goon - Edward Lee *h* 2698

Piper, Rick
Panic - Chris Curry *h* 1050

Poe, John Charles
Return to the House of Usher - Robert Poe *h* 3461

Prescott, Elaine
Soul Snatchers - Michael Cecilione *h* 768

Prosky, Ronald
The New Neighbor - Ray Garton *h* 1728

Quadrun, Ben
Nightmare Logic - Matthew Hall *h* 2000

Quinn
Silicon Embrace - John Shirley *s* 3996

Raleigh, David
Nightmare - S.K. Epperson *h* 1472

Ravanski, Magda
The Frighteners - Michael Jahn *h* 2273

Rebecca "Becca"
Briar Rose - Jane Yolen *f* 4806

Robbins, Maggie
The Dig - Alan Dean Foster *s* 1607

Roberts, Roy
Grave Markings - Michael A. Arnzen *h* 175

Roberts, Veronica "Ronnie"
Universal Soldier - Robert Tine *s* 4368

Rosen, Gerry
The Jericho Iteration - Allen Steele *s* 4182

Runyon, Damon
Nevermore - William Hjortsberg *h* 2150

Sawyer, Meredith
The Long Midnight - Daniel Ransom *h* 3572

Saxton, Drake
The Black Carousel - Charles L. Grant *h* 1846

Sloan, Susan
Beneath Still Waters - Matthew J. Costello *h* 964

Smithback, Bill
Relic - Douglas Preston *h* 3521

Spencer, Arlene
Revenge of the Seventh Carrier - Peter Albano *s* 39

Stevens, Jim
Reborn - F. Paul Wilson *h* 4691

Stiller, Dennis
The Nexus - Mike McQuay *f* 3075

Stone, Walker
Whipping Boy - John Byrne *h* 655

Suilin, Dick
Rolling Hot - David Drake *s* 1325

Sulaiman, Kahlili "Kay Bee" bint Munadi
Looking for the Mahdi - N. Lee Wood *s* 4753

Thaxton, Xavier
Count Geiger's Blues - Michael Bishop *s* 404

Theremon 762
Nightfall - Isaac Asimov *s* 207

Thomas, Fran
Winter Wolves - Earle Wescott *h* 4587

Thorne, Holly
Cold Fire - Dean R. Koontz *h* 2546

Tiernan, John
The Jericho Iteration - Allen Steele *s* 4182

Trask, Victor
Savant - Rex Miller *h* 3107

Tremaine, Bernard
Black Dogs - Ian McEwan *h* 3034

Tremaine, Ian
Carlucci's Edge - Richard Paul Russo *s* 3796

Vigeant, Alison
Angel Souls and Devil Hearts - Christopher Golden *h* 1810

Wallace, Ditsy
The Square Deal - David Drake *s* 1327

Webster, Torie
The Eyes of Torie Webster - Roy Sorrels *h* 4121

Wilson, Braemer
White Queen - Gwyneth Jones *s* 2355

Windsor, Marion
The Blood of the Lamb - Thomas F. Monteleone *h* 3150

Wing, Sue
The Summoning - Bentley Little *h* 2777

Woodbury, Gillian
Silent Moon - William Relling Jr. *h* 3616

Wright, Paul
Nightlight - Michael Cadnum *h* 664

Zarnicke, Marion
A World Lost - James B. Johnson *s* 2327

JUDGE

Acari, Stefan
The Beacon - Valerie J. Freireich *s* 1646

Brody, Aloysius
Pallas - L. Neil Smith *s* 4093

Candle, Martin
Blameless in Abaddon - James Morrow *f* 3209

Fastet, Meer
Exile - Michael P. Kube-McDowell *s* 2582

Gundhalinu, BZ
The Summer Queen - Joan D. Vinge *s* 4440

James, Dede
The Between - Tannarive Due *h* 1346

Mertz, Harry
A Covenant of Justice - David Gerrold *s* 1771

Phillips, Triune Adjudicator
Tangled Webs - Steve Mudd *s* 3220

Rile, Martin
Lunar Justice - Charles L. Harness *s* 2034

Svensdotter, Esther "Star"
Red Planet Run - Dana Stabenow *s* 4139

Tarkenton, Lewis
Echoes - Jackie Hyman *h* 2245

KIDNAPPER

Carton, Sidney "Sid"
North Wind - Gwyneth Jones *s* 2354

Pong, Mustapha
McCade's Bounty - William C. Dietz *s* 1252

Pook
Voices of Hope - David Feintuch *s* 1532

KNIGHT

Amaury
King & Raven - Cary James f 2275

Amfortas
The Grail of Hearts - Susan Shwartz f 4001

Bedwyr
The Last Pendragon - Robert Rice f 3661

Byron
Henry's Gift: The Magic Eye - David
  Worsick f 4759

Darius
Kaz the Minotaur - Richard A. Knaak f 2522

de Beq, Henri
Knights of the Blood - Scott MacMillan f 2862

de Courcy, Guiscard
King Javan's Year - Katherine Kurtz f 2591

de Verdeur, Michel "Raven"
King & Raven - Cary James f 2275

Drummond, Cathan
The Bastard Prince - Katherine Kurtz f 2588

Eckert, Jim
The Dragon and the Djinn - Gordon R.
  Dickson f 1233
The Dragon at War - Gordon R. Dickson f 1234
The Dragon on the Border - Gordon R.
  Dickson f 1236
The Dragon, the Earl, and the Troll - Gordon R.
  Dickson f 1237

Ector, Sir
The Dragon's Boy - Jane Yolen f 4807

Elric
The Spellkey Trilogy - Ann Downer f 1285

Falc of Risskor
Deathknight - Andrew J. Offutt f 3346

Fitz-Gerald, Ralf
Sherwood - Parke Godwin f 1806

Gawaine
Blood and Honor - Simon R. Green f 1893

Gilman
Pigs Don't Fly - Mary Brown f 594

Hawson, Jordan
The Forge of Virtue - Lynn Abbey f 14
The Temper of Wisdom - Lynn Abbey f 15

Jaqueth, Falcon
The Falcon and the Serpent - Cheryl A.
  Smith f 4068

Kaz
Kaz the Minotaur - Richard A. Knaak f 2522

Lancelot
The Child Queen - Nancy McKenzie f 3049
Chronicles of King Arthur - Andrea
  Hopkins f 2206
Guinevere: The Legend in Autumn - Persia
  Woolley f 4757
Queen of the Summer Stars - Persia
  Woolley f 4758

Launcelot
The King - Donald Barthelme f 313

mac Cuel, Ceilyn
The Work of the Sun - Teresa Edgerton f 1402

Morrough
StarSpawn - Kenneth Von Gunden s 4453

Neville-Smythe, Brian
The Dragon and the Djinn - Gordon R.
  Dickson f 1233
The Dragon, the Earl, and the Troll - Gordon R.
  Dickson f 1237

Odosson, William "Will"
Knight's Wyrd - Debra Doyle f 1294

Parsifal
Parsifal - Peter Vansittart f 4431

Ra-khir of Erythane
Beyond Ragnarok - Mickey Zucker Reichert f 3604

Rainaut, Valence
Crusader's Torch - Chelsea Quinn Yarbro h 4795

Simon "Seoman/Snowlock"
To Green Angel Tower - Tad Williams f 4645

Sparhawk
The Diamond Throne - David Eddings f 1389
Domes of Fire - David Eddings f 1390
The Hidden City - David Eddings f 1391
The Ruby Knight - David Eddings f 1392
The Sapphire Rose - David Eddings f 1393

Stardust, Baijon "Tiggy"
Archangel Blues - eluki bes shahar s 384
Darktraders - eluki bes shahar s 385

Tancred, Tolwyn
Storm Knights - Bill Slavicsek f 4059

Tawl
Master and Fool - J.V. Jones f 2358

William
Here There Be Dragons - Roger Zelazny f 4840

Woczniak, Hal
The Forever King - Molly Cochran f 879

LAIRD

Montana, Kent
668: The Neighbor of the Beast - Lionel
  Fenn h 1541
Kent Montana and the Really Ugly Thing From Mars -
  Lionel Fenn s 1542
Kent Montana and the Reasonably Invisible Man -
  Lionel Fenn s 1543
The Mark of the Moderately Vicious Vampire - Lionel
  Fenn h 1544

Tuchman, Ward
Enemy of My Enemy - Ben Ohlander s 3349

LANDLORD

Connaghan, Connor
Child of Shadows - John Coyne h 1001

Daez, Henry
Makoto - Kelley Wilde h 4619

Stone, David
Sati - Christopher Pike f 3449

LANDOWNER

Sylvie
Moonwise - Greer Ilene Gilman f 1799

Thinking Man of Moha
Fish Soup - Ursula K. Le Guin f 2688

Vehmund, Marsall
Heart Beast - Tanith Lee h 2713

Writing Woman of Maho
Fish Soup - Ursula K. Le Guin f 2688

LANDSCAPER

Lakeman, Max
Max Lakeman and the Beautiful Stranger - Jon
  Cohen f 883

LAWMAN

Adwon, Jay
Dusk - Ron Dee h 1185

Allen
The Persistence of Memory - Karen Ripley s 3669

Bill
Dusk - Ron Dee h 1185

Booth, Felix
Pitfall - Ronald Kelly h 2435

deLacey, William
Lady of the Forest - Jennifer Roberson f 3687

Erickson, Richard
Shadows Fall - Simon R. Green f 1903

Fitz-Gerald, Ralf
Sherwood - Parke Godwin f 1806

Kresh, Alvar
Caliban - Roger MacBride Allen s 63
Inferno - Roger MacBride Allen s 64

Laker, Tom
Among Madmen - Jim Starlin s 4156

Mark, Philip
The Sheriff of Nottingham - Richard Kluger f 2515

Narn, Roger K. "RK"
Mojo and the Pickle Jar - Douglas Bell f 357

Pale Boy
Batman: Captured by the Engines - Joe R.
  Lansdale h 2641

Presley, Elvis
Comeback Tour: The Sky Belongs to the Stars - Jack
  Yeovil s 4798

Smith, Alamo
Destination: Showdown - Jake Davis s 1131
The Last Rangers - Jake Davis s 1132

Watt, Al
Darkly the Thunder - William W.
  Johnstone h 2333

LAWYER

Adair, Hugh
Breeder - Douglas Clegg h 867

Adair, Rachel
Breeder - Douglas Clegg h 867

Allison, Harold
The Man Who Turned into Himself - David
  Ambrose h 74

Banner, Clint
Quake - Richard Laymon h 2681

Banning, Peter "Peter Pan"
Hook - Terry Brooks f 583

Beaumont, Greg
Midnight's Lair - Richard Laymon h 2680

Becker, Max
Second Contact - Mike Resnick s 3636

Bellman, Craig
The House That Jack Built - Graham
  Masterton h 2925

Birkett, Alison
Temporary Agency - Rachel Pollack f 3474

Burlingame, Gerald
Gerald's Game - Stephen King h 2486

Cray, Jennifer
One Land, One Duke - Ru Emerson f 1452
The Two in Hiding - Ru Emerson f 1454

Dad
Thor - Wayne Smith h 4106

LEADER

LESBIAN

LIBERAL

LIBRARIAN

MAIDEN

MAINTENANCE WORKER

Thorsen, Thorian "Torrie"
The Fire Duke - Joel Rosenberg f 3740
The Silver Stone - Joel Rosenberg f 3745

Topaz
Mistworld - Simon R. Green s 1902

Vader, Darth
Shadows of the Empire - Steve Perry s 3423

Vallaniri, Daner
The Raven Ring - Patricia C. Wrede f 4764

Veate
The Albino Knife - Steve Perry s 3415

Venabili, Dors
Forward the Foundation - Isaac Asimov s 195

Vree
Fifth Quarter - Tanya Huff f 2227
No Quarter - Tanya Huff f 2230

Wu, Kildee
Black Steel - Steve Perry s 3418

MASSEUSE

Galloway, Katt
Walking Wounded - Robert Devereaux h 1215

MATCHMAKER

Sparrow
Justice - David Drake s 1321

MECHANIC

Bowers, Sidney
Mojave Wells - L. Dean James s 2281

Cugnet, Vern
Stones of the Dalai Lama - Ken Mitchell f 3121

Frank
Spacer Dreams - Larry Segriff s 3923

Hummingbird, Kinsey
Drawing Blood - Poppy Z. Brite h 568

Petway, Boomer
Skinny Legs and All - Tom Robbins f 3684

Sam
The Unfinished - Jay B. Laws h 2676

Semmlar, Wayne
Near Dead - Stephen R. George h 1768

Solis, Rudy
Mother of Winter - Barbara Hambly f 2007

Tick-Tick
Finder - Emma Bull f 632

MENTALLY ILL PERSON

Calder, Reginald
No Blood Spilled - Les Daniels h 1083

Carol
Century 21 - Ewa Kuryluk s 2595

di Hoa, Barry
The Voices of Heaven - Frederik Pohl s 3470

Jack
Lunatics - Bradley Denton f 1205

Liddy, Mary
The Uprising - Brent Monahan h 3149

Tobias, Cameron
Making Love - Melanie Tem h 4327

Tobias, Robin
Strange Angels - Kathe Koja h 2543

Wade, Tamara
Bad Blood - D.A. Fowler h 1622

MERCENARY

Alon
The Nomad Queen - James Gordon White f 4607

Barek, A.E.
Created By - Richard Christian Matheson h 2937

Belmonte, Rodrigo
The Lions of Al-Rassan - Guy Gavriel Kay f 2403

Bruno
Harm's Way - Colin Greenland s 1934

Byrnison, Iorek
The Golden Compass - Philip Pullman f 3545

Calis
Shadow of a Dark Queen - Raymond E.
  Feist f 1538

Calmady, Pollexfen
The Architecture of Desire - Mary Gentle f 1761

Canby, Gordon
Canby's Legion - Bill Baldwin s 258

Carson, Chev
Warp Angel - Stuart Hopen s 2205

Clay, John Sebastian
A Landscape of Darkness - John Blair s 416

Cooke, Daniel
Surface Action - David Drake s 1329

dav Medroch, Cullin
Kingmaker's Sword - Ann Marston f 2887

Dawson, Jack
Hell-Storm - James A. Moore h 3174

de Garsenc, Blaise
A Song for Arbonne - Guy Gavriel Kay f 2404

d'Iste, Tiran
Dark Mirror, Dark Dreams - Sharon Green f 1889
Silver Princess, Golden Knight - Sharon
  Green f 1891

Falkenberg, John Christian
Prince of Mercenaries - Jerry Pournelle s 3490

Gordon, John
Surface Action - David Drake s 1329

Grover
Heroes, Inc. - Kyle Crocco f 1029
Heroes Wanted - Kyle Crocco f 1028

Horn, Alan
Star Bridge - James Gunn s 1970

Jill of Cerrmor
The Dragon Revenant - Katharine Kerr f 2445

kar Therma, Staffa
Relic of Empire - W. Michael Gear s 1742

Karolyi, Ignace
Traveling with the Dead - Barbara Hambly h 2012

Kerowyn
By the Sword - Mercedes Lackey f 2602

Korendir
The Master of Whitestorm - Janny Wurts f 4786

Latro
Soldier of Arete - Gene Wolfe f 4735

Lyma, Skyla
Relic of Empire - W. Michael Gear s 1742

Maelwaedd, Rhodry
Days of Air and Darkness - Katharine Kerr f 2443
Days of Blood and Fire - Katharine Kerr f 2444
The Dragon Revenant - Katharine Kerr f 2445
A Time of Exile - Katharine Kerr f 2452

Mark, Philip
The Sheriff of Nottingham - Richard Kluger f 2515

Matar, Kitiara "Kit"
Steel and Stone - Ellen Porath f 3481

Miri
Carpe Diem - Steve Miller s 3113

Morrison, Athol
When Heaven Fell - William Barton s 319

ni Errhyn, Bracht
Dark Magic - Angus Wells f 4569
Forbidden Magic - Angus Wells f 4572
Wild Magic - Angus Wells f 4576

Owensford, Peter
Go Tell the Spartans - Jerry Pournelle s 3488
Prince of Sparta - Jerry Pournelle s 3491

Parmenion
Lion of Macedon - David Gemmell f 1756

Ramok
Cat Scratch Fever - Tara K. Harper s 2037

Ranson, June
Rolling Hot - David Drake s 1325

Reece
War - Simon Hawke f 2099

Rhodry
A Time of Omens - Katharine Kerr f 2453

Rico
Fade to Black - Nyx Smith s 4095

Romlar, Artus
The Regiment's War - John Dalmas s 1072
The White Regiment - John Dalmas s 1073

Roshannon, Nikkael
Wheel of Dreams - Salinda Tyson f 4409

Sadi
Kaleidoscope Century - John Barnes s 294

Shaman
The Quick - Burt Cole s 896

Silverhorn, Aelfred
Into the Void - Nigel Findley f 1560

Starhawk
The Dark Hand of Magic - Barbara Hambly f 2004

Suilin, Dick
Rolling Hot - David Drake s 1325

Sumara
The Nomad Queen - James Gordon White f 4607

Sun Wolf
The Dark Hand of Magic - Barbara Hambly f 2004

Tarlach
Flight of Vengeance - Andre Norton f 3306
Storms of Victory - Andre Norton f 3315

Theisiger, Carlo
Enemy of My Enemy - Ben Ohlander s 3349

Wolf
Konrad - David Ferring f 1551

Xris
The Knights of the Black Earth - Margaret
  Weis s 4561

Zakalwe, Cheradenine
Use of Weapons - Iain M. Banks s 277

MERCHANT

Gragelouth
Son of Spellsinger - Alan Dean Foster f 1617

MILITARY PERSONNEL

Agesilaus, "Agis"
Spartan Run - David Robbins s 3679

Aidan
Way of the Clans - Robert Thurston s 4362

al-Schouki, Esoch
Foragers - Charles Oberndorf s 3334

Alaiya
The Return of the Breakneck Boys - Geary
  Gravel s 1868

Althor
Catch the Lightning - Catherine Asaro s 181

Amilcar
Pendragon - Stephen R. Lawhead f 2672

Andojar, Susan Smith
The Web of Spider - W. Michael Gear s 1744

Angelus, Lucifer "Luke"
Chains of Light - Quentin Thomas s 4347

Antero, Rali Emilie
The Warrior's Tale - Allan Cole f 895

Antilles, Wedge
Rogue Squadron - Michael A. Stackpole s 4152

Antonius, Marcus
Throne of Isis - Judith Tarr f 4305

Antonovich, Colonel
The Struggle - Jerry Ahern s 34

APU-805 "Bird Dog"
Destination: Showdown - Jake Davis s 1131
The Last Rangers - Jake Davis s 1132

Armstrong, Alexander "the Great"
Martian Rainbow - Robert L. Forward s 1594

Arthur
The Hawk's Gray Feather - Patricia
  Kennealy f 2439

Arvin, Andro
Starfire Down - Lee McKeone s 3052

Asado
The War of Don Emmanuel's Nether Parts - Louis de
  Bernieres f 1137

Asher, Anat
Signs of Life - Cherry Wilder s 4622

Atkins, Thomas "Soldier"
Genetic Soldier - George Turner s 4381

Atle
Silent Songs - A.C. Crispin s 1026

Atvar
Worldwar: Striking the Balance - Harry
  Turtledove s 4396
Worldwar: Upsetting the Balance - Harry
  Turtledove s 4398

Auganzar
Warlord of Heaven - Adrian Cole f 887

Augustine, Alexa
Dream of Glass - Jean Mark Gawron s 1734

Bammer, Mortimer
Kill Crazy - L.S. Riker s 3667

Bar-el, Shimon
Hero - Joel Rosenberg s 3741

Baranyk, Valentin
Cold Allies - Patricia Anthony s 128

Barnes, Randy
Sleipnir - Linda Evans f 1493

Bashir, Julian
Time's Enemy - L.A. Graf s 1842

Belkassem, Ferhat Ben
Path of the Fury - David Weber s 4527

Bezarian
Red Army - Ralph Peters s 3429

Bickerstaff, Robert Luther
Terraplane - Jack Womack s 4749

Bill, Corporal
Planet of the Robot Slaves - Harry Harrison s 2058

Birch, Wellington
Lurid Dreams - Charles L. Harness s 2035

Black, Frank
Dead Heat - Del Stone Jr. h 4239

Blackstone, Rex
Primary Inversion - Catherine Asaro s 182

Blade, Sonya
Mortal Kombat - Martin Delrio f 1199

Bloch, Jared
No Limits - Nigel Findley s 1561

Blount, Mikal
The Clouds of Saturn - Michael McCollum s 3001

Bonaparte, Napoleon
The Napoleon Wager - William R.
  Forstchen s 1589

Braan
Genellan: Planetfall - Scott G. Gier s 1786

Bradoukis, Matthew
Ground Zero - Kevin J. Anderson h 89

Brainard
The Jungle - David Drake s 1320

Brightlaw, Nic
The Cup of Morning Shadows - Rosemary
  Edghill f 1403

Brim, Wilf
The Defenders - Bill Baldwin s 259
The Defiance - Bill Baldwin s 260
The Mercenaries - Bill Baldwin s 261
The Siege - Bill Baldwin s 262

Britannicus, Caius
The Skystone - Jack Whyte f 4614

Broketail, Bazil
Battledragon - Christopher Rowley f 3756
Dragons of War - Christopher Rowley f 3758
A Sword for a Dragon - Christopher
  Rowley f 3760

Brutus, Marcus Junius
Child of the Eagle - Esther Friesner f 1668

Buccari, Sharl
Genellan: Planetfall - Scott G. Gier s 1786

Bueller
Aliens: Earth Hive - Steve Perry s 3416

Bushell, Thomas
The Two Georges - Richard Dreyfuss s 1335

Caceras, Mimla
Traitors from Within - R.A. Montgomery s 3157

Caillet, Bertrand
The Werewolf of Paris - Guy Endore h 1463

Calrissian, Lando
Before the Storm - Michael P. Kube-
  McDowell s 2581

Cameron, Dev
Warstrider - William H. Keith Jr. s 2421

Carlson, Curt
Blood Siege - G. Harry Stine s 4211
Force of Arms - G. Harry Stine s 4212
Guts and Glory - G. Harry Stine s 4213
Judgment Day - G. Harry Stine s 4214
Warrior Shield - G. Harry Stine s 4216

Carnes, Rebecca
Arc Riders - David Drake s 1314

Carrigan
The Unknown Soldier - Mickey Zucker
  Reichert s 3611

Cedric
One for the Morning Glory - John Barnes f 297

Centuri, Ariann
Half-Light - Denise Vitola s 4443

Chakotay
Ragnarok - Nathan Archer s 170

Chan
Dragon's Blood - Alex McDonough s 3025

Chaney
Crown of Empire - Chelsea Quinn Yarbro s 4794

Chapel, Christine
Crossroad - Barbara Hambly s 2003

Charlie
Chains of Light - Quentin Thomas s 4347

Chekov, Pavel
The Ashes of Eden - William Shatner s 3936
The Disinherited - Peter David s 1116
Traitor Winds - L.A. Graf s 1843
Windows on a Lost World - V.E. Mitchell s 3125

Chen, Kao
Beneath the Tree of Heaven - David
  Wingrove s 4710

Chibisov
Red Army - Ralph Peters s 3429

Christiansen, Mitch
Killjoy - Elizabeth Forrest h 1585

Cind
Empire's End - Allan Cole s 888

Clendannan, Cherrid ris
Death's Gray Land - Mike Shupp s 3998

Coke, Matthew
The Sharp End - David Drake s 1326

Collins, Lysander
Prince of Sparta - Jerry Pournelle s 3491

Connor, Islaen
Fire Planet - P.M. Griffin s 1949
Jungle Assault - P.M. Griffin s 1950

Coollege, Emma
Galactic MI - Kevin D. Randle s 3561

Corry, William M.
Starsea Invaders: First Action - G. Harry
  Stine s 4215

Court, Annalyn Reynolds
The Winds of Mars - H.M. Hoover s 2204

Courvossier, Raoul
The Honor of the Queen - David Weber s 4523

Creighton, Abe "TC"
Afrikorps - Bill Dolan s 1264
Cobra Curse - Bill Dolan s 1265
Iron Horse - Bill Dolan s 1266
White Rhino - Bill Dolan s 1267

Crisco, Bungeeman
Star Wreck 6: Geek Space Nine - Leah
  Rewolinski s 3642

Croaker
Bleak Seasons - Glen Cook f 925
Dreams of Steel - Glen Cook f 928

Crusher, Wesley
Balance of Power - Dafydd ab Hugh s 6

Dacham, Klaus
Partisan - S. Andrew Swann s 4276

Dai, David
Half the Day Is Night - Maureen F.
  McHugh s 3042

Damico, Mary
Dream Baby - Bruce McAllister s 2948

Danirov, Major
Suicide Attack - John Sievert s 4007

Danner, Hannah
Ammonite - Nicola Griffith s 1956

Data
The Devil's Heart - Carmen Carter s 748

Doomsday
The Death and Life of Superman - Roger Stern *s* 4198

Fades
The Eye of the World - Robert Jordan *f* 2381

Frankenstein's Monster
The Final Battle - Richard A. Lupoff *f* 2840

Frostwing
Frostwing - Richard A. Knaak *f* 2520

Graylord
Shadowlight - Jackie Hyman *f* 2246

Grendel
The Tower of Beowulf - Parke Godwin *f* 1808

Grundbur
Whose Song Is Sung - Frank Schaefer *f* 3897

Kaeot
A Whisper of Wings - Steven Ray Fulgham *h* 1684

Mama
India's Story - Kathlyn S. Starbuck *s* 4153

Nicodareus
Darkenheight - Douglas Niles *f* 3269

Poduano, Dominic
Shapes - Steve Vance *h* 4425

Shadowman
Dark Souls - Barry Porter *h* 3482

Shudde-M'ell
The Burrowers Beneath - Brian Lumley *h* 2823

Sikes, Jesse
Sins of the Flesh - Don Davis *h* 1130

Skogskra, Haakon
The Gnome's Engine - Teresa Edgerton *f* 1398

Utlunta
Stoneskin's Revenge - Tom Deitz *f* 1194

Verner, Janice
Find Your Own Truth - Robert N. Charrette *f* 787

Vril, Dietrich
The Armageddon Box - Robert Weinberg *h* 4536

Ward, Alan
Midsummer - Matthew J. Costello *h* 971

MORGUE ATTENDANT

Radburn, Adam
The Undead - Roxanne Longstreet *h* 2796

Washburn, Corky
Bring on the Night - Don Davis *h* 1129

MOUNTAIN MAN

Digby, Digger
The World Next Door - Brad Ferguson *s* 1548

Kindle, Tom
The Harvest - Robert Charles Wilson *s* 4703

Malone, Amos "Mad Amos"
Mad Amos - Alan Dean Foster *f* 1612

MOUNTAINEER

Appenfell, Rudgar "Rudy"
A Breach in the Watershed - Douglas Niles *f* 3267
Darkenheight - Douglas Niles *f* 3269

Glover, Tony
Snowbeast! - Peter Tremayne *h* 4373

MURDERER

Bates, Norman
Psycho - Robert Bloch *h* 440

Psycho II - Robert Bloch *h* 441

Bergeron, Carolyn
Nightmare Logic - Matthew Hall *h* 2000

Blade
Shadow Hunt - Anne Logston *f* 2791

Bothari
Barrayar - Lois McMaster Bujold *s* 620

Brandsetter, Earl
Lethal Interface - Mel Odom *s* 3338

Caiper, Watly
The Host - Peter R. Emshwiller *s* 1460

Cassidy, Lylah
Looker - Jorge Saralegui *h* 3859

Chandler, Joshua "the Whistler" Jeremiah
Oracle - Mike Resnick *s* 3632

Chucky
Child's Play III - Matthew J. Costello *h* 965

Dagon
Dead Boys - Richard Calder *s* 683

Dennis
Frisk - Dennis Cooper *h* 943

Ell, Pe
The Druid of Shannara - Terry Brooks *f* 580

Felmet
Wyrd Sisters - Terry Pratchett *f* 3512

Gaimes, Gary
House Haunted - Al Sarrantonio *h* 3868

Garrett, Carl
The Dead Man's Kiss - Robert Weinberg *h* 4541

Gavel, Kevin
Junkyard - Barry Porter *h* 3483

Helman, Granger
Bloodshift - Garfield Reeves-Stevens *h* 3597

Johnny
The Bad Thing - Michael O'Rourke *h* 3366

Kane
Kane - Douglas Borton *h* 472

King, Depard
Spindoc - Steve Perry *s* 3424

Laker, Maria
Among Madmen - Jim Starlin *s* 4156

Lector, Hannibal "Cannibal"
The Silence of the Lambs - Thomas Harris *h* 2051

Marrah, Rabh
The Light of Exile - Cheryl J. Franklin *s* 1637

Mishwe, Dajaj
ViraVax - Bill Ransom *s* 3570

Newman, Greg
Impulse - Rick Hautala *h* 2084

Ostrow, Henry
Clarke County, Space - Allen Steele *s* 4181

Page, Scott
This Side of Judgment - J.R. Dunn *s* 1364

Phoenix, Simon
Demolition Man - Richard Osborne *s* 3371

Primavera
Dead Girls - Richard Calder *s* 684

Reich, Ben
The Demolished Man - Alfred Bester *s* 388

Royal, Barton
Billy - Whitley Strieber *h* 4258

Saladin
The Forever King - Molly Cochran *f* 879

Sikes, Jesse
Sins of the Flesh - Don Davis *h* 1130

Stark, George
The Dark Half - Stephen King *h* 2481

Steve
Sacrifice - Richard Kinion *h* 2498

Succubus
The Hacker - Chet Day *h* 1135

Thibodeau, Skida "Skilly"
Prince of Sparta - Jerry Pournelle *s* 3491

Tomaso
Polar City Blues - Katharine Kerr *s* 2449

Two Feathers, Jimmy "the Injun"
Oracle - Mike Resnick *s* 3632

Walford, John
Walford's Oak - Jill M. Phillips *f* 3433

Wolf, Billy "Slider"
Dreamer - Peter James *h* 2288

MUSEUM CURATOR

Barton, Howard
The Paper Grail - James P. Blaylock *f* 424

Flannery, Kathleen
The Two Georges - Richard Dreyfuss *s* 1335

Hunt, Katie
Trickster - Muriel Gray *h* 1875

Jordan, Miles
End of an Era - Robert J. Sawyer *s* 3883

Kawakita, Gregory
Relic - Douglas Preston *h* 3521

Roberts, Karin
Blood Sabbath - Leigh Clark *h* 843

Schenk, Madeline Leuoir
Warsprite - Jefferson P. Swycaffer *s* 4285

Thackeray, Brandon
End of an Era - Robert J. Sawyer *s* 3883

Wisnewski, Leonard
Legion of the Dead - Geoffrey Caine *h* 681

Ystilog, Erpad
Brotherhood of the Stars - Kirby Greene *s* 1932

MUSICIAN

Alton, Margaret
Exile's Song - Marion Zimmer Bradley *s* 520

Alvarez, Dan
Bone Music - Alan Rodgers *h* 3718

Amy
Stranded - Camarin Grae *s* 1841

Angel Juan
Missing Angel Juan - Francesca Lia Block *f* 448

Arlen, Drew
Beggars and Choosers - Nancy Kress *s* 2573

Asgard, Paula
Carlucci's Edge - Richard Paul Russo *s* 3796

Banyon, Eric
Knight of Ghosts and Shadows - Mercedes Lackey *f* 2612
Summoned to Tourney - Mercedes Lackey *f* 2623

Bat, Cherokee
Cherokee Bat and the Goat Guys - Francesca Lia Block *f* 445

Batterberry, Lesli
Ghosts of Wind and Shadow - Charles de Lint *f* 1151

Bauer, Robert
Requiem - Clifford Mohr *h* 3146

Character Description Index

Pel of House Yendi
Five Hundred Years After - Steven Brust   f   607

Penward, Darren
Carnosaur - Harry Adam Knight   s   2538

Pjerin
Sing the Four Quarters - Tanya Huff   f   2231

Prosper
The Shining Company - Rosemary Sutcliff   f   4271

Quordane, Holis
Shadow of the Crown - Craig Mills   f   3119

Ranulf
Changing Fate - Elisabeth Waters   f   4485

Rap
The Living God - Dave Duncan   f   1354
The Stricken Field - Dave Duncan   f   1360

ReAth
Shaper's Legacy - Sheila Finch   s   1556

Robert "Robin Hood" of Locksley
Lady of the Forest - Jennifer Roberson   f   3687

Sadir
Canby's Legion - Bill Baldwin   s   258

Sakhalin, Anatoly
The Law of Becoming - Kate Elliott   s   1423

Santos, Ramon
Iceman - Cynthia Felice   s   1539

Sessine, Alandre VII
Feersum Endjinn - Iain M. Banks   s   274

Sethiyan, Hattim
The Usurper - Angus Wells   f   4574

Shinji, Matsumura
The Yngling in Yamato - John Dalmas   s   1075

Shonto
Gatherer of Clouds - Sean Russell   f   3792

Skogskra, Haakon
The Gnome's Engine - Teresa Edgerton   f   1398

sorMeklan, Driskolt "Dart"
Beneath the Web - Lynn Abbey   f   10

Stark, Eddard
A Game of Thrones - George R.R. Martin   f   2896

Steadford, Sir Harry
The Meddlesome Ghost - Sheila Rosalynd
   Allen   f   70

Strelsau, Mathias
Silk and Steel - Ron Miller   f   3111

Tarrant, Gerald
Black Sun Rising - C.S. Friedman   f   1653
When True Night Falls - C.S. Friedman   f   1656

Thann, Danilo "Dan"
Elfshadow - Elaine Cunningham   f   1045

Tremane
Storm Rising - Mercedes Lackey   f   2621

Valemar
Summer King, Winter Fool - Lisa Goldstein   f   1815

Vallaniri, Daner
The Raven Ring - Patricia C. Wrede   f   4764

Villette, Louis
The Judas Cross - Charles Sheffield   h   3958

Viroslav, Alexander
The Kiss - Kathryn Reines   h   3614

Volmar
Castle of Deception - Mercedes Lackey   f   2604

von Amerningen, Lutz
Cloud Castles - Michael Scott Rohan   f   3730

von Darkmoor, Erik
Rise of a Merchant Prince - Raymond E.
   Feist   f   1536

von Hessel
Escape From Loki - Philip Jose Farmer   f   1503

von Schuss, Nicholas
Kit's Book - C.J. Mills   s   3116

Vorkosigan, Aral
Barrayar - Lois McMaster Bujold   s   620

Vorkosigan, Miles
Cetaganda - Lois McMaster Bujold   s   622
Memory - Lois McMaster Bujold   s   624
Mirror Dance - Lois McMaster Bujold   s   625

Vorpatril, Ivan
Cetaganda - Lois McMaster Bujold   s   622
Memory - Lois McMaster Bujold   s   624

Xar
The Seventh Gate - Margaret Weis   f   4566

Young, Pavel
Field of Dishonor - David Weber   s   4519

Youngman, Cai
The Dragon's Boy - Jane Yolen   f   4807

zu Blas und Fiersing, Dalain "Wisp"
An Exchange of Gifts - Anne McCaffrey   f   2968

NOBLEWOMAN

Acila
Changing Fate - Elisabeth Waters   f   4485

Aiko
The Dragonstone - Dennis L. McKiernan   f   3054

al Jorddyn, Kerridwen
Kingmaker's Sword - Ann Marston   f   2887

Albain, Elandra
Reign of Shadows - Deborah Chester   f   819

Alice
The Prince and the Pilgrim - Mary Stewart   f   4205

Altunin, Roberta
Rock of Ages - Walter Jon Williams   s   4651

Amalayna
Chains of Darkness, Chains of Light - Michelle
   Sagara   f   3823

Amalia, Lady
The Interior Life - Katherine Blake   f   417

Aradia
A Heroine of the World - Tanith Lee   f   2714

Arin
The Dragonstone - Dennis L. McKiernan   f   3054

Aryton, Antonia
Whispers in the Dark - Jonathan Aycliffe   h   239

Avignon, Kitten "Our Lady of Roses"
Mage Heart - Jane Routley   f   3754

Bannering, Charlan "Arlin"
King of the Dead - R.A. MacAvoy   f   2846

Bathori, Elizabeth
Daughter of the Night - Elaine Bergstrom   h   379

Bathory, Elizabeth
Blood Countess - Andrei Codrescu   h   881

Beauty
Beauty - Sheri S. Tepper   f   4333

Catelyn
A Game of Thrones - George R.R. Martin   f   2896

Damarr, Amala
The Mace of Souls - Bruce Fergusson   f   1549

de Brus, Marjory
Quest for a Maid - Frances Mary Hendry   f   2124

de Marktos, Cecelia
Hunting Party - Elizabeth Moon   s   3159
Sporting Chance - Elizabeth Moon   s   3163
Winning Colors - Elizabeth Moon   s   3165

de Remy, Mireille
The Eight - Katherine Neville   f   3258

Eleighanaran "Leigh"
Shadows on the Hill - Jackie Cassada   f   758

Erzsebet
*The Secret Weavers: Stories of the Fantastic by Latin
   American Women* - Marjorie Agosin   f   33

FitzWalter, Marion "Marion of Ravenskeep"
Lady of the Forest - Jennifer Roberson   f   3687

Francine
Lord Conrad's Lady - Leo Frankowski   s   1644

Gallowglass, Cordelia
M'Lady Witch - Christopher Stasheff   f   4161

Graciosa
Child of Faerie, Child of Earth - Josepha
   Sherman   f   3976

Halarek, Kathryn "Kit" Magdalena Alysha
Kit's Book - C.J. Mills   s   3116

Harlan, Kathryn "Kit"
Zjhanne's Book - C.J. Mills   s   3117

Harrington, Honor
Field of Dishonor - David Weber   s   4519
Flag in Exile - David Weber   s   4520
Honor Among Enemies - David Weber   s   4522
The Honor of the Queen - David Weber   s   4523
On Basilisk Station - David Weber   s   4526
The Short Victorious War - David Weber   s   4528

Helen
The Princess and the Dragon - Roberto
   Pazzi   f   3402

Hutsenreiter, Skirlet
Night Lamp - Jack Vance   s   4422

Jaeme
Twisted Dragon - Kevin Stein   f   4188

Javere "Javerri"
Ladylord - Sasha Miller   f   3112

Katrina
War - Simon Hawke   f   2099

Kessallia
The Prince of Ill Luck - Susan Dexter   f   1220

Lohmatski, Natalya
Dancing Bears - Fred Saberhagen   f   3809

Lysia
Hammer and Anvil - Harry Turtledove   f   4387

Marian
The Outlaws of Sherwood - Robin
   McKinley   f   3065

Matilde
A Strange and Ancient Name - Josepha
   Sherman   f   3981

Melliandra "Melli"
The Baker's Boy - J.V. Jones   f   2356
A Man Betrayed - J.V. Jones   f   2357

Morgiana
The Dagger and the Cross: A Novel of the Crusades -
   Judith Tarr   f   4301

Morianna, Maigrey
King's Sacrifice - Margaret Weis   s   4560
The Lost King - Margaret Weis   s   4562

Naismith, Cordelia
Barrayar - Lois McMaster Bujold   s   620

Nordbo, Tyra
Inconstant Star - Poul Anderson   s   107

Pentacoste
Better in the Dark - Chelsea Quinn Yarbro   h   4792

Penward, Jan
Carnosaur - Harry Adam Knight   s   2538

Percy, Anne
The Spiral Dance - R. Garcia y Robertson   *f* 1704

Raine of the Three Waters
A Breach in the Watershed - Douglas Niles   *f* 3267
Darkenheight - Douglas Niles   *f* 3269

Ramkin, Sybil
Guards! Guards! - Terry Pratchett   *f* 3501

Rangegonda
Better in the Dark - Chelsea Quinn Yarbro   *h* 4792

Renya, Jacinta
Iceman - Cynthia Felice   *s* 1539

St. Du Lac, Lynn
The Lost History of Redwyn - William Jay   *f* 2299

Scatha
The Endless Knot - Stephen R. Lawhead   *f* 2671

Soerensen, Terese "Tess"
Jaran - Kate Elliott   *s* 1422

Soolis, Yveena
The Thirteenth Majestral - Hayford Peirce   *s* 3407

Valaise, Ailena
Kingdom of the Grail - A.A. Attanasio   *f* 226

Vantara
The Fugitive Worlds - Bob Shaw   *s* 3946

ViKay
Hour of the Octopus - Joel Rosenberg   *f* 3742

Viroslav, Maria
The Kiss - Kathryn Reines   *h* 3614

vo Derrivalle, Eliste
Illusion - Paula Volsky   *f* 4448

Voerster, Eliana Ehrengraf
Glory - Alfred Coppel   *s* 955

Volkova, Ekaterina Alexandrova
Glory's War - Alfred Coppel   *s* 957

von Alte, Erde
The Book of Earth - Marjorie Bradley
   Kellogg   *f* 2427

Yvette of Grintz
The Pixilated Peeress - L. Sprague de
   Camp   *f* 1141

Zaula
Requiem for Anthi - Jay D. Blakeney   *s* 419

Ziemann, Mia
Holy Fire - Bruce Sterling   *s* 4195

Zillabar
A Covenant of Justice - David Gerrold   *s* 1771

NURSE

Armstrong, Vera
Werewolf - Peter Rubie   *h* 3764

Barrett, Kitty
Night Music - Sheila Bristow Garner   *h* 1724

Boardman, Gillian
Stranger in a Strange Land - Robert A.
   Heinlein   *s* 2117

Chapel, Christine
Crossroad - Barbara Hambly   *s* 2003

Charlie
Chains of Light - Quentin Thomas   *s* 4347

Coughlin, Molly
Dry Skull Dreams - Michael Green   *h* 1879

Damico, Mary
Dream Baby - Bruce McAllister   *s* 2948

Everson, Kelly
Harmful Intent - Robin Cook   *s* 939

Fellowes, Edith
The Ugly Little Boy - Isaac Asimov   *s* 209

Halloran, Myrna
Flying in Place - Susan Palwick   *h* 3380

Kelly, Dorothea
Systems - W.T. Quick   *s* 3549

Kuttner, Dayne
Sympathy for the Devil - Holly Lisle   *f* 2771

Matheson, Honor
Fatal Outcome - Patricia Wallace   *h* 4479

McCulley, Kitty
The Healer's War - Elizabeth Ann
   Scarborough   *f* 3891

Prawdzik, Ed
Night Sounds - Warner Lee   *h* 2716

Sannazarro, Sally
Treasure Box - Orson Scott Card   *h* 729

Shikome, Lily
The Twelfth Child - Raymond Van Over   *h* 4415

Waller, Enid
Fiends - John Farris   *h* 1516

OCCULTIST

Alice, Ti
Tempter - Nancy A. Collins   *h* 907

Callow, John
Evil Intent - Bernard Taylor   *h* 4308

Mander, Otto
The Burning - Graham Masterton   *h* 2922

Mandrax
Master of Lies - Graham Masterton   *h* 2926

Miller, Quintus
Walkers - Graham Masterton   *h* 2927

Raeburn, Francis
The Lodge of the Lynx - Katherine Kurtz   *f* 2592

Talbot, David
The Tale of the Body Thief - Anne Rice   *h* 3655

OFFICE WORKER

Bobby
Steam - Jay B. Laws   *h* 2675

Carpenter, Paul
Hot Sky at Midnight - Robert Silverberg   *s* 4013

Craig, Alice
Down River - Stephen Gallagher   *h* 1696

Frankl, Victor
The Suiting - Kelley Wilde   *h* 4621

Harrison, Sally
The Eyes of the Beast - Steve Harris   *h* 2050

Kennedy, Jill
Insatiable - David Dvorkin   *h* 1370

Mick
Steam - Jay B. Laws   *h* 2675

Roode, Tanya
Lethal Delivery - J.G. Maxon   *h* 2939

Sciascia, Francesca
Catacomb - Andrew Laurance   *h* 2665

Thompson, Patty
Seed of Evil - Edmund Plante   *h* 3457

Toplin
Toplin - Michael McDowell   *h* 3033

OIL INDUSTRY WORKER

McFarland, Henry Lee
Petrogypsies - Rory Harper   *s* 2036

Miller, Doc
Petrogypsies - Rory Harper   *s* 2036

ORGANIZED CRIME FIGURE

Bey, Friedlander
The Exile Kiss - George Alec Effinger   *s* 1406

Catalano, Serena
Protektor - Charles Platt   *s* 3459

Gaetano, Rafaelo
Empire Builders - Ben Bova   *s* 479

Jabba the Hutt
Tales From Jabba's Palace - Kevin J.
   Anderson   *s* 95

Kyler, Vaughan
Blood on the Water - P.N. Elrod   *h* 1437

Paco, Frank
Bloodlist - P.N. Elrod   *h* 1438

Pruet, Maxine
Phule's Paradise - Robert Asprin   *s* 219

Raven
Snow Crash - Neal Stephenson   *s* 4191

Scanwell, Jane
Empire Builders - Ben Bova   *s* 479

Stoogeone, Anthony
Something Out There - Ronald Kelly   *h* 2437

Xisor
Shadows of the Empire - Steve Perry   *s* 3423

ORPHAN

a-Lagan, Meredydd
The Meri - Maya Kaathryn Bohnhoff   *f* 459

Blessing, Arthur
The Forever King - Molly Cochran   *f* 879

Brita
Conan the Rogue - John Maddox Roberts   *f* 3693

Buddy
Land O'Goshen - Charles McNair   *s* 3071

Calliope
Ecstasia - Francesca Lia Block   *f* 446

Chance, David
Brain Child - George Turner   *s* 4380

Concord, Tappuah "Tappy"
The Caterpillar's Question - Piers Anthony   *f* 134

Destree
Storms of Victory - Andre Norton   *f* 3315

Dillon, Ronny
Soulsmith - Tom Deitz   *f* 1193

Francie
In the Heart of the Valley of Love - Cynthia
   Kadohata   *s* 2387

Gael, Dorothy "Dotty"
Was - Geoff Ryman   *f* 3804

Gwyn, Angharad "the Rowan"
The Rowan - Anne McCaffrey   *s* 2980

Harris, Nora
Grandma's Little Darling - Stephen R.
   George   *h* 1767

Harth, Beren "Brat" SanDyllin
Wheel of Dreams - Salinda Tyson   *f* 4409

Hasmara, Faan "Fa"
The Magic Wars - Jo Clayton   *f* 860
Wildfire - Jo Clayton   *f* 865

Hawkins, Rosalind "Rose"
The Fire Rose - Mercedes Lackey   *f* 2608

Character Description Index (column 1)

Willson, Matthew
Dark Reunion - Stephen R. George h 1764

Windclan, Raincloud
Daughter of Elysium - Joan Slonczewski s 4062

Woody
My Stepfather Shrank! - Barbara Dillon s 1258

Zimmerman, Debra
Panda Ray - Michael Kandel s 2398

Zorba the Hutt
Zorba the Hutt's Revenge - Paul Davids s 1126

PASSENGER

Cline, Tara
Redshift Rendezvous - John E. Stith s 4232

Stripe
A Maze of Stars - John Brunner s 600

Volar
A Maze of Stars - John Brunner s 600

PATIENT

Adda
Flux - Stephen Baxter s 331

Andrews, Laura
Quarantine - Greg Egan s 1415

Billie
Aliens: Earth Hive - Steve Perry s 3416

Canary, Sarah
Sarah Canary - Karen Joy Fowler f 1628

Cleg, Dennis "Spider"
Spider - Patrick McGrath h 3039

Engel, Emily
Zod Wallop - William Browning Spencer h 4123

Fraser, Mike
Dark Silence - Rick Hautala h 2081

Griffith, Wally
Strange Invasion - Michael Kandel s 2399

Horsfall, Arne
Fiends - John Farris h 1516

Johnson, Laura
Door Number Three - Patrick O'Leary s 3355

Kevin
The Midnight Club - Christopher Pike h 3448

Lassiter, Charles
Hopeship - Simon Lang s 2637

Lockheart, Karen
Eden's Eyes - Sean Costello h 976

Owens, Tiffany "Tif"
Resurrection - Katharine Kerr s 2450

Pawluk, Ilonka
The Midnight Club - Christopher Pike h 3448

Story, Raymond
Zod Wallop - William Browning Spencer h 4123

Voisard, B.J.
Sarah Canary - Karen Joy Fowler f 1628

PATRIOT

Vivo, Dionisio
Senor Vivo and the Coca Lord - Louis de Bernieres f 1136

PAWNBROKER

Steiner, Bill
Rose Madder - Stephen King h 2492

PEDDLER

Crocken
The Wizard's Shadow - Susan Dexter f 1222

Gunn
Primavera - Francesca Lia Block f 449

PHARMACIST

Aiken, Robert
The Mysterium - Eric McCormack h 3008

Kole, Polly
Flesh - Gus Weill h 4531

Small, Elmo
The Devil's Cradle - Kate Stewart h 4204

PHILANTHROPIST

Cornish, Francis
The Cornish Trilogy - Robertson Davies f 1127

Dore, Michael
Lunar Justice - Charles L. Harness s 2034

Flitheimer, Samuel
Dr. Dimension - John DeChancie s 1176

Maule, Matthew
A Matter of Taste - Fred Saberhagen h 3814

PHILOSOPHER

Johnson, Mark "Hobbes"
Mosaic - Jeri Taylor s 4311

Malu
Children of the Mind - Orson Scott Card s 717

Tradescant, John
Sexing the Cherry - Jeanette Winterson f 4719

PHOTOGRAPHER

Brady, Mathew B.
The Gallery of His Dreams - Kristine Kathryn Rusch f 3775

Brenner, Robin
The Feeding - Leigh Clark h 845

Cadigan, Risha "Rusty"
Love Bite - Sherry Gottlieb h 1835

Castle, Charles
Photographing Fairies - Steve Szilagyi f 4289

Chase, Adam
Nocturnas - Shawn Ryan h 3801

Cotto, Grant
Strange Angels - Kathe Koja h 2543

Fender, Duncan
Suckers - Anne Billson h 397

Freeman, Claire
Candle Night - Phil Rickman h 3663

Gray, Doreen
Fire in the Blood - P.N. Elrod h 1441

Hazel
Belladonna - Michael Stewart h 4206

Hitchcock, Frank
The School - T.M. Wright h 4778

Landon, Harry
I'll Be Watching You - Samuel M. Key h 2463

Lewis, Dafydd
Naomi's Room - Jonathan Aycliffe h 237

Lewis, Leonard
Nightlight - Michael Cadnum h 664

Lucas, Annabel "Nan"
My Soul to Keep - Judith Hawkes h 2105

McClure, Katy
The Dwelling - Tom Elliott h 1424

McGann, Jim
From a Whisper to a Scream - Samuel M. Key h 2462

Pike, Eli
The Rim-World Legacy and Beyond - Frank A. Javor s 2298

Popman, Walker
Passive Intruder - Michael Upchurch h 4410

Preston, Natalie
Carrion Comfort - Dan Simmons h 4028

Rabjohns, Will
Sacrament - Clive Barker h 290

Ted
Thor - Wayne Smith h 4106

Williams, Stanley
The Undine - Michael O'Rourke h 3368

Zivic, Leland
From the Teeth of Angels - Jonathan Carroll h 744

PHOTOJOURNALIST

Nash, Scott
Lagoon - Alison Drake h 1313

Pike, Eli
The Ice Beast - Frank A. Javor s 2297

PILOT

Amaya, Anya
Glory's People - Alfred Coppel s 956

Antilles, Wedge
Rogue Squadron - Michael A. Stackpole s 4152

Arbok
Prison Ship - Martin Caidin s 676

Ashata/Maya
The Queen's Squadron - R.M. Meluch s 3087

Bass, Rocket Man
Voyage to the Red Planet - Terry Bisson s 412

Baxter, Carl
The Homecoming - Barry B. Longyear s 2798

Beautiful Maria
Angel Station - Walter Jon Williams s 4646

Bird, Morris
Heavy Time - C.J. Cherryh s 806

Blackstone, Rex
Primary Inversion - Catherine Asaro s 182

Bloodyluck, Kithri
Jaydium - Deborah Wheeler s 4601

Boggs, W. J.
Labyrinth of Night - Allen Steele s 4183

Buccari, Sharl
In the Shadow of the Moon - Scott G. Gier s 1787

Callista
Darksaber - Kevin J. Anderson s 86

Cargo
Cyberstealth - S.N. Lewitt s 2743
Dancing Vac - S.N. Lewitt s 2744

Chin, Gun Roh
The Run to Chaos Keep - Jack L. Chalker s 778

Collingwood, Max
Ancient Shores - Jack McDevitt s 3014

Davis, Kyra
Harvest of Stars - Poul Anderson s 105

Deering, Wilma
A Life in the Future - Martin Caidin s 675

Dekker, Paul
Heavy Time - C.J. Cherryh s 806
Hellburner - C.J. Cherryh s 807

di Hoa, Barry
The Voices of Heaven - Frederik Pohl s 3470

Dooley, Samantha "Sam"
No Limits - Nigel Findley s 1561

Dulcimer
Transcendence - Charles Sheffield s 3963

Falcon, Nikki
Falcon - Emma Bull s 631

Faulkner, William
The Wild Blue and the Gray - William Sanders s 3853

Gorbunova, Ludmila
Worldwar: Tilting the Balance - Harry Turtledove s 4397
Worldwar: Upsetting the Balance - Harry Turtledove s 4398

Hawksmoor, Nicholas
Berserker Kill - Fred Saberhagen s 3806

Hiller, Steven
Independence Day - Dean Devlin s 1216

Horn, Corran
Rogue Squadron - Michael A. Stackpole s 4152

Hutchins, Priscilla "Hutch"
The Engines of God - Jack McDevitt s 3015

Janusz, Pov
Siduri's Net - P.K. McAllister s 2951

Jetboy
Night of the Cooters - Howard Waldrop s 4472

Jian, Reverdy
Dreamships - Melissa Scott s 3910

Jiltanith
Mutineers' Moon - David Weber s 4524

Jute, Tabitha
Seasons of Plenty - Colin Greenland s 1935

Kaa
Infinity's Shore - David Brin s 565

Kady, Meg
Hellburner - C.J. Cherryh s 807

Kan-Kon
Dragon Rigger - Jeffrey A. Carver s 752

Keff
The Ship Errant - Jody Lynn Nye s 3327

Kruger, Clayton Allen
Deadly Breed - T.J. Kirby h 2505

Kustaa, Captain Fred
Under the Yoke - S.M. Stirling s 4229

Kymri
Grounded! - Chris Claremont s 840

LaBrae, Jael
Dragon Rigger - Jeffrey A. Carver s 752

Lando, Pik
Drifter's Run - William C. Dietz s 1246
Drifter's War - William C. Dietz s 1247

Low, Boston
The Dig - Alan Dean Foster s 1607

Lukas, Greg
Mind Light - Margaret Davis s 1133
Minds Apart - Margaret Davis s 1134

MacLoed, Alex
Fallen Angels - Larry Niven s 3279

Malone, Patrick
Alien Tongue - Stephen Leigh s 2722

Maraquine, Toller II
The Fugitive Worlds - Bob Shaw s 3946

Marconi, Maria
Buying Time - Joe Haldeman s 1993

Matthieson, Jonah
Man-Kzin Wars V - Larry Niven s 3284

McAlois, Lois
Tower of the Gods - Thomas A. Easton s 1384

Mendez, Sofia
The Sparrow - Mary Doria Russell s 3789

Michaelson, Kiley
Mind Light - Margaret Davis s 1133

Morales, Daire
Lethe - Tricia Sullivan s 4269

Morianna, Maigrey
King's Sacrifice - Margaret Weis s 4560
The Lost King - Margaret Weis s 4562

Newell, Charlie
Wildside - Steven Gould s 1837

Nguyen, Marie
Wildside - Steven Gould s 1837

Ninekiller, Amos
The Wild Blue and the Gray - William Sanders s 3853

Northfield, Anthony
War Birds - R.M. Meluch s 3088

O'Tennis, Ned
The Last Legends of Earth - A.A. Attanasio s 227

Owens, Tiffany "Tif"
Resurrection - Katharine Kerr s 2450

Pallas
Raft - Stephen Baxter s 332

Pollard, Ben
Heavy Time - C.J. Cherryh s 806
Hellburner - C.J. Cherryh s 807

Prentice, Clara
Wildside - Steven Gould s 1837

Randolph, Jake
The Torching - Marcy Heidish h 2110

Raqella
Sundowner - Chris Claremont s 841

Renner, Kevin
The Gripping Hand - Larry Niven s 3281

Ringess, Danlo
The Broken God - David Zindell s 4853
The Wild - David Zindell s 4854

Rogers, Buck
A Life in the Future - Martin Caidin s 675

Roy, Ubu
Angel Station - Walter Jon Williams s 4646

Ryder, Christine
The Tranquility Alternative - Allen Steele s 4187

St. John, Ian "Hunter"
Wing Commander: Freedom Flight - Mercedes Lackey s 2630

Sands, Larson Clarke
The Clouds of Saturn - Michael McCollum s 3001

Sangre, Ryne
A Roil of Stars - Don Wismer s 4722

Scoresby, Lee
The Golden Compass - Philip Pullman f 3545

Sebasten-Janurias
Mighty Good Road - Melissa Scott s 3911

Shea, Nicole
Grounded! - Chris Claremont s 840
Sundowner - Chris Claremont s 841

Siggerson, Olaf
Destination: Mutiny - Sean Dalton s 1078

Spinner-of-Rope
Ring - Stephen Baxter s 333

Thibodeaux, Suzanne "Suzy Falcon" Marie
Eternal Light - Paul J. McAuley s 2952

Toad of Toad Hall
The Willows in Winter - William Horwood f 2212

Trioran, Eril
Jaydium - Deborah Wheeler s 4601

Trudeau, Arielle
Return to Rocheworld - Robert L. Forward s 1596

Vantara
The Fugitive Worlds - Bob Shaw s 3946

Vaughan, James
Dr. Haggard's Disease - Patrick McGrath h 3037

von Richtofen, Manfred
The Bloody Red Baron - Kim Newman h 3261

Walthers, Audee
The Gateway Trip: Tales and Vignettes of the Heechee - Frederik Pohl s 3462

Yeager, Pauli
Heritage of Flight - Susan Shwartz s 4002

Young, "Mighty" Joe
Lunar Descent - Allen Steele s 4184

PIRATE

Blackstrap
Dinotopia Lost - Alan Dean Foster f 1608

de Wolf, Mike
Typewriter in the Sky - L. Ron Hubbard f 2224

Deadmon
Dragon's Plunder - Brad Strickland f 4256

Frank
Spacer Dreams - Larry Segriff s 3923

Gabool
Mariel of Redwall - Brian Jacques f 2268

Gregg, Stephen
Through the Breach - David Drake s 1330

Hook, James
Hook - Terry Brooks f 583

Islay, Arran
Henry Martyn - L. Neil Smith s 4092

Ivard
Ruler of Naught - Sherwood Smith s 4101

Khordas
Highlander: The Element of Fire - Jason Henderson f 2121

Kobir, Nikolai
Canby's Legion - Bill Baldwin s 258

Louchard, Onidi "Dinah O'Neill"
Power Play - Anne McCaffrey s 2977

Magon
The Warrior Returns - Allan Cole f 894

Marth, Jarem
Ash Ock - Christopher Hinz s 2148
The Paratwa - Christopher Hinz s 2149

McDonald
Cat's Gambit - Leslie Gadallah s 1690

Merrick the Blackbird
Sister Blood - Karen Haber s 1986

Mission
Ghost of Chance - William S. Burroughs s 637

Pong, Mustapha
McCade's Bounty - William C. Dietz s 1252

Hayden, Mark
Bats - William W. Johnstone *h* 2330

Hendricks, Clint
Stone Dead - Ellen Jamison *h* 2295

Hershey
Judge Dredd - Neal Barrett Jr. *s* 306

Huxley, Lenina
Demolition Man - Richard Osborne *s* 3371

Hyland, Morn
Forbidden Knowledge - Stephen R.
  Donaldson *s* 1269
The Gap into Conflict: The Real Story - Stephen R.
  Donaldson *s* 1270
The Gap into Madness: Chaos and Order - Stephen R.
  Donaldson *s* 1271
The Gap into Power: A Dark and Hungry God Arises
  - Stephen R. Donaldson *s* 1272
The Gap into Ruin: This Day All Gods Die - Stephen
  R. Donaldson *s* 1273

Ingalls, Ray
The Devil's Laughter - William W.
  Johnstone *h* 2334

Johnson, Greg
The Charm - Adam Niswander *h* 3272

Kastlin, Vask
Mainline - Deborah Christian *s* 828

Kelly, Bob
The Forbidden Zone - Whitley Strieber *h* 4259

Killany, Mark
Night Cruise - Billie Sue Mosiman *h* 3218

Killdeer, Hunter
Living with the Reptiles - Roger L.
  DiSilvestro *s* 1262

Kimball, Joel
Night - Alan Rodgers *h* 3722

Kimmler, Vic
Borderland - S.K. Epperson *h* 1468

Kirkpatrick, Stanley
*The Spider #8: The Devil's Paymaster/Legions of the
  Accursed Light* - Grant Stockbridge *f* 4236

Knudsen, Arne
Master of Lies - Graham Masterton *h* 2926

Kostal, Miriam
River of Dust - Alexander Jablokov *s* 2263

Lacey, Bobbie
Polar City Blues - Katharine Kerr *s* 2449

Laidlaw, Alison
Cloud Castles - Michael Scott Rohan *f* 3730

Langston, Fred
Blood - Ron Dee *h* 1182

Laughing More, Anna
Wake of the Werewolf - Geoffrey Caine *h* 682

Laverne, Vernon
The Death Prayer - David Bowker *h* 493

Lawson, John
Moonfall - Tamara Thorne *h* 4360

Llewellyn, George
Werewolf - Peter Rubie *h* 3764

Locke, Ryan
Bloody Valentine - Stephen R. George *h* 1763

Lockerman, John
Grave Markings - Michael A. Arnzen *h* 175

Luckinbill, Tom
Yellow Moon - David J. Searls *h* 3920

Lyon, Harry
Dragon Tears - Dean R. Koontz *h* 2548

Mahan, Sherry
The Bad Thing - Michael O'Rourke *h* 3366

Mallory, Thomas
The Wizard of Camelot - Simon Hawke *f* 2101

Marceline
Fools - Pat Cadigan *s* 657

March, Xavier
Fatherland - Robert Harris *s* 2049

Maxwell, Mahlon Sumner "Mama"
Dragon's Teeth - Lee Killough *s* 2470

Mays, Johnny
Down River - Stephen Gallagher *h* 1696

McCardle, Box "Texas"
Metal Angel - Nancy Springer *f* 4135

McElroy, Jud
The Headsman - James Neal Harvey *h* 2075

McGarvey, Jack
Winter Moon - Dean R. Koontz *h* 2558

McKinnan
The Third Beast - Peter Loughran *h* 2804

McLeod, Noel
The Adept - Katherine Kurtz *f* 2587
Dagger Magic - Katherine Kurtz *f* 2589

McRay, Kevin
Nine Levels Down - William Dantz *h* 1089

Meagher, Richard
The Uprising - Brent Monahan *h* 3149

Melrose, Frank
Dead Voices - Rick Hautala *h* 2082

Mullins, Lawrence
Creekers - Edward Lee *h* 2697

Munro, Dan
Reign - Chet Williamson *h* 4657

Nanopoulos, Sheila
Glass Houses - Laura J. Mixon *s* 3126

Obo
Mind Slayer - Kevin D. Randle *s* 3563

O'Brien, Ed
Leanna: Possession of a Woman - Marie
  Kiraly *h* 2501

O'Brien, Richard
The Crawling Dark - Pauline Dunn *h* 1366

O'Donnell, Erin
Deathwalker - Patrick Whalen *h* 4596

O'Hara, Frank
A Room for the Dead - Noel Hynd *h* 2250

Okata, Gail
Demon Fire - Gary L. Holleman *h* 2188

Ooljee, Paul
Cyber Way - Alan Dean Foster *s* 1605

Ortiveda, Phyllis
Ursus - David Dvorkin *s* 1371

Outhwaite, Terence
Virgins and Martyrs - Simon Maginn *h* 2867

Owldark, Fringe Dorwalk
Sideshow - Sheri S. Tepper *s* 4340

Packard, Nick
Wet Work - Philip Nutman *h* 3320

Pangborn, Alan
Needful Things - Stephen King *h* 2490

Parsons
Twisted - Sue Hollister Barr *h* 304

Payne
Running Wild - J.G. Ballard *h* 270

Peters, George
Offspring - Jack Ketchum *h* 2461

Plase, Janice
Kent Montana and the Reasonably Invisible Man -
  Lionel Fenn *s* 1543

Portlock, Ben
Dumford Blood - S.K. Epperson *h* 1469

Powell, Lincoln
The Demolished Man - Alfred Bester *s* 388

Prejean, Lani
Night Mask - William W. Johnstone *h* 2335

Rafin
Runes of Autumn - Larry Elmore *f* 1436

Ramsey, Quinn
Demon Fire - Gary L. Holleman *h* 2188

Randall, Mick
Shadows - Kimberly Rangel *h* 3565

Rathe, Nicolas "Nico"
Point of Hopes - Melissa Scott *f* 3913

Rossi, Eric
Domination - Michael Cecilione *h* 767

Rydell, Berry
Virtual Light - William Gibson *s* 1782

Sanders, John A.
Dark Visions - T. Lucien Wright *h* 4771

Sanders, Phillipe "Phil" Montoya
The Modular Man - Roger MacBride Allen *s* 65

Silver, David
Alien Blues - Lynn S. Hightower *s* 2142
Alien Eyes - Lynn S. Hightower *s* 2143
Alien Heat - Lynn S. Hightower *s* 2144
Alien Rites - Lynn S. Hightower *s* 2145

Sinclair, Travis
Prank Night - David Robbins *h* 3678

Singer, Helen
Symphony - Adrian Savage *h* 3880

Slaughter, Nathan
The Totem - David Morrell *h* 3193

Solo, Jay
The Nine Lives of Catseye Gomez - Simon
  Hawke *f* 2094

Stablits, Dothan
Hard Landing - Algis Budrys *s* 617

Stack, Nathan
Demon Download - Jack Yeovil *f* 4799

Stanley, Rodman
Night Beasts - T.W. Stetson *h* 4199

Stark, Emmett
The Headsman - James Neal Harvey *h* 2075

Starlen, Garett
Night Watch - Robin Wayne Bailey *f* 244

Stavrianos, Nick
Quarantine - Greg Egan *s* 1415

Stepovich, Mike
The Gypsy - Steven Brust *f* 608

Stone, Neil
Deathscape - Michael Cecilione *h* 766

Straker, Phil
Creekers - Edward Lee *h* 2697

Stratton, Dan
Night Hunter - Michael Reaves *h* 3587

String
Alien Blues - Lynn S. Hightower *s* 2142
Alien Eyes - Lynn S. Hightower *s* 2143
Alien Heat - Lynn S. Hightower *s* 2144
Alien Rites - Lynn S. Hightower *s* 2145

Sutton, Henry
Out of the Night - Patrick Whalen *h* 4598

POLITICAL FIGURE

Pickard, Joe
Echoes - Jackie Hyman h 2245

Polmaire
Deepwater Dreams - Sydney J. Van Scyoc s 4417

Prothore, Alfred
The Jekyll Legacy - Robert Bloch h 435

Purcell, Harry
Worlds Enough and Time - Joe Haldeman s 1996

Pyramors
Warlord of Heaven - Adrian Cole f 887

Reagan, Ronald
The Atrocity Exhibition - J.G. Ballard s 269

Reem "First Cousin Brother"
Brother Termite - Patricia Anthony s 127

Reeve, Todd
Treaty at Doona - Anne McCaffrey s 2985

Renier, Mordan
Ganwold's Child - Diann Thornley s 4361

Richmond, Eleanor Boxwood
Interface - Stephen Bury s 638

Rollie, Steve
Dark Tide - Elizabeth Forrest h 1584

Roosevelt, Franklin Delano
Triumph - Ben Bova s 491

Roosevelt, Theodore
1901 - Robert Conroy s 918
Bully! - Mike Resnick s 3622

Scanwell, Jane
Empire Builders - Ben Bova s 479

Shazad
Queens of Land and Sea - John Maddox
   Roberts f 3696

Sheba
Traitors - Kristine Kathryn Rusch f 3786

Shefferton, Jeffrey
The Argus Gambit - David D. Ross s 3750
The Eighth Rank - David D. Ross s 3751

Stane, Temelathe
Shadow Man - Melissa Scott s 3914

Tali
Brother Termite - Patricia Anthony s 127

Travassa, Daisainia
Legacies - Alison Sinclair s 4045

Verid
Daughter of Elysium - Joan Slonczewski s 4062

Wakefield, Nicole des Jardins
Rama Revealed - Arthur C. Clarke s 852

Welch, Lewis
Dreambuilder - Tom Deitz f 1190

Weston, Quinton
The Immortals - Tracy Hickman s 2141

Whitmore, Thomas
Independence Day - Dean Devlin s 1216

Womack, Jeff
Brother Termite - Patricia Anthony s 127

Zellorian
Warlord of Heaven - Adrian Cole f 887

PORNOGRAPHER

Shutterbug
Slippin' into Darkness - Norman Partridge h 3390

POSTAL WORKER

Bethune, Casey
The Black Carousel - Charles L. Grant h 1846

Chevette
Virtual Light - William Gibson s 1782

Jaffe, Randolph
The Great and Secret Show - Clive Barker h 286

Simon
Wishbringer - Craig Shaw Gardner f 1715

Smith, John
The Mailman - Bentley Little h 2775

PREHISTORIC HUMAN

Amgigh
My Sister the Moon - Sue Harrison f 2065

Ayla
The Plains of Passage - Jean M. Auel f 231

Bad Belly/Still Water
People of the Earth - W. Michael Gear f 1737

Ban-ya
The Edge of the World - William Sarabande f 3856

Brave Man
People of the Earth - W. Michael Gear f 1737

Catchstraw
People of the Sea - W. Michael Gear f 1740

Cha-kwena
The Edge of the World - William Sarabande f 3856
Thunder in the Sky - William Sarabande f 3858

Chagak
Mother Earth, Father Sky - Sue Harrison f 2064

Doban
Shiva: An Adventure of the Ice Age - J.H.
   Brennan f 548

Elk Charm
People of the Fire - W. Michael Gear f 1738

Fava
Serpent Catch - Dave Wolverton s 4745

Hawk
The Hunter Returns - David Drake f 1318

Helen
No Enemy but Time - Michael Bishop s 407

Heron
People of the Wolf - W. Michael Gear f 1741

Hiram
Shiva Accused: An Adventure of the Ice Age - J.H.
   Brennan f 546
Shiva: An Adventure of the Ice Age - J.H.
   Brennan f 548
Shiva's Challenge: An Adventure of the Ice Age - J.H.
   Brennan f 547

Jondalar
The Plains of Passage - Jean M. Auel f 231

Kestrel
People of the Sea - W. Michael Gear f 1740

Kiin
My Sister the Moon - Sue Harrison f 2065

Kori
The Animal Wife - Elizabeth Marshall
   Thomas f 4345

Little Dancer
People of the Fire - W. Michael Gear f 1738

Lolita
Cathouse - Dean Ing s 2252

Mah-ree
The Edge of the World - William Sarabande f 3856

Maliwal
The Sacred Stones - William Sarabande f 3857

Masau
The Sacred Stones - William Sarabande f 3857

Ozette, Ember
Ember From the Sun - Mark Canter s 706

Raven Hunter
People of the Wolf - W. Michael Gear f 1741

Runs in Light
People of the Wolf - W. Michael Gear f 1741

Samiq
My Sister the Moon - Sue Harrison f 2065

Shiva
Shiva Accused: An Adventure of the Ice Age - J.H.
   Brennan f 546
Shiva: An Adventure of the Ice Age - J.H.
   Brennan f 548
Shiva's Challenge: An Adventure of the Ice Age - J.H.
   Brennan f 547

Sunchaser
People of the Sea - W. Michael Gear f 1740

Swift
The Animal Wife - Elizabeth Marshall
   Thomas f 4345

Talker
Dawn Land - Joseph Bruchac f 597

Thag
Shiva's Challenge: An Adventure of the Ice Age - J.H.
   Brennan f 547

Timmie
The Ugly Little Boy - Isaac Asimov s 209

Tull
Serpent Catch - Dave Wolverton s 4745

White Ash
People of the Earth - W. Michael Gear f 1737

Willow
The Hunter Returns - David Drake f 1318

Wolf
The Hunter Returns - David Drake f 1318

Young Hunter
Dawn Land - Joseph Bruchac f 597

Ysuna
The Sacred Stones - William Sarabande f 3857

PRINCIPAL

Hanley, Matthew
The School - Ed Kelleher h 2425

Stiles
Mysteries of the Word - Stanley Wiater h 4616

PRINTER

Wolsey, Faye
The Palm Dome - Liz Fulton h 1686

PRISONER

Armand, Pamela
The Living Evil - Ruby Jean Jensen h 2312

Bowe-Hawkins, Thomas "Tom"
Tripoint - C.J. Cherryh s 814

Braldt
The Hunter on Arena - Rose Estes s 1478

Case, Jamie
Wheels of Fire - Mercedes Lackey f 2624

Chappy
The End of Alice - A.M. Homes h 2197

Coffey, John
The Green Mile - Stephen King h 2487

Dillon
Alien 3 - Alan Dean Foster s 1599

PSYCHOLOGIST

PUBLIC RELATIONS

Ogle, Cyrus "Cy"
Interface - Stephen Bury   s   638

Silk, Venture
The Forever Drug - Steve Perry   s   3422

Spano, Constance "Connie"
Independence Day - Dean Devlin   s   1216

Taylor
The Tenth Class - Karen Ripley   s   3671

Wishart, Adam
The Walking Shadow - Brian Stableford   s   4146

PUBLISHER

Dixon, Travis
Night Brothers - Sidney Williams   h   4639

Gibbs, Hank
Psycho House - Robert Bloch   h   442

Hamilton, Rick
The Man Who Turned into Himself - David Ambrose   h   74

James, Will
Warpath - Tony Daniel   s   1082

Seton, Winston
Naming the Flowers - Kate Wilhelm   s   4626

Sturdley, Harry
Crossover - Bill McCay   f   3000

Walton, Robert
Gothic Romance - Emmanuel Carrere   h   740

Wasserman, Janus Cornelius
The House of the Toad - Richard Tierney   h   4363

RACIST

Bracher, Frederick
Mark of the Werewolf - Jeffrey Sackett   h   3822

McKendree
Devil's Deal - Richard Austin   s   233

RADIO

Alexander, Sam
SETI - Frederick Fichman   s   1553

Hale, Dick
Night Mask - William W. Johnstone   h   2335

RADIO PERSONALITY

Cooley, Dan
The Devil and Dan Cooley - Holly Lisle   f   2766

Csejthe, Christopher
One Foot in the Grave - Wm. Mark Simmons   f   4039

Handler, Paul
Deathgrip - Brian Hodge   h   2156

Russie, Moishe
Worldwar: Striking the Balance - Harry Turtledove   s   4396

Scott, Aaron "Sunset"
Shock Radio - Leigh Clark   h   846

RAKE

Skelbrooke, Francis
The Gnome's Engine - Teresa Edgerton   f   1398

RANCHER

Abernathy, Tom
Thunder Road - Chris Curry   h   1051

Alfonso
Under the Shadow - Jane Toombs   h   4372

Fundan, Fair
To a Highland Nation - Christopher Rowley   s   3761

Hawkes, Benton "Ben"
Man o' War - William Shatner   s   3938

Kinner's Son, Kensher
The Blood of a Dragon - Lawrence Watt-Evans   f   4496

Reeve, Todd
Crisis on Doona - Anne McCaffrey   s   2962

Shade, John
Nightshade - Jack Butler   s   646

Spenotex, Arakaho Blundy
Stopping at Slowyear - Frederik Pohl   s   3469

Wiltin, Hof
To a Highland Nation - Christopher Rowley   s   3761

RANGER

De Brouchee, Montolio
Sojourn - R.A. Salvatore   f   3845

Linders, Martin
The Quiet - Patrick Billings   h   396

Norris, Robert
Vyrmin - Gene Lazuta   h   2686

Pirelli, Peter
Swamp - Peter Tremayne   h   4374

Tanner, John
The Quiet - Patrick Billings   h   396

REAL ESTATE AGENT

Barnes, Collee
Black Death - R. Karl Largent   h   2655

Chessner, Barbara
Infernal Affairs - Jane Heller   h   2118

Demos, Maria
Souls - Katina Alexis   h   58

Dvorak, Teresa
Frostwing - Richard A. Knaak   f   2520

Harker, Jonathan
Bram Stoker's Dracula - Fred Saberhagen   h   3808

Lutz, Frances
Infernal Affairs - Jane Heller   h   2118

Maxwell, Maureen
Relife - Dan Barton   h   314

Poker, Susan
The Hacker and the Ants - Rudy Rucker   s   3765

Roberts, Katie
The Haunting - Ruby Jean Jensen   h   2311

S———, Delia
First Love: A Gothic Tale - Joyce Carol Oates   f   3331

Stebbins, Ivy
All the Bells on Earth - James P. Blaylock   f   420

Willson, Andrea
Dark Reunion - Stephen R. George   h   1764

REANIMATED DEAD

Ash, Leanard
Shadows Fall - Simon R. Green   f   1903

Bogert, Norman
I, Robot: The Illustrated Screenplay - Harlan Ellison   s   1432

Cheops
The Mummy!: A Tale of the Twenty-Second Century - Jane Webb Loudon   h   2803

Clerval, Henry
Brittle Innings - Michael Bishop   h   403

Crea
The Darker Passions: Frankenstein - Amarantha Knight   h   2529

Daniels, Danny
Deadweight - Robert Devereaux   h   1214

Devreaux, Luc
Universal Soldier - Robert Tine   s   4368

Gorobec, Anton
I Am Frankenstein - C. Dean Andersson   h   116

Herrin, Ashley
Harrowgate - Daniel H. Gower   h   1838

Hitch
Dead Heat - Del Stone Jr.   h   4239

Keelie
The Jigsaw Woman - Kim Antieau   f   163

Merrick, Geoffrey Robert
Fear Itself - Ric Meyers   h   3092
Living Hell - Ric Meyers   h   3093
Worst Nightmare - Ric Meyers   h   3094

Nolan, Durk
Celia - Ruby Jean Jensen   h   2310

Nuwen, Pham
A Fire upon the Deep - Vernor Vinge   s   4441

Outis, Charles "Mr. Charlie"
Solis - A.A. Attanasio   s   229

Poons, Windle
Reaper Man - Terry Pratchett   f   3506

Ramses the Great
The Mummy, or Ramses the Damned - Anne Rice   h   3652

Scott, Andrew
Universal Soldier - Robert Tine   s   4368

Soo, Hannah
Take Back Plenty - Colin Greenland   s   1936

Zachary
Guilty Pleasures - Laurell K. Hamilton   f   2016

REBEL

Akma
Earthborn - Orson Scott Card   s   718

Falsche, Viktor
The Janus Mask - Richard A. Knaak   f   2521

Gi'Suei'Obodi'Sedon
The Last Dancer - Daniel Keys Moran   s   3177

Linn-Campbell, Neena
A Covenant of Justice - David Gerrold   s   1771

Maniakes
Hammer and Anvil - Harry Turtledove   f   4387

McCann, Rorin
Caledon of the Mists - Deborah Turner Harris   f   2045

Sobek, Yoo
Hostile Takeover - Jack McKinney   s   3067

RECEPTIONIST

Cobb, Phoebe
Everville - Clive Barker   h   284

Gregory, Libby
Ghost Boy - Jean Simon   h   4041

King, Ellen
The Faery Convention - Brett Davis f 1128

Pond, Susan
Passive Intruder - Michael Upchurch h 4410

RECLUSE

Haramis
Lady of the Trillium - Marion Zimmer
Bradley f 525

Kubick, Ruby
Glass Houses - Laura J. Mixon s 3126

Rushkin, Vincent Adjani
Memory and Dream - Charles de Lint f 1157

Smith, Brandon
Virtual Girl - Amy Thomson s 4358

Talbot, Edward "Eddie"
Her Monster - Jeff Collignon h 898

Wallace, Enoch
Way Station - Clifford D. Simak s 4027

Wolf, Behrooz "Bey"
Proteus in the Underworld - Charles
Sheffield s 3960

REFUGEE

Ayyah
Cat's Gambit - Leslie Gadallah s 1690

ben Sierra Nueva, Amos "Simeon"
The City Who Fought - Anne McCaffrey s 2961

Bishop, Toby
Furious Gulf - Gregory Benford s 367

Casey, Jerry
Cold Allies - Patricia Anthony s 128

Fileli, Mathembe
The Broken Land - Ian McDonald s 3017

Mondragon, Tom
Endgame - C.J. Cherryh s 800

ni Bron, Deir
Redmagic - Crawford Kilian f 2469

Russie, Moishe
Worldwar: Striking the Balance - Harry
Turtledove s 4396

Rusty
A Time for Dragons - Gary Gentile s 1759

Scott
A Time for Dragons - Gary Gentile s 1759

Waesc, Dorias
Reclamation - Sarah Zettel s 4850

Zwakh, Ignatz
Dead Boys - Richard Calder s 683

REINCARNATED PERSON

Severn, Joseph
The Fall of Hyperion - Dan Simmons s 4031

Thaxton, Wendall
The Higher Space - Jamil Nasir s 3241

Wiggin, Peter
Children of the Mind - Orson Scott Card s 717

RELATIVE

Casteel, Luke Jr.
Gates of Paradise - V.C. Andrews h 121

Claus, Bob "Santa"
Santa's Twin - Dean R. Koontz f 2556

Jack the Bodiless
Magnificat - Julian May s 2943

Madison, Jay
The Gryphon King - Tom Deitz f 1192

Marat, Beverly
Thirst of the Vampire - T. Lucien Wright h 4772

Miller, Calvin
Alvin Journeyman - Orson Scott Card f 715

Nahadeh, Nika
Ember From the Sun - Mark Canter s 706

Ratkay, Jet
Resurrection Man - Sean Stewart f 4210

Risinger, Werner
Oktober - Stephen Gallagher h 1698

Stout, Thomas A.
Humpty Dumpty: An Oval - Damon Knight s 2533

Susan
Fade - Robert Cormier h 961

Tolar, Rob
The Gryphon King - Tom Deitz f 1192

RELIGIOUS

Aenea
Endymion - Dan Simmons s 4030

Ainvar
Druids - Morgan Llywelyn f 2780

Akiba
Freeze Frames - Katharine Kerr s 2447

al'Vere, Egwene
A Crown of Swords - Robert Jordan f 2379
The Dragon Reborn - Robert Jordan f 2380

Anaral
An Acceptable Time - Madeleine L'Engle f 2732

Anthony, Father
Catacomb - Andrew Laurance h 2665

Arcangelo
Zaragoz - Brian Craig f 1006

Augustine
Blameless in Abaddon - James Morrow f 3209

Auk, Maytera
Exodus From the Long Sun - Gene Wolfe s 4732

Auriane
The Light Bearer - Donna Gillespie f 1791

Ayth, Argoth
Demon Moon - Jack Williamson s 4669

Bach, Arthur
Night Prophets - Paul F. Olson h 3357

Bain
The Thing That Darkness Hides - Robert
Morgan h 3188

Bardsey, Geoffrey
The Merlin Effect - T.A. Barron f 310

Barron, Paul
Wurm - Matthew J. Costello h 973

Barthlomew, Lucy
Moonfall - Tamara Thorne h 4360

Bayley, Frank
Unholy Fire - Whitley Strieber h 4261

Beatrice
Bright Messengers - Gentry Lee s 2701

Begg, Edwin
Lunching with the Antichrist - Michael
Moorcock f 3169

Belkin, Gregory
Servant of the Bones - Anne Rice h 3654

Ben Yussef, Essaj
The Riddled Man - Mark E. Rogers f 3726

Benedict
Sable, Shadow and Ice - Cheryl J. Franklin f 1638

Benjamin, Papa
The Black Lodge - Robert Weinberg h 4538

Boro
Brand New Cherry Flavor - Todd Grimson h 1960

Braco, Jag
Inquisitor - Ian Watson s 4493

Brendan, Father
The Book of Brendan - Ann Curry f 1049

Breyd
The Sword and the Lion - Roberta Cray f 1016

Bruno, Giordano
Love and Sleep - John Crowley f 1035

Brutha
Small Gods - Terry Pratchett f 3507

Bryce, Christopher
Storm Knights - Bill Slavicsek f 4059

Bryce, Pat
The Priest: A Gothic Romance - Thomas M.
Disch h 1261

Cadderly
In Sylvan Shadows - R.A. Salvatore f 3840

Cahill, Joseph
Midnight Mass - F. Paul Wilson h 4687

Caillean
The Forest House - Marion Zimmer Bradley f 521

Callahan
Aqua Sancta - Edward Bryant h 612

Calyx
Sunder, Eclipse and Seed - Elise Guttenberg f 1981

Carenza, Peter
The Blood of the Lamb - Thomas F.
Monteleone h 3150

Carpenter, Tom
Dark Fortune - Richard Lee Byers h 650

Carrie
Virgin - Mary Elizabeth Murphy h 3226

Cassia
The Cult of Loving Kindness - Paul Park s 3382

Catalina, Mother
Yesterday We Saw Mermaids - Esther
Friesner f 1680

Celeste
Private Demons - Robert Masello h 2909

Centuri, Ariann
Half-Light - Denise Vitola s 4443

Champion, Dragonbait
Masquerades - Kate Novak f 3318

Chomanche
A Miracle of Rare Design - Mike Resnick s 3631

Cincinnati, Chime
Last Refuge - Elizabeth Ann Scarborough f 3892

Clement VII, Pope
Scorpio - Alex McDonough s 3028

Cleopatra
Throne of Isis - Judith Tarr f 4305

Columcille
The Throne of Tara - John Desjarlais f 1209

Corey, Elizabeth "Betty"
The World on Blood - Jonathan Nasaw h 3240

Crookleg, Poilar
Kingdoms of the Wall - Robert Silverberg s 4014

Van Chou, Ngen
The Web of Spider - W. Michael Gear   s   1744

Vanelli, MONDO
How to Mutate and Take Over the World - R.U.
   Sirius   s   4050

Vierran
Hexwood - Diana Wynne Jones   s   2349

Washington, George
Two Crowns for America - Katherine Kurtz   f   2594

West, Kilimanjaro
Out on Blue Six - Ian McDonald   s   3020

Zeenoson, Dref
Illusion - Paula Volsky   f   4448

Zhu Wong
The Golden Nineties - Lisa Mason   s   2912

Zorin, Lavrenti Borisovich
Branch Point - Mona Clee   s   866

ROBOT

APU-805 "Bird Dog"
Destination: Showdown - Jake Davis   s   1131
The Last Rangers - Jake Davis   s   1132

Arthur
The Immortality Option - James P. Hogan   s   2175

Bailey, David "Herbert" Clancy
The Modular Man - Roger MacBride Allen   s   65

Bill
Hawaiian U.F.O. Aliens - Mel Gilden   s   1788
Tubular Android Superheroes - Mel Gilden   s   1790

C-3PO
The Glove of Darth Vader - Paul Davids   s   1124

Caliban
Inferno - Roger MacBride Allen   s   64
Utopia - Roger MacBride Allen   s   69

CBN-001 "Caliban"
Caliban - Roger MacBride Allen   s   63

Celia
Automated Alice - Jeff Noon   f   3292

Cge
Backblast - Lee McKeone   s   3050
The Clone Crisis - Lee McKeone   s   3051

Claude
Title Deleted for Security Reasons - Ed
   Blome   s   451

Delta
Warsprite - Jefferson P. Swycaffer   s   4285

Didi "Deeds"
Circle of One - Eric James Fullilove   s   1685

Doggie
Daughter of Elysium - Joan Slonczewski   s   4062

Eleanor of Aquitaine
Rama Revealed - Arthur C. Clarke   s   852

Elvis
The Man in the Moon Must Die - Jeff
   Bredenberg   s   545

Fess
The Warlock Insane - Christopher Stasheff   f   4168
The Warlock Rock - Christopher Stasheff   s   4169
A Wizard in Absentia - Christopher Stasheff   s   4172

Flere-Imsaho
The Player of Games - Iain M. Banks   s   275

Hunter
Dictator - William Wu   s   4780
Predator - William Wu   s   4782
Warrior - William Wu   s   4784

Jakobot "Jacko" 490,9000
*Extreme Paranoia: Nobody Knows the Trouble I've
   Shot* - Ken Rolston   s   3733

Jin the Plarnjarn
The Race for God - Brian Herbert   s   2128

Karli Dog
Vurt - Jeff Noon   s   3294

Kryten
Better than Life - Grant Naylor   s   3246

Mandrake
Nightshade - Jack Butler   s   646

Marble, Maytera
Lake of the Long Sun - Gene Wolfe   s   4733

Martin, Andrew
The Positronic Man - Isaac Asimov   s   208

Moses
Greenthieves - Alan Dean Foster   s   1610

Mthembu, Lucas "Venator"
Harvest the Fire - Poul Anderson   s   106

Nimrod
Solo - Robert Mason   s   2914

Norby
Norby and the Court Jester - Janet Asimov   s   211
Norby and the Oldest Dragon - Janet
   Asimov   s   212
Norby and Yobo's Great Adventure - Janet
   Asimov   s   213
Norby Down to Earth - Janet Asimov   s   214

Olivaw, R. Daneel "Eto Demerzel"
Forward the Foundation - Isaac Asimov   s   195

Oliver
Stationfall - Arthur Byron Cover   s   987

Prospero
Inferno - Roger MacBride Allen   s   64

RAMROD Mark I "Rod"
Cybernarc - Robert Cain   s   677
Endgame - Robert Cain   s   678
Gold Dragon - Robert Cain   s   679

Solo
Solo - Robert Mason   s   2914
Weapon - Robert Mason   s   2915

Spinner, Probe
Arachne - Lisa Mason   s   2910

Terminationer
Samurai Cat Goes to the Movies - Mark E.
   Rogers   s   3727

TW-O: 114-84-1311825
Cathedral of Thorns - Steven Frankos   f   1640

Unnamed Character
A Prophecy of Monsters - Clark Ashton
   Smith   h   4070

X41
Specterworld - Isidore Haiblum   s   1990

ROGUE

Crowley
Lady Cottington's Pressed Fairy Book - Terry
   Jones   f   2376

Elemak
The Ships of Earth - Orson Scott Card   s   728

ROYALTY

Adric
The White Mists of Power - Kristine Kathryn
   Rusch   f   3787

Aeid
O Greenest Branch! - Gael Baudino   f   328

Aidan
Alamut - Judith Tarr   f   4298
The Dagger and the Cross: A Novel of the Crusades -
   Judith Tarr   f   4301

al-Badr, Arwa Bint Muhammad
Guts and Glory - G. Harry Stine   s   4213

Alain
M'Lady Witch - Christopher Stasheff   f   4161

Albert Victor Christian Edward
The Women of Whitechapel and Jack the Ripper - Paul
   West   h   4590

Alderan, Kermiak
Rediscovery: A Novel of Darkover - Marion Zimmer
   Bradley   s   527

Alexander
The Floating Castle - Craig Mills   f   3118
The Prince and the Pilgrim - Mary Stewart   f   4205

Alexia
Dark Mirror, Dark Dreams - Sharon Green   f   1889
Silver Princess, Golden Knight - Sharon
   Green   f   1891
Wind Whispers, Shadow Shouts - Sharon
   Green   f   1892

Allic
The Crystal Sorcerers - William R.
   Forstchen   f   1588

Alya, Princess
Strings - Dave Duncan   s   1361

Amatus
One for the Morning Glory - John Barnes   f   297

Amelia
Dragon's Plunder - Brad Strickland   f   4256

Ancar
Winds of Fury - Mercedes Lackey   f   2629

Anghara, Princess
Nemesis - Louise Cooper   f   950

Anigel
Black Trillium - Marion Zimmer Bradley   f   518

Anlawdd
Arthur War Lord - Dafydd ab Hugh   f   5

Annice
Sing the Four Quarters - Tanya Huff   f   2231

ap Don, Gwydion
The Island of the Mighty - Evangeline
   Walton   f   4483

ap Hywel, Dafydd
The Dragon on the Border - Gordon R.
   Dickson   f   1236

ap Kian, Donaugh
The Western King - Ann Marston   f   2888

ap Kian, Tiernyn
The Western King - Ann Marston   f   2888

ap Mathonwy, Math
The Island of the Mighty - Evangeline
   Walton   f   4483

ap Medrault, Irion
The Last Pendragon - Robert Rice   f   3661

ap Nia, Aidan
King's Son, Magic's Son - Josepha Sherman   f   3977

Apuilana, Nialli
The New Springtime - Robert Silverberg   s   4020

Arbol
Split Heirs - Lawrence Watt-Evans   f   4505

Arianrhod
The Island of the Mighty - Evangeline
   Walton   f   4483

Artemisia
Split Heirs - Lawrence Watt-Evans   f   4505

Tamas of Maggiar
The Goblin Mirror - C.J. Cherryh   f   805

Theovere
The Eagle and the Nightingales - Mercedes Lackey   f   2607

Theseus
Whilom - Robert Watson   f   4495

Thorian
The Reaver Road - Dave Duncan   f   1359

Thuro "Uther Pendragon"
Ghost King - David Gemmell   f   1755

Tianna
Iron Dragons: Mountains and Madness - Rose Estes   f   1479

Toikella
The Mountains of Majipoor - Robert Silverberg   s   4017

Tolivar
Blood Trillium - Julian May   f   2940

Trelane, Athaya
Call of Madness - Julie Dean Smith   f   4086
Mission of Magic - Julie Dean Smith   f   4087
Sage of Sare - Julie Dean Smith   f   4088
The Wizard King - Julie Dean Smith   f   4089

Trelane, Durek
Mission of Magic - Julie Dean Smith   f   4087
Sage of Sare - Julie Dean Smith   f   4088

Trent
Castle Dreams - John DeChancie   s   1173
Castle Spellbound - John DeChancie   s   1174

Trerzian
Bewitchments of Love and Hate - Storm Constantine   s   919

Trusslo, Alix Amanda
Dragon Rescue - Don Callander   f   687

Tupac, Acanna
Mansions of Darkness - Chelsea Quinn Yarbro   h   4796

Tyner, Gil
The Hero King - Rick Shelley   f   3966
The Hero of Varay - Rick Shelley   f   3967

Valmar
Voima - C. Dale Brittain   f   575

Varis
The Wolf of Winter - Paula Volsky   f   4449

Venkatna
Justice - David Drake   s   1321

Veriam, Lizora "Lizra"
Gold Unicorn - Tanith Lee   f   2712

Victor
Blood and Honor - Simon R. Green   f   1893

Wenceslas, Rudyard "Waldo" Riding
The Wealdwife's Tale - Paul Hazel   f   2108

William
Robin and the King - Parke Godwin   f   1805

Willow
The Tangle Box - Terry Brooks   f   586

Wizenbeak
Lord of the Troll-Bats - Alexis A. Gilliland   f   1796

Wynett
The Usurper - Angus Wells   f   4574
The Way Beneath - Angus Wells   f   4575

Xena
The Empty Throne - Ru Emerson   f   1451

Yambu
Wayfinder's Story: The Seventh Book of Lost Swords - Fred Saberhagen   f   3820

Yamun
Horselords - David Cook   f   923

Ylon
Mirror of Destiny - Andre Norton   f   3312

Yuan, Li
The Middle Kingdom - David Wingrove   s   4712

Zeus
Sons of the Titans - Patrick H. Adkins   f   29

Zoltan
Wayfinder's Story: The Seventh Book of Lost Swords - Fred Saberhagen   f   3820

RULER

Agricola, Caesar Germanicus
Cry Republic - Kirk Mitchell   s   3122

Anadon, Oren
Exile - Michael P. Kube-McDowell   s   2582

Andry
The Dragon Token - Melanie Rawn   f   3577
Stronghold - Melanie Rawn   f   3583

Anthimos
Krispos Rising - Harry Turtledove   f   4390

ap Kian, Keylan
The Western King - Ann Marston   f   2888

Archon of Lycanth
The Warrior's Tale - Allan Cole   f   895

Arthur
The Autobiography of Santa Claus: It's Better to Give - Jeff Guinn   f   1967
The Child Queen - Nancy McKenzie   f   3049
Chronicles of King Arthur - Andrea Hopkins   f   2206
Guinevere: The Legend in Autumn - Persia Woolley   f   4757
King & Raven - Cary James   f   2275
Mordred's Curse - Ian McDowell   f   3032
Pendragon - Stephen R. Lawhead   f   2672
Queen of the Summer Stars - Persia Woolley   f   4758

Arthur "Artos"
A Prince Among Men - Robert N. Charrette   f   791

Atare, Darame "Silver" Meath
Hidden Fires - Katharine Eliska Kimbriel   s   2475

Atare, Sheen
Hidden Fires - Katharine Eliska Kimbriel   s   2475

Avril
A Sorcerer and a Gentleman - Elizabeth Willey   f   4629

Azoun
Crusade - James Lowder   f   2812

bad-Jam, Gilan "Gilan the Third"
The Swords of Zinjaban - L. Sprague de Camp   f   1143

Biilathkamoro, Chodrisei "Coso"
The Kalif's War - John Dalmas   s   1068

Bloat
Dealer's Choice - George R.R. Martin   s   2894
Jokertown Shuffle - George R.R. Martin   s   2897

Boncorro
The Secular Wizard - Christopher Stasheff   f   4165

Brandin of Ygrath
Tigana - Guy Gavriel Kay   f   2405

Brown, Pellimore "Pel"
The Reign of the Brown Magician - Lawrence Watt-Evans   f   4503

Charlemagne
His Majesty's Elephant - Judith Tarr   f   4302

Chevenga
Shadow's Son - Shirley Meier   f   3085

Chevenga, Fourth
Lion's Heart - Karen Wehrstein   f   4529
Lion's Soul - Karen Wehrstein   f   4530

The Computer
Extreme Paranoia: Nobody Knows the Trouble I've Shot - Ken Rolston   s   3733

Conan III
A Wild Dog and Lone - Dan Crawford   f   1014

Cornelian, Prime
Exile - Al Sarrantonio   s   3867

Darius
Fractal Mode - Piers Anthony   f   140
Virtual Mode - Piers Anthony   f   160

Diogenes, Romanus
Shards of Empire - Susan Shwartz   f   4003

d'Iste, Tiran
Wind Whispers, Shadow Shouts - Sharon Green   f   1892

Dy-Dybo
Fossil Hunter - Robert J. Sawyer   s   3885

Edward III
Chicago Red - R.M. Meluch   s   3086

Elessedil, Wren
The Talismans of Shannara - Terry Brooks   f   585

Elric
Elric: Song of the Black Sword - Michael Moorcock   f   3167

Emshander IV
Upland Outlaws - Dave Duncan   f   1362

Emshander V
The Living God - Dave Duncan   f   1354
The Stricken Field - Dave Duncan   f   1360

Estarion
Arrows of the Sun - Judith Tarr   f   4299

Friend
Swan Song - Robert R. McCammon   h   2990

Gampo, Songstan
The Yngling and the Circle of Power - John Dalmas   s   1074

Garden, Humility "Humi"
Delta City - Felicity Savage   f   3881

Gerin the Fox
Prince of the North - Harry Turtledove   f   4392

Gleese, Eacon
The Stone Movers - Patricia Mullen   f   3221

Greene, Andy "the Warden"
The Warden of Horses - Karen Ripley   s   3672

Gwenhwyvar
Pendragon - Stephen R. Lawhead   f   2672

Halarek, Karne
Brander's Book - C.J. Mills   s   3114
Egil's Book - C.J. Mills   s   3115
Kit's Book - C.J. Mills   s   3116
Zjhanne's Book - C.J. Mills   s   3117

Haldane, Rhys Michael Alister
The Bastard Prince - Katherine Kurtz   f   2588

Harold Bull-Roar
Byzantium - Stephen R. Lawhead   f   2670

Hemlock
Sweet MYTH-tery of Life - Robert Asprin   f   220

Holiday, Ben
The Tangle Box - Terry Brooks   f   586
Witches' Brew - Terry Brooks   f   587

Ilisidi
Inheritor - C.J. Cherryh   s   808

RUNAWAY

SAILOR

SALESMAN

SALOON HOSTESS

SALOON KEEPER/OWNER

SCAVENGER

SCHOLAR

SCIENTIST

Jack the Ripper
A Night in the Lonesome October - Roger
  Zelazny h 4843

Jarrow, Tod
Evil Reincarnate - Leigh Clark h 844

Kilpatrick, Mark Michael
Grave Markings - Michael A. Arnzen h 175

Lavanic, Cruise
Night Cruise - Billie Sue Mosiman h 3218

Ledbetter, Gary
A Room for the Dead - Noel Hynd h 2250

Lorelei
Lorelei - Mark A. Clements h 875

Lugosh, James D.
Order of the Arrow - Michael T.
  Hinkemeyer h 2147

Nasty Andrew
Bleeder - Gene Lazuta h 2684

Performer
Puppet Master - Barry T. Hawkins h 2106

Semmlar, Wayne
Near Dead - Stephen R. George h 1768

Spoda, Arthur
Iceman - Rex Miller h 3106

Turch, Averell "The Needle"
Soulcatchers - Jan Lara h 2654

Vassago
Hideaway - Dean R. Koontz h 2550

Vess, Edgler Foreman
Intensity - Dean R. Koontz h 2552

Zyto, Michael
Machine - Rene Belletto h 360

SERVANT

Avran
Aurian - Maggie Furey f 1687

Aziz
Crescent in the Sky - Donald Moffitt s 3143

Bascombe, Jeryline A.
Tales From the Crypt: Demon Knight - Randall
  Boyll h 507

Beeker
Phule's Company - Robert Asprin s 218

Caillet, Josephine
The Werewolf of Paris - Guy Endore h 1463

Dara
Guardian's Key - Anne Logston f 2788

Duvet, Berthe
The Porcelain Dove - Delia Sherman f 3974

Ember, Annie
Elephantasm - Tanith Lee h 2711

Fledge
The Grotesque - Patrick McGrath h 3038

Frike
Bring Me the Head of Prince Charming - Roger
  Zelazny f 4834

Gregor
Dr. Haggard's Disease - Patrick McGrath h 3037

Hornchurch, Anthony
The Devil You Say - Elisa DeCarlo f 1170
Strong Spirits - Elisa DeCarlo f 1171

Jaimah
The Apprentice - Deborah Talmadge-
  Bickmore f 4292

Jasper
Murder in Cormyr - Chet Williamson f 4656

Jeeves
Scream for Jeeves: A Parody - H.P.G.
  Wodehouse h 4723

Konrad
Konrad - David Ferring f 1551

Lewis
Prisoner of Dreams - Karen Ripley s 3670

Mafoo
The Remarkable Journey of Prince Jen - Lloyd
  Alexander f 56

Michael
Dark Dance - Tanith Lee h 2709

Miss Bird
The Gilda Stories - Jewelle Gomez h 1819

Polijn
The Sure Death of a Mouse - Dan Crawford f 1013

Pomegranate
Bronze Mirror - Jeanne Larsen f 2656

Reilly, Mary
Mary Reilly - Valerie Martin h 2903

Roman
Rock of Ages - Walter Jon Williams s 4651

Rufo
Glory Road - Robert A. Heinlein f 2112

Saluez
Shadow's End - Sheri S. Tepper s 4339

Singh, Ram
*The Spider #8: The Devil's Paymaster/Legions of the
  Accursed Light* - Grant Stockbridge f 4236

Sulula "Philiope"
Conan of the Red Brotherhood - Leonard
  Carpenter f 734

Underbridge, Kin
Thunder of the Captains - Holly Lisle f 2772

Valcourt, Guy-Luc
Adversary - Daniel Rhodes h 3648

Vierran
Hexwood - Diana Wynne Jones s 2349

Wang-mu
Xenocide - Orson Scott Card s 730

Zaman
Viper - Alan Riefe h 3666

SETTLER

Adair, Devon
Earth 2 - Melissa Crandall s 1010

Barrera, Ramis
Lifeline - Kevin J. Anderson s 92

Calhoun, Janey
Warpath - Tony Daniel s 1082

Dura
Flux - Stephen Baxter s 331

Gart, Maya
The Faces of Ceti - Mary Caraker s 712

Harris, James
Bright Angel - John Blair s 415

Hrriss
Crisis on Doona - Anne McCaffrey s 2962

Maddock, Yanaba
Power Lines - Anne McCaffrey s 2976

Magnus, Brock
The Faces of Ceti - Mary Caraker s 712

Metcalf, Elizabeth
Nadya: The Wolf Chronicles - Pat Murphy f 3228

O'Hara, Marianne
Worlds Enough and Time - Joe Haldeman s 1996

Raven, Jeff
The Rowan - Anne McCaffrey s 2980

Rourke, Buneka
Powers That Be - Anne McCaffrey s 2978

Tucker, Paris
Red Genesis - S.C. Sykes s 4287

Vega, Carlos
The Faces of Ceti - Mary Caraker s 712

Watanabe, Kenji
The Garden of Rama - Arthur C. Clarke s 848

SHAMAN

Alara
The Elvenbane - Andre Norton f 3303

Anasan
Sing for a Gentle Rain - J. Alison James f 2278

Asakeiri, Adline
The Watcher's Mask - Laurie J. Marks f 2883

Ata'al
The Watcher's Mask - Laurie J. Marks f 2883

Aurelio
The War of Don Emmanuel's Nether Parts - Louis de
  Bernieres f 1137

Ayla
The Plains of Passage - Jean M. Auel f 231

Bandit
Fade to Black - Nyx Smith s 4095

Bear, Tom
The Charm - Adam Niswander h 3272

Bitterhand, Calvin
Trickster - Muriel Gray h 1875

Broken-finger, Leonard
High Steel - Jack C. Haldeman II s 1992

Carver, Alison
Seed upon the Wind - Carole Nelson
  Douglas f 1278

Cha-kwena
The Edge of the World - William Sarabande f 3856
Thunder in the Sky - William Sarabande f 3858

Coyote
Cherokee Bat and the Goat Guys - Francesca Lia
  Block f 445

Crone
Shiva Accused: An Adventure of the Ice Age - J.H.
  Brennan f 546

de Marion, Auguste "White Bear"
Shaman - Robert Shea f 3948

Dibiaja, Mpu
The Painted Alphabet - Diana Darling f 1096

Dzaminid
Spirits of Cavern and Hearth - M. Coleman
  Easton f 1380

Gallegher, P. J.
Valentine - S.P. Somtow h 4118

Heron
People of the Wolf - W. Michael Gear f 1741

Little Dancer
People of the Fire - W. Michael Gear f 1738

Lorat
Rinn's Star - Paula King s 2479

McAusland, Louisa
Changeweaver - Margaret Ball f 263

Ouija
Cyberweb - Lisa Mason s 2911

Ravinga
The Mark of the Cat - Andre Norton f 3311

Ryson, Kerryl
The Thirteenth Majestral - Hayford Peirce   s   3407

Sadira
The Verdant Passage - Troy Denning   f   1201

Tiana
Songs of the Dancing Gods - Jack L. Chalker   f   780

Timkin
The Red King - Victor Kelleher   f   2426

Vashanna
Cat Scratch Fever - Tara K. Harper   s   2037

Willow Leaf
The Road to Underfall - Mike Jefferies   f   2304

Yaroslavich, Yuri
Terrible Swift Sword - William R. Forstchen   s   1591

SMUGGLER

Barabbas
Woman Without a Shadow - Karen Haber   s   1988

Dalamini, Ming
Crystal Witness - Kathy Tyers   s   4404

Hinton, Blackbird
Python Isle - Kenneth Robeson   f   3700

Iger
The War Minstrels - Karen Haber   s   1987

Lando, Pik
Drifter - William C. Dietz   s   1245
Drifter's Run - William C. Dietz   s   1246
Drifter's War - William C. Dietz   s   1247

Mogurn, Deuteronomous
Dragons in the Stars - Jeffrey A. Carver   s   753

Reed, Kayla
The War Minstrels - Karen Haber   s   1987

St. Cyr, Butterfly
Archangel Blues - eluki bes shahar   s   384
Darktraders - eluki bes shahar   s   385
Hellflower - Eluki bes Shahar   s   386

Tanner, Louis
Destroying Angel - Richard Paul Russo   s   3797

Valentine, Patrick
Prototype - Brian Hodge   h   2159

Vasquez, Juanita
Mojo and the Pickle Jar - Douglas Bell   f   357

X, Aaron
Conglomeros - Jesse Browner   f   595

SOCIAL WORKER

Block, Hillary
Deathchain - Ken Greenhall   h   1933

Fairfax, Eugenia
Black Night - S.J. Strayhorn   h   4255

Haberman
The Nihilesthete - Richard Kalich   h   2391

James, Hilton
The Between - Tannarive Due   h   1346

Janos, Teodor
The Death of Sleep - Anne McCaffrey   s   2966

Jo
The Parasite War - Tim Sullivan   s   4268

Johnston, Jerry
Prodigal - Melanie Tem   h   4328

Samson, Rosalie "Rose"
The Godmother - Elizabeth Ann Scarborough   f   3889

Stevens, Carol
Reborn - F. Paul Wilson   h   4691

Vaughn, Melissa
Child of Shadows - John Coyne   h   1001

Winchell, Anne
Bone - George C. Chesbro   h   817

SOCIALITE

Cobri, Amy
Sundowner - Chris Claremont   s   841

de Conde, Sarah Webster
Deep Freeze - Zach Hughes   s   2239

Evans, Constanza
The War of Don Emmanuel's Nether Parts - Louis de Bernieres   f   1137

Galinda "Glinda the Good"
Wicked: The Life and Times of the Wicked Witch of the West - Gregory Maguire   f   2869

Leyner, Mark
Et Tu, Babe - Mark Leyner   s   2747

Rogers, Troi
Treks Not Taken - Steven R. Boyett   s   497

Zant, Quasar
Quasar - Jamil Nasir   s   3242

SOCIOLOGIST

Baker, Jonathan
Red Genesis - S.C. Sykes   s   4287

Dove, Amy
God's World - Ian Watson   s   4492

Lixia, Li
A Woman of the Iron People - Eleanor Arnason   s   174

Massif, Sheila
The Living One - Lewis Gannett   h   1700

Morris, Claudia
Children of the Thunder - John Brunner   s   599

SONGWRITER

Bradley, Angela
Metal Angel - Nancy Springer   f   4135

SORCERER

Al-Ra,ma, Khaddam
The Riddled Man - Mark E. Rogers   f   3726

Asandir
Curse of the Mistwraith - Janny Wurts   f   4785

Avril
The Price of Blood and Honor - Elizabeth Willey   f   4628
A Sorcerer and a Gentleman - Elizabeth Willey   f   4629

Azrael
Evil Reincarnate - Leigh Clark   h   844

Baralis
The Baker's Boy - J.V. Jones   f   2356
Master and Fool - J.V. Jones   f   2358

Bariden
The Hidden Realms - Sharon Green   f   1890

Belgarath
Belgarath the Sorcerer - David Eddings   f   1388

ben Shaqar, Sharif
The Devouring Void - Mark E. Rogers   f   3725

Bonaduce, Aballister
Canticle - R.A. Salvatore   f   3835

Brandin of Ygrath
Tigana - Guy Gavriel Kay   f   2405

Brandis
Wind Whispers, Shadow Shouts - Sharon Green   f   1892

Caolin "Blood Lord"
The Jewel of Fire - Diana L. Paxson   f   3396

Constance
Down Among the Dead Men - Simon R. Green   f   1897

Creeping Sword
Spell of Apocalypse - Mayer Alan Brenner   f   551

Custer, George Armstrong
Devil's Tower - Mark Summer   f   4270

Darynson, Davyn "Davi"
Book of Stones - L. Dean James   f   2279

Deite, Manuel "Childe"
Raven - S.A. Swiniarski   h   4284

Dewar
The Price of Blood and Honor - Elizabeth Willey   f   4628
A Sorcerer and a Gentleman - Elizabeth Willey   f   4629

Drulethen "Dru"
The Qualinesti - Paul B. Thompson   f   4353

Dur
Drum Warning - Jo Clayton   f   858

Elena
The Fourth Guardian - Ronald Anthony Cross   s   1032
The Lost Guardian - Ronald Anthony Cross   s   1033

Elminster
Elminster: The Making of a Mage - Ed Greenwood   f   1941

Erwyn
Go Quest, Young Man - K.B. Bogen   f   455

Evander
Days of Air and Darkness - Katharine Kerr   f   2443

Gervinus
The Shattered Oath - Josepha Sherman   f   3980

Grandier, Urbain
The Element of Fire - Martha Wells   f   4582

Great Karlini
Spell of Apocalypse - Mayer Alan Brenner   f   551

Gwydion
The Well-Favored Man: The Tale of the Sorcerer's Nephew - Elizabeth Willey   f   4630

Jack
The Baker's Boy - J.V. Jones   f   2356
A Man Betrayed - J.V. Jones   f   2357
Master and Fool - J.V. Jones   f   2358

Jazen sr'Yat
The Fountains of Mirlacca - Ashley McConnell   f   3005

Kaftus
The Sure Death of a Mouse - Dan Crawford   f   1013

Klingsor
The Grail of Hearts - Susan Shwartz   f   4001

Lady
Dreams of Steel - Glen Cook   f   928

Litzenreich
Shadowbreed - David Ferring   f   1552

Lothor
Nightseer - Laurell K. Hamilton   f   2019

Lukasha
The Spirit Gate - Maya Kaathryn Bohnhoff   f   460

Macumba the Dark Man
Howl-O-Ween - Gary L. Holleman   h   2189

SORCERESS

SPACESHIP CAPTAIN

Mama Yaya
I, Tituba, Black Witch of Salem - Maryse Conde   f   911

Maybelle, Great Aunt
The Witch House - Norma Tadlock Johnson   f   2329

Miranda, Carmen
Carmen Miranda's Ghost Is Haunting Space Station Three - Don Sakers   s   3827

Mogget
Sabriel - Garth Nix   f   3288

Molly
Tex and Molly in the Afterlife - Richard Grant   f   1863

Orlene
And Eternity - Piers Anthony   f   132

Pascale
The Ghost Inside the Monitor - Margaret J. Anderson   f   101

Patience
A Witch Across Time - Gilbert B. Cross   f   1031

Peregrine
The Thread That Binds the Bones - Nina Kiriki Hoffman   f   2169

Queenie
The Influence - Ramsey Campbell   h   698

Ransome, Errec
The Long Hunt - Debra Doyle   s   1295

Raynor, Sara
Darkling - Michael O'Rourke   h   3367

Rohr, Gail
The Land of Nod - Mark A. Clements   h   874

Rowan, Jack
Dead Lines - John Skipp   h   4056

Scathach
The Scathach and the Maeve's Daughter - Mary Alexander Walker   f   4476

Scott, Walter
Picking the Ballad's Bones - Elizabeth Ann Scarborough   f   3895

Scrooge, Ebenezer
Carol for Another Christmas - Elizabeth Ann Scarborough   f   3888

Seth, Nguyen
Demon Download - Jack Yeovil   f   4799

Stanovich, Martin Philip
Ghost Boy - Jean Simon   h   4041

Steadford, Sir Harry
The Meddlesome Ghost - Sheila Rosalynd Allen   f   70

Tuggle, Mrs.
The Witch's Eye - Phyllis Reynolds Naylor   f   3250

Vivian
Black Snow Days - Claudia O'Keefe   s   3350

Walford, John
Walford's Oak - Jill M. Phillips   f   3433

Yang
Unicorn U. - Esther Friesner   f   1678

SPORTS FIGURE

Angel
Damnbanna - Nancy Springer   f   4131

Asakeiri, Adline
The Watcher's Mask - Laurie J. Marks   f   2883

Boles, Danny
Brittle Innings - Michael Bishop   h   403

Briggs, Timothy
Hence - Brad Leithauser   s   2727

Clerval, Henry
Brittle Innings - Michael Bishop   h   403

David
Gameplay - Kevin J. Anderson   f   88
Game's End - Kevin J. Anderson   f   87

Doyle, Irini
The Sweetheart Season - Karen Joy Fowler   f   1629

Drake, Tannim
Chrome Circle - Mercedes Lackey   f   2606

Goon
Goon - Edward Lee   h   2698

Greene, Harris
Doc Sidhe - Aaron Allston   f   71

Gurgeh, Jernau
The Player of Games - Iain M. Banks   s   275

Haas, Peter
Memento Mori - Shariann Lewitt   s   2746

Hoey, Buck
Brittle Innings - Michael Bishop   h   403

Knight, Aubrey
Gorgon Child - Steven Barnes   s   302

Lily
Ecstasia - Francesca Lia Block   f   446

Major, Cyrus "Cy" Lance
Zeus and Co. - David Lee Jones   f   2344

Melanie
Gameplay - Kevin J. Anderson   f   88
Game's End - Kevin J. Anderson   f   87

Parmenion
Lion of Macedon - David Gemmell   f   1756

Sands, Max
The Barsoom Project - Larry Niven   s   3275

Seavers, Kim
Beamriders! - Martin Caidin   s   672

Shomer, Jillian
Achilles' Choice - Larry Niven   s   3274

Silk, Venture
Spindoc - Steve Perry   s   3424

Sonnenberg, Bryce
The Ganymede Club - Charles Sheffield   s   3953

Tanner, Mark
Creature - John Saul   h   3873

SPOUSE

Adair, Hugh
Breeder - Douglas Clegg   h   867

Addams, Morticia
Addams Family Values - Todd Strasser   f   4246

Banner, Elizabeth "Betty Tanner"
What Savage Beast - Peter David   s   1122

Barton, Alex
The Circus of the Earth and Air - Brooke Stevens   f   4200

Bellman, Effie
The House That Jack Built - Graham Masterton   h   2925

Bellman, Kim
The Printer's Devil - Chico Kidd   f   2465

Bird, Marianne
Tap, Tap - David Martin   h   2891

Bonney, Isabel "Iz"
Elvissey - Jack Womack   s   4746

Bonney, John
Elvissey - Jack Womack   s   4746

Brady, Julia
The Gallery of His Dreams - Kristine Kathryn Rusch   f   3775

Carpenter, Rebecca
Dark Fortune - Richard Lee Byers   h   650

Casaubon, Lord-Architect
The Architecture of Desire - Mary Gentle   f   1761

Cedar, Janice
Fossil - Hal Clement   s   872

Cooper, Ellen
Earthbound - Richard Matheson   h   2930

Cortez, Rosita "Rose" Carmelita
Timemaster - Robert L. Forward   s   1598

Curtis, Richard
Dreamer - Peter James   h   2288

Dalton, Tom
Watchers in the Woods - William W. Johnstone   h   2340

Doreen
Flickering Shadows - Kwadwo Agymah Kamau   f   2395

Duke, Cindy
The Wild - Whitley Strieber   h   4262

Eichord, Donna
Iceman - Rex Miller   h   3106

Elizabeth
The Secret Life of Laszlo, Count Dracula - Roderick Anscombe   h   124

Elspeth
Thomas the Rhymer - Ellen Kushner   f   2596

Elvis
The Man in the Moon Must Die - Jeff Bredenberg   s   545

Francine
Lord Conrad's Lady - Leo Frankowski   s   1644

Gail
Nobody's Son - Sean Stewart   f   4208

Glivven, Miranda
Cat's Paw - L.A. Taylor   f   4316

Gold, Michael "Mike"
Unquenchable Fire - Rachel Pollack   f   3475

Guenevere
The Camelot Chronicles - Mike Ashley   f   186
Witch of the North - Courtway Jones   f   2342

Gwenhwyfar
Pendragon's Banner - Helen Hollick   f   2191

Harootunian, Geoffrey "Hoot"
Larque on the Wing - Nancy Springer   f   4134

Heln
Chimaera's Copper - Piers Anthony   f   136

Hillenbrand, Laura
Naomi's Room - Jonathan Aycliffe   h   237

Indian, John
I, Tituba, Black Witch of Salem - Maryse Conde   f   911

Julia
The Hellbound Heart - Clive Barker   h   287

Knight, Aubrey
Firedance - Steven Barnes   s   301

Laker, Maria
Among Madmen - Jim Starlin   s   4156

Larking, Lorien
Lorien Lost - Michael King   f   2477

Lilith
The Shape-Changer's Wife - Sharon Shinn   f   3990

Lowell, Janet
The Well - Michael B. Sirota   h   4053

Soothsayer - Mike Resnick   *s*   3638

Moonblade, Arilyn
Elfshadow - Elaine Cunningham   *f*   1045
Silver Shadows - Elaine Cunningham   *f*   1048

Morganstern, Jack
Dead Girls - Richard Calder   *s*   684

Morris "Mauricio di Mauro"
*The Night of Wishes: or The
   Satanarchaeolidealcohellish Notion Potion* - Michael
   Ende   *f*   1462

Multiple Entity "ME"
ME: A Novel of Self Discovery - Thomas T.
   Thomas   *s*   4350

Nash, August
Labyrinth of Night - Allen Steele   *s*   4183

Nivens, Sam
The Puppet Masters - Robert A. Heinlein   *s*   2114

Nysander
Luck in the Shadows - Lynn Flewelling   *f*   1572

Ochs, Thur
The Spirit Ring - Lois McMaster Bujold   *f*   626

Old Man
The Puppet Masters - Robert A. Heinlein   *s*   2114

Pulaski, Toya
Converse and Conflict - L. Neil Smith   *s*   4091

Quail, Douglas
*The Collected Stories of Philip K. Dick, Volume Two:
   We Can Remember It for You Wholesale* - Philip K.
   Dick   *s*   1226

Quinn "Nomad"
Nomad - David Alexander   *s*   54

Ramsey
Nomad - David Alexander   *s*   54

Relanj, Zia
The Forever Drug - Steve Perry   *s*   3422
Spindoc - Steve Perry   *s*   3424

Reydak, Karl
A Fearful Symmetry - James Luceno   *s*   2817

Rialla
Steal the Dragon - Patricia Briggs   *f*   561

Ring, Ethan
Scissors Cut Paper Wrap Stone - Ian
   McDonald   *s*   3021

Rourke, John T.
The Struggle - Jerry Ahern   *s*   34

Santoul, Remy
Illegal Alien - James Luceno   *s*   2818

Scribble, Jacob
*The Night of Wishes: or The
   Satanarchaeolidealcohellish Notion Potion* - Michael
   Ende   *f*   1462

Seavers, Kim
Beamriders! - Martin Caidin   *s*   672

Seregil
Luck in the Shadows - Lynn Flewelling   *f*   1572

Silver, Mier
Mission: Tori - Johanna Bolton   *s*   462

Sims, Dolores
Cradle of Splendor - Patricia Anthony   *s*   129

Sma, Diziet
Use of Weapons - Iain M. Banks   *s*   277

Somoroff, Peter
Red Devil - David Saperstein   *h*   3855

Steengo
The Stainless Steel Rat Sings the Blues - Harry
   Harrison   *s*   2060

Steiner, Clara
The Werewolf's Revenge - Richard Jaccoma   *h*   2264

Stone, Will
Majestic - Whitley Strieber   *s*   4260

Sutter, Frank
Innerverse - John DeChancie   *s*   1178

Tamara
On My Way to Paradise - Dave Wolverton   *s*   4744

Thann, Danilo "Dan"
Silver Shadows - Elaine Cunningham   *f*   1048

Tower, Josh
Systems - W.T. Quick   *s*   3549

Trask, Ben
Bloodwars - Brian Lumley   *h*   2822
The Last Aerie - Brian Lumley   *h*   2830

Trilling, Kate
The Invisible Company - Scott Russell
   Sanders   *s*   3852

Underhill, Jimmy
The Werewolf's Revenge - Richard Jaccoma   *h*   2264

Van Dorne, Chesna "Echo"
The Wolf's Hour - Robert R. McCammon   *h*   2992

Van Ryn, Rex
The Devil Rides Out - Dennis Wheatley   *h*   4600

Vear, Nick
The Ridge - Lisa Cantrell   *h*   708

Wei
Rule Golden and Double Meaning - Damon
   Knight   *s*   2536

Whitaker, Tomyris "Whit Hastings"
Return to Isis - Jean Stewart   *s*   4203

Winter, John
Deathwalker - Patrick Whalen   *h*   4596

Wright, Jimjoy Earle
The Ecolitan Operation - L.E. Modesitt Jr.   *s*   3129
The Ecologic Secession - L.E. Modesitt Jr.   *s*   3130

Xu-Tzu, Phan
Celestial Matters - Richard Garfinkle   *s*   1717

Zakalwe, Cheradenine
Use of Weapons - Iain M. Banks   *s*   277

STATISTICIAN

Tremaine, Elspeth "Beth"
The Convocation - John R. Holt   *h*   2192

STEP-PARENT

Branwen
The Lost Years of Merlin - T.A. Barron   *f*   309

Burrich
Assassin's Apprentice - Robin Hobb   *f*   2151

Cwenn
Suisan - Phyllis Carol Agins   *f*   32

Peter
Bones - Joyce Thompson   *h*   4351

Robin
Passager - Jane Yolen   *f*   4813

Sherwood, Iris "Butcher of Boston"
In the Cube - David Alexander Smith   *s*   4076

Wilkinson, Hilda
Spider - Patrick McGrath   *h*   3039

Willson, Andrea
Dark Reunion - Stephen R. George   *h*   1764

STEWARD

Lindgren, Anton
Carve the Sky - Alexander Jablokov   *s*   2260

McGulvey, Mr.
In between Dragons - Michael Kandel   *f*   2397

STOCK BROKER

Duke, Bob
The Wild - Whitley Strieber   *h*   4262

Mati, Gwendolyn "Gwen"
Half Asleep in Frog Pajamas - Tom
   Robbins   *s*   3683

Rotciv, Victor
The Convocation - John R. Holt   *h*   2192

STORE OWNER

Deeters, Nathan
Cross a Dark Bridge - Deborah Churchman   *h*   829

Gypsy Pete
Frisk - Dennis Cooper   *h*   943

Hodge, Benton
Sineater - Elizabeth Massie   *h*   2917

Jonah
Something Rich and Strange - Patricia A.
   McKillip   *f*   3060

Katts, Wesley
Anthony Shriek - Jessica Amanda
   Salmonson   *h*   3832

Kopp, Curly
Seaward - Brad Leithauser   *h*   2729

Markham, Dan
California Gothic - Dennis Etchison   *h*   1483

Markham, Evie
California Gothic - Dennis Etchison   *h*   1483

Moriarity, Pepper
The House That Jack Built - Graham
   Masterton   *h*   2925

Somersby, Nadine
Prank Night - David Robbins   *h*   3678

STORYTELLER

Dandilion
Tales From Watership Down - Richard Adams   *f*   25

Khalifa, Rashid
Haroun and the Sea of Stories - Salman
   Rushdie   *f*   3788

Magara
Shadow-Maze - Mark Smith   *f*   4094

Mikhailovych, Lixand
Shadow's Daughter - Shirley Meier   *f*   3084

Murphy, Buffy
Fair Peril - Nancy Springer   *f*   4132

Quijance, Natasha
Red Planet Run - Dana Stabenow   *s*   4139

Scheherazade
The Last Arabian Night - Craig Shaw
   Gardner   *f*   1712

STOWAWAY

Allaird, Margaret "Marnie"
Arrow From Earth - F.M. Busby   *s*   639

Chase-Frisson L'Zalle, Trevarre
Shivering World - Kathy Tyers   *s*   4406

Colter, Daniel
Into the Deep - Ken Grimwood   s   1962

STREETPERSON

Allen, Zadok
The Shadow over Innsmouth - H.P.
   Lovecraft   h   2809

Bone
Bone - George C. Chesbro   h   817
A Hidden Place - Robert Charles Wilson   s   4704

Elgin
Street - Jack Cady   h   671

Holt, Kenneth
Wyrm Wolf - Edo Van Belkom   h   4414

Julian
Wilding - Melanie Tem   h   4330

Peru, Mattie
Breeder - Douglas Clegg   h   867

Phousita
The Bohr Maker - Linda Nagata   s   3238

Pook
Voices of Hope - David Feintuch   s   1532

Silk
Street - Jack Cady   h   671

Symptomatic Nerve Gas
Street - Jack Cady   h   671

STUDENT

a-Lagan, Meredydd
The Meri - Maya Kaathryn Bohnhoff   f   459

Ahrens, Bleys
Young Bleys - Gordon R. Dickson   s   1243

Alderberry, Jane
The Iron Dragon's Daughter - Michael
   Swanwick   f   4282

Alexander, Ardeth
The Night Inside - Nancy Baker   h   252

Alnosha "Nosh"
The Hands of Lyr - Andre Norton   f   3308

Anderson, Marion
Flesh - Gus Weill   h   4531

Angelo, Jamie
Beauty - Brian D'Amato   h   1080

Ariadne, Helene
Light Raid - Connie Willis   s   4674

Ashenden, Turner
Views from the Oldest House - Richard
   Grant   s   1865

Attercop, Karen
Webs - Scott Baker   h   255

Aubrey
The Shape-Changer's Wife - Sharon Shinn   f   3990

Aurian
Aurian - Maggie Furey   f   1687

Bankhead, Tallulah "Tulley"
Beyond the Door - Gary L. Blackwood   s   413

Barclay, Andy
Child's Play III - Matthew J. Costello   h   965

Barrett, Jonathan
Red Death - P.N. Elrod   h   1443

Bittan, Rebecca
The Kiss - Kathryn Reines   h   3614

Blennerhassett, Daniel
Virgins and Martyrs - Simon Maginn   h   2867

Bradley, Alexander "Alex"
The Hollowing - Robert Holdstock   f   2184

Brown, Tim
The Select - F. Paul Wilson   h   4693

Bryant, Martin
The Crawling Dark - Pauline Dunn   h   1366

Burkhardt, Jared Jr.
First Love: A Gothic Tale - Joyce Carol
   Oates   h   3331

C.
Galatea 2.2 - Richard M. Powers   s   3493

Cadderly
Canticle - R.A. Salvatore   f   3835

Caeser, Justin
Flesh - Gus Weill   h   4531

Caldwell, Jay
Call to Battle - Doug Murray   h   3234

Campbell, Deirdre
Indiana Jones and the Dance of the Giants - Rob
   MacGregor   f   2853
Indiana Jones and the Seven Veils - Rob
   MacGregor   f   2857

Cannon, Ben
Cannon's Orb - L. Warren Douglas   s   1279

Cannon, Bobby
The School - Ed Kelleher   h   2425

Carter, Janet
Tam Lin - Pamela Dean   f   1166

Chios, Maia
Dragon Season - Michael Cassutt   f   759

Christie
The Informers - Brett Easton Ellis   h   1426

Cleary, Quinn
The Select - F. Paul Wilson   h   4693

Colette, Sianna
The Shattered Sphere - Roger MacBride Allen   s   67

Collins, Jack
A Logical Magician - Robert Weinberg   f   4543

Collins, Karen Cecile "Casey"
Islands of Tomorrow - F.M. Busby   s   640

Conti, Ned
Madeleine's Ghost - Robert Girardi   h   1801

Coughlan, Demeter
Man Plus - Frederik Pohl   s   3464

Crusher, Wesley
Debtors' Planet - William R. Thompson   s   4355

Daae, Christine
Phantom - Susan Kay   h   2407

Dain, Benn
Mazeway - Jack Williamson   s   4671

David
Gameplay - Kevin J. Anderson   f   88
Game's End - Kevin J. Anderson   f   87

Davis, Anne
Order of the Arrow - Michael T.
   Hinkemeyer   h   2147

de Kreshtur, Andrei
Blood Countess - Andrei Codrescu   h   881

DeWoe, Dekker
Mining the Oort - Frederik Pohl   s   3465

Dion
Mage Heart - Jane Routley   f   3754

Dougal, Duncan
My Teacher Fried My Brains - Bruce Coville   s   993

Doyle, Keith
Higher Mythology - Jody Lynn Nye   f   3322
Mythology Abroad - Jody Lynn Nye   f   3326

Drib
The Knights of Cawdor - Mike Jefferies   f   2302

Ehlers, Lou
Who Killed James Dean? - Warren Newton
   Beath   h   352

Ellerman, Amy
The Quiet - Patrick Billings   h   396

Engle, Kivrin
Doomsday Book - Connie Willis   s   4672

Exeter, Edward
Past Imperative - Dave Duncan   f   1356

Farley, Heather
Serpent's Gift - A.C. Crispin   s   1023

Forbes, Vanessa
The School - Ed Kelleher   h   2425

Gangle, Kendar "Ratwacker"
Majyk by Accident - Esther Friesner   f   1673

Gardner, Sam
Captain Quad - Sean Costello   h   974

Gates, John
Flicker - Theodore Roszak   h   3752

Gilbert, India
India's Story - Kathlyn S. Starbuck   s   4153

Ginny
Virago - Karen Marie Christa Minns   h   3120

Gorse
Wizard's Hall - Jane Yolen   f   4817

Green, Margo
Relic - Douglas Preston   h   3521

Grey, Liza
The Messenger - Donald Tyson   h   4408

Harper, Fay
Jinx High - Mercedes Lackey   h   2611

Harrison, Lee Anne
The Magic and the Healing - Nick
   O'Donohoe   f   3341
Under the Healing Sign - Nick O'Donohoe   f   3343

Harrison, Theophilius "Ted"
Orbital Resonance - John Barnes   s   298

Helit, Susan Sto
Soul Music - Terry Pratchett   f   3508

Helling, Suzanne "Alouzon"
Dragon Death - Gael Baudino   f   324
Duel of Dragons - Gael Baudino   f   325

Henry "Thornmallow"
Wizard's Hall - Jane Yolen   f   4817

Hoyland, Hugh
Silent Thunder/Universe - Dean Ing   s   2253

Hph-wayuo "Alvin"
Brightness Reef - David Brin   s   562

I
Ishmael - Daniel Quinn   s   3552

James, Mike
The Orchid Eater - Marc Laidlaw   h   2635

Jankowitz, Sheldon
User Unfriendly - Vivian Vande Velde   f   4429

Jasper
Murder in Cormyr - Chet Williamson   f   4656

Jennedote, Yaji
Fire in the Mist - Holly Lisle   f   2767

Joanna
The Time Tree - Enid Richemont   f   3662

Johnson, Sibyl
Far Edge of Darkness - Linda Evans   s   1492

Kane, Laura
Deathscape - Michael Cecilione   h   766

Theodora of Pyrene
The Gate of Ivory - Doris Egan   s   1411

Thompson, Peter
My Teacher Flunked the Planet - Bruce
   Coville   s   992
My Teacher Glows in the Dark - Bruce
   Coville   s   994

Tobin, Sara Ann
Angel Light - Andrew M. Greeley   f   1877

Tooley, Nick
Tam Lin - Pamela Dean   f   1166

Torres, Rogelio
Meridian 144 - Meg Files   s   1555

Trevisan, David
The Fair Rules of Evil - David C. Smith   h   4077

Tugelbend, Victor
Moving Pictures - Terry Pratchett   f   3505

Turch, Averell "The Needle"
Soulcatchers - Jan Lara   h   2654

Ulrich, Will
The Robin Hood Ambush - William Wu   s   4783

Voss, Dorn
Where the Ships Die - William C. Dietz   s   1254

Wae, Kiondili
Lightwing - Tara K. Harper   s   2038

Walthers, Danielle "Dani"
The Vampire Odyssey - Scott Ciencin   h   832
The Wildlings - Scott Ciencin   h   834

Washburn, Bob
The Robin Hood Ambush - William Wu   s   4783

Wells, Jeff
Norby and the Court Jester - Janet Asimov   s   211

Wilkinson, Steve
A Call to Arms - Thomas K. Martin   f   2901

Winter, James
Sing for a Gentle Rain - J. Alison James   f   2278

Wren
Wren's Quest - Sherwood Smith   f   4103

Zoe
The Silver Kiss - Annette Curtis Klause   f   2514

STUDENT—COLLEGE

Allie
Lost in Translation - Margaret Ball   f   265

Aylesworth, Jesse
An Exaltation of Larks - Robert Reed   s   3595

Bainbridge
Ferman's Devils - Joe Clifford Faust   s   1522

Bird, Marianne
Tap, Tap - David Martin   h   2891

Calderon, Miguel
Shango - James Roberto Curtis   h   1053

Caldwell, John
Mojave Wells - L. Dean James   s   2281

Callare, Jesse
Mother of Storms - John Barnes   s   296

Clark, Joe
Fiend - C. Dean Andersson   h   114

Collier, Marcy
Mythology 101 - Jody Lynn Nye   f   3325

Copley, Isabelle "Izzy"
Memory and Dream - Charles de Lint   f   1157

Crusher, Wesley
Balance of Power - Dafydd ab Hugh   s   6

Daniels, Aikin
Dreamseeker's Road - Tom Deitz   f   1191

Desmond, Timothy Alfred
Unicorn U. - Esther Friesner   f   1678

Devery, Nell
When Darkness Falls - Sidney Williams   h   4640

Domerc
Lost in Translation - Margaret Ball   f   265

Doyle, Keith
Mythology 101 - Jody Lynn Nye   f   3325

Faulkner, Sully
An Exaltation of Larks - Robert Reed   s   3595

Fortunato, Amelia
Dark Visions - T. Lucien Wright   h   4771

Harris, Tina
The Abductors: Conspiracy - Jonathan
   Frakes   s   1633

Jacoby, Darcy
Wendigo Border - Catherine Montrose   h   3158

Kaplan, T'ing Hau
Unicorn U. - Esther Friesner   f   1678

Lahikainen, Sarah
Cold Whisper - Rick Hautala   h   2080

Madison, Jay
The Gryphon King - Tom Deitz   f   1192

McLean, Alec
Dreamseeker's Road - Tom Deitz   f   1191

Murphy, Grey
Man From Mundania - Piers Anthony   f   148

Papen, Richard
The Secret History - Donna Tartt   h   4306

Rob
Agviq - Michael Armstrong   s   171

Roberts, Sheila
Into the Deep - Ken Grimwood   s   1962

Sullivan, David
Darkthunder's Way - Tom Deitz   f   1189
Dreamseeker's Road - Tom Deitz   f   1191
Sunshaker's War - Tom Deitz   f   1195

Swenson, Colter
Footprints of Thunder - James F. David   s   1115

Tolar, Rob
The Gryphon King - Tom Deitz   f   1192

Wilkinson, Steve
A Two-Edged Sword - Thomas K. Martin   f   2902

Winter, Henry
The Secret History - Donna Tartt   h   4306

Zalewski, Petra
Footprints of Thunder - James F. David   s   1115

STUDENT—EXCHANGE

Lonat, Bosanka
The Golden Thread - Suzy McKee Charnas   f   784

STUDENT—GRADUATE

Kaye, Peter
Chiller - Randall Boyll   h   500

Losmara, Rafe
Reprisal - F. Paul Wilson   h   4692

Shepherd, Chyna
Intensity - Dean R. Koontz   h   2552

Tabor, Lucian "Luke"
Islands of Tomorrow - F.M. Busby   s   640

Timmers, Lacy
Soulcatchers - Jan Lara   h   2654

Verruckt, Steven
Vampires Anonymous - Jeffrey N.
   McMahan   h   3070

Zolotin, Peter
Burster - Michael Capobianco   s   711

STUDENT—HIGH SCHOOL

Alexander, Sam
SETI - Frederick Fichman   s   1553

Angel
Damnbanna - Nancy Springer   f   4131

Bryge, Larry
Spirit Crossings - Claudia Peck   f   3405

"Damnbanna" Deil
Damnbanna - Nancy Springer   f   4131

Desmond, Timothy Alfred
Harpy High - Esther Friesner   f   1670

Dillon, Ronny
Soulsmith - Tom Deitz   f   1193

Marsh, Valentine
The Golden Thread - Suzy McKee Charnas   f   784

Martino, Chris
OtherSyde - J. Michael Straczynski   h   4245

Oakland, Brian
Stunts - Charles L. Grant   h   1857

Obst, Roger
OtherSyde - J. Michael Straczynski   h   4245

Roeder, Karel
Lights Out in the Reptile House - Jim
   Shepard   f   3969

Sherman
In between Dragons - Michael Kandel   f   2397

Welch, Lewis
Soulsmith - Tom Deitz   f   1193

STUDENT—JUNIOR HIGH SCHOOL

De Witt, Ryan
Red Wizard - Nancy Springer   f   4136

STUDENT—MIDDLE SCHOOL

Jeff
On Meeting Witches at Wells - Judith
   Gorog   f   1832

SUPERNATURAL BEING

Harkender, Jacob
The Carnival of Destruction - Brian
   Stableford   h   4142

James, Raglan
The Tale of the Body Thief - Anne Rice   h   3655

McGee, Rosa
Sacrament - Clive Barker   h   290

Pangloss
In the Blood - Nancy A. Collins   h   903

Steep, Jacob
Sacrament - Clive Barker   h   290

SURVIVOR

Laski, Saul
Carrion Comfort - Dan Simmons   h   4028

TAILOR

Mulvihill, Travest
The Ways of Magic - Scott Ciencin   *f*   833

TAXI DRIVER

Boda
Pollen - Jeff Noon   *s*   3293

Coyote
Pollen - Jeff Noon   *s*   3293

Spencer, Jake
Bloodlines - J.N. Williamson   *h*   4660

TAXIDERMIST

Reed, Matt
The Reckoning - Ruby Jean Jensen   *h*   2314

TEACHER

Al-Ra,ma, Khaddam
The Riddled Man - Mark E. Rogers   *f*   3726

Albin, Doug
The Mailman - Bentley Little   *h*   2775

Almond, Donna
Dead in the Water - Nancy Holder   *h*   2180

Anara
India's Story - Kathlyn S. Starbuck   *s*   4153

Anaxagoras
The Wizard's Apprentice - S.P. Somtow   *f*   4120

Anthony, Father
Catacomb - Andrew Laurance   *h*   2665

Archer, Ann
Otherworld - Kenneth C. Flint   *h*   1576

Baker, Bob
After Life - Andrew Neiderman   *h*   3252

Bevol, Israed
Taminy - Maya Kaathryn Bohnhoff   *f*   461

Bevol, Osraed
The Meri - Maya Kaathryn Bohnhoff   *f*   459

Bird, Roscoe
Tap, Tap - David Martin   *h*   2891

Bjornsen, Paula
Night Sounds - Warner Lee   *h*   2716

Bloch, Jared
No Limits - Nigel Findley   *s*   1561

Bodbmall
Master of Earth and Water - Diana L.
   Paxson   *f*   3397

Bolton, Jennifer
Cold White Fury - Beth Amos   *h*   81

Bowen, Tess
The Uprising - Abigail McDaniels   *h*   3013

Buchanan, Victoria
The Vampire Papers - Michael Romkey   *h*   3737

Callare, Jesse
Mother of Storms - John Barnes   *s*   296

Carter, Travis
Demon's Fright - Penelope Banka Kreps   *h*   2571

Chapin, Francis
Blood of Innocents - John Arbucci   *h*   168

Chen, Robert
Starseed - Spider Robinson   *s*   3717

Cierto, Hoja
Black Steel - Steve Perry   *s*   3418

Coffey, Malcolm "Cup"
Goat Dance - Douglas Clegg   *h*   870

Connely, Mary
Blood Feud - Sam Siciliano   *h*   4005

Craven, Tammy
Blood Kin - Ronald Kelly   *h*   2432

Crindle
Mysteries of the Word - Stanley Wiater   *h*   4616

Cruitaire, Christa
Gossamer Axe - Gael Baudino   *f*   326

Denisovitch, Pavel
The Nanotech Chronicles - Michael Flynn   *s*   1580

Dennehy, Nuala Maebh
The Rising of the Moon - Flynn Connolly   *s*   915

Drake, Christopher
Endgame - Robert Cain   *s*   678

Dunbar, Maggie
Dark Tide - Elizabeth Forrest   *h*   1584

Edhadeya
Earthborn - Orson Scott Card   *s*   718

Evans, Jonna
Monster - John Tigges   *h*   4366

Fast, Barry
Firestar - Michael Flynn   *s*   1579

Feinstein, Rose
The Magic Touch - Jody Lynn Nye   *f*   3323

Feraru, Michael
The Lost - Jonathan Aycliffe   *h*   235

Frame, Max
Dead End - Guy N. Smith   *h*   4083

Freleng, Rachel
Cries of the Children - Clare McNally   *h*   3072

Galbraith, Jenn
Good Night, Sweet Angel - Clare McNally   *h*   3073

Ghan
The Waterborn - J. Gregory Keyes   *f*   2464

Graham, Dexter
Mysterium - Robert Charles Wilson   *s*   4705

Graves, Elliott
Dark Lullaby - Jessica Palmer   *h*   3377

Grout
The Knights of Cawdor - Mike Jefferies   *f*   2302

Halver
The Dubious Hills - Pamela Dean   *f*   1165

Harker, Mina
Mina - Marie Kiraly   *h*   2503

Harper, Jim
Oktober - Stephen Gallagher   *h*   1698

Harris
The Rats - James Herbert   *h*   2132

Hawthorne, Sara
Moonfall - Tamara Thorne   *h*   4360

Heredes
A Passage of Stars - Alis A. Rasmussen   *s*   3574

Hickory, Magister
Wizard's Hall - Jane Yolen   *f*   4817

Holman, Guy
Charmed Life - Bernard Taylor   *h*   4307

Ironhart, Jim
Cold Fire - Dean R. Koontz   *h*   2546

Jackson, Andrew
Spirit Crossings - Claudia Peck   *f*   3405

John, Mortel
Commencement - Roby James   *s*   2294

Johnson, Harriette
Inagehi - Jack Cady   *h*   668

Johnson, Hildy
Steel Beach - John Varley   *s*   4436

Kallisti, Magdalen
Specters - J.M. Dillard   *h*   1255

Karpou, Betty Lou
My Teacher Fried My Brains - Bruce Coville   *s*   993

Kelys
In the Mothers' Land - Elisabeth Vonarburg   *s*   4455

Kendal, Evan
Stunts - Charles L. Grant   *h*   1857

Lasalle, Stevie
The Death Crystal - J. Edward Ames   *h*   75

Leigh, Makoto Shirata
Makoto - Kelley Wilde   *h*   4619

Leones, Giraut
A Million Open Doors - John Barnes   *s*   295

Lewes, Charlotte
John Dollar - Marianne Wiggins   *h*   4617

Linnie
The Wall at the Edge of the World - Jim
   Aikin   *s*   36

Logan, Diana
Eye Killers - A.A. Carr   *h*   739

Logan, Jennifer
Earthgrip - Harry Turtledove   *s*   4385

Lu
Sing the Light - Louise Marley   *s*   2884

Macaffrey, Lester Hill
Heathern - Jack Womack   *s*   4747

Manning, Kitty
Meridian 144 - Meg Files   *s*   1555

Martin, Paul
Shaman Woods - Morgan Fields   *h*   1554

McCarthy, Mary Margaret
Substitute Teacher - Jordan Storm   *h*   4240

McCormick, Lianne
When the Bough Breaks - Mercedes Lackey   *f*   2625

McCready
Damnbanna - Nancy Springer   *f*   4131

McPherson, Jim
The Gold Coast - Kim Stanley Robinson   *s*   3707

Milburn, Annie
Charmed Life - Bernard Taylor   *h*   4307

Mint, Maytera
Calde of the Long Sun - Gene Wolfe   *s*   4728

Morgasdotte, Roba
Bones of the Past - Holly Lisle   *f*   2765

Nailer, Steve
Grimm Memorials - R. Patrick Gates   *h*   1732

Neary, Mark
Billy - Whitley Strieber   *h*   4258

Nielson
When Darkness Falls - Sidney Williams   *h*   4640

Overstreet, Lee
After Life - Andrew Neiderman   *h*   3252

Oykib
Earthfall - Orson Scott Card   *s*   719

Paarman, Martin
Succumb - Ron Dee   *h*   1187

Palmer, Jane
Panda Ray - Michael Kandel   *s*   2398

Podlowski, Eric
Brothers of the Dragon - Robin Wayne
   Bailey   *f*   242

Powers, Richard
Galatea 2.2 - Richard M. Powers   *s*   3493

Powl
Lens of the World - R.A. MacAvoy   *f* 2847

Rakam, Radosse
Four Ways to Forgiveness - Ursula K. Le
   Guin   *s* 2690

Rasa
The Call of Earth - Orson Scott Card   *s* 716
The Memory of Earth - Orson Scott Card   *s* 725

Reeves, Gail
The Immaculate - Mark Morris   *h* 3204

Reichmann, Wolfgang "Wolfie"
Being of Two Minds - Pamela F. Service   *f* 3928

Rhymer, Catherine
Reluctant Voyagers - Elisabeth Vonarburg   *s* 4456

Richards, Neil
Sister, Sister - Andrew Neiderman   *h* 3257

Robinson, Sarah
Beyond the Shroud - Rick Hautala   *h* 2079

Ross, Angie
Impulse - Rick Hautala   *h* 2084

Scott, Michael
The Black School - J.N. Williamson   *h* 4659

Sensar
Minds Apart - Margaret Davis   *s* 1134

Sharpless, Carril
The Ragged World: A Novel of the Hefn on Earth -
   Judith Moffett   *s* 3140

Shelagh
Sweetheart, Sweetheart - Bernard Taylor   *h* 4310

Simms, Nanci
Deep Trek - James Axler   *s* 234

Strayhorn, Philip
Shock Lines - Warren Newton Beath   *h* 351

Succor-of-Yellowways-Sands
Nanoware Time/The Persistence of Vision - Ian
   Watson   *s* 4494

Sutton, Michael
Secrets of the Morning - V.C. Andrews   *h* 122

Tekkitho, Chin
Homegoing - Frederik Pohl   *s* 3463

Thakur
Ratha and Thistle-Chaser - Clare Bell   *f* 356

Tobias, Charlotte
Making Love - Melanie Tem   *h* 4327

Travis, Susanne
The One Safe Place - Ramsey Campbell   *h* 701

Von Karlsfeld, Hilda
Mordenheim - Chet Williamson   *h* 4655

Wallace, Brandy
Dreambuilder - Tom Deitz   *f* 1190

Warwick, David
Sweetheart, Sweetheart - Bernard Taylor   *h* 4310

Webster, Tom
Requiem - Graham Joyce   *h* 2386

Weir, Jacob
The Black School - J.N. Williamson   *h* 4659

Wells, Nancy
Dark Twilight - Joseph Citro   *h* 836

Wheeler, Kelly
Captain Quad - Sean Costello   *h* 974

Withrow, Dennis "Dennis Dithrovvu"
Mathemagics - Margaret Ball   *f* 266

Wu, Kildee
Black Steel - Steve Perry   *s* 3418

TECHNICIAN

Craig, James Christopher
Psychamok - Brian Lumley   *h* 2833

Karmade, Theodore "Ted"
Quasar - Jamil Nasir   *s* 3242

Lee, Wei
Red Dust - Paul J. McAuley   *s* 2956

Mirabara, Keishi
The Fortunate Fall - Raphael Carter   *s* 750

Ornis, Frederik Ry
Legacy - Greg Bear   *s* 344

Sharkey, Alex
Fairyland - Paul J. McAuley   *s* 2953

Sullivan, Pete
Expiration Date - Tim Powers   *f* 3494

Tamura, Eiko
Harvest of Stars - Poul Anderson   *s* 105

Trapp, Phillip
Blood Work - Fay Zachary   *h* 4823

TEENAGER

12
Random Acts of Senseless Violence - Jack
   Womack   *f* 4748

Aaron, Lincoln
After Silence - Jonathan Carroll   *h* 742

Adams, Nicola Chelsea "Niki"
From a Whisper to a Scream - Samuel M.
   Key   *h* 2462

Aguilar, Carlos
Days of the Dead - Ashley McConnell   *h* 3004

Aisling, Miranda
Voyage of the Basset - James C. Christensen   *f* 827

Alexander
The Prince and the Pilgrim - Mary Stewart   *f* 4205

Alice
The Prince and the Pilgrim - Mary Stewart   *f* 4205

Allaird, Margaret "Marnie"
Arrow From Earth - F.M. Busby   *s* 639

Alys
Dragon's Bait - Vivian Vande Velde   *f* 4427

Amy
The Kingdom of Kevin Malone - Suzy McKee
   Charnas   *f* 785

Anatole
Silicon Embrace - John Shirley   *s* 3996

Anderson, Aaron
Oasis - Brian Hodge   *h* 2158

Anderson, Chris
Oasis - Brian Hodge   *h* 2158

Anderson, Kelly
Darkness - John Saul   *h* 3874

Andrea
The Third Beast - Peter Loughran   *h* 2804

Angel Juan
Missing Angel Juan - Francesca Lia Block   *f* 448

Antero, Amalric
The Far Kingdoms - Allan Cole   *f* 889

Anthony
The First Horror - R.L. Stine   *h* 4219

Aradia
A Heroine of the World - Tanith Lee   *f* 2714

Arry
The Dubious Hills - Pamela Dean   *f* 1165

Aryl
Under Alien Stars - Pamela F. Service   *s* 3929

Atbin
The Promise - Monica Hughes   *s* 2237

Baldwin, Sean
Yon Ill Wind - Piers Anthony   *f* 162

Balter, Harry
Parable of the Sower - Octavia E. Butler   *s* 649

Barrow, Simon
The First Duelist - Rutledge Etheridge   *s* 1488

Basker, Tem
The Starlight Crystal - Christopher Pike   *s* 3452

Bat, Cherokee
Cherokee Bat and the Goat Guys - Francesca Lia
   Block   *f* 445

Battacharia, Rustum "Bat"
The Ganymede Club - Charles Sheffield   *s* 3953

Becky
See You Later - Christopher Pike   *f* 3451

Bellard, Fern
Something Stirs - Charles L. Grant   *h* 1856

Belle, Amy
Witch - Christopher Pike   *f* 3453

Bidding, Philippa
Rebel From Alphorion - Robyn Tallis   *s* 4291

Bishop, Bryan
Away Is a Strange Place to Be - H.M.
   Hoover   *s* 2202

Black, Charlie
When Darkness Falls - Sidney Williams   *h* 4640

Blade
Madman Run - David Robbins   *s* 3677

Blair, Tony
Boys of Life - Paul Russell   *h* 3790

Blake, Nick
Dragon Burning - Craig Shaw Gardner   *f* 1709
Dragon Sleeping - Craig Shaw Gardner   *f* 1710
Dragon Waking - Craig Shaw Gardner   *f* 1711

Bouriere, Tira
Crown of Empire - Chelsea Quinn Yarbro   *s* 4794

Bouriere, Wiley
Crown of Empire - Chelsea Quinn Yarbro   *s* 4794

Brandon "Brand" X
Killjoy - Elizabeth Forrest   *h* 1585

Brazil, Bubbles
Negrophobia: An Urban Parable - Darius
   James   *f* 2276

Bremmers, Lana
The Devil's End - D.A. Fowler   *h* 1624

Brett/Natalie
Holy Fire - Bruce Sterling   *s* 4195

Brewster, Mackenzie
The Witch of Maple Park - Stephanie S.
   Tolan   *f* 4370

Brightblade, Douglas
Pyromancer - Don Callander   *f* 689

Brill, Lucy
Prodigal - Melanie Tem   *h* 4328

Brill, Rae
Prodigal - Melanie Tem   *h* 4328

Brostek
Shadow-Maze - Mark Smith   *f* 4094

Brown, Max
Thrill - Patricia Wallace   *h* 4481

Bryge, Larry
Spirit Crossings - Claudia Peck   *f* 3405

Buckland, Ulysses
The Whims of Creation - Simon Hawke   s   2100

Buddy
Land O'Goshen - Charles McNair   s   3071

Buffy
Buffy the Vampire Slayer - Richie Tankersley Cusick   h   1056

Burroughs, Mahree
Starbridge - A.C. Crispin   s   1027

Byrns, Scott
Something Stirs - Charles L. Grant   h   1856

Caceras, Mimla
Traitors from Within - R.A. Montgomery   s   3157

Callahan, Jessica
Sweet Revenge - Jean Simon   h   4043

Campbell, Brianne
Journeyman Wizard - Mary Frances Zambreno   f   4830

Carpenter, Alison
Guardian - John Saul   h   3875

Carpenter, Corey
Dark Time - Maxine O'Callaghan   h   3336

Carruthers, Ronald "Ronnie"
Hunting Party - Elizabeth Moon   s   3159

Carson, Erin
Darkside - Dennis Etchison   h   1485

Cart
The Time of the Ghost - Diana Wynne Jones   f   2352

Carter, David
The Eyes of the Beast - Steve Harris   h   2050

Casad, Sasha
Bodyguard - William C. Dietz   s   1244

Casey, Jerry
Cold Allies - Patricia Anthony   s   128

Caspar
The Ogre Downstairs - Diana Wynne Jones   f   2350

Cassia
The Cult of Loving Kindness - Paul Park   s   3382

Cedric
Strings - Dave Duncan   s   1361

Chakallakak, Chakallakak "Chaka" ngha
The Long Hunt - Debra Doyle   s   1295

Challer, Bo
A Whisper of Wings - Steven Ray Fulgham   h   1684

Chang, Deanna
Scorpion Shards - Neal Shusterman   s   4000

Chase-Frisson L'Zalle, Trevarre
Shivering World - Kathy Tyers   s   4406

Christian, Paige
The Starlight Crystal - Christopher Pike   s   3452

Clemmy
The Fool's War - Lee Kisling   f   2511

Cofield, Aaron
Ray Bradbury Presents: Dinosaur Planet - Stephen Leigh   s   2724
Ray Bradbury Presents: Dinosaur World - Stephen Leigh   s   2725

Cole, Dillon
Scorpion Shards - Neal Shusterman   s   4000

Colene
Chaos Mode - Piers Anthony   f   135
Fractal Mode - Piers Anthony   f   140
Virtual Mode - Piers Anthony   f   160

Collins, Chad
Quozl - Alan Dean Foster   s   1615

Corrigan, Casey
The Witch of Maple Park - Stephanie S. Tolan   f   4370

Costello, Joey
Something Stirs - Charles L. Grant   h   1856

Cottington, Angelica
Lady Cottington's Pressed Fairy Book - Terry Jones   f   2376

Crandall, Raymond E. Jr.
The Magic Touch - Jody Lynn Nye   f   3323

Culley, Mance
The Living Dark - Stephen Gresham   h   1945

Curran, Baal
Killobyte - Piers Anthony   f   147

Cutler, Philip
Dawn - V.C. Andrews   h   120

Dafoe, Mary Lou "Merrilu"
Dragon Sleeping - Craig Shaw Gardner   f   1710

Daneam, Penelope
Dominion - Bentley Little   h   2774

Danilov, Justin
These Fallen Angels - Wendy Haley   h   1997

Danya
Vampire Diary: The Embrace - Robert Weinberg   h   4549

David
Medallion of the Black Hound - Shirley Rousseau Murphy   f   3231

Davidson, Troy
Liquid Diet - William Tedford   h   4324

Deal, Brian
The Square Deal - David Drake   s   1327

Deborah
Wilding - Melanie Tem   h   4330

Debra
The Sister - Elleston Trevor   h   4375

Delacroix, Ivy
Tunnelvision - R. Patrick Gates   h   1733

Delane, Ariel
Intensity - Dean R. Koontz   h   2552

Delgato, Amy
Dark Time - Maxine O'Callaghan   h   3336

Demarest, Patti
Demon's Fright - Penelope Banka Kreps   h   2571

Denison, Will
Dinotopia - James Gurney   f   1979

Dentata, Regina
Shock Lines - Warren Newton Beath   h   351

Desmond, Emily
King of Morning, Queen of Day - Ian McDonald   f   3019

Desmond, Timothy Alfred
Gnome Man's Land - Esther Friesner   f   1669

Doheny, Shannon
Elvira: Transylvania 90210 - Elvira   h   1445

Donatello, Kevin
The Uprising - Abigail McDaniels   h   3013

Doot
Wolf Flow - K.W. Jeter   h   2325

Douay, Deldragon Drakedon "Drake"
Lords of the Sword - Hugh Cook   f   933

D'Rosselin, Jens Metadi Jessan
The Long Hunt - Debra Doyle   s   1295

Duberville, Myron
Outer Space and All That Junk - Mel Gilden   s   1789

Dug
Demons Don't Dream - Piers Anthony   f   138

DuMar, Theresa "T.J." Jr.
T.J.'s Ghost - Shirley Climo   h   876

Dunbar, Lane
The Stake - Richard Laymon   h   2683

Eagen, Wesley
Hell-O-Ween - David Robbins   h   3675

Ella
I Feel Like the Morning Star - Gregory Maguire   s   2868

Elliott, Kate
Vision Quest - Pamela F. Service   f   3930

Ember, Annie
Elephantasm - Tanith Lee   h   2711

Emerson, Dirk
Demon's Fright - Penelope Banka Kreps   h   2571

Erik
The Lone Sentinel - Jo Dereske   s   1206

Esterbrook, Diana
The Higher Space - Jamil Nasir   s   3241

Etchison, Theo
Riverrun - S.P. Somtow   f   4117

Eva
Eva - Peter Dickinson   s   1231

Fels, Jimmy
Penance - Rick R. Reed   h   3591

Fleming, Cory
Hell-O-Ween - David Robbins   h   3675

Florence, Julia
Witch - Christopher Pike   f   3453

Fong, Jimmy
Vision Quest - Pamela F. Service   f   3930

Francie
In the Heart of the Valley of Love - Cynthia Kadohata   s   2387

Francy, Lizzie
Beggars Ride - Nancy Kress   s   2575

Frankel, Melissa
Roadkill - Richard Sanford   h   3854

Frankie
Collidescope - Grace Chetwin   s   820

Frasier, Cally
The First Horror - R.L. Stine   h   4219

Frasier, Cody
The First Horror - R.L. Stine   h   4219

Freeman, Justine
Perfect Little Angels - Andrew Neiderman   h   3256

French, Melissa
Liquid Diet - William Tedford   h   4324

Fuller, Stan
The Summoned - Steven Ray Fulgham   h   1683

Gale, C.J.
Little Boy Lost - T.M. Wright   h   4776

Garcia-Chase, Isabel
The Wall Around Eden - Joan Slonczewski   s   4063

Garfield, Joanne
Parable of the Sower - Octavia E. Butler   s   649

Gart, Maya
The Faces of Ceti - Mary Caraker   s   712

Gelly
Flight to Hollow Mountain - Mark Sebanc   f   3921

Geronimo
Madman Run - David Robbins   s   3677

Gilmour, Wendy
Nighteyes - Garfield Reeves-Stevens   s   3599

TELEPATH

Macintosh, Elizabeth
Rediscovery: A Novel of Darkover - Marion Zimmer Bradley s 527

Marbon, Doyce
Exiles' Return - Gayle Greeno s 1937
Finders-Seekers - Gayle Greeno s 1938
Mind-Speakers' Call - Gayle Greeno s 1939

McBan, Rod
Norstrilia - Cordwainer Smith s 4072

McCray, Jimmy
The Demons at Rainbow Bridge - Jack L. Chalker s 771
The Ninety Trillion Fausts - Jack L. Chalker s 776
The Run to Chaos Keep - Jack L. Chalker s 778

McCrea, Rinn
Rinn's Star - Paula King s 2479

Murrinder, Ainne
The Wall at the Edge of the World - Jim Aikin s 36

Naufts, Tom
The Gifted - Jack Caravela h 714

Nigheyes
Royal Assassin - Robin Hobb f 2152

Noelle
Starborne - Robert Silverberg s 4021

Owen, Rhyssa
Pegasus in Flight - Anne McCaffrey s 2975

Oykib
Earthfall - Orson Scott Card s 719

Pelleas
In the Shadow of the Oak King - Courtway Jones f 2341

Pellia
The Unicorn Solution - John Lee f 2703

Pendrake, Matthew
Mind Slayer - Kevin D. Randle s 3563

Rand, Aino
Marks of Our Brothers - Jane M. Lindskold s 2763

Ree, Danlo
The Wall at the Edge of the World - Jim Aikin s 36

Ripley, Ellen
Aliens: The Female War - Steve Perry s 3417

Rudolph "Rudy"
Being of Two Minds - Pamela F. Service f 3928

Sarrasri, Diane
The Realms of the Gods - Tamora Pierce f 3442
Wild Magic - Tamora Pierce f 3443
Wolf-Speaker - Tamora Pierce f 3444

Saturna
Saturn's Child - Nichelle Nichols s 3264

Seqiro
Chaos Mode - Piers Anthony f 135
Virtual Mode - Piers Anthony f 160

Smoke, Smokey
Smoke and Mirrors - Jane M. Lindskold s 2764

Sogan, Varn Tarl
Jungle Assault - P.M. Griffin s 1950

Starbuck, July
Double Trouble Squared - Kathryn Lasky f 2658
Shadows in the Water - Kathryn Lasky s 2659

Starbuck, Liberty
Double Trouble Squared - Kathryn Lasky f 2658
Shadows in the Water - Kathryn Lasky s 2659

Stewart, Guil
Rider at the Gate - C.J. Cherryh s 811

Stone, Richard
Psychamok - Brian Lumley h 2833

Streak
Shadows in the Water - Kathryn Lasky s 2659

Summer
Master of Many Treasures - Mary Brown f 593

Taylor, Jessica
Bureau 13 - Nick Pollotta f 3476
Full Moonster - Nick Pollotta f 3478

Tharion
Blindfold - Kevin J. Anderson s 84

Tharna
The Key of the Keplian - Andre Norton f 3310

Thorpe, Proserpine
The Reign of the Brown Magician - Lawrence Watt-Evans f 4503

Troi, Lwaxana
Q-in-Law - Peter David s 1118

Troit, Deanna "Dee"
Star Wreck IV: Live Long and Profit - Leah Rewolinski s 3645

Valdez, Maria
Under Fire - Kenneth Von Gunden s 4454

Wae, Kiondili
Lightwing - Tara K. Harper s 2038

Waterfall, Kylene
Death's Gray Land - Mike Shupp s 3998
The Last Reckoning - Mike Shupp s 3999

Weisser, Erich
Child of the Light - Janet Gluckman f 1803

Welch, Lewis
Dreambuilder - Tom Deitz f 1190

Welch, Lewis Owen
Wordwright - Tom Deitz f 1196

Weser, Erich "Erich Alois"
Child of the Journey - Janet Berliner f 381

Whitehorse, Janara
Enemy Unseen - V.E. Mitchell s 3123

Winters, Talia
Voices - John Vornholt s 4461

Wycherley, Jenret
Exiles' Return - Gayle Greeno s 1937
Mind-Speakers' Call - Gayle Greeno s 1939

TELEVISION

Allen, Sandy
Ancient Images - Ramsey Campbell h 693

Claypoole, Chester "Chet" W.
Live From Golgotha: A Novel - Gore Vidal s 4438

Franker, Edward "Eddie"
Pictures at 11 - Norman Spinrad s 4127

TELEVISION PERSONALITY

Collier, Samantha
Shock Radio - Leigh Clark h 846

Collins, Rikka
Satellite Night News - Jack Hopkins s 2208

Feirn
Hero - Dave Duncan s 1352

Figueroa, Calafia "Kali"
Kalifornia - Marc Laidlaw s 2634

Figueroa, Poppy
Kalifornia - Marc Laidlaw s 2634

Figueroa, Sandy
Kalifornia - Marc Laidlaw s 2634

Inman, Toby
Pictures at 11 - Norman Spinrad s 4127

Jeremy, Clark
Blood Siege - G. Harry Stine s 4211

Lyon, John
Bring Me Children - David Martin h 2889

Martens, Billy
The Wizard of Camelot - Simon Hawke f 2101

Mays, Randolph
The Diamond Moon - Paul Preuss s 3523

Mendoza, Carl
Pictures at 11 - Norman Spinrad s 4127

Snyder, Harry
Satellite Night News - Jack Hopkins s 2208

Wanda-Jean
The Feelies - Mick Farren s 1510

Waterhouse, Mary Ann "Synthi Venture"
Mother of Storms - John Barnes s 296

TERRORIST

Aarons, Keith "Pan"
Second Chance - Chet Williamson h 4658

al-Qurtubi
Name of the Beast - Daniel Easterman h 1379

Dread, Doctor
Revenge of the Fluffy Bunnies - Craig Shaw Gardner f 1714

Jeremiah
The Quiet Pools - Michael P. Kube-McDowell s 2583

Terrell, Mary "Merry Terror"
Mine - Robert R. McCammon h 2989

THIEF

Aaron
The Fire's Stone - Tanya Huff f 2228

Aladdin
A Bad Day for Ali Baba - Craig Shaw Gardner f 1706

Alderberry, Jane
The Iron Dragon's Daughter - Michael Swanwick f 4282

Asrubal
Night Lamp - Jack Vance s 4422

Aurelico, Karvonen
The Raven Ring - Patricia C. Wrede f 4764

Bagsby
Dragonspawn - Mark Acres f 21

Blaine, Cassandra "Cass"
Clipjoint - Wilhelmina Baird s 248
Crashcourse - Wilhelmina Baird s 249

Brayker, Silas
Tales From the Crypt: Demon Knight - Randall Boyll h 507

Brekke, Robbie
Brain Rose - Nancy Kress s 2576

Breks, Falca
The Mace of Souls - Bruce Fergusson f 1549

Brenn
A Sorcerer's Apprentice - Michael Williams f 4635

Castanaveras, Trent
The Long Run - Daniel Keys Moran s 3178

Cat
Mistworld - Simon R. Green s 1902

Crane, Mary
Psycho - Robert Bloch h 440

Cumberland, Jack
Mongster - Randall Boyll   *h*   506

Donya
Shadow - Anne Logston   *f*   2789
Shadow Dance - Anne Logston   *f*   2790

Etcher
Arc d'X - Steve Erickson   *f*   1475

Fafhrd
Ill Met in Lankhmar - Fritz Leiber   *f*   2718
Lean Times in Lankhmar - Fritz Leiber   *f*   2719

Father Christmas
The Widowmaker - Mike Resnick   *s*   3640

Faust, Johann
If at Faust You Don't Succeed - Roger
  Zelazny   *f*   4841

Felice
User Unfriendly - Vivian Vande Velde   *f*   4429

Garlthik
The Longing Ring - Christopher Kubasik   *f*   2580

Grey Mouser
Ill Met in Lankhmar - Fritz Leiber   *f*   2718
Lean Times in Lankhmar - Fritz Leiber   *f*   2719

Hammen
Arena - William R. Forstchen   *f*   1587

Hinckel, Hieronymus
Chorus Skating - Alan Dean Foster   *f*   1603

J'role
The Longing Ring - Christopher Kubasik   *f*   2580

Kemp, Jerod
Shadow of the Crown - Craig Mills   *f*   3119

Kiera
Orca - Steven Brust   *f*   609

Kwip
Castle Spellbound - John DeChancie   *s*   1174

Lucas, Prince
Rats and Gargoyles - Mary Gentle   *f*   1762

Lucy
But What of Earth? - Piers Anthony   *s*   133

Macero
Songs of the Dancing Gods - Jack L. Chalker   *f*   780

Maijstral, Drake
Rock of Ages - Walter Jon Williams   *s*   4651

Malkin
The Wizardry Consulted - Rick Cook   *f*   936

Medakan, Taziar
By Chaos Cursed - Mickey Zucker Reichert   *f*   3605
Shadow's Realm - Mickey Zucker Reichert   *f*   3610

Mouse
Soothsayer - Mike Resnick   *s*   3638

Mwili-Ferret
The 97th Step - Steve Perry   *s*   3414

Nightfall
The Legend of Nightfall - Mickey Zucker
  Reichert   *f*   3608

Orien
On Fortune's Wheel - Cynthia Voigt   *f*   4445

Petie
The Red King - Victor Kelleher   *f*   2426

Pinch "Janol"
King Pinch - David Cook   *f*   924

Pope, Justin
Mixed Doubles - Daniel Da Cruz   *s*   1057

Sataru, Hidaka
The Yngling in Yamato - John Dalmas   *s*   1075

Shadow
Dagger's Edge - Anne Logston   *f*   2786
Shadow - Anne Logston   *f*   2789

Shadow Dance - Anne Logston   *f*   2790
Shadow Hunt - Anne Logston   *f*   2791

Shadowspawn
The Shadow of Sorcery - Andrew J. Offutt   *f*   3347

Sharrow
Against a Dark Background - Iain M. Banks   *s*   272

Slash
Rememory - John Betancourt   *s*   391

Tabaea
The Spell of the Black Dagger - Lawrence Watt-
  Evans   *f*   4504

Tainharsdartter, Kevral
Beyond Ragnarok - Mickey Zucker Reichert   *f*   3604

Talen
The Ruby Knight - David Eddings   *f*   1392

Trace, Charlie
Demogorgon - Brian Lumley   *h*   2826

TIME TRAVELLER

Aburto, Manuel "Manny"
Tyrannosaurus Rex - J.F. Rivkin   *s*   3674

Antiope
Amazon: A Novel - Barbara G. Walker   *f*   4474

Bartlett, Tony "Antonius Caelerus"
Far Edge of Darkness - Linda Evans   *s*   1492

Basehart, Diana
Time Station London - David Evans   *s*   1491

Beauty
Beauty - Sheri S. Tepper   *f*   4333

Beckett, Sam
Knights of the Morningstar - Melanie Rawn   *s*   3579

Bentley, Abigail Porterhouse
Friends in Time - Grace Chetwin   *f*   821

Bento, Jake
The Virgin and the Dinosaur - R. Garcia y
  Robertson   *s*   1705

Birch, Wellington
Lurid Dreams - Charles L. Harness   *s*   2035

Blondell, Mark "Tony" Anthony
Tyrannosaurus Rex - J.F. Rivkin   *s*   3674

Bonney, Isabel "Iz"
Elvissey - Jack Womack   *s*   4746

Bonney, John
Elvissey - Jack Womack   *s*   4746

Borgel
Borgel - Daniel Manus Pinkwater   *f*   3456

Callahan, Mike
Callahan's Legacy - Spider Robinson   *s*   3714

Carelias, Caroline "Sarah"
Union Fires - John Barnes   *f*   299

Carnes, Rebecca
Arc Riders - David Drake   *s*   1314

Carrigan
The Unknown Soldier - Mickey Zucker
  Reichert   *s*   3611

Carson, Kenneth "Kit"
Time Scout - Robert Asprin   *s*   221

Chang, Steve
Warrior - William Wu   *s*   4784

Chiron Cat's Eye in Draco
Summer of Love - Lisa Mason   *s*   2913

Coconino
Children of the Earth - Catherine Wells   *s*   4578
The Earth Saver - Catherine Wells   *s*   4580

Cofield, Aaron
Ray Bradbury Presents: Dinosaur Planet - Stephen
  Leigh   *s*   2724
Ray Bradbury Presents: Dinosaur World - Stephen
  Leigh   *s*   2725

Cole, James
12 Monkeys - Elizabeth Hand   *s*   2025

Collier, Ben
A Bridge of Years - Robert Charles Wilson   *s*   4700

Collins, Karen Cecile "Casey"
Islands of Tomorrow - F.M. Busby   *s*   640

d'Anton, Charlotte Marie
The Virgin and the Dinosaur - R. Garcia y
  Robertson   *s*   1705

Davis, Edward
Thebes of the Hundred Gates - Robert
  Silverberg   *s*   4022

Devane, Elizabeth
The Trinity Paradox - Kevin J. Anderson   *s*   97

Diego
Time: The Semi-Final Frontier - Lionel
  Fenn   *s*   1545

DiFalco, Tiraena
Legacy - Steve White   *s*   4609

Diko
Pastwatch: The Redemption of Christopher Columbus -
  Orson Scott Card   *s*   726

Dobbs, Karl
The Lincoln Hunters - Wilson Tucker   *s*   4378

Donnelly, John
Door Number Three - Patrick O'Leary   *s*   3355

Dubchek, Jackson
Stranded! - Warren Norwood   *s*   3317

Durvash
Man-Kzin Wars V - Larry Niven   *s*   3284

Eakins, Daniel Jamieson
The Man Who Folded Himself - David
  Gerrold   *s*   1772

Eakins, Diane Jane
The Man Who Folded Himself - David
  Gerrold   *s*   1772

Engle, Kivrin
Doomsday Book - Connie Willis   *s*   4672

Fall-Levchenko, Anna Leah
Branch Point - Mona Clee   *s*   866

Fawcett, Christine
Tyrannosaurus Rex - J.F. Rivkin   *s*   3674

Fergus
The Lost Prince - Bridget Wood   *f*   4751

Flynn, Charlie
Far Edge of Darkness - Linda Evans   *s*   1492

Foster, Bass
Of Beginnings and Endings - Robert Adams   *s*   26

Gibbs, Rinpoche
Muddle Earth - John Brunner   *s*   601

Gibson, Emma
Friends in Time - Grace Chetwin   *f*   821

Gina
All's Faire - Pamela F. Service   *f*   3927

Grady, Joanna
Wolfking - Bridget Wood   *f*   4752

Grainger, Tim
Arc Riders - David Drake   *s*   1314
The Fourth Rome - David Drake   *s*   1317

Harper, Timothy
Death's Gray Land - Mike Shupp   *s*   3998
The Last Reckoning - Mike Shupp   *s*   3999

TINKER

TOUR GUIDE

TOURIST

Valdemar "Val"
Wayfinder's Story: The Seventh Book of Lost Swords - Fred Saberhagen   *f*   3820

Westriding, Margorie "Jory"
Sideshow - Sheri S. Tepper   *s*   4340

Whit, Beatrice
The Beacon - Valerie J. Freireich   *s*   1646

Ying, Soong Mei
The Discovery of Dragons - Graeme Base   *f*   320

Zoltan
Wayfinder's Story: The Seventh Book of Lost Swords - Fred Saberhagen   *f*   3820

TROUBLESHOOTER

Dearborn, Sondra
Proteus in the Underworld - Charles Sheffield   *s*   3960

Dinsman, Angela
Reefsong - Carol Severance   *s*   3933

Homer-R-ICK-3
Extreme Paranoia: Nobody Knows the Trouble I've Shot - Ken Rolston   *s*   3733

McCray, Tom
Protektor - Charles Platt   *s*   3459

Sheehan, Matt
Manhattan Transfer - John E. Stith   *s*   4231

Sparrow
Bone Dance - Emma Bull   *s*   629
Bone Dance - Will Shetterly   *s*   3982

TRUCK DRIVER

Cohen, Sophie
The Black Mariah - Jay R. Bonansinga   *h*   468

Crispian, Grace
Rune - Christopher Fowler   *h*   1621

Hardin, Charlie
Roadkill - Richard Sanford   *h*   3854

Hynde, Lucas
The Black Mariah - Jay R. Bonansinga   *h*   468

Ketter, Bill
Lot Lizards - Ray Garton   *h*   1726

Mel
Celia - Ruby Jean Jensen   *h*   2310

Winters, Michael
Sati - Christopher Pike   *f*   3449

TWIN

Akimura, Julian
Mutant Star - Karen Haber   *s*   1985

Alastair
The Heirs of Hammerfell - Marion Zimmer Bradley   *s*   524

Conn
The Heirs of Hammerfell - Marion Zimmer Bradley   *s*   524

Daniel
Dark Father - Tom Piccirilli   *h*   3435

de Conde, Sarah Webster
Deep Freeze - Zach Hughes   *s*   2239

Dennessy, Beth
The Darkness Within - Shawn MacDonald   *h*   2850

Dennessy, Carol
The Darkness Within - Shawn MacDonald   *h*   2850

Dion
Shadow Leader - Tara K. Harper   *f*   2039

Grason, Missy
Cross a Dark Bridge - Deborah Churchman   *h*   829

Harrah, Talia Crawford
The Lilith Factor - Jean Paiva   *h*   3376

Harvey, Emily
Memorymakers - Brian Herbert   *s*   2127

Harvey, Thomas
Memorymakers - Brian Herbert   *s*   2127

Keogh, Nathan
Bloodwars - Brian Lumley   *h*   2822

Kiklu, Nathan
Blood Brothers - Brian Lumley   *h*   2821
The Last Aerie - Brian Lumley   *h*   2830

Kiklu, Nestor
Blood Brothers - Brian Lumley   *h*   2821
Bloodwars - Brian Lumley   *h*   2822
The Last Aerie - Brian Lumley   *h*   2830

Korsyzczy, Nela Zy-Czorsky
Sideshow - Sheri S. Tepper   *s*   4340

Lamai, Leie
Glory Season - David Brin   *s*   564

Marshall, Olivia
Seeds of Evil - Margaret Bingley   *h*   398

Marshall, Orlando
Seeds of Evil - Margaret Bingley   *h*   398

Rhom
Shadow Leader - Tara K. Harper   *f*   2039

Samuel
Dark Father - Tom Piccirilli   *h*   3435

Starbuck, July
Double Trouble Squared - Kathryn Lasky   *f*   2658
Shadows in the Water - Kathryn Lasky   *s*   2659

Starbuck, Liberty
Double Trouble Squared - Kathryn Lasky   *f*   2658
Shadows in the Water - Kathryn Lasky   *s*   2659

Vaughan, Elsie Crawford
The Lilith Factor - Jean Paiva   *h*   3376

Wade, Arlo
Bad Blood - D.A. Fowler   *h*   1622

Wade, Austin
Bad Blood - D.A. Fowler   *h*   1622

Wade, Bree
Double Date - R.L. Stine   *h*   4218

Wade, Samantha
Double Date - R.L. Stine   *h*   4218

UNDERTAKER

Archway, Andy
The Unnatural - David Prill   *h*   3539

Diest, Vernon
The Moons of Summer - S.K. Epperson   *h*   1471

Grimm, Eleanor
Grimm Memorials - R. Patrick Gates   *h*   1732

Mitsumishi, Ecclesiastes
The Abraxis Marvel Circus - Stephen Leigh   *f*   2721

O'Shea, Patrick
Moon of the Werewolf - Ronald Kelly   *h*   2434

Rodgers, Franklin
Moon Walker - Rick Hautala   *h*   2085

Simpson, Beth Ann
Buried Screams - C. Dean Andersson   *h*   113

Sunnyside, P.T.
The Unnatural - David Prill   *h*   3539

UNEMPLOYED

Allen, Harrison
Dark Twilight - Joseph Citro   *h*   836

Ballard, Mitch
The Voice in the Basement - T. Chris Martindale   *h*   2906

Douglas, Doug
Slippin' into Darkness - Norman Partridge   *h*   3390

Nimitz, Brent
Dark Journey - A.R. Morlan   *h*   3192

VACATIONER

Baldwin, Sean
Yon Ill Wind - Piers Anthony   *f*   162

Deanna
A Well-Timed Enchantment - Vivian Vande Velde   *f*   4430

Heffer, John Wilson
The Feelies - Mick Farren   *s*   1510

VAGRANT

Flanders, Ted "Dead Ted"
Tower of Evil - James Kisner   *h*   2513

Frost, Joni
Stone Angels - Mike Jefferies   *h*   2305

Laurie
Dark Father - Tom Piccirilli   *h*   3435

Parsons, Ronna
Twisted - Sue Hollister Barr   *h*   304

Shustak, Evan "American Dream"
The Holy Terror - Wayne Allen Sallee   *h*   3829

VAMPIRE

Adler, Stephen
Less than Human - Gary L. Raisor   *h*   3558

Agenor, Roland
The Golden - Lucius Shepard   *h*   3971

Aguilana, Haros
King of the Grey - Richard A. Knaak   *f*   2523

Agyar, Janos "Jack"
Agyar - Steven Brust   *f*   604

Akasha
The Queen of the Damned - Anne Rice   *h*   3653

Aleron
Sex and the Single Vampire - Nancy Kilpatrick   *h*   2472

Allogiamento, Maria Theresa
The Vampire Journals - Traci Briery   *h*   557

Alucard, Sevil
Elvira: Transylvania 90210 - Elvira   *h*   1445

Angel
Dark Prince - Keith Herber   *h*   2125

Anyelet
Afterage - Yvonne Navarro   *h*   3243

Aragon, Julian
Thirst - Michael Cecilione   *h*   769

Astare, T.
Morningstar - Peter Atkins   *h*   223

Austra, Catherine
Daughter of the Night - Elaine Bergstrom   *h*   379

Austra, Laurence
Blood Alone - Elaine Bergstrom   *h*   378

Bach, Arthur
Night Prophets - Paul F. Olson   *h*   3357

Hercules
By the Sword - Timothy Boggs f 457

Hickock
Yellowstone Run - David Robbins s 3682

Hirsch, Magen
Warp Angel - Stuart Hopen s 2205

Holbian
The Road to Underfall - Mike Jefferies f 2304

Idera
Dark Legend - Jamake Highwater f 2146

Iowyn
Tears of Time - Nancy Asire f 215

Isaf
The Fortress of Eternity - Andrew Whitmore f 4612

Ivar
The Hammer and the Cross - Harry Harrison f 2055

Jaeme
Twisted Dragon - Kevin Stein f 4188

Jarnhann, Nils
The Yngling and the Circle of Power - John Dalmas s 1074
The Yngling in Yamato - John Dalmas s 1075

Jiana
Warriorwards - Dafydd ab Hugh f 9

Jones, Cory
City of Pain - John Terra f 4341

Kadumi
The Parched Sea - Troy Denning f 1200

Kahless
Kahless - Michael Jan Friedman s 1660

Kahn, Tae
Beyond Ragnarok - Mickey Zucker Reichert f 3604

Kahsir
Tears of Time - Nancy Asire f 215

Kairn
The Steel Kings - John Maddox Roberts f 3697

Kallmirsson, Rache
The Last of the Renshai - Mickey Zucker Reichert f 3607

Kardith
Northlight - Deborah Wheeler s 4602

Kashir
To Fall Like Stars - Nancy Asire f 216

Kastring
Shadowbreed - David Ferring f 1552

Kikun
Shadowkill - Jo Clayton s 861
Shadowplay - Jo Clayton s 862
Shadowspeer - Jo Clayton s 863

Kireyevsky, Vasily "Vasha"
The Law of Becoming - Kate Elliott s 1423

Kirha
Wing Commander: Freedom Flight - Mercedes Lackey s 2630

Kith-Kanan
The Kinslayer Wars - Douglas Niles f 3271
The Qualinesti - Paul B. Thompson f 4353

Konrad
Shadowbreed - David Ferring f 1552

Kruickshank, Jenny
The Whims of Creation - Simon Hawke s 2100

Kurosawa, Oishi
The Napoleon Wager - William R. Forstchen s 1589

Iach Feragh, Culain
Ghost King - David Gemmell f 1755

Lamaril
Golden Trillium - Andre Norton f 3307

Latticus, Gaarius "Gaar"
The Vampire Memoirs - Mara McCuniff h 3009

Llew Silver Hand
The Silver Hand - Stephen R. Lawhead f 2673

Loran, Luroc I
Firehand - Andre Norton s 3305

Lorhaiden
To Fall Like Stars - Nancy Asire f 216

mac Brian, Murcha
Brian Boru: Emperor of the Irish - Morgan Llywelyn f 2779

Mac Cool, Finn
Finn Mac Cool - Morgan Llywelyn f 2782

Mac Morna, Goll
Finn Mac Cool - Morgan Llywelyn f 2782

mac Mornas, Goll
The Shield between the Worlds - Diana L. Paxson f 3398

Macurdy, Curtis
The Lion of Farside - John Dalmas f 1070

Mad Mall
Chase the Morning - Michael Scott Rohan f 3729

Mana
Lion's Heart - Karen Wehrstein f 4529

Mandaka, Bukoba
Ivory: A Legend of Past and Future - Mike Resnick s 3629

Mano, Iuti
Demon Drums - Carol Severance f 3932
Storm Caller - Carol Severance f 3934

Margawt "The Morigu"
Morigu: The Dead - Mark C. Perry f 3412

Mariel
Mariel of Redwall - Brian Jacques f 2268

Matthias
Mattimeo - Brian Jacques f 2270

Mek Kermak's-kin, Shkai'ra
Saber & Shadow - S.M. Stirling f 4226
Snowbrother - S.M. Stirling f 4227

Melody
The Lion of Farside - John Dalmas f 1070

Miaowara Tomokato
Samurai Cat Goes to the Movies - Mark E. Rogers s 3727
The Sword of Samurai Cat - Mark E. Rogers s 3728

Minstrel Boy
The Last Stand of the DNA Cowboys - Mick Farren s 1511

Mitrian
The Last of the Renshai - Mickey Zucker Reichert f 3607

Moonblade, Arilyn
Elfshadow - Elaine Cunningham f 1045
Silver Shadows - Elaine Cunningham f 1048

Moondark, Gan
Warrior - Donald E. McQuinn s 3077
Witch - Donald E. McQuinn s 3078

Moore, Teldin
Into the Void - Nigel Findley f 1560

Morgis, Duke
Wolfhelm - Richard A. Knaak f 2525

Mwili-Ferret
The 97th Step - Steve Perry s 3414

Naguchi, Machiko
Hunter's Planet - David Bischoff s 399

Nazhuret
The Belly of the Wolf - R.A. MacAvoy f 2845
King of the Dead - R.A. MacAvoy f 2846
Lens of the World - R.A. MacAvoy f 2847

Nick
The Paratwa - Christopher Hinz s 2149

No-man's Son, Roric
Voima - C. Dale Brittain f 575

Oblivion, Billy
The Last Stand of the DNA Cowboys - Mick Farren s 1511

O'Day, Gallen
Beyond the Gate - Dave Wolverton s 4740
The Golden Queen - Dave Wolverton s 4742

Oghmal
Search for the Starblade - Keith Taylor f 4315

Ohaern
The Sage - Christopher Stasheff f 4164
The Shaman - Christopher Stasheff f 4166

O'Meara, Patrick
Masters of the Fist - Edward P. Hughes s 2234

Orion
Orion Among the Stars - Ben Bova s 483
Orion and the Conqueror - Ben Bova s 484
Orion in the Dying Time - Ben Bova s 485

O'Shay, Padrig
City of Pain - John Terra f 4341

Parmenion
Dark Prince - David Gemmell f 1754

Patterson, Gil
Mother of Winter - Barbara Hambly f 2007

Pendragon, Uther
The Dragon and the Unicorn - A.A. Attanasio f 224

Penthesilea
The Amazon Chronicles - Jane E.M. Robinson f 3703

Phillips, Mark
The Crystal Sorcerers - William R. Forstchen f 1588

Pirelli, Vince
Warlords of Jupiter - William H. Keith Jr. s 2420

Quinn "Nomad"
Desert Fire - David Alexander s 53
Nomad - David Alexander s 54

Raihna
Conan the Relentless - Roland J. Green f 1883

Ranji
The False Mirror - Alan Dean Foster s 1609

Rap
Emperor and Clown - Dave Duncan f 1350

Raven Hunter
People of the Wolf - W. Michael Gear f 1741

Renagi
Tegne: Soul Warrior - Richard La Plante f 2598

Renzie
Vanishing Point - Michaela Roessner s 3724

Rikki-Tikki-Tavi
Spartan Run - David Robbins s 3679

Rikus
The Verdant Passage - Troy Denning f 1201

Ripley, Ellen
Aliens: The Female War - Steve Perry s 3417

Rivakonneva "Riva"
Mathemagics - Margaret Ball f 266

WEALTHY

WEREWOLF

Cade, Skinner
Wild Blood - Nancy A. Collins   *h*   909

Caillet, Bertrand
The Werewolf of Paris - Guy Endore   *h*   1463

Caldwell, Jay
Call to Battle - Doug Murray   *h*   3234

Cameron, Jason
The Fire Rose - Mercedes Lackey   *f*   2608

Duke, Bob
The Wild - Whitley Strieber   *h*   4262

Gallatin, Michael
The Wolf's Hour - Robert R. McCammon   *h*   2992

Garou, Lupe
One Foot in the Grave - Wm. Mark
   Simmons   *f*   4039

Haal, Daetrin Ungashak To-Alym
The Madness Season - C.S. Friedman   *s*   1655

Halver
The Dubious Hills - Pamela Dean   *f*   1165

Ives, Bobby
The Nightwalker - Thomas Tessier   *h*   4343

Jez
Wild Blood - Nancy A. Collins   *h*   909

Jock o' the Syde
The Spiral Dance - R. Garcia y Robertson   *f*   1704

Kaldy, Janos
Mark of the Werewolf - Jeffrey Sackett   *h*   3822

Kinkaid, Johnny
Moon Dance - S.P. Somtow   *h*   4116

Koshka, Ulysses
Under the Shadow - Jane Toombs   *h*   4372

Leith
Tapestry of Dark Souls - Elaine Bergstrom   *h*   380

Lycaon
The Last World - Christoph Ransmayr   *f*   3567

mac Cuel, Ceilyn
The Work of the Sun - Teresa Edgerton   *f*   1402

Marley, Andrew
The Werewolf's Touch - Cheri Scotch   *h*   3908

Melvinge
Night of the Living 'Gator! - Richard A.
   Lupoff   *s*   2841
Night of the Living Rat! - Debra Doyle   *s*   1296
Night of the Living Shark! - David Bischoff   *s*   400

Nora
Animals - John Skipp   *h*   4054

Oldman, Wendel
Wyrm Wolf - Edo Van Belkom   *h*   4414

O'Shea, Devin
Moon of the Werewolf - Ronald Kelly   *h*   2434

O'Shea, Patrick
Moon of the Werewolf - Ronald Kelly   *h*   2434

O'Shea, Rosie
Moon of the Werewolf - Ronald Kelly   *h*   2434

Penz
Conan the Formidable - Steve Perry   *f*   3420

Rybak, Nadya
Nadya: The Wolf Chronicles - Pat Murphy   *f*   3228

Skillet, William "Billy"
Walking Wolf - Nancy A. Collins   *h*   908

Talbot, Larry
A Night in the Lonesome October - Roger
   Zelazny   *h*   4843

Ted
Thor - Wayne Smith   *h*   4106

Turner, Loraine "Phyllis"
The Werewolf Chronicles - Traci Briery   *h*   558
Wolfsong - Traci Briery   *h*   559

Unnamed Character
A Prophecy of Monsters - Clark Ashton
   Smith   *h*   4070

Vehmund, Daniel
Heart Beast - Tanith Lee   *h*   2713

Warhelski, Maxim
All Things under the Moon - Robert
   Morgan   *h*   3184

White, Alice
Wilderness - Dennis Danvers   *h*   1090

White, Gabriel
Hell-Storm - James A. Moore   *h*   3174

Zeeman, Richard
The Lunatic Cafe - Laurell K. Hamilton   *h*   2018

WIDOW(ER)

Aditi
Blood of the Goddess - Kara Dalkey   *f*   1066

Alderson, Charlotte
The Colors of Hell - Michael Paine   *h*   3374

Baxter, Anna Elizabeth
Sheltered Lives - Charles Oberndorf   *s*   3335

Bremen, Jeremy "Jerry"
The Hollow Man - Dan Simmons   *s*   4033

Brewer, Tom
Dreamthorp - Chet Williamson   *h*   4654

Deems, Ann
Reign - Chet Williamson   *h*   4657

deJanes, Ecktor
Adiamante - L.E. Modesitt Jr.   *s*   3127

Gormlaith
Pride of Lions - Morgan Llywelyn   *f*   2784

Hamilton, Ruth
Dead in the Water - Nancy Holder   *h*   2180

Heron, Madeleine
Green Lake - S.K. Epperson   *h*   1470

Hunsacker, Patty
Blind Hunger - David Darke   *h*   1092

Kimmler, Vic
Borderland - S.K. Epperson   *h*   1468

Kishida, Katie
Tech-Heaven - Linda Nagata   *s*   3239

Kung, Evelyn
The Lincoln Hunters - Wilson Tucker   *s*   4378

Lewes, Charlotte
John Dollar - Marianne Wiggins   *h*   4617

Lewis, Mary
Nightlight - Michael Cadnum   *h*   664

Merwoman, Mela
The Color of Her Panties - Piers Anthony   *f*   137

Miles, Dora
The Baby - Stephanie Kegan   *h*   2417

Mordance of Barquist
The Queen of Ashes - Deborah Turner
   Harris   *f*   2046

O'Hallahan, Emma Delaney
What's Wrong with America - Scott
   Bradfield   *h*   515

Ruha
The Parched Sea - Troy Denning   *f*   1200

Starbridge, Charity
Sugar Rain - Paul Park   *s*   3383

Stumpf, Cordie
Fires of Eden - Dan Simmons   *h*   4032

Telek, Kassia
The Spirit Gate - Maya Kaathryn Bohnhoff   *f*   460

Tenar
Tehanu: The Last Book of Earthsea - Ursula K. Le
   Guin   *f*   2693

Tyrell, Sarah
A Question of Time - Fred Saberhagen   *h*   3816

Ward, Donna
Heathen - Shaun Hutson   *h*   2244

WITCH

al'Vere, Egwene
A Crown of Swords - Robert Jordan   *f*   2379
The Dragon Reborn - Robert Jordan   *f*   2380

Antonia
Daughter of Magic - C. Dale Brittain   *f*   574

Ariodne
The Wolves of Autumn - Scott Ciencin   *f*   835

Avris
Songsmith - Andre Norton   *f*   3314

Baba Yaga
Harpy High - Esther Friesner   *f*   1670

Bedlam, Gwen
Wolfhelm - Richard A. Knaak   *f*   2525

Black, Angela
Fetish - Edward Bryant   *h*   613

Brevelan
The Glass Dragon - Irene Radford   *f*   3554

Caitlin
The Spellkey Trilogy - Ann Downer   *f*   1285

Carewe, Eliza "Bettina"
Absolute Power - Ray Russell   *h*   3791

Ceridwen
Dragonslayer's Return - R.A. Salvatore   *f*   3838

Civet
Dragon Cauldron - Laurence Yep   *f*   4802

Coxe, Rachel
Witches - Kathryn Meyer Griffith   *h*   1955

Curry, Rowan Mayfair
Lasher - Anne Rice   *h*   3650

Datu, Dayu
The Painted Alphabet - Diana Darling   *f*   1096

Demidas, Tanya
Cardinal's Sin - Raymond Buckland   *h*   615

Denton, Alba
Black Body - H.C. Turk   *h*   4379

Dorella
Dorella - Mark A. Garland   *f*   1719

Drake, Selma
The Quagmire - James Kisner   *h*   2512

Eithne
The Shattered Oath - Josepha Sherman   *f*   3980

Ela
The Goblin Mirror - C.J. Cherryh   *f*   805

Elayna
Heartstone and Silver - Jacqui Singleton   *f*   4047

Ellel, Quince
A Plague of Angels - Sheri S. Tepper   *f*   4337

Elphaba
*Wicked: The Life and Times of the Wicked Witch of
   the West* - Gregory Maguire   *f*   2869

Elspet
Coven - Steven William Rimmer   *h*   3668

Esk
Equal Rites - Terry Pratchett *f* 3498

Florence, Julia
Witch - Christopher Pike *f* 3453

Fuller, Maude
Slow Funeral - Rebecca Ore *f* 3365

Galinda "Glinda the Good"
Wicked: The Life and Times of the Wicked Witch of the West - Gregory Maguire *f* 2869

Gallowglass, Cordelia
M'Lady Witch - Christopher Stasheff *f* 4161

Gallowglass, Gwen
The Warlock Rock - Christopher Stasheff *s* 4169

Garlick, Magrat
Lords and Ladies - Terry Pratchett *f* 3502
Witches Abroad - Terry Pratchett *f* 3511

Givens, Amanda
Witches - Kathryn Meyer Griffith *h* 1955

Glendil
The Moon's Wife: A Hystery - A.A. Attanasio *f* 228

Gowdie, Maggie
The Rebirth of Wonder - Lawrence Watt-Evans *f* 4502

Grimm, Eleanor
Grimm Memorials - R. Patrick Gates *h* 1732

Gullone, Greta
The Witch Returns - Phyllis Reynolds Naylor *f* 3249

Hali
Witch and Wombat - Carolyn Cushman *f* 1054

Inge
Quest for a Maid - Frances Mary Hendry *f* 2124

Kadar
The Fagin - Pat Graversen *h* 1870

Latimer, Sarah
Witch Hill - Marion Zimmer Bradley *h* 536

Layla
Spyder - Norman Partridge *h* 3391

Lessis of Valmes
Bazil Broketail - Christopher Rowley *f* 3757

Luz, Gabriel
Witch-Light - Nancy Holder *h* 2181

Lydi
Shadow of the Seventh Moon - Nancy Varian Berberick *f* 375

Margery
Strange Devices of the Sun and Moon - Lisa Goldstein *f* 1814

Margrett
Coven - Steven William Rimmer *h* 3668

Mayfair, Rowan
The Witching Hour - Anne Rice *h* 3657

Medea
Fiend - C. Dean Andersson *h* 114

Moira
The Wizardry Cursed - Rick Cook *f* 937
The Wizardry Quested - Rick Cook *f* 938

Morwen
Calling on Dragons - Patricia C. Wrede *f* 4761

Musser, Joanie
Apocalypse - Nancy Springer *f* 4130

Naismith, Gladys
A Sudden Wild Magic - Diana Wynne Jones *f* 2351

Nessarose
Wicked: The Life and Times of the Wicked Witch of the West - Gregory Maguire *f* 2869

Niahrin
Aisling - Louise Cooper *f* 945

Norman, Eliza
Neighbors - Maureen S. Pusti *h* 3547

Norman, Rebecca
The Tallow Image - Jane Brindle *h* 567

Oakes
On Meeting Witches at Wells - Judith Gorog *f* 1832

Ogg, Nanny
Lords and Ladies - Terry Pratchett *f* 3502

Olon, Sammis Arloff
Timediver's Dawn - L.E. Modesitt Jr. *s* 3138

Partridge
Slow Funeral - Rebecca Ore *f* 3365

Prokash, Magda
Blood Sabbath - Leigh Clark *h* 843

Relorn, Wryan
Timediver's Dawn - L.E. Modesitt Jr. *s* 3138

Rowan
His Majesty's Elephant - Judith Tarr *f* 4302

Seraphina
The Memoirs of Elizabeth Frankenstein - Theodore Roszak *h* 3753

Skylda "Skyla"
The Clan of the Warlord - Elizabeth H. Boyer *f* 494

Smith, Evangeline
The Torching - Marcy Heidish *h* 2110

Telek, Kassia
The Spirit Gate - Maya Kaathryn Bohnhoff *f* 460

Teneria of Fishertown
The Blood of a Dragon - Lawrence Watt-Evans *f* 4496

Theodora
Daughter of Magic - C. Dale Brittain *f* 574
The Witch and the Cathedral - C. Dale Brittain *f* 576

Thunder, Anna
The Grass Dancer - Susan Power *f* 3492

Tituba
I, Tituba, Black Witch of Salem - Maryse Conde *f* 911

Tregarde, Diana
Jinx High - Mercedes Lackey *h* 2611

Tuggle, Mrs.
The Witch's Eye - Phyllis Reynolds Naylor *f* 3250

Tzigane
I Am Dracula - C. Dean Andersson *h* 115

Weatherwax, Granny
Lords and Ladies - Terry Pratchett *f* 3502
Witches Abroad - Terry Pratchett *f* 3511
Wyrd Sisters - Terry Pratchett *f* 3512

Wheeler, Yvonne
Witch Spell - Guy N. Smith *h* 4084

Wickes, Margaret
The Quagmire - James Kisner *h* 2512

Witch Baby
Cherokee Bat and the Goat Guys - Francesca Lia Block *f* 445

Zady
Mouvar's Magic - Piers Anthony *f* 150
Orc's Opal - Piers Anthony *f* 151

Zagala
Yesterday We Saw Mermaids - Esther Friesner *f* 1680

WIZARD

Aigar
Lost in Translation - Margaret Ball *f* 265

Ala-eh-din Beyh
Tower of Fear - Glen Cook *f* 932

Alamar
Voyage of the Fox Rider - Dennis L. McKiernan *f* 3057

Alfred
Fire Sea - Margaret Weis *f* 4557
Into the Labyrinth - Margaret Weis *f* 4559
Serpent Mage - Margaret Weis *f* 4565
The Seventh Gate - Margaret Weis *f* 4566

Alyna
Runes of Autumn - Larry Elmore *f* 1436

Ambrosius, Merlin
The Wizard of Camelot - Simon Hawke *f* 2101

Ambrosius, Merlinus "Myrddin/Lailoken"
The Dragon and the Unicorn - A.A. Attanasio *f* 224

an Jiar yn Aliria dur Hamley, Quinzaine
Fire Crossing - Cheryl J. Franklin *s* 1635

Anaxagoras
The Wizard's Apprentice - S.P. Somtow *f* 4120

Anderson, Richard
Bureau 13 - Nick Pollotta *f* 3476

Antero, Rali Emilie
The Warrior Returns - Allan Cole *f* 894

Ape
The Gates of Noon - Michael Scott Rohan *f* 3732

Archon of Lycanth
The Warrior's Tale - Allan Cole *f* 895

Aubrey
The Shape-Changer's Wife - Sharon Shinn *f* 3990

Bal-Simba
The Wizardry Cursed - Rick Cook *f* 937
The Wizardry Quested - Rick Cook *f* 938

Baloran
Shadow Hunt - Anne Logston *f* 2791

Barnard, Jacques
2XS - Nigel Findley *f* 1558

Bedlam, Cabe
The Crystal Dragon - Richard A. Knaak *f* 2517

Belevairn
A Two-Edged Sword - Thomas K. Martin *f* 2902

Benelaius
Murder in Cormyr - Chet Williamson *f* 4656

Beogoat
Heroes Wanted - Kyle Crocco *f* 1028

Black-Robe, Harvas
Krispos of Videssos - Harry Turtledove *f* 4389

Boncorro
The Secular Wizard - Christopher Stasheff *f* 4165

Bremen
First King of Shannara - Terry Brooks *f* 582

Bremener, Saul
The Witch Doctor - Christopher Stasheff *f* 4171

Brightglade, Douglas
Aquamancer - Don Callander *f* 685
Geomancer - Don Callander *f* 688

Buckland, Ulysses
The Whims of Creation - Simon Hawke *s* 2100

Carpenter, Aaron
The Hero King - Rick Shelley *f* 3966

Carpinski, Wyrdrune
The Samurai Wizard - Simon Hawke *f* 2097

WOODSMAN

WORKER

Sheldon, Peter
Lucifer's Eye - Hugh B. Cave *h* 765

Sheridan, Alan
Twisted Images - Don D'Ammassa *h* 1081

Sinbad the Porter
The Other Sinbad - Craig Shaw Gardner *f* 1713

Slonimsky, Waldo
The Burning - Graham Masterton *h* 2922

Sudek, Anna
The Amulet - A.R. Morlan *h* 3191

Sudek, Tina Miner
The Amulet - A.R. Morlan *h* 3191

Taylor, Gary
The Bridge - John Skipp *h* 4055

Weil, Gunther
Griffin's Egg - Michael Swanwick *s* 4281

Whitcomb, Johnny
Inagehi - Jack Cady *h* 668

Whitefeather, Matthew
The Last Vampire - Kathryn Meyer Griffith *h* 1953

Womack, Ewa
Chicago Loop - Paul Theroux *h* 4344

WRITER

Adams, Joseph
The Penultimate Truth - Philip K. Dick *s* 1228

Aesop
The Fabulist - John Vornholt *f* 4459

Albright, Steven
Bloodletter - Warren Newton Beath *h* 350

Alburton, Denso
Hidden Echoes - Mike Jefferies *f* 2301

Alderini, Delbert
Quest for Apollo - Michael Lahey *f* 2632

Angier, Rupert
The Prestige - Christopher Priest *s* 3534

Anglith of Arkraz, Omar "Trader of Tales"
The Hunters' Haunt - Dave Duncan *f* 1353
The Reaver Road - Dave Duncan *f* 1359

Ann
Gothic Romance - Emmanuel Carrere *h* 740

Aragon, Julian
Thirst - Michael Cecilione *h* 769

Aretino, Pietro
A Farce to Be Reckoned With - Roger Zelazny *f* 4835

Bandy, Emily
Bad Brains - Kathe Koja *h* 2540

Banning, Mitch
The Singularity Project - F.M. Busby *s* 641

Barnevelt, Dirk
The Hand of Zei - L. Sprague de Camp *s* 1139

Baum, L. Frank
Was - Geoff Ryman *f* 3804

Baylor, Katti
Rockabilly Limbo - William W. Johnstone *h* 2338

Beaumont, Thad
The Dark Half - Stephen King *h* 2481

Bell, Howard
A Key for the Nonesuch - Geary Gravel *s* 1866

Bellman, Alan
The Printer's Devil - Chico Kidd *f* 2465

Bennington, Jay Jay
Glenraven - Marion Zimmer Bradley *f* 523

Benson, E.F.
The Haunting of Lamb House - Joan Aiken *h* 35

Bishopric, Susan
The Night Mayor - Kim Newman *s* 3262

Black, Marguerita "Maggie"
The Wood Wife - Terri Windling *f* 4709

Blake, Jason
Moonbane - Al Sarrantonio *s* 3869

Blaylock, Morgan
The Devouring - Douglas D. Hawk *h* 2090

Borden, Alfred
The Prestige - Christopher Priest *s* 3534

Boscage, A.D.
The Priest: A Gothic Romance - Thomas M. Disch *h* 1261

Bramhall, Arthur
The Bear Went over the Mountain - William Kotzwinkle *f* 2561

Bugmeier, Neil
Horror Show - Greg Kihn *h* 2466

Byron, George Gordon
Lord of the Dead - Tom Holland *h* 2187
The Stress of Her Regard - Tim Powers *h* 3496

Carlson-Wade, Bruno David
Bereavement - Richard Lortz *h* 2802

Carrington, Charles Francis
Changeweaver - Margaret Ball *f* 263

Chasen, Liz
Demon Night - J. Michael Straczynski *h* 4244

Chekhov, Anton
Chekhov's Journey - Ian Watson *s* 4489

Clare, Peter
The Vanishment - Jonathan Aycliffe *h* 238

Clavel
North Wind - Gwyneth Jones *s* 2354

Clayburn, Karl Thomas
Buried Screams - C. Dean Andersson *h* 113

Colridge, Samuel Taylor
Walford's Oak - Jill M. Phillips *f* 3433

Connel, Eileen
October - Al Sarrantonio *h* 3870

Conner, Daphne "Dee"
Cat's Eye - William W. Johnstone *h* 2332

Cooper, Arlene
The Children of Hamelin - Norman Spinrad *s* 4124

Cooper, David
Earthbound - Richard Matheson *h* 2930

Corbett, Blake
Shapes - Steve Vance *h* 4425

Coventry, Martina
City of Truth - James Morrow *s* 3210

Crazy
Death Is a Lonely Business - Ray Bradbury *h* 508

Crowe, Derek
The 37th Mandala - Marc Laidlaw *h* 2633

Delacroix, Conway
Fetish - Edward Bryant *h* 613

Dero, Halleyne dar
Thunder of the Captains - Holly Lisle *f* 2772

Devereaux, Cleveland Carroll
Who Killed James Dean? - Warren Newton Beath *h* 352

Diane
Amazon: A Novel - Barbara G. Walker *h* 4474

Dickinson, Emily
The Steampunk Trilogy - Paul Di Filippo *s* 1224

Diehrenn
Encounter with Tiber - Buzz Aldrin *s* 52

Donner, Bruce
Stage Fright - Clare McNally *h* 3074

Donner, Greg
Dreamer - Daniel Quinn *h* 3551

Doughterty, Brian
Icebound - Dean R. Koontz *h* 2551

Doyle, Arthur Conan
Believe: A Novel - William Shatner *f* 3937
Nevermore - William Hjortsberg *h* 2150
Photographing Fairies - Steve Szilagyi *f* 4289

Dunbar, Larry
The Stake - Richard Laymon *h* 2683

Dunreith, Cassandra "Cass"
Dragon Moon - Chris Claremont *f* 839

Duvet, Berthe
The Porcelain Dove - Delia Sherman *f* 3974

Eliot, Ann
The Innsmouth Heritage - Brian Stableford *h* 4145

Endymion, Raul
Endymion - Dan Simmons *s* 4030

Esher, David
Unearthed - Ashley McConnell *h* 3007

Etchison, Phil
Forest of the Night - S.P. Somtow *f* 4114

Eupolis of Pallene
Goatsong - Tom Holt *f* 2194
The Walled Orchard - Tom Holt *f* 2195

Faulkner, William
The Wild Blue and the Gray - William Sanders *s* 3853

Fettle, Richard
Queen of Angels - Greg Bear *s* 347

Fitzroy, Henry
Blood Price - Tanya Huff *h* 2225
Blood Trail - Tanya Huff *h* 2226

Fleming, Paul
Demon Shadows - Michael B. Sirota *h* 4051

Flood, C. Thomas
Bloodsucking Fiends: A Love Story - Christopher Moore *h* 3172

Forrest, Jack
Evil Intent - Bernard Taylor *h* 4308

Fortizak "Zak"
Murder at the Galactic Writers' Society - Janet Asimov *s* 210

Fowler, Cassie
Towing Jehovah - James Morrow *f* 3215

Frisson
The Witch Doctor - Christopher Stasheff *f* 4171

Fronto
The Arkadians - Lloyd Alexander *f* 55

Gainsborough, Harry
Zod Wallop - William Browning Spencer *h* 4123

Galliez, Aymar
The Werewolf of Paris - Guy Endore *h* 1463

Gardner, Joe
The Children's Hour - Douglas Clegg *h* 868

Grey, Agnes
Pillow Friend - Lisa Tuttle *h* 4402

Grey, Alice
The Torching - Marcy Heidish *h* 2110

Grey, Marjorie
Pillow Friend - Lisa Tuttle *h* 4402

Guerreri, Karen Rohmer
Preternatural - Margaret Wander Bonanno *s* 466

Shields, Ben
Prank Night - David Robbins *h* 3678

Sierek, Detlef
Drachenfels - Jack Yeovil *f* 4800

Smith, Stephen
Where Does Kissing End? - Kate Pullinger *h* 3544

Speke, Hamilton
Ghostwright - Michael Cadnum *h* 661

Spenotex, Arakaho Blundy
Stopping at Slowyear - Frederik Pohl *s* 3469

Stenvall, Richard
The Night Seasons - J.N. Williamson *h* 4666

Sterling, Ben
Midnight Sun - Ramsey Campbell *h* 700

Stevens, Jim
Reborn - F. Paul Wilson *h* 4691

Stillwater, Marty
Mr. Murder - Dean R. Koontz *h* 2555

Stoker, Bram
Dracula Unbound - Brian W. Aldiss *h* 43

Stone, Jack
The Immaculate - Mark Morris *h* 3204

Storey, Graham
Pillow Friend - Lisa Tuttle *h* 4402

Strine, Arnold
The Fermata - Nicholson Baker *s* 253

Talbot, Edward "Eddie"
Her Monster - Jeff Collignon *h* 898

Taliesen
The Hawk's Gray Feather - Patricia
  Kennealy *f* 2439
The Hedge of Mist - Patricia Kennealy *s* 2440
The Oak Above the Kings: A Book of the Keltiad -
  Patricia Kennealy *s* 2441

Tichy, Ijon
Peace on Earth - Stanislaw Lem *s* 2731

Timmerson, Ray
Immortal - Jason Nickles *h* 3265

Timothy "Timmy"
Live From Golgotha: A Novel - Gore Vidal *s* 4438

Torrance, Jack
The Shining - Stephen King *h* 2494

Tregarde, Diana
Burning Water - Mercedes Lackey *h* 2601
Jinx High - Mercedes Lackey *h* 2611

Tremaine, June
Black Dogs - Ian McEwan *h* 3034

Underbridge, Kin
Thunder of the Captains - Holly Lisle *f* 2772

Underhill, Tim
Koko - Peter Straub *h* 4250
The Throat - Peter Straub *h* 4254

Virgil
Quest for Apollo - Michael Lahey *f* 2632

Wade, Kara
Sibs - F. Paul Wilson *h* 4694

Walker, David
Steam - Jay B. Laws *h* 2675

Walker, Hillary "Hilly"
The Forgotten - Stephen R. George *h* 1766

Wallace, Wendy
The Hunted - Kathryn Ptacek *h* 3542

Warren, Carol
In the Deep Woods - Nicholas Conde *h* 912

Watson, John H.
Sherlock Holmes in Orbit - Mike Resnick *s* 3637

Webster, Duncan
Cardinal's Sin - Raymond Buckland *h* 615
The Committee - Raymond Buckland *h* 616

Wheldrake
The Revenge of the Rose - Michael
  Moorcock *f* 3170

White, Alan
Created By - Richard Christian Matheson *h* 2937

Wilde, Oscar
The Hunger and Ecstasy of Vampires - Brian
  Stableford *h* 4144

Williams, Martin
Mirror - Graham Masterson *h* 2920

Wilson, Barry
The Fungus - Harry Adam Knight *h* 2539

Wollstonecraft, Mary
Wall, Stone, Craft - Walter Jon Williams *h* 4653

Writer
The Time Ships - Stephen Baxter *s* 334

Writing Woman of Maho
Fish Soup - Ursula K. Le Guin *f* 2688

Wulf
Wulfsyarn: A Mosaic - Phillip Mann *s* 2876

Young, Samson
London Fields - Martin Amis *s* 79

YOUNG MAN

Andrew
The Last Coin - James P. Blaylock *f* 421

Azod
The Forsaken - Steven Ray Fulgham *h* 1682

Baedecker, Scott
Phases of Gravity - Dan Simmons *s* 4036

Cade, Skinner
Wild Blood - Nancy A. Collins *h* 909

Casteel, Luke Jr.
Web of Dreams - V.C. Andrews *h* 123

Deeping, Gabriel
Gabriel's Body - Curt Siodmak *h* 4049

Donner, Mark
Disciples of Dread - Hugh B. Cave *h* 764

Drackman, Bryan "Ticktock"
Dragon Tears - Dean R. Koontz *h* 2548

Gray, Zachary
An Acceptable Time - Madeleine L'Engle *f* 2732

Grieg, Christian
Boundaries - T.M. Wright *h* 4774

Hawthorne, Royce
Chaingang - Rex Miller *h* 3105

Hightower, Fabian
Possession - Peter James *h* 2290

Jonathan
Tapestry of Dark Souls - Elaine Bergstrom *h* 380

Julian
Orphans - Jean Simon *h* 4042

Justin
The Living Evil - Ruby Jean Jensen *h* 2312

Lawrence, Mark
The Offspring - Kenneth McKenney *h* 3048

Lydyard, David
The Werewolves of London - Brian
  Stableford *h* 4147

Majeed
The Safety of Unknown Cities - Lucy
  Taylor *h* 4320

Matthews, Eric
Demon Night - J. Michael Straczynski *h* 4244

Michaels, Judge
The M.D.: A Horror Story - Thomas M.
  Disch *h* 1260

Radcliffe, Phillip
A Sharpness on the Neck - Fred
  Saberhagen *h* 3818

Rice, Doug
Blood of Mugwump - Doug Rice *h* 3658

Rork, Paddy
Signs of Life - Cherry Wilder *s* 4622

Saralyn, Paul
The Link - Andrew Laurance *h* 2666

Sikes, Stephen
Sins of the Flesh - Don Davis *h* 1130

Stranger
Black Sun - Douglas E. Winter *h* 4716

Thorsen, Thorian "Torrie"
The Fire Duke - Joel Rosenberg *f* 3740
The Silver Stone - Joel Rosenberg *f* 3745

Tsepesh, Arkady
Covenant with the Vampire - Jeanne
  Kalogridis *h* 2393

Van Buren, Peter
Silent Witness - Robert Arthur Smith *h* 4097

Washington, Sandy
Homegoing - Frederik Pohl *s* 3463

Wilkinson, Esau
The Hunger of the Beast - John Driver *h* 1336

YOUNG WOMAN

Adderstone, Susannah
The Vanishment - Jonathan Aycliffe *h* 238

Anghara, Princess
Nemesis - Louise Cooper *f* 950

Barrett, Elizabeth
Death Masque - P.N. Elrod *h* 1440

Barrington, Cathy
The Tallow Image - Jane Brindle *h* 567

Bell, Celina
The Unborn - Andrew Laurance *h* 2668

Blaise, Anna
A Hidden Place - Robert Charles Wilson *s* 4704

Caitlin
The Druid's Gift - Margaret J. Anderson *f* 100

Chen Li
Twisted Images - Don D'Ammassa *h* 1081

Conner, Katie
Dead Lines - John Skipp *h* 4056

Craig, Julie
Heathen - Shaun Hutson *h* 2244

Crawford, Oilvia
Blood Roots - Richie Tankersley Cusick *h* 1055

Cross, Jo
Garden - Matthew J. Costello *h* 968

Dalton, Jennifer "Darla"
Darkman #4: The Face of Death - Randall
  Boyll *h* 505

Donaldson, Pamela
Madeline: After the Fall of Usher - Marie
  Kiraly *h* 2502

Duffy, Karen
Boundaries - T.M. Wright *h* 4774

Dun Lady's Jess
Dun Lady's Jess - Doranna Durgin *f* 1368

ZOO KEEPER

Author Index

This index alphabetically lists authors of books featured or mentioned in entries in the main section of this book. For each author, the titles of books written and entry numbers are shown. A bold entry number indicates a featured main entry under the title and author in question; lightface numbers refer to main entries that mention the title in question under the rubric "Other books you might like."

A

Aakhus, Patricia
The Voyage of Mael Duin's Curragh **1**, 3065

Aamodt, Donald
A Name to Conjure With **2**, 550, 864, 2279, 3573, 4635
A Troubling Along the Border **3**, 552, 864

Aardema, Verna
Why Mosquitoes Buzz in People's Ears 2692

Aaron, Shale
Virtual Death **4**, 410

ab Hugh, Dafydd
Arthur War Lord **5**, 4609
Balance of Power **6**
Endgame 2756
Fallen Heroes **7**, 2324
Far Beyond the Wave 4609
The Final Fury **8**, 733, 1842, 4081
Knee Deep in the Dead 2756
Warriorwards **9**

Abbey, Lynn
Beneath the Web **10**, 4584
The Black Flame 4576
The Brazen Gambit **11**, 2098
Catwoman **12**, 1707, 1915, 1916, 3359
Cinnabar Shadows **13**
Daughter of the Bright Moon 1687, 2382, 3396, 4569
The Forge of Virtue **14**
The Temper of Wisdom **15**
Unicorn and Dragon 375, 4815
The Wooden Sword **16**, 1688, 2464, 3312, 3762

Abbott, Edwin A.
Flatland 3241

Abe, Kobo
The Face of Another **17**, 1080, 2407, 4049

Abella, Alex
The Killing of the Saints **18**, 1053, 1490, 1725, 2865

Abrahams, Roger D.
Afro-American Folk Tales 3352

Acker, Kathy
Empire of the Senseless 3658
Pussy, King of the Pirates 637

Ackerman, Forrest J.
I, Vampire: Interviews with the Undead **4217**
New Eves: Science Fiction about the Extraordinary Women of Today and Tomorrow **1634**

Ackroyd, Peter
First Light 666
Hawksmoor 881, 3169
The Trial of Elizabeth Cree **19**

Acres, Mark
Dark Divide **20**, 395, 1236, 1480
Dragonspawn **21**

Adair, Gilbert
Alice through the Needle's Eye: The Further Adventures of Lewis Carroll's "Alice" 3292, 4556

Adams, Douglas
Dirk Gently's Holistic Detective Agency 1173, 1543, 1790, 1990, 3500, 3501
The Hitchhiker's Guide to the Galaxy 392, 451, 601, 777, 987, 1173, 1175, 1176, 1179, 1213, 1542, 1545, 1604, 1652, 1669, 1706, 1713, 1714, 1715, 1743, 1772, 1788, 1868, 2052, 2053, 2096, 2193, 3246, 3247, 3499, 3642, 3643, 3644, 3645, 3646, 3727, 3733, 3827, 4052, 4791
The Illustrated Hitchhiker's Guide to the Galaxy **22**
Life, the Universe, and Everything 1542, 3247
The Long Dark Tea-Time of the Soul **23**, 1543, 1790, 3506
Mostly Harmless **24**
The Original Hitchhiker's Radio Scripts 1431
The Restaurant at the End of the Universe 400, 777, 1179, 1296, 1542, 1652, 1706, 1713, 3246, 3247, 4052
So Long, and Thanks for All the Fish 1542, 2841, 3247

Adams, Richard
Girl in a Swing 1620
Maia 2714, 3882
The Plague Dogs 2504, 2944
Shardik 3403, 3757
Tales From Watership Down **25**
Watership Down 356, 913, 2268, 2270, 2473, 3403

Adams, Robert
The Coming of the Horseclans 1920
Of Beginnings and Endings **26**
The Seven Magical Jewels of Ireland 3695
Stairway to Forever 3606

Adams, Terry A.
The Master of Chaos **27**

Adams, William
The Unwound Way **28**, 2983, 4148, 4150

Adkins, Patrick H.
Sons of the Titans **29**, 374, 1588, 2122

Adler, C.S.
Ghost Brother 1528

Adrian, Jack
Strange Tales from the Strand **30**

Aesop
Aesop's Fables **31**, 1959

Afanas'ev, Aleksandr
Russian Fairy Tales 2609

Agins, Phyllis Carol
Suisan **32**

Agosin, Marjorie
The Secret Weavers: Stories of the Fantastic by Latin American Women **33**, 41, 1136, 1137, 1459, 1634, 3321, 4631, 4632

Ahern, Jerry
Final Rain 233
The Quest 234
The Struggle **34**, 1548
To End All War 1861, 1862
Werewolves 2264

Aickman, Robert
Cold Hand in Mine 4251
The Fontana Book of Ghost Stories Series 1061
Pages From a Young Girl's Journal 4324
Painted Devils 4251

Unsettled Dust 4592, 4593, 4594
The Wine-Dark Sea 692, 703, 704, 705, 2753, 2754, 4251

Aiken, Joan
Black Hearts in Battersea 4763
The Haunting of Lamb House **35**, 4591
The Last Slice of Rainbow and Other Stories 2870
Nightbirds on Nantucket 4763
The Shadow Guests 3392

Aikin, Jim
Walk the Moon's Road 1932, 1962
The Wall at the Edge of the World **36**, 3570

Akers, Alan Burt
Arena of Antares 1587

Albano, Peter
Assault of the Super Carrier **37**
Ordeal of the Seventh Carrier **38**
Revenge of the Seventh Carrier **39**
Super Carrier: The Ultimate Secret Weapon **40**

Alcala, Kathleen
Mrs. Vargas and the Dead Naturalist **41**

Alcock, Vivian
The Haunting of Cassie Palmer 3392

Aldiss, Brian
An Island Called Moreau 4731
Last Rites 4731

Aldiss, Brian W.
Common Clay: 20 Odd Stories **42**
Cryptozoic 155
Dracula Unbound **43**, 2392, 3259, 3816
Frankenstein Unbound 116, 403, 740, 1057, 2406, 2529, 2886, 3496, 3753
Greybeard 2287
Helliconia Spring 3382, 4020, 4731
Helliconia Summer 718, 3382, 4020, 4731
The Helliconia Trilogy 3383
Helliconia Winter 3382, 4020, 4731
Hothouse 2266, 4512
Last Orders **44**
Man in His Time: The Best Science Fiction Stories of Brian W. Aldiss **45**, 102, 512, 4731

Author Index

Author Index

Author Index

Crandall, Melissa
Earth 2 **1010**
Search and Rescue 3579

Crawford, Betty Anne
The Bushido Incident **1011**, 3953

Crawford, Dan
Rouse a Sleeping Cat **1012**
The Sure Death of a Mouse **1013**
A Wild Dog and Lone **1014**

Crawford, F. Marion
For the Blood Is the Life and Other Stories **1015**

Cray, Roberta
The Sword and the Lion **1016**, 2598

Crean, Michelle Shirey
Dancer of the Sixth 182, 262, **1017**, 1291, 3159, 4519

Creighton, Lee
Two Queens of Lochrie 3573

Cresswell, Helen
A Game of Catch 1951
Moondial 820

Crichton, Michael
The Andromeda Strain 916, 939, 1366, 1646, 2145, 2389, 2655, 2675, 2946, 3193, 3520, 3828
Jurassic Park 476, 485, 732, **1018**, 1115, 1142, 1387, 1837, 2247, 2538, 2570, 3245, 3277, 3674, 3883, 4267
The Lost World **1019**, 1115
Sphere 362, 973, 3926
The Terminal Man 476, 939, 1089, 2289, 2544, 3373
Westworld 3277

Crider, Bill
Shotgun Saturday Night 1469

Crimmins, Cathy
Revenge of the Christmas Box **1020**, 2556

Crispin, A.C.
Ancestor's World **1021**, 1211
The Eyes of the Beholders 1121, 1661, 1663, 2801
Sarek 995, **1022**
Serpent's Gift 189, 872, **1023**
Shadow World **1024**, 1123
Silent Dances **1025**, 1123, 1287, 1499, 2037, 2985, 2999, 3287
Silent Songs **1026**, 1606, 4017
Songsmith **3314**
Starbridge 190, 419, **1027**, 1079, 1123, 2038, 2442, 3313, 3465, 4027
Time for Yesterday 428, 732, 748, 2638
V 1216, 2319, 2349, 4215, 4443
Yesterday's Son 428, 429, 748, 1117, 2638

Crocco, Kyle
Heroes, Inc. 137, 457, 979, **1029**, 1674, 2351, 3035, 3175, 3553, 4505, 4837
Heroes Wanted 220, **1028**, 3035, 4505

Crompton, Ann Eliot
Merlin's Harp **1030**

Crosland, Margaret
The Gothic Tales of the Marquis de Sade 4297

Cross, Gilbert B.
A Witch Across Time 101, 821, **1031**, 2738

Cross, John Keir
The Angry Planet 2115

Cross, Ronald Anthony
The Fourth Guardian **1032**, 2594
The Lost Guardian 880, **1033**
Prisoners of Paradise 46, 1363

Crowe, Catherine
Night-Side of Nature 1730

Crowley, John
Aegypt 420, 1177, 1814, 1865, 2955, 4456
Antiquities **1034**, 1155, 1817, 3803
Beasts 589, 3023, 3681
Little, Big 228, 280, 281, 282, 361, 446, 449, 669, 745, 856, 1127, 1148, 1692, 1694, 1799, 1865, 2026, 2161, 3017, 3019, 3169, 3474, 3494, 3567, 4719
Love and Sleep 537, **1035**
Novelty **1036**, 4489, 4736

Crowther, Peter
Blue Motel **1037**
Dante's Disciples **1038**
Escardy Gap **1039**
Heaven Sent: 18 Glorious Tales of the Angels **1040**, 1084, 1877, 4808
Narrow Houses **1041**, 1746, 3154, 4517
Tombs **2567**
Touch Wood **1042**

Crozier, Ouida
Shadows After Dark **1043**, 4047

Cuddon, J.A.
The Penguin Book of Ghost Stories 1061

Cunningham, Elaine
Daughter of the Drow **1044**
Elfshadow **1045**, 1200, 1201, 2813, 3840, 3843, 3844, 3846
Elfsong **1046**
The Radiant Dragon **1047**, 2219
Silver Shadows **1048**

Cunningham, Jere
The Abyss 1516

Curry, Ann
The Book of Brendan 309, **1049**, 3546, 4813

Curry, Chris
Haunted **4359**
Moonfall **4360**
Panic **1050**
Thunder Road **1051**
Trickster 351, **1052**

Curry, Jane Louise
Over the Sea's Edge 3927

Curtis, James Roberto
Shango **1053**

Cushman, Carolyn
Witch and Wombat 265, 574, 741, **1054**

Cusick, Richie Tankersley
Blood Roots **1055**, 2709
Buffy the Vampire Slayer 832, 834, **1056**, 1445, 4246
Vampire 3447

Cussler, Clive
Raise the Titanic! 4080

Da Cruz, Daniel
The Ayes of Texas 38, 39
Mixed Doubles 26, **1057**, 1192, 1543, 1642, 1643, 1645
Texas on the Rocks 37, 38, 39, 40, 54
Texas Triumphant 37, 38, 39, 40

Dahl, Roald
Charlie and the Chocolate Factory 3456
Roald Dahl's Book of Ghost Stories **1058**
The Witches 2350, 3249, 3250

Dalby, Richard
The Best of Ghosts and Scholars 2283
Chillers for Christmas **1059**
Dracula's Brood **1060**, 1099, 1108, 1912, 2371
Ghosts and Scholars 239
Ghosts for Christmas 3624, 3888
The Mammoth Book of Ghost Stories 999, 1058, **1061**, 1372
The Mammoth Book of Ghost Stories 2 999, 1372
The Mammoth Book of Victorian and Edwardian Ghost Stories **1062**
Mistletoe Mayhem **1063**
Modern Ghost Stories by Eminent Women Writers **1064**, 4631, 4632
Shivers for Christmas **1065**
Tales of Witchcraft 1373
Thrillers for Christmas 3624
Vampire Stories 4534
Victorian Ghost Stories by Eminent Women Writers 1000, 4631
The Virago Book of Ghost Stories 3543, 4403
The Virago Book of Ghost Stories: The Twentieth Century 3543

Daley, Brian
The Doomfarers of Coramonde 132, 858, 925, 1144, 1410, 1452, 1454, 1455, 2901, 2902, 3437, 3610
Fall of the White Ship Avatar 218, 219, 888, 891, 922, 1270
The Han Solo Adventures 62, 86, 91, 96, 2002, 2581, 4407, 4741, 4828
Han Solo and the Lost Legacy 4825, 4827
Han Solo at Star's End 4825, 4827
Han Solo's Revenge 4825, 4827
Jinx on a Terran Inheritance 218, 219, 891, 922, 1077, 1079, 1244, 1270, 1297, 1299, 3418, 4518
Requiem for a Ruler of Worlds 218, 219, 259, 262, 386, 891, 893, 922, 1270, 1560, 2970, 4518, 4794
Starfollowers of Coramonde 1410
A Tapestry of Magics 217, 611, 3739
Tron 4125, 4585

Dalkey, Kara
Blood of the Goddess **1066**
The Curse of Sagamore 1222, 3498
Euryale 2632
Goa 161
Little Sister **1067**, 1501, 2089, 3288
The Nightingale 32, 313, 1166, 1197, 4856, 4858
The Sword of Sagamore 1222

Dalmas, John
Fanglith 3027, 4453
Homecoming 719, 1609
The Kalif's War **1068**, 3975

The Lantern of God **1069**, 3113, 4453, 4696
The Lion of Farside **1070**
The Lizard War 934, **1071**, 1759, 1887, 4453, 4696, 4724
The Regiment 258, 483, 1248, 3491
The Regiment's War **1072**
The Walkaway Clause 955
The White Regiment **1073**, 3486, 4722
The Yngling 37, 40, 3677, 3679, 3695, 3697
The Yngling and the Circle of Power **1074**
The Yngling in Yamato **1075**

Dalton, Annie
Out of the Ordinary 990, **1076**

Dalton, Sean
Beyond the Void 752. **1077**, 2143
Destination: Mutiny **1078**
The Salukan Gambit **1079**

D'Amato, Brian
Beauty **1080**, 2542

D'Ammassa, Don
Twisted Images **1081**

Daniel, Les
Don Sebastian Series 3811

Daniel, Tony
Warpath **1082**, 4580

Daniell, Tina
The Companions 3481
Dark Heart 125, 2507, 3481

Daniels, Les
The Black Castle 379, 1442, 3426, 4793, 4795, 4796, 4797
The Chronicles of Don Sebastian 4143
Citizen Vampire 1439, 1440
No Blood Spilled **1083**, 3261, 3814, 4792
The Silver Skull 4796
Yellow Fog 2012

Daniels, Patricia
Sinbad the Sailor 312, 1713, 3788, 4855

Dann, Jack
Aliens! 3513
Angels! 1040, **1084**, 1877, 2766, 4808
Dinosaurs! 1911, 1979, 3626
Dinosaurs II 1911
Dragons! 1989, 3515, 4553
Hackers 1918
High Steel **1992**
Little People! **1085**, 3919, 3979
Magicats! 1107, 2687, 3300, 3301, 3403, 4189
Magicats II 3300, 4189
The Man Who Melted 1435
The Memory Cathedral **1086**
Run for the Stars/Echoes of Thunder 1435
Sorcerers! 2451
Unicorns! 338, 339, 1920, 2343, 4810
Unicorns II 338, 339, 989, **1087**, 2343, 4810
Wandering Stars: An Anthology of Jewish Fantasy and Science Fiction 1435

Dann, Jeanne Van Buren
In the Field of Fire 2948

Dantz, William
Hunger 311, 363, **1088**, 2570, 3180

Other **1241**
The Pritcher Mass 345, 4013
Secret Under the Caribbean 2659
Soldier, Ask Not 170, 416, 1651,
  1884, 2419, 3016, 3339, 3487,
  3490, 3560, 4362
The Space Swimmers 1962
Space Winners 2115, 2659, 2967
The Spirit of Dorsai 3490
The Tactics of Mistake 1068, 1072,
  1073, 1324, 1884, 1885, 1887,
  3016, 3088, 3562, 3741
Time Storm 109, 334, 1564, 1591,
  2237, 3125, 3138, 3999, 4059,
  4378, 4783
Way of the Pilgrim 110, 1206, 1423,
  1758, 2999, 3041, 4711, 4712
Wolf and Iron 171, 1074, **1242**,
  1478, 1555, 2078, 2759, 3077,
  3747
Wolfling 1288, 1601, 1609
Young Bleys **1243**

Dietz, William C.
Bodyguard **1244**
Cluster Command **1316**
Drifter 386, **1245**
Drifter's Run **1246**
Drifter's War **1247**
The Final Battle **1248**
Legion of the Damned **1249**, 2418,
  4519, 4561
Mars Prime **1250**, 3704, 3708
Matrix Man 249, **1251**, 1681, 4127
McCade's Bounty **1252**
Prison Planet 892, **1253**
War World 4722
Where the Ships Die **1254**

Dillard, Anne
Specters 1550, 4041

Dillard, J.M.
Emissary 1010, 1657, 2317, 4461
The Lost Years 1219, 1546, 1664,
  3936
Recovery 1573
Specters **1255**, 2042
Spectres 1625, 2850, 3542, 3591,
  4240
Star Trek V: The Final Frontier 1386,
  1582, 1658, 2128
*Star Trek VI: The Undiscovered
  Country* **1256**, 2630
Star Trek: Generations 1657, 1659
Star Trek: The Lost Years **1257**,
  1386, 1582, 1658

Dillon, Barbara
My Stepfather Shrank! **1258**

DiMarco, Jennifer
Escape to the Wind **1259**, 4154

Dimenstein, Catherine Wells
Children of the Earth 4578
The Earth Is All That Lasts 4579
The Earth Saver 4580

Disch, Thomas M.
*The Brave Little Toaster: A Bedtime
  Story for Small Appliances* 211
*The Brave Little Toaster Goes to
  Mars* 211
*The Businessman: A Tale of
  Terror* 515, 1347, 2438, 2909,
  3538
The Genocides 822, 2114, 2239
Getting into Death 283
The M.D.: A Horror Story 515, **1260**,
  2156, 2775, 3539
Mankind under the Leash 822, 4679

*The New Improved Sun: An Anthology
  of Utopian Science Fiction* 3957
The Priest: A Gothic Romance 515,
  1261
*The Ruins of Earth: An Anthology of
  the Immediate Future* 3957

DiSilvestro, Roger L.
Living with the Reptiles 53, 117, 118,
  119, 424, 1142, **1262**, 2724, 2725,
  3644, 4430
Ursula's Gift 4730

Dixon, Larry
The Black Gryphon **2599**
Born to Run **2600**
Chrome Circle **2606**
The Silver Gryphon **2619**
The White Gryphon **2626**

Doctorow, E.L.
The Waterworks 19, **1263**

Dodge, Jim
Stone Junction 3684

Dolan, Bill
Afrikorps 1131, **1264**, 3747
Cobra Curse **1265**, 2400
Iron Horse 1131, **1266**
White Rhino **1267**, 3627

Donaldson, D.J.
Blood on the Bayou 818, **1268**, 1716

Donaldson, Stephen R.
Chronicles of Thomas Covenant 727
Forbidden Knowledge **1269**
*The Gap into Conflict: The Real
  Story* **1270**
*The Gap into Madness: Chaos and
  Order* **1271**
*The Gap into Power: A Dark and
  Hungry God Arises* **1272**
*The Gap into Ruin: This Day All Gods
  Die* **1273**
*The Gap into Vision: Forbidden
  Knowledge* 753
The Illearth War 1538, 2303, 4175,
  4576, 4831
Lord Foul's Bane 15, 150, 583, 835,
  2304, 2382, 2846, 3195, 3607,
  3819, 3837, 3848, 4175, 4569,
  4645, 4714, 4715, 4831
The Mirror of Her Dreams 417,
  2006, 2008, 2908
The Power That Preserves 4175,
  4831
Strange Dreams **1274**
The Wounded Land 4645

Doohan, James
The Rising **1275**

Dorf, Fran
A Reasonable Madness **1276**

Dorfman, Ariel
Mascara 17, 1080, 4049

Douglas, Carole Nelson
Cup of Clay 242, 461, **1277**, 1641,
  1710, 1890, 2092
Keepers of Edanvant 1389
Keepers of the Edanvant 1392
Seed upon the Wind **1278**
Six of Swords 2004, 3690

Douglas, L. Warren
Bright Islands in a Dark Sea 1330,
  1613
Cannon's Orb 250, 344, 562, 565,
  756, 809, **1279**, 1611, 2109, 2141,
  2985, 3568, 3571, 4361

A Plague of Change **1280**, 1292,
  1611, 2109, 2354, 2763, 3716,
  4275, 4357
Stepwater 622, 1211, 1254, **1281**,
  1450, 3264, 4419
The Wells of Phyre **1282**

Douglas, Lauren Wright
In the Blood 60, 543, **1283**, 1378,
  1802, 2844, 3120

Douglis, Marjie
Matrix Witch 4418

Dowd, Tom
Night's Pawn **1284**, 4096

Downer, Ann
The Spellkey Trilogy **1285**

Downing, Paula E.
Fallway 1279, **1286**, 1786, 1787,
  1986, 2143, 2949, 2950, 2951,
  2962, 2985, 2993, 4361
Flare Star 807, **1287**, 1529, 2949,
  2950, 2951, 4311, 4836
Maia's Veil 2949
Rinn's Star 520, 728, 1422, 2950,
  2951, 3297
Siduri's Net **2951**
A Whisper of Time **1288**, 2949,
  2950, 2951, 3327, 4422

Doyle, Arthur Conan
*The Best Horror Stories of Arthur
  Conan Doyle* **1289**, 2938
*The Best Supernatural Tales of Arthur
  Conan Doyle* 2140, 2499, 3202
*The Horror of the Heights and Other
  Tales of Suspense* **1290**
The Lost World 256, 1019, 1115,
  1142, 1979, 3674, 4044

Doyle, Debra
By Honor Betray'd **1291**
The Gathering Flame **1292**
Groogleman **1293**
Knight's Wyrd **1294**
The Long Hunt **1295**
Night of the Living Rat! 400, **1296**,
  2841
The Price of the Stars 260, 752, 841,
  1212, 1254, **1297**, 1531, 1650,
  2961, 2982, 3955, 4098, 4099,
  4100, 4101, 4521, 4522, 4523,
  4527, 4528, 4854
School of Wizardry 689, **1298**, 4496,
  4817, 4830, 4831
Starpilot's Grave **1299**, 4523

Dozois, Gardner
Angels! **1084**
Down Among the Dead Men 4536
*Future Earths: Under African
  Skies* 3627
*Geodesic Dreams: The Best Short
  Fiction of Gardner Dozois* 49, 656,
  1300
Isaac Asimov's Aliens 3513
Isaac Asimov's Ghosts **1301**
Isaac Asimov's Vampires **1302**
Little People! **1085**
*Modern Classic Short Novels of Science
  Fiction* **1303**, 2691
*Modern Classics of Science
  Fiction* 205, 346, **1304**, 2066,
  2073, 2691
Ripper! 1416, 4590
Slow Dancing through Time **1305**
Strangers 648
Unicorns II **1087**

*The Year's Best Science Fiction: Eighth
  Annual Collection* 178, 1102,
  1306, 3211, 3639
*The Year's Best Science Fiction:
  Eleventh Annual Collection* **1307**,
  4025
*The Year's Best Science Fiction: Ninth
  Annual Collection* **1308**, 3212
*The Year's Best Science Fiction
  Series* 205, 1084, 2072, 2073,
  2074
*The Year's Best Science Fiction:
  Seventh Annual Collection* 177,
  197, 405, 406, 721, **1309**, 3783,
  4739
*The Year's Best Science Fiction: Tenth
  Annual Collection* 179, 1103,
  1104, **1310**
*The Year's Best Science Fiction:
  Thirteenth Annual Collection* **1311**
*The Year's Best Science Fiction:
  Twelfth Annual Collection* **1312**,
  2139, 2984

Drake, Alison
Lagoon **1313**, 1449, 4055

Drake, David
Arc Riders **1314**, 1491
At Any Price 258
Battlestation **1315**, 2421
Birds of Prey 1492
Cluster Command **1316**, 3487, 4794
Counter Attack 1526
Counting the Cost 1651, 3137
Cross the Stars 1609
Dagger 3347
The Dragon Lord 3032
Enemy of My Enemy **3349**
The Fleet 1526, 3486
The Fleet 1-6 4788
The Forlorn Hope 1073, 3741
Fortress 2851, 4228
The Fourth Rome **1317**
From the Heart of Darkness 2215,
  2218, 2986
Hammer's Slammers 1072, 1649,
  1651, 1860, 2234, 3339, 3429,
  3487, 3490, 3660
The Hammer's Slammers Series 3867
Heads to the Storm 2499, 2500
The Heart of Darkness 553, 554
An Honorable Defense **1333**, 4794
The Hunter Returns **1318**
Igniting the Reaches 258, **1319**,
  4224
The Jungle 1249, 1265, **1320**, 1901,
  1950, 3596, 4213
Justice **1321**, 3349
Northworld **1322**, 1340, 1497, 3349,
  4224
Old Nathan **1323**, 1897, 4270
Ranks of Bronze 170, 1589, 1591,
  1755
Redliners **1324**
Rolling Hot **1325**, 3429, 3490, 3741
The Sea Hag 1140
The Sharp End **1326**
The Square Deal 72, **1327**
Starliner 639, **1328**, 1650, 2637,
  3159, 3163, 3963, 4526
Surface Action **1329**, 3923
Target 3198
Through the Breach 258, **1330**
*The Undesired Princess and the
  Enchanted Bunny* **1144**
Vengeance **1331**, 3349
Vettius and His Friends 697, 895,
  2216, 4388
The Voyage **1332**

Author Index

Author Index

McCabe, Patrick
The Butcher Boy 701, **2957**

McCaffrey, Anne
Alchemy and Academe 550, 3504
All the Weyrs of Pern 2431, **2958**
Black Horses for the King **2959**,
  4614, 4813
*The Chronicles of Pern: First
  Fall* 1901, **2960**
The City Who Fought 69, **2961**
The Coelura 3060
Crisis on Doona 2442, **2962**, 3295,
  3296, 3322, 3328, 3424
Crystal Line **2963**
Crystal Singer 863, 1987, 1988,
  2613, 3095, 3896, 3986, 4601
Damia 84, 1988, **2964**, 3634, 4826
Damia's Children **2965**, 4521
The Death of Sleep 862, **2966**, 3322,
  3328
Decision at Doona 1025, 1288, 1938
Dinosaur Planet 1593, 2560
The Dolphins of Pern 1962, **2967**
Dragon Drums 991
Dragon Song 3986
Dragondrums 858
Dragonflight 184, 725, 811, 897,
  1635, 1938, 1939, 2427, 2509,
  3138, 3303, 3577, 3581, 3583,
  3584, 3757, 3758, 3760, 4551,
  4669
Dragonquest 3303, 3757, 3760
Dragonriders of Pern 686, 687, 3756
Dragonriders of Pern Series 2040,
  2616, 4643
Dragonsdawn 524, 797, 1010, 1901,
  2390
Dragonsinger 991, 3314
Dragonsong 991, 1617
Drangonsinger 1417
An Exchange of Gifts **2968**
Freedom's Landing 319, 344, 1211,
  1633, 1786, **2969**, 3276
Generation Warrior 862, **2970**
Get Off the Unicorn 3064
The Girl Who Heard Dragons **2971**
Killashandra 1422
Lyon's Pride **2972**
Moreta's Story 2427
Nerilka's Story 524
No One Noticed the Cat **2973**
PartnerShip 263, 265, **2974**
Pegasus in Flight 84, 1984, 1985,
  2975
Power Lines **2976**
Power Play **2977**
Powers That Be 247, 520, 1595,
  1613, 1986, 2674, 2781, **2978**,
  3470, 4337, 4339, 4580
The Renegades of Pern 524, **2979**
Restoree 1539
The Rowan 84, 181, 527, 535, 1934,
  1984, 1985, 1988, 2038, 2884,
  2885, 2943, **2980**, 3264, 4826
Sassinak 50, 621, 627, 840, 862,
  1949, 2630, **2981**, 3574
The Ship Who Sang 600, 1121,
  1315, 1936, 2306, 2422, 3095,
  3327, 4285, 4527
The Ship Who Searched 527, **2982**
The Ship Who Won **2983**, 3327
Space Opera **2984**
To Ride Pegasus 84, 526, 645, 1937,
  4153
Treaty at Doona 1021, 1026, 1248,
  1279, 1606, **2985**
The White Dragon 184, 3303, 3757,
  3760, 4496

McCammon, Robert R.
Blue World 572, 782, 1519, 1830,
  1858, 2491, 2557, 2642, 2652,
  2986, 3721, 4695
Boy's Life **2987**
Gone South **2988**
Mine 1483, 1697, 2041, 2483,
  2649, 2939, **2989**, 3903
Mystery Walk 1518, 3244, 4375,
  4376
The Night Boat 2559
Stinger 472, 507, 837, 1854, 2482
Swan Song 284, 286, 288, 426,
  2495, 2496, **2990**, 3720, 4142
They Thirst 1129, 1182, 1183, 1185,
  1514, 1726, 2493, 2495, 2824,
  2825, 2836, 2837, 3243, 3265,
  4116, 4177, 4597, 4687
Under the Fang 695, 1110, 1703,
  1855, 1912, **2991**, 4685
Usher's Passing 57, 1700, 1999,
  2043, 3678, 3680
The Wolf's Hour 378, 2264, **2992**,
  3764, 3822

McCarthy, Wil
Aggressor Six **2993**
The Fall of Sirius **2994**
Flies From the Amber **2995**
Murder in the Solid State **2996**

McCarty, Dennis
Across the Thlassa Mey **2997**
The Birth of the Blade **2998**

McCauley, Kirby
Dark Forces 1486, 1849, 2364
Frights 2364
Night Chills 1484, 2364, 2370

McCay, Bill
Chains of Command **2999**, 4355
Crossover **3000**

McCloy, Helen
Through a Glass Darkly 2047

McCollum, Michael
Antares Dawn 295, 716
Antares Passage 955, 1618
The Clouds of Saturn 1593, **3001**
A Greater Infinity 772, 2661
Life Probe 4611
The Sails of Tau Ceti **3002**
Thunder Strike! **3003**

McConchie, Lyn
The Key of the Keplian 3310

McConnell, Ashley
Days of the Dead 1518, 2181, 2313,
  3004, 3678, 3680, 4487
The Fountains of Mirlacca 2608,
  3005
Highlander: Scimitar 2121, 3686
The Itinerant Exorcist **3006**
Prelude 3579
Quantum Leap: The Novel 2756,
  3579
Too Close for Comfort 3579
Unearthed **3007**
The Wall 3579

McCormack, Eric
Inspecting the Vaults 514, 944
The Mysterium **3008**
The Paradise Motel 1187

McCrumb, Sharyn
Bimbos of the Death Sun 210, 266,
  466, 2052, 3279, 3628, 3827
*If Ever I Return, Pretty Peggy-
  O* 1469
Zombies of the Gene Pool 3279

McCullough, Colleen
A Creed for the Third Millenium 3747

McCuniff, Mara
The Vampire Memoirs 115, 1819,
  2471, 2503, **3009**, 3808, 3818,
  4796

McDaniels, Abigail
Althea **3010**
Dead Voices 2313, 2337, **3011**
Playmates 2295, 2312, **3012**
The Uprising 1550, 2248, 2337,
  3013, 4041

McDevitt, Jack
Ancient Shores 706, **3014**
The Engines of God 562, 1021,
  1211, 2995, **3015**, 3410
The Hercules Text 166
A Talent for War 365, 418, **3016**

McDonald, Ian
The Broken Land 2353, **3017**, 3381
Desolation Road 277, 446, 449, 669,
  1512, 1692, 2026, 4045
Empire Dreams 1036
Evolution's Shore 2764, **3018**
*King of Morning, Queen of
  Day* 1190, 1577, 1799, 2671,
  2672, 2759, **3019**
Out on Blue Six 1036, **3020**, 3798,
  4711, 4712
Scissors Cut Paper Wrap Stone **3021**,
  3422
Speaking in Tongues 2061, **3022**
Terminal Cafe 274, 683, 684, 1781,
  2575, **3023**, 3042, 3493, 4072,
  4190

McDonald, Thomas Liam
*Sea Cursed: Thirty Terrifying Tales of
  the Deep* 2180, **3024**

McDonough, Alex
Dragon's Blood **3025**
Dragon's Claw **3026**
Dragon's Eye **3027**
Scorpio 334, 1194, **3028**, 3425
Scorpio Descending **3029**
Scorpio Rising **3030**

McDonough, Thomas R.
The Missing Matter 1990, **3031**,
  3200

McDowell, Ian
Mordred's Curse **3032**

McDowell, Michael
The Amulet 976
Blackwater 57, 121, 123, 4718
The Blackwater Series 1055
Cold Moon over Babylon 1495
Toplin **3033**, 4249

McElroy, Joseph
Plus 3658

McEwan, Ian
Black Dogs **3034**
The Cement Garden 829, 1697
In Between the Sheets 514, 746

McFadden, Kevin
The Cold One 3446
The Last Vampire 3447
The Midnight Club 3448
Sati 3449
The Season of Passage 3450
See You Later 3451
The Starlight Crystal 3452
Witch 3453

McGann, Michael
The Ghost Warriors 1861, 1862

McGarry, Jim
Irish Tales of Terror 3348

McGinley, Phyllis
The Plain Princess 278

McGirt, Dan
Dirty Work **3035**, 4837
Jason Cosmo 796, 813, 1029, **3036**

McGrath, Patrick
*Blood and Water and Other
  Tales* 747, 3169, 3207
Dr. Haggard's Disease **3037**
The Grotesque 515, 1700, 2391,
  2934, **3038**, 3830
The New Gothic 3207
Spider 662, **3039**, 3333

McGraw, Charles G.
Demon Blade **1718**
Dorella **1719**

McGraw, Eloise Jarvis
Merry-Go-Round in Oz 2869
The Moorchild 1067, **3040**

McHugh, Maureen F.
China Mountain Zhang 750, 2353,
  2413, **3041**, 4190
Half the Day Is Night **3042**

McIntyre, Vonda N.
Aurora: Beyond Equality 3863, 3864
The Crystal Star 86, 91, 2002, **3043**,
  3423, 4407, 4741
Dreamsnake 526, 1380, 2235, 3328
Enterprise 427, 731
The Entropy Effect 427, 1120
The Exile Waiting 1987, 3219
The Girl Who Was Plugged In 4405
Metaphase 67, 272, 335, 852, 1079,
  1384, 1596, 1598, 2758, 2976,
  2978, 2982, **3044**, 3470, 3959,
  3963
Nautilus 3045
*Screwtop/The Girl Who Was Plugged
  In* 108
The Search for Spock 428, 1256
Star Trek II: The Wrath of Khan 427,
  1256
*Star Trek III: The Search for
  Spock* 1573
Star Trek IV: The Voyage Home 467,
  1256, 3403
Starfarers 538, 598, 1259, 1332,
  1361, 1527, 1845, 2261, **3046**,
  3759, 4140
Superluminal 149, 2261, 3465, 4769
Transition 67, 538, 848, 1256,
  1328, 1527, 1598, 1646, 1996,
  2260, 3031, **3047**, 3594

McKay, William
The Secret Peace 2819

McKee, Lynn Armistead
Woman of the Mists 597, 1737, 2274

McKenney, Kenneth
The Offspring **3048**

McKenzie, Nancy
The Child Queen **3049**

McKeone, Dixie
Greatheart 2099
The Spider's Test 2099

McKeone, Lee
Backblast **3050**
The Clone Crisis **3051**
Starfire Down **3052**

McKiernan, Dennis L.
Caverns of Socrates **3053**

Pfeffer, Susan Beth
Rewind to Yesterday 1341

Pfefferle, Seth
Stickman 4051

Phelps, Ethel Johnston
Tatterhood and Other Tales 232, 690, 1721, 1723, 2021, 2171, 3190, 3978, 4475, 4856, 4857

Philbrick, Rodman
Hunger **1088**
Nine Levels Down **1089**

Phillifent, John T.
The Man From U.N.C.L.E.: The Mad Scientist Affair 1491, 3422

Phillips, Jill M.
Walford's Oak 3405, **3433**

Phillips, Robert
The Omnibus of Twentieth Century Ghost Stories **3434**
Triumph of the Night 999, 1058, 1091, 2875, 3358, 4322

Piccirilli, Tom
Dark Father 1622, 1870, 3257, **3435**, 3785, 4511, 4770, 4776
Pentacle 2476, **3436**

Pierce, Constance
Elvis Rising: Stories on the King **4061**

Pierce, David
Forever Yours 3448

Pierce, J. Calvin
The Door to Ambermere **3437**
The Wizard of Ambermere **3438**

Pierce, Meredith Ann
The Dark-Angel 1165
The Pearl of the Soul of the World 134, 689, 2511, 3061, 3288, 3308, **3439**, 4761
The Son of Summer Stars **3440**
The Woman Who Loved Reindeer 547, 1737, 1738, 1739, 1740, 1741, 2064, 2065, **3441**

Pierce, Tamora
Alanna: The First Adventure 4485
The Realms of the Gods **3442**
Wild Magic **3443**
Wolf-Speaker **3444**

Piercy, Marge
He, She and It 1465, **3445**, 4348, 4455
Woman on the Edge of Time 417, 783, 911, 1475, 2879, 4134, 4700, 4702

Pike, Christopher
The Cold One **3446**, 3872
The Creature in the Teacher 882, 4221
The Eternal Enemy 466, 3355, 4000
The Last Vampire **3447**
The Midnight Club **3448**
Sati 1653, **3449**
The Season of Passage 163, **3450**
See You Later 1031, 1193, **3451**
The Starlight Crystal 163, 466, **3452**
The Tachyon Web 1837
Whisper of Death 537
Witch **3453**, 4370

Pine, Nicholas
The In Crowd 3448
The New Kid 4218
Night School 3447

Pines, T.
13 Tales of Horror 1919
Thirteen 1919

Pini, Richard
Against the Wind 3455
The Blood of Ten Chiefs 3455, 4788
Dark Hours **3454**, 3455
The Quest Begins 3455
Winds of Change 3455
Wolfsong 3455

Pini, Wendy
Elfquest: Journey to Sorrow's End 3454
The Quest Begins **3455**

Pinkwater, Daniel Manus
The Afterlife Diet 1863
Borgel 992, 994, 1296, 1715, 2841, **3456**, 3644
Lizard Music 988, 993
The Snarkout Boys and the Avocado of Death 994
Young Adults 444, 445, 448, 450

Piper, H. Beam
The Cosmic Computer 728
Fuzzies and Other People 371
Fuzzy Sapiens 4355
Little Fuzzy 189, 358, 371, 1025, 1288, 2203, 2763, 2800, 3115, 3403, 3535, 3536, 3537, 3635
Lord Kalvan of Otherwhen 117, 118, 119, 1262, 1314, 1644, 3217, 3317, 3998
The Other Human Race 371, 1025, 2638
Space Viking 107, 1319, 4100, 4636
Uller Uprising 3491

Plante, Edmund
Alone in the House 4219
Seed of Evil 2423, **3457**, 4082, 4309

Platt, Charles
Free Zone 1615, **3458**
Protektor **3459**
The Silicon Man **3460**

Poe, Edgar Allan
The Fall of the House of Usher 3037
Ligeia 3037
The Narrative of A. Gordon Pym 3484
The Science Fiction of Edgar Allan Poe 2500

Poe, Robert
Return to the House of Usher 2502, **3461**

Pogue, Bill
The Trikon Deception **490**

Pohl, Frederik
The Best Science Fiction for 1972 204
The Best Science Fiction From If 200
Beyond the Blue Event Horizon 3600
The Coming of the Quantum Cats 477, 4702
Drunkard's Walk 1993, 2326, 3852
The Eighth Galaxy Reader 202
Gateway 206, 367, 369, 1217, 3266, 3959
The Gateway Trip: Tales and Vignettes of the Heechee 2260, 3266, **3462**, 4183, 4725
Gladiator-at-Law 1448, 1478, 1864, 2034, 2208, 3021, 3566, 3733, 4458
Homegoing 3140, **3463**
Jem 207, 1418
Man Plus 481, 1418, 2263, 2956, 3350, **3464**, 3961, 4287

Midas World 1522
Mining the Oort 69, 345, 2204, **3465**, 3923, 3956, 3960
Narabedla, Ltd. 980, 1601, 3342, 3406, 4501
Nebula Winners 14 204
The Other End of Time 565, 1607, **3466**
Outnumbering the Dead **3467**, 3953
The Science Fiction Roll of Honor 204
The Seventh Galaxy Reader 201
The Singers of Time 1824, **3468**
The Space Merchants 486, 1522, 3020
Stopping at Slowyear 2235, 2450, 2532, 2574, 3324, 3328, **3469**, 3949, 3955, 4626, 4839
The Voices of Heaven 1364, 3276, **3470**
The World at the End of Time 600, **3471**, 3595
The Years of the City 1460, 1461, 4498

Polikarpus, Viido
Down Town 1482, 3322

Pollack, Rachel
Godmother Night **3472**
Tarot Tales **3473**
Temporary Agency 323, 2447, 3135, **3474**, 4409
Unquenchable Fire 2734, 3135, **3475**, 3706, 4105, 4409, 4456

Pollotta, Nick
Bureau 13 324, 577, 1128, 1586, 1850, 1859, 2017, 3337, 3427, **3476**, 3502, 4383
Doomsday Exam 935, 1586, 1850, 1859, 1895, **3477**
Full Moonster 2590, **3478**, 3502, 4383
Illegal Aliens 392, 1174, 1522, 1545, 1790, 3279, **3479**
Satellite Night News **2208**

Pope, Elizabeth Marie
The Perilous Gard 15, 267, 327, 2404, 3040, 3060, 3896
The Sherwood Ring 101, 1031, 3248

Popescu, Petru
In Hot Blood **3480**

Popkes, Steven
Caliban Landing 108, 4074
The Longest Voyage/Slow Lightning **108**
Slow Lightning 4074

Porath, Ellen
Kindred Spirits **125**
Steel and Stone **3481**, 3935

Porter, Barry
Dark Souls **3482**
Junkyard 311, **3483**, 3854

Posey, Ernest
Hormone Pirates of Xenobia and Dream Studs of Kama Loka 1702

Potocki, Jan
The Manuscript Found in Sragossa **3484**

Pournelle, Jerry
Beowulf's Children **3276**
Birth of Fire 345, 2204
The Children's Hour 1077, 2900, 3283, 3284, **3485**
CoDominium: Revolt on War World **3486**, 4222

Falkenberg's Legion 1068, 1072, 1073, 1248, 1742, 1885, 1887, 1948, 2419, **3487**, 3560, 3660, 3741, 4228, 4362
Fallen Angels **3279**
Go Tell the Spartans 1324, **3488**, 4222
The Gripping Hand **3281**
Higher Education **3956**
Janissaries 300, 1249, 1321, 1325, 1884, 3346
King David's Spaceship 295, 955
Life Among the Asteroids **3489**
Man-Kzin Wars III **3282**
The Mercenary 258, 1329, 1651
Oath of Fealty 1884
Prince of Mercenaries 107, 258, 896, 1316, 1325, 1333, 1530, 1651, 1884, 2915, **3490**, 4287
Prince of Sparta **3491**
War World 1609
War World I: The Burning Eye 4222
War World II: Death's Head Rebellion 4222
War World III: Sauron Dominion 4222
West of Honor 3956

Power, Susan
The Grass Dancer **3492**

Powers, Richard M.
Galatea 2.2 **3493**

Powers, Tim
The Anubis Gates 422, 784, 1177, 1226, 1263, 1305, 1671, 1865, 2035, 2477, 2720, 2859, 3025, 3028, 3029, 3030, 3534, 3545, 3729, 3730
Dinner at Deviant's Palace 1225
The Drawing of the Dark 774, 1814, 2590, 2955, 3032
Expiration Date **3494**
Last Call 73, 420, 1035, 2594, 3473, **3495**
On Stranger Tides 3732, 4653
The Stress of Her Regard 740, 1034, 1817, 2187, **3496**, 3628, 4031, 4472, 4473, 4653, 4797, 4800

Poyer, David C.
The Shiloh Project 4386

Pratchett, Terry
The Colour of Magic 143, 1669, 2091, 4651
Diggers 992, 993, 994, **3497**
Equal Rites 2058, 3194, **3498**
Eric 3323, **3499**
Feet of Clay **3500**
Good Omens: The Nice and Accurate Prophecies of Agnes Nutter, Witch **1693**
Guards! Guards! 978, 3175, **3501**, 4505
The Light Fantastic 297
Lords and Ladies **3502**
Men at Arms **3503**
Mort 1119, 3195, **3504**
Moving Pictures 2841, **3505**, 4677
Reaper Man 162, 1296, 1863, **3506**
Small Gods **3507**, 4173
Soul Music **3508**
Sourcery 148, 1708
Strata 2431
Truckers 992, 993, 994, 1258, **3509**
Wings 992, 993, 994, **3510**, 3536
Witches Abroad 154, 1722, **3511**
Wyrd Sisters 794, 842, 2193, 2344, 2454, **3512**, 4257

Author Index

Author Index

Twain, Mark
*The Adventures of Huckleberry
    Finn* 4202
*A Connecticut Yankee in King Arthur's
    Court* 1144, 1235, 1642, 1643,
    1645, 2091, 3967, 4813
Satires and Burlesques 1712

Tyers, Kathy
Crystal Witness 3220, **4404**
Firebird 1422
One Mind's Eye **4405**
Shivering World 190, 1448, 2978,
    3724, **4406**
The Truce at Bakura 91, 3423, **4407**,
    4828

Tyson, Donald
The Messenger **4408**

Tyson, Salinda
Wheel of Dreams 2357, **4409**

U

Upchurch, Michael
Passive Intruder 1801, **4410**

Updike, John
The Witches of Eastwick 613, 1955,
    3650, 3656, 4006, 4379

Ustinov, Peter
The Old Man and Mr. Smith **4411**,
    4438, 4595

Uttley, Alison
A Traveler in Time 2385, 2593

V

Vachss, Andrew
Born Bad 2166
A Flash of White 826

Vallejo, Doris
The Boy Who Saved the Stars 4847
*Ladies: Retold Tales of Goddesses and
    Heroines* **4412**

Van Allsburg, Chris
Two Bad Ants 2692

Van Asten, Gail
Charlemagne's Champion 3065,
    3606, **4413**

Van Belkom, Edo
Wyrm Wolf 3174, 3234, **4414**

Van Gores, Alida
Mermaid's Song 932

Van Hise, Della
Killing Time 731, 748, 1119, 1120,
    1219, 1842, 3409, 3939, 4079

Van Hise, James
Midnight Graffiti **2210**

Van Lustbader, Eric
Dai-San 1075
The Sunset Warrior 2908, 3168

Van Name, Mark L.
*Intersections: The Sycamore Hill
    Anthology* **2458**

Van Over, Raymond
The Twelfth Child **4415**
Whisper 1765, **4416**

Van Scyoc, Sydney J.
Assignment: Nor'Dyren 1932
Bluesong 3306
Cloudcry 1902
Darkchild 1288, 3986, 4422
Deepwater Dreams 51, 1962, 2659,
    2967, 3526, 3933, 4011, **4417**,
    4605
Feather Stroke 1413, 2614, 3315,
    3603, **4418**

van Vogt, A.E.
The Battle of Forever 1743
Null-A Three 1780, 4478
The Pawns of Null-A 4478
The Players of Null-A 1780
The Silkie 1188, 4417
Slan 463, 465, 526, 599, 1836,
    1937, 2034, 2127, 3177, 3178,
    3251, 3428, 3928

Van Vogt, A.E.
Slan 4019

van Vogt, A.E.
*The Voyage of the Space
    Beagle* 1332, 4027
The Weapon Makers 641, 888, 893,
    1502, 3274, 4419, 4670
The Weapon Shops of Isher 1229,
    1502, 3087, 3274, 4196, 4670
The World of Null-A 315, 1780,
    2942, 3051, 3751, 4478

Vance, Jack
Alastor 622, 717, **4419**, 4564
The Anome 1134, 2942, 4034
Araminta Station 3407
The Asutra 4034, 4091
Big Planet 728, 1363
The Book of Dreams 3407
The Brave Free Men 718, 1771
City of the Chasch 519
Cugel's Saga 3407
The Dragon Masters 822, 1655,
    1759, 3407, 4829
The Dying Earth 2509, 2510
The Dying Earth Series 3504
Ecce and Old Earth **4420**
Emphyrio 144, 1758, 2940, 4355
The Eyes of the Overworld 2510
The Five Gold Bands 1504
Galactic Effectuator 3407
The Green Pearl 4448
The Languages of Pao 4490
Lyonesse 518, 774, 2347, 2452,
    4448
Madouc 520, 1399, 2124, **4421**,
    4448, 4495
Night Lamp **4422**
Planet of Adventure 772
Servants of the Wankh 1075
Showboat World 1363, 2060, 3342,
    4034
Space Opera 3342, 4159
Space Pirate 1330
Suldrun's Garden 184
Throy **4423**
To Live Forever 1993, 2326, 3852
Trullion: Alastor 2262 1932, 3280,
    3709
When the Five Moons Rise **4424**

Vance, Steve
Shapes **4425**
Spook 898, 1080, 2407, **4426**

Vande Velde, Vivian
Dragon's Bait 1571, 4302, **4427**
*Tales From the Brothers Grimm and the
    Sisters Weird* 1105, **4428**

User Unfriendly 73, 147, 387, 411,
    988, 1181, 1293, 1506, 1676,
    2757, 2770, 3053, 3535, 3740,
    3931, 4040, **4429**
A Well-Timed Enchantment 821,
    4430, 4637

Vansittart, Peter
Parsifal 4112, **4431**

Vardeman, Robert E.
Ancient Heavens **4432**
Dark Legacy 2251
Death Channels **4433**
The Glass Warrior **4434**
The Infinity Plague 2632, **4435**
The Klingon Gambit 428, 1219
Mutiny on the Enterprise 429
Phantoms on the Wind 932, 1401

Varian, Nancy
Berberick, Stormblade 4563

Varley, John
*The Barbie Murders and Other
    Stories* 2589, 3425, 3489, 4073,
    4494
Blue Champagne 42, 49, 103, 131,
    193, 408, 512, 566, 633, 656, 691,
    1300, 1507, 2054, 2061, 2534,
    2631, 2839, 2899, 3241, 3278,
    3282, 3285, 3286, 3360, 3425,
    3489, 3641, 3711, 3717, 3767,
    3954, 3959, 4010, 4073, 4184,
    4186, 4193, 4265, 4280, 4424,
    4494, 4625, 4673
Demon 412, 1143, 4174, 4651
Millennium 97, 117, 118, 119, 221,
    672, 1262, 2035, 2756, 3946,
    3998, 4215, 4378
*Nanoware Time/The Persistence of
    Vision* **4494**
The Ophiuchi Hotline 274, 1606,
    1647, 1743, 2422, 3140, 3197,
    3939, 3960, 4269, 4405, 4671
The Persistence of Vision 131, 192,
    193, 368, 408, 545, 656, 854,
    1223, 1300, 1507, 1841, 1995,
    2061, 2117, 2123, 2172, 2532,
    2534, 2631, 2864, 2971, 3278,
    3282, 3285, 3286, 3462, 3489,
    3641, 3711, 3717, 3767, 3951,
    3959, 4073, 4184, 4193, 4263,
    4280, 4424, 4494, 4623, 4625
Press Enter/Hawksbill Station 108
Steel Beach 4, 63, 65, 106, 111,
    195, 208, 482, 1342, 1583, 1681,
    1781, 1969, 2063, 2113, 2595,
    2746, 2911, 3141, 3411, 3459,
    3464, 3806, 3887, 4182, 4187,
    4191, 4281, **4436**, 4441, 4670
Superheroes 996, 1122, 1345, 2706,
    4437
*Tango Charlie and Foxtrot Charlie/The
    Star Pit* 108
Titan 563, 773, 779, 1320, 1841,
    1901, 3161, 3266, 3409, 3523,
    3526, 3672, 3766, 3946, 4503
Wizard 848, 2431, 3989, 4014

Varma, Devendra P.
*Voices From the Vault: Authentic
    Vampire Tales* 1926, 4550

Vaughan, Ralph
*Sherlock Holmes in the Adventure of the
    Ancient Gods* 1494, 3799, 4723

Vercors
You Shall Know Them 1947

Verne, Jules
From the Earth to the Moon 330

*Journey to the Center of the
    Earth* 1979, 1980, 2855, 3766
Mysterious Island 4286
*Twenty Thousand Leagues under the
    Sea* 330, 362, 1344
Yesterday and Tomorrow 2500

Vidal, Gore
Live From Golgotha: A Novel **4438**
Messiah 3449
Visit to a Small Planet 995, 1119

Vidal, Harriette
Animus **2423**
Breeder **2424**
The School **2425**

Vinge, Joan D.
Catspaw 391, 2148, 2149, 2895,
    3414, 4019
Dreamfall 2294, **4439**
Mad Max Beyond Thunderdome 1327
The Outcasts of Heaven Belt 1116
Psion 1984, 1985, 2964, 2965,
    2975, 3912, 4019, 4826
Return to Oz 2869
The Snow Queen 144, 804, 949,
    2895, 4650
The Summer Queen 589, 622, 625,
    772, 773, 779, 1188, 1286, 1299,
    2967, 2978, 2983, 3786, 4422,
    4440, 4580

Vinge, Vernor
A Fire upon the Deep 36, 65, 67,
    195, 259, 272, 318, 333, 340, 384,
    389, 562, 565, 649, 717, 723, 756,
    757, 797, 803, 814, 852, 872, 956,
    957, 1026, 1079, 1082, 1178,
    1271, 1273, 1279, 1280, 1342,
    1385, 1461, 1596, 1598, 1599,
    1604, 1613, 1681, 2038, 2256,
    2758, 2876, 2961, 2963, 2976,
    2982, 2994, 3015, 3044, 3045,
    3281, 3296, 3419, 3470, 3592,
    3635, 3806, 3885, 3912, 3963,
    4030, 4098, 4100, 4191, 4196,
    4269, 4275, 4358, 4436, **4441**,
    4518, 4526, 4647, 4740, 4853,
    4854
Marooned in Realtime 332, 751, 754,
    848, 1593, 1864, 2078, 2589,
    2969, 3182, 3199, 3200, 3595,
    3724, 4022, 4044, 4513, 4703
The Peace War 2078, 2297, 3199,
    3893, 4022
Tatja Grimm's World 1288, 3786
Threats...and Other Promises 349

Vinicoff, Eric
The Weigher 649, 1017, 1956, 2109,
    2976, **4442**

Vitola, Denise
Half-Light 1650, 2281, 2349, 4215,
    4443

Vizenor, Gerald
*Dead Voices: Natural Agonies in the
    Real World* 156, 2146, 3352,
    3353, 3492, **4444**, 4583

Voigt, Cynthia
Jackaroo 3546
On Fortune's Wheel 794, **4445**

Vollman, William T.
Whores for Gloria 2676

Vollmann, William T.
The Ice-Shirt **4446**
You Bright and Risen Angels 637

Volsky, Paula
The Gates of Twilight **4447**

Author Index

Author Index

Title Index

This index alphabetically lists all titles featured or mentioned in entries in the main section of this book. Each title is followed by the name of the main author and the entry number(s) of the entry or entries where the title can be found. A bold entry number indicates that the title in question is a featured main entry; lightface numbers refer to entries for other books that mention the title in question under the rubric "Other books you might like."

A

2XS
Findley, Nigel   787, 789, 790, 1003, 1284, **1558**, 2579, 3860, 4095, 4096, 4567, 4798

5th Annual of the Year's Best S-F
Merril, Judith   199

6th Annual of the Year's Best S-F
Merril, Judith   200

7 Past Midnight
Matheson, Richard   3900

7 Seconds to Midnight
Matheson, Richard   74

7 Steps to Midnight
Matheson, Richard   **2928**

7th Annual of the Year's Best S-F
Merril, Judith   200

The 7th Guest
Costello, Matthew J.   **963**, 3118, 3586

8th Annual of the Year's Best S-F
Merril, Judith   201

9th Annual of the Year's Best S-F
Merril, Judith   202

12 Great Classics of Science Fiction
Conklin, Groff   199, 1304

12 Monkeys
Hand, Elizabeth   **2025**

13 Again
Finnis, A.   1919

The 13 Clocks
Thurber, James   1232

13 Plays of Ghosts and the Supernatural
Kaye, Marvin   1168

13 Short Horror Novels
Waugh, Charles G.   187, 2370

13 Tales of Horror
Pines, T.   1919

17 X Infinity
Conklin, Groff   201

28 Science Fiction Stories
Wells, H.G.   1290

The 37th Mandala
Laidlaw, Marc   537, 1785, **2633**

50 Great Ghost Stories
Canning, John   2032, 2111

65mm
Hoover, Dale   376, 874, 1093, **2200**, 2466

The 97th Step
Perry, Steve   475, 1297, 3298, 3370, **3414**, 3428, 3561, 4846

100 Creepy Little Creature Stories
Weinberg, Robert   3866, **4532**

100 Ghastly Little Ghost Stories
Dziemianowicz, Stefan   **1372**, 3866

100 Great Fantasy Short Short Stories
Asimov, Isaac   4533

100 Hair-Raising Little Horror Stories
Sarrantonio, Al   1372, **3866**, 4532, 4533

100 Tiny Tales of Terror
Weinberg, Robert   **4533**

100 Vicious Little Vampire Stories
Weinberg, Robert   1666, 4217, **4534**

100 Wicked Little Witch Stories
Dziemianowicz, Stefan   **1373**

100 Wild Little Weird Tales
Weinberg, Robert   390, 2412, **4535**

668: The Neighbor of the Beast
Fenn, Lionel   **1541**, 3505, 4843

1901
Conroy, Robert   **918**

1945
Gingrich, Newt   **1800**, 4396, 4397

1984
Orwell, George   470, 3969

The 1990 Annual World's Best Science Fiction
Wollheim, Donald A.   177, 178, 197, 198, 405, 406, 721, 1306, 1308, 1309, 3211, 3639, 3783, **4739**

2001: A Space Odyssey
Clarke, Arthur C.   317, 415, 3886, 3952, 3962

2010: Odyssey Two
Clarke, Arthur C.   317, 415, 3952, 3962

2041: Twelve Short Stories about the Future by Top Science Fiction Writers
Yolen, Jane   3639, 4178, **4805**

2061: Odyssey Three
Clarke, Arthur C.   317, 415, 3950, 3952, 3962

Abduction: The UFO Conspiracy
Bischoff, David   1633

The Abductors: Conspiracy
Frakes, Jonathan   1275, **1633**

Abel/Baker/Charley
Maxim, John R.   1466, 1763, 2088, 2481, 2684, 2937, 4327

The Abode of Life
Correy, Lee   427

Above the Lower Sky
Deitz, Tom   **1188**

The Abraxis Marvel Circus
Leigh, Stephen   424, 2613, **2721**

Absolute Power
Russell, Ray   2244, **3791**

The Abyss
Card, Orson Scott   268, 362, 855, 972, 973, 3926, 4215

The Abyss
Cunningham, Jere   1516

An Acceptable Time
L'Engle, Madeleine   310; 833; **2732**

Accusations
Tilton, Lois   307, 4461

Ace in the Hole
Martin, George R.R.   802, **2892**

Achilles' Choice
Niven, Larry   301, 893, 2746, **3274**, 3335, 4128

Across the Far Mountain
Hancock, Neil   2452

Across the Sea of Suns
Benford, Gregory   851, 1779, 2114

Across the Thlassa Mey
McCarty, Dennis   **2997**

Act of God
Kotani, Eric   479, 753

Act of Love
Lansdale, Joe R.   1471, 2551, 2552, **2640**

The Active-Enzyme Lemon-Freshened Junior High School Witch
Hildick, E.W.   2350, 4370

Addams Family Values
Strasser, Todd   **4246**

The Adept
Kurtz, Katherine   615, 1904, 2045, 2385, **2587**

Adiamante
Modesitt, L.E. Jr.   **3127**

The Admirer
Franklin, Debra   4218

Adulthood Rites
Butler, Octavia E.   383, 563, 1018, 1134, 1381, 1384, 1385, 1418, 1504, 1655, 1777, 1834, 2029, 2390, 2429, 2535, 3018, 3181, 3361, 3363, 3382, 4002, 4283, 4845

The Adventure of the Ectoplasmic Man
Stashower, Daniel   2150, 2934, 3461, 3937

Title Index

Title Index

Title Index

T

Z

Z for Zachariah
O'Brien, Robert C.   2849, 2868

Z Is for Zombie
Roscoe, Theodore   2865

The Zap Gun
Dick, Philip K.   **1229**

Zaragoz
Craig, Brian   **1006**, 3725, 4059

Zelerod's Doom
Lichtenberg, Jacqueline   3826

Zeta Base
Alguire, Judith   **60**, 543, 2814

Zeus and Co.
Jones, David Lee   2168, **2344**

Zjhanne's Book
Mills, C.J.   **3117**

Zod Wallop
Spencer, William Browning   874, **4123**

Zombie
Oates, Joyce Carol   2197, 2391, **3333**, 4248

Zombies of the Gene Pool
McCrumb, Sharyn   3279

Zone Yellow
Laumer, Keith   4091

Zoo 2000: Twelve Stories of Science Fiction and Fantasy Beasts
Yolen, Jane   2871

Zorba the Hutt's Revenge
Davids, Paul   **1126**

The Zork Chronicles
Effinger, George Alec   241, **1410**, 1479

The Zothique
Smith, Clark Ashton   3202